杨良宜 杨大明 杨大志 司嘉 贡航 王可心 | 著

合约的效力 上

虚假陈述、错误、非法、胁迫等的影响

法律出版社
LAW PRESS · CHINA
——北京——

图书在版编目(CIP)数据

合约的效力：上下册．虚假陈述、错误、非法、胁迫等的影响／杨良宜等著．--北京：法律出版社，2023

ISBN 978-7-5197-8303-7

Ⅰ．①合… Ⅱ．①杨… Ⅲ．①国际商法－研究 Ⅳ．①D996.1

中国国家版本馆CIP数据核字(2023)第166606号

合约的效力：虚假陈述、错误、非法、胁迫等的影响(上下册)
HEYUE DE XIAOLI：XUJIA CHENSHU、CUOWU、FEIFA、XIEPO DENG DE YINGXIANG (SHANGXIACE)

杨良宜 等 著

责任编辑 吴 昉
装帧设计 凌点工作室

出版发行 法律出版社
编辑统筹 法律教育出版分社
责任校对 郑怡萍
责任印制 刘晓伟
经　　销 新华书店

开本 710毫米×1000毫米 1/16
印张 85　　字数 1718千
版本 2023年9月第1版
印次 2023年9月第1次印刷
印刷 固安华明印业有限公司

地址：北京市丰台区莲花池西里7号(100073)
网址：www.lawpress.com.cn
投稿邮箱：info@lawpress.com.cn
举报盗版邮箱：jbwq@lawpress.com.cn
销售电话：010-83938349
客服电话：010-83938350
咨询电话：010-63939796

书号：ISBN 978-7-5197-8303-7
定价(上下册)：198.00元

序　一

自从 1979 年 10 月我第一次回到北京授课（当年主要讲授航运与外贸的 CIF/FOB 付运合约），我已经深深感受到内地同胞对学习国际商业规则的强烈兴趣。在接下来几乎没有任何间断的将近 45 年授课生涯中，我也感受到内地学习国际商业规则之路有些偏差，包括过度重视语言（主要是英语）与国际公法，而忽略私法。

但在国际商业活动中，所有活动都涉及国际私法（本文中指合约法、证据法与国际仲裁）。例如，所有的商业关系都是合约串起来。从 20 世纪 70 年代开始，随着全球化的不断发展，所有商业合约的争议都是以国际商事仲裁解决，而国际商事仲裁走的是复杂与昂贵的证据程序，仲裁庭作出的决定也必须是针对双方争辩的合约法与证据法的说理。可以说，国际商业环境是一个法治的环境。这法治环境也是深受普通法的影响，除了历史原因，也确实是在越来越复杂与变化万千的国际商业活动中累积了大量的经验，并且结合国际一流商业人士（无论是大陆法还是普通法背景）反复思考所发展起来的一套“最佳做法”（best practice）。

所以，我深深感觉到“走出去”的中国企业和自然人必须掌握这一套“最佳做法”的国际商业规则。无论是订立、履行或终止商业合约，他们才能与西方国家的企业平等对话，立于不败之地。如果中国“走出去”的企业与自然人掌握和熟悉这套现存的国际商业规则，还可以“以其人之道、还治其人之身”。

近年来，国内大力培养涉外法律人才。中国作为全球商贸大国，迫切需要培养精通国际私法的法律人才。对年轻一代而言，系统性地学好国际私法会带来不可估量的好处，包括中国在国际商贸活动中的地位代表着无穷尽的工作机会、大量与高层次高水平人士深入接触与交流对话的机会等，也因此带来我最重视的全面提高中国年轻一代国际思维的可能性。

早在 20 年前，我就从自己所走过的路中认识到学习这三门国际私法课题的重要性，并开始系统性地写作相关书籍。自 2006 年第一部《仲裁法：从 1996 年英国仲裁法到国际商务仲裁》，直到这一部《合约的效力：虚假陈述、错误、非法、胁迫等的影响》（上下册），已经有 8 部书籍，即 4 部关于合约法，2 部关于证据法，2 部关于国际仲裁。我认为学无止境，写书也同样无止境。我们的团队也在持续研究和写作，包括“财产法、衡平法与信托”“经济侵权”等合约法相关的课题。当然这些课题在 4 部有关合约法的书籍中已经有所涉及，在推广普通法系列课程与培养涉外法律人才方面业已足够，可为设立课程内容与大纲、不同授课老师备课、读者/学生进一步熟读与研究之用。可以说，没有这套书籍，我为培养尖端涉外法律人才而设计的系列课程是很难开设与推广的。所以，在此重要的里程碑时刻，我为自己这20年的写书道路与建立的学习体系而感到庆幸与无悔。

杨良宜
2023年8月

序　　二

Seldom, very seldom, does complete truth belong to any human disclosure; seldom can it happen that something is not a little disguised or a little mistaken.（人会绝少，非常绝少，透露全部事实；绝少不会有一些事情有小小的隐瞒或一小点的错误。）

——Jane Austen（简·奥斯汀）

Crime is common. Logic is rare. Therefore it is upon the logic rather than upon the crime that you should dwell.（犯罪是平常。逻辑是罕有。所以应该纠缠在逻辑而不是在犯罪上。）

——Sir Arthur Conan Doyle（亚瑟·伊格内修斯·柯南·道尔爵士）

If you demand money from someone in exchange for your silence, it's called 'blackmail'. If your lawyer demands money from someone in exchange for your silence, it's called a settlement.（如果您要求人付钱换取您的沉默，这就是"勒索"。如果您的律师要求人付钱换取您的沉默，这就是和解。）

——Arthur Baer（亚瑟·贝尔）

基本上在所有普通法体系中，合同法都拥有崇高的地位。很多人平常都不会把最真实的一面展现给别人，而是会留一手，关键是知道法律的边界在哪里。不完全合法的事情也每天都有，关键是知道如何影响合同的操作。合法和非法有的时候也就是一线之差。

我一直感到非常幸运，可以协助父亲杨良宜先生将合同法和其他普通法中的法律制度以最有效的方式，包括这套书籍和一系列的涉外法律人才培训课程带给大家。在此也感谢各位"战友"，包括我的弟弟杨大志先生、司嘉女士、王可心女士和贡航先生。

杨大明

2023年8月

序　　三

国际商业活动的世界是在合同的基础上建立的，普通法是其中所使用的主要法律体系之一。因此，了解普通法体系下的合同法是在国际贸易和国际金融领域取得成功的先决条件之一。很有意思的是，英国作为普通法体系的发源地，于 2021 年 10 月发布了一份关于英国合同法经济价值的报告（报告由 LegalUK 和咨询公司 Oxera 发布）。该报告强调，在很多国际商务领域（理论上当事人可以选择任何法律体系来管辖合同）中，绝大多数合同都受英国法管辖。这些商务领域包括：(1) 全球并购（交易额 23 亿元人民币）；(2) 全球金属交易（交易额 106 万亿元人民币）；(3) 场外衍生品交易（交易的名义金额为 5200 万亿元人民币）；(4) 保险合同（合同额度 7330 亿元人民币）；(5) 海事仲裁（占全球案件的 80%）。这些数字甚至还未将受美国法律管辖（在跨境贸易中并不常用）、新加坡法律管辖或者中国香港特区法律管辖的合同计算在内。

与此同时，令我感到非常惊讶的是，尽管在普通法下所进行的国际商务交易数额巨大，但有资格在英国法下执业的事务律师只有约 16 万名，诉讼律师则不到 2 万名。即便加上其他采用普通法体系的金融中心的所有律师（新加坡 6300 名、澳大利亚 83000 名、中国香港特区 13000 名），有资格根据普通法从事合同法业务的人也只有大约 28 万名。而且，即使有执业资格也不代表真的精通普通法，这要靠个人的勤奋与机遇。可想而知，这样的人才对企业与国家的价值。

当然，学习普通法系的合同法体系并不一定意味着要在普通法系国家取得执业资格，这也是我父亲杨良宜先生的普通法系合同法系列丛书以及多年来举办的系列讲座的理念所在。中国和很多其他贸易大国一样，亟须更多精通普通法/国际商法的人才（无论是法官、仲裁员、律师、法务人员、专家证人还是有关领域的政府官员）。我们为中国企业进军国际商业世界保驾护航，而如今中国企业所面临的国际商业环境并不尽如人意，我们的工作比以往任何时候都更具挑战性，但同时也更具价值。

杨大志

2023 年 8 月

序　　四

从 2005 年我在香港特区读研究生期间因实习与杨先生结缘,到毕业后加入杨先生团队边工作边学习,至今已经近 20 年的时间。回看走过的路,从学生到独立国际仲裁员,对于在成长道路上遇到好的老师领路,并且能够一直坚持走下来,我深感幸运。

2005 年我在杨先生办公室实习期间,杨先生正在撰写《仲裁法:从 1996 年英国仲裁法到国际商事仲裁》一书,而为杨先生写书提供协助也是当时我实习时的主要工作。现在看来,这本书是杨先生将写作领域从以海商、贸易法律为主转到以基础性的一般商业法律,包括合同法、证据法、仲裁法等为主的转折点。而这个转折也正好契合了国际仲裁随着全球化而蓬勃发展的轨迹,即从主要在海商、贸易领域发展到几乎所有的商业领域甚至非商业领域。

而当国际仲裁变为国际商业合同的"必需"之后,普通法也因历史的原因以及其肯定、务实与全面的优点而受到国际商业人士的欢迎与被选择作为合同的适用法。对越来越多参与国际商业活动的中国企业与律师来说,这类基础性的商业法律的重要性更加凸显,原因在于这套基础理念和规则贯穿在所有商业交易中。

本书是普通法系合同法系列书籍的第四部,可以说在完成本书后,合同法领域的主要课题已经全部覆盖。本书主要针对影响合同效力的因素,包括虚假陈述、错误、非法、胁迫、显失公平的交易等。虽然中国法中也有相关的立法条文与诚实信用的帝王条款来针对这些课题,但是因为缺少细节和指引,无法应付复杂商业交易中会发生的各种困难与刁钻的情况。本书希望通过展现这些课题的细节,令读者了解这些课题在实务中的应用与相互之间的区别,从而为进一步完善法律带来一些启发。

在多年参与写书的过程中,我深刻体会到写书是一个非常好的系统性学习的过程。系统性学习的重要性在于令知识更加体系化,在面对各种实际问题时,能够很快找到解决问题的方向。在普通法的先例原则下,每一个先例都在告诉你现实中的商业交往如何进行,会发生哪些争议以及法官如何分析问题与适用法律去解决问题。这些鲜活的案例让理论与实务很好地结合在一起,即使个人无法真正从事各行各业,也可以通过这些先例了解各行各业。这是一个非常有趣的过程。

在今天信息极端容易获得的情况下,希望有更多的读者能够通过阅读好的内容开启学习与了解普通法之旅。

最后，我也感谢杨先生一路的指导，家人一直以来对我工作的全力支持，以及团队伙伴们的同心协力。

司　嘉

2023年8月

序　五

我自2012年开始参与杨良宜先生书籍的撰写工作，从最早文字上的编辑核稿，针对个别案例的研究与分析，到后来开始搜集整理材料与拟定个别章节的初稿，到现在有幸可以作为共同作者参与成书，这十余年的经历弥足珍贵。也为自己在有时间、精力与热情的年纪，有机会为此事业做出贡献而深感荣幸。

普通法（以及国际仲裁）中，有大量的针对各个不同专项课题的英文权威书籍。在早期成书后，还有多批水平很高的作者每隔几年进行更新，如《Chitty on Contracts》与《Snell's Equity》均已出到了第34版。这些权威书籍在多年改版后已经面面俱到、字字珠玑，也因此不会有太多解释，实际是当作索引工具使用。而且这些权威书籍针对的都是有相当基础的人士，需要整套知识框架做基础并结合大量案例阅读与学习，才能读得明白。这导致对不少中国读者而言，想要真正理解与掌握并在实践中马上应用是存在困难的。

我碰到不少朋友都问，如何能"快速上手"，这是因为在"走出去"的过程中碰到了大量实践问题。尤其是在普通法占据主导地位的国际商业活动中，遇到对手"出招"时没有解决的思路，更谈不上解决的办法。甚至由于对这套游戏规则不了解，有时都不知道对手"出招"。所以，想要提高自己的水平，是否要硬着头皮去读这些英文的权威书籍？读不明白的话，是否应该去读普通法的学位，或者去获取普通法地区律师的执业资格？但即使获取了学位，考取了资格，能否在竞争激烈的国际商业活动中立足也是要打上问号的。因此，杨先生近年来致力于完成这一整套包括合约法、证据法与仲裁法在内的中文书籍，为读者打造一条学习的"捷径"。杨先生在2016年完成《提单与其他付运单证》一书的写作后，就提到这可能是他最后一本有关国际航运与贸易的书籍，将来要把主要的时间与精力放在完成整套书籍的愿景上。后来也确实如此，先是专门针对合同法补充了比较急需的弃权与禁反言内容；之后更是专门针对不同的课题——证据法完成了两部书籍。

本书主要针对影响合约效力的多种因素，这是过往书籍中没有详细针对，但在实践中非常重要的课题。有趣的内容很多，例如：（1）虚假陈述/失实陈述/误述，这是近年来诉讼中普遍与常见的争议，也是新闻中常常出现的热点话题；（2）非法理论，在涉外诉讼中，中方常提出"非法"的抗辩，但却因为对国际规则缺乏了解而甚少成功；（3）胁迫理论，尤其是了解在商业谈判中采取了威胁违约等"过火"的行为可能构成经济胁迫而影响合约效力。

“学海无涯，而吾生有涯，以有涯随无涯，殆矣”。更不用说国际商业规则实际上随着社会、科技、世界局势的发展而快速更新与发展。我自己的切身感受是，在阅读过程中，并不是要死板地学习知识，更重要的是读通与思考为什么这是最佳做法以及能被普通法系与大陆法系国家接受与认可，以及熟悉这套思考问题的方法。这样也就能够在遇到任何问题时，都有解决问题的思路。这也是杨先生常说的要提高“思维水平”，“一理通，百理明”。

感谢杨先生一路以来对我的信任。本书的撰写也感谢所有团队成员的通力合作，才能在新冠疫情期间成书。还要感谢在书籍撰写工作中对我给予支持与帮助的各位师长与亲友。最后则是写书占用了生活中的大量时间，要借此机会向在撰写期间支持与体谅我的太太王梦洁女士致意。

最后希望能承前人之志。也希望能与更多师长、朋友在这条路上携手前行。

贡　航

2023 年 8 月

序　　六

博学之，审问之，慎思之，明辨之，笃行之。

——《中庸》

杨先生在《合约的履行、弃权与禁反言》一书的序言中提到，这是英美合约法的最后一本。但在之后的实践与构建系统性学习国际合约法的框架时，杨先生认为有必要将本书针对的影响合约效力的因素这一部分补全。并且随着写作的逐渐深入，本书的篇幅也从计划中的一册变为上下两册。

从2012年加入杨先生团队到现在已经有11年，所做的工作也从当初简单的文字校对到成为本书的共同作者。一路走来，我感觉学习的过程正如开头引用的名言，首先要有耐心与恒心去持续与广泛地阅读和学习，对其中有疑问的地方有针对性地提问请教，然后谨慎地思考，并在消化吸收后辨明正确的内容，最后将已内化的知识系统性地表达出来与应用到实践中。

就我这些年来的观察与体会而言，当今在运行的国际商贸与金融制度，英国法为主的普通法在近几百年来通过对无数涉及方方面面的争议案件审理并以立法去解释、演绎、填补与完善这套制度，令很多十分细致或罕见的商业领域的疑点都在普通法下有了肯定的说法或法律地位。我深信，如果能掌握英国合约法，国际商事活动中出现的大多数的问题及其解决都将有答案。至于剩下的部分，往往只需要有限的信息去确定自己已经有了初步答案，如需要看有关的某外国国家的法律有什么具体不同的规定或某专业人士的意见。在缩小了范围后，也很容易知道向谁提问与怎么提问，对方提供了答案后，也可知道有否帮助或需要追问，甚至是否需要多寻找一个意见作为对比。但如果不了解英国合约法而对问题没有底，即使向称职的律师咨询，也会由于不知道真正的争议点在哪里与无法给出正确的信息，而得不到正确的答案。毕竟差之毫厘，谬以千里，错误的问题只能带来错误的答案。

在目前全球化的背景下，企业在全球进行投资与交易，中国企业需要的涉外法律人才是“指挥官”与统筹整场“商战”类型的人才，而要具备这项能力，掌握一套全面与适用广泛的规则（普通法）是基本的要求。俗话说“千军易得，良将难求”。所谓良将，要能判断谁是可以信赖与委以重任的士兵，在每场不同的战役中应该采取怎样的战术，就必须熟读兵法。在国际商事领域中，这兵法就是普通法/合约法。

有人说，人常常会高估自己一年可以完成的事，也常常会低估自己十年可以完成的事。也有人说，选择比坚持更关键，所以重要的是坚持走在正确的路上。有了杨先生这套系统介绍普通法最重要法律（合约法、证据法、仲裁法）的书籍，相信读者只要坚持学习与应用在实践中，十年内变为国际一流的"指挥官"是完全可能的。

王可心

2023 年 8 月

目　　录

第一章　误述或虚假/不正确陈述

不正确陈述或虚假陈述[1](misrepresentation 或 misstatement)(以下简称误述)是每一个人都会经常遇到的情况,不论是自己作为误述方(misrepresentor)或是作为接收别人误述的被误述方(misrepresentee)。这是因为误述在日常生活中、社交中或是商业活动中都会发生。不同情况下,误述会带来不同的法律后果,所以有必要去做出区分。总的来说在商业的范畴中,普通法下的误述可发生在以下几种情况中:

1. 误述令误述方与被误述方之间订立一个合约,这是最传统的误述,习惯上被称为可诉误述(actionable misrepresentation),也有相应的法律后果与救济,主要是在普通法下被误述方或受害方有权撤销(rescind)[2]该合约。即使误述方是完全无辜(innocent)作出误述,也不影响这个权利。毕竟,在误述下产生的合约显然本身有缺陷,难说是双方对整个合约的方方面面都有一致想法/意见(meeting of minds 或 ad idem)。

2. 误述并没有令误述方与被误述方订立合约,这就与合约关系无关,即使有可以索赔的诉因也是侵权。但普通法只要求对事实的一般陈述诚实(honest),因为如果不诚实就可能涉及欺骗的侵权(tort of deceit)。[3] 而如果没有不诚实,只是疏忽(无

---

〔1〕 中国内地读者比较习惯的叫法是虚假陈述或不实陈述。笔者在本书不使用这种叫法,因为虚假陈述或不实陈述有故意欺骗的感觉,也就是相等于本书中的欺诈性误述。但在现实中,很多情况是陈述方无心之失,诚实地(无论是疏忽或是无辜)作出了不正确的陈述。

〔2〕 误述撤销合约权利(rescission)与合约在其他情况下(如毁约/违约)被终止(terminate)也经常被说成是"rescind"带来了混乱,正如在 Mussen v. Van Dieman's Land Co(1938)Ch 253 先例中,Farwell 大法官说:"No doubt the word 'rescission' or the word 'rescind' is capable of two meanings. The rescission of a contract may mean **putting an end to it altogether, that is to say, making it null and void ab initio**, or it may mean putting an end to it except so far as any obligation or right which rises under the contract if and when so determined."(加黑部分是笔者的强调)

〔3〕 在 Vald. Nielsen Holding A/S v. Baldorino(2019)EWHC 1926(Comm)先例中,Jacobs 大法官在 130-159 段对"民事欺诈/欺骗侵权"有很详尽的总结,他指出欺诈/欺骗的基本要求就是被告对原告作出不正确的陈述,说:"The tort of deceit requires the claimant to show that: (i) the defendants made false representations to the claimants; (ii) the defendants knew the representations to be false, or had no belief in their truth, or were reckless as to whether they were true or false; (iii) the defendants intended the claimants to rely on the representations; (iv) the claimants did rely on the representations; and (v) as a result the claimants have suffered loss and damage …"另在 European Real Estate Debt Fund(Cayman)Ltd (In Liquidation) v. Treon(2021)EWHC 2866(Ch)先例中,Males 大法官也是同样判法。

心之失)甚至完全无辜的误述,就不会构成侵权并产生诉因。但如果误述方与被误述方之间存在一个法律认可的小心谨慎的责任(duty of care),这就需要误述方对自己在疏忽下做出的误述对被误述方负疏忽的侵权(tort of negligence)责任。

3. 合约已经存在,双方在履行时发生的疏忽或欺诈性误述。这往往也是违约(breach of contract)的情况,违反的会是明示条文,也会是法律默示的地位。[4] 后者如默示要求双方给予协助/合作让对方顺利履行合约,合约一方不能通过自己的错误获利,或在英国法下越来越多类别的合约有对善意(good - faith)的要求。在疏忽或欺诈性误述,除了违约外,也可能同时是构成侵权的言行。这样,就会带来同步责任(concurrent liability),导致合约与侵权的混合诉讼。

4. 在一般情况下随口或在商业社交场合上提供信息与事实,双方没有合约关系(contractual relationship)或特殊关系(special relationship),法律只要求诚实,即不要骗人就不会因提供错误信息与事实而负上法律/侵权的责任,否则就可能构成"欺诈/欺骗"(fraud/deceit)的侵权与/或刑事犯罪。因为合约关系有严格或绝对责任,而特殊关系下法律会强加一个小心谨慎责任,即使是无心之失也要承担责任。正如 Reid 勋爵在 Mutual Life and Citizens Assurance Co Ltd v. Evatt(1971)AC 793 枢密院先例中说:"… the first principle is that no duty beyond the duty to give an honest answer can arise when advice is given casually or in a social context, and the reason is that it would be quite unreasonable for the inquirer to expect more in such circumstances and quite unreasonable to impose any greater duty on the adviser. The law must keep in step with the habits of the reasonable man and consider whether ordinary people would think they had some obligation beyond merely giving an honest answer."

换言之,在这种明确的法律地位下,即使陈述方是一位顶尖专家,如果他/她只是在社交场合随口一提自己的专家意见,不严肃与不正规(这表示有错误或遗漏的机会也相对较高),第三人也不应过度依赖作出重要的决定,否则蒙受损失也不能要求该专家承担法律责任。

1. 误述导致一个合约产生

这种误述应是传统的合约法下的误述,是在订约前谈判的阶段,订约的一方对现在(present)或过去(past)的事实作出了不正确的陈述,而另一方完全或部分依赖(rely)该不正确的陈述("误述")达成合约,即已存在法律上认为的可诉误述。

在传统的普通法下,因误述的存在,订约双方在订约意图以及想法一致方面存在重大缺陷,很难说存在双方均对合约所有内容有全面、自主与知悉后的同意(full, free

[4] 关于合约的默示条文可见笔者《合约的解释:规则与应用》一书第七章。

and informed consent),所以他有权选择撤销(rescind)合约与复原(*restitutio in integrum*)[5]的做法,回复到没有这个有缺陷的合约的地位。误述导致或产生的合约是一个可使无效(voidable)的合约。其他同样是可使无效的合约的情形,如胁迫(duress)、[6]不当影响(undue influence)、[7]显失公平/不合情理交易(unconscionable bargain/contract),[8]自始无效(void ab intio)的合约情形,如错误(mistake),[9]或是有大同小异的后果的合约涉及非法/不法(illegal/unlawful),[10]都与误述产生的合约一样,可以因合约的订立本身存在重大缺陷或违反公共政策而被撤销或不被法院协助执行。

对于自始无效与可使无效这两种合约效力的区分,可节录《Chitty on Contracts》(2021 年,第 34 版)一书之 1 – 074 段所述:"A **void contract** is strictly a contradiction in terms, because if a contract is truely void it is not a contract at all; but the term is a useful one and well understood by lawyers. Properly speaking, a void contract should produce no legal effects whatsoever. Neither party should be able to sue the other on the contract. If goods have been delivered, they or their value should be recoverable by an action in tort, because the property will not pass. If money has been paid, it should be recoverable by an action in restitution, because the money was not due."

另 1 – 076 段所述如下:"A **voidable contract** is one where one or more of its parties have the power, by a manifestation of election to do so, to avoid the legal relations created by the contract; or by affirmation of the contract to extinguish the power of avoidance. In English law, contracts may be voidable, e. g. for misrepresentation, duress, undue influence, minority, lack of mental capacity, drunkenness or under statute. If the contract is wholly executory, the party entitled to avoid the contract can plead its voidability in an action against him. If it has been wholly or partly executed, he can claim to have set it aside and to be restored to his original position. But until the right of avoidance is exercised, the contract is valid."

---

〔5〕 撤销与复原的课题将在本书第三章详细探讨。

〔6〕 这个课题会在本书第十章介绍。

〔7〕 这个课题会在本书第十一章之 1 段介绍。

〔8〕 这个课题会在本书第十一章之 2 段介绍。

〔9〕 这个课题会在本书第七章介绍。

〔10〕 非法的一般后果是合约不可执行(non-enforceable),是程序问题而非实质问题,一方申请执行合约的要求不会得到法院支持。正如《Chitty on Contract》(2021 年,第 34 版)一书之 18 – 047 段所说如下:"The 'effect of illegality is not substantive but procedural', it prevents the plaintiff from enforcing the illegal transaction… illegal contracts are not devoid of legal effect, but the ex turpi causa maxim may entail that no action on the contract can be maintained."但也有一些自始无效的情况,如违反限制商贸(restraint of trade)的公共政策,或一些立法明确特定类型与情况的合约无效。这个课题会在本书第八章与第九章介绍。

在现实商业社会合约自始无效的情况不多，少数的情况如错误又很难成立。更多的情况是在订立时有缺陷的合约在现实上仍然可以履行，法律上给出的救济是可使无效的救济而不是自始无效的救济。而衡平法(equity law)的可使无效救济，由于法院有裁量权与可以灵活处理，兼顾所有当事人/有关人士的合法利益。其中一个主要的考虑是保护无辜第三方，另外在复原有困难的案件中去找出一个实际公平(practically just)的处理方法等。

在这些有重大缺陷的合约中，误述发生的频率比错误或非法、胁迫高得多，所以一直以来，特别是近年来大金额的商业交易如公司并购、金融投资/投机等发生频密，其中涉及误述争议的案件更是特别多。所以，本书前六章都针对误述，之后的章节会区别针对错误、胁迫与非法。

在普通法下，所谓的误述只针对导致合约产生的可诉误述，可简单节录《Chitty on Contracts》(2021 年，第 34 版)一书之 9－004 段所述："Before the Misrepresentation Act was passed, the law relating to misrepresentation was generally concerned solely with misrepresentations made before the contract was entered into, and not to misrepresentations which actually constituted contractual terms."

1.1　误述在法律上的演变

一直以来，普通法针对在欺诈性误述(fraudulent misrepresentation)诱导(induce)下订立的合约有额外的救济，在允许受害方撤销合约外，还可以欺骗侵权(tortious action of deceit)的诉因获得对蒙受的损失的赔偿。这很公道，的确有不少欺诈性误述根本是以骗人的手法诱导对方订立合约，本质与非法胁迫一样恶劣。但普通法对非欺诈性(non-fraudulent)误述(这包括真正的无辜误述与疏忽误述)没有任何救济，无论是撤销或是索赔损失。因为普通法不会在谈判时强加一个小心谨慎责任，[11] 只要求诚实。

到了 19 世纪，衡平法允许撤销非欺诈性误述诱导所产生的合约，但受害方无法进一步索赔金钱上的损失，因为赔偿金钱损失是普通法法院的权利：见 Attwood v. Small(1838)6 Cl. & F. 232 贵族院先例。这直到普通法法院与衡平法法院在《Judicature Acts 1873》下合并后，才不再需要区分去哪个法院寻求什么救济。只要是误述导致合约的产生，不管是欺诈性或非欺诈性，一概可让被误述方撤销合约。

非欺诈性误述会是真正的无辜误述(innocent misrepresentation)，即陈述方是在有完全合理依据(reasonable grounds)的情况下讲错了事实。但也包括更多会是疏忽的误述(negligent misrepresentation)，如没有合理小心谨慎查清楚与有了足够与合理的知识/能力就陈述，与/或作出的陈述没有合理依据。普通法没有对真正的无辜误

〔11〕 小心谨慎责任只适用在疏忽侵权(tort of negligence)，与欺诈/欺骗侵权(tort of deceit)没有关系。一旦发生涉及人为的事故去追究责任，总会能找到人为疏忽，分别只在多少或轻重。但不论疏忽程度，只要是造成事故的有效原因之一，在法律上都是违反小心谨慎责任。

述与疏忽误述作出区分，一并视为非欺诈性的无辜误述，直到重要的 Hedley Byrne v. Heller（1964）AC 465 贵族院先例与《Misrepresentation Act 1967》〔12〕的立法后才有了改变。

英国法律在 Hedley Byrne 先例前，对疏忽误述（无论是否产生合约）的说法既不重视也不接受，也只规定在误述诱导合约产生的情况可作出撤销合约的衡平救济，但不能索赔金钱损失。普通法也视合约的谈判中，订约双方之间对对方只有一个诚实责任不去欺诈/欺骗，并没有一个小心谨慎的责任去避免疏忽与错误让对方可以安心依赖。只有在双方有特殊关系（special relationship）或诚信关系（fiduciary relationship）时，普通法才认为在政策上强加一个小心谨慎的责任是公平合理。这种情况传统上主要是在享有专业或技巧的一方（他们会是专业人士或商业上关系）向另一方提供意见与信息，也可预期另一方很可能会依赖去作出重大决定时才会有此责任。例如他们是律师、会计师、经纪人等专业人士给客户提供意见。陈述方必须要小心谨慎与有合理依据支持这意见与信息是正确的，往往要"做功课"与深思熟虑后，才可以说这对一些复杂问题的回答是有合理依据，陈述方只是诚实并不够。

但如果双方没有合约或特殊关系，即使是这些专业人士，法律仍只要求诚实，即只要不要骗人就不会因提供错误信息与事实而负法律/侵权的责任。这表示如果并非专业或商业上被第三人要求提供信息与事实，如一位著名银行家或律师在晚宴中被同桌的一位朋友提出询问，他/她可以有三种恰当的应对。一是拒绝提供，二是提供并作出不承担任何责任的声明（disclaimer），三是诚实提供所知道的信息与事实。但他没有小心谨慎责任确认提供信息与事实的正确与完整，也不会预期对方会依赖他的陈述作出一个重大决定。

在 Hedley Byrne 贵族院先例中，Heller 银行在无偿的情况下向 Hedley Byrne 提供存户错误的资信，并导致 Hedley Byrne 蒙受金钱损失，贵族院判 Heller 银行有责任并要作出赔偿。这一重要先例带来很多改变，也显示了误述的适用是比传统的想法广泛得多。另也显示疏忽误述的危险与可以适用在纯经济损失（pure economical losses），〔13〕无论双方是否有合约关系或诚信关系，也无论陈述方是否是专业人士。充其量，Heller 银行有一些特殊的信息是被误述方不拥有的，否则对方也不会提问。但如果一方比另一方有较多信息就足以构成双方有"特殊关系"并产生小心谨慎的责

〔12〕《Misrepresentation Act 1967》立法在本书第四章有详细介绍。

〔13〕英国法律一直对侵权索赔纯经济损失很谨慎，主要是考虑到害怕打开泄洪阀（floodgate）导致没完没了的诉讼。被侵权方要索赔必须有实质损失（physical loss），然后才可以加上索赔间接经济损失（consequential economic loss）。实质损失也容易满足疏忽侵权对"邻近"（proximity）的要求。但纯经济损失就不一样了。疏忽言行中，语言上的疏忽往往只是造成纯经济损失，但疏忽行为则通常造成实质损失（不论是人命伤亡或财产）。所以前者的语言上疏忽侵权的诉讼大门在 Hedley Byrne 先例与《Misrepresentation Act 1967》立法后才打开。关于这方面可见本章之 2.2.1 段与本书第四章，另在笔者《损失赔偿与救济》一书第八章之 5 段有详细的介绍。

任,会否口子开得太大?

在接下来的 Mutual Life and Citizens Assurance Co Ltd v. Evatt(1971)AC 793 先例中,案情将在本章之 2.2.2 段介绍。枢密院(Privy Council)的多数意见的判决将重点放在了提供信息的一方到底是否经营这方面业务与/或拥有有关的技巧与能力,并且愿意尽职给出可靠意见,如果没有,就只有给出诚实回答的责任。枢密院的多数意见说这一点在 Hedley Byrne 先例里没有针对,等于避开了是否与 Hedley Byrne 先例持不同看法的问题。而少数意见认为在这问题上应该根据不同案情去弹性处理,不应该限制得这么紧。

由于枢密院的决定,不是贵族院,所以也不严格对英国下级法院有约束力(stare decisis doctrine),[14] 只能是有说服力(persuasive power)。所以在 Howard Marine and Dredging Co Ltd v. A Ogden & Sons(Excavations)Ltd(1978)QB 574 上诉庭先例中,Denning 勋爵选择依从 Mutual Life and Citizens Assurance Co Ltd v. Evatt 先例中的少数意见。区分有否像 Hedley Byrne 先例的陈述方提供信息与事实违反小心谨慎责任的侵权后果,是要看向误述方提问的严肃性(gravity of inquiry),即是否是严肃与正规提出,或只是在一个随意的场合(即使属于商业范畴)中大家在闲谈中提出的问题。另要看是否预期收到的回答会是一个深思熟虑的意见(considered advice)并且对方知道提问方会依赖它行事(act on it in a particular way)。这种不同案情的区分也区分了法律责任到底是需要小心谨慎(这往往表示需要调查取证、深思熟虑后才能提供,特别是复杂的信息与意见)或只需要诚实。

如果双方掌握的信息是一面倒,即订约的一方(如卖方对有关货物)有全面的信息与知识,而另一方完全要依赖对方提供的信息与协助来决定是否订约以及如何议价,纯是在合约谈判中,掌握信息的一方在陈述时也有一个小心谨慎的责任。当然这也要看谈判双方一问一答的情况与环境的严肃性,与所采用的措辞/文字(如是否是泛泛地提问或回答)等。这样,才考虑在个别案件是否例外地强加给陈述方一个小心谨慎责任,一旦违反就构成侵权。如 Esso Petroleum Co Ltd v. Mardon(1976)2 Lloyd's Rep 305;Howard Marine and Dredging Co Ltd v. A Ogden & Sons(Excavations)Ltd 等先例。

根据英国法律,在不属于例外的情况下,即使是疏忽误述,只要程度上没有达致欺诈性误述,受害方仍是只能寻求衡平法下撤销合约的救济,[15] 但无法索赔损失。无辜误述是更不用说了,索赔损失更是根本没有基础与可能,唯一的救济就是在衡平

---

[14] 见 Great Western Railway Co v. SS Mostyn(Owners)(1928)AC 57;Wilkinson v. Sisley(1932)1 KB 194 等先例。

[15] 衡平法下的救济与普通法下的救济不同。前者是侧重在损失赔偿不能弥补的情况,所以主要是撤销合约、颁布禁令、履约指令等,仅在有立法的情况下才有例外,例如会在本书第四章之 5.4.2 段介绍的《Lord Cairns' Act 1858》。

法下撤销有关被误导订立的合约。这是因为在普通法下,受害方只能索赔违约造成的金钱损失。而误述导致合约撤销,没有合约也就不存在违约一说。即使不撤销合约,订约前的误述也不属于履行中的违约,所以也就无法索赔了。至于欺诈性误述索赔金钱损失,不是以合约法为依据,而是欺骗侵权。

这导致受害方在非欺诈性误述(无辜或疏忽)下,向误述方索赔的唯一办法是成立一个附带协议或附带保证(collateral contract or warranty)。这方面在本章之2.5.2段有涉及,在此只是先强调要成立一个附带保证并非易事,但这不能无中生有,要有事实根据。比方买卖一辆车(也可以是一套房屋,或是一艘船舶),卖方说这车是新的,但事实上它是二手车,这即是误述。它可以是欺诈性的,卖方故意去欺骗买方。但它也可以是无辜的,比如卖方自己也是给供应汽车的车行和有关资料误导了。至于有否一个附带保证,只是没有记录在双方谈判后签署的文字合约内,是要看有关谈判的口头证据(parol evidence)去认定到底发生了什么。如果在谈判时,买方对此汽车是否全新有疑问,卖方为了成交,向买方说:"你只要肯买这车,我可保证这车是新的。"这很明显有一个附带保证或协议。但如果卖方只是将新车这项与其他很多关于该汽车的资料给买方看,这并不容易指称卖方对其中的一项误述是有一个附带保证或协议。

看来,法院是不愿意轻易认定有附带协议或保证把新内容增加在一份看来是完整记录的合约中。道理好像要求法院在一份合约双方合意签署,把双方所有在谈判中同意的条文细节全部记录在内的合约中,增加一条事实默示(implied by fact)的条文一样。类似的,法院也不会轻易认定合约记录有错,从而命令变更合约(rectification)。[16] 附带协议或保证虽然是另一种默示,但困难比默示条文有过之而无不及。双方肯定也是对此默示的附带协议或保证有异议,否则也不必打官司。但法院或仲裁庭又不是合约方,只是根据法律去自说自话在双方有争议的情况下增加内容。但如果不这样做,就无法在普通法下索赔一个看来是十分严重的疏忽误述(但仍证明不了是欺诈性误述)导致的损失。

这种种的困难,到了有了《Misrepresentation Act 1967》才得到改善。在该立法下,让无辜或疏忽的误述的受害方都可获得金钱损失的赔偿。该1967年立法的目的不是改变普通法/侵权法,而是企图去扩大受害方可以在各种不同的误述下获得损失赔偿的范围,正如Hamblen大法官在Cassa di Risparmio della Repubblica di San Marino SpA v. Barclays Bank Ltd(2011)EWHC 484(Comm)先例中说:"The fact that Parliament ... has thought it right to provide a broad measure of compensation where a contract has been made as a result of a misrepresentation should not affect the prior question whether there has been a misrepresentation."

---

〔16〕 关于合约变更可见笔者《合约的解释:规则与应用》一书第三章之13段的介绍,由于变更合约有重写(rewrite)双方订立的合约的风险,所以法院会十分谨慎。

需要强调的是，1967年的立法仍只是针对误述导致一个合约产生的情况，不针对非合约的误述如Hedley Byrne贵族院先例的误述，这仍是侵权法的范畴，根据公共政策考虑是否需要给特殊关系下的陈述方强加一个小心谨慎的责任。在《Misrepresentation Act 1967》之Sections 1、2(1)与2(2)都写明："Where a person has entered into a contract after a misrepresentation has been made to him ..."

最后跳到英国法律目前对误述的地位，这可节录Foxton大法官在近期的SK Shipping Plc v. Capital VLCC 3 Corp(2020) EWHC 3448(Comm)先例中所说如下：

"The general principles of the law relating to actionable misrepresentation were not substantially in dispute. I have gratefully adopted the following summary of the law from the judgment of Mr Justice Jacobs in Vald. Nielsen Holding A/S v. Baldorino [2019] EWHC 1926(Comm), ... which draws on earlier authority, and which I have supplemented by the further authority cited to me by the parties.

First, the defendant must establish that a representation was made(首先要证明对方有作出陈述)：

i) A representation is a statement of fact[17] made by the representor to the representee on which the representee is intended and entitled to rely[18] as a positive assertion that the fact is true.(陈述是陈述方向被陈述方作出的对事实的表述，被陈述方有意图与有权依赖陈述方主张的事实为真。)

ii) Determining whether any and if so what representation was made by a statement involves(1) construing the statement in the context in which it was made, and(2) interpreting the statement objectively according to the impact it might be expected to have on a reasonable representee in the position and with the known characteristics of those to whom the representation is being made. [决定是否存在陈述与陈述的具体内容时涉及：(1)根据表述的背景/语境解释表述的内容；(2)根据有关表述会对一位合理人士会造成什么影响，去客观解释有关表述。而该合理人士与被陈述方有同样的地位，也与被陈述方有一样的、且陈述方应知悉的特质。]

iii) A statement of opinion[19] is not in itself actionable but is invariably regarded as incorporating an assertion that the maker does actually hold that opinion. Further, at least where the facts are not equally well known to both sides, a statement of opinion by one who knows the facts best may carry with it a further implication of fact,[20] namely that the representor by expressing that opinion impliedly states that he believes that facts exist

---

〔17〕 见本书第二章之1.1段。

〔18〕 见本章之1.3段。

〔19〕 见本书第二章之2段。

〔20〕 见本书第二章之3.4段。

which reasonably justify it.（对意见的表述本身不会构成误述，但是这种表述同时包含了陈述方主张其确实持有这个意见。特别是当双方对事实的了解程度完全不对等时，更了解事实真相的一方的表述会默示其明示意见所基于的事实确实存在。）

iv) Silence by itself cannot found a claim in misrepresentation. But an express statement may impliedly represent something. In relation to implied representations the 'court has to consider what a reasonable person would have inferred was being implicitly represented by the representor's words and conduct in their context'〔21〕[Toulson J in IFE v. Goldman Sachs (2006) EWHC 2887 (Comm) ...]. That involves considering whether a reasonable representee in the position and with the known characteristics of the actual representee would reasonably have understood that an implied representation〔22〕 was being made and being made substantially in the terms or to the effect alleged.（沉默本身不会构成误述，但是明示的表述可以默示对某些事实作出了陈述。在决定是否存在默示陈述时，法院会考虑一位与被陈述方处于同样地位且有同样特质的合理人士会推断在有关的背景/语境下，陈述方的言行默示了什么。）

v) In a deceit case it is also necessary that the representor should understand that he is making the implied representation and that it had the misleading sense alleged. A person cannot make a fraudulent statement unless he is aware that he is making that statement.〔23〕To establish liability in deceit it is necessary 'to show that the representor intended his statement to be understood by the representee in the sense in which it was false' [Morritt LJ in Goose v. Wilson Sandford & Co (2001) Lloyd's Rep PN 189...].（要证明欺骗，也要证明陈述方知道自己作出了默示陈述并在误导被陈述方。如果陈述方没有意识到自己的陈述错误，就不能说他欺诈性误述。所以欺骗的责任要成立，就必须证明陈述方有意识地希望被陈述方对有关陈述的理解就是错误的事实。）

Second, the representation must be false. A representation may be true without being entirely correct, provided that it is substantially correct and the difference between what is represented and what is actually correct would not have been likely to induce a reasonable person in the position of the claimant to enter into the contracts: Rix J in Avon Insurance v. Swire Fraser [2000] Lloyd's Rep IR 535....（第二，有关陈述必须是错误的。一个陈述可能整体来说是真实的尽管细节并非完全正确，但只要实质上是正确的，其中与真相的差异一般不足以被认为会诱导一位合理人士订立原本不会订立的合约。）

Third, for the statement to have been made fraudulently（第三，对于欺诈性陈述）:

i) One of the two mental states established in Derry v. Peek (1889) 14 App Cas 337

---

〔21〕 见本书第二章之 1.4.1 段。

〔22〕 见本书第二章之 1.4 段。

〔23〕 见本书第三章之 8.2.1 段。

must be established:the statement must have been made knowing it is untrue,or recklessly, not caring whether it is true or not.[24](陈述方明确知道表述是错误或虚假,或鲁莽与不顾后果地不管真假执意作出自己的表述。这两种陈述方的心理状态或想法必须成立才构成欺诈性误述。)[25]

ii)The requirements for proving that a misrepresentation was made fraudulently must not be watered down into something akin to negligence,however gross. However,the unreasonableness of the grounds of the belief,though not of itself supporting an action for deceit,will be evidence from which fraud may be inferred.(对于欺诈性误述的要求不能被弱化为类似于疏忽,不管是多重大的疏忽。但是,如果客观看来陈述方认为陈述为真的理由并不合理与说不通,虽然这本身不能用来支持构成欺骗,但是可以作为推断存在欺诈性误述的证据之一。)

iii)Actionable fraud involves an intention on the part of the representor to induce the representee to act as he did. It is not necessary for the representor to intend to induce the specific action taken by the representee in reliance on the misrepresentation. It is only necessary that there should be an intention that the representation should be acted on.(欺诈性误述要求陈述方有意图诱导被陈述方作出有关行为。这不需要是某个特定行为,只要是陈述方有意图让被陈述方依赖有关错误陈述行事即可。)

iv)The standard of proof in a case of fraud is the balance of probabilities.[26](民事诉讼中欺诈的举证责任仍然是平衡的可能性。)

Fourth,the representee must show that he in fact understood the statement in the sense(so far as material)which the court ascribes to it,and that,having that understanding,he relied on it. The general principles applicable where a misrepresentation is said to have induced the making of a contract are set out in Chitty on Contracts...In this regard, it is important to keep two distinctions well in mind:the distinction between fraudulent and non-fraudulent misrepresentations;and the distinction between what the misrepresentee must establish in order to be in a position to rescind a contract for a pre-contractual misrepresentation and what must be shown in order to be able to recover damages for loss suffered as a result of entering into a contract.(第四,被陈述方必须证明他确实像法院认定的理解一样去理解有关的陈述/表述,并且依赖这个理解行事。救济方面有两方面的区分:一个是欺诈性误述与非欺诈性误述的区别;另一个是被陈述方想要撤销合约与想要索赔订立合约造成的损失时,要证明的事情的区别。)

---

〔24〕 见本书第三章之8.2段。

〔25〕 关于怎样证明思想状态,在笔者2021年出版的《证据法:基础理论、口头证据与专家证据》一书第十章有详论。

〔26〕 在笔者《证据法:基础理论、口头证据与专家证据》一书第七章之7.2.1.2段有详细介绍。

The principles are as follows:[27]（大原则如下）

i) For rescission, it is not necessary that the misrepresentation should be the sole cause which induced the representee to make the contract. It is sufficient if it can be shown to have been one of the inducing causes.（被陈述方想要撤销合约并不需要证明误述是导致其订立合约的唯一原因，只要证明是其中一个原因就已经足够。）

ii) However, where a party has entered a contract after a misrepresentation has been made to it other than fraudulently, it will not have a remedy unless it would not have entered the contract (or not on the same terms) but for the misrepresentation.［但如果是非欺诈性误述，除非被陈述方能证明如果不是有这个误述自己不会订立合约（或是不会接受同样的条件/条文），否则不会有救济。］

iii) In cases of fraud, however, if the representee seeks to rescind, it is no defence for the representor to show that if the misrepresentation had not been made, the misrepresentee might still have made the contract. It is sufficient if there is evidence to show that he was materially influenced by the misrepresentation in the sense that it had some impact on his thinking, or as it is sometimes put, 'was actively present to his mind': BV Nederlandse Industrie van Eidprodukten v. Rembrandt Enterprises Inc [2020] QB 551....（但欺诈性误述，如果被陈述方要求撤销合约，陈述方不能以就算没有该误述，被陈述方仍会订立合约抗辩。被陈述方只需要证明该误述对他的想法有影响就足够。）

iv) Once it is proved that a false statement was made which is 'material' in the sense that it was likely to induce the contract, and that the representee entered the contract, it is a fair inference of fact (though not an inference of law) that he was induced by the statement.［如果能够证明错误陈述是'重要'，也就是客观看可能导致一位合理人士订立合约，并且被陈述方确实订立了合约，可以作出是该误述诱导订立合约的事实推断（不是法律推断）。］

v) The inference is particularly strong where the misrepresentation is fraudulent. In BV Nederlandse Industrie Van Eidprodukten v. Rembrandt Enterprises Inc, ... the Court of Appeal held that in deceit cases 'there is an evidential presumption of fact (not law) that a representee will have been induced by a fraudulent misrepresentation intended to cause him to enter the contract and that the inference will be "very difficult to rebut"...'［特别是在欺诈性误述，存在误述方是希望诱导订立合约的事实推定，误述方要承担反驳的举证责任（该误述没有导致合约的订立），但这个事实推定很难推翻。］

vi) It is sometimes said that a misrepresentation will not be effective to ground relief in law unless it was material, in the sense that a reasonable person would have been influenced by it in deciding whether to enter into the contract, although there is no clear au-

---

〔27〕 以下有关诱导与依赖的介绍可见本章之1.3段。

thority denying relief to a representee who has in fact been influenced by a misrepresentation which would not have influenced a reasonable person. In cases of fraud, the representor is not permitted to argue that itwas unforeseeable that the representee would be influenced by the lie. [有说法是误述必须是重要,也就是一位合理人士(诉讼是由法官或仲裁员代入)在决定是否订立合约时会被影响。但目前没有明确先例否定当被陈述方确实受了一般合理人士不会被影响的陈述影响时,可以获得救济。但在欺诈性误述,陈述方不得争辩他无法预见被陈述方会受该谎言影响(例如说我的谎言与误述漏洞百出,真没想到对方会愚蠢到相信并依赖去行事)]。

vii) When a claimant seeks damages, whether for negligent or fraudulent misrepresentation, for loss which it alleges it has suffered by entering into a contract on particular terms as a result of that misrepresentation, the court must find that it would not have entered into the contract on those terms but for the misrepresentation: ... To this extent, in fraud cases there is a difference between what must be shown in order to obtain rescission of a contract, and what must be shown to recover damages. [如果被陈述方要索赔因订立合约而造成的金钱损失,无论是疏忽的误述还是欺诈性误述,[28]都要证明如果不是因为误述不会订立合约(或以同样的条件/条文订立合约)。对欺诈性误述来说,这与撤销合约的救济的举证责任不同与更高。]”

上述对英国法律针对误述的大原则的总结看来是冗长、复杂与令人似懂非懂。这是因为人性,加上国际商业社会越来越复杂,骗人与误导的手法也越来越多且越来越隐蔽,法律也必须与时俱进。看了本章更详尽的介绍后读者应该会更明了,希望中国读者在了解了这些内容后,能够在受英国法律很大影响的国际商业社会,更好掌握讲话与听取他人表述时轻重的技巧。

1.2 法律对误述的轻重掌握

对是否构成误述的轻重要掌握好,过了火会影响正常的社会活动,特别是商业活动,如没人敢做广告或是推销商品等。这也会影响法律在其他方面对风险的分摊,如货物买卖是要买方自己小心(let the buyers be aware 或拉丁文的 Caveat emptor)。[29]

但不过火之余,也要防止隐瞒短处,明知对方需要依赖仍提供明知不正确的信息与事实,甚至是无中生有或凭想象制造假消息。同时,也要兼顾社会上一般人的做法。例如,在一间二手房的买卖,卖方常会重新装修以吸引买方。对买方而言,也应知道老龄的二手房总有点毛病,在买方自己要小心的原则下,他应小心检查并知道检查什么地方,不应将卖方的新装修指责为误述。但如果卖方隐瞒了二手房的严重缺点(如用木板挡住破洞)或是误述这房子在 1 年前大修过等,后果就会不一样了。一

---

〔28〕 关于欺诈性误述的损失计算也可见本书第四章之 4.2.2 段。

〔29〕 这也是《Sale of Goods Act 1979》之 Section 14(1)的规定,在杨大明律师《国际货物买卖》一书第四章之 1 段有介绍。

般法律是以客观看一位诚实与合理人士（在诉讼中也就是法官、陪审团或仲裁员代人）会怎么认为与怎样做作为分水岭（watershed）/红线（red line）。

误述的法律也发展了很多方面的重要细节。例如传统的误述只能是针对事实，而不是法律（指英国法）方面。道理是每个人都应懂法［至少是一般法律（general law）］，而且法律是完全公开的资料，不像在事实方面那样。所以一方被对方误述法律而上当的，法律是保护不了的，无知并不是抗辩理由。但显然这种假设人人懂法并不贴合现实，也容易造成与鼓励懂法的人去误导不懂法的人但没有法律后果。所以在 Kleinwort Benson Ltd v. Lincoln City Council（1999）2 AC 349 贵族院先例后，这方面也有了改变，导致对法律的误述（即使是无辜或疏忽）也有法律后果，只要是对方作出依赖与误述方也预期对方会依赖。

至于事实的陈述，肯定是指对方不知悉的事实，所以才要依赖陈述方的陈述去订立合约。传统的说法是误述的事实也应只是过去（past）或现在（present）的事实，而不是针对将来的预测或预期。毕竟将来尚未发生，不会是事实，而且人生不如意之事十之八九，现实中预期落空大有所在。但这会带来不公平的情况，也允许懂法或精明的一方以预期的表达方式去接近欺骗另一方，并明知另一方会依赖，但没有任何后果。例如，甲与乙订立一个贷款合约，其中是乙借给甲一笔钱，甲告知乙预期利用这笔钱做一项有 20% 回报的投资，但根本不是这回事。

判断预测或预期是否构成误述的另一个困难是难以知道被指称误述的人士在预测或预期时脑袋里到底是在想什么。如果不知道与证明不了他是想骗人，就难以指控欺诈性误述让受害方可以索赔金钱损失。这在 Edgington v. Fitzmaurice（1885）29 Ch. D. 459 先例中有了指引，并在笔者 2021 年出版的《证据法：基础理论、口头证据与专家证据》一书第十章中有详论，此处不再重复。

接着笔者将举两个在中国十分频密发生的商业活动的例子，以加深上述有关误述的简介。

1.2.1 例子之一：海上货物保险

这种情况在很多商业活动会发生，如保险，很多情况是受保人（assured）在风险还没有开始时就需要投保，如一批货物需要付运去外国。所以受保人向保险人（insurer）披露的信息往往只能是预期的"事实"，以让保险人评估风险并考虑接不接受投保与/或多少保费（premium）。为了防止受保人不诚实或乱讲以蒙混过关，英国《Marine Insurance Act 1906》[30]之 section 20 规定说要求这些预期/预测是善意（good faith）作出："**Representations pending negotiation of contract.** (1) Every material representation made by the assured or his agent to the insurer during the negotiations for the contract, and before the contract is concluded, must be true. If it be untrue the in-

〔30〕《Insurance Act 2015》生效后已经对此立法有所改变，但该立法条文不受影响，因为其已经存在上百年，深入人心。

surer may avoid the contract. (2) A representation is material which would influence the judgment of a prudent insurer in fixing the premium, or determining whether he will take the risk. (3) **A representation may be** either a representation as to a matter of fact, or as to **a matter of expectation or belief.** (4) A representation as to a matter of fact is true, if it be substantially correct, that is to say, if the difference between what is represented and what is actually correct would not be considered material by a prudent insurer. (5) **A representation as to a matter of expectation or belief is true if it be made in good faith.** (6) A representation may be withdrawn or corrected before the contract is concluded. (7) Whether a particular representation be material or not is, in each case, a question of fact."（加黑部分是笔者的强调）

1.2.2　例子之二：公司上市与招股章程

简单举一个商业活动的例子，如私人公司申请上市（IPO）、上市公司集资与上市公司的年报等。由于这是面对公众，而有关公司的信息与事实一面倒掌握在公司手中，一般股民只能依赖公司的披露与正确且全面的陈述才有信心作决定，主要是是否投资或抛售股票。所以，上市公司受到的法律规管特别多且特别严厉。例如上市或集资规定要求公司提供的招股章程（prospectus）[31]与具有同样性质的文件，如公告、启事、通告、宣传册、广告等全面披露与陈述公司的业务、资产与负债、经济状况、公司管理、业务前景与盈利亏损等。这些资讯与事实就涉及了过往、现在与将来预期的"事实"。招股章程可视为邀请公众作出购买公司股票或债券的要约（offer）。一旦披露的信息与事实、意见或预期有错，公司董事与相关人士如发起人（promoter）、授权作出招股章程人士如保荐人（sponsor）等，会面对刑事与民事的责任。而民事责任就是普通法与立法[如香港特区的《公司（清盘及杂项条文）条例》与《证券及期货条例》]下的误述。

如果在招股章程预测或预期将来的公司业务与行为时，并没有真正意愿（will）或能力（ability）去付诸事实的想法，也证明不了，就会构成误述：见 Edgington v. Fitzmaurice（1885）29 Ch. D. 459 先例。

著名的 Derry v. Peek（1889）14 App Cas 337 贵族院先例对欺诈性误述下了定义，并且是十分严格包括在作出陈述时"明知不正确、或不相信它的真实性、或鲁莽不理会真假"。该先例涉及招股章程内有不正确的内容，就是"The company has the right to use steam or mechanical power instead of horses"的一句。该公司计划发展以蒸汽动力替代马匹拉车的业务，但根据当时立法《Tramways Act 1870》，这是需要政府贸易局（Board of Trade）批准，但这没有在招股章程说明或作出批注，反而以刚刚节录的一句话显示公司有一个绝对权利这样做。原告受到该招股章程的吸引，投资并认购

---

〔31〕 发行人（issuer）把自己的情况真实公之于众的文书，必须严格按照法律与证券交易所的规定进行。一旦被发觉文书上有虚假陈述的情况，发行人必须承担起刑事与民事的责任。

股票,但后来贸易局不批准,导致该公司倒闭清盘,也令原告的投资“打了水漂”。于是,原告向被告(该公司股票的发行人与股东)Peek 先生提起诉讼索赔损失。

在一审法院,Stirling 大法官认定的事实真相是被告是诚实相信有关陈述是正确,没有虚假陈述。但这被上诉庭推翻,认为被告作为公司董事没有合理依据去相信该招股章程的陈述。这带来被告向贵族院上诉,认为上诉庭把“欺诈”延伸得太广太宽,而证明欺诈就必须证明作出的言行有欺诈,不是一位诚实人士所为。即使是在言行中有错误与疏忽,也不会导致该言行变为欺诈。欺诈也涉及诱骗(tricking)第三人进行购买,例如知道是必须要有贸易局的批准但故意隐瞒以诱骗第三人或原告,但这不是一审法院认定的事实。

贵族院推翻了上诉庭判决并恢复一审判决。但贵族院对欺诈的权威定义仍相对广泛,其中包括了“鲁莽”(reckless)不理会陈述的真假。Herschell 勋爵说:“... fraud is proved when it is show that a false representation has been made knowingly; or(2) without belief in its truth; or(3) recklessly, careless whether it be true or false.”

这可节录《Chitty on Contracts》(2021 年,第 34 版)一书之 9-056 与 9-057 段的总结:“... The common law relating to fraud was established by the House of Lords in Derry v. Peek. It was there decided that in order for fraud to be established, it is necessary to prove the absence of an honest belief in the truth of that which has been stated. ...The converse of this is that however negligent a person may be, he cannot be liable for fraud, provided that his belief is honest; mere carelessness is not sufficient, although gross carelessness may justify an inference that he was not honest.

Absence of honest belief. That the claimant who alleges fraud must prove the absence of an honest belief is demonstrated by Derry v. Peek itself. ... In an action for deceit the House of Lords held that the directors were not liable in damages for fraudulent misrepresentation. The decisive factor, in Lord Herscell's words, was that 'they honestly believed that what they asserted was true'.”

在 Reese River Silver Mining Co Ltd v. Smith(1869) LR 4 HL 64 贵族院先例中,涉及董事在招股章程中有关在某矿场开展业务的好处有错误陈述,但自己没有事前查实陈述的真实性,不理真假就当作事实陈述,这被认定是欺诈/欺骗。Cairns 勋爵认为:“... if persons take upon themselves to make assertions as to which they are ignorant whether they are true or untrue, they must, in a civil point of view, be held as responsible, as if they had asserted that which they know to be untrue.”

这也无须去证明被告有不诚实的动机(motive),也不好证明:见 Polhill v. Walter (1832) 3 B & Ad 114; Standard Chartered Bank v. Pakistan National Shipping Corp & Ors. (1995) 2 Lloyd's Rep 365; Standard Chartered Bank v. Pakistan National Shipping Corp & Ors. (No. 2) (2000) 1 Lloyd's Rep 218; Gabriel v. Little (2013) EWCA Civ 1513; Morrell v. Stewart (2015) EWHC 962 (Ch) 等先例。在 Gabriel v. Little 上诉庭先

例中,Gloster 大法官说:

"It is trite law in this context that:'... **if fraud be proved, the motive of the person guilty of it is immaterial.** It matters not that there was no intention to cheat or injure a person to whom the statement was made.';

see e. g. Derry v. Peek(1889)14 App. Cas. 337 ... per Lord Herschell. ... As was stated in Barings plc v. Coopers & Lybrand(No 5)[2002] EWHC 461(Ch)lack of dishonest intent may be powerful evidence of a bona fide belief in the truth of the facts asserted by the defendant.

Thus, **whilst the motive of the representor is irrelevant, an intention to influence the mind of the representee must be shown if the requisite dishonest intention is to be established.** ..."(加黑部分是笔者的强调)

最后,民法与刑法对欺诈的证明并不一样,刑法更为严格,需要同时证明有关误述是不诚实与有欺诈的动机:见《Fraud Act 2006》之 section 2。

在笔者看来,上述介绍的先例显示了当时的背景/语境,也就是涉及了需要严格保证招股章程中的披露与陈述的正确性与真实性,以符合公众利益的政策。确实在当时开始萌芽的资本社会,已经有不少公司在招股章程中作出夸大或虚假的陈述。另是,当时的普通法也只有在欺诈性误述中才有权索赔损失,其他非欺诈性误述(包括疏忽误述)的受害方只有撤销合约的衡平救济。这对 Derry v. Peek 先例中的原告没有帮助,所以只能通过指控欺诈性误述才能向被告取回损失。这一法律地位直到在《Misrepresentation Act 1967》中才有了改变,让疏忽误述也有了损失赔偿的救济。

现在很多中国企业在境外上市,如果在招股章程里有错误或不全面的陈述,或在上市后没有及时披露应披露的事实就可能有严重后果。例如 2020 年蚂蚁集团上市被中国监管机构紧急叫停,阿里巴巴(在纽约证券交易所上市,所以受美国纽约南区联邦地区法院管辖)就面对了集体诉讼(class action)。作为投资者的原告指控阿里巴巴在蚂蚁集团 IPO 期间向公众隐瞒其知道或可以获得的不利事实,导致所作的陈述严重虚假与/或有误导性,即向公共投资者误述。2021 年,滴滴在上市不到 48 小时后,中国监管部门宣布对其实施网络安全审查,滴滴股价大跌。随后美国 Labaton Sucharow LLP 以及 Rosen Law Firm 宣布,其正在代表滴滴全球股份有限公司的股东调查潜在的证券索赔(也就是在调查取证),指滴滴可能向投资公众发布了有严重误导性的商业讯息。

面对这种天文数字的索赔,作为被告的中国公司的领导会需要出庭接受交叉盘问(cross-examination)。他们在回答一连串充满敌意与陷阱重重的问题时,清楚知道红线在哪里会是自保的重要条件,只有如此才不会令一个诚实与小心谨慎作出的陈述与预期被法院错误认定为疏忽甚至是欺诈,并导致惩罚性赔偿(punitive damages)。

1.3　诱导与依赖的重要性

可先节录《Misrepresentation, Mistake and Non-Disclosure》一书（2022 年，第 6 版）之 3 – 53 段如下：“**The requirement of a casual link between statement and loss** Whichever remedy is sought for misrepresentation, it will be necessary to establish an adequate link between the statement and the consequence from which the representee claims to be relieved. **If the claim is for damages, the question is whether the statement caused the loss. If the claim is for rescission of a contract, the inquiry is as to casual link between the statement and the claimant's entry into the contract.** ... A false statement, even one made fraudulently, will not be actionable as a misrepresentation by the person to whom it was addressed if it had no impact on his actions, nor otherwise caused him loss. This means that the statement must have been present to the claimant's mind at the time when he took the course of action on which he bases his claim (such as entering into the contract). A representee cannot normally succeed where he knows that the representation is false, although it has said that **it is not necessary, as a matter of law, for the claimant to prove that he believed that the statement was true: it is sufficient that the misrepresentation induced him** as a matter of fact ...”（加黑部分是笔者的强调）

说到“诱导”（inducement）与“依赖”（reliance）方面的因果关系（causation）要求，这也是追求法律的公道与符合基本人性。例如正常做广告、推销（sales talk）或是吹捧（puff）之所以不构成有法律后果的误述，就是因为一位合理人士一般不会去依赖。如 Carlsberg 啤酒声称“可能是全世界最好的啤酒”（probably the best lager in the world），除了无法证明这个事实的真假外，一般合理人士也不会严肃对待这个陈述（或误述）。又或是迪士尼乐园声称是“地球上最快乐的地方”（the happiest place on earth），也是同样道理，只会是骗骗小孩子，但不会被依赖而产生合约，即使被依赖而产生了合约也没有法律后果。一些空泛的推销语言也同样如此，例如说出售的房子是交通方便、环境美好舒适等。当然如果涉及特定情况就又会不同，例如买票时问售票人员迪士尼乐园里有没有某个特定游戏设备，一旦工作人员误述，就可能会产生法律后果。

如果双方都对一个事实有了解，有时甚至被误述方了解得比误述方更多，被误述方就说不上是依赖了误述。正如在 Sprecher Grier Halberstam LLP v. Walsh (2008) EWCA Civ 1324 上诉庭先例中，Ward 大法官说：“A man cannot be deceived if he knows the truth.”从另一个角度看，误述方也不会合理预期比自己知道得更多的对方会依赖有关的陈述。这不仅是无辜或疏忽误述，连欺诈性误述也需要满足因果关系。这因果关系在损失索赔中，就仍需要证明错误的陈述导致该损失。而在撤销合约中，就要证明该错误陈述与订立合约有一定的关系（casual link）。

所以在涉及各种各样的案情的误述案件，背景/语境（context）十分重要。如果同一句内容被指称是不正确的,在不同背景或在复杂的商业/专业下会得出不同的结论,如双方的水平高低(sophistication)、双方对有关误述的事实掌握与其他各种各样的因素。要构成误述,首先法官或仲裁员作为客观与合理的第三人解释陈述方的言行作出了怎样的陈述,之后被陈述方要证明他/她确实依赖了这个陈述或被该陈述诱导订立合约;否则双方"驴唇不对马嘴",被陈述方就说不上是依赖了该误述或被该陈述诱导订立合约:见在本章之3.4.1段介绍的Peek v. Gurney(1873)LR 6 HL 377等先例。

在进一步介绍前,可先节录《Chitty on Contracts》(2021年,第34版)一书之9-041与9-042段对诱导与依赖的如下总结:"**Inducement: representee unaware of representation or given correct information** It is essential if the misrepresentation is to have legal effect that it should have operated on the mind of the representee. It follows that if the misrepresentation did not affect the representee's mind, because he was unaware that it had been made,[32] or because he was not influenced by it,[33] he has no remedy. ... **Belief in truth of statement not necessary**In some cases the requirement of inducement may not be satisfied because the misrepresentee knew that the statement was false,[34] but it is not necessary that the misrepresentee believed that the claim made was true. In Hayward v. Zurich Insurance Co Plc(2015)EWCA Civ 327 the Supreme Court held that a settlement of an insurance claim could be avoided by the insurer when it discovered that the amount of loss had been exaggerated fraudulently, even though at the time of the settlement the insurer had doubts over the extent of the claim. It was sufficient that the false claim, which might influence the court that would fix the amount of recovery, influenced the insurer in the sum offered in settlement. The question is one of fact."

在Brown v. Innovator One Plc(2012)EWHC 1321(Comm)先例中,Hamblen大法官引用以上节录的总结,说:"In relation to reliance and inducement the position is conveniently summarised in Chitty as follows: (1) 'It is essential if the misrepresentation is to have legal effect that it should have operated on the mind of the representee. It follows that if the misrepresentation did not affect the representee's mind, because he was unaware that it had been made, or because he was not influenced by it, or because he knew it was false, he has no remedy' ... (2) 'It is not necessary that the misrepresentation should be the sole cause' of the claimant acting as he did. 'It is sufficient if it can be shown to be

---

〔32〕 见Horsfall v. Thomas(1862)158 ER 813先例。另在本书第三章之9.4.2段介绍的Leeds City Council and Ors v. Barclays Bank Plc and Ors(2021)EWHC 363(Comm)先例,也强调了这个"理解/意识因素"(understanding/awareness factor)的重要性。

〔33〕 见Attwood v. Small(1838)6 Cl. & F. 232;Jennings v. Broughton(1853)5 De G. M. & G. 126;Smith v. Chadwick(1884)9 App Cas 187;Holmes v. Jones(1907)4 CLR 1692等先例。

〔34〕 见Cooper v. Tamms(1988)1 EGLR 257先例。

one of the inducing causes.' ...(3) The normal rule is that 'where a party has entered a contract after a misrepresentation has been made to him, he will not have a remedy if it is shown that he would have entered the contract in any event'. This is not, however, necessary in cases of fraud. In such cases it 'is sufficient if there is evidence to show that he was materially influenced by the misrepresentation in the sense that it has some impact on his thinking, 'was actively present to his mind ...'"

以上简单提及的林林总总有关误述的各方面,会在后详细讲述,并多举实例案情以增强理解背后道理来活学活用,这里只先介绍一下这一大精神。

1.3.1 误述有否诱导与被依赖并产生合约与/或造成损失的举证责任

对误述(无辜、疏忽或欺诈)的举证责任(burden of proof),包括被陈述方要证明依赖与订立合约的因果关系,是要满足民事诉讼的平衡的可能性(balance of probabilities)的标准。早在 Arkwright v. Newbold(1881)17 Ch. D. 301 上诉庭先例中,Cotton 大法官说:"... in an action of deceit the Plaintiff cannot establish a title to relief simply by shewing that the Defendants have made a fraudulent statement: he must also shew that he was deceived by the statement, and acted upon it to his prejudice. But in this case, ... the Plaintiff does not carry the case further in his evidence. ... Therefore he does not allege that he relied on the prospectus ... In my opinion it would not be right in an action of deceit to give a plaintiff relief on the ground that a particular statement, according to the construction put on it by the Court, is false, when the plaintiff does not venture to swear that he understood the statement in the sense which the Court puts on it. If he did not, then, even if that construction may have been falsified by the facts, he was not deceived."

较近期在 Fitzroy Robinson Ltd v. Mentmore Towers Ltd (2009) EWHC 1552 (TCC)先例中,Coulson 大法官说到《Misrepresentation Act 1967》之 S. 2(1):"reliance needs to be proved to the civil standard."

现实中,举证责任对作为被误述方的原告的困难是订立一份合约往往是有很多因素。例如一个简单的货物买卖合约,买方的考虑因素就往往有为了预期的盈利、等着要用这种货物、预期市场价会上涨、有竞争对手想抢购这种货物、手头现金充足等。而卖方对有关货物的误述充其量只是导致该买卖合约(与相应的价格)的其中一个因素。如果虽然有其他考虑因素,但误述仍对决定是否订约有影响,则仍可能构成误述。但如果误述方能证明有关误述轻微到对订约与否的决定毫无影响,知道真相最多令被陈述方有点失望,就无法满足因果关系。在 HEB Fasteners v. Marks Bloom & Co(1983)1 All ER 583 先例中,Donaldson 大法官说:"... In real life decisions are made on the basis of a complex of assumptions of fact. Some of these may be fundamental to the validity of the decision. **'But for' that assumption, the decision would not be made**. Others may be important factors in reaching the decision and collectively, but **not**

individually, fundamental to its validity. Yet others may be subsidiary factors which **support or encourage** the taking of the decision. If these latter assumptions are falsified in the event, whether individually or collectively, this will be **a cause for disappointment** to the decision taker, **but will not affect the essential validity of his decision** in the sense that **if the truth had been known or suspected before the decision was taken, the same decision would still have been made**."（加黑部分是笔者的强调）

这简单的货物买卖的例子就可以显示需要原告满足"要不是"（but for）[35]的因果关系测试，也就是证明要不是这个误述（或至少是主要因素），他是不会订立有关的合约，或至少不会同意同样的条件如对价方面。在 Raiffeisen Zentralbank Osterreich AG v. Royal Bank of Scotland Plc（2010）EWHC 1392（Comm）先例中，Clarke 大法官说："'But for' causation means that unless the alleged cause（X）had come about the alleged result（Y）would not have occurred. ... [It] means showing that, unless the representee had had the representation made to him, he would not have contracted（or would not have done so on the same terms）."

提供证据去证明原告在订约时在考虑什么也是困难、不科学与不肯定的，正如 Cranworth 勋爵在 Reynell v. Sprye（1852）1 De G. M. & G. 660 先例中说："It is impossible so to analyse the operations of the human mind as to be able to say how far any particular representation may have led to the formation of any particular resolution, or the adoption of any particular line of conduct. No one can do this with certainty, even as to himself, still less as to another."

这可以笔者的一个中国香港特区仲裁案件为例。一家内地的上市公司意图以高价收购一家创新科技公司。在签署收购协议以及相关股东之间的股权转让协议（share transfer agreement）时，该科技公司的股东均对上市公司以及科技公司的其他股东作出其股权权属清晰、不存在争议或潜在争议的陈述与保证。后来，在收购交易提交证监会（securities regulatory commission）审查时，证监会收到举报人的举报信，举报人声称对科技公司的股份拥有所有权。这是因为该科技公司的一位股东 A 曾经将名下的股份部分转售给他，并作为他的股份代持人。在收购交易的谈判过程中，A 将该转售部分的股份买回，并在签署协议时作出了上述股权权属清晰、不存在争议或潜在争议的陈述。后来举报人发现该收购交易的存在便对 A 买回股份的价格提出争议，甚至开始了法院诉讼。证监会接到举报后要求上市公司对此争议进行进一步的调查与提供说明报告。虽然问题最后获得解决，但交易发生了延误。最终，上市公司宣告终止收购交易，这直接造成科技公司股东之间因收购交易失败而根据股东之间签署的股权转让协议产生相互追责的"内斗"。内斗涉及的他们之间的股权转让协议中也存在同样的陈述与保证，于是大股东就主张 A 存在欺诈性误述而令收购

[35] 见本书第十章之 9.1 段与笔者《损失赔偿与救济》一书第四章之 4 段对"要不是"测试的详细介绍。

交易失败,要A赔偿交易失败带来的损失。

本案涉及一个重要的争议是假如A的欺诈性误述成立,上市公司最终终止收购交易的原因与欺诈性误述之间是否满足“要不是”测试,只有满足该测试才能去谈损失计算的问题。这里涉及指控A的欺诈性误述导致大股东损失在举证方面的问题,而最终因为大股东在证据方面的严重不足与存在多处瑕疵,最后仲裁庭判因果关系不成立。这些包括:

1. A在文件披露程序中要求大股东披露能够证明上市公司终止收购交易真正原因的文件,但大股东主张这类文件在上市公司手中,而上市公司不是仲裁当事方而是第三人,他们无法从上市公司处取得文件。在A的请求下,仲裁庭也感觉这方面文件重要,曾经要求(但不是程序命令)该上市公司帮助提供有关的文件,如内部管理层对此收购交易的会议记录和与证监会的书信往来等文件。但被拒绝,这导致仲裁庭主要能够依赖与可信的文件是该上市公司年报(由A提供),其中有一小段说明终止收购的原因是内部的财政与市场问题。

2. 相信内地法院没有“第三方披露命令”(Norwich Pharmacal Order),否则A或是大股东只要向法院申请,就可以强制该上市公司提供相关的口头与文件证据了,不必请求其帮助。

3. 对仲裁庭而言,感觉上市公司行为前后矛盾与不相符的是在开庭审理前不久突然同意负责收购交易的高管作为证人出庭。该高管的证人证言中虽然附上了一些上市公司的内部文件,但并不完整,也并不是最关键。

4. 该高管证人的作证也说不上有说服力,只举两点:(1)他尽力解释所有上市公司的公开年报中向股民解释的原因通常不是真正的背后原因。但他不能解释为什么不能提供此收购终止的真正原因(A的欺诈性误述与造成证监会延误批准)的相关文件,毕竟仲裁是机密程序。(2)该高管在交叉盘问中也无法解释如果上市公司是因为欺诈性误述要终止交易,那为什么不在一发现此欺诈性误述的事实后就尽快或在合理时间终止,而是拖了近1年并在期间花费大量的金钱与人力去做调查、制作调查报告与不止一次回答证监会提出的问题等,并且在解决了证监会的问题后,在对收购协议作出修改并需要所有股东再次签署时才突然决定终止。

5. 针对欺诈性误述的责任与损失的问题,在本章之1.3.3段以及本书第三章与第四章有详论。这里只是简单提及,对于欺诈性误述是否诱导合约产生的责任问题,法律为了阻吓欺诈的行为,就假设只要存在欺诈,合约的订立就是该欺诈所导致。在索赔损失时,虽然仍然要满足“要不是”测试,但是会是较为宽松的对待。本仲裁案件中,大股东索赔损失没有成功的根本原因是没有证明上市公司终止收购与欺诈性误述(如果成立)之间的因果关系。

1.3.2 误述只需要是订立合约的有效因素之一

法律为了配合现实减轻原告举证责任的困难,承认订立合约会有很多不同考虑因素,误述充其量只是其中之一。此外,法院也不去区分(也区分不了)多个订约的因素的个别重要性,如 Ward 大法官在 Assicurazoni Generali SpA v. Arab Insurance Group(2003)1 All ER(Comm)140 上诉庭先例中说:"court does not allow an examination into the relative importance of contributory causes."

Halsbury 勋爵也早在 Arnison v. Smith(1889)41 Ch. D. 348 上诉庭先例中说:"you cannot weigh the elements by ounces."

针对无辜或疏忽误述,甚至是欺诈性误述的损失索赔,被误述方/受害方虽然仍需要满足"要不是"的因果关系测试去说明该误述是订立合约的其中一个有效因素(effective cause),也就是如果没有这个误述,他/她是不会订立有关的合约,或至少不会是以同样的条件如对价方面。至于同时有其他的有效因素去订立合约是没有关系或影响的,只要误述是有效因素之一。至于哪一个重量最高,是"最主要"因素,并不重要。在 Assicurazoni Generali SpA v. Arab Insurance Group 上诉庭先例中,Clarke 大法官说:"It seems to me that the true position is that **the misrepresentation must be an effective cause** of the particular insurer or reinsurer **entering into the contract but need not of course be the sole cause.** If the insurer would have entered into the contract on the same terms in any event, the representation or non-disclosure will not, however material, be an effective cause of the making of the contract and the insurer or reinsurer will not be entitled to avoid the contract. Thus **I agree with ... that, in this context at least, causation cannot exist when even the 'but for' test is not satisfied**..."(加黑部分是笔者的强调)

上诉庭 Ward 大法官也加了补充说:"I am happy to express my agreement with the analysis of the law conducted by Clarke L. J. subject to this reservation. I am not entirely sure that it is necessary to require the misrepresentation to be an effective cause of a party's entering into the contract on the terms on which he did. If by that qualification my Lord means no more than that **it did actually play upon his mind and influence his decision** then I have no argument. In other words **I readily accept it must have some causative effect. I would be concerned if the insistence on an effective cause were to lead to an evaluation of the weight placed by the representee upon the various matters which in combination lead to the agreement**. We must be careful not to be led back into the error that the cause has to be a decisive cause."(加黑部分是笔者的强调)

另在 Dadourian Group International Inc v. Simms(2006)EWHC 2973(Ch)先例中,Warren 大法官说:"(1)it is a question of fact whether a representee has been induced to enter into a transaction by a material misrepresentation intended by the representor to be relied upon by the representee;(2)if the misrepresentation is of such a nature that it would be likely to play a part in the decision of a reasonable person to enter into a transaction it will be presumed that it did so unless the representor satisfies the court to the contrary ...;(3)**the misrepresentation does not have to be the sole inducement for the**

representee to be able to rely on it:it is enough if the misrepresentation plays a real and substantial part, albeit not a decisive part, in inducing the representee to act; (4) the presumption of inducement is rebutted by the representor showing that the misrepresentation did not play a real and substantial part in the representee's decision to enter into the transaction; the representor does not have to go so far as to show that the misrepresentation played no part at all; and (5) the issue is **to be decided** by the court **on a balance of probabilities** on the whole of the evidence before it."(加黑部分是笔者的强调)

所以,误述方去争辩受害方即使没有这个误述亦会去订约,因为当时市场开始对受害方不利等,是不会成功的。毕竟,受害方即使去订约,可能在正确陈述下也会去争取不同的条件或价钱后才订约。故此受害方只需证明他曾受过这误述的诱导或影响,已足够构成"有效的误述"(operative misrepresentation)而可撤销合约并且索赔。所以,有说法是受害方的被误述方在这方面的举证责任"并不沉重"(is not a heavy one):见 Wise (Underwriting Agency) Ltd v. Grupo Nacional Provincial SA (2004) EWCA Civ 962 上诉庭先例。

1.3.3　无辜或疏忽误述下原告仍需要满足严格的"要不是"测试

"要不是"(but for)测试有不少先例是要证明要不是这个误述是不会订立有关合约的,这显然不容易。早在 Smith v. Kay (1859) 7 HL Cas 750 最高院先例中, Wensleydale 勋爵说:"where, unless it had been employed, the contract would never have been made."

较近期可见 Raiffeisen Zentralbank Osterreich AG v. Royal Bank of Scotland Plc (2010) EWHC 1392 (Comm) 与 Cassa di Risparmio della Repubblica di San Marino SpA v. Barclays Bank Ltd (2011) EWHC 484 (Comm) 等先例。只节录 Raiffeisen Zentralbank Osterreich AG v. Royal Bank of Scotland Plc 先例中, Christopher Clarke 大法官说:"The authorities show that inducement is, in essence, a question of causation and that the misrepresentation must be an effective cause of the representee entering into the contract in the 'but for' sense. 'But for' causation means that unless the alleged cause (X) had come about the alleged result (Y) would not have occurred."

更近期在 BV Nederlandse Industrie Van Eiprodukten v. Rembrandt Enterprises Inc (2019) EWCA Civ 596 上诉庭先例中,案情将在稍后介绍。虽然该先例是针对欺诈性误述,但判决中 Longmore 大法官说针对疏忽误述与无辜误述,是被误述方有证明诱导与依赖的举证责任,也就是要证明如果没有该误述不会订立合约:"the test for inducement in cases of innocent or negligent representation appears to be settled in the form that the representee has the burden of showing inducement in the sense that he has to show he would not have entered into the relevant contract had the representation not been made ..."

看来,不少权威先例(包括近期)对无辜或疏忽误述仍要求证明能够满足严格的"要不是"测试。但也有说法或呼声是去放宽,只要求满足有关误述对原告考虑是否订约有一定的影响。而如果没有该误述,原告"会有可能"有不一样的行动,即可能仍然会订立该合约,但也可能不会订立该合约。对原告来说,满足举证责任变得容易得多了,这令无辜或疏忽误述在诱导与依赖方面的举证责任与欺诈性误述变得相近或一致。正如在 Dadourian Group International Inc v. Simms(2006)EWHC 2973(Ch)先例中,Warren 大法官说:"It is sometimes said that the correct approach is to ask how the representee would have acted if the representation had not been made; and to say that, if he would have acted in exactly the same way, there is no inducement. In many cases, it may well be that that approach gives the correct answer. ..."

这可节录《Misrepresentation, Mistake and Non-Disclosure》一书(2022 年,第 6 版)之 3-58 段所述如下:"**The text of causation: 'but for'**? There is some disagreement in the authorities ... about now the test of causation should be applied. Some say that, if it is shown that the claimant would still have entered into the contract even if the misrepresentation had not been made, this misrepresentation cannot (on the 'but for' test of causation) have caused him to enter into the contract and therefore he has no remedy. Others say that if the representation was in fact present to the claimant's mind when he took the decision to enter into the contract and it did in fact contribute to his decision to contract, that is sufficient. In the recent cases this has been put as a distinction between requiring the claimant to show that he **would have acted differently** if the representation had not been made ('but for' causation) and it being sufficient that he can show that he **might have acted differently**. Given the difficulty of establishing the casual link between a misrepresentation and the decision to enter into the contract, one might expect the latter approaching generally to be preferred, since **as long as the misrepresentation in fact operated on the claimant's mind when he decided to enter into the contract, he did in fact rely on it**. However, the recent cases have drawn a distinction: that a strict 'but for' test is to be used in the case of innocent or negligent misrepresentations, but that the broader test may be appropriate where the misrepresentation was fraudulent, on the basis that, having intended to deceive, the defendant cannot be allowed to argue that his fraud did not achieve its object."(加黑部分是笔者的强调)

1.3.4 "要不是"测试的应对

实践中,实际情况很复杂,误述方/被告经常会在误述案件提出因果关系方面的争议,例如一种常见的争议是通过披露的文件与交叉盘问,去试图说服法院或仲裁庭在平衡的可能性下,就算没有这个误述,原告也会订立这个合约与同意相关的条件。

虽然在大部分的情况适用这样的测试会得出真相,但并不一定。举一个买卖房屋的简单例子,本来买方已经心动去支付了押金并委任了律师准备交割文件。但卖方多嘴或想讨好买方与坚定他的信心，多加了一句说有一位邻居是当红明星。但事实上该明星几个月前已经搬走，而且搬进来的新邻居是不良分子，是买方不想有的邻居。这也不是机密，一问隔壁邻居就可以查得出。这样卖方仅是证明在平衡的可能性下，没有这个误述，买方也会订立合约购买该房屋显然是不够的。卖方会要进一步证明有这误述后，买方也不理会新邻居是谁或知道是不良分子仍会订立合约，完成交割购买。

这样的测试也带来不必要与/或困难的揣测，例如在上市公司的招股章程中有严重的误述，被告代表律师去试图盘问原告："如果没有这个误述或有了这个披露你是否仍会认购这股票？"这可以带来一连串很复杂的问题，是一般的股民根本回答不了的。因为这是一个完全假设的问题，被盘问的原告也只能给出假设性的回答。被误述方只需要证明误述是诱导订立合约的其中一个因素，但不用证明是唯一因素。实际上盘问方根本不能盘问这个问题，所以原告代表律师应该反对，指出这不是正确的法律测试。而就算问了，原告回答"我不知道，我没有见过一份没有这误述的招股书"已经足够。这在 BP Exploration Operating Co Ltd v. Chevron Transport (Scotland) (2001) UKHL 50 先例中，Millett 勋爵说：

"I am satisfied that he **need not take this further step which involves a hypothetical inquiry which can never be answered precisely and may sometimes be incapable of being answered at all**. A representee can say why he acted as he did. He can say that it was, inter alia, because of the representation. But he can only speculate on what he would have done if the representation had not been made.

As a matter of English law, a representee must always be prepared to prove that the representation had an effect on his mind. But it is**sufficient for him to prove that the representation was an inducing cause** which led him to act as he did ... he need not prove that it was the inducing cause ... Whether, **if a full disclosure of the truth had been made, he would or would not have acted differently is a question to which English law does not require an answer; it is sufficient that he might have done so** ...

'Would you have taken the shares if something had been left out, and something else had been put in?' is**an extremely difficult question to answer**, and **one which the representor is not entitled to ask, and to which the representee can give a perfectly adequate reply by saying 'I cannot say; I have never seen such a prospectus'.**"（加黑部分是笔者的强调）

1.3.5　误述是否需要满足实质重要

对一个事实作出不正确的陈述，即会是构成"可诉误述"的第一步。而"实质重要"(material)的要求则是第二步，即客观看来该不正确陈述要对一位正常与合理的人士在决定会否订立合约与以什么条件订立合约时产生实质重要的影响。有该第二步的原因是被误述方一面之词说是主观上(subjectively)有被诱导与有去依赖该误述，对于误述方来说很难反驳，所以法律需要一个相对更为客观的标准或测试（objective standard/test）看待被误述方的证据是否可信。加上在一个决定去订立合约（特别在复杂的国际商业交易中），会涉及大量的因素，它们之间的重要性与各自造成的最后影响很难表达与衡量，也不科学。所以，被陈述方即使是出庭举证（主要会是口头证据声称他/她在订约时的主观想法），并接受交叉盘问，也难去认定是否有诱导与依赖。有关不正确陈述/表述是否"实质重要"测试的重要性就在这里。可以说，越是实质重要，也就越有可能被误述方确实被诱导与依赖。而实质重要到一个较高的程度，法院或仲裁庭就可以通过事实推断（infer）被误述方有被诱导与依赖，被误述方也无需对他/她的主观想法举证了。剩下是要误述方举证证明被误述方实际上没有被诱导，例如他/她曾经自己查核过并且根本就知道事实真相等，但误述方不容易抗辩成功。

这可先节录 Pan Atlantic Insurance Co Ltd v. Pine Top Insurance Co Ltd（1994）2 Lloyd's Rep 427 贵族院先例中，Mustill 勋爵说："… I have concluded that it is an answer to a defence of misrepresentation … that the act or omission complained of had no effect on the decision of the actual underwriter. As a matter of common sense however even where the underwriter is shown to have been careless in other respects the assured will have an uphill task in persuading the Court that the withholding or misstatement of circumstances satisfying the test materiality had no difference. There is ample material both in the general law and in the specialist works on insurance to suggest that there is a presumption in favour of a causative effect."

另 Moore-bick 大法官在 James v. CGU Insurance plc（2002）Lloyd's Rep 206 先例也说："The decision in Pan Atlantic v. Pine Top is … of importance，however，for the fact that their Lordships … held that there must be a causal connection between the non-disclosure（在保险法，因为是绝对善意合约，受保人不自动披露有实质重要信息等同是误述）and the making of the contract if the insurer is to be entitled to avoid the contract. In other words，the failure to disclose the fact in question must have induced the insurer to enter into the contract. Lord Mustill，with whom Lord Goff and Lord Slynn agreed，seems to have considered that on this issue the burden of proof falls on the insured（不自动披露的受保人）… to the effect that there is **ample material** to **suggest that there is a presumption in favour of a causative effect** and that **the insured is likely to have an uphill task in persuading the court that the withholding of circumstances satisfying the test of materiality made no difference**. The existence of **such a presumption** is further supported by the judgment of the Court of Appeal in St Paul Fire & Marine v McConnell Dowell [1995] 2 Lloyds Rep 116 where it was treated as **sufficient to discharge the burden of proof on the insurer in the absence of countervailing evidence**."（加黑部分是笔者的强调）

《Misrepresentation, Mistake and Non-Disclosure》一书(2022 年,第 6 版)之 5 – 25 段说:"**Proof of reliance**Once it is clear that the representee interpreted the representation in its false meaning, the question is whether the representee was in fact influenced by it. It is not necessary for the representee to give oral evidence to this effect and, indeed, oral evidence and cross – examination may not be conclusive because of the difficulty everyone has of explaining the impact on him of any particular representation, amongst the other factors which caused him to act. A broader enquiry is therefore necessary and if the representation was 'material' in the sense that it is of such a nature that it would be likely to induce a person in the representee's position to take the action he claims he took, the court is entitled to infer that the representation was an inducement to his action, unless the representor can show the contrary. The materiality of the statement places on the representor the burden of adducing evidence to rebut the inference."

对"实质重要"的定义,可先介绍在《Marine Insurance Act 1906》之 S. 18(2)与 S. 20(2)中有立法的解释,也就是以一位第三人的"谨慎的保险人"(prudent insurer)作为"正常与合理人士"去代入案件中的被告(说是受到受保人误述影响并试图去拒赔的真正有关保险人),客观测试是否会受该误述的影响,与会否接受承保或如果接受会收多少保费。立法 S. 18 是针对投保人(assured)的不披露(non-disclosure)。该立法之 S. 20 是针对误述。"实质重要"是在 S. 18(2)说:"Every circumstances is **material** which would influence the judgment of a prudent insurer in fixing the premium, or determining whether he will take the risk."而 S. 20 针对实质重要的测试是说:"(1) Every material representation made by the assured or his agent to the insurer during the negotiations for the contract, and before the contract is concluded, must be true. If it be untrue the insurer may avoid the contract. (2) **A representation is material which would influence the judgment of a prudent insurer in fixing the premium, or determining whether he will take the risk.**"(加黑部分是笔者的强调)

有关该海上保险立法下"实质重要"要求的受影响程度,在 Pan Atlantic Insurance Co Ltd v. Pine Top Insurance Co Ltd 贵族院先例中有详论,在本章的 1.3.5.3 段会进一步介绍。

1.3.5.1 客观第三人(审理法官或仲裁员)的测试

一个误述是否实质重要是以客观第三人来看,这才是所谓客观实质重要(objectively material),而不是任由受害方/被误述方自说自话说是实质重要。有关的测试是看一位客观第三人(也就是审理法官或仲裁员)在全面了解了当时有关的背景/环境、情况与事实后,代入考虑会否受到该指称的误述言行的诱导订立有关合约。如果会,就代表该误述是实质重要。

在合约解释(construction of contract)中,是不会考虑合约当事人的主观想法是什么，只是纯粹的客观测试（pure objective test）。[36] 所以，不会接受订约方的证据说他们在订约时脑袋在想什么或怎样理解有关的合约条文，这种证据被视为无关与不被采纳（inadmissible）。[37] 在开庭时的交叉盘问如果证人被问及或回答时涉及这方面，也会被阻示。正如 Staughton 大法官在 The"Amazonia"（1990）1 Lloyd's Rep 236 上诉庭先例中说："If the parties' correspondence and conduct shows … an intention（to make a contract）it will not，or may not，matter that neither privately intended to make a contract."

但一个误述是否实质重要与被误述方有否被诱导与依赖，与解释合约的纯客观测试不一样，加上了一些主观因素。被误述方要提供证据证明自己在订约时确有被对方的误述诱导与或多或少有依赖误述，并要接受交叉盘问。这也可以想得到，被误述方在订约时是否依赖了误述只有自己知道，本质上只有被误述方可举证，其他第三人无法代入。但对误述是否有实质重要性进行一并考虑，审理法官或仲裁员就可去代入考虑有关不正确陈述是否让一位正常与合理人士作出依赖，测试被误述方一面之词的主观证据的可信度。

毕竟不同的合约当事人的主观看法会有很大不同，而客观第三人的看法的重要性就在于，审理法官或仲裁员代入同样的背景/环境，对于一个陈述是否实质重要与被诱导的看法是相对稳定的。

至于有关误述是否被依赖的问题，从道理上说会需要同时考虑被误述方的主观想法，但这实际上借助客观的实质重要测试就可以事实推断会否有诱导与依赖，这会在下一段进行介绍。

1.3.5.2 实质重要与有否被诱导是否为相同情况

原告要证明有关误述是实质重要看来是与构成"可诉误述"的"诱导"（inducement）要件有所不同，前者是客观测试，而后者是主观测试（被误述方自己脑袋里的想法）。但也有说法认为在疏忽或无辜误述中，"诱导"与"实质重要"是同一码事。毕竟对一个不实质重要的陈述，可以很快去推断受害方/被误述方不像有被诱导与依赖订立合约。在 Museprime Properties Ltd v. Adhill Properties Ltd（1991）61 P & CR 111 先例中，Scott 大法官说：

"A representation is material，in my opinion，if it is something that induces the person to whom it is made，whether solely or in conjunction with other inducements，to contract on the terms on which he does contract. I would gratefully adopt the view expressed in Goff and Jones on the Law of Restitution，which reads：

'In our view any misrepresentation which induces a person to enter into a contract should be a ground for rescission of that contract. **If the misrepresentation would have**

---

〔36〕 见本书第七章之 6 段。

〔37〕 见笔者《证据法：基础理论、口头证据与专家证据》一书第九章之 4 段。

induced a reasonable person to enter into the contract then the court will, **as we have seen**, **presume that the representee was so induced** and the onus will be on the representor to show that the representee did not rely on the misrepresentation either wholly or in part. If, however, the misrepresentation would not have induced a reasonable person to contract, the onus will be on the representee to show that the misrepresentation induced him to act as he did. But these considerations relate to the onus of proof. **To disguise them under the cloak of materiality is misleading and unnecessary**. '

And, as the learned editors say a little way above that passage, the cases have tended to**treat materiality as synonymous with inducement**.

I respectfully agree with that view of the law and propose to apply it in this case. "（加黑部分是笔者的强调）

有说法是在疏忽误述或无辜误述下，原告是会需要证明该误述是实质重要。如果被否定是实质重要，就不是可诉误述了。但欺诈性误述中就不需要这一步的测试，存在一个事实推定（presumption）是实质重要，否则误述方何必有意作出一个虚假的事实陈述去骗人？可以说这种区分也配合政策上去阻吓与严惩欺诈/欺骗，但对一些微不足道与本质是诚实的无心之失则尽量设置障碍以减少令合约变得可使无效与撤销合约的情况。

早在 Smith v. Kay（1859）7 HL Cas 750 贵族院先例中，法院就拒绝了被告说有关的欺诈性误述"毫不重要"（wholly immaterial）的抗辩。另 Nicholas v. Thompson（1924）VLR 554 澳大利亚先例也说：

"Supposing defendant had admitted that the representation was made in order to induce, and that it did induce, could he insist that plaintiffs were bound to prove, in additional, ... that it was material? I do not think so."

而在一个疏忽或无辜误述的案件，原告需要同时满足有关误述是实质重要与被诱导。在 Macquarie Generation v. Peabody Resources Ltd（2000）NSWCA 361 新南威尔士上诉庭先例中，Beazley 大法官说："for an innocent misrepresentation to be actionable, the representee has to establish both materiality and inducement."

但也有说法认为是疏忽或无辜误述，只要有关误述是实质重要，被误述方被诱导也可以假设了，不必再去证明。在此先节录在 Pan Atlantic Insurance Co Ltd v. Pine Top Insurance Co Ltd（1994）2 Lloyd's Rep 427 贵族院先例中，Mustill 勋爵有提及："In the general law it is beyond doubt that even a fraudulent misrepresentation must be shown to have induced the contract before the promisor has a right to avoid, although the task of proof may be made more easy by a presumption of inducement. The case of innocent misrepresentation should surely be a fortiori, and yet **it is urged that so long as the representation is material no inducement need be shown**."（加黑部分是笔者的强调）

也有说法认为实质重要与诱导是两回事，毕竟实质重要充其量是间接证据（indirect evidence），而被误述方对自己被诱导与依赖提供的证据才是直接证据（direct evidence）。也会有被误述方在交叉盘问中承认或被认定是自己不小心、懒惰不用脑、无能、错误判断或其他私下原因去决定订立合约，是一位正常与合理的人士对有关误述是否实质重要并不知道与没有考虑在内。

这种争议特别是在保险合约，除了因为保险历史悠久有了不少有关先例外，也因为有《Marine Insurance Act 1906》立法规定有明示针对实质重要，但没有针对依赖。这样，例如一位谨慎保险人在考虑保费时，会考虑某 3 份文件，认为这些文件内容是重要的，所以不正确的陈述显然是有影响的。但是案件中真正的保险人因为当时赶着出门度假，根本没看就承保与确定了保费，也就是根本没有被这 3 份文件中的错误陈述诱导与依赖。所以，看来这两方面都应去考虑，不能视为同一码事。这可节录 Bennett 教授的《The Law of Marine Insurance》（2006）一书之 4.54 段：

"**The so-called 'presumption' of inducement**

...These references to a presumption of inducement flowing from proof of materiality have been taken at face value, but are apt to mislead. There is **no formal, legal presumption that requires a court, once the insurer has proved materiality, to find inducement** in the absence of convincing rebuttal evidence adduced by the assured. The idea of such a formal, legal presumption is a 'heresy ... long since exploded'（这是 Lloyd 勋爵在 Pan Atlantic Insurance Co Ltd v. Pine Top Insurance Co Ltd 先例所说）. Such a presumption would, moreover, be both illogical and undesirable. As a matter of logic, it simply does not follow that a circumstance that a prudent underwriter would consider relevant to assessing the risk would, if not disclosed or if misrepresented, cause the actual underwriter to decline the risk or accept only on different terms. ...

In truth, evidence of materiality has no special status in terms of proof of inducement. Its probative value in that regard depends entirely on the cogency and compelling nature of the evidence in question. **The stronger the case for materiality, the stronger the likelihood of inducement. Once evidence of materiality is sufficiently strong, it will logically follow that it is more likely than not that the actual underwriter would have taken a different decision in some way had the truth been known.** It is in this sense, but only in this sense, that an underwriter may be said to benefit from a 'fair inference of fact' flowing from evidence of materiality. ...

Where the**actual underwriter gives evidence to the court in person, there is little room for indirect evidence**. The court will normally draw a conclusion as to inducement from the underwriter's direct testimony. ...

In the absence of a good reason, **the failure on the part of the actual underwriter to testify may constitute evidence of lack of inducement**. The court may infer that the reason why the insurers did not produce the underwriter as a witness was because they lacked confidence that the underwriter could testify credibly of a difference in treatment of the risk and maintain that testimony under cross – examination. Again, however, there is no legal presumption, and the failure to produce the actual underwriter may be outweighed by other evidence. ...”(加黑部分是笔者的强调)

另在 Marc Rich & Co v. Portman & Ors(1996)1 Lloyd's Rep 430 先例中,案件涉及在一份“承租人责任保险”(charterer's liability insurance),保险人以误述与不自动披露拒赔。Longmore 大法官说:“Mr Kealey(原告受保人代表大律师)submitted that this presumption(指根据客观认定不自动披露或误述是实质重要后对有否误导与依赖的推定)is much diminished if it can be shown that the actual underwriter was careless in the writing of the very risk itself ... In my view, Mr Kealey is right about that. In most cases in which the actual underwriter is called to give evidence and is cross – examined, the Court will be able to make up its own mind on the question of inducement. The presumption will only come into play in those cases in which the underwriter cannot(for good reason)be called to give evidence and there is no reason to suppose that the actual underwriter acted other than prudently in writing the risk. In cases where he is called and the Court genuinely cannot make up its mind on the question of inducement, the insurer's defence of non-disclosure should fail because he will not have been able to show that he had been induced by the non-disclosure to enter into the insurance on the relevant terms. At the end of the day it is for the insurer to prove that the non-disclosure did induce the writing of the risk on the terms in which it was written.”

1.3.5.3 受一个实质重要误述(或不披露)影响或依赖的程度要求

在保险法下,作出对实质重要的认定,立法的定义要求必须引入专家证人(通常是劳合社资深的保险人)证明一位谨慎的保险人是否认为有关的误述(或不自动披露)是实质重要与会被影响。《Marine Insurance Act 1906》没有针对真正有关的保险人(actual insurer)也就是被陈述方是否有受到有关误述的影响,立法不针对真正有关保险人的主观想法与证据,针对的是一位“谨慎的保险人”。这不像普通法的“合理的正常与普通人士”,是可以让法官或仲裁员以自己为标准根据案情作出对某一个特别误述有否实质重要的认定,这涉及了立法下的误述(或不自动披露)要影响到什么程度才算是实质重要与有诱导。

早在 Ionides v. Pender(1874)LR 9 QB 531 先例中,审理法官就通过专家证据的帮助,判断一位谨慎的保险人会否受有关的误述(或不披露)影响,与受影响到什么程度才算是实质重要。这在笔者《海上货物保险》一书第二章之 4.3.2 段有详论。一个特定的误述对一位谨慎保险人会产生的影响(或诱导与依赖)的程度可以有三种不同测试如下:(1)决定性影响测试(decisive influence test);(2)增加风险测试(increase risk test);(3)纯粹会影响测试(mere influence test)/有兴趣知道测试(would be interested test)。

显然，影响程度定得太低就对受保人不利，因为保险人很容易以受到有关误述（或不披露）影响去拒赔。但程度定得太高则反过来对保险人不利，因为即使严重的误述（或不披露），也难以成功证明是决定性。

该书也提到这三种不同的测试会严重影响不同案件的结果，但在过往很多案例有不同说法并带来混乱，也没有定论。因为第一种（包括第二种）测试与承保的风险有关。在第一种中，保险人要证明如果受保人没有误述（或有自动披露有关信息与事实），保险人会拒绝承保或多收多少保费。因为这样该有关信息与事实才能算是有决定性的影响。但第三种测试保险人只需要证明他会希望知道该有关信息与事实，而知道了也不一定会受到影响，这也不必与承保的风险有关。可以说这是主观的说法，没有客观的标准与受保人难以提供证据去反驳，只要审理法官（通过专家证据的协助）代入保险人认为自己也会受影响或想知道即可满足有关信息与事实是实质重要的条件。

《海上货物保险》一书中举了不少案例，如适用第三种测试的 The"Dora"（1989）1 Lloyd's Rep 69 先例。案情涉及受保人在投保时对保险人误述令保险人以为将来会有更多生意，愉快地接受承保并在保费中打了折。这被判是误述与实质重要，虽然这与承保的风险没有关系，所针对的只是将来的生意。

另笔者《海上货物保险》一书第二章之4.3.4段的总结中也介绍了 Pan Atlantic Insurance Co Ltd v. Pine Top Insurance Co Ltd（1994）2 Lloyd's Rep 427 贵族院先例。在该先例中，要在决定性影响测试与真正诱导测试（actual inducement test）中作出选择。贵族院一致决定选择真正诱导的测试，主要是希望与普通法的可诉误述看齐。其中 Lloyd 勋爵说："In the case of a misrepresentation in the ordinary law of contract has always been necessary for the parties seeking to avoid the contract to show that he relied on the misrepresentation. It seems most unlikely that Parliament, by enacting（指《Marine Insurance Act 1906》立法）, intended to exclude this rule of common law for no apparent reason. It is much more likely that the intention was to codify the common law on materiality, without touching the common law on inducement."

另可节录 Goff 勋爵明确说明是实质重要下仍需要证明对真正保险人有诱导："I accept that the actual inducement test accurately represents the law. ... I conclude that there is to be implied in the Marine Insurance Act 1906 a requirement that a material misrepresentation will only entitle the insurer to avoid the policy if it induced the making of the contract...."

也就是根据立法一个实质重要的陈述会令保险人受到影响，而在 Pan Atlantic Insurance Co Ltd v. Pine Top Insurance Co Ltd 先例后，受影响程度的测试等同于普通法的诱导。

纯粹会影响测试/有兴趣知道测试，被视为对保险人太有利而且容易被滥用，特别是考虑到保险有广泛的自动披露责任，Templeman 勋爵说："...a circumstance was material if a prudent insurer would have 'wanted to know' or would have 'taken into account' that circumstance even though it would have made no difference to his acceptance of the risk or the amount of premium. If this is the result … then I must disapprove … If accepted, this submission would give carte blanche to the avoidance of insurance contracts on vague grounds of non-disclosure supported by vague evidence even though disclosure would not have made any difference. … there are no objective or rational grounds upon which this statement of belief can be tested."

在一般法律的误述中，Donaldson 大法官在 HEB Fasteners v. Marks Bloom & Co (1983) 1 All ER 583 先例中说，如果误述方能证明有关误述轻微到对订约与否的决定毫无影响，只是被误述方会想知道，而知道真相最多令被误述方有点失望，就无法满足诱导产生合约的因果关系。

而另一个极端的决定性影响测试，被视为对保险人太苛刻与不现实。其中 Lloyd 勋爵说："I am bound to say that in all but the most obvious cases the 'decisive influence' test faces them with an almost impossible task. How can they tell whether the proper disclosure would turn the scale? …"

这也配合普通法在一般法律下的误述，造成的影响无需是严重影响被误述方，而只要求被误述方有所依赖，并且只需要是其中一个影响合约产生的有效因素即可。这可节录《Misrepresentation, Mistake and Non-Disclosure》一书（2022 年，第 6 版）之 4－38段如下："**No requirement that the consequences of misrepresentation be substantial** Once it is shown that the representee relied on the statement in entering into the contract, the contract may … be rescinded. There is no requirement that the consequences of the misrepresentation must have been serious for the representee, who can therefore take advantage of a misrepresentation in order to rescind a contract even where his motives in rescinding are not related to the particular misrepresentation which founds the claim; and where the consequences of the misrepresentation are relatively minor in the context of the contract as a whole…."

看来，保险法与一般法律对依赖程度的要求是一致的。

1.3.5.4　举证责任

对举证责任的困难而言，原告作为被误述方有利之处是只要说服法院或仲裁庭认定被告曾经作出过一个实质重要的误述，也就是审理法官或仲裁员代入原告认定他们自己作为合理第三人会受到诱导，法院或仲裁庭就会以事实推断（infer in fact）[38]或推定（presume）[39]原告有依赖去订立合约。如此，轮到被告要推翻这个推断/推定，那就是证明原告并没有依赖有关的误述，可以说举证责任更加是难上加难，

〔38〕 关于事实推断可见笔者《证据法：基础理论、口头证据与专家证据》一书第八章之 1.1.3 段。

〔39〕 关于推定可见笔者《证据法：基础理论、口头证据与专家证据》一书第七章之 6 段。

特别是在欺诈性误述中，除非能找到一些明确不过的证据（例如找到被误述方的邮件说死活要这批货，货都不用看也不用检查了），否则推翻无望。

而反过来如果审理法官或仲裁员认定他们自己不会觉得有关误述是实质重要，也就是一位合理第三人不会受到有关误述的诱导，接下来的举证责任就是声称依赖了该误述的被陈述方证明（通过文件与/或口头证据）他确实有依赖。

在 Vraj Pankhania, Joshua Prakhania v. The London Borough of Hackney (2002) EWHC 2441 (Ch) 先例中，Rex Tedd Q. C. 大法官引用了 Scott 大法官在 Museprime Properties Ltd v. Adhill Properties Ltd (1990) 2 EGLR 196 上诉庭先例的说法："... If the misrepresentation **would have induced a reasonable person to enter into the contract then the court will, as we have seen, presume that the representee was so induced** and the onus will be on the representor to show that the representee did not rely on the misrepresentation either wholly or in part. **If, however, the misrepresentation would not have induced a reasonable person to contract, the onus will be on the representee to show that the misrepresentation induced him to act as he did**. But these considerations relate to the onus of proof. To disguise them under the cloak of 'materiality' is misleading and unnecessary. And as the learned editors say a little way above that passage; **the cases have tended to treat materiality as synonymous with inducement**."（加黑部分是笔者的强调）

这方面可节录《Misrepresentation, Mistake and Non-Disclosure》一书（2022 年，第 6 版）之 3 – 56 段如下所述：

"'**Materiality' of the statement and proof of reliance** The burden of proof of reliance is on the claimant（被陈述方）. But if a representation is such that it was likely that a person in the representee's position would rely on it-or, as is often said, the representation was 'material'-a court may find it easier to believe the representee's assertion that he did rely on it: the materiality of the statement is evidence that goes towards establishing reliance. ... It was once said that there is an inference in law that a statement, if material, was relied on by the person to whom it was addressed. But this has been rejected in favour of a rule, now well established in the context of a range of remedies for misrepresentation, that **materiality of a statement raises an inference in fact that it was relied on**. It was put by Jessel MR in Mathias v. Yetts (1882) 46 L. T. 496, CA in the context of the remedy of rescission:（这段大致上是说错误陈述的实质重要性，如果程度高，法院就更容易推断被误述方确实有依赖该误述。但这个推断并非法律推断而是事实推断，误述方可以相反的证据推翻这个推断。）

'**if a man has a material misstatement made to him which may, from its nature, induce him to enter into the contract, it is an inference that he is induced to enter into the contract by it. You need not prove it affirmatively.** The man who makes the material misstatement to induce the other to enter into the contract cannot be heard to say that he did not enter into it, to some extent, at all events, on the faith of that statement, **unless he can prove one of the two things**: either in fact that the man did not rely upon it, and made inquiries and got information which showed that the misstatement was untrue, and still went on with the contract, that is one thing; or else that he said, expressly or impliedly, "I do not care what your representations are; I shall not inquire about them, I shall enter into the contract taking the risk". '（误述方通常以两种办法推翻推定，证明虽然错误陈述有实质重要性，但是被误述方没有依赖。一种是被误述方曾经自己做过调查并查到信息能显示有关陈述是错误的，但仍订立合约。另一种是被误述方自己曾经明示或默示说过：'不管你的陈述正确与否，我都不关心也不会去调查，我会订立合约并承担风险。'）

The weight which such an inference of fact can carry will depend on the circumstances of the contract: the degree to which action by the representee on the basis of the particular misrepresentation was likely, and the available evidence of other grounds for the representee's actions. But**the effect of the rule is that, once a statement. Made to and understood by the representee, is shown to be material, the representor will have the burden of adducing evidence to rebut the inference that his representation was relied on by the representee**. It has sometimes been suggested that this inference (of fact) of inducement may be limited to cases of fraud; it may well be easy to establish the representee's reliance where that was the fraudulent representor's intention, but it is not limited to such cases.（有说法是对被误述方有依赖有关误述的推断应该只限于欺诈性误述，但如果误述的实质重要性高，一样可以推断被误述方确实依赖了误述，这个推断就改变了举证责任，要误述方举证反驳。）"（加黑部分是笔者的强调）

1.3.6　欺诈性误述下撤销合约在事实推定下对"要不是"测试举证责任的转移

如果涉及欺诈性误述让被误述方/受害方有权撤销合约，更是可以推定（presumption）有足够诱导与依赖，否则误述方何必刻意讲假话骗人？也就是被误述方如果想要撤销合约不需要满足"要不是"测试，而如果被误述方还想进一步以欺诈/欺骗的侵权（tort of deceit）向误述方索赔损失，则需要满足"要不是"测试（虽然对欺诈性误述这方面的要求会放宽，见本书第四章之4.2.2段/第十章之9.1.3段）。这可节录《Chitty on Contracts》（2021年，第34版）一书的9－047段所述："**'But for' causation not required for rescission for fraud.** In cases of fraud, in contrast, if the representee seeks to rescind, it is no defence for the representor to show that if the misrepresentation had not been made, the misrepresentee might still have made the contract. It is sufficient if there is evidence to show that he was materially influenced by the misrepresentation merely in the sense that it had some impact on his thinking, 'was actively present to his mind'. ... 'Once make out that there has been anything like deception, and no contract resting in any degree on that foundation can stand' ;per Lord Cranworth LJ in Reynell v. Sprye(1852)1 De G. M. & G 660'."

对欺诈性误述的推定,在 Barton v. County Natwest Ltd (2002) 4 All ER 494 (Note)上诉庭先例中,涉及原告(Barton)依赖了被告(银行)的欺诈性或疏忽误述为一笔贷款提供了个人担保(guarantee)。一审法院判是被告在知情或应该知情下误述但不认为原告有依赖。原告上诉并推翻了一审。原告指一审法院没有考虑到欺诈性误述应该作出"可反驳推定"(rebuttable presumption),这导致举证责任到了误述方。而误述方能够成功反驳只是三种情况:(1)被误述方签约前不知道有关误述(never knew of the statement until after he had entered into the contract);(2)被误述方签约前知道有关陈述是虚假(discovered before he entered into the contract that the statement was false);(3)明确证明被误述方的决定根本没有考虑有关误述(showed by words or clear conduct that the statement did not influence his decision)。

可见这三种情况都涉及误述方证明作为被误述方的原告没有被诱导,也没有作出过依赖,这十分不容易,因为欺诈性误述只要求原告在订约时对有关的误述有考虑并受到影响。[40] 在证据方面,这会是原告作为证人的一句话,作为误述方的被告就难以推翻。该先例的 Marriott 大法官说:

"The reasoning and conclusion of the judge are criticised by counsel for the Guarantors ... he contended that the **judge erred in failing to give any consideration to the rebuttable presumption which arises from the making of a fraudulent representation.** ... he submitted that in considering whether the Guarantors relied on the representation he overstated the requirement of reliance. I will consider each of those submissions in turn.

The... submission arises from the presumption that if the false statement is of such a nature that it would be likely to play a part in the decision of a reasonable person it will be presumed that it did unless the representor satisfies the court to the contrary. The continued existence of the presumption was reaffirmed by Lord Mustill in Pan Atlantic Insurance Co. Ltd v. Pine Top Insurance Ltd [1995] 1 AC 501...The nature and limits of the presumption appear from the speech of Lord Blackburn,... in Smith v. Chadwick(1884) 9 App. Cas. 187 ... Lord Blackburn said in relation to an allegation of deceit

'I think that if it is proved that the defendants with a view to induce the plaintiff to enter into a contract made a statement to the plaintiff**of such a nature as would be likely to induce a person to enter into a contract**, and it is proved that the plaintiff did enter into the contract, it is **a fair inference of fact that he was induced to do so by the statement**. ...'

... the presumption is one of fact and capable, like any other such presumption, of

---

〔40〕 见本书第十章之9.1.2段。

being rebutted. It would be dangerous in connection with any issue of fact to suggest that it may only be proved in certain specified ways. ...**The effect of the presumption is to alter the burden of proof**;the alteration remains unless and until the presumption is rebutted whether or not the representee gives evidence. ..."(加黑部分是笔者的强调)

在近期的 BV Nederlandse Industrie Van Eiprodukten v. Rembrandt Enterprises Inc (2019)EWCA Civ 596 先例〔41〕中,欺诈性误述的举证责任问题有了明确。该先例的案情涉及 2015 年美国禽流感大暴发导致被告 Rembrandt 的养鸡场一半母鸡被宰杀,鸡蛋的产量也相应大减。被告为了履行已经订立的合约,只能从外国进口鸡蛋。原告 BV Nederlandse Industrie Van Eiprodukten(以下简称 NIVE)是一家荷兰的供应商,双方订立了鸡蛋产品供应合约。但稍后不久,原告就发电邮给被告,说为了满足不可预见的法规要求而产生了额外费用,经过严格计算每千克要涨价 2.5 欧元,于是双方订立了第二份合约。〔42〕 合约开始履行一段时间后,被告以原告没有满足美国对鸡蛋进口的法规要求为由终止合约,原告于是开始诉讼索赔损失。合约约定的管辖法是英国法,英国法院拥有专属管辖权,所以虽然合约方一家是荷兰公司一家是美国公司,最后却由英国法院解决争议。

被告对违约/毁约的抗辩原因之一就是第二份合约是欺诈性误述,原告的陈述是涨价单纯是为了满足法规要求而产生的额外费用,但实际上还包括原告想要赚取更多利润的因素。而原告针对欺诈性误述的抗辩是被告非常需要鸡蛋,所以即使原告说了每公斤涨价 2.5 欧元中还包括赚取利润的考虑,被告仍然会同意订立第二份合约。也就是说并非该误述诱导订立合约,被告也没有真正去依赖过该误述。

一审法院不接受原告的抗辩,判原告的陈述是欺诈性误述。上诉庭支持了一审法院的判决,并对欺诈性误述诱导订立合约的举证责任作出了澄清。证明欺诈性误述导致订立合约的举证责任是在被陈述方,但是一旦存在欺诈性误述就有一个诱导订立合约的事实推定,也就是推定被陈述方已经满足了有关的举证责任,下一步是陈述方有举证责任推翻这个事实推定。Longmore 大法官说:"This to my mind shows that **if a representor fraudulently intends his words to be taken in a certain sense and the representee understands them in that sense and enters into a contract, it is likely to be inferred that the representee was induced to enter into the contract on the faith of the representor's statement. It is fair to call this a presumption of inducement**. But it is a presumption of fact which can be rebutted, not a presumption of law which cannot be rebutted or can only be rebutted in a particular way. The tribunal of fact has to make

---

〔41〕 针对 BV Nederlandse Industrie Van Eiprodukten v. Rembrandt Enterprises Inc(2019)EWCA Civ 596 先例的实体争议,可见本书第三章之 3.3 段的介绍。

〔42〕 很多时候这是以合约修改(amendment)的形式更改合约(variation)而非以订立第二个合约的形式,但合约更改也需要满足与合约订立同样的要件,所以道理是一样,也可以称其是一份新的合约。

up its mind on the question whether the representee was induced by the representation on the basis of all the evidence available to it. If a claimant does not give evidence, or if he does give evidence which is equivocal, that is part of the overall picture but is not conclusive. It also follows that the legal burden of proving inducement/reliance is on the representee and the fact that the court may start by making a presumption of fact in his favour does not change that position."(加黑部分是笔者的强调)

Longmore 大法官接着说被陈述方并不需要满足“要不是”的测试,只要证明对他的想法产生实质影响就已经足够,除了欺诈性误述还有其他因素导致订立合约并不意味着就没有被诱导:“... the **requirement of inducement in the tort of deceit and** in actions for **rescission for fraudulent misrepresentation** and could be stated as being that **the representee had to prove he had been materially ‘influenced’ by the representations in the sense that it was ‘actively present to his mind’** ...; that, whereas there is a presumption that a statement, likely to induce a representee to enter into a contract, did so induce him, that is merely a presumption of fact which is to be taken into account along with all the evidence. There was **no requirement as a matter of law, that the representee should state in terms that he would not have made the contract but for the misrepresentation**..."(加黑部分是笔者的强调)

最后,被误述方是否在知情与有意识下对欺诈性误述有作出过依赖,虽然在绝大部分的案件中显而易见是简单的“你骗人、我上当”,但在一些复杂的商业案件如涉及 LIBOR 丑闻的案件,会带来十分刁钻的“理解/意识因素”(understanding/awareness factor)争议。这在本书第三章之 9.4.2 段介绍的 Leeds City Council and Ors v. Barclays Bank Plc and Ors(2021)EWHC 363(Comm)先例中有介绍,不在此多讲。在 Barton v. County Natwest Ltd 先例中,虽然 Marriott 大法官不同意将对事实推定的反驳简单分为几类,但也同意想不出什么情况是不可以分进这三种的;而其中的说是被误述方订约前不知道有关的陈述就是“意识”的问题。这么看来只要存在欺诈性误述,证明被误述方没有意识到有关误述存在的举证责任在误述方。但 Leeds City Council and Ors v. Barclays Bank Plc and Ors 先例判即使是欺诈性误述,被误述方也需要先证明自己意识到有关误述存在,然后才是假设依赖的事实推定。

1.3.7 依赖误述是原告咎由自取(representee's own fault)

列举一个经常在“诱导”与“依赖”上起争议的商业情况。公司并购(merger & acquisition)或重大的买卖(如买二手船)就难免有尽职调查(due diligence investigation)或实地检验(actual inspection)。买方也就有机会核实卖方早前,例如在一份详尽的资料备忘录(information memorandum)或船舶详情(ship's particulars)等文件中作出的披露与陈述。这样,如果买方有做好尽职调查或实地检验,卖方也充分合作,买方之后(往往是有关市场逆转)能否指称误述导致合约产生而成功撤销合约?会否买方真正依赖的并不是卖方提供的信息或陈述,而是尽职调查或实地检验的结果?

正如 Park 大法官在一个涉及股权买卖合约的 Infiniteland Ltd v. Artisan Contracting Ltd(2004)EWHC 955 先例中说:"After all, a major reason why purchasers of companies carry out due diligence investigations is in order that they do not have to rely on what they have been told by the vendors, but can find things out for themselves before committing themselves to a contract."

但这种对误述的抗辩一般是不管用的,这好像罪犯以受害方为何不反抗或不逃跑作为抗辩。正如早在 Redgrave v. Hurd(1881)20 Ch. D. 1 先例中,上诉庭在推翻一审判决时说:"The person who has made the misrepresentation cannot be heard to say to the party to whom he has made that representation, 'You chose to believe me when you might have doubted me, and give further'."

在 Gould v. Vaggelas(1985)157 CLR 215 澳大利亚先例中,Brennan 大法官说:"a knave does not escape liability because he is dealing with a fool."

在 Jurong Town Corp v. Wishing Star Ltd(2005)3 SLR(R)283 新加坡先例中,Woo Bih Li 大法官说:"We see no logic, firstly, in penalising a party who has chosen to act carefully but failed, whether due to negligence or otherwise, to discover the fraud. But in another way, such a proposition would encourage the indolent. Secondly, such a proposition would also encourage fraud. It is our view that such a proposition cannot escape its consequences just because the innocent party has made his own inquiry or due diligence, unless the innocent party has come to learn of the misrepresentation before entering into the contract or does not rely on the misrepresentation when entering into the contract. This is all the more so when the representation is made fraudulently."

即使被陈述方已经提前被告知陈述的真实性有问题,但仍不去调查并作依赖,也不影响其主张可诉误述的权利。笔者的《提单与其他付运单证》(2016 年)一书第六章之 2.7.2.1 段(名为"第三人必须绝对明确提单陈述不准确"),其中介绍的 The "Johnstown"(1928)32 Lloyd's Rep 218 先例已很好说明。此先例中运输的是木材,装载作业中,船长曾书面抗议装载的木材受污染与有污泥,并且部分掉下海被冲走,但之后船长仍然签发了清洁提单。此先例中的货款支付是通过托收(collection)进行,而事实上在托收时买方手中同时有一份清洁提单与一份船长的书面抗议。所以船东(误述的被告)争辩说买方托收时已知真相,但仍作出支付,所以并没有真正地依赖提单上的不准确陈述。这一抗辩被法院驳回,认为这两份文件都出自船长,但内容相异,所以买方即使是半信半疑,选择去依赖提单对货物的表面状况描述也是合情合理。另法院也提到国际贸易的支付与提单的重要性,如果买方通过一些渠道知道或怀疑在装港签发的提单有不正确的陈述就可以合法拒绝支付,则会严重影响国际贸易。

话说回来,这种争议会是对案情的事实十分敏感(fact sensitive),永远会有极端情况对一般的大原则有偏离。相信如果没有对提单在政策上的考虑,加上告知有关文件上的陈述有虚假的渠道是十分可靠与可信,但被陈述方仍客观看来不合理地依赖就会有机会被认定为明知虚假,合理知道事实真相,对此就难说有依赖与无法证明因果关系了。

当然也难免不同审理法官或仲裁员在事实的认定会有不同看法,这是"诉讼风险"(litigation risk)。如在 Quah Poh Hoe Peter v. Probo Pacific Leasing Pte Ltd(1992) 3 SLR(R)400 新加坡先例中,案中被误述的内容是一间公司是否存在。被告误述方抗辩说公司的存续情况是公司注册处面向公众提供的资料,任何人士都可以轻而易举查询到,被误述方并不会依赖误述方的陈述。不过该案中作为原告的被误述方证明了自己确实没有机会去查询,而在误述作出之前该公司也确实存在,从而法院虽然认为对于这些面向公众的信息不应构成误述的对象,但是结合本案特定的案情,判误述仍然成立。

在30年后的今天,互联网发达,信息爆炸,资讯更加容易获取,但并不是说对于容易获取的信息的误述,尤其是带有欺骗目的的误述,误述方就可以轻易以被误述方能够获取这些信息就免责,这违反了法律要严惩欺诈的初衷。所以笔者并不认为上述新加坡案件的判决在这一点的认定上是主流的观点。

1.3.7.1 原告受害方可以或是自己作出调查去确定事实真相

误述方责怪原告被误述方是咎由自取虽然是不管用,例如很容易通过简单调查或检验就可以知道真相,但原告不去这样做,但现实中的误述案件(不论是欺诈性、疏忽或无辜)经常发生被误述方对"可诉误述"的"依赖"可否成立的争议。这可节录《Misrepresentation, Mistake and Non-Disclosure》一书(2022年,第6版)之3-59段所述:"**The claimant's own fault**In some cases, it has been argued that the representee could himself have discovered the truth, and that his failure to do so should count against him in his misrepresentation claim. ... **Generally it does not count against him: he is not deprived of the remedy of rescission just because he had the means of discovering that the statement was false; nor will the representee's own fault be counted against him in a claim in the tort of deceit**. ...This is so even where the representee deliberately chooses not to check the truth of the statement, although if he was on notice of the fact that the statement might not be true, he will not be allowed to base his claim on it. For this to apply, however, it seems that the representee must have had knowledge of facts from which he ought to have realised that the statement was false."(加黑部分是笔者的强调)

另也可继续节录该书之4-36段如下:"The representee is not deprived of the right to rescind just because he could have discovered the truth about the representor's statement-even where it might have been reasonable to expect him to make enquiries and discover the truth. There is no equivalent in the remedy of rescission to the defence of contributory negligence in a claim for damages in tort. ...This will not, however, apply in a case where **the falsity of the statement is obvious**,… Even if the representee makes some inquiries, but fails to pursue them with reasonable diligence and so fails to discover the truth, he is not necessarily prevented from rescinding. The question is always whether, as a matter of fact, he relied on the statement. **But if the representee's attempts to inquire into the truth demonstrated that he was relying on his own enquiries rather than the statement, rescission will not be available; not because of any doctrine of fault on the representee's part, but because one of the requirements of the remedy-reliance on the statement by the representee-is not satisfied.**"（加黑部分是笔者的强调）

上述的节录可总结如下几点。

1. 可诉误述能否成立的要素之一是被误述方有否依赖去订立合约。误述方对这一点的常见抗辩会是如：(1)你一听就知道我讲的是假话；(2)我讲话吞吞吐吐，你应该听得出可疑，我也叫你自己再去确认一下；(3)这事实的真假，一问就知道；(4)你如果确有进行详尽的尽职调查，没有道理查不出来；(5)你派来的检查员，只是喝酒与谈天，什么都没干，你是看了他乱写的报告才决定买；(6)你从来也没有相信过我；(7)其他各种各样的说法。

2. 作为起点，这都不影响可诉误述（特别是欺诈性，但也包括非欺诈性）是否成立。可诉误述是否成立，关键是看被误述方有否受到该虚假事实陈述或多或少的影响，不在于被误述方有没有错。所以被误述方在交叉盘问时不要乱讲，而要说一些有说服力与配合法律的回答，例如说：我是什么都不会尽信，我不会全信对方，所以派人去检查（或尽职调查），但也知道检查/调查是表面与会犯错，也不会尽信。最终决定签约是权衡后的决定，并且知道对方如果讲错也逃不掉，正如本诉讼的目的是可去向对方寻求救济。

3. 即使被误述方在特定情况确实或多或少值得责怪，但撤销合约的救济不像损失赔偿那样在疏忽的侵权下可以根据《Law Reform (Contributory Negligence) Act 1945》立法与误述方分摊损失，而只能是允许或不允许撤销。所以即使被误述方确实也严重犯错，只要认定有关误述的确在订约时有影响，仍是应该支持撤销该有缺陷合约的权利。正如上述节录的一句内容："no equivalent in the remedy of rescission to the defence of contributory negligence in a claim for damages in tort."

4. 但会有极端情况被法院（或仲裁庭）认定是没有依赖误述方的虚假陈述，如上述节录之4－36段加黑的第一部分说到法院也认同是客观看该有关"陈述"的虚假与不正确是明显不过，就是没有依赖。其中注脚提到在历史悠久的 Attwood v. Small (1838) 6 Cl. & F. 232 贵族院先例中，案情涉及卖方出售矿场时夸大了该矿场的收益能力，但之后买方请了专家在实地考察之后报告给买方的结论是确信卖方数字，其实专家也错了。之后，发现夸大真相，买方想去撤销合约。但贵族院说不行，因为买方未受误述影响，诱导合约的订立实是来自买方自己雇用的独立专家报告。Wynford

勋爵说："if the representations be of that nature, that by a view of the thing he can detect their falsehood, undoubtedly the party making the representations will not be answerable for that falsehood."

但一眼就看得出是虚假陈述在高水平(sophisticated)国际商业活动不多会出现。即使是有发生，如同在 The"Johnstown"(1928)32 Lloyd's Rep 218 先例中，在高水平的代表律师争辩下也不难解释过去为什么仍要依赖该误述。

5. 至于加黑的第二部分，也同样依赖 Attwood v. Small 贵族院先例，Wynford 勋爵说："Now suppose, instead of its having been made on the faith of the representation, the party had said, 'I draw so much beer in a month.' 'But,' says the other, 'I will not be satisfied with your telling me that; you will have no objection to verify and corroborate your statement of the draught, by giving me access to your beer books ....' ... And suppose the person had either gone and satisfied himself or sent his clerk, which clerk had made a report to him and said, I have looked through the books, and I am perfectly satisfied ..., and said, 'I see it is all right;' would he then be allowed six months after that to come and say, 'I will be off the bargain, because I find there is a less draught of beer than I expected?' ... 'No' my Lord Chief Justice would have said; 'how can I say that the purchase was made upon the faith of that representation, when I know that the purchase was made upon your own examination of the books ..., which report of your clerk was confirmed by your own ocular inspection'. ..."

这有关啤酒产量误述的例子没有太多意义，因为不同案件肯定有不同案情与背景/环境。但不排除会有极端案情被法院(或仲裁庭)认定被误述方只相信自己的非惯常的调查/检验，没有依赖、也从不相信对方的陈述。笔者相信特殊案情的案件才会被认定受害方/被误述方没有依赖对方陈述的虚假信息与事实去订立合约，所以《Misrepresentation, Mistake and Non-Disclosure》一书才只依赖这 1838 年的 Attwell v. Small 先例支持这个论点，这显示了这些年来没有同样说法或判决的重要案例，除了笔者看到的在 Hartlelid v. Sawyer & McClockin Real Estate Ltd.(1977)5 WWR 481 先例中，涉及一位地产代理误述了一间房子的车房(garage)的尺码大小，但买方曾经有过两次对房子非常详尽的检查才订约，法院判这误述没有造成影响或被依赖。笔者估计否定依赖案例不多的原因会是如下几点。

(1)否定依赖也就是否定可诉误述，即使明显在双方的谈判过程中有一个虚假的陈述，产生了一个有基本缺陷的合约。

(2)本来在国际商业活动中，双方当事人在商业交往中就是不会有尽信或完全不信，这包括在订约前的大量各种陈述/表述。对于会受较大影响的事实，被陈述方通常会承担费用去再次确认，如尽职调查、实地考察或对标的物测试检验等，甚至重复几次到自己满意为止。如果因为进行了这些惯常的调查/检验就会有失去误述救济的危险，那么会给商业活动带来严重后果，这是重视现实可行的英国法律不会做的事。

(3)所以只会在极端或特殊案情的个别案件认定受害方/被误述方没有依赖对方的虚假与不正确陈述订立合约。例如证人在交叉盘问承认没有依赖有关的误述，甚至证人一方的代表律师想补救在“再盘问”(re - examination)问证人是否有任何程度的影响(这会有诱导性问题的味道,但对方不一定会反对),证人仍不警觉说没有。[43] 也会是,披露的当场文件显示内部决定订立合约早于对方的误述,并显示毫不改变较早的决定。再另会是有证据证明受害方明知对方误述方是“外行”,他的陈述只是转达来源不明的信息与事实,所以受害方决定自己调查后下决定,甚至在谈判期间曾经纠正对方个别错误理解的陈述与/或因此压价等。

(4)确实今天有了《Misrepresentation Act 1967》之 S. 2(2)的立法条文,以轻微、不影响合约根基(root of the contract)的可诉误述(疏忽与无辜)作为借口去撤销合约,已经是此路不通。所以,根本无需去收紧受害方有否依赖(部分业已足够)的认定,进而否定一个可诉误述。

1.3.7.2　疏忽侵权以共同疏忽分摊损失

在疏忽误述(不是欺诈性误述)中,由于本质上是疏忽侵权(tort of negligence),在能够证明原告自己不去调查就贸然依赖是疏忽时,会可以共同疏忽(contributory negligence)并依赖《Law Reform(Contributory Negligence)Act 1945》立法要求分摊损失。[44] 这种抗辩在有关误述的诉讼十分常见,毕竟在商业交往,双方总能够互相挑出一些对方不小心的地方。

原告的疏忽也可以发生在另一种情况,就是确实去调查或检验(如进行尽职调查)了,但由于过程中有疏忽而导致没有找出很明显可以发觉的真相。这样不仅是分摊损失的问题,误述方会可去争辩原告根本没有依赖误述的错误事实,而是依赖了他自己疏忽调查或检验得出的错误事实。但上一段已经介绍,除非一些比较极端的情况,否则成功的机会不大。

但在欺诈性误述,由于1945年立法的措辞/文字是只针对“过错”(fault),所以不适用以共同疏忽去分摊损失。这可节录 Standard Chartered Bank v. Pakistan Nation-

---

[43] 关于交叉盘问与再盘问,可见笔者《证据法:基础理论、口头证据与专家证据》一书第三章。

[44] 见笔者《损失赔偿与救济》一书第八章之2.3段。简而言之,疏忽侵权早年的判决是一面倒,非黑即白。先是原告受害方如果在有关事故中自己也有共同疏忽(即使是十分轻微的程度),被告就可以此作为抗辩否定全部索赔。到了 Davies v. Mann(1842)10 M&W 546 先例中,法院发展出一条“最后机会规则”(last opportunity rule),也就是谁不疏忽才是避免事故发生的最后机会。例如原告不顾危险爬过栏杆在一条高速公路过马路,结果被不小心驾驶的被告撞伤,就会判被告仍是要100%赔偿原告,因为他的疏忽才是让避免此事故发生失去了最后的机会。但这种一面倒与非黑即白的疏忽责任分摊没有在海上船舶碰撞的疏忽侵权案件中被跟从:见 The“Eurymedon”(1938)p. 41 上诉庭先例(把碰撞责任50 - 50分摊)。这也与早期的国际公约《International Collision Convention 1910》一致。显然,对普通法的疏忽责任一刀切不满意,所以才有了此1945年的立法。

al Shipping Corp & Ors.（No. 2）（2002）UKHL 43 贵族院先例中，Hoffmann 勋爵所述的内容："In the case of fraudulent misrepresentation, however, I agree with Mummery J in Alliance & Leicester Building Society v. Edgestop Ltd（1993）1 WLR 1462 that there is no common law defence of contributory negligence. ... It follows that, in agreement with the majority in the Court of Appeal, I think that no apportionment under the 1945 Act is possible."

还可节录《Misrepresentation, Mistake and Non-Disclosure》一书（2022 年，第 6 版）之 6－50 段所述："The **defence of contributory negligence is available in the tort of negligence** where the claimant suffers damage as a result partly of his own fault and partly of the fault of the defendant. In such a case the court reduces the damage to such extent as it thinks just and equitable having regard to the claimant's share in the responsibility for the damage. The defence is therefore open to a defendant in a claim based on negligent misrepresentation. A claimant may be held to be contributorily negligent in relation to his own acts or omissions which, together with his reliance on the defendant's statement, caused his overall loss. **But it will generally not be possible to hold the claimant contributorily negligent simply by reason of his reliance on the defendant's statement**. ... It will therefore be **relatively rare** to find that, as a matter of fact, the duty was owed and broken and caused the claimant's loss, and yet the claimant was negligent in relying on the statement without taking further steps to verify it. **But it is possible for contributory negligence to be found on such a basis**."（加黑部分是笔者的强调）

成功以共同疏忽对索赔损失作出扣减的有 Barings Plc（In Liquidation）v. Coopers & Lybrand（No. 7）（2003）EWHC 1319；Speshal Investments Ltd v. Corby Kane Partnership Ltd（2003）EWHC 390（Ch）等先例。

1.3.8 完整合约条文与没有依赖条文

1.3.8.1 条文的作用

误述的争议是事实敏感，支持己方主张的事实的优质证据（不论是文件或口头）是至关重要的，这种诉讼也往往是昂贵且较难预料最后结果的。

所以，为了避免昂贵与费时的诉讼，今天有一条常被使用的惯用条文（boilerplate clause），也就是在笔者《合约的解释：规则与应用》一书第十三章之 2 段介绍的"完整合约条文"（Entire Agreement Clause）与专门针对谈判时误述的"没有依赖条文"（Non-reliance Clause）。后者在订约自由下有各种各样的写法，内容主要就是清楚说明双方没有依赖对方在谈判时作出的所有陈述或不存在附带协议（collateral contract）等。这往往不是事实真相，但由于条文构成了"合约性禁反言"（contractual estoppel),[45]所以真正有被误导的受害方就不能反悔。这也表示双方在有这种惯用条文的交易中,要更加小心不被对方的误述(通常是疏忽误述)诱导,对一些重要的事实尽量自己查明真相等;或者将实质重要的陈述与保证/预期以明示条文写在合约中,[46]变为合约责任。例如在一个公司并购交易中,增加条文说明无法达到谈判时陈述的预期就扣减收购价款,同时要求母公司提供担保等。

由于没有依赖条文在近年来的商业合约被广泛使用,也带来不少案例与文章质疑该条文的有效性。这在《合约的解释:规则与应用》一书第十三章之2.1段有详论,并介绍了如McGrath v. Shah(1987)57 P&CR 452;EA Grimstead & Son Ltd v. McGarrigan(1999)10 WLUK 818;Peekay Intermark Ltd v. Australia & New Zealand Banking Group Ltd(2006)2 Lloyd's Rep 511;North Eastern Properties v. Coleman(2010)3 All ER 528;Springwell v. JP Morgan(2010)EWCA Civ 1221[47]等先例,不在此重复。

1.3.8.2 没有依赖条文是否受1967年《Misrepresentation Act》的合理要求制约之争

由于大部分误述案件是无辜或疏忽,所以受害方试图向误述方索赔损失是要根据《Misrepresentation Act 1967》而不是普通法的侵权。但该立法之Section 3表述如下:"**Avoidance of provision excluding liability for misrepresentation.** (1)If a contract contains a term which would exclude or restrict—(a)any liability to which a party to a contract may be subject by reason of any misrepresentation made by him before the con-

---

〔45〕 在笔者的《合约的履行、弃权与禁反言》一书第八章有介绍。简而言之,"完整合约条文"与"没有依赖条文"即使并非事实(一方合约方确在谈判中误述并诱导合约的产生),仍是有效免责。Lewison大法官在First Tower Trustees Ltd v. CDS(Superstores International)Ltd(2018)EWCA Civ 1396上诉庭先例中说:"It is now firmly established at this level in the judicial hierarchy that parties can bind themselves by contract to accept a particular state of affairs if they know that state of affairs to be untrue. This is a particular form of estoppel which has been given the label **contractual estoppel**. Unlike most forms of estoppel it requires no proof of reliance other than entry into the contract itself. That as a matter of contract **parties can bind themselves at common law to a fictional state of affairs in which no representation have been made or, if made, have not been relied on**."(加黑部分是笔者的强调)这种条文只针对无辜与/或疏忽误述,但不针对欺诈性误述,在本书第三章之8.3段有介绍。在UBS AG v. Kommunale Wasserwerke Leipzig GmbH(2014)EWHC 3615(Comm)先例中,Males大法官说:"UBS accepts that the entire agreement and non-reliance clauses on which it relies cannot assist it to defeat a claim in fraud, and **would only be relevant if any misrepresentation was negligent or innocent**."(加黑部分是笔者的强调)。另在更近期的Aquila v. Onus Air(2018)EWHC 529(Comm)先例中,Cockerill大法官说:"Insofar as any fraudulent representation is properly pleaded and can arguably be established, it seems to me that the portions of the clauses relied upon by Aquila which relate to representations are highly unlikely to bite as a matter of law ... **The rationale behind this is that a party should not benefit from his fraud**."(加黑部分是笔者的强调)

〔46〕 见本书第二章之10.2段。

〔47〕 在《合约的解释:规则与应用》一书第十三章之2.4.9段有介绍。

tract was made;or(b)any remedy available to another party to the contract by reason of such a misrepresentation,

that term shall be of no effect except in so far as it satisfies the requirement of reasonableness as stated in section 11(1)of the Unfair Contract Terms Act 1977;and it is for those claiming that the term satisfies that requirement to show that it does. ..."(加黑部分是笔者的强调)

加黑部分显示没有依赖条文的有效性在1967年立法下,需要满足本来是针对消费者的《Unfair Contract Terms Act 1977》立法的对误述免责的条文必须"合理"的要求。[48] 例如,在Thomas Witter Ltd v. TBP Industries Ltd(1996)2 All ER 573先例中,一条没有依赖条文包括对所有的误述,包括欺诈性误述,其被法院视为不满足合理要求而无效。

在《合约的解释:规则与应用》一书没有来得及提在First Tower Trustees Ltd v. CDS(Superstores International)Ltd(2018)EWCA Civ 1396上诉庭先例中,看来与较早的Springwell v. JP Morgan(2010)EWCA Civ 1221上诉庭先例有矛盾,也否定了Thornbridge Ltd v. Barclays Bank Plc(2015)EWHC 3430(QB)与Sears v. Minco Plc(2016)EWHC 433(Ch)等一审先例认为没有依赖条文可以是一条针对双方相互承诺调节他们之间关系的条文(basis clause),不是一条免责条文(exclusion clause),不必满足1967年立法Section 3的合理要求。

在First Tower Trustees Ltd v. CDS(Superstores International)Ltd先例中,上诉庭认为任何排除立法的条文都应被视为免责条文。在该先例中,案情涉及仓库租赁,租客的代表律师在订约前询问房东仓库是否存在有害物质(包括石棉)的问题。房东回答据他所知不存在石棉与其他环境问题。但在这个回答之后租约订立之前,房东收到通知说仓库存在石棉问题,他应该即时通知租客,但他并没有。有关这持续性陈述(continuous representation)的问题,可见本书第二章之8段的介绍。一审法院判这构成误述,并且被告从表面看要负责。被告也接受这个认定,上诉的争议是被告在没有依赖条文下能否避免承担误述的责任。上诉庭最后判该没有依赖条文因不满足合理要求而无效。当然合理或不合理在每个不同案情的案件都会有不同结果,例如被陈述方是高水平与有议价能力,不像会被误述诱导的,就不应轻易以没有满足合理要求来否定他同意了的没有依赖条文,正如Lewison大法官说:"It will always be open to a contracting party seeking to rely on such a clause to establish that it was reasonable: and in cases involving the sale of complex financial products to sophisticated investors it may well be."

该案例曾经申请进一步上诉去最高院,但被拒绝。看来,在没有依赖条文到底是否是一条免责条文与要满足《Misrepresentation Act 1967》之section 3的合理的要求

---

[48] 这方面在本书第四章之6.2段有详论。

这一重要问题上,难免还会有进一步的发展。这在近期的 BNP Paribas SA v. Trattamento Rifiuti Metropolitani SpA(2020)EWHC 2436(Comm)先例中,涉及法院作出宣示判决(declaratory relief)判是在国际金融业务中被广泛使用的 1992 年 ISDA 主协议(ISDA Master Agreement)〔49〕中的没有依赖条文〔50〕有效,原告被禁反言,不得指称误述的 BNP Paribas 银行曾经作出误述并诱导订立一个对冲交易(hedging transaction)。在此先例中,Cockerill 大法官跟从 Springwell v. JP Morgan 上诉庭先例的判法而不是 First Tower Trustees Ltd v. CDS(Superstores International)Ltd 上诉庭先例,认为:

"The relevant authorities start with Springwell Navigation Corpn v. JP Morgan Chase Bank ... That case broadly supports the finding of contractual estoppels arising from such clauses. Aikens LJ said ... that: '**there is no legal principle that states that parties cannot agree to assume that a certain state of affairs is the case at the time the contract is concluded or has been so in the past, even if that is not the case, so that the contract is made upon the basis that the present or past facts are as stated and agreed by the parties.**' ...

TRM(被陈述方)pointed to the judgment of Leggatt LJ in First Tower Trustees and another v. CDS(Superstores International)Ltd ... as qualifying that approach and justifying a distinction between warranties/undertakings(which would give rise to an estoppel) from mere representations, which would not. In that case ... he stated that: '... I can see no reason in principle why it should not be possible for parties to an agreement to give up any right to assert that they were induced to enter into it by misrepresentation, provided that they make their intention clear. But I question whether a clause, ... which says simply that A 'acknowledges' that it has not entered into the contract in reliance on any representation made by B, clearly expresses such an intention. It seems to me that such wording is more naturally understood as stating a fact which may or may not be true. ... If what the parties wish to agree is that A will not assert in any future dispute that it relied on a

---

〔49〕 国际掉期与衍生工具协会(International Swap and Derivatives Association, ISDA)在 1985 年成立。它拟定的主协议(master agreement)是衍生性商品交易的重要标准文件,一般是银行或金融机构与交易对方订立所使用的框架协议(framework agreement),另加上一份双方谈判的附表(schedule)。

〔50〕 1992 年 ISDA 主协议中的"没有依赖条文"是:"**Non-Reliance.** It is acting for its own account, and it has made its own independent decisions to enter into that Transaction and as to whether that Transaction is appropriate or proper for it based upon its own judgment and upon advice from such advisers as it has deemed necessary. It is not relying on any communication(written or oral) of the other party as investment advice or as a recommendation to enter into that Transaction, it being understood that information and explanations related to the terms and conditions of a Transaction will not be considered investment advice or a recommendation to enter into that Transaction. No communication(written or oral) received from the other party will be deemed to be an assurance or guarantee as to the expected results of that Transaction."

representation made by B even if A did in fact rely on such a representation, then it seems to me that this is what the clause ought to say. ...'

It seems to me tolerably clear from this, that whatever**Leggatt LJ** ..., he **was not here purporting to or intending to overrule or qualify Springwell.** It is also worth bearing in mind that the factual situation there was very different...

As I have noted, **I am effectively bound by Springwell**. ...

That being the case one would be engaged not in discerning a dividing line between warranties and representations, but on that intention – an exercise into which the relevant background, including the nature and status of the ISDA would enter. On that basis even if Springwell were not binding, I would reach the same conclusion, namely that **a contractual estoppel exists**."(加黑部分是笔者的强调)

2. 误述带来法律责任所需要的关系

2.1 侵权概述

2.1.1 构成疏忽侵权的要件

误述的法律救济主要是依据侵权(tort)或针对合约关系的《Misrepresentation Act 1967》立法。当然,疏忽的侵权是要求双方(侵权方与受害方)有足够的邻近关系(necessary proximity or neighborhood)让侵权方可以合理预见到(foreseeable)自己不小心谨慎会令受害方受到伤害。另加上法院认为在公共政策(public policy)的考虑下,强加给在言行上犯错并导致其他人士受损的侵权人一个对无辜方/受害方小心谨慎的责任(duty of care)是公平、公正与合理(fair, just and reasonable)的。并且,如果违反了这个责任就要承担法律后果。至于什么情况下双方是有密切关系与强加小心谨慎责任是公平、公正与合理的,这涉及公共政策与方方面面的考虑。

"小心谨慎的责任"最著名的定义是 Atkins 勋爵在 Donoghue v. Stevenson(1932) AC 562 贵族院先例中所说:"The rule that you are to love your neighbour becomes, in law, 'You must not injure your neighbour', ... You must take reasonable care to avoid acts or omissions which you can reasonably foresee would be likely to injure your neighbour. Who, then in law is my neighbour? The answer seems to be persons who are so closely and directly affected by my act that I ought reasonably to have them in contemplation as being so affected when I am directing my mind to the act or omissions which are called in question."

法律对"邻居"的定义是在做任何行为时,可以合理预见到如果不小心谨慎会受影响的人士。简单的例子是驾驶车辆的司机与行人或其他车辆的,高空坠物的主人与楼下经过的人或摆放的财物(如一辆停泊的汽车)的主人。

接下来权威说法可节录 Dorset Yacht Co Ltd v. Home Office(1970)AC 1004 上诉庭先例中,Saville 大法官所述的内容:"... whatever the nature of the harm sustained by the plaintiff(被误述方),it is necessary to consider the matter not only by inquiring about **foreseeability** but also by considering the **nature of relationship** between the parties;and to be satisfied that in all the circumstances it is **fair,just and reasonable to impose a duty of care**. Of course ... these three matters overlap with each other and are really facets of the same thing. For example,the relationship between the parties may be such that it is obvious that a lack of care will create a risk of harm and that as a matter of common sense and justice a duty should be imposed ... Again **in most cases of the direct infliction of physical loss or injury through carelessness,it is self – evident that a civilised system of law should hold that a duty of care has been broken,whereas the infliction of financial harm may well pose a more difficult problem**. Thus the three so – called requirements for a duty of care are not to be treated as wholly separate and distinct requirements but rather as convenient and helpful approaches to the pragmatic question whether a duty should be imposed in any given case. ..."(加黑部分是笔者的强调)

Saville 大法官的说法在 The"Nicholas H"(1995)2 Lloyd's Rep 299 贵族院先例中被确认。Steyn 勋爵说:"That seems to me a correct summary of the law as it now stands."

普通法更愿意对造成实质损失(这包括人命伤亡与/或财产)的错误言行强加一个小心谨慎的责任,即使受害方同时索赔间接的经济损失。但对纯经济损失(pure economic losses)就比较有保留,原因大概是怕把侵权诉讼的口子开得太大,导致大量的侵权诉讼,这对整个社会也不是好事。[51] 所以早在疏忽侵权(tort of negligence)最著名的 Donoghue v. Stevenson 贵族院先例中,就确立对实质损失才有小心谨慎的责任。直到出现 Hedley Byrne v. Heller(1964)AC 465 贵族院先例,针对纯经济损失也有强加一个小心谨慎的责任。

最后,这也应是为什么虽然西方社会有这么多假消息在广泛流传,但除了政府当局的管制(这不容易做好与在不断变化的社会环境下难以在程度上掌握轻重),民事法律管不了。因为假消息虽然经常害人,而且可能会有大量受害方因为相信假消息而损失惨重,但他们往往与发布假消息的人或机构(如一些不负责的报刊)没有足够密切的关系,谈不上是"邻居",是无法提起民事诉讼索赔损失的。去强加一个小心谨慎的责任在政策上也不见得是好事,除了把侵权的口子开得太大,带来打开泄洪阀(floodgate)的后果,也会影响社会与言论自由(即使在程度上言论自由也并不是绝对),毕竟疏忽的言行是很容易发生的。

---

〔51〕 关于这方面也可见笔者《证据法:基础理论、口头证据与专家证据》一书第七章之 4.3.2.2.4 段介绍的 Alcock v. Chief Constable of South Yorkshire Police(1992)1 AC 310 贵族院先例。

2.1.2　合约谈判中的疏忽误述诱导产生合约一般不适用疏忽侵权而要以立法解决

至于合约关系，这显然是十分密切的关系。任何公司法人或自然人，只要有订约与履行合约的行为能力（capacity），在订约自由下都可以合意产生这种关系并同意分摊或承担责任。至于合约违约是否产生类似侵权的小心谨慎的责任，是要看合约的条文。在商业的范畴由于当事人之间都是合约关系，但如果涉及谈判时的误述，由于合约关系尚未产生，所以即使有一方的言行犯错，也只是侵权的范畴。例如，涉及欺诈性误述，就是欺诈/欺骗侵权。但如果是涉及疏忽误述，除非有法律强加谈判双方均有小心谨慎责任（但因为谈判涉及的范围太广，公共政策往往不会强加这样小心谨慎的责任），疏忽侵权是不适用。所以在商业上更多见，也较容易证明已成立的疏忽误述，在普通法的侵权是归类于非欺诈（non-fraudulent）性的无辜误述，只有在衡平救济有权撤销有关合约，但不能索赔损失（如果有）。

看来也是因为对普通法地位不满意，所以才会有《Misrepresentation Act 1967》立法让疏忽误述与无辜误述根据立法有机会索赔损失。[52] 这样，普通法对疏忽误述的重要性已经是减低。

2.1.3　欺诈性误述的被陈述方选择以立法误述或欺诈/欺骗侵权寻求救济

在误述的范畴，显然欺诈性误述是欺骗侵权行为。至于误述方与受害方之间是否有合约关系并不重要，只要他们之间是有法律承认的关系。此外如果欺诈性误述导致合约产生，受害方可能也会以《Misrepresentation Act 1967》之 section 2(1)起诉。因为显然一个欺诈性误述也难逃是一个疏忽的误述，也就是不满足小心谨慎责任也不会有合理依据（reasonable grounds）做出的陈述。

受害方这么选择有两个原因。

1. 举证责任：满足欺诈的举证责任（burden of proof）较为困难，但疏忽误述就相对容易了，而且在《Misrepresentation Act 1967》下是举证责任转移给误述方，由其证明作出错误的陈述是有合理依据。

这方面可节录《Chitty on Contracts》（2021 年，第 34 版）一书之 9－055 段表述："Where a person has been induced to enter into a contract as a result of a fraudulent misrepresentation by the other contracting party, he may rescind the contract, or claim damages, or both. … Misrepresentation Act 1967 … s. 2(1) of this Act allows a person who has been induced to enter into a contract by a misrepresentation to make a claim for damages as of right, … unless the representor 'proves that he had reasonable ground to believe and did believe up to the time the contract was made that the facts represented were true'. In an action under this subsection, **it is for the representor to disprove negligence, whereas in an action in fraud it is for the representee affirmatively to prove**

[52]　《Misrepresentation Act 1967》立法在本书第四章有详细介绍。

the fraud-and the burden is no light one …”(加黑部分是笔者的强调)

虽然一个错误陈述是欺诈性或只是疏忽,在民事诉讼的举证责任仍是根据双方当事人提供的证据以平衡的可能性认定事实真相,但显然成功说服法院(或仲裁庭)有关的言行构成疏忽比证明欺诈容易很多,这会是有这方面培训的法官或仲裁员在考虑证据时的直觉(instinct),欺诈也需要证明误述方主观上的不诚实(dishonest)意图。[53] 在 Dadourian Group International Inc v. Simms(2009)EWCA Civ 169 上诉庭先例中,Arden 大法官说:“Further,**the person alleging fraud must prove that the statement was made with intent that it should be acted upon by him** … **and that he did act in reliance upon it**. In considering whether a fraud has been established … Lord Nicholls in Re H(Minors)[1996] AC 563 …:‘The balance of probability standard means that a court is satisfied an event occurred if the court considers that on the evidence, the occurrence of the event was more likely than not. When assessing the probabilities the court will have in mind as a factor, to whatever extent is appropriate in the particular case, that **the more serious the allegation the less likely it is that the event occurred and, hence, the stronger should be the evidence before the court concludes that the allegation is established on a balance of probability**. **Fraud is usually less likely than negligence.**’ …”(加黑部分是笔者的强调)

2. 损失赔偿的计算不同:在侵权诉讼,是把受害方复原到侵权(也就是欺诈性误述)没有发生的地位。而且撤销合约是把该合约视为自始无效(void ab initio),好像什么都没有发生过,就带来复原(*restitutio in integrum*)的必要。所以在欺诈性误述中,损失计算会对受害方十分宽松。[54] 至于索赔损失,一般比合约的损失计算或把受害方复原到合约被履行的地位更优越。根据每一个不同案件,合约损失可能是零,但也可能是天文数字。例如,一个长达 20 年的昂贵合约,欺诈误述的受害方也不得不履行下去,那么合约损失索赔就会是一笔天文数字,比合约自始无效的复原或侵权更合算。这样,受害方可以在不同案件选择索赔合约损失或侵权复原损失。当然,能否以合约损失索赔要看有关的可诉误述有否成为后来产生的合约之条文,如有关的误述也加入一条“陈述与保证条文”(Representation and Warranty Clause);[55] 或是,有关的误述可构成“附带协议/保证”(collateral contract/warranty)。

至于立法的疏忽误述,在《Misrepresentation Act 1967》之 S. 2(1)下也可以向误述方提起索赔损失。在“拟制的欺诈”(fiction of fraud)[56] 下,也是以欺诈性误述的基

---

〔53〕 这在笔者《证据法:基础理论、口头证据与专家证据》一书第七章之 7.2.1 段有详细介绍,另也可见本书第三章之 8.2.3 段。

〔54〕 见本书第四章之 4.2.2 段。

〔55〕 见本书第二章之 10.2 段。

〔56〕 见本书第四章之 4.2.2.5 段。

础计算损失，比一般的普通法下索赔更宽松与优越。

以上的两个原因表示中国公司与代表律师应更多关注这立法或疏忽误述下提起损失赔偿的优点，而不是只关注中国法下的“虚假陈述”，相等于英国法的欺诈性误述。

2.2 非合约关系中或合约谈判中的误述

可先节录《Chitty on Contracts》(2021 年，第 34 版)一书之 9 - 101 段所说如下：“The principle of the Hedley Byrne case was somewhat limited by the majority decision of the Privy Council in Mutual Life and Citizen's Assurance Co Ltd v. Evatt(1971) AC 793 where it was held that in general there is no duty to take care in the making of statements unless the maker has held himself out as having some special skill or competence in the matter in question. **In general, it was held, the duty will only arise where the statement is made in the course of a business** ... It was decided by a bare majority and several judges have felt free to indicate their preference for the minority judgments of Lord Reid and Lord Morris. However, it has been pointed out that although the inflexible view of Mutual Life has been rejected, it remains the case that **a claimant is much more likely to be able to show that he is entitled to depend on a service or statement where the work is undertaken by a person who is exercising a special skill in a business context**.”(加黑部分是笔者的强调)

上述提到，普通法下一般的陈述/表述没有小心谨慎的责任。先去看在非商业(non-commercial)关系中作出的陈述，这是会发生在日常生活中。例如在路上向一位路人或一家商店的店员问路，但对方提供了一个错误的信息或事实。问题是可否以该路人或商店侵权误述为由，要求赔偿损失(时间上或金钱上)？答案显然是不能。普通法下侵权只分欺诈性误述与无辜误述两类，也只有欺诈性误述才在撤销误述导致的合约外，有权索赔损失。显然，指错路的误述既不会导致合约产生，也不会涉及欺诈，更不用说公共政策也不会强加路人在马路上被问路时，有小心谨慎的责任去回答与协助，否则有法律后果。这种日常或社交中的陈述，法律只要求诚实，不诚实变为欺诈/欺骗(fraud/deceit)才有法律责任。

但即使是商业上有很多活动也与非商业活动一样，商业朋友之间相互做出很多陈述，与普通法下只针对诱导合约产生的误述无关。例如在商业午餐或晚宴等活动上的陈述，更倾向于属于社交场合，是否只要求陈述方诚实？甚至在双方合约谈判期间共进晚餐时的陈述，是否也只要求陈述方诚实？如果是更严肃的场合，例如，商业伙伴写信咨询要求提供一些分公司的信息，之后也不一定会导致合约的产生，是否仍是只要求陈述方诚实？如果是这样，可以说被陈述方很难获得任何救济，毕竟证明陈述方欺诈是很困难的。

在接下来会介绍的 Hedley Byrne v. Heller(1964) AC 465 贵族院先例中，原则性地把提供事实或意见时小心谨慎的责任扩大至其他非合约的关系。这关系也不需要是诚信关系(fiduciary relationship)。至于这是怎样的关系,或可先节录 Pearce 勋爵在该先例所说的一句重要并后来被依赖的说法:"...To import such a duty [of care] the representation **must normally**, I think, **concern a business or professional transaction** whose nature **makes clear the gravity of the inquiry and the importance and influence attached to the answer** ... A most important circumstance is **the form of the inquiry and of the answer**."(加黑部分是笔者的强调)

2.2.1 Hedley Byrne v. Heller(1964)AC 465 贵族院先例

普通法自始以来将误述带来的侵权局限在双方具有特殊关系(如以下段节会提及的诚信责任),Hedley Byrne v. Heller 贵族院先例将这种特殊关系的范围进行了原则性扩大。该先例涉及的是银行就其客户的资信情况为咨询人提供参考意见。该提供参考意见的行为会在银行与咨询人之间建立一种特殊关系而令银行要对咨询人负上小心谨慎责任。如果银行提供的参考意见中存在无辜或疏忽的误述,并给依赖其参考意见的咨询人带来经济上的损失,银行要负责赔偿该损失。

该先例的案情是原告作为一家广告代理商,为其客户 Easipower Ltd 安排在电视与报纸上投放广告,并且在这些与电视台和报社的广告合约中对广告费承担责任。1958 年 11 月 4 日,原告要求自己的银行 National Provincial Bank Ltd 去调查 Easipower Ltd 公司的资信状况。原告的银行联系了 Easipower Ltd 公司有开户的银行,即被告 Heller 银行,并就 Easipower Ltd 的财务状况向被告提出了一系列问题,其中包括比较具体的问题如 Easipower Ltd 公司是否有财力每年投放价值 10 万英镑的广告。1958 年 11 月 11 日,被告回复称 Easipower Ltd 公司是一个"有声誉且日常经营状况良好的公司"(respectably constituted company, considered good for its ordinary business engagements)。原告依赖了被告对 Easipower Ltd 公司资信状况给出的意见并为 Easipower Ltd 公司安排投放了广告。随后 Easipower Ltd 公司很快破产的事实显示了被告作出的资信意见有误,原告因此损失了约 17,000 英镑并向被告索赔。

在高院,McNair 大法官认为原告与被告之间不存在普通法传统上诱导合约订立或者诚信责任的特殊关系,所以即使存在误述,也不用负责:"I am accordingly driven to the conclusion by authority binding upon me that no such action lies in the absence of contract or fiduciary relationship. On the facts before me there is clearly no contract, nor can I find a fiduciary relationship. It was urged on behalf of the plaintiff that the fact that Easipower Ltd. were heavily indebted to the defendants and that the defendants might benefit from the advertising campaign financed by the plaintiffs, were facts from which a special duty to exercise care might be inferred. In my judgment, however, **these facts, though clearly relevant on the question of honesty if this had been in issue, are not sufficient to establish any special relationship involving a duty of care even if it was open to me to extend the sphere of special relationship beyond that of contract and fiduciary relationship**."(加黑部分是笔者的强调)

2.2.1.1 特殊关系:自愿承担责任

但贵族院并没有认可该高院判决,贵族院认为如果一方有特别的技能(special skill)与知识(knowledge),用来给予意见(advice)或信息(information)协助另一方,他/她就有一个小心谨慎的责任(duty of care)。如果有疏忽,就违反了这责任,他/她应承担疏忽的侵权责任(liability in tort)。在是否构成特殊关系的问题上,该贵族院先例的判决中花费了不少篇幅分析被告银行是否在没有合约关系的情况下对原告"自愿承担责任"(voluntary assumption of responsibility)从而令双方拥有了满足侵权的"邻近"(proximity or neighborhood)要求的特殊关系。

有这样的要求也是考虑到类似银行等人士会时常提供陈述、建议/意见或信息,而如果是任何知悉该信息的人士都可以主张违反小心谨慎责任而索赔,甚至是索赔纯经济损失,这显然会导致这些人士面对过于广泛甚至是无边无际的风险。也因此必须对侵权责任加上邻近关系,自愿承担责任的要求。

过去当事人之间自愿向对方承担责任一贯是存在合约关系,并且是有对价(consideration)才被法律承认在违反时可去索赔纯经济损失,例如典型的专业人士为他们的客户提供意见与信息的做法。但此先例的情况不是合约关系,顶多是"等同于合约关系"(equivalent to contract),Heller 银行也不算是专业人士,顶多是拥有对方需要的信息,对此贵族院仍然确认这自愿承担责任的说法,的确把门开得很大。其中 Devlin 勋爵说:"The respondents in this case cannot deny that they were performing a service. Their sheet anchor is that they were performing it gratuitously and therefore no liability for its performance can arise. My Lords, in my opinion this is not the law. **A promise given without consideration to perform a service cannot be enforced as a contract** by the promisee; but if **the service is in fact performed and done negligently**, the promisee can recover in **an action in tort**. ...**It is a responsibility that is voluntarily accepted or undertaken**, either generally where a general relationship, such as that of solicitor and client or banker and customer, is created, or specifically in relation to a particular transaction. In the present case the appellants (Hedley Byrne) were not ... the customers or potential customers of the bank. Responsibility can attach only to the single act, that is, the giving of the reference, and only if the doing of that act implied a voluntary undertaking to assume responsibility. ...I think, therefore, that there is ample authority to justify your Lordships in saying now that **the categories of special relationships which may give rise to a duty to take care** in word as well as in deed **are not limited to contractual relationships or to relationships of fiduciary duty**, but **include also relationships** which ... **'equivalent to contract' that is, where there is an assumption of responsibility in circumstances in which, but for the absence of consideration, there would be a contract.** Where there is an express undertaking, an express warranty as distinct from mere representation, there can be little difficulty. The difficulty arises in discerning those cases in which the undertaking is to be implied. In this respect the absence of consideration is not irrelevant. **Payment for information or advice is very good evidence that it is being relied upon and that the informer or adviser knows that it is. Where there is no consideration, it will be necessary to exercise greater care in distinguishing between social and professional relationships and between those which are of a contractual character and those which are not.** It may often be **material to consider whether the adviser is acting purely out of good nature or whether he is getting his reward in some indirect form.** The service that a bank performs in giving a reference is not done simply out of a desire to assist commerce. It would discourage the customers of the bank if their deals fell through because the bank had refused to testify to their credit when it was good."(加黑部分是笔者的强调)

银行面对对其客户资信状况的咨询(不论是来自同行或是其他有关系的人士),可以选择不回答,但是如果选择回答,会有被认定为"自愿承担责任"的危险。但这并不是说任何在可以拒绝时回答的情况,都是自愿承担责任,例如路人被问路时指路。特殊关系不止包括合约关系或诚信关系,还可以包括可以"等同于合约"的关系,双方的交往中包括类似合约的因素,只是因为没有对价所以不构成合约(毕竟也有不少情况是给钱来购买信息)。是否会被认为是自愿承担责任的一个重要考虑因素是陈述方自愿提供信息,不是单纯出于好意(例如为路人指路),而是有其他等同于合约的考虑,例如,间接的好处如有将来的回报。这种考虑在商业与/或专业的活动中特别显著,即所谓的大家互相帮忙(scratch the back)。例如在此先例中,被告Heller银行是出于将来可能也需要对方银行提供资信信息的考虑,愿意给出对自己客户的资信意见。也会有情况是,一位资信状况良好的客户希望银行给出资信意见,如果银行拒绝会激怒客户。总之,都不是单纯出于好意,而是有商业上的考虑,只是不能在当时用金钱量化。

在该先例中,虽然判被告Heller银行对其出具的意见有小心谨慎的责任,但被告仍然最后胜诉,原因是在提供给原告的参考意见中有一免责条文说明本文件是"机密而且银行不负责任"(Confidential:For your private use and without responsibility on the part of this Bank and its officials)。这被认为银行提供的该参考意见并不是在非常严肃的情况下做出,例如律师在一份深思熟虑与严谨的法律意见中就不会加上这种批注。Pearce勋爵提出了"咨询的严肃性"(gravity of inquiry)的标准:"Was there such a special relationship in the present case as to impose on the defendants a duty of care to the plaintiffs as the undisclosed principals for whom the National Provincial Bank was making the enquiry? The answer to that question depends on the circumstances of the transaction. If, for instance, they disclosed a casual social approach to the enquiry no such special relationship or duty of care would be assumed … To import such a duty the representation must normally, I think, **concern a business or professional transaction whose**

nature makes clear the gravity of the enquiry and the importance and influence attached to the answer. … A most important circumstance is the form of the enquiry and of the answer. Both were here plainly stated to be without liability. Mr. Gardiner（原告代表大律师）argues that those words are not sufficiently precise to exclude liability for negligence. Nothing, however, except negligence could, in the facts of this case, create a liability（apart from fraud …）. I do not, therefore, accept that even if the parties were already in contractual or other special relationship the words would give no immunity to a negligent answer. But in any event **they clearly prevent a special relationship from arising**. They are part of the material from which one deduces whether a duty of care and a liability for negligence was assumed. If both parties say expressly … that there shall be no liability, I do not find it possible to say that a liability was assumed."（加黑部分是笔者的强调）

2.2.1.1.1 Caparo v. Dickman（1990）2 WLR 358 贵族院先例的指引

针对 Hedley Byrne 贵族院先例中所说的自愿承担责任时才有特殊关系，这到底是什么？又如何适用？在 Caparo v. Dickman 贵族院先例中给出了一些指引。

该先例的具体案情可见本章之 3.4.2 段的介绍。原告是一家上市公司的小股东，在看到会计师给上市公司提供的审计账目报告后，依赖该审计报告大量收购上市公司股票变成了大股东。但实际上该审计账目报告有错，导致原告蒙受巨大损失。这里的问题就是公司委任的会计师提供审计报告时，是否对公司个别股东自愿承担责任导致有小心谨慎责任？

Bridge 勋爵在总结了过往先例，尤其是 Hedley Byrne 贵族院先例后，给出了以下说法："The salient feature of all these cases is that **the defendant giving advice or information was fully aware of the nature of the transaction which the plaintiff had in contemplation, knew that the advice or information would be communicated to him directly or indirectly and knew that it was very likely that the plaintiff would rely on that advice or information in deciding whether or not to engage in the transaction in contemplation.** In these circumstances the defendant could clearly be expected, subject always to the effect of any disclaimer of responsibility, specifically to anticipate that the plaintiff would rely on the advice or information given by the defendant for the very purpose for which he did in the event rely on it."（加黑部分是笔者的强调）

除了上述 Bridge 勋爵的指引外，在 Caparo v. Dickman 先例中 Oliver 勋爵也给出了类似的说法，并加上了第 4 点，即被误述方确实依赖该陈述并导致损害，误述方才会有责任。也可以一并节录 Oliver 勋爵所说如下："What can be deduced from the Hedley Byrne case, therefore, is that **the necessary relationship between the maker of a statement or giver of advice**（'the adviser'）**and the recipient who acts in reliance upon it**（'the advisee'）may typically be held to exist where（1）the advice is required for a purpose, whether particularly specified or generally described, which is made known, either actually or inferentially, to the adviser at the time when the advice is given; (2) the adviser knows, either actually or inferentially, that his advice will be communicated to the advisee, either specifically or as a member of an ascertainable class, in order that it should be used by the advisee for that purpose; (3) it is known either actually or inferentially, that the advice so communicated is likely to be acted upon by the advisee for that purpose without independent inquiry; and (4) it is so acted upon by the advisee to his detriment. That is not, of course, to suggest that these conditions are either conclusive or exclusive, but merely that the actual decision in the case does not warrant any broader propositions."（加黑部分是笔者的强调）

Caparo v. Dickman 先例中给出的指引在后续一系列先例中被认为是更有帮助的说法，实践中认为 Hedley Byrne 贵族院先例中对于如何适用说得不够清楚，也就是错误陈述的被告什么时候需要承担小心谨慎责任，应该直接看 Caparo v. Dickman 先例中的指引。[57] 该指引在后续先例中也被反复提及与适用：见 James McNaughton Paper Group Ltd v. Hicks Anderson & Co (1991) 2 QB 113 上诉庭先例，Morgan Crucible Co Plc v. Hill, Samuel & Co Ltd (1991) Ch 295 上诉庭先例，以及近期的 Banca Nazionale del Lavoro SPA v. Playboy Club London Ltd & Ors (2018) UKSC 43 最高院先例等。

可以简单解释该指引中提到的以下几点：

1. 被告（误述方）了解原告（被误述方）想要进行什么交易，实际上也就是要看误述方陈述的目的到底是什么。

也因此在 Caporo v. Dickman 先例中，公司委任会计师是为了符合英国《Companies Act 1985》的要求而制作审计报告，贵族院认定此立法下审计报告的目的是让公司管治，完全不涉及提供信息给个别股东（甚至是外部人士），也因此会计师对个别股东投资公司行为不存在小心谨慎责任。

但这样的判法根据具体案情有时候会有些局限。显然文件目的到底有哪些，很依赖具体的案情而定。在后续的先例中就出现将陈述目的解释为有多重目的，也不

---

〔57〕 在 James McNaughton Paper Group Ltd v. Hicks Anderson & Co (1991) 2 QB 113 上诉庭先例中，Neill 大法官说："The natural starting point for this search for guidance is, of course, the Hedley Byrne case [1964] AC 465, but I do not propose to make any detailed reference to it for at least three reasons. In the first place, as Lord Oliver ... observed in the Caparo case...it is not easy to cull from the speeches in the Hedley Byrne case any clear attempt to define or classify the circumstances which give rise to the relationship of proximity. In the second place, the test which was suggested in some of the speeches in the Hedley Byrne case, the test of 'a voluntary assumption of responsibility' by the defendant, has been found to be unhelpful in more recent authorities: see, for example, per Lord Griffiths in Smith v. Eric S. Bush ... and per Lord Roskill in the Caparo case ... My third and most compelling reason for not making any detailed reference to the Hedley Byrne case is the fact that **Lord Oliver himself in the Caparo case ... set out, in words which I would gratefully adopt, the guidance which can be obtained from the Hedley Byrne case**."（加黑部分是笔者的强调）

需要主要目的涉及被误述方的交易,而只要有目的涉及就已经足够。

比如在 Morgan Crucible Co Plc v. Hill, Samuel & Co Ltd 上诉庭先例中,原告想要收购目标公司 First Castle Electronic Plc,而目标公司的董事、会计与金融顾问等人士向股东作出陈述,指出根据公司的盈利能力,建议不接受原告的收购。之后原告根据该陈述中的信息,提高了收购价,并成功完成收购。但实际该陈述的信息有错,原告也因此蒙受损失。原告想要向误述方索赔,显然困难就是目标公司董事、会计、金融顾问等人士与原告之间是否会有小心谨慎责任?

在此先例中,原告只不过是公司外部收购人。正常情况下,目标公司董事、会计、金融顾问等人士的建议也是提供给目标公司股东的,陈述或文件的目的应与外部收购人完全无关。但在此先例中的具体案情下,贵族院认定的事实是在原告已经出现与明确后,这些人士才给出的错误陈述,明确知道该陈述会被原告依赖用来收购。也因此就很弹性地将文件目的解释为,主要目的是向股东提供信息,但同时也有次要目的是向外部收购人抬价,这就足以在这些人士与原告之间建立小心谨慎责任了。

2. 知道有关陈述会被直接或间接交给被误述方,误述方能预见到对被误述方有小心谨慎责任。

这要求显然不是说误述方必须清楚知道被误述方的身份,而是误述方必须知道存在该类人士会依赖自己的陈述。例如,Hedley Byrne 先例中提供资信报告的被告银行未必知道原告的真实身份,但显然会知道资信报告是会被提供给其他人士依赖,也因此应该对自己的陈述加倍小心。

可能涉及的被误述方还可见本章之 3.1 段的介绍。

3. 被误述方很可能会依赖该陈述决定是否进行交易。也就是说,实际上误述方应该知道被误述方不会将该陈述不当回事,如被误述方自己本就不会进行独立的调查,反而会实际依赖误述方的陈述。站在被误述方的角度,则是自己依赖误述方的陈述是合情合理的。

虽然 Caporo v. Dickman 先例中专业人士无需承担责任,但在各种各样的案情下,适用有关指引后的结果可能有不同。在 Smith v. Eric S. Bush(1990)1 AC 831 先例中,希望购买房产的原告请自己的抵押贷款人 Abbey National Building Society(房屋互助协会)提供有关房屋的估值报告,房屋互助协会与被告测量师(Bush 先生)订立合约。被告的报告中称有关房屋无需大修,但是这并不是事实,有关房屋有结构缺陷。原告依赖被告的报告购买该房屋后不久,烟囱倒塌毁坏了房顶与阁楼。贵族院判被告对原告有小心谨慎责任。毕竟根据前述案情,显然估值报告的目的是让房屋互助协会判断是否发放贷款,也是让原告判断是否值得购买。

更重要的是,在这种小市民个人购买普通住宅的情况下,个人是可以合理依赖房屋互助协会委任的测量师出具的报告的,合理的测量师也能认识到这一点,事实上也就是自愿承担责任了。换个情况,如果是大型工业建设购买房产,大型开发商购买土地,或者是富豪购买顶级豪宅,此时就一般都会期待买家会独立调查情况来帮助买家了解价值与做商业上的判断，测量师完全可以合理估计买家并不会单纯依赖自己的报告进行交易。

可以节录 Templeman 勋爵所说如下："The valuer knows that the consideration which he receives derives from the purchaser and is passed on by the mortgagee, and the valuer also knows that the valuation will determine whether or not the purchaser buys the house."

还可以节录 Griffiths 勋爵所说如下："It must, however, be remembered that this is a decision in respect of a dwelling house of modest value in which it is widely recognised by surveyors that purchasers are in fact relying on their care and skill."

在 Morgan Crucible Co Plc v. Hill, Samuel & Co Ltd 先例中，Hoffman 大法官还指出了此先例为什么这样表面看来与 Caparo v. Dickman 先例不同判法的理由，强调了这背后经济上的原因。首先原告在此先例中支付了被告的费用，因此虽然严格来说在他们之间没有合约，但在他们之间是有一定关系的。其次 Caparo v. Dickman 先例中收购公司是高风险高回报的投资行为，在这类行为中并非所有人士都能通过投保保护自己面对的风险，而一旦出问题这些专业人士个人有可能因此大出血甚至倾家荡产；〔58〕而 Smith v. Eric S. Bush 先例中原告只是个人购买普通住宅，这类行为中的专业人士很容易投保来保护自己。最后则是从保险风险上来看，类似此先例中案件给专业人士加上小心谨慎责任，并不会显然增加专业人士投保责任保险风险。

2.2.1.1.2 免责声明

在本章之 2.2.1.1 段介绍 Hedley Byrne 贵族院先例时，提到了其中的免责声明。至于免责声明是否能减低咨询的严肃性，从而达到免于承担疏忽侵权责任的效果，根据 Smith v. Eric S. Bush(1990)1 AC 831 与 Harris v. Wyre Forest DC(1990)1 AC 831 等先例，针对消费者，除非可以满足《Unfair Contract Terms Act 1977》之 section 2(2)的合理要求，〔59〕否则作用有限。可先节录有关立法条文，以帮助读者理解："... In the case of other loss or damage, a person cannot so exclude or restrict his liability for negligence except in so far as the term or notice satisfies the requirement of reasonableness. ..."

在上一段介绍过的 Smith v. Eric S. Bush 贵族院先例中，原告与房屋互助协会的合约中说明房屋互助协会与被告都对提供给原告的报告内容免责："...neither the society nor the surveyor or the firm of surveyors will warrant, represent or give any assurance to me that the statements, conclusions and opinions expressed or implied in the report and mortgage evaluation will be accurate or valid and the surveyor's report will be

〔58〕 自贵族院的 South Australia Asset Management Corp v. York Montague Ltd(1997) AC 191 先例后，有了责任范围大原则的创新说法以限制专业人士的责任，这在本书第六章有详细介绍。

〔59〕 在本书第四章之 6 段对《Unfair Contract Terms Act 1977》之 section 2(2)的合理要求有详细介绍。

supplied without any acceptance of responsibility."贵族院判这种房屋价格相对较低，原告依赖估值报告作出决定是惯常做法，并非不合理。被告自愿承担责任，在 Hedley Byrne 先例下要对原告的损失负责。这个房屋可能是原告一辈子买过的最贵的东西，让专业人士测量师承担责任更合理。有关的免责条文不满足《Unfair Contract Terms Act 1977》之 section 2(2)的合理要求而无效。

同样情况也出现在 Harris v. Wyre Forest DC 先例中，涉及的免责条文是说："no responsibility ... for the value or condition of the property."

由于英国消费者的合约与立法的保护与中国公司关系不大，就此略过。只接下来只说在 Hedley Byrne 贵族院先例后，法律在这方面变得广泛得多了。这重大的改变，也带来实践中的难题。例如，如果一家银行对一位友好关系的客户或商业朋友(如另一家银行或金融机构)的一个咨询免费(不是合约关系，也没有对价)提供信息，如果法律下有小心谨慎责任，该银行是要做多少调查取证才算是尽了这个责任？会否因为这样"兴师动众"，该银行索性拒绝提供免费的信息？又或是，一个客户或商业朋友认为是简单的回答，但如果因为银行需要时间调查取证而迟迟无法回应，反而是"远水救不了近火"？这样，对整体的商业社会活动而言是不是好事？看来要由审理法院根据不同的案情有弹性地判断到底是否满足了小心谨慎的责任，不能上纲上线设立一个不现实的要求。

这类问题看来在《Chitty on Contracts》(2021 年，第 34 版)一书的 9-098 段有讨论："... It was ... said that a 'duty to be honest' is at least owed in such circumstances, though it is far from clear whether this is the same thing as the duty merely to abstain from fraud. If the 'duty to be honest' goes beyond liability in fraud, it would seem necessary to recognize a new form of liability midway between fraud and negligence, but it is submitted that this is a confusing and unnecessary conception. Since the duty of care means a duty to take such care as is reasonable in all the circumstances of the case, the law of negligence is already sufficiently flexible to cater for different degrees of care. There is, for instance, no reason why a court should not hold that a bank giving references about a customer does owe a duty of care to the representee, while at the same time recognizing that this duty does not require the banker to compile an exhaustive dossier on the customer's activities over a period of many years."

Goff 勋爵在多年后的 Henderson v. Merrett Syndicates Ltd(1995)2 AC 145 贵族院先例中说："The case(指 Hedley Byrne 贵族院先例)has always been regarded as important in that it established that, in certain circumstances, a duty may exist in respect of words as deeds, and further that liability may arise in negligence in respect of pure economic loss which is not parasitic upon physical damage."

2.2.1.2 疏忽侵权索赔纯经济损失

Hedley Byrne 贵族院先例带出来对传统普通法地位的另一重大改变是开放在疏

忽侵权的案件索赔纯经济损失。[60] 传统普通法下因疏忽侵权可以索赔经济损失只存在于三种情况:(1)双方有合约关系;(2)一方对另一方有诚信责任,例如律师、会计师与他们的客户;[61](3)双方之间存在邻近关系从而对对方有小心谨慎的责任。在第三种情况下,经济损失索赔的前提是该经济损失是侵权行为带来的实质损失(physical loss)所导致,例如开车撞伤人,伤者就医、无法工作等经济损失,而不包括伤者无法工作而给他就职的公司带来的纯经济损失。但是在本案中,贵族院的勋爵们认为现有的法律存在缺陷与不符合商业的发展,Delvin 勋爵解释了在 Hedley Byrne 贵族院先例前普通法疏忽的矛盾,并给了一个医生疏忽的例子说:"Today it is unthinkable that the law could permit directors to be as careless as they liked in the statements they made in a prospectus. ...This is why the distinction is now said to depend on whether financial loss is caused through physical injury or whether it is caused directly. The interposition of the physical injury is said to make a difference of principle. I can find neither logic nor common sense in this. If irrespective of contract, a doctor negligently advises a patient that he can safely pursue his occupation and he cannot and the patient's health suffers and he loses his livelihood, the patient has a remedy. But if the doctor negligently advises him that he cannot safely pursue his occupation when in fact he can and he loses his livelihood, there is said to be no remedy. Unless, of course, the patient was a private patient and the doctor accepted half a guinea for his trouble: then the patient can recover all. I am bound to say, my Lords, that I think this to be nonsense. It is not the sort of nonsense that can arise even in the best system of law out of the need to draw nice distinctions between borderline cases. It arises, if it is the law, simply out of a refusal to make sense. The line is not drawn on any intelligible principle. It just happens to be the line which those who have been driven from the extreme assertion that negligent statements in the absence of contractual or fiduciary duty give no cause of action have in the course of their retreat so far reached."

Pearce 勋爵也认为法律对于经济损失的保护已经落后于对于人身和财产伤害的实质损失的保护,但在当时法律没有开放纯经济损失索赔的口子,这主要是因为担心一旦开了口子将会产生大量的诉讼。此外,如果存在实质损失,也更容易证明确实存在邻近关系。但是 Pearce 勋爵认为在该先例的案情下因为双方之间存在邻近的特殊关系,所以可以索赔因 Heller 银行疏忽误述而带来的损失。毕竟从现实来讲,疏忽

---

〔60〕 关于传统的疏忽侵权(tort of negligence)只接受实质损失(physical loss)而不接受纯经济损失,可见本章之 2.2.1.2 段。

〔61〕 在 Nocton v. Lord Ashburton(1914) AC 932 先例中,贵族院用的词是"赔偿"(compensation)/衡平赔偿(equitable compensation)而不是"金钱损失"(damages),因为诚信责任是衡平法概念。有关衡平赔偿也可见本书第十章之 12.3.2 段。

误述只会带来经济损失而不会带来实质损失

后续案件中，更是根据 Hedley Byrne 贵族院先例的判法，也不仅仅是在错误陈述中，而是在各类行为，尤其是专业服务行为中，都以类似特殊关系下违背小心谨慎责任，索赔纯经济损失。近几十年来发生不少大型国际金融“诈骗”案件，在案件发生后，也产生了大量针对作为“中间人”的银行、金融顾问等人士进行索赔的诉讼，指他们违反小心谨慎责任给出错误的陈述、建议/意见或信息并向他们索赔。这类案件往往影响人士众多，涉案金额巨大。其中部分会涉及合约关系或信义/诚信关系，但如果没有或作为替代诉因，此时就可能需要考虑自 Hedley Byrne 贵族院先例以来的一系列先例判法考虑这些“中间人”是否自愿承担责任？

在此可节录 Henderson v. Merrett Syndicates Ltd(1995)2 AC 145 贵族院先例中，Browne – Wilkinson 勋爵说：

“**The law of England does not impose any general duty of care to avoid negligent misstatements or to avoid causing pure economic loss** even if economic damage to the plaintiff was foreseeable. However, such a duty of care will arise **if there is a special relationship between the parties**. Although the categories of cases in which such a special relationship can be held to exist are not closed, as yet only **two categories have been identified**, viz. (1) where there is a fiduciary relationship and (2) **where the defendant has voluntarily answered a question or tenders skilled advice or services in circumstances where he knows or ought to know that an identified plaintiff will rely on his answers or advice**.

In both these categories the **special relationship is created by the defendant voluntarily assuming to act in the matter by involving himself in the plaintiffs affairs or by choosing to speak.** If he does so assume to act or speak he is said to have assumed responsibility for carrying through the matter he has entered upon. ”(加黑部分是笔者的强调)

有关确认在“自愿承担责任”下索赔“纯经济损失”的贵族院先例还有 White v. Jones(1995)2 AC 207 先例与 Williams v. Natural Life Health Foods Ltd(1998)1 WLR 830 先例等。在后者，Steyn 勋爵说：“… a great many precedents were cited at first instance, in the Court of Appeal and in the printed cases lodged for the purpose of the present appeal. … The sole purpose of the citation of precedent is, or ought to be, the identification of a legal principle or rule which covers, or may arguably cover, the issue in the case to be decided. … **In this case the identification of the applicable principles is straightforward**. It is clear, and accepted by counsel on both sides, that the governing principles are … **First**, in Henderson’s case it was settled that the assumption of responsibility principle enunciated in Hedley Byrne & Co. Ltd. v. Heller & Partners Ltd. [1964] A. C. 465 is not confined to statements but may **apply to any assumption of responsibil-**

ity for the provision of services. The extended Hedley Byrne principle is the rationalisation or technique adopted by English law to provide **a remedy for the recovery of damages in respect of economic loss caused by the negligent performance of services**. **Secondly**, it was established that once a case is identified as falling within the extended Hedley Byrne principle, there is no need to embark on any further inquiry whether it is 'fair, just and reasonable' to impose liability for economic loss..."(加黑部分是笔者的强调)

2.2.2 Mutual Life and Citizens Assurance Co Ltd v. Evatt(1971) AC 793 枢密院先例

在接下来的 Mutual Life and Citizens Assurance Co Ltd v. Evatt 枢密院先例中,案情涉及澳大利亚的一家保险公司被一位客户(保单的受保人)Evatt 先生问及一家联营公司的财政状况。该保险公司免费提供了联营公司资产状况稳定的信息,也即是双方没有合约关系,情况与 Hedley Byrne 贵族院先例接近。由于信息错误,Evatt 先生向联营公司的投资蒙受经济损失,从而向保险公司提出索赔。Evatt 先生声称显然保险公司比他自己更能知道联营公司的有关信息,保险公司明知自己会依赖它提供的信息投资联营公司,仍然疏忽提供信息,并导致他蒙受损失,所以应该承担责任。

枢密院的多数意见是重点是提供信息的一方到底是否经营这方面业务与/或有有关的技巧与能力,并且愿意尽职给出可靠意见:"... in their Lordships' view the reference to 'such care as the circumstances require' presupposes an ascertainable standard of skill, competence and diligence with which the adviser is acquainted or has represented that he is. **Unless he carries on the business or profession of giving advice of that kind he cannot be reasonably expected to know whether any and if so what degree of skill, competence or diligence is called for**, and a fortiori, in their Lordships' view, he cannot be reasonably held to have accepted the responsibility of conforming to a standard of skill, competence and diligence of which he is unaware, simply because he answers the inquiry with knowledge that the advisee intends to rely on his answer. This passage should in their Lordships' view **be understood as restricted to advisers who carry on the business or profession of giving advice of the kind sought and to advice given by them in the course of that business.**"(加黑部分是笔者的强调)

而在该先例中,多数意见是保险公司经营的业务里不包括投资建议,也没有声称有相关的技巧与能力并且愿意尽职给出可靠建议,仅仅是知道 Evatt 先生会依赖它提供的信息并不够,保险公司只有诚实给出回答的责任。显然在该先例没有指控保险公司提供的信息不诚实,即不是欺诈/欺骗,所以保险公司对 Evatt 先生没有误述的责任。显然,多数意见是试图限制 Hedley Byrne 大原则的适用情况。这也有它的道理,举个生活中的例子帮助理解,在询问食评家某餐厅是不是好吃后,就有理由与合理去依赖他的回答。而如果同样的问题问个棺材铺老板,即使他热情回答,听者也应该对答案有保留。

但 Reid 勋爵与 Morris 勋爵不同意多数意见的判决。少数意见认为首先对于普通法是否强加小心谨慎的责任不应该设立死板的规则,应弹性处理。比较明确的是在一些日常或社交场合的陈述,只需要诚实。在该先例应考虑的问题是,这个陈述是否是在商业活动中作出的。可节录有关少数不同意见如下:

"**In our judgment it is not possible to lay down hard – and – fast rules** as to when a duty of care arises in this or in any other class of case where negligence is alleged. When, in the past, judges have attempted to lay down rigid rules or classifications or categories they have later had to be abandoned. But it is possible and necessary to determine the principles which have to be applied in determining whether in given circumstances any duty to take care arises.

In this class of case**the first principle is that no duty beyond the duty to give an honest answer can arise when advice is given casually or in a social context**, and the reason is that it would be quite unreasonable for the inquirer to expect more in such circumstances and quite unreasonable to impose any greater duty on the adviser. The law must keep in step with the habits of the reasonable man and consider whether ordinary people would think they had some obligation beyond merely giving an honest answer.

It may be going too far to say that a duty to take care can only arise where advice is sought and given in a business or professional context, for there might be unusual cases requiring a wider application of this principle. But for present purposes **we think that the appropriate question is whether this advice was given on a business occasion or in the course of the appellant's business activities.** ...

It appears to be**quite common practice for businesses to perform gratuitous services for their customers with the object of retaining or acquiring their goodwill**. If they incur expense in doing so it has never so far as we are aware been suggested that such expense is not a business expense and **we think that where companies do perform such service both they and their customers would be surprised to learn that the company is under no obligation to take any care in the matter.** "(加黑部分是笔者的强调)

少数意见认为只要是向商业人士在商业活动提出问题并寻求一个深思熟虑的意见(considered advice)或信息,并向商业人士表达将会依赖意见去做某些事情,而该商业人士如果提供(他/她当然可以拒绝提供,毕竟是免费提供的),就在道德上有了小心谨慎的责任。在 Hedley Byrne 贵族院先例中,只是通过指称双方有了特殊关系把道德上小心谨慎的责任转为是法律上。Reid 勋爵与 Morris 勋爵所说如下:"In our judgment when an inquirer consults a business man in the course of his business and makes it plain to him that he is seeking considered advice and intends to act on it in a particular way, any reasonable business man would realise that, if he chooses to give advice without any warning or qualification, he is putting himself under a moral obligation to take some care. It appears to us to be well within the principles established by the Hedley Byrne case to regard his action in giving such advice as creating a special relationship between him and the inquirer and to translate his moral obligation into a legal obligation to take such care as is reasonable in the whole circumstances."

看来,多数与少数意见的区别是:多数的判决是限制被指控是误述的被告的身份,原告问及与被告所提供的错误意见的内容必须是被告的业务范围,且客观看被告有相关方面的技巧与能力。只有这样,原告向被告提问才是"对口",也是合情合理可以去依赖,这才有特殊关系并在被告误述时可强加小心谨慎的责任。否则,原告问的不对口,自己也应该小心去通过其他渠道核实。这表示在 Hedley Byrne 贵族院先例中,提供客户的资信意见可以勉强说是被告 Heller 银行业务范围的一部分,所以错误的回答会是要对原告 Hedley Byrne 负责。但此先例是向保险公司问投资建议,被告就没有特殊关系下的小心谨慎责任。

看来多数意见与判决为了避免把这种侵权门开得太大,试图限制 Hedley Byrne 大原则的适用情况,甚至出现限制得太死的情况。毕竟在商业活动有真正技巧与能力并开门做生意提供信息与意见的是大批的专业人士如律师、会计师、专家等,在法律上也已经有在他们与客户之间强加小心谨慎责任的信义/诚信责任的说法。在此针对的只是一般商业人士对同行、客户或商业朋友免费提供信息与意见,而这种情况也经常发生。所以少数意见不同意多数意见所加的限制,认为只要是在商业活动上提供的意见,在恰当的情况下就可以适用 Hedley Byrne 大原则,对被告陈述方强加一个小心谨慎的责任。

总结说枢密院的多数意见与判决令法律地位更不肯定,特别是 3:2 的多数意见。毕竟,虽然枢密院的判决对英国法院没有约束,但十分有说服力,因为作出判决的与贵族院的大法官是同一批人。这方面的问题在后续先例有了进一步的明确与澄清。

2.2.3 后续案件之一:Esso Petroleum Co Ltd v. Mardon (1976) 2 Lloyd's Rep 305 上诉庭先例

接下来两个案例涉及的情况与 Hedley Byrne 贵族案先例与 Mutual Life and Citizens Assurance Co Ltd v. Evatt (1971) AC 793 先例本质上有一点区别,不再是免费向客户或商业朋友提供错误的信息与意见,而是涉及合约谈判过程中一方向另一方提供错误的信息或意见并造成另一方损失。

可先介绍 Esso Petroleum Co Ltd v. Mardon 先例的案情,原告 Esso (美国著名石油公司)在 1961 年想在英国的 Southport 建一个加油站,在当地进行选址之后看中了一个毗邻商业区主干道的地皮并就此选址做了详尽的调查。调查结果表明加油站如果建在此地皮上,开业第三年就可以达到每年出售汽油 20 万加仑的目标。但在向当局申请建造执照时,当地的规划局不批准加油站的加油桩与进入加油站的通道正对大马路,而是要将加油桩建在一个展示厅的后面背对大马路。这样,汽车要加油就要绕道旁边的小路才能进入加油站,这肯定会令加油站的生意受损。1963 年加油站建好后 Esso 与被告 Mardon 先生谈判将加油站租给 Mardon 先生经营,在谈判中 Esso 的代表仍然告知被告 Mardon 先生最初选址调查时得出的数据,即开始经营的第三年,每年就能出售 20 万加仑汽油,并将此数额作为双方谈判租金的一个重要依据。这令被告以较高的租金向 Esso 租用了这个加油站 3 年的经营权。在后来的经营中被告虽然想尽办法,但加油站出售的油量仍然与 20 万加仑差距甚远,每年仍只能出售约 8 万加仑的汽油,经营不断亏损。被告在苦心经营了 15 个月后在 1964 年 7 月实在坚持不下去,于是写信给 Esso 想终止租约。Esso 于是大幅降低了租金并留住 Mardon 先生继续经营。在 1967 年,Esso 向 Mardon 先生起诉追索欠下的油钱,而被告 Mardon 先生则向 Esso 反索赔这疏忽误述所带来的大笔损失。

因为这误述发生在 1963 年,所以《Misrepresentation Act 1967》尚未生效,只能以普通法寻求救济。但普通法下除非是欺诈性误述可以欺诈/欺骗侵权索赔金钱损失外,只有存在 Hedley Byrne 贵族院先例下的特殊关系并违反了因此产生的小心谨慎责任,也就是疏忽侵权的情况下,无辜方才可以索赔纯经济损失。但已经简单提过,不会对一般商业谈判一概强加对对方的小心谨慎责任。由于 Esso 的误述是发生在谈判期间,在时间上还没有合约,加上谈判不一定会产生合约,所以误述即使有责任,也不是合约责任,可索赔纯经济或金钱损失。

如果有附带协议/保证(collateral contract/warranty),这是相等于合约关系可索赔金钱损失。但在高院,Lawson 大法官判 Esso 胜诉,也判不存在一个附带协议或保证。所以,这道门也在一审被关上。

但去了上诉庭,一审判决被推翻,上诉庭一致判是 Esso 败诉,要赔 Mardon 先生一大笔钱。败诉原因之一是上诉庭认为 Esso 说加油站能够售出 20 万加仑汽油构成一个附带协议或保证。Denning 勋爵说虽然 Esso 从来没有保证能出售 20 万加仑汽油,但相对于 Mardon 先生来说,Esso 作为专业的石油巨头才是拥有全面资料并作出详细调查后得出该预测的一方,在双方的谈判中,证据清楚显示被告 Mardon 先生是不拥有这方面的专业知识与技能,完全依赖 Esso 提供的信息来订约与议价,这等于是 Esso 对 Mardon 先生作出的默示保证(implied warranty)。Denning 勋爵说:"Now, I would quite agree... that it did not guarantee that the throughput would be 200,000 gallons. But, nevertheless, it was a forecast made by a party-Esso-who had special knowledge and skill ... They knew the facts. They knew the traffic in town. They knew the throughput of comparable stations. They had much expertise and experience at their disposal. They were in a much better position than Mr Mardon to make a forecast. It seems to me that if such a person makes a forecast-intending that the other should act upon it and he does act upon it-it can well be interpreted as a warranty that the forecast is sound and reliable in this sense that they made it with reasonable care and skill. It is just as if Esso said to Mr. Mardon: Our forecast of throughput is 200,000 gallons. You can rely upon it as being a sound forecast of what the service station should do. The rent is calculated on that footing'."

Denning勋爵继续针对即使没有一个附带保证,Esso会否仍要赔偿Mardon先生的损失的问题,这就带出Hedley Byrne原则下的特殊关系会否适用在合约谈判并成功导致合约产生的情况。Denning勋爵对在这种一方完全依赖另一方提供的信息的情况下,Hedley Byrne原则是否适用在谈判的情况给出了定论,说:

"Assuming that there was no warranty, **the question arises whether Esso are liable for negligent mis－statement under the doctrine of Hedley Byrne** ... It has been suggested that Hedley Byrne cannot be used so as to impose liability for negligent pre－contract situation, the remedy (at any rate before the 1967 Act) was only in warranty or nothing. Thus, in Hedley Byrne itself Lord Reid said ...: '... Where there is a contract there is no difficulty as regards the contracting parties; the question is whether there is a warranty.' ... In arguing this point, (Esso代表大律师) submitted that, when the negotiations between two parties resulted in a contract between them, theirs rights and duties were governed by the law of contract and not by the law of tort. There was, therefore, no place in their relationship for Hedley Byrne, which was solely a liability in tort. ... But I venture to suggest ... **in the case of a professional man, the duty to use reasonable care arise not only in contract but is also imposed by the law apart from contract, and is therefore actionable in tort.** ... A professional man may give advice under a contract for reward; or without a contract, in pursuance of a voluntary assumption of responsibility, gratuitously without reward. In either case he is under one and the same duty to use reasonable care: see Cassidy v. Ministry of Health (1951) 2 KB 343 .... It follows that I cannot accept (Esso代表大律师) proposition.

It seems to me that**Hedley Byrne, properly understood, covers this particular proposition: If a man, who has or professes to have special knowledge or skill**, makes a representation by virtue thereof to another-be it advice, information or opinion-with the **intention of inducing him to enter into a contract** with him, **he is under a duty to use reasonable care** to see that the representation is correct, and that the advice, information or opinion is reliable. If he negligently gives unsound advice or misleading information or expresses an erroneous opinion, ... he is liable in damages ...

Applying this principle, it is plain that Esso professed to have-and did in fact have-special knowledge or skill in estimating the throughput of a filling station. They made the representation-.... They made it negligently. It was a 'fatal error'. And thereby induced Mr Mardon to enter into a contract of tenancy that was disastrous to him. For this misrepresentation they are liable in damages."(加黑部分是笔者的强调)

所以可以说,一般的商业谈判不会一概有小心谨慎的责任。毕竟有很多商业谈判会是漫长与随意的，如在午餐、晚宴或在高尔夫球场。但是如果一方有特殊的知识或技巧，而另一方要完全依赖该方的陈述，该方在作出有关的陈述时就会有小心谨慎的责任，好像专业人士在一个严肃情况下作出专业意见或陈述一样。

2.2.4　后续案件之二：Howard Marine and Dredging Co Ltd v. A Ogden & Sons (Excavations) Ltd (1978) QB 574 上诉庭先例

在 Howard Marine and Dredging Co Ltd v. A Ogden & Sons (Excavations) Ltd 上诉庭先例中，案情涉及一项英国 Tyneside 港排废水工程的挖泥合约，Ogden 作为承建商 (contractors) 要租挖泥船并公开邀请投标 (tender)。其中包括手上有两条挖泥船的 Howard Marine，其很想成功接标。Ogden 对船舶方面是外行（这也不幸代表容易出毛病），唯一关心的是能否装载足够的污泥去大海倾倒。在洽谈期间，Howard Marine 派出航运部经理 O' Loughlin 先生去 Ogden 办公楼。在谈到 Ogden 关心的装载量时，O' Loughlin 先生说每一艘挖泥船应可装载 850 立方米，这相当于可装载重约 1600 吨的污泥。这 1600 吨是如何得来的数字呢？是 O' Loughlin 先生查看了劳合社的记录 (Lloyd's Register)，说是该船舶的载重量 (deadweight) 是 1800 吨。所以很容易计算在减去燃油、食水等后确认应能够装载污泥约 1600 吨。

在接下来的公开投标，Howard Marine 在参与的 7 家公司中出的标价最低，并成功接标。在接下来的租约[以光船出租 (bareboat charter)]谈判，双方也一直没有发觉问题，特别是外行的 Ogden，根本连船舶的容量与载重量也分不清。虽有"以签署合约为准" (subject to contract) 的先决条件 (condition precedent)，[62] 最后整理好的光租租约，Ogden 并没有签妥。但由于双方已经开始履行并履行了好一阵子，所以最终也不争议双方是否有合约关系了。

劳合社的记录在航运界是出名可靠的，但在该案件，不幸的是记录出现罕有的错误。事实上，该挖泥船的真正载重量是 1194.94 吨，而不是 1800 吨。

这错误陈述在交船后才暴露，在履行期间，Ogden 发觉挖泥船只能装载 1055 吨污泥而不是 O' Loughlin 先生在洽谈/谈判时所陈述的 1600 吨，于是去单方面减付租金。Howard Marine 因此根据光租租约以承租人没有准时支付足数租金为由撤船，并起诉要取回欠下的 9 万多英镑租金。但 Ogden 以 Howard Marine 在订约前谈判的误述（即使是非欺诈性），并根据《Misrepresentation Act 1967》之 Section 2 (1) 反索赔损失 60 万英镑。另 Ogden 也指控 Howard Marine 对载重量的陈述实是作出一个附带协议/保证。

在一审，高院判 Howard Marine 胜诉，可取回 9 万多英镑租金加上利息。但 Ogden 上诉去了上诉庭，一审判决被推翻。

上诉庭同意一审认定 Howard Marine 没有对 Ogden 在装载污泥的载重量上有任

---

[62]　在笔者《合约的解释：规则与应用》一书第八章详细针对了包括先决条件与后续条件的变数条件条文，其中第 4 段详细介绍了"以签署合约为准"这一常见的先决条件。

何附带保证,因为附带保证是合约性保证(contractual warranty)需要有证据证明 Howard Marine 的误述是有合约意图与有约束力。但指称的误述是在公开投标前,而 Howard Marine 的标书有先决条件的"Subject to availability and contract"。所以不会是作出一个附带保证,也满足不了条件。

至于是否作出的误述是非欺诈性,在《Misrepresentation Act 1967》之 Section 2(1)下,Ogden 已经可以直接索赔无辜或疏忽误述带来的损失,而不必再依赖附带协议/保证,或是普通法下证明存在小心谨慎的责任,然后以疏忽侵权索赔损失。但 Section 2(1)的最后一句说明如果误述方有合理依据相信他/她的陈述是真实,其赔偿责任可以免除:[63]"... unless he proves that he had reasonable ground to believe, and did believe up to the time the contract was made that the facts represented were true."

照说,O'Loughlin 先生根据劳合社的记录作出的误述,在航运业人士看来应是挺无辜的,所以应该可以满足上述立法的有合理依据的要求。但在上诉庭,在这一点上 Howard Marine 以二比一(Denning 勋爵是少数意见,认为 O'Loughlin 先生有合理依据)败诉。多数意见(Bridge 与 Shaw 大法官)因为 O'Loughlin 先生在交叉盘问中承认曾经看过该挖泥船的文件(如船舶蓝图、舱容图、载重量曲线、船级证书等),显示了船舶的载重量是 1194.94 吨,不去查看船舶文件以核实而依据"间接"的劳合社记录就向 Ogden 作出陈述是谈不上有合理依据。

另一重要之处是租约内有一条文说明挖泥船在交船时被承租人(Ogden)接受,即表示已对船舶检验过并对一切满意,该条文表述如下:"On handing over by the owners, the vessel shall be tight, staunch and strong but charterers' acceptance of handing over the vessel shall be conclusive evidence that they have examined the vessel and found her to be in all respects seaworthy, in good order and condition and in all respects fit for the intended and contemplated use by the charterers and in every other way satisfactory to them."

Howard Marine 指出既然 Ogden 已无条件接受了挖泥船的交船,也曾经作了检验,并使用了 6 个月之久,在此条文下不能提出对载重量的异议。在此争议/争端,上诉庭也以如下两个理由判 Howard Marine 败诉:(1)合理解释该条文(本质上是免责条文),它只应包括在交船时 Ogden 可以通过表面检验看得见的问题。但船舶载重量的正确数字,并非从表面看得出来。(2)另《Misrepresentation Act 1967》之 Section 3 不承认这种条文,除非它是公平与合理的。而上诉庭不认为这条文可对载重量的误述免责是公平合理的。

最后针对的争议/争端是 O'Loughlin 先生的误述在普通法 Hedley Byrne 先例确立的"Hedley Byrne 原则"下,能否成立与 Ogden 有一个特殊关系,从而给 Howard Marine 强加一个侵权下的小心谨慎责任?这是《Misrepresentation Act 1967》外的另一个替代争议。这涉及伤脑筋的 Hedley Byrne 原则应定位在什么范围。正如

---

〔63〕 见本书第四章之 4.3 段。

Denning 勋爵说:"This raises the vexed question of the scope of the doctrine of Hedley Byrne."

面对 Mutual Life and Citizens Assurance Co Ltd v. Evatt(1971) AC 793 枢密院先例,Denning 勋爵对该先例中多数意见的严格判决不认同,反而接受少数意见(Reid 勋爵与 Morris 勋爵)的在不同案情的案件中弹性处理。Denning 勋爵指出少数意见的 Reid 勋爵与 Morris 勋爵说:"... when **an inquirer consults a business man in the course of his business and makes it plain to him that he is seeking considered advice and intended to act on it in a particular way** ... his action in giving such advice(gives rise to)... a legal obligation to take such care **as is reasonable in the whole circumstances**."(加黑部分是笔者的强调)

Denning 勋爵在该问题上的意见(另外两位大法官也同意)与 Pearce 勋爵在 Hedley Byrne 先例中提出的提问的严肃性(gravity of the inquiry)异曲同工。

所以这一法律原则适用在此先例中,首先是根据案情强加法律的小心谨慎责任是否合理。Denning 勋爵是认同 Howard Marine 代表大律师指出要小心会把侵权口子开得太大,例如在一般的谈判中都强加小心谨慎的责任:"This would be a tremendous impact if the law has gone so far as to say that every salesman in a precontractual situation, where people are normally exchanging information and asking questions which are answered with more or less care, is under a Hedley Byrne duty of care in everything he says."

所以在合约谈判中作出了不正确的陈述是否有法律责任是要根据个别案件的不同案情而定。首先是需要局限在商业活动,不是日常社交活动。这是常识,例如大家在家里或与家人/好友的闲谈一般都放松,对此就不适用,即使是商业午餐或晚宴并且涉及谈判,也远比不上在办公楼会议室的正式会谈。其次问答是否有特定的细节,是否是书面或有否文书记录,是否桌面上摆有档案、文件、电脑,回答有没有保留或免责声明等都是考虑提问与回答的严肃性的因素。

在此 Howard Marine 先例的案情下,Denning 勋爵觉得不足以强加给 O'Loughlin 先生一个小心谨慎责任,也就是他只需要诚实就足够了,并举了两个例子说电话口头交谈与谈的内容显示不够正规与严谨,让 O'Loughlin 先生有足够的警惕说:

"'...when an **inquirer consults a business man in the course of his business** and makes it **plain** to him that he **is seeking considered advice and intends to act on it** in a particular way ... his action in giving such advice...(gives rise to)...**a legal obligation to take such care** as is reasonable in the whole circumstances.'

Those principles speak of**the 'gravity of the inquiry'** and **the seeking of 'considered advice'**. Those words are used so as to exclude representations made during a casual conversation in the street; or in a railway carriage; or an impromptu opinion given offhand; or 'off the cuff' on the telephone. To put it more generally, the duty is one of honesty and no more whenever the opinion, information or advice is given in circumstances in which it appears that it is unconsidered and it would not be reasonable for the recipient to act on it without taking further steps to check it. …

Applying this test, it seems to me that at these various conversations Mr. O' Loughlin was under a duty to be honest, but no more. Take the first two conversations. They were on the telephone. The callers … wanted to know what was the capacity of the barges. Mr. O' Loughlin answered it offhand as best he could, without looking up the file. **If they had wanted considered advice, they should have written a letter and got it in writing.** Take the last conversation. It was on an occasion when Mr. O' Loughlin went up … to discuss all sorts of things. In the course of it, he was asked again the capacity of the barges. **He had not got the file** with him, so he answered as best he could from memory. To my mind in those circumstances it was not reasonable for Ogdens to act on his answers without checking them. They **ought either to have got him to put it in writing-that would have stressed the gravity and importance of it-or they ought to have got expert advice on their own behalf** -especially in a matter of such importance to them. So **I agree with the judge that there was not such a situation here as to give rise to a duty of care; or to make Howards liable for negligent misrepresentation at common law**."（加黑部分是笔者的强调）

2.3 双方在谈判中误述的特殊关系

较早前介绍的 Esso Petroleum Co Ltd v. Mardon (1976) 2 Lloyd' s Rep 305 与 Howard Marine and Dredging Co Ltd v. A Ogden & Sons (Excavations) Ltd (1978) QB 574 这两个上诉庭先例中，已经说明这种特殊关系（special relationship）会出现在合约谈判过程，给陈述事实或表达意见的一方的言行强加一个小心谨慎责任，让蒙受经济损失的被陈述方可以以侵权索赔金钱损失。

首先是一方在商业上的谈判过程中作出了大量的事实陈述或意见表述，但双方最终谈不拢。在一般情况下就是双方各行其道，但会有情况是在谈判过程中 A 向 B 作出了承诺、事实的陈述或意见的表述，B 也在完全合理的情况下依赖并蒙受损失。这样，就涉及 B 可否在普通法下向 A 取回这笔损失？

有关谈判中作出的承诺与陈述并被依赖，这已在笔者的《合约的履行、弃权与禁反言》一书第五章"承诺性禁反言"（promissory estoppel）有详论，其中 10.2 段针对合约谈判中会发生的误述与错误（mistake），有很多内容与此处想表达的是一致，很多介绍的先例也是本章介绍的，所以笔者尽量不去多重复。但承诺性禁反言是衡平法（law of equity），需要满足衡平法的条件。这样，在恰当的案件/案情，主要是涉及错误的陈述与表述，会是值得考虑以 Hedley Byrne 原则下的特殊关系存在小心谨慎的责任作为诉因或替代诉因（alternative cause of action）。

谈不拢的情况可节录《Chitty on Contracts》（2021 年，第 34 版）一书之 9 - 104 段

所说如下:"**Where negotiations do not lead to contract** In principle there seems no reason why a special relationship should not be held to exist between parties negotiating a contract even where the negotiations break down so that no contract is ultimately made. Indeed, this seems to have been the basis of the decision in Box v. Midland Bank Ltd (1979)2 Lloyd's Rep 391 where the plaintiff sought a large loan from his bankers. His bank manager told him that the loan would need approval from head office but gave the plaintiff to think that this was a formality; in the meantime, the plaintiff was permitted to overdraft facilities. The loan application was refused by head office and the plaintiff claimed that he had suffered loss through being led to believe that the loan would be forthcoming. The claim was, in part, upheld by Lloyd J. on the basis that the bank manager owed a duty not to mislead the plaintiff by careless advice as to the probable outcome of his loan application."

在上文提及的 Box v. Midland Bank 先例中,简单案情是原告的公司财务状况严峻,但手中有一份加拿大公司的合约并视为公司唯一希望。原告找被告银行要求贷款让公司可生存下去与履约,并展示了加拿大合约。原告被银行的 Brokenshire 先生误导说是没有问题,只要出口当局(Export Credit Guarantee Department, ECGD)批准后,批准贷款只是例行手续。但后来银行不批准贷款,这导致原告公司迅速发生经济困难,无法履行加拿大合约,并在不久后申请倒闭。原告向被告银行提起诉讼,声称被误导,并说是如果被告知真相,也就是不会拿到这笔贷款的批准,原告就可以想其他办法来挽救公司。原告 Box 先生主要的指控是在交叉盘问中说:"My claim is for the money I have lost through Mr Brokenshire not telling me that there was no hope of money being made available by the bank."

Lloyd 大法官判:"I can now summarise my views as follows. First, Mr Brokenshire, as manager of the Wells branch, was not obliged to predict the outcome of his application to regional head office for a loan to Mr Box of up to £ 45,000. But if he did predict the outcome he was under a duty to take reasonable care, since he knew that his prediction would be relied on. Secondly, Mr Brokenshire failed to exercise reasonable care — that is to say the care to be expected of an ordinary competent bank manager — in that he gave Mr Box the impression, as he intended, that the granting of a facility up to £ 45,000 would be a mere formality once the ECGD policy had been obtained, whereas there was never the prospect of the facility being made available, as Mr Brokenshire ought to have known. Thirdly, Mr Box did in fact rely on Mr Brokenshire's negligent prediction, ... thereby suffering damage. **Accordingly, the bank is liable on the Hedley Byrne principle**, ..."(加黑部分是笔者的强调)

多介绍另一个不同情况,不严格是涉及订约前的谈判,只是有关原告指称被告曾经作出过的一个默示承诺/保证(implied promise/warranty)。在 Argy Trading Development Co Ltd v. Lapid Developments Ltd(1977)1 WLR 444 先例中,案情涉及一个仓库的6年租赁合约。双方在1971年10月19日订立的租约中规定由租客投保火险,但是同时也约定如果业主为其拥有的物业一并投保,租客只需要支付给业主按比例分摊的保费。笔者估计这样保费会相比租客只为个别仓库投保便宜得多,而且一定是双方在谈判中就提到了这个方案才会在租约中约定。一开始租客也确实向业主支付了分摊的保费。但在1972年6月业主被苏格兰银行收购,而苏格兰银行在保险方面有自己的安排,加上认为应该是由租客投保,所以没有为有关仓库续保。道德上苏格兰银行应该通知租客让其自己安排,但忘了通知租客。不幸是仓库在1973年10月5日发生严重火灾,重新修复是需要一大笔钱。这本来是保险公司要赔付,但现在就要租客自己承担了。租客自己很想修复,因为还有4年的租期。但业主不想修复,因为想重建这块土地。

租客声称业主明示或默示承诺会为仓库购买火险并续保,而业主没有信守承诺,令租客失去了自己购买保险并获得保险公司赔付的机会,租客想要修复就必须自己出钱。看来,业主这个承诺不涉及诱导租客订立租赁合约,租客也没有想撤销该合约,只想索赔损失也就是这笔修复的费用。另是,已经提到租约约定是租客负责购买火险,这个租客声称的承诺没有被加在租赁合约,作为业主的一个持续性承诺或保证。租客的所有替代诉因或争议如承诺性禁反言、默示条文、合约性保证等都被法院否定,最后只剩下租客以 Hedley Byrne 原则指称与业主之间有特殊关系。Croom - Johnson 大法官否定了被告业主曾经作出一个默示承诺的事实,也进一步分析即使有默示承诺,被告也没有比原告多掌握信息与知识。被告也没有给出任何意见或信息,只是当时他的想法,而不是一个持续性的承诺。即使有小心谨慎的责任也只是在刚订立合约时,而不是在2年后。既然当时业主购买了火险是事实,就谈不上疏忽。虽然道德上被告应该通知租客,但应是租客自己至少每年确认一下是否仍有有效的火险保障。有关判决可节录如下:

"The plaintiffs'(租客)last line of attack is in tort. It is based upon Hedley Byrne ... They say that assuming there was no consideration and no contract, yet there was a duty of care owed by Lapid(业主)to the plaintiffs arising out of a special relationship between the parties and that Lapid broke it by not telling the plaintiffs that they were not renewing the insurance ... I have found that there was no contract here. All I need to do is to see whether there was a duty owed here in tort and, if so, whether it was broken.

What raises the duty? In Hedley Byrne ..., first of all there is postulated a special relationship, either general or particular. ...

In other words, ... there is a responsibility voluntarily accepted or undertaken, either expressly or impliedly. Lord Reid, after quoting a passage from a speech of Lord Haldane in another case, said: 'This passage makes it clear that Lord Haldane did not think that a duty to take care must be limited to cases of fiduciary relationship in the narrow sense of relationships … He speaks of other special relationships, and I can see no logical stopping place short of those relationships where it is plain that the party seeking information or advice was trusting the other to exercise such a degree of care as the circumstances required, where it was reasonable for him to do that, and where the other gave the information or advice when he knew or ought to have known that the inquirer was relying on him. …'

…. I have to decide three questions: (a) Was there such a special relationship as comes within the rule at all? (b) What duty, if any, was created? (c) Was any such duty broken?

As to (a) there was **undoubtedly a business relationship. But Mr. Cigman** (业主) **had no more skill than did the plaintiffs, nor did he have any knowledge which the plaintiffs did not have.** The only knowledge which he had and which the plaintiffs did not have was whether he really meant at that time to effect the insurance through the block policy. He could not know at that time whether he would change his mind later. If it had been the fact that he did not then do what he offered — namely, to effect the insurance on the plaintiffs' behalf at the end of 1971 — it might have been said that he misled Mr. Argy (租客). **Mr. Cigman was not offering advice. He was not giving information except as to his then state of mind.** Mr. Cigman in fact gave true information at that time. But supposing he had given false information? He would then at least have been liable for the tort of deceit, but that **does not mean when he gave information thought to be either true or false he was not entering into a special relationship with the plaintiffs for Hedley Byrne purposes.** …

…If special relationships in the Hedley Byrne sense are to be created in circumstances such as these, then the duty which is to be imposed must be circumscribed closely and ought to be limited to a duty to exercise care only at the time when the duty is purported to be discharged in the first place. **Of course, Lapid morally ought to have told the plaintiffs that they were not continuing with the insurance cover; but I cannot find that in failing to do so they were in breach of any duty laid on them by law.** After all, a reasonable man checks his insurances from time to time, at least annually. …. Lapid forgot to tell the plaintiffs who did not check their insurance as they should have done."(加黑部分是笔者的强调)

2.4 双方已经有合约的关系带来的同步/竞合责任

2.4.1 侵权与合约同步的发展

民事诉讼主要是侵权与合约的关系,而这两种关系有很重大的差异。第一,从这两种法律关系的出发点上来看,侵权关系下,当事人的权利与义务是法律赋予的,这是为了规范人们在社会中的行事标准与建立良好的社会秩序。而合约关系下,当事人的权利与义务则是完全由订约方自己商讨与确定的，法律对此予以尊重并帮助强制执行。从历史发展上来看，侵权在罗马法时期与刑法关系更为密切且有重叠，例如人身伤害、偷盗、抢劫这类对人身体和财产的侵犯，既属于刑法的范围，又涉及明显的侵权。在英国，12～13世纪时，侵权也是从属于刑法的概念，整个中世纪，侵权则主要集中在非法侵入(trespass)以及其他故意的行为；直到18世纪才出现对疏忽带来侵权的认定，这是在Coggs v. Bernard(1704)2 Ld Raym. 909先例中，Holt大法官援引罗马法原则，认定受托人对因他的疏忽而给托管(bailment)的货物带来的损坏与丢失负赔偿责任。本段中讨论的误述所带来的与合约关系共存(co－existence)或同步(concurrent)的侵权关系，是疏忽侵权(tort of negligence)。[64]

第二，侵权强调道德上的可归责性，所以行事中存在过错(fault)是构成侵权的前提条件。而合约义务是合约方自愿与主动承担的，所以是严格与绝对的责任，即使违约方没有疏忽或错误，只要无法严格履行自己的合约承诺就是违约，仍然需要负合约下的责任。

第三，侵权关系下，侵害方要弥补由其侵权行为所造成的损害，而合约关系下则是强调违约方要实现合约中所承诺或保证的能够为一方带来的利益。

根据以上对侵权与合约区别的罗列，可以对它们在具体适用上的不同进行举例说明，在诉因方面，合约关系是只要一方当事人违约就已经是有了诉因，受害方就可以向法院(或仲裁庭)提起诉讼并寻求救济，例如申请一个履约指令(specific performance)。但侵权并不是一旦发生了错误与疏忽的言行就已经是有了诉因，而是需要产生损失，且错误与疏忽之间需要满足因果关系(既要满足事实上的确是疏忽造成损失的“要不是”测试，也要满足索赔的是法律上所允许追回损失的可预见性、遥远性测试，例如通常是允许实质损失而不允许纯经济损失)。另一个例子是索赔时效(time limit)，虽然根据《Limitation Act 1980》，侵权诉讼的时效与一般合约诉讼的时效均是产生诉因后的6年。但除了因有订约自由，订约方可以在合约中明示约定与立法规定不同的合约时效(contractual time bar)之外，不同类别的违约与索赔也会受制于国际公约/本国立法，如货物在海上运输中的短缺损坏的索赔，在1924年《海牙规则》下，只有在卸货后(或应该卸货后)的1年时效。其他还有很多区别，如损失计算(measure of damages)、[65]只有合约权利可以转让(assignment)等就不展开谈了。

在现代商业活动中，商事活动主体之间几乎都存在合约关系的情况下，侵权责任是否可以与合约关系共存或同步颇具争议性。反对共存的最主要原因是合约是双方花费了大量时间、精力与金钱去特别定制的双方权利义务的产物，有了合约就没有理

---

[64] 本段不讨论欺诈性误述(fraudulent misrepresentation)是因为欺诈性误述其实就是欺骗。而根据“欺诈超越一切”(Fraud unravels all)的大原则，合约是无法通过明示条文去排除欺诈的责任的，也就不存在双方同步/并存的问题。这方面问题将在本书第三章之8.3段进行专门介绍。

[65] 关于侵权与合约损失计算方式等的不同，可见笔者《损失赔偿与救济》一书第一章之9段。

由对在合约的当事人强加适用一般法律对公众言行准则的要求。所以即使随后英国法确立了侵权与合约责任可以并存,但是合约的明示约定仍然对侵权责任是否被排除或被局限有很大的影响。在很长一段时期,尤其是20世纪最后的25年间,英国法律界对在有合约关系的情况下无辜方/受害方可否仍然主张对方的侵权责任这一问题有不同看法与相当多的争论,这也可以从随后介绍的一些不同判法的先例中窥见一斑。两种民事法律关系是差异极大,例如海上货物运输合约下的1年时效已逝,可否以享有6年时效的侵权起诉?毕竟,只要该合约在责任方面是与侵权同步与一致,是要求承运人或船东对船上托运的货物有一个小心处理(handling)与照顾(care for)的责任。这种在合约对履约方与/或法律对任何公众的言行提出的小心谨慎(或类似的措辞,反正是排除错误与疏忽)责任会在很多情况下出现,特别是针对专业人士(如律师、会计师、医生等)为客户提供服务的合约。

由于不论是大陆法系(civil law jurisdiction)或是普通法系(common law jurisdiction),其侵权法与合约法的发展都有着悠久的历史,所以都面对同样的问题。例如Jackson大法官在2014年10月30日发表的一篇名为"Concurrent Liability: Where have things gone wrong"的演讲稿中提到法国法与德国法中对侵权责任与合约责任是否可以同步的问题有不同对待。其中与罗马法一脉相承的法国法是不承认同步责任,这可节录该发言的相关部分如下:

"**The non-cumul principle.** In the late nineteenth century there was a debate about the classification of civil liability. Some argued that liability for non-performance of contracts and delictual liability were essentially the same. Others argued that there was a fundamental difference, namely that delict applied to everyone whereas contracts only bound the parties. The latter view prevailed. The principle noncumul des responsabilités contractualle et délictuelle was established and remains part of French law. The contracting parties cannot bring a separate or alternative delictual claim in respect of the same subject matter.

Justification of the non-cumul rule. The rationale of the rule is that the parties have chosen to be bound by the terms of their contract and the legal rules attaching to a contract of that type. Therefore the law of contract, not delict, should govern their rights and rcmcdics. A separate justification is that the tort provisions are so wide that if concurrency were not prohibited, contracting parties would at all times be able to resort to a tort claim."

而德国法则是承认同步责任,相关部分节录如下:"**Concurrent liability.** Unlike Roman and French law, German law allows concurrent liability. If D (Defendant) acts in breach of contract and his conduct also fulfils the definition of a tort, C (Claimant) may sue in contract and/or tort. There are, however, exceptions to this general rule (just as there are exceptions to the reverse rule-noncumul-in France). Sometimes the contractual relationship between the parties imposes restrictions upon what C can recover in tort. The caselaw in this area is not entirely consistent, but is broadly favourable to claimants."

今天在我国《民法典》第一编总则第八章第186条针对合约和侵权关系的竞合有规定[66]中,受损害方可以选择适合自己的救济途径,这一规定与德国法类似。可以节录该条文如下:

"因当事人一方的违约行为,损害对方人身权益、财产权益的,受损害方有权选择请求其承担违约责任或者侵权责任。"

特别值得一提的是,根据今天国内法院的判法来看,在合约当事人之间涉及真正的责任竞合时,即使申请人选择侵权之诉,仍然应当适用合约约定的仲裁管辖:见2004年最高人民法院《关于皇朝工程有限公司与西班牙奥安达电梯有限公司、广东奥安达电梯有限公司侵权纠纷管辖权异议一案的请示的复函》,2015年最高人民法院"厦门豪嘉利商贸发展有限公司与洋马发动机(上海)有限公司、洋马株式会社管辖权异议案"等。在后者案件中最高院给出的观点如下。

依照通常理解,该条款(指仲裁管辖条款)约定了两方面的条件:一是提交仲裁的争议性质为任何争议,[67]即不仅限于合同争议,也包括非合同性质的侵权争议或其他争议;二是在解释仲裁条款范围时,如侵权争议因违反合同义务而产生,违约责任和侵权责任有竞合关系,则原告即使选择以侵权为由提出诉讼,仍应受到合同仲裁条款的约束,不应允许当事人通过事后选择诉因来逃避仲裁条款的适用。

这样的说法,针对侵权责任与合约责任竞合,看来是与今天国际仲裁与普通法中的说法一致:见 Fiona Trust & Holding Corp v. Privalov(2007)UKHL 40 贵族院先例等。

2.4.2　疏忽侵权的构成要件

在进入疏忽误述的侵权与合约的同步责任这一课题前,首先需要明确疏忽误述构成侵权责任需要满足的要件。这可节录笔者所著的《损失赔偿与救济》第八章之4段提到的疏忽侵权的构成要件。

造成这种侵权需要四个要求如下:(1) the existence in law of a duty of care situation, i. e. one in which the law attaches liability to carelessness. There has to be recognition by law that the careless infliction of the kind of damage in suit on the class of person to which the claimant belongs by the class of person to which the defendant belongs is actionable[法律要求一类人士对另一类人士负有一个"小心谨慎的责任"(duty of care),[68]如果因为错误与疏忽前者没有尽到小心谨慎的责任并导致后者的损失,后者就会变了是原告,而前者变了是被告]。(2) breach of the duty of care by the de-

---

[66] 过去在《合同法》第122条有类似规定:"因当事人一方的违约行为,侵害对方人身、财产权益的,受损害方有权选择依照本法要求其承担违约责任或者依照其他法律要求其承担侵权责任。"

[67] 比如"执行本合同有关的一切争议"。

[68] 见 Donoghue v. Stevenson(1932) AC 562; Hedley Byrne v. Heller(1964) AC 465; Caparo v. Dickman (1990) 2 WLR 358 等贵族院先例。

fendant,i. e. that it failed to measure up to the standard set by law(就是被告违反了一个小心谨慎的责任,而是否小心谨慎是根据法律在不同情况下认定的标准)。(3)a causal connection between the defendant's careless conduct and the damage(被告的错误与疏忽与原告的损失有直接因果关系)。(4)that the particular kind of damage to the particular claimant is not so unforeseeable as to be too remote(原告的损失并非不能预见的,不会太遥远)。

在这里主要先去进一步解释法律在什么情况下会强加一个"小心谨慎的责任"(duty of care),这在著名的先例 Caparo Plc v. Dickman(1990)AC 605,贵族院的 Bridge 勋爵提了三个要求:[69] (1) foreseeability of damage arising from the negligent performance of the relevant operation(错误与疏忽的言行对所造成损失的可预见性)。(2)the existence of a sufficient relationship of proximity between the parties and(原告与被告之间的邻近关系)。(3)whether or not as a matter of legal policy it is"fair just and reasonable"that a duty of care should exist,the direct infliction of foreseeable physical damage is an established category of case where a duty exist(去强加这个小心谨慎的责任在被告的身上是否公平与合理,这涉及公共政策的考虑)。

2.4.3　英国法对疏忽误述是否能带来侵权与合约同步责任的不同看法

英国法在该问题的发展上也有不同看法,这在 Midland Bank Trust Co Ltd v. Hett,Stubbs & Kemp(1979)Ch 384 先例中首次有详尽的分析与介绍。虽然该先例只是高院的一审案例,但却是第一个仔细与深入地对合约与侵权同步责任的问题进行全面分析的先例。可以说该案例中的 Oliver 大法官将之前历史上相关与重要的案例全部都做了一次回顾与分析,只从中挑少量早期的先例介绍。

1. 在 Turner v. Stallibrass(1898)1 QB 56 上诉庭先例中,Collins MR 大法官区分什么情况下是合约关系或侵权关系,说:"I agree that the distinction between tort and contract is not a logical one,and that it is sometimes difficult to say whether a particular thing is a wrong or a breach of contract. If the claim of the plaintiff had been set out at large pointing to some particular stipulation in the contract,which stipulation had been broken,the action would be founded on contract;but where it is only necessary to refer to the contract to establish a relationship between the parties,and the claim goes on to aver a breach of duty arising out of that relationship,the action is one of tort."

2. 在 Groom v. Crocker(1939)1 KB 194 上诉庭先例中,Wilfred Greene MR 大法官认为律师和客户之间的关系只是合约关系,说:"In my opinion,**the cause of action is in contract and not in tort**. The duty of the appellants was to conduct the case properly on behalf of the respondent as their client,... The relationship of solicitor and client is a contractual one;... **It was by virtue of that relationship that the duty arose,and it**

---

〔69〕 Bridge 勋爵的这段话已经在本章稍早的 2.2.1.1.1 段节录。

has no existence apart from that relationship."(加黑部分是笔者的强调)

3. 在 Jarvis v. Moy, Davies, Smith, Vanderbilt & Co(1936)1 KB 399 上诉庭先例中,Greer 大法官说:"The distinction in the modern view, for this purpose, between contract and tort may be put thus: where breach of duty alleged arises out of a liability independently of the personal obligation undertaken by contract, it is tort, and it may be tort even though there may happen to be a contract between the parties, if the duty in fact arises independently of that contract. Breach of contract occurs where that which is complained of is a breach of duty arising out of the obligation undertaken by the contract."

4. 在 Clark v. Kirby - Smith(1964)Ch 596 上诉庭先例中,Diplock 大法官:"It seems to me that, in this case, the relationship which created the duty of exercising reasonable skill and care by the architects to their clients arose out of the contract and not otherwise. The complaint that is made against them is of a failure to do the very thing which they contracted to do. That was the relationship which gave rise to the duty which was broken. It was a contractual relationship, a contractual duty, and any action brought for failure to comply with that duty is, in my view, an action founded on contract. It is also, in my view, an action founded upon contract alone."

5. 到了 Esso Petroleum Co Ltd v. Mardon(1976)2 Lloyd's Rep 305 上诉庭先例中,根据本章之 2.2.3 段已经介绍过的案情与判决结果可知,上诉庭判 Esso 因在谈判中告知 Mardon 先生加油站在经营开始后很快就能达到 20 万加仑的年销量,不仅构成了合同上的附带保证并违反了该保证,也因该疏忽的陈述破坏了对 Mardon 先生负有的小心谨慎的侵权责任。[70] 该先例确立了订约前的陈述如果是错误的,会带来合约与侵权的同步责任。上诉庭的 Denning 勋爵说:"... He submitted that when the negotiations between two parties resulted in a contract between them, their rights and duties were governed by the law of contract and not by the law of tort. There was, therefore, no place in their relationship for Hedley Byrne ... which was solely on liability in tort. ... But I venture to suggest that ... in the case of a professional man, the duty to use reasonable care arises not only in contract, but is also imposed by the law apart from contract, and is therefore actionable in tort. It is comparable to the duty of reasonable care which is owned by a master to his servant, or vice versa. It can be put either in contract or in tort. ..."

---

〔70〕 本案在判损失赔偿的部分也体现了侵权与合约的不同。因为上诉庭同意 Esso 要对 Mardon 先生承担侵权的责任(疏忽侵权),所以损失赔偿就按照更为有利的侵权下的标准来厘定,即将受害方恢复到侵权行为没有发生的地位,也就是没有该误述就不会有合约。这样,Mardon 先生的损失除了多年间为加油站业务投入的资本,向银行的贷款等实际的付出,还包括如果他没有与 Esso 签订合约,这些年他通过正常的努力在其他工作与业务上会有的收入等,这些损失很明显在合约责任(违反附带保证)下是不能索赔的。

Ormrod 勋爵也支持合约与侵权责任可以并存，其认为："This is, I think, a difficult point for it is an attractive argument that, when a contract results, the rights of the parties should be governed by the terms agreed, ... There is no magic in the phrase 'special relationship'; it means no more than a relationship the nature of which is such that one party, for a variety of possible reasons, will be regarded by the law as under a duty of care to the other. In this case the plaintiffs had all the expertise, experience and authority of a large and efficient organisation carrying on the business of developing service stations to sell their petroleum products through dealers who were expected to invest a substantial amount of capital in the business and to observe the detailed trading requirements laid down in the tenancy agreements. There can be no doubt that the plaintiffs fulfilled the second condition for Hedley Byrne liability. On the evidence they clearly assumed responsibility for the reliability of their own e. a. c（汽油年耗量）."

在介绍了以上几个较早的先例后，可以回到 Midland Bank Trust Co Ltd v. Hett, Stubbs & Kemp 先例。该先例涉及的是律师为客户提供服务，在 1961 年 3 月，W 先生同意他的儿子 G 先生在支付 1 英镑的对价后，就有权在未来 10 年内选择以 75 英镑每英亩的价格购买 W 先生的 300 英亩农场，当时 G 先生是该 300 英亩农场的租户。被告律师事务所被聘请来帮助他们父子完成该交易的文件与手续。由于被告律师事务所律师的疏忽，该交易没有按照《Land Charges Act 1925》进行登记。随后，G 先生也时不时咨询该律所他是否要行使该期权/选择权。后来在 1967 年 W 先生想要废除该期权/选择权，在他咨询新的律师时发现该期权/选择权根本没有登记，于是就将该土地以 500 英镑的价格卖给了他的妻子。1967 年，G 先生正式发出了要行权的通知，结果 W 先生与妻子均没有遵循该通知将土地转让给 G 先生。1968 年时 W 先生的妻子去世，G 先生于是对他的父亲 W 先生与其妻子的遗嘱执行人提起诉讼，1972 年 W 先生也去世。G 先生在 W 先生去世后对当时帮助他们完成交易的律师事务所提起诉讼。G 先生在 1973 年也去世，所以本案的原告为 G 先生的遗嘱执行人。G 先生需要以合约与侵权同步作为诉因起诉，是因为合约时效的 6 年已经明显过了。Oliver 大法官在考虑了很多不同先例的决定之后认为没有哪一个先例有清晰与有约束力的指引，所以最终他决定允许原告将合约与侵权同步作为诉因来起诉。

Oliver 大法官说："In my judgment, the instant case is one in which there was clearly between the defendant firm and Geoffrey（G 先生）a relationship of the sort which gave rise to a duty of care under the Hedley Byrne principle. And, in my judgment, the interpretation of that principle by the Court of Appeal in Esso v. Mardon ... leads to the conclusion that there was here a liability in tort which arose when the damage occurred on August 7, 1967. Accordingly, the claim in my view is not barred by the Limitation Act 1939. I am, of course, conscious that, in reaching the conclusion to which I have felt compelled, **I am departing from what has long been considered a firm and settled rule of**

law. It is for that reason and because the point is obviously one of considerable importance both to clients and solicitors and to their insurers, that I have **felt it right to set out my reasoning in extension**."(加黑部分是笔者的强调)

但接下来的 Tai Hing Cotton Mills Ltd v. Liu Chong Hing Bank Ltd(1986) AC 80 枢密院先例则认为侵权与合约责任应该分开。该先例发生在香港特别行政区回归之前,该案当时从香港的上诉庭上诉去到英国的枢密院。该案的案情涉及非常常见的支票开立与在银行兑现的业务。Tai Hing 公司是 Liu Chong Hing 银行(香港廖创兴银行,在 2013 年被越秀集团收购,现为创兴银行)以及其他两家银行的客户,在 3 家银行均开立有支票户口。在 1974 年至 1978 年间,Tai Hing 公司的财务人员通过伪造总经理的签名签发了 300 多张支票,总金额约 550 万港币,而这三家银行均没有发现支票上的签名为伪造,并从 Tai Hing 公司的支票账户中兑现了该 300 多张支票。

本案的一个核心争议是客户在银行支票业务之中要负什么责任。首先,银行抗辩称客户与银行之间的服务合约与条款中有明示约定客户在收到月结单之后如果发现有错误要在规定的时间内将月结单上显示的错误及时通知银行。其次,银行主张客户对银行有一个小心谨慎责任,要为保护银行的利益而及时发现伪造的事实并告知银行。如果违反了这一小心谨慎责任,则要对银行负上侵权的责任。最后,枢密院否定了银行所有的主张。在服务合约方面,枢密院认为客户的责任仅在签发支票时需要认真仔细,不给欺诈或伪造留有空间,与发现有未授权的支取时立即通知银行。除此之外,客户无需承担采取措施防止伪造支票行为发生的责任,也不需要承担定期查看银行账户以检查是否有伪造或未授权行为发生与及时通知银行的责任。所以,由于服务合约中并未对此责任有明确的明示约定,也不能通过默示地位来添加这一责任。而针对侵权责任的问题,枢密院认为在双方订有服务合约的情况下,侵权不适用。

Scarman 勋爵说:"Their Lordships do not believe that there is anything to the advantage of the law's development in searching for a liability in tort where the parties are in a contractual relationship. This is particularly so in a commercial relationship. Though it is possible as a matter of legal semantics to conduct an analysis of the rights and duties inherent in some contractual relationships including that of banker and customer either as a matter of contract law when the question will be what, if any, terms are to be implied or as a matter of tort law when the task will be to identify a duty arising from the proximity and character of the relationship between the parties, their Lordships believe it to be correct in principle and necessary for the avoidance of confusion in the law to adhere to the contractual analysis: on principle because it is a relationship in which the parties have, subject to a few exceptions, the right to determine their obligations to each other, and for the avoidance of confusion because different consequences do follow according to whether liability arises from contract or tort, e. g. in the limitation of action."

Henderson v. Merrett Syndicates Ltd(1995)2 AC 145 贵族院先例对这一争议性的问题作出了权威的判决,并确立了在一方承担提供专业服务的责任时,如果另一方依赖了该服务,即使双方之间存在服务合约,也仍然会存在侵权中的小心谨慎的责任。但是该小心谨慎的侵权同步责任通常是在合约中没有将其明示排除的情况下才存在。所以,原告仍然不能将侵权与合约的诉因分开进行诉讼。该贵族院先例的案情是有关劳合社保险人与他的经纪人之间的争议。劳合社保险人通过他的经纪人去进行承保业务与建议投资项目,双方之间既有代理合约也有提供专业技术与知识的小心谨慎责任。

Goff 勋爵强调了同步侵权责任时对时效问题的重要性:"Foremost among these [practical considerations] is perhaps the question of limitation of actions. If concurrent liability in tort is not recognised, a claimant may find his claim barred at a time when he is unaware of its existence. This must moreover be a real possibility in the case of claims against professional men, such as solicitors or architects, since the consequences of their negligence may well not come to light until long after the lapse of six years from the date when the relevant breach of contract occurred."

Goff 勋爵认为疏忽侵权的责任是作为一般法适用在订约当事人之间,也就是承认同步责任。不过 Goff 勋爵同时也明确疏忽侵权的责任是否可以成立是受制于订约双方的明示约定:"Given that the tortious duty is imposed by the general law, and the contractual duty is attributable to the will of the parties, I do not find it objectionable that the claimant may be entitled to take advantage of the remedy which is most advantageous to him, subject only to ascertaining whether the tortious duty is so inconsistent with the applicable contract that, in accordance with ordinary principle, the parties must be taken to have agreed that the tortious remedy is to be limited or excluded."

经过之前长时间的争论、不稳定与不肯定,目前的英国法律地位可节录《Chitty on Contracts》(2021 年,第 34 版)一书之 9 - 105 段所说如下:"**Special relationship between parties already in contractual relationship** It is now clear that one party to a contractual relationship may owe duties in tort to the other; these duties may overlap with contractual duties, and where this is the case the claimant may have alternative causes of action in contract and in tort: Henderson v. Merrett Syndicates Ltd(1995)2 AC 145. It has also been held that damages may be obtainable for misrepresentations made in the course of renegotiating a contract already in existence, under the Misrepresentation Act, and there seems no reason to doubt that in appropriate case liability could also arise under the Hedley Byrne principle in such a situation."

2.4.4 同步/竞合责任为当事人带来的好处

同步责任的存在可以令当事人选择对自己更为有利的诉因起诉或者进行抗辩,对原告或被告的好处主要在以下两方面。

1. 索赔时效。虽然在民事诉讼,在《Limitation Act 1980》的立法下一般合约与侵权的时效均是6年,从有了诉因开始起算。但合约的诉因是在对方违约就产生,而侵权的诉因是第三人的疏忽言行并不够,而是必须导致损失才会有诉因。《Latent Damage Act 1986》[71]也只适用在侵权,不适用在合约。

在索赔时效,由于侵权的诉因是除了有疏忽的言行外,必须导致损失出现才产生,所以侵权的诉因通常比违反合约的诉因较晚。同样是《Limitation Act 1980》的6年时效,常会有情况合约索赔时效已过,但一些潜在的损失尚未发现,所以侵权的诉因尚未产生。Midland Bank Trust Co Ltd v. Hett, Stubbs & Kemp(1979)Ch 384先例正是这种情况,所以原告需要以损害真正出现时作为诉因产生的时间来计算时效。

2. 损失赔偿。合约对责任规定与疏忽侵权可能是一致,如1924年《海牙规则》之Article Ⅲ(2)对承运人/船东强加的责任也只是"妥善与小心"(properly and carefully)。侵权也会在合约关系外强加一个小心谨慎责任,如律师的委任合约(retainer agreement)。在同时存在侵权责任的情况下,可以根据双方诉讼方各自不同程度的疏忽在针对侵权的《Law Reform(Contributory Negligence)Act 1945》[72]立法下分摊损失,而不是根据平衡的可能性得出非黑即白的合约损失。

这方面最重要的是Vesta v. Butcher(1986)2 Lloyd's Rep 179先例,Hobhouse大法官认为《Law Reform(Contributory Negligence)Act 1945》立法并没有排除适用在合约的关系,其认为:"I do accept that the Act was not concerned with displacing contractual rights as is demonstrated by provisos(a)and(b)in s. 1(1), but these very provisos contemplate that the Act is capable of application where there is a contractual relationship between the parties..."

可以先简单介绍Vesta v. Butcher先例的案情,其是挪威一个养鱼场投保保险,其中一项保赔的是"任何原因导致的活鱼的损失"(loss of living fish from any cause whatsoever)。在该12个月的保单中,养鱼场做出一个承诺性保证(promissory war-

---

〔71〕 该立法针对建筑物因设计与建造中的疏忽而存在潜在缺陷并在之后造成损害的情况。该立法中主要针对时效问题的第1与第2条,也被并入了《Limitation Act 1980》作为14A与28A条。立法条文将时效放宽至发现潜在缺陷后的3年。

〔72〕 该立法旨在赋予法官权力让他们在对侵权行为带来的损失进行判决时,根据侵权人与被侵权人之间双方各自的过错程度来对损失进行按比例划分。其中该立法第1条是说:"Where any person suffers damage as the result partly of his own fault and partly of the fault of any other person or persons, a claim in respect of that damage shall not be defeated by reason of the fault of the person suffering damage, but the damages recoverable in respect thereof shall be reduced to such extent as the Court thinks just and equitable having regard to the claimant's share in the responsibility for the damage: Provided that -(a)this subsection shall not operate to defeat any defence arising under a contract. ..."可以举一个日常生活中的例子:一起车祸事故是由司机酒后驾驶与行人闯红灯共同酿成。这时法院在判决司机应承担的赔偿金额时,会考虑行人自身的过错,而按照行人与司机之间30:70或者20:80的比例进行划分,以扣减司机要赔偿的金额。

ranty)是每天24小时均有人在养鱼场当值。要知道,保险中的承诺性保证非同小可,它必须被严格执行,否则保险合约马上自动终止。

保险合约订立后,受保人(养鱼场主人)很快发觉这承诺性保证执行不了,于是向保险公司Vesta提出修改保单免去该承诺性保证。Vesta另叫他的保险经纪人Butcher向伦敦再保人提出同样的修改要求,但不知为何,保险经纪人忘了此事,而且大家都忘了去跟进,直至6个月后一场暴风雨令养鱼场遭到破坏,养鱼场的鱼全部流失。再保人拒赔,指是承诺性保证未被严格执行。这拒赔理由是完全能成立,但这样,Vesta夹在当中可就惨了。于是他向保险经纪人提出索赔,指出由于保险经纪人疏忽,没有尽到合理小心(reasonable care)的责任。

经纪人抗辩说他即使有错,Vesta也有错,他自己也忘了去跟进,所以在之后6个月未出事前Vesta明知这24小时承诺性保证仍未被修改,也没有跟进。法院判是双方都有过错,但Vesta的过错程度更高。Hobhouse大法官判是要保险经纪人承担1/4的责任,但Vesta承担3/4的责任。

接下来就要考虑在损失方面能否以1945年立法去分摊,因为如果不能,则Vesta要承担全部损失了。因为他的过错,才是出事的主因。

Hobhouse大法官认为1945年立法是否适用在根据合约提起的诉讼,这可以分以下三种情形。

(1)索赔所基于的合约条文不涉及被告是否有疏忽的问题。这合约责任与侵权责任无关,明显是1945年立法不适用。合约责任本来就是绝对或严格责任,[73]所以与侵权责任无关。只是在订约自由的大原则下,可把合约责任减轻为"小心谨慎"(exercise reasonable skill and care),即把合约责任变得与侵权责任一致。除了订约自由,国际公约或立法下也会对某些责任作同样的妥协,正如上述对《海牙规则》之Article Ⅲ(2)的介绍。订约自由下,合约条文甚至可以约定比小心谨慎更低的责任或免除责任,这样,合约责任更是与侵权责任无关。

(2)索赔所基于的合约条文明示约定被告有合理小心的责任,但这种以合约明示条文规定的合理小心的责任并不构成独立于合约关系的侵权责任下要求的小心谨慎的责任。换言之,一旦脱离了合约的关系,原告就不能以违反小心谨慎责任的疏忽侵权诉因向被告提出侵权索赔。典型的例子是总承建商在合约下对雇主承担小心谨慎的责任(或类似措辞/文字),但把工程分包后,分包商在施工的过程中因疏忽发生事故给雇主造成损失的,总承建商在合约下要对雇主负责,但造成损失的疏忽事故是由分包商具体操作,而总承建商针对分包商的工作对于雇主并没有侵权下的小心谨慎的责任,有的只是合约责任。在这一种情形,1945年立法也不适用。如果合约下的索赔时效已过,雇主就只能以疏忽侵权向分包商索赔,分包商不能以没有合约关系抗辩。这可见Colman大法官在Raflatac Ltd v. Eade and Ors(1999)1 Lloyd's Rep 5

[73] 见笔者《合约的履行、弃权与禁反言》一书第二章之2段。

先例中所说:“In the present case there is no doubt whatever that the first defendants(总承建商)were under a contractual obligation to exercise reasonable skill and care in the conduct of their work on the plaintiffs'(雇主)premises. But what was the actual relationship between them and the plaintiffs in respect of the carrying out of the work? It was quite simply that it was agreed that the first defendants would enter into a sub – contract with the second defendant(分包商)in order to provide the plaintiffs with the benefit of his knowledge and experience ... Thus, if one assumes no more than a voluntary undertaking in respect of the work in question, all the first defendant volunteered was at the highest to exercise reasonable care to procure the second defendant to carry out the works in question. ...There is no arguable basis on which it can be said that the first defendant owed to the plaintiffs a parallel duty of care in tort in respect of the conduct of the contract works. It follows that this is not a case to which the principles of contributory negligence apply."

(3)索赔基于的合约条文带来的责任与行为带来的侵权责任完全一致,两种责任也同时存在。这样,由于英国法律是承认同步责任,受害方可以选择对他最为有利的诉因去提起与推进诉讼,则 1945 年立法也应该适用。Hobhouse 大法官认为该第三类的情形去适用 1945 年立法分摊责任与损失是十分显著的,并说:“It is commonplace that actions are brought by persons who have suffered personal injuries as the result of the negligence of the person sued and that there is a contractual as well as tortious relationship. In such cases apportionment of blame is invariably adopted by the Court notwithstanding that the plaintiff could sue in contract as well as in tort. The example normally cited in the present context is the decision of the Court of Appeal in Sayers v. Harlow UDC(1958)1 WLR 623, which concerned a contractual visitor to premises(a lady who had paid to use a public lavatory). The Court of Appeal said it did not matter whether the cause of action was put in tort or in contract and proceeded to apportion blame awarding her three – quarters of her damages. This was a decision on a category(3)case."

在该 Vesta v. Butcher 先例中,Hobhouse 大法官判该案的是属于第三类情形,所以 1945 年立法适用。Hobhouse 大法官是这样说:“I consider that, in the present case and in any similar category(3)case where there is no express contractual provision which defines the parties' rights and liabilities in a different way, apportionment of blame and liability is open to the tribunal. My reasons are twofold. First, I am bound by the Court of Appeal so to decide in a category(3)case. Secondly, the correct analysis is that independently of contract there is a statutory or common law relationship which exists between the parties and which can then give rise to tortious liabilities which fall to be adjusted in accordance with the 1945 Act and the relevant question in any given case is whether the parties have by their contract varied that position. Here they patently have not."

该先例上诉到贵族院[1989) 1 Lloyd's Rep 331],但维持原判。

2.5 合约关系

合约关系在订约自由(freedom of contract)与订约方自治(party autonomy)等耳熟能详的说法下,与普通法的疏忽侵权是两码事。但在 Esso Petroleum Co Ltd v. Mardon(1976)2 Lloyd's Rep 305 上诉庭先例中,法院可以在合约关系下仍去强加一个 Hedley Byrne 原则的小心谨慎的责任,并与合约关系同步诉讼。但合约法下对承诺的履行责任是严格或绝对责任,仅是没有疏忽但履行不了仍是违约,所以合约下的违约与侵权是扯不上关系的,违约提起的诉讼/仲裁也无需涉及侵权与否。

另明示条文在订约方自治下是超越法律默示地位,而疏忽侵权正是法律的默示地位。所以在订约自由下,经常有明示条文去改变法律默示地位如即使疏忽仍不必负责,或反过来承担比疏忽更严格的责任,如严格或绝对责任。所以在订约自由下,合约的约定可以是各种各样的,任由合约双方通过谈判合意分摊责任与风险,法院或仲裁庭是管不了的。但侵权法不是"单对单"的私人合约,而是面对大众的(只要是侵权方与受害方有足够"邻近关系"),所以是否要承担侵权责任的标准就要统一,不像合约法下那样各种各样,要看合约怎样订。这标准就是在言行上有否疏忽(不再区分疏忽是严重或轻微)并对普通法承认的"邻居"造成伤害,特别传统上只局限在实质伤害上。

举一个旧版中介绍的航运与国际货物买卖的例子。法律(国际公约与国家立法)强制适用在提单合约(bills of lading)的 1924 年《海牙规则》的 Article Ⅲ(1)下,承运人或船东必须恪尽职责令船舶在装港启航前适航(seaworthy),[74] 这被视为接近绝对或严格的适航责任。而中国航运界经常使用的 GENCON 94 程租合约(voyage charter - party),由于有订约自由,对适航的责任就对船东非常有利,就算是船长疏忽船东也不用承担转承责任(vicarious liability):"The Owners are to be responsible for loss of or damage to the goods or for delay in delivery of the goods **only** in case the loss, damage or delay has been **caused by personal want of due diligence on the part of the Owners** ... And the Owners are responsible for **no** loss or damage or delay arising from **any other cause whatsoever**, even from the neglect or default of the Master or crew or some other person employed by the Owners on board or ashore ..."(加黑部分是笔者的强调)

反正这两份海上货物运输合约也会出现在同一货运航次,只是合约方有所不同。往往提单合约是在船东与收货人之间;程租合约是在船东与承租人(如是 CIF 或 CFR 的卖方或发货人)之间。但同样对同一艘船舶的适航责任,会是有天壤之别,而两个极端的合约责任也与疏忽侵权并不一致。

但除了船舶适航外,对于其他船东对货物的托管(bailment)与付运(shipment),

---

[74] 见 The"Manchester Castle"(1961)1 Lloyd's Rep 57 贵族院先例。

《海牙规则》对承运人/船东强加的责任是“妥善与小心”(properly and carefully),这是 Article III(2)所规定的:“the carrier shall properly and carefully load, handle, stow, carry, keep, care for, and discharge the goods carried.”这种措辞下的合约责任,应与疏忽侵权一致。如果船舶在运输途中托管货物期间犯错与疏忽并导致货损货差,就说不上有妥善与小心照顾货物。确实,最早带来侵权法律的 Coggs v. Bernard(1704) Ld Raym. 909 先例正是涉及索赔托管货物期间疏忽导致的货损。这样,提单合约强制合并在 1924 年《海牙规则》下对货物处理或照顾的违约与疏忽侵权是一致的,也就带来了上一小段介绍的同步责任的可能。

《海牙规则》之 Article IV(2)(a)规定对船舶的航行与管理的疏忽(“Act, neglect, or default of the master ... in the navigation or in the management of the ship”)免责,但没有对货物的妥善与小心照顾的责任有任何免责,所以不影响较早前的分析,也就是针对船东/承运人对货物的装卸与托管,必须妥善小心,不得对错误与疏忽免责。一旦疏忽导致货损货差甚至是连带造成船舶损坏(如在装卸货作业时货物从高处坠下砸坏甲板),如果只涉及船东/承运人的疏忽,索赔的收货人与/或承租人以提单(或程租)合约提起诉讼业已足够;但如果除了船东/承运人的过错与疏忽外,也同时涉及收货人与/或承租人的疏忽(例如在“free out”的条文下安排卸货),就会涉及提单(或程租)合约的违约与侵权同步审理。

2.5.1 根据合约明示或默示要求提供信息或意见的所谓“误述”实是违约

在合约履行,双方难免有大量的互动,包括向对方提供信息或意见。大量提供的信息或意见,特别是有时候时间很紧张,难免会有错误。这种情况下如果错误信息导致损失,提供方会要承担什么责任?

显然,普通法与/或《Misrepresentation Act 1967》都不适用在这种履行合约中的“误述”,也与诱导合约产生的误述无关,更与撤销合约的权利扯不上关系。所以,这种“误述”需要以合约法去解释看它的本质是什么与会有什么救济。

本质上发生在履约中的错误陈述(不论是无辜、疏忽或欺诈)常会是违约的情况,一般带来金钱赔偿的救济。但被称为误述应不是正确的说法。比如,在履约中会需要一方给另一方通知与提供信息,另一方才知道并能够准备他自己的履行。这样,合约会增加一条默示条文(implied term)。这在笔者《合约的解释:规则与应用》一书第七章之 10.1 段“默示条文例子一:履约需要对方先给通知”与 10.2 段“默示条文例子二:双方必须给予协助/合作让对方顺利履行合约”有介绍,可在此重复 Vyse v. Wakefield(1840)5 M & W 442 先例所说:“Where a party stipulates to a certain thing in a certain specific event which may become known to him, or with which he can make himself acquainted, he is not entitled to any notice, unless he stipulates for it; **but where it is to do a thing which lies within the peculiar knowledge of the opposite party, then notice ought to be given to him.**”(加黑部分是笔者的强调)

该段也介绍了国际货物买卖的 FOB,法律默示要求派船的买方通知卖方船舶到达装港并备妥装货,以让卖方去准备与安排交货。显然没有这个信息与事实的告知,卖方是不知道轮到他要履行合约下的承诺的。至于什么时候买方需要通知卖方,在合约没有明示规定的情况下,就以根据案件与案情而定的合理时间为准。这可能是船舶实际抵达装港后才需要与能够给的正确的通知,表明有关船舶已经抵达与备妥。在近代商业社会,时间就是金钱,必须要抓得很紧的情况下,这样一来,这种通知会来得太晚,从而导致卖方无法提早安排交货。所以 FOB 买卖合约会明示加上条文要求如 7 天、3 天不等的预期抵达与备妥日期通知。这样,如果届时卖方心急,10 天前就要求买方告知,买方在没有合约明示或法律默示要求的情况下,是没有必要作答的。但 7 天与 3 天不等的通知就必须作答,否则就是违约并会导致损失索赔,例如卖方来不及安排交货/装货。

这些通知或预期通知的法律要求是"诚实、善意并有合理基础"(honest, good faith and on reasonable ground),对此可见 The"Myrtos"(1984)2 Lloyd's Rep 449 先例。注意诚实与对事实真相坦率(truthful)不是同一回事。简而言之,诚实就代表不要说谎,要求有合理基础。但是这个 FOB 买方在作出通知或预期通知时的"合理"的尺度可以是宽松,如港口代理或船长的告知,但这不代表是事实真相。而对事实真相坦率不只要诚实,还要全面调查并掌握所有有关的真实情况,才能说出事实真相,否则"坦率"就无从说起。这往往需要时间去查明、讨论、研究、分析、合理化与反证等。

以一个诉讼为例,当事人代表律师必须对法院"诚实",不能对法院说谎,这是十分严格的法院规则与律师执业守则。但律师又无需坦率告诉法院"事实真相",因为这样才能替自己的客户扬长避短、避重就轻地表述己方的案件(present own case)。而法院是要在双方代表律师的"诚实"协助与不得误导法院的规定下(看来十分矛盾),寻找出双方争议背后的事实真相。

显然,FOB 买方的通知或预期通知可能错误。如果是无辜,例如错误是给了 3 天预期通知后发生意外,导致通知的抵达与备妥日期错误,这显然没有违反诚实的要求,往往合约内也有相关的免责条文(exception clause)可保护派船的买方。而如果通知或预期通知是欺诈/欺骗性,这显然违反了法律要求的诚实,这就是违约并带来损失赔偿的责任。这与撤销合约或更准确地终止合约无关,因为这种预期通知条文不会是合约的条件条文(condition),是法律认为非常重要,而且只是金钱损失的赔偿并不足以作为救济。至于预期通知是疏忽,是否满足诚实的要求要看情况而定,主要是看是什么原因造成疏忽与疏忽的程度。

但往往也无需深究到底是什么原因造成通知错误,因为会同时涉及合约其他条文强加的严格合约承诺。例如,在一个 FOB 买卖合约(或程租合约),除了通知或预期通知船舶抵达与备妥日期外,另有明示规定如"预计准备就绪装货日期"(expected ready to load)条文,[75]这被视为条件条文,其中包括船舶在上一个港口预留起航去

---

〔75〕 这课题在杨大明律师的《期租合同》一书第五篇之 5.2 段有详论。

装港时必须预留足够航行的时间，否则就是违约，对此见 The“Baleares”(1993) 1 Lloyd's Rep 215 先例。

另 Devlin 大法官在 Evera S. A. Commercial v. North Shipping Co Ltd (1956) 2 Lloyd's Rep 367 先例中提供了另一种情况，如下所述：“He enters into the obligation of making **an honest and reasonable statement about his position. That he discharged that is not questioned here.** But he also entered into an obligation, which is expressed in the ... charter, ... that the ship 'shall with all convenient speed sail and proceed to ...' It is for the breach of that obligation that the ship is being sued in this case ...”(加黑部分是笔者的强调)

船长如果“误述”了船舶可装载货物的数字，如计算错误，这是对船东在期租下允许承租方支配船上使用空间条文的违约，这条文在 2015 年纽约土产(NYPE)格式是 Cl. 2(c)，表述为：“The Vessel's holds shall be ... in all respect ready to receive ... any permissible cargo.”另 Cl. 8(a) 规定：“... The Master ... shall be under the orders and directions of the Charterers as regards employment and agency...”合约承诺是严格责任，也在这种违约没有免责条文可去保护船东。所以承租人根本无须关心船长的“误述”是否诚实、是否有疏忽。

总结以上，笔者想表达的是履约时经常会相互提供信息与事实陈述，如果是疏忽提供了虚假与不正确信息，虽然被通称为“误述”，但这实是违约，与本书针对的“误述”无关。当然是否违约仍要看有关合约的各种各样的约定，因为会有合约约定免除责任，例如约定一方合约方如果因代理人疏忽提供了不正确的信息则不必承担责任。

2.5.2 默示保证或附带协议/保证

已经在本章之1.1 段提到，在传统的普通法下受害方在非欺诈性误述(无辜或疏忽)下，向误述方索赔金钱损失的唯一办法是在谈判时对方曾经作出过一个附带协议或附带保证(collateral contract/warranty/promise)。现实中(包括在商业活动)，有不少口头协议或“部分文书、部分口头”协议/合约，对于这些合约，就不是附带协议或保证，而是合约的一部分，对此可见 Evans v. Merzario (1976) 2 Lloyd's Rep 165 先例。而对于看来是完整记录与被签署的合约(executed contract)，才有附带协议/保证一说，而法院通常是不愿意把新内容增加或强加进一份完整记录与被签署的合约的。但如果不这样做，就无法索赔一个对实质重要的事实的不正确陈述(明显是十分严重的疏忽误述，但仍证明不了是欺诈性误述)导致的损失，因为只有衡平法承认疏忽误述，但也只有撤销合约这唯一救济途径。要成立附带协议/保证被陈述方/受害方必须证明客观看陈述方有受该陈述或该陈述的真实性有合约效力与约束的意图，但这并不容易。这一情况直到《Misrepresentation Act 1967》生效后才得到改善，在该立法下无辜或疏忽误述的受害方都可获得损失赔偿。也因此在《Misrepresentation Act 1967》后，法院对通过事实的默示(implied by fact)去认定附带协议/保证的存在会更加谨慎与保守。正如 Denning 勋爵在 Esso Petroleum Co Ltd v. Mardon (1976)2 Lloyd's Rep 305 上诉庭先例中说:"more often than not the court elevated the innocent(这里的"无辜"是包括了疏忽误述)misrepresentation into a collateral warranty and thereby did justice — in advance of the Misrepresentation Act."

显然去证明有多一个主合约外附带合约/保证的默示不容易成立,故以明示的"陈述与保证条文"应是更佳选择。而有了明示条文在主合约,法律也不会再去增加默示的附带附议/保证。更不说今天不少合约也加上了"完整合约条文"(Entire Agreement clause)去明示排除或否定附带协议/保证的存在。

简而言之,附带协议/保证是指在谈判时作出的事实陈述,除了诱导对方依赖并订立合约外,客观上也看是陈述方有意图(相等于订约意图)把这些陈述作为有合约效力的保证(intended to guarantee the statement in the contract):见 Gee v. Lucas (1867)16 LT 357;Heilbut, Symons & Co v. Buckleton(1913)AC 30(HL);Oscar Chess Ltd v. Williams(1957)1 WLR 370(CA);Harlingdon and Leinster Enterprises Ltd v. Christopher Hull Fine Art Ltd(1991)1 QB 564(CA);Sabena Technics SA v. Singapore Airlines Ltd(2003)EWHC 1318(Comm)等先例。在 Sabena Technics SA v. Singapore Airlines Ltd 先例中,Colman 大法官说:"whether in all the circumstances of the statement by the representor would be understood by a reasonable representee in the precise position of the actual representee and with his knowledge of the negotiations as being made with **the intention that its truth could be relied upon as a matter protected by contractual enforcement**."(加黑部分是笔者的强调)

至于如何测试在谈判中对一个事实的陈述到底法律上是"陈述"(representation)或是"保证"(warranty),Denning 大法官在 Oscar Chess Ltd v. Williams 上诉庭先例中说得简单:"if an intelligent bystander would reasonably infer that a warranty was intended, that will suffice."

举一个例子说明,这就是通过广告(报刊、网站等)推销商品中对货物作出的陈述吸引或诱导潜在买方依赖并订购与产生买卖合约,这显然是保证,有合约效力:见 Dick Bentley Productions v. Harold(Motors)Ltd(1965)1 WLR 623(CA);Turner v. Anquetil(1953)NZLR 952(新西兰)等先例。如果将来的履行中有部分货物是货不对版,买方索赔损失,卖方不能抗辩说这是订立合约前的事实陈述,有了错误也只是"误述",买方在普通法下只能令该买卖合约无效或撤销合约,不得根据合约在《Sale of Goods Act 1979》下部分拒货并索赔损失。这显然说不过去,因为这属于合约保证而不是陈述。

在进一步去区分陈述与保证前,先说"附带"协议/保证不代表是在主合约(如果双方签订一份看来是完整的主合约)外另有一份独立的合约。这里的"附带"只代表是与主合约"同步"(concurrent),并带来对主合约的补充(addition)、更改(variation)甚至是否定(contradiction)。只有该保证是由第三人作出时,附带协议/保证才会被视为独立,如生产商作出对货物的陈述但主合约是分销商作为卖方与买方订立。这样,附带协议/保证也只是影响分销商与买方之间的合约,不代表与生产商有合约关系。

保护英国消费者的立法《Consumer Rights Act 2015》,已经明确与替代了这方面的普通法。由于与中国公司关系不大,只小部分与简单节录《Misrepresentation, Mistake and Non-Disclosure》一书(2022 年,第 6 版)之 8 – 17 段说:"**Consumer goods contracts** In the case of consumer goods contracts, where the goods are sold by description the contract is to be treat as including a term that the goods will match the description [这是在该立法的 S. 11(1)]. This will apply to incorporate certain pre-contractual representations into consumer goods contracts in similar way to s. 13 of the Sale of Goods Act 1979 in relation to non-consumer sale contracts. ..."

接下来再进一步但只是简略地分析"陈述"与"保证"的区分,这有以下一些考虑因素。

2.5.2.1 陈述/表述与附带保证区分之一:双方对事实真相的认知与理解

一个重要考虑因素是陈述方如果对有关事实的理解比被陈述方优越,令谈判中后者必须依赖前者,如货物买卖中买方必须依赖卖方对货物的陈述。这样这些对货物的陈述有很大的可能会被视为保证。相反,如果陈述方说明只是听回来的事实或被陈述方应该知道他不会知道事实真相,这些谈判中的陈述就不会是保证(除非特定说明愿意"打保票")。这可节录 Denning 大法官在 Oscar Chess Ltd v. Williams (1957) 1 WLR 370 上诉庭先例中说:"It is instructive to take some recent instances to show how the courts have approached this question. When the seller states a fact which is or should be within his own knowledge and of which the buyer is ignorant, intending that the buyer should act on it, and he does so, it is easy to infer a warranty ... But if the seller, when he states a fact, makes it clear that he has no knowledge of his own but has got his information elsewhere, and is merely passing it on, it is not so easy to imply a warranty. Such a case was Routledge v. McKay ... where the seller 'stated that it was a 1942 model and pointed to the corroboration to be found in the book', and it was held that there was no warranty."(加黑部分是笔者的强调)

在 Routledge v. McKay (1954) 1 WLR 615 先例中,Denning 大法官说:"it is important to remember that the seller, unless he is the first owner, is not the originator of the statement about the year. He does not know for himself, of his own knowledge, what year the car or cycle is. He has to accept it from the book, and he cannot be expected to warrant its accuracy, unless he in express terms makes himself responsible for it. In the ordinary way, therefore, the statement is only a representation and not a warranty."

在本章之 2.2.3 段介绍的 Esso Petroleum Co Ltd v. Mardon (1976) 2 Lloyd's Rep 305 上诉庭先例中,可重复 Denning 勋爵所说以显示这一方面是重要的考虑因素:"it was a forecast made by a party-Esso-who had special knowledge and skill. It was the yardstick … by which they measured the worth of a filling station. They knew the facts. They knew the traffic in the town. They knew the throughput of comparable stations. They had much experience and expertise at their disposal. **They were in a much better position than Mr Mardon to make a forecast**. It seems to me that if such a person makes a forecast, intending that the other should act upon it-and he does act upon it, **it can well be interpreted as a warranty** …"(加黑部分是笔者的强调)

2.5.2.2 陈述/表述与附带保证区分之二:陈述/表述的实质重要性

《Misrepresentation, Mistake and Non-Disclosure》一书(2022 年,第 6 版)之 8-09 段说:"**Significance of the statement** An important factor in determining whether the statement can be taken to have been intended to have contractual force is its significance: its seriousness, or importance. This has a number of interrelated aspects. …"

这个重要考虑因素可体现在 Harlingdon and Leinster Enterprises Ltd v. Christopher Hull Fine Art Ltd(1991)1 QB 564 上诉庭先例中,案情涉及两幅德国 20 世纪的一位表现主义(expressionist)画家,名为加布里埃莱·明特(Gabriele Munter)女士的画,该画在 1984 年被购买,但后来被买方发现是赝品,实际不值钱,这导致买方向卖方以《Sale of Goods Act 1979》的货不对版为由拒货,要求退还已经支付的每幅 6000 英镑,共 12,000 英镑的价款。但买方在上诉庭以多数意见(2:1)败诉,原因是买方自己小心(caveat emptor)。[76]

这里只提被告卖方的负责人 Hull 先生被认定不对这种画有培训、经验与知识(training, experience and skill)可去分辨出这两幅画的真伪。他是根据 1980 年的一次公开的拍卖目录(auction catalogue)的记载去陈述是 Munter 女士的画。相反,作为买方的原告的负责人 Holger Braasch 夫妻对德国艺术品的收藏有一定声誉,并对德国表现主义的画特别有兴趣,也在购买前检查过两幅画与拍卖目录。在涉及 Hull 先生对两幅画表述的归属(attribution),即是否是 Munter 女士的画,Nourse 大法官说:

"I desire to add some general observations about sales of pictures by one dealer to another where the seller makes an attribution to a recognised artist. The huge additional value of an authentic attribution has, from the earliest periods of European art, seduced a corresponding volume of skill and energy into the production of fakes, even in the lifetime of the artist. … With the great expansion in royal and noble collections which took place in the 18th century, faking became an art of its own. … Modern advances in technology, while in some respects increasing the possibilities of detection, have in others assisted the faker to apply his skill with ever increasing ingenuity. Even if fakes are put on one side, many old master paintings cannot be safely attributed to a particular member of a group of artists, some of whom may still remain obscure.

---

[76] 关于买方自己小心,可见杨大明律师《国际货物买卖》一书第四章。

All this is a matter of common knowledge amongst dealers in the art market and, I would expect, amongst all but the most inexperienced or naive of collectors. It means that almost any attribution to a recognised artist, especially of a picture whose provenance is unknown, may be arguable. In sales by auction, where the seller does not know who the buyer will be, the completeness with which the artist's name is stated in the catalogue, e. g. 'Peter Paul Rubens', 'P. P. Rubens' or 'Rubens', signifies in a descending scale the degree of confidence with which the attribution is made. Nowadays an auctioneer's conditions of sale usually, perhaps invariably, so declare and, further, that **any description is an opinion only**. But in **sales by private treaty by one dealer to another** there is no such practice. That would suggest that there **the seller's attribution is not a matter of importance**. ... He(专家证人) said that an art dealer's success depended on, and was judged by, his ability to exercise his own judgment. It was not customary for a dealer to rely in any way on the judgment or representations of the dealer from whom a picture was being purchased.

... **many dealers habitually deal with each other on the principle caveat emptor. ... The court ought to be exceedingly wary in giving a seller's attribution any contractual effect**. ..."(加黑部分是笔者的强调)

Nourse 大法官以上所说的大意是对画造假的现象非常普遍,甚至可以追溯到画家仍在世时,随着时代进步,检测是否是赝品的技术提高的同时,造假的技术也提高了。除了对艺术品市场交易毫无经验的菜鸟,这应是艺术品经销商间的共识。也就是说一幅画是否能归属于任何知名画家,特别是来源不明的画,都是可争议的。在公开拍卖,卖方不知道买方是谁,画的归属只是意见,拍卖目录上画家的名字的完整程度可以反映出卖方对画的真伪的信心。而在经销商间的私人交易,卖方说画归属于哪个画家根本不重要,这种陈述不会被当真,也就是不会被依赖。一个经销商依赖另一个经销商的判断并不是行业的惯常做法,而很多经销商也是以"买方自己小心"的大原则与对方做交易。所以法院不应该让卖方对归属的陈述有合约效力。

2.5.2.3　陈述/表述与附带保证区分之三:事实陈述与订立合约的相隔时间

《Misrepresentation, Mistake and Non-Disclosure》一书(2022 年,第 6 版)之 8 - 12 段说:"**Timing of the statement** A representation may become part of the terms of the contract even though it was made before the time at which the contract was concluded, but only where it is shown that the earlier statement was intended to continue into the discussions at the time of the contract itself. For example, a statement in an advertisement which caused the claimant to enter negotiations with the representor may be taken to have been intended to continue ... throughout the negotiations and become a term. However, it is undoubtedly easier to establish that a representation made at the time of the contract was intended to be part of the terms than in the case where there is a time gap between the making of a statement during the negotiations and the later conclusion of the contract."

理论上合约订立前甚至谈判开始前的陈述也可以构成合约的一部分，但必须证明该陈述是持续性陈述。例如原告看了被告的广告，令他找被告谈判并订立合约，广告中的陈述应该就属于持续性的陈述，并之后成为合约的一部分。因为谈判的内容，包括什么时候可以提供货物、广告的价格有否折扣、有否保证不会货不对版、如果货不对版能否退货等都会成为合约的一部分。当然，陈述离订约时越近，就越有可能属于合约的一部分。而如果陈述时间距开始谈判到最终订约还有一段时间，属于合约一部分的机会就大减。例如在本章之 2.2.4 段已经介绍过的 Howard Marine and Dredging Co Ltd v. A Ogden & Sons (Excavations) Ltd (1978) QB 574 上诉庭先例中，上诉庭认为考虑到相关事实发生的时间，这距离交船前 3 个月作出的陈述，不能构成合约的附带保证。

2.5.2.4　陈述/表述与附带保证区分之四：有关合约的形式

《Misrepresentation, Mistake and Non-Disclosure》一书（2022 年，第 6 版）之 8-13 段说："**Contracts in, or recorded in, writing** Where the parties have created a written document containing the terms of their agreement there will be an inference that statements, oral or written, which do not appear in the document were not intended to be incorporated as terms. … But **there is no absolute rule that a written contract, or a written document evidencing the terms of the contract, excludes the possibility of other contractually binding obligations**. In the case of a contract in writing, it may be necessary to hold that any such obligation is contained in a separate contract, collateral to the main written contract. Where there is no formal written contract, but only written evidence of the contract, the representation may be held simply to be one of the terms which were therefore not fully recorded in the written document. But **in all cases the question remains: even though the parties entered into a formal written contract, or one or both parties recorded their (informal) contract in writing, was a pre-contractual statement, which is not contained in the written document, intended by the parties to be warranted by the representator**?"（加黑部分是笔者的强调）

这一点已在本章多处提及，就是对一份（1）正式（formal）合约，无论是立法［如《Law of Property (Miscellaneous Provisions) Act 1989》、[77]《Statute of Frauds

[77] 《Law of Property (Miscellaneous Provisions) Act 1989》之 s. 2(1) 针对土地买卖规定："A contract for the sale or other disposition of an interest in land can only be made in writing and only by incorporating all the terms which the parties have expressly agreed in one document or, where contracts are exchanged, in each."

1677》[78]等]要求,或是双方同意完成合约订立必须签订一份正式文件(例如谈判中写明"以签订合约为准");[79](2)虽然不是正式合约,但看来是完整记录了双方同意的所有内容的合约(如一封电邮),法院是不愿意代替双方去增加或扣减合约的内容的。毕竟,双方会是有意不把谈判过的部分内容加入合约内。

如果合约的记录真有双方认同的错漏,问题也容易解决,双方大可以修改合约或重签一份合约替代。如果要惊动法院或仲裁庭,就表示只有一方合约方认为是有错漏,但另一方不这样认为。固然,认为有错漏的一方会觉得对方是乘机取巧、不合作。但对法院或仲裁庭而言,不会以"阴谋论"看待任何一方当事人,而往往会客观认为只是一方的错漏是有可能甚至很有可能的。在没有双方的共识下,法院或仲裁庭怎能凭单方面的主张任意增加或扣减合约内容? 而且,主张有错漏的一方往往唯一的解释是自己疏忽看漏了。这不是一个值得同情的理由,签署一份昂贵的商业合约是一件十分重大与严肃的事情。另是,主张错漏的一方往往是没有太优质的证据,通常是口头或加上不完整的文书证据。口头证据是谈不上优质,正如 Ormrod 大法官在 Esso Petroleum Co Ltd v. Mardon(1976)2 Lloyd's Rep 305 上诉庭先例中说:"The common law's mistrust of oral evidence, particularly of the parties themselves, and its reluctanceto impugn the certainty of the written word, comes into conflict with the principle that the law should so far as possible give effect to the presumed intentions of the parties."

也在本章多处提到,在《Misrepresentation Act 1967》立法生效前,由于法律对疏忽误述没有金钱赔偿的救济,所以法院为了个别案件的公平合理,会尽最大努力去挑出附带协议/保证。但在立法生效后,加上其他商业上越来越普遍的做法是加上一条"完整合约条文"与在部分合约类别(如并购合约、股权买卖合约等)中加上一条明示的"陈述与保证条文",默示的附带保证就不再有必要。

但这方面的法律仍是有效,社会上与商业上也仍有不少不完整的合约,如口头或部分口头部分书面的合约,也不会有之前提到的一些惯用条文(boiler - plate clause),所以仍会有附带保证/协议的争议。

2.5.2.5 陈述/表述与附带保证区分之五:其他个别案件的特定事实

这是各种各样,在每一个案件都会有不同的事实与证据。例如指称是附带保证的措辞/文字,一个极端是文件证据显示陈述方在谈判时另有说明"我保证""你可相信我说的话"等,而另一个极端是说"我无意给任何保证""这陈述不是承诺""我自

[78] 《Statute of Frauds 1677》之 s. 4 针对担保规定:"No Action shall be brought...whereby to charge the Defendant upon any special promise to answer for the debt default or miscarriages of another person ... unless the Agreement upon which such Action shall be brought or some Memorandum or Note thereof shall be in Writing and signed by the party to be charged therewith or some other person thereunto by him lawfully authorized."

[79] 见笔者《合约的解释:规则与应用》一书第八章之 4 段的介绍。

己也不肯定”等。又或是，在开庭审理时，误述方在回答原告的代表律师的交叉盘问时，承认对谈判时的有关陈述是愿意或有意图作为合约承诺或保证，以取得合约。这方面与误述方的陈述是否是欺诈、疏忽或无辜误述无关，所以交叉盘问不是为了寻找误述方是否知道或应知道陈述真伪的答案，这些只涉及侵权。在合约索赔下把谈判时的一些陈述作为附带保证是需要客观看误述方是否有订约意图，这涉及他个人的想法（state of mind）。当然涉及一个无辜误述，也往往是一些误述方自己也不会知道真相的事实，就可以推算到一般在这种情况误述方是不会愿意做出合约的承诺或保证。

2.6 善意责任关系

笔者在《合约的解释：规则与应用》一书第九章介绍了“善意”（good faith）的原则与要求，并提到除了某些合约与关系类别，如保险合约、[80]合伙人协议（partnership agreement）、[81]雇佣合约、[82]信托（trust）等，没有一般的善意要求。这在2014年写的书已经提到了Yam Seng Pte Ltd v. International Trade Corp Ltd（2013）EWHC 111（QB）先例，但没有进一步的介绍。该先例带来了创造性的善意原则可以默示条文（implied terms）强加在某类合约中的说法，这类合约可称为“关系合约”（relational contract）。这也在近10年来带来了针对方方面面的无数先例，有关的问题包括：是否支持这个一审判决；[83]善意是事实或是法律的默示；[84]明示善意条文；默示的善意责任对合约方的行为的要求的定义或标准，这显然也与误述/披露[85]的课题有关系，特别是在披露信息与事实方面，必须提供给对方合约方诚实与全面的信息与事实等。

另近10年来普通法/英国法律的善意原则对行使合约裁量权（discretion）、选择权（option）或权利（power/rights）有约束。在Braganza v. BP Shipping Ltd（2015）UKSC 17最高院先例后，开始有组织地通过默示强加一个可称为“Braganza责任”的善意责任在权利方（option-holder）/决策人（decision-maker）。在笔者看来，这方面的发展对“走出去”的中国公司影响比“关系合约”更严重。

本章与本书虽然不是针对善意的课题，但借这个机会补充《合约的解释：规则与应用》一书没有的内容，主要是英国法律在近期的重大发展，尽量不去重复。

---

〔80〕见本书第五章之6.1段。

〔81〕Hoffman勋爵在O’Neill v. Phillips（1999）1 WLR 1092先例中说是“contract of good faith”，见本书第五章之6.2段。

〔82〕见本书第五章之6.5.3段。

〔83〕Globe Motors Inc v. TRW LucasVarity Electric Steering Ltd（2016）EWCA Civ 396上诉庭先例看来有不同意见，但接下来的Amey Birmingham v. Birmingham City Council（2018）EWCA Civ 264与Candey Ltd v. Bosheh（2022）EWCA Civ 1103上诉庭先例是支持。

〔84〕见《合约的解释：规则与应用》一书第七章的介绍。

〔85〕关于误述的课题可见本书第一章至第四章，披露的课题可见本书第五章。

2.6.1 普通法与大陆法下善意原则或责任的巨大差异

英国合约法是不默示有善意要求,没有如欧洲大陆法国家[86]一样发展出一套完整与有组织的善意原则,甚至与同是普通法国家的美国也不一样。这里的原因一方面是“商场如战场”,在商业合约关系强加善意责任不现实。这可节录 Ackner 勋爵在 Walford v. Miles(1992)2 AC 128 贵族院先例的说法:“The concept of a duty to carry on negotiations in good faith is inherently repugnant to the adversarial position of the parties when involved in negotiations. Each party to the negotiations is entitled to pursue his(or her)own interest,... unworkable in practice as it is inherently inconsistent with the position of a negotiating party.”

虽然该先例针对的是谈判过程中的互锁协议(lock - out contract),但合约履行过程一样,都是各自谋利,唯一的区别是前者可以漫天开价而后者则受合约的约束。

另一方面是这与英国法强调的商业合约的“订约自由”与“肯定性”等大原则有冲突。合约谈判中价格等主要条文常常反而比较容易敲定,困难与耗时的往往是如何通过免责条文、不可抗力条文等分摊可以预见的风险。最后达成的合约可能因为双方谈判力量与知识水平悬殊而出现一面倒,但只要不涉及胁迫/不当影响[87]等,就是有效的商业合约。而如果有善意的“天条”,以合约不公平合理就更改双方辛苦谈判达成的条文,显然就会对订约自由与合约肯定性有影响。订约方不肯定自己能不能按照合约条文履行,而如果不能又何必谈判?

在 MSC Mediterranean Shipping Company SA v. Cottonex Anstalt(2016)EWCA Civ 789 上诉庭先例中,Moore - bick 大法官说:“There is in my view a real danger that if a general principle of good faith were established it would be invoked as often to undermine as to support the terms in which the parties have reached agreement. The danger is not dissimilar to that posed by too liberal an approach to construction, against which the Supreme Court warned in Arnold v Britton [2015] UKSC 36.”

在加拿大最高院的 Bhasin v. Hrynew(2014)3 SCR 494 先例中,也清楚说明了普通法反对善意原则的原因:“The first is that ‘good faith’ is an inherently unclear concept that will permit ad hoc judicial moralism to undermine the certainty of commercial transactions. The second is that imposing a duty of good faith is inconsistent with the basic principle of freedom of contract. ...”

对商业交易带来不肯定是因为善意如同“做好人”一样,只是抽象的做人大道

---

〔86〕 例如法国有大量针对善意的案例与法学学者的评论,如 Philippe Malaurie、Laurent Agnès 与 Philippe Stoffel - Munck 合著的《Droit Civil:Droit des Obligations》一书,就分别论述了合约法方方面面的善意议题,如合约谈判、合约形成、信息披露、免责条文、困难条文(hardship clause)、无法预见损失、复原、终止合约等。

〔87〕 见本书第十章与第十一章的详细介绍。

理，所以案件由不同待人处事、性格、道德标准、心境等的审理法官去决定，并让他们可去自由发挥，就很容易造成"棕榈树公正"（Palm tree justice），[88]破坏甚至无法建立与不断完善法律制度，并带来不肯定。

2.6.1.1　美国法/纽约州法下合约有默示的善意要求

在美国，合约法是由每个州自己管辖，除非是涉及联邦利益（uniquely federal interest）或与联邦的公共政策起重大冲突（significant conflict）。

在美国《Uniform Commercial Code》§1－304 中规定："every contract or duty within the Uniform Commercial Code imposes an obligation of good faith in its performance and enforcement."

《Restatement（Second）of Contracts》之 Section 205 也说："Every contract imposes upon each party a duty of good faith and fair dealing in its performance and its enforcement."

也有不少先例明确在美国法下合约有默示的善意要求，以与国际商业人士最有关系的纽约州法律为例，其在 511 W. 232nd Owners Corp. v. Jennifer Realty Co.，98 N. Y. 2d 144（2002）先例中说："In New York，all contracts imply a covenant of good faith and fair dealing in the course of performance. ... This covenant embraces a pledge that 'neither party shall do anything which will have the effect of destroying or injuring the right of the other party to receive the fruits of the contract'."

但上述善意原则对一些复杂与把双方对合约风险的分摊和各自的合约权利写得清楚明确的商业合约没有太多的影响。已有很多先例判善意与公平交易（fair dealing）的默示条文是不得插手或影响合约的明示规定与双方预期的合约成果。

以下简单介绍较近期的先例。第一个是在 Moran v. Erk，11 NY3d 452（2008）先例中，案情涉及房屋买卖，买卖合约中包括一条以律师批准为准[89]的条文。

双方签署的合约约定有关房屋的价格为 50.5 万美元，但之后买方 Erk 看中了另一套房屋，于是指示自己的律师不批准有关的合约，律师也根据指示在合约规定的期限内不批准合约。卖方 Moran 直到三年后才以 38.5 万美元的价格出售了房屋，于是开始诉讼向 Erk 索赔之间的差价与这三年为了出售房屋产生的费用。Moran 的主要争议是合约有默示的善意与公平交易的要求，对律师行使裁量权决定是否批准合约有约束。纽约州最高法院一审与上诉部门都接受了 Moran 的争辩，判如果卖方恶意指示律师不批准有关的合约，就视为对合约要经过律师批准的弃权，买卖合约成立，因此 Erk 要赔偿差价与支付利息。但这判决被纽约州上诉法院推翻，上诉法院认为

[88]　这比喻是来自阿拉伯与犹太文化中一位智者在棕榈树下为个别争议作出判决。这判决往往是不按照法律规则也不参考其他案件，而仅凭实用的常识在每个个案中发挥裁量权作出仅仅针对该个案是公平的判决。这种公正是无法建立一个普遍适用的法律制度，更不要说可以持续进行完善。

[89]　关于这类变数条件条文可见笔者《合约的解释：规则与应用》一书第八章的详细介绍。

这错误解释了纽约州法律的善意与公平交易的默示规定。

根据上述节录的511 W. 232nd Owners Corp. v. Jennifer Realty Co. 先例的说法，善意要求任何一方不得影响另一方享受合约的成果。而对于有关的买卖合约，合约的成果取决于律师是否批准。

此外，肯定性与可预测性对解释合约至关重要，而一审的所谓“恶意规则”显然对合约解释的肯定性与可预测性没有帮助，虽然上诉法院没有明说，但是相信这种以律师批准为准的条文在房屋买卖合约中非常常见也是考虑之一。

以此先例的案情为例，Erk 在 1995 年底指示律师不批准合约，并很快买了另一套房屋生活。对于 Erk 一家来说，之前的买卖合约已经因为律师不批准而无效。而三年后，Moran 开始了所谓的违约诉讼，在上诉法院审理时，时间更是已经过去了 10 年，而这只是因为当时与律师的一段对话。这带来的进一步的问题是，若每位不批准合约的律师都会被传召，提供当时客户给了什么指示、为什么不批准合约等的事实证据，则会与律师和客户之间的特免权〔90〕产生冲突。

在考虑了以上“恶意规则”会带来的缺点后，上诉法院最终判在有关的条文下，只要在规定时间内，律师可以任何理由或不给理由不批准合约。

接着纽约州最高法院在两个先例针对了善意与合约条文之间的关系。在第一个 ELBT Realty, LLC v. Mineola Garden City Co. ,144 A. D. 3d 1083(2nd Dep't 2016)先例，涉及一栋商业大厦的买卖合约，有明示条文说明买方“有全权裁量权”(in its sole discretion)与可以“以任何原因”(for any reason whatsoever)终止合约。买方行使裁量权终止合约后，卖方质疑买方终止合约是违反善意，并开始诉讼。法院判该条文有效，不受善意责任影响，说：“the plain language of the contract makes clear that termination of the contract was a possibility and the parties, who were sophisticated, counseled business entities negotiating at arm's length over a prolonged period of time, should have understood and expected that termination of the contract could occur during that specified window of time and that such decision was the purchaser's alone and did not need to be accompanied by any specific justification. To interpret section 3.01 as the seller asks(也就是有善意责任) would require adding terms to the contract and thereby make a new contract for the parties in the guise of interpreting the writing.”

第二个是 Transit Funding Associates LLC v. Capital One Taxi Medallion Finance, 149 AD 3d 23(1st Dep't 2017)先例，被告金融公司向原告作出循环贷款，原告可以定期向被告申请提款。有关贷款合约约定被告有“全权与绝对裁量权”是否批准申请。之后因为市场变差，被告不再批准原告的申请，原告生意进行不下去于是开始诉讼，指被告恶意拒绝批准。法院判：“the covenant of good faith and fair dealing cannot ne-

〔90〕 见笔者《证据法：国际规管与诉讼中的证据攻防》一书第九章的详细介绍，以法律业务特免权保密是至高无上的公共政策。

gate express provisions of the agreement ...where the contract terms unambiguously afford (被告)the right to exercise its absolute discretion to withhold the necessary approval."

法院也判无关被告的做法的真正意图或动机(motivation),这对笔者来说是与英国法律一致,以客观标准解释合约。

从以上介绍的纽约法院先例来看,美国法或纽约州法即使有善意的默示条文,但由于不得去超越合约的明示条文,所以在一份拟定得好与全面/完整的商业合约,解释起来与判决的结果与没有善意原则的英国法还是一样的。

2.6.1.2 法国/德国民法典视善意为公共政策

但这些美国先例如果在大陆法国家如法国审理,就有可能得出不同结果。在《法国民法典》之1104条,是把善意视为公共政策(ordre public),另在1102条规定订约自由不得超越公共政策。这可节录2022年11月发表的由Sir William Blair大法官主导的名为"Duties of Good Faith in Wholesale Financial Contracts"[91]报告中之3.2段:

"The French Code Civil sets out a somewhat different position: Article 1102 provides ...(Everyone is free to contract or not contract, to choose their contracting party and to decide on the content and form of the contract within the limits fixed by law. Freedom of contract does not permit derogation from rules of public policy).

The principal inroads into that freedom are those of good faith and measures to encourage performance. ...

In the modern systems the duty of good faith is enshrined in deceptively simple terms with a general duty.

Article 1104 of the French Code Civil provides...(Contracts must be negotiated, entered into and performed in good faith).

The statutory extension beyond their performance was added in 2016 but the courts had long since developed much the same concept in that regard. The provision is expressed to be one of public policy(ordre public) and so falls within the second sentence of Article 1102(see above) overriding freedom of contract.

The German civil code, the Bürgerliches Gesetzbuch(BGB) has an equally pithy provision in §242:...(the obligor is bound to ensure performance as may be required by good faith with regard to general custom and practice).(《德国民法典》在第242条也有同样的规定,合约的履行要求善意。)

In both France and Germany(and other civil law jurisdictions with regard to their equivalent provisions) these single sentences have evolved separately with extensive case

---

[91] 有兴趣的读者可在 https://fmlc.org/wp-content/uploads/2022/12/FMLC-Paper-Duties-of-Good-Faith-in-Wholesale-Financial-Contracts.pdf 下载全文。

law and academic commentary to which it is not possible to do justice here. **The good faith obligation permeates everything**. ...(法国与德国包括其他有同样规定的大陆法国家,对善意责任的要求渗透方方面面。)

... Breach of the duty of good faith can result in liability. Examples would include:

• breaking off negotiations before the contract is formed without proper cause, so that, contrary to English law, the reliance of the other party in the contract being concluded is protected;

• **failure to disclose material information prior to the contract**, so that, for example a market form of disclaimer effective under English law might be ineffective under a civil system. **The English basic view is that pre-contract disclosure is not mandatory**-if it were mandatory and was not done, there might, for example, be uncertainty about the validity of guarantees and of transactions in fast – moving derivative, securities and foreign exchange markets. By contrast, Article 1112 – 1 of the French Code Civil provides ...(The party who knows information which is of decisive importance for the consent of the other party, must inform him of it where the latter is legitimately unaware of this information or relies on the contracting party. However, this duty to inform does not apply to the estimation of the value of the performance). **The civil law systems may also have continuing disclosure obligations, which in English law depend on the agreed terms**; and (这个例子与本书第五章介绍的披露有关,英国法律在合约订立前没有主动披露的责任,合约履行时也没有披露的责任,除非合约中有相关规定。而大陆法国家无论在订立合约前还是合约履行期间都有披露责任。)

• inappropriate purported exercise of termination rights potentially resulting in both damages and enforced continuation of the contract. Hence, contrary to the English position, the courts could in some jurisdictions intervene to override an agreed immediate acceleration or close – out on an express event of default though clarity and detail in the drafting of causes of termination will often reduce this risk.

Motivation for the exercise of a right may be relevant. The extent to which a party observed good faith may affect the extent to which for example an exclusion clause is upheld or, in the case of restitution, the date from which interest accrues. ...(大陆法国家因为有善意的要求,善意针对是思想状态,所以行为的动机是有关的,但这方面取证并不容易。)"(加黑部分是笔者的强调)

2.6.1.3 加拿大 Bhasin v. Hrynew(2014)3 SCR 494 最高院先例确认善意原则

在加拿大最高院的 Bhasin v. Hrynew 先例中,原告 Bhasin 先生是作为共同被告的 Canadian American Financial Corporation(以下简称 Can – Am)公司的高级销售,双方为期三年的经销合约(dealership agreement)中有条文约定除非其中一方提前半年通知不续约,否则合约自动续约。Bhasin 的工作是为公司销售证券投资产品,业绩很依赖他自己手下的销售代理表现。另一个共同被告 Hrynew 先生也是 Can - Am 的高级销售，是 Bhasin 的竞争对手。Hrynew 拥有 Alberta 省最大的销售代理网络并且和监管部门 Alberta Securities Commission 的关系很好，所以在公司很有影响力。Hrynew 曾经向 Bhasin 提出想要合并 Bhasin 的销售代理（其实是想把 Bhasin 踢走），但被 Bhasin 拒绝，于是 Hrynew 又向公司施压，表示如果不合并就带着销售代理离开公司。

之后，监管部门开始关注 Can - Am 的高级销售们是否遵守证券法的问题，Can - Am为了应对监管部门的要求，委任 Hrynew 作为省交易主任（provincial trading officer）负责审计高级销售的记录。这意味着 Hrynew 可以查看所有高级销售的机密商业记录，可以想到知道 Hrynew 打算的 Bhasin 拒绝 Hrynew 查看自己的机密商业记录。

Can - Am 其实已经在考虑重组在 Alberta 省的代理体系，其中包括让 Bhasin 作为 Hrynew 手下的代理工作。Can - Am 借着调查之机，期间不断误导 Bhasin 说监管部门拒绝了 Can - Am 聘用外部省交易主任的提议，所以只能委任 Hrynew，而 Hrynew 作为省交易主任会对接触到的信息保密。甚至在 Bhasin 询问 Can - Am 是否已经决定合并自己的销售代理时，Can - Am 的回答也是含糊其词。随着 Bhasin 持续拒绝 Hrynew 审计他的记录，Can - Am 作出了不续约通知。而在合约结束时，Bhasin 手下的大部分销售代理都已经被 Hrynew 收入麾下。

Bhasin 于是开始对 Hrynew[92] 与 Can - Am 提起诉讼，案件一路打到加拿大最高院，其中最重要的争议之一就是 Can - Am 在经销合约下是否对 Bhasin 有善意责任。

Cromwell 大法官首先认为加拿大法下有一个一般性的诚实与善意履行合约的责任："... I would hold that there is **a general duty of honesty in contractual performance. This means simply that parties must not lie or otherwise knowingly mislead each other** about matters directly linked to the performance of the contract. This **does not impose a duty of loyalty or of disclosure or require a party to forego advantages flowing from the contract**; it is a simple requirement not to lie or mislead the other party about one's contractual performance. Recognizing a duty of honest performance flowing directly from the common law organizing principle of good faith is a modest, incremental step. The requirement to act honestly is one of the most widely recognized aspects of the organizing principle of good faith... There is **a longstanding debate about whether the duty of good faith arises as a term implied as a matter of fact or a term implied by law**... I am at this point concerned only with a new duty of honest performance and, **as I**

[92] 对 Hrynew 的诉因是诱导他人违约/毁约（induce a breach of contract），但这最终没有被法院支持。关于诱导他人违约/毁约等经济侵权（economic tort）可见本书第八章之 2.1 段的介绍。

see it, this should not be thought of as an implied term, but a general doctrine of contract law that imposes as a contractual duty a minimum standard of honest contractual performance. **It operates irrespective of the intentions of the parties**, and is to this extent analogous to equitable doctrines which impose limits on the freedom of contract, such as the doctrine of unconscionability. … The **precise content of honest performance will vary with context and the parties should be free in some contexts to relax the requirements of the doctrine** so long as they respect its minimum core requirements."(加黑部分是笔者的强调)

Cromwell 大法官接着说这种诚实与善意履行合约的责任不同于信义义务/诚信责任或披露责任:"The duty of honest performance that I propose **should not be confused with a duty of disclosure or of fiduciary loyalty**. A party to a contract has no general duty to subordinate his or her interest to that of the other party. However, contracting parties must be able to rely on a minimum standard of honesty from their contracting partner in relation to performing the contract as a reassurance that if the contract does not work out, they will have a fair opportunity to protect their interests. … But a clear distinction can be drawn between a failure to disclose a material fact, even a firm intention to end the contractual arrangement, and active dishonesty."(加黑部分是笔者的强调)

Cromwell 大法官最后总结说:"(1) There is a general organizing principle of good faith that underlies many facets of contract law. (2) In general, the particular implications of the broad principle for particular cases are determined by resorting to the body of doctrine that has developed which gives effect to aspects of that principle in particular types of situations and relationships. (3) It is appropriate to recognize a new common law duty that applies to all contracts as a manifestation of the general organizing principle of good faith: a duty of honest performance, which requires the parties to be honest with each other in relation to the performance of their contractual obligations."

最终最高院判 Can – Am 误导 Bhasin 的行为违反了善意履行合约的责任,要赔偿 Bhasin 的损失。

2.6.2 善意责任的定义或标准

对于普通法系的法律而言,善意也不是一个完全陌生的概念。善意在多种法律关系、多种立法中都有出现,而且各自都会有自己的含义与不同适用。在 Service Station Association Ltd v. Berg Bennett & Associates Pty Ltd (1993) FCA 638 澳大利亚先例中,Gummow 大法官介绍说:"The concept of 'good faith' appears in various areas of the law, in each case with a distinct body of authority as to its meaning and application.

The doctrine of the 'bona fide purchaser'[93] of the legal estate is one example. Another is the obligation of the fiduciary[94] to act in good faith towards the principal. The relationship of partners inter se calls for particular applications of this general fiduciary principle, even where there are written articles of partnership. Equity also imposes a particular obligation of good faith in the exercise of the powers of a mortgagee upon default[95] ... Another example may be equitable doctrines which are concerned with the setting aside of transactions(including contracts) by reason of misrepresentation,[96] presumed undue influence,[97] or illegitimate pressure,[98] or the like. The term 'good faith' also is used in important areas of statute law, for example bankruptcy law(e. g. Bankruptcy Act 1966, ss. 120,121,122,123,124) and insurance law(e. g. Insurance Contracts Act 1984, s. 13). ..."

2.6.2.1 立法中的善意

在立法方面,在美国《Uniform Commercial Code》(虽然不严格是立法)中, Section 1-201(20)的一般性规定对善意的定义是:"honesty in fact and the observance of reasonable commercial standards of fair dealing."同样是《Uniform Commercial Code》但针对特定货物买卖的 Section 2-103(1)(b)重复对善意的定义是:"'Good faith' in the case of a merchant means honesty in fact and the observance of reasonable commercial standards of fair dealing in the trade."也就是需要商业人士诚实,以及遵守惯常商业社会中的客观合理公平标准。

英国立法中也有善意的定义出现,例如在针对货物买卖的《Sale of Goods Act 1979》之 Section 61(3)中说:"A thing is deemed to be done in good faith within the meaning of this Act when it is in fact done honestly, whether it is done negligently or not."该立法只限于以是否诚实作为标准。

另对于针对海上保险的《Marine Insurance Act 1906》,显然在本质上这类合约关系对善意要求比大多数其他行业更高,所以立法也有不少具体的要求或善意的标准,如对有实质重要性的事实与信息自动披露的程度、对事实的正确陈述等,并且一旦违反就带来十分严重后果。这方面问题可见笔者的《海上货物保险》一书第二章,此处不予重复。

---

〔93〕"善意买方"(bona fide purchaser)必须不知情与支付合理价格,这方面可见笔者《证据法:基础理论、口头证据与专家证据》一书第十章之2段。另对善意买方的保护可见本书第三章之6.3段。

〔94〕见本章之2.7段。

〔95〕关于抵押权人/债权人/银行在出售被抵押的财产时的责任,可见笔者《船舶融资与抵押》一书第五章之4.3.1段与4.3.2段的详细介绍。

〔96〕见本书第一章至第四章。

〔97〕见本书第十一章之1.4.2段。

〔98〕见本书第十章之6段、7.2.2段与8.4.3段。

2.6.2.2　普通法要根据背景/语境来确定具体含义

至于在普通法下,已经有不少先例对"善意"有细化的定义,但其都是根据不同案件的案情而言,未必能套用在其他案件上。可以说是很难在法律上给"善意"以一般性(general)、公式化(formalistic)与肯定的定义或标准,因为很大程度是要根据不同案件各种各样的案情与背景/语境(context)考虑具体言行是否善意,例如有否不诚实的味道。

美国 American Law Institute 对本章之2.6.1.1 段节录的《Restatement(Second)of Contracts》之 Section 205,即合约中默示善意的问题进一步评论认为,善意的具体含义会根据具体的背景/语境而不同,但至少是必须忠于合约共同目的以及符合对方合约方的合法预期,以及至少从社会上客观的正直、公平、合理角度来看不属于恶意:"The phrase 'good faith' is used in a variety of contexts and its meaning varies somewhat with the context. Good faith performance or enforcement of a contract emphasises faithfulness to an agreed common purpose and consistency with the justified expectations of the other party; it excludes a variety of types of conduct characterised as involving 'bad faith' because they violate community standards of decency, fairness or reasonableness."

英国法下也是同样的大道理,必须结合背景/语境判断善意的含义。在稍后介绍的 Compound Photonics Group Ltd, Re(2022)EWCA Civ 1371 上诉庭先例中,更是指出由于英国法下的"善意",是来自双方合约的明示善意条文[99]或事实的默示,[100]而解释一份合约是要整体地解释。所以"善意"包括或不包括什么言行,在英国法下更有必要根据每一个不同合约的所有条文与特定案情的背景/语境来决定。

例如针对善意中英美法律下最核心的"诚实",表面看来"诚实"或"不诚实"应是黑白分明,例如在交往中说谎、给假文件就是不诚实;但在相对复杂的国际商业关系中,是不会非黑即白的。结合背景/语境,可以用一位"诚实"自然人的言行来说明"诚实"的不同程度。如面对的对象不同时对诚实的要求程度就可能不同,同样的言行有时就能够满足善意,有时就会由于善意的要求更高如涉及至亲家人的信托关系而不满足善意了。

这有时可以变得很复杂,例如在 Street v. Derbyshire Unemployed Workers' Centre(2004)EWCA Civ 964 先例中,案情涉及雇员在举报了上司的不当行为后被公司解雇,雇员就依赖《Employment Rights Act 1996》中保护吹哨人(whistleblower)的条文,主张自己采取的是受保护的举报行为,因此根据立法会推定之后被公司解雇属于不公平解雇(unfair dismissal)。而立法中保护的举报有"善意"要求,争议焦点就变成雇员的举报是否属于立法所要求的"善意"。但在有关的立法下,"善意"不仅要求吹

---

[99]　见笔者《合约的解释:规则与应用》一书第九章之5段。

[100]　见笔者《合约的解释:规则与应用》一书第七章之4.4段。

哨人要诚实(举报信息与实际事实相符或真实相信/有合理理由相信是真的),还有进一步的要求,如果吹哨人背后有其他恶劣目的,就不在立法想要保护的范围之内。这有点类似本书第十章之8.2.1段介绍的合法行为胁迫的敲诈勒索(blackmail)。法院判此先例中雇员举报的原因主要是对上司的个人恩怨、想要打击报复,因此即使雇员有合理理由真实相信自己举报内容为真,也不属于立法的背景/语境下的善意。

除了最基本的诚实以外,在保险领域中要求的最大善意(utmost good faith),可以说是最广泛地包括各种善意的要求,但仍然要根据具体言行当时背景/语境来看待,例如,在订约前的披露、订约后的披露与开始诉讼后的披露义务就有所不同:见The"Star Sea"(2001)UKHL 1 贵族院先例。[101] 例如一个极端是订约前,保险人决定是否承保与保费多少完全取决于投保人的坦诚与全面的披露,与在保险合约履行时受保人向保险人提出赔付的要求;而另一个极端就是他们在该保险合约下有了争议需要开始法院诉讼,在对抗制诉讼下就完全根据CPR规定行事,可以撇开善意责任。

也因此在Yam Seng Pte Ltd v. International Trade Corp Ltd(2013)EWHC 111(QB)先例中,Leggatt大法官说:"... the content of the duty to perform a contract in good faith is **dependent on context.**"(加黑部分是笔者的强调)

这根据不同背景/语境决定具体言行是否善意或有否违反善意责任是十分重要。Leggatt大法官另也说到有否违反善意责任的测试就是在解释合约,要采用客观测试:"...objective in the sense that it depends not on either party's perception of whether particular conduct is improper but on whether in the particular context the conduct would be regarded as commercially unacceptable by reasonable and honest people."

这样可以认为合约中什么是善意也在不同案件中有了不同要求。根据不同背景/语境,在商业合约下善意的精神包括:诚实(honest);合作(cooperative);任何决定与言行上关心与顾及对方合法与合约下的利益与合法预期(justified expectation),不只是保护自己;透明、不误导瞒骗、全面与坦率披露有关信息(full and frank disclosure);任何决定与言行关心、顾及与忠于合约精神及商业目的(这目的会明示或默示在合约约定,如合作/合资开拓欧洲市场或建造一项工程);不与第三人如竞争方在背后寻找合作机会;履约符合合理商业/行业标准(observe reasonable commercial standard);公平交易;遇到困难共同调查与解决;不启动任何压迫性的法律行动等。这方面过往先例中的说法可以简单举一些例子如下:

1. 双方有责任令自己在有关合约下的言行达到符合公平交易的合理商业标准,并忠于双方同意的共同目的与对方的合法预期。例如在Berkeley Community Villages Ltd v. Pullen(2007)EWHC 1330(Ch)先例中,在土地开发计划中,一片原本作为种植用途的土地可能重新被划分为住宅或商业用途。被告是拥有该片土地的农民,与作为原告的房地产开发顾问达成合约,原告会利用自己房地产开发的专业能力帮

---

[101] 有关课题可见《海上货物保险》一书第二章之4.1段。

助提升土地开发价值与前景，而在被告实际与开发商达成土地转让、开发的合约后，需要向原告支付特定数额的金钱作为报酬。在合约签订后原告已经花费了大量时间、金钱与精力，也确实让土地的价值得到实际提升，但是突然被告想要将土地出售给第三人。看来是第三人看到有机可乘，想要“截胡”。因为第三人不是开发商，所以原告拿不到报酬。于是原告开始诉讼，主张被告违反了合约中的善意条文。法院判此合约下双方的合约目的是帮助被告将土地以尽可能高的价格出售给开发商，因此被告将土地出售给第三人行为违反合约中的善意责任。

2. 在双方互动的交流中，最基本的要求就是诚实。在 Bristol Groundschool Ltd v. Intelligent Data Capture Ltd（2014）EWHC 2145（Ch）先例中，原告（BG）与被告（IDC）共同合作提供商业飞行员培训教材，BG 提供具体文本信息，IDC 提供软件、动画、平面设计等内容。在合作了 10 年后，双方关系破裂开始诉讼，互指对方违约/毁约。IDC 的一项主张就是在临近关系破裂前，BG 在未获得 IDC 许可的情况下，暗中甚至是黑入 IDC 的系统，下载了一些 IDC 保有知识产权的电子文件。法院判此先例属于本章之 2.6.5 段介绍的关系合约，并且有默示的善意责任。至于善意的含义到底是什么，虽然在不同情况下含义不同，但最基本的应该是诚实，Richard Spearman QC 大法官说：“good faith extends beyond, but at the very least includes, the requirement of honesty. The relevant test is that of conduct that would be regarded as ‘commercially unacceptable’ by reasonable and honest people in the particular context involved...”此先例中 BG 未获许可下载受保护信息的行为，就被认为不诚实与违反善意。

3. 在 CPC Group Ltd v. Qatari Diar Real Estates Investment Co（2010）EWHC 1535（Ch）先例中，原告 CPC 与被告 Qatari（卡塔尔国家基金控制的房地产开发公司）共同成立合资公司开发伦敦切尔西军营（chelsea barracks）的重建项目，并已经提交了著名设计师公司的重建计划等待审批。之后 Qatari 买断了 CPC 在合资公司的股权，而在股权转让协议（purchase and sale of shares agreement）中约定，CPC 除了首付款以外，之后只要现有的重建计划继续成功获批与发展还能继续获得最多 8100 多万英镑的收益。但是重建计划是现代主义设计风格，遭到了当时还不是国王的查尔斯王子的强烈反对，提出这一对于英国皇室与公众有历史意义的地区应该采用保守主义的建筑风格。被告与设计师公司修改了多版都未能成功，不得已之下只能撤回了重建计划并委任保守主义的设计师从头开始申请。这样 CPC 的 8100 多万英镑收益泡汤并开始诉讼，一个主张就是 Qatari 违反了合约中的明示善意条文，没有尽职推动与完成现有的重建计划。在根据背景/语境解释合约后，Vos 大法官认定 Qatari 在此股权转让协议的善意责任包括要忠于约定的共同目的，与双方的合法预期一致，根据合约精神采取一切合理商业审慎手段尽快继续推动现有的重建计划。Vos 大法官说：“... it seems to me that the content of the obligation of utmost good faith in the SPA was to adhere to the spirit of the contract, which was to seek to obtain planning consent ... in the shortest possible time, and to observe reasonable commercial standards of fair dealing, and

to be faithful to the agreed common purpose, and to act consistently with the justified expectations of the parties."

但是这并不意味着承担善意责任的 Qatari 不能考虑自己的利益,Qatari 不需要像信义/诚信关系中的受信人一样凡事都以 CPC 利益优先。因此在此先例中,法院判已经尽力与只是不得不重新开始设计与申请的 Qatari 情有可原,并没有违反善意责任。Vos 大法官针对此先例案情认可了 Barrett 大法官在澳大利亚 Overlook v. Foxtel(2002)NSWSC 17 先例的如下说法:"… the implied obligation of good faith underwrites the spirit of the contract and supports the integrity of its character. A party is **precluded from cynical resort to the black letter**. But **no party is fixed with the duty to subordinate self-interest entirely** which is the lot of the fiduciary … The duty is not a duty to prefer the interests of the other contracting party. **It is, rather, a duty to recognize and to have due regard to the legitimate interests of both the parties in the enjoyment of the fruits of the contract** as delineated by its term."(加黑部分是笔者的强调)

4. 在 New Balance Athletics Inc v. Liverpool Football Club and Athletic Grounds Ltd (2019)EWHC 2837(Comm)先例中,原告(New Balance, NB)在 2011 年与被告英超球队利物浦俱乐部签订赞助合约,自 2015 年起利物浦的有关球衣等球队周边产品会由 NB 在全球市场上出售,并在双方之间分成。双方之间的赞助合约约定了一条相称条文(matching clause),如果有第三人竞争赞助合约并给出要约时,只要 NB 也给出实质内容相称(要求"material, measurable and matchable")的要约,利物浦就应当继续与 NB 合作。由于 2019 到 2020 年赛季利物浦赢得了英超冠军,因此销售球队周边产品预计利润不菲,[102]而利物浦与 NB 当时的赞助合约将在 2020 年届满,因此耐克(Nike)就抛出橄榄枝。利物浦也倾向与耐克合作,但考虑到与 NB 之间相称条文的存在,因此特意在合约中设置了多项认为 NB 较难给出相称要约的条件,包括耐克保证在订约时与 2020 到 2021 赛季,至少全球有 6000 间门店销售利物浦周边产品。按合约要求,利物浦将耐克的要约通知了 NB,尽管 NB 回复说也将提供相称的要约,但被利物浦拒绝、不相信 NB 能真实提供相称条件、全球有这么多门店销售,因此最后仍然与耐克签约。NB 就向法院提起诉讼,要求执行相称条文。一个争议焦点在于 NB 与利物浦均同意赞助合约是本章之 2.6.5 段介绍的"关系合约"与默示善意,利物浦主张 NB 提供的要约根本是信口开河,不可能有这么多门店销售,违反善意条文。

高院 Teare 大法官的判法是,此先例中的善意条文要求当事人诚实与忠于合约目的/条件,如果 NB 确实知道或有合理理由知道自己提供的数据存在问题,就会是违反善意。但是此先例中根据证据显示 NB 在给相称的要约时,明知利物浦一定会

〔102〕 据称在 2021 年利物浦球衣在全球销量达到 245 万件,所有欧洲球队中排名第三。

"鸡蛋里挑骨头",因此事先特意进行了调查与进行了较为详细的记录,因此认定 NB 至少是有合理理由相信,并没有违反善意。[103]

2.6.2.3 善意的最低标准

在美国法下,由于所有商业合约默示善意,所以为了法律的肯定性,非常需要设定善意责任的标准或至少是最低标准(minimal standard),让商业人士可以跟从、适用与回避。在澳大利亚的 Anthony Mason 大法官的"Contract, Good Faith and Equitable Standards in Fair Dealing"(2000)116 LQR 66 一文中,针对美国法下的善意,提到了至少会包括以下三点:"(1) An obligation on the parties to co-operate in achieving the contractual objects(当事人之间应该合作达到合约目的);(2) Compliance with honest standards of conduct(行为满足诚实的要求);and(3) Compliance with standards of conduct that are reasonable having regard to the interests of the parties.(在考虑双方利益的前提下,行为符合客观合理的标准。)"

在澳大利亚的新南威尔士州也是类似美国法的地位:见 Burger King Corporation v. Hungry Jack's Pty Limited(2001) NSWCA 187;Overlook v. Foxtel(2002) NSWSC 17;Macquarie International Health Clinic v. Sydney South West Area Health Service (2010) NSWCA 268 等先例。例如在著名的有关善意的 Burger King v. Hungry Jack's Pty 先例中,涉及了全球著名快餐连锁公司汉堡王(Burger King)在澳大利亚授权特许经营/加盟(franchise)的问题。在 20 世纪六七十年代商人 Jack Cowin 就已经开始通过授权加盟汉堡王的方式在澳大利亚发展快餐连锁公司(Hungry Jack's,[104] 以下简称 HJ)。在汉堡王与 HJ 之间针对合作签订了一系列合约,包括在一份"发展合约"中约定了双方如何合作、HJ 如何申请与获得汉堡王授权加盟等。到了 20 世纪 90 年代,汉堡王开始逐步加强自己对澳大利亚市场的直接控制,并试图排挤 Jack Cowin/HJ,暗中挖墙脚(找 HJ 内部对澳大利亚市场有丰富经验的高管咨询与获取意见),直接与第三人合作排除 HJ 参与(包括原本与 HJ、壳牌讨论在壳牌加油站内开连锁餐厅的三方合作,但后来将 HJ 踢出自己与壳牌开展合作)、拒绝批准 HJ 加盟分店的新申请等,因此双方产生争议与诉讼。一个重要争议就是发展合约中是否默示善意,以及汉堡王是否违反善意,有说法是这是澳大利亚有史以来关于善意责任争辩最多也是最昂贵的争议。在此先例中澳大利亚新南威尔士州上诉庭参考了美国法下的做法,判合约有一般的默示善意与合理(in good faith and reasonably)责任后,有类似的最低标准,汉堡王不能阻碍(thwart)发展合约的目的、采取不合理行为,因此前述

---

[103] 但此先例中最后 NB 仍然败诉,因为针对耐克提出的其他条件,尤其是耐克承诺会找至少 3 位非足球明星参与宣传,如篮球明星勒布朗詹姆斯、网球明星小威、流行音乐明星 Drake 或同等咖位的其他明星,NB 并未给出相称的要约。但此问题与本章关系不大,不在这里详细展开。

[104] 在澳大利亚叫不同名称是因为在加盟时,汉堡王的商标已经被注册,因此澳大利亚的连锁加盟商只能采用了 Hungry Jack's 作为商标加盟营运。Hungry Jack's 一度是汉堡王在澳大利亚的独家经营/加盟店,发展到今天可能已经是澳大利亚最大的连锁餐厅。

行为被认为违反善意。判词中还给出理由:"...that people generally, including judges and other lawyers, from all strands of the community, have grown used to the courts applying standards of fairness to contract which are wholly consistent with the existence in **all contracts of a duty upon the parties of good faith and fair dealing in its performance**. In my view this is in these days **the expected standard, and anything less is contrary to prevailing community expectations**. ...That being so, it reinforces our view that (汉堡王) contractual powers ... are to be exercised in good faith and reasonably. That does not mean that(汉堡王) is not entitled to have regard only to its own legitimate interests in exercising its discretion. However, it must not do so for a purpose extraneous to the contract-for example, by withholding financial or operational approval where there is no basis to do so, so as to thwart(HJ) rights under the contract. In conclusion, therefore, we are of the opinion that the Development Agreement is subject to implied terms of reasonableness and good faith..."(加黑部分是笔者的强调)

在英国法下虽然没有一般性的善意要求去强加在所有的合约,而是以明示或默示条文去根据每个不同的合约解释善意以找出在有关合约下"善意"的含义,所以不存在一些放之四海皆准的标准或最低标准。但也有先例试图总结出一套类似标准。例如在 Unwin v. Bond(2020) EWHC 1768 (Comm) 先例中, Klein 大法官提出对善意可以设定一个最低标准,一旦在一个特定合约认定善意后,至少应该做到以下要求:"i) they must act honestly(诚实); ii) they must be faithful to the parties' agreed common purpose as derived from their agreement(忠于合约的共同目的); iii) they must not use their powers for an ulterior purpose(不应用自己的合约权利满足不可告人的目的); iv) when acting they must deal fairly and openly with the claimant(行使合约权利时需要对对方合约方公平与透明); v) they can consider and take into account their own interests but they must also have regard to the claimant's interest(在考虑自己利益时,也应照顾对方合约方的利益). These minimum standards are not entirely distinct from one another. Rather, they tend to overlap."

但 Compound Photonics Group Ltd, Re(2022) EWCA Civ 1371 上诉庭先例不认同英国法下有最低标准的说法。在此先例中涉及原告创立公司(Compound Photonics Group Ltd)后,被告认为原告能力强、运营的公司前景很好,因此注资成为大股东,并继续让原告运营公司。但多年后逼迫原告辞任董事会职务。原告作为小股东主张被告违反了股东协议与公司章程中的善意条文,属于《Companies Act 2006》之 Section 994 的不公平损害(unfairly prejudice)小股东利益。

英国高院的判法是,根据 Unwin v. Bond 先例中的善意的最低标准,此先例中的被告主要有两点未能满足善意要求:首先是在"赶走"原告的过程中,被告采取的是"突袭"的方式,在 16 年 3 月的董事会上突然给出要求原告辞职的最后通牒。而且明明被告在 16 年 5 月底前不会撤资,但在 3 月会议上威胁说如果原告不辞职就要马上撤资。这样的行为对原告不公平与透明,违反最低标准中的 iv)项,涉及程序上不公平(procedural unfairness)。其次根据股东协议与公司章程的措辞/文字,法院认定的事实是,虽然没有明确约定,但从措辞/文字来看很多内容都以原告创始人作为董事会主席或主导地位的背景/语境进行拟定,因此双方合作的条件或基石就是原告在董事会应有主导地位,事后被告将原告赶走就属于以上最低标准中的 ii)项,即未能忠于合约的共同目的。

但是这样的判法被上诉庭推翻。上诉庭指出善意的含义应该在每一个具体案件中根据事实情况考虑,即使是 Unwin v. Bond 先例中对善意的最低标准也不是一概适用在所有案件中。而且与美国法下在所有合约默示善意,因此为了法律的肯定性必须给予一个最低标准不同,英国法下的善意是个别案件中当事人之间明示或默示合约条文引入的。这纯粹是解释合约,而每一个案件中的合约本质与案情都不一样,强调根据具体情况具体分析,没有必要像美国法下一样订立一个最低标准。上诉庭的 Snowden 大法官说:"… apart from the very obvious point … that the core meaning of an obligation of good faith is an obligation to act honestly, it is very far from obvious why it is logical or appropriate to attempt to analyse other cases, decided on other facts, in order to deduce a number of further 'minimum standards' of conduct that a defendant must be taken to have agreed to comply with in every case in which a good faith clause has been used in a contract…

…Whilst the concepts and ideas advanced in other cases might well be useful analytical tools in the process of interpretation of a particular contract, in my view it is **not appropriate simply to apply them in a formulaic way in every case, irrespective of the context and the other terms of the agreement in issue**.

… those specific concepts originated in a commentary on **US contract law** … in the context of the imposition of terms requiring good faith in the performance of contracts as a matter of general law. They were not developed in the context of the interpretation of individually negotiated contracts. **It is entirely understandable that if a term is implied as a matter of law, it should have a single, clearly understood meaning**. However, I see **no sound juridical basis** for saying that all of **the same concepts should automatically be regarded as incorporated in a formulaic way whenever any contract governed by English law** contains an express term requiring the parties to act in good faith. Put into the context of this case, I do not see why the parties to an English law governed contract concerning an English company should automatically be presumed to have intended to incorporate such obligations, irrespective of the context given by the other terms of their contract."(加黑部分是笔者的强调)

否定最低标准的过程中,上诉庭指出了为什么不能一概适用的如下说法:

1. 针对最低标准的 iv)项,对对方公平与透明,一般在合伙人关系或准合伙关系

(quasi partnership)会有这样的要求:见 Mullins v. Laughton(2002)EWHC 2761(Ch);Audas Group,Re(2019)EWHC 2304(Ch)等先例。包括互相之间需要及时通知、互相咨询后,采用公平与透明的方式做决定。但是在一般的公司普通股东之间,各自根据自己持有的股权行权,即使是股东协议中有善意要求,也不意味着股东之间行权要公平与透明。商业现实是股东(尤其是一些专业投资人的股东)都会有自己的"小算盘",也不会期待所有情况下的股东之间可以完全坦诚。在股东会议上,固然股东之间可以互通有无、交流信息,但仅仅是广泛的要求善意的措辞/文字,并不要求必须这样做。

2. 针对 ii)项,即未能忠于合约的共同目的,或者是要善意合作为达成共同目的而努力等的义务,通常在一些长期的商业合约中较为常见。这类合约中由于合约时间长,在订约时难以预见履行时可能发生的问题,因此对当事人的善意会要求合作与追求"共赢"。例如在 Macquarie International Health Clinic v. Sydney South West Area Health Service 先例中,双方合作开发私家医院,由被告(政府医疗部门)提供土地,原告负责开发与经营,合约期长达 103 年。但被告计划在附近扩建另一家被告自己经营的公立医院,这显然影响合作的私家医院的利益,因此被告没有将此计划告知原告(如果告知肯定遭到原告反对),该行为就被认定为违反善意。

但是在 Compound Photonics Group Ltd,Re 先例中这种情况就与长期商业合作中的情况不同了,例如:(1)公司中的大股东与小股东关于董事会席位之争。公司股东如果不希望合作,完全可以选择撤资与退出,大家并非长期绑在一条船上。(2)公司的董事会的选择与任命,应该根据公司章程、有关公司法的规定作出,通常也都是时常发生变动与有弹性的,因此如果在公司运营过程中发生当初难以预料到的情况,可以通过股东投票决议的方式随时变化与作出应对(包括董事会成员变更甚至是改变公司章程)。但在商业合约中,并不存在这样的弹性应对机制。

因此从解释条文的角度来看,此类公司股东协议/公司章程并不需要善意条文来额外补充应对难以预见的问题,善意条文不需要解释为尽力合作达成最初的合约目的。而如果按照原告的说法,将善意条文解释为不得将原告赶出董事会,那么反而是限制了公司投票与运行的弹性机制,这样不合理的结果必须要有足够清楚与明确的条文。

Snowden 大法官也提到善意条文一般不意味着在合约条文的基础上额外给合约方强加义务或责任,而在有专业人士/称职律师帮助下拟定的合约(如果想强加额外义务或责任会有条文专门针对),或者是有完整合约条文[105]的合约中更是如此。Snowden 大法官说:"... although judges have, on occasions, used the expression 'the spirit of the contract' in the context of a good faith clause, I do not read that as an open invitation to the court to interpret a good faith clause as imposing additional substantive

---

[105] 见本章之 1.3.8 段与笔者《合约的解释:规则与应用》一书第十三章之 2 段。

obligations(or restrictions on action) outside the other terms of the contract. That must especially be so where(as in the instant case) the contract in question is professionally and comprehensively drafted, and contains an entire agreement clause."

而且再加上此先例中上诉庭也不认可根据股东协议与公司章程可以默示合约方订约时有共识是始终由原告占据董事会主导地位。如果当事人谈好的条件就是不应该赶走原告或改变其在董事会中的主导地位,就需要以足够清楚的措辞/文字予以明示,这也是常见的明示约定永久董事的做法,而不是非常笼统地事后将"善意"解释为包罗万象。

这样上诉庭既不认可根据股东协议与公司章程默示了保留原告在董事会主导地位的目的,也不认可事后被告行权剥夺原告在董事会中的权力违反善意责任。

3. 还有 v)项,针对合约履行过程中要照顾到对方合约方的利益的义务,此种义务可能会出现在商业合约中赋予一方合约方裁量权的情况:见本章之 2.6.4 段的介绍。但是公司股东的权利与义务依据股东协议、公司章程而定,股东根据自己的权利合法行权不需要特别照顾其他股东的利益,这也是一贯以来的长期地位:见 North-West Transportation Co Ltd v. Beatty(1887) 12 App Cas 589 先例与 Burland v. Earle (1902) AC 83 枢密院先例等。

针对股东投票的问题,一般而言,测试标准在于大股东投票是否真实为了公司的整体利益(bona fide for the benefit of the company as a whole),而不在于是否考虑了个别小股东的利益:见 Shuttleworth v. Cox Bros & Co(Maidenhead) Ltd(1927) 2 KB 9; Citco Banking Corporation v. Pusser's Ltd(2007) UKPC 13 等先例。

2.6.3 善意责任会否带来更多误述或不自动披露的争议

可诉误述(无论是欺诈性或非欺诈性)是针对在诱导与依赖的情况下令合约产生时,以普通法与立法的《Misrepresentation Act 1967》给予被误述方(representee)救济,如可使合约无效(voidable)。但善意责任,无论是通过明示条文或默示地位,只会适用在合约已经产生的情况,不适用在订约前的谈判。而英国法律一贯是十分抗拒对谈判强加善意责任:见 Walford v. Miles(1992) 2 AC 128 贵族院先例;也一贯不去插手双方的谈判,其认为法律是强制执行不了"协议将来达成协议"(agreement to agree)。而如果希望去约束对方或双方有诚意去谈判并努力去谈拢(这应算是对谈判的善意),在笔者的《合约的解释:规则与应用》一书第二章之 6 段,就介绍了"初步合约"(preliminary contract),以意向书(letter of intent)、安抚函(letter of comfort)、过渡合约(bridging or interim contract)或互锁合约(lock - out contract)等做法,去提升双方谈判的诚意或压力,这会是达成目标更肯定的做法。

但在合约产生后的履行,合约如果有明示或默示条文要求善意,履行时根据合约白纸黑字严格履行的心态就不够。这种有明示或默示善意责任的合约(如一个合资合约、中长期的合作协议等),往往在本质上是需要互信,大量交换意见、通讯往来、披露信息,共同承担与解决突发事件等的,即使合约写得很详细也无法包罗万象,这时就希望以这个善意责任去填补。但这也会带来更多潜在的误述与/或不披露或披露不足以的指控与争议。在 Yam Seng Pte Ltd v. International Trade Corp Ltd(2013) EWHC 111(QB)先例中,Leggatt 大法官也说到有善意条文的合约会要求高强度的沟通与合作:"Such 'relational' contracts, as they are sometimes called, may require a **high degree of communication**, **cooperation** and predictable performance based on mutual trust and confidence and involve expectations of loyalty which are not legislated for in the express terms of the contract but are implicit in the parties' understanding and necessary to give business efficacy to the arrangements."(加黑部分是笔者的强调)

在善意责任下,显然可以合理要求对方提供意见、信息与对事实的陈述,对方不能以合约没有明示或默示规定为由拒绝提供,因为善意的符合不能严格依赖合约白纸黑字的规定。至于怎样提出要求,这可以是以文书(如信函、电邮或微信)或是要求会面的方式。只要要求是合情合理与符合合约目的(consistent with contractual purpose)的,即使没有特定条文下,如果对方没有合理理由不理不睬导致延误与/或坏事,也会是违反善意责任的一种。正如 Jackson 大法官在他在 2017 年发表的"Does good faith have any role in construction contracts?"[106]的一文中所说:"A 'good faith' obligation in a … contract may encourage an arbitrator or judge called upon to construe the contract to be 'bold'; in other words, to be slightly more willing to give effect to the obvious purpose underlying the contract."

而书面或口头提供意见、信息与事实的同时,往往只是诚实、不说谎并不够。根据有关合约的背景/语境,善意会是要求合理、慎重、坦率、考虑对方的利益与共同目的等,这就表示提供信息的内容必须符合所有在善意关系下的要求。如果不这么做,信息就难免有错或遗漏,就会出现"误述"(对事实真相的陈述有了隐瞒、偏差与错误)的争议,即使严格来说这并非法律意义上的可诉误述,仅是违反了善意责任。

如果"误述"被证明是欺诈性,那肯定不会是善意,明显是违约。而如果"误述"是无辜,显然不影响善意的责任。但这种情况出现不多,而且一旦发现与事实真相有偏差,就必须马上向查问方更正。比较多的仍会是提供的事实真相有遗漏、偏差与错误是因为疏忽或不小心,这些是无心之失,看来与善意要求不像有冲突,但无心之失只代表诚实,善意要求的程度更高。看来这是要根据每一个案件的不同环境/背景与情况,去看会否违反了善意责任,包括好像是疏忽的严重性或程度、什么原因造成疏忽、业内其他同行的做法等。

与"误述"有紧密关系的是披露责任(duty to disclose),例如对善意要求最高的海上保险合约,受保人就在很长一段时期都要全面自动披露。这远远不止不能只把事实真相讲一半,"半真不假"(half - truth)的陈述在本质上仍是误导对方,属于"误

[106] 有兴趣的读者可以通过 < https://www.judiciary.uk/wp - content/uploads/2017/11/speech - lj - jackson - masons - lecture - hong - kong.pdf > 下载。

述”。善意责任要求的披露会是除了要提供对方要求的信息与事实外,对方没有要求的其他有关信息与事实,只要是善意关系下包括的内容也应一并全面披露。例如一旦知悉任何会影响对方合约利益或双方同意的共同目的的信息,就自动告知对方。否则,仍会违反善意责任。

即使是有善意责任的合约,披露的程度也是在不同类别的合约关系下有所不同。但没有善意责任的合约,如国际货物买卖或租船合约等,就没有自动披露的责任。这可节录《Chitty on Contracts》(2021 年,第 34 版)一书之 9 - 167 段所述:“... the extent of the duty to disclose and the remedies available seem to vary from type of contract to type of contract;... Therefore,it is more helpful to consider the extent of the duty and the remedies available in each type of case in which it has been held that there is some duty of disclosure. ... Contracts of service,contract of sale of goods and interest rate swap agreements have held not to be uberrimae fidei,so that there is no duty of disclosure.”

其他会违反善意责任的情况也是各种各样的,这种争议也很多,毕竟在一个唯利是图的商业环境与“顺境不持久”(good time never last long)的自然规律下,要求双方在一个中长期合约的任何时间都坚持善意对待对方与为共同目的和利益奋斗,在现实中并不现实。所以,判断是否违反善意责任必须要看有关言行的背景/语境。例如在合约期间双方因关系发生问题而谈判,这种背景对善意的要求也会与双方在顺利履行合约、计划开拓市场与/或发展业务的期间有所不同。

但与其在善意理论上纠缠,有水平的国际商业人士会更好地利用订约自由,以明示的合约条文防止对方不合作。例如通过在本书第二章之 10.2 段介绍的“陈述与保证条文”(Representation and Warranty Clause)。

反正在订约自由大原则下,只要懂有关业务与法律,知道自己会需要对方做什么或不做什么,只要想得到的事情,合约方或合约方的称职律师都能以文字正确表达出来。

在此多举一个例子,即与船舶保险有关。众所周知,保险人对承保的船舶完全不知情,也不会对船舶的营运有任何兴趣。只在船舶发生事故,保险人才会紧张,因为有了潜在的索赔风险。但保险人必须要尽快掌握当场证据与信息,才会知道是否在保单的承保风险范围内需要承担责任,也要跟进很多其他事故后的事情,例如船舶的救助、减损、修理等。这些信息与进一步的调查取证,完全要依赖船东,但船东实际与保险人有直接的利益冲突,一般不会提供帮助。所以在 2003 年,伦敦推出名为“International Hull Clauses(01/11/03)”[107] 的格式保单,其第 45 条文可节录如下:

“DUTIES OF THE ASSURED(受保人船东的责任)

45.1 The Assured shall,upon request and at their own expense,provide the Leading Underwriter(s) with all relevant documents and information that they might reasona-

---

〔107〕 参见杨良宜、汪鹏南:《英国海上保险条款详论》,大连海事大学出版社 2009 年版。

bly require to consider any claim.(船东在保险人要求下必须自费提供所有保险人合理认为是与索赔有关的文件与信息)

45.2 Upon reasonable request, the Assured shall also assist the Leading Underwriter(s) or their authorised agents in the investigation of any claim, including, but not limited to[在合理要求下,船东必须协助保险人或代理人(如被委任的律师)对索赔进行调查,包括以下方面]

45.2.1 interview(s) of any employee, ex-employee or agent of the Assured[与船东的雇员(主要是船舶发生事故时的船员)或前雇员或代理人会面查询]

45.2.2 interview(s) of any third party whom the Leading Underwriter(s) consider may knowledge of matters relevant to the claim(与任何其他会知道一些有关索赔事宜的信息的第三人会面查询)

45.2.3 survey(s) of the subject – matter insured(对投保船舶进行检验)

45.2.4 inspection(s) of the classification records of the vessel(检查船舶的船级社记录)

45.3 It shall be a condition precedent to the liability of the Underwriters that the Assured shall not at any stage prior to the commencement of legal proceedings knowingly or recklessly[作为保险人赔付责任的先决条件,船东在开始诉讼前(开始诉讼后是对抗制,所以诉讼开始后就不再存在善意责任与自动披露责任,一切要依照法院诉讼程序 CPR 去行事了),不得在知情或鲁莽的情况下做以下的两件事情]

45.3.1 mislead or attempt to mislead the Underwriters in the proper consideration of a claim or the settlement thereof by relying on any evidence which is false(提供虚假证据去误导或试图去误导保险人,企图能顺利获得赔付或和解)

45.3.2 conceal any circumstance or matter from the Underwriters material to the proper consideration of a claim or a defence to such a claim(向保险人隐瞒任何对索赔或抗辩该索赔是有关的情况或事情)

45.4 Clause 45.3 does not require the Assured at any stage to disclose to the Underwriters any document or matter which under English law is protected from disclosure by legal advice privilege or by litigation privilege.(船东无须在任何阶段向保险人披露在英国法律下可享有法律意见特免权或诉讼特免权的文件或信息。)"

从上述船舶保险的条文来看,根本不需要法律去强加善意责任(无论是通过立法、普通法的默示地位或明示条文),就可以订约自由把有关的责任全部清楚写明。所以笔者曾经听过部分法律专家建议不如不在合约中加入一条明示的善意条文,因为只要其他重要的条文写得好,善意条文起不到什么作用,只会带来更多的不肯定性与争议。

2.6.4 英国法律对善意责任的延伸之一:行使裁量权/选择权

从近年的发展来看,英国法也在试图扩展履行合约时对善意的默示要求而与其他国家的法律接近。这善意的要求主要体现在一方合约方行使合约赋予的裁量权、选择权或权利时与合约双方在一种名为“关系合约”的合约类型中履行合约时。

本小段首先针对行使裁量权或选择权(discretion/option)方面展开叙述,笔者感觉这是更重要与更影响国际商业活动,也是走出去的中国公司必须知悉的课题。

普通法是一贯不理会一方合约方怎样行使合约中规定的权利的,如是否合理、有否滥用、动机是否取巧或有否考虑对方利益会受影响等。这种情况十分普遍,合约经常约定一方合约方可在某些情况下行使裁量权或选择权,如终止合约或决定对价/报酬等,这些决定会严重影响另一方合约方。这种情况甚至出现在一些合约方谈判能力不对等的合约下,如雇佣合约明示规定雇主一面倒拥有大量在出现不同情况时的裁量权或选择权,如决定是否解雇、批准假期、要求加班、调整工资与职务、决定奖金金额等。银行的融资合约也是同样,例如银行可以调整利率、有权对抵押品估值、要求提前还款等。但只要有空间可以谈判,一般任何人订立合约都希望争取越多合约权利(无论是裁量权或选择权)越好,如此顶多是将来的情况变了,若是没有好处就不行使权利,但主动权还是掌握在自己手中的。

针对行使合约权利的约束(或没有约束),在近十几、二十年前看来没有一致的说法。例如一份贷款协议(loan agreement),在抵押(mortgage)[108]方面,很早就有法律不允许在抵押协议或契约中以合约条文形式去否定或剥夺债务人回赎的权利(right of redemption)。此外债权人(通常是银行)在处理抵押财产时要顾及债务人的利益,不得把财产半送半卖,只要足够清还债务等这种“苛刻与不合情理”(oppressive and unconscionable)行为:见 Marriott v. The Anchor Reversionary(Limited)(1860) 66 ER 191;Tse Kong Lam v. Wong Chit Sen(1983)1 WLR 1349(PC)等先例。但在同一份贷款协议,银行也另有很多其他的裁量权或权利,如要求提前还款(可以说是相等于终止合约),又或是债权人可去单方面调整利率:见 Lombard Tricity Finance Ltd v. Paton(1989)1 All ER 918(CA);Paragon Finance Plc v. Nash(2001)EWCA Civ 1466等先例。银行在行使这些权利或所有其他合约权利时,是否有同样的约束,如必须顾及债务人、不得独断专行(arbitrarily)、反复无常(capriciously)甚至是有更广泛的约束(如善意责任)?或是银行可以按照贷款协议一般的写法无拘无束、自由决定呢?在英国法不承认一般性的善意原则(general good faith doctrine)的情况下,就难免在不同合约权利有不同对待。

2.6.4.1 普通法对行使合约裁量权、选择权或权利的约束的演变

英国传统法律地位是不理会行使合约裁量权或选择权人士作出的决定在对方看来是否合理的,权利方/决策人也无需给出决定背后的原因,可以说只要不是恶意(maliciously),这裁量权是无拘无束(unfettered)的。这可节录 Reid 勋爵在 White & Carter(Councils)Limited v. McGregor(1962)AC 413 先例中所说:“It has never been

---

〔108〕 见本书第八章之9.4段的脚注。

the law that a person is only entitled to enforce his contractual rights in a reasonable way, and that a court will not support an attempt to enforce them in an unreasonable way. One reason why that is not the law is, no doubt, because it was thought that it would create too much uncertainty to require the court to decide whether it is reasonable or equitable to allow a party to enforce his full rights under a contract. ...”

但断断续续开始在一些较近期的案例对行使裁量权有了约束,如不能是恶意、要求公平合理等。这课题在笔者 2014 年写的《合约的解释:规则与应用》一书第九章之 3 段已经有详论,并区别介绍了 13 个针对行使合约裁量权必须考虑对方的利益与公平合理等的先例。

这里尽量不再重复,只略及其中较重要的 The“Product Star”(1993)1 Lloyd's Rep 397 上诉庭先例,该案涉及期租合约,其中有标准条文允许船长行使裁量权拒绝进入他们认为是危险的装港或卸港。当时是 1987 年,正是两伊战争(伊拉克与伊朗)期间,整个波斯湾都属于战区,船舶要支付战争加保费(war risks additional premium)才允许在区内航行。该期租合约的承租人是计划把“Product Star”轮从阿联酋的 Ruwais 港装运成品油去孟加拉国,并在 4 月底交船后航行了 4 个航次。但到了 8 月底的第五个航次,船长拒绝前往 Ruwais 港并指称该装港危险,要求承租人另指定其他安全装港。但承租人认为 Ruwais 港不会比订立期租合约时更危险,而订约时租约是说明会去阿联酋的港口如 Dubai、Abu Dhabi、Ruwais 等,也是船东同意的。另船舶也顺利航行了 4 个航次,所以船东在第五个航次改变主意是不合理也不诚实的,并非真正相信 Ruwais 港是危险的。但船东坚持船长行使的裁量权没有不诚实,就不应该质疑,否则就谈不上是裁量权了。这种困境也可以想到,船东一般只能支持船长的决定。至于船长为什么有不同的决定,理由可能有很多。例如虽然看来战争的大局是没有变化,但是身在战区时船员的心态可能产生变化,这变化甚至可能是因为一封家书劝说。一旦有部分船员或船长自己打退堂鼓,船长就会在去了 4 个航次后决定不再去该港口。

由于双方僵持,最终租约以双方相互指责对方违约/毁约(repudiatory breach)而被提前终止,双方也相互提出索赔与反索赔。一审法院认定 Ruwais 港并没有比订约时更危险的事实。例如,虽然在 8 月份多了油轮被袭击,但没有往返阿联酋港口的油轮受到过袭击,“Product Star”轮的船舶管理人同时允许另一艘“East Star”轮去波斯湾航行,但说不出有力理由为何区别对待。反正在一审与在上诉庭,船东都败诉,判船长行使裁量权是不合理与反复无常(unreasonable and capricious)的,因而被否定。

上诉庭的 Leggatt 大法官分析了较早的先例后总结说:“The essential question always is whether the relevant power has been abused. Where A and B contract with each other to confer a discretion on A, that does not render B subject to A's uninhibited whim. In my judgment, the authorities show that not only **must the discretion be exer-**

cised honestly and in good faith, but, having regard to the provisions of the contract by which it is conferred, it **must not be exercised arbitrarily, capriciously or unreasonably**. That entails a proper consideration of the matter after making only necessary inquiries. To these principles, little is added by the concept of fairness: it does no more than describe the result achieved by their applications. "(加黑部分是笔者的强调)

这方面的问题在《合约的解释:规则与应用》一书出版后的近十年有了进一步发展与明确的说法,特别是加上了善意的要求与责任,显示法院现在变得更愿意插手合约裁量权,也导致了哪些合约的选择权或裁量权是有善意的默示地位变得十分重要,因为所有类别的合约都会有(甚至是大量的)裁量权或选择权。

主要是法律已是明确对权利方/决策人自由行使在所有商业合约内都会有的权利(无论是裁量权、选择权或其他称呼)时,现在都有可能强加一个名为"The Socimer / Braganza implied term"[也被称为是"理性责任"(duty of rationality)或尽量在本段统一称为"Braganza 责任"]的默示地位的约束。

在此可介绍 Socimer International Bank Ltd v. Standard Bank London Ltd (2008) EWCA Civ 116 上诉庭先例,该先例原告与被告都是银行,双方签订了一份远期证券组合买卖合约(forward sale transaction)。原告 Socimer 是买方,被告 Standard 是卖方,但到期时 Socimer 没有履行合约购买证券,并在之后不久破产。合约中规定发生这种情况,Standard 有权将有关资产出售套现,而如果有超出合约下应付的部分,要退还给 Socimer:"The Seller may in its sole and absolute discretion sell the Designated Assets at such time, in such manner and at such price as it deems reasonable and appropriate. The value of any Designated Assets liquidated or retained and any losses, expenses or costs arising as a result of the termination or the sale of the Designated Assets shall be determined on the date of termination by the Seller."

Standard 在终止合约后没有立即对证券估价,而是在市场上出售这些证券。但因为证券组合中主要的两种证券的流通性很差,Standard 花了很久才分批售出有关证券,可想而知卖得不是一个好价钱。之后 Socimer 的破产管理人开始诉讼,索赔有关的证券在合约终止日的市场价值与出售的价格之间的差价。

诉讼的争议之一是 Standard 出售证券的决定显然会影响双方,Standard 的自由决定权是否应受到约束与受到什么约束?针对这个问题,上诉庭的 Rix 大法官考虑了 The"Product Star"等先例后,说:"It is plain from these authorities that a decision-maker's **discretion will be limited**, as a matter of necessary implication, **by concepts of honesty, good faith, and genuineness, and the need for the absence of arbitrariness, capriciousness, perversity and irrationality**. The concern is that the **discretion should not be abused**. Reasonableness and unreasonableness are also concepts deployed in this context, ..."(加黑部分是笔者的强调)

而在诚实与善意外,Rix 大法官拒绝再默示有进一步的约束,并说:"Implications

of good faith and rationality, and of lack of arbitrariness or perversity, are standard, for they represent the very essence of business (and other) relationships. Once one goes beyond them, however, the matter becomes much more uncertain. ... In my judgment, the implied term(超出诚实与理性)is not necessary or sufficiently certain and I would reject it. ..."

接下来介绍的是涉及雇佣合约与确立了在行使所有合约裁量权或选择权时都可能有的"Braganza 责任"的 Braganza v. BP Shipping Ltd(2015)UKSC 17 最高院先例,该案案情将在接下来之2.6.4.2.2 小段介绍。Hale 勋爵说强加法律默示的 Braganza 责任是为了防止在利益有严重冲突的情况下,权利方滥用他的权利:"Contractual terms in which one party to the contract is given the power to exercise a discretion, or to form an opinion as to relevant facts, are extremely common. It is not for the courts to re-write the parties' bargain for them, still less to substitute themselves for the contractually agreed decision-maker. Nevertheless, the party who is charged with making decisions which affect the rights of both parties to the contract has a clear conflict of interest. That conflict is heightened where there is a significant imbalance of power between the contracting parties as there often will be in an employment contract. The courts have therefore sought to ensure that such contractually powers are not abused. They have done so by implying a term as to the manner in which such powers may be exercised, a term which may vary according to the terms of the contract and the context in which the decision-making power is given. ..."

可以说权利方/决策人如果行使合约裁量权、选择权或权利有了 Braganza 责任的约束,就必须小心,不能独断专行,更不可以滥用权利。甚至为了小心行事,会在受影响的对方合约方反对下向法院(或仲裁庭)申请一个宣示判决/裁决,以免造成违约/毁约:见 TAQA Bratani Limited v. Rockrose UKCS8 LLC(2020)EWHC 58(Comm)先例。

其他需要跟进的工作包括:公司法务要考虑对行使裁量权与作出不同决定的公司部门与员工,如董事局、高管、人力资源部等,在这方面进行培训;拟定清单,针对不同的情况下作出决定必须考虑与不应考虑的各种因素等;要求必须留下当场证据如报告等。因为有了 Braganza 责任,行使裁量权作决定时需要经过深思熟虑,并且保留相关的证据来证明决策的过程,包括进行了什么调查、搜集了哪些信息、考虑了什么情况等。

2.6.4.2 行使裁量权的"Wednesbury 测试"与"Braganza 责任"

2.6.4.2.1 公法范畴的"Wednesbury 测试"

在公法(public law)的范畴,政府在作出各种行政决定时需要不断行使裁量权或权利。这种裁量权是否行使得当就会由法院通过司法复核(judicial review)来进行监督。[109] 法院会使用"Wednesbury 测试"来判断政府的行政决定是否合理,包括行政机关是否存在滥用权力、独断专行或有否考虑一般民众的利益等。

"Wednesbury 测试"来自 Associated Provincial Picture Houses Ltd v. Wednesbury Corps(1948)1 KB 223 上诉庭先例。该先例的案情是被告是在《Cinematograph Act 1909》立法下授权发放许可证的公共机构,原告拥有一家电影院,根据《Sunday Entertainments Act 1932》立法向被告申请在周日营业。被告批准了原告的申请,但附加了条件,即 15 岁以下的儿童无论是否有成年人的陪同,均不得在周日进入电影院观影。原告认为该附加的条件不合理且属于被告的越权行为,于是向法院申请对该决定进行司法复核。

法院的判决明确了法院作为司法机构,在对政府或公共机构等行政机关在有关立法的授权下行使裁量权进行监督时,只能审查行政机关在决策的过程中程序公正方面是否有欠缺或犯错,而不存在法院可从社会或道德层面客观看以自己认为更合理的决定去替代或改变行政机关的决定。

上诉庭的 Greene 勋爵明确了在三种情形下法院可以对决定作出干预,即(1)行政机关在行使裁量权时考虑了不应该考虑的事项;(2)行政机关在行使裁量权时拒绝考虑或忽略了应该考虑的事项;(3)行政机关行使裁量权所作出的决定太不合理,是任何其他合理的行政机关都不会作出的决定。其中前两种是针对行使裁量权的过程,而第三种是针对行使裁量权的结果。Greene 勋爵说:"... I will summarise once again the principle applicable. The court is entitled to investigate the action of the local authority with a view to seeing **whether** they have **taken into account matters which they ought not to take into account, or, conversely, have refused to take into account or neglected to take into account matters which they ought to take into account**. Once that question is answered in favour of the local authority, it may be still possible to say that, although the local authority have kept within the four corners of the matters which they ought to consider, they have nevertheless **come to a conclusion so unreasonable that no reasonable authority could ever have come to it**. In such a case, again, I think the court can interfere."(加黑部分是笔者的强调)

2.6.4.2.2 "Wednesbury 测试"适用在私法范畴的仲裁法

"Wednesbury 测试"虽然开始是针对公法范畴中行政机关的裁量权,但后来也被适用在私法领域的监督。笔者先针对程序方面进行探讨,例如上诉庭复核与监督一审判决的事实认定(finding of facts),或仲裁地监督法院复核与监督仲裁裁决书的事实认定。虽然后者在政策上约束法院尽量不去插手仲裁庭的决定是对是错(例如对有关证据给予的重量影响最后认定的争议"事实"),因为当事人在仲裁协议授权去对争议作决定的是双方委任的仲裁庭,但仲裁庭在合议与作决定的程序中必须是公

---

[109] 这方面可见笔者《合约的履行、弃权与禁反言》一书第四章之 5.4 段与第五章之 11 段。

正、没有过错或遗漏的。另是,裁决书一般要求仲裁庭全面考虑双方提供的有关争议事实的证据并排除一些不应该考虑的证据(如特免权文件),并在裁决书中解释他是如何作出决定的。

这可以节录权威的 Mustill & Boyd 之《Commercial Arbitration》(1989 年,第 2 版)一书之 561 页说:"It is conceivable that where the state of the evidence is such as to show, not merely that **no reasonable arbitrator would reach a particular conclusion of fact** upon the basis of it, but also that there **is no evidence at all to sustain the findings**, the award can be attacked-either on the ground that the arbitrator has acted unjudicially, or on the ground that by deciding that contrary to the obvious facts he has taken the parties by surprise, and hence been guilty of misconduct. "(加黑部分是笔者的强调)

在《Arbitration Act 1996》生效后,以仲裁庭错误认定事实为由去撤销裁决书更加困难。但在极端的情况下,仍可能以 Section 68 来撤销有关裁决书。这可节录在 Arduina Holdings BV v. Celtic Resources Holdings Plc(2006)EWHC 3155 先例中,Toulson 大法官说:"section 68 is available only in extreme cases where the arbitral process has gone wrong in such an exceptional way that justice demands its correction. ...The assertion that the arbitrator failed to take any or proper consider of the evidence could, **in an exceptional case**, give rise to a challenge under section 68, **based on the general duty of an arbitrator under section 33 if, for example, an arbitrator genuinely overlooked evidence that really mattered, or got the wrong end of the stick in misunderstanding it**. But there is all the difference in the world between such cases and an arbitrator evaluating evidence but reaching factual conclusions on it(as will happen in most arbitrations) which one party does not like. That cannot be the basis of a complaint under section 68. "(加黑部分是笔者的强调)

另在 Statoil v. Sonatrach(2014)EWHC 875 先例中,Flaux 大法官说:"The assertion that the arbitrator failed to take any or proper consideration of the evidence could, in an exceptional case, give rise to a challenge under section 68 ... if, for example, an arbitrator **genuinely overlooked evidence that really mattered, or got the wrong end of the stick in misunderstanding it**. ..."(加黑部分是笔者的强调)

以上是程序法,在实体法方面,涉及信托法的 Pitt v. Holt(2013)2 AC 108 最高院先例中,Walker 勋爵是不认同适用"Wednesbury 测试"的。他同意 Lightman 大法官在 2003 年的一个有关信托法的先例中指出的公法与私法对裁量权的监督有三个重要的不同之处,包括:(1)救济方式;(2)公法是以越权(ultra vires)令有关决定无效而不是以私法令合约无效或可使无效(void or voidable);(3)时效,所以不能乱套用,其认为:"There are superficial similarities between what the law requires of trustees in their decision-making and what it requires of decision-makers in the field of public law. ... The analogy cannot however be pressed too far. ... In Abacus Trust Co(Isle of Man)v Barr

[2003] Ch 409 … Lightman J identified three important differences as the discretionary nature of relief on judicial review, a different approach to nullity, and strict time limits."

2.6.4.2.3 Braganza v. BP Shipping Ltd (2015) UKSC 17 最高院先例的"Wednesbury/Braganza 测试"

Pitt v. Holt(2013)2 AC 108 最高院先例不再重要,因为在接下来的 Braganza v. BP Shipping Ltd 最高院先例中,就全盘接受"Wednesbury 测试"可以适用在法院审查私法领域一方当事人在行使裁量权时是否合理,间接改变了 Pitt v. Holt 先例在这方面的说法,这也可被称为"Wednesbury/Braganza 测试"。

该先例的案情是原告是 Braganza 先生的妻子,被告是英国石油公司(BP)。Braganza 先生受雇在 BP 的一艘油轮上担任轮机长,Braganza 先生在船上工作期间,于 2009 年 5 月 11 日凌晨 1 点至 7 点之间,油轮航行在北大西洋上时失踪。船上也没有任何人知道他到底发生了什么事情。作为雇主的 BP 经过调查后认为最有可能发生的事是 Braganza 先生跳海自杀。根据雇佣合约第 7.6.3 条,[110] 如果在 BP 或保险人看来,Braganza 先生的死因是自杀,那么 BP 与保险人就不必对 Braganza 先生的遗孀进行任何赔偿。Braganza 先生的妻子就将 BP 告上法庭,诉因包括作为雇主的 BP 存在疏忽管理从而导致其丈夫死亡以及 BP 不恰当行使了雇佣合约赋予它的裁量权。

BP 在事故发生后,成立了一个 5 人事故调查小组。该小组对事故的原因、目前工作制度中存在的漏洞以及可以如何进行改善进行了为期 4 个月的调查,并于 2009 年 9 月 17 日做出了一份调查报告。该调查报告列举了 6 个主要的证据来支持 Braganza 先生是故意跳海自杀,包括:(1)Braganza 先生的言行举止在开始最后这个航次时与之前不同,例如他变得沉默寡言、不修边幅与在工作中注意力不集中。(2)Braganza 先生失踪后,他在船上经常穿的鞋仍然留在他的房间。(3)一些 Braganza 先生与家人的邮件往来显示他正在忧虑一些家庭和财务上遇到的问题。例如妻子对 Braganza 先生写道:"I really cannot figure out what has shaken you out so much that you seem to be so afraid of life."(4)Braganza 先生在上船后发现船舶的情况不佳,有多处需要维修,从而不开心。(5)Braganza 先生认为他应该获得 2008 年的分红奖励,但后来该分红被公司取消。(6)在 Braganza 先生失踪前的那晚,右侧生活区通往上层甲板的水密舱门可能曾经被打开,但没有船员报告说曾打开过这个门。

该报告历经几个版本的草稿,其中第一版并没有提到自杀,调查小组在与 BP 的法务团队进行过沟通后,最后一版的报告中得出结论是,在考虑了所有证据后,调查小组认为最有可能的是 Braganza 先生故意跳海结束自己的生命。

---

[110] 该条文的相关内容是:"For the avoidance of doubt compensation for death, accidental injury or illness shall not be payable if, in the opinion of the Company or its insurers, the death, accidental injury or illness resulted from amongst other things, the Officer's wilful act, default or misconduct whether at sea or ashore …."

最高院的 Hale 勋爵认为 BP 根据调查报告就认为 Braganza 先生是自杀的决定是有问题的。首先,调查并非仅仅只是针对 Braganza 先生失踪的原因,也包括整个 BP 工作制度上存在的问题,以及对公司可以如何更好地帮助在经济和家庭上有困难的员工提出建议。BP 的决策部门在做决策时不能仅仅依靠该调查报告,而是应该在法务部门的帮助下更理性地考虑对于船员在工作中自杀这一非常少见的事件是否有非常有说服力的证据来证明,例如发现遗书,Braganza 先生正在承受明显的令人想要寻短见的生活或经济上的巨大压力,Braganza 先生有精神上的问题或郁郁寡欢的性格等。上述调查报告中的 6 个证据,在 Hale 勋爵看来顶多只是一些迹象或苗头,距离有说服力仍有距离。其中两个相对有说服力的证据,即 Braganza 先生在工作中心不在焉和家书的字里行间所反映的问题,BP 都没有进行进一步的深入调查和挖掘,甚至都没有询问过 Braganza 先生的妻子家书的内容具体是指什么。另外,考虑到 Braganza 先生完全有可能因为担心天气而在凌晨走上甲板查看从而意外落海,这与他是一个虔诚的天主教徒,而天主教视自杀为不可饶恕的大罪等因素相适应,BP 行使裁量权没有满足理性的测试,也即 Wednesbury/Braganza 测试。Hale 勋爵总结说:"Although I would not have phrased the correct approach exactly as Teare J(一审法官) phrased it, in my view he was right to conclude ... that the investigation team's report and conclusion could not be regarded as sufficiently cogent evidence to justify Mr Sullivan (BP 相关负责人), and hence BP, in forming the positive opinion that he had committed suicide. No – one suggests that his decision was "arbitrary, capricious or perverse", but in my view it was unreasonable in the Wednesbury sense, having been formed without taking relevant matters into account."

2.6.4.2.4 "Wednesbury/Braganza 测试"带来"Braganza 责任"对决策人行使合约裁量权、选择权或权利的约束

在 Braganza v. BP Shipping Ltd(2015)UKSC 17 先例中,最高院明确了法院并不是决策人,所以不应该用自己认为合理的决定去替代决策人的决定,但是法院可以从决定的过程和结果是否理性来进行审查,这包括两方面的要求。**(1)程序上**("Process"或 Braganza 1):决策人要把所有应该考虑的事情考虑在内,或是考虑所有有关的事情,但排除所有无关的事情(to consider all relevant matters and exclude all irrelevant matters)。**(2)结果上**("Outcome"或 Braganza 2):作出的决定的不合理程度是否是没有其他站在此地位的合理人士会作出同样决定(reach a decision which so unreasonable that no reasonable decision – maker could have come to it)。

这审查也被称为是"理性与善意责任"(rational and good faith duty)的测试。在 Braganza v. BP Shipping Ltd 先例中,Hale 勋爵说:"It is in my view ... part of a rational decision-making process to take into account those considerations which are obviously relevant to the decision in question. It is of the essence of 'Wednesbury reasonableness' ... review to consider the rationality of the decision-making process rather than to concentrate upon the outcome. Concentrating on the outcome runs the risk that the court will substitute its own decision for that of the primary decision – maker. ... the court will only imply a term that the decision-making process be lawful and rational in the public law sense, that the decision is made rationally(as well as in good faith) and consistently with its contractual purpose. ... But whatever term may be implied will depend upon the terms and the context of the particular contract involved. ”

在较早已提到,White & Carter(Councils) Limited v. McGregor(1962) AC 413 先例中的传统法律地位是法律不理会行使裁量权或选择权人士作出的决定在对方看来是否合理,决策人也无须就作出的决定给原因或作解释,只要不是恶意可以说裁量权是无拘无束的。而这“Wednesbury/Braganza 测试”或“Braganza 责任”显然是这传统法律地位的一个例外。

如此一来,针对商业合约中不同的裁量权或选择权,就有必要区分哪些是受 Braganza 责任约束,而哪些仍是适用传统法律地位。毕竟一旦涉及 Braganza 责任,在行使裁量权时就要谨慎,因为这责任的条件并不容易满足。

在 Braganza v. BP Shipping Ltd 先例中,笔者认为 BP 在做法上已经足够小心,但仍未满足 Braganza 责任。这未满足不是指在结果上或“Braganza 2”,而是在程序上没有考虑所有应该考虑的事情,如 Hale 勋爵提到的没有考虑有关因素如“Braganza 先生是天主教徒,不大可能会自杀”。这在笔者看来有些挑毛病的感觉,而且要挑总会挑到。正如 Neuberger 勋爵在该先例中提到的,由于雇佣合约中雇员与雇主之间谈判地位不对等,从而需要对雇主(BP)行使严重影响雇员(Braganza 先生)的裁量权增加约束的政策考虑。

笔者认为本来 Braganza v. BP Shipping Ltd 先例中,如果法院在决定时确实有一些政策上的考虑与倾向,法律的发展本可以将这个“Wednesbury/Braganza 测试”只限制在此类一面倒的合约中适用。但接下来的发展却将这个苛刻与不肯定的测试普遍适用在所有类型的合约,包括一贯视为双方有对等谈判力量的国际商业合约。这样,就带来了很大的问题,这将在接下来进一步介绍。

2.6.4.3 “履行/合约选择权”与“商业/真正选择权”

在此先指出在笔者的《合约的解释》一书第九章之 3.2 段与《合约的履行、弃权与禁反言》一书第三章之 3.3 段,有详尽介绍两种选择权(options),一种可称为是“履行/合约选择权”(performance/contractual option),另一种可称为是“商业选择权”或“真正/绝对选择权”(business/true option)。该书的分析主要是不少合约(特别是很多早年的先例涉及货物买卖合约与租船合约)的内容中有不少这两种不同的选择权。它们的不同主要体现在权利方/决策人需要怎样做才是恰当行使权利。前者完全是决策人自己在履行合约时方便,他可以完全自由决定与随时改变想法,不存在对方的利益会否受到影响,更不需要把决定提前通知对方(除非合约另有明示规定),直接履行即可。

例如买卖散货如石油的数量是“20 万至 25 万吨,卖方选择”。这样,卖方或发货人(shipper)可以决定交货或付运在这范围内任何数量的石油,买方不能有异议或抗拒。买方可以提出要求如“我的炼油厂因为库存受到限制,请只提供顶多是 20 万吨”或“由于气温暴跌,请付运 25 万吨应急”。但卖方不必理睬,反正付运任何在约定范围内重量的石油都属于履行合约承诺,若最终付运了 21.5 万吨(为例),买方不满或威胁提起诉讼/仲裁,都是乱来并会被提前撤销索赔(strike - out claim)。

但后一种选择权,在笔者的《合约的解释:规则与应用》一书被称为是“真正或绝对的商业上选择权”,权利方/决策人在这种选择权下没有责任以替代的选择履行合约,而合约只是根据一个原本在合约预先约定的方法履行,直到决策人纯粹是为了自己的利益行使了该选择权,令替代方法取代了原本约定的方法。

举一个简单的例子,在一个房屋租赁合约中,原来约定的是 1 年租期,但也有条文约定租客有选择权可延长 1 年。这样,如果租客不行使选择权,预先约定的是 1 年租约;如果租客行使选择权,则由 2 年的租约替代了 1 年的租约。

租客在行使选择权时也无需考虑对方房东的利益,例如地产市场猛涨或房东急需把房屋腾空出售或自住等。但与上述“履行选择权”主要的不同是需要及时行使选择权与清楚无误地通知对方,否则将被视为弃权(waiver)。

行使履行选择权是不需要通知的,正如在 The“Aspa Maria”(1976)2 Lloyd's Rep 643 上诉庭先例中,租船合约的租期届满,承租人还船有 30 天的宽限期,Denning 勋爵说:“It seems to me that the phrase ‘30 days more or less at charterers option’ was not a true option. It did not have to be exercised by express notice or declaration such as ... would be necessary for a true option.”

但行使一个商业/真正的选择权时必须及时且精准通知对方,而且一旦作出,就无法反悔去改变。Parker 大法官在 The“Trado”(1982)1 Lloyd's Rep 157 先例中说:“Those who have options in their favour must, if they wish to exercise them, exercise them in words which are not really capable of doubt. ... It is clear law that if a charterers has an option ... once exercised, is binding and is as if written into the charter party ...”

这样,区分两种选择权就很必要了。有情况是容易撇开合约的明示写法,同样是租期,1 年加选择延长 1 年就容易区分;但如果是 1 年加 1 个月的延长就不容易在本质上与 30 天的宽限期去作出区分了。这没有脱离大原则,同样的一个字或一句话还是要根据合约的背景/语境整体解释。

至于商业/真正选择权必须及时行使与精准通知对方,从弃权(waiver by election)的角度看完全说得通。毕竟这也是公平合理的,房东是需要及时知道租客选择的是 1 年或 2 年的租约,才能继续履行下去。否则房东会在 1 年即将届满,就寻找新租客并去订立下一份租约了。

从弃权的角度分析,涉及行使的权利与原来的权利是相互替代(alternate rights)并会带来两种对立的结果,权利方就有必要作出“走东或是走西”的选择。这也需要让对方合约方知悉,因为对方会受到影响。所以,权利方作出选择就需要根据合约规定的时限与通知形式(或根据法律的默示地位),及时以通知形式告知对方。而权利方作出选择就是终止,不得出尔反尔。这可节录《Chitty on Contracts》(2021 年,第 34 版)一书之 27 – 060 段说:"… ‘waiver by election’ …is here used to signify the ‘abandonment of a right which arises by virtue of a party making an election’. Thus it arises when a person is entitled to alternative rights inconsistent with one another and that person acts in a manner which is consistent only with his having chosen to rely on one of them."

显然,可以让权利方单方面选择要或不要(弃权)的权利,无论称为选择权或裁量权,这才是"真正"(real)或"绝对"(absolute)的权利。而履行选择权去交货或付运 20 万至 25 万吨石油,卖方就不存在选择要或不要这个权利,不要就是不交货了。而付运的 20 万吨、21.5 万吨或 25 万吨就谈不上是对立的权利。

这两种不同的权利在"Wednesbury/Braganza 测试"下的区分变得更加重要,因为一个真正或绝对权利(或选择权/裁量权)是不受这苛刻测试的约束的,如在 Monk v. Largo(2016)EWHC 1837 先例中,被告 Largo 工厂聘用原告 Monk 提供咨询服务,合约规定如果在 1 年后双方都满意,合约将再延长 2 年。但 1 年后,工厂决定不延长。法院判是不受 Braganza 责任的影响。权利方可以从自己的利益出发去行使裁量权,不必关心对方的利益与影响。当然上面已经提到对这种真正或绝对选择权,还有必须及时通知对方否则会构成弃权的说法。David Foxton QC 大法官说:"However, it is not every decision which a party to a contract makes which can properly be characterised as a contractual discretion and to which the principles identified in Socimer and Braganza apply. Where, for example, a commercial contract gives one party a right to terminate in certain circumstances, it will not ordinarily be appropriate to subject the exercise of that right to obligations of procedural or substantive fairness akin to the public law duties which apply to the decisions of the executive. …Similarly, where **a commercial contract gives one party an option to extend the contract, or as to the amount of goods to be supplied or acquired, or as to the ports or berths to or from which the cargo is to be shipped, that party will not ordinarily be under any duties of the kind recognised in Braganza** in relation to the exercise of that option."(加黑部分是笔者的强调)

2.6.4.4　适用 White & Charter 先例的无约束传统法律地位与默示"Braganza 责任"的权利的区分

问题是 Braganza 责任并非对行使所有合约下的权利都适用,所以近期不少先例在寻找分水岭在哪儿。看来在这方面的法律应该是在不断发展的。

另外,一种重要的例外情况是一条明确的明示条文允许一方合约方有终止合约的权利,不受 Braganza 责任的影响,例如可以想到的是银行的贷款合约通常会有的违约事件(events of default)条文。

在 Sir William Blair 大法官主导的名为"Duties of Good Faith in Wholesale Financial Contracts"报告中之5.3段说:"The good faith element of that duty is based on similar principles to those applicable to the implication of terms of good faith in other contractual situations ... **The key distinction in this context is between an absolute contractual right conferred on a party for their sole benefit**(and which can be exercised regardless of the other party's interests) and a discretion that must be exercised, rationally, in good faith and for the purpose for which it was conferred. Which category a particular example falls into is **a question of construction** but, in the absence of an express duty, the relevant factor is **essentially that one party is trusting the other to decide the matter with integrity and avoid sharp practice**(for example in setting the rate of interest payable under a contract or making a genuine attempt to come up with a proper valuation). ..."(加黑部分是笔者的强调)

该报告提供了不少在不同情况下行使商业合约(特别是金融合约)的裁量权或权利到底会否默示 Braganza 责任的案例,可介绍如下:

1. 在远期合约买方违约时,卖方有权决定远期合约中相关资产的估值,Braganza 责任适用:见 Socimer International Bank Ltd v. Standard Bank London Ltd(2008)EWCA Civ 116 先例。

2. 一方有权单方面设定或变更收费或利率时,Braganza 责任适用:见 Paragon Finance Plc v. Nash(2001)EWCA Civ 1466;British Telecommunications Plc v. Telefonica O2 UK Ltd(2014)UKSC 42;BHL v. Leumi ABL Ltd(2017)EWHC 1871 等先例。

3. 在认股权(share option)合约中,一方认股需要公司董事会大多数同意该方已经完成履行合约下的义务,董事会在决定是否给出该同意时有 Braganza 责任:见 Watson v. Watchfinder. co. uk Ltd(2017)EWHC 1275(Comm)先例。

4. 除非雇佣合约中有明示规定发放奖金的方式和计算办法,否则在雇主行使裁量权给员工发放奖金时,适用 Braganza 责任:见 Commerzbank AG v. Keen(2006)EWCA Civ 1536;Brogden v. Investec Bank plc(2016)EWCA Civ 1031 先例。

5. 合伙人之间分配利润也适用 Braganza 责任:见 Tribe v. Elborne Mitchell LLP(2021)EWHC 1863(Ch)先例。

6. 雇主决定员工离职前的带薪假期天数时,Braganza 责任适用:见 Faieta v. ICAP Management Services Ltd(2017)EWHC 2995(QB)先例。

7. 银行的贷款合约中有条文约定银行有权对抵押资产进行估值,并且估值所产生的费用由借款人承担,银行对是否需要进行估值做出决定时,Braganza 责任适用:见 Property Alliance Group Ltd v. Royal Bank of Scotland(2018)EWCA Civ 355 先例。

8. 建筑工程合约中总包商与分包商约定总包商拥有对应付工程款进行核算与要求归还多付的钱的裁量权,行使该权利时 Braganza 责任适用:见 Everwarm Ltd v. BN Rendering Ltd(2019)EWHC 3060(TCC)先例。

9. 根据保险合约中的约定,[111] 如果被保险人可以说服保险人自己的一些不披露是无辜而非故意欺诈,保险人有裁量权不撤销保险合约,保险人在决定是否被说服时 Braganza 责任适用:见 UK Acorn Finance Ltd v. Markel(UK)Ltd(2020)EWHC 922(Comm)先例。

10. 特许经营合约(franchise agreement)中的不可抗力条文约定:"This Agreement will be suspended during any period that either of the parties is prevented or hindered from complying with their respective obligations under any part of this Agreement by any cause which the Franchisor designates as force majeure including strikes, disruption to the supply chain, political unrest, financial distress, terrorism, fuel shortages, war, civil disorder, and natural disasters."授权人在决定有关事件是否属于条文中包括的不可抗力事项时,Braganza 责任适用:见 Dwyer(UK Franchising)Ltd v. Fredbar Ltd(2021)EWHC 1218(Ch)先例。

2.6.4.5 "Braganza 责任"可否以明示条文排除

在《合约的解释:规则与应用》一书第九章之 3.3 段曾说:在订约自由下,如果怕对这两种选择权的规定不清楚而令行使选择权或裁量权时被解释为要考虑对方的利益,大可以以文字/措辞加以改变。例如,在一个合约履行的选择权,有裁量权或选择权的一方完全可以像 Lymington Marina Ltd v. MacNamara(2007)Bus LR Digest D29 先例中一样写上"absolute discretion"或"the discretion is final and not open to challenge"。

但实践中看来不是这么简单,正如在 Mid Essex Hospital Services NHS Trust v. Compass Group UK and Ireland Ltd(2013)EWCA Civ 200 上诉庭先例中,Jackson 大法官说:"An important feature of the above line of authorities is that in each case the discretion did not involve a simple decision whether or not to exercise an absolute contractual right. **The discretion involved making an assessment or choosing from a range of options, taking into account the interests of both parties**. In any contract under which one party is permitted to exercise **such a discretion, there is an implied term**. The precise formulation of that term has been variously expressed in the authorities. In essence, however, it is that the relevant party will not exercise its discretion in an arbitrary, capricious or irrational manner. **Such a term is extremely difficult to exclude, although I would not say it is utterly impossible to do so**. ..."(加黑部分是笔者的强调)

另也可节录 David Pollard 大律师在 2020 年发表的"Applying Wednesbury reasonableness to legal review of trustee discretions after Braganza and Pitt v Holt" Tru. L. I.

[111] 关于保险合约中以明示条文要求被保险人披露,可见在本章之 2.6.3 段节录的"International Hull Clauses(01/11/03)"的格式保单第 45.3 条文(虽然不是责任保险合约,只是船舶保险)。在订约自由下,针对不同类别的保险可以有更针对性的措辞/文字。

2020,34(2),86 - 116 一文的有关部分,如下:

"Seemingly **a statement in the** relevant trust(or **contract**) **that the decision is 'absolute,final and unchallengeable' may be enough to exclude or modify review by the courts**.

Conversely some of the cases look at trusts where the trustee's decision is stated to be 'final'. Despite this the courts reviewed the decision on the irrationality basis. See for example Glidewell LJ in Harris v. Lord Shuttleworth(1994)ICR 991:'The trustees shall be empowered conclusively to determine all matters,questions,and disputes touching or in connection with the fund's affairs and all claims thereon ... every such determination shall be conclusive and binding on all parties.'

In Trustees of the Saffil Penson Scheme v. Curzon(2005)EWHC 293(Ch),the trust deed provided that 'the decision of the Trustees shall be final'. Despite this,in both cases the courts reviewed the decision on the irrationality basis.

Merely describing a power or discretion in the relevant contract or trust as 'absolute' or 'sole and absolute' may well not be enough to exclude the Braganza irrationality tests. There are a number of decisions where a power or discretion has been described as 'absolute' in the relevant instrument,but the courts have still applied review concepts:see, for example, Dundee General Hospitals Board of Management v. Walker (1952)1 All ER 896;TJH and Sons Consultancy Ltd v. CPP Group Plc(2017)EWCA Civ 46;... and Wellington City Council v. Local Government Mutual Funds Trustee Ltd (2017)NZHC 2901.

Conversely if**a discretion is not described as 'absolute' or 'uncontrollable' a court may be 'more willing' to intervene**:see Esso Australia Ltd v. Australian Petroleum Agents' & Distributors Association(1999)3 VR 642 ...

In the share option case,Mallone v. BOB Industries Ltd(2002)EWCA Civ 126,Rix LJ held that**a discretion was reviewable for being fully irrational even though it was described as absolute**. ...

Similarly,in British Telecommunications plc v. Telefonica O2 UK Ltd(2014)UKSC 42,Lord Sumption ... said this was a construction test. He held:'As a general rule,the scope of a contractual discretion**will depend on the nature of the discretion and the construction of the language conferring it**. But it is well established that in the **absence of very clear language to the contract,a contractual discretion must be exercised in good faith and not arbitrarily or capriciously**. This will normally mean that **it must be exercised consistently with its contractual purpose**."(加黑部分是笔者的强调)

最后介绍 Michael Bridge 教授 2019 年在"The exercise of contractual discretion" (2019)135 Law Quarterly Review 227 一文针对如何区分传统不受约束的绝对权利与

受到 Braganza 责任约束的权利:"... this article demonstrates that a difficult line has to be drawn between reviewable discretionary powers and what have been referred to as absolute rights."

Bridge 教授提及 Monde Petroleum SA v. WesternZagros Ltd(2016)EWHC 1472(Comm)先例的一审判决中,Salter QC 大法官提到他认为的一种区分是:"a contractual right to terminate a contract is, as the Court of Appeal noted in Lomas v. JFB Firth Rixson Inc(2012)EWCA Civ 419, not the exercise of a contractual discretion. Contractual discretions arise where there are **a range of options from which to choose. A contractual right to terminate involves a binary choice.**"(加黑部分是笔者的强调)

本段较早节录的 Jackson 大法官在 Mid Essex Hospital Services NHS Trust v. Compass Group UK and Ireland Ltd 上诉庭先例也有同样说法。

但 Bridge 教授在分析后认为这个区分没有帮助且并不正确,共在结论中说:"This is an unhelpful distinction in some respects since it deflects attention away from the hard work of construing the contract. It may be in some cases misleading to refer to the right to terminate a contract as definitively an absolute one. It is also unhelpful to locate the boundary of controlled discretion by reference to the difference between binary and multiple choices."

笔者也认为区分并非这么简单,例如如果租约是 1 年加 1 年,这应是很明确是一个真正或绝对选择权,不适用 Braganza 责任。但是如果条文更复杂,租约允许租客在半年内选择延长租期 1 年加 1 年、或 1 年加 2 年、又或 1 年加 3 年,每个选择都有不同的租金。这似乎并非二元的选择,而是在一个范围中选择。但这不应改变该权利的性质,其还是一个真正或绝对选择权。

至于以明示条文去把一些权利明确为权利方/决策人的"绝对"与不受法院监管的权利,似乎并不容易,因为解释合约是否加入默示的善意责任是要根据整体的背景/语境来看。例如在 Equitable Life Assurance Society v. Hyman(2000)UKHL 39 贵族院先例中,Cooke 勋爵说:"starting from the principle that no legal discretion, however widely worded[here, by article 65(1), the directors may apportion bonuses 'on such principles, and by such methods, as they may from time to time determine'], can be exercised for purposes contrary to those of the instrument by which it is conferred."

这背景/语境甚至会包括法院的政策性考虑,例如在 Mid Essex Hospital Services NHS Trust v. Compass Group UK and Ireland Ltd 上诉庭先例中,涉及一个原告(Compass Group)为被告(公立医院医管局或"Trust")提供长达 7 年的膳食与清洁服务的合约,但 Trust 以服务不佳为由行使合约权利扣费与终止合约。该合约的第 3.5 条文明示了双方要善意合作,而有关争议是 Trust 的合约权利是绝对或是可去默示 Braganza 责任。上诉庭判是绝对裁量权或权利,因为 Trust 作为公立医院,对其保护社会上的病弱人士有更严格的要求。换言之,合约的明示善意条文没有起作用。Jackson 大法官说:"The discretion which is entrusted to the Trust in relation to service failure points and deductions in the present case is very different … The Trust is a public authority delivering a vital service to vulnerable members of the public. It rightly demands high standards from all those with whom it contracts. … The discretion conferred by clause 5.8 simply permits the Trust to decide whether or not to exercise an absolute contractual right."

法院会根据政策倾向来进行判决也可见在本章之2.6.4.6.1段介绍的 Equitas Insurance Ltd v. Municipal Mutual Insurance Ltd(2019)EWCA Civ 718 上诉庭先例。

所以 Bridge 教授在文章中总结说绝对的裁量权与有 Braganza 责任约束的裁量权之间没有清楚的红线/分水岭，要根据每个不同案件的案情来定："It has been firmly asserted that there is no scope for treating the exercise of an 'absolute' right as subject to the controls that would otherwise govern the exercise of a discretion, but this of course does not help us to determine whether we are looking at a discretionary power or an absolute right. We might say that a right exists, absolute and non-reviewable, if the contract clearly so provides, but that approach could lead to circularity. If an implied term of the contract so provides, then we are looking instead at a discretionary power, and an implied term will so provide in the case of a discretionary power that is not an absolute right. Dependent as the question is on the intention of the parties, there is **no bright line test for distinguishing the absolute and the discretionary.**"（加黑部分是笔者的强调）

另在笔者看来，这与在《合约的解释：规则与应用》一书的第十二章之1.7.3段针对的试图以一条免责条文豁免己方疏忽、过错的责任有同样的困难。

更不用说明示豁免欺诈/欺骗更是不可能的事，因为该规则违反公共政策。[112]但在行使合约裁量权或权利时，看来是很难说得通可以上升到公共政策的层面，进而排除订约自由的豁免。但就像要明示写明才能免除疏忽的责任一样，要在合约中写明权利方/决策人可以独断专行、反复无常、非理性行使裁量权还希望对方能够接受，是不现实的。

虽然以上观点认为通过明示条文豁免 Braganza 责任有一定困难，但毕竟解释合约是要整体解释且要考虑背景/语境，所以也不是没有成功的先例。在本章之2.6.4.6.2段介绍的 TAQA Bratani Limited v. Rockrose UKCS8 LLC(2020)EWHC 58 (Comm)先例中，有关的联营协议(Joint Operation Agreement 或"JOAs")投票罢免经营人的条文的写法是："**Change of Operator** 19.1 Operator may be discharged; (a) at the end of any calendar month by the Operating Committee giving not less than ninety (90) days notice to it, provided that in respect of any vote of the Operating Committee on any such discharge under this Article 19.1(a) the voting interest of the Participant which is the Operator and the voting interest of any Participant which is an Affiliate of the Oper-

---

〔112〕见本书第三章之8.3段。

ator shall be ignored and the required percentage figure shall be One hundred per cent (100%) of the total votes available to the remaining Parties;…"

Pelling QC 大法官针对该条文解释说:"Absolute rights conferred by professionally drawn or standard form contracts including but not limited to absolute rights to terminate relationships and roles within relationships are an everyday feature of the contracts that govern commercial relationships and extending Braganza to such provisions would be an unwarranted interference in the freedom of parties to contract on the terms they choose, at any rate where **there is no fiduciary relationship created by the agreement** (as is the case with the JOAs because **the parties have agreed that the JOAs ' … shall not be construed as creating any partnership or association**[113] …' and the **members of the decision making body** are each required to ' … **act solely on behalf of the Party whom he represents** and not on behalf of the Participants as an entity …')."(加黑部分是笔者的强调)

2.6.4.6 涉及是否适用"Braganza 责任"争议的先例

在此挑选两个近期先例进行介绍,因为这类案件都涉及大量的事实要去认定,所以虽然是简介,内容仍较多,需要在针对 Braganza 责任的本段的最后去分段介绍。

2.6.4.6.1 先例之一:Equitas Insurance Ltd v. Municipal Mutual Insurance Ltd (2019) EWCA Civ 718 上诉庭先例

在 Equitas Insurance Ltd v. Municipal Mutual Insurance Ltd 上诉庭先例中,案情涉及在 20 世纪 80 年代的石棉(asbestos)污染带来的保险索赔,导致英国劳合社在 1990 年前后三年亏损于当时是天文数字的 60 亿英镑,面临严峻危机,在 1993 年通过对劳合社的一些结构性改变[114]才慢慢恢复。石棉可以令接触过石棉的工人(当年的工厂或其他工作环境如建造房屋普遍在使用石棉)罹患"间皮瘤"(mesothelioma),但潜伏期可以长达 40 年并在发病后很快死亡。这也带来损失计算的因果关系(causation)的问题,因为潜伏期间该工人已经在很多不同工厂工作过,甚至有自雇但也有接触石棉。这样,谁要为该工人的病危或死亡负责赔偿,在哪一家工厂的接触才是导致间皮瘤的罪魁祸首并无法确定。

由于无法解决普通法下因果关系的基本要求,但为了公共政策的规定要让受害工人获得赔偿,所以有了 Fairchild v. Glenhaven Funeral Services (2003) AC 32 贵族院先例与接下来的《The Compensation Act 2006》立法。该立法的 Section 3 说明有责任的被告(受害工人曾经工作过的工厂)导致或允许原告(受害工人)接触石棉,而原告

---

[113] 在本章之 2.6.5.2 段也提到在 Cathay Pacific Airways v. Lufthansa Technik AG (2020) EWHC 1789 (Ch) 先例,也有明示条文说明该 10 年的飞机维修合约不是合伙人协议(partnership agreement)或合资协议,以明示条文排除了合约属于关系合约,有善意责任。

[114] 见本书第三章之 6.3.2 段。

事后间皮瘤发作,但没有办法证明是否是被告导致的接触或是其他工厂或工作环境的接触引发疾病,被告依旧要负责任并需要负责原告所有的损失,这损失是连带性(joint and several liability)的。至于被告在赔偿原告后去找其他同样有侵权责任的第三人分摊,那是另一码事。这种做法或可称为"spiking of claims",允许受害工人向过去二三十年工作过的任何一家工厂或雇主(只要仍存在与有钱作出赔付)索赔所有损失。这显然十分偏帮受害工人,这一完全背离普通法的基本损失计算的大原则的立法也带来很多当时无法预见的困难。

这些内容已经在笔者的《损失赔偿与救济》一书第四章之4.3.3段有详细叙述,不多重复,而在此先例就涉及了其中一个无法预见的困难,就是再保险(reinsurance)。在一线的保险,也就是工厂如果投保了责任险(Employer's Liability 或"EL"),而该工厂过去二三十年分别向不同保险人/保险公司投保过同样保险(通常是1年的保单或保险合约),就会面对向哪个保险人/保险公司要求赔付的问题。接下来在 Durham v. BAI(Run Off) Ltd(2012) UKSC 14 与 International Energy Group Ltd v. Zurich Insurance Plc UK(2015) UKSC 33 最高院先例中,工厂也可以"spiking of claims"向任何一位保险人要求赔付所有损失(赔付给受害工人),然后保险人/保险公司再根据风险时间(time on risk)按比例向其他承保过风险的保险人/保险公司要求分摊。这可节录在 Equitas Insurance Ltd v. Municipal Mutual Insurance Ltd 先例中,Males 大法官对该 International Energy Group Ltd v. Zurich Insurance Plc UK 先例的介绍:"... the effect of the 'Trigger' litigation was that an insurer which had provided cover for only part of the period of the employee's exposure must meet the entirely of the employer's liability, recognising that this would enable the insured employer to select the insurer against which to claim. ... Although the solution adopted by the majority was to say that each insurer was liable in full and(in effect) that spiking was permitted, but that the spiked insurer would then have rights of contribution from other insurers ..."

但再保险是否可以"spiking",就从来没有出现过,Equitas Insurance Ltd v. Municipal Mutual Insurance Ltd 先例是首次。该先例也涉及了一线保险人可以向长达二三十年中的哪一位再保险人要求赔付的"分配"裁量权(deemed allocation),是一个没有约束的绝对权利或是有 Braganza 责任的问题。再保险人 Equitas 的代表大律师主张一线保险人 MMI 只应该按受害工人接触石棉的时间段去按比例分摊,不应该只挑选向 Equitas 要求赔付索赔所有的金额,特别是现在有了 Braganza 责任,说:"... in particular the ability of the insurer to select the policy to which a loss should be attached which is contrary to elementary principles of liability insurance. ... namely(1) the nature of an insurance or reinsurance contract as a contract of the utmost good faith, (2) cases which have held that contractual discretions must be exercised in good faith(or, more fully, in a manner which is not irrational, arbitrary or capricious ..."

在上诉庭,推翻了一审的仲裁裁决(仲裁员是 Flaux 大法官),判 MMI 在 Braganza

责任下是不应该在再保险允许“spiking”的 Males 大法官说：

“In my judgment there are powerful reasons to support the implication of a term in the very specific reinsurance context existing within the Fairchild enclave that the insurer's right to present its reinsurance claims **must be exercised in a manner which is not arbitrary, irrational or capricious, and that in that context rationality requires that they be presented by reference to each year's contribution to the risk**, which will normally be measured by reference to time on risk unless in the particular circumstances there is a good reason (such as differing intensity of exposure) for some other basis of presentation. That is because spiking is inconsistent with the presumed intentions and reasonable expectations of the parties at the time when the contracts were concluded. On that basis the insurer remains the decision – maker, so that a rational view that (for example) the intensity of exposure had been greater in one year than another could not be challenged, but the decision must be made by reference to each year's contribution to the risk.

In summary, the Fairchild jurisprudence ... It results in a situation, spiking, which does not accord with common law notions of fairness ... and is contrary to the underlying statistical reality that in fact the critical exposure(s) of employees to asbestos will not all have occurred in the same year. It is a situation in which there is**a clear conflict of interest between the parties and a significant imbalance of power between them**. That imbalance is not the result of a relationship such as employer and employee which existed in Braganza [2015] 1 WLR 1661, but arises out of the control which the insurer can exercise in allocating its inwards claims and its exclusive knowledge of its reinsurance arrangements over an extensive period.

In an area of the law in which considerations of fairness and policy have explicitly loomed larger than usual, and bearing in mind the willingness of the Supreme Court to 'strike new ground' if necessary to achieve a fair balance of all the interests concerned, I would hold that such a term should be implied. **The term can conveniently be described as requiring 'good faith', but this is merely a label**. Its content and rationale are as I have described. Such a term achieves an outcome which is as close as possible to what the parties can be taken to have intended if they had foreseen the development of the Fairchild jurisprudence.”(加黑部分是笔者的强调)

另 Leggatt 大法官也说：“At a higher level of abstraction, the justification for implying this term is that the implication is necessary to prevent the insurer's power to allocate its loss among policy years from being abused. The power to 'spike' a loss to a particular year is not one for which the reinsured can reasonably be said to have bargained since it was not within the reasonable contemplation of the parties when the reinsurance contracts were made that the reinsured might be able to choose the year to which a loss will attach.

Nor was it within the reasonable contemplation of the parties that the reinsured might be able to claim under a policy providing one year of cover loss that results from risks that arose in other policy years. Both these possibilities are inconsistent with the essential nature and purpose of the parties' agreement. In these circumstances **good faith requires that the reinsured should not exploit this power which it was not intended to have for its own commercial advantage but should exercise it in a way which is as consistent as possible with the assumption of risk for which the reinsurance premium was paid**."(加黑部分是笔者的强调)

上诉庭推翻 Flaux 大法官的裁决是认为 MMI 向再保险人 Equitas 行使要求赔付的"分配"裁量权,不应该允许"spiking",因为:(1)在 International Energy Group Ltd v. Zurich Insurance Plc UK 最高院先例中考虑的是一线的公共政策去偏帮间皮瘤受害的工人,如果工厂赔偿工人要面对"spiking",但去向保险人要求赔付就不能去"spiking",而是在要求赔付时要向二三十年间每年不同的保险人证明因果关系,等于是难以获得赔付,也会是无法去向受害工人赔付了。更不用说受害工人可以根据《Third Parties(Rights Against Insurers)Act 1930》直接向保险公司索赔损失,[115]这也难免要涉及"spiking"。所以,最高院心知肚明不去判可以"spiking",政府与议会也会跟随《Compensation Act 2006》去另外立法针对了。(2)但再保险是第二线,就不必考虑公共政策,而可以回归去更公平与配合订约(分保合约)时双方的合法预期与支付的保费。而如果允许一线保险人"spiking",而被"spiking"的再保保险人想找其他再保保险人分摊,也很难知道这长达二三十年的时间里一线保险人的再保险安排。

但在笔者看来,这判法仍是带来很多问题。例如在可高可低的免赔额(deductible),如果一线保险人可以"spiking",就只会面对一次的免赔额。但如果要去分开向每一年度的再保险人去区别要求赔付,撇开做法上的麻烦、工作量与费用,一线保险人要面对可能多达二三十次的免赔额,这笔账怎样算?这会否影响保险市场针对这种 EL 保险的萎缩等?看来这方方面面的问题还会继续发展,有兴趣的读者可以跟进。

2.6.4.6.2　先例之二:TAQA Bratani Limited v. Rockrose UKCS8 LLC(2020) EWHC 58(Comm)先例

在 TAQA Bratani Limited v. Rockrose UKCS8 LLC 先例中,案情有关北海油田的油气开发,原告与被告之间的联营协议(joint operation agreement)中有一条十分详尽的条文针对如何罢免被告作为经营人(operator)的职务。其中一种方式是所有联营协议下的非经营人(non-operators)投票并作出 90 天的通知。原告申请法院作出宣示判决已经成功罢免被告经营人的职务,而被告的抗辩主要是:(1)Braganza 责任适用,原告行使裁量权决定罢免被告经营人职务时有善意责任;(2)联营协议属于关系合约,有善意责任。

---

〔115〕　这方面可见笔者《损失赔偿与救济》一书第七章之 3.7 段的介绍。

高院首先分析了联营协议的明示条文,考虑到有关合约是由有经验的大公司聘请了律师经过深思熟虑的谈判达成,解释合约时应首先考虑条文的措辞/文字。该条文写得清楚无误,非经营人作出罢免决定与投票时没有任何约束,也没有证据显示根据背景/语境解释合约会与字面解释有不同。此外,从合约整体来看,这也与其他合约条文一致,例如合约其他条文明示说明合约方可以完全根据自己的利益投票。因此,Pelling QC 大法官判合约的明示条文下不存在善意责任的要求。

接着 Pelling QC 大法官分析了合约下是否默示了 Braganza 责任,结论是不适用。双方均是水平高的商业人士(sophisticated commercial parties),条文也写得非常清楚,如果这样都有 Braganza 责任,那基本上所有的合约下的条文都有 Braganza 责任。Pelling QC 大法官说:"Whilst I accept that the circumstances in which such terms can be implied into commercial agreements is an incrementally developing area of the law, I consider it clear that one the current state of the authorities, **the Braganza doctrine has no application to unqualified termination provisions within expertly drawn complex commercial agreements between sophisticated commercial parties such as those in this case**. … if a right of the sort being exercised by the claimants in this case was to attract a Braganza qualification, then there is almost no contractual provision that would not attract them. That would have profound implications for English commercial and contract law."(加黑部分是笔者的强调)

Pelling QC 大法官参考了有同样性质案情的 Reda v. Flag Limited (2002) UKPC 38; Lomas v. IFB Firth Rixson (2012) EWCA Civ 419; TSG Building Services Plc v. South Angelia Housing Limited (2013) EWHC 1151 (TCC); IBRC v. Camden Market Holdings Corp (2017) 2 All ER (Comm) 781 等先例,而这些先例都一致判如果合约中有一条明示的终止合约的条文,就应该根据合约行事,不适用 Braganza 责任:"In my judgment these authorities speak with a single voice — where the parties choose to include within their agreement a provision that entitles one or more of the parties to terminate the agreement between them, that cause takes effect in accordance with its terms."

而针对关系合约,Pelling QC 大法官同意有关的联营协议至少可以争辩说是关系合约,但这不表示非经营人根据合约行使权利投票罢免经营人时有默示的善意责任。已经提到,Pelling QC 大法官对合约明示条文的解释是这是绝对与没有约束的权利,因此,在双方已经有清楚无误的明示规定的情况下,不应该用默示善意加以约束。Pelling QC 大法官引用了 Beatson 大法官在 Globe Motors Inc v. TRW LucasVarity Electric Steering Ltd (2016) EWCA Civ 396 先例的说法:"Even in the case of such agreements, however, the position will depend on the terms of the particular contract. … an implication of a duty of good faith will only be possible where the language of the contract, viewed against its context, permits it. It is thus not a reflection of a special rule of interpretation for this category of contract."

2.6.4.6.3 笔者的中国香港特区仲裁案件

笔者近年处理的一个中国香港特区仲裁案件也涉及一方行使裁量权的问题。该案的案情是外国投资银行(以下简称外国投行)与一间在中国内地开设国际学校的教育公司订立股权协议,外国投行购买由教育公司100%控股的项目公司30%的股权,[116]该项目公司直接拥有国际学校与其他教育机构。股权协议中约定外国投行作为买方在教育公司发生违约事件(events of default)或者无法在规定的期限前完成项目公司上市时,有权行使股权的卖出选择权(put option),要求教育公司回购所有外国投行购买的股权。回购的价格是以外国投行购买股权所支付的价款为基础按照年内部回报率25%增长后计算出的金额。作为履约的担保,教育公司将持有的40%的项目公司的股权也质押给外国投行。

后来因为中国内地政府加大对教育行业的监管力度,限制外资进入与禁止教育机构上市,从而令双方合作想要项目公司上市的目的落空。这样,外国投行也不再希望通过上市发财,转而声称教育公司在履行中有发生多项合约约定的违约事件。众所周知,外国投行拟定得投资合约往往是密不透风,一面倒保护自己的利益与埋下不少"地雷",中国公司如果照单全收,是非常危险的。例如合约中会规定很多项违约事件,中国公司难逃有或轻或重的违反,这已足够令外国投行有权按照合约条文的明确规定去行使权利,如终止合约与行使卖出选择权等。

接下来外国投行先将教育公司质押的股权登记到自己名下(因为教育公司在签订股权质押协议时已签好了转股的表格,外国投行私下完成了转让,仲裁庭在仲裁后期才发觉)。在公司层面,外国投行以大股东的身份将教育公司创始人与他的家人从项目公司赶走。接着外国投行进一步启动仲裁要求行使卖出选择权,让教育公司回购这30%的股权。总之,外国投行投资约2亿元人民币,但通过行使一系列的权利后,算总账是可以把价值12亿元的整个教育公司"吞下",而且背后提供个人担保的公司创始人与家人还要欠投行一大笔债。

应该很明显看得出,教育公司质押的40%股权本质上是作为履行回购股权的担保,外国投行在私自实现了担保权益后,不能再进一步行使卖出选择权,要求教育公司回购股权。因为如果仲裁庭允许外国投行行使卖出选择权,外国投行一边以25%内部回报率的价格增长卖出30%的股权给教育公司,而另一边又已经获得项目公司40%的股权。这是最简单的数学计算问题,运用常识即可看出不妥。这也违背了复原的赔偿大原则,令教育公司遭受双重损失,而外国投行双重得利。

教育公司的内地代表律师虽然也看到了问题所在,但因为对英国法不了解,所以并没有提出行使选择权要受Braganza责任的约束,而只是泛泛用常识指出不公平与不合理,且其后缺席没有参与开庭。

---

[116] 教育与地产等行业都对外资有所限制,因此这里与本书第九章之4.7.4段提到的笔者另一个涉及地产行业香港仲裁案件一样,投资银行都通过类似手法钻我国立法的空子。

在后来仲裁庭的合议,笔者的两位共同仲裁员认为合约的条文中写的是外国投行的卖出选择权与其他权利可以"exercisable in its sole discretion",该文字的确是清楚无误的表达出外国投行是完全可以按照他想要的方式去行权。但笔者坚持这些文字是受到 Braganza 责任中善意、不能独断专行、反复无常与不理性地行使合约选择权,这是约束合约权利的大原则,即使是有清楚无误的措辞/文字。

但最后笔者无法说服两位共同仲裁员,其中首席曾经有一点摇摆不定,但最终还是决定由于教育公司的代表律师没有提出,所以不接受仲裁庭主动适用 Braganza 责任。笔者曾经希望仲裁庭同意通过询问制审理主动向双方当事人提出这个 Braganza 责任的问题,并要求双方递交进一步的陈词,但共同仲裁员反对。

最后,笔者只能出具一份不同意见。但因为当事人没有提出 Braganza 责任,所以笔者只能泛泛从合约整体解释的角度说不应该允许投行在教育公司发生违约事件时,同时行使不同合约条文赋予的不同权利而对教育公司造成双重损害。笔者也简略提到在 Braganza v. BP Shipping Ltd(2015)UKSC 17 先例后,行使裁量权或选择权要受 Braganza 责任的约束,即使合约对行权(无论是对质押股权与卖出选择权)写得清楚明确。

2.6.5 英国法律对善意责任的延伸之二:关系合约

可先节录《Chitty on Contracts》(2021 年,第 34 版)一书之 2 - 080 至 2 - 082 段所说如下:

"(cc) **Implied Terms Requiring Good Faith in Commercial Contracts More Generally**

Introduction Since the decision of Leggatt J in Yam Seng Pte Ltd v. International Trade Corp Ltd …, a number of courts at first instance have accepted his suggestion that some commercial contracts (which may be described as 'relational contracts') should contain an implied term requiring good faith in the contracting parties, but other courts at first instance have refused to accept such an implied term in the contract before them. Although, as will be seen, the Court of Appeal has commented on this development, no court higher than the High Court has yet accepted the implication of such a term in a contract on the basis of this particular line of authority.

Yam Seng Pte Ltd In Yam Seng Pte Ltd v. International Trade Corp Ltd, Leggatt J. held, though strictly obiter, that a contract for a license to distribute and for the supply of branded goods contained an implied term of good faith in its performance. The key significance of this implied term in the context was that one of the parties should not **knowingly** providing false information on which the other party was likely to rely. In so holding, Leggatt J recognised that the general view among commentators is that there is no legal principle of good faith of general application, but considered that: '… a duty of good faith is implied by law as an incident of certain categories of contract, for example contracts of employment and contracts between partners or others whose relationship is characterised as a fiduciary one.'

He continued：'I doubt that English law has reached the stage, however, where it is ready to recognise a requirement of good faith as a duty implied by law, even as a default rule, into all commercial contracts. Nevertheless, there seems to me to be no difficulty, following the established methodology of English law for the implication of terms in fact, in implying such a duty in any ordinary commercial contract based on the presumed intention of the parties.' ..."

2.6.5.1 开创关系合约说法的 Yam Seng Pte Ltd v. International Trade Corp Ltd (2013) EWHC 111 (QB) 先例

英国法律在 Yam Seng Pte Ltd v. International Trade Corp Ltd（以下简称 Yam Seng）先例首次提出在一些特殊商业关系的合约强加默示的善意责任。该先例中被告声称自己拥有耐克（Nike）与曼联（Manchester United）的授权，可以出售带有其商标的香氛产品。原告在该陈述下与被告订立了在一些地区免税店独家销售曼联品牌香氛产品的合约。在履约过程中，原告认为被告有多个违约，包括延迟付运与拒绝付运某些产品。原告后来也发现在与被告签订合约时，被告还没有取得曼联的授权，于是原告终止合约并向被告索赔。这种独家经销合约本质上要求合约双方有大量的合作与沟通。所以，Leggatt 大法官以双方在订约时可以假设他们认同是理所当然或异口同声地同意（presumed intention of the parties）这个合约的执行需要有善意或这种商业安排是商业效力所必要的（necessary to give business efficacy to the arrangements），[117] Leggatt 大法官说：

"**What good faith requires is sensitive to context. That includes the core value of honesty**. In any situation it is dishonest to deceive another person by making a statement of fact intending that other person to rely on it while knowing the statement to be untrue. **Frequently, however, the requirements of honesty go further.** For example, if A gives information to B knowing that B is likely to rely on the information and A believes the information to be true at the time it is given but afterwards discovers that the information was, or has since become, false, it may be dishonest for A to keep silent and not to disclose the true position to B. Another example of **conduct falling short of a lie which may, depending on the context, be dishonest is deliberately avoiding giving an answer, or giving an answer which is evasive, in response to a request for information**.

In some contractual contexts the relevant background expectations **may extend further to an expectation that the parties will share information relevant to the performance of the contract such that a deliberate omission to disclose such information may amount to bad faith**. English law has traditionally drawn a sharp distinction between cer-

---

[117] 有关事实默示（implied by fact）要件，可见《合约的解释》一书第七章之 4.4 段。

tain relationships-such as partnership, trusteeship and other fiduciary relationships-on the one hand, in which the parties owe onerous obligations of disclosure to each other, and other contractual relationships in which no duty of disclosure is supposed to operate. Arguably at least, that dichotomy is too simplistic. While it seems unlikely that any duty to disclose information in performance of the contract would be implied where the contract involves a simple exchange, many contracts do not fit this model and **involve a longer term relationship between the parties which they make a substantial commitment**. Such '**relational**' **contracts**, as they are sometimes called, **may require a high degree of communication, cooperation and predictable performance based on mutual trust and confidence and involve expectations of loyalty which are not legislated for in the express terms of the contract but are implicit in the parties' understanding and necessary to give business efficacy to the arrangements**. Examples of such relational contracts might include some joint venture agreements, franchise agreements and long – term distributorship agreements."(加黑部分是笔者的强调)

可以说,长期的联营协议(joint venture agreement)、许可协议(license agreement)或经销协议(distributorship agreement)等就是典型的关系合约(relational contract)。不少这类合约今天已经会加上一条明示的善意条文或进一步说明对合约双方的各种友好合作要求。但看来即使是没有明示条文,也会有默示条文。

这类合约的履行,往往需要双方大量的合作、交往、提供信息与事实等。显然,这一过程不容对信息与事实作出任何"误述"去误导对方,陈述方必须诚实,甚至有全面与坦率的披露责任,否则就会是对善意条文(明示或默示)的违约。而由于在将来的长时间履行会出现各种各样与预期不到的情况或困难,在这种合约下需要双方真心真意为共同目的与双方利益着想才能解决,所以无法以明示条文针对。这样,通过假设双方的订约意图去默示善意,就可以在将来出现问题时,根据不同的环境与情况决定某些言行是否对善意有违约。正如在 Cathay Pacific Airways v. Lufthansa Technik AG(2020)EWHC 1789(Ch)先例中,Kimbell QC 大法官说:"The test for incorporation as a matter of law is whether the contract is a long-term contract which requires the parties to collaborate in future in ways that respects the spirit and the objectives of their joint venture but which the parties have not specified or have been unable to specify in detail, the contract will also involve trust and confidence that each party will act with integrity and co-operatively."

Yam Seng 先例只是一审判决,接下来有很多一审先例也认同,虽然成功被认定为关系合约的案例并不多:见 Hamsard 3147 Ltd(t/a Mini Mode Childrenswear)v. Boots UK Ltd(2013)EWHC 3251(Pat);Bristol Groundschool Ltd v. Intelligent Data Capture Ltd(2014)EWHC 2145(Ch);Acer Investment Management Ltd v. Mansion Group Ltd(2014)EWHC 3011(QB);Carewatch Care Services Ltd v. Focus Caring Services Ltd(2014)EWHC 2313(Ch);D&G Cars Ltd v. Essex Police Authority(2015) EWHC 226(QB);Globe Motors Inc v. TRW LucasVarity Electric Steering Ltd(2016) EWCA Civ 396;National Private Air Transport Services Co(National Air Services)Ltd v. Creditrade LLP(2016)EWHC 2144(Comm);Apollo Window Blinds Ltd v. McNeil (2016)EWHC 2307(QB);Property Alliance Group Ltd v. Royal Bank of Scotland (2016)EWHC 3342(Ch);Astor Management AG v. Atalaya Mining Plc(2017)EWHC 425(Comm);Monde Petroleum SA v. WesternZagros Ltd(2018)EWCA 25;Amey Birmingham v. Birmingham City Council(2018)EWCA Civ 264;Al Nehayan v. Kent (2018)EWHC 333(Comm);UBS AG v. Rose Capital Ventures Ltd(2018)EWHC 3137 (Ch);New Balance Athletics Inc v. Liverpool Football Club and Athletic Grounds Ltd (2019)EWHC 2837(Comm);Bates v. Post Office(2019)EWHC 606(QB);Teesside Gas Transportation Ltd v. CATS North Sea Ltd(2019)EWHC 1220;UTB LLC v. Sheffield United Ltd(2019)EWHC 2322(Ch);Wales(t/a Selective Investment Services)v. CBRE Managed Services Ltd(2020)EWHC 16(Comm);Russell v. Cartwright(2020) EWHC 41(Ch);TAQA Bratani Limited v. Rockrose UKCS8 LLC(2020)EWHC 58 (Comm);Morley(t/a Morley Estates)v. Royal Bank of Scotland Plc(2020)EWHC 88 (Ch);Essex County Council v. UBB Waste(Essex)Ltd(2020)EWHC 1581(TCC);Cathay Pacific Airways v. Lufthansa Technik AG;Candey Ltd v. Bosheh(2022)EWCA Civ 1103;Stobart Capital Limited v. Esken Limited(2022)EWHC 1036(Ch);Perucci v. Orlean Investment Holding Ltd(2022)EWHC 2038 等先例。

Yam Seng 先例看来也在其他普通法管辖的国家或地区开始被接受,如新加坡的 The One Suites v. Pacific Motor Credit(2015)SGCA 21 上诉庭先例或我国香港特区的 Golden Miles Group Holdings v. Jacob & Co(2018)HKCFI 441 先例等。

Yam Seng 先例只是一审,早年由于没有更高的法院判决(上诉庭[118]或最高院),所以法律地位仍难说是肯定/稳定的,期间也有不少学者的争议,例如无需去默示善意,只要通过解释合约也可以解决。所以其他一审法院在审理特定案件时拒绝作出同样的善意责任默示,如 2014 年的 Greenclose Ltd v. National Westminster Bank Plc 先例中,Andrews 大法官说:"… there is no general doctrine of good faith in English contract law and such a term is unlikely to arise by way of necessary implication in a contract between two sophisticated commercial parties negotiating at arms' length."

另在 2016 年的 Globe Motors Inc v. TRW LucasVarity Electric Steering Ltd 上诉庭先例也不像是认同。Beatson 大法官说:"This is not the occasion to consider the poten-

---

[118] 只有一个上诉庭先例提到过,在 Mid Essex Hospital Services NHS Trust v. Compass Group UK and Ireland Ltd(2013)EWCA Civ 200 上诉庭先例中,Jackson 大法官说英国合约法没有善意的说法,但会有一些类别的合约默示有此责任,并以 Yam Seng 先例作为例子。

tial for implied duties of good faith in English law because the question in this case is one of interpretation or construction, and not one of implication."另也提到 Steyn 勋爵在 Total Gas Marketing Ltd v. Arco British Ltd(1998)2 Lloyd's Rep 209 贵族院先例所说："there are no special rules of interpretation applicable to long term contracts of a type that are sometimes called relational contracts. But in an appropriate case:'a court may ... take into account that, by reason of the changing conditions affecting such a contract, a flexible approach may best match the reasonable expectations of the parties. But, as in the case of all contracts, loyalty to the contractual text viewed against its relevant contextual background is the first principle of construction.'"

但在更近期的两个上诉庭先例中，是接受了关系合约的说法：见 2018 年的 Amey Birmingham v. Birmingham City Council 先例与 2022 年的 Candey Ltd v. Bosheh 先例。所以，可以说关系合约的法律地位已经明确。

2.6.5.2　总结认定关系合约的考虑因素的 Bates v. Post Office(2019)EWHC 606(QB)先例

在 Yam Seng 先例后，在不同案例也出现了怎样才会是"关系合约"可去默示善意的争议。一些先例在这方面提供了指引，其中在 Bates v. Post Office 先例中，Fraser 大法官给了 9 个不同的考虑因素并指出除了第一个(合约明示约定去否定)外，其余的 8 个考虑因素都不是决定性，只能说一个关系合约应该会满足好几个考虑因素：

"What then, are the specific characteristics that are expected to be present in order to determine whether a contract between commercial parties ought to be considered a relational contract? I consider the following characteristics are relevant as to whether a contract is a relational one or not:

1. There must be no specific express terms in the contract that prevents a duty of good faith being implied into the contract. [例如在 Cathay Pacific Airways v. Lufthansa Technik AG (2020) EWHC 1789 (Ch)先例有明示条文说明该 10 年的飞机维修合约不是合伙人协议(partnership agreement)[119]或合资协议。合约的条文主要重点在提

---

[119] 在《Lindley and Banks on Partnership》一书说合伙人协议是合约带出的关系(Partnership, although often called a contract, is more accurately described as a relationship **resulting** from a contract)。另说到合伙人关系的三个或四个要件，如涉及商业业务、两位以上合作进行有关业务[但有"幕后合伙人"(sleeping partner)说法]、为了赚取利润与分红："Section 1(1) of the Partnership Act 1890 provides as follows 'Partnership is the relationship which subsists between persons carrying on a business in common with a view of profit.' From this statutory definition it appears that before a partnership can be said to exist, three conditions must be satisfied, ie there must be(1) a business(2) which is carried on by two or more persons in common(3) with 'a view of profit'. Historically, views differed as to whether a fourth condition was also to be imported, namely an agreement to share any profits realized.."上述的粗略介绍是指出如果是合伙人协议就有衡平法下的信义/诚信责任，但一些法律上的要件与商业上如合资合约不容易区分。例如有说法是一个区分是合伙人的"业务"(business)会是重复(如律师或会计师的业务)，但合资合约通常只针对一个具体的目标，但这种区分就比较模糊了。所以在一些合资合约，只有大股东小股东，也可以是以合伙人协议合作，特别是大股东不想被强制诚信责任，就会有像 Cathay Pacific Airways v. Lufthansa Technik AG(2020)EWHC 1789(Ch)先例中一样去特别明示说明并非合伙人协议。

供的服务、标准、收取的费用与调整等,不是原告与被告之间的关系。一旦有明示条文就排除了默示地位。]

2. The contract will be a long - term one, with the mutual intention of the parties being that there will be a long - term relationship. [合约是长期合约,并且双方的共同意愿是建立长期关系。但合约仅是长期不足以构成关系合约,如在一些历史悠久与经常发生诉讼的行业中订立的合约,如租船合约(charter - party)或付运买卖合约(shipment sales contract)等,即使是长期,也不大可能被视为关系合约。如果这种合约(如供应合约)的合约方是比较重视长远关系的亚洲人,怕将来在履行时因为短期利益(例如市场波动)发生对抗、取巧与/或不合作,而更希望双方开诚布公坦率合作解决问题,可加上一条明示善意条文。]

3. The parties must intend that their respective roles be performed with integrity, and with fidelity to their bargain. (合约方应是希望双方在履约时正直与忠诚。)

4. The parties will be committed to collaborating with one another in the performance of the contract. (合约双方在履行合约时会是要相互协作。)

5. The spirits and objectives of their venture may not be capable of being expressed exhaustively in a written contract. (合约双方商业合作的精神与目的无法用文书合约充分与全面地表达。)

6. They will each repose trust and confidence in one another, but of a different kind to that involved in fiduciary relationships. (合约双方都要相互信任与有信心去依靠对方,但不等同于诚信关系。)

7. The contract in question will involve a high degree of communication, co - operation and predictable performance based on mutual trust and confidence, and expectations of loyalty. (有关合约会涉及大量通讯往来与合作,根据相互的信任与信心可预期合约的履行,也期望相互忠心。)

8. There may be a degree of significant investment by one party (or both) in the venture. This significant investment may be, in some cases, more accurately described as substantial financial commitment. (会涉及一方或合约双方的重大投资或金钱上的承诺。)

9. Exclusivity of the relationship may also be present. (会涉及独有的特权,例如对某产品专卖权。)

I hesitate to describe this as an exhaustive list. No single one of the above list is determinative, with the exception of the first one. This is because if the express terms prevent the implication of a duty of good faith, then that will be the end of the matter. However, many of these characteristics will be found to be present where a contract is a relational one. In other cases on entirely different facts, it may be that there are other features which I have not identified above which are relevant to those cases."

Bates v. Post Office 先例的 9 个考虑因素也在后来的先例被引用,如近期的

Wales(t/a Selective Investment Services) v. CBRE Managed Services Ltd(2020) EWHC 16(Comm); Stobart Capital Limited v. Esken Limited(2022) EWHC 1036(Ch); Perucci v. Orlean Investment Holding Ltd(2022) EWHC 2038 等先例。

2.6.5.3 对关系合约的小结

可对目前已经报道的关系合约的大量先例作出一些小结说:

1. 已经说过,成功被接受为关系合约的案例并不多,正如在 Candey Ltd v. Bosheh (2022) EWCA Civ 1103 上诉庭先例中,Coulson 大法官说:"there has been something of an avalanche of Claimant's in recent years trying to show that the contract into which they seek to imply the term is a relational contract, thereby bringing with it the implied obligation of good faith. Only a relatively few have succeeded. ... it might be said that the elusive concept of good faith should not be used to avoid orthodox and clear principles of English contract law."

2. 即使成功去默示善意责任,被认定违反善意的案例也往往是涉及极端的应受谴责的行为。例如在本章之 2.7.4.3 段介绍的 Al Nehayan v. Kent(2018) EWHC 333 (Comm)先例中,原告代表就威胁被告说不拿出钱来会见血。在 Bates v. Post Office (2019) EWHC 606(QB)先例中,案情涉及英国邮政丑闻,在 2000 年至 2014 年间因为新投入使用的电子会计系统有漏洞,导致英国邮政错误起诉全国各地 736 名邮政支局长监守自盗并被定罪。真相被曝光后,被认为是英国司法系统有史以来最大冤案,此先例就是 550 名邮政支局长向英国邮政起诉索赔。在 Bristol Groundschool Ltd v. Intelligent Data Capture Ltd(2014) EWHC 2145(Ch)先例中,原告与被告合作制作与销售商业飞行员的培训教材。在合约到期前,原告未经被告同意"黑入"被告的电脑系统下载电子文件,并在合约结束之后用在自己的培训教材上。在 D&G Cars Ltd v. Essex Police Authority(2015) EWHC 226(QB)先例中,原告与被告警局订立车辆回收合约,其中对处理回收车辆的程序有规定,包括部分车辆必须销毁以保证任何一部分都不会用在别的车上。但原告没有按规定销毁一辆车,还换了车牌与车辆的外壳伪装成其他车辆。

这些极端受谴责的行为,即使不是违反善意责任(因为没有默示),也可以根据其他的诉因如本书第十章之 12.2 段介绍的恐吓侵权(tort of intimidation)提起索赔或其他救济。

3. 对善意责任的默示本质上是法律或事实的默示(implied by law or by fact)在一审判决的层次看来仍有不同说法。照说只去适用或默示在关系合约这种类别合约,更接近是法律的默示。这在 UTB LLC v. Sheffield United Ltd(2019) EWHC 2322 (Ch)先例中有支持的观点,Fancourt 大法官是说:"... a later judgment of Leggatt LJ (sitting at first instance), ... Al Nehayan v Kent ... In that case, an oral joint venture had been agreed relating to the acquisition and operation of hotels, and part of the business was later demerged under a rudimentary framework agreement. The express terms were

very limited, and yet the joint venture had been intended as a long – term collaboration requiring the cooperation and commitment of both parties. It was based on a strong personal friendship between them. ... Leggatt LJ held that implication of an obligation to act in good faith was essential to give effect to the reasonable expectations of the parties, i. e. the term was implied in fact on the conventional approach. The contract was of course a 'relational' contract, and **Leggatt LJ held that the term would also have been implied as a matter of law, given the nature of the contract**."(加黑部分是笔者的强调)

另在 Cathay Pacific Airways v. Lufthansa Technik AG(2020)EWHC 1789(Ch)先例中,Kimbell QC 大法官也同意说:"... it is equally clear that Leggatt LJ was contemplating that **a good faith term may be implied as a matter of law in some relational contracts.** I reject CX's submission that this is a questionable proposition of law. Like Fancourt J. it seems to me that the type of contract in which that will be so will be ones in which the parties have not only entered into a long – term collaborative relationship but crucially where they have not specified(or have been unable to specify) in detail the terms governing their relationship."

但在 Russell v. Cartwright(2020)EWHC 41(Ch)先例中,Falk 大法官认为是事实的默示,说:"... rather than trying to identify first whether a contract is a 'relational contract' and for that reason includes an obligation of good faith, the better starting point ... is the application of the conventional tests for the implication of contractual terms, as authoritatively restated by Lord Neuberger in Marks and Spencer Plc v. BNP Paribas Securities Services Trust Co(Jersey)Ltd(2015)3 WLR 1843.[120] ... that is whether a reasonable reader would consider that an obligation of good faith was obviously meant, or the obligation was essential to the proper working of the contract since it would otherwise lack commercial or practical coherence(the business efficacy test)."

而 Sir William Blair 大法官主导的名为"Duties of Good Faith in Wholesale Financial Contracts"报告中之 5.2.1.1 段也认为是事实的默示:"For most contracts, a duty of good faith can only be implied if it meets the strict tests for the implication of terms in fact, set out in Marks & Spencer plc v BNP Paribas Securities Services Trust Company (Jersey)Ltd [2015] UKSC 72. Amongst other things, this means that the implied term must be so obvious that 'it goes without saying' or be necessary for business efficacy such that the contract would lack commercial or practical coherence without it ..."

但总而言之,既然是默示地位,就可以明示条文去超越。(1)在一份拟定得好的合约,清楚无误地全面针对了合约履行时会出现的方方面面问题,那就没有什么可以默示的了,特别是事实的默示。而即使是法律默示善意责任也起不了作用。可以从

---

〔120〕 见笔者《合约的履行、弃权与禁反言》一书第四章之 5.1 段。

先例中看到，要默示的关系合约往往写得很简单，例如 Yam Seng 先例与 Al Nehayan v. Kent 先例。(2)可以以明示条文排除善意的默示。当然在谈判一份长达 10 年、15 年的合约中，试图加入一条明示条文说明不适用善意或不是关系合约可能不现实。可以参考 Cathay Pacific Airways v. Lufthansa Technik AG 先例，或在个别一两个特别事项说明只在这方面适用善意责任，又或是给"善意"一个十分局限的定义。

4. 要小心不要乱主张善意责任，这会带来诉讼费用的惩罚。在有关一个长达 25 年的融资、建造、运营垃圾处理厂的合约 Essex County Council v. UBB Waste(Essex) Ltd(No. 3)(2020) EWHC 2387(TCC)先例中，Pepperall 大法官判主张善意责任失败的被告要承担"补偿基础"(indemnity basis)[121]的费用："Since questions of good faith are likely to be fact sensitive, it is difficult for a court to weed out hopeless allegations before trial. ... In my judgment, it is important ... that parties realise that they cannot make unjustifiable allegations of a lack of good faith with impunity. While I do not equate the allegations in this case with fraud, I nevertheless conclude that UBB's(主张原告违反善意责任作为抗辩但败诉的被告)conduct in making widespread allegations of a lack of good faith against the Authority(原告)and its officers without any proper foundation was 'out of the norm' and, of itself, justifies an order for costs on the indemnity basis."

2.6.6　对善意原则的总结

对适用英国法(或更正确地说是普通法，可包括我国香港特区、新加坡等)的国际商业合约，去默示一个一般性的善意原则是好是坏或是中性，笔者的看法是无所谓。关键仍是把合约订好，针对会在履行时出问题的方方面面，争取对己方有利的规定，以合约条文方式把风险分摊给对方。这样，将来有了争议，对方去求助于善意原则(如果有默示)，也是徒劳。因为清楚无误的明示与特定条文肯定超越默示地位，也对实际情况更有针对性，如较早介绍的船舶保险的 International Hull Clauses(01/11/03)的第 45 条文。只有在一份简单的合约，好像是 Yam Seng 先例中的合约，默示的一般性善意原则(如果有)才会有用武之地。

笔者也相信今天的国际商业活动，大部分的主流行业是英美(帝国)在过去两三百年建立与完善起来的。期间不断遇到问题，都在通过法律(普通法与立法)的发展去解决。虽然这个演变与完善的过程还在不断持续，但可以说商人在今天的国际商业活动中遇到的方方面面的问题，只要熟读普通法，其中 99% 都可以找到或推算出答案。这样如果善意原则从来没有在英国法下落地生根与发展起来，只要今天同样的国际商业活动仍是在持续，就表示这个原则即使在英国法下被接受，也只会是可有可无。

英国法或今天更适宜称为是普通法，虽然没有接受善意原则，但不表示就非黑即白地纵容恶意。法律只是配合现实去有针对性与精准地在无数不同方面弘扬善意或

---

[121] 见笔者《仲裁法：从开庭准备到裁决书的作出与执行》一书第一章之 5.4.3.2 段。

公平合理的精神。例如针对合约法的部分:

1. 本书第十一章介绍了在衡平法下可去撤销因不当影响(undue influence)产生的合约与不合情理交易(unconscionable bargain);本书第一至四章介绍的可诉误述(actionable misrepresentation)、第七章介绍的可诉错误(actionable mistake)与第十章介绍胁迫(duress),如果成立,可去撤销有关合约等。

2. 在笔者的《合约的解释:规则与应用》一书详细介绍了解释合约的精神与解释规则(rules of construction)。其中包括:解释合约的结果要尽量从客观看合理(假设双方是希望达成一个公平合理的合约);合约的默示条文(法律或事实)一定要合理;如果合约双方的订约意图确实是一个不合理结果,就必须在明示条文(如免责条文)中把这意图写得清楚无误才会被支持;法律默示合约双方必须相互给予协助/合作让对方顺利履行合约与任何合约方不能通过自己的过错获利等。

3. 在接下来的本章之2.7段会介绍有一些特殊的合约关系被解释为合约一方与另一方有"信义/诚信关系"(fiduciary relationship),这是有比善意责任更高的要求。另也有其他特殊类别的合约关系默示了善意责任,如保险、合伙人等。

4. 笔者的《合约的履行、弃权与禁反言》一书介绍了弃权(waiver)、各种不同的禁反言(estoppel)等说法,防止在合约履行时合约一方误导或出尔反尔,令对方蒙受不利或损害而造成不公平。

5. 在 Braganza v. BP Shipping Ltd(2015)UKSC 17 最高院先例后,在英国已经有超过50个先例依从;另有我国香港特区的 FWD Life Insurance Co(Bermuda)Ltd v. Poon Cindy (2019) HKCA 697; Chok Kin Ming v. Equal Opportunities Commission (2019) HKCFI 755; Global Gaming Philippines LLC v. Deutschmark Bank AG, HK Branch(2019)HKCFI 405; Invest Gain Ltd v. Novel Good Ltd(2019)HKCFI 1633; Pa Sam Nang v. The Hongkong and Shanghai Banking Corporation Ltd(2016)HKCFI 409等先例;新加坡的 Leiman, Ricardo v. Noble Resources Ltd(2018)SGHC 166 等先例;澳大利亚的 Mineralogy Pty Ltd v. Sino Iron Pty Ltd(No. 6)(2015)FCA 825, 329 ALR 1; Bartlett v. Australia & New Zealand Banking Corp Ltd(2016)NSWCA 30 等先例;新西兰的 Peregrine Estate Ltd v. Hay(2017)NZCA 496; Wellington City Council v. Local Government Mutual Funds Trustee Ltd(2017)NZHC 2901; Sharma v. Air New Zealand Ltd(2020)NZHC 230 等先例;牙买加的 Williamson v. Port Authority of Jamaica(2019) JMCA Civ 8 先例;斐济的 Fiji Times Ltd v. Solicitor General(2016)FJHC 548 先例。所以可以说普通法系已经针对性地确立了所有类别的合约在行使会影响对方合约方的裁量权或选择权时,具备善意与诚实,有不得独断专行(arbitrarily)、反复无常(capriciously)或不合理(unreasonably)情形的所谓"理性测试"(rational test)或 Braganza 责任。

可见,再去引入一般性的善意原则(general good faith principle),在"商场如战场"的背景下要求唯利是图的商人在商业交易与合约关系要"做好人",只是一个抽象、笼统、概括的大道理,实际作用不大。

另有几个现实方面问题:

1. 肯定与可预测的法律是对社会大众最公平的法律。朝令夕改是最可怕的,虽然这朝令夕改的决策人[在这里就是在“棕榈树公正”(Palm tree justice)下的审理法官了]肯定是真心实意认为自己是以该案件的特定案情,根据善意原则(双方都要做好人)去公平合理作出决定,如判所有说得出名堂的损失都是一人一半。但在决定的过程中,他可能既没有追究损失是谁的责任(这要看合约怎样分摊风险),也没有计算损失(这要看损失遥远性,如可否合理预见与因果关系等复杂的问题)。引入善意作为一般性与超越性原则就会有此危险。

“公平合理”虽然是大家都挂在口边的,但无法去准确定义,而是根据不同案件的案情各有不同。这在 Waaler v. Hounslow London Borough Council(2017)EWCA Civ 45 上诉庭先例中,Lewiston 大法官说:“the open textured nature of a test of reasonableness makes it dangerous even to attempt to be prescriptive. Factual situations are almost infinitely variable, and different considerations will come into play in different circumstances. Parliament has deliberately chosen an open ended and flexible test, and has left all factual determinations to the good sense ...”

肯定与可预测对国际商业合约尤其重要,毕竟很多是价值高昂与具有较长期限的。这种合约(如长期供货合约/买卖合约)经常会在履行过程中发生争议,需要以诉讼或仲裁方式去解决。如果适用的法律崇向与高调主张“善意”与公平合理原则,但没有细节,那么不管合约有没有约定或如何约定,会在每次大同小异的案情(如每次供货有或多或少的货损货差)下,因不同审理法官在善意原则下的自由发挥而得出不同结果。如虽然上一次是判损失一人一半,但下一次又判供货方不必赔偿。因为市场已经是货物短缺与价格高涨,供货方仍努力准时供货,收货方捡了大便宜等。从善意/公平合理的角度考虑,虽然有小小货差,但供货方已有极大诚意,所以不应该支持收货方仍去斤斤计较向供货方索赔损失。

国际商人不像一般社会大众,他们可以实际行为来投票,在他们的合约中去选择一套被视为肯定与可预测的合约适用法(governing law)。

2. 英国 Jackson 大法官在他 2017 年的“Does Good Faith Have Any Role in Construction Contracts?”一文中提到另一个重要考虑,就是一份商业合约或工程合约通常会涉及很多第三人参与履行,如承建商与分承建商的大量雇员。他们都没有参与工程合约的订立,但他们都必须要知道合约需要做什么或不允许做什么。他们只能去严格按照合约在文字上的规定,而不理会(也不知道)合约背后涉及的善意原则会涉及的“伦理”(ethics)或“形而上学”(metaphysics):“There is generally no reason to imply such a nebulous provision of little utility. There is also a wider consideration. A large number of individuals, who had nothing to do with drawing up the contract, have to operate in accordance with its provisions. Some may be employees of the building owner or

contractor. Others may be outsiders, such as certifiers or measurers or subcontractors. They all need to know what the contract requires and what the contract permits. To that end, they do not speculate about ethics or metaphysics. ... They look at the black letter provisions of the contract. That is what the court should do as well."

3. 行使合约裁量权、选择权或权利明示受善意约束，从本章之 2.6.4 段简单的介绍中就可以看到这会带来不确定，甚至是混乱。例如，对善意的最低标准也无法有共识，更谈不上如何划出一条分水岭/红线。所以在大量的先例中都可以看到判决上诉后被推翻的情况，包括 Braganza v. BP Shipping Ltd 最高院先例，还有诸如 Mid Essex Hospital Services NHS Trust v. Compass Group UK and Ireland Ltd (2013) EWCA Civ 200; Evangelou v. McNicol (2016) EWCA Civ 817; IBM UK Holdings Ltd v. Dalgleish & Ors (2017) EWCA Civ 1212; Equitas Insurance Ltd v. Municipal Mutual Insurance Ltd (2019) EWCA Civ 718; Compound Photonics Group Ltd, Re (2022) EWCA Civ 1371 等先例。

2.7 信义/诚信关系(fiduciary relationship)

英国法律很早以前就有了信义/诚信关系(fiduciary relationship)的说法。首先去解释什么是诚信关系这个衡平法规定(rule of equity)，这可节录《Chitty on Contracts》(2021 年，第 34 版)一书之 9 - 097 段所说如下："The fiduciary or confidential relationship necessary to bring this doctrine into operation extends to certain obvious ties, such as those between trustee and cestui que trust, solicitor and client, and parent and child. **But the courts have not fettered their jurisdiction by defining its limits, and are ready to interfere in order to protect the person who is under the influence of another.**"(加黑部分是笔者的强调)

在英国法律中，诚信关系可以说是一面倒对委托人/信托人(trustor)十分有利，但对受托人(trustee)就十分严格。这不只是合约的善意或疏忽侵权的小心谨慎责任，诚信关系的主要特点是受托人必须对信托人尽"效忠"/忠实(loyalty)的责任，正如 Millett 大法官在 Bristol and West Building Society v. Mothew (1998) Ch. 1 先例中说："**The distinguishing obligation of a fiduciary is the obligation of loyalty. The principal is entitled to the single-minded loyalty of his fiduciary**. This core liability has several facts. A fiduciary must act in good faith; he must not make a profit out of his trust; **he may not act for his own benefit** or the benefit of a third person without the informed consent of his principal."(加黑部分是笔者的强调)

另节录加拿大最高院的 Norberg v. Wynrib (1992) 2 SCR 226 先例中，McLachlin 大法官所说："In negligence and contract, the parties are taken to be independent and equal actors, concerned primarily with their own self - interest. ... The essence of a fiduciary relationship, by contrast, is that one party exercises power on behalf of another and pledges himself or herself to act in the best interests of the other. ... The fiduciary relationship has trust, not self – interest at its core ..."

基本上这种诚信关系是一方会受另一方的不当影响（undue influence），[122]往往是受益人/信托人自己无法充分（即使是有合约关系）保障自己的利益而完全依靠受托人去真心真意保护他/她的利益，受托人就在衡平法下被禁止滥用信托人的信心。诚信关系带来的责任要求受托人"无保留、全心全意与专一的效忠"（undivided, exclusive and single – minded loyalty），这无私与效忠的要求也带来受托人必须善意、小心谨慎与避免利益冲突（duty to avoid conflict of interest）的责任。正如 Tate v. Williams（1866）LR 2 Ch. App. 55 先例的名言如下："Wherever two persons stand in such a relation that, while it continues, confidence is necessarily reposed by one, and the influence which naturally grows out of that confidence is possessed by the other, and this confidence is abused, or the influence is exerted to obtain an advantage at the expense of the confiding party, the person so availing himself of his position will not be permitted to retain the advantage, although the transaction could not have been impeached if no such confidential relation had existed."

诚信关系也是存在于一些涉及"信任与信心"（trust and confidence）的关系，这会是父母与子女、合伙人、公司与董事（私人或上市公司）、律师与客户、信托人与受托人、代理人与委托人、[123]破产管理人/清盘人与债权人等之间的关系。甚至近期连出庭作证的专家证人（expert witness）也涉及是否对委任方的客户有一个诚信责任。[124]

2.7.1 诚信关系的例子：公司董事的诚信关系与责任

在很多已经是公认的诚信关系中，对诚信责任的大原则/大精神虽然一致，但因为关系不同，所以各有各的特点，去详谈每一个领域是需要另一本甚至几本书。所以本书只挑公司董事的诚信责任简单介绍，相信我国内地读者也会觉得有兴趣。毕竟今天中国公司与/或自然人对适用英国法的英属维尔京群岛（British Virgin Island, BVI）或开曼群岛（Cayman Islands）公司不会觉得陌生。在一些内地禁止或限制外商投资的行业中，中国公司要想取得海外融资就需要通过搭建可变利益实体［Various Interest Entity（VIE），又称协议控制］的公司架构去实现。考虑到税收与各种中国内地的政策法规，这种公司架构常见的形式是：第一层海外融资的主体往往是 BVI 公

---

〔122〕 这个课题会在本书第十一章之 1 段介绍。

〔123〕 代理人的言行会严重影响委托人的合法权利：见 Bristol and West Building Society v. Mothew（1998）Ch. 1 上诉庭先例等。

〔124〕 见 A Company v. X, Y, Z（2020）EWHC 809（TCC）；Secretariat Consulting Pte Ltd, Secretariat International UK Ltd, Secretariat Advisors LLC v. A Company（2021）EWCA Civ 6 等先例。这个问题英国法院以前没有面对过，但不在此多讨论。如果专家证人对客户有忠诚的诚信责任，那么会与在 CPR 下对法院的责任有严重矛盾。但也有说法认为这是可以协调的矛盾，例如代表律师也是对客户有诚信责任，但同时在证据方面是法院的官员，顶多是专家证人对法院的责任更多更高，必须提供独立与客观的专业意见。看来，这方面的法律仍会有发展。

司或开曼公司；而 BVI 公司或开曼公司再全资控股我国香港公司；我国香港公司再全资控股一家在我国境内设立的外商独资公司（Wholly Foreign Owned Enterprise, WFOE）；而 WFOE 再通过与真正在中国境内运营与赚钱的公司的所有股东签订一系列的协议，包括股权质押、独家购买权协议、股东表决权委托协议、独家技术咨询服务协议、商标许可协议、软件使用许可协议、配偶同意函等，来达到通过协议实际控制该中国境内实体运营的公司的结果。在该 VIE 架构下，真正重要的公司就是第一层负责海外融资的公司与在中国境内实体运营的公司，而其他层级的公司只是在税收与政策上的考虑下才设立，中国实体运营公司的创始人也是 BVI 公司或开曼公司的股东。在经营中，一旦股东之间在权益分配上发生争议，中方当事人无可避免要在第一层公司下解决，这就需要知悉以英国法为基础的 BVI 公司法或开曼公司法。

针对公司董事的诚信责任，英国公司法［《Companies Act 2006》之 S. 170（3）］将公司董事责任置于普通法与衡平法下去立法，要求公司董事作为受托人必须只为公司的利益着想，并在 S. 170（2）说明即使是辞去公司董事的职务，仍受到必须回避利益冲突与不得接受第三方好处的约束。

诚信关系带来的责任对公司董事在很多方面的细节都有要求，例如不得在没有披露与授权（如公司章程允准）下获取个人利益、避免关联交易、不参与有利益冲突的董事会决议、不能与公司做出任何在业务上的竞争等。这在《Companies Act 2006》之 S. 175"Duty to avoid conflicts of interest"有立法规定。另也表现在不得使用作为公司董事而获取的信息或地位为自己谋利或创造机会，如非法的内幕交易或收取佣金等。这在《Companies Act 2006》之 S. 176"Duty not accept benefits from third parties"有立法规定。但即使表面看来并非这样极端，是合法的且对公司并没有造成任何损失的，例如公司决定不插手的业务或订立的合约，董事自己觉得不错而事后插手或订立，甚至是辞去董事的职务才去跟进，也仍是法律不允许的：见 Industrial Development Consultants v. Cooley（1972）1 WLR 443；CMS Dolphin Ltd v. Simonet（2001）EWHC Ch 415 等先例。立法之 S. 175（2）也规定说："This applies in particular to the exploitation of any property, information or opportunity（and it is immaterial whether the company could take advantage of the property, information or opportunity）."

以上所讲的方方面面的诚信责任，都是严格责任，不只是诚实与善意就足够满足的。在 Regal（Hastings）v. Gulliver（1967）2 AC 134 贵族院先例中，Russell 勋爵说利用诚信关系赚钱的受托人，即使不涉及欺诈与是善意，也仍要交出获取的利润："The rule of equity which insists on those, who by use of a fiduciary position make a profit, being liable to account for that profit, in no way depends on fraud, or absence of bona fides; or upon such questions or considerations as whether the profit would or should otherwise have gone to the plaintiff, or whether he took a risk or as he did for the benefit of the plaintiff, or whether the plaintiff has in fact been damaged or benefitted by his decision. The liability arises from the mere fact of a profit having … been made. The profiteer, however honest and well – intentioned, cannot escape the risk of being called upon to account."

此处不是去讨论公司法,只在以下多举几个相关先例。

2.7.1.1 确认公司董事是受托人的早期先例:Aberdeen Railway Co v. Blocky Brothers(1854)1 Macq. 461

早在 Aberdeen Railway Co v. Blocky Brothers 先例中,判决提要(headnote)介绍说:"**The director** of a railway company **is a trustee**, and, as such, is precluded from dealing, on behalf of the company, with himself, or with a firm of which he is a partner."(加黑部分是笔者的强调)

另可节录 Cranworth 勋爵在该先例解释说公司法人通过代理人(也就是公司董事)才能操作,也必须有这些代理人的效忠、善意与小心谨慎才能保障公司利益,进而间接保护股东利益(私人公司会是有限人数的大股东、小股东,上市公司就会涉及广大民众,更是事关重大):"A corporate body can only act by agents, and it is of course the duty of those agents so to act as best to promote the interests of the corporation whose affairs they are conducting. Such agents have duties to discharge of a fiduciary nature towards their principal, and it is a rule of universal application that no one having such duties to discharge shall be allowed to enter into engagements in which he has, or can have, a personal interest conflicting, or which possibly may conflict, with the interests of those whom he is bound to protect."

2.7.1.2 确认公司董事对股东没有诚信责任的近期先例:Sharp v. Blank(2015) EWHC 3220(Ch)

在 Sharp v. Blank 先例中,案情涉及 Lloyds 银行收购 Halifax Bank of Scotland Plc(以下简称 HBOS)与相关的资产重组。该收购与资产重组是需要 Lloyds 银行的股东批准。股东声称 Lloyds 银行的董事建议收购与资产重组是符合他们的最佳利益,在提供误导性的信息与隐瞒了 HBOS 真正的财务情况的基础上获得股东的批准,违反了对股东的诚信责任与其他责任。此先例主要争议之一是作为被告的董事对股东是否有诚信责任。

Nugee 大法官首先总结了这方面的法律地位,也就是董事毋庸置疑对公司有诚信责任,但一般对股东没有诚信责任:

"The general principles are well established:

(1) The directors of a company owe fiduciary duties to the company. This is unexceptionable and flows from the fact that the directors are agents of the company and stewards of its affairs. .... the fiduciary duties owed by directors to the company 'arise from the relationship between the directors and the company directed and controlled by them'; it is the fact that they are directors of the company's affairs which by itself gives rise to their fiduciary duties.(公司董事对公司有诚信责任,没有例外情况。因为公司董事是

公司的代理人与公司事务的管理者,领导与控制公司,作为公司董事就难逃对公司有诚信责任。)

(2)But in general the directors do not, solely by virtue of their office of director, owe fiduciary duties to the shareholders, collectively or individually….(但一般来说,董事对股东,无论是股东个人或是整个股东集体都没有诚信责任。)

(3)The general principle that directors do not owe fiduciary duties to shareholders has also been said to be supported by a number of policy considerations. … only the company, not its members, can sue for wrongs done to the company …, and the principle that where a wrong has been done to a company, individual shareholders are not able to sue for losses which are merely derivative or reflective … this is of course not a complete explanation as some losses claimed by shareholders go beyond merely reflective loss(as indeed in the present case). … if the directors owed fiduciary duties to the shareholders they would be liable to harassing actions by minority shareholders, and exposed to a multiplicity of actions, each shareholder having his own personal claim. … it was important that directors are not over – exposed to the risk of multiple legal actions by dissenting minority shareholders. … to hold that a director owed some sort of general fiduciary duty to shareholders would involve placing an unfair, unrealistic and uncertain burden on a director, and would present him frequently with a position where his duty to shareholders would be in conflict with his undoubted duty to the company…[这有公共政策的考虑。首先只有公司(而不是公司股东)有权以公司的名义起诉做出错误行为的人士(这包括董事、高管与第三人)并索赔损失。至于股东对公司董事提起派生诉讼或索赔反映损失,可见本章下一段的介绍。如果董事对股东有诚信责任,无可避免会面对很多不同意公司决定的少数意见的股东的起诉,如一宗关联交易。这无疑是对董事的滋扰,也让董事承担了不公平、不现实与不肯定的责任。更不用说,如果董事对股东有诚信责任,就可能与对公司的诚信责任起冲突。因为诚信责任是要将信托方的利益摆在第一位,如果股东与公司都是信托方,而部分股东的利益与公司的利益不一致,就会有问题。]

(4)…**the general principle that directors do not owe fiduciary duties to their shareholders is confirmed by Peskin v. Anderson [2000] EWCA Civ 326 and is not in doubt.**"(加黑部分是笔者的强调)

Nugee 大法官接着说,要在董事与股东之间成立诚信责任,双方之间必须存在特殊关系(special relationship)。仅仅是董事比股东对公司事务知道得更多,或是董事的行为会对股东造成影响并不够。一般来说,要成立这种特殊关系,董事与股东之间必须有一些私人关系(比如家族企业中的亲戚关系),或是有特定的交易或安排。Nugee 大法官所说可节录如下:"I take it therefore to be established law, binding on me, that although a director of a company can owe fiduciary duties to the company's shareholders, he does not do so by the mere fact of being a director, but only where there is on the facts of the particular case a 'special relationship' between the director and the shareholders. It seems to me to follow that this special relationship must be something over and above the usual relationship that any director of a company has with its shareholders. It is not enough that the director, as a director, has more knowledge of the company's affairs than the shareholders have; since they direct and control the company's affairs this will almost inevitably be the case. Nor is it enough that the actions of the directors will have the potential to affect the shareholders-again this will always, or almost always, be the case. On the decided cases the sort of relationship that has given rise to a fiduciary duty has been where there has been some personal relationship or particular dealing or transaction between them."

Nugee 大法官判在此先例的案情下,董事与股东之间不存在特殊关系,董事对股东不存在诚信责任。

也就是说,一般情况下公司董事与股东之间没有任何关系,无论是合约关系还是诚信关系。当然这不代表公司董事对股东没有任何责任,在此先例的被告接受他们有向股东提供足够信息的责任(sufficient information duty),让股东有足够的信息对收购与重组作出知情决定。但这是出于公平与满足公司章程的规定,而不是因为对股东效忠,不属于诚信责任。

2.7.1.3　股东以公司董事违反诚信责任提起诉讼的例外

任何人为的社会科学的规则都难免要有例外,因为在各种各样的不同情况,硬性划一地适用一条规则总会带来不公平、不现实或违反公共政策的情况。当然这种例外不能有太多,否则规则就不再是规则,也失去了肯定性与稳定性。所以,例外不能为个别或少数案件开门,即使在该特殊与个别的案情看来,硬性使用有关规则并不公平。

以下介绍几种公司董事只对公司有诚信责任,但对股东没有责任的例外情况。

2.7.1.3.1　派生诉讼

公司股东的派生诉讼(derivative action)是公司的一位或多位股东(一般是小股东)代表公司起诉。被诉的对象一般是董事会成员、执行董事或高管,常见的让股东开始派生诉讼的原因包括:执行董事、董事总经理或其他董事会成员违反诚信责任,公司内部人士的行为是为了他们自己的最佳利益而不是公司的最佳利益,公司的非法、欺诈活动,内部高管利益与公司冲突,内部交易,财务问题(如误导或错误的财务报表),高管薪酬不当,内部高管的行为引起证券交易所(Securities and Exchange Commission, SEC)或司法部(Department of Justice)的调查等。派生诉讼存在的必要是公司董事、高管或控股股东不会代表公司起诉他们自己,所以只能是小股东在公司利益受损时以派生诉讼的形式代表公司起诉。如果胜诉,获得的赔偿也是归公司而不是起诉的小股东所有。

这种争议也可以发生在各种各样的情况中,例如笔者遇见过一个仲裁案件是一间公司C的大股东A在一个增资扩股协议下把大部分股权转让给B,于是B成为了C的大股东并控制C。但在增资扩股协议下,B要向C注资,但B在获得股权后并没有支付全部的股权转让款让C有钱解除A曾经为C向银行作出的个人担保。虽然C也是增资扩股协议的一方当事人,但显然在B的控制下,C是不会启动对B的诉讼,要求强制执行或赔偿损失的。这样,A要自己启动一个诉讼,而申请的救济是要B支付股权转让款给C。这虽然是一个合约诉讼/仲裁,但有派生诉讼的味道,双方之间的争议也正是派生诉讼的法律问题。

2.7.1.3.2 反映损失/反射损失

如果公司发生丑闻股价大跌甚至面临破产,代表公司提起派生诉讼可能对股东来说意义不大。一是清盘人可能自己会提起诉讼,这就不需要股东提起派生诉讼。更重要的是,派生诉讼拿回的钱属于公司,由所有债权人分,股东很可能"为人作嫁衣",所以其更希望以个人的身份向董事起诉。

Prudential Assurance v. Newman Industries(No. 2)(1982)1 Ch 204 上诉庭先例定下了这"反映损失/反射损失"(reflective loss)原则,也就是个别股东不能向犯错与对公司违反诚信责任的董事索赔他们的个人损失[避免双重赔偿(double recovery)、对所有股东与其他债权人公平对待等原因]的说法:"But what he(个别股东)cannot do is to recover damages merely because the company in which he is interested has suffered damage. He cannot recover a sum equal to the diminution in the market value of his shares, or equal to the likely diminution in dividend, because such a 'loss' is merely a reflection of the loss suffered by the company. ... The shareholder does not suffer any personal loss. His only 'loss' is through the company, in the diminution in value of the net assets of the company ... The plaintiff's shares are merely a right of participation in the company on the terms of the article of association. The shares themselves, his right of participation, are not directly affected by the wrongdoing. the plaintiff still holds all the shares as his own absolutely unencumbered property."

接下来在 Johnson v. Gore Wood(2002)2 AC 1 贵族院先例中,Bingham 勋爵明确了这原则:"(1) Where a company suffers loss caused by a breach of duty(指诚信责任)owed to it, only the company may sue in respect of that loss. No action lies at the suit of a shareholder suing in that capacity ..."

到了 Gardner v. Parker(2004)2 BCLC 554 上诉庭先例中,更是把反映损失原则扩大到包括公司的无担保债权人(unsecured creditors)。另在颇受批评的 Giles v. Rhind(2003)Ch 618 先例中,公司因各种原因不能向做出错误行为的人士提出索赔,法院允许股东提起诉讼作为反映损失原则的例外。

到了近期的 Sevilleja v. Marex Financial Limited(2020)UKSC 31 最高院先例中,是较罕见地由7位大法官审理,显示了该先例的重要性。案情涉及控制与拥有 BVI

公司的 Sevilleja 先生，被指称剥除公司财产并导致公司无法清还 Marex 胜诉的判决债务。所以，Marex 直接起诉 Sevilleja 先生，而 Sevilleja 先生的抗辩是这只是反映损失。当时也有大量未判的案件在等待最高院的判决结果，看是否会推翻 Johnson v. Gore Wood 先例。多数意见判公司法仍保留反映损失原则，但只局限在 Prudential Assurance v. Newman Industries（No. 2）先例针对的股东索赔股价下跌的损失的情况，不包括无担保债权人的所有其他损失。少数意见（Sales、Hale 与 Kitchin 勋爵）认为不应保留反映损失原则。

这最高院先例后有 Naibu Global International Company PLC and Ors v. Daniel Stewart & Company PLC and Ors（2020）EWHC 2719（Ch）；Nectrus Ltd v. UCP Plc（2021）EWCA Civ 57；Broadcasting Investment Group Ltd & Ors v. Smith and Ors（2021）EWCA Civ 912 等先例。但这里不再多谈，反正这方面仍会有发展，甚至最高院将来可能在一些合适的案件撤销反映损失原则的说法。这样，股东或债权人就可以直接向董事起诉。在经济走下坡的时期，很多私人公司都会面临经营不下去的困境。一旦出现倒闭的危机，公司控股股东或董事、高管转移公司资产的事情会经常发生。这也是人性，想从一艘下沉的船上跳船逃生，一点儿也不奇怪。而私人公司因为信息不透明也缺乏监管，等小股东发现时一切为时已晚，公司很可能只剩下一个空壳。这时反映损失的索赔对小股东（或债权人）来说是至关重要的，即使将来清盘人会向董事索赔，财产也可能早就被转移找不回来了。而如果法律允许，股东就可以马上采取行动，如追踪资产、〔125〕申请全球冻结令〔126〕等。

2.7.1.3.3　公司董事与个别股东有特殊关系

稍早已经提到在 Sharp v. Blank（2015）EWHC 3220（Ch）先例中，Nugee 大法官说董事要与股东有特殊关系（special relationship）才会需要承担诚信责任，也就是他们之间必须有一些私人关系或是有特定的交易或安排。

Nugee 大法官举的一个例子是家族企业中的亲戚关系，但股东与董事之间有亲戚关系也并不意味着就一定会有诚信责任，还是要根据不同案件的案情判断。在 De Sena v. Notaro（2020）EWHC 1031（Ch）先例中，第一原告与第一被告是姐弟，共同经营一家由他们的父亲创立的公司。他们的父亲去世后，由弟弟担任董事总经理并管理公司业务，姐姐则有参与公司行政管理。双方产生分歧并最终决定拆伙，姐姐放弃她持有的公司 31.25% 的股份，而作为交换，一部分公司财产转给姐姐所有与控制的公司，也就是第二原告。之后姐姐认为她有公司 31.25% 的股份，所以理应获得公司 31.25% 的资产，而她获得的资产没有这么多，所以开始诉讼。该先例的争议涉及不当影响、不当得利（unjust enrichment）、专业人士（会计师、律师）的责任等，这里只介绍在该先例的特定案情下，董事（弟弟）是否对股东（姐姐）有诚信责任。

---

〔125〕　见笔者《证据法：基础理论、口头证据与专家证据》一书第十章之 2.7.2 段的详细介绍。

〔126〕　见笔者《证据法：国际规管与诉讼中的证据攻防》一书第三章之 1 段的详细介绍。

法院没有支持原告的请求,判在此先例中弟弟对姐姐没有诚信责任。Sharp v. Blank 等先例已经明确,公司董事对股东没有诚信责任,除非双方之间存在特殊关系。一般来说,在存在特殊关系的案件中,股东都不会同时是董事,这会导致在权力与获取信息方面与董事出现严重不平衡。但此先例中并非如此,姐姐作为公司董事与弟弟有同样的获取公司信息与管理公司业务的权力,唯一的区别是弟弟是董事总经理,但这不会令弟弟对姐姐有诚信责任。姐姐知道她是作为一个商人在与另一个商人对她放弃公司股份进行谈判,他们的利益本质上是相冲突的。她不可能相信对方会把她的利益放在第一位而把公司与自己的利益放在第二位。任何一位合理的商业公司董事都不会这么认为,双方不存在特殊关系。Matthews 大法官说:

"Almost always in those cases where such a 'special relationship' is found to exist, the claimant is not a fellow director, but simply a fellow shareholder of the defendant, and there is a serious imbalance in power and access to information. That is not this case. In the present case, both the **first claimant(姐姐) and the first defendant(弟弟) had precisely the same access to information, and(as directors) precisely the same authority in relation to the conduct of the company's business**, save only that the first defendant was the managing director. There is no allegation made that the first defendant did anything as managing director(rather than as director) which caused a fiduciary relationship to arise with the first claimant.

But, in any event, the first claimant's claim suffers from the problem that she was (and she knew she was) in the position of a businesswoman negotiating against another businessman on the terms on which she would surrender her shares in the company. Accordingly, their interests were intrinsically opposed. **She cannot possibly have believed that the person with whom she was negotiating on behalf of the company owed a fiduciary duty to her to put her interests first and the company's(or his) interests second. That is just fantasy.** Even if somehow she believed it, it was not true. ... In my judgment, there was no 'special relationship' such as to call into existence a fiduciary duty owed by the first defendant to the first claimant."(加黑部分是笔者的强调)

姐姐的另一个替代争辩是公司属于"准合伙"(quasi - partnership),而合伙人之间公认有诚信责任,所以股东/董事互相之间有诚信责任。但这也不被法院接受,首先在某种情况下公司可以被视为属于准合伙不代表在任何其他情况下都可以被视为准合伙,包括令股东/董事互相之间像合伙人一样有诚信责任。其次,公司之前一直是由他们的父亲全权控制,没有和任何人合伙。他退休后把公司交给自己的孩子,之后姐弟也没有同意合伙。所以姐弟是在公司框架下经营生意,受公司章程与公司法管辖,没有理由认为存在合伙关系。Matthews 大法官说:

"By way of an alternative to the argument that there was here a 'special relationship' between a director and shareholder, the claimants argued that this company was akin to a quasi - partnership, and that therefore the shareholder/directors owed each other fiduciary duties. I reject this submission. First of all, even if the company could be regarded as a quasi partnership for one purpose (for example in considering the question whether a petition for the winding up the company on the just and equitable ground could be maintained), that does not mean that it would be a quasi partnership for any other, let alone all purposes, including ... the shareholder/directors owe each other fiduciary duties, just as if they were partners of a partnership.

Secondly, I do not accept that this company could properly be regarded as a quasi - partnership in any meaningful sense of the phrase. Although the very early history of the business carried on by Sabato Notaro(父亲) is not clear, the business certainly did not begin as a partnership between individuals, let alone as a partnership between the first claimant and the first defendant ... It is clear that, until he retired from the business, Sabato Notaro controlled everything. Thereafter, he left it to his children, who had never agreed to be partners in anything. They were accordingly from the beginning operating in a framework subject to corporate governance rules, including the articles of association and the general company law. There is no justification for seeking to treat this therefore as if it were a partnership. The rules of company law apply."

2.7.2 诚信关系与合约关系的融合

至于每种不同关系的诚信责任,虽然衡平法责任(equitable obligations)与侵权的小心谨慎责任的大原则是一致的,但它们之间在实质方面对什么可以做或什么不可以做是各有各的情况与细节的。正如 Browne - Wilkinson 勋爵在 Henderson v. Merrett Syndicates Ltd(1995)2 AC 145 先例中说:"The phrase 'fiduciary duties' is a dangerous one, giving rise to a mistaken assumption that all fiduciaries owe the same duties in all circumstances. That is not the case."

主要原因是在这方面会涉及合约关系、侵权关系(小心谨慎责任)与诚信关系的混合。这并不容易,因为合约关系本质上是各自以自己利益考虑,但诚信关系是为对方利益考虑。正如 McLachlin 大法官在 Norberg v. Wynrib(1992)2 SCR 226 先例中说:"In ... contract the parties are taken to be independent and equal actors, concerned primarily with their own self - interest ... The essence of a fiduciary relationship, by contrast, is that one party exercises power on behalf of another and pledges himself or herself to act in the best interests of the other ... The fiduciary relationship has trust, not self - interest at its core ..."

合约责任与诚信责任同时存在的重要性,可以一个托管一些特定财产或一笔社保基金的长期信托关系作为例子。虽然在合约关系下可把一些能够预见的事情对受托人的权限与责任作出明示规定/约定,但难去包罗万有地针对将来会发生的不可预见的情况。而在管理财产期间,受托人可能行使裁量权作出不计其数的决定,如果受托人有私心就可能带来严重后果。这样,有了诚信责任法律所确定下来的大原则,就可以有了指引与对受托人的约束,以保护"弱势"的信托人。

由于两者的混合相当于把合约法与衡平法去混合,也带来如何确定实质方面责任的问题。在订约自由的大原则下,显然分析是以合约规定为优先。最高院的 Sales 勋爵在 2019 年 8 月的"The Interface between Contract and Equity"一文中说:"Whether analysed as a duty of care owed by a fiduciary in tort or as an aspect of equitable obligations, the case indicates that the substantive content of the duty of care to be applied where all the duties-contract, tort and/or fiduciary-is to be derived from the terms of the contract. **The contract takes priority on this as a matter of analysis, because it is on the terms specified in the contract that the fiduciary has assumed the responsibility to act**."(加黑部分是笔者的强调)

所以在商业合约中,合约双方享有没有节制的订约自由,是可以把受托人在方方面面的权力与责任写清楚的,让衡平法的诚信责任没有作为默示地位加插在合约内的余地,如 Sales 勋爵说:"the principle of freedom of contract means that the parties are at liberty to specify not just the scope of the task to be performed, but also to specify with precision what their rights and obligations are to be, and it is possible that the degree of precision with which this is done is such that it excludes the possibility of an additional overlay of equitable obligation. In Breen v Williams (1997) 186 CLR 71 Gummow J said that 'a contractual term may be so precise in its regulation of what a party may do that there is no scope for the creation of a fiduciary duty'. The contract may be exhaustive."

Mason 大法官在 Hospital Products Ltd v. United States Surgical Corp (1984) 156 CLR 41 澳大利亚高院先例中也说,即使同时产生了诚信关系,仍是以合约明示条文优先或超越性,诚信责任不得去改变合约的规定:"That contractual and fiduciary relationships may co-exist between the same parties has never been doubted. ... in these situations it is the contractual foundation which is all important because it is the contract that regulates the basic rights and liabilities of the parties. The fiduciary relationship, if it is to exist at all, must accommodate itself to the terms of the contract so that it is consistent with, and conforms to, them. The fiduciary relationship cannot be superimposed upon the contract in such a way as to alter the operation which the contract was intended to have according to its true construction."

虽然不得改变合约规定,但诚信责任会增加合约责任,如在合约已经是终止后诚信责任依然会持续:见 Longstaff v. Birtles (2002) 1 WLR 470; Conway v. Ratiu (2005) EWCA Civ 1302 等先例。在 Conway v. Ratiu 上诉庭先例中,Auld 大法官说:"... whilst it subordinates the effect of a fiduciary relationship to the terms of any concurrent contract, it also acknowledges — depending upon the circumstances — the potential coming into being and continuation of a fiduciary obligation without or regardless of any contract. ”

接下来的问题是在商业合约，受托人可否以订约自由去豁免诚信责任？Sales 勋爵是这样说：“There is no conceptual difficulty about fiduciary duties existing alongside contractual ones. **The powerful moral imperative of honesty and self – denial reflected in equitable doctrine is such that a fiduciary duty of loyalty will not readily be found to be excluded**. Where the contract sets out a task in relation to which Equity would impose a fiduciary duty, that will only be excluded by very clear and very precise drafting in the contract. **The strong presumption is against exclusion**. It is, I would say, even stronger than the presumption that a contract does not remove ordinary common law remedies and the presumption that an exclusion clause in a contract does not affect rights apparently given by the contract itself. As often happens, it is in the interstices of interpretation that competing principles and interests are brought into account and balanced against each other. ”（加黑部分是笔者的强调）

也可节录在 Henderson v. Merrett Syndicates Ltd 贵族院先例中，Goff 勋爵以常见的“受托人有绝对的裁量权做任何事情”的措辞为例，说这也不足以豁免诚信责任：“a contractual statement that underwriting names could act according to their ‘absolute discretion’ did not exclude them from being subject to an implied or fiduciary duty to act with reasonable care. ”

结合上述，在一个明显是诚信关系的商业合约中，受托人如果想去明示豁免诚信责任会是十分困难的，甚至比去豁免其他法律责任更加困难。本来以明示条文去豁免法律责任（立法或普通法），只要不是强制性（mandatory）或违反公共政策，理论上都是可以的；但对法院或仲裁庭而言，在双方有争议时去解释有关条文就会先有一个推定（presumption），就是任何一位合理的合约方是不会愿意自动放弃法律给予的好处、保障与权利，特别是一个弱势的信托人。所以任何试图豁免衡平法所默示或强加的诚信责任的条文恐怕要写得非常清楚无误才有机会成功。笔者甚至怀疑明示规定合约双方不是诚信关系也不一定足够，因为还要看合约其他条文是什么，而解释是要全面去分析考虑的。笔者也相信如果涉及的事件是受托人不诚实违反诚信或善意责任，仅是一句不是诚信关系也不够。毕竟，事件的环境/背景是诚信关系，在解释合约时要将这点加入考虑。而不诚实构成欺骗/欺诈也不是任何免责条文可以豁免责任的，正是“欺诈超越一切”（Fraud unravels all）。[127]

2.7.3　诚信责任与善意责任的区别

诚信关系下的诚信责任与合约下的善意责任（不论是明示或默示）表面看来区别不大且会有重叠，但实际仍有重要差异。这在 Sheik Tahnoon v. Kent（2018）1 CLC 216 先例中，Leggatt 大法官说：“**it is a mistake to draw a simple dichotomy between**

---

〔127〕　见本书第三章之 8.3 段的介绍。

relationships which give rise to fiduciary duties and other contractual relationships and to treat the latter as all alike. In particular,(in Yam Seng)I drew attention to a category of contract in which the parties are committed to collaborating with each other,typically on a long term basis,in ways which respect the spirit and objectives of their venture but which they have not tried to specify,and which it may be impossible to specify,exhaustively in a written contract. **Such 'relational' contracts involve trust and confidence but of a different kind from that involved in fiduciary relationships. The trust is not in the loyal subordination by one party of its own interests to those of another. It is trust that the other party will act with integrity and in a spirit of cooperation**."(加黑部分是笔者的强调)

这进一步表示在诚信关系下,信托人即使是不善意、不合作或关系变坏,只要诚信关系未有终止,受托人仍必须严格处事。这主要就是无私为信托人或受益方的利益着想,受托人自己的利益就要回避。相比之下,善意关系虽然也是要考虑对方的利益,但无需牺牲自己的利益。另外,善意关系是双向的要求,而诚信关系只是单向的要求。正如在《Misrepresentation,Mistake and Non-Disclosure》一书(2022 年,第 6 版)之 17 - 39 段说:"Parties negotiating for a contract may already be in a relationship which imposes on one or both of them the duty **to disclose information during the negotiations**. The duties may be **mutual**-for example,in the case of dealings between partners, where the duty of good faith attaches to both parties in their mutual dealings during the partnership;**or unilateral**-for example,in the case of dealings between a trustee and the beneficiary of the trust,or between a person who owes fiduciary duties and the person to whom he owes those duties."

可见,诚信关系远超出了合约关系(合约方履行时只考虑自己的合法利益),即使合约有善意的责任与要求(只是要求考虑与平衡对方的利益但不要求牺牲自己的合法/合约利益)。在 Gold Group Properties Ltd v. BDW Trading Ltd(2010)EWHC 1632(TCC)先例中,Stephen Furst QC 大法官说:"... Thus good faith,whilst requiring the parties to act in a way that will allow both parties to enjoy the anticipated benefits of the contract, **does not require** either party to give up a freely negotiated financial advantage clearly embedded in the contract."(加黑部分是笔者的强调)

Stephen Furst QC 大法官也提到,Barrett 大法官在 Overlook v. Foxtel(2002) NSWSC 17 澳大利亚先例针对善意说:"... But no party is fixed with the duty to subordinate self - interest entirely which is the lot of **the fiduciary** ... The duty is **not a duty to prefer the interests of the other contracting party**. It is,rather,a duty to recognise and to have due regard to the legitimate interests of both the parties in the enjoyment of the fruits of the contract as delineated by its terms."(加黑部分是笔者的强调)

诚信关系甚至与雇佣合约(employment contract)也不同,虽然是法律默示在每一个雇佣合约有忠诚(fidelity)的责任,如要求雇员要为雇主的利益着想,不要让自己的利益与雇主的利益起冲突:见 University of Nottingham v. Fishel(2002)ICR 1462 先例。但这忠诚责任不等同于诚信责任:见 Ranson v. Customer Systems Plc(2012)EWCA Civ 841 上诉庭先例。在此先例中,上诉庭的 Lewison 大法官说:"It is not disputed that an employee has an obligation of fidelity towards his employer. If the obligation is not express, it will invariably be implied."另在"The difference between the contractual duty of fidelity and the duties of a fiduciary"的小标题下,Lewison 大法官支持与引用了 University of Nottingham v. Fishel 先例中一审的 Elias 大法官的判决观点:"... the hallmark of a fiduciary is a single - minded duty of loyalty. The duty of loyalty in that context has a precise meaning: 'namely the duty to act in the interests of another'. As mentioned, this is not a feature of any employment relationship. In the employment context the duty of loyalty, although given the same label, 'is one where each party must have regard to the interests of the other, but not that either must subjugate his interests to those of the other'. ... the obligation of loyalty is no more than an obligation loyally to carry out the job that the employee agreed to do. This ... is the result of Fishel. The University complained that Dr Fishel had undertaken work abroad which should have been passed on to the University. Elias J rejected that complaint. He said: '... The employee does not in general promise to give his employer the benefit of every opportunity falling within the scope of its business.' ... '... the duties of a director are in general higher than those imposed by law on an employee. This is because a director is not simply a senior manager of company. He is a fiduciary and with his fellow directors he is responsible for the success of the company's success.' ... I would endorse the general principle as stated by Elias J in Fishel."

2.7.4 商业关系中的诚信责任

不少商业关系,也会有诚信责任争议的出现。例如在一个商业合约中双方明示同意是合伙人关系或一方作为另一方的代理人。但除非合约以清楚无误的语言/文字引入诚信责任,无法有其他解释去否定,否则不能只因为在有关合约中,其中一方依赖另一方更多一些,就默示存在诚信责任,这只会令双方的合约关系变得复杂。正如在 Re Goldcorp Exchange Ltd(In Receivership)(1995)1 AC 74 枢密院先例中,案情涉及客户把金条存放在一家公司保管,也没有办法去核实,完全要信任公司,但枢密院不承认公司有诚信责任。Mustill 勋爵说:"Many commercial relationships involve just such a reliance by one party on the other, and to introduce the whole new dimension into such relationships which would flow from **giving them a fiduciary character would ... have adverse consequences** ... It is possible without misuse of language to say that the customers put faith in the company, and that they trust has not been repaid. But the vocabulary is misleading; **high expectations do not necessarily lead to equitable remedies**."

(加黑部分是笔者的强调)

在 Fujitsu Services Ltd v. IBM United Kingdom Ltd(2014)EWHC 752(TCC)先例中,Carr 大法官说:"the courtship **must be careful not to** distort the parties' contractual bargain by the **inappropriate introduction of equitable principles**. In a commercial context wider duties will not lightly be implied. Fiduciary duties do **not commonly arise outside the settled categories** of fiduciary relationships, not least because independently **contracting parties do not undertake normally to subordinate their own commercial interests to another.**"(加黑部分是笔者的强调)

而作为商业合约的订约方,也应尽量避免被默示为受托人,要向另一方承担诚信责任。因为正常的商业关系中,是很少有一方会愿意只考虑对方的利益而完全不考虑自己的利益,更加不会希望自己的每一个决定都要留下证据,以在对方拿着显微镜挑刺时显示确实是为了对方利益着想。由于现在英国法律在正常商业合约对诚信责任适用没有具体限制,也就带来了一定的不肯定。特别在长期关系合约(relational contract)等合约类型中,合约的主导方(往往也难以避免,例如负责管理、资金管账等)可能对默示的善意责任并不抗拒,因为善意是双向的,但诚信责任是单向的。合约的主导方为了避免承担诚信责任,可以在合约中明示写明不承担诚信责任,并且在条文中增加另一方的权利以作出平衡,例如对方可以通知要求查账、派人监督等。

特别是近年来关系合约已有法律或事实默示的善意责任,法院或仲裁庭就不应该轻易多去强加苛刻与严格的诚信责任在其中一方合约方。即使在合约中约定与履行是其中一方合约方的利益被交托给另一方,也不代表另一方就有了诚信责任。近期涉及这方面争议的有 Bristol and West Building Society v. Mothew(1998)Ch. 1;Murad v. Al - Saraj(2005)EWCA Civ 959;Ross River Ltd v. Waveley Commercial Ltd(2013)EWCA Civ 910;Al Nehayan v. Kent(2018)EWHC 333(Comm)等先例。

Dawson 大法官在澳大利亚的 Hospital Products Ltd v. United States Surgical Corp(1984)156 CLR 41 先例也说在正常的商业关系中一方毫无保留信赖对方但最后证明是信错人(这种情况在中国等发展中国家经常发生),[128] 也不会因此产生一个诚信关系:"A fiduciary relationship does not arise where, because one of the parties to a relationship has wrongly assessed the trustworthiness of another, he has reposed confidence in him which he would not have done had he known the true intentions of that other. **In ordinary business affairs persons who have dealings with one another frequently have confidence in each other and sometimes that confidence is misplaced. That does not make the relationship a fiduciary one.** A fiduciary relationship exists where one party is in a position of reliance upon the other because of the nature of the relationship and not

[128] 这种情况很多,例如将在本书第十一章之 1.7.3 段介绍的 The Libyan Investment Authority v. Goldman Sachs International(2016)EWHC 2530(Ch)先例等。

because of a wrong assessment of character or reliability."(加黑部分是笔者的强调)

在没有明示规定的一般情况下,在一些商业合约的关系是一方A极其需要另一方B在履行时顾及与保护A的利益而不是B自己的利益,但A是控制不了,完全要依靠B,此时法律就有可能会为B强加一个诚信责任。例如,A同意B去全权与单方面对合约针对的财产或事情进行管理与决策,而作出的决定显然是约束与严重影响另外不参与管理的A。但从合情合理的角度看来,B有必要对A有一定程度的"效忠"。这正如早已经被接受的律师与客户之间的诚信关系,客户会大程度受到律师的判断影响,这需要法律默示律师有一个没有异心的诚信责任。这可节录在Al Nehayan v. Kent先例中,Leggatt大法官说:"Thus, fiduciary duties typically arise where **one person undertakes and is entrusted with authority to manage the property or affairs of another and to make discretionary decisions on behalf of that person**. (Such duties may also arise where the responsibility undertaken does not directly involve making decisions but involves the giving of advice in a context, for example that of solicitor and client, where the adviser has a substantial degree of power over the other party's decision-making:... The essential idea is that a person in such a position is not permitted to use their position for their own private advantage but is required to act unselfishly in what they perceive to be the best interests of their principal. This is the core of the obligation of loyalty ... **Loyalty in this context means being guided solely by the interests of the principal and not by any consideration of the fiduciary's own interests**. To promote such decision-making, fiduciaries are required to act openly and honestly and must not (without the informed consent of their principal) place themselves in a position where their own interests or their duty to another party may conflict with their duty to pursue the interests of their principal. They are also liable to account for any profit obtained for themselves as a result of their position."(加黑部分是笔者的强调)

诚信关系必须是涉及"信任与信心"的关系,正如Millett大法官在Bristol and West Building Society v. Mothew上诉庭先例中对诚信关系讲述的名句:"someone who has undertaken to act for or on behalf of another in a particular matter in circumstances which give rise to a relationship of trust and confidence."但这不是主观测试,即一方合约方对另一方有完全的信任;而是一个客观的测试,双方约定的合约关系在法律与现实情况中是给了有"诚信责任"的一方滥用其权力的机会(the relationship ... is one which gives the fiduciary a special opportunity to exercise the power or discretion to the detriment of that other person who is accordingly vulnerable to abuse by the fiduciary of his position)。

2.7.4.1 案例之一:Ross River Ltd v. Waveley Commercial Ltd(2013)EWCA Civ 910上诉庭先例

Ross River Ltd v. Waveley Commercial Ltd先例涉及一个地产开发的项目,该地

产开发项目由 Barnett 先生和 Harney 先生发起,原告 Ross River 公司的负责人 York 先生经人介绍同意参与该地产项目并提供资金,于是 Barnett 先生和 Harney 先生专门成立了 Waveley Commercial Ltd 公司(本案的被告之一,以下简称 WCL)与 Ross River 于 2004 年 12 月 23 日订立了合资协议(joint venture agreement)发展该地产项目。合资协议的订约方除了 Ross River 与 WCL,还包括 WCL 的两位董事 Barnett 先生和 Harney 先生,后者的角色是作为履约的担保人。该地产项目在 2007 年完工,直到 2011 年所有的房产才售完。在整个地产项目的建设、发展与出售过程中,Ross River 的角色主要是提供资金,而其他的工作全部依靠 WCL,或者更具体说是 Barnett 先生。2008 年开始,Ross River 开始对 WCL 不满,认为整个项目推进的太慢,WCL 向他披露的项目的相关信息也越来越少,且甚至对一些 WCL 开展的交易产生怀疑。于是 Ross River 在 2009 年开始了对 WCL 与 Barnett 先生等的诉讼。双方争议的焦点在于 Ross River 最终可以从该地产开发项目中取得的净利润的数额。Ross River 认为合资协议中 WCL 是唯一负责管理项目、出售(时间是 WCL 决定)与分摊利润等事项的合约方,所以合资协议中存在一条 WCL 以及 Barnett 先生对 Ross River 负有诚信责任的默示地位,而 WCL 和 Barnett 先生进行了未经 Ross River 允许的交易与支出,部分支出还与 Barnett 先生自己的利益相关,这令 Ross River 最终可以从地产开发项目中分得的净利润大幅减少,所以 WCL 与 Barnett 先生违反了该诚信责任,要对 Ross River 承担赔偿责任。其中,Barnett 先生虽然是合资协议的订约方,但其责任仅限于担保事项,不存在争议。不过在 2011 年时,WCL 已经无法支付到期的债务,所以 Barnett 先生个人对 Ross River 是否负有诚信责任与赔偿责任的争议也显得更为重要。

WCL 与 Barnett 先生方面的主要抗辩是双方的权利义务全部写在也局限在合资协议的明示条文中,法院要严格限制去添加属于衡平法上的诚信责任的默示条文去改变双方的合约内容与令合约变得不肯定的规定。

一审的 Morgan 大法官认为在该合资协议下,因为 Ross River 对 WCL 有高程度的信赖(不仅仅是一般的合资协议这么简单),所以 WCL 与其负责人 Barnett 先生也有了一个诚信责任去善意对待 Ross River,不得做任何对 Ross River 不利的事情,包括令其可以获得的净利润减少。其中 Morgan 大法官说:"Under the JVA, as between Ross River and WCL, the latter had complete control over the operation of the joint venture, at any rate in the later stages following the sale of the supermarket site (which occurred in March 2006). Thus, WCL was to handle the disposals of the interests in the site. WCL was to receive the proceeds of those disposals. WCL was to incur the expenditure necessary for the purposes of the joint venture and it was to pay the sums due in those respects. WCL was to account to Ross River in relation to the Net Profits and to pay to Ross River the Development Profit. Some of the terms of the JVA are of particular relevance in this regard. The agreement was expressed to be 'a joint venture'. The objectives of the parties were to maximise profits from the development. The parties were to share in the profits from the development at the earliest possible time. WCL was to provide Ross River with all relevant invoices and accounts. Under clause 10.5, Ross River was entitled to receive Development Profit. ... Clause 10.5 appeared to contemplate that WCL was not entitled to pay itself out of the revenues of the development before it accounted to Ross River for its share of Net Profit. **Ross River had no control over most if not all of these matters. Ross River had no nominee director on the board of WCL and had no shares in WCL**. Mr Barnett accepted when cross-examined that Ross River 'reposed a very high degree of trust in [him] and Mr Harney to run the JV for the benefit of all parties' and that 'with that trust came duties which [he] owed, [he] and WCL owed, ...to the Ross River parties'. That answer by Mr Barnett partly concerns matters of fact and partly deals with the legal consequences of those facts. Mr Barnett accepted as a fact that Ross River placed a very high degree of trust in him and Mr Harney. He also accepted, seemingly as a legal consequence of that fact, that he and WCL owed duties to Ross River. I am not obliged to find as a matter of law that WCL(and Mr Barnett) did owe a fiduciary obligation of some sort to Ross River just because of that answer. **The issue is ultimately one of law and not one of fact. However, the issue of law is very sensitive to the particular facts of the case**. If I felt that Mr Barnett had been pressurised into giving this answer, I would pay little attention to it on its own. However, apart from the inevitable pressure of the process of cross – examination, Mr Barnett gave this evidence readily and freely. He did not make any attempt to quarrel with, or even qualify, the proposition that was put to him. **I am able to make a finding supported by this evidence that Ross River did have to trust WCL and Mr Barnett as to the operation of the joint venture and as to the necessary accounting process at the end of it**. Indeed, that finding is supported by all the evidence in the case. I am also entitled to bear in mind that **Mr Barnett freely accepted that he and WCL owed duties to Ross River as a result of the fact that Ross River placed trust and confidence in them**. ..."(加黑部分是笔者的强调)

上诉庭就是否存在诚信责任这一争议点结合了3个之前先例[129]的判法支持了一审的判决。其中Lloyd大法官认为应根据不同案件的事实而去认定是否存在诚信关系与责任:"Each relationship which is described as joint venture has to be examined on its own facts and terms to see whether it does carry any obligations of a fiduciary."

2.7.4.2 案例之二:Murad v. Al – Saraj(2005)EWCA Civ 959先例

另一个支持有诚信责任的是Murad v. Al – Saraj先例。案情涉及住在巴林(Bah-

---

[129] 分别是Murad v. Al – Saraj(2004)EWHC 1235(Ch);JD Wetherspoon plc v. Van de Berg & Co Ltd (2007)EWHC 1044(Ch);John v. James(1991)FSR 397先例。

rain)的 Murad 两姐妹(原告)希望在伦敦投资房地产,而被告(Al - Saraj 先生)是一位住在伦敦的伊拉克人,也是一位从事伦敦地产买卖的经纪人。被告的其中一位科威特客户曾经在 1995 年通过被告的协助以 270 万英镑购买了一家酒店,并且在之后,被告收取工资负责该酒店的管理。到了 1997 年,该科威特客户希望出售该酒店。这令被告希望自己能买下并与 Murad 姐妹联络上。双方最后同意以 410 万英镑买下酒店,其中 Murad 姐妹出资 100 万英镑,被告出资 50 万英镑,余下的 260 万英镑向科威特银行贷款。至于将来再出售能赚取的利润,就双方对半分摊,因为这投资机会是被告介绍的,且还需要被告管理直到出售。Murad 姐妹称被告说他会以现金支付这 50 万英镑,但被告说他告知 Murad 姐妹出售酒店的科威特客户欠他钱,所以这 50 万英镑不必去支付而只需要对冲(set - off)债务。事实上,后来的买卖(通过一家 Dabescroft 的直布罗陀公司去拥有)的文件如买卖合约与实际支付只是 360 万英镑。直到 2002 年,Murad 姐妹才首次看到买卖合约的价格是 360 万英镑而不是 410 万英镑。至于这 50 万英镑说是被告与科威特卖方的对冲,会是出售该酒店的佣金与欠下的一些管理费用。在 2004 年,该酒店成功出售,售价是 665 万英镑。

原告 Murad 姐妹向法院提起诉讼,指控被告的欺诈性误述诱导合约产生,要求一连串的普通法与衡平法救济,包括撤销合约(rescission)、赔偿损失、交出利润(account for profit)[130]等。一审法院认定被告误述,向 Murad 姐妹说支付现金 50 万英镑,而没有告知 Murad 姐妹只是对冲。毕竟如果告知真相,Murad 姐妹会进一步查询对冲的细节。但显然撤销合约已经是不可能,因为时间过了太久,且撤销也不会是 Murad 姐妹所希望的。一审法院也认定被告对 Murad 姐妹有诚信责任,并且是违反。所以支持衡平救济的交出利润来避免被告不当得利(unjust enrichment)。一审判决也被上诉庭支持。

2.7.4.3 案例之三:Al Nehayan v. Kent(2018)EWHC 333(Comm)先例

但在更近期的 Al Nehayan v. Kent 先例中,Leggatt 大法官就不支持引入诚信责任。案情涉及商业合约,双方是在阿联酋的原告(以下简称 Sheikh Tahnoon)与在希腊的被告(Kent)。被告在希腊成立与经营一个名为"Aquis"的酒店品牌,在 2008 年底,原告同意注资 3110 万欧元与被告成为 50 - 50 的股东。到了 2012 年 4 月,原告更是把持股量提升到 70%。但当时该酒店业务已经出现现金短缺情况,甚至面临倒闭,这导致原告改变主意,不想再继续投资支持,并有意向撤资离开,于是派出代表去希腊谈判。双方之后又签订了两份合约:一份是框架协议(Framework Agreement)去针对酒店业务的重整,并加上了被告作出一些承诺、保证与补偿(undertakings and indemnities);另一份是从 2013 年 11 月 1 日至 2018 年,被告每年签发 540 万欧元的本票(promissory note)。

---

[130] 这种交出利润的衡平救济是强制被告将自己的不当得利返还给受害方,这方面可见笔者《损失赔偿与救济》一书第一章之 7 段,以及本书第十章之 12.3.1 段。

但由于被告没有支付，于是原告提起诉讼。而被告提出的抗辩是这两份合约是有严重缺陷的，主要涉及“经济胁迫”（economic duress），[131] 以及原告代表暴力威胁。另被告的反索赔是根据指控原告违反了对被告的诚信责任与善意责任。在此只针对诚信责任，被告指称在 2008 年开始，双方已经是合伙关系（partnership）。即使仍只是合资（joint venture），也属于相互对对方的诚信责任的关系。这包括在需要时提供资金，不能在没有合理通知与合理的条件下单方面终止合资关系与善意行事。

原告否认有这些责任，声称如果合约有诚信责任也只是在被告，因他全权经营与管理酒店业务。

被告指称原告在 2008 年的一次会议，曾经口头承诺如果酒店业务无法从机构投资者处获得资金，原告会提供资金让酒店拓展业务。但这不被 Leggatt 大法官接受，其中重要的原因是双方后来几年的通讯往来的文件中从来没有记录或提及这个重要的口头承诺。而证据显示原告的几次注资都是个别的决定。Leggatt 大法官说：“In sum, the history of financial dealings between Sheikh Tahnoon and Mr Kent clearly shows the understanding between them to have been that: (i) Sheikh Tahnoon had no contractual obligation to make funds available for investment other than when on particular occasions in particular amounts and on particular terms he agreed to do so; ...”

另是，双方也不是合伙关系，毕竟他们不像律师或会计师那样是经营同一种业务（酒店业务）。这在《Partnership Act 1890》之 section 1(1) 中规定为：“the relationship which subsists between persons carrying on a business in common with a view to profit.” 充其量双方只是共同持股一家公司。另是没有证据显示合伙人的关系，例如双方一起作决定、相互代表与第三方订立合约、共同对产生的债务负责等。Leggatt 大法官说：“They did not themselves carry on any business in common — or for that matter individually — having chosen a corporate structure in which the relevant businesses were carried on by Aquis SA and other companies established for that purpose. ... Although there are no doubt cases where parties may be regarded as carrying on a business as partners notwithstanding their use of corporate vehicles, Aquis SA and the other trading companies were far from being creatures of their beneficial owners. Although Mr Kent was the driving force in the business, there were other directors ... who played an important part in decision - making. I see nothing in the fact of this case to suggest that any business was being carried on by Mr Kent and Sheikh Tahnoon over and above the business of Aquis and the other group companies. Furthermore, there is no suggestion that Mr Kent was authorities to enter into contracts which bound Sheikh Tahnoon or vice - versa, nor was there any intention that Sheikh Tahnoon or Mr Kent should be jointly liable for debts incurred or obligations undertaken by the other. In short, the allegation that there was a part-

---

[131] 见本书第十章之 5.4 段的介绍。

nership between them was untenable."

最后总结，Leggatt 大法官是不认同原告对被告有诚信责任的："... in the present case Sheikh Tahnoon did not undertake to act for or on behalf of Mr Kent in anyway, let alone in any management capacity. The main decisions that Shiekh Tahnoon was required to make were decisions about when, for what purposes and how much money to invest in the companies which Mr Kent was responsible for managing. ... His motive for investing was obviously the hope of making a profit and Mr Kent could have no legitimate expectation that Sheikh Tahnoon would subordinate that interest to the interests of Mr Kent ... The relationship was a commercial one in which Shiekh Tahnoon was entitled to decide whether to make further funds available on the basis of a judgment about what would be in his own best financial interests."

虽然原告对被告没有诚信责任，但 Leggatt 大法官同意本合约是一个典型的关系合约，应该默示双方之间有善意责任。

Leggatt 大法官认为本合约中，被告对原告有一个诚信责任，例如在对酒店业务作决定时，如果有好的机会出现，例如有第三人出高价租用酒店，被告把机会给对他有更大利益的其他酒店，而不是只占小股的 Aquis，就会是明确不过的违反了诚信责任。

2.7.5 总结诚信责任与误述的关系

去总结以上所讲，笔者是认为诚信关系与本章针对的误述的关系是明显的，因为有诚信责任的一方合约方符合诚信责任会需要作出大量陈述与披露，也因此要保留大量的证据以证明每一个决定与行动都满足诚信责任下的要求，如：(i)诚实与善意(honest and in good faith)；(ii)效忠/忠诚(loyalty/fidelity)；(iii)除非信托人同意，否则不把自己放在一个有个人利益冲突的地位；(iv)除非信托人同意，否则不得从关系中获利；(v)不要滥用信任；(vi)小心谨慎；(vii)自动披露自己(如雇员)犯错等：见 Sybron Corp v. Rochem Ltd(1984) Ch 112；Tesco Stores Ltd v. Pook(2004) IRLR 618 等先例。

3. 疏忽误述的责任的范围

疏忽行为如一宗车祸，受害方人数是有限的，可以索赔的范围也是有限的，这是政策上的考虑，如果放开会造成无边无际的索赔与诉讼，疏忽的一方或背后的保险公司也不可能赔得起。而一旦涉及实质损失也容易去认定疏忽的侵权方(tortfeasor)与受害方满足"邻近"测试，毕竟出事故时，大家在同一个地点。又例如在一个需要小心谨慎的环境下，如在装卸易燃气体，并有告示说明不得吸烟时，一位工人点燃香烟并导致爆炸造成重大实质损失(人命与财产)的，就可以毫无困难去认定该在事故现场的疏忽工人有且违反了小心谨慎责任。正如 Lloyd 勋爵在 The"Nicholas H"(1995)2 Lloyd's Rep 299 贵族院先例中说:"In physical damage cases proximity very often goes without saying. Where the facts cry out for the imposition of a duty of care between the parties,... it would require an exceptional case to refuse to impose a duty on the ground that it would not be fair,just and reasonable."

在较早前的 Dorset Yacht Co Ltd v. Home Office(1970)AC 1004 上诉庭先例中,Saville 大法官也解释说对于涉及实质损失的情况,很容易证明疏忽的一方存在小心谨慎责任。但对于纯经济损失,例如伤者的老板因为伤者无法上班导致的损失,政策上应如何避免将门开得太大就困难得多。Saville 大法官说:"... whatever the nature of the harm sustained by the plaintiff,it is necessary to consider the matter not only by inquiring about foreseeability but also by considering the nature of the relationship between the parties;and to be satisfied that in all the circumstances it is fair,just and reasonable to impose a duty of care. Of course ... these three matters overlap with each other and are really facets of the same thing. ... **Again in most cases of the direct infliction of physical loss or injury through carelessness,it is self – evident that a civilised system of law should hold that a duty of care has been broken,whereas the infliction of financial harm may well pose a more difficult problem.** Thus the three so – called requirements for a duty of care are not to be treated as wholly separate and distinct requirements but rather as convenient and helpful approaches to the pragmatic question whether a duty should be imposed in any given case. ..."(加黑部分是笔者的强调)

相比之下,误述涉及疏忽语言(文书或口头)更加危险,因为它范围更广、影响更深远。例如,一个错误的法律意见、会计报告或估值报告,会在所有利益相关的人群中流传并会有不少人依赖并订立合约、蒙受损失。理论上,被陈述方可以是所有人。另是,误述通常也只会导致纯经济损失而不会是实质损失。所以,有必要局限谁能在法律上依赖这误述自称为受害方向误述方索赔。

在此,可重复本章之2.4.2段所讲,Hedley Byrne v. Heller(1964)AC 465 与 Caparo v. Dickman(1990)2 WLR 358 等贵族院先例有重复提到只有在满足以下的三个要件(也在刚节录的 Saville 大法官判词中提到)的情况,法律才会强加疏忽侵权的"小心谨慎责任":(1)误述方可以合理预见(foreseeability)受害方会依赖这陈述,而且如果陈述错误,会蒙受损失。比如,Hedley Byrne 先例的银行可以预见原告会依赖这份资信意见,但如果这份文件由原告给了其他不知名的朋友来参考并依赖,就不应是银行可合理预见的了。(2)误述方与受害方之间有足够密切的邻近关系(necessary proximity or neighbourhood)。(3)客观看要求误述方向受害方尽小心谨慎的责任是公平、公正与合理的(just,fair and reasonable),这往往是政策上的考虑。

这三方面的测试也被通称为"Caparo Test",因为 Bridge 勋爵在 Caparo v. Dickman 贵族院先例中说到强加"小心谨慎责任"是:"What emerges ... is that,in addition to the **foreseeability of damage**, necessary ingredients in any situation giving rise to a duty of care are that there should exist between the party owing the duty and the party to whom it is owed **a relationship characterised by the law as one of 'proximity' or 'neighbourhood'** and that the situation should be one in which the court considers it **fair, just and reasonable** that the law should impose a duty of a given scope upon the one party for the benefit of the other."(加黑部分是笔者的强调)

3.1 三类被误述方

接下来探讨英国法律承认哪些依赖一份错误的法律意见、会计报告或估值报告而蒙受损失的被误述方可以合法向误述方寻求救济,而不是自己承担听信与依赖(relying at own perils)的风险。被误述方可以分三大类:(1)误述方直接(也可以是通过代理人)向被误述方提供错误信息与事实,这种情况显然是最常见的。(2)误述方预期他的错误陈述会被转告给作为第三人的被误述方,并会被依赖:见 Yianni v. Edwin Evans & Sons(1982)QB 438;Clef Aquitaine SARL v. Laporte Materials(Barrow) Ltd(2001)QB 488(CA)等先例。但如果不是误述方合理预期会被第三人依赖的用途,即使发生也不必负责:见 Peek v. Gurney(1873)LR 6 HL 377 贵族院先例与稍后会详述的 Banca Nazionale del Lavoro SpA v. Playboy Club London Ltd & Ors(2018)UKSC 43 最高院先例。(3)误述方是面对公众做出错误陈述,也预期被依赖或信赖,例如一位专业人士在一个会议或采访发表一些错误的意见或提供错误的信息与事实。这样,任何公众人士都是潜在的被误述方。如果他们可以排着队向误述方索赔损失,显然对社会带来的坏处远超于好坏。例如,会再也听不到意见或信息而成为"寂静社会";如果免费听取的专业意见与要支付昂贵费用才取得的专业意见(如律师意见)有同等的法律保护,谁会傻傻地付钱给专业人士;法院会因为太多的疏忽侵权案件而被挤爆等。所以法律必须控制针对怎样的错误陈述与哪些类别的公众人士才能获得救济,而不属于该类别的人士,即使是依赖了同一错误陈述也无权获得救济。而平衡对社会的利弊,决定哪些错误陈述需要阻吓与哪些类别的人士需要保护,就涉及公共政策的考虑,法律手段就是确认误述方与被误述方(特定类别人士)之间有"特殊关系"(special relationship),误述方违反小心谨慎责任。

在《Chitty on Contracts》(2021 年,第 34 版)一书之 9 – 037 段说:"In order to be entitled to relief in respect of misrepresentation, the person seeking relief must be able to demonstrate that he is a representee;... To put the matter another way, the claimant must show that it was intended that he should act on the representation, rather than it being aimed solely at someone else. There may be said to be **three types of representees: first**, persons to whom the representation is directly made and their principals; **secondly**, persons to whom the representor intended or expected the representation to be passed on; and **thirdly**, members of a class at which the representation was directed. If the representation is directed at a particular class of persons, the alleged representee must be able to bring himself within that class. ..."(加黑部分是笔者的强调)

3.2 误述方对预期会依赖其错误陈述的第三人有小心谨慎责任

接下来介绍一些先例进一步说明上述介绍的第二类被误述方,首先是 Yianni v. Edwin Evans & Sons(1982)QB 438 先例。案情涉及原告(Yianni 夫妇)向 Halifax Building Society 申请抵押贷款购买房屋,该房屋互助协会委任被告(一家测量师事务所)为房屋估价,以考虑贷款的金额。虽然在贷款的申请表格上有建议原告自己独立测量(independent survey),但原告因为需要额外花费而没有去做,只依赖了被告提供给房屋互助协会的估价。在买了两年多后,房屋出现严重缺陷并导致修理费用超出了买房的钱。于是原告向被告索赔损失。

早在同类情况但涉及的专业人士是一位会计师的 Le Lievre v. Gould(1893)1 QB 491 上诉庭先例中,就判这方面的法律是不必对明知道会作出依赖的第三人负责。这之后被 Candler v. Crane, Christmas & Co(1951)2 KB 164 上诉庭先例依从,案情也涉及会计师为一家有限责任公司做账不小心,有好几处是错误或虚假。该会计师也知道有潜在投资人会依赖,因为客户要求直接把该账目给有关投资人。事后该投资人投资该公司,但公司在1年后破产清盘,投资人血本无归。多数意见判会计师等专业人士只需要对他/她的雇主负责,而不必对第三人负责,但 Denning 大法官不同意多数判决:"... to whom do these professional people owe the duty? I will take accountants, but the same reasoning applies to others. They owe the duty, of course, to their employer or client; and also I think to any third person to whom they themselves show the accounts, or to whom they know their employer is going to show the accounts, so as to induce him to invest money or take some action on them. But I do not think the duty can be extended further so as to include strangers of whom they have heard nothing and to whom their employer without their knowledge may choose to show their accounts. Once the accountants have handed their accounts to their employer they are not, as a rule, responsible for what he does with them without their knowledge or consent."

接下来是在本章之2.2.1段详细介绍了的 Hedley Byrne v. Heller(1964)AC 465 重要贵族院先例中,案情虽然不一样,不涉及第三人,但上述的两个上诉庭先例仍被考虑。贵族院针对 Candler v. Crane, Christmas & Co 先例是支持 Denning 大法官的观点并认为多数判决是不应该支持的,只节录 Morris 勋爵如下所说:"It seems to me, therefore, that if A claims that he has suffered injury or loss as a result of acting upon some misstatement made by B who is not in any contractual or fiduciary relationship with him, the inquiry that is first raised is whether B owed any duty to A: if he did the further inquiry is raised as to the nature of the duty. There may be circumstances under which the only duty owed by B to A is the duty of being honest: there may be circumstances under which B owes to A the duty not only of being honest but also a duty of taking reasonable care. ... But apart from cases where there is some direct dealing there may be cases **where**

one person issues a document which should be the result of an exercise of the skill and judgment required by him in his calling and where he knows and intends that its accuracy will be relied upon by another."(加黑部分是笔者的强调)

在 Yianni v. Edwin Evans & Sons 先例中,Park 大法官根据 Hedley Byrne 先例,针对这种情况支持原告 Yianni 夫妇成功向被告测量师事务所索赔:"Accordingly guided by the passages in the judgment of Denning LJ in the Candler's case and the speeches in the House of Lords cases,I conclude that,in this case,the duty of care would arise if,on the evidence,I am satisfied that the defendants knew that their valuation … would be passed on to the plaintiffs,who,notwithstanding the building society's literature … in the defendant's reasonable contemplation would place reliance upon its correctness in making their decision to buy the house and mortgage it to the building society."

Park 大法官也平衡了政策方面的考虑与该案例的事实。这包括原告有不被质疑的证据显示在相对廉价的房屋的抵押,90%的普通小市民是只会依赖房屋互助协会的估值,不会另去进行独立测量,并认定被告不会不知道。至于是否需要担心测量与估价报告被房屋互助协会任意给第三人而导致测量师面对无限责任,Park 大法官认为只应局限在申请抵押类别人士(也就是邻近要求)。这与本章之 2.2.1.1.1 段介绍的 Smith v. Eric S. Bush(1990)1 AC 831 先例是大同小异的案件。

3.3 船级社对船舶检查与签发证书的错误陈述被预期第三人的依赖

较早介绍的 Yianni v. Edwin Evans & Sons(1982)QB 438 先例显示英国法下,误述方对预期会依赖他/她提供的意见、信息与事实行事的这类的公众时,会被法院强加一个小心谨慎责任。这涉及社会的公众政策的考虑,也就是上述所讲的"公平、公正与合理"。

本书旧版曾经详细介绍了 20 世纪 90 年代开始出现的一连串对船级社(classification society)的索赔诉讼。众所周知,船级社历史悠久,像英国劳合社(Lloyd's Classification Society)成立已有 200 年以上。中国现在也有中国船级社(China Classification Society),在国际航运享有颇高地位。船级社一般是非盈利机构,它们的收入主要是靠对船舶的各种检验收取合理费用。这各种检验主要是针对船舶安全方面,例如船舶的结构、主机、救生设备等。这些检验很多是来自很多国际公约下的要求,如 1974 年《海上人命安全公约》(Safety of Life at Sea Convention 或 SOLAS)与修订[如 1993 年的《International Safety Management(ISM)Code》、1966 年《International Convention on Load Lines》、1969 年《International Convention on Tonnage Measurement of Ships》等]。在个别国家根据国际公约立法后,由于政府自己执行监督的人手不够与/或缺乏相关专业知识,索性授权船级社去做。在不同的立法下去检验并且满意后,船级社会被政府授权给船舶发出各种证书。

多年来虽然有不少批评指船级社太商业化,对检验与签发证书的严格性与水准也在下降,但无可否认的事实是船级社对船舶的海上安全作出了莫大的贡献,这是目前没有其他人士或组织可去替代的。

而航运与国际贸易的相关业内人士，都无可避免要依赖船级社的检验报告与证书行事。例如，船东没有船级社对船舶结构与安全检验满意的证书是买不到船舶保险，进不了船东互保协会(P& I Club)去相互承保船舶在全球航行与营运带来的责任的等。而即使已有保险公司的承保，也会因失去船级社的有效证书而变得自动无效，出了意外事故也没有赔偿，因为保单上通常会有对保持船级社的有效证书的承诺性保证(promissory warranty)。另各国港口在船舶没有船级社有效证书时，会拒绝它进港，或是进去了出不来，船舶被扣。没有船级社有效证书的船舶，也找不到承租人(charterer)，因为船舶根本无法营运。例如货物无法装上这种没有船级社批准的船舶，货物会买不到保险，在货物买卖合约下也会违约。还有其他林林总总的麻烦，可见船级社对船东的重要性与在一般业内人士心目中的地位。也不可避免的是，业内人士，甚至是政府如港口当局，都依赖船级社证书中陈述的意见、信息与事实行事，包括订立大量不同的合约：如船舶或货物保险合约、付运货物买卖合约、租船合约、提单合约等。这种依赖已经有上百年的历史，船级社作为签发检验报告与签发证书的陈述方不会不知道或不可预期到。

问题是，船级社也难免会在繁多与复杂的检验中犯错，进而在签发的报告或证书中有疏忽误述。

为了避免在合约下承担责任，船级社会在它被委任(通常是与船东)的合约与签发的证书等中放进一条免责条文。劳合社的条文如下："… it is understood that neither the society nor any member of its committee not any of its officers, servants or surveyors is under any circumstances whatsoever to be held responsible or liable for any inaccuracy in any reports or certificates issued by its surveyors…or for any act or omission, default or negligence of any of its committee or any member thereof or any of the other officers or servants or agents of the society. …"

但这种免责条文对非合约方的第三人来说，并没有约束力。所以防止不了有依赖误述而蒙受损失的第三人在 Hedley Byrne v. Heller(1964) AC 465 贵族院先例后试图以侵权的疏忽误述向船级社起诉索赔。接下来介绍有关的先例。

3.3.1 The"Morning Watch"(1990) 1 Lloyd's Rep 548 先例

这应是在英国法院第一个起诉船级社的案例，在 The"Morning Watch"先例中，案情涉及一艘游艇。游艇在 4 年一次的特别检验(special survey)后不久，有买方购买了该游艇。买方的重要依赖是英国劳合社所签发的有效特别检验证书。但购买后，买方发觉甲板下严重生锈，结果要多花不少钱去更换。为此，买方向劳合社以侵权索赔损失，指劳合社疏忽误述。

但在高院，Phillips 大法官判劳合社胜诉，因为双方(劳合社与买方)根本没有足够的密切或邻近关系。这一结果与稍后本章之 3.4.2 段会介绍的 Caparo v. Dickman (1990) 2 WLR 358 贵族院先例的判决相当一致。

3.3.2 The"Nicholas H"(1995)2 Lloyd's Rep 299 贵族院先例

The"Nicholas H"重要案例控告日本船级社(Nippon Kaiji Kyokai 或简称"NKK"),一直上诉到了贵族院。该"Nicholas H"轮在1986年初从秘鲁 Callao 港与智利 Antofagasta 港装满了铅锌精矿(lead and zinc concentrate)开往意大利途中,发觉船旁出现裂缝,并需要绕航去波多黎各 San Juan 港避难。船东委任日本船级社前来检验,而在第一次检验后是要求船东作出永久修理,即要完全修妥才批准继续航行。但这样对船东非常不便而且价格昂贵,如当地或附近没有适当或廉价的修船设备,船舶已装满货物,要卸下部分才能修理等。于是船东派代表飞 San Juan 港与日本船级社检验师交涉,最后可能迫于压力,日本船级社把永久修理的要求改为暂时修理后即批准开航。

不幸在航行途中,裂缝扩大引致船舶沉没。看来,日本船级社这暂时修理的决定应是错误且有疏忽的。货物全损的货方(或代位求偿的货物保险公司)在向船东索赔并获得船东互保协会赔偿50万美元后(这金额是1924年《海牙规则》下的限额),对余下赔不到的550万美元向日本船级社以疏忽误述为由追偿。

在高院的一审,Hirst 大法官判日本船级社违反了小心谨慎责任,认为在本案特殊的情况下与第三人货方有足够密切的邻近关系,这是因为:(1)日本船级社完全可主宰船舶能否开航,非是船东可听可不听船级社的修理要求。(2)时间上非常接近,日本船级社犯了错误并有疏忽,船舶随即开航并很快沉没,不是几个航次后才出事。(3)检验师在犯错时,明知船舶上有货物,所以应合理预见到如果疏忽会对货物带来的后果,加上案情显示有足够的邻近关系,也就可以强加一个小心谨慎责任。

但这案件到了上诉庭与贵族院,日本船级社反败为胜。原因是:(1)主要在公共政策与公共利益大前提下不应强加船级社一个对货方的小心谨慎责任,这不是公平、公正与合理的法律。强加这个侵权责任等于打开泄洪阀,会失控,因为不知道责任会扩散到什么地步。例如,其他的受害方如船员、旅客、承租人、油污受害民众与国家等。而船级社以后处处防范甚至不能生存(正如日本船级社的副总裁 Mitsubishi Abe 先生的证言所说),整体而言对全球的国际贸易与航运绝非好事。(2)另一个重要的公共政策考虑是船东如果违约导致货损货差,已有国际公约对此作出规定,如1924年《海牙规则》,船舶可以吨位限制责任的1976年《International Convention on Limitation of Liability for Maritime Claims》等。如果允许船级社被货方起诉,将来船级社又会在替船东检验时要求给予补偿(indemnity)等,即会搞垮整个国际公约所建立起来的风险分摊制度。(3)要对船舶安全适航负责的主要是船东,不是船级社。

在贵族院是多数意见(Lloyd 勋爵持不同意见,其支持一审 Hirst 大法官的判决)认为在公共政策的考虑不应强加给船级社一个对货方(并可以延伸至所有其他第三人)的小心谨慎责任。代表多数意见或判决的 Steyn 勋爵说:"... I conclude that **the recognition of a duty would be unfair, unjust and unreasonable** as against the shipowners who would ultimately have to bear the cost of holding classification societies liable, such consequence being at variance with the bargain between shipowners and cargo-owners based on an internationally agreed contractual structure. It would also be unfair, unjust and unreasonable towards classification societies, notably because they act for the collective welfare and unlike shipowners they would not have the benefit of any limitation provisions. Looking at the matter from the point of view of cargo-owners, the existing system provides them with the protection of The Hague Rules or Hague-Visby Rules. But that protection is limited under such Rules and by tonnage limitation provisions. Under the existing system any shortfall is readily insurable. In my judgment the lesser injustice is done by not recognising a duty of care. ..."(加黑部分是笔者的强调)

少数不同意见的Lloyd勋爵将船级社与公立医院相比较,例如大家都是非盈利机构,大家都是为了大众服务且十分被重视等,但法律仍是强加给医院一个小心谨慎责任。所以,Lloyd勋爵不认为船级社可以这些理由不必承担对货方实质损失的赔偿:"... it was pointed out that classification societies are charitable non-profit making organisations, promoting collective welfare and fulfilling a public role. But why should this make any difference? Remedies in the law of tort are not discretionary. Hospitals also are charitable non-profit making organisations. But they are subject to the same common duty of care under the Occupier's Liability Acts, 1957 and 1984 as betting shops or brothels."

3.3.3 对船级社应否对第三人承担一个小心谨慎责任的看法

从英国公共政策或公共利益的角度来看,笔者认为Lloyd勋爵举的例子与Yianni v. Edwin Evans & Sons(1982)QB 438先例是完全说得通的,因为对医院与房屋互助协会聘用的测量师强加小心谨慎的责任是为了保护英国普罗大众的利益。但涉及船级社,考虑到英国作为国际航运、商务与保险业的中心,特别在软件服务的方面,强加小心谨慎责任并打击船级社以保护需要依赖船级社提供意见与信息的(在比例上绝大多数是外国的)业内人士与/或民众,显然不符合英国的公共利益。在The "Nicholas H"(1995)2 Lloyd's Rep 299先例中,多数意见或判决在行使他们的裁量权作出平衡时有否受到这方面的影响,笔者没有在判决中看见,这也不好去明说,笔者只想说英美法律在考虑公共政策或公共利益时,难免会有与其他国家不一致的情况。所以,学习与了解英国法律要分清轻重,无需照单全收,毕竟最主要目的是希望中国年轻一代通过学习与了解英国法律,充实思维模式,能够与西方国家做朋友时有共同语言(same page),做竞争对手时知己知彼。

在此也不进一步探讨船级社责任问题,毕竟这不是本章的针对重点。它们也面临着世界上不同国家法律的规管与影响,并带来了不同法院的判决,在此就不展开谈了。

3.4 不是误述方预期会被依赖的用途

一般而言,对误述责任警觉性高的人士(通常是专业人士)都不希望他们需要小心谨慎去提供的意见与信息,会随意被第三人依赖并做出相应的严肃行动。毕竟,除了误述的重大责任外,第三人通常不会支付费用,而提供的意见与信息也不一定对口。而面对客户就十分不一样,他们之间是有对价的合约关系,或即使免费也是为了将来的关系,对此陈述方会自愿承担责任(voluntary assumption of duty)。

所以有说法是陈述方不知道或不预期他的错误陈述会被第三人依赖,第三人应该不能成为原告提起索赔。这说法针对欺诈性误述应是没有疑问,骗子如果不预期他的误述会被依赖,怎会是欺诈/欺骗?但针对疏忽误述,这说法或要求就比较宽松,只要求被误述方合理依赖有关误述并导致合约与损失的产生,而该被误述方是误述方预期会依赖与有权依赖的人士。这方面可节录《Misrepresentation, Mistake and Non-Disclosure》(2022 年,第 6 版)一书之 3 – 52 段说:"**Intention that the representee act on the representation** It is sometimes said that all the remedies have a minimum requirement as to the defendant's(误述方)state of mind:he cannot be held responsible for the consequences of his statement unless he intended the representee(被陈述方)to act on it. This requirement should not, however, be viewed as a significant hurdle for the representee to overcome. It is usually stated most explicitly in relation to the tort of deceit, where the courts often couple it with the requirement to prove the defendant's fraud, and in that context it can be seen naturally to have a positive subjective content. However, in relation to the other remedies, it means only that the representor, in making the statement, realised that his statement would be received by the representee and that he might therefore act upon it. It serves more to define the range of potential claimants-defining those who are entitled to sue on the representation; the statement was consciously directed at the claimant. It is closely linked to the requirements that the representation be one on which the claimant was entitled to rely; and that the representee must have in fact relied upon it."

特别是对专业人士而言,现实中难防其提供的意见与信息会被流传给第三人,包括被客户转发。这样,除非意见与信息中有明示条文免责,否则就会需要靠法院根据个别案件的案情决定是否强加误述方一个对第三人小心谨慎的责任。这就代表了只要有错误或疏忽陈述,就难逃赔偿责任。虽然在本章之 3.2 段介绍的 Yianni v. Edwin Evans & Sons(1982)QB 438 先例给对第三人承担责任开了门,但看来法院是不希望延伸太广,有不少情况就从公共政策考虑角度去关上大门。在本章之 3.3 段有关船级社的叙述就是典型例子,船级社肯定知道与预期到它的陈述会被航运、国际贸易、保险、银行等依赖并进行商业活动与订立合约,但贵族院在 The "Nicholas H" (1995)2 Lloyd's Rep 299 先例中把被误述方要求索赔损失的大门关上,理由是根据公共政策,强加一个小心谨慎的责任是不公平、不公正,不合理的确定这些受害方是无权对有关误述提起诉讼。以下介绍几个著名案例与不同的情况。

3.4.1 Peek v. Gurney(1873)LR 6 HL 377 贵族院先例

首先在 Peek v. Gurney 贵族院先例中,案情涉及原告依赖错误与隐瞒重要事实真相的招股章程(prospectus)买了2000股,但公司在不到1年后破产清盘,原告蒙受损失并向公司董事索赔,指控被告欺诈性误述诱导原告订立合约在市场购买这些股票。但贵族院判招股章程是为了诱导认股方(allottee),而不是诱导像原告一样后来在市场向认股方买入的股民。其中Chelmsford勋爵说:"The last question to be considered is,(Peek)who alleges that he purchased his shares upon the faith of the prospectus,has a remedy against(Gurney)for the misrepresentations which it contains. (Peek) contends that the prospects being addressed to the public for the purpose of inducing them to join the proposed company,and any one of the public who is led by it to take shares, whether originally as an allotted,or by purchase of allotted shares upon the market,is entitled to relief against the person who issued the prospectus. There can be no doubt that the prospectus … is addressed from the temporary offices of the company for allotment and registration of shares. It states how much is to be paid upon application for shares,and how much upon allotment,and how and where the application for shares is to be made; and it gives the form of payment to the bankers and of the receipt to be given by them to the applicant for shares to be allotted. …I therefore think that(Peek)cannot make(Gurney)responsible to him for the loss he has sustained by trusting to the prospectus issued by them inviting the public to apply for allotments of share;…"

这方面的普通法地位已经被立法改变,先是《Directors' Liability Act 1890》,接下来可跳到目前的《Financial Services and Markets Act 2000》之section 90,内容稍长,根据该条文,任何因为依赖了招股章程或上市详情中的不正确或不完整信息而购买股票并蒙受损失的人士都可以获得赔偿(compensation is payable to any person who has acquired securities relying on incorrect or incomplete statements in the prospectus or listing particulars)。

3.4.2 Caparo v. Dickman(1990)2 WLR 358 贵族院先例

在Caparo v. Dickman先例中,原告Caparo本来已是一家公司的小股东,他在看了Dickman先生审计的公司账目报告后,收购了公司其他股票而变为大股东,结果这报告有错,引致Caparo先生投资损失。案中的问题是双方是否有足够密切的邻近关系?

上诉庭认为有,因为Caparo先生是股东之一,不是一些不知名的外来投资者,Dickman先生应充分预见到他的报告会被Caparo先生参阅。

但案子到了贵族院,这一上诉庭判决被推翻,而这邻近关系被进一步收紧。Oliver勋爵说误述方(Dickman先生)在陈述(给意见或出报告)时,必须知道依赖他的受害方(Caparo先生)要此陈述的目的,而他也乐于受害方为此目的而依赖他,甚至受害方不会再去另作调查。Jauncey勋爵也说这依赖(受害方依赖这报告或意见)达至某一目的必须是"极有可能"(highly probable)而不仅是"会有可能"(possible)才可要误述方负责。

换言之，若要 Dickman 先生负责，情况应是 Caparo 先生想去收购公司的股份而变为控股大股东，在进行收购前，先指示 Dickman 先生来审计一下公司的经济状况与业务前景。而如果 Dickman 先生在此报告中有错，则他对 Caparo 先生就有小心谨慎责任。但如果 Dickman 先生只是例行公事地每年出一个账目报告，如给股东大会所用，他是不必对 Caparo 先生私下用来决定增持股份，而且并不另作调查负任何责任的。

如此看来，这种侵权下的误述并不会无边无际，也不鼓励去延伸。确实，Millett 大法官在 Al Saudi Banquet v. Clark Pixel（1990）2 WLR 344 先例中说："In my judgment, Caparo marked the furthest limit to which the duty of care for negligent misstatement has so far been taken in England, and its reasoning does not encourage any further advance."

可简单节录《Chitty on Contracts》（2021 年，第 34 版）一书之 9 - 099 段说："**Statement in connection with particular transaction.** In Caparo Industries Plc v. Dickman（1990）2 AC 605, it was held that there will be no liability in tort for negligent misrepresentation unless the maker of the statement knew that the statement would be communicated to the person relying on it specifically in connection with a particular transaction or a transaction of a particular kind. In relation to misrepresentation as between contracting parties, this appears to mean that the misrepresentation must have been made in connection with the contract in respect of which relief is sought, or at least that reliance on the representation in connection with the contract was likely."

该先例虽然是以邻近关系为由拒绝了 Caparo 先生的索赔，但是本质上还是公共政策的考虑，即看强加这样一个小心谨慎的责任在陈述方是否是公平、公正与合理。

3.4.3 Banca Nazionale del Lavoro SPA v. Playboy Club London Ltd & Ors（2018）UKSC 43 最高院先例

在近期的 Banca Nazionale del Lavoro SPA v. Playboy Club London Ltd & Ors 最高院先例中，虽然案情非常像好莱坞电影，但是最高院所作的判决在法律原则上与 Hedley Byrne v. Heller（1963）1 Lloyd's Rep 483 先例和 Caparo v. Dickman（1990）2 WLR 358 先例没有区别。在该先例中 Barakat 先生是黎巴嫩赌场的常客，但很少在原告 Playboy Club London 赌场赌博。Barakat 先生经介绍在 Playboy Club London 赌场赌博，并被该赌场认为是个大顾客。Barakat 先生申请赌场 80 万英镑的支票兑现服务（check - cashing facility），就是赌场接受一些熟客的支票，在没有向银行提现的情况下就让熟客可以兑换最高不超过支票金额的筹码。使用这个服务需要价值客户提供的支票两倍的银行资信报告（credit reference）。为了避免泄露查询的用途，赌场一般会通过关联公司（在该先例是 Burlington Street Services Ltd）向客户的银行查询。Barakat 先生提供的银行是被告 Banca Nazionale del Lavoro（以下简称 BNL）银行。BNL 回复说 Barakat 先生在该银行有账户，并且值得信赖对其作出 160 万英镑的贷款。但其实这是错误的信息，Barakat 先生在两天后才在该银行开了账户，并且直到销户该账户中一直没钱。

在收到 BNL 的资信报告后，赌场接受了 Barakat 先生的支票并且之后把额度提升到了 125 万英镑。Barakat 先生在赌场赢了超过 42 万英镑，拿到钱就离开了伦敦再也没有去过原告赌场。之后，原告赌场发现 Barakat 先生提供的两张支票跳票，赌场总共损失了超过 80 万英镑，于是开始诉讼向 BNL 索赔损失。

诉讼的主要争议之一是 BNL 对原告赌场有没有小心谨慎责任。因为 BNL 对 Burlington Street Services Ltd 有小心谨慎责任是没有什么疑问，但是 Burlington Street Services Ltd 没有蒙受任何损失。原告赌场蒙受了损失，但是如果 BNL 对原告赌场没有小心谨慎的责任，就不用赔偿。一审法院认为 BNL 对原告赌场有小心谨慎的责任，因为没有证据显示如果是赌场而不是 Burlington Street Services Ltd 查询会对结果有什么影响，合法赌博的融资也不应与普通的商业交易的融资有什么不同。

BNL 提起上诉，上诉庭支持了上诉，认为 BNL 对原告没有小心谨慎的责任。因为赌场故意匿名躲在 Burlington Street Services Ltd 背后，BNL 对赌场的存在与查询的目的一无所知，不可能假设赌场会依赖自己的陈述，双方也不存在密切关系，因此让 BNL 承担小心谨慎的责任不合理。

原告上诉到了最高院，最高院支持了上诉庭的判法，在 BNL 不知道原告存在与不知道查询目的时，不可能假设其对原告有小心谨慎的责任。Sumption 勋爵说："The defendant's knowledge of the transaction in respect of which the statement is made is potentially relevant for three purposes:(i) to identify some specific person or group of persons to whom he can be said to assume responsibility; (ii) to demonstrate that the claimant's reliance on the statement will be financially significant; and (iii) to limit the degree of responsibility which the defendant is taken to assume if no financial limit is expressly mentioned. We are presently concerned with its significance for the first of these purposes, which will vary according to what is known about the person or group expected to rely on the statement.... It is impossible to feel much sympathy for BNL given the circumstances in which they came to give a favourable credit reference for some one with whom they appear to have had no relevant dealings. But they had no reason to suppose that Burlington was acting for some one else, and they knew nothing of the Playboy Club. In those circumstances, it is plain that they did not voluntarily assume any responsibility to the Club. It may well be, since they knew nothing of Burlington either, that they were indifferent to whom they were dealing with. But the fact that a representor may have been equally willing to assume a duty to some one else does not mean that he can be treated as if he had done so."

虽然该先例中银行胜诉，但是否有小心谨慎的责任非常依赖不同案件的案情，所以银行为了限制有小心谨慎责任的对象，可以在资信证明中明确只对特定接收方负责。

第二章　可 诉 陈 述

1. 可诉陈述概述

在本书第一章一开始就已经指出可诉误述是指陈述方(representor)向被陈述方(representee)做出不正确或虚假的事实陈述(false statement of fact)(误述),被陈述方依赖(rely)该误述订立合约并产生损失,被陈述方可以向陈述方就该误述(misrepresentation)主张法律上的救济,这主要包括撤销(rescind)在误述诱导下订立的合约,或加上索赔误述导致的金钱损失。由于商业关系都是由合约建立的,所以这种法律救济十分重要。现实中经常会发生一方订约方(如买卖合约下的买方)在谈判中相信了对方的事实陈述、意见、预期或承诺后订立合约,但之后甚至是在履行期间才发觉是误述,于是后悔并想脱离合约关系,或是在不想或无法脱离合约关系的情况下,索赔该误述带来的金钱损失。

首先有必要明确什么是被陈述方能够依赖的陈述,因为被陈述方相信或依赖无效/不可诉陈述(non-actionable representation)是没有法律保护的,属于自担风险。

所以清楚区分"有效"与"无效"的陈述是至关重要的,正如在 De Beers Abrasive Products Ltd v. International General Electric Co of New York Ltd(1975)1 WLR 972 先例中,Walton 大法官说:"it is a blinding glimpse of the obvious to say that there must be a dividing line between statements that are actionable and those which are not."

《Misrepresentation, Mistake and Non-Disclosure》(2022 年,第 6 版)一书之 3 - 14 段也说:"**The practical requirement of a statement of 'fact'**. It is often said that a misrepresentation, to be actionable, must have been one of (present) fact; and 'fact' is here commonly contrasted with belief or opinion, law, and future fact or intention. ... It is necessary to explore in some detail the reasoning of the courts in those cases which have drawn on the distinction between misrepresentations of fact and misrepresentations of opinion, law and intention. It will be seen that this requirement is based in general terms on the courts' desire to limit actionable misrepresentations to those on which a representee ought to be entitled to rely."

1.1　可诉陈述:对过去或现在事实的虚假或不正确陈述

传统上,可构成可诉误述的陈述只包括对"事实"的不正确陈述,而这里的事实是指做出陈述之前已经发生的(past)或当时正在发生的(present)事实。在国际贸易领域,最为人熟悉的误述是签发虚假或不正确的装船提单(bills of lading)。这些虚假的内容包括:货物有表面损坏但签发清洁提单(说是货物“表面状况良好”);货量短少(如装船只有10,000吨但提单上写12,000吨);倒签提单(把装货上船的日期写为更早的时间以配合买卖合约与/或信用证规定的最后付运日期);实际装港写成其他根本没有去过的港口以隐藏货物的来源等。这些都是针对过去与现在的事实,因为货物已经是装船,事实都已经发生。所以,这种虚假或不正确的陈述是典型的可诉误述。而且船东或代理人明知道事实真相仍做出虚假或不正确的陈述,这显然是欺诈性误述。

至于对将来(future)的事实的陈述,由于做出陈述时将来的事实尚未发生,无所谓“真假”,只是一个预测(prediction)或在没有法律约束下对将来会发生事情的估算,这不构成可诉误述。例如在一宗公司并购交易,卖方告知买方预测或估算未来几年内每年的营业额与纯利润每年会上升15%。买方如果想约束卖方,或试图要卖方认真与坦率地做出预测或估算(因为卖方掌控所有资料与信息),那最好要求将此预测或估算加入并购合约内作为保证条文(warranty)。

有大量权威先例区分误述的是过去或现在的事实还是将来的事实,如在Beattie v. Lord Ebury(1872)LR 7 Ch. App. 777上诉庭先例中,Mellish大法官说:“There is a clear difference between a misrepresentation in point of fact, a representation that something exists at that moment which does not exist, and a representation that something will be done in the future. Of course, a representation that something will be done in the future cannot either be true or false at the moment it is made, and although you may call it a representation, if it is anything, it is a contract or promise.”

另在British Airways Board v. Taylor(1976)1 WLR 13贵族院先例,Wilberforce勋爵说:“... the distinction in law between a promise as to future action, which may be broken or kept, and a statement as to existing fact, which may be true or false, is clear enough.”

由于作为一位合理人士大家都知道在现实中没有人有“神通”可以准确预测到将来,所以法律是不愿意把对将来事实的不正确陈述视为“误述”的,这在FoodCo UK LLP v. Henry Boot Developments Ltd(2010)EWHC 358(Ch)先例中有着很好说明,Lewison大法官说:“Outside the realms of mythology and literature, no one can foretell the future. Even in those realms the prophecies of the Oracle of Delphi[1] were al-

---

〔1〕 古希腊神话中著名的德尔斐神谕,德尔斐被古希腊人认为是世界的中心,也是阿波罗神女祭司皮媞亚的驻地,在这里神的话语通过皮媞亚下达到凡人。Lewison大法官说这些神谕往往比较含糊。

ways ambiguous, Cassandra[2] was never believed, and the prophecies of the witches of Macbeth[3] were downright obscure. The law has thus been wary of imposing liability for statements about the future."

另也有说法是对意见的表达(express of opinion of fact)也不能构成有法律后果的可诉陈述,也就是说意见通常不会构成可诉误述的对象。因为意见是非常主观的内容,也不存在真假之分,只是听者相信或不相信,或是否能被支持意见的理由说服的问题。笔者的《证据法:基础理论、口头证据与专家证据》一书第九章之1段对"事实"与"意见"的区别有详论,内容在此完全可适用,不去重复。

1.2 可诉陈述的复杂形式

在接下来分析什么才是可诉陈述前,可先节录近期的 Raiffeisen Zentralbank Osterreich AG v. Royal Bank of Scotland Plc(2010)EWHC 1392(Comm)先例,Christopher Clarke 大法官对一些重要先例中各种陈述的表现形式与判断标准做出的总结与提炼,以给读者一个概览,具体的内容会在接下来的段节详细分析:

"...Whether any and if so, what representation was made has to be '**judged objectively according to the impact that whatever is said may be expected to have on a reasonable representee in the position and with the known characteristics of the actual representee**' .... The reference to the characteristics of the representee is important. The Court may regard **a sophisticated commercial party** who is told that no representations are being made to him **quite differently than it would a consumer**.

In the case of**an express statement**, 'the court has to consider what a reasonable person would have understood from **the words used in the context** in which they were used' ... The answer to that question may depend on the **nature and content of the statement, the context in which it was made, the characteristics of the maker and of the person to whom it was made, and the relationship between them**.

...In the case of **an implied statement**, 'the court has to perform a similar task, except that it has to consider what a reasonable person would have inferred was being implicitly represented by the representor's words and conduct in their context' ...

Silence by itself cannot found a claim in misrepresentation(fraudulent or otherwise). But an express statement may impliedly represent something. **A possible implication of a statement may be that what has been expressly stated is complete**, i. e. covers everything material or relevant on a particular matter such that something which has not been referred to does not exist. It is, however, necessary to distinguish between what a

---

[2] 卡珊德拉,希腊、罗马神话中特洛伊的公主,阿波罗的祭司,有预言能力,但因抗拒阿波罗,预言不被人相信。

[3] 莎士比亚戏剧《麦克白》中的三女巫,作出了多个模棱两可的预言。

document does not say and what it impliedly represents.

The **essential question is whether** in all the circumstances it has been **impliedly represented by the defendant that there exists some state of facts different from the truth**. In evaluating the effect of what was said a helpful test is whether a reasonable representee would naturally assume that the true state of facts did not exist and that, had it existed, he would in all the circumstances necessarily have been informed of it: Geest plc v. Fyffes plc [1999] 1 All ER(Comm)672 … Further, if the claim is under s 2(1) of the Misrepresentation Act 1967, it is necessary to heed the warning of Rix J that because of the broad measure of damages currently available in the light of Royscot Trust Ltd v Rogerson [1991] 2 QB 297: 'where there is room for an exercise of judgement, a misrepresentation should not be too easily found' …

It is also necessary for the statement relied on to have **the character of a statement upon which the representee was intended, and was entitled, to rely**. In some cases the statement in question may have been accompanied by other **statements by way of qualification or explanation which would indicate to a reasonable person that the putative representor was not assuming a responsibility for the accuracy or completeness of the statement or was saying that no reliance can be placed upon it**. Thus the representor may qualify what might otherwise have been an outright statement of fact by saying that it is only a statement of belief, that it may not be accurate, that he has not verified its accuracy or completeness, or that it is not to be relied on.

Lastly the **claimant must show that he in fact understood the statement in the sense(so far as material) which the court ascribes to it**: Arkwright v Newbold(1881) 17 Ch D 301; Smith v Chadwick(1884)9 App. Cas 187; and that, having that understanding, he relied on it. This may be of particular significance in the case of implied statements."(加黑部分是笔者的强调)

日常生活(更不用说国际商业交往)中陈述可以以变化无穷的方式作出,这就令法院或仲裁庭根据证据认定有否可诉陈述也变得复杂。这里只指出如果被陈述方并不能够清楚与肯定地证明陈述方有否向他做出过一个可诉陈述,陈述的内容是什么或该陈述是否实质重要[4]等,法院或仲裁庭就尽量不会去轻易认定可诉误述成立,因为可诉误述一旦成立后果将十分严重。在欺诈性误述的情况下,无论是在损失赔偿方面还是对误述方的影响方面,后果严重当然是没得说。《Misrepresentation Act 1967》立法 Section 2(1)对误述方无法证明有诚实与合理依据(honest and reasonable

---

〔4〕 在本书第一章之1.3.5段有介绍,"实质重要"(materiality)是指法院或仲裁庭客观看来,会影响一位正常与合理人士(a normal and reasonable person)是否会订立合约与以什么条件订立的虚假或不正确陈述。

ground)下做出的误述,也适用欺诈性误述同样的损失赔偿[5]标准,这一规定看来也是相当苛刻。所以,正如上述节录中提到的 Royscot Trust Ltd v. Rogerson 先例就有说:"where there is room for an exercise of judgement, a misrepresentation should not be too easily found."

另在 Avon Insurance Plc v. Swire Fraser Ltd(2000)Lloyd's Rep IR 535 先例中,Rix 大法官也说:"The ... present state of the law, whereby any misrepresentation which induces a contract provides damages upon the fraud basis. Since that is the law which binds me, it ought in my view to follow that, where there is room for an exercise of judgment, a misrepresentation should not be too easily found. ..."

现实中陈述方做出的陈述会以各种不同的方式传达给被陈述方,这包括文书或语言的明示(express)、默示(implied)或行动(conduct),也往往会有这几个不同方式的结合。沉默(silence)一般不会是一个陈述,但这也难予以确定。例如,在一个商业谈判中一方被对方问及公司背后是否有某财团支持,对方不去否认,更不用说是加上一些行动如带有深意的微笑、点头或只可意会不可言传的眼神,都有可能因为传达给被陈述方与对他做出误导而构成一个有效的陈述。总而言之,判断的标准是去客观看被指称是误述方的被告在谈判中的一连串前后的言行结合起来,有否(无论是有意或无意)给了原告一个虚假或不正确的印象。

这可介绍 Curtis v. Chemical Cleaning and Dyeing Co Ltd(1951)1 KB 805 上诉庭先例,该案案情是原告把结婚礼服送去洗衣店清洗,被要求签署一份标准文件,原告问洗衣店助理签署文件会有什么后果,助理是"讲一半、不讲一半"的回答说是洗衣店对在清洗过程中衣服上装饰的闪光珠片的损坏不负责。但实际上该文件中是有一条洗衣店对清洗过程中衣服的任何损坏都不负责的广泛的免责条文。上诉庭认为洗衣店助理的回答构成可诉误述,结婚礼服被严重损坏(不只是衣服上的装饰),被告洗衣店要赔偿,不得依赖广泛的免责条文(注意当年仍没有保护消费者的立法)免于担责。Denning 大法官认为任何语言或行动,只要能够误导对方与致使对方存在一个对事实的不正确印象就已经足够构成一个对免责条文是否存在或免责去到什么程度的误述,他说:"In my opinion any behaviour, by words or conduct, is sufficient to be a misrepresentation if it is such as to mislead the other party about the existence or extent of the exemption. **If it conveys a false impression, that is enough**. If the false impression **is created knowingly, it is a fraudulent misrepresentation; if it is created unwittingly, it is an innocent misrepresentation**; ... The present case is a good illustration. The customer said in evidence: 'When I was asked to sign the document I asked why? The assistant said I was to accept any responsibility for damage to beads and sequins. I did not read it all before I signed it'. In those circumstances, by failing to draw attention to the width of

[5] 见本书第四章之4.2.2.5段。

the exemption clause, the assistant created the false impression that the exemption only related to the beads and sequins, and that it did not extend to the material of which the dress was made. It was done perfectly innocently, but nevertheless a false impression was created. … it was a sufficient misrepresentation to disentitle the cleaners from relying on the exemption, except in regard to beads and sequins."（加黑部分是笔者的强调）

对于陈述方的语言、行动或两者的混合是否构成一个有效的陈述（无论是明示还是默示），因为现实中有千变万化的情况，所以法院或仲裁庭会根据每一个案件的具体情况来具体做出判断。大多数用明确的语言或文字来做出的陈述是比较清楚的陈述，法院只需考虑一位合理人士在当时的环境/背景下是如何理解他听到或看到的内容。但是一旦涉及通过语言或行动来推断存在某些默示陈述（implied representation），情况就会变得比较复杂，法院除了考虑明示的语言/文字或行动，还要考虑在当时的环境/背景下，一位合理人士是否会从这些内容中推断出某些默示的内容。这正如 Toulson 大法官在 IFE Fund SA v. Goldman Sachs International（2006）EWHC 2887（Comm）先例中对明示和默示的陈述的观点："In determining whether there has been an express representation, and to what effect, the court has to consider what a reasonable person would have understood from the words used in the context in which they were used. In determining what, if any, implied representation has been made, the court has to perform a similar task, except that it has to consider what a reasonable person would have inferred was being implicitly represented by the representor's words and conduct in their context."

判断可诉陈述的复杂性除了体现在判断陈述方是如何作出一个陈述或作出一个怎样的陈述，还体现在判断被陈述方（背景、所处环境与水平不同）如何接受与理解该陈述。

1.3　不清楚的陈述

在多数情况下，被误述方都很容易指出误述方所传递给他的信息中哪些是虚假与不正确的。但也有情况下，陈述方在有意或无意的情况下做出模棱两可、可以有不同理解的对事实的陈述。当双方对通过语言或行动做出的陈述的理解有争议时，法院需要被误述方说明与证明在订约时误述方存在哪些语言或行动导致他所理解或相信的是不正确的事实，并且被陈述方根据他自身的情况与案件的事实背景去这样理解是合理的。这也是十分容易明白，如果原告连陈述方陈述的内容究竟是什么都说不清楚，他就不可能证明该陈述是错误的并且自己受到了误导。在《Misrepresentation, Mistake and Non-Disclosure》一书（2022 年，第 6 版）之 3 – 06 段说："In all cases of misrepresentation, the claimant must include in his particulars of claim the details of the misrepresentation on which he relies, and this will require him to give sufficient indication of the alleged inaccuracy in the statement. It is therefore necessary, in analysing a claim for misrepresentation, to identify the false statement for which the defendant is responsible, and was communicated to the representee. In most cases the falsehood and its communication to the representee can be easily identified from the defendant's words or actions. Sometimes, however, there is some doubt about the meaning which was, or might have been, conveyed to the representee ... the test is whether: (a) the words or conduct in fact led the representee to believe the alleged false fact, and (b) it was reasonable for the representee to believe it from the words or conduct as he perceived them. Where there is a dispute over the meaning of a statement, this is the approach the courts should use in determining whether it is to be treated as a misrepresentation. In applying this test, the characteristics of the representee are important."

早期的 Smith v. Chadwick(1884)9 App Cas 187 贵族院先例中就存在对不清楚陈述(ambiguous representations)的理解的争议。该案中原告投资人 Smith 先生主张被告 Chadwick 先生等人在招股章程(prospectus)中做出欺诈性误述,其中最实质重要的一项误述内容是招股章程中对公司名下的钢铁厂的年营业额或年产值的说明。该说明的内容是"the present value of the turnover or output of the entire works is over £ 1,000,000 sterling per annum"。对于该说明内容有两种理解是:(1)钢铁厂的营业额或年产值在过去的年份已经超过 100 万英镑,所以用英文的现在时态来表示持续到现在的情况也是如此;(2)钢铁厂目前的营业额或年产值最高能够达到 100 万英镑以上。结合事实情况来看,第一种理解与事实不相符,第二种理解才符合当时实际情况。

一审法院判原告胜诉,被告要赔偿原告投资的损失。被告上诉至上诉庭,上诉庭推翻了一审的判决,认为因为该说明文字的表述可以有两种理解,存在模糊与不清楚之处。原告要主张被告欺诈性误述,他需要证明被告的语言或行动令他对说明文字的理解是与事实不符的那一种。但原告并没有在文书请求中说清楚被告的哪些语言与行动令他得出的是不符合事实的那一种理解。上诉庭的 Jessel MR 大法官说如果原告只是泛泛说他依赖招股章程中的说明文字,无论该说明文字的意思是什么,法院无法查明他究竟是如何被诱导或欺骗,如果陈述方并没有表达错,而仅仅是他自己理解错了,是否仍然能够说他被欺骗?对此,Jessel MR 大法官说:"But if the plaintiff will not tell us what he relied on; if he says to the court 'Please to find out the meaning; I relied on the statements in the prospectus, and I relied upon them accordingly to their meaning, whatever that meaning is'; surely that will not do. How can the court find out that he has been deceived at all? The court may think it means the very thing the plaintiff did not think it meant, and then are they to say he has been deceived, because he took it in the wrong sense? That, of course, is impossible."

贵族院也支持了上诉庭的判决,并进一步分析即使存在这样的语言或行动,但结合原告本身是从事钢铁生产与贸易的业务,并且曾经对钢铁厂的产量提出过询问,根据他自身对钢铁产品市场价格的了解,他作为一个专业的商业人士是不会得出第一种与事实不符的理解的。

在近期的 Foster v. Action Aviation(2013) EWHC 2439(Comm)先例中,Hamblen 大法官说:"Unless one understands that a representation is being made it is difficult to see how it can be said to have been relied upon. Mr Foster's evidence was that had he known at the time that the factory had financial issues he would not have signed the contract. However, the case is one of positive representation, not non-disclosure. He gives no evidence that he understood that the defendants were representing to him or telling him that the factory had no financial issues, still less that they were making the more specific representations set out in the pleading. I am accordingly not satisfied that inducement has been sufficiently proved."

可另介绍一个新加坡 Chuan Bee Realty Pte Ltd v. Teo Chee Yeow Aloysius (1996)2 SLR(R)134 先例,该案案情涉及被告在报纸上刊登出售房屋的广告,对面积的陈述为"9000/5600 平方尺",这一对面积的表述并不清楚。原告根据广告支付了 35,000 新加坡币获得购买的选择权(option to purchase),但后来没有在该选择权的有效期届满前及时作出选择。被告不退还该 35,000 新加坡币。原告以被告在报纸上刊登的广告中存在误述去申请法院撤销合约,企图取回这笔钱。但原告不成功,因为他无法说明与证明他对该面积的表述的理解与该理解是与事实不符从而诱导了他。Lim Teong Qwee JC 大法官说:"The statement in the advertisement ... was certainly ambiguous and for the plaintiffs to succeed in misrepresentation there must be evidence as to the construction they put on it. They must say in what way they understood it. If they do not then it is impossible to say that the statement is false and that they have been induced by it to alter their position. I am unable to find any such evidence in this case ..."

1.4　默示陈述

在上面已经提到陈述不仅可以以明示的方式作出与传达给被陈述方,也可以通过陈述方的语言、文字或行动默示做出,甚至是在陈述方表达意见、意图或将来的事实这些本不属于可诉陈述的内容时也存在对现在事实的默示陈述(implied representations)。这里先将默示陈述主要的情形列举一下,在以下专门分析对意见的陈述、行动的陈述、对意图和将来事实的陈述时还会进一步分析这些陈述下存在默示陈述的问题。

1.4.1　明示陈述带出来的言下之意、潜台词或弦外之音

解释合约的原则首先要看合约条文本身所传达出来的意思,也就是字面的意思,只有在字面意思存在模糊或模棱两可的情况下,法院或仲裁庭才会去考虑其他因素(如订约时的背景/语境[6])来帮助解释。这一原则也适用在判断陈述的内容究竟

---

[6]　在笔者《合约的解释:规则与应用》一书第六章有详细介绍。

是什么意思这一问题上，即通常先去看语言或文字字面上最自然的意思。不过由于语言或文字可以是很有技巧，甚至经常被形容为是一门艺术，这时语言或文字除了字面的意思，仔细分析还会推断出存在有隐藏或暗含的意思，也就是通常所说的言下之意、潜台词或弦外之音。该语言或文字所暗含的意思通常也会跟随着语言与文字本身被传达给被陈述方，由此法律会将其视为一种默示陈述。如果语言或文字本身的内容是真实的，但其弦外之音会误导被陈述方，该弦外之音也属于可诉陈述。

这种默示陈述在国际商业交易中十分危险。熟悉国际游戏规则的高水平西方商人想要误导人时往往也会留一手，不会直说。所以为了保护自己，面对这种情况就要采取手段保留证据，例如在依赖言下之意订约前向对方文书记录自己的理解，他如果不作出更正将来就无法逃脱误导的责任。

先举几个默示陈述的例子。在一个土地买卖中，卖方的律师告诉买方他不知道存在任何会影响土地自由使用的限制性约定（restrictive covenants），如土地上不能建造砖厂。该陈述存在一个言下之意是该律师对土地是否有限制性约定进行过合理的调查，并且如果确实存在这类限制性约定该律师会披露给买方，所以他说不知道存在就等于是不存在：见 Nottingham Patent Brick and Tile Co v. Butler（1886）16 QBD 778 先例。

又或者卖方作出陈述说该房产在出售前不久还是以某一个不错的价格出租。不难看出卖方的潜台词是买方如果购入该房产，也能以差不多的租金价格出租出去：见 Dimmock v. Hallett（1866）LR 2 Ch. App. 21 先例。

这时，如果在上述两个先例中存在律师根本没有进行过调查；在之前租客离开之后卖方就再也找不到能够出此租金的租客的事实情况，看起来虽然明示陈述的表面意思都是没有问题，只是两者的弦外之音所构成的对现有事实的默示陈述是不正确的，而恰恰正是这默示陈述误导买方去作出签订买卖合约的决定。类似的争议也出现在 William Sindall Plc v. Cambridgeshire CC（1994）1 WLR 1016 与 Clinicare Ltd v. Orchard Homes and Development Ltd（2004）EWHC 1694（QB）等先例中。

1.4.2　法律没有自动披露责任但不披露会误导对方

默示陈述也可以通过行动构成，这行动包括主动隐瞒与掩盖不利事实或没有披露全面的事实，无论没有披露是故意还是疏忽。虽然在英国法下合约方在订约时通常没有自动披露的责任（no duty of disclosure），〔7〕但可想而知是不会什么都不披露就达成合约的。如果法律允许大家只披露好的，隐藏不好的，显然不仅会带来误导，也非常不利于商业社会的健康发展。于是，法律就设立这种默示陈述，从陈述方的明示陈述中去做出一些对某些事实存在或不存在的合理默示推断来构成默示陈述，这合理推断出的默示陈述也是可诉陈述，从而约束陈述方不能随意挑挑拣拣做出陈述去误导对方。

---

〔7〕 见本书第五章的详细介绍。

Property Alliance Group Ltd v. Royal Bank of Scotland(2018)EWCA Civ 355 先例,[8]第一次在上诉庭的层面考虑并确认了 Colman 大法官在 Geest Plc v. Fyffes Plc (1999)1 All ER(Comm)672 先例中所确立的测试标准,即是否会令一个合理的被陈述方从陈述方的言行中自然地就默示认为某个事实不存在。因为如果某事实存在,陈述方是有必要披露出来。Colman 大法官说:"whether a reasonable representee would naturally assume that the true state of facts did not exist and that, if it did, he would necessarily have been informed of it."

1.4.3　双方对相关事实与信息知悉程度不同时的默示陈述

通过表达意见(opinion)、意图(intention)或对将来事实(future facts)的预测可能会带出对事实的默示陈述。在本章一开始就已经提到这一类陈述的本身并不是对过去或现在事实的陈述,从而也不是可诉陈述。但实践中,表达严肃意见或对将来作出预测都不是毫无事实根据的,这时往往就会在陈述意见、意图或作出预测时,带出对过去或现在事实的默示陈述。

在 Smith v. Land and House Property Corporation(1884)28 Ch. D. 7 贵族院先例中,被告地产公司在一个拍卖中准备购买 Smith 先生名下的酒店,Smith 先生称酒店目前出租给一个非常令人满意的租客(a most desirable tenant)。Smith 先生对租客的评价意见中默示了一个过去与现在的事实是他与该租客之间没有发生过需要追讨租金之类的不令人满意的事情。但实际上该租客已经有好长时间没有准时支付过租金,仅在各种施压下才断断续续支付了少量租金。Bowen 大法官说经常会有一种错误的假设是意见的表述中不会涉及对事实的陈述。这种假设能够成立的前提条件是双方对相关的事实与信息具有同等的知悉程度。但如果双方并不具有这种同等的知悉程度,了解情况的一方做出的意见陈述,在不知悉事实的另一方的眼中就存在一个默示陈述是该意见有实质重要的事实作为依据,而不是乱说的。该先例中显然卖方与现有租客之间发生的事情只有卖方知道,而潜在的买方是不会知道的。Bowen 大法官说:"In considering whether there was a misrepresentation, … It is material to observe that it is often fallaciously assumed that a statement of opinion cannot involve the statement of a fact. **In a case where the facts are equally well known to both parties, what one of them says to the other is frequently nothing but an expression of opinion.** The statement of such opinion is in a sense a statement of a fact, about the condition of the man's own mind, but only of an irrelevant fact, for it is of no consequence what the opinion is. **But if the facts are not equally known to both sides, then a statement of opinion by one who knows the facts best involves very often a statement of a material fact, for he impliedly states that he knows facts which justify his opinion.** … Now are

[8]　该先例是操纵 LIBOR 丑闻爆出之后带来的一系列诉讼案例之一。对于是否构成默示陈述,该先例是试水的测试案件。稍后在本章之 1.4.5 段会详细述及。

the statements here statements which involve such a representation of material facts? They are statements on a subject as to which prima facie the vendors know everything and the purchasers nothing. The vendors state that the property is let to a most desirable tenant, what does that mean? I agree that it is not a guarantee that the tenant will go on paying his rent, but it is to my mind a guarantee of a different sort, and amounts **at least to an assertion that nothing has occurred in the relations between the landlords and the tenant which can be considered to make the tenant an unsatisfactory one. That is an assertion of a specific fact.**"（加黑部分是笔者的强调）

在较近期有相同说法的是 BG Plc v. Nelson Group Services (Maintenance) Ltd (2002) EWCA Civ 547 上诉庭先例中，Kennedy 大法官说："When an opinion is expressed, the person who express it either does or does not know facts which justify that opinion. The existence of those facts, and his state of knowledge in relation to them, are themselves facts capable of being misrepresented by implication by the expression of opinion ... Sometimes an expression of opinion may carry with it no implication other than that the opinion is genuinely held."

以上所讲可去举一个简单的例子令读者更容易明白。比方说如果双方都对某一房屋的情况十分了解，甚至均在里面住过，其中一方对另一方说该房屋住起来是十分舒适且生活便利就仅仅只是一个意见的表达，另一方如果不同意这个意见，也会提出不同的意见。但如果买方根本不了解该房屋的情况，卖方或他的经纪人向买方做出同样的评价，买方就会认为卖方是基于一定的事实才去作出这样的评价，例如他对房屋非常了解或者房屋附近步行十分钟的范围内就有超市、学校、公共交通等才能被称为生活便利。而这些事实就构成评价意见带出的默示陈述。如果经纪人根本没有亲自去看过这个房屋的情况就随便给出评价意见，例如距离该房屋最近的一个商店或公共交通站点要步行一个小时以上，这就令评价意见带出的默示陈述变得不正确，从而会构成可诉误述。

根据以上对由意见表述所带出的默示陈述的介绍，可以看到这类情形中对判断是否存在默示陈述的一个很重要的测试标准是看双方对相关事实与信息的知悉程度是否对等。双方在知悉程度上相差得越远，不掌握信息的一方会对掌握信息的一方的依赖程度越高，由此也越容易构成默示陈述。

1.4.4 商业案件中双方的言行带出来的默示陈述

默示陈述构成可诉误述的案件是有不少，在此不去逐一介绍，只挑几个商业案件去介绍。首先介绍 Credit Lyonnais Bank Nederland NV (now Generale Bank Nederland NV) v. Export Credits Guarantee Department (1996) 1 Lloyd's Rep 200 先例。政府机构 Export Credits Guarantee Department（"ECGD"）要对某进出口公司的信用状况作出评级。Credit Lyonnais Bank Nederland N. V（"银行"）则负责向"ECGD"提供该公司资信状况的信息。"银行"对该公司的评价为"respectable and trustworthy and had demonstrated that it was highly able and efficient"。该评价意见同时传递出来一个默示的陈述是该银行做出的评价意见是有合理的事实基础,例如该公司的经营状况良好、盈利丰厚、资信评级高等,反正肯定不是濒临破产等。但该评价意见后来因该公司很快就破产被证明是不正确的。这明显看出"银行"在给出评价意见时根本就没有相关的事实基础。这相当于你对一个根本不认识的人做出严肃(明知道对方会依赖)的评价意见说他是一个值得信赖的人。

另在 FoodCo UK LLP v. Henry Boot Developments Ltd(2010)EWHC 358(Ch)先例中,被告 Henry Boot 公司获得了一个开发高速公路服务区的项目,于是开始招商,并在招商手册中说明在服务区会设立多个便利设施,并根据一份由被告聘请的专业团队所作的调查报告预测将来到访服务区的人流量每周可达 88,000 人。于是 KFC 和 Burger King 这一类的快餐店决定加入。不过后来事实证明到访服务区的人流量仅有预测数量的 10% 左右。加入该项目的投资人以被告存在误述将被告诉至法院。该先例涉及的默示陈述是 Henry Boot 先生作为被告的董事默示陈述了他真诚与有合理理由相信调查报告中对人流量的保守估计是可靠与审慎的;同时也默示陈述自己是不知道任何可以对此报告中数据可靠性提出质疑的信息与事实。

Lewison 大法官也同意在对将来的预测中会存在对现在事实的默示陈述说:"while a forecast may carry with it an implicit representation about a present fact(e. g. that the forecaster believes the forecast or that he has taken reasonable care in making it) it is that implicit representation about a present fact rather than the forecast itself that constitutes the actionable representation."

1.4.5 有关 LIBOR 丑闻系列案件的复杂与富有想象力的默示陈述

伦敦银行同业间拆借利率(London Inter Bank Offered Rate,LIBOR)指的是伦敦一流银行之间无担保借款的利率,该利率反映了银行之间的信誉风险。这曾经是世界上使用最广泛的一个基准利率,是金融市场的重要基准指标,无数贷款、债券、金融衍生品合约与 LIBOR 挂钩。LIBOR 主要针对短期利率,包括一个月、三个月、六个月不等。LIBOR 体系包括美元、英镑、欧元、日元与瑞士法郎五种货币。LIBOR 产生的机制是由 20 家伦敦的一流国际银行每日向英国银行家协会提供借贷利率估值,然后英国银行家协会在去掉 25% 最高和 25% 最低的估值之后根据剩余的估值的平均值得出 LIBOR。在 2006 年美国次贷危机爆发后,由于次级债务和优良债务打包在一起,在金融市场流通,不同的银行之间都无法得知对方手中的次债的数量,所以市场上一夜之间 LIBOR 大涨,令整个金融市场的流动性降低,一些银行甚至出现借不到钱周转、资金链断裂而破产的情况。在次贷危机发生之后,大型银行操纵 LIBOR 的问题被放到聚光灯下,由 LIBOR 的产生机制可以看出只要有超过 25% 的银行参与共谋,LIBOR 是很容易受到影响。2012 年 6 月,英国巴克莱银行因操纵与虚假汇报 LIBOR 与欧元银行间同业拆借利率(EURIBOR)被英国与美国监管机构处以 4.5 亿美元罚款。在笔者《证据法:国际规管与诉讼中的证据攻防》一书第十三章之 1.2 段介绍的 Property Alliance Group Ltd v. Royal Bank of Scotland Plc(2015) EWHC 1557 (Ch)先例也是同样的背景。该先例的被告英国苏格兰皇家银行(RBS)也由于在2006年到2010年间参与操纵LIBOR受到美国有关机构与英国当时的金融监管局(FSA,在今天已经被金融行为监管局Financial Conduct Authority取代)调查,最后达成和解被罚款8.75亿英镑。

操纵LIBOR丑闻在全球持续发酵后,英国、美国、欧盟、日本、加拿大等多国监管机构先后介入调查,调查涉及数十家欧美金融机构。除了上述提到的巴克莱银行与苏格兰皇家银行,2012年12月,瑞银向美国、英国与瑞士的金融监管机构支付了共计15亿美元罚款,以了结对瑞银操纵LIBOR及其他利率的指控。2016年5月,因为未能很好地执行2012年有关LIBOR操纵的和解协议,瑞银被美国司法部门再次罚款2.03亿美元。2013年10月,荷兰合作银行也因操纵LIBOR与EURIBOR被英、美、荷三国监管机构处以10.7亿美元的罚款。2015年4月,德意志银行向美国监管机构支付21.75亿美元罚款,向英国FCA支付2.268亿英镑罚款,这在当时是金额最大的一笔罚款。2016年5月,美国花旗集团同意向美国监管机构支付4.25亿美元罚款,以了结针对该银行试图操纵全球重要基准利率的指控。

而在监管机构的巨额罚款外,各大银行还面临私人集体诉讼的民事索赔。据报道,场外交易/柜台买卖(OTC)投资人就银行间共谋操纵LIBOR在美国起诉,之后巴克莱银行以1.2亿美元、花旗集团以1.3亿美元、德意志银行以2.4亿美元和解。汇丰银行虽然否认不法行为,但是为了避免诉讼的风险、成本与造成的不安,因而决定以1亿美元和解。

可以说操纵LIBOR与其他利率丑闻暴露出全球金融体系存在普遍的系统性欺诈/欺骗与明显的监管漏洞,甚至严重挫伤公众对金融业的信心。市场参与者不再愿意使用该基准。与此同时,银行因为怕提供利率估值后承担监管的后果,也越来越不愿意向英国银行家协会提供自己的估值数据。这令LIBOR的产生开始依赖专家对市场和交易数据的判断,也即专家意见而不再是真实的交易数据进行活动,这进而影响了市场的流动性与稳定性。FCA在2017年7月,宣布其在2021年之后将不再强制要求报价行更新LIBOR报价,并建议金融市场的参与者使用另外一种替代的无风险利率(risk-free rate,简称RFRs)。[9]

FCA在2021年3月5日进一步确认,所有LIBOR设置将在下述日期后不再由

---

[9] RFRs是根据隔夜储蓄利率计算得出,因其是基于大量真实与可观测到的市场数据,所以可以说是最接近实际且没有风险的。不过相比于LIBOR,RFRs的使用有其自身的问题,这包括LIBOR是前瞻性的针对将来的利率,而RFRs则是基于已经发生过的交易,这令一项贷款无法在一开始就能计算出借款人将要支付的利息,从而会影响借款人现金流的管理;LIBOR针对五种货币都可以适用,而RFRs则只针对一种具体的货币,这就会给涉及多种货币的交易带来计算上的困难;LIBOR有考虑市场的流动性,而RFRs则没有这个考虑,所以实际的借款利率会高于RFRs,市场参与者还要另外想办法去弥补这种差别等。

任何执行机构提供报价或不再具代表性:(1)就所有英镑、欧元、瑞士法郎和日元设置,以及1周与2个月美元设置,有关日期为2021年12月31日;(2)就其余的美元设置,有关日期为2023年6月30日。

由于LIBOR取消的最后时间已经到来,金融市场上的多个行业协会都对如何做好这个过渡给出指引或制定标准的格式条款供市场参与者使用。而银行面对成千上万涉及以LIBOR作为基准的合约需要进行修改,由于这些标准合约中往往有不可口头修改的条文(no oral-amendment clause),[10]现实中对于成千上万的合约也做不到和每一个订约方都以书面修改,唯一可行的解决办法是发信函给所有客户,如果到了某一天对方没有书面提出异议就用视为同意(deem consent)的禁反言理论来解释,由于本书不是针对这个课题,所以在此就不再展开讲。

在上述介绍的背景下,本小节主要想讲LIBOR丑闻引发的大量民事索赔中有关贷款、金融衍生品合约这类大型商业案件,这些先例涉及方方面面的争议,其中误述(主要是默示误述)是一个共同且重要的争议,本书之后会介绍好几个这方面重要的先例。上面已经提到过Property Alliance Group Ltd v. Royal Bank of Scotland(2018) EWCA Civ 355上诉庭先例,接下来也有一系列先例有关LIBOR丑闻,并最终导致LIBOR的消失。在该系列先例中,原告贷款人为了控制融资成本往往会签订利率掉期合约(swap)以对冲利率变动带来的风险。被告银行往往以LIBOR作为利率基准来订约。英国几家主要银行参与操纵LIBOR的丑闻一经爆出,多个利率掉期合约中的贷款人纷纷提出银行要求使用LIBOR作为计息基准,就默示陈述了银行不存在操纵LIBOR的不当行为且也不会去参与操纵LIBOR。

由于这些跨国银行对法律的警觉性高与有高水平的法务团队,一般想在他们做出过的清楚无误的明示陈述中抓到把柄非常不容易,更不要说是在这种涉及金额庞大与复杂交往的商业交易中。原告往往只能依赖双方在漫长沟通中银行的一些明示陈述中存在某些默示陈述,而这些默示陈述是虚假与不正确的来作为诉因。笔者举一个简单例子,银行在贷款标准合约下提出使用LIBOR作为基准,甚至说LIBOR是最公道的,或客户要求银行解释LIBOR是怎样操作,银行也解答了,这就是一个明示陈述,但对真相只讲一半。而贷款人的争辩就是银行默示陈述没有参与也不会参与操纵LIBOR。但该系列案件中,法院在考虑大局的倾向性下均以各种理由判银行在订约时不存在这样的默示陈述。即使在非常具体的案情下,法院认为银行存在默示陈述,但也会因贷款人无法证明可诉误述的其他要件而败诉。如无法证明银行虽然存在默示陈述,但该默示陈述是错误的:见Property Alliance Group Ltd v. Royal Bank of Scotland先例;或即使假设银行存在该默示陈述,贷款人也根本没有意识到该默示陈述,从而更不存在依赖:见Leeds City Council and Ors v. Barclays Bank Plc and Ors (2021) EWHC 363(Comm)先例。

---

〔10〕 见笔者《合约的履行、弃权与禁反言》一书第三章之1段。

节录的 Graiseley Properties Limited & Ors v. Barclays Bank Plc(2013)EWCA Civ 1372 上诉庭先例中,Longmore 大法官提到 Cooke 大法官在 Deutsche Bank AG v. Unitech Global Ltd(2013)EWHC 471(Comm)先例中的判法:"... Cooke J then said that pleas ... sought to place in the mouth of one bank a statement about the overall integrity of the LIBOR system or of an individual bank's contributions to it which was unrealistic and did not meet Toulson J's test.[11] He accepted that ... in the context of the credit and the swap agreements no representation was being made in relation to the means by which the LIBOR figure was compiled. He was prepared to allow a plea of **an implied term that the bank would do nothing during the existence of the contracts to jeopardize the ordinary and proper assessment of the relevant LIBOR rate to which the transactions were linked but not the plea of an implied representation based merely on the fact that the bank was a panel bank and offered or made a financial transaction linked to LIBOR.** To imply such a representation would, he said, amount to a duty to disclose any information which the bank had which might undermine the integrity of LIBOR. ..."(加黑部分显示原告指称的默示陈述)

上述 LIBOR 丑闻系列先例中原告提出的默示陈述显示出在金额庞大与交往时间长的商业交易中,交易双方发生争议后往往会带出十分复杂与富想象力的争辩理由,例如结合案件事实背景提出对各种不同的事实的默示陈述/表述,这可见本书第三章之 4.3.2 段 Marme Inversiones 2007 SL v. NatWest Markets Plc(2019)EWHC 366(Comm)先例中提到的 5 个默示陈述。其他 LIBOR 系列案例所提出的默示陈述也大同小异。在涉及 LIBOR 丑闻的系列先例中,原告指控被告银行的默示陈述绝大部分都没有获得法院的支持,这显示了构成默示误述的困难。这也符合本章之 1.2 段所讲的法院会因有严重后果而不轻易判误述成立。该系列案件更是考虑涉及大局的问题,正如刚节录的 Cooke 大法官的最后一句"To imply such a representation ... might undermine the integrity of LIBOR"。

最后,由于本书多次提及 Property Alliance Group Ltd v. Royal Bank of Scotland 上诉庭先例,所以在此简单介绍一下该先例的案情。原告 Property Alliance Group Ltd 是一家地产投资与开发公司,它在 2003 年 5 月到 2014 年 7 月之间与被告苏格兰皇家银行订立了多份信贷合约。为了对冲利率变化的风险,在被告银行的要求下,双方在 2004 年 10 月至 2008 年 4 月期间也订立了 4 份利率掉期合约,计算利率的基准是 3 个月的英镑 LIBOR。2008 年金融海啸后,该 LIBOR 陡升。原告最终于 2010 年 6 月 7 日无力履行利率掉期合约而终止履约,给原告带来了 826 万英镑的损失。原告于是将被告诉至法院,并提出被告向原告作出过多达 10 项的误述。其中,也有关

---

[11] 见本章 1.2 段节录的 Toulson 大法官在 IFE Fund SA v. Goldman Sachs International(2007)1 Lloyd's Rep 264 先例中所说的测试标准。

于 LIBOR 的默示陈述，原告认为被告通过要求原告订立利率掉期合约的行为，默示做出了陈述。该先例是第一个法院判默示陈述存在的先例。但因为原告没有证明 RBS 操纵 LIBOR，所以这些陈述并非错误。

2. 对意见的表述

本段会分析如何区分对事实的陈述与对该事实发表的个人意见（statement of opinion），可先节录一些权威说法，《Chitty on Contracts》（2021 年，第 34 版）一书之 9－009 段说："**Puffs and statement of opinion**. Mere 'puffs' do not amount to representations. A mere statement of opinion which proves to have been unfounded, will not be treated as a misrepresentation; for as a general rule these cannot be regarded as representations of fact, except in so far as they show that the opinion or intention is held by the person expressing it."（加黑部分是笔者的强调）

另《Misrepresentation, Mistake and Non-Disclosure》一书（2022 年，第 6 版）之 3－15 段所说："**Sales talk**. Some statements made during the negotiations for a contract might be regarded as just 'sales talk': either the statements are, on their face, assertions of fact but they are only exaggerations, 'puffing the product' and not to be taken seriously; or they are **not sufficiently clear and precise to constitute actionable misrepresentations**. The circumstances of the contract and its negotiations have to be considered as a whole in order to decide whether the statement is to be regarded as actionable, and **the core question is whether the representee was entitled to take the statement seriously and so to rely on it in deciding whether to enter into the contract**. ...."（加黑部分是笔者的强调）

在笔者《证据法：基础理论、口头证据与专家证据》一书第九章之 1 段已经提到事实（fact）与意见（opinion）有重要的区别，但在千变万化的现实情况中不容易区分到底是对一个事实的陈述或是对该事实发表的个人意见。这种区分在误述的范畴会比证据（事实证据或意见证据）范畴更重要，因为直接决定了某些言行是否有法律后果。

可先以商业活动中最频繁发生的推销（sales talk）为例。推销不仅是针对任何商品的买卖，在今天竞争激烈的国际商业环境下，任何行业都需要推销与做广告，就连专业人士如律师、会计师、银行等也需要向潜在客户推销自己以求被委任去提供专业服务。在推销过程中，几乎无可避免地会对商品或自己的能力与水平夸大、避重就轻与吹捧性（puff）地"卖花赞花香"。既然是无可避免的人性，重视配合实际的英国法律显然不会唱高调。总之，只要是在做法上，推销方表现是在给意见，就不会带来法律责任。即使是有少数听众是"傻瓜"，会相信一般合理人士不会相信的而"受骗"，给意见的一方也不会有法律责任。比如,在做广告时自我吹嘘说:“我认为这个产品应该是全世界最好的。”这可能是事实真相,但在表达上是属于意见,法律上没有责任(既然是事实真相,本来也不会有责任)。一位合理谨慎的听众也不会依赖这句话,而会综合考虑通过各种渠道获得的信息才最终作出买还是不买的决定。

对于专业人士做出的会带来法律后果的“意见”,更是不容易给予一个准确的定义,需要根据不同案件的背景/语境去作出判断。[12] 在 Rubenstein v. HSBC Bank Ltd (2011) EWHC 2304 (QB)先例中,对于银行的投资部门做出的投资建议,Havelock - Allan QC 大法官认为去对“意见”下定义是不明智的,因为事实与意见总是混在一起。一个好的起点是看客户提出的是什么问题或查询什么东西。如果客户是希望银行从专业角度推荐一些投资产品,任何推荐都可能构成意见;而如果客户只是对一些具体信息与事实的查询,银行做出的回答就很可能只是提供信息与事实。Havelock - Allan QC 大法官说:

“The key to the giving of advice is that the information is either accompanied by a comment or value judgement on the relevance of that information to the client's investment decision, or is itself the product of a process of selection involving a value judgement so that the information will tend to influence the decision of the recipient.

To attempt **any greater definition of the giving of advice in an investment context would be unwise and is probably impossible**. I suggest, however, that **the starting point** of any inquiry as to whether what was said by an IFA(独立财务顾问) in a particular situation did or did not amount to advice **is to look at the inquiry to which he was responding**. If a client **asks for a recommendation, any response is likely to be regarded as advice** unless there is an express disclaimer to the effect that advice is not being given. On the other hand, if a client makes **a purely factual inquiry** such as 'What corporate bonds are currently yielding X%?' or 'How does this structured product work?', it is not difficult to conclude that **a reply which simply provides the relevant information is no more than that**.”(加黑部分是笔者的强调)

这些年来中国经济高速发展,财富不断累积,投资变为一个热门的课题,各种投资意见或建议“满天飞”。不少会被投资人依赖的意见或建议也是来自一般公众有信心的银行的理财或投资顾问(financial/investment adviser)。在这种投资活动,也常会涉及律师与会计师等专业人士。他们如果提供错误意见或虚假信息与事实固然可能构成可诉误述,因为这些意见与事实可能导致双方之间产生合约(如委托合约),但更多可能会发生的是错误意见或虚假信息导致受害方与其他第三人订立合约,如购买其他金融机构发行的不良金融产品,并蒙受损失。这样,受害方向提供错误投资建议的银行提起诉讼,就不能以可诉误述为诉因,并要求包括撤销合约(rescission of

---

〔12〕 有关专业人士提供专业意见的问题,在本书第六章有详论。

contract)与损失赔偿等普通法与《Misrepresentation Act 1967》立法对误述的救济,而是以银行在非一般关系(如诚信责任、特殊关系)下违反"小心谨慎责任"(duty of care)的疏忽侵权为诉因,索赔侵权导致受害方蒙受的经济损失。关于这方面的责任与损失,在贵族院的 South Australia Asset Management Corp v. York Montague Ltd (1997) AC 191 先例后,有了责任范围大原则的创新说法,可见本书第六章的详细介绍。

但正如在本书第一章之 2.2.1 段介绍的 Hedley Byrne v. Heller(1964) AC 465 贵族院先例显示,即使是专业人士也不是提供的所有意见都有法律后果,而是要有非一般关系,如"自愿承担责任"(voluntary assumption of responsibility)等。以银行为例,它们经常会面对很多客户的查询,银行自己也经常向新老客户推销各种金融产品。在 JP Morgan Chase Bank v. Springwell Navigation Corporation (2008) EWHC 1186 (Comm)先例中,对于涉及新兴市场的金融产品,Gloster 大法官说:"... indeed, the giving of advice, were part and parcel of the every day life of a salesman in emerging markets."

所以,需要区分什么才是有法律后果的意见,如 Hamblen 大法官在 Standard Chartered Bank v. Ceylon Petroleum Corporation (2011) EWHC 1785 (Comm)先例说:"there is a clear distinction between giving advice and assuming legal responsibility for that advice."

在更近期的 Thornbridge Ltd v. Barclays Bank Plc (2015) EWHC 3430 (QB)先例中,Moulder 大法官节录了 JP Morgan Chase Bank v. Springwell Navigation Corporation 先例中所说需要区分到底只是普通的销售投资产品还是自愿承担责任下对特定产品提供意见:"the fact that a person, in the capacity of a salesperson, gives investment advice, tells us nothing about what, if any, obligations were in fact owed... still less does it inform us to the extent of any such duties of care as were owed. In order to decide whether the advice given gave rise to obligations that went beyond the normal recommendations or 'advice', given in the daily interactions between an **institution's salesforce and a purchaser of its products**, so as to import obligations of the type owed by **a fully fledged investment advisor**, one needs to look at all aspects of the objective evidence of the relationship between the parties. ... it follows that **mere giving of advice, even specific investment advice, is not sufficient to establish a duty of care. This is the case even where the investment advice is relied upon by a customer**: the fact that... a salesman... was, in that capacity, giving such advice and making recommendations, and that the customer was taking the salesman's advice and recommendations into account... does not in my judgement predicate that a duty of care arises on the part of the salesmen. Reliance on its own, even if established, does not give rise to an advisory relationship, with consequential duties of care'."(加黑部分是笔者的强调)

3. 事实陈述与意见表述的区分

上一段提及推销自己想出售的商品、财产（如房屋）或提供的服务时会不可避免地进行夸大，这是人性与现实，也是法律可以容忍的。但推销与做广告不能太过火，否则就接近欺骗，这时法律就不能容忍了。这样过火的推销或广告被听众或商业交易的对方所依赖，并且由于过度夸大变为错误的陈述而给依赖一方造成损失的，推销一方就会产生法律责任。在案情千变万化的不同案件中区分推销或广告的特定言行是"事实陈述"还是"意见表述"，显然对个别案件与整个社会都重要。有了稳定与肯定的分水岭，一般的公众或商业人士也就知道哪些推销或做广告是可依赖的，哪些是要自己进一步调查的。

区分事实的陈述或意见的表述，甚至是否有误述的内容，显然是要看每一个案件的不同案情，如陈述/表述用的是什么话语或文字，如何客观理解，当时的环境（circumstance）/语境（context），不同行业的习惯做法等。随后段节会对此做进一步的探讨，只先节录在 Bankers Trust International v. PT Dharmala Sakti Sejahtera（1996）CLC 518 先例中，Mance 大法官提到的作出区分的主要考虑因素："... the potential relevance of the **parties' relationship** and the **surrounding circumstances** to a decision whether any and if so **what representation was made** in the particular case. The **meaning and effect of words** never falls to be viewed in a vacuum. It **is shaped by the context** of their communication, including the **parties respective positions, knowledge and experience**. A description or commendation which may be irrelevant or may even serve as a warning to one recipient, because of its generality, superficiality or laudatory nature, or because of the **recipient's own knowledge or sophisticated receiver**."（加黑部分是笔者的强调）

在 Kyle Bay Ltd（t/a Astons Nightclub）v. Underwriters（2007）EWCA Civ 57 上诉庭先例中，Neuberger 大法官也说到其中一些考虑因素："The question whether a statement can amount to a representation capable of founding a claim in misrepresentation **must depend on the words involved in the context in which they were so used**. Until one has decided that, in the circumstances of the particular case, the statement should be treated as a representation rather than, say, a contention or argument, any question of liability for misrepresentation cannot arise."（加黑部分是笔者的强调）

在 Raiffeisen Zentralbank Osterreich AG v. Royal Bank of Scotland Plc（2010）EWHC 1392（Comm）先例中，Christopher Clarke 大法官说："The answer to that question may depend on the nature and content of the statement, the context in which it was made, the characteristics of the maker and of the person to whom it was made, and the relationship between them."

3.1　区分之一:陈述/表述时的环境/语境

作出陈述当时的环境(circumstance)/语境(context)显然十分重要,例如即使是自我吹嘘说自己的商品或服务是"万能"的并花钱登广告,大家也知道市场上同类产品或服务很多。一般合理人士(审理法官或仲裁员会代入去从这方面考虑)是不会把广告或推销的吹嘘当真而严肃对待。但换了环境/语境,例如,有潜在客户上门并咨询有关产品或服务能否干某些事情,同样的吹嘘就有问题了。其他要考虑的重要环境/语境是该陈述/表述只是随口说说或是在严肃的环境下作出等。

方方面面的环境/语境也包括不同行业的话语或文字与一般理解是否不同。在本书第一章之2.5.2.2段介绍的Harlingdon and Leinster Enterprises Ltd v. Christopher Hull Fine Art Ltd(1991)1 QB 564上诉庭先例中,显示了在二手艺术品市场,对一幅名画的画家名字的陈述是不能去严肃对待的。另也可节录De Beers Abrasive Products Ltd v. International General Electric Co of New York Ltd(1975)1 WLR 972先例中,Walton大法官认为公开拍卖是做出的陈述/表述会不严格正确:"Principal among its applications has been the case of auctioneers, who, within limits, have always been allowed to use language which is strictly perhaps not literally true; thus, for example, to take note of one instance, in Hope v. Walter [1900] 1 Ch. 257, Lindley M. R. stated…: 'I do not attach any importance to the word "eligible": it is the ordinary auctioneer's language'."

Walton大法官提到的Hope v. Walter先例中,案情涉及公开拍卖房屋。在买卖双方都不知情的情况下,房屋现在的租客将房屋用来开妓院。该事实被买方在交割(closing)前查出,于是买方拒绝完成交割。这导致卖方向法院申请履约指令(specific performance)迫使买方完成交割,而买方以卖方对该房屋误述要求撤销合约。在公开拍卖中,该房屋一直被形容为是"合资格的永久产权与适合投资"(an eligible freehold fit and proper for investment),并提供了目前的租金金额与长租租期。但房屋用作开妓院是非法用途,在当时的《Criminal Law Amendment Act 1885》下出租房屋的业主也是刑事犯罪。这样,说是"合资格(作为投资)"(eligible)显然是误述,而卖方即使是无辜(或疏忽)误述,作为受害方的买方仍可撤销合约。针对履约指令,一审法院批准,但上诉庭推翻了该判决。这可以想到,履约指令是衡平救济(equitable remedy),迫使买方完成交割并同时犯罪是很难说得通。至于买方撤销合约的申请也被一审与上诉庭否定,理由是卖方对房屋"合资格"的陈述/表述虽然不完全正确,但是在公开拍卖中做出,这不是有法律后果的误述。笔者可以想到如果不是公开拍卖,而是普通房屋交易中卖方在一个严肃环境下做出的特定陈述,就会有不同结果。至于原告将来能不能索赔损失,该案例没有报道。

另多节录Hamblen大法官在Cassa di Risparmio della Repubblica di San Marino SpA v. Barclays Bank Ltd(2011)EWHC 484(Comm)先例中所说:"A representation is a statement of fact made by the representor to the representee on which the representee is intended and entitled to rely as a positive assertion that the fact is true. In order to determine whether any and if so what representation was made by a statement requires(1)**construing the statement in the context in which it was made**, and(2) interpreting the statement objectively according to **the impact it might be expected to have on a reasonable representee in the position and with the known characteristics of the actual representee**."(加黑部分是笔者的强调)

在 Mabanga v. Ophir Energy Plc(2012)EWHC 1589(QB)先例中,Christopher Clarke 大法官说:"In the case of an express statement,the court has to consider **what a reasonable person would have understood from the words used in the context in which they were used** ... The answer to that question will depend on **the nature and the content of the statement**,in **the context** in which it was made,**the characteristics of the maker and of the person to whom it was made** and **the relationship** between them ...In the case of an express statement which is made in a document,the context will include the other terms of the document and the terms of surrounding documents passing between the parties. When considering a written representation,the task is to determine how the words would have been understood by the parties,not in a vacuum,but having regard to all the surrounding circumstances known to the parties. It is important in this context,**just as when seeking to determine the true construction of a contract**,**to consider the full terms of the relevant document**,**not merely the extract which is said to contain the express statement amounting to a misrepresentation**. This is not some arbitrary rule of construction. It accords with the commercial expectations of businessmen. One sentence in a letter is not written or read in isolation. It is written or read in the context of the whole letter and would be intended and understood as such."(加黑部分是笔者的强调)

在 FoodCo UK LLP v. Henry Boot Developments Ltd(2010)EWHC 358(Ch)先例中,Lewison 大法官说:"it is dangerous to transpose a representation held to have been made on the particular facts of one case into the facts of another."

其中道理与解释合约时在特定背景/语境下客观考虑措辞/文字的意思是一样的,对此在笔者《合约的解释:规则与应用》一书第六章有详细介绍,不再重复。

3.2 区分之二:陈述/表述的措辞/文字

这方面的考虑是针对事实陈述或意见表述的内容与措辞/文字(language or words used)。例如,如果说是意见,是什么意见?是很细致或只是泛泛的意见?用字是否肯定、绝对且没有任何斟酌或限制(qualification)等。

泛泛或是特定与有针对性,可举例"我这商品是全世界最好"或"我这商品比你在使用的 X 牌子的商品防护力更好"。前者是一位合理的被陈述方不会当真去作出依赖的表述,因为太泛泛与不大可能和全球很多牌子的商品严肃比较过。但后者就会构成对事实的陈述,而误述会带来法律后果。

至于在对事实的陈述时加上斟酌或限制,这往往是指一些模棱两可的话(quibbles),如"我相信""我听说"等。因为当时双方只在谈判,不可能每次陈述前都加上合约中的"完整合约条文"或"没有依赖条文"[13]来为每一个事实陈述或意见表述免责。陈述方只能通过一些简短的模棱两可、有所保留的话来免责。在 Roe v. Bradshaw(1865 – 66)LR 1 Exch 106 上诉庭先例中,案件不是误述的争议,而是针对《Bills of Sale Act 1854》立法下要求以誓章(affidavit)形式对一些有关事实的确认。但誓章对有关事实确认后加上一句说"据我所信"(to the best of my belief)是否符合立法要求对事实的陈述。在此针对误述只作参考,也难保陈述方在对事实陈述后,加上同样的一句。

例如在 Hummingbird Motors Ltd v. Hobbs(1986)RTR 276 上诉庭先例中就发生了这种情况。案件涉及二手车买卖,被告在二手车拍卖中买下一辆看来状态良好的二手车。它的里程表(odometer)显示该车已经行驶了 34,900 里,但实际上是已行驶了 80,000 里,是原车主在里程表做了手脚后才在公开拍卖中出售给了被告。被告在转售给原告时,显然没有告知其里程表不正确,但有告知原告他不保证行驶里程。在签发的发票上也注明"mileage not warranted"。另在交付二手车时签的文件上更加上一句据他所知所信[to the best of(his)knowledge and belief]里程表显示的里数正确。一审法院判被告的明示陈述/表述或保证是诚实,因为被告根本不知道原车主对里程表做过手脚。但被告对不正确的陈述有疏忽,所以根据《Misrepresentation Act 1967》要赔偿原告损失。但被告上诉,成功推翻了一审。上诉庭认为被告根本没有误述,被告对行驶里程的陈述有限制,整句看不属于对事实的陈述,所以不构成误述,Kerr 大法官说:"... the Act of 1967 is irrelevant in the present case, because no misrepresentation has been established. The statement that the mileage was correct to the defendant's best knowledge and belief was not a misrepresentation on the findings made by the trial judge."

一种经常发生的情况是重复第三人提供的信息与/或事实的陈述,例如在本书第一章之 2.2.4 段介绍的 Howard Marine and Dredging Co Ltd v. A Ogden & Sons(Excavations)Ltd(1978)QB 574 上诉庭先例,该案案情涉及船东依赖劳合社的记录(Lloyd's Register)向承租人陈述船舶的载重量(deadweight),但由于劳合社记录有错误,导致确信记录并重复陈述的船东构成了误述。但可以想到,如果船东不是把劳合社记录的信息毫无保留地,甚至是在明示保证下重复给承租人,而去加上限制与保留,或甚至明示告知承租人这是来自劳合社的信息,对此船东无法肯定正确与不保证,就不会有责任了。

重复第三人提供的信息与事实陈述/表述在很多重要的商业活动频繁发生,也变

---

〔13〕 见本书第一章之 1.3.8 段。

得十分复杂,所以要稍后在本章之4段详论。

3.3 区分之三:陈述方与被陈述方有非一般的关系

陈述方与被陈述方之间是否有诚信关系或特殊关系也会影响是否可以构成误述。在本书第一章之2.7段已经对诚信关系或特殊关系作出了介绍,例如,双方是律师与客户关系、代理人与委托人关系等。因诚信关系或特殊关系中法律对陈述方会有额外要求,所以同样的陈述/表述在一般情况下不被认定构成误述,但在这种特殊关系下,却因为内容不完整,属于讲一半不讲一半,而构成误述。[14]

3.4 区分之四:陈述方与被陈述方的水平、经验或对事实的知悉程度的不同

一个重要考虑因素是谁是"被陈述方"与谁是"陈述方",他们在有关方面的水平是高是低、有没有相关经验等。毕竟在行业内有丰富经验的专业人员被一位新手误导去签订一份对自己不利的合约的可能性不大。相反,对有关产品或服务知道得更多的专业人员更容易误导一位新手。因为,专业人员表述的意见中言下之意传达了一个事实,就是他对有关的产品或服务知道得更多,所以有事实依据可以做出这样的意见,这就是本章之1.4段介绍的默示陈述。

除了水平与经验,这个重要区分的另一个考虑因素,是陈述方与被陈述方对有关陈述/表述的知悉程度。这方面在本章之1.4.3段介绍Smith v. Land and House Property Corporation(1884)28 Ch. D. 7贵族院先例时也已经阐明。表面看,卖方在出售他的酒店时指承租人是"称心如意"是卖方的一个意见,但法院认为只有卖方才了解他的租客,买方不了解,知道得更多的一方的意见表述就通常会被认为是因该意见中存在一个默示的对事实的陈述,所以构成可诉误述,买方可撤销合约。

在MCI WorldCom International Inc v. Primus Telecommunications Inc(2004)EWCA Civ 957上诉庭先例中,Mance大法官说:"**Judged objectively according to the impact that whatever is said may be expected to have on a reasonable representee in the position and with the known characteristics of the actual representee.** [just as contractual interpretation depends on ascertaining 'the meaning which the document would convey to a reasonable person having all the background knowledge which would reasonably have been available to the parties in the situation in which they were at the time of the contract': Investors Compensation Scheme Ltd. v. West Bromwich B. S. (1998) 1 WLR 896 ...]"(加黑部分是笔者的强调)

这说法也在后来的多个先例被采纳与引用,如Raiffeisen Zentralbank Osterreich AG v. Royal Bank of Scotland Plc(2010)EWHC 1392(Comm);Marme Inversiones 2007 SL v. NatWest Markets Plc(2019)EWHC 366(Comm)等。

这符合人性与实际,因为被陈诉方也知道或可以知道的事实,除了不存在依赖陈述方的陈述外,陈述方也不会傻到仍然以虚假陈述去诱导(induce)对方。举一个简

[14] 这在本书第五章有详论。

单的例子,卖方对买方说"这商品应可用在某用途"。如果买方对这种商品十分熟悉,甚至双方已经有了好几年对该商品的买卖与使用,这会只是卖方的意见。但同一句话对另一位新的买方,且他也从来没有用过这种商品时,这就会是卖方的事实陈述了。

一个经常被提及的经典先例是 Bisset v. Wilkinson(1927) AC 177 先例。该先例中,Bisset 先生想卖出一块在新西兰的土地,他告诉 Wilkinson 先生这块地能养 2000 只羊,但在这之前并没有任何人在这块地养过羊。在买下这块土地后,Wilkinson 先生发觉根本没法容纳与养活 2000 只羊。但枢密院判这只是意见的表述,不构成事实的陈述,因为大家知道这块地从未养过羊,何来事实?

已在本书第一章之 2.2.3 段有详尽介绍的 Esso Petroleum Co Ltd v. Mardon (1976)2 Lloyd's Rep 305 上诉庭先例中,也是明确显示了这原则,不去重复。该先例认定 Esso 误述,而且该误述也构成附带保证(collateral warranty)。有附带保证之争是因为该先例的案情发生在《Misrepresentation Act 1967》立法生效前,英国法律下一个可诉但"非欺诈性"(non-fraudulent)误述的受害方,是无权索赔金钱损失的。但撤销合约的救济在 Mardon 先生苦心经营几年,面对持续亏损要破产时对他根本没有用处。只再节录 Denning 勋爵所说:"Now, I would quite agree ... that it did not guarantee that the throughput would be 200,000 gallons. But, nevertheless, it was a forecast made by a party-ESSO-who had special knowledge and skill. ... They knew the facts. They knew the traffic in town. They knew the throughput of comparable stations. They had much expertise and experience at their disposal. They were in a much better position than Mr Mardon to make a forecast. It seems to me that if such a person makes a forecast —intending that the other should act upon it and he does act upon it —it can well be interpreted as a warranty that the forecast is sound and reliable in this sense that they made it with reasonable care and skill. It is just as if ESSO said to Mr. Mardon: 'Our forecast of throughput is 200,000 gallons. You can rely upon it as being a sound forecast of what the service station should do. The rent is calculated on that footing'."

3.5　区分之五:合理的被陈述方会否严肃依赖有关陈述/表述

客观看陈述方可否预期被陈述方会合理依赖这个错误陈述/表述去签订合约,或从另一个角度看被推销的被陈述方会否合理与有权依赖该陈述并决定订约是另外一个考虑因素。至于是否合理,则由审理法官/仲裁员根据所有的证据,在千变万化的案件中针对特定案情作出客观判断。正如在 De Beers Abrasive Products Ltd v. International General Electric Co of New York Ltd(1975)1 WLR 972 先例中,Walton 大法官说:"In the kind of situation where one expects, as a matter of ordinary common experience, a person to use a certain amount of hyperbole in the description of goods, property or services, **the courts will do what any ordinary reasonable man would do**, namely, ... **whether a reasonable man would take the claim as being a serious claim or not**."

这方面的举证责任是在被陈述方,即去证明他/她如何理解有关的陈述/表述,并合理视该陈述是一个严肃的陈述与作出依赖。

这个考虑因素在很多先例涉及是否有法律后果时都有提到,可部分介绍如下:

1. Denning 勋爵在 Dutton v. Bognor Regis Urban District Council(1972)1 QB 373 先例中说:"Nowadays since Hedley Byrne & Co. Ltd. v. Heller & Partners Ltd. [1964] A. C. 465 it is clear that a professional man who gives guidance to others owes a duty of care, not only to the client who employs him, but also to another who he knows is relying on his skill to save him from harm. It is certain that a banker or accountant is under such a duty. and I see no reason why a solicitor is not likewise. **The essence of this proposition, however, is the reliance**. In Hedley Byrne v. Heller it was stressed by Lord Reid ..., by Lord Morris ..., and by Lord Hodson ... **The professional man must know that the other is relying on his skill and the other must in fact rely on it**. "(加黑部分是笔者的强调)

2. 在 De Beers Abrasive Products Ltd v. International General Electric Co of New York Ltd 先例中,Walton 大法官说:

"What precisely is the law on this point? It is a blinding glimpse of the obvious to say that there must be **a dividing line between statements that are actionable and those which are not**; and the sole question upon a dry point of law such as we are discussing here is: **where does that line lie**? On the one hand, it appears to me that the law is that any trader is entitled to puff his own goods, even though such puff must, as a matter of pure logic, involve the denigration of his rival's goods. ...

... At the other end of the scale, if what is said is: 'My goods are better than X's, because X's are absolute rubbish,' then it is established by dicta of Lord Shand in the House of Lords in White v. Mellin [1895] A. C. 154 ..., which were accepted ... as stating the law, the statement would be actionable.

Between these two kinds of statements there is obviously still an extremely wide field; and it appears to me that, **in order to draw the line, one must apply this test, namely, whether a reasonable man would take the claim being made as being a serious claim or not.** "(加黑部分是笔者的强调)

3. 另在 Smith v. Eric S. Bush(1990)1 AC 831 贵族院先例中,案情涉及"自愿承担责任"(voluntary assumption of responsibility)的情况,也就是提供意见的人士(通常是专业人士)明知一些特定的第三人十分可能对此严肃地依赖。这样,不正确的意见就会构成误述与有法律后果。Templeman 勋爵说:"... to the question in what circumstances should the law deem those who give advice to have assumed responsibility to the person who acts upon the advice ... I would answer- **only if it is foreseeable that if the advice is negligent the recipient is likely to suffer damage** ... it should only be in

cases when the adviser knows that there is a high degree of probability that some other identifiable person will act upon the advice that a duty of care should be impose."(加黑部分是笔者的强调)

4. 在 IFE Fund SA v. Goldman Sachs International(2006)EWHC 2887(Comm)先例中,Toulson 大法官说:"In determining whether there has been an express representation, and to what effect, the court has to consider what **a reasonable person would have understood from the words used in the context** in which they were used. In determining what, if any, implied representation has been made, the court has to perform a similar task, except that it has to consider what **a reasonable person would have inferred was being implicitly represented by the representor's words and conduct in their context**."(加黑部分是笔者的强调)

5. 在 Raiffeisen Zentralbank Osterreich AG v. Royal Bank of Scotland Plc(2010) EWHC 1392(Comm)先例中,Christopher Clarke 大法官说:"… the claimant must show that he in fact understood the statement in the sense(so far as material) which the court ascribes to it: Arkwright v Newbold(1881)17 Ch D 301 13; Smith v Chadwick(1884)9 App. Cas 187; and that, having that understanding, he relied on it. This may be of particular significance in the case of implied statements."

4. 重复或转递第三人提供的信息与事实陈述

在不少重要的商业活动中,经常会发生需要重复第三人提供的信息与事实陈述的情况。例如在《合约的履行、弃权与禁反言》一书第十一章之 4 段介绍的银团贷款(syndicate loan)业务,通常由一家牵头银行(lead bank)来负责统一安排贷款的相关事项,特别是与贷款人(borrower)和其他有关人士沟通,再与银团中的其他银行成员沟通,包括转达贷款人(或其他有关人士)提供的信息与事实陈述。但牵头银行不会对这些信息与事实再自行去调查确定,只是相信贷款人的陈述/表述应是正确。但如果贷款人有误述(特别是欺诈性),牵头银行如果像 Howard Marine and Dredging Co Ltd v. A Ogden & Sons(Excavations)Ltd(1978)QB 574 上诉庭先例一样向其他银行成员重复与转达,该表述就会被当作牵头银行自己的陈述/表述,其就会有危险被夹在中间。

4.1　银团贷款/融资业务的 IFE Fund SA v. Goldman Sachs International (2007)EWCA Civ 811 先例

在 IFE Fund SA v. Goldman Sachs International 上诉庭先例中,案情涉及公司收购,一家法国公司 Autodis 考虑收购一家英国公司 Finelist。为此交易,Autodis 委任了安达信跨国会计师事务所进行尽职调查与 Goldman Sachs(以下简称 GS)安排这次收购的融资。为此，GS 邀请了一些银行去组织银团，成员包括了本案例的原告 IFE（全名是“Intermediate Finance Europe”，是一家比利时金融机构）。GS 向所有银团成员发送了一份名为“Syndicate Information Memorandum”以下简称 SIM，的文件，内容包括了 Finelist 的核算账目（audited account）与安达信的尽职调查报告，并表达了对收购 Finelist 乐观的意见。但这次收购是灾难性的，因为 Finelist 的财政并非如核算账目所显示的那般乐观。其中涉及 Finelist 集团公司管理层的欺诈与做假账，这导致收购后没几个月 Finelist 就被接管（receivership）。蒙受重大损失的 IFE 向 GS 提起诉讼，诉因是违反小心谨慎责任与疏忽误述（明示与/或默示），并要求以《Misrepresentation Act 1967》之 S.2(1)赔偿损失。IFE 声称是被 SG 在 SIM 的误述诱导下去参与银团贷款。

SIM 一开始是明示说明有“重要通知”（Important Notice），接下来有 3 页纸，其中包括大量的免责声明（disclaimer of responsibility）。对本案重要的是说明信息与事实陈述的来源与 GS 没有独立查明，所以不构成 GS 的明示陈述或保证等。相关内容可节录如下：“(i) The information contained in this Memorandum has been obtained from the Sponsors (various identified financial institutions), Autodis, Finelist, professional consultants and/or public sources ... None of this Memorandum, the information contained in it or any other information supplied in connection with the Facilities shall form the basis of any contract... (ii) The Arranger (GS) has not independently verified the information set out in this Memorandum. Accordingly, no representation, warranty or undertaking, express or implied, is made and no responsibility is accepted by GS... (iii) This Memorandum contains only summary information and does not purport to be comprehensive ...”

在一审[(2006) EWHC 2887 (Comm)]，Toulson 大法官不接受 GS 有 Hedley Byrne v. Heller (1964) AC 465 贵族院先例中确立的小心谨慎责任，因为 GS 不是作为 IFE（或其他银团成员）的顾问（advisor）去提供信息，不存在有自愿承担责任。GS 只是代表 Autodis 或保荐人（sponsor）。GS 与 IFE 之间只是一般的商业关系，要自己为自己利益小心谨慎。银团贷款或融资业务的习惯做法也是这样理解，这被 IFE 的主要证人在交叉盘问时接受。这可节录 Toulson 大法官的观点：

“Common features of such a syndication are that the parties introducing the equity into the venture ('the sponsors') retain a bank ('the arranger') (此先例也就是 GS) which arranges and sometimes underwrites the facilities; the arranger prepares a SIM; the debtor (IFE) accepts responsibility for the accuracy of the information contained in the SIM at that date; and the arranger disclaims any legal responsibility for its accuracy. Mr Mitjavile (IFE 主要证人) accepted in cross – examination that these were standard features of a syndication of credit facilities. Towards the end of the cross examination, Mr Howard (GS 代表大律师) put to Mr Mitjavile a number of short points as follows:

'Q I am going to make a number of short points to see whether we agree or disagree. The first thing is:you did not understand that Goldman Sachs had made any representations to you on which you could rely;Correct?

A I agree.

Q Secondly,you understood that Goldman Sachs were saying to you:I will have no legal responsibility to you in relation to your acquisition of these bonds?

A I agree.

Q Thirdly,Goldman Sachs were making it clear that if you suffered any loss as a result of relying on the syndication information memorandum or any other information that you were provided with they would not have any responsibility to you for that?

A I agree

Q You had no objection to proceeding on that basis;correct?

A I agree.

Q And the reason you had no objection was that this type of syndication information memorandum and there being no legal responsibility on the part of Goldman Sachs was something that you regarded as perfectly standard and acceptable?

A I agree. '"

上述节录的交叉盘问显然对 IFE 十分不利,因为显示了声称被误述诱导的 IFE 实是知道不能合理与有权依赖 GS 通过 SIM 传达过来的陈述。GS 的代表大律师在取得了 IFE 主要证人这些回答后,估计是知道胜券在握,所以接下来的开庭审理,也不去传召 GS 的证人,省得证人在交叉盘问中讲错话反而麻烦。

至于误述的指控,显然较早前节录的 SIM 中的"重要通知"至关重要。IFE 指称该条文或内容违反《Misrepresentation Act 1967》之 S. 3,[15]规定合约中对误述的免责条文必须满足合理的测试,否则无效。SIM 并不是合约,双方仍在谈判阶段。在谈判的陈述/表述也通常不会有免责条文,只会是有一些限制、保留或模棱两可的说法。但在此先例重要的是 SIM 的相关文字(撇开免责的内容)是说明 GS 提供的不是陈述、表述或保证,只是从其他第三人处取得的信息、事实与意见,并明确没有去核查,也就是没有自愿承担责任。同样重要是 IFE 的主要证人承认在收到 SIM 时没有当作是可诉陈述。所以根本不存在有任何可诉陈述,也就不会有误述了。Toulson 大法官说:"In determining whether there has been an express representation, and to what effect,the court has to consider what a reasonable person would have understood from the words used in the context in which they were used. In determining what,if any,implied representation has been made,the court has to perform a similar task,except that it has to consider what a reasonable person would have inferred was being implicitly represented by the representor's words and conduct in their context. ... The SIM has to be read as a

[15] 见本书第四章之 6 段的详细介绍。

whole in order to see what a reasonable participant would understand was the scope of the responsibility undertaken by the arranger in relation to its contents."

在默示陈述的层面,双方接受有一个诚实的默示陈述,也就是 GS 如果知道第三人的信息、事实与意见有问题、不可信,就不能无条件、无保留地转递与误导 IFE。但 IFE 没有办法证明 GS 在转递 SIM 时,对第三人的信息有任何怀疑。因为 GS 不知 SIM 中 Finelist 经济状况的信息与事实正确与否,无法知道安达信报告是否正确与表达的意见是否合理,GS 只能知道安达信是认为报告中的事实是正确与表达的意见是合理的。

在上诉庭,Waller 大法官同意一审判决:"The fundamental questions in this case are in my view whether in the light of the terms of the Important Notice IFE have established that GS made any representation of fact when handing over the SIM ... What IFE must first establish is a misrepresentation. In the context of this case that means first establishing that GS by issuing the SIM was expressly or by implication representing to IFE something as a fact ... It seems to me that IFE's suggested representations asserted ... involving representing facts or opinions which 'were or might be untrue' or opinions which 'were or might be unreasonable', are simply impossible to spell out of the supply of the SIM since GS make it clear by the 'Important Notice' that they have no obligation to check. As the judge said, an implied representation of the scope contended for ... would potentially require GS to do an evaluation contrary to the express terms of the SIM. For all the reasons given by the judge I would reject the implication of any representations as asserted ..."

4.2 重复或转递第三人提供的信息与事实陈述/表述的不同做法与相关法律责任

重复或转递第三人提供的信息在社会上(特别是商业社会)频繁发生,且远远不止上述介绍的银团贷款业务,而包括方方面面。包括如再保险业务,再保险人(reinsurer)要依赖一线保险人(insurer)重复与转递受保人(assured)提供的事实陈述与披露的实质重要信息(material fact):见 Anderson v. Pacific Fire and Marine Insurance Co (1872) LR 7 CP 65;Highlands Insurance Co v. Continental Insurance Co (1987) 1 Lloyd's Rep 109;Sirius International Insurance Corp v. Oriental Assurance Corp (1999) 1 All ER (Comm) 699 等先例。只节录在 Highlands Insurance Co v. Continental Insurance Co 先例中,Steyn 大法官所述:"... present understanding in the London market whereby reinsurers place reliance on a broker's presentation of 'Information' as recording statement of facts, unless qualifying language or the context indicates that a particular statement falls in a different category."

其他领域的近期相关先例可见:FoodCo UK LLP v. Henry Boot Developments Ltd (2010) EWHC 358 (Ch);Webster v. Liddington (2014) PNLR 26 等。但因为篇幅关系

不再详细介绍。

如何重复或转递第三人提供的信息才可以如 IFE Fund SA v. Goldman Sachs International(2007)EWCA Civ 811 上诉庭先例中那样无需承担虚假或不正确信息的责任,而不是如 Howard Marine and Dredging Co Ltd v. A Ogden & Sons(Excavations)Ltd (1978)QB 574 上诉庭先例那样被视为自己的事实陈述?这当然在现实中十分重要,因为来源可靠的第三人也常会提供不正确信息,更不要说是来源不可靠的第三人。今天假消息满天飞,如果重复或转递第三人骗子提供的假消息并带来责任,夹在当中后果将很严重。所以去探讨一下重复或转递第三人提供的信息的几种做法,与相应会带来的不同责任。

可先节录《Misrepresentation, Mistake and Non-Disclosure》一书(2022 年,第 6 版)之 3 – 20 段所说:"A question can sometimes arise as to whether a contracting party makes a representation when he simply passes on information which he received from another person who is not involved in the transaction. ... If the party makes clear that he is simply passing on information which he believes to be true but for which he cannot vouch, then the question will be one of his honesty in making the statement. But he may, by passing the information on, be seen as taking responsibility for it. Indeed, there is a range of possible forms of responsibility that may be taken where a person(X) passes on information produced by another(Y) to a person(Z) with whom he hopes to contract: (**i**) X may warrant to Z that the information is correct. X may thereby assume contractual liability to Z for the accuracy of the information. That liability may exist under the main contract or a collateral contract. (**ii**) X may adopt the information as his own, thereby taking on such responsibility as he would have if he were the maker of the statement. (**iii**) X may represent that he believes, on reasonable grounds, the information supplied by Y to be correct. That involves a lesser degree of responsibility than scenario(ii). (**iv**) X may simply pass on the information to Z as material coming from Y, about which X has no knowledge or belief. X then has no responsibility for the accuracy of the information beyond the ordinary duties of honesty and good faith."

上述的四种不同做法,其中(i)是对第三人提供的信息向对方合约方保证(不论是明示在一份完整的合约内或附带协议/保证)。显然信息错误会带来合约责任,损失赔偿也是根据合约的"复原大原则"("as far as money can do it, to be placed in the same position as if the contract had been performed"/"*restitutio in integrum*")。[16]

(ii)的做法就如同 Howard Marine and Dredging Co Ltd. v. A Ogden & Sons(Excavations)Ltd 先例,把劳合社记录的船舶载重量数字重复给承租人,这就成为一个可诉陈述。如果数字错误,也就变为可诉误述,将带来法律后果。毕竟,对承租人而言,他

〔16〕 在笔者《损失赔偿与救济》一书第一章有详细介绍。

也不会知道船东向他陈述的数字只是根据劳合社记录,而不是来自更准确的船图。

至于在救济方面是根据侵权,除了有撤销合约的衡平救济外,在损失赔偿方面,这种重复第三人的信息与事实陈述的疏忽或无辜误述在《Misrepresentation Act 1967》生效后也有了这种救济,并以侵权的"回复到侵权没有发生"的地位作为计算损失办法。

(iii)的做法是重复或转递第三人提供的信息去说明来源,但加上个人的意见说是自己相信该信息与有合理依据(reasonable ground)相信。这说法与《Misrepresentation Act 1967》之 S.2(1)一致,即以有合理依据相信作为对向被陈述方赔偿损失责任的抗辩。但要构成合理依据相信就代表已经做了一些合理的工作,去核实第三人提供的信息。如果有做到,即使有关的陈述/表述的确错误,也不必承担对可诉误述的责任;但在《Misrepresentation Act 1967》之 S.2(2)下,如果法院(或仲裁庭)行使裁量权认为应以损失赔偿代替(in lieu of)撤销合约,那么误述方仍要作出金钱赔偿,只是计算方式不同,甚至可能只是名义损失。

而(iv)的做法正是 IFE Fund SA v. Goldman Sachs International 先例中 GS 的做法,不必再去重复了。

在千变万化的商业社会,上述的四种做法只是最常见的做法,往往还会有其他不同做法的案件。正如在 Webster v. Liddington 上诉庭先例中,Jackson 大法官说:"**Those four scenarios are not a complete statement of the range of possibilities, there are other intermediate positions**. The test for determining which scenario applies is an objective one, as stated by Toulson J in IFE. The extent of X's responsibility for Y's information is that which a reasonable person in Z's position would (a) understand from X's words or (b) infer from X's conduct and all the circumstances."(加黑部分是笔者的强调)

5. 对意图或预期事实的表述

对意见的表述没有真假,而对意图(intention)或是预期事实(future fact)的表述,因为将来还没有来到,意图或是预期将会成真的机会反而不高。这样看来,对意图或预期事实的表述在做出陈述/表述时实是空话一句或至少无分真假,一般不构成可诉陈述。作为听众的被陈述方,也不会或不应该将任何人(如西方国家的政客)对意图或愿景的表述当真与作为做出重大决定的依据。

但凡事都有例外,对意图或预期事实的表述也会构成对事实的可诉误述或违约。第一种情况是普通法要求诚实,所以只要能证明陈述方在陈述时就不诚实(当然这很难证明)就会构成欺诈性误述。第二种情况是看陈述的是什么意图与预期,所以如果双方都没有经验,陈述的意图与预期是没有什么后果。但是如果陈述的一方有经验、数据等,例如在一个公司并购交易,卖方对公司将来预期利润的陈述,就要求对这个陈述有合理依据了。第三种情况是在合约条文中的意图或预期事实,还是以公司并购为例,如果合约中明示说明是保证将来的利润能达到某个金额那再清楚不过;但即使是没有明确说保证,把预期写入条文(订约自由下会有千变万化的写法)也会有一定的法律后果,因为在解释合约时尽量会给合约内的文字一定的解释,而不会解释为一句空话。这种合约保证的形式也会出现在谈判时对将来的意图/预期事实的陈述而被解释为构成附带协议/保证(collateral contract/warranty)。最后是对意图或预期事实的表述有时可以被解释为对过去或现在的事实的默示陈述,例如借钱时常会说"我预计1个月内就可以还清",这是对意图或预期事实的陈述,但这默示他讲这句话时是有意图与能力在1个月内还清的,否则就是可诉误述。

5.1 诚实作出对将来意图或预期事实的表述没有法律后果

所以一个诚实的预期只是一个没有法律后果的"预测"(prediction),不是一个可诉陈述。在 Bank Leumi Le Israel BM v. British National Insurance Co Ltd(1988)1 Lloyd's Rep 71 先例中,Saville 大法官说:"A statement as to a future state of affairs can in itself neither be true nor false at the time it is made, since the future cannot be foretold."

需要诚实的做出预期是可以想象得到,因为不诚实就构成欺诈/欺骗(tort of deceit)。这可以 The "Mihalis Angelos"(1970)2 Lloyd's Rep 43 上诉庭先例为例。

在 The "Mihalis Angelos" 先例中,Denning 勋爵说:"... he(船东)is making a representation as to his own state of mind; that is, of what he himself expects: and, what is more, he puts it in the contract as a term of it, binding himself to its truth. ... It is **at lowest a misrepresentation which entitles the other party to rescind**: and at highest a breach of contract which goes to the root of the matter. The charterer, who is misled by the statement is entitled, on discovering its falsity, to throw up the charter. It may, therefore, properly be described as a 'condition'."(加黑部分是笔者的强调)

另 Edmund Davies 大法官说:"These words mean that, in the light of the facts known to the owner at the time of making the contract, he **honestly expected** that the vessel would be ready as stated and, further, that such expectation was based on reasonable grounds."(加黑部分是笔者的强调)

至于表达意图,是说明将来会做些什么,这是一个将来才会兑现的"承诺"(promise)。显然也要求陈述方诚实表述,虽然在现实中证明陈述方的脑袋在做出表述时(这可能是出争议时的多年前)不诚实肯定不会容易。

对将来意图或预期事实的陈述在法律上只有诚实的要求,陈述方对将来意图或预期事实的表述等于对他/她在当时确实这么想的或确实是这么相信的做出了事实陈述,所以如果陈述方在当时就不诚实,就是对这个现在的事实的误述。在 FoodCo UK LLP v. Henry Boot Developments Ltd(2010)EWHC 358(Ch)先例中,Lewison 大法官也说："It would not, I think, be difficult to say that in most cases a prediction about the future (particularly in the context of contractual negotiations) would necessarily be understood as **implicitly representing that the maker of the prediction had an honest belief in it.** The existence (or otherwise) or a belief is a present fact at the moment that the prediction is uttered. **If, therefore, the maker of the prediction does not have an honest belief in the prediction at the time when he makes it, he will have made a false representation of fact.** In other cases, further implications may be appropriate. It may be that the representation would necessarily be understood as meaning that the prediction is based on reasonable grounds; or that the maker of the prediction has the present intention to do what he can to make it come true."（加黑部分是笔者的强调）

对上述的介绍，可举一个旧版《国际商业游戏规则：英国合约法》一书提到的伦敦海事仲裁案。该案内容是警告中国公司不要在国际商业活动中随便相信与依赖对方对将来意图的表述。例如在租船业务，不要因承租人在谈判时表述意图是让船舶装运棉花或散粮而忽略了对租约条文的重视，比如仍要明示订明禁止装废铁（scrap）、硫黄（sulphur）、其他的危险品或一些自己不想装的货物。笔者就经历过一艘新造船舶因为在期租合约没有明示去禁止，误信承租人对将来营运的计划，后来被要求去装废铁，否则构成违约并要赔偿承租人金钱损失，而且损失颇大，因为装运废铁承租人在分租约下可赚取的运费比较高。

另提到1980年"KW"轮的伦敦仲裁案件中，"KW"轮是中资公司拥有的一艘在香港特区管理的方便旗船舶，它被出租给一位美国承租人。订约前的谈判中承租人多次说他意图或计划把以"航次期租"（Time-Charter-Trip 或 TCT）租入的"KW"轮用在自美湾装散粮去意大利，结果租约条文订为："One time charter trip via safe port(s) berth(s) always afloat and always within Institute Warranty Limits. ..."而一般期租租约下，船东会谨慎地限制航区范围（trading limit）要排除战区与一些特定船东不肯去的以色列、伊拉克、古巴、朝鲜等国家，没有加入租约作为条文。原因是船东认为承租人既然是计划从美湾装散粮去意大利，就不必太关心排除不允许或不想去营运的航区或国家。结果货物在美湾装到一半时，该承租人才指示"KW"轮从美湾装运散粮去以色列，不是意大利。当时以"石油武器"称霸的阿拉伯国家严禁行走过以色列的船舶，否则会列入黑名单。所以一般船东不愿意去行走以色列以避免被永久列入黑名单，除非是很高的运费或租金可去平衡利益。例如有关船舶已经很高船龄，很快就要拆船也就无惧黑名单了。

仲裁结果是船东败诉，因为承租人只是表述意图而已，也很谨慎没有做出任何接近一个只去意大利的承诺或保证。这样，承租人可说是（或可能是）使用妙计用很低廉的租金租一艘船舶去转租用作可以赚取很高租金或运费的以色列航次。

理论上如果"KW"轮的船东能证明承租人在表述他的意图是装运散粮去意大利时，已经在说谎，根本没有愿望（will）或能力（ability）去化为事实，就会扭转乾坤；但证明美国承租人欺诈性误述非常困难,在国际仲裁更加是难上加难,因为文件披露比不上法院诉讼那样全面与严格。更不说用是该承租人在表述将来意图时,的确可能是诚实的。例如披露的文件显示当时唯一在洽谈的去意大利的生意在稍后告吹,令承租人另找了去以色列的一票生意让“KW”轮营运。

上述举的虽然是航运的例子,但是在任何行业都适用。在国际商业社会和成熟与精明的外国商人打交道时,对方最容易采取的误导中国(或其他发展中国家)商人的方式就是讲意图。如果相信了对方的意图,被对方画的大饼欺骗,就可能落入陷阱而没有任何法律救济。所以,如果外国商人有求于人,就会很主动建议飞到当地面谈,一是可以避免留下最有重量与难以反驳的文书证据,二是可以根据对方的反应调整自己的说法,以说服对方相信自己的意图而不必承担任何法律后果。

5.2 通过合约条文令意图或预期事实有法律保护

在合约谈判中对将来才会发生的意图或预期事实,由于其不是可诉的陈述,故对被陈述方而言没有保障。被陈述方想获得法律的保障,唯一办法是将该陈述加入合约条文作为合约的保证,说明将来会做什么或不会做什么。这样,表述将来意图或预期事实才受到约束,而且是严格责任。一旦不兑现,就是违约。这可节录少量的权威说法,在 Tudor Grange Holdings Ltd v. Citibank NA(1992)Ch 53 先例中,Browne-Wilkinson 大法官说:“A representation as to future conduct has no effect unless it constitutes a contract. ...”

另在《Misrepresentation,Mistake and Non-Disclosure》一书(2022 年,第 6 版)之 3-45 段说:“The mechanism provided by the law for remedying such mispredictions or promises is the contract itself. If a contract contains a term guaranteeing that a future event will happen,or that the party will do some identified act,then there will be a breach of contract if that event does not happen,or if the party fails to keep his promise. Put this way,it ought to be clear that a person who receives a statement of future fact or intention ought generally not be entitled to rely on it;if he wishes to obtain a remedy he should ask for a warranty in the contract to the effect that the fact will turn out as represented,or that the promise will be kept.”

在并购(M & A)或股权买卖(Share Purchase)中就经常会这样做。这在刚介绍的 Denning 勋爵在 The“Mihalis Angelos”(1970)2 Lloyd's Rep 43 上诉庭先例的判词中也有显示。

在保险合约中也经常这样做。考虑到证明表述将来意图是否诚实是不容易、不肯定的,所以重视这方面的合约方,如果做得到,最安全的还是较早提到的把对方的意图(与预期事实)加入合约作为“承诺性保证”(promissory warranty)。这在笔者的《海上货物保险》一书第四章之 2 段有详论,此处不再重复。在谈判中受保人对实质重要的信息与事实有必须尽量正确(substantially correct)、全面与坦率披露与陈述/表述的责任,应是众所周知的,这在《Marine Insurance Act 1906》与《The Insurance Act

2015》都有规定。但针对预期的将来事实,只能是要求受保人诚实与善意,这在《Marine Insurance Act 1906》之 S. 20(5)中说:"A representation as to a matter of expectation or belief is true if it be made in good faith."另在《The Insurance Act 2015》之 S. 3(3)(c)"duty of fair presentation"说:"fair presentation of the risk is one … in which every material representation as to a matter of fact is substantially correct, and every material representation as to a matter of expectation or belief is made in good faith."

但撇开对受保人在投保时的陈述/表述是否诚实与善意举证的困难与不肯定,即使是受保人确实百分之百诚实,对保险人(或保险公司)的保障仍是远远不足。因为在英国一个古老的 Baxendale v. Harvey(1859)157 ER 913 先例中,明确了受保人在保险合约生效的期间,有做一些会增加风险的事情的自由度。但承保的保险人最关心的是受保人在受保期间增加了的风险,是原先接受投保与确定保费时没有考虑到与包括在内的。例如在人寿险或医疗险,受保人投保时的陈述/表述是生活健康与不抽烟,这表述也是诚实与善意;但之后在受保期间,受保人开始生活不健康或者抽烟,对此保险人也没有办法拒赔。又或是在盗窃险中,一家珠宝店在投保时的陈述/表述是商店安装了先进完善的防盗设备。但之后在受保期间,难以防止受保人怠慢维修保养或是把防盗设备改装等行动,并因此增加风险。因为与上一段提到的"KW"轮的仲裁案件一样,对于意图的陈述只要作出时是善意与诚实即可,将来仍可以改变。

这样对保险人最好的保障仍是在保险合约增加一条承诺性保证条文,说明在受保期间,受保人什么能做与什么不能做等。在订约自由下,也无所谓去剥夺受保人的自由行动,反正是双方合意。如果受保人拒绝一些太苛刻的承诺性保证,保险人就可以拒绝承保或增加保费。可节录在《Marine Insurance Act 1906》之 S. 33 有关承诺性保证条文的解释与将来在受保期间受保人不严格履行的拒赔严重后果,内容如下:"A warranty … means a promissory warranty, that is to say, a warranty by which the assured undertake that some particular thing shall or shall not be done, or that some condition shall be fulfilled, or whereby he affirms or negatives the existence of a particular state of facts. (3) A warranty … is a condition which must be exactly complied with, whether it be material to the risk or not. If it be not so complied with, then, subject to any express provision in the policy, the insurer is discharged from liability as from the date of the breach of warranty …"

5.3　表面完整的书面合约才涉及谈判时有否附带协议/保证

有关附带协议/保证的课题在本书第一章之 2.5.2 段有针对,[17]此处不再重复。至于在谈判时出现的将来意图或承诺/安抚(promise 或 assurance),若事实上没有做到,也不会构成误述,只要在承诺/安抚时诚实,就没有法律责任。但会否可解释为是构成一个附带协议/保证,并带来责任？这方面在 Evans v. Merzario(1976)2 Lloyd's

---

〔17〕　附带保证/协议也在笔者的《合约的解释:规则与应用》一书第六章之 2.3.2 段有详论。

Rep 165 先例有涉及。

该先例的案情涉及在航运的集装箱运输(containerisation)的萌芽年代,提供这种服务的船公司与航线仍不多。英国的一家进口商(Evans)从意大利进口一台铸造机(moulding machine)并委托了被告作为货代(forwarding agent)安排运输。被告一直为原告安排的机械运输是以木板箱(crates)或货卡(trailers)装货并装在船舱内,这也是传统的航运做法,只有在非常特殊的情况下,才会把货物装在船舶的甲板上,因为对货物运输的风险会大很多。但被告企图转为集装箱运输,这让原告进口商表示担心,因为其知悉集装箱运输会把部分集装箱装在甲板上。在双方的谈判中,被告向原告承诺/安抚说公司的政策是货物一贯装在船舱,包括集装箱运输。当时在集装箱运输初期,的确是很多集装箱也只是装载在船舱内,不像现在专门设计与建造的集装箱船可以安装在甲板上。至于双方交谈中所用的明确措辞/文字,双方证人在开庭审理时都记不清楚了。但后来事与愿违,在被告无法控制的情况下,船舶公司把该集装箱装在一艘不是集装箱船舶的"Ruhr"轮的甲板上,并且在航次中遇上坏天气令集装箱被冲入海中而造成铸造机的全损。这导致后来保险公司代位求偿(subrogation)向被告索赔。

但在一审法院,Kerr 大法官不认为被告对铸造机不装在甲板上的承诺有一个法律约束的协议,谈不上是误述,也谈不上是一个附带协议/保证。这是通过分析双方在谈判时的言行,包括原告没有要被告担保货物一定装在船舱内;被告在后来发给原告的报价(运费)与标准合约,内有条文说明被告有完全的自由去决定怎样付运货物(在现实中被告作为货代也往往控制不了,在实际运输时会是船东/船长当场根据配货与船舶装载因素进行决定)与免责条文(要赔也很低的金额等)。

但去了上诉庭,一审判决被推翻,认定被告的承诺/安抚是双方合约条文的部分内容或其中一条条文。因为双方的付运合约是"部分文书、部分口头与部分行为",不是有一份整理出来的完整与双方签字的文书合约,记录了双方在谈判中同意的所有承诺与条件,才会有附带协议/保证之争。所以该口头承诺/安抚也不是一个附带协议/保证,而是付运合约的部分内容。Roskill 大法官说:"The matter was apparently argued ... **on the basis that the defendant's promise ... was that the lawyers sometimes call a collateral oral warranty**. That phrase is normally only applicable where the original promise was external to the main contract, that main contract being a contract in writing, so that usually parol evidence[18] cannot be given to contradict the terms of the written contract. ... But the doctrine, as it seems to me, has little or no application where one is not concerned with a contract in writing... but **with a contract** which, as I think, was **partly oral, partly in writing and partly by conduct**. In such a case **the Court does not require to have recourse to lawyer's devices such as collateral oral warranty** in

[18] 有关"口头证据规则"见笔者的《合约的解释:规则与应用》一书第六章之 2 段。

order to seek to adduce evidence which would not otherwise be admissible. **The Court is entitled to look at and should look at all the evidence from start to finish in order to see what the bargain that was struck between the parties** … Thus there was a breach of that contract by the defendants when this container was shipped on deck …"(加黑部分是笔者的强调)

总体来说,证明与成立一个附带协议/保证也不容易,[19] 特别是有了《Misrepresentation Act 1967》立法后,疏忽误述(但这不包括谈判时表达的将来意图或承诺/安抚)已经有了索赔损失的权利,再也无需像早期一样以附带协议/保证才能让无辜方有金钱赔偿的救济;所以已经是多处提到,法院也收紧了对附带协议/保证的认定。

总结以上所讲,会否认定在谈判时曾经做出过附带保证可节录 Lightman 大法官在 Inntrepreneur v. East Crown(2000)2 Lloyd's Rep 611 先例中所说:"The relevant legal principles regarding the recognition of pre-contractual promises or assurances as collateral warranties may be stated as follows:(1)a pre-contractual statement will only be treated as having contractual effect if the evidence shows that parties intended this to be the case. Intention is a question of fact to be decided by looking at the totality of the evidence;(2)the test is the ordinary objective test for the formation of a contract:what is relevant is not the subjective thought of one party but what a reasonable outside observer would infer from all the circumstances;(3)in deciding the question of intention,one important consideration will be whether the statement is followed by further negotiations and a written contract not containing any term corresponding to the statement. In such a case, it will be harder to infer that the statement was intended to have contractual effect because the prima facie assumption will be that the written contract includes all the terms the parties wanted to be binding between them;(4)a further important factor will be the lapse of time between the statement and the making of the formal contract. The longer the interval,the greater the presumption must be that the parties did not intend the statement to have contractual effect in relation to a subsequent deal;(5)**a representation of fact is much more likely intended to have contractual effect than a statement of future fact or a future forecast.**"(加黑部分是笔者的强调)

---

〔19〕 成立附带协议/保证本质上与合约变更(rectification)类似,而合约变更向来非常困难。在《Chitty on Contracts》(2021 年,第 34 版)一书之 5-095 段表述为:"The denial of one of the parties that the deed as it stands is contrary to his intention ought to have considerable weight. Indeed,it has been said that it is not sufficient that the written contract does not represent the true intention of the parties;it must be shown that the written contract was actually contrary to the intention of the parties. Where it is sought to rectify a document in accordance with a prior agreement between the parties,it must be shown that the intention of the parties continued unaltered up to the time of the execution of the document."关于合约变更可见笔者《合约的解释:规则与应用》一书第三章之 13 段。

5.4　证明陈述方陈述/表述意图或预期事实时想法不诚实

在商业活动的现实中有不少情况难免要依赖其他人意图与预期事实的表述去作出重大决定,但又无法在诱导产生的合约中把它加入成为合约的明示保证以有利受到法律保护。典型的例子就是公司上市或公司集资等的活动。本来,利益相关人士(如公司董事或推荐人)难免如兜售货物的卖方一样倾向夸大现在的事实(例如公司目前与近年来赚钱的能力),但也难逃要对公司的前景去表达自己的预期与计划,这往往涉及意图或愿望。在做法上,夸大现在的事实就不敢太乱来,因为有法律对可诉误述(特别是欺诈性)的责任;但对公司意图或预期事实,其夸大就没有太多限制了,有时甚至会接近欺诈/欺骗。

由于意图或预期事实的表述到底是真是假,利益相关人士的内心是否为想骗一般民众与股民,涉及了陈述方的想法,故外人无法取证,只有他自己才知道。但在 Edgington v. Fitzmaurice(1885)29 Ch. D. 459 上诉庭先例中,涉及某公司发出了一份招股章程,其中声明说公司意图将募得的金钱改建公司大楼,购买马和车辆的营运工具,以及其他方面发展公司业务的资金。但后来实际上筹集来的金钱被该公司用去还债。法院判公司董事要负上欺诈/欺骗的侵权责任(tort of deceit),上诉庭的 Bowen 大法官讲了一句名言如下:"There must be a misstatement of an existing fact:but the state of a man's mind is as much a fact as the state of his digestion ... A misrepresentation as to the state of a man's mind is,therefore,a misstatement of fact."

换言之,在表述这意图时,陈述方已是在讲假话,他在当时根本没有愿望或能力把这意图将来化为事实,这就是对现在事实的误述。至于怎样去证明,就要看接下来的行动与真正发生的事实与早前承诺的计划是否有偏差。例如公司的财务报表显示公司在集资后很快就花在还债(甚至是还给公司董事或其他关联公司)上,根本一毛钱也没有花在不久前表述的公司营运与业务方面。相反如果公司把相当部分的集资花在表述的公司营运与业务,在过了一段时间后才把其他部分花在还债,就比较困难去证明表述的董事在表述时的想法是没有诚意与善意的。

5.5　对意图或预期事实的表述被解释为对现在事实的默示陈述

《Chitty on Contracts》(2021 年,第 34 版)一书之 9－016 段形容这方面的默示陈述是说如果一个人在表达他的意图时就知道他根本不准备或没有能力去按照表达出来的意图行事,该对意图的陈述可以被视为对一个现有事实的误述。该段节可部分节录如下:"A statement of intention may be looked upon as a misrepresentation of existing fact if,at the time when it was made,the person making the statement did not in fact intend to do what he said or knew that he did not have the ability to put the intention into effect;..."

这背后的原因可举例说明,如在一个买卖或服务交易中,如果买方对卖方说他是在收到货物或服务后才支付价款,他在订购货物或服务时存在一个对现在事实的默示陈述,就是买方会有愿望与能力在将来作出支付。而如果后来的情况证明该默示陈述不正确,就构成误述,而且应是欺诈性误述。买方在取货时给了卖方一张空头支票,在取了货后就逃之夭夭,这肯定是欺诈性误述,而误述的言行是骗子没有愿望或能力为买的货物作出支付,但通过欺诈性误述去诱导卖方订立买卖合约,交出货物。至于骗子承诺卖方回公司后明天才会寄出该支票,这是将来意图或预期事实的表述;但只要这支票是空头的并且骗子逃之夭夭了,就显示骗子在较早取货时已经是不安好心,这不影响骗子的欺诈性误述。

很早已经有先例涉及这方面的问题。这可以 Re Shackleton Ex v. Whittaker (1875) LR 10 Ch. App. 446 先例作为介绍,该案案情涉及一批羊毛的买卖,当时买方已经处于经济困难境况,但卖方不知道,仍交出羊毛给买方,当时是周六。但到了下周一,买方宣布破产。这样,卖方就收不到货款了。但当时这批羊毛仍在买方仓库,所以卖方希望取回这批货物以保不失。但破产管理人认为在卖方交出羊毛时,货物产权已经转移给了买方。所以卖方只是一个普通债权人,无权取回已经不属于他的羊毛。这样,卖方能否证明买方取货时有一个欺诈性误述,也就是知道或估计到自己在下周一要破产,根本没有愿望与能力为这批羊毛作出支付。一旦能够证明,卖方就有权去撤销买卖合约,并要求回复到没有发生这欺诈/欺骗前的地位,[20] 也就是羊毛的产权仍在卖方的手中,也就有权把属于他的这批羊毛取回了。但由于证据不足(案例报告中不清楚破产买方 Shackleton 先生有否作证,但估计没有,因为破产管理人也没有出庭),卖方证明不了买方在取走羊毛时就意图不付钱(无论是通过其他办法支付这笔小钱或买方不能在最后关头避免破产),所以卖方没有成功。Mellish 大法官说:"We need not go into the question whether mere silence may not in some cases amount to a misrepresentation. It would be outrageous to hold that Shackleton, when he purchased, was bound to make any statement to the vendor as to his pecuniary circumstances, so there is nothing to affect the validity of the contract. It is true, indeed, that a party must not make any misrepresentation, express or implied, and as at present advised, I think **that Shackleton when he went for the goods must be taken to have made an implied representation that he intended to pay for them, and if it were clearly made out that at that time he did not intend to pay for them, I should consider that a case of fraudulent misrepresentation was shewn.** But I do not think this sufficiently made out. The debt for which he was proceeded against was a small one, and he did not attempt to raise money on these goods. I cannot say that he may not have thought that he could come to some terms with the petitioning creditor, and stop the bankruptcy proceedings."(加黑部分是笔者的强调)

在相对近期的 Director of Public Prosecutions v. Ray (1974) AC 370 贵族院先例中,该先例是一个涉及吃霸王餐被抓的刑事案件。被告 Ray 是大学生,他与 4 位同学

---

〔20〕 关于撤销合约与回复到原状,可见本书第三章之 5 段的介绍。

去一间中餐馆饱食一顿后，在侍应生进入厨房没有留意到他们时，他们未结账就跑出餐馆。贵族院判当被告 Ray 走进餐馆像一般客人一样坐下点餐时，这是告诉餐馆侍应生他意图付钱购买食物与服务，而该意图默示陈述了一个事实是他点餐与享用食物和服务时是有能力与愿意做出支付。这是一个对现在事实的默示陈述，并且随着他享用食物与服务，该意图是一个持续的表示。但他后来不付钱就逃跑的行为证明他在中途已经改变了意图，已经不打算再付钱，那这个持续意图表示所带出的对事实的默示陈述也构成是欺骗。于是贵族院判在《Theft Act 1968》下的“欺诈”(deception)罪名成立。

Re Gerald Cooper Chemicals Ltd(1978)Ch 262 先例涉及英国公司法下的欺诈性营运，这会带来民事与刑事责任。案情涉及生产靛青(用在牛仔裤的生产)的 Re Gerald Cooper Chemicals Ltd(以下简称 Cooper)在公司清盘前与本案例的原告 Harrisons 订立了买卖合约，约定将在 1 个月后交付 5000 公斤的靛青，并收取了 125,698.32英镑的预付货款。但 Cooper 随即把这笔钱用在归还给追债追得很紧的债权人 Jimlou，也是本案例的被告。但这样，Cooper 根本没有钱去生产这批靛青，也不可能把预付的货款归还，看来就是欺诈/欺骗了 Harrisons。在 Cooper 清盘后，Harrisons 对 Jimlou 与公司的两位董事提起诉讼，要求 Cooper 支付的这笔钱退还给 Harrisons，原因是参与欺诈/欺骗(这要看证据显示 Jimlou 是否知情，如参与 Cooper 的业务)或只是一位“推定信托人”(constructive trustee)。[21] 在此先例中，Jimlou 申请提前撤销原告的索赔(strike out claim as disclosing no cause of action)。[22] 但 Templeman 大法官不同意撤销，只提到 Jimlou 如果退还这笔钱，会否是退给 Cooper 的清盘人(liquidator)或 Harrisons，这是将来审理时要处理的。Templeman 大法官说：“(这是指当时生效的《Companies Act 1948》) Section 332(1) provides, inter alia: ‘If in the course of the winding up of a company it appears that any business of the company has been carried on with intent to defraud creditors of the company … or for any fraudulent purpose, the court, on the application of the official receiver, or the liquidator or any creditor or contributory of the company, may, if it thinks proper so to do, declare that any persons who were knowingly parties to the carrying on of the business in manner aforesaid shall be personally responsible, without any limitation of liability, for all or any of the debts or other liabilities of the company as the court may direct.’ … In my judgment, when Mr. Cooper on behalf of the Cooper companies sought from Harrisons an order for indigo on advance payment terms, Mr. Cooper was carrying on the business of the Cooper companies. When the Cooper companies accepted advance payment of £ 125,698 – odd, **Mr. Cooper knowing that there was no prospect, or no reasonable prospect or inten-**

---

〔21〕 见笔者《证据法：基础理论、口头证据与专家证据》一书第十章之 2.10 段的详细介绍。

〔22〕 见笔者《证据法：国际规管与诉讼中的证据攻防》一书第六章之 4 段的详细介绍。

tion of supplying indigo, and no intention of returning the money to Harrisons, the business of the Cooper companies was carried on fraudulently. The subsequent payment to Jimlou of £ 110,000 made the fraudulent carrying on of the business irremediable and constituted a fraud on the then creditor, Harrisons. The whole transaction between the Cooper companies and Harrisons constituted the carrying on of the business of the Cooper companies with intent to defraud a creditor of the company. Save that only one creditor was involved, the situation appears to meet the requirements of section 332 …"（加黑部分是笔者的强调）

最后，客观解释每个不同案件中涉及将来意图或预期事实的言行，也要小心不要太容易说成是也有一个默示的现在事实的陈述，它们毕竟在概念上是两码事，而且这种案件常会涉及刑事的严重后果，这与本章的 1.4.5 段提到的默示事实陈述不容易成立道理一样。这可节录 FoodCo UK LLP v. Henry Boot Developments Ltd (2010) EWHC 358 (Ch) 先例中，Lewison 大法官的警告："**Foretelling the future.** …, in Tudor Grange Holdings Ltd v Citibank NA (1992) Ch 53 … Browne-Wilkinson V-C said: '… Although **a bare prediction does not attract legal consequences**, a statement about the future **may implicitly contain a statement about the present**. But as with all cases in which **the court is asked to imply terms, the court must be cautious**. As Lord Wilberforce observed[23] …: 'My Lords, **the distinction in law between a promise as to future action, which may be broken or kept, and a statement as to existing fact, which may be true or false, is clear enough. There may be inherent in a promise an implied statement as to a fact**, and where this is really the case, the court can attach appropriate consequences to any falsity in, or recklessness in the making of, that statement. Everyone is familiar with the proposition that a statement of intention may itself be a statement of fact and so capable of being true or false. But **this proposition should not be used as a general solvent to transform the one type of assurance with another: the distinction is a real one and requires to be respected, particularly where the effect of treating an assurance as a statement is to attract criminal consequences**, …'.'"（加黑部分是笔者的强调）

6. 对法律的陈述

这课题在笔者《合约的履行、弃权与禁反言》一书第五章之 6.6 段已有涉及，在此只增加部分内容。传统的说法是对法律的陈述（statement of law）即使不正确，也

[23] 见 British Airways Board v. Taylor (1976) 1 WLR 13 贵族院先例。

不构成误述。这“对法律理解错误规则”(mistake of law rule)也不只是适用在误述法律导致合约产生的范畴,也适用在其他方面的民事诉讼,如“可诉错误”(actionable mistake)[24]与“复原”(restitution),[25]也当然适用刑事案件(criminal)。

6.1 “对法律理解错误规则”背后的原因

首先介绍有这条历史悠久“对法律理解错误规则”(mistake of law rule)的背后原因有以下几种。

1. 在法治社会,每一位人士都应懂法(这是指英国人要懂英国法),不存在民事诉讼可指交易的对方误述法律,自己作出依赖并蒙受损失,要求对方赔偿。早在 Bilbie v. Lumley(1802)2 East 469 先例中,Ellenborough 勋爵已经有说:“Every man must be taken to be cognisant of the law; otherwise there is no saying to what extent the excuse of ignorance might not be carried. It would be urged in almost every case.”

这精神源自罗马法的 ignorantia juris haud excusat,即“对法律的无知不是抗辩的理由”(ignorance of the law is no excuse)。这精神特别适用在刑法,所以很早就有这方面案例,也就是被告不得以对有关刑法无知(即使是真相)作为抗辩。但在民事/商事的范畴,对一般人的一般常识只是停留在“无知不是抗辩”的法律地位。

例外是有特殊的诚信关系(fiduciary duty),比如律师与他的客户。另也要去区分,刑事诉讼会有所谓“教唆犯罪”(aiding, abetting, counseling and procuring)的说法,但这与民事诉讼无关。

2. 良好法治社会的公共政策也应迫使每一位民众学法、懂法与守法。所以法律不应保障不懂法才被对方误述法律误导而蒙受损失的受害方。

3. 法律是完全公开的资料,双方要查阅,完全做得到。法律不像事实真相,例如在一宗买卖的交易中,卖方完全知悉有关标的(无论是商品、机械、房屋或是被并购的公司等)的事实真相,但买方要了解就不容易了。即使通过详细与不惜代价的全面检查或尽职调查,也不会比卖方对标的更熟悉。特别是在这种买卖合约中,英国法律视为无需默示善意(good faith),反而是默示要买家自己小心(caveat emptor)。[26]这样,加上人性,一位想成功出售标的的卖方难免扬长避短,也不会做“老实人”披露任何对自己不利的信息。这样,买方保护自己的法律武器就只能要求卖方提供足够的信息与事实,特别是在检查或尽职调查的过程中(也是在合约谈判的过程中)。面对买方的查询或要求信息,卖方如果希望交易顺利完成就必须回答。面对懂行与精明的买方,简单或模棱两可的回答也无法过关,买方会打破砂锅问到底。在一个复杂

---

〔24〕 见本书第七章。

〔25〕 见本书第三章关于撤销合约后复原以及笔者《合约的履行、弃权与禁反言》一书第五章之 4 段关于弄错事实/法律下付钱的复原的介绍。

〔26〕 这也是《Sale of Goods Act 1979》之 Section 14(1)的规定,在杨大明律师《国际货物买卖》一书第四章之 1 段有介绍。

的商业交易，如果之后发生争议，就会从这一连串与全面的问答（经常以书面往来以留下文件证据）中挑出卖方提供的不正确信息与事实，构成可诉误述。

4. 对法律的陈述与对意见的表述相同，因为懂法律的人知道不能把一个法律观点“说死”，不像是对过去或现在的事实可以明确真假。所以英国法院是不采纳英国法的专家证人的，因为这种意见不会对审理法官有帮助，他们应该自己去作出最后对英国法律的“意见”（opinion），也就是“判决”（judgment）。[27] 这可节录《Misrepresentation, Mistake and Non-Disclosure》（2022 年，第 6 版）一书之 3 - 33 段说：“It is sometimes said that the rule that a false statement of law cannot be an actionable misrepresentation is a sub-species of the rule that statements of opinion are not to be treated as ‘misrepresentation’; unlike fact, law is not something which can be stated with certainty; a statement of law is essentially the speaker's own assessment, or opinion, of what the law would say on the matter.”

另在 Spencer Bower 的《Actionable Misrepresentation》（2014 年，第 5 版）一书之 2.25 段说：“He who expresses his views on law to another is in the same position as one who expresses his views on any other question of science, or business, and the inquiry as to whether, and to what extent, his statement is a representation is governed by the same considerations.”

所以不正确的对英国法律的陈述，过往是不视为误述的：见 Rashdall v. Ford (1866) LR 2 Eq 750; Beattie v. Lord Ebury (1872) LR 7 Ch. App. 777; Harse v. Pearl Life Assurance Co (1904) 1 KB 558; Beesley v. Hallwood Estates Ltd (1960) 1 WLR 549 等先例。

6.2　对“对法律理解错误规则”不满意的原因

6.2.1　假设大家都懂法、有均等渠道熟悉法律是否现实？

上述“对法律理解错误规则”一直受到不少攻击。可节录在 Evans v. Bartlam (1937) AC 473 贵族院先例中，Atkin 勋爵说：“I am not prepared to accept the view that there is in law any presumption that anyone, even a judge, knows all the rules and orders of the Supreme Court.”

另在 Kiritimati Cotton Co Ltd v. Dewani (1960) AC 192 (PC) 先例中，Denning 勋爵说这规定只适用在违约方或侵权方（当然也包括罪犯）不得以自己不懂法律作为抗辩：“It is not correct to say that everyone is presumed to know the law. The true proposition is that no man can excuse himself from doing his duty by saying that he did not know the law on the matter. Ignorantia juris neminem excusat. ...”

也可节录《Misrepresentation, Mistake and Non-Disclosure》一书（2022 年，第 6 版）之 3 - 31 段说：“... a presumption that everyone knows the law. But this is **nothing more**

---

〔27〕 见笔者《证据法：基础理论、口头证据与专家证据》一书第五章之 11.1 段。

than a fiction which simply restates the general proposition that no one can plead mistake of law. … It is **unrealistic to expect every contracting party to be fully and accurately informed of every relevant question of law**. The quantity and complexity of primary and secondary legislation speak against it-to say nothing of the difficulties for the parties of answering with certainty questions of interpretation of statute and common law, particularly when the parties can be held to have been under a mistake of law because of a later judicial decision which has retrospective effect in changing the understanding of the law which was settled at the time the mistake was made. …"(加黑部分是笔者的强调)

撇开律师对客户错误陈述法律是有特殊关系与诚信关系针对,在一般民众之间,他们对法律了解程度很不一样,这条规则就会造成不公平,让懂法律的精明人士占尽便宜。同样重要的是这个法律规则不现实,即使是早期的英国法律相对比较简单,也不见得英国人是人人懂法。这样如果误述法律没有法律责任,容易造成更多精明商人通过对法律的误述去诱导/诱骗不懂的对方,而对方受骗也只能怪自己。

随着英国法律特别是商法的日趋复杂与广为国际贸易所用,这法律误述没有后果的规定显然更是造成不公平。英美商人特别是跨国公司肯定对英国法律较精通,但在国际商业上的活动面对的发展中国家对手(包括大部分的中国公司)往往不懂。他们也因为知道自己不懂,所以依赖对方西方国家的公司,例如习惯上使用对方草拟的文书合约或提供的范本。最多只是泛泛问草拟的合约是否是公平合理,对方也肯定会说"是",即使其中有多处地雷。由于只是泛泛地询问,好像正常做广告、推销的吹嘘,所以即使是事实陈述,也不构成可诉误述,更不说是法律的误述了,例如问西方公司合约条文要如何解释。但如果问得特定与具体,针对事实是会构成误述,但针对法律就没有后果了。

例如笔者记得发生在40年前的一件事情,涉及中国与美国一家著名公司订立一个技术专利转让合约。在该美国公司的标准合约中有一条是专利转让的惯用条文,内容是美国公司作为卖方向中方保证它拥有这个转让的专利,并承诺将来中方以此专利制造的产品/商品如果被第三人提起侵犯第三人专利权的诉讼,美国公司将赔偿中方所有的损失,包括预支对专利谁属的诉讼所产生的法律费用。据知,该美国公司为了进入中国市场,事前还商谈了哪些合约条文预计中方会为了自己的利益提出异议,并需要美国公司让步才会成交这笔金额庞大的专利转让交易。美国公司也有心理准备,例如对美国公司是至关重要的纽约或伦敦仲裁条文,准备中方如果坚持就让步去接受贸仲仲裁,毕竟当时美国公司很想进入中国市场。

但在双方谈判,中方只对此惯用条文有异议,声称将来不想涉及诉讼,所以如果有不知名的第三人起诉,必须只能告美国公司。美国公司解释英国法下第三人是没有诉因可直接告美国公司,因为被指控违反第三人专利的产品/商品是中方生产。但由于中方半信半疑,也对美国公司是否拥有专利有怀疑,美国公司建议了一条条文说明在有第三人将来提起专利诉讼时，美国公司将与中方“并肩”（side – by – side）作为被告，并全面负责与处理该诉讼与绝不干扰中方，并说这可以完全解除中方的忧虑，这为中方接受。笔者认为美国公司的打算是万一有第三人向中方提起专利权争议的诉讼，美国公司会与第三人直接接触，并以中方名义接管与第三人的诉讼，任何时候尽量不去麻烦中方。美国公司也可以假惺惺地要求第三人把它作为被告，但第三人应无法同意，因为根本没有诉因可以在法院向美国公司提起诉讼。但也能想到，如果出事时中方与美国公司关系转坏，美国公司不理睬第三人对中国公司的诉讼，中方就要自己上阵对抗。中方如果以美国公司误述诱导该技术专利转让合约的产生，美国公司就会以对法律的误述不能构成可诉误述作为抗辩了。

6.2.2 区分法律与事实的困难

在介绍区分法律与事实的困难前，先简单介绍两个早期先例。它们是 Bilbie v. Lumley（1802）2 East 469 先例与 Kelly v. Solari（1841）9 M & W 54 先例。两个先例都涉及保险人（insurers）错误赔付后企图以错误支付（payment under mistake）向受保人（assured/insured）索要回来，但因为错误是有法律与事实的区别，导致两个对一般人士看来是一模一样的案情有截然不同的结果。在 Bilbie v. Lumley 先例中，案情涉及船舶保险，保险人在赔付后企图根据复原原则取回这笔钱（£ 100），因为受保人在投保时没有披露一封有实质重要的信息的信函。但保险人败诉，因为错误支付是一个法律上的错误。

在 Kelly v. Solari 先例中，案情涉及一个人寿保险。受保人是在 1840 年 10 月 18 日去世，但在 9 月 3 日没有支付每一季度要准时支付的保费，这导致保险人的精算部门视该保单失效（lapsed），并告知了公司负责的两位董事。到了 1841 年 2 月 6 日，去世受保人的遗孀向保险人申请赔付，并很快在 2 月 13 日获得了保险人签发的 £ 9871.10 的支票。但事后两位董事声称是因为忘记了保单已经失效才错误支付，要求把这笔钱取回。

在法院，Abinger 勋爵说针对错误支付能否以复原原则取回有 3 种情况：“The safest rule however is, that if the party makes the payment with full knowledge of the facts, although under ignorance of the law, there being no fraud on the other side, he cannot recover it back again. There may also be cases in which, although he might by investigation learn the state of facts more accurately, he declines to do so, and chooses to pay the money notwithstanding; in that case there can be no doubt that he is equally bound. Then there is a third case, and the most difficult one, — where the parties had once a full knowledge of the facts, but has since forgotten them. ... I think the knowledge of the facts which disentitles the party from recovering, must mean a knowledge existing in the mind at the time of payment. I have little doubt in this case that the directors had forgotten the fact ...”

这说法也被其他上诉庭法院大法官同意，命令案件重审，让陪审团根据证据决定该两位董事是否在支付时真正忘掉了保单失效这个事实。显然如果是事实的错误，就可以取回这笔钱。

接下来可举三个方面(还有很多其他方面但不去多说)难以区分法律与事实的例子。

1. 合约或书面文件的解释是法律问题(issue of law)。但在笔者的《合约的解释:规则与应用》一书第五章之1段有介绍这是历史原因,因为早期的民事诉讼是有陪审团制度,而当时陪审团有相当部分人士是文盲,根本看不懂合约条文可当作“事实”决定。所以解释合约条文是由审理法官自己决定,虽然已经是明确解释,仍需要考虑订约时可能存在的大量“事实”,也就是背景/语境(context 或 factual matrix)。

可节录《Misrepresentation, Mistake and Non-Disclosure》(2022年,第6版)一书之3-26段说:“**Interpretation of documents.** The law/fact distinction appears to be rather unclear in its application to the interpretation of documents. One would expect the question of what the words of a document are to be a matter of fact, and the legal effect of those words to be a matter of law; but sometimes the courts have held mistakes or misrepresentations about the effect of a document to be mistakes or misrepresentations of fact; and the distinction between what a document says, and what it means, is not always easy to draws. ...”

2. 有不少问题是法律与事实的混合(mixed law and fact),如合约受阻(frustration)、弃权与禁反言(waiver and/or estoppel)等。在这种情况下,错误做出的陈述被对方合理依赖并产生合约(如双方达成和解协议),那么在不同案情下,区分何谓“法律”或“事实”的误述并不容易。另在笔者的《合约的解释:规则与应用》一书第二章之13.2段“解释部分文书部分口头合约是一个事实与法律问题的混合”,也提到这种问题,但在此不去重复。普通法也把它视为“对法律理解错误规则”的另一个例外,这在《Chitty on Contracts》(2021年,第34版)一书之9-020段说:“... It seems that the courts tend to regard statement of mixed law and fact, and statements capable of having either meaning, as statements of fact, and therefore as representations...”

3. 外国法律(foreign law)的问题。在英国法的角度,所有外国的法律被视为“事实”。所以在英国法院(或仲裁庭),一旦有外国法律的争议,都视为是事实的争议:见 The“Amazonia”(1990)1 Lloyd’s Rep 236 等先例。法院需要通过证据(主要是外国法的专家证人)并根据平衡的可能性作出事实的认定。这样,可以容易推算到一个对外国法律的不正确或虚假陈述可以构成可诉误述。

Andre v. Ets. Michel Blanc(1979)2 Lloyd’s Rep 427 先例是1973年6月因密西西比河泛滥引致农产品失收,美国政府作出被认为过火的对大豆禁运(禁止出口)决定,进而引致大豆市场价格急升的一连串案例之一。

卖方 Andre 在美国政府禁运后,告诉买方在禁令下只能有40%的货量供应,而其余的60%他不负责,因为买卖合约有一条说:“21. **Prohibition**: In case of prohibition of export .... preventing fulfilment, this contract or any unfulfilled portion thereof so affected shall be cancelled..."

同时卖方要求买方确认同意只要40%的货量即可算履约,因为这是美国政府禁令所要求。于是买方为了得到这"宝贵"的40%,同意并最后打了如下电文:"We hereby declare that under the legislation presently in force in the USA for the export of soya meals, we accept to receive 40% of the quantities contracted for shipment ... in total fulfilment of the above mentioned contracts."

在交付了40%大豆后,买方得知美国政府的禁令被卖方误述、曲解。例如禁令根本没有要求买方同意在合约中减少货量,否则什么都得不到。因此,买方向卖方起诉,追讨其余60%货量的差价。当然,买方也不接受卖方可对不交足货物免责。而卖方依赖的自然是双方已达成和解协议,同意只要交付40%的货物即可算是已经履约。

在一审[(1977) 2 Lloyd's Rep 166]先例中,高院的Ackner大法官判是卖方对美国法律误述。美国法律对在伦敦仲裁/英国法院审判而言是外国法,而外国法被当作"事实"处理,所以,误述美国法等于"误述事实"。而虽然卖方会是非欺诈性或是无辜误述,只是曲解了美国政府的禁令,但本案适用《Misrepresentation Act 1967》,在Section 2(1)下亦要求其对受害方买方负责。Ackner大法官说:"I have no hesitation in finding that ... the sellers materially misrepresented the situation and even if the misrepresentation was (which I doubt) [28] a representation of law, it was a representation of American law and is therefore treated by these Courts as a representation of fact."

至于合约21条的免责,Ackner大法官也判卖方不能依赖,因为他对有关事实没有足够的举证,如证明手上没有已装上驳船(lighter)的大豆,因为美国政府没有禁运这些已算是付运的"浮动货物"(floating cargo)。

这也带来另一个问题,就是有不少的"外国"是普通法系国家,在不少法律方面的问题与英国一致或十分接近。这样,如果在订约谈判时误述了英国法律,就不构成可诉误述;但如果误述了澳大利亚或新加坡法律,即使是同一码事,就变了是事实的误述,成为可诉误述。

总的来说,这"法律"与"事实"的区分受到不少质疑,如上诉庭的Denning勋爵在Andre v. Ets. Michel Blanc先例说:"... **the distinction between law and fact is very illusory. It is so difficult to define that I hope that the time will soon come when it will be disregarded.** It does not apply here for several reasons ... it seems to me not to be a misrepresentation of the general law, even if the United States. It is a misrepresenta-

---

[28] Achner大法官认为有疑问估计是认为卖方不是错误陈述法律,而是误述特定法律权利(legal rights)。这在普通法下早已被视为错误陈述事实,可以构成可诉误述;但Achner大法官无须去决定这一点,所以只表达了怀疑。

tion as to private rights in the United States … The real reason why in former days misrepresentations of law were accepted was because both parties were supposed to have equal access to the law and to have equal knowledge thereof. It is not right to say that everyone is presumed to know the law. **It is very proper, therefore, that the distinction between law and fact should soon be abandoned.**"(加黑部分是笔者的强调)

6.3 一般法律与特定法律权利的区分

上一小段已经提到,为了减少"对法律理解错误规则"的适用,有不少早期的先例设立例外,其中包括一般法律(general law)与特定法律权利(legal rights)的区分。对一般英国法律做出错误评论或概述,例如陈述方说订约后违约要赔偿损失也很有限甚至不需要赔,或大家合作打击对手也没有后果等,因为这些是法制环境下的基础与常识,被陈述对方应该知道,也应该知道不能依赖。如有疑问,对方也应该自己去咨询律师才去依赖。

但如果狭窄地针对英国法律下某一件事或对方有什么法律权利,例如:告诉交易的对方你是不需要向当局申请执照或批准,或这套房屋的产权属于某某人,或你只要做了A就可以合法做B与C等,而对方也合理依赖(如对方是有关行业的新手)的情况下,即使是涉及法律/法例,仍会构成可诉误述。

在 Cooper v. Phibbs(1867)L. R. 2 H. L. 149 贵族院先例中,Westbury 勋爵说:"It is said, 'Ignorantia juris haud excusat', but in that maxim the word 'jus' is used in the sense of denoting general law, the ordinary law of the country. But when the word 'jus' is used in the sense of denoting a private right, that maxim has no application. Private right of ownership is a matter of fact; it may be the result also of matter of law; but if parties contract under a mutual mistake and misapprehension as to their relative and respective rights, the result is, that that agreement is liable to be set aside as having proceeded upon a common mistake. Now, that was the case with these parties—the Respondents believed themselves to be entitled to the property, the Petitioner believed that he was a stranger to it, the mistake is discovered, and the agreement cannot stand."

在接下来的 Eaglesfield v. Marquis of Londonderry(1876)4 Ch. D. 693 先例中,Jessel MR 大法官也解释了特别法律权利本身是事实问题,只不过是涉及法律/法例:"It is not the less a fact because that fact involves some knowledge or relation of law. There is hardly any fact which does not involve it. If you state that a man is in possession of an estate of £ 10,000 a year, the notion of possession is a legal notion, and involves knowledge of law; nor can any other fact in connection with property be stated which does not involve such knowledge of law. To state that a man is entitled to £ 10,000 Consols involve all sorts of law."

可节录《Misrepresentation, Mistake and Non-Disclosure》(2022年,第6版)一书之3-27段:"**Mistake or misrepresentation of 'private rights'** Sometimes the courts have characterised what appears at first sight to be a ... misrepresentation of law as one of fact, on the basis that the rule applies only to issues of general law, and so ... misrepresentations of private rights are to be treated as issues of fact for this purpose. The origins of this distinction are contained in the speech of Lord Westbury in Cooper v. Phibbs, a case in which it was held that the question of the ownership of property of which the claimant took a lease, but which was found to belong to him already, was one of fact because the issue of his rights of ownership was one of his private rights. ... The principle stated in relation to mistake in Cooper v. Phibbs has been applied also to misrepresentation characterised as statements of 'private rights' rather than of the general law."

这方面也有其他先例,如 Laurence v. Lexcourt Holdings Ltd(1977)1 WLR 1128; Brikom Investments Ltd v. Seaford(1981)1 WLR 863; China Pacific SA v. Food Corp of India(1981)QB 403 等,但因为在下一段会介绍的"对法律理解错误规则"已经不复存在,所以就没必要多谈。

6.4 Kleinwort Benson Ltd v. Lincoln City Council(1999)2 AC 349 贵族院先例

早在 Brisbane v. Dacres(1813)5 Taunt 143 先例中,就在复原(restitution)设立了"对法律理解错误规则",也就是如果因为法律上(不是事实上)的错误自愿支付一笔钱,但后来发觉错误,就无权追讨这笔钱。简单举一个例子,雇主如果误以为法律(有关的劳工法或雇佣合约条文)是要对某离职的雇员支付 3 个月工资的遣散费,后来发觉法律已经改了或这一条文被错误理解,这 3 个月工资的遣散费就要不回来了。但如果是事实的错误,例如这笔钱本来是想汇给雇员 A,把银行账号搞错汇给了雇员 B,就可以向雇员 B 根据复原原则追讨回来。在 Brisbane v. Dacres 先例中,也讨论了允许法律错误下获得支付的被告取得这份财产在道德上是否公平合理。多数意见是没有不公平合理,因为收钱的被告会以为在法律下,他是有权收取这笔钱的。他甚至在原告要求复原时也已经花了部分,现在要求把这笔钱全数退还,反而有时候会造成不公平合理。法院确立了这"对法律理解错误规则",这可节录 Gibbs 大法官所说:"We must take this payment to have been made under a demand of right, and I think that where a man demands money of another as a matter of right, and that other, with a full knowledge of the facts upon which the demand is founded, has paid a sum, he never can recover back the sum he has so voluntarily paid. It may be, that upon a further view he may form a different opinion of the law, and it may be, his subsequent opinion may be the correct one. If we were to hold otherwise, I think that many inconveniences may arise; there are many doubtful questions of law; ..."

在复原法律后来的发展中,特别是在 Lipkin Gorman v. Karpnale Ltd(1991)2 AC 548 贵族院先例后的"改变地位"(change of position)中,就令复原请求能够更公平对待原告与被告,不再是以前的收钱的被告要么是成功以陈述性禁反言(estoppel by representation)可一毛钱也不退还给原告,要么就是不成功要全数退还,即使已经是花费了的部分金钱也要自己掏腰包退还。这可节录在笔者《合约的履行、弃权与禁反言》一书第五章之4段所说:"改变地位的抗辩不需要给错钱的一方做出任何错误陈述,也不需要收钱的一方有任何依赖并蒙受损害。"更明显的区别是后果不同,这显示在还钱时因为改变地位成为实质的抗辩(substantive defence),收钱的一方可以不用还钱(因为已经全部合理用掉)或只需要还一部分。但陈述性禁反言是程序上的抗辩(procedural defence),一旦成立给错钱的一方就一分钱都拿不回来,是没有中间地带,也不会考虑要求退还一部分没有合理用掉的钱是否公平。

这样,这"对法律理解错误规则"更是没有必要持续存在。这也是法律改革委员会的建议,可部分节录1991年的《Law Commission's Consultation Paper No. 120 on "Restitution of Payments made under a Mistake of Law"》的总结如下:

"**CONCLUSION AND SUMMARY OF CONSULTATION ISSUES**

5.1 In this paper we have considered the general rule that payments made under a mistake of law are irrecoverable and the position of ultra vires payments to and by public authorities. We have canvassed a number of possible reforms and have considered their implications. The case for reform is based on the fact that it is unjust that as between the parties the payee should be able to retain a payment received at the expense of the payer because of the payer's mistake. This basic principle is recognised in the law relating to payments made as a result of a mistake of fact. The different treatment given to mistakes of law and mistakes of fact is inconsistent and arbitrary, and these features of the law are exacerbated by the development of many exceptions to the mistake of law rule. There have, moreover, been important statutory modifications of the rule....

5.2 Our provisional conclusions on the main issues are as follows: (a) there is a case for abolishing the rule precluding the recovery of payments made as a result of a mistake of law so as to permit recovery in the same way that it is currently allowed where the payment is made under a mistake of fact..."

6.4.1 多数意见推翻"对法律理解错误规则"

接下来的发展可带出 Kleinwort Benson Ltd v. Lincoln City Council (1999) 2 AC 349 贵族院先例,该案案情涉及利率掉期(Interest Rate Swap)的交易,[29] 原告银行与作为被告的4个地方议会(Lincoln City Council、Birmingham City Council、Southwark London Borough Council 与 Kensington and Chelsea Royal London Borough Council)有3年—4年(1982至1985年)的交易,并总共在这些利率掉期合约下支付给了4位被告811,208英镑。但在1991年有了一个判决说这些政府机构没有被立法授权去订立这种对冲协议,这导致银行向这些地方议会提起诉讼,认为它们是越权(ultra vi-

[29] 这种对冲交易在本书第六章之9.1段介绍 Manchester Building Society v. Grant Thornton UK LLP (2021) UKSC 20 最高院先例中有介绍。

res)订立合约,所以合约是无效(void),而已经错误支付了的钱应该根据"复原"或"不当得利"(unjust enrichment)的法律原则退还给原告银行。但这样,就面对"对法律理解错误规则"的抗辩,也就是被告无需退还这笔钱。

"复原"与"不当得利"的法律原则在笔者《合约的履行、弃权与禁反言》一书第五章之4段有详论。在该章之6.6段的注脚54,也有简单提及此先例说:弄错事实下付钱可以根据复原从收钱的一方追回这笔钱。但在弄错法律下付钱,一贯以来的说法是复原不适用。在 Kleinwort Benson Ltd v. Lincoln City Council 先例中,贵族院拒绝对复原加以这样的限制,即弄错法律下付钱也可以根据复原追回。

贵族院的多数意见判原告银行胜诉,可以根据复原把这笔错误支付的钱取回,并明确推翻了"对法律理解错误规则"。以下可节录判决的摘要:"... application of the principle of unjust enrichment the rule precluding recovery of money paid under a mistake of law could no longer be maintained and recognition should be given to a general right to recover money paid under a mistake, whether of fact or law, subject to the defences available in the law of restitution; that money paid under a mistake of law was recoverable even where the payment had been made under a settled understanding of the law which was subsequently departed from by judicial decision or where the payment had been received by the recipient under an honest belief of an entitlement to retain the money; that there was no principle in English law that money paid under a void contract was irrecoverable on the ground of mistake of law where the contract had been fully performed according to its terms ..."

6.4.2 少数不同意见的反对原因

至于持不同意见的 Browne - Wilkinson 与 Lloyd 勋爵,倒也不是反对推翻"对法律理解错误规则",而是认为这个历史悠久、也已经有无数案例跟从的法律地位,应该是议会(Parliament)在整体考虑影响后通过立法作出改变,而不应由法院改变。

这是因为对重大与已经是长期被接受的法律地位,如果是由法院通过案例去作出法律改变,就会带出很多以前没有人想到会有机会成功的案件有了成功机会,只要不是时效已过或已经被判过(因为一事不再审)就可以开始诉讼。正如 Goff 勋爵在该先例所说:"... when judges state what the law is, their decisions do ... have a retrospective effect. That is, I believe, inevitable."

但通过议会立法就可以避免这种情况,因为改变了的法律地位往往说明从立法规定的生效日期起才适用。而且一般针对实体性的法律地位,立法作出改变不会有追溯权。此外立法改变法律地位还有其他好处,因为立法时会对各种情况全面考虑,而在个别案件中作出的法律改变不一定会或能够全面考虑其他情况并作出针对。

的确在几乎所有对法律地位有重大改变的贵族院或最高院案例中,都会有少数持不同意见的大法官,而持少数意见的大法官反对的原因也通常有认为这种重大法律的改变应通过立法去改变,而不是通过个别案例(judicial law - making)去改变或纠正。例如 Donoghue v. Stevenson(1932)AC 562 贵族院先例(3－2);Woolwich Equitable Building Society v. Inland Revenue Commissioners(1993)AC 70 贵族院先例(3－2);Campbell v. MGN Ltd(2004)2 AC 457 贵族院先例(3－2);Jones v. Kaney(2011)UKSC 13 最高院先例(5－2)等。

简单节录在 C(a minor)v. DPP(1996)AC 1 贵族院先例中,Lowry 勋爵提到的贵族院在发展普通法的过程中要节制,不要太轻易在个别案件去改变或纠正上百年来已经确立的法律地位,并指出 5 点需要考虑的内容:"I believe, however, that one can find in the authorities some aids to navigation across an uncertainly charted sea. (1) If the solution is doubtful, the judges should beware of imposing their own remedy. (2) Caution should prevail if Parliament has rejected opportunities of clearing up a known difficulty or has legislated, while leaving the difficulty untouched. (3) Disputed matters of social policy are less suitable areas for judicial intervention than purely legal problems. (4) Fundamental legal doctrines should not be lightly set aside. (5) Judges should not make a change unless they can achieve finality and certainty."〔30〕

6.5　"对法律理解错误规则"的小结

Kleinwort Benson Ltd v. Lincoln City Council(1999)2 AC 349 贵族院先例虽然只是针对"复原"并推翻了"对法律理解错误规则",但在之后的 Vraj Pankhania, Joshua Prakhania v. The London Borough of Hackney(2002)EWHC 2441(Ch)先例中,明确了英国法律下的"对法律错误理解规则"也不再适用在对法律误述的情况,而不只是错误支付。Treitel 教授说对法律误述的说法根据 Kleinwort Benson Ltd v. Lincoln City Council 先例已经有所改变,并在 Vraj Pankhania, Joshua Prakhania v. The London Borough of Hackney 先例被引用,Rex Tedd QC 大法官说:

"As to the origins of the 'misrepresentation of law' rule, Sir G Mellish L. J. said in Beattie-v-Lord Ebury [LR] 7 Ch. App. 777 … said that 'although I have found no case at law, there is a case in equity which clearly shows that a person cannot be made liable for making a misrepresentation unless it is a misrepresentation in point of fact, and not merely in point of law'. … Professor Treitel, at … his work, independently draws attention to the analogy, in this passage: 'The House of Lords has recently held that mistakes of law, no less than mistakes of fact, can give rise to a claim for the return of money paid under a mistake. Such a claim is analogous to one for the return of payments made under a contract which has been rescinded for misrepresentation, so that there is now a strong case for reconsidering the effects of the distinction in the context of restitution claims based on misrepresentation'. …

〔30〕 这 5 点在 Walker 勋爵发表的"Developing the Common Law: How Far Is Too Far?"(2013)37 MULR 232 一文中有详细讨论,与本书内容关系不大,不在此详论。

…I have concluded that the ' misrepresentation of law ' rule has not survived the decision in Kleinwort Benson Ltd-v-Lincoln City Council … Its historical origin is as an off – shoot of the ' mistake of law ' rule, created by analogy with it, and the two are logically inter – dependent. Both are grounded in the maxim ' ignorantia juris non excusat ', … The distinction between fact and law in the context of relief from misrepresentation has no more underlying principle to it than it does in the context of relief from mistake. Indeed, when the principles of mistake and misrepresentation are set side by side, there is a stronger case for granting relief against a party who has induced a mistaken belief as to law in another, than against one who has merely made the same mistake himself. **The rules of the common law should, so far as possible, be congruent with one another, and based on coherent principle. The survival of the ' misrepresentation of law ' rule following the demise of the ' mistake of law ' rule would be no more than a quixotic anachronism.** "(加黑部分是笔者的强调)

"对法律理解错误规则"目前的法律地位,在《Chitty on Contracts》(2021 年,第 34 版)一书之 9 – 020 段有较全面的总结,可节录如下:"**Statements of law.** It used commonly to be said that a statement of law cannot be treated as a misrepresentation. But the proposition was always in need of qualification and it is now more accurate to say that a statement of law will amount to a misrepresentation unless, in the circumstances, it reasonably appeared that the statement was put forward as nothing more than an opinion on which it would not be reasonable to rely.〔31〕 **First**, a statement of law may be regarded as a statement of opinion, but just as a statement of opinion may be a representation of fact, so too a statement of law may amount to a representation, or misrepresentation, as the case may be. So a wilful misstatement of law would always amount to a misrepresentation and even an innocent misstatement of law may do so where it carries an implication of fact which is itself untrue. **Secondly**, the question whether a statement is one of law or fact are so frequently no small difficulty, especially as statements of law and of fact are so frequently intermingled. … But **thirdly, in the law of restitution the distinction between a payment made under a mistake of fact and one made under a mistake of law has been held by the House of Lords not to be part of English law,〔32〕 and, in the light of this, it was held in Pankhania v. Hackney LBC that the ' misrepresentation of law ' rule is no longer good law.** Thus, for the purposes of the law of misrepresentation, the

---

〔31〕 例如,对一般法律的误述,如是 A 向 B 说签了合约也不会有责任,这只是一个错误的法律意见。但是一般人(特别是参与国际商业活动的 B)都应该了解这种一般法律,所以即使是依赖了错误的表述也是不合理,B 也不会有可诉误述的救济。

〔32〕 也就是 Kleinwort Benson Ltd v. Lincoln City Council(1999)AC 349 贵族院先例。

distinction between statements of law and statements of fact is no longer maintainable and that even an incorrect statement of an abstract proposition of law may amount to a misrepresentation unless it is apparent that all that is being offered is an opinion without implication that the speaker has reasonable grounds for that opinion. ..."(加黑部分是笔者的强调)

也就是在今天的法律地位下对法律的误述也可以构成可诉误述,除非是误述方只是给出个人的意见(无论是对是错),而且被误述方也应该知道有关的法律是一般的常识或应该很容易查问到正确的法律地位,那么再去依赖误述方的陈述就不合理。

7. 行动表示的陈述

社会上的一般性交易,常会见面洽谈并最后以言行达成合约。事后双方有了争议,比如是同意了什么,就只能以口头证据去让法院或仲裁庭根据平衡的可能性认定事实。同一道理下,在谈判过程中如果客观看某一方的眼色,或一个点头,或一个微笑,会造成误导对方的后果,这行动(如果被法院认定)即会是可诉误述。比如,买方问卖方这面包是否新鲜,在今天刚出炉?卖方固然会回答说"是"或"不是",但也会只是微笑点头。如果这并非事实,面包是隔夜面包,这明显是卖方的语言或行动构成可诉误述。但相信随着今天越来越多的以网购达成的远程合约(distance contract)的出现,买卖双方从不见面,这种行动上的误述会更少发生。而且这种日常生活中的交易虽然频繁,但通常涉及金额不大,有了争议也绝少会花费昂贵的律师费用去提起诉讼并成为先例。

这种行动表示的误述(representation by conduct)在比较承担得起诉讼费用的国际商业也发生不多,因为双方通过简单的面对面谈判就订立一个标的很高的商业合约的情形并不多。在如今(2020年全球新冠疫情暴发前)的国际商业谈判中,即使有面对面谈判,也会比较严谨并制造大量文件,例如会议记录、录音、事后的电文/电邮往来确定面对面谈判的重点等。反正不会涉及面谈中对方的点头、摇头、微笑等的"小动作"传达什么信息或事实。

这也解释了有关行动表示的误述案例很少,比较著名的只是19世纪寥寥无几的先例,今天更可能是在有关的背景/语境下,语言与行动加起来向对方作出一个默示陈述。可先节录《Chitty on Contracts》(2021年,34版)一书之9-022段说:"**Misrepresentation by conduct**. ... a person may be guilty of misrepresentation by conduct. It is sometimes hard to distinguish misrepresentation by conduct from implied representation, but normally it is unnecessary to do so. In the simplest case, conduct may be intended to convey information in precisely the same way as the written or spoken word. Thus a person who goes into a shop in a university town wearing cap and gown ... would be representing that he is an undergraduate; a person who sits down in a restaurant and orders a meal impliedly represents that he has the means to pay, and more generally it has been said in a well – known dictum that ' a nod or a wink or a shake of the head or a smile' may amount to a representation if it is intended to induce the other party to believe in a certain state of facts. ..."

另节录权威书籍《Misrepresentation, Mistake and Non-Disclosure》一书(2022 年,第6版)之 3 – 04 段所说:"**Misrepresentation by conduct** The false statement need not, however, be made through the medium of words, whether written or oral. What is required is that a falsehood be communicated to the claimant; and this can be done by his interpretation of the defendant's action as well as by his hearing or reading the defendant's words. A 'nod or a wink, or a shake of the head, or a smile from the purchaser intending to induce the vendor to believe the existence of a non-existent fact' can be enough. And other conduct not directed at the claimant as directly as a nod of the head but which has the effect of communicating to him a falsehood can equally well constitute a 'misrepresentation', such as the action of the agents of a lessor of a flat in covering up patches of dry rot, which has been held to be a misrepresentation to prospective tenants about the state of the property for the purposes of the tort of deceit. Most cases which reach the courts involve words, perhaps because a misrepresentation by words is the clearest form of false statement; there is a greater possibility for argument about the meaning which action can be taken to have communicated."

早期行动构成的误述,往往涉及在买卖交易中以行动隐藏一些货物的缺点,这可节录《Chitty on Contracts》(2021 年,34 版)一书之9 –023 段说:"**Conduct intended to conceal facts.** Conduct may amount to a representation where the conduct is not so much intended to convey information as to conceal facts from the other party. There are nineteenth-century cases in which a seller of goods was held guilty of misrepresentation where it was shown that he had deliberately concealed defects in the goods being sold, as, for instance, by nailing down planks and closing the seams of a rotten ship, or by plugging a hole in a gun with soft metal; and more recently the deliberate covering up of dry rot in a building was held to amount to fraud ..."

7.1 先例之一:Baglehole v. Walters(1811)3 Camp 154 先例

上述节录最后一句提到的情况是指两个古老先例,先是在 Baglehole v. Walters 先例中,卖方故意钉块木板挡住船舶腐烂的地方,不让买方检验时看到,此举即会构成误述。法院认为卖方即使对出售的货物有缺陷是知情(或不知情)的,但不主动告诉买方,也不是欺诈/欺骗。这是"买方要自己小心"(let the buyers beware,或是拉丁文的 Caveat emptor)[33] 的大原则。但卖方故意隐瞒缺点让小心谨慎的买方通过合理检验也不一定查得出来就不一样了，这是欺诈性误述。正如该先例的 Ellenborough 勋爵说："Where an article is sold with all faults, I think it is quite immaterial how many belonged to it within the knowledge of the seller, **unless he used some artifice to disguise them, and to prevent their being discovered by the purchaser**. The very object of introducing such a stipulation is to put the purchaser on his guard, and to throw upon him the burthen of examining all faults, both secret and apparent."（加黑部分是笔者的强调）

7.2 先例之二：Horsfall v. Thomas (1862) 158 ER 813 先例

另在 Horsfall v. Thomas 先例中，卖方将手枪的洞用东西塞住，作为遮掩。买方在没有检查的情况下（如果检查应可以发觉问题）使用，开枪时发生爆炸，并受了伤。法院判是卖方在出售货物时明知有潜在问题，如果该问题是买方在收货时小心检查可以发现的，但买方疏忽没有检查，卖方没有披露责任也不是欺诈性误述。但如果该问题是买方根本无法合理检查出来，卖方明知有潜在问题但不讲，就是构成欺诈性误述，因为对货物情况的陈述/表述只讲一半。Bramwell 大法官说："wherever a manufacturer makes for a purchaser a chattel, and there is a patent defect in it which either impairs its value or may render it worthless, although the purchaser has neglected to inspect it, if the manufacturer conceals the defect he is guilty of fraud. We are of opinion that no such proposition can be supported; and that it would be mischievous if it were so. **To constitute fraud, there must be an assertion of something false within the knowledge of the party asserting it, or the suppression of that which is true and which it was his duty to communicate**. Here there was no assertion of an untruth, and the only question is whether there was a suppression of anything which the plaintiffs were bound to make known to the defendant. Now, the manufacturer of an article is not always bound to point out its defects to the purchaser. **If, indeed, there be a defect known to the manufacturer, and which cannot be discovered on inspection, he is bound to point it out; but if there be a defect which is patent, and of which the purchaser is as capable of judging as the manufacturer, he is not bound to call the attention of the purchaser to it**. It would be mischievous if he were, for in such case he would be bound to point out everything which might by any possibility be considered a defect; ..."（加黑部分是笔者的强调）

7.3 先例之三：Gordon v. Selico (1986) 2 WLUK 192 先例

较近期的 Gordon v. Selico 上诉庭先例中，涉及房屋出租，房东刻意隐藏房屋的干腐问题。这在一审[(1985) 1 WLUK 774]与上诉庭被认定是欺诈性误述。一审的

---

[33] 这在杨大明律师《国际货物买卖》一书第四章之 1 段有介绍。

Goulding 大法官强调是否构成欺诈性误述要根据每个不同的案情而定，不能把每一个令标的物更容易出售或出租的行为，例如重新粉刷墙壁、更换装饰物等，都说成是欺诈性，即使有些吹毛求疵的人士会觉得这是不诚实的。有关判决可节录如下："The law must be careful not to run ahead of popular morality by stigmatising as fraudulent every trivial act designed to make buildings or goods more readily saleable, even if a highly scrupulous person might consider it dishonest. But it is to my mind **quite a different matter for an intending vendor to hide so sinister and menacing a defect as active dry rot**. The case is fairly comparable, in my view, with the concealment of cracks indicating the settlement of foundations, considered in Ridge v. Crawley, 172, Estates Gazette, 637 and, in the Court of Appeal… There the plaintiff relied on a combination of words and conduct, but **I believe it to be the law that conduct alone can constitute a fraudulent misrepresentation**. … In my judgment the concealment of dry rot … was a knowingly false representation that Flat C did not suffer from dry rot, which was intended to deceive purchasers, and did deceive the plaintiffs to their detriment. I am satisfied that the plaintiffs would not have entered into a contract or accepted the lease had they known there was dry rot inside Flat C. … I accordingly hold that the Lessor is liable to the plaintiffs in damages for deceit."（加黑部分是笔者的强调）

7.4 以行动作出可诉的默示陈述

行动表示的陈述也与"默示陈述"（implied representation）分不开，虽然往往也没有区分的必要。

例如，"表见授权"（ostensible authority）[34]的基础就是有关人士有授权代表委托人订立合约的默示陈述，被陈述方依赖了该陈述，并且委托人的行动令其被禁止否认该陈述的正确性，所以有关的合约有商业效力（to give business efficacy）。正如 Diplock 勋爵在 R. v. Charles (1977) AC 177 贵族院先例说："What creates ostensible authority in a person who purports to enter into a contract as agent for a principal is a representation made to the other party that he has the actual authority of the principal for whom he claims to be acting to enter into the contract on that person's behalf. If (1) the other party has believed the representation and on the faith of that belief has acted upon it and (2) the person represented to be his principal has so conducted himself towards that other party as to be estopped from denying the truth of the representation, then, and only then, is he bound by the contract purportedly made on his behalf. The whole foundation of liability under the doctrine of ostensible authority is a representation, believed by the person to whom it is made, that the person claiming to contract as agent for a principal has the actual authority of the principal to enter into the contract on his behalf."

---

〔34〕 见笔者《合约的履行、弃权与禁反言》一书第五章之 12.2 段。

行动表达的陈述如果是做出不正确事实的诱导,那就是误述了。例如银行的信用卡(credit card)就默示向有关的商店或餐馆等表示他们可以向持卡人订立合约去提供商品或饮食,并可稍后向发卡银行要求支付有关对价。这样,持卡人向商店或餐馆交出信用卡,是以行动表示了有发卡银行的授权。对有关商店或餐馆而言,持卡人的行动也就默示了他/她有发卡银行的表见授权。这可节录 R. v. Lambie(1982) AC 449 贵族院先例中,Roskill 勋爵的观点:"it is in my view clear that the representation arising from the presentation of a credit card has nothing to do with the respondent's(被告) credit standing at the bank but is a representation of actual authority to make the contract with, in this case, Mothercare(有关的商店) on the bank's(发卡银行) behalf that the bank will honour the voucher upon presentation. Upon that view, the existence and terms of the agreement between the bank and Mothercare are irrelevant, as is the fact that Mothercare, because of that agreement, would look to the bank for payment. That being **the representation to be implied from the respondent's actions** and use of the credit card, the only remaining question is whether Miss Rounding(商店的经理) was induced by that representation to complete the transaction and allow the respondent to take away the goods."(加黑部分是笔者的强调)

针对上述的关系,在千变万化的案情下,只去分析以下几种可能的情况。在正常情况下,商店或餐馆在向持卡人提供商品或饮食后,有权向发卡银行要求支付有关对价。银行在"禁反言"的大原则下,不论是"陈述性禁反言"[35]或"承诺性禁反言",[36]不得拒绝支付签信用卡欠下的钱。如果持卡人超额或逾期还款,银行只能自己采取法律行动,与商店或餐馆无关。但如果持卡人是骗子,例如信用卡是偷来,而有关的商店也在发卡银行给了该信用卡无效的通知后,仍是忽略了把商品(这可以是昂贵的商品,如珠宝名表)交出给骗子,商店如果反应快就可以持卡人以行动或默示欺诈性误述为由撤销合约,并在商品的产权(title)还没有转交给其他无辜买方前通过法律行动取回该商品;但如果商店知道持卡人是欺诈,仍把商品交出给骗子,认为反正有发卡银行的承诺会支付,这就会涉及商店本身也参与欺诈/欺骗,即触犯刑法。

以行为表示的误述也会发生在其他各种情况,这也经常和意图联系在一起,毕竟很多意图是通过行动来表示。例如在本章之 5.5 段已经介绍过的 Director of Public Prosecutions v. Ray(1974) AC 370 贵族院先例中走进餐馆点餐、享用食物与服务的行动就默示陈述了该顾客是有钱与有意图在饱腹后作出支付。Ex p. Whittaker(1875) LR 10 Ch. App. 4461 先例中买方取走货物的行为默示他准备支付货款。Eastgate, Re (1905) 1 KB 465 先例中双方为支付专门订立合约的行动默示了付款人是真诚的意

---

〔35〕 见笔者《合约的履行、弃权与禁反言》一书第五章。

〔36〕 见笔者《合约的履行、弃权与禁反言》一书第四章。

图与相信他能够支付。Lewin v. Barratt Homes Ltd(2000)1 EGLR 77 先例中在展厅中展示设计图的行动默示能够建造设计图中的房屋。Salmon Harvester Properties Ltd v. Metropolitan Police Authority(2004)EWHC 1159(QB)先例中被告去与原告订立合约是用行动默示他有授权订立合约。Advanced Industrial Technology Corp v. Bond Street Jewellers Ltd(2006)EWCA Civ 923 先例中被告去典当的行动默示他对典当物有产权,与出售货物的卖方是默示他拥有货物的产权一样。

通过行动作出的默示陈述也不容易成立,因为每一个行动都可以有多个不同解释,要具体分析每一个不同案件中的行动与行动发生的背景。例如在 Director of Public Prosecutions v. Ray 先例中,假设有证据显示 Ray 在进入餐馆与点餐时,他的一位同伴同学知道他没有钱也愿意借钱给他支付餐费,Ray 也不反对;但饭菜上桌后,Ray 的同学突然有急事匆匆走了,也没有留下钱。如果是这样的案情看来,Ray 点餐的行动所做出的愿意付钱的默示陈述并不构成误述,Ray 在《Theft Act 1968》下欺骗的刑事罪名就成立不了;此时即使最后 Ray 在结账时支付不了钱,也只能停留在民事的债务问题上。又或是在 Ex p. Whittaker 先例中,卖方最后无法成功证明买方在取走货物的那一刻就有意图不作出支付,虽然买方最后破产,但不代表他不能通过借钱等其他办法来作出支付或者买方可以在最后关头找到钱来成功避免破产,从而继续支付。

反正行动被认定为默示误述在今天常会制造大量文件证据的国际商业社会不大会发生,所以本文略过不谈。

8. 持续性的陈述

谈判会维持一段时间,这就涉及事实改变的可能,即在起初陈述时是正确无误或陈述方是有合理理据(reasonable ground)支持有关对事实的陈述,但之后在合约尚未确立时有了改变。这样,陈述方有责任马上或尽快更正,否则会构成可诉误述。

要是在订约后才发觉这事实改变呢?答案是不更正并不构成误述,毕竟是更正了也没有用,因为已有合约产生,原来的陈述也不涉及误述了。如果有关的陈述是被加入合约条文,如对标的的描述或作为明示保证(express warranty),在合约产生后有了改变可能构成违约(看合约条文与改变的原因等),无辜方可以索赔损失。但这救济与误述不一样,因为误述会让无辜方有权撤销(rescind)合约。它甚至不涉及损失赔偿的救济,例如无辜方没有损失或证明不了误述导致的损失或是涉及的重大误述是无辜作出。无辜方撤销合约的主要原因是市场下跌或有了重大逆转等,在此情形下借机脱身把市场风险甩给可能是无辜的误述方。

在《Chitty on Contracts》(2021 年,第 34 版)一书之 9 – 025 段是说:"**Representation ceases to be true.** A statement may be made which is true at the time but which subsequently ceases to be true to the knowledge of the representor before the contract is entered into. In such circumstances a failure to inform the representee of the change in circumstances will itself amount to a misrepresentation, unless in the context it is quite clear to the reasonable recipient of the information that the party who gives it accepts no responsibility for its accuracy or for reviewing it."

接下来 9 - 026 段说:"**Continuity of representations.** Representations are treated for many purposes as continuing in their effect until the contract between the parties is actually concluded. This is one reason why a statement which is true when made, but which ceases to be true to the knowledge of the representor before the contract is concluded, is treated as a misrepresentation unless the representor informs the representee of the change in circumstances. This principle may have other effects as well. First, as we have just seen, **if a representation is made innocently but falsely**, and facts later come to the knowledge of the representor which show that the statement was false, **a failure to inform the representee of the truth may convert what was originally an innocent misrepresentation into a fraudulent one**. Again, if a man truthfully states that he intends to do something but changes his mind at a later stage he may come under a duty to disclose that change. ..."(加黑部分是笔者的强调)

8.1 有关先例

8.1.1 先例之一:With v. O'Flanagan(1936)Ch 575 上诉庭先例

首先可介绍这方面的权威先例,在 With v. O'Flanagan 上诉庭先例中,案情涉及 O'Flanagan 先生想出售他的诊所,谈判从一月持续到五月。在一月,O'Flanagan 先生告诉原告 With 先生该诊所每年收入有近 2000 英镑,当时是正确或大致上正确的。但之后几个月,基于 O'Flanagan 先生生病等原因,收入剧减,到签约时(五月份)该诊所平均每周只能收入 5 英镑,也就是平均每年收入 260 英镑。但这变化没有向原告更正,法院判 O'Flanagan 先生误述。

除了陈述的持续性要求在陈述作出之后有了变化要及时更正,此先例对陈述不需要完全正确,只需要大致上正确也有权威说法。这就表示,如果在谈判过程中陈述只是有了轻微改动,仍是大致上正确,可以不用更正。毕竟,在较漫长的谈判,早期的陈述有了改动并不奇怪,例如在一个公司收购交易,不需要公司的营业额每天有了改变都要不断更正早期的陈述。只有较大的变化并明知道会合理影响对方与有关的交易才需要更正。Wright 勋爵说:"A representation is not like a warranty; it is not necessary it should be strictly construed or strictly complied with; it is enough if it is substantially true; it is enough if it is substantially complied with. If it is not substantially complied with then the court finds itself in the range of misrepresentation and must give effect to that position if it is satisfied that the plaintiffs acted upon the representation in concluding a bargain..."

例如在土地/房屋买卖中，如果卖方陈述的实用面积与真正实用面积只相差 2.3%，判不构成误述：见 Chuan Bee Realty Pte Ltd v. Teo Chee Yeow Aloysius (1996) 2 SLR(R) 134 新加坡先例。

8.1.2 先例之二：FoodCo UK LLP v. Henry Boot Developments Ltd (2010) EWHC 358 (Ch) 先例

持续性陈述的说法在较近期的 FoodCo UK LLP v. Henry Boot Developments Ltd 先例中，Lewison 大法官也有提及，可节录如下：

"It is well settled that **a representation made in the course of negotiations may be treated as a continuing representation**. The authoritative source of the principle in modern times is With v O'Flanagan [1936] Ch. 575. ... Lord Wright MR expressed his conclusion thus: 'I think that the change in circumstances ought to have been communicated to the plaintiffs before they were allowed to close the transaction.'

This, he said is based upon the duty to communicate the change of circumstances. However, as seen from the way in which he expressed his ultimate conclusion, the duty is**a duty to communicate before the transaction is closed.**

Romer LJ said: 'If A with a view to inducing B to enter into a contract makes a representation as to a material fact, then if at a later date and before the contract is actually entered into, owing to a change of circumstances, the representation then made would to the knowledge of A be untrue and B subsequently enters into the contract in ignorance of that change of circumstances and relying upon that representation, A cannot hold B to the bargain.'"（加黑部分是笔者的强调）

8.1.3 先例之三：Spice Girls Ltd v. Aprilia World Service BV (2002) EWCA Civ 15 上诉庭先例

另在 Spice Girls Ltd v. Aprilia World Service BV 上诉庭先例中，涉及了在 1994 年成立的英国"辣妹组合"（Spice Girls）。原告（一家意大利制造摩托车的公司）谈判有关赞助"辣妹组合"去欧洲与美国巡回演出的事宜。谈判长达两个月，1998 年 5 月 6 日才签署合约。合约说是"辣妹组合"有 5 位成员，这包括了本案例涉及的洁芮小姐（Geri Halliwell）。其他较出名的成员是 Victoria Beckham，她是英国足球明星贝克汉姆先生（David Beckham）的夫人。但在开始谈判后不久，洁芮小姐告诉了其他成员她希望在 1998 年 9 月底离开。在 1998 年 4 月 25 日与组合经纪人开会并确认离开。但被告一直没有把这件事告诉原告，而原告也不知情地签署了赞助合约。

一审与上诉庭判被告代表"辣妹组合"的公司误述，即使被告在洁芮小姐在 3 月告知希望离开组合时是不当真（法院不接受），但到了 4 月 25 日的会议后，就肯定明确了早前向原告说组合有 5 位成员的陈述不再正确，不尽快更正就构成可诉误述。根据《Misrepresentation Act 1967》之 S.2(1)，被告要赔偿原告的损失。一审的 Arden 大法官的判决可节录如下："Though the representation had to be one of fact, representations as to the future or of opinion frequently contained implied representations with regard to the present or the knowledge of the representation. Once made, a representation was likely to have a continuing effect. If made for the purpose of an intended transaction, it would continue until the transaction was completed or abandoned or the representation ceased to be operative on the mind of the representee. If at a time when it was continuing the representor discovered that the representation was false when made or had since become false, he should correct it. The meaning and effect of a statement or conduct had to be ascertained in the light of the circumstances pertaining at that time, which could include the course of the negotiations and any earlier representations."

8.2 谈判中意图改变是否需要更正

"事实改变"要及时更正已经是明确,但谈判期间的"意图改变"是否要更正？这方面很早已经有明确先例针对,大原则应该是没有不同,例如 Spice Girls Ltd v. Aprilia World Service BV(2002)EWCA Civ 15 上诉庭先例已经有涉及。但毕竟事实改变是赖不掉的,而意图是变得多与变得快,因为各种环境与情况都在不断发展与变化,很难证明意图在什么时候改变,也很难掌握什么时候应该披露。而谈判的对方可能不知道有这种意图的改变,所以要根据个别案情(如有关信息与事实是否一面倒只有陈述方知道)客观看是否公平与不披露会否构成误导,令不更正"意图改变"构成可诉误述。

早在 Traill v. Baring(1864)4 DJ & S 318 先例中,案情涉及一线保险人(insurer)在分保时告诉了分保人(reinsurer)他自己将会承保余下部分的风险,但在订约前,他改变主意把余下的风险也分保给了其他分保人,但没有把这改变的意图与做法告诉分保人,法院判是误述。原因是如果一线保险人自己承保余下的大部分风险,会让分保人对分保更有信心,因为显示了一线保险人觉得风险可控。而如果一线保险人把风险全部或大部分分保给了别人,则对分保人来说有很大不同。Turner 大法官认为如果一方对自己的意图做出陈述诱导谈判对方,而谈判对方相应进行了某行为,然后他知道对意图的陈述已有所变化,并且该变化会影响被陈述方(谈判对方)的行为,则陈述方有责任将变化通知被陈述方:

"The question really is, whether, representations having been made that a liability would be retained on the part of the Defendants, and **that intention having been changed before the liability attached upon the Plaintiffs** ... there ought not to have been a communication of that change of intention to the Plaintiffs before they undertook the liability for the £ 1000(分保金额)in question.

I take it to be quite clear, that if a person makes a representation by which he induces another to take a particular course, and the circumstances are afterwards altered to the knowledge of the party making the representation, but not to the knowledge of the party to whom the representation is made, and are so altered that the alteration of the circumstances may affect the course of conduct which may be pursued by the party to whom the representation is made it is the imperative duty of the party who has made the representation to communicate to the party to whom the representation has been made the alteration of those circumstances; and that this Court will not hold the party to whom the representation has been made bound unless such a communication has been made."(加黑部分是笔者的强调)

《Chitty on Contracts》(2021 年,第 34 版)一书之 9 - 183 段也提到有不同判例 Wales v. Wadham(1977)1 WLR 199 先例。案情涉及 Wales 夫妻离婚并需要分割财产,双方也往往会达成和解协议。Wales 先生从出售住所的钱中分给了他前妻 13,000 英镑。Wales 先生本来可以每一个月定期支付给前妻一笔赡养费,直至他的前妻再婚。但因为前妻曾许诺 Wales 先生不打算再婚,所以 Wales 先生决定一次过付一笔钱了结。在付款协议签订前,前妻决定再婚,嫁给 Wadham 先生。看来,Wales 先生上当,但法官接纳他前妻的说法是她不把这意图改变说出来,是因为不想 Wadham 先生卷进这场悲剧。看来,对为何不去更正"意图改变"是否有一个被审理法官接受的合理解释会是关键,又或是涉及家庭的案件会与商业的和解协议有不同对待。正如《Chitty on Contracts》一书也继续提到此先例的判法已被推翻:"... in Wales v. Wadham it was held that a wife was under no duty to disclose to her husband, ... However, Wales v. Wadham was overruled so far as it related to disclosure in proceedings for financial relief by the House of Lords in Livesey v. Jenkins(1985) AC 424. ... These decisions leave it uncertain whether the common law today recognises family settlements as contracts uberrimae fidei."

8.3　立法与其他相关法律的相同理念

以上的说法或做法与其他方面的法律也相互配合。例如在 1906 年的《海上保险法》,由于其是通过立法确定的"绝对善意"(utmost good - faith),所以除了与其他合约类别一样有针对误述的救济外,也多了受保人(assured)自动披露(disclosure)[37]对保险人(insurer)有实质重要性的信息与事实的要求。这要求也是持续性的,在 section 18 说:"..., the assured must disclose to the insurer, **before the contract is concluded**, every material circumstances which is known to the assured, ... If the assured fails to make such disclosure, the insurer may avoid the contract."(加黑部分是笔者的强调)

这在《Misrepresentation Act 1967》之 Section 2(1)最后一句也有同样说明:"... that person shall be so liable notwithstanding that the misrepresentation was not made fraudulently, unless he proves that he had reasonable ground to believe **and did believe up to the time the contract was made that the facts represented were true**."(加黑部分是笔者的强调)

---

〔37〕 见本书第五章之 1 段,有关普通法下没有自动披露的责任。

多举另一方面的法律,就是仲裁员对利益冲突的自动披露责任。这除了在一开始被委任时需要披露,仲裁员也有持续性责任要把后来发生的变化尽早向双方当事人与仲裁庭其他成员披露。这里并不涉及误述的问题,只是仲裁员要保证持续的独立与公正。这在 Halliburton v. Chubb(2020)UKSC 48 最高院先例中,Hodge 勋爵说:“When,on being asked to accept an appointment,an arbitrator knows of a matter which ought to be disclosed to the parties to the reference,prompt disclosure to those parties of that matter provides the safeguard as the quality of impartiality is shown to have been there from the beginning. But **the obligation of impartiality continues throughout the reference** and the emergence during the currency of the reference of matters which ought to be disclosed means that an arbitrator's prompt disclosure of those matters can enable him or her to maintain what Lord Hope calls the 'badge of impartiality'."(加黑部分是笔者的强调)

8.4 不更正早前陈述的危险:容易构成欺诈/欺骗

不更正早前陈述的危险是被视为欺诈性误述的机会大增,因为不更正已经变得是不正确的事实(或意见)陈述总难免是知道(knowingly)现在正确的事实与故意(deliberately)这么做,如想蒙混过关或害怕坏事。这种判决可见 Fitzroy Robinson Ltd v. Mentmore Towers Ltd(2009)EWHC 1552(TCC);FoodCo UK LLP v. Henry Boot Developments Ltd(2010)EWHC 358(Ch);Erlson Precision Holdings Ltd v. Hampson Industries Plc(2011)EWHC 1137(Comm)等先例。

只简单介绍 Erlson Precision Holdings Ltd v. Hampson Industries Plc 先例,该案案情涉及一个股权买卖合约(Share Purchase Agreement)。被告是一家涉及高科技的英国上市公司,它希望把集团下的一家名为 HPA 的附属公司出售,HPA 的业务是制造飞机的涡轮增压器的部件。为此,被告准备了一份详尽的资料备忘录(Information Memorandum),内容包括潜在买家会需要的信息与资料,如制造的产品,设备/设施,业务情况,主要客户名单,财务状况如营业额(revenue)、税息折旧及摊销前利润(EBITDA),营业利润(trading profit)等。这吸引了原告公司并最终与被告完成交易。在原告与被告谈判收购 HPA 期间,HPA 的一位主要客户 Cummins Turbo Technologies 告知其将停止采购。HPA 与 Cummins 这两家公司的主管也有就停止采购事宜通过电话,并在后来作为事实证人出庭接受盘问。HPA 的主管是说 Cummins 说要停止采购是一种通过商业压力去谈判的技巧,希望借此压低采购的售价,所以没有必要向原告披露。Cummins 是说 HPA 的主管要求 Cummins 把此事件保密,让他先向董事会交待与考虑对策,否则这信息将令 HPA 无法出售。法院最后采信 Cummins 的口头证据,可能是因为 Cummins 的立场中立,不涉及原告与被告之间的重大经济利益。而且这个改变是重要的,会导致备忘录中的部分陈述不正确。Field 大法官判被告误述(不更正主要客户名单)并诱导股权买卖合约的产生,而且这是欺诈性误述,所以原告可撤销合约与索赔损失,说:

"In my judgment, if an individual in the position of Mr. Ward; the CEO of a listed company(被告公司), knows that a forecast has been falsified by events to which he is privy but remains silent intending that the forecast should be relied on by persons to whom the forecast is directly communicated, dishonesty on the part of that individual will have been proved without it being necessary distinctly and separately to show a conscious awareness of a duty to correct the statement."

9. 只讲一半造成整体事实真相虚假或扭曲构成误述

在《Chitty on Contracts》(2021 年,34 版)一书之 9 - 024 段是说:"**Partial non-disclosure.** Although total non-disclosure does not amount to a misrepresentation, a partial non-disclosure may do so. This may happen in a number of different ways. Thus a statement may be a misrepresentation even though it is literally true if it implies certain additional facts which are themselves false. A striking instance of this possibility is Goldsmith v. Rodger(1962)2 Lloyd's Rep 249 in which the defendant who was negotiating for the purchase of the plaintiff's yacht informed the plaintiff, after paying a visit to the yacht, that she had rot in her keel. The Court of Appeal held that this statement implied that the defendant had actually examined the keel, and as he had not done so, this was itself a misrepresentation, whether or not the yacht did have rot in her keel. Again, a statement may amount to a misrepresentation if facts are omitted which render that which has actually been stated false or misleading in the contract in which it is made. So, for example, where a shop assistant told a customer that a receipt for the cleaning of a dress which she was required to sign excluded liability for damage to beads and sequins, and in fact the receipt excluded all liability, this was held to be a misrepresentation."[38]

本书第五章会详细介绍普通法下是没有自动披露的责任的,但如果不全部披露令整体的事实扭曲与引起对方合理误解,则构成可诉误述,而且会是欺诈性误述。例如告诉对方"我目前的身体状况很好,刚做了全身检查",但漏了一句是"但刚发现肝癌"。笔者以下会介绍几个先例中,希望能帮助读者更好地理解这种情况。

9.1 先例之一:Oakes v. Turquand(1867) LR 2 HL 325 贵族院先例

在 Oakes v. Turquand 贵族院先例中,案情涉及股民 Oakes 先生根据一家股份有限公司的招股章程(prospects)认购股票。公司不久后清盘,Oakes 先生发现有部分事实真相(主要是公司的财务信息)没有在招股章程中向公众披露,只是讲一半不讲一

[38] 见 Curtis v. Chemical Cleaning and Dyeing Co Ltd(1951)1 KB 805 先例。

半,造成整体的信息严重误导并构成欺诈性误述。Oakes 先生要求撤销股份认购合约,并申请衡平法法院把他从股东登记名册(Register)中除名或对公司出资人名单作出变更(rectification),这主要是为了取回其认购股份的出资。衡平法法院判该股份有限公司的股东隐藏信息的行为构成欺诈,Malins 大法官说:"Men who undertake duties so important as these should be made aware that truth should not so be trifled with, but that in commercial, as well as other transactions, it is a duty not to conceal facts from those whose vital interests are involved in their knowledge."

贵族院在这一点上也同意衡平法法院的判决。其中 Cranworth 勋爵说:"I must believe that the truth was intentionally concealed, and hopes held out which those who framed the prospectus must have known would deceive those who trusted to it. There were both suggestio falsi and suppressio veri."

9.2 先例之二:Barwick v. English Joint Stock Bank(1867) LR 2 Ex. 259 上诉庭先例

在 Barwick v. English Joint Stock Bank 先例中,案情涉及原告一直在供应货物(燕麦)给名为 J. Davies & Son 的顾客,让它履行一份向政府按月供应饲料(forage)的合约,并一直有被告银行的担保。在一次的担保谈判,被告银行的一位经理向原告承诺会保证 J. Davies & Son 向政府收取的钱除了归还银行外优先支付原告,以期原告同意被告赊账获得价值 1227 英镑的一批燕麦。确认担保的信函内容是:"Dear Sir,— Referring to our conversation of this morning, I beg to repeat that if you sell to, or purchase for, J. Davis and Son not exceeding 1000 quarters of oats for the use of their contract, I will honour the cheque of Messrs. J. Davis and Son in your favour in payment of the same, on receipt of the money from the commissariat(政府当局) in payment of forage supplied for the present month, **in priority to any other payment, except to this bank**; and provided, as I explained to you, that they, J. Davis and Son, are able to continue their contract, and are not made bankrupts. (Signed) Don. M. Dewar, Manager."(加黑部分是笔者的强调)

但银行经理没有告诉原告 J. Davies & Son 在当时已经欠下银行 12,000 英镑。这导致 J. Davies & Son 将政府支付的 2676 英镑归还给被告银行后,根本没有钱去支付赊账的货款给原告。

这在一审与上诉庭都判被告银行不去披露 J Davies & Son 欠下 12,000 英镑的事实,讲一半不讲另一半是欺诈性误述,而被告银行也要为它的经理承担替代责任/转承责任(vicarious liability)。

9.3 先例之三:Jewson & Sons Ltd v. Arcos Ltd(1933)47 Lloyd's Rep 93 上诉庭先例

在本书旧版《国际商务游戏规则:英国合约法》有介绍 Jewson & Sons Ltd v. Arcos Ltd 上诉庭先例。案件发生在 1930 年,当时英国的俄罗斯木材市场很萧条。英国进口商 Jewson 发现俄罗斯的供应商 Arcos 给他的货价高于他的竞争对手 Hillas,故而不再进货。从 5 月 14 日开始,Arcos 就以进口木材问题与 Jewson 展开谈判。Arcos 告诉了 Jewson 关于稳定市场的计划,该计划承诺至 1931 年 1 月之前,所有的木材买卖都基于一个标准的合约与价格。该计划从 5 月 28 日开始实施,Jewson 为此而与 Arcos 签订了进口木材合约。但 Jewson 不知道,Arcos 也没有讲的是 Arcos 与其竞争对手 Hillas 在 7 天前(5 月 21 日)签订了合约,货价低于标准价格。这样,Arcos 的进口木材面临 Hillas 的削价竞争,带来亏损。为此,Jewson 在发觉后向 Arcos 提起诉讼,以欺诈性误述的诉因索赔损失。这带来的争议是,在"买方自己要小心"的原则下,卖方是否要披露并自动提供自己认为是商业机密的信息?

上诉庭支持一审判决,认定 Arcos 要承担欺诈性误述的责任,因为没有披露 5 月 21 日与 Hillas 签订的合约在当时情况下去整体看是"讲一半不讲一半",不披露有诱导 Jewson 决定签订进口木材合约的迹象,这构成可诉误述。货物买卖合约不像保险合约(后者是绝对善意的合约)那样,一般没有自动披露的责任。虽然披露与误述是两回事,但针对事实的表述或陈述,如果只有一半是真的,而另一半被故意隐藏而令整个真相没有表达出来,这仍是欺诈性误述。

上诉庭的 Greer 大法官引用了当时著名的 Anson 的《Law of Contract》一书说:"… I think, accurately summed up in Anson on Contracts, … as follows: There must be an active attempt to deceive either by a statement which is false, or by **a statement not untrue in itself, but accompanied with such a suppression of facts as to convey a misleading impression**. Concealment of this kind is sometimes called 'active', 'aggressive', or 'industrious'; but perhaps the word itself, as opposed to non-disclosure, suggests the active element of deceit which **constitutes fraudulent misrepresentation**. The distinction between misrepresentation by non-disclosure, which can only affect contracts uberrimae fidei, and misrepresentation which gives rise to an action of deceit, is clearly pointed out by Lord Cairns in the case of Peek v. Gurney: 'Mere non-disclosure of material facts, however morally censurable, … ' would, in my opinion, form no ground for an action in the nature of an action for misrepresentation. 'There must, in my opinion, be some **active misstatement of fact, or**, at all events, such **a partial and fragmentary statement of fact, as that the withholding of that which is not stated makes that which is stated absolutely false**."(加黑部分是笔者的强调)

9.4 先例之四:Goldsmith v. Rodger (1962) 2 Lloyd's Rep 249 先例

在 Goldsmith v. Rodger 先例中,案情涉及双方在电话中谈判有关一艘名为"Atalanta"的渔船的买卖。卖方要价 400 英镑,但买方还价到 100 英镑,并在检查了船舶后说发觉该渔船船底腐烂生虫。但没有讲另一半的事实,就是实际上买方只是道听途说得知。对自己渔船情况不了解的卖方也就答应了以 100 英镑成交。但事后知悉买方在检查船舶时从来没看过船底,而不久前另一位买方看过船底并无此事。所以卖方拒以100英镑交船,买方起诉。但上诉庭判是买方这说法可解释为应是默示他确有检查过船底,不只是道听途说,所以即使是非欺诈性,可诉误述也成立,卖方可拒绝交船,撤销合约。

9.5 先例之五:Davis & Co. v. Afa – Minerva(1974)2 Lloyd's Rep 27 先例

Davis & Co. v. Afa – Minerva 先例已经适用《Misrepresentation Act 1967》立法。原告是一位零售商,他购买了被告的防盗设施,并由被告安装。但在一个周末,商店被盗,被大肆破坏之余,也被盗走一批存货。但期间防盗设施根本没有反应,也没有响。原告零售商于是提出索赔,指控被告曾有误述,声称该系统如果电线被弄断,它的警铃仍会响不停,没有办法弄停,而只要电池足够,可响足一天。但实际上该系统有一弱点,如果破坏了控制板再切断电线,警铃并不会响,这次盗窃也确是如此情况。这样,对警铃可响足一天无法去弄停的陈述是虚假或不正确是没有疑问的。在交叉盘问,被告承认这一方面是该防盗设施唯一的致命弱点(Achilles heel)但不大可能发生。Fay大法官也最后认定被告确曾作出相似的陈述,而即使陈述中只是部分正确,整体仍是不正确,仍属误述。

但在该先例中,原告没指控这误述是欺诈性,只当作是无辜的误述。反正在《Misrepresentation Act 1967》生效后,根据 Section 2(1)非欺诈性误述(non-fraudulent misrepresentation)也可以获得赔偿,而原告也没有要求撤销合约,因为在这种案情下是根本没有什么好去撤销了。

至于损失方面,法院认为商店被破坏与警铃不响(误述)无关,即使响也难免商店被破门而入的各种破坏。至于存货被盗的损失,法院判商店是因为对防盗设施有信心才在店内多放了存货,所以与误述有关联,可以索赔损失。

9.6 "只讲一半"视为误述而不是不披露的原因

只讲一半而不讲另一半和普通法下不要求自动披露(除非双方是有特殊关系,如诚信责任或善意责任)紧密联系但也有不同。前者针对的是陈述方在合约谈判时已经是明确做出了一定的事实陈述,但另有一些事实与已经陈述的事实有关,并会影响被陈述方对已经陈述事实的全面理解,但陈述方在刻意或无心遗漏下没有去同时做出披露,该不披露部分就会令被陈述方无法全面理解事实而产生误导/诱导被陈述方的效果,这就可构成可诉误述。而完全不披露因为从来没有提过任何相关的事实,则不会有该误导/诱导被陈述方的效果,也就没有法律责任与后果。在普通法下,到底是着重"讲一半"将其视为误述,或是着重"不讲一半"将其视为不披露,是没有区别的。但是在《Misrepresentation Act 1967》生效后,因为立法只针对误述但不针对不自动披露,非欺诈性误述为了索赔金钱损失,就应视为误述而不是不披露。

可先节录在 Banque Keyser Ullmann SA v. Skandia(UK)Insurance Co Ltd(1990)1 QB 665 上诉庭先例中,Slade大法官的观点:"…If section 2(1)is to apply at all, a misrepresentation has to have been 'made' to the complainant by the other party. The expression 'misrepresentation… made'(which is repeated in several later sections of the

Act of 1967) would, in our judgment, on the ordinary meaning of words be inapt to refer to a misrepresentation which had not been made in fact but was (at most) merely deemed by the common law to have been made. If it had been the intention of the legislature that a mere failure to discharge the duty of disclosure in the case of a contract uberrimae fidei would fall to be treated as the 'making' of a representation within the meaning of the Act of 1967, we are of the opinion that the legislature would have said so."

《Misrepresentation, Mistake and Non-Disclosure》(2022 年,第 6 版)一书之 4 - 68 段也说由于 1967 年立法只针对误述而不针对披露,所以把"讲一半、不讲一半"视为误述而不是将不讲的一半视为不披露,才可适用立法对非欺诈性误述提供比普通法(只针对欺诈性误述)与衡平法(只允许非欺诈性误述有撤销合约的救济)更进一步的救济(赔偿金钱损失的救济):"**Not applicable to cases of non-disclosure.** Since the subsection applies only where a 'misrepresentation has been made to' the representee, it has been held that it covers only cases of active misrepresentation, and not cases of non-disclosure. **Cases of 'half - truth' or where silence communicates a falsehood would, however, be included since they are regarded as 'misrepresentations' for the purpose of other remedies at common law and in equity.**"(加黑部分是笔者的强调)

在《Chitty on Contracts》(2021 年,34 版)一书之 9 - 24 段也有同样的说法:"... It will be observed that these cases of partial non-disclosure can either be explained as cases of actual misrepresentation, or as cases in which there is a duty to disclose certain facts by reason of the facts actually stated. Until the passing of the Misrepresentation Act 1967, it was immaterial which explanation was adopted since the effect of an actual misrepresentation and the breach of a duty to disclose (where such a duty exists) were generally the same. But since the passing of this Act this is no longer the case as the Act applies to misrepresentations, but not to the breach of duties of disclosure. It is thought that cases of partial non-disclosure will normally be treated as cases of actual misrepresentation falling within the Act, but it has been held that cases of complete non-disclosure will not."

10. 认定可诉陈述的困难

上述介绍的不同形式的陈述或表述如果虚假与不正确会否构成可诉误述,在早期相对简单与淳朴的社会,认定事实后作出判断并不困难。这在今天的大众社会,仍是同样的情况;但涉及国际商业社会,情况就复杂得多了,在本段与本章之 11 段会去介绍两种认定可诉陈述的困难情况。

10.1 事实陈述与合约保证的区别

可以构成误述的事实陈述(representation)(虽然对法律的陈述也可以,但主要是事实陈述）是对事实的表述（statement），诱导被陈述方依赖并订立合约。而合约保证（warranty）[39]属于合约中的条文，是一方合约方以合约条文的方式向对方作出承诺（promise、undertaking、assurance 或 obligation），即将来会做或会发生什么，以及不会做什么。会有部分内容涉及事实陈述（特别是对过去或现在的事实）但以合约保证的形式加进合约，即在订约前以陈述的形式，而在合约中同样的信息又被重复。理论上，如果该陈述是错误的，受害方可以误述诱导订立合约为由寻求救济（撤销合约以及复原，除非是欺诈性误述可以再索赔侵权的损失），也可以对方违反合约保证构成违约为由寻求救济（索赔合约的损失或严重情况下终止合约）。是否可行带来近期不少疑问，看来除了看表述的时间外，也要看背景（context）/环境（circumstances）去解释有争议的“保证”事项会否实是“陈述”；又或是，反过来去解释有争议的“陈述”，实是“保证”？接下来的段节会进一步分析。

对保证的违约与误述这是两个本质上完全不同的诉因（cause of actions），前者是合约诉因（contractual），后者是侵权/非合约诉因（tortious/non-contractual）。显然，它们带来的后果也不一样。而如果重叠，既能够证明是诱导合约产生的一个事实误述，又同时是明示的一个保证，就可以同步/竞合诉讼（concurrent action）进行。由于两者的不同，会给受害方原告带来很多重大好处，例如时效、撤销合约与终止合约的难易、损失计算等。[40]

正如在 Sycamore Bidco Ltd v. Breslin & Anor（2012）EWHC 3443（Ch）先例中，在一个股权买卖合约（share purchase agreement）[41]中，买方声称一个合约保证也是订约前的陈述或误述，以复原为由向卖方索赔，因为违约的损失计算只有 600 万英镑，但复原的计算高达 1600 万英镑。Mann 大法官说：“The point has a real significance in terms of the measure of damages（and also the date at which damages should or can be assessed），so it is necessary to deal with it. If the claimants are right about it，and can otherwise put their claim successfully in misrepresentation，then they may be entitled to recover damages which would not be available under a contractual claim. At their highest，the misrepresentation claim damages are equivalent to or exceed the consideration paid（approximately Pds. 16 million）. At its highest the warranty damages claim is about Pds. 6 million. Hence the point's importance.”

又或是在 Idemitsu Kosan Co Ltd v. Sumitomo Corp（2016）EWHC 1909（Comm）先例中，以违约索赔损失，但由于 18 个月的合约索赔时效已过而投诉无门，后以侵权

---

〔39〕 合约保证与保险的承诺性保证（promissory warranty）或合约中与条件条文（condition）相对应的保证条文（contractual warranty），虽然英文都是“warranty”，但是完全不同的概念。

〔40〕 见本书第一章之 2.4.4 段。

〔41〕 中国公司多年来经常涉及股权买卖合约与并购合约，其中误述是主要问题之一，即使有详尽的尽职调查也不能解决问题。

的可诉误述进行索赔,才有机会向被告"误述方"索赔上亿美元的庞大损失。

以违约与侵权索赔计算损失有这么大的区别,主要是因为违约的损失计算是将无辜方回复到合约被履行的地位,而侵权则是将受害方回复到侵权没有发生的地位,也就是没有订立合约。所以如果谈下来一个赚大钱的合约,是会以违约索赔更划算,但如果合约条件对自己不利,就以侵权索赔更划算。

事实陈述与合约保证本质上不同,其之间的关系在法律上是"楚河汉界",可先节录《Misrepresentation Mistake and Non-Disclosure》(2022 年,第 6 版)一书之 8 - 02 段:"'**Representations' and 'warranties' distinguished** There is a distinction in law between 'representation' and 'warranties'. A representation is a statement of fact (or law) which induces the representee to enter into the contract. A warranty is a provision in the contract: a promise made by one contracting party to the other as a term of the contract. The same information may be given both as a representation and as a warranty: it is given in the form of a representation if it is made before the contract was concluded, even if it might also then be repeated in the contract in the form of a warranty. If a statement is false — and is therefore a misrepresentation — remedies for misrepresentation are available by reason of the claimant's reliance on the false statement; and remedies for breach of contract are available by reason of the validity of the statement constituting a breach of a contractual undertaking given by the representor. Such claims must be kept separate, however, since many pre-contractual representations are not subsequently incorporated into the contract; and even if information is 'warranted' in the contract it might not also have been provided by way of pre-contractual representation."

上述对两者的区分带出不少问题,很多订约前在谈判中做出的陈述不会在之后被合并进合约,合约中保证条文的信息也不一定在谈判阶段以陈述的形式做出过。但仍有部分陈述的错误事实有重叠,会既是可诉误述,也是对合约保证的违约。在《Misrepresentation Act 1967》之 S. 1(a)的立法条文下,可诉误述被加进合约作为合约部分内容是不影响它仍是可诉误述的。

如果一方没有作出过对某一个特定事实的陈述,但在双方谈判保证条文时有针对该特定事实的保证,并将草稿相互交流去讨论措辞/用字。这样,如果保证条文中所针对的特定的过去或现在的事实错误,并且对受害方而言侵权的损失计算更为有利,他能否将对方发送该保证条文草稿的行为当作是做出了错误事实陈述? 毕竟此时合约还没订立。如果可以,岂非所有合约内的保证条文只要涉及过去或现在的事实也同时是谈判的事实陈述,因为保证条文不可能在双方没有谈判与同意后无端在一份合约出现。近期这可称为是"双重属性"有不少先例去探讨,并由于有不同案情所以有不同结论。

但主流的一审判决(没有进一步上诉)看来是倾向把合约内容中的陈述与保证当成是同一码事,如果虚假与不正确,受害方的则是合约而不是侵权。这主流一审判决的看法可以 Idemitsu Kosan Co Ltd v. Sumitomo Corp 先例为代表，Andrew Baker QC 大法官说："when a seller, by the terms of the contract under which he sells, 'warrants' something about the subject matter sold, he is making a contractual promise. Nothing less. But also I think (and all things being equal) nothing more. That is so just as much for a warranty as to some then present or past matter of fact as it is for a warranty as to the future. By contracting on terms by which he warrants something, the seller is not purporting to impart information; he is not making a statement to his buyer."

针对保证条文是否能"自动过档"成为合约陈述或误述的"双重属性"将在本章之10.3段详及。

但 Andrew Baker 大法官也说根据不同情况也会有不同区分："Language found in the communication of a negotiating position, or in draft wording for a contract, or in an entire draft contract, passing between the parties during the negotiation of a contract, might amount to or form the content of a pre-contractual representation capable of being actionable under the 1967 Act. ..."

这种在谈判后期在有关合约保证条文拟定时，该保证条文所针对的特定事情可以被视为同时做出了可诉误述情况的案例，也在本章之10.4段进行了介绍。

10.2　陈述与保证条文

近年来，越来越多不同类别的合约都加上了一条明示与详尽的"陈述与保证条文"(representation and warranty clause)，变为一条惯用条文(boiler - plate clause)。

原因之一是有不少合约今天已经加上"完整合约条文"(Entire Agreement clause)与"没有依赖条文"(Non-reliance clause)，[42] 被误述方不一定可以以订约前的误述提起诉讼，而且被误述方在很多情况下也不想撤销(rescind)合约。所以越来越多情况是在某些类别的合约中明示加上一条"保证条文"(Warranty Clause)或"陈述与保证条文"(Representation and Warranty Clause)[43] 把所有订约前实质重要的陈述，如过去与现在事实、对将来的预期与意见等，一并加进合约。例如在并购合约(Merger & Acquisition Agreement)或股权买卖合约中，就会包括公司过去3年的业务与盈利等、股份的所有权、来年的业务与估算盈利等。私人公司则包括方方面面的保证，因为其不像上市公司一样透明度高，保证条文会是内容详细与复杂得多。如果任何保证有错误或违反，则是严格责任的合约承诺，另一方可提出损失索赔。涉及收购卖方的整家公司，买方当然也要求卖方的母公司(parent company)或银行提供担保(guarantee)或补偿函(letter of indemnity)，或部分收购金额存入一个共同账号(escrow account)作为留置(retention)，以保证将来有钱赔偿。

---

〔42〕 见本书第一章之1.3.8段与笔者《合约的解释：规则与应用》一书第十三章之2段。

〔43〕 常会见到有些合约中把这种条文称为"Representation and Warranty Clause"，特别是美国律师，不理会在英国法下"陈述"与"保证"是两种不同概念，把它们当作同一码事。

另一个原因是订约前的陈述主要针对过去与现在事实的误述，对将来的意见或预期事实的陈述，如目标公司来年的业务与估算盈利、有否潜在的诉讼或仲裁等，就起不了作用。更要命的是，并购合约或股权买合约虽然会有昂贵与仔细的尽职调查，但在这些方面是尽职调查也查不出来的。这样，唯一保护买方的办法就是把它加在合约内作为一个这些将来的事实属实的保证。

再一个原因是误述争议的诉讼昂贵与不肯定，双方经常对在漫长的谈判中说过什么是各执一词。但违反合约保证就肯定得多，往往是违约责任没有什么好争，要争也是在损失计算方面。正如 Denning 大法官在 Oscar Chess Ltd v. Williams（1957）1 WLR 370 上诉庭先例说："everyone knows what a man means when he says 'I guarantee it' or 'I warrant it' or 'I give you my word on it'. He means that he binds himself to it."

以上解释了为何今天不少类别的合约中，特别是中国公司涉及很多的公司并购或股权买卖合约，一条"陈述与保证条文"已经是最重要的条文之一，也往往是争议与诉讼/仲裁的主要来源。现在也有保险（M&A Representations and Warranties Insurance）可去投保，不少著名保险公司有这种业务，如 AIG、Ambridge、AXA XL、Beasley、BlueChip、Chubb、Concord、Ethos、Everest Insurance、The Hartford、QBE、VALE 等。

例如在 Elaine Philp & Anor v. Cook（2017）EWHC 3023（QB）先例中，案情涉及原告与被告订立的一份股权买卖协议，其中第 7 条文与附录 3 就将部分谈判阶段的陈述变为了合约明示保证，并写明了误述的后果：

"7. Warranties

7.1 The Buyer is entering into this agreement on the basis of, and in reliance on, the Warranties.[44]

7.2 The Seller jointly and severally warrants and represents to the Buyer that each Warranty is true, accurate and not misleading on the date of this agreement.

7.3 Without prejudice to the right of the Buyer to claim on any other basis or take advantage of any other remedies available to it, if any Warranty is breached or proves to be untrue or misleading, the Sellers shall pay to the buyer on demand:[45]

7.3.1 the amount necessary to put the Company into the position they would have

---

〔44〕 虽然这里说是"保证"，但从条文的说法来看应该是订约前的"陈述"，这也显示了这方面的混乱与为什么会有这么多争议。

〔45〕 这是说如果卖方违反了保证就需要无条件对给买方带来的损失作出赔付。这种见索即付（on demand）的方式代表卖方一收到买方提出的要求就要无条件与无异议立即作出支付。这是对投资者利益保障的一种方式，可以通过在股权买卖合约中要求卖方提供独立于股权买卖合约，由金融机构或财力雄厚的母公司提供履约担保来实现。在最近的 Shanghai Shipyard Co Ltd v. Reignwood International Investment（Group）Co Ltd（2021）EWCA Civ 1147 上诉庭先例可以看出"见索即付"字样的重要性。

been in if the Warranty had not been breached or had not been untrue or misleading;

7.3.2　the amount necessary to compensate the Buyer if Warranty 2 (Sale Share constitutes all of the issued shares) is untrue or incorrect in any respect; and

7.3.3　all costs and expenses (including, without limitation, damages, claims, demands, proceedings, costs, legal and other professional fees and costs, penalties, expenses andconsequential losses whether directly or indirectly arising) incurred by the Buyer or the Company as a result of such breach of 7.3.1 or 7.3.2 or of the Warranty being untrue or misleading. ..."

10.3　合约保证条文是否有陈述与保证的双重属性

即使是有一条明示与完整的"陈述与保证条文",不少原告仍会提出该条文中有个别的保证同时是陈述,所以是有双重属性(dual quality)。也就是针对同一内容的不正确陈述(false statement)既是合约的保证,同时也是侵权的可诉误述。原告的主张显然是为了可以去同步诉讼或仲裁,可占尽合约与侵权的好处,如时效长短、更容易去撤销合约、或损失计算等。在正常情况下,能否这样做显然要看这两种不同的诉因是否能够成立。

首先是,有否一个特定的合约保证被违反应不难确定,根据有关的事实客观解释"陈述与保证条文"自然会有答案。而是否在订约前的谈判过程中做出过错误的陈述(刚好与保证的内容重叠)是根据有关证据去客观看各种成立误述的要求是否满足,如实质重要(materiality)、"要不是"(but for)测试、诱导(inducement)与依赖(reliance)等,这也可以做到。

举例说,A与B在一辆二手车的买卖中,A向B说这二手车已经走了5万里,并进一步说我愿意在将来的合约中保证这一点。这样,如果事实上车辆已经是走了10万里,B就同时有误述与违反保证的两个诉因。但在不同事实下,B可能只有误述或只有违反保证的一个诉因。前者是谈判中A只向B提供了5万里的信息,并没有提保证这回事。后者会在"买方自己小心"(caveat emptor)的大原则下比较罕见,是A没有说,B也没有问,但在后来作为走形式(formality)而签署的合约有提到5万里。

近年才兴起在某些类别合约中有详尽的"陈述与保证条文"的习惯做法也带来新问题与刁钻的争议。这是,合约内的保证条文(内容中肯定有不少是对过去或现在事实的保证)中有个别事项被发觉是虚假信息,但在订约前的谈判,双方并没有去讨论过,也没有证据显示卖方(如一宗公司并购交易)曾提供给买方有关虚假信息,并要求对方接受。但是在谈判后期,主要条件(main terms)已经是同意了双方去拟定合约时(在此阶段,主要在进行讨论的是双方代表或公司律师),才有了这一条完整的"陈述与保证条文"的定稿,其中内容包括该虚假信息。问题是,即使是谈判后期,仍是在订约前。这样,会否这对合约最后版本的通讯往来就可以构成订约前陈述(pre – contractual representation)? 毕竟这种情况"有效"陈述的特征并不明显,如卖方并不严格是向买方提供信息与事实,买方也没有提问,会只是在拟定的合约中有此一栏的事项要填上。此时卖方是否有意图诱导与买方有否依赖去订立合约，即使是有程度也不会高？如果这仍是属于可诉误述，岂非合约的保证条文不少内容可“自动过档”，导致一旦有违反保证，也成为是可诉误述？

这方面的案例近期有不少，如 Invertec Ltd v. De Mol Holding BV（2009）EWHC 2471（Ch）；Sycamore Bidco Ltd v. Breslin & Anor（2012）EWHC 3443（Ch）；Idemitsu Kosan Co Ltd v. Sumitomo Corp（2016）EWHC 1909（Comm）；Ivy Technology Ltd v. Martin（2020）EWHC 94（Comm）；Arani & Ors v. Cordic Group Ltd（2021）EWHC 829 等一审先例。其中 Invertec Ltd v. De Mol Holding BV 先例是认同这“自动过档”的说法，但后来的 4 个先例是不同意。以下简单介绍：

1. 在 Invertec Ltd v. De Mol Holding BV 先例中，Arnold 大法官认定在该股权买卖合约，被告既违反保证，也同时有误述：“Counsel for the Defendants（被告）argued that, because Invertec's claims are all framed by reference to warranties in the SPA, Invertec cannot have any claim for misrepresentation, fraudulent or otherwise, but only a claim for breach of contract. I do not accept this argument for the following reasons. First, two of the claims（... management accounts and its corporation tax liability）concern information which was supplied by（被告）to Invertec during the negotiations prior to the SPA, albeit that its correctness was warranted in the SPA. ... Secondly and more fundamentally, the warranties in question also amount to representations of fact ... **The warranties were negotiated between Invertec and（被告）over a considerable period prior to the execution of the SPA. As a result Invertec knew prior to signing that the agreement it was about to enter into contained those warranties. In those circumstances I cannot see any reason in principle why Invertec cannot claim that it was induced to enter into the agreement by the representations made by those warranties so as to found a misrepresentation claim if they were false**, particularly if they were fraudulently made.”（加黑部分是笔者的强调）

2. 接下来的 Sycamore Bidco Ltd v. Breslin & Anor 先例持不同看法，案情涉及收购公司的股权买卖合约。买方指控卖方违反了一项有关会计的保证（这种会计保证条文通常保证公司账目反映公司真实与客观现状，包括有关公司业务、资产与负债、盈亏，并遵守特定的会计准则等），把年度的营业额（turnover）错误地夸大，这也导致收购的价格受到了影响等。由于在损失计算中以侵权计算损失金额要大得多，所以买方作为原告也同时主张误述的诉因，指称保证条文中内容（包括公司账目）是卖方以一份“披露信函”（Disclosure Letter）的文件在订约前提供给买方的。但 Mann 大法官不同意 Invertec Ltd v. De Mol Holding BV 先例中 Arnold 大法官的看法，结果判被告卖方只是违反了保证，但没有误述。Mann 大法官不同意 Arnold 大法官看法的理由有 6 点，其中包括针对保证条文措辞/文字的解释只针对保证，根本不涉及订约前的陈述。但 Mann 大法官也承认这方面不重要，毕竟每个不同合约条文都会有不同写法。最重要的是对这方面的理念(conceptual),也就是保证条文能否“自动过档”与有双重属性。以下节录 Mann 大法官的主要理由:

“... **the claimants also run an additional case** in misrepresentation. It is said that the warranties are also capable of being representations so that, **if there is a contravention of their terms, there is also a misrepresentation**, and claims are made in the tort of negligent misrepresentation and under the Misrepresentation Act 1967. The defendants take the point that the warranties do not contain representations, ...

The point has a real significance in terms of the measure of damages (and also the date at which damages should or can be assessed), so it is necessary to deal with it. If the claimants are right about it, and can otherwise put their claim successfully in misrepresentation, then they may be entitled to recover damages which would not be available under a contractual claim. At their highest, the misrepresentation claim damages are equivalent to or exceed the consideration paid. At its highest the warranty damages claim is about £ 6 million. Hence the point's importance.

It is to be noted that**the claimants do not rely on anything other than the terms of the warranties in the SPA as amounting to representations for this purpose**. There is no reliance on any pre – contract representations; the warranties are relied on as both warranties and representations.

It does not seem to me that they have that dual quality. **I find that they are warranties only, and not representations**, for the following reasons:

(i) There is a clear distinction in law between representations and warranties, and that would be understood by the draftsman of the SPA. That is likely to be the case in any transaction of this nature, but is also apparent from the SPA itself....

(ii) The warranties in this case are clearly, and at all times, described as such, and are nowhere described as representations. Those giving the warranties are described as 'Warrantors' (again with a capital 'W'). The relevant wording is always in terms of warranties.

(iii)...

(v) Clause 8 of the SPA contains significant limitations on the liability under the 'Warranties'. It does not refer to representations. The clause is obviously a significant part of the overall structure of liability. If the warranties were capable of amounting to representations as well, then on the strict wording of this clause it would not apply to any such misrepresentation. The sellers would thus be deprived of a large part of their protection and limitation. That would be a strange and uncommercial state of affairs, and can hardly have been intended. This is strikingly so in relation to clause 8.2 containing the overall cap on recoveries and on what could be recovered from each warrantor, ...

(vi) There is**a conceptual problem in characterising provisions in the contract as being representations relied on in entering into the contract. The timing does not work**. The normal case in misrepresentation involves the making of a representation, and as a result the entering into of the contract. That does not work where the only representation is said to be in the contract itself. ..."(加黑部分是笔者的强调)

3. 再接下来是 Idemitsu Kosan Co Ltd v. Sumitomo Corp 先例,该案案情涉及 Sumitomo 集团旗下的一家能源公司的股权买卖合约,双方当事人都是日本公司。Idemitsu 声称 Sumitomo 在合约中的保证是错误的,但因为已经过了合约明示的 18 个月时效,所以成立误述的侵权责任在《Misrepresentation Act 1967》之 s. 2(2)下索赔损失(仍是上亿美元)变得至关重要。Idemitsu 以合约保证也属于陈述,构成《Misrepresentation Act 1967》下的误述为由起诉,以绕开时效的限制。而在修改后索赔请求中提供的误述详情(particulars)是被告 Sumitomo 对目标公司过去与现在事实的陈述不正确,而做出的时间是:"before (i) providing the Execution Copy as the contract to be signed by both parties on 12 November 2009; (ii) offering to sign the Execution Copy, or (iii) signing the Execution Copy."高院的 Andrew Baker QC 大法官同意 Mann 大法官的看法并对怎样区分给出了以下指引(部分已经在本章之 10.1 段节录):

(1)如果一方(如卖方)在有关合约(如股权买卖合约)中对合约的标的物(如公司股份)做出保证(无论是过去、现在或将来的事实),他/她并没有传递信息也没有向另一方(如买方)作出陈述,他/她只是作出受合约约束的承诺:"When a seller, by the terms of the contract under which he sells, 'warrants' something about the subject matter sold, he is making a contractual promise. Nothing less. But also ... nothing more. That is so just as much for a warranty as to some then present or past matter of fact as it is for a warranty as to the future. By contracting on terms by which he warrants something, the seller is not purporting to impart information; he is not making a statement to his buyer. He is making a promise, to which he will be held as a matter of contract in the sense that any breach of the warranty will be actionable as a breach of contract, subject to any other relevant terms of the contract and to general principles of the law of contract, for example as to remedies."

(2)订立的合约包括有关合约保证并不表示保证方向对方做出任何陈述,而是表示保证方承诺受合约条文约束:"I do not think that by concluding a contract on terms which include contractual warranties the warrantor makes any relevant statement to the counterparty. The act of concluding a contract is constituted by, and amounts to a communication only of, assent to and intention to be bound by the terms agreed."

(3)仅仅是该保证可以认为陈述并不够:"In order to make the relevant material a representation one has to find something in the SPA which is capable of doing that. It is not enough that the subject matter of the warranty is capable of being a representation.

One has to find out why those words are there."

(4)当然如果合约中明示写明合约保证也有陈述的效果(例如,对合约的"陈述与保证条文"加上说明对过去或现在事实的陈述如果不正确,即构成"可诉误述"),那么可以推翻上述(1)的说法,但这个文字必须清楚无误、没有歧义,笔者相信这在现实中很少出现:"In such a case,as I see it and have sought to explain above,there is no representation,at all events in the absence of some provision saying otherwise,i. e. saying ... that the warranty is also to take effect as,or to be treated as,a representation."

(5)理论上,双方交换的谈判中的通讯、合约的草稿或终稿中的语言/文字可能找得出能构成《Misrepresentation Act 1967》下的误述的陈述,但这完全取决于不同案件的特定案情:"It seems to me right in principle that language found in the communication of a negotiating position,or in draft wording for a contract,or in an entire draft contract,passing between the parties during the negotiation of a contract,might amount to or form the content of a pre-contractual representation capable of being actionable under the 1967 Act. That possibility was recognised by the Court of Appeal in Eurovideo Bildprogramm Gmbh v. Pulse Entertainment Ltd [2002] EWCA Civ 1235,to which Peter Gibson LJ referred in Leofelis v. Lonsdale, supra, at [141], where he emphasised that all would depend on the particular facts of any given case."

(6)无论如何,在此先例去区分陈述与保证也没有必要。根据有关股权买卖合约的"没有依赖条文",原告明示同意了没有依赖任何保证条文外的陈述或被诱导订立合约。有关条文可节录如下:"12.12.3 The Buyer acknowledges and agrees with the Sellers that:(a)it has not relied on,or been induced to enter into,this Agreement by any representations,warranties or undertakings of any kind other than the Warranties(as modified by the Disclosure Letter);and(b)the Sellers shall not be liable to the Buyer(whether in equity,contract,tort or under the Misrepresentation Act 1967 or otherwise)for any warranty or undertaking which is not set out in this Agreement and the Buyer shall not be entitled to terminate or rescind this Agreement as a result of a breach of this Agreement,including the Warranties(for which the Buyer's only remedy shall be in damages for breach of contract)."

4. 另在近期的 Ivy Technology Ltd v. Martin 先例中,涉及是否批准修改文书请求,Teare 大法官根据 Andrew Baker QC 大法官的指引拒绝了申请。

5. 而在更近期的 Arani & Ors v. Cordic Group Ltd 先例中,案情与 Idemitsu Kosan Co Ltd v. Sumitomo Corp 先例非常类似,也跟从了 Idemitsu Kosan Co Ltd v. Sumitomo Corp 先例的判决。高院判股权买卖合约中的保证条文只是合约承诺,不能作为订约前的误述。并且该合约也包括一条明示的完整合约条文,所以该先例买方的欺诈性误述索赔被简易撤销(summarily struck out)。但买方以欺诈性违反合约保证(fraudulent breach of warranty)为由的索赔被允许继续审理。

10.4 不同案情分析是可诉误述或违反合约保证的上诉庭先例

由于不同案件的案情千变万化,例如即使在谈判后期与在最后合约版本的讨论中,双方仍可能要求对方提供某些特定信息与事实等不同情况。而且,一审法院的主流看法也难以说是稳定权威的法律地位,需要更高层次的法院(上诉庭或最高院)对此问题作出决定才算数。所以,可预期这方面问题仍有发展空间。

10.4.1 Eurovideo Bildprogramm GMBH v. Pulse Entertainment Ltd (2002) EWCA Civ 1235 上诉庭先例

在 Eurovideo Bildprogramm GMBH v. Pulse Entertainment Ltd 上诉庭先例中,其实可以有不同的看法,因为上诉庭的判决主要在分析保证条文的文字与措辞的条件下得出结论是可诉误述;但如果结合具体的案情,可以见到双方在合约谈判与进行修改时有明显的陈述,而这有很强烈的构成可诉误述要件的诱导与依赖的倾向。所以这并不代表与上小段介绍的一连串一审判决有矛盾。

该先例涉及的是对一些录像的许可协议(license agreement)。有关争议是在合约内的第 8 条:"Representation and Warranties":"Licensor represents and warrants to Licensee as follows:...C. That Licensor has not entered into any agreement which conflicts with the rights granted herein to Licensee. Licensee has the exclusive first exploitation right in the licensed territory."

在合约的第一稿由许可人(Pulse)发给被许可人(Eurovideo)之后,Eurovideo 对合约草稿提出了一些修改意见,其中包括重复几次提到要将"exclusive right of first exploitation"的字样加进合约,而 Pulse 也回复说"accepted and amended",并反映在上述节录的第 8(C)条文中。Eurovideo 也在修改后的合约文本上签字。该措辞/文字是显示了 Pulse 没有与任何其他第三人在有关地区(欧洲德语区)订立任何与许可协议相冲突的协议,Eurovideo 享有专属(exclusive)的"第一使用权"(first exploitation right)。Eurovideo 赖此愿意订立合约。但是实际上 Pulse 在订约前已经将这些录像许可过给其他第三人。Eurovideo 发现后提起诉讼,一审 Crawford QC 大法官判这既构成违约,也构成误述。如果只是违约,Pulse 主张 Eurovideo 在合约下没有什么实质的损失,即使有也只是名义上的,第三人许可的存在也没有对 Eurovideo 有什么影响。但是如果误述成立,Eurovideo 可以主张撤销合约与复原或在《Misrepresentation Act 1967》下索赔损失。所以 Pulse 就是否构成误述进行了上诉。上诉庭的 Rix 大法官结合双方订约前的通讯支持了一审的判决,他从两个方面去分析该 8(C)条的文字与措辞,认为在订约前 Pulse 就已经有对 Eurovideo 的陈述。其中第一方面是该第 8 条上来就说是许可人向被许可人陈述与保证,这本身就包括了陈述和保证两种概念,而更为关键的是该 8(C)条的第一句就是一个对过去事实的陈述,即许可人没有订立过任何与本合约下赋予的权利相冲突的其他合约。第二方面是在该 8(C)条的第二句中提到专属优先使用权,这本身就是一个事实的陈述,陈述的内容是被许可人是专属的第一使用权人,而只有之前没有其他被许可人的才有可能构成专属与第一。如果 Pulse 是在订约之后才又许可了第三人使用这些录像，那毫无疑问是违约行为。但 Pulse 在订约之前就已经许可第三人使用，这使得专属与第一的描述在做出时已经与事实不相符，从而构成可诉误述。Rix 大法官说：

"The judge found that not only was there a breach of contract but that there had also been a misrepresentation of fact, to be found in the pre-contract exchange letters, to which I have referred, and also in the terms of the draft contract proffered for signature, to the effect that these license rights had not been previously granted to other distributors. The judge found that this was a misrepresentation of fact entitling Eurovideo to damages in misrepresentation or, alternatively, rights of restitution. ...

It seems to me**the judge was perfectly right to regard that language as containing representations of fact.** The introductory language emphasises that the parties are concerned in the representations as well as warranties. As for sub - clause C, **its first sentence is plainly a representation of fact relating to what the licensor has done up to the time of the contract**, that is to say, **a representation that the licensor 'has not entered into any agreement' which conflicts with the rights granted to the licensee**. One of the rights granted to the licensee, even assuming for the moment that that is purely a right of warranty and nothing more, is **a right of first exploitation**. In fact, the licensor had already entered into agreements which conflicted with that right of first exploitation because he had already granted rights of exploitation within the licensed territory in the relevant medium. **So there was a misrepresentation of fact there**.

In my judgment, however, there was**also a misrepresentation of fact involved inherently in the language of 'first exploitation'**. ... If a contractor promises a right of exclusive exploitation he is ... promising for the future that he will not grant a right of exploitation to others which impinges on that promise of exclusivity. If he has not previously granted a conflicting right of exploitation that promise operates only to govern the future. If then the licensor grants a conflicting licence in the future that is simply a question of a breach of warranty; no question of misrepresentation occurs. **If however he has already granted a conflicting right of exploitation which is still subsisting at the date of the contract, then**, as of that very moment, the moment ... as of making that contract, that **promise of exclusivity contains within it a false representation that there is no existing grant of the relevant exploitation rights to others which would prevent the contractual grant being exclusive**. That is an example of how ... **contractual language can exist both as a term and as a representation**. ...

Thus a promise of first exploitation necessarily, in my judgment, contains within it a representation of fact that the relevant exploitation rights have not previously been granted. That was a representation of fact which was implicit in the language of the contract. ...[46]

The question then arises **whether that representation of fact was a pre-contractual representation on the basis of which the contract was entered into**. It seems to me to be perfectly plain that it was. **It is a representation of fact** which was bargained for in the letters to which I have referred, which **Pulse agreed to give in its letter of 18th December by saying it accepted the amendment and which was duly set out in the amended draft contract proffered for signature** together with that letter and also in the complete form of contract re-sent in the following January."（加黑部分是笔者的强调）

10.4.2 Leofelis SA v. Lonsdale Sports Ltd(2008)EWCA Civ 640 上诉庭先例

另外一个上诉庭先例 Leofelis SA v. Lonsdale Sports Ltd 中一方主张在《Misrepresentation Act 1967》之 Section 2(1)下索赔损失的权利。而要依赖该立法条文索赔损失的前提条件是一方是在另外一方对他做出误述后订立合同(entered into a contract after a misrepresentation has been made to him)。这样，是否在订约前存在可诉误述的事实就变得十分重要。该上诉庭先例涉及原告 Leofelis 与名牌运动服饰 Lonsdale 之间一份时长 6 年的商标许可协议(Trade Mark License Agreement)。相关的案情与涉及的争议有不少，但和本课题相关的内容是许可人 Lonsdale 与被许可人 Leofelis 在 2002 年 11 月签订了商标许可协议，授权 Leofelis 在 2003 年 1 月 1 日起计的 6 年内除了现存的其他 3 项许可之外，对 Lonsdale 的商标在除了英国与爱尔兰以外的其他欧洲经济区国家或地区享有独家使用权。

在该 2002 年 11 月的许可协议中，Lonsdale 披露了 3 项签约时已经存在的其他许可，并指出 Lonsdale 已经向这 3 项许可下的被许可人发出终止通知，它们的许可会很快到期与终止。其中 Leofelis 提出争议的是 Lonsdale 与 Alavi 先生之间的许可协议。2002 年 11 月的许可协议中提到 Lonsdale 与 Alavi 先生之间的许可协议将于 2004 年 2 月终止。但在 2003 年初，Leofelis 才发现根据 Lonsdale 披露出的与 Alavi 先生之间的许可协议的解释，以及他们之间的关系来看，这并不是事实，Lonsdale 单方面的通知不能终止与 Alavi 先生的许可协议，Alavi 先生有权永远将许可协议持续下去。而且 Alavi 先生在另外一份协议下拥有向 Lonsdale 无限量以较低价格购买带有其商标的货品在英国销售，而根据欧洲经济区知识产权权利穷竭原则(Exhaustion Doctrine)这就有危险，因为这些在英国销售的货品可以进一步销往其他欧洲经济区的国家或地区，这就会破坏 Leofelis 在这些地区的独家商标使用权，这是从未曾披露过给 Leofelis 的信息。

Leofelis 还主张 Lonsdale 在合约的协商过程中存在误述，其中尤其是 2002 年 7 月 22 日双方在伦敦希斯罗机场附近的酒店内召开的一次会议上 Lonsdale 的代表口头上也向 Leofelis 的代表陈述与保证 Leofelis 取得的许可在相关的地区是独家的，其

[46] 也就是本章之 1.4 段介绍的默示的事实陈述。

他现存的许可都会在通知发出后较短的时间内终止。这也是 Leofelis 主张的订约前 Lonsdale 做出的可诉陈述。

一审法官同意了 Leofelis 有关误述与违约的主张，但在上诉庭，该决定被推翻。Lloyd 大法官不认为 Alavi 先生可以从 Lonsdale 处购买产品在英国销售的事实会对 Leofelis 的商标使用权有任何影响，所以不构成违约。而 Lonsdale 在 2002 年 7 月 22 日开会中口头做出与后来写入合约中的现存许可会在做出通知后很快可以成功终止的说法也不构成违约，因为这是他们当时真实的想法与相信的事情。

至于 Leofelis 想依赖《Misrepresentation Act 1967》之 Section 2(1)的条文来认定 2002 年 7 月 22 日 Lonsdale 做出的是可诉误述(Alavi 先生的许可协议终止不了)，要求法院命令其赔偿损失，并提出在上小段 Eurovideo Bildprogramm GMBH v. Pulse Entertainment Ltd(2002)EWCA Civ 1235 先例中认为合约条文中的陈述，也可被视为谈判时的可诉误述，Lloyd 大法官指出 7 月 22 日的事实在一审后期才作为一个争端提出，也没有被一审法院认定为事实，所以不接受："…(Leofelis 的代表律师) argued that representations are made in the draft of the contract, and that the representee enters into the contract in reliance on, and after, those statements made in draft form. It seems to me that the answer to that is that the draft is no more than a statement that, if and when the contract is entered into by all relevant parties, the particular party will make the statements in question, just as it will undertake obligations set out in the draft. … it seems to me that …(Lonsdale 的代表律师) is right to submit that **damages under section(1) of the 1967 Act are not recoverable in respect of a misrepresentation which is made in a contract, as distinct from one which is made before the contract** is entered into. … drew attention to the decision of the Court of Appeal in Eurovideo Bildprogramm Gmbh v. Pulse Entertainment Ltd, arguing that Rix LJ there held that language found in negotiations or in a draft contract can, depending on the particular wording involved, amount to a representation of fact. In a case in which the point matters, it would be **necessary to consider the details of the negotiations and the terms of any successive drafts, something that was not investigated in this case**. Since the Claimants did not rely on pre-contractual representations …, because that was not made until the trial, or shortly before it, by which time the misrepresentations relied on had long since been formulated in the Claimants' Particulars of Claim."(加黑部分是笔者的强调)

可以总结，上述 Eurovideo Bildprogramm GMBH v. Pulse Entertainment Ltd 上诉庭先例、Idemitsu Kosan Co Ltd v. Sumitomo Corp(2016)EWHC 1909(Comm)、Ivy Technology Ltd v. Martin(2020)EWHC 94(Comm)先例与 Arani & Ors v. Cordic Group Ltd(2021)EWHC 829 等一审先例主流看法应该是吻合的，就是单纯在谈判后期草拟的合约中包括陈述与保证条文，不构成可诉陈述，而是需要看双方之间是否存在做出可诉陈述的事实。例如草拟合约到最后定稿只是走程序，甚至只是双方代表

律师或经纪人去完成,而最后双方签字的版本有新的内容或事实,但在双方谈判没有涉及过,就不会是可诉陈述了。而如果一方修改对方的草稿并加入了新的事实,而对方也没有反对,就会是存在可诉陈述。

10.5　谈判期间的“陈述”是否为可诉陈述或将来合约内的履约保证

10.5.1　The“Larissa”(1983)2 Lloyd's Rep 325 先例

有关区分合约承诺(contractual promise/obligation)或合约保证(contractual warranty)与合约订立前的陈述(pre-contractual representation)的困难,上述已有介绍。在此介绍另一种看来是相反的情况,即不是合约承诺是否属于可诉陈述,而是合约谈判期间的“陈述”去进一步分析是否真的是对过去或现在事实的可诉陈述,或只是一个将来合约内的履约保证。

受害方/被误述方声称对方误述,显然先要说明对方到底陈述了什么信息以及证明事实是虚假与不正确的,接下来还要证明该不正确陈述是实质重要与有诱导或部分诱导合约产生等一连串确立对方作为误述方有责任的事宜。但在千变万化的商业活动下,仅是确立对方有否“误述”与误述了什么信息与事实都不容易。毕竟,在双方的谈判过程中,误述可以是从行动中默示,或是书信往来中的内容进行。但这声称的误述到底是否是一个可诉误述与误述了什么信息与事实,声称是受害方的一方是不是自己想歪了或是找借口,需要由法院(或仲裁庭)客观认定。法院在解释被指控误述的一方的行动或信函有否误述一个事实与是什么事实,并后来被证实是虚假与不正确时就好像解释合约一样,根据当时的环境/背景与谈判中所用的文字客观解释的。

在 The“Larissa”与 SK Shipping Plc v. Capital VLCC 3 Corp(2020)EWHC 3448(Comm)这两个租船合约的先例中,争议就涉及了谈判时“陈述”与“承诺”或“承诺保证”的区分。显然,后者即使是不正确,也只会构成违约,通常不容易去终止合约。但前者若虚假与不正确,就构成误述,可以带来严重得多的撤销合约的后果。

这两个先例都涉及了在租约谈判中的油耗保证(bunker consumption warranty)是否默示了船舶的实际油耗的事实陈述,如果不正确就构成误述。这信息往往是船东提供给承租人一份“船舶详述”(vessel's description)让后者考虑是否租入船舶与以什么租金租入。这船舶详述的内容有不少信息如船旗、船龄、船级、容积与载重量、有否受到国家抵制(boycott)、有否拥有某些批准(vetting)等是构成事实的陈述,一旦不正确与虚假即会构成误述。正如在 The“Lucy”(1983)1 Lloyd's Rep 188 先例所涉及的船舶航区(trading limit),也会是船舶详述的内容之一,虚假信息无疑构成可诉误述。

但涉及船速或油耗,船东提供给承租人考虑的信息则会有多方面的变数。例如,在表达时往往会说明“最低”,如“最低油耗为 40 吨燃油”(minimum fuel consumption 40 tons)。另是,如果涉及长期租约,由于租约往往要求船速与油耗是一个持续性保证(continuous warranty),所以船东提供的数字会较保守,以防在履行半年或 9 个月后船舶因污底而船速减慢或油耗升高。相反,在一个航次的期租(time-charter-trip)中,船东敢以目前(会根据刚完成的几次航次推算)船舶能达到的航速与油耗向承租人保证或陈述。另一种情况是船东提供信息时船舶严重污底,快要走不动了,但已经是计划进船坞清底,之后才交船给承租人,就应可履行正常航速与油耗。

更会是,由于期租合约也会有条文针对船舶如果履行超出或低于租约保证,将可以提高或扣减租金作为奖赏或惩罚,这特别是在油轮租约中,如著名的 Shelltime 标准格式期租租约就这样规定。船东也因此会在提供的数字上动脑筋,例如市场低迷导致租金低迷,但燃油价格高昂,就尽量把陈述或保证的油耗数字提高,务求在履行时会有节省而不被惩罚甚至反而有慷慨的奖赏。

这样,在谈判时船东提供了有关船舶的船速与/或油耗数字,如果视为对现在的事实的"陈述"且不正确,在不同的背景/语境下解释,会难以确定到底是针对何种现在的事实的陈述,如陈述时的真实/正确事实,还是 1 到 2 个月后交船时的将来事实?或如果该内容"不正确",应是什么误述。

在 The"Larissa"先例中,案情涉及一个 19 个月(10 个月加上 9 个月延长)的油轮租约并使用 Shelltime 3 的标准格式。其中有长篇幅的第 24 条文约定:"Owners warrant that at the date of delivery under this charter the vessel shall be of the description set out in Form B … attached hereto and … **Owners guarantee** that the **average speed** of the vessel **will not be less than** 14.6 knots … with a **maximum bunker consumption** of … 42 tons fuel oil per day … If during any year from the commencement of the charter period the vessel falls below or exceeds the performance guaranteed in this clause then(a)if such shortfalls … results … from a reduction … in the average speed of the vessel … in relation to the average speed guaranteed … then hire shall be reduced or increased … in an amount proportionate to the loss or gain in time involved;(b)if such shortfall … results … from a decrease in the vessel's average daily bunker consumption … in relation to the average daily consumption guaranteed … hire shall be reduced or increased … by an amount equivalent to the value of the excess or saving in bunkers involved based on the average price paid by Charterers for the vessel's bunkers in this period …"

在寻找租约的船东通过经纪人给承租人的一封 3 月 6 日有关航速与油耗的电文信息时说:"Owners to guarantee 14.6 knots in moderate weather … consumption of 42 Long Tons HVF."而最后订立的租约第 24 条文如上述部分节录变得更完整。显然,完整的租约条文多了好几个重要文字,如船速是"平均"(average)与"不少于"(will not be less than),或油耗最高(maximum consumption)是每天 42 吨燃油等。这样,可以说事实上船舶的实际油耗是 41、40、37、35 吨不等,都不是不正确与虚假的。而如果油耗事实上是 43、48 吨不等,由于有第 24 条文的调整,也难说 42 吨是诱导租约产生的虚假陈述。

该案案情是在租约履行完毕后,船舶的平均船速在第一年履行期间是 13.9914

节与延长租期期间为 13.74 节，这比租约保证的 14.6 节差劲，承租人可以扣减船速慢而多花时间的租金。但平均油耗是每天 31.899 吨与 31.36 吨，比租约保证的 42 吨要节省不少。感觉是船东刻意去这样做以赚取昂贵的燃油差价，对此如果真构成“误述”，会是欺诈性误述。反正是，船东计算出来的油耗奖赏扣掉船速慢的惩罚后约可以索赔 130,000 美元。但承租人抗拒与提出反索赔，其中一个主要理由是谈判时提供的船速与油耗量是对现在的事实的误述而不只是将来合约中的履行保证，谈判时 3 月 6 日电文中所陈述的 14.6 节与 42 吨的数字显然与后来履行的真实数字相比是虚假与不正确的。

在伦敦仲裁，仲裁庭视该 3 月 6 日电文确实是对船速与油耗的陈述，数字不正确也就构成了误述，并判承租人胜诉。但上诉（因为对 3 月 6 日电文的解释是法律问题，英国《Arbitration Act 1979》允许在批准下上诉）去了法院，这不为 Hobhouse 大法官接受，认为解释该电文的文字或用词，是要全面解释与配合背景/语境。而该 3 月 6 日电文中的内容也包括了 Shelltime 3，措词是“C/P Form：Shell time 3，1972 …”。这表示一并去解读或视为该电文的背景/语境，这 14.6 节的航速与 42 吨的油耗会加上“平均”“最低”等的限制，只是船东会以此指标履行并可最后调整的租约承诺（obligation），不能解读为是在 3 月 6 日做出对当时的事实陈述。

Hobhouse 大法官说：“… the arbitrator does not appear to have considered closely whether or not this telex contained a representation. **He appears to have assumed that it did rather than deciding that it did**. … In so far as the arbitrator appears to found himself upon the fact that the telex does not use the words ‘not less than’ or ‘maximum’ either in relation to the speed or in relation to the consumption figures, **in my judgment he is clearly failing to read the telex in its context**. The relevant words are introduced by **the phrase ‘Owners to guarantee’** and the words are clearly directed to cl. 24 of the Shelltime 3 form. In Shelltime 3 the words are ‘not less than’ blank ‘knots with a maximum bunker consumption of’ blank. Further the arbitrator does not … face up to the difficulty of deciding what the representation is. The representation cannot be that the vessel consumes exactly 42 long tons. It must on any view be open to the owner to leave himself a margin of error. Indeed, he would be unwise if he does not do so. **One of the difficulties in treating the telex as containing a representation is in deciding precisely what the representation is**. No clear answer to this problem was provided by charterers and this is a further reason against reading the wording of the telex as containing a representation.”（加黑部分是笔者的强调）

The“Larissa”先例后的一个涉及再保险（reinsurance）的 Kingscroft Insurance Co Ltd v. Nissan Fire & Marine Ins Co Ltd（1999）1 Lloyd’s Rep IR 603 先例中，Moore-Bick 大法官说：“The first is **whether by offering to contract on certain terms a person normally makes any representation about the particular subject matter of those terms**.

In my judgment he does not. He offers to become bound to certain obligations, but is not normally to be understood at the same time to be making statements about the subject matter of those obligations. ... The position would no doubt be different where the offer included terms which were intended to stand as representations in the contract as ultimately concluded, for example, statements of the kind which sometimes form part of the preamble to a formal contract. **Whether any particular term is a term of obligation or representation will be a matter of construction in each case**. A rather different question is whether simply by offering to contract on certain terms a person by implication represents that he intends to perform any contract made on those terms and believes that he is, or will be, able to do so. In principle I think he does. That, after all, is the basis on which he expects the offeree to judge his offer. However, it is important to understand exactly what representation the offeror is making. In most cases it is unlikely that he will be saying any more than that he intends to perform the obligations which, as he understands it, a contract in those terms would impose on him. He is unlikely to be saying that he intends to perform the contract in accordance with its true construction whatever that may in due course be held to be ... In practice, therefore, the representation is likely in most cases to come down to no more than one of honesty in entering into the bargain..."(加黑部分是笔者的强调)

Moore – Bick 大法官以上所讲是说要区分发出特定合约条文的要约是否表示对条文内容做出了陈述与是否默示陈述该合约方有意图根据合约条文的规定(或他/她认为的规定)履行合约。如果没有明示规定或并不在合约的前言部分,前者的答案一般是否定的,即订约方只是表示他/她愿意受某些合约责任约束,而不是针对有关责任的事实做出陈述。而后者的答案原则上来说是肯定的,实践中一般只是要求合约方在订约前谈判时诚实,也就是相信合约条文的规定可以做到。

10.5.2 SK Shipping Plc v. Capital VLCC 3 Corp(2020)EWHC 3448(Comm)先例

SK Shipping Plc v. Capital VLCC 3 Corp 先例涉及一艘名为“C Challenger”的超级油轮(VLCC),在 2016 年 12 月 6 日订立期租合约。事实上,船东拥有的另外 3 艘 VLCC:“C Spirit”、“C Innovator”与“C Progress”也租了给承租人。由于船舶之前是以航次出租,昂贵的燃油是船东自己承担,承租人无需关心。但由于船东公司决策改变,船东希望把船舶以长期期租合约出租,这时该 4 艘 VLCC 的“船速与油耗”信息就变得重要,因为承租人要承担营运与油耗的费用,这是承租人决定是否租入船舶的重要考虑因素。船东制作了一份电子数据表(spreadsheet),内有 4 个表格(table)。表格 1 中包括了船舶下水试航时、交船 6 个月和交船 12 个月(至 2013 年 8 月)这 3 个时间点的船舶油耗数字。表格 2 是在表格 1 中的数字上加多了 5.5 吨油耗,作为发电机与其他附属机器的油耗。而表格 3 与 4 则是在表格 2 的数字上多加了 4%。这简单划一的数据调整显然是粗糙,例如不区分"轻载"(ballast)或"满载"(fully laden),但肯定应该是较接近船舶的实际情况或真相。该电子数据表显示数据的更新截止至2014年10月。

反正从2016年11月7日开始,船东的租船部门向市场传递有关4艘VLCC的信息,包括重要的航速与油耗,数字是根据表格2提供。这在船东公司的内部,船管部门也认为租船部门保证的数字是错误的。最后船东与被告承租人订立2年加1年的期租合约,合约第24条文也是如同The"Larissa"(1983)2 Lloyd's Rep 325先例中Shelltime 3针对的船速与油耗的奖赏与惩罚的调整一样,只是在此先例是新版本的Shelltime 4。

船舶是在2017年2月7日交船,但被告在2016年12月1日就已经从另两艘VLCC"C Spirit"与"C Innovator"的每天"午间报告"(noon report),内容包括船舶位置、天气、过去24小时的航速与油耗中得知实际油耗比租约保证的数字大得多,并持续与船东交涉与扣租,而船东也反对扣租,其认为在第24条文是要6个月才根据平均的数字调整租金。而船长也在电文中确认保证数字是错误的并要求承租人与船东联络。承租人在2017年3月24日给船东的电文说:"this vessels misdescription is also advised several times by the Masters when asked about the high consumption stating that 'Seems that the data on the T/C description is different to actual consumption' i. e. admitting that the vessels are mispresented to the Charterer by Owners. With the misrepresented Speed and Consumption all voyage estimations made are based on unrealistic data leading to significant economic losses to the Charterers by Owners fault."

再到了7月21日,承租人发出指控船东误述的电文:"...(i) it had intentionally misdescribed the speed and consumption characteristics of all four VLCCs in the charters and/or was in breach of the speed and consumption warranty and clauses 1 and 3 of the charters so far as the VLCCs' performance was concerned; (ii) the masters of the "C SPIRIT" and "C INNOVATOR" had 'candidly confirmed that the Charterparty description of those vessels differs from their actual capability'; (iii) ... and that if these matters were not resolved within 7 days, the various charterparties would be rescinded and/or terminated. ..."

到了10月19日,承租人告知船东以船东误述撤销租约或船东违约/毁约终止租约。船东也在第二天回应说接受承租人的拒绝履行租约(renunciation of Charterparty)。

接下来船东提起诉讼,指称其在谈判中对船舶的船速与油耗并不是陈述而只是租约中的保证,并诚实相信可去合理做到。而承租人的抗辩是这些是"误述",而且是鲁莽与不理会真假(reckless, not caring whether they are true or not)[47]的欺诈性误

〔47〕 Derry v. Peek(1889)14 App Cas 337贵族院先例对什么构成欺诈的指引。

述,或是《Misrepresentation Act 1967》之 S. 2(1)下的疏忽误述,没有合理理据(reasonable ground)相信是真实/正确的。

油轮市场受国际政治、石油需求等因素影响波动很大,可以在短期内大涨大跌。在订约期间的 12 月 9 日,VLCC 市场租金是 37,027 美元一天;到了 12 月底已涨至 50,000 美元。但之后回落,到 2017 年 2 月底,市场租金只是 16,800 美元,之后更在 3 月中之后很长一段时间(只在 4、5 月有短暂的波动)市场租金是在 10,000 美元或更低。在这里提市场,纯粹是想表达从这个角度看,承租人拖了这么久也不像是想用误述取巧撤销租约。

高院的 Foxton 大法官不愿意偏离 The"Larissa"先例的判决,支持船东并详尽分析了为什么整体解释"船速与油耗保证"是不适合被视为谈判时的事实陈述的:

"the issue of whether the offer of a speed and consumption warranty generally involves a representation as to the vessel's current or recent performance is a key issue when undertaking the counterfactual enquiry which arises as part of the Charterer's misrepresentation case. …

I would have been reluctant to depart fromThe Larissa on this issue. The decision has stood for 37 years without criticism, and was cited with approval in Kingscroft. In any event, **I have concluded that there are good reasons why the mere offer of a speed and consumption warranty, and in particular of a continuing warranty as in this case, should not of itself be held to involve an implicit representation as to the vessel's current or recent performance**:

· i) The language of such an undertaking-a warranty-is inherently **promissory**, and is **expressed in relation to the future**(**performance during the chartered service**).

· ii) The attempt to imply such a representation raises **the difficulty of determining the date at which any particular level of performance is said to have been represented**, in circumstances in which a vessel's performance will change over time depending on matters such as hull fouling and the efficiency of the engine, and also the issue of whether any representation is made as to the position(i) at the date of the communication said to constitute the making of the representation, (ii) the date of the charter or(iii) the date the vessel enters the charterparty service. …

· iii) Speed and consumption warranties are frequently the **subject of negotiation**-for example as to the degree of margin, or the weather conditions in which the warranted performance is guaranteed … That is inconsistent with the offered warranties involving a representation as to a vessel's actual consumption.

· iv) The wordings of most tanker time charterparties … provide for some **off-setting of over-consumption and under – consumption over a set period**, with the result that the warranty given takes effect not so much as a warranty as to the vessel's capability at any particular point in time but as to its average performance over a longer period. It has been noted that such provisions：

· ... The Shelltime 4 form ... provided for an average over 6 months. As a result, a vessel which does not initially perform at the required level might ‘make up that performance’ ... such that there is no clause 24 claim. The intricacies of such a warranty make it difficult to spell out an implied representation from the fact of the promise alone."（加黑部分是笔者的强调）

笔者认为目前的法律地位对承租人不利，容易给“别有用心”的船东取巧，例如The“Larissa”先例中去提高油耗为将来履行赚取燃油差价。更或是，在争取一份好租约时刻意提高船速与压低油耗，宁可将来面对租约如 Shelltime 第 24 条文的惩罚，给潜在承租人一个假象是船舶比其他竞争对手更具吸相力。毕竟法律的地位是谈判时的船速与油耗本质上不会构成一个可诉陈述，就无所谓真假。但承租人就会上当，例如，营运需要一艘快船，如能有航速 15 节。但船东声称 15 节航速的船舶实际上只能有 12 节。这不是承租人可以在租金作出扣减去惩罚就可以令人满意的，承租人通常不会想与船东不断的争议与诉讼，租约约定的机制也不一定能够充分补偿承租人的损失。承租人也会把船东提供的“租约承诺/保证”中的航速（与油耗）作为对事实的陈述向第三人（如 CIF 买方或分承租人）提供，并在出了争议后被夹在当中。

但对懂行懂法律的承租人来说，总有办法解决。例如要求船东在提供船速与油耗外，提供过去 3 个或 5 个不等航次的细节。这是对过去事实的陈述，那么有虚假与偏差则难去争辩不是可诉误述。甚至，可以进一步把这陈述的事实加进租约并规定为明示条件条文。这样，承租人撤销合约或终止租约的普通法权利或合约权利就有保证与肯定了。

至于该先例另外两个重要争议，关于承租人有否通过继续营运船舶的言行选择了确认租约，可见本书第三章之 6.1.3 段，而关于受害方在自助撤销合约后，法院可否在《Misrepresentation Act 1967》之 S.2(2) 下否定撤销令合约重生，可见本书第四章之 5.3.2 段。

11. 向第三人做出或由第三人做出的陈述

可诉误述的起点是有关的虚假与不正确陈述被误述方确有收到并受到影响，否则也难说是有依赖并导致合约的产生。在社会上普通民众之间的误述，一般不会是复杂，往往是一方直接向另一方做出欺诈性或非欺诈性的误述，如一家黑店以虚假或半真不假的对货物质量或价格的标签去弄虚作假骗人。由于这种误述争议的价值不高，一般也不会带来可诉误述的民事诉讼。防止的方式往往是靠政府保护民众的立法或作出惩罚性规定与监督，如《商品说明条例》、消费者委员会等。

但一旦去到国际商业社会，情况就会复杂得多。其中一种情况是在商业活动，难免有第三人参与，这就会带来各种变数。例如一个虚假陈述会是来自一方陈述方并且原封不动通过第三人如代理人去转达给被陈述方，但也会有第三人转达并非原封不动而是添油加醋令一个原来非欺诈性变为欺诈性误述的情况。也会是第三人在委托人正式委托前或委托后不知情的情况下向对方做出虚假陈述。还会是第三人虽然是代理人，但是全权代表被陈述方，陈述方做出错误的事实陈述，第三人没有转达给对方就已经是代为拍板订立合约等。

更不说这第三人如经纪人一般，仅是他的身份就可以有很多变化。例如，陈述方委托，但也会是被陈述方委托，更会是他是完全独立于双方当事人。

11.1　向第三人做出的陈述

在国际商业社会，一个可诉误述有千变万化的情况可以涉及第三人。最常见的情况如陈述方向第三人（如代理人或经纪人，代理人也包括是公司法人的雇员）做出陈述，并授权与/或知道第三人会转达原告，并且第三人也确实转达了，因转达的陈述是虚假与不正确而被诱导或是受骗并蒙受损失的原告，作为被陈述方，也可以向陈述方主张可诉误述的救济，即撤销因误述订立的合约与/或索赔损失。另一种情况是，陈述方是向一类人做出的陈述，并没有特定的目标，如果这类人中有依赖（也是陈述方合理预期会依赖的人士）了误述并蒙受损失，也可以主张误述的救济。最典型的例子就是可转让的提单（negotiable bill of lading），背书（endorse）与交出（deliver）给任何潜在的买家，[48]这类人中最后的提单持有人就是提单上误述的受害方/被误述方了。

这可先节录《Chitty on Contracts》（2021 年，第 34 版）一书之 9－037 段："… To put the matter another way，the claimant must show that it was intended that he should act on the representation，rather than it being aimed solely at someone else. There may be said to be three types of representees：first，persons to whom the representation is directly made and their principals；secondly，persons to whom the representor intended or expected the representation to be passed on；and thirdly，members of a class at which the representation was directed … On the other hand，where a person makes a false statement in a document（such as a bill of lading）which he knows is going to be passed on to other people and relied on by them, any person who does in fact rely on the document will be a representee. …"

在 OMV Petrom SA v. Glencore International AG（2015）EWHC 666（Comm）先例中，原告是罗马尼亚的国有公司，负责进口原油。但实际进口是由原告的佣金代理人（commission agent）Petex 公司进行，在订立合约时，也是 Petex 公司自己与卖方订立合约。这看起来有点类似早期中国的外贸进口（如机械）必须依赖外贸代理商与外

---

〔48〕　见笔者《提单与其他付运单证》（2016 年）一书第二章之 3.1.5 段。

商之间签订合约，然后由外贸代理商把有关进口机械转交给中国的最终使用者（end user）。如果该机械有问题，最终使用者就会蒙受损失，甚至是严重损失。根据外贸代理商与外商的合约，外商有明确的责任，但问题是蒙受损失的是最终使用者而不是外贸代理商，最终使用者也往往不能或不敢向外贸代理商索赔，除非能够说服外贸代理商把诉权转让（assign）给他或允许他以代理商的名义根据与外商的合约向外商主张救济。如果由最终使用者以自己名义直接去向外商索赔，他们之间并没有合约关系，也不涉及侵权，就投诉无门了。但如果问题涉及误述（如外商把二手机械虚假陈述为新出厂机械），就涉及了最终使用者可否作为受害方/被误述方以外商欺诈性误述的欺诈/欺骗侵权（tort of deceit）行为（双方没有合约关系是不要紧），去直接提起诉讼并要求救济？

可以想到，外商的抗辩是误述只是向外贸代理商做出，与最终使用者无关。但外商的抗辩会站不住脚，因为误述虽然只是向外贸代理商做出，但应可以合理预期到会被转达与被最终使用者依赖。

在此先例正是如此，买卖合约中约定的原油是伊朗重油或 GOSM，但实际上货不对版，部分付运的原油中混有其他不同品质的原油。作为卖方的被告通过伪造付运文件在信用证下获得支付。原告发现后，立刻以欺诈性误述向被告索赔。被告承认自己的行为是欺诈性，但主要有两个抗辩，与本段有关的是虚假陈述只是做出给 Petex公司，不是给原告的，所以被告对原告没有责任。

但这抗辩没有被法院接受，Flaux 大法官说原告满足刚节录的《Chitty on Contracts》一书中提到的 3 类被陈述人中的每一类："In my judgment，Rafirom（原告改组前的前身）falls into each of the three categories of representee identified. The relevant representations were made by Glencore（被告）directly to Rafirom's agents，Petex（原告代理人，也是被误述方）and the banks which issued and confirmed the letters of credit. Even if the representations in question had never reached Rafirom，but only been relied upon by Petex and the banks as its agents（信用证结汇银行也是原告代理人，他们被误述诱导去产生合约，也是误述方知道的后果，原告即可以被误述方立场主张误述救济），Rafirom would be entitled to relief，as Chitty says. That Glencore knew that the banks were relying on the false representations … In fact however，the representations were passed on to Rafirom and the banks by Petex **as Glencore intended and expected. Glencore knew that Petex was passing on the representations**. … **Furthermore，Rafirom was clearly in the class of persons to whom the representations** in the shipping documents，commercial invoices and certificates of conformity **were directed**."（加黑部分是笔者的强调）

甚至在陈述方向第三人做出陈述时原告还不存在（如公司仍没有注册），也不影响原告之后以误述提起索赔，毕竟误述是持续性（continuous）的。在 Cramaso LLP v. Ogilvie - Grant，Earl of Seafield & Ors（Scotland）（2014）UKSC 9 先例中，争议是疏忽误述,与欺诈性误述道理一样。该先例的案情并不复杂。被告接触 Erskine 先生讨论出租自己的松鸡狩猎场。Erskine 先生对狩猎场内的松鸡数量表示担忧,害怕不够支撑狩猎季的计划。被告在电邮中说根据早些时候在狩猎场一个区域内统计出的松鸡数推测,整个狩猎场内的松鸡数量支撑狩猎季的计划完全没有问题。于是 Erskine 先生委任了律师,并通过律师通知希望以有限责任合伙(以下简称 LLP)公司订立租赁合约。之后 Erskine 先生成立了 Cramaso LLP(也就是原告)与被告订立了合约,但事后发现被告统计的松鸡数目的区域实际是松鸡最集中的区域,所以整个狩猎场内的松鸡数目远远少于推测出的数目。于是原告开始了诉讼,声称被告误述,故意诱导他订立租赁合约。

一审法院判 Erskine 先生是原告的主导意志(directing mind),被告的电邮构成重要的疏忽误述,且 Erskine 先生依赖该误述订立租赁合约,所以原告胜诉。但上诉庭认为原告 Cramaso LLP 在被告发出邮件时仍未成立,被告只能预见 Erskine 先生而不是原告会依赖这个陈述。所以被告在做出误述时与原告之间没有密切关系,对原告没有小心谨慎责任(duty of care),不存在有疏忽的误述责任,所以原告不能索赔损失。

原告上诉到英国最高院,最高院一致支持了原告的上诉,判原告可以获得损失赔偿。当可能的合约方仍是 Erskine 先生时,被告电邮中的陈述很明显是持续性的陈述。[49] 当原告成立后,被告仍然与 Erskine 先生(这时是作为原告代理人)谈判,被告没有撤回在电邮中对 Erskine 先生较早做出的虚假陈述,就等于默示向原告声明了陈述的准确性。Reed 勋爵类比了 Briess v. Woolley(1954) AC 333 先例的情况,在该先例中,公司的一名股东在与原告谈判出售公司股份时做出了欺诈性误述,而之后该股东又被其他股东委任作为代理人代表他们与原告谈判出售股份,贵族院最后判其他股东要作为共同侵权人为该股东的欺诈性误述承担责任,虽然当他做出该欺诈性误述时还没有成为代理人。Reed 勋爵说:

"Where the inference to be drawn is that a representation continued to be made until the contract was concluded, it may also be inferred that the risk of harm being suffered as a result of reliance upon it, in the event that it was inaccurate, continued to be foreseeable. In such circumstances, the representor may be taken to have assumed responsibility for the accuracy of the representation towards the contracting party who relied upon it, even though that person was not the original representee.

No authority has been cited in which the court has considered the liability of a contracting party for a representation inducing the conclusion of the contract by someone other than the original representee. The decision of the House of Lords in Briess v. Woolley … is however relevant. The case concerned a fraudulent misrepresentation made in the course

〔49〕 见本章之 8 段。

of pre-contractual discussions by a shareholder in a company. He was subsequently authorised by the other shareholders to continue the negotiations as their agent, and in due course a contract was concluded. The shareholders were held liable in damages to the other contracting party, notwithstanding that the representation had been made by the shareholder before he began to negotiate on their behalf. ...

The same principle should also apply in the converse situation, where the representation is made to (rather than by) the agent prior to the commencement of his agency. In such a situation, depending of course on the facts, the representor can equally be taken to be, by his conduct, implicitly repeating the representation previously made, and can therefore owe a duty in respect of the accuracy of the representation towards the agent's principal. ...

In the present case, the change in the identity of the prospective contracting party did not affect the continuing nature of the representation, or the respondents' continuing responsibility for its accuracy. ..."

11.2 由第三人做出的陈述

11.2.1 谁应对欺诈性误述负责:代理人、经纪人或原始的误述方或委托人

通过第三人表达一个可能是欺诈性误述的虚假事实在国际商业社会中经常会出现,例如,作为法人的有限公司就难免要通过代理人(特别是公司高管与雇员)去做每一件事或每一个决定。在国际商业活动,也经常通过经纪人或代理人的书信往来去谈拢并产生合约。例如受保人想在劳合社(Lloyd's)投保,必须经过劳合社经纪人(Lloyd's brokers):见 HIH Casualty and General Insurance Ltd v. Chase Manhattan Bank (2003) UKHL 6 贵族院先例。如果欺诈性误述成立,接下来的疑问是谁应该对有关的误述负责。被告(或代理人如公司的董事或高管)如果是自然人且被认定为是"骗子",撇开刑事后果,在民事上也可能有后果严重。[50]

如果委托人做出欺诈性误述,代理人原样转达给另一方合约方,就有疑问是代理人会否惹祸上身,即作为共同侵权人(joint tortfeasor)被索赔?获得公司授权(不论是真正授权或表见授权)的个别人士,特别是不知道也没有理由怀疑要转达的事实陈述是欺诈性的,会否不应该需要承担个人责任?毕竟,欺诈/欺骗侵权的指控需要证明被告的主观意图是想要欺诈或鲁莽不理会真假。

在千变万化的国际商业社会,也会出现委托人没有陈述某虚假信息或事实,但经

---

〔50〕 这可以我国香港特区的《香港联合交易所有限公司证券上市规则》为例。在该上市规则第 13.51 (2)条中,要求董事每年需要就若干问题作答复,其中包括:"阁下是否曾被法庭或仲裁机构判定阁下因不诚实行为而须承担任何欺诈、违反责任或其他不当行为的民事责任?(Have you been adjudged by a Court or arbitral body civilly liable for any fraud, breach of duty or other misconduct by you involving dishonesty?)"多举一个例子是针对专业人士如律师提起这严重的指控,即使只是民事诉讼但如果最后成功,也会导致律师协会纪律调查,最后结果甚至会把该律师除牌。

纪人或代理人希望成交以赚取佣金，从而在转达的信息与事实中添油加醋，加入虚假信息与事实（例如有其他买家出高价抢这批货）诱导了对方。这种情况中，委托人不应被指控为“骗子”，但也没有道理让他继续享有对方受误述误导而订立的合约。如果是代理人做出虚假陈述，在代理关系的要件都能满足的情况下，委托人是否要承担误述责任的转承责任（vicarious liability）？

在《Misrepresentation，Mistake and Non-Disclosure》一书（2022 年，第 6 版）之 5 - 21 段列举了三种不同的情况：

“（1）The defendant，D，authorises the statement to be made by his agent or employee，A. D knows that it is false. In this case there is no difficulty in establishing D' s liability in deceit. He is clearly fraudulent for the purposes of his primary liability under the tort：the fact that he uses an agent to make the statement does not prevent it being his representation for the purposes of the tort. If A also knows that the statement is false，or at least does not honestly believe that it is true，he too will be liable personally in deceit.

（2）D does not know that A is making the statement. A，who makes the statement，knows that it is false. Here D is not liable as a primary tortfeasor in deceit，because he does not personally have the necessary fraudulent state of mind. But the elements of the tort are satisfied as regards A，who is therefore personally liable in deceit. Whether D is liable，not as a primary tortfeasor but vicariously，depends on the application of the normal rules of agency and vicarious liability，which would normally provide that if A made the statement in the course of his employment or within the scope of his authority as agent，then D is liable. However，dishonest conduct perpetrated with no intention of benefiting the employer but solely with that of procuring a personal gain or advantage to the employee is governed，in the field of vicarious liability，by set of principles and a line of authority of peculiar application，which holds D liable only if A made the fraudulent statement within his actual or apparent authority as D' s agent. It makes no difference that D was not himself fraudulent，nor that … D did not gain personally by A' s tort.

（3）D does not know that A is making the statement. A，who makes the statement，does not know that it is false. But D does know the circumstances which made the statement false：that is，if D had known that the statement was being made，he would have known that it was false. The tort of deceit is not here committed at all. Neither D nor A has the necessary fraudulent state of mind. Even on the assumption that A' s statement was made in the course of his agency or employment，the fact that D would have had the necessary state of mind had he known that the statement was being made does not make him in fact fraudulent …”

以上是说：

1. 雇主/委托人 D 授权雇员或代理人 A 做出虚假陈述，且 D 知道该陈述是虚假的,让D承担欺诈/欺骗侵权的责任应该没有什么问题。D让A代为做出陈述的事实并不影响这是D的陈述:见 Cornfoot v. Fowke(1840)6 M & W 358 等先例。而A如果知道该陈述是虚假的,或至少不相信该陈述正确,则A个人也要承担欺诈/欺骗侵权的共同责任。

2. D不知道A做出了陈述,而A在做出陈述时知道陈述是虚假的。在这种情况下,D不会作为首要侵权人承担欺诈/欺骗侵权的责任,因为他本人没有欺诈的主观意图。但A满足构成欺诈/欺骗侵权的所有要件,要个人承担侵权责任。至于D要不要承担转承责任,就要看A是否是在受雇工作期间或授权范围(包括真正授权、默示授权与表见授权)内做出的陈述,如果是,则D要承担转承责任,否则就不用承担:见 Briess v. Woolley(1954)AC 333;Armagas Ltd v. Mundogas SA(1986)AC 717;Mercantile Credit Co Ltd v. Garrod(1962)3 All ER 1103;Alliance & Leicester Building Society v. Edgestop Ltd(1993)1 WLR 1462;Credit Lyonnais Bank Nederland NV(now Generale Bank Nederland NV)v. Export Credits Guarantee Department(2000)1 AC 486;Dubai Aluminium Co Ltd v. Salaam(2002)UKHL 48;Frederick v. Positive Solutions(Financial Services)Ltd(2018)EWCA Civ 431;Winter v. Hockley Mint Ltd(2018)EWCA Civ 2480 等先例。而A到底是为了自己的利益还是为了D的利益,D到底有没有在此过程中获益并不重要:见 Lloyd(Pauper)v. Grace, Smith & Co.(1912)AC 716 先例。但是这些涉及各种类型的代理(例如,拿佣金的经纪人或代理人与另一个极端的公司雇员)与复杂的代理方面的法律,在本章不深入探讨。

3. D不知道A做出了陈述,A在做出陈述时不知道是虚假的,而D如果知道A做出了这样的陈述就会知道这是虚假的。例如D向A做出陈述,但让A暂时不要告诉原告。D后来发觉该陈述是虚假的但以为没有什么关系,因为已经让A不要告诉原告。谁知A在不知道该陈述是虚假的情况下自作主张将该陈述告诉了原告。在这种情况下双方都不用承担欺诈/欺骗侵权的责任,因为A与D都没有欺诈的主观意图。即使A是在受雇工作期间或授权范围内做出的陈述,再加上D如果知道该陈述就会知道这是虚假的这个事实,并不能得出D事实上有欺诈的主观意图的结论。在 Armstrong v. Strain(1952)1 TLR 82 先例中,上诉庭确认了一审法院的 Devlin 大法官的判决:"There is no way of combining an innocent principal and agent so as to produce dishonesty. You may add knowledge to knowledge, or, … state of mind to state of mind. But you cannot add an innocent state of mind to an innocent state of mind and get as a result a dishonest state of mind."

最后可以节录 Supperstone 大法官在 Montpellier Estates Ltd v. Leeds City Council(2013)EWHC 166(QB)先例对以上所讲的总结:"An employer or principal is liable for torts committed by his employee or agent acting within his authority. Accordingly where an employee or agent makes a representation he knows to be false, and it was within his actual or ostensible authority to make that representation, the employer or principal will be liable even if personally entirely innocent. Conversely if the employer or principal expressly authorises his employee or agent to make a statement which he himself knows to be false, he is liable. However where a false representation has been made innocently by an agent acting within his authority, the mere fact that the principal knows the facts which render the representation false will not make the latter liable if he has not expressly authorised the representation or deliberately concealed facts from the agent with a view to the claimant being misled."

11.2.2　不针对欺诈性误述的《Misrepresentation Act 1967》之 S.2(1)下谁对疏忽误述负责

《Misrepresentation Act 1967》之 S.2(1)的立法条文针对的是做出误述的"人士"(person)要对疏忽误述负责,说:"if the **person making the misrepresentation** would be liable to damages."虽然在国际商业社会,订约的双方大部分都是公司法人,也可算是"人士",但同样也可以把"人士"解读为自然人。这样,在一个非欺诈性误述中,受害方除了向误述的对方合约方(商务上通常是有限公司)索赔外,可否也向疏忽提供或转达虚假与不正确信息与事实的第三人,例如代表误述方公司去实质参与谈判有关合约的公司(甚至是母公司)老板个人、董事或高管本人、经纪人、其他代理人索赔?

在这方面,《Misrepresentation, Mistake and Non-Disclosure》一书(2022 年,第 6 版)之 7 – 10 段,针对立法 S.2(1)的分析,有以下说法:"Where the misrepresentation is made by the contracting party personally, it is clear that s.2(1) can apply to make him personally liable. But where the misrepresentation is made by an agent of the contracting party acting in the course of his actual or ostensible authority, who is liable under the section: the agent, the contracting party, or both? **It has been held in such a case that the principal is liable under the section for a statement made by his agent, but the agent is not personally liable. Any liability of the agent must be established on other grounds, such as in the torts of deceit or negligence.** ..."(加黑部分是笔者的强调)

这也可见 Morin v. Bonhams & Brooks Ltd (2003) EWHC 467 先例中, Jonathan Hirst 大法官的观点:

"In Resolute Maritime Inc v Nippon Kaiji Kyokai [1983] 1 WLR 857, Mustill J... held that **the remedies under the Act applied only against the other contracting party**. His reasoning ... was as follows: '...Common sense suggests that if anyone is liable under a statute concerned with representations inducing a contract, it ought to be a principal as party to the contract.

It may, however, be objected that even if this is so, there is still room to read section 2(1) as creating an additional liability in the agent. I do not agree. The Act is concerned with representations made in the particular context of a contract, and it seems to me that it was aimed at the position of the parties to the contract. ... **The purpose of the Act was to fill a gap** which existed, or was believed to exist, **in the remedies of one contracting party for an innocent representation by the other**. But there was no such gap in the case of the agent; ... What purpose would there be in creating an entirely new absolute liability, independent of proof that the representee fell within the scope of a duty of care, simply because the representor happened to be an agent, concerned in the making of a contract, but not himself a party to it? I can see none; and, since, as I have suggested, the words of section 2(1) must be read as extending to the principal, I consider that their operation should be confined to him alone. '"(加黑部分是笔者的强调)

也就是说,一般只有委托人(也就是误述导致的合约的合约方)要承担误述的侵权责任,而合约责任更不用说了。毕竟,误述主要的救济,也就是撤销该有缺陷的合约,只能向他去主张,不会是向第三人。

受害方/被误述方也不能在《Misrepresentation Act 1967》之 S. 2(1)下向代理人/第三人索赔损失,这通过分析与解释该 S. 2 立法条文的文字/措辞就会清楚:(1)该立法只适用在误述导致合约产生的情况,S. 2(1)的用字"Where a person has entered into a contract after a misrepresentation has been made to him by another party thereto"应只局限在合约方,而不是合约方外的其他第三人。(2)该 S. 2(2)立法条文是说如果法院或仲裁庭认为公平合理(在误述不严重的情况下允许撤销合约的救济是不成比例的),可以金钱损失的赔偿替代(in lieu of)撤销合约的救济。Salt v. Stratstone Specialist Ltd(2015)EWCA Civ 745 上诉庭先例[51]已经明确说明如果没有一个普通法/衡平法下站得住脚与不被否定(bar)[52]的撤销合约的权利,就也不会有损失赔偿的救济。而合约方外的第三人显然是不可能撤销合约,也就是《Misrepresentation Act 1967》S. 2(1)(本意是允许疏忽误述索赔损失)不适用。

但万事总有例外,例如"未披露委托人"(undisclosed principal)[53]的代理人的情况下,受害人/被误述方对撤销合约的选择权利应不受影响。无论该有缺陷合约是与谁订立(因为代理人没有透露是另有委托人在背后),反正是因谈判时代理人误述(欺诈性或非欺诈性)诱导而产生,就有权使合约无效:可见 Garnac Grain Company Incorp. v. H. M. F. Fabre & Fairclough Ltd & Ors(1968)AC 1130 贵族院先例等。

但涉及受害人索赔损失的救济,未披露委托人的代理人不像其他一般受害方看得见有实际授权或表见授权的代理人,就有可能有个人责任赔偿疏忽误述导致受害

[51] 见本书第四章之 5.5.2 段。

[52] 见本书第三章之 6 段。

[53] 见笔者《提单及其他付运单证》(2016 年)一书第三章之 2.4 段与《损失赔偿与救济》一书第七章之 3.2 段的详细介绍。对于未披露委托人,未披露委托人与代理人都可以起诉与被诉:见 Siu Yin Kwan et al v. Eastern Insurance Co Ltd(1994)1 Lloyd's Rep 616 等先例。

人的损失。最明显的是该代理人从头到尾都没有透露背后谁是委托人的例子,那只能被视为他就是与受害人订立合约的合约方。但这不必是根据 1967 年立法之 S. 2(1)了,也可以是 S. 2(2)下法院行使权利否定受害方撤销合约权利并以金钱赔偿替代。

撇开未披露委托人的特殊情况,即使在一般的现实情况中,受害方可能确实有必要向第三人索赔损失。例如做出误述诱导合约的对方合约方已经破产或经济出问题,而代理人是一家大型经纪公司或律师事务所。又或是,交易谈判的人员/团队实际来自对方合约方的母公司等。在这种情况下,想要成功把第三人扯进来索赔误述损失,如作为共同被告,就需要以 1967 年立法外的普通法权利下的侵权支持,也就必须证明第三人欺诈/欺骗[54]或第三人在有一个小心谨慎责任(duty of care)的情况下疏忽侵权。[55]

11.3 第三人做出虚假陈述会有疏忽侵权责任的例外

如果第三人参与欺诈/欺骗,需要承担个人责任没有什么争议。而如果第三人(如代理人、经纪人与其他任何类别的第三人)没有欺诈/欺骗,只是疏忽陈述,在例外情况下也会对受害方/被误述方负上小心谨慎责任而需要对疏忽言行负责,即使疏忽言行源自背后的委托人/合约方。

想起诉直接做出疏忽侵权行为的第三人获得赔偿早有例可循,例如在海上付运合约,蒙受损失的货方希望以侵权向在货物托运期间有工作疏忽的船东/承运人的雇员与代理人索赔,以绕过提单合约的免责条文以及 1 年索赔时效与赔偿限额(package limitation):见货方取巧成功以疏忽侵权向船东/承运人雇用的装卸工人索赔货损的 Midland Silicones v. Scruttons(1961)2 Lloyd's Rep 365 先例[56]和带来了将免责扩大到雇员与代理人的"喜马拉雅条文"(Himalaya Clause)的 Adler v. Dickson (1954)2 Lloyd's Rep 267 先例。[57] 但这些案例都涉及人身或财产的实质损失(physical losses),容易满足侵权要求的邻近(proximity 或 neighbourhood)要求,让法院去强加给疏忽的第三人如雇员或代理人一个小心谨慎的责任。

但要求第三人负责的人士可能无边无际,必须划出一个分水岭。委托人与代理人之间的诚信关系与善意关系存在小心谨慎的责任理所当然,甚至他们之间的代理合约中也会明示针对。但如果把范围从委托人无限扩大到没有委托合约关系的其他人士,任何关系在任何情况下都有小心谨慎的责任,那显然就会乱套。

这方面之后也有所放宽,主要体现在本书第一章之 2. 2. 1 段介绍的 Hedley Byrne v. Heller(1964)AC 465 贵族院先例中语言上的疏忽陈述带来受害方纯经济损

---

[54] 见本书第三章之 8.2 段。

[55] 见本书第一章之 2.1 段。

[56] 见《提单与其他付运单证》(2016 年)一书第三章之 2.5.4.3 与 10.2.2 段。

[57] 见《提单与其他付运单证》(2016 年)一书第五章之 6.2 段。

失(pure economic losses)方面。这样，如果第三人在转达不正确陈述或做出其他言行时对没有委托关系的其他人有疏忽，会否带来侵权责任？例如，公司高管代表公司做出疏忽言行，但疏忽言行实是他本人的疏忽，因为公司法人只是一个虚拟的存在。如果受害方无法向公司索赔损失，例如公司倒闭，带来的问题是受害方能否向公司高管这个自然人以侵权索赔这笔纯经济损失？

这里主要是看法律能否强加一个小心谨慎责任在公司高管，这看来是有很大的疑问。Hedley Byrne 贵族院先例的小心谨慎责任，前提是自愿承担责任(voluntary assumption of responsibility)。说是高管对所有其他人士自愿承担责任恐怕很难说得通，更不用说他们也没有拥有什么特别技能可合理让其他人士去信赖。即使不是雇员的关系，而是公司的其他代理人如拥有专业知识的律师或财务顾问等，也很难说他们会对委托方的对手或任何其他人自愿承担责任并带来小心谨慎责任。这可以在接下来的段节举例说明。

11.3.1 交易/土地买卖代理律师对对方当事人的查询做出误述：Gran Gelato Ltd v. Richcliff(Group)Ltd(1992)Ch 560 先例

首先针对律师(也是代理人的一种)是否对客户外的其他人士有小心谨慎的责任，例如在一宗交易中，一方当事人向对方代表律师问有关法律或其他信息与事实，但对方律师因疏忽说错了。这会在现实发生，毕竟交易的谈判不像诉讼的对抗性，大家会在友好得多的情况下交谈并导致对对方律师有一定信任，为了避免自己花钱向其他律师询问法律意见，就干脆向对方律师查问。反正对方律师的误述会导致交易合约的产生，从而令合约方蒙受损失，也可以向对方合约方寻求救济。如果该律师的疏忽误述是向客户做出，毫无疑问他是有小心谨慎的责任要对这个疏忽负责(不论是普通法或他们之间的委托合约关系)。但律师要对对方当事人负有小心谨慎的责任，需要对他的疏忽负责赔偿，这就是大问题了。例如律师向客户(一家重要的企业)做出疏忽误述并导致客户向大量其他人士误述或作出错误决策，客户可向律师根据 SAMMCO 原则[58]索赔专业疏忽的损失自然是不在话下。其他因该企业误述或错误言行而蒙受损失的人士的正途是向该企业索赔，而即使疏忽与过错是源自律师，该企业仍是要承担转承责任。但可想象到，该企业倒闭或其他原因可以拒赔如合约时效已过或有合理的免责条文，这成千上万的人士如果可以疏忽侵权的诉因，指称律师除了对客户也同时欠他们一个小心谨慎责任，这就真正打开了泄洪阀，不是很不妥了。对于其他类别代理人[有些代理人也会涉及严重责任的工作，例如一个巨额的责任保险(liability insurance)的保险公司代理人]来说，大道理也是同样：见 McCullagh v. Lane Fox & Partner Ltd(1996)1 EGLR 35 等先例。

在 Gran Gelato Ltd v. Richcliff(Group)Ltd 先例中，Nicholls 大法官说对于一般直接做出虚假与不正确陈述的代理人(代理人的类别与职责范围可以很广泛而言，其

---

〔58〕 见本书第六章。

对被陈述方是否有责任，要看是否满足 Hedley Byrne v. Heller（1964）AC 465 贵族院先例下的特殊关系（special relationship）的要求，[59] 但对于处理地产转让业务的律师来说，只对自己客户有小心谨慎的责任：

"It is now established that the fact that **the person making the representation was acting for a known principal does not necessarily negative the existence of a duty of care owed by him to the representee**. … In such a case the representee can sue the agent at common law, in accordance with Hedley Byrne & Co. Ltd. v. Heller & Partners Ltd. principles.

That was in the context of agents generally. In the particular context of inquiries before contract in a normal conveyancing transaction, Morritt J. expressed a different view in Cemp Properties (UK) Ltd. v. Dentsply Research & Development Corporation [1989] 2 E. G. L. R. 205. He observed that it would be absurd if the solicitor for one party to the transaction owed a duty of care to another party as well as to his own client.

In my view, in normal conveyancing transactions**solicitors who are acting for a seller do not in general owe to the would – be buyer a duty of care** when answering inquiries before contract or the like. In reaching the conclusion that the law should not generally import a duty of care in such circumstances …"（加黑部分是笔者的强调）

11.3.2　遗嘱拟定律师对受益人负责的例外：White v. Jones（1995）2 AC 207 贵族院先例

之后在贵族院的 White v. Jones 先例中，案情涉及被告律师收到客户指示要修改遗嘱（will），将遗产留给两个女儿。但被告律师疏忽拖延，直到客户去世也没有修改遗嘱，导致两个女儿拿不到遗产。于是两个女儿起诉律师索赔损失。

在上诉庭，Nicholls 大法官说律师要遵守职业规则与标准，作为法院的官员[60] 对法院有责任，但是除此之外只对自己的客户有职业责任，包括小心谨慎的责任。但客户关于遗嘱的指示与其他指示不同，如果疏忽是在客户仍在世时发现，指定的受益人没有损失。但如果客户去世就不同，在这种特殊情况下，应该在该律师与失去继承权的受益人之间强加一个特殊关系，律师需要对后者负上小心谨慎的责任：

"In general, and always leaving reliance cases on one side, **a solicitor owes a professional duty of care to his client and no one else**. He is subject to professional rules and standards, and he owes duties to the court as one of its officers. But within that framework it is to his client alone that he owes a duty to exercise the standard of skill and care appropriate to his status as a solicitor. …

Instructions to prepare a will are different from other instructions to a solicitor. The

---

[59]　见本书第一章之 2.2.1 段的详细介绍。

[60]　见笔者《证据法：国际规管与诉讼中的证据攻防》一书第七章之 4 段。

failure to carry them out properly results in the client's purpose being thwarted but leaves the client's estate with no effective remedy. There is**good reason why the solicitor should be liable to a third party in this very special situation**. If the mistake, such as faulty witnessing, is discovered in the client's lifetime and corrected, the third party will suffer no loss. The cost of preparing and signing a new will would be recoverable by the client from the solicitor. But it is different if the client dies at a time when, because of a breach of the solicitor's professional duty, the will for whose preparation the solicitor was responsible has not been duly prepared and signed. Then it is **eminently fair, just and reasonable that the solicitor should be liable in damages to the intended beneficiary**. Otherwise there is no sanction in respect of the solicitor's breach in his professional duty. Thus **there is a special relationship between the solicitor and intended beneficiary which should attract a liability if the solicitor is negligent**."(加黑部分是笔者的强调)

贵族院支持上诉庭判决,Goff 勋爵同意 Nicholls 大法官说的一般律师只对客户有小心谨慎的责任,而对其他人士没有小心谨慎的责任,言行上即使疏忽也不负侵权责任:"First, the general rule is well established that a solicitor acting on behalf of a client owes a duty of care only to his client. The relationship between a solicitor and his client is nearly always contractual, and the scope of the solicitor's duties will be set by the terms of his retainer; but a duty of care owed by a solicitor to his client will arise concurrently in contract and in tort..."〔61〕

但在此先例这种特殊情况下,客户(已经去世)与失去继承权的人士(只是第三人)都不能起诉律师,等于律师完全不必为自己的疏忽言行或误述负责。法律应该填补这个漏洞,让律师对客户自愿承担责任扩大到客户希望指定为遗嘱受益人的人士,也就是强加 Hedley Byrne v. Heller(1964) AC 465 先例要求的特殊关系。

只简单指出:(1)如果客户没有去世,不会有此特殊关系产生。因为此时客户可以选择修改遗嘱将有关人士改为受益人,也可以改变主意不再修改遗嘱。因为律师拖延而没有成为受益人的有关人士不能说如果律师没有拖延而是及时改好遗嘱,那么自己就变为受益人,而客户很可能怕麻烦之后也就不会再进一步改动。(2)在此先例案情涉及的错误,也可能以其他形式出现,例如客户并非去世而是患上了阿尔茨海默病。所以不用纠结于案情稍有差别,重点还是要看疏忽的律师是否要承担责任,是否有法律漏洞需要以强加特殊关系填补。(3)如果受益人是因为其他原因而受到律师疏忽的影响,律师与受益人没有此特殊关系。例如律师在客户生前对客户处理资产作出建议,但因为疏忽导致资产贬值,对可能会受到不利影响的受益人没有小心谨慎的责任。Goff 勋爵说:"... it has been held that a solicitor advising a client about a

---

〔61〕 见本书第一章之 2.3 段。

proposed dealing with his property in his lifetime owes no duty of care to a prospective beneficiary under the client's then will who may be prejudicially affected: see Clarke v. Bruce Lance & Co. [1988] 1 W. L. R. 881."

12. 对可诉陈述的总结

上述介绍有关英国法律对怎样的言行构成可诉误述(actionable/operative misrepresentation)的历史,也反映了英美社会特别是商业社会在人与人之间交往的语言与表达方法的演变。在早年,法律看来是相当简单地划分欺诈性与非欺诈性(包括无心之失的疏忽),也就是对言行的陈述/表述只区分为诚实或不诚实,只有能够证明不诚实的欺诈/欺骗才有法律后果;另法律只针对对过去或现在事实(past or present fact)的不诚实,毕竟事实的真假容易证明。并且在简单与相对淳朴的社会,这区分也足够应对社会上大部分的事件。

而随着英国社会(包括商业社会)的演变与民众(特别是商人)的教育提升,语言与表达方法的艺术也相应提高,对讲话的轻重掌握得更好、更加含蓄,在对方不知不觉中起作用。而不安好心希望欺诈/欺骗或误导对方的"合法"技巧也肯定提升得更快。这特别是在"精英"与"豺狼"云集的国际商业社会,更是不会落后。早期显示什么是欺诈性误述的言行的典型先例中,如今在"高层次"的国际商业社会也被视为不屑去做的简陋、粗暴、直白与低档的谎言,但这不代表在道德上有任何提升。

所以,今天花得起高昂的诉讼费用并且作为被广泛报道的涉及欺诈性或其他可诉误述的诉讼案件的当事人很多是在商业金融等行业,而被指控误导的言行或是只讲一半不讲一半的沉默,往往是十分隐晦(subtle),审理法官或仲裁员需要从大量与十分复杂的事实(涉及漫长的谈判、大量文件证据与相互矛盾的证据等)中抽丝剥茧地分析是否有对过去或现在事实的误述。如果有误述也往往不会是一些低档的言行表达方式,而是通过意图(intention)、预测(prediction/forecast)、一连串在谈判中的间断言行讲一半不讲一半、不自动披露去澄清对方的不正确理解等,带来对过去与现在事实的错误默示。因为只有挑出有否与是什么对过去与现在事实的陈述,才可认定真假,再进一步认定有否默示误述。

当然,审理法官或仲裁员是不会主动为原告找出案件的案情是否有默示的对事实的误述,这是要熟悉案情、机灵与称职的原告代表律师去分析并证明被告(如一些高水平与精明的跨国商业机构或投资银行)在订约前的所有言行有否代表了对过去或现在事实的默示陈述与是什么内容、是否正确。[62] 当然也可挑出附带协议/保证(collateral contract/warranty),但由于今天的法院不是太愿意支持这个说法,加上今

〔62〕 见本章之1.4.5段的介绍。

天的合约往往有一条“完整合约条文”(entire agreement clause),所以这不会太管用。至于证明被告在表达意图或预测等时不诚实,这是十分难以满足的举证责任,特别是面对高水平与精明的被告更是不容易成功。当然这也可以通过合约明示条文的形式拆招,例如如今越来越常见的陈述与保证条文,[63]反正怎样谈判、订立与履行合约都是双方斗法。

这样就解释了今天大量涉及商业与金融的欺诈性误述案例,如几乎所有涉及LIBOR丑闻的案例,双方的争辩都是在针对默示误述。在每一个不同的案件与案情下,高水平与有创意的代表律师会指出各种对过去与现在事实的默示陈述。而一旦能找出来或挑出来,而且表面说得通,原告就有50%的机会可以说服审理法官或仲裁员。且如果被告委任的代表律师水平差(当然对跨国商业公司或银行而言,这是不大可能会发生),胜诉的机会就会提升至七八成或更高了。反之,若被告的代表律师水平高,一般默示误述的成功率是不会高的。

以上所讲可节录Rix大法官在Avon Insurance Plc v. Swire Fraser Ltd(2000) Lloyd's Rep IR 535先例中的总结:

“The law of misrepresentation has developed in fits and starts. **At one time a misrepresentation**(outside contractual or fiduciary relationships) only granted a remedy in two situations: a pre-contractual misrepresentation could be a ground for avoiding a contract; and a remedy in damages was available in the tort of deceit but **only of course if there was fraud. No damages were available for an innocent misrepresentation, not even if it was a negligent one**. Then in 1963 in Hedley Byrne & Co Ltd v. Heller and Partners Ltd [1964] AC 465 the House of Lords made it plain that **a duty of care to avoid negligent misstatements could arise between persons in a special relationship** and breach of that duty could found recovery in damages. Only a few years later in **1967 the Misrepresentation Act extended a right to damages** under section 2(1) in the case of **any misrepresentation inducing a contract** made by one party to another party to it where **the representor is unable to prove absence of negligence or bad faith**. In the meantime, the law of contract had developed the collateral warranty..., while the passing of the Act in 1967 with its alternative remedy under section 2(1) made the inference of a collateral contract less necessary. **Not**, however, **entirely unnecessary: for promissory representations or representations as to the future are harder to fit within the scope of the Act**, which has been interpreted as applying to the classic representation of present or past fact, as distinct from representations as to the future and statements of opinion, expectation, intention or law.

... it is the pressure of dishonesty which led to the doctrine that**statements of opin-**

[63] 见本章之10.2段。

ion or as to the future can be read as containing an implied statement of present fact as to a person's beliefs or intentions: see eg Edgington v. Fitzmaurice(1885)29 Ch D. 459 ('the state of a man's mind is as much a fact as the state of his digestion' per Bowen LJ, a case of fraud). That doctrine has led in turn to the **implication** that a representor **has reasonable grounds for his statement of belief or intention**: see eg Brown v. Raphael [1958] Ch 636, where the court of appeal stressed that **the representor was in a far better position to ascertain the facts than the representee.** In other situations, however, where fraud is not in issue, the courts have sometimes preferred to say that **statements of belief or as to the future, or promissory representations, should take effect as terms of the contract (or it might be said as collateral warranties) or not at all**: Economides v. Commercial Union Assurance Co plc(1998) QB 587 ..."(加黑部分是笔者的强调)

上述 Rix 大法官的总结已在本书各处详及,此处只简单指出如下几点。

1. 早期的法律或普通法,对订约前的误述给予受害方可使合约无效与索赔损失的救济,但受害方必须证明误述涉及欺诈/欺骗。但 Rix 大法官没有提到由于早年普通法法院为了追求法律的肯定去僵化处理,所以衡平法法院在一些没有救济是不合情理(unconscionable)的案件让非欺诈性误述也可以有撤销合约的救济,只要符合衡平法的一些理论即可,如受害方自己没有过错或做出过不公道的行为(he who comes to equity must come with clean hands; he who seeks equity must do equity);不作出任何救济在有关案件是不合情理(equity will not suffer a wrong to be within a remedy)的;受害方一发觉误述就马上寻求救济(delay defeats equity);不影响善意与不知情的第三人(bona fide purchaser for value without notice)等。但由于普通法法院与衡平法法院是分开的,给英国民众去哪里寻求救济带来很多不便与困扰,好像有两套不同的法律在实施,这最终导致了《Judicature Acts 1873》把英国普通法法院与衡平法法院合并在一起。

2. 1963 年的 Hedley Byrne v. Heller(1964) AC 465 贵族院先例[64]确认双方在特殊关系下有小心谨慎责任,不正确的陈述/表达也会带来法律责任与需要赔偿纯经济损失。但在所有合约的谈判都强加一个特殊关系很难说得通,所以很快,就有了《Misrepresentation Act 1967》,所有误述方如果无法举证说明有关误述是没有疏忽或是善意,就要赔偿受害方金钱损失。这样,过去唯一令非欺诈性误述的受害方可以获得金钱赔偿救济的附带协议/保证[65]就变得不再重要了。

3. 但也不是完全不再需要附带协议/保证,因为《Misrepresentation Act 1967》只

---

[64] 见本书第一章之 2.2.1 段。

[65] 见本书第一章之 2.5.2 段。

针对非欺诈性误述传统的对过去或现在事实的陈述,[66]不针对意图或预期事实。越来越多(特别是懂法律后果与语言艺术的国际商业人士)的"误述"是以将来意图或预期事实的形式作出,法律对付的办法(视不同案情而定)包括:(1)证明不诚实:见 Edgington v. Fitzmaurice(1885)29 Ch. D. 459 上诉庭先例;(2)推断有默示对过去或现在事实的陈述;(3)可解释为附属协议/保证。

〔66〕 见本章之1.1段。

第三章　误述的救济之一:撤销合约

1. 对误述撤销合约的救济简介

在英国普通法与衡平法下,无论是欺诈性(fraudulent)、疏忽(negligent)或是无辜(innocent),只要是误述(misrepresentation),即陈述了不正确的信息与事实(false statement of fact),被陈述方(representee)都有救济去撤销依赖(reliance)误述而产生的合约。毕竟就算误述的程度轻微(但也需要满足诱导与依赖的要求),也会导致合约的构成出现缺陷,毕竟说不上是合约双方对每一点达成一致想法,所以撤销合约也被视为对误述最恰当与正常的救济。

这早在涉及欺诈/欺诈性误述(fraudulent misrepresentation)的 Derry v. Peek (1889)14 App Cas 337 贵族院先例中,Herschell 勋爵有说:"Where rescission(on the ground of misrepresentation of a material fact) is claimed it is only necessary to prove that there was a misrepresentation; then, **however honestly it may have been made, however free from blame the person who made it**, the contract, having been obtained by misrepresentation, cannot stand."(加黑部分是笔者的强调)

这在近期针对非欺诈性误述(non-fraudulent misrepresentation)的 Salt v. Stratstone Specialist Ltd(2015)EWCA Civ 745 上诉庭先例有重复,Longmore 大法官说:"The normal remedy for misrepresentation is rescission … This remedy should be awarded if possible, …"

另在 SK Shipping Plc v. Capital VLCC 3 Corp(2022)EWCA Civ 231 上诉庭先例中,Males 大法官同意说:"… rescission is the normal remedy, … It should at least be a strong starting point."

当然,会有风险受害方/被误述方撤销(rescission)合约后,在后来的诉讼中被法院或仲裁庭认定没有一个可诉误述。这样,早前的撤销合约就会是变为拒绝履行合约(renunciation/repudiatory breach)。[1] 但任何撤销合约[如以胁迫(duress)、[2] 不

---

〔1〕 见笔者《合约的履行、弃权与禁反言》一书第一章之3段。

〔2〕 见本书第十章。

当影响（undue influence）〔3〕等］或终止合约（接受对方违约/毁约或拒绝履行合约、违反合约明示或默示条件条文〔4〕等）的决定都会有这诉讼风险。相信在普通法/衡平法下，以可诉误述撤销合约已经是相对肯定与简单。因为只要对方在谈判中做出过陈述（在国际商业活动这种陈述一般都会有文件证明），事后发觉并可以证明陈述的事实虚假或不正确，就已经可以相对肯定有一个可诉误述可去采取行动。因为无论对方对不正确的信息与事实有任何解释都不会有用，无论是欺诈性、疏忽或完全无辜，被误述方在普通法/衡平法下一律可去撤销合约。

如果受害方/被误述方自己手中的证据并不肯定可去成立可诉误述（如对方只是一个模棱两可的言行或自己不像有依赖）或撤销合约权利会被其他原因否定，加上涉及庞大金额（如撤销的是一个价值高昂的长期合约），可以尝试与对方达成"无损害"（without prejudice）协议，就如 The"Lucy"（1983）1 Lloyd' s Rep 188 先例一样。但能否成功除了要看不同案情，也要看对方是否合作与明智。但无论成功与否，都不代表撤销合约的权利要在法院（或仲裁庭）命令下才能行使，更不代表这救济不能由受害方自助的以通知方式撤销（rescission with notice），而变为是法院命令撤销（judicial rescission）救济。真正的关系可节录《Misrepresentation, Mistake and Non-Disclosure》（2022 年，第 6 版）一书之 4 – 19 段说："A court may of course become involved in determining a dispute between the representor and the representee as to whether there was a right to rescind, but if it decides that rescission was justified, the court order does not constitute the rescission: it merely confirms that the earlier act of election by the representee did validly rescind the contract, and then gives effect to it and makes any appropriate consequential orders. Even if there was no sufficient act of election before the proceedings were begun, the plea in the action that the contract has been or should be set aside will suffice, and therefore any order of the court will relate back at the latest to that time."

上述节录是说如果受害方自助撤销合约后，在后来的诉讼被法院确认是有权撤销合约，事情就告一段落。但如果不被法院确认，认定这不是一个可诉误述、或无法复原/反复原、又或不利影响无辜第三人等，就表示较早前撤销合约实是拒绝履行合约。如果受害方没有向误述方作出通知去自助撤销合约，而是在知悉误述的事实与自己的权利后，启动诉讼或在抗辩误述方的索赔时要求法院宣告他有权撤销合约，这也相等于是给误述方的撤销通知。而在等待法院审理与作出判决的期间，双方当事人即使仍在"无损害"的安排下履约，也不会被视为确认（affirm）合约的存在。但也要考虑如果后来法院确认受害方的撤销救济，就需要双方回归到零，双方在等待结果期间的一切因履约从对方获取的好处都需要去回归（unwind）或以金钱替代。

---

〔3〕 见本书第十一章。

〔4〕 见笔者《合约的履行、弃权与禁反言》一书第一章之 1 段。

1.1　普通法撤销与衡平法撤销的不同

在《Judicature Acts 1873》把英国普通法法院（Court of Law）与衡平法法院（Court of Equity）合并在一起前，普通法法院只承认欺诈性误述，并给予撤销合约与金钱赔偿的救济。这在 Redgrave v. Hurd（1881）20 Ch. D. 1 上诉庭先例中，Jessel 大法官有提起说："at common law rescission extended only to a misrepresentation where the representor knew it to be false, or was 'reckless, and without care, whether it was true or false, and not with the belief that it was true'."

衡平法法院则处理非欺诈性误述，因为衡平法法院是无权作出金钱赔偿判决的，所以"撤销"（rescission）是衡平法法院能对这类误述（包括疏忽与/或无辜误述）诱导产生的"可使无效合约"（voidable contract）作出的唯一救济。

普通法撤销（common law rescission）与衡平法撤销（equitable rescission）由于历史上的区分与各自发展，相关说法在不少地方都有不同，[5] 例如普通法撤销针对的只是欺诈性误述［以及胁迫（duress）］的普通法诉因（cause of action），而衡平法撤销可以针对包括欺诈性误述在内的各种类型的误述［以及其他衡平法撤销的理由，如有关的案情不给予救济是显失公平/不合情理（unconscionable）等］。衡平法撤销也会涉及衡平法法院拒绝行使裁量权的一些考虑，比如是怠慢理论（doctrine of laches）、保护不知情无辜第三人等。

1.1.1　主要不同之一：撤销是否为自助救济

普通法撤销合约的选择（election）通常是受害方/被误述方自己决定与行使，所谓的"自助救济"（self-help remedy）。如在 Drake Insurance Plc v. Provident Insurance Plc（2003）EWCA Civ 1834 上诉庭先例中，Rix 大法官说："In any event an exercise of avoidance does not depend on the court's assistance or declaration. In all these matters the insurer's right to avoid is like any other case of rescission of a contract."

只有在误述方对于撤销权提出争议时，才涉及法院审理。但如果法院审理认为并不存在撤销权，就变成受害方的违约/毁约。

而衡平法撤销就有一些争议到底是否为自助救济，毕竟衡平救济需要法院行使裁量权，而不是让当事人自说自话，在 Erlanger v. New Sombrero Phosphate Co（1878）3 App Cas 1218 先例中，Blackburn 勋爵就说："a Court of Equity requires that those who come to it to ask its active interposition to give them relief..."

但现在的案例是有不同说法，如在 Drake Insurance Plc v. Provident Insurance Plc 先例一审［（2003）EWHC 109（Comm）］中，Moore-Bick 大法官说："modern authorities do not suggest that a distinction is to be drawn between the principles that apply to the exercise of that right in different cases."

虽然实际做法上撤销合约都是被陈述方的自助救济，他是不会去客观分析到底

---

〔5〕 这在本书第十章之 12.1 段有更详尽的介绍。

有关的误述是欺诈性或只是疏忽(非误欺性),在接下去的诉讼,他也把两种不同诉因作为替代诉因作出请求。也就是,证据说服不了审理法官(或仲裁员)是欺诈性误述,会退而求其次认定是疏忽误述。被陈述方心里是想去撤销合约(通常是不利的合约),一旦抓到对方误述,总会是自助救济尽快作出选择,向陈述方或误述方作出通知撤销合约。一旦延误,即使原本有权撤销合约,也会变成因为选择确认(affirmation)合约而弃权,与加大了无辜第三人介入的风险。至于在后来的诉讼,被陈述方会根据案情主张欺诈性误述、非欺诈性误述(包括疏忽或无辜)等。即使最终被法院(或仲裁庭)认定没有欺诈性误述,也没有非欺诈性误述,或有非欺诈性误述的疏忽误述但法院不行使裁量权允许撤销合约,都不影响合约已实际上被"自助"撤销了。这无可避免带来了被陈述方的错误"自助救济"变为是"违约/毁约"。被陈述方自助救济的决定是正确的情况只有法院认定,包括:(1)欺诈性误述;(2)非欺诈性误述,并且行使裁量权去撤销合约。本章与第四章提到的"自助救济",主要针对的是一般商业人士的实际做法,不是普通法撤销或衡平法撤销在法律上的微妙区分。

1.1.2 主要不同之二:回复到原状的严格或宽松

另一个重要区别,是过去普通法撤销合约有各种障碍,特别是能否做到"回复到原状"(restitutio in integrum)或复原。在追求法律肯定性与可预测性的普通法下,对待这些障碍是相对僵化与严格的。即使涉及的是欺诈,法院想要更优待受害方,[6]但如果是回复到原状有困难,就无法寻求普通法撤销,而只能寻求衡平法撤销:见HMRC v. IGE USA Investments Ltd(2021)EWCA Civ 534 上诉庭先例等。

但如果案件的情况是无法令双方当事人去复原/反复原(impossibility of restitution/counter - restitution),也就要否定撤销合约的救济了。但这也难免会不令人满意,迫使受害方/被误述方接受与履行一个通常是对他不利并且明显有严重缺陷(defective)的合约。笔者感觉在一些类别的案件,如家事案件,这种情况会更多。而在今天的商业合约,则大多可以金钱量化以达到复原与反复原。

而衡平法法院为了对双方公平合理,有更大的灵活性与裁量权作出一个对受害方或是对双方当事人公平合理的救济方案。有裁量权为达至个别案件公平合理去撤销合约并回复到原状(即使不是百分百的原状),灵活与有弹性地量身定做不同的安排,只要求做到"实际公平"(practical justice)。

至于什么是实际公平则可见 Blackburn 勋爵在 Erlanger v. New Sombrero Phosphate Co(1878)3 App Cas 1218 贵族院先例中的名言:"**A Court of Equity could not**

---

〔6〕 只有一些案情十分特殊的案件中,涉及的反复原也意义不大,法院会有一些变通做法。例如,在Hulton v. Hulton(1917)1 KB 813 先例中,夫妻签署分居契据(deed of separation),丈夫答应妻子在世与未再婚嫁期间每年支付一笔费用,但妻子不得为过去婚姻期间的一些事件起诉丈夫,并必须销毁所有双方之间过往的信件。事后,妻子提出丈夫存在欺诈性误述要求撤销合约,丈夫提出撤销必须将已经销毁的契据一并恢复,但被法院拒绝。

give damages, and, unless it can rescind the contract, can give no relief. And, on the other hand, it can take accounts of profits, and make allowance for deterioration. And I think the practice has always been for a Court of Equity to give this relief whenever, by the exercise of its powers, it **can do what is practically just, though it cannot restore the parties precisely to the state they were in before the contract**."（加黑部分是笔者的强调）

1.2 普通法法院与衡平法法院合并后的变化

在《Judicature Acts 1873》后，S. 25(11)规定两个法院合并后有冲突时衡平法优先于普通法，并在《Senior Court Act 1981》之 Section 9 与《Constitutional Reform Act 2005 Schedule 11》重复说："... whenever there is any conflict or variance between the rules of equity and the common law with reference to the same matter, the rules of equity shall prevail."所以有说法是衡平救济，包括误述带来的撤销合约救济，在英国法院与普通法下的撤销合约与金钱损失赔偿（局限在欺诈性误述）一并审理了。但这种说法也带来一定程度的混乱，到今天还没有明确。

看来也是因为这个，今天普通法撤销也开始试图改变自己僵化处理复原与反复原的不利之处，偏向衡平法撤销的实际公平的做法。例如，原告获得的交易标的是被告提供的服务，交易完成、服务已经（或部分）提供后显然这不可能实物复原，但因此就不给予救济说不过去。例如一方向另一方提供装饰，撤销合约后也不必要将已经完成的装饰部分拆除，但允许对冲需要返还的费用：见 Do Ferguson & Associates v. Sohl (1992) 62 BLR 95 先例等。又例如涉及的有同类型的替代（如公开交易的股票）时，贵族院先例中的附带意见提到有可能可以在市场上购买股票替代：见 Smith New Court Securities Ltd v. Scrimgeour Vickers (Asset Management) Ltd (1994) 1 WLR 1271 先例。[7] 但相对而言普通法撤销由于很多过往先例的判法并没有被改判，所以仍然相比衡平法撤销面对的阻碍要大得多。

也正是由于普通法撤销合约适用范围的相对狭窄与面对的障碍众多，如今主要是在有恢复原状可能的待履行的合约（executory contract）、保险合约（insurance）以及货物买卖中才仍然考虑普通法撤销。而绝大部分撤销合约实际上都是考虑只需要实际公平的衡平法撤销了。这可见在近期的 Wood v. Commercial First Business Ltd (2021) EWCA Civ 471 上诉庭先例中，David Richards 大法官说："Rescission was then, and remains, a remedy available both at law and in equity. ... Similar but distinct remedies developed at law and in equity. Owing to its greater flexibility, the equitable remedy is now predominant except in relation to executory contracts, insurance and the sale of goods.' The greater flexibility in large part lay in equity's ability to provide satisfactory substitutes for the precise restitutio in integrum required by the common law. Rescission is

---

〔7〕 此先例还可见本章之 5.3.1 段的介绍。

also available in a wider range of cases in equity than at law, but it clearly is available at law in the case of fraud..."

也因此在本章后文中,除了少数特别作出区分的课题外,并没有严格区分这两者。后文中主要介绍的是衡平法撤销的衡平救济。加上在《Judicature Acts 1873》后,在诉讼过程中完全可以将之一同作为主张或替代主张的理由,在本书讨论中也没有必要再特别严格区分。

最后,对于可诉胁迫(actionable duress)产生的合约也有同样的普通法撤销与衡平法撤销的问题,对于问题的成因、目前的做法与将来的展望,将在本书第十章之12.1段有详细介绍。

2. 撤销与终止的区别

一个合约无论是1年、2年或是长达10年、20年在履行完毕前终止,会有各种不同与混乱的叫法或称呼,这也出现在很多早年的先例中。这包括被称为合约被"撤销""终止""卸下"(discharge)、"取消"(cancel)等。这并非好事,毕竟案例中使用的是被视为法律名词,如果有混乱就难免令法治社会的民众思维混乱。这好像是"弃权"(waiver)与"禁反言"(estoppels)早年经常被混为一谈,直到Goff勋爵在The "Kanchenjunga"(1990)1 Lloyd's Rep 391贵族院先例中区分两者不同的要件与后果后才明确下来。[8] 而"撤销"(rescission)合约与"终止"(termination)合约的区分与双者不同的要件与后果也是在Johnson v. Agnew(1980) AC 367贵族院先例与另一个Photo Production Ltd v. Securicor Transport Ltd(1980)1 Lloyd's Rep 545贵族院先例后,才明确下来。Wilberforce勋爵后一个先例说:

"... I have, indeed, been unable to understand how the doctrine can be reconciled with the well accepted principle of law, stated by the highest modern authority, that when in the context of a breach of contract one speaks of 'termination', what is meant is no more than that the innocent party or, in some cases, both parties, are excused from further performance. Damages, in such cases, are then claimed under the contract, so what reason in principle can there be for disregarding what the contract itself says about damages-whether it 'liquidates' them, or limits them, or excludes them? These **difficulties arise in part from uncertain or inconsistent terminology. A vast number of expressions are used to describe situations where a breach has been committed by one party of such a character as to entitle the other party to refuse further performance: discharge, rescission, termination, the contract is at an end, or dead, or displaced; clauses cannot**

---

〔8〕 见笔者《合约的履行、弃权与禁反言》一书第三章之5.2.2段。

survive, or simply go. I have come to think that some of these difficulties can be avoided; in particular the use of 'rescission', even if distinguished from rescission ab initio, as an equivalent for discharge, though justifiable in some contexts ... may lead to confusion in others. **To plead for complete uniformity may be to cry for the moon. But what can and ought to be avoided is to make use of these confusions in order to produce a concealed and unreasoned legal innovation**. ...

...I venture with apology to relate the classic passages. In Heyman v. Darwins Ltd. [1942] A. C. 356 ... Lord Porter said: 'To say that the contract is rescinded or has come to an end or has ceased to exist may in individual cases convey the truth with sufficient accuracy, but the fuller expression that the injured party is thereby absolved from future performance of his obligations under the contract is a more exact description of the position. **Strictly speaking, to say that on acceptance of the renunciation of a contract the contract is rescinded is incorrect**. In such a case the injured party may accept the renunciation as a breach going to the root of the whole of the consideration. **By that acceptance he is discharged from further performance and may bring an action for damages, but the contract itself is not rescinded**. "(加黑部分是笔者的强调)

在 Wilberforce 勋爵的呼吁后,之后的案例也比较稳定地在各自不同的案情下使用"撤销"或"终止"合约这两种不同概念的措辞。

这可节录在《Chitty on Contracts》(2021 年,第 34 版)一书之 9 - 123 段说:"**Rescission and termination** Since the decision of the House of Lords in Johnson v. Agnew a much clearer and sharper distinction has been drawn between rescission of a contract ab initio and termination of the contract for subsequent breach. The former generally has retrospective effect, while the latter does not; indeed, termination usually affects only some of the obligations under the contract and it is strictly incorrect to speak of the contract ceasing to exist through termination. It is clear from Johnson v. Agnew itself that rescission for fraud is rescission ab initio, and will therefore prima facie have retrospective effect, though it has already been submitted that such rescission will not deprive the representee of a right to damages for fraud. Because that right arises in tort, and not out of the contract. ..."

另也可节录《Misrepresentation, Mistake and Non-Disclosure》(2022 年,第 6 版)一书之 8 - 43 段说:"**The preferred (but not unanimous) terminology in the modern law**. More recently, the House of Lords made clear that the potential confusion arising out of this ambiguity is such that the use of the term 'rescission' should be restricted to the remedy of avoidance of the contract ab initio. In Photo Production Ltd v. Securicor Transport Ltd (1980) AC 827, HL, Lord Wilberforce recognised that 'to plead for complete uniformity may be to cry for the moon', but he urged the use of such words as 'discharge' or 'termination' to describe the remedy by which the unaccrued obligations under the contract are released by reason of a breach of contract, without the contract being avoided ab initio. This has led to a greater consistency of usage of language in the recent cases ..."

也就是说,因欺诈性误述而带来的撤销,是消除(wipe out)整个合约的存在,令双方回复到订约前各自的地位,即所谓"rescission of a contract ab initio"。所以有说法是撤销合约是一个"有追溯力的救济"(retrospective remedy),或也被称为是把已经履行了部分或甚至是全部的合约"反向履行"(reverse performance),又或是被称为"复原"(restitution)。例如在一个简单的买卖合约,复原到订约前的地位就要求买卖双方把各自获得的利益退还给对方。这代表买方退还有关货物,卖方退还收到的货价。这并不涉及在终止合约总会带来的金钱损失索赔,虽然表面看来是很难去区分。例如欺诈性误述说是可以索赔所有因欺诈/欺骗侵权所带来的损失,但本质仍是去复原,把受害方复原到欺诈/欺骗前的经济地位。

读者可以马上想到会有情况是一方当事人或甚至是双方无法去复原,例如买方已经把货物处理了才发觉卖方对货物有误述。这也表示撤销合约的救济行不通。这样除非卖方的误述涉及并能证明是欺诈性,普通法下买方才可以通过索赔金钱损失回复到没有被欺骗前的经济地位。但如果卖方是无辜误述,在无法复原失去了撤销合约的救济后,买方即使有损失,也没有了救济。在《Misrepresentation Act 1967》立法生效后,在S.2(2)条下法院是有裁量权决定是否以赔偿一定的金额代替撤销合约的救济。但如果买方无法复原而失去了撤销合约的救济,是否仍会在S.2(2)条下有金钱赔偿救济,不同一审法院有不同看法:见Thomas Witter Ltd v. TBP Industries Ltd (1996)2 All ER 573;Zanzibar v. British Aerospace(Lancaster House)Ltd(2000)1 WLR 2333;Floods of Queensferry Ltd v. Shane Construction Ltd(2000)BLR 81 等先例。在近期的Salt v. Stratstone Specialist Ltd(2015)EWCA Civ 745 上诉庭先例有了说法,会在接下去分段详论。如果无法复原而法院在S.2(2)条下无权给予金钱赔偿,等于是回到普通法地位了,就是无辜误述的受害方不能撤销合约就什么救济都没有了。

但终止合约,主要是履约时拒绝履行或违反条件条文(condition),也就是违约/毁约(repudiatory breach),[9]并不意味着合约从来都不存在,不能追溯到未订约前的地位。换言之,在合约仍存在时履约所支付的金钱如租金或货价、财产的转移、违约等,合约的终止都不影响已经是发生了的事实,不存在追溯。已经是欠下的债务或是发生了的违约/毁约,合约终止后仍可以通过法律行动去追债或索赔损失。而损失的计算办法是以合约法去计算,那就是让无辜方回复到合约被履行的经济地位。这与撤销合约是复原到误述前没有订立合约的经济地位的计算办法完全不一样。可以想到,如果合约本身是对受害方不利,以合约索赔可能只有名义损失,但是侵权下回复

---

〔9〕 见笔者《合约的履行、弃权与禁反言》第一章。

到没有合约的地位(特别是已经亏了一大笔钱的情况下)可以拿回一大笔钱。例如在 Sycamore Bidco Ltd v. Breslin & Anor(2012)EWHC 3443(Ch)先例中,违约的损失计算只有 600 万英镑,但以复原计算高达 1600 万英镑。

也可从另一个角度解释两者的区别。合约的首要合约义务(primary obligation)是指严格按照合约明示与默示的规定/承诺做一些事情;而次要合约义务(secondary obligation)就是指做出承诺的合约方违反了他的首要合约义务,不履行或是有缺陷履行首要合约义务,就会带来法律默示的次要合约义务,也就是对这个违约产生的损失向受害方做出金钱上的赔偿。可节录 Diplock 勋爵在 Photo Production Ltd v. Securicor Transport Ltd 先例中针对首要合约义务与次要合约义务的著名说法:"Leaving aside those comparatively rare cases in which the Court is able to enforce a primary obligation by decreeing specific performance of it, breaches of primary obligations give rise to substituted or secondary obligations on the part of the party in default, and, in some cases, may entitle the other party to be relieved from further performance of his own primary obligations. These secondary obligations of the contract breaker and any concomitant relief of the other party from his own primary obligations also arise by implication of law-generally common law, but sometimes statute, as in the case of codifying statutes passed at the turn of the century, notably the Sale of Goods Act 1893. The contract, however, is just as much the source of secondary obligations as it is of primary obligations; and like primary obligations that are implied by law, secondary obligations too can be modified by agreement between the parties, although, for reasons to be mentioned later, they cannot, in my view, be totally excluded. In the instant case, the only secondary obligations and concomitant reliefs that are applicable arise by implication of the common law as modified by the express words of the contract... Every failure to perform a primary obligation is a breach of contract. The secondary obligation on the part of the contract breaker to which it gives rise by implication of the common law is to pay monetary compensation to the other party for the loss sustained by him in consequence of the breach..."

所以终止合约,是无辜方在违约方违反首要合约义务后,要求违约方履行次要合约义务作为替代;而撤销合约是将合约的首要合约义务当作从未存在过。

这个区别在欺诈/欺骗侵权(tort of deceit)关系密切,因为这与欺诈性误述关联在一起。如果要骗人,怎会不需要讲谎言,把虚假事实与/或承诺说到天花乱坠去诱导受害方?这样,如果骗子把财产(这可以是货物或金钱)骗到手,是不大可能把财产留在自己名下的,而是会尽快脱手或转售。如果受害方不警觉受骗或动作慢,没有在骗子要转售前撤销合约,这货物的产权就会因为合约的存在合法转让(transfer)给了另一位无辜的第三人或新买方。但如果受害方及时撤销合约,骗子之后才成功把货物脱手转售,由于产权在此时,已经因复原而自动回归(revesting title)受害方,所以骗子在自己没有货物产权的情况下,也无法成功通过转售把货物产权合约转移。

这就轮到新买方惨了，因为他再也无法向骗子要回货款。因为既然是骗子，他肯定已经失踪了。这看来对新买方很不公平，但双方遇到骗子受骗，两位都是无辜，由于骗子已经逃之夭夭，所以他们之间的争夺总难免其中有一位是要受到损害。这方面的案件多不胜数，如 Car and Universal Finance Ltd v. Caldwell(1965)1 QB 525 先例，对此将在本章之 6.3.1 段进一步详及。

至于被骗走的是金钱，由于金钱没有独特性(identifiable)，产权问题与其他财产的产权不一样。在合法与自愿交出的情况下，新主人对这笔钱的产权是"衍生获取"(derivatively acquired)，是新产生的产权，比原来的主人或任何其他人有更高与更优先的权利。所以受害方如果希望取回终止合约前已经支付了给骗子的钱，只能通过索赔损失而不是回归产权，这显然会是一场空。但如果是撤销合约，就可以开始追索(restitutionary action)是属于受害方的这笔被骗的钱或用这笔钱购买的其他财产，这就会涉及资产追踪(asset tracing)的课题。这可见笔者《证据法：基础理论、口头证据与专家证据》一书第十章之 2.7 段，不去重复。

3. 误述诱导产生的合约更改

在一个合约履行的过程中，经常会因为情况有改变而需要更改合约，就是合约双方合意对原合约的部分内容作出有约束力的改变。在英国法下，合约的实质性权利的更改或修改(amendment)是要求满足与订立原来有效的合约一样的要件，如双方的订约意图(contractual intention)、对价(consideration)、要约(offer)与接受(acceptance)等。所以，合约的更改(variation of contract and misrepresentation)会对原合约多改或少改，多改更会是改到原合约面目全非，更改后的合约会被视为一份新合约，虽然也会有只是以一个原合约的附件(addenda)的形式去更改部分内容的情况，但都遵循订约自由的大原则。[10]

3.1 因误述撤销的是更改后的整个新合约还是只是更改的部分

显然，合约更改也必须有一个谈判(negotiation)的过程，也会有一方向另一方做出了误述去诱导这个合约更改的产生。这样，如果另一方发觉了这个误述，他会有什么救济？如果是误述的正常救济，也就是撤销合约，会是撤销整个更改过的新合约还只是更改了原合约的部分？由于原合约在发生误述时已经是在履行，这会否是违约/毁约可享有终止合约的救济？但这误述是与原合约的条文并没有关系，所以也说不通。

这方面可先节录在《Misrepresentation, Mistake and Non-Disclosure》(2022 年，第 6 版)一书之 4－16 段说："**Rescission of a contract which itself varied an earlier contract.** The variation of a contract is effected by a new contract: the variation must itself

[10] 有关合约更改的课题，在笔者《合约履行、弃权与禁反言》一书第三章之 2 段有详论，此处不重复。

satisfy the same rules as are set for the formation and validity of a contract if the variation is to have the same binding force as the initial contract so as to modify or supersede it. Variations may take various different forms. The contract of variation may discharge the initial contract and replace it with a new contract, or simply modify one or more terms of the contract; or it may even simply discharge the initial contract without replacing it with a fresh contract; or it may take the form of a tripartite agreement of novation, under which a new party take the place of one of the existing parties, and the retiring party is released. **If the contract of variation is induced by misrepresentation, and if it is rescinded, the contract of variation retrospectively avoided, with the consequence that the original contract is resurrected.** ”(加黑部分是笔者的强调)

以上节录加黑的最后一句是说如果合约更改是由于误述的诱导所产生(这种情况在国际商业活动经常有),并且被误述方选择撤销,就会回复到没有更改前的情况,也就是只有原合约仍在。这表示即使更改后是新合约替代了原合约,在撤销后也令原合约“复生”(resurrect)。

稍后介绍的案例会令对这方面更明了,但不妨也先节录另一本权威书籍的说法。在《Chitty on Contracts》(2021 年,第 34 版)一书之 9 – 123 段说:“... Problems may well arise in deciding whether a refusal to continue with the contract in such circumstances amounts to a rescission or only a termination. It has been held that where a variation of a contract has been induced by fraud, the innocent party may rescind the variation ab initio, with the effect that the original contract is retrospectively revived. ”

3.2 The“Siboen”and The“Sibotre”(1976)1 Lloyd's Rep 293 先例

上述节录后可先介绍一个海事案件,在 The“Siboen”and The“Sibotre”先例中,该案案情涉及两艘 76,000 吨的油矿两用挪威旗船舶在 1970 年 8 月订立了长达 3 年的期租合约,承租人是西方石油公司(Occidental Petroleum Inc,以下简称 Oxy)[11] 集团下负责租船业务的利比利亚(Liberia)注册的附属公司,名为 Concord Petroleum Corp(以下简称 Concord)。同期间(1970 年 5 月至 1971 年 1 月),Oxy 也另租入大批船舶,共有 39 艘油轮(包括此先例中的两艘)。油轮市场是著名的会在短期内大起大落的市场,尤其是在对主要石油出口地的中东政治局势特别敏感的时期。之后由于油轮市场下跌,在 1971 年初 Oxy 就在这个雄心勃勃的租船计划中蒙受重大亏损,并需要紧急救亡。这亏损程度的严重性可以油轮现货市场的运费费率的世界标准(Worldscale,以下简称 WS)[12] 显示:在 1972 年春,油轮市场跌至历史性低点的 WS30。但到了 1973 年的夏天,油轮市场上升至 WS430。

---

〔11〕 西方石油公司于 1920 年成立,总部在美国洛杉矶,是美国第四大石油与天然气公司。

〔12〕 有关油轮市场的世界标准制度,参见杨良宜:《航运实务丛谈:程租合约》(第 7 册),大连海事大学出版社 1998 年版。

1971 年的救亡行动,主要是在两个方面。一方面就是在 3 月份成立一家新的利比利亚公司名为 New Concord,由集团公司直接控制,并且将 Concord 的大量资产与现金转移给 New Concord。这些行动是高度机密,外边的船东(租入的船舶)都不知道,以为仍是与以前资金雄厚的 Concord 在打交道,但实际上 Concord 已经变为是一家皮包公司。但这不表示 Oxy 可以脱身,因为 Concord 即使倒闭,船东们仍可以有办法去对付 Oxy,Oxy 只能是拖时间与增加船东追债的难度。例如,可以通过"撕破公司面纱"(lifting the corporate veil)去找上 Oxy,因为整个公司重组(reorganisation)是一个为了避债的骗局(sham)。这种剥离资产(assets stripping)的做法也具有欺诈性,只要追究起来就有严重后果,毕竟 Oxy 是美国一家上市公司。

所以,救亡行动的另一方面是与船东谈判减租金,并以承租人会马上倒闭,一拍两散作为威胁或增加压力。这样,船东为了保住这个宝贵的租船合约,就可能会让步。1972 年 3 月,承租人与船东在巴黎见面商谈。谈判期间,也可以想到承租人会讲什么来威胁,并会显示部分文件证据证明自己的困难,如会计师的财务报告等,但其中有不少"事实"是半真半假。例如:(1)承租人没有资产与蒙受严重亏损,随时会倒闭。(2)承租人目前就是靠 Oxy 的输血生存。(3)Oxy 也决定如果在这次的谈判无法将租金减下来就会让承租人倒闭。(4)显示承租人已经是亏损了 1.2 亿美元,但实际上有 6500 万美元只是亏损拨备,等于把租金减下来就不会有这一笔损失。(5)其他。之后,船东在无可奈何的情况下同意减租,并以 Oxy 集团公司做出履约担保作为交换或对价,并签署了附件确定减租金。

主要的上述陈述被 Kerr 大法官认定为欺诈性误述,其认为:"It … follows that during the Paris meeting misrepresentations to the following effect were made. First, fraudulent misrepresentations to the effect that the charterers had no substantial assets; that they depended on the support of the parent company and required the continuation of its support for survival; and there was no difficulty about letting them go bankrupt. If various owners, including the defendants in this action, did not agree to renegotiation the charters; and that there was a real possibility that the charterers would be allowed to go bankrupt if the owners did not agree. …"

但船东的让步并没有带来双方的友好,这也是对抗性的本质与商人贪利的国际商业环境的现实。以 1973 年 4 月市场状况为例,当时油轮市场已经在上升,为 WS 110,相当于两艘油轮在原租约的租金。而且船东看到 Oxy 的公司年报后,发觉它的租船业务根本不是在巴黎谈判时所表达的严重亏损,甚至还有一点盈利,所以就写了一封很强硬与不客气的信给 Oxy 要求回复到原租约的租金,也就是去撤销同意减租的附件。但 Oxy 拒绝,并坚持严格按租约加上附件去履行。这最终导致船东将两艘油轮撤船以终止两份租约。在撤船后,油轮市场持续上升并在 1973 年达到 WS 430。承租人或 Oxy 于是向船东提起金额很大的损失索赔,这也被 Kerr 大法官认定船东的单方面撤船是违约/毁约,需要对承租人作出赔偿。但这不是本段的针对,所以略过不多谈。

回到巴黎和谈中被认定的欺诈性误述，其带来的救济是船东有权撤销减租的附件。这也表示船东可以向承租人索赔因为附件带来的减租而少收的租金差额。但这不影响在附件前或附件后双方履行原租约的责任与产生的索赔权利，包括在附件后船东的单方面撤船违约事件，只不过在赔偿方面可以与船东之前少交的租金对冲。

3.3　BV Nederlandse Industrie Van Eiprodukten v. Rembrandt Enterprises Inc (2018) EWHC 1857(Comm)先例

另举近期的 BV Nederlandse Industrie Van Eiprodukten v. Rembrandt Enterprises Inc 先例，[13] 案情涉及美国 2015 年因禽流感(avian flu)宰杀大量母鸡导致鸡蛋供应短缺，这令鸡蛋市场价格上涨。被告(Rembrandt)美国鸡蛋供应商于是与原告荷兰鸡蛋供应商(Nederlandse，以下简称 NIVE)在 2015 年 5 月 13 日订立了 2 年的供应合约，其中同意了不同鸡蛋产品的供应数量与价格。供应合约中 NIVE 也保证(warrant)鸡蛋产品符合规格(但没有说明什么规格)与必须获得美国农业部(USDA)/食品安全与检查(FSIS)的进口批准。

开始供应是在美国 USDA/FSIS 与荷兰当局批准进出口为准，但当局如何检查进口鸡蛋仍未有定局，这涉及美国当局与荷兰当局的商讨。到了 2015 年 6 月 1 日美国 FSIS 才正式批准或承认荷兰当局对鸡蛋产品的检查。

在 2015 年 5 月 21 日，NIVE 首次被荷兰当局告知进口美国需要做的事情，NIVE 发觉这额外费用会增加成本并导致失去利润，所以希望把这笔不可预见的额外费用转移给 Rembrandt。到了 6 月 12 日，在 Rembrandt 对 NIVE 供应鸡蛋产品的催促下，NIVE 以电邮回应说："no inspectors for grading and processing processes had yet been appointed and only after that could start shipping ... we also still need to agree on the cost for grading and inspection, which we have estimated as EUR 2.5/kg..."

Rembrandt 前初是抗拒，在 6 月 13 日的电邮中说："we have to say we have a contract, willing to talk but the economics of the present requests are off the table."

而当时美国与欧洲的鸡蛋市场价格正在急升，Rembrandt 也急需鸡蛋产品的供应。总之在双方一轮的谈判后，最终在 2015 年 6 月 24 日双方签订了一个新合约，将每公斤的鸡蛋产品价格提高了 2.5 欧元，说是单纯是为了满足美国进口要求而产生的额外费用，但 NIVE 证人在开庭的交叉盘问中承认实际上还包括原告想要赚取更多利润的因素。

但市场急升也会暴跌，到了 2015 年 9 月初，Rembrandt 认为合约价格太高并试图让 NIVE 减低价格，但不成功。再到了该年 11 月，美国市场有谣言说是荷兰的产品并不符合美国的规定要求，并引起民众的关心。这导致 Rembrandt 在 2016 年 1 月 26

〔13〕 BV Nederlandse Industrie Van Eiprodukten v. Rembrandt Enterprises Inc(2019) EWCA Civ 596 先例也针对欺诈性误述的举证责任，可见本书第一章之 1.3.6 段。

日以鸡蛋产品不符合供应合约的保证为由拒绝接收鸡蛋产品,最终导致供应合约的终止。

NIVE 根据合约的英国法院专属管辖条文(exclusive jurisdiction clause)以 Rembrandt 的违约/毁约提起诉讼索赔损失,但 Rembrandt 以 NIVE 对美国进口检查费用的 EUR 2.5/kg 的欺诈性误述与违反对鸡蛋的质量保证为由抗辩。Rembrandt 同时反索赔或要求退还合约终止前以高价供应与接受了的鸡蛋产品,因为如果被法院认定有误述与可撤销合约,就要回复到双方没有订立合约的地位。

法院判 NIVE 并没有违反保证,但这与本段题目无关,所以在此不展开论述。但 NIVE 误述成立,Teare 大法官在聆听了开庭审理双方证人的盘问后认定:

"It seems to me that what was said about the additional costs was a negotiating device used to persuade Rembrandt to agree an increase to the already agreed price. **The EUR 2.50 per kg. was not believed by NIVE to be a genuine estimate of the additional costs**. That is why Jasper van Loon(NIVE 的证人)described it as 'merely' the price increase which was being sought. That is why he found himself unable to say that it was a genuine estimate of the additional cost. **He knew that it contained additional profit. It must follow that NIVE misrepresented a fact, namely, that NIVE believed that the figures were a genuine estimate of the additional costs.** Counsel for NIVE fairly accepted in his closing oral submissions that he could not argue the contrary. ...

More recent authority explains that the test is whether the representee is entitled to take the statement seriously rather than with a pinch of salt ... Having regard to the number of times that NIVE raised the question of additional costs and NIVE's provision, in response to a request, of a 'calculation' of such costs I find it impossible to say that Rembrandt was not entitled to take what NIVE said seriously. Rembrandt was intended by NIVE to regard the figures as a genuine estimate of cost. ...

The conclusion I have reached is that, whilst Mr. Rettig(Rembrandt 的证人)**might have agreed** to the requested price increase, NIVE cannot show that he **would have agreed** to the requested price increase. The **fraudulent misrepresentation** as to the additional costs of complying with the US regulations **was made for the very purpose of persuading Rembrandt to agree the requested price increase**. That end was achieved. **Very strong evidence is required to rebut the presumption or inference of inducement in such a case**. Whilst there is evidence that ... Rembrandt, might have agreed to the requested price increase had the misrepresentation not been made I do not consider that that evidence has the clarity and cogency necessary to enable NIVE to persuade the court that Mr. Rettig would in fact have agreed to the requested price increase even if the misrepresentation had not been made."(加黑部分是笔者的强调)

在救济方面,由于是以新合约提高价格,而新合约因为误述被撤销后原合约"复生”,NIVE 可以违约/毁约索赔损失,但是计算金额是要根据原合约中较低的价格计算。Teare 大法官说:“It is now accepted that the effect of rescinding the revised contract is that the original contract is resurrected. The original contract had been brought to an end by the operation of … the revised contract. Once the revised contract is rescinded, it cannot now be regarded as having brought the original contract to an end. Thus …, that the effect of rescission is that NIVE can still recover damages for breach of the original contract(the original contract having been entered into freely and unaffected by any misrepresentation …). Such damages must be assessed upon the basis of the originally agreed prices, …”

之后 NIVE 上诉,上诉庭[(2019) EWCA Civ 596]也支持了一审判决。

4. 撤销的是全部或只是部分合约

大原则是误述的撤销合约是只能去撤销全部或整份的合约,而不能只是部分。这也完全合理,因为误述导致整份合约的产生有缺陷而可使合约无效,而撤销一个无效的合约也就需要去回复到原状,让双方回复到没有合约产生过的地位,而不是不伦不类的有半份合约被撤销(有关误述所针对或有关联部分),但另半份合约处于被保留的地位。

所以,只部分撤销是说不通也行不通。例如因为卖方对货物有误述就有权撤销并无需履行,但买方支付货价不涉及误述就不去撤销并需要履行与作出支付。说不通与不合理之处自然是显而易见的,而行不通是这两部分的合约内容不可分割,如货价是需要卖方实际供应或付运多少货量后才算得出来。真正能够被分割出来不受撤销合约影响的,只会是仲裁条文(arbitration clause)或专属管辖条文(exclusive jurisdiction clause)。换言之,如果双方对是否发生过误述与被陈述方有否依赖、是否正确撤销合约或实是毁约/违约等有争议,在双方有一条有效的仲裁条文的情况下,需要通过仲裁去解决争议。这也是所谓的仲裁条文独立原则(separation principle)。[14]

针对这上述介绍的大原则,接下去的分段将探讨在各种不同的情况下如何适用。可先节录一些权威书籍的说法。

在《Misrepresentation, Mistake and Non-Disclosure》(2022 年,第 6 版)一书之 4－13 段中说:“**Rescission of the whole contract; rescission of part of the contract** The general rule is that if rescission operates, the contract is set aside in its entirety: it is not simply set aside as regards a limited part of the contract which was directly affected by the misrepresentation relied upon to claim the remedy. This rule has two dimensions.

〔14〕 关于独立原则可见笔者《仲裁法:从 1996 年英国仲裁法到国际商务仲裁》一书第五章之 8.4 段。

First, the representee must rescind the whole contract or none of it: he cannot elect to rescind only the part affected by the misrepresentation, whilst retaining the advantage of the remainder of the contract. The bar on partial rescission applies not only to inseverable parts of a single contract, but also to contracts which form part of an indivisible bargain. Similarly, if the representee is unable to make restitution of part of the benefits obtained under the contract, he cannot rescind as regards the remaining part: if a contract cannot be rescinded in toto it cannot be rescinded at all ...

Secondly, the representor cannot resist rescission of the whole of the contract if the representee has a valid claim for rescission ... It flows from the fact that the remedy for rescission of the contract for misrepresentation is not within the discretion of the court, but is available as of right to a representee who satisfies the requirements of the remedy ... As long as there is no impediment to rescission, such as the representee not being able and willing to make restitution of benefits obtained under the contract, the representor has no choice but to submit to rescission of the entire contract."

4.1 不可分割合约或可分割合约的撤销

这可先节录《Misrepresentation, Mistake and Non-Disclosure》(2022 年,第 6 版)一书之 4 - 14 段的观点:"**Severable contracts** ... If what appears to be a single contract should properly be construed as severable into separate contracts, rescission will be available of the whole of each separate contract which is affected by the relevant misrepresentation. For example, a single insurance policy may be written so as to separate the risks into separate contracts, with the result that a misrepresentation with respect to one risk will vitiate only the contract relating to that risk. And a composite insurance policy-a single insurance policy which insures two or more persons with separate interests (such as the landlord and tenant of property) - will generally be treated as containing separate contracts, so that a pre - contractual misrepresentation by one insured will allow the insurer to rescind the policy only as far as it relates to that insured. A contract for the allotment of shares in a company has also been held to be a severable contract, so that the shareholder could rescind in relation to the shares he still held where he had parted with part of the shareholding before discovering the fraud which induced him to take the shares."

有关一个合约记录在一份完整的文件是可分割(divisible/severable contract)或不可分割(indivisible),在笔者其他的书籍多处有涉及或详论。例如在《合约的履行、弃权与禁反言》一书第一章之 3.5.4 段与第二章之 8 段均有涉及,分别去探讨毁约/违约令合约终止(termination by repudiatory breach)与合约受阻(frustration)对可分割或不可分割合约的差异。由于内容太多,不会在此再重复,只简单重复少数对这一点的权威说法。

在 Larrinaga v. Soc. Franco – Americaine des Phosphates (1923) 14 Lloyd's Rep 457

贵族院先例中，Sumner 勋爵说 6 个可分割的程租合约，只不过被包括在一个包运合约或框架协议中，这完全是可以的：“The charter-party provides for six separate voyages, each being a distinct commercial adventure. There is no reason why a single contract should not provide for many adventures, nor why these adventures should not be entirely independent of one another.”

另是在 The“Nema”(1980)2 Lloyd's Rep 83 贵族院先例的一审中，Goff 大法官说：“... in my judgment, where a single contractual document provides for what Lord Atkinson called：'six wholly distinct, separate and severable adventures between which there was no interdependence in the sense that the carrying out of any one of them was made to depend in any way upon the carrying out or abandonment of any of the others ...' That this transaction has in law no different effect from a divisible contract as I have described it, viz. a single transaction, contained in one contractual document, which provides for a number of contracts. In both cases, ... anticipatory repudiation or fundamental breach, will be considered in relation to each adventure or separate contract independently; and likewise so will be frustration. ...”

可以与毁约/违约而终止合约或合约受阻同样的道理或精神去分析因误述撤销合约的情况。例如在一个 10 年的煤炭供应合约中，期间每个月付运一次 5 万吨的煤炭，供应合约的条文没有把每月的付运串起来，如没有说明从上一次成功付运起算的 1 个月后才付运下一次等，明显每个月的付运就是可分割的独立、自主的合约。毕竟在订约自由下，双方也可以其他形式去签订 10 年的煤炭供应，如有一份框架协议(framework agreement)，然后每月一次的付运，就签一份针对性的付运合约。

这样，如果在履行期间发生了可以令该合约短期受阻的事件，如中国法律禁止煤炭进口 3 个月，显然不足以令一个 10 年的供应合约受阻，也不是中国进口商希望的结果，但足以保护中国进口商可以主张这 3 个月共 3 次的付运无法履行是由于可分割而去各自受阻。相反，如果该供应合约不可分割，由于履行合约承诺在英国法律下是绝对或具有严格责任的，而中国进口商无法履行这 3 次的付运是明显的违约，需要赔偿供应商的损失主要就是这 3 次付运的预期利润了。

在同样道理下，这 3 次或某次的付运，也可能会发生可诉误述。例如供应商对中国进口商误述付运船舶或付运日期等，并导致后者同意该次付运，也可以撤销该次受误述影响的付运，但不撤销整个在几年前订立，并没有任何误述的 10 年供应合约，或是其他不涉及有关误述的付运。

上述节录的《Misrepresentation, Mistake and Non-Disclosure》一书的内容中介绍了英国保险合约或保单(policy)是一种典型的可分割合约，这又是与刚才举的 10 年供应合约不同的情况。伦敦的保险市场是一个“签名认数市场”(subscription market)，这已是好几百年的做法，被视为有很多好处，主要是保险就是为了分散风险，“再保”(reinsurance)故然是一个重要的分散风险做法，但即使是一线的保险，也往往是面对一票巨大的承保风险,根本不是一位保险人或一家保险公司能吃得下,然后再安排再保的。

伦敦的签名认数市场就解决了这方面的问题。做法就是通过受保人(insured/assured)委任的保险经纪人去对某特定风险(如一艘或多艘船舶、飞机或一项工程等)的投保作安排。保险经纪人就会定一份恰当的承保条(slip),[15]并接下去寻找一个带头人(leader 或 leading underwriter)。这带头保险人会是在承保某类风险有经验、有名气、受尊重与有专业知识的人士。双方根据承保条的内容谈判后,确定承保风险应支付的保费费率与其他条件,他会在承保条签字确认愿意"认数",也就是接受承保风险的百分比,如 3% 或 5% 不等,这也是受保人与带头保险人之间有法律约束力的保险合约了。早在 Ionides v. Pacific Fire & Marine Insurance Co(1871)LR 6 QB 674 先例中,Blackburn 大法官说:"The slip is, in practice, and according to the understanding of those engaged in marine insurance, the complete and final contract between the parties, fixing the terms of the insurance and the premium, and neither party can, without the assent of the other, deviate from the terms thus agreed on without a breach of faith, …"

之后,保险经纪人就会以该份只是开了头的承保单去寻找其他凭经纪人的经验知道会相信带头保险人对有关风险的专业判断的其他保险人,不论是劳合社的其他承保小组(syndicate)、伦敦或全球保险公司,看他们各自是否愿意认数以及认数多少百分比,直到 100% 都有了认数,就表示保险经纪人投保有关风险的任务已是大功告成。这表示一份承保条会有好几十家不同的保险人/保险公司区别签字去认数承保一定百分比的承保风险,各自享有按比例的好处(分摊的保费)与出现承保风险的事故与蒙受的损失,承担按比例的赔偿责任。也表示这一份承保条(或在可能长达几个月后拟定的一份保单),实际上是包括了有几十份独立与不同合约方(因为不同保险人/保险公司)的保险合约。[16] 这在 American Airlines v. Hope(1974)2 Lloyd's Rep 301 贵族院先例中,Diplock 勋爵有说:"The broker takes the slip in the first instance to an underwriter whom he has selected to deal with as a leading underwriter, ie, one who has a reputation in the market as an expert in the kind of cover required and whose lead is likely to be followed by other insurers in the market. If it is the first contract of insurance covering that risk in which a particular underwriter has acted as leading underwriter it is treated as an original insurance. The broker and the leading underwriter

---

[15] 在 2002 年 2 月生效与使用的承保条标准格式 LMP BRAT form(代表 London Market Practice, Broker Reform Action Team)中,有四部分,包括:(1)风险的细节(包括与标准合约相同与不同的合约条文);(2)签名认数合约;(3)信息(所有需要自动披露给保险人考虑是否接受承保与厘定保费费率的有实质重要性的有关投保风险的信息与事实);(4)财务与法规事宜。

[16] 见 The"Zephyr"(1985)2 Lloyd's Rep 529; Aneco Reinsurance Underwriting Ltd v. Johnson & Higgins Ltd(2001)UKHL 51 等先例。

go through the slip together. They agree on any amendments to the broker's draft and fix the premium. When agreement has been reached the leading underwriter initials the slip for his proportion of the cover and the broker then takes the initialled slip round the market to other insurers who initial it for such proportion of the cover as each is willing to accept. For practical purposes all the negotiations about the terms of the insurance and the rate of premium are carried on between the broker and the leading underwriter alone."

由于同一份保单/保险合约可以分割为多份不同与独立的保险合约,每一位保险人/保险公司为他们愿意认数的百分比承担赔付责任,如果发生拒赔,受保人也需要把所有认数的保险人/保险公司一并作为共同被告(可能会有几十个被告)去提起诉讼索偿。理论上有可能各保险人/保险公司会有自己的盘算与不同做法,但由于伦敦保险市场有悠久历史与既定的游戏规则,所以也不会给受保人带来困难与混乱。一般就是跟着带头人(follow the leader),不论是愿意赔付或是拒赔或是在诉讼中达成部分赔付的和解,所有保险人/保险公司都是以带头人的决定为准。也是在理论上,保险经纪人会在寻找不同保险人/保险公司去洽谈以完成100%的承保时,对个别不同的保险人/保险公司做出误述并导致个别主张撤销该占一定百分比的保险合约。但这只是理论上,在专业的保险经纪人与伦敦市场的做法下,很少发生此情况。因为对整个承保风险的谈判只是在保险经纪人与带头保险人之间才会发生,也只有在谈判时才会出现误述或是不披露信息与事实的情况。但这也不是不可能发生,例如保险经纪人无法达成100%的认数,于是找到其中一间保险公司说:"这次承保的风险确实没什么油水,但是如果你再认数剩下的几个百分比,之后我会再给你几票好生意来补偿。"而之后保险经纪人并没有给该保险公司什么好生意,该保险公司就可以误述撤销合约,但撤销的只能是之后多认购的部分,也不影响带头人、其他保险公司的合约。

4.2 合约链中多份相关合约

首先节录《Misrepresentation, Mistake and Non-Disclosure》(2022年,第6版)一书之4-15段:"**Rescission of chains of contracts and of related contracts** Sometimes there will be a chain of contracts, such as where A sells goods to B, which B sells on to C. If B has a claim against A to rescind the first contract, its exercise is likely to be dependent on C first rescinding his contract with B, since it will generally be impossible for B to restore the goods as long as the contract with C is outstanding. However, if C is willing and able to rescind that contract, B is reinvested with the rights of property in the goods, so allowing the exercise of his right of rescission against A. However, for each link in the chain of contracts the requirements of rescission must be satisfied and the remedy sought by the party with the right to it. So, to take a different example, if by a misrepresentation X induces Y to buy goods, and Y later transfers the goods to Z, Z's remedy of rescission is normally only available against Y. He has no right as against X to require him to take back the goods and hand over the purchase price he received from Y. The misrepresentation made by X to Y is spent when Y buys the property, and Z must find a separate claim, based on Y's own misrepresentation to him, in order to rescind the contract with Y."

其次谈谈合约链，这经常发生的情况对很多商业人士都不会陌生。在国际商品买卖中，同一个交易与同一票货物几乎大多数都涉及合约链：A 以 FOB 卖给 B，B 以 CIF 转卖给 C，C 也会以不同价格再以 CIF 转卖给 D，反正这种合约链屡见不鲜。但显然每一个合约都是独立，更是涉及不同的合约方。所以，误述会只发生在个别的合约中但不影响合约链的其他合约。毕竟，可诉误述除了错误的信息与事实外，还有其他要件，如诱导与依赖。所以即使是对货物质量或特征的误述，也会是只与 A 与 B 之间的合约有关，让 B 有一个裁量权去撤销合约，使其无效。但问题是，B 已经把货物转卖给了 C，C 再转卖给了 D。这些相关合约不一定有发生过相同的可诉误述，而即使是有，C 或 D 也不见得想撤销合约。这表示即使是 B 想撤销合约（例如 B 是以高价购买，并在转卖中因市场下跌而亏损），也无法去把货物归还给 A，并让双方回复到订约前的地位了。所以有说法是在这种国际货物或商品买卖的合约链，B 一旦把货物转售与交出，B 对 A 撤销合约的救济就已经是"作废"（spent）。

但正如 Blackburn 勋爵在 Erlanger v. New Sombrero Phosphate Co（1878）3 App Cas 1218 贵族院先例说，衡平救济虽然不涉及金钱损失的赔偿，但可以为达到公平（也就是在误述下撤销合约能够尽量做到复原）去尽量灵活处理。已经在本章之 3.3 段详细介绍的 BV Nederlandse Industrie Van Eiprodukten v. Rembrandt Enterprises Inc（2018）EWHC 1857（Comm）先例中，Rembrandt 希望以 NIVE 对美国进口检查费用的误述为由去撤销原合约，但由于已经付运了部分鸡蛋产品并且被转卖，加上可以想到这种货物的寿命（shelf - life）不长，肯定已经被处理了。这代表无法复原去退回鸡蛋产品给 NIVE，所以 Rembrandt 想出"以钱代货"并创造一个"pecuniary counter-restitution"的新名词，把早前转卖的售价退回给 NIVE，说这可以在现实做到复原（practically just）。但该先例最后无须对这个争议去作出决定，所以没有定论或说法。Teare 大法官说："Rembrandt is so entitled so long it is able to provide restitution of the egg product supplied to it between September 2015 and January 2016. That cannot do because the egg product has been sold by Rembrandt. It was therefore submitted on behalf of NIVE that rescission was not available. In response it was submitted on behalf of Rembrandt that it can give 'pecuniary counter-restitution' in the form of the proceeds of selling the egg product. It was submitted that that was permissible because it was 'practically just', notwithstanding that it would not 'restore the parties precisely to the state they were in before the contract' … On behalf of NIVE it was said that English law does not permit 'substitute counter restitution' by paying over the value of the goods supplied instead of returning the goods themselves. … it is not necessary for the court to resolve the interesting questions of law as to the extent to which, if at all, a party seeking rescission may give 'pecuniary counter restitution' where return of the goods themselves is not possible."

如果"以钱代货"的"pecuniary counter - restitution"的说法可以确立,就等于完全改变了历史悠久的英国法律地位,清除了撤销合约最主要的一个障碍,即本章之5段将介绍的回复到双方没有产生合约的地位。这样几乎所有的商业合约都可以撤销,再也不存在买方一旦把货物转卖,撤销合约的救济就作废的说法,因为买方是乐得将亏了一大笔的转卖费用"归还"给误述的卖方。在此先例,因为撤销的是之后每千克涨价2.5欧元的合约可以与违约/毁约的损失对冲,所以Teare大法官无需对这个问题作出决定。而即使案情需要,一审法院也只能跟从过去的先例,要最高院才能改变这个历史悠久的法律地位;甚至即使最高院认为需要改变,也可能不愿改变,而最好是交由议会立法改变。这是因为立法还有其他好处,不仅可以借机全面针对这个问题,也可以因其没有追溯力,而只影响将来的合约或争议;而普通法不同,如果最高院改变了这个法律地位,会带来大量本来已经无望放弃但时效未过的诉讼。

4.3　一个不可分割交易中多份相关合约

可节录O'Sullivan, Zakrzewski & Elliott合著的*The Law of Rescission*(2014年,第2版)一书之19 - 05段:

"The rule against partial rescission applies to bargains rather than individual contracts. Rescission will accordingly be refused where the contract in question is part of a wider transaction, the components of which are commercially interdependent in the sense that they were contracted each in consideration or contemplation of the others and were intended to be performed together. For example, in Maguire v. Makaronis (1997) 188 CLR 449 the High Court of Australia reversed the decision of the court below, which had been to rescind a mortgage while leaving the underlying contractual covenants intact. The effect of that had been to leave the borrower in possession of the loan money while depriving the lender of his security. The High Court considered this to involve an impermissible reformation of a single bargain comprised of two instruments.

By contrast, where a contract or wider transaction is severable according to conventional principles, there is usually no difficulty with rescinding one severable part and leaving the remainder on foot. In effect the court must find that the obligations in respect of which rescission is claimed form a self - contained bargain. There may be cases, however, in which a defendant would suffer unjustified prejudice if one agreement were set aside in circumstances where a second independent agreement remained on foot, such that substantial restitutio in integrum is not possible."

以上节录是说不可分割的合约不可部分撤销的原则也适用在一个不可分割的交易中,即使是该交易涉及多份有关与相互依赖(inter - dependent)的合约。也就是说,一旦发生误述,即使只影响其中一份合约,撤销的救济也是要么全部撤销,要么就不能撤销。毕竟撤销是衡平法救济,涉及法院的裁量权,不是一定要去作出撤销的救济。法院更是要考虑撤销是否能够基本上做到把双方复原到交易前的地位,不会让其中一方在交易中去撤销个别不利的合约取巧,或因此受到严重损害甚至使交易推进不下去。

而如果这交易涉及的多份合约是可以分割与独立对待,就不影响对受到误述诱导的个别独立合约去主张撤销的救济了。这可以一个简单的日常生活的例子帮助理解,例如在商场买了电冰箱和扫地机器人,销售人员误述扫地机器人是扫拖一体的,但是其实根本不能拖地,顾客可以撤销购买扫地机器人的合约。但是电冰箱是一个完全可以分割的合约,就不能撤销。但如果顾客买的是扫地机器人和相关配件,显然双方都明白这是一个不可分割的买卖交易,就可以同时撤销这两份合约。这可节录《Misrepresentation, Mistake and Non-Disclosure》(2022 年,第 6 版)一书之 4 - 15 段:"Where there are two or more related contracts, each must normally be considered separately as regards any claim for rescission. So if a purchaser buys two separate items, under two separate contracts from the same vendor, e. g. separate lots at auction, a misrepresentation by the vendor as to one of the items will not normally allow the purchaser to rescind also the second contract, unless both parties knew and understood that the two contracts were interdependent."

4.3.1 同一个交易中涉及多份关联与相互依赖的合约/协议难以分割的现实

显然,这在每一个交易,所签订的多份合约到底是相互依赖或是可以分割与独立,就要看个别案件的案情了。可以说,在今天复杂的国际商业交易如公司并购(M& A transaction)或国际融资合约中,都会涉及多份合约,绝少双方当事人之间只有一份合约。也可以说,这多份合约几乎肯定相互依赖或有关联,很少能够从整个交易中分割出来,允许只撤销受误述影响的个别合约。例如在一个国际融资并涉及通过搭建可变利益实体[Various Interest Entity(VIE),又称协议控制]的公司架构〔17〕中,是不可能把这些串在一起的合约进行个别撤销。甚至是如果不适合撤销的救济,笔者怀疑法院在认定有否误述时也会受潜移默化的影响变得更严格。

上述节录所提到的 Maguire v. Makaronis(1997)188 CLR 449 澳大利亚先例中,谈不上是一个复杂的国际商业交易,最高院也推翻了一审与上诉庭的判决,不允许在一个贷款的交易中撤销抵押,因为这等于剥夺了原告作为抵押权人的担保,让现实上无法还债的被告无需继续还债。案情为被告 Makaronis 夫妻以自己的房屋作为抵押向原告 Maguire(也是被告的律师)以短期高息(达 24%)贷款购买一个养鸡的农场,但因为经营不善无法还债,导致原告向法院申请占有抵押的房屋。被告的抗辩是原告有一个"诚信责任"(fiduciary duty)与"小心谨慎责任"(duty of care),但没有向他

〔17〕 这种做法在本书第一章之 2.7.1 段有详细介绍。

们披露贷款的钱来自他自己而不是来自银行等，这相当于误述。一审法院也认定了原告违反了诚信责任，并撤销抵押与有关的登记。这判决最后被最高院推翻，因为除了做不到回复到交易前的原状外，对确实是贷了款的原告也不公平合理。所以把案件发还（remit）给上诉庭考虑判决要求被告在命令后30天内清还债务与利息，否则原告可占有抵押与登记了抵押权的房屋。

在更复杂的商业交易中，只会有更多关联性的合约/协议针对方方面面的问题。例如NGM Sustainable Developments v. Wallis（2015）EWHC 2089（Ch）先例中，涉及原告想以165万英镑的价格购买一块土地开发的融资贷款交易，该交易涉及了9个关联合约，后来原告以被告欺诈性误述要求撤销其中的4个合约，并取回押记作为担保的专利（涉及漂浮建筑的浮力基底或平台结构与如何建设），并索赔失去开发土地的机会损失。[18] 审理的Peter Smith大法官不认为指控的误述成立，而即使成立，针对部分撤销也不认同说："It seems to me that one cannot pick and choose from the suite of documents in respect to which rescission is sought. It is partial rescission. It cannot be right for NCM（原告）to seek to retain the Patent without unscrambling all the transactions. ..."

同样说法也可见Deutsche Bank AG v. Unitech Global Ltd（2017）EWHC 1381（Comm）先例[19]的一审，Cooke大法官说："The rule against partial rescission applies, it is said, to bargains rather than merely to individual contracts. Rescission will be refused where a contract in question is part of a wider transaction, the components of which are commercially inter - dependent, in the sense that they were contracted each in consideration or contemplation of the others and were intended to be performed together."

4.3.2 Marme Inversiones 2007 SL v. NatWest Markets Plc（2019）EWHC 366（Comm）先例

接下去笔者在此较全面介绍与上一小段内容相关的一个重要近期先例。在Marme Inversiones 2007 SL v. NatWest Markets Plc先例[20]中，Picken大法官说："It is clear, therefore, that the bar on partial rescission applies not only to inseverable parts of a single contract but also to contracts which form part of an indivisible bargain. The underlying principle is that a party seeking rescission should not be allowed to pick and choose which parts of the transaction to perform since that would involve rewriting the parties' bargain."

该先例中发生争议的合约是利率掉期合约，但在介绍该利率掉期合约之前，为了帮助读者理解整个交易安排，先将该利率掉期合约发生的背景介绍一下。原告

---

〔18〕 关于机会损失可见笔者《损失赔偿与救济》一书第六章之4段。

〔19〕 该先例的事实背景可见本书第五章之6.3.3.3.2段，此先例是另一个卫星诉讼。

〔20〕 这也是在本书第二章之1.4.5段提到的与LIBOR丑闻有关的一系列先例中的一个。

Marme 是荷兰公司 Ramblas 为了完成在西班牙的地产交易而专门在西班牙设立的特殊目的公司(special purpose vehicle)。Marme 与西班牙最大的国际银行桑坦德银行(Santander)就一个在西班牙首都马德里的名为金融城的地产项目进行磋商。双方于 2008 年 1 月 25 日签署了一个买卖回租协议(Sale and Leaseback Agreement),该协议约定 Marme 以 19 亿欧元的价格从桑坦德银行处收购金融城地产项目,而桑坦德银行承诺将会租用金融城 40 年,每年的租金最初约定为 7408 万欧元,后来上调至每年 8200 多万欧元。该交易被指是当时欧洲最大的地产交易,涉及巨额融资。

Marme 本来想将每年会收到的租金做成资产包以发行债券的形式在金融市场上进行融资,但因为 2008 年金融海啸带来的信贷危机,这种做法显然不是一个好的选择。后来,Marme 为收购金融城地产项目达成的融资安排主要包括以下三项:(1)与8 家银行组成的银团(包括 Bayerische Landesbank、HSH Nordbank AG、The Royal Bank of Scotland plc、ING Real Estate Finance SE E. F. C. ,S. A. 、ING Bank N. V. 、Caixa d'Estalvis i Pensions de Barcelona、Raiffeisen Zentralbank Österreich Aktiengesellschaft、Deutsche Postbank AG)达成了一份 5 年期总额为 15.75 亿欧元的银团贷款合约,贷款利息为欧元同业银行间拆借利率(EURIBOR) +1.6%;(2)由苏格兰皇家银行(The Royal Bank of Scotland,以下简称 RBS)提供 2 亿欧元的夹层初级贷款(mezzanine junior loan)作为给 Marme 母公司 Ramblas 的续贷;(3)由 Ramblas 的两位股东 Maud 先生与 Quinlan 先生注资 1.5 亿欧元。后来,RBS 更是为 Maud 先生与 Quinlan 先生负责注资的 1.5 亿欧元向他们提供了 7500 万欧元的个人贷款。

银团贷款协议约定 Marme 要安排利率掉期以对冲利率变化带来的风险。这才带来本案例中起争议的利率掉期合约。Marme 与 RBS 作为牵头银行的银团包括:(1)Natwest Markets Plc(RBS 旗下负责投资银行业务的子公司,也即代表 RBS);(2)HSH Nordbank AG;(3)Bayerische Landesbank;(4)ING Bank NV;(5)Caixabank SA 等5 家银行商讨利率掉期的安排,并于2008 年9 月 12 日与 RBS 订立了利率掉期合约,而 RBS 随后也与其他 4 家银行订立了背靠背的利率掉期合约,该合约使用的是著名的国际掉期与衍生工具协会(International Swaps and Derivatives Association,以下简称 ISDA)的标准合约格式。掉期安排为 Marme 从掉期合约订立起至 2023 年 8 月 20 日期间以固定的 3.3030% 的年利率向 RBS 支付利息,该固定利率逐年增加,直至达到最高的 6.7635%。而 RBS 则是按照 3 个月的浮动 EURIBOR 利率支付给 Marme。

随着 2008 年金融海啸席卷全球,Marme 最终在无法取得进一步融资的情况下无力偿还在银团贷款下 2013 年 9 月 13 日到期的那一笔分期还款而在银团贷款协议下违约。随后 Marme 向西班牙法院申请了自愿破产。RBS 与其他 4 家银行在利率掉期合约下向 Marme 索赔共计 7.1 亿欧元。Marme 则以 RBS 存在默示误述(implied misrepresentation)〔21〕为由要求撤销利率掉期合约。在本案中作为原告的 Marme 指称:曾经在英国巴克莱银行任职的 Philippe Moryoussef 先生由于在巴克莱银行任职期间参与操纵 EURIBOR 利率,在 2008 年金融海啸开始后被调查,并于 2018 年以串谋与欺诈罪被判监 8 年;而在 2007 年 8 月至 2009 年 9 月期间,Moryoussef 先生在 RBS 担任其欧元利率衍生品部门的主管,Marme 与 RBS 商谈利率掉期合约的相关时间也在这个期间内,Moryoussef 先生在 RBS 工作期间,RBS 也有参与操纵 EURIBOR 或至少通过 Moryoussef 先生知道有此操纵行为的存在;RBS 在与 Marme 订立利率掉期合约期间对 Marme 存在他自己是诚实与没有参与操纵 EURIBOR 的默示陈述,而该默示陈述不正确。Marme 进而以 RBS 存在误述与自己有依赖主张撤销利率掉期合约。Marme 指称 RBS 做出的不正确的默示陈述主要包括以下五项内容:(1)在与 Marme 订立利率掉期合约的相关时间与订约的日期,RBS 没有参与操纵 EURIBOR。(2)在与 Marme 订立利率掉期合约的相关时间与订约的日期,RBS 没有理由认为银团中其他银行有参与操纵 EURIBOR。(3)在与 Marme 订立利率掉期合约的相关时间与订约的日期,RBS 没有进行任何会破坏 EURIBOR 公信力的行为,并且也无意在将来进行该破坏行为。(4)在与 Marme 订立利率掉期合约的相关时间与订约的日期,RBS 没有理由认为银团中其他银行有进行任何会破坏 EURIBOR 公信力的行为,并且也无意在将来进行该破坏行为。(5)在与 Marme 订立利率掉期合约的相关时间与订约的日期,在确定 EURIBOR 的程序中,RBS 始终都是诚实行事,并且将会一直诚实行事。

Picken 大法官否定了 Marme 主张的 RBS 存在不正确的默示陈述。而关于利率掉期合约是否可以被撤销,其中一个争议就是该利率掉期合约与银团贷款合约是否可以被视为完全独立与相互之间没有依赖性。Picken 大法官在分析了双方的证人证言之后认定利率掉期合约与银团贷款合约之间存在相互依赖的关系,正如银团贷款合约中各银行的证人出庭作证时所说,在银团贷款合约中有明示的条文约定 Marme 要作出对利率掉期的安排以对冲风险,并且有条文要求 Marme 保证最低利息保障倍数〔22〕(minimum interest cover rate)在 105%,而只有通过利率掉期的安排,才有可能对冲 EURIBOR 变动的风险与确保最低利息保障倍数的实现。所以,利率掉期合约与银团贷款合约之间是相互依赖与完全不可分割的,也即是无论默示误述能否成立,利率掉期合约都不可以单独被撤销。

4.3.3 同一个交易中多份关联合约启动多个仲裁会带来的困境

本段一开始节录的 O'Sullivan, Zakrzewski 与 Elliott 合著的《The Law of Rescis-

〔21〕 见本书第二章之 1.4 段。

〔22〕 根据维基百科的解释,利息保障倍数,也称已获利息倍数,是指息税前利润对利息费用的倍数。利息保障倍数被认为是分析企业长期偿债能力的指标,利息保障倍数越大,说明企业通过营运利润来支付利息费用的能力越强;反之,则说明企业的债务压力越大。

sion》一书是针对所有的撤销合约,这除了是误述可使有关合约无效外,还有不当影响(可使无效)、胁迫(可使无效)与非法(无效/不可执行)。在英国法院诉讼,审理法官就可以全盘去考虑,不会容许单独撤销一个交易中有关联与相互依赖的合约中的个别合约而令这个衡平救济出现不公平,甚至是令双方当事人无所适从,不知道这个交易怎么样走下一步。

但这个危险存在于仲裁中,因为即使同一个交易的不同合约,合约双方也会错误地约定不同的仲裁条文。即使是相同的仲裁条文,例如都是北仲、上仲、贸仲、SIAC或 HKIAC 机构仲裁,今天在 Halliburton v. Chubb(2020) UKSC 48 最高院先例与大气候下抗拒不同的相关合约下的关联仲裁案件中重复委任同一位做共同仲裁员(common arbitrator),仲裁机构〔23〕也一般会委任不同的仲裁员或至少是不同的首席。这样,就会有很大的危险导致在同一个交易中两个密切关联与相互依赖的合约,会得出矛盾与不一致的裁决结果。如果矛盾与不一致只涉及金钱,例如对损失的计算,这造成的不公平与不合理应该不会致命。但如果矛盾与不一致是在一个仲裁去作出履约指令(specific performance)或禁令(injunction),但另一密切关联与相互依赖的合约被仲裁庭判是可使无效并撤销,问题可就大了,双方当事人会对这个交易怎么样走下去就无所适从。

5. 回复到原状

行使撤销合约的救济(不论是衡平法或是普通法的救济)是必须能够把双方当事人回复到原状(restitutio in integrum),否则就失去了这撤销合约的权利。两者捆绑在一起,英文可以表述为"rescission – restitution tie"。

早期的权威先例就已经把这个大原则说得十分清楚,可部分节录作为引子。首先是在 Clarke v. Dickson(1858)120 ER 463 先例中,案情涉及保险人以受保人欺诈性误述拒赔,但对是否需要退还已支付的保费的争议,Crompton 大法官说:"... If you are fraudulently induced to buy a cake you may return it and get back the price; but you cannot both eat your cake and return your cake."

接下去在 Western Bank of Scotland v. Addie(1867)5 M. (H. L.)80 贵族院(苏格兰)先例中,Cranworth 勋爵说:"Relief ..., which is what ... is designated restitutio in

〔23〕 这可见 Anaklia Development Consortium LLC(Georgia) v. The Government of Georgia, ICC Case No. 25542/HBH, ICC 国际仲裁院认为多次委任的仲裁员有"不自觉的偏袒"(unconscious bias),因为:"With respect to the asymmetry of information, ... the Court considered that Mr Sachs(被赶走的仲裁员) may have access to information that will not be available to his fellow arbitrators in the ICC proceedings, who will not participate to the ISCID case ..."

integrum, can only be had where the party seeking it is able to put those against whom it is asked in the same situation in which they stood when the contract was entered into."

另是 Blackburn 勋爵在 Erlanger v. New Sombrero Phosphate Co(1878)3 App Cas 1218 贵族院先例中说:"It is, I think, clear on principles of general justice, that as a condition to a rescission there must be a restitutio in integrum. The parties must be put in status quo. ... It is a doctrine which has often been acted upon both at law and in equity."

另在 Newbigging v. Adam(1886)34 Ch. D. 582 上诉庭先例中, Bowen 大法官说: "... there ought ... to be a giving back and a taking back on both sides."

在较近期的先例也是同样说法,首先介绍 TSB Bank Plc v. Camfield(1995)1 WLR 430 上诉庭先例中, Nourse 大法官说:"... she(被误述方 Camfield 夫人)is in my judgment entitled to, is to set aside the transaction which, to my mind, is **an all or nothing process**. This is consistent with the fact that a party who complains of having entered into a transaction on the basis of a misrepresentation is saying that if he had been aware of the truth, he would not have entered into the transaction. If this claim is upheld, the court seeks to put that party into the position in which he would have been if the representation had not been made. **This involves ascertaining what the position would have been if the transaction had not taken place**. It does not involve reforming the transaction to accord with the representation."(加黑部分是笔者的强调)

另是在 De Molestina v. Ponton(2001)CLC 1412 先例中, Colman 大法官有很清楚的解说:"... **there cannot be rescission unless there can be restitutio in integrum**. Further, that requirement is the conceptual consequence of the basic nature of the remedy of rescission which is to discharge all the parties from the bargain into which the misrepresentor has induced them to enter. It is not and **never has had the function of providing compensation for the misrepresentation or some hybrid solution to reflect what would be fair between the parties having regard to the nature of the representation and the extent to which one party has been misled by another**. Consistently with that, the court has no power to create a new bargain for the parties. What has been induced is the original bargain and it is the purpose of the remedy to return the parties to their position before that particular bargain was made. There is therefore **no room for any form of equitable engineering directed to re-constructing the fabric of the original contract.**"(加黑部分是笔者的强调)

5.1　撤销合约的救济只为了回复到原状,不考虑惩罚也不调整合约以达到公平合理

因误述(不论是无辜、疏忽或是欺诈)而撤销合约的救济在逻辑上很容易理解,就是既然该合约是有缺陷的合约,在被误述方发觉了误述后说"我如果知道真相就不会订这个合约了"的情况下,就应该让双方(不论是误述方或是被误述方)回复到

原来没有产生合约的地位。这不是针对性改造有缺陷的合约让它变得更公平合理,不存在去重写(rewrite)合约。这也不是去惩罚误述方,因为有可能是无辜误述,而欺诈性误述也另有欺诈/欺骗侵权的索赔金钱损失的救济,无须在撤销合约的救济中“越俎代庖”。

但在很多案件中回复到原状是谈何容易,很多时候都做不到。受害方/被误述方往往在合约已经部分甚至是全部被双方当事人履行后才发觉误述(特别是欺诈性),想让双方当事人回复到什么都没有发生过的地位,把所有履行与发生了的事情抹掉,几乎不可能。

如果双方都已经履行了合约的部分或全部,各自享受了对方提供的好处,例如服务或供应,但也会是蒙受了损害。这些说不清与可能是大量的“恩怨情仇”都要量化并将时间拨回(unwind),在把双方当事人回复到合约产生前的原状时应尽量做到公平合理。

在近年来全球化带来的复杂国际商业案件中,发生可诉误述去诱导合约产生的情况更多了,例如公司并购、股权买卖、银行融资、投资、保险等重大交易,误述都是“热点争议”。参与这些交易的人士往往都是手段更高明的国际商业人士,即使是有意识的误述也懂得包装。这些案件的案情也更复杂,往往涉及专业与商业知识,法院或仲裁庭要全盘掌控不同案件的背景/语境后仔细分析才清楚有否可诉明示或默示误述等。如果可诉误述可以成立,被误述方就要决定是否终止合约。这时常取决于市场、整体经济环境与政治环境。如果这些因素都是积极的,例如购买了一家公司并在发现误述前已经经营了半年或一年的被误述方,可能决定不终止合约并继续拥有与经营公司。当然如果是欺诈性误述,或是有关的误述被包括在了一条陈述与保证条文中,也就是构成违约,被误述方仍可以索赔损失。但损失可能金额不高(现实中有些人可能对一些鸡毛蒜皮的事也撒谎),或是很难证明。而如果市场、经济与政治环境都在被误述方购买公司后转差或是突变,被误述方将尽一切努力摆脱这个错误的投资决定。但因为被误述方已经经营了半年或一年,期间有无数事项需要回归以做到回复到原状。这些误述争议往往涉及天文数字,国际上有大量这种高价值的“大案子”在法院或仲裁审理。但偏偏在这种复杂案件中,即使在衡平法下可以尽量灵活与弹性处理复原与反复原,也难以在方方面面回复到原状,这比国际商品买卖合约等涉及的有形标的物(tangible assets)的复原要困难得多。

如果是源于普通法的复原救济,例如由于普通法过错(common law wrong)(如欺诈性误述),或者是普通法的错误(mistake)理论,回复原状或复原就比较死板或僵化,例如要求“实物归还”(restitution in specie),正如在 Smith New Court Securities Ltd v. Scrimgeour Vickers (Asset Management) Ltd (1994) 1 WLR 1271 上诉庭先例中,Nourse 大法官说:“The **remedies** available to a party who has been induced to enter into a contract by **a fraudulent misrepresentation are rescission and damages**. Rescission is a restitutionary remedy which allows the defrauded party to recover the property with which he has parted under the contract and return the benefit which he received. It is however **a necessary condition of this remedy in English law that the plaintiff should be able to make substantial restitution in specie of the property** which he has received."(加黑部分是笔者的强调)

但如果是源于衡平法的复原救济,例如案件由于衡平法过错(equitable wrong)的救济,就会在复原方面处理起来有弹性得多。权威的 Erlanger v. New Sombrero Phosphate Co(1878)3 App Cas 1218 贵族院先例(涉及是违反信义/诚信责任)可以显示衡平法下不追求精确回复到原状,只要达至"实际公平"(practical just)即可。这是因为衡平法涉及在不同案件的裁量权,法院可以灵活决定行使或不行使或如何行使裁量权。但普通法是要严格按照已经确立的法律、法规或立法去作出决定,无法在不同案件去灵活处理务求对该特定案件做到公平合理。

接下来会先随意挑三个有关衡平法复原的先例进行介绍:Erlanger v. New Sombrero Phosphate Co;O'Sullivan v. Management Agency and Music Ltd(1985)QB 428(涉及衡平法过错的不当影响)与 Mahoney v. Parnell(1996)3 All ER 61(也涉及不当影响)先例。

再接下去介绍有关普通法复原并显示了其中的困难的 3 个先例:Smith New Court Securities Ltd v. Scrimgeour Vickers(Asset Management)Ltd;Crystal Palace FC(2000)Limited v. Iain Dowie(2007)EWHC 1392 与 Halpern v. Halpern(2007)EWCA Civ 291 先例。

这两种有重大不同的撤销合约与复原在本章之 1 段与本书第十章之 12.1.1 段有详论。

5.2 衡平法复原:法院灵活行使裁量权追求实际公平复原的案例介绍

5.2.1 Erlanger v. New Sombrero Phosphate Co(1878)3 App Cas 1218 贵族院先例

在 Erlanger v. New Sombrero Phosphate Co 贵族院先例中,一家名为 The Sombrero Company 的公司从英国政府手中以每年 1000 英镑的租金承租了西印度群岛中的一个名为 Sombrero 的小岛,租期为 1865 年起算的 21 年。该公司主要的业务是开采 Sombrero 岛上丰富的磷酸盐矿。后该公司进入破产程序,破产清算人将该公司最有价值的这份租赁合约进行转让。Erlanger 先生是巴黎的一个银行家,他与他的合伙人从该破产清算人处以 55,000 英镑购买了该租赁合约,Erlanger 先生后来想以公司的名义去开发该小岛上的磷酸盐矿与执行该租赁合约,于是成立了 New Sombrero Phosphate Co 公司。Erlanger 先生委任了 5 位董事,其中有 2 位董事在国外,而另外 3 位董事中有 2 位都是在他的控制下。New Sombrero Phosphate Co 公司后来进行公开的招股。Erlanger 先生通过一个代理人以 11 万英镑的价格转让了该租赁合约给 New Sombrero Phosphate Co 公司。8 个月后,公司的股东发现 Erlanger 先生购买该租赁合约的实际价格,于是代表公司起诉 Erlanger 先生要求撤销该转让合约,原因是在该转让交易中 Erlanger 先生作为公司的创始人对公司负有诚信责任(fiduciary duty),[24]而他向其他股东隐瞒了自己其实是该转让租赁合约交易的合约相对方与该租赁合约的实际价格,是违反了诚信责任。而 New Sombrero Phosphate Co 公司也从来没有在该交易达成前对该租赁合约的价值进行调查与评估。该案一个重要的争议是撤销合约是否能够复原的问题,因为 New Sombrero Phosphate Co 公司已经对小岛上的磷酸盐矿进行了开采的工作并且有获利。

法院同意 New Sombrero Phosphate Co 可撤销合约,退还矿场给 Erlanger 先生,虽然该公司已经对矿场进行了开采的工作,但可以通过折旧与退还利润弥补,做到实际公平。Blackburn 勋爵说:"It(衡平法院)can take account of profits and make allowance for deterioration. And I think **the practice has always been for a court of equity to give this relief whenever**, by the exercise of its powers, it can do what is **practically just**, though it cannot restore the parties precisely to the state they were in before the contract."(加黑部分是笔者的强调)

也如 Roche 大法官在 Compagnie Chemin de Fer Paris-Orleans v. Leeston Shipping Co(1919)36 TLR 68 先例中所说:"The principle of restitutio in integrum did not require that a person should be put back into the same position as before; it meant that he should be put into as good a position as before."

5.2.2 O'Sullivan v. Management Agency and Music Ltd(1985)QB 428 先例

在此先举一个较近期与著名的例子,在 O'Sullivan v. Management Agency and Music Ltd 先例中,可显示可使合约无效(voidable contract)独有的让受害方/被误述方有撤销合约的权利但同时必须要去复原与反复原相比合约自始无效(void ab initio 或英文"treated as invalid from the outset")更灵活与公平合理,因为衡平救济涉及裁量权,法院可以设定复原与反复原的条件以达到实际公平合理,包括对第三人。

案情涉及的原告 Gilbert O'Sullivan 是世界知名歌星,他遇到第三被告 Mills 先生前(第一被告是 Mills 控制的 MAM 公司,其余的 4 位被告区别是 MAM 的其他联营公司/分公司),虽然也已与 April Music 公司订立版权管理合约并与 CBS 订立了唱片合约,但写的歌与发行的专辑都默默无闻。Mills 是国际知名的经纪人与唱片制作人,旗下艺人包括 Tom Jones 与 Engelbert Humperdinck 等当红歌星。O'Sullivan 很快与 Mills 订立了经纪合约,也很快与第一被告 MAM 订立了独家代理合约,与第二被告订立了版权管理合约,与第五被告订立了唱片合约,与第四被告(为了收取艺人的海外收入专门成立的联营公司)订立了雇佣合约。O'Sullivan 作为一位涉世未深的没有任何商业知识的年轻人,出于对 Mills 的信任签署文件,当时也没有被建议要获得任何独立法律意见。

到了 1970 年底,O'Sullivan 开始有热门单曲登上英国榜单。1972 年,凭借一首

[24] 信义/诚信责任是衡平法理论,可见本书第一章之 2.7 段。

他自己创作的著名歌曲“Alone Again Naturally”，O’Sullivan 的事业飞升，迅速成为炙手可热的歌星，横扫各国各大榜单。但好景不长，随着几次合约结构变动，O’Sullivan 觉得自己赚得更少花得更多，大部分钱都进了 Mills 与有关公司的口袋。在咨询了独立法律意见后，O’Sullivan 在 1979 年年中开始了诉讼，声称以上所有的合约都是违反公共政策与非法的。虽然在开庭时，所有的有关合约都已经履行完毕。

一审法院判以上的合约都是限制商贸/就业的（restraint of trade），[25] 虽然并没有以此认定合约非法，而是判 Mills 和其他被告与 O’Sullivan 之间存在诚信关系，[26] O’Sullivan 是在被告的不当影响（undue influence）下订立合约，故合约自始无效，Mills 与其他被告要交出从 O’ Sullivan 身上赚取的利润（account for profit）。

之后被告们上诉，上诉庭部分推翻了一审的判决，判是原被告之间确实存在诚信关系与 O’Sullivan 是在这种“特殊关系”（special relationship）下受不当影响，才会去订立这些合约。不当影响是衡平法过错，救济应是可使无效而非自始无效。只有可使无效，才会涉及撤销合约的权利并需要实际可行去在复原与反复原对双方当事人（包括 Mills 与其他被告）做到公平合理。

接下来上诉庭要处理的争议就是，被告声称因为合约已经全部履行完毕，双方改变地位已是不现实，不可能回复到没有订立合约的地位，所以 O’Sullivan 不能撤销合约只能向被告索赔金钱损失。显然被告的算盘是在金钱损失赔偿下，O’ Sullivan 要去证明他提出的每一项索赔的损失，加上计算的复杂性与局限如可否合理预见（reasonable foreseeability）、因果关系（causation）、合理减损（mitigation）等，就会令 O’ Sullivan 面对一场漫长、艰辛与庞大诉讼费用的诉讼。这就可把 O’ Sullivan 拖垮或在几年折磨后心力交瘁，会愿意以一笔小钱接受庭外和解。

上诉庭判虽然双方诉讼方无法回复到原本的地位，但在衡平法下对于不当影响产生的合约，应该是可使合约无效。这样，即使是撤销已经履行了的合约，仍可以通过金钱量化去复原与反复原以回复到合约没有产生的地位。法院有裁量权在双方当事人之间的复原与反复原有可行性地主持公道，做到实际公平。在此先例就是撤销所有合约，让被告交出在 O’ Sullivan 身上赚取的利润。但是同时被告为推广 O’Sullivan 的作品提供了技术与作出了努力，对 O’Sullivan 的成功有巨大贡献（O’Sullivan 在和 Mills 合作前与在同 Mills 产生分歧最终闹翻后都没有什么十分热门的歌曲），被告可以为此获得合理报酬（remuneration）包括赚取一定利润。当然这远远低于被告这些年实际赚的钱，但相信仍是一笔可观的钱要扣除，毕竟 Mills 是一位国际知名经纪人。

上诉庭的 Fox 大法官说：“... it seems to me that the principle that the court will do

---

〔25〕 可见本书第八章之 11.2 段与《合约的解释：规则与应用》一书第七章之 3.3.1 段的详细介绍。

〔26〕 对于互相之间有信任与信心（trust and confidence）的诚信关系（fiduciary relationship），就可能法律推定存在不当影响（undue influence），这在本书第十一章之 1.4.2.2.1 段有介绍。

what is practically just as between the parties is applicable to a case of undue influence even though the parties cannot be restored to their original position. That is, in my view, applicable to the present case. The question is not whether the parties can be restored to their original position; it is what does the justice of the case require? That approach is quite wide enough, if it be necessary in the individual case, to accommodate the protection of third parties. The rights of a bona fide purchaser for value without notice would not in any event be affected. "

另 Dunn 大法官说："...the principle of restitutio in integrum is not applied with its full rigour in equity in relation to transactions entered into by persons in breach of a fiduciary relationship, and that **such transactions may be set aside even though it is impossible to place the parties precisely in the position in which they were before, provided that the court can achieve practical justice** between the parties by obliging the wrongdoer to give up his profits and advantages, while at the same time compensating him for any work that he has actually performed pursuant to the transaction.... I do not think that equity requires such a narrow approach. ...In my judgment **the judge was right to set the agreements aside and to order an account of the profits and payment of the sums found due on the taking of the account. But in taking the account the defendants are entitled to an allowance** ... for reasonable remuneration including a profit element for all work done in promoting and exploiting O'Sullivan and his compositions, whether such work was done pursuant to a contractual obligation or gratuitously. What constitutes 'reasonable remuneration' will depend on evidence on the taking of the account..."（加黑部分是笔者的强调）

另外，此先例还涉及第三人权益的问题，例如 CBS 与 MAM 的协议让 CBS 全权在美国销售 O'Sullivan 的歌曲，这涉及版权与交出母带（master recording/master tapes）的问题。一审法院判合约自始无效，等于合约从来没有存在过，显然与 CBS 的协议也从来不会存在。这也表示转让的版权与母带都要归还给 O'Sullivan，一审法院就作出了"交出命令"（order for delivery up）。

但上诉庭改判为可使无效，CBS 与 MAM 订立的协议也就是在合约仍是有效的履行期间发生。这样，在 CBS 对 O'Sullivan 是受到不当影响订立合约不知情，也没有被通知的情况下，类似货物买卖在可使无效的合约下合法的转移产权，第三人作为"善意买方"（bona fide purchaser）是有优先的权利。所以，上诉庭改判 CBS 与 MAM 的协议仍是有效，CBS 无需交出母带，但被告从 CBS 收取的版权费等金钱，是属于 O'Sullivan 所有。Dunn 大法官说："... The defect of the agreement with CBS Inc was to give CBS Inc the right to exploit records already in existence and made ... and other records to be made during the continuance of the agreement. Pursuant to the agreement master tapes were actually sent to CBS Inc. ...The situation therefore is that CBS inc acquired the tapes and the right to exploit them for good consideration without knowledge of undue influence by any of the defendants. In those circumstances on well established principles they are entitled to retain the tapes pursuant to the terms of their agreement with the first defendant, … The order for delivery up of the master tapes should be amended accordingly. … under the terms of the order which I propose the defendants will be bound to account to O'Sullivan for all sums received from … CBS Inc, credit being given for reasonable remuneration to the defendants for work done on O'Sullivan's behalf."

5.2.3　Mahoney v. Parnell(1996)3 All ER 61 先例

在 Mahoney v. Parnell 先例中，案情涉及原告与被告是翁婿关系，双方合伙拥有与经营一家酒店。在被告的不当影响下，在 1988 年原告以酒店估值为 20 万英镑的基础出售了他的 50% 股权给被告。在 1989 年，公司以 327.5 万英镑出售该酒店。原告主张不当影响，要求撤销 1988 年股份出售合约，虽然公司已经清盘，无法回复到原状，但 May 大法官仍是"以钱代货"，根据 1988 年酒店的真正估值算出一笔补偿给原告。这是以对等的金钱复原，可称为"衡平法赔偿"(equitable compensation)，[27] 而不是索赔与计算损失，因为衡平法是不能作出金钱损失的救济的。

在《Chitty on Contracts》(2021 年，第 34 版)一书之 10 - 136 段，针对 Mahoney v. Parnell 先例说："It has been held that if restitutio in integrum is no longer possible, and the defendant does not retain any profits for which he may be made to account, the claimant may still be given 'compensation in equity'. In Mahoney v. Purnell, May J held that equitable compensation … is also available in such circumstances and the plaintiff could recover the value of what he had transferred, giving credit for what he had received. …. It has been argued persuasively that 'equitable compensation' in this context should be understood as referring to pecuniary restitution of any unjust enrichment, which is appropriate in cases of undue influence. **The case shows not that equitable compensation may be given when restitution is impossible, so much as that rescission need not be prevented by the fact that property cannot be returned in specie; as between the parties it may be effected in money**."(加黑部分是笔者的强调)

5.2.4　衡平法复原的小结

衡平法复原在每个案件中针对不同情况的灵活处理，往往量身定做给出解决方案。作为小结可先节录一些权威说法提到的一些达至实际公平复原的做法。

先是在较近期的 De Molestina v. Ponton(2001)CLC 1412 先例中，Colman 大法官说：

"… Consideration of those authorities which have been concerned with restitutio in integrum shows that **rescission will not be withheld where substantial restitution is pos-**

---

〔27〕 见本书第十章之 12.3 段。

sible, but this remedy is not fettered by some overriding equitable test as to whether the consequences would work unfairly to the misrepresentor. ... there is **undoubtedly a degree of flexibility in the approach to restitution**. It has to be possible to achieve substantial restitution, albeit precise restitution of what passed under the contract may no longer be possible. What the courts are doing in those cases where they deploy that flexibility which involves, for example, the taking of an account or an order for the payment of compensation or an indemnity, is to make adjustments ancillary to and in aid of restitution to take account of changes to property or benefits derived from the contract by one side or another during the period between the making of the contract and the proceedings for rescission. This is clearly reflected in the speech of Lord Wright in Spence v. Crawford [1939] 3 Al ER 271 ...

'**The remedy is equitable. Its application is discretionary, and, where the remedy is applied, it must be moulded in accordance with the exigencies of the particular case**. The general principal is authoritatively stated in a few words by Lord Blackburn in Erlanger v. New Sombrero Phosphate Co, ...

In that case, Lord Blackburn is careful not to seek to tie the hands of the court by attempting to form any rigid rules. The court must fix its eyes on the goal of doing '**what is practically just**'. How that goal may be reached must depend on the circumstances of the case, ...

.... The purpose of the relief is not punishment, but compensation. **The rule is stated as requiring the restoration of both parties to the status quo ante**..."(加黑部分是笔者的强调)

另在本章稍后的6.2.2段将介绍案情的Salt v. Stratstone Specialist Ltd(2015) EWCA Civ 745上诉庭先例中,Longmore大法官说:"Rescission is prima facie available if '**practical justice**' can be done. If '**practical justice**' **requires a representor to be compensated for depreciation, it is for the representor so to assert and prove**; likewise if the representor asserts that use of the car is to be taken into account, which may well be difficult if the car was as 'troublesome' ... The absence of evidence about depreciation or the value of the use of the car should not operate to the disadvantage of the representee who should never have been put in the position of having a troublesome old car rather than a brand new one."(加黑部分是笔者的强调)

衡平法为了要把双方回复到原状就要在每个不同案件都有不同设计、灵活处理或甚至要创新。这在O'Sullivan v. Management Agency and Music Ltd(1985) QB 428先例就能明显看到。在比较简单的有形财产交易如货物或房屋买卖中,如果要求撤销救济的被误述方是买方,他就要能够归还(revesting)在误述下购买的标的物与它的产权。

归还务求回复到原状不仅是如货物或房屋的标的物，也可以是任何其他有形或无形的财产，如股权、一家公司、专利或知识产权等。例如在 Erlanger v. New Sombrero Phosphate Co(1878)3 App Cas 1218 先例中，就涉及归还整个矿场给 Erlanger 先生，虽然该公司已经对矿场进行了开采的工作，但可以通过折旧与退还利润的方式弥补。或是，归还股权的同时，买方也应归还在合约撤销前收到的派息(dividends)。又例如标的物是一家餐馆或一个游乐场，在撤销前已经享用了一段时间或在经营中赚了些钱，衡平法下这需要去"反复原"把这笔钱退还给误述方以保证公平与合理，甚至可以估计一笔金钱作为补偿。

为了保证复原，法院也可以在判决中附加条件，例如在 30 天内原告支付了反复原计算的衡平法赔偿后才撤销合约、改变财产的产权登记等。这种精准的做法，在 O'Sullivan v. Management Agency and Music Ltd 先例中也清楚显示出来，如命令从 CBS 处收取的版权费要支付给 O' Sullivan 等。

5.3　普通法复原的案例介绍

5.3.1　Smith New Court Securities Ltd v. Scrimgeour Vickers(Asset Management) Ltd(1994)1 WLR 1271 先例

在 Smith New Court Securities Ltd v. Scrimgeour Vickers(Asset Management)Ltd 上诉庭先例[28]中，案情涉及原告在被告花旗银行的欺诈性误述的诱导下，向被告买入一家名为 Ferranti 公司价值高达 23,141,424 英镑的 28,141,424 股股票。但不久后该公司出了丑闻(涉及内部雇员欺诈/欺骗的名为"Guerin fraud"的事件)，导致股价在市场大跌。原告看到市场的走势不妙，决定尽快出售脱身。反正最后结算差价是损失了 11,353,220 英镑。原告要求撤销合约去复原。虽然原告也可以被告的欺诈/欺骗索赔损失，但这会是不利的。因为 Guerin fraud 导致的损失不是来自被告的误述，而是原告作为买方自己应承担的市场下跌风险。只有在撤销合约下复原，原告才可以把这风险转回给被告卖方。

但由于 Ferranti 股票已被原告出售，所以复原只能去市场以低价另买入同样的股票。但上诉庭说这不是英国传统法律，因为这不是原来的一批股票去复原，但当事人没有再要求复原，上诉庭也无需对这一点做决定或改变过去地位。Nourse 大法官说："The remedies available to a party who has been induced to enter into a contract by a fraudulent misrepresentation are rescission and damages. Rescission is a restitutionary remedy which allows the defrauded party to recover the property with which he has parted under the contract and return the benefit which he received. It is however **a necessary condition of this remedy in English law that the plaintiff should be able to make sub-**

---

[28] Smith New Court Securities Ltd v. Scrimgeour Vickers(Asset Management)Ltd(1996)3 WLR 1051 贵族院先例中关于目前英国法律下有关欺诈/欺骗侵权(tort of deceit)与一般的民事错误(违约、疏忽侵权)不同的损失计算方式的权威说法，可见本书第四章之 4.2.2 段的详细介绍。

stantial restitution in specie of the property which he has received. If SNC(原告)had retained the shares, it would have been able to return them and claim repayment of the full price, even though the value of the shares had fallen. But, no doubt after weighing the commercial risks of winning the action against the possibility of a further decline in the Ferranti share(欺诈性误述诱导产生的合约的标的)price, it decided to sell. Thereby it lost the right to rescission. **In the case of a fungible asset like quoted shares, the rule which requires restitution in specie is a hard one.** Not every legal system would insist upon it, particularly in a case of fraud. But SNC accepted that it could not pursue the claim to restitution and abandoned it at the trial. "(加黑是笔者的强调)

此先例上诉去了贵族院[(1996) 3 WLR 1051],贵族院看来也有点不认同,但没有下任何定论,因为在该先例无需对这一点作出决定。Browne-Wilkinson 勋爵说:"...first, the denial of rescission where a plaintiff cannot return in specie the very shares which were the subject matter of the fraudulent sale ... if the current law in fact provides (as the Court of Appeal thought) that there is no right to rescind the contract for the sale of quoted shares once the specific shares purchased have been sold, the law will need to be closely looked at hereafter. Since in such a case other, identical, shares can be purchased on the market, the defrauded purchaser can offer substantial restitutio in integrum which is normally sufficient."

这样看来,对归还需要是同一标的物或股票有严格要求,如果标的物在实质上已经不与原状一模一样,例如股票在价格上贬值,但股票仍是同样的股票,仍是可以反复原,正如在 Armstrong v. Jackson(1917)2 KB 822 先例中,说:"the market valuation of the shares has greatly dropped, but the shares are the same shares."但如果股票已经出售,就无法归还来复原了。这不是可以从市场另买入同样的股票可以补救的,否则世界上大部分的货物商品,即使已经毁掉、吃掉、用掉或转售了,仍可以在市场或其他渠道找另一批来替代归还,因此也就不必再追求归还来复原的问题了。倒不如以对等的金钱来替代股票复原更干净利落,但这不是目前英国实物复原的法律地位。

5.3.2 Crystal Palace FC(2000)Limited v. Iain Dowie(2007)EWHC 1392 先例

在 Crystal Palace FC(2000)Limited v. Iain Dowie 先例中,案情涉及雇佣合约。被告 Dowie 先生是一名成功的职业足球运动员,曾效力于英国著名的职业足球队水晶宫足球俱乐部。他退役之后开始担任足球经理,于 2003 年与水晶宫足球俱乐部签订雇佣合约,受雇作为俱乐部的经理管理球队,聘用期至 2008 年 6 月 30 日。在雇佣合约中有条文约定,如果 Dowie 先生在合约期未届满前离职,需要赔偿给俱乐部 100 万英镑。在 2006 年,水晶宫足球俱乐部在晋级赛中输给了沃特福德足球俱乐部。可能是因为该原因,Dowie 先生希望去成绩更好的足球俱乐部任职,而事实上也确实有其他俱乐部以更好的条件在招揽他。于是 Dowie 先生在雇佣合约期未届满前向俱乐部提出离职请求,理由是想要和家人团聚。俱乐部与 Dowie 先生在 2006 年 5 月 22

日签署了终止雇佣合约的和解协议，该和解协议豁免了 Dowie 先生按照雇佣合约应该支付给俱乐部的 100 万英镑的赔偿。

在和解协议签署与召开新闻发布会宣布离开后刚一个星期的 2006 年 5 月 30 日，另外一家英国职业足球俱乐部查尔顿竞技足球俱乐部就宣布委任 Dowie 先生为球队的经理。水晶宫足球俱乐部于是起诉 Dowie 先生，主张和解协议是在 Dowie 先生以和家人团聚的欺诈性误述下签署，并要求(a)将和解协议撤销，(b) Dowie 先生根据雇佣合约赔偿 100 万英镑，(c)或替代地以赔偿损失代替撤销和解协议。

法院审理后认为 Dowie 先生存在欺诈性误述，但是撤销和解协议意味着 Dowie 先生和水晶宫足球俱乐部的雇佣合约没有终止仍然有效。这样，在“一仆难侍二主”的情况下，对于 Dowie 先生的新雇主查尔顿竞技足球俱乐部来说就十分不公平了。法院在权衡后认为从实际公平的角度让 Dowie 先生按照与水晶宫足球俱乐部的雇佣合约中提前解约的赔偿对其作出金钱上的赔偿是一个更为合适的救济。

欺诈性误述通常是要撤销合约，因为即使不撤销合约也很难让受害人与骗子继续合作。而在上述水晶宫足球俱乐部的案件中，虽然法院判不撤销和解协议，但这在本质上其实是一样不让受害人与骗子继续合作。因为一旦撤销和解协议，就表示原合约继续存在，但想来 Dowie 先生不会尽心尽力，水晶宫足球俱乐部也不会安心。

5.3.3　Halpern v. Halpern (2007) EWCA Civ 291 先例

在 Halpern v. Halpern 先例中，涉及双方当事人在达成和解协议后根据约定把所有有关文件毁掉。但之后原告提出在谈判和解有胁迫(duress)，[29] 这导致原告要求撤销和解协议。但问题是撤销后双方仍存在的争议与诉讼怎么办，因为再也没有有关文件可以作为证据去重新推进与开庭审理。在复原的问题更是毁掉的文件如何去“实物归还”(restitution in specie)？

为了寻找解决办法，上诉庭看来认同 Trietel 教授在《Law of Contract》(2003 年，第 11 版)一书第 380 页的看法，就是不必太计较把双方当事人回复到原来没有该和解协议的地位，特别对误述方的反复原只是次要考虑，只要不让被误述方不当得利即可，Waller 大法官说：“... perhaps, that for the purpose of ‘practical justice’, the primary objective may not always need to be to restore both parties to their previous positions. As Professor Treitel has said ... ‘the essential point is that the representee should not be unjustly enriched at the representor's expense; that the representor should not be prejudiced is a secondary consideration, which is only taken into account when some benefit has been received by the representee.”

重要与特别的是在此先例中，上诉庭认为普通法过错的“胁迫”与衡平法过错的

[29] 关于胁迫的课题可见本书第十章。

"不当影响"本质上是同一事项,[30]而根据《Senior Court Act 1981》之 Section 9,针对同一事项,如果有了冲突就以衡平法优先。这样上诉庭就可以引入衡平法救济的复原,逃避实物归还,例如灵活以金钱替代被毁掉的文件。[31] 但该先例是处理简易判决的申请,所以没有针对具体怎么确定赔偿的金额,要留待将来的案件审理。这计算虽然不容易,但也并非不可能,例如争议金额是确定的情况下,完全可以机会损失(loss of chance)[32]的计算方式根据这些文件证据的关联性与重要性进行计算。反正只要大致上做到实际公平即可,毕竟这是唯一解决办法。

5.4 对撤销与复原困境的解决办法的探讨

读者不必为在这课题上看来是十分复杂难明的英国法律感到困扰,这种衡平法与普通法之间的不协调只是英国历史的包袱。同样的社会问题在中国也会发生,但中国法律没有这种包袱,可以轻装上路,发展出一套一致性地针对所有情况、更完善与配合国际的法律制度的法律。

接下来继续看英国法律对怎样解决这普通法复原与衡平法复原,与无法复原的情况下如何给予撤销合约救济的困境的探讨。毕竟有些情况下,合约的缺陷很严重,令合约方/受害方继续履行合约是不公平的,此时撤销合约才是唯一恰当的救济。

5.4.1 解决办法之一:接受部分撤销的 Vadasz v. Pioneer Concrete (SA) Pty Ltd (1995) 184 CLR 102 澳大利亚先例

一种解决办法改变英国法律,不再要求撤销全部合约,而允许部分撤销,也就是只允许能够回复到原状的部分撤销,南澳大利亚最高院的 Vadasz v. Pioneer Concrete (SA) Pty Ltd 先例就是这样判的。该先例的背景是 Vadipile 是一间建筑公司,而 Pioneer 水泥公司是该建筑公司的水泥供应商。因为 Vadipile 的经济状况变坏,陆续欠下 Pioneer 公司 20 万澳元的水泥货款。双方经过协商达成了还款协议。对于将来的供货,Pioneer 的负责人告知 Vadipile 公司的股东兼董事 Vadasz 先生,Pioneer 在他对未来供货的货款提供个人担保之后才会继续供货。Vadasz 先生相信了该负责人的说法,在没有阅读个人担保合约条文的情况下就签署了该个人担保,该个人担保措辞如下:"IN CONSIDERATION of you having agreed or agreeing to sell goods or to provide services granting or giving credit to VADIPILE DRILLING PTY LTD hereinafter called 'The Company'... at my request and forbearing for the time being to sue the Company for the recovery of monies owing by it to you, I, ... HEREBY jointly and severally for ourselves and our respective Executors and Administrators UNCONDITIONALLY AND IRREVOCABLY GUARANTEE to you the due and punctual payment of **all monies which are now or**

---

〔30〕 在本书第十章之 1.1 段提到,直到 20 世纪 70 年代有了"经济胁迫"(economic duress)前,由于早年的胁迫由于太过局限,所以经常要以不当影响寻求衡平救济。

〔31〕 见本书第十章之 12.1.2 段的详细介绍。

〔32〕 见笔者《损失赔偿与救济》一书第六章之 4 段。

may at any time until we are released be owing to you by the Company including all costs, charges and expenses of every description which may be incurred by you in the exercise or attempted exercise of any power or remedy AND UNDERTAKE as a separate and additional obligation under this Instrument and as a principal Debtor to indemnify and to keep you indemnified against any loss that you incur as a consequence of the failure for whatever reason of the due and punctual payment by the Company of any monies due to you as aforesaid."(加黑部分是笔者的强调)

Pioneer 也确实继续供货给 Vadipile。但 Vadipile 的经济状况一直没有起色，不仅无法偿还个人担保合约订立之前欠下的货款，也无法支付个人担保合约签订之后欠下的货款，最后破产。Pioneer 根据个人担保合约的条文对 Vadasz 先生提起诉讼要求他承担 Vadipile 欠下的全部约 36 万澳元的货款。一审法院判 Pioneer 确实是希望 Vadasz 先生对所有欠款提供担保，但为了不将 Vadasz 先生吓退或鼓励他提供个人担保，Pioneer 的负责人在要求 Vadasz 先生提供个人担保时对该个人担保的范围存在误述，令 Vadasz 先生以为他签署的个人担保只是针对未来供货的货款，而不包括已经欠下的 20 万澳元的货款。针对该误述的救济，一审法院接受了 Pioneer 的主张，说 Vadasz 先生本来就愿意为将来的货款提供个人担保，所以该个人担保并非全部不可以履行，进而一审法院判该个人担保合约仅部分被撤销，签署个人担保合约后欠下的货款部分仍然要履行。

Vadasz 先生认为一审法院仅部分撤销合约的决定是在法律适用上存在错误，所以上诉。南澳大利亚最高院同意一审法院的判决，并认为撤销合约是衡平法上的救济，法官拥有裁量权，并要兼顾各方的利益。在该案中，无论是一审还是最高法院都没有对该误述到底是欺诈性误述还是无辜误述或疏忽误述进行判定，因为法院认为无论是哪一种误述，都不影响判决的结果。

显然这与其在英国的法律地位，如 TSB Bank Plc v. Camfield(1995)1 WLR 430 上诉庭先例的判决不同，即如果合约存在误述，那整个合约都应被撤销，而不是部分(all or nothing)。该先例的案情涉及两位被告 Camfield 夫妻把他们共同拥有的房屋作为担保物向原告银行借贷 3 万英镑，作为 Camfield 先生与其他人士合伙经营租用车辆业务的资金。Camfield 先生在说服妻子把房屋以押记做担保时，曾经告诉她作为担保人的责任封顶在 1.5 万英镑。这是误述，其实作为共同担保人责任是无限的。在借贷 3 万英镑后，Camfield 先生有持续的借贷。最后 Camfield 先生的生意失败，也没有清还债务的能力，这导致银行向 Camfield 夫妻(债务人与担保人)追债并要求占有房屋。Camfield 太太虽然曾经被银行作出过例行的警告，要在委任自己的律师并咨询后再签署担保协议，但她并没有这样做。在面对银行的索赔与执行担保时，Camfield 太太作为第二被告并不是指称原告对她有误述或没有披露"不寻常事宜"(unusual features)，而是以她的丈夫(第一被告 Camfield 先生)对她的误述(接受是无辜做出)作为抗辩。[33] 这导致一审的 Meier 法官判 Camfield 先生赔偿 47,315 英镑，Camfield 太太赔偿 1.5 万英镑。这显然是认为 Camfield 太太本来是愿意担保 1.5 万英镑，所以赔这笔钱是公平合理。另也作出占有房屋命令(order for possession)，除非判决债务在 6 个月付清。

但这一审判决被上诉庭推翻，理由是一审法院无权根据误述的程度与本质以自己的裁量权(discretion)改造在客观看来是公平合理的救济，只能在认定有误述的事实后，撤销担保协议，让被误述方全身而退。除了在本章之 5 段已节录的 Nourse 大法官的判词，Roch 大法官也说："The right to set aside or rescind the transaction is that of the representee, not that of the court. The court's role in a disputed case will be to decide whether the representee has lawfully rescinded the transaction or is entitled to rescind it. Normally, if the representee is entitled to rescind the legal charge, that will have been effected by the representee's pleading that the transaction has been or should be set aside; that is to say, the transaction would have been set aside before the matter reaches the court. The court is not being asked to grant equitable relief; nor is it, in my view, granting equitable relief to which terms may be attached. ...In this case Judge Meier did not consider it appropriate to declare the contract to be subsisting and to award damages, although he gave no reason for that conclusion. The absence of reasons, in my view, is explained by the fact that in this case an award of damages against Mr. Camfield would have been an empty remedy, ...The loss to the wife by upholding the legal charge in exchange for an award of damages against her husband would have far outweighed the loss that rescission would cause to Mr. Camfield. The judge decided to limit the extent to which the transaction — that is to say, the legal charge — was enforceable by the bank against the wife, namely, to the extent of £ 15,000. The judge was, in effect, declaring the legal charge to be subsisting and depriving the wife of her right to rescind it on terms that the enforceability of the charge against her would be limited to £ 15,000. In my judgment the judge has no power to do that. Once it was proved that the wife had the right to rescind the transaction, she could not be deprived of that right by the court ..."

5.4.2 解决办法之二:接受以对等的金钱复原

另一个普通法撤销与复原的改革会是完全可用对等的金钱(money – equivalent)来替代有形(tangible)或无形(intangible)标的物复原。这也是在本章之 3.3 段提到的 BV Nederlandse Industrie Van Eiprodukten v. Rembrandt Enterprises Inc (2018)

[33] 还涉及一个问题，就是此先例中是丈夫对妻子的误述，怎么会影响到银行的担保合约以及银行对房屋的权利?今天主要是在 Barclays Bank Plc v. O'Brien(1994)1 AC 180 先例后，特别针对债务人与担保人有非商业关系的情况(如夫妻关系)下，如果银行未能履行查问义务(duty of inquiry)，会推定银行对第三人(丈夫或妻子)的错误行为(以误述、不当影响等诱导作出担保)知情，并导致担保合约也可撤销。这些内容可见本书第五章之 6.3.1 段的介绍。

EWHC 1857(Comm)先例中提出的"以钱代货"的"pecuniary counter - restitution"的说法。

但即使英国法律有这方面改革,也解决不了社会上千变万化的所有不同情况,因为有一些情况无法以钱代货。例如对有形标的而言,有所谓的独一无二的货物(unique goods)。这在杨大明律师的《国际货物买卖》一书第八章之3段与笔者《损失赔偿与救济》一书第十二章之4.4段有介绍,在此只说没有市场可找替代与估值,甚至会是掺杂个人感情的货物,如"蒙娜丽莎"名画的买卖。

另一个问题是即使法律改变,允许以钱代货,但被误述方如买方,既无法实质把标的物去复原,也没有钱去代替对标的物的复原。而如果以无法复原为由不准撤销合约,只是个无关紧要的误述倒还好,但对欺诈性误述,甚至是暴力胁迫、不当影响下产生令人不齿的合约,受害方是否就只能被迫履行一个有严重缺陷与不利的合约?这会否带来更不公平合理的结果?

5.4.3　解决办法之三:不再把"撤销—复原"捆绑在一起

这里的说法就是把撤销与复原分开来对待,也就是一旦发生了误述、胁迫、不当影响等可使合约无效的情况,受害方就有了撤销合约的自助救济。在当今的英国法律下,撤销合约谈不上是一种真正"自助"的救济,因为普通法撤销与复原和反复原捆绑在一起,而衡平法撤销也一贯取决于法院的裁量权,令受害方为了安全需要法院以一个"宣示判决"(declaratory judgment)去命令撤销。这就要法院为每一个案件的不同案情去量身定做,甚至因为无法复原或反复原而否定撤销的救济。这也表示即使法院最后支持撤销合约,也因诉讼需要时间而迫使受害方继续履行一个严重缺陷与不利的合约,直到判决(或仲裁裁决)有了最终结果。虽然理论上是这样,但这种情况实际不会发生。因为正如在本章之1.1.1段所讲,受害方或被误述方会在发现误述的第一时间就撤销合约,但如果后来被法院认定因无法复原而否定撤销的救济,受害方较早前的自助撤销行为就有危险变为违约/毁约(repudiatory breach),虽然这方面还没有定论。《Misrepresentation Act 1967》的适用令这方面变得更加复杂。[34]

这显然不是一个对受害方理想的法律地位,但一"松绑"就可以解决这问题。一旦有可使合约无效的情况,受害方(在误述就是被误述方)就可立即自助行使权利选择撤销合约[或反过来确认(affirm)合约],不再需要履行原本要严格履行的有缺陷的合约下的合约责任。至于在复原部分,就是另一个稍后进行的不同诉因的诉讼,以法律(这不是合约法或侵权法,因为届时双方已经没有合约存在),也就是以已经成熟的"不当得利"(unjust enrichment)[35]与"改变地位"(change of position)理论处理。

不当得利理论是Goff勋爵在Lipkin Gorman v. Karpnale Ltd(1991)2 AC 548贵

---

〔34〕 见本书第四章之5.3段。

〔35〕 有关这一个课题,可见本书第七章之7.1段与本书第十章之11.2段与笔者的《合约的履行、弃权与禁反言》一书第五章之4段的详细介绍。

族院先例后发展起来的,并把在此之前 150 年以来各种不同名称或理由的复原案例归纳在此理论内。复原的救济与传统的合约与侵权的救济不同。如果 A 在弄错事实(或法律)的情况下将一笔金钱支付给了 B,经常 A 与 B 是没有合约关系的,而 B 也没有因为将天上掉下来这笔钱花掉了一部分而对 A 有了侵权的责任;所以 A 如果想通过法律向 B 要回这笔钱,唯一就是靠复原索赔(restitutionary claim)。这种情况在社会上多得很,例如银行错误汇款或双方算账算错导致多付了钱等。

复原的索赔通常要满足三个要件:(1)被告 B 必须得利(enrichment);(2)在 A 的受损下(at the expense of the claimant)B 才得利(不论是金钱或其他的利益);(3)让B 保留这笔钱或其他利益是不公平与不合情理的。所以复原的法律现在是被称为不当得利的法律(law of unjust enrichment)。在 Fibrosa Spolka Akcyjna v. Fairbairn Lawson Combe Barbour Ltd(1943)AC 32 先例,Wright 勋爵说:"It is clear that any civilized system of law is bound to provide remedies for cases of what has been called unjust enrichment or unjust benefit,that is to prevent a man from retaining the money of or some benefit derived from another which it is against conscience that he should keep. Such remedies in English law are generically different from remedies in contract or in tort,and are now recognized to fall within a third category of the common law which has been called quasi - contract or restitution. "

如果已经将钱花掉了一部分,面对这些困难,收到好处的一方有两个可能的抗辩。一个是传统的陈述性禁反言(estoppel by representation),另一个是较近期才发展起来的改变地位。根据重要的 Lipkin Gorman v. Karpnale Ltd 贵族院先例,针对弄错事实下给钱的一方要求复原的请求,如果让收钱的一方归还全部或部分会造成不公平,收钱的一方就可以改变地位作为抗辩。

当然,收钱的一方如果依赖改变地位的抗辩,就必须面对证明让他还钱是不公平(因为他已经合理花掉)的困难。换言之,就是要证明改变地位带来的损害。如果被告无法证明改变地位或带来的损害到什么程度(合理花掉了多少钱),则法院没有裁量权进行决定,正如 May 大法官在 Filby v. Mortgage Express(No. 2)(2004)EWCA Civ 759 先例中说:"... there is no residual general discretion to withhold the remedy nor to modify it simply to avoid harsh reality. "

正如 Slade 大法官在 Avon County Council v. Howlett(1983)1 WLR 605 先例所说,收钱的一方在计错数或者汇错钱也没有人来找的情况下经常会认为他是完全有权拥有这笔钱,直到被告知道事实并非如此。他收到钱后可能生活方式发生改变,做出了其他承诺或达成了其他交易,而这些都是他没有收到这笔钱是不会做的。但要事后让他去提供细节证明这些改变或达成的交易是如果没有这笔钱就不会发生的是很困难的。尤其是生活方式的改变,举个简单的例子,去的餐厅提高了一个档次,出门坐地铁变为打车等,这些都不会保留证据,也很难证明是因为得到了这笔钱才会有的改变。但这是另一个在考虑改变地位以去扣减归还的问题,就不再探讨或重复了。

至于还不起钱之类的问题，在“松绑”的情况下就只是执行金钱判决（money judgment）的问题。之后会是破产清盘还是其他执行手段［如指定破产接管人（receiver）等］，至少受害方不会因为无法复原或反复原而无法撤销可能是很不公平的合约，只能硬着头皮继续履行。

6. 撤销合约的其他障碍

已经详尽介绍了被误述方在发觉了误述后最正常与重要的救济是行使撤销有关合约的权利，否定这种救济的最重要的理由是不能回复到没有该合约产生的地位，也就是无法复原/反复原。可在接下来的段节区别探讨其他可否定被误述方这个救济的理由。可以说，也就是有这些问题，所以误述只是可使合约无效（voidable），不是自动就变无效（void）。

6.1　其他障碍之一：确认合约

“确认合约”（affirmation of contract）实际与“弃权与禁反言”的原理相近，这方面在笔者《合约的履行、弃权与禁反言》一书也已经有详论：第一章之7段就是针对在履行中发生违约/毁约（repudiatory breach），受害方选择（election）接受（acceptance）去终止合约或确认合约去坚持合约继续有效；另在第三章之3段更详尽针对“因选择而弃权”（waiver by election），是在面对两个完全对立的合约与法律权利（inconsistent rights）时，有权选择的一方要在规定或法律默示的合理时间内做出选择。同样的大道理/大原则也适用在受害方/被误述方有权去撤销或确认一个因误述诱导而产生的合约的情况。显然，这两个权利是完全对立的。由于针对如何才算是做出选择的法律已经有详论，不去重复，只在此小段针对误述方面稍作介绍。

确认的情况是受害方/被误述方在知悉了误述［或任何其他可使合约无效或可以终止（terminate）合约的毁约/违约等］后，不去发出撤销（或终止）合约通知，而是做出了一些客观看应被视为他/她放弃了这撤销（或终止）权利的言行。受害方在知悉了他有两个完全对立（也就是使合约无效或让合约有效，双方必须继续履行）的权利后，法律就要受害方必须在合理的时间内选择并告知对方（误述方）受害方的决定。毕竟，对方也会因受害方的选择而受到重大影响，所以应该让对方尽快知悉。

这与自始无效的合约无关，因为自始无效不涉及受害方或任何人有权利去选择并确认一份严重共同错误（例如标的房屋在订约时已经被烧毁）的合约有效。但法律下合约自始无效的情况不多，只有少数的情况，[36]如错误。但有法律后果的错误（actionable mistake）很难成立，所以在现实商业社会合约自始无效的情况不多。从以

〔36〕　也会有其他情况，如在本书第八章介绍的一些公共政策如限制贸易（restraint of trade），还如有一些其他立法规定无效的情况等。

下权威说法可见，法律规定大部分在订立时有缺陷的合约（但现实上仍然可以履行）是可使无效的救济而不是自始无效的救济，其中一个主要的考虑是保护无辜第三人。

6.1.1　权威说法

这在《Chitty on Contracts》（2021 年，第 34 版）一书之 9 – 141 段：“**Affirmation of the contract** If the representee, having discovered the misrepresentation, either expressly declares his intention to proceed with the contract, or does some act inconsistent with an intention to rescind the contract, he is bound by his affirmation. Thus a shareholder's right to claim rescission of a contract to take shares, made on the strength of a misrepresentation in the prospectus, **may be lost if, after discovering the facts**, he carries on the business of which the shares give him control, or if he attends a shareholders' meeting or tries to sell the shares; for by such acts he is taken to have affirmed the contract. But, where rescission cannot in fact be made without the co-operation of the representor, affirmation is not to be inferred merely because the representee continues to enjoy the fruits of the contract. ... **Each case is decided on its own facts, and the courts may pay particular attention to the nature of the contract, to any lapse of time which may have occurred, and to the question whether the representor has changed his position in reliance on the absence of a protest by the representee, or whether third parties have been affected by this.**”（加黑部分是笔者的强调）

另可节录《Misrepresentation, Mistake and Non-Disclosure》（2022 年，第 6 版）一书之 4 – 40 段说：“**The representee may elect to affirm or rescind** Since misrepresentation renders the contract not void but voidable at the instance of the representee, it gives the representee an election: the right to decide whether to rescind or not-and this means affirming or rescinding the whole contract: ... If the representee elects not to rescind, he affirms the contract. As long as the representee has not yet elected to exercise his right to rescind or his right to affirm the contract, and as long as none of the other bars to rescission ... has arisen, the election remains exercisable, and the contract remains on foot but voidable.”

6.1.2　受害方/被陈述方会构成选择确认合约的言行

在一个完美的情况下，即使合约的达成有十分严重的缺陷与对受害方不利，如好莱坞电影《教父》中的名言“make an offer that one cannot refuse”（拿枪指着头要对方签署的非法胁迫合约），或是严重的欺诈性误述诱导产生的合约，客观看来让这种有严重缺陷的合约有效存在并可以寻求法律强制执行的救济是无论如何都说不通的。但受害方在完全知情与知道自己权利，也不再有任何压力的情况下，明确向胁迫方或误述方说：“我确认这合约有效，双方应继续履行。”这样，法律何必再去理会是否应该强制使这有严重缺陷的合约无效？毕竟，这是合约双方的自治，任何第三人包括法院也管不了。至于背后的原因，除非是非法（例如胁迫继续存在），否则也就不必深究了,如商业或政治决定,又或是市场有重大改变等,受害方在权衡下想合约继续有效。

但问题是经常不是完美的情况,确认经常涉及受害方/被误述方做出的言行客观看来是有意识选择继续履行该误述导致的合约。但如果受害方虽然是已经知道了误述的事实,但不知道自己的法律权利与面对一个选择必须尽快决定是撤销或是确认该合约,没有意识下做出的言行在客观看来是确认合约,这样受害方就会惨了,在受害方后来才发觉自己错失良机去撤销一份有缺陷与不利的合约时,就只剩下一个昂贵与胜负难料的诉讼或仲裁去认定做出的言行是否是一个清楚无误的确认。

需要去客观认定受害方/被误述方的特定言行是否是一个确认而不是撤销合约的合理性是显而易见的。要知道这言行传递的讯号会对误述方造成不公平,确认或撤销合约的选择是完全对立的,任何一种选择都严重影响对方。但误述方只能客观看受害方的言行去分析与理解他的决定是什么,无法知道受害方的脑袋里在想什么(可能受害方的脑袋里根本没有在想什么,因为他不知道自己的法律权利)。所以审理法官或仲裁员也应该客观分析受害方特定的言行应是选择确认还是撤销合约,毕竟法律是针对懂法律的人士设计的,无意也无法去针对或保护不懂的人士。例如,受害方在知悉误述的事实后,要求误述方为接下去一年的履行提前作出准备与配合,这言行是怎样看都是确认而不会是撤销合约。

6.1.3　“无损害”的言行被解读为选择确认合约(或撤销合约)能起的作用

一种避免决定撤销合约前的言行被解释为作出确认合约的选择的保护做法是受害方在作出一些模棱两可的言行的同时明示加上“无损害”(without prejudice),但这个做法也是要懂法律的当事人才能恰到好处地做到。“无损害”[或同义词如“保留权利”(reserve rights)或“抗议下”(under protest)]作为保护自己的利益与权利能够起到的作用与局限在笔者其他的书籍已经有详论,如《证据法:国际规管与诉讼中的证据攻防》一书第十三章与《合约的履行、弃权与禁反言》一书第四章之6.5段。前一本书是针对双方有争议时试图和解,但为了防止双方谈不拢需要启动或继续诉讼或仲裁程序时,对方把有关和谈的内容向法院或仲裁庭披露,这种在和解谈判(也包括调解)中试图解决争议的“无损害”言行在证据规则下是不允许抖出来的,可享有特免权(privilege)。这种“无损害”与本小段关系不大。

但后一本书有所不同,其是针对面对一个合约或法律下的不同权利的选择时,需要决定要么走东,要么走西。这样,有权选择的一方就必须在合理时间内决定,并需要以清楚的言行通知对方自己选择走东或走西。否则,在合理时间过后就会失去选择权,选择了走东或走西后也再也不能回头。而如果在合理时间内仍未最后决定(如仍在确定有关事件的真相或仍在询问法律意见),由于双方仍在互动,如合约仍在履行,有权选择的一方为了避免自己的言行被误解或误读为作出选择的言行,就可以加上“无损害”的标签。例如《合约的履行、弃权与禁反言》一书的第四章之6.5.1.2段针对的有权终止合约,这权利可来自:(1)法律,如对方违约/毁约或拒绝履行合约，自己可去"接受"[37]并终止合约或坚持对方履行（甚至威胁向法院申请履行指令）；[38]或是（2）来自合约的明示条文，如银行的借贷合约经常有一条文列出大量的违约事项，并说明一旦发生，银行有权选择终止合约。这样，终止的权利一旦出现，法律就默示有权选择的一方必须合理作出选择：是终止合约，或是确认合约继续履行，放弃终止合约权利。

这与本段所针对的可诉误述（无论是欺诈性、疏忽或是无辜）带来了受害方/被误述方的选择权，他可去选择走东（撤销合约）或走西（确认合约仍是有效）是同样道理。所以，无需重复已有详尽针对的内容。在近期的 SK Shipping Plc v. Capital VLCC 3 Corp（2020）EWHC 3448（Comm）先例中，也涉及了这方面的争议（与其他重要争议，在本书第二章之 10.5.2 段与第四章之 5.3.2 段有不同针对），并给出了一些实用的指引。

案情涉及十分常见的航运争议。原告船东在 2016 年 11 月在市场上放出"C Challenger"轮的信息（其中包括该船舶的船速与油耗）以寻求长期租约。在 2016 年 12 月，被告承租人与船东订立了 2 年加 1 年的期租合约，标准合约中包括一条详尽的船速与油耗保证。承租人不久后发觉船舶的油耗超过了船东在谈判时提供的信息与租约中的保证。并从 2017 年 3 月开始向船东投诉对油耗的误述。虽然承租人不断重复这个说法，并且从 2017 年 6 月起不再支付租金，但还是一直继续租用与营运该船舶。2017 年 10 月，承租人通知船东决定以误述撤销合约或以违约/毁约终止合约。[39] 而船东认为承租人的通知构成拒绝履行合约，接受并终止合约。在之后的诉讼，其中一个争议是如果承租人对船东欺诈性误述船舶的船速与油耗以诱导订立租约的指控能够成立，承租人有否通过继续营运船舶的言行选择了确认租约？承租人声称因为自己与船东的书信往来都明示保留了权利，说明"无损害"，所以没有清楚无误地确认租约。但法院并没有支持承租人的说法，法院认为虽然保留权利可以令有关言行不被解释为选择确认租约，但这并不是绝对的。因为在每一个争议，都需要去看是什么言行并根据当时的背景/环境去客观解释。这言行会是模棱两可，也会是明确了承租人不选择撤销租约，然后再去比较泛泛的"无损害"措辞，看看孰轻孰重。有时候，行胜于言（actions speak louder than words），但有时也会是言胜于行（words speak louder than actions）。

例如，如果受害方/被误述方是在履行自己的合约义务或向对方要求信息时保留撤销合约的权利，很有可能可以成功保留自己撤销合约的选择权。因为可以解读为

---

〔37〕 见笔者《合约的履行、弃权与禁反言》一书第一章之 7 段。

〔38〕 见笔者《损失赔偿与救济》一书第十二章。

〔39〕 船速与油耗虽然属于租约保证，但违反的后果可以轻微或严重，属于中间条文，见 The"Hong Kong Fir"（1962）2 QB 26 贵族院先例。因为英国法不鼓励随便终止合约，所以想要以对船速与油耗的保证终止租约有困难。这也是为什么承租人要同时提起误述撤销合约与违约/毁约的替代争辩，只要成立可诉误述，选择行使撤销合约的权利就容易很多。

受害方仍在对发生的误述与是否能够构成可诉误述在调查取证或咨询律师，而在此期间，由于合约尚未变为无效，显然仍需要履行。例如，承租人到时间支付 15 天租金，如果不准时支付就会让船东根据合约条文撤船或甚是因承租人拒绝支付租金去接受违约/毁约。所以，承租人还要硬着头皮支付租金，但为了不被视为此行为是放弃对可诉误述（当时承租人会是已经提出航速与油耗误述）的撤销合约权利，选择了确认租约，就应该在通知船东支付了租金的同时，加上“无损害”的措辞以保护承租人自己。

但如果是其他千变万化的行为，例如受害方承租人要求船东履行租约下保持船舶状况（maintenance of vessel）的条文，进坞清洁船底，去改善航速与油耗，以利在分租约下交船，船东也就安排了。为此，船东也产生了额外使费。这样，就有危险不会仅仅因为承租人在提出要求时泛泛保留了权利，此言行就不被解读为确认租约。

在该先例中，可节录 Foxton 大法官所说如下：“I have concluded that while … a reservation of rights will often have the effect of preventing subsequent conduct constituting an election, this is not an invariable rule. In the final analysis, the issue of whether there has been an election requires the court to have regard to all the material, including any reservations which have been communicated. **Where conduct is consistent with the reservation of a right to rescind**, but also consistent with the continuation of the contract, then an express reservation will preclude the making of an election. This is likely to be the case where there is a reservation of rights accompanying the exercise of a contractual right **to obtain information** as to a party's rights, **or** where a party is **performing its own obligations while assessing its position**. However, where a party **makes an unconditional demand of substantial contractual performance of a kind which will lead the counterparty and/or third parties to alter their positions in significant respects**, such conduct may be wholly incompatible with the reservation of some kinds of rights, even if the party demanding performance purports at the same time to reserve them.”（加黑部分是笔者的强调）

6.1.4 受害方/被误述方知悉误述的事实与法律权利后的言行才会被视为确认合约

这先节录近期的 Leeds City Council and Ors v. Barclays Bank Plc and Ors（2021）EWHC 363（Comm）先例中，Cockerill 大法官所说：

“The fundamentals of the law on affirmation were not in dispute. A contract tainted by misrepresentation is voidable ab initio at the instance of the representee. In other words **the innocent party can choose whether to rescind the contract or insist on performance**. Since the **two rights are mutually inconsistent**, **the representee must make an irrevocable choice**. If he chooses to affirm the contract, he cannot later change his mind and opt for rescission instead.

But the representee**cannot exercise his right to rescind unless he knows that such a right has accrued to him**;hence,what is required is **informed election**. First,the representee must have sufficient knowledge of its right to rescind the contract,and then he must **manifest the election to affirm through words or conduct which,objectively construed,evince such an election**.

The parties hotly dispute whether the claimants' conduct can be taken as affirmatory,what amounts to sufficient knowledge,and whether sufficient knowledge can be inferred or attributed to the claimants in these proceedings."(加黑部分是笔者的强调)

当然,在受害方/被误述方不肯定是否有可诉误述,只是有了猜疑时,需要进一步调查事实真相。如果期间受害方继续在履约,这算不算是确认的行为是要看不同案件的案情。毕竟,受害方会对继续履约的行为合理化,如受害方在当时仍未完全肯定误述的事实与肯定自己应有撤销合约的权利,所以不去"打草惊蛇",直到肯定。毕竟对任何这种争辩都是认定事实后客观分析来认定有关的言行是否应被视为受害方选择确认该有缺陷合约,或在当时的背景/环境下难去说死。

例如在 Senanayake v. Cheng(1966)AC 63 枢密院先例中,是新加坡上诉的案件,案情涉及误述。误述方 S 是一家马来西亚股票经纪公司的主要合伙人,他向一位犹疑未决的新合伙人(Cheng)游说公司业务前景极好,导致新合伙人出资 20,000 元加入该合伙公司。但不久后的 5 月底/6 月初主要合伙人出门度假,Cheng 有机会多看公司文件才知悉公司很有问题,债台高筑(如向银行透支 250,000 元等)。接下去在 7 月 1 日,Cheng 委托律师写信给公司要求归还 20,000 元,并在 7 月 21 日提起诉讼。而公司也在 7 月上旬正式结业并指定了接管人(receivers)。被告误述方在枢密院的主要抗辩是 Cheng 确认了误述导致的加入合伙的合约,因为她发觉了误述后仍在任职,并在 6 月 29 日召开合伙人会议,这是明确确认的言行。Cheng 的解释是她不尽快辞退合伙人是因为想等主要合伙人度假结束后回来,而合伙人会议谈的是有关她投诉主要合伙人向其他合伙人隐瞒信息与几位合伙人注资去挽救公司,但谈不拢。枢密院的 Morris 勋爵在考虑证据显示的事实后,不认为 Cheng 有确认的言行:"A consideration of the course of events leads their Lordships to the view that it is quite impossible to say that the plaintiff affirmed the contract or that she is in any way precluded herself from taking the course that she adopted."

显然,这种争议十分事实敏感(facts - sensitive)。笔者估计如果 Cheng 召开的合伙人会议谈的是发展公司业务;或 Cheng 不在会议没有结果后很快委托律师明确说明撤销合约的立场而是拖拖拉拉再上班一两个月;又或是 Cheng 不能提供可信证据(这会是口头证据,优质可信证据就会是 Cheng 能够应对交叉盘问并获审理法官相信)等,就不见得会胜诉。

另在 Coastal Estates Pty Ltd v. Melevende(1965)VR 433 澳大利亚先例中,案件涉及土地买卖的一个欺诈性误述。被误述方买方在知悉了该虚假陈述后,仍向误述方卖方作出一些支付。独立去看，这支付的言行明显是去履行合约下的支付责任或承诺，等同或更接近是确认合约而不是撤销合约。但澳大利亚法院认为知悉除了是误述的事实外，还包括了被误述方的法律权利，也就是他有权去撤销合约。毕竟这是有严重后果的一步，被误述方的谨慎是完全合理。所以在涉及较复杂的情况时，被误述方需要查询称职律师才算是知悉。而在真正知悉前被误述方履行合约的言行，不应该被轻易定性为确认的言行。在该先例中，Herring 大法官说："... It is conduct no doubt that could have properly been put forward as evidence that the plaintiff had resolved to affirm, if he had known he had a right of election. But of course in the present case his conduct has to be looked at on the basis that **he did not have any such knowledge, and so looked at it would not appear conduct of such an unequivocal character as to preclude the plaintiff from exercising his right to rescind**. By paying the instalments and interest payable under the contract and the rates that the contract required him to pay, the plaintiff was doing nothing inconsistent with disaffirmance. He was doing no more than fulfilling his own obligations under the contract. He was not seeking to exercise rights under the contract adverse to the defendant as vendor, nor was he seeking to gain advantages for himself. **He did not do anything that unequivocally involved an affirmative of the contract** ..."（加黑部分是笔者的强调）

Adam 大法官也说："The conclusion I have reached ... is that the ultimate question to be answered in cases where affirmation is relied upon as a defence to a rescission is whether the representee has after discovery of the falsity of the relevant misrepresentations, in truth elected to affirm the contract and thereby elected not to avoid it. Because the making of **an election necessarily presupposes a knowledge that a choice between alternative courses is open, in general, no question of affirmation can arise in the absence of such knowledge**. ..."（加黑部分是笔者的强调）

Peyman v. Lanjani（1985）Ch 457 上诉庭先例很大程度参考了 Coastal Estates Pty Ltd v. Melevende 澳大利亚先例，重申只有受害方在清楚知道误述的事实也同时了解他有撤销合约的法律权利后的言行，才会被视为确认的言行。笔者只节录会更清楚的判决提要如下："Where a party to a contract was faced with the choice whether to affirm or rescind the contract, in order to render his election irrevocable he had to have knowledge not only of the fact which gave rise to the election but also of the right of election itself; that a person could not be treated as having elected to affirm a contract unless he had unequivocally demonstrated to the other party that he intended to proceed with it; that the issue of election was a question of fact to be decided on the evidence.... "

6.1.5　证明受害方/被误述方知悉事实与法律权利的困难

在一个严重的欺诈性误述下受骗，很难想象有太多受害方/被误述方会在知悉受骗后真心真意告知误述方："我确认这个不利的合约，我愿意受骗。"当然万事也会有例外,如事后由于情况的变化,导致合约下受害方会利润丰厚,显然受害方不会愿意撤销合约。然而这例外不多,也很容易想到欺诈性误述(或如胁迫)诱导产生的合约,通常是对受害方非常不利的。

问题是受害方必须知悉误述的事实以及知悉法律权利后的言行才会被视为或解释为确认合约,如果受害方不懂法律或游戏规则,又不肯花钱调查或咨询称职律师,这样该受害方永远不会事实上真的知悉(actual knowledge)有关事实与法律权利,难道他所有的言行都不会构成确认吗?例如误述方直接问受害方是否确认合约,受害方回答说"可以""你要我确认我就确认吧",之后受害方委任律师可否说受害方一直不知悉自己的权利,所以即使是这样明白的言行都不是确认合约?这对误述方公平合理吗?毕竟可以肯定被受害方这样言行误导,误述方可以以为是合约被确认。

上述情形除了是对误述方不公平,也在鼓励愚昧。因此做法上会是误述方可以提供证据,例如受害方曾经获取过律师意见,这就可能足以让法官或仲裁员根据事实推断(inferred)受害方知悉;或者可以事实推定(evidential presumption)[40]受害方知悉事实与法律权利,此时就轮到受害方提供证据反驳(rebut)事实推定,做不到的话即认定受害方知悉。再加上若事后受害方其他的言行也可分析为更接近确认合约,其就有危险被认定为确认合约。

至于是否愿意作出推断或推定知悉,就完全是审理法官或仲裁员自己的裁量权了。如何根据事实认定,很大程度上是依据审理法官或仲裁员的个人看法,换个人就可能完全不同。所以上诉庭也会自制,不会去质疑一审对事实的认定。这也要看具体的证据,显示出事情发生的内在可能性(inherent probability)等问题。在 Yukon's Line Ltd of Korea v. Rendsburg Investment Corporation(1996)2 Lloyd's Rep 604 先例中,Moore - Bick 大法官提醒法官或仲裁员不要轻易作出这样的认定,因为现实是不会有太多例外情况是受骗的受害方会真正愿意确认合约的:"In my view, the Court should generally be slow to accept that the injured party has committed himself irrevocably to continuing with the contract in the knowledge that if, without finally committing himself, the injured party has made an unequivocal statement of some kind on which the party in repudiation has, the doctrine relied of estoppel is likely to prevent any injustice being done."(加黑部分是笔者的强调)

这个道理与解释合约一条经常被引用的主要解释规则类似,如果解释条文/文字会带来一个不合理的结果,越不合理的结果就表示越不可能是双方在订立合约时的共同订约意图,而如果这的确是他们的订约意图,就必须把这个意图写得清清楚楚。Reid 勋爵在 L Schuler AG v. Wickman Machine Tool Sales Ltd(1973)2 Lloyd's Rep 53 先例中说:"The fact that a particular construction leads to a very unreasonable result must be a relevant consideration. The more unreasonable the result the more unlikely it is

---

〔40〕 有关事实推定可见《证据法:基础理论、口头证据与专家证据》一书第七章之 6.1 段。

that the parties can have intended it, and if they do intend it the more necessary it is that they shall make that intention abundantly clear."

6.1.6 确认合约要求受害方/被误述方知悉事实与权利的例外:禁反言与其他情况

由于社会上会发生千变万化的不同案件,所以任何原则或规定都会有例外,难以在所有情况适用。

首先介绍重要的例外是禁反言(estoppels)。众所周知,禁反言(不论是陈述性禁反言或是承诺性禁反言)并不像弃权,不要求被禁反言的一方做出有关的言行时知悉他的法律权利,而是主要看该言行有否对另一方造成损害。

在 Coastal Estates Pty Ltd v. Melevende(1965) VR 433 澳大利亚先例中,Adam 大法官说:"In the case of a representee unaware of his right of election there is, I consider, **a distinction to be drawn between acts** done by him in exercise of rights under the contract **adversely to the other party** which, were the contract not on foot, could not be justified, **and acts which** do no more than show that the representee recognised the contract as still subsisting, but **are not prejudicial or adverse to the other party**. Such a distinction may be explained as an application of the **doctrine of estoppel** ..."(加黑部分是笔者的强调)

Sholl 大法官也说:

"If the defrauded party does not know that he has a legal right to rescind, he is not bound by acts which on the face of them are referable only to an intention to affirm the contract, **unless those acts are 'adverse to' the opposite party, i. e., unless they involve something to the other party's prejudice or detriment**, ... **This a form of estoppel**, for the other party has in such a case acted to his prejudice upon a representation, made by the defrauded party's conduct, that the latter is going on with the contract. The law does not require the representor in such a case to inquire of the representee whether he knows his legal rights.

Acts of the defrauded party which are not adverse in the above sense, such as payments made by him to the other party ... They **may, however, form part of the foundation for an estoppel**, e. g., if the opposite party, misled by such an act into supposing that the other is proceeding with the contract, refuses a more advantages offer for the property. ... or otherwise acts to his prejudice."(加黑部分是笔者的强调)

这可去简单举例,如在本章之6.1.3段举的受害方承租人在对撤销或确认租约犹疑不决期间,要求船东进坞清洁船底去改善航速与油耗,船东也就安排了的例子。船东因此产生了额外使费,因为原本可以留待其他方便与便宜的时机再清洁,也就是依赖了承租人的言行(不论承租人当时对能否撤销合约的事实与法律是否知情)蒙受了损害。在这种情况下,承租人作为受害方就会因言行构成陈述性禁反言,不能以船东误述船舶的船速与油耗去撤销租约。

另多介绍一种较次要与特定案件(case specific)的例外情况,是去撤销合约非要误述方合作不可,但误述方不合作,迫使受害方被迫履行下去,这种言行不能算确认,毕竟受害方选择了撤销的意图已是清楚表达给了误述方。这方面可介绍 Kupchak v. Dayson Holdings Co Ltd(1965)53 DLR(2d)482 加拿大先例中,涉及原告(Kupchak)买入被告(是一家经营汽车旅馆的公司)的股票并加入董事会,但后来发觉被告的过往利润其实有很大水分以存在作假,从而以欺诈性误述以由去撤销合约。但在此期间的几个月,原告被指称不去归还股票与保留董事职位构成确认合约的言行,而原告的解释是没有被告的合作(如需要被告的签字)做不到。当然这不能是原告空口讲或推搪,只说加拿大英属哥伦比亚上诉庭最后认定这些言行不构成确认合约。

6.2 其他障碍之二:时隔太久/怠慢理论

延误撤销可使无效的合约不适用索赔损失的时效,如《Limitation Act 1980》的 6 年立法时效。但如果延误过了合理时间,会因在衡平法救济要求尽快以保证对双方当事人都尽量持平的"怠慢理论"下而失去,这也可视为弃权或禁反言(早年并没有做区分)的一种"沉默性弃权/禁反言"(waiver/estoppel by acquiescence)。[41]

"时隔太久"(lapse of time/delay)是事实,也是中性的描述,会是不同原因造成。但"怠慢理论"(doctrine of laches)是衡平法理论,在 Lindsay Petroleum Co v. Hurd (1874) LR 5 PC 221 枢密院先例中有针对,指的是"有关行为或不为,即使不是弃权,但如果之后在主张权利时给予救济,会导致另一方处于不合理的地位"(by his conduct and neglect … has, though perhaps not waiving that remedy, yet put the other party in a situation in which it would not be reasonable to place him if the remedy were afterwards to be asserted)。

在此先例中,Barnes Peacock 大法官说到两方面的考虑,延误的程度与延误期间的行为对双方当事人的影响,在做出救济时进行权衡以达到对双方公平:"two circumstances, always important in such cases, are, the length of the delay and the nature of the acts done during the interval, which might affect either party and cause a balance of justice or injustice in taking the one course or the other, so far as relates to the remedy."

同样说法可先节录较近期的 Salt v. Stratstone Specialist Ltd (2015) EWCA Civ 745 上诉庭先例中,Roth 大法官说:"… **rescission for misrepresentation is an equitable remedy**. Absent a statutory bar, an objection to rescission must therefore rest on equitable basis. Accordingly, it is something of a misnomer to say that rescission may be barred by lapse of time. It is only **the lapse of a reasonable time** such that it would be **inequitable in all the circumstances to grant rescission** which constitutes a bar to remedy. This is in essence the principle of laches, which accordingly requires close attention to

---

〔41〕 见笔者《合约的履行、弃权与禁反言》一书第五章之 10 段的详细介绍。

the facts of the case."(加黑部分是笔者的强调)

同样的精神,即"有权不用、过期作废"也在其他情况适用。如针对违约/毁约或任何其他出现相对权利的选择时要求受害方或有权选择方尽快在合理时间内行使权利,作出最后选择。或是在货不对版下拒货,正如在《Sale of Goods Act 1979》之 S.35 中说如果买方在合理时间后仍然保留货物,没有通知卖方拒货,就视为买方接受了有关货物:"after the lapse of a reasonable time, he retains the goods without intimating to the seller that he has rejected them."

《Chitty on Contracts》(2021 年,第 34 版)一书之 9 - 145 段针对延误撤销误述导致的合约说:"**Lapse of time** Lapse of time after discovery that there has been a misrepresentation may be evidence of affirmation. ... This is especially true of contracts for the sale or allotment of shares in companies, where the utmost promptness is required. In such a case a delay of even a few weeks after discovery of the misrepresentation is usually fatal, and there cannot, in any event, be rescission of an allotment after the company has gone into liquidation. ..."

6.2.1 Leaf v. International Galleries(1950)2 KB 86 上诉庭先例

上述节录提到 Leaf v. International Galleries 上诉庭先例中,误述的受害方买方是在订立合约的 5 年后才主张撤销合约,这被上诉庭否决。Jenkins 大法官说:"contracts such as this cannot be kept open and subject to the possibility of rescission indefinitely ... I think that, at all events, it behoves the purchaser either to verify, or, as the case may be, to disapprove the representation within a reasonable time, or else stand or fall by it. If he is allowed to wait five, ten or twenty years and then reopen the bargain, there can be no finality at all."

该先例买卖的是一幅名画,买方在买了 5 年后想通过佳士得拍卖行出售才发觉是假画,所以晚了去撤销 5 年前的合约。买方希望根据复原原则向原卖方取回货价。由于这被认定为无辜误述,所以买方不存在可以索赔损失(在 1967 年立法生效前,非欺诈性误述只有撤销合约的衡平救济而没有索赔损失的救济)的情形,能够撤销买卖合约并取回货价是买方唯一的救济。

实践中对此先例不无质疑,因为虽然延误 5 年,但原因是 5 年后买方才对误述知情。《Chitty on Contracts》(2021 年,第 34 版)一书之 9 - 145 段说:"... **But there can normally be no affirmation where the representee is ignorant of the truth and therefore of this right to rescind**, and the inference of affirmation from lapse of time should therefore be rebuttable by proof of lack of knowledge of the untruth. In Leaf v. International Galleries(1950)2 KB 86 the right to rescind a contract for the sale of goods was held barred by five years' delay **despite the fact that the representee only discovered the truth shortly before the proceedings** but that was a case in which the delay would have amounted to acceptance of the goods and appears to be **an exception to the general**

rule;and,as we have seen,in the Court of Appeal〔42〕 it has been questioned whether Leaf v. International Galleries is good law after the enactment of s. 1 of the Misrepresentation Act 1967. **It seems doubtful whether mere lapse of time will bar rescission in other cases of completely innocent misrepresentation**, and this will not be so in cases of fraud, nor where there has been breach of a fiduciary duty, at least until the fraud or breach has been discovered. "(加黑部分是笔者的强调)

笔者也质疑此先例与选择有直接矛盾,因为在一个可使无效的合约中,受害方可选择撤销或确认该合约,这是无可置疑的法律地位。而作出选择,是需要受害方知悉误述的事实,但这显然不是 Leaf v. International Galleries 先例的案情。

看来在《Misrepresentation Act 1967》立法后,这 Leaf v. International Galleries 上诉庭先例的判法也存在其他问题,这在本章下一段将进行讲述。

6.2.2 Salt v. Stratstone Specialist Ltd(2015)EWCA Civ 745 上诉庭先例

接下来介绍的 Salt v. Stratstone Specialist Ltd 上诉庭先例中,案情是 Salt 先生是一个豪车与跑车的狂热爱好者,拥有凯迪拉克、宝马与捷豹等品牌的多辆汽车。2007 年 9 月初被告 Stratstone Specialist Limited 公司的销售人员向 Salt 先生推荐了一款凯迪拉克的跑车,并声称该车是全新的(brand new)。2007 年 9 月 7 日,Salt 先生在与该销售人员的电话通话中同意以 21,895 英镑的价格购买该车。2007 年 9 月 29 日该车交付给 Salt 先生。Salt 先生在开始驾驶该车之后,该车的点火装置、电池、卫星导航系统、雨刮器、加油提示灯等零部件均先后出现了问题,甚至有一次 Salt 先生在驾驶途中被困在车内出不来。被告通过修理解决了该车的部分问题。但 Salt 先生实在忍无可忍,于 2008 年 9 月 16 日要求将该车退回被告并想要拿回买车支付的全部价款,被告拒绝了该退款的要求。2009 年 3 月 24 日 Salt 先生开始了对被告的诉讼,主张货物在买卖合约下不符可商售质量(merchantable quality)而索赔损失。2009 年 9 月 Salt 先生也停止使用该汽车。在双方诉讼过程中,经过共同专家对车辆情况提交专家报告与文件披露程序,Salt 先生发现该车的出厂日期在 2005 年,并于 2005 年 3 月交付给被告,该车虽然在登记机关从来没有登记车主的记录,但在 2005 年至 2006 年间却被多次修理,并且还发生过一次严重的碰撞损毁。这与被告的销售人员所说的该车是全新的描述根本不符,这构成误述。Salt 先生在 2011 年 5 月 19 日修改了索赔请求书,〔43〕将不符可商售质量索赔损失变更为误述〔44〕与撤销合约。

地区法院的 Hickman 法官判他无法给予 Salt 先生撤销合约的救济,因为 Salt 先生已经无法使双方复原到合约没有订立前的状态。首先,Salt 先生登记了该车辆在

〔42〕 将在本章下一段详细介绍的 Salt v. Stratstone Specialist Ltd(2015)EWCA Civ 745 上诉庭先例。

〔43〕 见笔者《证据法:国际规管与诉讼中的证据攻防》一书第七章之 6.1 段与 6.6 段。

〔44〕 从案情来说很可能是欺诈性误述,但是从报道出来的上诉庭先例的判决来看,Longmore 大法官针对的是《Misrepresentation Act 1967》之 S. 2,看来案件中应该是将误述定性为无辜误述与/或疏忽误述。

他的名下,该车无法复原到交付给他时的没有登记车主的状况。其次,也已经时隔太久。Hickman 法官也无法计算出要扣减多少金钱可以对应 Salt 先生收到汽车与使用汽车后而给汽车带来的价值上的贬损与享受上的增加,也就是无法计算反复原(counter - restitution)。所以 Hickman 法官最后判 Salt 先生的救济只能局限在损失赔偿,而根据专家的报告与多次维修给 Salt 先生带来的不便,Hickman 法官确定损失金额为 3250 英镑。

Salt 先生将案件上诉至巡回法院,Charles Harris QC 大法官推翻了 Hickman 法官的判决,认为双方的地位完全可能复原,汽车仍然存在,被登记了车主与时隔太久并不能成为撤销买卖合约的障碍,而任何汽车价值的贬损的计算应该对误述方不利而不是对被误述方不利。结果 Charles Harris QC 大法官判合约被撤销而 Salt 先生可以拿回买车所支付的价款。被告收到该截然相反的判决结果之后进一步上诉。

上诉庭的 Longmore 大法官支持了巡回法院 Charles Harris QC 大法官的判法,Longmore 大法官认为复原是可以做到的,对车辆登记车主是法律上的概念,而并不会影响车辆本身,并且买卖标的物价值上的贬损可以根据 Erlanger v. New Sombrero Phosphate Co(1878)3 App Cas 1218 先例确立的实际公平原则通过扣除标的物价格的方法解决。

本案中一个重要的争议是时隔太久是否构成对撤销合约的障碍。Longmore 大法官与 Roth 大法官对此都进行了分析。他们均认为时隔太久本身并不能构成对撤销合约的障碍,而是要看具体的情况,特别是受害方需要时间才能发现撤销合约的理由。本案中 Salt 先生修改索赔请求并不是他自己存在怠慢,而是因为他是在诉讼过程中才发现了误述的存在。

其中针对在此问题上的权威先例 Leaf v. International Galleries(1950)2 KB 86 先例中,该先例中名画的买家在购买 5 年后才发现画作并非画廊声称的画家所作并主张画廊存在无辜误述而要撤销合约的救济。Denning 大法官认为在该案涉及的买卖名画的交易中,该画的作者构成了买卖合约的条件条文。而后来证实作者并非合约中所标明,该条件条文被违反,而根据《Sale of Goods Act 1893》立法的规定,买方拒货与索赔货款要在合理的时间内,5 年的时间已经不能算合理时间。因此,如果允许买方以无辜误述去撤销合约,买方就会得到比主张违反条件条文更好的救济。而显然违反条件条文是触及合约的根本,是比无辜误述的后果更为严重。所以买方不被允许获得撤销合约的救济。

Longmore 大法官认为在《Misrepresentation Act 1967》通过之后,其 S. 1 已经明确写明误述的内容成为合约的条文也并不影响可以适用误述的救济。Leaf v. International Galleries 先例确立的原则看来已经并不是一个好的法律原则了,其说:"It must, moreover, be remembered that Leaf was decided well before the Misrepresentation Act was passed. It must be doubtful whether since the enactment of section 1 it is still good law that a representor should be in no worse position than if the representation had become a term of the contract, particularly if the representor takes no steps to prove that he was not negligent."

因为 Leaf v. International Galleries 先例是一个上诉庭的先例中，所以在普通法先例规则下如果要改变该先例确立的原则需要有最高院的判例。即使本先例同为上诉庭先例中，但仍无法对此问题作出改变。Longmore 大法官只能通过案情不同以做出区分(distinguish)的方法来解决。

Roth 大法官则认为时隔太久本身并不会构成怠慢而给撤销合约的救济带来障碍，他援引 Lindsay Petroleum Co v. Hurd(1874) LR 5 PC 221 枢密院先例中 Selborne 勋爵的说法如下："Now the doctrine of laches in Courts of Equity is not an arbitrary or a technical doctrine. Where it would be **practically unjust to give a remedy, either because** the party has, by his conduct, done that which might fairly be regarded as equivalent to **a waiver of it, or** where by his conduct and neglect he has, though perhaps not waiving that remedy, yet **put the other party in a situation in which it would not be reasonable to place him if the remedy were afterwards to be asserted**, in either of these cases, lapse of time and delay are most material. But in every case, if an argument against relief, which otherwise would be just, is founded upon mere delay, that delay of course not amounting to a bar by any statute of limitations, the validity of that defence must be tried upon principles substantially equitable. **Two circumstances, always important in such cases, are, the length of the delay and the nature of the acts done during the interval**, which might affect either party and cause **a balance of justice or injustice in taking the one course or the other**, so far as relates to the remedy."(加黑部分是笔者的强调)

Selborne 勋爵该段权威的判词，也被贵族院的 Fisher v. Brooker(2009) UKHL 41 先例所确认。这里提到时隔太久是否能够构成怠慢主要看两个方面：一方面就是看间隔的时间长度，另一方面看在该时间间隔中当事人的行为。而构成怠慢往往会带来两种结果：一种是从公平来看当事人已经构成弃权，[45]另一种是在该段时间内一方当事人的行为令另外一方在依赖后地位改变，从而构成禁反言。[46]

6.2.3 合理时间

合理时间(reasonable time)的课题在笔者《合约的解释：规则与应用》一书第十章之 4.2.1 段有详细介绍，所以这里只简单介绍尽量不重复。

在 Torrance v. Bolton(1872) LR 8 Ch. App. 118 上诉庭先例中，James 大法官说："a right to a reasonable time to ascertain his position, and to take advice from persons capable of advising him as to what he ought to do."

---

[45] 见笔者《合约的履行、弃权与禁反言》一书第三章。

[46] 见笔者《合约的履行、弃权与禁反言》一书第四章与第五章。

在 Newbigging v. Adam(1888)13 App Cas 308 贵族院先例中,涉及 Adam 向 Newbigging 误述(没有指控是欺诈性)诱导 Newbigging 注资成为合伙人[不参与公司管理的隐名合伙人(sleeping partner)]。Newbigging 在 1883 年初已经发觉合伙业务有问题,但在 Adam 的解释下,多待了一年多才警觉严重性,开始诉讼要求撤销合约的救济。法院不认同过了合理时间,Watson 勋爵说:"He relied,and was entitled to rely,upon the assurances which he had received,as to the satisfactory condition of the business,until he became aware of the true state of the facts. **It cannot be reasonably suggested that he ought to have known these facts before his suspicions were awakened** in August 1884;and he then made a searching investigation of the affairs of the partnership,which resulted in his bringing this suit against the appellants in November 1884."(加黑部分是笔者的强调)

至于什么是"合理时间",而延误错过合理时间与沉默性弃权视为确认的道理大同小异。确认往往是指受害方有行动而这行动客观上看是知道了误述事实与自己的法律权利后,但更想履行而不想撤销合约。而知道了权利后时隔太久则是没有任何行动或语言下,过了合理时间,被误述方仍不撤销合约,坐在那里不动,也往往是对另一方误述方不公平或造成影响。例如,订约后但仍未开始履约,被误述方的不行动令误述方不得不继续履约并导致劳民伤财或错过其他交易机会。另外,合理时间的长短要看个别案件。有些市场短期会浮动很大,如股票买卖、航运、商品等市场,被误述方在发觉误述后一两个星期仍不行动,他就会是失去撤销合约的权利。看合理时间也要去看延误是否会对误述方造成不公平、误述的性质等因素。

最后可节录《Misrepresentation,Mistake and Non-Disclosure》(2020 年,第 6 版)一书之 4-51 段说:"The length of time within which the representee must rescind cannot be stated with precision,because what is 'reasonable' must be determined in the light of the particular contract. ... the time to which the representee is entitled will depend on the nature of the contract,its subject-matter and the representations that were made. In the case of a contract to purchase a perishable commodity,or where the nature of the subject-matter and the representation in issue are such that the representee ought easily to have been able to discover the truth soon after the contract was concluded,the time within which he is expected to exercise his right to rescind will be relatively short. But if it is reasonable for him to remain in ignorance for an extended period,he may be able still to rescind after that time."

6.2.4 无辜误述与欺诈性误述在怠慢理论上的区别

有说法是非欺诈性误述更会受时隔太久的影响而导致失去撤销合约的权利,毕竟这是衡平法救济,而衡平法下一个基本理论是受害方一发觉就马上寻求救济(delay defeats equity)。正如 Blackburn 勋爵在 Erlanger v. New Sombrero Phosphate Co (1878)3 App Cas 1218 贵族院先例说:"a Court of Equity requires that those who come to it to ask for its active interposition to give them relief, should use due diligence, after there has been such notice of knowledge as to make it inequitable to lie by."

这可节录《Misrepresentation, Mistake and Non-Disclosure》(2022年，第6版)一书之4－52段说："Lapse of time ... can **operate as a bar to rescission in the case of a non-fraudulent misrepresentation**, and in that context the courts ask whether the representee has rescinded within a reasonable time from the contract. It is often said that lapse of time operates as a bar only to rescission for non-fraudulent misrepresentation; **lapse of time may be evidence of affirmation of the contract in a case of fraud, but does not of itself bar rescission**. It is clear that, in a case of fraud, time does not run against the representee as long as he remains, without any fault on his part, in ignorance of the fraud. But the equitable doctrine of laches operates in cases of fraud; and it seems preferable to say that time does run against the representee, even in a case of a fraudulent misrepresentation, but then only from the time he **discovered** it (or perhaps **ought to have discovered** it, if it is by his fault that he failed to do so). ..."(加黑部分是笔者的强调)

以上节录是说，在 Leaf v. International Galleries (1950) 2 KB 86 上诉庭先例中，针对非欺诈性误述，是否时隔太久是从合约订立时开始考虑。但欺诈性误述就不一样，是从被误述方发现或应该发现时开始考虑。但已经介绍过，随着《Misrepresentation Act 1967》立法生效与在 Salt v. Stratstone Specialist Ltd (2015) EWCA Civ 745 上诉庭先例后，Leaf v. International Galleries 先例在这方面的参考意义已经不大。表面看，现在在是否时隔太久方面，对于欺诈性误述与非欺诈性误述已经没有区别。但笔者相信对一些严重与隐蔽的欺诈性误述，基于惩奸除恶的心态，法院会更宽松对待时间延误的问题。

上述主要针对在发觉误述的时隔太久问题，至于从发觉欺诈后多少时间之内必须采取行动去主张撤销合约，这方面法律看来仍然在不断发展。目前针对欺诈性误述的衡平法撤销，在 HMRC v. IGE USA Investments Ltd (2021) EWCA Civ 534 上诉庭先例中判可以类比(analogy)欺诈/欺骗侵权(tort of deceit)，因此根据《Limitation Act 1980》之 Section 36[47]有6年时效，不会在之前被判是怠慢。而非欺诈性误述的衡平法撤销看来就未必有这样的类比，仍然是根据每个案件看是否存在怠慢。当然在实践操作中，两者未必会导致重大区分，都要考虑是否有怠慢。这在 P&O Nedlloyd v. Arab Metals (No. 2) (2006) EWCA Civ 1717 上诉庭先例中，Moore－Bick 大法官说：

---

〔47〕 可以节录该条文如下："**Equitable jurisdiction and remedies**. The following time limits under this Act, that is to say—the time limit... shall not apply to any claim for specific performance of a contract or for an injunction or **for other equitable relief, except in so far as any such time limit may be applied by the court by analogy in like manner as the corresponding time limit** under any enactment repealed by the Limitation Act 1939 was applied before 1st July 1940."(加黑部分是笔者的强调)

"... could see no reason in principle why, in a case where a limitation period does apply, unjustified delay coupled with an adverse effect of some kind on the defendant or a third party should not be capable of providing a defence in the form of laches even before the expiration of the limitation period. The question for the court in each case is simply whether, having regard to the delay, its extent, the reasons for it and its consequences, it would be inequitable to grant the claimant the relief he seeks."

6.3 其他障碍之三:伤害不知情无辜第三人

可先节录《Chitty on Contracts》(2021 年,第 34 版)一书之 9 - 147 段的观点:"**Third - party rights** The intervention of a third party may prevent the misrepresentee from rescinding the contract and reclaiming property transferred under it. This is one of the risks run by the injured party if he delays in taking action, for if a third party acquires an interest in the subject matter of the contract before the contract has been avoided a claim for rescission will not lie, provided that the third party acted in good faith and gave consideration. Thus, although there may be no duty to act within a prescribed time, it is in the representee's interest to act promptly, for the longer the delay, the greater the possibility of a third party acquiring rights in the subject-matter of the contract. This rule does not apply to void contracts, for in such cases the transferee has no title to pass to the third party; it does apply to voidable contracts, for here the transferee has a good title until the contract is avoided ..."

另节录《Misrepresentation, Mistake and Non-Disclosure》(2022 年,第 6 版)一书之 4 - 63 段的观点:"**Rescission is barred if third parties would be prejudiced** Rescission will generally be barred if it would prejudice the rights of third parties. For example, a contract between a Lloyd's Name and certain Lloyd's companies authorising the companies to enter into settlements on behalf of the Name could not be rescinded for fraudulent misrepresentation because rescission would affect third parties with whom settlements had been entered into. ..."

以上节录是说受害方/被误述方如果选择撤销合约是会影响第三人的合法权利,就"可能"(may)或"通常"(generally)会被否定。"通常"是因为在衡平法的灵活性与弹性下,在个别案件表面看来会影响第三人的合法权利时,法院可以为其量身定做去设计方案解决,即可让受害方的选择权不受影响,但同时也不影响第三人。在本章之 5.2.2 段介绍的 O'Sullivan v. Management Agency and Music Ltd(1985)QB 428 先例就是一个很好的例子,显示受害方撤销合约的权利可以被确认,并附上条件(on terms),令第三人不受影响。在该先例中,在一系列的合约安排后,O'Sullivan 部分作品的母带被交给了另两间音乐公司,法院判这两间音乐公司支付了不菲的对价也是因为这两间音乐公司对 O'Sullivan 与被告之间的不当影响毫不知情,所以不用交还母带。

另外,法院对救济附上条件除了可以避免影响第三人,也可以避免好像 Re Petro China International(Hong Kong)Corp Ltd(2011)4 HKLRD 604 香港特区先例面对的问题。在该先例虽然是执行裁决书,但道理是一样。贸仲裁决书中判买方胜诉,要退回不符合货物描述的货物(硫),而卖方要退回货价。卖方声称退回货价的前提是买方退回货物,但买方否认裁决书的裁决中有此前提。双方在这个问题上纠缠了好几年,据知最后的解决办法是把钱放进法院,在卖方确认收到货物后法院把钱交给买方,对此,如果裁决书中写明条件就不会有这个问题。特别是复原与反复原相比裁决书的执行更加复杂,如果让复原(如回归或退回货物与产权)与反复原(如退回货价)去区别执行,就很容易带来困难如不公平。例如复原的一方是在容易被执行的管辖地,但反复原一方则不是。

6.3.1 财产/货物与产权转移:保护善意第三人不受影响

法律有必要保护善意第三人以保护正常商业市场的信心与运作。这第三人一般是有缺陷的,如可使无效合约中的标的物(如一辆汽车)的下一手买方(C)获得货物的产权,只要该买方 C 没有收到关于 A(被误述方)与 B(误述方)的合约有缺陷的通知(真正或推定通知),是完全不知情与诚实的,也在一个公平交易下付出合理对价,C 即是善意第三人。

如果 A 与 B 的合约是自始无效,因为 B 从来不拥有 A 通过有效合约合法转让的产权,自然也不会有产权再转让给 C:见 Candy v. Lindsay(1878)3 App Cas 459;Ingram v. Little(1961)1 QB 31;Shogun Finance Ltd v. Hudson(2003)UKHL 62[48]等先例。也可见英国的《Sale of Goods Act 1979》之 S.21(1)有说明:"**Sale by person not the owner.** (1) Subject to this Act, where goods are sold by a person who is not their owner, and who does not sell them under the authority or with the consent of the owner, the buyer acquires no better title to the goods than the seller had, unless the owner of the goods is by his conduct precluded from denying the seller's authority to sell."

当然,这不能防止 B 在 A 能够采取行动前出售给善意第三人 C。但这样,如同 B 是把有关标的物从 A 那里偷来抢来后出售给 C 一样,B 是从来没有合法产权。所以,不影响 A 可向 C 要回有关标的物,否则是侵占(conversion)[49]行为。

但如果是可使无效合约,在 A 撤销合约之前,该可使无效合约是有效,B 可以合法拥有由 A 转让的财产/货物上的财产性权利(proprietary right)并获得产权(title),

---

〔48〕 此贵族院先例是针对错误理解对方订约方身份(mistake in identity)的权威先例中,在本书第七章之12段详论。这里只说可诉错误的救济一贯是令合约自始无效,原因是错误的本质是无法让一方当事人选择"合约"有效履行,但这往往会伤害不知情的无辜第三人。在该先例中,贵族院以 3:2 多数判错误理解对方订约方身份的救济是一贯的合约自始无效。但 Millett 与 Nicholls 勋爵的少数意见认为救济应是可使无效,因为保护无辜第三人更重要与更公平合理。而可诉误述中,救济是合约可使无效,才可去保障不伤害无辜第三人。

〔49〕 有关侵占的课题与严重后果,在笔者的《提单与其他付运单证》(2016 年)一书第二章有详论。

还可以进一步通过出售合法转让财产性权利给C,然后C可能会再合法出售给D、E、F等。此时A对财产/货物没有产权,只是因为合约可撤销,A对财产/货物有"单纯衡平权利"(mere equity)。[50] 所谓的"单纯衡平权利",简单而言是A可以行使权利撤销合约并重新获得财产性权利,因此也有说法将此称为"衡平撤销权"(equity to rescind)。《Chitty on Contracts》(2021年,第34版)一书之9-149段说:

"Until the contract is rescinded, the accepted view is that the misrepresentee has no proprietary right in the property transferred but only a 'mere equity'."

而在A撤销合约后,如果财产/货物仍在误述方如买方的手中,就要回归(re-vest)给受害方A。此时会存在以下情况。

1. 针对欺诈性误述的普通法撤销,此时如果涉及的是一般货物等财产,受害方选择撤销合约,财产的法律产权(legal title)自动回归:见Load v. Green(1846)15 M&W 216;Car and Universal Finance Ltd v. Caldwell(1965)1 QB 525先例等。这普通法救济是自助,[51] 因此只要以各种形式作出选择/通知,财产即自动回归。此时受害方可以要求误述方归还占有的财产,否则也就是刚才提到的侵占行为。

但这是普通法做法,因此只能处理不需要当事人行动或特定形式就可以处理法律产权的财产,而一旦涉及了如公司股份交易、土地交易[52]等情况,就无法采用普通法处理了。

2. 衡平法撤销,影响不了法律产权,但可以回归财产的衡平法财产性权利(equitable proprietary right),如由A获得衡平法产权,这样就在A与占有财产的B之间建立信托(trust)关系,在这个信托关系中受托人B只单纯有义务将占有的财产交还给A,例如交还占有的货物,或者涉及登记就要注销登记(de-register),国际货物买卖就要把产权证明(document of title)的一套提单背书(endorse)退还等。但在期间B对A并没有一般信托下的诚信义务(fiduciary duty),因此也有说法将之称为单纯信托

---

〔50〕 采用这样的说法是因为要区分于衡平法财产性权利(equitable proprietary right)。也只有对财产有普通法/衡平法的财产性权利时才可以追踪财产去向,并最后找恰当的救济取回财产,见《证据法:基础理论、口头证据与专家证据》一书第十章之2.7.2段。

〔51〕 见本书第四章之5.1段。

〔52〕 英国针对土地有立法规定,尤其是关于衡平权利与已经登记产权土地之间的关系。但这部分与本书的中国读者关系不大,在本书中也不会多作介绍。

(bare trust)。[53]

这衡平法救济下,在什么时间点衡平法财产性权利回归 A 是有疑问的,是 A 选择撤销时,还是在财产交给 B 时就已经产生信托关系?今天一般看法,看来应该是在 A 选择撤销时(各种方式的通知,或提起诉讼默示通知)财产性权利就回归:见 Allcard v. Skinner(1887)36 Ch. D. 145;Shalson v. Russo(2003)EWHC 1637(Ch);National Crime Agency v. Robb(2014)EWHC 4384(Ch)等先例。今天更麻烦的问题是,这权利是否仍属自助也是有疑问的,尤其是在《Misrepresentation Act 1967》S. 2(2)后,因为该立法写得不明确,所以有争议是否需要等到法院先认定才能实现财产性权利回归并不明确。这也带来了如果涉及必须由法院裁量的衡平法撤销是否应当是法院认定后才能真正确认与撤销的问题,有关内容见本书第四章之 5.1 段与 SK Shipping Plc v. Capital VLCC 3 Corp(2022)EWCA Civ 231 先例,此处不多做介绍。

需要关注财产性权利(无论是法律产权,还是衡平财产性权利)回归的时间点,有多方面的重要原因。一个重要原因就是,在 B 将财产转让给第三人后,如果 A 想要追回财产,是否有足够与第三人对抗的产权要求交还财产?

如果是在撤销前转让,后果是有恰当产权的 B 合法销售给支付了对价的善意第三人 C,C 也获得恰当的合法产权,此时撤销 A 与 B 之间的合约,A 也无法要求 C 交还财产,否则是影响了第三人利益。英国的《Sale of Goods Act 1979》之 S. 23 说:"**Sale under voidable title.** When the seller of goods has a voidable title to them, but his title has not been avoided at the time of the sale, the buyer acquires a good title to the goods, provided he buys them in good faith and without notice of the seller's defect of title."

如果是在撤销后才转让财产:

1. 普通法救济下,由于 B 已经没有法律产权,第三人 C(或后续的 D、E、F、G)也

---

[53] 此时信托的性质看来有争议。例如在美国法或澳大利亚法律下,由于认可救济性推定信托(remedial constructive trust),即可以事后由法院/仲裁庭判决将信托作为救济的一种手段,因此认为此时是推定信托。但在英国法律下只认可实体性推定信托(institutional constructive trust),即只要有关事实发生,信托关系就根据法律产生,而不是一种事后根据判决/裁决赋予的救济手段,英国法下的推定信托仅仅被用作法律认定当事人转让衡平权益的意图,或者剥夺有衡平法过错行为人士的获利等情况:见 Westdeutsche Landesbank Girozentrale v. Islington LBC(1996)AC 669 贵族院先例。因此有说法是英国法下此类信托关系应属于回归信托(resulting trust),即将财产的衡平法产权退回(jump back)给转让人,可见在 El Ajou v. Dollar Land Holdings Plc(No. 1)(1993)3 All ER 717 先例中,Millett 大法官说:"They can rescind the purchases for fraud, and he for the bribery of his agent; and each can then invoke the assistance of equity to follow property of which he is the equitable owner. But, if this is correct, as I think it is, then the trust which is operating in these cases is not some new model remedial constructive trust, but an old-fashioned institutional resulting trust."但至少在本章要针对的课题上,无论定义为哪一种信托,在撤销后给予受害方的权利是一致的,因此也不对此进行仔细区分,概称"信托"。

不会有法律产权，这是 nemo dat 规则。[54] A 看来可以向实际占有货物的人士（C 或 D、E、F、G）要求交回财产，否则就可以起诉侵占，向法院申请交回财产。

2. 衡平法救济下，撤销后 A 有衡平产权可以要求交还财产，但这受限于实际获得了财产（或其他财产性权利，如接受了财产作为抵押担保的第三人银行等）的第三人针对衡平权利的抗辩。这些抗辩主要是第三人是否是不知情的善意第三人，例如支付了对价的不知情善意买方（bona fide purchaser for value without notice）等。甚至如果可以证明第三人有衡平法下显失公平/不合情理行为，可能与第三人之间建立推定信托（constructive trust）的关系，并要求第三人承担个人责任或交回财产。

也正是因为有财产性权利的回归，A 才可以追回（follow）或追踪（tracing）财产去向，并通过其他法律行动如第三方披露令（Norwich Pharmacal Order）、[55] 搜查令（Search Order）、[56] 冻结令（Freezing Order）[57] 等的协助下，最终能追踪到全球任何地方的 F 或 G，并以侵占的威吓或法律行动把标的物取回。这方面可节录一个较近期的 Shalson v. Russo 先例中，Rimer 大法官的观点："As Lord Millett explained in Foskett v McKeown and others [2001] 1 AC 102 …, tracing is neither a claim nor a remedy. It is the process by which a claimant seeks to show that **an interest he had in an asset has become represented by an interest in a different asset**. Typically, he will seek to show that his share of the proceeds of the original asset has been applied in the acquisition of the different asset. **Having shown that, he will endeavour to maintain a proprietary interest in the different asset** referable to the application of his property into it. But an ability to trace into the different asset will not automatically entitle him to maintain his claim to such an interest. The legal owner of that asset may have one or more defences to it, for example that of a good faith purchaser for value. **Considerations such as this will raise questions as to whether, having established his tracing claim, the claimant can assert his proprietary claim in respect of the different asset**. But the first question is whether he can trace into the asset at all."（加黑部分是笔者的强调）

这也表示 A 在知悉误述的事实与自己的法律权利后，应尽快行使撤销合约的权利。越是延误、犹豫不决，B（或 C、D、E、F 或 G 之间）让善意第三人介入的可能性越大。这在一个严重欺诈性误述，例如 B 是以一张空头支票把汽车骗到手，A 显然要尽快撤销合约，因为如果比 B 出售给善意第三人 C（或 B 赠送给了 C，C 再出售给善意第三人 D）慢了半步，就会失去汽车。而 A 对骗子 B，在因为无法复原而失去撤

---

〔54〕 见《国际货物买卖》一书第七章之 3 段的介绍。另在本章之 2 段已经提到如果涉及的财产是金钱，地位有所不同，即使在普通法下善意第三人也可以获得完整与恰当的法律产权，这不是本书重点也不在此针对。

〔55〕 见《证据法：国际规管与诉讼中的证据攻防》一书第二章之 4 段。

〔56〕 见《证据法：国际规管与诉讼中的证据攻防》一书第二章之 3 段。

〔57〕 见《证据法：国际规管与诉讼中的证据攻防》一书第三章。

销合约并恢复原状的良机后,以欺诈/欺骗侵权去索赔金钱损失也很肯定是一场空。

在 Shalson v. Russo 先例中,也可节录 Rimer 大法官的观点:"Rescission is an act of the parties which, when validly effected, entitles the party rescinding to be put in the position he would have been in if no contract had been entered into in the first place. It involves a giving and taking back on both sides. If it is necessary to have recourse to an action in order to implement the rescission, the court will make such orders as are necessary to put both contracting parties into the position they were in before the contract was made. There is, however, also a line of authority supporting the proposition that, **upon rescission of a contract for fraudulent misrepresentation, the beneficial title which passed to the representor under the contract revests in the representee. The representee then enjoys a sufficient proprietary title to enable him to trace**, follow and recover what, by virtue of such revesting, can be regarded as having always been in equity his own property. This may be an essential means of achieving a proper restoration of the original position if **the representor has in the meantime parted with the property and is ostensibly a man of straw**(这里是说被告是光棍一条)**unable to satisfy the court's orders for restoration of the original position.**"(加黑部分是笔者的强调)

除此以外,必须尽快行动的另一个原因,会是无法追踪到第三人或被第三人成功抗辩,那就只能向 B 要求金钱复原或赔偿,或者是要 B 承担个人责任。但如果 B 破产,而此时还没有撤销合约,如有先例判如果作为公司[58]的 B 破产后,受害方 A 才撤销合约,A 也只能是像其他普通债权人(ordinary creditors)一样排队与按比例索赔债务,毕竟在撤销前公司 B 对财产有法律与衡平产权,由此有关财产属于公司财产,破产后公司财产需要在所有债权人之间分配,允许 A 对财产有产权、可以直接取回财产就会影响所有其他债权人的利益:见 Crown Holdings(London)Ltd(In Liquidation),Re(2015)EWHC 1876(Ch)先例。

6.3.1.1 需要给误述方通知以显示撤销合约的选择

撤销要求给误述方通知以显示撤销的决定,这通知只需要简单告诉对方自己决定撤销合约即可,不必要有严格格式。

在《Misrepresentation, Mistake and Non-Disclosure》(2022 年,第 6 版)一书之 4 -

---

[58] 在 Crown Holdings(London)Ltd(In Liquidation),Re(2015)EWHC 1876(Ch)先例中,Murray Rosen QC 大法官提到由于《Insolvency Act 1986》立法条文针对自然人破产的规则与公司有差异,因此自然人破产时地位不同,受害方撤销合约后,针对自然人的破产财产可以要求交回财产。这方面问题与本书关系不大,也不在此详细介绍。只简单地说法官的此说法只是附带意见,为何这样区分的理由看来也并不十分清楚,与有待后续先例澄清,可节录《Goff & Jones:The Law of Unjust Enrichment》(2016 年,第 9 版)一书之 40 - 27 段所说:"The justification for this distinction is far from obvious, and it remains to be seen whether the judge's analysis will be accepted in later cases."

20 段说:"… what constitutes a sufficient 'unequivocal act of election' by the representee. A formal notice to the representor that the representee now treats the contract as rescinded will normally suffice and will take effect, at the latest, at the moment of its receipt by the representor. Similarly, any informal notice or any act by the representee which sufficiently communicates his decision to rescind will suffice."

一般撤销合约只由受害方/被误述方自己决定与行动即可,不必惊动法院或仲裁庭(虽然衡平法下仍有争议)。这样看来,这种选择与其他的"选择"是一样,是自助。只有在双方当事人对是否有权撤销合约有争议时,才会需要法院插手。这方面可节录 Drake Insurance Plc v. Provident Insurance Plc(2003)EWHC 109(Comm)先例中,Moore – Bick 大法官所说:"a right to rescind the contract and its exercise is subject to the same principles as apply to the exercise of the right to rescind generally. Although equity recognised a right of rescission in a wider range of circumstances than did the common law, modern authorities do not suggest that a distinction is to be drawn between the principles that apply to the exercise of that right in different cases. Whenever **a right to rescind arises it is exercisable at the election of the injured party. Moreover, it does not require the intervention of the court but is effective immediately upon the communication by the injured party of his decision to rescind the contract**:…In Horsler v Zorro [1975] Ch 302 … Megarry J summarised the position in this way: '… **the process of rescission is essentially the act of the party rescinding, and not of the court.** Of course, if matters are disputed, the dispute may have to be determined by the court, and until the decision is given it will not be known whether or not there has been a proper and effectual rescission: but **that does not mean that there is no rescission until the court speaks**'."(加黑部分是笔者的强调)

这方面被上诉庭[(2003) EWCA Civ 1834]认同,Rix 大法官说:"Once an insurance contract has been properly avoided, there is no duty to reconsider or to reinstate the contract by reason of knowledge only acquired after avoidance. In any event an exercise of avoidance does not depend on the court's assistance or declaration. In all these matters the insurer's right to avoid is like any other case of rescission of a contract."

此先例虽然是保险合约,但在这方面是与其他合约的选择撤销一样,撤销后也不存在法院可稍后令合约"重生"。如果自助的撤销被判是错误的,只会视为违约/毁约,撤销的受害方要赔偿损失(见本书第四章之5.3段)。

严重的欺诈性误述在社会上无处不在,骗子在成功把财产/货物骗到手后往往就不知所踪。这样,受害方的撤销合约通知在送达(service)时就有困难。在 Car and Universal Finance Ltd v. Caldwell(1965)1 QB 525 先例中,是可以见到英国法律为了配合现实在通知无法送达给骗子方面颇有弹性处理。在该先例中,Caldwell 先生被骗,Norris 用空头支票与欺诈性误述把 Caldwell 的汽车骗到了手。Caldwell 在发觉支票跳票后赶紧设法撤销合约,取回汽车的产权,但因找不到 Norris,没法发出通知。Caldwell 只好通知警察与汽车会(Automobile Association),法院判这已是足够的行动去视为通知他的撤销合约决定。Denning 勋爵说:"In principle, it seems to me that a seller can avoid a contract by an unequivocal act of election which demonstrates clearly that he elects to rescind it and to be no longer bound by it. It is sufficient if he asserts his intention to rescind 'in the plainest and most open manner competent to him.' … I would ask this simple question:'How is a man in the position of Caldwell ever to be able to rescind the contract when a fraudulent person absconds as Norris did here?' If his right to rescind is to be a real right, when the rogue absconds, it must be sufficient if he does all that he can in the circumstances unequivocally to make it known. It is not sufficient for him, of course, to keep it in his own mind or write down a note in his own private sitting room. However, conduct such as we have here, namely, telling the bank, the police and the A. A., 'Find this car if you possibly can. Get it back. It is mine,' seems to me an unequivocal act of rescission."

6.3.1.2 推定信托(constructive trust)

较早有提到如果误述方能够把财产/货物的产权回归给受害方/被误述方,在走程序注销登记的期间,双方是存在信托的关系,即误述方只是作为受托人(trustee)持有产权,而受害方是信托人(trustor)。这种信托的情况其实十分普遍,例如在无效合约,或在可使无效合约在受害方撤销合约后,财产/货物仍被出售或转让给第三人。往往是该无辜第三人与受害方/被误述方都被误述方骗了,但法律总得挑一位去承受损失,这分水岭就是一个可使无效合约被撤销的前后。如果出售是在撤销后,该无辜第三人对有关财产/货物就不是合法所有人而只是信托受托人。

另也常会发生是出售或转让给说不上也证明不了是无辜与诚实的第三人。这种第三人并非参与欺诈/欺骗,否则他/她也变了是同谋(accomplice),要一并承担民事侵权与刑事责任的后果。但该第三人通过出售与转让而取得的有关财产/货物,事前已经是对有关产权的问题有了通知或推定通知。这通知的重要性在 Car and Universal Finance Ltd v. Caldwell(1965)1 QB 525 先例已是清楚明了。还有很多同一原则的例子,例如在《提单与其他付运单证》一书,就有多处提及,在该书第六章之 2.7.2 段是说:"船东/承运人一发觉承租人(或代理人)背后代船长签发的一套提单上的陈述与事实不符,一般的做法是尽快……通知所有会受到提单不准确陈述影响的有关人士。如果第三人及时收到这个通知并知情,之后看来就不能再依赖提单上的记载了……"换言之,该第三人再也不是无辜、诚实与善意第三人了。

上述例子是真正通知或知情(actual notice),[59]另第三人可以有推定知情(constructive notice)。这就是根据不同情况法律推定第三人应该是对事实真相知情,只要他/她作为一位合理第三人应该去调查、应该有怀疑,更不说是“视而不见”(turn a blind eye knowledge)或蓄意与鲁莽不去查问的极端情况。反正这样,法律是不会去保护这种第三人的。例如,一位欺诈/欺骗的误述方把骗来的财产/货物以不可思议的价格卖给了第三人,如将一辆名牌汽车以100元卖给第三人,恐怕该第三人很难会被法院接受是善意买方。这样,该名牌汽车虽然在第三人的名下,但他/她只会是信托受托人,被骗的受害方可随时向该第三人取回,抗拒是构成侵占。

在笔者的《证据法:基础理论、口头证据与专家证据》一书的第十章,有介绍推定信托可以分成两大类别。第一类不严格是信托但十分接近,也就是本就作为受托人行事,只是没有正式委任的人士,如公司董事去管理与处置公司资产,一旦涉及他们违反对公司的诚信义务(fiduciary duty),在向他们寻求救济时就将他们类同为正式受托人一样看待。例如,违背诚信义务收受贿赂与/或秘密佣金的政府公务员、公司高管或代理人等。

第二类则针对实际上是陌生人(strangers)的第三人,这类人士涉及:(1)不诚实地帮助(dishonest assist)/知情帮助(knowing assist)他人违背信托义务挪用信托资产,如帮助洗钱:见 Stanford International Bank Ltd(In Liquidation)v. HSBC Bank Plc(2021)EWCA Civ 535 等先例。(2)对违反信托义务的情况知情或应该有怀疑但不查问,这会构成是知情接收(knowing receipt)信托资产。例如,骗子把欺诈行为骗取的一大笔异常的金钱存入银行账户,或者是骗取的货物以不可思议的低价转售给第三人买方后,从银行或第三人买方知情或推定知情开始即可属于此类。

这类人士从没想要作为受托人管理资产,但是在他人违反信托义务挪用信托资产后,在上述两种情况下,衡平法给予欺诈的受害方作为信托受益人针对不诚实帮助或知情接收人士救济。在救济中将他们视为像有信托义务一样看待,也就是推定信托的关系。由于受害方与第三人不相识,一般不存在合约(contract)与侵权(tort)的关系与诉因,只能对第三人合法拥有与已经是改头换面的资产/新资产以推定信托的诉因起诉。

这第二类推定信托在今天大量国际欺诈案件(其中不少是商业案件)中,常常会涉及欺诈等行为后的洗钱。例如在 Sino Iron Pty Ltd v. Worldwide Wagering Pty Ltd(2017)VSC 101 澳大利亚先例中,作为受害方的原告被骗子骗走的资产被存入被告

---

[59] 在笔者的《证据法:基础理论、口头证据与专家证据》一书的第十章,有详尽介绍各种不同类别或程度的知情,在从正常的商业交易到欺诈的不同类别的案件判断是否满足“知情”要求时作为参考。Baden v. Societe Generale pour Favoriser le Development du Commerce et de l' Industrie en France SA(1993)1 WLR 509 先例的5类“Baden 知情”是包括:(1)真正知情;(2)视而不见;(3)蓄意与鲁莽不去查问;(4)与(5)为稍有不同的推定知情。

银行的账户,被告从知情/应当知情或推定知情这笔金钱有问题后,就开始承担类似信托人的义务,对之后这笔金钱的流失要承担衡平法责任了。

显然在第二类推定信托中,无论是不诚实帮助还是知情接收,都要求第三人对挪用(这包括是欺诈、不诚实等手段得来)的信托资产的情况有一定程度的知情,问题是这应当到什么程度呢? 在分析这问题时,“Baden 知情”就是一个很好的判断标准,看公共政策之下需要对信托受益人或资产的实际所有人的衡平法权利保护到什么程度。这需要平衡与考虑各类公共政策,包括要打击欺诈与洗钱等不法活动,帮助追讨因为不法的欺诈、不诚实行为导致的损失,也要保护无辜、毫不知情的第三人,保障商业社会的正常与顺畅运转[60]等。

6.3.2 其他情况的撤销合约会伤害无辜或善意第三人

在与有形财产(tangible asset)买卖无关的其他情况,包括在本章稍早的5.2.2段提到的 O'Sullivan v. Management Agency and Music Ltd(1985)QB 428 先例的情况,道理也是一样,受害方/被误述方选择撤销合约不能影响其他无辜第三人的合法利益。

在本章较早的6.3段节录《Misrepresentation, Mistake and Non-Disclosure》(2022年,第6版)一书之4-63段中提到一个保险的案例支持这个观点,这是著名的 Society of Lloyd's v. Leighs(1997)CLC 1398 上诉庭先例,可在此多作介绍。该先例的案情背景是20世纪80年代,英国劳合社的保险人因为大量来自美国的石棉污染的再保赔付而严重亏损,整个劳合社几乎要因为没有能力赔付而破产。由于劳合社的做法是以个人名义(name)去参与各种辛迪加/保险小组(syndicate),而个人名义承保,不像有限公司可以法人局限损失,所以保险人要承担无限责任。当年这种巨额赔付导致好几个保险人自杀与/或破产。为了改变这种情况,劳合社在1993年委任了新的主席与首席执行官,并开始做出一些基本性的改革,实施了“重建更新计划”(Reconstruction and Renewal Plan)。改革的一个令人瞩目的措施便是向劳合社引入了公司成员(member),允许公司资本(corporate capital)进入劳合社,打破了劳合社成员只允许是自然人的传统惯例。在成功吸收了有限公司的大量资本后,劳合社这才慢慢恢复元气。

重建更新计划中的一个核心安排是把劳合社所有1992年及以前年度的非寿险

---

[60] 这是 Sanders v. MaClean(1883)11 QBD 327 先例中 Bowen 大法官所说:“But the practice of merchants, it is never superfluous to remark, is not based on the supposition of possible frauds. The object of mercantile usages is to prevent the risk of insolvency, not of fraud; and any one who attempts to follow and understand the law merchant will soon find himself lost if he begins by assuming that merchants conduct their business on the basis of attempting to insure themselves against fraudulent dealing. The contrary is the case. Credit, not distrust, is the basis of commercial dealings…”

责任再保给 Equitas,[61] 同时任命 Equitas 为这些责任自然结清的代理(run - off agent)。劳合社 95% 收到这个解决方案的成员接受了该提议,因此劳合社根据《Lloyd' s Act 1982》强制所有的成员都把他们 1992 年及以前年度的非寿险责任再保给 Equitas。在 1996 年,劳合社代表所有成员与 Equitas 订立了再保与自然结清责任合约,Equitas 将再保保费转让(assign)给了劳合社。

这个案例是劳合社向几位拒绝接受解决方案的成员索赔欠下的再保保费的一个试探性的先行案例。被告的抗辩理由之一是当时是基于劳合社的欺诈性误述才成为劳合社成员,所以要撤销与劳合社的合约,这样劳合社就没有该成员的授权与 Equitas 订立再保合约。虽然劳合社不承认有欺诈性误述,但是为了这个简易判决,双方同意应假设欺诈性误述成立,该成员能否撤销合约,或是只能索赔损失。上诉庭判因为会影响第三人的利益,双方不可能回复到没有合约的地位,所以不能撤销合约。其中最重要的是该成员在加入劳合社后,劳合社代表成员以个人名义承保。如果撤销合约,则劳合社没有授权代表订立这些保单。而根据《Insurance Companies Act 1982》,如果个人不是劳合社成员,则他就不能从事保险业务。这势必影响这些保单下的受保人,所以无法复原。上诉庭说:"We believe that there is a more general and equally fundamental reason why it was not open to names to rescind their general undertakings. Membership of Lloyd's is the foundation of the insurance business that has been carried on by names, and must necessarily be carried on by them until all their liabilities to policy holders are discharged. As a matter of law, membership of Lloyd's is essential if the names are not to infringe the provisions of s. 2(1) of the Insurance Companies Act 1982. These forbid unauthorised persons to carry on insurance business in the UK. Authorisation has only been granted to individuals who are members of Lloyd's. In practice, the names have only been able to conduct insurance business and will only be able to run - off that business by taking advantage of the complex structure of the Lloyd's market which enables policy holders to transact business as if with a corporate entity rather than with a large number of individuals. The rules and regulations of Lloyd's have enabled this business to be transacted on behalf of and with the authority of the names. It is fundamentally incompatible with the business that has been carried on for names to withdraw, retroactively, from membership of Lloyd's. **It is impossible to sever the contracts under which the names became members of Lloyd's from the business that has been carried on, and the contracts that have been concluded, by virtue of that membership. Restitutio in integrum is impossible.**"(加黑部分是笔者的强调)

---

〔61〕 Equitas 是劳合社为了这个重建更新计划处理 1992 年及以前的非寿险保单导致的巨额债务而专门成立的独立保险公司。

7. 撤销合约的障碍之五:《Misrepresentation Act 1967》之 S. 2(2)

在介绍以上普通法与衡平法的四种撤销合约的障碍,即确认合约、时隔太久、伤害不知情无辜第三人与最重要的无法复原外,笔者接下去会介绍《Misrepresentation Act 1967》之 S. 2(2)立法条文带来的障碍。

在分析该立法条文前,可先节录《Chitty on Contracts》(2021 年,第 34 版)一书之 9-112 段[内容中也节录了立法之 S. 2(2)条文]说:"**Misrepresentation Act section 2(2)** This subsection reads as follows:'Where a person has entered into a contract after **a misrepresentation** has been made to him **otherwise than fraudulently**, and **he would be entitled, by reason of the misrepresentation, to rescind the contract**, then, if it is claimed, in any proceedings arising out of the contract, that the contract ought to be or has been rescinded, **the court or arbitrator may declare the contract subsisting and award damages in lieu of rescission, if of opinion that it would be equitable to do so**, having regard to the nature of the misrepresentation and the loss that would be caused by it if the contract were upheld, as well as to the loss that rescission would cause to the other party.'

It will be seen that this subsection does not give a representee any right to claim damages, but it enables**the court, in its discretion, to grant damages to the representee in lieu of rescinding the contract.** It seems probable that the subsection was intended principally for the benefit of the representor, so that a contract need not be rescinded where the court feels that the representee can be adequately compensated in damages. But cases may well occur in which damages would be the preferable remedy for the representee. In this event there seems nothing to prevent the representee from claiming the right to rescind but then inviting the court to award damages in lieu. Nor does there seems to be anything which would prevent the court from taking this course over the protests of the representor, who may prefer rescission to an award of damages."(加黑部分是笔者的强调)

另也节录《Misrepresentation, Mistake and Non-Disclosure》(2022 年,第 6 版)一书之 4-19 段说:"**Since 1967 the court has had a statutory discretion to declare the contract subsisting and to award damages in lieu of rescission** in certain circumstances. This emphasises that, but for the statute, the court has no power to declare the contract subsisting when the representee has exercised his right to rescind. And since rescission is available as of right to a representee who can show that the requirements of the remedy ... have been satisfied, the court has no general power to impose terms on the grant of the remedy."(加黑部分是笔者的强调)

根据以上所说,《Misrepresentation Act 1967》不适用在欺诈性误述,这种误述在普通法下的欺诈/欺骗侵权(tort of deceit)早有了全面的救济,即撤销合约与索赔所有的损失:见 Attwood v. Small(1838)6 Cl. & F. 232;Newbigging v. Adam(1888)13 App Cas 308 等先例。立法是为了扩大非欺诈性(这包括无辜与疏忽)误述的救济,让受害方/被误述方获得金钱损失的赔偿。而以前衡平法下,受害方/被误述方只被给予了撤销合约的衡平救济,不会有金钱的赔偿。当然,受害方也不是只有好处,立法之 S. 2(2)条文规定由法院决定如何对撤销合约或损失赔偿的两种救济进行选择。

这代表在以前只要是有了一个可诉误述,即使误述方是完全无辜的,有关的误述只是鸡毛蒜皮的小事情与涉及小金额,被误述方仍会实际上借机自助撤销一个高价值与长期的商业合约,特别是在市场逆转令履行该合约对被误述方不利时。但在立法 S. 2(2)的措辞(可去重复是"the court or arbitrator may declare the contract subsisting and award damages **in lieu of** rescission, if of opinion that it would be equitable to do so")下,应会是法院(或仲裁庭)不再允许受害方/被误述方去取巧。误述可以是很轻微(当然也会在不同案件是很严重),只有极小的诱导或影响去导致合约的产生。如果一视同仁可去撤销合约,不论误述是疏忽或是无辜,往往会带来不公道。毕竟有很多撤销合约是基于订约后市场逆转对受害方/被误述方不利,或是发觉自己错误去订了一个亏本的合约,想利用误述去脱身。在 William Sindall Plc v. Cambridgeshire CC(1994)1 WLR 1016 上诉庭先例中,Evans 大法官说让受害方/被误述方脱身不公平,这是立法不想见到的:"The starting point for the application of the sub - section is the situation where a plaintiff has established right to rescind the contract on grounds of innocent misrepresentation: its objection is to ameliorate for the innocent misrepresentor the harsh consequences of rescission for a wholly innocent ... misrepresentor, in a case where it is fairer to uphold the contract and award damages against him."

所以,S. 2(2)不像 S. 2(1),其主要是去保护误述方(特别是疏忽但实是轻微与无辜的误述)让法院有裁量权剥夺受害方/被误述方在衡平法下撤销合约的救济。这可见立法 S. 2(2)所依据的 Tenth Report of the Law Reform Committee,(1962) Cmnd. 1782 之 11 - 12 段。[62]

所以可总结在立法下,非欺诈性误述的地位是在疏忽误述中,受害方在 S. 2(1)下肯定有权索赔损失,但在 S. 2(2)下撤销合约就要看法院(或仲裁庭)了。而无辜误述是肯定不会两者救济兼得,完全要看法院的裁量权。而法院也只会在很极端的案件才会给予无辜误述的受害方损失赔偿,一般只是获得赔偿范围比损失窄的补偿(indemnity),甚至只有名义损失(nominal damages)。这可节录《Chitty on Contracts》

---

〔62〕 见本书第四章之 5.4 段。

(2021年,第34版)一书之9-113段,说:"... In the case of a negligent misrepresentation, the representee can claim both rescission and damages, but whereas his claim to damages under s. 2(1) is as of right, his claim to rescission is now subject to the discretion of the court under s. 2(2). But in the case of an innocent misrepresentation, the representee cannot get both rescission and damages, nor can he claim either remedy as of right."

关于《Misrepresentation Act 1967》立法,将在本书第四章详论。

8. 撤销合约的障碍之六:免责条文

在订约自由的大原则/大精神下,以免责条文去豁免误述导致的严重后果(撤销合约与/或损失赔偿的救济)与责任是有必要的。但针对可诉误述的豁免,在普通法与立法(《Misrepresentation Act 1967》之S. 3)下,并不容易,这会在本段与本书第四章之6段去介绍与分析。显然,如果免责条文被判合理有效,自然是可以否定一个本来可以成立的可诉误述与相应的撤销合约的救济。这样就回复不到没有订立合约之前的地位,而令一个有缺陷的合约有效与必须被继续严格履行。这方面稍后会分段详论,在此可先节录《Misrepresentation, Mistake and Non-Disclosure》(2022年,第6版)一书之9-01段说:"**Varieties of exclusion and limitation clause** A person may, by the use of a contractual term or a non-contractual notice, seek to exclude or limit the liability or the range of remedies to which he would otherwise be exposed ... in the context of liability for misrepresentation. There is a wide range of types of clause and notice in common use, and a range of techniques available to the courts to control them. A clause in a contract may seek to exclude altogether, or to limit in some way, a liability which arises either under the contract or outside the contract (for example, in tort). ..."

8.1 普通法下是否允许豁免非欺诈性误述

在The Huntsworth Wine Company Limited v. London City Bond Limited (2021) EWHC 2831 (Comm)先例中,Pearce大法官对近50年来普通法针对任何形式的豁免条文(exclusion clause)或免责条文(exemption/exception clause)的发展简短介绍说:

"The approach of the courts to the interpretation of exclusion clauses (including clauses limiting liability) in commercial contracts has changed markedly in the last 50 years. **Two forces have been at work. One has been the impact of the Unfair Contract Terms Act 1977**, which provided a direct means of controlling unreasonable exclusion clauses and removed the need for courts to resort to artificial rules of interpretation to get around them ... This change of attitude was heralded by the decision of the House of Lords in Photo Production Ltd v Securicor Transport Ltd [1980] AC 827. The **second**

force has been the development of the modern approach in English law to contractual interpretation, with its emphasis on context and objective meaning and deprecation of special ' rules' of interpretation-encapsulated by Lord Hoffmann's announcement in Investors Compensation Scheme Ltd v West Bromwich Building Society [1998] 1 WLR 896 ... that ' almost all the old intellectual baggage of ' legal' interpretation has been discarded'.

The modern view is accordingly to recognise that commercial parties are free to make their own bargains and allocate risks as they think fit, and that the task of the court is to interpret the words used fairly applying the ordinary methods of contractual interpretation. It also remains necessary, however, to recognise that **a vital part of the setting in which parties contract is a framework of rights and obligations established by the common law**(and often now codified in statute). These **comprise duties imposed by the law of tort and also norms of commerce** which have come to be recognised as ordinary incidents of particular types of contracts or relationship and which often take the form of **terms implied in the contract by law**. Although its strength will vary according to the circumstances of the case, the court in construing the contract **starts from the assumption that in the absence of clear words the parties did not intend the contract to derogate from these normal rights and obligations.**

The first and still perhaps the leading statement of this principle is that in Modern Engineering(Bristol)Ltd v Gilbert - Ash(Northern)Ltd [1974] AC 689 ... Lord Diplock said:

' It is, of course, open to parties to a contract for sale of goods or for work and labour or for both to exclude by express agreement a remedy for its breach which would otherwise arise by operation of law ... But in construing such a contract **one starts with the presumption that neither party intends to abandon any remedies for its breach arising by operation of law**, and clear express words must be used in order to rebut this presumption. '

InPhoto Production Ltd v. Securicor Transport Ltd ..., Lord Diplock returned to this principle and explained its rationale more fully:

' Since **the presumption is that the parties by entering into the contract intended to accept the implied obligations exclusion clauses are to be construed strictly and the degree of strictness** appropriate to be applied to their construction may properly **depend upon the extent to which they involve departure from the implied obligations**. Since the obligations implied by law in a commercial contract are those which, by judicial consensus over the years or by Parliament in passing a statute, have been regarded as obligations which a reasonable businessman would realise that he was accepting when he entered into a contract of a particular kind, the court's view of the reasonableness of any departure from the implied obligations which would be involved in construing the express words of an exclusion clause in one sense that they are capable of bearing rather than another, is a relevant consideration in deciding what meaning the words were intended by the parties to bear. But this **does not entitle the court to reject the exclusion clause, however unreasonable the court itself may think it is, if the words are clear and fairly susceptible of one meaning only**. '

... Moore - Bick LJ in the Court of Appeal ... Stocznia Gdynia SA v Gearbulk Holdings Ltd [2009] EWCA Civ 75 ... he said:

'The court is unlikely to be satisfied that a party to a contract has abandoned valuable rights arising by operation of law unless the terms of the contract make it sufficiently clear that that was intended. **The more valuable the right, the clearer the language will need to be**. ' ..."(加黑部分是笔者的强调)

另在近期的 Triple Point Technology Inc v. PTT Public Co Ltd(2021) UKSC 29 最高院先例中,Leggatt 勋爵也有同样说法:"... clear words are necessary before the court will hold that a contract has taken away valuable rights or remedies which one of the parties to it would have had at common law(or pursuant to statute)."

上述介绍的近期先例显示了在50年间法院严格针对与敌视豁免或免责条文的态度有了重大的改变,主要是来自以下两个方面:

1. 有了保护英国普通老百姓/消费者的《Unfair Contract Terms Act 1977》立法去否定消费合约的豁免/免责条文,除非是满足公平合理的要求。在针对非欺诈性误述的《Misrepresentation Act 1967》之 S. 3 也有同样的立法条文,这方面将在本书第四章之6段讨论。

针对所有其他不涉及英国消费者的合约,特别是国际商业合约,Diplock 勋爵在 Modern Engineering(Bristol)Ltd v. Gilbert - Ash(Northern)Ltd 与 Photo Production Ltd v. Securicor Transport Ltd(1980)1 Lloyd's Rep 545 这两个贵族院先例的呼吁后,普通法已经是摒弃了以往敌对解释豁免/免责条文的态度,而是任由合约双方自由订约,双方怎样同意豁免/免责条文的措辞/文字,就怎样解释与强制执行。

即使是对已经过时的"基本违约"(fundamental breach)与"故意违约"(deliberate and wilful breach),也是一样,完全可以去豁免/免责:见 Photo Production Ltd v. Securicor Transport Ltd 与 Mott MacDonald Ltd v. Trant Engineering Ltd(2021)EWHC 754 (TCC)等先例。在后一个先例中,Eyre QC 大法官说:"In my judgement the correct approach is accordingly that the position remains as set out in Photo Production ... **Exemption clauses including those purporting to exclude or limit liability for deliberate and repudiatory breaches are to be construed by reference to the normal principles of contractual construction** without the imposition of a presumption and without requiring any particular form of words or level of language to achieve the effect of excluding liability. ... The court is to construe the contract so as to give effect to the parties' intention as disclosed by the language read in context. In that exercise the court is to be conscious that the exclusion of a liability which would otherwise and ordinarily arise is to that extent a departure from the norm ... That has the consequence that it will be inherently less likely ... unless it is clear from the language when properly interpreted in context that it has that effect. ..."

2. 近30年有了不少相关的重要先例,特别是从著名的 Investors Compensation Scheme Ltd v. West Bromwich Building Society(1998)1 WLR 896 贵族院先例出台后,解释合约逐渐从严格的合约措辞/文字(textual)解释改变为着重背景/语境(contextual)。这并不代表普通法在解释合约或任何其他文书文件时有什么方向性的改变,顶多只是一个持续的演变。而两种解释合约的不同方向,其实也没有矛盾,都是法院在面对不同案件的案情时可以拿来使用与达到自己认为在该案件公平合理的结果的工具。例如如果是有双方律师帮助草拟与经过多轮修改的合约,法院或仲裁庭就会着重措辞/文字解释,而如果是由没有什么法律知识的当事人自己订立的合约,法院或仲裁庭就会着重考虑背景/语境,以作出一个客观看来是公平合理的解释。正如 Hodge 勋爵在 Wood v. Capita Insurance Services Ltd(2017)UKSC 24 最高院先例说:"Textualism and contextualism are not conflicting paradigms in a battle for exclusive occupation the field of contractual interpretation. Rather, the lawyer and the judge, when interpreting any contract, can use them as tools to ascertain the objective meaning of the language which the parties have chosen to express their agreement. The extent to which each tool will assist the court in its task will vary according to the circumstances of the particular agreement or agreements. Some agreements may be successfully interpreted principally by textual analysis, for example because of their sophistication and complexity and because they have been negotiated and prepared with the assistance of skilled professionals. The correct interpretation of other contracts may be achieved by a greater emphasis on the factual matrix, for example because of their informality, brevity or the absence of skilled professional assistance. But negotiators of complex formal contracts may often not achieve a logical and coherent text because of, for example, the conflicting aims of the parties, failures of communication, differing drafting practices, or deadlines which require the parties to compromise in order to reach agreement. There may often therefore be provisions in a detailed professionally drawn contract which lack clarity and the lawyer or judge in interpreting such provisions may be particularly helped by considering the factual matrix and the purpose of similar provisions in contracts of the same type..."

但确有说法是解释豁免/免责条文是要比一般合约条文较严格。这不是因为适用好像传统的“针对规则”(contra proferentem rule)[63]去针对免责条文的获利方,而是因为解释的起点是假设双方都不会轻易答应去放弃他们的法律默示(implied by law)[64]地位。

法律通过立法与无数案件建立起来,针对无论在合约关系或侵权关系下会在现实中出现的方方面面的问题,是一套被视为客观、肯定、可预测与相对公平合理的体系或游戏规则。所以,假设合约方选择适用的是英国法(或其他普通法),就是希望在他们的合约内适用这一套公平合理的游戏规则。但如果不想照单全收,有个别的默示规定不想适用,在订约自由下双方是完全可以同意以明示文字(express wording)改变。豁免/免责条文正是有此假设作为解释的前提,因为双方都假设适用法律默示规定如果在合约严格责任下疏忽或在侵权的“小心谨慎责任”关系下疏忽,并导致对方损失,就要赔偿对方。在 Photo Production Ltd v. Securicor Transport Ltd 先例后,如果合约双方要改变或去局限赔偿金额,法院不会在解释的过程中再针对任何一方去敌意解释,而是看有关条文是否写得足够明确与清楚让法院(或仲裁庭)可以给予支持。毕竟商业活动就是为了赚钱,同意将对方的风险转移到自己身上的内在可能性较低,所以免责条文越是放弃重要的权利,措辞/文字就越是要写得清楚明确才会被法院(或仲裁庭)支持。

有关免责条文在普通法下的解释,在笔者《合约的解释:规则与应用》一书第十二章之1段有详细介绍,不再重复。

8.2 民事/商事欺诈

民事/商事欺诈(civil fraud/commercial fraud)是英国普通法与公共政策(public policy)不容,这默示的重大原则不是订约自由可去超越的。如何给它一个定义并不容易,因为范围太广,在社会人士(特别是经验丰富的国际商人)的丰富想象力、创新与政府试图通过立法反制的拉扯下,会不断有千变万化的情况出现。在 William Holdsworth 的《A History of English Law》(1972)一书提到 Hardwicke 勋爵在 1759 年说:“Fraud is infinite, and were a court once to lay down rules, ... to define strictly the species of evidences of it, the jurisdiction would be cramped, and perpetually eluded by new schemes which the fertility of man's invention would contrive.”

虽然本段是主要针对欺诈性误述,但常发生的民事/商事的欺诈/欺骗还有其他主要类别,部分并不涉及误述但肯定涉及不诚实,如:不导致误述方与被误述方之间

---

〔63〕 见笔者《合约的解释:规则与应用》一书第四章之5段。

〔64〕 包括针对各种类别行业的合约与不同形式的合理商业做法有针对性的默示,如货物买卖合约的“满意质量”与“货物适合买方用途”;租船合约的“船舶必须适航”等的默示:见笔者《合约的解释:规则与应用》一书第七章之3段。

产生合约的欺诈/欺骗；[65] 经济性串谋（economic conspiracy）；[66] 诱导他人违约（inducing breach of contract）；[67] 行贿受贿（bribery）；刻意违反诚信责任（deliberate breach of fiduciary duty）；欺诈营商（fraudulent trading），例如明知还不上钱还利用信息差大肆向债权人借钱，或是明知不能支付对价还欺骗对方订立合约，[68] 转移财产，欺骗债权人；[69] 知情帮助与知情接收的从犯责任（secondary liability for breach of trust in dishonest assistance and knowing receipt），[70] 例如帮助洗钱；虚假提单或任何其他文件等。

所以如果是要求去给一份清单列出商业欺诈的类别，不如看在任何个别不同案情的案件是否能够证明满足欺诈/欺骗侵权的要件。首先现代欺骗侵权的起源一般被认为是在 Pasley v. Freeman（1789）3 TR 51 先例中，而关于欺骗侵权的基本原则之后也没有大的发展与改变。在该先例中，原告向被告询问第三人的信用情况，被告明知不是事实但仍对原告说第三人信用良好。于是原告依赖被告的陈述向第三人赊售（sale on credit）了一批货物，结果没有收回货款。原告以欺骗侵权向被告索赔，并获得了法院的支持："A false affirmation, made by the defendant with intent to defraud the plaintiff, whereby the plaintiff receives damage, is the ground of an action upon the case

---

〔65〕 例在 Osteopathic Education and Research Ltd v. Purfleet Office Systems Ltd（2010）EWHC 1801（QB）先例中，被告欺诈性诱导原告与第三人产生合约。这不是可诉误述或是可使无效合约，也不是《Misrepresentation Act 1967》立法的问题，只能算是欺诈/欺骗侵权。

〔66〕 见笔者《禁令》一书第二章之 3.2.3.1 段。

〔67〕 见笔者《禁令》一书第二章之 3.2.3.2 段。

〔68〕 在我国香港特区，近年来社会经济下滑陆续有商店倒闭。一些商店在倒闭前仍向一般消费者出售代金券，导致事后商店老板或公司董事被警察拘捕的案件频频发生。根据我国香港《商品说明条例》（第 362 章）之第 13L 条，这属于不当接受付款的犯罪行为。有关条文规定："如任何商户就某产品（有关产品）接受付款或其他代价，而在接受时（a）该商户意图不供应有关产品；（b）该商户意图供应与有关产品有重大分别的产品；或（c）没有合理理由相信该商户将能（i）在其接受该付款或代价之时或之前所指明的期间内，供应有关产品；或（ii）（如在接受该付款或代价之时或之前没有指明期间）在合理时间内，供应有关产品，则该商户即属不当地就有关产品接受付款。"

〔69〕 在 BTI 2014 LLC v. Sequana SA（2022）UKSC 25 先例中，最高院确认当公司董事知道或应该知道公司破产或接近破产或很可能破产时，就要考虑债权人的利益。但 Hodge 勋爵也说很多时候当公司接近破产时，不代表一刀切要终止所有商业活动。董事要在债权人与股东的利益之间权衡并作出商业决定，拯救公司的合理商业决定不会违反对债权人的责任。有关判决可节录如下："In many cases when a company is bordering on insolvency, an obligation to consider the interests of a company's creditors and balance them against the interests of the shareholders will involve directors in making a commercial judgment about the benefits and risks of a transaction or course of action which may not readily be impugned. A reasonable decision by directors to attempt to rescue a company's business in the interests of both its members and its creditors would not in my view involve a breach of the common law duty."这表示董事在公司接近破产时的商业决定最好留下证据，显示自己的决定考虑了债权人的利益与是合理的商业决定。

〔70〕 见笔者《证据法：基础理论、口头证据与专家证据》一书第十章之 2.11 段与 2.12 段。

in the nature of deceit. In such an action, it is not necessary that the defendant should be benefited by the deceit, or that he should collude with the person who is."

在较近期的 The"Kriti Palm"(2006)EWCA Civ 1601 上诉庭先例中,Rix 大法官简要总结了欺骗侵权的四个要件:"The elements of the tort of deceit are well known. In essence they require(1)a representation, which is(2)false,(3)dishonestly made, and (4)intended to be relied on and in fact relied on."

另 Buxton 大法官也说:"The tort [of deceit] involves a perfectly general principle. Where a defendant makes a false representation, knowing it to be untrue, or being reckless as to whether it is true, and intends that the claimant should act in reliance on it, then in so far as the latter does so and suffers loss the defendant is liable for that loss."

在 Templeton Insurance Ltd v. Motorcare Warranties Ltd (2010) EWHC 3113 (Comm)先例中,Simon 大法官说:"The elements of the tort of deceit are well established. A defendant is liable where(i)it makes a representation which is false,(ii)knowing it to be false, or reckless as to whether it is true or not,(iii)intending that the claimant should act in reliance on it,(iv)the claimant does act in reliance on it and(v)suffers loss thereby."

在更近期的 Eco 3 Capital Ltd and others v. Ludsin Overseas Ltd(2013)EWCA Civ 413 上诉庭先例中,Jackson 大法官也有同样的说法:"...the tort of deceit contains four ingredients, namely:i)The defendant makes a false representation to the claimant. ii)The defendant knows that the representation is false, alternatively he is reckless as to whether it is true or false. iii)The defendant intends that the claimant should act in reliance on it. iv)The claimant does act in reliance on the representation and in consequence suffers loss. Ingredient(i)describes what the defendant does. Ingredients(ii)and(iii)describe the defendant's state of mind. Ingredient(iv)describes what the claimant does."

也就是说欺骗侵权是指陈述方对被陈述方做出了明知是虚假的陈述或者不理会陈述真假,并希望被陈述方依赖,而被陈述方确实依赖该虚假陈述并蒙受损失。如果虚假陈述是合约一方在订约前的谈判阶段故意做出,并且被陈述方被该虚假陈述诱导订立合约,就构成欺诈性误述或其他商业欺诈。

至于欺诈性误述的定义,可以节录 Nigel Cooper K. C. 大法官在 Bell v. Singh (2022)EWHC 3272(Comm)的说法,如下:

"The elements of the tort of fraudulent misrepresentation are well – known and have been recently set out by Andrew Baker J in Pisante v. Logothetis [2022] EWHC 161 (Comm) at §6.

i)There must be a false representation of fact, made with the intention that it be relied on, that was in fact relied on;

ii)A statement of opinion, therefore, is not actionable save in so far as it incorporates or implies a representation of fact;

iii) A representation as to the future is not actionable save insofar as it incorporates or implies a representation as to present intention or presently held opinion; made either expressly or impliedly from words or conduct;

iv) A representation may be made expressly or may be implied from words or conduct. However, clear words or conduct are required for the implication of a representation, reflecting the principle that there is no duty to disclose;

v) A representation is not to be implied, therefore, from conduct the tenor of which is vague, uncertain imprecise or elastic;

vi) In consequence, where a representation is said to be implied, particular care is needed to identify with precision the content of the representation and how it is said to have been made;

vii) A representation cannot be inferred from mere silence;

viii) What (if any) representation has been made is ascertained objectively and construing the representation fairly in its context, but a) Where a representation is ambiguous, the claimant must prove that the representor intended their statement to be understood by representee in the sense in which it was false and that the representee did understand the statement in that sense; Cassa di Risparmio della Republica di San Marino Spa. v. Barclays Bank Ltd [2011] EWHC 484 (Comm) at [221]. b) For a claimant to establish reliance he will have to show that he understood the representation in the sense alleged; and c) In order to establish deceit, the claimant must show that the defendant understood they were making the allegation representation, i. e. that they were conveying to the defendant that which was in fact untrue;

ix) The test for deceit, then, is whether the representor knew the representation to be false, did not believe it to be true, or was reckless as to whether it was true or false; and

x) The representation is intended to be relied on and was in fact relied on; and

xi) While the standard of proof remains the balance of probabilities, more convincing evidence is required to establish fraud than is true of other types of allegation because the law considers there to be a strong inherent improbability that a party would dissemble to persuade a counterparty to enter into a contract.

The fraudulent representation must also cause loss."

8.2.1 对陈述不诚实的思想状态

不同类别的商业欺诈/欺骗最主要的共通点是被告有意图欺骗(actual intention to deceive)原告受害方或一类人(member of a class)。对"一类人"的受害方，可节录 Abu Dhabi Investment Co v. H Clarkson Ltd (2008) EWCA Civ 699 上诉讼先例的观点：
"The precise identity of the Claimant need not be known when the false representation is

made, provided that he belongs to a class of persons within the contemplation of the Defendant as likely and intended to be deceived by the misrepresentation."

《Chitty on Contracts》(2021 年,第 34 版)一书之 9 – 057 段说:"**Absence of honest belief.** That the claimant **who alleges fraud must prove the absence of an honest belief** is demonstrated by Derry v. Peek (1889) 14 App. Cas. 337 itself. A company issued a prospectus stating that it was entitled to use steam power to run trams; the respondents obtained shares on the strength of this representation, which was in fact false, although at the time the company had reason to believe that permission would be granted by the Board of Trade as a matter of course. Permission to use steam power was, however, not granted and the company was wound up. In an action for deceit the House of Lords held that the directors were not liable in damages for fraudulent misrepresentation. **The decisive factor**, in Lord Herschell's words, was that '**they honestly believed that what they asserted was true**'."(加黑部分是笔者的强调)

指控被告"意图骗人"就代表要让法院(或仲裁庭)客观认定被告的主观思想状态不诚实(subjective state of mind was dishonest)。这也是原告最不容易满足的举证责任。这也是为什么在20世纪七八十年代全球开始涌现大量商业欺诈/欺骗后,英国法院发明了很多"核武器",特别是冻结令与附属的资产披露令、[71]搜查令、第三方披露令等"诉前披露"(pre – action discovery)[72]做法,以应对并非正常披露可以解决的问题。否则受害方根本不知道谁是骗子,或即使知道,也无法满足成功指控被告意图骗他的举证责任。

不诚实是被告的主观思想状态,但是法院(或仲裁庭)根据一般社会上诚实第三人的标准与看法判断,所以说这是主观与客观的一并测试。由于这已经在笔者《证据法:基础理论、口头证据与专家证据》一书第十章之5段有详细介绍,此处不再重复。只节录在 Possfund Custodian Trustee Ltd v. Diamond (1996) 1 WLR 1351 先例中,Lightman 大法官的观点:"Whether or not theoretically a subjective intention is sufficient, for all practical purposes … the intention must in all cases be objectively established. Such intent is objectively established if the representor expressly communicates intent to the representee. On the other hand, where it is not expressly communicated, the representee must establish that he reasonably relied on the representation and that he reasonably believed that the representor intended him to act upon it."

需要证明被告的主观上不诚实,首先是他自己是知道有关的陈述/表述是虚假/不正确或不关心真假。这带来的问题是在国际商业谈判中,很多有心误导或欺骗对方的较高水平人士(尤其是对手水平不高,容易受骗),会是把欺诈性误述包装得更

---

[71] 见笔者《证据法:国际规管与诉讼中的证据攻防》一书第三章。

[72] 见笔者《证据法:国际规管与诉讼中的证据攻防》一书第二章。

为隐蔽、模棱两可与间接去表达,令该陈述可以有不同解释。[73] 这样,即使被陈述方与法院(或仲裁庭)认定有关陈述/表述为虚假或不正确,这对无辜误述已经足够,但对成功指控欺诈性误述来说仍不够,必须进一步证明被告误述方知道是虚假或不正确或不合理,但希望原告相信这陈述是真实或正确。这可节录 Cassa di Risparmio della Repubblica di San Marino SpA v. Barclays Bank Ltd(2011)EWHC 484(Comm)先例中,Hamblen 大法官说:"In a deceit case it is also necessary that the representor should understand that he is making the implied representation and that it had the misleading sense alleged. A person cannot make a fraudulent statement unless **he is aware that he is making that statement. To establish liability in deceit it is necessary 'to show that the representor intended his statement to be understood by the representee in the sense in which it was false'** ...In other cases of misrepresentation this is not a requirement, but one would generally expect it to be reasonably apparent to both representor and representee that the implied representation alleged was being made."(加黑部分是笔者的强调)

8.2.2 不考虑的因素:欺诈/欺骗背后的动机、无心伤害受害方等

被告的动机并不重要,例如不是为了自己获利,是为了原告受害方好或无心去伤害他。可重复 Herschell 勋爵在 Derry v. Peek(1889)14 App Cas 337 贵族院先例的说法:"Thirdly, if fraud be proved, the motive of the person guilty of it is immaterial. It matters not that there was no intention to cheat or injure the person to whom the statement was made."

在民事诉讼中,是不像刑法那样要在一个不诚实的陈述(dishonest statement)中进一步要求原告证明被告有骗人的意图。这可节录在近期的 Vald. Nielsen Holding A/S v. Baldorino(2019)EWHC 1926(Comm)先例中,Jacob 大法官说:"It is **not necessary that the maker of the statement was 'dishonest' as that word is used in the criminal law...Nor is the defendant's motive in making the representation relevant**. 'If fraud be established it is immaterial that there was no intention to cheat or injure the person to whom the false statement was made' ... **What is required is dishonest knowledge, in the sense of an absence of belief in truth** ... It is in that sense that I use the word 'dishonest' in this judgment."(加黑部分是笔者的强调)

另在较早的 Gabriel v. Little(2013)EWCA Civ 1513 上诉庭先例中,Gloster 大法官说:"It is trite law in this context that: '... if fraud be proved, the motive of the person guilty of it is immaterial. It matters not that there was no intention to cheat or injure a person to whom the statement was made.'."

相比之下,刑法需要证明被告有意图骗人,可节录《Fraud Act 2006》之 section 2 针对虚假陈述时的说法:"(1) A person is in breach of this section if he —(a) dishon-

---

[73] 这带来意识(awareness)与理解(understand)的问题,将在本章之 9.4.2 段介绍。

estly makes a false representation, and(b) **intends, by making the representation —(i) to make a gain for himself or another, or(ii) to cause loss to another or to expose another to a risk of loss.** (2) A representation is false if —(a) it is untrue or misleading, and(b) the person making it knows that it is, or might be, untrue or misleading."(加黑部分是笔者的强调)

以下介绍两个案件来显示这一点。首先是 Polhill v. Walter(1832)3 B & Ad 114 先例这个古老的先例中,被告为同住的 Hancorne 先生代签一份汇票。被告只是为了帮 Hancorne 先生的忙,虽然知道自己没有授权,但理所当然地认为他的代签会被追认(ratify),汇票会获得支付。但是之后出事,原告蒙受巨额损失,于是起诉被告。法院判虽然被告的动机是为 Hancorne 先生好而不是为了自己受益或为了伤害原告,但只要被告明知做出的陈述是错误的,并且希望对方依赖,对方也确实依赖并蒙受损害,就构成欺诈。Tenterden 勋爵说:"... it is not necessary to prove that the false representation was made from a corrupt motive of gain to the defendant, or a wicked motive of injury to the plaintiff: it was said to be enough if a representation is made which the party making it knows to be untrue, and which is intended by him, or which, from the mode in which it is made, is calculated, to induce another to act on the faith of it, in such a way as that he may incur damage, and that damage is actually incurred. A wilful falsehood of such a nature was contended to be, in the legal sense of the word, a fraud ..."

从上面这个古老先例可以看出代签文件的风险。当然在现实生活中的一些小事,如为同住室友代签信件或代签包裹等,问题不大,因为一般不会有人依赖这个代签而蒙受损害。但对一些严肃的商业文件就完全不一样了,以提单为例,一些公司乱签提单的情况可以说是屡见不鲜。为不清洁货物签发清洁提单(clean bill of lading)或倒签提单(back - dated bill of lading)常常并非为了船东自己的利益,也经常见到许多船东以此抗辩,但这是在刑事欺诈才会有关的抗辩,而并非民事欺诈的抗辩。甚至有情况是不止卖方要求,买方为了避免修改信用证的麻烦与费用也同意,也仍然会有危险。因为如果买方转卖,分买方仍会依赖造假的提单并可能蒙受损失。即使不转卖,银行也依赖这份文件来支付货款。事实上,不应该签署任何虚假文件,因为法律要求诚实,为什么要签一些与事实不符的文件呢?即使是为了帮朋友忙的推荐信、履历证明或收据等经常会接触的文件,如果明知或应该知道其中包括了不正确的内容,也不应该同意签字,因为肯定有人会依赖这些文件并会带来后患而被认定为"骗子"。

另可以介绍近期大量在国际上被报道的 RBRG Trading(UK) Ltd v. Sinocore International Co Ltd(2018) EWCA Civ 838 上诉庭先例,[74] 该案涉及一个中国贸仲的仲裁裁决书在英国的承认与执行。在贸仲仲裁中,案情涉及中国卖方 S 与英国买方 R

---

〔74〕 此先例在本书第九章之 6.9.5 段有更详细的案情介绍。

一票钢材的买卖。在准备货物的过程中,R 突然单方面修改信用证,合约中对付运日期的规定是在 7 月 30 日之前,而单方修改后的信用证中却规定付运日期为 7 月 20 日—7 月 30 日。在笔者看来,该行为是因为当时钢材市场大跌,不安好心的英国买方想要摆脱合约从而设置陷阱来试探中国卖方是否会上当或知道如何应对。

S 在 7 月 6 日货物全部装船之后就将装船通知发给了英国买方,正确付运日期为 7 月 6 日。这本来符合买卖合约与原信用证的付运日期,但修改的 20 日至 30 日之间日期就不符了。在收到开证银行通知信用证被 R 单方面修改后,S 没有向银行主张不接受修改,因为信用证是双方之间的合约不能单方面改变。而 S 在仲裁中说为了方便,也为大家(包括 R 与开证银行)省钱,在知道事实真相下不必再修改信用证,就把提单上的装船日期改为 7 月 20 日以配合修改后的信用证。

但 R 早有准备,在开证行通知卖方结汇的同时,以提交的一套提单付运日期加上较早的装船通知,马上在开证行所在地的荷兰法院获得对开证行的止付禁令(anti - payment injunction)。S 拿不到货款下与 R 交涉,最终双方相互指称对方违约/毁约并在北京贸仲提起仲裁。而船上一批的钢材最终在美国被 S 转卖,S 几乎是颗粒无收,但也必须如此才能把租用的船舶还船。

长话短说,包括笔者的仲裁庭认定 R 全面知道装货的安排与进展,S 也告知了货物真正装船的日期。所以在买卖双方的买卖合约下,S 对 R 不存在欺诈/欺骗或任何欺诈性误述,更不用说是 R 根本说不出对它有什么诱导或依赖。正如在 Sprecher Grier Halberstam LLP v. Walsh (2008) EWCA Civ 1324 上诉庭先例中,Ward 大法官说:"A man cannot be deceived if he knows the truth."结果是贸仲仲裁庭不接受 R 的争辩,也就是 S 制造假提单构成违约/毁约的行为。

至于 S 确实制造了假提单的事实,仲裁庭的解释是欺诈/欺骗只在信用证合约关系下针对荷兰开证行。但信用证是独立的合约关系不影响买卖合约下双方的履行情况,案件也在其他法院处理中,与本仲裁无关。所以,最终 S 在仲裁中以它指控 R 单方面修改不符合买卖合约付运日期的信用证的违约行为成功而胜诉。关键是仲裁庭预计该裁决书的执行会有问题,所以在原因部分(就是裁决书最有含金量的部分)长篇大论(100 页中的 65 页)分析为什么在假提单/假文件的事实下,制作的 S 仍不构成买卖合约下的欺诈/欺骗,并且引经据典陈述了大量普通法理念。

S 最后按照《New York Convention 1958》将裁决书拿到英国执行。R 大力抗拒,主张执行这个被欺诈污染的裁决书违反英国的公共政策。但是英国一审法院与上诉庭最终一致决定执行该贸仲裁决书,判决的原因是配合裁决书的原因部分。毕竟如果拒绝执行,英国法院要给充分原因去否定裁决书中的原因,这是困难的。此先例也显示了仲裁庭需要在裁决书给原因(而且是优质与有说服力的原因)的理由之一,就是去协助执行。

本仲裁案件中,S 的上策是按照《跟单信用证统一惯例》(UCP600)的规定去直接拒绝接受开证银行修改信用证,毕竟银行不像 R 会不安好心,肯定按照规则

(UCP600)做。当然S也可以回去与R交涉,要它再改回信用证,否则就属于违约/毁约。但这已经是中策了,因为明知R是不安好心,而货物已经装船,即使接受违约/毁约也是于事无补。也可以选择让船舶返回装港,换掉部分货物,然后在7月20日再签发提单。但由于日期差得太远,所以也是中下策。但S偏偏选择了下下策,还以为是最省事与走捷径的解决问题的方法。虽然仲裁庭接受这背后的动机是无心伤害或欺骗R或开证银行,但很不明智。

8.2.3 欺诈性误述的不诚实思想状态的种类

欺诈性误述的不诚实思想状态,可节录Herschell勋爵在Derry v. Peek(1889)14 App Cas 337贵族院先例中所说:"First, in order to sustain an action in deceit, there must be proof of fraud and nothing short of that will suffice. **Secondly**, fraud is proved when it is shown that a false representation has been made (i) **knowingly**, (ii) **without belief in its truth**, or (iii) **recklessly, careless whether it be true or false**. Although I have treated the second as distinct cases, I think the third is but an instance of the second, for one who makes a statement under such circumstances can have no belief in the truth of what he states. **To prevent a false statement being fraudulent, there must, I think, always be an honest belief in its truth**. ... Thirdly, if fraud be proved, the motive of the person guilty of it is immaterial. It matters not that there was no intention to cheat or injure the person to whom the statement was made."(加黑部分是笔者的强调)

8.2.3.1 第一种:真正知道/知情

上述经典节录是说欺骗侵权/欺诈性误述有三种,第一种是知情(knowingly)或真正知道(actual knowledge)是虚假与不正确的事实,但因为希望对方会受诱导并依赖去产生合约(或其他符合己方的目的)仍去陈述,这应是容易理解的情况。

在Armstrong v. Strain(1951)1 TLR 856先例中,Devlin大法官强调了对第一类欺诈性误述,误述方必须对虚假事实是完全知情,并且是处于"邪恶"(wickedness)与不诚实的主观思想状态,也就是意图骗人:"A man may be said to know a fact when once he has been told it and pigeon – holed it somewhere in his brain where it is more or less accessible in case of need. In another sense of the word **a man knows a fact only when he is fully conscious of it**. For an action of deceit there must be knowledge in the narrower sense; and **conscious knowledge of falsity must always amount to wickedness and dishonesty**. When judges say, therefore, **that wickedness and dishonesty must be present**, they are not requiring a new ingredient for the tort of deceit so much as describing the sort of knowledge which is necessary."(加黑是笔者的强调)

即使在Derry v. Peek(1889)14 App Cas 337贵族院先例中,假设当时当局的回复不是报道中说的批准没问题而是有50%的可能批准,但被告仍在招股章程中陈述当局会批准,同样也是明知陈述不正确。

这种真正知道自己在说谎去骗人的欺诈性误述案件在商业社会虽然不少,并且会是同时构成刑事犯罪(见《Fraud Act 2006》之 s. 2),但在高水平与更隐蔽的国际商业社会,会更多是第二种的欺诈性误述,这在下一段介绍。

8.2.3.2 第二种:鲁莽、不相信/不理会真假

至于第二种的是不真正相信是真实(without belief or caring in its truth)与第三种的鲁莽(reckless)的陈述,实是同一码事。鲁莽不去理会真假是需要分析被告当时的思想状态,这与疏忽甚至是严重疏忽(gross negligence)不涉及主观上的不诚实不一样。当然证明被告在误述时与订立合约期间的思想状态不可能,但 Herchell 勋爵在 Derry v. Peek(1889)14 App Cas 337 贵族院先例中有说:"where the fact that an alleged belief was destitute of all reasonable foundations would suffice of itself to convince a court that it was not really entertained, and that the representation was a fraudulent one." 也就是,被告如果想抗辩这方面的指控,就要证明他不知情或不真正知道事实的真相,即需有一个说得通的理由去支持他相信这陈述应是真实。如果被告说不出一个或更多他相信陈述为真的合理理由,就有危险被认定为第二种的欺诈性误述了。

随便举一个例子,就是被告向原告做出的误述,是一个网上流传的信息。但众所周知,网上流传的信息十之八九是虚假信息与事实。被告不假思索也不进一步调查或没有可靠源头的信息相互印证就拿来用,不加以限制(如说明是网上的消息)就当作是事实向原告做出陈述,这就会是第二类的欺诈性误述。相反如果信息与事实的渠道可靠,甚至被告自己也曾经同样依赖作决定,这样即使没有进一步调查确认就向原告当作事实做出陈述是有错,也会被视为只是疏忽或违反《Misrepresentation Act 1967》S. 2(1),虽没有合理理由(reasonable ground)相信,但不会上升到欺诈/欺骗。

多举一个例子是在商业社会经常会发生不少工作繁忙的公司高管会被同事、雇员或朋友告知某些事实,又或是看过某份文件。但时间一久(可以只是一两个月或更短),就已经记得不清楚甚至是忘掉。但在合约谈判中,该高管仍是凭模糊的记忆或是已经忘了但乱猜(blind guess),然后当成是事实向对方陈述。即使他打个电话问问或翻查文件就很容易知道真相,但也贪方便不去做。或是,心底里不想查问,因为害怕事实的真相不会对己方有利,真正知道反而令自己不知讲或不讲。这些千变万化的情况,也因人而异,到底算是严重疏忽或是鲁莽,或是属于欺诈性误述的鲁莽不理会真假?

毕竟它们在犯错的程度上看来不像有大多不同,但法律上是不同。正如 Bowen 大法官在 Le Lievre v. Gould(1893)1 QB 491 上诉庭先例强调严重疏忽不代表不诚实。不诚实的不关心陈述事实的真假是"not taking care to find out whether the statement was true or false; it meant not caring in the man's own heart and conscience whether it was true or false."

在近期的 Sears v. Minco Plc(2016)EWHC 433(Ch)先例中,案情涉及私人投资人 Sears 先生指控被告欺诈性误述(有关 Minco 的持股量)诱导被告入股 Minco(一家爱尔兰矿业公司)的 800 万股,结果损失惨重,特别是对比这一笔钱如果花在替代

投资能获得的收益。Hodge QC 大法官接受被告的抗辩,认为这不是不诚实的欺诈性误述:"that while recklessness may be evidence of dishonesty, it is no substitute for that state of mind, and that even gross carelessness cannot be equated with indifference as to the truth of a representation ..."

看来,欺诈性误述要成立关键是要证明被告的思想状态有不诚实,无论有关误述是标签为疏忽、严重疏忽还是鲁莽的陈述。有时候这也很难区分,所以很多索赔欺诈性误述的原告会加上一个替代诉因,即在本书第四章介绍的《Misrepresentation Act 1967》之 S.2(1)的立法误述(本质类似疏忽误述)。

在较早举的商业社会常发生的例子,笔者可去推算不同案情会带来的不同决定。如果公司高管自信过高认为自己的记忆力应是错不了,或该高管在做出陈述前曾想查问但被告知要较长时间才能确认事实,或有向雇员查问但被告知错误信息等,这些犯错均应是疏忽。或这些错误程度严重,可标签为严重疏忽或甚是鲁莽,但都没有认定被告在当时的思想状态是不诚实。

但有一种情况会是思想状态涉及不诚实,即该高管心底里不想查问也不去查问,这可以是懒惰、省钱或以免知道事实真相后不知道讲或是不讲,心底里也知道自己不确定陈述的真假。这种不理会,不想/不敢面对可能的真相就当作"事实真相"去陈述应是 Derry v. Peek 贵族院先例的第二种欺诈性误述了。显然,在民事诉讼中也无须达到刑法的要求要证明被告有骗人的动机,但必须让法官或仲裁员客观认定陈述方根本不在乎真假,但希望被陈述方认为陈述为真。看来,最关键的区分还是该高管是否有能被接受的合理理由不去查问事实真相。

Sears v. Minco Plc 先例的判词在这方面会更清楚,该先例被法院认定欺诈性误述不成立,原告败诉。因为审理法官认定误述方虽然可去轻易查获事实真相,但疏忽没有去做,而一旦接受误述方认为陈述为真有说得通的基础或至少是没有合理理由去怀疑是不正确,就不会构成欺诈性误述。有关的判词是:"... the re-re-amended defence, which pleads that both Mr McKillen(Minco 的 CEO,被指控欺诈性误述的被告主要证人)and Mr Varma(Minco 的 CFO)'did not have a perfect recall of the terms of the JVA(合资协议)and would have needed to see the terms of the JVA to refresh their memory as to its terms or to ascertain the precise terms relating to Minco's entitlement(有关的误述事实)'. But ... no admission or acknowledgment that either Mr McKillen or Mr Varma **knew that they did not have a perfect recall of the terms of the JVA and would have needed to see that document to refresh their memory** in order to ascertain the precise terms relating to Minco's entitlement ... The defendants' case, which I find to be made out on the evidence, is that both Mr McKillen and Mr Varma **genuinely believed that the former sufficiently knew the terms of the JVA governing**(误述的事实), and that Mr McKillen was simply, but **genuinely, mistaken as to what those terms were. I hold that that is not sufficient to justify a finding of fraud or deceit**; and I reject the claimants' case on fraud and deceit. I do not find that Mr McKillen(still less Mr Varma) consciously appreciated that Mr McKillen's understanding of the … provisions of the JVA was wrong. Nor is this a case where either of them simply did not give a damn about what those provisions were. I find that Mr McKillen had no reason to suspect that his understanding of … of the JVA was inaccurate, and he had no reason to consider that he needed to consult or refer to the JVA to confirm that or to check whether his understanding was correct. I find that Mr Varma had no reason to suspect that anything that Mr McKillen had said was inaccurate, or founded upon inadequate knowledge, still less to challenge any of Mr McKillen's statements in any respect. "(加黑部分是笔者的强调)

笔者重复成功指控被告欺诈性误述必须证明思想状态,不仅是去比较一般合理做法是严重疏忽甚至是极度严重疏忽的鲁莽不理会真假就足够,还必须判断与认定被告误述方在思维上刻意鲁莽(deliberate recklessness),程度达到根本不想知道真相,虽然两者之间的分水岭并不明显。正如在 Angus v. Clifford(1891)2 Ch 449 先例中,Bowen 大法官说:"**Not caring**, in that context, did not mean not taking care, **it meant indifference to the truth**, the moral obliguity of which consists in a wilful disregard of the importance of truth, and unless you keep it clear that this is the true meaning. Of the term, you are constantly in danger of confusing the evidence from which the inference of dishonesty in the mind may be drawn—or of dishonesty itself, which has to be drawn after you have weighed all the evidence. "(加黑部分是笔者的强调)

在我国香港上诉庭的 Lee Yuk Shing v. Dianoor International Ltd(2016)HKEC 1139 先例中,笔者认为比刚介绍的英国 Sears v. Minco Plc 先例更好地说明了两者微妙与不明显的分水岭。我国香港特区的一审先例中,认定被告曾作出欺诈性误述,但这被上诉庭推翻,指一审判决/判词显示一审法官执着于误述方被告是否严重疏忽不去理会陈述事实的真假,但这并不正确,应该针对与认定被告在做出陈述/误述时思想状态是刻意不理会真假。香港上诉庭的关大法官说:

"There is clearly a difference between the test for recklessness in common law deceit … It would appear that the judge(一审大法官)had applied the wrong legal test for recklessness in fraudulent misrepresentation. The representor will be fraudulent if he made the statement 'recklessly, careless whether it be true or false' … **Lord Herschell in Derry v Peek was at pains to emphasise that negligence is not sufficient for deceit**, since recklessness involves not caring whether the statement is true: an indifference to the truth …. The expression **'not caring' had nothing to do with not taking care, it meant not caring in one's own heart and conscience whether the statement is true or false**. It is well established that **to establish common law deceit, a degree of dishonesty or moral turpitude has to be present**. In this context, the **moral obliquity consists of an indifference to the truth, a wilful disregard of the importance of the truth**(Joliffe v Baker

(1883)11 QBD 255 at 275; Angus v Clifford [1891] 2 Ch 449 at 471; Le Lievre and Dennes v Gould [1893] 1 QB 491 at 501; Thomas Witter Ltd v TBP Industries Ltd [1996] 2 All ER 573 at 587g to h).

The judge is wrong in law in holding that recklessness for fraudulent misrepresentation will be established even if it cannot be shown that the defendant was **deliberately closing its eyes to the truth or that it had any kind of dishonest mind**. The judge framed the 'crucial issue' and his finding in this context in § 117: 'the Liquidators had done nothing or nothing adequate to ensure no representations or warranties as to the authenticity of the items to be auctioned was given.' In the judge's discussion of the issue of recklessness of the liquidators, he repeatedly described the liquidators as being 'negligent', 'grossly negligent', not taking steps which 'any reasonable liquidator' would have taken, going 'far beyond the realm of gross negligence' ... **He was assessing the liquidators' conduct against the notions of negligence, reasonableness and not taking care. He had not directed his mind to the correct legal test for recklessness in this context**.

...**I do not agree with his submissions.** I do not think the passages emphasised by Mr Wong(原告代表大律师) would go to show that the judge had approached the matter correctly with the view to ascertain whether there was any degree of dishonesty or moral turpitude of the liquidators. **Gross want of caution on their part cannot be stretched to constitute wilful or wicked indifference that is necessary for a fraudulent state of mind**. The finding of recklessness of the liquidators' conduct cannot be sustained."(加黑是笔者的强调)

8.2.4　指控对方欺诈/欺骗的诉讼程序上的问题

针对原告必须证明被告欺诈/欺骗的程序与证据方面的问题,只提以下几点:

1. 英国法院会严肃对待民事/商事欺诈案件,这反映在大律师公会的规则(Bar Code of Conduct)之Para. 704(c)中说:"A barrister ... must not draft any statement of case, witness statement, affidavit, notice of appeal or other document containing: ...(c) any allegation of fraud unless he has clear instructions to make such allegation and has before him reasonably credible material which as it stands establishes a prima facie case of fraud."

我国香港特区大律师的执业守则中也有类似的规定:"10.23 A practising barrister instructed to draft or settle a court document(be it a pleading, affidavit, witness statement, notice of appeal or other document) is under responsibilities to the Court as well as to his client. He may not: - ...(b) allege fraud unless he has clear instructions to make such allegation and he has before him reasonably credible material which, as it stands, establishes a prima facie case of fraud; ..."

英国与我国香港事务律师协会(Law Society)也有类同规定,不节录。有规则就会有新问题,即什么才算是足够的关于欺诈/欺骗的"可信材料"(credible material)。毕竟在现实中,有经验的律师一收到新客户的委任与被告知相关问题,如果感觉可能涉及欺诈/欺骗与欺诈性误述,就会意识到要尽快行动才能保护客户利益,如撤销合约、冻结令、搜查令等。但冻结令等的法律行动是难免要拟定一连串的文件如证人证言(witness statement)、宣誓书(affidavit)等。但很可能在当时,律师只是听客户的一面之词(这顶多是传闻证据与有很大的主观性)与很有限的几份文件,而认定欺诈/欺骗是需要比指控一般民事过错更多与更完整的文件证据。这样,会陷入两难的境地,对此律师需要平衡与准确判断。

在 Medcalf v. Mardell(2003)1 AC 120 贵族院先例中,涉及法院对一位代表律师作出要他个人负责的"浪费费用命令"(wasted costs order),[75] 因为不当提出欺诈/欺骗的指控。在贵族院,Bingham 勋爵说:"While counsel should never lend his name to such allegations unless instructed to do so, the receipt of instructions is not of itself enough. **Counsel is bound to exercise an objective professional judgment whether it is in all the circumstances proper to lend his name to the allegation.** As the rule recognises, counsel could not properly judge it proper to make such an allegation unless he had material before him which he judged to be reasonably credible and which appeared to justify the allegation. **At the hearing stage, counsel cannot properly make or persist in an allegation which is unsupported by admissible evidence**, since if there is not admissible evidence to support the allegation the court cannot be invited to find that it has been proved, and if the court cannot be invited to find that the allegation has been proved the allegation should not be made or should be withdrawn. I would however agree ... that **at the preparatory stage the requirement is not that counsel should necessarily have before him evidence in admissible form but that he should have material of such a character as to lead responsible counsel to conclude that serious allegations could properly be based upon it**. I could not think, for example, that it would be professionally improper for counsel to plead allegations, however serious, based on the documented conclusions of a DTI(政府商务部) inspector or a public inquiry, even though counsel had no access to the documents referred to and the findings in question were inadmissible hearsay."(加黑部分是笔者的强调)

换言之,什么才是足够的可信材料去支持欺诈/欺骗的指控需要灵活处理,按照不同时间与案件的进度而异,在准备的早期与开庭审理时会是很不一样的。中国少部分律师动辄就指控对方欺诈/欺骗,又没有充分证据支持,这在国际诉讼或仲裁要小心。

---

〔75〕 见笔者《证据法:国际规管与诉讼中的证据攻防》一书第三章之 1.7.1.7.2 段。

2. 在民事诉讼中，即使是涉及一个严重的欺诈/欺骗指控，也依然根据平衡的可能性（balance of probability）认定事实。但平衡可能性是一个弹性的理念，特别是去证明一个"虚无缥缈"的思想状态。所以由于欺诈/欺骗的严重性与发生的内在可能性，需要更多可信（cogent）的证据才会能说服审理法官（或仲裁庭）。正如 Hoffmann 勋爵在 Re B（children）（sexual abuse：standard of proof）（2008）4 All ER 1 贵族院先例说："There is only one rule of law, namely that the occurrence of the fact in issue must be proved to have been more probable than not. Common sense, not law, requires that in deciding this question, regard should be had, to whatever extent appropriate, to inherent probabilities."

3. 由于大部分的民事/商事欺诈案件，涉及的被告更狡猾与水平高，欺诈更隐蔽，如果涉及跨境取证也更困难，所以证明被告的不诚实思想状态不容易，特别是指控的不诚实是 Derry v. Peek（1889）14 App Cas 337 贵族院先例的第二种"不理会真假的鲁莽"的思想状态。所以，受害方原告经常需要邀请法院去根据证据（包括相似事实证据）[76] 展示的案情去推断内在可能性。

不像刑事案件，虽然举证责任是更高，但因为往往是本土案件不涉及跨境取证，犯罪嫌疑人很多也水平有限，证明不诚实的思想状态反而相对容易。

4. 也因为如此，试图在欺诈/欺骗案件中提早处理争议（early disposal）如申请简易判决（summary judgment）或撤销索赔请求（strike out claim）会十分困难。这类案件本质上有迫切原因（compelling reason）在考虑了所有有关证据（特别是对有关当事人的交叉盘问/口头证据）后才作出决定。在 Wrexham AFC Ltd v. Crucialmove Ltd（2007）BCC 139 上诉庭先例中，Gibson 大法官说："Experience teaches us that on occasion apparently overwhelming cases of fraud and dishonesty somehow inexplicably disintegrate. In short, oral testimony may show that some such cases are only tissue paper strong."

当然也不是没有成功申请简易判决的先例，如 Cheshire Building Society v. Dunlop Haywards（DHL）Ltd（2008）PNLR 19 先例。看来在以下罕有的情况下才会成功：（i）已经有刑事定罪的可采纳证据；[77]（ii）极端与明确的当场证据可去毫无疑点地证明被告的不诚实。

同样道理下，被告申请简易撤销欺诈/欺骗的指控也往往需要指出原告指控的详情（particulars）不够，与/或提及与依赖的证据是不可靠，甚至是不正确的：见 Bleas-

---

[76] 相似事实证据（similar facts evidence）可见笔者《证据法：基础理论、口头证据与专家证据》一书第九章之 2.5 段。较近期的 Abbey National plc v. JSF Finance & Currency Exchange Co Ltd（2006）EWCA Civ 328 上诉庭先例中，法院允许原告以过去 2 年发生的同类事件支持申请禁令，以证明被告对有关的欺诈/欺骗是"视而不见"或"鲁莽不去查问"。

[77] 见笔者《证据法：基础理论、口头证据与专家证据》一书第九章之 1.3.2.1 段。

dale v. Forster(2011)EWHC 416(Ch)等先例。

5. 即使有足够证据相信可去提出欺诈/欺骗的指控,CPR Part 16 规定原告在索赔请求中必须将欺诈/欺骗指控的详情全部列出。这在 Three Rivers District Council v. Bank of England(No. 3)(2001)UKHL 16 贵族院先例中,Hope 勋爵说:"(13)... as a general rule, the more serious the allegation of misconduct, the greater is the need for particulars to be given which explains the basis for the allegation. This is especially so where the allegation that is being made is of bad faith or dishonesty. (15) Of course, the allegation of fraud, dishonesty or bad faith must be supported by particulars. The other party is entitled to notice of the particulars on which the allegation is based. If they are not capable of supporting the allegation, the allegation itself may be struck out."

这方面十分复杂,需要在本章之 9 段另行介绍。

8.2.5 指控欺诈性误述的好处

上述看来,成功指控对方欺诈/欺骗在实质与程序上均不是容易的一件事,特别是证明对方的思想状态是不容易与不肯定。但这方面好处也不少,如下所述。

1. 首先在调查取证,如果争议/争端涉及欺诈/欺骗,并且显示的案情是一个表面良好的案件,可以说服法院或仲裁庭下令对方披露即使是主张诉讼特免权的文件:见笔者《证据法:国际规管与诉讼中的证据攻防》一书第十一章之 1.2.4 段。

2. 时效更宽松:虽然英国针对合约与侵权的立法时效一般长达事发也就是有了诉因(cause of action)后的 6 年,但仍有不少错过时效而失去索赔权利的情况。一种情况是对方欺诈/欺骗,而涉及欺诈/欺骗通常都是隐蔽的,令受害方不知道或不肯定自己索赔的权利或诉因,或因为没有足够详情与证据而无法启动诉讼以保护时效。英国立法对这方面有作出救济,针对这种涉及不诚实与欺诈的案件在受害方发现或合理可以发现时[78]才开始起算时效。《Limitation Act 1980》之 section 32,可节录如下:"(1) Subject to ..., where in the case of any action for which a period of limitation is prescribed by this Act, either—(a) the action is based upon the fraud of the defendant; or ... the period of limitation shall not begin to run until the plaintiff has discovered the fraud, concealment or mistake (as the case may be) or could with reasonable diligence have discovered it."

这意味着无辜方只要不是因为自己的疏忽才没有发现欺诈,时效可能就一直不

---

〔78〕 例如近期就有 European Real Estate Debt Fund(Cayman)Ltd(In Liquidation)v. Treon(2021)EWHC 2866(Ch)先例判受害方从合理应当知道欺诈存在开始已经超过 6 年,因此超出索赔时效了。此先例中较为特别的是受害方其实是在损失产生前就合理可以知道真实情况,但只要受害方并非真正知道实情,看来是不会影响欺诈性误述的存在,但在时效上仍然是从应当合理知情开始计算。Miles 大法官说:"If a claimant could reasonably have discovered the fraud by virtue of events and circumstances occurring before it actually suffered a loss, there was no principled rationale for allowing it the indulgence of more than the normal six years' period to bring its claim."

起算。相比之下,错误(mistake)同样会在后来才被发现,例如,公司之间的账目有错漏,时效就会严格得多:见 Phillips - Higgins v. Harper(1954)1 QB 411 上诉庭先例。[79]

3. 在受害方/被陈述方也有部分过错(如疏忽不去做或疏忽执行一些例行的调查或测试,否则很容易知道对方骗人的事实真相),在《Misrepresentation Act 1967》下的非欺诈性误述是可以根据《Law Reform(Contributory Negligence)Act 1945》分摊损失,但欺诈性误述不适用。在 Alliance & Leicester Building Society v. Edgestop Ltd (1993)1 WLR 1462 先例中,Mummery 大法官说:"In brief, a person liable for deceit, whether personally or vicariously, is not entitled as a matter of law to deny by a plea of contributory negligence, that his deceit was the sole effective cause of the damage suffered by his victim. Nothing in the Act or on authority entitles a person liable for deceit to plead contributory negligence."

4. 更容易申请撤销合约,毕竟在《Misrepresentation Act 1967》之 S. 2(2)下,法院可以对不严重的疏忽或无辜误述以赔偿损失替代(in lieu of)撤销合约的救济。可以说这立法剥夺了大量这种非欺诈性误述本来自动拥有的撤销合约的衡平法救济,只有立法管不到的欺诈性误述才会肯定这普通法救济不受影响:见 SK Shipping Plc v. Capital VLCC 3 Corp(2020)EWHC 3448(Comm)先例。

5. 损失计算比一般正常的计算宽松多了:见 Doyle v. Olby(Ironmongers)Ltd (1969)2 QB 158 上诉庭先例与 Smith New Court Securities Ltd v. Scrimgeour Vickers (Asset Management)Ltd(1996)3 WLR 1051 贵族院先例。这将在本书第四章之 4.2.2段详细分析。

6. 普通法下不允许对欺诈性误述责任以合约条文豁免,这会在下一段接下去讲。

8.3 普通法下不允许豁免欺诈性误述责任

可先节录《Misrepresentation, Mistake and Non-Disclosure》(2022 年,第 6 版)一书之 9 - 13 段说:"**Exclusion of liability for fraudulent misrepresentation** A clause might attempt to limit or exclude a person's liability for fraudulent misrepresentation either by expressly referring to liability for fraud, or by being drafted so wide as apparently to cover fraudulent, as well as non-fraudulent, misrepresentations. It is generally accepted, however, that a clause which expressly excludes or limits a party's personal liability for fraud would be held ineffective at common law. At least until the enactment of the Misrepresentation Act 1967 the courts used to construe widely - drafted exclusion clauses so that they did not apply to fraud; they presumed that the parties must have intended the clause only to apply to liability arising from honest (non-fraudulent) misrepresentations. It has been said that such a construction is now no longer necessary, since a clause which is suffi-

[79] 见本书第七章之 17.2 段。

ciently general to cover liability for fraud can instead be held unreasonable,…"

这方面的权威先例是早期的 S. Pearson & Son Ltd. v. Dublin Corporation(1907) AC 351 贵族院先例中,案情是有关被告雇主欺诈性提供了有关工地的信息,但合约有条文说明是原告承建商自己要理解与满意工程涉及的工作,而且雇主对提供的信息的正确性不负责。这条文本质上与今天国际商业合约中常有的"没有依赖条文"(Non-reliance Clause)一致。但贵族院判该免责或豁免条文对欺诈/欺骗无效,Loreburn L. C. 勋爵说:"Now it seems clear that **no one can escape liability for his own fraudulent statements by inserting in a contract a clause that the other party shall not rely upon them**. I will not say that a man himself innocent may not under any circumstances, however peculiar, guard himself by apt and express clauses from liability for the fraud of his own agents. It suffices to say that in my opinion the clauses before us do not admit of such a construction. They **contemplate honesty on both sides and protect only against honest mistakes**."(加黑部分是笔者的强调)

另 Halsbury 伯爵也说:"The action is based on the allegation of fraud, and no subtlety of language, no craft or machinery in the form of contract, can estop a person who complains that he has been defrauded from having that question of fact submitted to a jury."

最后节录 James 勋爵的观点:"Such a clause would be good protection against any mistake or miscalculation, but **fraud vitiates every contract and every clause in it.**"(加黑部分是笔者的强调)

8.3.1　不允许的原因

由于欺诈/欺骗为公共政策不容,所以试图去以合约明示条文豁免责任也因违反公共政策而无效。豁免欺诈性误述责任的条文如果有效也必须是双方有订约意图,大家有一致想法(meeting of minds/consent)。但难以想象一方合约方是有订约意图或同意在对方欺骗自己的情况下(可以是严重),仍免除对方的责任。以上说法在 HIH Casualty and General Insurance Ltd v. Chase Manhattan Bank(2003) UKHL 6 贵族院先例中,Bingham 勋爵说:"It reflects an **old legal rule that fraud unravels all**: fraus omnia corrumpit. It also reflects the practical basis of commercial intercourse. **Once fraud is proved, 'it vitiates judgments, contracts and all transactions whatsoever'** … Parties entering into a commercial contract will no doubt recognise and accept the risk of errors and omissions in the preceding negotiations, even negligent errors and omissions. But each party will assume the honesty and good faith of the other; absent such an assumption they would not deal. … **It is clear that the law, on public policy grounds, does not permit a contracting party to exclude liability for his own fraud in inducing the making of the contract**."(加黑部分是笔者的强调)

在同一先例中 Hobhouse 勋爵从订约意图上去否定对欺诈的免责条文说:

"Where a contract has been procured by the material fraud of one party (or of the agent he has employed to make the contract), **the party deceived has not given a true consent to be bound by the contract**. He is entitled at common law to avoid the contract when he discovers the deceit."(加黑部分是笔者的强调)

8.3.2 委托人可否以合约条文有效豁免不涉及委托人的代理人的欺诈性误述责任

本书第二章之11段已经讨论了通过第三人做出欺诈性误述的责任与救济。在这里针对如果合约中的特定条文明示写明了可以豁免欺诈性误述的转承责任(对并非自己公司雇员的代理人),在一方合约方A委托的代理人或经纪人向对方合约方B做出了欺诈性误述时,面对B以该误述选择撤销合约与索赔欺诈/欺骗带来的损失,A能否依赖该条文否定这些救济?毕竟,代理人或经纪人在委托人不知情的情况下,为了成功交易以赚取佣金而私下做出欺诈性误述的情形并不是没有听说过。

解决这种第三人(代理人或经纪人)的欺诈/欺骗把合约双方害苦的情况,会面临两难的局面。如果不允许受害方B撤销被代理人或经纪人诱导而产生的合约,因为合约只是与A订立,就对B十分不公平。毕竟,B要被迫继续履行的合约可能由于欺诈性误述而存在极严重的缺陷。而让A可享有通过代理人或经纪人以欺诈/欺骗手段(即使A不知情)获得的合约果实也说不通。再说,A本来也应该承担转承责任,即使A控制不了代理人甚至分代理人。

但如果法律允许B撤销合约又会对A不公平,因为有时A对代理人或经纪人的欺诈/欺骗根本不知情,在欺骗侵权方面也无须对B承担责任,怎会去让B可享有撤销合约的救济?再说,也完全有可能欺诈性误述涉及的只是一些微不足道的事实,但B借此误述在市场逆转的情形下去撤销与赖掉一个变为严重亏损的长期合约。

更复杂的还会有经纪人或其他第三人完全独立的情况,此时A与B又该如何分配风险?而这份确实存在缺陷的合约,又能否被撤销?

所以订下一条肯定的法律原则或默示地位去适用在案情完全不一样的不同案件实并不容易,不论是左是右都容易受批评。这样在订约自由的大原则下,A去豁免自己做出的欺诈性误述的责任因违反公共政策而不被允许,这是已经明确的且完全有说得通的道理。但是否允许A在合约中豁免它委任的或独立的代理人或经纪人做出A不知情的欺诈性误述的责任就难以决定了。毕竟法律如果允许,可以订约自由的大原则作为理由。但不允许就难以有说得通的道理,因为上述介绍有两难局面,这应该不会构成公共政策。

这方面的法律看来并不明确,但在美国纽约州的法律中是允许的。在Chase Manhattan Bank v. AXA Reinsurance UK plc (unreported, index number 603080/00, 26 July 2001)先例中,Gammerman大法官说:"Under well-established New York law, such express, detailed disclaimers preclude a claim of fraud based on misrepresentations within the scope of the disclaimers ..."

另在 Chase Manhattan Bank v. New Hampshire Insurance Company and AXA Reassurance SA(unreported,index number 602759/01)先例中,也是 Gammerman 大法官说:"The clauses are drafted with great precision. Each sentence and word within each clause serves a separate function. Some portions of the clauses are limited to representations/omissions about the risk,while others are not. Given the sophistication of the parties,I decline to read into the contractual language limitations that are not stated in the plain text of the parties' agreements."

而在英国法律下,在 HIH Casualty and General Insurance Ltd v. Chase Manhattan Bank(2003)UKHL 6 贵族院先例也有这方面的替代争议/争端。虽然最终无须法院去作出判决,但贵族院的大法官仍表达了不同的看法。如 Hoffmann 勋爵看来是不支持 A 可用合约条文去豁免委任代理人或经纪人的欺诈/欺骗的:"There is no doubt that a party cannot contract that he shall not be liable for his own fraud. But whether he can contract that he should not be liable for his agent's fraud is less clear. Mr Sumption (Chase 的代表大律师)submitted that although he might be able to exclude liability for the fraud of an agent in the performance of a contract,**he could not exclude the right of the other party to rescind for the fraud of an agent in inducing the conclusion of the contract. It would be contrary to public policy to allow him to enforce a contractual advantage which had been obtained for him by the fraud of his agent**."(加黑部分是笔者的强调)

但看来 Scott 勋爵持不同意见说:"I would,for my part,be content to accept the need for and the existence of such a rule. If the truth of statement clause in the present case had contained a phrase expressed to exonerate Chase from any liability for fraudulent representations made by itself,Chase could not have relied on the phrase to bar an action based on its own fraudulent misrepresentation. I can,however,for my part see no reason of public policy why a party should not exclude his contractual liability for fraudulent misrepresentation by his agent. And **I can see no reason of public policy why parties should be unable by contract to exclude a right of rescission for misrepresentation by an agent,whether the misrepresentation** be innocent,negligent **or fraudulent**. Public policy would,in my view,come into play only where the agent's principal knew of or was otherwise complicit in the fraud or where the agent was the alter ego of the principal,as an executive director may be of his company."(加黑部分是笔者的强调)

在笔者看来,即使委托人可以依赖合约条文豁免欺诈性误述的转承责任,受害方仍可以其他理由,如没有一致想法要求法院判合约无效。虽然这样无法索赔损失,但是至少不用继续履行一个可能有严重缺陷的合约。至于损失,可以向做出欺诈性误述的代理人或经纪人以欺诈/欺骗侵权索赔(如果还能找得到以及他是有资产可以赔的情况下),但因为委托人不知情所以不能以欺诈性误述向委托人索赔损失。

8.4 总结普通法下允许对非欺诈性误述责任作出豁免的地位与《Misrepresentation Act 1967》的地位

只简短总结说本章之8.1段显示了在普通法的订约自由大原则下,只要不影响公共政策,一条清楚无误的豁免误述的条文如广泛在使用的没有依赖条文(Non-reliance Clause)是完全有效的。这种条文虽然有不同写法,但都是为了豁免与否定可诉误述的存在。可少量节录一些近期案例中的相关条文:

在 Trident Turboprop(Dublin)Ltd v. First Flight Couriers Ltd(2009)EWCA Civ 290 上诉庭先例是:"The Lessee [First Flight Couriers] also agrees and acknowledges that save as expressly stated in this Agreement and the other Transaction Documents to which the Lessor is a party, the Lessor has not and shall not be deemed to have made any warranties or representations, express or implied, about the Aircraft, including but not limited to the matters referred to above."

在 Government of Zanzibar v. British Aerospace(Lancaster House)Ltd(2000)1 WLR 2333 先例是:"[A] The parties have negotiated this contract on the basis that the terms and conditions set out herein represent the entire agreement between them relating in any way whatsoever to the aircraft and the initial and continuing spares which form the subject matter of this contract and [B] accordingly they agree that all liabilities for and remedies in respect of any representations made are excluded save in so far as provided in this contract. [C] The parties further agree that neither party has placed any reliance whatsoever on any representations agreements statements or understandings whether oral or in writing made prior to the date of this contract other than those expressly incorporated or recited in this contract."

在 EA Grimstead & Son Ltd v. McGarrigan(1999)10 WLUK 818 上诉庭先例是:"The Purchaser confirms that it has not relied on any warranty, representation or undertaking of or on behalf of the Vendors ... or of any other person in respect of the subject matter of this Agreement save for any representation or warranty or undertaking expressly set out in the body of this Agreement."

在 Thomas Witter Ltd v. TBP Industries Ltd(1996)2 All ER 573 先例是:"the Purchaser acknowledges that it has not been induced to enter into this Agreement by any representation or warranty other than the statements contained or referred to (in a Schedule)."

在 McCullagh v. Lane Fox & Partners Ltd(1996)1 EGLR 35 上诉庭先例是:"None of the statements contained in these particulars as to this property are to be relied on as statements or representations of fact. Any intending purchaser must satisfy themselves by inspection or otherwise as to the correctness of each of the statements contained in these particulars."

由于豁免欺诈性误述因违反公共政策而无效,这也解释了一些广泛的豁免条文害怕法院解释为包括欺诈性误述令整条条文无效,刻意加上一句说明本条文不包括或不适用在欺诈性误述,反正写清楚也没有牺牲什么,乐得大方。例如在 Armitage v. Nurse(1998)Ch 241 上诉庭先例中的免责条文就是如此:"No trustee shall be liable for any loss or damage which may happen to Paula's fund or any part thereof or the income thereof at any time or from any cause whatsoever **unless such loss or damage shall be caused by his own actual fraud**..."

在本章之 8.1 段解释了目前普通法地位是因为豁免/免责条文(只要不是针对欺诈性误述)内在可能性更低,所以会相比其他合约的一般条文稍微严格与狭窄解释,但一条广泛的条文只要写的清楚无误就会被法院或仲裁庭支持。

但撇开普通法,与疏忽或无辜误述更有关的是《Misrepresentation Act 1967》立法之 S.3 的管制,这会在本书第四章之 6 段讨论。

9. 指控欺诈性误述的索赔请求或抗辩书要满足的要求

9.1　文书请求/案件陈述的作用

有关文书请求(pleadings)或 CPR 下的案件陈述(statement of case)的课题,在笔者《证据法:国际规管与诉讼中的证据攻防》一书第七章之 6 段有详细介绍。诉讼的第一步程序就是双方当事人把他们之间的争议/争端(issues)是什么记录与明确下来让法院(或仲裁庭)与对方当事人知道。通常的做法是原告先提交一份索赔请求(statement of claim),接下去被告针对该索赔请求提交一份抗辩书(statement of defence)。这些双方提出的指控(allegations),无论是索赔或是抗辩,都要有事实基础从而能够在法律上站得住脚。例如,索赔是违约/毁约就有必要明确说明有一份有效的合约存在、被告在合约下有什么承诺与责任、做了什么言行构成法律上的违约/毁约等。当事人要对这些事实[只要求主要事实(material/primary facts)]提供足够的详情与细节(particularise the stated facts with sufficient details),让对方当事人能够明白并在接下去的程序中有针对性与精准地进行调查取证,并在相互文件披露或交换证人证言时提供有关与足够的反驳证据针锋相对。例如,原告主张双方签订了一份有效合约,原告就需要说明如:(1)合约是口头或文书;(2)订约日期;(3)谁与谁订立该合约;(4)合约的相关内容等。

这些主张的事实需要足够支撑索赔或抗辩在法律上站得住脚。至于那些有争议的"事实",双方当事人谁对谁错、证据的强弱,这要看走下去的证据程序与最后的开庭审理双方的争辩了。而如果一方当事人在文书请求中没有说明令有关索赔或抗辩在法律上站得住脚的某些重要事实,甚至在对方要求其提供事实的详情(request for particulars）的情况下，也无法提供，可推断该索赔或抗辩成功的机会不大或甚至是无望。在英国法院，对方当事人就会向法院申请，提前去撤销（strike out）该索赔（或抗辩）。毕竟将无望的索赔或抗辩拖到开庭审理后败诉才告一段落，是浪费法院宝贵的资源，对双方当事人而言也是劳民伤财。

欺诈性误述在英国法下是十分严重的指控，所以有严格的要求/要件，需要在文书请求中提出大量的主要事实，如什么虚假/不正确的事实陈述、被告如何表述给原告、被告的不诚实思想状态、被告希望原告相信、原告也作出依赖（而且是在理解与有意识下依赖）并导致损失。这每一个要件都需要通过说明主要的事实去满足，才可以成功指控被告欺诈性误述。这些指控的主要事实无需去标签“欺诈/欺骗”或不诚实，除非碰巧有发生过的事实是被告曾经在某天的电邮中承认自己欺诈/欺骗。关键是这些主要事实（如果后来能够证明）可去推断有一个表面看来可成立（当然要看后来双方的证据强弱）的欺诈性误述。提出欺诈性误述的原告，如果在文书请求做不到，就难逃会被被告向法院申请提前撤销有关的索赔。由于欺诈性误述或欺诈/欺骗的严格要求，提出指控的原告如果没有明确的事实可去支撑每一个要件更是容易被提前撤销。

《Bullen & Leake & Jacob's Hong Kong Precedents of Pleading》（2020 年，第三版）一书之 21 - 01 段：“In order to sustain the common law action of deceit, the following facts must be established, that is they must be pleaded and proved, namely: (1) there must be a representation of fact made by words or conduct and mere silence is not enough; (2) the representation must be made with knowledge that it is false, that is it must be wilfully false or at least made in the absence of any genuine belief that it is true, or recklessly, that is without caring whether it is true or false; (3) the representation must be made with the intention that it should be acted upon by the Claimant, or by a class of persons which will include the claimant, in the manner which caused damage to him; (4) it must be proved that the Claimant acted upon the false statement; and (5) it must be proved that the Claimant has sustained damage by doing so.”

对上述所讲的有关文书请求或案件陈述这一步诉讼程序的作用，可先简单节录几个权威说法。首先是在我国香港的 ADS v. Wheelock Marden & Co Ltd & Ors (1994) 2 HKC 264 上诉庭先例中，Bokhary 大法官说：“... it is important to remember this. Our procedure aims to ensure that litigation, particularly the trial itself, is conducted fairly, openly, free from surprise, and without unnecessary delay or expense. In the attainment of that objective, pleadings have a fundamental role to play. Accordingly, there are a number of things which pleadings should do. Ideally, they would do them from the outset. ...What those things are is to be gathered from the decided cases. ... 1 thereof, the things which properly particularized pleadings must do are to: (1) inform the other side of the nature of the case they have to meet as distinguished from the mode in which that case is to be proved;(2)prevent the other side from being taken by surprise at the trial;(3)enable the other side to know what evidence they ought to be prepared with and to prepare for trial;(4)limit the generality of the pleadings,the claim and the evidence;(5)limit and define the issues to be tried,and as to which discovery is required,and the hands of the party so that he cannot without leave go into any matters not included(although if the opponent omits to ask for particulars,evidence may be given which supports any material allegation in the pleadings)."

另可节录在 Al Ravi v. Security Service(2010)EWCA Civ 482 上诉庭先例中,Neuberger 勋爵说:"a civil claim should be conducted on the basis that **a party is entered to know**,normally **through a statement of case,the essentials of its opponent's case in advance**,so that the trial can be fairly conducted,and,in particular,the parties can properly prepare their respective evidence and arguments at trial."(加黑部分是笔者的强调)

最后节录在 Towler v. Wills(2010)EWHC 1209(Comm)先例中,Teare 大法官说:"**The purpose of a pleading or statement of case is to inform the other party what the case is that is being brought against him**. It is necessary that the other party understands the case which is being brought against him so that he may plead to it in response,disclose those of his documents which are relevant to that case and prepare witness statements which support his defence. If the case which is bought against him is vague or incoherent he will not,or may not,be able to do any of those things. Time and costs will,or may,be wasted if the defendant seeks to respond to a vague and incoherent case. It is also necessary for the Court to understand the case which is brought so that it may fairly and expeditiously decide the case and in a manner which saves unnecessary expense,for these reasons **it is necessary that a party's pleaded case is a concise and clear statement of the facts on which he relies**."(加黑部分是笔者的强调)

9.2 对欺诈性误述或其他不诚实行为的指控必须全面与清楚说明所依据的主要事实,否则请求将被提前撤销

这样,如果在文书请求或案件陈述去提出与指控对方曾经作出一个十分严重的欺诈性误述(或其他不诚实行为的指控,如故意违反诚信责任等),就更是必须在索赔请求或抗辩书(看是原告或被告提出指控)中把支持与证明此严重指控的主要事实精准(precise)、明确(distinct)、清楚(clear)、详尽(detail)与全面(fully)地说明,以让对方知道他面对的是一个严重的欺诈性误述的指控(而不是其他,如无辜的误述),与根据什么主要事实作为合理基础。

这些主要事实是无需去说明是欺诈或不诚实,因为除非对方事实上曾经在文书或口头承认是不诚实,否则也只是指控方或原告的个人意见。审理法官(或仲裁庭)是要通过一连串被证明的主要事实后,才可去得出欺诈/欺骗与否的推断(inference)

与认定。

如果在文书请求或案件陈述中主张是欺诈性误述,但说明的主要事实却不能去表面或初步推断是有不诚实(强弱是另一码事),或有关事实虽然可以推断出会是不诚实但也可能会是疏忽或是无辜,就会有危险被对方提前撤销索赔或抗辩。在后者的情况,法院更是会同时作出简易判决(summary judgment)。

CPR Rule 3.4(2)(a)说:"The court may strike out a statement of case if it appears to the court —(a) that the statement of case discloses no reasonable grounds for bringing or defending the claim;..."另在 CPR Rule 3.4(1)中,说是包括了案件陈述部分内容的撤销。所以,如果索赔请求或抗辩书显示不了主张有合理基础的事实支持,则可以去提前撤销。而即使是没有被提前撤销(如对方没有采取行动),在开庭审理也时也没有用处,因为在文书请求说明的事实若不能推断出欺诈性误述,那么没有在文书请求说明的事实是不会允许在开庭时提出的,这是突袭(ambush),对没有准备与没有走过证据程序的对方是十分不公平。

一个简单的例子是在本书第二章之 5.5 段介绍的 Re Shackleton Ex p. Whittaker (1875) LR 10 Ch. App. 446 先例中,假设索赔请求指控的主要事实只是买方在周六赊账下取走了羊毛的货物,在下周一就宣布破产,这会可以推断是欺诈营商(fraudulent trading)。[80] 欺诈营商在《Insolvency Act 1986》之 S. 213 的定义是公司继续营运的意图是欺骗债权人(any company business has been carried on with intent to defraud its creditors)。但如果买方在赊账的情况下把货物取走并在两周后破产,仍可能是欺诈营商但也可能有其他非欺诈的原因,如融资银行因内部原因宣布不再支持。所以,会需要进一步指控与证明该先例的买方在周六取走货物时已经是知道公司经济很差、随时要面临破产,是不可能在 1 个月后支付赊的货款,这才足够说明欺诈营商/欺诈性误述的主要事实。

这特别是在复杂与高端的国际商业合约中,即使是不安好心的欺诈或不诚实,在言行上也包装得很好,法院需要客观与深入考虑所有的有关证据,推敲与分析后才能认定是欺诈还是严重疏忽。所以在证据与事实比较模棱两可的情况下,在文书请求或案件陈述中去指控对方的欺诈性误述,但同时以疏忽误述作为替代诉因,会更稳妥,也不存在内在矛盾。这在 Abbar v. Saudi Economic & Development Company Real Estate (2010) EWHC 2131 (Ch) 先例中,Nicholas Strauss QC 大法官说:"In the present case, the claimants have alleged fraud and, in the alternative, negligence. Mr Reed(撤销申请人的代表大律师)submitted that this, by itself, must mean that the primary facts were consistent with honesty, and that fraud therefore could not be pleaded. This, if cor-

---

〔80〕 在英国《Companies Act 2006》之 Chapter 2 有关公司董事个人责任,172(3)条文就要求考虑公司债权人的利益。这特别在知道或应该知道公司会破产(insolvent):见 BTI 2014 LLC v. Sequana SA (2022) UKSC 25 最高院先例。

rect, would apply to all cases, and it would never be open to a claimant to plead alternative claims for fraud and negligence. Such alternative claims are of course commonplace, and this submission is wrong. If there are facts which 'tilt the balance' and justify an inference of dishonesty, then dishonesty may be alleged. Alleging negligence in the alternative involves no inconsistency: it simply recognises that the court may find that the defendant was not dishonest but merely negligent."

这严格的文书请求规则也不是技术性要求,而是为了实质性的公平审理(fair trial)。这可节录 Millett 勋爵在 Three Rivers District Council v. Bank of England(No. 3)(2001) UKHL 16 贵族院先例中的观点:"… **an allegation of fraud or dishonesty must be sufficiently particularised**, and that **particulars of facts which are consistent with honesty are not sufficient**. This is only partly a matter of pleading. It is also **a matter of substance**. As I have said, the defendant is entitled to know the case he has to meet. But since **dishonesty is usually a matter of inference from primary facts**, this involves knowing not only that he is alleged to have acted dishonestly, but also the primary facts which will be relied upon at trial to justify the inference. At trial the court will normally allow proof of primary facts which have not been pleaded, and will not do so in a case of fraud. It is **not open to the court to infer dishonesty from facts which have not be pleaded, or from facts which have been pleaded but are consistent with honesty. These must be some fact which titles the balance and justifies an inference of dishonesty, and this fact must be both pleaded and proved.**"(加黑部分是笔者的强调)

另在香港特区的 Liang Jun Xian v. Tsui Hin Chi(2011) HKEC 124 先例中, Suffiad 大法官也说:"None of the basic rules of pleadings have anything to do with technicality. All of them have everything to do with practical justice. They have always been of importance. Never before as much as now. For these days, there are more and more cases so vast and so complex that they push practicality to its limit our system's capacity effectively to cope with them…"

由于在不少复杂的商业案件会涉及大量的事实,所以在文书请求或案件陈述中把所有可推断为不诚实的主要事实清楚与不含糊地说明并不容易,对方往往能挑得出一些毛病并向法院申请部分或全部撤销索赔或抗辩请求。但只要对方指出,往往己方是可以通过修改(amendment of pleadings)去说清楚或澄清。

所以,法院通常不会马上去提前撤销,而是会给一段时间作出修改。如果修改后仍令法院不满意,其就会把索赔或抗辩撤销了。正如潘大法官在香港特区的 Total Lubricants Hong Kong Ltd v. Christophe de la Crote de Chanterac HCA1694/2008(unreported, 15 December 2009)先例中所说:"if a pleading is capable of being cured by amendments, it should not be struck out. An opportunity to amend should be given instead. However, if the pleading is so defective that no amendment can cure it or if the proposed amendment is incapable of improving the defects, the pleading is liable to be struck out ..."

在更近期的权威说法可节录新加坡的 BOM v. BOK(2018) SGCA 83 上诉庭先例中, Andrew Phang Boon Leong 大法官说:"It is **a trite principle that allegations of fraud must be pleaded with sufficient particularity**. This principle finds statutory expression in O 18 r 12(1) of the Rules of Court(Cap 332, R 5, 2014 Rev Ed). It is **a principle of natural justice that the court painstakingly upholds so as to ensure that the defendant knows the case it has to meet**: ... Accordingly, where a plaintiff succeeds on findings of fact that were not pleaded, the Court of Appeal will not allow the judgment to stand: see Sheagar s/o T M Veloo v Belfield International(Hong Kong) Ltd [2014] 3 SLR 524 ... But **one must also be careful not to descend blindly into technicalities when assessing the adequacy of pleadings, and to always bear in mind that their ultimate purpose is** to define the scope of the issues arising for the court's determination and **to ensure that the parties are not taken by surprise and deprived of the opportunity to adduce the relevant evidence** ... It is for this reason that we observed in OMG Holdings Pte Ltd v Pos Ad Sdn Bhd [2012] 4 SLR 231 that 'evidence given at trial can, where appropriate, overcome defects in the pleadings provided that the other party is not taken by surprise or irreparably prejudiced'."(加黑部分是笔者的强调)

9.3 必须知道欺诈性误述成立的法律要件才能全面清楚说明主要事实详情

欺诈性误述的诉因成立需要满足一定的要求或先决条件[在本书有详尽介绍,特别是 Derry v. Peek (1889) 14 App Cas 337 贵族院先例的权威说法中],因此在文书请求中就有必要针对这些法律要求去详细说明有关的事实,并在开庭审理时证明。这包括:(1)对方曾做出过一个虚假/不正确事实或法律的陈述。(2)对方在做出陈述时知道是虚假,也就是故意说谎,或最起码是并不真正相信该陈述是正确,又或是鲁莽不理会真假。所以应说明有关的事实,以支持与证明对方是知情。在 Belmont Finance Corp Ltd v. Williams Furniture Ltd(1979) Ch 250 上诉庭先例中,指出是必须说明对方是"一定知情",而不是模棱两可的"一定或应该知情"(knew or ought to have known)。(3)对方是希望该虚假陈述被己方依赖并造成预期的损失。(4)己方也真正依赖了该虚假陈述订立合约。(5)己方依赖该虚假陈述蒙受损失。

可节录《Bullen & Leake & Jacob's Hong Kong Precedents of Pleading》(2020 年,第三版)一书之 21-21 段至 21-22 段,以补充针对上述五个要件,在索赔(或抗辩)请求中指控被告(或原告)欺诈性误述必须说明哪些主要事实,如下所述:

"21-21 It may not be necessary in all cases to use the word 'fraud'. An allegation that the defendant made to the claimant, representations on which he intended the claimant to act or rely on, which representations were untrue, and known to the defendant to be untrue or false(which may be pleaded in the alternative), is sufficient.

21 - 22 The particulars of claim must also(i) state the representation and show the nature and extent of each alleged misrepresentation and(ii) contain particulars showing when, where(if relevant) by whom and to whom it was made, and how it was made, whether orally or in writing, and if in writing, identifying the relevant document; (iii) state it's falsity; (iv) state the inducement; (v) state the intention of the defendant that the claimant should rely and act on it; (vi) state the fact showing the reliance by the claimant upon the representation(eg alteration by the claimant of his position in reliance upon the representation); (vii) where appropriate and necessary, state the relationship between the defendant and the claimant which gives rise to a duty of care owed by the defendant to the claimant(and hence may also support why the claimant relies on the representation); (viii) state the facts that are relevant to the relief claimed."

在 Armitage v. Nurse(1998) Ch 241 上诉庭先例中,Millet 大法官提到欺诈/欺骗应该如何去请求,认为:

"The general principle is well known. Fraud must be distinctly alleged and as distinctly proved: Davy v. Garrett(1878) 7 Ch. D. 473 ... per Thesiger LJ It is not necessary to use the word 'fraud' or 'dishonesty' if the facts which make the conduct complained of fraudulent are pleaded; but, **if the facts pleaded are consistent with innocence, then it is not open to the court to find fraud**. As Buckley LJ said in Belmont Finance Corporation Ltd. v. Williams Furniture Ltd. [1979] Ch. 250: 'An allegation of dishonesty must be pleaded clearly and with particularity. That is laid down by the rules and it is a well - recognised rule of practice. This does not import that the word "fraud" or the word "dishonesty" must be necessarily used ... The facts alleged may sufficiently demonstrate that dishonesty is allegedly involved, but where the facts are complicated this may not be so clear, and in such a case it is incumbent upon the pleader to make it clear when dishonesty is alleged. **If he uses language which is equivocal, rendering it doubtful whether he is in fact relying on the alleged dishonesty of the transaction, this will be fatal; the allegation of its dishonest nature will not have been pleaded with sufficient clarity.**'

That case is authority for the proposition that **an allegation that the defendant 'knew or ought to have known' is not a clear and unequivocal allegation of actual knowledge and will not support a finding of fraud**. It is not treated as making two alternative allegations, i. e. an allegation(i) that the defendant actually knew with an alternative allegation(ii) that he ought to have known; but rather a single allegation that he ought to have known(and may even have known - though it is not necessary to allege this).

Before turning to the pleadings I would add one thing more. In order to allege fraud it is not sufficient to sprinkle a pleading with words like 'wilfully' and 'recklessly' (but not 'fraudulently' or 'dishonestly'). This may still leave it in doubt whether the words are being used in a technical sense or merely to give colour by way of pejorative emphasis to the complaint."(加黑部分是笔者的强调)

另在CPR生效后,这方面没有改变,在近期的Robert Sofer v. Swissindependent Trustees SA(2020)EWCA Civ 699上诉庭先例中,Arnold大法官总结说:

"i)Fraud or dishonesty must be specifically alleged and sufficiently particularised,and will not be sufficiently particularised if the facts alleged are consistent with innocence ...

ii)Dishonesty can be inferred from primary facts,provided that those primary facts are themselves pleaded. There must be some fact which tilts the balance and justifies an inference of dishonesty,and this fact must be pleaded ...

iii)The claimant does not have to plead primary facts which are only consistent with dishonesty. The correct test is whether or not,on the basis of the primary facts pleaded,an inference of dishonesty is more likely than one of innocence or negligence:JSC Bank of Moscow v Kekhman [2015] EWHC 3073(Comm)...

iv)Particulars of dishonesty must be read as a whole and in context:Walker v Stones [2001] QB 902...

To these principles there should be added the following general points about particulars:i)The purpose of giving particulars is to allow the defendant to know the case he has to meet...ii)When giving particulars,no more than a concise statement of the facts relied upon is required ... iii)Unless there is some obvious purpose to be served by fighting over the precise terms of a pleading,contests over their terms are to be discouraged..."

9.4 因主要事实详情不够而被法院提前撤销的先例

早在Salaman v. Warner(1891)65 LT 132 CA上诉庭先例中,就已经有了因索赔请求中没有事实或事实不足以指控有关被告的意图而被撤销的做法。

笔者接下去只在大量涉及提前撤销索赔或抗辩并作出简易判决的先例(不少是欺诈性误述的指控),如较近期的JSC Bank of Moscow v. Kekhman(2015)EWHC 3073(Comm);Terry v. BCS Corporate Acceptances Ltd(2018)EWCA Civ 2422;Stanford International Bank Ltd(In Liquidation)v. HSBC Bank Plc(2020)EWHC 2232(Ch);Blockchain Optimization SA v. LFE Market Ltd(2020)EWHC 2027(Comm);King v. Stiefel(2021)EWHC 1045(Comm);Maranello Rosso Ltd v. Lohomij BV(2021)EWHC 2452(Ch);Crypton Digital Assets Ltd v. Blockchain Luxembourg SA(2021)EWHC 3194(Ch);Cayman Music Ltd v. Blue Mountain Music Ltd(2022)EWHC 1469;Michael Wilson & Partners Ltd v. Emmott(2022)EWHC 1481(Comm);Chandler v. Wright(2022)EWHC 2205(Ch)等先例中,挑一两个介绍。

9.4.1 先例一:Liang Jun Xian v. Tsui Hin Chi(2011)HKEC 124中国香港特区先例

在中国香港特区的Liang Jun Xian v. Tsui Hin Chi先例中,案情涉及公司股份所有权的争议。原告在2005年想要投资广州德政南路19－49号重建工程,当时这个重建工程是属于广州远兴房产有限公司(以下简称远兴)。2005年11月3日,原告在香港特区成立了China Investment Group International Finance Limited(以下简称CIGIF)并100%控股。原告的意图是与一家名为广东中大中鑫投资策划有限公司(以下简称中鑫)联营,拍得远兴100%的股份,其中60%的股份由CIGIF持有,另外40%由中鑫持有,当时原告也是中鑫的控股股东。

2006年中,原告为了联营融资时认识了被告。2006年10月,被告口头同意为联营提供5000万人民币。被告在11月20日,向原告汇了首期1000万港币,作为对向原告的承诺的部分履行。12月6日,原告与被告订立合作协议,同意被告出资5000万人民币,并在买下远兴公司后获得40%的股份,原告负责余下的资金并将获得剩余的60%的股份,原告还承诺将多给被告2%的股份作为收益。2007年1月,CIGIF与中鑫成功拍下远兴的股份。被告在2月转给原告剩下的4000万港元。

原告主张被告在合约协议下投资的5000万人民币是借贷而不是投资。被告多次要求原告质押(pledge)CIGIF的40%股份与将其委任为CIGIF的董事作为对他在合作协议下远兴42%的股份的担保。2007年2月与8月,被告要求原告签署几份英文文件,说这只是质押与委任为董事的文件,并且他只是为了给自己担保不会影响原告对CIGIF的营运与所有权。原告因为不懂英语所以依赖被告对文件内容的陈述后,并签署有关文件。但后来才发觉其实自己签的文件是股权买卖与转让协议,并已经将CIGIF的所有股权转让给了被告。原告还发觉她已经被被告解除了CIGIF董事的职位,而由Mok与另一位人士替代。因此原告开始诉讼,主张被告欺诈性误述诱导她订立股权买卖与转让协议,要求法院宣告她是CIGIF的100%所有人。

此先例是有关原告申请将Mok加入作为第二被告与申请修改索赔请求。被告与Mok是表兄弟,被告曾经向原告介绍Mok希望作为投资者加入联营,但被原告拒绝。原告通过向公司注册处查询后发现被告已经将CIGIF全部股份转让给Mok(看来这个做法是为了引入一个"善意第三人",让原告无法追回CIGIF的股份)。原告主张这显示了被告与Mok串谋(conspiracy),被告与Mok之间的股权转让完全是一个骗局(sham),Mok知道或应该知道被告整个的欺诈计划并协助或参与。

法院判,第一,原告没有在文书请求/索赔请求说明Mok的哪一个特定行为可以显示或者推断出Mok与被告串谋共同欺诈原告。而原告依赖的行为,包括Mok被转让股份与委任为公司董事都发生在原告主张的被告的欺诈性误述之后。第二,这些行为虽然可以是串谋,但也可能Mok完全不知情。第三,原告也没有提供任何详情显示Mok与被告的交易只是一个骗局,Mok知道或应该知道被告的欺诈计划并协助或参与。所以,原告将Mok加入作为第二被告的申请没有被批准。

而原告的另一个修改索赔请求的申请,其中针对Mok的部分,因为法院拒绝将Mok加入作为第二被告,显然就同样拒绝该修改索赔请求的申请,而双方的争议是原告能否将原本的"原告不会读或写英语"修改为"原告只会读或理解简单的英语"。

被告反对是因为原告的主张一直是不会英语,所以完全要依赖被告对文件内容的口头陈述,而被告欺诈性误述让原告以为文件内容是质押而不是转让。而修改后显然与原告的案件不符,也与原告的真实声明(statement of truth)起冲突。但法院并没有支持被告的抗辩,认为只要对另一方诉讼方没有不公平,就可以修改案件陈述,即使是与原本的有冲突,这也只是影响将来审理法官对原告证据可信度与重量的认定。

9.4.2 先例二:Leeds City Council and Ors v. Barclays Bank Plc and Ors(2021) EWHC 363(Comm)先例

最后是介绍 Leeds City Council and Ors v. Barclays Bank Plc and Ors 先例,该案案情与操纵伦敦银行间同业拆借利率(LIBOR)有关。有关银行操纵 LIBOR 与其他利率的丑闻与原告指称存在的默示误述在本书第二章之 1.4.5 段有详细介绍,不再重复。

在此先例中,原告是英国利兹市议会等地方政府,被告是 Barclays 银行与附属机构。原告与被告订立了 60 至 70 年的长期 Lender Option-Borrower Option(LOBO)贷款,贷款人可以在双方约定的特定时间选择调整贷款的利率,而借款人可以选择接受新利率或提前还款(可能要交一笔提前退出的罚金),LIBOR 作为双方贷款合约中利率的参考。在操纵 LIBOR 丑闻爆出后,原告起诉被告银行要求撤销合约与/或赔偿损失,而被告以原告没有可争辩的案件(arguable case)的理由向法院申请撤销索赔。[81]

此先例为了决定原告是否有一个可争辩案件去避免被法院撤销索赔请求,双方同意假设银行确实曾经做出了没有也无意在将来操纵 LIBOR 的虚假陈述。而被告的主张是,在此假设下索赔请求中的主要事实也不能证明原告确实依赖该虚假陈述,因为原告想要证明依赖,是要先证明其在当时意识到(awareness)或如何理解(understanding)这个陈述。

这“理解/意识因素”(understanding/awareness factor)的重要性可先去介绍一些权威说法。首先针对“理解”,不同人士对一个复杂与模棱两可的陈述可以有不同理解,所以被误述方需要在文书请求或案件陈述中说明与证明他对陈述方做出的陈述的理解是什么,并且该理解是与事实不符从而构成误述。即使是以文书形式如在电文中做出一个明示陈述,如果使用的文字/措辞有一定的含糊,也会带来陈述方有自己的解释并且在这解释下并非误述。但被陈述方肯定有不同的解释与理解而令陈述变为是虚假或不正确。这样,法院(或仲裁庭)就需要去客观解释对陈述的理解。而

---

[81] 在该先例中,被告的另一个申请是即使原告可以撤销合约,原告的言行也确认了该合约,严格来说这是一个简易判决而不是撤销起诉的申请,但双方同意可以一并处理。关于确认合约的争议,因为与本章介绍的内容关系不大且只很简单针对,所以这里不介绍,感兴趣的读者可以看笔者《合约的履行、弃权与禁反言》一书第一章之 7 段。关于撤销起诉与简易判决可见笔者《证据法:国际规管与诉讼仲裁中的证据攻防》第六章之 4 段。

如果法院得出的结论是与被陈述方一致,也就是陈述确是虚假,被陈述方只要有依赖就构成可诉误述。而针对默示陈述,即使有部分是以文字做出,但更多会是通过行动做出。如果双方当事人对陈述为何有不同理解,法院也是要同样的处理。这种情况的一个好例子是在本书第二章之 1.3 段介绍的 William Smith v. David Chadwick (1884)9 App Cas 187 贵族院先例中有所体现。

在 IFE Fund SA v. Goldman Sachs International(2006)EWHC 2887(Comm)先例中,Toulson 大法官说:"In determining whether there has been an express representation, and to what effect, the court has to consider **what a reasonable person would have understood from the words used in the context** in which they were used. In determining what, if any, implied representation has been made, the court has to perform a similar task, except that it has to consider **what a reasonable person would have inferred was being implicitly represented by the representor's words and conduct in their context**."(加黑部分是笔者的强调)

另在 Cassa di Risparmio della Repubblica di San Marino SpA v Barclays Bank Ltd (2011)EWHC 484(Comm)先例中,Hamblen 大法官说:"… the claimant must show that he in fact understood the statement in the sense(so far as material) which the court ascribes to it; and that, having that understanding, he relied on it. Analytically, this is probably not a separate requirement of a misrepresentation claim but rather is part of what the claimant needs to show in order to prove inducement."

再是 Foster v. Action Aviation(2013)EWHC 2439(Comm)先例中,Hamblen 大法官说:"Unless one understands that a representation is being made it is difficult to see how it can be said to have been relied upon. …"

最后在 Leni Gas & Oil Investment Ltd v. Malta Oil Pty Ltd(2014)EWHC 893 (Comm)先例中,Males 大法官说:"a claimant must show that it understood that the representation alleged was being made to it. Without such an understanding, there can be no question of any reliance on the representation."

"意识"更会是涉及知不知道对方曾经做出过误述。如果是双方当事人都不在一个频道的"鸡同鸭讲",一方做出了一个误述,但另一方根本没意识到有这个误述,也不会存在依赖了。更不要说误述是发生在被误述方不在场的时刻,正如 Cockerill 大法官在此先例说:"… the step which forms the logical bridge between the representation and reliance is merely the awareness of the representation as something which was made. **If there is no awareness of the making of the representation, logically it cannot operate**. For example, suppose a very clear representation was made just at the moment when a meeting participant's wifi dropped out momentarily; or if a pneumatic drill started up outside her window so that she could not hear anything but that noise for the crucial 30 seconds. If however there is an awareness, the court then has to try to unpick, based on other evidence (such as evidence as to what the representee would have done in other circumstances) whether, taken in the round, inducement is made out."(加黑部分是笔者的强调)

最后可节录 Cockerill 大法官对此 Leeds City Council and Ors v. Barclays Bank Plc and Ors 先例的总结，如下所述：

"... That there is **some requirement of awareness ... is established by the authorities. Often that requirement will not be in issue**; but that does not mean that it is not a requirement; just that in some cases that it is so obvious that the parties do not bother to argue about it. And when that requirement is in issue, in some cases **the question will be what the claimant consciously thought**, but in other cases it may be better expressed by a focus on active presence.

I am of the opinion that there will... be cases where the **element of awareness will come very close to** something which might loosely ... be characterised as **assumption** and which is most obviously derived from conduct. ... **the dividing line** between giving contemporaneous **conscious thought to the conduct** and contemporaneous **conscious thought to the representation may-in some cases-be thin to non-existent**. In some cases ... specific conduct may precisely and inevitably equate to a representation, without any room for ambiguity. ... Thus, for example, in the case of a bidder at an auction raising a paddle, representing a willingness and ability to pay a certain sum. In such a case a requirement for separate or distinct understanding or thought to the representations would be artificial. ...

...**the fact that awareness has been found to be required in the cases of Marme**[82] **and PAG**,[83] which relate to alleged representations which are effectively identical. This, it seems to me, **is key in the present case**. ...

The Leeds Claimants have also pleaded that it would be sufficient to establish reliance if a representee was 'influenced or affected' by the pleaded LIBOR Representations, 'in the sense that **the LIBOR Representations operated on their minds, whether consciously or subconsciously**. ... However **the Leeds Claimants do not go on to plead**

---

〔82〕 本章之 4.3.2 段介绍的 Marme Inversiones 2007 SL v. NatWest Markets Plc (2019) EWHC 366 (Comm) 先例。

〔83〕 在本书第二章之 1.4.5 段介绍的 Property Alliance Group Ltd v. Royal Bank of Scotland (2018) EWCA Civ 355 先例的一审[(2016) EWHC 3342 (Ch)]。虽然该先例上诉庭推翻了一审，认定存在默示陈述，但是因为一审法院同时认定原告没有证明银行操纵 LIBOR 的事实，所以该默示陈述并非虚假。这样上诉庭就无需决定原告是否依赖该陈述的问题，所以在 Leeds City Council and Ors v. Barclays Bank Plc and Ors 先例中，考虑的仍是一审的决定，也就是即使存在默示的虚假陈述，原告也没有依赖。

any conscious operation on anyone's mind;...

Further I am persuaded that... indicate clearly that in **a case of this sort more is needed than an assertion of subconscious operation**. It follows that the Leeds Claimants' pleaded case, even if proved, has no real prospect of success, and that it falls to be struck out."(加黑部分是笔者的强调)

根据此先例中，误述的要件"诱导"(induce)是将被告/误述方的行为(做出虚假或不正确的陈述)与原告/被误述方的行为(依赖订立合约)建立因果关系。而"诱导"可被分为"意识/理解"与"依赖"两个部分，被误述方必须先证明自己意识到或如何理解有关的陈述，然后再证明自己确实依赖了有关误述订立合约。虽然欺诈性误述(fraudulent misrepresentation)一直在事实上推定(presumption of facts)被误述方对误述存在依赖，[84]但被误述方仍必须先证明"意识/理解"，然后才能推定确实依赖了该误述。

在此先例中，法院最后判原告在索赔请求中的主要事实即使被证明为真，也无法推断出在订约时原告意识到银行做出默示的虚假陈述，因此索赔被撤销。也可以看出，只有明白有关主张成立需要满足什么要件，才能在索赔请求中指出有关的主要事实来满足该要件。如果原告不是没有满足"诱导"的请求要求，即除了"依赖"外要主张与证明他确实"意识"或"理解"有关陈述，那么就不会被提早撤销索赔了。但笔者感觉这也并非原告律师疏忽，而是因为原告无法主张与证明自己当时意识到或怎样理解有关"陈述"。如果有不同的案情，被告银行在贷款标准合约下明确提出过使用 LIBOR 作为基准，并说 LIBOR 是最公道与透明的机制，又或是客户曾要求银行解释 LIBOR 是怎样操作，银行也解答了，这就是一个明示或默示的误述。若把这些发生过的主要事实在索赔请求说明，原告也就不会被提前撤销索赔了。

但现实是绝大部分的案件是大家对 LIBOR 有信心，以为是公道与透明的机制，在此假设下将其作为金融合约中利率的基准。这就有问题了，作为被误述方的原告很难把这背景说成是被告银行的误述(欺诈性或疏忽)，因为银行在谈判时什么都没有说过、做过或以行动作出过诱导，且被原告"意识"到并去依赖。毕竟，误述是要误述方有一个主动的行动(positive act)，这与不自动披露(non-disclosure)的完全不作为(不构成误述)是两码事。[85]

换一个话题是在笔者看来法院这种严格的判法也涉及政策上的考虑，笔者不知道有指控银行操纵 LIBOR 存在默示误述成功撤销合约的先例。在以上节录的 Cockerill 大法官的判决中也说，如果不是因为有 Marme Inversiones 2007 SL v. NatWest Markets Plc 与 Property Alliance Group Ltd v. Royal Bank of Scotland (2016) EWHC 3342 (Ch) 先例的判决，她可能会对"意识/理解"采用一种更宽松的测试。但一旦被

---

〔84〕 见本书第一章之 1.3.6 段。

〔85〕 见本书第五章的详细介绍。

先例确定,就变为了普通法,会约束其他类别的案件。因此将来一些复杂与涉及巨额索赔的先例中,即使与银行操纵 LIBOR 无关,也可能有类似的争议。

除了操纵 LIBOR 这种复杂的争议,难以证明“意识/理解”的另一个极端是原告说是(也感觉上是)被被告骗了,但自己也说不清是被被告的什么虚假言行骗了。又或是,被告在半年前另一个交易曾对原告做出过一个正确的事实陈述。在半年后该有关事实已不再是正确,但原告问也不问就假设事实没有变化去订立另一个交易的合约。这不是本书第二章之 8 段的在同一个交易谈判过程中的持续性的陈述(continuous representation),被告也会忘掉半年前讲过什么,他也没有自动披露的责任。这样,又会是原告难以证明“意识/理解”了被告在谈判中有什么误述。这会是原告自己粗心大意、想当然、把事情想得简单或对有关业务或事务不了解等的原因,根本不能有条有理地说是什么欺诈性误述。

最后,与本段的文书请求有更密切关系是 Cockerill 大法官在此先例并没有说文书请求必须去区别主张“意识/理解”与“依赖”,因为绝大多数的误述案件涉及的都是明显的误述,两者是走在一起的,无须去区别主张。例如陈述是“我这一辆车子只行走了 1000 公里”,依赖的买方对陈述的意识/理解与依赖也就是这句话。Cockerill 大法官在上述节录也举了一个在公开拍卖去高举名牌被意识与理解为愿意出价与有财力去作出支付的例子,拍卖官的“意识/理解与依赖”也是走在一起的。只有复杂的案件涉及通过隐蔽的言行做出默示误述,才有原告作为被误述方到底如何意识与理解这些言行的质疑。

这在欺诈性误述中尤其重要,因为在“要不是”测试与依赖中有一个事实推定,把举证责任转移给被告(被指控的误述方),而被告往往是无法证明对方没有依赖。所以,在复杂与不明显的默示误述的案件中,被告要更主动去要求原告提供进一步的信息与详情(CPR Part 18“Further Information”),务求在文书请求或索赔请求中讲清楚有关其“意识”与“理解”被告做出的到底是什么误述。这是因为 Cockerill 大法官说在绝大部分的案件是没有必要区分得这么清楚而没有讲清楚,原告会在索赔请求好像本先例一样对“依赖”简单带过。

9.5 对国际仲裁的启示

国际仲裁虽然没有跟从法院诉讼程序中严格的文书请求规则(pleadings rules),往往是以书面形式的陈述书(submissions)如索赔请求或抗辩书或请愿书(memorial)去替代法院正式的文书请求或案件陈述,[86]但自然公正(natural justice)与程序公平(due process)仍是仲裁员要遵守的“天条”,仲裁员仍要做到同样的公平审理。这样,原告如果在索赔请求(claim submissions)或索赔请愿书(claim memorial)中看来只是不起眼地随意一提对方说谎话,根本没有将欺诈/欺骗要成立的各项要求/要件(或红线)是区别基于什么主要事实与有关详情进行说明,这就会导致被告不警觉与没

---

〔86〕 见笔者《证据法:国际规管与诉讼中的证据攻防》一书第七章之 6.5 段的详细介绍。

有机会为抗辩作出准备，如调查取证。到了最后开庭审理时原告才提出指控的事实（无论是真是假），但对被告来说是为时太晚，如果仲裁庭仍是受理或接受原告的指控就会产生仲裁程序的不公平。

随着国际仲裁不断吸收法院的做法，不只是没有在文书请求或案件陈述中说明足够主要事实详情的欺诈/欺骗指控在开庭时会最终败诉的问题，更会提前到在案件陈述的阶段就已经面临被提前撤销的危险。SIAC 与 HKIAC[87]相继在 2016 年与 2018 年引入了提前决定争议的新规定，之后 LCIA、ICC、ICSID 也在 2020 年至 2022 年陆续加入了相关规定。英国法律委员会（Law Commission）在 2022 年 9 月 22 日发表的对《Arbitration Act 1996》的修改咨询，[88]主要内容之一是增加提前撤销与简易裁决（summary award）。看来这类修改是大势所趋，这在笔者的《证据法：国际规管与诉讼中的证据攻防》一书第六章之 4.4 段已有介绍并讲到提前决定争议的简易裁决的新规定会带来的问题。显然这新规定是与提前撤销索赔或抗辩的请求走在一起的，包括在本段介绍的情况，就是在欺诈性误述的诉因下，在案件陈述中主要事实的详情不够或不清楚。

本来这也不足为怪，国际仲裁由英美律师与仲裁员主导。英国法院是解决国际商事争议最有经验的法院，且其不断为了配合国际商业做法进行改革，所以一些被视为好的英国法院做法，这些律师与仲裁员肯定会想引入国际仲裁，只是难免在时间上会要慢一步。

中国的仲裁机构要配合国际做法，难免将来也要对仲裁规则做相应的修改，而想要修改好，就不能简单照抄，必须知道背后的道理。中国涉外律师与仲裁员，看来也是有必要去掌握这些合约法、证据法的知识。而因为学习需要时间，再等待就来不及了。今天看到很多中国律师在国际仲裁只是泛泛指控对方欺诈/欺骗或非法等，但没有或没有足够的主要事实的详情，在案件陈述中也只是只各说各的，不去点对点针对对方当事人的事实指控。这在将来的国际仲裁都会被提前撤销，无论是索赔或抗辩。

---

〔87〕 只以 HKIAC 规则有关提前决定争议（Early Determination Procedure）作为代表，在第 43 条说："The arbitral tribunal shall have the power, at the request of any party and after consulting with all other parties, to decide one or more points of law or fact by way of early determination procedure, on the basis that: (a) such points of law or fact are manifestly without merit; or (b) such points of law or fact are manifestly outside the arbitral tribunal's jurisdiction; ...

43.3 Any request for early determination procedure shall be made as promptly as possible after the relevant points of law or fact are submitted ...

43.5 After providing all other parties with an opportunity to submit comments on the request, the arbitral tribunal shall issue a decision either dismissing the request or allowing the request to proceed ... The arbitral tribunal shall make such decision within 30 days from the date of filing the request. ..."

〔88〕 见 https://s3-eu-west-2.amazonaws.com/lawcom-prod-storage-11jsxou24uy7q/uploads/2022/09/Arbitration-Consultation-Paper.pdf。

第四章 《Misrepresentation Act 1967》

1. 概　　述

《Misrepresentation Act 1967》立法在多处说明是不适用在欺诈性误述(fraudulent misrepresentation),包括在 S. 1 之“without alleging fraud”;S. 2(1)之“notwithstanding that the misrepresentation was not made fraudulently”;S. 2(2)之“otherwise than fraudulently”等。这是因为欺诈性误述构成欺诈/欺骗的侵权(tort of deceit),普通法下早就有了全面的救济,即撤销合约与宽松对待所有索赔的损失:见 Attwood v. Small (1838)6 Cl. & F. 232;Newbigging v. Adam(1886)34 Ch. D. 582 与确认的 Newbigging v. Adam(1888)13 App Cas 308 等先例。此立法只是为了去针对非欺诈性误述(non-fraudulent misrepresentation),这包括了疏忽误述(negligent misrepresentation)与真正的无辜误述(innocent misrepresentation)。普通法(也包括在《Judicature Acts 1873》之后的衡平法)针对这种误述的地位在很多方面并不令人满意,所以以立法去解决。

立法针对的是普通法认为的诚实(honest)误述,而疏忽误述也是诚实误述,只是不小心而已。只有合约双方有法律在公共政策的考虑下强加了小心谨慎责任(duty of care)的特殊关系(special relationship)[1]时,疏忽侵权(tort of negligence)才适用,也令疏忽误述有法律责任。所以,在早期的案例,判词中提及的“无辜误述”(innocent misrepresentation)一词,读者要小心区分。在《Misrepresentation Act 1967》立法前,普通法下这是指包括了疏忽误述与真正的无辜误述的“非欺诈性误述”(non-fraudulent misrepresentation)。但有了立法后,把疏忽误述与无辜误述区分,无辜误述一词才变为真正“无辜”,碰上了谁也怪不了谁,只应算是双方当事人的坏运气。在国际商业活动,真正的无辜误述虽然是有,但不会太多,更多数是疏忽误述。

在立法前,普通法下是一概不允许非欺诈性误述的被误述方(misrepresentee)或受害方索赔金钱损失。这可节录早在 Heilbut, Symonds & Co v. Buckleton(1913) AC 30 贵族院先例中,Moulton 勋爵说:“It is, my Lords, of the greatest importance, in my opinion, that this House should maintain in its full integrity the principle that a person is not liable in damages for an innocent misrepresentation, no matter in what way or under

---

〔1〕 见本书第一章之 2.2 段。

what form the attack is made."

这带来很多不令人满意之处，毕竟疏忽误述可以是严重疏忽(gross negligence)，[2]其与欺诈性误述的鲁莽(reckless)只有一线之隔，只是证明不了误述方(misrepresentor)的思想状态(state of mind)是不诚实而已。这导致英国政府在1959年成立一个法律改革委员会并提出了一个问题："whether any alterations were necessary or desirable in the law relating to innocent misrepresentation and the remedies available for such misrepresentation?"

之后 Tenth Report of the Law Reform Committee(1962)Cmnd. 1782 的立法报告向政府作出的建议是："Where a person has, either by himself or his agent, induced another to enter into a contract with him(including a contract relating to land) by an untrue representation made for the purpose of inducing the contract he should be liable in damages for any loss suffered in consequence of the representation unless he proves that up to the time the contract was made he(or his agent, if the representation was made by him) believed the representation to be true and had reasonable grounds for his belief."

而1967年立法之S.2(1)条文是对此建议照单全收，本章稍后详论。法律改革委员会针对的另一个不满意之处是普通法虽然不给予非欺诈性误述任何救济，但衡平法(equity)给予被误述方有撤销合约(rescission of contract)选择权的救济。这代表在以前只要是有了一个可诉误述(actionable misrepresentation)，即使误述方是完全无辜，另外有关的误述也只是小事情以及涉及小金额，被误述方仍会实际上借机自助(self-help)撤销一个高价值与长期的商业合约，特别是在市场或商业环境逆转令履行该合约对被误述方不利时。这的确是严重的问题，特别是面临越来越复杂的国际商业合约，在漫长的谈判过程中一方或合约双方会向对方做出过无数的事实陈述、披露(主动或在对方查问下)、预测与意见等。即使是没有任何欺诈/欺骗的意图，也会在这些表述/表达中犯错或有轻微的差异。所以在很多这种复杂交易带来的诉讼/仲裁中，原告(或是被告)经常会提出涉及各种方面的多个误述的指控。可以想到如果任何一个误述成立，被误述方就有权撤销合约，那对国际商业社会就影响大了。例如明明是因为新冠疫情导致履行合约会造成严重亏损，但为了将市场损失转嫁给对方，就在谈判中找几个无关痛痒的误述以撤销合约。

所以，法律改革是希望收紧这方面的权利，立法之S.2(2)条文是让法院根据每个案件的公平合理在撤销合约或损失赔偿这两种救济中选择。可以想象得到，法院是不会允许被误述方以一个无关紧要或技术性的误述取巧，而会决定以损失赔偿作为救济。而往往被误述方也没有什么损失可以证明，这等于什么救济都没有。当然从另一个角度讲，对真正的无辜误述的受害方来说，如果能证明损失，现在也能在立法下获得赔偿。

---

[2] 见《证据法：基础理论、口头证据与专家证据》一书第十章之3.2.1段。

这可节录在 William Sindall Plc v. Cambridgeshire CC(1994)1 WLR 1016 上诉庭先例中,Evans 大法官说:"The starting point for the application of the sub-section is the situation where a plaintiff has established right to rescind the contract on grounds of innocent misrepresentation:its objection is to ameliorate for the innocent misrepresentor the harsh consequences of rescission for a wholly innocent ... misrepresentor,in a case where it is fairer to uphold the contract and award damages against him."

1967 年立法短短的 3 条立法条文之 s. 3 在普通法的订约自由(freedom of contract)的大原则下,出现了大量豁免误述责任与救济的合约条文。普通法能做到的只是以欺诈侵权限制对不诚实的欺诈性误述的免责或豁免条文,但对非欺诈性误述就无能为力了。这对每天都发生大量误述事件的英国社会中的小市民与消费者不公平,但法律并没有救济。例如任何一家消费品公司只要在相关买卖合约中加上一条误述的免责或豁免条文,就可以通过把话说得天花乱坠去以次充好(但证明不了欺诈),且可以不用承担责任。

所以,S. 3 加上一条立法条文限制对非欺诈性误述免责或豁免条文,除非该条文能满足法院客观认定合理(reasonable)的要求。但在保护英国消费者的《Unfair Contract Terms 1977》[3]与后来修订的《Consumer Rights Act 2015》[4]立法后,1967 年立法之 S. 3 只适用在非消费者(non-consumer)之间的合约。这也包括了国际商业合约的外国(中国公司)合约方,只要合约适用英国法。S. 3 也会在稍后详论,在此只介绍立法条文的来龙去脉以及希望以条文解决的普通法的不足。

---

[3] 《Unfair Contract Terms 1977》之 Section 8(1)规定:"In the Misrepresentation Act 1967,the following is substituted for section 3—

'3 Avoidance of provision excluding liability for misrepresentation.

If a contract contains a term which would exclude or restrict—

(a) any liability to which a party to a contract may be subject by reason of any misrepresentation made by him before the contract was made;or

(b) any remedy available to another party to the contract by reason of such a misrepresentation,that term shall be of no effect except in so far as it satisfies the requirement of reasonableness as stated in section 11(1) of the Unfair Contract Terms Act 1977;and it is for those claiming that the term satisfies that requirement to show that it does.'."

[4] 《Consumer Rights Act 2015》中 Schedule 4 Section 1 规定:"Section 3 of the Misrepresentation Act 1967 (avoidance of provision excluding liability for misrepresentation) is amended as follows. ...

(3) At the end insert—'(2) This section does not apply to a term in a consumer contract within the meaning of Part 2 of the Consumer Rights Act 2015(but see the provision made about such contracts in section 62 of that Act).'"

2. 立法条文的节录

先节录《Misrepresentation Act 1967》[5]不长的立法条文如下：

"An Act to amend the law relating to innocent misrepresentations and to amend sections 11 and 35 of the Sale of Goods Act 1893.

1 Removal of certain bars to rescission for innocent misrepresentation.

Where a person has entered into a contract after a misrepresentation has been made to him, and—(a) the misrepresentation has become a term of the contract; or (b) the contract has been performed; or both, then, if otherwise he would be entitled to rescind the contract without alleging fraud, he shall be so entitled, subject to the provisions of this Act, notwithstanding the matters mentioned in paragraphs (a) and (b) of this section.

2 Damages for misrepresentation.

(1) Where a person has entered into a contract after a misrepresentation has been made to him by another party thereto and as a result thereof he has suffered loss, then, if the person making the misrepresentation would be liable to damages in respect thereof had the misrepresentation been made fraudulently, that person shall be so liable notwithstanding that the misrepresentation was not made fraudulently, unless he proves that he had reasonable ground to believe and did believe up to the time the contract was made the facts represented were true.

(2) Where a person has entered into a contract after a misrepresentation has been made to him otherwise than fraudulently, and he would be entitled, by reason of the misrepresentation, to rescind the contract, then, if it is claimed, in any proceedings arising out of the contract, that the contract ought to be or has been rescinded, the court or arbitrator may declare the contract subsisting and award damages in lieu of rescission, if of opinion that it would be equitable to do so, having regard to the nature of the misrepresentation and the loss that would be caused by it if the contract were upheld, as well as to the loss that rescission would cause to the other party.

(3) Damages may be awarded against a person under subsection (2) of this section whether or not he is liable to damages under subsection (1) thereof, but where he is so liable any award under the said subsection (2) shall be taken into account in assessing his liability under the said subsection (1).

---

[5] 该立法在2014年有一次修改加上了新的2(4)条文针对有关消费者的《Consumer Protection from Unfair Trading Regulations 2008》。但与中国公司关系不大，这里略过。

3 Avoidance of provision excluding liability for misrepresentation.

If a contract contains a term which would exclude or restrict—(a) any liability to which a party to a contract may be subject by reason of any misrepresentation made by him before the contract was made; or(b) any remedy available to another party to the contract by reason of such a misrepresentation, that term shall be of no effect except in so far as it satisfies the requirement of reasonableness as stated in section 11(1) of the Unfair Contract Terms Act 1977; and it is for those claiming that the term satisfies that requirement to show that it does.

[This section does not apply to a term in a consumer contract within the meaning of Part 2 of the Consumer Rights Act 2015(but see the provision made about such contracts in section 62 of that Act).]"

由于我国香港特区与内地的公司/企业在商业、金融、争议解决等方面关系密切。很多这方面的商贸活动(如IPO、收购公司、股权转让、融资、投资、仲裁、货物买卖等)都是与误述的课题有紧密联系甚至可以带来严重后果。在笔者参与的香港特区仲裁中,误述争议也与损失计算争议一样,频频出现,而且感觉作为当事人的中国内地公司与他们的法律代表在处理这个复杂的误述争议时往往有不足之处。在此只说在这方面的法律,我国香港特区作为普通法管辖(common law jurisdiction)地区是与英国较为一致。所以,也有雷同英国1967年立法的立法,可以节录中文版本如下:

"香港特区的《失实陈述条例》(第284章)

1. 简称

本条例可引称为《失实陈述条例》。

2. 除去某些阻止因无意的失实陈述而撤销合约的障碍

凡任何人在别人向他作出失实陈述后订立合约,但同时有下述情况或其中一项情况——(a)该失实陈述已成为合约中的一项条款;或(b)该合约已履行,而假若无上述情况,该人是无须指称有欺诈情况而即有权撤销合约的,则即使有(a)及(b)段所提及的情况,他在符合本条例的规定下仍无须指称有欺诈情况而如上述般有权撤销合约。

3. 失实陈述的损害赔偿

(1) 凡任何人在立约的另一方向他作出失实陈述后订立合约,结果因此蒙受损失,又若该失实陈述是欺诈地作出,会引致作出失实陈述的人要承担损害赔偿的法律责任,则即使该失实陈述并非欺诈地作出,该人亦须承担该损害赔偿的法律责任,但如他证明他有合理理由相信,而且至立约时他仍相信所陈述的事为真实,则属例外。

(2) 凡任何人在别人向他作出并非欺诈地作出的失实陈述后订立合约,而他是可以失实陈述为理由而有权撤销合约的,则在该合约引起的法律程序中,如有声称指该合约应予撤销或已遭撤销,法庭或仲裁人在顾及失实陈述的性质,和顾及若维持合约效力,失实陈述会造成的损失及撤销合约对另一方可造成的损失后,认为合约继续生效并判给损害赔偿以代替撤销合约属公正的,可宣布合约继续生效,并如上所述般判给损害赔偿以代替撤销合约。

(3) 根据第(2)款可判给损害赔偿由任何人作出,不论该人是否须承担根据第(1)款的损害赔偿法律责任,但凡他须承担该项法律责任,则在根据第(1)款评估他所须承担的法律责任时须考虑到根据第(2)款而作出的任何判给。

4. 免除失实陈述的法律责任的条文属于无效

如合约载有条款免除或限制——(a)立约的一方因在立约前作出失实陈述以致可能承担的法律责任;或(b)立约的另一方因该项失实陈述而可获得补救,则该条款即告无效,但如该条款符合《管制免责条款条例》(第71章)第3(1)条所述的合理标准,则不在此限;而任何人如声称该条款符合合理标准,须负责证明如是。"

此外,很多其他普通法国家/地区也有类似的立法,如中国公司也经常去诉讼或仲裁的新加坡的《Misrepresentation Act》(Cap. 390)等。

3. 立法条文 S.1 的分析

《Misrepresentation Act 1967》之 S.1,在这较简单的立法条文的(a)与(b)中区别针对了两种原本不明确的情况能否构成可诉误述并享有误述的救济,主要就是可选择该有缺陷的合约无效的权利。

3.1 立法 S.1(a)谈判中的可诉误述不受误述变为合约内容/条文的影响

在 S.1(a)中,也就是谈判时对一些信息与事实的虚假陈述(误述)也被加进合约作为合约部分内容后,还算不算是误述?这种情况在现实中经常发生,例如在本书第二章之10.2段就介绍了在公司并购合约(merger & acquisition agreement)或股权买卖合约(share purchase agreement)等合约中,经常有一条陈述与保证条文(representation and warranty clause)把所有或大部分订约前实质重要的陈述,主要是过去与现存事实与对将来的预期、意见等一并加入合约,作为一条重要的合约条文。例如会包括公司过去3年的业务与盈利等、股份的所有权、主要的客户名单、估算的来年业务与盈利、对公司将来发展的其他意见、有否潜在的诉讼或仲裁、有否受到规管调查等。

这样,一旦在谈判中对这些内容有虚假陈述,并出现在合约内,即可视为违约。但进一步分析,由于谈判时仍没有合约关系,所以谈判时的误述是侵权行为,而普通法法院只对欺诈性误述有救济。至于非欺诈性误述,受害方/被误述方更是要依赖衡平法才有撤销合约的救济。在谈判时的误述摇身一变成为了合约条文后,普通法也可去处理本来是非欺诈性误述的陈述并给予合约的救济。根据违约是"保证条文"(warranty)或是"条件条文"(condition)等,普通法可以给予金钱赔偿(以合约的损失计算办法)或加上终止合约的救济,无须再理会衡平法的救济了。关于误述与合约的同步/竞合责任(concurrent liability)在本书第一章之2.4段已有详细针对,这也配合在笔者《损失赔偿与救济》一书第八章之3段介绍的普通法下针对违约与侵权的竞合责任,允许作为受害方的原告自由选择根据违约或是侵权起诉,而如果原告以侵权起诉,法院或仲裁庭就必须去看双方有关的合约中是否约定了与以侵权为诉因时法律地位不同的条文(例如有更短的时效或赔偿金额限制)。如果有,就以双方约定的条文为准。

但这并不公平合理,毕竟确实发生了可诉误述诱导合约产生的事实,这可以是十分严重的虚假陈述(即使证明不了是欺诈),如果没有该误述受害方/被误述方根本不会订立该不利的合约。而违约与误述对受害方的救济很不一样,特别是在撤销或终止该合约方面。误述的撤销合约的救济是相对容易,而一旦变为终止合约,就会困难重重了,毕竟合约法下英国法律是不鼓励太容易让任何一方终止合约,正如Roskill大法官在The"Hansa Nord"(1975)2 Lloyd's Rep 445先例中说:"In principle contracts are made to be performed and not to be avoided according to the whims of market fluctuation and where there is a free choice between two possible constructions. I think the Court should tend to prefer that construction which will ensure performance and not encourage avoidance of contractual obligations."

对谈判时的误述变为合约条文说是受害方只能以违约起诉,只有是谈判中的误述与没有加进合约内才是可诉误述的说法可见The"Vendemiaire"(1936)55 Lloyd's Rep 271先例。在该先例中,Branson大法官说背后的道理是"衡平法跟从普通法"(equity follows the law)。对于非欺诈性误述撤销是衡平法救济,而如果误述被写进合约,就会有普通法对违约的救济,此时衡平法就应该靠边站。有关判决可节录如下:"... in Anson on Contract ... it is there pointed out that at common law if an innocent misrepresentation did not afterwards become part of the contract its untruth was immaterial. In such a case equity might intervene to avoid or rescind the contract. But where the representation has been embodied in the contract, there the Courts of Common Law could deal with it according to whether it was a condition entitling the injured party to repudiate the contract or a warranty giving rise only to an action ... for damages. The representation thus becomes merged in the higher contractual right and there was no need to resort to equity for rescission."

所以,《Misrepresentation Act 1967》的S.1(a)明确了立法地位,可重复节录:"**Removal of certain bars to rescission for innocent misrepresentation.** Where a person has entered into a contract after a misrepresentation has been made to him, and—(**a**) **the misrepresentation has become a term of the contract**..., if otherwise he would be entitled to rescind the contract without alleging fraud, **he shall be so entitled**, ..."(加黑部分是笔者的强调)

此立法之S.1(a)将误述内容变为合约条文的情况也涵盖在立法中,这也带来在本书第三章之6.2.2段介绍的Salt v. Stratstone Specialist Ltd(2015)EWCA Civ 745上诉庭先例中,Longmore大法官说此立法生效后就可以消除Leaf v. International Galleries(1950)2 KB 86上诉庭先例中的顾虑。后者涉及在买画5年后才发现作者并非谈判中陈述与合约中标明的,Jenkins大法官将无辜误述与违反合约的条件条文进行比较(因为两种都可以终止或撤销合约),认为条件条文都是涉及合约根本的内容,所以违反条件条文的后果比无辜误述的后果要严重。既然违反条件条文要终止合约不能"时隔太久"(lapse of time/delay),否则构成弃权。无辜误述自然也不能时隔太久,即使多年后才发现误述的存在。

3.2 立法S.1(b)可诉误述导致的缺陷合约已被部分或全部履行不受影响

至于S.1(b)是针对另一种不明确与不令人满意的情况,就是曾经有一些古老的案例有不同说法是如果该有缺陷的合约已经被履行了就不应该被允许撤销了。例如在Leaf v. International Galleries(1950)2 KB 86先例中就提到Wilde v. Gibson(1848)1 HLC 605;Seddon v. North Eastern Salt Co Ltd(1905)1 Ch 326;Redgrave v. Hurd(1881)20 Ch. D. 1;Whittington v. Seale - Hayne(1900)82 LT 49;Angel v. Jay(1911)1 KB 666等先例。

这也可节录《Misrepresentation,Mistake and Non-Disclosure》(2022年,第6版)一书之4-09段的观点:"The mere fact that the contract has been partly or even fully performed by one or both parties is not a bar to rescission."并在脚注说明:"Although there was some judicial authority before 1967 that performance of the contract might bar rescission,the Misrepresentation Act 1967 s.1(b),provides that it does not."

误述的撤销合约救济不应该受到合约被履行的影响是合理与现实的,因为谈判中的误述,即使是非欺诈性,也往往是在履行合约期间甚至是履行完毕才被受害方发现。而且,撤销合约的衡平法救济是一个"有追溯力的救济"(retrospective remedy)去回复到订约前的地位,只要能够去复原(restitution)与反复原(counter restitution),该有缺陷的合约无论是履行了多少,甚至是履行完毕,也不影响撤销合约的权利,只要受害方一旦发现了误述的事实后尽快作出选择撤销合约的决定,不去怠慢。

4. 立法条文S.2(1)的分析

在本书第一章之1.1段与本章之1段已经提到,普通法下无辜与疏忽的非欺诈性误述的受害方/被误述方不能向误述方索赔损失,只在衡平法下有撤销合约的救济。因为首先在谈判时双方没有合约,所以没有合约责任。而普通法下合约的谈判中,订约双方之间对对方只有一个诚实的责任,并没有一个小心谨慎的责任去避免疏忽与错误让对方可以安心依赖,所以即使存在疏忽误述(negligent misrepresentation)也不能以疏忽的侵权索赔损失。以前这迫使无辜与疏忽误述下被否定撤销合约的救济或不想撤销合约的受害方,如果希望索赔金钱损失,只能通过成功主张有一个附带协议或保证(collateral contract/guarantee)。[6]

4.1 S.2(1)的立法误述等同普通法下疏忽误述

但在《Misrepresentation Act 1967》立法通过后,情况得到改善,因为S.2(1)创造了一种"立法误述"(statutory misrepresentation)的表达,本质与疏忽误述十分接近。虽然在该立法没出现过"疏忽"一词,但在很多先例中,把这立法误述与疏忽误述相提并论:见Howard Marine and Dredging Co Ltd v. A Ogden & Sons(Excavations)Ltd (1978) QB 574;HIH Casualty and General Insurance Ltd v. Chase Manhattan Bank (2003) UKHL 6;Taberna Europe CDO II Plc v Selskabet AF1 (2016) EWCA Civ 1262等先例。

在Howard Marine and Dredging Co Ltd v. A Ogden & Sons(Excavations)Ltd上诉庭先例中,3位大法官都判误述方船东在疏忽侵权与1967年立法下都有责任。

在HIH Casualty and General Insurance Ltd v. Chase Manhattan Bank贵族院先例中,Bingham勋爵说:"... the right to damages given by s.2(1) of the Misrepresentation Act 1967 to the victim of a negligent misrepresentation; and the right to recover damages for deceit given by common law to the victim of a fraudulent misrepresentation."

在Taberna Europe CDO II Plc v Selskabet AF1上诉庭先例中,Moore - Bick大法官说:"Section 2(1) of the Misrepresentation Act 1967 creates a form of statutory liability sounding in negligence. In principle, therefore, contributory negligence ought to be available as a defence."

上一段节录的判词提到被告可以要求原告为原告自己也在同一事件有过错(fault)去分摊部分责任与损失是依据《Civil Liability (Contribution) Act 1978》立法。该立法之S.4对"过错"的定义就是疏忽侵权:"Negligence, breach of statutory duty or other act or omission which gives rise to liability in tort."

在贵族院对1967年立法的第二次辩论的记录中(Hansard, HL Vol. 274, Cols 922),Wilberforce勋爵批评立法误述太广,等于把所有合约订立前谈判中的陈述/表述,都强加了小心谨慎的侵权责任,一旦有错误就是疏忽:"to impose generally a duty of care, in relation to all contracts."

4.2 立法误述的优越之处之一:损失计算

接近归接近,立法误述与疏忽侵权(也包括疏忽误述)仍是有不同。例如在同一个误述的事实下,以普通法起诉,原告就要先证明被告(比如是以前委任的代理人或律师等)对原告有小心谨慎的责任与违反了这个责任。但在S.2(1)的立法误述下,原告就无需证明被告对他有一个小心谨慎的责任,只要说明与证明订立合约前的陈述/表述的信息与事实是虚假或不正确,就马上轮到被告去证明他这个陈述/表述是

---

[6] 见本书第一章之2.5.2段。

诚实与有合理依据(honest and reasonable ground)的。所以即使也可以以普通法下的疏忽误述起诉被告,以 S. 2(1)的立法误述也会容易成功得多。所以今天受害方如果不想撤销合约或是合约已经履行完毕,只想索赔损失,绝大部分情况都应该以 S. 2(1)提起诉讼。

另一个立法误述比普通法下疏忽误述的优越之处是在损失赔偿的救济方面,这可先节录《Misrepresentation, Mistake and Non-Disclosure》(2022 年,第 6 版)一书之 7 –46 段说:"**Comparison with the tort of negligence** Although the section does not use the word ' negligence', the claim for damages under s. 2(1) is, in substance, a claim for damages for negligent misrepresentation. The obvious point of reference for the statutory claim amongst the other **remedies is therefore the claim for damages in the tort of negligence. However, the remedy is not identical to that awarded in the tort of negligence, but**, at least on the authorities as they currently stand, is **more closely linked to the tort of deceit**. Since there will be cases where a claimant has the choice between a claim under the statute and a claim in negligence, it is necessary to be clear about the points of comparison between the two remedies. **Where the claimant has such a choice it is generally to his advantage to pursue the remedy under the statute**. "(加黑部分是笔者的强调)

这是说 S. 2(1)立法误述虽然本质上是普通法的疏忽误述,但在损失计算方面,S. 2(1)立法本意与不少先例判一样是以欺诈/欺骗侵权去计算。这在 Royscot Trust Ltd v. Rogerson(1991)2 QB 297 上诉庭先例中,案情涉及第一被告 Rogerson 先生从第二被告 Maidenhead Honda Centre Limited 车行处以租购(hire purchase)的方式购买一辆二手本田轿车,该轿车售价为 7600 英镑,Rogerson 先生支付了第一期的 1200 英镑,该付款金额占总价款 15.8%。原告是一家金融机构,业务是为租购协议提供贷款,它为该笔交易剩余的价款提供贷款。车行在替 Rogerson 先生填写贷款申请时对交易的情况做出误述,包括将轿车的售价填写为 8000 英镑与将 Rogerson 先生已经支付的金额填写为 1600 英镑,因为原告金融机构的政策是不会为已支付金额低于总价 20% 的租购交易提供贷款。后来,Rogerson 先生的经济出问题,他背地里将该轿车出售,并最终于 1988 年 9 月终止向原告金融机构支付余下的贷款。对原告金融机构来说,既失去了轿车,又产生了 3000 多英镑未支付的贷款金额。原告起诉两位被告,虽然根据案情来看很明显被告车行是有欺骗原告金融机构的做法,但因为证明欺诈的举证难度较高,所以原告金融机构仍只是根据 S. 2(1)向被告索赔损失,估计是想根据立法绕过艰难的对欺诈思想状态的证明。

该案中 Balcombe 大法官在谈到损失的计算是以合约还是侵权为基础时说:"... the measure of damages recoverable for innocent misrepresentation under section 2(1) of the Act of 1967, which was the tortious measure rather than the contractual one, was, on the true construction of section 2(1), the measure for fraudulent misrepresentation rather than that for negligence at common law ..."

S.2(1)的文字与措辞对如何计算损失说得确实并不清楚,从表面看来应是与欺诈性误述一致,可先重复节录有关内容说:"... if the person making the misrepresentation would be liable to damages in respect thereof had the misrepresentation been made fraudulently, that person shall be so liable notwithstanding that the misrepresentation was not made fraudulently."

在此之后有不少先例跟从与受到约束,这带来了"拟制的欺诈"(fiction of fraud)的说法而且颇受批评,对此会稍后详论。

换言之,可以同时以普通法的疏忽误述与S.2(1)立法误述作为诉因的案件,其中以后者计算损失划算得多。为了方便读者理解,可以先在接下来的段节介绍在疏忽侵权下的损失计算与欺诈/欺骗侵权下的不同。

4.2.1 对非欺诈性误述的损失计算:立法是否以欺诈性误述为准

这对"无辜"的非欺诈性误述与欺诈性误述一视同仁的立法规定,可去重温在普通法下非欺诈性误述(包括疏忽误述)是没有任何救济(除非双方的关系本来就有小心谨慎的责任)的,只有衡平法下的裁量权才有撤销合约的救济。而通过这立法之S.2(1)就可以令非欺诈性误述(无法证明有关陈述是有合理依据)等同欺诈性误述,在撤销合约的救济外[立法之S.2(2)针对],有权(as of right)索赔损失。在Avon Insurance Plc v. Swire Fraser Ltd(2000) Lloyd's Rep IR 535先例中,Rix大法官就同样提到有说法是:"it is arguable that the words in s.2(1) 'that person shall be so liable' etc. mean merely that 'that person shall be liable in damages notwithstanding that at common law damages were only available for misrepresentations proved to be fraudulent."

但误述的问题极其复杂,S.2(1)立法条文没有进一步写清楚有关细节,一个重要细节就是如果索赔损失的权利可以等同,损失的计算是否也是等同?在阻吓越来越多的民事欺诈案件的公共政策下,计算欺诈性误述的损失时会刻意放宽与弹性对待受害方因欺诈所蒙受的直接(direct)与间接损失(indirect / consequential damages),不管损失类别是否可以合理预见(foreseeable);也会宽松对待损失是否满足"要不是"(but for)测试由违约或错误直接与自然导致,务求受害方能够取回该交易所导致的所有损失。这可节录在Smith New Court Securities Ltd v. Scrimgeour Vickers(Asset Management) Ltd(1996) 3 WLR 1051贵族院先例中,Steyn勋爵说:"Such a policy of imposing more stringent remedies on an intentional wrongdoer serves two purposes. First it serves a deterrent purpose in discouraging fraud. Counsel for Citibank(欺诈性误述的被告) argued that the sole purpose of the law of tort generally, and the tort of deceit in particular, should be to compensate the victims of civil wrongs. That is far too narrow a view. ... And in the battles against fraud civil remedies can play a useful and beneficial role. Secondly, as between the fraudster and the innocent party, moral considerations militate in favour of requiring the fraudster to bear the risk of misfortunes directly caused by his fraud."

这与对待疏忽误述这种一般民事错误(civil wrong)很不一样。后者没有公共政策的考虑,所以为了法律的肯定与可预测性,更适合订立一套稳定的损失计算规则与限制,务求达至赔偿受害方损失的地位。正如 Steyn 勋爵说:"It may be said that logical symmetry and a policy of not punishing intentional wrongdoers by civil remedies favour uniform rule."

这个在政策上不同对待两种(无意的疏忽与故意的欺诈/欺骗)在本质上都属于侵权行为与民事错误的行为也很早就已明确。Blackburn 勋爵在 Livingstone v. Rawyards Coal Co(1880)5 App Cas 25 先例说:"There could be no doubt that there you would say that thing would be taken into view that would go most against the wilful wrongdoer — many things which you would properly allow in favour of an innocent mistaken trespasser would be disallowed as against a wilful and intentional trespasser on the ground that he must not qualify his own wrong, and various things of that sort."

由于欺诈性误述与疏忽误述在损失计算与理念上有这么大的差异,所以如果《Misrepresentation Act 1967》的立法意图确实是希望令疏忽误述的损失计算办法等同于欺诈性误述,就应该把立法文字写得更清楚,其道理与订立一个昂贵与重要的商业合约一样。但看来该立法没有做到,这带来广泛的批评。

然而,很不幸在富争议性但仍是有效与有约束力的 Royscot Trust Ltd v. Rogerson (1991)2 QB 297 上诉庭先例中,确认 S. 2(1)下疏忽误述是以与欺诈性误述同样的方法计算损失。Balcombe 大法官说:"The first main issue before us was: accepting that the tortious measure is the right measure, is it the measure where the tort is that of fraudulent misrepresentation, or is it the measure where the tort is negligence at common law? The difference is that in cases of fraud a plaintiff is entitled to any loss which flowed from the defendant's fraud, even if the loss could not have been foreseen .... **In my judgment the wording of the subsection is clear: the person making the innocent misrepresentation shall be 'so liable,' i. e., liable to damages as if the representation had been made fraudulently**. ... With all respect to the various learned authors whose works I have cited above, it seems to me that to suggest that a different measure of damage applies to an action for innocent misrepresentation under the section than that which applies to an action for fraudulent misrepresentation (deceit) at common law is to ignore the plain words of the subsection and is inconsistent with the cases to which I have referred."(加黑部分是笔者的强调)

Gibson 大法官说:"... in my judgment, entitled to recover the loss suffered by it as a result of entering into the two contracts as if the misrepresentation had been made fraudulently. That seems to me to be the plain meaning of section 2 of the Act of 1967 as explained by Balcombe L. J. **I find it impossible to attribute to Parliament the intention**,

by the use of the words in section 2(1), of causing the maker of such a representation to be liable as for a negligent statement. If that had been the intention I have no doubt whatever that apt words would have been used to express it. Liability as for a fraudulent misrepresentation is **to make reparation for all the actual damage directly flowing from the fraudulent inducement** … subject, of course, to remoteness."(加黑部分是笔者的强调)

在接下来的 Smith New Court Securities Ltd v. Scrimgeour Vickers(Asset Management)Ltd 贵族院先例中，由于这方面不是争议点，从而失去了澄清或推翻 Royscot Trust Ltd v. Rogerson 上诉庭先例的机会。但看来贵族院对该上诉庭先例是有保留，Browne-Wilkinson 勋爵提到此先例说："I express no view on the correctness of that decision."

而 Steyn 勋爵虽然也说不需要决定，但更详尽地显示了他对此有保留的观点："At the risk of being side - tracked I must now refer to two Court of Appeal decisions which were discussed in argument. In Royscot Trust Ltd. v. Rogerson … the Court of Appeal held that under section 2(1) of the Misrepresentation Act 1967 damages in respect of an honest but careless representation are to be calculated as if the representation had been made fraudulently. **The question is whether the rather loose wording of the statute compels the court to treat a person who was morally innocent as if he was guilty of fraud when it comes to the measure of damages**. There has been trenchant academic criticism of the Royscot case. … Since this point does not directly arise in the present case, I express no concluded view on the correctness of the decision in the Royscot case."(加黑部分是笔者的强调)

Royscot Trust Ltd v. Rogerson 先例也被学术界严厉批评，被 Atiyah 与 Treitel 教授称为"拟制的欺诈"(fiction of fraud)把"一位无辜人士(即使是疏忽也仍是道德上无辜)在法律上视为骗子"(effect of treating an innocent person as if he was fraudulent)并去阻吓性计算所有损失：见 Doyle v. Olay(Ironmongers)Ltd(1969)2 QB 158；East v. Maurer(1991)1 WLR 461 等先例。接下来一连串的案例都无法摆脱 Royscot Trust Ltd v. Rogerson 上诉庭先例的约束，如：Gran Gelato Ltd v. Richcliff(Group)Ltd (1992)Ch 560；Garden Neptune Shipping v. Occidental Worldwide(1990)1 Lloyd's Rep 330；Avon Insurance Plc v. Swire Fraser Ltd 等先例。

这是此立法在这方面受到批评的主要原因之一，正如 Atiyah 与 Treitel 教授在《Misrepresentation Act 1967》(1967)30 MLR 369 一文说："The Act has altogether failed to simplify the law. It has left in force many of the distinctions which existed before and has superimposed its own structure upon them. The resulting state of the law is almost incredibly complex."

Treitel 教授在《The Law of Contract》(1987 年，第 7 版)一书之 278 页中说：

"Where the action is brought under section 2(1) of the Misrepresentation Act, one possible view is that the deceit rule will be applied by virtue of the fiction of fraud. But the preferable view is that the severity of the deceit rule can only be justified in cases of actual fraud and that remoteness under section 2(1) should depend, as in actions based on negligence, on the test of foreseeability."

4.2.2 欺诈性误述的损失计算

已经在本书第三章之8.2段提到,在道德层面与必须阻吓越来越多的民事欺诈案件的公共政策下,欺诈性误述可以撤销合约与宽松、灵活对待一切损失索赔。早在Quinn v. Leathem(1901) AC 191贵族院先例中,Lindley勋爵已说:"the intention to injure the plaintiff ... disposes of any question of remoteness of damage."

这导致很多在笔者的《损失赔偿与救济》一书所针对一般违约或疏忽侵权的损失计算大原则与限制都有所改变,例如在损失可否合理预见(foreseeability),[7]违约一天计算损失(breach date rule),[8]非金钱损失(non-pecuniary loss)如痛苦、受难、精神压力等,[9]惩罚性损失(punitive/exemplary damages),[10]机会损失(loss of chance),[11]分摊责任与损失(contributory negligence),[12]交出利润(account for profits)[13]等。

可先节录《Chitty on Contracts》(2021年,第34版)一书之9-068段针对欺诈性误述计算损失的大原则的观点:"In Smith New Court Securities Ltd v. Scrimgeour Vickers (Asset Management) Ltd (1997) AC 254, Lord Browne-Wilkinson described Doyle v. Olby (Ironmongers) Ltd as restating the law correctly. He stated the principles applicable in assessing damages where a party has been induced by a fraudulent misrepresentation to buy property as follows: (1) The defendant(误述方) is bound to make reparation for all the damage directly flowing from the transaction(误述导致的交易); (2) Although such damage need not have been foreseeable, it must have been directly caused by the transaction; (3) In assessing such damage, the plaintiff(受害方/被误述方) is entitled to recover by way of damages the full price paid by him, but he must give credit for any benefits which he received as a result of the transaction; (4) As a general rule, the benefits received by him include the market value of the property acquired at the date of the transaction; but such general rule is not to be inflexibly applied where to do so

[7] 见笔者《损失赔偿与救济》一书第三章。
[8] 见笔者《损失赔偿与救济》一书第十三章。
[9] 见笔者《损失赔偿与救济》一书第二章之15段。
[10] 见笔者《损失赔偿与救济》一书第一章之6段。
[11] 见笔者《损失赔偿与救济》一书第六章之4-7段。
[12] 见笔者《损失赔偿与救济》一书第八章。
[13] 见笔者《损失赔偿与救济》一书第一章之7段。

would prevent him obtaining full compensation for the wrong suffered;(5) Although the circumstances in which the general rule should not apply cannot be comprehensively stated, it will normally not apply where either(a) the misrepresentation has continued to operate after the date of the acquisition of the asset so as to induce the plaintiff to retain the asset or(b) the circumstances of the case are such that the plaintiff is, by reason of the fraud, locked into the property;(6) In addition, the plaintiff is entitled to recover consequential losses caused by the transaction;(7) The plaintiff must take all reasonable steps to mitigate[14] his loss once he has discovered the fraud."

上述节录也在该贵族院先例被其他大法官所认同,如 Mustill 勋爵说:"For my part, I would suggest that in the future when faced with situations such as the present courts would do well to be guided by the seven propositions set out by my noble and learned friend, Lord Browne-Wilkinson ..."

接下来会介绍 Doyle v. Olby(Ironmongers) Ltd(1969)2 QB 158 上诉庭先例与 Smith New Court Securities Ltd v. Scrimgeour Vickers(Asset Management) Ltd 贵族院先例的案情,将更清楚展示在目前的英国法律下对待欺诈性误述如何宽松计算损失。

4.2.2.1 Doyle v. Olby(Ironmongers) Ltd(1969)2 QB 158 上诉庭先例

在 Doyle v. Olby(Ironmongers) Ltd 先例中,案情是原告(Doyle 先生)1963 年在报纸上看到被告要出售五金店业务(包括剩下的租约、业务与商誉),价格是 4500 英镑,店内库存价格另算。原告于是向被告咨询更多信息,被告的董事 Olby 先生(第二被告)提供了五金店前三年的收益:1960 年是 1921 英镑,1961 年是 1749 英镑,1962 年是 1361 英镑。Doyle 也咨询了五金店的雇员,Olby 先生的兄弟 Cecil Olby 先生(第三被告)生意的来源。Cecil Olby 先生说:"三分之二是零售,三分之一是批发,都是柜台生意。"

于是 Doyle 决定以 4500 英镑买下五金店业务,并且同时以 5000 英镑购买店内库存。Doyle 也从作为房东的 Olby 先生处以更高的价格获得更长的租约,但同时约定被告 5 年内不能在方圆 10 英里的范围内开展类似业务。[15] 为了支付这笔钱,Doyle 不仅掏空了积蓄,还贷款了 3000 英镑。

但事与愿违,Doyle 发现五金店的营业额远远低于被告的陈述,事实上店里一半的生意是批发,这需要聘请旅行推销员(travelling salesman)上门推销招揽生意,但 Doyle 根本请不起,于是失去了这些生意。Cecil Olby 先生也对此完全知情,因为他自己就是原本的兼职旅行推销员,每年的报酬是 555 英镑。整个交易对 Doyle 来说完全是一场灾难,而雪上加霜的是,不久后被告就在另外的区域开了一家经营类似业

---

〔14〕 见笔者《损失赔偿与救济》一书第五章。

〔15〕 关于这类限制商贸/就业契约/条文(restraint of trade clause)可见本书第八章之 11.2 段与笔者《合约的解释:规则与应用》一书第七章之 3.3.1 段。

务的店铺(第四被告),派出旅行推销员去招揽五金店的前客户。

1964 年 5 月,Doyle 起诉共同被告欺诈与串谋并索赔损失,但诉讼期间 Doyle 努力继续经营五金店业务。Doyle 试图转售五金店,但面对了很多困难,其中包括 Olby 先生作为房东不准他将租约转让。这等于 Doyle 被锁死在这个亏本的生意里无法减损与脱身,直到 3 年后,Doyle 以约 3500 英镑出售了五金店业务,以约 800 英镑出售了店内库存。在用这笔钱还掉贷款后,Doyle 的负债仍高达 4000 英镑,因为还不起债务被多个债权人告上法院。

在此先例中,一审法院判虽然被告开新店不违反双方之间的限制商贸条文(上诉庭的 Denning 勋爵对此决定有疑问,但上诉不涉及质疑这个决定),但谈判时被告存在欺骗/欺诈性误述,而赔偿以一般民事错误计算去把原告回复到误述没有发生或应是正确的地位。这可以有两种计算方法,一种是对比五金店卖给原告的售价与如果没有误述的售价的差别,另一种是聘请旅行推销员才能达至陈述是正确的地位要付出的成本,算出来差不多都是 1500 英镑,所以一审法院判被告赔偿 1500 英镑。

原告认为这个赔偿金额太低,提起上诉,上诉庭同意原告欺诈的损失计算不能以一般违约或疏忽侵权损失赔偿的复原大原则来计算,而是应赔付受害方原告所有因欺诈带来的损失,不管是否是可预见的间接损失。Denning 勋爵说:

"On principle the distinction seems to be this: in contract, the defendant has made a promise and broken it. The object of damages is to put the plaintiff in as good a position, as far as money can do it, as if the promise had been performed. In fraud, the defendant has been guilty of a deliberate wrong by inducing the plaintiff to act to his detriment. ... In contract, the damages are limited to what may reasonably be supposed to have been in the contemplation of the parties. **In fraud, they are not so limited. The defendant is bound to make reparation for all the actual damages directly flowing from the fraudulent inducement**. The person who has been defrauded is entitled to say: 'I would not have entered into this bargain at all but for your representation. Owing to your fraud, I have not only lost all the money I paid you, but, what is more, I have been put to a large amount of extra expense as well and suffered this or that extra damages.'

All such damages can be recovered: and**it does not lie in the mouth of the fraudulent person to say that they could not reasonably have been foreseen**. For instance, in this very case Mr. Doyle has not only lost the money which he paid for the business, which he would never have done if there had been no fraud: he put all that money in and lost it; but also he has been put to expense and loss in trying to run a business which has turned out to be a disaster for him. He is entitled to damages for all his loss, subject, of course to giving credit for any benefit that he has received. There is nothing to be taken off in mitigation: for there is nothing more that he could have done to reduce his loss. He did all that he could reasonably be expected to do."(加黑部分是笔者的强调)

Sachs 大法官说："If the purchase is one of a business which the plaintiff but for the fraud would not have acquired at all, the objective of the court is to put the plaintiff, so far as it is possible, into the same position financially as if he had not entered into the contract at all; in other words, one must look at the end result of his having entered into the transaction and find out what was his loss over all. ..."

Winn 大法官也有同样的说法，并举了个例子说："If a man in this country is made **the victim of a fraudulent misrepresentation that a business in Bangkok, Hongkong, Manila or the Fiji Islands** has certain equipment, certain assets, certain goodwill, certain trade contracts and profits, and is thereby induced to pay for that business, it being, of course, understood by both parties to the transaction of sale, for the procurement of which a fraudulent misrepresentation is made, that **he will set out to that remote place with his family and, it may be, his household goods, at very considerable expense, and on arrival will acquire living accommodation and, perhaps, have to buy additional furniture and engage staff or servants; and if he acts upon the representations and incurs all such expenses**, and the business is found to be very different from that which it was fraudulently represented to be, so that he cannot survive out in the remote place to which he has gone, and is bound to come back again, then **I, speaking for myself, would not hesitate to give him all the outgoings from his pocket of the kinds which I have indicated**, up to such time as he should sensibly have come home again, and had the money to come back again, less, of course, by way of set-off, any benefit which he has derived from the exploitation of such assets as he found there upon his arrival."[16]（加黑部分是笔者的强调）

针对此案的具体赔偿金额，Winn 大法官的分析是：(1)原告购买五金店业务与库存支付了 9500 英镑；(2)原告以约 3500 英镑出售了五金店业务，约 800 英镑出售了店内库存；(3)原告每周从五金店支取 10 英镑用于生活，原告与妻子住在店内可以不用额外支付租金，这些好处加起来约 2500 英镑。上述三项计算的结果约 2500 英镑（单纯数学计算应该是 2700 英镑，但是因为都是粗略地估计，Winn 大法官减到了 2500 英镑）。此外，在经营五金店期间原告一直亏损，而为了应付亏损，原告四处借钱并支付利息［这在一般民事错误的损失计算，会被视为因果关系是来自原告的

---

〔16〕 根据 Winn 大法官举的例子，如果一位商人因为欺诈性误述搬到中国香港做生意，之后发现生意并非陈述中的情况而最终做不下去要搬回英国，在计算损失时来回搬家、买家具、请佣人等的费用都可以包括在内，但要扣减商人获得的好处。这样，假设商人来中国香港时买房（如果以为可以有长期生意这决定也是合理），但最后离开时房价大跌，其中的差价在合约或一般民事错误下是不可能获得赔偿，因为无法合理预见，但在欺诈/欺骗下这应是可以被包括在内。而如果反过来，房价大涨，商人获得的好处也要从损失中扣减。

"贫穷"(impecuniosity)而不是被告的民事错误,[17]但无可否认这是欺诈性误述带来的损失]。Winn 大法官估计这部分共约 3000 英镑,所以最后加起来是5500 英镑,是一审判决的好几倍。

总之,这个案件的大原则是要尽量宽松与灵活地对待欺诈性误述的受害方蒙受的所有损失,让受害方回到没有被欺诈性误述/欺骗所影响的地位。所以,只要受害方有合理减损与对冲掉从中获得的好处(如最终出售五金店与店内库存),受害方的所有损失无论是否可以预见,或个别损失是否严格满足因果关系的测试,都可以获得赔偿。

4.2.2.2 Smith New Court Securities Ltd v. Scrimgeour Vickers(Asset Management)Ltd(1996)3 WLR 1051 贵族院先例

Smith New Court Ltd v. Scrimgeour Vickers(Asset Management)Ltd 贵族院先例在本书第三章之 5.4.2 段有关以对等的金钱复原部分已经略及,但在此会更详尽分析另一个方面,也就是目前英国法律下有关欺诈/欺骗侵权与一般的民事错误(违约、疏忽侵权)不同的损失计算方式的权威说法。

在该案中,因客户无法偿还贷款,美国花旗银行(第二被告 Citibank)通过它自己的股票经纪人(第一被告)的负责人 Roberts 先生出售用来为该笔贷款抵押的 28,000,000 股Ferranti 股票。当时市场这股票应值 78 便士,但 Citibank 与经纪人被指控作出欺诈性误述,结果在 1989 年 7 月 21 日以高价的 82.25 便士成功出售了该批股票给受害方原告并希望作为投资长期拥有。被指称的误述是:(i)有其他两位人士在争购这批股票;(ii)已有其他人在出价要买;(iii)这些出价在 81 便士不等。其实这些是谎言。这欺诈性误述也被一审法院认定,可名为"Roberts fraud"。

该批股票买了后不久,在1989 年9 月 11 日,Ferranti 的董事局在市场上宣告有内部欺诈(可名为"Guerin fraud")令公司蒙受严重亏损的丑闻,并申请市场停止买卖,停牌到了 10 月 3 日才复牌。在 11 月 7 日,Ferranti 公布了公司账目,显示 Guerin fraud 造成的损失比之前的估计更严重。在整个期间,股票价值波动与大跌。最终原告是在 11 月 20 日开始分批出售(笔者估计分批是市场低微时,买方不多,所以只能耐心等待,一有买方出现想买多少就脱手多少),而价格只能以 30 便士至 49 便士之间,直至 1990 年 4 月 30 日才完全把手中的 Ferranti 股票脱手,可谓是损失惨重。原告于是以欺诈性误述向被告索赔所有的损失,高达 11,353,220 英镑。而被告计算的办法是英国法律的"违约一天规则"(breach date rule)[18]加上"市场规则"(market rule),[19]因为上市公司的股票价值有市场可参考。在误述的范畴就是误述方在做出了误述并且被依赖导致损失产生的一天。例如在货物买卖,如果买方以交付的货物

[17] 关于受害方的贫穷打断因果关系,可见笔者《损失赔偿与救济》一书第四章之 9.2.2 段的介绍。

[18] 见笔者《损失赔偿与救济》一书第十三章与第十四章。

[19] 见笔者《损失赔偿与救济》一书第十五章与第十六章。

是“货不对版”,本质上是对货物有误述,而拒绝接收货物。卖方不同意并向买方索赔损失,损失计算在《Sale of Goods Act 1979》之 S. 50 有立法规定了表面规则是违约一天规则与市场规则,说:“(1) Where the buyer wrongfully … refused to accept and pay for goods, … (3) Where there is an available market for the goods in question the measure of damages is prima facie to be ascertained by the difference between the contract price and the market … price at the time or times when the goods ought to have been accepted or(if no time was fixed for acceptance) at the time of the refusal to accept.”

因为在买方拒货后,卖方在减损要求下与在有市场的情况下,应尽快转售被拒货物。显然转售价格会比买卖合约价格低,所以卖方在该天(或临近的时间)产生了差价的损失。又例如在频频发生误述的公司并购(M & A)中,由于签订合约后会有很多程序要走(如尽职调查、政府批准、股东大会批准、双方履行各种要件等),时间会拖长。所以双方会同意一个公司价格但以交割(closing/completion)一天的估值调整为准。所以,如果卖方的误述对买方造成损失,也就会是在交易交割一天。

而该 Ferranti 股票在欺诈性误述诱导合约产生的一天市场价格是 78 便士,然后去比较合约价格的 82.25 便士。这样按照市场规则,原告能获得赔偿的损失显然是远比不上所有损失,因为原告是以 30 至 49 便士之间的价格把 Ferranti 股票脱手,不是 78 便士。

高院判欺诈性误述成立。在损失计算上,Chadwick 大法官不接受被告的争辩,认为 Ferranti 股票在违约一天的规则下,也就是订约当天该股票真正的市场价格并不是 78 便士一股。因为当时存在公司内部欺诈的 Guerin fraud 与严重亏损,Ferranti 公司股票的真正价值未在市场价格上反映,市场只是假象,只是因为坏消息仍未抖出来。Chadwick 大法官的估计(根据后来披露的信息与事实)是订约当天真正市场价格应为 44 便士,所以被告应赔偿的损失是 82.25 便士与 44 便士的差价。

到了上诉庭,这方面被推翻,而去更改为 82.25 便士与 78 便士的差别。上诉庭根据早在 Waddell v. Blockey(1879)4 QBD 678 先例的“违约一天规则”与“市场规则”的计算方法,认为 78 便士的市场价格并没有因欺诈性误述的 Roberts fraud 而变得不反映当时市场。至于估计的真正价值 44 便士,是由于后来曝光的 Guerin fraud 所导致,与 Roberts fraud 扯不上因果关系,而此先例的诉因只是针对 Roberts fraud 的欺诈性误述诱导原告同意购买这批 Ferranti 股票。所以损失计算是违约一天的市场价格的 78 便士与原告在合约下支付的 82.25 便士之间的差价,并一下子将一审判决赔偿的 10,764,005 英镑减为接近十分之一的 1,196,010 英镑。

上诉庭也理解在交易后才曝光的 Guerin fraud 的不可预见与灾难性事故要受骗的原告承担恶果并不公平合理,但由于受到两条法律原则(原告已经将股票脱手导致无法“实物归还”复原与违约一天的市场规则)约束不得不如此判。这在贵族院的 Browne-Wilkinson 勋爵的判词中有提道:“The Court of Appeal was conscious that, in so holding, they were throwing the whole risk of catastrophic events onto the innocent purchaser rather than the fraudulent vendor. But they held that such injustice stemmed from the rigidity of two rules(both of which had been common ground before them): first, the denial of rescission where a plaintiff cannot return in specie the very shares which were the subject matter of the fraudulent sale; second, the rule which requires the damages to be calculated as at the date of sale."

最后上诉到了贵族院,据报道针对这一方面的争议是第一次上到贵族院。受害方的争辩是在欺诈/欺骗的侵权行为中,被告误述方要负责所有损失,不论能否预见(比如本案的 Ferranti 公司内部欺诈,在订约时并不为外人所知道)。没有欺诈性误述,原告也不会购买这批股票。这样,无论 Guerin fraud 对 Ferranti 造成任何严重的亏损,也与原告无关,原告只会当作花边新闻。但不幸的是原告因欺诈性误述而购入股票,就与 Guerin fraud 有关系与受影响了,这带来的损失显然是误述的直接后果与被包括在误述造成的所有损失中。而误述方的争辩是"违约一天计算"办法,而且没有这误述,受害方也会以 78 便士买这 Ferranti 股票。之后他不尽快转售,而去继续持有,带来后来股价严重下挫的风险,是受害方自己的决定,不能赖误述方。

贵族院又推翻上诉庭决定,支持了 Chadwick 大法官的判决。贵族院不接受受违约一天计算办法的限制,认为可非常弹性地给予受害方所有因误述带来的直接损失,不论可否预见,以及可充分考虑因误述买进了一样东西,但没法再出售而被捆住(locked into),被迫随着市场下跌等无法减损的情况。

此重要先例对欺诈/欺骗侵权与欺诈性误述的损失计算有很清楚的指引,以下予以分别介绍。

1. 侵权的损失赔偿目的是把双方当事人回复到侵权(包括误述)没有发生的地位,正如 Blackburn 勋爵在 Livingstone v. Rawyards Coal Co(1880)5 App Cas 25 先例说:"… a general rule that, where any injury is to be compensated by damages, in settling the sum of money to be given for reparation of damages you should as nearly as possible get that sum of money which will put the party who has been injured, or who has suffered, in the same position as he would have been in if he had not sustained the wrong for which he is now getting his compensation or reparation."

这涉及复原/反复原(restitution/counter restitution),已经在本书第三章之 5 段有详论,不重复。在此先例中,由于案件的标的物 Ferranti 股票已经转售,原告无法去"实物归还"复原(restitution in specie),而要通过困难重重的索赔损失途径。否则在反复原下,被告要回归整批 Ferranti 股票的 82.25 便士对价也就是"完璧归赵",不再有金钱上损失的争议了。

2. 在损失赔偿,以违约一天规则与市场规则计算损失的好处就是简单与可以避免真正损失会带来的复杂争议如因果关系与减损。例如在此先例中,这假设是既然有市场的买卖可把 Ferranti 股票以 78 便士出售,原告就假设在违约一天以 78 便士出售,这就是原告的假设损失了。但如果以真正损失,也就是在 11 月 20 日才开始在市场分批出售(或在相反的情况是受害方可去买入),就会带来很多损失计算的争议。例如,原告在 9 月 20 日就发觉 Guerin fraud,为何不在 Ferranti 股票在 10 月 3 日复牌后尽快出售,而要拖拖拉拉多等 2 个月在市场更低微时才抛售,令损失更为严重。欺诈性误述在损失计算仍受到因果关系与减损这两个限制的约束,所以被告在此做文章。

3. 但违约一天规则与市场规则计算本来也不是绝对规则(absolute rule),只是表面规则(prima facie rule),需要配合赔偿大原则去调整,见 The "Golden Victory" (2007) UKHL 12 先例。正如 County Personnel (Employment Agency) Ltd v. Alan R Pulver & Co (1987) 1 WLR 916 上诉庭先例中,Bingham 大法官所说:"While the general rule undoubtedly is that damages for tort or breach of contract are assessed as at the date of the breach ... this rule also should not be mechanistically applied in circumstances where assessment at another date may more accurately reflect the overriding compensatory rule."

特别是对欺诈性误述,赔偿大原则更是需要宽松与灵活让受害方不蒙受任何欺诈带来的损失。所以如果受骗买入的房屋(举例)市场价格一直在下跌(无论这下跌是否由同一欺诈造成),在过了一段时间(特别是受害方被锁死无法合理脱手)后才能脱手转卖,差价扩大,法院也会选择后来任何的一天的市场价格来比较受害方受骗付出的价格,务求在案件中赔偿受害方所有因为欺诈性误述而蒙受的损失。

Browne – Wilkinson 勋爵说:"The old 'inflexible rule' is both wrong in principle and capable of producing manifest injustice. The defendant's fraud may have an effect continuing after the transaction is completed, e. g. if a sale of gold shares was induced by a misrepresentation that a new find had been made which was to be announced later it would plainly be wrong to assume that the plaintiff should have sold the shares before the announcement should have been made. Again, the acquisition of the asset may ... lock the purchaser into continuing to hold the asset until he can effect a resale. To say that in such a case the plaintiff has obtained the value of the asset at the transaction date and must therefore bring it into account flies in the face of common sense: how can he be said to have received such a value, if, despite his efforts, he has been unable to sell. ... in East v. Maurer (1991) 1 WLR 461 and Downs v. Chappell (1996) CLC 1492 ... both cases the plaintiffs had purchased a business as a going concern in reliance on the defendant's fraudulent misrepresentation. In each case after discovery of the fraud they sold business at a loss and recovered by way of damages the difference between the original purchase and the price eventually realised on a resale, i. e. The old date of transaction rule was not applied."

4. 至于原告不及时把 Ferranti 股票出售涉及的因果关系与减损原则,鉴于原告在受骗的情况下的做法被认定没有不合理,Browne – Wilkinson 勋爵说:"Can it then be

said that the loss flowed not from Smith's(原告)acquisition but from Smith's decision to retain the shares? In my judgment it cannot. ... Smith could not dispose of them on 21 July otherwise than at a loss. Smith were in a special sense locked into the shares having brought them for a purpose and at a price which precluded them from sensibly disposing them. It was not alleged or found that Smith acted unreasonably in retaining the shares for as long as they did or in realising them in the manner in which they did."

5. 而 Steyn 勋爵认为因果关系与减损即使在欺诈/欺骗的案件中仍是有必要去保证骗子赔偿的损失是符合现实与理性的,但一般的"要不是"测试因果关系不一定在所有不同案情的案件都能够得出正确结果,需要宽松对待,会以一般常识看在每一个不同案件,判断最后造成的损失与欺诈/欺骗侵权行为是否能扯得上一定的关系(sufficient casual connection)。而在这个案件的案情,原告基本上是被迫与标的物 Ferranti 股票锁在一起无法脱身,在这种情况下,即使有其他无关欺诈性误述的事情(Guerin fraud)在同时或交易后发生,也不会构成新的因素去打断 Roberts fraud 所无可避免导致的损失与结果。Steyn 勋爵说:

"It is now necessary to consider separately the three limiting principles which, even in a case of deceit, serve to keep wrongdoer's liability within practical and sensible limits. ... For present purposes, causation is the most important. The major issue in the present case is whether there is a casual link between the fraud and the loss arising by reason of the pre-existing fraud perpetrated on Ferranti. ... What was further been established is that **the 'but for' test, although it often yields the right answer, does not always do so**. That has led judges to apply the pragmatic test whether the condition in question was a substantial factor in producing the result. On other occasions judges assert that the guiding criterion is whether in **common sense terms there is a sufficient casual connection** ...

The distinctive features of the case are —(1) that the fraud of Mr Roberts induced Smith to buy the Ferranti shares, the value of which were already at the date of sale doomed to collapse due to the fraud practiced on the company by a third party; and (2) that by reason of the fraud of Mr Roberts, Smith was induced to buy the shares as a market making risk, i, e. to hold on to the shares for sale at a later stage.

In these circumstances**Smith was truly locked into the transaction by reason of the fraud perpetrated on it. And the causative influence of the fraud is not significantly attenuated or diluted by other causative factors acting simultaneously with or subsequently to the fraud**. ...

In the actual circumstances of this case I am satisfied that there was a sufficient casual link between the fraudand the Smith's loss. Moreover, for substantially the same reasons, I would hold that Smith's losses, calculated on the basis of the difference between the price paid and the proceeds of subsequent realisation, flowing directly from the fraud.

In my view Smith would on this bases be entitled to recover the sum of about £ 11.3m."(加黑部分是笔者的强调)

6. 至于损失计算的"可预见性",在欺诈/欺骗中是不管用的,已经在很多先例有提及。在此只简单节录 Steyn 勋爵的观点:"On any view it is clear that ... the law imposes liability in an action for deceit for some consequences that were unforeseen and unforeseeable when the tortfeasor committed the wrong."

7. 在此先例中,贵族院推翻了上诉庭判决并支持一审 Chadwick 大法官判的10,764,005英镑,比根据最后原告把整批 Ferranti 股票出售后总损失的 1130 万英镑要低,但差不多。原因是原告上诉只要求贵族院支持一审判决,而一审判决是另一种对欺诈性误述造成损失的计算办法。这早在 Twycross v. Grant(1877)2 CPD 469 先例中,Cockburn CJ 大法官举了一个例子说:"If a man buys a horse, as a racehorse, on the false representation that it has won some great race, while in reality it is a horse of very inferior speed, and he pays ten or twenty times as much as much as the horse is worth, and after the buyer has got the animal home it dies of some latent disease inherent in its system at the time he bought it, he may claim the entire price he gave; the horse was by reason of the latent mischief worth less when he bought; but if it catches some disease and dies, the buyer cannot claim the entire value of the horse, which he is no longer in a condition to restore, but only the different between the price he gave and the real value at the time he bought."

把此例子适用在本先例的事实,由于在原告购买 Ferranti 股票时,Guerin fraud 已经存在,这相当于例子的赛马有潜在疾病并后来导致死亡,令受害方/被误述方无法完璧归赵,就可以索赔支付所有的对价,看来与反复原的地位一样。而如果赛马是买卖交易后才染病并导致死亡,则误述的损失计算可以是受害方真正支付的对价与该赛马如果没有该误述的真正价值之间的差价。这也正是此先例一审的 Chadwick 大法官的计算办法,认为市场的 78 便士是虚假市场,Ferranti 股票的真正价值只是 44 便士。看来,这另类的计算办法也被贵族院认可。

8. 一审判决的较低金额(10,764,005 英镑)与贵族院认定的金额(1130 万英镑),在笔者看来后者是根据原告的真正损失。这判法与 East v. Maurer 与 Downs v. Chappell 先例一致。但如果标的物无法出售与脱手,估计原告因欺诈性误述导致的所有损失就会以一审判法了。看来由于在此先例中的两个金额相差不远,加上是原告上诉要求的赔偿金额,所以贵族院也就支持了一审判决的金额。

4.2.2.3 对不同损失类别的针对

正如在本章之4.2.2 段提到,针对部分损失类别对欺诈性误述导致的与其他民事错误导致的有不同的态度,接下来可介绍没有在上述详及的损失类别:

4.2.2.3.1 非金钱损失如痛苦、受难、精神压力等

痛苦、受难、精神压力等非金钱的损失(damages for non-pecuniary loss)需要量化

才能做出金钱上的赔偿,这一直以来是属于侵权的范畴,而对合约违约在英国法下传统只允许向违约方索赔经济损失,而对非金钱损失有所抗拒,虽然近年来有所放宽。[20] 对于欺诈性误述,受害方/被误述方可以在欺诈/欺骗侵权下获得非金钱损失的赔偿。在《Chitty on Contracts》(2021 年,第 34 版)一书之 9 – 077 段说:"Damages for worry and inconvenience and for mental and physical suffering have been awarded in actions based on fraud."

这可见:McNally v. Welltrade International Ltd(1978)IRLR 497(误述产生雇佣合约,雇主的赔偿包括给雇员带来的精神压力与不便);Shelley v. Paddock(1980)QB 348(房屋买卖合约,实际不拥有房屋的卖方要赔偿买方包括精神压力在内的损失);Jones v. Emerton – Court(1983)CLY 982(房屋买卖合约,卖方要赔偿给买方造成的不便);Archer v. Brown(1985)QB 401(股份买卖合约,卖方将同样的股份多次买卖,法院判在欺诈/欺骗下,卖方不仅要赔偿买方支付的股价,还要赔偿向银行贷款要支付的利息,买方失业与要重新找工作的损失与感情上受伤的损失);Saunders v. Edwards(1987)1 WLR 1116(房屋买卖合约,卖方误述公寓包括屋顶花园,法院判卖方要作出的赔偿包括买方的不便与失望)等先例。

4.2.2.3.2 惩罚性损失

英国法律对违约或侵权的民事诉讼,损失赔偿的大原则是"赔偿性复原"(compensatory principle),不允许赔偿惩罚性损失(punitive/exemplary damages),认为这是刑事诉讼的范畴。

在《损失赔偿与救济》一书第一章之 6.1 段,详细介绍了 Rookes v. Barnard (1964)AC 1129 贵族院先例中,明确了民事诉讼只在 3 种例外情况允许作出惩罚性损失赔偿:(1)政府官员的压迫性、随意性或违反宪法的行为;(2)侵权行为是侵权方计算过好处大过坏处(例如汽车公司明知车辆有缺陷,但计算过赚到的利润多过出事要作出的赔偿,所以拒绝召回);(3)立法规定。

显然,只是(2)侵权行为是侵权方计算过好处大过坏处与欺诈性误述可否作出惩罚性赔偿最有关系。但在 AB v. South West Water Services Ltd(1993)QB 507 上诉庭先例中,认为 Rookes v. Barnard 先例只适用在该先例前的侵权案件。另加上有看法是欺诈性误述如果在刑事诉讼下被定罪(欺诈是侵权外,也可能犯了刑法),就不应该在同一事项去惩罚两次(double jeopardy)。所以,以前版本的《Chitty on Contracts》欺诈/欺骗与欺诈性误述是不能获得惩罚性损失的赔偿的。

但在 AB v. South West Water Services Ltd 先例被 Kuddas v. Chief Constable of Leicestershire Constabulary(2001)UKHL 29 贵族院先例推翻与 AXA Insurance UK Plc v. Financial Claims Solutions Ltd(2018)EWCA Civ 1330 上诉庭先例出现后,这本权威书籍有了不同说法。

---

[20] 见笔者《损失赔偿与救济》一书第二章之 15 段。

上述简介可节录《Chitty on Contracts》(2021 年，第 34 版)一书之 9－079 段说："It is **not yet wholly clear if exemplary damages can be awarded for fraud**. Until recently it seems very unlikely. Even if fraud could be brought within the first or second of Lord Devlin's three categories in Rookes v. Barnard (1964) AC 1129, namely, first, oppressive, arbitrary or unconstitutional action by the servants of government or, secondly, cases in which the defendant's conduct has been calculated to make a profit for himself which may well exceed the compensation payable to the plaintiff, the interpretation of those categories by the House of Lords in Cassell & Co Ltd v. Broome (1972) AC 1027 and by the Court of Appeal in AB v. South West Water Services Ltd (1993) QB 507 required that for exemplary damages to be awarded the tort must be one in respect of which such an award had been made prior to 1964, and deceit is not such a tort. However in Kuddas v. Chief Constable of Leicestershire Constabulary (2001) UKHL 29, the House of Lords held that the power to award exemplary damages is not limited to those cases in which such awards had been made before 1964. AB v. South West Water Services Ltd was overruled. **This seems to open the way for awards of exemplary damages in respect of deceit which falls into Lord Devlin's first two categories**. … the growth of remedies for unjust enrichment may make Lord Devlin's second category of less importance as the defendant's profit may be removed without an award of exemplary damages,[21] **exemplary damages were awarded in a case involving fraudulent insurance claims** where the anticipated profit would have exceeded the loss: AXA Insurance UK Plc v. Financial Claims Solutions Ltd (2018) EWCA Civ 1330. The argument (made in previous editions of this work) that it would be wrong to award exemplary where the defendant has already been convicted and imprisoned for the same fraud, because would infringe the basic principle that a person should not be punished twice for the same offence, has been rejected. …"(加黑部分是笔者的强调)

在 AXA Insurance UK Plc v. Financial Claims Solutions Ltd 上诉庭先例中，涉及被告以虚假交通事故向保险公司欺诈性索偿(显然与欺诈性误述走在一起)，Flaux 大法官接受 Rix 大法官在 Borders (UK) Ltd v. Commissioner of Police of the Metropolis (2005) EWCA Civ 197 上诉庭先例中所说的宽松解释 Rookes v. Barnard 贵族院先例的第二个例外情况就会可以适用在一些欺诈/欺骗案件作出惩罚性损失赔偿。Flaux

[21] 在本书第三章之 5 段也已经提到了，涉及可使无效合约时，如果选择撤销合约，必须进行复原，在完全恢复原状有困难时，今天也存在有弹性的做法只需要达到实际公平(practical justice)。这会包括很多手段，其中就包括要求误述方交出利润(account for profits)等。这些手段并非损失计算，而只是辅助复原的手段。但很多时候被误述方选择确认(affirm)合约，只索赔损失，如合约已经履行了一段时间，被误述方也不希望撤销合约。此时就难以依赖前述手段索赔对方的利润，而需要依赖这里所提到的惩罚性损失赔偿了。

大法官(上诉庭也同意)说:

"Rix LJ said:'**Exemplary damages no doubt remain a controversial topic** … In my judgment, however, … controversial as they are, they are **not to be contained in a form of straight – jacket**, but can be awarded, ultimately in the interests of justice, to punish and deter outrageous conduct on the part of a defendant. As long therefore as the power to award exemplary damages remains, it is not inappropriate in a case such as this, … '

Provided that it is recognised that the criterion which Lord Devlin(Rookes v. Barnard 贵族院先例)identified, that the wrongdoer has calculated that the profit to be made from the wrongdoing may well exceed any compensation he has to pay the claimant, must have been satisfied for exemplary damages in the second category to be available, this seems to me to be **an appropriate statement of the approach to be adopted to the award of exemplary damages in this category**.

Applying that approach, **in my judgment the present case(in which, as I have stated, the criterion which Lord Devlin identified is satisfied)is a paradigm case for the award of exemplary damages.** This was a sophisticated and sustained fraud **involving deceit and fraudulent misrepresentation** from the outset. The accidents were faked. False documentation, such as the hire agreements and medical reports, was created. The claimants themselves may not have existed. …

Contrary to the view of the judge, it is nothing to the point that criminal proceedings could have been brought(and indeed were brought against the third respondent). That was precisely what had occurred in theBorders(UK)Ltd v. Commissioner of Police of the Metropolis case, where the appellant had been tried and convicted of fraud and sentenced to 30 months imprisonment. … As in **the present case, confiscation proceedings were pending at the time of the hearing in this Court. The existence of the criminal proceedings and, in particular, the confiscation proceedings was not considered by this Court to affect the award of exemplary damages if appropriate and the argument of double jeopardy was rejected**."(加黑部分是笔者的强调)

4.2.2.3.3 机会损失

这看来是与《损失赔偿与救济》一书第六章之4至7段介绍的违约导致的机会损失(lost opportunity/chance)的大道理是一样。只要能证明是欺诈性误述导致的利润损失,例如因为买了这个公司而失去了购买另一家公司的机会,或是这几年不能在其他公司工作赚取工资等,就可以索赔损失。如果涉及第三人的变数,可以根据有关证据认定几率作出相应的扣减。在《Chitty on Contracts》(2021年,第34版)一书之9-065段说:"The points that damages for fraud will not compensate the claimant for loss of bargain but **may cover loss caused by passing up other profitable opportunities**

are well illustrated by East v. Maurer(1991)1 WLR 461. The plaintiffs bought a hairdressing business in reliance on a false representation that the defendant had no intention of working regularly at a second hairdressing business he owned in the same town. In fact he continued to work at the second business and the plaintiffs were forced to resell the business they had bought at a substantial loss. They were awarded damages for the difference between the price they had paid and the price they received on resale, plus expenditures wasted in attempting to improve the business and in other ways. **They were also awarded the sum they could have expected to make as profit had they bought another similar business in the same area.** ... **Damages for lost opportunity may be recovered even though they may have to be discounted on the ground that it was not certain that the claimant would have been able to take up the opportunity**, e. g. if the owner of the alternative business might not have agreed to sell. It is not necessary to show that the alternative deal would necessarily have been profitable; if necessary the amount can be discounted to reflect the element of risk. "(加黑部分是笔者的强调)

在上面提到的 East v. Maurer 先例中，被告是一位著名的发型师，在邻近区域经营两家美发沙龙。原告向被告购买了其中一家美发沙龙自己经营，虽然非常努力经营但始终赚不到钱，客户也流失得很快。原告后来发现虽然被告在谈判期间向原告误述他本人不会在另一家美发沙龙里接待客户，但实际上被告在另一家美发沙龙里全职工作。原告于是开始诉讼声称被告欺骗侵权，同时也试图将生意转手，但直到 3 年后才卖出去。上诉庭支持了一审法院的判决，认定在欺诈性误述原告可以索赔利润损失(loss of profit)。上诉庭在考虑了这笔钱放在银行的收益，原告如果这 3 年在别的美发沙龙打工可以赚的钱等因素后，认定原告的利润损失为 10,000 英镑。

Baldem 大法官说："But as to the statements of principle to which I have referred, it seems to me clear that there is no basis upon which one could say that loss of profits incurred whilst waiting for an opportunity to realise to its best advantage a business which has been purchased, are irrecoverable. It is conceded that losses made in the course of running the business of a company, are recoverable. If in fact the plaintiffs lost the profits which they could reasonably have expected from running a business in the area of a kind similar to the business in this case, I can see no reason why those do not fall within the words of Lord Atkin in Clark v. Urquhart [1930] A. C. 28 ..., 'actual damage directly flowing from the fraudulent inducement.'

So I consider that on the facts found by the judge in the present case, the plaintiffs did establish that they had suffered a loss due to the defendants' misrepresentation which arose from their inability to earn the profits in the business which they hoped to buy in the ... area."

之后的 4 Eng Ltd v. Harper(2008)EWHC 915(Ch)先例中，双方的争议之一是原

告能否索赔因为欺诈性误述而失去的购买 Tarvail Ltd 的机会及由此带来的利润损失与增值损失。针对 Tarvail Ltd 的股东会否同意将公司出售给原告的变数,David Richards 大法官认为看不到什么原则性的理由不能以机会损失的方法计算:"It does not seem to me to be an objection that the loss is assessed as a loss of chance, not as a loss established on the balance of probabilities.[22] It is true that it does not previously appear to have been decided that damages for loss of a chance are recoverable for deceit, but there is in my judgment no objection in principle. If damages for loss of a chance are recoverable in negligence, why should they not also be recoverable in deceit?"

高院根据证据最终认定有 80% 的机会 Tarvail Ltd 会被出售给原告,也就是要对如果购买 Tarvail Ltd 会带来的估计的利润与增值作出 20% 的扣减。

4.2.2.3.4 受害方/被误述方本来就可能会订立另一个亏本交易

这个课题的关系是既然在欺诈性误述是可以让受害方/被误述方获得其他赚钱机会的损失,同样道理下误述方如果能够证明(虽然举证不容易)受害方不订立这个欺诈性误述导致的有缺陷合约,也会订立另一个同样亏本的合约,在计算损失时就应该扣减或对冲另外的亏本。正如在 Yam Seng Pte Ltd v. International Trade Corp Ltd (2013) EWHC 111(QB)先例中,Leggatt 大法官说:"In my view ... In circumstances where it is established that the claimant can recover a profit that would have been obtained from entering into some other transaction, it must be in principle be equally relevant to take account of any loss."

这种情况的出现会是误述方在谈判时就知道受害方与另一位第三人在同时谈判(如买卖同一类商品或公司),如果不是与误述方订约也会与第三人订约。而订约后不久,遇上金融海啸或新冠疫情暴发或相关法律的改变等,导致订任何一份合约都是亏本。受害方以误述方的欺诈性误述索赔损失,误述方就会要求对金融海啸或新冠疫情暴发或相关法律的改变导致的损失作出扣减或对冲。在《Chitty on Contracts》(2021 年,第 34 版)一书之 9-075 段说:

"**Claimant would have entered another losing transaction**. As mentioned earlier, in fraud cases it is presumed that had it not been for fraud, the claimant would not have entered the contract. In Downs v. Chappell(1997)1 WLR 426, it has said that a party who has been induced to enter a contract by fraud and who seeks damages need not show that, had he known the truth, he would not have entered the transaction. He need only show that he was induced to enter the contract by a material misrepresentation and the loss that flowed from entering it. Where the misrepresentee claims to rescind the contract, it is irrelevant that he might have entered a contract with the misrepresentor even if the fraudu-

---

[22] 在笔者《损失赔偿与救济》一书第六章之 4.1.3 段与 4.1.4 段就提到,在计算涉及第三人变数的损失时,因果关系方面不需要达到 50% 以上的平衡的可能性。

lent misrepresentation had not been made:it need only have been one of the factors which influenced him. **But what the misrepresentee would have done will normally be relevant to a claim for damages,since he must show a casual connection between the misrepresentation and the loss claimed;and if it is shown that he would have entered another losing transaction,this should be taken into account**. This is certainly the case when the claim is one for negligence. ... The same rule should apply in cases of fraud, even though,according to Lord Steyn ' s speech in the Smith New Court Securities v. Scrimgeour Vickers(Asset Management)Ltd(1997)AC 254,the rule of causation are applied differently and:' ... it is not necessary for the judge to embark on a hypothetical reconstruction of what the parties would have agreed had the deceit not occurred. '

In Yam Seng Pte Ltd v. International Trade Corp Ltd(2013)EWHC 111(QB),Leggatt J held that although there is some authority for ignoring the fact that, but for the fraudulent misrepresentation, **the claimant might have entered another losing transaction,such a rule would be logically indefensible when profits that the claimant might have made are to be taken into account in assessing damages for fraud.** ... It is therefore **open to a defendant to show that, had the representation not been made, the claimant would have entered another losing transaction.** The evidential burden will be on the defendant,and in seeking to discharge this burden,the defendant(unlike the claimant)does not have the benefit of the principle that if the financial outcome of the alternative transaction is uncertain the court will make reasonable assumptions in its favour(for example by allowing damages to be calculated a loss of a chance basis)to assist in the proof of loss. "(加黑部分是笔者的强调)

法律为了阻吓欺诈的行为,将欺诈性误述与合约产生之间的因果关系的标准定得比较低,只要扯得上一定关系就可以,甚至法律默示一个假设就是如果没有欺诈性误述,合约就不会订立,从而令被误述方无需去证明要是没有该欺诈性误述就不会与误述方订立合约。但是在具体核算损失金额时,不能不考虑即使不在欺诈性误述下订立合约,订立其他合约也一样会带来损失。以上节录的《Chitty on Contracts》部分就是在 Yam Seng Pte Ltd v. International Trade Corp Ltd 先例中的表述,虽然该先例是在确立关系合约(relationship contract)有善意责任[23]方面更为著名,但是其中也有关于误述的争议。该案中关于误述带来的损失,被告主张原告根本没有任何损失,如果一定要说有损失,顶多就是加快了订立合约的时间,因为原告在被告取得曼联授权之后仍然会与被告订立合约。对于是否要看如果没有误述原告会有什么样的行为,高院的 Leggatt 大法官在分析了 East v. Maurer(1991)1 WLR 461 与 4 Eng Ltd v. Har-

〔23〕 关于关系合约的善意责任与 Yam Seng Pte Ltd v. International Trade Corp Ltd 先例的案情可见本书第一章之2.6.5段。

per(2008)EWHC 915(Ch)先例后认为,既然法院允许被误述方取回如果没有误述他能够在其他地方获得的利润,如果在其他地方有损失,也是因为同样的道理要考虑进来。不过对于如果没有误述被误述方会有的损失的证明责任在误述方,对于这种损失的证明有任何的不确定,都是因误述方没有尽到举证责任而败诉。

有关损失与欺诈性误述之间的因果关系,虽然较早前谈到会宽松对待,但还是适用在欺诈/欺骗中,否则这损失计算起来就无边无际了。这可节录《Chitty on Contracts》(2021 年,第 34 版)一书之 9 - 062 段说:"**Causation in damages for fraud**. As stated earlier, when the claimant seeks damages for fraud as opposed to rescission, the normal 'but for' rule of causation seems to apply. Thus if the claimant would have entered the contract on the same terms even if the misrepresentation had not been made, his claim for damages will fail. ... if the misrepresentor can definitely show that this is what the misrepresentee would have done. ..."

4.2.2.3.5 本来是亏本交易

在一般的交易中,也会有好/坏或稳赚/稳亏的交易。如果误述诱导产生的原本的合约是一个坏交易或亏本交易(bad bargain),以合约的违约/毁约(误述被合并在合约,发觉后受害方以此合法终止合约)去计算损失,即把受害方回复到误述或违约没有发生的地位。但在这地位下,有关误述事实如果真实,受害方也难逃因为他投资决定错误的坏交易所面对的损失,这损失也与误述或违约没有因果关系。所以,以合约计算违约/毁约损失就会是零(看坏交易坏到什么程度)。相反,如果是好交易或赚钱生意(如顺利履行估算可赚 1000 万美元),在计算误述或违约导致的损失时,是可以索赔利润损失(loss of profit),也就是这 1000 万美元就可作为损失的一部分向误述方/违约方索赔。

若是以误述去复原,让受害方/被误述方回复到没有发生误述的地位,是可以把一个坏交易或亏本生意赖掉,去把错误投资决定的风险转嫁给误述方的。所以如果原本的合约是个好交易与赚钱生意,以合约索赔损失是好于误述,但如果误述诱导产生的原本的合约是一个坏交易或亏本生意,则相反。

因此,如果有关的陈述既构成可诉误述,又被包括在合约的陈述与保证条文(Representation and Warranty Clause),[24] 原告就要考虑以哪一个诉因(可诉误述或违反合约的陈述与保证条文)索赔更为划算,这显然取决于这个交易是不是一个好交易。这可节录在《Chitty on Contracts》(2021 年,第 34 版)一书之 9 - 066 段说:"**Not loss of bargain** It follows that in many cases the measure of damages for breach of contract will be higher than that for fraud, as it will include the profit that would have been made on the contract in question had the representation been true. If as a result of a fraudulent misrepresentation the claimant has bought a property, but the property appears

---

〔24〕 见本书第二章之 10.2 段。

to be worth the price paid for it and there is no wasted expenditure or loss of a more valuable opportunity, the claimant damages according to the tort measure would appear to be nil."

另在《Chitty on Contracts》(2021 年,第 34 版)一书之 9 - 067 段说:"**Property worth less than paid for it.** While the claimant in an action for fraud cannot claim to be put into the position he would have been in if the fact represented were true, a claimant who made a bad bargain, in the sense that even if what he had been told were true, at the time the contract is made the property he is induced to buy would have been worth less than he has agreed to pay for it, will be better off under the tortious measure than the contractual one."

在 Wemyss v. Karim(2016)EWCA Civ 27 上诉庭先例中,Lewison 大法官说:

"In the case of a claim that there has been a breach of warranty about the quality of an asset that is sold, the measure of damages is the difference between the true value of the asset and its value with the quality as warranted. But in the case of a claim in tort, the measure of damages is the difference between the true value of the asset and the price paid. The point was put clearly by Lord Denning MR in Doyle v Olby(Ironmongers)Ltd [1969] 2 QB 158:'On principle the distinction seems to be this: in contract, the defendant has made a promise and broken it. The object of damages is to put the plaintiff in as good a position, as far as money can do it, as if the promise had been performed. **In fraud, the defendant has been guilty of a deliberate wrong by inducing the plaintiff to act to his detriment. The object of damages is to compensate the plaintiff for all the loss he has suffered**, so far, again, as money can do it.'

As Prof Treitel explained in 'Damages for Deceit' (1969) 32 M. L. R. 556 ... in a passage approved by Lord Steyn in Smith New Court Ltd v Citibank NA [1997] AC 254 ...: '**If the plaintiff's bargain would have been a bad one**, even on the assumption that the representation was true, **he will do best under the tortious measure**. If, on the assumption that the representation was true, his bargain would have been a good one, he will do best under the first contractual measure (under which he may recover something even if the actual value of what he has recovered is greater than the price).'"(加黑部分是笔者的强调)

最后可以 Lewison 大法官在该先例举的例子帮助理解。假设原告花了 8000 英镑向被告购买一幅画,被告告诉原告这幅画是一位著名画家所作。如果是真的,这幅画会价值 10,000 英镑,但事实上这幅画并非该著名画家所作,只值 100 英镑。如果原告可以证明被告的陈述构成买卖合约的附带保证(collateral warranty),甚至被写进了买卖合约,原告可以索赔 10,000 - 100 = 9900 英镑的损失。但如果只能证明被告误述,原告只能索赔 8000 - 100 = 7900 英镑的损失。而假设的事实稍有改变,例如被告向原告保证这幅画价值10,000英镑,但实际只值8000英镑,而原告花了8000英镑买画。在违约下,原告可以索赔2000英镑,但在误述下,原告没有损失。

4.2.2.3.6 交出利润

一般损失计算关注的是受害方/被误述方的损失,让受害方/被误述方回复到没有发生误述的地位,而不是误述方的利润。针对欺诈性误述的损失计算也是如此,法院一般不会让误述方交出利润(account of profits)。要区分的是,这里指的是损失计算,而不是撤销合约带来的复原的辅助手段。在《Chitty on Contracts》(2021年,第34版)一书之9-078段说:"**No account of profits**. The victim of fraud may not obtain an account of profits made by the fraudulent party, at least where the victim has affirmed the contract and has suffered no loss. The House of Lords in AG v. Blake(2001)AC 268[25] held that, in certain circumstances, the victim of a breach of contract may obtain an account of the profit made by the other party through his breach. This is undoubtedly a relaxation of the rule in cases of breach of contract and it may be asked whether the rule that an account of profits is not available in case of fraud will continue to be applied. However, the conditions which the House of Lords laid down for an account of profits in breach of contract cases-broadly, that the claimant has a legitimate interest in the promised performance which an award of damages will not satisfy because the breach will not necessarily cause a loss-are less likely to occur in cases of fraud, since damages for fraud by definition do not include the gain the claimant would have made(the 'expectation')had the statement made been true. Thus the claimant is entitled only to be put into the position he would have been in had the misrepresentation not been made, and it is suggested that damages will normally be adequate for this purpose. To award the victim of a fraud an account of profit would be to allow him a fully restitutionary claim, and in Halifax Building Society v. Thomas(1996)Ch. 217, that was held by the Court of Appeal not to be available."

在关于欺诈性误述下交出利润的著名先例Murad v. Al-Saraj(2005)EWCA Civ 959先例[26]中,Arden大法官说这个做法不是由于欺诈侵权而是由于双方存在诚信关系:"It would be tempting to jump to the conclusion from paragraph 347 of the judge's judgment(一审法院的判决)... that in this case the judge took the novel step of awarding the equitable remedy of account for the common law tort of deceit ..., but that is not in my judgment the true interpretation of the judge's judgment. **The judge gave a remedy of account because there was a fiduciary relationship**. For wrongs in the context of such a relationship, an order for an account of profits is a conventional remedy. ..."(加黑

〔25〕 在笔者《损失赔偿与救济》一书第一章之7.3.2段对该贵族院先例有介绍。

〔26〕 见本书第一章之2.7.4.2段的详细介绍。

部分是笔者的强调)

在之后的 Renault UK Ltd v. FleetPro Technical Services Ltd(2007)EWHC 2541(QB)先例中,Richard Seymour QC 大法官认同以上判决,认为不应该支持在欺诈性误述下要求被告交出利润。

也就是说如果要让法院判误述方要交出利润,就要证明误述方与被误述方之间存在诚信关系,[27]且误述方利用该诚信关系获利。

4.2.2.3.7 共同疏忽下分摊责任与损失

根据《Law Reform(Contributory Negligence)Act 1945》立法的文字,该立法只适用在疏忽侵权的情况,所以共同疏忽在普通法下与《Law Reform(Contributory Negligence)Act 1945》立法下都不是欺诈/欺骗侵权的抗辩,所以即使受害方有自己疏忽或粗心大意导致受骗的情况,欺诈性误述的误述方也不能以共同疏忽要求被误述方/受害方分摊责任与损失。

在《Chitty on Contracts》(2021 年,第 34 版)一书之 9 - 080 段说:"Contributory negligence is **not a defence to an action of deceit and the Law Reform(Contributory Negligence)Act 1945 does not apply**. Section 1(1)of the … Act applies 'when any person suffers damage as the result partly of his own fault and partly of the fault of any other person'. Section 4 defines 'fault' as:'… negligence,breach of statutory duty or other act or omission which gives rise to liability in tort or would,apart from this Act,give rise to the defence of contributory negligence.'

Thus for the Act to apply,the claimant's conduct must either be an act giving rise to liability to the defendant in tort or be one which at common law would have given rise to the defence of contributory negligence. It has been held that at common law contributory negligence is not a defence to fraud and that therefore the … Act does not apply to fraud: Alliance and Leicester Building Society v. Edgestop Ltd(1993)1 WLR 1462;Corp Nacional del Cobre de Chile v. Sogemin Metals Ltd(1997)2 All ER 917;Standard Chartered Bank v. Pakistan National Shipping Corp(No. 2)(2002)UKHL 43."(加黑部分是笔者的强调)

4.2.2.3.8 与非法合约的关系

在《Chitty on Contracts》(2021 年,第 34 版)一书之 9 - 082 段说:"**Illegality.** It has been held that payments made under a contract which was illegal(though not to the

---

[27] 见本书第一章之 2.7 段。在本书第十一章之 1.5 段会介绍,违背诚信义务时会有衡平法救济,如滥用信任(abuse of confidence)。此时未能履行应尽义务的受托人的行为被认为是衡平法过错行为,可以给予衡平法赔偿(equitable compensation),在衡平法赔偿下法院可以给予返还性损失赔偿(restitutionary damages)。所谓返还性损失赔偿,目的在于当受害方自己的损害不多甚至没有时,以受托人获取的利益作为计算损失的依据,或称之为"返还"。这类损害赔偿的叫法也是在近 30 年才确立起来,见 AG v. Blake(2001)AC 268 先例等。

knowledge of the plaintiff) would be recovered in an action of fraud, though the contract itself could not be sued upon because of the illegality: Saunders v. Edwards (1987) 1 WLR 1116. Further, damages for fraud may be recovered even where the contract was known by the plaintiffs to be illegal, if the fraud and the illegality were quite unconnected. In The 'Siben' (No. 2) (1996) 1 Lloyd's Rep 35, the misrepresentee was permitted to claim damages for fraud although part of the business transferred to him was used for immoral purposes, as it was said that he did not have to rely on the illegal contract. ..."

不难推算，即使是非法的合约，只要欺诈性误述的争议与救济（撤销合约与/或损失赔偿）不直接涉及非法部分，是不受影响的，笔者接下来将继续举例说明。

在上述《Chitty on Contracts》的节录中提到的The"Siben"（No. 2）先例中，交易的部分对价涉及一家妓院，这是非法。但有关欺诈性误述的争议与妓院没有直接关系，所以无须依赖非法诉因的欺诈性误述，在普通法下的索赔损失不受影响。而如果争议是有关妓院如何分红或分工管理的履行，这就直接有关并是因非法无法获法院协助执行了。但在撤销合约与复原方面，因为是衡平法救济而对价涉及非法，就会因为"净手原则"（clean hand policy）受影响了。

先介绍The"Siben"先例的案情，这是通过报刊广告，原告与被告达成买卖合约，被告以在葡萄牙的一家夜店（discotheque）与一间在营运陪游服务（escort services）的别墅以货易货，交换原告营运的一艘名为"Siben"的游艇、一辆名车与一笔85,000英镑（其中50,000英镑在交付游艇后12个月支付）。但被告在谈判时有两个误述：其一是说他拥有这家夜店，但其实该店由第三人拥有，被告只是在安排买过来，然后才能去转交给原告；其二是指这夜店每星期周末可赚高达1500英镑，其实差很远，而这对原告十分重要，因为他将以此谋生。

双方同意后不久，原告把"Siben"轮与名车交付给了被告，但被告无法交出夜店，也稍后明确了根本在每周末赚不了1500英镑。原告于是拒绝支付余下的50,000英镑，并以欺诈性误述要求法院命令撤销合约，把价值显然是最高（估值为750,000美元）的"Siben"轮的产权回归（revert）给原告。

Clarke大法官在听取大量证据（主要是口头证据）后，认定被告欺诈性误述，但有关撤销合约并回归"Siben"轮产权方面，法院并不支持。原因如下：

1. 这是与本小段有关的原因，就是营运陪游服务的别墅实是提供娼妓服务，这在英国法下是非法。而这部分的对价在整个交易中不可分割（non-severable），[28] 所以也无法把合法与非法部分分割。因为没有在合约中对夜店与别墅区别估价，所以根据普通法去作出撤销合约的救济，这是去协助非法而违反"非法理论"（doctrine of illegality）[29] 的大原则。而如果退一步去求助衡平法救济去撤销合约与复原，让原告

---

〔28〕 见本书第八章之11段。

〔29〕 见本书第八章。

可取回 The“Siben”轮,在衡平法的“净手原则”下,更是不能用在救济非法的交易中。Clarke 大法官说:“... the Villas Rouges business was part of the property to be swapped ... It follows that it was part of the consideration for the agreement as a whole even though no separate figure was attached to it. A significant part of the Villas Rouges business was the provision of girls for money... I accept ... that the contract between the parties was illegal on the ground that it was in part for immoral purposes. ... I do not think that the position can be any different because the prostitutes were to be provided in Portugal. **I do not think that a Court of Equity should make an order which would in principle have the effect of transferring an illegal business from one party to another.** It follows that I shall not order rescission. ”(加黑部分是笔者的强调)

2. 时隔已久,交易发生在 1991 年,原告提出申请撤销合约是在 1993 年 5 月。期间,该别墅已被原告转售,无法回归给被告去复原。

所以即使法院在欺诈性误述下可以有很大的弹性去处理救济,以达到个别案件的公平合理结果,Clarke 大法官在平衡后还是认为在此先例不适合允许撤销合约与下令回归“Siben”轮的产权,并决定以金钱损失赔偿作为替代,帮原告在经济上回复到合约没有订立前,也就是欺诈性误述没有发生的地位。这表示非法只影响撤销合约的救济,在普通法下的金钱赔偿救济不受影响。

虽然在判决中没有说明,但笔者可以想到金钱赔偿对原告不利之处是不一定很快能够成功去执行,甚至最后在无法执行的情况之下,胜诉判决只是空话一句。但如果下令回归“Siben”轮的产权,只要没有被被告转售给无辜第三人买方,这是对原告更快与更有保障的救济。

接下来《Chitty on Contracts》中提到的另一个案件 Saunders v. Edwards 先例的案情涉及房屋买卖,卖方误述公寓包含屋顶花园,但其实没有。此案涉及非法的部分是买方为了少交一些印花税,把购买房屋的 45,000 英镑拆成了两部分,一部分是房价 40,000 英镑,另一部分是家具装饰等 5000 英镑,但实际上,这些家具装饰只值不到 1000 英镑。房屋没有花园的估价是 40,650 英镑,因此卖方抗辩说买方不能依赖自己欺骗政府的非法目的说付出了 45,000 英镑,而以 40,000 英镑算,买方根本没有损失。上诉庭不接受卖方的抗辩,Nicholls 大法官说在该先例买方是索赔欺骗导致的损失,而不是要执行合约:“The plaintiffs' claim is for damages for deceit. The claim is not to enforce the contract, nor is the claim one which is, strictly, based on the contract, although the contract is a material part of the history. The claim is simply that in November 1983, by reason of a fraudulent misrepresentation, the plaintiffs paid to the defendant a sum (including the deposit) of £ 45000. But for that misrepresentation that payment would not have been made. In claiming damages for fraud, credit has to be given for the true market value of what the plaintiffs in fact received from the defendant. Thus, although one of the provisions in the contract (the apportionment of the price) had an unlawful purpose, analogous to the splitting up of one transaction into two documents for a fraudulent purpose..., the plaintiffs do not, strictly speaking, rely on that contract in the present proceedings."

Nicholls 大法官接着说要考虑所有的情况，在不能鼓励买方逃税行为与不能让卖方保留自己欺诈性误述从买方那里骗来的钱这两个公共政策之间作出权衡。买方只逃了几百英镑的税与根据有关法律罚款很少显然是一个重要考虑，而如果案情有所改变，法院的判决也可能不同。Nicholls 大法官说："Applying that test, in this case there has been illegality of which the court should take notice. It is not a matter to which the court should turn a blind eye. However, when one comes to weigh, on the one hand, the extent to which it might seem that by granting these plaintiffs relief the court is indirectly encouraging these plaintiffs in their tax evasion activity, or indirectly encouraging others in other cases to proceed similarly when apportioning a purchase price, against, on the other hand, permitting a fraudulent defendant to retain money which he has received from the plaintiffs and which represents a financial loss suffered by the plaintiffs directly as a result of the fraudulent misrepresentation, I have no doubt on which side the scales fall. I have no hesitation in concluding that, on the facts of this case, granting to these plaintiffs relief against the defendant would not be an affront to the public conscience. The plaintiffs' loss, flowing from the defendant's fraud, would have been the same irrespective of the precise way in which the price was apportioned between the flat and the chattels. .... Although the deliberate overstatement of the price being paid for the chattels, and hence the deliberate understatement of the consideration being paid for the flat, have not affected the outcome of the plaintiffs' claim in this action, it should not be assumed that this will always be so in other cases where such deliberate misstatements are present...."

在 Patel v. Mirza(2016) UKSC 42 最高院先例〔30〕后，非法的课题有了重大的改变。而 The"Siben"(No. 2)与 Saunders v. Edwards 先例都是以前的案件，在 Patel v. Mirza 先例后非法与欺诈性误述的关系会有什么改变，尚待后来的先例中再做进一步分析。

4.2.2.4 对欺诈性误述(包括其他政策上要阻吓的欺诈/欺骗)损失计算总结

在上述详尽介绍的 Smith New Court Securities Ltd v. Scrimgeour Vickers(Asset Management) Ltd(1996) 3 WLR 1051 贵族院先例中，相信读者对欺诈/欺骗与欺诈性误述的损失计算的灵活性有所认识，例如，偏离计算损失的一般原则与限制，务求把受害方/被误述方蒙受的所有损失转嫁给误述方骗子。读者也可更深入理解本章之 4.2.2 段节录的《Chitty on Contracts》(2021 年，第 34 版)一书之 9-068 段中 Browne-Wilkinson 勋爵说的 7 个原则。笔者只针对不肯定与要估计的损失多去强调以下几

---

〔30〕 见本书第八章之 7.5 段。

个方面，并且这些方面会是对欺诈/欺骗案件更加适合：

1. 在《Chitty on Contracts》（2021 年，第 34 版）一书之 29 – 019 段说："**Difficulty of assessment** The fact that damages are difficult to assess does not disentitle the claimant to compensation for loss resulting from the defendant's breach of contract. Where it is clear that the claimant has suffered substantial loss, but the evidence does not enable it to be precisely quantified, the court will assess damages as best it can on the available evidence. The fact that the amount of that loss cannot be precisely ascertained does not deprive the claimant of a remedy. The loss of profits suffered by a claimant as the result of the defendant's breach of contract frequently depends on many speculative factors, but the courts will always attempt to assess the amount of the loss."

2. 在欺诈/欺骗的案件中，即使是发现了被骗如欺诈性误述，也不会一下子真相大白。骗子的谎言会持续，受害方也会有幻想而不会当机立断去减损，受害方也会如 Doyle v. Olby (Ironmongers) Ltd (1969) 2 QB 158 先例的案情一样被锁死，无法脱身而要持续亏损营运等。所以以违约一天计算损失[31]在欺诈/欺骗案件并不一定公平合理，而以受害方真正把受骗购买的标的物在往后出售或处理所得的价钱才是更能代表真正损失的。这是减损的问题，虽然欺诈性误述的受害方仍要在发现受骗后承担减损的责任，但是判断受害方是否合理减损会是很灵活。在《Chitty on Contracts》（2021 年，第 34 版）一书之 9 – 070 段说："As Lord Brown-Wilkinson's fourth proposition indicates, the damages are normally to be calculated according to the difference between the contract price and the value of the property at the time of the contract. This seems to follow from the rule that the loss must flow directly from the transaction. But this is **only a prima facie rule**; as Lord Steyn put it, **the date of transaction rule is simply a second – order rule** applicable only if the valuation method is followed, and **the court is entitled to assess the loss flowing directly from the fraud without any reference to the date of the transaction or indeed any particular date**. In some situations, the claimant may recover the difference between the contract price and **the value of the property at a later date**. This is so when the fall in value is due to the discovery of the defendant's fraud, which has also deceived others in the market. However, it may **also apply even if the reduction of value is not the result of fraud**."（加黑部分是笔者的强调）

3. 对于欺诈/欺骗，即使是不可预见的损失也会被宽松对待。在 Doyle v. Olby (Ironmongers) Ltd 上诉庭先例中已经明确，除了 Denning 勋爵所说，另是如 Winn 大法官举的例子受害方在欺诈性误述下买下了在外国的业务，并举家搬迁去外地（曼谷、香港、马尼拉或斐济）而花费了很多费用也可以向骗子取回。正如在《Chitty on

[31] 见笔者《损失赔偿与救济》一书第十三章。

Contracts》(2021 年,第 34 版)一书之 9 - 064 段说:"**Unforeseeable losses**. In Doyle v. Olby(Ironmongers)Ltd, it was held that in cases of fraud the plaintiff was entitled to damages for any such loss which flowed from the defendants' fraud, even if the loss could not have been foreseen by the latter. Thus the claimant may recover not only the difference between the price paid and the value of what he received but also expenditure wasted in reliance on the contract and compensation for other opportunities passed over in reliance on it."

4. 欺诈/欺骗案件的受害方在特别/间接损失(special/consequential damages)的计算中经常会遇到困难,往往是证据不足或只能去粗略估计,但这不应该影响尽量赔偿受害方欺诈/欺骗导致的所有损失的大原则。在一个较近期的涉及欺诈/欺骗与欺诈性误述的 Parabola Investments Ltd v. Browallia Cal Ltd(2010)EWCA Civ 486 上诉庭先例中,Toulson 大法官说对于部分间接损失甚至可以不用满足平衡的可能性:"Some claims for consequential loss are capable of being established with precision(for example, expenses incurred prior to the date of trial). Other forms of consequential loss are not capable of similarly precise calculation because they involve the attempted measurement of things which would or might have happened(or might not have happened)but for the defendant's wrongful conduct, as distinct from things which have happened. In such a situation the law does not require a claimant to perform the impossible, **nor does it apply the balance of probability test to the measurement of the loss**."(加黑部分是笔者的强调)

5. 欺诈/欺骗的案件在损失计算方面也经常面对证据不全,特别是被告不合作的情况下。这样,在对受害方损失(特别是特别/间接损失)估计时,可以对被告作出推定(presumption)与不利推断(adverse inference),这在《证据法:基础理论、口头证据与专家证据》一书第七章之 8.4 段有介绍,包括古老的 Armory v. Delamirie(1722)93 ER 664(KB)先例。在近期的 One Step(Support)Ltd v. Morris - Garner and another(2018)UKSC 20 最高院先例中,此古老先例被作为依据,Reed 勋爵说:"**In so far as the defendant may have destroyed or wrongfully prevented or impeded the claimant from adducing relevant evidence, the court can make presumptions in favour of the claimant**. The point is illustrated by Armory v Delamirie(1721)1 Str 505, where a chimney sweep's boy found a jewel and took it to the defendant's shop to find out what it was. The defendant returned only the empty socket, and was held liable to pay damages to the boy. Experts gave evidence about the value of the jewel which the socket could have accommodated, and Pratt CJ directed the jury: 'that, **unless the defendant did produce the jewel, and shew it not to be of the finest water, they should presume the strongest against him, and make the value of the best jewels the measure of their damages**: which they accordingly did'."(加黑部分是笔者的强调)

6. 在同一 Armory v. Delamirie 先例有说到需要给原告一个“顺风原则”(fair wind principle)与于举证上有利的推定:“raises an evidential(i. e. rebuttable) presumption in favour of the claimant a fair wind in establishing the value of what he has lost.”

这在近期的 Gul Bottlers(PVT)Limited v. Nichols plc(2014)EWHC 2173(Comm)先例中,Cooke 大法官也对受害方损失的估计说到了“fair wind”原则,对任何不肯定之处(毕竟是由被告的欺诈/欺骗引起)是要对原告受害方作尽量宽松或慷慨的推定,即使估计错误,也错在多赔而不是少赔给受害方:“I bear in mind the ‘fair wind’ principle set out … in Yam Seng Pte Ltd v International Trade Corp Ltd [2013] 1 CLC 662 by Leggatt J at 709A:‘… it is fair to resolve uncertainties about what would have happened but for the defendant's wrongdoing by making reasonable assumptions which err, if anything, on the side of generosity to the claimant where it is the defendant's wrongdoing which has created those uncertainties’.”

7. 最后笔者多举一个简单例子,在损失计算最著名的 Hadley v. Baxendale(1854)9 Ex. 341 贵族院先例中,虽然与欺诈性误述没有关系而只是一般的违约案件,但可以说,如果该著名先例是一个欺诈性误述案件,就不会有“一般损失”(ordinary damage)与订约时无法预见的损失类别的“特别损失”(special damage 或有时候称为 consequential damage)的区分了,反正误述方骗子导致的所有损失都要赔。

再多举一个例子,受害方在欺诈性误述下购买了一家公司,如果“东窗事发”后该公司清盘倒闭,受害方所有的投资付之东流,就应可索赔所有的投资损失甚至为这项投资所花费的使费。如果该公司仍可以低价出售脱手,并且成功,受害方应可以索赔购买所支付的对价减去低价出售所得价格。而在出售前的期间发生其他外来因素导致公司最后出售价格更低,例如,整体的市场变坏或其他千变万化因素,这种市场风险或不幸,只要不涉及受害方的过错或疏忽(毕竟受害方仍需合理减损),都可转移给误述方骗子承担。因为没有该欺诈性误述,受害方根本不会购买该公司,自然也不会与后来的市场变坏或不幸有任何关系。

如果该公司无法出售脱手并仍是在营运,受害方可以假设没有该欺诈性误述,公司在购买时应该值多少钱的真正价值(估值),然后比较受害方支付给误述的卖方的金额,其差价即是可以索赔的损失。

当然,这也不影响受害方如果没有被否定撤销合约与复原的权利,可以把该公司回归给骗子卖方,并取回支付的对价。但在千变万化的情况下,会有很多情况是无法(如公司引入新股东或有了重大改组)复原或受害方不愿意去复原的,并希望继续营运该公司,这就涉及复杂的损失计算了。

8. 在 Smith New Court Securities Ltd v. Scrimgeour Vickers(Asset Management)Ltd 贵族院先例中,Browne - Wilkinson 勋爵的 7 条欺诈性误述损失计算的指引,也在后来被很多案例依从,在此只提部分:Spice Girls Ltd v. Aprilia World Service BV(Damages)(2001)EMLR 8;Chef Aquitaine Sarl v. Laporte Materials(Barrow)Ltd

(2001)QB 488;Great Future International Ltd v. Sealand Housing Corp(In Liquidation)(2002)EWHC 2454(Ch);Pankhania v. Hackney LBC(Damages)(2004)EWHC 323(Ch);Halston Holdings v. Simons(2005)EWHC 30(QB);Veitch v. Avery(2007)EWCA Civ 711;4 Eng Ltd v. Harper(2008)EWHC 915(Ch);Dadourian Group International Inc v. Simms(2009)EWCA Civ 169;Parabola Investments Ltd v. Browallia Cal Ltd(2009)EWHC 901(Comm);Invertec Ltd v. De Mol Holding BV(2009)EWHC 2471(Ch);Murfin v. Campbell(2011)EWHC 1475(Ch);Butler-Creagh v. Hersham(2011)EWHC 2525(QB);OMV Petrom SA v. Glencore International AG(2015)EWHC 666(Comm);HQ Accountancy Solutions Ltd v. Polo/Lauren Co LP(2016)3 WLUK 236;Khakshouri v. Jimenez(2017)EWHC 3392(QB);Inter Export LLC v. Townley(2018)EWCA Civ 2068;Playboy Club London v. Blanca Nationals deal Lavora SpA(2019)EWHC 303(Comm);Vald. Nielsen Holding A/S v. Baldorino(2019)EWHC 1926(Comm);Glossop Cartons and Print Ltd v. Contact(Print and Packaging)Ltd(2021)EWCA Civ 639;Cahane v. The Investigative Journal Ltd(2021)EWHC 2344(QB)等先例。这足可见欺诈性误述争议发生的频密程度,也显示了国际商业的险恶(其中很多先例都是商业争议),但至少法律比较肯定宽松计算欺诈/欺骗导致的损失。

4.2.2.5 "拟制的欺诈"(fiction of fraud)

再重复 S.2(1)立法条文,对立法误述的损失计算的措辞/文字是:"would be liable to damages in respect thereof had the misrepresentation been made fraudulently, that person shall be so liable notwithstanding that the misrepresentation was not made fraudulently ..."

这是把 S.2(1)的立法误述的损失以欺诈性误述来核算(assess),这看来十分奇怪,毕竟立法误述等同于疏忽误述,误述方在道德上是诚实的,只是无心犯错。

但这立法的措辞/文字不是笔误,而是有意参考了《Companies Act 1948》之 S.43,[32] 而这条立法可以追溯到《Directors Liability Act 1890》之 S.3,其目的是保证公司的招股章程(prospectus)中所有的陈述的正确性。只要董事无法证明自己有合理依据相信有关陈述为真,就会被视为欺诈,以让董事更加谨慎。正如 Atkin 勋爵在 Clark v. Urquhart(1930)AC 28 贵族院先例说:"... the effect of the section in the original Directors Liability Act was merely to eliminate the element of fraud from the cause of action based on misrepresentation in a prospectus, and to give the same remedy in the statutory conditions for an untrue misrepresentation as for a fraudulent misrepresentation."

所以在 Tenth Report of the Law Reform Committee(1962)Cmnd. 1782 立法报告中有说明 S.2(1)的立法损失的救济是"欺骗但不需要有欺诈意图"(deceit without the fraud),其中也提到立法想构建整个误述的框架,所有关于误述的索赔都在立法框架下

〔32〕 现在生效的对应立法应该是《Financial Services and Markets Act 2000》之 S.90。

进行,不用再依赖欺诈/欺骗:"We appreciate that the independent remedy in damages which we have recommended will be available in any case in which, under the present law, fraud has to be proved. The damages obtainable for misrepresentation will be no less extensive and the plaintiff's burden of proof very much lighter. It may be therefore that, so far as misrepresentations inducing a contract are concerned, actions for fraud will fall into disuse and be replaced by our proposed remedy … The tort of deceit will still be needed for those cases where a fraudulent statement has induced a person to act to his detriment otherwise than by entering into a contract …"

有了上述有关1967年立法之s. 2(1)的立法历史的介绍,可以理解较早节录的Royscot Trust Ltd v. Rogerson(1991)2 QB 297上诉庭先例中Balcombe大法官所说,因为法院必须严格按照议会立法意图(不论法院是否同意)去解释立法条文并加以适用。

很多受Royscot Trust Ltd v. Rogerson上诉庭先例约束的一审或上诉庭先例,[33]被迫"错判",笔者只介绍在判词中有简单提到立法历史的Raiffeisen Zentralbank Osterreich AG v. Royal Bank of Scotland Plc(2010)EWHC 1392(Comm)先例中,Christopher Clarke大法官说:"… as the law now stands RZB(原告被误述方)is entitled to recover the loss which it has suffered as a result of entering into the contract. That is the measure of recovery in an action for deceit … In Royscot Trust Ltd v. Rogerson … the Court of Appeal held that **the measure of damages in an action under section 2(1) of the Misrepresentation Act is the same as in an action for deceit**. The measure is not, as it would be in a case of negligence, the loss which flows from the inaccuracy of the information: South Australia Asset Management Corporation v. York Montague Ltd(1997)1 AC 191 … **Royscot has been subject to strong academic criticism**. Equally, it has been said that the Court of Appeal was bound to reach the conclusion that it did having regard to the decision of the House of Lords in Clark v. Urquhart(1930)1 AC 28 in relation to section 3 of the Directors' Liability Act 1890 … RBS, **whilst submitting that it was wrongly decided, recognises that I am bound by it**. …"(加黑部分是笔者的强调)

目前的英国法律,也让受害方/被误述方有机会取巧,正如在《Misrepresentation, Mistake and Non-Disclosure》(2022年,第6版)一书之7-46段针对立法误述与普通法下的疏忽误述的比较说,如果作为受害方的原告有选择,就应以立法误述谋求最大利益:"Where the claimant has such a choice it is generally to his advantage to pursue the

---

〔33〕 见Andre v. Ets Michel Blanc(1979)2 Lloyd's Rep 427;Chesneau v. Interhome Ltd(1983)CAT 238(CA);Cemp Properties(UK)Ltd v. Dentsply Research & Development Corp(No. 2)(1989)36 EG 90;Bridgegrove Ltd v. Smith(1997)2 EGLR 40(CA);Showan v. Yapp(unreported, 3 November 1998);Avon Insurance Plc v. Swire Fraser Ltd(2000)Lloyd's Rep IR 535;Forest International Gaskets Ltd v. Fosters Marketing Ltd(2005)EWCA Civ 700;Cheltenham BC v. Laird(2009)EWHC 1253(QB);Cassa di Risparmio della Repubblica di San Marino SpA v. Barclays Bank Ltd(2011)EWHC 484(Comm)等先例。

remedy under the statute."

但笔者认为不只是普通法的疏忽误述(如果误述方有"小心谨慎责任"),连欺诈性误述也应以立法误述去起诉。这就可以避免最困难的举证责任,要去证明被告在误述时有不诚实的思想状态。除非欺诈性误述的受害方本意是想撤销合约,如果仅是想索赔损失,那么在目前的法律地位下,通过 S.2(1)的立法误述索赔损失是可以获得同样宽松的损失计算/核算。所以中国公司如果在伦敦、中国香港特区或新加坡仲裁,大可以在指称对方欺诈性误述外,再加上一个立法误述作为替代争议(alternative claim)。

虽然目前对这方面法律不满意,但想要推翻 Royscot Trust Ltd v. Rogerson 上诉庭先例只能是通过最高院或是英国议会修改 1967 年立法。这都不是容易事,也要等待机会。例如最高院就需要有针对这一问题的争议上诉,并有机会(例如双方当事人不会在审前庭外和解)去作出判决。而有了机会和条件,还需要最高院的多数大法官愿意与能够对 S.2(1)立法条文作出与 Royscot Trust Ltd v. Rogerson 先例不同的解释,毕竟最高院也同样必须按照议会立法的意图解释。当然也会有最高院大法官愿意偏离,理由就是该立法条文简短与不够清楚,为不同解释留有余地,这可节录 Steyn 勋爵在 Smith New Court Securities Ltd v. Scrimgeour Vickers(Asset Management)Ltd(1996)3 WLR 1051 贵族院先例说:"whether the rather loose wording of the statute compels the court to treat a person who was morally innocent as if he was guilty of fraud when it comes to the measure of damages."

现代误述的法律越来越复杂,不仅法律渊源来自普通法、衡平法与成文立法,而且还既涉及侵权责任又涉及合约的责任。根据本章的介绍,立法并没有完全达到其目的,甚至带来与普通法甚至常识之间矛盾冲突的地方。笔者认为如果对整个误述课题足够了解,那中国在完全没有历史包袱的情况下,完全可以订立一套全新的、更完整、更符合国际商业实际的立法。

4.3 立法误述的优越之处之二:举证责任

原告被误述方指控被告做出可诉误述,在"谁主张、谁举证"的原则下有举证责任。但在 S.2(1)的立法误述中,立法条文等于把举证责任转嫁给了误述方,在原告证明有一个虚假或不正确的事实陈述后,就轮到误述方证明该错误陈述有"合理依据"(reasonable ground)。只在误述方成功证明自己的错误陈述有合理依据时,才可避免以"拟制的欺诈"去计算损失赔偿。

该立法的本意是为了扩大非欺诈性(这包括无辜与疏忽)误述的救济,让没有合理依据误述(在本章之 4.1 段也解释了是相等于疏忽误述)的受害方/被误述方获得金钱损失的赔偿。而在以前衡平法下,受害方/被误述方只被给予了撤销合约的衡平救济,不会有金钱的赔偿。立法之 S.2(1)也说明误述方如果能够证明他/她有合理依据相信陈述是正确(had reasonable ground to believe... the facts represented were true)的则可免除赔偿损失责任。一般的疏忽误述没有"合理"依据,而无辜误述是有合理依据。这表示 S.2(1)开了门让非欺诈性误述也可以向误述方索赔损失只针对疏忽误述,不包括真正无辜的误述。

4.3.1 合理依据

陈述方要证明他有合理依据相信陈述为真，这应该是纯客观的考验（objective test）还是也有主观因素（subjective element）并不清楚，但看来应该是有一定的主观因素的。有关的考验不是广泛的合理人士会否相信陈述为真，而是特定的被告是否有合理依据相信陈述为真，所以要问的问题是，根据该陈述方的所有情况（陈述方知悉哪些信息，信息来源，陈述方的能力、水平、专业等），一位合理人士（审理法官或仲裁员）认为陈述方在当时理应了解事实到什么程度，才属于有合理依据。因此陈述方信息的来源与陈述方本身的水平都是相关的，例如一个普通人按照一篇科普文章做出错误陈述，可以认为是有合理依据。但如果是该领域的专家做出同样的错误陈述，就明显不会是有合理依据。正如 Atiyah 与 Treitel 教授在《Misrepresentation Act 1967》（1967）30 MLR 369 一文说："Thus the actual knowledge of the representor are relevant in determining whether he has satisfied the burden of proof under section 2(1)：a layman may succeed here where an expert would fail."

已经在本章之 4.2.2.5 段提到 S.2（1）立法时参考了《Directors Liability Act 1890》之 S.3。早在 Alman v. Oppert（1901）2 KB 576 先例中，上诉庭就判针对《Directors Liability Act 1890》之 S.3，公司董事声称自己有合理依据时，应该提供合理依据到底是什么与有关详情。显然普通股民与小股东对公司的了解与公司董事不可同日而语，所以他们指称公司董事在招股章程中误述时，让他们根据"谁主张，谁举证"证明公司董事做出有关陈述时是没有合理依据相信为是刁难行为。Collins 大法官说："In my opinion, having regard to the provisions of the Act, **particulars ought to be given by the defendants. The question is whether they had reasonable grounds for believing the statements in the prospectus to be true**. That being so, it would be very strange that the person whose business it will be to dispute the reasonableness of the grounds of belief should not be entitled to know beforehand what those grounds were. **A man who sets up as his defence that he believed a statement and had reasonable grounds for so doing can hardly say that it would be an intolerable burden to state the grounds of his belief, and I do not think it would be unfair to impose that burden on him**. I can quite understand that there may be difficulties in the way of stating the grounds of belief; but I do not think the task is insuperable...."（加黑部分是笔者的强调）

在 Adams v. Thrift（1915）2 Ch 21 先例中，一审法院与上诉庭都确认陈述方必须提供证据证明已经采取了行动，并使用可行的调查手段检查了陈述的真实性。在近期的立法《Financial Services and Markets Act 2000》之 Schedule 10 para. 1（2）也明确了进行合理调查的要求，认为："(2) A person does not incur any liability under section 90(1) for loss caused by a statement if he satisfies the court that, at the time when the listing particulars were submitted to the FCA, he reasonably believed (**having made such enquiries, if**

any, as were reasonable) that—(a) the statement was true and not misleading, or(b) the matter whose omission caused the loss was properly omitted, and that one or more of the conditions set out in sub-paragraph(3) are satisfied."(加黑是笔者的强调)

针对在该1967年立法之S.2(1)下,误述方能否满足合理依据的要求,显然相比招股书中的误述有更千变万化的情况。误述方到底是否有合理依据相信陈述为真,也要根据每个特定案件的案情而定,而要证明有合理依据的事实,就要有完整证据支持。此外,不同的审理法官/仲裁员虽然都要客观认定是否有合理依据,但毕竟每个人对某些特定情况合理与否的尺度会有差异,最终的结果会不肯定。尤其是在三位仲裁员组成的仲裁庭,在认定是否有合理依据时可能有不同看法,需要相互协调才会有一致的决定。

这也是为什么虽然有很多案件存在这方面的争议,如稍后会介绍的SK Shipping Plc v. Capital VLCC 3 Corp(2020)EWHC 3448(Comm)先例中,但专门针对这一点的研究不多,其中比较常被提到的案件是在本书第一章之2.2.4段详细介绍的Howard Marine and Dredging Co Ltd v. A Ogden & Sons(Excavations)Ltd(1978)QB 574上诉庭先例。在该先例中,O'Loughlin先生根据劳合社的记录做出的误述,按理来说应该可以满足合理依据的要求。但在上诉庭中,在这一点上Howard Marine以二比一败诉。多数意见认为O'Loughlin先生在交叉盘问中承认曾经看过该挖泥船的文件(如船舶蓝图、舱容图、载重量曲线、船级证书等),显示了船舶的载重量是1194.94吨与劳合社记录不符,所以O'Loughlin先生不查看船舶文件以核实而依据"间接"的劳合社记录向Ogden做出错误陈述谈不上有合理依据。

另在Cooper v. Tamms(1988)1 EGLR 257先例中,原告想买被告的公寓,在谈判期间原告拿到测量师一份有限的测量报告,说公寓有轻微的木材湿腐(wet rot)问题,如果没有卖方的担保就需要请专业团队检查,但也不可能看到地板下的情况。被告卖方因此减价500英镑。之后被告回答订约前询问时说她不知道公寓有任何湿腐问题。在双方完成交易后,原告发现地板下有严重的湿腐问题,于是以《Misrepresentation Act 1967》之S.2(1)下的误述与普通法下的疏忽起诉。PJ Crawford QC大法官判原告明知被告的陈述是错误的,故没有依赖被告的陈述,而是依赖的测量师报告与律师意见。此外PJ Crawford QC大法官的附带意见(obiter)说因为独立测量师给被告的意见是这个问题大概花500到600英镑可以修好,最好就是减价,而她也确实这么做了,所以被告也有合理依据相信她的陈述正确。

在中国香港特区的Li Kwok Heem John v. Standard Chartered International(USA) Ltd(2016)HKEC 7先例中,案情涉及原告在被告渣打银行的建议下购买了Fairfield Sentry Fund基金,但之后证明该基金是前纳斯达克主席Bernard Madoff经营的庞氏骗局之一。2008年骗局曝光后,原告血本无归,起诉被告渣打银行并索赔损失,其中包括以《失实陈述条例》(第254章)第3(1)条向被告在订约前对基金做出的误述索赔。法院同意银行对基金做出了误述,但该误述并非一个可诉误述,因为虽然被告渣打银行对原告客户有小心谨慎的责任，但银行没有疏忽或有合理依据相信陈述为真。银行分析了基金收益并与其他产品进行了对比，结论是该基金回报良好，但也没有到令人震惊的地步。银行的资深职员与基金公司的投资经理会面并讨论了基金的投资策略与操作。银行也审查了基金公司准备的尽职调查问卷答案与普华永道审计的该基金过去 12 年的财务报表。此外，尽管 Bernard Madoff 一般不与投资者会面，被告渣打银行会每六个月与 Bernard Madoff 进行一次会面，而直到 2008 年 4 月的最后一次会面，这些会面本身与银行之后跟进的查询都没有什么可疑之处。法院判被告银行已经以合理的谨慎与技术进行了尽职调查，没有发现有关基金是庞氏骗局不属于疏忽。法院在平衡的可能性下认定被告有合理依据相信并且直到骗局被发现前都确实相信有关陈述为真。

4.3.2　证明合理依据的举证责任在误述方

S.2(1)也规定了只要是有了误述(虚假的事实)而蒙受损失，即使是非欺诈性误述，也被推定为误述方如欺诈性误述一样要承担赔偿损失的责任。这表示误述方要抗拒赔偿损失的责任，就有举证责任去推翻这个法定推定(legal presumption)，[34]也就是证明他在做出误述时，有合理依据相信陈述的真实性。如果成功证明，就代表了误述是无辜。如果证明不了，就代表立法误述成立。这在上一段节录的 Collins 大法官在 Alman v. Oppert(1901)2 KB 576 先例中的判决(特别在加黑的部分)已是很清楚。在此节录《Chitty on Contracts》(2021 年，第 34 版)一书之 9 - 092 段说：“**Burden of proof** Once the representee proves that the statement was in fact false, the burden under the subsection shifts to the representor to prove that he had reasonable ground to believe and did believe up to the time the contract was made[35] that the facts represented were true. Where the negotiations for a contract have continued over a substantial time, and the misrepresentation was made some while before the contract was finally entered into, this burden may indeed prove a heavy one. It will not be sufficient for the representor to prove that he had reasonable grounds to believe the statement was true when made; he will have to go on to prove that he had reasonable grounds to believe and did believe the statement was true when the contract was made.”

这样，对受害方/被误述方带来以下几个好处：(1)这“合理依据”在先例看来很严格针对误述方。(2)一般民事诉讼的侵权是受害方/被误述方对误述方犯错(civil wrong)或疏忽的主张有举证责任，所谓的“谁主张，谁举证”。这法定的举证责任在部分误述争议案件会是容易，因为事实摆在眼前[36]就是欺诈/欺骗。但也有不少复杂与有漫长谈判过程的商业案件，受害方去证明误述方有疏忽误述[这会先要证明双方有“特殊关系”(special relationship)，带来“小心谨慎责任”(duty of care)]会是不容易，更

---

〔34〕 见笔者《证据法：基础理论、口头证据与专家证据》一书第七章之 6 段。

〔35〕 这就是在本书第二章之 8 段介绍的持续性的陈述。

〔36〕 见笔者《证据法：基础理论、口头证据与专家证据》一书第七章之 6.2 段。

不用说是证明欺诈性误述。例如在一个公司并购的交易中,显示有虚假或不正确的事实会是不难,但进一步证明被告在做出误述时是欺诈性与/或疏忽就十分困难。除了会面对被告自我保护(self - serving)或被隐瞒(如 CCTV 记录被销毁)的文件证据外,也需要依赖大量口头证据去说明双方在漫长谈判中的言行证明直到订约前该陈述仍是虚假(变为虚假或没有改正),也往往会遇上西方公司精明与懂法律的当事人能在交叉盘问时掌握好轻重。但在《Misrepresentation Act 1967》之 S. 2(1)的立法误述下,受害方/被误述方的困难就得以大程度解决。(3)再就是可以看到在先例中很少有被告会根据 S. 2(1)中提到的合理依据的例外作为抗辩,笔者觉得这原因也很容易想得到,就是大部分的误述从表面来看陈述方都是有刻意做出误述的味道。但是对于被误述方来说,要证明这种刻意并不容易。但是如果根据 S. 2(1)起诉,就会将这举证不足的风险大大降低,而将证明有合理依据的责任转移到误述方,而误述方在一看上去就是刻意欺骗的事实背景下甚至都不敢去提合理依据的问题:见 Royscot Trust Ltd v. Rogerson(1991)2 QB 297 先例。

4.3.3 中国公司应该多利用立法误述的优越性

笔者感觉在处理的仲裁案件中,经常见到中国公司只提出欺诈性误述的指控,即使证据完全不足。毕竟要构成欺诈性误述,必须证明误述方的思想状态是不诚实,也就是要满足 Derry v. Peek(1889)14 App Cas 337 贵族院先例设立的三种或严格来说是两种标准。如果是真的认为对方欺诈性误述,在文书请求(pleading)/案件陈述(statement of case)阶段就必须非常注意,要满足在本书第三章之 9 段的所有要求,包含构成误述要件的事实详情与相应的证据,特别是最困难的证明误述方做出误述时的思想状态的证据。

但即使是认为自己有足够的证据去支持对方欺诈性误述的主张,为了保险也应该同时根据中国香港特区《失实陈述条例》(第 254 章)第 3(1)条作为替代诉因(alternative case)主张损失赔偿。已经介绍过,根据该立法条文,举证责任就从作为受害方的中国公司转移到被指控做出误述的对方,后者必须举证证明自己有合理依据相信自己做出的陈述为真。

也已经提到过,如果能成功证明立法误述,损失计算是类似欺诈性误述宽松对待。虽然中国香港特区法院不受 Royscot Trust Ltd v. Rogerson(1991)2 QB 297 上诉庭先例的约束,该先例只是有说服力,但是中国香港特区《失实陈述条例》(第 254 章)第 3(1)条的文字与英国《Misrepresentation Act 1967》中 s. 2(1)文字完全一样,相信中国香港法院不会偏离。

但在笔者的经验中,中国公司虽然常有仲裁案件涉及误述的争议,但很少有提出与依赖《失实陈述条例》的立法误述。如果原告在指控欺诈性误述的同时,主张被告在第 3(1)条文下构成立法误述作为替代,胜诉机会就大得多。虽然被告有可能主张他做出的误述是有合理依据,但这可能不被仲裁庭接受为“合理”。

4.4 S.2(1)立法误述只适用在误述导致合约产生的情况

疏忽误述可以发生在很多并不涉及合约产生的情况,例如合约已经订立,双方履行合约时交流互动的情况下错误陈述信息与事实。也可以是如著名的 Hedley Byrne v. Heller(1964) AC 465 贵族院先例[37]一样,如果普通法不去强加双方一个特殊关系并带来小心谨慎责任,被告错误提供信息与事实就不会对原告有责任。这种类别的疏忽误述不是导致合约产生的可诉误述,前者例子只是带来违约责任,后者 Hedley Byrne 先例只是侵权关系下违反小心谨慎责任。

而 S.2(1)的立法条文说明只适用误述导致合约产生的情况,可节录其中有关的一句话:"Where a person **has entered into a contract after a misrepresentation** has been made to him by another party thereto and as a result thereof he has suffered loss ..."(加黑部分是笔者的强调)

所以在 William Sindall Plc v. Cambridgeshire CC(1994)1 WLR 1016 上诉庭先例中,Hoffmann 大法官说:"First, section 2(1) provides for damages to be awarded to a person who 'has entered into a contract after a misrepresentation has been made to him by another party and as a result thereof'—sc of having entered into the contract—'he has suffered loss'. In contrast, section 2(2) speaks of 'the loss which would be caused by it'—sc the misrepresentation—'if the contract were upheld'. **In my view, section 2(1) is concerned with the damage flowing from having entered into the contract ...**."(加黑部分是笔者的强调)

另在本书第二章之 10.4.2 段详细介绍的 Leofelis SA v. Lonsdale Sports Ltd(2008) EWCA Civ 640 上诉庭先例中,Lloyd 大法官说:"... it seems to me that ... damages under s.2(1) of the 1967 Act are not recoverable in respect of a misrepresentation which is made in a contract, as distinct from one which is made before the contract is entered into."

在 Taberna Europe CDO II Plc v Selskabet AF1(2016) EWCA Civ 1262 上诉庭先例中,案情涉及原告 Taberna 是一家在爱尔兰成立的投资公司,名下掌管不同金融产品的投资组合。被告在 2008 年金融海啸之前名为 Rosklide,是一家成功的丹麦银行。因有融资的需要,Rosklide 于 2006 年发行了票面价值 8000 万欧元的次级债券给美林银行,债券 2014 年到期。美林银行又进一步将债券在二级市场发售。Taberna 在 2008 年 2 月从德意志银行手中购买了其中票面值 2700 万欧元的次级债券。随着 2008 年金融海啸的爆发,Rosklide 的经济恶化,Rosklide 将名下除了次级债券部分的资产与债务转去另外一家新的银行(也就是本案的被告)后,最终于 2009 年 2 月进入破产程序。

Taberna 认为自己持有的次级债券作为债务留在进入破产程序的 Rosklide,最后很可能是血本无归,于是想将该新的银行作为索赔对象,因为相信新银行接收了不少 Rosklide 名下优良的资产。在这种转移索赔对象的策略下,Taberna 不主张自己在次级

[37] 见本书第一章之 2.2.1 段的详细介绍。

债券下的债权,而是声称自己是看到 Rosklide 在网站上发布给投资者的对该笔次级债券的介绍并依赖其中陈述的信息后才购买了该笔次级债券。在该网站介绍中,Rosklide 对其持有的未还款的贷款金额做出错误陈述,将实际上是 35 亿丹麦克朗的未还款贷款虚报为仅有 5700 万丹麦克朗。该陈述构成欺诈性或疏忽误述,而因误述带来的侵权责任与损失赔偿不应划归于次级债券的部分留在 Rosklide,而是应该根据资产与债务转移的安排被转入新银行的名下。

一审法院的 Eder 大法官判 Taberna 胜诉,支持了 Rosklide 在网站上发布的给投资者的介绍中误述,而 Taberna 也依赖了该误述。Taberna 主张根据《Misrepresentation Act 1967》之 S.2(1)去索赔也被 Eder 大法官支持,他认为该立法条文也适用在误述方是合约方(Taberna 与德意志银行的买卖合约)以外的第三方(Rosklide)的情况。

但去了上诉庭,Eder 大法官有关 S.2(1)的适用的判决被推翻,Moore - Bick 大法官澄清 S.2(1)仅适用在误述方与被误述方均为合约方,且被误述方是在依赖误述方的误述才订约的情况,说:"In my view, the background to the legislation and the language of section 2(1) itself read in the context of section 2(2) point to the conclusion that it is concerned only with representations made by a person who enters into a contract with the representee and with losses arising as a result of entering into that contract. ... For all these reasons I have reached the clear conclusion that section 2(1) of the 1967 Act entitles the representee to recover only such damages as flow from his having entered into a contract with the representor."

4.5 对 S.2(1)的总结

S.2(1)立法条文的很多其他措辞/文字都没有给定义与解释,这是因为它只对普通法的非欺诈性误述/无辜误述作出改变,并不是对普通法下所有针对误述的方方面面都有了改变。正如在 Andre v. Ets Michel Blanc(1979)2 Lloyd's Rep 427 上诉庭先例中,Geoffrey Lane 大法官说:"it is plain from the title to the Act that it is an Act to amend the law relating to innocent misrepresentation ... So it seems to be based upon the assumption that the common law rules shall be the foundation of the amendments which the Act proposes."

这表示本书所针对的普通法下有关误述这个大课题的方方面面的细节,只要与 1967 年立法没有矛盾,仍继续适用。例如,何谓"误述"、陈述的信息与事实必须是虚假与不正确、误述的时间与持续性误述等。例如在疏忽侵权(或合约规定有相同的责任)中,被告可以《Civil Liability(Contribution)Act 1978》去要求与原告分摊责任与损失,这在 S.2(1)的损失赔偿也同样适用。在 Gran Gelato Ltd v. Richcliff(Group)Ltd(1992) Ch 560 先例中,Donald Nicholls VC 大法官说:"liability under the Misrepresentation Act 1967 is essentially founded on negligence ... This being so, it would be very odd if the defence of contributory negligence were not available to a claim based on a breach of a duty to take care in and about the making of a particular representation, but not available to a claim for damages under the Act in respect of the same representation."

至于误述是一个虚假事实,这毫无疑问是1967年立法所针对的,因为在S.2(1)的最后几个字是"... the facts represented were true"。但这一表述遭到批评,因为这个立法定义相比千变万化的误述太局限,是否包括意图(intention)、意见(opinion)或法律(law)的误述并不肯定。毕竟,在有立法的情况下,法院只能去解释与依从。而解释立法条文好像解释合约条文一样,必须忠于立法意图如同订约意图。而1967年立法时,普通法针对误述案件主要针对的的确是过去或现在的事实(past or existing facts)。对虚假的将来意图[38]或意见[39]会在特定的案件/案情下(例如双方对有关事实的了解是一面倒,受害方必须信赖误述方的意图或意见等)可以构成误述,或错误法律的表述[40]可以构成误述[Kleinwort Benson Ltd v. Lincoln City Council & Ors (1999) 2 AC 349 贵族院先例带来变化]等,都是1967年立法后发展起来的。而1967年立法时,商业社会相比今天也相对简单。

介绍这方面的不肯定可先节录《Misrepresentation, Mistake and Non-Disclosure》(2022年,第6版)一书之7-11至7-12段说:

"**Representation of fact**? ... In the tort of deceit, fraudulent misrepresentations of intention, law and opinion are actionable; it might be thought that all such misrepresentations are therefore within the scope of s.2(1) ... one might expect the section to be limited to misrepresentation of fact. This is not simply because there would otherwise be a much wider liability for misrepresentations of opinion and intention which would, in effect, involve ascribing to the word 'misrepresentation' a meaning which it does not generally bear at common law; but also **because the language of the section itself shows that the draftsman had in mind the restricted meaning of 'misrepresentation', as a misrepresentation of fact. The closing words of the section** refer to the defendant proving that he believed, on reasonable grounds, 'that the facts represented were true', and this makes sense only if the actionable representations for the purposes of the section are restricted to representation of fact.

Representation of law ... the courts(主要是指 Kleinwort Benson Ltd v. Lincoln City Council & Ors 贵族院先例与之后依从的先例) have now abandoned the formal distinction between misrepresentations of law and misrepresentations of fact, and in Pankhania v. Hackney LBC (2002) EWHC 2441 (Ch), the judge held that, in light of these general developments, a misrepresentation of law is now sufficient to form the basis of a claim for damages under s.2(1) of the Misrepresentation Act 1967. **This decision sits somewhat uncomforta-**

---

[38] 见本书第二章之5段。

[39] 见本书第二章之2段。

[40] 见本书第二章之6段。

bly with closing words of the subsection..."(加黑部分是笔者的强调)

上述节录的第一段还可以稍多介绍以利理解。欺诈性误述除了包括过去与现在的事实外,也包括误述方对意图、意见与法律的虚假表述。这是因为欺诈/欺骗的重点是在证明误述方在陈述/表述时,并不真诚相信陈述/表述是正确的(absence of an honest belief in the truth of that which has been stated)。正如在 Derry v. Peek(1889)14 App Cas 337 贵族院先例中,判决是对被告(公司董事)的欺诈性误述指控败诉,因为 Herschell 勋爵认定"they honestly believed that what they asserted was true"。

但针对非欺诈性误述的 1967 年立法之 S.2(1)条文是无法去等同解释为包括对意图或意见的虚假陈述/表述,因为这会把门开得太宽,远超出普通法目前会把意图或意见的虚假陈述/表述局限在本书第二章之 3.3 段介绍的"陈述方与被陈述方有非一般的关系""对比下陈述方与被陈述方的水平、经验或对事实的了解""证明陈述方陈述/表述将来意图或预期事实时想法不诚实""对将来意图或预期事实的表述言行被解释为对现在事实的陈述"等特定情况。显然,S.2(1)立法条文是没有也不可能解释为这么细致。而如果真的在立法加上"意图"与"意见"字样,而不去加上细致的局限(面对千变万化的情况也很难做到),就打开了泄洪阀(floodgate)。

这方面的不肯定也反映在 Avon Insurance Plc v. Swire Fraser Ltd(2000)Lloyd's Rep IR 535 先例中,Rix 大法官说:"... in 1967 the Misrepresentation Act extended a right to damages under section 2(1) in the case of any misrepresentation inducing a contract made by one party to another party to it where the representor is unable to prove absence of negligence or bad faith. ... for promissory representations or representations as to the future are harder to fit within the scope of the Act, which has been interpreted as applying to the classic representation of present or past fact, as distinct from representations as to the future and statements of opinion, expectation, intention or law. ..."

但如果意见来自只有他才会知道的事实,这意见可解释为是一个对事实的"默示陈述"(implied representation)。这在 Lancaster City Council v. Unique Group Ltd(unreported, 15 December 1995); Inntrepreneur Pub Company and Ors v. D. Sweeney(2002) EWHC 1060(Ch); Springwell v. JP Morgan(2010)EWCA Civ 1221 等先例中,都认为这种意见表述可以构成 1967 年立法 S.2(1)下的立法误述。

在 Inntrepreneur Pub Company and Ors v. D. Sweeney 先例中,Park 大法官说:"Sometimes an expression of opinion may carry with it no implication other than that the opinion is genuinely held.[41] But on other occasions, as in this case, the circumstances may be such as to give rise to the implied representation that the person knew of facts which justified his opinion. In such a case I see no reason why the representee should not rely upon s.2(1)."

〔41〕 见著名的 Edgington v. Fitzmaurice(1885)29 Ch D.459 上诉庭先例。

在 Springwell v. JP Morgan 上诉庭先例中,Aikens 大法官说:"Therefore, because the Misrepresentation Act 1967 is concerned with representations of fact, not opinion, in respect of the Misrepresentation Act claim ... Mr Brindle(原告被陈述方代表大律师)had to argue before the judge that each time JA(被告银行雇员)gave an opinion on the nature of ..., it carried with it an implied statement of fact by JA that he had reasonable grounds for holding that opinion."

5. 立法条文 S.2(2)的分析

面对复杂的误述课题,《Misrepresentation Act 1967》之 S.2(2)简短的立法条文又是看来很不足。在接下来的段节会介绍几个至今仍难拆解的重大疑点。

5.1 撤销合约是否为"自助救济"

在 TSB Bank Plc v. Camfield(1995)1 WLR 430 上诉庭先例中,Nourse 大法官说:"the right to set aside or rescind the transaction is that of the representee, not that of the court."而在选择撤销合约的做法上是去给误述方一个清楚无误的通知(notice),正如 Denning 勋爵在 Car and Universal Finance Ltd v. Caldwell(1965)1 QB 525 上诉庭先例说:"by an unequivocal act of election(被误述方作出)which demonstrates clearly that he elects to rescind(有关误述的合约)and to be no longer bound by it."

这显示了在误述导致一个可使无效的合约产生时,受害方/被误述方选择撤销该合约的救济在本质上是自助救济,除了给误述方通知外,无须法院(或仲裁庭)的命令。也就是说欺诈性误述在普通法下无须法院(或仲裁庭)命令,反正法院是无权去剥夺受害方在一个可使无效合约中行使撤销合约权利的,法院命令也只是走个形式,没有实质意义。

但因为有否定的机制,特别是撤销一个已经是部分或全部履行了的合约就必定会涉及复原/反复原(restitution / counter restitution)的问题,会需要法院去决定。而在衡平救济下,法院也会加上条件,正如 Nourse 大法官在 Killick v. Roberts(1991)1 WLR 1146 上诉庭先例说:"an equitable remedy ... sometimes granted only on terms."但因为衡平法有广泛的裁量权与重视公平合理,所以如果受害方已经在开始诉讼前"自助"撤销,除非误述的指控不成立或涉及第三人利益,且完全没有其他办法补救,否则一般不会没有办法去调整复原/反复原而需要判不可以撤销,令已经撤销合约的受害方变成违约/毁约。所以在实际上衡平法救济是否"自助"的争议在实际上也没有影响受害方"自助"撤销合约。这可节录在《Chitty on Contracts》(2021 年,第 34 版)一书之 9-128 段的脚注 597:"Rescission was available for fraud at common law, but subject to precise restitution being available. It seems likely that a court order is not necessary even when the party rescinding is relying on the wider equitable notion of rescission(这是指依赖衡平救济去撤销合约的非欺诈性误述)that would,for example,allow the defrauded party to rescind even though they are not able to restore the property in its original condition and would have to make an allowance for depreciation;it is thought that a notice of rescission coupled with an offer of an appropriate amount,or even stating a willingness to make an allowance,would effect rescission..."

非欺诈性误述有了 1967 年立法之 S.2 进行规定,但 S.2(2)认可受害方的自助救济的同时,认为法院或仲裁庭有权在损失赔偿与撤销合约之间二选一,决定以损失赔偿替代撤销合约:"... the court or arbitrator may declare the contract subsisting and award damages in lieu of rescission."

有内部矛盾(internal inconsistency)的立法条文没有澄清,如果有关合约早已经是被受害方自助撤销(实际也通常是如此),那么法院在审理后作出判决时会否失去这立法赋予的选择什么救济的权力?这个疑问会稍后针对。

虽然 1967 年立法没有说清楚立法针对的"撤销合约"到底是基于普通法的自助撤销还是衡平法的由法院行使裁量权,但在 S.2(2)立法条文的措辞/用字"or has been rescinded",也显示在法院审理案件后最后决定以损失赔偿替代(in lieu of)撤销合约时,该合约可以早已被受害方/被陈述方撤销。可见,1967 年立法是无意改变这普通法下自助救济的权利。正如在《Chitty on Contracts》(2021 年,第 34 版)一书之 9 - 128 段,说:"**Court order not required** Although it is common to speak of a court 'setting aside' or rescinding a contract for misrepresentation,a court order is not necessary when a contract is rescinded for fraud. In cases of non-fraudulent misrepresentation the balance of authority suggests that the remedy is not necessarily a judicial one ... the wording of s.2(2)of the Misrepresentation Act 1967,'if it is claimed ... that the contract ought to be **or has been rescinded**' would seem inappropriate a court order is required. ... In other words,a representee is entitled to rescind for misrepresentation **without invoking the assistance of the court at all.**"(加黑部分是笔者的强调)

虽然有了 1967 年立法,但仍可以说针对误述,即使是非欺诈性的可诉误述,一般的救济仍主要是撤销合约。正如在 Salt v. Stratstone Specialist Ltd(2015)EWCA Civ 745 上诉庭先例中,Longmore 大法官说:"it still remains a general proposition that the remedy for misrepresentation is rescission of the contract."

5.2 立法 S.2(2):法院可否定撤销合约救济以损失赔偿替代的立法原因与带来的问题

但注意《Misrepresentation Act 1967》立法生效后,上一小段介绍的法律地位在针对非欺诈性误述在衡平法下撤销合约方面有了巨大的变化。这个重要的改变在本章之 1 段已有略及,在此进一步详论并介绍该 1967 年立法所带来的问题。为了方便阅读,可重复节录有关的 S.2(2)并加黑重点如下:"Where a person has entered into a contract after a misrepresentation has been made to him otherwise than fraudulent,and **he would be**

entitled, by reason of the misrepresentation, to rescind the contract, then, if it is claimed, in any proceedings arising out of the contract, that the contract ought to be or has been rescinded, **the court or arbitrator may declare the contract subsisting and award damages in lieu of rescission, if of opinion that it would be equitable to do so**, having regard to the nature of the misrepresentation and the loss that would be caused by it if the contract were upheld, as well as the loss that rescission would cause to the other party"（加黑部分是笔者的强调）

在立法 S. 2(2)的措辞下，应会是法院（或仲裁庭）不再允许受害方/被误述方去取巧。在误述很轻微（当然也会在不同案件是很严重），即只有极小的诱导或影响导致合约的产生的情况下，如果一视同仁可去撤销合约，不论误述是欺诈、疏忽或是无辜，往往带来不公道。毕竟有很多的撤销合约是基于订约后市场逆转，受害方发觉履行下去对自己不利，或是发觉自己错误去订了一个亏本的合约，想利用误述去脱身。在 William Sindall Plc v. Cambridgeshire CC(1994)1 WLR 1016 上诉庭先例中，Evans 大法官说让受害方脱身是不公平的，这是立法不想见到的："The starting point for the application of the sub – section is the situation where a plaintiff has established right to rescind the contract on grounds of innocent misrepresentation：its objection is to ameliorate for the innocent misrepresentor the harsh consequences of rescission for a wholly innocent … misrepresentor, in a case where it is fairer to uphold the contract and award damages against him."

所以，S. 2(2)立法条文与 S. 2(1)不同，它主要是去保护误述方（特别是疏忽但实是轻微与真正无辜的误述），让法院（或仲裁庭）有裁量权剥夺受害方在衡平法下撤销合约的救济。这可见 S. 2(2)所依据的 Tenth Report of the Law Reform Committee (1962)Cmnd. 1782 立法报告之 11 至 12 段（本章稍后的 5.4.2 段有节录）。

但 S. 2(2)没有针对如何协调普通法/衡平法下受害方实际"自助"撤销合约给出任何指引。例如，如果受害方一旦发觉误述马上撤销合约，而在后来的诉讼中，被认定无法满足对欺诈性误述的举证责任，而只是成立一个立法误述。但由于已经撤销了合约，法院（仲裁庭）在实质上已经没法选择了，这种情况下该怎么办？毕竟，在很多情况下感觉不妥或较严重误述的受害方是需要尽快行动以保护自己的。这会包括在本书第三章之 6.3 段介绍的在买卖合约阻止货物产权转让给无辜第三人（good faith third parties），第三章之 6.2 段介绍的必须在可能是短暂的合理时间内选择是撤销合约或是不撤销等。

以上述介绍的情况，受害方一旦发觉误述（即使是相对轻微）马上撤销合约后，才启动诉讼索赔损失，诉因只是以普通法的欺诈侵权与/或 1967 年立法之 S. 2(1)。这样，只要被告误述方不能满足证明错误陈述是有合理依据的，就可能获得以欺诈侵权计算的损失赔偿。如此，岂非不必是欺诈性误述而是根据 1967 年立法，也可以撤销合约后同时索赔损失。报道不详的较早期 F&H Entertainments Ltd v. Leisure Enterprises Ltd (1976)120 SJ 331 先例中，看来就是一个两种救济都获得的案例。该先例涉及原告在被告说业主不涨租金的误述下从被告那里接手了一个房屋的租约,并花费 4000 英镑对该房屋进行装修与配备设施。后来,原告发现业主曾经发出过涨租通知给被告,于是原告从房屋中搬走,向被告主张撤销合约与根据 1967 年立法之 s. 2 索赔装修带来的花费,两个主张均得到支持。Walton 大法官说:"On the question of damages ... no case had been made out that the defendants had reasonable grounds to believe that the representation was true and they did not, therefore, come within the proviso to section 2 of the Misrepresentation Act 1967. ... **So the measure of damages under section 2 was clearly the same as in an action for damages for deceit**. ... The proper measure of damages covered all expenditure properly and not prematurely or extravagantly incurred."(加黑部分是笔者的强调)

要重申 1967 年立法的本意是不允许受害方取巧,减少目前太多与太轻易撤销合约的情况,所以 S. 2(2)立法条文赋予法院或仲裁庭在撤销合约与损失赔偿两种救济中二选一的权力。而既然受害方在 S. 2(1)下可以获得两种救济,是否要误述方在诉讼的抗辩与反索赔请求中提出 S. 2(2),才会成为一个争端(issue)并让法院或仲裁庭去考虑?特别是在 SK Shipping Plc v. Capital VLCC 3 Corp (2020) EWHC 3448 (Comm)先例(稍后介绍)中,绝大部分受害方较早前撤销合约的决定会因为有关误述本质上不会影响合约的根基(go to the root of contract)而被法院或仲裁庭在 S. 2(2)下否定,导致受害方较早前的撤销合约从合法撤销变为是拒绝履行合约。这样,会否 1967 年立法令非欺诈性误述的受害方在实际做法上不再可以自助撤销?

看来,1967 年立法的简单处理在面对现实社会(特别是复杂的国际商业社会)出现的千变万化的情况,以及与已有悠长历史的普通法与衡平法协调时,严重不足。

至于在另一个撤销合约外的救济,就是受害方损失的索赔中,可总结在 1967 年立法下,非欺诈性误述的"疏忽误述"(或无法满足有合理依据的"立法误述"),受害方肯定在 S. 2(1)下有权索赔损失(as of right),也是以欺诈性误述的损失计算为准。但在 S. 2(2)下,无论是疏忽误述或真正无辜误述,受害方想去撤销合约就要说服法院(或仲裁庭)接受这是在该案件/案情下公平合理的做法的说法。但这不容易成功,这带来的结果是疏忽误述仍在 S. 2(1)下可以索赔损失,但真正无辜误述就只能依赖在 S. 2(2)下法院(或仲裁庭)行使裁量权以损失赔偿替代撤销合约的救济。这可节录《Chitty on Contracts》(2021 年,第 34 版)一书之 9 - 113 段:"... In the case of a negligent misrepresentation, the representee can claim both rescission and damages, but whereas his claim to damages under s. 2(1) is as of right, his claim to rescission is now subject to the discretion of the court under s. 2(2). But in the case of an innocent misrepresentation, the representee cannot get both rescission and damages, nor can he claim either remedy as of right."

但毕竟这是真正无辜的误述,法院会怎样决定这"立法损失赔偿"?显然这不会以 S. 2(1)的"拟制的欺诈"的损失计算,以疏忽侵权的损失计算办法也说不通,真正无辜与疏忽侵权是扯不上关系的。会否法院只会在很极端的案件中才会给予真正无辜误述的受害方损失赔偿，一般只是能获得赔偿范围比损失窄的补偿（indemnity），甚至是名义损失（nominal damages）[42]？

至于疏忽误述或没有合理依据的立法误述，会否在S.2(1)有权以欺诈侵权索赔宽松计算的损失，在S.2(2)下只会是一面倒吃亏？受害方只会被法院或仲裁庭否定撤销合约权利，而因为在S.2(1)已经索赔了所有损失，所以作为替代撤销的立法损失根本是不是不会有一分钱？因为S.2(3)也说了："Damages may be awarded against a person under subsection(2) of this section whether or not he is liable to damages under subsection(1) thereof, but where he is so liable any award under the said subsection(2) shall be taken into account in assessing his liability under the said subsection(1)."

所以疏忽误述或立法误述的受害方为了获得两种救济看来最好就是先撤销合约，然后在法院（或仲裁庭）以S.2(1)索赔损失，完全不提S.2(2)。如果误述方不懂，也不提S.2(2)，这就不会是一个需要法院（或仲裁庭）决定的争端。但是也要警惕，这是假设对方不懂甚至缺席，正常情况下只要对方提出S.2(2)的争议，就有可能被法院或仲裁庭判应以损失赔偿替代撤销合约，此时较早的撤销就会变为违约/毁约。

另在S.2(2)立法条文下所说的损失是以法院（或仲裁庭）行使裁量权替代撤销合约的权利所导致的损失，还是该无辜误述直接导致的损失？另外，是否应以违约或侵权去计算此立法损失？

最后S.2(2)立法条文带来的问题是，既然损失赔偿是作为替代（in lieu of），这样如果撤销合约的权利被其他原因否定（如无法复原、时隔太久、免责条文等），[43]会否再也没有什么好去替代或需要替代？这个疑问在一审先例中一直有矛盾，直到近期才看到主流的判法。

接下来的段节会进一步探讨上述介绍的S.2(2)立法条文的三个重大疑点或立法本身的内部矛盾。

---

〔42〕 在近期的Ceviz v. Frawley(2021) EWHC 8(Ch)先例中，Keyser QC大法官说："... it confers a power on the court that can be exercised if the court considers it equitable to do so. I should have considered it equitable to uphold the Agreement. I should also **have considered that nominal damages would suffice. There is nothing in section 2(2) to require that damages awarded in lieu of rescission be substantial**; of course, in most cases they will be, but I cannot see that it is axiomatic that they must be. As I have observed, the defendants' pleaded case on misrepresentation does not justify the conclusion than they are in any materially different position from that in which they expected to be. The court is directed to have regard to 'the loss that would be caused by [the misrepresentation] if the contract were upheld'. But(a) any 'loss' to the defendants would be caused not by the misrepresentation but by their inability ..."（加黑部分是笔者的强调）

〔43〕 见本书第三章之5至8段。

5.3 立法 S.2(2)带来的疑点之一:受害方撤销合约后,法院可否否定撤销令合约重生

这立法条文与一直以来误述可以自助撤销合约的实际做法的关系没有说得太清楚。立法可去超越普通法与衡平法地位是没有疑问,但正如合约明示条文(express clause)清楚无误才可去超越默示条文(implied clause)的道理一样,立法也必须清楚无误。但 S.2(2)谈不上是清楚无误地剥夺了被误述方自己撤销合约的权利,或与立法给予法院裁量权去决定以损失赔偿替代(in lieu of)撤销合约之间如何协调。所以有疑问的是,如受害方撤销合约后,法院根据立法之 S.2(2)的裁量权去否定撤销合约的救济而以金钱赔偿替代,那这较早的撤销会怎样看待,会否是拒绝履行合约的违约/毁约?这方面稍后去分析并介绍近期的 SK Shipping Plc v. Capital VLCC 3 Corp (2020) EWHC 3448(Comm)先例一审给了一个解答,但上诉庭[(2022) EWCA Civ 231]看来并不认同。

在法院行使裁量权否决撤销合约权利并以损失赔偿代替时,轻微的误述是不会导致太高的金钱赔偿的。但这也带来另一个疑问,就是无辜方一旦发觉误述(无辜或疏忽)就马上去撤销合约,毕竟如果拖太久可能会构成弃权(waiver);接下来处理诉讼需要时间,如果最后虽然法院(或仲裁庭)认为误述相对轻微,但当时合约已经被撤销,还能否选择以金钱赔偿误述带来有限的损失去替代早已经发生了的撤销合约?这在 The"Lucy"(1983)1 Lloyd's Rep 188 先例中,Mustill 大法官说:"there are some formidable difficulties in the practical application of this discretion to a case where the court is not asked to order rescission as a direct and immediate remedy, but is invited to validate a rescission which has already been effected as a measure of self-help. ... It seems to me that in such a case the words 'or has been rescinded' in s.2(2) must be read as entitling the Court to annul retrospectively a rescission which has taken place in the past, and to compel the injured party to accept damages in lieu. ..."

5.3.1 The"Lucy"(1983)1 Lloyd's Rep 188 先例

在 The"Lucy"先例中,船舶被期租 3 年。在谈判时,双方说明条文按照原租约(head charter party)条文。明显是,在此先例的船东实是二船东(disponent owner),他会尽量去将分租约(sub-charter party)内容与原租约(二船东跟原船东订的)背靠背保持一致,以免夹在当中。二船东也确实送了一份原租约给承租人,作为谈判基础。但在船舶允许的航区(trading limit)方面,二船东实际上与原船东另有了追加协议,允许的航区实际比原租约看到的要窄,但二船东忘了告诉承租人这件小事。结果这分租约在航区上虽然订得与原租约基本上是一样,但还是有出入。

在顺利营运 9 个月后,运费市场大跌。看来承租人就想取巧,也不知是真是假,说当时才发觉有这个对航区的误述,并要去行使权利撤销这份分租约。但最后双方总算没有过分反应,同意这分租约仍继续履行,然后在"无损害"(without prejudice)基础下尽快去诉讼,看有否一个可诉误述与承租人可否去撤销分租约。一般这种过

渡性协议会约定如果判决是可去撤销,则从分租约订立或无损害协议那天(这反正是订约自由)开始,租金调低至市场租金,当作是原来的分租约被撤销,并以一份按照市场租金的新分租约替代。而如果法院判不能撤销,原租约不变,仍是照原来租金支付去继续履行。这种赌博,肯定是对承租人有百利而无一害。

在高院,Mustill 大法官判是:(1)二船东给承租人一份原租约,却没有同时说明对航区的另外协议,这等于是对信息与事实"讲一半、不讲另一半",[44]构成可诉误述。即使这是非欺诈性的误述,承租人在衡平法下也可去撤销分租约。(2)如果可去撤销合约,这分租约已被履行了9个月并没有重大关系。只要承租人一旦发现误述并尽快行动,这撤销的权利就不会失去。(3)但在此先例中,这航区的差别很小,证据看来承租人在订立租约后进行营运时根本不关心。这航区的差别也不会造成与当时同意的每天租金有所差别。(4)即使有较小(trivial)的依赖,在立法 S.2(2)条文下法院仍有权以赔偿损失(在本案应是没有实质损失,所以只能是名义损失)来替代撤销合约。

在此先例中,Mustill 大法官也指出了 S.2(2)不好处理之处。因为虽然审理法官或仲裁员有此法定裁量权去决定以赔偿损失替代撤销合约,也可以在此先例中以此裁量权主持公道,不让承租人在市场不利时取巧撤销分租约,但这是因为有此"无损害"过渡性的安排。要是没有,承租人一旦发现误述已在第一时间把分租约撤销。这样,后来的诉讼审理法官应怎样办?难道判承租人败诉,指他不应该撤销,要赔偿二船东被提前终止分租约的损失?但毕竟,承租人是误述的受害方,二船东才是误述方;或可试图把已发生的撤销合约判是无效,让"时光倒流"令分租约"重生"。但如果相隔时间已久,甚至可能"Lucy"轮已沉没。这方方面面的疑点在近期的 SK Shipping Plc v. Capital VLCC 3 Corp(2020)EWHC 3448(Comm)先例中给了一个解答,但上诉庭[(2022) EWCA Civ 231]看来并不认同,等于还没有解答。

这困难在南澳大利亚的立法《Misrepresentation Act 1972》之 section 7(5)已有刻意针对,其在同样的立法条文中多加了一句说:"where a contract has been rescinded but is subsequently declared to be subsisting under section(3),the respective rights and liabilities of the contracting parties will be determined in all respects as if the contract had never been rescinded."但这有否解决问题,就不去深究了。

5.3.2　SK Shipping Plc v. Capital VLCC 3 Corp(2022)EWCA Civ 231 上诉庭先例

在近期的 SK Shipping Plc v. Capital VLCC 3 Corp 先例中,案情涉及十分常见的航运争议,对此在本书第二章之10.5.2段有详细介绍。原告船东在2016年11月在市场上放出"C Challenger"轮的信息(其中包括对承租人十分重要的船速与油耗)以寻求长期租约。在2016年12月,被告承租人与船东订立了两年的期租合约,标准合

---

〔44〕 见本书第二章之9段。

约中包括一条油耗保证(bunker consumption warranty)。船东在2017年2月交船,在履行租约期间船舶油耗超过了租约中的保证。承租人从2017年3月开始向船东投诉对油耗的误述。虽然承租人不断重复这个指控,并且从2017年6月起不再支付租金,但它还是一直继续履行租约并向船长作出营运命令。到了2017年10月,承租人通知船东决定以误述撤销合约或以违反油耗保证构成违约/毁约终止合约。而船东认为承租人的通知构成拒绝履行(repudiatory breach)合约,船东接受并终止合约。之后船东开始诉讼,起诉违约/毁约造成的损失,而承租人以船东欺诈性误述船舶的油耗诱导订立租约作为抗辩与反索赔。

该先例的一审[(2020) EWHC 3448 (Comm)]判决长达100多页,其中有很多争议只适用在该先例特别的案情,对整个误述的课题来说比较重要的主要争议之一[45]就是本小段关注的疑点之一,也就是如果法院判承租人有权去撤销租约,是否仍会行使S.2(2)下的立法裁量权,以损失索赔替代撤销合约的权利。面对这个争议,法院首先要考虑的是在承租人已经选择撤销合约时要不要行使裁量权。因为如果行使了裁量权,会否变成无辜的承租人违约/毁约?这个问题在以前的先例中没有直接被考虑过,高院最后判说这不属于法院拒绝行使立法裁量权以损失索赔代替撤销合约的理由。这有两方面的原因:(1)高院认为S.2(2)中的金钱赔偿的金额并不等同于撤销合约,在该先例就是租约的租金与如果没有误述的租金之间的差价。因为主要是考虑到S.2(2)的目的是在某些情况撤销合约对误述方/船东来说太严苛,承租人往往是取巧将市场下跌或商业谈判不利的后果转嫁给了船东。而且从立法条文的用字上来说,也没有提到法院在行使立法裁量权要考虑否定让承租人已经是撤销了合约会对承租人带来的后果。(2)高院判除了欺诈性误述,非欺诈性误述下撤销合约应由法院确认有效的衡平救济,而不是承租人可以自助的衡平救济。承租人选择先早一步撤销合约要自行承担后来被法院否定而变为违约/毁约的风险。

Foxton大法官在该先例中讲了一大堆该案件案情的特定理由去支持他否定较早前承租人的自助撤销租约:"... this would have been a clear case for the exercise of the court's power to declare the contract as subsisting: i) The misrepresentation, while not trivial, was not one which could be said to strike 'to the root of the bargain' ... In particular, the speed and consumption warranty in the Charterparty provided substantial, albeit as I have found not complete, protection to the Charterer with regard to the subject-matter of the misrepresentation. ii) While the misrepresentation was made without reasonable grounds for believing in its truth, ...iii) There was a substantial fall in the tanker charterparty market in the period between the date when the Charterparty was concluded and the date of the purported rescission. ...iv) The Charterer does not contend that it paid more

---

[45] 关于是否存在事实陈述或只是合约保证,可见本书第二章之10.3段。关于承租人有否通过继续营运船舶的言行选择了确认租约,可见本书第三章之6.1.3段。

under the Charterparty than the market value of what it received, and its claim for damages for misrepresentation claims no wider or different loss than that recoverable in contract under the Charterparty. v) I have found that the impact of disclosing the true position on the contractual terms agreed would have been limited to a relatively small reduction in the hire rate. vi) The Charterer has accepted, through its own calculation of damages for misrepresentation, that even if it had not entered into the Charterparty, it would have entered into a charterparty with another owner at or around the same rate, and been exposed to the same market fall."

5.3.3 上诉庭不同意但没有作出解答与对目前法律地位的批评

可先节录《Chitty on Contracts》(2021 年,第 34 版)一书之 9－119 段对 SK Shipping Plc v. Capital VLCC 3 Corp(2020) EWHC 3448(Comm)先例的严厉批评:"When a misrepresentee purports to rescind a contract for non-fraudulent misrepresentation, but the court exercises its discretion to declare the contract subsisting, the effect is not wholly clear. In SK Shipping, in which the misrepresentee … had purported to rescind … Foxton J said that the result of declaring the contract subsisting would be that the misrepresentee was in repudiatory breach of contract. **The judge seemed to base this conclusion principally on his view that rescission for non-fraudulent misrepresentation requires a court order, and so by proceeding without obtaining one the charterer took the risk**, though the judge said that the outcome would be the same even if he was incorrect about the need for a court order. **With respect**, when a misrepresentee has given a proper notice of rescission but the court has in its discretion declared the contract subsisting, **it seems incorrect to treat the misrepresentee as having repudiated the contract**, unless the misrepresentee were to refuse to perform despite the court order. As we will see below, **the judge's argument that rescission for non-fraudulent misrepresentation requires a court order seems contrary to the bulk of authority and inconsistent with s. 2(2)** itself. And if the misrepresentee can indeed effect rescission by giving notice, **it seems unlikely that Parliament intended that by doing so the misrepresentee might become liable for breach of contract …**"(加黑部分是笔者的强调)

根据 Foxton 大法官在 SK Shipping Plc v. Capital VLCC 3 Corp 先例中的判决,非欺诈性误述撤销合约并非自主救济,而是需要法院确认,所以如果被误述方贸贸然撤销合约,就要承担撤销合约的救济被法院否定的风险。而如果法院行使裁量权让合约重生,则已经撤销合约的被误述方就变为违约/毁约。但《Chitty on Contracts》一书显然不同意 Foxton 大法官的判决,认为如果被误述方通过合理通知撤销了合约,即使法院行使裁量权让合约重生,也不应将被误述方之前撤销合约的言行视为违约/毁约,除非被误述方在有了法院命令后仍然拒绝履行合约。Foxton 大法官认为的非欺诈性误述下撤销合约需要法院命令的看法(只在衡平法救济存在这种争议)也和众多先例与1967年立法之S.2(2)的措辞存在冲突。而如果被误述方仍可以通过通知自助撤销合约,英国议会立法时应该不太可能希望被误述方会因为根据衡平法撤销合约变为违约/毁约。

在笔者看来,SK Shipping Plc v. Capital VLCC 3 Corp先例否定了历史悠久的非欺诈性误述实际可以自助撤销合约的法律地位。被误述方发现了误述后会陷入左右为难的境地,如果继续履行合约可能构成确认合约,如果撤销合约可能最后因为法院行使裁量权而变为违约/毁约。如果必须影响到合约根基法院才会同意被误述方撤销合约而不是行使裁量权以损失赔偿替代,参考著名的The"Hong Kong Fir"(1961) EWCA Civ 7先例[46]就可知道,想要达到影响合约根基的程度是非常难的。也不是每次都能像The"Lucy"(1983)1 Lloyd's Rep 188先例一样,在"无损害"的基础上继续履行合约,因为这需要双方合作。这导致误述方刚发现误述时,只能肯定有关陈述不正确,需要尽快行动去撤销合约与避免无辜第三人的介入。但到底这是欺诈性误述、疏忽误述或对方会有"合理依据"的无辜误述,与最后法院(仲裁庭)会怎样认定是难以预测。这样,结果可能是可以在欺诈性误述或立法S.2(1)的"拟制的欺诈"下拿到一大笔赔偿与撤销两种救济,也可能是因为S.2(2)被否定撤销而变为违约/毁约要赔给对方误述方一大笔钱,面对的是完全不肯定与天差地别的情况。所以,这种牵一发而动全身的法律地位改变,仅仅是Foxton大法官的理由显然是不够的。

当然,SK Shipping Plc v. Capital VLCC 3 Corp先例只是一审先例中,其他的一审法院大法官未必跟从Foxton大法官的说法。该先例上诉到上诉庭[(2022) EWCA Civ 231]后,可惜因为双方没有对这个法律观点提出上诉,所以上诉庭并不需要对这点作出决定,但看来上诉庭并不认同Foxton大法官的看法,Males大法官说:"it is apparent that the judge's approach was coloured by his view that rescission for misrepresentation is not a self-help remedy available to a representee, but depends on the representee obtaining an order for rescission from the court, even though in the end he said that this issue was not decisive. This is itself a highly controversial question, on which we did not hear argument. I note, however, that section 2(2) appears to be drafted on the basis that, at least in some circumstances, rescission does not depend on obtaining a court order. Hence the language 'claimed ... that the contract ought to be or has been rescinded'."

另Males大法官也认为被误述方去自助撤销合约的救济不应轻易在立法误述上被剥夺:"... rescission is the normal remedy, ... It should at least be a strong starting point."

可以说目前这种疑点仍然存在,等待有合适的案件到上诉庭甚至是最高院进一步澄清。笔者也相信在《Chitty on Contracts》等权威学术著作的批评下,上诉庭与最高院肯定会很小心。

---

[46] 见笔者《合约的履行、弃权与禁反言》一书第一章之3.5段。

5.4 立法 S.2(2)带来的疑点之二:替代撤销合约的"损失赔偿"针对何损失

在上述本章之 5.2 段已经对此疑点有了简单的介绍。虽然 1967 年立法之 S.2(2)说明法院或仲裁庭为了保持公平,有裁量权让误述方以赔偿被误述方损失的方式来替代撤销合约的救济,但该立法条文写得过于简单,并没有针对替代撤销合约的损失赔偿是按照什么标准来计算与具体包括哪些类别的损失等细节的问题。这也带来实际适用该立法条文时的不确定以及与 S.2(1)条文下疏忽误述的损失赔偿内容之间的关系为何的疑问。

5.4.1 立法 S.2(2)与 S.2(1)下损失的关系

对于 S.2(2)下针对的损失赔偿问题,《Chitty on Contracts》(2021 年,第 34 版)一书之 9 - 115 段说:"**Measure of damages under s.2(2)**. Section 2(2) does not state the measure of damages to be awarded. It is possible that the measure of damages which may be awarded under subs. (2) is intended to be lower than the measure of damages for fraudulent misrepresentation under s.2(1). This possibility is suggested by subs. (3) of the same section which provides that damages may be awarded under subs. (2) whether or not the representor is liable for damages under subs. (1) (i. e. whether or not he has been negligent), but goes on to provide that any damages awarded under subs. (2) shall be taken into account in assessing liability under subs. (1). This seems to indicate that the damages awarded under subs. (2) may be lower than the damages awarded under subs. (1), and there might be something to be said for this since the representor may be wholly innocent in a case under subs. (2). But the Act gives no clue as to how damages are to be assessed under this subsection if they are not to be assessed in the same way as under subs. (1). It has already been seen that damages under subs. (1) are tortious rather than contractual. It would seem a fortiori the damages under subs. (2) would not be at the contractual level. The alternatives then would seem to be to award either the tort measure or a special measure designed to compensate the representee for the loss resulting from his inability to obtain rescission. Whereas the result of the misrepresentation the misrepresentee has given up some other right, the damages should be the value of that other right. ..."

根据上述的节录,首先明确的是 S.2(2)和 S.2(1)下损失计算的标准是一样的,即以侵权为标准而不是以合约为标准。[47] 这在《Misrepresentation, Mistake and Non-Disclosure》(2022 年,第 6 版)一书之 4 - 76 段也有同样的结论如下:"...The words of the subsection itself which indicate the answer are 'loss that would be caused by [the Misrepresentation] if the contract were upheld'. This suggests that the purpose of the damages is to compensate the claimant for not being allowed to exercise his right to rescind: that is, damages to put him in the financial position in which he would have been if the

---

〔47〕 关于两者的区别,可见本章之 4.2.2.3.5 段。

contract had been rescinded. This points more towards the tort measure of damages than the contract measure."

有关S.2(2)与S.2(1)下损失的关系的问题,既然S.2(2)与S.2(1)均是根据侵权责任来计算损失,两个条文区别是在什么情况下适用以及两个条文中所包括的损失之间是否有重叠?这问题在解释了S.2(2)具体适用的情况之后,再去看上述节录的《Chitty on Contracts》一书之9-115段的相关部分就会更加清晰。该节录部分从1967年立法之S.2(3)的措辞/文字入手去分析,在该S.2(3)下,法院可以在S.2(2)下行使裁量权判决误述方赔偿被误述方损失,无论该误述方是否同时在S.2(1)下都要赔偿被误述方的损失,而在根据S.2(1)判决损失时,任何在S.2(2)下被判决的损失数额都不能再重复计算。这显示了S.2(1)与S.2(2)的计算方法不同,并且S.2(1)的损失金额应该比S.2(2)大。这也可以理解,毕竟已经在本章之4.2段介绍S.2(1)是根据"拟制的欺诈"来计算损失,而众所周知欺诈计算损失时是很宽松。

5.4.2 立法S.2(2)下的赔偿不应是令被误述方回复到合约被撤销的地位

S.2(2)看来是想要用损失赔偿去补偿被误述方不能撤销合约的损失。这个损失赔偿的结果是否需要令被误述方回复到合约被撤销的地位?在立法本身没有写清楚时,法院在适用立法时经常要从记录了立法原意的报告中去找答案。在William Sindall Plc v. Cambridgeshire CC(1994)1 WLR 1016上诉庭先例中,Hoffmann大法官在谈到适用S.2(2)的问题时,首先援引了Tenth Report of the Law Reform Committee (1962)Cmnd. 1782立法报告中谈到订立S.2(2)的背景与立法意图:

"11. A more fundamental objection which may be advanced against our recommendation [to abolish the bar on rescission after completion] concerns the drastic character of the remedy to which the plaintiff would be entitled. Unless the court's power to grant rescission is made more elastic than it is at present, the court will not be able to take account of the relative importance or unimportance of the facts which have been misrepresented. A car might be returned to the vendor because of a misrepresentation about the mileage done since the engine was last overhauled, or a transfer of shares rescinded on account of an incorrect statement about the right to receive the current dividend. In some cases the result could be as harsh on the representor as the absence of a right to rescind under the current law can be on the representee. Moreover, the conflict between remedies for misrepresentation and those for breach of contract would be aggravated. There is already the anomaly that a statement embodied in the contract and constituting a minor term of it is treated as a warranty, the breach of which gives only a right to damages, whereas the same statement as a representation inducing the contract enables the latter to be rescinded. Before the contract is executed and at a time when the parties can be relatively easily restored to their original positions, this anomaly may not matter very much, but the position would be very different if the court had no option but to order rescission after the contract had been executed.

12. To meet these objections we recommend that wherever the court has power to order rescission it should, as an alternative, have a discretionary power to award damages if it is satisfied that these would afford adequate compensation to the plaintiff, having regard to the nature of the misrepresentation, and the fact that the injury suffered by the plaintiff is small compared with what rescission would involve. The courts were given power to award damages in addition to or in substitution for an injunction or a decree of specific performance by Section 2 of Lord Cairns' Act (the Chancery Procedure Amendment Act 1858) and since the decision of the House of Lords in Leeds Industrial Cooperative Society Limited v. Slack [1924] AC 851, the power has been exercised on principles similar to those we have just mentioned."

该立法记录用了两个类比去说明订立 S. 2(2)的原因。第一个类比是普通法根据合约条文内容对合约的重要性将合约条文区分为条件条文(condition)与保证条文(warranty)。保证条文是针对不太重要的合约内容,对保证条文的违反,能够得到的救济就只有索赔损失,而不能终止合约。众所周知,可以构成合约条件条文的内容并不多,通常是涉及合约根基的内容,其他绝大部分的内容都是合约的保证条文或在 The "Hong Kong Fir" (1961) EWCA Civ 7 先例确立的中间条文(intermediate term)。[48] 这样,如果一个误述的内容变为合约的条文(如一条陈述与保证条文),通常只可以被视为保证条文,可以获得的救济只有损失赔偿,但在误述下,同样的内容根据误述就可以撤销合约,这从救济方面来看显然是很不对等的。

第二个类比是《Lord Cairns' Act 1858》立法的 Section 2。该 Section 2 的内容如下:"2. In all cases in which the Court of Chancery has jurisdiction to entertain an application for an injunction against a breach of any covenant, contract, or agreement, or against the commission or continuance of any wrongful act, or for the specific performance of any covenant, contract, or agreement, it shall be lawful for the same Court, if it shall think fit, to award damages to the party injured, either in addition to or in substitution for such injunction or specific performance; and such damages may be assessed in such manner as the Court shall direct."

《Lord Cairns' Act 1858》立法的背景是传统上英国衡平法法院只能给予禁令(injunction)或履约指令(specific performance)的衡平救济,而不能判决损失的金钱赔偿救济,这只是普通法法院在法律下的权力。但是随着社会和法律的发展,出现了禁令或履约指令无法被履行或执行而要以损失赔偿来替代的情况,这可见《损失赔偿与救济》一书第十二章之 1.3 至 1.5 段。该立法正是为了赋予衡平法法院针对这种情况判决金钱损失赔偿(equitable damages)救济的权力而制定。而 Section 2,也是该立

[48] 见笔者《合约的履行、弃权与禁反言》一书第一章之 3.5 段。

法的核心条文,即允许衡平法法院用损失赔偿替代禁令或履约指令的救济,而损失也是实质性补偿无辜方无法取得禁令或履约指令救济的损失。

去类比《Lord Cairns' Act 1858》的原因是,非欺诈性误述下撤销合约的救济属于衡平法范畴,而《Lord Cairns' Act 1858》正是说明了在衡平法领域以损失赔偿替代衡平救济已经有先例可循。

通过以上两个类比,1967 年立法小组意图将 S. 2(2)适用在一些较轻微的误述中。该误述对合约的履行仅仅带来较小的影响,而且用较少的金钱就能补救误述的内容,令合约恢复正常履行,相对而言若是撤销合约给误述方带来的损失更为巨大,这时对于误述方来说,如果撤销合约,对他的惩罚与他的过错之间就不成比例。这时法院或仲裁庭考虑了 S. 2(2)中提到的三个因素:(1)误述的性质,也就是说误述的内容是否重要以及对于合约履行的影响;(2)如果合约不被撤销,被误述方的损失是多少;(3)如果合约被撤销,误述方会产生的损失,就可以根据 S. 2(2)来行使裁量权平衡双方的利益后决定以损失赔偿去替代撤销合约。而且赔偿的标准只是补救误述给被误述方带来的麻烦与损失。

5.4.2.1 William Sindall Plc v. Cambridgeshire CC(1994)1 WLR 1016 上诉庭先例

William SindallPlc v. Cambridgeshire CC 上诉庭先例就是一个很典型的例子。该先例中被告地方议会需要筹集一笔资金,于是招投标出售一块土地给地产开发商。原告以 5,082,500 英镑的价格中标,并于 1989 年 3 月 28 日与地方议会订立了土地买卖合约。原告计划在该土地上建造 60 幢别墅和 30 间公寓,结果当地规划部门反对原告建造计划中的部分内容,原告经过 18 个月的上诉与努力后才取得全部的批准。然而在此期间,地产市场发生急剧逆转,到 1990 年 10 月时,该土地的市价已经低于中标价格的一半。而原告为了发展此地产项目,向银行借了高息贷款,在取得全部的批准后,原告公司也决定不再投入更多资金进该项目,而只是希望将正在建设的部分尽快建好出售以取得资金回笼。不过在当时的市场上,已经很少有买家。在此事实背景下,原告在建造房屋进行勘探时发现地底下铺设有一个相邻住宅小区的污水管道对角线穿过该土地,连接到另一个排污主管道。这是在土地买卖合约中没有提到过的,也即原告在订约时并不知道的。由于污水管道的周围要预留一些空间,建房时就要考虑避开这些地方,所以该污水管道的存在,破坏了原告的建造计划。被告得知后与原告进行磋商并提出各种解决方案,但原告均拒绝接受,并以被告存在误述要求撤销该土地买卖合约。

一审法院判被告在合约中对土地的描述详情中存在误述,双方对于污水管道的存在也构成共同错误(common mistake),[49] 所以原告可以撤销合约。该判决在上诉庭被推翻,上诉庭的 Hoffmann 大法官认为被告不存在误述,而对于共同错误这一点,

〔49〕 见本书第七章的详细介绍。

由于合约中写明了任何被告不知道的地役权(easement)的存在的风险在买方,所以即使有共同错误,被告也没有责任。对于一审法院在1967年立法之S.2(2)下行使裁量权不去以金钱损失赔偿替代撤销合约的救济,Hoffmann大法官说基于他认定被告不存在误述的决定,本来可以不用再考虑损失赔偿的问题,但是考虑到该案进一步上诉的可能性,他还是对此问题进行了详细的分析。

Hoffmann大法官认为一审法院高估了污水管道的存在对整个合约履行的影响。因为原告要修正该污水管道带来的问题只需花费18,000英镑,以及工程延误每天产生的2000英镑的利息。而另一方面,如果撤销合约,对于被告来说,其要恢复原状所要付出的是退还原告购买土地的金钱与利息共计800万英镑。这误述(即使存在)的严重性与修正误述所花费的金额同撤销合约的后果比较来看是非常不成比例的。而且在案件上诉到上诉庭时,被告已经自己花费54,000英镑将该邻近小区的污水管道进行了改道。Hoffmann大法官认为S.2(2)立法的初衷就是针对这种不成比例的情况,判原告只能取回补救所花费的费用。

Evans大法官也同意Hoffmann大法官的判决,Evans大法官还进一步分析了如果根据原告提出的在1967年立法S.2(1)去进行金钱赔偿,包括土地价格的变动,这实际上等同于撤销合约的结果,显然与S.2(2)相矛盾。而原告在地价上的损失,跟误述根本无关,是因为市场的变化令一个好的交易变为亏大本的买卖,但原告不能通过误述来将这市场损失转嫁给误述方。

5.4.2.2 SK Shipping Plc v. Capital VLCC 3 Corp(2020)EWHC 3448(Comm)先例

已经在本章之5.3.2段介绍的SK Shipping Plc v. Capital VLCC 3 Corp先例中,其中一个重要之处就是对立法S.2(2)的该疑点给了一个解答。Foxton大法官除了依从William Sindall Plc v. Cambridgeshire CC(1994)1 WLR 1016上诉庭先例的判决外,也强调了Hoffmann大法官一个十分有说服力的理由去支持他的决定,这就是,众所周知S.2(2)的立法本意就是去阻止太多被滥用的“自助”救济,以一些无伤大雅的非欺诈性误述/真正无辜误述去撤销一个亏本的交易/合约,带来对诚实的误述方完全不成比例(disproportionate)的伤害。所以通过立法把撤销合约的裁量权从被误述方的手里交给法院或仲裁庭去决定,也可以想到在这种不成比例去伤害诚实的误述方是不会被允许的。在这个立法背景下,法院或仲裁庭决定的去替代撤销合约的损失赔偿不可能金额太大或同样不成比例,即不会是以金钱赔偿让被误述方回复到合约被撤销的地位。可以说在多数无伤大雅的真正无辜误述,法院会只去作出名义损失(nominal damages)的赔偿,见:UCB Corporate Services Ltd v. Thomason & Anor(2005)EWCA Civ 225;Ceviz v. Frawley(2021)EWHC 8(Ch)等先例。

这可见上述提到的《Lord Cairns' Act 1858》类比在损失计算上完全不适用于S.2(2)。在William Sindall Plc v. Cambridgeshire CC先例中,Hoffmann大法官同意这类比在某些方面正确,但不适用在损失方面的计算:“The Law Reform Committee drew the analogy with Lord Cairns' Act and in some respects this analogy is a good one. But it breaks down when one comes to decide the measure of damages. Under Lord Cairns' Act, the plaintiff who is refused specific performance or an injunction is left to his damages in contract or tort. The measure of such damages is exactly what it would be at common law [see Johnson v. Agnew (1980) AC 367…]. The only change made by the Act was to give a remedy for purely equitable rights, such as breach of a restrictive covenant to which the plaintiff was not a party. But in such cases the common law analogy enabled a suitable measure of damages to be devised. Section 2(2), on the other hand, creates a power to award damages in a wholly new situation."

以下节录 SK Shipping Plc v. Capital VLCC 3 Corp 先例中,Foxton 大法官相关的判决:

"It is noteworthy that s2(2) does not expressly provide that the court is to consider the effect of declaring the contract subsisting on the party entitled to rescission when assessing damages,…

However, **I am satisfied** that I should approach the issue on the basis that damages under **s2(2) are not intended to constitute the monetary equivalent of rescission**:

i) There is authority in the Court of Appeal, which although not binding[50] is highly persuasive, and which ought in my view to be followed at first instance, that s2(2) is not concerned with awarding the monetary equivalent of rescission: William Sindall plc v Cambridgeshire CC [1994] 1 WLR 1016: a)… Hoffmann LJ stated: 'The Law Reform Committee report makes it clear that **section 2(2) was enacted because it was thought that it might be a hardship to the representor to be deprived of the whole benefit of the bargain on account of a minor misrepresentation. It could not possibly have intended the damages in lieu to be assessed on a principle which would invariably have the same effect.'** ….

iii) As noted above, s2(2) asks the court to consider the effect of rescission on the misrepresentor, but expressly addresses the issue of loss to the misrepresentee resulting from the refusal of rescission only by reference to loss caused by the misrepresentation, not that which will follow from the refusal of rescission.

iv) Approached purposively, the Court of Appeal's conclusion inWilliam Sindall, seems (with respect) intrinsically right. As both Hoffmann LJ and Evans LJ noted, if the discretion exists because, **in many cases, the remedy of rescission will have dispropor-**

---

〔50〕 根据上面的介绍,Hoffmann 大法官在 William Sindall Plc v. Cambridgeshire CC 上诉庭先例认为基于他认定被告不存在误述的决定,本来可以不用再考虑损失赔偿的问题,但是考虑到该案进一步上诉的可能性,他还是对此问题进行了详细的分析,所以这只是附带意见(obiter)。

tionate consequences, it would seem wrong in principle for damages in lieu to be assessed on a basis which seeks to replicate those disproportionate consequences of rescission in monetary terms. ..."(加黑部分是笔者的强调)

5.5 立法 S.2(2)带来的疑点之三:如果受害方撤销合约的权利因其他原因被否定,法院/仲裁庭是否仍可给予损失赔偿去"替代"

该疑点是一个已经有很多讨论的话题。一审法院层面针对《Misrepresentation Act 1967》之 S.2(2)的适用就持有两种不同看法。

主流看法认为 S.2(2)下,法院可以判决损失的前提是撤销合约的救济可以成立,如果撤销合约因为某些限制无法成立,就不存在以损失替代(in lieu of)撤销合约的做法:见 Alton House Garages(Bromley)Ltd v. Monk(unreported, 31 July 1981); Atlantis Lines and Navigation Co Inc v. Hallam Ltd(1983)1 Lloyd's Rep 188; Floods of Queensferry Ltd v. Shand Construction Ltd(2000)BLR 81; Zanzibar v British Aerospace (Lancaster House) Ltd(2000)1 WLR 2333; Pankhania v. London Borough of Hackney (2002)EWHC 2441(Ch)等先例。

5.5.1 认为不影响可以作出损失赔偿的 Thomas Witter Ltd v. TBP Industries Ltd(1996)2 All ER 573 先例

也有看法认为 S.2(2)并没有将撤销合约作为判决损失赔偿的前提,即使撤销合约的权利因为误述后的其他原因被否定(如无法复原、时隔太久、免责条文等),[51] 法院也仍然可以判决损失赔偿。在 Thomas Witter Ltd v. TBP Industries Ltd 先例中,原告的代表律师从议会在讨论通过《Misrepresentation Act 1967》立法时的会议记录(通常在立法条文的文意解释有争议时会通过查询立法过程的会议记录来搞清楚立法的原意)中,挖掘出时任副检察长的 Dingle Foot 爵士的一段发言,来说服 Jacob 大法官该 S.2(2)下法院作出判决时合约可以被撤销并不是去判决损失的前提条件,而是法院可以在撤销合约与判决损失上行使裁量权来进行选择的方式。Dingle Foot 爵士的该段发言可节录如下:

"I come now to the other point which was raised by(其他议会同僚)...They were particularly concerned with transactions in real property, and ... put to me the case of the sale of a house. He asked me to suppose that there had been a sale of a house, some defect was discovered afterwards, it might be that a third party had come into the matter, and it might be entirely unjust or inequitable to insist on recission in such a case. I suggest that in such a case, ... **the conveyance is unlikely to be rescinded because of the impossibility of restitution.**

My answer is that a case of that sort would be covered by Clause 2(2) which says: Where a person has entered into a contract after a misrepresentation has been made

[51] 见本书第三章之5至8段。

to him otherwise than fraudulently, and he would be entitled, by reason of the misrepresentation, to rescind the contract, then, if it is claimed, in any proceedings arising out of the contract, that the contract ought to be or has been rescinded the court or arbitrator may declare the contract subsisting and award damages in lieu of rescission.... That is **the option which is given to the court**, and in the sort of case which has been put to me by(其他议会同僚), it would follow **that the court or arbitrator would almost certainly award damages in lieu of rescission**. Therefore that matter is really fully covered."(加黑部分是笔者的强调)

Jacob 大法官说:"the power to award damages under **section 2(2) does not depend upon an extant right to rescission-it only depends upon a right having existed in the past.** Whether it depends upon such a right existing at any time, or depends upon such a right subsisting at the time when the representee first claims rescission, I do not have to decide ... In principle, however, I would have thought that it is enough that at any time a right to rescind subsisted. **It is damages in lieu of that right(even if barred by later events or lapse of time) which can be awarded**."(加黑部分是笔者的强调)

5.5.2 认为只有撤销合约权利没有被否定才能以损失赔偿替代的其他先例

Hugh Beale 教授(是《Chitty on Contracts》的总编辑)在 1995 年发表名为《Points on misrepresentation》(1995) 111 LQR 385 的对 Thomas Witter Ltd v. TBP Industries Ltd(1996)2 All ER 573 先例的案例评述,他说解读议会在立法过程中的会议记录并不是容易的事情,因为立法过程中讨论的内容非常多,不能只是单独把其中 Dingle Foot 爵士的部分发言抽出来,而且该发言中也并不是没有任何模糊的地方。Hugh Beale 教授特意指出 Dingle Foot 爵士是在议会从前一天早晨开始讨论直到第二天凌晨 3 点 17 分时的发言,暗示该发言也并不是在头脑十分清晰的情况下做出的,即使有模糊也毫不奇怪。这估计也是 Floods of Queensferry Ltd v. Shand Construction (2000) BLR 81; Zanzibar v British Aerospace (Lancaster House) Ltd (2000) 1 WLR 2333; Pankhania v. London Borough of Hackney(2002) EWHC 2441 (Ch) 等先例认为法律条文本身已经写得十分清楚是"替代",而并没有跟从 Thomas Witter Ltd v. TBP Industries Ltd 先例的判法的原因。

在 Salt v. Stratstone Specialist Ltd(2015) EWCA Civ 745 上诉庭先例中, Longmore 大法官在列举了上述持不同观点高院的先例后,对此点作出认定,并同意多数先例与 Hugh Beale 教授的观点,认为:"The point appears to be open at the level of the Court of Appeal. The words of the statute are 'if it is claimed ... that the contract ought to be or has been rescinded the court ... may declare the contract subsisting and award damages in lieu of rescission'. No doubt a claimant can be said to make a claim even if he is subsequently held not to be entitled to do so. But the words 'in lieu of rescission' must, **in my view, carry with them the implication that rescission is available(or was available at**

the time the contract was rescinded). If it is not(or was not available in law) because e. g. the contract has been affirmed, third party rights have intervened, an excessive time has elapsed or restitution has become impossible, rescission is not available and damages cannot be said to be awarded 'in lieu of rescission'."(加黑部分是笔者的强调)

综上来看,目前针对此疑点,较主流、权威与有约束力的看法就是上诉庭 Longmore 大法官的观点。如果撤销合约的权利被否定,法院就没有权再去以判决损失替代撤销合约。上述所讲在《Chitty on Contracts》(2021 年,第 34 版)一书之 9 – 114 段有说:"A ... limitation on the subsection is that **the power to grant damages** is, on the balance of authority, **available only where the remedy of rescission would still be available at the time of the court's order**. The court may award damages in lieu of rescission wherever the representee 'would be entitled ... to rescind the contract'. **The question is whether this means: 'would be entitled at the time of the court's order', or 'would have been entitled after representation was made'.** Purely linguistic considerations suggest that the former meaning is the correct one ... nonetheless earlier editions of this Work suggested that the wording was ambiguous. In Thomas Witter v. TBP Industries Ltd, Jacob J expressed the view that damages could have been awarded under s. 2(2) even though the misrepresentee had lost the right to rescind. But the suggestion that the words were unclear was disapproved in Zanzibar v. British Aerospace (Lancaster House) Ltd in which Judge Jack QC held that the power to award damages is an alternative to damages and no longer existed when the right to rescission had been lost. The same conclusion had been reached earlier by Judge Humphrey Lloyd QC in Floods of Queensferry Ltd v. Shane Construction Ltd, who refused to follow the decision in the Thomas Witter case. **The Court of Appeal has now confirmed that there is no power to award damages under s. 2(2) if the claimant has lost the right to rescind**."(加黑部分是笔者的强调)

5.5.3　不能以 S. 2(2)向没有撤销合约权利的第三人索赔损失

在有权去撤销合约(没有被其他原因否定)的前提下才存在法院或仲裁庭可在 S. 2(2)下行使裁量权以损失赔偿作为替代,也可去解释其他不同的情况。一种情况是一位独立的中间人的误述(疏忽或欺诈性)导致受害方/被误述方与其他第三人订立了一个有严重缺陷的合约。例如,受害方在银行的投资建议下通过银行从第三人处买入亏本的金融产品或土地。此时,受害方不能以 S. 2(2)向做出误述的中间人索赔损失,因为大前提是双方之间没有因误述产生的合约可供受害方撤销。这表示受害方/被误述方如果向作为中间人/误述方的银行索赔损失,就要根据其他的诉因了。如果误述是欺诈性,就以欺诈/欺骗侵权(tort of deceit)。如果误述只是疏忽,就要看双方关系,撇开合约(不一定有)就要看侵权下是否有小心谨慎的责任,如果没有,就是受害方自己"误信",损失也要自认倒霉了,而借助 S. 2(1)去回避受害方需要承担的证明中间人的欺诈意图或疏忽的举证责任也就走不通了。

这可节录《Chitty on Contracts》(2021 年,第 34 版)一书之 9 - 129 段,说:"**Rescission not available except against contracting party** It seems clear that rescission is prima facie a remedy which is only available against the other party to the contract. In Northern Bank Finance Corp Ltd v. Charlton(1979)IR 149, this principle was affirmed by a bare majority of the Supreme Court of Eire in a case in which the plaintiff had been induced by the fraud of a bank to pay various sums to the bank in order that these sums should be used by the bank to purchase various properties on behalf of the plaintiff. The properties were in fact so purchased from third parties. The plaintiff claimed rescission of the contracts of purchase but the majority of the court held that rescission was not available as against the bank since the properties were not bought from the bank itself. Rescission would in fact have amounted to a sort of compulsory subrogation under which the bank would have taken over the properties and refunded the purchase price to the plaintiff."

6. 立法条文 S.3 的分析

在普通法的订约自由与合约方自主的大原则下,在商业合约去加上一条免责条文/豁免条文(exception clause/exclusion clause)已是早有的做法,也是完全合法,这已在本书第三章之 8 段介绍。在此只节录《Chitty on Contracts》(2021 年,第 34 版)一书之 9 - 153 段去把此小段串起来:"**Position at common law** At common law a person could not contract out of liability for fraud inducing the making of a contract with him, at least where the fraud was his own. It is, however, possible that he could do so where the fraud was that of his employees or agents and there seems no doubt that it was possible, by a provision of the contract itself, to exclude or modify the normal consequences of innocent or negligent misrepresentation. Such clauses are, however, subject to the normal principles of construction common to all exemption clauses. Any exclusion of liability for misrepresentation must be clearly stated. ..."

6.1 普通法下对免责条文的控制或限制

在普通法下,传统对免责条文的控制或限制就只能通过严格与针对性(contra proferentem)地解释条文。有说法是如果免责条文不明示说明对"疏忽"免责,那么就不会被解释为疏忽被包括在免责范围。在 Gillespie Bros & Co Ltd v. Roy Bowles Transport Ltd(1973)QB 400 上诉庭先例中,Buckley 大法官说:"It is inherently improbable that one party to the contract should intend to absolve the other party from the consequences of the latter's own negligence. The intention to do so must therefore be made perfectly clear, for otherwise the court will conclude that the exempted party was only intended to be free from liability in respect of damage occasioned by causes other than negligence for which he is answerable."

但在保护英国消费者的《Unfair Contract Terms Act 1977》生效后,法院对商业合约针对疏忽的免责条文的解释开始放宽。正如在 Taberna Europe CDO II Plc v Selskabet AF1(2016)EWCA Civ 1262 上诉庭先例中,Moore-Bick 大法官说:"the law has moved on ... The authorities show that there has been an increasing willingness in recent years to recognise the parties to commercial contracts are entitled to determine for themselves the term on which they will do business."

另在 Persimmon Homes Ltd v. Ove Arun & Partners Ltd(2017)EWCA Civ 373 上诉庭先例中,Jackson 大法官说:

"The contra proferentem rule requires any ambiguity in an exemption clause to be resolved against the party who put the clause forward and relies upon it. In relation to commercial contracts, negotiated between parties of equal bargaining power, that rule now has a very limited role.

Lord Neuberger MR summarised the position succinctly inK/S Victoria Street v House of Fraser(Stores Management)Ltd [2011] EWCA Civ 904..:'Quite apart from raising abstruse issues as to who is the proferens...,'rules' of interpretation such as contra proferentem are rarely decisive as to the meaning of any provisions of a commercial contract. The words used, commercial sense, and the documentary and factual context, are, and should be, normally enough to determine the meaning of a contractual provision."

6.2 针对误述的免责条文要求符合"合理"要求的原因

但普通法放宽了控制或限制,针对可诉误述/立法误述还有《Misrepresentation Act 1967》之 S.3 的一关要通过才会是有效去保护疏忽的误述方。这是通过立法去否定任何逃避即使是非欺诈性误述(也就是立法针对的疏忽与真正的无辜误述)责任的"免责条文",除非该条文能符合"合理"(reasonable)的要求。

在不少人看来,英国法律高度重视订约自由,要求订约方自己掌控合约的命运,特别是有了保护英国消费者的《Unfair Contract Terms Act 1977》立法后,怎会允许这立法 S.3 继续存在,并强制适用在其他非消费者(non-consumer)的合约中,甚至是适用英国法的国际商业合约中呢?毕竟在国际商业社会,英国法院一直(错误)假设不论来自任何国家(西方或发展中国家)的订约方都是有同等的法律水平去保护自己的,会毫不迟疑协助强制执行一个发展中国家因为不懂而签订的可能让自己送命的商业合约,又怎会立法在误述方面作出 S.3 的保护?

针对误述以立法形式否定订约自由的原因可节录近期重要的 First Tower Trustees Ltd v. CDS(Superstores International)Ltd(2018)EWCA Civ 1396 上诉庭先例中,

Leggatt 大法官的观点："The decision to make section 3 applicable to all contracts induced by misrepresentation, irrespective of the nature and subject matter of the contract and the identity of the contracting parties, is readily understandable. The importance which English law attaches to the freedom of parties to contract on whatever terms they choose depends on crucially the assumption that their consent to the terms of the contract has been obtained fairly. That is not the case where one party's consent has been induced by a misrepresentation made by the other contracting party. Misrepresentation is a paradigm 'vitiating factor' which undermines the validity of a contract. This does not mean that a party cannot choose to give up the right to complain that its consent to the terms of the contract was obtained by misrepresentation. But in so far as a contract term is said to have removed that right, a control mechanism is needed to ensure that this term was a fair and reasonable one to include. That, at all events, is the policy which Parliament has thought it right to adopt. It is the duty of the courts to uphold and not to subvert that policy choice."

当然，1967 年立法之 S. 3 也在后来排除了对部分国际商业合约的保护，这可节录《Chitty on Contracts》(2021 年，第 34 版)一书之 9 - 159 段："**International supply contracts and s. 3** Section 3 does not apply if the contract is an 'international supply contract' within the meaning of the Unfair Contract Terms Act 1977 s. 26. This is because s. 3 subjects the relevant clauses to the requirement of reasonableness under s. 11 of the 1977 Act and s. 26 of the 1977 Act provides that the requirement of reasonableness does not apply to exclusions or restrictions of liability arising under contracts with s. 26."

也就是说，可以不受 S. 3 立法管控的对误述免责的条文是《Unfair Contract Terms Act 1977》之 S. 26 豁免的国际供应合约(international supply contract)。这种合约在 S. 26(3) - (4)被定义为："(3) Subject to subsection(4), that description of contract is one whose characteristics are the following—(a) either it is a contract of sale of goods or it is one under or in pursuance of which the possession or ownership of goods passes; and (b) it is made by parties whose places of business (or, if they have none, habitual residences) are in the territories of different states... (4) A contract falls within subsection(3) above only if either—(a) the goods in question are, at the time of the conclusion of the contract, in the course of carriage, or will be carried, from the territory of one state to the territory of another; or (b) the acts constituting the offer and acceptance have been done in the territories of different states; or (c) the contract provides for the goods to be delivered to the territory of a state other than that within whose territory those acts were done."

在此不去进一步分析此立法的"国际供应合约"所包括的范围，只说在 Amiri Flight Authority v. BAE Systems Plc(2004) 1 All ER(Comm) 385 先例中是包括了国际货物买卖的付运合约(shipment sales contracts)，Mance 大法官说："... Without going into its precise limits, one classical example within section 26(4)(a) would be the sale of goods on CIF or FOB terms. The supplier thereby undertakes to ship goods, or to give the receiver the benefit of a shipping contract, without undertaking that the goods will actually be delivered by the carrier to their overseas destination."

在 Trident Turboprop (Dublin) Ltd v. First Flight Couriers Ltd (2009) EWCA Civ 290 上诉庭先例中,案件涉及在英国交飞机飞去印度的飞机租赁合约(aircraft operating lease agreement)的争议,也被判为包括在这一类合约内。也就是说这一类合约中的对疏忽误述免责的条文,不受 1967 年立法之 S. 3 对"合理"的要求的管控,完全有订约自由。

6.3 "合理"的免责条文

S. 3 明示"合理"的要求是《Unfair Contract Terms Act 1977》之 S. 11(1)的定义:"In relation to a contract term, the requirement of reasonableness for the purposes of this Part of this Act, section 3 of the Misrepresentation Act 1967 … is that the term shall have been a fair and reasonable one to be included having regard to the circumstances which were, or ought reasonably to have been, known to or in the contemplation of the parties when the contract was made."

众所周知,什么是"合理"或"不合理"要视双方订约当时所有的情况而定,正如立法条文说的"the circumstances which were, or ought reasonably to have been, known to or in the contemplation of the parties when the contract was made"。这已经显示了一些重要因素如合约双方(特别是质疑免责条文是否合理的一方)的水平高低、有否律师代表或协助、双方是否有谈判讨价还价(特别是对有关免责条文)、是否是一个公平交易(arm – length transaction)等,因为这可客观判断有关免责条文是否为双方在订约时知悉(known to)与深思熟虑(in the contemplation)后才接受。这些考虑因素与《Unfair Contract Terms Act 1977》之 S. 11(2)提到的 schedule 2 对合理与否的指引接近,这包括:"(a) the strength of the bargaining positions of the parties relative to each other, taking into account (among other things) alternative means by which the customer's requirements could have been met; (b) whether the customer received an inducement to agree to the term, or in accepting it had an opportunity of entering into a similar contract with other persons, but without having a similar term; (c) whether the customer knew or ought reasonably to have known of the existence and the extent of the term (having regard, among other things, to any custom of the trade and any previous course of dealing between the parties); (d) where the term excludes or restricts any relevant liability if some condition was not complied with, whether it was reasonable at the time of the contract to expect that compliance with that condition would be practicable; …"

当然,合理与否也要看不同案件其他订约时的背景/语境、免责条文本身与有关交易等的特定因素。可先节录《Misrepresentation, Mistake and Non-Disclosure》(2022

年,第6版)一书之9-30段提到一些考虑是否“合理”的因素:“In deciding whether a clause satisfies the reasonableness test, the courts consider not only the substance of the clause but also the circumstances in which it was included in the contract, such as the relative bargaining positions of the two particular parties. So, for example, courts have held that a clause fails to satisfy the reasonableness test because it is too widely drafted; or because the circumstances in which the claimant has been induced to agree to the clause render the clause unreasonable. But they have indicated that a clause is more likely to be held to be reasonable where it is negotiated between the two contracting parties, especially where the parties are of equal bargaining power and have the benefit of professional advice; in such cases, the parties are likely to prefer commercial certainty, and are likely to have included the existence and enforceability of the exclusion or limitation clause in their assessment of the balance of risk in the contract.”

由于“合理”与否的考虑是要针对特定案件的案情而定(case-specific),合理与否也就不能一概而论。可能同一条免责条文,例如标准格式合约的一条对误述免责的条文,在一个案件被视为合理,但在另一个案件不被视为合理。这可以是因为不同订约方相互之间的谈判力量有了变化。这也在《Misrepresentation, Mistake and Non-Disclosure》(2022年,第6版)一书之9-30段有提道:“So it is not sufficient to show that a clause is a standard form exclusion which is commonly used between other parties in similar contracts, unless it can be shown that it is reasonable in the context of the contract in issue.”

已经有不少先例针对在S.3下考虑“合理”与否时要考虑哪些因素作出分析,但很多是取决于不同案件的特定案情,不同的审理法官或仲裁员也会对不同案件合理与否得出不同结论。这种对事实与证据作出最后的认定是一审法院(或仲裁庭)的工作与责任,上诉庭与最高院也管不了,所以不能明确。在George Mitchell (Chesterhall) Ltd v. Finney Lock Seeds Ltd (1983) 2 AC 803贵族院先例中,Bridge勋爵有很好去说明如下:“But the several provisions of the Unfair Contract Terms Act 1977 which depend on ‘the requirement of reasonableness,… are **likely to come before the courts with increasing frequency**. It may, therefore, be appropriate to consider how an original decision as to what is ‘fair and reasonable’ made in the application of any of these provisions should be approached by an appellate court. …, the court **must entertain a whole range of considerations, put them in the scales on one side or the other**, and decide at the end of the day on which side the balance comes down. There will sometimes be **room for a legitimate difference of judicial opinion as to what the answer should be**, where it will be impossible to say that one view is demonstrably wrong and the other demonstrably right. It must follow, in my view, that, when asked to review such a decision on appeal, the appellate court should treat the original decision with the utmost respect and refrain from interference with it unless satisfied that it proceeded upon some erroneous principle or was plainly and obviously wrong."(加黑部分是笔者的强调)

6.4 有关免责条文"合理与否"的先例

针对误述的免责条文主要就是"没有依赖条文"(Non-reliance clause),只随意挑几个先例介绍,并加黑个别先例中法院认为是考虑合理与否的重点:

1. 在 FoodCo UK LLP v. Henry Boot Developments Ltd(2010)EWHC 358(Ch)先例中,Lewison 大法官针对房屋租赁合约中的一条"没有依赖条文"的合理与否进行表述:"I have no doubt that the non-reliance clause in the present case satisfies the requirement of reasonableness. I say that for the following reasons:i)The **aspiration of certainty** is a reasonable one for the parties to adopt. In most cases it will have the effect of avoiding a twelve day trial such as this one. ii)There was **no substantial imbalance of bargaining power between the parties**. Each of the tenants was a commercial and substantial concern. ...iii)Each of the tenants was **advised by solicitors**... iv)The term itself was **open to negotiation**,..."

2. 在 Lloyd v. Browning(2013)EWCA Civ 1637 上诉庭先例中,Davis 大法官说:

"... as I see it,other matters also strongly indicating that this condition was a reasonable and fair one to be introduced into this particular contract:(1)First,**each side had**, and as they each knew,**legal advisers**. That was,as the judge duly found,**plainly material as to the reasonableness** of including this particular condition into the contract. Moreover,it was the case,as was known to all concerned,that the claimants had **in addition instructed architects and planning consultants**. That was a relevant factor,too. (2)Second,the contract was one for the sale of land. It is generally well known that such contracts do indeed,as the judge put it,have **a status of 'formality'** about them. Contracts relating to the disposition of property are designed by law to require that all the agreed terms are set out in one contractual document signed by each party. (3)Third,this condition was **not a 'take it or leave it' condition of the kind** sometimes imposed in small print on consumers,acting without legal advice,in consumer transactions. It was **a special condition agreed by the parties' lawyers in circumstances where the parties had equal and corresponding negotiating positions**. Moreover,such condition had the general imprimatur of the Eastbourne Law Society and was,it is to be inferred,**in common use. That,too,is a further factor indicating reasonableness**. (4)Fourth and I think this is **a particular striking feature in the present case** the condition,expressly by its terms,**permitted the claimants to rely on written statements made by the defendants' solicitors** in replying to pre-contract enquiries or otherwise in correspondence. Thus,if the claimants wished to rely on what had been said to them orally the means for giving legal effect to that were readily available:that is,by an appropriate written pre-contract enquiry or solicitor's letter. Such a request would reveal just what the defendant vendors were prepared formally to commit themselves to."

3. 在 Hardy v. Griffiths(2014)EWHC 3947(Ch)先例中,Amanda Tipples QC 大法官说:"...The approach set out in Foodco v. Henry Boot is,it seems to me,the correct approach in the present circumstances and I find that special condition 10 is fair and reasonable. This is because:(1)It **provides certainty and the aspiration of certainty** is a reasonable one for the parties to adopt. (2)There was **no imbalance of bargaining power between the parties**. Indeed,Mr Hardy is an experienced businessman. The Defendants are both experienced lawyers. The parties were in an equal bargaining position. (3)The parties were **each advised by conveyancing solicitors** in relation to the Contract. (4)**Clause 10 was a special condition,and was open to negotiation**. ...(5)**The clause expressly permitted reliance on any reply given by the Claimants' solicitors**. If,therefore,something of importance had been stated in the course of negotiations upon which the Defendants wished to rely,the Defendants' solicitors only had to ask the Claimants' solicitors the relevant question. That would have revealed whether the Claimants were prepared to formalise the statement so that the Defendants could rely on it or whether the Defendants would have to undertake their own due diligence."

4. 在 EA Grimstead & Son Ltd v. McGarrigan(1999)10 WLUK 818 上诉庭先例中,Chadwick 大法官认为商业合约中,有两个原因应该支持一条"没有依赖条文"的有效性,也就是合约的肯定性与商业合约中往往已经以价格反映了风险的转移:"There are,as it seems to me,at least **two good reasons** why the courts should not refuse to give effect to an acknowledgement of non-reliance in **a commercial contract between experienced parties of equal bargaining power**-a fortiori,where those **parties have the benefit of professional advice**. First,it is reasonable to assume that **the parties desire commercial certainty**. They want to order their affairs on the basis that the bargain between them can be found within the document which they have signed. They want to **avoid the uncertainty of litigation** based on allegations as to the content of oral discussions at pre-contractual meetings. Second,it is reasonable to assume that **the price to be paid reflects the commercial risk which each party** - or,more usually,the purchaser-**is willing to accept**. The risk is determined,in part at least,**by the warranties which the vendor is prepared to give**. The tighter the warranties,the less the risk and(in principle at least)the greater the price the vendor will require and which the purchaser will be prepared to pay. It is legitimate and commercially desirable,that both parties should be able to measure the risk,and agree the price,on the basis of the warranties which have been given and accepted."

该先例也另有支持"没有依赖条文"满足 S.3 的合理要求的特定案情,Chadwick

大法官另说:"In the present case the evidence showed that the draft accounts were available;and that **the purchaser had had the opportunity to investigate the company's books and records, if it had chosen to do so**. The parties entered the agreement… with the benefit of advice**… it would have been clear that Mr. McGarrigan**(被告)**was only prepared to enter into the agreement on the basis that the purchaser relied on its own investigations and judgment**. In such a case it seems to me wholly fair and reasonable that the purchaser should seek his remedies(if any) within the four corners of the agreement;and should not be permitted to rely on pre-contractual representations which are, deliberately, not reflected in contractual warranties. That is **a decision on the particular facts of the case as they had emerged during the trial.**"

5. 在 First Tower Trustees Ltd v. CDS(Superstores International) Ltd(2018) EWCA Civ 1396 上诉庭先例中,看来涉及的误述的本质(是真正的无辜误述)与重要性(已经要求被误述方自己确认陈述是否正确)也是合理与否的考虑之一。Lewison 大法官说:"The landlords(被一审认定误述的业主) argue that because the **misrepresentation was an innocent one**, and CDS(原告) was told to satisfy itself that there were no environmental problems, the judge should have held that the clause was reasonable 'in so far as' it related to that misrepresentation. … if, … it means non-culpable or non-negligent that would have required a factual finding from the judge. Since no one from the landlords gave evidence at trial and no one attempted to explain … the factual premise on which the argument is based is unsound. … The landlords also argue that all the factors that I considered in FoodCo … were presented in this case … **a court should be very wary of saying contract terms negotiated by commercial parties are unreasonable.** …"

6. 除非是在个别的案件有特殊的情况,例如一个争议的误述是一方特定向对方查问时对方的回答(有些行业交易中是有这样的习惯,例如土地买卖或保险),对方就不能在"没有依赖条文"下逃避责任。否则这个查问就没有意义,因为对方可以误述然后依赖"没有依赖条文"。正如 Lewison 大法官在 First Tower Trustees Ltd v. CDS(Superstores International) Ltd 先例中说:"In my judgment, he(一审法官) was right to stress the **importance of pre – contract enquiries** in the field of conveyancing; and right in the conclusion to which he came. As the judge said, if clause 5.8(没有依赖条文) governs the landlords' liability the important function of replies to enquiries before contract becomes worthless."

7. 在 Schenkers v. Overland Shoes(1998) 1 Lloyd's Rep 498 上诉庭先例中,Pill 大法官说只有双方的谈判地位完全不平等,一般的商业习惯做法才会被视为不合理:"In my judgement, the plaintiffs have satisfied the burden upon them of establishing that Clause 23(A) in the circumstances satisfies the requirement of reasonableness. The clause

was in common use and well known in the trade following comprehensive discussions between reputable and representative bodies mindful of the considerations involved. It reflects a general view as to what is reasonable in the trade concerned. ... In a situation in which there **was no significant inequality of bargaining position, the customs of the trade were an important factor**. ..."

8. Cleaver v. Schyde(2011)EWCA Civ 929 上诉庭先例也涉及标准格式合约的免责条文,但因为案件有特定案情(买卖双方都知道对土地开发计划的陈述会严重影响买方的决定),所以得出与 Schenkers v. Overland Shoes 先例不同的判决。Longmore 大法官说:

"This case is a good example of the width of the interference with freedom of contract generated by s. 11 of the Unfair Contract Terms Act 1977. My initial reaction was that a term restricting rescission(in non-fraudulent cases)to instances where the property differed substantially in quantity, quality or tenure from what it had been represented to be was, in general, a reasonable clause. The Law Society(with, of course, no axe to grind on behalf of either vendors or purchasers)had promulgated the clause, taking into account judicial criticism of its predecessors.

But **the question is not whether the clause is, in general, a reasonable clause. The question is whether it was a reasonable clause in the contract made between this vendor and this purchaser at the time when the contract was made**. On the particular facts of this case both parties were aware of and wished(if possible)to exploit the development potential of the property. The planning position(and any change to it between the answer to enquiries and completion)was of obvious materiality. Yet the mere existence of an application for planning permission can hardly be said to make the property different in quantity, quality or tenure from what it had been represented to be.

It is therefore **difficult to criticise a judge who hears all the evidence and concludes that, in the particular circumstances of this particular case, the vendor had not satisfied him that cl. 7. 1. 3 was a reasonable clause to have included in the contract at the time when it was made**."

6.5 被告误述方主张依赖合约中的免责条文须注意的实体与程序方面问题

这样看来,在英国法院(或仲裁庭)假设参与国际商务游戏的中国公司是与西方公司有同样水平与有委任(或可以去委任)律师的情况下,加上"没有依赖条文"对中国公司也有好处因为可以避免谈判时有否可诉误述的昂贵与耗时争议以及带来肯定性(certainty),一条"没有依赖条文"很可能被视为合理。虽然本质上该条文是一条 S. 3 要管控的免责条文,但中国公司很难在发生诉讼时攻击其有效性。可以说"没有依赖条文"是一把双刃剑:一方面中国公司要特别小心对方在谈判阶段误述或误导但依赖该条文逃避责任(除非能证明欺诈性误述,但这是很难);另一方面如果中国公司有水平，如果曾经在谈判过程中向对方做出过非欺诈性误述，就可以利用一条满足 S. 3 对"合理"要求的广泛的条文免除误述责任。

误述的争议因为涉及大量的事实证据，所以在文书请求/案件陈述中要特别小心。在本书第三章之 9 段针对作为受害方/误述方指控欺诈性误述的文书请求/案件陈述要满足的要求进行描述，这里要针对的是作为误述方要满足哪些要求。

如果中国公司被指控误述并以《Misrepresentation Act 1967》的立法误述作为诉因起诉，中国公司想依赖一条免责条文（在不少国际商业合约会有），就要记得在抗辩书（statement of defence）中提出，并最好要指出在 S. 3 立法条文下符合"合理"测试的案情事实，因为被告误述方有举证责任。这才可让原告在答辩书（statement of reply）中同意、不同意或否认有关请求的事实，[52] 并指出该免责条文"不合理"的新的有关事实。当然，原告也可能会申请要被告提供有关主张免责条文"合理"的进一步详情（application for further and better particulars 或 clarifications），[53] 以确定有关的争议事实包括什么并准备相应证据。

这可节录《Misrepresentation, Mistake and Non-Disclosure》（2022 年，第 6 版）一书之 9 – 27 段所说："**Pleading and proving reasonableness** Since it is the defendant who must show that the reasonableness test is satisfied, it is he who must plead the circumstances which render the clause reasonable. Where the pleading makes it clear that the defendant will rely upon an exclusion clause, then it is implicit in that pleading that the defendant is asserting that the clause is reasonable. But the better practice is to include in the defence a statement that the standard conditions relied upon are reasonable." 这样，也可以避免原告去提前要求撤销抗辩（strike – out application）并申请简易判决（summary judgment）。[54] 在该权威书籍同一段接下来说："... the court will not normally decide the issue of reasonableness on a strike – out application since it cannot decide whether the term was a fair and reasonable one, having regard to all the circumstances, without hearing evidence: the issue is a broad issue of fact which can normally only be dealt with at the trial of the action."

在 Sheffield v. Pickfords Ltd（1997）CLC 648 上诉庭先例中，Woolf 勋爵解释被告要依赖免责条文的先决条件是在文书请求中说明条文合理性并提供详情的原因时说：

"... Because the language of s. 3 is explicit and clear, the other party to a contract cannot exclude liability in respect of the breach, or restrict liability, except in so far as the contract terms satisfy the requirement of reasonableness. In other words, the requirement

---

〔52〕 见笔者《证据法：国际规管与诉讼中的证据攻防》一书第七章之 6. 1 段。

〔53〕 见笔者《证据法：国际规管与诉讼中的证据攻防》一书第七章之 10. 1 段。

〔54〕 见笔者《证据法：国际规管与诉讼中的证据攻防》一书第六章之 4 段。

of reasonableness is a condition precedent to the reliance upon the standard conditions which are being prayed in aid. …

I am satisfied that at least… that there is an implication,…. I would go further and say that I can see advantages in a defendant setting out squarely and clearly that they contend that the contract provisions are reasonable. They can then require the plaintiff to clarify his or her position and say whether or not they are taking the point. If they are taking the point, then the defendants are in a position to have the necessary evidence at the hearing to establish their case on reasonableness. …

I am of the view that it is much better for the defendants to be certain as to what is required of them and not to be in any doubt in the matter, than to have a situation where they are not clear whether they are going to have to call evidence or not. If the position is clarified, at least in some cases, plaintiffs will not be challenging the reasonableness and that being so the evidence will not be necessary."

6.6 "完整合约条文"与"没有依赖条文"

在本书第一章之1.3.8段已提到此类条文,在笔者《合约的解释:规则与应用》一书第十三章之2段也已有介绍,但讲得不完整,特别是不包括《Misrepresentation Act 1967》之S.3对这类条文的管控与该书在2014年出版后的重要先例中,所以在此加以补充。

《Misrepresentation, Mistake and Non-Disclosure》(2022年,第6版)一书之9-06段说到解释一条一般措辞/文字的"完整合约条文"(Entire Agreement Clause)会是只否定谈判时曾经做出过"附带协议/保证"(collateral contract/warranty),[55]但不包括否定谈判时曾经做出过可诉误述:"'**Entire agreement' clauses** It is not uncommon for a commercial contract to contain an 'entire agreement' clause …. It only denies contractual force to statements which are not contained in the contract; it does not purport to affect the status of any statement as a (pre-contractual) misrepresentation."

另在该书之9-12段说:"'**Entire agreement' clauses** It is well established that a clause in a written contract providing that the contract constitutes the 'entire agreement' between the parties normally has the effect that the parties' contractual obligations are **to be found only in the written contract itself** and not, for example, in **any side agreement or collateral contract. But it goes no further than this**. This is simply the natural interpretation of the clause: if it were to be intended to have any wider effect, such as to exclude liability for misrepresentation, or even to exclude all remedies which are not expressly provided for in the contract, clear words would have to be used. … **the words 'this contract comprises the entire agreement between the parties' simply do not**

[55] 见本书第一章之2.5.2段。

themselves exclude misrepresentation."（加黑部分是笔者的强调）

可简单重复"完整合约条文"的本意是局限或排除一份全面拟定与双方签署了的合约内明示条文/文字以外的合约争议。这主要包括在双方谈判时会（或没有）发生过的如附带协议/保证、默示条文、商业习惯做法/惯例等。做法是通过合约双方同意，所有合约内容全部在该合约的"四个角"内，这无论是对错，双方都睁着眼睛同意这是事实，也就是任何一方以后都不能回头，去提出还有谈判中达成的其他合约内容被没有被加进合约。

但谈判如果发生过可诉误述，那么其在本质上就不可能加在一份完整合约中。[56] 所以如果想排除误述，"完整合约条文"就需要加上一条"没有依赖条文"（Non-reliance Clause），正如在 Watford Electronic Ltd v. Sanderson CFL Ltd（2001）EWCA Civ 317 上诉庭先例中的条文："（1）The parties agree that these terms and conditions... represents the entire agreement between the parties ... and（2）that no statement or representation made by either party have been relied upon by the other in agreeing to enter into the Contract."

《合约的解释：规则与应用》一书也提到对该条文的质疑，说："有逻辑不通之处，就是在较早谈判时涉及的如果合约是依赖严重的误述而产生，而没有依赖条文只是该合约的条文之一，会否整个合约包括没有依赖条文都一并无效？"

或说得更极端，一方被骗订立合约，合约中的惯用条文说明"我没有受骗去签下这份合约"。但如果有证据证明该方确实是被骗签下这份合约，包括此条文，又应在这背景/语境下如何解释此条文？可节录 Moore - Bick 大法官在 Peekay Intermark Ltd v. Australia & New Zealand Banking Group Ltd（2006）2 Lloyd's Rep 511 先例中所说："The effectiveness of（没有依赖条文）may be challenged on the grounds that the contract as a whole, including the clause in question, can be avoided if in fact one or either party was induced to enter into it by misrepresentation."

书中也说到在一些先例，如 EA Grimstead & Son Ltd v. McGarrigan（1999）10 WLUK 818 与 Watford Electronics Ltd v. Sanderson CL Ltd 等先例，"没有依赖条文"曾经被视为判了死刑。但在之后的 Peekay Intermark Ltd v. Australia & New Zealand Banking Group Ltd 与 Springwell v. JP Morgan（2010）EWCA Civ 1212 上诉庭先例中，又被判有效而"复生"。

不多去重复这些普通法/案例法下的内容，接下来是从《Misrepresentation Act 1967》之 S. 3 条文去分析立法地位如何影响普通法地位，S. 3 会否否定这一条主要针对谈判时可诉误述免责、也富争议的"没有依赖条文"。接下的小段会介绍近期对该条文两方面的攻击。

---

〔56〕 即使合约中有一条在本书第二章之 10.2 段介绍的陈述与保证条文（Representation and Warranty Clause），作用也不一样，条文内容也不会针对谈判中的所有误述。

6.6.1 “没有依赖条文”本质上是免责条文还是基础条文

在普通法下,“没有依赖条文”的理据是“合约性禁反言”(contractual estoppel),[57]也就是谈判过程中确实发生过可诉误述,并且被误述方依赖产生合约,但由于合约明示约定是没有依赖,这双方同意去认定的历史事实(rewrite history)即使是错误也构成了双方之间的禁反言,禁止被误述方事后提出误述的争议,也就是说即使能够证明事实是错误,双方也同意不能推翻或反口。

6.6.1.1 “没有依赖条文”在普通法下的地位与在立法 S.3 下的关系

只随意挑 Thornbridge Ltd v. Barclays Bank plc(2015)EWHC 3430(QB)先例去支持上述介绍的合约性禁反言的普通法地位,也就是双方可以同意将不存在依赖的事实(即使是错误)作为双方订约的基础。Moulder 大法官说:“In my view recent authorities have been very clear that **parties may agree the basis on which they are entering into a relationship.** The effect of such a clause is that the party is contractually estopped from denying to the contrary. This is so even where for example parties agree that one party has not made any pre – contract representations about a particular matter and both parties knew that such representations have in fact been made … this is **the basis on which the parties agreed to enter into the relationship**. ”(加黑部分是笔者的强调)

但普通法下说得通的“合约性禁反言”不代表 1967 立法之 S.3 管控不了,正如在 First Tower Trustees Ltd v. CDS(Superstores International)Ltd(2018)EWCA Civ 1396 上诉庭先例中,Lewison 大法官说:

“… in my judgment, that **the label ‘basis clause’** in some of the cases is to be understood. The label means no more than that the clauses in question are defining the parties’ primary obligations. …

It is now firmly established at this level in the judicial hierarchy that parties can bind themselves by contract to accept a particular state of affairs even if they know that state of affairs to be untrue. This is a particular form of estoppel which has been given the label ‘contractual estoppel’. Unlike most forms of estoppel it requires no proof of reliance other than entry into the contract itself. Thus as a matter of contract **parties can bind themselves at common law to a fictional state of affairs in which no representations have been made** or, if made, have not been relied on. Aikens LJ put the point thus in Springwell Navigation Corpn v JP Morgan Chase Bank [2010] 2 CLC 705: ‘If A and B enter into a contract then, unless there is some principle of law or statute to the contrary, they are entitled to agree what they like. … there is **no legal principle that states that parties cannot agree to assume that a certain state of affairs is the case at the time the contract is concluded or has been so in the past, even if that is not the case**, so that the

[57] 见笔者《合约的履行、弃权与禁反言》一书第八章。

contract is made upon the basis that the present or past facts are as stated and agreed by the parties.' ...

However, as Aikens LJ recognised ..., **the position at common law is not the end of the inquiry. There remains for consideration whether there is a 'statute to the contrary'. Whether section 3 of the 1967 is such a statute is a question not of the interpretation of the contract but of the interpretation of the statute**. The fact that ... a contractual estoppel does not prevent consideration of this question; not least because section 3 is expressly directed at contract terms."(加黑部分是笔者的强调)

另 Leggatt 大法官也同意说:"I would hold that whenever a contracting party relies on the principle of contractual estoppel to argue that, by reason of a contract term, the other party to the contract is prevented from asserting a fact which is necessary to establish liability for a pre – contractual misrepresentation, the term falls within section 3 of the Misrepresentation Act 1967."

6.6.1.2 免责条文与基础条文的区分

在"道高一尺、魔高一丈"的斗法下,带来了能否说一条"没有依赖条文"不是一条免责条文,而只是双方规定合约过去事实或历史背景的"基础条文"(basis clause)的争议。如果是后者,即使双方同意的事实有对有错,在普通法下也是禁反言,1967年立法之 S.3 并不针对基础条文,所以也就管不了。但如果这"没有依赖条文"本质上是免责条文,S.3 就要看其是否符合"合理"的要求了。

"基础条文"与"免责条文"的不同在 JP Morgan Chase Bank v. Springwell Navigation Corporation(2008) EWHC 1186 (Comm) 先例中有所体现,Gloster 大法官说:"There is a clear distinction between clauses which exclude liability and clauses which define the terms upon which the parties are conducting their business; in other words, clauses which prevent an obligation from arising in the first place. ...

这两者的区别也可以 Christopher Clarke 大法官在 Raiffeisen Zentralbank Osterreich AG v. Royal Bank of Scotland Plc(2010) EWHC 1392(Comm) 先例中说:"... the essential question is whether the clause in question goes to whether the alleged representation was made (or, I would add, was intended to be understood and acted on as a representation), or whether it excludes or restricts liability in respect of representations made, intended to be acted on and in fact acted on; and that **question is one of substance not form**. ... Per contra, to tell the man in the street that the car you are selling him is perfect and then agree that the basis of your contract is that no representations have been made or relied on, may be nothing more than **an attempt retrospectively to alter the character and effect of what has gone beforehand in substance an attempt to exclude or restrict liability**."(加黑部分是笔者的强调)

6.6.1.3 是免责条文还是基础条文的判断依据为谈判时是否发生误述

Christopher Clarke 大法官在 Raiffeisen Zentralbank Osterreich AG v. Royal Bank of Scotland Plc(2010)EWHC 1392(Comm)先例中解释说有关的条文到底是免责条文还是基础条文要看实质,而不是简单的贴标签。也就是要看是否确实发生了误述,并且误述方需要以"没有依赖条文"免除误述责任。Christopher Clarke 大法官以 Toulson 大法官在另一个 IFE Fund SA v. Goldman Sachs International 先例中举的例子为例,也就是一辆二手车卖方向潜在的买方陈述,说:"我买这辆车时是一手车并且之后一直是我拥有,它的记录仪器说行走了 20,000 英里是准确。"后来的文书合约加上"没有依赖条文",如果这确实是虚假陈述,这条文就是免责条文,在 S.3 下可能被视为不合理而无效。但如果卖方在谈判时是另一种说法陈述这虚假/错误的 20,000 英里的事实,说:"记录仪器是 20,000 英里,但我不知道准确与否。"这样,同样的一条"没有依赖条文"就与免责条文无关。有关判词说:

"Toulson J observed that **the question was** whether the challenged clauses were properly to be understood,not as excluding a liability for misrepresentation,but rather as going to the question **whether the alleged representation was made at all**. If the latter, neither the Misrepresentation Act 1967,section 3,nor UCTA section 2,had any relevance to them...

He rejected the claimant's challenge to the clauses**holding that the question was one of substance and not form** ... so that **a party cannot by a carefully chosen form of wording circumvent the statutory controls on exclusion of liability for a representation which on a proper analysis has been made**.

He gave the example of the seller of a car who says to a buyer 'I have serviced the car since it was new,it has had only one owner and the clock reading is accurate'. **Such statements would be representations and would remain so even if the seller had added the words' but those statements are not statements on which you can rely'.**

By contrast,if the seller of the car said 'The clock reading is 20,000 miles,but I have no knowledge whether the reading is true or false' the position would be different because the qualifying words could not fairly be regarded as an attempt to exclude liability for a false representation arising from the first half of the sentence."(加黑部分是笔者的强调)

Jack QC 大法官在较早前的 Zanzibar v British Aerospace(Lancaster House)Ltd (2000)1 WLR 2333 先例中也有类似的说法,并强调不可以这么容易就回避掉立法管控对误述免责的条文的意图:

"**Part C of clause 23**. ... however the present term operates,in my view it **comes within section 3 of the Act. I assume that a representation was made,and I assume that it was in fact relied on by Zanzibar.** Part C is then 'a term [of the contract] which would exclude or restrict—(a) any liability to which a party to [the] contract may be subject by reason of any misrepresentation made by him before the contract was made:' ...

A term which negates a reliance which in fact existed is a term which excludes a liability which the representor would otherwise be subject to by reason of the representation. If that were wrong, it would mean that section 3 could always be defeated by including an appropriate non-reliance clause in the contract, however unreasonable that might be. So I consider that **part C of clause 23 has to satisfy the requirement of reasonableness.** ..."(加黑部分是笔者的强调)

这样看来,如果的确在谈判时发生了可诉误述,误述方就要以"没有依赖条文"作为抗辩。但此时"没有依赖条文"就被视为免责条文,不会被当作基础条文以回避1967年立法S.3的管控。也就是说,该条文要通过S.3对"合理"与否的测试,如果通过,该条文才能保护误述方。

6.6.1.4 小结

在《Misrepresentation, Mistake and Non-Disclosure》(2022年,第6版)一书之9-21段对目前英国法律地位有更全面的总结,其认为:"... Sometimes **a clause has to be analysed very carefully to check whether in substance**, even if not by its literal language, **it excludes or restricts liability or a remedy for misrepresentation**. So a clause which seeks to negative an element of a claim for misrepresentation might, **in substance**, be a clause which excludes the liability which would otherwise have existed. Where, therefore, **a misrepresentation was made and was in fact relied upon by the claimant, it was held** that a clause which sought to negate the claimant's reliance was a term which excluded a liability to which the representor would otherwise be subject by reason of the representation, and therefore was **regulated by s. 3**: otherwise the section could always be defeated by including an appropriate non-reliance clause in the contract, however unreasonable that might be. This is not to say that an appropriately-drawn clause cannot effectively prevent a claim arising and therefore avoid the operation of s. 3. For example, a clause which genuinely prevents there being a misrepresentation at all by, for example, making clear that **a statement is only one of the defendant's opinions on which the claimant is not entitled to rely, ought to be unaffected by s. 3**; the cases in which such clauses have been subjected to s. 3 have been ones in which there was in fact a misrepresentation on which the claimant relied, but a clause was being used to seek to deny those facts. It has also been held that a clause by which the defendant limits the authority of his agent, and therefore successfully at common law ensures that he is not liable for his agent's representations outside the scope of that authority, is unaffected by s. 3: **the section only applies to a provision which would exclude or restrict liability for a misrepresentation made by a party or his duly authorised agent**, but does not qualify the right of a principal publicly to limit the otherwise ostensible authority of his agent. ..."(加黑部分是笔者的强调)

正如在《Chitty on Contracts》(2021年,第34版)一书之9-154段说:"... However,unless the party to whom the statement was made(or possibly subsequently but before the agreement was concluded)that the statement was not one in which the party was entitled to rely,the clause(指一条"不可依赖条文")is likely to be interpreted as an attempt to exclude or restrict liability for misrepresentation and thus subject to statutory control."

6.6.2 广泛免责条文如可被解释为包括豁免欺诈性误述是不合理条文

《Misrepresentation,Mistake and Non-Disclosure》(2022年,第6版)一书之9-24段说:"Section 3 provides that a term to which it applies is of no effect except in so far as it satisfies the requirement of reasonableness. This has been interpreted to mean that,**if unreasonable,the whole term is of no effect**,... the court cannot rewrite the term so that it constitutes only a reasonable exclusion or limitation clause,even if(so rewritten)it would then apply to the case in hand. **So,for example,a clause which is drafted widely so as to exclude all liability for misrepresentation might be held to be ineffective on the basis that it covered fraudulent misrepresentations**,even where the claim against which the defendant seeks to use the clause is based on a non-fraudulent misrepresentation. In drafting an exclusion or limitation clause great care must be taken to ensure that the clause might not be **held ineffective because it covers liabilities which render the whole clause unreasonable**. Although a court might sometimes be able to sever the provisions of an exclusion clause and so to hold there to be separate 'terms' which can be separately upheld or struck down under s. 3,the better advice is to review an exclusion or limitation clause carefully to ensure that it covers as precisely as possible the liabilities or remedies which are intended to be excluded or limited,and to structure the clause in such a way that it can be treated as severable ...."

上述是说去豁免欺诈性误述的免责条文,在S.3下被视为不合理而无效。但本来在普通法下,去豁免欺诈/欺骗侵权就因违反公共政策而无效,[58]何必烦劳S.3去视为不合理而无效?毕竟,这公共政策为绝大多数商业人士熟悉,所以在现实中也绝少会见到有合约条文去明目张胆对欺诈免责。

危险是在一条广泛的条文中,例如粗略例子是说"双方(或一方)不必对误述负责",但没有被局限的"误述"一词是包括欺诈性与非欺诈性误述,就相当于包括了欺诈性误述了。或说,可否把该条文解释为只包括非欺诈性误述的疏忽误述,把欺诈性误述分割(sever)出来否定掉?但这一句很难分割,硬去扭曲等同于法院或仲裁庭代

---

〔58〕 见本书第三章之8.3段。

合约双方将合约条文重写为“双方不必对误述(除了欺诈性)负责”,这违反了双方意思自治的基础合约法精神,法院或仲裁庭是万万不该做的。

一般去豁免误述就是一条“没有依赖条文”,在 Thomas Witter Ltd v. TBP Industries Ltd(1996)2 All ER 573 先例中,Jacob 大法官判一条广泛的条文因为可解释为是包括欺诈性误述而无效以及在 S. 3 下是不合理,其认为:“But I have to say that even if clause 17. 2 had exclusionary effect it would to my mind be **neither fair nor reasonable. The problem is its scope**. The Act of 1967 calls for consideration of the term as such. And it refers to ‘any liability’ and ‘any misrepresentation.’ It does not call for consideration of the term so far as it applies to the misrepresentation in question or the kind of misrepresentation in question. **The term is not severable**: it is either reasonable as a whole or not. So one must consider its every potential effect. **The clause does not distinguish between fraudulent, negligent, or innocent misrepresentation**. If it excludes liability for one kind of misrepresentation it does so for all. I cannot think it reasonable to exclude liability for fraudulent misrepresentation ... It may well be, with a different clause, reasonable to exclude liability for innocent misrepresentation or even negligent misrepresentation. But **since the width of this clause is too great I would have held it failed the requirement of reasonableness and so was of no effect**. ... A possible route around this latter objection would be to construe the clause so that it did not apply to a fraudulent misrepresentation. This approach is artificial. ... The construction involves creating an implied exception in the case of fraud. What about an implied exclusion of negligence? Or gross negligence? **It is not for the law to fudge a way for an exclusion clause to be valid. If a party wants to exclude liability for certain sorts of misrepresentations, it must spell those sorts out clearly**.”(加黑部分是笔者的强调)

但接下来在 Zanzibar v British Aerospace(Lancaster House)Ltd(2000)1 WLR 2333 先例中有不同判法,合约有一条用字十分广泛的“完整合约条文”加上“没有依赖条文”,可节录如下:“[A] The parties have negotiated this contract on the basis that the terms and conditions set out herein represent the **entire agreement between them relating in any way whatsoever** ... which form the subject matter of this contract and [B] accordingly they agree that **all liabilities for and remedies in respect of any representations made are excluded** save in so far as provided in this contract. [C] The parties further agree that neither party has placed **any reliance whatsoever on any representations agreements statements or understandings whether oral or in writing made prior to the date of this contract** other than those expressly incorporated or recited in this contract.”(加黑部分是笔者的强调)

Jack QC 大法官在解释这同样广泛的“没有依赖条文”就不认同 Jacob 大法官在 Thomas Witter Ltd v. TBP Industries Ltd 先例中的判决,他认为:“Part A is what is often called an entire agreement clause. The wording of this part of clause 23 does not affect Zanzibar's right to rely on any misrepresentations. ... And even in the contracts of today it surely has the ring of common sense that clauses dealing with representations are not intended by the parties to apply where a representation has been fraudulently made. I respectfully differ from Jacob J. and **I hold that clause 23**(节录的"完整合约条文"加上"没有依赖条文")**would not apply where fraud is alleged. I should say that there is no suggestion of fraud here.** ..."(加黑部分是笔者的强调)

也就是说 Jack QC 大法官在 Zanzibar v British Aerospace(Lancaster House)Ltd 先例中解释一条广泛的"没有依赖条文"并不包括欺诈性误述,不认为合约双方在同意该条文时有去包括欺诈性误述的订约意图,而该案例也不涉及欺诈性误述的指控。在 Six Continents Hotels Inc v. Event Hotels GmbH(2006)EWHC 2317(QB)先例中,Gloster 大法官也更倾向于 Jack QC 大法官的判法。

一条广泛的"没有依赖条文"显然对陈述方有好处,为了避免这些冲突的一审判例造成的不肯定,《Misrepresentation,Mistake and Non-Disclosure》(2022 年,第 6 版)一书建议说不如直接在条文中明示规定不包括欺诈性误述,这样更为明确。反正欺诈性误述本来也无法免责,写清楚不会损失什么,还可以完全避免条文被解释为包括欺诈性误述而不"合理"的可能。这可节录该书之 9 - 14 段说:"**Exclusion of liability except for fraud** In order to avoid a successful challenge to a clause on the basis that it is sufficiently wide to contravene either the common law rule that a party cannot exclude liability for its own fraud, or that the clause, by extending to claims for fraud, might thereby be held unreasonable within the statutory controls on exclusion clauses, it is not uncommon for a well - drawn exclusion clause to provide expressly that the clause does not seek to exclude or limit the parties' liability for fraud. The precise scope of such a clause depends on the language used, ..."

但只在免责条文中简单写排除"欺诈"(fraud),会有可能实际排除了所有涉及不诚实的行为,因此用一条更小心拟定只排除欺骗侵权(tort of deceit)与欺诈性误述的条文会更好。例如在 Cavell USA Inc v. Seaton Insurance Co(2009)EWCA Civ 1363 上诉庭先例中,有关的和解协中的第 13 条排除了原告"欺诈"的诉讼:"(被告)**hereby releases and forever discharges**(原告)**of and from all actions, causes of action, suits, claims and demands whatsoever**, whether at law or equity, whether known or unknown, suspected or unsuspected, disclosed or undisclosed, fixed or contingent, accrued or unaccrued, asserted or unasserted, which(原告)ever had, now has or hereafter can, shall or may have against(原告)for, upon, or by reason of any matter, cause or thing whatsoever arising out of or in connection with any business, commercial, contractual or other arrangements between or involving either of them as at the date of this Term Sheet(和解协议), **save**(i)in respect of any obligations expressly set out in this Term Sheet,(ii)in respect of any actions, causes of action, suits, claims, and demands arising from any breach by(原告) of any provision of this Term Sheet, and (**iii**) **in the case of fraud on the part of**(原告)."(加黑部分是笔者的强调)

之后被告以原告不诚实滥用诚信地位(dishonest abuse of fiduciary position)在纽约法院开始诉讼,而原告则在英国法院开始诉讼,请求法院作出宣告判决,阻止被告在纽约法院的诉讼。

Longmore 大法官通过分析和解协议第 13 条的"欺诈"是否包括不诚实滥用诚信地位,说:"… in the commercial context of this case the concept of 'fraud' is wider than the concept of the tort of deceit where a fraudulent misrepresentation(or equivalent) is required. …the exception 'in case of fraud' in clause 13 of the Term Sheet is not confined to claims in deceit but extends to at least some cases of dishonest abuse of fiduciary position."

7. 总　　结

由于中国公司近年来大量参与的国际商业活动都有可诉误述的风险,所以相关合约内(如工程合约、金融协议、联营协议、股份买卖合约、VIE 框架下的协议等)难逃有一条惯用的"没有依赖条文",合约适用法定为英国法或其他普通法国家/地区法律,外国公司或己方在有了误述指控后试图以"没有依赖条文"免责等关联问题都接踵而来。笔者可以中国公司被指控是误述方为例,对本章所讲的地位与应对作一个小结如下。

1. 抗拒欺诈性误述的指控,当然这首先要求在国际商业活动时应习惯性尽量避免做出任何不诚实的陈述/表述。不能光靠抗拒,因为不会经常抗拒成功,即便成功也是劳民伤财。

2. 针对替代指控的疏忽误述,对方被误述方会以《Misrepresentation Act 1967》之 S. 2(1)要求损失赔偿,并在该立法条文下以"拟制的欺诈"(fiction of fraud)宽松计算损失。中国公司可试图以有关陈述/误述是有"合理依据"(reasonable ground)与具体是什么合理依据抗辩,能否成功就要看有关的案情与有否证据支持。

3. 无论如何,有"没有依赖条文"可对有关非欺诈性误述豁免或免责。虽然在 1967 年立法之 S. 3 下会难逃被定性为"免责条文"而受到管控,但中国公司可以证明在有关交易与谈判的过程中,该免责条文也可以满足"合理"的要求。毕竟在国际商业交易中,特别是大公司之间,英国法院一直(错误)假设订约方不论是来自任何国家(西方或不发达国家)都有同等水平去保护自己,从而会迟疑作出 S. 3 的保护。换言之,如果满足"合理"的测试,中国公司可以依赖"没有依赖条文"不必承担可诉误述的责任。

4. 如果对方被误述方企图以误述指控提早"自助"撤销合约取巧(例如市场因疫

情而逆转），可以立法之 S. 2(2)与 SK Shipping Plc v. Capital VLCC 3 Corp(2020) EWHC 3448(Comm)先例[59]警告其可能构成违约/毁约(repudiatory breach)，也可试图达成像 The"Lucy"(1983)1 Lloyd's Rep 188 先例一样的"无损害"(without prejudice)的过渡协议。

5. 对误述的文书请求(pleadings)也十分重要，特别是法院诉讼，但在国际仲裁中也不能掉以轻心。例如上述提到的"合理依据"或"合理"免责条文认定合理与否都涉及事实。如果不在文书请求中把这些详情(particulars)写上，就没有证据的披露、提供与准备。在开庭时提出这些事实以支持合理与否，对方就会提出抗议，也确实会违反自然公正。而法院或仲裁庭也无法最后对这些事实作出对中国公司有利的决定。

---

[59] 这是一审判决，但由于双方没有对这个法律观点提出上诉，所以没有被上诉庭推翻(只是不像是认同)，目前也没有其他高院判决有不同判法，故其仍处于有效的法律地位。

第五章　自动披露责任、沉默与隐瞒

1. 普通法不要求自动披露,也不构成可诉误述

英国普通法下合约双方在谈判时是没有自动披露的责任,也完全可以保持沉默,即使知道另一方合约方需要知道这些信息与事实,而且知道了就很可能不会订立有关合约,或会坚持不同对价与/或条件。这隐瞒在道德上说不过去或违反善意(good faith),但在法律上却没有后果。英国法律在这方面的理念与其他方面上"没有责任去救援"(no duty to rescue)也是一致。[1] 正如 Steyn 大法官在 Banque Keyser Ullmann SA v. Skandia(UK) Insurance Co Ltd(1990) 1 QB 665 上诉庭先例的一审说:"English law has always adopted a robust approach to any suggestion that, in the absence of a special relationship, somebody owes a legal duty to rescue another from physical harm or financial ruin. That is so no matter how simple and easy the intervention to rescue the other might be: In Dorset Yacht Co. Ltd. v. Home Office [1970] A. C. 1004 ..."

换言之,即使对危难中的第三人作出生死之别的援助只是举手之劳,英国法律下的不作为(omission)仍是无罪。这看来更是道德不容,所以在商业合约谈判双方有利益冲突的情况下,没有法律责任向对方自动披露肯定对对方有利的信息与事实,也就觉得是理所当然了。

在英国的合约法下是没有善意的默示要求,因为这被认为是与现实不配合地唱高调。没有善意要求的英国法律地位最明确显示在合约谈判的双方没有自动披露责任。但即使是有个别合约要求善意,如通过明示(订约方去加入一条善意条文)或对某些类别合约的默示,也不适用在尚没有合约关系的谈判。谈判只属于侵权的范畴,而英国的侵权法去区分了"误述"导致合约的产生是有救济,因为合约成立(formation of contract)的要件是有缺陷,但不自动披露或隐瞒就没有救济。这奇怪的区分在 Banque Keyser Ullmann SA v. Skandia(UK) Insurance Co Ltd 先例中,上诉庭的 Slade 大法官解释说:"For better or worse, our law of tort draws a fundamental distinc-

---

[1] 但在海上却因为条件与环境的特殊,为了鼓励自发救援而在海事法(admiralty law)并在国际公约的《1910 年统一海难援助和救助某些法律规定公约》要求救援财产(主要是遇上海难的船舶与货物)与设立救援奖金,甚至后来有国际公约(《1989 年国际救助公约》)去强制海上救助人命。

tion between the legal effects of acts on the one hand and omissions on the other. ... in Yuen Kun Yeu v. Attorney – General of Hong Kong [1988] AC 175, Lord Keith said: 'Foreseeability of harm is a necessary ingredient of such a relationship, but it is not the only one. Otherwise there would be liability in negligence on the part of one who sees another about to walk over a cliff with his head in the air, and forbears to shout a warning.' ... The example given by Lord Keith is of a failure to prevent physical harm. But the same **reluctance on the part of the courts to give a remedy in tort for pure omission applies**-perhaps even more so-when the omission is a failure to prevent economic harm. As will appear below, a corresponding **distinction is drawn by the law of contract which in general imposes no liability by virtue of a failure to speak, as opposed to a misrepresentation.** ...The general principle that there is **no obligation to speak within the context of negotiations for an ordinary commercial contract** (though qualified by the well known special principles relating to contracts uberrimae fidei, fraud, undue influence, fiduciary duty, etc.) is **one of the foundations of our law of contract**, and must have been the basis of many decisions over the years. There are countless cases in which one party to a contract has in the course of negotiations failed to disclose a fact known to him which the other party would have regarded as highly material, if it had been revealed. However, ordinarily in the absence of misrepresentation, our law leaves that other party entirely without remedy."(加黑部分是笔者的强调)

相比之下,欧洲大陆法(包括中国法律)有善意的要求,[2]就在自动披露有不一样的对待。例如,法国有"pre – contractual liability"的侵权责任,会在要求善意谈判时包括了自动披露的责任。《French Code Civil》之 Article 1112 – 1 说:"The party who knows information which is of decisive importance for the consent of the other party, must inform him of it where the latter is legitimately unaware of this information or relies on the contracting party. However, this duty to inform does not apply to the estimation of the value of the performance."

这方面不多讲,有兴趣的读者可参阅如《Precontractual Liability in European Private Law》(Cambridge University Press, 2009);《Precontractual Liability》(Kluwer, Deventer, 1990);《A Role for Tort in Pre-Contractual Negotiation? An Examination of English, French and Canadian Law》(2003)52 I. C. L. Q. 969 等。

英国普通法对谈判时的误述诱导合约产生有很严格的救济,特别是欺诈性误述。但即使针对的是无辜误述,衡平法也有让受害方/被误述方选择撤销合约的救济。而在《Misrepresentation Act 1967》的立法下,更加可以让受害方取得金钱上的赔偿。但不自动披露,即使是"欺诈性"地不披露,仍是没有法律后果,这显然是与误述有完全

---

〔2〕 关于普通法与大陆法下善意原则或责任的巨大差异,可见本书第一章之 2.6.1 段。

不同的对待。其中一个重要的解释就是误述涉及误述方采取了行动(positive act)以言行诱导受害方,所以法律应该阻止。但在被动的(passive)不自动披露中,对方根本什么都没有做,只是受害方自己不知道应该知道的信息与事实而吃亏,所以不能怪罪于对方。

重要与必须知道不自动披露与保持沉默,可区分为两类:一类是保持沉默会误导(mislead)对方,这仍会构成可诉误述(actionable misrepresentation)并有法律后果。另一类的保持沉默只是不告诉对方他很想知道的事实或情况,但并没有任何行动误导对方。前一类包括沉默的同时或以前有一些"小动作"、讲一半不讲一半或曾经让对方有过一种理解但对后来的情况改变保持沉默[3]等。

很早已有说法在货物买卖时要求买方自己小心,[4]卖方不会有向买方自动披露的责任。例如,对有关商品,卖方自己的售价比不远的商店价格贵,或该商品有什么缺点。而货物买卖的交易是社会上最频密、普及与重要的商业活动,早年是如此,今天在国际商业社会仍是如此。又例如在土地/房屋买卖中,有关土地/房屋的弱点与潜在问题明确适用买方自己小心(caveat emptor)的原则,正如英国政府在《Reforming the Home Buying and Selling Process in England and Wales:Contents of the Home Information Pack》(Consultation Paper, Office of the Deputy Prime Minister, March 2003)的7.5段确认说:"We do not intend, however, to change the principle of caveat emptor(let the buyer beware)."

表面看来确实对买方有点不公道,在很大部分情况下,买方会是卖方无需自动披露信息与事实的受害方,因为只有卖方才会知道任何有关土地/房屋的弱点与潜在的问题。但反过来测试公道与否,如果买方私下知道该土地所在地区会被政府计划大力发展或建造主要干道,又或是地下应有金矿,买方也无需自动向卖方披露。正如在Jewson & Sons Ltd v. Arcos Ltd(1933)45 Lloyd's Rep 326先例中,一审Branson大法官说:"The case put of the purchase of an estate, in which there is a mine under the surface, but the fact is unknown to the seller, is one in which a man of tender conscience or high honour would be unwilling to take advantage of the ignorance of the seller; but there can be no doubt that the contract for the sale of the estate would be binding."

"caveat emptor"的说法或原则也不只是适用在货物买卖或土地买卖等合约上,而是一般适用在所有其他的商业合约关系上,正如Atkin勋爵在Bell v. Lever Brothers Ltd(1932)AC 161贵族院先例说:"The principle of caveat emptor applies outside

---

[3] 见Spice Girls Ltd v. Aprilia World Service BV(2002)EWCA Civ 15上诉庭先例与Erlson Precision Holdings Ltd v. Hampson Industries Plc(2011)EWHC 1137(Comm)先例,这已经在本书第二章之8段与9段有介绍。

[4] 这也是《Sale of Goods Act 1979》之Section 14(1)的规定(早在《Sale of Goods Act 1893》就已有类似规定),在杨大明律师《国际货物买卖》一书第四章之1段有介绍。

contracts of sale."

虽然英国法律不保护受害方的地位，也就是不要求自动披露对方很想知道的信息与事实，确实会在极端的情况下令一般人士觉得道德不容。但从整体上去看，这个普通法地位是保护交易的双方。只要是双方自己小心谨慎，能调查到的相关信息与事实，就自己尽量去做好。如果自己调查有困难或花费高/耗时长，就尽量向对方提问，要求对方回答与详尽陈述直到自己满意才订立合约。而如果对方在回答时误述，就会有法律后果了。对方当然可以选择不回答，但这样，最终是否还能订立合约就有了疑问。对方如果不在乎交易是否成功，或自己有垄断性地位就可以拒绝或减少回答，不理不睬。能够做好这些工作就可以避免自己成为对方不自动披露或隐瞒的受害方了。正如在 Terrene Ltd v. Nelson(1937)3 All ER 739 先例中，Farwell 大法官说："In the ordinary case, a purchaser has to go for his information to the vendor, but, bearing in mind **the principle of caveat emptor**, he is bound to make proper inquiries for himself. But he must, in almost every case, in the first instance, at any rate, **seek his information from the vendor, who knows the facts**, whereas the purchaser probably does not know them. When a purchaser, with a possible view of making an off for the property, seeks information from the vendor, **the vendor, of course, is bound to the best of his ability to supply him with accurate information**."(加黑部分是笔者的强调)

针对不自动披露，《Chitty on Contracts》(2021 年，第 34 版)一书之 9 - 021 段有如下说明："**Non-disclosure** The general rule is that mere non-disclosure does not constitute misrepresentation, for there is, in general, no duty on the parties to a contract to disclose material facts to each other, however dishonest such non-disclosure may be in particular circumstances. ... Tacit acquiescence in another's self - deception does not itself amount to a misrepresentation, provided that it has not previouy been caused by a positive misrepresentation. ..."

另本章所针对的是合约前的披露(pre - contractual disclosure)。对合约履行过程中披露信息与事实，要根据每个合约不同的明示或默示条文，本章不去针对，顶多只会提到。

2. 法律强加"披露责任"的例外

无需自动披露的法律地位也有不少例外，这包括是通过立法或是来自普通法对某些类别的合约[例如关系合约(relational contract)][5]作出例外，强加一个披露责任(duty of disclosure)。一旦有了披露责任，在合约关系的范畴就会因不自动披露而

[5] 见本书第一章之 2.6.5 段。

构成了误述,正如 Jonathan Parker 大法官在 Conlon v. Simms(2006) EWCA Civ 1749 上诉庭先例中说:"Non-disclosure where there is a duty to disclose is tantamount to an implied representation that there is nothing relevant to disclose."

这也带来误述导致合约产生的救济同样适用在违反披露责任,如有权撤销合约、[6]以欺诈/欺骗侵权(tort of deceit)[7]或《Misrepresentation Act 1967》[8]索赔金钱损失等。

在有披露责任下刻意隐藏信息与事实,也很可能构成欺诈/欺骗与欺诈性误述,正如早在 Brownlie v. Campbell(1890)5 App Cas 925 先例中,Blackburn 勋爵说:"I go on further still to say, what is perhaps not quite so clear, but certainly it is in my opinion, where there is a duty or an obligation to speak, and a man in breach of that duty or obligation holds his tongue and does not speak, and does not say the thing he was bound to say, if that was done with the intention of inducing the other party to act upon the belief that the reason why he did not speak was because he had nothing to say, I should be inclined myself to hold that that was fraud also."

另在 Conlon v. Simms 先例的一审中,Lawrence Collins 大法官说:"It is clear that where there is a duty to disclose, and the failure to disclose is fraudulent, there will be an action in deceit and damages will be an available remedy. In such cases 'the non-disclosure assumes the character of fraudulent concealment, or amounts to fraudulent misrepresentation, or is otherwise founded on, or characterised and accompanied by, fraud."

3. 内幕交易与不自动披露

现代商业交易中最常见的一种交易就是公司股票的买卖,这包括上市公司的股票和私人公司的股份。影响股票价格的因素有很多,包括公司的业绩,公司管理层的素质,公司业务所在行业的发展,政府的政策与法规对相关业务是支持还是制约甚至是禁止,公司得到或失去一个巨额订单、项目或重要合作伙伴,公司的产品在技术上有历史性的突破,公司进行收购或者被收购等。对于股票交易的双方来说,如果他们在对这些会影响股票价格的信息享有同样的掌握程度的情况下订立买卖合约,可以说这个交易是双方在权衡过各种信息与利弊之后合意公平达成的交易,无论该交易的价格或其他条文如何。

但是现实中,这种理想与公平的状态常常达不到或被破坏,其中一个很常见的情

---

[6] 见本书第三章。

[7] 见本书第三章之8.2段。

[8] 见本书第四章。

况就是交易的一方知道一些对方不知道的非公开的信息，而该信息会对股票的价格有重大的影响。交易一方就凭借这种信息的不对称，在交易中取巧，使对方同意以一个相比于他知道这些信息后会同意的价格更高或更低的价格达成交易。

3.1　公司董事一般情况下对公司股东没有诚信责任而无需披露内幕信息

这种信息不对称最常见的情况是出现在公司的董事、高管以及其他雇员买卖自己公司的股票。早在 Percival v. Wright(1902)2 Ch 401 先例中，就出现公司股东在将股份卖给公司董事之后才获悉公司将被收购的消息，该收购公司股份的价格明显高于其卖给董事的价格。英国普通法对订约当事人没有强加自动披露的要求，这种不披露就不会有法律后果，除非当事人之间有特殊的关系，例如诚信责任。[9] 这也正是本案中股东主张的董事对股东负有诚信责任，在这种特殊的关系下，董事需要披露。不过法院并没有支持股东这种主张，在该先例明确了公司的董事只是公司法人的受托人(trustee)而不是公司股东的受托人，所以只对公司负诚信责任而不对公司的股东负诚信责任。该高院判决的判决提要(headnote)说："The directors of a company are not trustees for individual shareholders, and may purchase their shares without disclosing pending negotiations for the sale of the company's undertaking."

Percival v. Wright 先例确立的公司董事只对公司负有诚信责任的大原则直到今天仍然适用，已经被写进英国《Company Act 2006》的第 170 条。这背后的道理也是完全可以理解的。诚信责任的本质是委托人(trustor)完全信任与依赖受托人，而受托人则效忠委托人，所作所为完全为委托人着想，保护委托人的利益。但是在公司与公司股东之间，针对某一具体的交易或决策事项，公司的利益与个别股东的利益完全有可能不一致，大股东与小股东的利益也可能不一致，这样，就不可能要求董事对所有人都负诚信责任。

但该董事不对股东负诚信责任的一般性原则并不是绝对的，随后已经有先例在案情上与 Percival v. Wright 先例做出区分，在适当的情况(主要是一方对另一方完全信任或会产生不当影响的情况)偏离该一般原则。首先是在新西兰上诉庭 Coleman v. Myers(1977)2 NZLR 225 先例中，Myers 父子是一间私人公司的董事，儿子是公司的董事总经理(managing director)与股东，父亲则是公司的主席(chairman)，整个私人公司是家族企业，很多股东都是他们的亲戚。儿子希望以每股 4.8 美元的价格收购其他股东手中的股份，进而变为公司的唯一拥有者。遂以董事的身份向股东发出收购股份的要约，并用公司的资产去支付收购所需的价款，在收购完成后将完全控制公司。Coleman 先生作为小股东抗拒这种做法并起诉 Myers 父子，声称在收购股份时，他们并没有披露一些显示公司资产真正价值的内部信息，并在劝说其他股东出卖股份时做出欺诈性或疏忽误述。上诉庭判 Coleman 先生这两个主张都败诉，其中针对误述是因为证据不足失败，而关于没有披露的内部信息，上诉庭认为 Coleman 先生

---

[9]　这可见本书第一章之 2.7.1.2 段。

指出的都是一些很不重要的信息,并不会实质影响公司资产的价值进而影响股份的价值。但是对于在本案中 Myers 父子作为董事是否对 Coleman 先生作为股东负有诚信责任而要进行披露,上诉庭则是批评了 Percival v. Wright 先例中的判决后认为考虑到本案的特殊情况,董事对股东负有诚信责任并且应该进行披露。本案的特殊情况包括公司是家族企业,其他股东非常信任与依赖 Myers 父子对公司的管理,Myers 父子高度独占公司内部信息,该交易完全就是为了他们个人的利益以及他们在收购公司股份时对小股东进行各种游说等因素,令整个交易看来非常类似一方在另一方不当影响(undue influence)[10]下做出决定,所以 Myers 父子作为公司的董事对股东负有诚信责任。不过上诉庭拒绝去设立任何判断的标准,而只是根据个案的案情来进行判断。

接下来在澳大利亚的 Brunninghausen v. Glavanics(1999)46 NSWLR 538 先例中,法院也是同样采用从具体的案情出发来进行判断。本案中的原告与被告也是亲戚关系,他们既是家族公司的董事也是该公司的股东。后因双方发生矛盾与产生不同意见,G 先生就不再参与公司的事务,后来 G 先生将其手中的股份转给 B 先生。不过在转卖股份时,B 先生并没有向 G 先生透露公司正在谈判一个收购计划。之后公司以一个不错的价格被卖出去,而股份的价格是明显高于 B 先生从 G 先生处购买的价格。法院判考虑到 G 先生退出公司事务之后他是无法得知公司的经营情况与该收购信息,自然也就无法知道他手中股份的真正价值。所以 B 先生对 G 先生负有诚信责任而需要将公司正在谈判中的收购事宜告知 G 先生。

最后介绍英国较近期的 Peskin v. Anderson(2000)EWCA Civ 326 上诉庭先例中,案情涉及英国皇家汽车俱乐部(Royal Automobile Club)的 4 位会员起诉该俱乐部的董事。英国皇家汽车俱乐部隶属于英国皇家汽车俱乐部有限公司,该俱乐部的会员也是该公司的股东。该 4 位会员指称他们退出会籍时公司的董事没有向他们披露公司正在商谈将旗下的部分业务出售的信息,因此损失了出售该业务后股东应该得到的分成。一审法院的 Neuberger 大法官与上诉庭的 Mummery 大法官均判英国普通法下公司的董事对股东没有诚信责任,所以无需进行披露。在上诉庭,Mummery 大法官提到了上述介绍的新西兰与澳大利亚的两个先例,并同意在案情非常特殊的情况下,一般的原则会有例外,也即董事对股东有诚信责任。Mummery 大法官说:"The court has been referred to the valuable and detailed surveys of the authorities, expounding the special circumstances which justify the imposition of fiduciary duties on directors to individual shareholders, in the judgments of Court of Appeal in New Zealand in Coleman v. Myers … and of the Court of Appeal of New South Wales in Brunninghausen v. Glavanics … In both of those cases fiduciary duties of directors to shareholders were established in the specially strong context of the familial relationships of the directors and

〔10〕 见本书第十一章。

shareholders and their relative personal positions of influence in the company concerned."

这种内幕交易在现实中经常发生，其之所以会大行其道，其中一个重要的普通法上的支持就是订立合约时订约方没有披露的责任。笔者也曾经见过不少涉及这类情况的案件，公司的大股东本身也是高管，知悉一家上市公司有意以非常优越的价格收购自己的公司，在其他小股东尚未得知此消息时，该大股东主动要求购买小股东手里的股票，并在不披露该收购事宜的情况下将购买的价格定得远远低于上市公司收购时为公司股票做出的定价。如果这种情况适用英国普通法，该小股东即使之后发现该收购交易，也只能怪自己不去查清楚，或者不去向大股东问清楚。可是如果同样的情况发生在要求订约方有善意责任的地方就会有所不同。

3.2 对上市公司要披露内幕信息的立法监管

随着后来金融证券业的发展，尤其是上市公司的大量涌现，公司从公众处吸收资金，其业务也会影响公众利益。这种公司内部人员（insider）或掌握了某些内部信息的人士因为信息的不对称从中取巧去损害交易对方利益的做法，不仅道德难容，更是对整个市场秩序有着极大的破坏性，以及打击投资者的积极性。所以，世界各国家和地区纷纷通过立法来打击这种内幕交易，参与内幕交易的人士除了要对受损害的交易对方承担民事上的赔偿责任之外，甚至还需要承担罚款与监禁的刑事责任。

美国作为金融证券业务发展得最早与最快的国家，内幕交易在其《The Securities Exchange Act of 1934》中已经被提出。英国则是在《Company Act 1980》中首次将内幕交易提升至刑事犯罪的高度。随后英国的《Criminal Justice Act 1993》也明确写明内幕交易在刑法下的责任，见 Section 52"The offence of insider dealing"。很多中国公司都选择去上市的香港特别行政区也有立法针对内幕交易，这可见《Security and Future Ordinance》（第 571 章）。这些立法中都对什么是内幕交易行为、内幕消息、内部人员，民事责任有哪些，刑事责任是什么等问题作出了详细的规定，因为本书的课题不是内幕交易，所以在此就不再展开来讲。目前针对上市公司，因为其行为影响面广，所以各国（地区）的证券交易法与交易所规则都对公司的各种信息披露做出详细规定与严格的规管，内幕交易更是被严格禁止。

不过英国的《Criminal Justice Act 1993》Section 63（2）却也同时明确写明"No contract shall be void or unenforceable by reason only of section 52"。我国香港特区的《Security and Future Ordinance》第 280 条与第 304 条也有同样的说法。这表示虽然内幕交易被禁止，但内幕交易下订立的非法合约并不会无效或不能强制执行。通常英国立法都会考虑多个公共政策以及普通法的地位，结合本章的课题，这等于说其中一个考虑是立法无意去影响普通法下订立合约时无需披露的一般大原则，从而不会令合约因为订约方没有披露就无效。笔者将在本书第八章 5.2 段从非法的角度再来分析内幕交易的课题与该立法。

4. 其他通过立法要求自动披露的例子

这方面例子很多,例如刚提到的《Company Act 1980》与《Criminal Justice Act 1993》,或稍后会介绍的《Marine Insurance Act 1906》之 S. 18 等的立法,都是给有关人士强加一个披露责任的典型例子。这些自动披露责任甚至不只是针对受影响类别的合约在订立前的谈判,更会延伸至合约履行或其他千变万化的情况。

再提一些其他立法,以让读者有一个较为全面的概念,虽然与走出去的中国公司关系不大。英国的《Housing Act 1985(as amended)》立法之 S. 125 名为"Landlord's notice of purchase price and other matters",S. 125(4A)要求屋主自动向租客披露知悉的房屋结构性缺陷。《Estate Agents Act 1979》之 S. 18 也规定了地产中介向客户对收取佣金的披露责任等。

有关公司挂牌上市或上市公司发行债券的手续,英国《Financial Services and Markets Act 2000》立法针对发行人(issuer)在递交了上市详情(listing particulars)后,如果其中的事项如公司资产、负债、财政状况、利润亏损、招股章程(prospectus)等变化,是需要追加一份附加上市详情(supplementary list particulars)。

这方面广为公众所知的还有各种保护消费者的立法,成为涉及消费者合约的默示地位/条文(implied term)。这可节录《Misrepresentation, Mistake and Non-Disclosure》一书(2022 年,第 6 版)之 17 - 60 段说:"**Duties of disclosure under the Consumer Contracts (Information, Cancellation and Additional Charges) Regulations 2013** Part 2 ... requires a trader to provide certain specified information to a consumer with whom the trader contracts. In relation to the information that must be provided, the Regulations differentiate between an on - premises contract,[11] an off-premises

[11] 立法的定义是:"a contract between a trader and a consumer which is neither a distance contract nor an off - premises contract."即除以下两个脚注介绍的合约类型外的合约,最常见的就是消费者在商店里购买有关产品。这里要强调立法要适用,买卖双方必须满足立法对供应商(trader)与消费者(consumer)的定义,这显示是不会包括国际货物买卖合约。

contract[12] and a distance contract[13] ...The information to be provided is more extensive for off - premises contracts and distance contracts than for on - premises contracts, but for all three types of contract, where the duty arises it requires the trader to give information in a clear and comprehensive manner about such things as the main characteristics of the goods, services or digital content, the price, and details about the trader (including his identity). In the case of off - premises and distance contracts the consumer generally has a right to cancel the contract, and in such cases the information to be provided by the trader includes information about the cancellation right and its method of exercise."

《Consumer Contracts (Information, Cancellation and Additional Charges) Regulations 2013》将合约分为三类,其中第一类合约消费者在供应商的商业处所购买有关产品,因为亲自看过、检查过,毕竟普通法的大原则是买方自己小心,所以供应商的披露责任比另两类要低。而在后两类合约,特别是双方完全没有面对面地远程订立合约,因为消费者非常依赖供应商的陈述,所以供应商的披露责任也相应升高,包括要告知消费者有权取消合约与如何取消。

在法院程序方面,法律也会对一些向法院申请的禁令如冻结令(Freezing Injunction)[14]与搜查令(Search Order)[15]强加申请人自动披露的责任。因为这是涉及单方面(ex partes)申请,所以法院很担心申请人与他的代表律师误述与/或不披露/隐瞒重要(对法院的决定而言)的事实真相,不作出全面与坦率的披露,误导了法院对不知情的被申请人作出会有严重不良后果的禁令。在 Steven Gee QC 的《Commercial Injunctions》(2016 年,第 6 版)一书之 8 - 014 段说:"**The Lawyers' duties to the**

---

〔12〕 立法的定义是:"a contract between a trader and a consumer which is any of these—(a) a contract concluded in the simultaneous physical presence of the trader and the consumer, in a place which is not the business premises of the trader; (b) a contract for which an offer was made by the consumer in the simultaneous physical presence of the trader and the consumer, in a place which is not the business premises of the trader; (c) a contract concluded on the business premises of the trader or through any means of distance communication immediately after the consumer was personally and individually addressed in a place which is not the business premises of the trader in the simultaneous physical presence of the trader and the consumer; (d) a contract concluded during an excursion organised by the trader with the aim or effect of promoting and selling goods or services to the consumer."就是买卖双方在供应商的商业处所(包括永久性与临时摊位)外,面对面订立的合约。最常见的就是上门推销订立的合约,也包括把消费者请到生产产品的工厂参观并订立合约等。

〔13〕 立法的定义是:"a contract concluded between a trader and a consumer under an organized sales or service - provision scheme without the simultaneous physical presence of the trader and the consumer, with the exclusive use of one or more means of distance communication up to and including the time at which the contract is concluded."也就是买卖双方没有面对面见过面,只是使用一种或多种远程通讯方式订立的合约,例如电话购物与现在非常常见的网购等。

〔14〕 见笔者《证据法:国际规管与诉讼中的证据攻防》一书第三章之 1 段。

〔15〕 见笔者《证据法:国际规管与诉讼中的证据攻防》一书第二章之 3 段。

Court-The fair presentation of the Application The application in all its aspects must be made fairly, accurately, without misrepresentation, **or non-disclosure of anything which may be material whether of fact, law, practice or expectations**. This includes **full disclosure of material facts and matters** and the duty of fair and accurate presentation of the application to the court. Materiality is to be assessed by the court and not by the applicant. ..."（加黑部分是笔者的强调）

这方面在笔者《证据法：国际规管与诉讼中的证据攻防》一书第三章之1.7.1段有详细介绍。

5. 普通法下不要求披露的先例

可多举一些先例说明，先是Keates v. The Earl of Cadogan(1851)138 ER 234先例中，该先例涉及原告向被告租用3年房屋用于居住。但在没有任何信息、事前通知或警告下，该房屋因为失修根本无法居住，而且随时有倒塌危险。原告在没有事前进行检查下就搬了进去，结果出事并向被告提起诉讼，指称被告欺诈性误述并索赔损失（包括原告妻子受伤等）。但原告败诉，Jarvis大法官说："... I think this declaration does not disclose a sufficient cause of action. It is not pretended that there was any warranty, express or implied, that the house was fit for immediate occupation: but it is said, that because the defendant knew that the plaintiff wanted it for immediate occupation, and knew that it was in an unfit and dangerous state, and did not disclose that fact to the plaintiff, an action of deceit will lie. The declaration does not allege that the defendant made any misrepresentation, or that he had reason to suppose that the plaintiff would not do what any man in his senses would do, viz, make proper investigation, and satisfy himself as to the condition of the house before he entered upon the occupation of it. There is nothing amounting to deceit: it was a mere ordinary transaction of letting and hiring. The defendant is entitled to judgment."

这种情况在不断发生，无论是在20多年前旧书《国际商务游戏规则：英国合约法》已经介绍过的案件，还是笔者近期处理的仲裁案件。例如在旧书中就介绍过一些简单的例子说明，可以在这里重述。第一个例子是一家中国公司买入一艘二手船舶，但没有检查就确定买卖，只凭一些船舶的照片（笔者怀疑这些漂亮的照片会否是多年前新船下水时拍的）就买了一艘船。但在交船后开始营运，买方才发现船舶问题很大，根本不值买入所支付的价格，于是向卖方提起诉讼，指卖方误述、欺诈/欺骗与隐瞒。但笔者作为仲裁员看不到任何证据显示卖方有作出过任何可以构成误述（特别是欺诈性）的言行（positive act），而隐瞒却是没有疑问。但在英国法律下，卖方是没有自动披露的责任，即使知道中国买方根据照片以相对高价买入了他的船舶是不值得的。

第二个例子也是笔者作为仲裁员处理的仲裁案件。案情是船东出租船舶给承租人,并提供了正确的船舶载重量(deadweight)与容积(capacity)等。但在租约订立前航次的承租人已经告知船东计划去装运10,000吨棉花。精明的西方船东马上知道该出租船舶是装不下这批货物,估计承租人可能是外行,所以即使有了船舶的数据(特别是容积)仍看不出问题。在装货过程中,船舶只能装载约3000吨的棉花,这短装也对承租人带来颇大的损失与不便。但在仲裁中,笔者看不出船东有任何误述(无辜或疏忽误述,更不说是欺诈性)。船东针对船舶的载重量与容积数据的陈述,这些事实完全正确,有大量的船舶证书与船图可证明。如果说误述是对船舶能否装载10,000吨计划的棉花,笔者看不到有这方面的证据显示船东有说过这样的话。而在英国法律下,船东在谈判过程中知悉了承租人的装货计划后,明知道承租人会掉进坑里,仍是没有责任去告知承租人,可以保持沉默。

第三个例子涉及一个租约谈判,船东知悉承租人要租他的船舶去装钢管,也知道该船的吊杆无法吊起钢管与装港不一定有岸吊,所以会有大麻烦。但船东当时没有为船舶找到其他生意,也就乐得让承租人上当,不自动披露这个"缺点"。显然,英国法律也不会因为船东不自动披露(或隐瞒)而构成可诉误述。所以承租人会蒙受重大损失与难逃败诉。

撇开道德方面(特别是在极端的案件)与立法有针对的特定领域(如消费者保护),在一般的商业交易中,如果要求自动披露与不得保持沉默,不但防止不了争议,甚至会大幅度增加在每一个不同案件到底应该自动披露什么与披露到什么程度的争议。也导致如果其中一方合约方因为没有经验或自己不小心,不去检查甚至也不多向对方合约方提出特定问题以澄清,在将来履行时出了事故就责怪对方没有自动在事前通知或提出警告,将风险转移到水平高的一方,这显然在全局考虑不是好事。

在本章之1段介绍的普通法大原则是源自 Smith v. Hughes(1871)LR 6 QB 597 先例中,这也被很多后来的先例如 Bell v. Lever Brothers Ltd(1932)AC 161 贵族院先例与 Jewson & Sons Ltd v. Arcos Ltd(1933)45 Lloyd's Rep 326 一审先例引用与认同。在后一先例中,Branson 大法官说:

"... the decision of Chief Justice Cockborn in the case of Smith v. Hughes ... '**The general rule, both of law and equity, in respect to concealment, is that mere silence with regard to a material fact, which there is no legal obligation to divulge, will not avoid a contract**, ... although a vendor is bound to employ no artifice or disguise for the purpose of concealing defects in the article sold, since that would amount to a positive fraud on the vendee; yet, **under the general doctrine of caveat emptor, he is not ordinarily, bound to disclose every defect of which he may be cognizant, although his silence may operate virtually to deceive the vendee**.'

And he concludes 'that mere silence as to anything which the other party might by proper diligence have discovered, and which is open to his examination, is not fraudulent, unless a special trust or confidence exist between the parties, or be implied from the circumstances of the case;' In the doctrine thus laid down **I entirely agree**."(加黑部分是笔者的强调)

也就是说一般人看来在道德上难容的"隐瞒"事实真相,如果仅是被动(passive)保持沉默,在普通法或衡平法下是没有法律后果的,对方也不可以把沉默视为可诉误述去试图撤销合同。这也不是欺诈/欺骗,特别是在对方花点功夫就能查出来的事实,不论是自己通过其他渠道去查还是通过向沉默方查问。

6. 善意责任与有披露责任的合约类别

一般的商业合约(如买卖合约等)只是要求诚实(honest),根本不要求合约双方的善意。[16] 正如 Atkin 勋爵在 Bell v. Lever Brothers Ltd(1932) AC 161 贵族院先例中说:"Ordinarily the failure to disclose a material fact which might influence the mind of a prudent contractor does not give the right to avoid the contract. The principle of caveat emptor applies outside contracts of sale. **There are certain contracts expressed by the law to be contracts of the utmost good faith, where material facts must be disclosed; if not, the contract is voidable**. Apart from special fiduciary relationships, contracts for partnership and contracts of insurance are the leading instances. In such cases the duty does not arise out of contract; the duty of a person proposing an insurance arises before a contract is made, so of an intending partner."(加黑部分是笔者的强调)

在《Chitty on Contracts》(2021 年,第 34 版)一书之 9-167 段有如下说明:"**Non-disclosure** Mere non-disclosure of fact, material or not, does not ordinarily amount to misrepresentation, and the general rule is that in order to be actionable a representation must take an active form. But in certain cases a stricter rule is enforced. The most important of these are the contracts uberrimae fidei in which knowledge of the material facts generally lies with one party alone; that party is under a duty to make a full disclose of these facts, and failure to do so makes the contract voidable. ..."

另也想在开始说清楚的是,即使是合约有明示或默示的善意责任(例如今天常会见到双方在订约时加上一条善意条文或普通法近年发展起来的"关系合约"),这往往只是针对合约的履行或部分履行[虽然其间也会有各种谈判针对个别事情如对

---

[16] 笔者《海上货物保险》一书第二章与《合约的解释:规则与应用》一书第九章对英国在合约法下否定商业合约谈判与履行的善意责任有详论,主要原因是被视为与订约自由以及各自谋利的商业现实有直接冲突。

原合约的更改(variation)、协议将来达成协议(agreement to agree)[17]等],但不会针对原合约的谈判。此时双方之间没有合约关系,所以即使在谈判时发生误述并导致合约的产生,也归纳为侵权[如欺诈性误述是“欺骗侵权”(tort of deceit)]的范围。而且,在英国法律是原则性把双方在商业合约的谈判视为对抗与各自谋利的现实,更是难接受善意的说法。正如在 Walford v. Miles(1992)2 AC 128 贵族院先例中,[18] Ackner 勋爵说:“... duty to carry on negotiations in good faith is inherently repugnant to the adversarial position of the parties when involved in negotiations, each party to the negotiations is entitled to pursue his or her own interest, so long as he avoids making misrepresentations.”

笔者想表达的理念是,即使在商业合约的履行中有善意责任(duty of good faith)与披露责任(duty to disclosure),需要自动披露对方应该知道与对合约共同目的有关的信息与事实,也不代表在合约谈判时有同样的披露责任。《Misrepresentation, Mistake and Non-Disclosure》(2022 年,第 6 版)一书之 17 – 45 段说:“**No general contractual warranty of disclosure** Given the general position taken by English law that there is no obligation to disclosure between negotiating parties, it follows that there is no general implied contractual promise by each party to the other that material matters have been disclosed. Even where the contract is one uberrimae fidei and has associated duties of disclosure in the information of contract, there is not thereby any implied contractual warranty that disclosure has been made...”

6.1 保险合约(insurance policy / contract)

最为一般人士熟悉的海上保险合约,很早已经在普通法要求受保人(assured)在订约前向保险人(或保险公司)自动披露所有实质重要(也就是会影响保险人并增加风险)的情况与事实(material circumstances and facts),以利后者决定是否或以什么条件与多少保费接受投保去订立保险合约。这要求可以理解,因为对投保标的(不论是船舶、运输的货物还是其他标的)一切有关风险是保险人不知情的,也在早年无法去自己调查,反倒要依赖受保人的披露。虽然保险人可以向受保人提出问题要求提供信息,受保人也就有了责任去准备回答,否则会构成可诉误述,并受到普通法与衡平法下可撤销保险合约的救济。但主要的问题是保险人对投保船舶,即将付运的货物与有关航次一无所知也无从问起。这样不像开庭审理时的交叉盘问(cross – examination)是盘问律师在完全掌握有关事实情况下向证人提出针对性的问题,保险人充其量也只能向受保人提出一些泛泛与不着边际的问题。

在 Carter v. Boehm(1766)3 Burr. 1905 先例中,Mansfield 勋爵说要求受保人自动披露实质重要的情况与事实的原因:“Insurance is a contract upon speculation. The spe-

[17] 见笔者《合约的解释:规则与应用》一书第三章之 12.1.3 段与第九章之 5.2.4 段。

[18] 有关案情可见笔者《合约的解释:规则与应用》一书第九章之 2 段。

cial facts, upon which the contingent chance is to be computed, lie most commonly in the knowledge of the insured only: the underwriter trusts to his representation, and proceeds upon confidence that he does not keep back any circumstances in his knowledge, to mislead the underwriter into a belief that the circumstance does not exist, and to induce him to estimate the risque, as if it did not exist. The keeping back such circumstance is a fraud, and therefore the policy is void. Although the suppression should happen through mistake, without any fraudulent intention; yet still the underwriter is deceived, and the policy is void; because the risque run is really different from the risque understood and intended to be run, at the time of the agreement."

之后《Marine Insurance Act 1906》立法把普通法发展起来的先例编集成法典(codify),在 S. 18 中说:"Subject to the provisions of this section, the assured must disclose to the insurer, before the contract is concluded, every material circumstance which is known to the assured, and the assured is deemed to know every circumstance which, in the ordinary course of business, ought to be known by him. If the assured fails to make such disclosure, the insurer may avoid the contract."

在该立法下,保险合约也被定名为"绝对善意"(uberrimae fidei 或 utmost good faith)的合约:见《Marine Insurance Act 1906》之 S. 17 与 Pan Atlantic Insurance Co Ltd v. Pine Top Insurance Co Ltd(1994)2 Lloyd's Rep 427 等大量先例。

但 2013 年 4 月生效的《Consumer Insurance(Disclosure and Representations) Act 2012》已经废除了消费者作为受保人要在投保时自动作出"全面与坦率地披露"(full and frank disclosure)的责任。替代的只是要消费者合理小心不得对保险人的提问作出虚假回答而构成误述。有关这方面的法律改革背后原因,在笔者的《海上货物保险》第二章之 10 段有详论,不在此重复。其中一个考虑是消费者涉及的不同险种比较单一,保险人可以拟定一系列要求消费者提供的信息与事实的列表,要求消费者在投保时回答。也由于本书不针对英国消费者,所以不多花篇幅探讨这方面,只节录英国议会在讨论这个立法时,在这一点发表的笔记(notes),说:"Clause 2 abolishes the duty of disclosure in consumer insurance contracts and replaces it with the duty 'to take reasonable care not to make a misrepresentation'. This removes the consumer's duty to volunteer information to the insurer. Instead, consumers are required to answer insurers' questions honestly and to take reasonable care that their replies are accurate and complete. If consumers do provide insurers with information which was not asked for, they must do so honestly and carefully."

至于不是消费者(non-consumer)的保险,也就是中国公司涉及英国保险(不止局限在海商的保险)的情况,也有在 2016 年 8 月生效的《Insurance Act 2015》。该立法废除了《Marine Insurance Act 1906》之 S. 18(Insurance is uberrimae fidei)、S. 19(Disclosure by assured)与 S. 20(Disclosure by agent effecting insurance),替代的做法是受

保人有一个向保险人“公平表述有关投保风险”(fair presentation of the risk)的责任。至于这与以前的必须向保险人自动“全面与坦率地披露”“实质重要的情况与事实”的责任有什么不同,可以简单节录《Misrepresentation, Mistake and Non-Disclosure》(2022年,第6版)一书之17-23段:

“**Non-consumer insurance contracts: the content of the new statutory duty of disclosure** The disclosure required by the 2015 Act, in order to fulfil the insured's duty to make to the insurer a fair presentation of the risk, is as follows: '(a) disclosure of every material circumstance which the insured knows or ought to know, or (b) failing that, disclosure which gives the insurer sufficient information to put a prudent insurer on notice that it needs to make further enquiries for the purpose of revealing those material circumstances' in a manner which would be reasonably clear and accessible to a prudent insurer. In the absence of enquiry, however, this does not require the insured to disclose a circumstance if it diminishes the risk, the insurer knows it, the insurer ought to know it, the insurer is presumed to know it, or it is something as to which the insurer waives information.

The materiality of a circumstance is determined by whether 'it would influence the judgment of a prudent insurer in determining whether to take the risk and, if so, on what terms.'

... The Act gives examples of things which may be material circumstances: special or unusual facts relating to the risk, any particular concerns which led the insured to seek insurance cover for the risk, and anything which those concerned with the class of insurance and field of activity inquestion would generally understand as being something that should be dealt with in a fair presentation of risks of the type in question. ...”

同样重要或是更重要的是有关不履行披露责任的救济,这在以前被视为一面倒倾向保险人利益的法律,违反的后果极其严重,保险人可撤销保险合约,也就是拒赔。至于违反披露责任是否是欺诈,或只是疏忽,甚至是无辜,这不影响保险人有同样的救济。但《Insurance Act 2015》立法在这方面有了重大的改变,对受保人的利益有了更好的平衡。

首先,保险人要证明如果没有违反,保险人是不会接受承保的,或接受也是以不同的条件或对价,这才会有法院的救济。有关立法条文是在S.8(1):“The insurer has a remedy against the insured for a breach of the duty of fair presentation only if the insurer shows that, but for the breach, the insurer—(a) would not have entered into the contract of insurance at all, or (b) would have done so only on different terms.”也只有这些被证明可享有救济的违反,才算是“适格的违反”(qualifying breach)。

立法把这“适格的违反”区分为欺诈性与非欺诈性的违反披露责任。欺诈性的违反在立法之S.8(5):“A qualifying breach is deliberate or reckless if the insured (a) knew that it was in breach of the duty of fair presentation, or, (b) did not care whether or not it was in breach of that duty."这是采纳在 Derry v. Peek(1889)14 App Cas 337 贵族院先例中对欺诈/欺骗或欺诈性误述的定义。

如果是这种违反,保险人在立法之 Sch. 1, Para. 2 的规定下可去撤销保险合约与拒赔,并且不必退回已经收取的保费。但如果违反是非欺诈性,在 Sch. 1, Para. 4,只有保险人能够证明如果受保人公平表述有关投保风险,他是不会承保该风险时,他才可以撤销保险合约,但同时必须退还所有已经收取的保费。这等于是可以撤销合约但金钱上复原(rescission of the contract with restitution),立法条文是:"4 If, in the absence of the qualifying breach, the insurer would not have entered into the contract on any terms, the insurer may avoid the contract and refuse all claims, but must in that event return the premiums paid."

但如果保险人只能证明如果受保人公平表述有关投保风险,他仍会承保该风险,只是承保会有不同的保费与条件,根据立法之 Sch. 1, Paras. 5-6 是不能撤销合约,只是按比例赔偿(如果承保是会收取更高保费)或按照会接受的条件[例如,会要求有更高的免赔额(deductible)]理赔。这可节录立法条文:

"5 . If the insurer would have entered into the contract, but on different terms (other than terms relating to the premium), the contract is to be treated as if it had been entered into on those different terms if the insurer so requires.

6(1) In addition, if the insurer would have entered into the contract (whether the terms relating to matters other than the premium would have been the same or different), but would have charged a higher premium, the insurer may reduce proportionately the amount to be paid on a claim. (2) In sub-paragraph (1), 'reduce proportionately' means that the insurer need pay on the claim only X% of what it would otherwise have been under an obligation to pay under the terms of the contract (or, if applicable, under the different terms provided for by virtue of paragraph 5),

Where — X = Premium actually charged / Higher premium ×100."

上述的介绍可简单节录《Chitty on Contracts》(2021 年,第 34 版)一书之 9 - 177 段有关违反披露责任对保险人的救济,说:"**Remedies for non-disclosure** Traditionally, the insurer's remedy for breach of the duty of disclosure by the insured was to rescind (or 'avoid') the contract. Under both the Consumer Insurance (Disclosure and Representations) Act 2012 and the Insurance Act 2015, if the breach of the relevant duty by the insured was deliberate or reckless, the insurer may avoid the policy and refuse all claims, and may not have to return the premium; but in other cases the insurer may avoid the contract only if, in the absence of the breach the insurer would not have entered the contract on any terms. If the insurer would have entered the contract but on different terms, then the contract is to be treated as if it contained those terms; if at a different premium, then the insurer may reduce the amount paid on the claim proportionately."

面对英国上述对保险法律的改革,英国保险市场使用的标准格式合约也需要有相应的应对。例如,保险人需要受保人自动对承保风险披露有关与实质重要的信息与事实不只在订立保险合约前,也包括在履行时,特别是受保人发生了受保风险(insured perils)有关的事故带来潜在的理赔与向第三人抗辩或代位求偿(subrogation)等法律行动,保险人(或再保险人)都需要受保人披露大量有关事故的信息与事实。本来保险合约关系被法律规定在"绝对善意"的地位下,保险人有默示的权利要求受保人提供。正如 Longmore 大法官在 The"Mercandian Continent"(2001)2 Lloyd's Rep 563 上诉庭先例中说:"His(一审的大法官)view was that there was a continuing duty on the assured to refrain from a deliberate act or omission intended to deceive the insurer through either positive misrepresentation or concealment of material facts and would only be material for the purpose if they had ultimate legal relevance to a defence under the policy. I agree with the Judge's conclusion … I would conclude that the giving of information, pursuant to an express or an implied obligation to do so in the contract of insurance, is an occasion when good faith should be exercised. Since, however, the giving of information is essentially an obligation stemming from contract, the remedy for the insured fraudulently misinforming the insurer must be commensurate with the insurer's remedies for breach of contract. The insurer will not, therefore, be able to avoid the contract of insurance with retrospective effect …"

但英国法律对"绝对善意"有了改变,保险合约中就需要有更有针对性与详尽的明示条文要求受保人自动披露与提供有关信息与事实,以及一旦违约的后果。但笔者不去进一步详谈这方面的发展了。

6.2 合伙人协议(partnership agreement)

合伙人协议,也是普通法要求双方在合约履行期间也即合伙人关系存续期间绝对善意,互相之间有自动披露实质重要的信息与事实的责任:见 Green v. Howell (1910)1 Ch 594(CA);Law v. Law(1905)1 Ch 140(CA);Bell v. Lever Brothers Ltd (1932)AC 161(HL)等先例。

在《Limited Liability Partnerships Act 2000》立法下成立的"有限法律责任合伙"(limited liability partnership, LLP)则有不同。在该立法下 LLP 是独立于合伙人(member)的法律实体,每一位合伙人都被认为是 LLP 的代理人。犯错或疏忽的合伙人要承担个人责任,LLP 也要共同为合伙人的错误或疏忽承担责任。但没有错误或疏忽的合伙人只需要承担有关合伙协议下的责任,而不用承担个人责任。也就是说,像有限责任公司一样,LLP 下没有犯错或疏忽的合伙人不需要承担超出他/她的投资的责任。LLP 比较适合知识服务行业的公司,很多律师事务所、会计师事务所与顾问公司都转为了 LLP。这与现在专业人士责任越来越重与赔偿金额越来越大有关,这方面可见本书第六章介绍的 SAAMCO 大原则。在 F&C Alternative Investments

(Holdings) Ltd v. Barthelemy (No. 2) (2011) EWHC 1731 (Ch)先例中，Sales大法官针对LLP中合伙人是否互相之间有诚信责任说："A limited liability partnership is not **a partnership in the traditional sense**, in which the **individual partners owe fiduciary duties to each other** in relation to the management of the affairs of the partnership and when acting as agents for the partners. The LLPA(指《Limited Liability Partnerships Act 2000》立法) has established a new form of entity, with its own separate legal personality: section 1(1)(2). Such an entity may be expected to have its own corporate governance structures. Except to the limited extent that it is preserved by the new legislation, the general law relating to partnerships does not apply to it: section 1(5). The **LLPA** and the associated regulations **do not provide for the members in a limited liability partnership to owe each other fiduciary duties**. They lay down a minimal legal framework for the operation of a limited liability partnership, leaving most of the detailed rules for the operation of such an entity to be worked out by the parties to the agreement which establishes it, with a considerable degree of freedom of contract."(加黑部分是笔者的强调)

再回去谈本小段针对的一般合伙人协议，固然在这种合约类别下在履行期间有善意与诚信责任已是明确，但在双方谈判时，仍未有合约关系，是否有此法律责任去自动披露一直看来是不明确。这可节录《Misrepresentation, Mistake and Non-Disclosure》(2022年，第6版)一书之17-26段的说明："**Prospective partners have mutual duties of disclosure** It has long been clear that partners owe each other duties of good faith and disclosure during the currency of the partnership. Until recently there was no clear authority on whether the duty extended to the pre-contractual negotiations, but it has now been settled by the Court of Appeal that in negotiating a partnership agreement a party owes a duty to the other negotiating parties to disclose all material facts of which he has knowledge and of which the other negotiating parties may not be aware."

直到近期的Conlon v. Simms (2006) EWCA Civ 1749上诉庭先例明确了这一点。案情涉及一家律师事务所，原告与被告(Simms先生)在谈判2000年至2002年合伙人协议与2002年5月的另一份协议时，被告没有披露曾在1997年初涉及不诚实行为并被律师协会调查，最终在2004年2月2日被律师协会除名。原告知悉后显然希望撤销与被告的合伙人协议，否则会令律师事务所名誉扫地与影响业务。理由是被告在谈判中没有自动披露在1997年的不诚实事件，被告有披露责任下不这样做相等于欺诈性误述或欺诈/欺骗，原告有权撤销不自动披露诱导产生的合伙人协议。被告提出多方面的抗辩，例如，过去律师协会与后来法院对他在1997年不诚实行为的认定不能在此案例被采纳作为他不诚实的证据，[19] 在谈判时没有自动披露的责任等。但被告的抗辩在一审与上诉庭都被否定，其中有关在谈判时的自动披露责任，上诉庭的 Jonathan Parker 大法官引述一审 Lawrence Collins 大法官所说："**The most fundamental obligation which the law imposes on a partner is the duty to display complete good faith towards his co-partners in all partnership dealings and transactions …**

…It follows that when co-partners are **negotiating between each other** in relation to partnership assets, **each partner must put the others in possession of all material facts with reference to the partnership assets, and not to conceal what he alone knows**: Maddeford v Austwick (1826) 1 Sim 92; Law v Law [1905] 1 Ch 140 …

It has been said that the duty of good faith exists not only as between persons who are actually in partnership together, but also as between persons who are negotiating their entry into partnership ….

…In Bell v Lever Bros Ltd [1932] AC 161 …, Lord Atkin assumed that an intending partner had a duty of disclosure. He said: 'Fraudulent concealment has been negatived by the jury; this claim is based upon the contention that Bell owed a duty to Levers to disclose his misconduct, and that in default of disclosure the contract was voidable. Ordinarily the failure to disclose a material fact which might influence the mind of a prudent contractor does not give the right to avoid the contract. The principle of caveat emptor applies outside contracts of sale. There are certain contracts expressed by the law to be **contracts of the utmost good faith, where material facts must be disclosed; if not, the contract is voidable**. Apart from special fiduciary relationships, **contracts for partnership** and contracts of insurance **are the leading instances**. In such cases **the duty does not arise out of contract; the duty** of a person proposing an insurance **arises before a contract is made, so of an intending partner**.'

I am satisfied on principle and authority that prospective partners have a duty to disclose material matters."（加黑部分是笔者的强调）

6.3　担保合约（surety contract/guarantee contract）

担保合约的担保人只对债务承担次要责任（secondary liability），被担保人（债务人）才承担主要责任（primary liability）。担保合约依附（accessory）在债权人（credi-

---

〔19〕 较早前判决、裁决或其他司法认定的事实在他案可否采纳的问题在笔者《证据法：基础理论、口头证据与专家证据》一书第九章之 1.3 段有详细介绍，其中 1.3、2.2 段也简单提到了 Conlon v. Simms (2006) EWCA Civ 1749 上诉庭先例。被告提出这个争辩是如果有关 1997 年不诚实的定罪证据不被采纳，就等于他是否曾经有过不诚实的事实尚待证明，是要在这一个案件重审一次，而不能视为已经被法院在较早前案例认定的事实。

tor)与债务人(debtor)之间的主合约,也受到《Statute of Frauds 1677》[20]的规管。这些都是与另一类的补偿合约(letter of indemnity)或保函的主要不同之处。而在本段针对探讨的只是担保合约。

针对本段的自动披露信息与事实,可先节录《Misrepresentation, Mistake and Non-Disclosure》(2022年,第6版)一书之17-28段与17-29段说:"**Surety contracts are not contracts 'uberrimae fidei'** It is well established now that surety contracts are not contracts uberrimae fidei. The courts have made this clear in order to emphasise that the **creditor under a surety contract does not have a general duty of disclosure to the surety.** However, **a surety contract by its very nature** does carry **obligations for the creditor to make disclosure to the surety in certain situations**, and therefore the creditor under a surety contract has more extensive duties than a party to a normal commercial contract. ...**The creditor's duty of disclosure** Although a surety is, in general, expected to inform himself about the risks he is undertaking under the contract, the creditor is under a duty to disclose to the surety **any unusual feature of the contract** between the creditor and the debtor which makes it materially different in a potentially disadvantageous respect from what the surety might expect. ..."(加黑部分是笔者的强调)

以上是一般情形,债权人对担保人是没有披露责任,担保人要自己确定与了解自己将面临的风险。但在一些特定情况下,债权人有责任向担保人披露主合约中一些会对担保人不利的不寻常事宜。这在接下来的段节会详细介绍。

6.3.1 要求债权人在担保合约产生前向担保人自动披露的原因

担保合约不是绝对善意合约,这不像保险合约或合伙人协议,虽然在早期有把担保合约与保险合约视为在本质上是雷同。担保合约有很多不同形式,简单举例,A(银行或其他债权人)贷款或融资给B(债务人),并由C(担保人)向A担保这笔债务。C会是政府当局(例如中国对出口商提供担保的中国进出口银行)、B的母公司、父母、夫妻、好友、另一家银行或是有其他关系的自然人或法人。由于没有绝对善意的法律地位,照说大家也就没有自动披露责任。作为担保人,C也就要自己小心谨慎去了解自己会面对的风险才去承诺作为担保人。但C作为担保人,由于不是像A与B作为贷款或融资合约[可称为"主合约"(principal agreement)]的订约方与履约方一样,所以会对他承诺担保的一些隐蔽的风险不充分了解。毕竟,主合约与担保合约是两份独立与不同内容的文件,C对于A与B之间的主合约不一定是完全了解,而A则是肯定知道两份合约的当事人。而B虽然也知道两份合约,但他作为想要拿到

---

[20] 这1677年的立法在s.4规定担保合约必须以文书形式与有担保人签字才有效:"... no action shall be brought ... whereby to charge the defendant upon any special promise to answer for the debt default or miscarriage of another person ... unless the agreement upon which such action shall be brought or some memorandum or note thereof shall be in writing and signed by the party to be charged therewith ..."

担保的人士,会向担保人 C 隐瞒一些潜在的风险也是完全可以理解的。

所以法律在一些情况下会强加一个自动披露责任在债权人 A,要他自动披露与 B 之间的主合约中任何会对 C 有不利影响的“不寻常事宜”(unusual features),否则就将 A 与 C 之间的担保合约视为误述导致,C 可以撤销担保合约。

这个法律地位可从另一个角度了解其重要性,就是这种合约关系对英国社会或家庭的影响。英国社会或家庭经常签这种担保合约,也就是 C 为另一位家庭成员或朋友 B 向银行或其他融资机构 A 作出债务的担保,并以 C 的资产(如居住的房屋)作为担保物(security)通过抵押(mortgage)或押记(charge)等方法给银行。但经常是 C 并不知道或不完全知道所面对的风险,因为 B 会通过误述或不当影响(undue influence)去说服 C 作为担保人,不论是为 B 欠 A 的一笔债务并承诺分期还款,或是一笔贷款或信用额度,又或是为了一个项目的融资等。这种在社会或家庭层面的误述是 B 对 C 说:“你尽管放心,我肯定有钱归还这个债务,只不过暂时要你出面去挂个名。”又或是,受不当影响的 C 是 B 年迈的父母或非常相信他的妻子。

这样,要求 C 从 B 获取足够的信息以深思熟虑去衡量自己作为担保人的风险并不现实。为了不给社会与/或家庭带来太大的不良影响,也只能以法律强加 A 在订立担保合约前向 C 作出自动披露让 C 更好了解会在担保合约下面对的风险与责任。可以说,B 如果对 C 曾经有过误述或不当影响,是要 A 向 C 披露与解释,以作出化解。

这理念也在其他方面配合去保护担保人,例如笔者《合约的解释:规则与应用》一书第五章之 6.6.1 段的最后提到担保合约必须与主合约共存(co - existence),只能依附于主合约。如果作为主债务人的 B 因为各种合法理由不必对 A 负责,作为担保人的 C 也不必负责。另如果 A 与 B 在履行时对主合约有任何更改(variation),都必须向 C 披露以获得同意,才能令担保合约持续有效。可举一个极端的例子说明,如果银行或联营公司担保合约是涉及购买一艘船舶,但因为航运市场逆转或其他商业原因,A 与 B 私下把主合约更改为购买一架飞机或一个海上钻井平台。这是完全不同的风险,所以除非预先得到作为担保人 C 的同意,否则这个担保合约就会因为主合约的更改而变为无法执行。这主合约不得私下更改的说法是被严格执行,不管个别案件的担保风险实际上有否增加或改变。可简单节录《Chitty on Contracts》(2015 年,第 32 版)一书之 45 - 104 段的说明:“**Variation of Contract between creditor and debtor**. It is well established and strictly applied principle that any variation in the terms of the agreement between the creditor and the debtor which could prejudice the surety will, unless he consents thereto, discharge him from liability, unless the contract of suretyship provides to the contrary. It is immaterial that the variation has not in fact prejudiced the surety, or that the likelihood that it may do so is remote. …”

在介绍 Royal Bank of Scotland Plc v. Etridge(No. 2)(2001)UKHL 44 贵族院先例的案情后,就会明白这种经常在英国社会与家庭发生的案件,相信这种情况在中国发生的也不少。一位受到丈夫不当影响的女士作为担保人为丈夫的债务向银行作出担保,并把她居住的房屋作为担保物的押记。显然,丈夫无法还债后,银行就行使它在担保合约下的权利申请占有该房屋,也无可避免令该女士(与她的子女)流离失所了。所以,该女士非得要去合法撤销该担保合约,令其无效,才保得住她的房屋。在该先例中,Scott 勋爵说:"A surety contract **is not a contract uberrinae fidei**. In Seaton v. Heath(1899)1 QB 782,Romer LJ said:'The risk undertaken is generally known to the surety,and the circumstances generally point to the view that as between the creditor and surety it was contemplated and intended that the surety should take upon himself to ascertain exactly what risk he was taking upon himself. ' But although **a would-be surety is, in general, expected to acquaint himself with the risk he is undertaking, the creditor is under an obligation to disclose to the intending surety 'anything that might not naturally be expected to take place between the parties who are concerned in the transaction**, that is, whether there be a contract between the debtor and the creditor, to the effect that his position shall be different from that which the surety might naturally expect'(per Lord Campbell in Hamilton v. Watson(1845)12 Cl & F 109 ...)This passage ... was cited by Vaughan Williams LJ in London General Omnibus Co Ltd v. Holloway (1912)2 KB 72 ... 'Lord Campbell, it is true, takes as his example of **what might not be naturally expected an unusual contract** between creditor and debtor whose debt the surety guarantees, ... **the general proposition that a creditor must reveal to the surety every fact which under the circumstances the surety would expect not to exist, for the omission to mention that such a fact does exist is an implied representation**[21] **that it does not**. ' ..."(加黑部分是笔者的强调)

而如果债权人没有向担保人自动披露的信息与事实客观看是对担保人重要但其并不知道的"不寻常事宜",是担保人在知悉后会不愿意在相同条件下做担保人,就会有权撤销担保合约。Newey 大法官在 North Shore Ventures Ltd v. Anstead Holdings Inc(2010)EWHC 1485(Ch)先例中说:"... a guarantee can be avoided only if the non-disclosure was in fact significant to the guarantor. A contract cannot be rescinded for misrepresentation unless the representee was induced to enter into the contract by the representation. Surely, a surety cannot avoid a guarantee for non-disclosure by the creditor unless disclosure of the relevant information would have made a difference to him. ..."

6.3.2 债权人需要披露的范围

在理解了债权人有法律责任向担保人自动披露信息与事实的原因后,实际操作的真正困难就来了。即什么是自动披露的范围(extent of disclosure)?分水岭划在哪里?毕竟,法律的肯定性与稳定性对整个社会(特别是商业社会与银行)至关重要。

---

〔21〕 有关默示陈述可见本书第二章之1.4段的介绍。

如果要求披露责任太广,很容易因为一个遗漏而导致对债权人至关重要的担保合约失效,最常见的是对整个商业社会最重要的债权人银行就会不干了。正如在 Hamilton v. Watson(1845)12 Cl. & F. 109 贵族院先例中,Campbell 勋爵早就提道:"... no bankers would rest satisfied that they had a security for the advance they made, if, ... it is essentially necessary that everything should be disclosed by the creditor that is material for the surety to know. If such was the rule, it would be indispensably necessary for the bankers to whom the security is to be given, to state how the account has been kept; whether the debtor was in the habit of overdrawing; whether he was punctual in his dealings; whether he performed his promises in an honourable manner;—for all these things are extremely material for the surety to know."

另 Blackburn 大法官也在 Lee v. Jones(1864)17 CBNS 482 先例中说:"... I think that great practical mischief would ensue **if the creditor were by law required to disclose everything material known to him, as in a case of insurance**. If it were, no creditor could rely upon a contract of guarantee, unless he communicated to the proposed sureties everything relating to his dealings with the principal, to an extent which would in the ordinary course of things be so vexatious and annoying to the principal and his friends, the intended sureties, that **such a rule of law would practically prohibit the obtaining of contracts of surety in matters of business**."(加黑部分是笔者的强调)

以下探讨这方面的一般原则性(general principle)说法。在最初有此说法的 Hamilton v. Watson 贵族院先例中,Campbell 勋爵就针对需要向担保人在他/她签订担保合约前披露什么信息与事实说:"I should think that this might be considered as the criterion whether such disclosure ought to be made voluntarily, namely, whether there is anything that might not naturally be expected to take place between the parties who are concerned in the transaction, that is, **whether there be a contract between the debtor and the creditor, to the effect that his position should be different from that which the surety might naturally expect; and, if, so, the surety is to see whether that is disclosed to him**. But if there be nothing which might not naturally take place between the parties, then, if the surety would guard against particular perils, he must put his question, and he must gain the information which he requires."(加黑部分是笔者的强调)

这是指债权人 A 与债务人 B 之间的主合约如果有内容是担保人 C 无法自然(naturally)可预期到的,A 就有责任向 C 自动披露。至于什么内容是 C 自然可以预期到的,法院会根据不同案件的事实去客观认定。例如一个重要变数是看担保人是谁,一家跨国银行与一位不识字的年迈父母作为担保人对什么是可以预期到的事情就不一样。从 Campbell 勋爵的说法看来自动披露责任应只是局限在 A 与 B 之间的主合约,内容也肯定与 C 的担保合约有不同与部分内容会影响担保人要承担的风险。而 A 需要自动披露的范围如果局限在主合约内容,在笔者看来较容易满足,A

干脆把与 B 的主合约(如果有一份整理过的书面合约)给 C 一份就会安全。即使今天解释合约从早年的“字面解释”(literal interpretation)或“四个角内规则”(four corners rule)变为今天的“语境解释”(contextual construction),[22] A 顶多向 C 自动披露更多有关谈判时会影响解释有关合约条文的信息与事实,也就应该是安全了。

在接下来可介绍较近期的先例中,首先是 Scott 勋爵在 Royal Bank of Scotland Plc v. Etridge(No. 2)(2001)UKHL 44 贵族院先例中引用了 King 大法官在 Pooraka Holdings Pty Ltd v. Participation Nominees Pty Ltd(1991)58 SASR 184 澳大利亚先例中的说法:“The duty of disclosure, said King CJ, extends to **any unusual feature** surrounding the transaction between the creditor and the surety (**a**) of which the creditor is or ought to be aware, (**b**) of which the surety is unaware, and (**c**) which the creditor appreciates, or in the circumstances ought to appreciate, might be unknown to the surety and might affect the surety's decision to become a surety. This statement of the extent of the disclosure obligation may be too wide. But at least, in my opinion, the **obligation should extend to unusual features of the contractual relationship between the creditor and the principal debtor, or between the creditor and other creditors of the principal debtor, that would or might affect the rights of the surety**.”(加黑部分是笔者的强调)

另也有其他先例对“不寻常事宜”的披露范围有较为狭窄的定义,将在稍后的段节介绍,先节录其中一个是 Michael Burton QC 大法官在 Levett v. Barclays Bank Plc (1995)1 WLR 1260 先例说:“... I propose to deal first with the non-disclosure claim. Applying these principles as I seek to do, it then becomes **simply a question of fact** by reference to the circumstances of this case. The principle of the cases as formulated ... was suggested to be as follows: the creditor is under a duty to the surety to **disclose to the surety contractual arrangements made between the principal debtor and the creditor** which both (**a**) make the terms of the principal contract something different from those which the surety might naturally expect and (**b**) materially affect the degree of the surety's responsibility. I propose to abbreviate that and run it together, still by reference to the ‘contractual arrangements’ to which he refers, as follows: the creditor is under a duty to the surety to disclose to the surety contractual arrangements made between the principal debtor and the creditor which make the terms of the principal contract something materially different in a potentially disadvantageous respect from those which the surety might naturally expect.”(加黑部分是笔者的强调)

6.3.3 需要披露的“不寻常事宜”范围不明确

什么事宜才算是“不寻常”而需要自动披露,这当然要看每一个不同案件千变万

[22] 见笔者《合约的解释:规则与应用》一书第六章。

化的事实,并由审理法官或仲裁员客观做出认定。但可以澳大利亚高院的 Behan v. Obelon Pty Ltd(1985)157 CLR 326 先例为例。案情涉及两位共同担保人向债权人作出共同与连带(jointly and severally)的担保,但其中一位担保人(F 先生)没有资产,只有 F 先生引入的作为共同担保人的 Behan 女士有资产。面对 Obelon 在担保合约下的索赔,Behan 女士的抗辩是 Obelon 作为债权人应事前向她自动披露另一位共同担保人 F 先生是"光杆司令"。但澳大利亚高院不认为这事有什么不寻常,因为一般情况下共同担保人与要求提供担保的债权人一样,都会先查查谁是另一位担保人,他是否有钱做担保人等,说:"... there is the circumstance that, generally speaking, a co-surety as well as the creditor may reasonably be expected to make his or her own inquiries about the financial worth or standing of another co-surety and to form an opinion on the basis of those inquiries. In this situation information possessed by the creditor concerning **the financial worth or standing of one co-surety could not ordinarily be regarded as information about an unusual and unexpected feature of the transaction which would require disclosure by the creditor to the other co-surety**."(加黑部分是笔者的强调)

但债权人(很多是银行)进一步面对更大的困难是在千变万化的不同案件中去肯定什么信息与事实(即使肯定是不寻常事宜)是要自动披露的范围或分水岭(watersheds)。这并不明确,包括以下几个原因。

6.3.3.1 不同类别与本质的担保合约

担保合约有很多不同的类别与本质,如"忠诚担保"(fidelity guarantee)是针对被担保人的不诚实行为带来的经济权益损失,或是"贷款担保"(loan guarantee)是针对被担保人或债务人的一笔债务的偿还,又或是"对某交易或项目的履行或财务担保"(guarantee of a particular transaction)等。显然,不同类别与本质的担保合约都对自动披露有不同程度的要求。

6.3.3.1.1 忠诚担保

可先介绍 London General Omnibus Co Ltd v. Holloway(1912)2 KB 72 上诉庭先例,案情涉及"忠诚担保"。原告在 1903 年就雇用了一位 L 先生负责收钱,但在 1905 年原告发觉 L 盗窃公款。结果在 L 的亲属代为赔付下不了了之。原告同意继续雇用 L,条件是 L 本人加上第三人担保或保证 L 会诚实与不行差踏错。而很快 L 也取得他一位亲属(也就是被告)签妥的担保。但到了 1909 年,L 又再度被发觉盗窃至少 100 英镑的公款。这最后导致原告向作为担保人的被告提起诉讼,要求赔偿损失。而被告的抗辩是原告应该事先披露 L 曾经有盗窃公款的不诚实记录,如果原告披露,被告对签署一个忠诚担保就会有顾虑而改变决定。这被一审与上诉庭认可。一审法院认定原告漏了向被告披露有关 L 不诚实不涉及欺诈,但被告仍被允许撤销该忠诚担保。在此先例前,由于担保合约不是 uberrimae fidei 合约,而一般法律在 caveat emptor 原则下是不要求自动披露,所以有关这方面的案件都是涉及欺诈/欺骗担保人,才允许担保人撤销担保合约。但一审的判法改变了担保合约的法律地位,只要不向担保人自动披露实质重要的信息,即使是非欺诈性或无辜,担保人也有权撤销担保合约。这带来原告的上诉,但上诉庭维持原判并确认了这个法律地位。上诉庭的 Farwell 大法官指出忠诚担保与贷款担保本质上不一样,说:"There is a wide distinction between a case like the present and the cases which have been cited of guarantees for overdrafts given to bankers,... Dishonesty may occur, and the guarantee is given to insure against the chance, but guarantees for overdrafts are required for the purpose, and not on the chance, of being used. ... it is perfectly legitimate and usual for a man to carry on his business on borrowed money, including money borrowed from his bankers by way of overdraft, and the surety knows this, and becomes surety for the very purpose of enabling him to do so. There is nothing in such a case which the surety does not know as well as any other member of the community, and nothing therefore which needs to be disclosed of him. **The surety may well complain 'I did not know that your servant was a thief'; but he cannot be heard to complain 'I did not know your customer had been overdrawing his account or what the nature of his business was'.**"(加黑部分是笔者的强调)

另 Kennedy 大法官也解释债务人的诚信品格是忠诚担保的"本质"(intrinsic),但对贷款担保而言只是"非本质"(extrinsic)。除了保险合约外,法律没有在其他类别的合约强加自动披露只是属于非本质信息与事实的责任。换言之,贷款合约只需要披露主合约的不寻常事宜,而不需要披露其他非担保合约本质的事宜,例如债务人曾经有数次不能按时还债等,这些需要担保人自己向债务人与债权人查问。而因为 L 曾经有过不诚实的行为才需要这个忠诚担保,所以 L 的不诚实行为是忠诚担保的本质,需要披露。Kennedy 大法官的判决可节录如下:

"... the difference between intrinsic and extrinsic circumstances, the first forming the very ingredients of the contract, and the latter forming no part of it, but only incidentally connected with it,... In regard to such extrinsic circumstances, **no class of case** occurs to my mind in which our law regards **mere non-disclosure as a ground for invalidating the contract, except in the case of insurance.** ...

...**in the present case, the honesty of the servant**, which is the subject - matter of the suretyship bond, **is plainly an intrinsic circumstance** ... the peculiar relation created by the guarantee, between the surety, who gives, and the employer, who takes, the suretyship bond, **justifies the importation into such a contract, as a condition of the liability of the surety**, of the disclosure by the employer to the surety of any previous dishonesty of the servant known to the employer. ...

On the other hand, in the case of the **suretyship or guarantee of a financial account**, the previous pecuniary dealings between the creditor and the person whose future liability the surety is invited to secure **constitute only extrinsic circumstances**. They may be material circumstances, … in the language of Sir Frederick Pollock (Principles of Contract, 8th ed., p. 568), 'the creditor is **not bound to volunteer information as to the general credit of the debtor or anything else which is not part of the transaction itself** to which the suretyship relates; and on this point there is no difference between law and equity. …"(加黑部分是笔者的强调)

这在 National Provincial Bank of England Ltd v. Glanusk (1913) 3 KB 335 先例中也是同样判法, Horridge 大法官说:"It was contended before me that on the principle of the cases dealing with fidelity guarantees, … the bank ought to have informed the defendant of any facts which might indicate that his agent was behaving improperly towards him, but I do not think the principle of these cases applies to a bank guarantee."

6.3.3.1.2 针对一笔债务偿还的担保

对于非忠诚担保的其他债务担保,当事人的品格顶多只能算是其中一个考虑因素,甚至是不重要与非本质的因素。

这方面的案例看来仍是不断,如 Redmond v. Allied Irish Banks Plc (1987) FLR 307; Barclays Bank Plc v. Khaira (1992) 1 WLR 623; Barclays Bank Plc v. O'Brien (1994) 1 AC 180; Royal Bank of Scotland Plc v. Etridge (No. 2) (2001) UKHL 44; North Shore Ventures Ltd v. Anstead Holdings Inc (2011) EWCA Civ 230 等先例。但不多去探讨,近期的 North Shore Ventures Ltd v. Anstead Holdings Inc 上诉庭先例明确说是贷款担保除了债权人与债务人之间的主合约关系上的"不寻常事宜"外,没有其他法律责任去自动披露,因为这不是主合约的不寻常事宜,说:"… not a contract uberrimae fidei but a loan guarantee. The authorities are clear in such a case the duty of disclosure does not go further than the limit set by Lord Campbell in Hamilton v. Watson and by Lord Scott … in Royal Bank of Scotland plc v. Etridge (No. 2). Accordingly there is no duty to disclose facts or matters which are not unusual features of the contractual relationship between the creditor and the debtor, or between the creditor and other creditors of the debtor. …"

《Chitty on Contracts》(2015 年,第 32 版)一书之 45 - 038 段有说该上诉庭先例的案情涉及债务人被调查挪用公款与账户曾被扣押,但债权人仍没有法律责任向担保人自动披露:"The Court of Appeal therefore held the contract of guarantee binding on the surety, even though the creditor had failed to disclose that the principal debtors were investigated for embezzlement and that their bank accounts had been frozen as these were not 'unusual features of the contractual relationship between the creditor and the debtor. …"

这样看来,虽然该上诉庭先例在这方面的法律地位仍不算是有定论,可以说作为债权人的银行通常是不必对担保人自动披露有关债务人的贫困、过往打交道的不良记录、目前的经济状况或对品格的怀疑[23]等。这除了上述先例的分析外,也可以理解:(1)法律不想强加太多太重不现实的披露责任在银行而扼杀这个至关重要的行业;(2)可以想到贷款担保既然有担保人的要求,债务人的经济状况与诚信度或还债能力估计也不会好到哪里去;(3)愿意做担保人也肯定知道或假设可以知道债务人的有关资料才会承诺做担保人;(4)法律不要求银行自动披露并不代表担保人不可以自己向有关银行进一步查问债务人的信息。

即使是妻子或年迈父母作为担保人的贷款担保,也会在本质上有了不同而令债权人自动披露的责任有所改变。这在本章接下来的6.3.3.2段有详论,可先节录在Royal Bank of Scotland Plc v. Etridge(No.2)贵族院先例中,Bingham勋爵说:

"As to **the type of transactions where a bank is put on inquiry**, the case where a wife becomes surety for her husband's debts is, in this context, a straightforward case. **The bank is put on inquiry**. On the other side of the line is the case where **money is being advanced, or has been advanced, to husband and wife jointly. In such a case the bank is not put on inquiry**, unless the bank is aware the loan is being made for the husband's purposes, as distinct from their joint purposes. That was decided in CIBC Mortgages plc v Pitt [1994] 1 AC 200.

Less clear cut is the case where the wife becomes surety for the debts of a company whose shares are held by her and her husband. Her shareholding may be nominal, or she may have a minority shareholding or an equal shareholding with her husband. In my view **the bank is put on inquiry in such cases**, even when the wife is a director or secretary of the company. Such cases cannot be equated with joint loans. The shareholding interests, and the identity of the directors, are not a reliable guide to the identity of the persons who actually have the conduct of the company's business."(加黑部分是笔者的强调)

6.3.3.1.3　对某交易或项目的履行或财务担保

"对交易或项目担保"看来与债权人的自动披露关系不大,毕竟会涉及的担保人与债务人(往往也是法人而不是自然人)的关系,往往是集团公司与子公司或要贷款融资的公司与老板等。因此担保人会对有关交易或项目的方方面面都熟悉,不存在被债务人误述与不当影响的可能性,对债务人的品格方面的了解也不会比不上债权人。涉及的人士的层次也不会欠缺法律知识,特别是作为担保人会带来的如倾家荡产的严重后果。

但不表示这类别的担保合约没有在其他方面要求债权人自动披露信息与事实的争议,例如稍后介绍的North Shore Ventures Ltd v. Anstead Holdings Inc(2011)EWCA

---

[23] Credit Lyonnais Bank Nederland NV(now Generale Bank Nederland NV)v. Export Credits Guarantee Department(1996)1 Lloyd's Rep 200 先例判债权人银行没有责任披露它的怀疑。

Civ 230 上诉庭先例与 Deutsche Bank AG v. Unitech Global Ltd(2016)EWCA Civ 119 上诉庭先例就涉及这类担保,并且金额庞大。

6.3.3.2 潜在的担保人是谁

在这方面的一个极端是高水平的跨国公司为其一个新项目或附属公司的一笔贷款做担保人,并且对有关项目或附属公司十分熟悉并有参与。这样,作为债权人的银行或银团(syndicate)恐怕没有什么"不寻常"的信息与事实需要向担保人披露了。正如在 North Shore Ventures Ltd v. Anstead Holdings Inc(2010)EWHC 1485(Ch)先例中,一审的 Newey 大法官说:"… a creditor need not … disclose anything which the prospective guarantor could reasonably be expected to know. A creditor is not, as it seems to me, to be taken to have made a representation in respect of a matter unless he can expect the guarantor not to know it. The fact that a loan creditor is not normally under an obligation to disclose matters bearing on the principal's creditworthiness can be explained on this basis. … in other words, the guarantor can be expected to know that there is reason for concern as to the principal's creditworthiness. … Again, in Shivas v. Bank of New Zealand(1990)2 NZLR 327 the creditor was not obliged to disclose matters with which a surety could have been expected to be familiar as the principal debtor's accountant or which the other co-plaintiff could have been expected to discover from her co-trustee. … it is immaterial that a prospective surety could be expected to be ignorant of a particular matter if he could be expected to know of the risk in general terms."

当然如果债权人预期担保人是应该知道有关的不寻常信息与事实,后来证明这预期是不对的,债权人还是要承担没有向担保人自动披露的后果。正如上诉庭的 Andrew Morritt C 大法官在该先例中说:"…I would reject … the creditor is absolved from his duty of disclosure because he reasonably believes that the surety knows of it already. … If the belief of the creditor turns out to be not well founded then, … he should suffer the consequences not the surety…"

而另一个极端是一些水平不高的妻子(只是一个普通的家庭主妇)作为担保人(surety wives)的案件(年迈父母是同样道理):见 Cooper v. National Provincial Bank Ltd(1946)KB 1;National Westminster Bank Plc v. Morgan(1985)AC 686(HL);Midland Bank Plc. v. Sheppard(1988)3 All ER 17;Barclays Bank Plc v. O'Brien(1994)1 AC 180;Barclays Bank Plc v. Khaira(1992)1 WLR 623;Royal Bank of Scotland Plc v. Etridge(No. 2)(2001)UKHL 44 等先例。这种案件的担保人常会是法律知识贫乏、水平很有限的家庭主妇。如果问她借 1 万元,她很可能坚决拒绝,但反而有可能说服她让她将自己唯一的财产(自己住的价值 100 万元的房屋)拿出来作担保。而且,往往后果对整个社会影响很不好。所以法院对这类别的案件,要求债权人 A 自动披露的信息与事实就严格得多。这可部分节录《Misrepresentation, Mistake and Non-Disclosure》(2022 年,第 6 版)一书之 17 – 31 段如下:"**Disclosure to surety wives** …

where the surety contract is one under which a wife guarantees her husband's debt or those of his company, the courts have taken a different approach. ... the courts have in effect imposed a higher obligation in circumstances where the creditor has actual or constructive notice that the husband may be making misrepresentations to the wife, or subjecting her to undue influence, in order to induce her to enter into the surety contract. ... the bank which is on notice of the risk of the debtor's misconduct towards the surety is required to take certain steps to satisfy itself that the surety has had brought home to her the practical implications of the surety contract, ... What is required will depend on the facts, but ordinarily it will include information on the purpose for which the loan which is to be guaranteed has been requested by the debtor, the current amount of the debtor's indebtedness, the amount of the current loan facility, and the amount and terms of any new facility."

在 Barclays Bank Plc v. Khaira 先例中,Thomas Morison QC 大法官虽然没有说银行有法律责任去这样做,但银行应建议担保人妻子在签署担保合约前,先自己委任律师取得独立法律意见与解释担保合约的本质与后果,如担保合约被执行她会失去多年来一直居住的房屋或倾家荡产等。另外重要的是委任了律师可以有效中止丈夫对她持续的误述与/或不当影响。当然,该妻子会否舍得花钱委任律师、会否找到适合的律师等一连串的后续问题,也就管不了太多,法律能够做到的保护也是有限的。Thomas Morison QC 大法官说:"In my judgment, in the normal course of events, the bank owes no duty of care in tort or contract to proffer explanations or to advise the taking of independent advice to those who come to their premises to sign securities. That said, banks would be well advised to ensure that wives who sign documents for their husband's benefit should routinely be asked to take independent advice, since otherwise they will be exposed to the risk of being saddled with a charge which in equity the court is not prepared to enforce because of the husband's undue influence. Further, in my judgment, banks should be encouraged, as a matter of good business practice, to explain to those who have come to their premises to sign securities the nature and effect of the document to be signed..."

这也会是在 Royal Bank of Scotland Plc v. Etridge (No. 2) 贵族院先例中,Nichols 勋爵提到把这种案件区分为"商业"与"非商业"两种,后者是银行必须要评估它的客户(也就是申请贷款的丈夫或其他人士)对潜在担保人会有的影响并作出相应的"需要进一步查问"(put on inquiry)的责任,说:"... if a bank is not to be required to evaluate the extent to which its customer has influence over a proposed guarantor, the only practical way forward is to regard banks as 'put on inquiry' in every case where the relationship between the surety and the debtor is non-commercial."

但法律也没有这样发展,相信也解决不了问题。毕竟怎么样区分商业与非商业案件也不容易,妻子可以在丈夫(或其他家属)的同样的误述与不当影响下为一家在破产边缘但属于商业范畴的公司做担保人。例如,在 Lloyds Bank Ltd v. Bundy (1975) QB 326 上诉庭先例中就涉及一位年迈的农夫把他唯一的财产农场作担保物为儿子的公司担保。又或者是在类似 Royal Bank of Scotland Plc v. Etridge 先例中,虽然妻子作为公司董事或股东为公司担保,但公司的实际控制人其实是丈夫,妻子完全不参与公司营运与管理,本质仍是妻子把自己的住所押上为丈夫担保。

6.3.3.3 银行作为债权人自动披露责任局限在主合约条文或包括所有其他与合约关系有关的信息与事实的疑问

6.3.3.3.1 North Shore Ventures Ltd v. Anstead Holdings Inc (2011) EWCA Civ 230 上诉庭先例

在近期的 North Shore Ventures Ltd v. Anstead Holdings Inc 上诉庭先例中,在同样的案情下,上诉庭与一审针对这自动披露范围的争议/争端作出了不同决定。在此先例中,涉及两家 BVI 公司之间的 5000 万美元的借贷,原告 North Shore 公司(背后老板是 Boris Berezovsky 或简称 B 先生)向第一被告 Anstead 作出这笔贷款用来进行俄罗斯粮油与肉食生意营运,以赚取合约约定的高息(15% 与 20%)与复息(compound interest)。[24] Anstead 背后的老板与控制人,也就是本先例的第二被告(F 先生)与第三被告(P 先生)对这笔债务向原告作出担保。虽然本金 5000 万美元被归还,但原告仍索偿约 3500 万美元的利息,并提起诉讼。由于第一被告不出庭,英国法院作出"缺席判决"(default judgment)。此时,再加上利息,金额或判决债务(judgment debt)变得比本金还要大,约 5250 万美元。

原告向 F 先生与 P 先生两位担保人索赔,两位被告提出抗辩,其中一个主要抗辩是原告作为债权人没有提前披露 B 先生被瑞士当局调查有关洗钱、挪用公款(会是

---

〔24〕 这种"国际高利贷"的高息借贷或融资在现实中也经常见到,尤其是目前国际上热钱非常多,投资活动十分频繁,而一间公司要发展壮大,都离不开资本的投入。对于借贷协议,尚有立法会在有限范围内对利息做出限制,例如我国香港特别行政区的《放债人条例》第 12 条与第 24 条就将借贷给股本低于 100 万港币的公司的利息上限规定为年利率不得高于 60%。但是对于大公司与国际性的借贷,从公共政策上来看,也无需立法的保护与完全放任,美其名曰是保护商业的自由与订约的意思自治。除了借贷之外,目前很多投资银行、投资基金或者其他投资者都是以购买目标公司股份的形式对公司进行融资,也就是现在的"以股代债""名股实债"。这种协议本质上也是借贷,但显然就不适用立法对借贷的规管,双方之间的权利与义务完全以商业合约中的内容来确定。其中为了保障投资人的投资回报可以实现,想要融资的公司除了会答应苛刻的赔偿条款之外,也往往会提供给投资人各种担保或者质押公司股份给投资人。这样一旦发生会影响投资人投资回报的违约事件(在订约自由下可以是针对十分轻微的违反,务求容易抓到把柄),借款人不仅要偿还投资人的本金,还要支付高额的利息。笔者就处理过目标公司在违约后根据股份买卖合约中常见的卖出选择权(put option)条文,以 20% 或 25% 内部回报率(internal return rate)与复息作为利率计算,短短两年时间,目标公司就要偿还两倍于投资额的款项给投资人。也见过国际高利贷商人以 70%—80% 不等的利率与复息作出借贷的仲裁案件。这种案件可能是借贷 500 万美元,但结果是吃掉价值 1 亿美元的公司。

涉及以前在俄罗斯航空 Aeroflot 的工作)与账号被当局扣押(sequestration)。这给整个 5000 万美元贷款的交易也带来风险,因为 F 先生曾是 B 先生同事(associate),而借贷的5000 万美元是在贷款合约中约定汇入一家瑞士银行。所以有这重关系,很容易被瑞士当局同时调查、追踪与扣押这些钱,并在 Anstead 要动用这笔货款时发现用不了。被告指这是"不寻常事宜",原告应有责任披露,即:"(a)Boris Berezovsky and his associates were being investigated by the Swiss authorities in relation to alleged embezzlement of moneys due to Aeroflot,(b)the bank accounts of Boris Berezovsky and his associates had been frozen by the Swiss authorities and(c)consequently there was a substantial risk that money paid to an associate of Boris Berezovsky in Switzerland would be frozen."

对原告是否有法律责任去披露这些与主合约(贷款合约)没有本质上的关系但是对整体交易十分有关的不寻常信息与事实,一审认定是有。否则从保护担保人的角度去看,只要求披露主合约的不寻常事宜,但不要求披露其他有关整个交易与会影响担保人的不寻常事宜如债务人的欺诈/欺骗行为,实在是说不通。但在该先例的案情下,一审认为 F 先生知道此事宜与 P 先生应该可以知道,所以原告不去主动披露,不构成误述,也谈不上有诱导与/或依赖。一审的 Newey 大法官说:"First,the obligation of a creditor to make **disclosure to a prospective guarantor need not,even in the case of a guarantee for a loan,be limited … to features of the contract between the creditor and the principal debtor**. In London General Omnibus Company Ltd v. Holloway(1912)2 KB 72,Vaughan Williams LJ treated … 'whether there be a contract between the debtor and the creditor,to the effect that his position shall be different from that which surety might expect' as 'only an example of **the general proposition that a creditor must reveal to the surety every fact which under the circumstances the surety would expect not to exist**.' Vaughan Williams LJ's remarks were,… quoted with apparent approval by Lord Scott in both the Royal Bank of Scotland v. Etridge(No. 2)(2002)2 AC 773 and Estate of Palmer v. Cornerstone Investments & Finance Co Ltd(Jamaica)(2007)UKPC 49 cases. In Etridge,Lord Scott also said that the disclosure obligation should 'at least' extend to unusual features of 'the contractual relationship … between the creditor and other creditors' as well as of that between the creditor and the principal debtor,… Further,it would,as it seems to me,be **surprising if a loan creditor never had to disclose anything other than a feature of the contract between himself and the principal debtor** … 'it would be somewhat odd if the creditor was obliged to disclose an unusual contractual term of the principal agreement,but not the fraudulent practices of the principal'. … **On balance,I consider that the better view is that even a loan creditor can have an obligation to disclose an unusual feature other than of the contract with the principal debtor**."(加黑部分是笔者的强调)

但上诉庭在分析同样的先例与解释它们的判词时，得出不同结论，认为只是主合约关系的“不寻常事宜”才需要向担保人自动披露。这显然是大幅度局限了债权人向担保人披露的范围。上诉庭的 Andrew Morritt C 大法官说：

“I acknowledge the care with which the judge(一审的 Newey 大法官) approached the problem but I cannot agree with his conclusion. ...

It is well established that a guarantee is not, as such, a contract uberrimae fidei. Consequentlyin addition the duty of disclosure is an essential element in proving **the creditor is not obliged to disclose all matters relevant to a decision of the surety whether or not to enter into the guarantee....** a misrepresentation inducing the contract of guarantee where no other ground exists. ...

For these reasons I do not agree that the grounds given by Newey J ... justify his conclusion. The Guarantee was not a contract uberrimae fidei but was a loan guarantee. The authorities are clear that in such a case the duty of disclosure does not go further than the limit set by Lord Campbell in Hamilton v. Watson ... and by Lord Scott in Royal Bank of Scotland Plc v. Etridge ... Accordingly **there is no duty to disclose facts or matters which are not unusual features of the contractual relationship between the creditor and the debtor, or between the creditor and other creditors of the debtor.**

It is not disputed that the matters on which the Guarantors(两位被告) rely ... are not unusual features of the contractual relationship between the creditor and the debtor, or between the creditor and other creditors of the debtor. It follows that North Shore was not under any duty to disclose them to the Guarantors. ...”(加黑部分是笔者的强调)

对笔者而言，一审的 Newey 大法官与他判决的理由是十分有说服力。也就是说，只向担保人披露主合约的不寻常事宜，但无需披露被担保人/债务人的欺诈/欺骗行为，既保护不了担保人，也很可笑与说不通。此外，上述节录的上诉庭的 Andrew Morritt C 大法官也提到债权人与债务人的其他债权人的关系(“between the creditor and the other creditors of the debtor”)也要主动向担保人披露。例如，债务人 B 除了担保人 C 向债权人 A 担保的一笔债务外，还欠下了其他银行 E、F 与 G 一系列的债务。但问题是这往往也不严格属于主合约的不寻常事宜，更会是整个交易的不寻常事宜。但目前权威的法律地位是只局限这两方面的不寻常事宜需要向担保人披露。

可见这个问题是不肯定与不稳定的，但在关键时这担保合约是否有效对债权人(主要是银行)至关重要，这也是英国即使在商业担保上的态度也摇摆不定的原因。

6.3.3.3.2 Deutsche Bank AG v. Unitech Global Ltd(2016) EWCA Civ 119 上诉庭先例

在 Deutsche Bank AG v. Unitech Global Ltd 上诉庭先例中，案情涉及原告德意志银行(Deutsche Bank)与被告 Unitech Global Ltd(UGL)订立了 1.5 亿美元信用贷款

合约(credit facility agreement)与利率掉期合约(interest swap),信用贷款合约与利率掉期合约都与伦敦银行同业间拆借利率(London Inter Bank Offered Rate,LIBOR)挂钩。被告的核心抗辩是原告参与操纵 LIBOR,[25]构成违约或误述。

如果被告能证明银行操纵 LIBOR 违反合约,就可以获得赔偿,但赔偿只是实际 LIBOR 数额与没有被操纵下 LIBOR 的数额之间的差别。如果被告能证明银行误述诱导订立合约,就可以撤销合约,令其回到合约没有订立的地位。所以诉讼方的第一个卫星诉讼(satellite litigation)就是银行作为原告申请简易判决(声称只是简单的债务问题),[26]而被告申请修改抗辩,加上误述的抗辩。上诉庭[(2013) EWCA Civ 1372]同意被告的申请,并认为误述的抗辩有胜诉机会,所以拒绝作出简易判决。

而与本段内容有关的此先例中,是另一个卫星诉讼。共同被告 Unitech 作为 UGL 的母公司为 UGL 在信用贷款合约与利率掉期合约下作担保,Unitech 申请修改抗辩,其中包括原告银行没有向作为担保人的 Unitech 披露信用贷款合约中不寻常事宜:(1)银行明知道利率掉期合约实际上不适合 UGL 用来对冲信用贷款合约下利率浮动的风险;(2)LIBOR 被操纵,其实并不真实;(3)银行自己参与操纵 LIBOR。而银行则称披露的责任只限于合约本身。

Longmore 大法官说"不寻常事宜原则"仍在发展,没有定论:"**The doctrine of unusual features is** something of **a developing doctrine whose ambit is perhaps not entirely clear from the authorities**. It can be said with considerable force that Unitech(担保人,是债务人的母公司)knew the terms of the credit agreement with UGL(债务人) perfectly well since it was a party to the agreement. Both UGL and Unitech were able to take a view about the suitability of the agreement for UGL. But,if the doctrine extends to the contractual relationship rather than just the terms of the contract itself(as the decision in North Shore Venture Ltd ... might suggest), it is arguable that manipulation by the Bank of a rate by reference to which interest was calculated would be a most unusual feature. It is therefore necessary to consider whether clause 15.1(c) precludes the application of the doctrine."(加黑部分是笔者的强调)

Longmore 大法官提到的 clause 15.1(c)可节录如下:

"**15.1 Guarantee and indemnity**

The Guarantor irrevocably and unconditionally:...(c) agrees with each Finance Party that if,for any reason,any amount claimed by a Finance Party under this Clause is not recoverable from the Guarantor on the basis of a guarantee,then the Guarantor will be liable as a principal debtor and primary obligor to indemnify that Finance Party in respect of any loss it incurs as a result of the Company failing to pay any amount expressed to be

---

[25] 有关这个课题可见本书第二章之 1.4.5 段。

[26] 见笔者《证据法:国际规管与诉讼中的证据攻防》一书第六章之 4 段。

payable by it under a Finance Document on the date when it ought to have been paid. The amount payable by the Guarantor under this indemnity will not exceed the amount it would have had to pay under this Clause had the amount claimed been recoverable on the basis of a guarantee."

也就是说,clause 15.1(c)通过明示条文排除了"不寻常事宜原则"的适用,因为无论任何原因令被担保人无法在担保合约下获得赔偿,担保人都会转为"主债务人"(principal debtor)要承担补偿的首要责任,不再受到需要披露不寻常事宜的困扰。至于担保合约与补偿的区别,在本章之6.3段一开始就已经简单介绍过。也就是说,即使法院支持了Unitech增加的不寻常事宜抗辩也于事无补,所以拒绝了Unitech的修改请求。

可见在合约中有一条对自己有利的条文是多么重要。这种跨国银行的标准合约经过无数的案例与顶级律师的不断修改,可以说是面面俱到,用尽各种办法确保能在各种情况下都保护自己的利益,中国的各大银行尤其是在做国际业务时应该参考。

最后,在此先例中,银行向法院申请命令被告提前将1.2亿美元支付到法院账户(payment into court),[27]作为可以误述抗辩的前提条件。因为即使被告的抗辩被法院接受,双方恢复到没有合约的地位(*restitutio in integrum*),[28]被告仍然要把银行贷款给它的本金退还给银行,双方同意还没还的部分是1.2亿美元。上诉庭支持了银行的申请,但这样被告要一下子拿出来这么一大笔钱,可以说是非要与原告和解或本质上投降了。

6.4 关系合约(relational contract)

随着今天有越来越多的商业合约明示加上一条善意条文,[29]普通法也在Yam Seng Pte Ltd v. International Trade Corp Ltd(2013)EWHC 111(QB)先例后有了所谓的"关系合约"[30]去默示善意的责任。但普通法在这方面仍在发展与不是太肯定,例如哪些合约是属于或不属于"关系合约"的分水岭仍待进一步明确。这在Bates v. Post Office(2019)EWHC 606(QB)先例中,Fraser大法官指出一般商业合约没有善意责任,但有些合约根据它们的环境/背景与其他条文,可以合约双方假设的订约意图去看是否为"关系合约",说:"These cases, both appellate and first instance, all demonstrate in my judgment that there is no general duty of good faith in all commercial contracts, but that such **a duty could be implied into some contracts**, where it was in accordance **with the presumed intention of the parties**. **Whether any contract is relational is heavily dependent upon context, as well as the terms**. The circumstances of the

---

〔27〕 在笔者《仲裁法:从开庭审理到裁决书的作出与执行》一书第一章之5.3.3.3.6.1段有介绍。

〔28〕 有关这个课题可见本书第三章之5段。

〔29〕 在笔者《合约的解释:规则与应用》一书第九章有详细介绍。

〔30〕 见本书第一章之2.6.5段。

relationship, defined by the terms of the agreement, set in its commercial context, is what decides whether a contract is relational or not. "(加黑部分是笔者的强调)

善意要求的起点是 Mansfield 勋爵早在 Carter v. Boehm(1766)3 Burr. 1905 先例中就说到。善意是禁止一方当事人隐瞒一些对方不知道的事实,甚至是在相信并非事实的情况下,利用对方对此事实的无知订立合约:"Good faith forbids either party by concealing what he privately knows, to draw the other into a bargain, from his ignorance of that fact, and his believing the contrary."

这显示如果一旦被认定是关系合约与默示善意,就会在履行或部分履行(其间合约双方仍会不断有针对个别方面的谈判或作出对合约的更改)需要向对方坦率披露或不隐瞒一些信息与事实,因为善意要求不仅要考虑自己的利益还要考虑对方的利益。这可节录《Misrepresentation, Mistake and Non-Disclosure》(2022 年,第 6 版)一书之 17 – 40 段说:"**The content of the duty depends on the relationship** The nature of the relationship between the parties must always be examined, to see what duty is imposed:… Similarly, even where the relationship does not fall within an established category of fiduciary relationship the court may decide that the relationship on the facts carried duties of confidence and disclosure. For example, **where the relationship falls short of partnership, but has elements of joint enterprise or joint venture, there is no hard and fast rule as to whether the parties owe each other duties of good faith, fiduciary duties or duties of disclosure: each case depends on its facts**, but **the terms of the contract which regulates the relationship will be of primary importance to decide whether** one party's actions under the contract can properly be said to have been for the purpose **of serving the parties' joint interests, rather than its own separate interest, and therefore the party can be held to have owed a duty of good faith to the other** during the performance of the contract. …The scope of the duty of disclosure owed as a result of such a duty of good faith will depend on the facts and on the terms of the contract between the parties. "(加黑部分是笔者的强调)

上述节录的加黑部分是针对 Ross River Ltd v. Cambridge City Football Club Ltd (2008)1 All ER 1004 先例中,简单案情是有关被告(剑桥足球俱乐部)(Club)因为财政困难把它拥有的剑桥足球场土地以 130 万英镑出售给原告(Ross River)以重新发展为房屋。这土地买卖合约针对土地溢价(overage)约定平分,这表示将来土地的发展带来升值,如政府当局批准发展(planning permission)、土地高价转售、或建造了的房屋出售等带来的利润等,Club 有权分享 50%。由于 Club 持续的财政困难,之后又有了 Ross River 出资买入 Club 对土地溢价的 50% 权益,并以 90 万英镑成交。Ross River 在买下土地(但 Club 有 5 年的租用期)后为发展该土地做了大量工作,所以对土地发展后的真正价值一直十分了解,但没有与 Club 分享。双方在谈判土地溢价的 50% 权益买卖时,一方(Club)在暗、另一方(Ross River)在明。这导致 Club 后来发现自己在售价吃亏后，以 Ross River 不披露的误述（因为对该土地发展的真正价值有一个披露责任）诱导该合约的产生，要求撤销这个合约。Briggs 大法官支持 Club 的请求，说：

"In my judgment the project for the realisation of the development value of the Ground（足球场土地）constituted by the mutual obligations of the Club and Ross River set out in the Sale Agreements had enough about it **in the nature of a joint venture to require the parties to conduct themselves with mutual good faith** in relation both to the carrying out of their various obligations, and **in relation to any negotiations for a buy - out of either party's share in the hope — for Overage.** Clearly, the project was to be carried out for their mutual benefit, as sharers in the anticipated profit, and the costs of the exercise (as Planning and Development Costs) were in substance to be shared by way of deduction before distribution of profits, ...

Furthermore, for the parties' mutual benefit, the Sale Agreements clearly imposed upon Ross River in its conduct of the lion's share of the work necessary to realise the Overage, obligations to obtain best value and to minimise costs.

...my appraisal of the rights, powers, duties and discretions given to Ross River under the Sale Agreements indicates decisively that **the role of Ross River in taking steps** and obtaining information for the purpose of developing the Scheme, obtaining the Planning Permission and satisfying the Development Conditions can properly be said to have been **for the purpose of serving the parties' joint interests, rather than simply the separate interests of Ross River**, ...

In particular, I accept... that **it makes no sense at all** to conclude ... that, when it came to a negotiation of a buy - out of the Club's financial interest in the project, **Ross River was at liberty to use, conceal or otherwise deal with information which it had obtained from outside professionals at an expense which was to be shared by the parties as a deduction from their profits, purely for the separate interests of Ross River**.

I prefer to describe**that duty as being a duty of good faith**, by analogy with the well known obligation that subsists between partners, than as a fiduciary duty, albeit that it has an element of fiduciary obligation embedded in it.

I am not however persuaded that the Sale Agreements, and the relationship thereby created between the parties, **imposed a positive obligation upon Ross River to volunteer disclosure of all the information which it had gained** in discharging its function under the Sale Agreements, once a negotiation for a buyout of the Club's interest started. The Sale Agreements made detailed provision for the stages in the project at which, either expressly or by necessary implication, Ross River was to make disclosure to the Club. Those stages were（接下来针对合约的明示与默示要披露的 5 个阶段的信息与事实，但没有

必要详及)…"(加黑部分是笔者的强调)

6.5 和解协议(settlement agreement/release of claims agreement)

双方发生争议甚至已经在诉讼过程中,这时已经完全是敌对的状态,在和解(放弃诉讼请求/解除责任)谈判中没有披露的一般性责任,毕竟很多和解谈判是在对抗性(adversarial)诉讼过程中边打边谈,要求善意不现实。法院鼓励诉讼方通过和解谈判解决争议的公共政策也令法院不愿意插手双方的和解谈判:见 Simantob v. Shavleyan(2019)EWCA Civ 1105 等先例。

甚至即使合约本身有善意的要求例如本质上是"关系合约",当诉讼开始也不再要求善意,而是变为受 CPR 程序规则与法院命令约束,也就是说,合约方没有自动披露的责任,更不用提醒对方还有什么别的诉讼请求或抗辩漏了没提。在 The"Star Sea"(2001)UKHL 1 贵族院先例中,Hobhouse 勋爵说:"When a writ is issued the rights of the parties are crystallised. The function of the litigation is to ascertain what those rights are and grant the appropriate remedy…. It cannot be disputed that there are important changes in the parties' relationship that come about when the litigation starts. There is no longer a community of interest. The parties are in dispute and their interests are opposed. Their relationship and rights are now governed by the rules of procedure and the orders which the court makes on the application of one or the other party. The battle lines have been drawn and new remedies are available to the parties. …"

6.5.1 和解协议谈判双方掌握信息不均等的先例

这可以古老的 Turner v. Green(1895)2 Ch 205 先例为例,案情涉及双方通过律师在谈判和解,原告律师早一步比被告律师知道了法院在早一天对原告作出的预先争议(preliminary issue)申请给了不利的意见,并在"一方明、一方暗"的情况下签署了和解协议。这在早年通讯(通常以电报)较困难与缓慢的年代是不奇怪的。被告声称原告应该披露这实质重要的信息,保持沉默是"欺诈性沉默"(fraudulent silence),因为被告如果知道是不会签署此和解协议,并要求法院宣告无效。Chitty 大法官不同意被告的说法,认为在土地或货物买卖时是没有自动披露的责任与可以保持沉默的法律地位已是明确。只要不同时做出一些"小动作"如点头摇头去试图误导对方,就不会构成可诉误述而带来法律后果。而此法律地位也适用在其他一般情况,如本先例涉及的一个和解协议。

可节录 Chitty 大法官所说:"In Walters v. Morgan 3 D. F. & J. 718. where specific performance of an agreement for a lease was being sought, Campbell L. C. said: 'There being no fiduciary relation between vendor and purchaser in the negotiation, **the purchaser** (也可以是卖方) **is not bound to disclose any fact exclusively within his knowledge which might reasonably be expected to influence the price of the subject to be sold. Simple reticence does not amount to legal fraud, however it may be viewed by moralists**. But a single word, or(I may add) a nod or a wink, or a shake of the head, or a smile from the purchaser intended to induce the vendor to believe the existence of a non-existing fact, which might influence the price of the subject to be sold, would be sufficient ground for a Court of Equity to refuse a decree for a specific performance of the agreement.' That is **a correct statement of the law, and one which, it appears to me, is not to be confined to the sale of lands or goods, but is of general application**, except perhaps in the case of contracts requiring uberrima fides, which involve a duty to make full disclosure."(加黑部分是笔者的强调)

另在较近期的 Silver Queen Maritime Ltd v. Persia Petroleum Services Plc(2010) EWHC 2867(QB)先例中,案情涉及被告与伊朗国家石油公司的分公司 Iranian Offshore Oil Company(IOOC)订立提供波斯湾海底石油勘探服务的合约,并把海底地质研究的部分分包给了原告。之后 IOOC 停止代被告向原告支付费用,原告开始向被告起诉支付将近 1000 万欧元的拖欠费用。原告与被告最终达成和解,金额约为 810 万欧元。原告已经在和解契约上签字,并发给被告要求被告签字。这时被告发现原告曾经直接与 IOOC 谈判,并主动提出了 750 万欧元的要约之后甚至降到了 650 万欧元,但没有与 IOOC 达成协议。这显示被告这 810 万欧元是给多了,于是被告拒绝签署并要撤销和解契约,理由是原告没有披露它曾经向 IOOC 作出过更低的要约。但法院判原告没有责任向被告披露之前向 IOOC 作出过更低的要约。原告不是代表被告与 IOOC 谈判,不是代理人,所以对被告没有诚信责任。即使有诚信责任,在双方的诉讼过程中,这个诚信责任也不再存在了。

Lindblom 大法官说:"In my judgment, however, it does not follow that in such a case, where hostile litigation is in progress and one party knows that the other is ignorant of the real limits upon his own source of funds, there arises an 'unusual circumstances' obligation on the first party to tell the second what he knows. The proposition seems to run counter to the basic principle that parties to hostile litigation are entitled not to disclose, during settlement negotiations, information relating to the claim..."

6.5.2 家事案件强制要求当事人全面与坦率披露财务/资产信息

但和解协议也不仅是针对双方在诉讼或仲裁中的争议,虽然这是商业人士最熟悉的一种和解协议。在商业社会(特别是国际),由于假设双方水平均等与有渠道掌握均等的信息,所以一般不会好像社会上会发生的信息严重失衡下所订立的合约,需要以"不合情理"(unconscionable)等理由去撤销该合约,和解协议也是同一道理。而且从上一段介绍的两个先例可见,在商业社会往往是可以获取信息,如可以等待知道法院对预先争议的意见后再决定是否签订和解协议,或在达成和解前先向关系友好的第三方询问(事实证明也确实可以问到,只是太迟),只是因为存在一定程度的疏忽就匆匆与对方签订和解协议,但这与信息失衡是两回事。

但在其他范畴的和解协议,主要是涉及家事问题,例如在夫妻离婚时,通常发生的问题是一方(有经济能力)或双方隐瞒自己的财务/资产信息(这包括隐瞒除了正职外其他收入、夸大负债与将来的支出、建立外国银行户口与信托、转移给其他家人或好友代为托管财产/资产等),以避免分身家或需要支付更高的赡养费。但这就会带来不必要敌意的诉讼以及其他恶果与不公平,如对小孩的照顾方面。所以有法律与/或诉讼程序去针对当事人必须全面与坦率(full and frank)向对方自动披露财务/资产信息,违反被视为欺诈性不披露(fraudulent non-disclosure):见 Young v. Young (2013) EWHC 3637 (Fam); Sharland v. Sharland (2015) UKSC 60; Gohil v. Gohil (2015) UKSC 61;香港特区的 TCP v. KLS (2020) HKCU 675; SPY v. KYH (2021) HKCU 1424 等先例。

6.5.3 雇佣合约之和解协议/解除责任协议谈判的披露问题

另是涉及雇佣合约(employment contract),这是默示雇主/公司与雇员之间有信任与信心(trust and confidence),也要求雇员对雇主/公司效忠(loyalty)与忠诚(fidelity)的合约关系。如果雇员是高层如聘用的董事,更是对雇主/公司有更高的诚信责任(fiduciary duty):见 Horace Ltd v. Garland (1983) BCLC 60; Item Software (UK) Ltd v. Fassihi and Ors (2004) EWCA Civ 1244 等先例。在 Item Software (UK) Ltd v. Fassihi and Ors 上诉庭先例中,Arden 大法官说:"... the duties of a director are in general higher than those imposed by law on an employee. This is because a director is not simply a senior manager of company. He is a fiduciary and with his fellow directors he is responsible for the success of the company's business."

为了尽这效忠/忠诚的默示责任,雇员为了保护雇主/公司的财产,会在知悉有同事偷取雇主/公司的财产时,需要向雇主/公司披露或通报:见 Sybron Corp v. Rochem Ltd (1984) Ch 112 等先例。现在很多大公司/上市公司都会有"吹哨人"制度,要求雇员向公司汇报。会有一些雇员内心抗拒,感觉是要自己打小报告,但其实作为雇员在效忠/忠诚的默示责任下本身就有披露的责任。

但如果是该雇员自己偷取,强加一个自动披露责任就是违反人性与不现实,除非雇佣合约有明确规定。这可介绍 Bell v. Lever Brothers Ltd (1932) AC 161 贵族院先例。该贵族院先例的案情不复杂,涉及 Bell 先生与另一位共同原告 Snelling 先生被 Lever Brothers 聘用为西非公司的主席与副主席。但后来由于公司的合并而不再需要两位原告的服务,要终止雇佣关系。在双方的和解协议中,Lever Brothers 向 Bell 作出一笔在当年看来相当丰厚的补偿(5 万英镑)。但之后发觉 Bell 在职时曾有以公司名义做不恰当事宜(涉及投机倒把为自己谋利),根据雇佣合约完全可以作为辞退的理由,于是企图以该和解协议无效(void)向 Bell 取回这 5 万英镑的补偿,理由是这 5 万英镑的支付是"可诉错误"(actionable mistake)[31] 与 Bell 应该在达成和解协议前自动披露他所做过的不恰当或违反雇佣合约的事情。法院判共同错误不成立,笔者在本书第七章之 13.2 段对此课题有详细介绍,就不在这里展开。而针对披露责任,

---

[31] 见本书第七章。

上诉庭认定有披露责任，但在贵族院被推翻，不认为 Bell 作为雇员有此责任。其中可节录 Atkin 勋爵解释这不可行与违反人性说：“It is said that there is a contractual duty of the servant to disclose his past faults. I am satisfied that to imply such a duty would be a departure from the well established usage of mankind and would be to create obligations entirely outside the normal contemplation of the parties concerned. If a man agrees to raise his butler's wages, must the butler disclose that two years ago he received a secret commission from the wine merchant; and if the master discovers it, can he, without dismissal or after the servant has left, avoid the agreement for the increase in salary and recover back the extra wages paid? If he gives his cook a month's wages in lieu of notice can he, on discovering that the cook has been pilfering the tea and sugar, claim the return of the month's wages? I think not. He takes the risk; if he wishes to protect himself he can question his servant, and will then be protected by the truth or otherwise of the answers.”

6.5.4 全面和解协议谈判涉及卑鄙狡诈行为会有披露责任说法

接下来介绍 BCCI v. Ali(2001) UKHL 8 贵族院先例。该重要先例在笔者《合约的解释：规则与应用》一书第一章之 8.4 段有详细介绍，只简单概括案情以帮助读者理解。在 1991 年，巴基斯坦的著名国际银行 Bank of Credit and Commerce International SA(BCCI)被指称业务广泛涉及欺诈、洗钱与贪污，这导致了该银行在全球出现问题并被英国当局下令清盘。有一位伦敦 BCCI 雇用的巴基斯坦裔雇员在丑闻爆发之前，已被银行裁员。当时 BCCI 是清付了所有的遣散费与工资还多给了一个月的工资作为优惠赔偿，双方也签了一份和解协议，确认是全面与最终的和解(full and final settlement)与双方友好分手，并同意放弃所有对雇主“存在或可能存在的索赔诉因，无论是怎样的性质”(“of whatever nature that exist or may exist”)，可以说是用字十分广泛。

在清盘过程中，有其他雇员成功以 BCCI 违反了一位负责任的雇主有不做非法与不道德的事情令雇员名誉受损而找不到工作面临损失的默示责任，并获得贵族院的支持可索赔这种所谓“烙印损失”(stigma damages)：见 Mahmud v. BCCI(1998) AC 20 先例。这是原来没有的法律地位，在笔者的《损失赔偿与救济》一书第二章之 15.4.4 段说社会名誉的降低或名誉损失是普通法不接受的损失类别，认为是太投机与难以量化，除非是一些特殊的诉讼如诽谤(defamation)。显然，烙印损失也应是这种损失类别。另外，在传统说法下，雇主对雇员的小心谨慎责任主要在安全与工作环境方面，如安全的工作地点与其他方面，如设备/设施、合理薪酬与假期、平等对待与升迁机会、上班不会受到骚扰等。

有了这个普通法地位的改变,[32]也提供给了 BCCI 前雇员(或任何其他被严重丑闻拖垮的公司的前雇员,因为有此工作记录而在寻找新工作时有或多或少的困难)一个新诉因。BCCI v. Ali 先例中的部分雇员于是开始诉讼指称 BCCI 违反该默示责任索赔烙印损失,因为他们也同样面对找不到工作的困境与损失。

双方的争议之一是上述的全面和解协议是否可以被解释为包括这个在订约时根本不知道,也没有考虑过的烙印索赔权利。贵族院的多数判决是双方的和解协议中并不包括在 Mahmud v. BCCI 先例后新出现法律改变导致有了新诉因可向 BCCI 索赔损失的权利,这在订约时,双方根本不可能预见后来普通法有这样的改变与这种索赔。所以和解协议即使用字十分广泛也不包括这种索赔,因为没有这个订约的意图。这可节录在《Chitty on Contracts》(2021 年,第 34 版)一书第 25 - 020 段说:"**The scope of a general release** The scope of a release drafted in general terms may be limited either by the existence of a dispute between the parties or by the parties' knowledge, at the time of entry into the release, of the existence of the claim where the parties have a particular dispute in mind when entering into the release, the scope of the dispute 'provides a limiting background context to the document'. Even where the parties do not have a particular dispute in mind, the circumstances in which the release was given may suggest that the release should only apply to a particular subject matter. An illustration of this is provided by Bank of Credit and Commerce International SA v Ali where a very broadly worded release was held, as a matter of construction, to be confined to matters relating to the termination of the employment relationship and did not encompass a claim for stigma damages arising out of an alleged breach of an implied duty owed to the employees not to carry out a dishonest or corrupt business. **An important factor which influenced the conclusion that the release did not extend to a claim for stigma damages was the fact that the existence of such a claim, as a matter of law, was unknown at the time of entry into the release.**"

双方另一个与本章有关的替代争议(alternative dispute)是在谈判全面和解协议,BCCI 是否有向雇员披露的责任?这披露责任是在和解谈判一方知道但也明知道另一方不知道的情况下,不去自动披露会让和解协议包括了一些对方不知道将来会有的特定索赔权利,糊里糊涂签订了和解协议而失去了该权利。在本先例中,就是 BCCI 或它的董事局是知道银行的全球业务广泛涉及欺诈、洗钱与贪污,但原告作为一般雇员是不会知道,而这会是将来对他的事业有不良影响与带来一些特定权利。

---

[32] 对重大与已经是长期被接受的法律地位,如果是由法院通过案例作出法律改变,就会令很多当事人将自己以前被认为是没有机会成功的诉求而诉诸法院。但通过议会立法就可以避免这种情况,因为改变了的法律地位往往是说明从立法规定的生效日期起才适用。而且一般针对实体性的法律地位,立法作出改变是不会有溯及力。

但在此先例中,贵族院判双方在订立全面和解协议时都没有意识到和解协议包括这个新的索赔权利,所以 BCCI 不存在有什么可以或需要披露。但看来是认同如果是在知道一些信息与事实是会带来一些特定责任与/或权利,而对方雇员是不知道的情况下签订全面的和解协议,这会被视为"卑鄙狡诈行为"(sharp practice),雇主是有自动披露的责任。其中 Nicholls 勋爵说:

"Thus far I have been considering the case where both parties were unaware of a claim which subsequently came to light. Materially different is the case where the party to whom the release was given knew that the other party had or might have a claim and knew also that the other party was ignorant of this. **In some circumstances seeking and taking a general release in such a case, without disclosing the existence of the claim or possible claim, could be unacceptable sharp practice. When this is so, the law would be defective if it did not provide a remedy.**

That is not the present case. Although the bank through its officers may be fixed with knowledge of the corrupt activities taking place within the bank, officers of the bank and, through them, the bank itself, were not aware that these activities might give bank employees a claim for damages for breach of their contracts of employment. ... This being so, I prefer to leave discussion of the route by which the law provides a remedy where there has been sharp practice to a case where that issue arises for decision. That **there is a remedy in such cases I do not for one moment doubt**. "(加黑部分是笔者的强调)

在同一先例中,Hoffmann 勋爵说:"A transaction in which one party agrees in general terms to release another from any claims upon him has special features. **It is not difficult to imply an obligation upon the beneficiary of such a release to disclose the existence of claims of which he actually knows and which he also realises may not be known to the other party.** There are different ways in which it can be put. One may say, for example, that inviting a person to enter into a release in general terms implies a representation that one is not aware of any specific claims which the other party may not know about. That would preserve the purity of the principle that there is no positive duty of disclosure. Or one could say, as the old Chancery judges did, that reliance upon such a release is against conscience when the beneficiary has been guilty of a suppressio veri or suggestio falsi. On a principle of law like this, I think it is legitimate to go back to authority, to Lord Keeper Henley in Salkeld v Vernon 1 Eden 64 ... where he said: 'no rule is better established than that every deed obtained on suggestio falsi, or suppressio veri, is an imposition in a court of conscience.' ... **a person cannot be allowed to rely upon a release in general terms if he knew that the other party had a claim and knew that the other party was not aware that he had a claim.** I do not propose any wider principle: there is obviously room in the dealings of the market for legitimately taking advantage of the known ignorance of the other party. But, both on principle and authority, I think that a release of rights is a situation in which the court should not allow a party to do so. On the other hand, if the context shows that the parties intended a general release for good consideration of rights unknown to both of them, I can see nothing unfair in such a transaction."(加黑部分是笔者的强调)

上述有关谈判和解协议的披露责任,可见《Chitty on Contracts》(2021年,第34版)一书之8-007段"Mistake and unconscionability",另可节录9-192段针对全面和解协议/解除责任协议说是会有此披露责任,虽然在该BCCI v. Ali先例中是无需去决定这一点:"In(BCCI v. Ali) Lord Nicholls said that where the party to whom a general release was given knew that the other party has or might have a claim and knew that the other party was ignorant of this, to take the release without disclosing the existence of the claim or possible claim could be unacceptable sharp practice. The law would be defective if it did not provide a remedy, and while the case did not raise the issue, he had no doubt that the law would provide a remedy.... **Whatever the basis on which this is to be explained, it would amount to creating a duty on a party negotiating for a general release to disclose a claim that he knows the other has or may have and which he knows the other is not aware of.**"(加黑部分是笔者的强调)

6.6 不同合约类别的披露责任小结

从上述段节对五种不同类别与不同性质的合约(保险、合伙人、担保、关系合约与和解协议)的介绍中,可见到它们对披露信息与事实,不论是在谈判合约或是在履行合约的不同阶段,都分别有所不同。这不是简单划分有关合约是否属于绝对善意或绝对有披露责任。正如《Chitty on Contracts》(2021年,第34版)一书之9-167段有如下说明:"... **the extent of the duty to disclose and the remedies available seem to vary from type of contract to type of contract**;... Therefore, it is more helpful to consider the extent of the duty and the remedies available in each type of case in which it has been held that there is some duty of disclosure. These include contracts to subscribe for shares in a company, family settlements, contracts for the sale of land, contracts for suretyship and partnerships. To this list may be added general releases and contracts where the parties are in a relationship of trust and confidence. **Contracts of service, contract of sale of goods and interest rate swap agreements have held not to be uberrimae fidei, so that there is no duty of disclosure.**"(加黑部分是笔者的强调)

7. 信义/诚信关系的合约类别

首先可节录《Misrepresentation, Mistake and Non-Disclosure》(2022年,第6版)一书之17-40段说:"... But in various contexts the courts have held that a consequence of characterising the relationship between the parties as fiduciary is that **the party owing fiduciary duties is required to make full disclosure of relevant matters, and that in the event of non-disclosure the other party may avoid the contract.** Similarly, even where the relationship does not fall within an established category of fiduciary relationship, the court may decide that the relationship on the facts carried duties of confidence and disclosure. ..."(加黑部分是笔者的强调)

这是说诚信责任是要求受托人(trustee)对信托人(trustor)或受益人(beneficiary)的利益"无保留、全心全意与专一的效忠"(undivided, exclusive and single-minded loyalty),也完全不能考虑自己的利益。可以说,这比善意的要求更进一步。在商业合约如果被默示一方对另一方有诚信责任,并要求一面倒以对方的利益为依归,会在不同的案情与不同的环境/背景下,要求双方在谈判与履行时:诚实(honest)、合作(cooperative)、言行上关心与顾及对方合法利益与合法预期(justified expectation)、透明(transparency)、不误导瞒骗、合理或甚至是只要涉及信托人或受益人的利益相关事宜,去全面与坦率披露有关信息(full and frank disclosure)等。

有说法是在诚信责任下,再也无需另有一个独立的披露责任了,因为已经被包括在诚信责任内。在Item Software(UK) Ltd v. Fassihi and Ors(2004) EWCA Civ 1244上诉庭先例中,Arden大法官说:"For my part, I do not consider that it is correct to infer from the cases to which I have referred that a fiduciary owes a separate and independent duty to disclose his own misconduct to his principal or more generally information of relevance and concern to it. So to hold would lead to a proliferation of duties and arguments about their breadth. I prefer to base my conclusion in this case on the fundamental duty to which a director is subject, that is the duty to act in what he in good faith considers to be the best interests of his company."

在本章之6.4段介绍的Ross River Ltd v. Cambridge City Football Club Ltd (2008) 1 All ER 1004先例中,Briggs大法官说不必认定Ross River对Club在买卖土地溢价权益方面是否有诚信责任,仅是默示的善意责任已经足够命令Ross River作出披露。可见,如果默示有诚信责任,更是难逃要披露本来想隐藏的信息与事实。在本章之6.2段介绍的Conlon v. Simms(2006) EWCA Civ 1749上诉庭先例中,就说到在合伙人协议的谈判阶段就有自动披露的责任。

7.1 Nocton v. Lord Ashburton(1914)AC 932 贵族院先例

首先在《Chitty on Contracts》(2021 年,第 34 版)一书之 9 - 095 段有说到在一个早年的先例中,确认在有法律强加的小心谨慎责任(duty of care),[33] 例如诚信责任时,疏忽误述也可以带来金钱损失的索赔,这是与当时如果没有这种特殊关系不能索赔金钱损失的普通法地位不一样:"... Since the decisions in Nocton v. Lord Ashburton (1914)AC 932 ... it is clear that **an action will lie in tort for negligent misrepresentation causing loss to the representee where the relationship of the parties is such as to give rise to a duty of care**. The former case establishes that such a duty may arise(even apart from contract) out of a fiduciary relationship, such as that of solicitor and client, principal and agent, or trustee and beneficiary ..."

在 Nocton v. Lord Ashburton 贵族院先例中,案情涉及伦敦一块土地的买卖与开发交易,Nocton 律师也在该交易中有利益。Nocton 律师是 Ashburton 勋爵的家庭律师,他成功说服 Ashburton 勋爵贷款给开发商以供开发建屋之用,并以建造的房屋作为抵押。之后为了让开发商能够顺利向民众出售房屋,Nocton 律师再说服 Ashburton 勋爵自动把抵押撤销。结果出了事,Ashburton 勋爵因为担保不足以保护借出的金钱而蒙受损失,于是向 Nocton 律师索赔损失,诉因是错误提供法律意见,而且是"欺诈性误述"(fraudulent misrepresentation)。在本书第二章之 2 段提到这种错误的专业"意见"是可以被视为可诉误述(actionable misrepresentation)。由于在当时的年代没有《Misrepresentation Act 1967》立法,误述只区分为两种并且只有"欺诈性误述"才让被误述方(misrepresentee)除了有权在欺诈/欺骗侵权(tort of deceit)下撤销有关的合约外,还可以同时索赔金钱的损失。但疏忽误述就只在衡平法下有撤销合约的救济,无法索赔损失。所以 Ashburton 勋爵只有以欺诈性误述作为诉因,才能索赔损失。

但在一审中,Nocton 律师被认定是没有欺诈/欺骗,只是疏忽误述,所以 Ashburton 勋爵败诉。去了上诉庭,一审结果被改变,判是有欺诈性误述。最后贵族院认为上诉庭推翻一审对事实的认定(就是 Nocton 律师是否有欺诈性误述)是应该避免,毕竟是一审法院才处理证据(例如对有关证人的盘问)。但一审与上诉庭都不应该只针对误述是否欺诈/欺骗,而是应该针对 Nocton 律师作为 Ashburton 勋爵的家庭律师是有诚信责任,这种特殊关系是有小心谨慎责任。所以在本案的事实下,不需要再去区分是欺诈性误述或非欺诈性误述,Nocton 律师在利益冲突下提供错误法律意见显然是违反诚信责任,需要赔偿 Ashburton 勋爵的损失。贵族院的 Haldane 子爵说:"I think that Neville J(一审大法官)was wrong in treating this case as if it were based on substance only in deceit and intention to cheat. No doubt a good deal was said both in argument and in cross-examination which, if established, would have afford proof of actual fraud. But that was no reason for treating the action as launched wholly on this

---

[33] 见本书第一章之 2.1 段。

foundation. It was really an action based on the exclusive jurisdiction of **a Court of Equity over a defendant in a fiduciary position in respect of matters which at law would also have given a right to damages for negligence.** ... My Lords, the conclusion at which I have arrived is that this action ought properly to have been treated as one in which the plaintiff had made out **a claim for compensation** either for loss arising from misrepresentation made in breach of fiduciary duty or for breach of contract to exercise due care and skill. ..."

《Chitty on Contracts》(2021 年,第 34 版)一书之 9 – 097 段的脚注 452 看来对这个先例的判法有点质疑,说诚信责任是衡平法概念,而衡平法下是不能判金钱损失的救济,因为这是普通法法院的权利,所以贵族院在该先例用的词是"赔偿"(compensation)/衡平赔偿(equitable compensation)[34] 而不是"金钱损失"(damages)。但在今天这类案件中已不再重要,因为有先例支持在这种专业关系下有小心谨慎的责任,而侵权是可以赔偿金钱损失。[35] 有关内容可节录如下:"It is perhaps not strictly accurate to refer to an action for 'damages' for negligence in breach of a fiduciary relationship, for this was an equitable remedy and equity did not award damages. In Nocton v. Ashburton ... the House of Lords spoke of an action for 'compensation' and it may be that the measure of damages which they had in mind as appropriate in that case would have been lower than the usual tort measure. But today it is at least clear that a fiduciary relationship arising out of a professional relationship will ordinarily support a duty of care in tort for which ordinary tort damages will be recoverable, see eg Arenson v. Arenson (1977) AC 405; Midland Bank v. Hett, Stubbs and Kemp (1979) Ch. 384."

7.2　默示诚信责任合约在履行时的自动披露责任

接下来可先简单介绍小部分有关在诚信责任下的披露责任,这方面有很多先例是涉及高管/董事对受聘公司的诚信责任。例如在 Shepherds Investments v. Walters (2007) IRLR 110 先例中,被告受聘为原告公司的董事,负责销售人寿保险。但被告另去成立将来会正面竞争抢客的公司,这被指控违反诚信责任。被告抗辩说只是做准备工作,离职后才会实际行动。但 Etherton 大法官判被告败诉,说:"a fiduciary's duty to disclose his own misconduct to his principal or, more generally, information of relevance and concern to his principal, the single and overriding touchstone was the fundamental duty of a director to act in what he considered in good faith to be in the best interests of the company. There was no separate and independent duty of disclosure. ... Even if there had been no obligation to disclose their own 'preparatory' activity, each of the in-

---

〔34〕 有关衡平法赔偿在本书第三章之 5.2.3 段也有提到,还可见本书第十章之 12.3.2 段的介绍。

〔35〕 在本书第一章之 2.2.1 段介绍的 Hedley Byrne v. Heller (1964) AC 465 贵族院先例后,疏忽侵权也可以索赔纯经济损失(pure economic loss)。

dividual defendants was obliged, by August 12, 2003 at the latest, to disclose to Financial or Investments the actual or threatened activity of the others to set up the competing business."

这方面还有很多其他案例如 British Midland Tools v. Midland International Tooling(2003)2 BCLC 523; Ranson v. Customer Systems Plc(2012)EWCA Civ 841 等先例,不去多讲。

而如果涉及的不是有诚信责任的高管或董事,而是只有效忠与忠诚责任的一般雇员,看来就不需要披露将来离职后的打算。

7.3 默示诚信责任合约在谈判时的自动披露责任

现在回到本段针对的双方有诚信关系下,在谈判合约过程中要求自动披露或不得保持沉默的问题。在本章之6.2段介绍的 Conlon v. Simms(2006)EWCA Civ 1749 上诉庭先例中,Jonathan Parker 大法官明确说明在一个有诚信关系的合伙人协议中,无论在谈判时(双方仍没有诚信关系合约的产生)或在履行时都有这方面的责任,说:"In my judgment there can be no doubt that the principle of caveat emptor does not apply to the making of a partnership agreement, and that in negotiating such an agreement a party owes a duty to the other negotiating parties to disclose all material facts of which he has knowledge and of which the other negotiating parties may not be aware. ..."

接下来在 JD Wetherspoon Plc v. Van de Berg & Co Ltd(2007)EWHC 1044(Ch)先例中,针对的是被告(Van de Berg)向法院申请以各种理由提早把原告(JD)的索赔撤销(strike out),[36]但这被 Lewison 大法官拒绝。但由于不是全面的审理,只能看到简单的案情。Van de Berg 是以固定的年度聘费加上交易成功的奖金被 JD 聘用为地产经纪人(estate agent)去寻找恰当的地方开酒吧。Van de Berg 找到适当的地方,本来是可以购买,但只告诉 JD 可以租用。而在 JD 决定租用后,因为可以保证这物业有投资价值,被告就私下以关联或背后控制的公司把该物业买入,并以高价连有稳定租金收入的租赁合约一并转售。这种赚取"秘密利润"(secret profit)的手法也已经发生了好几宗,只是 JD 很晚才发觉(所以本案其中一个争议是索赔是否已经错过了6年的时效)。在发觉后,JD 向 Van de Berg 与公司的3位董事作为第一至第四被告,提起了诉讼索赔,诉因包括违反了委托人与代理人之间的诚信责任、欺诈/欺骗、欺诈性误述、非法隐瞒等,并索赔损失与要求返还秘密利润等。

只针对 Van de Berg 被控的欺诈性误述,从索赔请求所写的重要事实(material facts)与提供的详情(particulars)来看,[37]指控的谎言主要是对第三人讲而不是对 JD 讲。所以法院认为表面看来,JD 的欺诈/欺骗指控会是不容易成立,因为谎言不是对 JD 说,JD 也谈不上有对谎言作出过依赖。但非法隐瞒/不去诚实自动披露,告诉 JD

〔36〕 见笔者《证据法:国际规管与诉讼中的证据攻防》一书第六章之4段。

〔37〕 见本书第三章之9段。

有关物业除了租赁之外也可以购买与 Van de Berg 有利益冲突的事实,就会是违反了诚信责任下要求的自动披露,并会是欺诈性误述。Lewison 大法官也跟从了 Conlon v. Simms 先例,说:"Although the Particulars of Claim in the present case contain numerous allegations that the defendants told lies, they are all allegations that the defendants told lies, not to JD Wetherspoon, but to other people. JD Wetherspoon had no knowledge of the lies at the time, and therefore did not rely on them. Miss Newman(JD 的代表大律师)accepts that the mere fact that the defendants told lies to third parties(assuming for the sake of argument that they did)does not give JD Wetherspoon a cause of action in deceit. JD Wetherspoon's real complaint is not that it was told lies at the time of the relevant transactions, but that the defendants kept silent about what was really going on. As a general rule mere silence, however morally wrong, will not support an action for deceit: Bradford Third Equitable Benefit Building Society v Borders [1941] 2 All ER 205. However, there are exceptions to that general rule. One such exception is(or at least may be)where the person against whom the claim is made has a duty of disclosure and fraudulently fails to do so: Conlon v Simms [2006] 2 All ER 1024. Viewed in that way it seems to me that there is an arguable cause of action in deceit if: i) Any particular defendant had fiduciary obligations to JD Wetherspoon; ii) Those obligations included an obligation to disclose either(a)the availability of freeholds or(b)the defendants' own financial interests in transactions relating to those freeholds; and iii) The defendants dishonestly failed to make disclosure. ..."

8. 有责任说清楚/沉默性禁反言

这课题已经在笔者的《合约的履行、弃权与禁反言》一书的第五章之 10 段有详论,并介绍了 Mangles v. Dixon(1852)3 HL Cas 702; Hartog v. Colin and Shields(1939)3 All ER 566; The "Nai Genova"(1984)1 Lloyd's Rep 353; The "Stolt Loyalty"(1993)2 Lloyd's Rep 281; OT Africa Line Ltd v. Vickers plc(1996)1 Lloyd's Rep 700; Thames Trains Ltd v. Adams(2006)EWHC 3291(QB); MIOM 1 Ltd v. Sea Echo ENE(No. 2)(2012)1 Lloyd's Rep 140 等有关先例。

这里尽量不再重复,该书介绍了会在一些特定的案情下有责任说清楚(duty to speak)或要自动披露,如在 10.1.1 段的"产权人知道另一方对所有权有了错误理解";在 10.1.2 段的"委托人有责任说明代理人授权的局限";在 10.1.3 段的"陈述方有责任通知原本的陈述已经改变";在 10.1.4 段的"银行的客户有责任通知银行"与在 10.1.5 段的"其他情况"。

其他情况可以在任何商业合约的谈判或履行时发生,只要是知道对方有了错误理解但刻意不去提出。但照理说,在英国普通法不要求善意、买方自己小心(caveat emptor)与没有自动披露的大原则下,应是不必向对方提出或提醒。所以,针对会构成有这个说清楚或披露责任的要件,Christopher Clarke 大法官在 Ted Baker Plc v. AXA Insurance UK Plc(2017)EWCA Civ 4096 上诉庭先例中说:"the duty necessary to found an estoppel by silence or acquiescence arose where a reasonable man would expect the person against whom the estoppel was raised acting **honestly and responsibly** to bring the true facts to the attention of the other party known by him to be under a mistake as to their respective rights and obligations."(加黑部分是笔者的强调)

也就是说,在有关情况下,任何一位合理人士都可预期 A 会诚实与负责地告知对方 B 有关事实真相,但 A 保持沉默,这是不合情理与可以构成禁反言。这里简单介绍案情。原告 Ted Baker 是著名的服装连锁品牌,发现自己的一名员工大量盗窃库存从而导致损失,于是在营业中断险(business interruption insurance)下向 AXA 要求赔付。AXA 在保险合约的 2(b)条文下要求原告提供大量文件,其中包括公司的损益表(profit and loss accounts)与管理会计报表(management accounts)。原告称准备这些文件很花时间与很昂贵,根据保险合约下的 Professional Accountants Clause 要求 AXA 提供合理费用。AXA 不接受,原告表示除非 AXA 在责任方面原则上愿意赔付(有关文件只与决定金额有关),否则不会自己花钱准备与提供这些文件。而在等待 AXA 决定是否在 Professional Accountants Clause 下承担费用期间,2(b)条文下提供文件的时限已经过去,后来 AXA 也没再坚持向原告要这些文件。AXA 主张原告没有提供有关文件是没有满足保险合约要求赔付的先决条件,于是拒赔。高院一审支持了 AXA 的主张,但被上诉庭推翻。上诉庭判虽然一般保险公司没有责任提醒受保人满足先决条件的重要性,特别是在此先例中,原告请了非常有经验的保险经纪作为代理人,但是此先例的特别之处在于如果 AXA 仍认为需要有关文件,而不是双方暂时搁置,应该对原告说清楚。

此先例也涉及上述加黑的"诚实"的说法是否要求不诚实或欺诈性的不披露(fraudulent concealment)与沉默才会是禁反言的争议,也就是 AXA 是否故意保持沉默蒙蔽原告让其来不及即时提供文件。Christopher Clarke 大法官说是不必与欺诈/欺骗扯在一起,只需要这不披露与沉默在当时的案情下是"不恰当"(impropriety),说:"The reference to 'acting honestly' did not ... mean that the party against whom estoppel was asserted had to be guilty of actual dishonesty in the sense of acting fraudulently. ... absent a relationship of good faith or partnership or something akin to a joint enterprise the courts would not impose a duty to speak in the absence of impropriety of some description by the person alleged to be estoppel. That impropriety might, however, come from the act of staying silent itself, as where a reasonable person would expect the person who is alleged to be estoppel, acting honestly and responsibly, to bring the true facts to the attention of the other party known to him to be under a mistake as to their respective rights and obligations."

另一个笔者觉得十分典型的情况是在 Eminence Property Developments Limited v. Kevin Christopher Heaney(2010)EWCA Civ 1168 先例中。案情有关房产买卖,但在金融海啸后市场大跌,买方经济情况也出现问题,向卖方要求减价但被拒绝。根据有关的房产合约规定,卖方在给买方的通知中要求在 2008 年 12 月 15 日前完成交易,但这是算错了时间,正确的时间应是 12 月 18 日。卖方在 12 月 17 日向买方做出终止合约的通知,买方看来早有准备马上接受了卖方违约/毁约。双方的争议是原告是否是诚实误解(honest misapprehension),[38] 并没有提到禁反言的问题,但从 Etherton 大法官的判决理由看,应是觉得在这种情况下,买方有责任向卖方指出这明显的计算错误,有关部分可节录如下:"(4)... In the present case, as a reasonable person in Mr Heaney's(买方代表)position would have realised, there was a simple error of calculation by Eminence's(卖方)solicitors, analogous to a clerical error, which, once pointed out, would have been(as it was)conceded immediately. The consequence of pointing it out, as the reasonable person would have appreciated, was that the rescission notices would have been treated, as they were in law, as ineffective, and Eminence would have waited until the expiry of the notices to complete before deciding whether or not to treat the contracts as at an end. ..."

所以在此先例中,如果卖方争辩有责任说清楚或沉默性禁反言,应该也可以成功。

[38] 见笔者《合约的履行、弃权与禁反言》一书的第一章之 3.6.4 段。

第六章　疏忽或欺诈意见

1. 专业人士提供意见与服务时的小心谨慎责任

继之前几章对误述课题的讨论，本章会针对专业人士因疏忽而提供了错误意见或服务这个更具体的课题展开讨论。在本书第一章中也提到，提供专业服务的专业人士（如律师、医生、经纪人、会计师、估价师、测量师、建筑师、财务顾问、银行家等）对委任方/客户在合约与侵权的法律关系下都负有小心谨慎责任（duty of care），Bridge 勋爵在 Caparo v. Dickman（1990）2 WLR 358 贵族院先例中给出了一个经典说法："In advising the client who employs him, a professional man owes **a duty to exercise that standard of skill and care** appropriate to his professional status and will be **liable in contract and in tort for all losses** which his client may suffer **by reason of any breach of that duty**."（加黑部分是笔者的强调）

这也在英国的立法中有针对，如《Financial Services and Markets Act 2000》修改后增加《Financial Services Duty of Care Bill》针对给一般消费者提供金融服务的专业人才，并将小心谨慎的责任定义为"an obligation to exercise reasonable care and skill when providing a product or service"。还有各种专业的专业守则（code of conduct）也对专业人士的小心谨慎责任与标准有规定。例如在《Code of Conduct for Healthcare Support Workers and Adult Social Care Workers in England》中说："You are responsible for, and have a duty of care to ensure that your conduct does not fall below the standards detailed in the Code."

1.1　在侵权与合约两种不同法律关系下法律强加的小心谨慎责任

"小心谨慎责任"是构成侵权的要件，在本书第一章之 2.1.1 段已有详及，这包括的要件是双方有邻近（proximity）关系，一方可合理预见到自己不小心会给另一方造成损失或伤害以及法律强加这个小心谨慎的责任在一方，公共政策上考虑是公平、公正与合理（fair, just and reasonable），并在违反后作为受害方的原告可主张疏忽侵权（negligence tort）。

而如果没有法律强加的小心谨慎的责任，仅是不小心（carelessness）是不会带来疏忽的侵权责任。

在普通法下，专业人士一直以来都毫无疑问对他们的客户有小心谨慎责任。在合约下这是来自法律的默示(implied by law)地位，虽然在订约自由的大原则下可以明示条文豁免或减轻小心谨慎的责任。但会有立法或个别专业的守则禁止这样做，加上委任这些专业人士的客户也会抗拒。而在侵权中，是在 Donoghue v. Stevenson (1932) AC 562 贵族院先例中确立了在双方没有合约关系下也会有小心谨慎责任，违反并造成人身或财产损失就构成疏忽侵权。在接下来的 Hedley Byrne v. Heller (1964) AC 465 贵族院先例中，更进一步判违反小心谨慎责任造成纯经济损失也可以构成疏忽侵权。

法院认为正是因为专业人士在特定的领域有特殊的技能与经验，所以作为外行人的客户更可能依赖专业人士的意见行事。这也是法律愿意在这一类提供专业服务的合约默示小心谨慎责任的原因。只节录少量权威说法，在 Hedley Byrne v. Heller 贵族院先例中，Hodson 勋爵说："Where a person is so placed that others could reasonably rely upon his judgment or his skill or upon his ability to make careful inquiry, and a person takes upon himself to give information or advice to, or allows his information or advice to be passed on to, another person who, as he knows or should know, will place reliance upon it, then a duty of care arise."

另在 Caparo v. Dickman (1990) 2 WLR 358 贵族院先例中，Oliver 勋爵说："What can be deduced from the Hedley Byrne case, therefore, is that the necessary relationship between the maker of a statement or giver of advice (the adviser) and the recipient who acts in reliance on it (the advisee) may typically be held to exist where (1) the advice is required for a purpose, whether particularly specified or generally described, which is made known, either actually or inferentially, to the adviser at the time when the advice is given, (2) the adviser knows, either actually or inferentially, that his advice will be communicated to the advisee, either specifically or as a member of an ascertainable class, in order that it should be used by the advisee for that purpose, (3) it is known, either actually or inferentially, that the advice so communicated is likely to be acted on by the advisee for that purpose without independent inquiry and (4) it is so acted on by the advisee to his detriment."

1.2 专业人士小心谨慎责任的测试标准

当然，专业人士对客户(或其他"邻居")的小心谨慎责任也只是以有关专业标准(professional standard)所要求的合理技能与谨慎去提供专业服务，并不要求完美或要保证特定结果/成果。

针对以什么技能与谨慎的标准去衡量被告专业人士是否存在疏忽的问题，法院决定什么是"合理"标准时会让原告引入相同专业或行业的专家证人去对被告的言行挑毛病。这些专家证人往往是专业内的顶尖人士，也确实会挑出毛病，如有更好的意见或做法，甚至会挑出不小心之处。但问题是在任何专业，意见或做法都不会只有一个答案。可能会是原告专家证人与被告以及他的专家证人,虽然是各持己见,但大家的意见都是正确的或不能算是错误。至于谁在有关专业有更高的地位与更多经验,并不代表什么。

例如,当事人有一个合约条文如何解释的法律的争议,一种经常会有的做法就是去向大律师寻求法律意见。如果对取得的第一个法律意见不满意或不放心,会去向另一位大律师寻求法律意见。但经常会是两份大律师意见有差异,甚至有完全不同的看法。但两位大律师都是根据合约解释的规则去说理与分析,并得出自己的结论。也会是,其中一位大律师找出了一个年代古老的事实相同与有说服力的案例,而另一位大律师没有提到,但这过错或不小心也不代表专业上有了疏忽。毕竟在同样专业再多找十位八位大律师,会有一半以上也不会找出该古老案例,更说不定会有个别大律师多挑出了几个其他会扯得上关系的新案例。更不要说,在浩如烟海的案例中,大家对某一个案例是否适用在该客户的咨询中还会有不同的看法。所以在该两位被委任去提供法律意见的大律师是无法说谁对谁错,谁有了疏忽或遗漏的责任,只是大家有不同的法律意见。

当然,也的确会有大律师在他提供的法律意见中存在专业疏忽,但这带来一个问题:应以什么基准(benchmark)或标准(standard)去衡量他是否是达标?显然,这标准不会看某一个特定专业人士的水准,无论是顶尖还是一般的相同专业人士。而应是该专业/行业被普遍接受的标准。不少专业/行业机构,都会有它们的专业守则,往往是规定了业内能够接受的最低专业标准。这样,如上一段作为例子的大律师意见,如果他的意见被法院认定为对相关事宜的意见说的是外行话,加上他确实无法证明他对法律意见有关的事情有什么经验与了解(如非诉律师提供商事仲裁的意见与服务),就会违反了专业守则。例如,他对某一领域的权威先例与法律地位根本都不知道,自己知道对委任事项是不称职或没有足够经验而不应该接受。

这带来在笔者《证据法:基础理论、口头证据与专家证据》一书第六章之5.3段介绍的判断医疗疏忽的"Bolam 考验",就是适用这个标准去衡量被告医生是否专业疏忽,即涉案的医生的行为如果符合了行业负责机构(如医学会)的要求就并非疏忽。即使是同一专业/行业内实际上有其他(甚至可能是有更多其他机构或主流看法)不同、更高的标准也是一样并非法律上的疏忽。在该著名的 Bolam v. Friern Hospital Management Committee(1957)1 WLR 582 先例中,[1] McNair 大法官说有关的考验是:"I must tell you what in law we mean by 'negligence' ... there is ample scope for genuine difference of opinion and one man clearly is not negligent merely because his conclusion differs from that of other professional men. ... [被告专业人士] is not guilty

[1] 该先例的争议是医生在使用电休克疗法治疗病人的精神疾病时,没有注射肌肉松弛剂或束缚住病人,导致病人骨折是否是疏忽,McNair 大法官最终判医生的做法在医疗专业机构的标准看可以接受,因此没有疏忽。

of negligence if he has acted in accordance with a practice accepted as proper by a responsible body of medical men skilled in that particular art … Putting in the other way round, a man is not negligent, if he is acting in accordance with such a practice, merely because there is a body of opinion who would take a contrary view. …"

这一审的 Bolam 考验在 Marynard v. West Midlands RHA(1984)1 WLR 634 贵族院先例中被确认而成为权威说法，Scarman 勋爵说："Differences of opinion and practice exist, and will always exist, in the medical as in other professions. There is seldom only one answer exclusive of all others to problems of professional judgment. A Court may prefer one body of opinion to the other, but that is no basis for a conclusion of negligence."

在接下来有多不胜数的案例中适用 Bolam 考验作为标准判断专业人士（特别是医务人员）在有关的特定案情中是否存在疏忽：Anderson v. Lyotier (t/a Snowbizz)(2008) EWHC 2790(QB)（滑雪教练）；Richards v. Speechley Bircham LLP(2021) UKSC 20（事务律师）；Hart v. Large(2020) EWHC 985(TCC)（测量师）；Charles B Lawrence & Associates v. Intercommercial Bank Ltd(2021) UKPC 30（估价师）；Martlet Homes Ltd v. Mulalley & Co Ltd(2022) EWHC 1813(TCC)（承建商）等。这甚至对政府在行政上有否疏忽的案件：见 Phelps v. Hillingdon Borough Council(2001)2 AC 619(HL)；David Leslie Smith v. London Borough of Havering(2004) EWHC 599(QB)；Watts v. Secretary of State for Health(2016) EWHC 2835(QB)；Williams v. Betsy Cadwaladr University Local Health Board(2022) EWHC 455(QB)；Hoyle v. Hampshire CC(2022) EWHC 934(QB)等先例。

在 David Goldstein v. Levy Gee(A Firm)(2003) EWHC 1574(Ch)先例中，原告原本是公司董事，被告是审计师，原告聘用被告对公司股本估值，以确定原告所持公司股票的价格。原告指称被告因疏忽低估了股价，导致他蒙受损失，但没有获得支持。Lewison 大法官针对判断审计师是否疏忽的标准说：

"In Zubaida v. Hargreaves [1995] 1 EGLR 127 Hoffmann LJ said: 'In an action for negligence against an expert, it is not enough to show that another expert would have given a different answer. Valuation is not an exact science, it involves questions of judgment on which experts may differ without forfeiting their claim to professional competence. The fact that a judge may think one approach better than another is therefore irrelevant … **The issue is not whether the expert's valuation was right, in the sense of being the figure which a judge after hearing the evidence would determine. It is whether he has acted in accordance with practices which are regarded as acceptable by a respectable body of opinion in his profession**: see Bolam v. Friern Hospital Management Committee [1957] 1 WLR 582 …'

This is in line with the general principle that a professional does not warrant a result.

He agrees only to use reasonable skill and care in forming his opinion or giving his advice. In other words**it is the process that must be examined rather than simply the end result**. That is not to say that the end result is irrelevant. First, the end result may be very far from opinions given by other experts, or may be falsified by some empirical outcome, with the result that one must infer that something has gone wrong with the process. Second, a professional may have a duty, as part of the process, to stand back and look at the end result in the round to see if it accords with his instinctive feel. "（加黑部分是笔者的强调）

另在 199 Knightsbridge Development Ltd v. WSP UK Ltd（2014）EWHC 43（TCC）先例中，案情涉及被告的设计工程师被指控对供水系统设计不当导致建筑被水淹造成严重损失。法院判被告疏忽，但是即使没有疏忽给出了恰当的建议也无法改变水淹的结果，因此不满足因果关系。Edwards - Stuart 大法官总结了 Bolam 考验与其他相关案例的原则说："I draw the following principles from the authorities that I have cited. i) A professional man does not warrant that the course of action that he takes or advises his client to follow will be successful. …ii) If a professional man adopts or advises a course of action which although unsuccessful or shown to be wrong is a course of action that was **in accord with or was adopted at the time by a responsible body of opinion held by practitioners in that discipline, he will not be negligent provided that that body of opinion has a logical or rational basis**…iii) If the exponents of the 'responsible body of opinion' relied on cannot demonstrate that the opinion has a logical or rational basis, the defence will be unlikely to succeed …iv) If the reason why the impugned course of action or advice was wrong is that the professional man in question and others in his position did not identify or foresee a particular risk or sequence of events, then there is probably no room for the application of the Bolam test …"（加黑部分是笔者的强调）

在较少有的情况下，会有案件是法院认为专业成员自己设立的专业守则等标准过低或没有给客户提供足够保护而不合理，即使专业人士遵循了行业指引，也可以判他要承担专业疏忽的责任。毕竟，专业成员组成的团体可能因为主观、保护主义或故步自封跟不上时代等原因，以及自己设立的标准并不合理，所以为了社会整体的进步，法院会通过判例去推动有关的专业/行业设立更高的标准。

在 Bolitho v. City & Hackney Health Authority（1998）AC 232 贵族院先例中，Browne - Wilkinson 勋爵说法院可以认为专业人士的观点不符合逻辑与不合理，但只有在极少的情况下法院才会这样做，毕竟这里涉及法院不熟悉的专业或行业知识：

"there are cases where, despite a body of professional opinion sanctioning the defendant's conduct, the defendant can properly be held liable for negligence … In my judgment that is because, in some cases, it cannot be demonstrated to the judge's satisfaction that the body of opinion relied upon is reasonable or responsible. In the vast majority of cases the fact that distinguished experts in the field are of a particular opinion will demonstrate the reasonableness of that opinion. In particular, where there are questions of assessment of the relative risks and benefits of adopting a particular medical practice, a reasonable view necessarily presupposes that the relative risks and benefits have been weighed by the experts in forming their opinions. **But if, in a rare case, it can be demonstrated that the professional opinion is not capable of withstanding logical analysis, the judge is entitled to hold that the body of opinion is not reasonable or responsible.**

I emphasise that in my view it will very seldom be right for a judge to reach the conclusion that views genuinely held by a competent medical expert are unreasonable.... It is **only where a judge can be satisfied that the body of expert opinion cannot be logically supported at all that such opinion will not provide the benchmark by reference to which the defendant's conduct falls to be assessed.**"(加黑部分是笔者的强调)

这种少见的情况就出现在了 Edward Wong Finance Co Ltd v. Johnson Stokes & Master(1984)AC 296 先例中,案情涉及香港(当时还没有回归,所以上诉到了英国枢密院)的地产交易。对于地产交易,英国的惯常做法是买卖双方的律师同时交换最后一笔钱与产权转移的有关文件。但香港的做法都是买方的律师先将钱交给卖方的律师,卖方律师担保会在一定时间内将产权有关文件交给买方律师。在此先例中,在买方律师将钱交给卖方律师后,卖方律师卷款逃跑,交易无法完成。买方于是起诉自己的律师专业疏忽,法院虽然认定了几乎所有的香港地产交易都是采用这种做法。专家意见说是99%的交易都是这样操作,这是因为当初香港做地产交易的律师有限,所有人都相互认识,而这是地产交易第一次出现因为律师卷款逃跑而交易无法达成的情况。但是鉴于卖方律师欺诈侵占的风险是可以合理预见的,所以枢密院认为买方律师的做法不能说是合理与负责。加上即使这种是香港行业做法,律师也可以采取其他预防措施防范这种风险。例如,向卖方确认律师有权代他收钱,或是与卖方同意支票抬头不要写律师事务所而是写当初给卖方提供贷款的银行。因此,虽然律师只是根据香港的行业做法操作,但依然是专业疏忽并要赔偿客户因为疏忽导致的损失。

总而言之,法律并不要求完美,也同意很多专业人士的意见的性质决定了不可能保证最后能取得特定的结果。律师不能保证会赢得法院案件,投资顾问也不能保证客户在某个投资一定能取得多少回报。他们无法保证并不代表他们没有以合理技能与谨慎提供服务。类似的,专业人士犯错或有遗漏也并不意味着就一定是疏忽或没有以合理技能与谨慎提供服务,法院会考虑是否在目前专业或行业可以合理接受的范围内。

1.3 违约或疏忽侵权与损失的关联性

因果关系(causation)的问题,也在笔者的《损失赔偿与救济》一书的第四章有详论,尽量不重复。对合约而言,违约的言行(例如违反小心谨慎责任的默示要求)是“前因”,而受害方蒙受的损失为“后果”,它们两者之间必须有关联性(casual connection)。这可节录在《Chitty on Contracts》(2021 年,第 34 版)一书之 29 – 073 段如下:

“**Requirement of a casual connection**. Although the issue of remoteness-whether a particular loss was within the reasonable contemplation of the parties-tends to the prominent one in cases of liability for damage in the law of contract,before any issue of remoteness can arise causation must first be proved:there must be a casual connection between the defendant' s breach of contract and the claimant' s loss. ...The answer to whether the breach was the cause of the loss or merely the occasion for the loss must ‘in the end’ depend on ‘the court' s commonsense’ in interpreting the facts. So where a company continued to trade after a negligent audit by the defendant failed to reveal the true financial position of the company,the Court of Appeal held that the auditor' s breach of contract gave the company ‘the opportunity ... to incur ... trading losses:it did not cause those trading losses’. The trading losses flowed from trading,not auditing.”

针对合约下专业疏忽与造成的损失的问题,在实务中有时并不容易将有因果关系的损失从所有的损失中区分出来。有时专业疏忽只是为进一步的损失创造了机会,但并不是直接造成了损失,这时是否要将这部分损失算在专业人士?

在 Galoo and Gamine v. Bright Grahame Murray(1994)1 WLR 1360 先例中,被告是会计师事务所,而第一与第二原告是被审计账目的公司,实际上是代表所有债权人的公司清盘人。第一与第二原告其中的一个主张是,如果被告没有在服务合约下疏忽/违约,就会发现公司账目的虚假之处。这样,公司早就破产也就不会蒙受之后生意亏本的损失。但这没有被法院支持,会计师事务所的疏忽只是为公司继续经营创造了机会。Glidewell 大法官针对因果关系说:

“The passages ... make it clear that if a breach of contract by a defendant is to be held to entitle the plaintiff to claim damages,it must first be held to have been an ‘effective’ or ‘dominant’ cause of his loss. The test in Quinn v. Burch Bros. (Builders) Ltd. [1966] 2 QB 370 that it is necessary to distinguish between a breach of contract which causes a loss to the plaintiff and one which merely gives the opportunity for him to sustain the loss,is helpful but still leaves the question to be answered ‘How does the court decide whether the breach of duty was the cause of the loss or merely the occasion for the loss?’

The answer in my judgment ... is ‘By the application of the court's common sense.’

Doing my best to apply this test,I have no doubt that the deputy judge arrived at a correct conclusion on this issue. The breach of duty by the defendants gave the opportunity to Galoo and Gamine(第一与第二原告)to incur and to continue to incur trading losses;

it did not cause those trading losses, in the sense in which the word 'cause' is used in law."

侵权的因果关系或关联性与合约也是大致相同,但会有自己的复杂之处。这可先节录《Chitty on Contracts》(2021 年,第 34 版)一书之 20-161 段如下:"**Lack of casual connection**. First, the tort is not committed if the defendant's interference was not the cause of the claimant's loss. ... Similarly, where breach of the contract has already been induced by C's acquisition of the property from B, there will be no tort liability for inducing breach of contract on D, who subsequently buys the property from C, even with knowledge of the contract between A & B, for D's conduct will not have played any part in inducing the original breach. Nor will D in such a case be liable for interference with the remedies arising out of the broken contract between A and B."

1.3.1 必须造成有关联性的损失才有侵权的诉因

上述《Chitty on Contracts》节录的第一句就说明对疏忽侵权而言,成立一个诉因(cause of action)的前提是已经造成有关联性的损失(无论是人身/财产的实质损害还是纯经济损失)。指控侵权的原告仅是能证明被告侵权方在言行中有过错或疏忽,并违反了小心谨慎责任,仍是不够。这与违约的诉因是在发生违约事件时就已经存在并不一样,合约关系下即使无法证明损失也可判违约方赔偿名义损失(nominal damages)。

侵权的诉因必须是责任(疏忽)与损失走在一起,只有疏忽(甚至是严重疏忽)但没有造成任何损失是不构成侵权的。这在 Cartledge v. E Joplin & Sons Ltd(1963) AC 758 先例中, Reid 勋爵说:"a cause of action accrues as soon as a wrongful act has caused personal injury beyond what can be regarded as negligible."

另在 Watson v. Fram Reinforced Concrete Co(Scotland) Ltd(1960) SC HL 92 苏格兰案例中, Reid 勋爵也有同样说法:"The ground of any action based on negligence is the concurrence of breach of duty and damage ..."

再是在 The "Wagon Mound" (1961) 1 Lloyd's Rep 1 枢密院先例中, Simonds 子爵说:"But there can be no liability until the damage has been done. It is not the act but the consequences on which tortious liability is founded. Just as ... there is no such thing as negligence in the air, so there is no such thing as liability in the air ... it is, vain to isolate the liability from its context and to say that B is or is not liable, and then to ask for what damage he is liable. For his liability is in respect of that damage and no other."

更近期可节录 Hoffmann 勋爵在 Rothwell v. Chemical & Insulating Co Ltd(2007) UKHL 39 先例中说:"a claim in tort based on negligence is incomplete without proof of damage. Damage in this sense is an abstract concept of being worse off, physically or economically, so that compensation is an appropriate remedy. ..."

但这给某些类别的案件(如人身伤亡)带来困难,如在发生错误与疏忽的言行后，损失不会马上出现，甚至是过了6年的法定时效才出现。一个典型的例子是笔者在《损失赔偿与救济》一书第四章之4.3.3段介绍的工人因接触石棉而导致患上间皮瘤（mesothelioma），而间皮瘤的潜伏期可以长达40年。专业人士的疏忽也会带来这类的案件。这方面的困难已经有立法作出明示规定，《Latent Damage Act 1986》之section 1引进《Limitation Act 1980》之section 14A，针对非人身伤害的案件，允许原告在无法知道他们是否有诉因但事实上已经是存在的情况下，可享有另一段从原告首度发现有诉因开始计算的额外3年时间。但这仍有一个15年的时效，即疏忽行为发生15年后无论如何都不能再起诉。而针对人身伤害，在《Limitation Act 1980》之section 11，也有类似的规定。

在专业人士疏忽的案件中，如著名的South Australia Asset Management Corp v. York Montague Ltd（1997）AC 191（以下简称"SAAMCO"）先例（后详）涉及对房屋物业估价的估价师（valuer）因为高估物业的价值而令依赖估价报告的银行或融资机构蒙受损失或担保有了短缺（under – secure）。在后者的情况也并非真正有金钱上的损失，除非把担保变为现金后才算得出到底短缺了多少钱。

这带出另一个现实困难，就是原告真正蒙受的损失金额是不肯定的，直至把有关被抵押（mortgaged）作为担保的房屋收回并成功出售后，根据取回的金额才算得出真正损失数字（如果有损失），这才对被告估价师有了侵权的诉因。

但会有情况在房地产市场低落的大环境下，无法找到买家，能找到也会需时很久。如果因为不肯定有否损失而没有诉因向疏忽提供错误信息的估价师提起诉讼，撇开时效的问题，蒙受损失的银行或融资机构也不愿意漫长地等下去。但Nicholls勋爵在Nykredit Mortgage Bank Plc v. Edward Erdman Group Ltd（No. 2）（1997）1 WLR 1627贵族院先例中说这不是问题。同样的疏忽如果是以合约索赔，在估价师疏忽的一刻就已经有了诉因，根本不需要银行将房屋出售，法院也会尽最大努力通过专家意见证据等去核算真正损失，而不会只需要赔偿名义损失。同样的疏忽以侵权索赔（如果与专业人士没有合约关系）也应该是同样的做法。Nicholls勋爵的判决可部分节录如下："Indeed, for the cause of action to arise only when the lender realises his security would be a highly unattractive proposition. It would mean that, however obvious it may be that the lender will not recover his money, he cannot start proceedings. He must wait until he manages to sell the property, a process which may be protracted. This would be a surprising stance for the law to take. **It would be all the more surprising** when one has in mind **that a lender's cause of action against his negligent valuer for breach of contract, as distinct from a claim in tort, arises when the negligent valuation is given. If** disaster were evident and **the lender were to sue his valuer for breach of contract without waiting until he had realised his security, it is inconceivable that the court would award only nominal damages. The court would do its best to assess the loss.** This prompted the trenchant observation of Bingham LJ in D. W. Moore & Co. Ltd. v.

Ferrier [1988] 1 WLR 267:'If, in a contractual claim for negligence, the court would have awarded other than nominal damages, **I do not see how it can be said that an action in tort based on the same negligence would have been bound to fail for want of any damage** as an essential ingredient of the cause of action'."(加黑部分是笔者的强调)

1.3.2 The"Empire Jamaica"(1957) AC 386(HL)贵族院先例

无论是违约或疏忽侵权因果关系或关联性通常是以"要不是"(but for)测试[2]去分析有关案件的事实,即简单问:"如果不是被告的疏忽行为,原告会否蒙受这种损失(but for the defendant's breach of duty, the claimant would not have suffered the loss)?"在《McGregor on Damages》(2020年,第21版)一书之8-003段有说到这"要不是"测试是一个分水岭测试(a threshold test):"The defendant's wrongful conduct is a cause of the claimant's harm if such harm would not have occurred without it; 'but for' it."

也就是说,被告的过错或疏忽与原告的损失在事实上或按照常理分析是有因果关系。The"Empire Jamaica"贵族院先例是早期有关何谓"有效或重要关联性"的重要案件,"Empire Jamaica"轮由于航行疏忽导致船舶碰撞,并造成重大损失。"Empire Jamaica"轮的船东在承认责任后提出申请责任限制。这历史悠久的允许限制海事事故赔偿责任以鼓励商人投资航运是早有立法针对,英国本土立法是《Merchant Shipping Act 1864》,国际公约则是当今生效的《1976 Convention on Limitation of Liability for Maritime Claims》,有关课题在笔者的《海事法》(1999年,大连海事大学出版社)一书有详论。但当年要成功申请让法院颁布允许责任限制,是需要"Empire Jamaica"轮的船东证明他本人(不是船长/船员)对该事故与所造成的损失没有错与并不知情(actual fault and privity)。这样,本来"Empire Jamaica"轮的航行疏忽是不影响这申请,因为只是在碰撞时当值的二副疏忽。但挑出来的问题是该二副没有执照,虽然他本人是被认定有能力担当这职务。这样,"Empire Jamaica"轮船东被指称有错与知情,因为雇用了没有合格执照的二副。显然船东在立法规管的层面是会受到英国有关当局的惩罚,但在此碰撞事故中,这过错或知情是否扯得上关联性?毕竟,该二副即使是有执照,也会发生碰撞。他当时的航行疏忽(甚至极端一点的例子是喝醉了酒)与他是否有执照是没有足够有效与重要的关联性。这是一审法院的判决,也被贵族院确认。

1.3.3 Bolitho v. City & Hackney Health Authority(1998) AC 232 贵族院先例

另在 Bolitho v. City & Hackney Health Authority 贵族院先例中,案情有关医疗疏

---

[2] 关于"要不是"测试在本书第一章之1.3段有更详细的介绍。这因果关系的测试是:"要不是被告的违反责任,原告就不会蒙受损失"(but for the defendant's breach of duty, the claimant would not have suffered the loss)。

忽。一名两岁的儿童因为呼吸困难入院,半夜两次病情恶化时护士打电话通知医生,但医生都没有去看患儿的情况。之后患儿呼吸与心脏骤停,并导致了脑损伤。于是患儿与其父母开始诉讼,法院判医生疏忽,双方的争议是医生没有去看患儿与脑损伤之间能否满足因果关系。原告的主张是在第二次病情恶化时,正常的医生如果去看了患儿都会给患儿施行预防性气管插管,这样就不会出现之后的心脏骤停与脑损伤,所以满足因果关系。但是被告则主张,就算医生去看了患儿,也不会给他进行气管插管。这也是被告专家证人的说法,根据患儿当时的症状与指标,气管插管并非恰当的治疗方法。一审法院与上诉庭都接受了被告的主张,判医生虽然疏忽但因为与损失之间的因果关系不成立,所以不构成疏忽侵权。

双方的其中一个争议是,法院在决定损失计算的因果关系时是否应该适用 Bolam 考验。Browne – Wilkinson 勋爵解释说并非在因果关系适用 Bolam 考验,而是在此先例中,决定是否有因果关系需要考虑两个问题:(1)医生如果去看了患儿的情况,会不会决定插管;(2)如果医生决定不插管,是否属于疏忽? 而在决定第二个问题时,Bolam 考验适用。Browne – Wilkinson 勋爵说:“Where … a breach of a duty of care is proved or admitted, the burden still lies on the plaintiff to prove that such breach caused the injury suffered… In all cases the primary question is one of fact: did the wrongful act cause the injury? But in cases where the breach of duty consists of an omission to do an act which ought to be done … that factual inquiry is, by definition, in the realms of hypothesis. The question is what would have happened if an event which by definition did not occur had occurred…There were, therefore, two questions for the judge to decide on causation. (1) What would Dr. Horn(医生) have done, or authorised to be done, if she had attended Patrick(患儿)? and(2) if she would not have intubated, would that have been negligent? The Bolam test has no relevance to the first of those questions but is central to the second.”

而在此先例中,一审法院与上诉庭接受被告专家证人的说法的决定是没有不合理。因为根据患儿的情况,两次呼吸困难之后都自主恢复,发生全面呼吸骤停的可能性较小。而且插管本身也有风险,特别是考虑到患儿只有两岁。所以假设医生去看了患儿的情况并决定不插管,也是符合行业标准,不属于疏忽。这样,该患儿的呼吸、心脏骤停与随之带来的脑损伤仍会发生,所以因果关系不成立。

2. 合约或侵权不同诉因下索赔纯经济损失

专业人士对客户的小心谨慎责任一般是来自双方订立的服务合约(service contract),但专业人士也会面对没有合约关系的情况。例如,律师常会在被正式委任前(可能之后不会被委任)对一位潜在客户(informal clients 或 quasi – clients)的电话咨询给出一些初步意见,这表示律师如果提供疏忽意见,该潜在客户只有以侵权向他索赔损失了。

或是,私人/家庭医生与病人之间也会有合约关系,但公立医院的医生与病人之间就不会有:见 Hutson v. East Berkshire(1987)AC 750 贵族院先例。

这也类同在 Woodland v. Essex County Council(2013)UKSC 66 最高院先例中的情况,涉及私立学校的学生就有合约关系,但免费的公立学校学生就没有。这导致学生在学校发生意外事故,学生就要以不同的诉因起诉疏忽照顾的学校,并会带来不同的结果如损失赔偿的高低。正如 Sumption 勋爵说:"there seems to be no rational reason why the mere absence of consideration should lead to an entirely different result when comparable services are provided by a public authority."

但直到 Hedley Byrne v. Heller(1964)AC 465(HL)(以下简称"Hedley Byrne")贵族院先例对纯经济损失(pure economic loss)放宽后,以前涉及律师(与类同的专业人士如会计师或审计师等)的专业疏忽,都是以服务合约提起诉讼,因为错误的法律意见或处理法律事务通常只会带来纯经济的损失。正如在 Candler v. Crane, Christmas & Co(1951)2 KB 164 上诉庭先例中,原告 A 是一位潜在投资人要求准备投资的公司 B 提供公司的账目,B 命令独立会计师事务所 C 尽快准备一份公司全面的账目。但 C 准备的账目有严重的不正确信息,虽然最后被认定不涉及欺诈/欺骗,但疏忽是无可置疑。A 根据该错误的公司账目作出投资,但 B 在 1 个月后倒闭,导致 A 的投资泡汤。A 向 C 以疏忽侵权/疏忽误述索赔蒙受的经济损失,毕竟他们之间没有合约关系,因为 A 蒙受的是纯经济损失所以败诉。

在本书第四章之 1 段已经有介绍,在《Misrepresentation Act 1967》前的疏忽误述在普通法下是没有金钱赔偿的救济,除非误述方对被误述方有一个小心谨慎的责任,这才满足了疏忽侵权的要件。在此 Candler v. Crane, Christmas & Co 先例的一审与上诉庭多数认为对"邻居"的小心谨慎的责任只适用在人身或财产的实质损伤,不适用在纯经济损失。Asquith 与 Cohen 大法官(Denning 大法官不同意)判:"following Derry v. Peek(1889)14 App. Cas. 337 and Le Lievre v. Gould(1893)1 QB 491 ... that a false statement, carelessly, as contrasted with fraudulently, made by one person to another, though acted on by that other to his detriment, was not actionable in the absence of any contractual or fiduciary relationship between the parties, and that this principle had in no way been qualified by the decision of the majority in Donoghue v. Stevenson(1932)AC 562."

所以,以前是不能以疏忽侵权向律师索赔的,因为律师不会像医生的疏忽会带来人身伤亡或建筑师/工程师疏忽会带来财产的实质损失。但在 Hedley Byrne 贵族院先例中革命性的开了头,就打开了疏忽侵权可以索赔纯经济损失的"泄洪阀",这特别影响专业人士如律师、会计师等。

律师给的是法律意见,这不像疏忽驾驶的不当行为,即使是十分严重的事故也只会造成十位八位行人伤亡，法律上强加在司机的小心谨慎责任可预期的“邻居”会是有限。但疏忽作出的法律意见（或其他专业意见）是可以一传十、十传百，也会没完没了地被依赖并造成无数人士的经济损失，是专业人士与背后的责任保险人根本赔不起。所以必须收紧给意见时的小心谨慎责任的范围与限制错误意见或陈述（misstatement）与疏忽造成的纯经济损失，这也解释了发展到 Caparo v. Dickman（1990）2 WLR 358 贵族院先例对近代疏忽言行会要去强加小心谨慎的责任的“Caparo 测试”：（1）造成伤害是可以合理预期；（2）双方有邻近关系；（3）强加小心谨慎的责任是公平、公正与合理的。

这第三个要件是为了去控制对纯经济损失索赔是否强加小心谨慎责任的宽紧的公共政策的考虑，在疏忽造成人身/财产的实质损失是不必考虑的。

革命性的 Hedley Byrne 先例对专业人士如律师带来至少两大新问题，接下来介绍。

2.1 免费咨询

传统的说法是错误意见只要是免费的就不会有责任，因为免费就没有对价（consideration）而构成不了合约关系。且这也构成不了侵权关系，因为侵权是不承认纯经济损失的索赔。但 Hedley Byrne 贵族院先例确立了即使没有对价，提供意见与服务的人士自愿承担责任（voluntary assumption of liability）下，法律强加给他一个小心谨慎的责任的说法或诉因，[3] 在违反这个小心谨慎责任下，依赖意见与服务的受害方可以索赔纯经济损失。这种在合约与侵权夹缝的关系是 Devlin 勋爵在 Hedley Byrne 先例中所说的：“a promise given without consideration to perform a service cannot be enforced as a contract by the promisee; but if the service is in fact performed and done negligently, the promisee can recover in an action in tort”与“relationships which ... are ‘equivalent to contract’.”

这样，免费咨询（gratuitous consultation/advice）时提供错误法律意见也是可以带来法律责任。另是，律师在提供免费的咨询有错漏的机会比正式委任后客户花钱收到的律师深思熟虑的意见（considered opinion）更是大得多。所以，虽然许多律师都会面对免费咨询并且是非要提供意见（即使只是简短）不可，最安全的做法仍是婉拒。但由于这并不现实，就只能建议好像 Hedley Byrne 先例的 Heller 银行一样在提供的信息中加上一个“免责声明”（disclaimer）说“机密而且银行不负责任”（Confidential: For your private use and without responsibility on the part of this Bank and its officials）。

笔者记得早年在 Hedley Byrne 先例后不久，Mustill 勋爵（当年是执业的御用大

---

〔3〕 见 Hedley Byrne 先例后针对“自愿承担责任”方面问题有 Henderson v. Merrett Syndicates Ltd（1995）2 AC 145; Commissioners of Customs and Excuse v. Barclays Bank（2007）1 AC 181; Lejonvarn v. Burgess（2017）EWCA Civ 254; Tindall v. Chief Constable of Thames Valley（2022）EWCA Civ 25 等先例。

律师)在一次会议发言中曾针对这方面的重大改变,并在发言后与听众的问答环节开玩笑[4]说:"我会以合理技能与谨慎来免费回答你们的问题,但不接受任何导致的损失或损害的责任(I will give answers gratuitously with such skill and care as I can command, but accepting no liability for loss or damage, however caused)。"

即使在日常生活中,同样的道理也适用。例如在 Burgess v. Lejonvarn (2016) EWHC 40 (TCC) 先例中,案情涉及原告想修整花园,一开始找的景观设计师报价太高,就找了他们的朋友(被告)。双方没有签订合约也没有讨论报酬,但被告实际提供了项目管理服务。之后因为预算等原因,原告和被告关系破裂,原告又重新找了一开始的景观设计师做工程并多花了一大笔钱。于是原告起诉被告,要求赔偿损失。Alexander Nissen QC 大法官考虑了提供服务的时长、性质、严肃性等方面后,认定虽然没有正式合约,被告也没有收取报酬,但被告仍有小心谨慎责任并在疏忽侵权下需要赔偿金钱损失,说:"I am also satisfied that the circumstances are such that it is appropriate for a tortious remedy to apply in law. This was a significant project, **albeit in a residential setting, and was being approached in a professional way**. This was not a piece of brief ad hoc advice of the type occasionally proffered by professional people in a less formal context. Instead, the services were provided over **a relatively lengthy period of time and involved considerable input and commitment on both sides**. ..."(加黑部分是笔者的强调)

2.2 对第三人负有金钱赔偿的责任

第二个新问题是专业人士也会对有合约关系的客户以外的第三人有专业疏忽。传统的疏忽侵权的受害方如交通事故的行人或路边的商店,总会有人身或财产的伤害。但其他受影响的第三人如受害方的家人或公司,有损害也只会是纯经济损失。在 Hedley Byrne 贵族院先例后,可以索赔纯经济损失的疏忽侵权大门一打开,要再去收紧看来只能去靠 Caparo 测试引入的公共政策方面的考虑了。

在商业范围内,涉及的都是金钱,方方面面的影响显然会更大。简单与经常发生的例子是像 Candler v. Crane, Christmas & Co (1951) 2 KB 164 上诉庭先例的 A 问 B 要意见或陈述,B 要 C 提供专业意见或陈述,C 也知道给 B 的意见或陈述会转发给 A,并会令 A 作出依赖。这样,即使是造成纯经济损失,C 也在疏忽侵权关系下有小心谨慎的责任。当然,A 是可以更直接要求有合约关系的 B 负责赔偿,但 B 会倒闭变成光棍或其他原因令此路不通,只能以侵权起诉 C。

在 Ross v. Caunters (1979) 3 All ER 580 先例中,律师没有提醒客户不能由受益人的配偶见证遗嘱,结果客户签署遗嘱时有一名见证人是遗嘱中其中一位剩余财产受

---

[4] 在本书第一章之 2.2 段提到了 Pearce 勋爵在 Hedley Byrne 先例说的提问的严肃性(gravity of the inquiry)是决定是否有法律责任的因素之一。只是在会议上的问答,Mustill 勋爵是不会承担责任,但如果同样的问答发生在 Mustill 勋爵的大律师事务所就不同。

益人(residue beneficiary)的丈夫。客户去世后,因为《Wills Act 1837》之 S. 15 的规定,遗嘱中对该受益人的馈赠失效。于是该受益人起诉律师疏忽,要求赔偿她原本在遗嘱下可获得的利益。律师承认疏忽,但是指称只对客户有小心谨慎的责任,而对受益人没有责任,所以受益人不能以侵权索赔。但这不被法院接受,根据 Donoghue v. Stevenson(1932)AC 562 与 Hedley Byrne 贵族院先例,律师不仅对自己的疏忽要对客户承担合约与侵权责任,也要对其他第三人承担侵权责任,只要满足在本书第一章之 2.1.1 段介绍的构成疏忽侵权的要件。

这判法也在 White v. Jones(1995)2 AC 207 先例中[5]被确认,之后在 Carr-Glynn v. Frearsons(A Firm)(1999)2 WLR 1046 先例中,这对遗嘱受益人的责任被进一步扩大。该先例的客户要订立遗嘱,死后将自己与外甥共同拥有的房产中自己的 50% 份额给外甥女。律师对客户解释了联权共有(Joint Tenancy)与分权共有(Tenancy in Common)的区别。前者是房产的共同所有人以联名的方式持有房产,共同拥有该资产的全部。如其中一名所有人离世,房产会由仍在世的其他所有人拥有。而后者是共同所有人按比例持有房产。举个简单的例子,如果夫妻以联权共有的形式共同拥有房产,如果丈夫去世,妻子自动拥有 100% 的房产。而如果是以分权共有的形式,各自拥有 50% 的房产(也可以是 30% 与 70% 等),丈夫去世后,丈夫 50% 的房产就是他的遗产,妻子原本 50% 的房产不受影响。所以如果此先例的客户希望将 50% 的房产份额留给外甥女,首先要确定自己与外甥共同拥有房产的方式。客户说要回去确认,但是在签署遗嘱时并没有确认,律师没有自己去确认也没有提醒客户如果是联权共有就要立刻作出分割业权通知书(Notice of severance),改为分权共有。客户去世后,因为是联权共有,房产自动变为外甥 100% 所有,这等于遗嘱这部分无效。外甥女于是起诉律师索赔损失。上诉庭推翻了一审判决,判根据此先例的案件,作出分割业权通知书是整个订立遗嘱过程中的一部分,律师疏忽导致无法达成客户希望遗嘱能起到的作用,根据 White v. Jones 的精神,律师应对应是受益人的原告承担疏忽侵权责任。

3. 订约自由大原则下的免责或限定赔偿责任条文的有效性

一般被委任的专业人士与客户都是有合约关系,并会有正规的文件如律师的委任书(engagement letter)。这种服务合约会在许多方面有明示规定,如专业人士的收费、约定被委任的责任范围等。但一般是不会,有关法律或专业守则也不允许去明示排除专业人士在提供意见或服务时过错与疏忽的责任,虽然可能会去限制责任。但

[5] 在本书第二章之 11.3.2 段有详细介绍。

在服务合约明示限制责任,也不完全是订约自由。除了需要与客户自愿外,也会有专业守则甚至是法律的规范。

以事务律师为例,根据《Solicitor Indemnity Insurance Rules》规定,英国强制购买责任保险,有限责任合伙的律师事务所不低于300万英镑,其余不低于200万英镑。Rule 3.2规定,律师事务所限制责任时,不能低于这个金额。但这只是最低的标准,知悉不少大型跨国律师事务所,往往是有更高金额的责任保险。这样,服务合约中的限制责任金额也相应提高,如3500万至4000万英镑或美元不等。

爱尔兰也有类似的规定,律师可以在与客户的合约中限制自己的责任,但不能低于法律规定的最低责任保险,也就是150万欧元。爱尔兰律师协会建议的限制责任条文可节录如下:"**Limitation of our liability** Our liability(and that of our present and former partners and employees) to you arising out of, or in connection with, our engagement(whether for breach of contract or of statutory duty, negligence, or otherwise) will be limited to [the higher of(a) the minimum amount of the professional indemnity insurance cover from time to time required to be maintained by us under applicable law; or(b) [具体金额]]. Nothing in this letter shall limit our liability to you(a) for fraud or fraudulent concealment[6] or(b) to the extent that under any applicable law liability may not be limited."

香港特别行政区的《律师(专业弥偿)规则》(第159M章)也规定事务律师/律师事务所强制购买责任保险,赔偿限额为2000万港币。根据香港特区律师协议的操作指引(practice direction)M,虽然律师不能排除对客户的责任,但可以限制对非诉业务法律责任(也就是说,对诉讼业务是无法限制责任的),责任限制不得低于专业弥偿计划要求的最低保障水平(目前是2000万港币)。

例如,一家著名律师事务所的服务合约中的限制责任条文说:

"14. 法律责任的限度……

14.2　双方能于一开始就本行的潜在法律责任上限达成协议是合理的,惟有关限制须属公平。阁下及本行现同意在此协议本行在本聘用下承担法律责任的程度,是双方共同判断确定为合理的。阁下及本行现同意,考虑到该等服务的范围及规模,与本行在提供该等服务时承受的风险与将收取的费用的对比,该责任上限是公平的。

14.3　在法律允许范围内,除此等聘用条款明文所列外,本行豁除所有保证、条件或条款,包括但不限于所有由事实或法律隐含的保证、条件或条款。

14.4　除非聘用函内另有规定,在法律允许范围内,就所有非争讼事务而言,本

---

〔6〕在本书第四章之6.6.2段介绍了广泛免责条文如可被解释为包括豁免欺诈性误述是不合理条文,有危险令整条条文不合理,因为违反公共政策。所以干脆明示写明不包括欺诈、欺诈性误述,落得大方。

行对阁下因本聘用所造成、导致或与之有关的损失或损害(包括间接和后果性的损失或损害)(包括不论是因违约、疏忽或任何其他侵权行为(不论是否在衡平法上)所致,亦不论本行有否获通知该损失或损害的可能性)的法律责任上限为(a)阁下向本行支付本聘用当中引起法律责任该部分之费用(为免生疑问,不含开支)的三倍,或(b)不时适用于及经《律师(专业弥偿)规则》要求的最低保障水平,以较高者为准。……"

会计师特别是审计师(auditor)的服务合约中限制责任的条文更是非常普遍,在英国《Company Act 2006》专门有一章针对审计师的责任,包括免除责任条文无效(S. 532),但是限制责任的条文只要满足有关要求就是有效的(SS. 534-538)。英国财务汇报局(Financial Reporting Council)对审计师限制赔偿金额给出了一条示范条文如下:

"Clause A: This Agreement limits the amount of any liability owed to the Company by the Auditor in respect of any negligence, default, [or] breach of duty [, or breach of trust,], occurring in the course of the audit of the accounts for the financial year [beginning/ending] [insert date] pursuant to [this Letter of Engagement or the Letter of Engagement entered into on [date]] of which the Auditor may be guilty in relation to the Company ("the Auditor's Liability").

Clause B: This Agreement shall not limit the amount of any liability of the Auditor for its fraud or dishonesty] or any other liability that cannot be excluded or restricted by applicable laws or regulations.

Clause C: The maximum aggregate amount of the Auditor's Liability to the Company shall not exceed (1) the sum of [具体数字] times the fees payable (excluding expenses and Value Added Tax) under the Engagement Letter referable to the financial year in question, or (2) £ [具体金额], whichever is the lesser amount. ...

Clause D: In accordance with section 537 of the Companies Act 2006, if the effect of Clause C of this Liability Limitation Agreement would be to limit the Auditor's Liability to less than such amount as is fair and reasonable, as determined in accordance with that section this Liability Limitation Agreement shall have effect as if it limited the Auditor's Liability to such amount as is fair and reasonable, as so determined.

Clause E: In Clauses [A, B, C and D] of this Agreement, the 'Auditor' means [insert the name of the audit firm] and includes any of its [members,] partners, employees, consultants [and agents] and any other person for whom [insert the name of the audit firm] is vicariously liable."

4. 合约与侵权的同步责任下去分摊损失

在 Hedley Byrne 贵族院先例中，Devlin 勋爵就批评说在同一因疏忽导致的事故在违约与侵权不同的诉因会有不同救济是可笑的(nonsense)与不符合逻辑与常理："lacking neither logic nor common sense to distinguish sharply between advice given by an NHS doctor and by a doctor whose private patient paid half a Guinea for his trouble."

所以法律是一直试图把违约与侵权的损失赔偿的计算去拉平(levelling)，但这是不容易的，毕竟合约在订约自由大原则下是可以有无穷无尽变化的条文去针对损失赔偿与救济。例如上一段介绍的限制责任条文，显然就无法适用在疏忽侵权的损失赔偿中。

只以机会损失(loss of chance)为例，在笔者《损失赔偿与救济》一书第六章之4.4 段介绍的 Allied Maples Group Ltd v. Simmons & Simmons(a firm)(1995)1 WLR 1602 先例中带来的以机会损失计算律师的专业疏忽所导致的损失，显然是减轻了律师(与他们背后的保险人)的赔偿责任。但在今天标的高昂的国际商业案件中，律师或责任保险人赔起来会是沉重负担。例如，在一个标的是 1 亿美元的诉讼中(这种案件在国际商业中也非常常见)，即使是有 25% 的胜诉机会，也要赔 2500 万美元。

在 Hutson v. East Berkshire(1987)AC 750 贵族院先例中有关机会损失是否除了合约关系也可适用在侵权的损失计算，上诉庭的 Donaldson 大法官说："unable to detect any rational basis for a distinction between NHS tort liability and contract claims in private medicine."但这最终在 Gregg v. Scott(2005)UKHL 2 贵族院先例中，[7] 拒绝把机会损失去适用在侵权的案件。

另是，律师疏忽提供意见与服务会存在合约与侵权的同步责任/竞合责任(concurrent liability)的问题，这在本书第一章之 2.4 段与笔者《损失赔偿与救济》一书第八章有详细介绍，不再重复。在 Vesta v. Butcher(1989)1 Lloyd's Rep 331 上诉庭先例中，合约条文带来的责任与侵权行为责任完全一致，两种责任也同时存在，如疏忽误述。Henderson v. Merrett Syndicates Ltd(1995)2 AC 145 贵族院先例也确认英国法律是承认同步责任，受害方可以选择对他最为有利的办法去提起诉讼。所以虽然

---

〔7〕 在笔者《损失赔偿与救济》一书第六章之 6 段对该先例有详细介绍，拒绝适用机会损失的其中一个重要的政策原因是如果打开泄洪闸容许机会损失的索赔，就会令英国的国家医疗服务(National Health Service)与保险公司面临大量的索赔从而在财政上无法负担。但会否不是公立医院，而是合约关系的私家医院/私人医生，机会损失仍是适用?

《Law Reform [Contributory Negligence] Act 1945》立法[8]只是针对侵权，在同步责任下该立法也应该适用。而如果合约责任与侵权责任有冲突，例如合约明示对疏忽免责或限制损失，则以合约规定为准。所以客户不可以以疏忽侵权或违反诚信责任(fiduciary duty)来绕过服务合约的明示责任限制，但其他没有合约关系的第三人反而不会受此限制责任条文的约束，不存在同步责任的问题。

5. 专业人士违约与侵权的复原或赔偿大原则

5.1 复原或赔偿大原则

专业人士在服务合约违约(违反了小心谨慎责任的默示条文)的损失计算，与其他商业合约违约的损失计算没有不同，就是"尽量用金钱来令受害方恢复到一个合约被履行的地位"(as far as money can do it, to be placed, in the same position as if the contract had been performed)。这也是复原或赔偿大原则的拉丁文"*restitutio in integrum*"或英文的"compensatory principle"，在笔者的《损失赔偿与救济》一书有详论，不重复。只节录在 Robinson v. Harman(1848)1 Ex. 850 先例中，Parke B 大法官说："The rule of the common law is, there where a party sustains a loss by reason of a breach of contract, he is, so far as money can do it, to be placed in the same situation, with respect to damages, as if the contract had been performed."

对疏忽侵权，在损失计算方面也是与违约一样，在损失赔偿的复原大原则下，也是为了让受害方的原告恢复到侵权没有发生的经济地位，正如在 Robinson v. Harman 先例中说："place plaintiffs in the position they would have occupied had they not been injured."

另在 Livingstone v. Rawyards Coal Co(1880)5 App Cas 25 先例中，Blackburn 勋爵说："I do not think there is any difference of opinion as to its being a general rule that, where any injury is to be compensated by damages, in settling the sum of money to be given for reparation of damages you should as nearly as possible get at that sum of money which will put the party who has been injured, or who has suffered, in the same position as he would have been in if he had not sustained the wrong for which he is now getting his compensation or reparation"

---

[8] 该立法之 section 1(1)规定："Where any person suffers damage as the result partly of his own fault and partly of the fault of any other person or persons, a claim in respect of that damage shall not be defeated by reason of the fault of the person suffering the damage, but the damages recoverable in respect thereof shall be reduced to such extent as the court thinks just and equitable having regard to the claimant's share in the responsibility for the damage..."

在 Nykredit Mortgage Bank Plc v. Edward Erdman Group Ltd(No. 2)(1997)1 WLR 1627 贵族院先例中,Nicholls 勋爵说如果涉及专业人士的专业意见,一般情况是客户在听取后才安心去完成有关交易或投资决定。所以侵权(服务合约违约也一样)下基本计算损失会是去让客户恢复到此错误与疏忽意见没有发生的经济地位,也就是不会进行这一严重亏本(否则客户也不会因为错误与疏忽意见而向有关的专业人士提起诉讼)的交易或投资:"... to identify the relevant measure of loss. It is axiomatic that in assessing loss caused by the defendant's negligence **the basic measure is the comparison between(a)what the plaintiff's position would have been if the defendant had fulfilled his duty of care and(b)the plaintiff's actual position.** Frequently, but not always, the plaintiff would not have entered into the relevant transaction had the defendant fulfilled his duty of care and advised the plaintiff, for instance, of the true value of the property. **When this is so, a professional negligence claim calls for a comparison between the plaintiff's position had he not entered into the transaction in question and his position under the transaction. That is the basic comparison.** Thus, typically in the case of a negligent valuation of an intended loan security, the basic comparison called for is between(a)the amount of money lent by the plaintiff, which he would still have had in the absence of the loan transaction, plus interest at a proper rate, and(b)the value of the rights acquired, namely the borrower's covenant and the true value of the overvalued property."(加黑部分是笔者的强调)

5.2 传统的损失计算

违约方或侵权人以金钱赔偿让被违约或被侵权的受害方复原是损失赔偿的大原则,该原则的适用会给违约方或侵权人带来沉重的经济负担。英国法律早已发展出一些限制损失计算的原则。这主要包括:损失遥远性(remoteness)中的因果关系与可预见性(foreseeability)、减损(mitigation)、自甘风险原则(Volenti non fit injuria)、侵权的责任范围(scope of duty)、原告的连带疏忽(contributory negligence)等的原则。这些限制与它们之间的交错关系在千变万化的不同案件下也是损失计算这个困难的课题(往往比认定责任方面困难得多)中最复杂与最有挑战性的部分。

传统分析的做法是一旦认定被告有过错或疏忽,并违反了对原告的小心谨慎责任,就要通过"要不是"测试看原告的损失是否与过错或疏忽串得起来(有关联性),也就是建立因果关系(causation)。如果能串起来,而且没有其他可以去中断因果关系的事件,加上损失的类别不是不可预见,被告的过错或疏忽就被视为造成损失的"有效原因/主因"(effective and predominant cause),并要被告赔偿所有的损失。

这可节录在 Yorkshire Dale Steamship Co Ltd v. Minister of War Transport(1942) AC 691 贵族院先例中,Simond 子爵说:"... one has to ask oneself what was the effective and predominant cause of the accident that happened, whatever the nature of that accident may be."

另在 Roe v. Minister of Health(1954)2 QB 66 先例中,Denning 大法官说:"Starting with the proposition that a negligent person should be liable, within reason, for the consequences of his conduct, the extent of his liability is to be found by asking the one question: Is the consequence fairly to be regarded as within the risk created by the negligence? If so, the negligent person is liable for it: but otherwise not."

即使再复杂的案情,这因果关系仍只是以普通人的常识去分析,正如 Wright 勋爵在 Yorkshire Dale Steamship Co Ltd v. Minister of War Transport 先例中说:"This choice of the real or effective cause from out of the whole complex of the facts must be made by applying common sense standards. Causation is to be understood as the man in the street, and not as either the scientist or the metaphysician, would understand it."

在任何重大的商业交易、借贷或投资中,买方、金融机构或投资方都会委任一大批不同专业人士为他们服务,包括提供意见与信息,如会计师、审计师、财务顾问、律师、估价师、测量师等。可以说,这些专业人士中只要是任何一位出错(特别是大错),都有可能对买方、金融机构或投资方(51%的可能性即满足举证责任)是否去完成交易有直接的影响。毕竟对客户而言,专业服务与意见如果对是否完成交易或决定是否提供贷款只是可有可无,没有太多关联性,这些客户怎会愿意花这么多钱去聘请昂贵的专业人士?

所以,在"要不是"测试下,把专业人士的违约或疏忽侵权与亏本甚至血本无归的结果串起来,一般并不困难。这样,在传统的损失计算下,也就是去分析"要不是因果关系"(but for causation),买方、金融机构或投资方有很大机会成功说服法院要不是估价高了、或尽职调查遗漏了重要信息、或律师对税务的法律意见有重大错误等,我是不会去完成此交易的。

虽然损失遥远性除了分析因果关系外,也要接下来分析损失的可预见性。损失可否合理预见在合约关系下是著名的 Hadley v. Baxendale(1854)9 Ex. 341 贵族院先例,[9] 只随意多介绍较近期 Supershield Ltd v. Siemens Building Technologies FE Ltd(2010) EWCA Civ 7 先例,Toulson 大法官说:"Hadley v. Baxendale(1854)9 Exch 341 remains a standard rule but it **has been rationalised on the basis that reflects the expectation to be imputed to the parties** in the ordinary case, i. e. that a contract breaker should ordinarily be liable to the other party for damage resulting from the breach if, but only if, **at the**

---

〔9〕 Hadley v. Baxendale(1854)9 Ex. 341 先例是英国关于损失计算最著名的、在诉讼中被引用最多的先例。它就损失类别的合理预见性问题确立了一套基本的理论,有关违约损失赔偿的判定以双方订约时能否合理预见作为标准把损失分为两类。一类是一般损失(ordinary damage,有时被称为 general damage 或 incidental damage),或违约/毁约会造成的自然与一般性后果,违约方要赔;另一类是特别损失(special damage,有时候被称为 consequential damage),或称非一般后果,除非订约当时或之前受害方已将会产生特别损失的后果告诉了违约方,否则违约方不用赔。该先例在笔者《损失赔偿与救济》一书第三章之2段有详细介绍。

time of making the contract a reasonable person in his shoes **would have had damage of that kind in mind as not unlikely to result from a breach.** "(加黑部分是笔者的强调)

而在侵权关系下考虑损失可预见性或侵权时"合理料想得到"(reasonable contemplation)是根据The"Wagon Mound"(1961)1 Lloyd's Rep 1枢密院先例确立的法律地位。这都在笔者的《损失赔偿与救济》一书第三章有详论,不重复,只节录Simonds子爵说:"It is a principle of civil liability ... that a man must be considered to be responsible for **the probable consequences of his act**. To demand more of him is too harsh a rule, to demand less is to ignore that civilised order requires the observance of a minimum standard of behaviour. "(加黑部分是笔者的强调)

虽然文字上稍有不同,现实上"可预见"或"料想得到"是同一码事,正如Bingham大法官在Banque Bruxelles Lambert SA v. Eagle Star Insurance Co Ltd & Ors (1995) QB 375上诉庭先例中说:"It is trite law that a plaintiff may not recover damages which are held to be too remote from the breach of duty of which he complains. Somewhat different language has been used to define the test in contract and tort, but **the essence of the test is the same in each case**. The test is whether, **at the date of the contract or tort, damage of the kind** for which the plaintiff claims compensation **was a reasonably foreseeable consequence** of the breach of contract or tortious conduct of which the plaintiff complains. If the kind of damage was reasonably foreseeable it is immaterial that the extent of the damage was not. "(加黑部分是笔者的强调)

但可否在订约时或疏忽侵权时合理预见是针对损失的类别,不追究在个别案件损失的程度严重或不严重。所以被视为商业风险(commercial risk)的市场损失(market loss),一贯被视为可以合理预见到的损失类别。在著名的The"Heron II"(1969)1 AC 350贵族院先例中,[10]法院判在一个租船合约下,市场下跌是可预见的损失类别。这种合约的本质与参与其中的商人在订约时都不会不知道或可预期到有关市场(租船市场、船舶市场、燃油市场、运载的商品市场等)的波动,即使波动很大。所以这种市场上涨或下跌所导致的损失都是可合理预见到的损失类别。只有在针对一份不同性质而且特殊的合约与/或不理解市场运作的合约当事人,才可能会得出不同结论。

即使市场波动很大甚至是崩溃而导致损失惨重,但市场损失仍是属于可预见的损失类别,仍然要包括在赔偿范围内。Hoffmann勋爵在The"Achilleas"(2009)1 AC 61贵族院先例中说:"It is generally accepted that a contracting party will be liable for damages for losses which are unforeseeably large, if loss of that type or kind fell within one or other of the rules in Hadley v. Baxendale ... That is generally an inclusive princi-

〔10〕 该先例在笔者《损失赔偿与救济》一书第三章之4段有详细介绍。

ple: if losses of that type are foreseeable, damages will include compensation for those losses, however large."(加黑部分是笔者的强调)

回到专业人士在为一个重大的商业交易或投资提供服务和意见时犯错的情况,如果要专业人士承担客户所有因交易产生的损失是显然不成比例,因为不是所有的损失都与他们的错误/疏忽有直接关系。就以市场波动带来的损失为例,这显然是与委任专业人士的客户的商业决定与愿意冒商业风险更有关系。更不说是亏本与血本无归经常是由许多其他分拆不出来的因素如卖方欺诈/欺骗如虚假陈述或误导,买方/投资方自己管理不善,自己的资产状况、融资情况、投资环境、有关法律有重大逆转等原因所共同导致。这正是本书第十章之9.1.4段提到的多重原因与同步原因的问题,也可见《损失赔偿与救济》一书第四章第12段。这些原因任何一个单独拿出来可以说都能够与投资失败之间满足要不是测试的因果关系。

这表示即使作为被告的专业人士在责任范围内犯错与疏忽只是造成最终的灾难性后果的部分原因,但无法以传统损失计算的方法去过滤(filtering)损失,也就是无法以损失的遥远性去排除其他分拆不出来的因素所带来的损失赔偿。所以要对专业人士公平,就需要对只有一笔但金额巨大的损失作出扣减。但扣减多少不能是没有合理与肯定的理据而让审理法官或仲裁员拍脑袋。

如果客户的交易或投资严重亏本或血本无归是因为房地产泡沫破裂、雷曼兄弟倒闭等经济或市场崩溃所导致,这是市场或投资的风险,但在传统的"要不是因果关系"与复原大原则不容易区分下仍会被转嫁给专业人士。正如在 Hughes - Holland v. BPE Solicitors(2017)UKSC 21 最高院先例中,Sumption 勋爵说:"if the adviser has **negligently assessed risk A**, the result is that the overall riskiness of the transaction has been understated. If the client would not have entered into the transaction on a careful assessment of its overall merits, the fact that **the loss may have resulted from risks B, C or D should not matter**."(加黑部分是笔者的强调)

历史上对律师疏忽所要赔偿的金额是十分严苛的,如果律师疏忽(如错过时效),要赔偿前客户原本可以向其他人索赔的全部金额(虽然今天也有了机会损失的计算办法),除非律师可以证明前客户的索赔诉因是没有机会成功,也就是他根本没有损失:见 Aitcheson v. Madock(1792)170 ER 135 先例或近期的 Mount v. Barker Austin(1998)PNLR 493 上诉庭先例。

5.3 非常特殊与极端情况才会是不可预见的损失:Camerata Property Inc v. Credit Suisse Securities(Europe)Ltd(No.2)(2012)EWHC 7(Comm)先例

这里可介绍 Camerata Property Inc v. Credit Suisse Securities(Europe)Ltd 先例,也是涉及雷曼兄弟的倒闭。案情是原告(一家在伯利兹注册的投资公司,背后是一位希腊船东富商)2007 年中在被告瑞士信贷银行的财富管理经理 S 先生的推荐下投资了由雷曼兄弟附属公司签发的票据(note),票据是和美元与欧元汇率挂钩。如果不是雷曼兄弟在 2008 年 9 月倒闭,这票据在 2009 年到期就会带来丰厚的利润,但可惜雷曼兄弟倒闭就令这笔投资打水漂。这导致原告向被告提出损失索赔，指称被告疏忽建议这笔中高风险的投资。因为被告明知原告接受的投资风险只是保守型，所以这种进取型的投资并不适合。另在 2008 年被告已经知道雷曼兄弟财政不稳时，应该建议原告抛售这些票据。

在针对部分票据的第一个诉讼 Camerata Property Inc v. Credit Suisse Securities (Europe) Ltd (No. 1) (2011) EWHC 479 (Comm) 中，法院判原告败诉，并认定被告没有疏忽。原告针对其他票据开始了第二个诉讼，并提出新主张指被告违反了《Financial Services and Markets Act 2000》之 S. 150，但这也被法院否定，因为立法只是保护本质上是消费者的"个人"(private person)。另外，原告的做法也涉及了滥用司法程序(abuse of process)。[11] 但笔者在这里要针对的是被告的代表大律师提出即使被告有疏忽，雷曼兄弟的倒闭也是不可预见的，说："… even if Camerata could establish its general wrong advice case and even if it could show that it would not have invested in the Note had it been given the right advice, the claim for damages would still fail because **the actual cause of the loss was issuer default as a consequence of the collapse of Lehman Brothers, which was wholly unexpected and unforeseeable**."(加黑部分是笔者的强调)

对被告大律师提出的说法，Flaux 大法官说本案由于在责任方面原告已经败诉，所以无需对他提出的损失作出决定，看来 Flaux 大法官是同意这个说法，说："It seems to me that, in principle, this argument is correct. Were it not for the **unforeseeable bankruptcy of Lehman Brothers**, Credit Suisse would have had a complete answer to Camerata's case that, but for the wrong advice, it would not have entered into the transaction. That answer would have been that the transaction had in fact been profitable, so that any negligence or breach of contract had not in fact caused any loss. **In other words, the only reason why Camerata has suffered any loss** at all, as opposed to making a substantial profit, **is because of the collapse of Lehman Brothers, which was unforeseeable.**" (加黑部分是笔者的强调)

5.4 专业人士的责任范围与只负责赔偿疏忽造成的损失在"要不是"测试下的问题

侵权与违约下被告的损失赔偿需要考虑被告承担的责任范围的说法早已有之。针对疏忽侵权，Simonds 子爵在 The "Wagon Mound" (1961) 1 Lloyd's Rep 1 枢密院先例中说："It is, no doubt proper when considering tortious liability for negligence to analyse its elements and to say that the **plaintiff must prove a duty owed to him** by the defendant, **a breach of that duty** by the defendant, **and consequent damage**."(加黑部分是笔者的强调)

---

[11] 在笔者《合约的履行、弃权与禁反言》一书第九章之 8 段有详细介绍。

针对合约的违约,在 Caparo v. Dickman(1990)2 WLR 358 贵族院先例中,Bridge 勋爵说得很直白:"It is never sufficient to ask simply whether A owes B a duty of care. It is always necessary to determine **the scope of the duty by reference to the kind of damage** from which A must take care to save B harmless."(加黑部分是笔者的强调)

另 Oliver 勋爵也说:"It has to be borne in mind that the duty of care is inseparable from the damage which the plaintiff claims to have suffered from its breach. It is **not a duty to take care in the abstract** but **a duty to avoid causing to the particular plaintiff damage of the particular kind** which he has in fact sustained."(加黑部分是笔者的强调)

不涉及专业人士的这种案例也不是没有。在 Greenway v. Johnson Matthey (2016)EWCA Civ 408 上诉庭先例中,案情涉及 Johnson Matthey 工厂生产催化转换器(catalytic converters),而生产过程是要使用铂金盐(platinum salts),这会导致工人铂金过敏(platinum allergy)。原告 Greenway 是受雇的工人,并在工作一段时间后的定期检查中发觉患上轻微的铂金过敏。这样,Greenway 就在生产岗位做不下去了,而被调职去另一个不接触铂金盐的部门工作。Greenway 的工资因此大幅降低。Greenway 向 Johnson Matthey 提出侵权与/或雇佣合约的索赔,指控雇主没有尽小心谨慎的责任,导致自己无法赚取更高的工资而蒙受经济损失。在责任方面 Johnson Matthey 也承认了没有尽到小心谨慎责任去为工人在立法、侵权与合约下提供一个安全工作的地点与环境,但 Greenway 在一审与上诉庭均在损失方面败诉。法院判雇主对雇员安全的小心谨慎责任只包括免于受实质伤害,不包括影响经济收益(纯经济损失),而铂金过敏的生理变化不属于实质伤害。

对专业人士在传统损失计算的不成比例与不公平,也是同样道理。他们各自在收取费用的服务合约下承担的合约责任或风险,不应包括导致整个商业交易或投资亏本甚至血本无归的损失。这往往是包括了许多其他因素或风险,并非有关专业人士同意承担的小心谨慎责任所覆盖的范畴。只是,这些风险是订立服务合约时可以合理预见会发生(如市场大跌)与因果关系没有中断,加上整个交易或投资的损失是无法像 Greenway v. Johnson Matthey 先例一样去拆分成两种不同的损失类别。

另可举 Hoffmann 勋爵在 SAAMCO 先例中的著名比喻,之后也在多个案例中被提到。如在 Hughes - Holland v. BPE Solicitors(2017)UKSC 21 最高院先例中,Sumption 勋爵说:"… one of the most celebrated legal parables of modern times, the story of the mountaineer's knee devised by Lord Hoffmann … Like all parables, this one … serves the purpose which its author intended, of introducing one of the main dilemmas of the law of damages."

Hoffmann 勋爵的比喻是一位认为自己膝盖有问题的病人(一位登山运动员)去造访医生,但医生疏忽并错误告知他的膝盖没有问题。这导致不久后该登山运动员安心去登山,结果遇上意外。问题是该医生是否要对该意外负责,毕竟如果医生正确告知病人膝盖有问题,病人是不会出发去参加这次登山。根据 SAAMCO 原则,医生的责任范围只在膝盖有没有问题,过错与疏忽只针对这方面。而该病人决定去登山往往会涉及多方面因素,被错误告知膝盖没有问题只是一个方面。至于在登山过程中遇上的意外,如果是因膝盖问题所导致,这是医生应该承担的后果,需要作出赔偿,因为这是他的责任范围,他犯的过错与疏忽与损失能直接串得起来。但如果是遇上其他意外,如雪崩、天气问题、设备问题、突发疾病来不及救治等,这都与医生没有直接关系。他的责任范围只针对该病人的膝盖,不包括他在登山中遇到的雪崩、坏天气、设备故障或甚至是他个人运气不佳。

这个"登山运动员膝盖"(mountaineer's knee)的例子是至少可以用传统的损失计算与损失遥远性去化解对医生的不公平。例如,医生并没有被告知病人要登山或建议病人可以放心去登山,所以登山遇上的意外并非医生可合理预见。另是,意外是雪崩、坏天气或是病人自己疏忽如设备不足,也可以是外来介入原因(intervening act)打断了医生疏忽诊断意见与最终意外造成的损失之间的因果链。

但这往往是不适用于不少商业交易或投资的专业人士。首先专业人士会预见到如果他们正确提供服务与意见,客户是不会完成交易的。其次,专业人士提供的疏忽服务与意见,在时间上会与客户拍板确定订约十分接近,没有让其他外来介入原因去打断因果链的机会或可能。

5.5 专业人士在"不会有交易"类别的案件中要赔偿所有可预见的交易损失

恰到好处与成比例计算专业人士疏忽所造成的损失的困难可以在 Banque Bruxelles Lambert SA v. Eagle Star Insurance Co Ltd & Ors(1995)QB 375 上诉庭先例中看到。在一审(unreported,21 December 1993),Phillips 大法官认为原告是自承房屋市场下跌的风险,后来的市场下跌损失与第五被告估价师疏忽高估了房屋价格无关,说:"… BBL(原告)will not recover as damages that part of their loss which is attributable to the collapse of the property market. It does not seem to me that such loss can fairly and reasonably be considered as resulting naturally from John D Wood's(第五被告)failure to report as they should have done. Where a party is contemplating a commercial venture that involves a number of heads of risk and obtains professional advice in respect of one head of risk before embarking on the adventure, I do not see why negligent advice in respect of that head of risk should, in effect, make the adviser the underwriter of the entire adventure."

但一审的判决在上诉庭被否定,上诉庭判第五被告要赔偿原告所有的损失。这涉及专业意见是"不影响交易"(successful transaction)或是"不会有交易"(no transaction)类别的案件。前者的类别是指专业意见的对错不会影响交易的达成,而后者是指专业意见的对错会直接影响交易是否能够达成。

专业人士疏忽的案例有不少,不少都是属于"不影响交易"的类别,损失计算只针对特定的疏忽所带来的损失:见 Philips v. Ward(1956)1 WLR 471;Pilkington v. Wood(1953)Ch 770;Food v. White & Co(1964)1 WLR 885;Singer & Friedlander Ltd v. John D

Wood & Co(1977)234 EG 212;Corisand Investments Ltd v. Druce & Co(1978)EGD 769;Perry v. Sidney Phillips & Son(1982)1 WLR 1297;Watt v. Morrow(1991)1 WLR 1421 等先例。如 Watts v. Morrow 上诉庭先例中测量师的报告中漏了针对有关房屋的一些缺陷如烟囱、窗台、地板等。上诉庭判损失赔偿不是实质的修理费用(actual cost of repair),而是该房屋因为有这些缺陷的贬值(diminution of value)。[12]

但一旦去针对“不会有交易”的案件,仍是用同样的方式计算损失就说不通了。这早在 Baxter v. FW Gapp & Co Ltd(1939)2 All ER 752 上诉庭先例中,原告说如果被告估价师没有犯错,他是不会买入该房屋。虽然在上诉庭被告有争辩说损失应局限在修理费用,但被法院拒绝,原告成功取回所有损失。

跳到更近期的 Hayes v. James & Charles Dodd(1990)2 All ER 815 上诉庭先例中,涉及事务律师在房屋买卖交易中的疏忽,法院就认定是“不会有交易”案件。Staughton 大法官说:“I am quite satisfied that Hirst J(一审法官)was entitled to award damages in this case on the no – transaction basis, and that he was right to do so ... So they should recover all the money which they spent, less anything which they subsequently recovered, provided always that they acted reasonably in mitigating their loss.”

接下来的 Swingcastle Ltd v. Alastair Gibson(1991)2 AC 223 贵族院先例,看来接受“不会有交易”或“不影响交易”是两种不同类别的案件,但说 Baxter v. FW Gapp & Co Ltd 上诉庭先例是一个“不太受欢迎的约束性先例”(not an attractive precedent)。

这带来在 SAAMCO 贵族院先例在上诉庭判决阶段,Bingham 大法官的判决是以“不会有交易”或“不影响交易”去计算损失,认为 Baxter v. FW Gapp & Co Ltd 与 Swingcastle Ltd v. Alastair Gibson 先例对他有约束力,说:“It does not appear to us that the authority of Baxter v. FW Gapp & Co. Ltd. [1939] 2 All ER 752 is in any way impaired by subsequent authority ... The decision has been held to be binding on the Court of Appeal, and we must apply the principle it laid down. ... If the valuer overvalued the land it was **foreseeable that the lender would lend on inadequate security**, perhaps in circumstances **where(properly advised)he would not lend at all**. It was foreseeable that the borrower might default, and if he did the lender's recovery would depend on **what the land might fetch at the time of realisation**. This would, **foreseeably, depend on how the market moved**. We agree, of course, that the valuer in no sense guaranteed or underwrote the lender's business investment. Had the valuer valued the land competently, he would have been under no liability to the lender no matter how disastrous the investment proved. But once it is established that the valuer's negligence led the lender to make a loan he would not otherwise have made it seems to us that the lender is entitled to be compensa-

〔12〕 有关修理费用或有缺陷财产在市场价格的贬值的课题,在笔者的《损失赔偿与救济》一书第二章之 13 段有针对,包括著名的 Ruxley Electronics and Construction Ltd v. Forsyth(1995)All ER 1936 先例。

ted for all the damage he has suffered. If the market moves upwards, the valuer reaps the benefit; if it moves downwards, he stands the loss. ..."(加黑部分是笔者的强调)

这样表示高估了价格的估价师要承担客户整个交易的损失,因为所有的损失,包括市场下跌的损失都是违约或侵权时可预见的。但最后上诉去了贵族院,上诉庭的判决又被否定,贵族院也否定了用"不会有交易"或"不影响交易"这两种不同类别的案件去计算损失。

6."责任范围原则"的创新说法

South Australia Asset Management Corp v. York Montague Ltd (1997) AC 191 ("SAAMCO")贵族院先例确立了专业人士提供意见与服务的责任范围(scope of duty)[13]的创新说法。专业人士如果因疏忽提供了不正确的专业意见与服务,损失的计算只是局限在他的责任范围。这看来是对专业人士更公平合理的做法。此贵族院先例创造的 SAAMCO 原则实是对传统损失计算的办法,也就是只看专业人士的过错或疏忽(不论错多错少)与最后客户蒙受损失之间的因果关系(causation),只要符合"要不是"的测试就均要赔偿的原则的一种调整,调整的办法就是在稍后 6.3 段会介绍的 SAAMCO 原则与 SAAMCO 反事实分析(SAAMCO Counterfactual)了。

在 Hughes - Holland v. BPE Solicitors (2017) UKSC 21 最高院先例中, Sumption 勋爵对 SAAMCO 原则去进一步解释与澄清:"**the principle has nothing to do with the causation of loss as that expression is usually understood in the law**. Lord Hoffmann made this point ... 'It is important to emphasise that this is a consequence of the limited way in which the House defined the valuer's duty of care and has nothing to do with questions of causation or any limit or 'cap' imposed upon damages which would otherwise be recoverable. It was accepted that the whole loss suffered by reason of the fall in the property market was, as a matter of causation, properly attributable to the lender having entered into the transaction and that, but for the negligent valuation, he would not have done so. It was not suggested that the possibility of a fall in the market was unforeseeable or that there was any other factor which negatived the causal connection between lending and losing the money ... Nor, if one started from the proposition that the valuer was responsible for the consequences of the loan being made, could there be any logical

---

[13] 这里的责任范围与传统疏忽侵权的责任范围有很大区别。疏忽侵权的责任范围是指双方之间有足够的密切关系,否则就无法满足"邻近原则";损失类别必须可预见与满足因果关系:Caparo v. Dickman (1990) 2 WLR 358 贵族院先例;不能索赔纯经济损失等。这里的责任范围是指专业人士提供意见或服务时就其意见和服务对客户所承担的责任范围。

basis for limiting the recoverable damages to the amount of the overvaluation. The essence of the decision was that this is not where one starts and that the valuer is responsible only for the consequences of the lender having too little security.'"(加黑部分是笔者的强调)

以上节录的英文是说这个SAAMCO原则并不是偏离损失计算的基本原则包括可预见性与有因果关系等,也不是对应该赔偿的损失强加一个封顶或限制。而是分析问题的起点应该是估价师要负责的范围只在因为它错误的估值令贷款人取得的担保价值太少而不够抵偿借款这个后果上。这是把考虑损失的时间点放到服务合约订立时,客观看他们收取的费用与承担的责任范围。

另在SAAMCO先例中,Hoffmann勋爵把专业人士在一开始愿意承担责任范围区分为愿意提供的是第一类(Category 1)"信息"(information)或第二类(Category 2)"意见"(advice)。这不同的分类会分别带来的赔偿损失责任有天渊之别。这方面会在稍后详细介绍。

6.1 South Australia Asset Management Corp v. York Montague Ltd(1997)AC 191("SAAMCO")先例

可先介绍大量这类案件的背景,美国在20世纪80年代末房地产泡沫破裂,并引发了储蓄和贷款危机,英国(也包括世界其他国家)也在这段时间(1989~1993年)出现严重经济衰退与房地产市场崩溃。在此情况下,大量购买房屋自住或投资的借款人无法还债,贷款的银行或金融机构被迫要把抵押的房屋收回拍卖,显然拍卖能取回的金钱就不足清还所欠的债务而蒙受损失了。

为了转嫁这笔损失,贷款人就会动脑筋向提供专业服务与意见的专业人士转嫁损失,如高估了房屋价格的估价师或提供错误法律意见的事务律师。往往是一审法院认定估价师确实疏忽高估的事实,违约(小心谨慎责任)与/或侵权已是定局,但更大的问题是被告应赔的金额。这是因为原告的损失是来自多个因素,疏忽高估了房屋价值只是其中一个。其他因素包括重要的房地产市场崩溃、借款人违反贷款合约拒绝还债等。这样,是否被告仍要赔偿所有损失?

SAAMCO先例实是涉及三个一并上诉到贵族院的同类型案例,作为原告的不同银行或金融机构向房屋买方作出融资并以有关的房屋作为抵押。[14] 为了决定融资多少钱,他们都会先对有关的房屋估值,也就是在当时市场上该房屋值多少钱。被告是原告委任的估价师,原告指控被告疏忽高估了房屋市场价格,这也被一审法院认定为事实,而且被认定如果没有发生高估的情况,原告是不会作出这笔贷款的。

显然,如果市场稳定与/或买方经济稳定没有违反贷款合约准时分期还债,被告即使高估了房屋价格也无所谓,也不会造成原告任何金钱上的损失。因为充其量只是令原告对他们的贷款,实际上在担保价值上是偏低了,但这并不代表借款人在贷款

〔14〕 见笔者《船舶融资与抵押》一书第三章之7段。

合约下会赖账与违约。正如 Nicholls 勋爵在 Nykredit Mortgage Bank Plc v. Edward Erdman Group Ltd(No. 2)(1997)1 WLR 1627 先例中说:"More difficult is the case where, as a result of negligent advice, property is acquired as security. In one sense the lender undoubtedly suffers detriment when the loan transaction is completed. He parts with his money, which he would not have done had he been properly advised. In another sense he may suffer no loss at that stage because often there will be no certainty he will actually lose any of his money: the borrower may not default. Financial loss is possible, but not certain. Indeed, it may not even be likely. Further, in some cases, and depending on the facts, even if the borrower does default the overvalued security may still be sufficient."

在 SAAMCO 先例涉及的三宗不同案件,其中两宗被上诉庭根据传统分析一致判被告需要赔偿原告所有的损失。而第三宗案件的一审法院也跟从作出同样判决。

在损失赔偿的复原大原则下,不论是侵权还是违约都是让受害的原告恢复到侵权没有发生或合约被履行的地位。由于一审法院认定房屋的价值若没有被疏忽高估,原告是不会提供这笔贷款,所以要恢复至没有作出贷款的地位也即代表要被告承担所有可预见的损失的赔偿。

另是,被告并没有以损失遥远性作为抗辩减少赔偿金额,但笔者也相信即使是去提出也难以成功。因为市场的涨跌(即使是暴涨暴跌)与暴跌后借款人会无法还债也是本质上可以预见会发生的事情。

再另是,其他造成原告损失的因素扯不上原告的过错与疏忽,否则或可借助《Law Reform(Contributory Negligence) Act 1945》立法减少赔偿。SAAMCO 先例涉及的三个案件,都是在美国储蓄和贷款危机以致房地产市场崩溃的背景下,原告蒙受巨大损失。这虽然是"人祸",但谈不上是原告的过错与疏忽。除非原告在贷款决策中曾经做出了什么疏忽或鲁莽的决定,否则是谈不上共同疏忽可请求法院分摊责任,如原告被告各承担一半损失。

但最后上诉去了贵族院,有了重大的改变,普遍说法是贵族院对这方面有了政策上的改变或创新。在 SAAMCO 先例中,Hoffmann 勋爵在所有其他大法官同意下作出唯一的判词。他批评上诉庭的判法,认为分析的起点(starting point)应是先看被告估价师的责任范围(scope of duty),以确定他应负责的损失类别(kind of loss),之后才考虑损失计算(measure of damages)。他说:"A duty of care such as the valuer owes does not ... exist in the abstract. A plaintiff who sues for breach of a duty imposed by the law (whether in contract or tort or under statute) must do more than prove that the defendant has failed to comply. He must show that the duty was owed to him and that it was a duty in respect of the kind of loss which he has suffered."

至于什么是责任范围与损失类别,Hoffmann 勋爵说:"Rules which make the wrongdoer liable for all the consequences of his wrongful conduct are exceptional and need to be justified by some special policy. Normally the law limits liability to those consequences which are attributable to that which made the act wrongful. . **In the case of liability in negligence for providing inaccurate information, this would mean liability for the consequences of the information being inaccurate.**"（加黑部分是笔者的强调）

接下来 Hoffmann 勋爵带出专业人士提供的服务可归为两类：一类是信息，另一类是意见。它们之间的分别是在："The principle thus stated distinguishes between **a duty to provide information** for the purpose of enabling someone else to decide upon a course of action **and a duty to advise someone as to what course of action he should take**. If the duty is to advise whether or not a course of action should be taken, the adviser must take reasonable care to consider all the potential consequences of that course of action. If he is negligent, he will therefore be responsible for all the foreseeable loss which is a consequence of that course of action having been taken. If his duty is only to supply information, he must take reasonable care to ensure that the information is correct and, if he is negligent, will be responsible for all the foreseeable consequences of the information being wrong."（加黑部分是笔者的强调）

可以说 Hoffmann 勋爵把专业服务区分为两类不同的责任范围，即提供"信息"或"意见"。前者只是提供信息让客户或其他人士（如客户委任的其他专业人士）做出进一步的行动，如是否完成一个交易。而后者是更全面提供意见给客户去完成一个交易。提供这两类服务的专业人士或任何有合理小心谨慎责任的人士都必须尽到责任，否则就会构成疏忽并带来服务合约下赔偿损失的次要责任（secondary obligation）。[15] 在 SAAMCO 先例与后续大量的先例中，提供疏忽信息要负责的损失类别只是局限在假设提供的错误信息是正确的可合理预见的损失（如果有），而其他类别的关联损失即使可预见也不必负责。

但提供疏忽意见就很不一样了，疏忽意见的责任范围会令损失类别扩大至整个交易所有可预见的损失，因为要把受害方客户恢复到疏忽没有发生的地位，也就是有关的亏损交易没有发生过。

或者举一个简单例子会更能说清楚两种不同责任范围的服务会带来全然不同的结果。例如，一位估价师对一处房屋（也可以是一家公司）的估值被认定为疏忽高估（也可以是低估）。属于提供信息，只需要赔偿高估的部分。但如果该专业人士是客户的置业顾问，在考虑了所有因素，包括估价师的报告、将来的法律风险（如是否存在产权争议）、转售的可能性、房地产市场的动向、政府规划等，建议客户购买该房屋，那就属于提供了意见，需要赔偿客户所有损失包括市场下跌的损失。

---

〔15〕 关于首要合约责任（primary obligation）与次要合约责任可见笔者《损失赔偿与救济》一书第十一章之1.1段。

6.2 SAAMCO先例的三个案件的结果

回到SAAMCO先例的三个同类的案件，可简单介绍有关的事实与最高院的判决。首先是South Australia Asset Management Corporation v. York Montague Ltd案件，原告在1990年8月3日根据房屋高达1500万英镑的估值提供了1100万英镑的贷款。一审的May大法官认定该房屋在当时实际上只值500万英镑，显然被严重高估了1000万英镑。在房地产市场崩溃后，原告行使抵押权把房屋收回出售，只卖了247.7万英镑。可以说，如果没有被高估了1000万英镑，原告是不会有损失的。贵族院支持原告可以索赔所有损失，并被核算为9,753,927.99英镑（这是低于高估的1000万英镑），但由于原告的共同疏忽进一步又扣减了25%。

在第二宗United Bank of Kuwait Plc v. Prudential Property Services Ltd案件中，原告根据房屋250万英镑的估值在1990年10月19日提供175万英镑贷款。一审大法官认定正确的估值只是在180万至185万英镑之间。原告把房屋收回后出售，只取得95万英镑。一审法院与上诉庭核算并认定原告在此交易的全部损失是1,309,876.46英镑（这包括借款人违约没有支付利息等损失），并全数要被告赔偿，但这不被贵族院支持。

Hoffmann勋爵说被疏忽高估的房屋只是令原告丧失了自以为拥有的大概65万至70万英镑的担保，所以充其量原告的损失只能局限在高估的价格与正确的价格的差价。原告指出高估的后果不仅是减少了担保，也令借款人违约的风险（risk of default）增加。但Hoffmann勋爵指出被告估价师并没有提供有关违约风险方面的“意见”，他只提供对有关房屋估值的“信息”。毕竟，被告也没有足够的证据去了解与提供这方面的意见，例如借款人是否个人财力雄厚与声誉良好，抵押房屋的担保只是例行公事、可有可无。而这些事实或资料，只有原告自己拥有，去决定是否完成交易。

最后第三宗Nykredit Mortgage Bank Plc v. Edward Erdman Group Ltd案件，案情比较复杂。原告是根据房屋350万英镑的估值在1990年3月12日提供了245万英镑的贷款。但正确的价值被一审法院认定为200万至顶多为237.5万英镑（这在后来被双方当事人同意为210万英镑）。换言之，有关房屋被高估了140万英镑。但在房地产市场崩溃后，原告在1993年初把抵押房屋收回后公开拍卖只取回34.5万英镑，可以说原告损失惨重，总损失被一审法院核算与认定为3,058,555.52英镑（也包括如借款人欠下的利息等损失），被告需要负责。但贵族院不支持这判法，认为被告估价师封顶的赔偿是被高估的140万英镑。

Nicholls勋爵在之后的Nykredit Mortgage Bank Plc v. Edward Erdman Group Ltd (No. 2) (1997) 1 WLR 1627先例中说：“Typically, the answer to this further inquiry will correspond with **the amount of the loss as shown by the basic comparison**, for the lender would not have entered into the transaction had he been properly advised, **but limited to the extent of the overvaluation**. This was the measure applied in the present case. Nykredit suffered a loss, including unpaid interest, of over £ 3m. Of this loss the amount attributable to Erdman's incorrect valuation was **£ 1. 4m. , being the extent of the over – valuation**. "（加黑部分是笔者的强调）

6.3 SAAMCO 原则与 SAAMCO 反事实分析

可以说在上小段介绍的先例中，已经显示了 SAAMCO 原则的精神。可以说传统的损失计算是违反小心谨慎责任后，分析造成的损失能否与被告的错误与疏忽串得起来，这容易导致专业人士狭窄与轻微地违反小心谨慎责任，也会因与后来金额巨大且虽然是由很多原因造成但是无法区分的损失可以联系上因果关系与可合理预见，而需要赔偿所有损失。

但 SAAMCO 原则变了是分析违反小心谨慎责任的起源而不是违反的后果，也就是有关专业人士在服务合约愿意承担的责任范围（scope of duty）。这责任范围可宽可窄，最肯定的是在服务合约中明确约定。但没有明示，就可以该专业人士一般被理解的会提供的服务与意见的责任范围为准，例如估价师就是为房屋估价，税务律师就为税务的法律问题提供意见等。也可能是 Caparo v. Dickman（1990）2 WLR 358 贵族院先例中立法确定的公司审计师的责任范围。正如 Leggatt 勋爵在 Manchester Building Society v. Grant Thornton UK LLP（2021）UKSC 20 先例中说："Ascertaining the scope of the defendant's duty in such cases depends on identifying the matters relevant to a decision to be taken by the claimant which the defendant has undertaken responsibility for assessing and advising the claimant about. The **extent of those matters may be defined by express agreement** or, in the absence of such an agreement, is **implied from the role of a doctor or other professional person as that role is conventionally understood**（or in the case of an auditor prescribed by statute）**and by the objective purpose of the advice**（which … is not necessarily coextensive with the purposes for which the claimant intends to rely on the advice）. "（加黑部分是笔者的强调）

有情况是在计算损失时很容易看出某些损失是不属于专业人士提供意见与服务的责任范围，但也有不少情况是并不容易根据责任范围对损失进行划分，这时就需要"SAAMCO 反事实分析"作为再次确认（double – check）的办法。又或是，以此去过滤传统违约或侵权中因果关系与可预见损失计算出来的金额，以保证专业人士只赔偿他们责任范围内的损失（可称为法律过滤器"legal filter"）。另也有将错误意见与正确意见量化为金钱（如果可以做得到）后的差别作为最后要负责赔偿的金额封顶（可称为"SAAMCO Cap"）。正如在 Manchester Building Society v. Grant Thornton UK LLP 最高院先例中，Hodge 与 Sales 勋爵说："… the question posed by the scope of duty principle as illustrated by SAAMCO is **not one of causation in the conventional sense of identifying the consequences which flow from a breach of duty, but 'rather whether the loss flowed from the right thing**, ie from the particular feature of the defendant's conduct which made it wrongful. That turns on an analysis of what did make it wrongful'. "（加黑部分是笔者的强调）

以上所讲可举简单的例子来说明，就是估价师对一栋房屋作出了高的估值报告，就以涉及的疏忽也就是估值报告中高估的差价在损失赔偿中封顶。如只值 100 万元的房屋被高估为 150 万元，50 万元就是损失赔偿的封顶。如果客户在整个交易中的损失只是 25 万元（这较低的损失可以是各种原因造成的，如房产市场没有大跌、借款人已经还了大部分债务才违约、银行把房屋收回后拍卖了一个好价钱等），估价师也就赔这笔钱。但如果以传统计算方法得出客户损失最终是 100 万元（因为房价市场大跌与其他各种原因），只去适用 SAAMCO Cap 就代表估价师只需要赔 50 万元，其余的损失是其他并非估价师所愿意承担与在责任范围外的因素所导致。

在 Khan v. Meadows（2021）UKSC 21 最高院先例中，Hodge 勋爵与 Sales 勋爵代表多数意见说反事实分析要问的问题是"假设被告实际上提供的信息（错误的）是正确的，原告会承担怎样的损失"。这不是问如果被告提供的错误信息是正确的，原告会不会有不同的做法，而是看原告在既有行为下会不会蒙受同样的损失。有关判决可节录如下：

"The mechanism by which the duty nexus question is addressed in the value Rs' negligence cases is **to ask a counterfactual question：what would the claimant's loss have been if the information which the defendant in fact gave had been correct**? We refer to that question as 'the SAAMCO counterfactual'. It is sometimes misunderstood. **The question is not whether the claimant would have behaved differently if the advice provided by the defendant had been correct**. Rather, the counterfactual assumes that the claimant would behave as he did in fact behave and asks whether, if the advice had been correct, the claimant would have resulted in the same loss. By this means, the court can ascertain the loss which is attributable to that information being wrong.

Where the counterfactual is applied in negligent overvaluation, the tool used to give effect to the answer to the counterfactual question has been**to limit the damages awarded to the difference between the valuation and the true value of the property at the time of the negligent valuation**. As Lord Sumption has explained in Hughes - Holland, ..., this tool has been criticised for its imprecision but, as he observed, mathematical precision is not always attainable in the law of damages. ... that **the SAAMCO counterfactual and cap are a robust way of applying the scope of duty principle**."（加黑部分是笔者的强调）

另 Burrows 勋爵也说，反事实分析是问如果被告提供的错误信息是正确的，原告是否也会有同样的损失？如果答案是"会"，这个损失就不在原告的责任范围之内。如果答案是"不会"，这个损失就在原告的责任范围之内。Burrows 勋爵的判词可节录如下："A counterfactual test can assist as a flexible cross - check in deciding on the scope of duty of care. **Applying the counterfactual test, one asks, would the claimant have suffered the same loss if the information/advice had been true**? If the answer is 'yes', the scope of the duty does not extend to the recovery of that loss. If the answer is 'no', the scope of the duty does extend to the recovery of that loss. ... what may be said is that **the more limited the advice or information being provided**-in the sense that the more the claimant has to decide on – **the more appropriate the counterfactual test is likely to be**."(加黑部分是笔者的强调)

以上所讲可以所谓的"不会有交易"(no transaction)的案件为例,即证据显示如果没有这错误的专业人士服务与意见(如会计师疏忽的尽职调查或律师的错误税务法律意见),原告不会收购该公司。如果按照传统的分析,在疏忽责任被认定后,即转向损失计算。由于这疏忽对整个交易至关重要,应是很容易满足因果关系的"要不是"测试。只要因果关系串得起来,在平衡的可能性(balance of probability)下专业人士的疏忽(即使疏忽程度不高,如估值只高估了10%)是会被宽松认定是达成交易的有效原因(effective cause),被告专业人士就难逃要负责所有交易的损失。这就会导致疏忽尽职调查的会计师(或税务律师等)要承担整个交易带来的损失。但很明显交易失败的损失虽然是一笔过的损失,往往主要是因为其他原因,如金融海啸带来的市场暴跌。

这是因为一般普通人的逻辑与常识就是如果没有这个错误或疏忽就不会有这个交易(至于如果没有这个过错与疏忽,双方会不会通过及时的谈判达成另一个不同对价的交易与是怎样的对价就不必去猜测了),而市场波动(不论是什么原因造成)又属于可预见的损失类别,即使损失出乎意料得巨大,也不影响疏忽的有关专业人士作为被告的赔偿责任,因为法律上只要满足损失遥远性中的因果关系与可预见性的要求,计算损失时在金额上是没有封顶或上限。这表示疏忽的会计师或律师,会要面对最后失败交易的所有损失,这可以是上千万元甚至上亿元。

但在SAAMCO原则与反事实分析下,假设专业人士的错误意见是正确的,原告就仍会达成这个交易,仍会蒙受因金融海啸导致市场衰退带来的巨额损失。这样就可以说这些损失不在专业人士的责任范围之内,或者这些损失与专业人士的责任范围没有关系。而在责任范围内,损失的计算仍是传统的损失计算,这也是为什么说SAAMCO原则只是改变了计算损失的起点,而不是改变了传统损失计算的大原则或在以传统方式计算损失后强加一个封顶。这个SAAMCO反事实分析原则或测试的确是有点绕,不容易活学活用。希望读者在阅读接下来介绍的各种千变万化案情的先例中,更是可以从方方面面不同的角度掌握怎样适用SAAMCO原则。另是,这SAAMCO反事实分析也受到批评,认为是在有些案情下不适用,甚至是误导,如有关的交易或投资本来就是亏本难逃,失败是必然。

所以在本章之9.3段介绍的Charles B Lawrence & Associates v. Intercommercial Bank Ltd(2021)UKPC 30枢密院先例中批评了反事实分析,认为用反事实分析得出的结论与枢密院的判决不符。虽然可以通过调整反事实分析的问题来得到"正确"的答案,但反事实分析只是对照核查的工具,重要的还是看责任的目的与责任范围。

6.4 SAAMCO 先例否定了“不影响交易”或“不会有交易”类别的案件

在本章之5.5段介绍的有关“不会有交易”(no transaction)类别案件去考虑与分析专业人士如果没有违反小心谨慎责任,客户是不会有交易,所以要承担所有在因果关系串得起来的交易损失的法律地位,在 SAAMCO 先例被否定。Hoffmann 勋爵说:“The distinction between the 'no-transaction' and 'successful trans - action' cases is of course quite irrelevant to the scope of the duty of care. ...The distinction is not based on any principle and should in my view be abandoned.”

但当案情足够明确时,即使被告专业人士自愿承担的责任范围只是提供部分专业服务与意见,也只收取一般的费用而并没有愿意承担更大的后果或责任,但在有关专业人士从本质与程度上看是犯了严重的疏忽,确实影响了客户决定是否进行交易的情况下,法院仍会以传统的“不会有交易”去计算损失。即使在 SAAMCO 先例后,仍是有这种案例。

在 Bristol and West Building Society v. Fancy & Jackson(a firm)(1997)4 All ER 582(Ch)先例中,Chadwick 大法官就是这样的判法。有关案情是原告金融机构在房地产市场崩溃后提起了87个诉讼,分别控告律师提供错误与疏忽意见或信息,并要求赔偿所有贷款变成坏账的损失,其中挑了8个代表性案件在此先例审理。审理当时前的几个月贵族院已经作出了 SAAMCO 先例的判决。Chadwick 大法官判其中三个案件是原告如果知道了正确意见或信息是不会考虑贷款的“不会有交易”案件,并不适用 SAAMCO 原则。至于为什么判如果没有错误与疏忽意见或信息是不会有交易,就要看各种证据。例如,原告公司有政策是只对价值500万元以上的房产提供贷款,而有关的房产被高估为550万元但实际价值其实只有400万元。

在接下来的 Portman Building Society v. Bevan Ashford(a firm)(2000)PNLR 344 上诉庭先例中,专业人士涉及的案件也被认定为“不会有交易”案件,Otton 大法官说:“where a negligent solicitor fails to provide information which shows that the transaction is not viable or which tends to reveal an actual or potential fraud on the part of the borrowers, the lender is entitled to recover the whole of his loss. In other words, the whole is his loss suffered by the lender is within the scope of the solicitor's duty and is properly recoverable.

... I am also satisfied that far from being an incorrect application of the SAAMCO principle, the decision of Chadwick J. is a proper application of the principle. If the whole of the loss suffered by the lender is within the scope of the relevant duty, he should be entitled to recover the whole of the loss.

On this analysis, I do not consider it necessary to consider whether BA(被告的律师) gave advice rather than information.”

另 Schiemann 大法官说:“These solicitors were under an obligation to draw to the attention of the lender a matter which cast doubt upon the reliability of the borrowers. The reason why this duty is imposed upon them is to protect the lender against greater exposure to risk of damage occasioned by the failure of the borrowers to honour their covenants to repay than it would willingly have assumed, in any event at the rate at which it lent. Any lender is exposed to a risk that the borrower will default. Its willingness to expose itself to that risk in return for a particular consideration depends on its assessment of the chance of the borrower defaulting. In part, that assessment depends on the borrower's financial situation and honesty. In the present case the financial situation and honesty of the borrowers were misrepresented to the lender due to the negligence of the solicitors. The lender clearly would not have lent had the borrowers' true situation been made clear to it. It is right that in those circumstances the solicitors should pay for the damage resulting from the fact that the lender made a loan which otherwise it would not have made."

但上述两个仍然认定"不会有交易"的案件被认为是对 SAAMCO 先例很好的总结与澄清的 Hughes – Holland v. BPE Solicitors(2017) UKSC 21 最高院先例所否定,最高院认为上述的判法不是从责任范围来判断损失的计算,而仍是考虑本质与程度上疏忽是否严重,Sumption 勋爵说:

"I respectfully doubt whether these are rational distinctions. In all three cases,[16] the solicitors were on the face of it supplying specific information in accordance with the lender's standard reporting instructions. The lender would in due course take it into account in deciding whether and if so how much to lend, along with other important information for which the solicitors had no responsibility, such as the valuation of the property, the amount of the loan, and the borrower's capacity to service it. **The solicitors had not assumed responsibility for identifying all the matters relevant to the lender's decision or for advising them whether to proceed. That was a matter for the lender**, and would depend not just on the whole of the material before it but on its internal guidelines and lending policies and the judgment of individual loan officers. **All of these cases therefore came within Lord Hoffmann's 'information' category**.

...**The duty of the solicitors depended on their retainer, which was agreed before any breach of duty occurred** and appears to have been in substantially similar terms in both cases.[17] In both cases, it extended to the care with which the solicitor answered the questions in the lender's standard reporting instructions, but not to the decision whether to proceed with the transaction. It followed that the loss flowing from the decision to lend could not as such be within the scope of their duty. **Chadwick J's approach was to**

---

〔16〕 指 Bristol and West Building Society v. Fancy & Jackson(a firm)先例中的三个同类案件。

〔17〕 指 Bristol and West Building Society v. Fancy & Jackson(a firm)先例中的 Steggles Palmer 与 Colin Bishop,Chadwick 大法官区分了两者的案情,前者律师要承担所有的损失,而后者不用。

make the measure of damages depend not on the scope of the duty but on the gravity of the particular breach and on his assessment of the objective quality of the reasons why the lender would have responded by refusing to proceed. In effect, he reverted ... to the distinction between 'no transaction' and 'successful transaction' cases which had been rejected in SAAMCO. **His observation that the lender had been deprived of the opportunity to make the decision that he would have made is only another way of saying that this was a 'no transaction' case.**"(加黑部分是笔者的强调)

6.5 SAAMCO先例区分不同案件的责任范围是提供"信息"或"意见"

在SAAMCO先例中,Hoffmann勋爵把专业人士在订立服务合约时愿意承担的责任范围区分为提供的是第一类(Category 1)"信息"(information)或第二类(Category 2)"意见"(advice)。这在Hughes – Holland v. BPE Solicitors(2017)UKSC 21最高院先例中,Sumption勋爵有解释说:"The SAAMCO principle has led to a distinction being drawn between 'advice' cases(sometimes referred to as '**category 2 cases**') and 'information' cases(sometimes referred to as '**category 1 cases**'). It has also given rise to what is generally referred to as the '**SAAMCO cap**', namely the principle that in an 'information' case the recoverable damages exclude losses which would still have been suffered even if the erroneous information had been correct."

这两种不同类别的自愿承担责任范围如果只限于"信息",如明显的例子是估价师只限于针对房屋当时的市场价值,或税务律师只限于针对某国的税务问题,这可以明确专业人士只是属于提供信息。如果该信息有错漏,该专业人士负责赔偿的损失只局限在该错误信息在整个交易或买卖过程中造成的部分损失。

但如果提供的是"意见",也即该专业人士是针对客户在一个商业交易或投资的每一步,更广泛与全面地去考虑会影响客户决定的关键事项。该专业人士自愿承担小心谨慎责任参与客户作出决定的整个过程的所有有关的事项,而不只是在作出决定的过程中某项特定的事项。这样,如果意见有错漏,该专业人士应负责赔偿整个交易带来的可合理预见的损失。

这两类不同的专业人士自愿承担的责任范围与带来的不同损失赔偿,可节录Sumption勋爵在Hughes – Holland v. BPE Solicitors最高院先例中所说:"(1)It is **first necessary to consider whether it is an 'advice' case or an 'information' case. This is a necessary first step because the scope of the duty, and therefore the measure of liability, is different in the two cases.** (2)It will be an 'advice' case if it can be shown that it has been 'left to the adviser to consider what matters should be taken into account in deciding whether to enter into the transaction', that 'his duty is to consider all relevant matters and not only specific matters in the decision' and that he is 'responsible for guiding the whole decision – making process'. (3)If it is **an 'advice' case, then the negligent adviser will have assumed responsibility for the decision to enter the trans-**

action and will be responsible for all the foreseeable financial consequences of entering into the transaction. (4) If it is not an 'advice' case, then it is an 'information' case and responsibility will not have been assumed for the decision to enter the transaction. (5) If it is **an 'information' case, the negligent adviser/information provider will only be responsible for the foreseeable financial consequences of the advice and/or information being wrong.** (6) This involves a consideration of what losses would have been suffered if the advice and/or information had been correct. It is only losses which would not have been suffered in such circumstances that are recoverable."（加黑部分是笔者的强调）

根据上述说法，看来专业人士只在对整个交易的方方面面都有参与并作出建议的"意见"类别案件，才会对整个失败的商业交易或投资的所有可预见的损失负责，对损失赔偿可在 SAAMCO 原则下封顶的只是"信息"类别案件。所以在 Aneco Reinsurance Underwriting Ltd v. Johnson & Higgins Ltd（2001）UKHL 51 先例中，Lloyd 勋爵说"意见"类别的案件仍适用传统对损失计算的分析，适用 SAAMCO 原则的只是"信息"类别的案件。

按理来说，"意见"类别的案件在专业人士的服务中比较少有，毕竟在一些复杂的商业交易或投资中，涉及方方面面（包括经济、政治、社会环境、法律、人事、信任、业务等）的考虑与判断，很少有只在一方面有专长的专业人士会全程参与一个复杂交易的决策与决定并提供方方面面的建议。只会在如投资顾问/银行对一个没有投资经验与水平不高的客户，作出了错误的投资建议或安排，才会是较明确的"意见"类别案件。有关投资顾问/银行的参与要到什么程度才算给出的是"意见"，可见 Springwell v. JP Morgan（2010）EWCA Civ 1221 上诉庭先例。

这也代表了大部分涉及专业人士疏忽的案件，都应是属于"信息"类别案件，正如 Manchester Building Society v. Grant Thornton UK LLP（2019）EWCA Civ 40 上诉庭先例中，Hamblen 大法官说："… unless the adviser is 'responsible for guiding the whole decision – making process' in the way described (in Hughes – Holland), it is an 'information' case."

但在 SAAMCO 先例后的案件在适用 SAAMCO 原则时，最困难与富争议性的就是去区分第一类的信息或是第二类的意见。可以说是比在证据法下区分"事实"（fact）与"意见"（opinion）更是困难得多。这是很明显，毕竟两者不是相互排斥（mutually exclusive），甚至往往是关系密切或是同一回事，即专业意见中往往有大量信息，而提供专业信息中也往往有个人意见。但在 SAAMCO 原则下，非要先以"法律过滤器"将两者分开，因为两者带来极不一样的经济后果。

这导致在 SAAMCO 先例后有大量的案例去澄清在不同的案情下到底是标签为"信息"或"意见"，也经常出现不稳定的判决。不少案例都是上诉后推翻了原来的判决。

只在一些极端案件中才能明确专业人士提供的到底是“信息”还是“意见”。前者往往是专业人士参与的只是对整个决策过程的一件特定工作或事情提供信息,而且是责任范围越窄越少就越明确是“信息”。例如,做一个检验、调查某一件事情等。好像 SAAMCO 先例的房屋估值与作出报告以供银行或金融机构考虑是否对该房屋做出贷款以及决定借贷的金额,就是典型的“信息”案件。

但每个案件都会有千变万化的案情,区分专业人士的所作所为与自愿承担的责任范围并给出标签是不容易的且富争议性。大部分的案件都处于“光谱”(spectrum)中间,要分析到底这个专业意见或专业信息是为了什么用途,以及实际上发生了什么,如专业人士确实给出了什么意见或信息。为了在每一个不同案件的特定案情中尽量做到公平合理,甚至会考虑其他各种因素:如商业交易或投资本身的复杂性与由多少/哪些方面决定、是否有其他专业人士参与、客户的水平高低与对专业人士的依赖程度、专业人士被认定错误与疏忽的程度是否严重等。这也代表了除非是极端例子(如证明被告只参与交易决策过程中极少与片面的工作),否则就像 Sumption 勋爵在 Hughes – Holland v. BPE Solicitors 最高院先例中说是无法再给出更清楚的指引,如果区分太僵化,可能对个别案件造成不公平:“between these extremes, every case is likely to depend on the range of matters for which the defendant assumed responsibility and no more exact rule can be stated.”

对这方面的批评,也就是一开始要去标签“信息”或“意见”类别案件,在 Manchester Building Society v. Grant Thornton UK LLP(2021)UKSC 20 最高院先例中,代表多数意见的 Hodge 勋爵与 Sales 勋爵提出了批评,并调整为专业人士提供的无论是“信息”还是“意见”是什么目的或与避什么风险,说:“The distinction drawn by Lord Hoffmann in SAAMCO between ‘advice’ cases and ‘information’ cases has not proved to be satisfactory. Put shortly, as explained by Lord Sumption in Hughes-Holland ..., the distinction is too rigid and, as such, it is liable to mislead. In reality, as Lord Sumption emphasises ..., the whole varied range of cases constitutes a spectrum. At one extreme will be pure ‘advice’ cases, in which on analysis the adviser has assumed responsibility for every aspect of a transaction in prospect for his client. At another extreme will be cases where the professional adviser contributes only a small part of the material on which the client relies in deciding how to act. In some cases (such as those involving valuers) it is readily possible to say that the purpose of the advice given is limited and that the adviser has assumed responsibility under a duty the scope of which is delimited by that purpose, which Lord Hoffmann called an ‘information’ case. However, Lord Sumption observed ... ‘[b]etween these extremes, every case is likely to depend on the range of matters for which the defendant assumed responsibility and no more exact rule can be stated’.”

实际上该先例就涉及这方面的争议,原告(Manchester Building Society)主张是

“意见”案件,但上诉庭判是“信息”案件,这将在稍后介绍案例时详及。

6.6 订约自由下订约方愿意在合约中承担的责任

SAAMCO 原则确立的专业人士的服务合约合理默示(如果没有明示说明)了专业人士愿意对客户承担的责任或风险(assumption of contractual liability or risks)的范围,这也影响了其他不涉及专业人士的商业合约。航运人士十分熟悉的 The“Achilleas”(2009)1 AC 61 贵族院先例,[18] 就是著名例子。

众所周知,商业合约中双方订约方相互做出了许多合约承诺,这些承诺是承诺方有责任去严格履行,否则构成违约,并带来后续赔偿与支付因违约所导致的经济损失的责任。这两个履行与赔偿的责任或义务被称为“首要义务”(primary obligation)与“次要义务”(secondary obligation)。[19] 这是英国法律默示的地位,正如 Hoffmann 勋爵说:“Every failure to perform a primary obligation is a breach of contract. The secondary obligation on the part of the contract breaker to which it gives rise by implication of the common law is to pay monetary compensation to the other party for the loss sustained by him in consequence of the breach.”

但法律的默示地位是可以明示条文去超越与否定,而在现实中也确实如此。例如,以明示条文如“免责条文”(exception clause)或“限制赔偿条文”讲明不赔利润损失(loss of profit)等去减轻或否定作为次要义务的赔偿责任。

在 SAAMCO 先例中,Hoffmann 勋爵认为先要看被告(也就是估价师)在合约中愿意承担的责任,之后再核算损失,说:“that which the law regards as best giving effect to the express obligations assumed by the valuer(and) not extending them so as to impose on the valuer **a liability greater than he could reasonably have thought he was undertaking.**”(加黑部分是笔者的强调)

这 SAAMCO 先例中说法在后来的 The“Achilleas”先例中被认同与被引用,说:“to exclude from liability the damages attributable to a fall in the property market notwithstanding that those losses were foreseeable in the sense of being ‘not unlikely’(property values go down as well as up) and had been caused by the negligent valuation in the sense that, but for the valuation, the bank would not have lent at all and there was no evidence to show that it would have lost its money in some other way. It was excluded on the ground that it was **outside the scope of the liability which the parties would reasonably have considered that the valuer was undertaking.**”(加黑部分是笔者的强调)

在 The“Achilleas”贵族院先例中,案情涉及一个 5—7 个月的期租合约,且后来再续期 5—7 个月,租金是每天 16,750 美元。计算出来的最后还船日期(terminal rede-

---

〔18〕 见笔者《损失赔偿与救济》一书第三章之 8 段的详细介绍。

〔19〕 见笔者《损失赔偿与救济》一书第十一章之 1.1 段。

livery date)是2004年5月2日。在4月20日,承租人给了还船通知说是在4月30日至5月2日之间还船。这样,船东就在市场订下了下一个4—6个月的期租合约,租金是每天39,500美元,而销约期是5月8日。可以说如果承租人能准时在5月2日还船,赶下一个租约的销约期可以说是绰绰有余。但最终船舶是在5月11日才在日本的大分港(Oita)卸清了煤炭并去还船给船东。这样超出或延迟的时间是9天,比较与市场租金的差价后损失应是158,301.17美元。但实际上船东的损失远不止此数,这是因为延迟至5月11日还船就错过了下一个租约的5月8日的销约期,而当时市场租金急剧下挫,这导致了船东最终被下一个租约承租人从39,500美元压价到31,500美元才保住了这份租约。这等于每天损失8000美元,再乘以至少4个月的租约期,船东真正的损失就变成了1,364,584.37美元。

双方开始为这笔钱去伦敦仲裁,仲裁庭的少数意见(dissenting opinion)是认为承租人不应该负责,原因是两个:(1)在期租的租船市场上一般认为是承租人只需要对超期使用船舶的损失或市场差价负责赔偿。这在实务中确实如此处理,但这一点并没有有关先例去明确。(2)任何一位合理的承租人不会在一个期租合约去接受这种无边无际的赔偿责任。因为承租人不知道也无法控制船东私下订下怎样的租约,例如,如果船东私下订下的下一个租约长达10年,而市场下跌的幅度更大,这笔损失可能是上亿美元。但根据损失计算的大原则,损失是不能封顶的,而船东会在交船前在市场上寻找下一个租约/长期租约是可以预见的事情,并非不太可能发生。

多数的仲裁裁决,也是船东胜诉成功索赔后续191天租约的损失在高院与上诉庭均获得支持,但最后去了贵族院被推翻。因为船东有一个默示的承担责任的合理范围,不会同意无边无际的赔偿责任。Hoffmann勋爵说:"is the rule that a party may recover losses which were foreseeable('not unlikely') an external rule of law, imposed upon the parties to every contract in default of express provision to the contrary, **or is it a prima facile assumption about what the parties may be taken to have intended**, no doubt applicable in the great majority of cases but capable of rebuttal in cases in which the context, surrounding circumstances or general understanding in the relevant market **show that a party would not reasonably have been regarded as assuming responsibility for such losses**."(加黑部分是笔者的强调)

这是说在考虑损失计算中损失类别的遥远性,除了因果关系与可预见性外,也要考虑与受限于违约方被告合理愿意在有关合约承担的责任。这在后来的Supershield Ltd v. Siemens Building Technologies FE Ltd(2010) EWCA Civ 7上诉庭先例中有提到,Toulson大法官说:"**The law on remoteness of damage** in relation to claims for breach of contract is grounded on the policy that the loss recoverable by the victim **should be limited to loss from which the party in breach may reasonably be taken to have assumed a responsibility to protect the victim**. It follows that the question of remoteness cannot be isolated from consideration of the purpose of the contract and the scope of the contractual obligation. The underlying policy is implicit in Lord Reid's speech in C Czarnikow Ltd v. Koufos ... it has been made more explicit in the decisions of the House of Lords(in SAAMCO and the 'Achilleas')..."(加黑部分是笔者的强调)

7. SAAMCO 反事实分析在某些情况下不适用

简单重温,SAAMCO 反事实分析是去问原告如果被告专业人士的错误服务与意见是正确的,原告会否仍蒙受同样的损失?如果答案是"会",就表示原告的损失与被告的疏忽无关,不在被告的责任范围之内。如果答案是"不会",如意见正确就可以减少一半损失,有关的损失就在被告的责任范围内。

估价师对土地或房屋的错误高估或低估是简单明了的案件,但如果是较复杂的专业意见(这经常会在商业中发生)有错误与疏忽,就不会这么容易通过 SAAMCO 反事实分析去量化专业人士疏忽所导致的金钱损失了。例如 Leggatt 勋爵在 Manchester Building Society v. Grant Thornton UK LLP(2021)UKSC 20 最高院先例中给了一个例子说:"As an example,... a hypothetical case in which a company's audited accounts show a profit of £ 50m when, on a true and fair view, its profit was nil. In reliance on the auditor's report, the company pays a dividend of £ 25m. It is established law that in such a case, where a dividend is paid out of capital and not out of distributable profits, the company(at least where it is insolvent) is entitled to recover the amount of the dividend as damages from its auditor:... However, counsel for the society submitted that limiting the auditor's liability to loss that would have occurred if the auditor's advice had been correct would defeat that claim, since, if the advice had been correct, the company would still have paid out the dividend and suffered the same loss. They argued that the fact that such a conclusion is plainly wrong shows that the counterfactual question articulated in SAAMCO is not applicable to auditor's negligent cases. ... Thus, in the example given ... above where a company pays a dividend of £ 25m in reliance on the auditor's negligent advice that there were distributable profits of £ 50m available, when on a true view there were none, the payment of the dividend causes an actionable loss to the company of £ 25m. **Applying the counterfactual test, the relevant question is whether the payment of the dividend would have resulted in the same actionable loss if the auditor's advice had been correct** and the company's financial position had been as represented in its audited accounts. In that situation the company would indeed have had profits of £ 50m out of which it could lawfully pay the dividend. Paying the dividend would therefore not have caused an actionable loss to the company. **Accordingly, the loss incurred by paying the unlawful dividend is not excluded by applying the counterfactu-**

al test."(加黑部分是笔者的强调)

简单介绍上述例子,就是审计师的年度核算报告中错误与疏忽得出客户上市公司有可分配利润5000万英镑,但其实根本没有这笔利润。公司管理层根据此报告与其他考量,决定派息给股东,总金额达2500万英镑。但如果没有审计师的这个错误,公司管理层就不会作出这笔派息或分红,否则就是蚕食公司资本而不合法了。但向审计师索赔损失,是否就是这2500万英镑?原告 Manchester Building Society 的代表大律师说如果以 SAAMCO 反事实分析,就是错误的年度核算报告是正确的,是有5000万英镑的利润,结果也是派息2500万英镑,公司的行为不会有任何改变。这样,根据 SAAMCO 原则岂非审计师的过错与疏忽没有造成损失,但这明显有问题,所以 SAAMCO 原则不应该适用。但这被 Leggatt 勋爵否定,说正确的反事实分析并非原告的行为会否改变,而是原告是否会蒙受同样的损失。公司没有可分配利润但非法派息2500万英镑,会造成公司2500万英镑可追讨的损失。但如果确实赚取利润5000万英镑,就是合法派息,则不会有可追讨的损失。因此在反事实分析下这笔非法派息不会被排除,也不代表原告没有损失。

在 Hughes - Holland v. BPE Solicitors(2017)UKSC 21 最高院先例中,关键的争议不在于被告律师的过错与疏忽的严重性与导致原告贷款,而在于原告借贷的20万英镑对一项一开始就是被原告过分乐观而错误估计的失败地产发展项目是否有影响。上诉庭与最高院根据 SAAMCO 反事实分析,看来得出的结论是即使假设被告律师实际上作出的错误专业意见是正确的,对这项"先天不足"的失败投资项目仍是于事无补。Sumption 勋爵说:"Mr Gabriel would still have lost his money because the expenditure of £ 200,000 would not have enhanced the value of the property. The development would have been left incomplete, the loan unpaid and the property substantially worthless when it came to be sold into a depressed market under the chargee's power of sale. None of the loss which Mr Gabriel suffered was within the scope of BPE's duty. None of it was loss against which BPE was duty bound to take reasonable care to protect him. It arose from commercial misjudgements which were no concern of theirs."

对笔者带来的疑问是,会否对一项"先天不足"的注定失败的投资或贷款,专业人士提供"信息"(如尽职调查)错误与疏忽,甚至是严重疏忽,在 SAAMCO 反事实分析下都无须对客户在投资或贷款失败后巨大的损失承担任何赔偿责任?如果是,会否看来,这 SAAMCO 反事实分析不是对每个千变万化案情的案件(即使都是针对专业人士的疏忽案件)都适用。

而另在大部分其他类别的疏忽侵权的案件中,如交通意外或医疗疏忽案件,也不需要进行 SAAMCO 反事实分析。这会使这些案件责任范围比较单一,复杂的往往只在损失计算的遥远性(因果关系与可预见)、减损、自甘风险等方面。Hodge 与 Sales 勋爵在 Khan v. Meadows(2021)UKSC 21 最高院先例中说:"In many, and probably a large majority of, cases of clinical negligence the application of the scope of duty principle results in the conclusion that a type of loss or an element of a claimant's loss is within the scope of the defendant's duty, without the court having to address the SAAMCO counterfactual. Where a surgeon negligently performs an operation and causes both physical injury and consequent economic loss to the patient, both types of loss will normally be within the scope of the defendant's duty of care. In other words, by undertaking the operation on the patient the surgeon takes responsibility for physical harm caused by any lack of skill and care in performing the operation and for consequential economic loss. Similarly, when a general medical practitioner negligently prescribes unsuitable medication, thereby causing injury or failing to prevent the development of an otherwise preventable medical condition, both the injury or condition and the consequential economic loss will generally be within the scope of the defendant's duty."

最后是针对"多重侵权人"(multi – tortfeasor)[20]的案件。这种案件经常发生在串谋(conspiracy)或欺诈(fraud)类别的侵权但也可是任何其他类别的侵权案件,如一个简单的交通意外事故,SAAMCO原则也不适用。不会因为被告只是其中的一位侵权人,甚至过错与疏忽占造成有关的意外事故份额不多,而可以减低赔偿。在普通法中,早在Merryweather v. Nixan(1799)1 ER 1337先例中已确认受害方可以向任何一位侵权人取回所有损失,毕竟受害方也往往不会知道背后的其他共同侵权人。另是在多位共同侵权人之间,已经通过立法有了一套分摊(contribution)机制。

8. SAAMCO先例后判断专业人士责任的案例

这些案例不少,如 Nykredit Mortgage Bank Plc v. Edward Erdman Group Ltd

---

〔20〕 简而言之,就是有多于一位的侵权人的过错与疏忽结合导致原告受害人的损失。这样,各侵权人或疏忽行为人要承担"共同与连带"(joint and several)的责任赔偿受害人的所有损失。原告可以只向其中一位侵权人提起诉讼并索赔所有损失,而被告在该意外事故只是有部分责任,可申请法院把其他知道的共同侵权人加入为共同被告,并要求法院在一次过审理时一并考虑如果原告索赔成功,如何在多名被告之间根据他们的疏忽程度分摊各自要承担损失的金额。被告也可以在原告索赔成功后,再向其他的共同侵权人要求补偿他们共同疏忽导致的部分赔偿责任。这课题在笔者《提单及其他付运单证》一书第五章之17.2.9.4段有详及。英国有关立法之《Civil Liability(Contribution)Act 1978》之S.1(1)说:"... any person liable in respect of any damage suffered by another person may recover contribution from any other person liable in respect of the same damage(whether jointly with him or otherwise)...."另S.2(1)说:"... in any proceedings for contribution ... the amount of the contribution recoverable from any person shall be such as may be found by the court to be just and equitable having regard to the extent of the person's responsibility for the damage in question."S.3说:"Judgment recovered against any person liable in respect of any debt or damage shall not be a bar to an action, or to the continuance of an action, against any other person who is(apart from any such bar)jointly liable with him in respect of the same debt or damage."另在S.6(1)说明立法适用在侵权或违约("whatever the legal basis of his liability, whether tort, breach of contract, breach of trust or otherwise.")

(No. 2)(1997)1 WLR 1627(估价师);Bristol and West Building Society v. May, May & Merrimans(1996)2 All ER 801(律师);Bristol and West Building Society v. Fancy & Jackson(a firm)(1997)4 All ER 582(律师);Nationwide Building Society v. Balmer Radmore(1999)Lloyd's Rep PN 241(律师);Omega Trust Co v. Wright Son & Pepper (1998)PNLR 337(律师);Portman Building Society v. Bevan Ashford(a firm)(2000) PNLR 344(律师);Platform Home Loans Ltd v. Oyston Shipways Ltd(2000)2 AC 190 (测量师);Lloyds Bank Plc v. Burd Pearse(2001)EWCA Civ 366(律师);Aneco Reinsurance Underwriting Ltd v. Johnson & Higgins Ltd(2001)UKHL 51(保险经纪);Haugesund Kommune v. Depfa ACS Bank(Wikborg Rein & Co, Part 20 defendant)(No. 2) (2011)EWCA Civ 33(律师);Makar v. Pricewaterhousecoopers LLP(2011)EWHC 3835(Comm)(公司审计师);Capita Alternative Fund Services v. Drivers Jonas(A Firm)(2011)EWHC 2336(Comm)(测量师);Astle v. CBRE Ltd(2015)EWHC 3189 (Ch)(测量师);O'Hare v. Coutts and Co(2016)EWHC 2224(QB)(投资顾问); LSREF III Wight Ltd v. Gateley LLP(2016)EWCA Civ 359(律师);Halsall v. Champion Consulting Ltd(2017)EWHC 1079(QB)(税务顾问);Bank of Ireland v. Watts Group Plc(2017)EWHC 1667(TCC)(工料测量师);Lloyds Bank Plc v. McBains Cooper Consulting Ltd(2018)EWCA Civ 452(工程监督);AssetCo Plc v. Grant Thornton UK LLP(2020)EWCA Civ 1151(审计师);Hughes - Holland v. BPE Solicitors (2017)UKSC 21(律师);Ahmad v. Wood(2018)EWHC 996(QB)(律师);LIV Bridging Finance Ltd v. EAD Solicitors LLP(2020)EWHC 1590(Ch)(律师);Large v. Hart (2021)EWCA Civ 24(测量师);Multiplex Construction Europe Ltd v. Bathgate Realisations Civil Engineering Ltd(2021)EWHC 590(TCC)(顾问工程师)等先例。以下段节只随意挑少数几个先例作简单介绍,希望显示在不同案情下决定专业人士是否要赔偿特定损失或属于"信息"或"意见"类别案例的困难与不稳定。

8.1 案例之一:Rubenstein v. HSBC Bank Ltd(2012)EWCA Civ 1184 上诉庭先例

在 Rubenstein v. HSBC Bank Ltd 上诉庭先例中,案情涉及原告 Rubenstein 先生卖房后,想把这笔钱先存在一个安全的地方,等他找好满意的新房屋后再买房。所以 Rubenstein 先生是明确告知了被告 HSBC 的雇员,他不希望有任何投资风险。而被告疏忽建议客户投资 AIG Life 的一种债券(bond investment),声称如现金存款一样安全,但实际上债券的价值是随着市场波动有市场风险。在 2008 年美国雷曼兄弟(Lehman Brothers)破产前的周末,加上 AIG Life 的母公司 AIG 也同时被怀疑有破产风险,Rubenstein 先生决定将钱从债券投资中取出来,但因为同时有太多人提现,AIG Life 暂时停止了这个项目的取现并在之后提出了新的取现计划。最终原告蒙受了约 18 万英镑的损失,而原告声称如果将这笔钱存在银行同样时间,是可以得到约 18.7 万英镑的收益。

一审法院判虽然被告的建议疏忽且原告依赖了被告的建议,但是原告的损失是当时前所未有的市场动荡所导致,而并非被告的疏忽建议导致,所以是不可预见的与太遥远。一审法院最后判原告只能获得名义损失。

上诉庭推翻了一审判决,判被告要赔偿原告的损失。首先 SAAMCO 先例中著名的登山运动员的例子不适用在此案,医生只是告诉病人他的膝盖良好,并没有建议他去登山,但是被告不止建议了原告投资,还建议了特定产品。如果最后投资失败,是应由法院决定这损失是否在被告的责任范围之内。Rix 大法官说:"(HSBC) not only advised Mr Rubenstein on the investment of his capital, he recommended a particular investment. He, so to speak, put him in it. If such an investment goes wrong, there will nearly always be other causes (bad management, bad markets, fraud, political change etc): but it will be an exercise in legal judgment to decide whether some change in markets is so extraneous to the validity of the investment advice as to absolve the adviser for failing to carry out his duty or duties on the basis that the result was not within the scope of those duties."

原告 Rubenstein 先生已经明示不希望承担任何投资风险,是被告错误建议并误导了原告,让他以为投资产品没有风险。所以与 SAAMCO 先例中登山运动员的例子不一样,原告的损失与错误建议之间并非没有关联,原告的损失并非被告责任范围外的不可预见的因素造成。被告的责任范围包括保护原告无需面对市场波动的风险,在这种情况下让被告不必承担市场波动导致的风险是错误的。Rix 大法官说:"Against the background of the facts found and of the origin of the transaction, and the scope of HSBC's duties, what connected the erroneous advice and the loss was the combination of putting Mr Rubenstein into a fund which was subject to market losses while at the same time misleading him by telling him that his investment was the same as a cash deposit, when it was not. Therefore, the correct selection of the cause of Mr Rubenstein's loss was the loss in value of the assets in which the EVRF(有关的投资产品)... was invested. Therefore, unlike the case of the mountaineer's knee, advice and the loss were not disconnected by an unforeseeable event beyond the scope of the bank's duty. It was the bank's duty to protect Mr Rubenstein from exposure to market forces when he made clear that he wanted an investment which was without any risk (and when the bank told him that his investment was the same as a cash deposit). It is wrong in such a context to say that when the risk from exposure to market forces arises, the bank is free of responsibility because the incidence of market loss was unexpected."

8.2 案例之二:Hughes - Holland v. BPE Solicitors (2017) UKSC 21 最高院先例

接下来的 Hughes - Holland v. BPE Solicitors 最高院先例,在确认 SAAMCO 先例外,进一步对"信息"与"意见"的区分提供了指引。案情涉及借款人 Little 先生对出借人 Gabriel 先生(后来破产,原告 Hughes-Holland 是破产受托人)说要为一个将一座荒废了的热水塔(heating tower)重建与发展为写字楼的地产项目(称为"Building 428")贷款20 万英镑。Little 先生说发展有关的地产项目预计要使用20 万,于是 Gabriel 先生认为这 20 万英镑是用于发展地产项目,虽然他并没有被明确告知这 20 万英镑具体会如何使用。之后 Gabriel 先生委任了被告律师所负责拟定贷款协议与对热水塔进行押记登记。但负责处理文件的 Spencer 律师实际收到的具体指示是来自 Little 先生而不是 Gabriel 先生。Little 先生曾经向银行贷款15 万英镑,在热水塔上设立押记作为担保。Little 先生准备用现在这笔 20 万英镑贷款偿还银行这笔 15 万英镑的贷款后解除热水塔的押记,并将热水塔产权转移给自己控制的 SPV 公司。Little 先生在给 Spencer 律师的电话留言与指示里只说他要将热水塔出售给一个 SPV 公司,并且 Gabriel 先生会借给他 20 万英镑,并没有提及该贷款是用于发展地产项目所需资金或是用于偿还贷款。Spencer 律师没有向 Gabriel 先生确认这个指示。Spencer 律师使用了一份在另一宗贷款交易的文本,内有文字说明这笔贷款的目的与用途是提供该地产项目所需资金(will be made available as a contribution to the costs of the development of the property),虽然在 Spencer 律师收到的指示里并不包括这一点,但 Spencer 律师没有发现并删除这句话,而这恰好又符合 Gabriel 先生自以为是地认为这 20 万英镑会被用在发展地产项目上的想法。看来这中间不涉及欺骗或是不诚实,只是 Little 先生与 Gabriel 先生之间的沟通有误解与 Spencer 律师疏忽错误使用另一宗交易的贷款确认函文本。

此地产发展项目由于 Little 先生大大低估了工程所需费用与其他的错误估计和管理不善,最后导致项目失败,也没有推进重建。最后该荒废的热水塔以低价公开拍卖,所得的款项连拍卖的费用也不足以支付。这表示原告的 20 万英镑贷款全数打了水漂。原告对借款人 Little 先生、他的地产发展项目公司与被告律师以欺诈误述等诉因起诉,但只有被告律师的疏忽判成立。这带来被告应承担的后果的争议,毕竟被告所承担的责任范围只在贷款确认函的拟定与押记。

一审法院判原告胜诉,被告除了扣减部分共同疏忽(contributory negligence)与减损(mitigation)后,要赔偿原告所有损失。但上诉庭推翻并改判是原告自己对发展项目的错误判断导致损失 20 万英镑贷款,被告律师事务所无须赔偿。

最后在最高院,除了全面针对了对 SAAMCO 原则的各种批评与进一步澄清有关"信息"与"意见"的区分外,支持了上诉庭的判决。Sumption 勋爵说:"The first question is whether BPE Solicitors assumed responsibility for Mr Gabriel's decision to lend money to Mr Little. In my judgment, it **is clear that they did not. Their instructions were to draw up the facility agreement and the charge, nothing more.** Mr Spencer did not know and did not need to know what had passed between Mr Gabriel and Mr Little, except that they had agreed upon a loan of £200,000 secured by a charge on Building 428. He knew nothing about the nature of the proposed development, its likely cost, the financial capacity of Mr Little to fund it without Mr Gabriel's loan or the value of the property in its developed or undeveloped state. Indeed, he does not even appear to have known of Mr Gabriel's assumption about the use to be made of the loan moneys. He simply included in the draft facility agreement by oversight language which by an unhappy chance confirmed that assumption. ... On the footing that BPE was not legally responsible for Mr Gabriel's decision to lend the money, but only for confirming his assumption about one of a number of factors in his assessment of the project, the next question is what if any loss was attributable to that assumption being wrong. The answer is that if it had been right, Mr Gabriel would still have lost his money because the expenditure of £ 200,000 would not have enhanced the value of the property. The development would have been left incomplete, the loan unpaid and the property substantially worthless when it came to be sold into a depressed market under the chargee's power of sale. **None of the loss which Mr Gabriel suffered was within the scope of BPE's duty.** None of it was loss against which BPE was duty bound to take reasonable care to protect him. **It arose from commercial misjudgements which were no concern of theirs.**"(加黑部分是笔者的强调)

8.3 案例之三:Lloyds Bank Plc v. McBains Cooper Consulting Ltd(2018) EWCA Civ 452 上诉庭先例

借款人向银行(Lloyds Bank)借款用于重新开发教堂,银行委任了 McBains 监督工程并定期向银行作出报告,报告的内容包括工程进度与质量、批准支取借款的申请、确保支取的金额在借款合约下是合理、是否存在对银行不利的事项、未支取的金额是否足够完成剩余的重建工程等。虽然 McBains 的报告中提到了借款人要再额外建造三楼与正在借款合约外寻找其他资助,但银行没有调查,仍在 McBains 的建议下同意了支取申请。后来银行发现整个工程完全失控了,为了减少损失,银行提前终止了借款合约。因为担保不够,银行以 McBains 疏忽提起诉讼索赔损失,指 McBains 没有警告银行余下的未支取借款不足以完成剩余重建工程,也不应建议银行同意支取额外建造三楼的费用。

一审法院判银行胜诉,即如果 McBains 没有疏忽银行会更早终止借款合约,因此 McBains 要承担之后的所有损失。McBains 上诉,指这是"信息"而不是"意见",所以只应该负责进度报告错误导致的损失。

上诉庭同意一审法院认为不用执着于标签到底是"信息"还是"意见"案件的观点,并引用了 Hughes - Holland v. BPE Solicitors(2017) UKSC 21 最高院先例。Longmore 大法官说:"Although there is now much learning on the distinction between information and advice in the SAAMCO line of cases and it is sometimes necessary to ascertain whether information provided by a defendant is the sole input into a claimant making a decision or part only of a number of considerations which a claimant will take into account in making a decision, I do not think that learning assists in this case. … In Hughes-Holland v BPE Solicitors Lord Sumption said … that the labels of advice and information are:— 'neither distinct nor mutually exclusive categories. Information given by a professional man to his client is usually a specific form of advice, and most advice will involve conveying information. Neither label really corresponds to the contents of the bottle.' I respectfully agree."

但上诉庭不认同一审法院的判决，上诉庭认为除了建造三楼的费用外，银行在这个借款合约下蒙受的其他损失主要是因为银行一开始就明知有短缺但仍然愿意借钱并继续借钱给借款人，而不是因为 McBains 对支取建造三楼的费用的申请给了任何错误信息或意见，因此 McBains 只需要对多支取的建造三楼的费用负责。Longmore 大法官说："But, with respect, that is illogical because **the bank was going to lose those sums, apart from the sums paid for the third floor, in any event**. The bank, …, **knew** from **the inception of the loan that there was to be a serious shortfall** between the sums payable under the building contract and the amount of the facility. … The cause of the bank paying out amounts pursuant to Progress Reports 14 – 17 (McBains 的报告) was not the fact that McBains gave wrong information or advice to the bank in relation to sums claimed for the third floor; it was the fact that the bank agreed to lend (and continued to fund) a project which was never financially viable. …"

这看来与 Hughes – Holland v. BPE Solicitors 最高院先例的精神一样，即如果一个交易是"先天不足"，则不能争辩属于"意见"的案件而将损失转嫁给专业人士。此外上诉庭也改变了一审法院对共同疏忽的责任分摊，认为银行知道借款不足以完成重建工程，没有调查额外建造三楼的情况与要求借款人自己支付费用，允许借款人减少担保，没有向 McBains 提供借款合约等。所以银行不应该只承担一审法院认定的 1/3 的共同疏忽责任，而应该是 2/3。这样可以说是大幅扣减了 McBains 需要赔偿的金额。

8.4 案例之四：AssetCo Plc v. Grant Thornton UK LLP (2020) EWCA Civ 1151 上诉庭先例

原告 AssetCo 是一家经营消防与救援业务的公司，被告 Grant Thornton (GT) 是原告的审计师。在 2009 年 GT 的审计报告中说原告的业务很成功并且可以赚取很多利润，但是原告的首席财务官与首席执行官欺诈做了假账，直到两年后原告才发现真相。原告以疏忽向 GT 索赔提起诉讼，指 GT 的疏忽导致原告失去在两年前重组 (也意味着可以避免之后的损失) 的机会。

GT 承认在审计工作中疏忽，特别是没有发现原告高管欺诈，但不承认因果关系与损失。双方同意如果 GT 没有疏忽，原告在 2009 年就会发现公司的真实情况，开始破产管理与重组以避免清盘。但 GT 主张原告的损失主要是因为做的生意亏本，而这不在 GT 的责任范围之内。此外 GT 也否认原告在 2009 年失去真实与实质性的机会进行重组避免清盘。

一审法院拒绝了 GT 的抗辩，在扣除了原告 25% 的共同疏忽后判 GT 要赔偿原告 2336 万英镑的损失。GT 提起上诉，指一审法院错误认定原告的损失在 GT 的责任范围之内。

对于第一个争议，在一审双方都没有提出要适用 SAAMCO 原则，是在上诉时被告更换了律师团队，才提出这个核心争议。原告主张 SAAMCO 原则只适用于审计师针对某一个特定交易给出信息或意见以让客户作出决定的案件。但是审计报告是不针对任何特定的交易，没有必要区分到底是"信息"还是"意见"，而应该适用普通的因果关系与遥远性等。上诉庭没有接受原告的主张，认为 SAAMCO 原则在一般的涉及审计师的责任时都适用，Richards 大法官说："Nonetheless, I do not see any substantial reason why the SAAMCO principle cannot or should not, in most circumstances, be applied to determine whether particular losses come within the scope of the auditor's duty when signing an unqualified audit certificate. Its purpose … is to distinguish the negligent audit that is merely the occasion for the loss from the negligent audit that gives rise to a liability to make good the loss. It is capable of being effectively applied to most types of loss that may be claimed in respect of a negligent audit. …."

针对原告在 2010 年与 2011 年的损失是否在被告的责任范围内，一审法院在认定事实时考虑了被告的疏忽不只是令原告有机会继续经营而在之后蒙受交易损失，[21] 而是被告说原告的业务很成功并且可以赚取很多利润，原告的管理没有问题，令原告继续以原本的方式经营而蒙受了损失。所以被告的疏忽十分严重，违反了审计师最基本的责任，也是造成原告损失的直接主要原因。一审法院的有关判决可节录如下："The losses that were suffered were not suffered simply because the company remained in existence and carried on trading, but rather as a result of AssetCo continuing to trade in a particular fashion in reliance on the (negligent) audit."

上诉庭也没有分析这到底是一个"信息"或"意见"的案件，只是支持了一审判决，认为原告的损失在 GT 的责任范围内：

"This is not just a case of 'but for' causation, with the audit certificate providing the occasion for losses subsequently suffered. GT here failed to detect the dishonest concealment of the substantial losses made in FY2009 and the group's insolvency, which continued in FY2010 and FY2011 resulting in the losses claimed by AssetCo, or most of them. This failure deprived AssetCo (whether acting by its shareholders collectively in general meeting or by its non-executive directors) of the opportunity to call the senior management to account and to ensure that errors in management are corrected. … this is a principal purpose of an audit and, a… the scope of an auditor's duty is determined by ref-

---

〔21〕 见本章之 1.3 段的介绍。

erence to the purposes of the statutory requirement for an audit. Liability for the losses suffered in FY2010 and FY2011 is ‘liability for the consequences of the information being inaccurate’…

… By failing to detect that the accounts were prepared, and deliberately prepared, by management on a wholly false basis, presenting an insolvent company and group as successful and profitable, GT deprived AssetCo of the very information that would have caused it to cease its loss – making activities and to take the steps necessary to regain its solvency…. GT's negligence was not therefore merely the occasion for the losses which AssetCo continued to incur but was a substantial cause of those losses.

In my judgment, the judge was therefore right to conclude that GT was liable for the losses …"

唯一被上诉庭排除认为 GT 不用负责的是原告的一位董事为了自身利益挪用了一部分公司资产，上诉庭认为这与 GT 的疏忽没有足够联系。

9. 对 SAAMCO 原则与问题作出总结的最高院先例

SAAMCO 先例后的 20 多年来，特别是 SAAMCO 原则被 2017 年 Hughes – Holland v. BPE Solicitors(2017) UKSC 21 最高院先例再度确认与澄清后，一直被英国法院依从。但 SAAMCO 原则仍有不少不明朗之处，也一直面对批评。这导致最高院由同样的 7 位（一般都是 5 位）大法官（分别是 Reed、Hodge、Black、Kitchin、Sales、Leggatt 与 Burrows 勋爵）审理了两个案件，并在 2021 年 6 月 18 日同时作出判决（以起到相互呼应与参考作用）。鉴于这两个先例的重要性与特殊性，可以断言恐怕有很长一段时间不会改变它们定下来的英国法律地位。以下会介绍两个最高院先例，看如何对 SAAMCO 原则的问题作出进一步的帮助。

9.1　案例之一：Manchester Building Society v. Grant Thornton UK LLP (2021) UKSC 20 最高院先例

在 Manchester Building Society v. Grant Thornton UK LLP 最高院先例中，原告是英国一个小型的房屋互助协会（mutual building society）。在英国，原告这种互助协会是属于金融机构，主要业务包括接受储蓄、提供住房信贷等。从 1997 年到 2012 年，原告的会计账目都由被告 Grant Thornton 会计师事务所（以下简称 GT）审计。在进行一些借贷业务时，原告想要通过订立利率掉期合约来对冲利率波动带来的风险。但如果根据法律要求所使用的国际财务报表准则（International Financial Reporting Standards, IFRS）来准备账目，利率的波动会令会计报表上原告的财务状况也相应波动，立法会要求原告增加资本金，这显然是原告想要避免的。2006 年 4 月，GT 在了解原告的目的与需求后，建议原告可以使用《国际会计准则第 39 号——金融工具：确认和计量》(International Accounting Standard 39,IAS 39)下的套期保值会计规则〔22〕来在账面上减少利率波动对财务状况的影响。原告根据 GT 的建议在 2006 年至 2011 年年底准备自己的财务报表,并在此期间订立了更多的利率掉期合约。

在 2013 年 3 月,GT 通知原告自己在 2006 年作出的专业意见与之后的审计意见错误,原告在准备财务报表时不可以使用套期保值会计。双方同意 GT 的疏忽或错误主要在两个方面:一是原告的业务不满足 IAS 39 下使用套期保值会计的前提条件;二是原告的财务报表实际上有严重错误,对被套期项目的现存价值调整有缺陷。

GT 错误建议原告使用套期保值会计带来的影响是,原告重新作出 2011 年的财务报表,结果是由盈利 635 万英镑变为亏损 1144 万英镑,净资产从 3840 万英镑变为 970 万英镑。而纠正后,原告就不再满足立法的最低资产要求。

为了摆脱这种困境,原告提前终止了所有利率掉期合约并蒙受约 3200 万英镑的损失,其中包括因提前终止利率掉期合约而支付的约 30 万英镑的交易成本。

原告向 GT 索赔因依赖 GT 错误或疏忽的专业意见而导致的损失,其中最主要的(也是最后一路打到了最高院的)损失就是在 2013 年提前终止利率掉期合约时蒙受的损失。

一审法院[(2018) EWHC 963 (Comm)]认定如果不是 GT 在 2006 年 4 月的疏忽意见,原告之后不会再订立更多并会终止之前已经订立的长期利率掉期合约,也就不会蒙受在 2013 年终止利率掉期合约的约 3200 万英镑的损失。一审法官判 GT 的疏忽是原告损失的主因,损失类别是可预见的,因此并非太遥远,属于可索赔的损失。但是一审法官接着根据 SAAMCO 原则判金融海啸导致的损失并不在 GT 提供意见时承担的责任范围之内,所以只需要赔偿约 30 万英镑的损失,这主要反映了提前终止利率掉期合约的交易成本。

此外,一审法官还在万一他以上的结论错误的假设下,认定原告证明了如果 GT 的建议正确,原告可以不必提前终止有关的利率掉期合约,也就是不会蒙受这笔 3200 万英镑的损失。但同时原告有 50% 的共同错误,一是错误决定订立的利率掉期合约的合约期,二是原告的财务总监准备财务报表时有疏忽,应该知道原告的财务报表不符合 IAS 39 的要求。所以就算 GT 要承担提前终止有关的利率掉期合约的损失(与一审法官的判决结果相反),也只需要承担 50%。

原告向上诉庭上诉,理由可简单总结如下:(1)一审法官基于 GT 愿意承担的责任范围,而不是 SAAMCO 原则的"信息"与"意见"案件的分类,适用法律错误。(2)正确的分析应是 GT 向原告提供能否使用套期保值会计的专业意见,属于"意见"类别的案件。所以 GT 要为可预见的原告的所有损失负责,也就是包括利率掉期合约的市值下跌的损失。(3)即使这是"信息"类的案件,一审法官的决定也是错误

---

〔22〕 这种会计规则下的记账方式是在同一期计入套期保值产生的盈亏与被套期保值项目价格变化,这两者的损益可以相互抵消。

的。一审法院既然认定了如果 GT 的建议正确,原告不用蒙受这笔损失,有关的损失就应该是 GT 责任范围内可预见的损失。

上诉庭[(2019) EWCA Civ 40]同意一审法院错误偏离了应先去区分案件是归类“意见”或“信息”案件,但结论正确,此案件的正确归类是属于“信息”案件。

上诉庭还判一审法官错误认定如果 GT 的建议正确,原告就可以避免蒙受有关损失。Hamblen 大法官说要证明原告提前终止利率掉期合约蒙受损失,必须证明原告继续持有有关合约是比提前终止有好处,但原告没有证明这一点。因此上诉庭驳回了原告的上诉请求。

原告再上诉到了最高院,最高院的 7 位大法官一致决定支持了原告 3200 万英镑损失索赔的上诉请求,但原告要承担 50% 的共同疏忽责任。主要原因是 GT 在提供建议时是完全知道原告需要专业意见的目的,GT 疏忽的建议令原告不仅达不到目的还蒙受了这笔损失。可先节录最高院的 Hodge 与 Sales 勋爵的总结如下:“In summary,our view is that(i) the scope of duty question should be located within a general conceptual framework in the law of the tort of negligence;(ii) the scope of the duty of care assumed by a professional adviser is governed by the purpose of the duty,judged on an objective basis by reference to the purpose for which the advice is being given …;(iii) …,the distinction between ‘advice’ cases and ‘information’ cases drawn by Lord Hoffmann in his speech in SAAMCO should not be treated as a rigid straitjacket;and,following on from this,(iv) counterfactual analysis of the kind proposed by Lord Hoffmann in SAAMCO should be regarded only as a tool to cross – check the result given pursuant to analysis of the purpose of the duty at(ii),but one which is subordinate to that analysis and which should not supplant or subsume it.”

笔者在以下的段落会分析最高院的最后决定是如何支持与调整了主导这方面法律地位的 SAAMCO 原则,并加上自己的一些想法。

9.1.1　总结之一

最高院认同 SAAMCO 先例后才带出的“责任范围”的概念应该被纳入考虑疏忽侵权的框架内,要先考虑被告在法律或合约中应该对原告承担什么责任或风险,之后再分析与计算违反此责任所带来的损失。

这样,传统对疏忽侵权的考虑与分析的四个方面问题,[23]显然需要有所增加。Hodge 与 Sales 勋爵在 Manchester Building Society v. Grant Thornton UK LLP(2021)

---

〔23〕　根据传统对疏忽侵权的分析,责任成立需要证明:(1)有小心谨慎责任(a duty of care)的情况出现;(2)违反了该责任(breach of duty of care);(3)这不谨慎的言行与主张的损失有因果关系(a casual connection between the careless conduct and the damage);(4)这种损失的类别是可预见的(the existence of a particular kind of damage to the claimant is not so unforeseeable as to be too remote)。这在本书第一章之2.4.2段有介绍,也可参阅《Clerk and Lindsell on Torts》(2020 年,第23 版)一书之7 – 04段。

UKSC 20 最高院先例中总结对疏忽侵权的分析需要考虑以下的六个问题:

"...it is helpful to analyse the place of the scope of duty principle in the tort of negligence in the following way. When a claimant seeks damages from a defendant in the tort of negligence, a series of questions arise:

1) Is the harm (loss, injury and damage) which is the subject matter of the claim actionable in negligence? (**the actionability question**)

2) **What are the risks of harm to the claimant against which the law imposes on the defendant a duty to take care**? (**the scope of duty question**)

3) Did the defendant breach his or her duty by his or her act or omission? (**the breach question**)

4) Is the loss for which the claimant seeks damages the consequence of the defendant's act or omission? (**the factual causation question**)

5) Is there a sufficient nexus between a particular element of the harm for which the claimant seeks damages and the subject matter of **the defendant's duty of care as analysed at stage 2 above**? (**the duty nexus question**)

6) Is a particular element of the harm for which the claimant seeks damages irrecoverable because it is **too remote**, or because there is a **different effective cause** (including novus actus interveniens) in relation to it or because the claimant has mitigated his or her loss or has **failed to avoid loss** which he or she could reasonably have been expected to avoid? (**the legal responsibility question**)

Application of this analysis gives the value of the claimant's claim for damages in accordance with the principle that the law in awarding damages seeks, so far as money can, to place the claimant in the position he or she would have been in absent the defendant's negligence."(加黑部分是笔者的强调)

其中,(2)的"Scope of duty"就需要在损失计算前考虑。而(5)的"duty nexus"就需要损失与(2)的责任范围有足够的联系。这等于认同 SAAMCO 原则。

9.1.2 总结之二

专业人士的责任范围是取决于他们被委任的目的,也是为了达到这些目的他们需要提供小心谨慎的服务。这是许多这方面的重要先例中的说法,可更好与更直接去称为"责任的目的"(purpose of the duty)。在 SAAMCO 先例中,被告估价师的责任是对房屋估值,而估价师也合理知道估值的目的是保证原告银行对作出的贷款有足够的担保,也知道自己提供的信息或意见必须正确以保障原告免受损害。所以,估价师高估房屋价值的过错与疏忽只对担保不够的部分负责。

Hodge 与 Sales 勋爵说:

"In our respectful opinion, the scope of duty question can and should be approached in a more straightforward way ... In our view, the scope of the duty of care assumed by a professional adviser **is governed by the purpose of the duty**,judged on an objective basis by reference to the reason why the advice is being given(and,as is often the position,including in the present case,paid for). ...

The other leading authorities confirm that this is the proper approach. All the speeches in Caparo emphasised that the scope of the auditor's duty of care in that case was to be derived from an examination of the purpose served by the duty to audit the accounts of the company. ...

... Therefore,in our view,in the case of negligent advice given by a professional adviser one looks to see**what risk the duty was supposed to guard against and then looks to see whether the loss suffered represented the fruition of that risk**."(加黑部分是笔者的强调)

在 Manchester Building Society v. Grant Thornton UK LLP(2021)UKSC 20 最高院先例中,最高院认定原告向 GT 寻求专业意见的目的与这个建议对原告决定建立终身抵押贷款与利率掉期协议之间的套期关系至关重要的原因,是套期保值会计对原告满足立法的资本要求的影响。使用套期保值会计可以使原告在满足立法的资本要求的基础上,进行原本不可以的交易。原告的目的也是 GT 知道的,在这种情况下,原告为了满足立法的资本要求被迫提前终止利率掉期合约造成的损失应该在 GT 的责任范围与责任的目的之内。Hodge 与 Sales 勋爵说:"But for the purposes of analysing whether the loss suffered by the society fell within the scope of the duty of care owed by Grant Thornton we think it is important to have regard to the commercial reason,as appreciated by Grant Thornton,why advice about this was being sought and why this was fundamental to the society's decision to engage in the business of matching swaps and mortgages. That reason was the impact of hedge accounting on the society's regulatory capital position. Use of hedge accounting allowed the society to make the assessment that,in terms of the constraints imposed on it by the regulatory capital requirements to which it was subject,it had the capacity to proceed with that business whereas otherwise it did not. In our opinion,reference to the reason the advice was sought and given is important,because that is the foundation for the conclusion that the purpose of the advice was to deal with the issue of hedge accounting in the context of its implications for the society's regulatory capital. It is not in dispute that the loss in issue formed part of the society's 'basic loss' flowing from Grant Thornton's negligent advice. Examination of the purpose for which that advice was given shows that the loss fell within the scope of their duty of care. Having regard to that purpose,we consider that Grant Thornton in 2006 in effect informed the society that hedge accounting could enable it to have sufficient capital resources to carry on the business of matching swaps and mortgages,when in reality it did not."

9.1.3 总结之三

SAAMCO先例带出来的第一类“信息”与第二类“意见”两类案件被批评太僵化，不少千变万化案情的案件是需要去硬套，好像是一件紧身衣（straight jacket）束缚了发展。因为大部分案件都不是处于光谱两端的极端案件，而是处于中间，所以可以看到很多先例在上诉过程中不断被推翻。就像在此先例中，上诉庭的节录是“信息”的案件，而原告以这应是“意见”的案件上诉。最终这方面的法律被最高院否定，转而要在不同的案件中分析责任的目的是什么，与违反责任带来的后果与损失，也就是不再理会与分类区分专业人士给的是信息还是意见。

Hodge与Sales勋爵说：“In our view, for the purposes of accurate analysis, rather than starting with the distinction between ‘advice’ and ‘information’ cases and trying to shoe-horn a particular case into one or other of these categories, **the focus should be on identifying the purpose to be served by the duty of care assumed by the defendant**: see section (ii) above. Ascribing a case to one or other of these categories seems to us to be a conclusion to be drawn as a result of examination of that prior question.”（加黑部分是笔者的强调）

9.1.4 总结之四

有关Hoffmann勋爵在SAAMCO先例中创新的“SAAMCO反事实”（SAAMCO counterfactual）分析，最高院说在Hughes-Holland v. BPE Solicitors（2017）UKSC 21最高院先例中，Sumption勋爵已经指出这只是为了区分被告疏忽提供错误信息导致的损失（也就是被告责任范围内的损失）与原告订立合约导致的所有损失（也就是传统的“要不是”测试）。Hoffmann勋爵在SAAMCO先例中创立这个说法也只是为了强调责任范围的重要性。“SAAMCO反事实”分析对决定是“信息”或是“意见”的案件分类没有帮助，而且还有通过设定“反事实”的情况操纵是否属于被告疏忽导致的损失的危险。所以，最高院认为“SAAMCO反事实”分析只是一个对照核查的工具，不应该被认为可以替代对责任范围与责任的目的的分析，也不一定在部分案件可以适用。[24]

Hodge与Sales勋爵说：“As Lord Sumption said in Hughes-Holland … this is ‘simply a tool for giving effect to the distinction between (i) loss flowing from the fact that as a result of the defendant's negligence the information was wrong [ie the loss falling within the scope of the defendant's duty] and (ii) loss flowing from the decision to enter into the transaction at all [ie by application of a simple ‘but for’ test]’. As so explained, it is clear that the use and, in particular, the correct framing of the counterfactual scenario follows from the prior question, which is, what purpose was the duty of care assumed by the defendant supposed to serve? In that regard, we agree … that the counter-

〔24〕 见本章之7段。

factual test may be regarded as a useful cross – check in most cases, but that it should not be regarded as replacing the decision that needs to be made as to the scope of the duty of care…Another problem associated with counterfactual analysis of this kind is the danger of manipulation, in argument, of the parameters of the counterfactual world. Lord Leggatt points out … that the counterfactual test can yield the right result if it is properly applied. However, the more one moves from the comparatively straightforward type of situation in the valuer cases, as illustrated by SAAMCO, the greater scope there may be for abstruse and highly debatable arguments to be deployed about how the counterfactual world should be conceived.

9.2　案例之二:Khan v. Meadows(2021)UKSC 21 最高院先例

Khan v. Meadows 最高院先例与 Manchester Building Society v. Grant Thornton UK LLP(2021)UKSC 20 最高院先例是在同一天作出判决。该先例的案情相对简单,涉及原告 Meadows 夫人因为她的侄女出生后被诊断患有血友病(haemophilia)[25]而担心自己与自己想生的子女。所以去见了一位普通科医生看自己是否有血友病的基因,并抽血作了检测。之后另去咨询了本案的被告 Khan 医生(也是普通科医生),并被 Khan 医生告知血液检测一切正常。这导致 Meadows 夫人安心认为她如果生孩子是不会有得血友病的风险。但其实是否有血友病基因,靠血液检验是查不出来的,是需要 Khan 医生转介去另一位血液专科医生(haematologist)做基因检测才能发觉。结果不久 Meadows 夫人怀孕并生下儿子取名 Adejuwon,但不幸被诊断为患上遗传而且是严重的血友病。更不幸的是,他也被诊断患上自闭症(autism)。[26] 这可说是"屋漏偏逢连夜雨",因为自闭症会令治疗血友病变得更加复杂与困难。例如,他不会把流血或疼痛的感觉告诉母亲,他不会自我照顾例如准时打针与吃药,他也不能自力更生,更不说是去工作谋生了。

Meadows 夫人因此向 Khan 医生提起诉讼,指称如果 Khan 医生没有疏忽并能够及时通过正确的基因检测发觉她带有血友病基因,她是不会怀孕并生下 Adejuwon。Khan 医生也承认责任,所以争议只在将来要长期照顾与治疗 Adejuwon 的赔偿金额。双方同意针对血友病,只需要 140 万英镑,而自闭症是昂贵多了,高达 760 万英镑,所以如果法院判 Khan 医生要全部负责,总共有 900 万英镑。

---

〔25〕 血友病(haemophilia)是基因疾病,患者由于基因异常,身体无法制造足够的凝血因子,因而发生持续性出血症状,并危及生命。血友病目前尚无法完全根治,主要的治疗方法仍是以注射凝血因子为主,再搭配药物治疗。有血友病家族史的孕妇在怀孕期可接受诊断,籍以判定胎儿是否为血友病患者。在产检时,医生会视情况采用不同检验方法。怀孕 10 周时为绒毛采样术;怀孕满 16 周羊水较多时,可做羊膜穿刺术;而怀孕 18 周时会以脐带血采样,务求取得胎儿的染色体,进行基因检测。

〔26〕 自闭症(autism)也是影响终身的发展障碍,主因是神经系统失调影响大脑功能所造成。也是与遗传有关,概率是 1 万新生儿中有 10 ~ 15 例。自闭症行为包括社交反应差、语言沟通能力差、兴趣狭窄、经常与外事隔绝不理会外界发生的事情,需要特殊教育。

显然,争议是 Khan 医生愿意赔偿针对血友病的治疗费用,因为是在自己的责任范围内,即 Meadows 夫人就是为此事去看医生,希望找出她是否带有血友病的基因。但责任范围并不包括 Adejuwon 患自闭症的风险。她当时没有怀孕,看医生不是为了咨询有关怀孕的风险,包括新生儿会否有自闭症的风险,更谈不上 Khan 医生曾在这方面有过任何疏忽或过错。另外这两种病是没有相互关系,不会因为有血友病而提升自闭症的几率。

所以以“SAAMCO 反事实”分析,在不改变 Adejuwon 已经出生这个无可扭转的事实下,假设 Khan 医生在当时的咨询中是没有犯错与疏忽,也就是告诉 Meadows 夫人她不带有血友病基因是正确的话,会有什么结果。答案应是明显,就是 Adejuwon 会被生下并患有自闭症。这样,就明确显示自闭症与 Khan 医生的疏忽无关。正如 Burrows 勋爵说:“Applying the SAAMCO counterfactual test as a cross-check, it supports a decision that the autism losses were outside the scope of the doctor's duty of care. If we ask the question, would the claimant have suffered the same loss had the information /advice been true, the answer is ‘yes’ as regards the autism losses (so that the scope of the duty of care does not extend to the recovery of the autism losses) but ‘no’ as regards the haemophiliac losses (so that the scope of the duty of care does extend to the recovery of the haemophiliac losses). This is because had the information/advice that the claimant was not a carrier of haemophilia been correct, the claimant would still have given birth to an autistic child but would not have given birth to a child with haemophilia. Applying the counterfactual test therefore supports the view that the autism losses were outside the scope of the doctor's duty of care.”

但 Meadows 夫人是索赔 900 万英镑的赔偿,在一审法院以“要不是”测试,判 Khan 医生要负责赔偿 Meadows 夫人这笔损失,因为“要不是 Khan 医生疏忽,就不会生下 Adejuwon”。

但 Khan 医生上诉去了上诉庭,一审判决被推翻。上诉庭判决被最高院介绍为:“... the focus of the consultation, advice and appropriate testing was directed to the issue of whether Ms Meadows was a carrier of the haemophilia gene and not the wider issue of whether she should become pregnant. The scope of duty test which Lord Hoffmann identified in SAAMCO was determinative of the issues ... In short, Dr Khan was not liable for the costs associated with Adejuwon's autism because that type of loss was not within the scope of the risks which she had undertaken to protect Ms Meadows against and therefore was not within the scope of her duty of care. The purpose of the consultation was to put Ms Meadows in a position to make an informed decision in relation to a child which she conceived which was discovered to carry the haemophilia gene. Secondly, the doctor was liable for the risk of the mother giving birth to a child with haemophilia because there had been no foetal testing and consequently no termination of the pregnancy. But the mother would take the risks of all other potential difficulties of the pregnancy and birth, both to herself and to her child. The third factor, applying the SAAMCO counterfactual …, is that if the information which the defendant imparted had been correct, ie that Ms Meadows did not carry the haemophilia gene, the result would have been that the child would have been born with autism. ”

本先例的重点是 SAAMCO 原则是否适用在医疗案件,毕竟这种案件在本质上与商业案件只涉及纯经济损失很不一样,会延伸去人身伤亡等考虑,最高院判责任的目的的分析同样适用在医疗案件,并支持了上诉庭的判决。

9.3 案例之三:Charles B Lawrence & Associates v. Intercommercial Bank Ltd (2021) UKPC 30 枢密院先例

此枢密院案例是紧跟着 Manchester Building Society v. Grant Thornton UK LLP (2021) UKSC 20 与 Khan v. Meadows (2021) UKSC 21 最高院先例,所以去独立介绍。案情涉及与 SAAMCO 先例一样的估价师把土地价值高估,把一块只能用做发展住宅的土地错误当作商业土地去估值,这块只是价值 237.5 万美元的土地被高估为 1500 万美元。

原告银行根据借款人 R 提供的这份估值报告贷款 300 万美元。R 作为债务的担保人也把他委任被告估值的这块土地抵押给银行。但结果是 R 一分钱都没有归还,迫使银行委任接管人(receiver)去把抵押的土地收回来拍卖,但发觉最高的竞标也只是 200 万美元,但即使是愿意亏本出售(土地应值 237.5 万美元)也不能,因为银行发觉了 R 实际不拥有这块土地的产权(title)。这导致银行向疏忽没有查清土地产权的律师起诉,并在不久后双方以 240 万美元达成和解。

银行同时以疏忽侵权起诉被告估价师,这带来损失如何计算的问题。在责任方面,一审的特立尼达(Trinidad)法院已经认定估价师在土地估值有疏忽。一审判被告要对银行所有的损失负责,再减去和解所得的 240 万美元,金额约是 236 万美元。

之后上诉到特立尼达上诉庭,除了对利率下调外,主要被改变的是扣除了 20% 的损失分摊,要银行自己承担。这是因为银行有疏忽,没有派人去该土地视察,否则就可以看到问题,如有其他人占用土地。这样,银行的损失调整后变为是 207 万美元。

之后被告上诉到枢密院,指一审与上诉庭在法律方面犯错,没有适用 SAAMCO 原则计算损失。在此案例中,是分别有两方面的损失:(1)是错误高估了土地价格,这是在被告自愿承担小心谨慎责任的范围内;(2)是土地产权有缺陷,这部分并非被告的责任范围。

这表示被告的损失计算应是借贷的 300 万美元减去土地的真正价值的 237.5 万美元,等于是 62.5 万美元。这笔损失去扣除 20% 后再加上利息,应该赔偿的是 833,204 美元。

被告的损失计算被枢密院一致支持。Burrows 勋爵说:

"... it has been made clear by the Supreme Court in Manchester Building Society v Grant Thornton UK LLP and Khan v Meadows that, **in determining the scope of the duty of care, it is particularly important to consider the purpose of the advice or information being given**. As Lord Hodge and Lord Sales said in their leading judgment in the former case (agreed with by Lord Reed, Lady Black and Lord Kitchin) [2021] UKSC 20 at [4] 'the scope of the duty of care assumed by a professional adviser is governed by the purpose of the duty, judged on an objective basis by reference to the purpose for which the advice is being given ...'.

And again, at [17], they said 'in the case of negligent advice given by a professional adviser one looks to see what risk the duty was supposed to guard against and then looks to see whether the loss suffered represented the fruition of that risk'.

Similarly, in their leading judgment inKhan v Meadows ..., Lords Hodge and Sales (with whom Lord Reed, Lady Black and Lord Kitchin agreed) said at [41]: 'In addressing the scope of duty question in the context of the provision of advice or information, the court seeks to identify the purpose for which that advice or information was given. Where the claimant has asked for advice about a risk or about a proposed activity which involved that risk, the court asks: "what was the risk which the advice or information was intended and was reasonably understood to address?".'

It is clear, not least from the assumptions expressly specified by Lawrence(被告估价师) in the valuation report, that **the purpose of Lawrence's report was to value the property on the assumption that there was good legal title to the land. It was not the purpose of Lawrence's report to advise on, or give information about, the title to the land**. It is clear that the bank was not looking to Lawrence's report to advise on, or give information about, **the title to the land**. That **was a matter for a lawyer not a valuer**.

The board(枢密院) is therefore seeking to exclude from **the total loss factually caused to the bank by Lawrence's negligence that element of the loss that is outside the scope of Lawrence's duty of care because it is attributable to the defect in title rather than to the overvaluation being based on commercial not residential use**. That exclusion is satisfactorily achieved on these facts by taking as the starting point the loan made ($3 million) and deducting the actual residential value of the land at the date of the loan on the assumption that there was good title to the land ($2,375,000). ...

... **Comparing Khan v Meadows to the facts of this case, one can see that, just as the haemophilia loss, but not the autism loss, was within the scope of the doctor's duty of care** so here the commercial, rather than residential, overvaluation loss, but not the defective title loss, was within the scope of the valuer's duty of care. And in each case that conclusion follows from the purpose of the advice or information given by the professional and hence the risk that was being guarded against."

Burrows 勋爵认为本案与银行和律师达成的关于土地产权的和解无关,不应扯在一起造成混乱,这正是特立尼达一审与上诉庭犯的毛病。这和解的金额,明显没有超出银行在土地产权问题的损失,律师也不会笨到去多赔,所以不存在双重赔偿的担心,更是不应扯进来,说:"What is the relevance, if any, of the Bank's settlement with its conveyance attorneys LC ... for \$2.4m? ...Once one correctly applies the scope of duty principle, It can be seen that the settlement with LC is irrelevant. This is because the loss attributable to the defective title was outside the scope of Lawrence(被告) duty of care. ... There is no prospect of doubt recovery, given that it is not suggested that the sum received from LC exceeded the loss properly attributable to the defective title. The fact that the Bank managed to obtain a settlement with LC a in relation to its negligence in respect of the defective title is, therefore, irrelevant."(加黑部分是笔者的强调)

这个先例也可以看出 SAAMCO 原则并不是以传统方式计算损失并加上一个封顶,因为在此先例所谓的"SAAMCO Cap"超过 1250 万美元,而以传统损失计算出来的损失仅为 236 万美元。但是 Burrows 勋爵强调被告的责任范围只是提供正确的估价,因此只有估价错误令原告没有足够的担保导致的损失才与被告的责任范围有关联,即借贷的 300 万美元与土地真正价值的 237.5 万美元之间的差额。

Burrows 勋爵也批评了反事实分析可能带来的混乱与错误,并再次强调了反事实分析只能作为再次确认专业人士的责任范围的工具,并非在所有案件都适用:

"The Supreme Court in Manchester Building Society v Grant Thornton UK LLP(at paras 23 – 27) and Meadows v Khan(at para 53) explained that the counterfactual test, put forward by Lord Hoffmann in SAAMCO, should be regarded as a flexible and useful cross – check for deciding on the scope of the duty of care in most but not all cases. In applying the counterfactual test(and extending it to advice as well as information in line with the Supreme Court's criticism of that distinction), one asks, in summary, would the claimant still have suffered the same loss if the information or advice had been true? If the answer is 'yes', the scope of the duty does not extend to the recovery of that loss. If the answer is 'no', the scope of the duty does extend to the recovery of that loss.

Applying that counterfactual test to the facts of this case would contradict our view, set out above, that the defective title loss was outside the scope of Lawrence's duty of care. Had Lawrence's valuation of \$15m been correct, the Bank would still have entered into the loan, taking the mortgage over the Land as security, but would not have suffered the same(or indeed any) loss. This is because, as the Land would have been worth \$15m (assuming no defect in title), the Bank would have had adequate security to cover the guarantor's default in repaying the loan. It may be that one could modify the counterfactual in order to reach the 'correct' result but, in our view, this merely serves to reinforce the point made by the Supreme Court that the counterfactual is of second – order importance as regards establishing the scope of the duty and is a helpful cross – check of that scope in most but not all cases. This is one of the cases where it is unhelpful. ”

10. 新冠疫情与责任的目的分析

新冠疫情席卷全球期间，经济崩溃，无数大小公司无法生存与/或遭受庞大损失。而新冠疫情前订立的交易（不论是投资收购还是其他），也几乎可以肯定订约时的美好预期很难实现。过往多次由天灾人祸造成的经济危机后，蒙受严重损失的当事人肯定希望把这个无法预料的风险转嫁给其他人，不论是谁。第一个主要对象显然是交易的对手，但很多情况是有关合约赖不掉或为时已晚，如果硬来只会面对诉讼败诉或禁令等，令该当事人输得更惨。第二个转嫁风险的对象会是保险人，新冠疫情中也带来不少这方面的诉讼，如 Financial Conduct Authority v. Arch Insurance（UK Ltd）& Ors（2021）UKSC 1 最高院先例。但很多时候此路也行不通，毕竟许多交易是不会投保这种新冠疫情或相关风险，如瘟疫（pandemic）、疾病（disease）或检疫（quarantine）等，而投保了也往往只针对财产损失，而不是受保人的纯经济损失。这样，第三个转嫁风险的对象就会是对该交易提供信息、建议与意见的人士（都是对有关交易有专长的专业人士）如银行、投资顾问、会计师、交易律师、有关专家等，希望只要能够挑出他们的意见是对风险 A 有疏忽，结果有了不可预见的风险 B（也就是新冠疫情），提供该疏忽意见的人士仍要赔偿全部的损失，让当事人在损失赔偿的复原大原则下恢复到违约或侵权没有发生的地位，成功转移风险 B。这对当事人来说也很有吸引力，因为这些专业人士往往很有钱，也购买了责任保险并赔得起，所以可预期这场新冠疫情会带来大量在这方面的诉讼。

虽然最新的两个最高院先例已经调整了“SAAMCO 原则”，并替代为“责任范围”（scope of duty）与“责任的目的”（purpose of duty），也明确了在一开始的违约或侵权诉因就应去考虑，再分析导致的损失。也就是认同了 Hoffmann 勋爵在 SAAMCO 先例中说的这是分析疏忽侵权的更好的起点（starting point），可以说除了排除了硬性划分“信息”与“意见”，以利在不同案件更有弹性与灵活地处理外，与 SAAMCO 原则在精神与本质上没有区别。

但更有弹性与灵活处理每个不同案情的案件会否令“no transaction”与“successful transaction”的区分复活，毕竟这更符合普遍的思维方法？但从 Khan v. Meadows（2021）UKSC 21 最高院先例的判决看，并非如此。因为 Khan 医生如果作出了正确的诊断意见，Meadows 女士是不会怀孕的。这应是“no transaction”类别的案件，但这不影响最高院的重点仍是在分析 Khan 医生的责任范围与责任的目的。

这样看来，专业人士很需要在被委任时通过合约条文明确责任范围与责任的目的,并有证据证明。例如,交易律师就可以在他们的委任书(engagement/ retainer letter)中明确他们的责任范围与责任的目的。据知已经有一些跨国律师所在委任书中加上条文明示说明。另要小心律师与客户之间,会被假设前者对后者有“不当影响”(undue influence),所以在拟定委任书时要小心。另外,最好另加上一条禁止口头更改合约的“无口头修改条文”(No oral amendment clause)。[27] 当然,专业人士与律师在之后与客户的互动中也要言行一致,避免产生衡平法禁反言(equitable estoppel)[28] 等的争议。

11. 衡平救济是否适用 SAAMCO 原则/责任范围原则

SAAMCO 原则/责任范围原则是普通法对专业人士违反了小心谨慎责任时应该赔偿客户(或其他可预见会依赖的第三人)多少损失的法律过滤器。但这原则在衡平法是否适用,在稍后介绍的 Main v. Giambrone & Law(2017)EWCA Civ 1193 上诉庭先例与 LIV Bridging Finance Ltd v. EAD Solicitors LLP(2020)EWHC 1590(Ch)先例中有针对。

首先会涉及衡平法是因为部分专业人士经常会是商业信托(commercial trust)的受托人(trustee),这特别是事务律师(solicitors)。他们经常会在房屋(或其他财产)的买卖为客户买方(或融资银行)托管买卖的金钱,在完成交易时或其他双方同意下去支付给卖方(或按照委托人指示的其他人士)。这只是其中一个例子,还有许多其他情况如双方争议的金额或和解的金钱都会存放在作为受托人的律师处等。

如果作为受托人的律师违反信托,一般是错误支配了信托的金钱或财产,例如提前把钱交给了卖方,当然会也有较少发生的私下挪用的不诚实情况。受托人在责任方面是严格的,举证责任是在受托人去证明自己是诚实与合理等。在《Trustee Act 1925》之 S. 61 中说:“**Power to relieve trustee from personal liability.** If it appears to the court that a trustee, whether appointed by the court or otherwise, is or may be personally liable for any breach of trust, whether the transaction alleged to be a breach of trust

---

〔27〕 这类条文除非以书面形式修改合约,否则修改无效,以确保其合约规定的内容不会被后来在履行时的言行(往往事实真相双方当事人有不同版本)非正式修改并带来争议。这方面不展开讨论,近期重要的英国最高院先例是 Rock Advertising Ltd v. MWB Business Exchange Centres Ltd(2018)UKSC 24;之后有 NHS Commissioning Board v. Dr Manjul Vasant(2020)1 All ER(Comm)799;Great Dunmow Estates Ltd v. Crest Nicholson Operations Ltd(2020)2 All ER(Comm)97;James v. Hertsmere BC(2020)1 WLR 3606;Kabab – Ji SAL(Lebanon)v. Kout Food Group(Kuwait)(2020)EWCA Civ 6;CIS General Insurance Limited v. IBM United Kingdom Limited(2021)EWHC 347(TCC)等先例。另有新加坡稍不同判法的 Charles Lim Teng Siang v. Hong Choon Hau(2021)SGCA 43 上诉庭先例。

〔28〕 见笔者《合约的履行、弃权与禁反言》一书第四章与第五章的介绍。

occurred before or after the commencement of this Act, but has acted honestly and reasonably, and ought fairly to be excused for the breach of trust and for omitting to obtain the directions of the court in the matter in which he committed such breach, then the court may relieve him either wholly or partly from personal liability for the same."

违反信托也带来衡平救济（equitable remedies），目的是复原（restitution）与复位（restoration）因违反信托而令信托人（trustor）失去的财产。在赔偿大原则下，如果财产无法去实质复原，就要以金钱作为"衡平赔偿"（equitable compensation）。这可节录在 Auden McKenzie（Pharma Division）Limited v. Amit Patel（2019）EWCA Civ 2291 上诉庭先例中，David Richards 大法官说："Equitable compensation is the personal remedy（as opposed to a tracing or proprietary remedy）available against trustees, or others in a fiduciary position, whose acts or omissions amount to a breach of trust or fiduciary duty. Breaches of duty may take many forms, but in broad terms they are often with good reason analysed as falling within one of three main categories: **first**, transactions involving the unauthorised payment or disposal of or damage to trust assets, causing loss to the trust; **second**, breaches of duties of loyalty, involving the trustee in making profits at the expense of the trust or by the use of information or opportunities available to the trustee in that capacity; **third, breaches of duties of skill and care, resulting in loss to the trust**. In the case of breaches in the second category, an account of profits may be the appropriate remedy, and is the only remedy where the trust could not itself have made the profit."（加黑部分是笔者的强调）

看来专业人士违反信托责任应该属于第三种。计算衡平救济在本质与精神上与普通法以金钱赔偿损失的救济是一致，但两者在计算的原则上有很大的不同。这可先节录 Browne - Wilkinson 勋爵在 Target Holdings Ltd v. Redfern（1996）AC 421 贵族院先例中说：

"At common law there are two principles fundamental to the award of damages. First, that the defendant's wrongful act must cause the damage complained of. Second, that the plaintiff is to be put 'in the same position as he would have been in if he had not sustained the wrong for which he is now getting his compensation or reparation' ... Although, as will appear, in many ways equity approaches liability for making good a breach of trust from a different starting point, in my judgment those two principles are applicable as much in equity as at common law. **Under both systems liability is fault - based: the defendant is only liable for the consequences of the legal wrong he has done to the plaintiff and to make good the damage caused by such wrong**. He is not responsible for damage not caused by his wrong or to pay by way of compensation more than the loss suffered from such wrong. **The detailed rules of equity as to causation and the quantification of loss differ**, at least ostensibly, **from those applicable at common law. But**

the principles underlying both systems are the same. …

The equitable rules of compensation for breach of trust have been largely developed in relation to such traditional trusts, where the only way in which all the beneficiaries' rights can be protected is to restore to the trust fund what ought to be there. In such a case **the basic rule is that a trustee in breach of trust must restore or pay to the trust estate either the assets which have been lost to the estate by reason of the breach or compensation for such loss.** Courts of Equity did not award damages but, acting in personam, ordered the defaulting trustee to restore the trust estate … **If specific restitution of the trust property is not possible, then the liability of the trustee is to pay sufficient compensation to the trust estate to put it back to what it would have been had the breach not been committed**: …, the trustee is liable to make good that loss to the trust estate if, but for the breach, such loss would not have occurred: … Thus, the common law rules of remoteness of damage and causation do not apply. However there does have to be some causal connection between the breach of trust and the loss to the trust estate for which compensation is recoverable, viz. the fact that the loss would not have occurred but for the breach: …

But **the basic equitable principle applicable to breach of trust is that the beneficiary is entitled to be compensated for any loss he would not have suffered but for the breach**…

…the fact that there is an accrued cause of action as soon as the breach is committed does not in my judgment mean that the quantum of the compensation payable is ultimately fixed as at the date when the breach occurred. **The quantum is fixed at the date of judgment at which date… the compensation is assessed** at the figure then necessary to put the trust estate or the beneficiary back into the position it would have been in had there been no breach."（加黑部分是笔者的强调）

上述节录带来的问题是，违反信托与疏忽侵权或违反合约的小心谨慎责任是两码事，正如在 Main v. Giambrone & Law 上诉庭先例中，Jackson 大法官说："It follows that the liability of a trustee for breach of trust, even **where the trust arises in the context of a commercial transaction which is otherwise regulated by contract, is not generally the same as a liability in damages for tort or breach of contract.**[29] Of course, the aim of equitable compensation is to compensate: that is to say, provide a monetary equivalent of what has been lost as a result of a breach of duty. At that level of generality, it has the same aim as most awards of damages for tort or breach of contract. Equally,

〔29〕 可见 Target Holdings Ltd v. Redfern（1996）AC 421 贵族院先例与 AIB Group（UK）Plc v. Mark Redler & Co（2014）UKSC 58 最高院先例。

since the concept of loss necessarily involves the concept of causation, and that concept in turn inevitably involves a consideration of the necessary connection between the breach of duty and a postulated consequence (and therefore of such questions as whether a consequence flows 'directly' from the breach of duty, and whether loss should be attributed to the conduct of third parties, or to the conduct of the person to whom the duty is owed), there are some structural similarities between the assessment of equitable compensation and the assessment of common law damages. Those structural similarities do not however entail that the relevant rules are identical; ..."

而在普通法对赔偿大原则的损失计算的限制,如损失的遥远性与因果关系,特别是普通法的"违约一天计算损失"规则(breach date rule),也不完全适用在衡平赔偿。这带来的疑问是普通法发展起来的 SAAMCO 原则/责任范围原则是否适用在衡平赔偿的计算。而对原告的客户而言,会否对被告的律师以违反信托以取得衡平赔偿的救济会比违反合约的小心谨慎责任与/或疏忽侵权以索赔普通法的损失更为优越?

11.1 Main v. Giambrone & Law(2017)EWCA Civ 1193 上诉庭先例

在 Main v. Giambrone & Law 上诉庭先例中,被告是一家在英国与意大利均有分所的意大利律师事务所,经开发商的推荐,代表上百位买方向开发商购买位于意大利的度假屋期房。在每一份委任函(engagement/retainer letter)中,被告都声称自己专长于处理意大利不动产交易和购买期房交易,将会对有关的期房项目完成独立的尽职调查,并确保开发商向买方提供意大利立法强制要求的银行担保,以在开发商破产清盘的情况下也可以退还定金以保障买方的利益。之后被告向客户/买方出具了调查报告,并表示审核了购房合约。在购房合约下,买方向被告支付了定金,被告写信向买方确认在收到开发商签署的购房合约与银行担保后,才会将定金转给开发商。但实际上被告根本没有收到开发商提供的符合立法要求的银行担保就将定金转给了开发商。之后在只有一小部分房屋建好时,意大利警方怀疑这个地产项目是爱尔兰共和军(IRA)与意大利黑手党用来洗钱的,遂查封了整个地产项目。买方虽然取消了合约,但并无可执行的银行担保从而取回定金,所以对被告开始了集体诉讼。

上诉庭支持了一审法院[(2015) EWHC 1946 (QB)]的判决,驳回了被告的上诉。针对"衡平赔偿",双方同意即使原告拥有银行的担保,但银行仅在开发商破产时才需履行担保人的责任,而在本案中只是地产项目被查封,开发商并没有破产。因此,被告指称原告的地位不会因取得银行担保而有任何改变。但原告认为,被告的责任不是主动获得担保,而是在没有获得担保时不应将钱给开发商。因此,如果不是被告违反了信托责任与合约责任,这笔钱根本就不会给开发商,原告也就不会蒙受损失。Jackson 大法官支持了原告的主张,说:

"Let me now apply the principles emerging from those authorities. The first task is to identify the duty which has been breached or the content of the obligation which has not been performed. Mr Flenley(被告代表大律师)says that the duty or obligation was to procure guarantees which complied with Decree 122. Ms Bhaloo and Mr Majumdar(两位都是原告代表大律师)say that it was the duty of the developers, not the solicitors, to provide compliant guarantees. The duty or obligation of the solicitors was to receive deposits from purchasers and to hold that money as custodians until the developers provided compliant guarantees.

On this issue I accept the submissions of(原告). ... It was not the function of Giambrone to liaise with the providers of the guarantees. Giambrone had no input into the drafting of the guarantees or any of the other formalities under Italian law. Giambrone' s role was to receive whatever guarantees the developers provided and to check whether or not they complied with Decree 122. If(and only if)the guarantees did comply, then the solicitors were under a duty to release the deposits. …

In the circumstances which unfolded in the present case, I would characterise**the solicitors' obligation as an obligation to act as custodians of the deposit monies indefinitely**. Compliant guarantees never appeared. Therefore Giambrone should have remained as custodians of the deposit monies until the preliminary contracts were rescinded, and then paid those monies back to their clients.

… In the present case **the trust was part of the machinery for the performance of the solicitors' contract of retainer**. Giambrone's breach of contract consisted of wrongfully paying out deposit monies which it had undertaken to keep safe. The contractual measure of damages is the amount of the deposits, because those monies have now vanished. This is **a case where equitable compensation and contractual damages run in tandem.** "(加黑部分是笔者的强调)

针对 SAAMCO 原则,上诉庭判这是一个"意见"类的案件,所以被告要承担原告所有的损失。这可节录上诉庭 Jackson 大法官的判词如下:"The claimants were buying properties in Italy and had no knowledge of Italian law and conveyancing procedures. Giambrone decided what information the claimants needed and provided that information to them … Giambrone were(albeit imperfectly)guiding the whole decision - making process. They were telling the clients what protection they needed, what sums they should pay out and when it was safe to pay those sums out. … in my view **this is a category 2 case**. Obviously the claimants decided whether or not they wanted to buy holiday homes in Southern Italy. But having taken that primary decision, they put themselves into the hands of Giambrone as their experienced Anglo-Italian lawyers. "(加黑部分是笔者的强调)

但这方面有不同意见,因为律师通常只是对整个交易的特定部分提供法律服务与意见,在本章之 6.4 段已经引用了 Sumption 勋爵在 Hughes - Holland v. BPE Solicitors(2017)UKSC 21 最高院先例中的判词,批评了在 Bristol and West Building Society

v. Fancy & Jackson(a firm)(1997)4 All ER 582(Ch)先例与 Portman Building Society v. Bevan Ashford(a firm)(2000)PNLR 344 上诉庭先例判律师是第二类(category 2)提供的是“意见”。Sumption 勋爵认为即使律师违反小心谨慎的责任是十分严重与信息或意见对客户是否进行有关交易是十分关键,也不会把第一类变了为第二类。

在此先例中,显然案情显示被告 Giambrone 只是在买方支付了 3000 欧元订金后才被委任,被告也不可能对整个房屋买卖提供一些非意大利法律的服务与意见。至于 Jackson 大法官认定被告自愿承担更大的责任(much wider obligations),说是因为:“were telling the clients what protection they needed, what sums they should pay out and when it was safe to pay those sums out.”

但这种意见出自律师应是十分正常与一般,不应变为第二类“意见”的案件。会否是这先例显示律师在面对不熟悉与不了解当地情况的外国客户进行跨境交易时,小心谨慎的责任范围相比于面对本地客户或熟悉有关情况的客户会扩大。该先例也显示了虽然在做广告时自我吹嘘是很正常,但如果过分与没有在委任书中限制责任范围,就可能面对严重后果。在该先例中,会否也是因为被告不断强调自己是在英国执业的顶级意大利律所,在期房交易很有经验,保证会尽职调查等,而令买方认为被告所做的会超出简单的处理购房的有关法律手续?

11.2　LIV Bridging Finance Ltd v. EAD Solicitors LLP(2020)EWHC 1590 (Ch)先例

原告 LIV 是一家小型财务公司,主要经营短期商业贷款业务。被告 EAD 是一家律师事务所,在此先例涉及的 4 笔贷款(加起来约 80 万英镑)中代表原告。LIV 指称 EAD(通过雇员 Gorman 律师)违反了指示,在没有获得有关房地产的第一法定押记(first legal charge)作为担保的情况下就将钱出借给了借款人。之后借款人没有还款,原告也没有担保,LIV 以违反信托责任起诉 EAD,索赔贷款总金额扣除其中两笔已归还的部分加上根据合约利率计算出的利息总共约 90 万英镑并申请简易判决。

Halliwell 大法官说针对第二笔与第三笔贷款,EAD 是没有机会抗辩成功,因此作出简易判决。而第一笔与第四笔贷款因为已经归还了一部分,需要全面开庭审理应如何计算利息等的争议,因此没有成功申请到简易判决。

针对衡平救济是否适用 SAAMCO 原则,Halliwell 大法官跟从了 Main v. Giambrone & Law(2017)EWCA Civ 1193 上诉庭先例认为适用,要看 EAD 的责任范围也就是 EAD 扮演的角色到底是指导整个商业决策过程,还是只提供特定信息,[30] 如果

---

〔30〕 这 Main v. Giambrone & Law(2017)EWCA Civ 1193 先例与 LIV Bridging Finance Ltd v. EAD Solicitors LLP(2020)EWHC 1590(Ch)还在纠缠到底是“信息”或是“意见”类的案件是因为是在 Manchester Building Society v. Grant Thornton UK LLP(2021)UKSC 20 最高院先例认为更好与更直接应是分析“责任的目的”(无论是信息或是意见)之前。

是后者，原告就只能获得责任范围内的衡平赔偿，说："In Main v Giambrone & Law … the Court of Appeal were satisfied that, whilst the SAAMCO principle was applicable, it did not operate so as to limit or restrict the measure of damages recoverable. However, Jackson LJ's judgment must be treated as a persuasive statement of the law and, in quantifying the amounts, if any, to which LIV is entitled as equitable compensation, I must address the scope of EAD's duty and ask whether its role was to guide the decision-making process or merely to provide part of the material on which LIV was to rely. If it was the latter, equitable compensation must be limited to the ambit of the specific duty."

接下来针对 EAD 的角色，Halliwell 大法官说 EAD 只是根据指示获得第一法定押记，而并非指导整个商业决策过程，因此对于如果 LIV 获得第一法定押记仍会蒙受的损失就不用赔偿。但在此先例中，因为 EAD 没有提供证据证明如果 LIV 获得第一法定押记的担保仍会蒙受损失（如市场会大幅下跌导致房产价值下跌而不足以支付贷款），所以要赔偿第二与第三笔贷款的总额共 25 万英镑。Halliwell 大法官的判决可节录如下：

"EAD's role in the present case, was to implement（原告的）specific instructions and, pursuant to such instructions, to provide specific advice by confirming LIV had acquired a first charge over the relevant properties. ... in my judgment, this does not support any suggestion（被告）was expected to guide the whole decision – making process. Consistently, with Hughes-Holland v. BPE Solicitors... and Main v. Giambrone & Law ... equitable compensation is thus limited to the losses falling with the scope of EAD's narrower duty to obtain a first charge and confirm that it has been obtained. LIV is not entitled to recover all the losses that it would have sustained on the hypothesis LIV had, indeed, obtained a first charge over the relevant properties and EAD acted consistently with their instructions.

In the present case, LIV advanced the sums of £ 100,000 and £ 150,000 … under the Second and Third Loans without obtaining security. … It is correct that LIV is not entitled to recover losses that it would have sustained in the event that it had obtained a first charge … However, in thehypothetical event LIV had obtained a first charge, there is no reason to believe LIV would then have sustained a loss. There is no evidence, for example, to suggest that the market value of the properties was less than the amounts advanced or subsequently diminished so as to be less than those amounts. Since it is LIV's stated case that, before advancing funds,（原告）took steps to satisfy himself about the sale value and development costs of each property and LIV was aware that the loan to site value was intended to be less than 50%, it is inherently unlikely that the market value was less than the amounts advanced and it is thus for EAD to suggest at least some reason to the contrary. Whilst LIV bears the persuasive burden of proof, there is at least an evidential burden on EAD to show that the market value of the properties might have been less than the amount advanced to advance such a case. In the present case, EAD has failed to do so. In my judgment, LIV can thus be taken to have sustained losses under the Second and Third Loans of £ 100,000 and £ 150,000, amounting in total to some £ 250,000. ”

杨良宜 杨大明 杨大志 司嘉 贡航 王可心 | 著

合约的效力（下）

虚假陈述、错误、非法、胁迫等的影响

法律出版社
LAW PRESS · CHINA
北京

目　　录

第七章　错　　误

1. 错误的定义

"错误"(mistake)是一个十分通用的词语,被使用在不同的情况。《牛津字典》(Oxford English Dictionary)对"错误"的定义为:"a. A misconception about the meaning of something;a thing incorrectly done or thought;an error of judgment. … c. In generalised use:misapprehension,misunderstanding;error,misjudgment."

在 Phillips-Higgins v. Harper(1954)1 QB 411 上诉庭先例中,Pearson 大法官提到一些常见的有法律救济的错误的例子说:"Familiar examples are,first,money paid in consequence of a mistake:in such a case the mistake is made,in consequence of the mistake the money is paid,and the action is to recover that money back. Secondly,there may be a contract entered into in consequence of a mistake,and the action is to obtain the rescission or,in some cases,the rectification of such a contract. Thirdly,there may be an account settled in consequence of mistakes;if the mistakes are sufficiently serious there can be a reopening of the account."

错误的定义显然十分广泛,不是法律可以作出救济[就是会令有关合约自始无效(void ab initio)]的"可诉错误"(actionable/operative mistake)。在商业的范畴,一个合约的订立与在之后的履行,难免有一合约方会感觉到亏了或赚得不够,这可以是市场并非如订约时的预期而有了逆转,或是订约时因己方水平不够、欠缺经验、疏忽大意或判断错误去接受了不利的合约条件/条文。如果这些单方面错误都有法律救济,也就再也不会有合约约束的保障(security of contract)与"合约的神圣性"(sanctity of contracts)的说法,也会严重影响合约必须要严格履行的肯定性(certainty)与可预测性(predictability),并会影响依赖该合约的无辜第三人如融资银行、供应商、生产商等。这个大原则或大道理有无数的权威说法,在此只节录著名的有关错误的 Bell v. Lever Brothers Ltd(1932)AC 161 贵族院先例,Atkin 勋爵说:"It is of paramount importance that contracts should be observed,and that if parties honestly comply with the essentials of the formation of contracts — i. e. agree in the same terms on the same subject matter — they are bound,and must rely on the stipulations of the contract for protection from the effect of facts unknown to them … it is far greater importance that well established principles of contract should be maintained than that a particular hardship should be redressed;..."

本章针对的"错误"是可诉错误,指的是在订约时订约方在没有过错(fault)的情况下,单方面(unilateral)或共同/共享(common /shared)或本质上是单方面的相互(mutual[1])对当时某个特定的(specific)现存事实(existing fact)或法律(existing law)有了肯定/确信想法(positive state of mind),而这种想法是错误的(erroneous belief),如果在正确理解下是不会订立该合约的。但这仍是不够,因为错误会是针对次要的合约内容,而可诉错误针对的内容则必须是一个会令合约自始无效的根本性或严重的错误(fundamental or material mistake)。客观(objectively)看来订约双方是难说在足够了解合约条件下,你情我愿地同意了该合约,也就是达成一致想法(英文的"meeting of minds"或拉丁文的"consensus ad idem")。又或是,这错误理解导致订立的合约根本是空的或无法履行,典型的例子是双方在不知情下买卖根本不存在的特定货物,合约订立后即使想去履行也无法启动。这样,法律除了去把该合约视为自始无效外也没有其他办法。

这种订约时的错误可以令一个表面看来已经是生效的合约变为无效,因为法律承认并会协助执行的合约要求双方在订立合约时符合订约自由的大原则,完全自愿、自由,知道自己所订立的所有内容,包括合约的对手[不少合约会涉及信任与信心(trust and confidence)]、标的/目的、相互的承诺与责任等。但如果有了一个重大或根本性的错误理解或假设,特别不是由于错误方的过错、无知或健忘所带来的单方面错误,就表示这表面看来有效的合约有极大的缺陷,双方实质上没有真正达成一个有效的合约,法律也就会否定(negative)这种表面看来达成但实际并非如此的"一致想法"。

而另外一种订约时的错误是双方虽然达成了一致想法,但该一致想法是错误的,所以是共同/共享。合约的成立是不成问题,但由于这错误的理解或假设是重大与根本的,令合约的标的或目的变为空的或无法履行,这样,法律也需要将本来有效的合约废除(nullify)。反正无论是否定还是废除,结果都会令合约自始无效。这可节录《Misrepresentation, Mistake and Non-Disclosure》(2022 年,第 6 版)一书之 12 - 10 段说:"A ... distinction that can be drawn between different categories of mistake ... is be-

[1] 英文的"common mistake" /"shared mistake"与"mutual mistake"的区别是前者对同一件事情有共同错误理解,这同一件事情可以是双方以为买卖标的/货物持续存在(continuous existence),却不知道在订约时该货物实是已经灭失/全损。而后者的错误是对订立合约是否已经成立,或如果成立,是什么内容与条件,双方各有各的不同主观想法或订约意图,造成"鸡同鸭讲"的"相互误解"(cross purposes):在订约时是 A 想买鸡、B 以为 A 想买鸭,造成双方订约时想法根本没有一致。基本所有对合约订立的条件/条文有不同解释的争议,都会是这种错误,或可称为"相互错误"。在法院或仲裁庭客观解释与审理后,最终只会支持 A 或 B 的其中一位的主观想法。这样,相互错误本质上仍是单方面错误,是败诉的 A 或 B 的主观想法不被支持,相等于单方面对订立合约的内容有了错误理解。

tween mistakes which ‘negative’ the parties’ consent; and mistakes which ‘nullify’ the consent. A mistake ‘negatives’ consent if it prevents the parties from coming to any agreement: for example, they are at cross-purposes as to the very terms of the contract so that there is never a sufficient agreement for the contract to be formed. A mistake ‘nullifies’ consent if, although the parties reach agreement about the terms of the contract, that agreement was based on a sufficiently serious mistake to allow the mistaken party to say that he should not be bound by it. This difference in language therefore describes different ways in which the mistake operates, and different reasons for the contract being void.”

最后强调的是轻易令合约自始无效，让错误方复原(restitution)或恢复到原状(restitutio in integrum)，重新再来，只是免费吸取了一个教训，并不是好事，这也变为法律不鼓励商人在做决定时要小心谨慎。显然，在这个大原则考虑下，必须严格限制这种有法律救济的可诉错误，这特别是在更常会发生的单方面错误。这可先简单节录《Misrepresentation, Mistake and Non-Disclosure》(2022 年，第 6 版)一书之 12 - 01 段说：“We shall see that English law is reluctant to give remedies for mistake.”接下来的段节会解释英国法律如何局限或收窄法律承认与会给予救济的可诉错误。

2. 法律承认的不是对将来情况的估计错误

对将来的事实或法律“估计错误”就不严格可视为“错误”，更应是作出估计的当事人对将来无可避免会有的变化的判断，而将来的变化如果不如意，就是自己在作出估计时应该与自愿承担的风险。正如在 P. Birks 的《An Introduction to the Law of Restitution》(1985)一书之 147 页说：“A mistake as to the future, a misprediction, does not show that the plaintiff’s judgment was vitiated, only that as things turned out it was incorrectly exercised. A prediction is an exercise of judgment. To act on the basis of a prediction is to accept the risk of disappointment. If you then complain of having been mistaken you are merely asking to be relieved of a risk knowingly run.”

另在《Misrepresentation, Mistake and Non-Disclosure》(2022 年，第 6 版)一书之 12 - 05 段说：“An incorrect belief or understanding is a **‘mistake’ for the purposes of remedies** discussed in this book **only if it relates to the present, and not the future**. A mistake is fundamentally different from a misprediction. … a statement by one party to the other during the negotiations is not a misrepresentation if it is only a statement of what will happen in the future.[2] If the representee wishes to hold the representor to liability in the event that the prediction is not borne out by the facts as to the future finds them, he

〔2〕 见本书第二章之 5 段。

must secure a warranty, in the contract, that the facts will turn out as represented.[3] ... However, when we consider the different categories of mistake, we shall see that a mistake may be made not only about the facts at the time of the formation of the contract, but also about content of the other party's promises. The **law of mistake** here becomes **entwined with the fundamental rules for the formation of the of the contract** – the test for deciding whether the parties have reached a sufficient agreement to form a contract, and the content of that contract. But **even here the 'mistake' relates to the present, and is not simply a misprediction or a misunderstanding about the future**. If the claimant is allowed to say that he made a mistake about the terms of the contract, he is asserting that he misunderstood the other party's proposal for the contract as it was at the moment when he gave his assent to the formation of the contract. If, on the other hand, his complaint is that, after the contract has been formed, the other party has not kept his promise, that is a claim for breach of contract, not for mistake."(加黑部分是笔者的强调)

在近期的 Jazztel Plc v. Revenue and Customs Commissioners(2017) EWHC 677 (Ch)先例中,案情涉及买卖股票时搞错了要缴纳的印花税储备税(stamp duty reserve tax)的税率(应为0.5%还是1.5%)的争议,Marcus Smith 大法官说:"**Mistakes must be distinguished from mispredictions**. A misprediction is a present belief or assumption about a future state of affairs, which is subsequently falsified; whereas a mistake involves the vitiation of the claimant's judgment at the time the enrichment is conferred. Put another way, **a mistake operates only as regards the present or the past, whereas a prediction, by definition, involves the future. Whereas mistake constitutes a ground for restitution, misprediction does not.**"(加黑部分是笔者的强调)

另在 Pitt v. Holt(2013) UKSC 26 最高院先例中,Walker 勋爵说对将来可能发生的事情的估计错误与对过去或现在事实或法律的错误理解的区分在实际案例的适用中有时是十分困难与有争议性,并以在本书第二章之6.4段介绍过的贵族院先例 Kleinwort Benson Ltd v. Lincoln City Council(1999) 2 AC 349(以下简称"Kleinwort Benson")为例。在 Kleinwort Benson 先例中原告银行在一个利率掉期合约下向被告作出支付,根据付钱时的法律是正确做法。但后来法律有了改变(案例法下有了不同判决,推翻以前的法律地位),显示原告作出的支付是错误的,这导致原告向被告起诉以支付是存在法律的错误要求法院判支付无效并把支付的钱退还复原。贵族院勋爵们以3:2的多数意见判可诉错误成立,多数与少数意见的分歧主要是后者认为根据原告同意作出支付时的法律作出支付是正确做法,何错之有?但多数意见认为法律只有一套原则与道理,只是在不同时间被不同法院的审理法官做出不同的演绎,而会有一些先例作出错误的演绎并在后来被上级法院推翻与纠正。所以,原告的支

---

〔3〕 见本书第二章之10.1段。这些道理本质上与误述是一样的。

付是在法律错误理解下作出,只要索赔时效(6 年立法时效)没有过,可以以可诉错误要求复原。

Walker 勋爵所说可节录如下:"**A misprediction relates to some possible future event, whereas a legally significant mistake normally relates to some past or present matter of fact or law**. But here too the distinction may not be clear on the facts of a particular case. The issue which divided the House of Lords in Kleinwort Benson Ltd v. Lincoln City Council[1999]2 AC 349 was whether … the correct view was that, 'a person who pays in accordance with what was then a settled view of the law has not made a mistake' and 'that his state of mind could be better described as a failure to predict the outcome of some future event … than a mistake about the existing state of the law'. …"(加黑部分是笔者的强调)

这可举一个简单例子来解释估计错误与错误的区别:如果买卖双方订立一个买卖合约,标的物可以是一栋在外国的特定房屋或一幅名画。显然双方都对这个标的物有一个肯定的想法是该标的物完好存在与法律允许这个交易。但如在订约前不久或甚至在同时,在双方不知情的情况下,该标的物受到意外事故如火灾的根本性毁坏,或是法律有了改变如不再容许外国人拥有当地的物业,这就是典型法律承认的"可诉错误"了。后果是订立的合约无效(void),不只是可使无效(voidable)。因为该"买卖合约"根本是无法履行下去,所以不存在其中一方当事人有选择权撤销(rescind)合约或坚持合约的履行。再说,既然是双方的共同错误理解,也不存在哪一方当事人算是无辜方可以有此选择权。

这可节录在 Bell v. Lever Brothers Ltd(1932)AC 161 贵族院先例中,Atkin 勋爵说:"So the agreement of A and B to purchase a specific article is void if in fact the article has perished before the date of sale. In this case, although the parties in fact were agreed about the subject-matter, yet consent to transfer or take delivery of something not existent is deemed useless, the consent is nullified. As codified in the Sale of Goods Act the contract is expressed to be void if the seller was in ignorance of the destruction of the specific chattel.[4] … This is a case where mutual mistake(在今天清楚的法律地位下,应该归类为"common mistake")certainly and … will prevent a contract from arising."

但如果标的物受到影响如法律的改变是发生在买卖合约订立后,如通过立法对外国人拥有本国房屋加征重税,又或是买卖的标的物在产权转移给买方后发生损毁

---

〔4〕 可节录《Sale of Goods Act 1979》之 Section 6:"Goods which have perished. Where there is a contract for the sale of specific goods, and the goods without the knowledge of the seller have perished at the time when the contract is made, the contract is void."还可顺便同时节录 Section 7:"Goods perishing before sale but after agreement to sell. Where there is an agreement to sell specific goods and subsequently the goods, without any fault on the part of the seller or buyer, perish before the risk passes to the buyer, the agreement is avoided."

与灭失,这就不涉及可诉错误,即使受到不良影响的一方当事人(通常是买方)仍是会泛泛觉得买错了或对这项交易作出了错误判断。这种情况也不影响有关买卖合约可以履行,即卖方可以交付,买方也可以接收,根本无须把该合约视为无效。这可以从两方面分析:(1)是订立合约后的事实或法律的改变是"将来",这错误理解不是订约时的"现存"。这与对事实的可诉误述只局限在现存事实,而对将来的事实只是没有法律后果的意见(opinion),无所谓真假之分是同样道理。(2)涉及风险(risk)的分摊。在合约关系中,通常通过明示或默示条文,会把合约的风险分摊。这样,风险一旦发生,就由承担风险的一方当事人承担恶果,不存在可寻求法律救济如错误去令合约无效,实质上把恶果转嫁给对方。这重要方面将在下小段详及。

3. 可诉错误针对的是没有在合约中分摊的风险

法律承认并给予相对十分极端的令合约自始无效(void ab initio)的救济只局限在可诉错误。虽然主张可诉错误的案件很常见,成功被法院或仲裁庭接受的却是极少。主要的原因是一般的国际商业合约对可预见与一般会发生的风险都已经通过明示(express)或默示(implied)条文[5]有了分摊。显然,在当事人意思自治(party autonomy)与订约自由等大原则下,双方在你情我愿下分摊了风险,就不应该支持在发生了风险后,如合约标的物灭失,要承担风险的合约方去主张可诉错误以逃避合约责任。

这样,可以考虑法律救济的可诉错误只局限在合约没有去分摊或针对的风险。正如《Chitty on Contracts》(2021 年,第 34 版)一书之 8 - 014 段所讲:" ... one must first determine whether the contract itself, by express or implied condition or otherwise, provides who bears the risk of the relevant mistake. Only if the contract is silent on the point is there scope for invoking the doctrine of mistake."

另在 The "Great Peace"(2002)EWCA Civ 1407 上诉庭先例中,Phillips 勋爵说:" ... the English doctrine of mistake ... fills a gap in the contract where it transpires that it is impossible of performance without the fault of either party, and the parties have not, expressly or impliedly, dealt with their rights and obligations in that eventuality."

3.1 合约风险的分摊导致可诉错误成功的案件不多

任何合约的内容是由明示与默示(法律或事实默示)的条文构成,如果双方对合约在某方面是如何规定或什么订约意图有了争议,法院或仲裁庭也是综合考虑明示与默示条文以客观找出与确定这个订约意图。在一个价值高昂的国际商业合约的漫长谈判中,订约方主要谈判的内容是针对可预见会存在或会出现的各种风险如何进

---

[5] 见笔者《合约的解释:规则与应用》一书第七章。

行分摊。英国法律已经通过大量的先例对很多不同类别的合约与情况确立了默示地位去分摊风险。但订约方如果对默示地位不满意或认为不够明确,就会通过明示条文去改变或将风险推给对方。对方会抗拒,但最终为了合约谈判能够继续下去,双方可能各让一步妥协,也或是一方订约方退让。

明示条文在订约自由下可以是千变万化。例如,在上述买卖外国房屋的例子,如果买方因为听到一些传闻担心法律改变去禁止自己这种外国人士买入房屋,遂要求卖方在房屋交割完成前保证法律不会改变,否则卖方要承担所有的损失。又例如买卖的特定标的物是 A,合约加上了明示条文约定如果 A 灭失或损毁,卖方可以交付标的物 B 作为替代,这类似著名的 The "Super Servant Two" (1990) 1 Lloyd's Rep 1 先例的情况。这些都是通过明示条文把会造成可诉错误的风险转移给其中一方合约方。

反正一个完整的国际商业合约会有大量条文都是针对预计可能会发生的风险的分摊,如免责条文(exception clause)、不可抗力条文(force majeure clause)、保证条文(warranty clause)、停租条文(off-hire clause)等。

至于默示条文或法律默示地位在买卖合约或很多其他类别的商业合约,英国法律下是要买方承担风险("let the buyers be aware"/*Caveat emptor*)。这表示在大量社会上的买卖交易,小至菜市场买卖或大至公司企业的并购,买错或买贵了标的物都是买方的风险,不是法律会救济的可诉错误。这历史悠久与至关重要的法律大原则会在下一小段详及。

在 CIF 或 FOB 的国际货物买卖中,这种付运合约(shipment contracts)的法律默示地位是在货物付运后(也就是货物装上船舶后),货物的风险就转移给了买方,除非合约有明示条文去改变这个法律地位。例如在信用证开出时或结汇时买方发觉船货已是全损,他也不能以共同错误为由拒付。又如典型的分配了风险的针对货物的保险合约。这类保险合约存在付运后真正合约才达成的情况,如在开口/敞口保单(open cover)或独立投保的情况下,货方宣告具体货物的时间是在付运后。但问题是当时货物可能已经灭失。因此做法上就是除非在投保时被保险人已经明知货物灭失,否则在合约下保险人会承担在合约订立前货物已经灭失的风险,无论真正订约时货物是否已经灭失(lost or not lost)。在立法《Marine Insurance Act 1906》之 Section 6 中这样规定:"Provided that where the subject-matter is insured 'lost or not lost,' the assured may recover although he may not have acquired his interest until after the loss, unless at the time of effecting the contract of insurance the assured was aware of the loss, and the insurer was not."

今天针对货物保险使用的标准合约格式 Institute Cargo Clause 之 Article 11.2 有明示条文:"... the Assured shall be entitled to recover for insured loss occurring during the period covered by this insurance, notwithstanding that the loss occurred before the contract of insurance was concluded, unless the Assured were aware of the loss and the Insurers were not.”

反正在这种情况下，保险人都不能以货物灭失为由，主张可诉错误导致保险合约无效：见 Wunsche Handelsgesellschaft International mbH v. Tai Ping Insurance Co Ltd (1998) 2 Lloyd's Rep 8 先例。

这表示可诉错误是合约内容没有明示或默示条文所针对的现存事实或法律问题，因为一旦有针对，就要以合约的规定为准，而规定也往往是分摊了合约风险。这可节录在 Dana Gas PJSC v. Dana Gas Sukuk Ltd(2017) EWHC 2928(Comm)先例中，Leggatt 大法官说："Where this leaves the common law doctrine of mistake, as it seems to me, is as follows. First, the doctrine is not based on an inquiry into the subjective beliefs of the parties but on an objective analysis of what they agreed. Second, the doctrine does not rest on the notion that the parties have impliedly agreed what is to happen in the event that an assumption underlying the contract proves to be false. It does, however, involve a question of construction of the contract. It is only where it is to be inferred from the terms of the contract or the surrounding circumstances that the contract was never intended to apply in the situation which in reality existed when the contract was made that the doctrine will apply. Such an inference will be drawn only if the difference between the state of affairs on which the contract was premised and the actual state of affairs is sufficiently fundamental. Thus, **the doctrine of mistake can only apply if there is a gap in the contract. If the parties have expressly or impliedly agreed what is to happen if they turn out to have been mistaken about the matter in question-in other words, if the risk of the mistake has been allocated by their contract-there is no scope for the doctrine** ..."（加黑部分是笔者的强调）

一份正式与小心拟定的商业合约会对绝大部分在现实履行中会遇上的风险都在订约方之间进行分摊与/或针对。这不仅仅是以明示条文，更是英国法院上百年来通过无数各自有独特事实、案情与合约条件/条文的案件，确立的法律对风险分摊的默示地位，就是合约双方对某些风险谁要承担后果。所以涉及可诉错误争议的新案件，通过分析有关合约的明示与默示条文（法律或事实默示），参阅与跟从以往先例对风险分摊的法律默示地位，就往往能够在新案件中去决定哪一方要承担风险，而无须以可诉错误这个最后的救济手段（remedy of last resort）令合约无效。这也正是虽然当事人经常提出可诉错误的主张，以为很容易成立，但真正能成功被接受的案例绝少的原因。

3.2 法律默示或明示条文分摊风险的例子

可先举早期著名的 McRae v. Commonwealth Disposals Commission (1951) 84 CLR 377 HCA 澳大利亚先例作为例子。案情涉及被告（政府机构）通过招标去出售一艘搁浅在新几内亚（New Guinea）100 海里外的某处珊瑚礁的油轮，并说明听说油轮上是有石油（"an oil tanker wrecked on the Journaund Reef approximate 100 miles north

Samarai. The vessel is said to contain oil")。最后原告中标,并组织了一批负责打捞的人员出发去该油轮希望掘金。但去到目的地,怎么样也找不到该油轮。后来事实证明,该油轮根本不存在,是被告听回来的错误信息。这导致原告以违约与欺诈性误述〔6〕向被告索赔依赖损失(reliance loss),〔7〕也就是组织打捞团队并白走一次所浪费的费用。但被告以标的在订约时不存在的共同/共享错误作为抗辩,主张合约应是自始无效。在一审,法院判是被告胜诉,合约无效与从未成立过。原告上诉后,一审判决被改变过来,判被告违约,要赔偿原告损失。而主要理由是对合约的解释,被告有保证该油轮的存在。这样,如果油轮并不存在,这是被告明示愿意接受的风险,也构成违约而不是可诉错误了。Dixon 大法官与 Fullagar 大法官说:"The buyers relied upon, and acted upon, the assertion of the seller that there was a tanker in existence. ... The only proper construction of the contract is that it included a promise by the Commission(被告)that there was a tanker in the position specified. The Commission contracted that there was a tanker there."

至于该油轮(如果存在)是否有石油在船上,被告并没有做出任何保证或承诺,只说是"听说是有"(said to contain)。这样原告愿意去投标买入,如果结果找到油轮但石油已经漏光,这是分摊给原告的风险了,也不是可诉错误。

另去举一个较近期的例子,在 William Sindall Plc v. Cambridgeshire CC(1994)1 WLR 1016 上诉庭先例中,〔8〕案情涉及土地的地役权(easement),但合约第 14 条将地役权的风险分摊给买方,Hoffmann 大法官说:"Without prejudice to the duty of the vendor to disclose all latent easements and latent liabilities known to the vendor to affect the property, the property is sold subject to any rights of way and water, rights of common and other rights, easements, quasi-easements, liabilities and public rights affecting the same."

Hoffmann 大法官说合约已经明示把风险分摊给了买方,不再存在订约时对地役权的错误理解去撤销合约令其无效,说:"In this case the contract says in express terms that it is subject to all easements other than those of which the vendor knows or has the means of knowledge. This allocates the risk of such incumbrances to the buyer and leaves no room for rescission on the grounds of mistake."

再多举一个以明示条文分摊风险的例子可以是 Standard Chartered Bank v. Ban-

---

〔6〕 如果在今天,原告 McRae 的诉因不必是欺诈性误述,因为被告没有不诚实的意图,也证明不了。但在当年,既没有类似《Misrepresentation Act 1967》的立法去允许疏忽误述索赔损失,另也是到了 Hedley Byrne v. Heller(1964)AC 465 贵族院先例才有了侵权也可以索赔纯经济损失(pure economic loss)的说法。

〔7〕 这课题可见笔者的《损失赔偿与救济》一书第二章之 4 段。在此先例中,由于油轮根本不存在,无法比较,所以原告 McRae 无法计算出他的预期损失(expectation loss)或利润损失(loss of profit)。

〔8〕 在本书第四章之 5.4.2.1 段对案情有详细介绍。

que Marocaine du Commerce Exterieur(2006)EWHC 413(Ch)先例。在该先例中,原告渣打银行为一家名为 Parmalat Brazil 的巴西公司的食品生意提供约 670 万美元的融资,该食品公司开出了 7 份每份约 100 万美元的本票(promissory note),本票上也写明"The financing evidenced by this promissory note is in support of the purchase and sales of foodstuff by Parmalat SpA(母公司)subsidiaries and/or affiliates in Latin America",即融资的目的是支持其在拉丁美洲的食品生意,其母公司也提供担保。针对该融资项目,位于法国巴黎的银行,也即本案的被告 BMCE,与渣打银行订立了一份分担坏账风险的同意协议(Acceptance Agreement),协议约定在 BMCE 收取一定费用的基础上,为其中 4 张本票提供进一步的担保。后来食品公司无法履行本票下的偿还义务,其母公司也破产而无法履行担保合约。渣打银行要求 BMCE 在分担风险的同意协议下支付 4 张本票的金额。BMCE 的抗辩是食品公司对融资的目的做出欺诈性误述,名为发展食品生意,实际是为了偿还债务与夸大资产来欺骗股东。这样,它和渣打银行是在对食品公司融资的目的存在共同/共享错误下签署了分担坏账风险的同意协议,如果它知道真正的融资目的是不会签署同意协议,从而要求法院判该协议无效。但法院并不接受该抗辩,因为分担坏账风险的同意协议中有明示条文[9]将这种债务人误述的风险分摊给 BMCE,其中 Gloster 大法官说:"As Steyn J ... said in Associated Japanese Bank(International)Limited v Credit du Nord SA[1989]1 WLR 255 ...:'**Where the contract in question allocates the risk of mistake to one of the parties, there is no scope for the application of the doctrine of common mistake.**' Here, in my judgment, that, in respect of its participation, to BMCE. The risk that Parmalat Brazil and indeed **risk was clearly allocated** Parmalat SpA would not pay up on the promissory notes which was aggravated by the alleged misapplication for fraudulent purposes of the funds advanced or likewise was aggravated by the fraudulent misrepresentation if it existed, **is exactly the risk that BMCE in my judgment agreed to bear when entering into the acceptance agreement**.... The contract in my judgment clearly **allocates the risk of non-payment or the increased risk of non-payment for either of these**

---

[9] 有关条文可节录如下:"6.3 Responsibilities: In respect of any Acceptance Agreement, **the Grantor**(渣打银行)**makes no representation or warranty** ... with respect to, and the Participant(BMCE)confirms that it has made and will continue to **make its own independent appraisal of, and has not and will not rely on the Grantor** as to: a. the due execution, legality, validity, adequacy or enforceability of the Documents; b. the recoverability of any sum due under the Documents; c. the current or future financial condition of each Obligor(食品公司)and Security Party(食品公司的母公司); d. the performance by the Obligor and any Security Party of their respective obligations under any Document; e. **the accuracy of any representation or warranty made by the Obligor or any Security Party in any Document**; and f. the accuracy of any opinions or certificates delivered or to be delivered under or in connection with any Document."(加黑部分是笔者的强调)

reasons to BMCE.... Accordingly, in my judgment as I have said, any defence or counterclaim based on common mistake must fail."(加黑部分是笔者的强调)

合约即使是有明示条文针对，是否真有分摊风险或针对某方面的理解或假设的事实有了错误应如何处理，仍是需要通过合约的解释去分析后才能有答案：见 John Lobb Ltd v. John Lobb SAS(2022)EWHC 2306(Ch)先例。这正如国际商业合约普遍会有一条泛泛的不可抗力条文，总会提到战争等事项。这不该被解释为排除了合约受阻。

3.3　权威先例说法

一旦有了明示或默示条文去分摊现存与将来的法律风险，就会排除了默示的可诉错误令合约无效或受阻(frustration)令合约终止(terminate)的适用。一旦出现风险，就是去解释合约看看哪一方要承担该风险。而同意承担风险的一方当事人，如果风险果真发生，即使他本来是认为这风险是不会发生，也不是可诉错误而是估计错误，正如在《Misrepresentation, Mistake and Non-Disclosure》(2022 年，第 6 版)一书之 12 – 06 段中说："**Risk-taking contrasted with mistake.** A party who takes a risk as to whether a fact is true cannot be heard to say that he made a mistake as long as the facts are within the range of the risk. If a party knows that the facts might be(x)or(y), then as long as they are either(x)or(y), he simply has not made a mistake. This is so, even if he thinks that the facts are(x), but has a residual doubt about whether they might be(y): for example, if he buys a painting believing it to be a genuine work by a particular seventeenth century artist, whilst knowing that there is a minority opinion amongst art historians that it might have been painted by another artist of the same school. However, if the party holds a positive belief that the facts are(x)or(y)and not(z), he may be allowed to assert that he made a mistake if(z)is shown to be the true state of affairs: to continue the example, if the buyer of the painting has a positive belief that it must at least be a genuine seventeenth century work, but in reality it is a modern forgery. ..."

以下节录部分权威先例对这一点同样的说法，首先介绍是 Associated Japanese Bank(International)Ltd v. Credit du Nord SA(1989)1 WLR 255 先例，Steyn 大法官说："Logically, before one can turn to the rules as to mistake, whether at common law or in equity, one must first determine whether the contract itself, by express or implied condition precedent or otherwise, provides who bears the risk of the relevant mistake. It is at this hurdle that many pleas of mistake will either fail or prove to have been unnecessary. Only if the contract is silent on the point, is there scope of invoking mistake. ..."

在 William Sindall Plc v. Cambridgeshire CC(1994)1 WLR 1016 上诉庭先例中，Hoffmann 大法官说："When the judge speaks of the contract allocating risk 'by express or implied condition precedent or otherwise' I think he includes **rules of general law applicable to the contract** and which, for example, provide that, **in the absence of express**

warranty, the law is caveat emptor. This would, in my view, **allocate the risk of an unknown defect in goods to the buyer**, even though it is not mentioned in the contract. Similarly, the rule in Hill v. Harris [1965] 2 Q. B. 601 that a lessor or vendor does not impliedly warrant that the premises are fit for any particular purpose means that the contract allocates the risk of the premises being unfit for such purpose."（加黑部分是笔者的强调）

在 The "Great Peace"(2002) EWCA Civ 1407 上诉庭先例中，Phillips 勋爵说："**Circumstances where a contract is void as a result of common mistake are likely to be less common than instances of frustration**. Supervening events which defeat the contractual adventure will frequently not be the responsibility of either party. Where, however, the parties agree that something shall be done which is impossible at the time of making the agreement, it is **much more likely that, on true construction of the agreement, one or other will have undertaken responsibility for the mistaken state of affairs. This may well explain why cases where contracts have been found to be void in consequence of common mistake are few and far between**."（加黑部分是笔者的强调）

另在近期的 Triple Seven MSN 27251 Ltd v. Azman Air Services Ltd (2018) EWHC 1348 (Comm) 先例中，MacDonald Eggers QC 大法官说："**The main reason why pleas of mistake seldom succeed is that the risk of a mistake is usually allocated by the contract to one of the parties**. Plainly, there is no room for the doctrine to operate if the contract states expressly what is to happen if the relevant assumption proves to be false. It may be harder to determine whether the contract impliedly allocates the risk ... In practice in such a case the answer is likely to be found through construction of the contract."（加黑部分是笔者的强调）

最后节录《Misrepresentation, Mistake and Non – Disclosure》(2022 年，第 6 版) 一书之 15 – 15 段去总结这方面的法律地位，说："**Risk-taking excludes mistake**... the mistake about the subject-matter of the contract inevitably raises questions of the contractual allocation of risk. The courts in discussing cases of alleged mistakes about the subject-matter have not always addressed this question openly, or even at all; but it is clear that this question is logically prior to any analysis based on mistake. If the contract expressly or implied provides for the circumstances as they have now been found to be, but were believed by the parties to be otherwise, then the matter is concluded by the provision contained in the contract. There is no 'mistake' at all. The common law rules for mistake are, in this sense, rules of last resort which come into play only if there is no solution in the contract itself. ...."

4. 买卖合约的风险分摊:"买方自己小心"

众所周知,一般的买卖是要买方承担风险,所谓"买方自己小心"(let the buyers be aware/*Caveat emptor*。所以除非卖方有误述(misrepresentation)的情况,或是违反了一些默示条件(如对货物拥有主权/产权),[10]买方对买卖合约的条件与内容(不是标的物是否存在,而是如货物的质量、特征、价格等)的错误要自己承担风险,如买贵了或是买错了等。毕竟,这种合约不是无法履行。

这"*Caveat emptor*"的说法或原则也不只是适用在货物买卖或土地买卖等合约中,而是适用在所有其他的商业合约关系,如租赁合约、投资合约等。正如 Atkin 勋爵在 Bell v. Lever Brothers Ltd(1932) AC 161 贵族院先例中说:"The principle of caveat emptor applies outside contracts of sale."

以买卖合约为例,如果买方买了一只自以为是黄金的戒指,实质它是铜的,只要卖方没有误述,买方要为这错误付出代价,不能以搞错为由要求法院判这交易无效,然后要回已经付出的货价。即使卖方怀疑买方是搞错了,把铜戒指当作金戒指,法律地位仍是一样。因为卖方不讲话怎会有误述?[11]至于要卖方主动提醒买方要小心别搞错,这是颠倒了承担风险的责任,英国法律也没有自动披露的责任。

这表示买方要自己小心,主要是主动问清楚,如问卖方这是铜戒指还是金戒指。要是卖方讲假话,说是金戒指,这才是误述。这可节录《Misrepresentation, Mistake and Non-Disclosure》(2022 年,第 6 版)一书之 15 - 13 段说:"**A unilateral mistake which is caused by the other party is actionable as a fraudulent misrepresentation, but not as a mistake**. ... It is clear in the modern law that a contract can be avoided for innocent, as well as fraudulent, misrepresentation, although for the resulting mistake to be unilateral, the misrepresentation will be fraudulent. But it should be remembered that the effect of a misrepresentation, even a fraudulent misrepresentation, is to render the contract voida-

---

〔10〕 有关产权的默示条文可节录《Sale of Goods Act 1979》之 Section 12(1):"In a contract of sale ... there is an implied term on the part of the seller that in the case of a sale he has a right to sell the goods, and in the case of an agreement to sell he will have such a right at the time when the property is to pass...",以及在 Section 12(5A)规定为条件条文:"As regards England and Wales and Northern Ireland, the term implied by subsection(1) above is a condition..."这方面可见杨大明律师的《国际货物买卖》一书第七章。在该立法下还有各类其他默示条件,如 Section 13 规定以货物描述进行买卖,则货物必须符合合约描述(correspond with description);Section 14 规定货物有"可商售质量"(merchantable quality)/在 1994 年立法改为"满意质量"(satisfactory quality),特定情况货物需要适合特别用途(fitness for particular purpose);Section 15 规定以样本进行买卖,则货物也必须符合样本(correspond with sample)等。这方面可见《国际货物买卖》一书第四章。

〔11〕 见本书第五章之 1 段。

ble, not void. If, therefore, the (unilateral) mistake is induced by a fraudulent misrepresentation, the claimant (受害人买方) can avoid the contract — but in so doing he relies upon the misrepresentation, not the mistake…."(加黑部分是笔者的强调)

又如买方主观是想买烧鹅但买了烧鸭，如果对方/卖方不知道买方的想法(也就是想买烧鹅)，卖方自己是知道他出售的是烧鸭，也就不会是一个共同/共享错误，但也仍是远不足以成为一个可诉的单方面错误。正如在 Smith v. Hughes (1871) LR 6 QB 597 上诉庭先例中，案情涉及买方想购买"老燕麦"(old oat)给他饲养的马匹吃，但结果卖方交付了的是"新燕麦"，买方想以单方面错误去令买卖合约无效。Cockburn 大法官判说："I take the true rule to be, that where a specific article is offered for sale, without express warranty, or without circumstances from which the law will imply a warranty … and **the buyer has full opportunity of inspecting and forming his own judgment, if he chooses to act in his judgement, the rule caveat emptor applies**. If he gets the article he contracted to buy, and that article corresponds with what bit was sold as, he gets all he is entitled to, and is bound by the contract. Here the defendant (买方) agreed to buy a specific parcel of oats. The oats were what they were sold as, namely, good oats according to the sample. The buyer persuaded himself they were old oats, when they were not so; but the seller neither said nor did anything to contribute to his deception. He has himself to blame."(加黑部分是笔者的强调)

这个早期先例一直被视为正确的英国法律原则并被跟从，正如在 The "Harriette N" (2008) EWHC 2257 (Comm) 先例中，Aikens 大法官说："the correctness of the decision in Smith v. Hughes, and analysis in it, has never been doubted."

这也是 Atkin 勋爵在 Bell v. Lever Brothers Ltd 贵族院先例中所做的两个大同小异的比喻，第一个是一匹马的买卖，买方以为以好价钱买了一匹骏马，而实是跛马。在卖方没有误述的情况下，买方是自负恶果，风险是买方的，说："A buys B's horse: he thinks the horse is sound and he pays the price of a sound horse; he would certainly not have bought the horse if he had known the fact that the horse is unsound, if B has made no representation as to soundness and has not contracted that the horse is sound, A is bound and cannot recover back the price …"

Atkin 勋爵另一个比喻说："A agrees to take on lease or to buy from B an unfurnished dwelling-house. The house is in fact uninhabitable. A would never have entered into the bargain if he had known the fact. A has no remedy, and the position is the same whether B knew the facts or not, so long as he made no representation or gave no warranty. …"

这看来对买方十分苛刻的法律地位有以下几方面的考虑：

1. 默示法律地位是"买方自己小心"。对标的货物(可以是任何买卖，包括公司并购)的本质或特质、是否适合自己用途、价格是否划算等，只有买方自己最清楚，所以全要靠买方自己的判断,并会通过检查或尽职调查等帮助自己作出准确的判断。如果还不放心,买方可咨询卖方或要求卖方作出担保。如果判断错误,如没有小心检查,买方要自己承担风险。所以,如果法律允许一方以判断错误令合约无效,被视为干预与重写(rewrite)双方同意的合约条件(这包括明示与默示条文对风险的分摊),这是违反合约解释的大原则。

这可节录在 Grains & Fourrages SA v. Huyton(1997)1 Lloyd's Rep 628 先例中,Mance 大法官说:"If the buyers had made their proposal in terms, or on a basis, which amounted to an acceptance of risk on their part that the facts might turn out differently, then of course I would accept that they could not and should not be allowed to reopen the matter."

《Sale of Goods Act 1893》与发展到今天的《Sale of Goods Act 1979》的部分内容以及其他保护消费者的立法,都可以说是不遗余力在加强保护买方,也在一定程度上削弱了"买方自己小心"大原则的肯定性。这与中国公司参与的国际商业合约的关系并不大,所以只节录 Steyn 勋爵在 Slater v. Finning Ltd(1997)AC 473 贵族院先例中所说:"Outside the field of private sales the shift from caveat emptor to caveat venditor in relation to the implied condition of fitness for purpose〔12〕 has been a notable feature of the development of our commercial law."

2. 英国合约法下没有"善意"(good-faith)的法律默示要求,也没有自动披露(voluntary disclosure)的法律责任,〔13〕例如要求卖方自动告知买方:"我的商品比对面马路的商店质量差多了,我知道你是不知道与怕你会有错误理解,你还要不要买?"显然,这是可笑与并不符合人性与实际的。

在 Smith v. Hughes 先例中,Blackburn 大法官也说明这一点:"... I agree that even if the vendor was aware that the purchaser thought that the article possessed that quality, and would not have entered into the contract unless he had so thought, still the purchaser is bound, unless the vendor was guilty of some fraud or deceit upon him, ... for, whatever may be the case in a court of morals, there is no legal obligation on the vendor to inform the purchaser that he is under a mistake, not induced by the act of the vendor."

这道理不只适用于买卖关系,而是适用于所有其他商业关系。显然,在对卖方没有善意与自动披露的要求的情况下,买方当然只能是自己订立合约并对接受的条件与承担的义务和责任需要自己小心并承担错误的风险。正如在《Chitty on Contracts》(2021 年,第 34 版)一书之 8-06 段中说:"... for the principle that in relation to sale is

---

〔12〕 这包括货物需要符合一般用途(common purpose),或者是商业交易中买方明确告知了卖方、需要依赖卖方判断将货物用于非一般用途(uncommon purposes)。《Sale of Goods Act 1979》之 Section 14(3)等默示货物必须符合买方用途的情况可见杨大明律师的《国际货物买卖》一书第四章之 6 段。

〔13〕 见本书第五章的详细介绍。

referred to as caveat emptor（'let the buyer beware'）is still the starting point of the English law of contract."，并在脚注提到了 Bell v. Lever Brothers Ltd 贵族院先例。

3. 虽然在上述的节录中 Blackburn 大法官有提到不知道"良心法院"[a court of moral，应是指衡平法法院（court of equity）]会不会有不同看法，因为 Smith v. Hughes 先例是在普通法法院审理。但笔者相信即使是在衡平法法院审理，也不会改变买方自己小心与卖方知道对方犯错也不主动提醒的地位。

衡平法法院在早期不像普通法法院追求法律的肯定性（certainty）与可预测性（predictable），而是看个别案件根据普通法判决的结果是否是不合情理（unconscionable）而试图作出衡平救济（equitable remedy）。随着衡平法的发展，虽然核心思想仍只是针对不公平与/或不合情理的案件，但不是"拍拍脑袋"，也像普通法一样去遵从先例并受约束与发展出一整套的理论（doctrines），务求有一定程度的肯定。此外，它仍是必须让法律先行，后果是不合情理才能插手，所谓"equity must follow the law"。

对可诉错误的衡平救济，稍后在本章之 14 段会详细介绍。在 Hutton SA v. Distribuidora Internacional De Productos Agricolas SA（2002）EWHC 2088（Comm）先例中，Andrew Smith 大法官有提到衡平救济，说："I conclude，in view of the relative insignificance of the mistaken belief and the lack of demonstrable hardship to Huyton（卖方）in holding them to the SA（买卖合约），that it would be equitable for the court to enforce it."

但这不被后来的 Aikens 大法官在 The"Harriette N"先例中认同，因为较早前 The"Great Peace"（2002）EWCA Civ 1407 上诉庭先例已经否定了可诉错误可以获得衡平救济说："With respect to Andrew Smith J.，I must disagree with his conclusion that there is an equitable jurisdiction to grant rescission of a contract where one party has made a unilateral mistake as to a fact or state of affairs which is the basis upon which the terms of the contract are agreed，but that assumption does not become a term of the contract. None of the cases he cites … is authority for the existence of that jurisdiction. The Great Peace decision strongly suggests that there is no such jurisdiction in the case of a unilateral mistake. If there is no such jurisdiction in the case of a common mistake，I fear I am unable to see how，in logic，one can devise a rationale for an equitable jurisdiction in the case of a unilateral mistake，at least where there has been no misrepresentation by the other party."

5. 可诉错误必须不是错误方的过错、不小心、疏忽、无知或健忘

这是排除日常生活（特别是在商业社会）中无时不在发生的人为过失或犯错的

错误,这种错误往往是单方面搞错或遗漏,特别是对订立合约的条件。这早在 Barrow v. Isaac & Son(1891)1 QB 417 上诉庭先例中,Esher 勋爵说到健忘带来的遗漏并不是可诉错误,因为在订约时根本没有想过的事实(或法律),又何来错误之有,说:"Can you, in English, say, 'I forgot,' and is that the same thing as saying, 'I was mistaken'? I think not. Both those questions depend on something happening in the mind of the person, and you have to see what it is that happens in his mind. If he merely forgets, he does not assume that one state of things exists whereas some other state of things exists: it is mere passive state of mind; he has forgotten - he has not thought that one thing was in existence, whereas something else was existence. I should say that mere forgetfulness is not mistake at all in ordinary language."

一般出现的现实情况是:错误方 A 在谈判时坚持订立的重要合约条件,例如在买卖合约下针对标的物的描述(descriptions)、价格(price)、质量(quality)或数量(quantity)、交付时间、支付货价办法(信用证、托收、结账或分期支付)等,是 x。但对方 B 却坚持是 y。这样,双方没有达成有效合约,因为还没有一致想法(meeting of minds 或 consensus ad idem)。

但如果 A 与 B 达成一份合约,表面看来是双方同意与接受了某条件(不论是 x 还是 y),在你情我愿下已经达成一个有效合约。但实际上仍是 A 以为是 x,而 B 以为是 y。造成这种错误会是 A 传达给 B 的信息不清楚或有错,也会是 B 对 A 传达的正确信息有了误解。另会是 B 不坚持谈下去并转了去谈其他方面,让 A 以为 x 已经被接受,但 B 并不是这样认为,因为他坚持 y 是一直没有放弃过。在合约订立时双方来回修改合约会出现的格式之争(battle of forms)也是类似情况,各自把自己的惯用合约格式发送给对方,卖方说是"以我的附件合约格式卖给你",买方以同样方式回复说"以我的附件合约格式向你买"。之后卖方就付运货物,买方也接受并支付了货款。在多个月后,双方有了争议,例如货物有缺陷,才带出了以哪一个合约格式为准,因为各自有不同的明示条文,例如不同的索赔时效或其他问题。

或是在合约履行过程中,双方才发现对合约条件如支付货款办法有不同理解。这在他们主观看来,显然是没有一致想法。但由于已经履行了部分,说是双方因尚未有一致想法而没有合约关系也不是可行的解决办法。

这种情况正是 Blackburn 大法官在 Smith v. Hughes(1871) LR 6 QB 597 先例中说:"If one of the parties intends to make a contract on one set of terms, and the other intends to make a contract on another set of terms, or, as it is sometimes expressed, if the parties are not ad idem, there is no contract, unless the circumstances are such as to preclude one of the parties from denying that he has agreed to the terms of the other. The rule of law is that stated in Freeman v. Cooke(1848)2 Exch 654. If, whatever a man's real intention may be, he so conducts himself that a reasonable man would believe that he was assenting to the terms proposed by the other party, and that other party upon that belief enters into the contract with him, the man thus conducting himself would be equally bound as if he had intended to agree to the other party's terms."

5.1 双方对合约的条件有不同理解通常不是可诉错误

这种谈判的主观错误理解,通常本质实是由于错误方(A 或 B)自己的过错(fault)、不小心(careless)或疏忽(negligence),如不清楚(unawareness)、无知(ignorance)、不注意(inadvertence)所导致。

在 The "Harriette N"(2008) EWHC 2257 (Comm)先例中,虽然 Aikens 大法官针对的是法院有否对单方面错误作出衡平救济的权力,并确认没有这权力,但也说到了如果有,也不会行使这权力,因为涉及的错误理解是由于一方当事人不小心所造成,说:"I would be inclined to say that in this case it would not be proper to exercise the jurisdiction... **The mistake was entirely the result of carelessness by Mr Rostrup**(原告证人),**as he was constrained to admit in cross examination.** If I had held there was jurisdiction to grant rescission, I would have held, on the facts of this case that **it would not be just and equitable to grant it**."(加黑部分是笔者的强调)

接受主观想法除了是各说各的不解决问题外,也带来滥用(abuses)与欺诈(fraud)。这是因为只有 A 与 B 两位当事人能为自己的主观想法提供证据。在重大利益冲突下,他们肯定是各说各的,更会容易带来狡猾的证人欺骗法院或仲裁庭并成功蒙混过关。这在早期的 Tamplin v. James (1880) 15 Ch. D. 215 上诉庭先例中,Baggallay 大法官说:"he is not entitled to say any effectual purpose that he was under a mistake, when he did not think it worth while to read the particulars and look at the plans. If that were to be allowed, **a person might always escape from completing a contract by swearing that he was mistaken as to what he bought, and great temptation to perjury** would be offered."(加黑部分是笔者的强调)

另 James 大法官也说:"It is not enough for a purchaser to swear, 'I thought the farm sold contained twelve fields which I knew, and I find it does not include them all', or, 'I thought it contained 100 acres and it only contains eighty'. **It would open the door to fraud if such a defence was to be allowed**."(加黑部分是笔者的强调)

5.2 英国法律解决办法:客观解释双方合约有否成立与成立条件

英国法律解决的办法是法院或仲裁庭对有关争议作出的解释是客观测试(objective test),不去理会也不采纳双方订约方的主观想法,也不理会这主观的错误理解是否由于不小心或疏忽所导致。所以如果判决或裁决是 x,错误传达或错误理解为合约同意的条件是 y 的 B 就要承担后果。而如果判决或裁决是 y,错误传达或错误理解为 x 的 A 就要承担后果了。

在《Misrepresentation, Mistake and Non-Disclosure》(2022 年,第 6 版)一书之 13-12 段中说:"**The objective element of the test** The test set out by Blackburn J relies heavily on objective criteria. Given that it is to be used in a case where the parties were not, in fact, in agreement, it must be applying an objective test to override a party's lack of subjective agreement. This is seen in the words of the test ...: 'whatever a man's real intention may be, he so conducts himself that a reasonable man would believe that he was assenting to the terms proposed by the other party.'"

5.2.1 被告的过错或不小心造成的错误

在《Misrepresentation, Mistake and Non-Disclosure》(2022 年,第 6 版)一书之 13-25 段中说:"**The defendant's 'fault'** There are a number of cases in which the defendant might be said to have been at fault – with the consequence that he cannot deny that he is bound to the contract on the claimant's terms, even though he in fact made a mistake. In one sense, the very basis of the 'objective test' is the defendant's fault: the reason that the defendant's subjective misunderstanding about the terms of the contract is overridden in favour of the claimant's understanding is that he has behaved in such a way as to entitle the claimant to misunderstand him. **If the defendant had not failed properly to communicate his own intentions, the problem would not have arisen.** So, typically, where the defendant's misunderstanding about the terms was **neither caused by the claimant, nor arose in circumstances where the external observer in the claimant's position would have realised that there was a mistake, the defendant is bound because he has no one to blame but himself**. For example, where the defendant bids at auction for the wrong property, and the auctioneer (on behalf of the claimant) has no way of knowing that the defendant did not fully understand what he was doing, there is no basis on which the defendant can be heard to say that he misunderstood which property was the subject matter of the sale. Or where the defendant writes to the claimant in terms which contain a proposal as to price which is clear, and the claimant cannot be expected in the circumstances to realise that the defendant has made a mistake when he wrote the price into the letter, the defendant will be bound to the price he has written. In both of these cases the defendant can be said to be at fault, in failing to take the proper precaution to protect his own interests. ..."(加黑部分是笔者的强调)

针对被告的过失、不小心造成的错误(被告会在面对违约与索赔时抗辩提出可诉错误令合约无效),可先举早期的 Malins v. Freeman (1837) 48 ER 537 先例,被告本来受雇拍下另一块土地,但是因为他搞错了,把原告的土地当成了他应拍下的土地而匆忙出价,以对原告的土地来说不合理的 1400 英镑高价拍下。拍卖结束后,被告以错误令合约无效而拒绝支付,原告则申请法院作出履约指令(specific performance)。法院虽然拒绝作出履约指令,但仍判被告应赔偿损失。

同类型的案例另有 Tamplin v. James (1880) 15 Ch. D. 215 上诉庭先例,被告拍下了一块土地,因为他知道土地后的院子一直被租客占用,所以就理所当然地以为院子也属于他拍下的土地,而并没有看对土地的描述和有关的地图,但事实并非如此。被告之后拒绝履行并希望以错误令合约无效,法院最后也判被告败诉,要赔偿损失。

另在不涉及拍卖的 Scott v. Littledale(1858)120 ER 304 先例中,案情涉及凭样品出售货物(sale by sample),但作为卖方的被告搞错了样品,样品与实际货物完全不是同一种茶叶,法院判被告仍要承担责任。虽然有“买方自己小心”的大原则,但该大原则不适用于卖方自己疏忽提供了错误的样品的情况。

在 Centrovincial Estates Plc v. Merchant Investors Assurance Co Ltd(1983)Com LR 158 上诉庭先例中,案情涉及房屋租赁,原告作为新房东向被告租客书面提议新租金应为每年 6.5 万英镑,而当时被告给前房东的租金已经是每年约 6.8 万英镑,因此被告很高兴地接受了原告的要约。但是其实原告希望提出的要约是每年 12.6 万英镑,但是写错了,被告拒绝修改已经达成的新租约。法院判如果一方明知或应该知道对方犯错,不会构成有效合约。但是在该先例中,没有证据显示被告知道或应该知道原告的本意并非如此。Slade 大法官说:“in the absence of any proof ... that the(tenant) either knew or ought reasonably to have known of the(landlord's)offer, why should the (landlord) now be allowed to resile from that offer?”

最后在 OT Africa Line Ltd v. Vickers Plc(1996)1 Lloyd's Rep 700 先例中,原告在诉讼中索赔 70 万美元。在法院审理中途,被告把 10.3 万美元支付给法院(payment into court)作为和解金额。原告反要约的金额是 18.5 万美元加上 28 万美元的诉讼费用。双方持续的谈判后被告律师作出一个 15 万英镑的要约,这包括已经支付法院的一笔钱。但这里被告律师犯错,实际上被告愿意作出和解的是美元而不是英镑,但发传真时把“ $ ”写成了“£ ”,要约也被原告接受。被告试图以单方面错误从和解协议中脱身,但 Mance 大法官不认为原告知道被告的错误,所以就不成立可诉错误。但如果事实稍有变动就可能有很不同的结果。例如,原告提出和解的金额是 30 万美元,被告的反要约是 29 万英镑,折算为美元比 30 万美元更多。这样原告不可能不知道或合理看应该知道被告存在单方面的错误,如果取巧接受并坚持这个 29 万英镑的和解协议,法律就很有可能做出救济,判原告有责任说清楚,[14] 向被告指出他的错误。

5.2.2 原告的过错或不小心造成的错误

在《Misrepresentation, Mistake and Non-Disclosure》(2022 年,第 6 版)一书之 13-26 段中说:“**The claimant's 'fault'** On the other hand, there are cases in which the claimant might be said to have been at fault-with the consequence that he cannot enforce the contract on the terms as he intended them. ... where the claimant can be said-more or less precisely-to have been at fault, it will be found that he fails to satisfy the objective test, either because in fact he knew about the other party's different intentions as to the

〔14〕 关于有责任说清楚/沉默性禁反言,可见笔者《合约的履行、弃权与禁反言》一书第五章之 10 段的详细介绍。

terms of the contract, or because he should have done-and so a reasonable person in his position would not have misunderstood the defendant. Where, for example, his 'fault' consists of having induced the mistake in the other party, either deliberately or at least carelessly, he will not be allowed to enforce a contract on his own terms-but in such a case it can be said either that he knew, or at least that he reasonably ought to have known, that the defendant's expression of assent did not accord with his real intentions."

在 Scriven Bros & Co v. Hindley & Co(1913)3 KB 564 早期先例中,案情与上一段介绍的早期先例类似,涉及一次货物拍卖中,卖方委托拍卖人去卖出一批麻和麻屑(麻经过梳理后掉下来的碎屑),拍卖名册中仅仅只是指出这批货分属不同的拍卖编号,不同编号的货物上的唛头是一样的,并没有显示出哪些是麻,哪些是麻屑。买方只是想买麻而根本不想买麻屑,所以在拍卖中,他以为是在竞拍麻,进而给出一个对麻屑来说是天价的价格(就好像以金价去购买铜),并顺利拍得货物。但后来才发现他竞拍的那个编号的货物是麻屑,从而拒绝付款。Lawrence 大法官判因为原告卖方的疏忽,导致被告买方错误理解货物的种类,双方根本没有达成一致想法(consensus ad idem),卖方要自己承担责任,说:"such a contract cannot arise when the person seeking to enforce it has by his own negligence or by that of those for whom he is responsible caused, or contributed to cause, the mistake."

在 Lloyds Bank Plc v. Waterhouse(1993)2 FLR 97 上诉庭先例中,父亲和他的兄弟一起经营农场,一开始是租用,后来贷款买下农场。儿子在大学学习了农业专业,并在父亲的农场工作一段时间后,想要自立门户,购买自己的农场。于是不识字但会写自己名字的父亲在儿子的煽动以及银行的诱导下在儿子购买农场的交易中为交易签下了担保合约。但父亲因为不识字以及对担保的错误理解,不清楚自己的担保责任是什么。而且当时父亲也刚刚贷款买下自己之前和兄弟一起租赁的农场,根本也无力再为其他贷款提供抵押与担保。当原告银行后来要执行担保合约时,父亲才发现自己在担保合约下的担保责任远远超过自己愿意承担的范围,从而抗拒履约。Eveleigh 大法官在考虑了所有的事实之后认定在订立担保合约时银行知道或应该知道父亲对担保责任有错误理解,判银行败诉,说:"in all the circumstances, the manager ought to have known that the defendant was not aware of the extent of the obligation in the guarantee, that the defendant would only be willing to undertake a(less extensive) liability ... Consequently, in my opinion, the guarantee was signed under a mistake which was negligently induced by the manager and, therefore, the mistake prevents the signature from having a binding effect inter partes: see Scriven Bros v. Hindley & Co."

5.3 在没有对价或名义对价的合约/契约中,法律对当事人过错、不小心、疏忽、无知或健忘有更大宽容

以上针对的是有对价(consideration)的商业合约,但在 Pitt v. Holt(2013)UKSC 26 最高院先例中,针对的不是有对价的合约,而是涉及错误理解遗产税而成立信托。

在该先例中 Walker 勋爵说:

"For present purposes a **mistake must be distinguished from mere ignorance or inadvertence**,... The editors of Goff & Jones, The Law of Unjust Enrichment, 8th ed (2011), para 9-11 comment that the distinction between mistake and misprediction can lead to 'some uncomfortably fine distinctions', and **the same is true of the distinction between mistake and ignorance**.

Forgetfulness, inadvertence or ignorance is not, as such, a mistake, but it can lead to a false belief or assumption which the law will recognise as a mistake. The Court of Appeal of Victoria has held that mistake certainly comprehends 'a mistaken belief arising from inadvertence to or ignorance of a specific fact or legal requirement': Ormiston JA in Hookway v. Racing Victoria Ltd(2005)13 VR 444,...

The best-known English authority on this point isLady Hood of Avalon v. Mackinnon[1909]1 Ch 476.... Eve J granted relief, stating ...: 'Having regard to the facts which I have stated, I must assume that **Lady Hood, intending only to bring about equality between her daughters, was labouring under a mistake** when she thought that equality would be brought about by the execution of the deed appointing £ 8,600 to her elder daughter. **It was obviously a mistake**, because the effect of the execution of that deed was to bring about that which Lady Hood never intended and never contemplated.'

In his judgment Eve J referred at length to the decision of the Court of Appeal in Barrow v. Isaacs & Son[1891]1 QB 417. In that case the Court of Appeal declined to grant relief, on the ground of mistake, from forfeiture of a lease for breach of a covenant against underletting. The solicitors acting for a respectable tenant **had overlooked** the covenant and the premises had been sublet to a respectable subtenant.... Lord Esher MR said,... that the head tenant had had '**a mere passive state of mind**': 'I should say that **mere forgetfulness is not mistake at all** in ordinary language. ...'

The fullest academic treatment of this topic is in Goff & Jones, The Law of Unjust Enrichment, 8th ed, paras 9-32 - 9 - 42. The editors distinguish**between incorrect conscious beliefs, incorrect tacit assumptions, and true cases of mere causative ignorance** ('causative' in the sense that but for his ignorance the person in question would not have acted as he did). The deputy judge's first instance decision in Pitt v. Holt ... is suggested as **an example of mere causative ignorance: 'If someone does not apply his mind to a point at all, it is difficult to say that there has been some real mistake about the point'**. The Court of Appeal adopted a different view of the facts, treating the case ... as one of an incorrect conscious belief on the part of Mrs Pitt...**The editors of Goff & Jones are, on balance, in favour of treating mere causative ignorance as sufficient.** ..."(加黑部分是笔者的强调)

上述 Walker 勋爵所讲可作以下的解释：

1. 健忘、不注意或无知不是错误。例如，对某方面的无知就会与有关的错误理解扯不上关系，因为想也没有想过的事情，就不存在对错的问题。正如在 Pitt v. Holt 先例的一审中所说："If someone does not apply his mind to a point at all, it is difficult to say that there has been some real mistake about the point."

但这些方面也往往会导致错误方对现存事实或法律的错误理解，例如在 Hookway v. Racing Victoria Ltd(2005) 13 VR 444 澳大利亚先例中，涉及在一场赛马比赛中，主办方因为不知道上诉机制规则的改变以为冠军已经决定，就派发了冠军奖金，但选手上诉后排名被改变，主办方发现后以错误为由向原本的冠军取回奖金。这就涉及了对赛马会上诉机制改变的不注意或无知是否仍能以错误获得救济的争议。上诉庭最终判主办方可以向原本的冠军取回奖金。

2. 在英国有类似的 Lady Hood of Avalon v. Mackinnon(1909) 1 Ch 476 先例，简单案情涉及 Lady Hood 给两位女儿分财产。在 1888 年大女儿结婚时财产已经分过一次给她。但到 1904 年去再分财产时，Lady Hood 希望平等对待两位女儿，但她忘记了 16 年前已经分过一部分财产给大女儿。随后，她在分给每人 8600 英镑后，才想起 1888 年的事情，就以错误为诉因向大女儿成功取回这笔钱。

3. 导致错误的无知(causative ignorance)与刻意错误相信或假设(conscious mistaken belief/assumption)不容易区分，Walker 勋爵是说仅是无知，即使导致错误，仍不足以构成法律承认的可诉错误。

4. 要注意是所提及的案例如 Hookway v. Racing Victoria Ltd, Lady Hood of Avalon v. Mackinnon 与 Pitt v. Holt 先例，都不是本章针对的一份有对价的合约，如国际商业合约。针对没有对价的合约/契约如捐赠或设立信托，由于没有政策上需要考虑合约约束的保障(security of contract)与神圣性(sanctity)，也不影响可能依赖有关合约的第三人等方面，也就对单方面搞错，包括涉及健忘、不注意或无知是否构成可诉错误会有所放宽。正如在 Pitt v. Holt 最高院先例中，Walker 勋爵说："… It **does not matter if the mistake is due to carelessness** on the part of the person making the **voluntary disposition**, unless the circumstances are such as to show that he deliberately ran the risk, or must be taken to have run the risk, of being wrong. …. Nor need the mistake be known to (still less induced by) the person or persons taking a benefit under the disposition. **The fact that a unilateral mistake is sufficient** (without the additional ingredient of misrepresentation or fraud) **to make a gift voidable has been attributed to gifts being outside the law's special concern for the sanctity of contracts** … Conversely, the fact that a purely unilateral mistake may be sufficient to find relief is arguably a good reason for the court to apply a more stringent test as to the seriousness of the mistake before granting relief."(加黑部分是笔者的强调)

6. 以客观测试决定合约是否成立与合约条件/条文

经常会出现的相互错误（mutual mistake）争议是双方对合约是否成立，或如果成立合约的内容、条件/条文（terms）是什么有不同的主观理解。例如A是理解合约已经成立，合约条件（这可以包括合约的方方面面）是x。但对方B却认为合约尚未成立，或即使是成立了，合约条件也只会是y。

这种争议经常在双方以言行/书信往来谈判达成（或尚未达成）合约的情况下出现。双方经过整理后共同在一份完整与正式的合约签字的情况下，这种争议会相对较少，毕竟自愿下去签字就代表了同意该正式合约的正确与完整。

这种对有根本重要性的合约条件的相互错误理解与其他可诉错误有一个很大的不同。在其他如共同错误或对对方身份有单方面错误，是令一个表面有效的合约自始无效。但在这种对合约条件的相互错误，如果对有根本重要性的条件是一方主观认为是x而另一方主观认为是y，而法院或仲裁庭客观看是确定不了双方同意的是x或是y，就代表合约根本尚未成立，不是令合约无效的问题。这也可先节录《Misrepresentation，Mistake and Non-Disclosure》（2022年，第6版）一书之13-28段说："**Mistake by the defendant which is not overridden by the objective test** Where the claimant fails to satisfy the objective test，he has failed to establish the contract that he alleges. But it is important to recognise the limitations of such a decision. The claimant was seeking to prove that the defendant was bound to a contract on terms（x）. He fails. This only proves that there was no contract on terms（x）. … it is not necessarily clear whether there was no contract …；or whether there was a contract but on terms（y）. …"

以上所说可以《Misrepresentation，Mistake and Non-Disclosure》（2022年，第6版）一书之13-01段去总结说："'**Mistake' in this context** At first sight，the language of mistake fits rather uncomfortably … To say that a party to a contract make a mistake is to say that he misunderstood something：that he had a belief，or misunderstanding，that was incorrect. But how can one party be mistaken about the terms of the contract? If they are the terms of the contract，then he must surely，in law，have agreed to them. If he agreed to them，he did not make a mistake about them. This appears to be a fundamental enquiry about whether the contract was formed at all，rather than whether the（formed）contract was vitiated by a defect in consent. This difficulty does not arise in relation to written contracts，where the document is the contract-and one or both of the parties can have misunderstood what the document contained when he gave his consent to it. … It is more difficult to speak of 'mistake' in relation to contracts which are not reduced to writing，and which are formed through discussions between the parties who exchange communications until there is an expression of final assent by one party to the latest proposal of the other. But even here the enquiry is essentially the same: the communications are to be analysed to determine whether there is a contract, and (if so) on what terms. If, at the end of that analysis the conclusion is that there is a contract on a set of terms (x); but one of the parties believed either that there was no contract, or that there was a contract but on a set of terms (y), then we can say that that party was mistaken about the terms of the contract."

对这种单方面或相互错误理解合约条件,可举已经介绍过的买方对购买的货物(燕麦)的品种或描述有了主观错误理解的 Smith v. Hughes (1871) LR 6 QB 597 早期先例为例。买方以为买的是"老燕麦",卖方知道自己出售的是"新燕麦",[15] 双方在鸡同鸭讲下同意了买卖合约。从他们的主观想法看来,显然是双方根本没有想法一致(consensus ad idem),应是买卖合约仍未算是成立。但双方的言行却是已经达成合约,例如在书面的往来中清楚表达了要约(offer)与无条件地接受(acceptance),甚至相互祝贺达成合约。虽然在 Smith v. Hughes 先例中,买方以交付的不是老燕麦而拒收,但这种案件会是双方进一步在履行中才发现这对合约条件的相互错误。

解决这种错误的办法已经多次重复(如在笔者的《合约的解释:规则与应用》一书),解释合约是纯客观的做法(也就是法院或仲裁庭去客观解释),完全不理会双方订约方对他们的主观想法提供的证据。这些证据不会被采纳,如果证人在开庭接受盘问时想提供主观想法的口头证据也往往会被对方代表律师或法官/仲裁员阻止。否则,双方有了争议肯定会各说各的,即使真正在订约时(可能是不久前但也会是多年前),双方对"想法不一致"的争议的合约内容、条文/条件实是没有去深思熟虑过,或根本不记得。但这样,在双方坚持想法不一致的证据下,去考虑主观想法,岂非合约会因在订约时双方想法不一致而无效?但这在合约已经部分或全部履行时并不现实,加上这种情况实在太多会导致大量合约变为无效令这样的做法更不现实。正如 Donaldson 大法官在 Summit Investment Inc v. British Steel Corp (1987) 1 Lloyd's Rep 230 先例中说:"... their actual intentions are happily irrelevant, since, were it otherwise, many, and perhaps most, disputes upon points of construction would be resolved by holding that the parties are not ad idem..."

---

[15] 在很多情况下,卖方是不知道买方的特定要求是什么,就算知道,在买方自己小心的大原则(例如,应该查问清楚才确定买,或对想买的燕麦应描述得更详尽)与卖方在没有自动披露责任的大原则下,也不用提醒买方。在《Sale of Goods Act 1979》之 Section 14(1)就说:"Except as provided by this section and section 15 below and subject to any other enactment, there is no implied about the quality or fitness for any particular purpose of goods supplied under a contract of sale."一般情况下就只要符合该类货物的一般用途。但在 Section 14(3)也针对了商业交易中,如果买方明示或默示告诉了卖方自己的需求,并且能合理依赖卖方的判断货物是否适合时,才会默示货物适合买方特别用途(fitness for particular purpose),这方面可见杨大明律师的《国际货物买卖》一书第四章之6段。

6.1 合约成立与否的客观测试

英国法律是以客观测试(objective test)来确定双方当事人在合约谈判中的言行与书信往来,以解决这种争议,这包括有效合约有否在双方想法一致与你情我愿下成立,如果合约成立,是以什么条件/条文成立。

在英国法律下对有否成立了一个有约束力的合约在笔者的《合约的解释:规则与应用》一书第二章"合约的达成与内容"中已有详论,在此不去重复或多讲。有关如何通过客观测试来看待双方谈判言行与书信往来的证据以找出他们主张的合约条件与内容最后双方是否达成一致想法,可先节录一些权威说法。首先是 The "Hannah Blumenthal"(1983)1 AC 854 贵族院先例中,Diplock 勋爵说:

"To create a contract by exchange of promises between two parties where the promise of each party constitutes the consideration for the promise of the other, what is necessary is that the intention of each as it has been communicated to and understood by the other(even though that which has been communicated does not represent the actual state of mind of the communicator) should coincide. That is what English lawyers mean when they resort to the Latin phrase consensus ad idem and the words … are essential to the concept of consensus ad idem, the lack of which prevents the formation of a binding contract in English law.

Thus if A(the offeror) makes a communication to B(the offeree) whether in writing, orally or by conduct, which in the circumstances at the time the communication was received, (1) B, if he were a reasonable man, would understand as stating A's intention to act or refrain from acting in some specified manner if B will promise on his part to act or refrain from acting in some manner also specified in the offer, and (2) B does in fact understand A's communication to mean this, and in his turn makes to A a communication conveying his willingness so to act or to refrain from acting which mutates mutant is satisfies the same two conditions as respects A, the consensus ad idem essential to the formation of a contract under English law is complete."

另是 Shogun Finance Ltd v. Hudson(2003)UKHL 62 贵族院先例中,Phillips 勋爵说:"A contract is normally concluded when an offer made by one party('the offeror') is accepted by the party to whom the offer has been made('the offeree'). Normally the contract is only concluded when the acceptance is communicated by the offeree to the offeror. **A contract will not be concluded unless the parties are agreed as to its material terms**. There must be 'consensus ad idem'. **Whether the parties have reached agreement on the terms is not determined by evidence of the subjective intention of each party. It is, in large measure, determined by making an objective appraisal of the exchanges between the parties**. If an offeree understands an offer in accordance with its natural meaning and accepts it, the offeror cannot be heard to say that he intended the words of his offer to have a different meaning. The contract stands according to the natural meaning of the words used."(加黑部分是笔者的强调)

但现实中有各种各样的情况出现,所以决定双方有否成立有效合约与双方想法一致,不严格是要每次去找出双方是否曾经有要约与接受去显示双方合意与想法一致。只介绍Denning勋爵在Gibson v. Manchester City Council(1978)1 WLR 520上诉庭先例中说:"... as I understand the law, there is no need to look for a strict offer and acceptance. You should look at the correspondence as a whole and at the conduct of the parties and see therefrom whether the parties have come to an agreement on everything that was material. If by their correspondence and their conduct you can see an agreement on all material terms — which was intended thenceforward to be binding — then there is a binding contract in law even though all the formalities have not been gone through."

另一种情况是双方谈判中的言行与书信往来,除了不显示有过要约与接受外,连双方有否谈妥了所有希望谈拢的合约条件也无法确定,但双方已经迫不及待开始履行合约。如在一个国际货物买卖合约中,虽然双方看来仍在谈判中,但买方已经向卖方开出信用证或卖方已经交付货物。这样,说是双方没有订约意图去达成有效合约,或是因双方谈妥的合约条件不足够、含糊不清与不肯定,令合约无效,就不现实了。法院或仲裁庭更应该做的是客观去看在双方没有谈妥的合约条件,或是含糊不清与不肯定之处,能否以默示条文填补,或将双方觉得没有谈妥的条文视为并不重要,谈不拢也罢。这可节录在G Percy Trentham Ltd v. Archital Luxfer Ltd(1993)1 Lloyd's Rep 25上诉庭先例中,Steyn大法官说:"... it is true that the coincidence of offer and acceptance will in the vast majority of cases represent the mechanism of contract formation. It is so in the case of a contract alleged to have been made by an exchange of correspondence. But it is not necessarily so in the case of a contract alleged to have come into existence during and as a result of performance.... **The fact that the transaction was performed on both sides will often make it unrealistic to argue that there was no intention to enter into legal relations**. It will often make it difficult to submit that the contract is void for vagueness or uncertainty. Specifically, **the fact that the transaction is executed makes it easier to imply a term resolving any uncertainty, or, alternatively, it may make it possible to treat a matter not finalised in negotiations as inessential**."(加黑部分是笔者的强调)

6.2 国际商业合约的谈判与订立

合约可以通过不同的手段或方式来订立。在今天的国际商业社会,订约方谈判的方式往往是通过电邮、微信等电子通信;或是部分电子文书往来、部分口头(电话、微信电话等);又或是口头但间中有文书确认谈了或同意了什么条件/条文。反正整个可以是漫长与艰辛的谈判过程就是双方通过相互或一方的让步、谈判技巧、说服力、各自的估算等,并由言行或书信往来显示双方已经对要谈妥的方方面面逐步达成一致想法，而这些同意了的方面也已经是足以履行该合约（任何合约都不可能涵盖将来会发生的所有事情，其中总会有遗漏或欠缺。如果将来出现了合约遗漏或欠缺的问题，默示条文或地位就会填补与解释），这样有效合约也就成立了。在很多国际商业领域中，当事人也是大量以这种形式去订立合约，如在国际大量的货物/商品买卖、租船合约等。

但在不少的国际商业谈判中，订约双方会多走一步，把谈判直到最后双方通过言行与书信往来在方方面面达成的一致想法整理出来一份完整与正式（formal）的合约文件，并且在双方检查与满意后轮流或同时签字。这会涉及大量额外的工作，所以只在一些需要一份正式合约的商业活动才这样多走一步，如一份昂贵与重要的合约，特别是涉及第三人（如融资银行、集团公司、政府机构、合伙人、担保人等），或履行期限较长与涉及其他执行合约义务的人士（如员工、管理人等）的合约与其他各种不同的情形。显然，不整理出一份完整与正式的合约，而只告诉其他有关的第三人："合约已经订立，而有关的内容可以给你 5 个文件夹，加上 3 份参与谈判的相关人士对同意了什么的记录，你去从中寻找。"这显然不是可被接受的做法。

为了避免对有效与约束性合约在什么时候订立有争议，到底是在言行或书信往来显示了双方已经对要谈妥的方方面面达成一致想法的一刻，或是在后来如相隔 1 个月后才整理出一份完整合约签字的一刻？如果是以前者的时间为准，后来准备一份签字合约就被视为例行手续（formality）。但如果是以后者的时间为准，如在谈妥前说明是"以合约为准"（subject contract），[16] 在整理完整合约的时间就仍会视为在谈判，任何一方可以改变订约意图而没有法律后果。也会在整理时挑出双方在谈判过程中以为是同意了的方面但其实不是，或是出了新的问题需要重新启动谈判并达成妥协（或无法妥协）。

在一个漫长与复杂的国际商业合约的谈判后，整理出一份完整与正式签字的合约是有好处或必要性的。否则在履行时发现谈判的内容有欠缺，如模糊、不肯定或双方的同意不完整，双方在有了争议后再去在零散的言行与书信往来中找出双方到底同意了什么殊非易事，而且在每一个方面都有得争与结果不肯定。在整理一份完整合约时由于双方当时有共同利益希望促成合约，如果发现对是否同意了 x 仍有疑问，双方就会在整理时搞清楚，也一般不会有异议。但如果后来履行出了问题与发生利益冲突，在没有正式合约的情况下，就会有一方当事人坚持双方在订约时同意的是 y 了。可见，整理一份完整合约时，将这些欠缺或尚未完全谈妥的地方找出来。这就比在将来履行时才发现会好得多。

6.2.1 通过言行与书信往来达成合约

在《Misrepresentation, Mistake and Non-Disclosure》（2022 年，第 6 版）一书之 13–19 段中说：

---

〔16〕 见笔者《合约的解释：规则与应用》一书第八章之 4 段。

"**Summary of the test to be applied** … it will be useful to summarise the test that the courts will apply in order to ascertain whether there is a contract, and (if so) on what terms, in a case where the contract is alleged to have been formed by successive communications between the parties. It can be put in the following propositions:[17] (针对双方在一连串言行的交流后被指称订立了合约,法院认定双方有否真正订立合约与如果有是以什么条件订立,可以根据以下的步骤去分析:)

1. The first question is whether the parties were in fact (subjectively) in agreement on the existence and terms of the contract. If they were, that should be determinative. (第一个问题是双方当事人是否主观同意有合约存在与基于什么条件存在。如果是,这就是决定性,不存在法院去质疑。这通常在文书请求/案件陈述中原告主张有合约关系,被告对这一点是同意。)

2. If the parties were not, in fact, in agreement then-in the case where the claimant is seeking to rely on there being a contract on terms (x), and the defendant is either denying that there is a contract at all, or is asserting that there is a contract on terms (y) — the question becomes whether the claimant can in law hold the defendant to have agreed to a contract on terms (x). (如果双方在主观上是不同意有否合约存在[18]或基于什么条件存在 — 原告主张合约存在并且是条件 x,但被告主张合约并不存在,而即使存在,合约条件是 y — 这样就要看原告能否说服法院根据法律判被告是同意了合约并且是条件 x)

He may do so if: (原告是要成立:) (a) The defendant's words, conduct or (exceptionally) silence would have led a reasonable person in the claimant's position to believe that the defendant was agreeing to (x); and [被告的言行或沉默(例外情况如沉默造成误导)让原告作为一位'合理人士'是去相信被告同意了合约条件 x] (b) The claimant in fact believed that the defendant was

---

[17] 见 DNA Productions (Europe) Ltd v. Manoukian (2008) EWHC 943 (Ch) 先例。

[18] 在 Maple Leaf Macro Volitality Master Fund v. Rouvroy (2009) EWHC 257 (Comm) 先例中,Andrew Smith 大法官说:"I conclude that on an objective assessment the parties … evinced an intention to be bound contractually by its terms. … However, there are circumstances in which the parties to what would **objectively be held to be contractual are not legally bound by it under English law**. If the other parties actually and reasonably believed that the defendants intended to make a contract, there would be a concluded contract, **but not if the other parties knew or would reasonably have believed that that was not the defendants' intention and not, in my judgment, if the other parties had simply formed no view one way or the other as to whether the defendants so intended**. That is the opinion expressed by Professor Sir Gunter Treitel in Chitty on Contracts, (2008) 30th Ed at para 2 - 004, and I agree with it." (加黑部分是笔者的强调)

agreeing to(x).(原告也在当时确实相信被告同意了合约条件 x,而不是知道或合理知道对方其实并不是这样的想法。)

3. If the claimant succeeds in showing that he can hold the defendant to a contract on terms(x)in accordance with proposition 2, he has established a contract on terms(x)**unless** the defendant can rebut this by showing that the claimant's conduct, words or(exceptionally)silence would have led a reasonable person in his position to believe that the claimant was agreeing to(y), and that the defendant in fact believed that the claimant was agreeing to(y). In such a case, there is no contract. [被告如果反驳,就需要提供证据显示原告的言行或沉默(例外情况如沉默造成误导)让被告作为一位'合理人士'是去相信原告同意了合约条件 y]"

显然,最后是审理法官或仲裁员作为合理与客观的人士在考虑双方提供的证据后,认定原告或被告的主张哪个更为合理与实际,也就决定了合约条件是 x 或是 y。

最后可以节录《Misrepresentation, Mistake and Non-Disclosure》(2022 年,第 6 版)一书之 13 – 35 段说:"**Interpretation of communications, and interpretation of the written contract**. ... it could be said that the objective test is the rule of interpretation of communications; that is, when the question is whether the parties by their communications have come to an agreement, the courts will interpret those communications objectively, from the perspective of the parties. What the defendant is taken to have agreed to is not what he intended his communication to convey but what it would have conveyed to a reasonable person in the claimant's position-and it is binding if the claimant in fact so understood it. ..."

6.2.2 完整与正式签字的合约

在《Misrepresentation, Mistake and Non-Disclosure》(2022 年,第 6 版)一书之 13 – 33 段中说:"**Contracts in writing**. The objective significance of writing is even stronger where the parties have not only used writing as a means of communication during their negotiations, but have, on conclusion of their agreement, decided that the agreement should be put into a written document, to which they will both then give their assent(typically, by signing it). ... The purpose of such practice is clarity and certainty. If each party has given his assent to a single, written statement of the terms, there is much less room for doubt or argument about the fact that both parties have agreed to the contract(their signatures show it); and what they have agreed to(the document is to be conclusive)—all the more so if the written contract makes clear that it is the complete agreement.[19] ..."

---

〔19〕 这特别是合约加上一条"完整合约条文"(Entire agreement clause),可见本书第一章之 1.3.8 段、第四章之 6.6 段与笔者《合约的解释:规则与应用》一书第十三章之 2 段。

也就是说，如果订约双方多走一步把通过言行与书信往来达成的合约整理出来成为一份完整与正式的合约文件并签字，除了在极大程度上排除了双方是否有订约意图与是否达成一致想法的争议，解释合约条件/条文的重心也转移至该正式的合约，而不再理会较早在谈判中与在言行/书信往来中同意了什么条件，这些谈判的证据已经是无关，也已经被该正式合约替代或超越。

这可节录部分权威说法，首先是早在苏格兰最高民事法院的 A & J Inglis v. John Buttery & Co(1877)5 R. 58 先例中，Gifford 勋爵的说法。这在上诉去了贵族院[(1878)3 App Cas 552]后，也被 Blackburn 勋爵确认。Gifford 勋爵说："Now, I think it is quite fixed ... that where parties agree to embody, and do actually embody, their contract in a formal written deed, then **in determining what the contract really was and really meant, a court must look to the formal deed and to that deed alone. This is only carrying out the will of the parties**. The only meaning of adjusting a formal contract is, that **the formal contract shall supersede all loose and preliminary negotiations** — that there shall be no room for misunderstandings which may often arise, and which do constantly arise, in the course of long, and it may be desultory conversations, or in the course of correspondence or negotiations during which the parties are often widely at issue as to what they will insist on and what they will concede. The **very purpose of a formal contract is to put an end to the disputes which would inevitably arise if the matter were left upon verbal negotiations or upon mixed communings partly consisting of letters and partly of conversations**. The written contract is that which is to be appealed to by both parties, however different it may be from their previous demands or stipulations, whether contained in letters or in verbal conversation. There can be **no doubt that this is the general rule** ...."（加黑部分是笔者的强调）

较近期的 Prenn v. Simmonds(1971)1 WLR 1381 贵族院先例，再次确认 A & J Inglis v. John Buttery & Co 先例。其间也有不少争论认为这所谓的"口头证据规则"(Parol Evidence Rule)[20]有太多例外，不如干脆推翻。其中 Wilberforce 勋爵也说了仍支持这解释合约规则不变的理由："**The reason for not admitting evidence of these exchanges is not a technical one or even mainly one of convenience, (though the attempt to admit it did greatly prolong the case and add to its expense). It is simply that such evidence is unhelpful.** By the nature of things, where negotiations are difficult, the parties' positions, with each passing letter, are changing and until the final agreement, though converging, still divergent. It is **only the final document which records a consensus**. If the previous documents use different expressions, how does construction of those expressions, itself a doubtful process, help on the construction of the contractual

[20]　在笔者《合约的解释：规则与应用》一书第六章之 2 段有详细介绍。

words? If the same expressions are used, nothing is gained by looking back: indeed, something may be lost since the relevant surrounding circumstances may be different. And at this stage there is no consensus of the parties to appeal to. It may be said that previous documents may be looked at to explain the aims of the parties. In a limited sense this is true: the commercial, or business object, of the transaction, objectively ascertained, may be a surrounding fact. ... And if it can be shown that one interpretation completely frustrates that object, to the extent of rendering the contract futile, that may be a strong argument for an alternative interpretation, if that can reasonably be found. [21] But beyond that it may be difficult to go: it may be a matter of degree, or of judgment, how far one interpretation, or another, gives effect to a common intention: the parties, indeed, may be pursuing that intention with differing emphasis, and hoping to achieve it to an extent which may differ, and in different ways. The words used may, and often do, represent a formula which means different things to each side, yet may be accepted because that is the only way to get 'agreement' and in the hope that disputes will not arise. The only course then can be to try to ascertain the 'natural' meaning. Far more, and indeed **totally, dangerous is it to admit evidence of one party's objective, even if this is known to the other party**. However strongly pursued this may be, the other party may only be willing to give it partial recognition, and **in a world of give and take, men often have to be satisfied with less than they want**. So, again, it would be a matter of speculation how far the common intention was that the particular objective should be realised."(加黑部分是笔者的强调)

Wilberforce 勋爵提出支持口头证据规则不变的理由包括:

1. 如果采纳合约双方漫长与艰辛的谈判过程中所有的言行或书信往来,会有大量的证据(文件与口头)。这显然会让法院诉讼/仲裁变得更耗时与更昂贵。

2. 采纳这种谈判的"口头证据"对客观解释双方的订约意图与同意了什么也没有帮助。因为在谈判过程中,双方曾经表达过的订约意图或是坚持的立场也只是暂时性与经常会变来变去,甚至在最后一刻作出重大让步。曾经同意过的事情与之后订立与签字的正式合约,即使是同样的文字,在不同的背景/语境(context)下也会完全不同。例如,在谈判表达同意时的20天前市场看涨,但订约时刚出了"黑天鹅"事件导致市场看跌。更不说谈判过程中的用字或表达如果与正式合约不一样,应是更

---

〔21〕 Wilberforce 勋爵是说只在一些特殊的情况下,需要看双方谈判中的证据找出合约的真正解释,也就是口头证据规则的例外情况:见笔者《合约的解释:规则与应用》一书第六章之2.3段。Wilberforce勋爵提的例外是如果一份正式的签字合约的字面解释会令合约完全失去目的,除此之外还有合约变更(rectification)、私人字典(private dictionary)、商业习惯做法/惯例或术语、附带保证/协议、有关合约标的或订约方身份等的例外情况,都会需要考虑谈判时的"口头证据",光靠解释一份正式的签字合约是无法解释与确定双方的订约意图与同意了什么。

难对合约解释有帮助了。

谈判过程中也会有一方当事人为了避免在某一方面(如出了某些事情风险谁去承担)谈得太僵,也觉得合约履行如果顺利该事情应是不会发生,所以不再坚持而改了谈判的话题。表面看来,该当事人好像是以行为或沉默同意了对方坚持的立场,但实质并没有同意或在将来事情发生时有争议。

这林林总总的问题,都显示了在谈判过程中寻找双方的订约意图与一致看法是没有帮助,反而会带来混乱。要寻找什么是双方最后的订约意图与达成的一致想法,最好与最肯定是只局限在解释双方签字确认的一份看来是完整内容的正式合约。

3. 如果采纳谈判过程中的"口头证据",有更大危险引入双方订约方的主观想法证据并会带来已经提到的滥用、欺诈与伪证(perjury)。

接下来的 Chartbrook Ltd v. Persimmon Homes Ltd(2009)1 AC 1101 贵族院先例也有同样的针对与说法。如 Hoffmann 勋爵说:"The rule that pre-contractual negotiations are inadmissible was clearly reaffirmed by this House in Prenn v. Simmonds[1971] 1 WLR 1381 ... where Lord Wilberforce said that earlier authorities 'contain little to encourage, and much to discourage, evidence of negotiation or of the parties' subjective intentions'. It is clear that the rule of inadmissibility has been established for a very long time."

Rodger 勋爵也说:"Like Lord Hoffmann, I would decline counsel's elegant but, in the event, unnecessary invitation to revisit the rule in Prenn v. Simmonds ... No one could possibly say that the rule is based on some error of law or misconception. On the contrary, the main pros and cons of having regard to prior negotiations when interpreting a formal contract have been known and discussed for centuries... Some 60 years later, with rather more deliberation, the House affirmed that approach in A & J Inglis v. John Buttery & Co ... and, a century after that, reaffirmed it in Prenn v. Simmonds ... The rule could scarcely be more firmly embedded in our law."

4. 如果采纳谈判过程中的"口头证据",也影响一份正式合约的肯定性。而商业合约的肯定性至关重要,也是英国法律在国际商业社会受欢迎的主要原因。在 Shogun Finance Ltd v. Hudson(2003)UKHL 62 贵族院先例中,Hobhouse 勋爵说:"The rule that other evidence may not be adduced to contradict the provisions of a contract contained in a written document is fundamental to the mercantile law of the country; the bargain is the document; the certainty of the contract depends on it. ...The rule is one of the great strengths of English commercial law and is one of the main reasons for the international success of English law in preference to laxer systems which do not provide the same certainty."

有关解释合约的大量解释规则(rules of construction),读者可参阅笔者的《合约的解释:规则与应用》一书。

7. 可诉错误与怀疑的关系

如果一方当事人 A 怀疑或明知道现存事实或法律有可能并非如此,但认为相比搞错的几率,有其他因素如带来的好处使得他值得冒险,那只要事实没有超出 A 愿意承担的风险范围,只是结果猜错了,就不能算是可诉错误。

如果 A 知道事实可能是 x 也可能是 y,只要事实确实是 x 或 y,A 只是押宝 x 但结果是 y,就谈不上 A 有任何错误。只有在结果既不是 x,也不是 y,而是 z 时,才会是错误。

简单举一个例子,在一个艺术品的买卖中,如一幅书法作品说是王羲之的真迹,但市场上也有说法这不是出自王羲之而是唐代的摹本。这样,在该买卖中,买方 A 以高价向 B 买入但后来该书法作品在权威的鉴定后被确认为唐代摹本,导致价格大幅下调。但 A 不能以可诉错误去向 B 主张买卖合约自始无效,要求复原。因为 A 作为一位合理买方是知道市场上有这个怀疑并带着怀疑买入,加上在"买方自己小心"(caveat emptor)的大原则下,这不是错误。

但换一个情况,该书法作品被鉴定为现代仿造品,既不是真迹也不是唐代摹本,一文不值。这样,A 就有机会成功向 B 主张可诉错误了。

有关怀疑不是错误的权威说法,可节录在 Kleinwort Benson Ltd v. Lincoln City Council(1999)2 AC 349 贵族院先例中,Hope 勋爵说:"A state of doubt is different from that of mistake. A person who pays when in doubt takes the risk that he may be wrong-and that is so whether the issue is one of fact or one of laws."这是说在对事实或法律有怀疑的情况下去做的任何事情都要对最终怀疑成真自担风险。

怀疑与错误也不是绝对不相容。例如,在上述的王羲之书法真迹例子中,A 以高价买入除了是考虑到会是唐代摹本的风险外,也有怀疑会可能是现代仿造品,只是可能性极低如 0.1% 或 0.2%,与买入价格等因素总体平衡后,决定买入。显然如果真是现代仿造品,不应该因为 A 有稍许的怀疑而否定是错误。

在复杂与多变的国际商业社会,确有不少精明的商人在订立一份昂贵合约或支付一笔大钱时,都会思前想后,对每件事都有怀疑顾虑。他们对将来情况的估计,已在本章之 2 段解释是不被视为可诉错误。但即使对现存事实或法律,也应会有怀疑顾虑。在复杂的国际商业环境下是不容易全盘掌握现存事实真相,而在英国的普通法体系下虽然尽力追求肯定与可预测,法律仍会被将来的案例改变并且有追溯力,令现存的法律从正确变为错误。只能说对一位谨慎、有经验与称职的商人来说,他们在商业活动中通常是在认为错误与怀疑的风险是极低与可控下才会做出决定。

显然,如果法律对两种极端情况不做区分,一律作出可诉错误的法律救济去令合约无效,这并不是公平合理与现实的做法。

这样,法律为了肯定,就需要对什么程度的怀疑可以构成法律承认的错误,与什么程度不再是错误而是"明知山有虎,偏向虎山行"的自愿冒险,划出分水岭。显然,怀疑程度低的是可以与错误共存,但怀疑程度高的就不行了。这可节录在 Jazztel Plc v. Revenue and Customs Commissioners(2017)EWHC 677(Ch)先例中,Marcus Smith 大法官说:"... Mistake can co-exist with an element of doubt. By 'doubt' is meant the claimant's conscious appreciation that the facts or law may not be as he or she believes them to be. ... For example, a claimant may (wrongly) believe that he or she is legally obliged to make a payment, whilst at the same time appreciating that there is an argument that he or she is not in fact obliged to make the payment at all. Such **doubts are not inconsistent with mistake, provided the doubt does not overwhelm the mistake** ..."(加黑部分是笔者的强调)

这个问题对国际商业活动影响最大与带来最多困难的是在两方面,这将在以下段节针对:(1)是错误作出支付(wrongful payment)并在后来发现试图去向收款人(payee)或得利方(enriched party)取回来;(2)是订立和解协议(compromise/settlement agreement)后发现订约时对现存的事实或法律有错误理解或估算,试图以可诉错误令和解协议无效。

7.1 错误支付以不当得利要求归还

错误支付(mistaken payment)是指如果在支付方(payor)A 知道或应该知道现存的正确事实或法律地位(也就是不必支付)的情况下是不会去支付的,这才突显了"错误"。

任何人士如果发现他在对现存事实或法律的错误理解下支付金钱后,想向对方取回这笔钱,英国法律下错误支付的 A 是可以不当得利(unjust enrichment),[22] 要求对方收款人(payee)B 退回这笔付错的金钱。在 Jazztel Plc v. Revenue and Customs Commissioners(2017)EWHC 677(Ch)先例中,Marcus Smith 大法官简单针对错误支付以不当得利的诉因向收款人取回说:

"In short, in order to establish a prima facie claim to restitution of an enrichment, all a claimant need show is that: (i) at the time the enrichment was conferred, the claimant was mistaken; and (ii) the mistake caused the enrichment to be conferred (in the sense that, **but for** the mistaken, the enrichment would not have been conferred)."(加黑部分是笔者的强调)

除非 B 乖乖退回给 A 这笔错误支付的金钱,否则 A 会要通过法律向 B 要回这笔钱,这在本质上是一个复原的索偿(restitutionary claim)。复原或不当得利作为诉因的索偿通常要满足三个要件:(1)是被告 B 必须得利(enrichment);(2)A 受损下(at

〔22〕 这课题在本书第三章之 5.4.3 段、第十章之 11.2 段与笔者的《合约的履行、弃权与禁反言》一书第五章之 4 段有详细介绍。

the expense of the claimant）B 才得利（不论是钱或其他的利益）；（3）让 B 保留这笔钱或其他利益是不公平的。

在近期的 Robert Stevens 教授的《The Laws of Restitution》（2023 年，第 1 版）一书中，Reed 勋爵也在序言中提到不当得利的要件说："The creation of the legal category of unjust enrichment，with a conceptual structure based on the four elements of（1）enrichment of the defendant，（2）at the expense of the claimant，（3）an unjust factor，and（4）the absence of a defence，is arguably the most remarkable development in English law in recent times."

可以说，不当得利的 B 也难以抗拒，不得把原告错误支付的钱视为天上掉馅饼去占有，除非可用改变地位（change of position）作为抗辩，证明这笔付错的钱已经被合理处理掉，只能部分归还或全部不归还。

早在 Fibrosa Spolka Akcyjna v. Fairbairn Lawson Combe Barbour Ltd（1943）AC 32 贵族院先例中已经有提到不当得利的诉因，并说是有别于合约或侵权，Wright 勋爵说："It is clear that any civilized system of law is bound to provide remedies for cases of what has been called unjust enrichment or unjust benefit，that is to prevent a man from retaining the money of or some benefit derived from another which it is against conscience that he should keep. Such remedies in English law are generically different from remedies in contract or in tort，and are now recognized to fall within a third category of the common law which has been called quasi-contract or restitution."

Wright 勋爵在上述节录的最后一句提到"准合约"（quasi-contract）或"复原"（restitution），是以前的叫法。直到较近期才试图将过往在方方方面有不同说法但本质上是复原索偿的案件归类为不当得利，并建立自己的一套理论。这主要的推动是来自 Peter Birks 教授，他在 2003 年出版的《Unjust Enrichment》一书据称是第一本以不当得利为名的书籍。在 1966 年出版第 1 版有关复原的权威书籍《The Law of Restitution》，也在 2016 年的第 9 版改名为《The Law of Unjust Enrichment》，该书的 2022 年第 10 版被本书各章节多处节录与引用。

本书主要针对各种影响合约效力的因素（vitiating factors），如误述（misrepresentation）、错误（mistake）、胁迫（duress）、不当得利（undue influence）、不合情理/显失公平交易（unconscionable bargain）或非法（illegality）等，无效或可使无效都难免带来复原或恢复到原状（restititio in integrum）的问题。复原也在其他方方面面涉及，包括合约、侵权、信托、财产等。本段针对的错误支付只是一方面，现在都可归类在"不当得利"。

7.1.1 怀疑下作出的支付是错误支付还是自愿支付

在 Woolwich Equitable Building Society v. Inland Revenue Commissioners（1993）AC 70 贵族院先例中，Goff 勋爵详尽分析了不同类别、性质或情况下的错误支付，哪

些是可以要求收款人归还,哪些是不可以。其中提到自愿支付(voluntary payment)[23]是无法要求收款人归还,说:"Where **a sum has been paid which is not due**, but it has **not been paid under a mistake of fact or under compulsion** …, it is generally **not recoverable**. Such a payment has often been called a voluntary payment. In particular, a payment is regarded as **a voluntary payment and so as irrecoverable** in the following circumstances. …(b) The payer has the opportunity of contesting his liability in proceedings, but instead gives way and pays… So **where money has been paid under pressure of actual or threatened legal proceedings for its recovery**, the payer cannot say that for that reason the money has been paid under compulsion and is therefore recoverable by him. If he chooses to give way and pay, rather than obtain the decision of the court on the question whether the money is due, **his payment is regarded as voluntary and so is not recoverable**: see e. g., William Whiteley Ltd. v. The King, 101 L. T. 741…. "(加黑部分是笔者的强调)

早在 Maskell v. Horner(1915)3 KB 106 上诉庭先例中,Reading 勋爵就提到了自愿支付好像是赠送礼物或捐款一样,给出去就不存在可复原索偿,因为收款人/受礼人不存在有任何"不当"(unjust)。Reading 勋爵说:"If a person **with knowledge** of the facts pays money, which **he is not in law bound to pay, and in circumstances implying that he is paying it voluntarily to close the transaction, he cannot recover it**. Such a payment is in law like a gift, and the transaction cannot be reopened. If a person pays money, which he is not bound to pay, under the compulsion of urgent and pressing necessity or of seizure, actual or threatened, of his goods he can recover it as money had and received. …"(加黑部分是笔者的强调)

也就是说,支付方明知道法律是不必支付,但仍这样做,就视为自愿支付,将来是无法以复原索偿去取回了。这在国际商业活动中也不乏例子,背后原因可以有很多,如有了争议但为了将来的友好合作、维持关系、在对方合法压力下让步等。在这种情况下,如果在支付之后仍不解决问题,又或是因为换了负责人,又或是在咨询律师意见后,发现已经作出的支付有问题,想要拿回来。这时就要面对已经作出的支付是属于自愿支付还是在错误下作出的支付的争议,只有在后者的情况下才能以不当得利复原。

自愿支付与怀疑之间的关系是如果怀疑程度极高,就等同在对现存事实或法律的正确地位(无需作出支付)知情下但仍去支付。

在本书第二章之 6.4 段介绍的 Kleinwort Benson Ltd v. Lincoln City Council

---

[23] Goff 勋爵的说法是在贵族院的 Kleinwort Benson Ltd v. Lincoln City Council(1999)2 AC 349 先例之前,所以把错误理解法律下支付也当作自愿支付的一种,无法取回。但在 Kleinwort Benson 先例后,这法律地位已经有了改变,现在法律错误与事实错误下的支付都可向收款人以不当得利取回。

(1999)2 AC 349 贵族院先例中,Hope 勋爵说:"Cases where the payer was aware that there was an issue of law which was relevant but, being in doubt as to what the law was, paid without waiting to resolve that doubt may be left on one side. **A state of doubt is different from that of mistake.** A person who pays when in doubt takes the risk that he may be wrong-and that is so whether the issue is one of fact or one of law."(加黑部分是笔者的强调)

Hope 勋爵把错误与怀疑区分为两码事,就带来对任何错误支付的复原索偿案件,被告收款人就质疑原告在作出支付时有否对现存的事实或法律的任何怀疑。如果有,就代表这不是可诉错误,而是原告自担风险去自愿支付。

这在近期不少先例,希望走出这个法律困境。毕竟不让错误支付的当事人有复原救济只因有或多或少的怀疑,而让收款人不当得利,也是说不过去。在接下来的小段,会介绍部分先例。

7.1.2 Marine Trade SA v. Pioneer Freight Futures Co Ltd BVI(2010)1 Lloyd's Rep 631 先例

可先介绍 Marine Trade SA v. Pioneer Freight Futures Co Ltd BVI 先例,案情涉及原告和被告在 2007 年 5 月至 2008 年 9 月之间签署的 14 份远期运费协议(Forward Freight Agreement, FFA)。FFA 是基于波动剧烈的运费市场而产生的一种运费风险管理工具。简而言之,FFA 中的买方和卖方就某航线在未来某一个时间点的运费价格进行约定,然后收取或支付该预测价格与在该时间点波罗的海航运交易所(Baltic Exchange)发布的运费指数价格的差额。

2008 年金融海啸席卷全球,也给运费市场带来巨变,在很短的时间内有些运费指数甚至下跌了 90% 以上。很多 FFA 的订约方都面临要在 FFA 下支付大笔的现金进行结算,从而给公司运营带来现金流方面的巨大压力以及各种违约,甚至最终资金链断裂进而破产。本案中的原告与被告所签署的 FFA 中有违约终止与提早终止条文,可节录如下:

"5. **Events of Default and Termination Events**

(a) Events of Default. ... such party of any of the following events constitutes an event of default ...: -(i) Failure to Pay or Deliver. **Failure by the party to make, when due, any payment under this Agreement** or delivery under Section 2(a)(i) or 2(e) required to be made by it **if such failure is not remedied on or before the third Local Business Day after notice of such failure is given to the party**; (vii) Bankruptcy. ...

(2) **becomes insolvent or is unable to pay its debts or fails or admits in writing its inability generally to pay its debts as they become due**;

6. **Early Termination**

(a) **Right to Terminate Following Event of Default.** If at any time an Event of Default with respect to a party (the "Defaulting Party") has occurred and is then continuing, the other party (**the 'Non-defaulting Party'**) **may, by not more than 20 days notice to the Defaulting Party** specifying the relevant Event of Default, designate a day not earlier than the day such notice is effective as **an Early Termination Date in respect of all outstanding Transactions. ...**"(加黑部分是笔者的强调)

2009 年 1 月,在多份 FFA 中双方进行结算,发现被告作为卖方的 FFA 中,原告要支付给被告 1200 多万美元,而原告作为卖方的 FFA 中,被告要向原告支付 700 多万美元,相互扣抵之后,原告最终要向被告支付 500 多万美元。原告根据当时市场中的各种信息高度怀疑被告符合 FFA 中 5(a)(vii)(2)规定的无力偿还债务的违约事项,从而无需向被告支付 1200 多万美元。但是被告仍要向他支付 700 多万美元,于是在 2009 年 1 月底向被告开出了支付 700 多万美元的发票。而被告则在 2009 年 2 月 1 日向原告开出要求支付扣抵后的 500 多万美元的发票,并要求原告在 2009 年 2 月 6 日前支付。原告没有按时支付,被告又于 2009 年 2 月 9 日向原告发出 5(a)(i)下的通知。

原告担心被告在发出该通知后,进一步根据 6(a)提早结束条文而将所有尚未结算的交易都终止。于是原告向高院申请一个保持现状的中间禁令(interim injunction maintaining status quo)。[24] 高院的 Field 大法官拒绝了该会给被告公司的现金流带来灾难性效果的禁令。原告为了避免被告以提早终止条文去终止所有交易,在抗议下于 2009 年 2 月 13 日向被告支付 500 多万美元,但随后向法院提起诉讼要求被告向他支付 700 多万美元。

本案中的一个争议是,原告是否可以根据错误理解的合约条文(被告有权提早终止所有交易),在有怀疑与抗议下作出支付而在复原大原则下要求被告退还错误支付的 500 多万美元。Flaux 大法官认为在支付方当时的主观想法下,这笔钱不是错误支付,而是在预料之中的自愿支付,所以无法去复原把这笔钱要回来。他说:

"Mr Baker(原告代表大律师) submitted that **the case raised the issue of what degree of doubt on the part of the paying party will negative mistake, an issue on which there was no authority** binding on the court. However, Mr Baker conceded that if the law was that the 'mistake' argument was only available where the degree of doubt in the payer's mind was such that he thought he was probably liable to pay, Marine Trade could not satisfy that test. This was because Mr Baker accepted, realistically in my view, that the highest he could put Mr Arnese's(原告的证人与作出支付的决策人) evidence was that Mr Arnese thought, at the time of payment, that Marine Trade was probably not liable to pay. However, **Mr Baker submitted that the law** did not require the paying party to demonstrate that, notwithstanding any doubt, he still thought he was liable to pay and that, as a matter of principle, **there was no maximum amount of permissible doubt.**

---

[24] 见笔者《禁令》一书第三章对中间禁令的介绍。

Mr Ashcroft(被告代表大律师)... **submitted that the law was that any substantial degree of doubt was inconsistent with mistake** and, if he was wrong about this, his **fallback position was that the payer could not establish payment by mistake if he paid thinking that payment was probably not due**....

Speaking for myself I am not convinced that, even if Lord Hope... was going any further than saying that there may be cases in which **it can still be said that the payer was under a mistake, even if he had a degree of doubt as to the position**. However, in my judgment, **nothing in the speeches** of their Lordships who touched on this issue **supports Mr Baker's proposition that a payer can still be making a payment by mistake, when his state of mind is that he thinks it more likely than not that he is not liable to pay**."(加黑部分是笔者的强调)

从该案例的案情可以看到,支付之前一定要想清楚,原告明显是迫于压力,而且还在支付前向法院申请禁令,不成功下才作出支付,也仍然被后来的法院认定为是自愿支付。

7.1.3 Deutsche Morgan Grenfell Group plc v. Inland Revenue Commissioners (2006) UKHL 49 贵族院先例

在 Deutsche Morgan Grenfell Group plc v. Inland Revenue Commissioners 贵族院先例中,案情涉及英国税法,如果母公司和子公司都在英国,在集团公司合并报税下,子公司向母公司支付股息时是豁免缴纳预先公司税(advanced corporation tax),但对母公司在英国以外其他欧盟成员国的公司则没有这种豁免。2001 年 3 月 8 日欧盟法院(Court of Justice for the European Communities)在 Metallgesellschaft Ltd v. Inland Revenue Commissioners(Joined Cases C-397 and C-410/98)(2001) Ch 620 一案中判这种区别对待是违反欧洲联盟条约而不合法的。看来欧盟因为将成员国看成是一个大家庭,不能存在这种区别对待,所以该案例是约束当时仍是欧盟成员国的英国。这一判决结果在英国带来了大量的诉讼,母公司在英国以外其他成员国的英国子公司纷纷要求英国税务局退还之前缴纳的预先公司税。

该系列案例[25]中很多都涉及索赔的退税款项是否仍在时效内的问题。而时效问题又进而带出具体诉因是什么的问题。英国《Limitation Act 1980》规定,普通民商事案件的时效是诉因发生后的 6 年,而针对一些特别的情况会有特殊的规定,其中诉因如果因为错误、刻意隐瞒或欺诈而不能及时知道,则是从发现(或合理应该发现)

[25] 关于税务问题的系列案件可见本书第十章之 11 段。

错误、刻意隐瞒或欺诈时开始计的6年。[26] 这方面问题在本章之17段与本书第十章之11.5段详细介绍。

本案中也涉及时效方面的问题，如果诉因不是在搞错法律下错误支付，已经缴付超过6年的税款就会因时效已过并不得延后起算而无法取回。

本先例中一个争议是DMG在作出支付时对当时的英国法律确信自己的支付是正确做法，但事后这法律地位被推翻，导致本来以为正确的法律地位变为不再正确。毕竟，错误支付就是DMG如果知道或应该知道后来被纠正的正确税法地位（不必支付）下是不会支付的，这才是"错误"。但争议是在DMG作出支付时，有关的税法地位正在欧盟法院上诉。显然如果上诉成功，就会对有关集团公司的英国税法地位有改变。这表示DMG在支付时，肯定对当时的税法是否正确有一定的怀疑。这就涉及Hope勋爵在Kleinwort Benson贵族院先例中说错误与怀疑是两码事的问题，抗拒退还税款的英国税务局指称这不是DMG错误支付，而是怀疑下自愿支付，没有什么"不当"（unjust），不适用不当得利的救济。

在贵族院，Hoffmann勋爵在分析时就DMG在做出支付时存在怀疑以及怀疑的程度是否是自担风险还是能够构成错误说：

"I do not think that Lord Hope could have meant that a state of doubt was actually inconsistent with making a mistake（这是去对Hope勋爵在Kleinwort Benson先例说怀疑不是错误的起点，去作出调整说它们是可以共存的）. Contestants in quiz shows may have doubts about the answer（'it sounds like Haydn, but then it may be Mozart'）but if they then give the wrong answer, they have made a mistake. The real point is whether the person who made the payment took the risk that he might be wrong. If he did, then he cannot recover the money.（关键是在错误支付时，支付方的怀疑如果去到一个程度是他明知道会是错误但为了其他原因甚至是刻意去冒这个风险，自愿作出支付，就不能以错误支付取回了）Speaking for myself, I think that there is a parallel here with the question of whether a common mistake vitiates a contract. ...

Likewise, the circumstances in which a payment is made may show that the person who made the payment took the risk that, if the question was fully litigated, it might turn out that he did not owe the money. Payment under a compromise is an obvious example: see Brennan v. Bolt Burdon [2005] QB 303. I would not regard the fact that the person making the payment had doubts about his liability as conclusive of the question of wheth-

---

〔26〕 见英国《Limitation Act 1980》之Section 32（1）（c）："where in the case of any action for which a period of limitation is prescribed by this Act, either—（a）the action is based upon the fraud of the defendant; or （b）any fact relevant to the plaintiff's right of action has been deliberately concealed from him by the defendant; or （c）**the action is for relief from the consequences of a mistake; the period of limitation shall not begin to run until the plaintiff has discovered** the fraud, concealment or **mistake**（as the case may be）or could with reasonable diligence have discovered it."（加黑部分是笔者的强调）

er he took the risk, particularly if the existence of these doubts was unknown to the receiving party. It would be strange if a party whose lawyer had raised a doubt on the question but who decided nevertheless that he had better pay should be in a worse position than a party who had no doubts because he had never taken any advice, particularly if the receiving party had no idea that there was any difference in the circumstances in which the two payments had been made. It would be more rational if the question of whether a party should be treated as having taken the risk depended upon the objective circumstances surrounding the payment as they could reasonably have been known to both parties, including of course the extent to which the law was known to be in doubt（法律对这方面仍是不肯定，Hoffmann 勋爵举的例子是怀疑是主观的。如果一个人比较小心，先咨询了律师，律师提出了一些疑问，但是他在其他考虑下还是决定支付比较保险，而另一个人无知无畏就作出了支付。是否前者就是自愿支付，而后者就是错误支付？这显然是不合理。Hoffmann 勋爵认为更恰当的区分是客观看根据当时的环境，支付的目的到底是什么。接下来一段会引用 Peter Birks 教授所著的《Unjust Enrichment》一书为依据）.

These thoughts may be said to support the view of Professor Birks that English law should be less concerned with whether the person who paid the money made a mistake (involving an inquiry into his subjective state of mind) than with whether there was a valid cause for the payment, such as a debt, compromise or gift, these being matters of objective inquiry into the circumstances of the payment as they would have been known to both parties.... Mr Thomason, the head of taxation at DMG, gave evidence about his state of mind when it paid the ACT. He said:

'At all times prior to the determination of the European court in the Hoechst case（这就是上述提到的欧盟法院的案例，DMG 在作出支付时该案正在上诉，而原告知道或是应该知道这个事实。这也是被告英国税务局说原告 DMG 在作出支付时应该对法律地位有怀疑的原因，故此不能以错误支付复原），I believed that the United Kingdom statute denying the ability to make a group income election was the law and that I was bound to act in accordance with this law ... It did not occur to me that I could ignore the law as it stood for the simple reason that the law is the law. Just because another taxpayer challenged the law that did not mean that I could or should ignore it.'

Park J accepted this evidence as showing that, whether or not a state of doubt was consistent with making a mistake, DMG, in the person of Mr Thomason, was not in a state of doubt.（在此先例中，一审法院的 Parker 大法官接受 DMG 的证人 Thomason 先生的证人证言，并认定在作出支付时他对当时的法律地位毫不怀疑，毕竟它是要依照现行的法律地位交税，不因为知道有其他人士在法院质疑这个法律地位而有所改变。所以是在错误理解法律下作出支付，可以复原。）Jonathan Parker LJ agreed. He said: 'I accept … that **mere knowledge that the statutory provisions in question are under challenge is not to be equated with a state of doubt** as to the validity of those provisions. In any event, as I have already pointed out, Mr Thomason's evidence was that he was in no doubt that the ACT was payable, whatever the decision in the Metallgesellschaft case.'

Buxton and Rix LJJ, on the other hand, doubted whether this could be reconciled with the observations of Lord Hope which I have cited above.（上诉庭的 Buxton 与 Rix 大法官受到 Hope 勋爵在 Kleinwort Benson 贵族院先例中判怀疑与错误是两码事的影响，决定在受约束下推翻一审法院的判决）But I do not understand why this should be so. The judge attributed Mr Thomason's state of mind to DMG and found as a fact that he was not in doubt. He thought that DMG had to pay. Someone with a more sophisticated approach to the law might have had doubts-might even have thought that Hoechst had a good case and that the European Court of Justice ruling would apply retrospectively-but not Mr Thomason. I would therefore agree with the judge … that on any view of the law on this point, he made a mistake.（在贵族院 Hoffmann 与其他 4 位勋爵再度推翻上诉庭的判决，认为本案中即使原告知道欧盟法院的案例正在上诉，但这带来的怀疑不足以排除可诉错误，DMG 有权向税务局追回已缴税款。）"

Hope 勋爵在本案中也对他自己在之前的 Kleinwort Benson 贵族院先例中的判决作出调整，认为错误与怀疑可以共存，而最难的地方是在怀疑到什么程度才能排除错误。Hope 勋爵说：

"… reference is made to what I said in Kleinwort Benson(1999)2 AC 349 about the state of mind of the payer who claims to have made a payment under a mistake. I said … that **cases of mistake could vary from complete ignorance to a state of ample knowledge but a misapplication of what was known to the facts-from sheer ignorance to positive but incorrect belief**…But I also said that a state of doubt was different from a mistake, and that **a person who pays when in doubt takes the risk that he may be wrong. I ended this passage … by saying that the critical question was whether the payer would have made the payment if he had known what he is now being told was the law.**

These propositions are capable of further refinement…**The difficult question is what degree of doubt is compatible with a mistake claim**, …I see the issue as being **essentially one of causation**. What was the effect of the mistake on the payer? But the basic principle is, of course, that of unjust enrichment. At what point can it be said that the payee has been unjustly enriched? The answer to these questions will depend on the facts of the case. One can leave on one side cases where there is another ground on which the payee was entitled to be paid…As for the rest, the payer's reason for making the payment despite his doubt will have a part to play in resolving the issue as to whether the payer, who would not have made the payment had he known the true state of the facts or the law at the time of the payment, should bear the risk or can recover on the ground that he was mistaken."（加黑部分是笔者的强调）

7.1.4 BP Oil International Ltd v. Target Shipping Ltd (2012) EWHC 1590 (Comm)先例

BP Oil International Ltd v. Target Shipping Ltd 先例涉及租船合约，承租人 BP 在错误计算下多支付了 100 万美元运费，他发现后要求被告船东退还。在此不多介绍案情，只说 Andrew Smith 大法官支持 BP 胜诉，他有谈到 Hope 勋爵在 Kleinwort Benson 贵族院先例中有关"错误与怀疑是两码事"的名言带来有怀疑的错误支付就是支付方自担风险，不再是可诉错误。而 Hoffmann 勋爵在 Deutsche Morgan Grenfell Group plc v. Inland Revenue Commissioners (2006) UKHL 49 贵族院先例中的说法只是他对如何绕过这个困境的看法与建议。Andrew Smith 大法官说："Mr Berry（被告船东的代表大律师）also referred to the remarks of Lord Hoffmann in his speech in the Deutsche Morgan Grenfell case ... Lord Hoffmann floated the suggestion that, in cases where a payor was in doubt whether he was liable, the law might adopt an objective test to determine whether he should be regarded as having made the payment by mistake: that **the question whether the payor should be treated as having taken the risk of paying when not liable should depend upon 'the objective circumstances surrounding the payment as they could reasonably have been known to both parties'**. The Owners' argument does not exactly reflect the thinking of Lord Hoffmann, who was contemplating **a test depending on the view of an objective observer rather than what a reasonable recipient might think**. More importantly, Lord Hoffmann ... was digressing in his speech to introduce thinking about how the law might engage with the problem encapsulated in **Lord Hope's now famous remark in the Kleinwort Benson case ... that a state of doubt and mistake are different and a payor who has doubts assumes the risk that he might be wrong**. Lord Hoffmann pointed to a possible path for the development of the law ..., but his thinking does not represent the present law and Lord Hoffmann did not suggest otherwise. In any case, these questions arise where **a paying party**, or some relevant agent of the paying party, **has material doubts about whether there is liability**, and that is not the position in this case."（加黑部分是笔者的强调）

7.1.5 Jazztel Plc v. Revenue and Customs Commissioners (2017) EWHC 677 (Ch)先例

Jazztel Plc v. Revenue and Customs Commissioners 先例也是向税务局追回已缴税款的同类型案件，案情在本书第十章之 11.5.2.6 段有详细介绍。Marcus Smith 大法官就怀疑的程度给了一个 50% 的分水岭，认为怀疑的程度低于 50% 才会与错误共存,他说:"In my judgment,the furthest that a court of first instance could or should go as to the current state of law is that there may be cases in which a payer can still be said to be under a mistake,even if he has doubts,provided that he paid concluding that it was more likely than not that he was liable to pay …' … **In my judgment,provided the level of subjective doubt remains below the 50% threshold,a mistake can still exist.** …"(加黑部分是笔者的强调)

笔者看来,这50%不应是错误与怀疑两者的红线,或是更好的表述是类似民事诉讼举证责任(burden of proof)的平衡的可能性(balance of probability)。也就是说,根据每一个不同案情,如果怀疑的程度接近50%,作出支付时还有其他的考虑,这到底是自担风险的自愿支付还是错误支付,看来并不是这么清晰。

笔者也认为在这些案例如Deutsche Morgan Grenfell Group plc v. Inland Revenue Commissioners(2006)UKHL 49贵族院先例中,如果因为怀疑就剥夺对付错的支付方的复原救济也不公道。毕竟,直到税法真被改变,即使有关法律正在上诉最高院,并在一审与上诉庭都判是现存税法在有关方面是错误,而最高院会去扭转判法也不被普遍看好,从客观看来,应是对现存法律有错误的怀疑超出50%或平衡的可能性,但对付错的DMG来说,它能够拒不支付到期的税款吗?充其量是向税务局说明是"抗议下支付"(pay the under protest)或"保留权利"(reserve rights),以表达对目前税法的怀疑。所以以怀疑程度的高低去决定支付方或DMG的命运,对笔者而言不太公平与现实。

7.1.6 公司法人的错误以哪位雇员的主观怀疑为准

由于商业案件涉及的当事人绝大多数是公司法人,不是自然人。这样,在本课题下,就需要错误作出支付(或订立合约,如和解协议)的经办人与决策人出庭接受盘问,看他在采取支付行动时对有关错误理解事宜(现存事实或法律)是否有(或应该有)怀疑与去到什么程度。但一家大公司或企业对任何重要事情都会有多名代理人、经办人与决策人参与,如像BP Oil International Ltd v. Target Shipping Ltd(2012)EWHC 1590(Comm)先例中的英国石油公司。确定谁在作出支付时的"怀疑"才作准也不容易。另也会有情况是决策人没有(或微不足道的)怀疑,但经办人却有很大怀疑,或倒过来的情况。这样,都涉及了谁的怀疑才作准可去算是公司法人的"怀疑"?

在Jazztel Plc v. Revenue and Customs Commissioners(2017)EWHC 677(Ch)先例中,Marcus Smith大法官说:"… Mistakes by corporations. It can be particularly difficult to ascertain whether a mistake made within a legal person,like a corporation,constitutes a ground for restitution,as where one employee or agent of the corporation pays under a mistake,in circumstances where another employee or agent knows the true position. Goff & Jones,para 9 – 79 suggests that such cases are to be resolved by the rules relating to the attribution of knowledge within a corporation,albeit that this statement of the law was doubted by Andrew Smith J in BP Oil International Ltd v. Target Shipping Ltd ... It will be necessary to consider the distinction between mistakes and mispredictions and the ability of mistake to co-exist with doubt in the context of the precise facts of this case. However, although Jazztel is a legal and not a natural person, and although Jazztel acted through multiple different persons when making the Payments and when receiving ... advice as to whether those Payments should be made, it is not necessary, for the purposes of this judgment, to consider the correct approach to the mistake of a corporation. That is because, in this case, even though Jazztel acted through multiple natural persons, there is nothing in the evidence that I have seen to suggest any material difference in the subjective states of mind of these different actors."

上述判词是说此先例无需决定这一点，但提到《Goff & Jones：The Law of Unjust Enrichment》（2016 年，第 9 版）权威书籍建议是以公司法中“谁的言行能够代表公司的言行”的“问责制”或“归责制”（rule of attribution）[27]去针对。该权威书籍的最新版（2022 年，第 10 版）之 9－83 段仍有同样建议。这样看来，如果公司付错了一笔巨额款项，是公司 CEO 才能决定，就会是以 CEO 在决定时的思想状态（state of mind）[28]为准，也就是用他当时对现存的有关事实或法律是否有怀疑与什么程度的怀疑，考虑与平衡是否可排除错误。但如果公司付错了一笔金额不大的钱，付款的权限只是停留在部门经理，就是以该部门经理的思想状态为准了。

7.2 诉讼/仲裁签订妥协/和解协议时的怀疑与估算

带有怀疑但愿意自担风险去订立的国际商业合约有不少，但大部分的风险都是在本章之 2 段提及的对将来事实或法律的失算/估计错误（misprediction as to the future），如对市场风险、金融风险、贸易风险、法律风险、政治风险、币值波动、通货膨胀等。至于订约时对现存的事实或法律的假设错误，也经常会是涉及本章之 5 段的过错或不小心。加上法律的默示地位通常已经是分摊了风险，如“买方自己小心”（Caveat emptor）大原则，更不会接受这种估计错误或假设错误是可诉错误导致合约无效。所以，大部分国际商业合约都不存在因为有各种怀疑而带来可诉错误的争议。

但有一种类别的合约，就是妥协/和解协议（litigation compromise/settlement agreement），经常是在订约时对现存的事实或法律有怀疑，并由于后来发现错误（事实或法律）而产生纠纷。和解协议的谈判经常会涉及一方甚至双方的吹牛（bluff），夸大一些在法院诉讼不敢提起的所谓“事实”，因为证明不了或知道靠不住等，务求诱使对方让步妥协。在这种情况下订立的和解协议，难免事后会有争议是一方应该

〔27〕 这方面的近期重要案例有 Bilta（UK）Ltd（In Liquidation）v. Nazir（2015）UKSC 23；UBS AG（London Branch）and another v. Kommunale Wasserwerke Leipzig（2017）EWCA Civ 1567；Singularis Holdings Ltd v. Daiwa Capital Markets Europe Ltd（2019）UKSC 50 等上诉庭与最高院先例。

〔28〕 关于怎样认定思想状态可见笔者《证据法：基础理论、口头证据与专家证据》一书第十章。

知道对方在接受和解时是“受错误的困扰”(labouring under mistake)。这错误可以是事实真相在和解协议后才冒出来,如发现了新的证据。错误也可以是在法律方面,如在和解协议后有了新的权威案例推翻以前的法律地位,导致和解协议下支付给对方的钱实际上是应该对方支付给己方才对。

的确,试图以错误令和解协议变为无效的案例有不少,包括是在这课题最权威与主导的 Bell v. Lever Brothers Ltd(1932)AC 161 与 BCCI v. Ali(2001)UKHL 8 等贵族院先例与很多其他近期相关先例如 Champion Investments Ltd v. Ahmed(2004)EWHC 1956(QB);Brennan v. Bolt Burdon(2004)EWCA Civ 1017;Kyle Bay Ltd(t/a Astons Nightclub)v. Underwriters(2007)EWCA Civ 57;Elston v. King(2020)EWHC 55(Ch);Tatishev v. Zimmerz Management LP(2021)EWHC 2611(Ch)等。

和解协议大量出现在双方当事人之间已经产生争议,甚至是已经启动了法院诉讼或仲裁,但中途达成和解。毕竟没有争议谈何和解,真正你情我愿、各让一步的和解协议都必须在考虑到某些争议的基础上。简而言之,这争议范围可以很广泛,无论是目前的争议或将来的潜在争议。也不必要开始诉讼,只要是当事人之间想得到或应该可以想得到,一旦和解不成功就可能会开始诉讼都能算是争议。这在《证据法:国际规管与诉讼中的证据攻防》一书第十三章之 3.1 段有介绍。

在一般涉及争议的和解协议(litigation compromise)中,双方当事人总难免评估诉讼风险,主要是审理法官或仲裁员会对争议的事实或法律(经常是对合约条文的解释)如何认定(finding)与裁定(holding),并据此评估谈判相应的和解比例。例如,被告认为自己对欠下的债务或要承担的损失只有把握在金额上砍掉一半,但责任难逃,就会希望通过和解谈判达到赔偿一半或以下金额的结果。显然,原告也会同样评估诉讼风险,结论可能与被告接近,但也可能相差很远。如果相差很远,就表示和解谈判很难成功。反正是双方都是在估算胜诉/败诉的几率,也难逃对现存的正确事实或法律有怀疑,因为“正确”的事实或法律就是法院或仲裁庭尚未认定/裁定的事实或法律。

和解协议也不仅是有可诉错误与怀疑的冲突,还加上了其他的公共政策考虑,如法律鼓励诉讼方和解,避免劳民伤财和浪费有限的法院资源,所以绞尽脑汁要鼓励双方去和解,如强制或鼓励先去调解(mediation)。此外,当事人自己也会考虑有竹篮打水一场空的风险,而各自愿意对双方争议的事实与法律各让一步(give-and-take)去自担风险,有怀疑但不再追求最后的“正确答案”(判决/裁决)。这就表示更抗拒让可诉错误导致和解协议无效。

当然,妥协/和解协议也不仅是争议才有。大量其他的类似和解协议(non-litigation compromise)也在国际商业活动中存在。例如,双方在一个交易终结时,在结算总账后会约定一个“全面与最终的结算”(full and final settlement);雇员在离职时与公司结算工资、花红与其他赔偿后,此时可能也产生争论,但无论如何最后是签署了一份表示满意结算与放弃(release)一切将来索赔权利的文件等。这种类别的和解协议与上一段介绍的争议带来的和解协议的区别就是因为没有特定的争议与各让一步,所以没有上一段提到的种种考虑。

在政策上,法律是保护所有类别(涉及争议或非诉)的妥协/和解协议,不会轻易让可诉错误令协议无效,这与保护合约的保障性与神圣性是一样道理。

针对以上的介绍,接下来进一步详谈。

7.2.1　争议双方对现存事实或法律存有怀疑时合意各让一步承担风险的和解协议

对现存的事实或法律有怀疑并不代表是错误,在自己有怀疑的情况下仍然订立合约,就是愿意与应该承担怀疑中的不正确结果出现,一般是自己愿意承担风险。这道理特别会影响双方考虑到了争议(或潜在争议)后试图达成和解协议的情况。

双方谁也不知道打到底最后真正结果如何,如基于已经较为明确的事实,法院(或仲裁庭)最后会如何解释合约在没打到底时谁也不知道。因此和解协议中这很难说是谁吃了亏,会是基于和解协议双方就此罢手。

但往往会事后出现一些情况发现自己和解时对现存事实或法律有错误理解,就觉得自己吃了亏,因此想要事后推翻和解协议,比如:(1)一方当事人后来拿到的新证据发现在和解协议时对事实有重大错误理解。(2)一些集体诉讼中,在被告与个别原告和解后,其他原告仍然坚持打到底,这样经过整个诉讼过程披露的事实与法律争辩后,法院给出判决。已经和解的部分原告就可能发现自己吃了大亏。(3)当事人在签订和解协议时对法律地位有一些共同理解。但后来发现理解是错误的,或者是后来有新的有追溯力的判决改变了签约时的法律地位。这样就肯定会有一方吃亏了。

和解协议也是一种合约,因此一样可能因为错误而无效。但与一般合约不同,有说法就是和解协议的本质,是在双方已经有争议的基础上,各自都不同意对方说法与坚持主张自己的权利,但是对于此权利是否能得到法院(或仲裁庭)支持总是有疑虑/怀疑的,双方根据掌握的案件事实与对法律的了解各自猜测法院(或仲裁庭)可能会如何判,并双方你情我愿各让一步。

在 Elston v. King(2020)EWHC 55(Ch)先例中,Marcus Smith 大法官这样描述:

"Compromise agreements—by which I mean an agreement whereby a pre-existing dispute between parties is settled by agreement—are contracts like any other. The difference between a compromise agreement and other contracts is that—unlike with other contracts—the parties reach a consensus ad idem in relation to a matter on which they disagree. The nature of that disagreement will, of course, vary from case-to-case, but oftentimes, the parties' individual expectations, and so the compromise, will be informed by their individual assessment of what a court might do were the matter to be litigated. Inevitably, this involves reaching a view not on what the facts are or what the law is, but on how the court (often a particular court) will determine certain factual and/or legal questions.

It is the overtness of such disagreements which as a matter of fact, if not as a matter of law, renders compromises different to other contracts. Not only is there a public interest in the finality of litigation but, more importantly for present purposes, the parties will be approaching the compromise not from a common perspective but actually from a divergent one. It is precisely this divergence which the compromise resolves, not by determining it… but by reaching an accommodation which both sides find acceptable."

而这样通过在各自的不同怀疑的前提下,再各让一步的协议中,多半可以说,或者法院会倾向于将协议解释为当事人实际上各自承担各自"押宝"的对象不正确的风险(risk-taking),[29]这就并不是可诉错误。

以上所说也与 Kleinwort Benson 贵族院先例中提到的公共政策要保护妥协与和解(compromise and settlement)、和解与清偿(accord and satisfaction)的终局性相配合。在该先例中,Goff 勋爵说:"I recognise that the law of restitution must embody specific defences which are concerned to protect the stability of closed transactions. The defence of change of position is one such defence; the defences of compromise, and settlement of an honest claim (the scope of which is a matter of debate) are others."

Hope 勋爵说:"Then there is the defence that the money was paid as, or as part of, a compromise. Brennan J in [David Securities Pty Ltd v. Commonwealth Bank of Australia (1992) 175 CLR 353]… said that, where a claim is satisfied by accord and satisfaction, a payment made in satisfaction is made in discharge of an obligation created by the accord; it is unaffected by any mistake as to the validity of the compromise. That must be so, irrespective whether the mistake is as to the facts or the law regarding its validity. In the Ontario Hydro case [1982] 1 SCR 347… Dickson J said that there was a head of public policy which recognised that there was a need to preserve the validity of compromises freely entered into with advice. I think that it is possible to find a more principled basis for the defence … But my main point is that it is available irrespective of the nature of the mistake."

毕竟如果觉得自己胜诉机会很大,而对方在和解协议中的让步很不让人满意,大可以拒绝和解协议,把诉讼进行到底,在有了更充分的事实披露、更多的法律争辩后,看看到底谁赢谁输。

如果双方水平对等时,即使对方的和解要约比自己估计的还要稍低一些,但考虑到可以省下时间、精力与诉讼费用,再加上自己估计的法院(或仲裁庭)判法毕竟只是个概率事件,可能发生的事情谁也说不准。比如有出乎意料的事实、法律争辩,或者法院(或仲裁庭)的态度问题、可能的错判等,因此愿意做出一些让步。如果真打

---

[29] 这相当于本章之 3 段中所讲的风险分摊了,预期的风险一旦发生也不再是可诉错误。

到底可能确实比和解协议中能拿回更多金钱,但这是自己愿意承担的风险。

或者是一方觉得自己胜诉机会一般,但对方给出的和解要约比自己预计的要丰厚,这看来要不是自己搞错了什么,要不就是对方掌握了什么自己不知道的情况,此时愿意与对方达成和解协议,就是自愿承担了之后可能知道了更多信息,确实是自己对事实或法律的了解不够充分,该协议中自己吃了亏的风险。

在 Huddersfield Banking Co Ltd v. Henry Lister & Son Ltd(No. 2)(1895)2 Ch 273 上诉庭先例中,银行是某不动产的抵押权人,而拥有该不动产的人士还对债权人欠下债务。银行与债权人均同意该不动产中的一批织布机(loom)并不是固定在不动产上的,因此属于动产(chattels)而非不动产附着物(fixture),并由法院给出了同意命令(consent order)。因此债权人得以要求变卖这些动产实现债权,而不需要与针对不动产有权利的银行起什么冲突。但问题是后来银行发现,这些织布机原本被买入后是固定在不动产上,应属于不动产附着物即属于不动产的一部分,只是后来不知道什么原因被错误取下。因此银行以共同错误为由申请撤销同意命令,看来随后要开始诉讼主张自己对变卖织布机所得利益的权利了。上诉庭指出,经过当事人协议的同意命令,也会与合约一样被错误等问题影响效力:"...can be impeached, not only on the ground of fraud, but upon any grounds which invalidate the agreement it expresses."

而至于具体到此先例中的情况,当事人之间虽然同意了有关事实,但这是因为当事人之间误以为对这事实不存在任何争议,所以并不涉及什么妥协/和解,也没有你情我愿、各让一步。也因此后来发现的事实显示当事人当时的共同错误,足以导致协议(指同意命令)无效。一审的 Vaughan William 大法官说:"... I agree that **if the arrangement come to was a compromise of doubtful rights and a give-and-take arrangement, parties to it could not afterwards have the compromise set aside because upon obtaining fuller information they thought they had made a bad bargain.** But having regard to the evidence, I am of opinion that this arrangement was not a compromise or give-and-take arrangement of the sort I have referred to. The arrangement was not that one side should give way as to some of the machines and the other side as to the rest of them; and that being so, I have nothing further to dispose of before I deal with the question whether the machines were included in the mortgage."(加黑部分是笔者的强调)

上诉庭的 Kay 大法官也说:"A compromise takes place when there is a question of doubt and the parties agree not to try it out, but to settle it between themselves by a give-and-take arrangement. I quite agree that if this was a case of that kind it would be extremely difficult to interfere with the order."

但需要再次指出的是,和解协议也是合约,只要能够符合错误的要件,如本章之 13.4 段介绍的 The "Great Peace"(2002) EWCA Civ 1407 上诉庭先例中提出共同错误需要满足的五个要件，[30] 和解协议也是一样可以被推翻的。对于事实的认定，取决于证据甚至证人的表现，因此有诉讼风险，双方对此达成的和解协议是你情我愿各让一步，这就不能以共同错误推翻。但针对法律问题时，当事人如果在订立和解协议时都理解某个已经有悠久历史与稳定的法律问题（但不是指新法律或尚未确立的法律观点，可见本章之7.2.3段）法院会给出特定判法，并且基于此判法签订和解协议。这就不涉及诉讼风险与各让一步，因为审理法官都要基于这个法律地位作出裁定，如果错误适用法律也可以上诉。这样，如果事后法律地位改变（如最高院改判或澄清了过往的先例判法）导致和解协议中的一方吃大亏，理论上就有机会推翻和解协议。这问题并不简单，有关将来法律地位改变的问题可见本章之7.2.3段的介绍。

7.2.2 非诉和解协议中并没有怀疑、根本没有考虑过的争议不涉及当事人自担风险

作为对比，国际商业活动中双方也经常会在方方面面达成“和解”，但协议不涉及对权利或法院（或仲裁庭）判法的怀疑，也没有你情我愿、在已经知道的事实与法律的争议与各自坚持不同立场下各让一步，承担自己立场可能会错误但也怀疑对方立场的风险。此种妥协/和解协议与其他合约一样，符合可诉错误的要件仍然可以用来推翻协议。

例如双方在一个交易中结算总账（full and final settlement），这类和解协议通常不涉及考虑一些不知道但实际存在的事实或法律，及其带来的新争议。既然没有考虑过，也不存在合意各让一步。作为合约解释，“全面与最终和解”的措辞/文字也不应该包括双方没有考虑过与不知道的新争议，这不是订约意图。

也因此只要事后发现在协议中没有包括的争议，仍然可以提出。在笔者看来，这实际上更多的是解释合约的问题，要看在签订协议时到底当事人是怎么想的，意图是什么，是否已经包括了这些将来的情况，是否是在考虑了有关事实和法律后作出的决定。

例如上一段提到的 Huddersfield Banking Co Ltd v. Henry Lister & Son Ltd（No. 2）（1895）2 Ch 273 上诉庭先例，就说当事人其实根本没有想到有关争议的存在，只不过是同意了一些误以为不需要争议的事实。事后也因此可以在有新证据时重新提出争议。

还如在本书第五章之6.5.4段已经详细介绍的 BCCI v. Ali（2001）UKHL 8 先例中。Ali 先生是被 BCCI 解雇的前雇员，向 BCCI 提起诉讼。双方之间签订了协议放

---

[30] 在此只简单节录这五个要件：“（1）There must be a common assumption as to the existence of a state of affairs.（2）There must be no warranty by either party that that state of affairs exists.（3）The non-existence of the state of affairs must not be attributable to the fault of either party.（4）The non-existence of the state of affairs must render performance of the contract impossible.（5）The state of affairs may be the existence, or a vital attribute, of the consideration to be provided or circumstances which must subsist if performance of the contractual venture is to be possible.”

弃诉讼权利(release),措辞/文字写得非常广泛:"… in full and final settlement of all or any claims…. of whatsoever nature that exist or may exist…"但问题是原告当时还不知道 BCCI 存在严重的腐败与不诚实问题,这问题也从未在社会上曝光。后来 BCCI 金融帝国破产,事情曝光后,作为 BCCI 前雇员的原告很难再找到下一份工作,因此起诉 BCCI 的破产清算人(liquidator)。此时原告就要面对前述放弃诉讼权利协议的问题了。贵族院的判法是,这与普通合约没什么不同,一样是客观来解释当事人的订约意图到底是什么,是否包括现在面对的争议? 此先例中在订约时,BCCI 与 Ali 先生显然都没有考虑过现在这种因为 BCCI 的坏名声导致 Ali 先生找不到工作的情况。也因此协议并不能阻碍 Ali 先生索赔烙印损失(stigma damages)。在此只节录 Bingham 勋爵所说:"A party may, at any rate in a compromise agreement supported by valuable consideration, agree to release claims or rights of which he is unaware and of which he could not be aware, **even claims which could not on the facts known to the parties have been imagined, if appropriate language is used to make plain that that is his intention** … but a long and in my view salutary line of authority shows that, in the absence of clear language, the court will be very slow to infer that a party intended to surrender rights and claims of which he was unaware and could not have been aware."(加黑部分是笔者的强调)

这两种不同情况的区分还可见 Brennan v. Bolt Burdon(2004) EWCA Civ 1017 上诉庭先例中 Maurice Kay 大法官说:"Whilst **a general release executed in a prospective or nascent dispute requires clear language** to justify an influence of an intention to surrender rights of which the releases was unaware and could not have been aware …, **different considerations arise in relation to the compromise of litigation which the parties have agreed to settle in a give-and-take basis** …"(加黑部分是笔者的强调)

这也看到了这类非诉和解协议中如何解释条文的重要性。一般而言是会被非常严格解释,只有明确写明放弃的权利才会被放弃。但这是强求,也不现实,因为既然是订约方不可预见将来会出现的权利,也就无法明确放弃。这也表示和解协议无论用如何广泛的文字,也很难去清楚无误地包括对不可预见的将来争议(在此先例就是法律之前没有的烙印损失)的放弃。

这种在和解协议上没有预见与考虑到的事情本质上与非诉和解协议一样,不存在对特定争议各让一步,即没有怀疑与自担风险,所以可诉错误是有适用的空间。

7.2.3 将来法律地位改变对诉讼/仲裁签订妥协/和解协议的影响

针对争议的和解协议,一个并不罕见的情况是在和解协议签订后,普通法经过判例的发展导致原本双方在和解时所假设的法律地位发生改变,令一方在和解协议下吃了大亏,例如本来要承担责任变成无需承担。毕竟众所周知普通法是通过案例在不断发展与进化的,即使是长期、稳定与众所周知的法律地位也难免会被后来更高的法院推翻。

有争议是这到底算是事实错误还是法律错误,而较近期的 Elston v. King(2020) EWHC 55(Ch)先例中 Marcus Smith 大法官的说法(见本章之 7.2.1 段的节录)看来是说和解协议中实际上是双方基于对法院(或仲裁庭)如何判的看法,因此属于事实错误。本章之 2 段介绍的 Kleinwort Benson 贵族院先例中已经说过无需这样区分,在本章之 7 段也已经节录 Hope 勋爵所说,不在此重复。

法律变化是发生在和解协议订立之后带来的问题就是,既然和解协议与其他任何协议一样可能由于错误导致无效,而且将来法律地位改变可能有追溯力影响之前订立和解协议时的法律地位,那岂不是说将来法律地位改变,可能导致原先订立的大量和解协议都因共同错误理解订约时的法律而自动无效?Kleinwort Benson 贵族院先例就是典型例子,推翻了早在 Brisbane v. Dacres(1813)5 Taunt 143 先例中确立的"对法律理解错误规则"(mistake of law rule)。这就影响无数的案件,即使早已经是生效判决,甚至已经履行/执行了。也幸亏有 6 年的立法时效,否则是更不得了。但仅是 6 年内判下的案例也很多,都会以错误理解法律为由寻求翻案。难怪在 Kleinwort Benson 先例中,Brown-Wilkinson 与 Lloyd 勋爵持不同意见,认为应通过立法改变就可以避开普通法的追溯力的问题。

当然这错误必须能够符合可诉错误令合约无效的一些要件,比如共同错误的 The "Great Peace"(2002)EWCA Civ 1407 上诉庭先例中提出需要满足的五个要件等。

7.2.3.1 法律改变:立法或普通法的区别

普通法或案例法的法律改变所带来的问题,已经在本书中多处提到,如第二章之 6.4 段。Kleinwort Benson 贵族院先例就解释说普通法判法发生变化的法律改变就有追溯力,可以影响之前的法律地位,即有追溯性的宣示理论(retrospective "declaratory" theory),在此仅节录 Goff 勋爵所说如下:"It is in this context that we have to reinterpret the declaratory theory of judicial decision. We can see that, in fact, it does not presume the existence of an ideal system of the common law, which the judges from time to time reveal in their decisions. The historical theory of judicial decision, though it may in the past have served its purpose, was indeed a fiction. But it does mean that, when the judges state what the law is, their decisions do, in the sense I have described, have a retrospective effect. That is, I believe, inevitable. It is inevitable in relation to the particular case before the court, in which the events must have occurred some time, perhaps some years, before the judge's decision is made. But it is also inevitable in relation to other cases in which the law as so stated will in future fall to be applied. I must confess that I cannot imagine how a common law system, or indeed any legal system, can operate otherwise if the law is be applied equally to all and yet be capable of organic change."

这问题包括已经有了判决结果的大量先例[在本章之 14.3.1 段介绍的"先例理论"(doctrine of precedent)],在败诉方看来是错判,但因为一事不再审(Res judicata)

与时效已过，所以无法翻案。更现实的问题是针对还没有过立法时效的争议，即使双方已经达成和解协议（这不是一事不再审，但数量会比打到底有判决的先例更多），感觉吃亏了的一方可以双方对法律地位的可诉共同错误去撤销和解协议，而这些案件会是大量与影响重大，毕竟当事人会在和解后做了跟进的事情，如销毁争议证据，所以是无法回头。

更深层次了解这个大问题，在于法院只是解释法律，而“法律改变”只是以前“错判”的先例被现在的判决“纠正”（配合社会发展而不断进化）过来。这也解释了为何普通法对法律的改变，不算是“真改”，所以是有追溯力。另外 Goff 勋爵提到判决针对的事实已经发生了一段时间（甚至可能已经是十几年前），法院根据判决时认为正确的法律判孰是孰非，而不是事实发生时的法律，这本身就是有追溯力。

7.2.3.2　法律地位改变不会轻易影响争议的和解协议

Brennan v. Bolt Burdon (2004) EWCA Civ 1017 上诉庭先例就是很好的例子。此先例中人身伤害案件的受害人作为原告提起诉讼。根据 CPR 的规定，原告在颁布诉状/诉讼立案（issue of claim form）后 4 个月内必须送达诉状（service of claim form）。原告在 2001 年 6 月 7 日立案，在 2001 年 10 月 6 日实际送达诉状。但问题是 10 月 6 日是星期六，根据当时多个有争议先例对生效了没多久的 CPR[31] 的解释与判法，会算作在下一个工作日，即 10 月 8 日星期一才视为正式送达的时间，这样就超过 4 个月时间了。在被告的申请下，法院也给出命令确认没有在规定时间内送达，并且撤销（strike out）了原告的索赔诉讼。[32] 在此基础上，双方当事人达成妥协/和解协议，约定双方各自承担自己的诉讼费用，就此终止诉讼。

但不久之后，前述多个先例中对 CPR 的解释与判法被改判，这也意味着在 10 月 6 日实际送达的诉状应该仍然算作在时效内送达。这样原告马上上诉，并主张和解协议因为错误而无效。

Maurice Kay 大法官提出了以下针对和解协议中发生法律地位改变，应该如何考虑的说法：

“It is apparent … that principles have been developed … but that different principles have been articulated in different types of case, sometimes without cross-reference to each other. For example, Kleinwort Benson, a seminal case on mistake of law, was not cited or

---

〔31〕 当时 CPR 之 Rule 7.5(2) 这样写：“(2) The general rule is that a claim form must be served within 4 months after the date of issue.”但后来已经明确作出更改，仅仅节录修改后的 CPR 下针对域内送达的 Rule 7.5(1) 这样写：“Where the claim form is served within the jurisdiction, the claimant must complete the step required by the following table in relation to the particular method of service chosen, before **12.00 midnight on the calendar day four months** after the date of issue of the claim form.”（加黑部分是笔者的强调）也因此不再有此先例中的问题了。

〔32〕 这也是法院非常严格跟从法院规则的做法。如果是在仲裁中，就不会有这样的问题，仲裁能撤销索赔的只有仲裁法规定的两种特定情形（原告延误推进仲裁程序与原告无法或拒绝提供费用担保）。

referred to in Ali(BCCI v. Ali[2001]UKHL 8 贵族院先例),which was decided on construction but perhaps also had the potential for consideration on the basis of a mistake of fact and law. ... What principles relevant to the resolution of the present appeal can be extracted from these rather diverse authorities? In my judgment,the following propositions emerge:(1)As with any other contracts,compromises or consent orders may be vitiated by a common mistake of law. (2)It is initially a question of construction as to whether the alleged mistake has that consequence. (3)Whilst a general release executed in a prospective or nascent dispute requires clear language to justify an influence of an intention to surrender rights of which the releases was unaware and could not have been aware (Ali),different considerations arise in relation to the compromise of litigation which the parties have agreed to settle in a give-and-take basis(Huddersfield Banking). (4)For a common mistake of fact or law to vitiate a contract of any kind,it must render the performance of the contract impossible(The Great Peace)."

这四条被 Maurice Kay 大法官总结的内容相信在阅读了本章之前两段,以及结合本章之 13.4 段介绍的 The "Great Peace"(2002)EWCA Civ 1407 上诉庭先例后应该比较容易理解。是不是可以说,如果经过解释和解协议后,当事人在订约时确实对当时的法律地位有共同理解,[33] 但在后来这法律地位被改判,就可以满足这个要件?[34] 如果答案是肯定,就有机会广泛地影响几乎所有已经达成的大量和解协议的稳定性了。

因此,上诉庭的大法官们纷纷表示了自己的忧虑与反对,一致认为一般情况下不应该允许因为后续法律变化而以法律错误影响早前的和解协议。毕竟双方当事人都了解当时存在的事实/法律、在你情我愿各让一步的和解协议中,即使后续法律发生变化,法院也不倾向于解释为是真正错误,而更像是单纯的"押宝"出错,双方愿意自担风险。[35] 在 Deutsche Morgan Grenfell Group plc v. Inland Revenue Commissioners (2006)UKHL 49 先例中原告即使已经知道有欧盟法院的案件正在上诉,都仍然被法院判怀疑程度不足以排除可诉错误,那对于虚无缥缈的怀疑将来法律会改变,就更加不会去排除可诉错误。所以,最主要还是双方各让一步下的怀疑与自担风险才可以排除可诉错误。

但上诉庭的三位大法官也各自对这问题如何解决,提出了自己的看法:

1. Maurice Kay 大法官说这类和解协议中,如果一方当事人(被撤销索赔的原告)知道有关事实,但觉得后续法律变化会影响和解协议,该当事人就应该在和解协

---

〔33〕 这也是 The "Great Peace"(2002)EWCA Civ 1407 上诉庭先例中五个要件的第一点。

〔34〕 在笔者看来,满足其他一些要件仍然存在障碍,如合约不可能履行(impossible to perform),但和解协议看来大多都仍然应该可以履行。

〔35〕 见本章之 7.2.1 段。

议中以明示条文针对如保留权利："... the correct approach to the construction of compromises. Their essence in finality. There is a real difference between the situation where the compromise is agreed in ignorance of significant facts and the law which would be applicable to them (as in BCCI v. Ali) and the situation in which **the compromise is agreed with no misapprehension of the facts at all (as in the present case), just an erroneous assumption about the law**. This is not to reintroduce the distinction between mistake of fact and mistake of law. It is to require that, **where a party wishes to reserve his rights in the event of subsequent judicial decision** in a future case to which he is not a party, it is **he who should seek and secure a term to that effect**, not his opponent who should have to stipulate for protection notwithstanding the possibility of such a subsequent decision. Such a requirement is consistent with the policy of encouraging settlements and respecting their finality. I do not consider it to be in conflict with BCCI v. Ali."（加黑部分是笔者的强调）

2. Bodey 大法官与 Sedley 大法官则特别强调了本章之 7.2.1 段提到的 Kleinwort Benson 贵族院先例中指出的保护妥协与和解、和解与清偿终局性的重要性。

Bodey 大法官主张众所周知普通法都是不断在发展的，当事人在拟定和解协议时其实是对将来法律地位的变化存在怀疑，但仍愿意订立和解协议表示已经自担风险。可以节录 Bodey 大法官所说："There is not an operative common mistake where there is doubt as to the law concerned and where the party wishing to reopen the contract went ahead with it (the contract) anyway, As Lord Hope ... said in Kleinwort Benson: 'Cases where the payer was aware that there was an issue of law which was relevant but, being in doubt as to what the law was, paid without waiting to resolve that doubt may be left on one side. A state of doubt is different with that of mistake. A person who pays when in doubt takes the risk that he may be wrong — and that is so whether the issue is one of fact or one of law' ... **in contract of compromise each party normally takes a risk that the law may change**. Whichever **party would be favoured** by a subsequent retrospective change of law must therefore, so it seems to me, **be taken to have assumed the risk that he or she would have done better by not compromising**."（加黑部分是笔者的强调）

3. Sedley 大法官主张在和解协议订立时双方对现存法律地位与将来此法律地位会变化应是知道，这是订约时的全面事实背景/语境（factual matrix）[36] 的部分。在解释该协议时予以考虑，即可去默示双方是不会因将来法律变化去令合约无效。可以节录 Sedley 大法官所说如下："..., like Maurice Kay LJ and Bodey J, I see no

---

〔36〕 这在笔者《合约的解释：规则与应用》一书第六章有详细介绍，特别是重要的 Investors Compensation Scheme Ltd v. West Bromwich Building Society (1998) 1 WLR 896 贵族院先例。

choice in the present case. The law must be taken to have been what it was only later declared to be, but the putative mistake created by this shift **cannot be allowed to undo a compromise of litigation entered into in the knowledge both of how the law now stood** and of the fact-for it is always a fact-**that it might not remain so**. While I am not happy about translating such knowledge into **an implied term that the settlement is to stand notwithstanding any future change in the understanding of the law**, I have less difficulty in recognising it as part of the matrix of fact in which a litigation compromise is cast."(加黑部分是笔者的强调)

也因此结合其他成立可诉错误的因素来看,合约仍然可以被履行(在此先例被撤销索赔的原告完全可以选择上诉去推翻一审决定,但就此罢手),以及在这个事件中原告多少有一些可怪罪的地方[当时对于 CPR 之 Rule 7.5(2)的争议焦点,原告委任的大律师都建议原告上诉,但出于费用以及与律师关系的考虑原告并没有这样做]等。[37] 反正最后原告败诉,该罢手和解协议(也就是不再索赔的"drop-hand settlement")的效力并没有被影响。

7.2.3.3 两步骤测试

更近期的 Elston v. King(2020)EWHC 55(Ch)先例有非常类似的案情。Elston 先生已经破产,并已经有破产管理人(trustee)被委任。根据《Insolvency Act 1986》之 Section 310 的规定,破产人的收入(income)可以被用来还债。而此先例涉及的问题是破产人的养老金(pension)是否属于立法下的收入的问题。根据 2012 年的高院判法,养老金属于收入。也因此破产人与破产管理人签订协议"Income Payments Agreement"或称 IPA,效果就是允许破产管理人使用尚未提取的养老金还债。但 IPA 签订 1 个月后,高院有了与 2012 年案件不同的判法,后来还得到了上诉庭的确认,也即养老金中还未提取的部分不属于收入。这样破产人马上开始诉讼,主张错误导致 IPA 无效,因此破产管理人需要归还不当得利。

一审法院就通过事实认定此先例中的 IPA 属于和解协议的一种,当事人在订约过程中是考虑过可能的争议,并且是在考虑了事实与法律之后,你情我愿各让一步订立。如果达不成这样的协议,势必破产管理人会向法院申请法院命令("Income Payments Order"或称 IPO)。高院认可了郡法院的 George 法官的判法如下:"There was **a potential dispute between the parties** in this case. (破产管理人) told (破产人) that following(2012 年先例) the court could order him to make payment from his pensions. (破产管理人) said he wanted him to agree to such payments otherwise he would apply to the court. He made it clear that solicitors were instructed. (破产人) gave various reasons that led him to agree to sign the (IPA). In my judgment, there was **a compromise of the**

---

[37] 当事人的过错,合约是否还能履行等区别是 The "Great Peace"(2002)EWCA Civ 1407 上诉庭先例中五个要件的第三点与第四点。

potential dispute which may have given rise to litigation if(破产人)had not acquiesced to the agreement. This is **not a situation where there was no give-or-take as in the Hudderfield Banking case**. In that case, there was a dispute as to fact in respect of the subject-matter of the contract. In this case, the subject-matter of the contract was the payment of income from(破产人)pensions. The trustee said he was entitled to seek(IPA). (破产人)raised certain issues, but for a variety of reasons he has articulated he decided to enter into the agreement. **The parties decided to settle the issue between themselves and not go to court.** The consideration was the forbearance of the trustee not to bring proceedings. **I find that this was a compromise.** "(加黑部分是笔者的强调)

也因此接下来的问题就是该和解协议是否会因为之后法律地位的变化而受到影响？此先例中 Marcus Smith 大法官给了一个两步骤的分析方法。可以节录 Marcus Smith 大法官所说如下：

"**In cases where it is asserted that a compromise agreement should be set aside on grounds of this sort of mistake of law**, it seems to me that the following process must be undertaken:

(1) The compromise agreement must be construed so as to understand its true meaning and effect, including as to any **implied terms which may or may not exist**. Naturally, that **will involve examining the 'factual matrix'**, which in such cases will involve particular consideration of the nature of the dispute that the parties thought they were settling. To the extent that that dispute turns on points of law, it will be necessary to consider quite carefully the points at issue, **including the status of any judicial decision being relied upon by the parties**. To take **a crude example**, **there is all the difference in the world between** an agreement where the parties are **considering a first instance decision determining a novel point of law(at one extreme) and an established rule of law**, asserted and re-asserted by many courts, including the highest courts (**at the other extreme**).

It may be that such an assessment results in**a construction of the contract where it is found that one or other party has assumed the risk of the law changing in the future, whether by way of an express or an implied term. If so, then the inquiry is at an end.** The answer to the effect of a mistake will be found in the risk allocation adopted by the parties to the compromise agreement.

(2) In those cases where the contract does not provide the answer, it will be necessary to consider the nature of the change in law relied upon by the party seeking to set aside the compromise agreement, and ask 'Does this retrospective change in the law give rise to a common mistake, or did one or both of the parties simply make a misprediction about the course of future legal events?' Reverting to my crude example in the preceding

sub-paragraph, **a mistake will more likely arise where a well-established and unquestioned rule of law is dramatically overturned than where a single decision on a new and difficult point is overruled.** The latter case, …, the parties to a compromise should not be treated as ignorant of the fact that the common law develops …, is **a case of misprediction**."(加黑部分是笔者的强调)

Marcus Smith 大法官看来是认同了 Bodey 与 Sedley 两位大法官在 Brennan v. Bolt Burdon 上诉庭先例中的看法,以两步骤分析这方面的问题,区别是:(1)根据订约时的事实背景/语境去解释和解协议,看当事人是否明示或默示分摊了对现存法律地位将来会有改变的风险。(2)如果根据(1)难以判断是否分摊了风险,还要进一步看改变的法律的性质,如果是一个长期的、稳定的法律地位突然有了重大改变,就更有可能属于错误。但如果只是一个单一案例对一个困难的新争议的判决被推翻,就更像是自愿承担对将来的错误估计的风险。本质上是类似在本章之 7.2.1 段所讲的在事实争议方面你情我愿各让一步的相互妥协。

这两个步骤看来都需要找出双方争议的关键法律问题是什么,在诉讼或仲裁过程中双方当事人通常也会引经据典去提出、依赖或反驳各自所基于的法律或先例是什么。这关键的法律问题会是两个极端:(1)一个极端是争议的法律问题客观看来是基于一个已经长期与稳定确立的法律地位,比如是等级较高的上级法院,如上诉庭或贵族院/最高院的判决,而且经过长期不同先例的不同案情的反复检验与精炼。此时就更可能被认为双方没有怀疑与自担风险,毕竟这种情况下双方更应会是认为法律地位不存在改变的风险。即使双方当事人作为常识知道普通法会发展变化,但可能性极低,也就代表怀疑程度很低。这样如果真的发生,就可以与错误共存,容易被认为在订立和解协议时是存在对法律理解的可诉错误。(2)另一个极端就是争议的是非常新颖的法律问题,普通法也难说是有权威定论,双方依赖或反驳的也是基于一两个基层法院的观点,甚至判法会有不一致。这样,可以客观去推断双方当事人是明知有关法律问题仍然在发展,很可能有变化,但双方仍决定就此罢手,也不上诉(或等待其他同类案件的上诉结果)去追求更权威法院的判决。从怀疑的程度去分析,也代表对现存法律会改变的怀疑程度很高,就更像是自愿承担法律变化几率高的风险,这就无法与错误共存了。

而回到此 Jeremy Philip Elston v. Lawrence King, Sue Roscoe(trustees in bankruptcy of Jeremy Philip Elston)先例的案情,法院详细审视了在订约时当事人的想法和意图。根据各类证据,法院认定的事实是破产管理人威胁要开始申请 IPO 时,破产人完全可以获取律师的法律意见。但因为各种原因,如害怕资金不够,过往几次败诉带来了惨痛经验等,破产人没有这样做。尤其是在破产人阅读了 2012 年的判决与一些评论文章后认为根据该判法,法院是有管辖权对未提取养老金作出 IPO 的。但破产管理人对该案件的理解不同,破产管理人认为其实这只是从没被后续先例审视过的一审案件,该新法律观点尚待发展与确立。这样双方根本没有对法律问题的共同理解

(common assumption of law),更加谈不上是共同错误了,可以说连 The "Great Peace" (2002) EWCA Civ 1407 上诉庭先例中,Phillips 勋爵确立的五个要件中的第一个条件都没办法满足。也不用再进一步分析可否以共同错误理解法律为由去令和解协议无效了。[38] 因此原告败诉,IPA 并没有因为错误而被推翻。

7.2.4 对争议的和解协议的小结

笔者可对各让一步与自承风险下所签订的和解协议的问题作一个小结。公共政策要求要保证和解协议的终局性,所以只有以下的情况是例外:(1)历史悠久的普通法地位被之后的先例改变(这一般是最高院才能改),而这是有追溯力。但是立法的改变就不会影响和解协议,因为立法改变通常没有追溯力。(2)尽管 BCCI v. Ali (2001) UKHL 8 先例是适用在出现了非诉和解协议(non-litigation compromise)中没有考虑过的新法律观点的情况,但笔者看来对诉讼和解协议也应该同样适用。因为双方在你情我愿各让一步承担风险时,是根本没有考虑过这种新的法律问题。(3)和解协议也是合约,影响合约效力的因素(vitiating factor)理论上都适用,如误述、胁迫、恐吓侵权、不当影响或不合情理/显失公平交易。但在诉讼或仲裁中,绝大部分情况下诉讼方是有代表律师(都被假设为有同等法律水平与称职,即使这不是实际情况)的协助,所以上面提到的大部分因素都失去了适用空间。例如,诉讼双方都会对所有相关的事实调查取证,了解自己案件的强弱,以最终达成合理的和解协议解决争议。所以很难说服法院或仲裁庭对方对有关事实作出误述,而己方是依赖了对方的误述并被诱导订立了和解协议。又如胁迫,诉讼方完全可以打到底等待法院或仲裁庭的最终判决,而不是妥协订立一份城下之盟,因此很难满足经济胁迫的没有其他合理选择的要求。

8. 可诉错误只针对有根本重要性的事情

在可诉错误,已经很明确成立的要件之一是有关错误必须是对订约时现存的事实或法律有了严重的错误理解(mistaken misapprehension)或错误假设(mistaken assumption),严重的程度是足够令合约标的或目的有了根本性不同,或令合约自始无效。这是与违约/毁约必须是违反有根本重要性的条件条文(contractual condition)[39] 或是合约受阻(frustration of contract)中的突发事件必须对合约有根本性影

[38] 但除此以外,法院也提到了履行问题。即使是法律错误,也并没有阻止 IPA 的履行,毕竟该合约关键是破产人让步将养老金算作收入,破产管理人则不向法院起诉申请 IPO 将破产人卷入官司,这看来没有受到法律错误的影响。毕竟共同错误是针对会令合约不可能履行的内容,例如标的物灭失。

[39] 见笔者《合约的履行、弃权与禁反言》一书第一章之 3.5 段。

响[40]的道理是一致的。这有很多不同的说法去表述,例如在《Chitty on Contracts》(2021年,第34版)一书之27-043段中针对违反中间条文(intermediate term)可以终止合约需要达到的严重程度说是要"going to the root of the contract"或"to deprive ... substantially the whole benefit which it was the intention of the parties as expressed in the contract..."

至于在一些案例,这可节录 Davis Contractors Ltd v. Fareham UDC(1956)AC 696 贵族院先例中,Radcliffe 勋爵说:"Frustration occurs whenever the law recognizes that without default of either party a contractual obligation has become incapable of being performed because the circumstances in which performance is called for would render it **a thing radically different from that which was undertaken by the contract**. Non haec in foedera veni. It was not that I promised to do."(加黑部分是笔者的强调)

这也符合常理,毕竟可诉错误的救济是令合约自始无效,等于双方从来没有订立过这一份合约,所以不可能是小错误就带来这么严重的后果。毕竟针对次要的共同错误或是单方面错误,可以通过合约变更(rectification)[41]去作出救济,而不会是令整个合约无效。

在早期的 Kennedy v. Panama, New Zealand and Australian Royal Mail Co Ltd (1867) LR 2 QB 580 先例中,案情会稍后在本章之15.1段介绍,在此只说 Blackburn 大法官判共同错误不成立,因为股票仍是股票,只是价值大幅度下跌,说:"An innocent misrepresentation or misapprehension did not give the right to rescind at common law, **unless** it is such as to shew that there was **a complete difference in substance between what was supposed to be** and what was taken, so as to constitute a failure of consideration."(加黑部分是笔者的强调)

接下来在 Bell v. Lever Brothers Ltd(1932)AC 161 贵族院先例中,在上诉庭时 Scrutton 大法官说:"In my opinion, the present law is that where at the time of making the contract the circumstances are such that the continuance of a particular state of things is in the contemplation of both parties **fundamental to the continued validity of the contract**, and that state of things **substantially ceases to exist** without fault of either party, the contract becomes void from the time of such cessation, the loss falling where it lies. ..."(加黑部分是笔者的强调)

另 Greer 大法官也同意说:"But it is not, in my judgment, the law that the only mutual mistakes that will avoid an agreement are mistakes as to the existence or identity of the subject matter of the contract. I think **a mistake as to the fundamental character of the subject matter of the contract is one which, if mutual, the law will regard as ren-**

[40] 见笔者《合约的履行、弃权与禁反言》一书第二章之7.3段。

[41] 见本章之11.3段与笔者的《合约的解释:规则与应用》一书第三章之13段的详细介绍。

dering the contract void. ..."（加黑部分是笔者的强调）

再接下来在 Shogun Finance Ltd v. Hudson（2003）UKHL 62 贵族院先例中，Hobhouse 勋爵说："the identity of the customer is **fundamental to the whole transaction** because it is essential to the checking of the credit rating of the applicant borrower."（加黑部分是笔者的强调）

另 Millett 勋爵也说："The problem is sometimes mentioned in the textbooks in the section which deals with the formation of contract, where the question is whether a contract has been concluded; but it is more usually dealt with in the section which is concerned with the effect of mistake and in particular 'mistaken identity', where the question is said to turn on whether **A's identity is**（i）**'fundamental'**（in which case the contract is completely void）or（ii）**'material' but not 'fundamental'**（in which case the contract is merely voidable）."（加黑部分是笔者的强调）

英国同样说法的先例多不胜数，无法一一节录。在此可以介绍其他普通法管辖区的同样判法。在 Chwee Kin Keong v. Digilandmall. com Pte Ltd（2005）1 SLR 502 新加坡先例中，一审的 VK Rajah 大法官也有说："As the law now stands, **mistakes that are not fundamental or which do not relate to an essential term do not vitiate consent**. Mistakes that negative consent do not inexorably result in contracts being declared void."（加黑部分是笔者的强调）

最后详细介绍一下近期的 Triple Seven MSN 27251 Ltd v. Azman Air Services Ltd（2018）EWHC 1348（Comm）先例，该先例涉及两架飞机的租赁协议。原告拥有两架波音 777－200 飞机，于 2016 年 6 月 20 日租给被告用于接载位于非洲西部地区的伊斯兰教徒往返于沙特阿拉伯麦加参加朝圣活动，租期 5 年。2016 年 6 月 11 日，被告获得了尼日利亚国家麦加朝圣委员会的批准参与到为朝圣活动提供空运服务的计划中。除了本国的批准，被告同时需要获得沙特阿拉伯民航局的批准。2016 年 6 月 15 日，朝圣委员会向被告发送了一封信，告知被告因它没有满足沙特阿拉伯政府方面对经济和安全的要求，从而被排除在空运服务商名单外。但是被告与原告签订飞机租赁协议的几个小时后才收到这封信。被告收到信后，仍然努力尝试说服沙特阿拉伯方面改变主意，不过这些努力均不成功。与此同时，原告于 6 月 28 日与 7 月 4 日要将两架飞机交付给被告。被告于 7 月 6 日至 7 日之间通知原告他无法接受飞机，因为他没有被沙特阿拉伯允许为朝圣活动提供空运服务，而这也正是他租用这两架飞机最主要的目的。原告继续坚持要被告履约不果后，起诉被告违约/毁约与要求赔偿损失。被告将共同错误作为抗辩理由要求令合约无效。

MacDonald Eggers QC 大法官在认定事实方面是同意双方在订约时存在共同错误，因为双方订约时并不知道沙特阿拉伯方面已经公布将被告排除在空运服务商名单外，但 MacDonald Eggers QC 大法官在考虑了一系列之前先例所确立的法律地位后，认为即使存在共同错误，该错误也并没有严重到令整个合约自始无效（radically different from what the parties believed to be the case at the time of the conclusion of the contract),因为整个租约是5年期,只是2016年至2017年被排除在空运服务商名单外并不必然会令被告在接下来的年份仍然被排除。而且根据专家的估算,如果被告在接下来的年份能够取得沙特阿拉伯的批准,每年运营这两架飞机都会带来上千万甚至数千万美元的获利。

另外,虽然双方如果在订约前就获悉被告没有获得沙特阿拉伯的批准,就不会签订租赁合约,但只有这一点也不足以以共同错误令合约无效。MacDonald Eggers QC 大法官总结说:

"I consider that the test determining the application of the doctrine of common mistake is best applied by (a) **assessing the fundamental nature of the shared assumption to the contract**, and (b) **comparing the disparity between the assumed state of affairs and the actual state of affairs and analysing whether that disparity is sufficiently fundamental or essential or radical**.[适用共同错误要满足的测试是:(1)评估双方对合约的共同假设是什么;(2)比较假设的情形与实际的情形之间不一致的程度,进一步分析该不一致的程度是否足够令合约标的或目的有了根本性不同。]

The doctrine of**common mistake is not meant to apply to** those cases where the shared assumption is not sufficiently fundamental and/or where the difference between the assumed and actual states of affairs is **anything less than fundamental or essential or radical**. If it were otherwise, the value of certainty attached to a contract would be unjustifiably undermined. ...(共同错误不适用在不触及合约根本的共同假设,也不适用在假设的情形与实际情形不一致的程度并不实质重要的情况。否则合约的肯定性就会因合约动辄被判无效而被不恰当的破坏。)

There is no precise test to measure what constitutes a fundamental assumption underlying the contract and what constitutes a fundamental or essential or radical difference between the assumed and actual state of affairs. It is obviously a question of degree, but the nature of the test is such that it necessarily applies to a small number of cases, given that the doctrine applies in circumstances which ... are 'unexpected and wholly exceptional' ...(对于什么是对合约根本的假设以及假设的情况与实际情况不一致的程度是根本性没有准确的衡量标准,都是根据不同案情而变化。这明显是一个程度的问题,而且本质只应该适用在少量出乎预料与非常例外的案件。)

Moreover, the fundamental nature of the common mistake is not one necessarily to be equated with the inducing effect of the commonly shared assumption upon the parties. In other words, it is**not sufficient if both parties would not have entered into the contract had they known of the true state of affairs**. If such were the test, it might well be on the facts of the particular case that both **parties might not have entered into the contract had they known the true state of affairs**, **even where the commonly shared as-**

sumption related to a less important or non-fundamental matter. Therefore, if there had been a misrepresentation by one of the parties, the fact that the representee would not have entered into the contract had the misrepresentation not been made, is not necessarily indicative of the importance or fundamental nature of the representation itself. The reason for this is simple. Unlike misrepresentation or a unilateral mistake known or encouraged by one of the parties, a common mistake exists where neither party is at fault for the mistaken assumption, and **the contract** which they have voluntarily concluded **should not be disturbed unless that assumption renders the contract wholly different from what they understood the case to be**. [什么是有根本重要性,不能只是看双方的共同假设是否'诱导'(induce)合约产生。换言之,双方如果知道真实的情况就不会订约,这就足以被认为是诱导,但并不足以构成有根本重要性的共同错误。因为如果这可以作为测试标准,对于一些并不触及合约根本或稍微不根本性的事实的错误理解也一样会产生如果理解正确双方就不会订立合约的效果。但在误述中,如果不是一方存在误述另一方就不会订立合约中误述的事项并不一定要求触及合约根本。这种区别的原因也很容易理解。因为共同错误与误述或单方面错误不同,后者是在一方(如误述方)知情或应该知情与鼓励下订立的合约,多少有问责的味道。而前者则是订约双方均对错误假设没有过错,而是双方你情我愿的订立合约。所以,这种你情我愿订立的合约不应该被打扰,除非这种共同错误是令合约根本性改变。]"

如果该先例涉及合约受阻,因为法律的改变导致合约一两年无法履行,也是因为严重程度达不到触及合约的根本或令合约自始无效而不能令合约受阻下自动终止。这可以看出受阻与可诉错误的相通之处。看来如果被告要避免这种厄运,只有在合约中加入一条免责条文或不可抗力条文,在万一发生沙特阿拉伯不批准或其他战乱、天气、瘟疫等情况下,被告无需履行与承担责任。

9. 错误经常被主张但极少成功的原因

本章(如在 3.1 段)提到有说法是有不少案件诉讼方会提出可诉错误作为诉因或抗辩,但成功被法院(或仲裁庭)接受的先例是寥寥可数。并已经有提及背后原因,其中主要是英国法律是极不愿意为可以是广泛与无处不在的错误去提供救济,特别是普通法下对可诉错误是给予令合约自始无效(void ab initio)的极严重救济。这与保护合约的肯定性、保障性与神圣性的主要公共政策,显然是背道而驰的。另也会有其他无辜第三人如融资银行、供应商、生产商等受影响去承受主合约变为无效的恶果。

法律特别严格对待错误理解订立合约的一方当事人(这是单方面错误),背后原因也涉及几方面的考虑。

1. 以一个买卖合约为例,如果错误不是卖方的过错导致(如卖方误述或其他在本章之5.2.1与5.2.2段举例的原因导致),令买卖合约无效,让买方以他自己单方面的对事实或法律的重大错误理解从合约脱身,对卖方是否公道?毕竟,卖方对这个达成的买卖合约是有他的合法与合理的预期(lawful / reasonable expectation)。所以,这代表要严格与狭窄去处理单方面错误,并需要考虑对方的利益,也就是非错误方(non – mistaken party)的卖方对该笔交易的合理预期。

毕竟不像是误述,错误的买方在自己错误理解下订立买卖合约往往是与卖方无关。所以在《Misrepresentation,Mistake and Non – Disclosure》(2022年,第6版)一书之12 – 15段中说到英国法院在考虑错误的案件,总会先想到非错误方,也就是在这买卖合约例子的卖方的利益,令合约无效是否对他不公道,说:"… Put rather simplistically,it could be said that,when considering mistake,the judge does not begin by assuming that the mistake should release the mistaken party from the contract. He is more inclined to ask:**why should the non-mistaken party lose the contract**?"(加黑部分是笔者的强调)

很多先例有相同说法,如在Tamplin v. James(1880)15 Ch. D. 215上诉庭先例中,James大法官说:"It is said that it is hard to hold a man to a bargain entered into under a mistake,**but we must consider the hardship on the other side.** … If a man makes a mistake of this kind without any reasonable excuse he ought to be held to his bargain."(加黑部分是笔者的强调)

在G Percy Trentham Ltd v. Archital Luxfer Ltd(1993)1 Lloyd's Rep 25上诉庭先例中,Steyn大法官说:"English law generally adopts an objective theory of contract formation. That means that in practice our law generally ignores the subjective expectations and the unexpressed mental reservations of the parties. Instead **the governing criterion is the reasonable expectations of honest men …**"(加黑部分是笔者的强调)

在笔者的《合约的履行、弃权与禁反言》一书第五章之10.2.2段"单方面错误之二:合约内容或条件搞错"也有涉及。

2. 在证据方面,错误与可诉误述相比,后者要去证明对方卖方曾经在谈判时为诱导买方订约而作出虚假与不正确陈述,并被买方依赖而订立这一份买卖合约,是可以做得到。但针对买方主张他在订约时单方面有错误理解买卖合约的条件,证据会只是买方的一面之词,也是非错误方的卖方无法或很难去反证的。所以,对错误的主张与提供的证据就不理想与必须严格对待。如在Tamplin v. James上诉庭先例中,James大法官说:"It is not enough for a purchaser to swear,'I thought the farm sold contained twelve fields which I knew,and I find it does not include them all',or,'I thought it contained 100 acres and it only contains eighty'. **It would open the door to fraud if such a defence was to be allowed**."(加黑部分是笔者的强调)

3. 主要在单方面错误,但也在双方相互错误,只是错误方自己主观对有关合约条件有了错误理解。但在英国合约法中，一贯是审理法官或仲裁员纯粹以客观角度去看待合约是否达成或如何解释合约条件/条文，不理会任何一方当事人在订约时的主观想法。这就已经是把大量商业人士挂在口边的错误排除在可诉错误外。

4. 在买卖合约中，买方的错误理解是可以来自不同渠道，并以此去作出订约的决定，在发现真相才后悔莫及。常见是买方出高价以为买了正货，但实是不值钱的次货。或是买了根本不是买方想买的与所需的货物、商品、设备、艺术品、专利、技术、股权或公司等。

这错误若是卖方的误述所导致，可让买方有权去撤销合约，令该买卖合约无效（voidable），也就无需求助更难成功的可诉错误了。

但更常见的是买方的错误理解是自己的原因所导致，如买方为了省钱省事，疏于调查取证并在没有合理依据下草草以错误的假设去订立合约。即使买方在订立合约（如收购公司）前做了检查或尽职调查，但核查人员在工作中犯错或纯粹是看不了太多/太细。买方本来也可通过向卖方查问并要求详尽陈述甚至保证，但没有去做或做得不够。这些原因导致买方的错误理解与假设，都涉及买方的过错、不小心、疏忽或无知，这在本章之5段已经说是错误方的买方要自己承担恶果。

但即使买方已经是无懈可击尽了合理努力下仍发生错误理解，也不代表买方可以他的单方面错误去令买卖合约无效。这里涉及法律对风险的分摊。在买卖合约中，对标的的质量与/或合约条件有错误理解，即使是十分严重，在"买方自己小心"（let the buyer be aware 或 Caveat emptor）的大原则下，风险是默示分摊在买方。卖方即使明知买方有错误理解，也可以保持沉默无需披露。所以买方无辜"上当"，法律仍不会接受以错误去令合约无效。毕竟这是与"买方自己小心"唱反调，会对同样是无辜与不承担风险的卖方不公平。

5. 英国法律在政策上把可诉错误局限得十分严格与狭窄，特别是单方面错误，但双方的共同错误也好不了太多。英国合约法对错误严格的政策与欧洲大陆法（相信中国法律也是一样）的宽松政策很不一样，例如法国《民法典》第1104条规定双方在合约谈判就有善意责任（这包括了披露责任）。这可简单节录《Chitty on Contracts》（2021年，第34版）一书之8-006段说："**Underlying policy**. ... a **mistake about the facts** surrounding the contract **is relevant only if it is made by both parties and is fundamental**. A mistake as to the facts made by party A only is legally irrelevant, even if the other party B knows of it, unless the mistake was caused by a misrepresentation by B. Mere silence as regards a material fact which the one party is not bound to disclose to the other is not a ground of invalidity, for the principle that in relation to sale is referred to as caveat emptor ... is still the starting point of English law of contract. This sets **English law apart from many of the continental systems**, which not only seem to give relief in cases of shared mistake more readily than does English law but which also may allow a party who has made a unilateral mistake about the subject-matter to avoid the contract

provided the mistake was sufficiently serious. **The restrictive approach to mistake seems to represent a strong policy underlying English contract law**. As Lord Atkin(在 Bell v. Lever Brothers Ltd[1932]AC 161 贵族院先例)said:'It is of paramount importance that contracts should be observed, and that if parties honestly comply with the essentials of the formation of contracts-i. e. agree in the same terms on the same subject-matter-they are bound, and must rely on the stipulations of the contract for protection from the effect of facts unknown to them'."(加黑部分是笔者的强调)

6. 在接下来的段节,读者会看到单方面错误在英国法律下基本不会成立,除非涉及欺诈/欺骗或取巧的案件。单方面错误下在合约承诺了一些实际上是不可能做到的事情,在英国合约法下仍是需要严格履行,只是履行的是次要合约责任(secondary obligation),[42]也就是赔偿金钱损失。正如早在 Thornborow v. Whitacre(1705)92 ER 270 先例中,Holt 大法官说:"where a man will for a valuable consideration undertake to do an impossible thing, though it cannot be performed, yet he shall answer damages."

只有是共同/共享错误,也就是订立合约的双方对现存(existence)的标的或目的有了错误假设,但订约时其实已经不再存在(non-existence)。例如,双方假设存在的标的已经刚刚灭失、合约目的如合作开发项目但因法律改变被禁止等情况,就是典型的共同错误。毕竟在这种情况下,双方订约方想去履行合约也无法做到。当然,成功成立法律承认的可诉共同错误还有其他关卡,如这不再存在的标的或目的是否是因一方订约方的过错所导致,或是否已经通过明示或默示分摊了这个风险。可以说,成立可诉共同错误去令合约自始无效与合约受阻的要件基本一致。众所周知,合约受阻想要成功十分困难,而可诉共同错误因时间短暂,会出现的几率比合约受阻更罕见。正如 Phillips 勋爵在 The "Great Peace"(2002)EWCA Civ 1407 上诉庭先例中说:"Circumstances where a contract is void as a result of common mistake are likely to be less common than instances of frustration …"

在本章之 14 段介绍的衡平法错误(mistake in equity)也被 The "Great Peace"上诉庭先例否定,更是把可诉共同错误的大门几乎关上,顶多只是留下一条狭窄的门缝。这导致英国法律在这方面不但与欧洲大陆法的宽松对待不一样,甚至与普通法的美国也不一样。

可诉错误虽然极少成功,但双方有争议时仍经常去主张。毕竟对不想或无法履行的一方订约方,去令合约自始无效,不存在损失赔偿的说法,是十分有吸引力的法律救济。这样,审理法官或仲裁员也有必要去掌握这个困难的课题,以避免错判。

本章以上在原则性介绍了可诉错误后,接下来各段会介绍可诉错误的类别与实际会发生的情况。首先介绍普通法下的单方面错误(unilateral mistake)与相互错误(mutual mistake),接下来是共同/共享错误(common/shared mistake),之后是衡平法错误。

---

[42] 关于次要合约责任可见笔者《损失赔偿与救济》一书第十一章之 1.1 段。

10. 单方面错误、相互错误与共同/共享错误

可诉错误的分类有不同说法。例如在权威的《Chitty on Contracts》(2021 年，第 34 版)一书，就把错误分两种类别："对合约条件或身份错误理解"(mistake as to the terms or identity)与"对同一个事实或法律有根本的共同/共享错误"(shared and fundamental misapprehension as to the facts or the law)。

该权威书籍甚至在不同的两章去针对上述两类错误，好像它们之间的不同是黑白分明，但实际上它们本质上的区别就是本章之 1 段已经讲过的，是否定(negative)合约与废除(nullify)合约的区别。这可节录《Chitty on Contracts》(2021 年，第 34 版)一书之 5 - 001 段(在 8 - 001 段也有同样的说法)说："**Types of mistake**. The doctrine of mistake in the law of contract deals with two rather different situations. In **the first, there is some mistake or misunderstanding in the communications between the parties which prevents there being an effective** agreement (for instance, if the parties misunderstand each other) **or at least means that there is no agreement on the terms apparently stated** (for instance, if one party in an offer states terms which the other party knows the first party does not intend, but nonetheless the other purports to accept). This first category of mistake, which can generally be referred to as '**mistake as to the terms or identity**', includes 'mutual misunderstanding', where each is mistaken as to the terms intended by the other, and 'unilateral mistake', where only one of the parties is mistaken, over the terms of the contract or the identity of the other party. **In the second situation, the parties are agreed on the terms of the contract but have entered it under a shared and fundamental misapprehension as to the facts or the law**. Cases in this category are now usually referred to as '**common' mistake**, for normally the mistake is legally relevant only if both parties have contracted under the same misapprehension."(加黑部分是笔者的强调)

在另一本权威书籍《Misrepresentation, Mistake and Non-Disclosure》(2022 年，第 6 版)中也是分为两类：单方面错误与双方共享的错误。这可节录该书之 12 - 09 段说："**Unilateral mistake or shared mistake**. ... it is significant to establish whether the claimant(声称错误理解的原告) alone made the mistake, or whether the other party shared it — and so they both made the same mistake. In the case of a mistake of identity, the answer is obvious: the defendant can hardly have misunderstood his own identity, and so the mistake will of its nature be unilateral. Mistakes about the subject-matter, however, may be either unilateral or shared; and ... a unilateral mistake about the subject-matter does not normally affect the validity of the contract, whereas a common mistake might.

And even a mistake about the terms of the contract may be shared, although it is more common for such a mistake to be unilateral. ”

在本章,笔者也先区分“单方面”错误与“共同”错误,前者包括相互(mutual)的“鸡同鸭讲”的错误,而后者是双方在订约时对根本性事实或法律的假设有了真正是共同(common)或共享(shared)的错误。笔者在本章稍后会再把这两类(或三类)可能有法律救济的错误适用在商业活动经常发生的三种情况:(1)对方订约方的“身份”(identity);(2)合约的标的/目的(subject-matter/objective);(3)合约的内容、条件/条文(terms of the contract)。

10.1 分类的必要性

笔者相信读者在细读并思考后就会明白这个复杂,又不容易成功成立的合约法课题。只先说这三类不同错误的区别与分类的必要性:

1. 相互错误(mutual mistake)是双方在订约时对合约有根本重要性的内容或条件有了相互主观上的误解。但他们当时并不觉察,A 以为是 x,B 以为是 y,正是鸡同鸭讲的自以为是。如果最后法院或仲裁庭客观认定合约条件是 x 而不是 y,本质上也是 B 的单方面错误。实际上现在对合约解释的争议大部分都是这种情况。另纯粹的单方面错误也会发生在误解对方合约方的身份的情况下,因为对方是不会对自己身份有错误理解的。

2. 错误不发生在双方当事人之间的谈判交流,而是双方同时对与合约有关的重大事实或法律有了同样的错误假设的共同/共享错误(common/shared mistake)。典型例子是双方洽谈并订立买卖合约,但订约时在不知情下对事实(或法律)有了错误假设,卖方以为可按照合约履行去如期交出买卖标的,买方也可去接收并支付对价。但是这假设后来发现是错误,因为在订约时该标的因天灾而灭失(或是法律有了重大改变不准有关的标的进行买卖)。另如,双方在洽谈一批特定(如某农场饲养)的活鸡买卖,大家都没有主观上对对方的身份、买卖标的与合约条件有错误理解(所以不是相互错误)。但在订约时该农场暴发禽流感,需要马上把所有活鸡宰杀。这就会令该买卖合约因共同/共享错误变为无效了。

3. 读者或可见到上述介绍的相互错误在大部分情况下是可以通过法院或仲裁庭的客观测试去解决,如合约条件应是 x 或是 y,让合约有效存在并去履行。但在共同/共享错误下,合约是无法履行的。如果可诉错误成立(如双方错误理解的法律与事实是有根本重要性),法律救济就只能是判合约自始无效了。所以,分类是有必要的。

10.2 不同情况下可诉错误需要给予或抗拒法律救济的原因

首先单方面错误有法律救济是由于错误造成表面看来有效合约的基础或成立的要件有了重大缺陷,就是客观看双方订约时没有对该合约的所有条件/条文达成一致的想法(consensus ad idem),所以合约自动无效。

例如,错误理解对方身份肯定是单方面错误,一般情况会是一位骗子 C 冒充为 B

去试图诱导/诱骗错误方A。显然骗子是不会不知道自己真正是谁,也就是自己的身份。即使不涉及欺诈/欺骗,也只是单方面错误。例如A想与B订立合约,但结果与C订了合约,因为B与C两家公司名字(或电邮地址)十分相似/接近,令A有了错误理解与C电邮往来但以为是与B订立一份简式合约(simple contract)。当然,也会是A由于其他自己各种各样的过错、不小心或疏忽造成对对方身份的误解。

自始至终的订约过程,C是不会对自己的身份或"我是谁"有错误理解的。其间,如果C只是感觉到或怀疑A搞错了自己的身份,但不去向A指出,这也不影响搞错对方C身份只是A的单方面错误,怪不了C不去提醒。毕竟英国合约关系没有默示善意责任,更不会在谈判合约通过默示强加善意要求。也就是在本章之5段说的,如果是自己的过错、不小心或疏忽造成的错误,是没有法律救济。

但会有情况也是怪不了A,他错误理解C的身份并不涉及他的过错、不小心或疏忽。毕竟这种把对方身份搞错的案件很多是涉及欺诈/欺骗,如骗子C冒充为名牌公司B以诱使A与他订立合约。这样,法律必须给予这种单方面错误理解了对方身份的A救济了。

另错误理解有关合约的标的,在"买方自己小心"的大原则下,搞错的风险已经是默示加在买方。[43] 买方在这方面因自己错误理解而"上当",法律是不会接受买方的单方面错误去给予救济令合约无效。所以,这种对合约标的或目的的可诉错误,主要局限在双方的共同/共享错误(common /shared mistake)。例如,买卖双方在订约时不知道买卖的海上运输中的浮动货物(floating cargo)[44]或储藏在仓库里的一批特定货物刚遇上事故(如海难或火灾)而灭失,[45]不再实质存在。或是,法律刚有了重大改变令买卖无法履行。在双方的合约根本履行不了,双方也都没有过错与可怪罪谁的情况下,唯一也只能令合约自始无效,各自承担已造成的损失。

至于对合约有根本重要性的内容与条件的错误理解可否成立可诉错误更是经常会见到的争议,也产生大量的先例:如Bell v. Lever Brothers Ltd(1932)AC 161(涉及雇佣合约);The "Great Peace"(2002)EWCA Civ 1407(涉及租船合约);Triple Seven MSN 27251 Ltd v. Azman Air Services Ltd(2018)EWHC 1348(Comm)(涉及飞机租赁合约);OT Africa Line Ltd v. Vickers Plc(1996)1 Lloyd's Rep 700,Brennan v. Bolt Burdon(2004)EWCA Civ 1017与Elston v. King(2020)EWHC 55(Ch)(都涉及和解协议)等先例。

订约时对有否达成有效合约或合约内容与条件的错误理解通常是鸡同鸭讲的相互错误,双方在订约时对某些重要条件在主观上没有一致的想法。这种错误理解经

---

〔43〕 类似的,如果错误理解有关的合约目的(objective of contract),如建造一个工程,法律也已经默示规定了各自要承担的风险。

〔44〕 见Couturier v. Hastie(1856)10 ER 1065先例。

〔45〕 见Barrow,Lane & Ballard Ltd. v. Phillip Phillips & Co.(1929)1 KB 574先例。

常是双方谈判时的言行/书信往来所造成,往往法院或仲裁庭以客观测试就可解决争议。

但会有情况是客观测试也解决不了双方相互的主观错误理解。这在著名的 Raffles v. Wichelhaus(1864)2 H & C 906 早期先例中显示双方在谈判时鸡同鸭讲而需要判合约无效。在该先例中,被告向原告买了已装在船上的棉花,该船舶名为“Peerless”轮,所以买卖的特定货物被描述为“cotton to arrive ex-Peerless from Bombay”。但原来有两艘船舶都名为“Peerless”轮(这在悬挂不同船旗的情况下会发生),而且巧的是它们都刚好装了棉花自孟买开出:一艘“Peerless”轮在十月份开出,另一艘在12 月开出。被告心目中是 10 月的一船货,但原告心目中则是 12 月的一船货。对不少商品,付运的时间早晚至关重要。显然,双方订约时根本是鸡同鸭讲。在这种巧合下谁也没有过错或可以责怪,但造成的后果就是双方并没有一致想法。法院同意在这种情况下,不存在有效合约。

如果允许本质是单方面错误理解的相互错误可以订约时想法不一致为由令合约无效,就会有大量的合约无效了。在订约后 A 或 B 一旦发觉合约部分内容对它不利,就可以指称是与对方订约时产生相互错误理解(会是根本没有想清楚、不小心、疏懒或是不懂)。而且这与合约条件/条文的解释与是否成立是纯客观的测试,也就是作为一位合理人士(reasonable man)的审理法官或仲裁员从双方的用字与言行去推论(deduce)他们的订约意图,不理会 A 或 B 的主观理解。就表示在双方对某特定合约条件有了不同解释的“x”或“y”的争议,法院判是“y”,持“x”看法的 A 以他主观理解去主张合约无效去脱身就不可能了。在对抗制下,法院或仲裁庭一般会接受其中一方的主张,也就是 x 或 y,而不会自己去找一个不同于任何一方的答案 z。但实务中也存在 Raffles v. Wichelhaus 先例中没有任何理据去支持到底是 x 还是 y,法院或仲裁庭只能判双方没有合约。

这一点早在本章之 6 段有详及,在 Smith v. Hughes(1871)LR 6 QB 597 上诉庭先例中,Blackburn 大法官已说清楚如下:“if one of the parties intends to make a contract on one set of terms, and the other intends to make a contract on another set of terms, as it is sometimes expressed, if the parties are not ad idem, there is no contract … If, whatever a man's real intention may be, he so conducts himself that a reasonable man would believe that he was assenting to the terms proposed by the other party, and that other party upon that belief enters into the contract with him, the man thus conducting himself would be equally bound as if he had intended to agree to the other party's terms.”

总而言之,对这种订约时双方对合约内容与条件有不同理解的相互错误,本质是单方面错误,法律会卡得更严。除了上述提到的“Peerless”轮这种在今天绝少会发生的情况,法律给予救济的唯一例外情况是:A 的单方面错误是对方 B 知道或应该知道,并且 B 知道正确的情况不会是 A 的订约意图。特别是 B 知道 A 搞错了,取巧赶紧在 A 没有发觉与纠正前确立合约。这是从商业道德上也说不过去的。

至于双方对合约内容或条件是共同/共享错误,相对法律没有卡得这么紧。当然,在现实中发生的情况也比单方面错误或相互错误少得多。但总的说仍是关卡重重,目前的法律地位是 The "Great Peace" 上诉庭先例中,Phillips 勋爵总结了五个要去成功证明才能成立可诉的共同/共享错误的要件或因素。这也会在稍后详论。

这以上的分类将在接下来段节去进一步分析与介绍相关的先例。

11. 单方面错误之一:对合约条件错误理解

在 Thomson Reuters 的 UK Practical Law [46] 中对单方面错误的简单定义是:"Unilateral mistake(where one party is mistaken and the other knows or ought to have known of the mistake). If the mistake relates to the fundamental nature of the offer the contract can be avoided."

对合约标的(subject-matter)与/或合约内容与条件(terms)的单方面错误,包括与对方在订约时有不同理解但在客观测试下认定是己方的理解错误的相互错误,已经在本章之 3 段与 4 段的明示或默示的合约风险分摊,5 段的不涉及错误方的过错、不小心、疏忽或无知与 6 段的客观测试中多次强调,可以说是绝大部分的单方面错误与相互错误,都不是法律会给予救济的可诉错误。

本章下去针对可诉单方面错误会介绍:(1)会有法律救济(令合约无效或作出变更)的唯一例外;(2)错误理解对方合约方的身份;(3)少数有关与重要先例。

11.1 唯一例外:单方面错误是对方知道或应该知道可令合约无效

法律对可诉单方面错误给予救济卡得紧,唯一例外就是要求 A 的单方面错误是对方非错误方 B 知道或应该知道,并且 B 知道这错误不会是 A 的订约意图。这样,就谈不上 A 与 B 对合约的所有条件是在你情我愿下达成一致想法(consensus ad idem)了。这往往代表 A 的单方面错误必须是十分严重与明显的错误理解才可让 B 知道不是 A 的订约意图。

早在本章之4 段介绍的 Smith v. Hughes(1871)LR 6 QB 597 上诉庭先例中,案情涉及买方想购买"老燕麦",但搞错去买了"新燕麦",Hannen 大法官就说得很清楚在这种单方面错误与"买方自己小心"的大原则下,买方要自己承担责任。但 Hannen 大法官也提到了买方会有法律救济的例外情况,说:"But one of the parties to an apparent contract may, by his own fault, be precluded from setting up that he had entered into it in a different sense to that in which it was understood by the other party. ...The rule of law applicable to such a case is a corollary from the rule of morality...may be thus ex-

[46] https://uk.practicallaw.thomsonreuters.com/Browse/Home/PracticalLaw?transitionType=Default&contextData=(sc.Default)&comp=pluk&firstPage=true.

pressed：'The promiser is not bound to fulfil a promise in a sense in which the promisee knew at the time the promiser did not intend it.' … **If by any means he knows that there was no real agreement between him and the promiser, he is not entitled to insist that the promise shall be fulfilled in a sense to which the mind of the promiser did not assent**. … but a belief on the part of the plaintiff（卖方）that the defendant（买方）was making a contract to buy the oats, of which he offered him a sample, under a mistaken belief that they were old, would not relieve the defendant from liability **unless** his mistaken belief were **induced by some misrepresentation** of the plaintiff, **or concealment** by him of a fact which it became his duty to communicate. In order to relieve the defendant it was necessary that the jury should find **not merely that the plaintiff believed the defendant to believe that he was buying old oats, but that he believed the defendant to believe that he, the plaintiff, was contracting to sell old oats**."（加黑部分是笔者的强调）

在一般的商业活动中会出现这种唯一例外情况，可先介绍 Chwee Kin Keong v. Digilandmall. com Pte Ltd（2005）1 SLR 502 新加坡上诉庭先例。案情涉及被告在网站以 66 新币出售共 1606 台 Hewlett Packard 彩色激光打印机，而市场上一台该打印机的一般售价是 3854 新币。这吸引了不少买方在网上定购，但被告发觉标价错误想去反悔，不少买方也接受被告卖方更正价格，但除了 6 位买方，这 6 位提起诉讼迫使被告履行合约去交付打印机。但这被一审法院与上诉庭判是 6 位原告真正知道（actual knowledge）被告单方面错误（一审的 VK Rajah 大法官认为应该知道也是足够，而上诉庭不同意，虽然不影响判决结果），所以合约无效。

显然，如果单方面错误不太严重，假设是打印机市场上售价只是 150 新币，买方是知道被告定价在 66 新币是比较便宜，但这可以有其他解释而不会令买方明确知道这不是被告的订约意图。即使怀疑对方出错，但怀疑仍是不足以构成知道或应该知道。而且买方也没有责任去主动向卖方澄清与帮助去纠正他的错误。

针对同样道理，英国有不少先例，如重要的 Hartog v. Colin and Shields（1939）3 All ER 566 先例。在该案中，被告卖给原告 3000 块兔皮。谈判前一段双方谈到的价钱是指每一块多少钱，这也是该行业订兔皮价格的一贯做法，但在提出要约时，被告错误地写了价格是 10 便士 1 磅，而他的主观想法是 10 便士 1 块。原告估计也看到这个被告的错误，马上就去接受，希望拣个大便宜。被告发觉后拒绝履行，原告起诉索赔。法院判是原告一定会知道这个要约不代表被告的真正意图，谈不上订约时双方想法一致，所以合约无效。Singleton 大法官说："I am satisfied … from the evidence given to me, that the plaintiff must have realised, and did in fact know, that a mistake had occurred."

另在 Centrovincial Estates Plc v. Merchant Investors Assurance Co Ltd（1983）Com LR 158 上诉庭先例中，案情已经在本章之 5.2.1 段介绍，没有证据显示租客是知道或应该知道新房东搞错了房租。所以 Slade 大法官说："written proposal by landlord that new rent should be £ 65,000 a year,instead of(as intended)£ 126,000. The existing rent was already £ 68,320, but ' in the absence of any proof.., that the tenant either knew or ought reasonably to have known of the landlord's error at the time when they purposed to accept the landlord's offer,why should the landlord now be allowed to reside from that offer?"

在更近期的 OT Africa Line Ltd v. Vickers Plc(1996)1 Lloyd's Rep 700 先例中，案情也已经在本章之5.2.1段介绍。Mance大法官也说只有在对方知道或应该知道律师搞错了货币符号时，错误方才能不受和解协议约束："On any objective approach there was an agreement to settle at £ 150,000 ... In the light of the dicta in the Centrovincial case and The 'Antclizo'(1987)2 Lloyd's Rep 130 ... I ... proceed on the basis that Vickers would not be bound if they could show that OTAL, or those acting for OTAL,either knew or ought reasonably to have known that there had been a mistake by Vickers or those acting for Vickers..."

最后介绍一个笔者知悉的近期在结构性票据市场发生的事件，该事件涉及一家银行发行结构性票据(structured notes)。该银行委托某国际律师事务所处理相关文件，结果该律所准备交易合约文件时将计算票据回购价格的回购公式(redemption formulae)中的某个乘除关系搞反了。后来东窗事发，发行结构性票据的银行固然面对投资者要求的天文数字的回购金额，涉事的律师事务所也面对天文数字的专业疏忽的指控。据知，银行是以"明显错误"作为与投资者的谈判筹码，最后以不公布的金额和解了事。虽然这错误可能在任何有商业常识的人来看是很明显的错误，但是票据一旦在市场上发行，不同的投资者进行交易，银行仅仅靠法律争辩是很难理清全部的纠纷，为了维护银行的声誉以及与投资者的关系，看来银行和解也是有必要。

根据以上例子的介绍，可以看到明显错误在商业活动中带来的后果可大可小。作为总结，可节录Phillips勋爵在 Shogun Finance Ltd v. Hudson(2003)UKHL 62 贵族院先例中说："There is one important exception to this principle. If the offeree knows that the offeror does not intend the terms of the offer to be those that the natural meaning of the words would suggest,he cannot,by purporting to accept the offer,bind the offeror to a contract — Hartog v Colin and Shields[1939]3 All ER 566;Smith v Hughes(1871)LR 6 QB 597. Thus the task of ascertaining whether the parties have reached agreement as to the terms of a contract can involve quite a complex amalgam of the objective and the subjective and involve the application of a principle that bears close comparison with the doctrine of estoppel."

另可节录《Misrepresentation,Mistake and Non-Disclosure》(2022年，第6版)一书之13-21与13-22段说：

"**Mistake of one party known by the other**. Under this test a party cannot enforce a contract on his own terms,even if it appears on the objective evidence to have been concluded, where he knows that the other party was mistaken about the terms. … This is the basis on which it is sometimes said that a party will not be allowed to 'snap at' an offer; that is, if he receives an offer which he knows contains a mistake about a term — for example, the price stated in the offer is lower than the offeror intended the contract to prescribe — he cannot by accepting the offer before the offeror has discovered his mistake conclude a binding contract at the lower price. The fact that he knew that the offeror made a mistake in his letter of offer means that he cannot show that he in fact believed that it reflected the offeror's true intentions.

Mistake if one party that the other should have known about. Similarly, a party cannot enforce a contract on terms which he should have known did not reflect the other party's true intentions. … in practice, it may be easier to rely on this ground to avoid the contract, rather than proving that the other party actually knew about the mistake, because it is easier to prove what reasonable person would have understood than what the other party actually did understand."

在英国法下没有自动披露的义务,所以一方知道另一方搞错了某些事实也没有责任去提醒。这看来与上述介绍的有法律救济的例外情况区别不大与带来困扰。看来它们的分水岭/红线是在知道对方或应该知道对方搞错的程度,如前者可归类在怀疑(甚至可能深信但还没到知道的程度),但后者是在知道对方"受错误的困扰"(labouring under mistake)的情况下订立合约,即双方没有一致想法(consensus ad idem)。另是后者往往涉及对方取巧或是在衡平法看来"不合情理"(unconscionable),这就可让后者情况更是严格与两者之间有更明显区分。本章之4段提到的金戒指与铜戒指就可以作为例子,即使卖方怀疑甚至是深信买方搞错,但只要卖方不涉及任何取巧的言行,买方仍是不会有救济。

11.1.1 真正知道和应该知道的区别

区分两者的轻微差别并不容易,虽然理论上是有不同的测试。真正知道(actually know)就要去认定非错误方的主观意图,也只有他自己才能提供证据。除非他自己承认,否则审理法官或仲裁员只能从案件的所有情况(all surrounding circumstances),包括该非错误方的水平、经验与特质等,去作出推断(infer)他应否在该情况下知道对方有了错误理解。换言之,仍是需要一个客观的合理分析。

而应该知道(should have known)或"推定知情"(constructive knowledge)的认定就完全是客观去看待,审理法官或仲裁员自己代入作为一个合理第三人在该情况下是否应该知道对方有了错误理解。甚至审理法官可以引入专家证据帮助作出正确决定,例如在 Hartog v. Colin & Shields(1939)3 All ER 566 先例中,就有行业内的专家证人去提供专家证据有关什么是行业内合理人士应该或不应该知道。

这两种"知道"只是程度上的差异,不在本质。应该知道的程度越高就可以推定为真正知道了。正如《Misrepresentation, Mistake and Non-Disclosure》(2022 年,第6

版)一书之13-22段所说,应该知道应是较容易成立:“In practice, it may be easier to rely on this ground to avoid the contract, rather than proving that the party actually knew about the mistake, because it is easier to prove what a reasonable person would have understood than what the other party actually did understand.”

在英国法律中,看来是不区分真正知道或应该知道。反正一认定非错误方是知道(真正或应该)对方在订约时有了根本性的错误理解或假设,就可以判一个表面是完全有效的合约变为无效。只节录在 OT Africa Line Ltd v. Vickers Plc(1996)1 Lloyd's Rep 700 先例中,Mance 大法官说:“I further proceed on the basis that Vickers would not be bound if they could show that OTAL, or those acting for OTAL, **either knew or ought reasonably to have known that there had been a mistake** by Vickers or those acting for Vickers. I put the onus that way round, as it appears so in the authorities, but it would not make any difference in this case if it were the other way round. ... Here, there is objectively agreement on a particular sum. The question is what is capable of displacing that apparent agreement. **The answer on the authorities is a mistake by one party of which the other knew or ought reasonably to have known**. I accept that this is capable of including circumstances in which a person refrains from or simply fails to make enquiries for which the situation reasonably calls and which would have led to discovery of the mistake. But there would have, at least, to be **some real reason to suppose the existence of a mistake before it could be incumbent on one party or solicitor in the course of negotiations to question whether another party or solicitor meant what he or she said**.”(加黑部分是笔者的强调)

加拿大先例 McMaster University v. Wilchar Construction Ltd(1971)22 DLR(3d)9 看来也是与英国法律一致,说:“In my view, this is truly a case of unilateral mistake ... [F]rom the circumstances, the plaintiff must, in any event, be taken to have known of the mistake before acceptance of the offer. In this context, it should be stressed that one is taken to have known that which would have been obvious to a reasonable person in the light of the surrounding circumstances: see Hartog v Colin and Shields ...”

但 Chwee Kin Keong v. Digilandmall. com Pte Ltd(2005)1 SLR 502 新加坡上诉庭先例是不同意一审在这方面持与英国判例一致看法,认为在普通法下,标准是真正知道才能令合约自始无效(void ab initio)。而只是应该知道的推定知情,特别是在非错误方的取巧是不合情理(unconscionable),就应是衡平救济即合约可使无效(voidable)。[47] 尽量减少合约自始无效的主要考虑应是不影响无辜第三人,如善意的第三人买方,这只在衡平法的救济下才会一并考虑。

---

〔47〕 但在英国,衡平法错误在 The “Great Peace”(2002)EWCA Civ 1407 上诉庭先例被否定,这方面在本章稍后的14段有详细介绍。

上诉庭的 Chao Hing Tin 大法官说："While we recognise that the distinction between actual knowledge and constructive knowledge can be a fine one and can often be difficult to discern… once the court should hold that a contract comes within the common law principle of unilateral mistake, it is void ab initio for all purposes. Moreover, as pointed out earlier, the line between actual knowledge and constructive knowledge may often be hard to draw. In a difficult case where the court is not convinced that the non-mistaken party has actual knowledge but is well satisfied that there is constructive knowledge and where there is evidence of unconscionable conduct or sharp practice on the part of the non-mistaken party, relief in equity may be granted on terms to ensure that justice is attained with regard to all affected parties."

另在 Wellmix Organics(International) Pte Ltd v. Lau Yu Man(2006)2 SLR(R)117 新加坡先例中，Phang 大法官也说这个区别其实不重要，无论是真正知道还是应该知道，都已经足够认定可诉的单方面错误："One approach might be to accept that whilst the practical-as opposed to the conceptual-distinction between actual and constructive knowledge might not be as clear as we would like it to be, the difference is … one of degree rather than kind. However, that still does not resolve the difficulties that will invariably arise in marginal cases where the objective evidence is such that it is difficult to decide, on the balance of probabilities, precisely what type of knowledge the contracting party concerned had. But that is perhaps inherent in the imperfection that is part of life and of the law itself. What is important and practical, however, is that **regardless of whether or not actual or constructive knowledge is found by the court in the case concerned, the requirement of knowledge is satisfied and that justice is thereby achieved**, assuming that the other necessary elements relating to the doctrine of unilateral mistake have been satisfied."（加黑部分是笔者的强调）

11.1.2 是否要求非错误方有取巧

考虑非错误方是否取巧是因为法律对单方面错误给予救济卡得很紧，如果非错误方取巧(sharp practice)，从公平合理的角度更容易被法院认为应该给予救济。另外，如果非错误方取巧，也会更容易认定其知道或应该知道错误方的单方面错误。这种情况的出现也是千变万化，分享一个笔者（杨良宜）早年在租船业务的经验。租船业务经常是船东与承租人通过信函、电报与长途电话的谈判后达成协议，然后由经纪人草拟一份正式并让双方轮流签署的租约。租约条文显然是根据双方在谈判中所同意的内容，但用字显然会是由有关经纪人调整，也会有所遗漏。如果一方没有小心检查或甚是因为自己水平不足没能警觉到不妥，就会签署一份错误记录了双方谈判后同意的内容的租约。出问题后处于严重不利的一方，显然就希望能够对有关的条文作出变更(rectification)。但显然在对方抗拒下这并不容易，毕竟一份正式与双方签署的合约是一个显示双方最后同意内容的很强的表面证据。

所以在 The "Nai Genova" and The "Nai Superba"(1984)1 Lloyd's Rep 353 上诉庭先例中,涉及长期租约中"通货膨胀条文"(escalation clause)因币值的改变而令船东处于严重不利的地位,船东要以单方面错误将租约中约定的意大利里拉变更为美元,主张租约中的意大利里拉是错误的记录,但不成功。因为法院判承租人不真正或应该知道船东单方面错误,也不会预测到将来里拉会大幅度贬值,自然不涉及取巧。而上诉庭 Slade 大法官认为船东单方面错误是他自己不小心:"The loss which the plaintiffs have sustained in this case, though most unfortunate for them, is in my opinion not attributable to the defendants. It is attributable solely to the plaintiff's own carelessness in failing properly to read the provisions of the charter-party ..."

但如果案情稍有改变,也是笔者遇过好几次的早年经验是对方(船东或承租人)轮流签署租约时发觉了有关的单方面错误,但由于对他有利,所以取巧故意不指出这明显错误(如运费写少了一个零,但承租人不向船东指出而签署)。显然对这种客观看来很不公平的情况,即合约一方明知对方有了单方面错误去乘机取巧,法律就往往有所救济,即允许合约变更。

对这个要件,早在英国的 Hartog v. Colin & Shields(1939)3 All ER 566 先例中,Singleton 大法官说到非错误方的买家有取巧去抓紧卖方犯错的机会,即"snap at an offer"。这也在后来的案例中被提及,如在 Ram Lubhaya v. John Stanley(2014)WL 6633395 郡法院判例中,Falvey 法官说:"I should say that it is very clear from the judgment that Mr Justice Singleton found that there was, if not actual dishonesty, at least a degree of unethical practice on the part of the party seeking to take advantage of the mistake in that case."

在 Riverlate Properties Ltd v. Paul(1975)Ch 133 上诉庭先例中,Russell 大法官说:"... it appears to us that there is no justification, assuming a mistake on the side of the lessor, for rectification either on the ground of a common mistake, or on the ground of knowledge on the lessee's side at the time of execution of the contract or the lease that the lessor in putting forward the lease in its particular form was making a mistake. ... Whether there was in any particular case knowledge of the intention and mistake of the other party must be a question of fact to be decided upon the evidence. Basically it appears to us that **it must be such as to involve the lessee in a degree of sharp practice.**"(加黑部分是笔者的强调)

另在 Thomas Bates & Son Ltd v. Wyndham's(Lingerie)Ltd(1981)1 WLR 505 上诉庭先例中,案情涉及工厂厂房的租赁协议。双方于 1956 年订立了工厂厂房的租赁协议,该租赁协议中有一条续约选择权条文以及双方在不能同意续约租金时的租金调整条文(rent review clause)。承租人有权在租约到期前的 6 个月内通知房东,选择继续租赁 7 年或 14 年。如果双方不能同意续租的租金,该租金的数额由皇家特许测量师协会的主席作为独任仲裁员来决定。双方在 1963 年与 1970 年分别签订了续租协议。在 1963 年续租协议中,只是将 7 年或 14 年的时间调整为 7 年,租金调整条文不变。在 1970 年的续约协议中,承租人与房东同意再租 14 年,而房东提出在第 5 年与第 10 年分别对租金进行评估与调整,而不是在第 7 年。不过在该 1970 年的租赁协议中,秘书通过打字机打出来的租约中遗漏了双方不能同意租金时的租金调整条文。在 5 年租约期满时,房东要调整租金,也发现遗漏了该租金调整条文,于是要求承租人签订一份租金调整条文作为租约的附件,但承租人却不同意,认为双方同意的租金就是 1970 年协议中提到的金额。于是房东提起诉讼以错误要求变更租约。Buckley 大法官在总结单方面错误去给予变更救济的四个要件时,提到第四个要件是非错误方的被告可以从中获利(mistake must be one calculated to benefit),而这是法院认为不公平(inequitable)的。

其他的有关先例如刚介绍的 The "Nai Genova" and The "Nai Superba"上诉庭先例都有不能容许非错误方去取巧的说法,也就不多去介绍了。

在 Chwee Kin Keong v. Digilandmall. com Pte Ltd(2005)1 SLR 502 新加坡先例中,一审的 VK Rajah 大法官也有提到非错误方的买方有"掠夺性"(predatory)。

看来在这方面,法院是去考虑衡平法下的"不合情理"(unconscionability),[48] 否则就难以去作出区分。因为已在本章多处如第 10 段提及单方面错误,非错误方只要不存在误述或其他不当行为去影响错误方,是可在明知道对方有了单方面错误的情况下,去保持沉默不去指出。也或可看来,这不合情理是针对非错误方在对方的特殊不利地位(special disability)下,坚持取巧从中获利。这可节录在《Chitty on Contracts》(2021 年,第 34 版)一书之 8 - 007 段中说:"**Mistake and unconscionability**. A qualification must be made to **the general rule that a mistake as to the facts that is not shared, and was not induced by a misrepresentation by the other party, is legally irrelevant**. Facts that bring a case within the category covered by the rules on 'mistake' may, in an extreme case, give one party the right to avoid the contract on the ground of unconscionability. Broadly if one party is suffering from what is sometimes termed a 'specially disability', such as 'poverty, or ignorance, or lack of advice', and the other party consciously takes advantage of the disability, the first party may be entitled to avoid the contract. In many unconscionability cases the first party was in fact making the contract under a misapprehension as to the facts, typically as to the value of the property he was selling. **There is some suggestion that the doctrine may sometimes be used more**

---

[48] 衡平法下的不合情理/显失公平理论(unconscionable doctrine),一般而言要影响合约效力,必须满足:(1)一方当事人有特殊不利地位(special disadvantage/disability);(2)另一方当事人采用不道德/应受谴责的方式(reprehensible mean/morally culpable manner)利用对方劣势;(3)交易内容对劣势方非常过分、震惊法院良心(shock the conscience of the court)。这方面的说法,以及权威的 Alec Lobb v. Total Oil GB(1983)1 WLR 87 与 PIAC v. Times Travel(2021)UKSC 40 先例等见本书第十一章之 2 段的介绍。

broadly to prevent one party taking unconscientious advantage of the other's mistake. ... It is obvious that the unconscionability doctrine has the potential to **undermine the principle that a mistake as to the factual circumstances is irrelevant unless it is a common mistake**, and the courts will **no doubt restrict it to cases of 'special disability'**."(加黑部分是笔者的强调)

另在权威书籍《Misrepresentation, Mistake and Non-Disclosure》(2022 年,第 6 版)一书中是说案情如果显示被告或非错误方有取巧、不公平与不合情理的行为,错误方单方面错误也可以变更合约作出救济(Remedying Mistake by Rectification: Unilateral Mistakes)。在该书之 13 - 51 段中说:"**Inequity or unconscionability.** It is not sufficient that the defendant knew of the claimant's mistake. In addition, the court must be satisfied that in the circumstances it would be inequitable for the defendant to resist rectification into the terms as the claimant believed them to be. ... This test may be satisfied by **proof of unconscionable conduct, or unfair dealing: some positive conduct by the defendant** which either causes the mistaken belief about the contents of the document or (without causing the mistake) is calculated to divert the claimant from discovering the truth about it; or **taking advantage of the claimant's misunderstanding about the document when the defendant knows that he is making such a mistake**."(加黑部分是笔者的强调)

脚注也引述了 Commission for the New Towns v. Cooper (Great Britain) Ltd (1995) Ch 259 上诉庭先例。在该先例中,Stuart-Smith 大法官说:"I would hold that where A intends B to be mistaken as to the construction of the agreement, so conducts himself that he diverts B's attention from discovering the mistake by making false and misleading statements, and B in fact makes the very mistake that A intends, then notwithstanding that A does not actually know, but merely suspects, that B is mistaken, and it cannot be shown that the mistake was induced by any misrepresentation, rectification may be granted. **A's conduct is unconscionable** and he cannot insist on performance in accordance to the strict letter of the contract; that is sufficient for rescission. But **it may also not be unjust or inequitable to insist that the contract be performed according to B's understanding**, where that was the meaning that A intended that B should put upon it."(加黑部分是笔者的强调)

11.2 可诉单方面错误的另类救济:变更合约

11.2.1 合约无效不可行时的另类救济

单方面错误一般没有法律救济,除非对方知道或应该知道这单方面错误。而救济除了因双方没有达成一致想法而可令合约无效外,也可以有变更合约(rectification)的救济。需要有此特殊的救济显然是有情况令合约无效并非好的可行做法,例如单方面错误是在合约履行后期才发现,此时合约双方都不会希望合约无效。

一个典型的例子就是在 A Roberts & Co Ltd v. Leicestershire County Council (1961) Ch 555 先例中,案情涉及被告地方议会为建造一家学校去公开招标,原告投的标书是£ 165,910,并承诺在 1954 年 3 月 31 日的限期前动工以保证能够获得英国教育部的资助,但没有说工程需要多久。之后,原告被告知标书可被考虑但仍要求再压低工程价格以符合教育部的预算。这导致原告把工程价格减至£ 138,399,并在标书中说明工程将在 78 周或 18 个月内完成,完工日期预计为 1955 年 9 月 30 日。但在被告的内部讨论中认为 18 个月的时间不够,决定将合约中的完工时间改为 30 个月,足足把完工日期延长了 1 年至 1956 年 9 月 30 日。但由于没有告知原告,而原告自己也没有在准备签署的建造合约中发现这个改动,公司董事没有细看合约就签了名,但私下自以为工程完成是 18 个月。到了 1955 年 2 月,动工了近 1 年,原告董事才发现了此错误并发信给被告说:"We are very concerned to discover that there would appear to be a clerical error on the form of contract for the above, in that the date for completing is given as September 30, 1956 instead of September 30, 1955, which is the correct date. ... we shall, therefore, be glad if you will kindly arrange for the date on the contract documents to be corrected and initialled by the parties."

显然,如果真的是笔误,被告不会抗拒。但真正的情况是被告内部讨论后在合约内对工期作出修改,所以不会同意原告修改的要求,最终带来诉讼。原告向法院请求变更,把签字的正式合约的完工日期从 1956 年 9 月 30 日变更为 1955 年 9 月 30 日。在该先例中,显示了行业内工程完成时间越长,工程造价就越高的共识。

这是原告单方面不看清楚就签字的错误是没有疑问,但问题是被告是否知道或应该知道原告的错误。Pennycuik 大法官在审理后认定被告的证人 Smith 先生应该知道原告在签署合约时有了单方面错误,以为完工是在 18 个月后的 1955 年 9 月 30 日。Smith 先生也知道他的同事 Collins 先生决定把完工日期改为 1956 年 9 月 30 日,但没有去提醒原告。Smith 先生作为一位有经验的建筑师,也应该知道如果是 30 个月完工,原告是要支付更高的工程造价,这看来是暗示被告取巧。

被告代表大律师指称 Smith 先生没有动机去取巧,Pennycuik 大法官回应说:"It is also contended that Smith had no motive for acting as he did. No one suggests that he had any corrupt personal motive, but, as a loyal officer of the council he must have recognised that it would be extremely inconvenient if the contract were to go off, bearing in mind that work under it must begin by the end of March, 1954, in order to qualify for the Ministry grant."

最后,法院认定被告应该知道,说:"Only if he was unusually stupid or unusually heedless could he have failed to understand the company's state of mind at least by the end of this meeting. I am satisfied he was neither stupid nor heedless, and it seems to me he did realise the company's mistake. It is contended that it would be inconceivable for an official of Smith's position, if he did realise the company's mistake, to stand by without bringing it to the company's notice; but after hearing Smith's evidence, and in particular his views upon the propriety of inserting a new date for completion in the contract without communication with the company, I am unable to attribute any weight to this argument."

总而言之,Pennycuik 大法官最后命令合约变更。

11.2.2 变更合约本意是针对正式合约错误记录双方在谈判中同意之处

变更合约的课题在笔者的《合约的解释:规则与应用》一书第三章之 13 段有详论,在此只说是针对一份双方签署的合约后来被发觉在某些内容或条文并不正确记录合约双方在谈判时直到确定合约所同意的内容。显然,蒙受不利的一方会希望法院或仲裁庭插手去变更合约,把错误纠正,而对方会抗拒,坚持没有纠正的合约才是正确记录了双方同意的内容。对法院来说,双方签署的合约理所当然是很强的表面证据(prima facie evidence)去显示双方所同意的内容,这代表了要求变更合约的一方需要提供很明确的证据显示双方直到订约的一刻所同意的真正内容,毕竟在谈判早期所同意的内容,会在谈判持续的期间有所改变。这也是《合约的解释:规则与应用》一书中第六章之 2.3.3 段提到的口头证据规则(parol evidence rule)的主要例外之一。

在此只说,通过法院变更合约将错误记录改为双方谈判时真正同意的合约内容显然是配合共同错误,因为这是双方签字下共同都没有发现的记录错误。正如 Brightman 大法官在 Thomas Bates & Son Ltd v. Wyndham's (Lingerie) Ltd (1981) 1 WLR 505 先例中,说:"As the alleged common intention ex hypothesi contradicts the written instrument, convincing proof is required in order to counteract the cogent evidence of the parties' intention displayed by the instrument itself. ... the evidential requirement needed to counteract the inherent probability that the written instrument truly represents the parties' intention because it is a document signed by the parties."

但针对单方面错误就有点难以适用了。因为单方面错误就表示对方当事人并没有同意一方单方面错误理解的合约内容。这代表如果法院或仲裁庭同意把一份双方签署的合约变更为一方合约方主观理解的合约内容,更像是重写(rewrite)双方的合约。所以不可以太轻易以这种单方面错误变更合约。这可节录 Burrows 教授在《Construction and Rectification》(2007)一书中的解释,说:"... it appears to be **a serious flaw** in many contract textbooks that **unilateral mistake rectification is treated as if the same basic requirements apply as for common mistake rectification**. In particular, while there may be a continuing common intention and a unilateral mistake by one party, known about by the other, in not realising that the written contract has been inaccurately drawn up so as not to reflect that common intention, this is not the usual situation. Hence a number of leading cases have not been concerned with a mistake in the recording of the agreement. Rather one party has been mistaken during the negotiations and the other party has known about that mistake and has not pointed it out. Therefore the objection is **not**

that the written contract inaccurately reflects a previous common intention and that one party did not spot this inaccuracy while the other did. **On the contrary, the written contract accurately reflects the fact that, in the previous negotiations, one party was mistaken on a serious matter** and the mistake was **known about by the other. It is the bad faith or**, if one insists on using that most slippery of words, **the 'unconscionability' of the non-mistaken party** that leads to the mistaken party being able to insist on the contract being upheld on the basis of its own understanding of the contract …"(加黑部分是笔者的强调)

11.2.3 单方面错误去变更合约是特殊与例外的救济并适用于不变更不合情理的情况

在没有明确证据显示合约错误记录了双方谈判中同意的内容时,如果只是根据单方面指称合约存在记录错误,那就等于是重写合约,变更后就将不利之处强加在非错误方。在订约自由大原则下,显然这是不应该做的事情,所以说这种救济是特殊与例外,举证责任也较重。如在 George Wimpey UK Ltd v. VI Construction Ltd(2005) EWCA Civ 77 上诉庭先例中,Blackburne 大法官说:"it is an exceptional jurisdiction to rectify for unilateral mistake."

所以,错误方希望能够成功获得法院给予变更或重写合约的救济,是要迈过不少关卡。Buckley 大法官在 Thomas Bates & Son Ltd v. Wyndham's(Lingerie)Ltd(1981) 1 WLR 505 先例中就总结了四个要件,说:"I think it must be shown: **first**, that one party A erroneously believed that the document sought to be rectified contained a particular term or provision, or possibly did not contain a particular term or provision which, mistakenly, it did contain; **secondly**, that the other party B was aware of the omission or the inclusion and that it was due to a mistake on the part of A; **thirdly**, that B has omitted to draw the mistake to the notice of A. And I think there must be a **fourth** element involved, namely, that the **mistake must be one calculated to benefit B**. If these requirements are satisfied, the court may regard it as **inequitable to allow B to resist rectification** to give effect to A's intention on the ground that the mistake was not, at the time of execution of the document, a mutual mistake."(加黑部分是笔者的强调)

上述要件基本上已经谈到过,也与法院会否给予合约无效的救济的要件或考虑因素是大同小异。变更合约的救济会是比合约无效的救济更进一步,在本质上是重写合约后强制非错误方去履行。而非错误方肯定就会说:重写的合约是我从来没有同意过,错误方的犯错也是与我毫无关系,怎能去把他认为正确的理解变了是合约内容,当作是我同意的?所以,Buckley 大法官说的第四个要件,即拒绝作出变更让非错误方明知道错误方在订约时有了错误理解而仍享有好处会是不合情理,就是在这方面的平衡,十分重要。所以,以单方面错误去变更合约是一种衡平救济(equitable remedy),可归类为一种衡平法禁反言(equitable estoppel):见《Snell's Equity》(2019

年,第34版)之§16-019.33段。这样衡平法的说法或原则适用,如一旦发觉尽快申请变更合约、变更不影响无辜第三人等:见Liberty Mercian Ltd v. Cuddy Civil Engineering Ltd(2013)EWHC 2688(TCC)等先例。

接下来可以节录《Misrepresentation, Mistake and Non-Disclosure》(2022年,第6版)一书之13-47段说:"**The aim of rectification for material mistake** Where a party to a written contract claims rectification on the basis of unilateral mistake, he does not say that he did not agree to the written document; nor that the document fails to reflect the terms as the defendant intended them; but simply that the document does not reflect his own intentions. Given the significance that the law places on written documents as prima facie evidence of the intention of the parties, and given that — unlike in a case of common mistake — The claimant cannot argue that the document is itself written in error, failing properly to record the agreement that was reached, it will be evident that the courts are reluctant to rectify a contract where the mistake is only unilateral. ...But if the defendant knew about the claimant' s mistake about the terms, or if ... a reasonable person in his position would have realised that the claimant was making a mistake, the common law would say that the defendant is not entitled to hold the claimant to terms ... A claim for rectification, however, goes further than this. The claimant who gave his assent to a written document is not simply seeking to avoid the transaction on the basis of his mistake; he is seeking to enforce the transaction on the terms as he understood them. He seeks the court to rewrite the document...Rectification for unilateral mistake therefore involves depriving the defendant of the terms of the contract that he had intended, and to which the claimant had in fact agreed, and requiring the defendant to submit to a contract on the claimant' s own terms. ..."

11.2.4 部分有关先例的相同说法

这种现代单方面错误可以变更合约的理论首先在Riverlate Properties Ltd v. Paul (1975)Ch 133上诉庭先例中建立,Russell大法官在考虑了大量的先例如Garrard v. Frankel(1862)30 Beav. 445; Harris v. Pepperell(1867)LR 5 Eq 1; Paget v. Marshall (1884)28 Ch. D. 255; May v. Platt(1900)1 Ch 616等后,认为单方面错误也可去变更合约,说:"It may be that the **original conception of an instrument by rectification was based solely upon common mistake**: but certainly in these days **rectification may be based upon such knowledge on the part of the lessee**: ...Whether there was in any particular case knowledge of the intention and mistake of the other party must be a question of fact to be decided upon the evidence. Basically it appears to us that it must be such as to **involve** the lessee in **a degree of sharp practice**."(加黑部分是笔者的强调)

在此上诉庭先例中,Brightman大法官也针对了虽然举证责任仍是平衡的可能性,但因为考虑到双方签署了一份正式合约,其中的内容代表了双方最终同意的条件的内在可能性[49]更高,所以要推翻需要更有说服力的证据,说:"The standard of proof required in an action of rectification to establish the common intention of the parties is, in my view, the civil standard of balance of probability. But as the alleged common intention ex hypothesi contradicts the written instrument, convincing proof is required in order to counteract the cogent evidence of the parties' intention displayed by the instrument itself. It is not, I think, the standard of proof which is high, so differing from the normal civil standard, but **the evidential requirement needed to counteract the inherent probability that the written instrument truly represents the parties' intention because it is a document signed by the parties**. The standard of proof is no different in a case of so-called unilateral mistake such as the present."

在 George Wimpey UK Ltd v. VI Construction Ltd(2005)EWCA Civ 77 上诉庭先例中,案情涉及原告是一家大型的住宅发展商,它想从被告处购买土地开发住宅公寓。原告计划在购买的土地上建造 231 个公寓,根据计划建造的公寓数量与面积计算,双方同意将 20,610,090 英镑作为一个将来原告卖楼收入的基准数。双方约定原告购买土地的价格除了 265 万英镑外,还要再加上住宅建好后原告卖楼超过基准数 20,610,090 英镑部分的 50%。

由于建筑图纸在实际报规划部门审批时,难免会发生原有的设计计划需要改变,包括可能增加公寓的面积与数量,从而会带来比原计划价格的"溢价"(overage)。而且,在卖楼时,江景房、地下车库、层高都会作为公寓增值部分(enhancement)而令公寓的售价增加。考虑到这些不可避免地会令卖楼收入增加的部分,双方在土地买卖合约中为 20,610,090 英镑的基准数增加了一个溢价条文,也即最终的土地售价为 265 万英镑 +(实际售价 - 20,610,090 英镑 - 溢价)×50%。根据该公式可以看到,原告希望溢价部分越高越好,而被告希望溢价部分越低越好。

双方经过多轮谈判后确定了一个双方都满意的计算溢价的公式。在之前交换的合约草稿的版本中计算溢价的公式中均有公寓增值部分这个计算因子"+E",但在双方最后对溢价公式改变后的一版的合约中溢价公式中这个"+E"的计算因子不见了,原告在没有觉察下签署了合约。这样,原告在土地购买价格上就吃亏了。原告向法院以相互错误或单方面错误提出要求变更合约的溢价条文。

一审法院支持了原告变更合约条文的申请。但上诉庭却推翻了一审的判决,上诉庭认为虽然原告存在错误,该错误也给它带来不小的损失,但是它无法证明被告是

---

[49] 关于内在可能性在笔者《证据法:基础理论、口头证据与专家证据》一书第七章之 7.2.1.2 段中有详细介绍。Hale 勋爵在 B(Children)(Sexual Abuse:Standard of Proof), Re(2008)UKHL 35 先例举例中说,如果是在常见遛狗公园里看见犬类动物的身影闪过,这犬类动物是狗的内在可能性就更高,相反如果是动物园里的笼子被打开,动物园通知狮子脱逃疏散游客,此时看到大型动物的身影,它是狮子的内在可能性相比是一只大狗的可能性就会更高。

知道它的错误并从中取巧。毕竟原告是一家大型的房地产开发商,该合约是经过原告董事会的审核与批准,而且原告也专门聘请了律师给它提供专业的意见,很难说原告会是在被告取巧下订立合约。

原告的主张是:“i)Wimpey had failed to notice the omission from the overage formula of “ +E”,as put forward by VIC …;ii)VIC became aware of Wimpey's mistake but said nothing;iii)the contract,as executed,omitted “ +E” from the overage formula; iv)Wimpey entered into the contract mistakenly believing that the formula included “ +E” whereas VIC entered into it knowing(a)that it did not and(b)that Wimpey mistakenly believed that it did;and v)the contract as executed gave to VIC a significant financial advantage which VIC would not have had if “ +E” had been included in the formula.”

上诉庭的 Peter Gibson 大法官说:“I cannot see that Wimpey has discharged the onus on it of providing convincing proof that VIC did have knowledge in either of categories(ii)and(iii)of Wimpey's mistake. These were **arm's length negotiations for the sale of property for residential development** between,on the one hand,**VIC,with no relevant experience** and,on the other,**Wimpey with its vast experience. It is a ‘heavy-weight'**… He(原告证人)was an experienced negotiator and said in cross-examination:

Q. ‘When you are buying a piece of land,it is your responsibility to make sure that everything is as you are happy with,not what individuals are telling you,because people do tend to tell you things which aren't 100 per cent.

And that makes you particularly cautious,does it?

A Yes,it does. …

… in that case,it is significant that Mr. Ketteridge(原告证人)acquitted Mr. Youens (VIC 证人)of any intention to mislead. **In truth,it was a mistake by Mr. Ketteridge not to see what is obvious,that the formula inserted in cl. 16. 10. 2(溢价条文)did not contain “ + E”**. I acknowledge that VIC's conduct comes near to crossing the line. However,in the light of all the circumstances,in my judgment,Wimpey has **failed to provide convincing evidence that VIC shut its eyes to the obvious or wilfully and recklessly failed to do what an honest and reasonable person would have done** in the circumstances,and it would not be inequitable to allow VIC to resist the claim for rectification.” (加黑部分是笔者的强调)

另 Sedley 大法官说:“There are at least two kinds of mistake. One is a literal misunderstanding of some fact material to the proposed contract. The other is an error of judgment in entering into the contract. I find it difficult to think that the second kind has any relevance to the law of unilateral mistake. Nobody is bound,even in honour,to help his opposite number to negotiate to the best advantage. What then was the material fact that Wimpey misunderstood? That +E was omitted? They had only to look at VIC's draft to see that it was. Their mistake was failing to renegotiate it, and that seems to me an error of judgment, not of fact."

从以上的判决可以看出至少在单方面错误要求变更已经签署了的正式合约方面,大公司要特别小心不要犯错。因为一个成熟且有律师帮助的大公司,很难说服法院自己被对方一个甚至可能没有律师帮助的小公司取巧。更有可能的情况是大公司自己判断错误或疏忽,这是不会有衡平救济的。这可以说是公开的法院审理中的锄强扶弱,法律面前人人平等的典型例子。

Rowallan Group Ltd v. Edgehill Portfolio No 1 Ltd(2007)EWHC 32(Ch)先例也是同样的例子,文书请求中根本显示不了非错误方知道或应该知道错误方犯错或非错误方有什么取巧,因此案件被提前撤销。Lightman 大法官说:"In my judgment the Claimant has no real prospect of establishing his pleaded case claiming rectification on grounds of unilateral mistake. The amendment on its face plainly and unequivocally imposed the obligation on the Claimant to pay the Instalment.... There was no sharp practice on the part of the Defendant...Likewise there was no reason why the Defendant could or should have known or even suspected the pleaded mistake on the part of the Claimant.... There is no reason why this hopeless case should proceed to trial."

在更近期的 FSHC Group Holdings Ltd v. GLAS Trust Corp Ltd(2019)EWCA Civ 1361 上诉庭先例中,Leggatt 大法官说:"It has come to be accepted that the jurisdiction to rectify a written contract is not limited to cases where there was a common mistake and that in certain circumstances rectification may be granted even though at the time of execution of the contract only one of the parties was mistaken about its terms or effect. The development of the modern doctrine stems from the approval in A Roberts & Co Ltd v Leicestershire County Council[1961]Ch 555 ... of the following statement of principle in Snell's Equity, 25th ed(1960): 'a party is entitled to rectification of a contract upon proof that he believed a particular term to be included in the contract, and that the other party concluded the contract with the omission or a variation of that term in the knowledge that the first party believed the term to be included.' **The precise scope of this principle remains controversial**. But there is no doubt that it covers at least a case, such as the facts found in Thomas Bates & Son Ltd v Wyndham's(Lingerie)Ltd[1981]1 WLR 505, where the parties had a common intention that each had communicated to the other but one party before executing the contract realised that the document did not give effect to that intention and changed their mind without telling the other party."(加黑部分是笔者的强调)

最后是近期的 Caledonian Maritime Assets Ltd v. HCC International Insurance Co Plc(2022)EWHC 164(Ch)先例,原告是在苏格兰经营轮渡业务的公司,苏格兰政府是它的唯一股东。原告于 2015 年向 Ferguson 船厂订购建造两艘渡轮。被告为 Ferguson 船厂提供信用保险(credit insurance)[50]的同时,也要求 Ferguson 船厂为信用保险下的责任向他提供各种担保,其中也包括与 Ferguson 船厂同属一个集团的姐妹公司 Mackellar 公司提供的担保。可以想到这些担保的措辞都是非常广泛且同样都是针对被告在信用保险下所有的责任。Ferguson 船厂除了被告,还有其他债权人,包括苏格兰政府。在 2019 年 2 月,Ferguson 船厂的经营状况不佳,债权人之间签署了一个债权人间的契约(intercreditor deed),就将来 Ferguson 集团(包括 Ferguson 船厂与 Mackellar 公司)偿还债务的先后顺序做出约定,被告是第一被偿还顺位的债权人,苏格兰政府是第二被偿还顺位的债权人。也就是说根据该债权人间的契约,任何顺位靠后的债权人从 Ferguson 集团获得的钱都要转交给被告,直到 Ferguson 集团还清欠被告的债务为止。

后来在 2019 年 5 月,建造渡轮的进度大幅度落后于合约约定的销约期,从而原告可向 Ferguson 船厂主张终止造船合约与在信用保险下向被告要回预付款 2450 万英镑。但是这样,被告在支付后就会进一步向 Ferguson 船厂主张担保权益,从而 Ferguson 船厂就会彻底经营不下去而破产,建造中的渡轮永远也无法交船。相比于终止造船合约,原告还是希望 Ferguson 船厂能够最终将渡轮建好并交船,以减少损失。所以,原告与被告达成和解协议,要求被告仅支付 485 万英镑后就从原有的 2450 万英镑的信用保险的责任中完全脱离出来,而被告也放弃 Ferguson 船厂向它提供的担保。该和解协议也是本案中原告要求变更的协议。原告主张经过该和解协议,被告从信用保险中脱离出来,也不再是 Ferguson 船厂的债权人,所以也应该从债权人间的契约中脱离出来。但该和解协议中没有考虑到 Mackellar 公司提供的担保。

Ferguson 船厂进入破产管理人程序后,苏格兰政府作为船厂原有的债权人决定买下它。本来苏格兰政府的如意算盘是政府买下该破产船厂的钱,将会偿还给作为债权人的苏格兰政府,就相当于从左口袋拿出这笔钱又装进了右口袋。但破产管理人却认为被告是在信用保险下作出的支付,根据 Mackellar 公司提供的担保,被告仍然可以作为债权人间的契约下的第一偿还顺位的债权人从苏格兰政府处获得转交的 485 万英镑以及一些使费共计 500 多万英镑的偿付。这令苏格兰政府的如意算盘落空与相当于多花 500 多万英镑购买船厂。于是作为原告唯一股东的苏格兰政府,希望从原告这方面变更和解协议下手。原告主张在签署和解协议时存在单方面错误,要求变更和解协议。被告抗辩说原告根本知悉 Mackellar 公司的担保,是自己看漏了,所以不存在错误。

Simon Gleeson 大法官说变更只是针对字词的错误以及会带来的法律后果,而不包括一份商业协议会带来的商业后果,所以拒绝变更,说:“... in order for unilateral rectification to be available ‘the mistake must be as to either the words used or their legal effect’. Where the mistake is as to neither the words used nor their legal effect, but as to

[50] 相当于造船合约下的还款担保(refund guarantee),可见笔者《造船合约》一书第十九章之 5 段。

the commercial outcome of the agreement actually made as a result of subsequent developments which were not foreordained at the time of the agreement, I do not accept that this is a ground for unilateral rectification. Another way of putting this is that there is no such thing as retrospective rectification-a party or parties are not entitled to rectification of a document which accurately reflected their intentions at the time that it was entered into, but whose terms have turned out to have unexpected consequences. If this were the case, the commercial reliability of English deeds would receive a significant body-blow which it does not need or deserve."

11.3 可诉错误在有对价与没有对价合约/契约的区别

有对价的合约与没有对价合约的区别,在本章之5.3段已经提过。没有对价往往涉及一些赠与合约,这种合约[会是通过契约(deed)形式订立]也会出现赠与方事后以自己有了错误(可以是对事实或法律的错误)为由令赠与无效,希望取回赠与的礼物或资产的情况。看来,赠与方单方面错误下作出赠与,如果总体看来错误是足够严重,受赠与方不去退回也不公平合理或不合情理,法院是有衡平法权力令合约无效,或是对该赠与合约作出变更。这就不用仅仅限制在上述所讲的一方知道对方犯错想取巧的唯一例外。

赠与本质上是本章之7.1.1段介绍的自愿支付(voluntary payment)的一种,赠与方不能够随便将赠与的东西拿回来。毕竟,受赠与方的合法利益或合理预期也受到法律保护,但保护的强度就比不上普通法管辖下的有对价合约,这主要是通过普通法对可诉错误的狭窄与严格的解释。这里的原因正是在本章之5.3段介绍的Pitt v. Holt(2013)UKSC 26最高院先例中Walker勋爵提到的要保护合约的肯定性、保障性与神圣性。

在近期的Van der Merwe v. Goldman(2016)EWHC 790(Ch)先例中,Morgan大法官更是说清楚这个区分,即有对价合约受普通法管辖(重视法律肯定性),而没有对价合约或契约受衡平法管辖(重视个别案件的公平合理),说:"the difference between the case where the equitable rules apply and those where they do not turns on whether consideration has been given for the benefit conferred by the transaction. If the effect of rescission(or a declaration that a transaction is void) would deprive a party of a benefit for which he gave consideration, then the common law rules apply and there is no separate equitable jurisdiction to order rescission. Conversely, if the effect of rescission would deprive a party of a benefit for which he gave no consideration, then there is a separate equitable to order rescission."

针对没有对价合约,通常是赠与方可主张单方面错误令合约无效。先节录Ogilvie v. Littleboy(1897)13 TLR 399先例中,案情涉及一位十分富有的Ogilvie女士在1887年以两份契约把一大笔财产捐赠作为慈善之用,但在7年后以五个不同理由(主要说是她自己搞错,受到募捐方的干扰与没有获得全面与恰当的法律咨询等),

申请法院把两份契约确定无效,以取回财产。但她在一审、上诉庭与贵族院都败诉。在一审法院,Byrne 大法官指出这是根本不构成订立的合约有缺陷,如欺诈、不当影响、隐瞒事实等,说:"The case is entirely wanting in any of those elements of fraud, undue influence, concealments of facts from the donor, want of separate and independent advice, surprise or pressure, which, or some of which, are commonly to be met with in cases of attempts to set aside or rectify voluntary instruments."

在上诉庭,Lindsey 大法官说:"Gifts cannot be revoked, nor can deeds of gift be set aside, simply because the donors wish they had not made them and would like to have back the property given. Where there is no fraud, no undue influence, no fiduciary relation between the donor and donee, no mistake induced by those who derive any benefit of it, **a gift, whether by mere delivery or by deed, is binding on the donor**. ... In the absence of all circumstances of suspicion **a donor can only obtain back property which he has given away by showing that he was under some mistake of so serious a character as to render it unjust on the part of the donee to retain the property given to him**."(加黑部分是笔者的强调)

贵族院是完全支持上诉庭的判决,Halsbury 勋爵说:"The appellant, a lady, was desirous of establishing certain charities, and she now contends that, though she did intend to devote her money to charity, certain specific intentions as to management, control, independence of control, and the like were such essential and important considerations to her mind that in these respects she was misled, and now seeks to get rid of the effect of her deeds upon that allegation. Such questions, doubtless, may arise under circumstances where misunderstanding on both sides may render it unjust to the giver that the gift should be retained. It appears to me that there are no such circumstances here. ..."

除非在很特殊的情况下,要求无辜的受赠与方(没有对赠与方误述、欺诈、不当影响、隐瞒事实等不当的游说募捐)去退回赠与财产(或变更赠与合约的条件)是并不公平合理。因为很可能有部分钱已经被受赠与方用来买物资或作为其他用途,即使没有使用,至少也是打乱受赠与方的计划,空欢喜一场。

所以,即使是没有对价的赠与合约/契约也不是任意可令它无效。首先是这可诉错误必须是严重与确实对现存事实或法律有错误理解才会有法律救济,对将来情况的错误估计并不是可诉错误。例如作出赠与后,赠与方的经济状况变坏不想捐了,甚至希望能以单方面错误令赠与合约/契约无效,可取回已经是给出去的赠与财产。这种情况也涉及了赠与方在自愿支付下自己承担风险(这已在本章之 3 段与 4 段详及),即使是面对没有对价的合约/契约,也可以否定或排除可诉错误。这也不是本章之 7.1 段说的不当得利,因为受赠与方没有任何"不当"。

另是,这是衡平法管辖,法院有裁量权。所以对个别案件的案情都会加以考虑,例如赠与方的单方面错误是什么错误、过错或不小心的严重与可归责程度、赠与方与受赠与方两者的水平对比、受赠与方保留不退回赠与财产是否不合情理等。

所以不要动歪脑筋，以为可以作出一大笔的捐赠，出出风头之后，再以单方面错误试图去令赠与合约/契约无效，并取回这笔捐赠。

除了赠与/捐赠外，在信托下也同样会出现以单方面错误去令信托无效的争议。例如在 Bainbridge v. Bainbridge(2016) EWHC 898(Ch)先例中，原告父子共同拥有农场与土地，因为怕将来有其他人争产，如儿子如果离婚，他的前妻。所以在律师建议下把农场与土地的产权转移给了一个自由裁量信托(discretionary trust)。但原告不知道设立信托需要向税务局缴付财产收益税(capital gain tax)20 万英镑。原告知道后希望以错误去令信托无效，因为在普通法下，这相当于整件事没有发生过，也就不存在财产收益税这码事了。正如 Matthews 大法官说："... the effect of an equitable rescission for mistake is to undo the transaction from the beginning. It is thereafter treated for the purposes of the general law as if it never took place... Whether it has the same effect for the purposes of tax law must however depend on the true construction of the tax law in question. The ordinary or default position would be that the tax(whatever it was) should be exigible only where the act or event is ultimately held to be valid and effective under the general law. So under the default position, if the act or event is ultimately held not to be valid and effective under the general law, it is also not treated as a taxable event either.... "

此先例虽然涉及原告(或他们的律师)的无知与不小心，但仍可以可诉错误令信托无效。只要不是原告刻意自愿承担风险(本案不是这种情况)，在这种没有对价的合约/契约，不存在需要考虑在本章之 9 段提到的考虑之一，即非错误方的合理预期与利益，也不涉及退还农场与土地是否合情理，所以法院同意这是可诉错误与可去令转移农场与土地产权的信托无效。Matthews 大法官援引了 Etherton 大法官在 Kennedy v. Kennedy(2014) EWHC 4129(Ch)先例中对 Pitt v. Holt 最高院先例对此问题的总结，说："(1) There must be a distinct mistake as distinguished from mere ignorance or inadvertence or what unjust enrichment scholars call a 'misprediction' relating to some possible future event.... (2) A mistake **may still be a relevant mistake even if it was due to carelessness on the part of the person making the voluntary disposition**, unless the circumstances are such as to show that he or she deliberately ran the risk, or must be taken to have run the risk, of being wrong. (3) The causative mistake must be sufficiently grave as to make it unconscionable on the part of the donee to retain the property. That test will normally be satisfied only when there is a mistake either as to the legal character or nature of a transaction or as to some matter of fact or law which is basic to the transaction.... (4) **The injustice(or unfairness or unconscionableness) of leaving a mistaken disposition uncorrected** must be evaluated objectively but with an intense focus on the facts of the particular case.... "(加黑部分是笔者的强调)

国际商业合约绝大部分是有对价合约,所以本段只粗略提及没有对价的合约,这可能包括如财产托管建立信托、自愿财产支配或转让(voluntary disposition)、赠与(gift)等。在有对价合约中,正如在本章之5.3段所讲错误方自己的遗忘(forgetfulness)、疏漏(inadvertence)或无知(ignorance),通常不被接受为是可诉错误而令合约无效。但没有对价的合约在这方面就较为宽松,只要错误足够严重,以及对方不退还财产是不公平合理与/或不合情理,就可以获得救济。

最后可节录《Misrepresentation, Mistake and Non-Disclosure》(2022年,第6版)一书之15-12段说:"Unilateral mistake may be sufficient to allow rescission in equity of a voluntary transaction but, given the different policies relating to security of transactions in the cases of unilateral voluntary transactions and bilateral contracts, this is clearly distinct from the rules governing the impact of mistake on contracts."

12. 单方面错误之二:对对方订约方的身份有错误理解

在进一步分析前,可先参阅笔者《合约的履行、弃权与禁反言》一书第五章之10.2.1段"单方面错误之一:身份搞错"的相关内容。

12.1 错误理解订约方身份与错误理解合约条件的区别

首先说明在搞错对方订约方的身份(identity)与搞错了合约条件这两种情况下,能够成立可诉单方面错误的都是要求非错误方是知道错误方的错误。因为只有这样,才能被认为双方没有达成一致想法,而令合约的成立要件有缺陷,从而合约无效。

如果A意图是与B订立合约,并以电文形式向B发出了一个十分优惠的要约(offer)。但不小心将电文发错给了C,C在看到B的抬头下仍然马上回复A接受了这个要约。这样可否说A与C之间产生或成立了一个合约呢?这显然是说不通的,因为即使C有订约意图,A也没有与C的订约意图。他们之间不会有一致想法。正如Atkin勋爵在Bell v. Lever Brothers Ltd(1932)AC 161贵族院先例中说:"A mistaken belief by A, that he is contracting with B, whereas in fact he is contracting with C, will negative consent where it is clear that the intention of A, was to contract only with B."

另在Shogun Finance Ltd v. Hudson(2003)UKHL 62贵族院先例中,Phillips勋爵也说:"Just as the parties must be shown to have agreed on the terms of the contract, so they must also be shown to have agreed the one with the other. If A makes an offer to B, but C purports to accept it, there will be no contract. Equally, if A makes an offer to B and B addresses his acceptance to C there will be no contract. ..."

但把对方身份搞错,与对合约内容与条件有了单方面错误理解,仍然会有一些区分。这首先是订约方的身份并不属于合约的条件,也有说法是订约方的身份是比一般合约条件更为根本。另外更为重要的就是搞错身份的案件多是发生在货物买卖中,并且多与欺诈/欺骗有关。明知对方搞错合约条件还与对方订约,通常涉及取巧,而明知对方搞错身份还与对方订约则往往涉及欺诈/欺骗,不只是取巧这么简单。并且在搞错身份的欺诈/欺骗案件中,通常骗子会很快将骗到手的货物转卖给第三人。这时经过买卖合约而合法转移货物的产权,如果令合约自始无效,就会影响无辜第三人。这个严重的问题至今也没有解决,这些内容在接下来的段节会重点分析。

针对订约方的身份是比一般合约条件更为重要,正如 Millett 勋爵在 The "Starsin"(2003) UKHL 12 贵族院先例中说:"**The identity of the parties to a contract is fundamental**. It is not simply a term or condition of the contract. It goes to the very existence of the contract itself. If it is uncertain, there is no contract. Where there is an issue as to whether two persons have reached an agreement, the one with the other, the courts have tended to adopt the same approach to resolving that issue as they adopt when considering whether there has been agreement as to the terms of the contract. **The court asks the question whether each intended, or must be deemed to have intended, to contract with the other**. That approach give rise to a problem where one person is mistaken as to the identity of the person with whom he is dealing, as the cases demonstrate."(加黑部分是笔者的强调)

另在《Misrepresentation, Mistake and Non-Disclosure》(2022 年,第 6 版)一书之 14 – 04 段中提到搞错身份与搞错合约条件的其他不同,说:"**Identity is not a term of the contract** The identity of the parties to a contract is not a term of the contract. The parties do not exchange promises about their respective identities. If one is not who he claims to be, it is not a breach of contract. On the other hand it has been suggested that the same approach can be taken to identity and terms. ... where the parties are not in fact in agreement about the terms of the contract, the subjective understanding may be overridden by the objective test: but under this test one party cannot hold the other to have agreed to terms where he either knew, or ought reasonably to have known, that the latter was making a mistake."

以上节录说合约条件涉及双方相互交换合约承诺,如卖方承诺交付货物、货物的描述与数量、何时交付等。而买方承诺支付货价与如何支付,如开出信用证等。但订约方身份并非一种合约的承诺,而订约方身份不正确的结果也不是违反合约条件中作出的承诺的结果,即赔偿损失或加上可去终止合约,而是合约变了是自始无效。

虽然,针对合约条件或订约方身份的争议解决,做法上是一致,也是以客观的角度去解释双方的通讯往来或一份正式合约,而不理会两位订约方主观的看法/说法。但只要是对方订约方的 C 是知道,或应该知道 A 对 C 的身份有了错误理解,如错误以为 C 就是 B,就不再是你情我愿去达成了一致想法了,也就不会产生有效合约了。也就是在本章之 11.1.2 段所说的错误理解合约条件需要订约方明知对方搞错仍取巧(sharp practice 或 unfair dealing)。而搞错订约方身份,往往不涉及订约方取巧,只要他明知对方搞错了自己的身份,就等于知道了双方没有一致想法,也就是没有合约产生。这种案件多数是涉及欺诈/欺骗,所以 A 证明 C 作为骗子是知道或应该知道 A 对 C 搞错了身份,误以为他是 B,应该是容易的。

最后可节录一些对这方面的权威说法,在 Ingram v. Little(1961)1 QB 31 上诉庭先例中,Pearce 大法官说:"Has it been sufficiently shown in the particular circumstances that,contrary to the prima facie presumption,a party was not contracting with the physical person to whom he uttered the offer,but with another individual whom(**as the other party ought to have understood**)he believed to be the physical person present. The answer to that question is a finding of fact."(加黑部分是笔者的强调)

另在新西兰上诉庭的 Fawcett v. Star Car Sales Ltd(1960)NZLR 406 先例中,Gresson P 大法官说:"if it is established that **A did not intend** to make a contract with B,and **B was aware of this fact**,then the apparent contract is void for mistake ..."(加黑部分是笔者的强调)

12.2 错误理解订约方身份的救济是否应为合约自始无效或可使无效

由于对订约方身份有错误理解的案件绝大部分涉及货物买卖与欺诈/欺骗,所以经常会影响无辜第三人。这种情况是可想而知,一位骗子通过以虚假名字冒充别人(法人或自然人)的方式把货物骗到手,就会尽快把这些赃物脱手去转卖给其他不知情的无辜第三人,然后自己失踪,剩下两位无辜人士(受骗原卖方与无辜第三人)去争夺有关货物的产权。法院或仲裁庭在面对这种案件时,难免感到左右为难,正如在 Cundy v. Lindsay(1878)3 App Cas 459 贵族院先例中,Cairns 勋爵说:"My Lords,you have in this case to discharge a duty which is always a disagreeable one for any Court,to determine as between two parties,both of whom are perfectly innocent,upon which of the two the consequences of a fraud practised upon both of them must fall."

在本书第三章之6.3 段中有介绍,合约如果是自始无效(void ab inition)就会让不幸的无辜第三人蒙受损失,因为私有财产(personal property)是不会无端转让给了第三人。这可节录在新西兰的 Fawcett v. Star Car Sales Ltd(1960)NZLR 406 先例中,Gresson P 大法官说:"In this case,the delivery which was made purported to be made in performance of the apparent contract;if this was a nullity,there is nothing to support the delivery."

但如果合约只是可使无效(voidable),就代表直至合约被撤销并恢复原状前,有效合约仍是存在,骗子 B 是可以合法把来自 A 的私有财产与产权转卖给无辜第三人 C,让 C 去拥有该财产的法定产权(legal title),而没有收到货价的 A,充其量也是对该财产有次要的衡平产权(equitable title)。对私有财产而言,也只能通过有效的合约在你情我愿下去转让私有财产,正如 Cairns 勋爵在 Cundy v. Lindsay 贵族院先例中说:"If the property in the goods in question passed,it could only pass by way of contract;there is nothing else which could have passed the property."

这就表示除非可诉错误的法律救济好像可诉误述的救济一样是可使无效,才会在涉及无辜第三人的情况下,阻止受骗原卖方主张货物产权,进而保护了无辜第三人对有关货物的产权。在较近期的先例中,法官们对此问题的看法就并不一致,部分法官认为可使合约无效的救济更为公平合理,务求不会影响无辜第三人。但这样,从纯理论角度看来是难以说得通的,因为受骗原卖方与骗子是不可能有一致想法,这显然也是目前的法律地位。

首先在 Lewis v. Averay(1972)1 QB 198 上诉庭先例中,Denning 勋爵认为在买卖合约下,即使是搞错对方订约方身份仍是可使无效的救济更为公平合理,且不会影响无辜第三人,说:"I felt it wrong that an innocent purchaser(who knew nothing of what passed between the seller and the rogue) should have his title depend on such refinements. After all, he has acted with complete circumspection and in entire good faith: whereas it was the seller who let the rogue have the goods and thus enabled him to commit the fraud.... It is this: When two parties have come to a contract——or rather what appears, on the face of it, to be a contract-the fact that one party is **mistaken as to the identity** of the other **does not mean that there is no contract, or that the contract is a nullity and void from the beginning. It only means that the contract is voidable**, that is, liable to be set aside at the instance of the mistaken person, so long as he does so before third parties have in good faith acquired rights under it."(加黑部分是笔者的强调)

另在 Shogun Finance Ltd v. Hudson(2003) UKHL 62 贵族院先例中,少数意见也有同样说法,认为受骗原卖方而不是无辜第三人更应承担损失。Millett 勋爵说:"... it is surely fairer that the party who was actually swindled and who had an opportunity to uncover the fraud should bear the loss rather than a party who entered the picture only after the swindle had been carried out and who had none."

另 Nicholls 勋爵说:"As between two innocent persons the loss is more appropriately borne by the person who takes the risks inherent in parting with his goods without receiving payment."

但在 3:2 多数意见的判决中对此问题有了定论,也就是在对订约方的身份有了错误理解时,合约自始无效。多数意见中的 Hobhouse 勋爵说:"... the approach and dicta of Lord Denning MR in Lewis v. Averay ... are misplaced and wrong."

最后可节录《Misrepresentation, Mistake and Non-Disclosure》(2022 年,第 6 版)一书之 14-09 段说:"**The contract entered into under a mistake of identity is void** We shall see that the disagreement amongst judges in recent years over mistake of identity has focused on this issue. Some have argued that a mistake of identity should not make the contract void, because of the drastic consequences which follow upon such a finding; and that it is better to hold that the effect of the mistake should be no more than to render the contract voidable. However, the majority of the House of Lords in Shogun Finance Ltd v.

Hudson has confirmed the earlier authorities that held that, if the mistake is sufficient to constitute an actionable mistake of identity, the consequence is that the contract is void."

12.3 错误理解订约方身份是单方面错误

错误理解身份显然是单方面错误,因为被错误理解身份的对方订约方,是不会不知道自己真正是谁。

在英国法律中,单方面错误理解对方订约方的身份一般是没有法律的救济。这道理是显而易见:(1)如果给予法律救济去令合约无效,等于让订约方说一句"我搞错了对象"就走掉,赖掉一个表面看来是他在你情我愿下订立的合约,令清楚知道自己是谁与以为订立了有效合约的无辜对方订约方承担损失与不便。(2)在买方自己小心的原则延伸下,查清楚与了解订约的对方是谁,是错误方应该承担的风险。(3)如果错误方闭着眼睛与对方订合约,也往往会涉及自己的过错、不小心或无知。(4)在上述的情况下,绝大部分也不是属于对订约方身份的错误。说到有错误,就代表错误方的A早就已经有了目标对象,如有特定原因只与B订约,例如在Boulton v. Jones(1857)157 ER 232先例中,Jones只是想与Brocklehurst买货,因为双方有流水账(running account),不必马上支付。但Brocklehurst被Boulton收购后,Jones就要马上支付,所以Jones提出他是向Brocklehurst订购而不是Boulton,是把对方订约方的身份搞错了。只是在后来阴差阳错的情况下,A与C订立了合约而不是B,这才能说是A搞错了对方身份。在同样例子中,如果A是不介意与B或C订立合约,结果在与C订立合约后才发觉C的财政状况与可信度(creditworthiness)远不如B而后悔,或甚是C在履约时倒闭。这会涉及A的过错或不小心,没有查清楚C就贸然订约,但不是搞错身份,因为原来就没有"非卿不嫁"的订约目标对象,何错之有?另是,A搞错的是C的特质/属性(attributes/ characteristics),即他的财力与可信度,不是身份。如果C的财政状况与可信度没有出问题,A是不会有异议的。

当然,如果错误理解了对方身份是由于对方的误述或诱导,通常是欺诈性误述(典型是以言行去假冒身份),这就变成是一个欺诈/欺骗(tort of deceit)的侵权案件了。这也符合在本章之11.1段所讲的单方面错误的唯一例外,也就是一方知道对方是在搞错了他的身份的情况下与自己订立合约,也就表示双方在合约身份方面从来没有一致想法。可节录在《Misrepresentation, Mistake and Non-Disclosure》(2022年,第6版)一书之14-06段中说:"... it is not sufficient in English law for a party to avoid a contract by simply showing that he made a mistake. In addition, it must be shown why the other party should lose the contract; because he caused or contributed to the mistake, or knew or at least ought to have known about it. [51]"

---

[51] 在Boulton v. Jones(1857)157 ER 232先例中,简单案情在上一小段有介绍,该先例中Boulton上午收购了Brocklehurst,下午收到Jones的订单,该订单上写的是给Brocklehurst,所以Boulton应该知道Jones搞错了他的身份。但此先例不涉及欺诈/欺骗,完全是个正常交易,只是其中一方换了老板。

从上述介绍可见，绝大部分可能会有法律救济的搞错对方订约方身份的案件，都涉及欺诈/欺骗。一般涉及这种案件，都会有骗子 C 作出欺诈性误述冒充 B 去诱导 A。这样，A 以欺诈性误述作为诉因更容易取得法律救济，包括宽松的损失计算。但 A 仍去主张对身份的单方面错误往往是因为案件涉及了无辜第三人，只有合约自始无效的救济才能去摆脱这些无辜第三人。这可节录《Misrepresentation, Mistake and Non-Disclosure》(2022 年，第 6 版)一书之 14 – 08 段说："**Mistakes of identity are normally unilateral and induced by fraud** In every reported case the alleged mistake of identity has been unilateral. This is inevitable in the normal case, because A may be mistaken about B's identity; but it is difficult to see how B could be equally mistaken. He may share A's mistake about some of his own characteristics, less than a mistake of identity-such as whether he has authority to enter into the contract. …Moreover, **in almost every case the mistake of identity was induced by the other party's misrepresentation**; and such a misrepresentation **is generally fraudulent**. The purpose of misleading another party about one's own identity is commonly to practise some form of deception; … The party who is misled about the other's intention by his misrepresentation will therefore have a range of remedies arising from the misrepresentation: the contract is voidable; and damages can be obtained for loss caused by reliance on the misrepresentation of identity-typically, this means that the losses flowing from entering into the contract. The fact that the misrepresentation is fraudulent can in some respects strengthen the claim for these remedies. The question, therefore, is **why a party needs to establish not only that he was misled** by the other party about his identity; **but also that the mistake was itself sufficient to give rise to a remedy. In most cases, this is because he needs to show that the contract was not just voidable, but void**."(加黑部分是笔者的强调)

12.4　身份与特质/属性的区别

身份对于法人或自然人来说只是一个名字(name)或一个标签(label)，到底名字的背后真正是谁往往不容易去调查请楚。显然，与来历不明与不知特质/属性(attributes/characteristics)的人士，只凭他的名字或标签去订立商业合约，可以说是十分危险。但现实中即使在国际商业活动，也往往只是依靠业界朋友之间的口口相传就进行交易，如国际货物买卖，并在几次交易后就成为外国"老朋友"或"老关系"，甚至会推荐给业界朋友，虽然双方可能还没有亲自见过，更没有紧密的调查与跟进对方不断在改变的财政状况与商业信用。

例如，在较近期的 P&P Property Ltd v. Owen White & Catlin LLP (2018) EWCA Civ 1082 上诉庭先例中，就是被告(竟然是一位律师)只凭一个名字，没有或难以调查到对方的特质/属性，结果上当。案情显示在真正的商业交易中，骗子的行骗手法层出不穷。该案涉及一幢在伦敦的房屋，房屋登记注册上显示该房屋从 1989 年开始由 Clifford Harper 先生拥有，但他本人没有居住在该房屋，而是将房屋出租出去。

2013 年 11 月 20 日，一位自称是 Clifford Harper 的人士（以下简称卖方，后来也被证实是骗子）打电话给本案的被告律师所，委托被告帮他完成一项以该房屋为抵押的融资交易。卖方声称想要购买另外一座房屋，希望在 10 日内以该价值 120 万英镑的房屋为抵押融资到 80 万英镑。被告于 11 月 29 日在律师所与卖方会面后，开始对其进行身份验证，卖方自己主张当时是工作与生活在迪拜。后来因为贷款机构要被告提供在迪拜的住址、工作合约与银行的月结单，卖方转而告诉被告他怕麻烦不准备抵押贷款而是要卖出该房屋。本案的原告在 12 月 4 日出价 103 万英镑购买，该价格虽然低于 120 万英镑不少，但是卖方说他要完成另外一项物业交易所以急需现金，在原告愿意支付现金的前提下，他也接受这低于市价的价格。原告在 12 月 12 日支付了全部的 103 万英镑后，于 2014 年 1 月去办理过户时才发现卖方是骗子。这时骗子和 103 万英镑也早已一起不见踪影了。原告没有起诉自己委托的律师，而是将卖方也就是骗子的律师告上法庭，主张被告律师所违反了授权与承诺、存在疏忽与违反信托等。

原告在上诉庭就违反信托与违反承诺胜诉，被告律师所因违反了英国律师协会制定的房屋交易过户行为守则《Law Society Code for Completion by Post》，在没有完成过户就过早地将买房款转给自己的客户，这里不再展开具体来讲。只是说针对国际欺诈，在现实中非常多，而且也防不胜防，任何疏漏都会给骗子可乘之机。被告律师所是有根据英国的反洗钱相关法律设立的多个要求去对卖方的身份进行核实与验证，包括核对卖方护照、要求卖方提供住址证明、通过反洗钱调查对其进行身份验证、甚至是要求迪拜的律师为骗子卖方出具身份证明等，但在进行验证的过程中存在疏忽，尤其是事后来看在几个环节都存在问题，包括卖方提供的银行月结单只有封面而没有内容，没有确认卖方当时在英国的住址、迪拜律师（后来被发现在 2011 年已经被除牌）为卖方提供的身份证明也是虚假的、反洗钱调查的结果是无法根据卖方提供的地址确认该卖方的唯一身份、卖方在交易文件上的签名与护照签名不一致等。

名字与标签并不代表什么，真正重要的是名字与标签后面的特质/属性（如可信度）才是决定是否订约的关键，而这两者显然是不同的。身份（名字或标签）与他的特质/属性不同在 Lewis v. Averay（1972）1 QB 198 上诉庭先例中，Denning 勋爵已有批评，说："It has been suggested that a mistake as to the identity of a person is one thing: and a mistake as to his attributes is another. A mistake as to identity, it is said, avoids a contract: whereas a mistake as to attributes does not. But this is a distinction without a difference. A man's very name is one of his attributes. It is also a key to his identity. If then, he gives a false name, is it a mistake as to his identity? or a mistake as to his attributes? These fine distinctions do no good to the law."

Denning 勋爵对两者的区分看来并不友善，但 Denning 勋爵是在该上诉庭先例认为对订约方身份的搞错，法律救济应该是可使无效而不是自始无效的背景下做出该批评。反正在英国法律中，这两者的区分仍是存在，对待身份错误与特质/属性错误是截然不同的救济,这在稍后会详及。正如在《Misrepresentation, Mistake and Non-Disclosure》(2022 年,第 6 版)一书之 14 – 13 段中说:"… Although the distinction between a person's identity and his attributes if often, on the facts, not easy to make, it is still valid, … And we have seen that the other party's name can have quite different significance to the claimant in negotiating a contract: it might be just a label, an identifier. But, more than that, it might identify the person (and, let us say, the **only** person) with whom he is prepared to enter into the present contract. This is what lies at the heart of the difficulty of establishing whether the claimant really made a mistake of 'identity', and sometimes it will help to exclude an alleged mistake by characterising it as only a mistake about the person's attributes."(加黑部分是笔者的强调)

12.4.1 商业人士一般不关心对方的名字而是关心特质/属性

在现实的社会或国际商业活动中,商业人士对对方订约方的名字或标签,往往是不太重视,更重视的是对方在方方面面的特质/属性,其中最重要的是已经多次提到的财政状况与商业信用。例如,一般商业人士是不介意与一家来历不明的皮包公司订立一个昂贵的合约,只要它背后有财雄势大的母公司,更不要说该母公司还愿意提供履约担保(performance guarantee)与合约有利可图。

在本土商业社会中,一般商店或超级市场是不介意与任何顾客去订立买卖合约,反正是一手交钱、一手交货,连顾客的财政状况或信用也不必关心。正如在 Dennant v. Skinner and Collom (1948) 2 KB 164 先例中, Hallet 大法官说:"In normal times a shopkeeper is not usually concerned with the identity of the customer when deciding whether he is willing to sell his goods to him, although he may be concerned with that matter when deciding whether, having effected the sale, he should give the purchaser credit."

今天的网上买卖或拍卖等,卖方更是没有兴趣知道对方订约方的身份,只要买方提供的信用卡或银行卡可以支付到位,根本不会有搞错了对方订约方身份的问题。

在国际商业社会中,虽然交易往往涉及的金额会大得多,但有不少行业参与的商业人士,对对方订约方的身份也是十分随意。例如租船合约,在一些案例中可以很明显看到这种随意的做法。而且,租船合约经常没有一个正式的合约,只是本章之 6.2.1 段介绍的以言行/书信往来达成合约。这就比整理出一份完整与正式签字的租船合约更容易发生并且不及时觉察这种名字搞错/误名(misnomer)的情况。在 The "Rhodian River" (1984) 1 Lloyd's Rep 373 先例中,双方是在所有重要的核心条件同意后,也就是已经有了一个有效的租约,承租人才问到底谁是船东(full style of owners)。另在 The "Double Happiness" (2007) 2 Lloyd's Rep 131 先例中,承租人更是可以接受"whoever was the disponent owner",只要是"a member of Golden Ocean group"。

另在 TTMI Sarl v. Statoil ASA (2011) EWHC 1150 (Comm) 先例中,涉及 TTMI 背

后的集团公司 Sempra Energy(美国加利福尼亚的一家石油公司)委任一家在伦敦的著名船舶经纪人把集团租入但一时运力过剩的“Sibohelle”轮分租出去。结果经纪人成功把该油轮转租给了挪威的 Statoil,并顺利履行了一个航次。问题是经纪人在指定谁是船东或二船东时搞错了,说成 Sempra Energy 是二船东或“T/C owner”。但作为集团公司,Sempra Energy 不管油轮业务,集团中负责的是原告 TTMI。这导致在租约履行后的滞期费(demurrage)结算,就有了谁是船东,谁有诉权向 Statoil 索赔滞期费等的争议。

在国际货物买卖与航运的提单合约(bill of lading)中,由于装船提单是船上货物的产权凭证(document of title),更是会被频频转卖,导致船舶抵达卸港时,船东或承运人根本不会知道在提单合约下的对方合约方是谁。这也带来大量的质疑诉权(title to sue)的争议,迫使英国需要以立法去解决这个问题。[52]

这种订约方的名字被搞错/误名的案件也发生在其他行业。在 Hamid(t/a Hamid Properties) v. Francis Bradshaw Partnership(2013) EWCA Civ 470 上诉庭先例中,案情涉及 Chad 家具店的展馆(furniture showroom)的工程合约。双方没有签订一份正式的合约,所以对订约方的身份约定并不明确,被告承建商质疑原告的身份,到底是 Chad 还是它的老板 Hamid 先生?

多举一个例子,在 Dumford Trading AG v. OAO Atlantrybflot(2004) EWHC 1099 (Comm)先例中,案情涉及原告贷款给 Shelley 公司,并由被告作出两份担保合约,写的都是 ZAO Atlantrybflot。ZAO 在俄语中应是“有限公司”(Ltd.),它是 OAO Atlantrybflot 的附属公司,OAO 在俄语是“上市公司”(plc.)。争议谁是担保人:ZAO 或 OAO? 因为上市公司财雄势大,而附属的有限公司的经济状况就不是同一码事了。

这种订约方“名字搞错”的案件多不胜数,而且往往是在合约被履行或部分被履行后双方有了争议时被一方当事人(通常是被告)提出来质疑对方(原告)的身份与诉权或对方搞错了被告的真正身份并不是合约方。背后的原因也往往是策略性(tactical),如以此质疑仲裁庭的管辖权(jurisdiction challenge);原告身份如果改了,其他人会出现时效已过或无法证明有蒙受损失;被告身份如果改了,其他人或附属公司会是皮包公司可以赖掉欠债等。

12.4.2 名字搞错案件:以特质/属性协助确定订约方真正的身份

名字搞错(misnomer)/误名与本段主要介绍的身份搞错令合约无效,是不同的身份争议,因为这类争议并不存在一个“非卿不可”的对象。可以说合约的成立如果是双方书信往来,对谁是正确的订约方有争议应在本质上是相互(mutual)或单方面错误,需要法院或仲裁庭从双方的言行与书信往来,通过背景/语境去客观认定订约方的身份。如果有一份正式合约,争议本质是共同/共享错误,因为双方记录错误了在谈判达成的约定或共识。在认定双方的共识(谁是订约方)后,救济就要进一步变

---

〔52〕 这一个课题可参阅笔者的《提单与其他付运合约》(2016 年)一书第三章之 14 段与 15 段。

更正式合约。相反如果无法认定双方在谈判时有共识,变更合约申请也就不成功了,名字就只能以正式合约记录为准。

这些"名字搞错"的争议也经常引用 Shogun Finance Ltd v. Hudson(2003)UKHL 62 贵族院先例中 Phillips 勋爵的名言说:

"This area of the law has developed because of confusion about names and it may be helpful at the outset to reflect on the nature of a name. Words in a language have one or more ordinary meaning, which will be known to anyone who speaks that language. Names are not those kind of words. **A name is a word, or a series of words, that is used to identify a specific individual. It can be described as a label. Whenever a name is used, extrinsic evidence, or additional information, will be required in order to identify the specific individual that the user of the name intends to identify by the name** — the person to whom he intends to attach the label. Almost all individuals have two or more names which they use to identify themselves and where a name is mentioned in a particular context, or a particular milieu, those who hear it may have the additional information that they need to identify to whom the speaker is referring.

Where a name appears in a written document, the document itself may contain additional information which will enable the reader to identify the individual to whom the writer intended to refer when he wrote the name."(加黑部分是笔者的强调)

针对在一份正式合约或书信往来中,如何客观解释与找出合约方的正确身份,上述判决中说到名字是说明或标签一位特定人士(法人或自然人),但名字如果不清楚是谁,就需要从其他的背景/语境,以及提供的特质/属性才能去确定真正身份。

例如,一个法人或自然人的名字,加上了他的住址或注册地,就更好地说明他的身份。正如在 Dumford Trading AG v. OAO Atlantrybflot(2004)EWHC 1099(Comm)先例中,虽然担保中是 ZAO,但地址是 OAO,Chambers 大法官说:"In the present case there could be no good reason for stating the address except to constitute it a part of the label. The guarantees make separate provision both for the address for service of demands or notices and for service of proceedings. The address ...is the company's registered address at '19 K. Marks Str.' ...The address is as much part of the identity of the guarantor as is its name or the fact that it is a company incorporated under the laws of Russia. ..."

针对这方面只多节录 Nicholls 勋爵在 Shogun Finance Ltd v. Hudson 贵族院先例中说:"... **a person may be identified by reference to any one of his attributes**. He may be identified as 'the person in the room', 'the person who spoke on the telephone', 'the person who appended the illegible signature', 'the writer of the letter under reply', or 'the person who made the offer'; but he may also be identified, and sometimes more relevantly, as 'the person whose creditworthiness has been checked and found to be satisfactory'. Any of these may be the means of identifying a unique person. ..."(加黑部

分是笔者的强调）

一个名字代表的真正身份可以从提供的特质/属性去确定当然，在国际化的商业环境中，全球调查取证找出一个名字背后的特质/属性又谈何容易。这特别是在名字的背后是一个骗子时，他会刻意隐瞒他的特质/属性，正如在本章之12.4段中介绍的P& P Property Ltd v. Owen White & Catlin LLP（2018）EWCA Civ 1082上诉庭先例。

名字搞错的商业案例也有不少，但不是本章要详及的错误类别，所以只说在较近期的Liberty Mercian Ltd v. Cuddy Civil Engineering Ltd（2013）EWHC 2688（TCC）重要先例中，Ramsey大法官详细针对了这一课题（名字搞错与合约变更）。该先例涉及超市的工程合约，并由一家名为“Cuddy Group”的承建商承建。这名字显然只是集团的商号（trading name）。之后，虽然工程是由集团下的Cuddy Demolition履行与签发发票（invoices），但双方在文件（如担保与正式合约）上都写的是集团下另一家名为Cuddy Engineering的休眠公司（dormant company）。后来工程不顺利发生争议，双方相互指称对方违约/毁约。Liberty Mercian以单方面错误或共同错误造成了“名字搞错”，向法院申请变更合约的订约方，把Cuddy Engineering改为Cuddy Demolition。

但该申请败诉，Ramsey大法官不同意双方直到订约前都有一个持续的共同订约意图是合约方是Cuddy Demolition，只是在合约中记录错误。而单方面错误虽然也可以变更合约，但要求被告是知道Liberty Mercian有了错误理解。〔53〕显然，这不是本案的事实，Liberty Mercian也证明不了Cuddy Group或Cuddy Engineering知道该错误理解。

所以，搞错对方订约方的名字想申请变更也并非容易。

12.5 不同对待搞错身份与搞错特质/属性的不妥之处

A搞错了对方订约方B的“身份”与A搞错了B的“特质/属性”有不同对待，只有前者才算是可诉错误可去判合约自始无效，而后者是不能。即使涉及欺诈性误述，例如骗子B的误导令A搞错了对方的特质/属性（如欺诈性误述了他的财力，令A信赖后上当），法律救济充其量也只是合约可使无效。而自始无效（void）与可使无效（voidable）之间文字上的区别并不明显，但后果极其严重，特别是在货物买卖合约下影响不知情的无辜第三人。

英国在这方面的法律并不令人满意，这可节录Nicholls勋爵在Shogun Finance Ltd v. Hudson（2003）UKHL 62贵族院先例中说：

“… The seller wants to be sure he will be paid for the goods he is handing over. Here the common law seems to have drawn a distinction between two kinds of fraudulent misrepresentation. The common law distinguished between a case （1） **where a crook fraudulently asserts he is creditworthy** and a case （2） **where a crook fraudulently as-**

---

〔53〕 见本章之11.1段的介绍，包括Ingram v. Little（1961）1 QB 31与Fawcett v. Star Car Sales Ltd（1960）NZLR 406，NZCA等先例。

serts he is someone else known to be creditworthy. One might suppose there is no difference of substance between these two cases. These are merely two ways a crook may assert a spurious creditworthiness. But, historically, the law seems to have been otherwise. In case(1), when the seller parts with his goods he does so pursuant to **a voidable contract**. This is said to be **a case of mistake as to a person's attributes**. In case(2), in some circumstances but not all, the seller has been held to part with his goods pursuant to **a void contract**, that is, no contract at all. This is said to be **a case of mistake as to a person's identity**. ...(虽然骗子向受害方欺诈性误述他是可信任与冒充其他可信任人士以获得受害方放心交出货物在本质上区别不大,但普通法却把它们视为有很大不同,前者是欺诈性误述,合约可使无效,而后者是错误,合约自始无效。)

The distinction in outcome thus drawn between these two kinds of fraudulent misrepresentation, one as to 'attributes' and the other as to 'identity', **is unconvincing**. ...(区别对待欺诈性误述导致受害方搞错"特质/属性"与搞错"身份"是没有说服力,因为两者之间根本不是黑白分明。)

A contract of sale and purchase, like any other contract, requires agreement, a meeting of minds. The seller must intend, or appear to intend, to sell the goods, and the buyer must intend, or appear to intend, to buy the goods on the agreed terms. The presence of fraud does not negative the existence of such an intention on the part of either party. **Fraud does not negative intention**. A person's intention is a state of mind. Fraud does not negative a state of mind.... Fraud enables the victim of the fraud to decline to proceed with a contract into which, by reason of the fraudulent misrepresentation, he was induced to enter, and he has a claim for damages for any loss he may suffer. But fraud does not have the consequence of negativing the formation of a contract. ...(货物买卖合约也是合约的一种,法律要求双方订约时有一致想法。即使涉及欺诈,这不影响客观认定成立了一个有效合约,也就是受害方与骗子在你情我愿下对有关买卖合约有了一致想法。骗子根本不打算履行,也就是不会支付货价,只是骗子的主观思想状态,解释合约有否成立或以什么条件成立是纯客观测试,不理会一方或双方各自的主观想法。所以,骗子不支付货价只是违约/毁约,误信了骗子说自己可信的受害方只可索赔损失,与合约无效没有关系。)

Thus, if a person is induced to buy goods by a fraudulent misrepresentation that the goods are sound, in law a contract to buy the goods is created even though the goods are different from the goods the buyer intends to buy and even though the other party knows this. **The fact that the goods are different in quality** from the goods which, as the crook knows, the victim wishes to buy **is not regarded by the law as meaning that no contract was made**. ...(以货物质量为例,如果不良商人通过欺诈性误述把次货当作高档货出售,根本不是受害方想买的,这不代表该买卖合约是自始无效,从来没有过合约

关系。受害方的救济是索赔损失,但会在欺诈性误述下可使合约无效去撤销,只要是没有本书第三章提到的各种障碍,特别是不能影响无辜第三人。)

The position is similar if the owner of goods agrees to sell them to a prospective buyer on the basis of a fraudulent assertion of his financial reliability. The buyer's fraudulent statement about himself does not negative the seller's intention to sell the goods to the crook on the agreed terms. Nor does it negative the fact that, when the crook acquired the goods from the seller, he did so with the seller's consent. The fraud means only that the seller's contractual intention was formed, and his consent to hand over the goods obtained, on a fraud-induced basis. There is a contract, but it may be avoided on discovery of the fraud. (骗子主张自己的财力可信任以欺诈性误述骗了受害方订立买卖合约,道理也是与货物质量一样。受害方有同样的法律救济,但不是合约自始无效。)"

相比对方订约方的特质/属性,对方身份(名字与标签)如果是搞错就有完全不同的分析了。身份搞错是影响双方达成一致想法,进而否定(negative)有效合约的成立。这与在本章之 12.1 段说的错误理解身份与错误理解合约条件(contractual terms)的道理一样,不去重复。

A 是一开始就把信誉良好或有某方面特殊技术的 B 视为订约的目标对象,但 A 误以为 C 是 B 去订立合约。这可以是 A 自己不小心,例如 C 与 B 的名字十分接近,甚至是关系密切,A 在没有查清楚之下,一厢情愿就贸然去确定了合约。这样,客观看 A 与 C 是你情我愿地达成一致想法,A 的主观想法是与 B 而不是 C 订约在客观测试下不必考虑。

但换了不同案情,C 是骗子冒充 B 并向 A 作出欺诈性陈述。又或是 C 是明知道 A 不小心贸然把它当作 B 去订立合约,如果向 A 说明就不会有该合约了。在这两种情况下,撇开违约或谁对谁错的问题,仅是在有效合约成立的要件下去分析,就难以客观得出结论说:A 与 C 是你情我愿与完全明白他们要订立的合约。

总结来说,上述的区分分析起来是很有道理,但其不妥之处在于实际中很多情况并不是黑白分明,这就会带来争议,由于两种情况下的不同救济差别太大也会带来不肯定。

12.6　英国早期的先例与立法未果的尝试

在上小段说到的硬将"身份"与"特质/属性"进行区分不令人满意,这主要是在早期的一些先例建立起来。早年一直至今,买卖均是社会与商业上最主要的活动,在该问题上的先例并不算多。而且看来判决相互矛盾,因为"身份"与"特质/属性"的区分并不明显,只是凭很轻微差异的不同事实得出不同结果。但 Cundy v. Lindsay (1878)3 App Cas 459 贵族院先例确立的法律地位,在这 100 多年来一直是英国法律的地位。直到在 Shogun Finance Ltd v. Hudson(2003) UKHL 62 先例中,贵族院才再有了机会去重新考虑这方面的问题。笔者接下来简单介绍五个重要的早年先例去说明。

12.6.1 Cundy v. Lindsay(1878)3 App Cas 459 贵族院先例

在 Cundy v. Lindsay 贵族院先例中,案情涉及名为 Blenkarn 的骗子冒充另一家著名的公司 Blenkiron & Company,以信函向 Lindsay 购买一批货物(手帕)。Lindsay 久闻 Blenkiron & Company 大名,不以为意之下向这骗子提供了一批货物,以为是交货给 Blenkiron & Company,大可以放心。骗子取得货物之后自然从来没有向原告付款,并将其中 3000 张手帕转卖给了此先例中不知情的善意第三人(bona fide purchaser for value without notice)Cundy。骗局不久后曝光,Lindsay 向骗子 Blenkarn 以民事诉讼索赔欠下的货款难免是一场空,事实上骗子 Blenkarn 也被警察以欺诈/欺骗拘捕并被法院判了刑。这样,Lindsay 以侵占(conversion)向 Cundy 起诉,要求归还货物。

贵族院的判法是原告与骗子的合约无效,因为 Lindsay 的订约意图是希望与著名的 Blenkiron & Company 打交道与订约,所以在订约时把对方"身份"搞错了,合约也就因为这个单方面错误而没有"一致想法"无效。

贵族院的 Cairn 勋爵说:"... It is that Blenkarn(骗子)— the dishonest man, as I call him—was acting here just in the same way as if he had forged the signature of Blenkiron & Co., the respectable firm, to the applications for goods, and as if, when, in return, the goods were forwarded and letters were sent, accompanying them, he had intercepted the goods and intercepted the letters, and had taken possession of the goods, and of the letters which were addressed to, and intended for, not himself but, the firm of Blenkiron & Co. Now, ... I ask the question, how is it possible to imagine that in that state of things any contract could have arisen between (Lindsay) and Blenkarn, the dishonest man? Of him(骗子) they knew nothing, and of him they never thought. With him they never intended to deal. Their minds never, even for an instant of time rested upon him, and as between him and them **there was no consensus of mind which could lead to any agreement or any contract whatever**. As between him and them there was merely the one side to a contract, where, **in order to produce a contract, two sides would be required**. With the firm of Blenkiron & Co. of course there was no contract, for as to them the matter was entirely unknown, and therefore **the pretence of a contract was a failure.**

The result, therefore, my Lords, is this, that your Lordships have not here to deal with one of those cases in which there is de facto a contract made which may afterwards be impeached andset aside, on the ground of fraud; but you have to deal with a case which ranges itself under a completely different chapter of law, the case namely in which **the contract never comes into existence.** My Lords, that being so, it is idle to talk of the property passing. **The property**(3000 条手帕的产权)**remained, as it originally had been, the property of the Respondents, and the title which was attempted to be given to the Appellants**(Cundy)**was a title which could not be given to them.**"(加黑部分

是笔者的强调)

另节录 Hatherley 勋爵相似的说法如下:“from beginning to end(Lindsay) believed they were dealing with Blenkiron & Co. , they made out their invoices to Blenkiron & Co, they supposed, they sold to Blenkiron & Co, they never sold in any way to Alfred Blenkarn(骗子); and therefore Alfred Blenkarn cannot, by so obtaining the goods, have by possibility made a good title to a purchaser, as against the owners of the goods, who had never in any shape or way parted with the property nor with anything more than the possession of it.”

Penzance 勋爵认为此先例与较早的 Hardman v. Booth(1863)158 ER 1107 先例的道理是一致,该先例也是判原告卖方只想卖给一家 Thomas Gandell 公司,从来没有想去卖给骗子 Edward Gandell。而 Thomas Gandell 公司也从来没有想买,因为不知道也从未授权 Edward Gandell 去买。所以双方从未有一致的想法(“there never were two consenting minds”)。Penzance 勋爵说:“I am unable to distinguish this case in principle from that of Hardman v. Booth, to which reference has been made. In that case Edward Gandell, who obtained possession of the Plaintiff's goods, pretended to have authority to order goods for Thomas Gandell & Co. , which he had not, and then intercepted the goods and made away with them; the Court held that there was no contract with Thomas Gandell & Co. as they had given no authority, and none with Edward Gandell, who had ordered the goods, as the Plaintiffs never intended to deal with him.”

这也是可以理解,因为骗子不会在骗来之后就对货物拥有产权与可以合法转卖给第三人。而第三人也不应该变为合法拥有货物。

12.6.2 King's Norton Metal Co. v. Edridge, Merrett & Co. Ltd. (1897) 14 TLR 98 上诉庭先例

在案情看来相近的 King's Norton Metal Co. v. Edridge, Merrett & Co. Ltd. 上诉庭先例中,判决的结果却是与 Cundy v. Lindsay(1878)3 App Cas 459 贵族院先例不一致。该案例涉及的骗子(名为 Wallis 先生)是以一家名为 Hallam & Co 的公司行骗。Wallis 说 Hallam & Co 是一家大公司,但该公司其实根本不存在。法院判原告只是想与通信的骗子 Wallis 先生与 Hallam & Co 公司(不管真正是谁)订约,证明不了有任何其他想要订约的特定对象(other identifiable person),所以从未搞错对象或对方的“身份”。原告错误理解的只是 Wallis 先生与 Hallam & Co 公司的“特质/属性”,即到底是大公司还是不可信任与虚构的。所以,合约不是自始无效。上诉庭的 A. L. Smith 大法官说:“The question was, with whom, upon this evidence, ... did the plaintiffs contract to sell the goods? **Clearly with the writer of the letters**. If it could have been shown that there was a separate entity called Hallam & Co and another entity called Willis(骗子) then the case might have come within the decision in Cundy v. Lindsay ... In his opinion there was a contract by the plaintiffs with the person who wrote the letters, by which the property passed to him. **There was only one entity,trading it might be under an alias**,and there was a contract by which the property passed to him. "(加黑部分是笔者的强调)

在《Misrepresentation,Mistake and Non-Disclosure》(2022 年,第 6 版)一书之 14－21 段中将这先例与"有特定与明确对象下的错误"的 Cundy v. Lindsay 贵族院先例进行区分,称是"没有特定与明确对象下的错误",在该先例原告因为和谁订约都行,结果被骗的只能是搞错对方的特质/属性,说:"**The 'mistake' where there is no identifiable,distinct person** A different situation arises,however,where 'X' is simply a name used as an alias by Y. The claimant,who says that he was mistaken in that he believed that he was dealing with X,cannot show a mistake of identity at all-he cannot show that he was intending to deal with another person. In King's Norton Metal Co Ltd v. Edridge, Merrett and Co Ltd,the claimant received an order to sell a ton of brass rivet wire to 'Hallam & Co', although there was no such entity separate from the person who was writing the letters-a man called Wallis who had assumed the business name, and used printed notepaper which made him sound more respectable, A. L. Smith LJ distinguished Cundy v. Lindsay:...In short,then,there can be **a mistake of identity only if the claimant had a positive belief that he was dealing with X, and intended his communications to be addressed to and responded to by X;but in fact the other party was not X,but a distinct and identifiable person,Y.** "(加黑部分是笔者的强调)

该案与 Cundy v. Lindsay 先例判法不一致也是可以理解。因为该案的事实显示受害方根本没有搞错骗子的身份,只是在没有调查清楚对方的特质/属性下与对方订约。这也在商业社会中经常见到一方可能因为懒惰、不想花钱、愚蠢从而与皮包公司做生意,但这就不能令合约自始无效,更不能令不知情的第三人受影响。

12.6.3 Phillips v. Brooks(1919)2 KB 243 先例

在面对面(face-to-face)的交易中,有一个表面推断(prima facie presumption)是他们各自是想与对面的另一方订约。这在国际商业中比较少见,但在社会上经常会有,例如去菜市场或奢侈品店买东西,都是面对面交易。但社会上还是有不少并不是这种面对面的交易,好像 Cundy v. Lindsay(1878)3 App Cas 459 贵族院先例的 Lindsay 与骗子订立合约,双方就从来没有见过面而是通过信函来下订单。又或是现在流行的网上购物,双方也从来没有面对面过。

第一宗面对面的案件是 Phillips v. Brooks 先例。一位名为 North 的骗子,自称是社会名流 George Bullough 爵士,在原告(有听说过该名流)的珠宝店以空头支票换取了一个名贵戒指,再去转售给被告(无辜第三人买方)。表面看来该案的案情与 Cundy v. Lindsay 先例一样,原告其实是想与 George Bullough 爵士订约。但法院判原告没有搞错对象,他只是意图与他面对面的骗子交易。Horridge 大法官说:"I have carefully considered the evidence of the plaintiff, and have come to the conclusion that, although he believed the person to whom he was handing the ring was Sir George Bullough, he is in fact contracted to sell and deliver it to the person who came into his shop, and who was not Sir George Bullough, but a man of the name of North, who obtained the sale and delivery by means of the false pretence that he was Sir George Bullough. It is quite true the plaintiff in re-examination said he had no intention of making any contract with any other person than Sir George Bullough; but I think I have myself to decide what is the proper inference to draw where a verbal contact is made and an article delivered to an individual describing himself as somebody else."

以上 Horridge 大法官认为面对面交易和只是以文书往来交易是有区别的，通过文书往来进行的买卖，受害方（根据订立的合约把货物与产权交出给骗子但没有获得货价的卖方）只能从文书上对谁是买方（无论是冒充其他人或是使用假名）作出判断。而面对面交易不一样的地方是受害方可以亲自见到、听到与感觉到对方更多的特质/属性，并在感觉良好下才会订立合约。可以说，在见过骗子本人后，骗子的身份或名字对受骗方来说也变得是次要了。

在国际商业社会中，面对面显然会令双方增加信任感，所以商人仍然愿意全球旅行去见客户，以增加双方相互对对方特质/属性的了解。这样，确定对方的身份就不只是看文件往来中对方的名字或商号或其他非常有限的特质/属性，如地址等。

该 Phillips v. Brooks 先例确立了面对面交易中搞错对象问题的判断原则，也就是在面对面交易中，即使骗子是冒充别人来与受害方订约，受害方仍然被推断是与对面的骗子订约。

最后，该先例在 Shogun Finance Ltd v. Hudson（2003）UKHL 62 贵族院先例中被提到，Phillips 勋爵是说："Phillips v. Brooks Ltd well illustrates the conundrum that the application of the test of intention raises when terms are negotiated between two persons who are face to face ... Horridge J solved the conundrum by drawing an 'inference' that the plaintiff intended to contract with the rogue（骗子 North），who was present, and not with the individual（George Bullough 爵士）whose identity the rogue had assumed."

12.6.4　Ingram v. Little（1961）1 QB 31 上诉庭先例

Ingram v. Little 上诉庭先例是另一个面对面的交易，案情基本上与 Phillips v. Brooks（1919）2 KB 243 先例相似，原告（Ingram 女士）被一位骗子游说卖她的车给他，Ingram 女士不肯答应除非先付现金。骗子再三游说并自称是一位 Hutchinson 先生，住在某处（换言之是有名有姓，将来追究是可以找得到的人）。Ingram 女士也在查了电话簿对此资料确实后，同意把车卖给这骗子，并接受了一张支票。后果可想而知是空头支票，而骗子又很快把车转售了给无辜的第三人，也就是被告 Little 先生。

在这场诉讼中都碰上了骗子的 Ingram 女士与 Little 先生，都很倒霉。但判决与 Phillips v. Brooks 先例又有相反结果，多数意见认为虽然面对面订约有一个推断是 Ingram 女士意图与亲眼见到与有亲身感受的对方骗子订约，但这推断可在不同案情的事实下被推翻。在此先例中,一审法院认定 Ingram 女士做了很大努力去确实骗子身份才同意卖车,只是最终仍是上当,他根本不是 Hutchinson 先生。但证据显示 Ingram 女士对 Hutchinson 先生这个身份十分重视,所以这是好像在 Cundy v. Lindsay (1878)3 App Cas 459 贵族院先例中,搞错了对方的"身份"的案件,合约应是无效。

上诉庭支持了一审判决,Sellers 大法官看来不认同 Phillips v. Brooks Ltd 先例的判决,说:"It is not authority to establish that where an offer or acceptance is addressed to a person(although under a mistake as to his identity) who is present in person, then it must in all circumstances be treated as it actually addressed to him."

虽然上诉庭三位大法官一致同意,面对面交易有一个表面推断是他们各自是想与对面的另一方订约。但 Pearce 大法官与 Sellers 大法官认为这是一个事实推断(presumption of fact),并非不可反驳的,根据有关的案情可以推翻。而作为少数意见的 Devlin 大法官,认为这应是法律推断(presumption of law),只有证明属于另一类的案件才能被反驳与推翻,只是以不同案件的事实是无法推翻。在《Misrepresentation, Mistake and Non-Disclosure》(2022 年,第 6 版)一书之 14 - 27 段中评述该案例说:

"All three members of the Court of Appeal in Ingram v. Little agreed that **the proper approach in a face-to-face contract is to require the claimant to rebut the presumption that he intended to deal with the person physically present**; but there was a significant disagreement as to how this test should be formulated and applied. ...

On first reading, this(Devlin 大法官的少数意见) may appear to be consistent with the reasoning in the other judgment in the case. But it is significantly different, in that it treats the question of identity as not simply one of fact, to be inferred from the face-to-face dealings(a factual presumption) but capable of rebuttal by evidence from the claimant as of his contrary(factual) intention. Rather, it takes the position that the claimant cannot normally lead evidence of the fact of his intention which will prevail over the(legal) presumption. This intention is inferred as a matter of law from the face-to-face dealings, and this can be overcome only in exceptional types of case, not simply by showing contrary facts.

The ratio of Ingram v. Little, therefore, is contained in the judgments of Sellers and Pearce LLJ, who also(contrary to Devlin LJ) held that, on the facts, the presumption **had been rebutted**. ..."(加黑部分是笔者的强调)

12.6.5 Lewis v. Averay(1972)1 QB 198 上诉庭先例

在 Lewis v. Averay 上诉庭先例中,虽然又是面对面订约,但判决结果又倒转过来。一位骗子向原告(Lewis 先生)买他的车,在付款时给了一张支票,Lewis 先生起初坚持先要把这张私人支票兑现后才容许骗子把车子开走。但骗子继续游说与坚持,并自称是一位著名的电影明星,又提供了一份进出片场的批文去证明他就是这位明星,结果 Lewis 先生就让骗子把车子开走了。骗子之后以 Lewis 先生的名义把车子转售给了被告(Averay 先生),并就此失踪,连警察也找不到他。

Denning 勋爵认为 Phillips v. Brooks(1919)2 KB 243 与 Ingram v. Little(1961)1 QB 31 两个先例在事实上难以区分,但判决结果完全相反。如果作出选择,Denning 勋爵选 Phillips v. Brooks 先例,也就是不去令合约自始无效而影响无辜第三人 Averay 先生。法院不应该看 Lewis 先生的意图或者他脑子的想法,而只看表面,Lewis 先生是与和他面对面的这个骗子订立了合约。而骗子对自己的身份误述,合约也仍然存在,只是可使无效。Denning 勋爵说:"When two parties have come to a contract ... the fact that one party is mistaken as to the identity of the other does not mean that there is no contract, or that the contract is a nullify and void from the beginning. It only means that the contract is voidable, that is, liable to be set aside at the instance of the mistaken person, so long as he does so before third parties have in good faith acquired rights under it ... In this case Mr Lewis's made a contract of sale with the very man, the rogue ... I say that he 'made a contract' because in this regard **we do not look into his intentions, or into his mind to know what he was thinking or into the mind of the rouge. We look to the outward appearances.** On the face of the dealing, Mr Lewis's made a contract under which he sold the car to the rogue, delivered the car ... to him, and took a cheque in return. The contract is evidenced by the receipts which were signed. It was, of course induced by fraud. **The rogue made false representations as to his identity. But it was still a contract, though voidable for fraud**. It was a contract under which this property passed to the rogue, and in due course passed from the rogue to Mr Averay(作为被告的善意第三人买方), before the contract was avoided."(加黑部分是笔者的强调)

在《Misrepresentation, Mistake and Non-Disclosure》(2022 年,第 6 版)一书之 14-28 段中说虽然该先例三位大法官得出了同样的结论,但理由各不相同。Denning 勋爵的分析是基于 Devlin 大法官在 Ingram v. Little 上诉庭先例中的理由,即认为面对面交易是想与对方订约是一个法律推断,并且更进一步,是任何不同的案情也推翻不了的不可反驳与推翻的法律推断。而 Phillimore 大法官则支持 Pearce 大法官在 Ingram v. Little 先例的判决,也就是认为应是事实推断。Megaw 大法官甚至根本不认同这个推断,而是从卖方是否认为买方的身份重要的角度分析。可节录有关部分如下:"In Lewis v. Averay the Court of Appeal again considered the test that should be applied in face-to-face transactions. The case again involved the sale of a car, following a newspaper advertisement, when the purchaser gave the name and other details of another person(冒充的电影明星), and thereby obtained the car in return for a worthless cheque. On this occasion, the contract was held not to be void for mistake of identity. The court was unanimous in the result, although again the reasoning varied. ... **Lord Denning's view is based on the approach taken by Devlin LJ in Ingram v. Little; but he appears to go even further. It is a 'presumption in law'**; but it appears to be an irrebuttable presumption. **Phillimore LJ, by contrast, quoted and applied the presumption of fact** in Pearce LJ's judgment. **Megaw LJ approached the matter more broadly**, and discussed whether, **on the facts, the claimant regarded the identity of the other party as a matter of vital importance**; ... It is therefore not easy to find a ratio in Lewis v. Averay as to the test to apply. But it is clear from the judgments of Phillimore and Megaw LJJ that a mistake of identity can make a contract void in a face-to-face transaction; but whether there is a sufficient mistake is a question as to the intention of the claimant; and this is a matter of fact."(加黑部分是笔者的强调)

Phillips v. Brooks、Ingram v. Little 与 Lewis v. Averay 三个先例都是面对面交易与订约,虽然都基本上同意是有一个推断是双方是意图与见到面的对方订约,但大法官们对到底是事实的推断还是法律的推断,到底是否可反驳与推翻有不同意见。

12.6.6 Hector v. Lyons(1989)58 P & CR 156 上诉庭先例

在 Hector v. Lyons 上诉庭先例中,案情非常特殊,想要依赖错误的不是错误方而是非错误方。该先例的原告是父亲,和被告卖方谈判购买一套伦敦的房屋。一直以来和被告接触的都是父亲,被告也一直以为买方是父亲。但是实际上父亲委任律师时一直让律师以为客户是他未满 18 岁的儿子(看来是没有订立此合约的行为能力),律师也是在买方是儿子的基础上准备与交换了合约。合约是父亲签的,但并没有在律师面前签,而且也不是父亲自己的惯常签名。看来伦敦房价上涨,于是原告向法院申请有关房屋买卖合约的履约指令,一审法院认定合约的买方是儿子,所以父亲不是合约方不能申请强制执行合约。父亲上诉,理由是父亲与卖方的共同意图是父亲作为买方,合约中出现的是儿子的名字只是一个不重要的错误。和卖方面对面谈判的一直是父亲,根据 Lewis v. Averay(1972)1 QB 198 上诉庭先例,真正的合约方应该是父亲而不是儿子。

但上诉庭不支持父亲的主张,原因主要是有一份双方签字的正式合约。在这种情况下,只需要解释正式合约中记录的真正订约方到底是谁,实际是一个误名(misnomer)的案件。面对面谈判与订约方是想与谁订立合约属于口头证据的一部分,受口头证据规则(parol evidence rule)约束,不可采纳。Browne-Wilkinson 大法官说:

"Mr. Cogley(Hector 代表大律师)relies on the line of cases dealing with unilateral mistake. In those cases, typically goods are sold by a vendor V, to a purchaser P, under the mistake that P is someone else, X.... Normally the case is that the purchaser P makes a fraudulent representation to the vendor that he, P, is some other person, X. In the case of **a face to face sale, where the sale is over a counter or between two individuals, the law is well established that the mere fact that the vendor V is under a misapprehension as to the identity of the person in front of him does not operate so as to render the contract void for mistake**, it being a mere unilateral mistake as to a quality of the purchaser; only in cases where the identity of the purchaser is of direct and important materiality in inducing the vendor to enter into the contract is a mistake of that kind capable of avoiding the contract.

With one exception those cases are entirely concerned with transactions between two individuals face to face entering into oral agreement. In my judgment**the principle there enunciated has no application to a case** such as the present **where there is a contract and wholly in writing**. There the identity of the vendor and of the purchaser is established by the names of the parties included in the written contract. **Once those names are there in the contract, the only question for the court is to identify who they are**."（加黑部分是笔者的强调）

上诉庭的附带意见（obiter）说卖方一直以为买方是父亲对父亲申请履约指令没有帮助，但是如果反过来，是卖方想向父亲执行买卖合约，父亲可能被禁反言（estoppel），不能否认自己是合约方。

12.6.7 立法未果的尝试

Delvin 大法官在 Ingram v. Little（1961）1 QB 31 上诉庭先例中曾建议对于这类案件，两位完全无辜的原告（受骗的卖方）与被告（不知情的无辜第三人买方）平均分摊损失会是最公道，说："For the doing of justice, the relevant question in this sort of case is not whether the contract was void or voidable, but which of the two innocent parties shall suffer for the fraud of a third. The plain answer is that the loss should be divided between them in such proportion as is just in all the circumstances. If it be mere misfortune, the loss should be borne equally; if the fault or imprudence of either party has caused or contributed to the loss, it should be borne by that party in the whole or in the greater part."

但要这样做在普通法下没有依据，英国法律界需要考虑这是否是最好的解决办法或有其他更好的办法从而去立法。这在法律改革委员会第 12 期报告（1965 – 1967 年）名为"Transfer of Title to Chattels"中有考虑 Devlin 大法官的建议，但被委员会拒绝。

在 Law Commission Ninth Programme of Law Reform（2005）中，这问题被包括在未来法律改革的计划中。但 Eleventh Programme of Law Reform, Law Comm No. 330（2011）之 3.4-3.6 段提到现实中大家对这个问题的解决没有显示出太大的热诚与期待，决定暂不去处理，所以立法不了了之。

12.7 Shogun Finance Ltd v. Hudson（2003）UKHL 62 贵族院先例

回到普通法层面，在著名的 Shogun Finance Ltd v. Hudson 贵族院先例中，有机会去重新考虑 Cundy v. Lindsay（1878）3 App Cas 459 贵族院先例确立的上百年的法律地位。

12.7.1 案情与贵族院的多数意见判决

此先例的案情是一位 Durlabh Patel 先生的驾驶执照被一个不知名的骗子偷到手

后,骗子冒充 Patel 先生去一家车行以租购方式(hire purchase)买下在陈列的价值 22,250英镑的车辆(型号为 Mitsubishi Shogun)。骗子签署了租购合约与支付了(以少数现金与支票,但支票后来无法兑现)10% 的车辆价款作为首期付款,并把车开走。其间,在骗子取走车辆前,车行找了为租购交易提供融资支持的原告(一家专门为这种型号的车辆提供融资服务的名为 Shogun Finance 的日本财务公司),让它赶紧在电脑的资料中查了 Patel 先生的资信、工作单位与住址,并发觉一切正常。车行也比较了 Patel 先生驾驶执照上的签名与骗子在租购合约的签名,发觉表面相符。

骗子把车辆开走后很快以£ 17,000 英镑转售给了一位被认定是不知情的善意第三人买方(Hudson 先生),之后就销声匿迹。所以到了东窗事发时,剩下两位都是属于无辜的受害方在争夺车辆的合法产权。

贵族院以轻微的多数(3:2)判 Shogun Finance 胜诉,Hudson 先生败诉,也就是车辆的产权没有合法转让给 Hudson 先生。Shogun Finance 与骗子签署租购合约与提供融资服务时搞错了对方身份,在谈不上有过错或不小心的情况下,在方方面面的调查后,错误深信对方是 Patel 先生。虽然实际上签合约的并不是 Patel 先生,而是一位他不知情也从未授权的骗子。

多数意见的 Hobhouse 勋爵(Walker 勋爵与 Phillips 勋爵同意)说第一个原因是这不是面对面订立合约,而是一份正式合约。客观解释,Shogun Finance 在合约的目标对象清楚无误是 Patel 先生,不是不知名的骗子。Hudson 先生争辩说车行曾经与骗子面对面打过交道。但这是在订约前,引进这些谈判的口头证据不被允许。后来东窗事发,不知情与从未授权的 Patel 先生显然不会是你情我愿达成一致想法的订约方。但 Shogun Finance 的合约目标对象却只是 Patel 先生。所以,只能是跟从 Cundy v. Lindsay(1878)3 App Cas 459 贵族院先例的判法,判租购合约自始无效。这样,车辆的产权从来没有转移给骗子,骗子再转售给 Hudson 先生也是空的。所以没有合法产权的 Hudson 先生必须要归还车辆给 Shogun Finance,否则是侵占。Hobhouse 勋爵说:

"… is a matter of written document. It admits of only one conclusion. There is no mention in the document of anyone other than Mr Durlabh Patel. The language used is clear and specific, both in the substance of the identification — name and address and license number and age …

Mr Hudson seeks not escape from this conclusion by saying: 'but the rogue was the person who came into the dealer's office and negotiated a price with the dealer and signed the form in the presence of the dealer who then witnessed it'. … The gist of the argument is that oral evidence may be adduced to contradict the agreement contained in a written … contract. The agreement is a written agreement with Mr Durlabh Patel. … The rule that other evidence may not be adduced to contradict the provisions of a contract contained in a written document is fundamental to the mercantile law of this country … the certainty of the contract depends on it. …

… The argument also fails on another ground. There was no consensus ad idem between the finance company and the rogue. … the hire-purchase ‘agreement’ to which Mr Hudson pins his argument was one purportedly made by the acceptance by the finance company, by signing the creditor's box in the form, of a written offer by Mr Durlabh Patel to enter into the hire-purchase agreement. This faces Mr Hudson with a dilemma: either the contract created by that acceptance was a contract with Mr Durlabh Patel or there was no consensus ad idem, the rogue having no honest belief or contractual intent whatsoever and the finance company believing that it was accepting an offer by Mr Durlabh Patel. On neither alternative was there a hire-purchaseagreement with the rogue."

但该先例的少数意见(Nicholls 勋爵与 Millett 勋爵)十分强烈反对多数的判决与错误理解对方订约方身份的原则或说法。他们认为应该改变 Cundy v. Lindsay 贵族院先例的法律地位,不再区分面对面或文书合约的不同订约方式,而一概以"欺诈性误述身份令合约可使无效"(voidable for fraudulent misrepresentation of identity)去替代目前的"错误令合约自始无效"(void ab initio for mistake)。这样,也就再也不会影响不知情的无辜第三人了。

两位勋爵认为没有必要区分面对面或文书合约。也就是在受害方与骗子有直接交流(direct dealing)的情况下,无论双方是以面对面或文书方式达成合约,都存在一个难以推翻的推断是受害方的意图是与骗子订约。另也不再理会骗子的欺骗手法中是否包括了冒充一位受害方想去或以为在打交道的目标对象。如果有,也是骗子对他身份的欺诈性误述去诱导受害方与他订立合约。这样就可以排除这历史悠久与不令人满意的错误理解的到底是对方订约方的"身份"还是"特质/属性"的区分。如 Nicholls 勋爵说:"The legal principle applicable in these cases cannot sensibly differ according to whether the transaction is negotiated face to face, or by letter, or by fax, or by e-mail, or over the telephone or by video link or video telephone. …A person is presumed to intend to contract with the person with whom he is actually dealing, whatever be the mode of communication."

另 Millett 勋爵说:"But the real objection to the present state of the law, in my view, is that the distinction between the face-to-face contract and other contracts is unrealistic. … in truth the distinction was always unsound. If the offeree's words of acceptance are taken to be addressed to the physical person standing in his presence who made the offer, why is the contract entered into by correspondence different? Why is the offeree's letter of acceptance not taken to be addressed to the physical person who made the written offer which he is accepting? The offeree addresses the offeror by his assumed name in both cases. Why should this be treated as decisive in the one case and disregarded in the other? …"

12.7.2　此先例前的英国法律地位

有了上一小段对 Shogun Finance Ltd v. Hudson(2003)UKHL 62 贵族院先例的介绍,应该容易理解在《Misrepresentation, Mistake and Non-Disclosure》(2022 年,第 6 版)一书之 14－33 段中所说的英国法律在此先例前的法律地位,也是上百年来唯一个贵族院先例的 Cundy v. Lindsay(1878)3 App Cas 459 先例确立的,说:

"We can summarise the position of the law as it stood before the decision of the House of Lords in Shogun Finance Ltd v. Hudson as follows:

1. Where the alleged contract was formed by communications between the parties in circumstances where one ultimately accepted an offer made by the other, the contract will be validly formed if each party intended to deal with the other. Even if one party(A)misunderstood with whom he was dealing, the other(B)is entitled to hold that party to having intended to contract with him, if B could reasonably believe that he was the intended recipient of A' scommunications, and in fact so believed.

2. Therefore, for A to say that he made a mistake about the other's identity, and did not intend to deal with the person who was in fact communicating with him, he must show(i)that he made a mistake of identity, that is, he intended to deal with another, distinct person whom he can identify; and(ii)that his subjective mistake should be allowed to prevail, that is, that B knew about it, or ought to have known about it(in practice, (ii) is often easy to established because the mistake in most cases is caused by B's deception as to his own identity).

3. Where the alleged contract was formed by communications between the parties who did not meet, the application of 2. depends on a proper construction of the communications themselves in order to determine A's intention. Where the alleged contract was formed between the parties in a face-to-face transaction, there is a presumption that A intended to deal with the person physically present, but whatever name or other information he identified himself; but this is rebuttable by A showing that, on the facts, he did make a mistake of identity.

4. Where the alleged contract was formed in writing, by the execution of a single, agreed document, the identity of the parties to the contract is to be determined by the objective construction of the document itself."

在上述节录的第二点中,A 如声称错误理解对方订约方 B 的"身份"必须证明两点:(1)A 是意图与其他人订约,并明确该其他人是谁,反正不是 B。(2)虽然这是 A 主观的单方面错误,但因为可以证明 B 是知道或应该知道 A 是搞错了 B 的真正身份,所以从合约成立的角度看双方是没有一致想法。这与本章之 11.1 段介绍的对合约条件的单方面错误的例外是同样道理。

显然,这两个条件是为欺诈/欺骗案件量身定做,条件(2)更是完全配合,B 如果是骗A应是理所当然知道A把B的身份搞错了。

但如果是作为卖方的A欠缺经验与不小心与B交易，而B是光棍的皮包公司，虽然当时市场上也有其他买方如E、F与G，但其实A可以卖给任何人，也就是谈不上有一个除了B以外的特定与明确(identifiable and distinct)对象。而且，B虽然知道自己是光棍，对A肯与他订立合约，也不要求B提供履约担保而感到奇怪与惊喜。但这不代表知道A搞错了B的身份，充其量只是搞错了B的特质/属性与选错了交易对象。

所以，"走出去"的中国公司在这种复杂的国际商业环境中，必须要小心与懂行，不要犯错，否则学费高昂。而且英国法律是不会轻易给这种单方面错误任何救济。

12.7.3　此先例后的英国法律地位

在Shogun Finance Ltd v. Hudson(2003)UKHL 62贵族院先例后，英国法律地位在这个问题上没有什么改变。当然如果是Nicholls勋爵与Millett勋爵的意见成为判决，法律的改动就会是根本性。但历史没有"如果"，所以如果英国法律再想要在这方面重大改动，恐怕是要法律改革委员会重新有兴趣考虑这个议题并立法。这可节录《Misrepresentation，Mistake and Non-Disclosure》(2022年，第6版)一书之14－43段说："**The current state of the law on mistake about the identity of the other party** The law as it stood before Shogun is summarised above. We have seen that this would have been fundamentally changed if the approach preferred by Lord Nicholls and Lord Millett had been adopted. As it is, the decision of the House is narrow and, strictly, deals only with the case of written contracts; and in this it confirms earlier position — where a contract is concluded in writing, the identity of the parties is to be determined by the objective construction of the document itself; and where the contract is formed by written communications, the intentions of each party as to the person with whom he is intending to deal is to be determined by the objective construction of the document from the recipient's perspective. The decision in Shogun does not formally touch on the approach to face-to-face contracts, but it appears that the presumption should be retained for such cases; and that, although there are some contrary views amongst the speeches in Shogun, the better approach is to continue to view the presumption as one of fact, albeit a presumption not in practice easy to rebut."

13. 双方共同错误：对订约时有根本重要性的事实或法律的共享错误

这类错误与上述介绍的错误有本质性不同。共同/共享错误(common/shared mistake)不像在本章之6段介绍的相互错误(mutual mistake)或是在11段与12段介绍的单方面错误(unilateral mistake)。这种单方面错误,常被另称为“对合约条件或身份的错误”(mistake as to the terms or identity),给予法律救济(令合约自始无效或是在特殊的情况下变更合约)是基于双方在订约时没有达成一致想法。

但共同错误不是这样,在合约订立时完全满足了一个有效合约成立所需要的要件。既然是“共同”或“共享”,就代表了双方订约方达成一致想法是毫无疑问。而问题是出在他们共享的合约基础(basis of the contract)上,这会是合约的标的或主要合约目的因为双方对事实或法律有了错误的假设(mistaken assumption),并严重到令合约无法履行或即使履行也不再是双方原来的订约意图。

一个明显与典型的共同/共享错误就是英国《Sale of Goods Act 1979》之 section 6 所针对的订约时买卖合约的特定标的(如一架飞机或一艘油轮等)因天灾人祸(这“人祸”当然不是指合约方的过错,所以立法要求卖方不知情,而买方是更不可能知情了)而灭失,合约就自始无效,说:“**Goods which have perished.** Where there is a contract for the sale of specific goods, and the goods without the knowledge of the seller have perished at the time when the contract is made, the contract is void.”

此外,一份正式与签字合约错误记录了双方在谈判时同意的事项或持续的共同意图需要变更(rectification)[54]本质也是共同/共享错误,正如在 Frederick E Rose (London) Ltd v. William H Pim Junior & Co Ltd (1953) 2 QB 450 上诉庭先例中,Denning 大法官说:“In order to get rectification, it is necessary to show that the parties were in complete agreement on the terms of their contract, but by an error wrote them down wrongly … If you can predicate with certainty what their contract was, and that it is, **by a common mistake wrongly expressed in the document, then you rectify the document**.”(加黑部分是笔者的强调)

可先节录对共同/共享错误的部分权威说法,《Anson's Law of Contract》(2020年,第31版)之296页对共同错误的定义是:“… **both parties make the same mistake of fact or law** relating to the subject-matter or the facts surrounding the formation of the contract.”(加黑部分是笔者的强调)

《Chitty on Contracts》(2021年,第34版)一书之8-015段说:“**Common mistake.** Where the mistake is common, that is shared by both parties, there is consensus ad idem, but the law may nullify this consent if the parties are mistaken as to some fact or point of law which lies at the basis of the contract. In summary, if: (i) the parties have entered a contract under a shared and self-induced mistake as to the facts or law affecting the contract; (ii) under the express or implied terms of the contract neither party is treated as taking the risk of the situation being as it really is; (iii) neither party was responsible for or should have known of the true state of affairs; and (iv) the mistake is so fundamen-

---

〔54〕 见笔者《合约的解释:规则与应用》一书第三章之13.1段的详细介绍。

tal that it makes the ‘contractual adventure’ impossible, or makes performance essentially different to what the parties anticipated, the contract will be void.”

13.1　对合约标的或主要合约目的有错误理解

对合约标的(subject-matter)的错误最常会发生在买卖合约(任何类型的货物商品、飞机、船舶、车辆等)或类似的合约(如买卖一家公司的并购合约,买卖股票的投资合约,买卖专利的专利转让合约等)。错误会在方方面面,如:

1. 订约时买卖的标的是否存在?会否遇到天灾人祸而灭失、或从来没有存在过:见 Couturier v. Hastie(1856)10 ER 1065; McRae v. Commonwealth Disposals Commission(1951)84 CLR 377 HCA; Associated Japanese Bank(International) Ltd v. Credit du Nord SA(1989)1 WLR 255 等先例。

2. 有关标的如货物是否拥有某一些基本性的特征或品质要求,但实际上是欠缺:见 Smith v. Hughes(1871)LR 6 QB 597 上诉庭先例。

3. 卖方是否拥有标的如货物的产权,可合法转让给买方?甚至是买方自己早已拥有产权,但不知道或搞错:见 Cooper v. Phibbs(1867)LR 2 HL 149 贵族院先例。该先例的案情是经过几代的遗产继承以及继承协议的签订,原告的叔叔拥有位于爱尔兰的一个三文鱼渔场,原告从他叔叔那里租入该三文鱼渔场经营,在叔叔去世后,渔场的租约也到期,于是原告与婶婶和叔叔的女儿订立了新的租约。但随后,原告发现根据 1827 年由原告爷爷与原告的父亲和叔叔所签署的一份继承和解协议,渔场的继承顺位是叔叔、父亲、叔叔的男性子嗣以及父亲的男性子嗣,因为叔叔没有儿子,只有 5 个女儿,所以叔叔去世时,原告的父亲也在之前去世,原告作为男性子嗣,变为渔场的主人,根本无需再订立该新租约。于是原告起诉要求法院判新租约无效,法院同意基于错误令租约无效。

4. 以为买卖是合法,后来发觉其实是非法或禁止买卖。同样道理也在所有其他的合约关系:见 Kleinwort Benson Ltd v. Lincoln City Council(1999)2 AC 349; Brennan v. Bolt Burdon(2004)EWCA Civ 1017 等先例。

很多对合约标的有错误理解或假设是单方面错误,错误的原因如买方自己一时冲动没有想清楚就订约购买,没有好好地对标的进行尽职调查或检查,错误理解了尽职调查或检查的结果,只是凭第三人朋友的不完整建议就订约等各种各样原因的错误。这些买方的错误并不是对方卖方会知道,所以不是“共同”或“共享”。而卖方即使知道,在没有法律责任去自动披露的情况下,只要卖方是没有取巧或甚是误述,法律也管不了。所以在“买方自己小心”与不能因为自己的过错或不小心获利的大原则下,这种单方面错误是没有法律救济。

显然,如果买方的单方面错误是由卖方的虚假陈述/误述或其他过错造成,这是会有不同的救济如可使合约无效(voidable),但与单方面错误就无关了。

当然,卖方也会发生上述方方面面的单方面错误。例如,标的在订约时并不存在或卖方实没有合法产权可转让给买方,但只要合约有明示或默示条文去针对,就会是风险已经分摊给了卖方,当然也会是卖方自己的过错或不小心导致。这样,又不会是可诉单方面错误,而是卖方的违约/毁约。

以上导致单方面错误的原因可节录《Misrepresentation, Mistake and Non-Disclosure》(2022 年,第 6 版)一书之 15 - 09 段说:"... A mistake about the subject-matter may be unilateral, or common (shared). We have seen that the source of the mistake may be the claimant's own spontaneous assumptions or his incorrect interpretation of the results of his investigations, or incorrect information provided by a third party. In such cases, he may well make a mistake which is not shared by the other party to the contract. The other party may be ignorant of the fact that the claimant is acting under a mistake; but, on the other hand, he may know about the claimant's mistake, but may not disabuse him of it; or he may even have caused it by deliberately misleading the claimant. The mistake in all such cases is unilateral."

这种对合约标的的单方面错误是不会有法律救济,原因已在本章多处提及。所以,只简单节录《Misrepresentation, Mistake and Non-Disclosure》(2022 年,第 6 版)一书之 15 - 10 段的部分内容:"The judgment in Smith v. Hughes make clear that **a unilateral mistake** about the subject-matter is **not in itself sufficient** to allow the mistaken party **to avoid the contract**. ...This makes clear that a mistake made by the claimant relating to the factual qualities or characteristics of the subject-matter which is not provided for expressly or impliedly in the contract, and where the other party has not contributed to the mistake, has **no legal consequence. The claimant is simply bound by the contract**. ..."(加黑部分是笔者的强调)

所以针对合约标的或目的,只有共同/共享错误才会有机会获得法律救济,但并不容易成功。在共同/共享错误下,本章之 5 段所讲的错误方的过错、不小心或疏忽导致错误应不适用。因为既然是共同/共享,有过错也是彼此彼此,大家谁都怪不了谁。即使错误是合约其中一方的误述所导致,也必须是他有合理依据(reasonable ground)的无辜误述(innocent misrepresentation)。[55]

但本章之 3 段介绍的风险分摊就不同,因为即使是共同/共享错误,还是要看这错误理解的事情是否在合约中有明示或默示条文去针对。一旦有针对,就要根据合约条文的解释处理了,也就是双方在合约把有关风险分摊了。这在 McRae v. Commonwealth Disposals Commission 澳大利亚先例中已经有介绍。

而本章之 8 段也是十分有关,就是错误必须是涉及了有根本重要性的事情,严重的程度是足够令合约标的或目的有了根本性不同,或令合约自始无效。正如 Associated Japanese Bank (International) Ltd v. Credit du Nord SA 说:"a mistake might render a contract void provided it rendered the subject-matter essentially and radically different

---

〔55〕 见本书第四章之 4.3 段。

from what the parties believed to have existed."

Solle v. Butcher(1950)1 KB 671 上诉庭先例曾经试图以衡平救济去针对一些不满足普通法对错误程度的根本重要性的要求,但不作出救济又是不合情理(unconscionable)的案件。但衡平法错误(mistake in equity)已在 The "Great Peace"(2002) EWCA Civ 1407 上诉庭先例中被否定,这会在本章之 14 段介绍。

以上所讲,可节录《Misrepresentation, Mistake and Non-Disclosure》(2022 年,第 6 版)一书之 15 – 14 段说:"**A common(shared) mistake about the subject-matter may be sufficient** We shall see ... that **a common(shared) mistake about the subject-matter**-a mistake of fact or law which bears upon the subject-matter of the obligations of one of the parties-**may be sufficient to render the contract void** at common law. This is only the case, however, in **very limited circumstances**. If the parties have expressly or impliedly made provision in the contract for the so-called mistake-or, in other words, if there is a contractual allocation the risk of the mistake-then the contract governs. If, however, the contract is silent about the matter, the courts may be persuaded to hold that the contract is void-but only if the mistake is of a degree of seriousness which, as we shall see, is not easy to define, nor(if it can be put into words) is the test for such an operative mistake always easy to apply. ... during the second half of the twentieth century the courts were prepared to hold that a common mistake, of a lesser degree of seriousness than that accepted by the common law authorities, could render a contract voidable in equity; but that this has now been rejected."(加黑部分是笔者的强调)

接下来会区别介绍三个共同/共享错误最重要的先例。

13.2 Bell v. Lever Brothers Ltd(1932)AC 161 贵族院先例

共同错误的课题中最重要的先例是已提到的 Bell v. Lever Brothers Ltd 贵族院先例。在该先例中,原告 Lever Bros 试图向被告 Bell 追回支付给他的大笔遣散费。Lever Bros 在非洲成立一家公司管理在非洲的业务,并与被告签订了服务合约,委任被告为该非洲公司的主席。合约要求被告全心全意为公司服务,但实际上被告在雇佣期间曾经利用公司关系偷偷牟利,而原告 Lever Bros 被蒙在鼓里。被告显然是违反对 Lever Bros 与非洲公司的诚信(fiduciary)或效忠(loyalty)责任。

后来 Lever Bros 对非洲业务有新的安排(与竞争对手合并),不再需要被告的服务。于是为了提早终止服务合约,Lever Bros 与被告谈判后付出给他一大笔遣散费。但支付了之后才发觉被告原先违约牟取私人的秘密利润,严重程度足可让 Lever Bros 单方面就能终止这服务合约,无需赔偿任何遣散费。这样,Lever Bros 起诉向被告追回这笔已付出的钱,理由是这遣散合约(severance contract)订立时,双方有一个错误假设,即认为服务合约没有被告的同意不能提前终止,而支付遣散费获得被告的同意是合约提前终止的唯一合法方法。

虽然在高院与上诉庭,Lever Bros 胜诉,但贵族院却是以 3 比 2 的多数推翻了原判,判 Lever Bros 最后败诉。表面看来这结果不太公道,因为被告可以同时赚取不应该赚的秘密利润与一大笔的遣散费(所谓的"golden handshake")。确实所有不同级别的法院与所有审理法官都认为被告不应该被允许这样做,Lever Bros 原则上是可以取回错误与冤枉支付的遣散费。但是否构成可诉错误是要看每个先例不同的案情,而此先例的案情看来没有满足可诉错误下错误必须有根本重要性的要件。贵族院认为 Lever Bros 当时非常心急要另作安排,所以即使 Lever Bros 知悉了被告的违约(秘密牟利),为了顺利合并与让被告在合并时合作,仍有可能与被告达成遣散合约来提早终止服务合约。换言之,这共同假设的错误并非足够重要到令遣散合约有本质不同,或者说是动摇整个遣散合约存在或继续有效的根基。

这方面可节录在接下来的 Associated Japanese Bank (International) Ltd v. Credit du Nord SA(1989)1 WLR 255 先例中,Steyn 大法官对该案判决的观察与分析,说:"Bell v. Lever Brothers Ltd ... was a quite exceptional case...The speeches do not suggest that the employees were entitled to keep both the gains secretly made and the 'golden handshakes.' The former were clearly recoverable from them.... But there are indications in the speeches that the so-called 'merits' were not all in favour of Lever Brothers. **The company was most anxious, because of a corporate merger, to terminate the two service agreements**. There was apparently **a doubt** as to whether the voidability of the service agreements if revealed to the company at the time of the severance contract would have affected the company's decision. Lord Thankerton said,...: '... I do not find sufficient material to compel the inference that the appellants, at the time of the contract, regarded the indefeasibility of the service agreements as an essential and integral element in the subject matter of the bargain.' ...It is noteworthy that Lord Atkin commented upon the scarcity of evidence as to the subsidiaries from the boards of which the two employees resigned...Lord Blanesburgh's speech ... did, however, make clear that 'The mistake must go to the whole consideration,' and pointed to the advantages (other than the release from the service agreements) which Lever Brothers received ... Lord Blanesburgh emphasised that Lever Brothers **secured the future co-operation of the two employees for the carrying through of the amalgamation**..."(加黑部分是笔者的强调)

总结说,该贵族院先例显示了普通法下的共同/共享错误能够成功的机会是非常低,这也带来了 Solle v. Butcher(1950)1 KB 671 上诉庭"衡平法错误"的说法,试图为一些错误程度稍低但结果令人感到不合情理的案件获得可使合约无效的救济。而且,也获得一定的支持,如 Steyn 大法官在 Associated Japanese Bank (International) Ltd v. Credit du Nord SA 先例中说:"... a narrow doctrine of common law mistake (as enunciated in Bell v Lever Bros Ltd ...), supplemented by the more flexible doctrine of mistake in equity ..., seems to me to be an entirely sensible and satisfactory state of the law ..."

但两者在对合约标的的共同/共享错误理解在程度上的差异,即衡平法错误的"基本"(fundamental)与普通法错误的"变为与预期的标的有了根本性不同"(essentially different from the thing believed to be/anticipated)在每个案件的不同事实下也不容易区分,只能粗略说衡平法错误在程度上的要求是较低。Phillips 勋爵在 The "Great Peace"(2002) EWCA Civ 1407 上诉庭先例中就批评说:"In Solle v. Butcher Denning LJ identified the requirement of a common misapprehension that was 'fundamental', and that adjective has been used to describe the mistake in those cases which have followed Solle v. Butcher. We do not find it possible to distinguish, by a process of definition, a mistake which is 'fundamental' from Lord Atkin's mistake as to quality which 'makes the thing contracted for essentially different from the thing that it was believed to be'. ..."

13.3 Associated Japanese Bank (International) Ltd v. Credit du Nord SA (1989) 1 WLR 255 先例

Associated Japanese Bank (International) Ltd v. Credit du Nord SA 先例的简单案情涉及 4 台机械设备的售后回租(sale and lease-back)交易。Bennett 先生把 4 台机械设备以 100 万英镑出售给原告,然后租回来使用并支付租金给原告,这种交易下无需实质交付机械设备给原告。被告是担保人,为 Bennett 先生准时支付租金提供担保。Bennett 先生在支付了一期租金后就被警察逮捕与在不久后破产。原告调查后发现这 4 台机械设备根本不存在,整件事情是一个骗局。而留下来的烂摊子就是原告与被告两位无辜人士之间的诉讼,各自希望把损失转嫁给对方。原告根据担保合约向被告索赔余下的租金。而因为担保的 4 台机械设备根本不存在,被告就抗辩说双方对标的物的存在与否的事实有了共同错误理解,要求令担保合约无效。

Steyn 大法官判担保合约在普通法的共同错误下无效,说:

"The **first** imperative must be that the law ought to uphold rather than destroy apparent contracts. **Secondly**, the common law rules as to a mistake regarding the quality of the subject matter, like the common law rules regarding commercial frustration, are designed to cope with the impact of unexpected and wholly exceptional circumstances on apparent contracts. **Thirdly**, such a mistake in order to attract legal consequences must substantially be shared by both parties, and must relate to facts as they existed at the time the contract was made. **Fourthly**, and this is the point established by Bell v. Lever Brothers Ltd. [1932] AC 161, the mistake must render the subject matter of the contract essentially and radically different from the subject matter which the parties believed to exist. ... **Fifthly**, there is a requirement which was not specifically discussed in Bell v. Lever Brothers Ltd. What happens if the party, who is seeking to rely on the mistake, had no reasonable grounds for his belief? An extreme example is that of the man who makes a contract with minimal knowledge of the facts to which the mistake relates but is content that it is a good speculative risk. In my judgment a party cannot be allowed to rely on a common mistake where the mistake consists of a belief which is entertained by him without any reasonable grounds for such belief: cf. McRae v. Commonwealth Disposals Commission (1951) 84 CLR 377, 408. That is not because principles such as estoppel or negligence require it, but simply because policy and good sense dictate that the positive rules regarding common mistake should be so qualified. …(共同错误的考虑之一是法律应该承认一个表面看来有效的合约而不是去毁掉它;二是共同错误与合约受阻的道理一样,是去应对合约标的受不可预期与完全是例外的事件的冲击的情况;三错误是双方订约方共享的,并且是针对订约时的现存事实;四 Belle v. Lever Bros Ltd 先例明确,错误是令合约的标的与订约方预期的有根本性不同;五主张共同错误必须是有合理依据去支持错误理解或假设,如果没有合理依据就去作出对一个现存'事实'的假设,即使缺乏合理依据不是主张共同错误方的过错或不小心导致,也更像是投机性的自担风险。)

… It is clear, of course, that in this case both parties — the creditors and the guarantors — acted on the assumption that the lease related to existing machines. If they had been informed that the machines might not exist, neither the plaintiffs nor the defendants would for one moment have contemplated entering into the transaction. That by itself, I accept, is not enough to sustain the plea of common law mistake. I am also satisfied that the defendants had reasonable grounds for believing that the machines existed. That belief was based on the defendants' discussions with Mr. Bennett, information supplied by National Leasing, a respectable firm of lease brokers, and the confidence created by the fact that the plaintiffs were the lessors. The real question is whether the subject matter of the guarantee (as opposed to the sale and lease) was essentially different from what it was reasonably believed to be. **The real security of the guarantors was the machines. The existence of the machines**, being profit-earning chattels, **made it more likely that the debtor would be able to service the debt**. More importantly, if the debtor defaulted, and the creditors repossessed the machines the creditors had to give credit for 97 1/2 per cent. of the value of the machines. If the creditors sued the guarantors first, and the guarantors paid, the guarantors were entitled to be subrogated to the creditors' rights in respect of recovery against the debtor: …No doubt the guarantors relied to some extent on the creditworthiness of Mr. Bennett. But I find that the prime security to which the guarantors looked was the existence of the four machines as described to both parties. **For both parties the guarantee of obligations under a lease with non-existent machines was essentially different from a guarantee of a lease with four machines which both parties at the time of the contract believed to exist**. The guarantee is an accessory contract. **The non-existence of the subject matter of the principal contract is therefore of fundamental importance**. … In my judgment the stringent test of common law mistake is satisfied：**the guarantee is void ab initio.**”（加黑部分是笔者的强调）

上述引用是分析该先例的事实证据来认定这4台机械设备的存在与否是否令有关的担保合约有根本性不同。显然，如果这是4台机械设备的买卖合约，作为标的的4台机械设备不存在肯定是令买卖合约有根本性不同。但此先例争议涉及担保合约，这4台机械设备谈不上是担保合约的对价物或担保物，主要是被告知道有这4台机械设备在，租金的支付就有保障，担保合约的风险也可控。

虽然，被告如果知道4台机械设备在订约时根本不存在，肯定不愿意订立这个担保合约。但这不足以构成可诉错误，因为4台变成只有3台或2台，被告也不会愿意去签订这个担保合约。而如果订约时4台机械设备只有3台，因为1台坏了，这在程度上是无法满足可诉错误（或合约履行期间构成受阻）。又如，被告为 Bennett 先生提供担保也获得 Bennett 先生提供其他的担保物如 Bennett 先生住的房屋，显然也不会因为4台机械设备的不存在（不存在的原因不一定是此先例的 Bennett 先生是骗子，可以是因为天灾而灭失）而令担保合约自始无效。所以此先例的案情下对可诉错误是否满足必须有根本性重要的要件有可争议之处，尽管最终 Steyn 大法官还是判满足普通法对错误的要求，可令该担保自始无效。

在该先例中，审理的 Steyn 大法官也提到即使程度上不满足普通法的共同错误，也可以衡平法错误去让担保合约无效。

13.4 The“Great Peace”(2002) EWCA Civ 1407 上诉庭先例

The“Great Peace”上诉庭先例是目前针对共同/共享错误重要的权威先例。不妨先简单介绍有关的案情，该案涉及有悠久历史的船舶海难救助（salvage）问题，这专业课题在笔者的《海事法》（大连海事大学出版社1999年版）一书第五章有详论，不去重复。出事的船舶是“Cape Providence”轮，该轮从巴西满载铁矿石前往中国，但在南印度洋发生严重船体损坏而需要紧急救援，船东于是与本案被告 Tsavliris Salvage 专业救助公司（professional salvor）签订了救助合约，以劳氏救助合约格式（Lloyd's Open Form 或 LOF）[56]为准。救助任务主要是拖带失去动力的“Cape

---

〔56〕 LOF著名之处是救助人的收费是根据“无效果，无报酬”（no cure, no pay），也就是救援不成功，即船货全损，没有有价值的海上财产被成功救回到安全港口，救助公司/救助人就白干。但如果救援成功或部分成功，就容许救助人从救回的财产中分摊部分作为报酬，分摊多少就根据每一次救助的危险性与复杂程度、及时性、最后成功的程度（如大部分或只是小部分财产救回）、救助人花费的成本/时间、专业水平与技能、冒险程度、是否值得额外鼓励（如专业救助人在没有救助任务时仍有高昂的成本、有否成功保护人命等）等来决定。但这些考虑救助人应该多少报酬的因素都是很专业与每一次的救助任务都是不同的，根本无法在事前预测去确定一笔适当的金额。所以LOF的“无效果，无报酬”有吸引力之处是救助成功后，根据LOF的仲裁条文由专业仲裁员最后根据整个救助行动的事实裁定报酬的金额。对救助人而言，知道只要把救助任务做好，加上运气好救助成功，将来由专业仲裁员裁定的报酬就不会被亏待。另一方被施加援手的船舶与货物背后的船东、货主与保险人，也满意这个安排，即在什么财产都救不回的情况下，无需再掏钱；在救回全部或部分财产的情况下，由专业与客观的仲裁员去裁定一个宽待但不会离谱的救助报酬。

Providence”轮去安全港口修理,但 Tsavliris Salvage 找到的拖轮(tug)是在新加坡,需要5～6天的航程才能抵达“Cape Providence”轮进行拖带。由于该轮的危险状况,在等待的5～6天内会随时沉没,并造成船员伤亡。所以,Tsavliris Salvage 决定找一艘在“Cape Providence”轮附近的商船,在旁准备,一旦“Cape Providence”轮在拖轮抵达前沉没,该商船可接收船员,保证人命不会有伤亡。

Tsavliris Salvage 通过 Ocean Routes(一家为船舶提供天气卫星导航服务的公司),找到一艘名为“Great Peace”的商船。Tsavliris Salvage 与该船船东就救援事宜接洽,并与船东订立了为期最少5天,每天租金16,500美元的租约。Tsavliris Salvage 从 Ocean Routes 处获悉“Great Peace”轮是距离“Cape Providence”轮最近的商船,距离约35海里,但在订立租约后两艘船舶直接联络时才知道实际相距410海里,需要39小时航行才能抵达现场,可见当时的卫星定位技术还并不准确。这样,租用船舶的目的大部分落空。而刚好 Tsavliris Salvage 被“Cape Providence”轮的承租人告知附近有他租用的另一艘“Nordfarer”轮可以同样施以援手,所以 Tsavliris Salvage 决定取消“Great Peace”轮的租约。

这导致“Great Peace”轮的船东索赔82,500美元(16,500美元×5天)的租金,而 Tsavliris Salvage 作为被告以双方对租用船舶的目的存在共同错误为由要求令租约无效。

从上述的案情介绍看来,普通法下可诉错误令合约无效是十分明显无法成功。虽然在订约时,双方有共同的错误假设,但其他要成立共同/共享错误的要件是难以满足。这包括在期租合约,需要更多航行时间的风险(risk of time lost)是由 Tsavliris Salvage 作为承租人承担。而“Nordfarer”轮同样可以施以援手从而不再需要“Great Peace”轮的情况是出现在订约后。租约有明示条文规定 Tsavliris Salvage 如果不再需要“Great Peace”轮的服务可支付5天租金作为销约金(cancellation fees)等。

但最关键是该共同错误的程度是否严重至双方订约意图全部落空或根本性改变,这明显是差得很远。一审的 Toulson 大法官说:“Was the Great Peace so far away from the Cape Providence at the time of the contract as to **defeat the contractual purpose**—or in other words to turn it into something essentially different from that for which the parties bargained? This is **a question of fact and degree**, but in my view **the answer is No**.... A telling point is the reaction of the defendants on learning the true positions of the vessels. They did not want to cancel the agreement until they knew if they could find a nearer vessel to assist. Evidently the defendants did not regard the contract as devoid of purpose, or they would have cancelled at once.”(加黑部分是笔者的强调)

上诉庭支持了一审判决,Phillips 勋爵说:

“It was unquestionably a common assumption of both parties when the contract was concluded that the two vessels were in sufficiently close proximity to enable the Great Peace to carry out the service that she was engaged to perform. Was the distance between the two vessels so great as to confound that assumption and to render the contractual adventure impossible of performance? If so, the defendants would have an arguable case that the contract was void under the principle in Bell v Lever Bros Ltd[1932]AC 161 …

…the fact that the vessels were considerably further apart than the defendants had believed did not mean that the services that the Great Peace was in a position to provide were essentially different from those which the parties had envisaged when the contract was concluded. The Great Peace would arrive in time to provide several days of escort service. The defendants would have wished the contract to be performed but for the adventitious arrival on the scene of a vessel(指的是"Nordfarer"轮)prepared to perform the same services. The fact that the vessels were further apart than both parties had appreciated did not mean that it was impossible to perform the contractual adventure. …

The parties entered into a binding contract for the hire of the Great Peace. That contract gave the defendants an express right to cancel the contract subject to the obligation to pay the'cancellation fee' of five days' hire. When they engaged the Nordfarer they cancelled the Great Peace. They became liable in consequence to pay the cancellation fee. There is no injustice in this result."

在 The "Great Peace"上诉庭先例中,Phillips 勋爵总结了五个构成可诉共同错误的要件:"(i)there must be a common assumption as to the existence of a state of affairs;[双方在订约时对现存的情况(事实或法律)有一个共同/共享的假设](ii)there must be no warranty by either party that state of affairs exists;(任何一方订约方都没有向对方保证该现存情况存在)(iii)the non-existence of the state of affairs must not be attributable to the fault of either party;(该现存情况不存在并非其中一方订约方的过错所导致)(iv)the non-existence of the state of affairs must render performance of the contract impossible;(该现存情况的不存在令合约无法履行[57])(v)the state of affairs may be the existence, or a vital attribute, if the consideration to be provided or circumstances which must subsist if performance of the contractual adventure is to be possible.[该现存情况(标的)的存在或主要属性,是履行该合约必须的]"

在 The "Great Peace"上诉庭先例后,很多涉及共同错误的案件都以该五个要件作为测试共同/共享错误能否成立的标准,如:Champion Investments Ltd v. Ahmed (2004)EWHC 1956(QB);Standard Chartered Bank v. Banque Marocaine du Commerce

---

[57] 单方面错误的错误方承诺了无法履行的事项,也不会令合约无效。履行合约的责任仍然在该错误方,如果无法按照合约约定履行,则用赔偿金钱损失的替代履行方法来履行。正如 Holt 大法官在 Thornborow v. Whitacre(1705)92 ER 270 先例中所说:"where a man will for a valuable consideration undertake to do an impossible thing, though it cannot be performed, yet he shall answer damages."这方面可见笔者《合约的履行、弃权与禁反言》一书第二章之 2 段。

Exterieur(2006)EWHC 413(Ch);John Lobb Ltd v. John Lobb SAS(2022)EWHC 2306(Ch)等先例;香港特区的 Bank of China(HK)Ltd v. Keen Lloyd Energy Ltd(2012)HKEC 421;Lo Shing Kin v. Shy Chin Ming Stephen(2012)HKEC 682 等上诉庭先例。

笔者可以一个简单例子去分析上述五个要件的测试,如租用一艘名为“No Peace”(举例)的船舶,为期 3 年,承租人与船东都知道是用来在 A 国与 B 国之间运输原油。但在订约时,“No Peace”轮遇上事故沉没,这是较容易成立的共同错误,双方订约的共同标的/目的是租用“No Peace”轮,肯定订约时假设船舶存在。但它的沉没令双方对租约标的/目的有根本重要性的共同错误理解或假设,这是典型的共同错误。

但一样的案件案情有了变化,就会不能满足上述的五个要件了。例如船舶沉没是船东不能免责的过错如船舶失修不适航引致,这就不满足要件(iii)了,不再是令租约无效的共同错误(不涉及金钱损失的索赔),而是船东的违约/毁约要面对承租人的损失索赔了。

假设另一个变化是船舶只是严重损坏,不是沉没全损,需要修理 6 个月。这样,要件(iv)就不能满足了,因为 3 年的租约不会因 6 个月的修理而无法履行。会是,租期只是 3 个月或 6 个月才可以满足这个要件。

再假设租约没有写明特定租用“No Peace”轮,而是稍后由船东指定(nominate)一艘符合一定规格的船舶去履行租约,或好像在 The “Super Servant Two”(1990)1 Lloyd’s Rep 1 贵族院先例中,“No Peace”轮只是租约中特定的两艘履行船舶中的一艘,稍后由船东决定。这样,“No Peace”轮就不是租约的标的(或主要的标的)了。双方订约方对“No Peace”轮在订约时存在的事实也不存在共同的错误理解或假设,承租人很可能没有听说过这艘船舶。该船舶也谈不上是该租约的属性/特性,租约完全可以其他船舶去履行。失去了“No Peace”轮也不会令租约无法履行。这样,要件(i)、(iv)与(v)都无法满足。

上述的情况也可以解释为要件(ii)也无法满足,也就是船东默示保证租约有船舶提供给承租人履行,并承担任何一艘想指定履行的船舶在尚未正式指定前不再存在的风险。

另在本章之 8 段有介绍详细案情的 Triple Seven MSN 27251 Ltd v. Azman Air Services Ltd(2018)EWHC 1348(Comm)先例中,MacDonald Eggers QC 大法官总结之前重要先例所确立的法律原则说:“the elements of a common mistake which has the effect of rendering the contract based on that common mistake void are as follows:(1)There must have been,at the time of the conclusion of the contract,an assumption as to the existence of a state of affairs substantially shared between the parties.(2)The assumption itself must have been fundamental to the contract.(3)That assumption must have been wrong at the time of the conclusion of the contract.(4)By reason of the assumption being wrong,the contract or its performance would be essentially and radically different from what the parties believed to be the case at the time of the conclusion of the contract; alternatively, the contract must be impossible to perform having regard to or in accordance with the common assumption. In other words, there must be a fundamental difference between the assumed and actual states of affairs. (5) The parties, or at least the party relying on the common mistake, would not have entered into the contract had the parties been aware that the common assumption was wrong. (6) The contract must not have made provision in the event that the common assumption was mistaken."

根据该先例的案情与法官的考虑,该先例主要是无法满足第四个要件。也即5年的飞机租赁协议只是一年因被告无法取得批准而无法达到订约的目的,也不能成立共同错误。这也可以看到普通法下要成立共同错误的难度是非常大。

最后,在The "Great Peace"上诉庭先例中总结的共同/共享错误的五个要件,虽然在之后同类的案件被跟从或适用。但在不同案件仍会有发展,正如John Lobb Ltd v. John Lobb SAS(2021) EWHC 1226(Ch)先例说:"I do not consider the doctrine is sufficiently settled ... in the judgment of Lord Phillips MR ... in The Great Peace and simply apply them as if they were part of a statute. The approach adopted to the doctrine in Chitty and the judgment of Mr McDonald Eggers in Triple Seven v. Azman Air suggest that the law is continuing to refine and develop."

13.5 与共同/共享错误有类似效果的说法:完全得不到对价的好处与默示先决条件

除了共同错误令一个有效的合约无效外,还有两种不同的说法可达成同样让一方当事人逃脱合约与类似复原一样去取回支付的金钱或转移的好处的效果。

在《Chitty on Contracts》(2021年,第34版)一书之8-016段中说:"**Different conceptual bases**. While it is clear on the authorities that a doctrine of common mistake exists in English law, the situation is complicated by the fact that there are three possible conceptual routes which have been employed in considering whether a fundamental mistake has the result that a party can in effect escape from the contract and recover any payment made or other benefit transferred: (1) that there has been a total failure of consideration; (2) that the contract is subject to an express or implied condition that the facts were as the parties believed them to be, or ... that it would be invalid if, on the true construction of the contract, the essence of the obligations are impossible to perform; and (3) that there is a separate doctrine of mistake. ..."

最典型的"完全得不到对价的好处"(total failure of consideration)或"失去基础"(failure of basis)的案件就是买方预付了货价,但卖方不交付货物:见BP Oil International Ltd v. Vega Petroleum Ltd & Ors(2021) EWHC 1363(Comm)等先例。这样,如果卖方是违约不去交付货物,买方可根据买卖合约在普通法向卖方索赔损失。但会有情况是不涉及违约,如合约受阻或免责,买方就会以"完全得不到对价的好处"要求卖方去退还预付的货价(这与损失是两回事,例如损失可加上预期的合理利润)。[58] 这个救济在《Sale of Goods Act 1979》立法之 Section 54 中也有规定说:"Nothing in this Act affects the right of the buyer ... to recover money paid where the consideration for the payment of it has failed."

另在《Benjamin's Sale of Goods》(2020 年,第 11 版)一书之 § 12 – 069-079 中有解释说:"Where, after the buyer has paid the price (or part of it) to the seller, the seller fails to deliver the goods ... he may either sue for damages, or for restitution of the money paid to the seller ... if he sues for restitution. He can avoid the rules of damages, since his claim is for return of the precise sum of money which he paid to the seller, but he must terminate the contract."

这种救济只需要满足两个要件,正如 Cockerill 大法官在 BP Oil International Ltd v. Vega Petroleum Ltd & Ors 先例中说:"Technically the hurdles to establishing this are simply that: **a.** BPOI(原告买方)has not received any consideration ... for the payments it has made; and **b.** The contracts have been terminated/determined/discharged."

当然,作为衡平救济,也受到其他衡平法理论的约束,如原告自己不能有过错导致"完全得不到对价的好处"。在 Stray v. Russell (1859) 120 ER 1144 先例中,买方拒绝接受卖给他的股票而在事后以"完全得不到对价的好处"要求对方退还已经支付的金钱就不成功。这也是完全合理,否则市场货价暴跌,预付货价的买方都可以违约/毁约,拒绝接收货物,并以"完全得不到对价的好处"向卖方主张复原与要求退还预付货款了。

以上简单介绍可看到"完全得不到对价的好处"的说法是不能替代共同错误:(1)后者是否定(nullify)合约的有效存在,与前者终止合约不同;(2)前者是衡平法,后者是普通法。

至于另一个说法是解释双方订立的合约中包括明示或默示条文,即合约的先决条件是双方当事人错误理解的事实为真,所以合约因无法满足先决条件而无法成立。但这看来并不现实,因为对订约时存在的事实或法律有共同/共享错误理解都会是一些不可预见的事故/事件导致。很难假设在双方订约时,会有一个好事第三人问:"你们假设天不会塌下来,但如果真的发生了,你们会怎么办?"然后双方回答:"那合约当然就无效了。"但双方更可能会说该好事第三人是胡思乱想。正如在 The "Great Peace" (2002) EWCA Civ 1407 上诉庭先例中,Phillips 勋爵说:"... the theory of the implied term is as unrealistic when considering common mistake as when considering frustration. Where the fundamental assumption upon which an agreement is founded proves to be mistaken, it is not realistic to ask whether the parties impliedly agreed that in those circumstances the contract would not be binding."

另一个在这个基础上发展起来的更现代的说法是,解释合约包括一条默示条文

---

[58] 见笔者《合约的履行、弃权与禁反言》第二章之 9 段。

是如果有关的错误令该合约重要义务(essential obligations)不可能履行,合约就无效。这个说法与合约受阻非常类似,区别只在共同错误是发生在订约前,而受阻事件是发生在订约后。

14. 衡平法错误

首先节录权威书籍的一些说法,《Misrepresentation, Mistake and Non-Disclosure》(2022 年,第 6 版)一书之 12 – 10 段提到直到较近期,对可诉错误导致的合约,英国法院会在普通法下判自始无效(void ab initio)或在衡平法下判可使无效(voidable),说:"... a mistake generally renders the contract void. Until recently, the courts recognised circumstances in which a mistake might make a contract voidable(in equity), as well as circumstances in which it might make the contract void(at common law). This doctrine of mistake in equity appears now to have been rejected, thus simplifying one aspect of the law of mistake. However, there are other equitable rules and doctrines governing mistake (如本章 11.2 段提到的变更合约或稍后会介绍的履约指令等的情况), ..."

另在《Chitty on Contracts》(2021 年,第 34 版)一书之 8 – 009 段中也有类似的说法如下:"**Common law and equity**. Until recently it could be argued that what has been said ... about the circumstances in which the law takes account of a mistake by both parties to a contract represented the position in common law; and that the rules of equity 'cut across this distinction'. This referred to the line of cases to the effect that in some circumstances a common mistake would give either party the right to avoid a contract that was not void for mistake at common law based on a rule of equity. Now that these cases have been disapproved. ..."

上述书籍提到直到较近期这有了改变,是指 The "Great Peace" (2002) EWCA Civ 1407 上诉庭先例否定了衡平法下对可诉错误的救济,即让有关合约的非错误方可使合约无效,也就是有权撤销合约(rescission),并恢复到原状(restitutio in integrum)。这表示直到 The "Great Peace" 上诉庭先例被最高院改变或否定,英国法律对可诉错误的救济只有普通法的令有关合约自始无效。这令本章之 9 段的"错误经常被主张但成功极少"的说法更是正确,毕竟本章已经是方方面面介绍了普通法下对可诉错误的局限与大政策是保护有对价合约的保障性(security of contract)与神圣性(sanctity),尽量保证履约。政策上收紧错误的必要性在 Bell v. Lever Brothers Ltd (1932) AC 161 贵族院先例中,Atkin 勋爵说:"It is of **paramount importance that contracts should be observed**, and that if parties honestly comply with the essentials of the formation of contracts-i. e. agree in the same terms on the same subject-matter-they are bound, and must rely on the stipulations of the contract for protection from the effect of facts unknown to them. … I see no way of giving relief to the plaintiffs in the present circumstances except by confiding to the Courts loose powers of introducing terms into contracts which would only serve to introduce doubt and confusion **where certainty is essential**."(加黑部分是笔者的强调)

14.1 衡平法下的可诉错误

也是因为政策如此,所以有了衡平法下的错误(mistake in equity)。正如在其他所有的课题或概念中,如在本书第一章之1.1段介绍的非欺诈性误述(non-fraudulent misrepresentation),由于在普通法下没有任何救济,所以需要衡平法去插手给予被误述方可使合约无效去撤销的权利,直到第四章详论的《Misrepresentation Act 1967》的立法生效后去替代。

衡平法是希望在个别案件为严格与主旨是追求法律的肯定性与可预测性的普通法下的合约法带来一点灵活性,虽然衡平法追求个案的公平合理,但也不是泛泛的一句,而是有不少的理论(doctrines)或原则(principles),务求在肯定性与公平合理间有一个平衡。

在《Judicature Act 1873》立法后,原来独立操作的普通法法院与衡平法法院被合并在一起。英国法院也就同时考虑,而如果案件在普通法下无法获得救济,但客观看来不合情理,审理法官去考虑衡平救济的可能性。而同一审理法官可以作出金钱赔偿的普通法/法律救济,也可以作出履约指令或禁令的衡平救济。

这在普通法下对共同错误是特别重要,因为法律在Kennedy v. Panama, New Zealand and Australian Royal Mail Co Ltd(1867)LR 2 QB 580先例与Bell v. Lever Brothers Ltd(1932)AC 161贵族院先例变得十分严格。合约的标的如买卖合约的货物灭失或根本上改变,才会是可诉错误(或在有了合约后才发生事故就会是合约受阻)。换言之,普通法是不理会错误发生在货物的质量的差别,所以无论质量的差别如何严重,只要不是变为与原来货物完全不同的垃圾或废铁,仍不会是可诉错误(或受阻事件)。在Bell v. Lever Brothers Ltd贵族院先例中,3∶2多数的Atkin勋爵是说:"a mistake will not affect assent unless it is the mistake of both parties, and is as to the existence of some quality which makes the thing without the quality essentially different from the thing as it was believed to be."

另Thankerton勋爵也说:"can only properly relate to something which both must necessarily have accepted in their minds as an essential and integral element of the subject matter."

共同错误在理论上是根据双方在买卖合约中达成一致想法,但该想法是根本性错误而判合约无效,所以有此"一刀切"的严格判法也不足为奇。一旦涉及货物质量问题,什么是严重或不严重的错误?分水岭划分在哪里就不好确定,这正是普通法所避忌的不肯定法律地位。这样如果只是针对极端的垃圾与废铁的情况,那适用的范围也是非常狭窄。

但这也带来其他的疑问。例如，完全得不到对价的好处（total failure of consideration）的说法本来就可产生与令合约无效同样的效果。这样，有否必要多一种共同错误的说法而把法律搞得更复杂与混乱？正如 Steyn 大法官在 Associated Japanese Bank（International）Ltd v. Credit du Nord SA（1989）1 WLR 255 先例中说："He（原告代表大律师）submitted that at common law a mistake even as to an essential quality of the subject matter of the contract would not affect the contract unless it resulted in a total failure of consideration. It was not clear to me that this formulation left any meaningful and independent scope for the application of common law rules in this area of the law."

在可诉错误方面，普通法与衡平法两者之间的关系是 Steyn 大法官在 Associated Japanese Bank（International）Ltd v. Credit du Nord SA 先例中所说的：法院应先去以普通法看看合约是否因错误而自始无效？如果是，再不必去理会衡平法。如果不是（如订约时双方对合约标的有一个共同/共享错误不是根本性，但仍是极其严重），则要以衡平法来看待这错误可否令合约无效。换言之，衡平法是辅助普通法。Steyn 大法官说："No one could fairly suggest that in this difficult area of the law there is only one correct approach or solution. But a narrow doctrine of common law mistake（as enunciated in Bell v. Lever Brothers Ltd…），supplemented by the more flexible doctrine of mistake in equity（as developed in Solle v. Butcher [1950] 1 K. B. 671 and later cases），seems to me to be an entirely sensible and satisfactory state of the law …It might be useful if I now summarised what appears to me to be a satisfactory way of approaching this subject. Logically, before one can turn to the rules as to mistake, whether at common law or in equity, one must **first determine** whether the contract itself, by express or implied condition precedent or otherwise, provides **who bears the risk of the relevant mistake.** [59] It is at this hurdle that many pleas of mistake will either fail or prove to have been unnecessary. **Only if the contract is silent on the point, is there scope for invoking mistake**. That brings me to **the relationship between common law mistake and mistake in equity. Where common law mistake has been pleaded, the court must first consider this plea. If the contract is held to be void, no question of mistake in equity arises. But, if the contract is held to be valid, a plea of mistake in equity may still have to be considered**."（加黑部分是笔者的强调）

Steyn 大法官判担保合约在普通法的共同错误下无效，这样再也没有必要考虑衡平法下的救济。但也提到如果普通法错误因太狭窄无法成立，也会在此案中以衡平法错误去令合约无效，说："Having concluded that the guarantee is void ab initio at common law, it is strictly unnecessary to examine the question of equitable mistake. Equity will give relief against common mistake in cases where the common law will not, and it

---

[59] 见本章之 3 段。

provides more flexible remedies including the power to set aside the contract on terms. It is not necessary to repeat my findings of fact save to record again the fundamental nature of the common mistake, and that the defendants were not at fault in any way. If I had not decided in favour of the defendants on construction and common law mistake, I would have held that the guarantee must be set aside on equitable principles."

除了在程度上衡平法会比普通法较为宽松外，在 William Sindall plc v. Cambridgeshire CC(1994)1 WLR 1016 上诉庭先例中，Evans 大法官也提到除了针对合约标的外，衡平法错误也对合约目的与条件的严重错误有更广泛的适用，说："The difference may be that the common law rule is limited to mistakes with regard to the subject matter of the contract, whilst equity can have regard to a wider and perhaps unlimited category of 'fundamental' mistake."

但衡平法下，也不是合约方订立了一个不利的合约可随意脱身。衡平法错误仍需要共同错误是"基本"(fundamental)的错误。另也需要法院认为让另一方获利、占便宜是不合情理，正如 Denning 大法官在 Solle v. Butcher(1950)1 KB 671 上诉庭先例中说："The court … had power to set aside the contract whenever it was of opinion that it was unconscientious for the other party to avail himself of the legal advantage which he had obtained."

因为衡平法不像普通法一样严格，后者一旦认定是可诉共同/共享错误即判合约自始是空的、无效的，而前者只是法院有权使合约无效。这就能保证不会影响无辜第三人，在本书第三章之6.3段已详及。

因为衡平法涉及法院的裁量权，所以在适当案件/案情中，法院可去订下条件才使合约无效。例如在 Grist v. Bailey(1967)Ch 532 先例中，被告作为业主以850英镑把一幢房屋卖给原告。订约时双方以为有一位受保护的租客(protected tenant)[60]住在该房屋。谁知道在订约时该租客已经死亡，这样，没有了租金受限的租约的该房屋可值2250英镑的市价，被告卖方显然想从合约脱身。原告起诉被告申请履约指令，要求被告以850英镑出售，但 Goff 大法官以衡平法错误判合约无效。但订下条件是被告要优先给原告一个机会以适当价格(proper vacant possession price)购买这房屋，当然这条件是否能起作用则无法得知了。

衡平法对错误的灵活处理显然会对一些案件是更公平合理，正如在 West Sussex Properties Ltd v. Chichester District Council(2000)NPC 74 上诉庭先例中，Staughton 大法官说："It is a matter of some satisfaction, in my view, that we can and do regard ourselves as bound by the decision in Solle v Butcher. That decision has now stood for over 50 years. Despite scholarly criticism it remains unchallenged in a higher court; indeed there have been remarkably few reported cases where it has been considered during that

〔60〕 即法例不准业主乱加租金从而保障该租客。

long period. **As this case shows, it can on occasion be the passport to a just result.**"（加黑部分是笔者的强调）

14.2 以衡平救济改变普通法在 Bell v. Lever Brothers Ltd 贵族院先例地位的 Solle v. Butcher (1950) 1 KB 671 上诉庭先例

衡平法下对错误的救济开始于 Solle v. Butcher 上诉庭先例。案情涉及一个公寓租赁协议。原告是一位建筑测量师，他与被告在 1947 年合伙开展地产经纪业务。被告在 1947 年长租了一幢有 5 个公寓的住宅楼。该住宅楼在第二次世界大战期间受附近地雷爆炸的波及，严重受损。于是被告与原告就该住宅楼的修缮与租金问题进行讨论。该住宅楼的一号公寓在 1938 年根据《Rent Restriction Act》立法，以标准租金 140 英镑一年出租过给一个租客，租期 3 年。1947 年时整个住宅楼都是空置的。原告告知被告如果按照计划对住宅楼进行修缮、改建与重新装修，整个住宅楼将会因比原来的住宅楼有了较大改变，而在身份上变为一幢新的住宅楼，从而不受原来立法对租金的限制。而且，根据《Rent and Mortgage Interest (Restriction) Act 1938》立法，新住宅楼的年租金将提升为 250 英镑。被告也认为 140 英镑的年租金将不再适用。于是被告花大价钱对住宅楼进行修缮、改建与装修，并且作为房东，将一号公寓以 250 英镑的年租金租给原告，租期为 7 年。后来，原告发现正确的法律地位是住宅楼在修缮、改建与重新装修后租金仍受限制，向被告提出年租金应为 140 英镑，而不是 250 英镑。被告不同意，于是原告起诉被告，要求法院确认公寓的年租金为 140 英镑与被告归还原告多付的租金。被告则反请求要求法院根据共同错误的理论将租约撤销，也提到原告曾经告知他 140 英镑的租金不再适用，新租金应为 250 英镑构成被告无辜误述与禁反言。但在该案当时的年代，普通法对无辜误述是没有救济，这直到《Misrepresentation Act 1967》才有了改变。所以无辜误述与共同错误是没有矛盾。而针对法律问题的禁反言，在 Kleinwort Benson Ltd v. Lincoln City Council (1999) 2 AC 349 先例前也是没有救济。

该案上诉至上诉庭，首先 3 位大法官一致支持了原告虽然对住宅楼（包括一号公寓）进行了较大规模的修缮、改建与装修，但这仍然是原来的住宅楼，而不是一幢新的住宅楼的主张。即使一号公寓的租约中还加入了 1938 年租约中不曾有的对车库的使用权，年租金也仍然受立法中标准租金的约束，即应为 140 英镑。接着多数意见（包括 Denning 大法官与 Bucknill 大法官）支持被告的反请求，即在衡平法下，双方存在可诉共同错误，该共同错误是触及合约的根本。被告对公寓楼进行大笔投资后，是不可能仍然愿意以年租金 140 英镑的价格出租公寓 7 年给原告，在被告自己没有过错的情况下，如果不允许撤销租约是不公平的。与此同时，Denning 大法官从实际公平 (practical just)〔61〕的角度出发，为撤销合约设立了条件 (on terms)，〔62〕即被告要保

〔61〕 见本书第三章之 5.2 段。

〔62〕 见本书第三章之 5.2.3 段。

证允许原告继续留在公寓里，并在原告向他发出书面通知后的一个月内与原告订立新的租约，年租金不超过 250 英镑。

在该先例中，Denning 大法官说："... it is necessary to remember that mistake is of two kinds: first, mistake which renders the contract void, that is, a nullity from the beginning, which is the kind of mistake which was dealt with by the courts of common law; and, secondly, mistake which renders the contract not void, but voidable, that is, liable to be set aside on such terms as the court thinks fit, which is the kind of mistake which was dealt with by the courts of equity. Much of the difficulty which has attended this subject has arisen because, before the fusion of law and equity, the courts of common law, in order to do justice in the case in hand, extended this doctrine of mistake beyond its proper limits and held contracts to be void which were really only voidable...

Applying these principles, it is clear that here there was a contract. The parties agreed in the same terms on the same subject-matter. It is true that the landlord was under a mistake which was to him fundamental: he would not for one moment have considered letting the flat for seven years if it meant that he could only charge 140l. a year for it. He made the fundamental mistake of believing that the rent he could charge was not tied down to a controlled rent; but, whether it was his own mistake or a mistake common to both him and the tenant, it is not a ground for saying that the lease was from the beginning a nullity. ...

Let me next consider mistakes which render a contract voidable, that is, liable tobe set aside on some equitable ground. Whilst presupposing that a contract was good at law, or at any rate not void, the court of equity would often relieve a party from the consequences of his own mistake, so long as it could do so without injustice to third parties. The court, it was said, had power to set aside the contract whenever it was of opinion that it was unconscientious for the other party to avail himself of the legal advantage which he had obtained ...

The court had, of course, to define whatit considered to be unconscientious, ... It is now clear that a contract will be set aside if the mistake of the one party has been induced by a material misrepresentation of the other, even though it was not fraudulent or fundamental; or **if one party, knowing that the other is mistaken** about the terms of an offer, or the identity of the person by whom it is made, **lets him remain under his delusion and concludes a contract on the mistaken terms instead of pointing out the mistake**....

A contract is also liable in equity to be set aside if **the parties were under a common misapprehension** either as to facts or as to their relative and respective rights, **provided that the misapprehension was fundamental** and that the **party seeking to set it aside was not himself at fault**."（加黑部分是笔者的强调）

接下来的 Grist v. Bailey (1967) Ch 532; Magee v. Pennine Insurance Co. Ltd. (1969)2 QB 507 等先例都是同样判法,直到 The "Great Peace" (2002) EWCA Civ 1407 先例才有了根本性改变,正是较早前节录的权威书籍所写的。

14.3 否定衡平法错误的 The "Great Peace" (2002) EWCA Civ 1407 上诉庭先例

在本章之 13.4 段已经介绍过 The "Great Peace"先例的被告 Tsavliris Salvage 在普通法错误过不了关,要以错误程度较宽松与更灵活处理的衡平法错误作为替代争议。在此先例中,一审与上诉庭都认为在 Solle v. Butcher(1950)1 KB 671 上诉庭先例确立的衡平法错误是错判,是 Denning 大法官在该上诉庭先例以不同说法或理论去绕过 Bell v. Lever Brothers Ltd(1932) AC 161 贵族院先例对他的约束。另是 Bell v. Lever Brothers Ltd 贵族院先例定下的大原则是共同/共享错误必须十分狭窄以保护普通法下错误的肯定性,也保护合约的保障性与神圣性。这样,以衡平法错误去另开一个门唱反调是不应该的。

Phillips 勋爵说:"... **Toulson J. described this decision by Lord Denning as one which 'sought to outflank Bell v. Lever Brothers'**. We think that this was fair comment. It was not realistic to treat the House of Lords in Bell v Lever Brothers as oblivious to principles of equity, nor to suggest that 'if it had been considered on equitable grounds the result might have been different'. ... The common law has drawn the line in Bell v Lever Brothers. The effect of Solle v Butcher is not to supplement or mitigate the common law; it is to say that Bell v Lever Brothers was wrongly decided. ... Our conclusion is that **it is impossible to reconcile Solle v Butcher with Bell v Lever Brothers**. ..."(加黑部分是笔者的强调)

14.3.1 先例理论

在此不妨先介绍另一个与衡平法错误无关的课题,也就是英国判例法下的"先例理论"(doctrine of precedent/rule of stare decisis)。此理论或法律制度,是普通法的大精神,也是与大陆法的主要不同,对绝大部分人士来说这是常识。只简单节录一些阐述此理论的优越性的说法,如美国的 Kavanaugh 大法官在 Evangelisti Ramos v. Louisiana 590 U. S. (2020)先例中说,对社会上(或商业上)发生的同样问题,先例理论下可集合过去多位审理法官的智慧与博学找出解决办法:"respect for the accumulated wisdom of judges who have previously tried to solve the same problem."

另英国最高院的 Rose 勋爵在 2022 年 5 月 23 日针对英国退出欧盟后英国普通法的情况的发言中说到英国比美国对先例理论更加执着,因为这带来了法律的肯定性与稳定性,说:"A general reluctance to overturn previous decisions is influenced by the importance of precedent in the common law system of judicial decision making. It has been described as **the cement of legal principle, as providing the necessary stability to a common law** in a constant state of adaptation and repair. Judges in the US Supreme

Court have been more forthright than justices here in their approach to overturning earlier decisions even though they also operate in a precedent based system."(加黑部分是笔者的强调)

有说法是为了社会民众对法律可预期(如商业合约就是合约双方根据法律默示地位谈判与最后以明示条文调控与分担风险与责任),即使是可以改变法律与推翻先例的贵族院或最高院,也不应只是在认为以前约束性先例是错判或不满意就去改变。正如 Diplock 勋爵在 Geelong Harbor Trust Commissioners v. Gibbs Bright & Co(a firm)(Australian)(1974)UKPC 2 枢密院先例中说:"The law laid down by a judicial decision, even though erroneous, may work in practice to the satisfaction of those who are affected by it, particularly where it concerns the allocation of the burden of unavoidable risks between parties engaged in trade or commerce and their insurers. If it has given general satisfaction and caused no difficulties in practice, this is an important factor to be weighed against the more theoretical interests of legal science in determining whether the law so laid down ought now to be changed by judicial decision."

Reed 勋爵在 2023 年 1 月 23 日针对这方面的发言"Departing from Precedent: The Experience of the UK Supreme Court"中提到从 19 世纪末直至 1966 年,贵族院自己在先例理论下也不能偏离早前贵族院已经作出的判决。这里的主要考虑或作出的权衡是改判贵族院作为英国最终法院确立了的法律地位会严重影响民众对法律的信心。如果因为个别案件在严格法律规定下看来造成苛刻结果就允许改判或带来例外,就会令每一个案情不一样的案件都重启对法律的争辩。正如在 London Tramways v. London County Council(1898)AC 375 贵族院先例中,Halsbury 勋爵说:"the disastrous inconvenience ... of having each question subject to being reargued and the dealings of mankind rendered doubtful by reason of different situations."

在 1966 年 7 月 26 日,贵族院有了一份名为"Practice Statement(HL: Judicial Precedent)"(1966)1 WLR 1234〔63〕的指引,可以说想法是让作为最终法院的贵族院变得更有弹性去改变法律以让普通法随着社会的改变去发展。在该指引下,要求贵族院一般仍需要遵从较早的贵族院先例所确立的法律地位,但如果在贵族院看来是"正确做法",是可以去偏离或改判。

---

〔63〕 在 2009 年 10 月 1 日,贵族院改为最高院,上述 1966 年指引也在《Constitutional Reform Act 2005》之 Section 40 下在最高院同样适用:见 https://www.supremecourt.uk/procedures/practice-direction-03.html。在 Austin v. Mayor and Burgesses of the London Borough of Southwark(2010)UKSC 28 最高院先例中,Hope 勋爵说:"the House of Lords issued a Practice Statement on 26 July 1966 which stated that it would still treat former decisions of the House as normally binding, but that it would depart from a previous decision when it appeared right to do so... It was part of the established jurisprudence relating to the conduct of appeals in the House of Lords which was transferred to this Court by section 40 of the Constitutional Reform Act 2005."

但怎样才是正确做法,答案是"情况不多"。一般想法仍是不能削弱民众长期形成的对先例理论带来的英国法律肯定性与可预测性的信心。所以,如果要改变比较复杂的法律,贵族院或今天的最高院会在判决中遵从先例,但呼吁政府通过立法改变。[64] 只在最高院认为早前贵族院或最高院作出的判例是妨碍法律的发展[65]或明显会带来不肯定、[66]行政困难或对个人的不公正[67]时,最高院才会重新考虑有关的法律地位。而如果涉及考虑是否改变法律地位,就会根据"Panel numbers criteria-The Supreme Court"从一般的5位大法官变为7位大法官,一个这种罕见情况的例子,就是在本书第十章之11段介绍的Test Claimants in the FII Group Litigation v. Revenue and Customs Commissioners系列先例。

最后可节录在Alan Paterson的《The Law Lords》(London:Macmillan,1982)一书之156页中说:"a. the Practice Statement should be used sparingly and only very rarely to be used to change the interpretation of legislation or documents;b. it ought not to be used where it would upset the legitimate expectations of people who had arranged their affairs in reliance on the existing law or where it is difficult to foresee the consequences; c. it ought not to be used where the Law Lords merely consider that the earlier decision is wrong;d. On the other hand,it ought to be used to overrule a decision that has caused great uncertainty;or to overrule a decision that is not in keeping with some broad consideration of justice or with contemporary social conditions or modern perceptions of public policy."

14.3.2 The "Great Peace"上诉庭先例有否遵从先例理论的质疑

在要求严格按照先例理论下,The "Great Peace"(2002)EWCA Civ 1407先例的一审与上诉庭可否偏离Solle v. Butcher(1950)1 KB 671上诉庭先例,指称该先例与更高级别的Bell v. Lever Brothers Ltd(1932)AC 161贵族院先例有不一致?毕竟,只能是贵族院或最高院才能推翻Solle v. Butcher上诉庭先例,对后续的上诉庭案件也是有约束力与需要遵从,不能因为认为是判错或不满意就去改变。在这方面,上诉庭也不是乱来,有考虑在Noble v. South Railway Company(1940)AC 53贵族院先例中,Wright勋爵说:"What a court should do when faced with a decision of the Court of Appeal manifestly inconsistent with the decisions of the House is a problem of some difficulty in the doctrine of precedent. I incline to think it should apply the law laid down by the House and refuse to follow the erroneous decision."

---

[64] 例如在本书第八章之7.3段提到,在Tinsley v. Milligan(1994)1 AC 340贵族院先例中,少数意见的Goff勋爵反对多数意见判决的一个理由是不应该以判例改变已经有200多年历史与复杂的"公序良俗测试",而建议法律委员会(Legal Commission)全面审核非法理论。

[65] 见R v. National Insurance Commissioner,ex parte Hudson(1972)AC 944先例。

[66] 见Oldendorff v. Tradax Export(1974)AC 479先例。

[67] 见R v. National Insurance Commissioner,ex parte Hudson(1972)AC 944先例。

这说法也被Lane勋爵在Holden & Co v. Crown Prosecution Service(1990)2 QB 261上诉庭先例中接受。

但在The“Great Peace”先例中,上诉庭不像有考虑另两个在先例理论十分重要的Young v. Bristol Aeroplane Co(1944)KB 718上诉庭先例与Miliangos v. Frank(1976)AC 443贵族院先例。这种问题往往是出在双方代表大律师没有向法院提出,这样审理法官(或仲裁员)不是无所不知或万能。当然,双方代表大律师也不是无所不知或万能的。但他们在准备案件时应该已花费大量时间去钻研与考虑,更加可能且也有责任收集所有有帮助与有关的先例(与其他资料如权威书籍)向法院陈述。这是审理法官或仲裁员在开庭前不会做的事,即使为案件做准备也顶多稍加阅读一些有关的主合约、文书请求、证人证言等文件稍加阅读。

这两个上诉庭没有考虑的先例,在第一个上诉庭先例中,Greene勋爵提到了四种情况可不去跟从较早的上诉庭判例。第一种与本段无关,可以不理,而与本段有关的是:(1)有两个起冲突的上诉庭先例(where there is such a conflicting decision);(2)上一个上诉庭先例被后来的贵族院先例视为不正确,即使没有去正式推翻(this court comes to the conclusion that a previous decision, although not expressly overruled, cannot stand with a subsequent decision of the House of Lords);(3)上一个上诉庭先例是一个疏忽大意的判例(per incuriam 或“through lack of care”),就是该上诉庭判决没有考虑一些相关先例或立法,而如果考虑了会对判决有影响。

至于第二个的Miliangos v. Franks贵族院先例,案情在笔者的《仲裁法:从1996年英国仲裁法到国际商务仲裁》一书第九章之3.31段与《仲裁法:从开庭审理到裁决书的作出与执行》一书第六章之3.1.1段有简单的介绍,在此不重复。该先例也涉及了同样问题,也就是在较早的Re United Railways of Havana and Regla Warehouses Ltd(1961)AC 1007贵族院先例中,判法院(包括仲裁庭)不能以外币作出判决(或裁决),只能是以英镑(这有缅怀大英帝国时代的味道)。

但接下来的Schorsch Meier GmbH v. Hennin(1975)QB 416上诉庭先例没有跟从,认为世界变了与英镑的价值无法保证,所以会造成不公平合理,例如在该先例中就是如此。但这不是上诉庭该去决定的,不知道会否有部分原因是该先例的被告没有出庭作出抗辩。反正这样,在Miliangos v. Franks先例一审中,Bristow大法官就有了矛盾,结果决定仍是去跟从贵族院先例。但在上诉庭,包括了审理了Schorsch Meier GmbH v. Hennin先例的Denning勋爵在内的大法官们推翻了一审。再到了贵族院,针对这一点,Simon勋爵认为一审的Bristow大法官应该跟从Schorsch Meier GmbH v. Hennin上诉庭先例,并假设它已经考虑了更早的贵族院先例并成功作出区分。Bristow大法官不应该分析该上诉庭先例(这等同去批判),然后选择跟从较早的Re United Railways of Havana and Regla Warehouses Ltd贵族院先例。应该做的是跟从Schorsch Meier GmbH v. Hennin上诉庭先例,但可在判决中说明他受先例理论的约束,即使该上诉庭先例看来是违反先例理论。这就有机会让一审判决直接跳过上诉庭(leap-frogging)直接去贵族院作最后的决定。因为即使去了同一级别的上诉庭，也应该与一审有同样的考虑。

以上的简单介绍，可足够清楚看到 The "Great Peace" 上诉庭的判决会有几个问题：(1) The "Great Peace" 先例判决没有考虑 Young v. Bristol Aeroplane Co 上诉庭先例与 Miliangos v. Frank 先例是有疏忽大意（如代表律师有所遗漏）的味道。(2) The "Great Peace" 的上诉庭是否应该去跟从 Solle v. Butcher 上诉庭先例，但指出与 Bell v. Lever Brothers Ltd 贵族院先例的不一致，然后让贵族院（后来改为最高院）去最后拍板。(3) 在 The "Great Peace" 上诉庭先例接下来的同样案件（涉及是否可去对"衡平法错误"作出救济），看来一审法院安全做法是跟从 The "Great Peace" 先例。但在上诉庭的级别，根据 Young v. Bristol Aeroplane Co 上诉庭先例的疏忽大意的例外，会是可从 The "Great Peace" 或 Solle v. Butcher 两个起冲突的上诉庭先例中选择一个跟从。

14.4 衡平法可诉错误被否定的现状

在 The "Great Peace" (2002) EWCA Civ 1407 上诉庭先例中，Phillips 勋爵也不否定普通法错误是可以变得更为灵活，但去改变 Bell v. Lever Brothers Ltd (1932) AC 161 贵族院先例确定下来的政策是应该好像普通法的受阻理论通过《Law Reform (Frustrated Contract) Act 1943》改变一样，由立法去考虑与改变，说："... We can understand why the decision in Bell v Lever Brothers Ltd did not find favour with Lord Denning. **An equitable jurisdiction to grant rescission on terms** where a common fundamental mistake has induced a contract **gives greater flexibility than a doctrine of common law** which holds the contract void in such circumstances. Just as the Law Reform (Frustrated Contracts) Act 1943 was needed to temper the effect of the common law doctrine of frustration, so there is scope for legislation to give greater flexibility to our law of mistake than the common law allows."（加黑部分是笔者的强调）

在其他普通法国家，看来对"衡平法错误"的救济比较宽松。如美国，在 Treitel 教授的《The Law of Contract》(2020 年，第 15 版）一书之 8－031 段中说："it may be, however, that the need for certainty is over-stated. This is suggested by the fact that the American rules on this subject are much closer to those of English equity than those of the English common law, and do not seem to have caused widespread inconvenience."

在新加坡，在本章之 11.1.1 段介绍的看来，仍是有"衡平法错误"的说法。

衡平法与普通法的错误课题仍是有关，首先在本章之 11.1.2 段涉及的单方面错误是对方知道但趁机去取巧的情况可使合约无效或变更，正如在《Chitty on Contracts》(2021 年，第 34 版）一书之 8－009 段中说："... Equity will on occasion supplement the remedies available at common law: for example, a mistake may entitle a party to a contract that has been reduced to writing to have the document rectified if it is not expressed in accordance with the parties' true intentions, or does not reflect the terms that the claimant intended and the other party knew him to intend."

另是,如果普通法的错误不成立,如共同或单方面错误没有根本重要性,合约继续存在,在救济方面就可能涉及衡平救济如履约指令。此时错误方仍然可以不合情理抗辩,履约指令作为衡平法救济是法院的裁量权,如果法院同意会导致不合情理的后果就可以拒绝作出履约指令。这只是行使裁量权,不代表支持有衡平法错误。这在该权威书籍之 8 – 010 段说:"The only apparent 'divergence' between the treatment of mistake cases in common law and in equity is that the hardship that would be caused by granting specific performance of a contract made under either unilateral or common mistake may lead to the court refusing specific performance as a matter of discretion even though the mistake does not render the contract void or have any other effect at common law. As this is merely the denial of a particular remedy, and the contract remains binding in other respects (e. g. the claimant would still be entitled to damages if the contract were not performed) this is not a contradiction of the common law rules. Thus in cases of contractual mistake, common law and equity are consistent and equity plays only a minor role...."

另在接下来的 8 – 061 段说:"The decision in **The Great Peace does not prevent a common mistake that is not sufficient to make the contract void being used as a defence to an action for specific performance**. A specific performance is **a discretionary remedy**, and in the exercise of its discretion, a court may refuse an order for specific performance on the ground of a mistake by the defendant. Although the cases are nearly all ones in which the defendant unilaterally misunderstood the terms, it is submitted that the same approach should apply in a case in which the contract has been made under **a common mistake that was not sufficient to invalidate the contract at common law, if to enforce the contract specifically would cause particular hardship to the defendant**."(加黑部分是笔者的强调)

并在脚注介绍了 Heath v. Heath(2009)EWHC 1908(Ch)先例中,Purle QC 大法官说:"Considerations of this kind may justify the court in refusing the remedy of specific performance. Mistake as a vitiating element has been eliminated as a separate equitable doctrine by Great Peace Shipping Ltd v Tsavliris Salvage(International)Ltd...Nevertheless, specific performance is a discretionary remedy and mistake may in my judgment still be a relevant factor in refusing equitable relief, at all events where the mistake has been induced by the words or conduct of the person seeking specific performance. In such a case, of which I consider the present to be one, the mistake may also amount to, or be practically indistinguishable from, a misrepresentation.... It would not be right or fair, in those circumstances, for the agreement now to be specifically enforced."

另在稍后会简单介绍案情的 UTB LLC v. Sheffield United Ltd(2019)EWHC 2322

(Ch)先例中，也有同样说法，就是法院可以在不合情理的案件中拒绝作出履约指令。

最后只重提在上小段提 The “Great Peace”上诉庭先例可能在“先例理论”(doctrine of precedent)有疏忽大意(per incuriam)的问题，会否将来会有先例在适合的案情下(错误的程度无法达到普通法的要求令合约标的或目的有了根本性不同，但造成的结果又是十分不合情理)，其他的上诉庭或甚是高院以 The “Great Peace”与 Solle v. Butcher(1950)1 KB 671 先例有直接冲突或以 The “Great Peace”是疏忽大意为由，仍作出“衡平法错误”的救济？

15. 可诉错误的案例介绍

最后介绍一些会涉及可诉错误(无论是相互、单方面或是共同/共享)的案件，以显示这个法律说法的广泛适用性。虽然这个主张(或替代主张)是不容易成功，但在困境时提出仍是常见。或也可见到在战略上的好处，毕竟大部分的国际商业争议的最后解决仍是庭外和解，而在现实中也经常会遇到对手(或他们的代表律师)对这可诉错误的原则与说法只是似懂非懂。

读者较深入研究这些先例，需要考虑它们不同的时间段。例如在共同/共享错误，到了 Bell v. Lever Brothers Ltd(1932)AC 161 贵族院先例中，有了政策上的改变，目的是保证合约的肯定性与神圣性而收紧可诉错误的门槛。The “Great Peace”(2002)EWCA Civ 1407 上诉庭先例延续了这个政策，同时去否定了衡平法错误，可以说是更加收紧了错误的大门。

以下先节录部分在笔者的《合同法：国际商业游戏规则》(2000 年)旧版所介绍的较有关的案例，然后再介绍部分在 The “Great Peace”上诉庭先例后的近期先例。

15.1 《合同法：国际商业游戏规则》(2000 年)介绍的案例

1. 在 Kennedy v. Panama, New Zealand and Australian Royal Mail Co Ltd(1867)LR 2 QB 580 上诉庭先例中，被告的招股书(prospectus)提到需要资金去执行另一个利润很高的新西兰邮政服务合约。原告被招股书吸引去买进新发行的股票，但事后发觉该新西兰邮政合约是未得授权订立的，而新西兰政府也不肯去追认(ratify)。原告要求法院判这股票买卖自始无效，因为合约标的/目的在本质上搞错了。但高院认为既没有欺诈性误述，被告也没有对这邮政服务合约作出过任何保证。而在双方共同/共享错误方面(当年仍没有这种错误类别的区分)，该批新发行的股票与招股书所针对的公司股票并非有根本不同，仍是有价值的股票，被告公司仍在营业与赚取利润(只是没有原告期望的这么高)，而原告也已经拿到股票。所以，原告看来是因为没有满足本章之 8 段的要件而败诉。

2. Frederick E Rose(London)Ltd v. William H Pim Junior & Co Ltd(1953)2 QB 450 上诉庭先例，是一个对口头的买卖合约的标的有了共同/共享错误的例子。在一

个买卖合约,买方问能否提供"up to five hundred tons Moroccan horsebeans described here feveroles. please offer CIF Port Said"。

显然有关货物或商品是一种豆叫"horsebeans",但北非种植的 horsebeans 有好几种。英文只有这个字的统称,但法文却分为大果名为"feves"、小果名为"fevettes"、中果才称为"feveroles"。卖方不知道法文的"feveroles"的意思,就在收到买方的咨询后问了买方代表,在双方均是无辜的情况下,卖方以为他可提供的"North African horsebeans,fair average quality"就是买方要的商品品种,并作出付运,也通过信用证获得货款。但在卸港,买方发觉付运的是"feves",实与买方所需的"feveroles"大不相同,价值也有差别。由于买方已经支付,所以无意去要求令合约无效,只要求法院去变更(rectify)合约的货物描述,以利买方向卖方索赔金钱损失。一审法院同意去变更合约,但上诉庭推翻判决。上诉庭认为变更并不涉及双方主观的订约意图(想买卖"feveroles",不只是 horsebeans),而只客观看双方的言行/书信往来达成的合约同意了什么,正式合约是否有了共同错误即不正确记录需要变更。但在此案件并非这种情况,正如 Denning 大法官说:"Their agreement,as outwardly expressed,both orally and in writing,was for 'horsebeans'. That is all that the defendants ever committed themselves to supply,and all they should be bound to. There was,no doubt,an erroneous assumption underlying the contract-an assumption for which it might have been set aside on the ground of misrepresentation or mistake-but that is very different from an erroneous expression of the contract,such as to give rise to rectification."

3. 在 Oscar Chess Ltd v. Williams(1957)1 WLR 370 上诉庭先例中,案情涉及一个车辆的租购合约(hire-purchase contract),但 8 个月后原告才发觉 1939 年的车辆被误认为是 1948 年的车辆,这欺诈性改动车辆的记录是以前不知名人士干的并遗留下来,而现在的原告(一家车行)只是无辜误述。上诉庭认为双方有一个有根本重要性的对标的的错误理解,如果不是这么晚才发觉,错误足可以令合约无效。

4. 在 Scott v. Coulson(1903)2 Ch 249 上诉庭先例中,案情涉及一份人寿保险的合约被判为共同错误而自始无效,因为投保时保险的受保人已经死亡。

5. 在 Sheikh Bros Ltd v. Ochsner(1957)AC 136 枢密院先例中,案情涉及一个本质上是联营(joint venture)的许可合约(license agreement),Sheikh Bros 容许 Ochsber 进入它在肯尼亚的约 5000 亩土地去收割与生产一种制绳的麻(sisal),交换条件或对价是 Ochsner 要支付一笔钱加上每月交出 50 吨的麻。但双方在订约时不知道的事实是该块土地连 50 吨的麻也生产不出来,所以合约无法履行。这看来又是双方对订约时的事实有了共同/共享的错误假设,而合约中也没有规定谁要承担风险,所以贵族院判是合约自始无效。

6. 在 Amalgamated Investment and Property Co Ltd v. John Walker & Sons Ltd (1977)1 WLR 164 上诉庭先例中,案情是关系到一座建筑物(一个旧仓库)的买卖。合约订立之后,该座仓库被当局"列名"为(listed)受保护的建筑。这样,无法去重建,该仓库价值马上大跌，相差150万英镑之多。买方自然想去赖掉这个合约，但无法在受阻的原则下成立；因为有证据是买方订约前已知悉将来会面对这风险。“列名”为保护建筑不是无法预见的事件，估计只是买方没想到会这么早发生而已，想买了马上拆除后再重建，但措手不及。买方根据共同/共享错误主张合约自始无效，因为双方有一个错误假设该座仓库在订约时未被“列名”为保护建筑。

这关系到哪一天算是被“列名”为保护建筑。政府当局是在1973年8月22日内定该仓库被“列名”为保护建筑，双方订约是在9月25日，当局在9月26日出信通知这座仓库被“列名”为保护建筑，在9月27日生效。买方指“列名”的正确日期应算是8月22日，订约时双方已经是错误理解或假设了这个存在的事实，所以合约无效。

但上诉庭认为客观看何时被“列名”为保护建筑，肯定是指它公布生效的日期，不会是当局内定但外人并不知情的一天。所以判这先例所涉及的只是受阻的问题，但受阻并不能成立。

7. 在The “Amazonia”（1990）1 Lloyd's Rep 236先例中，案情涉及租船合约。租约内第33条合并了澳大利亚的《海上运输法》（这是澳大利亚引入1924年《海牙规则》）。在该立法下，Section 9是澳大利亚立法的特殊规定，规定货物装自澳大利亚必须受它的法院管辖，任何条文去否定会是“非法、空的与无效”（illegal, null and void and of no effect）。

但该租约内亦同时另有第34条说明双方有了争议去伦敦仲裁，并以英国法律作为租约适用法。可是因为有刚提到的立法，这伦敦仲裁条文其实被澳大利亚视为空的与无效。但双方的船东与承租人却不警觉，在真正出了争议后双方同意指定在伦敦的一名海事仲裁员为独任仲裁员。在过了一段长时间，尤其是已经超过了《海牙维斯比规则》下的索赔时效后，船东（在伦敦仲裁的被告）才发觉这个空子并企图取巧，向法院申请给予一个宣告（declaration）判仲裁协议被合约第33条合并的澳大利亚立法Section 9超越而无效。

承租人的主张是即使租约第34条无效，双方后来实际上通过言行达成另一份不受制于租约第33条，独立但内容与租约仲裁条文一致的临时仲裁合约开始伦敦仲裁。对于此主张，船东提出的一项重要争辩〔68〕就是即使存在临时仲裁合约，也是因为当事人错误理解在他们之间存在有效的租约仲裁条文，才会采取这样的言行（开始与推进仲裁），因此临时仲裁合约属于共同/共享错误无效。

上诉庭判对于英国法院而言，澳大利亚法律应属外国法，而当事人对外国法的错

〔68〕　其他主张，如假设适用英国法，是否仍然因为违反澳大利亚法律而在英国法律下不可执行，这可见本书第九章之4.2段的介绍。

误认知属于事实错误,[69]再加上承租人也没有针对错误进行实质性争辩与提交证据,因此上诉庭判无论是否达成一份独立的临时仲裁协议,都因为共同/共享错误而无效。

但是此先例中承租人还有另一个主张,即由于双方基于仲裁条文有效的共识,开始与推进一段长时间仲裁,而如果违背此共识承租人会受损害(索赔时效已经届满了),船东此时再要主张仲裁协议无效是不合情理/显失公平(unconscionable),因此船东被禁反言(estoppel)[70]不被允许这样取巧。

类似的租约/提单中合并的仲裁条文与立法冲突的情况,还有在 Indussa Corp. v. Ranborg(1967)2 Lloyd's Rep 101 先例中,美国上诉庭判提单内的一条挪威法院管辖权条文因违反了美国 1936 年的《海上运输法》无效。但之后美国最高院在 The "Sky Reefer"(1995)63 USLW 4617 先例中明确承认提单合约合并的东京仲裁条文并不违反 1936 年《海上运输法》。而即使是有违反,由于美国在更后的时间接受 1958 年《纽约公约》,而《纽约公约》要求缔约国接受有效的仲裁条文,因此如果这两个规则有冲突,也是要以后者即《纽约公约》为准。另 The "Tuapse"(2005)658 LMLN 2 先例也是涉及仲裁条文是否因加拿大立法的规定(与澳大利亚相同)而无效的争议。这方面在笔者《仲裁法:从 1996 年英国仲裁法到国际商务仲裁》一书第六章之 7.5 段与《提单与其他付运单证》(2016 年)一书第四章之 2.5.1 段有详细介绍。

8. 笔者(杨良宜)在 1992 年的一个伦敦海事仲裁,涉及一个 20 天左右的航次期租(Time-Charter-Trip),意图是去印度的 Mangalore 装运矿砂去中国。在刚订约后,双方才发觉唯一的装港 Mangalore 发生严重水灾并导致需要全港封闭,无限期拒绝船舶进港装矿砂。承租人以租约的共同/共享错误或受阻为由,指租约无效而不必履行与也履行不了。至于是"可诉错误"或是"合约受阻"的大原则适用,这主要是看政府封港的正式时间是早于还是晚于订约时间。

最后的裁决书是判可诉错误或受阻都不能成立,这租约为航次期租是主要原因。既然本质是期租,承租人在船舶的营运是有较大的灵活性,即使订约意图是去 Mangalore 装运矿砂,但短期内去不了也不代表不能去其他装港。加上严重水灾这种天气因素所导致的问题,一般也不会是拖太久,带来的困难只是短暂的。而且涉及延误,在一个期租合约下,时间损失的风险已经在明示条文或默示地位有很清楚的约定/规定,是承租人要去承担这方面的风险。

9. 在 Grains & Fourrages SA v. Huyton(1997)1 Lloyd's Rep 628 先例中,一艘名为"Ince"的船舶自中国装两票货去土耳其的 Izmir 港。这两票货的卸量是:(1)Chi-

---

〔69〕 当时还没有承认对法律的错误理解可以构成可诉错误,直到 Kleinwort Benson Ltd v. Lincoln City Council(1999)2 AC 349 贵族院先例改变了这个法律地位,现在事实或法律的错误都可以成立可诉错误。

〔70〕 这可见《合约的履行、弃权与禁反言》一书第六章之 7.5 段。

nese cotton seed expellers 12,717.71 吨；(2) Chinese cotton seed extracts 10,012.39 吨。

在 Izmir 港，买方聘请一家验货师去取了样本并出了两份针对两票货的证明，内容包括货量、水分、蛋白质、纤维等。其中与这争议有关是：(1) Chinese cottonseed expellers — 10,012.31 吨；oil (on a dry basis) 5.81%。(2) Chinese cottonseed extracts — 12,770.71 吨；oil (on a dry basis) 1.27%。

读者可注意到这两份证明的吨数看来与两票货的卸量并不配合。卖方收到这两份证明后先是不满意，但在进一步查询后双方认为是打错字(typing error)而同意把检验结果替换为：(1) Chinese cottonseed expellers—12,770.71 吨；oil 1.27%；(2) Chinese cottonseed extracts—10,012.31 吨；oil 5.81%。双方以此结果达成和解协议。

但事后买方不满意这和解协议。认为原先的协议有一个共同与根本性的错误假设，以为把检验证明的结果替换就可以了，殊不知技术上 Chinese cottonseed expellers 根本不可能有如此低的含油量(oil)。买方要是能去把和解协议变为无效，他的新索赔金额则会大大提高。

在 GAFTA 的仲裁庭，买方败诉，判他受原先和解协议约束。但上诉到法院，Mance 大法官同意有一个共同与根本性的错误假设，进而判买方胜诉，说："where the parties had sought to rectify the mistake, they were both mistaken as to the real error. Therefore, to enforce the rectification agreement would be contrary to the purpose of that agreement, namely to remove the mistake. The mistake was fundamental. There was no evidence that either party had accepted the risk of such mistake. Therefore, the contract was not binding on the parties."

15.2 John Lobb Ltd v. John Lobb SAS (2022) EWHC 2306 (Ch) 先例

接下来是在较近期被报道的先例中，首先介绍的是 John Lobb Ltd v. John Lobb SAS 先例。案情涉及 John Lobb 英国名牌皮鞋，自 1972 年，Lobb 家族的 Eric Lobb 先生就在英国与巴黎成立公司(区别是原告与被告)。到了 1976 年，被告巴黎公司被出售给法国的爱马仕(Hermes Paris)。在 1992 年，原告、被告与 Eric 达成一个长达 15 年的合约(可名为 Radlett 合约)，目的是合作在全球推广销售产品。在地理范围上是英国市场由原告负责，包括制造产品、推广与销售。而被告就负责在法国与全球的市场，被告也要负责登记与保护不断推出带有 John Lobb 商标的不同产品(如皮带、皮箱、鞋油等)。

到了 2006 年，Radlett 合约将要届满，双方开始谈判延续合作并最后达成了一个"2008 年合约"。该 2008 年合约中说明被告是 John Lobb 商标在全球除了英国外的"法律与实益所有权人"(legal and beneficial ownership)，并有附件说明在全球多处登记的商标详情。

但在 2008 年合约履行了 9 年后，原告有了异议，并在 2017 年 4 月 19 日通过律师将被告按照 2008 年合约按年支付的钱退还给被告。到了 2020 年中，原告也开始诉讼要求以共同/共享错误令 2008 年合约自始无效,并宣示 John Lobb 商标在全球(只除了法国)是原告所拥有。

而共同错误是双方在订立 2008 年合约时对谁是 John Lobb 商标的拥有人有错误理解或假设,特别原告说是受到代表被告的欧华律师事务所(DLA)的来函中对 John Lobb 商标的说法的影响,[71] 错误以为是共同拥有,是在此错误理解下,才会去订立这 2008 年合约。这显然也是被告的理解,所以是共同错误。

在此先例中,被告申请法院提前撤销索赔(strike out),[72] 原因是:(1)2008 年合约已经有同意与保证有关商标所有权的明示条文,也就是 The "Great Peace"(2002) EWCA Civ 1407 先例的第二个要件。而共同错误只是针对明示或默示没有针对风险分摊的事宜,如 Phillips 勋爵在 The "Great Peace" 上诉庭先例中说:"... the English doctrine of mistake ... fills a gap in the contract where it transpires that it is impossible of performance without the fault of either party, and the parties have not, expressly or impliedly, dealt with their rights and obligations in that eventuality."(2)合约不因这个共同错误(如果成立)而无法履行,也就是 The "Great Peace" 先例的第四个要件。这也表示该错误没有根本严重性,能够令合约自始无效。

一审[(2021) EWHC 1226(Ch)]被告的申请被法院拒绝,认为诉讼争议如双方在订立 2008 年合约前对 John Lobb 商标的共同假设到底是什么是事实敏感(fact-sensitive),需要开庭审理,在看了所有证据后才能去认定,不能在初步阶段提前去草率处理。至于对被告提的两点,Marsh 大法官不同意,说:

"I turn briefly to deal with the two elements that are relied upon by the Defendant.

The first element relates to whether there is a 'warranty' that the state of affairs, which is said to have been the common understanding of the parties, exists. The starting point is the contract itself. The court must be in a position to construe the terms of the contract and to determine whether it deals with who bears the risk of the relevant mistake. As the element is described in Chitty, it is that neither party bears the risk of the situation being as it really proves to be.

The common understanding relied upon by the claimant is that the defendant held the legal and beneficial ownership of the Mark. The defendant says that there is no gap in the contract and the 2008 Agreement contains a 'warranty' about the legal and beneficial ownership of the Mark being vested in the defendant. Recital G of the agreement states in terms that this is so and the terms of the contract are clearly based upon this premise. In clause 1.3 the claimant acknowledges the defendant's 'ownership rights in the Mark'. ...

---

[71] 所以这个案件也涉及在本书第十一章介绍的不当影响的争议。

[72] 这课题在笔者的《证据法:国际规管与诉讼中的证据攻防》一书第六章之 4 段有详论。

As it seems to me, it is not possible to construe the 2008 Agreement as containing a warranty by the claimant that the defendant is the legal and beneficial owner of the Mark, or for the contract be taken to allocate the risk in the event that the assumption is wrong. The common understanding is clear from Recital G and clause 1. 3**. The contract does not go on to specify what is to happen if that understanding proves to be wrong**.

It is impossible to conclude that the claimant's case on this point is bound to fail and the claimant has a real prospect of showing that there is no allocation of risk between the parties about how the 2008 Agreement is to operate if the common understanding proves to be wrong.(以上是说2008年合约虽然有针对商标,写明共同的理解是被告对商标有法律与实益所有权,但没有针对如果后来发觉这共同理解错误,应如何处理,谁承担这错误的风险。)

I turn to**the second element** that Mr Davies(被告代表大律师)says is absent. Mr Mill(原告代表大律师)accepts that the contract was not impossible to perform. The defendant has made substantial payments to the claimant which it has accepted, the defendant has continued to take steps to protect the Marks and the parties together have respected the operation of the agreement that leaves the UK market to the claimant. If it is the case that impossibility of performance is a sine qua non, then it must follow that the claim is bound to fail.

It is clear, however, that**impossibility of performance may need to be measured against the common assumption**; the test may also be that performance is essentially different to that common assumption. If that is the test, the defendant is unable to show that the claimant's case with regard to the second element that is relied upon is bound to fail.(原告代表大律师同意2008年合约确实可以被履行,例如被告不断在支付钱给原告;被告不断在全球登记与保护商标等。而法院认为这里可能被作为测试标准的,是不以当事人的共同错误假设就无法履行,或者是履行会与以当事人的共同错误假设履行有本质不同。在此先例中,双方共同假设被告拥有商标权益,所以被告支付钱给原告并在全球登记与保护商标等。但如果被告不拥有商标权益,就无法这样履行合约。被告无法说明原告在这一点上一定败诉。)"(加黑部分是笔者的强调)

本案不是一个全面审理的案件,而只是针对提前撤销索赔申请的审理,所以不会全面分析这些争议。以上只是展示错误在实际案例中是怎么来的。类似的情况相信中国公司也会遇到,也就是听对方律师的解释,签对方准备好的合约,事后才发现有问题。

但之后被告上诉,并获得了撤销索赔的命令。法院仍然根据The "Great Peace"先例的五个要件判断。针对第一个被告的第一个问题,认为合约条文已经明示将对商标所有权的共同假设错误的风险分摊给了原告:"The answer to that question, as a matter of construction of the 2008 Agreement in general, and Clause 1 in particular seems to me to be obvious.(原告)was being required to agree,in terms,that(被告)did indeed own the Trade Marks;in other words that the Assumed State of Affairs did in fact exist. By this means the parties secured the assumption which underlay Clause 1;namely that the(被告)was in a position to licence the use of the Trade Marks to(原告)in the manner set out in Clause 1. As I have said, the parties might have left this assumption unexpressed. Instead,(原告)was required to acknowledge that the Assumed State of Affairs was correct. As such,it seems to me that the risk of the Assumed State of Affairs turning out to be wrong was allocated to(原告)."

这样,原告就没有机会成功以共同错误撤销合约:"Drawing together all of the above discussion I conclude that the Respondent has no real,or indeed any prospect of succeeding in its claim to avoid the 2008 Agreement on the basis of common mistake. I reach this conclusion on the basis that,as a matter of construction of the 2008 Agreement, the risk of the Assumed State of Affairs turning out to be wrong was allocated to the Respondent."

而针对被告的第二点,法院也接受共同错误并没有令合约无法履行。Edwin Johnson 大法官首先总结了过往先例中,说第四个要件的判断标准是:(1)是否令合约无法履行;或(2)是否令合约的标的或目的有了本质不同。Edwin Johnson 大法官说:"It seems to me that the effect of these authorities is that the test which falls to be applied,in relation to the Fourth Element identified by Lord Phillips,can legitimately be framed in two alternative ways;as a test of impossibility of performance or as a test of essential and radical difference in the subject matter of the relevant contract. It also seems to me that there is not,and is not intended to be a material difference between these two tests."

但"令合约的标的或目的有本质不同"与一审的 Marsh 大法官"履行有本质不同"是不同的测试:"I do not think that the Fourth Element test is whether 'performance is essentially different to that common assumption'. The alternative test to impossibility of performance is whether the relevant mistake renders the relevant subject matter of the contract essentially and radically different from the subject matter which the parties believed to exist. The difference in wording may be said not to be significant,but in my view it matters,because of the importance,in the present case,of concentrating upon the subject matter of the 2008 Agreement,and asking the question whether the mistake which the parties must be assumed to have made as to the ownership of the Trade Marks had the effect of rendering that subject matter essentially and radically different from the subject matter which the parties believed to exist. In order to answer that question it is essential to examine what the parties agreed to do under the 2008 Agreement."

而双方对商标所有权的错误假设(如果有),并没有令合约的标的或目的有本质

不同。Edwin Johnson 大法官说:

"The subject matter of the 2008 Agreement was not the equivalent of a transaction comprising a transfer of title to property. The 2008 Agreement regulated the future business relationship between the parties principally, but not exclusively, in relation to the future use of the Trade Marks. The subject matter of the 2008 Agreement is not easily reduced to any brief words of description, because it contains a suite of rights and obligations, ranging from rights and obligations concerning the use of the Trade Marks, through financial rights and obligations, to rights and obligations of pre-emption. So far as the subject matter of the 2008 Agreement can be reduced to brief words of description, the subject matter of the 2008 Agreement was concerned with the regulation of the future business relationship between the parties, including their respective spheres of operation.

There are various ways in which this can be illustrated. All of the provisions of the 2008 Agreement have been and remain perfectly capable of operation by reference to the True State of Affairs (meaning the state of affairs which must be assumed to be the true state of affairs for present purposes). If one considers whether the mistake of the parties has robbed the 2008 Agreement of its essential purpose, the answer seems to me to be in the negative. The essential purpose, or more accurately the essential purposes of the 2008 Agreement can still be served, by reference to the True State of Affairs. The subject matter of the 2008 Agreement, comprising the suite of rights and obligations contained therein, is still intact, notwithstanding that the Assumed State of Affairs has turned out to be wrong."

最后 Edwin Johnson 大法官也不认为有关的争议是事实敏感,而完全是解释合约的问题,因此最后作出了撤销索赔的简易判决。

15.3 Green v. Petfre (Gibraltar) Ltd (t/a Betfred) (2021) EWHC 842 (QB) 先例

在 Green v. Petfre (Gibraltar) Ltd (t/a Betfred) 先例中,涉及网络赌博,原告网上玩了 5.5 个小时,赢了 170 多万英镑。被告拒付,指出电脑出错,这导致原告提起诉讼。被告提出的抗辩包括了共同/共享错误。法院根据 The "Great Peace" (2002) EWCA Civ 1407 上诉庭先例不接受错误的抗辩,因为错误并没有导致合约不能履行,只不过令被告在财务上吃亏。而电脑出错亦可以算是被告自己的过错(与风险)。Foster 大法官判没有错误说:"Mr Osborne (被告代表大律师) argued that Nr Green (原告) and Bedfred (被告) proceeded on a shared but mistaken belief that the Game was functioning properly according to its intended design and the rules. ... Mr Courser (原告代表大律师) submits that ... it just cannot be said that the performance of the contract was rendered impossible by the alleged mistake. I agree. The contract of gaming were performed, albeit not as profitably to Betfred as they believed they would be. Further, it cannot properly be said in my view that the state of affairs was not the fault of the provider of the gaming services, Bedfred … the mistake did not render the contract incapable of performance, just less advantageous to one party."

15.4 UTB LLC v. Sheffield United Ltd(2019)EWHC 2322(Ch)先例

此先例案情涉及英国谢菲尔德联足俱乐部的股权买卖。被告的实际控制人是一位居住在英国南约克郡谢菲尔德的商人,他在20世纪90年代买下该俱乐部,但到了满65岁后,想要脱身并为俱乐部寻找新的投资者。当时在2012、2013年时俱乐部还只是在踢英国甲级联赛,不是一个赚钱的俱乐部,并且在新的投资者注资后仍然会亏损,直到俱乐部能够晋级英超联赛才会赚大钱(数据显示两个赛季就会有3亿英镑收入)。被告为了令俱乐部的交易价格不要太高,从而看起来更吸引投资者,成立了一家新公司Blades,将名下所有俱乐部的股权转给该新公司。但与俱乐部相关的5项物业,包括体育场、酒店、训练场地与办公楼,仍然留在被告自己的名下,等将来新的投资者通过继续注资或者行使购买选择权(call option)等方式获得超过75%的股权或俱乐部晋级到英超联赛后,该5项物业再转给俱乐部。

原告公司(UTB)背后的控制人是沙特阿拉伯的王子Abdullah bin Mosaad bin Abdulaziz al Saud,他通过UTB与被告在2013年订立了投资与股东协议(Investment and Shareholder Agreement, ISA)。原告在两年内分期共注资1000万英镑入股Blades公司,获得50%股份。在ISA内有两条重要的条文:一条是购买选择权条文,在该条文下双方可以行使选择权购买对方手中持有的股份;另一条为物业购买权(property assets option)条文,也就是如果UTB行使了购买选择权买入被告持有的50%股份后持有超过75%的股份,又或是俱乐部晋级到英超联赛(届时收入大增),UTB就必须以一笔高昂的价格买回该5项物业。显然这样的设计或安排也是配合被告背后的英国商人想赚一大笔从俱乐部脱身,实现真正退休的意愿。

双方各持Blades的50%股份,类似是以合伙人关系来共同运营这个亏本并仍停留在甲级联赛的俱乐部。在过程中,双方也开始在继续注资与管理权问题上不断发生争议,直到2017年11月关系彻底破裂。被告行使ISA中的购买选择权,向UTB发出行权通知,要以500万英镑的价格买回原告名下的50%的股份。根据ISA中购买选择权条文的规定,UTB如果在收到行权通知后的一个月内,向被告发出反行权通知,则被告要将名下50%的股份卖给UTB。所以在UTB收到被告行权通知后,被迫向被告发出了反行权通知,双方达成了股权转让协议。但为了避免因此而成为超过75%股份的持有人而要根据ISA下的物业购买权条文以高昂价格买回有关的5项物业,UTB耍了一个小聪明(其实是没有用)——在收到被告行权通知后的一个月内,UTB成立了一家新公司,并以1英镑的名义对价将40%的Blades股权转给该新成立的公司,并且在支付500万英镑给被告时,要求被告直接将30%的Blades股权转给他的律师和10%的Blades股权转给另外一位沙特王子(UTB背后老板的兄弟)。这样,名义上UTB从来没有拥有超过75%的Blades股权,不会触发必须以高价买回 5 项物业的物业购买权条文。

此先例的诉讼很复杂，双方涉及多项不同争议/争端。而可诉错误只是其中一个次要的争议/争端。这是被告提出的一个抗辩，指他存在单方面错误(unilateral mistake)，要求法院判合约无效。这单方面错误理解或假设是 UTB 在取得全部的股权后会按照 ISA 的约定同时让俱乐部履行购买 5 项物业的义务。而 UTB 根本就是知道被告的想法，从而故意安排分散股权导致不能达到 ISA 中约定的持股比例的 75%，存在取巧(sharp practice)。

高院的 Fancourt 大法官判 UTB 分散股权的行为不影响他实际上满足 75% 持股比例的条件，俱乐部仍然要根据 ISA 履行购买 5 项物业的义务。但是 Fancourt 大法官拒绝了被告提出的单方面错误的抗辩，说只有在搞错了对方订约方的身份(identity)[73]与合约内容或条件(terms)，[74]而对方也是知道的情况下，法律才会有救济，但不是在单方面搞错了其他的事实/事情(购买 5 项物业是 ISA 下的事情，不是股权转让合约下的事情，所以充其量只是有关系)，如对方 UTB 的动机，被告没有想到 UTB 会通过分散股权而令 ISA 中的物业购买权条文中的条件不能被满足。这不属于普通法承认的可以给予法律救济的单方面错误的类别。

Fancourt 大法官在判词中节录 Aikens 大法官在 The "Harriette N"(2008) EWHC 2257(Comm)案例中对此问题的总结说：

"...The general rule at common law is that if one party has made a mistake as to the terms of the contract and that mistake is known to the other party, then the contract is not binding. The reasoning is that although the parties appear, objectively, to have agreed terms, it is clear that they are not in agreement. Therefore the normal rule of looking only at the objective agreement of the parties is displaced and the court admits evidence to show what each side subjectively intended to agree by way of terms. If it is clear from such evidence that there was no consensus, then there can be no contract, because the parties have not truly agreed on the terms. Some of the cases talk of such a contract being 'void', but I think it is clearer to say that there was never a contract at all.

However, if one party has made a mistake about a fact on which he bases his decision to enter into the contract, but that fact does not form a term of the contract itself then, even if the other party knows that the first is mistaken as to this fact, the contract will be binding. That was the effect of the decision... in Smith v Hughes(1871) LR 6 QB 597, ...The correctness of that decision and the analysis in it has never been doubted."

15.5 British Red Cross v. Werry(2017) EWHC 875(Ch)先例

在 British Red Cross v. Werry 先例中，案情涉及两位长期同居的男女，男士(H)

---

〔73〕 见本章第 12 段介绍。

〔74〕 见本章第 11 段介绍。

在2008年突然死亡。在以为没有留下遗嘱的情况下,H的遗产继承人是H的15位亲属如侄子侄女,但什么也没有留给多年共同生活的女士(D)。之后继承人与D在2011年达成庭外和解,包括D可以在H拥有的房屋中住下去。H的遗产也为此成立了一个信托(trust)。D在2014年死亡,并在她的遗嘱中将财产捐了给5家慈善机构(包括红十字会、动物保护协会等)。这难免又带来5家慈善机构与H遗产的信托人之间的争议。其间,在清理D死亡后的房屋时找出了H的一份遗嘱,其中清楚地将所有的财产都留给了D。这样,5家慈善机构实是应该获得所有财产,并申请法院宣告2011年的庭外和解协议无效,因为双方(D与H的亲属)有共同/共享错误。Elizabeth Cooke大法官同意,说:"The appellants say that the settlement agreement was entered into in ignorance on the part of all parties of the vital fact that Mr. Harding(**H**)had left the property to Miss Deeley(**D**)in his will. The will gave her far more than she received under that agreement,and it is perfectly obvious that the agreement would not have been made had the will been discovered. The mistake is as fundamental as that referred to by Lord Atkin in Bell v Lever Bros[1932]AC 161,where a party contracted to purchase land that he or she already owned."

15.6 Credit Suisse AG v. Up Energy Group Ltd(2013)EWHC 3611(Comm)先例

该案中原告瑞信与被告有中方背景的公司UEGL订立了一份买卖合约,买卖的标的为被告子公司发行的面值1.5亿港币的可转换公司债券,该子公司为中国香港上市公司。与此同时,瑞信又与UEGL订立了一份回购选择权契约。该契约约定瑞信可以行使选择权要求UEGL回购该笔可转换公司债券。本案中双方对买卖合约没有争议,而争议的焦点在于该契约。瑞信要求UEGL根据契约的规定回购该笔可转换公司债券,在被拒绝后,向法院申请简易判决[75]要求UEGL履行契约下的债务。

UEGL最主要的抗辩为在订立契约时双方存在共同/共享错误。该共同错误是指双方均错误以为UEGL可以回购该笔可转换公司债券,但实际上UEGL并不能购买。因为债券的第2.4条规定这些债券不能转给发行公司的关联人[2.4 The permitted assignment or transfer of this Note…may only be made to person(s)which are not connected persons of the Company(as defined in the Listing Rules)]。而根据港交所上市规则,UEGL是它子公司的关联人。这样,UEGL根本无法回购该笔可转换公司债券。

瑞信的一个主要的反驳是共同错误不成立,因为契约的第7.2(b)(ii)条约定UEGL在回购时可以要求瑞信将该笔债券转给UEGL自己或者是UEGL指定的人选。UEGL完全可以将该笔债券卖给其他不是发行公司关联人的第三人,进而要求瑞信将该笔债券转给该第三人即可。UEGL抗辩说瑞信提出的交易方法根本不是双

---

〔75〕 这课题在笔者的《证据法:国际规管与诉讼中的证据攻防》一书第六章之4段有详论。

方订约时的想法,也与契约中约定的根本不同。整个契约就是为了让 UEGL 而不是其他第三人来回购。至于第 7.2(b)(ii)条中提到的 UEGL 指定的人选(as it may direct)是指由 UEGL 指定的名义持有人,而这些名义持有人也一样会被视为关联人,从而无法履行。瑞信另外也提出契约中全面保护它利益的有关条文也已经明确了相关的风险是在 UEGL。

高院的 Hamblen 大法官同意 UEGL 的立场,即瑞信提出的将债权卖给非关联人的第三人的交易方式与契约根本性不同,而契约条文也并没有清楚无误地将 UEGL 不能回购这个问题的风险转给 UEGL,要解释契约条文与探究双方订立契约时的共同想法,需要进一步的证据与审理,从而原告简易判决的申请被拒绝。

15.7 Dany Lions Ltd v. Bristol Cars Ltd(2013)EWHC 2997(QB)先例

在 Dany Lions Ltd v. Bristol Cars Ltd 先例中,案情是涉及一辆原告购买的限量古董汽车(在 60 年前只制造了 43 辆)并与被告订约以 15.3 万英镑的对价对该汽车进行全面改装,其中部分重要工作是在该汽车上安装一个自动变速箱(automatic gearbox)。但后来工作没有推进,因为发觉不能安装自动变速箱,否则会影响该汽车的性能。这导致双方的诉讼并带来了该改装合约是否因共同/共享错误而自始无效的争议。这共同错误就是双方在订约时错误假设以为可以改装与履行该合约。这可节录被告在抗辩请求说:"The said … agreement was entered into on the basis of a fundamental shared mistake between the parties, that it was possible to convert the car's transmission to automatic whilst retaining the car's full functionality. It would not in fact have been possible to do so. The car has a high-revving engine, which is not suitable to conversion to automatic transmission. The works were therefore impossible to perform and the agreement was void for common mistake."

针对该不成功的共同错误抗辩,一方面是在该合约中,被告有保证并承担这方面的合约责任(风险),Seymour 大法官说:"the Defendant has warranted that it would be possible to perform the relevant contractual obligation, which is to fix an automatic gearbox. …was there a common assumption as to the existence of a state of affairs such as to give rise potentially to a mistake? I think the answer obviously is no, the position simply was that the Defendant assumed a contractual obligation to supply and fit an automatic gearbox."

另一方面是安装自动变速箱只是合约标的/目的(车辆改装)的部分工作,Seymour 大法官说:"the inability… to perform its contractual obligation without adverse consequences for the performance of the car did not render performance of the contract impossible. The greater part of the contract was wholly unaffected by whether the automatic gearbox could be supplied and fitted or not."

也就是说,如果合约继续存在而被告又确实实际上不能安装自动变速箱,就构成违约,要对这部分的无法履行作出金钱赔偿。

15.8 Golden Ocean Group Ltd v. Humpuss Intermoda Transportasi Tbk Ltd & Genuine Maritime Ltd(2013)EWHC 1240(Comm)先例

此先例是一个在本章之12.4.1段介绍的名字搞错/误名(misnomer)的案例。原告(挪威公司)作为承租人期租了“Barito”轮,为期1年,但结果是早了4个月还船。原告向作为二船东(disponent owner)的被告(第一被告HIT是印尼上市公司,第二被告Genuine是HIT的新加坡子公司HST拥有的另一家巴拿马公司)索赔多支付的租金与还船时的船上燃油共180万美元,但被告向原告反索赔600万美元,作为提早还船的损失赔偿。[76] 原告根据书信往来中达成的租约(fixture)启动了伦敦仲裁,但被告(以Genuine的名义)在印尼法院提起了向原告的诉讼。其间双方也各自向对方提前取得担保:原告在美国纽约通过Rule B Attachment[77]的手段,而被告通过扣押(arrest in rem)[78]了一艘原告租用的“Golden Joy”轮。

双方试图达成和解,但谈判并不成功。双方(原告与Genuine)也达成一个协议,以附件(addendum)同意各自终止伦敦仲裁与印尼法院诉讼,并去新加坡仲裁解决双方争议。

但之后原告再向HIT启动伦敦仲裁,也拒绝参与Genuine启动的新加坡仲裁,理由是双方有了相互错误(mutual mistake)或共同错误(common mistake)。因为实际上原告一开始就告诉经纪人只愿意与HIT订约,因为是上市公司,财雄势大,所以租约中的二船东应该是HIT而不是Genuine。而约定去新加坡仲裁的附件是原告与Genuine之间订立的,属于对租约的订约方有错误理解,应是自始无效。原告同时向英国法院申请:(1)宣告期租合约是与HIT订立;(2)对Genuine启动的新加坡仲裁作出一个禁止仲裁的禁令(anti-arbitration injunction);(3)其他救济,但与可诉错误无关,不多去介绍。

法院认为在这个中间申请中决定是否存在错误是不可能的,应留待将来的全面审理,现在原告已经证明了此争议有可能成功。此外在考虑了各种因素之后,法院决定给出临时禁止仲裁的禁令,但因为与可诉错误无关,所以不详细介绍。

15.9 Apvodedo NV v. Collins(2008)EWHC 775(Ch)先例

此先例的案情涉及买卖伦敦丽兹酒店(Ritz Hotel)的骗局。丽兹酒店是全世界知名的酒店品牌,而位于伦敦的丽兹酒店更是久负盛名。一位姓Lee的先生与本案的被告Collins先生就买卖丽兹酒店的交易进行接洽。在交易当时,市场上公开知道丽兹酒店是属于亿万富翁Barclay兄弟。Barclay兄弟一向行事神秘与低调,所以Lee先生就自称是Barclay兄弟的生意伙伴,现在准备以2亿英镑从Barclay兄弟处买入丽兹酒店,并愿意以2.5亿英镑的价格进一步卖给被告所在的房地产投资公司

---

〔76〕 杨大明律师《期租合同》一书第六篇之6.5段。

〔77〕 在笔者《仲裁法:从开庭审理到裁决书的作出与执行》一书第三章之3.9段有简单提及。

〔78〕 见杨良宜《海事法》(1999年)一书第一章之6-18段的详细介绍。

LAH。在双方商谈的过程中,Lee 先生声称另有买家愿意出更高的价格来购买丽兹酒店,不过 Lee 先生仍然愿意按照之前谈好的价格以 2.5 亿英镑与 LAH 订约。但是 Lee 先生提出为了显示 LAH 有充足的资金来履行价格高昂的合约与将相关的文件(装满了 27 个纸箱,包括买卖丽兹酒店所做过的尽职调查文件、将会取得的买卖丽兹酒店的合约与有关的产权文件等,Lee 先生声称大部分摆放在他律师的办公室)转交给 LAH,LAH 需要先支付 100 万英镑,如果 Lee 先生与 Barclay 兄弟的交易不成功,他会将这 100 万英镑归还给 LAH。LAH 没有这么多的资金在手中,而且它购买丽兹酒店也并不是为了自己经营,而是再进一步找买家,从中赚取差价。

于是被告就找到了原告。原告是荷兰的公司,它准备买入丽兹酒店并自己经营。于是被告与原告就订立了一份独家协议(exclusivity agreement)。[79] 该独家协议是在 6 个星期的时间内,被告只与原告独家谈判以 2.585 亿英镑的价格出售丽兹酒店的交易。该协议中在本案最关键的一个条文是第 10 条,该条文约定原告支付给 Lee 先生 100 万英镑以换取 Lee 先生将 27 箱文件交给原告,如果在一个固定的时间之前 Lee 先生没有成功购买丽兹酒店,被告就会归还这 100 万英镑给原告。

在原告支付了 100 万英镑给 Lee 先生之后,Lee 先生的骗局被揭发,因为根本不存在这 27 箱文件,所以 Lee 先生也无法转交这些不存在的文件给原告。Lee 先生的真实身份是一个失业的货车司机,并且在与 LAH 谈判期间,他一直是被宣告破产的债务人。

原告于是申请法院的简易判决,要求被告履行独家协议的第 10 条归还 100 万英镑。被告作为同样受骗上当的人士,提出了双方对 27 箱文件是否存在的事实有一个共同的错误理解,所以根据共同错误,独家协议是无效的。而原告则对比 The "Great Peace"(2002)EWCA Civ 1407 上诉庭先例中确立的五个条件,认为其中第 1、4 与 5 都不成立。第 10 条已经明确对 Lee 先生交不出文件的风险进行分摊,即被告要归还 100 万英镑。而且即使搞错了 27 箱文件是否存在,也不会令被告根本无法履行归还 100 万英镑的合约义务。

Henderson 大法官倾向于认为表面看来确实有共同错误的存在,这包括其中双方确实都搞错了 27 箱文件是否存在的事实。而且根据案情和本案非常类似的 Associated Japanese Bank International Ltd. v. Credit du Nord SA(1989)1 WLR 225 先例,[80] 一方能够履约并不代表不能成立共同错误。至于独家协议的明示条文是否没有任何限制地将风险放在被告的身上与合约条文是否反映了双方对存在骗局这一风险有充分考虑,则是需要进一步的证明。所以,整体来看,被告提出的共同错误抗辩并非完全站不住脚,而需要进一步根据双方提供口头证词说明当时到底是如何理解这个问

---

〔79〕 这看来有互锁协议(lock-out contract)的意思,有关互锁协议可见笔者《合约的解释:规则与应用》一书第二章之 6.4 段的介绍。

〔80〕 该先例在本章之 13.3 段有介绍。

题与全面的文件披露来进行全面的审理。所以并不适合以简易判决的程序来做决定。

该案例与本章稍早的15.2段与15.8段介绍的案例一样,法院只是初步对错误的问题表达看法,而不会在有进一步的审理前做任何决定。由于错误和欺诈的争议一样,都会涉及大量事实的认定,所以通过预先程序来判决的机会不大。但是不少诉讼方仍然会走这个预先程序,例如尝试申请简易判决。背后的原因可能是策略性的,在笔者《证据法:国际规管与诉讼中的证据攻防》一书第六章之4.3.4段有介绍。

15.10 Champion Investments Ltd v. Ahmed(2004)EWHC 1956(QB)先例

此先例的案情涉及在本书第五章之6.3.3.3.1段脚注有提及的合法高利贷与"汤姆林命令"(Tomlin Order)[81]等课题。原告向被告分两期作出共100万英镑的短期借贷,据说是给被告用作炒股投机(share speculation)。显然,这在2003年7月15日订立的合约利息是十分高昂并在不同的时间段有不同的利息:第一个月的月息是8%,之后的周息是2.5%,到了10月6日(也是应该归还本金一天)后的周息是4%。

被告没有全数还债,只是断断续续地多次归还部分,直到9月19日总共还了88万英镑。在11月6日,原告启动诉讼程序,索赔余下欠款(至11月4日)391,071.33英镑。原告也很快为这笔欠债向法院申请一个简易判决(summary judgment),但早一天,被告通过代表律师向原告律师以支票归还了12万英镑。可以说至此,本金已经是全数归还,剩下的只是部分欠下的利息。这利息不容易计算,除了不同期间的不同利率,借贷与归还都涉及了很多不同日期,并且归还的部分中多少是本金与多少是利息是有争议,需要以Excel表格去计算。

反正双方代表律师告诉法院他们需要时间探讨能否达成和解。原告希望以利率稍作让步去和解,但被告则希望以一笔固定金额和解。这得出一个55,000英镑的金额,根据被告律师准备的Excel表格显示这大约相等于45%年利率。双方也以此达成和解,并获法院批准去作出汤姆林命令,中止诉讼。

但由于Excel表格中提取贷款日期填错,所以55,000英镑只应是33%年利率,而按45%利率计算应该是89,250英镑。原告在发觉错误后,向法院申请撤销汤姆林命令,也相当于令和解协议无效。原告是以共同/共享错误或单方面错误为依据,但都不被法院支持。其中针对共同错误,不被支持的理由是错误并没有令和解协议有了根本性不同,即错误严重程度不够,不至于和解协议自始无效。另是,和解协议仍可以履行。Blair QC大法官说:"In my view, the mistake in the parties' understanding in that regard did not prevent a contract from coming into existence. Nor, applying the tests set out in Bell v Lever, and the Great Peace, did it make the settlement of the interest claim essentially different from what the parties believed it to be, nor did it render per-

---

〔81〕 这课题在笔者的《证据法:国际规管与诉讼中的证据攻防》一书第四章之1.7.6段有详论。

formance of the contract impossible."

至于单方面错误，不被支持的理由是原告主张的单方面错误要成立必须是被告知道或应该知道原告搞错，并有取巧的味道令客观看来不作出救济是不合情理。但在此先例中，被告律师对他准备的 Excel 表格内的错误并不知情。Blair QC 大法官说："a contract may be affected by unilateral mistake on the part of one party if the other party ought reasonably to have known of the mistake, even if he did not in fact know of it. Mance J（这是指在 OT Africa Line Ltd v. Vickers Plc [1996] 1 Lloyd's Rep 700 先例）was however discussing the situation in which a settlement offer had been made by the solicitor for one party, the question being whether the solicitor for the other party should have realised that a mistake had been made in the terms of the offer. In the present case, Mr Fenwick（被告代表律师）created his spreadsheet in November 2003, as part of preparing the defence ... has submitted that even if (as I have held) Mr Fenwick did not in fact realise that the drawdown period was earlier..."

15.11　Bank of China (HK) Ltd v. Keen Lloyd Energy Ltd (2012) HKEC 421 中国香港特区上诉庭先例

此先例涉及中国银行（香港）[前身为新华银行，在 2001 年和宝生银行与其他 9 家中资银行合并成为中国银行（香港）]向被告追偿一笔巨额坏账，金额为 564,896,223.78 港元。被告公司背后的集团主席钱锦超在 1998 年 11 月至 1999 年 4 月期间向新华银行根据他们之间的信贷（banking facilities）申请与开出信用证（Letter of Credit），并以假文件结汇（因为背后没有真正的交易），欺骗新华银行，也因此后来在 2004 年 3 月被香港特区法院判刑事串谋（连同新华银行 4 位管理人员）欺诈/欺骗新华银行，判监禁 6 年半。

被告（公司清盘人）以非法与共同/共享错误作为抗辩。非法是指新华银行的贷款远超出中国《商业银行法》第 39 条第 4 款，对同一借款人的贷款余额与商业银行资本余额的比例不得超 10%。香港特区《银行业条例》第 81(1) 条也有类似规定，在香港特区注册成立的认可机构必须遵守法定限额，对任何一个人或一组相关人士的总财务风险不得超过认可机构资本基础的 25%。虽然该法不适用于在内地注册的银行（新华银行总部在上海），但立法精神同样适用，银行需要严格管理其信贷风险，避免风险高度集中于任何特定借款人。事实上，香港特区金管局曾机密发函给中国银行总行的一个独立办事处 HKMRO（该办事处负责管理、监督与协调中国银行集团在港澳特区的银行），该 1998 年 4 月 16 日的机密信函指出 Keen Lloyd Group 在 1998 年 2 月底为止，已获新华银行授予的信贷总额为 18.27 亿港元，已成为新华银行最大借款人，总风险敞口占其资本基础的 25%。

在此诉讼中，这非法的抗辩不被接受。原因是案件发生在香港特区，借贷也只是香港特区法律适用与管辖。但这方面与另一个共同错误的抗辩有关。

这共同错误是指原告（前新华银行）的信贷是双方合约的标的，而双方订约时对原告这样做是合法有共同错误理解与假设,但其实不是,被告也是后来才知悉。但这被法院拒绝,第一点是共同错误必须不涉及双方的过错或不小心,但原告显然是有过错(更不说是已经提及新华银行有4个前管理人员因串谋而判刑)。上诉庭说:"the 1st defendant is unable to satisfy on the pleadings the requirement that the 'non-existence of the state of affairs must not be attributable to the fault of either party' because according to the 1st defendant, it was the plaintiff's lending which breached the prescribed ratio. Hence the non-existence of the state of affairs was attributable to the fault of the plaintiff."

此外,被告也无法满足共同错误的另一个要件,就是错误的理解与假设令合约无法履行。但在此先例中,借贷合约是完全履行了。上诉庭说:"The 1st defendant only relied on mistake 14 years after the facilities were granted and after it had enjoyed the benefit of millions of dollars of facilities. This only shows that the 1st defendant is unable to fulfilled another essential requirement of common mistake, namely, that the non-existence of affairs(信贷违法) must render contractual performance impossible. In this case there was performance of the contract."

另是银行的信贷是随时可以撤回,新华银行可以在香港特区金管局于1998年4月16日作出信函忠告时或其他时间去撤回违法信贷。所以共同错误令借贷合约自始无效是不被接受。

上诉庭最后的理由是此案件已经是诉讼连绵,涉及十多次不同方面的诉讼。被告不在较早之前的诉讼中去提出这个共同错误,而在多年后才提出,显然是"事后诸葛亮"(after-thought),并构成"一事不再审"(issue estoppel)。[82]

16. 这并非我的协议(*non est factum*)

这种错误是一方当事人在合约签了字,然后说他签错了,要推翻签署了的合约,说这合约并非我同意的协议(this is not my deed),也是拉丁文的所谓 *non est factum*。

但照说一方当事人在一份签了字的正式合约中,[83]是不能以自己搞错了条文、没有细看、不懂英文、无知等理由去推翻合约。所以 *non est factum* 这类错误只是局限适用在因一方当事人有特殊不利地位(special disability)[84],所以他签字的合约与他当时以为他所签的合约并不是同一回事的情况。

---

〔82〕 见可见笔者《合约的履行、弃权与禁反言》一书第九章之7段。

〔83〕 本章之6.2.2段已有详论。

〔84〕 这与本书第十一章之2段介绍的不合情理/显失公平交易(unconscionable bargain)中一方是处于明显的特殊不利地位是类似。

这情况不少是发生在欺诈/欺骗特殊认知障碍人士,例如在 Saunders v. Anglia Building Society(1971)AC 1004 贵族院先例中,老妇以为她签的字是把房子作为礼物给她的侄子,但其实根本不是这回事。但也不一定是与欺诈有关才会适用 *non est factum* 原则。这在 Foster v. Mackinnon(1869)LR 4 CP 704 先例中,Byles 大法官说:"... it is invalid not merely on the ground of fraud, where fraud exists, but on the ground that the mind of the signor did not accompany the signature; in other words, that he never intended to sign, and therefore in contemplation of law never did sign, the contract to which his name is appended."

照说在这种情况下,会否本章之 11.1 段提到的可诉单方面错误让订立的合约无效就能够保护认知障碍人士,而无需再适用 *non est factum* 原则? 由于可诉单方面错误是要求对方合约方真正或应该知道才会成立,这在欺诈/欺骗特殊认知障碍的人士时就显然是毫无疑问。但在社会上各种各样的事情都会发生,法律需要能够填补每一个漏洞,显然就会有情况是对方合约方不一定知道或能够证明对方知道错误方的认知障碍。

如在 Lloyds Bank Plc v. Waterhouse(1993)2 FLR 97 上诉庭先例中,案情涉及被告成功以 *non est factum* 令他向原告银行签署的为他儿子债务作出的个人担保被判无效,Purchas 大法官说他没有责任去自动披露他是文盲。

16.1 *non est factum* 原则的主要目的:保护社会上特殊不利地位人士

non est factum 的原则主要是对有特殊认知障碍的人士在没有搞清楚下就签署一份合约或其他有法律后果的文件做出救济。这种情况在当今的国际商业环境是不大可能会发生,所以"走出去"的中国公司不必太关心这方面的法律,因为英国法院将这些公司都假设为英国合约法的一流专家。但在英国本土,即使今天文盲已经是很难找到,社会上仍经常会有莫名其妙订立合约的情况,需要法律保护。

在《Chitty on Contracts》(2021 年,第 34 版)一书之 5-005 段中说:"**Non est factum.** There is a third type of mistake which may be seen as a variant of unilateral mistake, ... It is peculiar to the law of written contracts, and it allows a party who has executed a document under a fundamental misappropriation as to its nature to plead that it is 'not his deed'. This is the defence of non est factum."

另该书接下来在 5-056 段说到 *non est factum* 原则是很少会保护没有认知障碍的人士:"... It will be a rare case in which a person who does not suffer from a disability will be able to plead non est factum when he has signed a document without checking to see what it is, or in what capacity he is signing it."

Saunders v. Anglia Building Society(1971)AC 1004 贵族院先例的说法也反映了这一点,现代社会虽然文盲已经几乎消失,但也会存在繁忙的人士不仔细看文件就签字的情况。这种随便签错字的人士就不能依赖 *non est factum* 原则。Wilberforce 勋爵说:"In my opinion, the correct rule, ..., is that, ..., a person who signs a document, and parts with it so that it may come into other hands, has a responsibility, that of the normal man of prudence, to take care what he signs, which, if neglected, prevents him from denying his liability under the document according to its tenor. I would add that the onus of proof in this matter rests upon him, i. e. , to prove that he acted carefully, and not upon the third party to prove the contrary. ... The preceding paragraphs contemplate persons who are adult and literate: the conclusion as to such persons is that, while there are cases in which they may successfully plead non est factum these cases will, **in modern times, be rare**. "(加黑部分是笔者的强调)

虽然数量很少,但也不是没有签错字的人士并非认知障碍而成功依赖了 *non est factum* 原则的案件。如在 Beardsley Theobalds Retirement Benefit Scheme Trustees v. Yardley(2011)EWHC 1380(QB)先例中,一位公司雇员为公司签了一份文件,以为自己只是作为见证人,但实际上是担保人。他成功以不当影响(undue influence)[85]与 *non est factum* 作出抗辩。

16.1.1　何为认知障碍的签字人士(disable signer)

可先节录《Misrepresentation, Mistake and Non-Disclosure》(2022 年,第 6 版)一书之 13 - 59 段说:"**Permanent or temporary inability to understand the document** The plead of non est factum allows a party to say that, by reason of some disability, he could not understand the document. In the early law, this was applied to parties who were blind or illiterate, and so could not read it themselves, and had to trust someone else to tell them what they were signing-and where they were misled about the document. **In the modern law, however, this extends also to other 'disabilities', whether from defective education, illness or innate incapacity. The disability may be permanent or temporary**: the question is whether it rendered the party incapable of both reading and sufficiently understanding the deed or other document to be signed; that is, incapable of understanding it at least to the point of detecting the fundamental difference between the actual document and the document as he had believed it to be. **It is not necessary that the other party to the document knew, or ought to have known, about the disability**. "(加黑部分是笔者的强调)

上述提到的确立了这一课题的当今法律地位(modern law)的重要先例是 Saunders v. Anglia Building Society(1971)AC 1004 贵族院先例。Reid 勋爵说:"Originally the extension(of the plea)appears to have been made in favour of those who were unable to read owing to blindness or illiteracy and who therefore had to trust someone to tell them what they were signing. I think it must also apply in favour of those who are permanently or temporarily unable through no fault of their own to have without explanation

---

〔85〕 见本书第十一章之 1 段。

any real understanding of the purport of a particular document, whether that be from defective education, illness or innate incapacity."

上述是说早期 *non est factum* 原则只适用在眼盲或文盲人士,这些人要依赖其他第三人去念给他们听才知道要签署的文件是什么内容,但过程中被第三人误导(有心或无心)而错误理解文件的性质(nature)或内容(contents)。

随着时代的进步,文盲人士在英国恐怕不容易找了。但在 Saunders v. Anglia Building Society 贵族院先例中,已经是将 *non est factum* 原则发展至把有认知障碍人士扩大或延伸至其他人士。只要该签字人士被影响而不能正确与充分理解他们在签什么文件,或者未能及时觉察签的文件与他们以为在签的文件有根本性差异的情况都可以适用该原则。这包括方方面面,如文化水平低,签字方在没有不小心的情况下签的文件中存在需要专业知识(包括法律)才会觉察出重大差异的内容。或是因为生病,如精神病是典型的例子。根据上述 Reid 勋爵的说法,看来认知障碍的人士是与"行为能力"(capacity)也有关系。在英国法律下,失去行为能力(incapacity)主要是指未成年人、失去认知能力与醉酒(也应包括吸毒)的人。这可节录《Chitty on Contracts》(2021 年,第 34 版)一书之 11 - 001 段说:"In English law, three classes of individuals are subject to some degree of personal contractual incapacity. These are minors, persons lacking the requisite mental capacity and drunken persons. ..."

这三种失去行为能力人士,未成年人士与商业活动没有太大关系。精神方面与醉酒是同一回事,都会令签字方不只是没法正确与充分理解他们在签什么文件,也会令他失去一般正常人士的警觉与自己没法理解自己在做什么。正如在 Barclays Bank Plc v. Schwartz(1995)6 WLUK 247 上诉庭先例中,Millett 大法官说:"... mental incapacity and drunkenness(may) not only deprive the sufferer of understanding the transaction, but also deprive him of the awareness that he(does) not understand it."

因精神问题失去认知能力的人士会闯的祸也不只局限在乱签合约或有法律后果文件,而是包括其他方方面面的行为。英国也已有立法针对这方面的保护:见《Mental Capacity Act 2005》。但不去扯开话题,不再去探讨这方面。

另是在衡平法下,对一些不合情理/显失公平交易(unconscionable bargains),包括对一些在谈判中处于不利地位的人士,作出衡平救济,就是让受害方有权使合约无效(voidable),可撤销合约,这方面问题会在本书第十一章之 2 段较详细讨论。Fry v. Lane(1888)40 Ch. D. 312 先例就是针对"贫穷与无知"(poor and ignorant)。这后来扩大了保护,Blomley v. Ryan(1956)99 CLR 362 先例对无能力(disability)有了延伸,Fullagar 大法官说:"... poverty or need of any kind, sickness, age, sex, infirmity of body or mind, drunkenness, illiteracy or lack of education, lack of assistance or explanation where assistance or explanatory is necessary."

在 Alec Lobb v. Total Oil GB(1983)1 WLR 87 先例中,Peter Millett QC 大法官说:"... one party has been at a serious disadvantage to the other, whether through poverty or ignorance, or lack of advice, or otherwise, so that circumstances existed of which unfair advantage could be taken."

另在 Barclays Bank Plc v. Schwartz 上诉庭先例中，Millett 大法官也有说到一方去占另一方是文盲或不懂英语的便宜而签下的合约可以以不合情理被撤销。

在澳大利亚的 Commercial Bank of Australia v. Amadio(1983)151 CLR 447 高院先例中，案件涉及一位年迈的意大利移民不太懂英语，但与银行签订合约抵押他的物业为儿子的债务提供担保。高院的多数判决是该担保不合情理而被撤销，其中 Deane 大法官说："... as extending generally to circumstances in which ... a party to a transaction was under a special disability in dealing with the other party with the consequences that there was an absence of any reasonable degree of equality between them."

16.1.2 *non est factum* 原则的问题

上述可见，*non est factum* 原则与很多普通法与衡平法下已经有的诉因与救济，如可诉错误、可诉误述与/或无行为能力等重叠或纠缠不清。也见到不少案例诉因被认为是可诉误述可使合约无效，而不应是 *non est factum* 原则等。此外，也可能有与不合情理/显失公平交易、不当影响、欺诈/欺骗等重叠的情况。但除了可诉错误外，其他诉因的救济都是可使合约无效，受害方有权撤销合约，而 *non est factum* 原则的救济却是令合约自始无效。如果合约自始无效，就等于失去了保护经常会涉及的无辜第三人的利益的机会，这不是法院愿意见到的。所以 *non est factum* 原则只适用在十分极端，没有其他诉因与救济的情况。

《Misrepresentation, Mistake and Non-Disclosure》(2022 年，第 6 版)一书之 13 - 64 段就说出了这方面的混乱："**Unresolved tension: the relationship between non est factum, mistake, misrepresentation and incapacity** The doctrine of non est factum fits uncomfortably in the English law of contract. It is based on a combination of a disability-the inability to understand the document-and a very serious mistake about the terms of the document. We have seen that a mistake about the terms may make a contract void; but that where the party has signed a document the courts are very reluctant to allow the signer to escape the apparent consequences of his signature, although they may do so where the other party knows or ought to know that the signature does not in fact signify consent. In the case of non est factum, the claim is more extreme: that the contract is void by reason of the mere disability which gave rise to a mistake about the document, without the other party necessarily knowing it or having caused it. At first sight it appears that the doctrine is designed to protect the disabled party against the consequences of his disability. But again, **it does not fit comfortably with the general approach of the law to contractual disabilities. Where, for example, a party lacks mental capacity a contract which he enters into is not void; it is voidable**-and only if the handicap is known to the other party. So the defendant can normally hold the claimant to a contract that he has signed, however serious the claimant's mistake may have been about the terms of the document, where the defendant did not know (nor should have known) about the mistake; and the contract is not even voidable for the claimant's mistake or disability unless the defendant caused the mistake (by making a misrepresentation) or knew about the disability. However, the approach taken to a plea of non est factum appears to run counter to the policies underlying the law of mistake, misrepresentation and incapacity, and to hold that a contract can be void (not merely voidable) where the other contracting party played no part in the creation of mistake, nor did he at the time of the contract have actual or constructive notice of the defect in consent. As we have seen, **the courts reserve this consequence for the most extreme cases: only where the consequences of the mistake are very serious-the document is 'radically' different from the document as it was believed to be; and the party is not at fault**. But it is an area of the law of mistake which may merits further review."（加黑部分是笔者的强调）

16.1.3 不查看文件内容乱签或在白纸上签字的危险

上述讲到的情况会发生在社会家庭，而本段所讲的情况则是在商业上出现。在 Saunders v. Anglia Building Society (1971) AC 1004 贵族院先例中，Wilberforce 勋爵也说到另一种情况适用这个原则，也就是一方当事人在一张白纸上签字，带来他没有预期到的法律后果："… persons who may be tricked into putting their signature on a piece of paper which has legal consequences totally different from anything they intended."

这种情况可以是一方当事人去签了一张白纸，或半张白纸，然后让其他人把他意图的细节填妥。相信不少工作繁忙人士都会遇到过这种情况，就是先签了字，而文件内容让助手或秘书去填上。但结果是被填上的细节完全不是签字方所想的，而且内容有了重大不同，如"no"写成是"yes"。这出错会涉及欺诈/欺骗，但也可以是完全无关，只是误解或不小心出错。这样，签字方常会希望依赖 *non est factum* 原则推翻该签署的文件，但这是不容易成功。一个没有认知障碍的成年人去盲目签署（blind signing）文件并带来法律后果，会被视为他自己冒险或不小心，满足不了 *non est factum* 原则的要件。

例如在 United Dominions Trust v. Western (1976) QB 513 上诉庭先例中，涉及一辆新车的租购合约（hire-purchase agreement），被告买方向车行购买时同意的价格是 550 英镑，并在一份原告金融公司的标准表格上签上了名字，让车行填上其他细节。但后来原告向被告要求执行的租购合约变为 750 英镑，以 35 个月分期付款。被告以 *non est factum* 原则抗辩，但不成功。上诉庭一致跟从 Wilberforce 勋爵在 Saunders v. Anglia Building Society (1971) AC 1004 贵族院先例中的说法："...a man cannot escape from the consequences, as regards innocent third parties, of signing a document if, being a man of ordinary education and competence, he chooses to sign it without informing himself of its purport and effect..."

Scarman 大法官说到工作繁忙的高管领导在文件签字后让助手或秘书填上内容的做法的危险之处,说:"… a busy managing director who has a pile of documents to be signed in a few minutes before his next meeting and his secretary arranges them for maximum speed with only the spaces for signature exposed; and the managing director signs them 'blind'. Lord Pearson(在 Saunders v. Anglia Building Society 先例)comments … that he may be exercising a wise economy of time and energy: 'but the person who signs documents in this way ought to be held bound by them, and ought not to be entitled to avoid liability so as to shift the burden of loss on to an innocent third party. The whole object of having documents signed by him is that he makes them his documents and takes responsibility for them. He takes the chance of a fraudulent substitution…'."

Reid 勋爵在 Saunders v. Anglia Building Society 先例中说:"I do not say that the remedy can never be available to a man of full capacity. But that could only be in very exceptional circumstances: certainly not where his reason for not scrutinising the document before signing it was that he was too busy or too lazy."

笔者也遇到过在机构仲裁或临时仲裁的首席仲裁员,在仲裁庭成员(可能住在全球各地)提前在单独的签字页上完成签署之后,办案秘书(或首席的秘书)将签字页附在裁决书后面发出裁决书时,将仲裁庭合议期间的初稿(内容与终稿有重大不同)错误地作为最终定稿的版本发出给双方当事人。这样,如果一方当事人不合作,坚持错误发送的版本就是最后裁决书,仲裁庭就可以提出 *non est factum* 原则。毕竟这错误不是可归咎于仲裁员,特别是边裁的,而且这种预先签署方法与发放裁决书的方式也是惯常做法。

最后针对这方面可节录《Chitty on Contracts》(2021 年,第 34 版)一书之 5 – 053 段说:"The plead of non est factum is … potentially applicable where one person signs a document in blank and hands it to another, leaving him to fill in the details and complete the transaction. However, where erroneous details are inserted which are not in accord with the instructions of the person executing the document. He may yet be liable if the transaction which the document purports to effect is not essentially different in substance or in kind from the transaction intended. Moreover, the onus is on the person signing the document to show that he has acted carefully, and if he fails to discharge that onus he will be bound."

16.2 要件之一:签错字的合约方不能自己有疏忽大意

《Chitty on Contracts》(2021 年,第 34 版)一书之 5 – 054 段说:"A person who signs a document **may not be permitted to raise the defence of non est factum where he has been guilty of negligence in appending his signature**. …the House of Lords in Saunders v. Anglia Building Society … held that no matter what class of document was in question, negligence or carelessness on the part of the person signing the document would exclude the defence of non est factum. This does not depend on the principle of estoppel but on **the principle that no man can take advantage of his own wrong**. "（加黑部分是笔者的强调）

在 Saunders v. Anglia Building Society（1971）AC 1004 贵族院先例中的 87 岁与眼镜坏了的老妇，曾被指控应该在签字前要求对方把内容念给她听，就不会乱签了，以此显示她有过错。最后贵族院判合约有效，*non est factum* 原则不适用。可以看出，即使有轻微的疏忽或过错，也会令 *non est factum* 原则不适用。

另多介绍在 CF Asset Finance Ltd v. Okonji（2014）CTLC 218 上诉庭先例中，Dyson 勋爵说："It is clear from the case law, including the leading authority of Gallie v Lee [1971] A. C. 1004, [86] that a person **may not raise the defence** of non est factum **if he has been guilty of negligence in appending his signature to the document which he wishes to disown…There is a heavy burden** on the person who seeks to invoke the remedy. He must prove that he took 'all reasonable precautions in the circumstances'. …"

本小段只多节录《Misrepresentation, Mistake and Non-Disclosure》（2022 年，第 6 版）一书之 13 – 61 段说："**The person signing must not have been careless** In addition to the disability of the party, and the very serious degree of his mistake about the document, it must be shown that he was not careless. … Much emphasis is placed on this requirement, and the heavy burden on the party to show that he was not careless. Lord Wilberforce（在 Saunders v. Anglia Building Society 贵族院先例）said：'A person who signs a document, and parts with it so that it may come into other hands, has a responsibility, that of the normal man of prudence, to take care what he signs, which, if neglected, prevents him from denying his liability under the document according to its tenor. I would add that the onus of proof in this matter rests upon him, i. e. , to prove that he acted carefully, and not upon the third party to prove the contrary.' What is expected of the party by way of care will depend on the facts; and will relate also to the nature of the disability and the nature of the transaction. But it is not easy to establish that sufficient care has been taken. **In particular, a party fails to read the document or to ask for an explanation of it, he will normally be held to have failed to exercise sufficient care.** "（加黑部分是笔者的强调）

可见在这权威说法下，*non est factum* 原则与国际商业没有太大关系。因为在商业活动中在一份重要文件中签错字，通常就是涉及签字方太忙与/或懒得去全面仔细检查了文件后才签字。虽然经常发生，但没有法律救济。

16.3 要件之二：错签的文件必须与本来想签的文件有根本性不同

这与本章之 8 段所讲的是一样道理或精神，也就是错签的文件带来后果的严重

〔86〕 与 Saunders v. Anglia Building Society（1971）AC 1004 贵族院先例是同一个先例。

程度是与本来想签的文件有根本性不同。这根本性不同本来曾被认为这只是针对错签文件的属性/本质(character/nature),不包括文件的内容(contents)。例如在Beardsley Theobalds Retirement Benefit Scheme Trustees v. Yardley(2011)EWHC 1380(QB)先例中,以为是作为见证人,但实是作为担保人。但在Saunders v. Anglia Building Society(1971)AC 1004贵族院先例后,*non est factum*原则也适用在文件内容,例如本来就是准备去签一份担保,错签的仍是一份担保,只错在本来只是担保10元,但错签的担保是1000元。只要在严重程度上有根本性不同,仍是可提出适用*non est factum*原则。

这可节录《Misrepresentation, Mistake and Non-Disclosure》(2022年,第6版)一书之13-60段说:"**The document must be 'fundamentally', 'radically' or 'totally' different** The speeches of the House of Lords used a variety of words to describe and emphasise the degree of difference that must be shown between the actual document, and the document as the party believed it to be. The question here is the party's subjective understanding, and so we are certainly within the realm of a party's mistake about the terms of the contract. But there must be a 'radical difference' between what he signed and what he thought he was signing; or it must be 'essentially different in substance or kind'; or the difference must 'go to the substance of the whole consideration or to the root of the matter'; or the actual document must be 'basically', or 'fundamentally', or 'seriously', or 'very substantially' or 'totally' different. In using such a test, the House rejected a tendency in the earlier cases to draw a firm distinction between (a) a difference in character of the document (which had been held to be sufficient for the plea of non est factum) and (b) a difference only in contents (which had been held not to be sufficient). This distinction may work in many cases, but it is not a formal part of the test. As Lord Reid said in Saunders v. Anglia Building Society ...: 'if a man thinks he is signing a document which will cost him £ 10 and the actual document would cost him £ 1,000 it could not be right to deny him this remedy simply because the legal character of the two was the same. It is true that we must then deal with questions of degree, but that is a familiar task for the courts and I would not expect it to give rise to a flood of litigation.'"

多介绍在CF Asset Finance Ltd v. Okonji(2014)CTLC 218上诉庭先例中,Dyson勋爵说:"The remedy of non est factum is usually invoked where a party signs a document which is essentially different in character or contents from that which he intends to sign. **In most cases, the issue is whether the difference is sufficiently fundamental or radical to invalidate the transaction**...."(加黑部分是笔者的强调)

17.《Limitation Act 1980》S. 32(1)(c)立法延长时效

针对民事诉讼的立法时效，如果诉因是错误，可以根据《Limitation Act 1980》之S. 32(1)(c)获得时效的延长。[87] 有关条文内容可节录如下："... where in the case of any action for which a period of limitation is prescribed by this Act, either—(a) the action is based upon the fraud of the defendant; or (b) any fact relevant to the plaintiff's right of action has been deliberately concealed from him by the defendant; or (c) **the action is for relief from the consequences of a mistake; the period of limitation shall not begin to run until the plaintiff has discovered the** fraud, concealment or **mistake** (as the case may be) or could with reasonable diligence have discovered it."（加黑部分是笔者的强调）

17.1 《Limitation Act 1980》S. 32(1)(c)立法的本意

时效的本意是阻止一些拖延太久的民事索赔(stale claims)，也就是在一般的合约下从有了诉因(cause of action)起算的6年，如果不启动法院诉讼或仲裁，就会过了时效。

但显然在各种各样的情况下需要有例外，而一种重要的例外就是欺诈、隐瞒与错误的情况，允许延后至发现(或合理勤勉可以发现)有关的欺诈、隐瞒与错误时才起算这6年时效。这很有必要，因为很多欺诈、隐瞒与错误会是在事件发生多年后才被受害人原告发现。如果6年立法时效是从发生欺诈、隐瞒或错误事件起算，原告发现时可能已是6年后。所以需要有这例外去将时效延至发现(或合理勤勉可以发现)后才起算。这也带来了无数先例发展起来的"发现理论"(discoverability doctrine)。

立法的措辞中可以明显注意到与(a)欺诈、(b)隐瞒相比，(c)错误的用字很不一样，是"为救济错误所导致的结果"(for relief from the consequences of a mistake)，不是简单的好像(a)"欺诈"一样说"the action is based upon the fraud"。这显示立法是不一样地对待错误，把可延后立法时效的起算日期的情况只局限在需要法律救济的可诉错误。

对"错误"给了一个局限或狭窄的解释是可以想到的。相比欺诈与隐瞒，"错误"对大众来说是可以十分广泛，任何做或不做的事情或任何决定，只要结果不理想就会被视为错误。即使是涉及了错误方的不小心、疏忽大意、无知愚昧、冒险、投机等的因素，仍可去说是错误。所以，如果让任何广泛字义的"错误"都去延后立法时效，大门广开，就会是没有立法时效这回事了。毕竟，错过了立法时效往往也会与原告的错误有关，没有及时采取行动保护自己索赔的权利。

---

[87] 这方面在本书第十章之11.5段也有详细介绍。

另是在《Limitation Act 1939》立法时,法律改革委员会(Law Revision Committee)在1936年报告中就指出"错误"(当时普通法只针对事实错误有救济)与S.32[1939年立法是S.26(c)]所针对的另两种情况的"欺诈"与"隐瞒"在本质与政策上很不一样。在后两种情况是"it is obviously unjust that a defendant should be permitted to rely upon a lapse of time created by his own misconduct",但错误就往往是扯不上被告有做任何事情令原告过了6年时效才发现错误。

所以在Phillips-Higgins v. Harper(1954)1 QB 411先例中,Pearson大法官就指出针对错误的时效需要狭窄解释说:"No doubt it was intended to be a narrow provision, because any wider provision would have opened too wide a door of escape from the general principle of limitation by six years' lapse of time, which is, of course, a reasonable and normally salutary principle, ..."

另在Test Claimants in the FII Group Litigation v. Revenue and Customs Commissioners(2012)UKSC 19最高院先例中,Walker勋爵也说:"As to policy, departure from Pearson J's relatively narrow interpretation would bring a real risk ... that 'the scope of [section 32(1)(c)] might be expanded dangerously close to the basic rule of common law limitation that ignorance of the existence of a cause of action does not prevent time from running'. It would be difficult to find any principled stopping-place for the expansion."

在此纠缠了20多年涉及金额高达50亿英镑,另加复息的退还多缴纳或错付公司税的集体诉讼案件,仅是在不同方面的法律就三次上诉去了最高院,在Test Claimants in the FII Group Litigation v. Revenue and Customs Commissioners(2020)UKSC 47最高院先例中,也是针对1980年立法之S.32(1)(c),也成为对解释S.32(1)(c)最重要的先例之一。案件主要针对的是S.32(1)(c)的延长时效是否在法律错误(这是在Kleinwort Benson Ltd v. Lincoln City Council[1999]2 AC 349先例后才发展起来的)也适用的问题,这将在本书第十章之11.5段详细介绍。

17.2 可诉错误可延后立法时效启动的权威先例

在Phillips-Higgins v. Harper(1954)1 QB 411先例中,一审的Pearson大法官有针对这一点,并给了"错误"可延后立法时效启动的情况一个局限或狭窄的解释,说:

"In construing the section it is to be observed that fraud and mistake are dealt with quite differently. ... In regard to fraud, there is provision(a) where the action is based upon fraud-for instance, if an action is to recover damages for fraudulent misrepresentation-or(b), that very wide provision, where the right of action (which may be wholly independent of fraud) is concealed by the fraud of 'any such person as aforesaid,' that is to say, the defendant or a person claiming through him; but **there is not in respect of mistake any provision similar to(b)**. The section does not apply to the case of a right of action which is concealed from the plaintiff by a mistake. What, then, is the meaning of provision(c)? **The right of action is for relief from the consequences of a mistake. It seems to me that this wording is carefully chosen to indicate a class of actions where a mistake has been made which has had certain consequences and the plaintiff seeks to be relieved from those consequences.** Familiar examples are, **first**, money paid in consequence of a mistake: in such a case the mistake is made, in consequence of the mistake the money is paid, and the action is to recover that money back. **Secondly**, there may be a contract entered into in consequence of a mistake, and the action is to obtain the rescission or, in some cases, the rectification of such a contract. **Thirdly**, there may be an account settled in consequence of mistakes; if the mistakes are sufficiently serious there can be a reopening of the account.

In my opinion, the mere operation of the Limitation Act unless excluded by this section is not a relevant consequence for the purpose of the section. If it were, then any concealment of a right of action from the plaintiff by a mistake would be intended to be covered by this section and the provision(b) in respect of fraud should have been applied to mistake also. Moreover, I think that it is right to say that if there would be no consequence except the operation of the Limitation Act, and the operation of the Limitation Act is excluded, then there is no consequence at all.... **Probably provision(c) applies only where the mistake is an essential ingredient of the cause of action, so that the statement of claim sets out, or should set out, the mistake and its consequences and pray for relief from those consequences.** ..."(加黑是笔者的强调)

这一 1954 年的 Phillips-Higgins v. Harper 先例,被较近期的 Test Claimants in the Franked Investment Group Litigation v Revenue and Customs Commissioners (2012) UKSC 19 最高院先例确认。

Phillips-Higgins v. Harper 先例的案情是原告受雇于被告律师事务所,1938 年至 1950 年是助理律师(assistant solicitor),之后升职为授薪合伙人(salaried partner)。但因为双方有了争议,所以只干了 1 年。原告指称双方早在 1938 年就有口头协议,被告承诺除了固定工资外,会每年有一笔奖金去把年收入升至被告总收入的 1/3。之后从 1938 年至 1950 年,原告的确每年收到一笔奖金。但到了 1951 年才发现这些年来的支付是少了。被告的抗辩是原来的口头协议不是 1/3,是 1/4。这显然是双方对口头协议的条件有主观的不同理解,正如本章之 6.2.1 段的介绍,是由法院(或仲裁庭)根据双方的证据去客观认定到底双方同意的是 1/3 还是 1/4(x 或是 y)。

被告也提出了立法时效已过的抗辩,这表示只有 1944 年至 1950 年的索赔才是在 6 年的立法时效内。而 1938 年至 1944 年部分的索赔是时效已过。原告对此点的答辩是由于错误少了支付在 1951 年才被发现,所以 6 年立法时效应是刚不久才起算。

Pearson 大法官在该先例中,根据立法的措辞与用字,判由于原告启动诉讼是想追回被告在口头协议下多年来少付的款项,所以原告的诉因其实是违反该口头协议的约定,错误不是违反的重要或相关因素,所以立法下延长时效的条文不适用。

这样解释立法,就带来说不通之处。如果是错误去多支付,在多年后发现错误就可享有延后立法时效向被告索赔,因为诉因与寻求的救济就是错误支付(mistaken payment)导致的结果。但如果是少了支付,如少了支付货价,在发现错误后索赔的诉因与寻求的救济就变了是尚欠下的货价了,延后立法时效就不适用了。就"少付"及"多付"这两个情况,在 Test Claimants in the Franked Investment Group Litigation v. Revenue and Customs Commissioners 最高院先例中有解释如下:"It has been suggested by academic commentators that this result may be anomalous, in that the extended period of limitation applies to a claim to recover a mistaken overpayment of a debt but not to a claim to recover a mistaken underpayment... The difference simply arises from the fact that if the claimant is underpaid and sues for the balance, he is enforcing the obligation that gave rise to the debt, whereas if he is overpaid (sic) then that obligation will have been discharged, so that he needs some other legal basis for getting it back."

这一方面在 Phillips-Higgins v. Harper 先例中也提到,说这看来不通或有矛盾之处是立法的问题,法院只能按照立法的措辞与文字合理解释,并必须跟从。这与解释合约的道理一样,就是法院或仲裁庭只能受限于合约的文字与措辞,只要写得足够明确,就不管解释的结果是否合理。Pearson 大法官说:"No doubt there are certain anomalies which result. ..., it is odd that a person who has by mistake paid too much can take advantage of the section whereas a person who has by mistake received too little and made no protest cannot take advantage of the section. There may be other anomalies also. But, in my judgment, the carefully chosen wording of the provision (c) must have its proper effect notwithstanding any resulting anomalies."

18. 错误与误述的关系

这两个诉因同时存在是不足为奇,毕竟,一方订约方对有关合约的标的或目的有了错误是可以来自不同渠道。以一个简单的例子,一位买方出高价以为买了"正货"(这标的可以是一间公司或一项价值连城的专利),但实是不值钱的垃圾或严重至根本谈不上是买方想买与所需的货物。这错误是对方卖方的误述(misrepresentation)所导致,这样根据可诉误述在法律下可使该买卖合约无效,买方可去撤销合约(rescission of contract),也就不需要求助更困难成立的可诉错误了。正如在本章之 3.3 段提到,错误是最后的救济手段(remedy of last resort)。

现实中订约方对一件现存的事实或法律有了一个共同/共享的错误理解或假设,有更大的可能是其中一方向另一方提供了错误的信息,而不是各自从第三人或其他渠道取得同样对事实或法律错误的信息。所以错误与误述经常走在一起,虽然成立误述的案件远比成立错误要来得多。正如在《Chitty on Contracts》(2021 年,第 34 版)一书之 8 - 013 段中说:"there are relatively few cases in which a party seeks to escape from a contract on the ground of common mistake: they will often be able to rescind the contract for misrepresentation, ..."

18.1 会与可诉错误走在一起的误述

由于可诉的共同/共享错误(common/shared mistake)的要件之一是双方必须有一个肯定与确信的共同想法(mutual positive state of mind),所以共同错误与欺诈性误述并无关系。在后者诉因,必须涉及误述方的不诚实,或者是明知道事实真相但刻意去误述或说一半、不说一半,或者是不理会事实真假。这样,对有关的错误理解(事实或法律)就不会是共同错误,也满足不了 The "Great Peace" (2002) EWCA Civ 1407 上诉庭先例的五个要件之(i)与(iii)了。

疏忽误述涉及了误述方的过错与不小心,不构成可诉错误。看来,可去成立共同/共享错误只会在误述方是真正无辜的误述(innocent misrepresentation)。这样,才会出现订约双方无辜去错误理解或假设合约的标的是正货,但事实上是垃圾,因为无辜误述方也在有合理依据(reasonable ground)下被上一位卖方或其他第三人欺骗或误导了。

欺诈性误述与可诉错误在单方面错误(unilateral mistake)上是不起冲突。法律对单方面错误理解了合约标的并构成订约时双方不是一致想法(consensus ad idem)的情况,在误述上也可以是误述方订约时是知道或应该知道被误述方对有关的现存事实或法律是有了错误理解,只是不主动提醒,而且是取巧去推波助澜加深买方的错误理解尽快订立合约。[88]

18.2 对原告来说可诉错误与可诉误述的优劣

《Misrepresentation, Mistake and Non-Disclosure》(2022 年,第 6 版)一书之 12 - 20 段说:"**Advantages for the claimant in showing that the contract is void for mistake** From the claimant's point of view, it can be difficult to show that the contract is void for mistake, given the limited scope of the doctrine, and the reluctance of the courts to find a sufficient mistake. In many cases, where the mistake was caused by information provided by the defendant, the claimant can more easily show that the contract was voidable for misrepresentation. However, even in such a case it may still be in his interest to go further and establish the mistake: for example, if rescission of the (voidable) contract has now become barred. Resorting to a claim for mistake in order to avoid being met by a bar to rescission for misrepresentation, may be an attempt to avoid policies, set by the law of misrepresentation, limiting the claimant's rights to escape the contract. However, where the

[88] 这正是本章之 11.1 段讲的情况。

reason that rescission is barred is that an innocent third party would thereby be prejudiced, establishing an actionable mistake can be a way of avoiding the policy underlying the rule which is designed to protect third parties. ...Where, however, the claimant's mistake was not induced by the other party's misrepresentation, he will be driven to prove mistake if he wishes to avoid the contract. This will happen where the mistake was based on the claimant's own investigations or assumptions, and not caused by the receipt of inaccurate information; or where it was caused by his reliance on information but where the source of the information was a third party for whom the other contracting party had no responsibility. In such a case, the claimant is not necessarily interested in establishing that the contract was void rather than voidable: he seeks to show that it is void because that is the legal consequence of the mistake, and it is mistake alone on which, on the facts, he can rely."

可诉误述远比可诉错误容易成立,这主要是在程度方面。错误针对的内容的重要性要令合约标的有了根本性不同或合约自始无效,但误述(无论是欺诈性、疏忽还是无辜)针对的内容就只需对合约的产生有一定的重要性(materiality),而且要求被误述方只是部分依赖就足够。但如果以误述为诉因有了困难,例如时效已过,就只剩下了错误才可能让无辜方有法律救济。这样,以错误作为诉因的优点就显示出来,如下:

1. 本书第三章详细介绍了在一个可使无效合约,说是被误述方有权撤销合约,但在复原(restitutio in integrum)会遇上困难,加上其他原因导致无法使合约无效。这特别在非欺诈性的疏忽误述,在本书第四章的《Misrepresentation Act 1967》立法下,撤销合约使合约无效更是困难,弄不好会构成被误述方的毁约/违约(repudiatory breach):见 SK Shipping Plc v. Capital VLCC 3 Corp(2022)EWCA Civ 231 先例。但在特别情况下,误述的受害方只希望从合约脱身,无意索赔损失(或也索赔不了多少钱),如果能在替代诉因的可诉错误成功,就肯定是合约自始无效,可以脱身了。

2. 本书第三章之6.3 段提到可诉误述使合约无效会遇上不知情的无辜第三人(innocent third-party without notice)如善意买方(bona fide purchaser),这是法律更希望保护的对象,导致受害方/被误述方对有关货物或资产的产权(title)受影响。但一旦是可诉错误成立,判合约从未生效,这不知情无辜第三人规则就不适用了。此时适用的是 *nemo dat* 规则,错误方原告对有关货物/资产的产权就动摇不了,不受任何影响。

以上所讲,特别是第一点,可以一个经常发生的日常事件为例,就是在一些贵重商品标价上大字写上 100 元,另有看不清的小字写上"每两"或甚是不写单位。这就可能吸引了一些粗心大意或赶时间的顾客以为很便宜,就拿了去柜台准备结账。而该商店也会把有关的商品切割好与包装,然后要求结账 1600 元。这样,顾客如果想从该买卖合约脱身,会依赖误述(应该是欺诈性误述)。但这会困难重重,如怎么样证明该标价是一个清楚无误的误述,毕竟在"买方自己小心"(Caveat emptor)的风险分摊大原则下,难免被质疑为什么不看清楚或多向卖方问几句才决定买。所以,以错误(单方面错误)与卖方知道或合理可以知道买方有了错误理解,会是更容易更简单去判买卖合约无效。反正买方也不会有损失需要索赔,因为可诉错误是没有这个救济的。

3. 对一个自始无效(void ab initio)的合约,即使合约中有明示与更短的时效(contractual time bar),也不用担心,因为从来就没有合约。针对民事诉讼的立法时效,如果诉因是错误,可以根据《Limitation Act 1980》之 s. 32(1)(c)获得时效的延长。

但涉及可诉误述的可使无效(voidable)合约,合约明示与立法时效(至少在非欺诈性误述)或怠慢理论(doctrine of laches)均适用。这在本书第三章之 6.2 段有详论,不重复。

19. 错误与合约受阻的关系

合约受阻(frustration)在笔者的《合约的履行、弃权与禁反言》一书第二章有详细介绍。可以说,在该书介绍的构成合约受阻的要件或因素是与构成可诉错误相当一致的。例如,7.1 段的"合约受阻是法律问题,但仍需要(法院与)仲裁员认定事实";7.3 段的"受阻事件必须为外来的突发事件,令整个合约无法履行或是与订约时的共同目的有根本性不同";7.4 段的"多花钱、多花时间以及赚钱变亏本都不足以令合约受阻";与 7.5 段的"受阻事件的产生不涉及任何一方的责任或过错或出自他的原因"。另在 9 段介绍合约受阻后的法律后果,也是合约自动终止。

在此只重复合约受阻的经典权威定义,也就是在 National Carriers Ltd v. Panalpina(Northern)Ltd(1981) AC 675 贵族院先例中,Simon 勋爵说:"Frustration of a contract takes place when there supervenes an event(without default of either party and for which the contract makes no sufficient provision) which so significantly changes the nature(not merely the expense or onerousness) of the outstanding contractual rights and/or obligations from what the parties could reasonably have contemplated at the time of its execution that it would be unjust to hold them to the literal sense of its stipulations in the new circumstances; in such case the law declares both parties to be discharged from further performance."

有说法是共同/共享错误与合约受阻是一脉相承,同一个理论发展起来,也确实看来十分相似。这在 The "Great Peace"(2002) EWCA Civ 1407 上诉庭先例中,Phillips 勋爵说:"At the time of Bell v. Lever Bros Ltd(1932) AC 161 the law of frustration and common mistake had advanced hand in hand on the foundation of a common principle. Thereafter frustration proved a more fertile ground for the development of this principle than common mistake, and consideration of the development of the law of frustration assists with the analysis of the law of common mistake."

Phillips 勋爵给了一个例子，就是共同错误与合约受阻都是针对合约双方完全预见不到的事情（指对现存事实或法律），所以合约不会有针对。一旦合约有明示或默示条文去针对，如一方向另一方担保合约标的存在或承诺合约可以履行，也就是本章之 3 段所讲的双方已经在合约中分摊了有关的风险。这样就根据合约规定，法律不会再插手对共同错误或合约受阻给予救济了。Phillips 勋爵说："Just as the doctrine of frustration only applies if the contract contains no provision that covers the situation, the same should be true of common mistake, If, on the true construction of the contract, a party warrants that the subject matter of the contract exists,[89] or that it will be possible to perform the contract, there will be no scope to hold the contract void on the ground of common mistake."

至于共同错误与合约受阻的适用，差别只在有关不可预见的事情是发生在订约前或订约后。这在本章之 15.1 段的（六）所介绍的 Amalgamated Investment and Property Co Ltd v. John Walker & Sons Ltd（1977）1 WLR 164 上诉庭先例就很好地说明了这一点，不去重复。

由于订约后的时间段，是指合约的履行，这在一个中长期合约的履行会是很长的时间段。所以相比订约前的一段后期谈判的时间（今天通讯快捷是不会在订约时不知道），肯定是长得多。所以会发生不可预见的事情，并且是严重影响至合约自始无效，肯定更多发生在合约受阻的漫长时间段，不是在共同错误的短暂时间段。这也是在较早节录的 Phillips 勋爵在 The "Great Peace" 上诉庭先例中所说的 "frustration provided a more fertile ground for the development"。

有关共同错误案件比合约受阻案件更少有，在 The "Great Peace" 上诉庭先例中，Phillips 勋爵从另外角度去分析，说："Circumstances where a contract is void as a result of **common mistake are likely to be less common than instances of frustration**. Supervening events which defeat the contractual adventure will frequently not be the responsibility of either party. Where, however, the parties agree that something shall be done which is impossible at the time of making the agreement, it is much more likely that, in true construction of the agreement, one or other will have undertaken responsibility for the mistaken state of affairs. This may well explain why cases where **contracts have been found to be void in consequence of common mistake are few and far between**."（加黑部分是笔者的强调）

另是法律后果也不一致，就是可诉错误会涉及订约双方没有一致想法，这是构成有效与约束性合约的要件。所以，可诉错误产生的"合约"是一开始就是无效（void ab initio），双方从来没有发生过合约关系。这不像合约受阻，受阻前的合约关系不受影响，账目与责任仍得算清楚。

---

[89] 见 McRae v. Commonwealth Disposals Commission（1951）84 CLR 377 HCA 澳大利亚先例。

第八章　非　　法

1. 非 法 理 论

本章针对的不是刑事，而是民事，主要是合约的非法（illegality），也包括侵权（tort）与“准合约”（quasi-contract）关系的复原（restitution）/不当得利（unjust enrichment）涉及非法。民事诉讼的合约关系只涉及私人的权利义务（private rights）的约定，在订约自由（freedom of contract）的大原则、大政策下，法律认可与乐意协助执行合约的各种相互承诺（mutual promises）。即合约当事人在对方不履行合约的承诺时，可以向法院申请执行，也就是以各种方式［包括履约指令（specific performance），[1]或者是更常见的以金钱赔偿损失的方式替代合约履行等］强制对方合约方履行合约的首要（primary）或次要（secondary）承诺。

如果合约涉及非法，就会导致法律不认可这样对私权的约定，有关合约即使拿到法院申请执行，也不会得到法院支持。毕竟经典的普通法法律格言（maxim）是“违背道德的对价不生诉权”［ex turpi causa（ex dolo malo）non oritur action］，最早的名言是来自 Holman v. Johnson（1775）1 Cowp 341 先例中，Mansfield 勋爵说：“ex dolo malo non oritur action. **No court will lend its aid to a man who founds his cause of action upon an immoral or illegal act.** If, from the plaintiff's own stating or otherwise, the cause of action appears to arise ex turpi causa, or the transgression of a positive law of this country, there the court says he has no right to be assisted. It is upon that ground the court goes; not for the sake of the defendant, but because they will not lend their aid to such a plaintiff. So if the plaintiff and defendant were to change sides, and the defendant was to bring his action against the plaintiff, the latter would then have the advantage of it; for **where both are equally in fault, potior est conditio defendentis.**”[2]（加黑部分是

---

〔1〕 见笔者《损失赔偿与救济》一书的介绍，其中第十二章针对衡平救济的履约指令。

〔2〕 拉丁文是指双方对非法行为均有过错，被告地位更强。也就是指被告可以非法抗辩（illegal defence）成功击退索赔，即使被告也与原告一样是涉及非法行为。所以，澳大利亚的 Nelson v. Nelson（1995）HCA 25 先例曾建议面对非法争议左右为难时，一种解决办法是把非法获利交出给政府，法院才会协助原告执行并给予救济。但这建议不像有进一步的跟进，看来把公权与私权混在一起也不被视为可行。

笔者的强调)

英国法下什么情况具体被称为违背道德的对价不生诉权,在 Hardy v. Motor Insurers' Bureau(1964)2 QB 745 先例中,Diplock 勋爵这样介绍:"The rule of law on which the major premise is based-ex turpi causa non oritur actio-is concerned not specifically with the lawfulness of contracts but generally with the enforcement of rights by the courts, whether or not such rights arise under contract. **All that the rule means is that the courts will not enforce a right which would otherwise be enforceable** if the right arises out of an act committed by the person asserting the right ... which is regarded by the court as **sufficiently anti-social** to justify the court's refusing to enforce that right."(加黑部分是笔者的强调)

在 Safeway Stores v. Twigger(2010)EWCA Civ 1472 上诉庭先例中,Longmore 大法官解释说这说法的意义在于,任何人不能从这些侵犯了公共利益的非法行为中获利,以及不能就自己错误的后果(如因为刑事犯罪丧失人身自由、被罚款等)向他人要求赔偿。可以节录 Longmore 大法官所说如下:"... maxim goes back at least as far as the judgment of Lord Mansfield CJ in Holman v Johnson(1775)1 Cowp 341, its modern application dates from Tinsley v Milligan[1994]AC 340, which held, overruling Euro-Diam v Bathurst[1990]1 QB 1, that **the courts had no discretion in relation to the maxim**. The modern law has now culminated in Gray v Thames Trains Ltd[2009]1 AC 1339[3] when Lord Hoffmann said that it expressed not so much a principle as a policy and that it was a rule which may be stated in a narrower form and a wider form. In its narrower form it is that a claimant cannot recover for damage which is the consequence of a sentence imposed upon him for a criminal act; in its wider version it is that a claimant may not recover for damage which is the consequence of his own criminal act."(加黑部分是笔者的强调)

本章主要针对涉及私权的民事的非法,怎样结合涉及公权的刑事的非法,以达到整个法律体系的一致性与正直完善是非常复杂与困难的,英国几百年来通过无数先例的实践也没有得出一个比较完美的答案。

1.1 建立非法理论的理由

为什么要建立这困难与复杂的"非法理论",则可节录 Toulson 大法官在 Patel v. Mirza(2016)UKSC 42 最高院先例中,认可在本章之 7.3 段会介绍的法律委员会(Law Committee)给出的咨询报告《The Illegality Defence: A Consultative Report》(2009, Consultation Paper No 189)之 2.5 段的内容如下:"From its study of the case law and academic writing, the Commission identified the principal policy rationales for the illegality doctrine as 1) furthering the purpose of the rule infringed by the claimant's

---

〔3〕 此先例可见本章之 9.5 段的介绍。

behaviour,2) consistency,3) prevention of profit from the claimant's wrongdoing,4) deterrence and 5) maintaining the integrity of the legal system. It observed that these rationales were not mutually exclusive but overlapped to a greater or lesser degree."[4]

这是列举了需要在政策上有一套完善的"非法理论"的五大理由:

1. 延续法律(立法或普通法)禁止或不允许有关行为(可以是任何一方合约方做出)的目的,如建立廉洁、公义、正直与守法的社会等,即使只涉及双方私权范畴的民法。

2. 普通法法律体系下的一致性(coherence/consistency)与正直(integrity),不要在刑事诉讼下被惩罚,但在民事诉讼又获得法院支持与协助。例如,刑法下走私贩毒肯定是非法并且会被严惩,但民事诉讼下法院却协助原告毒枭向另一个毒枭作出履约指令,这就太不一致与可笑了。正如在加拿大最高院的 Hall v. Hebert (1993) 2 SCR 159 先例中,McLachlin 大法官说:"It is particularly important in this context that we bear in mind that the law must aspire to be a unified institution, the parts of which-contract, tort, the criminal law-must be in essential harmony. For the courts to punish conduct with the one hand while rewarding it with the other would be to 'create an intolerable fissure in the law's conceptually seamless web'."另是,在同一宗犯法行为中,如果在刑事诉讼中已被惩罚,就要在民事诉讼中避免再去"惩罚",以免造成双重损害(double jeopardy)。本来民事诉讼就不存在法院可以做出惩罚,但有些非法案件,完全不支持或协助原告让被告得益就会带来这种后果。

一致性也需要在民事诉讼有不同诉因时体现,如原告在非法合约下是无法索赔成功,但在一个同步/竞合责任(concurrent liability)[5]下可以以侵权索赔成功也是同样的不一致与可笑了。

3. 不允许原告在自己非法犯错的情况下获利,可以成功向被告[即使是亦有参与非法行为,过错对等(*pari delicto*)[6]]索赔或追回债务/财产。英国普通法下与此大同小异的原则与精神在笔者的《合约的解释:规则与应用》一书第四章之 10 段"假设订约方不能从自己的错误行为中获利"(presumption that contracting party cannot take advantage of its own wrong)也已经详及。衡平法下的"净手理论"(clean hands doctrine)也是一样的道理,所以原告也不会成功申请到衡平法救济,如禁令或履约指令等。

---

〔4〕 在咨询报告中还提到了第 6 点的理由,即希望对非法行为作出惩罚(punishment)。但多数意见认为该点主要是刑事范畴,而在民事案件中无需理会,甚至要小心不要造成刑事与民事的双重损害。也因此 Toulson 勋爵说:"A sixth possible rationale, punishment, was controversial. The large majority of consultees considered that punishment was a matter for the criminal courts (to which one might add regulators) and should not be invoked in determining parties' civil disputes."

〔5〕 见本书第一章之 2.4 段。

〔6〕 见本章之 10.1 段。

4. 阻吓民众与商业人士要小心非法行为的严重后果，从而避免参与或涉及任何可能是违法或违反公共政策的行为，如订立非法合约（无论在合约形成、目的与/或履行）。即使是不知道、不懂法、不熟悉英国公共政策，这也不是可以被接受的理由或借口。更应该是在做出行为（如订立一份商业合约）之前小心调查与咨询称职律师该合约是否完全合法。这样才可保证对整个商业社会而言，非法交易会大幅度减少。只会有少数案件，如完全是一个骗局，原告作为受害方很明显是因为受骗才订立的非法合约，才可以 *pari delicto* 理论不适用而获得法院的协助。

5. 维护英国普通法系统的公平合理、诚实、公义与正直。也就是在一套大家可以接受是完整、完善、肯定、可预测、合理与可行的法律（无论是通过立法还是普通法）明确下来后，民众就必须依法行事。

1.2 非法理论的适用

当然从上段的法律格言也可以看到，非法理论不仅仅是适用在合约法中，一般民事法律关系下任何请求都可能用非法理论来抗辩。例如 Tinsley v. Milligan（1994）1 AC 340 贵族院先例涉及的是财产与信托权利（trust and property rights）。Murphy v. Culhane（1977）QB 94；Revill v. Newbery（1996）QB 567；Clunis v. Camden and Islington Health Authority（1998）QB 978；Hounga v. Allen（2014）UKSC 47 等先例涉及的是侵权（tortious rights）。近期的 Patel v. Mirza（2016）UKSC 42 权威最高院先例涉及的是不当得利与复原（unjust enrichment /restitution）等。可以节录 Patel v. Mirza 先例中 Toulson 勋爵所说如下："Illegality has the potential to provide a defence to civil claims of all sorts，whether relating to contract，property，tort，or unjust enrichment，and in a wide variety of circumstances. "

以非法理论说服法院（或仲裁庭）不协助执行本来有的合约、侵权或其他诉因的权利（rights），会主要是由被告提出作为对原告索赔的抗辩。这像是在仲裁案件，会对管辖权提出质疑的大多数都是被告，不会是主动启动仲裁的原告。所以，这理论也常被称为"非法抗辩"（illegality defence）或"ex turpi causa defence"。

这主要是根据两个非法的大原则，也是拉丁文的格言：（1）"ex turpi causa（ex dolo malo）non oritur actio"（"no action arises from a disgraceful cause"或是中文的"违背道德的对价不生诉权"）。（2）"in pari delicto potior est conditio defendentis"（"where both parties are equally in the wrong the position of the defendant is the stronger"或是中文的"双方当事人的过错相等，被告地位更强"）。也就是既然合约非法，双方都做错，任何一方都无法在合约下成功向另一方索赔。

在后一个法律格言中，可以解释为何"非法理论"被视为"非法抗辩"。例如 A 与 B 在一个非法的交易订立的合约，如果双方有了争议是 A 要向 B 索赔损失或追回一笔债务或财产，B 就可以去亮出"非法理论"抗辩。相反，如果是 B 要向 A 索赔或追债，就轮到 A 可以去亮出"非法理论"了。反正如果是能够成立非法理论，法院就不再理会，不会协助执行一个非法的合约。这造成的结果是 Eldon 勋爵在

Muckleston v. Brown(1801)31 ER 934 先例中所说的:“Let the estate lie where it falls.”

非法抗辩主要是出现在合约的案件,而涉及侵权就相对少。这可节录 Asquith 勋爵在 National Coal Board v. England(1954)AC 403 贵族院先例中说:“The **vast majority of cases** in which the maxim has been applied have been cases where, there being **an illegal agreement** between A and B, either seeks to sue the other for its enforcement or for damages for its breach.... Cases where **an action in tort has been defeated by the maxim are exceedingly rare**.”(加黑部分是笔者的强调)

但即使是当事人都没有用“非法理论”提出抗辩,只要根据当事人披露的事实被法院发现合约非法,就不应该执行合约:见 Scott v. Brown, Doering, McNab & Co (1892)2 QB 724;[7] Chettiar v. Chettiar(1962)AC 294[8] 等先例。这早在 Langton v. Hughes(1813)105 ER 222 先例中,Ellenborough 大法官说:“What is done in contravention of the provisions of an Act of Parliament, cannot be made the subject-matter of an action.”

在 Patel v. Mirza 最高院先例中,Sumption 勋爵解释了背后的原因,说:“Whatever rationale one adopts for the illegality principle, it is manifestly designed to vindicate the public interest as against the interests and legal rights of the parties. That is why the judge is required to take the point of his own motion even if the parties have not raised it ...”

这种情况更容易发生在立法禁止某些交易与合约时,但也可以是普通法禁止。这样,法院在了解案件的案情后(如涉及通敌的买卖或串谋损害第三人权利),法院就可以拒绝协助执行,即使双方当事人都没有提出非法理论。

这可举 Mahmoud and Ispahani, Re(1921)2 KB 716 上诉庭先例为例,案情涉及《Seeds, Oils and Fats Order 1919》立法是禁止双方在没有牌照下进行买卖。原告卖方自己是有牌照,并且在订立买卖 150 吨的亚麻籽油前曾经问被告买方是否有牌照,买

---

[7] 该先例中,投资人起诉股票经纪人,主张经纪人并没有履行经纪人职责,即在公开市场上购买某公司股票出售给投资人,而是经纪人将自己持有的股票出售给了投资人。但在披露当事人之间的详细交易后,法院发现当事人之间的协议涉嫌投资人与经纪人约定,让经纪人用一笔资金伪造(forgery)该公司股票存在大量交易。这样,虽然双方当事人均没有提出非法问题,但仍然被法院认定合约非法与不会被执行。

[8] 当时马来西亚的《Rubber Regulations of 1934》立法规定超过 100 亩土地的橡胶生产要经过国家审核委员会的批准,而 100 亩土地以下的生产只要本地的有关机构批准即可。此先例中父亲拥有 139 亩土地生产橡胶,纯粹是为了避开立法中国家审核委员会的审核,将其中 40 亩土地在没有对价的情况下转让给了儿子,并完成了恰当的手续(如登记等)。事后父亲想要将全部土地出售给第三人,要求儿子办理土地转让手续,但遭到儿子拒绝,父亲就起诉要求法院认定儿子只是 40 亩土地的受托人(trustee)。但父亲要说明这点,不可避免地陈述了自己为什么这么做,导致欺骗当局的事实曝光在法院面前。虽然双方都没有提出非法理论的问题,但枢密院仍然指出父亲与儿子之间的安排非法,并且不会执行父亲的诉求。

方回答是有，但其实是没有，这显然是误述（misrepresentation）。之后买方拒绝收货（这种情况很多是因为市场有了变化），买方抗辩理由是合约非法（实是依赖自己非法）。一审判决卖方胜诉，他有牌照也只是被买方误导了才令买卖合约非法。这一审判法可说在任何合理第三人看来也是完全公平合理，但在上诉庭被推翻。原因可节录 Scrutton 大法官说：

"I think the law is laid down in Cope v. Rowlands (1836) 2 M&W 149, where Parke B., delivering the judgment of the Court, said: 'It is perfectly settled, that where the contract which the plaintiff seeks to enforce, be it express or implied, is expressly or by implication forbidden by the common or statute law, **no Court will lend its assistance to give it effect. It is equally clear that a contract is void**[9] **if prohibited by a statute**, ... if the contract be rendered illegal, it can make no difference, in point of law, whether the statute which makes it so has in view the protection of the revenue, or any other object. **The sole question is, whether the statute means to prohibit the contract**?'

If the contract is prohibited by statute, the Court is bound not to render assistance in enforcing an illegal contract.

As I understand, two reasons are given why in this case the Court should enforce this contract. First of all, it is said that the Court will not listen to a person who says, 'Protect me from my own illegality.' In my view **the Court is bound, once it knows that the contract is illegal, to take the objection and to refuse to enforce the contract**, whether its knowledge comes from the statement of the party who was guilty of the illegality, **or whether its knowledge comes from outside sources.** The Court does not sit to enforce illegal contracts. ... it is for the protection of the public that the Court refuses to enforce such a contract."（加黑部分是笔者的强调）

针对非法理论经常会适用的情况，Kerr 大法官在 Euro-Diam Ltd v. Bathurst (1990) 1 QB 1 上诉庭先例中总结说："The authorities show that in a number of situations the ex turpi causa defence will prima facie succeed. The main ones are: (i) where the plaintiff seeks to, or is forced to, found his claim on an illegal contract or to plead its illegality in order to support his claim ... For that purpose it makes no difference whether the illegality is raised in the plaintiff's claim or by way of a reply to a ground of defence... (ii) Where the grant of relief to the plaintiff would enable him to benefit from his criminal conduct ... (iii) Where, even though neither (i) nor (ii) is applicable to the plaintiff's claim, the situation is nevertheless residually covered by the general principle summarised in (i) above. ... This is most recently illustrated by the judgment of Hutchison J. in Thack-

---

〔9〕 关于无效（void）与可使无效（voidable）的区别，可见本书第三章之6.3.1段。这里要强调的是，合约因非法而"无效"或更正确的是法院不予执行，有关的分析可见本章之12段。

well v. Barclays Bank Plc[1986]1 All ER 676 …, as approved by this court in Saunders v. Edwards[1987]1 WLR 1116 … However, the ex turpi causa defence must be approached pragmatically and with caution, depending on the circumstances… This applies in particular to cases which at first sight appear to fall within 2(i) or(ii) above. Thus: (a) situations covered by (2)(i) above must be distinguished from others where the plaintiff's claim is not founded on any illegal act, but where some reprehensible conduct on his part is disclosed in the course of the proceedings, whether by the plaintiff himself or otherwise: see e. g. Pye Ltd. v. BG Transport Service Ltd. [1966]2 Lloyd's Rep. 300 … In such cases the ex turpi causa defence will not succeed."

1.3 非法理论与例外

上一段 Mahmoud and Ispahani, Re(1921)2 KB 716 上诉庭先例的判决可见到"非法理论"是太严格(strict)、太苛刻(harsh)与欠缺弹性(inflexible),并在很多个别案件看来判决是不公平合理。例如,双方都在非法合约下有过错,但支持被告的非法抗辩是会对非法的"主犯"太宽待而反过来对"从犯"原告太苛刻,特别是原告寻求法院协助的诉因是不当得利,如原告作为买家向被告购买违禁品并做出了支付,但被告既不交付货物,也不退还这一笔"完全得不到对价的好处"的货价。但在非法理论下,法院是不会考虑与审理案件双方当事人相互的强弱或错多错少,也不会有法律的分水岭(thresholds)是多少百分比以下的非法过错就可以协助执行。本来非法理论作为法律规定(rule of law)适用也简单:在非法合约或行为下,被告提出了非法抗辩,法院就要撒手不理,不予协助执行,没有其他的裁量权。正如在 Les Laboratoires Servier v. Apotex Inc(2014)UKSC 55 最高院先例中,Sumption 勋爵说:"two features of this area of law have been characteristic of it from the outset. First, it is a rule of law and not a mere discretionary power. …"

另普通法的发展也确立了一些对非法理论的例外,[10]其中一种例外是双方非但不是"过错对等",甚至是原告根本谈不上有任何非法的过错。这主要是原告因为被告的虚假陈述诱导(并且原告被诱导与依赖是完全合理)[11]、胁迫(duress)[12]或错误(mistake)[13]才订立非法合约,见 Ashley v. Reynolds(1731)2 Str 815; Hughes v. Liverpool Victoria Legal Friendly Society(1916)2 KB 482; Shelley v. Paddock(1980) QB 348 等先例。

另一种非法理论的例外是在 Kiriri Cotton Co Ltd v. Dewani(1960)2 WLR 127 枢密院先例中,案情涉及乌干达的立法《Rent Restriction Ordinance》写得不清楚,在房东

---

〔10〕 见本章之 10 段的详细介绍。

〔11〕 见本书第一章的介绍。

〔12〕 见本书第十章的介绍。

〔13〕 见本书第七章的介绍。

与租客对立法的共同错误理解下,房东非法向租客多收取了费用。在租客知道了情况后,向房东索赔并要求归还多收了的费用,但房东提出非法抗辩。在非法理论下,照说是双方应都是(或都不是)"过错对等"。但上诉庭判守法(乌干达立法)是房东的责任,所以双方并非"过错对等",租客胜诉。Denning 勋爵说:

"Nevertheless, no matter whether the mistake was excusable or inexcusable, or the premium fair or extortionate, the fact remains that the landlord received a premium contrary to the provisions of the Ordinance: and the question is whether the tenant can recover it back-remembering always that there is nothing in the Uganda Ordinance, comparable to the English Acts, enabling a premium to be recovered back. ...

It is clear that in the present case the illegal transaction was fully executed and carried out. The money was paid. The lease was granted. It was and still is vested in the plaintiff. In order to recover the premium, therefore, the plaintiff must show that he was not in pari delicto with the defendant. That was, indeed, the way he put his claim in the pleadings. ...

They were both equally supposed to know the law. They both equally mistook it and were thus in pari delicto. ...

The most important thing to observe is that the Rent Restriction Ordinance was intended to protect tenants from being exploited by landlords in days of housing shortage. ... **the Rent Restriction Ordinance was enacted so as to protect tenants from exploitation of that kind**.... It may be that the tenant who pays money is an accomplice or an aider and abettor ..., but **he can hardly be said to be in pari delicto** with the landlord. The duty of observing the law is firmly placed by the Ordinance on the shoulders of the landlord for the protection of the tenant: and **if the law is broken, the landlord must take the primary responsibility**."(加黑部分是笔者的强调)

看来,此先例是偏离了非法理论的法律规定,而考虑案件双方当事人相互的强弱或错多错少,如被告房东是有主要责任的"主犯",而原告租客顶多是"从犯"而不是"过错对等"。涉及立法下的非法,还要看看立法的本意是为了保护哪一类的当事人。如果受保护方即使对非法有一定程度过错,也不算是"过错对等"。这个例外在 Browing v. Morris(1788)2 Cowp 790 先例中,Mansfield 勋爵就已经提出过:"Where contracts or transactions are prohibited by positive statutes, for the sake of protecting one set of men from another set of men; the one, from their situation and condition, being liable to be oppressed or imposed upon by the other; there, the parties are not in pari delicto; and in furtherance of these statutes, the person injured, after the transaction is finished and completed, may bring his action and defeat the contract."

最后重提有说法是不少案件没有区分非法到底是"非法诉因"还是"非法抗辩",令这方面的法律更加困难与混乱。这照说也很有道理,法院看到一个明显与凭常识知道是严重非法的案件如杀人贩毒，是不会因为被告不提出非法抗辩而去协助执行。在 Mahmoud and Ispahani, Re 上诉庭先例中，Scrutton 大法官也有说到法院是可以由任何渠道知悉非法（whether the knowledge comes from outside sources），就一概不协助。但这带来的混乱会是方方面面，如以仲裁为例，非法诉因会是管辖权问题，而非法抗辩只是一项争议/争端。会否被告忘了提出非法抗辩，但在败诉后挑战这一裁决书的管辖权？

1.4 非法与公共政策

有说法是"非法理论"背后的原理可以广泛都归结于违反公共政策（public policy）。[14] Mansfield 勋爵在古老的 Holman v. Johnson（1775）1 Cowp 341 先例中，已经是明确了这一点，另也可节录在 Mogul Steamship Co Ltd v. McGregor Gow & Co（1892）AC 25 先例中，Halsbury 勋爵说："Some such contracts may be void on the ground of immorality; some on the ground that they are contrary to public policy; as, for example, in restraint of trade: and contracts so tainted the law will not lend its aid to enforce. It treats them as if they had not been made at all."

从广义上讲，非法理论涉及的都是对公共政策的违反。虽然买凶杀人、走私贩毒的严重刑事犯罪肯定是违反公共政策与公共利益，但违反公共政策是远不止这些行为。公共政策是十分模糊、多变、可紧可宽的概念，被形容为"一匹没有被驯服的野马"（an unruly horse）。英国的公共政策涉及英国的历史、文化、政治、经济、公众利益、道德等方方面面。依赖公共政策去判断非法影响合约效力的一个问题是带来合约的不肯定性。例如，公共政策会随着时代、环境、道德观念或国际形势的变化而发生变化。不少行为在过去的公共政策下禁止，但在今天已经放开；也会是过去允许但在今天禁止。如针对烟草问题，从过去的放任，到后来开始为保护人民健康而逐步收紧，在 2021 年底有新闻报道新西兰开始禁止年轻人购买烟草。这些例子是数不胜数，与这些行为有关系的合约都会是"非法理论"的范畴。可举几个不同例子：

1. 在笔者旧版的《国际商业游戏规则：英国合约法》一书曾介绍的一种情况也是与刑事犯罪无关，但在民事中就视为违法的非法例子，如侵权（tort）。在商业范畴，经常会发生的是在合约约定经济侵权（economic torts），[15] 就会带来非法理论的适用，如侵占（conversion）第三人货物。

2. 不少其他的违反公共政策也与刑事犯罪无关与/或刑法也管不了这么多、这么

---

〔14〕 "公共政策"的定义在笔者的《仲裁法：从开庭审理到裁决书的作出与执行》一书第十二章有详细介绍。

〔15〕 见本章之 2.1 段。

细。例如,Halsbury 勋爵提到的限制贸易(restraint of trade)[16]就经常在雇佣合约或其他各种类别的商业合约(如收/并购或合资等)限制"分手"后的商业竞争。这种条文会以各种形式出现,主要是禁止另一方的行为,主要是:(1)禁止竞争条文(non-compete restraint clauses);(2)禁止接触一些有关系的人士如某些客户、供应商、公司雇员或其他人士的条文(non-solicit restraint clauses);(3)禁止使用某些商业机密信息或知识产权、禁止披露的条文(non-disclosure clauses)。但这会是违反公共政策,因为利用合约把对方捆绑得太紧会影响对方的谋生与职业自由。例如,雇佣技术人员在雇佣合约加上条文限制如果其离职,今后 10 年或 20 年不得在全球同类技术的其他公司就职。这是把他们捆绑一生,一旦离职就必须退休,因为他们一辈子只懂这种技术与专业。而对公共利益而言,社会也可能失去了一位极其需要的技术人才等。

3. 另举一个与商业活动没有关系而是有关自杀的公共政策方面的议题。英国普通法一直视自杀为不道德、违反公共利益与犯罪行为。原因是每一位自然人都应该热爱自己的生命;每一位自然人都是社会一份子,无权自己决定剥夺生命;生命是上帝赐予等。这直到《Suicide Act 1961》的立法后,自杀才不再被视为非法。

在 Beresford v. Royal Insurance Company Limited(1938)AC 568 贵族院先例中,涉及一份人寿保险合约/保单。该保单有条文针对受保人的有意识的自杀(sane suicide),说明在承保 1 年后即使这种自杀也可以获得理赔。当然,这赔付只是会赔给保单的受益人(如妻子、子女等)或自杀的受保人的遗产执行人等。至于保险人为何愿意承保这种风险(类似承保船舶被船东刻意凿沉船的风险),显然是为了提升人寿保险的吸引力。加上衡量风险不会大,绝少会有人 1 年前就计划好自杀。而即使计划,也很有可能之后会转变想法,如经济改善、寻找到新的人生目标或信仰、找到新欢等。

在该先例的年代,自杀仍是犯罪/非法行为。该保单的受保人在投保 1 年后自杀。但保单的受益人与该非法行为无关,也不涉及协助或知道受保人自杀。根据保单明示条文,保险人履行合约责任作出理赔更是清楚无误。但在普通法的非法理论下,原告是不能从自己的非法行为中获利。虽然在此先例中,原告受益人不是自己犯罪,但仍是从受保人的非法行为中获利。这利益是通过自杀获得保单赔付就增加了他的遗产,让他的受益人(如妻子、子女等)受惠。

至于在当年将自杀视为非法与保单的明示条文起冲突,毕竟支持合约的肯定性也是英国法律的重要公共政策。但在权衡两个起冲突的公共政策后,显然保单的受保人 1 年后自杀条文是要让路给将自杀视为非法的公共政策,条文是无效。众所周

---

〔16〕 限制贸易的公共政策在普通法下有悠久的历史,是普通法下最早一批发展起来的公共政策,也在此公共政策下促进了英国贸易的发展与繁荣。在 Tillman v. Egon Zehnder(2019)UKSC 32 最高院先例中,Wilson 勋爵这样介绍说:"The doctrine is one of the earliest products of the common law. It epitomises the nation which developed it:a nation which has ascribed central importance to the freedom of all of us to work-in the interests both of the self-sufficiency of ourselves and our families and of our common prosperity."这也可见本章之 2.2 段与 11.2 段的介绍。

知,订约自由是不能超越公共政策的。所以贵族院判原告在非法理论下败诉,不获保险赔付。但这个问题在《Suicide Act 1961》的立法后就不再存在。

4. 最后再多举一个例子是国与国之间的公共政策可能有很大差异。英国法院也面对大量的涉外合约(foreign-related contracts)前来要求作出各种协助执行,往往合约的适用法/准据法(proper law/applicable law)也是外国法。所以,这只涉及英国国际睦仪/礼让(international comity)的公共政策,如涉外合约违反外国友好国家的法律或公共政策,英国法院是不予协助执行:见 Foster v. Driscoll(1929)1 KB 470 与 Ralli Brothers v. Compania Naviera Sota Y Aznar(1920)2 KB 287 等上诉庭先例。

公共政策问题是一个复杂多变也没有边际的课题,笔者无意在此讨论太多,只希望上面的介绍已经清楚地将违反公共政策与违反英国法律区分出来。

1.5 非法理论与其他不同公共政策之间的对抗

在权威的 Patel v. Mirza(2016)UKSC 42 最高院先例中,Toulson 勋爵总结非法理论不予执行合约(或其他索赔)背后的公共政策为以下两方面:(1)任何人士不能从自己的错误行为中获利。这与"违背道德的对价不生诉权"的政策性法律规则是同一码事,无论是谁作为原告去要求法院协助执行一份非法合约都不会成功。(2)法律不能轻易容忍非法,必须要保持一致性,不能自我阻碍。例如,不能"右手"禁止非法,"左手"又允许执行涉及非法行为的合约。

Toulson 勋爵还指出了非法理论背后的大精神是维护英国法律整体的正直、提升英国社会道德,说:"... there are two broad discernible policy reasons for the common law doctrine of illegality as a defence to a civil claim. One is that a person should not be allowed to profit from his own wrongdoing. The other, linked, consideration is that the law should be coherent and not self-defeating, condoning illegality by giving with the left hand what it takes with the right hand... The essential rationale of the illegality doctrine is that it would be contrary to the public interest to enforce a claim if to do so would be harmful to the integrity of the legal system(or, possibly, certain aspects of public morality, the boundaries of which have never been made entirely clear ...)."

显然非法理论所涉及的两条主要的公共政策在适用时会与其他公共政策起冲突。因为这两条公共政策是至高无上的,所以很少有其他公共政策能抗衡。毕竟即使维护法治社会运行而需要将法律业务特免权(legal professional privilege)提升为绝对性权利(absolute right),[17]也有罪行原则(iniquity principle)[18]的例外。以下针对不同公共政策之间权衡问题。

1.5.1 适用非法理论是对不同公共政策冲突的权衡

一旦涉及非法理论的诉讼,往往会有其他背后的公共政策与上一段 Toulson 勋

---

〔17〕 见笔者《证据法:国际规管与诉讼中的证据攻防》一书第九章之 2.3 段。

〔18〕 见笔者《证据法:国际规管与诉讼中的证据攻防》一书第十一章之 1.2 段。

爵所说的公共政策相对抗。而公共政策之间除非涉及特别考虑,否则实际上都是对有冲突的公共政策之间进行轻重的权衡。这就是 Patel v. Mirza(2016)UKSC 42 最高院先例中确立的三阶段测试(three-stage test)中第二阶段测试(stage B test)必须考虑以非法理论否定了原告的索赔并不予执行权利会对其他有关公共政策造成的影响("to consider any other relevant public policy on which the denial of the claim may have an impact"),也是目前普通法判断非法理论是否适用的一个重要测试。这会在本章之7.5.3段详细介绍,在此不再展开。只多节录在 Hounga v. Allen(2014)UKSC 47 最高院先例中,Wilson 勋爵说:"The defence of illegality rests upon the foundation of public policy... So it is necessary, first, to ask 'What is the aspect of public policy which founds the defence?' and, second, to ask 'But is there another aspect of public policy to which application of the defence would run counter'?"

R(Best) v. Chief Land Registrar(2015)EWCA Civ 17 上诉庭先例显示了不同公共政策起冲突时的权衡。此先例中,一名"擅自占地人"(squatter)在没有得到不动产产权人(地主)同意的情况下在1997年侵占一幢空置与破损的房屋,之后进行了大量工程修缮与让房屋恢复到适合居住的状态,并在2001年开始以自己的名义居住在该房屋内。在2012年1月,该人士试图以逆权侵占(adverse possession)[19]为由将房产登记在自己名下。问题是在2012年生效的《Legal Aid, Sentencing and Punishment of Offenders Act 2012》立法中,擅自占地人的行为属于该立法之 Section 144 下规定的刑事犯罪行为。[20] 这就带来争议,是否适用非法理论,擅自占地人不能通过自己的刑事犯罪行为成为不动产产权人?

法院在此先例中,就考虑了两个不同的公共政策:(1)当事人不能从自己的刑事行为中获利;与(2)公共利益下应该允许逆权侵占。[21] 最后给出是即使擅自占地人的行为非法,仍然可根据逆权侵占获得不动产产权。可以节录 Sales 大法官所说如下:"... the wider idea that a person should not benefit from his own wrong has not prevented the law of adverse possession from operating. Adverse possession is, of course,

---

[19] 简单而言,是本没有占有权的擅自占地人,像不动产产权人一样,对地产事实上、持续性、公开与明显地占有,意图排除其他人(包括原本真正不动产产权人)的权利。在经过一段时间之后,擅自占地人也可以变成不动产产权人。今天英国法下采取土地登记制度后,在《Land Registration Act 2002》下规定擅自占地人可以提出申请,由登记官(registrar)通知相关人士后,再决定是否登记其为不动产产权人。这看来比只是事实上的占有更进一步,就是法律允许通过登记而令占有人变为土地的合法产权人,可以将来转卖、遗产继承等。

[20] 可节录该条文如下:"(1) A person commits an offence if—(a) the person is in a residential building as a trespasser having entered it as a trespasser, (b) the person knows or ought to know that he or she is a trespasser, and (c) the person is living in the building or intends to live there for any period..."

[21] 逆权侵占的制度看来是与资本主义下产权神圣的公共政策相矛盾,所以并不会轻易成立。其背后的公共政策是避免有限与宝贵的土地资源的浪费,打击囤积土地的行为。中国香港特区也有一样的制度,占有人占有土地超过12年,占有人就可以用逆权侵占去抗辩真正产权人要回土地的诉讼。

founded on the tort of trespass to land. **The public interest in having land put to good use and in having clear rules to govern acquisition of title to land which has been abandoned has been taken to override the general concern that a person should not benefit from their unlawful actions**. Since 1833, the balance of public interest has been expressed in statutory form by the law of limitation in relation to unregistered land, which is now set out in section 15 and 17 of Limitation Act 1980. Since 1925, the same balance of public interest has been expressed by similar provision allowing for title to registered land to be acquired by adverse possession, as now set out in the relevant provisions of the LRA."

在美国法下也有类似需要权衡公共政策的说法,可见 Restatement(2nd) of Contracts(1981)之 Para 178(1):"A promise or other term of an agreement is unenforceable on grounds of public policy if legislation provides that it is unenforceable or the interest in its enforcement is clearly outweighed in the circumstances by a public policy against the enforcement in such terms."

1.5.2 非法理论与合约订约自由和合约神圣性公共政策的冲突

支持双方的订约自由与合约神圣性本身也是非常重要的公共政策。而如果有其他公共政策会影响合约效力,就必然与此公共政策产生冲突。由于合约订约自由大原则与合约神圣性的首要地位,一般在权衡之下都是优先的,法院不会轻易用非法理论影响合约的效力与执行。这方面可见 Printing and Numerical Registering Co v. Sampson(1875)3 WLUK 22 先例中,Jessel 大法官说:"It must not be forgotten that you are not to extend arbitrarily those rules which say that a given contract is void as being against public policy, because if there is one thing which more than another public policy requires it is that men of full age and competent understanding shall have the utmost liberty of contracting, and that their contracts when entered into freely and voluntarily shall be held sacred and shall be enforced by Courts of justice. Therefore, you have this paramount public policy to consider—that you are not lightly to interfere with this freedom of contract."

不妨简单举两个例子来显示法院在有可能解释得通时,就尽量避免认定为非法合约。法院的处理办法包括对合约条文进行宽松解释,与看能否适用本章之 10 段会介绍的各种非法的例外(exceptions)等。这也配合笔者《合约的解释:规则与应用》一书第四章之 12 段介绍的"假设合约是合法"(presumption of legality)的解释规则的精神与原则,也与 6 段的解释规则,即解释合约尽量令它有效而不是无效(Ut res magis valeat quam pereat)的道理一样。

1. 首先介绍是 Fielding & Platt Ltd v. Najjar(1969)1 WLR 357 上诉庭先例。此先例中原告是一家英国的机器制造公司,被告是一家黎巴嫩公司的董事总经理。原告作为卖方与黎巴嫩公司作为买方就一台价值 23.5 万英镑的铝挤压机(aluminium ex-

trusion press)订立生产与销售合约,合约约定付款方式是由被告个人按照铝挤压机生产的进度分期开出六张本票。但该黎巴嫩公司在黎巴嫩法律下无权进口该类机器,被告因此希望原告将发票上的货品名称写为黎巴嫩公司有权进口的轧钢机(rolling mill)部件,这看来是用来欺骗黎巴嫩有关当局。合约开始履行后,英国公司也按照黎巴嫩公司的要求开出发票,但黎巴嫩公司未能按期付款,原告提起诉讼。被告提出因为采用虚假发票而合约非法。上诉庭判非法理论不适用,Denning 勋爵首先将被告的抗辩定性为他违反自己国家法律的行为,并想要通过将英国公司卷入该非法行为从而不能在合约下寻求救济。接下来 Denning 勋爵通过逐步扩大的分析从各方面排除非法理论的适用。这三个层层推进式的理由是:(1)合约中并没有条文要求卖方英国公司开出虚假发票,从而令合约不能够被合法履行。(2)即使合约中有这样的条文,被告还要证明原告英国公司知悉这种安排在黎巴嫩法律下是非法的,并且积极参与到该非法的行为中。但从当事人之间的通信往来看,英国公司对这样开发票在黎巴嫩法律下构成非法并不知情,[22]只是知道这样做对于黎巴嫩公司来说较为方便在本地使用。(3)即使退一万步来说,合约中有一条条文明确写明是为了欺骗黎巴嫩当局,卖方英国公司要开出虚假发票,虽然该条文自身会因非法而无效,但开发票是相对独立的行为,显然可以与其他合约条文的内容进行分割(severable),[23]从而令其他合约条文不受非法的影响而可以被履行。经过分割之后,英国公司就可以依约以 FOB 在英国装港交货,并开出真实的发票给黎巴嫩公司。被告也要依约去付款,而不能说“合约条文约定的是开出虚假发票,你没有依约履行”,因为该条文已经因为非法而无效。

Denning 勋爵说:“He(被告黎巴嫩公司)says:‘I asked you to invoice the press as part of a rolling-mill, and you agreed to it, and, therefore, you cannot recover anything.’ That defence does not commend itself to me. **Here is a man who prays in aid his own illegality** — he admits he was trying to evade the laws of his own country — and he seeks to implicate the English company in it.

In order for this to be any kind of defence, **he must show first of all that the contract contained a term that the English company were to give a false invoice**: so that it could not lawfully be performed.... **I do not think there was any such term**. ...

In the second place, even if it were a term, the defendant would have to show that the English company **were implicated in this illegality**, that is, **that they had knowledge of it and were actively participating in it** ... I can see no evidence worthy of the name to suggest that the English company knew of this illegality. The only evidence is contained in a cable about the import licence. On June 16, 1965, the English company said they were

---

〔22〕 见本章之 10.1.2 与 10.1.3 段。

〔23〕 见本章之 11 段。

agreeable to the proposed contract ' subject to evidence of satisfactory importing licence arrangements. ' The Lebanese company replied:...

I do not think that cable was enough to give the English company knowledge of the illegality. It only shows that the Lebanese company thought it convenient, for local consumption,...

There is another point: even if there was a term that these goods should be invoiced falsely in order to deceive the Lebanese authorities, I do not think it would render the whole contract void. **That term would be void for illegality. But it can clearly be severed from the rest of the contract.** It can be rejected, leaving the rest of the contract good and enforceable. The English company would be entitled, despite the illegal term, to deliver the goods f. o. b. English port, and send a true and accurate invoice to the Lebanese buyer. The Lebanese buyer could not refuse the goods by saying ' I stipulated for a false invoice. ' He could not rely on his own iniquity so as to refuse payment. "(加黑部分是笔者的强调)

2. Waugh v. Morris(1873)LR 8 QB 202 先例涉及从法国运输干草前往伦敦的租约,订约方不知道当时在《Cattle Diseases Act 1869》立法下法国已成为疫区,伦敦码头禁止卸载来自法国的干草。在船舶到达伦敦双方发现问题后,干草只能被转运去其他国家港口。其间船舶产生延误,船东索赔滞期费(demurrage),承租人以租约的目的是非法进行抗辩。

法院判虽然双方订约方在租约订立时并不知道合约的目的非法不是一个可以接受的理由,但由于最后租约被合法履行,这表示租约是可以合法履行的,也表示船东订立租约时的目的是预期承租人可以合法履行。这样承租人如果想以非法抗辩,去逃避租约下支付滞期费的责任,就需要证明船东在订立租约时是知道这个立法与有非法目的才可以。这显然是与事实不符,也证明不了,所以承租人败诉。Blackburn 大法官说:

"... in the present case the shipowner never did even contemplate or believe that the defendant would violate the law. He contemplated that the defendant would land the goods which he thought was lawful; but if he had thought at all of the possibility of the landing being prohibited, he would probably have expected that the defendant would in that case not violate the law. And he would have been right in fact in that expectation, for the defendant did not attempt to land the goods.

We quite agree, that, **where a contract is to do a thing which cannot be performed without a violation of the law it is void, whether the parties knew the law or not**. But we think, that in order **to avoid a contract which can be legally performed, on the ground that there was an intention to perform it in an illegal manner**, it is necessary to shew that there was the wicked intention to break the law; and, if this be so, the knowledge of what the law is becomes of great importance.

No one could for a moment contend, that if everything which happened in France had happened within the jurisdiction of our country, the plaintiff and defendant's agent could have been successfully indicted for a conspiracy to violate the law by landing these goods: for there would have been a want of mens rea. And it seems to us that the mens rea is as necessary to avoid a contract, which can be legally performed, because when it was made it was with the object of satisfying an illegal purpose, as it is to render the parties criminally responsible."(加黑部分是笔者的强调)

但在以上先例英国法院只是在解释合约时尽量宽松,不会"重写"合约令合约变为合法与更加合理。加拿大法院看来在这方面走得更远,在 Transport North American Express Inc v. New Solutions Financial Corp(2004)1 SCR 248 加拿大最高院先例中,涉及一笔贷款的利息约定得太高,违反了立法规定的60%年利率的上限。上诉庭以分割非法部分理论否定掉贷款合约的利息条文,只协助执行本金的归还,没有利息。但去了最高院,上诉庭的判决被否定,改为"重写"合约把利息支付定在立法上限的60%年利率。

最后,即使针对的并非合约而是侵权问题,普通法的态度看来也一样是尽量避免用非法理论去影响本可以要求的赔偿。在 Hall v. Hebert(1993)2 SCR 159 加拿大最高院先例[24]中,McLachlin 大法官就提到法院要保护法律系统整体的正直与公义,不允许一个人从自己的非法或错误行为中获利。而在侵权关系,尤其是疏忽侵权中,一般涉及的实际上是对损失的赔偿而不是获利,因此一般也谈不上涉及非法理论。

2. 非法合约与行为的类型

对几百年来林林总总的非法案件,《Chitty on Contracts》(2021 年,第 34 版)一书之 18-001 段将涉及"非法理论"的案件分成三大类。可先节录该段说法如下:"Within the heading of 'illegality' there is a distinction between cases in which the claims will not be enforced on the grounds of illegality in a narrow sense of being contrary to public policy because the contract somehow involves **the commission of a legal wrong**, and cases in which the claim may not be enforced for reasons of **public policy even though no otherwise unlawful act is involved**. Further, for reasons that may also be described broadly as a public policy, some contractual claims are rendered unenforceable

---

〔24〕 涉及的案情简单而言是汽车车主与乘客都喝了酒。在行使中途,汽车熄火,但车主又找不到钥匙,因此打算推动启动(roll starting)。在乘客的要求下,车主允许乘客在推动启动时坐上驾驶位控制汽车方向。结果汽车翻车,导致该乘客受伤,乘客即向车主索赔侵权导致的人身伤害损失。

by statute(**statutory illegality**)."(加黑部分是笔者的强调)

以下区别介绍这三大类(其中难免有重叠)在非法理论下属于非法的情况。

2.1 触犯法律(legal wrong)

可以说任何涉及违反立法与/或普通法的都是触犯法律,也因此触犯法律针对的范围十分广泛与数不胜数。与非法理论关系密切的,就会是违法的刑事犯罪行为,或者是涉及欺诈/欺骗(fraud/deceit)、不诚实(dishonest)行为,侵犯第三人权利的侵权等民事错误行为等。

可节录《Chitty on Contracts》(2021 年,第 34 版)一书之 18-058 至 18-062 段介绍的一些触犯法律并会影响合约的行为如下:

"**Examples of criminality** Criminal acts or objects which disentitle a party to contractual relief include doing something forbidden by statute, or delegated legislation,[25] such as infringing food and drug legislation or exchange control legislation, and the commission of offences at common law[26] such as publication of a criminal libel and blasphemy. A fortiori the courts will not enforce a contract the object of which is such as to render the contract a criminal conspiracy, e. g. to corrupt public morals or to rig the market for shares in a company...[27]

Fraud Where the object of a contract is the perpetration of a fraud, e. g. upon prospective shareholders in a company or upon the Government, or a trader the contract is illegal. Such frauds are usually criminal but the rule appears to be general; thus a creditor cannot enforce an agreement with an insolvent debtor under which the latter is to pay him an amount in excess of his share under a composition agreement since the agreement to do so is a fraud upon the other parties to the composition agreement. Likewise it is against public policy to enforce an agreement where the purpose of both parties was to defeat the proper claims of the Commissioners of Inland Revenue or of a rating authority...

Other civil wrongs If a contract has as its object the deliberate commission of a tort, it would seem that the contract is illegal, even though no criminality or fraud is involved.[28] Thus a printer cannot recover the cost of printing matter which he knew to be

---

〔25〕 这是一些立法的刑事犯罪。包括英国议会的立法,以及委任立法/次级立法(delegated legislation/secondary legislation)。次级立法即被英国议会授权或委任给政府部门或其他有关机构订立的法律,往往是议会立法给出大原则与方向后,由次级立法补充其中的细节。常见的政府部门等制定的各类法规、规章等多属于次级立法。

〔26〕 也会是一些普通法刑事犯罪,如刑事诽谤(criminal libel)、亵渎神明(blasphemy)等。

〔27〕 刑事串谋(criminal conspiracy)犯罪。例如在 Slaughter & May v. Brown Doering McNab & Co(1892)2 QB 724 先例中当事人约定刑事串谋伪造交易抬高股价的行为。

〔28〕 例如,在早期的 Allen v. Rescous(1676)2 Lev 174 先例中,涉及约定殴打第三人,这虽然没有达到刑事犯罪程度,但构成暴力威胁(assault)的民事侵权而非法。

libellous and the purchaser cannot recover a sum of money deposited with the printer on account of the cost to be incurred in printing it.[29] ..."

英国刑事犯罪的范围很广,从最严重的买凶杀人,到大量规章中涉及商业行为的轻微罪行都属于刑事犯罪。

以上节录段落中提到的民事错误行为在社会与商业活动中常见的涉及非法问题是欺诈/欺骗与不诚实的行为。这种例子多不胜数,有些也已经有刑事法律针对,另也是民事法律下的侵权与错误行为。其中欺诈/欺骗行为可随手举几个例子:虚报财产如不动产价值的逃税漏税行为;借用第三人名义获取贷款或提供虚假文件如阴阳合约骗取贷款的贷款欺诈/骗贷(mortgage fraud)行为;或是在明知会损害其他债权人利益的情况下将破产人士优先对待个别友好债权人的欺诈性优待(fraudulent preference)行为等。

本质相同并在商业活动常见的是合约因为涉及有目的地侵犯第三人权利而非法。在 Brown Jenkinson & Co Ltd v. Percy Dalton(London)Ltd(1957)2 QB 621 先例中涉及的是船东明知付运的货物在装船时已经损坏,但仍然在发货人签发保函(letter of indemnity)的情况下出具清洁提单(clean bill of lading),这清洁提单显然是被用来"欺骗"结汇银行与/或收货人。因此事后船东在赔付收货人损失后,想要在保函下向发货人寻求救济时,就涉及保函属于欺骗侵权(tort of deceit)而不可执行。Morris 大法官提到合约用于侵权目的时,会由于非法导致法院不协助执行,而且判词的措辞/文字写得宽泛也没有限定只是在欺骗侵权,说:"It is, I think, clear that the plaintiffs did not desire that anyone should be defrauded. In agreeing with the defendants, they did not have any such desire as their real purpose... But the question which here arises is whether the contract sued upon was founded upon an illegal consideration. **An agreement is illegal and unenforceable if it has as its object the commission of a tort.**"(加黑部分是笔者的强调)

与商业活动关系密切的侵权是一些主要保障营商不受非法干预(tortious interference with trade and business)的经济侵权(economic torts),以保护个人财富或预期经济利益。

普通法一贯认可市场竞争的正当性,认为优胜劣汰是市场经济(尤其是资本主义经济)发展的核心推动力。而市场竞争是非常无情的,有人获利就通常意味着有其他人士失去获利机会甚至是蒙受损失。但普通法的态度是法院会尽量避免限制一般与正常的竞争行为,即使社会有需要也是立法机构(英国议会)去解决问题。在 Swedac Ltd v. Magnet & Southerns Plc(1989)1 FSR 243 先例中,Harman 大法官说:"... the damage by one trader to another's trade is the essence of the results of competition. The man who makes a better mousetrap, leading to people beating a path to his door

---

〔29〕 这针对的是早期的 Apthorp v. Neville & Co(1907)23 TLR 575 先例,双方都知道印刷用作诽谤仍然继续推进合约而非法。

to buy it, will inevitably damage the business of the makers of the earlier, worse mousetraps; they will, perhaps sadly, go out of business unless they are backed; but that is what competition is about; and that is what has been the driving force for the success of the capitalist world. It is an absolutely fundamental proposition … that this alleged tort really amounts to saying that there has been competition, and adding the old nursery cry 'It's unfair!' To that I would only cite my nanny's great nursery proposition: 'The world is a very unfair place and the sooner you get to know it the better.'"

但这些竞争行为也不能无限制。很显然如果采用暴力威胁、欺诈,或联合起来形成大势力欺压等手段就是不会被接受的。例如,英国普通法的经济侵权早期的很多发展针对的是英国工会组织的蓬勃发展和变得越来越强大。工会组织的各种罢工与联合抵制的手段都会严重影响商业社会与社会民生,并构成各种侵权行为(如呼吁消费者不要再去某商家购物,要求在职的公会成员罢工/怠工,逼迫企业解雇非工会成员等)。工会的发展需要立法的保护(如《Trade Union and Labour Relations Act 1974》之 Sections 13 & 14 等),才可以对这些经济侵权免责。这些立法条文是扩张还是收紧限制也成为当年英国政治斗争的焦点。在近 100 年来国际贸易商业社会的发展中,也出现越来越多各种不同形式侵害他人营商、经济利益的不恰当行为[如限制贸易行为,行业内通过卡特尔协议(cartel agreements)等方式操纵、垄断市场等]。近年来,还出现了形形色色的设立离岸公司后,母公司或公司董事任意操纵离岸公司躲避债务、转移资产、减免自己对第三人的侵权责任(如严重环境污染或危险工作环境造成的侵权)等行为。因此,英国法院发展了经济侵权的制度允许一定程度限制竞争。在 Mogul Steamship Co Ltd v. McGregor Gow & Co(1892) AC 25 贵族院先例的二审[(1889) 23 QBD 598]中,上诉庭的 Bowen 大法官说:"What, then, are the limitations which the law imposes on a trader in the conduct of his business as between himself and other traders? There seem to be no burdens or restrictions in law upon a trader which arise merely from the fact that he is a trader, and which are not equally laid on all other… His right to trade freely is a right which the law recognises and encourages, but it is one which places him at no special disadvantage as compared with others. No man, whether trader or not, can, however, justify **damaging another in his commercial business by fraud or misrepresentation. Intimidation, obstruction, and molestation are forbidden; so is the intentional procurement of a violation of individual rights, contractual or other**, assuming always that there is **no just cause** for it …"(加黑部分是笔者的强调)

需要采用经济侵权,就是因为真正采取行动而且有财力值得被起诉的人士往往与受损害人士之间不存在合约关系,如在背后主导的工会与受损害的公司或雇员个人。而且为了尽量避免影响一般与正常的竞争,法院会考虑很多因素,例如侵权人是否存在恶意(malice)或意图(intention)针对性伤害他人经济利益,又如会考虑是否采取了不受法律保护的不法行为(unlawful act)等。

但一方面是应该认可市场竞争正当性尽量避免干预,另一方面是为了公平正义的目标阻止一些竞争行为,在这两者对抗之下法院过去一度有比较混乱的判法,经过经济侵权行为的权威 OBG Ltd v. Allan(2007)UKHL 21 贵族院先例后才逐渐稳定。本书并不针对侵权法律,因此也不打算一一详细针对各种不同经济侵权行为的构成要件。只节录在《Clerk & Lindsell on Torts》(2020 年,第23 版)一书之23 -01 段中这样介绍经济侵权:"The torts of procuring a breach of contract,intimidation,causing loss by unlawful means and the two forms of conspiracy are generally described today as 'the economic torts'. They form the core of the tort liabilities for intentional disruption of economic interests and the principles governing them are interrelated.... The term 'economic tort' is also applied more widely to other torts,such as passing off,malicious falsehood,slander of title,and wrongs in respect of patents,trademarks or breach of copyright(often referred to as wrongs to 'intellectual property') with which the core economic torts are frequently contiguous. The core economic torts also exist in parallel with,and sometimes overlap with,equitable wrongs such as 'knowing receipt' and 'knowing assistance'."

以上提到狭义的经济侵权,针对意图就是伤害他人的行为,主要是诱导他人违约/毁约(induce a breach of contract)、[30]恐吓(intimidation)、[31]采用不法方式造成他人经济损失(causing loss by unlawful means/unlawful interference with trade)[32]以

---

〔30〕 诱导他人违约/毁约侵权也被称为次要/从犯责任(accessory liability),针对的是在没有正当理由的情况下,侵权人/合约第三人知情(knowledge)与意图(intention)直接诱导一方合约方采取违约/毁约行为,造成违约/毁约后果与合约无辜方损失,此时侵权人要承担合约违约/毁约的次要/从犯责任:见 Lumley v. Gye(1853)2 El & Bl 216;Allen v. Flood(1898)AC 1;Said v. Butt(1920)3 KB 497;DC Thomson & Co Ltd v. Deakin(1952)Ch 646;OBG Ltd v. Allan(2007)UKHL 21;Palmer Birch(a partnership)v. Lloyd(2018)EWHC 2316(TCC)等先例。背后的原理主要是任何人士都应该有与他人订约、履行合约的自由与权利,法律也保护这样的权利不被侵犯。但也会有一些允许侵犯的正当理由,如货物卖方一物两卖,签订最初买卖合约的买方 A 为了在市场短缺的情况下让自己的合约被履行,给额外的好处压倒后一个买方 B 的价格,保证 A、C 之间的合约被履行,就可以抗辩说有合理理由。但如果是 B 在知道 A 与 C 已经签订合约的情况下,故意出高价、允诺会补偿 C 需要赔偿给 A 的损失等方式,诱导 C 对 A 违约/毁约,损害 A 的经济利益,这就是经济侵权行为了。今天这类侵权也会包括如公司作为法院判决债务人时,公司老板转移公司资产逃避债务的侵权行为(Marex tort):见 Marex Financial Limited v. Sevilleja(2017)EWHC 918(Comm)等先例。

〔31〕 恐吓侵权包括采取各种刑事犯罪行为、侵权行为或甚至是违约行为,导致被恐吓人作为/不作为,并导致被恐吓人或第三人产生损失。典型的恐吓就是暴力威胁,也会如工会威胁公司必须解雇(或不得解雇)特定非工会成员,否则就号召工会成员非法罢工。这方面先例可见 Garret v. Taylor(1620)Cro Jac 567;Tarleton v. McGawley(1793)170 ER 153;Rookes v. Barnard(1964)AC 1129 先例等。但在 OBG Ltd v. Allan(2007)UKHL 21 先例后,有说法是这类侵权应该一并归入"采用不法方式造成他人经济损失"的侵权。恐吓侵权在本书第十章之 12.2 段已有涉及。

〔32〕 采用不法方式造成他人经济损失,既需要侵权人意图损害被侵权人的经济利益,还需要侵权人采取了不被法律支持的不法行为或方式,并实际造成了被侵权人的损失。这类案件可见 National Phonograph Co Ltd v. Edison Bell Co Ltd(1908)1 Ch 335;Rookes v. Barnard(1964)AC 1129;Lonrho Ltd v. Shell Petroleum Co Ltd(1982)AC 173;Secretary of State for Health v. Servier Laboratories Ltd(2021)UKSC 24 等先例。什么是这里所说的不法行为或方式还会在稍后介绍。

及串谋(conspiracy)。[33]

除此以外,还有更广义的经济侵权,可以包括其他任何各种形式的侵权行为,只要能够造成经济利益损失的后果。例如,欺骗侵权,仿冒(passing off),[34]诽谤行为如恶意虚假陈述(malicious falsehood)与产权诽谤(slander of title),[35]各类侵犯知识产权如专利(patent)、商标(trademark)与著作权(copy right),还可能包括破坏机密(breach of confidence),[36]或者今天的抢占域名(cyber/domain squatting)等。还有在今天一些疏忽侵权(negligence tort)行为在 Hedley Byrne v. Heller(1964)AC 465 先例后,也会涉及影响了营商,因此索赔纯经济损失(pure economic losses)。[37]

为了不让经济侵权的范围过于广泛,法院常常考虑的问题是是否存在不法行为或方式,如采用不法方式造成他人经济损失,或者是不法方式的串谋侵权都必须涉及不法行为或方式。但这问题看来尚有争议。

过去有很广泛的说法,不法行为或方式应该是广泛包括任何法律下不会支持从事的行为,例如 OBG Ltd v. Allan 先例中给出少数意见的 Nicholls 勋爵说:"'unlawful means' embraces all acts a defendant is not permitted to do, whether by the civil law or the criminal law."因此会包括任何普通法或立法侵权、刑事犯罪、违约/毁约、违反信托与衡平责任、违背信赖义务等("It covers common law torts, statutory torts, crimes,

---

〔33〕 串谋侵权必须涉及两人或以上的侵权人士联合(combine)或达成协议(agreement)。而具体的侵权行为主要包括两种:(1)串谋伤害(conspiracy to injure)或合法方式的串谋(lawful means conspiracy),也就是主要目的就是意图伤害被侵权人并造成损失,此时无论行为本身是否不法,均会构成侵权。例如在 Quinn v. Leathem(1901)AC 496 先例中,工会施加合法压力,要求商家开除非工会成员的雇员,但是这些雇员想要加入工会都被拒绝,这就变成纯粹是为了私仇要伤害这些雇员,而不是为了公会成员的利益了。然而今天社会上常见的商业竞争,这种没有任何自己经济利益、纯粹伤害他人的行为看来并不容易证明。(2)不法方式的串谋(unlawful means conspiracy),即串谋以不法方式造成被侵权人损失,此时由于属于不法方式,也就显然是不正当的行为,也不要求行为的主要目的是伤害被侵权人了。这方面可见 OBG Ltd v. Allan(2007)UKHL 21;Customs and Excise Commissioners v. Total Network SL(2008)UKHL 19;Fish & Fish Ltd v. Sea Shepherd UK(2015)UKSC 10 等先例。这两种串谋的区别可见 Rookes v. Barnard(1964)AC 1129;Lonrho Ltd v. Shell Petroleum Co Ltd(1982)AC 173;Kuwait Oil Tanker v. Al Bader(2000)2 All ER(Comm)271 等先例。

〔34〕 仿冒经营,主要是一方仿冒成另一方提供的产品或服务,例如,采用类似的名字或标志导致仿冒与误导。如在笔者的《证据法:国际规管与诉讼中的证据攻防》一书第五章之 7.5.1 段中介绍的涉及伦敦旅游巴士的 London General Omnibus Company v. Lavell(1901)1 Ch 135 著名先例等。

〔35〕 恶意虚假陈述,即恶意刊登对被侵权人的商业、财产等经济利益不利的虚假陈述,例如,诋毁说竞争对手的产品存在重大缺陷容易造成危害,并给对手带来经济损害,有关先例可见 London Ferro-Concrete Co Ltd v. Justicz(1951)68 RPC 261 上诉庭先例等。产权诽谤(slender of title),就是针对财产的产权恶意虚假陈述,造成财产的转让交易无法正常完成:见 Green v. Button(1835)2 CM & 707 先例等。

〔36〕 见 Campbell v. MGN Ltd(2004)UKHL 22 最高院先例中,Douglas v. Hello! Ltd(No. 3)(2005)EWCA Civ 595 上诉庭先例等。

〔37〕 见本书第一章之 2.2.1.2 段。

breaches of contract, breaches of trust and equitable obligations, breaches of confidence, and so on")。

但 OBG Ltd v. Allan 贵族院先例中多数意见的 Hoffmann 勋爵,针对什么是"不法",说应该限制在受害方本就有独立诉因可以提起诉讼(或只是由于没有损失而没有诉因)的情况:"In my opinion, and subject to one qualification, acts against a third party count as unlawful means only if they are actionable by that third party. The qualification is that they will also be unlawful means if the only reason why they are not actionable is because the third party has suffered no loss..."

这样也就大大限制了不法的范围,但是也带来了很多问题。例如,一个重要问题是这看来就排除了应该由政府的检控机关提起的刑事诉讼,Hoffmann 勋爵对此解释说法院不应该自己为这些议会权衡后设立的刑事后果还额外设立民事诉因:"it is not for the courts to create a cause of action out of a ... criminal statute which Parliament did not intend to be actionable in private law."

但很快在后来由不同的大法官们审理的 Revenue and Customs Comrs v. Total Network SL(2008) UKHL 19 贵族院先例中,针对串谋侵权明确指出串谋采取刑事犯罪行为可以构成串谋侵权。在更近期的 JSC BTA Bank v. Khrapunov(2018) UKSC 19 最高院先例中也看来至少是在串谋侵权中采取的是相对宽松的态度,不严格必须是第三人能独立提起诉讼,Sumption 勋爵与 Lloyd-Jones 勋爵这样说:"Conspiracy being a tort of primary liability, the question what constitute unlawful means cannot depend on whether their use would give rise to a different cause of action independent of conspiracy. The real test is whether there is a just cause or excuse for combining to use unlawful means. That depends on(i) the nature of the unlawfulness, and(ii) its relationship with the resultant damage to the claimant."

针对这方面看来还有待后续先例的澄清。

从过往先例中来看,具体而言这些不法行为包括:(1)暴力或威胁暴力行为。见 Garret v. Taylor(1620) Cro Jac 567; Tarleton v. McGawley(1793) 170 ER 153 等先例。(2)欺诈与误述。见 National Phonograph Co Ltd v. Edison Bell Co Ltd(1908) 1 Ch 335; Lonrho v. Fayed(1990) 2 QB 479 等先例。(3)违约或威胁违约行为。见 Rookes v. Barnard(1964) AC 1129 等先例。(4)串谋采取违反竞争法的行为。见 WH Newson Holding Ltd v. IMI Plc(2013) EWCA Civ 1377; Emerald Supplies Limited v. British Airways Plc(2015) EWCA Civ 1024 等先例。(5)董事操纵公司破产逃避公司对债权人的债务。见 Palmer Birch(a partnership) v. Lloyd(2018) EWHC 2316(TCC) 等先例。(6)帮助冻结令/资产披露令的被申请人、判决债务人转移与隐藏资产,串谋藐视法院。见 JSC BTA Bank v. Khrapunov 最高院先例等。

而与本段课题关系比较密切的问题,是通常而言,狭义的经济侵权一般都要涉及中间人(intermediary)并造成第三人的经济损失。例如,在诱导他人违约/毁约的

Lumley v. Gye(1853)2 El & Bl 216 先例中,案情是今天仍经常在发生的“挖角”行为,被告 B 以金钱诱导一位歌星 C 违反与原告 A 的表演合约改去为 B 表演。在这种情况下,A 的损失固然在合约下可向 C 索赔,但法律也允许 A 以经济侵权向第三人的 B 索赔。[38] 如果 B 向 C 允诺说:“只要你违约/毁约,我会给你更好的代价,也补偿你对 A 造成的损失。”这 B 与 C 之间的约定,就可能由于涉及这类侵权行为的非法而不可执行了:见 British Homophone Ltd v. Kunz(1935)All ER Rep 627 先例。[39]

总而言之,国际上所有的商业行为都是通过一个个合约串联起来,这带来以上各种经济侵权行为所涉及的各种相关合约,都可能面临非法理论的抗辩。

2.2 违反公共政策(public policy)

这主要针对的是并非刑事犯罪或者其他民事触犯法律行为,但违反了广泛的公共政策的情况。对于所有可能超越合约订约大原则的公共政策,在《Chitty on Contracts》(2021 年,第 34 版)一书之 18 - 013 段中并不穷尽地总结为以下五大类。因为这里针对的是所有公共政策,所以与普通法非法与稍后会介绍的立法非法等部分有一些重叠。普通法非法与立法非法能够超越合约订约自由大原则、合约神圣性,也是因为背后有此公共政策。可节录有关内容如下:“Objects which on grounds of public policy invalidate contracts may, for convenience, be generally classified into five groups: **first**, objects which are illegal by common law or by legislation; **secondly**, objects injurious to good government either in the field of domestic or foreign affairs; [40] **thirdly**, objects which interfere with the proper working of the machinery of justice; [41] **fourthly**, objects injurious to marriage and morality; [42] and **fifthly**, objects economically against

---

〔38〕 需要采用侵权向第三人索赔的原因很多,主要就是违约/毁约方无力支付赔偿,也会是无辜方想要索赔违约损失中不会包括的非金钱损失(non-pecuniary loss)等。

〔39〕 此先例中,Du Parcq 大法官在附带意见中就说:“It seems to be consistent with principle that an agreement to do a legal wrong to a third party should be unenforceable by reason of its illegality.”

〔40〕 影响恰当执政(injurious to good government),这会包括内政(domestic affair)中的卖官鬻爵、贪污腐败、玩忽职守、采取不当手段影响履行公职等行为。也会包括对外事务(foreign affairs)中的通敌卖国行为等。例如与敌人交易非法,见 Ertel Bieber & Co v. Rio Tinto co(1918)AC 260 先例。令敌人获益也是非法,见 Kuenigl v. Donnersmarck(1955)1 QB 515; Bevan v. Bevan(1955)2 QB 227 等先例。保险合约所保的货物运自敌方港口,虽然船是中立国的,也仍然非法,见 Potts v. Bell(1800)8 TR 548 先例。

〔41〕 妨碍实现社会的公平正义。例如,在合约中约定对他人的非法行为保密。又如,任何滥用或阻碍司法公正的行为。还如,意图排除司法管辖权(ouster of jurisdiction),如离婚时的分居协议(deed of separation)约定一方不得去法院寻求进一步的司法救济(如要求法院重新审核抚养费等):见 Hyman v. Hyman(1929)AC 601; Bennett v. Bennett(1952)1 KB 249; Sutton v. Sutton(1984)Ch 184 等先例。也会包括不得助讼与揽讼(maintenance and champerty)等。

〔42〕 影响社会道德与婚姻(morality and marriage),这类案件就包括以性服务为对价签订的合约即卖淫嫖娼。以同居作为对价的合约,见 Tanner v. Tanner(1975)1 WLR 1346 先例。以及各类合约对价涉及影响婚姻关系的行为,如允诺结婚、限制结婚、不撤销遗嘱、父母责任,或者是为骗取签证假结婚等。

the public interest. [43] This classification is adopted primarily for ease of exposition. Certain cases do not fit clearly into any of these five categories."

在本章之1.4段已简单介绍了非法与公共政策的问题,不在这里进行太多介绍。

最后只在此多举一个例子来显示公共政策与违反英国法律非法的区别,就是普通法下有悠久历史的限制贸易(restraint of trade)公共政策。有关限制贸易的课题在本章稍后的11.2段有详论,另在笔者《合约的解释:规则与应用》一书第七章之3.3.1段与《禁令》一书第二章之3.1.6段中也有介绍。什么是限制贸易的定义,可见Diplock大法官在Petrofina v. Martin(1966)Ch 146先例中所说:"A contract in restraint of trade is one in which a party agrees with other party to restrict his liberty in the future to carry on trade with other persons not parties to the contract in such manner as he chooses."

涉及限制贸易的例子很多,常见的如收/并购(M&A)交易中被收购方的董事高管或雇佣合约中的雇员的竞业禁止条文(non-competition clause),工会与雇主组织中的成员受到工会的限制要求,供应货物或服务合约中的捆绑条文(solus tie),不动产的限制性约定(restrictive covenants)等。

例如,在雇佣合约的竞业禁止条文中限制离职雇员的自由,就涉及了好几个不同与起直接冲突的公共政策/公共利益:(1)不能剥夺雇员在离职或被解雇后的就业谋生与其他方面的人身自由,如工作自由。(2)不能让雇主妨碍社会进步,严重限制有能力或甚至有特殊技术的雇员继续工作或发展,为社会创造财富。(3)当然也要保障雇主的商业机密、商业关系(如客户名单、供应商等),防止前雇员调转矛头来恶性竞争与维持在职雇员的稳定(如不必怕在花费大量精力/财力培训雇员后,被竞争同行高薪挖走)等的合法利益。

在早期有很长一段时间,普通的低级雇员在面对雇主时处在非常不利的地位,往往面对雇主拿出来的非常偏向雇主利益的标准格式雇佣合约也被迫接受,这导致法院必须用公共政策来调整这样签订的合约,不允许无限制的订约自由。近年来即使有不少高管等雇员有水平与有谈判地位能够与雇主协商谈判约定一份更为公平的合约,但对于普通低级雇员而言,地位并没有太大改变。

简而言之,公共政策的大原则是任何人都应该有权利自由选择从事任何行业、贸易与专业,因此限制贸易的条文会是表面无效(prima facie void)。但是在社会现实下,又不得不允许一定程度的合理限制贸易,否则如收购方花费大量金钱收购竞争对手的生意,甚至通过原本的人脉挖走被收购公司的客户,这看来是说不通的,因此对这些行为可以允许一定限制。但由于这仅仅是大原则的例外,因此限制贸易的条文只能限于保护合法利益所必要,根据具体行业内的做法与习惯、在公共利益的角度上

---

〔43〕 这也会包括一般的欺诈(fraud)、限制贸易(restraint of trade)、仿冒(passing off)等影响社会整体经济效益的情况。

认为是合理(如时间上、范围上)的程度。早在 Mitchel v. Reynolds(1711)1 PWms 181 先例中,Parker 大法官就说:"To conclude, in all restraints of trade where nothing more appears, the law presumes them bad; but if the circumstances are set forth that presumption is excluded and the court is to judge of those circumstances, and determine accordingly. If on them, it appears to be a just and honest contract, it ought to be maintained."

还可见在 Nordenfelt v. Maxim Nordenfelt Guns and Ammunition Co(1894)AC 535 先例中,Macnaghten 勋爵说:"The true view at the present time, I think, is this: The public have an interest in every person's carrying on his trade freely ... All interference with individual liberty of action in trading, and **all restraints of trade of themselves ... are contrary to public policy, and therefore void. That is the general rule**. But there are exceptions: restraints of trade and interference with individual liberty of action may be justified by the special circumstances of a particular case. It is a sufficient ..., indeed, ... the only justification, if the restriction is reasonable—reasonable, that is, **in reference to the interests of the parties concerned and reasonable in reference to the interests of the public**, so framed and so guarded as to afford adequate protection to the party in whose favour it is imposed, while at the same time it is **in no way injurious to the public**."(加黑部分是笔者的强调)

以上普通法限制贸易完全是法律调整私人之间的法律关系,但今天限制贸易课题更是广泛,针对各类垄断市场、限制竞争的行为,涉及政府插手、公权力介入不允许、惩罚这类行为。美国早在 1890 年就有著名的反垄断法《Sherman Antitrust Act》,后来还有《The Federal Trade Commission Act》与《The Clayton Act》等联邦立法。今天英国这方面的立法是《Competition Act 1998》。主要禁止一系列限制市场竞争、有害社会公共利益的行为,包括:(1)联合一批人士达成垄断或限制竞争的协议(anti-competition agreements),也就是通常所称的卡特尔协议(cartel agreements),这会是竞争公司之间联合达成的垄断协议,也会是竞争公司与产业链上下游公司联合达成的垄断协议。(2)大型公司滥用市场支配地位(abuse of dominant position)。具体的行为也多种多样,如供货商的独家供货、最低供货义务的限制,或者拒绝供货、抬高或压低供货价格等行为;或是针对销售,要求"配货",捆绑销售,或者是设定高昂价格或价格歧视等行为;又如阻止市场发展、限制新技术开发等。这些具体行为并非本书重点,不在这里详细针对。对于第一类的联合垄断协议,《Competition Act 1998》明确规定该协议无效:"Any agreement or decision which is prohibited by subsection(1)(第一类被禁止的协议)is void."而针对第二类的滥用市场支配地位行为,则涉及对公司的罚款、禁止公司董事担任公司高管等职务、允许申请禁令阻止、允许蒙受损害的第三人索赔等救济手段。

3. 立 法 非 法

本段所针对的立法非法属于在本章之2段节录的《Chitty on Contracts》(2021年,第34版)一书之18－001段中提到的非法案件的第三类,因为内容较多,所以独立一段。立法是由英国议会(Parliament)及其授权的机构(如政府部门)制定,为了公共利益(public interest)、适用在所有公民的法律,而订立合约是个体公民之间对私权(private rights)的约定。这种公与私的区别,就从本质上决定了保护公共利益的立法是不会有很多针对合约私权的内容。只有在议会有意图令立法去影响当事人之间的私权时,合约的效力才会因非法而受影响。法院在面对合约因涉及违反立法而变为非法进而不可执行的抗辩时,就往往需要在立法没有规定的情况下,判断立法是否有意图或目的影响合约的私权。

立法非法中最多与最常见的会是针对合约的形成或目的非法的情况,也即立法明示或默示禁止当事人订立此类合约。但也会有少部分立法是针对合约履行的问题,如合约没有按照合法的方式来履行,该合约可能就会变成一个被立法禁止的合约,这也就是在The "St John"(1956)2 Lloyd's Rep 413先例中,Delvin大法官所说:"… the contract was performed turned into the sort of contract that was prohibited by statute…"

在《Illegality and Public Policy》(2020年,第5版)一书之1－14段中根据立法与合约的关系将立法条文分为三类,先节录该段如下:"It is necessary to distinguish broadly between three types of statutory provision. **First**, a criminal statute may prohibit certain activities and render them punishable. Those activities, which constitute the great majority of crimes, may not necessarily have any obvious relationship with contracts; that is it may be perfectly possible and usual for them to be engaged in without entering into any kind of contract. **Secondly**, a statute may refer to contracts or to commercial activity in defining the conduct to be penalised; but fail to state whether contravention of the statute is to have any effect upon the enforceability of the contracts in question, or whether the criminal penalties stipulated should be the only sanctions to be imposed. **Thirdly**, a statute may provide that contracts to which it refers should, as such, actually be 'void' or unenforceable."(加黑部分是笔者的强调)

3.1　立法非法的三种类型

上一段英文节录中三类立法条文是:

1. 刑事立法。这类立法所禁止并且处罚的行为,是我们平时所说的罪行(offence)。但对于大部分的刑事犯罪行为来说,并不会与合约有太大的关系。

2. 立法条文显示其惩罚的行为会涉及合约与商业活动,但并没有写明违反该立法的后果是否会令有关的合约也被禁止与不可执行。这就需要法院对立法进行解释。

例如,Bedford Insurance Co v. Instituto de Resseguros do Brasil(1985)QB 966 先例涉及《Insurance Companies Act 1974》立法之 Section 2(1)规定没有批文不得在英国从事海事保险业务:[44]"No person shall **carry on in Great Britain**[**marine insurance business**]...except -(a)a body corporate...authorised under section 3...to carry on business of that class;..."该立法条文禁止在没有批文下经营保险业务,但并没有写明如果在没有批文下接受投保,保险合约的效力如何。这带来的问题是投保人在遇险时是否可以索赔或者没有批文的保险人是否可以向投保人索赔尚未支付的保费。

在《Illegality and Public Policy》(2020 年,第 5 版)一书之 1-16 段中针对的是立法条文没有明确规定有关合约效力的情况,说尽管立法经常会带来一些不清楚的地方,但是权威说法认为,只有是在被刑事处罚的行为需要在合约的背景下发生,才可以默示推断立法是认为合约非法从而被禁止执行。可以节录有关部分如下:"Notwithstanding confusionin the reasoning in some cases, a close reading of the authorities supports the view that a contractual claim can only properly be said to have been implied prohibited by statute when the legislation which imposes criminal penalties upon activities necessarily contemplates those activities being done in a contractual context..."

今天英国各类法律法规、规章制度越来越多,其中大部分都不会涉及合约的效力问题。所以该类条文也是法院在面对非法争议时最主要要解释的立法条文,而解释立法条文也变成法院主要的工作,据知最高院有 75% 的案例是涉及这方面。

3. 立法明确规定违反会令有关合约无效或不可执行,或反过来明确规定即使发生了立法要禁止的行为,与该禁止行为有关的合约效力不受影响。

例如《Marine Insurance Act 1906》之 Section 4(1)规定投保人在没有保险利益(insurable interest)下去投保实际是在赌博,如读者为巴菲特的寿命投保,这整个合约都无效:"Every contract of marine insurance by way of gaming or wagering is void."

又如针对海上货物运输的 1924 年《海牙规则》/1968 年《海牙维斯比规则》之 Article III.8 规定任何减轻船方在海上运输时小心谨慎义务的条文或协议无效:"Any clause, covenant, or agreement in a contract of carriage relieving the carrier or the ship from liability for loss or damage to, or in connection with, goods arising from negligence, fault, or failure in the duties and obligations provided in this article or lessening such liability otherwise than as provided in these Rules, shall be null and void and of no effect."

立法写明违反的后果就好很多。如果规定合约无效,效果也是合约自始无效,即使在该非法合约下有转让财产等行为,财产的产权也不会真正转移给任何第三人。

---

[44] 见本书第九章之 6.3 段提到的 Harbour Assurance Co(UK)Ltd v. Kansa General International Insurance Co Ltd(1993)QB 701 先例。

除了有写明合约本身无效或不可执行的立法外，也有立法明确规定虽然立法禁止某些行为，如果违反会有惩罚，但该违反并不导致与该行为有关的合约无效或不可执行。例如在《Criminal Justice Act 1993》中 Section 63(2)中就规定内幕交易不影响相关的合约，说："no contract shall be void or unenforceable by reason only of section 52."有关的先例可见 Chase Manhattan Equities Ltd v. Goodman(1991)BCC 308[45]与 Patel v. Mirza(2016)UKSC 42 等。

类似的还有在 SCF Finance Co Ltd v. Masri(No. 2)(1987)QB 1002 先例中，原告与被告的交易涉及原告将金钱交给被告进行期货交易，问题是这行为是否属于英国当时在《Banking Act 1979》下的接受存款业务。如果是，被告主张他需要先申请批文才能从事接受存款业务，而他没有申请批文，因此合约非法不可执行。法院解释立法后认定原告与被告之间的交往并非接受存款业务，并不违反规定。而即使认为属于接受存款业务，根据《Banking Act 1979》之 Section 1(8)，违法接受存款并不会影响当事人之间因存款或存入的款项而产生的民事责任："The fact that a deposit is taken in contravention of this section shall not affect any civil liability arising in respect of the deposit or the money deposited."这是说当事人因存款所订立的合约的效力并不因此受影响。

但需要注意的是，如果立法规定的是合约有效，与合约无效或不可执行一样，法院是再也没有什么裁量权。但对于立法写明效力并不受影响的合约，虽然并不在立法下不可执行，但仍要考虑是否构成普通法下的非法。

上述所讲的三种分类，其中第二类应该是最多的情况，这就带来了如何解释立法的重要课题。

3.2 对立法的解释

在以上介绍的三种分类，如果是第三种立法明示了合约的后果，那显然很清楚的是一旦符合立法中规定的情形，法院也没有选择，只能跟从立法的要求。而如果是第二种立法针对了与合约或商业活动有关的行为，但没有明确写明有关合约的效力，法院就需要解释立法背后会对私权有什么想法。例如在其他各类惩罚(如罚金甚至监禁)的基础上，合约是否也要被禁止？还是其他的各种惩罚就已经足够，而合约仍然有效？甚至是禁止合约是否反而会违反立法的意图或目的？

立法的解释是一个内容很丰富与十分重要的课题。但如何解释立法并非本书的重点。法院在解释立法条文时会采取的几种方式是：

1. 字面解释(literal rule)。如 Esher 勋爵在 R v. Judge of the City of London Court (1892)1 QB 273 先例中说："If the words of an Act are clear then you must follow them even though they lead to a manifest absurdity. The court has nothing to do with the ques-

---

〔45〕 该先例涉及的《Company Securities(Insider Dealing)Act 1985》以及 Section 8(3)下有关内幕交易的内容，今天英国法下已经废除，并重新以《Criminal Justice Act 1993》之 Section 63(2)立法针对。

tion whether the legislature has committed an absurdity."

这种方式的好处是立法更加肯定明了。但坏处也有不少,如立法怎样小心拟定也会有漏洞或缺陷,立法总有滞后性也无法包罗万象,文字/措辞可以有多于一种解释,字面解释会在个别案件带来可笑与不公平的结果。

例如在 London & North Eastern Railway Co v. Berriman(1946)AC 278 先例中,铁路工人在为路轨与设备加润滑油时被火车撞死,他的遗孀根据《Fatal Accidents Act》向火车公司提起疏忽诉讼,因为公司没有按照《Prevention of Accidents Rules 1902》要求为工人提供警示。但该立法只针对工人在车轨从事继电保护与维修("for the purposes of relaying or repairing it")的工作,字面解释下不包括加润滑油,所以遗孀败诉。这显然是可笑与不公平的。

2. 黄金规则(golden rule)/当然解释。这是让法院有限度通过弹性解释立法文字去避免可笑与不公平结果。如在 Adler v. George(1964)2 QB 7 先例中,在《Official Secrets Act 1920》立法,在军营禁区"附近"(in the vicinity)阻碍办公是非法。但该先例的被告指称自己是在空军基地禁区"内部"阻碍办公,并非如立法规定的"附近"。但法院解释为立法中"附近"已经不行,"内部"只能是更加严重,所以立法应包括禁区内或禁区附近("in or in the vicinity of"),否则就会导致可笑的结果,并最终判被告犯法。但这种方式的缺点是很少去适用,也带来能否说服法院适用与到什么程度的不肯定。

3. 论理解释(mischief rule)。这种方式让法院在解释时有更大的弹性,即看立法前普通法案例带来了什么无法解决的问题,所以需要议会通过立法解决。这在一个十分古老的 Heydon's case(1584)76 ER 637 先例中,指出法院要考虑以下四点:"1st. What was the common law before the making of the Act. 2nd. What was the mischief and defect for which the common law did not provide. 3rd What remedy the Parliament hath resolved and appointed to cure the disease of the commonwealth. And,4th. The true reason of the remedy..."

在 Smith v. Hughes(1960)1 WLR 830 先例中,有 6 名女性在《Street Offences Act 1959》下被检控在街头卖淫。该立法的文字是"to loiter or solicit in a street or public place",但被告抗辩她们不是在街道或公共区域拉客,而是在阳台或窗口。法院判被告有罪,因为立法目的是防止路过的行人被拉客骚扰,这样只要她们的目标是街上的行人,是在街道或公共区域还是通过阳台或窗台没有区别。

这规则的好处是促进立法的本意,令立法变得更有效。但缺点是带来法院立法(judicial law-making)的危险及更大程度的不肯定,因为不是看了立法条文就明确了什么是该做与不该做;相比下一种方式的"目的解释"(purposive approach)较狭窄,因为只限于根据立法前的地位看立法要解决的是什么问题。

4. 目的解释(purposive approach)[46]。这可先节录 Burrows 勋爵在 2022 年 3 月 24 日的"Statutory Interpretation in the Courts Today"一文说:"Sometimes students are taught that there are three rules of statutory interpretation which the courts can choose between. The literal rule, the golden rule and the mischief rule. I think that is very misleading because there is only one correct modern approach — that one must ascertain the meaning of the words in the light of their context and the purpose of the provision — and none of those three rules quite captures that approach, albeit that the mischief rule perhaps comes the closest."

在英国加入欧盟的《European Communities Act 1972》立法,就规定针对欧盟法律,必须是一致以目的解释立法。这也影响了法院一般的立法解释,如在 R(Quintavalle) v. Secretary of State for Health(2003) UKHL 13 贵族院先例中,Steyn 勋爵说:"The pendulum has swung towards purposive methods of construction. This change … has been accelerated by European ideas … Nowadays the shift towards purposive interpretation is not in doubt."

另在澳大利亚,《(Commonwealth) Acts Interpretation Act 1901 (as amended)》在 1981 年新加入了 S. 15AA 条说:"In interpreting a provision of an Act, the interpretation that would best achieve the purpose or object of the Act … is to be preferred to each other interpretation."

也就是说在今天考虑立法的措辞/文字的文义解释作为起点外,还要更宽松地从立法的目的去解释。可多节录一些近年有关"目的解释"立法的权威说法,这在 R (Quintavalle) v. Secretary of State for Health 贵族院先例中,Bingham 勋爵说:"The court's task, within the permissible bounds of interpretation, is to give effect to Parliament's purpose. So the controversial provisions should be read in the context of the statute as a whole, and the statute as a whole should be read in the historical context of the situation which led to its enactment."

另在 Test Claimants in the FII Group Litigation v. Revenue and Customs Commissioners(2020) UKSC 47 最高院先例中,Reed 与 Hodge 勋爵说:"It is the duty of the court, in accordance with ordinary principle of statutory interpretation, to favour an interpretation of legislation which gives effect to its purpose rather than defeating it."

最后可节录在 Kostal UK Ltd v. Dunkley(2021) UKSC 39 最高院先例中,Arden 与 Burrows 两位勋爵说到现代解释立法往往会参考立法报告与记录以找出立法目的:"The modern approach to statutory interpretation requires the courts to ascertain the meaning of the words in a statute in the light of their context and purpose … in carrying

[46] 如何解释立法与解释一份复杂的完整商业合约看来是大同小异,这与在笔者的《合约的解释:规则与应用》一书第一章之 8 段中介绍的现在解释合约的"目的解释"是类似。

out their interpretative role, the courts can look not only at the statute but also, for example, at the explanatory notes to the statute, at relevant consultation papers, and, within the parameters set by Pepper v. Hart … a ministerial statements reported in Hansard."

总结这方面可简单节录《Chitty on Contracts》(2021 年,第 34 版)一书之 18 – 195 至 199 段部分内容如下:

"If, on the true construction of the statute '… the contract be rendered illegal, it can make no difference, in point of law, whether the statute which makes it so has in mind the protection of the revenue or any other object. The sole question is whether the statute means to prohibit the contract.'(唯一的问题是要看立法是否意图要禁止该合约。如果通过解释立法后发现合约确实属于立法非法,从法律上来看,该立法令合约非法是为了保护什么利益就变得没有太大区别。)

If, on the other hand, the object of the statute is the protection of the public from possible injury or fraud, or is the promotion of some object of public policy, the inference is that contracts made in the contravention of its provisions are prohibited…[如果从另一个方面考虑,立法的目的是保护公众不受侵害或欺骗(例如食品安全),或者是为了鼓励某种公共政策,就会存在一个推断是合约一旦违反立法条文就要被禁止。]

… it has also been suggested that '… not a bad test to apply is to see whether penalty in the Act[47] is imposed once for all, or whether it is a recurrent penalty imposed as often as the act is done. If it be the later, then the act is a prohibited act…(还有一个同样也不错的测试是看立法下的惩罚是一次性的还是每次发生该行为都会被处罚。如果是后者,看来立法是禁止该行为,从而约定了该行为的合约也是被禁止的。例如,每次违反食品安全的行为都会被处罚,而合约如果约定涉及不安全食品,该合约就应该是被禁止。)

The courts have also been reluctant to find contracts unenforceable because the illegality doctrine operates in an all or nothing way and there is no proportionality between the loss ensuing from non-enforcement and the breach of statute. This is to be contrasted with fines for criminal acts where some proportionality does pertain…(法院不太愿意认定合约因非法而不可执行。因为相对于刑法可以根据非法行为的轻重来成比例地做出惩罚,合约一旦被认定为非法,整个合约就不能被执行,不存在要比较不执行合约的后果与违反立法的后果来给予成比例的救济,这会给合约权利带来全有或全无的后果。)

… The courts have also been sensitive to the fact that non-enforcement may also result in unjust enrichment to the party to the contract who has not performed his part of the

〔47〕 这里节录的是 Victorian Daylesford Syndicate Ltd v. Dott(1905)2 Ch 624 先例的判词,有关的立法是《Money-lenders Act 1900》。

bargain but who has benefited from the performance by the other party...(如果合约不可执行,会存在合约一方在不履行自己义务的同时享有对方履行带来的好处的情况,例如涉及非法的买卖合约下买方付了货价但卖方不交货,法院也会尽量避免发生这种不当得利的情况。)

The Courts have also appreciated that the growth in statutory law(including delegated legislation)can result in the unwitting and quite innocent breach of the statute...[法院也要考虑现在立法越来越多(包括委任立法/次级立法),这会带来很多无辜的违反,也即因为不知道有此立法而违法,虽然在普通法下对法律无知并不是抗辩的理由。]

Although the court have recognised 'the desirability of(their)... assisting to enforce a statute',the consequence of this in driving from the seat of judgment sometimes innocentsupplicants has also to be weighed in the balance...(尽管法院认可他们要执行立法的规定,但仍会与对无辜方造成的后果做出权衡。)"

最后只节录的美国《Restatement(Second)of Contracts》之 § 179,这是美国解释立法的现代做法。有关公共政策方面的问题大部分是由立法者而不是法院来决定,因为立法者有资源去做出更多的事实调查与更好地回应公众的需求。但是立法者制定立法去禁止某些社会上的行为时,很少会针对这些行为所涉及的合约的效力问题,其实通常是因为国会根本就没有想过合约是否可执行:"**Modern role of legislation**. The declaration of public policy has now become largely the province of legislators rather than judges. This is in part because legislators are supported by facilities for factual investigations and can be more responsive to the general public. When proscribing conduct, however, legislators seldom address themselves explicitly to the problems of contract law that may arise in connection with such conduct... Usually they do not even have these problems in mind and say nothing as to the enforceability of terms. **In such situations it is pointless to search for the 'intention of the legislature,' and the court's task is to determine on its own whether it should, by refusing to enforce the promise, add a sanction to those already provided by the legislature**. This is a question of 'law,' in the conventional sense, rather than one of 'fact.' The legislation is significant, not as controlling the disposition of the case, but as enlightening the court concerning some specific policy to which it is relevant. A court will examine the particular statute **in the light of the whole legislative scheme in the jurisdiction** to see, for example, if similar statutes in the same area contain explicit provisions making comparable promises unenforceable. It will look to the **purpose and history of the statute.** The fact that the **statute explicitly prohibits the making of a promise or the engaging in the promised conduct** may be persuasive in showing a policy against enforcement of a promise but it is not necessarily conclusive. On the other hand, the fact that the **statute provides a civil sanction, whether in addition to a criminal penalty or not**, may suggest that no other civil sanction such as unenforceability is intended, but this is not necessarily conclusive either... Furthermore, even though a field is the subject of legislation, a court may decide that the **legislature has not entirely occupied the field** and may refuse to enforce a term on grounds of a judicially developed public policy even though there is no contravention of the legislation. ... Although no attempt is made in this Restatement to state rules to deal with any of the myriad of specific pieces of legislation that may be involved in such controversies..."(加黑部分是笔者的强调)

以上针对一般性对立法的解释,接下来的段节是针对非法理论,法院在解释立法时,会特别考虑的若干重要因素。

3.2.1 解释立法之一:如果立法目的只是增加收入,可以默示不影响合约的有效性

有不少立法涉及规管或统筹某些商业活动或行业,会要求事前申请牌照、批文、许可等的做法。如果不这样做,就会被视为违法或非法,并会带来罚款与/或其他惩罚。但显然,罚款是为政府带来进账。这虽然不是立法的目的或主要目的,但显然是带来这个结果。在早期的 Smith v. Mawhood(1845)14 M & W 452 先例中,案情涉及原告 Smith 先生作为烟草商没有按照《Excise License Act》立法的要求取得牌照后才售卖烟草而被政府罚款 200 英镑。Smith 先生没有收到卖给被告 Mawhood 先生的烟草的货款而提起诉讼,但 Mawhood 先生提出了非法抗辩去拒绝支付,指称买卖合约非法,因为 Smith 先生没有牌照。但法院判 Smith 先生胜诉。其中 Anderson 大法官说:"The question is, does the legislature mean to prohibit the act done or not? If it does, whether it be for the purposes of revenue or otherwise, then the doing of the act is a breach of the law, and no right of action can arise out of it. But here the legislature has merely said, that where a party carries on the trade or business of a dealer in or seller of tobacco, he shall be liable to a certain penalty, ... It seems to me, therefore, that there is nothing in the act of Parliament to prohibit every act of sale, but that its only effect is to impose a penalty, for the purpose of the revenue, on the carrying on of the trade without complying with its requisites.... "

另 Parke 大法官说:"Looking at the act of Parliament, I think its object was not to vitiate the contract itself, but only to impose a penalty upon the party offending, for the purpose of revenue. "

这里整体的公平合理很容易看到,这包括是:(1)原告 Smith 先生已经被政府当局惩罚,没有道理在私权的买卖合约下因为法院不协助执行而收不回欠款被再罚一次,为同一次的违法/非法承受双重损害(double jeopardy);(2)政府当局收取的罚款是进入库房,但如果 Mawhood 先生可乘机赖掉欠款,这只是他个人获利,与公共利益毫无关系;(3)法院如果因为非法而不去执行 Smith 先生向 Mawhood 先生追偿的欠款,究竟是维护了什么公共政策?如果买卖的不是烟草而是海洛因,这涉及公共政策

是可以理解。但这里买卖的是烟草,法律没有禁止买卖,立法只要求烟草商人需要取得牌照。

以上可以多举一个较后期的 The "St John"(1956)2 Lloyd's Rep 413 先例。案情是船舶超载并违反了《Merchant Shipping(Safety and Load line Conventions) Act 1932》,船东/船长也因此被政府当局罚了 1200 英镑。但货方趁机以非法提单为由,拒绝支付超载部分货物的运费。该先例又是同样情况,是明眼人客观看明显不公平合理。在立法没有明示下,议会是不会有立法意图去让私人提单合约不可执行,让货方可以一分钱运费也不用支付,这对船东而言是过于严重的双重损害。在此先例中,Delvin 大法官说:"To nullify a bargain in such circumstances frequently means that in a case-perhaps of such triviality that no authority would have felt it worth while to prosecute—a seller, because he cannot enforce his civil rights, may forfeit a sum vastly in excess of any penalty that a criminal court would impose; and **the sum forfeited will not go into the public purse but into the pockets of someone who is lucky enough to pick up the windfall or astute enough to have contrived to get it.** It is questionable how far this contributes to public morality."(加黑部分是笔者的强调)

3.2.2 解释立法之二:履行合约是否等于完成立法禁止的行为

这方面可以一个简单的例子说明,如立法明示禁止贩卖濒危动物与饲养濒危动物,前者的贩卖行为显然必须与买卖合约(不论是以口头、行为或文书)有所关联。这样既然立法背后的公共政策是为了保护濒危动物与地球的生态环境,就算不在立法明示,也可以通过默示得出结论是买卖合约或与其有所关联的合约都是包括在内,是被禁止的非法合约。

但立法禁止饲养濒危动物就不一定涉及合约了,也表示不能以默示立法去禁止与此非法行为有所关联的合约。

可以说前者例子,合约被立法同时禁止是"必要的推断"(necessary implication)。这在 The "St John"(1956)2 Lloyd's Rep 413 先例中,Delvin 大法官有很好的解释如下:"A court **should not hold that any contract or class of contracts is prohibited by statute unless there is a clear implication, or 'necessary inference,'** ... that the statute so intended. If a contract has as its whole object the doing of the very act which the statute prohibits, it can be argued that you **can hardly make sense of a statute which forbids an act and yet permits to be made a contract to do it**; that is a clear implication. **But unless you get a clear implication of that sort, I think that a court ought to be very slow to hold that a statute intends to interfere with the rights and remedies given by the ordinary law of contract**. Caution in this respect is, I think, especially necessary in these times when so much of commercial life is governed by regulations of one sort or another, which may easily be broken without wicked intent. Persons who deliberately set out to break the law cannot expect to be aided in a court of justice, but it is a different matter when the law is unwittingly broken. To nullify a bargain in such circumstances frequently means that in a case—perhaps of such triviality that no authority would have felt it worth while to prosecute…”（加黑部分是笔者的强调）

另在 Okedina v. Chikale（2019）EWCA Civ 1393 上诉庭先例中，Underhill 大法官也说是议会通常不会在立法下想去禁止与干预在合约下的私权，所以只有在立法的默示十分清楚无误时，法院才可以作出推断有关立法禁止的行为也禁止了某类为了完成这种行为的特定合约，说：“in the absence of an express prohibition a court should only find that Parliament has intended to prohibit a contract of a particular kind，or in particular circumstances，where the implication is clear…”

说到底，就是尽量避免解释立法是有意图去禁止有关合约，因为立法的重心是在公共利益，而不是合约的私权。立法者如果有此禁止合约的意图，正常情况是不会忘记去明示。另外支持双方有订约自由与合约神圣性这是非常重要的公共政策，这大精神/大原则在本章之 1.5.2 段已详及，虽然针对的是合约条文，而不是立法条文的解释，但目的一致：避免其他公共政策影响合约效力。这可见在 Vita Food Products Inc v. Unus Shipping Co Ltd（1939）AC 277 先例中，Wright 勋爵说：“Nor must it be forgotten that the rule by which contracts not expressly forbidden by statute or declared to be void are in proper cases nullified for disobedience to a statute is a rule of public policy only，and public policy understood in a wider sense may at times be better served by refusing to nullify a bargain save on serious and sufficient grounds.”

3.2.3　解释立法之三：立法只惩罚一方当事人

如果可以将立法解释为只惩罚一方当事人（即使可能是刑事犯罪后果），针对的也只是交易中的一种特定履行方式（能找出其他合法办法履行），这就有机会避开合约不可执行的后果。可以说此时立法并没有影响合约效力，或甚至只是排除被惩罚的当事人执行合约权利，而不影响无辜方的合约权利。[48]

在 Phoenix Insurance v. Helvanon Insurance（1988）QB 216 先例中，Kerr 大法官说如果立法只是禁止与处罚订约一方在没有批文下去订立合约，该单方面的禁止与处罚并不默示合约因非法而不可执行。否则，就会变为是“处罚”向没有批文的被告追讨欠款或索赔损失的无辜合约方了。至于判断立法是否只是想要达到惩罚一方的效果，那要综合考虑立法的语言、范围、目的、给无辜方带来的后果以及任何其他相关的因素，来决定立法要保护的公共政策与防止的侵害。具体到此先例中，这些因素包括：（1）是否会导致产生实质上的不公平；（2）被告是造成非法问题的罪魁祸首，而原告纯粹是无辜的“受害人”，但是被告想要用自己造成的非法来主张合约不可执行与抗辩原告的索赔。Kerr 大法官说：“… But where a statute merely prohibits one party from entering into a contract without authority，and/or imposes a penalty upon him if he

〔48〕 这看来与本章之 10.1 段介绍的对非法不是“过错对等”（pari delicto）是同样的道理。

does so(i. e. **a unilateral prohibition**) **it does not follow that the contract itself is impliedly prohibited so as to render it illegal and void**. Whether or not the statute has this effect depends upon considerations of public policy in the light of the mischief which the statute is designed to prevent, its language, scope and purpose, the consequences for the innocent party, and any other relevant considerations. ..."(加黑部分是笔者的强调)

在这里可以先以美国《Restatement(Second) of Contracts》之 Section 179 作为一个很好的例子,就是立法为了保护雇员的身心健康,规定雇员每天最长工作时间不得超过 8 小时,如果雇主和雇员违反该规定,则构成刑事犯罪,但并没有说明违反雇佣合约的后果是什么。这时如果雇主 A 雇佣雇员 B 并承诺 B 如果他每天工作 10 小时,而不是立法要求的 8 小时,则会就加班部分支付双倍工资给 B。之后 B 也确实每天工作 10 小时,但 A 却拒绝支付加班工资给 B。双方在法院诉讼,法院解释立法时会从立法的目的着手,因为立法的目的是保护一类人(雇员)的利益不受另一类人(雇主)的侵害,所以执行雇主的承诺也是符合保护雇员利益这个公共政策,雇主支付双倍加班工资的承诺仍然有效。

在本章之 1. 3 段中介绍的 Browing v. Morris(1788)2 Cowp 790 先例与 Kiriri Cotton Co Ltd v. Dewani(1960)2 WLR 127 枢密院先例也是同样的说法。可再多举几个先例,在 Hughes v. Asset Managers Plc(1995)3 All ER 669 先例中,投资人与证券交易人签署多份投资管理协议,投资人将 300 万英镑交给这些证券交易人投资股票。这笔投资非常失败,1 个月后股票大跌到价值不到 100 万英镑。投资人即开始起诉申请简易判决(summary judgment),主张所有的投资管理协议都因为非法而无效,希望拿回损失的钱。

根据当时《Prevention of Fraud(Investments) Act 1958》之 Section 1(1)规定,立法下定义的证券交易人士及其代理人都需要各自持有牌照:"no person shall...(a) carry on or purport to carry on the business of dealing in securities...(b) in the capacity of a servant or agent of any person carrying on or purporting to carry on that business, deal or purport to deal in securities except under the authority of a representative's licence..."

此先例中的证券交易人持有牌照,但是代表他们与投资人谈判、签订协议与做事情的代理人都没有牌照。而且在后续立法条文中还明确规定违反此规定的证券交易人或代理人属于犯下罪行,可能被处以监禁或罚款。

法院解释立法说并没有明确默示/必要推断合约不可执行或无效,也因此原告的申请被驳回。法院考虑的因素包括:(1)立法措辞/文字本身只惩罚交易人或其代理人,而完全没有针对交易合约或交易的履行;(2)立法完全没有针对有关交易的合约双方,而只是针对交易人或其代理人;(3)立法中规定的惩罚已经足够保护公共利益;(4)证券行业的情况与有关的公共政策等。Saville 大法官说:"I can see no basis in either the words the legislature has used or the type of prohibition under discussion, or in considerations of public policy ..., for the assertion that Parliament must be taken to have intended that such protection required(over and above criminal sanctions) that any deals effected through the agency of unlicensed persons should automatically be struck down and rendered ineffective. On the contrary, it seems to me that not only is there really no good reason why Parliament should have taken up this stance, but good reason why Parliament should have held the contrary view."

从这先例也显示出法院在解释立法时只要还能令人信服地避开不可执行的后果,有解释的余地,都会尽量解释为没有默示规定不可执行。

另在 Anandh v. Barnet Primary Health Care Trust(2004)EWCA Civ 5 上诉庭先例中也有类似情况,涉及在《Opticians Act 1989》立法〔49〕下医生/验光师有严格责任必须有恰当牌照才能检查视力。而一名医生被错误地颁发了牌照,事后牌照问题曝光。有病人主张自己与医生之前视力检查的合约因此非法,想要医生退还自己支付的金钱,并成功获得一审法院的简易判决。但上诉庭解释立法后,认为既没有明示也没有明确默示/必要推断禁止合约,不应该不允许医生在稍后的全面审理中进行抗辩而用简易判决处理。表面看来,立法下的无牌医生在非法行医的过程中会与大量的无辜人士订立合约,无论是病人或是护士等。如果立法被解释为禁止执行这些合约,就会大量影响这些无辜人士。Arden 大法官说:"There is good reason for section 24 of the 1989 Act to criminalise the performance of eye tests by an unqualified person rather than the formation of contracts for the provision of sight tests while unqualified. If the performance of such tests is not criminalised, there would be no criminal sanction for the gratuitous provision of eye tests while unqualified, and this would be anomalous. If the making of contracts for eye tests to be provided by an unqualified person is also impliedly prohibited, neither a paying customer nor the public nurse could recover the cost … This result would be to the detriment of innocent parties… In conclusion, I do not consider that the… 1989 Act of itself makes contracts for the provision of eye tests by an unqualified person unlawful."

再是在 Okedina v. Chikale(2019)EWCA Civ 1393 上诉庭先例中,双方都是马拉维共和国(Malawian)公民,被告带原告来英国做家庭佣工,但原告签证期满后仍然继续从事此工作直到双方关系破裂,原告向被告提起雇佣合约下的索赔。此先例中就需要解释《Immigration, Asylum and Nationality Act 2006》立法下是否雇佣合约非法(雇员没有恰当移民身份),也就是剥夺了雇员索赔的权利。上诉庭判立法没有这样做,Underhill 大法官主要的判决思路如下:(1)立法中没有明示措辞/文字禁止雇佣合约,立法中也仅仅单方面惩罚雇主。因此需要进一步在公共政策下解释立法是否有明确默示/必要推断。(2)立法背后的公共政策其实是想要禁止什么? 此先例中

---

〔49〕 有关的 Section 24 可节录如下:"… a person who is not a registered medical practitioner or registered [optometrist] shall not test the sight of another person."

的立法显然不是为了保护没有恰当移民身份的雇员,反而是阻止没有恰当移民身份的人士在英国做“黑工”。(3)立法目的也并非结论性因素。Underhill 大法官尤其考虑了很多情况,雇员其实是“无辜”的,如可能是被人口贩卖、被迫工作,或者可能是被他人告知后真实相信自己有恰当移民身份,或纯粹是搞错了事实或法律。[50] 而公共政策看来并没有打算硬性剥夺这些无辜雇员在合约下的索赔权利。(4)至于如果雇员并非真正无辜,则大可以在普通法非法理论下不予执行,而不是在立法下全面禁止。

最后可节录《Chitty on Contracts》(2021 年,第 34 版)一书之 18 - 206 至 207 段作为总结。针对立法只惩罚一方当事人和惩罚双方当事人的不同情况,前者看来会被解释为只会导致过错方在合约下的权利不被执行,而后者情况下才是包括“无辜”当事人在内的双方合约权利都不会被执行。可以节录有关部分如下:“Statutes which prohibit certain contracts often impliedly recognise, for example by punishing only one of the parties, that the parties are not equally at fault, and therefore on their true construction only one of the parties to the contract is prevented from suing upon it...In certain cases a statute may be construed to prohibit both parties from suing on a contract of the sort in question, e. g. since it makes them both guilty of a criminal offence in entering into the contract. In such cases, no matter how much more culpable one party is than the other, both are equally unable to sue upon the contract; and this is so even though the party who seeks to sue on the contract was at the time it was made ignorant of the facts which brought the contract within the statutory prohibition...”

前者情况只惩罚一方当事人与他的合约权利不被执行,正是本段前述介绍的三个先例。而后者情况在立法非法下双方合约权利都不被执行会在下一小段介绍。

在此只多说一点去针对前者情况的举证责任方面,在《Illegality and Public Policy》(2020 年,第 5 版)一书之 2 - 17 段中提出的说法是根据过往先例应该认为存在一个可反驳的推定(rebuttable presumption):[51] (1)只是立法下会受惩罚的一方才无法获得法院执行合约下的权利,以及(2)无辜方的权利是不会受到影响。可以节录 2 - 17 段所说如下:“It is suggested that an underlying principle can be derived from the majority of the cases as follows: there is a rebuttable presumption that a criminal statute which defines the offence it creates in terms of contractual activity (a) impliedly prohibits enforceability of contracts by the party subject to the penalty but (b) leaves unaffected the

---

〔50〕 有关错误(mistake)的课题,可见本书第七章。

〔51〕 法律推定是根据法律的规定,一旦发生某类一致的事实或情况时,就可以对事实进行推定。可反驳的法律推定是指虽然推定事实存在,但允许提出证据反驳。本章之 7.2.2 段介绍的“赠与推定”(presumption of advancement)就是一种可反驳的推定。关于这方面可见笔者《证据法:基础理论、口头证据与专家证据》一书第七章之 6.1 段。

rights of the other party."

3.2.4 解释立法之四:禁止合约双方都不能执行

有情况是立法时就考虑到了私权的问题,直接在立法条文中明确写明后果。例如在本章之3.1段节录的《Marine Insurance Act 1906》之 Section 4(1)规定投保人在没有保险利益下去投保,整个合约都无效。至于立法背后的原因,在这里无需深究。而即使法院不认同立法背后的原因,也只是立法的问题,法院是无能为力仍要遵从去解释。看来如果涉及一些要保护社会上的广泛公共利益(public interest)的重要公共政策,如要保障公共安全、健康等问题,立法就更有可能禁止合约,合约双方都不可执行。

在这方面著名的 Mahmoud and Ispahani, Re(1921)2 KB 716 先例中,涉及当时的《Seeds, Oils and Fats Order 1919》规定购买或出售特定类型的货物(如一些种子、食用油等)必须先申请批文,可以节录立法措辞/文字如下:"a person shall not either on his own behalf or on behalf of any other person buy or sell or otherwise deal in .... any of the articles specified in the schedule hereto, whether situated within or without the United Kingdom, except under and in accordance with the terms of a licence issued by or under the authority of the Food Controller."

原告持有合法批文出售受该立法规管的亚麻籽油(Linseed oil)。而被告声称自己有合法批文可以购买该亚麻籽油。原告真实相信了被告的说法,并与被告达成销售亚麻籽油的买卖合约。但事实上,被告根本没有批文。事后被告拒绝接收亚麻籽油,原告就索赔买卖合约下的损失,被告以非法作为抗辩。

这就造成了一个奇怪的情况,被告是造成非法问题的罪魁祸首,而原告纯粹是无辜的"受害人",但是现在是被告想要用自己造成的非法主张合约不可执行与抗辩原告的索赔。最后法院仍然判在立法下合约非法与不予执行。主要的理由看来就是因为解释该立法得出的结论,是立法要保护公众免受这类食品安全的风险,严格禁止买卖双方在没有批文的情况下订立买卖合约。因此只要是属于立法下禁止的合约,也无论当事人双方的情况如何、是否真的无辜,都不会予以执行。Scrutton 大法官说:"... in my view, if an act is prohibited by statute for the public benefit, the Court must enforce the prohibition, even though the person breaking the law relies upon his own illegality."

这样的判法从双方当事人之间的公平的角度上来看是有疑问的,但在涉及立法非法的情况下,一旦将立法解释为禁止合约,也就不再考虑个别案件中千变万化的案情下,严格适用立法会造成的实质不公平。

还如在 Yin v. Sam(1962)AC 304 枢密院先例中,当时马来西亚的《Rubber Supervision Enactment 1937》之 Section 5 规定购买橡胶必须持有批文,在立法中还特别规定如果涉及合伙人,牌照中必须将所有合伙人的姓名都列出:"(i)...no person shall purchase...rubber...unless he shall have been duly licensed in that behalf under this

Enactment. (ii) Every licence shall be in the prescribed form..."

而 Section 16 规定批文专属并且不得转让:"(ii) No licence shall be assignable... (iii) A licence is personal..."

此先例中就是橡胶生产商销售一批橡胶给合伙企业。但在合伙企业中只有一位合伙人持有私人批文,其他合伙人并未列出在该合伙人的批文中。生产商明知自己是与合伙企业交易,但没有进一步查问合约企业是否有恰当批文。事后合伙企业欠下部分款项未支付,生产商在买卖合约下提出索赔。但遇到合伙企业抗辩说没有恰当批文,整个橡胶交易合约非法。枢密院的判法就与 Mahmoud and Ispahani, Re 先例类似,认定合伙企业没有恰当批文,而与生产商之间的合约是由合伙企业作为合约当事人,这样该合约即属于被禁止的非法合约。再加上解释立法目的是保护广泛的公共利益,这就导致合约不可执行。生产商是否知道、是否真实相信合伙企业有恰当批文都与合约是否非法无关。生产商即使真的无辜,在合约下也无法获得救济。

读者可能觉得这些结果很不合理也很不公道,但实际上只要懂得立法规定的立场,就可以避免陷入这种困境。例如,如果明知立法有批文的要求且如果对方没有批文合约会被禁止,那就不能只听对方说自己有批文,必须要求对方拿出符合立法规定的批文,或者将对方有批文设为合约的先决条件或后续条件(如对方必须在合约订立后的30天内拿到批文)。

3.3 中国法律下的违反公序良俗

在梁慧星教授的《市场经济与公序良俗原则》(载《中国社会科学院研究生院学报》1993年第6期)一文中,将违反公序良俗的行为类型化为以下十种:(1)危害国家公序型,如以从事犯罪或者帮助犯罪行为为内容的合同;(2)危害家庭关系型,如约定断绝亲子关系的协议;(3)违反道德型,如开设妓院的合同,实践中以性行为为对价获得借款的情形;(4)射幸行为型,如赌博、巨奖销售变相赌博等;(5)违反人权和人格尊严行为型,如过分限制人身自由换取借款的情形;(6)限制经济自由型,如利用互相借款扩大资金实力以分割市场、封锁市场的协议;(7)违反公平竞争型;(8)违反消费者保护型;(9)违反劳动者保护型;(10)暴利行为型。

这看来是与普通法下的三大类的触犯法律、违反公共政策与立法非法大同小异。这十大类中多项可归类为违反公共政策,但应不会有普通法非法。作为成文法国家,中国的立法非法会如何影响合约关系/私权尤其重要。

笔者感觉近年来中国公司在国际仲裁中作为被告更多地提出非法的抗辩。但对中国公司或代表律师而言,如果合约适用英国法/普通法,不宜把太大希望寄托在用非法理论作为不履行合约的借口与抗辩。这些中国立法禁止的行为,除了少数国际认可的严重犯罪,一般针对的都是配合中国国情的规定。这在适用英国法的合约就只是合约履行或目的非法。这样,在一个国际仲裁中,需要考虑与权衡只是在英国公共政策下针对外国法非法的国际睦仪/礼让(international comity)。

即使有关合约的适用法是中国法,要提出非法理论也难逃如何解释这些立法的技术性问题,主要是要主张与证明立法机关已经明示或默示[“必要的推断”(necessary implication)]立法意图让有关合约无效与不可执行。另也需要进一步提供足够证据让仲裁庭能够判断有关立法是否强制性适用而没有当事人订约自由的余地,有关非法行为的严重性与后果是什么等。这都是需要找高水平的中国法律专家作为专家证人解释,并且说理能力能压倒对方专家证人,才能成功说服仲裁庭,否则非法抗辩估计是难以成功的。

4. 非 法 合 约

4.1 合约形成非法(illegality as to formation)

合约形成非法,也称合约本身非法。主要是合约在形成/订立时,就已经不可避免必须采取非法行为才能去履行(违反法律或公共政策)。在这种合约下,如果后来有一方当事人想以合法行为履行(即使是能够做到),也会是违反双方的约定而构成违约/毁约了,但不会改变合约形成是非法的本质。

重点在于通过解释合约,当事人的明示或默示条文要求实施非法行为。比如合约约定行为涉及触犯刑法,或者约定侵犯第三人权利,或者其他各种法律法规、规章制度等,如商业上常见的立法规定某种交易必须获得批文才可进行,但合约方因为不符合条件完全不可能获得批文。

在古老的 Levy v. Yates(1838)8 A&E 129 先例中,当时法律规定在伦敦 20 英里内演出必须符合特定条件与取得皇家许可,但一个剧院与演出主办方签订合约在剧场制作演出歌剧。法院认定他们在实际不可能获取有关许可的情况下不可避免要非法(“the agreement could not be carried into effect without a contravention of the law”),也因此合约非法。现实中也会发生订约时当事人都不知道法律的存在,约定的合约无法合法履行,这也会构成共同错误(common mistake)导致无效。[52]

在 Colen v. Cebrian(2003)EWCA Civ 1676 上诉庭先例中,Waller 大法官说:“... an analysis needs to be done as to what the party's intentions were from time to time. If the contract was unlawful at its formation or if there was an intention to perform the contract unlawfully as at the date of the contract, then the contract will be unenforceable.”

也可以节录《Chitty on Contracts》(2021 年,第 34 版)一书之 18 - 050 段所说:“**Illegality as to formation**Contracts may be illegal when entered into because they cannot be performed in accordance with their terms without the commission of an illegal act. Thus the contract may involve a breach of the criminal law, statutory or otherwise, or alternatively it may be a statutory requirement that the parties to the transaction possess a li-

---

〔52〕 见本书第七章之 13.1 段。

cence and where they do not the contract will be illegal as formed... Where a contract can only be carried out by the performance of an illegal act, it is illegal as to formation..."

4.2 合约履行非法(illegality as to performance)

合约形成非法,实际上也就是合约当事人约定做非法的事情(被立法禁止、普通法非法、或其他公共政策所不允许)。而履行合约非法针对的情况就有所不同,即合约实际可以被合法履行,只是在履行合约时,当事人采取(或意图采取)非法的方式履行。

例如在英国的 Sewell v. Royal Exchange Assurance Co(1813)4 Taunt 856 先例中,租约约定前往伦敦卸货,但该类货物必须先获取批文后才可以在伦敦卸货。Mansfield 大法官就判只要在真正卸货之前拿到批文就已经足够,而不需要认定合约非法。当然,如果合约方完全可以申请获得批文但实际履行时为了省钱或省麻烦等各种原因没有去申请就偷偷履行,这就属于合约履行非法而不是合约形成非法。

一度有说法是履行合约由于并不涉及合约本身,毕竟合约本身合法成立,当事人仅仅是履行过程中的非法,因此不应该影响合约的有效性与可被协助执行:见 Coral Leisure Group v. Burnett(1981)ICR 503 先例等。

但今天更被接受的是不应该如此严格区分合约形成与合约履行,合约履行中的非法只要达到一定程度,或者说严重到合约被污染(tainted),也会导致合约不可执行:见 B & B Viennese Fashions v. Losame(1952)1 All ER 909;Colen v. Cebrian(2003) EWCA Civ 1676 与 ParkingEye Ltd v. Somerfield Stores Ltd(2012)EWCA Civ 1338 等先例。在 Colen v. Cebrian 上诉庭先例中,Waller 大法官说得很清楚:"If the contract was unlawful at its formation or if there was an intention to perform the contract unlawfully as at the date of the contract, then the contract will be unenforceable. If at the date of the contract the contract was perfectly lawful and it was intended to perform it lawfully, the effect of some act of illegal performance is not automatically to render the contract unenforceable. If the contract is ultimately performed illegally and the party seeking to enforce takes part in the illegality, that may render the contract unenforceable at his instigation. But not every act of illegality in performance even participated in by the enforcer, will have that effect. If the person seeking to enforce the contract has to rely on his illegal action in order to succeed then the court will not assist him. But if he does not have to do so, then in my view the question is **whether the method of performance chosen and the degree of participation in that illegal performance is such as to 'turn the contract into an illegal contract'.**"(加黑部分是笔者的强调)

在本章较早提到的 The "St John"(1956)2 Lloyd's Rep 413 先例中,约定从美国运输货物去伦敦的租约本身完全合法,租约也没有约定超载,只是履行过程中因为各种原因船舶实际运输超载违反《Merchant Shipping(Safety and Load Line Conventions)Act 1932》下的规定而非法。但因为非法的程度很轻微,不应该影响合约本身的有效性。但如果有关的合约原本是买卖烟草并且获得了批文,这是完全合法的。可是在履行过程中,在双方都知情的情况下,烟草中混入大麻一起买卖,这就严重到令整个合约受到了"污染",合约本身也不可执行。

过往先例中对于合约履行非法,申请救济的当事人是否对非法情况知情有区分对待。例如一方采取非法方式履行,此时另一方无辜、完全不知情相比于知情并且有参与,会有不同对待。不知情是对非法"过错对等"(pari delicto)的例外,这可见本章之10.1段的介绍。在此先节录《Chitty on Contracts》(2021年,第34版)一书之18-051段中所说如下:"**Illegality as to performance**The illegality may arise because both or one of the parties may intend to perform the contract in an illegal manner... The court may deny its assistance where both or one of the parties intended to perform the contract in an illegal manner or to effect some illegal purpose. In this situation it is customary to distinguish between the situation where they are known only to one. For the illegality as to performance rule to apply there is no requirement that the illegal performance be intended from the time the contract is entered into;the formation of the intention after the execution of the contract can bring the rule into play."

4.3 合约目的非法(illegal purpose)

这类情况的经典例子就是Pearce v. Brooks(1866)LR 1 Ex 213先例。该先例中原告是马车制造商,而被告是一名性工作者。原告向被告租售一架特别定制的有棚四轮马车(brougham),但被告未能按约定支付租金,因此起诉被告。

表面看来,该先例不像是合约形成非法,租售马车本身并不涉及非法。同时该合约也不涉及履行非法,双方之间的交易是支付金钱与转让马车的使用权/产权,没有什么非法的。但是一个重要之处是在订立合约时,原告明知被告是性工作者,而且租售马车的目的就是要在马车中招揽顾客。而在当时英国社会与法律对于这类卖淫的行为严格反对,公共政策认为是不道德与非法。这先例结果是法院判签订该合约背后是非法目的,因此不协助原告拿回欠下的租金。

这样判法背后的一个重要理由,看来就是原告明知是非法目的,仍然提供特别的马车帮助被告实现非法目的,这其实也就是法院不会帮助基于自己不道德或非法行为的诉因("No court will lend its aid to a man who founds his cause of action upon an immoral or an illegal act.")。在该先例中,Pollock大法官说:"I have always considered it as settled law,that any person who contributes to the performance of an illegal act by supplying a thing with the knowledge that it is going to be used for that purpose,cannot recover the price of the thing so supplied... the rule which is applicable to the matter is,Ex turpi causa non oritur action..."

在确定合约有否非法目的时,相信该先例的马车租售金额会是丰厚,可去推断原告除了明知道被告的非法目的外,也有一定程度的参与。这在后来的JM Allan(Merchandising)v. Cloke(1963)2 QB 340上诉庭先例中,Denning勋爵提到此先例时带出了“共同策划”(common design)的说法,说:“I would take a comparable case where there is a common design to use a subject-matter for an immoral purpose. If a landlord lets a flat to a prostitute at **a rent beyond any normal commercial rent**,... it may fairly be inferred that it was their common design that it should be used for an immoral purpose. The letting is unlawful and he cannot recover the rent or hire. It is different with the washerwoman who washes the clothes of the prostitute or the butcher who supplies her with meat. They may know of her trade but they **charge her normal commercial prices. There is there no common design**.”(加黑部分是笔者的强调)

类似的情况还可见 Biggs v. Lawrence(1789)3 TR 454 与 Waymell v. Reed(1794) 5 TR 599 先例的买卖合约,卖方明知买方买走货物之后是为了走私去英国,但照样签订了合约,并且在此基础上还特别将货物包装得容易夹带与方便走私。有关这类明知并且参与的情况还可见本章之 10.1.3 段的介绍。

5. 普通法非法与立法非法的区分

有必要介绍一下英国法下一贯对于违反普通法与违反立法的区别。由于今天商业社会针对方方面面都有法律法规、规章制度,所以经常会有合约的订立或履行违反某些特定立法的情况。而非法(无论是普通法或立法)的实际后果一样,法院不会愿意协助执行/合约无效。

这两种不同非法的区别可以先节录 Okedina v. Chikale(2019)EWCA Civ 1393 上诉庭先例中,Underhill 大法官的说法[53]如下:“The essential starting point is to recognise that there are two distinct bases on which a claim under,or arising out of,a contract may be defeated on the ground of illegality. These are nowadays generally referred to as ‘statutory’ and ‘common law’ illegality. Put very briefly:(1)Statutory illegality applies where a legislative provision either(a)prohibits the making of a contract so that it is unenforceable by either party or(b)provides that it,or some particular term,is unenforceable by one or other party. The underlying principle is straightforward:if the legislation itself has provided that the contract is unenforceable,in full or in the relevant respect,the court is bound to respect that provision. That being the rationale,the knowledge or culpability of the party who is prevented from recovering is irrelevant:it is a simple matter of obeying the statute. (2)Common law illegality arises where the formation,purpose or performance of the contract involves conduct that is illegal or contrary to public policy and where to deny enforcement to one or other party is an appropriate response to that

〔53〕 主要的措辞/文字看来是《A Restatement of the English Law of Contract》(2016)一书的说法。

conduct.... ”

5.1 区分的原因

首先的问题是为什么要区分这两者？答案是因为英国法院在这两者的情况下，判断非法的方式有很大的不同。

在普通法非法下，法院一贯有相对大的空间去决定审理中案件的法律地位，如是否非法。当然审理法院是受到在本书第七章之 14.3.1 段的先例理论（doctrine of precedent/rule of stare decisis）的约束，不得偏离已经在先例中确立下来的法律地位。在本章介绍的有关非法的法律与先例中，主要是普通法非法。这包括稍后会详及的非法理论在这约 250 年以来从 Holman v. Johnson（1775）1 Cowp 341 先例发展到目前法律地位的 Patel v. Mirza（2016）UKSC 42 先例。在这 250 年间，也有无数的先例在面对千变万化案件下去完善与全面建立普通法下的非法理论。这包括非法如何确立，如看合约的形成（formation）、目的（purpose）或履行（performance）是否违背公共政策的约定或行为；非法理论的一些例外（exceptions），这包括撤回/悔改（repentance）、当事人原告对非法是否知情（knowledge）、参与的程度（participation）、对非法并非“过错对等”（pari delicto）等方面；通过分割理论（doctrine of severance）限制非法理论的适用；非法合约或行为的后果等。

在本章之 3 段已经详细解释过在立法非法下，法院的作用是解释立法条文与背后的目的，并适用在具体案件的事实中。但即使法院判不构成立法非法，这也不代表合约方就可以高枕无忧，因为法院仍会考虑有关的交易或合约是否构成普通法非法。在 Archbolds（Freightage）Ltd v. S Spanglett Ltd（1961）1 QB 374 先例中，Delvin 大法官说：“If the court too readily implies that a contract is forbidden by statute, it takes it out of its own power（so far as that contract is concerned）to discriminate between guilt and innocence. But if the court makes no such implication, it still leaves itself with the general power, based on public policy, to hold those contracts unenforceable which are ex facie unlawful, and also to refuse its aid to guilty parties in respect of contracts which to the knowledge of both can only be performed by a contravention of the statute ... or which though apparently lawful are intended to be performed illegally or for an illegal purpose .... ”

5.2 两者的区分与重叠

两者有时区分会是比较明显，尤其是在一些没有特定的立法针对的普通法下的犯罪、侵权或违反公共政策的行为，此时就显然只需考虑普通法非法。

但也有很多时候这两者之间不容易区分，并且是存在重叠的。毕竟普通法涉嫌非法的部分，背后其实违反的就是立法规定，此时就有机会要同时考虑两者，即既要解释立法条文看是否明示或默示排除合约的执行，又要根据案件情况分析是否存在普通法非法导致合约不可执行。也有情况是立法写明违反某立法条文不影响合约效力，但在该情况下仍然有适用普通法非法的空间。

尤其是本章之 3.2 段介绍的一些情况，在解释立法条文时，考虑到如果令合约不可执行或无效,原告会蒙受巨大不利(甚至是在刑法和民法下的双重损害),从而将立法条文解释为并没有默示合约不可执行或无效。

两者之间的关系从 Trietel 教授所著的《Law of Contract》一书中将非法的合约分为触犯法律的合约与违反公共政策的合约两大类也能够看得出来。公共政策相对于法律显然是一个更广的概念,包括宗教、家庭、种族、社会和谐、国家安全与国际睦仪/礼让等。会违反这些公共政策的合约各种各样,但并不是每一种都有立法来针对。有立法针对的,就适用立法;而没有立法针对的,这时法院就会在审理案件中通过普通法的先例来明确某种行为所涉及的不道德与对合约的后果。

另再多提一点,如果当事人约定采取特定合法方式"绕过"立法规定,如避开立法所采用的措辞/文字并可以解释(特别是以字面解释或当然解释)为并不被立法禁止,用这种方法实施了立法想要阻止的行为,一般情况下并不会属于前述非法。例如,合法避税,就不会适用非法理论。在 DPP v. Bhagwan(1972) AC 60 先例中,Diplock 勋爵这样说:"I know of no authority which would justify your Lordships in holding it to be a criminal offence for any person, whether or not acting in concert with others, to do acts which are neither prohibited by Act of Parliament nor at common law, and do not involve dishonesty or fraud or deception, merely because the object which Parliament hoped to achieve by the Act may be thereby thwarted."

对于立法非法与普通法非法的适用,可以 Chase Manhattan Equities Ltd v. Goodman(1991) BCC 308 先例为例帮助读者理解。该先例的案情涉及被告进行内幕交易,而根据当时的《Company Securities(Insider Dealing) Act 1985》立法,该行为涉嫌犯罪,原告的一项主张是合约因涉及非法而不可执行。但在该立法之 Section 8(3)[54] 明示这类内幕交易行为虽然涉嫌犯罪,但交易中所签订的有关合约并不因此无效或不可执行,也因此不存在立法非法的问题。但法院仍然认定执行被告在合约下的权利,实际等于让被告从非法行为中获利,也因此属于普通法非法,不予执行该合约。

同样的情况就是在本章之 7.5 段介绍的 Patel v. Mirza(2016) UKSC 42 最高院先例中,内幕交易问题并不影响合约的效力与执行,因此涉及的非法其实是普通法非法的问题。

这方面的推理、逻辑与思维是与合约在默示条文/法律赋予的权利与明示条文/合约赋予的权利之间的矛盾与重叠是一致的。笔者的《合约的履行、弃权与禁反言》一书第一章之 6.2 段有详论,并介绍了这方面包括 Stocznia Gdynia SA v. Gearbulk Holdings Ltd(2009) EWCA Civ 75 上诉庭先例。

---

[54] 《Company Securities(Insider Dealing) Act 1985》以及 Section 8(3)下有关内幕交易的内容,今天英国法下已经废除,并重新以《Criminal Justice Act 1993》之 Section 63(2)立法针对。在涉及合约效力的条文上几乎一样,可见本章之 3.1 段的节录。

6. 非法理论:困难与混乱的课题

首先节录《Restatement of the English Law of Contract》(2016 年)一书中,Burrows 教授(今天是英国最高院的 Burrows 勋爵)指出过去先例中从没有清楚明确的指示非法理论(特别是普通法下的非法)如何适用,而带来此课题的一片混乱。Burrows 教授说:"Leaving aside the law on what one can loosely label 'statutory illegality' [cases where a statute makes a contract or a contract term unenforceable by either or one party] the law on the effect of **illegality in contract** (which one may loosely refer to as 'the common law of illegality') **is in a state of flux** ...Traditionally, **two Latin maxims** have often been referred to without greatly illuminating the legal position: ex turpi causa non oritur actio ('no action arises from a disgraceful cause') and in pari delicto potior est conditio defendentis ('where both parties are equally in the wrong the position of the defendant is the stronger'). As previously understood, **illegality in the law of contract-as developed from those Latin maxims**-was governed by a series of rules which tended to distinguish, for example, between **illegality in formation and illegality in performance**. Unfortunately, commentators and courts have found it **very difficult to state those rules with confidence and precision.** Hence the textbook treatments not only differ from each other but are characterised by long-winded attempts to explain the law. Sharp propositions when offered by the courts or the books have to be qualified by reference to cases or hypothetical examples that do not fit those rules; and convincing justifications of those rules have proved elusive. **More recently**, therefore, and in line with a similar trend in respect of illegality as a defence in tort, **some courts have favoured greater flexibility culminating in a 'range of factors' approach aimed at achieving a proportionate response to contractual illegality in preference to the traditional rule-based approach**."(加黑部分是笔者的强调)

6.1 旧时的政策性非法理论适用在现代社会的困难

这方面的麻烦在于,今天的法律远比 Holman v. Johnson (1775) 1 Cowp 341 先例时期的法律复杂与繁多。尤其在近几十年,英国各类规章(regulations)的制定针对的范围越来越广,内容越来越多,细节越来越复杂。在今天看来,"违背道德的对价不生诉权"(ex turpi causa non oritur actio)与衍生出的"公序良俗测试"(public conscience test)法律规则(rule of law)对于维持一套正直、完善与一致的法律制度仍是真理。但这些原则之前所包括的具体的细节是否仍然适应社会的发展与现在的环境是要打上一个很大的问号。这在较近期的 Nelson v. Nelson (1995) HCA 25 澳大利亚先例中,McHugh 大法官有很好的表述,可节录如下:"The doctrine of illegality expounded in Holman was formulated in a society that was vastly different from that which exists today. It was a society that was much less regulated. With the rapid expansion of regulation, it is undeniable that the legal environment in which the doctrine of illegality operates has changed. The underlying policy of Holman is still valid today—the courts must not condone or assist a breach of statute, nor must they help to frustrate the operation of a statute … However, the Holman rule, stated in the bald dictum: 'No court will lend its aid to a man who founds his cause of action upon an immoral or an illegal act' is too extreme and inflexible to represent sound legal policy in the late twentieth century even when account is taken of the recognised exceptions to this dictum."

笔者完全认同已经多次节录的 Mansfield 勋爵在 Holman v. Johnson 先例中的名言,但在今天 21 世纪仍然要严格遵从,在不少千变万化的案件中难免是太极端与欠缺弹性了。

6.2 造成非法理论困难与混乱的主要原因

最后不妨总结英国非法理论在这些年来的困难与混乱的主要原因是:

1."非法"的定义太广、延伸的范围也十分广。今天方方面面的立法,特别是在国际的层面,太多与太细,无法合理掌控。这导致"非法理论"与现实中商业活动的情况脱节,让很多无意违法、正规与懂法的商人也会"身陷法网"。

2.非法理论的核心是英国法院要保护法律体系的一致性(coherence/ consistency)与正直(integrity),不能允许任何非法/违法人士逃避或转嫁刑事后果。否则变成一边刑法作出惩罚,但另一边他可以民事手段(无论是以合约、侵权或复原)通过法院协助取回损失、财产或获得赔偿/补偿。但这里的问题之一是刑法与民法无法同步。刑法对不同的违法有不同的惩罚,考虑了不同非法行为的严重性。但民法的私权下,只要有关合约是非法,无论严重与否,法律只能"一刀切"把非法合约视为无效,而法院也是一样,只能不对执行该非法合约作出任何协助。

3.刑法与民法是无法同步,硬去套用非法理论在民法就会难逃被批评是太严格、太苛刻、太含糊、欠缺弹性以及在千变万化的案件中经常造成不公平合理的判决。正如在 Tinsley v. Milligan(1994)1 AC 340 贵族院先例中,Goff 勋爵说:"(非法理论)not a principle of justice; it is a principle of policy, whose application is indiscriminate and so can lead to unfair consequences as between the parties to litigation."

4.非法理论是建立在一些格言之上,其中最重要的是"违背道德的对价不生诉权",并衍生出 Holman v. Johnson(1775)1 Cowp 341 先例的"公序良俗测试"(public conscience test)。用这种泛泛的格言去管治当今复杂的商业社会,就难逃会有不如意后果。这种批评在早期的 Yarmouth v. France(1887)19 QBD 647 先例中,Esher 勋爵说:"I detest the attempt to fetter the law by maxims. They are almost invariably misleading: they are for the most part so large and general in their language that they always include something which really is not intended to be included in them."在 Lissenden v. C

A V Bosch Ltd(1940) AC 412 先例中，Wright 勋爵同意上述说法，说："Indeed these general formulae are found in experience often to distract the court's mind from the actual exigencies of the case, and to induce the court to quote them as offering a ready made solution."

5. 如果不死板套用非法理论，而是让法院在个别不同案件的案情下行使裁量权，主要就是要看合约双方在非法方面的过错是否严重、是否过错对等、知情与参与程度多寡等多方面因素后，才作出对有关案件较为恰当与公平合理的判决。这就难免带来另一类危险，即涉及非法的大量案件会是由无数的一审法院在多方面考虑与做出权衡后判决。这就难逃审理法官会错判，令有关案件变得不可预测与不肯定。更重要的是个别案件会不可避免的偏离非法理论最基本的政策与法律规则，也会有个别案件与刑法产生不一致与矛盾等问题。这种没有止境的多因素判断(unlimited range of factors test)在重要的 Patel v. Mirza(2016) UKSC 42 最高院先例中，就被少数不同意见的大法官批评，其中 Sumption 勋爵说："I would not deny that in the past the law of illegality has been a mess. The proper response of this court is not to leave the problem to case by case evaluation by the lower courts by reference to a potentially unlimited range of factors, but to address the problem by supplying a framework of principle which accommodates legitimate concerns about the present law. We would be doing no service to the coherent development of the law if we simply substituted a new mess for the old one."

6. 以上所讲就是英国法院在很多涉及非法抗辩的案件都面对两难，这特别是在复原/不当得利(restitution/unjust enrichment)的案件，[55] 即如果支持非法抗辩，就让同样是非法(甚至比原告错得更多)的被告捡了大便宜。但如果不支持非法抗辩，就会有协助原告执行非法之嫌。这在本章之 7.3 段介绍的法律委员会的《The Illegality Defence》中提到了这两难局面，说："If the courts accept the illegality defence, it often involves granting an unjustified windfall to the defendant, who may be equally implicated in the illegality. However, if the courts refuse, they may be seen to be helping a claimant who has behaved illegally." Nicholls 大法官在 Tinsley v. Milligan 上诉庭先例中说："the underlying principle is the so-called public conscience test. The court must weigh, or balance, the adverse consequences of granting relief against the adverse consequences of refusing relief. The ultimate decision calls for a value judgment." 也就是法官个人的价值判断看支持原告或被告会是更加冒犯了公序良俗。而这带来的问题就是法律不成体系与不可预测。

7. 英国法院也不是没有尝试过去偏离，如 Saunders v. Edwards(1987) 1 WLR 1116；Euro-Diam Ltd v. Bathurst(1990) 1 QB 1；Pitts v. Hunt(1991) 1 QB 24 等先例以

---

[55] 这在本章之 12.2 段有针对，特别是 Patel v. Mirza(2016) UKSC 42 最高院先例如何解决这问题。

一种名为“直接/偶然性测试”(direct/incidental test)去替代长远以来传统的“公序良俗测试”,即有关非法与原告的索赔是没有直接关系,只是偶然或不经意涉及关系,就不能让非法去否定原告的索赔。在 Saunders v. Edwards 上诉庭先例中,Bingham 大法官就指出了有必要去偏离传统做法以达至公平合理,说:“Where issues of illegality are raised,the courts have … to steer a middle course between two unacceptable positions. On the one hand it is unacceptable that any court of law should aid or lend it's authority to a party seeking to pursue or enforce an object or agreement which the law prohibits. On the other hand,it is unacceptable that the court should,on the first indication of unlawfulness affecting any aspect of a transaction,draw up its skirts and refuse all assistance to the plaintiff,no matter how serious his loss nor how disproportionate his loss to the unlawfulness of his conduct.”

“直接/偶然性测试”令部分案件的判决更公平合理在 Euro-Diam Ltd v. Bathurst 先例中就明显可以看到。该先例涉及原告作为批发商把一批钻石运送到德国给一家后来清盘的 Verena 公司去转售/零售给最终的买方。履行期间,Verena 要求原告在发票中把钻石价格压低(undervalue),原告也这样做了。这是 Verena 为了逃税去欺骗德国税局,是非法行为。原告虽然声称他不知情,只以为是应 Verena 的审计要求去帮助与合作,但这不被法院相信。在运送期间,部分钻石在德国仓库被偷。原告已是为这批钻石在劳合社投保,所以是完全正常地向保险人要求赔偿钻石被盗窃的损失。但被告保险人以非法抗辩拒赔,而涉及的非法也就是刚介绍的行为。但在一审与上诉庭都判原告胜诉,认为有关非法行为与保单以及钻石被偷是相隔太远,与非法无关。原告向保险人提起的索赔无需依赖有关的非法行为,在索赔请求中也根本没有提起。保险人向原告赔付也不存在让原告从自己的非法行为中获利。可以说,对原告的赔付根本没有违反任何对非法重要与原则性的公共政策。想得再远一点,保险人的代位求偿(subrogation)[56]权利也没有受到非法行为的影响。代位求偿虽然是有了一点困难,但这是由于德国买方财力出问题而清盘,与有关非法行为一点关系都没有。

但这“直接/偶然性测试”已被 Tinsley v. Milligan 贵族院先例否定。这在 Patel v. Mirza 最高院先例中被 Sumption 勋爵提及:“The main justification for the ‘range of factors’ test has always been that it enables the court to avoid inflicting loss on the claimant disproportionate to the measure of his badness. This was the instinct that led the Court of Appeal in Euro-Diam Ltd v Bathurst … to propose that the illegality principle should be applied only where the alternative would be shocking to the public conscience. That concept was rejected in Tinsley v Milligan …”

8. 看来“非法理论”必须综合与协调考虑早在 1775 年 Holman v. Johnson 先例中

[56] 见笔者《海上货物保险》一书第十三章的详细介绍。

确立下来的政策与法律规则与个别案件不同案情中非法的严重性与各种其他因素。其中,对非法理论的基本性政策必须是优先考虑,在过了这关卡后,才考虑个别案件的其他因素与其严重性。这本来是希望通过立法解决,但这做法被否决,毕竟这么面广、困难与复杂的事情不是写几句或几章法条就可以解决所有问题。英国法律委员会试图以立法改变非法理论,但最后放弃,估计就是这个原因,这方面可见本章之7.3段的介绍。

幸亏涉及非法的案件十分多,没有等待太久,英国最高院就有了全面改变非法理论的机会(在先例理论下只有最高院才能改变),这就是将在本章7.5段详细介绍的Patel v. Mirza 最高院先例。至于该重要先例确立的多因素判断(factors-based approach)与三阶段测试(three-stages test)是否是非法理论良好的新篇章、新开始,笔者也在接下来的段节区别介绍一些Patel v. Mirza先例后的判例与如何适用这三阶段测试。

7. 建立非法理论的历史路程

在较近期的Patel v. Mirza(2016)UKSC 42先例中,英国最高院对非法理论背后的大原则与考虑方式明确了一些目前英国法下的地位。虽然该先例针对的只是普通法非法,但对于立法非法或违反其他公共政策都有借鉴意义。

Patel v. Mirza先例确立了基于多因素判断测试(factors-based approach),否定了此前的公序良俗测试(public conscience test)与依赖测试(reliance test)。但可以先从这些过去的测试标准开始,介绍这方面的历史与背景,以便读者理解。

7.1 Holman v. Johnson(1775)1 Cowp 341 先例:公序良俗测试(public conscience test)

在早期的案件中,这种测试下审理法官只考虑两个问题:(1)有关案件是否涉及非法;如果是,(2)如果法院仍给予救济,会否被视为协助或鼓励原告非法行为而导致违背公序良俗。

这可节录Hutchison大法官在Thackwell v. Barclays Bank plc(1986)1 All ER 676先例中的说法:"the court looking at the quality of the illegality relied on by the defendant and all the surrounding circumstances, without fine distinctions, and seeking to answer two questions: first, whether there had been illegality of which the court should take notice and, second, whether in all the circumstances it would be an affront to the public conscience if by affording him the relief sought the court was seen to be indirectly assisting or encouraging the plaintiff in his criminal act."

Hutchison大法官在该先例中还说如果给予原告救济,会变相地间接帮助或鼓励原告采取非法犯罪行为:"... affront to the public conscience if by affording him the relief sought the court was seen to be indirectly assisting or encouraging the plaintiff in his criminal act…"

在 Euro-Diam Ltd v. Bathurst(1990)1 QB 1 上诉庭先例中,Kerr 大法官也对此测试说:"in all the circumstances it would be an affront to the public conscience to grant the plaintiff the relief which he seeks because the court would thereby appear to assist or encourage the plaintiff in his illegal conduct or to encourage others in similar acts."

这背后的大原则固然正确,也可以清楚无误与严厉地阻吓任何形式的非法合约或行为。但是这公序良俗测试也被视为太严格、太苛刻、欠缺弹性以及在千变万化的案件中可能造成不公平合理(主要是对原告)的结果。这种测试标准也被批评过于不肯定与不可预测,每一个审理法官的判断都可能不同。

在 Les Laboratoires Servier v. Apotex Inc(2014)UKSC 55 最高院先例中,提到这种不如意主要体现在两方面,Sumption 勋爵说:"two features of this area of law have been characteristic of it from the outset. First, it is a rule of law and not a mere discretionary power. Secondly, it is based on public policy, and not on the perceived balance of merits between the parties to any particular dispute."

也就是说,公序良俗测试是基于英国公共政策的法律规定,不是追求司法公平,所以不涉及审理法官在不同情况下有裁量权或可权衡双方当事人案件的强弱,而是一律套用。这在 Tribe v. Tribe(1996)Ch 107 上诉庭先例中,Nourse 大法官说:"The rule that no court will lend its aid to a man who founds his cause of action on an immoral or illegal act has often led to seemingly unjust results. That is because, as Lord Mansfield C. J. made clear when stating the rule in regard to contracts in Holman v. Johnson(1775) 1 Cowp. 341… it is not a principle of justice; it is a principle of policy, whose application is indiscriminate and so can lead to unfair consequences as between the parties to litigation …"

毕竟非法与公共政策涉及极广,可大可小。双方当事人在非法程度上也可以是有极大差异,如相对无辜卷进去,也可以是"主犯"与"从犯"等。例如,"老实人"A 在 B 的误导与诱惑下把积蓄交出给 B 放高利贷,以为会有可观的收益。后来 A 不想继续投资,希望从 B 那里取回这笔钱,但遭到拒绝后需要提起诉讼。B 以非法作为抗辩。法院在"公序良俗测试"下也就只能考虑非法与公共政策这方面,但不能考虑该案件任何其他方面如是否涉及可诉欺诈性误述与 A 是相对无辜。

这测试标准也已经在 Tinsley v. Milligan(1994)1 AC 340 贵族院先例中被否定。在该贵族院先例中,也谈到这方面的问题,说:"…not to say that 'affront to the public conscience' is either a desirable or indeed a workable test. A clear and strict rule maximises the deterrent effect, whilst flexibility gives hope. The 'public conscience' test is inherently uncertain in its application; …The very uncertainty of this test will serve only to encourage more protracted and uncertain litigation in future cases. Moreover, it is particularly important for property law to be clear and not dependent upon unpredictable judicial decision making. The subject is entitled to know the extent of his rights, in and over property, as accurately as possible. That greater justice more than compensates for the 'injustice' of not relieving the fraudulent from the consequences of their own folly. ... The 'public conscience test' inevitably calls ... as 'a value judgment.' Such an exercise imposes standards which are not merely variable but are not readily ascertainable. How are the dictates of 'public conscience' to be ascertained? ...It is no proper function of the court to be grading illegalities 'according to moral turpitude.' In truth, the 'public conscience test' simply substitutes for the civil conscience of parliamentary legislation and the established rules of the common law the subjective private conscience of the judge. In place of the fixed and rational standards required by the rule of law, litigants will ... be judged by a standard varying with each judge...A just and workable rule ought to be reasonably sound, and depend upon categories of case, rather than a subjective judgment upon the particular circumstances of the individual case."

由于"公序良俗测试"太严格与太苛刻,法院在很长的一段时间中面对不同的案件与案情,为了达致公平合理的结果,也建立了非法理论的一些例外(exceptions)与适用的限制,主要是:(1)"撤回权"(locus poenitentiae 或"an opportunity to withdraw from a contract or obligation before it is completed or to decide not to commit an intended crime"),即当事人或原告在非法合约履行完毕前退出或在犯罪完成前放弃犯罪意图;(2)对非法行为的事实或法律不知情(ignorance)或没有参与(participation);(3)立法本意只惩罚一方当事人的类别人士;(4)可与非法部分分割(severance)。

但这些例外与限制的适用都十分严格,因为担心越界,与非法理论的基本大原则起冲突,所以仍然无法解决非法理论过于严格与苛刻的问题。

这些例外不因为有了 Patel v. Mirza 最高院先例而变为过时。相反,它们在"多因素判断测试"的成比例(proportionality)考虑下是非常重要的因素。这会在本章之10 段与 11 段分段介绍。

7.2 Tinsley v. Milligan (1994) 1 AC 340 贵族院先例:依赖测试(reliance test)

在 Tinsley v. Milligan 贵族院先例中,Tinsley 女士与 Milligan 女士共同出资购买了一处房产,实际共同拥有房产的衡平权益(equitable interest),而房产只登记在 Tinsley 女士一个人名下,即法律产权(legal title)由 Tinsley 女士独自持有。这种安排虽然十分平常,但此先例涉及一个非法目的,就是明面上没有房产的 Milligan 女士可以领取国家社会福利。在 Tinsley 女士的默许下,Milligan 女士确实领取了多年福利。但后来 Milligan 女士选择向有关机构坦白,并与有关机构达成和解。

此先例的问题是 Tinsley 女士与 Milligan 女士之间关系破裂,持有法律产权的 Tinsley 女士要把 Milligan 女士赶走。Milligan 女士则根据她拥有衡平产权(equitable title),要求法院宣告房产是由 Tinsley 女士作为信托人(trustee)持有,实际应由两人平分房产。这带来的问题,就是是否因为双方的约定/交易非法(目的是瞒报信息领取社会福利),导致 Milligan 女士的要求无法被法院协助执行?

上诉庭的判法是采用了"公序良俗测试",即有关行为是否冒犯了公序良俗。而此先例中涉及的行为被认为并没有到这个程度,因此判 Milligan 女士胜诉。

虽然贵族院也认为 Milligan 女士胜诉,但一致否定采用公序良俗测试。至于应如何考虑这问题,贵族院则产生分歧。多数意见的判法是,即使是不可执行的非法合约,已经发生的财产法律产权转让仍然有效,非法理论是否适用要看主张权利的一方是否必须依赖非法行为。在此先例中,Milligan 女士要求法院宣告该房产的信托关系,这种默示信托(implied trust)是否产生纯粹是看购买时双方出资的事实以及当时双方的意图。换言之,只要能够通过证据显示当时 Milligan 女士参与出资,而且双方共同理解大家是一起共享衡平权益,这就已经足够认为信托关系的存在,Milligan 女士不需要主张当事人之间存在什么合约如明示信托(express trust)。这样,Milligan 女士胜诉。

7.2.1 非法不影响普通法产权的 Bowmakers Ltd v. Barnet Instruments Ltd (1945) KB 65 上诉庭先例

更好地理解 Tinsley v. Milligan(1994)1 AC 340 贵族院先例在讲什么,就需要区分普通法下的法律产权(legal title)与衡平法下的衡平产权(equitable title)。[57] 这是因为涉及非法理论的大量案件,双方争议的往往不是合约权利,而是争夺在非法合约或合约目的下被占有或被转让的有关财产。在前者,主张合约权利就不能回避非法合约,也就绕不过非法理论了。但在后者的争夺财产中,就有可能绕过非法理论,原告只向被告(或任何第三人)主张他对有关财产的产权,就不必依赖非法合约了。这也是 Tinsley v. Milligan 贵族院先例的所谓"依赖测试"。而该先例被批评的主要原因也在以财产法的产权回避非法理论与程序上的依赖测试只会带来不肯定,在不同案情下稍有变化就有不同判法,不解决非法理论的大问题。

简而言之,非法合约或行为不影响法律产权。这正是 Eldon 勋爵在 Muckleston v. Brown(1801)31 ER 934 先例中所说的:"Let the estate lie where it falls."在 Patel v. Mirza(2016)UKSC 42 最高院先例中,Toulson 勋爵说:"Unless a statute provides otherwise(expressly or by necessary implication), property can pass under a transaction which is illegal as a contract."

现实情况经常是,A 把自己的财产(房产、股权、珠宝、古董名画、货物等)在各种交易或安排下(包括是买卖)转交了给 B,A 事后需要如本书第七章之 13.5 段的"完全得不到对价的好处"(total failure of consideration)或其他要求复原/不当得利的理由向 B 取回。但 B 如果不合作并挑出有关的交易或安排有过任何蛛丝马迹的猫腻,就会提出非法抗辩。这样,如果财产的法律产权是在 A 或 B 的名下就决定财产归

---

[57] 见本书第三章之 6.3.1 的详细介绍。

谁。这纯粹是财产法下谁有更优越的产权(better title),没去理会非法理论,也更不理会案件双方当事人之间的公道与否。民事法院是不会没收(confiscate)A 名下的财产给 B,或反过来做。即使非法买卖合约下 A 把财产如房产转交给了 B,但 B 的律师忘了登记办手续,财产的法律产权仍是属于 A,B 的损失只能向他的律师追偿:见 Stoffel & Co v. Grondona(2020)UKSC 42 最高院先例。

这可介绍 Bowmakers Ltd v. Barnet Instruments Ltd 上诉庭先例,案情是被告想要使用几套机械设备,就与原告达成融资租购合约。根据约定原告购买设备后会出租给被告,并允许被告在多年后以特定金额购买这几套设备。然而在履行过程中,被告侵占(conversion)了这批设备,并将设备出售给第三人,在起争执后拒绝将设备交还给原告。原告即起诉被告,而被告提出租购协议非法。涉及的法律是当时世界大战期间,政府设立规章制度限制一些战时资源的使用。根据《Defence(General)Regulations 1939》,此先例中的设备应受规管,尤其针对出租给被告的交易,是必须先向政府申请并获得批准。然而原告没有申请与获批,因此该交易非法。针对非法理论的问题,上诉庭就指出,原告的请求是根据自己对设备的法律产权主张被告侵占。该请求不需要依赖非法合约,财产的产权归属也与非法理论无关,因此诉讼请求可以被执行。上诉庭的 Du Parcq 大法官这样说:"In our opinion, a man's right to possess his own chattels will as a general rule be enforced against one who, without any claim of right, is detaining them, or has converted them to his own use, even though it may appear either from the pleadings, or in the course of the trial, that the chattels in question came into the defendant's possession by reason of an illegal contract between himself and the plaintiff, **provided that the plaintiff does not seek, and is not forced, either to found his claim on the illegal contract or to plead its illegality in order to support his claim.**"(加黑部分是笔者的强调)

但以上针对的是普通法下的法律产权,而在 Tinsley v. Milligan 贵族院先例中针对的是衡平产权。简单而言这规则就是要看索赔请求是否需要"依赖"非法行为。不妨举两种情况来显示这个规则的使用。

7.2.2　受非法影响的衡平产权(equity title)

非法的交易或行为经常涉及财产的转让,如果 A 希望把没有被履行或只是部分被履行的非法合约解开/拆散,把属于自己的财产(或蒙受的损失)向 B 要回来。但 A 也知道以双方的非法合约去寻求法院协助,是肯定会面对 B 的非法抗辩,结果是一场空。所以在涉及财产转让或支付给 B 的钱完全得不到对价的好处等的案件,就只能求助衡平法的复原(restitution)或不当得利(unjust enrichment)的救济了。照理来说,寻求衡平救济有"净手规则"(clean-hand doctrine),涉及非法合约或行为的申请人就难逃不是"净手"。但在"依赖测试"下,就可在技术上说是申请人,也就是 Tinsley v. Milligan(1994)1 AC 340 贵族院先例的 Milligan 女士,无须依赖非法而不属于非法理论,看来也会同样被认为就是"净手"了。

衡平产权是需要根据有关案件的事实去推定这个产权,好像 Tinsley v. Milligan 贵族院先例需要认定 Milligan 女士有参与出资购买了该房产等的事实。这样,如果这安排背后确实有非法目的,如 A 把财产在没有对价或只是名义对价(nominal consideration)下转让给 B,是为了成立一个虚假信托(sham trust)用来逃税、欺骗债权人(creditors)或其他千奇百怪的非法目的,法院需要在认定案件的事实去推定 A 是否在 B 手中的财产有一个衡平产权,就难逃要面对这非法合约与行为(信托协议与安排)了。

在家庭法下,家庭成员把财产在无对价下转让更是频繁发生,这里就涉及赠与(voluntary gift)[58] 与信托的区分。赠与/自愿支付一般在支付方 A 想清楚的支付后是无法向收款人 B 取回。但如果 A 只是想 B 作为他财产的受托人(trustee)去无对价转让/支付金钱,A 是随时可向 B 取回受托财产,而 B 对 A 是有一个信义/诚信责任(fiduciary duty)[59] 去处理好受托财产,完全不可以据为己有。

但一般民众不会记录下来一份完整合约。没有明示的情况下,法院就只能依赖默示去从整件事情所发生的事实作出推断。这就发展出来可名为“赠与推定”(presumption of advancement)的法律推定。这也是人类的经验与常识,父亲在无对价下转让财产给子女,可推定或假设为赠与。如果父亲不是这样想法,他需要保留证据证明只是信托与为什么要建立这个信托(如目的是非法地骗政府或债权人或合法避税等)并将来在需要时到法院向子女取回。但如果是隔了一层关系的亲友的第三人,就更有可能是信托而不是无端的赠与。第三人要证明这财产是赠与,就要提供证据了。

赠与推定可追溯到在 1677 年出现的与没有对价下转移金钱或其他财产有关的法律推定。从广义上讲,该推定规定,如果丈夫将财产转让给妻子,或父亲将财产转让给子女,在没有其他证据的情况下,法院将推定转让是通过赠与的方式进行的。在我国香港特区的 Suen Shu Tai v. Tam Fung Tai(2014)HKEC 1125 先例中,上诉庭在附带意见中更倾向于现代男女平等的看法,在母亲将财产转让给子女的情况下,推定同样适用。

该推定可通过证据反驳,在 Pettitt v. Pettitt(1970)AC 777 贵族院先例中,Hodson 勋爵指出该推定的分量非常轻,并且可能会被最轻微的证据反驳。但在没有任何其他证据的情况下,该推定仍然适用。

这里与非法理论有关的是:原告 A 如果是把有关财产(如股权)在无对价下转移给任何第三人,法院就可以推定或假设是信托关系,A 向作为受托人的第三人 B 去取回股权就相对简单。但如果被告 C 是 A 的儿子,就适用了赠与推定。而 A 提供证据予以反驳此法律推定,就会要涉及该行为(转移股权)的非法目的,如向债权人隐

---

〔58〕 这课题在本书第七章之 11.3 段有详论,不重复。

〔59〕 见本书第一章之 2.7 段。

瞒财产，并带来 C 的非法抗辩了。

相信在上述介绍后可以更了解 Tinsley v. Milligan 贵族院先例的针对。在该先例赠与推定也是重点，原告（Milligan 女士）与被告（Tinsley 女士）并不是夫妻或父子关系，不适用赠与推定，Milligan 女士只要证明她有共同出资购买该房产即可让法院认定有信托关系。但如果适用赠与推定，Milligan 女士就要依赖非法行为反驳她的出资是赠与/自愿支付了，并在 Tinsley 女士的非法抗辩下败诉。

可以说，Milligan 女士只需要依赖有关的事实构成信托关系，而这是与非法行为无关，不需捆绑在一起，即可以满足该先例确立的"依赖测试"，法院就可以给予衡平法或普通法救济。

7.2.3 依赖测试的弊端

由于 Tinsley v. Milligan（1994）1 AC 340 贵族院先例确立的替代了"公序良俗测试"的"依赖测试"已经很快被 Patel v. Mirza（2016）UKSC 42 最高院先例否定。有不少批评这依赖测试只是在程序上（procedurally）做文章，没有解决不同案件在非法程度严重或轻微、非法是否是核心问题或只是与索赔沾边的"擦边球"，更不解决非法理论带来的所有问题。在此只挑两个批评与反对理由：

1. 在该先例贵族院的少数意见对以依赖测试进行对非法的测试表示反对。Goff 勋爵就说不应该根据是否存在技术上不用依赖非法去判断是否协助原告取回财产，而不考虑非法的严重性。Goff 勋爵举了一个例子，如果劫匪以第三人名义（他对严重非法不知情）购买了一座房产作为犯罪基地，岂非在依赖测试下可以主张他们对房产的衡平产权并可以获得法院的衡平救济去协助劫匪把房产取回？只因请求不涉及非法行为可获得救济，这自我阻碍（self-stultification）[60] 是说不通的。Goff 勋爵给了这样的例子："if A puts property in the name of B intending to conceal his（A's）interest in the property for a fraudulent or illegal purpose, neither law nor equity will allow A to recover the property, and equity will not assist him in asserting an equitable interest in it. This principle applies whether the transaction takes the form of a transfer of property by A to B, or the purchase by A of property in the name of B."

2. Tinsley v. Milligan 贵族院先例的当事人关系只要有了改变，在完全一样的事实下就得出完全相反的结果，这是不理想与说不通的。如果此先例中两个朋友（Tinsley 女士与 Milligan 女士）合资购买房产的情况，改变为父亲与子女或夫妻合资购买，就会存在赠与的初步推定。既然是赠与，父亲也不会对该房产有衡平权益。如果

---

〔60〕 主要提出此说法的是 Birks 教授的"Recovering Value Transferred Under an Illegal Contract"（2000）1 Theoretical Inquiries in Law 155 一文，说："'To stultify' is to 'to make a fool of' or 'to make nonsense of'. It is important that the law as stated in one area should not make nonsense of the law as stated in another… Whether allowing the claim in unjust enrichment would make nonsense of the law's condemnation of the illegal contract in question and of its refusal to enforce the illegal contract."

父亲想要主张衡平权益,就要拿出证据反驳与解释为什么这样做,这一去依赖非法,就带来非法抗辩与法院不去协助。

但依赖测试也不是没有支持,在 Patel v. Mirza 最高院先例中,虽然多数意见的判决给出了今天权威的基于多因素判断的测试,但 Patel v. Mirza 先例中持少数意见的 Sumption 勋爵倾向于应该支持依赖测试。Sumption 勋爵指出依赖测试是非法理论与原告索赔请求与救济最狭窄的联系(narrowest connection),并可以:(1)确保当事人不能从自己的非法行为中获利;(2)明确了非法行为与对救济的请求之间的直接联系,因此如果只是细枝末节、背景事实中的非法行为就可以与此区分开来;(3)狭窄的范围确保了不容易造成滥杀(overkill),剥夺了太多本应可以获得的法律权利。可以节录 Sumption 勋爵所说如下:"... the reliance test accords with principle. **First**, it gives effect to the basic principle that a person may not derive a legal right from his own illegal act. **Second**, it establishes a direct causal link between the illegality and the claim, distinguishing between those illegal acts which are collateral or matters of background only, and those from which the legal right asserted can be said to result. **Third**, it ensures that the illegality principle applies no more widely than is necessary to give effect to its purpose of preventing legal rights from being derived from illegal acts. **The reliance test is the narrowest test of connection available**. Every alternative test which has been proposed would widen the application of the defence as well as render its application more uncertain."(加黑部分是笔者的强调)

7.3 英国法律委员会的建议

在 Tinsley v. Milligan(1994)1 AC 340 贵族院先例中,少数意见的 Goff 勋爵反对多数意见判决的另一个理由是不应该改变已经有 200 多年历史的在 Holman v. Johnson(1775)1 Cowp 341 先例中确立的"公序良俗测试",建议法律委员会(Legal Commission)[61]全面审核英国法律对非法理论的优劣,并可在参阅新西兰于 1970 年通过立法做出的重大改革后,以立法解决这方面的问题。Goff 勋爵说:

"... I have well in mind the reform introduced in New Zealand by the New Zealand Illegal Contracts Act 1970, which in section 6 provides that 'every illegal contract shall be of no effect and no person shall become entitled to any property under a disposition made by or pursuant to any such contract ...' and in section 7 confers on the court the power to grant relief: 'by way of restitution, compensation, variation of the contract, validation of the contract in whole or part or for any particular purpose, or otherwise howsoever as the court in its discretion thinks just.'

---

[61] 英国法律委员会是根据《Law Commissions Act 1965》成立的独立官方组织,职责是检讨英国的法律,并在需要时建议英国政府改革或修改有关法律,务求英国法律更容易让人获得公平、具成本效益与追得上时代。

These provisions of the Act demonstrate how sweeping a reform was considered necessary by the New Zealand legislature... Your Lordships have no means of ascertaining how successful the Act has proved to be in practice... In truth, everything points to the conclusion that, if there is to be a reform aimed at substituting a system of discretionary relief for the present rules, the reform is one which should only be instituted by the legislature, after a full inquiry into the matter by the Law Commission, such inquiry to embrace not only the perceived advantages and disadvantages of the present law, but also the likely advantages and disadvantages of a system of discretionary relief, no doubt with particular reference to the New Zealand experience. The real criticism of the present rules is not that they are unprincipled, but rather that they are indiscriminate in their effect, and are capable therefore of producing injustice. ... speaking for myself, I would welcome an investigation by the Law Commission, ... and that I would be more than happy if a new system could be evolved which was both satisfactory in its effect and capable of avoiding the kind of result which flows from the established rules of law in cases such as the present."

根据上一段所介绍的Goff勋爵的建议,英国专门成立法律委员会,并给出了一系列咨询报告,[62]包括《The Effect of Illegality on Contracts and Trusts》(1999, Consultation Paper No 154),《the Illegality Defence In Tort》(2001, Consultation Paper No 160),《The Illegality Defence: A Consultative Report》(2009, Consultation Paper No 189),《The Illegality Defence》(2010, Law Com No 320)。

在初期的报告中,立法委员会针对合约中的非法理论,一度建议可以按照过往先例中的判法,进行立法针对合约的形成、目的或履行中的非法。但这样的立法被认为非常困难,很难草拟一条具有足够肯定性的硬性规则。在后来的报告中也转换方向,认为违约、侵权、不当得利等案件中的非法理论不应该进行立法规定,转而建议让法院根据具体案件进行考虑。而立法委员会对目前"一刀切"处理非法合约明确不认同,在《The Illegality Defence: A Consultative Report》(2009, Consultation Paper No 189)之3.31段中说:"However it clearly cannot be in every case that a contract is unlawfully performed, even where this was the original intention, that the offending party loses his or her remedies. Such a proposition would result in the widespread forfeiture of contractual remedies as a result of minor and incidental transgressions. Although there is general agreement on this point amongst academic commentators, there is surprisingly little authority."

在此只节录法律委员会在最后报告《The Illegality Defence》之1.2至1.4段中提到,认为很难设定广泛适用的严格法律规则,而是建议最好由法院根据个案的情况予以权衡的说法:

---

〔62〕 具体报告的详情与内容,有兴趣的读者可参考:https://www.lawcom.gov.uk/project/illegality/。

"The illegality defence arises when the defendant in a private law action argues that the claimant should not be entitled to their normal rights or remedies because they have been involved in illegal conduct which is linked to the claim. **If the courts accept the illegality defence, it often involves granting an unjustified windfall to the defendant, who may be equally implicated in the illegality. However, if the courts refuse, they may be seen to be helping a claimant who has behaved illegally.**

The courts have attempted to set out rules to govern this area. However, the rules are complex and confused. This is because of the breadth of circumstances in which the issue arises. It may arise in many different areas of law, including contract, tort, unjust enrichment, property rights or trusts law. It may involve a wide variety of illegal behaviour, from parking offences to serious crime. The conduct may be integrally linked to the claim (as where a contract is to carry out a crime); or it may be just one of many background facts (as where a speed limit is broken in the performance of a contract). The consequences may be borne by the wrongdoer personally, or by a third party (such as the wrongdoer's creditors).

We have reached the conclusion that it is not possible to lay down strict rules about when the illegality defence should apply. Instead, the courts should consider the policy rationales that underlie the defence and apply them to the facts of the case. On the one hand, the courts should attempt to do justice between the parties, enforcing the rights set down by law. **On the other hand, the courts must not permit a claimant to profit from a wrong. They should deter illegal conduct and not allow the legal system to be abused by criminals.** "(加黑部分是笔者的强调)

针对非法理论是弹性处理还是严格政策性处理的矛盾,法律委员会拒绝以立法解决非法理论,英国政府也在2012年宣告不再考虑立法,[63]所以本章不多讲。但对非法这个课题有兴趣的读者,建议去找这些法律委员会发布的报告深入研究,会更深刻了解非法理论的课题。

在立法方面有所更改让法院弹性处理非法问题的只有《Financial Services and Markets Act 2000》之 Section 28(3):"(3) If the court is satisfied that it is just and equitable in the circumstances of the case, it may allow—(a) the agreement to be enforced; or (b) money and property paid or transferred under the agreement to be retained."

7.4 其他普通法国家对非法理论的立法或判例法的改革或倡议

已经有很多其他普通法国家对传统非法理论开始通过立法与/或案例作出改革,

---

〔63〕 "Report on the implementation of Law Commission proposals" (March 2012)。另外,针对法律委员会在中期报告废除赠与推定(presumption of advancement)的建议,英国政府已经在《Equality Act 2010》之 Section 199 拟定了立法条文,但是该条文并没有被推出生效,将来是否会生效也尚未可知。

试图摆脱传统“非法理论”下非法合约无法执行的“纯真理”(doctrinal purity),并让审理法官有更大的弹性去成比例处理个别案件。

这些改革涉及立法是刚刚已经提到的新西兰的《Illegal Contracts Act 1970》,现在已合并在《Contract and Commercial Law Act 2017》。其他立法改革的建议有:澳大利亚南澳大利亚州法律改革委员会 1977 年的“Thirty-Seventh Report Relating to the Doctrines of Frustration and Illegality in the Law of Contract”;[64] 加拿大英属哥伦比亚省 1983 年的“Report on Illegal Transaction”;[65] 加拿大安大略省 1984 年的“Amendment of the Law of Contract”第 11 章之“Contracts that Infringe Public Policy”;[66] 新加坡 2002 年 7 月 5 日的“Relief from Unenforceability of Illegal Contracts and Trusts”。[67]

而在判例法方面,可举两个先例,一个是加拿大联邦上诉庭的 Re Still v. Minister of National Revenue(1997)154 DLR(4th)229 先例,另一个是澳大利亚高院的 Nelson v. Nelson(1995)HCA 25 先例。

在前者,涉及加拿大合法移民(原告)不知道有关立法下是需要工作许可才能正式受雇工作。开始一切顺利,原告也在任职期间按时支付政府的退休金与劳工保险。但之后原告失业,在申请失业救济金时以非法受雇被拒。这导致原告向法院申请司法复核。上诉到联邦上诉庭,判是在传统的非法理论(classical model of illegality)下,原告是不知情的善意违法,反正就是非法。但在现在的非法理论(modern approach)下,这善意违法就是一个重要的考虑因素。再加上有关立法的背后目的(显然不是为了针对合法移民)与拒绝支付原告失业救济金会否是一个对违反立法完全不成比例的惩罚等因素,最后判原告胜诉。

在后者,案情是与英国的 Tribe v. Tribe(1996)Ch 107 上诉庭先例大致相同,就是原告(母亲)把她的房屋产权转让给了被告(女儿),以利以无产者身份根据立法向澳大利亚政府申请“二战”后军人遗孀购买住处的资助。这是欺骗政府的非法行为,在被告把转让的房屋出售后,原告要求把钱归还给她。被告提出非法抗辩,但不被支持,高院的 MuHugh 大法官说:“... courts should not refuse to enforce legal or equitable rights simply because they arose out of or were associated with an unlawful purpose unless:(a) the statute discloses an intention that those rights should be unenforceable in all circumstances;or(b)(i) the sanction of refusing to enforce those rights is not dispropor-

〔64〕 https://law. adelaide. edu. au/system/files/2019 - 02/37 - Doctrines - of - Frustration - and - Illegality - in - the - Law - of - Contract. pdf.

〔65〕 https://www. canlii. org/en/commentary/doc/1983CanLIIDocs2#! fragment//BQCwhgziBcwMYgK4DsDWszIQewE4BUBTADwBdoByCgSgBpltTCIBFRQ3AT0otokLC4EbDtyp8BQkAGU8pAEL-cASgFEAMioBqAQQByAYRW1SYAEbRS2ONWpA.

〔66〕 https://archive. org/stream/reportonamendmen00onta/reportonamendmen00onta_djvu. txt.

〔67〕 http://www. commonlii. org/sg/other/SGLRC/report/R9/9. pdf.

tionate to the seriousness of the unlawful conduct;(ii)the imposition of the sanction is necessary,having regards to the terms of the statute,to protect its objects or policies;and (iii)the statute does not disclose an intention that the sanctions and remedies contained in the statute are to be the only legal consequences of a breach of the statute or the frustration of its policies."

目前唯一生效的新西兰立法,对中国的相关立法会更有帮助。可节录在《Contract and Commercial Law Act 2017》之 S. 71(1)中对"非法合约"的定义:"(a)means any contract governed by New Zealand law that is illegal at law or in equity,whether the illegality arises from the creation or performance of the contract;and(b)includes a contract which contains an illegal provision,whether that provision is severable or not."

S. 72 是去收窄 S. 71(1)所针对的合约非法履行,说:"A contract lawfully entered into shall not become illegal or unenforceable by any party by reason of the fact that it's performance is in breach of any enactment,unless the enactment expressly so provides or its object clearly so requires."

接下来 s. 73 明确了非法合约的起点是无效,说:"73(1)Every illegal contract is of no effect. (2)No person is entitled to any property under a disposition made by or under an illegal contract."

但再接下来就给了审理法院十分广泛与有弹性的裁量权去改变这个无效的起点,S. 75 与 S. 76 说:

"**Who may be granted relief**

Relief under s. 76 may be granted to—(a)a party to an illegal contract;or(b)a party to a contract who is disqualified from enforcing it because of the commission of an illegal act in the course of its performance;or(c)a person claiming through or under a party referred to in paragraph(a)or(b)."

"**Court may grant relief**

76(1)The court may grant a person referred to in s. 75 any relief that the court thanks just, including (without limitation)—(a) restitution; or (b) compensation; or (c)variation of the contract;or(d)validation of the contract in whole or in part for any particular purpose."

新西兰的立法也无可避免地带来不少先例去解释、分析与适用。但由于篇幅,只能先提部分,例如:Evans v. Credit Services(1975)2 NZLR 560;Harding v. Coburn (1976)2 NZLR 577;Mall Finance & Investment Co Ltd v. Slater(1976)2 NZLR 685; Coleman v. Myers(1977)2 NZLR 225;Bardsell v. Kerr(1979)2 NZLR 731;Parker v. Rock Finance Corporation Ltd(1981)1 NZLR 488;Hurrell v. Townend(1982)1 NZLR 536;Leith v. Gould(1986)1 NZLR 760;France v. Might(1987)2 NZLR 38;Catley v. Herbert(1988)1 NZLR 606;Euro-National Corporation v. NZI Bank Ltd(1992)2 NZLR

739；Howick Building Co Ltd v. Howick Parklands Ltd（1993）1 NZLR 759；Supercool Refrigeration and Air Conditioning v. Hoverd Industries Ltd（1994）3 NZLR 300；Bevin v. Smith（1994）3 NZLR 648；Duncan v. McDonald（1997）3 NZLR 669 等。

可以说，以上介绍也对英国法院有了一定的压力，在英国法律委员会拒绝以立法针对下，在接下来的一段会详细介绍的 Patel v. Mirza（2016）UKSC 42 最高院先例就是摆脱非法理论下非法合约无法执行的严格与苛刻的政策性法律规则（rule of law），并让审理法官有更大的弹性成比例处理个别案件的英国回应。

7.5 Patel v. Mirza（2016）UKSC 42 最高院先例：多因素判断测试（factors-based approach）

法律委员会的建议看来并没有解决问题。在接下来的 Hounga v. Allen（2014）UKSC 47；Les Laboratoires Servier v. Apotex Inc（2014）UKSC 55 以及 Bilta（UK）Ltd（In Liquidation）v. Nazir（2015）UKSC 23 这三个最高院先例中，最高院的多名大法官对于适用"非法理论"具体应该如何应对，仍有巨大分歧。在 Les Laboratoires Servier v. Apotex Inc 最高院先例中，多数意见看来是支持"基于规则"（rule-based），而另两个最高院先例则支持所谓"基于多因素"（factors-based 或 range of factors）。

这两种意见主要不同是基于规则的方法，主要目的看来是尽可能减少审理法官在不同案件的裁量权空间。他们必须根据一套既定规则［当时主要是 Tinsley v. Milligan（1994）1 AC 340 贵族院先例的"依赖测试"］或公式进行判断，如果具体案情符合，就应该得到特定结果。审理法官（或仲裁员）在其中要做的并不是权衡公共政策或考虑案件的公平合理，而只是解释有关规则的内容，看特定的抗辩是否符合规则。理论上这样的做法应当能得到更肯定的结果，毕竟不涉及个别法官的裁量、不需要进行什么权衡，而纯粹是客观解释。但也有批评说这种基于规则的方法也不一定能够带来肯定性，如 Burrows 教授在《Restatement of the English Law of Contract 2016》一书中说："although a purported advantage of firm rules is greater certainty, the cases do not always fit the rules because courts have often sought ways around them when they do not like the consequence. The flexible approach would not only produce more acceptable results, but would in practice be no less certain than the rule-based approach."

至于多因素考虑，是涉及审理法官在不同案件去考虑很多不同因素，权衡轻重优劣，并最后行使裁量权去决定是否接受非法抗辩。这正是最后在 Patel v. Mirza 最高院先例中的多数判决所认同的方法。在此，在持同样意见的 ParkingEye Ltd v. Somerfield Stores Ltd（2012）EWCA Civ 1338 上诉庭先例中，粗略介绍了多因素考虑下的重要因素包括非法的严重性、合约方的目的与是否知情、非法行为是否有核心地位、拒绝非法抗辩会带来的后果、已经对非法行为作出的刑事/行政惩罚会否带来双重损害等，并建议审理法官在个别案件有弹性的考虑。Jacob 大法官说："... although Lord Mansfield made it clear in Holman v. Johnson that the illegality defence operates as a rule of public policy and is not designed to achieve justice between the parties, that does not mean that any result, however arbitrary, is acceptable. The law should strive for the most desirable policy outcome, and **it may be that it is best achieved by taking into account a range of factors.** ... although it may be argued that if there are deficiencies in the traditional rules, the way forward is to refine the rules to remove the deficiencies by appropriate exceptions, that task is one which has never been satisfactorily accomplished. The reason is that there are so many variables, for example, in **seriousness of the illegality, the knowledge and intentions of the parties, the centrality of the illegality, the effect of denying the defence and the sanctions which the law already imposes.** To reach the best result in terms of policy, the judges need to have the flexibility to consider and weigh a range of factors in the light of the facts of the particular case before them. ”(加黑部分是笔者的强调)

7.5.1 基于多因素判断的三阶段测试(three-stages test)

在 Patel v. Mirza(2016)UKSC 42 最高院先例中,案情是被告声称自己在苏格兰银行(Royal Bank of Scotland, RBS)中有“关系”,可以获悉 RBS 的内幕消息,认为在近期政府会公布某有关消息抬升 RBS 股价,因此原告与被告达成协议,原告支付了 62 万英镑给被告,被告则会用这笔钱买入 RBS 股票获利。但后续消息显示不会有能抬升股价的政府消息,因此也没能实际进行交易。但被告没有退钱给原告,因此开始诉讼。

原告要证明自己白白给出了 62 万英镑,难以避免地披露出了转账给被告的原因是双方约定利用内幕消息进行交易的实情。法院认定这约定属于《Criminal Justice Act 1993》之 Section 52 禁止的内幕交易(insider dealing),是刑事犯罪行为。同时当事人之间的合约还属于《Criminal Law Act 1977》之 Section 1 的串谋(conspiracy)犯罪行为。问题在于,原告主张不当得利(unjust enrichment),想要拿回自己的 62 万英镑,是否因为原告涉及了前述非法行为而不可执行?

贵族院的多数意见(Toulson 勋爵、Kerr 勋爵、Hale 勋爵、Wilson 勋爵与 Hodge 勋爵)明确否定了 Tinsley v. Milligan(1994)1 AC 340 贵族院先例中的依赖测试,不接受被告的非法抗辩,并根据不当得利判被告需要返还。他们更倾向于不用死板、公式化的规则,而是要求法官在考虑一系列因素的基础上,有弹性地权衡。但是又不希望因此导致审理法官裁量权过大而造成案件判法上的不一致,偏离 Mansfield 勋爵在 Holman v. Johnson(1775)1 Cowp 341 先例中确立的、在今天仍然是真理的法律规则(rule of law),因此设定了三个阶段的测试作为指引。

Patel v. Mirza 最高院先例中的少数意见(Mance 勋爵、Clarke 勋爵与 Sumption 勋爵)对于采用基于多因素的判断方法持反对意见。已经在本章之 7.2.3 段提到 Sumption 勋爵支持采用依赖测试,相关理由与说法不在此重复。Sumption 勋爵批评基于多因素的判断方法没什么帮助,让一审法院在过去原本就混乱的非法理论的基础上行使裁量权,并不会带来所希望的肯定性与一致性。可以节录 Sumption 勋爵所说如下："In my opinion, this is **far too vague and potentially far too wide** to serve as the basis on which a person may be denied his legal rights. It **converts a legal principle into an exercise of judicial discretion**, in the process exhibiting all the vices of '**complexity, uncertainty, arbitrariness and lack of transparency**' which Lord Toulson attributes to the present law. I would not deny that in the past the law of illegality has been a mess. The proper response of this court is not to leave the problem to case by case evaluation by the lower courts by reference to a potentially unlimited range of factors, but to address the problem by supplying a framework of principle which accommodates legitimate concerns about the present law. We would be doing no service to the coherent development of the law if we simply substituted a new mess for the old one."（加黑部分是笔者的强调）

还可以节录 Mance 勋爵反对理由如下："What is apparent is that **this approach**, **would introduce not only a new era but entirely novel dimensions into any issue of illegality. Courts would be required to make a value judgment, by reference to a widely spread mélange of ingredients, about the overall 'merits' or strengths**, in a highly unspecific non-legal sense, of the respective claims of the public interest and of each of the parties. But courts could only do so, by either allowing or disallowing enforcement of the contract as between the two parties to it, unless they were able (if and when this was possible) to adopt the yet further novelty, **pioneered by the majority of the Australian court in Nelson v Nelson, of requiring the account to the public for any profit unjustifiably made at the public expense, as a condition of obtaining relief**."（加黑部分是笔者的强调）

但即使有强烈反对的少数意见与将来改革的建议（如 Mance 勋爵提到澳大利亚最高院提出的一种可行的改革是法院帮助执行合约私权的前提条件是原告上交所有的非法获利），目前的权威与有约束力的说法仍然是 Patel v. Mirza 先例中的多数意见，在后续先例包括一些最高院先例中也开始采用基于多因素判断的方法。

7.5.1.1　何为三阶段测试

可先节录 Toulson 勋爵在 Patel v. Mirza (2016) UKSC 42 先例中所提到的三阶段测试如下：

"The essential rationale of the illegality doctrine is that it would be contrary to the public interest to enforce a claim if to do so would be harmful to the integrity of the legal system...In assessing whether the public interest would be harmed in that way, it is necessary: a) to consider the underlying purpose of the prohibition which has been transgressed and whether that purpose will be enhanced by denial of the claim, [在第一个阶段先考虑，为什么法律（特别是立法）禁止有关行为，背后的目的是什么。不予执行索赔是否有助于促进此目的？] b) to consider any other relevant public policy on which the denial of the claim may have an impact(在第二个阶段考虑,如果不予执行是否会影响一些其他的公共政策,除了最基本的影响了合约神圣性外,还有具体案件的大量不同公共政策,如会影响律师勤勉尽责与保护财产权的公共政策等,并作出权衡)and c) to consider whether denial of the claim would be a proportionate response to the illegality, bearing in mind that punishment is a matter for the criminal courts.(第三个阶段则要考虑个别案件各种因素成比例的问题,不能因为任何程度的非法就都一致不予执行。也要注意当事人主要应由刑事法院惩罚,而不是通过民事案件来惩罚。)

Within that framework, various factors may be relevant, but it would be a mistake to suggest that the court is free to decide a case in an undisciplined way. The public interest is best served by a principled and transparent assessment of the considerations identified, rather by than the application of a formal approach capable of producing results which may appear arbitrary, unjust or disproportionate."

Toulson 勋爵在最后一段中说,在这几个步骤中,有很多因素都可能有关与需要被考虑,但法院并非任意地做决定。而相比于采用死板的规则可能造成武断、不公平、不成比例的后果,还是这样设定好权衡的原则、公开透明地对于找出来的因素予以权衡,更能符合公共利益。

此先例中 Toulson 勋爵在另一段也有类似说法:"I would say that one cannot judge whether allowing a claim which is in some way tainted by illegality would be contrary to the public interest, because it would be harmful to the integrity of the legal system, without a) considering the underlying purpose of the prohibition which has been transgressed, b) considering conversely any other relevant public policies which may be rendered ineffective or less effective by denial of the claim, and c) keeping in mind the possibility of overkill unless the law is applied with a due sense of proportionality. We are, after all, in the area of public policy. That trio of necessary considerations can be found in the case law."

7.5.1.2 后续先例对三阶段测试的解读

对于三阶段测试的说法在本章后文中还会分段详细介绍。在此先节录近期的 Stoffel & Co v. Grondona(2020) UKSC 42 最高院先例中给出的进一步解读(此先例的具体案情会在本章稍后之9.1段详细介绍)。第一阶段(a)与第二阶段(b)是一般性的政策考虑,这是相对高层次的考虑,也不需要双方提供证据,只是审理法官权衡支持非法抗辩是否会与公共政策相冲突,是否会影响法律系统的正直与公义。只有答案是否定的情况下,才会考虑第三阶段(c)的测试,审理法官根据证据仔细考虑特定案件中的各种因素,权衡支持非法抗辩是否成比例。Lloyd-Jones 勋爵说:

"It is important to bear in mind when applying the 'trio of necessary considerations' described by Lord Toulson in Patel that they are relevant not because it may be considered desirable that a given policy should be promoted but because of their bearing on determining whether to allow a claim would damage the integrity of the law by permitting incoherent contradictions. Equally such an evaluation of policy considerations, while necessarily structured, must not be permitted to become another mechanistic process. **In the application of stages(a) and(b) of this trio a court will be concerned to identify the relevant policy considerations at a relatively high level of generality** before considering their application to the situation before the court. In particular, I would not normally expect a court to admit or to address evidence on matters such as the effectiveness of the criminal law in particular situations or the likely social consequences of permitting a claim in specified circumstances. **The essential question is whether to allow the claim would damage the integrity of the legal system. The answer will depend on whether it would be inconsistent with the policies to which the legal system gives effect**. The court is not concerned here to evaluate the policies in play or to carry out a policy-based evaluation of the relevant laws. It is simply seeking to identify the policies to which the law gives effect which are engaged by the question whether to allow the claim, **to ascertain whether to allow it would be inconsistent with those policies or, where the policies compete, where the overall balance lies.**

In considering proportionality at stage(c), by contrast, it is likely that the court will have to **give close scrutiny to the detail of the case in hand**. Finally, in this regard, since the overriding consideration is the damage that might be done to the integrity of the legal system by its adopting contradictory positions, it may not be necessary in every case to complete an exhaustive examination of all stages of the trio of considerations. **If, on an examination of the relevant policy considerations, the clear conclusion emerges that the defence should not be allowed, there will be no need to go on to consider proportionality**, because there is no risk of disproportionate harm to the claimant by refusing relief to which he or she would otherwise be entitled. **If**, on the other hand, **a balancing of the policy considerations suggests a denial of the claim, it will be necessary to go on to consider proportionality**."(加黑部分是笔者的强调)

另在 Henderson v. Dorset Healthcare University NHS Foundation Trust(2020) UKSC 43 最高院先例中，解释说在第一阶段和第二阶段主要是针对执行与不予执行背后对抗的公共政策之间进行大原则上的考虑与权衡（不用太关注具体案件的情况），而在第三阶段才根据具体案件情况考虑成比例问题。可以节录 Hamblen 勋爵所说如下："... questions arise as to exactly how under the trio of considerations approach relevant policy considerations are to be weighed. It appears that this must involve a balancing between considerations arising at the first and second stages; the third stage relates to proportionality and factors specific to the case rather than general policy considerations. Stage(a) is directed at policy reasons which support denial of the claim and stage(b) is directed at policy reasons which support denial of the illegality defence… stage(b) is meant to operate 'conversely' to stage(a)… It follows that stage(a) should not be interpreted as being confined to the specific purpose of the prohibition transgressed. Whilst that is of great importance, other general policy considerations that impact on the consistency of the law and the integrity of the legal system also fall to be taken into account."

也因此经过这样三个阶段基于多因素判断，尤其是让法院权衡公共政策与个别案件的不同因素的做法，就与基于规则的方法区分了开来，在《Chitty on Contracts》（2021 年，第 34 版）一书之 18－029 段中说："Thus the law in illegality in contract is no longer a prescriptive, mechanical rule but rather involves a determination of whether the policy underlying a particular rule would be advanced or frustrated by the application of the rule. The court granted restitutionary recovery to prevent the unjust enrichment of the defendant. This emphasis on restitutionary relief, coupled with a requirement of 'proportionality' is a development of considerable significance introduced by Patel v. Mirza."

7.5.1.3　三阶段测试考虑的因素

至于具体需要考虑的因素，可以节录 Patel v. Mirza(2016) UKSC 42 先例中节录的 Burrows 教授在《Restatement of the English Law of Contract》(2016)一书中所说如下："If a 'range of factors' approach were preferred, Professor Burrows suggested… that a possible formulation would read as follows: 'If the formation, purpose or performance of a contract involves conduct that is illegal (such as a crime) or contrary to public policy (such as a restraint of trade), the contract is unenforceable by one or either party if to deny enforcement would be an appropriate response to that conduct, taking into account where relevant—(a) how seriously illegal or contrary to public policy the conduct was（非法行为的严重性如何）;(b) whether the party seeking enforcement knew of, or intended, the conduct（寻求救济，想要法院执行合约的一方是否知道或目的就是采取该非法行为）;(c) how central to the contract or its performance the conduct was（非法行为与索赔所基于的合约之间关系是否密切）;(d) how serious a sanction the denial of enforcement is for the party seeking enforcement（拒绝执行会给寻求救济的原告带来怎样的影响）;(e) whether denying enforcement will further the purpose of the rule which the conduct has infringed（拒绝执行是否促进禁止非法行为背后公共政策的目的）;(f) whether denying enforcement will act as a deterrent to conduct that is illegal or contrary to public policy（拒绝执行是否会有阻吓力，明确此类非法行为不被接受）;(g) whether denying enforcement will ensure that the party seeking enforcement does not profit from the conduct（拒绝执行是否使得原告不会从自己错误行为中获利）;(h) whether denying enforcement will avoid inconsistency in the law thereby maintaining the integrity of the legal system（拒绝执行是否能避免法律的不一致，以保证法律体系的正直与公义）'。"

这些因素并不穷尽，而只是进行了一个列举。对于每一项的具体内容如何，看来也还纷纷有待后续先例进行解释。尤其是对于其中有些因素是否应当纳入考虑也尚有争议，简单节录《Chitty on Contracts》(2021 年，第 34 版)一书之 18－042 段，对 Sumption 勋爵针对这一系列因素反对意见的评论："He considered the factor(g) of the Burrows schema('whether denying enforcement will ensure that the party seeking enforcement does not profit from his conduct') was 'fundamental to the principle of consistency, and not just a factor to be weighed against others'. Lord Sumption also strongly objected to factor(a)('how seriously illegal or contrary to public policy the conduct was') as it was: '... difficult to reconcile with any kind of principle the notion that there may be degrees of illegality as Professor Burrows' factor(a) seems to envisage'..."

但需要理解 Burrows 教授以上所说是在 Patel v. Mirza 先例确立的三阶段测试之前，的确其中部分政策性的考虑已经包括在第一阶段与第二阶段，不是第三阶段考虑的因素。此外，这三阶段的考虑因素也可能会有重叠，例如上述节录的(c)，非法行为与索赔所基于的合约之间关系是否密切，是否是索赔的核心，看来应属于第三阶段要考虑的因素，但是其实在第二阶段也会有影响。道理是很简单，非法行为与索赔隔得越远，不予执行就越可能与其他公共政策起冲突(如合约的神圣性)。以 Stoffel & Co v. Grondona(2020) UKSC 42 最高院先例为例，如果该律师并非疏忽没有向土地注册的有关机构登记租赁产权的变更，以及登记 BM 对土地的抵押权利，而是直接帮助 Grondona 女士骗贷，Grondona 女士向律师的索赔就很可能失败。但在此先例中，对律师疏忽的索赔与骗贷没有直接关系，不让 Grondona 女士索赔会与律师应该勤勉尽职履行职责与应该允许客户向未能履行职责的律师提起民事诉讼与索赔的公共政策有冲突。

针对第三阶段成比例的说法可以节录 Toulson 勋爵在 Patel v. Mirza 先例中说："In considering whether it would be **disproportionate to refuse relief to which the claimant would otherwise be entitled**, as a matter of public policy, various factors may be relevant. Professor Burrows' list is helpful but I would not attempt to lay down a prescriptive or definitive list because of the infinite possible variety of cases. **Potentially relevant factors include the seriousness of the conduct, its centrality to the contract, whether it was intentional and whether there was marked disparity in the parties' respective culpability.**"(加黑部分是笔者的强调)

涉及哪些因素也显然非常依赖具体案件的案情，Patel v. Mirza 先例中 Neuberger 勋爵甚至认为不需要通过先例列举所有因素让审理法官在每个案件跟从，只要让审理法官在具体案件考虑所有有关因素[如 Jacob 大法官在 Parking Eye Ltd v. Somerfield Stores Ltd(2012) EWCA Civ 1338 上诉庭先例中提到的 5 个因素]并在权衡后给予恰当的重量。由于审理法官都是接受过同样的一套法律教育的称职法官，所以他们行使裁量权作出的判决的区别是有限的，不会影响法律的一致性。Neuberger 勋爵说:“I am not convinced that it is helpful to list all the potentially relevant factors and say that it is a matter for the court in each case to decide which of those factors apply in that case and what weight to give them. Once a judge is required to take into account a significant number of relevant factors, and the question of how much weight to give each of them is a matter for the judge, the difference between judgment and discretion is, I think, in practice pretty slight.”

7.5.2　阶段一:不予执行是否促进法律禁止有关行为的目的

第一个阶段也就是要先考虑为什么法律(普通法或立法)需要禁止有关合约与行为,禁止背后的目的和道理是什么。这样也就可以考虑如果支持非法抗辩去驳回索赔、不予执行合约与其他主张的权利,能否促进这个目的?如果可以促进或没有影响,法院在这一阶段的测试中根据非法理论驳回索赔请求、不予执行不会有障碍。但有时驳回索赔会妨碍有关法律背后的目的,甚至予以执行才有助于促进该目的。

不妨举两个例子,虽然这两个先例是在 Patel v. Mirza(2016) UKSC 42 先例之前,所以没有适用三阶段测试,但道理是一样。在本章之 3.2.1 段已经介绍过的 The “St John”(1956) 2 Lloyd's Rep 413 先例中,案情涉及船舶运输货物在冬天航行大西洋会在载重线有更大限制,在装港不小心计算多装了货物就会在船舶进入大西洋航区出现超载。这在当时的英国《Merchant Shipping (Safety and Load Line Conventions) Act 1932》立法下属于刑事罪行,船长也因此获罪并被罚了 1200 英镑。但其实船舶在从美湾去英国的航程中并未出问题,货物(谷物)也安全运送到卸港,货方想要依赖运输的非法履行而拒付运费。如果套用三阶段测试,在第一阶段,立法禁止超载的目的是保护货物与人命安全。但是船长的违反在现实中经常会发生,而且往往是不严重,加上现在港口的监管越来越严,真正会影响货物与人命安全的超载情况可以说船舶是根本开不出港口。所以如果仅仅因为不严重的超载,法院就不执行租约让船东收取运费,再加上已经就超载行为作出了罚款,说不上是能促进立法目的,也完全不成比例。

另在 Hardy v. Motor Insurers' Bureau (1964) 2 QB 745 先例中,原告是工厂的安保人员,拦下肇事人的车辆进行盘查时,肇事人突然加速并导致原告被车辆拖行,造成原告严重身体伤害,肇事人后来因此获刑。但问题是原告的损失如何处理?

这问题来源是英国《Road Traffic Act 1960》要求所有机动车都要投保在道路上造成人身伤亡的保险,但肇事人并没有投保,也无力偿还。幸好是英国还有特别方案针对此问题,英国有专门的机动车保险局(Motor Insurers' Bureau, MIB)会补偿受害人在恰当强制险下本可以获得的金钱赔偿。

原告因此先在针对肇事人的索赔胜诉后,找 MIB 要求补偿。MIB 提出肇事人故意犯罪,对于故意犯罪行为不应该受保,即使原本有保险也会因为故意犯罪行为而不可执行。但这样的抗辩被 Diplock 大法官拒绝。重要原因就是通过解释《Road Traffic Act 1960》下规定强制机动车保险的目的,是为了保护受到机动车驾驶错误行为影响的受害人。如果驾驶员只要存在非法犯罪行为,就认为保险失效,岂不是意味着以后驾驶员但凡涉及驾驶的犯罪(危险驾驶、酒后驾驶等),受害人都无法受到保护?此先例这种情况,就是执行才能促进立法目的。

7.5.3 阶段二:不予执行会影响其他的公共政策

由于公共政策太多太广,所以每一个案件都会涉及方方面面的不同公共政策,需要去做出权衡。例如在本章之 9.1 段介绍的 Stoffel & Co v. Grondona(2020) UKSC 42 最高院先例中,法院就认为不予执行会影响律师勤勉尽责与保护财产权的公共政策,也与律师疏忽的受害者应获得赔偿的公共政策有冲突。

除了 Stoffel & Co v. Grondona 先例外,在本章之 9 段介绍的另外 8 个先例中,法院在适用 Patel 指引时,也都有针对在有关的案情下的其他公共政策,并作出权衡。而因为案情不同这些公共政策也各不相同,根本无法列出一张完整清单。在法院权衡后,给这些公共政策的重量也不同。

7.5.4 阶段三:成比例

首先可以重复说,阶段三的测试是在权衡过公共政策后,根据案情的细节考虑不予执行是否成比例(proportionality)。如果在阶段一的衡量中不予执行并不能促进禁止行为背后的目的,在阶段二的衡量中不予执行又会妨碍其他公共政策,就可以不用进行阶段三的测试。正如在 Stoffel & Co v. Grondona(2020) UKSC 42 最高院先例中,Lloyd-Jones 勋爵说:“… I pause at this point in the process of addressing Lord Toulson's trio of relevant considerations. **To permit the respondent's claim in the particular circumstances of this case would not undermine the public policies** underlying the criminalisation of mortgage fraud and could, indeed, operate in a way which would protect the interests of the victim of the fraud, ie the mortgagee. **Furthermore, to deny the respondent's claim would run counter to other important public policies**. It would be inconsistent with the policy that the victims of solicitors' negligence should be compensated for their loss. It would be a disincentive to the diligent performance by solicitors of their duties. It would also result in an incoherent contradiction given the law's acknowledgment that an equitable property right vested in the respondent. **In these circumstances, it is not strictly necessary to go on to consider the third of the trio of considerations, namely whether denial of the claim would be a proportionate response to the illegality**, …”(加黑部分是笔者的强调)

在 Henderson v. Dorset Healthcare University NHS Foundation Trust(2020) UKSC 43 最高院先例中,Hamblen 勋爵也说:“… questions arise as to whether proportionality always has to be considered and as to how it is to be addressed. In some cases, … it may be apparent that the balancing of policy considerations comes down firmly against denial of the claim. If so, it will not be necessary to go on to the third stage and the issue of proportionality.”

至于第三阶段考虑成比例时一般要考虑哪些因素，已经在本章之7.5.1.3段介绍，这里不再重复。简而言之，如果涉及的是严重的非法，即使不是索赔核心或并非故意，法院也会支持非法抗辩。而如果虽然涉及的是不怎么重要的非法，但非法是索赔的核心或是故意做出非法行为，法院也可能支持非法抗辩。总之，在不同的案件中各种不同因素综合考虑与权衡轻重，无论是要考虑的因素还是给予的轻重都不能一概而论，目的是希望在每个不同的案件中，尽量做到成比例与在当事人之间的公平。

7.5.5　小结

Patel v. Mirza(2016) UKSC 42先例看来是公序良俗测试与其他所有不同说法的先例之间的妥协，特别表现在：

1. 法院可以有条有理与有弹性地根据三阶段测试决定是否支持非法抗辩，不予执行索赔。

2. 指引虽然没有违反非法理论的基本原则，但因为多因素考虑与成比例规则，审理法官对整体公共政策的权衡与对特定案件的不同考虑因素的裁量权占据重要地位。这样，不同案件的结果会是十分依赖审理法官在起冲突的不同公共政策和特定案件的所有因素中权衡轻重，并行使裁量权得出结论。这可能带来非法理论更大的不肯定与不可预测，但相信这失控的危险在英国法院会比较低。当然这只是理论，具体实践中Patel v. Mirza先例的三阶段测试是否恰当仍有待时间验证，现在说Patel v. Mirza先例已经解决了非法理论的问题是为时尚早。另一个笔者的担心是，现在很多争议是由仲裁解决。而国际仲裁涉及大量不同背景的仲裁员，在适用法是英国法的情况下，他们在审理非法理论的争议时面对各种起冲突的公共政策的权衡，且目前仍没有明确界限的所有不同因素去考虑成比例问题，相信分歧会比英国法院法官之间更大，也会给针对非法争议的仲裁带来更大的不肯定性。

3. Patel v. Mirza先例之前的先例仍然相关，只是在参考时会采取三阶段测试，基于多因素判断而不是规则判断。Patel v. Mirza先例之前的先例仍有先例价值，除非能证明与Patel v. Mirza先例不匹配。

4. Patel v. Mirza先例并没有偏离"违背道德的对价不生诉权"与"不能从自己的非法行为获利"的基本原则。只是现在法院可以在前两个阶段都有公共政策(包括这两个基本原则)支持非法抗辩后，最后在第三阶段再多考虑根据所有的因素不支持原告的请求是否成比例，务求行使裁量权达至一个在双方当事人之间更公平公正的结果。

5. 并非所有的案件都需要完整考虑三个阶段的测试。如果在考虑过前两个阶段的公共政策后，非法抗辩不应予以支持，就没必要考虑第三阶段的测试，可去支持原告了。

6. 对复原/不当得利，不再适用Tinsley v. Milligan(1994) 1 AC 340贵族院先例的"依赖测试"，而是假设法院可协助取消(undo)非法交易或合约并复原，除非涉及十分严重的非法(heinous crime)。这也大幅度简化了这种频密发生在非法合约下的复原/不当得利争议。

8. Patel v. Mirza 先例的影响

8.1 适用于所有普通法非法案件但不否定过往先例中的衡量

由于 Patel v. Mirza(2016)UKSC 42 最高院先例确定基于多因素判断与三阶段测试的方法[可称为"Patel 指引"(Patel guidelines)],与过去大量先例所采用的方法未必一致。这些过往先例如何考虑与处理?显然在普通法的先例理论(doctrine of precedent/rule of stare decisis)下,不会轻易地就将这些过往先例弃之不顾。在过往先例中,如果完全根据 Tinsley v. Milligan(1994)1 AC 340 贵族院先例的依赖测试就决定了案件的先例的意义不大,但如果涉及了法院权衡了不同公共政策后作出的决定,就仍然有重要的参考价值。

针对 Patel v. Mirza 先例普通法非法案件的影响,将在本章之 9.2 段介绍的 Henderson v. Dorset Healthcare University NHS Foundation Trust(2020)UKSC 43 最高院先例中明确三方面影响,可以节录 Hamblen 勋爵所说如下:

"First, it should be emphasised that Patel concerned common law illegality rather than statutory illegality. Where the effects of the illegality are dealt with by statute then the statute should be applied. As Lord Toulson stated …: 'The courts must obviously abide by the terms of any statute' …(Patel v. Mirza 先例的判法只针对普通法非法,而立法非法则要看具体立法条文的规定。毕竟立法条文如果明确后果,实际上可以认为是公共政策下已经由议会进行了权衡。法院此时只是纯粹解释立法条文是否适用与按照立法条文执行。)

Secondly, Patel concerned a claim in unjust enrichment, but there can be little doubt that it was intended to provide guidance as to the proper approach to the common law illegality defence across civil law more generally…(虽然 Patel v. Mirza 先例涉及的案情与索赔请求是基于不当得利,但该判法会广泛适用在所有的一般民事案件中,无论是合约、侵权还是不当得利等。)

Thirdly, that does not mean that Patel represents 'year zero' and that in all future illegality cases it is Patel and only Patel that is to be considered and applied. That would be to disregard the value of precedent built up in various areas of the law to address particular factual situations giving rise to the illegality defence. **Those decisions remain of precedential value unless it can be shown that they are not compatible with the approach set out in Patel in the sense that they cannot stand with the reasoning in Patel or were wrongly decided in the light of that reasoning.** Lord Toulson made it clear in

Patel that the principles he identified were to be found in the existing case law. [尽管 Patel v. Mirza 先例采用的基于多因素判断的方法与过往先例中的很多采用的规则不同(如依赖测试等),但这不意味着 Patel v. Mirza 先例之前的先例都可以弃之不顾。过去先例对于具体案件事实进行过的衡量仍然有重要参考价值。]"(加黑部分是笔者的强调)

虽然在上一段说 Patel 指引广泛适用于所有涉及非法的一般民事案件,但在 Harcus Sinclair LLP v. Your Lawyers Ltd(2021)UKSC 32 最高院先例中给出的目前权威说法,违反限制贸易的公共政策[68]已经有一套有弹性、灵活应对的办法。例如,考虑个案的情况与是否配合公共利益考虑合理性,以及考虑是否可以分割等办法。所以在限制贸易的案件不需要再适用 Patel v. Mirza 先例根据个案的多因素去成比例权衡。可以节录多数意见(Briggs 勋爵、Hamblen 勋爵与 Burrows 勋爵)的判词如下:"One might think that the recent series of Supreme Court cases analysing the law on illegality…is also relevant. This is not least because, in the contract textbooks, illegality is usually closely linked with public policy so that, for example, contracts involving crimes are usually examined alongside contracts that are contrary to public policy, such as contracts involving sexual immorality or contracts interfering with the administration of justice or contracts in restraint of trade. But the principles governing contracts in restraint of trade are well-established and(with the exception of the rules on severance) self-contained and already reflect the type of flexibility that Patel v Mirza has brought to the law on contracts affected by illegality. It seems preferable, therefore, to treat the law on the enforceability of contracts in restraint of trade as being separate from, albeit similar to, the law on the enforceability of contracts affected by illegality as laid down in Patel v Mirza."

8.2　Patel 指引对立法非法的影响

已经介绍过 Patel v. Mirza(2016)UKSC 42 最高院先例,该先例中确立的基于多因素判断的方法并不直接适用于立法非法,[69] Toulson 勋爵说:"The courts must obviously abide by the terms of any statute, but I conclude that it is right for a court which is considering the application of the common law doctrine of illegality to have regard to the policy factors involved and to the nature and circumstances of the illegal conduct in determining whether the public interest in preserving the integrity of the justice system should result in denial of the relief claimed. I put it in that way rather than whether the contract should be regarded as tainted by illegality, because the question is whether the relief claimed should be granted."

Burrows 教授在"A New Dawn for the Law of Illegality"一文中针对 Patel v. Mirza

---

[68]　关于限制贸易可见本章之 11.2 段的详细介绍。

[69]　关于立法非法可见本章之 3 段的介绍。

先例说,如果立法写明了非法行为(无论是合约、侵权、不当得利或是财产权)的后果,审理法官只能跟从立法的规定,这就只是一般解释立法的问题。或者也有情况是立法禁止某些行为默示了有关的合约也同样被禁止,所以任何一方都不能执行该合约,但这种情况相对罕见。因为议会在立法时主要针对的是社会层面,很少考虑合约私权的问题,所以大部分情况是立法没有针对民事后果。这时就需要根据普通法非法来决定,Patel 指引适用。可节录有关内容如下:"The first is that the debate about illegality that we are here concerned with concerns what is usually termed ' common law illegality'. That is to be distinguished from what is often termed ' statutory illegality'. It is crucial to understand that those labels are not concerned with whether the illegality in question is a common law illegality or, as is usually the case, a statutory illegality. Rather those labels are concerned with the effects of the illegality. It may be that where the illegality is statutory, the effects of the illegality(whether for contractual enforcement or tort or unjust enrichment or property law) have been laid down in the relevant statute. Where that is so, clearly the statute governs. That is all a question of normal statutory interpretation. It has most commonly arisen where a statute prohibits conduct which, by implication, means that the making of a contract involving that prohibited conduct is also prohibited so that neither party can enforce that contract. **But in general this is, and should be recognised as being, rare. In the vast majority of cases, it is a fiction to imagine that Parliament in a statute has dealt with the civil law effects of the illegality and, where the statute runs out, the common law must take over**. It is the common law on illegality that has given rise to so much controversy. In other words, everything said in Patel v Mirza is about common law illegality and assumes that statute has not dealt with the question. As Lord Toulson said, ' The courts must obviously abide by the terms of any statute'. He then went on in the same paragraph to set out his preferred approach to ' the common law doctrine of illegality'."(加黑部分是笔者的强调)

Energizer Supermarket Ltd v. Holiday Snacks Ltd(Trinidad and Tobago)(2022) UKPC 16 枢密院先例就是一个很好的例子。该先例涉及特立尼达和多巴哥共和国一块土地上的地役权(easement)[70]的争议。虽然是特立尼达和多巴哥法律的非法问题,但因为该国是英联邦国家,且法律也是跟从英国法,双方当事人的争辩与枢密院完全是按照分析本国法非法的思路去进行判决,所以不在本章之 8.3 段和本书第

---

〔70〕 要满足地役权,在 In re Ellenborough Park(1956)Ch 131 先例中上诉庭的 Evershed 勋爵引用了 Geoffrey Chevalier Cheshire 与 Edward Hector Burn 所著的《Cheshire's Modern Law of Real Property》(第七版)一书,第456 页说:"The essential qualities of an easement are(1)there must be a dominant and a servient tenement;(2)an easement must accommodate the dominant tenement, that is, be connected with its enjoyment and for its benefit;(3)the dominant and servient owners must be different persons; and(4)the right claimed must be capable of forming the subject-matter of a grant …"

九章针对。

原告 Holiday Snacks 的母公司 Kiss Baking 与自己拥有的土地相邻的另一块土地的所有人 Boodhai 先生在 1986 年 3 月达成书面的输气管道协议，Boodhai 先生允许 Kiss Baking 在一次性支付 12,000 美元后在他的土地下铺设输气管道连接至 Kiss Baking 所拥有的土地，并允许 Kiss Baking 在日后派人对管道进行维修保养。该输气管道协议下有关的权利与义务之后被转让给了 Holiday Snacks。在 1993 年 10 月，Boodhai 先生将他的土地卖给了被告 Energizer 用于建造一间超市，并通知原告双方早前的输气管道协议终止。之后因这些输气管道的存在，被告在土地上建造超市的申请被规划部门拒绝。被告要求原告拆除这些管道。

在 2006 年 12 月，原告开始诉讼要求法院宣告自己通过之前的输气管道协议而对这块土地享有地役权与申请禁令禁止被告阻挠自己使用输气管道。而被告的抗辩之一就是因为原告没有按照特立尼达和多巴哥共和国的石油法（Petroleum Act）的要求申请批文，所以原告与 Boodhai 先生达成的输气管道协议因非法而无效。

该先例最重要的和本段有关的争议是原告是否因为非法而不能行使在有关土地上使用输气管道的地役权。一审判原告没有申请批文属于非法，但不会令输气管道协议无效或不可执行，所以支持了原告的请求。被告上诉，上诉庭认为原告与 Boodhai 先生都不属于立法中的从事石油作业（petroleum operations）的人士，所以不用申请批文，从而不涉及非法。因此虽然与一审法官是不同的理由，但上诉庭也支持了原告的请求，于是被告上诉到了英国枢密院。

针对原告是否需要申请批文，枢密院同意一审法院的判法，判原告没有申请批文违反立法规定。接下来枢密院区别针对了立法非法与普通法非法下是否支持被告的非法抗辩。

枢密院首先判输气管道协议不会因为立法非法而无效或不可执行，原因如下：(1)原告与 Boodhai 先生在输气管道协议下铺设与使用输气管道的合约和财产权利与申请批文完全可以分开。原告与 Boodhai 先生没有获得批文与输气管道协议（和协议中的权利）的有效性是可以分开的独立事件。例如，原告完全可以与可能在订立输气管道协议后再去申请批文。(2)此先例与本章之 3.2.4 段介绍的 Mahmoud and Ispahani, Re(1921)2 KB 716 先例不同。因为后者立法明确写明了没有批文的合约无效，但此先例并非如此。只要事后申请批文，有关输气管道协议完全可以合法履行，因此输气管道协议没有被立法完全禁止（absolutely prohibited）。(3)输气管道协议并非要求 Boodhai 先生铺设管道，而是要求 Boodhai 先生允许原告在他的土地上铺设与维修管道。所以没有因为执行输气管道协议而强迫一个没有批文的人铺设管道的问题。(4)如果双方的协议不是原告获得铺设输气管道的地役权而是转让土地给原告，而原告的意图是在这块土地下铺设管道，土地转让协议显然不会因为后来原告没有申请批文而无效。那该地役权的协议也应是一样。(5)立法条文的目的是强调安全与效率的重要性，支持地役权并不会损害这个目的。特别是在此先例中有关的管道一直由国有企业所有，原告也在输气管道协议中同意会满足该国有企业所有安全方面的要求，所以安全性应该有保障。(6)根据立法条文的措辞/文字与目的，没有申请批文的惩罚由刑事法律决定，但地役权的合约与财产权利仍由一般的民事法律处理。

在认定了立法没有明示或默示禁止执行地役权，也就是立法非法的抗辩不成功后，枢密院接下来考虑被告普通法非法的抗辩并适用了 Patel 指引。

对阶段一与阶段二的问题，尽管不执行地役权可以说在某种程度上促进了石油法立法背后的目的，但枢密院认为还有更重要的公共政策支持执行地役权（也就是不支持普通法非法的抗辩）与执行地役权不会令法律的一致性与正直受损。如执行地役权可以保证财产法适用的肯定性；已经在立法非法部分提到的执行地役权与申请批文是独立的两件事；执行地役权不会强迫一个没有批文的人铺设管道；不会违背立法强调安全与效率的重要性的目的；没有证据显示在已经有刑法惩罚的情况下，拒绝执行地役权会鼓励其他人申请批文；立法下的罚款很高；管道一直由国有企业所有，在某种程度上减轻了非法性。

因为前两阶段都是否定的答案，所以可以不用考虑阶段三的问题，即使考虑，枢密院也认为拒绝执行地役权是不成比例的。第一，申请批文与输气管道协议是独立的，也不是该协议的核心。第二，尽管没有申请批文的罚款很高，但是罪行本身不是严重的犯罪。第三，地役权对原告的生意非常重要，没有燃气原告的生意就进行不下去。

因此，枢密院判被告在立法非法与普通法非法下的抗辩都不成功。

8.3 Patel 指引对外国法非法的影响

Patel v. Mirza(2016) UKSC 42 最高院先例是针对英国普通法下本土的非法，主要考虑的公共政策是在本章之 1.5 段提到的维护英国法律体系整体的一致性。但涉及外国的非法（foreign illegality），主要考虑的公共政策是国际睦仪/礼让（international comity）。但显然它们完全是两码事，所以 Patel 指引是无法去套用在外国法非法与违反公共政策上的。例如，在涉及外国法非法的 Foster v. Driscoll(1929) 1 KB 470 与 Ralli Brothers v. Compania Naviera Sota Y Aznar(1920) 2 KB 287 等经典上诉庭先例中，英国法院关心的是如果去协助执行有关的外国法非法合约是否会引起外交风波，友好国家是否会提出外交抗议。

Patel 指引的“三阶段测试”下的阶段一之“不予执行是否促进法律禁止有关行为的目的”与阶段二之“不予执行会影响的其他的公共政策”英国法院根本无法去考虑。这是外国的公共政策，涉及很多不同国家的历史、文化、政治、经济、公众利益、道德等方方面面，英国法院根本不能去对这些不同的公共政策作出轻重优劣的权衡。但这是三阶段测试中重要的测试，如果阶段一或阶段二的公共政策考虑能够对协助执行合约的决定有了定论，就根本无需去考虑阶段三的“成比例”（proportionality）。

但非法理论如果是英国与外国的非法差异太大，无法协调，这不是好事。例如，英国非法理论变得更有弹性，但外国法非法理论则是欠缺弹性。正如 Cockerill 大法官在 Magdeev v. Tsvetkov(2020) EWHC 887(Comm)先例中说:"a perverse dichotomy with a flexible rule in one context and a rigid and inflexible rule in another."

在 Patel v. Mirza 最高院先例后的 Magdeev v. Tsvetkov 先例中,才首次有了机会去看看 Patel 指引对外国法非法是否或能否延伸适用,把英国本土的非法理论与外国的非法理论变得更一致。〔71〕

在此只说此先例中投资人(Magdeev)向珠宝商(Tsvetkov)提供了一笔贷款,借贷合约本身没有约定利息的支付,但是通过签订另一份雇佣合约,在雇佣合约中以薪水的形式支付利息,同时也以雇佣合约帮助投资人获取当地(阿联酋)的工作签证。后来投资人在英国法院向珠宝商提起诉讼追偿贷款,后者以非法作为抗辩,指称雇佣合约是虚假(sham)的,用以取得工作签证,这违反阿联酋法律。

Cockerill 大法官在审理后认定这是骗取工作签证,但不认为在整体的权衡下协助执行贷款合约是违反公平正义。这权衡就是 Patel 指引之阶段三"成比例"的四方面因素,也就是:(1)非法行为的严重性;(2)非法行为与需要被执行的合约之间的关系是否密切;(3)当事人的主观意图如何,是否意图非法;(4)当事人之间应受谴责的程度(culpability)是否有所区别,即原告涉及的程度十分轻微因此不应该用非法理论拒绝执行?

针对(1)的严重程度,Cockerill 大法官同意以假文件骗取工作签证,在英国是十分严重的罪行,也有立法清楚规定,这不是一般的违反行政命令。但仍接受了专家证人的意见证据是阿联酋在实际做法上会宽待财力雄厚的公司/个人通过这种非法手段取得签证,也没有证据显示阿联酋曾经对这类非法案件提出过检控。Cockerill 大法官说:

"As to seriousness, there is some difficulty. On the one hand I have clear evidence as to the sanctions applicable to forgery: it is an offence which can result in **imprisonment for up to ten years**.... That speaks on its face of a degree of seriousness. So it is not possible to say here ... that these were mere administrative contraventions.

There is then the related question of 'iniquity'. Here, ... I would be minded to conclude that there was a degree of iniquity. **Visa fraud is a serious matter; ...It is a crime which has the capacity to affect not just the economy of a state but also its national security.**

On the other I have**no evidence about how serious or iniquitous that makes the conduct so far as UAE law is concerned**-where on the scale of seriousness it ranks. I have the sentencing range; but it would be a false analogy to compare the sentencing equivalents in this jurisdiction, because **UAE law may operate on a different scale of seriousness**. I have no evidence which enables me to decode this. As in Ryder, there has **ap-**

〔71〕 关于 Patel 指引对外国法非法的影响也可见本书第九章之 4.7 段。

parently been no prosecution or enforcement proceedings by the UAE authorities. …

Professor Al Aidarous' evidence(专家证人意见),which was not challenged,that **the UAE authorities might not take this kind of breach too seriously.** In one passage of his evidence he contrasted the position of Mr Magdeev,who was in a position to invest US $ 40 million …"(加黑部分是笔者的强调)

至于"成比例"考虑因素之(2)的关系密切程度,Cockerill 大法官就指出整套贷款交易的核心(central)是贷款合约。非法的雇佣合约只是与贷款交易有一点关联(incidental),是可有可无(optional extra)的。所以,不严重至令贷款合约不予协助执行。这可以节录 Cockerill 大法官所说如下:"For Mr Magdeev(投资人的争辩)it was argued that even if the employment contracts were illegal as a matter of UAE law,… it was contended that the principle was inapplicable where what was being sought to be performed was not the employment contract(performed and terminated)but a separate loan agreement. … that **the main purpose or intention was the loan-which was not illegal**. The use of the **employment contract was incidental-an 'optional extra'** and not,in the words used in Foster v Driscoll 'the whole adventure'. …For much of this argument I find myself in sympathy with the contentions advanced skilfully by … Mr Magdeev. To the extent that the submission … that the Employment Agreement was central to the adventure I would reject that submission firmly. **This was not a relationship about an employment contract**;the employment contract was used essentially synergistically-**it was a pleasant add-on or fringe benefit**. While structuring the parties' real deal,for the loan,it was possible also to give Mr Magdeev something which he valued,namely the visa. **The essence of the agreement was the loan. The employment relationship facilitates an additional benefit**."(加黑部分是笔者的强调)

至于"成比例"考虑因素之(3)与(4)有关是否意图非法与应受谴责的程度,Cockerill 大法官认为是不影响她协助执行贷款合约的决定,说:"In the present case the focus is very much on maximising benefit to the parties,with no positive intent to deceive that has emerged in the evidence…. Even looking at the agreement as originally concluded the intent and the illegal action is sufficiently far from the centre of gravity of the transaction to make it inappropriate to refuse enforcement."

9. Patel v. Mirza 先例后的非法案例

9.1 Stoffel & Co v. Grondona(2020)UKSC 42 最高院先例

Stoffel & Co v. Grondona 最高院先例就遵循了 Patel v. Mirza 先例中的三阶段测试详细考虑了非法理论适用的问题。

此先例中，Mitchell 先生在 2002 年 7 月以 3 万英镑的对价获得一处不动产 125 年的租赁产权（leasehold）。几个月后 Mitchell 先生想要进一步借助此租赁产权融资，但是 Mitchell 先生自己进一步获取贷款有困难，因此与 Grondona 女士签订了一份协议。根据此协议，Grondona 女士会通过向金融机构 Birmingham Midshires（BM）抵押贷款购买 Mitchell 先生的租赁产权，对价为 9 万英镑。但实际上不动产始终完全都由 Mitchell 先生控制与处置（包括 Mitchell 先生实际上将不动产用来放租），贷款也是由 Mitchell 先生偿还。Grondona 女士的好处看来只是在将来 Mitchell 先生出售不动产时收取净收益的 50%。这样做的目的就是借用了 Grondona 女士的名义从 BM 处借到贷款。而在贷款申请过程中，当事人的行为还涉及不诚实陈述，如否认此交易是双方私下磋商交易（private sale）、陈述 Grondona 女士会管理不动产等。

在这个不动产交易中，律师（Stoffel & Co）同时作为买方 Grondona 女士、卖方 Mitchell 先生及 BM 的代表律师。在完成交易后，律师应该向土地注册的有关机构登记租赁产权的变更，以及登记 BM 对土地的抵押权利，但是律师未进行相关登记。这导致 Mitchell 先生仍然是租赁产权的产权人。Mitchell 先生还利用产权进一步抵押贷款。Mitchell 先生后来还未能向 BM 按时还贷，BM 因此起诉贷款合约的借款人 Grondona 女士。面对索赔的 Grondona 女士被起诉才发现自己没有对不动产的登记产权，面对 BM 的索赔变成可能全部需要自己偿还。[72] 因此 Grondona 女士向律师索赔因其职业疏忽带来的损失。

律师承认未能登记不动产变更信息是未能履行自己的职责，但提出 Grondona 女士与 Mitchell 先生这整套交易，目的都是骗取 BM 的贷款，这是属于抵押贷款欺诈/骗贷（mortgage fraud）的犯罪行为，而律师自己对此犯罪行为并不知情或不参与。如果此说法能够成立，这套交易就无法得到法院执行，包括当事人委任律师的合约也一样不会被执行，这样也就不存在损失的问题。因此在最高院的审理中，法院详细地分阶段考虑了此问题。

9.1.1 阶段一：不予执行是否有助于达到禁止骗贷的目的

不予执行对于达到禁止贷款欺诈的目的并没有什么帮助。甚至是允许索赔、予以执行反而有助于保护设立贷款欺诈犯罪想要保护的贷款人。因此在阶段一来看，是不应该以非法理论驳回 Grondona 女士向律师的索赔。Lloyd-Jones 勋爵说：

“There clearly exists an important policy that the law should condemn mortgage

---

〔72〕 英国法下对于已经有登记的土地（registered land）而言，不动产的法律产权（legal title）在登记时转让。而类似 Grondona 女士这种交易完成但是没有登记的情况，只转让了对不动产的衡平租赁产权（equitable leasehold title），无法对抗不知情的善意第三人。而对 BM 而言，根据协议获取了对不动产的抵押权，但一样会由于未登记难以对抗不知情的善意第三人。可以想到 Mitchell 先生利用不动产反复融资行为，在后来多半是有已经登记了抵押权利的不知情的银行，这才导致 BM 实际无法实现对不动产的抵押权利，也因此需要针对 Grondona 女士个人索赔金钱。本书不针对英国土地产权问题，不在这里赘述。

frauds which are serious criminal offences. The appellants（作为被告的律师）correctly identify deterrence as one underlying policy of the criminal law against fraud. I doubt, however, that permitting a civil remedy to persons in the position of the respondent（Grondona 女士）would undermine that policy to any significant extent. The risk that they may be left without a remedy if their solicitor should prove negligent in registering the transaction is most unlikely to feature in their thinking.（禁止骗贷的一个目的，是用刑事法律阻吓这类欺诈行为。而对于涉嫌欺诈交易中 Grondona 女士的情况，允许其向律师民事索赔对此目的并没有什么严重影响。骗子在考虑欺诈行为时，事后是否会被禁止向律师索赔显然不在其考虑范围之内。）

A further underlying purpose of the prohibition against mortgage fraud is correctly identified by… the respondent as the protection of the public, and in particular mortgagees, from suffering loss. Viewed from this perspective, it is difficult to see how refusing the respondent a civil remedy against her solicitors for their negligence in failing to register the transfer would enhance that protection. Registration of the transactions could only take place after the completion of the conveyance. By the time of the negligent breach of duty the loan had already been advanced by BM and received by the respondent. The required registration was not a necessary step in perpetrating the fraud and, by the time of the negligent failure to register the transfer, the fraud was complete. In these circumstances, denying a remedy to the respondent in respect of negligence in what occurred subsequently would not afford any protection to BM.（禁止骗贷的另一个目的，是防止公众尤其是出借人/银行蒙受损害。针对这个目的而言，即使允许骗子向其律师索赔未能登记不动产变更的职业疏忽带来的损失，也没有影响。毕竟在登记不动产变更时，骗贷早就已经完成了。）

On the contrary, as the respondent points out, not only was the required registration of the transfer to the respondent in the interests of the respondent, but it was also in the interests of the mortgagee, BM, both during the currency of the mortgage and following its discharge, that the transfer should be registered in addition to the mortgagee's charge. … While BM had, in these circumstances, an independent claim for negligent breach of duty against the appellants, it can at the very least be said that the denial of such a claim by the respondent against the appellants would not enhance the protection afforded by the law to mortgagees. It was, therefore, in the interests not only of the respondent but also of BM for the appellants to have complied with their duties to the respondent…（而且类似此先例中这种律师协助不动产交易未能登记的职业疏忽应该可以被索赔，不仅仅是为了 Grondona 女士的利益，也与骗贷受害方 BM 息息相关。无法实现自己抵押权利的 BM，完全可能单独向律师以同样的理由索赔。因此允许向律师索赔不仅仅不妨碍实现保护银行的目的，反而是有助于实现此目的。）”

9.1.2　阶段二:不予执行会影响律师勤勉尽责与保护财产权的公共政策

Grondona 女士索赔理由是律师未能履行自己职责,显然不予执行会影响的一个公共政策就是律师应该勤勉尽职履行职责。一般情况下也都应该允许客户向未能履行职责的律师提起民事诉讼与索赔。不应该律师事后发现交易本身有猫腻,就可以因此逃脱自己未能尽职的责任。更不用说根据此先例中的案情(律师同时代理了不动产交易双方甚至是贷款人,而 Mitchell 先生刚买不动产没多久就马上出售,价格甚至变成了买入价格的三倍等)来看,律师应该注意到交易有猫腻,更是不应该让律师轻易逃脱自己应承担的责任。

另一个方面,即使交易本身非法,在交易中已经转让的财产权利应不受影响。在此先例中的情况下,虽然由于未登记 Grondona 女士未能获得不动产的法律产权,但是仍然获得了衡平财产性权利,应该支持 Grondona 女士维护自己的财产而起诉律师。否则就变成一边允许即使是非法合约下财产也可以转移,另一边则是不允许当事人保护自己的财产,这是有自我矛盾的,不予执行影响了 Grondona 女士的财产权。

9.1.3　阶段三:成比例

已经在本章之 7.5.4 段介绍过,实际上在第一阶段与第二阶段区别衡量后,既然不予执行看来只有弊端,那也没有什么冲突问题,不需要进一步考虑成比例问题了。但由于当事人对这方面进行了激烈争辩,因此最高院仍然继续讨论了是否成比例的问题。

当事人也提到相当多的因素,如提出索赔的 Grondona 女士一方就提到受害方 BM 都没有主张欺诈,也从来没有纯粹骗钱、在订约时是意图按约还钱等,但这些因素都被认为没什么重量。最高院在此先例中更看重起到较为重要作用的因素,是非法行为与 Grondona 女士索赔之间的关系,或者说是非法行为是否有核心地位。

而在此先例中的情况来看,Grondona 女士向律师索赔的是未能履行职责登记不动产变更导致的损失,至于在不动产交易中涉及贷款欺诈问题,只不过是 Grondona 女士索赔的事实背景,关系也并不紧密。毕竟一方面是在律师应该履行职责时,欺诈行为早已经完成了。另一方面则是无论是否有贷款欺诈,事实上 Grondona 女士已经获得了针对不动产的权利,律师有义务协助完成不动产变更登记。因此在成比例下也就不应该因为涉及贷款欺诈就拒绝 Grondona 女士的索赔。Lloyd-Jones 勋爵说:"... The appellants' breach of duty related to the registration of title and the way in which the respondent had procured the finance to obtain that title was irrelevant to the appellants' obligation to register the title. **Two features** of the present case, to which reference has already been made, **demonstrate the lack of centrality of the illegality to the breach of duty** of which the respondent complains. **First**, by the time the appellants were required to register the transactions the loan had been advanced... The defrauding of BM had been achieved. **Secondly**, by that time equitable title to the property had already passed to the respondent. Although legal title could pass to her only on registration of the transfer, she was already the owner in equity... These matters serve to distance the appellants' negligence from the respondent's fraud... As a result of the change in the law brought about by Patel v Mirza, the question whether a claimant must rely upon illegal conduct to establish a cause of action is no longer determinative of an illegality defence. Nevertheless, **the question of reliance may have a bearing on the issue of centrality**. In the present case it is significant that, as the decision at first instance on the basis of Tinsley v Milligan demonstrates, the essential facts founding the claim can be established without reference to the illegality. The respondent's claim for **breach of duty against her solicitors is conceptually entirely separate from her fraud on the mortgagee**."（加黑部分是笔者的强调）

9.2 Henderson v. Dorset Healthcare University NHS Foundation Trust (2020) UKSC 43 最高院先例

在 Henderson v. Dorset Healthcare University NHS Foundation Trust 先例中，原告患有偏执型精神分裂（schizophrenia with paranoia），被告（Dorset Healthcare University NHS Foundation Trust）负责派遣社区心理健康团队管理与照顾原告。但不幸的是原告刺死了自己的母亲，由于有精神问题仅被判过失杀人（manslaughter），需要在强制医疗机构接受严密控制与治疗。而在此民事诉讼中，原告（经由他人代表）主张被告未能在自己心理状况恶化的情况下及时采取更有效的医疗措施管理与控制，属于被告的过失行为，因此向被告索赔自己丧失自由与生活便利、病情加重、由于弑母导致丧失遗产继承权等损失。被告承认自己确实违反应尽义务/失职（breach of duty），但提出的一个重要主张，是由于原告的损失涉及刑事案件判决，因此无论如何在非法理论/公共政策下都不能通过民事诉讼向他人索赔这些损失。[73]

最高院一致认定非法理论适用，原告不得向被告索赔这一系列损失。该先例对三阶段测试的解读已经在本章之 7.5.1.2 段节录，这里不再重复。针对阶段一，最重要的考虑就是避免与刑法的不一致的公共政策。虽然因为精神问题责任从谋杀减为过失杀人，但仍是犯罪，且要承担刑事责任。针对阶段二，有关的公共政策是要求被告作为公共机构要向原告这类弱势群体提供称职的服务，尽到小心谨慎责任。如果被告违反应尽义务/失职，应该让作为受害者的原告获得赔偿。

接下来针对阶段三的成比例问题，最高院认定以非法否定原告的索赔并非不成比例。最高院对于 Toulson 勋爵提出的四点考虑因素进行了如下权衡：（1）从行为严

〔73〕 这方面还可见本章之 1.4 段介绍的 Beresford v. Royal Insurance Company Limited (1938) AC 568 贵族院先例与 9.5 段会介绍的 Gray v. Thames Trains Ltd (2009) UKHL 33 贵族院先例，主要涉及的公共政策是：（1）任何人不能从自己的不法行为中获利；（2）因为不法行为（unlawful）而受到法律的惩罚（如丧失人身自由、罚款等），不能向他人索赔。毕竟法律针对特定对象进行惩罚，如果可以通过事后向他人索赔、转移惩罚，这看来与法律背后权衡了公共政策选定的惩罚对象自我矛盾、自我阻碍。

重性问题上,显然此先例中涉及的是最严重的非法杀人行为。(2)从行为与索赔之间的密切程度上来看,也很显然杀人行为正是后续损失的有效原因(effective cause)。(3)在是否故意的问题上,原告确实是故意,只不过由于是精神问题才降低为过失杀人。(4)在当事人之间应受谴责的程度上,原告确实实施了故意杀人行为,而被告相比之下仅仅存在疏忽。

9.3 Singularis Holdings Ltd v. Daiwa Capital Markets Europe Ltd(2019)UKSC 50 最高院先例

在 Singularis Holdings Ltd v. Daiwa Capital Markets Europe Ltd 最高院先例中,原告 Singularis 是一家在开曼群岛注册的公司,为 Al Sanea 先生持有的私人资产。Al Sanea 先生是公司的股东与董事。Singularis 在被告 Daiwa 银行有账户,账户里有大量资金。从 2009 年 6 月 12 日到 7 月 27 日期间,Al Sanea 先生给了 Daiwa 银行 8 个不同的付款指示,总共从 Singularis 的账户里转出了约 2.04 亿美元支付给 Saad 集团的不同公司,而这些公司都是由 Al Sanea 先生拥有与控制的,这些指示都是 Al Sanea 先生伪造的。当时 Singularis 已经在破产边缘,Daiwa 银行内部曾对 Singularis 的经济状况与 Al Sanea 先生的私人财产被冻结的情况表示担心。在 Al Sanea 先生作出这些虚假付款指示前,Daiwa 银行的合规部门曾经发邮件警告对于有关人士或公司的指示必须小心,必须确保有恰当授权,如果有任何怀疑要立即联系法律与合规部门。但尽管如此,Al Sanea 先生的这些指示要么完全没有被要求提供任何解释,要么基于一些表面看上去就有问题的解释就被执行了。

之后 Singularis 因为无法向债权人偿还债款破产,清盘人开始诉讼向 Daiwa 银行索赔 Al Sanea 先生欺诈转出的全部金额,理由是:(1)知情帮助(dishonest assistance)[74] Al Sanea 先生违反诚信责任;(2)违反了对 Singularis 的 Quincecare 责任(Quincecare duty)。[75]

一审法院驳回了知情帮助的索赔,但判 Daiwa 银行违反对 Singularis 的 Quincecare 责任,只是在分摊责任时认为 Singularis 让 Al Sanea 先生可以肆意行事也有疏忽,所以作出了 25% 的扣减。上诉庭与最高院都支持了一审法院的判决。与本段内容有关的是 Daiwa 银行提出了非法的抗辩,简单说是因为 Singularis 是一人公司,[76] 所以 Al Sanea 先生对银行的欺诈应被认为是 Singularis 欺诈银行,所以 Singularis 就因为非法无法起诉 Daiwa 银行并拿回这笔钱。

一审的 Rose 大法官判 Al Sanea 先生的欺诈不应被认为是 Singularis 欺诈,也就

---

〔74〕 在笔者《证据法:基础理论、口头证据与专家证据》一书第十章之 2.11 段有详细介绍。

〔75〕 在笔者《证据法:基础理论、口头证据与专家证据》一书第十章之 2.7.2.1 段有简单介绍。另在近期的 Philipp v. Barclays Bank Plc(2022)EWCA Civ 318 先例中,这个 Quincecare 责任的范围又被拓宽。

〔76〕 关于一人公司,在笔者《证据法:国际规管与诉讼中的证据攻防》一书第七章之 8.6.1 段有详细介绍。

是说 Daiwa 银行不能以非法作为抗辩。虽然法院因此已经无需再决定非法的争议,但因为双方花了大量时间金钱争辩,Rose 大法官也简单进行了分析。即使法院在上一个争议中错判,Al Sanea 先生的欺诈应该被认为是 Singularis 欺诈,在适用 Patel 指引后,也不影响 Singularis 索赔。

针对阶段一的测试,Rose 大法官说禁止雇员违反诚信责任的目的是保护公司不成为公司雇员错误行使权利的受害者。不让 Singularis 拿回这笔钱,等于让 Singularis 成为 Al Sanea 先生的欺诈行为的受害者。禁止雇员违反诚信责任的目的对此案来说:一是保护银行不被欺骗,二是保护公司的钱不被挪用。尽管不让 Singularis 索赔可以说促进了保护银行的目的,但这个目的已经通过银行只有在违反了 Quincecare 责任时才需要对钱被挪用负责实现。Quincecare 责任就是法律在客户与银行的利益之间作出的权衡,显然不让 Singularis 索赔不会促进法律的正直。而且不让 Singularis 索赔也不会对 Al Sanea 先生之类的董事的不诚实行为有什么影响。

针对阶段二是否会影响其他公共政策的测试,Rose 大法官说不让 Singularis 索赔显然会影响让银行在发现经济犯罪与洗钱行为时扮演重要角色的公共政策。

针对阶段三成比例的测试,Rose 大法官说不让 Singularis 拿回这笔钱也对 Singularis 不公平与不成比例。虽然 Singularis 让 Al Sanea 先生可以肆意行事可以说是有错,但是法院以共同侵权分摊责任并扣减部分索赔金额调整显然是更合适的。

最高院的 Hale 勋爵完全支持了一审判决,说:

"... The judge held that the purpose of the prohibition of breach of fiduciary obligation was to protect the company from becoming the victim of the wrongful exercise of power by officers of the company. That purpose would certainly not be enhanced by preventing the company from getting back the money which had been wrongfully removed from its account. The purpose of the prohibition of making false statements was both to protect the bank from being deceived and the company from having its funds misappropriated. Although the purpose of protecting the bank would be enhanced by denial of the claim, that purpose was achieved by ensuring that the bank was only liable to repay the money if the Quincecare duty was breached: that duty struck a careful balance between the interests of the customer and the interests of the bank. 'It would not enhance the integrity of the law to undermine that balance by denying the claim on grounds of illegality in a case where, ex hypothesi, the exceptional circumstances needed for the duty to arise and be breached are found to be present.' ...

Turning to whether there might be any other relevant public interests, she(一审的 Rose 大法官)held that denial of the claim would have a material impact upon the growing reliance on banks and other financial institutions to play an important part in reducing and uncovering financial crime and money laundering. If a regulated entity could escape from the consequences of failing to identify and prevent financial crime by casting on the customer the illegal conduct of its employees that policy would be undermined...

Finally, denial of the claim would be an unfair and disproportionate response to any wrongdoing on the part of Singularis. The possibility of making a deduction for contributory negligence on the customer's part enables the court to make a more appropriate adjustment than the rather blunt instrument of the illegality defence...

Daiwa's arguments necessarily depend upon a finding that Mr Al Sanea's fraud was the company's fraud ... But even if it was, in my view the judge's conclusion was correct for the reasons she gave. ..."

9.4　Bank St Petersburg PJSC v. Arkhangelsky (2020) EWCA Civ 408 上诉庭先例

Bank St Petersburg PJSC v. Arkhangelsky 上诉庭先例涉及俄罗斯企业家 Vitaly Arkhangelsky 先生和他所控制的 Oslo Marine Group 集团公司（以下简称 OMG 公司）与俄罗斯西北部地区最大的私人银行之间的争议。OMG 公司的主营业务是航运、码头、保险等。原告银行对 OMG 公司提供大量贷款，相对应 OMG 公司与 Arkhangelsky 先生以公司资产与个人资产作为抵押或质押提供了多份公司和个人担保。2008 年金融海啸后，OMG 公司的主营业务遭受重创，无力偿还银行的贷款与利息，甚至为了获得延期还款而将 OMG 公司的股权抵押给银行。在延期也仍然无法支付后，银行开始执行在多个担保合约下的担保权益，包括解除 Arkhangelsky 先生董事的职务、控制 OMG 公司、处置 OMG 公司的资产、在防暴警察的协助下占有 OMG 公司名下的港口、闯入 OMG 公司的办公室拿走所有文件等。在一系列动作后，银行进一步主张 OMG 公司的资产仍然不足以清偿贷款与利息，进而起诉 Arkhangelsky 先生个人，要求执行银行在个人担保合约下的权益。

Arkhangelsky 夫妻在俄罗斯法院也对银行开始了多个诉讼，但在检控部门启动对他的刑事检控后逃去法国并获得政治庇护。在该银行根据个人担保合约启动的英国诉讼中，Arkhangelsky 先生提出反索赔，主张 OMG 公司是很值钱的公司，银行和俄罗斯政府勾结通过欺诈和不诚实的行为将他的资产不正当处置与侵占。他索赔被侵占的资产扣减了贷款和利息之后多出来的部分，价值约 5 亿美元。其中 OMG 公司名下最值钱的是圣彼得堡西部港口的发展项目。银行针对该反索赔的抗辩是 Arkhangelsky 先生在一审做供时清楚承认 OMG 公司为了取得该西部港口的发展项目，曾经花费 1.6 亿美元去贿赂相关的政府官员。该贿赂行为是非法的，而整个 Arkhangelsky 先生反索赔中最值钱的资产就是该港口项目，从而 Arkhangelsky 先生的反索赔因为被非法所"污染"，不能被支持。

该案一审开庭时，大家知悉 Patel v. Mirza (2016) UKSC 42 最高院判决很快就会做出，于是双方均保留了判决做出后发表进一步意见的权利。在 Patel v. Mirza 最高院判决做出后，双方同意无需再开庭，而仅以提交书面陈词的形式来就该最高院判决如何适用在本案发表意见。本案涉及很多争议点，重点的争议是 Arkhangelsky 先生提出的银行的欺诈、不诚实处置与侵占[77]OMG 公司的资产。非法只是其中一个针对反索赔的争议,并不是整个案件的重点。不过从时间上来看,该案是 Patel v. Mirza 最高院先例判决做出后最早受影响的先例。

双方针对非法的争议均按照 Patel 指引进行了争辩。银行针对第一阶段测试主张贿赂是非常严重的非法行为,是会动摇文明社会的根本,无论是在英国还是在俄罗斯都是应该被谴责的,如果允许 Arkhangelsky 先生的反索赔那将会令他从自己的非法行为中获利。第二阶段是如果拒绝了 Arkhangelsky 先生的反索赔并不会令任何其他的公共政策受损。第三阶段是看不出来针对这么严重的非法行为,拒绝 Arkhangelsky 先生的反索赔有什么不成比例的地方。

Arkhangelsky 先生针对这三阶段测试的抗辩是:第一阶段他的行贿行为与他在本案中银行通过欺诈与不诚实的手段变卖资产的主张是无关的;第二阶段如果拒绝了他的主张打击欺诈和不诚实的行为的公共政策将会受损;第三阶段是如果以与银行的交易完全无关的行贿就拒绝了他全部的反索赔是不成比例。

一审的[(2018)EWHC 1077(Ch)]Hildyard 大法官在权衡了双方针对非法理论是否适用的争辩后,认为行贿发生在前,而反索赔在银行欺诈与不诚实的处置资产之

---

〔77〕 关于抵押权人/债权人/银行在出售被抵押的财产时的责任,可见笔者《船舶融资与抵押》一书第五章之 4.3.1 段与 4.3.2 段的详细介绍。这里只简单节录在加拿大的 Oak Orchard Developments Ltd v. Iseman(1987)OJ No. 361(Ont HC);aff'd(1989)O. J. No. 2394(Ont. C. A.)先例中,Saunders 大法官参考了英国上诉庭的 Cuckmere Brick Co Ltd v. Mutual Finance Ltd(1971)Ch 949 先例中,将抵押权人行使权利时的责任程度与大精神总结如下:"1. The mortgagee selling under a power of sale is under a duty to take reasonable precautions to obtain the true market value of the mortgaged property at the date on which he decides to sell. This does not mean that the mortgagee must in fact obtain the true value.[抵押权人有责任合理谨慎地按照真正市场价格出售被抵押的财产(不能因为欠的债务不多,而草草以低价贱卖财产)。但这也并不代表他一定要卖出真正的市场价格。]2. The duty of the mortgagee is only to take reasonable precautions. Perfection is not required. Some latitude is allowed to a mortgagee.(抵押权人的责任只是合理谨慎,并不需要完美。抵押权人有一定的合理弹性空间。)3. In deciding whether a mortgagee has fallen short of his duty the facts must be looked at broadly and he will not be adjudged to be in default unless he is plainly on the wrong side of the line.(在决定抵押权人是否尽责时,应广泛考虑各种事实,除非明显越过了分水岭,否则不会被判是违反了合理谨慎的责任。)4. The mortgagee is entitled to exercise an accrued power of sale for his own purposes whenever he chooses to do so. It matters not that the moment may be unpropitious and that by waiting, a higher price could be obtained.(抵押权人可为他自己的利益选择任何时间去行使出售的权利,即使时间选得不令抵押人满意,因为再等会有更高的价格。)5. The mortgagee can accept the best price he can obtain in an adverse market provided that none of the adverse factors are due to fault on his part.(抵押权人可以在市场低迷时以最好的价格出售被抵押的财产,只要他自己对这种低价出售没有任何过错。)6. Even if the duty to take reasonable precautions is breached, the mortgagor must show that a higher price would have been obtained but for the breach in order to be compensated in damages.(即使抵押权人违反了合理谨慎的责任,抵押人也要证明要不是因为抵押权人违反了合理谨慎责任本可以取得一个更高的价格,才能获得损失赔偿。)"

后,非法与反索赔的关系比较遥远,并不是索赔请求的核心,所以他认为非法理论并不适用,他说:

"Turning to my assessment of these competing arguments, I must admit to some anxiety about the apparent breadth of the discretion conferred upon the Court in determining whether an illegal act is of a quality and closeness to the claim that a person should be deprived of his legal rights ... The fact that, as Millett LJ ... noted in Tribe v Tribe [1996] Ch 107 ... the ex turpi causa rule is 'not a principle of justice but a principle of policy' adds to the anxiety, since the exercise of discretion as to policy is not a customary role for a judge; ...

Whether or not a product of gut instinct, I consider that in a non-contractual case, where the Court is not being asked to enforce an illegal contract, and in a case where the Court is not in effect being asked to grant relief in the teeth of a statutory prohibition, it will be rare indeed that the Court will refuse a person the opportunity to vindicate a right on the grounds that the integrity of the system may thereby be imperilled. To warrant the Court 'drawing up its skirts and refusing all assistance' **... the illegal conduct** would, to my mind, **have to be not only serious but also central: the springboard for the claim sought to be pursued**.

Furthermore, in this case, what the Claimants are in effect contending, at least in the context of the claims in respect of the assets sales, is that the Counterclaimants should be prevented from vindicating their rights in respect of dishonest dealings with their property (or their equity of redemption[78]). Their property was not obtained illegally. On that basis, ... this case seems to me some distance from an appropriate case in which to deprive the Counterclaimants and insulate the Claimants in the name of preserving the integrity of the judicial process."(加黑部分是笔者的强调)

上诉庭援引了 Singularis Holdings Ltd v. Daiwa Capital Markets Europe Ltd(2018) EWCA Civ 84 先例中的说法,针对非法的问题不应该觉得自己对多因素的权衡会做出不一样的判断就轻易干预下级法院行使裁量权根据 Patel 指引作出的决定,只有下级法院在法律适用上出错才会干预:"In Singularis Holdings Ltd (In Official Liquidation) v. Daiwa Capital Markets Europe Ltd ... the Court of Appeal (Vos C, with whom Gloster and McCombe LJJ agreed) suggested ... that 'an appellate court should not inter-

---

〔78〕 这是指债务人有权回赎,即把所欠款项付清回赎抵押的财产。债权人不得拒绝,即使在这之前债务人有违约行为。要知道,多数情况是抵押的财产比欠的债务价值高,更不用说债务人往往已经向债权人/银行偿还了部分,甚至基本已偿还。英国法律禁止在抵押协议或契约上以明示条文阻止回赎。只要抵押的财产仍未出售,时间上来得及,抵押权人/银行自行安排出售或通过法院拍卖抵押的财产都不能剥夺债务人回赎的基本权利。

fere[in a lower court's decision on illegality under Patel v. Mirza] merely because it would have taken a different view had it been undertaking the evaluation. The test involves balancing multiple policy considerations and applying a proportionality approach. Accordingly, an appellate court should only interfere if the first instance judge has proceeded on an erroneous legal basis, taken into account matters that were legally irrelevant, or failed to take into account matters that were legally relevant. '"

上诉庭的 Coulson 大法官进一步说他完全支持一审法官拒绝接受适用非法理论的判决,认为一审法官在 Patel 指引下作出了非常恰当的权衡:"In my judgment, the judge's evaluation was a proper application of the tests in Patel v. Mirza. It would do nothing to prevent or discourage bribery to deny the appellants' claim for damages for a subsequent dishonest conspiracy. The two events are not as closely connected as the respondents contend. Secondly, there is a strong additional public policy in allowing the appellants to vindicate their rights (if they are shown to be entitled to do so) for the respondents' dishonest conspiracy to remove their property. Finally, in my judgment, the denial of the appellants' counterclaim would not be a proportionate response to the illegality, bearing specifically in mind that punishment for bribery is generally a matter for the criminal courts."

9.5 Day v. Womble Bond Dickinson(2020)EWCA Civ 447 上诉庭先例

Day v. Womble Bond Dickinson 上诉庭先例的案情是 Day 先生买了一块临近自然保护林区的土地,并在没有授权下砍伐了保护区内的 43 颗树木并开辟了一条车道。在当地其他居民的举报下,政府的环保部门将 Day 先生告上法院。法院判 Day 先生在《Wildlife and Countryside Act 1981》之 section 28P(1)下罪名成立,并对其处以刑事罚金 45 万英镑,与此同时还命令 Day 先生要赔偿环保部门的诉讼费用 457317 英镑。Day 先生针对该判决结果上诉不果后,转而以职业疏忽的侵权起诉在刑事诉讼程序中自己的代表律师 Womble Bond Dickinson(UK)LLP。Day 先生主张如果自己的代表律师没有在程序中疏忽,他的罪名应该不成立,不用支付罚金,更不用去赔偿环保部门一大笔律师费。

一审法官适用非法理论驳回 Day 先生的诉求,认为他是在滥用程序,想要将刑法对他的处罚通过民事诉讼转嫁给其他人。如果 Day 先生认为自己的代表律师在程序上存在疏忽,他更应该做的是在刑事诉讼中去上诉,从而推翻对他的刑事判决结果。Day 先生认为一审法官错误地适用了非法理论,进而将案件上诉到上诉庭。上诉庭的 Coulson 大法官重点根据 Gray v. Thames Trains Ltd(2009)UKHL 33 与 Patel v. Mirza(2016)UKSC 42 这两个最高院先例对非法理论的适用进行了分析。

根据 Patel 指引,Coulson 大法官认为第一阶段的公共政策是不允许原告将他自己的犯罪行为带来的惩罚通过民事诉讼滥用程序转嫁给其他人,这正如 Toulson 勋爵在 Patel v. Mizra 先例中所说的:"Looking behind the maxims, there are two broad discernible policy reasons for the common law doctrine of illegality as a defence to a civil claim. One is that a person should not be allowed to profit from his own wrongdoing. The other, linked, consideration is that the law should be coherent and not self-defeating, condoning illegality by giving with the left hand what it takes with the right hand."

例如在 Gray v. Thames Trains Ltd 先例中涉及英国 20 世纪最严重的火车事故之一,伦敦拉德布鲁克格罗夫火车撞车事件。原告是这次事故的幸存者,但患上了严重的 PTSD,并在遭受 PTSD 折磨期间杀了人,也对自己过失杀人的事实供认不讳。法院判决原告要在戒备森严的精神病医院羁押 6 年。原告于是起诉火车管理公司,主张如果没有火车事故给他带来的精神问题,他不会误杀他人,也不需要赔偿受害者亲属及因被羁押在精神病医院而丧失工作收入。最高院根据非法理论判原告不能取回任何因为他自己的犯罪行为而带来的损失。

至于第二阶段测试是如果拒绝原告的诉求是否会令其他公共政策受损,这里律师职业疏忽的索赔会涉及的公共政策是不能对于错判的刑事案件不给救济,而原告在此案中主张的就是没有被告律师的疏忽他就不会被定罪。其中 Coulson 大法官援引 Smith v. Linskills(1996)1 WLR 763 上诉庭先例(被定抢劫罪的被告在刑满释放后告他的代表律师职业疏忽)中 Bingham 大法官说:"We cannot of course shut our eyes to the possibility that a criminal defendant may be wrongly convicted, perhaps because his defence was ineptly prepared or conducted. When that occurs, it represents an obvious and serious injustice. There are two possible solutions. One is to relax the present restraint on seeking to establish that injustice by civil action. The other is to ensure that, in appropriate cases, the conviction itself can be reviewed. It seems to us clear that it is this second solution which has, over the past century, been favoured: by giving a criminal defendant a right of appeal; by providing a relatively low standard for the admission of fresh evidence on appeal; by empowering the appellate court to order a new trial; by giving the Home Secretary power to refer a case back to the Court of Appeal; and by proposals to establish a new review body."

但是 Coulson 大法官不认为本案中原告 Day 先生能够证明刑事判决有任何的不公平与错判。砍树和建车道都是 Day 先生自己的行为,律师在程序中的疏忽(即使有)并不会改变这个事实。所以上述 Bingham 大法官所说的第一种解决办法不适用。

至于第三阶段测试的成比例问题,Coulson 大法官说:"To the extent that it is necessary or appropriate, I should say that I consider this to be a fair and proportionate result (using the analysis outlined by Lord Toulson in Patel v Mizra). It is in accordance with the doctrine of illegality; it avoids an abusive collateral attack on the appellant's conviction; and it avoids both inconsistency and incoherence. There is no public policy which strongly suggests a different outcome; even the complaint that WBD(作为被告的律师)

would avoid liability for their own default(which I accept is in play) does not go very far, since the appellant had an opportunity to do something about that in the CACD(刑事法院上诉庭) and failed to take it."

因此,原告的索赔败诉。

9.6 Robinson v. HRH Al Qasim(2021) EWCA Civ 862 上诉庭先例

Robinson v. HRH Al Qasim 上诉庭先例涉及被告(阿拉伯皇室)雇佣原告从事一系列工作(如照顾被告在伦敦的财产等),在雇佣合约中约定原告需要自己缴税,但在 2009 年到 2014 年原告完全没有缴税。到了 2017 年,被告以原告不缴税为由解雇了原告。原告就在雇佣合约下指称属于不公平、错误解雇,并提出索赔。被告则提出偷税漏税的非法作为抗辩。

上诉庭明确说在今天基于多因素判断的方法下,雇佣合约中有一方实施非法行为是导致非法与不可执行的必要不充分条件,雇佣合约是否真的不可执行仍然需要结合多因素予以考虑。包括非法的程度、严重性,非法与索赔之间的关系是否紧密等,需要给一个根据具体的案情成比例的结果。

而此先例中一审的劳资审裁法庭(Employment Tribunal)判决的理由,是根据过去的 Quashie v. Stringfellow Restaurants Ltd(2012) IRLR 536 先例判只要雇员不对自己的薪水缴税,在雇佣合约下的索赔就不会得到法院支持,因此原告败诉。在二审劳资审裁上诉庭改判,这样死板、机械化的判法与今天基于多因素的判断方法不符,将案件发回重审。劳资审裁上诉庭针对非法问题的决定被进一步上诉到上诉庭,上诉庭指出整体阅读了劳资审裁上诉庭的判决后,虽然不是逐一考虑 Patel 指引中的每个步骤、针对每一个因素都仔细考虑与权衡,但总体来看是考虑了 Patel 指引,以及基于多因素、考虑成比例问题下得出的结论,并没有什么法律错误,也因此予以支持。

9.7 Al-Dowaisan v. Al-Salam(2019) EWHC 301(Ch)先例

Al-Dowaisan v. Al-Salam 先例中,原告是一名有钱有势的科威特牙医(Abdullah Al-Dowaisan 医生)。而被告(Imad Abdul Al-Salam 先生等)是住在英国的房地产开发商,在曼彻斯特、摩洛哥等多地开发地产。在过去十几年间,原告与被告之间关系密切,原告长期向被告投资。但是后来当事人之间关系破裂,在方方面面都产生争议并开始诉讼。

此先例中涉及的非法争议,是被告在地产开发时会找一些并非居住(domicile)在英国的海外人士作为明面上的项目持股人,但背后的实际受益人都是被告。让这些海外人士开设银行账户后,签署授权书将账户交给被告使用,被告就可以通过这些海外人士作为持股人的银行账户收取项目收益,事后实际则由被告使用。其中有一个银行账号,是原告在国民西敏寺银行(NatWest)开设的,在此账号下原告收到过 40

万英镑。[79] 在此先例中,被告就主张这笔金钱不属于原告,原告应该退还或赔偿。

法院审理后认定,这套做法的目的,是通过由不居住在英国的海外人士持股的方式非法逃避英国税务。[80] 住在英国的被告对此心知肚明,也明白这做法见不得光,因此为了实现非法目的,还有进一步的各种行为。例如,在各类税务报告中都隐瞒了这些账号下的资产,在第三人的刑事案件中给出虚假陈述,说自己并非这笔金钱的受益人/实益权利人,甚至对自己的律师也完全闭口不谈等。这也就带来了此先例中被告这种非法偷税漏税行为,是否导致不应该得到法院救济的问题。

Hodge 大法官根据 Patel 指引,判被告败诉,判决思路是这样的:(1)在今天将税务机关收到应缴税款的公共利益抬到了很高的地位。而此先例中这种情况如果不予执行被告的索赔,可以对社会大众起到警示作用。采取非法逃税行为将来可能会连原本的金钱都拿不回来。这就有助于保证税务机关收到应缴税款。此先例中,被告对警方虚假陈述的行为还影响到了刑事诉讼。通过不予执行,有助于警示社会大众,保证与刑事诉讼的和谐,促进刑事诉讼法律的正直。通过不帮助类似被告这样为了偷税漏税而给虚假陈述的人士以救济,是对这些不诚实的人士的阻吓。(2)不予执行显然会影响的是被告对这笔金钱的财产性权利,这笔金钱照理说确实本应属于被告。(3)但是权衡之下,不予执行仍然是成比例。被告的行为已经造成了偷税漏税的结果,也已经造成了刑事案件中未能将有关嫌疑人定罪的严重后果。这种扰乱了税务与法律正直的非法行为,即使会影响财产权,不给予救济也被认为是公道的结果。

在笔者看来,此案件中并无疑问的是这笔金钱本应该属于被告,而对财产权的保护照理说是有非常高的地位。而且在阶段一的测试中,会是与 Patel v. Mirza(2016) UKSC 42 先例类似,即使不予执行被告的索赔,对保证税务机关收取应缴税款看来并没什么直接影响。现在这样的判法,反而有点类似 Patel v. Mirza 先例中 Toulson 勋爵所反对的,在民事法院通过不予执行的方式,变相惩罚被告的非法行为。在此案件中即使是被告提供虚假陈述造成刑事案件的混乱,看来也应该是用留待伪证、藐视法院等方式来阻吓,而此先例中这样通过民事索赔案件中不予执行的方式来警示公众,还是有一些疑问的。当然此先例中,Hodge 大法官强调今天保护税收政策的重要性,也强调了此案件中被告的行为扰乱了刑事案件审理,以此合理化最后的判法。这也显示出了今天基于多因素判断方法的弹性,变得让审理法官可以根据具体案件给

---

〔79〕 这背后还有复杂的案情,如这 40 万被原告收取而不是实际操作账户的被告,起因是被告的私人助理 Hamond 女士伪造签字取走了 40 万英镑,在认定 Hamond 女士伪造行为后,NatWest 与作为账户户主的原告达成和解退还了 40 万英镑给原告。而原告在收取这笔金钱后离奇地将这笔金钱交给了 Hamond 女士及其律师,这也造成了原告与被告之间关系的决裂。但这与本章重点无关,就此略过。

〔80〕 简单而言,英国针对是否居住(domicile)在英国的人士,税务有不同对待。如果是居住在英国的人士,英国可能会对其全球收入征税。而非居住在英国的人士,就可能只对其汇入英国境内使用的部分征税。笔者在此不针对此问题详细展开。

一个在他看来最公道的结果。

9.8 Grove Park Properties Ltd v. The Royal Bank of Scotland Plc(2018) EWHC 3521(Comm)先例

Grove Park Properties Ltd v. The Royal Bank of Scotland Plc 先例的事实背景是原告 Grove Park Properties 的董事 Wyatt 先生在 2007 年 10 月 30 日代表原告与被告银行订立了一系列的合约:(1)1050 万英镑只还利息贷款[81](首期贷款);(2)190 万英镑只还利息贷款,还款期是 2008 年 5 月 1 日(第二期贷款);(3)10 万英镑的授权透支服务;(4)10 年的利率掉期协议(Interest Rate Swap)。

双方对于首期贷款的还款期有争议,原告说双方口头同意 10 年,和利率掉期协议同时结束,但被告银行说双方同意的是 5 年。双方同意首期贷款协议是银行起草的,协议的 5.1 条文显示还款期是 2012 年 11 月 1 日(也就是 5 年)。原告声称当时 Wyatt 先生向代表银行的 Bradstock 先生指出还款时间的问题,Bradstock 先生说是笔误,[82] Wyatt 先生改正为 2017 年并在旁边签上了姓名的首字母。银行不接受 Bradstock 先生或其他人士有权代表其同意修改还款期。双方也同意后来这份首期贷款合约被银行再次修改,从 2017 年改回了 2012 年。

原告的主张是根据 Pigot's Case(1614)77 ER 1177 先例与 Master v. Miller (1791)4 TR 320 先例中,银行欺诈性修改了首期贷款合约,整份合约变为无效,而第二期贷款、授权透支服务与利率掉期协议作为整个交易的一部分也同样无效。因此,原告没有责任归还 1250 万英镑的本金与利息,已经归还的部分可以复原。而被告银行的主张首先是首期贷款合约有效,即使无效,银行也可以反索赔,在普通法下要求复原在贷款协议下已经给原告的本金。

因为 Wyatt 先生在首期贷款协议下提供了个人担保,所以在银行要求还款时开始诉讼要求法院宣告他没有还款责任。在该诉讼的过程中,银行先提供 Bradstock 先生与另一位银行职员的证人证言,主张 Wyatt 先生欺诈,但之后因为与其他证人证言冲突撤回了 Wyatt 先生欺诈的主张并与 Wyatt 先生和解。

此先例针对的是法院是否批准原告申请修改文书请求依赖银行在 Wyatt 先生的诉讼程序中的不诚实与误导法院的错误行为。与本章内容有关的是原告希望依赖银行在 Wyatt 先生的诉讼程序中的错误行为作为对银行的复原反索赔的抗辩。原告主张被告银行的复原反索赔因为非法与违反公共政策而注定失败,而非法不仅是指银行欺诈性修改首期贷款合约,也包括银行在 Wyatt 先生的诉讼程序中的错误行为,属于向法院提供虚假证据,所以非法。

高院适用了 Patel 指引,Males 大法官说:

"The first consideration is the underlying purpose of the prohibition and whether it

---

〔81〕 只还利息贷款,就是指在约定的期限内只偿还贷款所产生的利息部分,从而降低最小还款额。

〔82〕 见本书第七章之 11.2 段的介绍。

will be enhanced by denial of the claim for restitution. If the relevant prohibition is the prohibition on the unauthorised alteration of contractual documents, its purpose … is to punish and deter fraud in commercial dealings. However, at this stage of the argument, the working assumption is that the bank has in principle a valid claim in restitution, so that denial of that restitutionary claim is not required by reason of the alteration itself. If alternatively the relevant prohibition is the prohibition on fraudulent claims or defences in legal proceedings, the position which the law generally adopts is that such conduct does not debar a valid claim and can be both punished and deterred in other ways, for example in costs or by proceedings for contempt of court…

Turning to the second consideration, whether there is any other relevant public policy, the policies which are relevant are those already identified (punishment and deterrence of fraud and good faith in the conduct of legal proceedings). It is not suggested that there is any other policy on which denial of the claim in restitution would have an impact.

Finally, the third consideration is proportionality. Here too the stage at which the argument arises is important. If it is assumed that the claim in restitution is not barred as a result of the fraudulent alteration of the Primary Loan document in 2007 itself, to hold that the bank must be deprived of an otherwise valid claim for £ 16 million in this action as a result of the conduct of (albeit closely related) proceedings to which the claimant was not a party would inevitably be a severe and disproportionate punishment. That is particularly so when what is assumed to be the particularly egregious conduct of the bank, the making of a false allegation of forgery and fraud against Mr Wyatt, was eventually withdrawn and the case settled on terms which, although not disclosed to me, can be taken to have been satisfactory to Mr Wyatt."

也就是说，在多因素考虑后，银行在 Wyatt 先生的诉讼程序中的非法行为不会令被告银行被禁止索赔，所以高院不批准原告修改对反索赔的抗辩。这里对中国读者可能重要的是不止在实体争议上的非法，在恰当的案情下，在诉讼案件程序中的非法也可以作为对索赔的抗辩。

10. 非 法 例 外

由于“违背道德的对价不生诉权”(ex turpi causa non oritur actio)与其衍生出 Holman v. Johnson (1775) 1 Cowp 341 先例的“公序良俗测试”(public conscience test)，作为政策性的法律规则严格套用在所有不同案情事实的案件，对部分案件造成了明显的不公平合理的结果，就难免在此长达 250 年时间内在普通法体系发展出一些例外，务求让部分案件能够有更公平合理的判决。在不违反“非法理论”的政策性法律规则下,也被接受为非法的例外(exceptions to illegality)。这可节录在 Bigos v. Bousted(1951)1 All ER 92 先例中,Pritchard 大法官总结了非法的两个重要例外,说:"The following propositions of law apply where a person seeks to recover property with which he has parted pursuant to an agreement which is tainted with illegality:(1)the general rule is that the person resisting the claim possesses the advantage over the person making it,or,in other words,in pari delicto potior est conditio defendentis;(2)there is **an exception to this rule** which applies to cases in which it can be said that **the parties are not in pari delicto**;(3)the point of time to which one has to look when one is deciding whether two people are in pari delicto is the time at which they enter into the illegal agreement;(4)there is **another exception to the rule in some cases where the contract is still executory, and where a party is allowed a locus poeitentioe**;and may recover money or property delivered to the other party, provided that he takes proceedings before the illegal purpose has been substantially performed;(5)in these cases the question is not one of the merit, or of the comparative merit, of the plaintiff and the defendant. What the court has to consider is purely and simply the demerit of the person seeking to recover money or property, without comparing his conduct with that of the other party to the agreement,..."(加黑部分是笔者的强调)

要注意以上所讲是指复原或不当得利时的情况,让原告可以拿回金钱或财产,法院在不违反非法理论的情况下,适用这两个例外。法院此时只是考虑原告在非法合约下支付或转让给被告的财产应该归谁的问题,并不关心双方之间错多错少。在接下来的段节会去进一步区别介绍这两个重要的非法例外。

10.1 非法例外之一:双方对非法不是"过错对等"(pari delicto)

Mansfield 勋爵在 Holman v. Johnson(1775)1 Cowp 341 先例中确定下来的政策性法律规则部分内容是说:法院不协助原告执行非法合约不是为了偏帮被告,如果他们变换身份,被告先提起诉讼要求协助执行,法院一样是撒手不理,因为他们两人对非法都有过错。重复这部分的名言如下:"... the court goes;not for the sake of the defendant, but because they will not lend their aid to such a plaintiff. So if the plaintiff and defendant were to change sides, and the defendant was to bring his action against the plaintiff, the latter would then have the advantage of it;for **where both were equally in fault, potior est conditio defendentis**."(加黑部分是笔者的强调)

确实,通常非法合约的形成必定是你情我愿。顶多是合约双方对非法的过错在程度上有所不同,但这是不必去区分的,因为不影响双方对该非法合约均有过错。

10.1.1 欺诈/欺骗、欺诈性误述、共同错误与胁迫导致不是过错对等

但当非法合约是通过一方当事人的错误行为诱导或威逼而订立,被诱导或被胁迫的对方当事人就通常是无辜方,难说是过错对等,要求法院协助与救济就不会是因为有关合约的非法而被法院拒之门外。这就是本书多处针对的欺诈/欺骗、欺诈性误

述、共同错误与胁迫。这种情况下，无辜方如果是原告向被告索赔，被告以非法合约作为抗辩，原告即可以他不是"过错对等"，对非法完全无辜，作为对非法抗辩的答辩。

涉及欺诈/欺骗与欺诈性误述，可介绍三个先例或例子，首先是在 Hughes v. Liverpool Victoria Legal Friendly Society（1916）2 KB 482 上诉庭先例中，涉及 5 份人寿保单以前的受保人断供，被告保险经纪人以欺诈性误述诱导原告 Hughes 夫人接手并继续支付保费。但其实这是非法，因为立法规定受保人如果没有保险利益（insurable interest），保单就是非法且无效。原告后来知悉向被告索赔要取回支付的保费，并在一审与上诉庭都成功。上诉庭的 Bankes 大法官说："Given fraud, the authorities seem to me to be all one way, namely, that an innocent plaintiff is entitled to say that he is not in pari delicto with the defendants whose agents by a false and fraudulent representation induced him to believe that the transaction was an innocent one, and one which was enforceable in law."

接下来介绍在 Shelley v. Paddock（1980）QB 348 上诉庭先例中，一审的 Bristow 大法官将此先例与 JM Allan（Merchandising）v. Cloke（1963）2 QB 340 上诉庭先例的区分是在后者双方都不知道合约的非法，而对法律无知并不是一个对抗非法的借口。但在此先例中，涉及被告欺诈/欺骗与欺诈性误述。原告与被告订立房屋买卖合约，但其实被告既不拥有房屋也没有被授权出售。原告起诉取回定金，但被告以原告支付定金的方式违反了英国的《Exchange Control Act 1947》立法，整个交易非法抗辩。外国原告对违反《Exchange Control Act 1947》立法并不知情。一审与上诉庭多数都支持原告索赔欺诈性误述的损失，而上诉庭主要是根据原告的不知情是双方并非"过错对等"。Denning 勋爵说：

"The point raised on their behalf is that this was an illegal transaction. It was in breach of the Exchange Control Act 1947. Miss Shelley（原告）did not know that she was breaking the Exchange Control Act when she paid the money into the bank account ...: but, even though she did not know that, it was an illegal transaction. It is said that under English law no person can recover on a transaction which is illegal. For that proposition the cases go back to a statement by Lord Mansfield in Holman v. Johnson ...

It is said that Miss Shelley founds her cause of action upon an illegal act, namely, that she paid the money to the bank ... without exchange control permission, contrary to the Exchange Control Act.... Therefore she cannot recover on an illegal act.

The judge rejected that argument on the ground that the Paddocks（被告骗子）were guilty of a fraud all the way through.... It is plain from the judge's findings that the Paddocks were swindlers right from the beginning who dishonestly obtained £ 9,500 from Miss Shelley.

In those circumstances, it seems to me that the principle stated by Lord Mansfield does not apply. ...

It is better to allow Miss Shelley to recover here rather than to allow the Paddocks to remain in possession of their unlawful gains. ...

It seems to me plain on each of those principles that these parties are not in pari delicto."

第三个作为例子介绍的是 Hewison v. Meridian Shipping Services Pte Ltd and others (2002) EWCA Civ 1821 先例,案情涉及原告(Hewison 先生)向被告雇主隐瞒他的癫痫病以获得聘用在一艘电缆船做吊车操作员。原告欺骗雇主而获得雇佣合约是属于《Theft Act 1968》之 S. 16 中规定的以欺骗手段获得经济利益的犯罪。但在工作期间,原告因雇主存在《Employers Liability (Defective Equipment) Act 1969》立法中规定的违规与疏忽而因公受伤。原告以侵权向被告索赔损失,但被告的抗辩是原告在欺骗下获得雇佣合约与薪水,因此不能在以自己的错误行为获得雇佣合约下索赔因为工伤而被迫提早退休的工资损失。

在上诉庭,多数意见判原告败诉,因为如果继续工作下去赚取工资,他就必须持续就他的病情对雇主做出欺诈。所以这项损失是原告以谎言与欺骗才可以赚取,判原告胜诉就违反非法理论的"任何人士不能从自己的错误行为中获利"与/或"违背道德的对价不生诉权"的政策性法律规则。

如果倒过来雇主向 Hewison 先生索赔,如他没有尽职令公司蒙受损失,Hewison 先生就无法以合约非法不可执行作为抗辩,因为不是"过错对等"。否则让他抗辩成功可逃避赔偿损失就违反了"任何人士不能从自己的错误行为中获利"的政策性法律规则。

至于胁迫下订立非法合约,也不是"过错对等"。例如,非法居住被业主榨取的钱,租客后来是可以要求退还,例如在 Kiriri Cotton Co Ltd v. Dewani (1960) 2 WLR 127 枢密院先例中提到的 Smith v. Bromley (1760) 2 Doug KB 696 先例。

可举一个早年的 Davies v. London and Provincial Marine Insurance Co (1878) 8 Ch. D. 469 先例为例,公司(London and Provincial)有一位雇员(Evans 先生)挪用了公司财物,公司的言行让雇员及其朋友(Davies 先生)以为将会面对侵占(embezzlement)公司资产的刑事指控。朋友为了帮助该雇员免于被指控,与公司约定并支付了 2000 英镑作为存款以备将来雇员需要补偿公司损失。但事后发现根本不构成侵占的罪行,朋友就要求退还这笔支付的金钱。看来,这种争议本质上是在本书第八章之 7.1 段的错误(是对法律的错误理解)作出支付的类别,但此先例也涉及非法行为,就是面对私了刑事罪行的非法。但法院仍然支持了公司需要退还这笔金钱的复原请求,重要理由就是这笔金钱的支付是在公司言行胁迫指控的情况下所支付,因此并非过错对等。Fry 大法官说:"... it appears to me to be clear that illegality resulting from pressure and illegality resulting from an attempt to stifle a prosecution do not fall within that class of illegalities which induces the Court to stay its hand, but are of a class in which the Court has actively given its assistance in favour of the oppressed party, by directing the money to be repaid."

10.1.2 对非法行为的事实与/或法律不知情导致不是过错对等

这是"过错对等"的延伸,例如在上小段介绍的 Shelley v. Paddock(1980)QB 348 上诉庭先例中,虽然是被告的欺诈性误述导致订立了一份非法合约,但也是原告对有关立法不知情才会被诱导与去依赖[83]订立合约。

显然,对非法知情与不知情(knowledge)在不同案件中是会出现千变万化的情况,但大致上会是:(1)双方都对非法知情;(2)双方都对非法不知情;(3)有一方知情,但另一方并不知情。此外,也会衍生很多有关的争议,如原告为了对抗被告的非法抗辩,说"我对有关法律无知,不知道该行为是非法",或是"我的知情程度低,与被告对有关非法的知情是完全不成比例"等。以下会展开讨论。

10.1.2.1 双方都对非法知情

针对合约双方都对有关非法知情去订立或履行合约,也就是"过错对等"(both were equally in fault 或 pari delicto),这是典型的非法合约,也是公共政策下要去阻吓的行为与拒绝协助执行以保证英国法律系统的正直与公义。

一方明知对方非法目的,并"参与"非法行为就导致不可执行。这早在 Hodgson v. Temple(1813)5 Taunt 181 先例中 Mansfield 勋爵就提出了参与非法交易(a sharer in the illegal transaction)的说法,或者在 JM Allan(Merchandising) v. Cloke(1963)2 QB 340 先例中 Denning 勋爵非法目的、主动参与(unlawful purpose, active participation)的说法等。

不妨先节录权威的《Chitty on Contracts》(2021 年,第 34 版)一书之 18-053 段,它把这种非法的后果说得很清楚:"**Both parties aware of legally objectionable features** Neither party can sue upon a contract if:(a) Both knew that its performance necessarily involved the commission of an act which, to their knowledge, is legally objectionable, that it is illegal or otherwise against public policy; or(双方都知道合约履行必然涉及特定行为,也都对该行为非法知情。这是合约形成非法的情况。)(b) Both knew that the contract is intended to be performed in a manner which, to their knowledge is legally objectionable in that sense; or(双方都意图采取特定方式履行,并且对该方式非法知情。)(c) The purpose of the contract is legally objectionable and that purpose is shared by both parties; or(合约的目的非法,双方都有参与。)(d) Both participate in performing the contract in a manner which they know to be legally objectionable.(在实际履行过程采取了非法行为,双方也都知道行为非法。)..."

作为对比则可见 JM Allan(Merchandising) v. Cloke 上诉庭先例,此先例的事件发生在 1962 年 6 月,原告与被告(一家俱乐部)签订租赁协议,原告出租用于轮盘赌博

[83] 可参阅本书第一章之 1.3 段。

游戏(roulette royale)的设备给被告，约定可以根据原告公司提供的规则娱乐。其中一条规则说这种娱乐方式是设计用来配合《Betting and Gaming Act 1960》的规定，显示双方无意违法/非法。但在当年8月底，类似的娱乐方式被法院判在前述立法下属非法行为。知道情况后原告马上也与被告"通气"，并建议使用另一种变更方式的娱乐规则，提出这样就合法了。但是被告看来仍然觉得风险太大，要求退还设备并拒绝继续支付租金。原告因此向被告提出租赁合约下的索赔，面对的就是被告以合约非法抗辩。

这里的问题是，能否说双方在订立合约时对于非法并不知情，而事后在知道行为非法后，马上就停止，因此合约下的索赔仍然可以被支持？法院的判法是在非法抗辩下，原告败诉。法院认定租赁合约就是为了让被告可以用该非法的规则进行娱乐，也因此合约形成非法。一旦合约形成非法就是米已成炊，事后再放弃非法行为并试图通过合约更改去改变非法并不能挽救本身不会被执行的非法合约。另是，对立法无知也不是可接受的理由。Denning 勋爵说："I desire to say that where two people together have the common design to use a subject-matter for an unlawful purpose, so that each participates in the unlawful purpose, then that **contract is illegal in its formation**: and **it is no answer for them to say that they did not know the law on the matter.**"(加黑部分是笔者的强调)

在 Ashmore, Benson, Pease & Co Ltd v. A V Dawson Ltd (1973) 1 WLR 828 上诉庭先例中，涉及的背景是根据《Road Traffic Act 1960》与《Motor Vehicles (Construction and Use) Regulations 1966》，某特定种类拖车运输载重不得超过30吨(包括车身重量)，这些立法背后的原因会有很多，例如这种拖车载重过重伤害路面、容易危害道路安全等。而此先例中约定由车方运送货方的两个重量为25吨的锅炉前往码头。因此可以说合约的形成与订立本身并不非法，例如完全可以安排高载重的拖车等方式履行。

但是问题出在实际运输的车辆正是前述立法中载重上限为30吨的拖车，而该拖车不载重的重量就有10吨。而且之后在双方均有熟悉业务的人士在场时，明显知道实际称重超出30吨达到35吨，这就超出立法允许载重上限。但双方均没有对此表示任何异议，继续履行合约。最后在运输途中有一辆拖车不幸翻倒导致锅炉损坏。

在此先例中，法院根据证据认定双方(尤其是货方)知道有关立法的存在，而且货方不仅仅是知道，甚至参与了该非法行为。这样，因为履行合约的方式导致合约也变为非法。[84] 法院也因此拒绝执行原告的索赔请求。

---

〔84〕 合约履行非法，要看选择履行的方式与请求法院救济一方参与的程度是否足以使得合约变成非法合约("whether the method of performance chosen and the degree of participation in that illegal performance is such as to turn the contract into an illegal contract")，见本章之4.2段。

10.1.2.2 双方都对非法不知情

就大原则上而言,非法合约并不会简单因为合约双方无知、不知道该行为非法就将合约合法化。而且英国法下也期待每个人都应合法行事,不能说因为我是“法盲”,我就可以随便做什么事情都无需承担后果。正如在 Waugh v. Morris(1873) LR 8 QB 202 先例中,Blackburn 大法官说:“... where a contract is to do a thing which cannot be performed without a violation of the law it is void, **whether the parties knew the law or not.** But we think, that in order to avoid a contract which can be legally performed, on the ground that there was **an intention to perform it in an illegal manner, it is necessary to shew that there was the wicked intention to break the law**; and, if this be so, the knowledge of what the law is becomes of great importance.”(加黑部分是笔者的强调)

立法的非法也是一样,当事人对法律无知不是借口:见 Kiriri Cotton Co Ltd v. Dewani(1960)2 WLR 127; Mahmoud and Ispahani, Re(1921)2 KB 716 先例等。在本章之1.3段介绍的 Kiriri Cotton Co Ltd v. Dewan 枢密院先例中,案情涉及乌干达的立法《Rent Restriction Ordinance》,Denning 勋爵说:“It is not correct to say that everyone is presumed to know the law. The true proposition is that **no man can excuse himself from doing his duty by saying that he did not know the law on the matter. Ignorantia juris neminem excusat.** ...”(加黑部分是笔者的强调)

合约形成非法与合约履行非法都是一样的道理,双方当事人是否知道有关的法律或是否意图违反法律并不重要。只有在合约目的非法时,需要证明双方确实有非法意图,这样双方是否知道是非法就变得十分重要。只有证明双方知道是非法,但仍订立合约时,合约目的非法才能成立。

10.1.2.2.1 与共同错误的关系及对产权的影响

上小段介绍的 JM Allan(Merchandising) v. Cloke(1963)2 QB 340 上诉庭先例的案情,显示双方在订立合约时明显不想违法,只是错误理解了《Betting and Gaming Act 1960》的立法规定。但双方对法律无知不是对非法的借口,所以面对非法抗辩原告不会获得执行仍是难免。此外虽然被告律师没有主张共同错误(common mistake),[85] 但双方订约时共同对法律错误理解,而且没有其他合法方式去履行合约(除非双方同意去变更合约),就正是共同错误可去令合约自始无效(void ab initio),可以达到同样的结果。

非法理论相比适用错误理论,会在少数情况下带来更多麻烦。例如,涉及货物产权(legal title)的问题时,非法不影响法律产权的转移,如果货物产权被转移给了第三人,主张拥有货物产权的一方不能向无辜第三人取回。但如果是共同错误,合约自始

---

〔85〕 有关对订约时双方对法律有共同错误,可见本书第七章之13段。

无效,货物产权从未被转移,在"nemo dat"规则下可以取回货物。[86]

对此仅简单节录《Illegality and Public Policy》(2020 年,第 5 版)一书之 3-06 段所说如下:"... A different approach to the problem in Allan... might have been to consider whether the contract was void for mistake on the ground that its subject-matter was fundamentally different from that which the parties had assumed... irrespective of the likely outcome via that approach, the crucial point is that the case should be perceived as having raised an issue on the law which applies when a state of affairs exists which is different from that which was in contemplation when the contract was made. To invoke illegality in such circumstances, with its focus upon the public interest rather than that of the parties, could potentially have quite inappropriate consequences. Difficulties might arise in a similar case, for example, in relation to recovery by the owner of goods transferred under the contract of hire."

10.1.2.2.2 订约时对非法无知的例外

但双方对非法无知有一种例外,即如果合约并非形成非法及可以有合法方式履行,只是双方原本因为对法律的无知而预期以非法方式履行。但在了解到真正法律地位后放弃此预期,而是转而采取合法方式履行合约。此时该合约就实际上与非法理论完全无关,纯粹是当事人一开始曾经在不知情下有过不合法意图,不会因此导致不可执行。

对这问题在《Illegality and Public Policy》(2020 年,第 5 版)一书之 3-02 段中说得很清楚:"In some cases one or both of the parties may intend that an otherwise lawful contract should be performed in a manner which would in fact involve contravention of the law. If this intention was formed **through ignorance of the surrounding circumstances, and was abandoned immediately the true position was ascertained so that the agreement was performed lawfully**, illegality as such should not, in principle, be relevant to the resolution of any dispute which might subsequently occur between the parties."(加黑部分是笔者的强调)

另在《Chitty on Contracts》(2021 年,第 34 版)一书之 18-055 段中说:"... where the contract is not unlawful on its face and is **capable of performance in a lawful way** and the parties merely contemplate that it will be performed in a particular way which would be unlawful, the parties, **through ignorance of the law**, failing to appreciate that fact, the contract may be enforced on the ground that **there was never a 'fixed intention'** to do that which was later discovered to be lawful and that while the parties 'contemplated' such an unlawful act, they did not 'intend' to do it. In other words, **knowledge of the law is of evidential significance with respect to the parties' intended**

〔86〕 关于这方面可见本书第七章之 18.2 段。

mode of performance…”(加黑部分是笔者的强调)

典型的例子就是在本章之1.5.2段已经介绍过的Waugh v. Morris(1873)LR 8 QB 202先例,双方约定从法国运输干草前往伦敦的租约,但不知道当时在《Cattle Diseases Act 1869》立法下法国已成为疫区,伦敦码头禁止卸载来自法国的干草。在船舶到达伦敦双方发现问题后,双方没有非法卸载而是马上安排转运去其他国家港口卸货。船东成功向承租人索赔其间船舶产生延误的滞期费(demurrage),承租人无法证明当事人在订约时知情而形成非法(这与事实不符也很难证明),而且在发现约定非法后马上悔改并可以用合法方式履行,并不真正有履行非法,因此承租人以租约目的非法的抗辩并不能成功。

10.1.2.3 单方面对非法不知情

这种情况很多,也就是非法合约双方只是单方面知道合约的目的或履行非法,但另一方不知道。在不知情下,另一方也算是无辜方,谈不上双方"过错对等"了。在这种情况下,无辜方向对非法知情的合约方索赔损失或寻求法院救济是不成问题,后者可成功提出非法抗辩是完全说不通的。

但反过来,对非法知情的原告向无辜方索赔损失,就有问题了,因为这违反了最基本的非法理论,也就是"违背道德的对价不生诉权"与"任何人不能从自己的不法行为中获利"。

这可节录权威书籍《Chitty on Contracts》(2021年,第34版)一书之18–054段说:"**Legally objectionable features unknown to one party**It follows what has been said that,if the performance of a contract necessarily and to the knowledge of the plaintiff involves or has as its object the commission by one or both parties of an act known to be legally objectionable,the plaintiff cannot sue on the contract and this is so irrespective of the state of knowledge of the defendant. **But when the contract does not necessarily involve the commission of legally objectionable act and the legally objectionable intention or purpose of one party is unknown to the other,the latter is not precluded from enforcing the contract.**"(加黑部分是笔者的强调)

在本章之1.3段介绍的Kiriri Cotton Co Ltd v. Dewani(1960)2 WLR 127枢密院先例中,Denning勋爵说:"… if there is something in the defendant's conduct which shows that,of the two of them,he is the one primarily responsible for the mistake-then it may be recovered back. Thus,if as between the two of them **the duty of observing the law is placed on the shoulders of the one rather than the other** - it being imposed on him specially for the protection of the other then **they are not in pari delicto** and the money can be recovered back…Likewise,if the responsibility for the mistake lies more on the one than the other-because **he has misled the other when he ought to know better-then again they are not in pari delicto** and the money can be recovered back…These propositions are in full accord with the principles laid down by Lord Mansfield relating to the action for money had and received. ...Seeing then that the parties are **not in pari delicto, the tenant is entitled to recover the premium by the common law: and it is not necessary to find a remedy given by the Ordinance**, either expressly or by implication. The omission of a statutory remedy does not, in cases of this kind, exclude the remedy by money had and received."(加黑部分是笔者的强调)

接下来不妨随便挑两个先例来介绍,显示履行合约过程中知情与否带来的区别。

在 Best v. Glenville(1960)1 WLR 1198 上诉庭先例中,原告出租一处房屋给被告开俱乐部,双方都知道根据《Town and Country Planning Act 1947》立法,这需要获取政府的批文。因此在谈判过程中,被告就已经开始进行申请,在此基础上双方达成租赁协议。后来被告在租赁协议下已经进驻场地并开始装修,但申请批文未能成功,而被告仍然继续用该房屋开俱乐部。事后被告欠下租金未支付,原告因此起诉,被告主张没有合法批文的非法抗辩,这被法院驳回。

此先例中的租赁协议本身并不存在形成或目的非法,单纯是原告出租房屋给被告用来开俱乐部,只是在实际开俱乐部之前必须先获得批文。根据双方的证据来看,在索赔之前双方(尤其是原告)也是意图合法履行的,被告也确实在谈判中就已经开始申请。原告还提供证人的可信证言,显示他如果知道该处会被在没有批文情况下就非法开俱乐部,是不会出租的。因此,原告作为不知情的无辜方,索赔欠下租金仍然得到法院协助执行。Ormerod 大法官说:"I find it very hard to see what there is **illegal in the contract so far as the plaintiff is concerned**. He let the premises for a perfectly proper purpose, that is, for their use as a club... There was no duty on him to obtain planning permission. It was unnecessary, in the circumstances, for him to say, as it was suggested he should have said: 'These premises are let only on the understanding that if they are for the use of a club there must be planning permission,' because that was something which had already come to the knowledge of the defendant, and was something which she was prepared to deal with by applying for planning permission. In those circumstances why should this be an illegal agreement? **If neither party took the trouble to take any steps to obtain planning permission, or if each party knew that no steps were to be taken, it might well be the case, if proved, that there was something unlawful in this agreement**. But that is not this case and I can see no reason why the plaintiff should be held to have entered into an illegal agreement."(加黑部分是笔者的强调)

接下来介绍在 Archbolds(Freightage)Ltd v. S Spanglett Ltd(1961)1 QB 374 上诉庭先例中,涉及当时在《Road and Rail Traffic Act 1933》立法下,A 类牌照的货车可以用来运输他人货物获利,而 C 类牌照只可以用来运输自己的货物但不能运输他人货物获利。被告是家具生产商,名下有 C 类牌照货车。原告是运输公司,用 A 类牌照货车从事货物运输业务。经过与被告公司电话交流后,原告以为被告公司也有 A 类牌照货车,就雇佣被告运输一部分自己招揽到的货物。但运输途中被告司机疏忽,导致货物被偷走,原告因此向被告索赔。

在此先例中的情况,运输合约本身并不非法,使用C类牌照货车运输他人货物获利才是非法行为。原告并不知情以为被告确实有A类牌照货车,因此之后实际装车等行为并不是在协助(aiding or abetting)非法履行。法院在综合考虑后驳回了被告依赖非法理论的抗辩,允许索赔。

说实在如果一方单方面知道自己以非法手段履约就可导致合约因非法理论而不可执行,就可去故意行差踏错赖掉欠不知情的对方的债务,很容易带来欺诈/欺骗与不诚实行为。这也会导致社会方方面面的问题:例如叫网约车出行时,岂不是要逼迫乘客在上车前要求司机拿出所有有效证件,以免行程中司机把乘客载到半途丢下或疏忽驾驶导致乘客受伤,乘客因非法理论无处申冤。

此先例的Pearce大法官说:"This view is **supported by common sense and convenience**. If the other view were held it would have far-reaching effects. For instance, if a carrier induces me (who am in fact ignorant of any illegality) to entrust goods to him and negligently destroys them, he would only have to show that (though unknown to me) his licence had expired, or did not properly cover the transportation, or that he was uninsured, and I should then be without a remedy against him. Or, again, if I ride in a taxicab and the driver leaves me stranded in some deserted spot, he would only have to show that he was (though unknown to me) unlicensed or uninsured, and I should be without remedy. … if both parties had that knowledge the contract would be unenforceable as being a contract which to their knowledge could not be carried out without a violation of the law; see per Lord Blackburn in Waugh v. Morris. … But where **one party is ignorant of the fact that will make the performance illegal, is it established that the innocent party cannot obtain relief against the guilty party**? The case has been argued with skill and care on both sides, and yet **no case has been cited to us establishing the proposition that where a contract is on the face of it legal and is not forbidden by statute, but must in fact produce illegality by reason of a circumstance known to one party only, it should be held illegal so as to debar the innocent party from relief.** In the absence of such a case I do not feel compelled to **so unsatisfactory a conclusion, which would injure the innocent, benefit the guilty, and put a premium on deceit.** … an extension of the law in this direction would be more harmful than beneficial. No question of moral turpitude arises here. … **The plaintiffs were never in delicto since they did not know the vital fact that would make the performance of the contract illegal.**"(加黑部分是笔者的强调)

10.1.3 知情与参与

10.1.3.1 仅仅知情未必足够的说法

有说法是仅仅知情未必足够,一方面是在Patel v. Mirza(2016) UKSC 42最高院先例中引入成比例(proportionality)说法之前,早已经有说法就是除了知情以外,还需要考虑有关非法行为在性质上的严重程度,对方非法行为越是严重危害社会的犯罪行为,越是可能导致合约在非法理论下不可执行。这看来如果非法行为在性质上非常轻微,一方当事人在正常商业往来中对对方的一些猫腻或擦边球行为去睁一只眼闭一只眼,也不应该影响其合约权利。但如果非法程度很高,如恐怖袭击、卖国通敌行为,任何形式的商业交易只要沾上了都会是非法合约或行为。

在美国《Restatement(Second)of Contracts》之§182 中就提出这要看是否有严重的社会危害(grave social harm),并给了一个很好的例子。如 A 销售一把霰弹枪给 B,如果知道 B 是要用来非法捕猎,他们之间的合约可能仍然有效。而如果 A 是知道 B 要用来杀人抢劫,A 就可能无法执行合约权利如追讨货价了。可节录部分内容如下:"If the promisee has substantially performed, enforcement of a promise is not precluded on grounds of public policy because of some improper use that the promisor intends to make of what he obtains unless the promisee(a) acted for the purpose of furthering the improper use, or(b) **knew of the use and the use involves grave social harm**... Illustrations: 1. A sells and delivers to B a shotgun on credit. The sale of firearms is legal, but B plans to use the gun in hunting without a license required by law and A knows this. Enforcement of B's promise to pay the price is not precluded on grounds of public policy. If B planned to use the gun to commit a robbery and A knew this, B's promise to pay the price would be unenforceable on those grounds."(加黑部分是笔者的强调)

另一方面是已经在本段一开始提到,这里的是否过错对等不能以非法行为错多错少去区分。否则就会导致除非能各错 50% 就再也没有非法理论的可笑情况,因为无法去划分一条分水岭/红线,如"主犯"与"从犯"的参与程度九一分或是只要超过了 50% 就是"主犯"。另是如果"从犯"过错很少就可算是无辜,可适用过错对等的例外,也无法划分一条分水岭/红线到底过错多少才能算很少。更不用说,这也违反非法理论的政策性法律规则。但现实中也确实经常存在合约一方(通常是原告)相对无辜(如对非法行为的过错只是 5%),如果不执行合约让 95% 过错的"主犯"获利是不公平合理的情况,就带来另一个希望达至同样目的的"从犯"在非法行为有否真正"参与"(participation)的说法。

例如在本章之 10.1.2.1 段介绍的 JM Allan(Merchandising) v. Cloke(1963)2 QB 340 先例中,Denning 勋爵说:"There is no participation in the **immoral purpose**, but **merely knowledge of it**, and that **is no bar to recovering the price**. Likewise with an **unlawful purpose, active participation debars, but knowledge by itself does not**. ...In this case, however, there was participation. The common design was that a game should be played which was in fact unlawful. I hold that such a contract is unlawful: and it is no answer for those concerned to say that they did not know the law."(加黑部分是笔者的强调)

Denning 勋爵另以已经在本章之 4.3 段中介绍的 Pearce v. Brooks(1866)LR 1 Ex

213 先例,妓女向原告租售一架特别定制的有棚四轮马车(brougham)的案件作为例子,就是房东以高价出租房屋给一位妓女会被推断为非法。特别是向她收取较高的租金,就可去推断是知道用来做不法用途,也表示房东在知情外,有一定程度的参与。但换了是清洁/洗衣工人或卖给妓女食物的商人,收取的费用只是正常的价格。这样即使他们知道该妓女是干什么的,但这知情并没有参与,不会令他们之间的合约变为非法而无法执行。Denning 勋爵说:"I would take a comparable case where there is a common design to use a subject-matter for an immoral purpose. If a landlord lets a flat to a prostitute at **a rent beyond any normal commercial rent**,... it may fairly be **inferred that it was their common design that it should be used for an immoral purpose**. The letting is unlawful and he cannot recover the rent or hire. It is different with **the washer-woman** who washes the clothes of the prostitute or **the butcher** who supplies her with meat. They may know of her trade but they **charge her normal commercial prices. There is there no common design**."(加黑部分是笔者的强调)

在本章之 10.1.2.1 介绍的 Ashmore, Benson, Pease & Co Ltd v. A V Dawson Ltd (1973)1 WLR 828 上诉庭先例中,货方在现场看到超载的情况下对仍然继续装载没有任何异议,这样的行为加上对非法的事实知情,就导致了原本无辜的货方也就无法执行合约权利。Scarman 大法官这样说:"The question now arises, and it is really a question of law, whether, Mr. Bulmer being the transport manager of Ashmores(货方/原告), his knowledge would be sufficient to impose upon Ashmores the consequences of being parties to an illegal performance of the contract. Mr. Bulmer was their responsible official. **But knowledge by itself is not, I think, enough. There must be knowledge plus participation**...In the present case Mr. Bulmer could have stopped the loading when he went down to watch it being done. He did not do so with all his knowledge and experience; and I am driven to the conclusion that he was a participator in the illegality...For these reasons I think the performance was illegal and that Ashmores, through Mr. Bulmer, participated in that illegal performance."(加黑部分是笔者的强调)

10.1.3.2　参与的认定

进一步的问题就是,什么情况可以认为是有"参与"导致原本无辜方成为"过错对等"(pari delicto)? 过往大量先例中有多种多样的复杂情况。

如果当事人会从违法行为中获利,比如在 Ashmore, Benson, Pease & Co Ltd v. A V Dawson Ltd(1973)1 WLR 828 先例中用 30 吨载重拖车运送 35 吨的货物,明显就是节省了运费,当事人也因此属于参与而无法执行自己的合约权利。

即使是一方当事人并不会从违法行为中"获利",如果是实际参与也是一样。对于此问题在早期的 Hodgson v. Temple(1813)5 Taunt 181 先例中,当时立法禁止蒸馏酒(spirituous liquors)零售商参与蒸馏酒的提纯行业,而一个蒸馏酒买卖中的卖方其实多半知道买方买蒸馏酒是要在工厂里提纯的,但卖方索赔合约下的损失赔偿仍然成功,卖方仅仅是知情而没有参与。Mansfield 勋爵就提出了必须是参与非法交易(a sharer in the illegal transaction)才会导致合约无法执行:“... The merely selling goods, knowing that the buyer will make an illegal use of them, is not sufficient to deprive the vendor of his just right of payment, but to effect that, it is necessary that the vendor should be a sharer in the illegal transaction.”

对比的例子就例如在 Waymell v. Reed(1794)5 TR 599 先例中,涉及的是蕾丝(lace)产品买卖,买方先在法国收货,然后再走私前往英国销售。但与 Hodgson v. Temple 先例不同的是,卖方根据买方的指示对产品采取了特别包装,使货品更容易隐藏,且在走私中不容易发现。该行为就会被认为是有参与,也导致在此先例中卖方由于非法理论无法执行合约权利。

另一种情况则会是同一个交易存在多个有关系的合约,其中有一个合约非法,其他合约也会由于当事人的知情与参与,或者说是被“污染”(tainted)而导致一整套交易都不可执行。例如,贷款合约,出借人的动机(motive)就是让借款人得以推进特定非法行为,借钱用来贩卖毒品、实施恐怖活动等,此时就会污染导致贷款合约都不可执行:见 Cannan v. Bryce(1819)106 ER 628 与 Spector v. Ageda(1973)Ch 30 等先例。

在 Patel v. Mirza(2016)UKSC 42 最高院先例后,是否被污染导致一整套交易不可执行更加要考虑非法的合约在整个交易中是否属于核心及非法是否严重。在本书第九章之 4.7.1 段介绍的 Magdeev v. Tsvetkov(2020)EWHC 887(Comm)先例中,虽然涉及的是外国法非法,但分析的道理是一样。在该先例中双方当事人同时订立了贷款合约与雇佣合约,而雇佣合约的目的是支付贷款合约的利息与让原告获得迪拜签证。之后原告要求被告还款,被告就以贷款合约非法抗辩。英国高院考虑全盘事实后认定整个交易真正与实质的主要目的是贷款,而雇佣合约纯粹是附带(如果不是雇佣合约有一部分是为了支付利息,就会变成另一个独立合约)。虽然以欺诈方式获取签证在英国法下被认为是严重的不法行为,但在阿联酋法律下即使涉及伪造文件不属于特别严重,专家证人就提到这种行为在阿联酋法律下未必会被严肃处理与对待,而且最后事情曝光看来阿联酋政府也确实没有采取什么刑事调查或检控的行为。因此英国高院最后判该贷款合约可以执行。

又如在一些保险案件中,国际货物买卖或运输合约中涉及非法行为,导致在货物的保险合约下也无法索赔。在 Geismar v. Sun Insurance(1978)QB 383 先例中涉及走私货物,货物被偷窃后走私方就想要找保险人索赔,但法院拒绝执行。但这要看具体的案情情况,如在 Euro-Diam Ltd v. Bathurst(1990)1 QB 1 先例中,涉及的是买卖/运输合约下进口方要求出口方提供虚假面值的发票(invoice),欺骗进口的有关当局逃避税务或规管,但在货物受损或遗失后,出口方想要向保险人索赔,法院判非法行为纯粹是为了进口方的利益,对于出口方而言没什么好处,该行为并没有“污染”保险合约。而在今天的 Patel 指引下,这类案件更是要考虑所有因素,比如有关非法行为在整个交易中是否是核心或关键,如走私货物在整个交易中是核心问题,给进口方的发票就可能只是一个附带的问题,对保险合约没什么影响。也有说法是今天这类案件中要看有关保险合约是否是该类行业中的惯常做法,如果是,即使实际交易中存在非法也倾向于不影响保险合约的执行。这可见《Illegality and Public Policy》(2020年,第5版)一书之4-21段的评论:"The appropriate question to ask may be whether taking out insurance would have been a routine and common practice irrespective of the nature of the activity. If so, the policy should in most cases be unobjectionable."

10.2 非法例外之二:撤回权理论

拉丁文的"*locus poenitentiae*"英文解释可以是:"an opportunity to withdraw from a contract or obligation before it is completed or to decide not to commit an intended crime."也就是当事人或原告在非法合约履行完毕前退出或在犯罪完成前放弃犯罪意图,就可以作为非法理论的例外情况。这例外在本质上也没有偏离非法理论的"违背道德的对价不生诉权"的政策性法律规则。

显然在普通法下去建立这例外说法是完全说得通,也不算是"例外",而是符合同一精神的公共政策。这就是去鼓励在有了非法的预谋或计划后,能够在实施非法行为或履行非法合约前,尚没有对其他第三人造成损害或自己非法获利的情况下,悬崖勒马或及时悔改(repentance)。但如果非法计划或合约已经付诸行动,原告也已经获得了部分或全部的非法利益才撤回,岂非骗了第三人,又可以向被告根据衡平法的复原/不当得利取回财产,这显然是违反法律与公共政策的。

这种情况在现实中不少,也就是双方订立了一份非法合约,但在真正履行违法行为前,其中一方的A想法或现实上有了改变,希望退出。如果订立的是一份合法合约,A想单方面退出倒也不容易,因为将面对对方B的损失赔偿的索赔。但订立的是一份非法合约,不会有法院的协助执行,所以这方面至少不必要担心。但很多情况是A已经是在非法合约下作出了部分的支付或贷款,或提供一些财产[如Oom v. Bruce(1810)12 East 225;Kiriri Cotton Co Ltd v. Dewani(1960)2 WLR 127;Shelley v. Paddock(1980)QB 348;Tribe v. Tribe(1996)Ch 107;Patel v. Mirza(2016)UKSC 42等先例]。这样,A如果去向B要求偿还/退还,就会面对B作为被告提出的非法抗辩。此时,A就会需要以"撤回权理论"作为答辩以对抗被告。这是因为非法合约的订立与形成,甚至双方都有非法目的,是已经发生了与摆在眼前的事实。

在Tribe v. Tribe上诉庭先例中,Millett大法官说:"The doctrine of the locus poenitentiae is **an exception which operates to mitigate the harshness of the primary rule**. It enables the court to do justice between the parties even though, in order to do so, it must allow a plaintiff to give evidence of his own dishonest intent. **But he must have withdrawn from the transaction while his dishonesty still lay in intention only**. The law draws the line once the intention has been wholly or partly carried into effect. Seen in this light the doctrine of the locus poenitentiae, **although an exception to the primary rule, is not inconsistent with the policy which underlies it**."(加黑部分是笔者的

强调）

至于A为何改变想法退出非法合约或行为可以有千奇百怪的原因。道德上悔改当然是最好，如订立一份在严重违法的合约后心里害怕并在家人劝阻下改变想法。又或是在不知情下订立一份在立法规定下是无法合法履行的合约，问了律师知情后改变想法。这种情况当然是值得鼓励与支持的，法院是没有理由不支持原告A，反而让“死不悔改”的被告B可以非法抗辩去获利。

但这种及时悔改在现实中肯定绝少，特别是在国际商业活动中，订约方都会深思熟虑后订立一份昂贵合约。所以在订立非法合约后直到要开始履行这个短暂与非常狭窄的窗口，是不大可能会发生有一方合约方有了真正悔改，改变了想法决定去退出。

更多的情况是导致非法合约的情况有了改变，再也无须去这样做了。例如，买凶杀人但目标人物因病死亡。或是，买卖违禁品但法律突然放宽。这样显然是非法合约并没有履行，但这与道德上真心真意悔改去退出非法合约是没有关系的。

非法理论下的撤回权理论与道德有关系首先是在 Parkinson v. College of Ambulance Ltd（1925）2 KB 1 先例中，Lush 大法官指出没有悔改就不适用撤回权理论，说：“The first difficulty in the plaintiff's way is that he is not in truth resiling from the contract at all. He is really bringing this action because he has failed to obtain the promised title. It seems to be something like an abuse of language to say that he is resiling from the contract，... If there is any locus poenitentiæ in a case like this，which I do not think there is，there has been no poenitentia.”

在接下来一连串的案例中，也是同样判法。这包括 Symes v. Hughes（1870）LR 9 Eq 475；Taylor v. Bowers（1876）1 QBD 291；Kearley v. Thomson（1890）24 QBD 742；Alexander v. Rayson（1936）1 KB 169；Berg v. Sadler & Moore（1937）2 KB 158；Bigos v. Bousted（1951）1 All ER 92 等先例。其中在 Bigos v. Bousted 先例中，Pritchard 大法官说：“If a particular case may be held to fall within the category of repentance cases，I think the law is that the court will help a person who repents，provided his repentance comes before the illegal purpose has been substantially performed. If I were able，in this case，to take the view that the defendant had brought himself within that sphere of the authorities，it might well be that I would have been able to help him by saying that his repentance had come before the illegal purpose had been substantially performed，but I do not take that view. I think，however，that this case falls within the category of cases which I call the frustration cases.”[87]

这带来在 Tinsley v. Milligan（1994）1 AC 340 贵族院先例中，Browne-Wilkinson

---

〔87〕 在该先例中，非法合约（涉及“套汇”并违反《Exchange Control Act 1947》立法）没有被履行不是因为有一方当事人真正悔改，而是因为非法合约因情势变更而不再需要这样做的受阻（frustration）。

勋爵提到这个撤回权理论说是普通法与衡平法都要求原告悔改,说:"There was originally a difference of view as to whether a transaction entered into for an illegal purpose would be enforced at law or in equity if the party had repented of his illegal purpose before it had been put into operation, ie the doctrine of locus poenitentiae. It was eventually recognised both at law and in equity that if the plaintiff had repented before the illegal purpose was carried through, he could recover his property."

但将撤回权理论这一例外与道德联系在一起并不是好事,原告 A 在企图退出非法合约时是否真正悔改是他的心理状态,只有他自己知道与可去提供证据。这并不理想,也会带来更多谎言/伪证的风险。另是,这撤回权理论如果只适用于 A 真正悔改就会带来实用性不高,因为现实很少会出现这种情况,B 也难去反证。

这与道德捆绑在一起要求原告真正悔改的法律地位,在后来的 Tribe v. Tribe 上诉庭先例被否定。案情涉及作为原告父亲为了非法向债权人隐瞒财产,在没有真正支付对价的情况下把家族公司股票转给他的儿子(也就是被告)。[88] 但事后父亲与债权人达成和解协议,在向被告要求归还股票时被拒,只能提起诉讼,而被告则提出非法抗辩。其中涉及撤回权理论,毕竟此先例中对债权人没有造成任何伤害,债权人也根本不知情。

但被告代表大律师指出:"The locus poenitentiae is repentance allowing the court to overlook the original illegality of a party's act. But the plaintiff could not repent if (i) the threat from the creditors had passed, or (ii) after harm had been done to the creditors, or (iii) after the illegal act had been partly performed."

也就是,被告主张一旦原告与债权人达成和解,危险已过,就不再需要非法以虚假信托(sham trust)去隐瞒财产,届时才悬崖勒马或悔改已经太迟。被告也引经据典去依赖 Bigos v. Bousted 与 Alexander v. Rayson 等先例。

但上诉庭判原告父亲胜诉,推翻了 Bigos v. Bousted 先例,其中 Millett 大法官说:"It is impossible to reconcile all the authorities on the circumstances in which a party to an illegal contract is permitted to withdraw from it. At one time he was allowed to withdraw so long as the contract had not been completely performed; but later it was held that recovery was barred once it had been partly performed: see Kearley v. Thomson (1890) 24 QBD 742. **It is clear that he must withdraw voluntarily**, and that **it is not sufficient that he is forced to do so** because his plan has been discovered. In Bigos v. Bousted [1951] 1 All ER 92 this was ... extended to prevent withdrawal where the scheme has been frustrated by the refusal of the other party to carry out his part.... I would draw back from any such attempt. But **I would hold that genuine repentance is not required**. **Justice is not a reward for merit; restitution should not be confined to the penitent**. I

---

〔88〕 这里涉及本章之 7.2.2 段介绍的"赠与推定"(presumption of advancement)的法律推定。

would also hold that voluntary withdrawal from an illegal transaction when it has ceased to be needed is sufficient. It is true that this is not necessary to encourage withdrawal, but a rule to the opposite effect could lead to bizarre results. Suppose, for example, that in Bigos v. Bousted ... exchange control had been abolished before the foreign currency was made available: it is absurd to suppose that the plaintiff should have been denied restitution. I do not agree that it was correct ... for the court to withhold its assistance from the plaintiff because 'if the crime has not been completed, the merit was not his'. "(加黑部分是笔者的强调)

此先例的判法就将撤回权理论适用的范围放宽了很多,重要的是撤回权不必与道德扯在一起,正如 Millett 大法官所说并在后来的案例中有援引,如 Bird 大法官在 RO v. Freddy Gray(2021) EWHC 2770(QB)先例中说:"It is important to remember that, as Millett LJ said in Tribe v. Tribe ... 'justice is not reword for merit'."。

在 Patel v. Mirza 最高院先例中,上诉庭[(2014) EWCA Civ 1047]的 Rimer 大法官也认同 Millett 大法官,说:"... I would regard as unattractive a distinction between cases (**a**) where the withdrawal is from an illegal agreement that is no longer needed for the purpose for which it was designed, and (**b**) where the withdrawal is from an illegal agreement that cannot be or is anyway not going to be performed. The drawing of any such distinction would, I consider, depend on holding that 'genuine repentance' on the part of the withdrawer is required. But I would take my lead from Millett LJ in Tribe and hold, in respectful agreement with him, that such repentance is not required. **I consider that if, as in Tribe, voluntary withdrawal from an illegal agreement when it had ceased to be needed is sufficient to entitle the claimant to recover**, it would be an odd distinction if a claimant were nevertheless not entitled to recover by relying on an illegal agreement that neither was performed nor could be performed. To recognise such a distinction would, I consider, require proof of a true sense of penitence, something that was not required or expected of the successful claimant in Tribe.... It appears to me, however, that the essence of what can be derived from Tribe is that, **so long as the illegal agreement has not been carried into effect to any extent, the claimant can rely on it and recover. That is this case**. "(加黑部分是笔者的强调)

在最高院,也可节录 Clarke 勋爵权威性认可说:"The courts began to treat the right of restitution as depending on the moral quality of the plaintiff's decision to withdraw. They reasoned that if the object of allowing restitution was to encourage withdrawal from an illegal venture, it ought to be withheld if the claimant had withdrawn involuntarily, for example because the other party withdrew first or the venture became impossible or failed for some reason other than his genuine regret. ...**It was rejected, rightly to my mind, by Millett LJ in Tribe v. Tribe** ... 'Justice is not a reward for merit', he said:

'restitution should not be confined to the penitent.' **I agree**. But for the same reason I would reject the suggestion that Millett LJ went on to make that the right to restitution should still depend on the voluntary character of the plaintiff's withdrawal. As with the notion of penitence, this is to put a moral gloss on **a principle that depends simply on the right to restitution that in principle follows from the legal ineffectiveness of the contract under or in anticipation of which the money was paid**."(加黑部分是笔者的强调)

10.3 非法例外之三:原告属于立法本意保护的一类当事人

在今天无数的立法下,如果原告属于立法本意保护的一类当事人,这样即使对非法有一定程度过错,也不算是"过错对等",非法理论不适用。这早在 Browing v. Morris(1788)2 Cowp 790 先例中,Mansfield 勋爵就已经提出过:"Where contracts or transactions are prohibited by positive statutes, for the sake of protecting one set of men from another set of men; the one, from their situation and condition, being liable to be oppressed or imposed upon by the other; there, the parties are not in pari delicto; and in furtherance of these statutes, the person injured, after the transaction is finished and completed, may bring his action and defeat the contract."

另在 Kearley v. Thomson(1890)23 QBD 742 上诉庭先例中,Fry 大法官也说:"there are other illegalities which arise where a statute has been intended to protect a class of persons, and the person seeking to recover is a member of the protected class.... In these cases of oppressor and oppressed, or of a class protected by statute, the one may recover from the other, notwithstanding that both have been parties to the illegal contract."

这个非法例外已经在本章之 1.3 段介绍 Kiriri Cotton Co Ltd v. Dewani(1960)2 WLR 127 枢密院先例时有详尽介绍。另在本章之 3.2.3 段中也介绍了其他先例,如 Anandh v. Barnet Primary Health Care Trust(2004)EWCA Civ 5 上诉庭先例等,不在此重复叙述。

11. 分割非法部分理论

鉴于 Holman v. Johnson(1775)1 Cowp 341 先例对非法的"公序良俗测试"法律规则太极端与欠缺弹性,加上涉及太广与判决只能是一刀切去接受或不接受非法抗辩,经常导致不少涉及非法的案件难以得出令审理法官满意与感觉到是公平合理的判决。比如去接受明知是罪魁祸首的被告,可以非法抗辩取巧去成功霸占原告的好处。

这样,为了不让非法理论过度影响合约有效性,很早就已经有了分割合约(severance)的非法部分不予协助执行,但剩余合法部分法院仍协助执行的做法。这种做法丝毫不违背非法理论,但同时不会去"滥杀",让合约的少许非法部分杀死整份合约。如果能分割开,就可以挽救剩下的有效部分认为仍然可以执行。

11.1 分割非法部分以免"滥杀"合约合法部分的有效性

在很多早期先例中就已经有分割非法部分的做法,如在 Chesman v. Nainby (1726)2 Ld Raym 1456 先例判词中说:"if a bond is given, with condition to do several things, and some are agreeable to law, and some against the common law; the bond shall be good as to the doing the things agreeable to law, and only void as to those that are against the law."

另在 Pickering v. Ilfracombe Railway Co(1868) LR 3 CP 235 先例中, Willes 大法官说:"Where you cannot sever the illegal from the legal part of a covenant, the contract is altogether void; but, where you can sever them, whether the illegality be created by statute or by the common law, you may reject the bad part and retain the good."

有一些古老案件,还涉及立法非法与普通法非法的区别,立法非法的情况下就不能分割。但在今天看来,这应该仍然是解释立法的问题。毕竟解释立法到底禁止什么之后,会是对某类合约完全的禁止(显然此时在立法规定下就不存在法院的分割),或者只是对特定条文的禁止,或者可能只是禁止特定人士不得执行合约权利。在《Chitty on Contracts》(2021 年,第 34 版)一书之 18 - 253 段中这样说:"It was laid down in some of the older cases that there is a distinction between a deed or condition which is void in part by statute and one which is void in part at common law. This distinction must now be understood to apply only to cases where as a matter of construction the statute enacts that an agreement or deed made in violation of its provisions shall be wholly void."

分割合约理论经常适用在各类限制贸易的竞业禁止条文(如 non-compete clauses/non-solicit clauses/non-disclosure clauses)的案件中,早期普通法就有针对。在今天,这类条文广泛出现在各类商业合约中,已经在本章之 1.4 段提到一些例子,如普通的雇佣合约,收/并购合约(被收/并购方被禁止另起炉灶设立竞争公司),供应货物或服务合约中的捆绑条文,不动产的限制性约定,知识产权的授权限制(如被授权人同意以一笔金钱为代价,不推销竞争公司的产品,或只在特定区域内销售)等。

又如禁止披露条文,在雇佣合约下很容易理解,公司显然不会希望自己的员工跳槽后将公司的机密带去给竞争对手,包括公司客户信息、公司战略等。但如果限制过分,如包括一些员工在工作过程中获得的经验、技巧,就可能构成限制贸易了。另在公司收/并购或专利买卖交易中,也是同样道理。在双方订立正式的合约前已经要向对方披露一些机密信息,此时披露的一方除了不希望对方使用这些信息与自己竞争外,也有必要禁止对方向任何第三人披露有关机密信息,此时就需要签订一份机密协议。或者是反过来,收/并购或专利买卖交易的买方除了上一段说的不希望卖方之后重起炉灶设立竞争公司之外,也不希望卖方向第三人披露有关信息与自己竞争,因此在最终的合约中设立一条禁止披露条文。这种机密协议或是禁止披露条文如果过分,限制了一些完全合理的情况,就可能构成限制贸易。这里不再进一步展开,关于什么是"机密信息"的写法可以是:"在机密情况下披露的、或双方根据合理的商业判断应理解为机密信息的,带有'机密'、'内参'或'由卖方、或其他第三人所有'标记的,与卖方或目标公司业务相关的所有商业、科技、营销或其他信息,包括但不限于专有技术、配方、数据、生产程序、工艺、产品设计、图纸、参数、图片、软件程序、样品等。卖方的代理、律师、会计师或其他顾问披露的保密信息也应视为由该方披露。"

在构成限制贸易时,虽然已经在本章之 8.1 段介绍不需要适用 Patel v. Mirza (2016) UKSC 42 后的违法理论的三阶段测试来考虑,而是有自己的一套标准考虑何时适用公共政策,以及何时能够满足公共政策要求的必要合理,但对于分割理论的做法,看来与一般非法理论的做法是一致的。在 Putsman v. Taylor (1927) 1 KB 637 先例中 Talbot 大法官这样说:"I know of no ground for saying that the law in this respect is not precisely the same as to contracts illegal as being in restraint of trade and contracts illegal in any other respect."

例如,雇佣合约早期就出现大量此类争议,在今天也仍然有大量是否属于限制贸易的案例。在这些案例中往往都有是否可以分割竞业禁止条文的争议,虽然分割理论不仅仅适用在雇佣合约中,但这类案例为能否分割带来大量的指引,今天有关分割的一些权威判法也出自雇佣合约案例。可以简单列举一些此类案例,如:Colgate v. Bacheler (1601) Cro Eliz 872; Chesman v. Nainby; Nordenfelt v. Maxim Nordenfelt Guns and Ammunition Co Ltd (1894) AC 535; Mason v. Provident Clothing and Supply Co Ltd (1913) AC 724; Attwood v. Lamont (1920) 3 KB 571; M&S Drapers v. Reynolds (1957) 1 WLR 9; Scully UK Ltd v. Lee (1998) IRLR 259; TFS Derivatives Ltd v. Morgan (2004) EWHC 3181 (QB); Thomas v. Farr Plc (2007) EWCA Civ 118; Intercall Conferencing Services Ltd v. Steer (2007) EWHC 519 (QB); Extec Screens & Crushers Ltd v. Rice (2007) EWHC 1043 (QB); Beckett Investment Management Group Ltd v. Hall (2007) EWCA Civ 613; Monster Vision UK Ltd v. McKie (2011) EWHC 3772 (QB); JM Finn & Co Ltd v. Holliday (2013) EWHC 3450 (QB); Croesus Financial Services Ltd v. Bradshaw (2013) EWHC 3685 (QB); Merlin Financial consultants Ltd v. Cooper (2014) EWHC 1196 (QB); Dyson Technology Ltd v. Pellerey (2015) EWHC 3000 (Ch); ICAP Management Services Ltd v. Berry (2017) EWHC 1321 (QB); Freshasia Foods Limited v. Jing Lu (2019) EWHC 638 (Ch); Tillman v. Egon Zehnder (2019) UKSC 32 等。

11.2 限制贸易/竞业禁止条文

已经在本章之 1.4 段简单介绍限制贸易的公共政策,以及普通法下限制贸易的条文属于表面无效(prima facie void)的条文,只限于保护合法利益所必要的内容才会有效与被法院支持:见 Mitchel v. Reynolds (1711) 1 PWms 181 先例与 Nordenfelt v.

Maxim Nordenfelt Guns and Ammunition Co(1894)AC 535 先例。不仅在过去几百年时间里限制贸易条文(restraint of trade clause)的案例无数，在 2019 年至 2021 的短短几年间，还陆续有三个案件上诉到最高院。它们是：(1) Tillman v. Egon Zehnder (2019)UKSC 32 先例(涉及雇佣合约下的竞业禁止条文)权威性针对分割理论，并明确推翻了这方面的 Attwood v. Lamont(1920)3 KB 571 上诉庭先例；(2) Peninsula Securities Ltd v. Dunnes Stores(Bangor)Ltd(2020)UKSC 36 最高院先例[涉及商场开发商为吸引重要的锚定租户(anchor tenant)而限制其他店铺入驻的限制性约定]，权威性针对何时需要考虑限制贸易理论；(3) Harcus Sinclair LLP v. Your Lawyers Ltd (2021)UKSC 32 最高院先例(涉及一个预期将会针对德国大众汽车公司的集体诉讼，律师事务所之间承诺除非获得对方同意否则不得抢集体诉讼的原告受害人，而这承诺是否属于限制竞争的争议)。可见，这方面在今天仍是普通法非常重要的课题，与商业活动尤其关系密切。

笔者可以一个简单的对比，显示限制贸易理论的必要性。如果是限制人身自由(physical restraint)，如雇主把雇员关在工厂里，不准他和自己的竞争对手接触，这显然非法且不会被现代社会接受。而如果换成以合约限制雇员，例如一辈子只能为自己工作，辞职就必须退休，这虽然不是人身监禁，但实质上是一样的效果，所以也必须加以限制。

11.2.1　限制贸易理论何时适用

如果适用限制贸易理论，就会导致有关条文表面无效，依赖条文申请救济(典型的做法就是申请禁令阻止另一方的竞争行为)的申请人必须证明条文是保护合法利益所必要的内容。但问题是什么时候应该算作限制了贸易，需要适用该理论？毕竟广泛地来说，合约本身就是限制合约双方必须在互相之间进行有关的交易，但显然不是所有合约都需要当事人来证明合理性。限制贸易公共政策要保护的是对整个社会而言的公共利益。而至于订立合约的个人，如果事后反悔自己订立的合约，就动辄以限制贸易理论来要求对方证明合理性是不应该被允许的。

也因此限制贸易理论并非一致在所有不同合约中都适用，需要根据具体案件情况来判断。但是普通法下看来刻意没有给出明确的标准。例如在 Esso Petroleum Co Ltd v. Harper's Garage(Stourport)Ltd(1968)AC 269 贵族院先例中，Reid 勋爵说他不会试图划出何时适用的分水岭："would not attempt to define the dividing line between the contracts which are and contracts which are not in restraint of trade..." Wilberforce 勋爵也说："...no exhaustive test can be stated-probably no precise non-exhaustive test."

在近期的 Peninsula Securities Ltd v. Dunnes Stores(Bangor)Ltd(2020)UKSC 36 最高院先例中，Wilson 勋爵说："... the common law had often thrived on ambiguity; that, even if it were possible, it would be mistaken to try to crystallise the rules of the doctrine into neat propositions; and that the doctrine had to be applied to factual situations with a broad and flexible rule of reason.... ."

这带来了很多并不足够明确的“灰色地带”，甚至这方面的法律被称为不肯定与有疏漏（“uncertain and porous”）。关键是要根据具体合约的内容与性质，判断在公共政策下是否应该要求证明有关禁止贸易条文内容的合理性。例如，有关条文是否本就是该合约涉及的行业内与社会上普遍接受的措辞/文字与内容、也没有什么特别之处（如时间非同一般的长或限制的范围特别广等），是否损害了社会上的公共利益（如有益于社会的技术被限制不得发展等），有关合约的订立过程中是否存在压迫，双方谈判地位或知识水平是否对等问题。

对这方面问题，可以节录 Carr 大法官在 Quantum Actuarial LLP v. Quantum Advisory Ltd（2021）EWCA Civ 227 上诉庭先例中总结的 8 个原则，并区别如下：

1. “The doctrine is not confined to immutable boundaries or rigid categorisation, but there are certain categories of covenants to which the doctrine traditionally applies, in particular those by which an employee undertakes not to compete with his employer after leaving the employer's service and those by which a trader who has sold his business agrees not thereafter to compete with the purchaser of the business. The doctrine has been held to apply to franchise agreements, share-purchase agreements and the assignment of a patent;”

限制贸易理论的适用不限于特定类型的合约，也难以明确地分类哪些合约会适用。传统上经常适用的情况，包括雇佣合约中的雇员允诺在离职后不会与雇主竞争，以及收/并购交易后被收/并购一方（主要是公司的董事、高管）允诺不会与收/并购一方竞争等。今天还常见的适用情况，包括特许经营协议不允许被授权人在特许经营终止后从事竞争业务，收购股权后出售方限制竞争，专利授权与转让等案件中的各类限制等。

2. “There are no clear limits on the scope of the doctrine and no precise or exhaustive test can be stated. The doctrine is to be applied to factual situations with a broad and flexible rule of reason … The question is whether or not in all the circumstances the contract should be excluded from the application of the doctrine or, as Lord Wilberforce put it in Esso[89] … whether it is appropriate to dispense the contract ‘from the necessity of justification under a public policy test of reasonableness’;”

具体什么时候适用限制贸易理论，并没有精确、能全面适用在所有案件的测试标准，也不会限于一些特定类型的合约。需要看具体案件的事实情况，根据公共政策来看是否不需要让当事人证明合理性。

3. “Contractual restraining provisions which are of a sort which have become part of the accepted machinery of a type of transaction which have generally been found acceptable and necessary-reflecting the accepted and normal currency of commercial or contractu-

---

〔89〕 这是指 Esso Petroleum Co Ltd v. Harper's Garage（Stourport）Ltd（1968）AC 269 贵族院先例。

al conveyancing relations-will generally fall outside the scope of the doctrine…；”

如果在有关行业中，这种限制性约定属于被广泛认为必要与被接受的机制，就一般不会适用限制贸易理论。在 Peninsula Securities Ltd v. Dunnes Stores（Bangor）Ltd 最高院先例中称之为“交易社会测试”（trading society test）[90]。

但是，交易社会测试是很模糊的，对于什么是行业内认为必要、被接受的机制、什么时候就有特别之处等问题都有非常大的可解释的空间。而且会有案件跨行业，或者有的行业本身非常狭窄或是新型/专精，导致根本没有这些机制，岂不是变成每一个当事人之间量身定制、根据具体情况拟定的条文，都必须证明条文的合理性，证明合理性本来就是昂贵且结果不肯定、不稳定。在 Quantum Actuarial LLP v. Quantum Advisory Ltd 先例中 Carr 大法官也明确说这并非一个普适的测试标准：“Whilst it is clear that the Supreme Court in Peninsula Securities rejected the ‘pre-existing freedom’ test[91] in the context of the doctrine as a whole …，I reject the submission that at the same time it laid down the ‘trading society’ test… as the single test of universal application in determining whether or not the doctrine is engaged.”

针对这方面问题不妨举两个近期先例作为例子来说明。

（1）Peninsula Securities Ltd v. Dunnes Stores（Bangor）Ltd 最高院先例中涉及的是地产开发商与锚定租户（anchor tenant）之间关于商场内店铺租赁的限制性约定。在购物中心的开发中，通常都会找一些知名度高、声誉良好的公司（如大型连锁商店、超市等）进驻作为锚定租户，甚至后续的开发建造、寻找后续租户都会围绕这些锚定租户来进行。锚定租户往往租用面积大、租期长，也能够吸引到大量人流，尤其是有助于吸引后续小商户进驻租赁。因此锚定租户对于开发商而言非常重要，也会有较强的谈判力量。而此先例中开发商找到了被告（北爱尔兰著名的超市 Dunnes Stores）作为锚定租户进驻，被告除了拿到较为便宜的租金外，也成功加入限制性约定，在购物中心中不允许有其他超过 3000 平方英尺的销售食品或服装的店铺，这样在此购物中心就不会有其他竞争对手抢生意。数年后，购物中心生意并没有发展起来（人流不高、拉不到好的商户入驻租赁等），开发商把问题怪罪在与被告之间的限制性约定上，就向法院申请救济宣告限制性约定因为限制贸易非法而无效/不可执行。最高院就认定这类商业地产开发与锚定租户的交易中，通常都会加入限制性约

---

[90] Wilson 勋爵这样说“… provisions of contracts which reflected the accepted and normal currency of commercial relations had come to fall outside the scope of the doctrine because，moulded under the pressures of negotiation，competition and public opinion，they had assumed a form which satisfied the test of public policy as understood at that time.”

[91] 过去一度有 Esso Petroleum Co Ltd v. Harper’s Garage（Stourport）Ltd（1968）AC 269 贵族院先例判只有在条文中一方当事人放弃了原本享有的自由才涉及限制贸易。换言之，如果当事人根本没有放弃任何贸易的自由，或者放弃的内容原本就不是当事人可以享有的权利，就根本谈不上限制贸易，这也被称为“既有自由测试”（pre-existing freedom test）。

定保护锚定租户的利益,此先例中的限制性约定也没有任何特别之处导致需要根据限制贸易理论让被告证明属于必要合理。所以原告败诉。

(2)在 Quantum Actuarial LLP v. Quantum Advisory Ltd 先例中,一批会计、精算等专业人士开创了一系列公司(统称 Quad)专门从事养老保险基金的管理、精算等业务。后来一位主要创始人 Coombes 先生想要拓展公司业务领域,但其他人士不愿意拓展,这样导致公司需要重组与分家。而在 Quad 中 Coombes 先生的股权占比太高,难以买断,大家也有保护现有公司已经建立起来的商誉与客户群等商业考虑,因此解决办法是不愿意扩张的人士设立一家新公司(Quantum Actuarial LLP, LLP)接收 Quad 现有的人员团队、办公场所等资源,而 Quad 老客户的服务会被外包给 LLP。LLP 与 Quad 之间签订服务协议,Quad 向客户收取服务费用后按比例分给 LLP。Coombes 先生则购买与接手 Quad 的股权并整合成自己的公司(Quantum Advisory Ltd),按自己的意图发展。这样做对 Coombes 先生的重要好处就是仍然可以收到过去 Quad 老客户的收益,对 LLP 的好处则是不需要"白手起家",有一整套已经建立好的团队与资源,也有前期的稳定收入,方便开发后续的新客户。

也能想到,在服务协议中有限制性约定,在合约期与解约后 1 年内 LLP 不得绕过利润分配约定直接与 Quad 老客户签约。但问题是最后签订的服务协议的期限被约定为 99 年。这样在双方履约多年后,LLP 的合伙人大多都已经"换血"变成新合伙人,新合伙人对服务协议非常不满,毕竟工作都是 LLP 在做,但却要分利润出去,而且更关键的是这份合约期限很长,岂不是这么长时间都是 LLP 在为别人打工。因此 LLP 主张条文限制贸易而无效/不可执行。

上诉庭就认为此先例中这种量身定制的合约,尽管不会在行业中有什么惯常标准做法,但在性质上与收/并购交易中出售公司的情况有类似之处。而且尤其考虑到双方当事人都是有经验与水平的商业人士、谈判力量对等;合约的签订是当事人之间为了 Quad 的重组量身定制的条文;合约期限改为 99 年后,也给了 LLP 充足的时间与机会考虑,LLP 经过深思熟虑后选择接受;从商业背景来看,限制性约定也符合双方的利益;而且当事人在当时的书信往来中也显示均认可这样的安排公平合理等。在这个基础上认定公共政策下没什么理由需要适用限制贸易理论让 Coombes 先生或 Quad/Quantum Advisory Ltd 证明合理性。[92]

4. "Determining whether contractual restraints fall outside the range of a normal commercial contract imposing restrictions on a contracting party's ability to carry on a business activity is a question of evaluating all the relevant factors to be assessed cumulatively …;"

什么时候合约条文不属于一般、正常的商业合约限制,需要考虑完整的事实背景。例如,Proactive Sports Management Ltd v. Rooney(2011)EWCA Civ 1444 先例中,

---

〔92〕 此先例中也判即使限制贸易理论适用,有关条文也会被认为有合理性。

涉及作为被告的著名足球明星鲁尼在17岁时与原告Proactive签订肖像权代理合约,让Proactive开发、利用他的肖像权。之后双方关系破裂,Proactive向鲁尼追讨拖欠的分成。争议之一是合约中约定的很多限制是否构成限制贸易,如没有Proactive同意鲁尼不得找其他人开发利用,鲁尼在合约期间内所有的广告、代理等肖像权收益均要按比例向Proactive分成,如果鲁尼提前解约要支付高昂补偿金等。这类条文在肖像权代理合约中并不罕见,也是惯常做法,但问题是法院认定此代理合约时间长达8年,远远超出了一般正常肖像权代理合约的时间,再加上签约时鲁尼年仅17岁,鲁尼与帮助他订立合约的父母都不谙法律与商业知识,没有经验,也没有律师代表或获取独立法律意见等。综合之下法院判这超出了一般该类合约中的限制的情况,因此限制贸易理论适用,公司必须证明有关条文是必要合理才有效。

5. "The assessment of application of the doctrine is to be carried out by reference to the position as at the time that the contract is made(not by reference to subsequent performance and events)...;"

考虑是否适用限制贸易理论,要看订约时的事实情况。例如同样是著作权、肖像权等代理开发协议,约定的违约金是年收入的2%(举例),而这是行业惯常做法,但因为有关的作品或明星出名后收入变为天文数字,导致代理协议解约时要付很大一笔钱,但订约后发生的事情不是要考虑的问题。

6. "The application depends less on legal niceties or theoretical possibilities than on the practical effect of the restraint in hampering the freedom to trade... It is a question of substance not form;"

是否真的限制了贸易,要看是否实际产生了影响,而不是一些法律细节或者是理论上的可能性,形式上是否有限制不重要。例如在Stenhouse Australia v. Phillips (1974) AC 391枢密院先例中,保险公司的前雇员与保险公司约定,在一定时间内如果招揽自己在保险公司就职时的旧客户,需要退还在职时赚取的佣金的一半,从措辞/文字上并没有"限制"或禁止前雇员抢客户,但在实际效果上是一样。

7. "The doctrine can apply to restraints operating during the currency of the contract, as well as post-contractually. However, the distinction between pre-and post-termination restraints is not without relevance. The fact that a restraint is limited to the period of the contract may be a factor in favour of excluding the doctrine(or a factor to be brought into account on the side of justification)...;"

限制并不区分是在合约期间的限制或合约结束后的限制。但是相比之下合约期内的限制更容易被认为是合理的,也能想得到合约结束后的限制是更大地影响了对方自由。

8. "As already set out above, where the doctrine applies, the contractual restraints are prima facie unenforceable but all, whether partial or total, are enforceable if reasonable."

如果限制贸易理论适用,后果就是表面不可执行。只有限制权一方在证明条文合理性后才可以被依赖与请求救济。

11.2.2 如何判断必要合理

已经介绍过限制贸易理论的核心问题是贸易自由(freedom to trade)与订约自由(freedom to contract)的冲突,在当事人的订约自由与不能因此危害公共利益之间找到平衡点。这也逐渐变成了今天的标准:(1)对双方当事人而言只限于保护必要合理私人的合法利益;(2)对于社会而言不应该影响第三人利益、公共利益。在 Nordenfelt v. Maxim Nordenfelt Guns and Ammunition Co(1894)AC 535 先例中,Macnaghten 勋爵说:"reasonable, that is, in reference to the interests of the parties concerned and reasonable in reference to the interests of the public, so framed and so guarded as to afford adequate protection to the party in whose favour it is imposed, while at the same time it is no way injurious to the public."

也因此在绝大部分情况中,如果当事人地位与谈判力量也对等,经过商业考虑后达成的合约,法院是尽量不希望事后以自己客观看待之下是否合理,来替代当事人在订约时的想法。也因此过往先例中显示出会考虑的因素非常多,包括商业行为的类型与社会对这类限制的认知与接受程度,是否有其他不需要如此广泛的保护方式,对于限制是否会有额外补偿,限制的时间长短,双方之间的谈判力量是否对等,限制贸易的条文是否是格式合约中的条文,限制是否仅限于合约履行期间还是会在合约履行完毕后继续限制,整个合约的背景事实等:见 Nordenfelt v. Maxim Nordenfelt Guns and Ammunition Co;Esso Petroleum Co Ltd v. Harper's Garage(Stourport)Ltd(1968)AC 269;Stenhouse Australia v. Phillips(1974)AC 391;A Schroeder Music Publishing Co Ltd v. Macaulay(1974)1 WLR 1308;Office Angels Ltd v. Rainer Thomas and O'Connor(1991)IRLR 214;Panayiotou v. Sony Music Entertainment(1994)EMLR 229;Quantum Actuarial LLP v. Quantum Advisory Ltd(2021)EWCA Civ 227;Dwyer(UK Franchising)Ltd v. Fredbar Ltd(2022)EWCA Civ 889 等先例。

具体考虑的方法,近期的 Harcus Sinclair LLP v. Your Lawyers Ltd(2021)UKSC 32 最高院先例跟从了 Macnaghten 勋爵的说法,给出了两个大原则:(1)对当事人之间而言,有关限制合理,这包括限制竞争的承诺是保护了被承诺人的合法利益(legitimate interests),有关的限制是保护这些合法利益所合理必要(necessary),以及承诺愿意被限制是否与承诺人获得的利益相称(commensurate)。(2)对社会而言,对其中一方的限制并不会影响社会大众的利益。

多数意见(Briggs 勋爵、Hamblen 勋爵与 Burrows 勋爵)的判词可以节录如下:"The first principle is that it is for the promisee … to establish that the non-compete undertaking is reasonable as between the parties. To satisfy this burden, the promisee must show, first, that the non-compete undertaking protects legitimate interests of the promisee and, secondly, that the non-compete undertaking goes no further than is reasonably necessary to protect those interests. There also appears to be a third element which the courts below in this case ... referred to as the promisee needing to show that the restriction is commensurate with the benefits secured to the promisor under the contract. ...The second principle is that, if the promisee succeeds in establishing that the non-compete undertaking is reasonable as between the parties, the burden shifts to the promisor to establish that the undertaking is unreasonable as being contrary to the public interest."

另外,被承诺人可去保护的合法利益并不限于合约中约定的利益,而是更广义的可能会有的利益。在最高院的判词中这样说:"In determining the legitimate interests of the promisee one can take into account what the parties (objectively) intended or contemplated, consequent on the contract, at the time the contract was made as well as the contract terms."

这可以 Harcus Sinclair LLP v. Your Lawyers Ltd 先例说明。原告律师事务所准备针对大众汽车提起集体诉讼,而被告律师事务所是一家著名的有大量集体诉讼经验的律师事务所,因此原告想要与被告合作。在尚未具体谈妥合作协议时,原告与被告共享部分信息与一些工作成果,为了保证机密性与被告签订协议保密,而且为了不让被告了解情况后就把原告一脚踢开自己主导集体诉讼,被告在协议中承诺在没有原告批准的情况下不会接受来自此集体诉讼任何当事人的委托。后来被告仍然拉拢了大量客户,并主张协议下此条文限制贸易而无效/不可执行。在上诉庭的判法就认为原告与被告并未达成合作协议,没有合约约定的利益,就没有合法利益,但这被最高院驳回。合法利益包括的不仅仅是合约下的利益,而是广泛地包括意图或预期可能会有的任何合法利益。此先例中也就是虽然目前双方仅仅签订保密协议,还没有签订合作协议约定如何分配工作及集体诉讼客户的委托与收益,但签订保密协议后原告已经可以预期很可能可以作为主导的律师事务所开始集体诉讼,这已经足够是合法利益。可以根据这个广义的合法利益考虑限制被告的有关条文是否合理。因此最高院判有关条文并非限制贸易且可以被执行。

11.2.3 条文的分割

也正是因为在这类案件中,需要看有关条文是否必要合理,因此产生了非常多部分条文属于必要合理,而又有部分不合理的情况。这会限制贸易的条文中常常涉及限制的时间、地域范围、行业种类等"过分"的情况。而一旦"过分",这些不合理的部分如果不能从限制贸易的条文中分割,就会导致整个限制贸易条文失效,连本来可以合理保护的部分也失效。甚至如果限制贸易条文无法整个从合约中分割,就可能污染整个合约导致整个合约都失效。在《Chitty on Contracts》(2021 年,第 34 版)一书之 18-123 段中有:"Unless the reasonable term can be severed from the rest of the contract to protect the contract from failing as a whole or the objectional parts of the clause can be severed from the rest of the clause, the entire contract is unenforceable."

例如常见的雇佣合约中的竞业禁止条文,限制性约定雇主在职期间及离职后一定时间不得在一定区域内从事竞争性行业。这里涉及了好几个不同与起直接冲突的公共政策/公共利益:(1) 不能剥夺雇主在离职或被解雇后的就业谋生与其他方面的人身自由,如工作自由。(2) 不能让雇主妨碍社会进步,严重限制有能力或有特殊技术的雇员工作或发展、为社会创造财富。(3) 当然也要保障雇主的商业机密、商业关系(如客户名单、供应商等)与维持雇员的稳定(如不必怕在花费大量精力/财力培训雇员后,被同行高薪挖走)等的合理/合法利益。(4)如果不允许雇主订立这些限制性条文,会导致雇主倾向于只雇佣少数值得信任的人士,减少了就业机会,也减少了雇员的发展机会。

实际上大部分的雇主拟定的条文都是"过分"的。这也不只是雇主偷懒,"一刀切"地订立一些格式化的雇佣合约。而是要求雇主能够在权衡了所有有关的公共政策后掌握轻重,拟定一条恰到好处的竞业禁止条文是不现实的。所以法院在面对这种对雇员是不合理与违反公共政策的条文时,如果简单地否定,拒绝协助雇主执行,就会忽视了雇主的合法利益,这也是公共利益的一部分。

也因此在限制贸易的领域,发展了有弹性的判断标准与做法,尤其是大量发展了分割非法部分的理论,在一条"过分"与"一刀切"的竞业禁止条文中分割一些法院视为违反对雇员保护的公共政策的部分内容。如果无法分割一条不合理的条文,法院才否定与不协助执行。这套做法与一般商业合约非法部分的分割理论也是一致的。

这些大量先例的案情虽然涉及不同的背景事实,但本质上换汤不换药。例如,一条竞业禁止条文中规定离职雇员"不允许在北京、上海、深圳开展同类业务",但法院认为雇员只是在北京受聘,业务也在北京展开,因此这地域限制并非必要合理。就可以划掉不合理部分[见本章之 11.5.1 段的"蓝色铅笔测试"(blue pencil test)],变成"不允许在北京、上海、深圳开展同类业务"。作为对比,如果条文是禁止"在全球开展同类业务",此时法院无法划掉"全球",也不能重写(rewrite)雇佣合约,以"北京"替代"全球"。这样法院就只能否定与不协助执行这一条不合理与违反公共政策的竞业禁止条文了。

在新西兰已经有立法针对,赋予法院裁量权完全改写/重写一条不合理的限制贸易条文或竞业禁止条文。在《Contract and Commercial Law Act 2017》之 Section 83 中说:"**83 Restraints of trade** (1) The court may, if a provision of a contract constitutes an unreasonable restraint of trade,—(a) delete the provision and give effect to the contract as amended; or (b) modify the provision so that, at the time the contract was entered into, the provision as modified would have been reasonable, and give effect to the contract as modified; or (c) decline to enforce the contract if the deletion or modification of the provision would so alter the bargain between the parties that it would be unreasonable to allow the contract to stand. (2) The court may modify a provision even if the modification cannot be effected by deleting words from the provision."

由于什么是必要合理要看审理法官的态度与看法。因此很多这类条文都会加入一条明示条文允许分割(severability clause)。这虽然是重复了法律默示的地位,但强调了希望在审理时应该尽量予以分割，避免“一刀切”地判全部条文可执行或不可执行。例如在 Tillman v. Egon Zehnder(2019) UKSC 32 最高院先例中，有关雇佣合约就有一条分割条文，专门约定如果竞业禁止条文中有任何部分被认为不合理限制贸易而无效，允许分割、删除不合理部分，以使剩下条文可执行：“If any of the restrictions or obligations contained in this clause 13(包括竞业禁止条文在内的条文) is held not to be valid as going beyond what is reasonable for the protection of the goodwill and interest of the company … but would be valid if part of the wording were deleted, then such restriction or obligation shall apply with such modifications as may be necessary to make it enforceable.”

这也给了审理法院更高的责任解释是否可以分割，如果法院作出决定不可以分割，要令竞业禁止条文甚至整份合约不可执行/没有意义，就要给出更多与更有说服力的理由。

11.3　雇佣合约与商业合约的不同对待

一般来说，对于商业合约中出现非法部分时，法院往往愿意分割非法部分，让剩余合约内容得到执行。在 Carney v. Herbert(1985) AC 301 枢密院先例中 Brightman 勋爵就提出一般大原则是，如果一份合法合约中的部分内容或条文非法，但只是原告的独家利益(如该非法条文是给原告一个选择权，但这是违反某立法)，原告放弃，[93] 只要求法院协助执行合法部分内容，就可以得到执行：“Subject to a caveat that it is undesirable, if not impossible, to lay down any principles which will cover all problems in this field, their Lordships venture to suggest that, **as a general rule**, where parties enter into a lawful contract of, for example, sale and purchase, and **there is an ancillary provision which is illegal but exists for the exclusive benefit of the plaintiff, the court** may and probably will, if the justice of the case so requires, and there is no public policy objection, **permit the plaintiff if he so wishes to enforce the contract without the illegal provision.**”(加黑部分是笔者的强调)

但在不允许不合理限制贸易的公共政策下，法院会根据具体的行业状况、对限制的接受程度来判断是否合理。而对于不同类型的行业也能想到就会有不一样的态度。在 Quantum Actuarial LLP v. Quantum Advisory Ltd(2021) EWCA Civ 227 上诉庭先例中，Carr 大法官说：“How these freedoms are reconciled may depend on the type of contract in question. By way of example, between employer and employee, the court more jealously guards the freedom of an employee to earn a livelihood elsewhere; in other cases, more weight is given to the ‘policy of the law that contracts freely entered into should, prima facie, be enforced’.”

---

〔93〕 有关条文是一方单方面的权利或利益可以提前放弃的课题，可参阅笔者的《合约的履行、弃权与禁反言》一书第三章之 3.3.4 段。

而在以上节录段落就提到在不少早期案件中,都出现了大量法院对待雇佣合约中竞业禁止条文是否可分割,比一般商业合约更严格的判法。这是因为在当时的公共政策下,是同情处在弱势地位、没有立法与/或工会保护的普通雇员。他们在面对强势雇主时没什么选择而被迫接受签订严苛的竞业禁止条文,而这些非常过分的条文并非为了保护雇主合理的商业利益,而是为了强迫雇员永远没法离职。例如,条文约定雇员在离职后在全球永远不能在同样与相关行业为同业的公司工作或自己创业。雇员一旦离职就失去了主要谋生手段,想要推翻雇佣合约中的竞业禁止条文,就被迫开始昂贵而漫长的诉讼争辩。这对一般的普通中下级雇员而言是过于困难,属于限制贸易的非法。雇主的心态是既然可以分割,与其在订约时对不同雇员量身定制一条适合的条文,不如"漫天开价",反正雇员大多不敢或没有条件开始一个昂贵的诉讼,雇主的目的就可以得逞。即使开始诉讼,至多就是法院将其余不合理的部分分割出来不可执行,雇主也没有什么损失。因此为了有利于保护往往处在弱势地位的雇员,在雇主订立的竞业禁止条文过于广泛、超出合理必要时,倾向于解释说整个竞业禁止条文非法与无效/不可执行。在 Mason v. Provident Clothing and Supply Co Ltd(1913)AC 724 贵族院先例中,Moulton 勋爵说:"It was suggested in the argument that even if the covenant was, as a whole, too wide, the Court might enforce restrictions which it might consider reasonable …, provided they were within its ambit. My Lords, I do not doubt that **the Court may**, and in some cases will, **enforce a part of a covenant in restraint of trade, even though taken as a whole the covenant exceeds what is reasonable**…. It would in my opinion be pessimi exempli if, when an employer had exacted a covenant deliberately framed in unreasonably wide terms, the Courts were to come to his assistance and, by applying their ingenuity and knowledge of the law, carve out of this void covenant the maximum of what he might validly have required. It must be remembered that **the real sanction at the back of these covenants is the terror and expense of litigation, in which the servant is usually at a great disadvantage**, in view of the longer purse of his master. … the hardship imposed by the exaction of unreasonable covenants by employers would be greatly increased if they could continue the practice with the expectation that, having exposed the servant to the anxiety and expense of litigation, the Court would in the end enable them to obtain everything which they could have obtained by acting reasonably. It is evident that those **who drafted this covenant aimed at making it a penal rather than a protective covenant**, and that they hoped by means of it to paralyse the earning capabilities of the man if and when he left their service, and were not thinking of what would be a reasonable protection to their business, …"(加黑部分是笔者的强调)

但到了今天,看来这非常偏向雇员的地位又已经不完全一样。不少法院的判例中都显示出了对雇主多少有点矫枉过正的味道。在 Tillman v. Egon Zehnder(2019)

UKSC 32 最高院先例中，Wilson 勋爵就提到在绝大部分情况下，公司的普通雇员是无力对抗且只能接受公司强加的这类条文。但有时候涉及的是非常高级别的雇员，例如已经是公司的董事总经理，此时与公司签订协议时通常有足够的谈判地位和能力保护自己的利益。Wilson 勋爵说："**High-ranking employees can do particular damage to the legitimate interests of their employers following termination of their employment**；and it may be that，when they enter into their post-employment covenants，they are able to negotiate with their employers on nearly an equal footing.... It is clearly common practice for an employer to present a prospective employee with a substantial written contract，many terms of which，including those imposing post-employment restraints...It is as valid in 2019 as it was in 1913 to infer that most prospective employees will not be able，even if minded，to decline to accept such terms，still less，following the end of their employment，to defend a claim that they are in breach of them. **The courts must continue to adopt a cautious approach to the severance of post-employment restraints.**"（加黑部分是笔者的强调）

也因此可以说法院的态度仍然是要保护弱势雇员，但已经不太会像早期先例一样采取截然不同的判断标准对待是否可分割的问题，特别是在涉及高级与强势的雇员时。在 T Lucas & Co Ltd v. Mitchell（1974）Ch 129；Sadler v. Imperial Life Assurance Co of Canada Ltd（1988）IRLR 388；Beckett Investment Management Group Ltd v. Hall（2007）EWCA Civ 613；Tillman v. Egon Zehnder 等先例中均允许分割雇佣合约中的竞业禁止条文。无论是雇佣合约还是商业合约，是否可分割的关键问题都是能否满足本章之 11.5 段介绍的三个条件，在判断标准上应该是一致的。

11.4　早期的 Attwood 标准

在早期对大量竞业禁止条文采用了各种非常严苛的标准，一般都不允许分割。看来是当时在公共政策下较为同情处在弱势地位的雇员，他们在面对强势雇主时没什么选择而被迫签订严苛的竞业禁止条文，这些非常过分的条文并非为了保护合理的商业利益，因此不怀好意的雇主就必须承担这类条文不容易分割的后果。也是想要推动社会进步，不允许雇主偷懒，"一刀切"地订立一些格式化的雇佣合约，让弱势的雇员因此受到严重限制。而且这样严苛的测试标准也配合允许竞业禁止条文是不得限制贸易大原则的例外的说法。

在 Mason v. Provident Clothing and Supply Co Ltd（1913）AC 724 贵族院先例中，雇佣合约下约定了竞业禁止条文，禁止雇员在雇主任何一个店铺周边 25 英里内从事竞争性行业，雇员被解雇后转投并不远的一家竞争公司，雇主就根据雇佣合约申请禁令阻止。贵族院 Moulton 勋爵提出针对分割问题可考虑的测试标准包括：（1）非常明确在措辞/文字上容易分割；（2）能分割的只是不重要（trivial importance）与仅仅是技术性（mere technical）的条文。这样其实能分割的情况就非常少了，而且既然要求不重要或仅仅技术性，在大部分情况下也看来不太会是争议的焦点问题。Moulton 勋爵说:"I do not doubt that the court may, and in some cases will, enforce a part of a covenant in restraint of trade, even though taken as a whole the covenant exceeds what is reasonable. But, in my opinion, that ought **only to be done in cases where the part so enforceable is clearly severable**, and even so **only in cases where the excess is of trivial importance, or merely technical, and not a part of the main purport and substance of the clause.**"(加黑部分是笔者的强调)

在 Attwood v. Lamont(1920)3 KB 571 先例中,雇主开了一家在英国小镇提供布艺、裁缝定制、服装等多种业务的商铺,雇佣了作为被告的雇员在裁缝部从事设计与度量的裁缝定制工作。雇佣协议中约定雇员离职后不得在小镇 10 英里内从事以下一系列广泛的业务:"... tailor, dressmaker, general draper, milliner, hatter, haberdasher, gentlemen's, ladies' or children's outfitter"雇员离职后确实在小镇 10 英里外开了一家裁缝定制店,但问题是该雇员到 10 英里内拉客户、接订单,雇主向法院申请禁令阻止。一审法院与二审[(1920)2 KB 146]的高院均认为这条文针对的业务过于广泛而不合理,但同时认为此条文中这些用逗号隔开的多种业务,可以进行分割,判允许保留禁止裁缝定制这一种业务,雇主也因此成功申请到禁令。

但这判法在上诉庭被驳回,上诉庭一致认为此条文不可分割。此先例中这种情况,虽然表面上布艺、裁缝、服装等不同业务放在一起并用逗号隔开,语句上可以分割。但是解释雇佣合约下的真实意思,是雇主不允许自己任何业务部门的雇员离职后与自己进行任何业务上的竞争,如果允许分割,就事实上改变了当事人的订约意图,变成新合约了。也因此尽管表面看来可分割,但法院可行使裁量权拒绝分割,此条文违反公共政策、法院不会给禁令的救济。Sterndale 勋爵说:"I think it is quite clear that this agreement was part of a scheme by which every head of a department was to be restrained from competition with the plaintiff even in the business of departments with which he had no connection and with the customers of which he was never brought into contact. If this be the true meaning of the agreement, it was, as it is described, an agreement not to trade in opposition and not an agreement to restrain the unfair use of secrets or knowledge of customers acquired by the servant in the employer's service. To effect this object the retention of the restraint to the business of all the departments is necessary, and I think that to strike out all but the tailoring department is not merely to remove one of several covenants, each directed to the legitimate object of preventing unfair competition, but to alter entirely the scope and intention of the agreement. It is thereby sought to be converted from an agreement to restrain general competition into an agreement which will conform to the requirements of the cases to which I have referred."

但已经在本章之 11.3 段介绍过,雇佣合约中严苛对待竞业禁止条文的态度已经有改变。这也带来了今天英国法下统一对待非法与违反公共政策时是否可分割的问题。

11.5 现在英国法的地位与测试标准

在早期允许分割条文的 S Nevanas & Co v. Walker and Foreman(1914)1 Ch 413 先例中,Sargant 大法官曾经说如果非常清楚本质上是针对两码事,只不过是被写在同一个条文,还是可以分割的:"I do not think that those remarks(本章上一段节录的 Moulton 勋爵的说法)were intended to be applicable to cases where the two parts of a covenant are expressed in such a way as to amount to a clear severance by the parties themselves, and as to be **substantially equivalent to two separate covenants**."(加黑部分是笔者的强调)

而在今天针对这方面的法律地位,主要是在 Sadler v. Imperial Life Assurance Co of Canada Ltd(1988)IRLR 388 先例中,Peter Crawford QC 大法官提出的三个条件的测试。该测试标准还得到了 Beckett Investment Management Group Ltd v. Hall(2007)EWCA Civ 613 上诉庭先例的认可,并且在较近期的 Tillman v. Egon Zehnder(2019)UKSC 32 最高院先例中得到确认。在本段后文内容中,也将区别针对这些问题分开讨论,但可以先简单介绍这几点区别是:

1. 不可执行的非法/违反公共政策部分可以直接删除而无需增补或修改剩余条文内容("the unenforceable provision is capable of being removed without the necessity of adding to or modifying the wording of what remains")。

2. 剩余条文仍然有足够对价支持("the remaining terms continue to be supported by adequate consideration")。

3. 在 Sadler v. Imperial Life Assurance Co of Canada Ltd 先例中说是删除不可执行部分不会改变原合约的性质("the removal of the unenforceable provision does not so change the character of the contract that it becomes 'not the sort of contract that the parties entered into at all.'")。在 Tillman v. Egon Zehnder 先例中说是删除条文后不会导致竞业禁止条文主要法律效果有重大改变("whether removal of the provision would not generate any major change in the overall effect of all the post-employment restraints in the contract.")。换言之,不能将有关部分分割之后,合约改头换面变成了新合约。

除此以外,在 Marshall v. NM Financial Management Ltd(1997)1 WLR 1527 上诉庭先例的一审[(1995)1 WLR 1461]中,Jonathan Sumption QC 大法官还加上也经常被考虑的第四个条件。

4. 分割条文的行为与认为有关部分非法背后的公共政策相互配合("the severance must be consistent with the public policy underlying the avoidance of the offending part")。或者换言之一旦涉及某些严重非法的公共政策,导致合约完全不能执行,不能通过分割条文来将合约合法化,如约定买凶杀人,不能仅仅删除买凶杀人的部分,而留下剩余部分。

另外需要特别指出的是，在对非法条文的分割方面，目前普通法也仍然处在积极的发展阶段，有不少问题都没有明确的答案。[94] 而且今天这类案件会非常依赖个案的情况如何，如当事人是否有做的不对的地方，或者是非法背后的公共政策如何等。从竞业禁止条文这类案件对待分割的态度上也可以看到，这非常依赖社会公共政策的大方向的变化，因此要结合具体公共政策做判断。对此仅节录《Illegality and Public Policy》（2020 年，第 5 版）一书之 19 - 26 段的说法如下："There is continuing scope for further judicial clarification of the doctrine of severance in illegality cases. There is, of course, an unavoidable degree of uncertainty resulting from the need to consider each contract individually. Nevertheless, this is one of those areas where the persistent reticence of the English judiciary with respect to the overt discussion of policy issues is particularly damaging. The temptation simply to manipulate formalistic tests, in order to produce a desired result, still has the potential to cause additional, avoidable, uncertainty."

11.5.1　条件之一：文字/措辞是否可以分割：蓝色铅笔测试

蓝色铅笔测试（blue pencil test）的说法可见 Attwood v. Lamont（1920）3 KB 571 上诉庭先例 Sterndale 勋爵的说法："...the severance can be effected when the part severed can be removed by running a blue pencil through it."

在 Sadler v. Imperial Life Assurance Co of Canada Ltd（1988）IRLR 388 先例与 Tillman v. Egon Zehnder（2019）UKSC 32 最高院先例中说，不可执行的部分可以直接删除而无需增补或修改剩余条文内容（"the unenforceable provision is capable of being removed without the necessity of adding to or modifying the wording of what remains"）。无需增补或修改剩余条文也是法院不应该重写合约的大原则，如果分割以后剩下部分说不通，必须进行增补或修改也就变成"重写"[95] 了。

在 Tillman v. Egon Zehnder 最高院先例中明确了蓝色铅笔测试作为是否可以分割的第一个条件，并同时说明除非立法改变法律地位，否则法院不会为了让合约剩下部分公平合理就重写合约。Wilson 勋爵说："The distinction is indeed settled. It is in-

---

[94] 例如，在本章后文中会讨论的主要都是在一份合约中，有条文或条文中的一部分涉及非法，是否可以将该条文或该条文的一部分分割出去，并仍然执行剩余部分的问题。但如果是涉及一个交易中的多个合约，如今天公司架构中常见的复杂结构，或者是各种工程合作项目中复杂得多合约互相配合的情况，如果是其中一份合约非法，是否"污染"并导致所有合约都非法等，这在目前看来都并没有明确解答，这会在本章之 12.3 段讨论。当然在笔者看来这会是非常类似于合约因为各种原因可使无效（如因为误述问题可使无效）时，是否会引起一连串交易中都可使无效的情况，这已经在本书第三章之 4 段介绍，不在这里重复。

[95] 虽然在 Transport North American Express Inc v. New Solutions Financial Corp（2004）1 SCR 248 加拿大最高院先例中，认为分割本身就是去重写双方当事人的非法合约了。另可见在本章之 11.2.3 段介绍的新西兰的《Contract and Commercial Law Act 2017》立法。

herent in the word ‘severance’ itself, which means cutting things up and does not extend to adding things in. The ‘blue pencil’ criterion is a significant brake on application of the principle; and, although it can work arbitrarily, it is in my view an appropriate brake on the ability of employers to secure severance of an unreasonable restraint customarily devised by themselves. Were it ever to be thought appropriate to confer on the court a power to rewrite a restraint so as to make it reasonable, it would surely have to be achieved by legislation.”

简单而言,就是单纯看是否能够用一支蓝色铅笔在条文中划去一部分。例如,在本章之11.2.3段提到的条文中规定了“不允许在北京开展同类业务”,用蓝色铅笔可以将上海与深圳划掉,变成“不允许在北京、上海、深圳开展同类业务”,这仍然说得通,不需要增补或修改任何其他内容,这就能通过蓝色铅笔测试。

相反,如果条文是“不允许在全中国开展同类业务”,用蓝色铅笔将“全中国”划掉,反而改变/增加“北京”,让剩余条文说得通与公平合理,这就是不能满足蓝色铅笔测试,也就是重写了合约内容。

可以再多举一个例子,如果条文中规定的是“雇主在上海陆家嘴的旗舰店周围25公里内不能开展同类业务”,即使法院认为这里规定的25公里过于广泛,5~10公里才是合理,但由于难以用蓝色铅笔划掉其中一部分,这就无法通过蓝色铅笔测试。

这样的做法也会有一些疑问,会需要弹性地对待。毕竟这是在解释合约,注重的应该是当事人的订约意图到底是什么。例如,如果写的是以陆家嘴为中心的25公里区域,但换成当事人分别列出了从近到远的地区,最终覆盖了整个25公里区域,前者无法通过蓝色铅笔测试,后者就能通过,看来就不太合理。当然可以说蓝色铅笔测试毕竟只是第一步、针对措辞/文字本身是否可分割的测试。这类问题看来也是过往先例中不允许单纯凭借蓝色铅笔测试来判断是否可分割的理由之一。在今天而言,这类问题完全可以根据删除后改变了当事人的目的、变成了一个新合约等理由来拒绝分割。

另外,虽然要求“无需增补或修改剩余条文内容”,但这也会被弹性对待,允许用被删除部分的内容来解释剩余条文。例如,在T Lucas & Co Ltd v. Mitchell(1974)Ch 129先例中,雇主是某种肉类生产添加剂的供应商,在雇佣合约中有一条竞业禁止条文,(1)前半句针对禁止交易(deal)该类产品,(2)后半句针对揽客或供应(solicit orders for or supply)该类产品。但问题是对产品的定义只写在了针对交易的前半句,而针对后半句揽客或供应只简单以“任何此类货物”替代。[96] 这样删除了前半句,

〔96〕 有关条文是:“within the allocated districts as existing at the termination of his employment **deal in any goods similar to or capable of being used in place of the allocated articles** or **solicit orders for or supply any such goods** to any person firm or company carrying on business within the allocated districts as existing at the termination of his employment…to whom the company has supplied any of the allocated articles during the 12 months preceding such determination.”(加黑部分是笔者的强调)

后半句就会需要增补才能说得通这里货物指代的到底是什么。法院仍然认为能够通过蓝色铅笔测试,因为虽然被分割的前半句已经不可执行,但被允许用来解释后半句内容。

11.5.2 条件之二:剩余部分仍然有对价支持

第二个条件就是剩余条文是否仍然有足够对价支持("the remaining terms continue to be supported by adequate consideration")。

对价是除了契约以外一般合约的要件,有关这方面问题可见《国际商务游戏规则:英国合约法》第二章。但对于非法合约的分割中的问题是,早期有一些案件涉及如果对价中有一部分非法,就会导致整个合约不被执行。但今天的法律地位是,即使对价涉及非法内容,在可以分割的前提下,只有被分割部分是其中一方当事人所给出的全部或主要对价,一旦被分割,剩余部分就没有足够对价支持,才会导致不允许分割。

可以节录《Chitty on Contracts》(2021 年,第 34 版)一书之 18 - 260 段如下:"Many of the older authorities laid down that if a contract was made on several considerations, one of which was illegal, the whole contract was unenforceable and severance was impossible. Such a test is unworkable and, as has been recognised in more modern decisions, the partial illegality, and hence unenforceability, is only relevant in one of two ways. First, the severance of the offending clause may so alter the scope of the whole contract as to make it a new contract. The true test under this head is therefore **whether illegal promise is substantially the whole or main consideration for the promise now sought to be enforced. If it is, then the court will not server it, leaving only a small part of the consideration to support the promise of the defendant; otherwise it may**."(加黑部分是笔者的强调)

在 Bennett v. Bennett(1952)1 KB 249 先例中,打算离婚的夫妻签订和解协议,约定丈夫向妻子(与子女)提供经济帮助,但妻子一方的对价是同意完全排除法院对于赡养费的管辖权(一般这类条文的写法可以简单是"任何一方不得向法院提起诉讼")。之后丈夫没有按约支付,妻子向法院申请要求丈夫按和解协议支付。英国公共政策下不允许完全排除法院管辖权,因此妻子提供的对价非法。但一旦允许分割非法部分,就变成妻子一方完全没有提供任何对价作为交换,因此无法将此非法部分从和解协议中分割,和解协议全部无法执行,妻子也因此可以向法院提起诉讼要求丈夫支付赡养费等而完全不受到和解协议的影响。

作为对比可见 Goodinson v. Goodinson(1954)2 QB 118 上诉庭先例,该先例与 Bennett v. Bennett 先例有非常类似的案情,只是当事人的和解协议中妻子除了同意排除法院管辖权外,还额外规定妻子需要补偿丈夫为了妻子而产生的债务。这样即使分割了非法部分,和解协议下妻子还仍然有其他对价作为交换,就足以支持剩余部分继续执行。

在 Alec Lobb v. Total Oil GB(1985)1 WLR 173 先例中,Dunn 大法官总结说:"… if the valid promises are supported by sufficient consideration, then the invalid promises can be severed from the valid even though the consideration also supports the invalid promises. On the other hand if the invalid promise is substantially the whole or main consideration for the agreement then there will be no severance."

有效合约中对价的要求并不高,不需要双方交换的对价相称,也因此有很多合约只要有名义上的对价就已经足够在法律上有效。也因此笔者看来在大部分情况中,关键还是解释合约,看被分割的部分是否属于"全部或主要对价",从而变成新合约。

例如,在竞业禁止条文中,一般而言雇员一方的对价主要是在受雇期间所提供的服务,而雇主作为交换的对价则是薪水、奖金等。涉及执行竞业禁止条文的时间,往往是在雇员离职后参与竞争工作时,此时雇员的对价早已经交换完成。即使分割了部分条文内容或完全分割了竞业禁止条文,也很难说雇员就完全没有对价。例如,在 Sadler v. Imperial Life Assurance Co of Canada Ltd(1988)IRLR 388 先例中,保险代理人(insurance agent)为保险人揽客拉生意,并会在被保险人前 10 年缴纳的保费中抽成,但有条件是一旦离职转投其他保险人,就不得继续抽成。代理人离职后仍然想要继续收取佣金,就主张此条件限制贸易应属非法并且可以分割,这个说法得到法院支持,法院在给出 3 个条件的测试标准时,针对对价问题指出从整个合约来看,代理人招揽客户是其主要对价,而此对价早已经交换,即使允许分割也不会影响剩余合约的对价问题。

类似案件还可见在 Marshall v. NM Financial Management Ltd(1997)1 WLR 1527 先例中也是保险代理人从招揽的被保险人支付的保费中抽成,在合约中约定条件必须是代理人离职后 1 年内不参与竞争工作,或者是代理人年满 65 岁则即使离职也可以继续抽成。此先例中代理人 40 岁离职后为其他保险人从事竞争工作。法院认定此条件属于限制竞争而非法,但是允许分割,道理一样是从整体上解释剩余合约有对价支持,并且早已经交换。

而且也能想到会有不同的情况,如高管/技术人员(或被收购公司的董事等情况),在雇佣合约中与对方约定,自己在特定时间内不会从事行业内竞争工作,针对此问题对方将支付一笔额外金钱。竞业禁止条文涉及违反公共政策,高管/技术人员就可能无法要求执行这笔额外金钱的给付了,毕竟这笔金钱的对价会被解释为纯粹是承诺不参与竞争的行为(或其他非法目的)。在近期的 Tillman v. Egon Zehnder (2019) UKSC 32 最高院先例中,Wilson 勋爵特别指出固然合约的对价问题是必须考虑的,但是一般针对雇佣合约终止后的竞业禁止条文的对价的争议绝少。

还可以再举一个对价要求并不高的例子。在 Mansell v. Robinson(2007) EWHC 101(QB)先例中 Williams 先生在早年与时代华纳关于蝙蝠侠漫画的收益分配产生争议但在诉讼中败诉,在被告的帮助下正打算调查翻案。于是他们找上了作为独立记者的原告,委任原告作为调查员调查线索。问题是委任合约中向原告支付的报酬包括:(1)每周250英镑固定薪资;(2)最后成功索赔后收益的1%。但最后向时代华纳的诉讼并未推进,被告也没有按约支付每周固定薪资,原告即在委任合约下向被告索赔。问题是由于报酬涉及诉讼收益1%,因此涉嫌揽讼(champerty)的非法。在一审认定确属揽讼且非法,每周250英镑与最后收益的1%又属于一揽子的整套报酬体系,一旦分割就导致变成了新合约因此不允许分割,原告也因此败诉。

但一审判决在二审高院被驳回,一方面是今天对待揽讼的严苛态度已经与过去有所不同,[97]上诉庭认定事实并不属于揽讼。另一方面是针对分割方面,即使属于揽讼,报酬中分割收益1%部分是允许的,虽然这整套报酬才是被告提供的对价,但分割其中一部分并未改变其性质,也谈不上切除了全部或根本性的主要对价,只不过是报酬变少了而已。Underhill 大法官说:"The fact that the two covenants may commercially have formed part of a single 'package' does not matter. Such a result would in no way prejudice the Defendant by leaving him with a fundamentally different bargain than that which he entered: it would simply mean that he was liable to a pay a lesser price than he had bargained for."

11.5.3 条件之三:是否改变合约的性质与当事人的合约目的

第三个条件在 Sadler v. Imperial Life Assurance Co of Canada Ltd(1988) IRLR 388

---

[97] 曾经在普通法下防止助讼与揽讼(maintenance and champerty)是重要的公共政策。过去很长一段时间助讼与揽讼无论是在普通法还是成文立法下均属于刑事犯罪行为。简单而言,助讼是毫无理由地擅自、肆意介入自己并无利益的他人诉讼,为一方提供帮助。而揽讼可以说是助讼的一种情况,特别针对了帮助一方当事人打官司,并且从争议财产中收取一部分作为报酬。也因此例如律师不能随意"拉客"到处找人打官司,又如不得任意转让诉权。这做法看来是很早期时,防止富人肆意欺压穷人,防止任意开始过多不必要的诉讼,也防止以争议财产作为报酬可能诱导人们妨碍司法公正、用司法裁决结果来进行非法交易或赌博等行为,这对整个司法系统与社会都会造成危害。在古老案件中的对待非常严格,甚至是证人如果并非接受法院的传召,否则不能提供证言。但在近代而言,这些古老的做法在今天由于社会与现实的需要已经不再如此严格。在 Sibthorpe v. Southwark LBC(2011) EWCA Civ 25 上诉庭先例中,Neuberger 勋爵指出在21世纪不应该再扩张助讼与揽讼的公共政策("it would be inappropriate in the 21st century to extend the law of champerty")。而英国在《Criminal Law Act 1967》中就废除了这类刑事犯罪,并且同时废除了这类行为带来的民事侵权责任。在近年来更是开放了律师可以有限制地(根据与客户的协议)订立按条件根据诉讼结果收费协议(Conditional Fee Agreement, CFA);诉讼费用的事后保险(After The Event Insurance, ATE 保险);以及第三方诉讼基金(third party funding)等做法。但助讼与揽讼的公共政策仍然存在,而且在《Criminal Law Act 1967》之 Section 14(2)中明示保留了这类公共政策在非法理论时的适用:"The abolition of criminal and civil liability under the law of England and Wales for maintenance and champerty shall not affect any rule of that law as to the cases in which a contract is to be treated as contrary to public policy or otherwise illegal."因此如果被认为属于助讼与揽讼,就可能导致有关合约不可执行。这方面的近期先例还可见 Chapelegate Credit Opportunity Master Fund Ltd v. Money(2020) EWCA Civ 246 上诉庭先例与 Diag Human SE & Anor v. Volterra Fietta(A Firm)(2022) EWHC 2054(QB)先例等。

先例中说是删除不可执行部分不会改变原合约的性质("the removal of the unenforceable provision does not so change the character of the contract that it becomes 'not the sort of contract that the parties entered into at all.'")。

而到了 Tillman v. Egon Zehnder(2019)UKSC 32 最高院先例中,Wilson 勋爵稍微更改了以下措辞/文字变为删除条文后不会导致竞业禁止条文主要法律效果有重大改变("whether removal of the provision would not generate any major change in the overall effect of all the post-employment restraints in the contract.")

这道理也是容易理解的,合约的大原则是当事人的意思自治,即使出现非法问题,法院(或仲裁庭)分割合约条文后如果会导致完全变成一个新合约,根本不是当事人想要订立的合约,这就变成法院重写合约,强加了一个新合约给当事人。例如,如毒枭将房屋出租给租客用来种植大麻并要每个月"上供",此时种植大麻与上供的部分如果分割出去,单纯变成一个出租房屋的合约,这就是完全改变了双方的合约目的,改变了合约的性质了。

11.5.3.1　是否改变性质依赖具体案情与法院/仲裁庭的看法

尽管有此大道理,关键问题就是一个合约什么时候在分割后会被认为变成了新合约,或者是改变了合约的性质,这是要根据个案不同案情让审理法院判断。过往各种先例中给出的判断描述很多,仅仅列举一部分例子如下:(1)Pigot's Case(1614)77 ER 1177 先例中指出要看剩余部分是否"依赖"被分割部分("if the part which is good depends upon that which is bad, the whole instrument is void");(2)Mason v. Provident Clothing and Supply Co Ltd(1913)AC 724 先例中 Moulton 勋爵说要看这是否属于有关条文中主要目的与实质内容的一部分("part of the main purport and substance of the clause");(3)Attwood v. Lamont(1920)3 KB 571 先例中 Sterndale 勋爵说的是要看是否导致整个合约的范围与目的都发生改变("alter entirely the scope and intention of the agreement?");(4)British Reinforced Concrete Engineering Co v. Schelff(1921)2 Ch 563 先例中 Younger 大法官说是看有关限制是否是有关交易中的重要部分:"Its application does not authorize the making of a new contract for the parties and the particular clause now in question is really a principal if not the main approach to the business..."(5)Bennett v. Bennett(1952)1 KB 249 先例中 Denning 勋爵说剩下部分是否仍然对当事人来说属于合理安排("leave the rest of the deed a reasonable arrangement between the parties?")。

但这些说法看来都比较概念性,也不是具体的测试标准。很大程度上仍然是要看特定法官(或仲裁员)根据具体的案件事实会得出什么看法。在解释合约的过程中,本会默示当事人意图是合约中的条文都有意义,而且应该是意图条文都可以被执行,而不应该是约定非法条文。因此条文的一部分或者干脆是一些条文被分割,除非是"不重要或技术性"的,否则必然导致合约发生一定程度的改变。也就必然导致当事人的订约意图被一定程度地扭曲,只不过是程度的问题。另外如果合约目的本就是要实施非常严重的违法犯罪行为,分割其中约定的非法部分就必然改变合约的性质,这方面还可见本章之 11.5.4 段的介绍。

只能说很显然的是,分割出去的部分对整个合约而言越是重要,越是不会允许分割。而且今天更关键的是看整体合约是否因此改变,而不仅仅只关注被分割的条文本身:见本章之 11.5.3.4 段会介绍的 Brand Studio Ltd v. St John Knits Inc(2015) EWHC 3143(QB)先例。

也因此由于具体案件中案情的千变万化,不打算过多详细讨论。仅仅简单介绍以下几个先例中法院如何考虑。

11.5.3.2 例子之一:独家经销协议中的捆绑条文(solus tie)

一个著名的案件是涉及特许独家经销协议(solus agreement)的 Amoco Australian Pty Ltd v. Rocca Bros Motor Engineering Co Pty Ltd(1975) AC 561 枢密院先例。此先例中是当年的阿莫科石油公司(Amoco)与被告(一家澳大利亚加油站)签订协议,被告提供土地与服务站,Amoco 则会铺设管道、油泵等设施。并且双方达成如下租赁协议:(1)被告将加油站租赁给 Amoco,为期 15 年,租金为 1 英镑,并要按每年实际提供石油数量按比例支付额外金钱。(2) Amoco 将加油站转租回给被告的董事,为期 15 年减 1 天,租金 1 英镑。并且在转租协议中加入限制性条文(restrictive covenants)规定,加油站每年从 Amoco 购买的石油必须达到某最低标准,加油站所有石油产品("petrol, oil and other petroleum products")只能从 Amoco 购买,没有 Amoco 的同意只能从事加油服务站业务。[98]

或许有读者会有疑问,为什么要进行如此麻烦的租赁与转租?实际上背后的原因有很多,例如会在租赁后 Amoco 才在自己有租赁产权(leasehold title)的土地上建设价值不菲的管道与油泵。还例如有一个在笔者看来会是更重要的原因,实际上是 Amoco 为了更牢固地掌控加油站。毕竟如果 Amoco 由于土地与财产并没有产权,对加油站行为其实是失控的:即使加油站不遵守合约行事,土地和财产的产权也属于加油站,Amoco 只能主张对方违约要求法院救济,但履约指令等救济并不容易申请,最后可能可以拿回的是一些金钱赔偿,这并不能达到长久与稳定的控制的目的。但是

---

〔98〕 在此节录有关条文方便有兴趣的读者阅读:"(g) To carry on and conduct in a proper manner in and upon the demised premises during all lawful trading hours the business of a petrol service station only and not to use same for any other business or purpose whatsoever and not during the continuance of this lease to cease to carry on the said business without the prior written consent of the lessor...(h) To purchase exclusively from the lessor all petrol, motor oil, lubricants and other petroleum products required for sale on the demised premises and not directly or indirectly to buy, receive, use, sell, store or dispose of or permit to be bought, received, used, sold, stored or disposed of at or upon the demised premises or any part thereof any petroleum products not actually purchased by the lessee from the lessor provided that the lessor is able to supply same...(i) To purchase at least 8,000 gallons of petrol and at least 140 gallons of motor oil from the lessor in every month during the term of this lease."

通过先获取对土地与财产的租赁产权,此时减少 1 天的租期恰当地转租给加油站,并且在转租协议中加上限制性约定。这样,加油站是在转租协议下照常运作,但只要加油站违反了转租协议中的限制性约定,违背 Amoco 的意愿行为(如销售其他公司的石油产品),石油公司就可以行使自己租赁产权的权利,针对土地和财产做文章,更容易申请禁令阻止加油站的行为,甚至根据协议条文的规定可以有权收回土地和财产。

回到这里的课题,被告顺利运营加油站多年后,通知 Amoco 自己打算与 Amoco 的竞争对手合作。Amoco 就马上申请禁令阻止。被告就主张在转租中的限制性约定属于不合理限制贸易,导致整个转租约以及连带租约都一并不可执行/无效。

枢密院的判法是这几个条文根本是整套做法运作的核心与灵魂("heart and soul"),因此拒绝分割此限制贸易的条文。Amoco 愿意推进整套交易,关键就是因为有这些限制性约定。Cross 勋爵尤其指出这情况其实仍然是要解释当事人订约时的目的或意愿到底是什么。看来也就是看分割条文后,是否导致这些目的或意愿发生根本性改变。Cross 勋爵这样说:"As ... in Brooks v. Burns Philp Trustee Co Ltd (1969)121 CLR 432...:'Questions of severability are often difficult.' **The answer depends on the intention of the parties as disclosed by the agreement into which they have entered; but generally, of course, they have not foreseen that one or more of the provisions in their agreement will be unenforceable.** It is inconceivable that any petrol company would grant a dealer a lease at a nominal rent of a site on which it had spent a substantial sum in installing pumps and other equipment without imposing on the dealer any obligation to buy petrol from it or even to carry on the business of a petrol station on the demised premises. (转租约中的有关条文) were **the heart and soul of the under-lease...**"(加黑部分是笔者的强调)

也因此枢密院认定条文不可分割,转租协议因为限制贸易而非法,租赁协议也被认定为一整套协议中的一部分,因此一并无效或不可执行。被告胜诉与逃离了 Amoco 的控制。

作为对比可见 Alec Lobb v. Total Oil GB(1985)1 WLR 173 上诉庭先例中,与 Amoco Australian Pty Ltd v. Rocca Bros Motor Engineering Co Pty Ltd 先例有类似的捆绑条文,但在不同的特定案情下认定捆绑条文并非交易的"核心与灵魂"。此先例中原告 Alec Lobb 经营一家加油站(也提供汽车修理服务),与被告法国石油公司 Total 签订独家经销协议与捆绑条文。Total 还向 Alec Lobb 提供了一笔贷款,加油站的一些资产作为抵押担保,多年来大家也没有争议。

之后在捆绑条文还剩没几年时,由于 Alec Lobb 的加油站遇上经济问题,没有资金难以继续经营,Alec Lobb 就找上了 Total 帮忙,双方之间达成了如下安排:(1)加油站被出租给 Total,租约时间 51 年,每年只收象征性的租金。但是在租约签订时,Total 将一次性支付 3.5 万磅。这笔金钱被法院认定基本与当时 51 年租约的市场租金价值相等。(2)加油站会被转租回给 Alec Lobb 的董事,租约时间 21 年,租金为每年 2250 英镑。转租中加入了限制性约定,包括 Alec Lobb 有权在一定时间后审视是否继续转租。也非常重要的是将独家销售作为条件,如果违反 Total 有权结束租约收回加油站。

这样等于是 Alec Lobb 的捆绑条文被通过这一次交易延长了。Alec Lobb 经过一次性的 3.5 万英镑"续命"经营 10 年后,想要拿回自己的资产。重要主张就是交易不合理限制了贸易,因此租约与转租约非法而无效/不可执行。

上诉庭的判法是由于此先例中的特殊情况,考虑到是 Total 帮助 Alec Lobb 渡过难关、一次性支付 51 年租约的费用。加油站也早已经在捆绑条文下运行多年、没有争议。即使没有这套交易,本来的独家经销协议与捆绑条文也可能继续延续等。综合之下认为并没有不合理,也就不存在限制贸易的非法/不可执行问题。

上诉庭也将此先例与 Amoco Australian Pty Ltd v. Rocca Bros Motor Engineering Co Pty Ltd 先例进行了区分。已经介绍过在该先例中,捆绑条文是整个合约的灵魂或核心内容,整套交易都是围绕捆绑条文而进行的。但在此先例中的情况,签订租约/转租约时 Total 本就尚有数年剩余的独家经销协议与捆绑条文,之后还可能继续续签,而租约/转租约的核心与主要目的是马上提供融资、让 Alec Lobb"续命"。也因此即使分割也没有涉及合约的灵魂或核心。

Alec Lobb 还提出 Total 如果没有此捆绑条文是不会签订租赁/转租交易的合约,一旦分割就导致根本性改变了合约,因此捆绑条文其实应该是交易的核心与灵魂。这说法也被法院驳回,Dillon 大法官这样说:"The contract is of course changed by the excision of the tie(分割捆绑条文),and obviously Total would not have granted a lease-back which did not contain such a tie. But I do not think that is good enough to prevent severance and lead to the conclusion that the whole of the lease and lease-back is void. A mortgage to a petrol company containing a tie would,in my judgment,remain in all other respects valid despite the invalidity of the tie as an unreasonable restraint of trade, **although the petrol company would not have contemplated making any advance on mortgage to a dealer without a tie.**"(加黑部分是笔者的强调)

换言之,考虑能否分割条文是不会考虑如果没有捆绑条文,当事人是否愿意签订合约。毕竟解释合约是纯客观,是不理会订约前当事人单方面的动机与主观理解。这可节录《Illegality and Public Policy》(2020 年,第 5 版)一书之 19 - 11 段的评论如下:"Provided that consideration to support the contract does remain,and provided also that severance does not alter the essential character of the agreement,enforceability cannot be resisted simply because one of the parties would not have chosen to enter into the contract in the absence of the deleted clause. At first glance this might seem surprising,but the motives of the parties for entering into an agreement are distinct from the concluded contract itself. Moreover,if the law were otherwise,the resulting denial of enforceability might sometimes lead to very unfair results."

11.5.3.3 例子之二:收回成本的主要方式被分割

还可以介绍 Credit Suisse v. Allerdale Borough Council(1997)QB 306 先例,此先例中被告地方议会(Council)根据立法赋予的权限要在当地修建泳池,成立了一家专门用于此目的的公司。之后在议会提供担保的情况下,公司从原告银行获取了贷款,用于建设休闲泳池与一些度假屋,打算事后出售度假屋收回成本。但事后度假屋销售不理想,公司破产。银行因此找上了作为担保人的议会。其中一项争议〔99〕就是,根据明确的立法,议会只能建造休闲泳池,但并没有建造度假屋的权力,因此是否可以将度假屋的部分从整个合约中分割开来变成争议焦点。

Neill 大法官就判度假屋的建造是整个建造中的核心部分,关键就是要出售度假屋收回成本,没有度假屋可以说这个项目根本不会推进。分割度假屋部分就变成了完全不同的新合约,因此不允许分割。这样由于议会没有建造度假屋的法定权力,整个合约非法,即银行败诉,法院不会帮助执行。Neill 大法官说:"How then is the possibility of severance to be approached? The answer is to be found by **considering whether if one isolated that part of the company's indebtedness which related to the leisure pool a fundamentally different contract would result**... In the present case the provision of the time-share units(度假屋)was an integral part of the scheme. Indeed the scheme would not and could not have gone ahead without the time-share development. In these circumstances it seems to me that **the contract without the time-share development would have been a quite different contract.** The leisure pool development was inextricably linked with the development which, it was hoped, would provide the finance. The guarantee was part of one composite scheme. On the facts of the present case I am quite satisfied that if a question of severance were a relevant consideration it would not be possible to enforce the guarantee pro tanto."(加黑部分是笔者的强调)

笔者的看法是,这会是非常依赖个案的事实情况,如果一个大型的社区建造计划中也加入了部分度假屋建造,但并不是期待用建造度假屋来帮助建造计划回本,而只是考虑到将来的运营对行政费用有所帮助,这样个别法官的看法就可能有所不同,愿意分割度假屋的部分,让剩余合法部分被执行。

11.5.3.4 例子之三:关注整个合约性质而非特定条文意义

这个问题在中国也经常发生,就是改革开放后有大量中国公司作为代理人与国际上的品牌公司签署代理协议,帮助品牌公司在中国经销代理、拓宽市场。有不少情况中国公司在市场开拓中立下汗马功劳,也投入大量成本、时间与精力,如建立整个团队、基本设施,还有大量的市场研究与宣发工作等。在刚开始品牌公司尚未打开市

〔99〕 此先例中最后银行败诉的原因很多,除了前文提到的度假屋无法与剩余合约分割开来以外,还包括根据立法议会根本没有为公司借贷提供担保的权力等。

场时，中国代理人根据销售赚取佣金的报酬是很有限的。但在市场开拓后，外国品牌公司就以对代理不满意或其他各种问题为名，把代理人踢开。中国代理人就需要特别小心这种情况的发生，订立代理协议就必须留意合约的内容，来保证：(1)如果外国公司这样做需要付出很大代价，如议定赔偿，以足够保护中国公司不受损而且有报酬，也起到阻吓作用不让外国公司轻易动歪脑筋。(2)将来合约容易执行，如中国法如果对自己有利而且有肯定性，就要坚持中国法院管辖而不是去国际仲裁，否则无论是申请禁令还是经过审理后的损失赔偿都要花费大量时间，还需要花费大量的金钱与精力，让外国公司觉得中国公司可能会怕麻烦而有机可乘。受到中国法院管辖的外国公司在中国打开市场后也就不敢轻易采取行动。(3)其他根据个案性质与特定案情对自己的必要保护。

也有国家或地区的法律会考虑到不是每一家当地公司都有足够的水平与谈判力量面对国际上的大型跨国品牌公司，难以订好能恰当保护自己的代理协议。因此通过立法规定一些必要的保护，帮助弱势的本地代理人，也在一定程度上保护本地市场。很好的例子就是欧盟的《Commercial Agents (Council Directive) Regulations 1993/3053》立法，针对的就是本地销售代理人帮助海外品牌拓展本地市场，立法规定这类代理人在代理协议被终止后有权获得补偿(indemnity)或赔偿(compensation)，并各自有不同判断标准。

简而言之，补偿主要是看代理人为委托人带来多少好处(看代理人带来了多少新客户或提升了多少销量等)，但在立法规定中限定上限是代理人过去5年的年平均收益。而赔偿则是看代理人蒙受多少损失，如英国在 Lonsdale v. Howard & Hallam (2007) UKHL 32 贵族院先例中判这赔偿参考解约时代理业务的价值(看将来预期的收益有多少，如果出售代理业务市场上的出价会是多少等)，而且赔偿并没有上限限制。这样两者之间可能差距巨大，如在 Shearman (trading as Charles Shearman Agencies) v. Hunter Boot Ltd (2014) EWHC 47 (QB) 先例中，补偿方式按年平均收益的上限只有20.4万英镑，但如果按赔偿方式算可以超过145.4万英镑。

欧盟立法中规定除非在当事人的协议中另有约定("otherwise provide")，否则默示是赔偿。英国在欧盟时就引入了此立法规定，并且为了保护代理人的利益及本地市场的公共利益，有先例判不允许品牌公司在代理协议中约定采用两种方式之间金额更低的方式：见 Shearman (trading as Charles Shearman Agencies) v. Hunter Boot Ltd 先例。这种约定属于非法/不可执行，作为不存在"另有约定"对待，也就此时会强制适用默示的赔偿方式。

在 Brand Studio Ltd v. St John Knits Inc (2015) EWHC 3143 (QB) 先例中，美国加州一家设计、生产、零售奢侈品的女装公司(St John Knits Inc)与一家英国销售代理签订代理协议，由英国销售代理在整个欧盟等地区零售美国公司的服装，并根据销售额赚取佣金。

美国公司与销售代理的协议中约定了一条6.3(a)条文：终止代理协议后，除非赔偿的金额更低，否则采用补偿。换言之，该条文的效力就是在最后美国公司总是可以用最“廉价”的方式甩开销售代理。该条文说：“6.3 Upon expiry or termination of this agreement for any reason：(a) If and to the extent that the ... Regulations apply，[销售代理] shall (if and to the extent so entitled in accordance with the provisions of the Regulations) have the right to be indemnified as provided for in regulation 17 of those Regulations. For the avoidance of doubt，[销售代理] shall have no right to any compensation under those Regulations upon termination or expiry of this Agreement provided that if the amount payable by way of indemnity under this clause would be greater than the amount payable by way of compensation，[销售代理] shall ... have the right to receive compensation instead of an indemnity under the Regulations ...”

这样在此先例中也就产生纠纷了，显然是因为此案件中赔偿方式能够拿到更多金钱，因此英国销售代理主张非法，应根据立法采用默示的赔偿。

而美国公司则主张合约中有一条明示可分割条文，规定一旦任何条文无效或不可执行，应当视为被分割，可节录该条文如下：“In the event that any provision of this agreement is held to be invalid or unenforceable，such provision will be deemed to have been severed from the Agreement，while the remained of the agreement will remain in full force and effect.”而只要将6.3(a)条文分割成前后两部分，前半部分约定补偿方式优先仍然留下，但排除后半部分允许赔偿金额更低时采用赔偿等的措辞/文字。这样就不再非法，剩下部分属于“另有约定”，应采用补偿。

对于能够分割条文的三个条件，前两个条件双方都没什么争议。关键的争议焦点就在于分割后半部分会否导致条文性质改变。而根据此先例中的案情来看，6.3(a)条文一旦将后半部分分割，显然意思就改变了，原本是从两种方式里选择金额较低的一种，分割后就变成选定了采用补偿方式。

但是高院的Teare大法官指出不能仅仅看特定条文是否因为分割而意思发生变化，而要看是否改变了“性质”。并认为此先例中的情况是原本美国公司就同意采用补偿方式，只是加上了非法的但书。Teare大法官就认为分割非法的但书后，并没有改变同意补偿的性质。也因此允许分割。Teare大法官说：“... **The question for the court is whether the removal of the unenforceable part so changes the character of the contract that it becomes ‘not the sort of contract that the parties entered into’.** The sort of contract into which the parties entered into was one in which the agent purported to accept an indemnity rather than compensation in the event that the agency was terminated. Had that been the effect of the clause as a whole the agent's acceptance of an indemnity would have been valid and enforceable. However，because of the proviso，that was not the effect of the clause as a whole. The proviso had the effect that the agent only agreed to accept an indemnity so long as the measure of an indemnity was less than the measure of compensation. If it was greater then he had to accept the lesser amount of compensation. **To remove the proviso certainly changes the meaning of the clause as a whole but I am not persuaded that it so changes the character of the contract that it becomes not the sort of contract that the parties entered into.** Before severance of the proviso it was an agency contract in which the agent had purported to accept an indemnity but had in addition agreed to accept compensation if that was a lesser sum. After severance it is an agency contract in which the agency has agreed to accept an indemnity whether or not compensation would be a lesser sum. In my judgment the contract remains, after severance, 'the sort of contract that the parties had entered into'."(加黑部分是笔者的强调)

11.5.4 公共政策下整个合约是否被非法"污染"(tainted)

在 Marshall v. NM Financial Management Ltd(1997)1 WLR 1527 上诉庭先例的一审[(1995)1 WLR 1461]中,Jonathan Sumption QC 大法官在认可与适用了 Sadler v. Imperial Life Assurance Co of Canada Ltd(1988)IRLR 388 先例中三个条件的基础上,还加上了第四个条件:"The first of these propositions is the 'blue pencil' test which for many years has been accepted as a necessary although not a sufficient condition for severance.... It is altogether more satisfactory than the more traditional and question-begging statement of the test: whether there is one obligation or more than one. To these three propositions there should perhaps be added a fourth, namely that **the severance must be consistent with the public policy underlying the avoidance of the offending part.**"(加黑部分是笔者的强调)

这主要针对的情况是,所涉及的非法违反了一些异常重要的公共政策,导致一旦涉及就无论如何不会允许合约继续执行,也无论是否可以分割。

这涉及考虑非法的程度、公共政策的问题,在 Goodinson v. Goodinson(1954)2 QB 118 上诉庭先例中,Somervell 大法官就提到说不同的非法会有不同的后果,而此先例中的非法是排除了法院管辖权,并没达到特别严重的程度,因此允许分割了非法部分,执行剩余部分。Somervell 大法官说:"In Bennett v. Bennett,[100] it was pointed out that there are two kinds of illegality of differing effect. **The first is where the illegality is criminal, or contra bonos mores**, and in those cases, which I will not attempt to enumerate or further classify, **such a provision, if an ingredient in a contract, will invalidate the whole**, although there may be many other provisions in it. **There is a second kind of illegality which has no such taint; the other terms in the contract stand if the illegal portion can be severed, the illegal portion being a provision which the court, on grounds of public policy, will not enforce**. The simplest and most common example of the latter class of illegality is a contract for the sale of a business which contains a pro-

[100] 在 Bennett v. Bennett(1952)1 KB 249 先例中,Somervell 大法官给出过类似的说法。

vision restricting the vendor from competing in or engaging in trade for a certain period or within a certain area. There are many cases in the books where, without in any way impugning the contract of sale, some provision restricting competition has been regarded as in restraint of trade and contrary to public policy. There are many cases where not only has the main contract to purchase been left standing but part of the clause restricting competition has been allowed to stand."(加黑部分是笔者的强调)

在笔者看来这也与今天 Patel v. Mirza(2016) UKSC 42 先例的基于多因素判断的方法所配合，需要看具体非法的严重程度，成比例地来看待问题。如果是严重的非法行为"污染"了整个合约，就会导致整个合约都无法执行，不允许分割。

11.5.4.1　严重且"污染"了整个合约的情形

严重的非法行为"污染"了整个合约的情况就会导致整个合约无效，在公共政策下也不应该把合约分割开来，允许合约部分有效。这是容易理解的，假设合约中约定买凶杀人，或者是通敌卖国，很显然这些合约都不能说只把非法部分分割后，还能允许执行剩余部分，这被"污染"的合约应该全部都无法被执行。

过去被判由于涉及商业的非法行为导致"污染"了整个合约的情况包括：(1)与敌对国家交易，见 Kuenigl v. Donnersmarck(1955)1 QB 515 先例等；(2)欺诈国家财政收入(defraud the revenue)的非法行为；见 Miller v. Karlinski(1945)62 TLR 85；Napier v. National Business Agency Ltd(1951)2 All ER 264 先例等。比如 Miller v. Karlinski 先例中有关合约就涉及有部分是为了骗税虚增公司的开支，导致被法院认定整个合约都被"污染"。

但这里的重要问题是什么时候才会"污染"整个合约？英国法下对这个问题并没有清楚地解答。上一小段节录了 Somervell 大法官在 Goodinson v. Goodinson (1954)2 QB 118 先例中提到的刑事犯罪(criminal)违反社会公共道德(contra bonos mores)的非法行为。这仍然是非常笼统的说法，毕竟即使是刑事犯罪也存在非常严重的刑事犯罪，如买凶杀人、卖国投敌行为，也会有非常轻微的刑事犯罪，尤其是今天英国法下有大量立法将一些商业行为都视为刑事罪行(offence)，甚至有一些是不需要犯罪的主观意图的严格责任罪行。

但如果有关合约中的非法部分本就并非合约的重要部分，看来并没什么理由不允许分割。例如本章之 1.5.2 段已经介绍过的 Fielding & Platt Ltd v. Najjar(1969)1 WLR 357 先例，英国公司出口机械给黎巴嫩公司，在黎巴嫩公司的要求下改了发票上的商品名称，目的是骗过黎巴嫩进出口的有关部门逃避责任。此先例中就判即使修改发票名称也是合约条文，也应该允许分割此条文，让英国公司回到合法地位并履行剩余合约。毕竟这本身是一个 FOB 买卖合约，分割此条文后不会改变合约本质，条文约定的只是合约履行的一小部分，没有严重到"污染"买卖合约。Denning 勋爵这样说："There is another point: **even if there was a term that these goods should be invoiced falsely in order to deceive the Lebanese authorities**, I do not think it would render the whole contract void. That term would be void for illegality. But it can clearly be severed from the rest of the contract. It can be rejected, leaving the rest of the contract good and enforceable. The English company would be entitled, despite the illegal term, to deliver the goods f. o. b. English port, and send a true and accurate invoice to the Lebanese buyer. The Lebanese buyer could not refuse the goods by saying 'I stipulated for a false invoice.' He could not rely on his own iniquity so as to refuse payment."(加黑部分是笔者的强调)

从这也能看出,即使是类似案件也要看具体情况有弹性判断,可以说审理法官应该是有一定裁量权空间,而不是光凭非法行为的类型就做决定。即使确实是罪行,甚至是可以够得上监禁的罪行,也未必就一定导致在公共政策下不可分割。看来只能说越严重危害社会的非法行为,越是容易被认为"污染"了合约。对此问题不妨简单节录《Illegality and Public Policy》(2020 年,第 5 版)一书之 19 – 23 段作为小结:"The English authorities since Bennett v. Bennett remain scanty but, such as they are, they establish that the mere fact that a stipulation provides for the commission of a criminal offence, even one technically punishable by imprisonment, will not ipso facto[101] contaminate the rest of the contract and render it unenforceable. The court will evidently exercise a measure of discretion, and will probably confine the rejection of severance, and total denial of enforceability, to provisions which contemplate the more serious varieties of criminality."

11.5.4.2　允许分割的例子:收/并购中的经济援助不够严重

不妨简单介绍两个涉及公司收/并购或股份出售交易中,出售子公司股份一方,通过子公司直接或间接向购买股份一方提供经济援助,帮助收购子公司股份的案件。这些行为在公司法下会是被禁止的行为,甚至可能有罚款或监禁后果,例如,英国的《Companies Act 1985》之 Section 151 规定:"If a company acts in contravention of this section, it is liable to a fine, and every officer of it who is in default is liable to imprisonment or a fine, or both."毕竟这会损害公司债权人或目标公司中持有各种不同意见的小股东等人士的利益:见 Chaston v. SWP Group Plc(2002)EWCA Civ 199 先例与 Anglo-Petroleum v. TFB(Mortgages)(2007)EWCA Civ 456 先例等。但此立法下的非法,在过去先例中的判法来看,并不会严重到"污染"整个合约导致不允许分割。

首先在 South Western Mineral Water Co Ltd v. Ashmore(1967)1 WLR 1110 先例中,收购方 Ashmore 先生与出售方 Mineral Water Co 签订协议,涉及对出售方子公司 Solent 全部股权的交易。约定的交易方式是,一次性支付首付后,剩余债务在 8 年内逐步付清,并由子公司提供以其资产为担保的债权(debenture),除此以外收购方还提供个人担保及一些证券作为担保。收购方支付首付后就获得对资产的占有权。

---

[101] 拉丁文 *ipso facto*,中文可以理解为事实上。

但当事人之间后来产生争议,出售方拒绝转交/过户资产,而收购方则停止分期付款,各自都要求对方先履行。出售方就提起诉讼,要求要不撤销合约,要不就给履约指令。这里的重要争议是,如果 Solent 为自己被收购的交易提供担保,是否属于经济援助的非法,导致整个合约无效/不可执行。

虽然经济援助的后果严重到会包括监禁,但 Cross 大法官仍然愿意分割这非法部分,让当事人如果想要继续履行,可以继续履行完成交易。这也是法院尽量支持商业合约完成的大原则。Cross 大法官说:"I cannot take the view and do not take the view that the fact that the granting of this debenture(以子公司资产为担保的债券) would be a criminal offence by Solent(子公司) made the whole of this agreement absolutely null and void so that the courts will not allow anybody to rely on any of its provisions. No case that has been cited to me suggests that I am obliged to arrive at so ridiculous a conclusion. The position was this, I think, that if the company(出售方) were prepared to waive the obligation of Solent to provide the debenture and were prepared to complete the transaction on the footing that they merely had the personal undertaking of Mr. Ashmore(收购方) to pay the £ 36,500(剩余债务) over eight years with 8 per cent interest secured only by the £ 9,000 securities(证券担保) and without any charge on the assets taken over by Solent, they were at liberty to enforce the contract on that basis."

又如在 Carney v. Herbert(1985) AC 301 枢密院先例中,涉及澳大利亚新南威尔士针对类似案情的上诉,枢密院一样认为此时完全可以将非法部分分割,即使在当地立法下该行为属于罪行,公共政策并不禁止分割并执行剩下整个股份出售的交易。Bingham 勋爵这样说:"In the light of the law … their Lordships feel no doubt in the instant case that the illegal provision of the debentures can be severed from the composite transaction, leaving the plaintiffs free to enforce the sale agreements … and the guarantee… and that **the nature of the illegality is not such as to preclude the plaintiffs on the ground of public policy from enforcing their rights under those documents.**"(加黑部分是笔者的强调)

11.5.4.3 出于非法目的签订的整个交易不允许分割

这些情况主要是设计出多份合约来完成交易,但交易涉及了某些非法目的,这样就可能导致整个交易中所有合约都被"污染"而不可执行,不存在从中分割出个别合约,剩下其他合约可执行的说法。

早在 Alexander v. Rayson(1936) 1 KB 169 先例中就出现过这类情况,涉及的是租赁一处公寓,而房东则会在租赁期间提供一些简单的服务,总价为一年 1200 镑。但问题在于当事人将合约分拆成了 750 镑 1 年的租赁合约,以及一份 450 镑 1 年的服务合约。实际上房东能提供的服务显然远远低于此价值,这样分拆纯粹是为了降低公寓的征税估定价值/应课差饷值(rateable value),目的看来就是用来欺骗政府、偷税漏税。也因此认定确实存在非法后,整个交易的内容都没有被执行。上诉庭说:

"In the present case, however, the documents themselves were dangerous in the sense that they could be and were intended to be used for a fraudulent purpose, without alteration, and **the splitting of the transaction into the two documents was an overt step in carrying out the fraud**. We cannot think that the plaintiff is entitled to bring these documents into a court of justice and ask the Court to assist him in carrying them into effect."(加黑部分是笔者的强调)

类似的是在 Mitsubishi v. Alafouzos(1988)1 Lloyd's Rep 191 先例中,买方/船东与船厂(Mitsubishi)以 40 亿日元价格签订造船合约,约定英国法院管辖与适用英国法。而买方的主要股东(Alafouzos)作为担保人签订担保合约。由于买方未能按期付款,船厂即开始向担保人索赔。在诉讼过程中披露出双方看来还另外签订了附带协议降低了造船价格,真实价格是不到 37 亿日元,但这协议没有放到明面上来,目的可能是欺骗当时日本有关机构以获取有关的批准。担保人即主张因此导致造船合约与担保合约均非法。

此时显然合约本身都没什么非法问题,无论是造船合约、担保合约,还是降低售价都是正常的商业行为。但是如果通过事实认定当事人目的非法是欺骗日本当局,并且被认为属于非法行为,[102] 这样进一步的问题就会是能否分割合约,仅仅分割掉非法部分(如分割掉降价部分)? 审理案件的 Steyn 大法官表达了自己的看法,认为在当时国际欺诈横行、愈演愈烈的情况下,法院的态度是如果实现整个欺诈性交易的手段,是通过多个不同合约来完成,法院不会轻易放过这类行为,会使所有密切相关的合约都不可执行。Steyn 大法官说:"... in an age in which commercial fraud is increasing, it seems imperative that the Court should refuse to allow a party to rely on a contract which was drafted or structured to deceive third parties. And the fact that what is alleged to have happened in this case is by no means unknown in the shipbuilding trade makes the stringent application of that public policy in this area a matter of the first importance ..."

这里非法是否严重的问题针对的是分割理论,但在 Patel v. Mirza(2016)UKSC 42 先例后实际上是否非法本身也要考虑严重性问题,这不可避免涉及审理法官的裁量权,也会由于不同案件案情的千变万化而带来不肯定性。例如在本章之 1.5.2 段介绍过的 Fielding & Platt Ltd v. Najjar(1969)1 WLR 357 先例中改写发票货品名称欺骗黎巴嫩政府被认为不够严重,而 Mitsubishi v. Alafouzos 先例中欺骗日本政府被认为足够严重。虽然两个案件都涉及假文件欺骗友好外国政府,而欺骗政府显然是严重侵犯了公共利益的行为,但在判法上就有不同结果。

11.5.4.4 分割理论中公共政策的小结

经过以上介绍,也就能比较容易理解《Chitty on Contracts》(2021 年,第 34 版)一

[102] 这是属于外国法非法的案件,见本书第九章之 5.5.5 段的介绍。

书之 18 – 261 段对此问题的介绍。可以节录该段内容如下:"**Severance and public policy The court will not sever the bad from the good unless this accords with public policy.** For example, part of the consideration for the promise of either party may be such as so gravely to taint the whole contract that there is no ground of public policy requiring the courts to assist either party by severing the offending parts: 'in all the cases a distinction is taken between a merely void and an illegal consideration'. In this context illegal means that which amounts to a criminal offence or is contra bonos mores, where, on ground of public policy, the illegality may, though does not invariably, preclude severance. Agreements the object of which is to defraud the Revenue, or which involve trading with enemy, have been held to be incapable of severance. On the other hand, examples of mere voidness on grounds of public policy are agreements to oust the jurisdiction of the court and agreements which are merely in restraint of trade."

11.6 Tillman v. Egon Zehnder(2019)UKSC 32 最高院先例

在本章之 11.5 段已经提到 Tillman v. Egon Zehnder 最高院先例确立了今天分割理论的地位与测试标准,不妨单独介绍此先例来总结刚刚已经介绍过的条件。

此先例中涉及的案件是瑞士专门从事管理咨询和猎头业务的亿康先达(Egon Zehnder)的英国分公司,在 2003 年签订雇佣合约,作为雇主聘用作为雇员的 Tillman 女士。职位一开始是公司金融服务部门的顾问,后来一路升职,到 2012 年时成为金融服务部门的联合全球主管。在与公司的雇佣合约之 13 条,规定了离职后 6 个月内不得从事多项业务的竞业禁止条文。之后还有一条分割条文,一旦任何部分被认为不合理限制贸易而无效,允许分割、删除不合理部分,使剩下条文可执行。在此仅节录争议焦点 13.2.3 条这样说:"(Tillman 女士)shall not without the prior written consent of the company directly or indirectly, either alone or jointly with or on behalf of any third party and whether as principal, manager, employee, contractor, consultant, agent or otherwise howsoever ... directly or indirectly engage or be concerned **or interested in any business** carried on in competition with any of the businesses of the company or any group company..."(加黑部分是争议焦点)

Tillman 女士在 2017 年 1 月底与公司的雇佣期届满,并打算在当年 5 月开始在一家有直接竞争关系的公司开始工作。前雇主因此申请禁令阻止。这也就带来了刚刚节录的 13.2.3 条是否不合理限制贸易,从而导致合约无效/不可执行的争议。上诉庭认定该条文中"or interested in"的措辞/文字的效果是,Tillman 女士不仅仅是不能亲自工作进行竞争,甚至 Tillman 女士不得成为任何竞争公司的股东,这就变得过于广泛。也可以想到的,即使在任职期间,也没有禁止 Tillman 女士如购买竞争对手的股票。这也并非保护前雇主利益所必要,要保护的只不过是 Tillman 女士在职期间通过工作获取的知识、人脉、技巧等不应该被用来与前雇主竞争。因此该条文确属不合理限制贸易,这样问题就变成该条文是否能够被分割出去,使剩余条文仍然有效了。如果可以分割,剩下部分足以支持法院作出禁令禁止 Tillman 女士的行为。如果不能分割,整个竞业禁止条文无效,禁令不会被支持了。

首先关注的就是公共政策下是否允许分割,是否整个合约都被"污染"。此先例涉及的是竞业禁止条文,仅仅是这部分限制贸易的非法看来并不会严重到整个雇佣合约都无效的地步。

接下来对于能否分割条文的三个条件,Wilson 勋爵的判法是这样的:

1. 蓝色铅笔测试,就是看能否直接删除部分内容。而此先例中前述节录条文中的加黑部分完全可以删除就已经足够,也不需要什么增补或修改。因此可以满足第一个条件。

2. 剩余条文仍然有足够对价支持。已经在本章之 11.5.2 段介绍过,在雇佣合约中,雇主禁止前雇员从事竞争行业的情况时,此条文看来应该关系不大,毕竟雇佣合约下双方的对价,主要是在雇佣合约履行期间提供服务与给付薪水,早已经交换完成。此先例中实际不存在对价问题。

3. 删除不可执行部分不会改变原合约的性质。Wilson 勋爵强调重点在于删除条文后不会导致竞业禁止条文主要的法律效果有重大改变。而且一般情况下应该是由希望申请禁令禁止雇员行为的前雇主来证明可以分割。Wilson 勋爵说:"This is the crucial criterion… In my view this third criterion was rightly imported into the general jurisprudence by the Beckett case [Beckett Investment Management Group Ltd v. Hall (2007) EWCA Civ 613 上诉庭先例] and has rightly been applied by our courts ever since then…But I suggest, with respect, that the criterion would better be expressed as being **whether removal of the provision would not generate any major change in the overall effect of all the post-employment restraints in the contract.** It is for the employer to establish that its removal would not do so. The focus is on the legal effect of the restraints, which will remain constant, not on their perhaps changing significance for the parties and in particular for the employee."(加黑部分是笔者的强调)

而此先例中仅仅是删除"or interested in"的措辞/文字,看来并不会有什么特别的影响,只不过是减少了一部分限制,没有改变条文的性质。剩余部分的法律效力仍然是稳定的,不会有什么特别的歧义、需要解释等问题。

这样,在以上三点都能满足的情况下,此先例中前雇主也得以将被认为非法的部分分割开来,剩下的部分就可以有效执行,因此成功申请到了针对 Tillman 女士的禁令。笔者也感觉到这类涉及高级雇员的雇佣合约中,法官是比较持平来看待双方的雇佣合约条文,认为双方订约时有对等的知识水平、谈判力量,也因此不会特意善待雇员,在条件满足时愿意给禁令阻止雇员违约行为。

12. 非法合约的后果

关于非法合约的后果的说法一直很混乱,有些说法是非法合约无效,也有说法是非法合约有效,只是不会被法院协助执行,也有将两者混为一谈并不区分的。毕竟“非法”覆盖的面很广。有情况是双方当事人都知情,就是为了非法交易订立的合约;也有情况是双方并非过错对等,一方无辜订立了非法合约,或是合约本身并不非法,只是一方在另一方不知情的情况下以非法方式履行等。

经典说法是 Archbolds(Freightage)Ltd v. S Spanglett Ltd(1961)1 QB 374 上诉庭先例中,Delvin 大法官说非法合约的后果可分为以下三种:(1)如果在订约时一方就意图通过不法方式履行合约,虽然合约仍然存在,但该订约方不能执行合约。而如果双方都有同样的意图以不法方式履行,双方都不能执行合约。笔者可举一个简单的例子:一个房租是正常的市场价格的房屋租约,租客在订约时或者后来打算用来种大麻,房东知道后换了门锁把租客赶走。租客就不能去法院申请执行租约,但房东可以执行租约要求租客支付拖欠的房租。但如果房东以高价租给租客种植大麻,双方都不能执行租约。(2)如果原告要证明他在合约下的权利必须依赖他自己的非法行为,就无法获得赔偿,即使他对非法不知情也不是抗辩理由。[103] (3)因为立法的明示或默示禁止或因为违反公共政策,合约自始无效。

Delvin 大法官说:“The effect of illegality upon a contract may be threefold. If at the time of making the contract there is an intent to perform it in an unlawful way, the contract, although it remains alive, is unenforceable at the suit of the party having that intent; if the intent is held in common, it is not enforceable at all. Another effect of illegality is to prevent a plaintiff from recovering under a contract if in order to prove his rights under it he has to rely upon his own illegal act; he may not do that even though he can show that at the time of making the contract he had no intent to break the law and that at the time of performance he did not know that what he was doing was illegal. The third effect of illegality is to avoid the contract ab initio and that arises if the making of the contract is expressly or impliedly prohibited by statute or is otherwise contrary to public policy.”

12.1 非法合约在程序上无法获得协助执行

简单而言,除非是立法中明确规定或默示有关合约是无效,或是仅仅无法执行,否则非法的后果需要看法院如何解释。而普通法下非法理论适用的后果,一般而言是法院不会执行该权利来帮助原告。换言之,一般情况下合约效力本身并不因为非法而无效,只是无法通过法院程序来获得执行了。

---

〔103〕 见本章之 10.1.2 段。

什么是执行可见 Royal Boskalis Westminster NV v. Mountain(1999)QB 674 先例中,Stuart-Smith 大法官所说:"Enforcement means compelling compliance with, in this case, contractual obligations. The court or tribunal compels compliance by its order or judgment."

而不可执行,就是法院(或仲裁庭)不会以命令或判决(或裁决)方式强制执行。如果涉及非法合约,导致适格法院(或仲裁庭)不予协助执行,后果将十分严重且代价高昂。

也因此有说法认为非法理论其实纯粹只是程序上的权利,即只是法院(或仲裁庭)不会协助执行,而没有影响实体权利,合约本身仍是一个有效合约,因为满足了合约构成的所有要件,特别是合约双方有一致想法(consensus ad idem 或 meeting of mind)。例如在 Hardy v. Motor Insurers' Bureau(1964)2 QB 745 先例中,Diplock 大法官说:"The rule of law on which the major premise is based-exturpi causa non oritur action-is concerned **not specifically with the lawfulness of contracts but generally with the enforcement of rights by the courts**, whether or not such rights arise under contract. All that the rule mean is that the courts will not enforce a right which would otherwise be enforceable if the right arises out of an act committed by the person asserting the right … which is regarded by the court as **sufficiently anti-social to justify the court's refusing to enforce that right**."(加黑部分是笔者的强调)

在 Tinsley v. Milligan(1994)1 AC 340 贵族院先例中,Browne-Wilkinson 勋爵也肯定了这样的说法:"The effect of illegality is not substantive but procedural. The question therefore is, 'In what circumstances will equity refuse to enforce equitable rights which undoubtedly exist.'"

还可见更近期的 Mohammad Saeed v. Mohammad Ibrahim(2018)EWHC 1804(Ch)先例中,Simon Barker QC 大法官也说:… the question was whether consideration of the policy factors and of the nature and circumstances of the illegality should result, given the public interest in preserving the integrity of the justice system, in the denial of the relief claimed."

最后可节录《Chitty on Contracts》(2021 年,第 34 版)一书之 18 - 047 段所说如下:"The 'effect of illegality is not substantive but procedural', it prevents the plaintiff from enforcing the illegal transaction… illegal contracts are not devoid of legal effect, but the ex turpi causa maxim may entail that no action on the contract can be maintained…."

虽然很多情况下非法合约无效与不可执行的这种区分在实质结果上并不明显,但也有很多情况会有明显区别,在本章下一段与 12.2.3 段提到的涉及第三人的产权问题就是一个很好的例子。

12.2　能否在非法合约中要求复原

以上区分了非法合约(无论是合约的形成或目的非法还是履行非法)理应是无

法执行而不是无效,可以对复原或不当得利进行进一步分析与说明。

如果非法合约是自始无效,也就是该合约从来不存在,就难逃与其他情况下的合约无效(无论是自始无效与可使无效)有同样的后果,也就是在本书第三章之5段的回复到原状(restitutio in integrum)了。这更会带来其他方方面面的严重后果,如本书第三章之6.3段介绍的无辜第三人会受影响。也就是在一个非法合约下的财产转移给无辜第三人或无辜买方,会因为非法合约是无效导致法律产权(legal title)从来没有在无效合约或从来不存在的合约下有过转移。

但如果非法合约不可执行,就有了很大的不同。在本章一开始讲到非法理论时节录Mansfield勋爵的经典法律格言"违背道德的对价不生诉权"[ex turpi causa(ex dolo malo)non oritur action]。这样,不管诉因是合约、侵权或不当得利,都是一视同仁了。在不当得利的衡平法救济下,在一个过错对等(pari delicto)的非法合约中,更是谈不上有什么"不当"。更不用说在净手理论(clean hand doctrine)下,法院不应该协助并非"净手"的原告向得利的被告取回财产。

但同样在经典法律格言后半部分的"in pari delicto potior est conditio defendentis"或是中文的"双方当事人的过错对等,被告地位更强"就带来在很多非法案件中令法院左右为难的情况。典型例子是被告对有关非法是责任更重大,是"主犯",而原告只是"从犯"。这样,支持非法抗辩就让被告可把原告转交给他的财产袋袋平安(如一笔非法高利贷或内幕交易的涉案金钱),岂非很不公平合理。所以早在Smith v. Bromley(1760)2 Doug KB 696先例中,Mansfield勋爵就提到说非法合约下允许复原,也是另一种形式的阻吓,让收钱的被告知道这笔钱在手上拿不稳:"Upon the whole,I am persuaded it is necessary,for the better support and maintenance of the law,to allow this action;for no man will venture to take,if he knows he is liable to refund."

也由于经常有不少案件令审理法院左右为难,所以法院就试图尽量不严格依照非法理论的"过错对等,被告地位更强"裁判,而是想要不支持被告的非法抗辩,转而去支持过错较低的原告取回金钱/财产。这也带来非法的例外。例如认定或解释说双方对非法不是"过错对等"(pari delicto),与带来撤回权理论(locus poenitentiae)。

而很多著名非法先例都是有关非法合约下,原告请求法院要求被告退还与复原支付或转移给了他的金钱/财产,如:Oom v. Bruce(1810)12 East 225;Davies v. London and Provincial Marine Insurance Co(1878)8 Ch. D. 469;Kiriri Cotton Co Ltd v. Dewani(1960)2 WLR 127;JM Allan(Merchandising)v. Cloke(1963)2 QB 340;Shelley v. Paddock(1980)QB 348;Tinsley v. Milligan(1994)1 AC 340;Tribe v. Tribe(1996)Ch 107;Patel v. Mirza(2016)UKSC 42等先例。

接下来会进一步区别针对上述提及的课题。

12.2.1 非法合约中复原/不当得利的例外

英国法院传统的做法中,法院针对有关的非法合约与行为,只有在原告比起被告的过错是不成比例[在Patel v. Mirza(2016)UKSC 42最高院先例前],顶多是"从犯"

而不是“主犯”时,才会支持原告复原/不当得利请求。所以希望去尽量支持原告去向被告取回金钱/财产。但法院要是严格根据“过错对等,被告地位更强”认定双方当事人过错是否对等,只有原告是过错较少一方而且过错是少得可去漠视时,才允许给予这类复原的救济。因为在非法理论下是不区分错多错少的,这也不是能够去分得清、分得细,而且确立一个百分比作为分水岭也只会带来法律的不确定与产生更多的诉讼。

所以,本章 10.1 段详细介绍了过往先例中对于什么时候才解释为“过错较少”应严格按照以下三个标准:(1)欺诈性误述、胁迫、不当影响等诱导合约产生;(2)原告对于非法不知情;(3)原告属于立法所保护的一方当事人。

这可先节录《The Illegality Defence: A Consultative Report》(2009, Consultation Paper No 189)之 4.3 - 4.4 段,对过去的法律地位的总结:

“one might have expected to find that illegality has little role to play as a defence to a claim for the restitution of benefits conferred under a contract that is unenforceable because of illegality. After all, the claimant is seeking to ‘undo’ the contract rather than execute it. **However, after a more liberal start, the courts adopted a much tougher stance**, and in cases involving illegality, the traditional approach is to apply the Latin maxim ‘in pari delicto, potior est conditio defendentis’ (when the parties are equally blameworthy, the defendant has the stronger position). The restitutionary remedy will only be allowed where the claimant is the ‘less blameworthy’ party... Furthermore, the courts have been inflexible in balancing the guilt of the parties.

Rather than enquiring into the facts of the particular case, a more formal, technical approach is adopted. **A claimant will only be regarded as less blameworthy-and therefore recovery allowed** - where he or she falls into one of **three main categories**. That is where the claimant (**i**) was induced to enter into the contract as a result of the duress of the other party; (**ii**) was ignorant of a fact or, probably, law that rendered the contract illegal; or, possibly, (**iii**) belonged to a vulnerable class protected by statute. This means that illegality generally acts as a defence to claims based on failure of consideration, but not to claims based on other grounds such as duress, mistake or vulnerability. ...”(加黑部分是笔者的强调)

法院之所以严格根据“过错对等,被告地位更强”,是因为传统的复原救济被视为合约的默示条文,即“完全得不到对价的好处”就默示需要去复原。因此,给予复原救济就是执行部分非法合约。虽然复原后来演变成为不当得利(unjust enrichment)的独立理论[104],与传统的合约与侵权的救济不同。但在涉及非法合约时,法

[104] 简而言之,不当得利理论是 Goff 勋爵在 Lipkin Gorman v. Karpnale Ltd(1991)2 AC 548 贵族院先例后发展起来的,并把 150 年以来各种不同名称或理由的复原案例归纳在此理论。

院仍不敢判决可在新诉因下返还。这可节录《Illegality and Public Policy》(2020 年,第 5 版)一书之 17 - 02 段如下:"Where the contract was not merely void, but **unenforceable for illegality, English law formerly adopted a rather narrow view of the scope of restitutionary relief**. Indeed the application of the law of restitution in this area was long inhibited by the fiction that restitution was founded upon an ' imputed promise' : if the contract was unenforceable for illegality it was difficult to see how there could be any basis for enforcing an implied term. But even after that fiction passed into history, the courts remained cautious about expanding the scope of restitution significantly in illegality cases. This perhaps reflected **a fear that its availability might provide an incentive to perform the forbidden contract itself, in order to avoid having to restore benefits received; or a belief that the contract was so abhorrent that the court should not assist the parties to it in any way...**"(加黑部分是笔者的强调)

12.2.2 Patel v. Mirza 最高院先例后一般允许复原/不当得利

在非法交易中已经将金钱/财产转让或支付,既然交易本身不可执行,是否可以要求复原或不当得利的问题,已经提及早在 Smith v. Bromley(1760)2 Doug KB 696 先例中,Mansfield 勋爵就提到说非法合约下允许原告向被告取回转移的财产或支付的金钱,也是另一种形式的阻吓非法。这也符合公共政策,即不让过错对等的被告间接从自己的非法行为中获利。

例如贪污受贿,纯粹从公共利益的角度出发,相比于允许行贿人拿回金钱而言,允许贿赂留在受贿人的手中看来更令人不满意。早在 Walker v. Chapman(1773) Lofft 342 先例中,就涉及贿赂他人以获取公职(海关工作),但没能成功拿到职位,行贿的原告就想要取回贿赂的金钱,Mansfield 勋爵给出了允许的判决,不支持非法抗辩。在 Patel v. Mirza(2016)UKSC 42 最高院先例中,Toulson 勋爵也提到说:"Bribes of all kinds are odious and corrupting, but it does not follow that it is in the public interest to prevent their repayment. There are two sides to the equation. If today it transpired that a bribe had been paid to a political party, a charity or a holder of public office, it might be regarded it as more repugnant to the public interest that the recipient should keep it than that it should be returned."

同样的说法也早已有不少,如在 Neville v. Wilkinson(1782)1 Bro CC 543 先例中,Thurlow 勋爵说:"... In all cases where money was paid for an unlawful purpose, the party, though particeps criminis, might recover at law; and that the reason was, that if courts of justice mean to prevent the perpetration of crimes, it must be not by allowing a man who has got possession to remain in possession, but by putting the parties back to the state in which they were before."

另在 Taylor v. Bowers(1876)1 QBD 291 上诉庭先例中,Mellish 大法官说去将双方当事人复原并不是执行他们之间的非法合约,没什么不妥。"To hold that the plaintiff is enabled to recover does not carry out the illegal transaction, but the effect is to put everybody in the same situation as they were before the illegal transaction was determined upon, and before the parties took any steps to carry it out..."

这到了近期的 Patel v. Mirza 最高院先例中, Mance 勋爵对非法合约的复原也有了同样说法:"I consider that there is **no reason why rescission should necessarily be restricted**, as it was even in these earlier authorities, by reference to a test of execution or carrying out of the illegal purpose. The logic of the principle is that the **illegal transaction should be disregarded, and the parties restored to the position in which they would have been, had they never entered into it**. If and to the extent that the rescission on that basis remains possible, then prima facie it should be available."(加黑部分是笔者的强调)

可以说在 Patel v. Mirza 最高先例中,特别是在多因素判断测试的成比例(proportionality)下,已经明确了非法理论(但会有罕见的例外如立法规定或涉及严重非法/犯法与不道德)一般是不影响复原/不当得利的。Toulson 勋爵的判决代表了今天的多数意见:"I would hold that a person who satisfies the ordinary requirements of a claim in unjust enrichment will not prima facie be debarred from recovering money paid or property transferred by reason of the fact that the consideration which has failed was an unlawful consideration. I do not exclude the possibility that there may be particular reason for the court to refuse its assistance to the claimant, ..., just as there may be a particular reason for the court to refuse to assist an owner to enforce his title to property, but such cases are likely to be rare."

Patel v. Mirza 最高院先例中少数意见实际上也支持在该先例的案情下应当复原,但给出了不同理由。简单介绍 Neuberger 勋爵与 Sumption 勋爵不同说法如下:

1. Neuberger 勋爵认为一般情况下即使涉及非法交易/合约,当事人要求复原的请求也应该被支持。针对非法合约而且原告已经向被告支付了金钱,在本章之 10.2 段的"撤回权理论"下,非法行为尚未实际履行的情况下是可以让原告要求退还金钱。但 Neuberger 勋爵认为即使是部分或全部履行,只要仍能复原,就不受非法理论影响:"The present appeal concerns a claim for the return of money paid by the claimant to the defendant pursuant to a contract to carry out an illegal activity, and the illegal activity is not in the event proceeded with owing to matters beyond the control of either party... In such a case, the **general rule should in my view be that the claimant is entitled to the return of the money which he has paid.** ... In effect, the reasons supporting the application of the Rule in cases where the illegal activity has not occurred, apply for the same reasons to contracts where the contemplated illegal activity has been wholly or partly performed. ... **I can see no good reason for not extending the rule to partly or even wholly performed contracts** where restitutio in integrum can be achieved in practical

terms and would be **consistent with policy and proportionality.**"(加黑部分是笔者的强调)

2. Sumption 勋爵则认为协助执行复原/不当得利根本没有违反非法理论可节录如下:"Of course, in order to demonstrate that the basis for the payment had failed, Mr Patel must say what that basis was, which would necessarily disclose its illegality. In my opinion, the reason why **the law should nevertheless allow restitution in such a case is that it does not offend the principle applicable to illegal contracts**. That principle, as I have suggested above, is that **the courts will not give effect to an illegal transaction or to a right derived from it**. But **restitution does not do that**. It merely recognises the ineffectiveness of the transaction and gives effect to the ordinary legal consequences of that state of affairs. The effect is to put the parties in the position in which they would have been if they had never entered into the illegal transaction, which in the eyes of the law is the position which they should always have been in."(加黑部分是笔者的强调)

Sumption 勋爵也不认同多数意见提及的例外,也就是严重非法(heinous crime)(如较早提到的贩卖毒品或买凶杀人)可去影响复原或不当得利,因为法律为了肯定与可预测性,需要确立在千变万化的非法案件什么是严重与什么是不严重,在后者才支持原告的复原请求。但这里的界限是难以确立,Sumption 勋爵以买凶杀人的非法交易或合约为例:如果 A 支付 1 万英镑雇佣杀手 B 杀掉敌人(如商业上的竞争对手)。此时 A 不应该支付 1 万英镑,B 也不应该实施杀人的行为。如果 B 不实施作为对价的杀人行为,也没有理由继续保留 A 支付的金钱。至于 B 是否实施杀人行为的问题,如果实施了就难逃刑法制裁,也不会涉及民法的复原/不当得利。但如果 B 没有实施,则应该停止行动,但也不影响 A 根据撤回权理论要求 B 退还这 1 万英镑。当然会有立法明确会没收作案工具、非法交易的金钱等,但那是另一回事了。Sumption 勋爵说:"I would also reject ... that there may be some crimes so heinous that the courts will decline to award restitution in any circumstances. There are difficulties about distinguishing between degrees of illegality on what must inevitably be a purely subjective basis. But the suggestion is in any event contrary to principle. If I pay £ 10,000 to a hitman to kill my enemy, he should not kill my enemy and should not have £ 10,000. The fact that when it comes to the point he is unwilling or unable to kill my enemy does not give him any legal or moral entitlement to keep the £ 10,000. If he does kill him, the rational response is the same. He should be convicted of murder, but he should never have received the money for such a purpose and by the same token should not be allowed to retain it."

但对此针对严重非法的说法看来有一些批评,主要是认为这样做法会带来 A 既能派遣杀手,又不用支付金钱的后果。简单节录《Chitty on Contracts》(2021 年,第 34 版)一书之 18-046 段:"This is rightly criticised ... as being an inappropriate response to the extreme illegality involved and would entail that the party arranging the murder would gain what he wanted at no cost..."

当然,这种极端严重非法在现实中不会出现在法院的民事诉讼中。这种事情通常涉及黑社会,他们会有自己的执行非法合约履行的手段,不会委任律师向法院提起诉讼,并且向社会公开为他们的非法行为做广告。

看来,非法理论已经不再影响复原/不当得利的请求,虽然在 Patel v. Mirza 最高院的 9 位大法官都有不同理由,但结论都是得出了这个当今的法律地位。最后可节录《Illegality and Public Policy》(2020 年,第 5 版)一书之 17 – 02 段,对涉及非法的案件原告以复原/不当得利请求法院救济进行阐释:"Patel v. Mirza... The fact that the Supreme Court was unanimous in the result it reached, against the background of the more restrictive approach which applied previously ..., demonstrates vividly in itself that **the law has now changed and that restitutionary relief is to be granted more widely in situations involving illegality**. Nevertheless the precise extent of the change is not easy to state in detail. This is because **the nine Justices differed in their reasons**. Those who focused specifically on unjust enrichment were in a minority. The majority used their judgments to restructure the law relating to illegality generally, so that their frame of reference extended well beyond unjust enrichment and the situation in the particular case. This restructuring involved, as explained earlier in this book, the adoption of an overtly policy-based approach to which the minority were opposed. **In practice, however, it seems unlikely that this difference of approach, although it might be fundamental in other contexts involving illegality, will often lead to different results in the context of restitution**."(加黑部分是笔者的强调)

12.2.3 非法合约下的财产转移带来的产权归属问题

不协助执行与合约无效的区分对非法合约下的财产产权有否转移也是至关重要。在本书第三章之 6.3 段已经详细提及:如果通过各自与 B 订立你情我愿的买卖合约,私人财产的产权从 A 合法转移给不知情的善意第三人 C。之后有关财产就是在 C 的名下,C 已经有了法律产权,即使在 A 与 B 之间的合约,A 仍会对该财产有一定的合约权利[如买卖合约有一条"保留产权条文"(retention of title clause)][105]或衡平法产权。

在一个从来不存在的无效合约中[或是一份可使无效(voidable)并已经是去令该合约无效了],有关的财产就不可以合法转移。这样,A 就可以向 C 取回该财产,他们之间也不存在非法合约的问题,纯粹是产权问题。

但非法合约不是"无效",只是不予协助执行,这也解释了为什么产权在非法合约下可以转移,正如 Toulson 勋爵在 Patel v. Mirza(2016) UKSC 42 贵族院先例中所说:"**Unless a statute provides otherwise (expressly or by necessary implication)**,

〔105〕 在杨大明律师《国际货物买卖》一书第五章之 1.4 段有详细介绍。

property can pass under a transaction which is illegal as a contract. There may be circumstances in which a court will refuse to lend its assistance to an owner to enforce his title as, for example, where to do so would be to assist the claimant in a drug trafficking operation, but the outcome should not depend on a procedural question."(加黑部分是笔者的强调)

Toulson 勋爵也提到了在类似贩毒这种严重犯罪中,产权不能合法转移的例外,虽然大体上很容易理解,但是具体的分界在哪儿,仍需要先例进一步澄清。

另在 Tinsley v. Milligan(1994)1 AC 340 贵族院先例中,Browne-Wilkinson 勋爵也说:"Neither at law nor in equity will the court enforce an illegal contract which has been partially, but not fully, performed. However, it does not follow that all acts done under a partially performed contract are of no effect. In particular it is now clearly established that at law(as opposed to in equity), property in goods or land can pass under, or pursuant to, such a contract. If so, the rights of the owner of the legal title thereby acquired will be enforced, provided that the plaintiff can establish such title without pleading or leading evidence of the illegality. **It is said that the property lies where it falls, even though legal title to the property was acquired as a result of the property passing under the illegal contract itself**."(加黑部分是笔者的强调)

也就是说一般情况下,A 与 B 订立非法合约将财产转移给 B,A 仍是有机会向 B 以复原/不当得利取回财产,特别是上一段已经提到在 Patel v. Mirza 先例后,一般都允许复原/不当得利。但如果 B 再将财产转移给无辜第三人 C,A 就不能向 C 以侵权的侵占(conversion)去要求 C 交出财产。因为即使是非法合约,由于只是不可执行而不是无效,B 在非法合约下获得产权后再转移给 C,仍是合法与有效的,不存在 A 可去向 C 主张已经失去的产权。

12.3 涉及多个关联合约的交易中有一个非法合约

如果一个交易的意图是非法,整个交易下的所有关联合约都会被污染而变为非法(即使部分合约单独看是完全合法)。只有在原告对非法不知情或是虽然知情但没有参与的例外情况,可以说是对非法不是"过错对等"(parı delicto),有关关联合约才能说没有被非法污染从而可以被执行。在《Chitty on Contracts》(2021 年,第 34 版)一书之 18-047 段说:"... If the parties' unlawful conduct is part of a scheme involving a number of contracts, it may not be necessary to establish that each contract is unlawful as each may be unenforceable by virtue of being part of the unlawful scheme."

在 Patel v. Mirza(2016)UKSC 42 最高院先例的基于多因素判断(factors-based approach)的三阶段测试(three-stages test)下,决定一个关联合约是否被整个交易的非法污染也要考虑是否成比例:非法目的或行为的严重性,非法是否处于合约的核心地位,是否故意,双方各自的犯错程度是否有差异等。在本章之 8.3 段介绍的 Magdeev v. Tsvetkov(2020)EWHC 887(Comm)先例就是个很好的例子,虽然该先例针对的是外国法非法合约。

这方面更大的问题是在国际仲裁程序。在 Halliburton v. Chubb(2020) UKSC 48 先例中,Hodge 勋爵判仲裁员不应该在多个涉及相同或有重叠的事宜的仲裁中,重复接受同一方当事人的委任:"... the inequality of knowledge between the common party and the other party or parties has the potential to confer an unfair advantage ... I therefore agree ... that where an arbitrator accepts appointments in multiple references concerning the same or overlapping matter with only one common party, this may... give rise to an appearance of bias."

支持这种判法的主要原因是这种重复委任会带来对一方当事人不公平的争议,也就是被重复委任的仲裁员从其他案件获得信息,从而与其他两位仲裁员和没有参与其他仲裁的对方当事人信息不对称。

但这无疑会带来在同一个交易下的不同合约有不同裁决结果的危险,并可能产生严重后果。例如在一个背靠背合约的合约链中,相对无辜的买方 B 在与 A 的合约下被仲裁庭要求支付全部货款,但在与下一手分买方 C 的合约下被另一个完全不同的仲裁庭裁决因为货物质量,C 可以拒货。更严重的是一个交易有几个相关合约,例如一个开发项目下的建筑合约、贷款合约与担保合约,如果贷款合约被判非法,担保合约与建筑合约是否应该继续严格履行?虽然大家都知道法律是社会科学,不存在一个绝对正确的答案,但是这种相互矛盾的判决结果,仍会影响民众对司法的信任,这也是英国司法系统最忌讳的。为了避免这种后果,英国法院诉讼可以将所有当事方加入(joinder)一次过一并审理。但在国际仲裁,因为仲裁庭的权力来自合约,所以无法做到跨合约把所有当事人拉在一起。在 Abu Dhabi Gas Liquefaction Co Ltd v. Eastern Bechtel Corporation(1982)2 Lloyd's Rep 425 上诉庭先例中,案情涉及建造储存液化天然气的罐子。Denning 勋爵说为了避免有不一致的结果,应该委任相同的仲裁员:"This is the application which is made before us. It seems to me that there is ample power in the Court to appoint in each arbitration the same arbitrator. It seems to me **highly desirable that it should be done so to avoid inconsistent findings**. On the other hand, it is equally desirable that it should not be done so that neither party should feel that any issue has been decided against them beforehand; or without their having an opportunity of being heard in the case. ..."(加黑部分是笔者的强调)

Fox 大法官也说:"... First, I am not myself convinced that ... the risk of such an event occurring is other than slight. If in fact he(相同仲裁员)feels that there is a possibility of prejudice at the time he has completed the first arbitration, or at some point of time before that, he can himself seek release from the second arbitration. ... In the circumstances it seems to me that **the general advantages of a single arbitrator are very considerable and that the disadvantage** which is primarily relied upon **is very unlikely to exist** ..."(加黑部分是笔者的强调)

正因为仲裁无法像诉讼一样完美解决这类问题，也导致在一个针对多份密切相关、相互依赖的合约的独立仲裁中，惧怕不同裁决导致整个交易出现一些尴尬情况的谨慎的当事人，除了试图向仲裁管理机构（arbitral institution）申请合并仲裁等办法外，也只能在不同独立但密切相关的仲裁案件去委任同一位仲裁员（common arbitrator）。但即便如此，仍不保证结果令人满意，正如我国香港特区的 W v. AW（2021）HKCFI 1707 先例中，陈美兰法官在罕有撤销（set aside）后一个不同裁决结果的裁决书时，介绍有关案情说：

"Disputes arose between the parties under the two agreements, and such matters were referred to arbitration … The tribunal in Arbitration 1 consisted of Mr Anthony Neoh SC, Mr Tao and Mr Philip Yang ("Tribunal 1"). The tribunal in Arbitration 2 consisted of Ms Winnie Tam SC, Mr Tao, and Mr Ing Loong Yang ("Tribunal 2"). The common arbitrator was Mr Tao.

On 13 March 2020, the award in Arbitration 1 was handed down ("Award 1"). On 13 July 2020, the award in Arbitration 2 was handed down ("Award 2"). In Award 1, the tribunal found in favour of … W on their claims against the Respondents for breach of the Framework Agreement, and dismissed the Respondents' Counterclaim, that the Framework Agreement had been induced by misrepresentations made by … W. In Award 2, the tribunal found in favour of AW's claim of misrepresentation, and allowed AW to rescind the Share Redemption Agreement. …

On 12 October 2020, W applied in these proceedings to set aside the award in Arbitration 2, on the ground (inter alia) that Award 2 is in conflict with the public policy of Hong Kong, in that contrary to principles of fairness, due process and justice, the tribunal ignored findings on common issues which were already determined in Award 1, and instead made findings which were inconsistent with the findings made in Award 1 on the same issues between the same parties. The findings were essentially as to whether misrepresentations had been made …

… Counsel forAW argued that arbitration proceedings are adversarial. The tribunal can only decide on the issues raised and pleaded, on submissions made by the parties to the arbitration. Tribunal 2 cannot be expected to deal with the issues decided in Award 1, when issue estoppel was not pleaded, and when the Tribunal was not informed of Award 1….

W argued that it was only after Award 2 was handed down that it was made aware of the findings made by Tribunal 2 and that such findings were inconsistent with those made in Award 1. … throughout the course of the hearing in Arbitration 2, W had advised Tribunal 2 that there were concurrent arbitration proceedings between the parties, and that there was a risk of inconsistent findings being made on the issues. Counsel for W highlighted the distinguishing feature in this case, that Mr Tao on Tribunal 2 was also a member of Tribunal 1, and that Mr Tao was obviously aware of the issues decided in Award 1. Mr Tao must be aware that Award 1 contained findings on the essential ingredients and conditions necessary for the findings on misrepresentations which were made in Award 2. Mr Tao did not issue any dissenting decision in Award 1, nor in Award 2. This meant that Mr Tao himself made inconsistent findings on the same facts which called for decision in the 2 Arbitrations."

另外,在同一个交易中,不同(但是密切相关)的多份合约应被视为只有一份合约。所以不应该在一份非法合约如买卖毒品中,拒绝执行卖方交付毒品,但协助执行买方支付货款。显然,这两件事紧密联系,支付货款严重被非法污染,也不可适用分割理论,所以整份合约都因为非法而不被协助执行。同样道理与推理也适用在同个交易中但涉及多份相互依赖去支持整个交易履行的相关合约的情况。正如在 Deutsche Bank AG v. Unitech Global Ltd(2017)EWHC 1381(Comm)先例中,虽然针对的是撤销合约,但同样的道理也适用在非法合约中,Cooke 大法官说:"The rule against partial rescission applies, it is said, to bargains rather than merely to individual contracts. Rescission will be refused where a contract in question is part of a wider transaction, the components of which are commercially inter-dependent, in the sense that they were contracted each in consideration or contemplation of the others and were intended to be performed together."

另在 Marme Inversiones 2007 SL v. NatWest Markets Plc (2019) EWHC 366 (Comm)先例中,Picken 大法官说:"It is clear, therefore, that the bar on partial rescission applies not only to inseverable parts of a single contract but also to contracts which form part of an indivisible bargain. The underlying principle is that a party seeking rescission should not be allowed to pick and choose which parts of the transaction to perform since that would involve rewriting the parties' bargain."

但如果涉及的只是一份非法合约,有了争议去仲裁只会有一个仲裁庭。所以该仲裁庭在一份严重非法合约如贩卖毒品中,是不会犯低级错误去判一个严重非法合约部分可以执行,但其余相关部分不予协助执行的。同样道理也适用在一个交易涉及的相关与相互依赖的多份合约。但一旦这些合约由不同成员的仲裁庭区别审理,就会出现这种低级与尴尬的情况了,正如本书第九章之4.7.3段介绍的仲裁案件。

由于非法合约的问题覆盖面太广,带来的这种问题也特别严重。在一个交易中的其中一份相关合约被挑出非法因素时,就带来该合约的无效或不可执行(在此无需区分),但其他有关合约在不同的仲裁庭审理下仍是有效与必须严格履行的尴尬局面。而在 Halliburton v. Chubb 最高院先例后,在普通法地区进行的仲裁中这种风险有增无减。[106]

---

[106] 这方面也可见本书第三章之4.3.3段。

第九章 外国法或域外法非法

1. 外国法或域外法与本地法

需要首先指出的是，这里所说的域外法，指代的是与法院地法不同的法律。例如，一国两制下中国内地法律与中国香港特区法律，就是不同的法律制度。

今天的国际商业活动中，有不少合约约定的适用法/准据法(proper law /applicable law)都是英国法，此时遇到合约的非法问题，本书第八章中介绍的英国法非法理论(doctrine of illegality)就完全适用。与此同时，英国法院也会面对大量涉及外国因素的案件，这包括合约的适用法/准据法并不是英国法，或者是合约有相当部分(甚至全部)的履行发生在外国的情况。面对这种涉外合约，英国法院仍然可能行使裁量权认为自己对实体争议有管辖权(如双方约定英国法院有专属管辖权或一方当事人在伦敦等)。又或者虽然英国法院对实体争议没有管辖权但当事人希望在英国法院申请诉前担保、禁令、全球冻结令(worldwide freezing injunction)、资产披露令(asset disclosure order)等，或通过第三方披露令(Norwich Pharmacal order)、搜查令(search order)等获取证据，或胜诉方在英国法院申请执行国际仲裁裁决书或外国法院判决。[1]

此时麻烦的问题就在于英国法院(或国际仲裁的仲裁庭)会否执行或协助执行这些可能在外国法下非法的合约。还有进一步更麻烦的问题，如涉外合约适用法是外国法，在外国法下合法有效，但该合约在英国法下会违反英国本地的公共政策[2](public policy)，此时英国法院是否可以与应该执行或协助执行该合约呢？目前，世界各国法律方面冲突的问题越加严峻。例如在一个国家视为合法的商业行为，就会被另一个国家视为非法，此时应该如何处理与考虑国际睦仪/礼让(international comity)呢？

---

[1] 见 Macartney(No. 2),Re(1921)1 Ch 522;Israel Discount Bank of New York v. Hadjipateras(1984)1 WLR 137;Lenkor Energy Trading DMCC v. Puri(2021)EWCA Civ 770 等先例。

[2] "公共政策"的定义在笔者的《仲裁法:从开庭审理到裁决书的作出与执行》一书第十二章有详细介绍。公共政策是十分模糊、多变化、可紧可宽的概念，被形容为"一匹没有驯服的野马"(an unruly horse)。由于公共政策的形成与一国的历史、文化、政治、经济、公众利益、道德甚至是外交等有关，所以国与国之间的公共政策可以有很大的不同或差异。

在这里只说近年更灵活处理外国法的做法。众所周知对于英国法来说,外国法律(包括在外国法下是否非法)实际上是一个事实问题(issue of fact),是需要当事人予以举证进行证明,然后由法院进行认定的。早在 Sussex Peerage Case(1844)11 Cl & Fin 85 先例,Brougham 勋爵就说:"... the judge has not organs to know and to deal with the text of the foreign law, and therefore requires the assistance of a lawyer who knows how to interpret it."

在《Dicey, Morris & Collins on the Conflict of Laws》(2018 年,第 15 版)一书之 9-002 段说:"... The principle that, in an English court, **foreign law is a matter of fact has long been well established: it must be pleaded, and it must be proved**: ...It follows that a representation of foreign law is a representation of fact ... and a finding upon foreign law made by arbitrators is a finding of fact which may not form the basis of an appeal on a point of law under s. 69 of the Arbitration Act 1996..."(加黑部分是笔者的强调)

根据 Leggatt 勋爵在 FS Cairo(Nile Plaza)LLC v. Brownlie(2021)UKSC 45 最高院先例的判决,在这个过程中,有两条规则:(1)默认规则(default rule),即如果当事人没有在文书请求中提到外国法,就默认英国法适用。例如,合约中约定的适用法是法国法,但是双方在文书请求中都没有提到法国法,法院就会适用英国法。背后的原因就是如果双方都没有提到外国法,就等于事实上达成了一个协议以英国法解决他们之间的争议。(2)类似推定(presumption of similarity),即虽然适用外国法,但如果因为某些原因当事人没有举证,会推定外国法与英国法一致。[3]

关于外国法专家证人,在笔者《证据法:基础理论、口头证据与专家证据》一书第五章之 11 段已经有详细介绍,这里只针对 FS Cairo(Nile Plaza)LLC v. Brownlie 最高院先例与之后的一些新发展。在该最高院先例中,Leggatt 勋爵针对类似推定的附带意见(obiter)说,现在能在网上十分方便地找到外国法律的文本,在一些案件没有必要非要外国法律的专家证人:"The old notion that foreign legal materials can only ever be brought before the court as part of the evidence of an expert witness is outdated. Whether the court will require evidence from an expert witness should depend on the nature of the issue and of the relevant foreign law. In an age when so much information is readily available through the internet, there may be no need to consult a foreign lawyer in order to find the text of a relevant foreign law. On some occasions the text may require skilled exegesis of a kind which only a lawyer expert in the foreign system of law can provide. But in other cases it may be sufficient to know what the text says. ... producing a copy of the relevant foreign legislation (with, if necessary, an English translation) is a much more secure basis for a finding than presuming that the foreign law is the same as

---

〔3〕 见《仲裁法:从 1996 年英国仲裁法到国际商务仲裁》一书第四章之 2.3.5.2.2.1 段。

the English law. Of course, a judge needs to be alert to whether the text relied on is current. But even if that cannot be guaranteed, the presumption of continuity may be a more reliable foundation in the absence of contrary evidence than the presumption of similarity."

虽然 Leggatt 勋爵的以上判词只是附带意见，但是 2022 年推出的第 11 版英国《Commercial Court Guide》特别提到这段判词，并鼓励当事人与他们的代表律师利用法院对案件的管理权力来灵活处理外国法律专家证据。《Commercial Court Guide》之 H3.3 段提供的选择包括但不限于：

"(a) The Court can direct an exchange (simultaneous or sequential) of expert reports, an experts' meeting and joint memorandum, and (if strictly required) supplemental reports following the joint memorandum, from experts to be called to give oral evidence at trial if their evidence is not agreed. (双方交换完整的专家报告，但只针对双方专家证人无法同意的部分提供口头证据。)

(b) The Court can direct such an exchange of reports (etc), but on the basis that the experts will not give evidence at trial although their evidence is not agreed, or do so only on some of the matters covered by their reports although their evidence on other matters is also not agreed, with the advocates making submissions at trial by reference to the reports and foreign law materials filed. (双方交换专家报告，但是不提供口头证据，而是由双方的代表律师根据专家报告与有关的外国法资料作出陈述。)

(c) The Court can limit the expert evidence to identification of the relevant sources of foreign law, and of any legal principles as to the interpretation and status of those sources, with the advocates making submissions at trial as to the relevant content of foreign law by reference to the sources thus identified. (限制专家证据只确认外国法法源与提供有关的解释规则，由代表律师在开庭时作出陈述。)

(d) In some cases, the Court may be prepared to take judicial notice, or accept the agreement of the parties, as to the nature and importance of sources of foreign law, and have the advocates make submissions at trial as to the relevant content of foreign law by reference to the sources thus identified, providing the source materials from their own researches. (没有专家证据，通过司法认知/司法通知[4]或双方同意确认有关的外国法法源，由双方代表律师在开庭时作出陈述。)"

《Commercial Court Guide》之 H3.4 段接下来说在决定采取哪种方式时的考虑因素有："(a) How much of the content of the relevant foreign law is in issue (as distinct from its application to the facts of the case, which is for argument not evidence). (有关的外国法内容有多少。) (b) How important those points of difference are to the issues to

---

〔4〕 见笔者《证据法：基础理论、口头证据与专家证据》一书第七章之 5 段。

be determined at trial.（双方对外国法的分歧对决定争议的重要性。）(c) The time and cost efficiency of different approaches (particularly having regard to the amount in issue in the proceedings which is affected by the issues of foreign law).（时间与费用要成比例，特别是要考虑涉及外国法的争议对最终判决金额的影响。）(d) The nature of the issues and the legal sources in issue. For example, the approach in H3.3(c) or H3.3(d) may be more appropriate when the foreign law issues relate to a common law system or a system of law with which the Court has familiarity from other cases.（有关外国法的性质，如如果外国法也是普通法体系，法院十分熟悉，就更适合采取上述提到的后两种处理方式。）(e) Whether there is already an English law decision on the relevant point of foreign law (which is admissible under s.4 CEA 1972).（之前是否有针对有关外国法的判决。[5]）"

在近期的 Suppipat v. Narongdej (2022) EWHC 1806 (Comm) 先例中，Calver 大法官在庭审前复核（Pre-Trial Review）的决定中就强调了当事人与代表律师要跟从新版《Commercial Court Guide》的建议。在该先例中，有关争议涉及新加坡法、泰国法与中国法。双方对这三种外国法律都交换了专家报告，但 Calver 大法官决定只有泰国法与中国法专家要给口头证据。而新加坡法因仅与小部分争议有关，加上也是普通法体系，所以只需要根据双方代表律师的陈述来处理。

笔者只提一点，本章针对的外国法或域外法非法与违反其他国家或地区公共政策，并非一般的法律争议，不能用这些灵活的简单做法去处理，而要采取惯常的由双方专家证人在开庭时被交叉盘问的做法。

2. 因外国法或域外法非法与本地法非法不予执行合约背后不同的政策考量

即使认定的事实是涉及外国法或域外法非法，而且该行为在法院看来足以在本地法律下也不予执行，这看来与纯粹的本地法非法仍然有根本上的区别：

1. 因本地法下的非法或违反公共政策而拒绝执行涉外合约或判决的原因，在 Patel v. Mirza (2016) UKSC 42 最高院先例中已经介绍过，是不能让当事人从非法行为中获利、违背道德的对价不生诉权（ex turpi causa non oritur action），以及保护英国法律制度的公正（integrity of the legal system）。

可介绍 Israel Discount Bank of New York v. Hadjipateras (1984) 1 WLR 137 上诉庭先例。该先例是向英国法院申请协助执行一份纽约法院对担保合约的判决。在该先例中，两位被告是父子，银行在纽约法院获得胜诉判决后在英国法院申请执行，作

[5] 见笔者《证据法：基础理论、口头证据与专家证据》一书第七章之 5.2.3 段。

为第二被告的儿子提出担保合约是在他父亲的不当影响（undue influence）[6]下订立的抗辩，上诉庭说可因不当影响而拒绝执行一份涉外合约。但在该先例中，是儿子自己选择没有在纽约法院提出不当影响的抗辩，所以不能在英国法院协助执行时才提出。Stephenson 大法官说：“**I do not doubt that an agreement obtained by undue influence, like an agreement obtained by duress or coercion, may be treated by our courts as invalidating a foreign judgment based upon the agreement, or as a ground for not enforcing it as contrary to the distinctive public policy of this country**. We have to assume that the original guarantee and its jurisdiction clause were arguably so obtained, presumably by the plaintiff or with the plaintiff's connivance or knowledge, ...But what is plain here is that in those cases to which we have been referred **the public policy involved was what English courts considered to be the distinctive public policy of this country**, and it was only because the law or practice of the foreign country, ... differed from that policy that the question of the validity of the contract or judgment was raised in the courts of this country. ”（加黑部分是笔者的强调）

2. 但拒绝执行外国法非法背后，显然英国法院对于不在它管辖权内的非法行为并非出于想要帮助执行外国法律、实现外国政府的各种公共政策的目的，不予执行的原因仍然主要是来源于英国自己的本地公共政策中对友好国家的国际睦仪/礼让。

在 Magdeev v. Tsvetkov（2020）EWHC 887（Comm）先例中，Cockerill 大法官说：“The public policy underpinning the law relating to domestic illegality is as noted above: ex turpi causa and consistency. But that underpinning both Ralli and Foster v Driscoll is international comity. ”

“国际睦仪/礼让”被理解为是国与国之间的相互与对等的行为。它高于国家之间的礼节，但低于国际公法如国与国之间签订的条约。这可以节录《Dicey, Morris & Collins on the Conflict of Laws》（第 15 版，2012 年）一书之 1 – 008 段的介绍：“**Comity** ... Comity is a term of very elastic content. Sometimes it connotes courtesy or the need for reciprocity; at other times it is used as a synonym for the rules of public international law. Thus ... referred to the rules of comity as the ‘accepted rules of mutual conduct as between state and state which each state adopts in relation to other states and expects other states to adopt in relation to itself.’ Story[7] used it to mean more than mere courtesy, but something rather less than equivalent to international law. ”

---

〔6〕 受胁迫（duress）、不当影响（undue influence）产生的合约的效力都会受影响，今天认为这些属于可使无效（voidable）的合约。这方面可见本书第十章与第十一章的介绍。

〔7〕 这是指 Joseph Story 先生，他在 1811 至 1845 年任美国最高院大法官。Story 先生根据美国与英国先例在 1834 至 1883 年间出版过多版的《Commentaries on the Conflict of Law》，可以说是《Dicey, Morris & Collins on the Conflict of Laws》一书之前普通法在法律冲突方面最重要的权威书籍。

也因此在这类外国法非法案件中需要考虑的因素以及法院的态度，与单纯英国本地法非法的因素会有所不同。

尤其需要强调的是涉及外国法问题时，当事人的举证会更重要，因为完全需要当事人通过各类文书证据尤其是专家证人显示外国法下这些非法的严重性等时，才有机会在国际礼让下让法院作出不予执行的决定。毕竟法院难以对外国的公共政策到底如何进行判断。这与涉及英国自己的法律制度、公共政策时，当事人只要援引过往先例后进行说理论证，审理法官就可以进行衡量，是存在重大差别的。

3. 外国法或域外法非法在过往先例中原则的小结

在 MacKender v. Feldia AG(1967)2 QB 590 先例中，Diplock 大法官总结了三种情况下英国法院不会协助执行涉外合约：(1) 无论合约适用法是什么，该合约在英国法下非法；(2) 即使在英国法下不是非法，但在合约的适用法下非法而无效；(3) 无论适用法是什么，合约要求的履行行为在有关的履行地非法。可以节录 Diplock 大法官的言论如下："**English courts will not enforce an agreement, whatever be its proper law, if it is contrary to English law**, whether statute law or common law; nor will they enforce it even though it is not contrary to English law **if it is void for illegality under the proper law of the contract**. Furthermore, subject to one exception, the English courts will not enforce **performance or give damages for non-performance of an act** required to be done under a contract, **whatever be the proper law of the contract, if the act would be illegal in the country in which it is required to be performed**. The exception, the precise scope of which is unsettled and need not be determined in the present case, is where the illegality is a breach of a revenue or fiscal law of a foreign state."(加黑部分是笔者的强调)

在较为近期的 Ryder Industries Limited v. Chan Wui Woo(2015)18 HKCFAR 544 中国香港特区终审法院先例[8]中，香港特区终审法庭的非常任法官 Collins 勋爵(也是冲突法方面权威书籍《Dicey, Morris & Collins on the Conflict of Laws》在现代的主要作者)在先明确了中国香港特区与中国内地均属于一个国家，但这类民事行为中适用的法律有所不同后，肯定了《Conflict of Laws in Hong Kong》(2012 年，第 2 版)一书中所总结的中国香港特区法律下，关于合约约定行为在履行地法律(香港特区这类案件主要会涉及内地)非法的问题。该总结较为清晰，可以节录如下：

"此先例中涉及的是合约适用法为中国香港特区法律，而合约实际履

〔8〕 此先例的案情会在本章之 4.5 段介绍。

行基本都在中国内地(深圳)……

接下来介绍的原则代表在各类不同情况下香港特区法律的地位,这是同时考虑国际礼让与香港特区本地公共政策后的结果。

第一个原则是合约在其(无论是当事人约定还是根据冲突法认定的)适用法下不可执行,香港特区法院就不会执行该合约。这是无论适用法中违法或非法的严重性如何(如无论是严重刑事犯罪,还是轻微的行政违法;也无论这些法律在香港特区是否相同)。笔者可以简单举一个例子,如合约约定适用中国法,合约约定要在上海开赌场,由于中国法下这属于禁止与非法行为,香港特区法院不会执行。

第二个原则是无论合约的适用法是什么,只要合约要求或实质需要的履行在履行地法律下非法,香港特区法院就不会执行合约。这可简单沿用上述例子,合约约定在上海开赌场,由于在履行地非法,香港特区法院也不会执行,即使合约适用法是中国澳门特区法律,而中国澳门特区允许此类行为,但不会改变此合约在香港特区法院不可执行的地位。

第三个原则是无论合约的适用法是什么,订约时当事人的真实目的是要采取违反当地法律的行为。换言之这并非第一或第二个原则下令合约形成非法(包括合约约定的履行非法),而是针对当事人目的非法的情况,此时也会不予执行。例如,当事人在合约中只约定了要在亚洲开赌场。此时合约本身并没有要求必须在中国内地开赌场,因此合约实际上可以合法履行(例如在中国澳门特区开赌场)。但是根据证据显示当事人在订约时目的就是在上海开地下赌场,此时香港特区法院也不会予以执行。

第四个原则则是既非合约形成非法,也非合约目的非法,但履行过程中采取了在履行地属于非法的行为,这要看履行地非法背后的公共政策的严重性。例如,当事人在合约中约定了在韩国开赌场,也没有证据能显示当事人目的涉及在中国开展业务。但是在实际赌场运营过程中,业务拓展到中国东北的地下赌场,这样就变成在履行过程中采取了履行地非法的行为。但是并不能说因为在履行过程中有一方(或双方)当事人采取了触犯法律(legal wrong)行为,就必然导致不可执行。这需要结合在履行地非法背后公共政策是否视为严重等考虑,才能有弹性与成比例地得出是否不予执行的决定。

以上这些不同情况下的四个原则,与域外法是否在合约形成时已经存在无关。例如,原本订约时合法的行为,因为环境改变后来在履行时变为非法,此时与订约时是否已经非法无关。”

对于以上内容将在以下段落中分段进一步介绍。但在此可以再次重复强调的是,尽管存在多种会拒绝执行合约的情况,但普通法下的态度仍然是尽量支持当事人之间订立的合约，[9]这也体现了合约约束的保障性（security）、神圣性（sanctity），以及合约必须要严格履行的肯定性（certainty）与可预测性（predictability）的精神。因此会有多种有理有据的办法绕过这些所谓的非法。

例如由于外国法域外法是事实问题，因此需要当事人予以举证，法院就可以根据证据认定当事人举证不够，并没有证明外国法域外法下的非法，就完全避免了以上问题。或者是涉及履行非法的问题时，法院可以通过解释合约，认定一些履行（尤其是金钱的支付）并不涉及在外国法域外法下的履行，也就可以避免履行非法。

又如在涉及违反域外公共政策时，是否属于域外公共政策下足够“严重”、结合礼让来看是否应该不予执行的问题上，法院也可以认定并没能显示足够严重、结合礼让来看不需要拒绝执行。

4. 合约在外国法或域外法下非法

本段想要讨论的合约涉及对英国法而言的外国法，并不特别针对合约适用法本就是外国法的情况，而更关注的是合约涉及在外国履行或者是合约目的涉及了与外国有关的因素的情况。例如：（1）合约约定的履行行为在外国法下非法；（2）当事人的目的是要采取外国法下非法的行为（如向外国走私货物、向外国政府官员行贿、逃避外国关税等）。

很显然这些情况中的外国法非法，会因为外国法律或公共政策的情况而千变万化。各个国家或地区也区别有自己比较特别的一些当地法律规定，会根据本地的公序良俗而区别有各自背后的社会公共政策，也会因为政府执政的策略与想法而执行有自己特色的法律法规、规章制度。但问题是在遇上这些情况时，审理的英国法院（或伦敦仲裁庭）应该如何看待？此时一般而言有两个步骤：

1. 当事人先要通过举证证明外国法下确实存在非法，否则根本不会有本段后文中的问题。而如果不仅仅是合约要求的履行方式或者当事人实际采取的履行方式违反外国法，而涉及的是当事人打算采取非法行为，则还涉及证明当事人的非法合约目的。

2. 权衡外国法非法背后的公共政策，以及英国法下国际礼让的公共政策后，英国法院是否仍愿意执行当事人的涉外合约？这不是认为外国法律有跨境适用的效力（extraterritorial effect），而是在国际礼让下英国法律不支持当事人约定在外国的非法行为。在 Ispahani v. Bank Melli Iran（1998）Lloyd’s Rep Bank 133 上诉庭先例中，Walker 大法官说：“However, the absence of a reported decision clearly demonstrating the point ought not in my view to deter this court from affirming that the **carrying out of**

---

〔9〕 见本书第八章之 1.5.2 段。

prohibited acts within the territory in question is an essential and necessary element of the principle stated … in Foster v Driscoll[1929]1 KB 470 … approved by the House of Lords in Regazzoni v Sethia[1958]AC 301. Apart from the formidable weight of judicial opinion behind that formulation of the principle, there are to my mind two compelling reasons against regarding as irrelevant the place where the prohibited acts are carried out. One reason is that **international comity is naturally much readier to accept that a country's laws ought to be obeyed within its own territory, than to recognise them as having extraterritorial effect**. The other reason is that the Ralli Brothers principle, although now regarded as a distinct principle, grows from the same rootstock. In the Ralli Brothers line of authority it is clear beyond argument that **it must be the law of the place of performance that prohibits the act of performance**…"(加黑部分是笔者的强调)

4.1 在合约的适用法/准据法下非法

显然有不少涉外合约,明确适用法是外国法,比如合约的实体争议会明示适用美国法或中国法,或者不少离岸公司的公司股权等争议会约定适用公司注册地法律(如开曼群岛等),或者有一些在海外的建筑工程或矿产、渔业、资源等合约可能也会约定适用当地法律。如果是合约内容违反了这些适用法/准据法(proper law / applicable law),合约会根据适用法/准据法如何处理而决定,英国法下一般也会尊重外国法。

例如,Kahler v. Midland Bank Ltd(1950)AC 24 与 Zivnostenska Banka National Corp v. Frankman(1950)AC 57 贵族院先例都涉及在当时捷克的《Foreign Exchange Law of 1946》立法下,捷克人与非捷克人交易外汇、证券等业务必须先获得捷克国家银行的批准。但看来不少捷克人设立的资产信托的受益人(或者遗产继承人)已经不是捷克人,如移民到英国或欧洲其他地方。但这些资产仍然存放在捷克的各大银行(如两个先例中区别是 Midland Bank Ltd 与 Zivnostenska Banka National Corp)在伦敦的分行,也因此这些捷克银行中的资产仍然受到捷克法律的影响。这样由于这些银行尚未获得捷克国家银行批准,在伦敦的资产就无法转出(transfer)给作为非捷克人的受益人。这也导致了受益人开始在英国法院起诉要求银行支付。法院的判法都是根据事实与法律冲突规则[10](conflict of law rules)认定适用法是捷克法后,由于捷克法下未经批准私自转出属于非法行为,因此不会给命令强制要求银行从事非法行为。

---

[10] 法律冲突(conflict of law),主要适用在涉及外国因素的情况中,解决是否有管辖权,以及针对特定争议应该适用什么法律的问题。在《Dicey, Morris & Collins on the Conflict of Laws》(第 15 版,2012 年)一书之 1-001 到 1-003 段这样描述:"The branch of English law known as the conflict of laws is that part of the law of England which deals with cases having a foreign element. By a 'foreign element' is meant simply a contract with some system of law other than English law… The questions that arise in conflict of laws cases are of two main types: first, has the English court jurisdiction to determine this case? And secondly, if so, what law should it apply?"

类似的是在 Lord Cable(Deceased),Re(1977)1 WLR 7 先例中,涉及 Cable 勋爵在印度居住时设立遗嘱并去世,遗产主要被设立为(印度)信托投资英国证券,信托受益人(或继承人)也全都是英国人。印度《Foreign Exchange Regulation Act 1947》立法后,印度有关机构要求将印度信托的资产转移回印度。受益人就担心资产回到印度以后再要出国就会困难重重,因此申请中间禁令阻止受托人转移资产。与本段内容有关的是,Slade 大法官在认定遗嘱以及根据遗嘱设立的信托应该适用印度法后,拒绝颁布禁令。因为虽然英国法院不太会帮助执行他国的财政立法(fiscal legislation),[11] 但英国法院可以允许当事人采取外国法合规行为,给禁令反而意味着强制要求当事人违反印度法。Slade 大法官说:"It is one thing for the court to intervene by requiring trustees to comply with foreign fiscal legislation;it is quite another thing for it to decline to prevent trustees of a foreign trust from complying with fiscal legislation of the country of the proper law,which under such foreign law they are entitled and indeed obliged to obey."

最后可以节录《Chitty on Contracts》(2021 年,第 34 版)一书之 18 – 071 段的说法如下:"Where the contract is governed by system of law other than English… the law governing the contract is foreign,and the contract is unenforceable for illegality under the relevant doctrine of the foreign system,the contract is also unenforceable in England,unless the vitiating illegality under the governing law is one that the English court declines to recognise…"

4.2　适用法/准据法是英国法但合约要求的履行在履行地非法

4.2.1　Ralli Brothers v. Compania Naviera Sota Y Aznar(1920)2 KB 287 上诉庭先例与后续案例

这方面的权威说法可见 Ralli Brothers v. Compania Naviera Sota Y Aznar 上诉庭先例。在此先例中英国承租人与西班牙船东签订租约,约定从加尔各答运输黄麻(jute)前往巴塞罗那。一半运费在船舶驶往加尔各答装港时,在伦敦由承租人支付。另一半则在船舶到达巴塞罗那卸港并开始卸货后,在巴塞罗那由收货人代为支付。租约是在伦敦签订,适用英国法,约定了伦敦仲裁条文。这是国际上典型的所谓"英国法合约"(English law contract)。

问题在于根据西班牙当时的立法,运输黄麻有最高费率限制,而此租约中的运费看来是远远超出了此费率限制。也因此船舶装载货物到达卸港卸货后,收货人拒绝

[11] 毕竟财产与税务问题每个国家都不一样,各自根据本地情况制定法律,一个国家也没理由帮助他国执行这类法律。在早期的 Holman v. Johnson(1775)1 Cowp 341 先例,Mansfield 勋爵说:"… no country ever takes notice of the revenue laws of another."当然今天对于这类立法下的外国法非法,法院未必会像以前一样不加理会,也有先例中涉及违反外国的财政、税务法律,也被认为属于非法而不可执行,如本章之 4.3.2 段介绍的 Regazzoni v. KC Sethia(1944)Ltd(1958)AC 301 先例等。

支付超过西班牙费率限制的运费。这样,船东就找上了承租人要求承担租约下在卸港欠下的部分运费。

法院的判法就是虽然租约适用英国法、伦敦仲裁管辖,但英国法不会支持执行要求当事人从事在履行地非法的行为,也因此船东无法取回超出西班牙卸港规定的最高运费。[12] Scrutton 大法官说:"... **where a contract requires an act to be done in a foreign country**, it is, in the absence of very special circumstance, an implied term of the continuing validity of such a provision that the act to be done in the foreign country shall not be illegal by the law of that country. **This country should not in my opinion assist or sanction the breach of the laws of other independent States.**"(加黑部分是笔者的强调)

这种情况下的关键是合约要求的履行方式,必然涉及在履行地的非法行为,这就类似于本书第八章之 4.1 段介绍的合约形成非法的情况。在这种情况下,当事人是否有进行非法行为的意图,或者当事人是否对非法的情况知情都是无关、不需要考虑的。[13] 这可见 Magdeev v. Tsvetkov (2020) EWHC 887 (Comm) 先例中,Cockerill 大法官所说:"... Ralli Bros v Compania Naviera Sotay Aznar [1920] 2 KB 287. It is authority for the proposition that the Court will not enforce a contract if **the performance of that contract necessarily requires an act in a friendly foreign state which would be unlawful** by the law of that state. The rule does not require the parties to intend the illegality or even to be aware of the fact that what they have bargained for will involve an act unlawful by the place of performance. It simply requires it to be established that their bargain necessarily involves such an act."(加黑部分是笔者的强调)

还可以介绍一个近期的 Dana Gas PJSC v. Dana Gas Sukuk Ltd (2017) EWHC 1896 (Comm) 先例,此先例涉及伊斯兰债券苏库克的发行与相关的法律。原告与被告为发行苏库克而签订了两份协议,一份为穆达拉巴协议 (Mudarabah Agreement),另一份为购买协议。穆达拉巴协议是以股权为基础的合伙协议,订约方共同分享利

---

[12] 笔者可进一步解释在程租合约的惯常做法,在早年的 FOB 买卖中,由于在装港的卖方更方便去安排恰当的船舶运输,所以常会代买方去租船。至于在租约中约定的运费,作为承租人的卖方会通过租约中的"中止责任与留置条文"(Cesser and Lien Clause),强制船东去在卸港向买方(也是收货人)收取。只有在卸港不是因为船东的错误(如不去留置货物)下收不到全部或部分的运费,才可在租约下向承租人通过仲裁要求支付。关于这种条文的做法与作用可见笔者《程租合约》(大连海事大学出版社 1998 年版)一书第十二章。笔者相信在此先例虽然没有一条中止责任条文,租约也是类似的安排,而船东 Compania Naviera Sota Y Azner 向承租人 Ralli Brothers 在伦敦仲裁要求在西班牙卸港因非法向收货人收不到的部分运费,承租人提出非法抗辩。

[13] 如果双方没有非法意图只是无知,之后咨询律师后同意改为合法方式履行,这当然是可以,因为技术上讲这是双方同意,达成了一个新的合法合约替代了非法合约。但如果双方无法达成协议,一方试图单方面以合法方式履行合约,就涉及违约。只不过因为是违反了一个非法合约,对方无法执行。例如双方合约约定买卖大麻,但卖方最后供应的是烟草。

润，但对于损失则是提供劳务（此先例中是原告）一方只承担劳务损失，而提供资金一方（此先例中是被告）则承担投资亏损，这也是伊斯兰法下强制要求，违反会带来非法的问题，穆达拉巴协议约定适用阿联酋法律/伊斯兰法律。

但双方同时签订的购买协议中约定了原告作为债券的发起人（originator）不仅要向被告债券发行人（issuer）按期支付一定的金额，还需要在特定事项（破产、无法支付到期金额、亏损严重等不好的事情）发生时，不管合伙的盈亏情况而以固定的价格收购被告在合伙中的全部份额。这也可以理解，被告只是作为债券的发行人（在泽西岛成立的公司），而真正使用募集来的资金的是原告，所以被告需要购买协议来保护自己的利益。购买协议约定适用英国法。

上述的简单介绍可以看出购买协议的订立实际上是改变了伊斯兰法律对穆达拉巴协议下提供劳务一方当事人只承担劳务损失的规定。而当债券投资发生亏损时，被告要求原告履行购买协议下以固定金额收购被告占股份额的义务。而原告也提出一个重要抗辩，就是在伊斯兰法的穆达拉巴协议下，如果经营失败不是由于原告的疏忽或过错，原告承担的风险只是劳务损失。此先例中原告在阿联酋法院以及在英国法院同时申请了中间禁令，阻止被告在案件争议没有得到审理前要求在购买协议下行使权利，要求原告收购被告在合伙中的全部份额。

此先例与 Ralli Brothers v. Compania Naviera Sota Y Aznar 上诉庭先例的情况非常类似，即购买协议适用法为英国法，但是在合约履行地有关交易属于非法。因此原告成功申请了中间禁令，审理的 Waksman QC 大法官说："The Ralli principle is that as a matter of English domestic law the court will not enforce here a particular obligation of a contract even when governed by English law if that contract requires the performance of an obligation in a jurisdiction where that performance would itself be illegal under local law."

4.2.2　通过严格解释履行地绕过非法

在 Ralli Brothers v. Compania Naviera Sota Y Aznar（1920）2 KB 287 先例的判决后，显然在履行地法律下是否非法就会变成争议焦点。当事人互相会需要提供证据，如有关外国法的法律专家证人来显示履行地法律到底如何，毕竟这会决定了英国法院（或适用英国法的仲裁庭）是否愿意执行合约。

但这些外国的法律显然会涉及外国社会上的方方面面与外国政府的各种考量，这些因素未必是英国愿意接受的内容。例如，过去有案件中，英国法院都显示出不会考虑、也拒绝帮助执行外国财政法律/税法（revenue law）或政治方面的法律（political law）。也因此今天不少情况中，英国法院采取的办法是，严格地解释合约要求的"履行地"，例如需要付款时，一方当事人例如收款人在伦敦，就可以解释为付款步骤的履行地是在伦敦，这样就绕过了很多如果在外国付款会在当地非法的情况，如根据外国法（甚至可能是突然颁布的临时性法律）必须先申请并获得外国政府批准等要求但当事人未能成功获得批准。

在 Kleinwort Sons & Co v. Ungarische Baumwolle Industrie Aktiengesellschaft (1939)2 KB 678 上诉庭先例中,伦敦的银行承兑了由匈牙利公司作为出票人并由匈牙利银行作为保兑行(confirming bank)的汇票(bill of exchange),付款日期在3个月后。匈牙利公司与银行还写了一封声明给伦敦银行(看来是预感到国内立法规定可能有影响),警告说到期日(maturity)时必须是符合匈牙利国内关于外汇立法规定他们才能向境外支付。结果后来果然匈牙利立法规定必须先获得匈牙利国家银行同意,匈牙利主体才能向境外支付,而有关匈牙利公司与银行均未获得批准。这样伦敦银行就起诉匈牙利公司与银行要求赔偿。

上诉庭认为此先例中汇票下作为出票人的承诺或保兑行支付金钱的地点是在伦敦。因此既然合约适用法是英国法、支付行为也发生在英国,与 Ralli Brothers v. Compania Naviera Sota Y Aznar 上诉庭先例的情况并不一样(该先例中约定的收取运费的履行完全发生在西班牙卸港),不能套用该先例中的判法。至于一方当事人如何真正做到合约要求的合法支付,并不在法院的考虑范围内。也就是即使匈牙利公司与银行因为支付这笔金钱,事后会在匈牙利属于非法,甚至看来就算是偷来、骗来的金钱,这也与英国法院在此先例中考虑的问题无关。Atkinson 大法官说:"In this contract the obligation is to pay certain money in London, and the contract is not concerned with the steps which the debtors may have to take to put themselves in a position to pay. It is concerned only with the payment itself, which is to be made in this country. This contractual obligation, in my view, does not come within the exception to the rule stated in ... by Scrutton LJ. in Ralli's case..."

在有完全相同判法的 Toprak Mahsulleri v. Finagrain(1979)2 Lloyd's Rep 98 先例中,涉及的事实背景是1974年土耳其粮食短缺,土耳其政府通过国有企业(Toprak Mahsulleri)作为买方招标大量收购小麦。此先例中,一个瑞士公司出售35万吨左右小麦,C & F 土耳其港口。合约约定的付款方式是由土耳其买方开出美国或西欧一流银行保兑的信用证,[14]交易货币采用瑞士法郎。之后卖方已经开始履行合约与租船,土耳其国有企业也实际上积极在努力推动想要进口这批小麦。但问题在于当时小麦价格大跌,土耳其政府内部看来产生了严重分歧,土耳其买方根据土耳其立法规定向当地政府申请外汇交易许可,反复警告无法获得许可卖方会在合约下索赔,并导致最后损失仍然由土耳其国企承担,但财政部迟迟不批准而且最后拒绝给予许可。这样卖方就根据合约开始了伦敦仲裁,在土耳其买方缺席的情况下,仲裁庭显然给出了对土耳其买方不利的裁决。而到了执行时土耳其买方才开始应诉,重要主张就是履行地非法(或实际无法履行)。

但上诉庭认定付款方式的条文中,如何付款明确说的是通过美国或西欧银行保

[14] 有关措辞/文字是:"Payment: by letter of credit to be opened in[买方]favour with and confirmed by a first class U. S. or West European Bank. Letter of credit shall be opened by March 31,1975, the latest."

兑信用证,因此可以说这部分(如果保兑银行要在如开证行倒闭下行使支付义务)并非在土耳其履行,也就不需要考虑土耳其本地法律下是否非法等问题了。这就与 Kleinwort Sons & Co v. Ungarische Baumwolle Industrie Aktiengesellschaft 先例中的情况类似,既然合约本身约定的付款方式不涉及土耳其而且收钱在瑞士也是合法,合约就可以执行,而土耳其公司如何完成自己的合约义务不是法院考虑的问题。Denning 勋爵说:"... the place of performance was not Turkey. Illegality by the law of Turkey is no answer whatever to this claim. The letter of credit had to be a confirmed letter of credit, confirmed by a first-class West European or US bank. The sellers were not concerned with the machinery by which the Turkish state enterprise provided that letter of credit at all. ... the sellers are not in the least concerned as to the method by which the Turkish buyers are to provide that letter of credit. Any troubles or difficulties in Turkey are extraneous to the matter and do not afford any defence to an English contract, performance to be by a confirmed letter of credit."

这看来就是通过严格解释履行地点到底是哪里,以达到支持合约有效的目的。这样一来,确实很多合约要求的履行即使涉及外国因素,也不会因为涉及外国法非法而无法执行。但实际上在笔者看来,对受影响的外国当事人而言,可能由于受到本国法律限制而实际上属于不可能履行的合约,但是在英国法院这样解释下就根本不会考虑不可履行,而是将受影响的当事人视为违约。正如早在 Thornborow v. Whitacre (1705)92 ER 270 先例,Holt 大法官说:"where a man will for a valuable consideration undertake to do an impossible thing, though it cannot be performed, yet he shall answer damages."

在较近期的 Deutsche Bank AG v. Unitech Global Ltd(2013)EWHC 2793(Comm)先例中,银行(Deutche Bank AG)与印度公司(Unitech)之间签订金融协议[包括借贷协议以及利率掉期协议(interest rate swap agreement)]。在协议中约定适用法是英国法、英国法院有专属管辖权,并写明了履行地点在纽约。之后看来印度公司在这些协议下欠了钱,因此银行开始诉讼。印度公司的抗辩内容很多,如操纵伦敦银行同业拆借利率(LIBOR)与默示误述(implied misrepresentation),[15]违反竞争法因此合约无效[16]等。而此先例中案件尚在银行申请简易判决的早期阶段。印度公司提出,假设在印度法下(印度公司的注册地)不允许印度公司将资金转移到纽约,即无法履行合约下的支付义务,并假设美国纽约州法院不会强制要求印度公司采取违反印度法规定的行为履行合约,这样根据 Ralli Brothers v. Compania Naviera Sota Y Aznar 先例的判法,既然在履行地(纽约)该行为不会被执行,在伦敦法院该行为一样不应该得到执行,至少也不是在早期阶段没有充分证据证明前述事实(包括印度法下不允许

〔15〕 见本书第二章之 1.4.5 段。

〔16〕 见本书第八章之 11.2 段。

转移、纽约法院不会强制要求违反印度法履约)的情况下给简易判决。

Teare 大法官先总结过往先例中的判法就说 Ralli Brothers v. Compania Naviera Sota Y Aznar 先例与 Kleinwort Sons & Co v. Ungarische Baumwolle Industrie Aktiengesellschaft 先例的区别正是在于后者的情况中如果做出支付,匈牙利公司在匈牙利最终会被认为非法,但实际支付的地点在伦敦,而在伦敦该行为并不非法,这就足以允许法院要求合约下该行为被履行。而且明确指出即使最后有关当事人在其本地可能属于非法,这并不在法院考虑的范围内,英国法院单纯只考虑在双方约定的履行地是否非法(此先例中也就是纽约),无论纽约法院怎么考虑印度法问题,不改变纽约法下支付是合法的。Teare 大法官说:"The decisions in Ralli Brothers and Kleinwort establish that the **English law of conflicts excuses performance of an obligation where performance would be illegal by the law of the country where the obligation is to be performed** but does not excuse performance where, although performance of the obligation is not illegal in the country where performance is to take place, steps necessary to enable a party to perform its obligation would be illegal in the country where such steps would be taken... Performance of an obligation governed by English law is unenforceable where the contract requires an act to be done which would infringe the laws of the country where that obligation must be performed. **The fact that a party may have to take a step which is unlawful in its own country in order to be able to perform its obligation does not excuse performance of that obligation if its own country is not the place of performance.**"(加黑部分是笔者的强调)

4.3 无论适用法是否英国法,合约目的是在友好国家采取非法行为

4.3.1 Foster v. Driscoll(1929)1 KB 470 上诉庭先例:合约目的违反友好外国法律不被执行

这方面的典型例子是 Foster v. Driscoll 上诉庭先例。此先例发生时正处于美国禁酒时期,这也导致了美国黑市中的酒价格飞涨。除了美国本地的私酿酒外,从海外走私的正规厂家酿制的酒更是能卖到天价,也带来了大量从加拿大等地走私酒入境美国的不法生意。此先例中就是多个英国当事人想要走私威士忌去美国获取高额利润。但后来酒还没能真正走私到美国,当事人之间已经开始争议,主要的出资人想要拿回自己的金钱,[17] 主张当事人之间的一系列合约安排均属非法。

上诉庭持少数意见的 Scrutton 大法官就提出,该走私的一整个交易安排中,有一部分合约本身是可以合法履行的,例如纯粹在英国供应威士忌的合约、装船开航后运输到加拿大的租约、雇佣装卸工人的合约等。至于后续走私的事情由当地的第三人

〔17〕 看来这是在非法合约下以不当得利(unjust enrichment)要求返还的争议。如果是英国法非法,就会涉及在本书第八章之 10.2 段介绍的撤回权理论(locus poenitentiae)。但是因为此先例是外国法非法,法院在决定是否执行时,这不是主要考虑。

(比如当地黑帮)负责,与之前合约的内容无关。这样此先例中的当事人们就仅仅是知道有关非法的情况,而没有实际参与,也因此合约本身并不非法,可以执行。[18]

但多数意见在事实上有不同认定,多数意见根据证据认定这一系列当事人之间根本像是合伙一样在做这个走私生意,有人出资,有人负责供应威士忌,有人负责运输,有人负责在美国的出售与收钱等。也因此虽然走私尚未完成甚至没有开始真正走私,即使合约的形成或履行未必非法,但整体来看所有人都参与在这个目的是走私去美国的交易。[19] 这样也就不用区分是否仅仅知情了,可以说所有人都是参与人,顶多是或多或少的区别。唯一问题就在于目的是违反外国法律是否也足以让英国法院不予执行?

上诉庭给出的答案是肯定的,重要的理由就是国际礼让的公共政策。Lawrence 大法官说:"I am clearly of opinion that **a partnership formed for the main purpose of deriving profit from the commission of a criminal offence in a foreign and friendly country is illegal**, even although the parties have not succeeded in carrying out their enterprise, and no such criminal offence has in fact been committed; and none the less so because the parties may have contemplated that if they could not successfully arrange to commit the offence themselves they **would instigate or aid and abet some other person to commit it**. The ground upon which I rest my judgment that such a partnership is illegal is that its recognition by our Courts would furnish **a just cause for complaint by the United States Government against our Government** (of which the partners are subjects), and would be contrary to our **obligation of international comity** as now understood and recognized, and therefore would offend against our notions of public morality."(加黑部分是笔者的强调)

Sankey 大法官也说:"… the mere fact that a vendor of goods knows that the purchaser proposes to run them into a country where they are prohibited by some revenue law is not sufficient to render the contract of sale illegal, but **if beyond mere knowledge the vendor actively engages in an adventure to get the goods into such country**, the Court will not assist the parties to the adventure by entertaining or settling any dispute between the parties arising out of the contract … [**T**]**he Courts of this country are not bound to entertain such actions in view of the obligations of international comity**… in my view an English contract should and will be held invalid on account of illegality **if the real object and intention of the parties necessitates them joining in an endeavour to perform in a foreign and friendly country** some act which is illegal by the law of such country

[18] 有关合约目的非法时,过往先例中对当事人仅仅知道(mere knowledge)与实际参与的区分,可见本书第八章之10.1.3段的介绍,不在这里重复。

[19] 这种一个不可分割交易中多份相关合约的情况,也可见本书第八章之12.3段。

notwithstanding the fact that there may be, in a certain event, alternative modes or places of performing which permit the contract to be performed legally."（加黑部分是笔者的强调）

4.3.2 区分 Ralli Brothers v. Compania Naviera Sota Y Aznar 先例

与本章之4.2.1段介绍的 Ralli Brothers v. Compania Naviera Sota Y Aznar (1920)2 KB 287 上诉庭先例相比，Foster v. Driscoll(1929)1 KB 470 上诉庭先例实际上是针对了不同方面的外国法非法。在前者的情况中，合约要求的履行必然导致在外国法下非法，这看来可以类比合约形成非法。而在后者的情况中，无论当事人的合约形成或履行是否非法，其实合约的形成甚至履行可能没有非法因素或可以合法履行（如 Foster v. Driscoll 先例中仅仅供应威士忌前往加拿大），针对的是当事人订约时的合约目的是在友好国家实施违反当地法律的行为。

在 Ispahani v. Bank Melli Iran (1998) Lloyd's Rep Bank 133 先例，Walker 大法官就总结两种不同的原则为区别针对了合约履行与合约目的。可以节录 Walker 大法官的言论如下："There are two associated principles. One is that where a contract is to be performed in a country where its **performance is unlawful by the law of that country** (lex loci solutionis), it will not be enforced by the English court. This principle is often identified with the well-known decision of this court in Ralli Brothers v Compania Naviera ... which was a case of supervening illegality. But the same (or a closely similar) principle applies to existing illegality: see ... Toprak Mahsulleri v Finagrain ... In this context **'performance' does not mean any activity required or contemplated by the contract; it has a relatively narrow and technical meaning** ...The other principle was stated as follows...in Foster v Driscoll ...: 'An English contract should and will be held invalid on account of illegality if the **real object and intention of the parties** necessitates them **joining in an endeavour to perform in a foreign and friendly country some act which is illegal** by the law of such country notwithstanding the fact that there may be, in a certain event, alternative modes or places of performing which permit the contract to be performed legally.'"（加黑部分是笔者的强调）

在 Magdeev v. Tsvetkov (2020) EWHC 887 (Comm) 先例中，Cockerill 大法官说 Ralli Brothers v. Compania Naviera Sota Y Aznar 上诉庭先例的非法针对的是合约要求的履行必然会涉及在履行地非法，无论合约的目的是什么；而 Foster v. Driscoll 上诉庭先例的非法只针对合约目的，不理会合约要求的履行是否在履行地非法。Cockerill 大法官说："The Foster v Driscoll and Ralli Bros principles differ in this way: the latter is concerned only with whether the contract between the parties necessarily involves performance of an act which is illegal by the law of the place of performance, irrespective of the object and intention of the parties; the former is only concerned with whether the object and intention of the parties is to perform their agreement in a manner which involves an illegal act in the place of performance, and is not concerned with whether the contract necessitates the undertaking of such an act."

也因此能够理解在不同案件的案情下，法院（或仲裁庭）在考虑"非法"的争议时会需要同时判断这几条路线的法律原则去区别测试能不能行得通。

例如在 Regazzoni v. KC Sethia（1944）Ltd（1958）AC 301 贵族院先例中，涉及的也是印度的黄麻（jute）出口生意。此先例中双方签订从印度出口黄麻袋（jute bags）的 CIF 买卖合约，最终的目的地是南非。双方也都知道印度政府立法禁止向南非出口黄麻，因此计划是先将货物运输到意大利热那亚，再转运前往南非，来回避印度的法律。买卖合约的适用法是英国法。订约后卖方反悔与违约，并主张该合约非法。最终上诉到贵族院后判有关合约非法/不可执行。

此先例的"非法"显然并非本书第八章之 4.1 段的合约形成（formation of contract）非法，因为在适用法即英国法下，从来没有禁止货物销售与运输前往友好国家南非，只是另一个友好国家印度禁止货物运输前往南非。至于一个友好国家针对另一个友好国家的禁运法律是否应该被支持，英国法院不应理会这类涉及政治的议题。Keith 勋爵说："The English courts cannot be called on to adjudicate upon political issues between India and South Africa. ... It is the illegality under the foreign law that is to be considered and not the effect of the foreign law on another country."

贵族院的大法官们虽然看来区别是考虑了不同的法律原则。例如 Simond 勋爵主要依据的是 Ralli Brothers v. Compania Naviera Sota Y Aznar 先例，认为在订约时当事人约定的就是在印度法律下非法的行为。Keith 勋爵则看来认为这更像 Foster v. Driscoll 先例中的情况，合约目的非法。而 Reid 勋爵则是同时依赖这两方面的途径。这里主要就是早期转运与三角贸易都不明确到底是合约约定的履行非法还是合约目的非法，但无论是哪种情况都会因非法无法执行。

当然无论到底是采取哪一种途径，都绕不开的问题，也是这类问题的核心是国际礼让的公共政策。也就是英国法院在什么情况下、为什么会考虑外国法怎么处理。

这种政治问题是一直在困扰国际商贸，20 世纪 50 年代美国对中国禁运，在 Regazzoni v. KC Sethia 先例的判词中就有提到英国会保持中立说："For instance, an English trader might buy goods from a French trader, knowing that they were from the United States and were ultimately for China. United States law prohibits export to China, but English law does not. The question would arise whether that prohibition would bar an action by the purchaser if the goods were not delivered."

到了今天越加复杂的国际政治局面，英国法院也不像早年尽量对外国法律保持中立。通过 Regazzoni v. KC Sethia 贵族院先例中这种转运贸易的做法来回避制裁或禁止贸易,在今天更全面的规管[20]下已经是行不通。至于相关合约非法与否,即使有关合约的形成或履行不严格是非法,但双方的合约目的是非法就已足够让法院否定执行了,也可以想到英国法院会是严格对待,对任何转运违反联合国禁运规定,都可能认为是非法、应该不予执行。

4.4 对友好国家的国际睦仪/礼让(international comity)

在 Regazzoni v. KC Sethia(1944)Ltd(1958)AC 301 贵族院先例中,会因为合约要求的履行必然涉及从印度出口黄麻而在履行地(印度)法律下非法,也会因为目的是违反友好国家的法律而不可执行。其中考虑到的是如果协助执行,印度政府就会向英国政府提出抗议,Keith 勋爵说:"I see no escape from the view that to recognize the contract between the appellant and the respondent as an enforceable contract would give a just cause for complaint by the Government of India and should be regarded as **contrary to conceptions of international comity. On grounds of public policy, therefore, this is a contract which our courts ought not to recognize.** It is said that the Indian legislation is discriminatory legislation against a country which is a member of the Commonwealth and with which this country is on friendly terms. But that, in my opinion, is irrelevant. The English courts cannot be called on to adjudicate upon political issues between India and South Africa. The Indian law is not a law repugnant to English conceptions of what may be regarded as within the ordinary field of legislation or administrative order even in this country. It is the illegality under the foreign law that is to be considered and not the effect of the foreign law on another country."(加黑部分是笔者的强调)

这个测试在 Foster v. Driscoll(1929)1 KB 470 上诉庭先例也有提到,Lawrence 大法官说:"The ground upon which I rest my judgment that such a partnership is illegal is that it's recognition by our Courts would furnish a just cause for complaint by the United States Government against our Government ... and would be contrary to our obligation of international comity as now understood and recognised ..."

在 Regazzoni v. KC Sethia 先例中,Simonds 勋爵还特别强调了必须针对的是"友好"国家,而不仅仅是任何外国:"When I say 'foreign country' I mean a foreign and

---

[20] 例如美国针对本国的商品、软件、科技等出口限制,会包括不允许转口,在美国《Export Administration Regulations》(15 CFR Chapter VII,以下简称 EAR)中称之为"Reexport"(定义可见 § 734.14)。很多出口限制的一般规定中都会包括禁止转口贸易,如针对特定列明国家贸易禁止的 §736.2(b)(1):"**General Prohibition One**-Export and reexport of controlled items to listed countries(Exports and Reexports). You may not, without a license or License Exception, export any item subject to the EAR to another country or reexport any item of U. S. -origin..."又例如针对特定实体贸易禁止的 §736.2(b)(5):"**General Prohibition Five**-Export or reexport to prohibited end-uses or end-users(End-Use End-User). You may not, without a license, knowingly export or reexport any item subject to the EAR to an end-user or end-use that is prohibited by part 744 of the EAR."

friendly country and will not repeat the phrase. In the statement of the question I call particular attention to the words 'the doing in a foreign country,' for it may well be that different considerations will arise and a different conclusion will be reached if the law of the contract is English and the contract can be wholly performed in England, or at least in some other country than that whose law makes the act illegal (see Kleinwort, Sons & Co. v. Ungarische Baumwolle Industrie Aktiengesellschaft[21]). There are points at which the two questions appear to touch each other, and sometimes the one proposition has been treated as an exception on the other. But there is, I think, a fundamental difference. It can hardly be regarded as a matter of comity that the courts of this country will not entertain a suit by a foreign State to enforce its revenue laws. It is, on the other hand, nothing else than comity which has influenced our courts to refuse as a matter of public policy to enforce, or to award damages for the breach of, a contract which involves the violation of foreign law on foreign soil, and it is the limits of this principle that we have to examine. If the principle is, as I think it clearly is, based on public policy, your Lordships will not hesitate, while disclaiming any intention to create any new head of public policy, to apply an old principle to new circumstances."

4.5 违反的外国法或域外法是否严重:Ryder Industries Limited v. Chan Wui Woo(2015)18 HKCFAR 544 先例

非法是否严重的课题已在本书第八章多处提到,也是权威的 Patel v. Mirza (2016) UKSC 42 最高院先例的三阶段测试的第三阶段"成比例"(proportionality)中重要的考虑因素。正如 Devlin 大法官在 The "St John"(1956)2 Lloyd's Rep 413 先例中所讲:"whether public policy is well served by driving from the seat of judgment everyone who has been guilty of a minor transgression."

另 Bingham 大法官在 Saunders v. Edwards(1987)1 WLR 1116 上诉庭先例中说:"Where issues of illegality are raised, the courts have ... to steer a middle course between two unacceptable positions. On the one hand it is unacceptable that any court of law should aid or lend its authority to a party seeking to pursue or enforce an object or agreement which the law prohibits. On the other hand, it is unacceptable that the court should, on the first indication of unlawfulness affecting any aspect of a transaction, draw up its skirts and refuse all assistance to the plaintiff, no matter how serious his loss nor how disproportionate his loss to the unlawfulness of his conduct."

这英国法合约下的"成比例"的道理在外国法或域外法非法也同样适用。在本段开头已经提到了较近期的 Ryder Industries Limited v. Chan Wui Woo 中国香港特区终审法院先例。从此先例中可以看到,尽管法院的确会因为合约的目的是在域外法

---

〔21〕 通过严格解释履行地来绕开非法问题的做法,可见本章之 4.2.2 段的介绍。

下从事非法行为而拒绝执行,但法院通过严格对域外法的事实认定以及对合约的解释,仍然会倾向于执行合约。

此先例中原告 Ryder Industries Limited(原名赛钛客 Saitek,消费电子产品品牌赛钛客就是来自于此)是中国香港特区注册的公司。该公司很早就已经在中国内地开展业务,包括在深圳宝安区与深圳政府合作成立合作公司,并且拥有大量工厂厂房。赛钛客还单独在深圳设立有一家外商独资公司。此先例中第一被告 Timely Electronics Co Ltd(Timely)也是香港注册的公司。第二被告陈先生(Chan Wui Woo)是 Timely 的主要股东。

在 2005 年时,Timely 看来是找到了一批客户需要制造手机,就找上了电子制造的大厂赛钛客合作。然而赛钛客并不是手机厂家,并不熟悉手机生产业务,当时拥有的设备也不足以生产手机,并且也不打算购置专门设备。因此在最后的合作协议中,赛钛客提供场地(合作公司的工厂)、部分设备与材料进行生产等,而 Timely 则向赛钛客支付工厂场地费用、提供另一部分设备、负责手机生产的管理和监督以及与客户对接、向客户收款等,并且最后从客户收取的款项中按比例分给赛钛客。该合作协议约定适用法是中国香港特区法律。

到了 2006 年中期,Timely 已经欠下了大量应付给赛钛客的账款。而陈先生作为担保人提供个人担保,但后来 Timely 与陈先生干脆明确拒绝支付,理由就是合作协议因为违反中国法而无效。

被主张非法的有多处问题,次要的略过。法院经过当事人的举证,尤其是双方中国法专家证人的争辩与帮助后,认定确实可能导致无效(或不可执行)的非法是赛钛客在深圳有两家主要公司,此先例中提供厂房、生产等的是赛钛客与深圳政府的合作公司。而赛钛客的独资公司也经营加工贸易,可以免税进口物料(电子元件)、在加工后出口境外,但是在没有获得海关批准前这些物料必须在独资公司的仓库中自己使用。而在此先例中独资公司进口的免税物料是给合作公司用于在 Timely 的合约下生产手机,这是违反了中国内地法律的行为。

在此先例中,虽然合作协议与后续有关还款、利息等问题的补充协议均是中国香港特区公司签订,也适用中国香港特区法律。而在中国香港特区本地法律下并不认为前述行为非法,也因此并非本章之 4.1 段介绍的在适用法下非法的问题。接下来就变成了合约的形成是否必然非法,看来也未必,毕竟当事人如果完全遵守规定,可以自己用不涉及免税的物料。而且即使必须使用免税物料,中国内地法律并没有完全禁止,只是需要按规定行事,先向海关提出申请。因此这也并非合约形成时就必然非法。但问题在于此时如果当事人订约时目的违反中国内地法律行事,仍然可能被认为合约非法。

而香港特区终审法院先是明确了多种导致合约不可执行的情况,接着明确了在域外法下也不是违反任何法律都会被认为“非法”。英国法在 Patel v. Mirza 最高院先例后,针对英国普通法非法问题采取的是基于多因素判断是否属于非法。在本书

第八章之 3 段也介绍了即使是违反了明确的立法规定，也往往是只有立法明示规定或通过必要的推断违反立法后果是合约不可执行（或无效）法院才会这样认定。针对事实问题的外国法或域外法，看来法院同样会采取类似的态度。

而在此先例中，当事人（尤其是 Timely 与陈先生）并没能提供足够证据说明中国内地法下此类违法的严重性。但法院能看到的是，中国内地的立法下违反这类法律时，针对合约并没有什么后果，尽管对当事人会有惩罚也并不严重，而主要是一些行政或经济上的后果。这样香港特区终审法院就从常识的角度认为在中国内地法律下这些违规行为不可以与严重非法行为相提并论，所以不能够在本案所适用的香港特区法律下，根据一国两制下礼让的公共政策不予执行，毕竟香港特区的普通法有保护合约神圣性的公共政策。

至于什么时候属于严重的问题，本就是在所有类别的外国法或域外法非法都需要考虑的，这就需要依赖专家证人就有关的非法的来龙去脉与后果提供证据。

4.6　外国法非法是否适用在非合约索赔

本段针对在涉及外国法非法时应该如何处理的问题，因为这不涉及保护英国法律对非法的公正、一致、和谐与完善，不能自我矛盾或阻碍〔22〕（self-stultified）。通常当事人之间产生争议，并非只有合约这一种索赔诉因，而经常会有替代诉因，如侵权〔23〕与复原/不当得利。〔24〕 在上一章针对的英国本地法非法，已是很明确在法律不能自我阻碍与不能让一方因自己的非法行为获利的大原则下，不会容许这种非合约索赔（non-contractual claims）。重复节录在 Patel v. Mirza（2016）UKSC 42 最高院先例中，Toulson 勋爵说："Looking behind the maxims, there are two broad discernible policy reasons for the common law doctrine of illegality as a defence to a civil claim. One is that a person should not be allowed to profit from his own wrongdoing. The other, linked, consideration is that **the law should be coherent and not self-defeating, condoning illegality by giving with the left hand what it takes with the right hand.**"（加黑部分是笔者的强调）

但涉及不当得利时，英国法院经常在不同个别案件面对左右为难，因为觉得支持非法抗辩让被告获得赃款比不支持非法抗辩让原告成功复原更不理想或不符合公共利益。所以在本书第八章之 12.2.2 段已经介绍了在 Patel v. Mirza 最高院先例一致

---

〔22〕 "自我阻碍"已经在本书第八章之 1.5 段与 7.2.3 段有介绍，包括其出处是来自 Peter Birks 教授的 "Recovering Value Transferred Under an Illegal Contract"（2000）1 Theoretical Inquiries in Law 155 一文。Birks 教授认为在一个非法合法下，知道与参与非法的一方当事人可通过法院协助去以不当得利成功取回金钱是荒谬的，说："important that the law as stated in one area should not make nonsense of the law as stated in another."

〔23〕 有关合约与侵权的同步责任问题，可见本书第一章之 2.4 段。

〔24〕 有关不当得利问题，可见本书第三章之 5.4.3 段、第七章之 7.1 段、第十章之 11.2 段与笔者《合约的履行、弃权与禁反言》一书第五章之 4 段。

认为非法理论不影响原告的不当得利的诉因。

但这是英国法律,在外国法非法时不直接适用。在目前说法看来,Foster v. Driscoll(1929)1 KB 470 上诉庭先例的判决针对的只是合约的执行问题。而如果是非合约索赔,即使后果会达到与执行合约类似效果,也并不因 Foster v. Driscoll 先例的判法而被法院不予执行。

以下先介绍两个先例。

4.6.1 Lilly Icos LLC v. 8PM Chemists Ltd(2009)EWHC 1905(Ch)先例

在 Lilly Icos LLC v. 8PM Chemists Ltd 先例中,涉及的问题是当时美国由于 20 世纪 90 年代后严苛的药物规管,有大量美国人选择从加拿大网上药店购买包括处方药在内的各种药物运输到美国,后来该行为还逐渐扩大,供货地开始逐渐拓展到全球,先是英国、澳大利亚,后来还进一步包括土耳其等地区。但事实上在美国法律下,进口药物也有各类规管,而以这样的方式进口的药物大多是违反法律的。

此先例中就涉及的是英国的药品供货商从土耳其购买药品,各类药品会先运送到英国,在英国免税仓打包后,再一起发往加拿大或美国。但药品在运输到英国免税仓后,主张是商标权利人的 Lilly 提出其中有一部分涉及商标侵权问题,因此在提供交叉担保(cross-undertaking)的前提下法院批准颁布了中间禁令[25]阻止进一步处置这些药品。但后来经过法院认定,由于药品到英国纯粹是在免税仓内打包,并不涉及在英国的任何流转,而不涉及商标侵权,因此解除了中间禁令。

这样,英国的药品供货商就提出索赔 Lilly 申请禁令带来的损失。Lilly 的一项主要抗辩,就是英国药品供应商一连串交易安排的目的是实施违反美国法的行为。但 Arnold 大法官判 Lilly 败诉,重要原因就指出药品供货商的索赔并非基于当事人之间的合约,而是基于 Lilly 在申请禁令所提供给法院的交叉担保,因为禁令最终被解除,需要赔偿对方当事人因禁令带来的损失,而在本章前文中介绍的 Ralli Brothers v. Compania Naviera Sota Y Aznar(1920)2 KB 287 先例或 Foster v. Driscoll(1929)1 KB 470 先例中都只是适用在针对执行外国法非法合约的情况。而此交叉担保与非法是完全谈不上任何关系,即使合约非法也不应该"诛九族"。可以节录 Arnold 大法官所说如下:"A more fundamental limit of both the Ralli Bros principle and the Foster principle is that they only apply to claims to enforce a contract. Since the defendants are not seeking to enforce any contract, but rather an undertaking to the court enforceable in equity, it follows that neither principle applies to the present case.... "

4.6.2 Jonathan Ang v. Lyu Yan(2021)SGCA 12 新加坡上诉庭先例

不妨再介绍一个近期的 Jonathan Ang v. Lyu Yan 新加坡上诉庭先例。此先例中一名中国公民(Lyu Yan)是法国巴黎银行新加坡分行(BNP' Paribas Singapore,或以下简称 BNP)的私人银行客户。由于需要逃避中国的外汇管制从自己的中国账户转

---

〔25〕 见《仲裁法:从 1996 年英国仲裁法到国际商务仲裁》一书第十章之 2.2.1.2.5 段。

移金钱到新加坡,经过 BNP 介绍认识了一位 Joseph Lim 先生。第一次交易时 Joseph 找了一家印尼的汇款公司,具体交易方式是 Lyu 先在中国将钱汇入 Joseph(实际上是印尼公司)指定的中国账户,事后会有一笔等值的钱汇入 Lyu 在新加坡的账号,此次交易价值 300 万美元并且顺利完成。

之后 Lyu 再次寻求 Joseph 的帮助,又需要汇款等值 300 万美元的人民币。但这次 Joseph 找的不是印尼公司,而是两位个人:Jonathan Ang 与 Derek Lim。原本预计做法应该与第一次汇款类似,Lyu 先将钱在中国汇入指定账号,之后在海外会有钱直接汇入 Lyu 在新加坡的账号。但是这一次 Lyu 在中国本地汇款后,迟迟未能在新加坡账户中收到钱。显然非常着急的 Lyu 向 Joseph 追讨,而 Joseph 则向 Jonathan 与 Derek 追讨。这样就披露出来,据说在后面还有一位"Allen",而 Allen 才是真正允诺在境外汇款的人士,然而在中国境内人民币汇款给 Allen 后,Allen 已经消失不见了。这看来是遇上了骗子,Lyu 因此针对 Joseph、Jonathan 与 Derek,以侵权与不当得利为由开始索赔。

在上诉庭的审理中首先认定的事实问题,是 Jonathan 与 Derek 未能提供足够证据证明 Allen 的存在,[26] 在这样的认定下 Jonathan 与 Derek 也就变成了"骗子",要承担责任了。而 Jonathan 与 Derek 提出的抗辩,则是当事人之间的协议实际上目的是逃避中国对外汇管制、资金出境的有关法律,因此协议非法。当事人的索赔无论是什么形式,都应该被一致不予执行,否则这会有悖于新加坡法律中(与英国一致的)不能自我阻碍原则,不能因为采取了非合约的索赔就变得与法院执行非法合约有一样的经济后果。

回到本段课题,上诉庭实际上在考虑了当事人提供的证据后,认定 Lyu 并不知情、更不用说是目的是采取中国法下的非法行为了,[27] 事实上就不适用 Foster v. Driscoll(1929)1 KB 470 上诉庭先例。但上诉庭接下来进一步考虑了 Foster v. Driscoll 先例到底能否适用在非合约索赔的课题。新加坡上诉庭给出的答案是否定的。

在这一点上新加坡上诉庭支持了 Lilly Icos LLC v. 8PM Chemists Ltd(2009) EWHC 1905(Ch)先例的判法,认为 Foster v. Driscoll 先例只适用在合约索赔的争议中。换言之,即使由于合约目的违反外国法导致合约不可执行,当事人其他的侵权、不当得利返还等主张并不因此不可执行。Andrew Phang Boon Leong 大法官这样说:

---

〔26〕 最后实际提供证据的责任在 Jonathan 与 Derek 身上,这出于多方面原因。包括是他们主张存在一位真正的骗子 Allen;以及包括钱实际被打给他们,是他们将钱转出的,这可以推断他们很可能是骗子,因此应该由他们来举证反驳;相比之下,由他们证明 Allen 的存在是更合适的,毕竟要受害人 Lyu 证明 Allen 不存在会违背了证有不证无的原理。有关举证责任问题可见《证据法:基础理论、口头证据与专家证据》一书第七章。

〔27〕 虽然这样用"地下钱庄"转移资产出境的行为看来显然目的是采取非法行为。但此先例中法院这样的判法应是根据特定的案件事实,以及当事人所提供(或未能提供或被告缺席)的证据进行的认定。

"... according to Jonathan and Derek, the contract between A and B is void and unenforceable. A thus cannot claim against B in contract. Further, A also cannot claim against B for non-contractual causes of action, if these non-contractual claims have the economic effect of enforcing the void and unenforceable contract... **This argument fails, because the rule in Foster v Driscoll can only be used to defeat a claim in contract, and is not applicable in relation to non-contractual claims**: see, for example, the English High Court decision of Lilly Icos LLC v 8PM Chemists Ltd ... In other words, if only the rule in Foster v Driscoll applies, **A will generally be allowed to make non-contractual claims against B, even though these non-contractual claims have the economic effect of enforcing the void and unenforceable contract.**"（加黑部分是笔者的强调）

照说新加坡法与英国法均有不能自我阻碍的说法，即对于涉及非法合约而产生的侵权、不当得利等索赔，需要考虑导致合约非法背后的公共政策。如果支持侵权、不当得利等索赔会阻碍公共政策，法院在衡量之下就也不会予以执行。在 Ochroid Trading Ltd v. Chua Siok Lui（2018）SGCA 5 新加坡上诉庭先例，Andrew Phang Boon Leong 大法官说："To reiterate, where a plaintiff brings an independent claim in unjust enrichment for the recovery of benefits conferred under an illegal and prohibited contract, the question which the court has to answer is whether to allow the claim would **undermine the fundamental policy that rendered the underlying contract void and unenforceable in the first place.**"（加黑部分是原文的强调）

在涉及外国法非法去适用 Foster v. Driscoll 先例时，已经在上一段介绍过是不影响当事人主张侵权、不当得利返还的非合约索赔的诉因。其中侵权的独立诉因在涉及非法合约争议的案件也很少涉及，这里就不再深究了。而针对不当得利，看来在适用法是新加坡法（即使是涉外合约）的情况下，如果合约非法，Ochroid Trading Ltd v. Chua Siok Lui 先例判不当得利作为独立诉因不会受影响，除非与基本性的公共政策起冲突。已经在本书第八章之 12.2.2 段介绍，Patel v. Mirza（2016）UKSC 42 最高院先例已经是明确了在英国法下不是主张非法合约权利而是以不当得利作为诉因，一般是不受影响。这样看来虽然该新加坡先例拒绝适用 Patel v. Mirza 先例的基于多因素判断的三阶段测试，但在不当得利作为诉因的情况下与 Patel v. Mirza 先例没有本质区别。

假设有一份买卖海洛因的合约适用新加坡法，在外国履行地也是非法。而新加坡有严苛的禁毒法律与公共政策，显然会导致合约非法/不可执行。这样即使是买家付了钱没收到货，事后以不当得利要求贩毒的卖方返还金钱，新加坡法院考虑到新加坡法律下禁止此类合约背后的公共政策，在不能自我阻碍的原则下，也考虑到非法的严重性，不会执行不当得利返还的索赔。相信在英国也是一样的判法。

至于适用法是外国法，即使 Foster v. Driscoll 先例不适用在非合约索赔，看来也会因为违反新加坡的基本性公共政策而不可执行了。这样，两者在这种严重案件的后果将没有区别。

4.7　涉及外国法非法的案件受 Patel v. Mirza 最高院先例的影响

在本书第八章之 7.5 段介绍了在 Patel v. Mirza（2016）UKSC 42 最高院先例中，已经权威性地针对了英国普通法非法的民事案件如何考虑，并确立了基于多因素判断（factors-based approach）的三阶段测试（three-stages test）。

涉及外国法非法，英国法院主要考虑的公共政策就是国际睦仪/礼让（international comity），可以说这方面与 Patel v. Mirza 最高院先例毫无关系。其他方面的考量也不一样，如英国法院不会关心外国法律是否完整、公正，也管不了。英国法院也难以分析、无法考虑外国千变万化的不同非法背后的公共政策是什么。因此，如自我阻碍原则或成比例原则等在考虑外国法非法时就不会有什么关系了。但在 Patel v. Mirza 最高院先例的权威判决作出之后，该先例考虑的一些重要因素即使在外国非法的案件仍是同样重要，典型的就是在本章之 4.5 段已经提到的违反的外国法是否严重的问题。

关于 Patel v. Mirza 最高院先例对外国法非法的影响，已经在本书第八章之 8.3 段简单介绍，这里尽量不再重复。只在简单介绍两个近期先例与笔者的一个仲裁案件，来显示 Patel v. Mirza 先例的精神的影响与可以考虑的一些因素。

4.7.1　Magdeev v. Tsvetkov（2020）EWHC 887（Comm）先例

Magdeev v. Tsvetkov 先例已经在本书第八章之 8.3 段有介绍，特别是分析与结论方面，但针对案情介绍不多，所以在此重点去更详尽针对案情以减少重复。在 Magdeev v. Tsvetkov 先例中，投资人（Magdeevis 先生）与珠宝商（Tsvetkov 先生）是关系非常好、胜似亲兄弟的朋友。在 2011 年前后，珠宝商由于与英国著名钻石珠宝品牌格拉夫（Graff）的格拉夫家族的关系，拿到长期的固定优惠（一般珠宝首饰 50%，GIA 认证的钻石有 37.5%），这样珠宝商就开始做起了珠宝首饰生意，专门设立了迪拜公司（EK Diamonds DMCC，或 Equix Dubai）经营生意，在迪拜和塞浦路斯销售珠宝首饰。到了 2014 年，为了扩张生意，当事人之间签订了如下适用英国法的合约：（1）贷款合约：投资人作为出借人出借 1000 万美元给作为借款人的迪拜公司，为期 3 年，无利息，并由珠宝商提供个人担保。（2）雇佣合约：迪拜公司将雇佣投资人，为期 3 年，薪资大约是贷款金额的 15%。然而虽然投资人会时不时介绍客户，但并不会真正为迪拜公司工作。

如此看来雇佣合约并非真正雇佣，实际上是以薪资为名、向投资人支付“利息”。而至于当事人之间为什么这么做，原因可能很多，至少其中一个原因看来是投资人需要获得迪拜的签证，而通过与迪拜公司签订雇佣合约，作为雇员就可以获得这样的签证。之后投资人与珠宝商之间还有一系列的合作，投资人与珠宝商在这种商业关系下最后反目成仇，双方对于一系列合作都产生严重争议。

争议主要针对的是非法的课题，涉及的问题是投资人在 2017 年要求偿还贷款，而珠宝商提出的一个重要抗辩是在 2014 年的贷款合约违反阿联酋法律。

法院认定雇佣合约的真正目的与意图是为了帮助投资人申请签证，不是真正的雇佣合约，也认定了这种行为违反了阿联酋法律。这样问题就是法院是否应该继续执行当事人之间的整个交易中不可分割的所有相关合约。这整个交易中，雇佣合约实际是用来支付贷款合约下的利息，但雇佣合约又有一部分涉及阿联酋法律非法。如果雇佣合约非法而无效/不可执行，由于难以与整个交易分割，会导致贷款合约也受影响。[28]

而且与 Ralli Brothers v. Compania Naviera Sota Y Aznar（1920）2 KB 287 先例以及 Foster v. Driscoll（1929）1 KB 470 先例相比，此先例是在 Patel v. Mirza（2016）UKSC 42 最高院先例后进行审理，也因此考虑这最高权威的 Patel v. Mirza 先例对外国非法案件的影响就显得异常重要。尤其是此先例针对的情况，有关涉外合约适用英国法，但合约的履行在阿联酋非法或者是合约目的是欺骗阿联酋政府。Cockerill 大法官一开始就提出了这种情况显然不能照搬 Patel v. Mirza 先例中的考虑因素。但 Cockerill 大法官接着明确指出 Patel v. Mirza 先例中的精神与弹性处理非法仍然是应当参考的，也就是要基于多因素来进行考虑与衡量了。

而 Cockerill 大法官在判决时，首先是认为 Patel v. Mirza 先例中提到的多因素中，成比例在涉及外国法时是非常难以考虑的，毕竟英国法院无法权衡外国法下这些非法问题背后的各种不同公共政策或者是考虑因素与背景。但 Cockerill 大法官仍然提供了一些可供参考的因素，其思路与考虑的因素包括以下内容：

1. 两份合约的主要目的是贷款，并不属于非法。Cockerill 大法官的思路是首先认定当事人这套交易的核心到底是什么。通过考虑全盘事实后认定其实整个交易的真正与实质的主要目的是贷款，而雇佣合约纯粹是附带（哪怕雇佣合约也有一部分是为了支付利息，否则就变成另一个独立合约）。而交易的主要目的并不涉及任何非法问题。

2. 当事人订立雇佣合约时的目的可能涉及非法。虽然通过双方当事人各自对抗的举证，并没有明显证据显示当事人对非法明确知情，但是从事实本身来看，以合法雇佣合约的手段掩盖欺骗当局骗取签证的实质，这很大程度上可以推断当事人知道这行为非法，尤其是其中还会涉及各种向政府提交文件的过程中需要进行虚假陈述

---

〔28〕 此交易中欺骗阿联酋政府的手段，是通过分开两份合约来完成的，因此如果一份合约不可执行，整个交易难以分割（non-severable），会导致其他合约也无法执行。Cockerill 大法官这样说："Where the deceptive drafting or structure involves splitting the contact into two parts and documents with deceptive intent, no part of the contract is enforceable, and severance is impossible. Thus, in Alexander v Rayson both the lease and the services agreement were unenforceable and in Mitsubishi v Alafouzos the shipbuilding contract (without the side letter) would have been unenforceable." Alexander v. Rayson（1936）1 KB 169 先例以及 Mitsubishi v. Alafouzos（1988）1 Lloyd's Rep 191 先例可见本书第八章之 11.5.4.3 段的介绍，不在这里重复。这种一个不可分割交易中多份相关合约的情况也可见本书第三章之 4.3 段。

等情况。

3. 非法的严重性与国际礼让的平衡。虽然涉及外国法的非法，不是根据成比例原则来判断是否非法而不予执行，也非常难以考虑外国法是否在外国公共政策下成比例。在本案看来，欺诈方式获取签证在英国法下被认为是严重的，毕竟会影响国家的经济和安全问题。

然而这是否严重仍然只是法院在英国法下的看法，现在要处理的是在履行地即阿联酋法律下是否认为这行为严重，但对此当事人没有提供什么证据。Cockerill 大法官说自己不能也不应该凭空揣测，毕竟阿联酋法律下完全可能有一套不同的标准。虽然阿联酋法律下伪造文件的后果甚至可以判处 10 年监禁，但欺诈方法获取签证即使涉及伪造文件看来不视为特别严重，原告专家证人就提到说这种行为在阿联酋法律下未必会被严肃处理与对待，而且最后事情曝光看来阿联酋政府也确实没有真正采取什么刑事调查或检控的行为。

因此最后 Cockerill 大法官总结了以上各种考虑因素，经过权衡之后，认为尽管当事人意图采取外国法非法行为，但交易只是部分附带内容非法、当事人也没能证明外国法下该非法的严重性，因此在国际礼让的公共政策下并不认为交易由于外国法非法而导致贷款合约不可执行。可节录 Cockerill 大法官所说如下："...However **in the overall balance in the light of the requirements of comity, the fact of the intent to deceive** in the context of what is plainly some way more than an administrative default **is outweighed by the fact that this was a small incident of a perfectly legitimate transaction** and with no apparent intent to break the UAE's laws, which has attracted no sanction from the UAE authorities. That balance indicates that **it would be contrary to justice to refuse enforcement** in this case-even on the basis of the contract as originally envisaged, and not as it was later amended to be. If one looks at it from the latter perspective, the position is a fortiori."（加黑部分是笔者的强调）

4.7.2　Haddad v. Rostamani（2021）EWHC 1892（Ch）先例

还可以介绍一个更近期的 Haddad v. Rostamani 先例。此先例中的共同被告主要是来自阿联酋的商业家族罗斯塔马尼（Al Rostamani）家族成员，以及一位向他们提供法律服务的阿联酋律师。原告是一位英国公民（Haddad 先生），曾经与第一被告（罗斯塔马尼家族的 Khulood 女士）关系很好，并且之后开始合伙经营房地产开发生意。

根据 Haddad 先生的指称，他在 2002 年与 Khulood 女士在伦敦达成口头合伙协议，之后还订立了书面合伙协议。合约中双方约定各自持有 50% 合伙资产，以英国作为合伙企业的总部，但具体的房地产开发项目则不仅仅是伦敦地产，也包括设立阿联酋公司开发阿联酋迪拜等地的项目。合伙协议约定适用英国法，并约定英国法院专属管辖。

但之后 Haddad 先生与 Khulood 女士关系破裂，原告指称 Khulood 女士（以及在其他被告的帮助下）以各种方式挪用（misappropriation）了超过13.5亿英镑的合伙资产，因此在英国法院针对被告提起诉讼。此先例中则是Haddad先生已经申请到了法院允许域外送达（service out of jurisdiction）诉状的命令，而被告则申请撤销此命令。被告的一个主要主张〔29〕是合伙协议意图违反阿联酋法律，因此合约无效/不可执行，显然没有域外送达的必要。

具体而言，阿联酋法律下有一段时期禁止非迪拜公民拥有迪拜土地，以及根据阿联酋公司法规定阿联酋股东在阿联酋外资公司中的持股比例不得低于51%。而合伙协议就是意图规避这些法律规定，约定由Khulood女士或她安排的其他家族成员作为名义上的开发商。

由于案件还没到最终审理，只是处于考虑是否允许域外送达阶段，因此并没全面审理所有证据与进行认定。但是法院首先指出即使由于合约目的确实是意图违反阿联酋法律，这类涉及外国法非法的问题中，也会采取类似Patel v. Mirza（2016）UKSC 42先例比较宽松的基于多因素判断的方法来考虑是否无效/不可执行，不会说只要意图违反外国法，就必然产生无效/不予执行的后果。Zacaroli大法官说："The defendants rightly point out that Patel v Mirza does not directly apply to a case where the relevant illegality is the breach of a foreign country's laws. Nevertheless, it has recently been held that a similar balancing exercise is appropriate in determining whether public policy requires the English court wholly to refuse to enforce a contract entered into with the intention of breaching a foreign law: see Magdeev v Tsvetkov ... I respectfully adopt Cockerill J's analysis. Lord Toulson's comment in Patel v Mirza, justifying a more flexible approach in the context of domestic illegality, that 'we are, after all, in the area of public policy' holds good in the case of foreign illegality. It is just that the public policies are different... Under the flexible approach which I consider the more recent authorities mandate, a finding of such illegality no longer leads inevitably to the contract being void for all purposes."

接下来回到此先例的案情，纯粹从已经提供的证据上来看，阿联酋法律下即使违反公司法中针对外国股东持股最高49%的规定，也只是按比例返还资本；针对必须阿联酋公民才能拥有土地的规定也只维持了一段时间。因此完全可以说即使意图违反这些法律，也并非严重非法，权衡之后英国法院仍然可能愿意执行。当然至于最后如何权衡，具体有哪些因素会影响法院的权衡，在此阶段还未能全都明确，但至少显示Haddad先生完全有可争辩的良好案件（good arguable case），也确实存在待审理的严肃争议（serious issue to be tried），因此在此阶段Haddad先生胜诉。

---

〔29〕　被告还有另一项主要主张是有关争议已经在迪拜法院审理，这有关争端的禁反言（issue estoppel）的问题不是本章重点，不在这里介绍。有兴趣的读者可参考《合约的履行、弃权与禁反言》一书第九章之7.2段。

4.7.3 涉及中国法非法的仲裁案件

目前中国公司无论是走出去海外投资还是在中国与来华投资者做生意，都会涉及是否符合中国法要求的问题。中国仲裁想要扩大国际影响力，也应该向国际做法靠拢。中国企业或律师了解英国法如何看待与处理非法问题的意义在于当中国企业在外国（尤其是普通法国家或地区）法院或仲裁庭想以中国法非法作为抗辩而否定与外国公司订立的合约时，需要知道从哪些考虑因素来争辩，包括如何首先说服法院或仲裁庭在中国法下非法是否成立的问题。

笔者以不久前处理过的涉及中国法非法的仲裁案件为例。该仲裁案件涉及欧洲的A公司拥有处理某些危险品业务的专长，投资并准备去自己营运一家在中国的工厂。该交易涉及多份合约，发生争议提交仲裁的合约有两份，一份是与该中国工厂的中国投资方B公司之间订立的股权转让合约，另一份是在股权转让后B公司移交工厂给A公司的管理合约。A公司在两个仲裁都委任了笔者作为仲裁员，这显然是希望两个密切相关与相互依赖的合约有一致与兼容的仲裁裁决结果。不过后来两个案件的进展不同，也在仲裁机构的介入下委任了不同的首席仲裁员。前者针对股权转让合约的仲裁动得较快，仲裁庭作出了针对A公司的履约指令（specific performance）。但在后者的管理合约，争议涉及B公司拒不移交工厂给A公司，这从案情、证据与合约条文看，B公司是完全站不住脚的。但B公司却提出了唯一的非法抗辩，说是营运该工厂是需要有关当局对营运主体进行资质批准，但A公司没有获得该批准。

在非法的问题上，笔者与两位共同仲裁员产生了严重分歧，对笔者来说，这一非法抗辩十分牵强，完全站不住脚。理由十分简单，具体如下：

1. 立法只要求营运主体获得资质批准，没有任何证据显示A公司是无法获得批准，例如该批准只颁发给中国公司。A公司在移交工厂前没有获得批准在笔者的解读只是因为他仍不是营运主体，但没有任何证据显示A公司在接管工厂后不能很快申请到批准。

2. 这从商业常识上来看也符合内在可能性，因为A公司在中国其他地区有投资与营运的同类工厂多达6个。A公司作为一家跨国公司，如果事前对中国有关当局会批准他作为合资质的营运主体没有充分把握，也不会贸然就作出这么大笔的投资。换言之，A公司很快获得批准应不是问题。

3. 移交工厂的管理合约虽然要求A公司在移交时拥有所有有关的合法证件，但没有明确说明这包括营运主体资质的批准，并且该批准是合约成立或继续履行的先决条件。笔者也相信如果双方在谈判合约时A公司也不会同意，因为在B公司没有移交工厂之前它与工厂一点关系也没有，是不用也不会取得批准的。

4. 更关键的是争议只针对B公司应否按照合约把工厂移交给A公司。移交工厂与A公司有否拥有资质批准是相互独立的事情，批准与否和移交工厂是没有关系的。至于移交后A公司的营运到底会是合法或非法（A公司拿不到资质批准但偷偷去营运),根本是将来的变数,不是本仲裁的争议点。B 公司没有或无法证明 A 公司是永远申请不到批准。

笔者在合议时向共同仲裁员指出如果在本仲裁判移交工厂的管理合约因非法而无效,是与另外一个仲裁的履约指令直接矛盾,而会令整个交易形成僵局与令交易方变得无所适从,因为一个交易的多份密切相关、相互依赖的合约本质上应统筹去对待,不该轻易抽出部分判是无效而令整个交易都无法进行,这与本书第三章之 4.3 段中所讲的在同一不可分割的交易不能部分撤销某一合约的道理一样。

但首席仲裁员坚持是每一个仲裁都是独立考虑,这是笔者同时作为两个仲裁案件的仲裁员所不认同的。最近在香港特区高等法院 W v. AW(2021)HKCFI 1707 先例中,两个涉及同一交易的仲裁案件,被重复委任在两个案件的一位共同仲裁员针对同样的事实问题在先后做出的两份裁决书中做出截然相反的决定而令后一个案件的仲裁裁决书被高等法院以违反自然公正而撤销。这也带来启示是如果两个涉及同一交易、事实背景相同、当事人也相同,只是针对不同合约的仲裁案件,被重复委任在两个案件的共同仲裁员在独立审理的基础上需要提醒其他非共同仲裁员要统筹考虑整个交易与其他直接相关的案件的结果。

至于首席仲裁员提出的独立审理的问题,是针对不同案件即使涉及同一交易,也有可能是在不同的当事人之间,或者不同的律师代表,提出的争议不同、提交的证据也不同等,这都是要完全独立审理。在现实中即使涉及同一交易或同样的事实背景,但因为时间不同与争议金额不同,完全有可能出现上述提到的不同因素。这就肯定是要独立审理与考虑证据,而不会受前一个仲裁的影响。当然共同仲裁员也需要在裁决书中写明强有力的理由支持自己就相同的争议做出截然相反的决定。

笔者参与的该两个仲裁案件涉及同一个交易,同样的当事人与相同的律师团队,只是两个仲裁所基于的两份相关联的合约一个是关于投资金额的支付,而另一个是关于工厂的移交,所以争议的合约侧重点不同。即使笔者不是共同仲裁员,而只是涉及该管理合约争议的仲裁员,笔者也会裁定非法的抗辩是无法成立。所以,不存在首席仲裁员独立考虑,笔者不独立考虑的问题。

5. 外国法合法但违反英国公共政策

本段要讨论的是另一方面的问题,也就是在外国法下合约的产生或履行或合约目的,都没有任何非法之处。但在英国的法律或公共政策下被认为非法。在部分或全部是涉外的合约,是否会被英国法院执行或协助执行(如申请各种禁令、承认与执行该合约下外国仲裁裁决书或外国法院判决等)?

这里针对的不是较早介绍的英国法合约在形成或履行是否在英国本地或外国法律下非法的问题了,而是看外国法合法下是否违反了英国公共政策。这不严格或不一定是违反明确法律规定的情况，虽然两者是经常相提并论。一般来说，与认可的公共政策相悖，会被认为属于非法与不被英国法院执行。

5.1　英国法院考虑英国公共政策的权力来源

英国法院目前考虑涉外合约的英国公共政策原则与权力来源是英国立法《Contracts(Applicable Law) Act 1990》中所引入的1980年《罗马公约》条文：[30] (1) Article 7(2)："Nothing in this Convention shall restrict the application of the rules of the law of the forum in a situation where they are mandatory irrespective of the law otherwise applicable to the contract.（无论适用法为何，英国法中强制性适用的部分仍然必须适用）"(2) Article 16："The application of a rule of the law of any country specified by this Convention may be refused only if such application **is manifestly incompatible with the public policy('ordre public') of the forum**.（任何外国的适用法下合法的合约，仍然可以因为与英国公共政策不符而被不予执行）"（加黑部分是笔者的强调）

也就是无论合约在外国适用法下是否合法，英国法院总可以有最后的机会考虑是否在英国本地的某些公共政策下，可以拒绝执行该合约。可以说，这是为英国法院提供了一个"安全阀"(safety valve)。

而执行外国仲裁裁决书也是同样的原则，英国法院的权力来源是英国《Arbitration Act 1996》。该立法之Section 100(1)对外国"公约裁决书"(New York Convention award)的定义为："an award made, in pursuance of an arbitration agreement, in the territory of a state(other than the United Kingdom) which is a party to the New York Convention"。接下来Section 101(2)说明在英国法院批准下(by leave)，一份公约裁决书可以在英国如同英国法院的判决一样强制执行："A New York Convention award may, by leave of the court, be enforced in the same manner as a judgment or order of the court to the same effect."

与本章课题有关的是针对英国法院可以拒绝承认或协助执行公约裁决书的有限例外或事由的是Section 103，其中(3)说："Recognition or enforcement of the award may also be refused if the award is in respect of a matter which is not capable of settlement by arbitration, or if **it would be contrary to public policy to recognise or enforce the award**."（加黑部分是笔者的强调）

这立法是根据1958年《纽约公约》之Article V(2)(b)同样提供给执行地法院的安全阀："2. Recognition and enforcement of an arbitral award **may** also be refused if the

---

[30] 在2009年12月17日之后，1980年《罗马公约》已经被"The Rome I Regulation"(Regulation(EC) No 593/2008)取代。在Rome I Regulation下有类似条文，区别可见Article 9与Article 21。在英国脱欧后，根据《The Law Applicable to Contractual Obligations and Non-Contractual Obligations(Amendment etc.)(EU Exit) Regulations 2019》与《The Jurisdiction, Judgments and Applicable Law(Amendment)(EU Exit) Regulations 2020》保留了绝大部分Rome I Regulation中的内容。

competent authority in the country where recognition and enforcement is sought finds that:...(b)The recognition or enforcement of the award **would be contrary to the public policy of that country.**"(加黑部分是笔者的强调)

5.2 足够重要可以不予执行或协助执行涉外合约的英国公共政策

即使是涉外合约(外国适用法与外国履行的合约),需要在英国法院寻求协助或执行,仍然需要考虑英国本地的公共政策。显然英国与不少外国的公共政策有相悖之处,各个国家或地区都会有自己的一套公共政策与/或法律,毕竟这与各个国家或地区的国情,包括历史、宗教、种族、政治、文化背景、经济条件、社会发展等因素息息相关。例如在 Cheni v. Cheni(1965)P 85 先例涉及叔叔与侄女结婚,之后他们移居英国,侄女向法院申请宣示婚姻无效。背后的原因不必深究,例如想再婚、财产分配等。这婚姻关系在埃及法下是被认可的,但在英国的《Sexual Offences Act 2003》立法下被视为乱伦而被禁止。这就带来英国法院在不同的公共政策下是否去认可这个婚姻的争议。

显然,如果是足够重要的英国公共政策,就很可能被不予执行。问题是哪些公共政策是足够重要?固然常见有"公共秩序"(ordre public)或者是"违反公序良俗"(contra bonos mores)等说法,但这些说法到底指的是哪些内容,能涵盖哪些范畴?这问题看来仍然尚待澄清,在千变万化的情况下也很难去一概而论。但可以节录《Chitty on Contracts》(2021 年,第 34 版)一书之 18-073 段如下:"Under the previous law it was clear that if the contract involved criminality either by statute or at common law, then it might be unenforceable in England despite its validity under the governing law and it may be that this is still so if the criminality is serious enough. Where, however, the contract, though not involving criminality, is alleged to offend against one of the recognised heads of English public policy, great care should be exercised by the courts in determining whether the domestic policy demands the non-enforcement of a contract with substantial or even exclusive foreign elements which is valid under the system of law with which it has the closest connection...Where again the contract is valid by its foreign governing law, but fails to comply with an English regulatory statute rendering similar domestic contracts void or unenforceable but not illegal, the courts have sometimes enforced the agreement, sometimes not. It is sought that the proper principle is that such agreements should be enforced unless the social policy expressed in the English statute is of such paramount importance that it must be applied even to a transaction with foreign elements or unless the contract, or its breach, has a substantial contact with England."

上述节录的权威书籍的说法可总结为:

1. 一旦涉及英国立法或普通法下的刑事犯罪的非法,特别是比较严重的犯罪,一般涉外合约也就不会被协助执行,即使它们在外国法下会是合法。

2. 即使不是违反英国刑法,但违反了英国承认的其中一项本地的公共政策,此时英国法院就要非常仔细考虑具体案件情况。例如,要看案件涉及的英国因素与外国因素的多寡(可以只是部分或全部涉外合约),并考虑英国公共政策下是否要求不予执行。这也意味着一个完全在外国形成、订立与履行的涉外合约,只是在英国解决争议如伦敦仲裁或申请英国法院协助执行,英国本地的公共政策就不应该有太多参与或插手的空间。

3. 英国目前对商业活动有大量规管的规章制度,如果是英国本地合约会被认为无效或不予执行但不一定是非法,但该涉外合约在它受管辖的外国法(无论是适用法或履行地)下被视为有效。这种情况可以如英国规管某些行业或交易,要求向相关机构登记与批准才能进行,否则有关合约无效。但涉外合约受管辖的法律都没有同样的规定。这样,除非是英国立法明确说明即使是外国合约也要适用同样规管(例如《Bribery Act 2010》),或者是合约实质上是英国法合约,否则都应该尽量支持或协助该涉外合约的执行。

上述《Chitty on Contracts》一书所说去套用在国际商业(特别是涉及发展中国家)的范畴,涉外合约违反一些英国认同的道德价值与英国的公共政策,并且同时涉及英国法律下的严重刑事犯罪的行为,如伪造文件(false documentation)去欺诈/欺骗[31](fraud/deceit)与/或贪污腐败[32](corruption & bribery)也很常见。在(一)的说法下,这些合约是不会被英国法院执行或协助。正如在本章之5.5.6段介绍的Lemenda Trading Co Ltd v. African Middle East Petroleum Co Ltd(1988)QB 448上诉庭先例中,Phillips大法官说:"Some heads of public policy are based on **universal principles of morality** ... Where a contract infringes such a rule of public policy the **English court will not enforce it, whatever the proper law of the contract and wherever the place of performance**. Other principles of public policy may be based on considerations which are purely domestic. In such a case there would seem no good reason why they should be a bar to the enforcement of a contract to be performed abroad."(加黑部分是笔者的强调)

但在不是刑事犯罪而只是违反公共政策的情况下,英国法院就要考虑各种因素,权衡后决定是否协助执行涉外合约。例如,不严格涉及或没有足够证据证明贪污腐败/以不正当手段疏通关系就会带来这种矛盾的Westacre Investments Inc v. Jugoimport SPDR Holding Co Ltd(1999)QB 740先例中,Colman大法官说:"it is difficult to see why anything short of corruption or fraud in international commerce should invite the attention of English public policy in relation to contracts which are not performed within the jurisdiction of the English courts. That it should be the policy of the English courts to deter the exercise of personal influence short of corruption and fraud to obtain valuable

---

〔31〕 见本书第八章之11.5.4.3段介绍的Mitsubishi v. Alafouzos(1988)1 Lloyd's Rep 191先例等。

〔32〕 见Lemenda Trading Co Ltd v. African Middle East Petroleum Co Ltd(1988)QB 448上诉庭先例等。

contracts in foreign countries ..."

5.3 国际商业的贪污腐败/以不正当手段疏通关系/ 游说

欺诈/欺骗与贪污腐败[33]也包括了以不正当手段去疏通关系人士（influence peddling），游说（lobbying）政府官员或企业领导，以谋取商业上的方便或好处并达成利润丰厚的合约。这种主合约（main contract）也往往不严格是普通法下的"非法"[34]，如一份供油合约或租船合约，猫腻只是在它的售价或租金只是市场的一半或1/3。但普通法是不理会对价的高低，该合约约定的履行与合约目的在合约的适用法/准据法下也是正常的商业活动——买卖石油与船舶的租用营运。但以这种不当手段获取的合约在任何角度去看都是败坏国际商业道德与诚实正直、公平竞争、透明与良好营商环境的行为，也严重违反有国际共识的公共政策。而合约即使不严格是非法，但通过贪污腐败的手段去获取合约，也难逃是可让受害的无辜方在证明合约是通过欺诈/欺骗的贪污腐败行为促成与诱导产生后，去撤销合约（rescission）并复原（restitutio in integrum）[35]。

这种贪污腐败/以不正当手段疏通关系在国际商业活动盛行，但现实中绝大部分情况是通过代理人或中间人向有关的政府官员用各种手法行贿与疏通。这也就令国际贪污腐败的案件很难会有直接与清楚无误的证据（direct and clear evidence）去证明这种严重的非法罪行。

所以一般英美的规管如美国的《海外反腐败法》（《The Foreign Corrupt Practices Act 1977》或简称 FCPA），认定是否有这种贪污腐败的行为就要依赖环境证据（circumstantial evidence），也就是所谓的"红旗测试"（Red Flags test）的说法。这些环境证据包括代理人或中间人的声誉与历史；外国公司在雇佣前有否对这些人士做出尽职调查；是否通过皮包公司或空壳公司操作；是否与某些重要的政府官员有关联；外国公司怎样支付这些代理人或中间人，如支付多少钱或是交易的百分比、钱支付到的账号（如海外的空壳公司账号）等；所做的合法工作与贡献是否与收费成正比；实际工作是什么，如真正不断向外国公司对当地知识做报告与提建议等，或只是停留在泛泛的"公关"（public relationship）或"市场营销"（marketing）等，实是向政府官员或企业疏通关系与游说。环境证据可以进一步去看整个交易，如交易如果涉及投标，就可看投标是否公开透明、程序流程是否正当、有否对投标公司尽职调查、决定是否做得太快等。

---

[33] 关于贪污腐败的定义可见本章之 3 段的脚注。

[34] 见 National Iranian Oil Co v. Crescent Petroleum Co International Ltd（2016）EWHC 510（Comm）；Honeywell International Middle East Ltd v. Meydan Group LLC（2014）EWHC 1344（TCC）；Wilson v. Hurstanger（2007）1 WLR 2351 等先例。

[35] 欺诈/欺骗与欺诈性误述等诱导产生的合约可使无效，无辜方可撤销合约并复原在本书第三与四章有详论。

5.3.1 不合法的疏通关系/游说政府是非法与违反公共政策

在 Omnium de Traitement et de Valorisation SA v. Hilmarton Ltd(1999)2 Lloyd's Rep 222 先例中,Timothy Walker 大法官已经说非法与违反公共政策根本就是同一码事。

针对这种不正当手段,在 Lemenda Trading Co Ltd v. African Middle East Petroleum Co Ltd(1988)QB 448 先例中,Phillips 大法官有说在英国公共政策下,这种行为针对英国政府官员或国有企业都是不允许的:"Had the agreement related to the procurement of a contract from a British Government department or a state-owned industry, I am in no doubt that it would have been unenforceable by reason of English public policy."

这种不当行为在英国法下被视为违反公共政策,在早期的 Montefiore v. Monday Motor Corporation Co Ltd(1918)2 KB 241 先例中,Shearman 大法官说:"... In my judgment it is contrary to public policy that a person should be hired for money or valuable consideration when he has access to persons of influence to use his position and interest to procure a benefit from the government."

另一个早期的 Parkinson v. College of Ambulance Ltd(1925)2 KB 1 先例中,涉及原告在被告会为他取得英皇的封爵(knighthood)的承诺下支付了 3000 英镑,但后来并没有成功。原告以被告欺诈性误述(fraudulent misrepresentation)向被告索赔取回这笔钱,但不成功。Lush 大法官判这种购买爵位的合约是违反英国公共政策与非法,法院不予执行。

这种不正当手段的疏通关系或游说即使是完全涉外的合约(适用法与履行地都是外国),英国法院也视为违反公共政策而拒绝执行。在本章稍后的 5.5.6 段会介绍 Lemenda Trading Co Ltd v. African Middle East Petroleum Co Ltd 先例,涉及适用法卡塔尔法是把原告作为中间人去疏通官员获取石油供应合约并从中抽取佣金视为违反公共政策。而英国法律下,这种行为也是违反公共政策。所以判该佣金合约的目的与约定的履行是在外国非法与/或违反英国公共政策不予协助。Phillips 大法官说:"In my judgment, the English courts should not enforce an English law contract which falls to be performed abroad where: (i) it relates to an adventure which is contrary to a head of English public policy which is founded on general principles of morality, and (ii) the same public policy applies to the country of performance so that the agreement would not be enforced under the law of that country. In such a situation **international comity combines with English domestic public policy to militate against enforcement.**"(加黑部分是笔者的强调)

这样,如果是一份适用英国法的合约,而合约履行地是在英国,并涉及违反这类的公共政策,英国法院显然不会协助执行合约。而如果合约的履行地是外国,而该外国也是有同样的社会道德大原则或公共政策,也不会有疑问英国法院不会协助执行合约。

但如果是一份适用外国法，合约的形成或履行地也是外国的完全涉外的合约，违反了英国这类公共政策，英国法院就不容易决定是否执行有关的合约了。这不只是考虑合约在外国适用法下或履行地是否合法的问题，而是有更基本需要考虑的问题。这就是在违反英国社会道德的公共政策下，是否应该去协助执行。如果不协助执行，除了友好国家的国际睦仪/礼让的考虑，另外也有会否把英国的公共政策或价值观强加于外国的嫌疑？

此外在这问题上难免涉及其他的公共政策需要去权衡，这主要是英国法律对合约有约束力的保障与合约神圣性[36]也是公共政策。这本来也就是与不协助执行合约的非法理论对立的公共政策。

5.3.2　合法的疏通关系/游说政府

当然，“游说”一词本身是中性的而且在现实世界是难以避免的。例如，美国就是一个允许在政治上游说的国家。它的合法性是根据美国《宪法第一修正案》的言论自由（freedom of speech）与有权向政府申诉（the right to petition the Government for a redress of grievances）。所以在美国向参众两院与政府进言，并提供更多更全面的专业与第一手信息，进而影响立法与政策等重大方面是完全合法。负责游说的人士（lobbyists）很多会是以前的参众两院议员或政府官员，甚至级别是高至前众参议员或前部长，被笑称为“旋转门”（revolving door）做法。要雇佣这些人士的有外国政府、各种行业联盟、私营公司、非营利团体等。这种活动受到规管，如《Lobbying Disclosure Act 1995》的立法，如需要登记、规定哪些行为是可以与不可以做等。立法的主要目的是保证游说活动尽量透明，让公众去衡量与监督某些行为是否不恰当影响政府的决定，不允许“黑箱”作业等。

在这方面，英国也是有类似立法，这是在《Transparency of Lobbying, Non-Party Campaigning and Trade Union Administration Act 2014》。另在欧盟，在2018年于欧洲议会（European Parliament）表决通过了一份程序规则，首次强制性要求议员公开自己受到过的游说。[37]

在国际商业社会，为了私利有更多这种疏通关系或是游说的行为在发生，往往是涉及私人公司/企业，除了在商业活动中有必要性外，也与公共利益无关，根本就没必要去关联非法或违反公共政策。有说法是在针对全球的商业活动，英国公共政策的考虑面更应是“现实”（pragmatism）、不只是道德（morality）。

---

〔36〕 拉丁文“*pacta sunt servanda*”的原则可以解释为有约必守或者是合约必须被守信执行。

〔37〕 有关会议报告《REPORT on amendments to Parliament's Rules of Procedure affecting Chapters 1 and 4 of Title I; Chapter 3 of Title V; Chapters 4 and 5 of Title VII; Chapter 1 of Title VIII; Title XII; Title XIV and Annex II》[2018/2170(REG)]文本可见：https://www.europarl.europa.eu/doceo/document/A-8-2018-0462_EN.pdf。

5.3.3　国际情况的改变导致公私不分下的态度转变

在近几十年来,国际情况有了改变,政府行使职能与从事商业活动越来越难区分。

美英也不是没有对这种败坏国际道德的行为去作出阻吓,如美国的《海外反腐败法》(以下简称 FCPA)与英国的《Bribery Act 2010》。为了应对立法,大部分在外国有业务的英美公司或其他在英美有业务的跨国公司只能在做法上更小心。常见的做法是通过中间人或代理人[称为顾问(consultant/advisor)或调解人(mediator)并订立合约]去达成交易,甚至对中间人或代理人做尽职调查并留下完整的记录。虽然这些中间人仍会或有很大可能会在疏通关系时涉及贪污腐败,但这已经不是该公司直接行贿,要搜集行贿的证据也会更难。而这些操作慢慢也开始被接受。

这种公私不分或难分的情况在 Tekron Resources Limited v. Guinea Investment Company Limited(2003)EWHC 2577(QB)先例中也有涉及。案情涉及原告 Tekron 是 BVI 公司,背后是 3 位自然人,他们与西非的几内亚政府(特别是矿务部长)关系很好。在他们的关系下,成功把几内亚的一个铝土(bauxite)矿场与提炼工厂把铝土变为铝材(alumina)的业务引入外资与借助美国的 Reynolds Metals(全球第三大的铝业公司)去成功重整,并为此成立一家在马绍尔群岛(Marshall Islands)注册的公司简称为"ACG"接管该提炼工厂,为期 25 年。ACG 是由被告(以下简称 GIC)、几内亚政府与 Reynolds Metals 共同拥有。而 GIC 是一家开曼群岛注册的公司,背后是一些希腊的富有船东与 Reynolds Metals 的高管。Tekron 与 GIC 签的代表协议(Representation Agreement)应是 GIC 背后的人士为了支付 Tekron 去介绍这项投资和疏通与几内亚政府的关系的报酬。该代表协议说明 Tekron 的主要责任是:"assist GIC in maintaining good commercial and political relations with the government of Guinea and all regulatory authorities in Guinea."在 GIC 与 ACG 的 25 年合约生效后的 30 天内,就要马上支付 40 万美元给 Tekron。而整个 25 年的代表协议如果一切顺利,估计要支付给 Tekron 高达 9000 万美元。审理的 Jack 大法官也感觉到 Tekron 从几内亚这种赤贫的发展中国家出售有限的自然资源以赚取微利的交易中去"榨取"这笔钱是不合理,说:"On any view the payments provided for by the representation agreement are very large. Some may find it objectionable on moral grounds that such large sums should be earned, effectively by three individuals, for services such as provided here, in particular in the context of the impoverished state of Guinea."

但好景不长,3 年后 GIC 与 Reynolds Metals 在 ACG 的所有股权被俄罗斯铝业公司(RusAl)收购。RusAl 拒绝在代表协议下向 Tekron 继续作出支付,并威胁要把已经支付的费用取回,理由就是合约非法与违反英国公共政策。该代表协议是英国法合约,明示约定适用法是英国法,并由英国法院管辖。

在该先例中,Jack 大法官认为现代的国际情况变得公私不分,本应是针对政府官员的不合法游说与以不正当手段疏通关系,违反英国公共政策的大原则不应去延伸。

因为在国际商业活动，总是难免需要在外国做生意要有中介人士去牵线才会能达成一个交易。而这些交易是不能因为有当地政府的参与而变为非法或违反公共政策。Jack 大法官支持 Tekron 的索赔，说：

"... the ambit of the principle of public policy which he advanced was limited to matters involving public bodies and their officials. **The justification was that with public bodies the public interest is engaged**. The distinction between public and private bodies seems to me to be today less clear than perhaps once it was. In addition there may well today be a considerable public interest in the activities of substantial private bodies which provide public services.

In my view it would be a substantial extension of the ambit of public policy as established... It would prevent the use of intermediaries in numerous situations where their use is now well-established in commercial situations, whether or not a 'public' body is involved. It would also bring in a serious element of uncertainty as to where the line was to be drawn. At what point would an intermediary cease to be able to negotiate fresh transactions with a particular third party? What happens when a position of 'influence' develops during a negotiation? The previous authorities which I have considered were concerned with what I may call the sale of influence and only influence, and in circumstances in which it could be considered that the use of the influence would involve some impropriety. ...

I will not repeat what I have said already as to the nature and substance of the representation agreement. **It is not by reason of that to be treated as contrary to public policy under English law**."（加黑部分是笔者的强调）

5.4 公约裁决书涉及不合法疏通关系/游说政府的执行

在本章之 5.1 段有关英国法院的权力来源，有节录 1958 年《纽约公约》之 Article V(2)(b)是允许国际仲裁裁决书的执行地国家法院以本地的公共政策为由考虑拒绝承认与执行有关的公约裁决书（convention award）。但众所周知，在一些倾向协助执行以支持国际仲裁的法院（如英国、美国纽约、新加坡）视执行公约裁决书为至关重要的公共政策。说法是来自《纽约公约》所建立的架构，这可节录 Diag Human SE v. Czech Republic(2014) EWHC 1639(Comm)先例中 Eder 大法官的小结，具体如下：

"... **the Convention comprises an 'overall scheme' for 'the facilitation of the enforcement of an award.' 'The scheme reflects a "pro-enforcement bias" ... or ... constitutes a praesumptio juris tantum, for the enforceability of an award ...' This pro-enforcement bias is recognised in England.** An award creditor seeking to enforce a Convention award in England under s101 "has a prima facie right to recognition and enforcement": Dardana v Yukos [2002] 2 Lloyd's Rep 326, per Mance LJ... To similar effect is the statement of Gross J in IPCO (Nigeria) Ltd v Nigerian National Petroleum Corp

[2005]EWHC 726(Comm)…:'… there can be no realistic doubt that section 103 of the Act embodies a predisposition to favour enforcement of New York Convention Awards,reflecting the underlying purpose of the New York Convention itself' …"(加黑部分是笔者的强调)

所以在英国《Arbitration Act 1996》之 Section 103 引入《纽约公约》之 Article V (2)(b),英国法院的理念与做法体现在 IPCO(Nigeria) v. Nigerian National Petroleum Corp(2005)EWHC 726(Comm)先例中,Gross 大法官这样说:"… there can be no realistic doubt that section 103 of the Act embodies a pre-disposition to favour enforcement of New York Convention Awards, reflecting the underlying purpose of the New York Convention itself;indeed, **even when a ground for refusing enforcement is established, the court retains a discretion to enforce the award**… considerations of public policy,if relied upon to resist enforcement of an award, should be approached with extreme caution:DST v Rakoil[1987]2 Lloyd's Rep. 246…The reference to public policy in s. 103 (3)was **not intended to furnish an open-ended escape route** for refusing enforcement of New York Convention awards. Instead,the public policy exception in s. 103(3)is **confined to the public policy of England** (as the country in which enforcement is sought)in **maintaining the fair and orderly administration of justice.** "(加黑部分是笔者的强调)

只有在狭窄的英国公共政策下,英国法院才会十分谨慎地允许仲裁裁决书的败诉方有一个"逃生门"(escape route),即拒绝协助裁决书的胜诉方执行。至于怎样的英国公共政策会被考虑,有不少不同说法。例如《纽约公约》是国际公约,所以针对的应该是国际性认同而不只是本国的公共政策。其他的说法有如"违反最根本性的道德与公平"(violates the forum's most basic notion of morality and justice);行为是"震惊法院的良心"(shock the conscience)、"清楚是对公众带来损害"(clearly injurious to the public good)、"知情与合理的公众会反感与抗拒"(wholly offensive to the ordinary reasonable and fully informed members of the public)等,英国法院才会考虑拒绝执行一个公约裁决书。

最符合以上所说的"违反最根本性的道德与公平"的,就是欺诈与贪污腐败。在 Attorney-General for Hong Kong v. Reid(1994)1 AC 324 枢密院先例中,Templeman 勋爵称政府官员的贪污腐败行为为:"an evil practice which threatens the foundations of any civilised society."

这样,一个国际商业合约涉及贪污腐败、不合法疏通关系或游说政府官员应是明确违反英国公共政策,否则《Arbitration Act 1996》之 Section 103 也就无用武之地了。这也会进一步令国际商业社会更加干净、公平与按照透明的秩序运转。但现实情况并不是这么简单,这会稍后在本章之 6 段去进一步做针对性探讨。

5.5　英国法院以本地公共政策为由考虑是否协助执行涉外合约的重要先例

本章之 5.2 段也有说到全球所有的不同国家或地区各有各的国情,这表示英国如果在协助执行涉外合约时过分考虑本地的公共政策并频频拒绝协助执行，就成为不了全球的法律中心（包括提供法律服务、法院申请协助如各种禁令、诉讼与仲裁等）。

这方面轻重的考虑，从下列介绍的先例可以看到，只有英国法院认为涉外合约涉及的非法是违反了任何文明社会都认可的公共政策，并且会一致不去协助执行（无论在合约关联的特定外国是否视为合法）时，英国法院才可以拒绝执行或协助执行。早在 Missouri Steamship Co, Re (1889) 42 Ch. D. 321 上诉庭先例非法就被局限在"刑事犯罪、邪恶与不道德"。西方国家认为的"文明社会"与其他发展中国家肯定有差异。这会否令同样是普通法体系的新加坡、印度、巴基斯坦、马来西亚、中国香港特区等国家和地区的法院，面对本地的公共政策的考量时与英国法院有不同的判断？

在接下来介绍的先例，首先针对胁迫（duress）导致的涉外合约。这包括 Kaufman v. Garson (1904) 1 KB 591；The "Evia Luck" (1992) 2 AC 152；Royal Boskalis Westminster NV v. Mountain (1999) QB 674；Kuwait Airways Corp v. Iraqi Airways Co (No. 6) (2002) UKHL 19 等先例。

5.5.1 Missouri Steamship Co, Re (1889) 42 Ch. D. 321 上诉庭先例

早在 Missouri Steamship Co, Re 上诉庭先例中，美国发货人与英国船东签订海上运输合约（提单合约），从波士顿付运一批活牛前往英国。在该提单合约中有一条船东对船长或船员疏忽的免责条文："Ship not accountable for the acts of God, …, whether arising from the negligence, default, or error in judgment of the master, mariners, engineers, or others of the crew, or otherwise howsoever, …, nor for collision, stranding, or any other accident or peril of the seas, rivers, and steam navigation, of what nature or kind, howsoever such collision, stranding, or other accident or peril may be caused."

这种免责条文在当时的英国法[38]下是有效的。但在波士顿的法律下此条文被视为违反公共政策而无效。船舶在半途遇上搁浅海难导致船上所有的活牛全部溺死，货方向船东索赔损失，该免责条文能否有效保护船东变为争议的关键。

英国法院根据法律冲突规则（如船旗是英国、搁浅地点在英国海域与提单合约的其他内容等）认定英国法为适用法，提单合约是一份英国法合约。但这也带来如何平衡作为部分履行地的美国波士顿的法律下是违反公共政策的问题。

一审的 Chitty 大法官判决免责条文有效，不受美国法律的影响，这毕竟不是涉及刑事犯罪、邪恶或不道德的事情需要所有有同样价值观的文明国家去一致拒绝执行，说："… **the stipulations are not impeached on the ground that they are of a criminal**

[38] 该年代英国主要代表船东利益与美国主要代表货方利益起的冲突与对抗，在笔者的《提单与其他付运单证》（2016 年）一书第五章有详尽介绍。英美之间对提单合约在海上运输的免责条文在有了 1924 年《海牙规则》并区别在 1924 年与 1936 年英美各自依据此国际公约立法后才有了一致的法律地位。

or wicked or immoral nature, or such as ought not to be permitted according to the law of civilized countries; they are impeached solely on the ground that they are void, as being disallowed by the law of the place where the contracts were made, which law considers them contrary to its own views of the public policy that ought to prevail within the limits of its own territorial jurisdiction. …, I cannot find any sufficient reason for saying it would hold them void in the case of a contract … was to be governed by the law of the country to which the ship belonged, and the law of such country allowed the stipulations to be valid."(加黑部分是笔者的强调)

上诉庭支持一审判决,同意如果是某些行为非常严重地触犯了一般文明社会的道德底线,就无论如何(无论适用法与履行地法是否认为合法)都不会被执行。毕竟这种法律与公共政策部分可以执行,但部分不可以执行,就不理想。Halsbury 勋爵说:"Where a contract is void on the ground of immorality, or is contrary to such positive law as would prohibit the making of such a contract at all, then the contract would be void all over the world, and no civilised country would be called on to enforce it."

5.5.2　Kaufman v. Gerson(1904)1 KB 591 先例

在 Kaufman v. Gerson 先例中,Kaufman 先生是一名住在法国的英国人。Kaufman 将一笔钱交予法国人 Gerson 先生,用于在法国开展一些特定生意。但 Gerson 挪用了这笔钱,在法国法下此行为会构成刑事犯罪。Gerson 的太太有不少个人财产,在 Kaufman 威胁说不还钱就要举报的情况下,为了防止 Gerson 被刑事控诉后给家族带来污名影响子女,Gerson 的太太与 Kaufman 在巴黎签订协议。根据协议内容 Kaufman 不会采取进一步行动,而 Gerson 的太太则会在 3 年内清偿被挪用的钱。后来由于 Gerson 的太太没能按协议还钱,因此 Kaufman 在英国法院起诉要求 Gerson 的太太根据协议还钱。

尽管此协议涉及当事人私下对刑事诉讼进行和解,还涉及胁迫或不当影响之下签订合约,但根据当事人提供的专家证据来看,双方对于此合约在法国法下是有效的并没有太大争议。因此案件的一个争议焦点就变成该合约是否会由于违背英国法下的公共政策,尤其是试图和解刑事指控而属于妨碍司法公正(interfere with the proper working of the machinery of justice),以及由于是胁迫下的合约而属于损害社会道德(moral coercion amounting to duress)。

在一审[(1903)2 KB 114]中,Wright 大法官执行了该涉外合约。但到了上诉庭被推翻,上诉庭的判法主要是认为胁迫行为而产生合约是损害社会道德,而不是妨碍外国的司法公正。[39] 这些可以导致不执行的原因应该是一些放之四海皆准的公共

---

〔39〕 当事人在适用外国法的合约中私下和解外国刑事诉讼,如果外国法下不认为非法,英国法院看来也不会认为是违反本地的公共政策要拒绝执行,特别是一些次要的刑事罪行。这种情况也出现在 Addison v. Brown(1954)1 WLR 779 等先例中。

政策或社会道德。Collins 大法官说："... where an English Court is asked to enforce a contract made in a foreign country, it is entitled to inquire whether, though the contract may be valid according to the laws of that country, it **violates some moral principle**, which, if it is not, **ought to be universally recognised**. I think that in this case, as in other cases, the principle applies that a plaintiff, who seeks the assistance of the Court, must come with clean hands; and, if the plaintiff is setting up a contract obtained in a manner which, **in the case of an English contract, the law deems contrary to morality, an English Court will not help him to enforce it, whatever may be the law of the country in which the contract was made.**"（加黑部分是笔者的强调）

Romer 大法官说："I think that to enforce a contract so procured would be to contravene what by the law of this country is deemed an **essential moral interest**; and therefore that **the Court ought not**, at the instance of the plaintiff, to **assist him in this case to enforce a contract which he has obtained by such means.**"（加黑部分是笔者的强调）

5.5.3 Royal Boskalis Westminster NV v. Mountain（1999）QB 674 上诉庭先例

在稍近期的 Royal Boskalis Westminster NV v. Mountain 上诉庭先例中，荷兰船东拥有多艘工程挖泥船（dredger），这些挖泥船均投保了战争险（war risk），[40]并且保险合约中有一条施救条文（sue and labour clause），[41]作用是为了鼓励船长在海上遇上海难时会尽一切努力与花费挽救挖泥船。而即使施救失败，保险人也会在赔付挖泥船的全损外加上赔付施救失败所花费的金钱。保险合约使用的是历史悠久的伦敦劳合社 SG 保单格式，[42]适用法是英国法。

荷兰船东与伊拉克当局成立合资公司，并在 1989 年 10 月通过合资公司与伊拉克政府签订合约，参与伊拉克境内港口的工程。工程合约约定了适用法是伊拉克法与巴黎仲裁。但在合约履行期间并预期在 1990 年 9 月可完成工程，不幸的在 1990 年 8 月海湾战争爆发。当时联合国安理会通过决议制裁伊拉克，并且希望成员国在国内立法中体现此制裁。不少国家纷纷进行立法，其中包括荷兰。而伊拉克也很快反制，通过伊拉克法律规定将会扣押、没收所有制裁伊拉克国家的公司的资产。这样荷兰船东就必须与伊拉克政府谈判和解，试图把在伊拉克境内扣押的挖泥船与雇员接出来。荷兰船东在压力下与伊拉克萨达姆政府达成解决方案（finalisation agreement），允许荷兰公司接走挖泥船与雇员，交换条件是荷兰船东要：(1)退回一大笔伊拉克公司为了工程预付的金钱；(2)放弃所有在工程合约下可以索赔的工程费。该解决方案也包括了荷兰公司承诺不向外界披露这个解决方案。这也导致荷兰船东没有及时向保险人披露有关信息，并带来荷兰船东与保险人之间复杂的争议。

---

[40] 见笔者《海上货物保险》一书第九章之 1 段。

[41] 见笔者《海上货物保险》一书第七章之 4.4 段。

[42] 见笔者《英国海上保险条款详论》（第二版）一书。

后来荷兰公司向伦敦保险人提出要求赔付挖泥船的推定全损(constructive total loss)与施救费用,这笔施救费用就是在放弃工程合约下,可以通过巴黎仲裁索赔的工程费。荷兰船东认为这笔损失好像支付海盗的赎金一样,非要这样才能去把挖泥船与雇员安全接回来。

这是一个非常复杂的案件,在此不展开讲。在一审,荷兰船东的推定全损索赔失败,但施救费用索赔成功。Rix 大法官说:"if the waiver of the joint venture's claims can, as I believe, properly be regarded as the payment of a ransom, it matters not that there may be good legal remedies for the recovery of that ransom. In seeking to render the plaintiffs' sue and labour claim valueless on the ground that the finalisation agreement, although valid by its proper law, would not be enforced by a Paris arbitration tribunal... There are many factors which might affect the value of such remedies. They do not, it seems to me, affect the essential existence of the sue and labour expense or the validity of the sue and labour claims."

但在上诉庭中,一审判决被推翻,施救费用的索赔也失败。原因与本章的内容有关,也就是该解决方案显然是在非法胁迫下订立的,这违反了英国公共政策不会被执行。这也很可能在巴黎仲裁中不被仲裁庭接受,因为也应该违反了法国的公共政策。这意味着荷兰船东可以去启动与推进巴黎仲裁,不存在一个有效的对索赔工程费的弃权,也就没有损失或任何真正的施救费用。上诉庭的 Stuart-Smith 大法官说:"The judge also seems to have thought that the fact that the finalisation agreement was valid by its foreign law, i. e. Iraqi law, was a sufficient answer to the defendants' contention. Again **I cannot agree**. The plaintiffs only had valuable claims in so far as they could be enforced in a Paris arbitration. Their **loss under the sue and labour clause could only be established in so far as they could show that Paris arbitrators would give effect to the waiver**. The fact that it was valid by Iraqi law was no doubt essential, but it was not sufficient if by the curial law the arbitrators would not enforce it. ...Mr. Aikens(荷兰船东代表大律师)did not seriously dispute that as a matter of English public policy an English court would not give effect to the finalisation agreement and the waiver of claims at the behest of the Iraqis. The principle was established in Kaufman v. Gerson[1904]1 K. B. 591. Moreover, whether or not a court today would regard the degree of coercion exercised in that case as sufficient to constitute duress and so affect the enforceability of the contract, there can be no doubt the degree of duress was so great in the present case that it comes within any application of the principles. Indeed I think that **any civilised tribunal**(这是指巴黎仲裁的仲裁员,他们必须遵守仲裁地法国的公共政策)**would refuse to give effect to it. In my opinion this affords a complete answer to the plaintiffs' claim on the basis that they failed to prove that they had suffered any effective loss to form the basis of their sue and labour charge**."(加黑部分是笔者的强调)

上诉庭的 Phillips 大法官也判"挟持"挖泥船与雇员的行为是非常极端的胁迫行为，也应属于被国际广泛认可的公共政策："The threat to use a large number of personnel as human shields was about as cogent and unconscionable a form of duress as one can imagine… **I do not believe that any civilised system of jurisprudence would recognise the effect of such an agreement**."（加黑部分是笔者的强调）

5.5.4　Kuwait Airways Corp v. Iraqi Airways Co（No. 6）（2002）UKHL 19 贵族院先例

Kuwait Airways Corp v. Iraqi Airways Co（No. 6）贵族院先例涉及的是 1990 年伊拉克入侵科威特后，侵占了科威特航空公司的飞机，事后伊拉克还试图通过立法合法化此行为。贵族院的判法是，一般情况下，外国法律即使是将其境内资产国有化，也与英国公共政策无关，即使有英国资产被波及，英国法院在英国公共政策下也不会因此就提出什么反对。但针对此先例中的特定情况，伊拉克政府行为被认为是违反了联合国宪章精神、违反国际法的行为，因此也无论在适用法下（如资产所在地的伊拉克法律）是否合法，英国法院在这种根本性地违反英国公共政策的情况下也总是可以拒绝执行。Hope 勋爵说：

"There is nothing in this case which connects the laws of this country with the events constituting the alleged tort, other than the fact that this is the country where the proceedings were brought. … this is **an action in tort that has nothing whatever to do with England**. So I would have no difficulty in holding that, in a case of this kind, **a principle of English public policy which was purely domestic or parochial in character would not provide clear and satisfying grounds for disapplying the primary rule which favours the lex loci delicti.**

But the public policy objection which is raised in this case is plainly not of that character. It is based on the Charter of the United Nations and the resolutions which were made under it. It is founded on a principle of public policy which places［有关立法］firmly into its international context. There is **a clear point of contact between this part of the lex loci delicti and the breaches of international law to which our courts are entitled to decline to give effect on grounds of public policy**."（加黑部分是笔者的强调）

此先例涉及的并非涉外合约而是涉外的侵权行为，但与本地法院是否愿意执行合约的原则本质上应是一样的，拒绝执行也是公平合理的。在《Illegality and Public Policy》（2020 年，第 5 版）一书之 10 – 11 段说："This decision has been much criticised, and does seem questionable on its particular facts. Nevertheless the broad principle that, **if severe pressure is exerted upon a party, the resulting contract will be unenforceable in England, must be correct.** The application of physical violence, or the threat of such violence, will clearly have that effect."（加黑部分是笔者的强调）

5.5.5　Mitsubishi v. Alafouzos(1988)1 Lloyd's Rep 191 先例

在 Mitsubishi v. Alafouzos 先例中,造船合约下买方与船厂约定在日本造船,但订立阴阳合约(yin yang contract/duplicate contracts)虚构造船价格。[43] 此先例在笔者的《造船合约》一书第三章之 10.2.3.3 段有详细介绍。

这里只说虽然该先例未对订立阴阳合约的行为在履行地日本是否非法进行详细论证(此先例中只涉及是否撤销索赔的初步争议,并非最后的实质审理),但 Steyn 大法官仍然表达了英国公共政策下对这种情况的看法,并指出这种欺诈行为是国际商业社会上都极为反对的,英国法院不会执行。可以节录 Steyn 大法官所说如下:"It would be extraordinary if public policy, in the context of international business transactions, condemned such conduct in this country but allowed the coercive power of the state to be enlisted if the deception was practised abroad. I hold, without hesitation, that the public conscience does not permit our Courts to show a larger tolerance to the enforcement of a deceiving transaction if it took place abroad..."

5.5.6　Lemenda Trading Co Ltd v. African Middle East Petroleum Co Ltd(1988) QB 448 上诉庭先例

Lemenda Trading Co Ltd v. African Middle East Petroleum Co Ltd 先例是今天这方面的权威先例。在此先例中,埃及商人通过自己设立的伦敦公司(African Middle East Petroleum Co Ltd)专门从事长期石油供应贸易。另有一名沙特商人自称通过设立的巴哈马公司(Lemenda Trading Co Ltd)在石油行业中做顾问。但实际看来沙特商人做的是中间人的生意,尤其是疏通政府官员拿到石油供应合约,并从中抽取佣金作为好处。

埃及商人原本与卡塔尔国有石油公司 Qatar General Petroleum Co(以下简称 QGPC)签订供应合约,自 1984 年 10 月 1 日起,QGPC 每个月都以 FOB 方式供应 75 万桶原油,但之后定期审核并考虑是否续约。合约明确约定卡塔尔法律作为适用法,在卡塔尔法律下 QGPC 供应石油不允许用需要支付佣金的代理人/中间人,卡塔尔法律下合约违反公共政策的后果是无效与不可执行。并且在合约中埃及商人还签署过一份附加协议,其中包括确认此协议的签订不涉及任何代理人/经纪人,也不会因此合

[43] 这种阴阳合约在中国也很普遍,例如大家都十分熟悉的房产买卖、艺人酬金等,为了贷款或税收上的好处而欺骗银行或政府。如果这只是发生在中国,那完全适用中国法。但一旦涉及需要英国协助执行的部分,如担保合约,英国法院将以违反英国公共政策为由不协助执行这种本来与英国无关的涉外欺诈/欺骗。其他如新加坡等法院,也会是同样的结果。这是非法应是毫无疑问:见 Scott v. Brown, Doering, McNab & Co(1892)2 QB 724; Alexander v. Rayson(1936)1 KB 169 等先例。

约支付佣金/折扣给其他人士〔44〕的谎言。

后来在1985年7月，埃及商人与QGPC的合约续约1年，供应量还提高到了每天3万桶。沙特商人就主张自己有权按每桶30美分获取佣金，并与埃及商人产生争议，之后开始诉讼，索赔的总金额超过了200万美元。双方达成了一份佣金协议，约定由沙特商人去游说QGPC高层，以帮助埃及商人拿到合约与石油供应，并可以因此获得佣金，而这份佣金协议约定适用法是英国法。

显然一旦涉及佣金并适用卡塔尔法律管辖时，在卡塔尔履行的供应合约就会违反卡塔尔公共政策，但严格来说其未必真正违反了哪一条具体的法律法规、规章制度。此时佣金协议适用英国法，法院会如何考虑此问题呢？

上诉庭的Phillips大法官首先指出过往先例在这些情况中并不适用，并且Phillips大法官接下来说卡塔尔本地的公共政策本身未必与英国有什么关系，至于英国法院是否愿意执行则要在国际睦仪/礼让的英国公共政策下进行权衡。Phillips大法官说："**There is a clear distinction between acts which infringe public policy and acts which violate provisions of law**. I have been referred to no decided case that supports the proposition that the English courts should, as a matter of comity, refuse to enforce an English law contract on the sole ground that performance would be contrary to the public policy of the country of performance. **The public policy of Qatar cannot, of itself, constitute any bar to the enforcement of the agreement in this case. It may, however, be a relevant factor when considering whether the court ought to refuse to enforce the agreement in this case under principles of English public policy**（这是指国际睦仪/礼让）."（加黑部分是笔者的强调）

接下来Phillips大法官指出此先例中的特别情况是卡塔尔法律下这种不应该利用自己（对政府）的影响力向第三人获取利益的公共政策，这种情况在英国法下实际上也一样存在。也因此英国法院在这种情况下，实际上是结合了国际礼让以及英国国内自己完全相同的公共政策，才做出不予执行的决定。Phillips大法官同时给出了一个必须同时满足的两个测试标准。可先节录Phillips大法官所说如下：

"The principles underlying the **public policy in the present case are essentially**

〔44〕 可以节录该部分措辞/文字如下："With reference to crude oil sales contract concluded between [QGPC] and your company on 28 August 1984, we should like you to note and confirm the following: 1. That this contract has been negotiated directly with your company and us without involvement of any agent/brokers. 2. That during the tenure of this contract or thereafter no commissions/discounts have been paid or will be paid to an agent/broker or any other person in receiving/obtaining benefits and consideration. 3. That any contravention of above would not only lead to termination of the contract, but also shall entitle the seller to take all necessary measures to remedy any loss/damage caused as a consequence thereof. All the above-mentioned points are considered integral part to the crude oil sales contract, and your signature on copy of this letter is binding on your part."

principles of morality of general application. The practice of exacting payment for the use of personal influence, particularly when the person to be influenced is likely to be unaware of the pecuniary motive involved, is unattractive whatever the context. Yet **it is questionable whether the moral principles involved are so weighty as to lead an English court to refuse to enforce an agreement regardless of the country of performance and regardless of the attitude of that country to such a practice.** The later English decisions were influenced, at least in part, by the effect of the practice in question upon good government in England. It is at this stage that, in my judgment, it becomes relevant to consider the law of Qatar. ... In the present case Qatar, the country in which the agreement was to be performed and with which, in my view, **the agreement had the closest connection, has the same public policy as that which prevails in England**. Because of that policy, the courts of Qatar would not enforce the agreement.

In my judgment, **the English courts should not enforce an English law contract which falls to be performed abroad where: (i) it relates to an adventure which is contrary to a head of English public policy which is founded on general principles of morality, and (ii) the same public policy applies to the country of performance so that the agreement would not be enforceable under the law of that country.**

In such a situation**international comity combines with English domestic public policy to militate against enforcement.**"(加黑部分是笔者的强调)

在前述节录内容中,Phillips 大法官就提到并不是说单纯违反英国法下公共政策就足够让合约无法执行,关键的是必须结合作为履行地法的外国法下的公共政策,以及英国公共政策,同时满足两者才能作出这样的认定。这也就是前述加黑部分的两个标准:(1)在英国的公共政策下来看,涉嫌违法的行为也不被一般社会道德认可;(2)履行地的外国也有一样的公共政策。

除此以外还需要强调的是,国际礼让不是说随便违反什么公共政策都会导致不予执行交易/合约,毕竟也有重要的公共政策是不轻易影响合约执行。也因此前文节录的 Phillips 大法官的言论也提到公共政策分量必须非常重("so weighty")才行。

5.5.7 Marlwood Commercial Inc v. Kozeny(2006) EWHC 872(Comm)先例

在 Marlwood Commercial Inc v. Kozeny 先例中,案情的背景是苏联解体后,苏联国有企业私有化。被告 Kozeny 是捷克人,在捷克的股权凭证私有化(voucher privatization)过程中,利用一些非常有争议性的手段大量购买捷克公民手上的凭证,从而获取了巨额利益。之后 Kozeny 想在阿塞拜疆的私有化过程中故技重施。阿塞拜疆发给每位合资格的公民 1 本共 4 张私有化股权凭证(privatisation voucher),当国有企业私有化时,公民可以凭证认购股份。该凭证可以自由流通买卖,虽然规定了每人/每机构不能超过 10 万本,但是这个限制完全可以通过控制不同的公司避开。外国人/机构也可以购买该凭证,但是还需要额外向阿塞拜疆政府购买期权(options)才能在国有企业私有化时认购股份。阿塞拜疆富含石油资源，所以在私有化过程中备受关注的就是阿塞拜疆国有石油公司（State Oil Company of Azerbaijan，以下简称SOCAR）。Kozeny想拉更多投资者入伙，这样就能一起控制私有化后的SOCAR，于是联系到了此先例的原告（包括最终损失最大的Omega Advisors、知名的AIG Global、哥伦比亚大学或它们控制的公司等）并签订了协议。在该协议下，Kozeny控制的公司作为代理为投资人直接从阿塞拜疆政府购买凭证与期权，协议中明确规定该协议的目的并非让Kozeny或他控制的公司赚取利润，而是为了有足够的资金购买期权与凭证在SOCAR私有化时获得控制权益。原告的总投资超过1.8亿美元但最终惨败，SOCAR没有私有化，凭证与期权变得毫无价值，原告血本无归。而Kozeny没有归还原告的投资，而是逃到了避税天堂巴哈马。原告发现期权实际并非从阿塞拜疆政府直接购买，而是从Kozeny控制的公司购买，于是以被告欺骗侵权与欺诈性误述开始诉讼。

Kozeny曾经口头承诺过阿塞拜疆的一位政府高官，会将手中2/3的凭证转给他，以确保共同投资的原被告可以继续购买凭证与期权，并且让该高官有动力推进SOCAR的私有化以获得好处。在美国的刑事诉讼中，Kozeny被判向该政府高官行贿。Omega Advisors的一位董事也承认他知道Kozeny与该政府高官协议达成的安排，并且也被定罪行贿。

此先例中Kozeny主张原告的诉讼没有机会成功，申请撤销索赔，[45]这是因为：（1）Omega Advisors的欺骗侵权的诉讼注定失败，因为董事在早期就知道了Kozeny与政府高官的安排。而既然双方知道这种非法的安排，合约就因为合约目的非法而无法执行，也就不存在误述诱导订立合约的问题。（2）即使Omega Advisors与其他原告不知道行贿的安排，也知道Kozeny与政府官员有不合法疏通关系，这令双方之间的合约违反公共政策。

法院最后判虽然Kozeny肯定向政府高官行贿，但是仍要决定是否与其达成了转让2/3的凭证与期权的协议。而Omega Advisors董事的知情能否被推定为公司法人知情[46]也需要法院认定，如果是，合约履行就与Kozeny和政府高官之间的非法往来密不可分。在违背道德的对价不生诉权的原则下，法院不能执行一个非法的合约，欺骗侵权的索赔失败。此外，原告仅仅知道Kozeny与政府关系良好不代表履行合约就一定会违反公共政策，这也是需要法院认定的事实。这些复杂的事实争议显然不适合在一个撤销索赔的申请中决定，因此法院驳回了Kozeny撤销索赔的请求，允许全面审理。

与本段内容有关的是，英国《Public Bodies Corrupt Practices Act 1889》之section 1（2）与《Prevention of Corruption Act 1906》之section 1（1）对海外的行贿不适用，直到

---

〔45〕见笔者《证据法：国际规管与诉讼中的证据攻防》一书第六章之4.3段。

〔46〕见笔者《证据法：基础理论、口头证据与专家证据》一书第十章之2.14段。

2002 年 2 月 14 日《Anti-Terrorism,Crime & Security Act 2001》之 section 108(2)、(3)修改生效。但这已经是在此先例发生后了,也就是说有关的非法安排,当时在英国法下并不非法。但法院认为即使如此,行贿也不道德与违反英国的公共政策,Jonathan Hirst QC 大法官说:

"However, whilst this may mean that **Mr Kozeny committed no criminal offence in English law, it is abundantly clear that in civil law this corruption would be regarded as immoral and contrary to English public policy**. In Lemenda Trading Co Ltd v. Africa Middle East Petroleum Co [1988] QB 448, Phillips J. held that a contract to use personal influence on a foreign official, particularly where it was not apparent to the official that the person using his influence was charging for doing so, was contrary to English public policy if the same public policy applied in the country of performance.... The Court held the contract to be unenforceable.

If a contract as in Lemenda is unenforceable, a fortiori a contract to bribe a foreign officialwould be void as contrary to English public policy. It matters not that at the time it did not constitute a criminal offence in this jurisdiction. Further, even at this stage, I would assume that bribery was a criminal offence in Azerbaijan — no evidence to the contrary has been proffered. **This Court will not enforce a contract the performance of which involves an unlawful act in a foreign and friendly country**.... An English contract will also be held invalid on account of illegality if the real object and the intention of the parties necessitates them joining in an endeavour to perform in a foreign and friendly country some act which is illegal by the law of that country notwithstanding the fact that there may be, in a certain event, alternative modes or places of performing which permit the contract to be performed legally: Foster v. Driscoll [1929] 1 K. B. 470."(加黑部分是笔者的强调)

5.5.8　Glencore International v. Metro Trading International (2001) 1 Lloyd's Rep 284 先例

在 Glencore International v. Metro Trading International 先例中,阿联酋一位销售与存储石油的商人(Metro Trading International)在阿联酋的富查伊拉(Fujairah)存储了 Glencore 的一些石油。但后来石油商人破产,石油被破产管理人出售与转让给第三人。此先例的争议是谁对这些石油有更高的产权?在英国法律下 Glencore 对这些石油一直有良好产权,因此 Glencore 可以主张返还石油(或出售所得金钱),拒绝返还就属于侵占。但法院认定有关的出售与转让交易应适用阿联酋法律,而在阿联酋法律下这些产权是合法转让,也就不存在侵占。这带来的问题就是虽然在阿联酋法律下合法,但是否因为在英国法下实际被视为侵占、违背禁止侵占背后的公共政策而不可执行。Moore-Bick 大法官指出如果达到"道德上令人反感"(morally repugnant)的程度就可以违反公共政策为由不予认可,但此先例中的情况并没有到这个程度。

Moore-Bick 大法官这样说:"... even if the lex situs rule applies to the passing of property between the immediate parties to the transaction, the court will not give effect to the relevant rules of the lex situs where they would be regarded as contrary to English public policy...I can say at once, however, that there is nothing about the relevant rules of the law of Fujairah which in my view would justify the court in treating them as morally repugnant or refusing to recognise them on any other grounds of public policy.... "

5.5.9 Pencil Hill Ltd v. US Citta Di Palermo SpA(2016)1 WLUK 262 先例

虽然这是一个外国仲裁裁决书在英国法院寻求协助执行的案件,但不留待在本章之6段介绍,是因为此先例不涉及贪污腐败或以不正当手段疏通政府官员关系的根本性的公共政策。

此先例中,涉及原告(Pencil Hill Ltd)将球员转会到被告(意大利巴勒莫足球俱乐部),被告承诺支付转会费。在合约中约定,如果被告在到期日前未能完成支付,需要双倍偿还欠下的债务。在合约中还约定争议交由国际体育仲裁庭(Court of Arbitration for Sport, CAS)在瑞士仲裁,适用法也是瑞士法。后来被告完全没有进行任何支付,原告因此开始 CAS 仲裁。

英国法不允许合约中约定违约方承担与无辜方的合法利益不成比例的责任的惩罚条文[47](penalty clause),这在今天明确是一项公共政策。在近期的 Cavendish Square Holdings BV v. Makdessi(2015)UKSC 67 最高院先例中,Hodge 勋爵这样说:"The rule against penalties is a rule of contract law based on public policy. It is a question of construction of the parties' contract judged by reference to the circumstances at the time of contracting; the public policy is that the courts will not enforce a stipulation for punishment for breach of contract. "

但在瑞士法下根据《Swiss Code of Obligations》之 Art. 163.3,审理的法院(或仲

〔47〕 惩罚条文的问题在笔者《损失赔偿与救济》一书第一章之6段有介绍。什么时候属于惩罚条文在 Cavendish Square Holdings BV v. Makdessi(2015)UKSC 67 最高院先例中,Neuberger 勋爵、Sumption 勋爵与 Carnworth 勋爵说关键是违约方需要承担的责任与无辜方的合法利益完全不成比例:"... the real question when a contractual provision is challenged as a penalty is whether it is penal, not whether it is a pre-estimate of loss. These are not natural opposites or mutually exclusive categories .... The true test is whether the impugned provision is a secondary obligation which imposes a detriment on the contract breaker out of all proportion to any legitimate interest of the innocent party in the enforcement of the primary obligation. The innocent party can have no proper interest in simply punishing the defaulter. "也可见 Hodge 勋爵说:"... whether the sum or remedy stipulated as a consequence of a breach of contract is exorbitant or unconscionable when regard is had to the innocent party's interest in the performance of the contract..."

裁庭)有权限制、调整被认为过分的合约惩罚条文。[48] 而此先例中的仲裁庭就认为合约约定的欠债翻倍的条文不成比例与不公平,因此行使裁量权将其缩减到欠债的25%。也就是原告胜诉后,除了本金外,只能额外拿回25%作为赔偿(而不是合约约定的翻倍)。被告还在瑞士的监督法院(supervising court)上诉,但瑞士法院支持了仲裁庭的裁决。

原告接下来就在作为执行法院的英国法院申请执行,这就遇到了是否因为合约约定了惩罚条文,违背了英国的公共政策,导致在英国不可执行。法院在权衡之下,完全支持了仲裁裁决的执行。

最重要的原因就是支持仲裁裁决执行的公共政策超越了不允许惩罚条文的公共政策。Bird 大法官说:"I have come to the conclusion that the award should be enforced in its entirety. The authorities are clear. There is a strong leaning towards the enforcement of foreign arbitral awards and the circumstances in which the English Court may refuse enforcement are narrow. I am satisfied that the **important public policy against enforcement of penalty clauses is not sufficient to permit me to refuse enforcement. The rule does not in my judgment protect a 'universal principle of morality'. It is not so clearly 'injurious to the public good' that enforcement should, without more, be refused.** ... In my judgment the public policy of upholding international arbitral awards, ... outweighs the public policy of refusing to enforce penalty clauses. The scales are tipped heavily in favour of enforcement."(加黑部分是笔者的强调)

再加上此先例中适用法是瑞士法,仲裁庭在审理中已经根据瑞士法限制了原本过分、不合情理/显失公平的惩罚条文。这本就是仲裁庭的职责,与执行法院无关,也不是执行法院应该干预的。更不用说还存在争端禁反言(issue estoppel)[49] 的问题,也令英国法院不应该重新考虑是否属于惩罚条文。如果不是仲裁裁决,而是一个美国法院作出的3倍赔偿损失的惩罚性判决来英国要求执行,英国法院就会以违反英国公共政策而拒绝。

---

[48] 中国法下也有类似规定,如《民法典》第585条第2款规定:"约定的违约金低于造成的损失的,人民法院或者仲裁机构可以根据当事人的请求予以增加;约定的违约金过分高于造成的损失的,人民法院或者仲裁机构可以根据当事人的请求予以适当减少。"

[49] 有关争端的禁反言问题可见笔者《合约的履行、弃权与禁反言》一书第九章之7段的介绍。在此只节录在 Virgin Atlantic Airways Ltd v. Zodiac Seats UK Ltd(2013)UKSC 46 最高院先例,Sumption 勋爵说:"Except in special circumstances where this would cause injustice, issue estoppel bars the raising in subsequent proceedings of points which(i)were not raised in the earlier proceedings or(ii)were raised but unsuccessfully. If the relevant point was not raised, the bar will usually be absolute if it could with reasonable diligence and should in all the circumstances have been raised."

6. 仲裁裁决书的执行

仲裁裁决书的执行在国际仲裁盛行的今天是一个至关重要的课题,笔者已经在《仲裁法:从开庭审理到裁决书的作出与执行》一书第十章至第十四章详细提及,其中第十二章更是针对以违反公共政策为由抗拒执行裁决书的课题。所以,笔者无意在此重复,只对此课题多增加一些特别是针对仲裁中的商业合约涉及政府官员或国企公职人员贪污腐败、以不正当手段疏通关系以及其他在中国法律下是非法的行为。

首先,英国与其他普通法国家或地区的相关法律是中国政府(如涉及投资仲裁或国企的重大仲裁案件)、中国公司与律师必须要熟悉的。即使不是境外的仲裁中心的仲裁,也往往与英国或其他普通法国家或地区(主要是中国香港特区)有密切关系,因为需要在这些法院寻求协助与执行。当事人会需要通过当地法院的协助取得诉前担保、向敌对方施加压力或执行胜诉裁决书。除了仲裁的敌对方或败诉方在这些地方可能有资产外,更有可能在这些普通法管辖地能申请到全球冻结令[50](worldwide freezing injunction)、资产披露令[51](asset disclosure order)、第三方披露令[52](Norwich Pharmacal order)、搜查令[53](search order)等有效手段迫使对方投降或仲裁败诉方支付裁决债务。这样,一旦发展到双方有争议,被告或被申请人出面抗拒,就难免要提出非法与/或违反公共政策的抗辩,要求法院不予协助或执行。

中国仲裁裁决在域外寻求协助或执行的著名案例数不胜数,如:Lin Chien-Hsiang v. Lin Hsiu-Fen(2022)HKCFI 1270(SHAC 裁决书在中国香港特区执行);Kei Kin Hung v. Hua She Asset Management(Shanghai)Company Limited(2022)EWHC 662(Comm)(SHIAC 裁决书在英国执行);La Dolce Vita Fine Dining Co Ltd v. Zhang Lan(2019)HKCFI 618(CIETAC 仲裁在中国香港特区申请全球冻结令与资产披露令);RBRG v. Sinocore International(2018)EWCA Civ 838(CIETAC 裁决书在英国执行);GKML(2018)(BAC 紧急仲裁员裁决书在中国香港特区执行);In re Application of Hanwei Guo,2019 WL 917076(S. D. N. Y. Feb. 25,2019)(CIETAC 仲裁在美国调查取证);HRC-Hainan Holding Company,LLC v. Hu,Case No. 19-mc-80277-TSH(CIETAC 仲裁在美国调查取证);ZF Automotive US, Inc. v. Luxshare, Ltd 21 - 401(2022)(中方原告在德国慕尼黑仲裁,美国取证)等。

英国法院决定是否为涉外合约下的外国仲裁提供协助的权力来源是《Arbitration

[50] 见笔者《证据法:国际规管与诉讼中的证据攻防》一书第三章之1段。
[51] 见笔者《证据法:国际规管与诉讼中的证据攻防》一书第三章之2段。
[52] 见笔者《证据法:国际规管与诉讼中的证据攻防》一书第二章之4段。
[53] 见笔者《证据法:国际规管与诉讼中的证据攻防》一书第二章之3段。

Act 1996》之 Section 44(2)与《Senior Courts Act 1981》之 Section 37:见 A and B v. C, D and E(2020)EWCA Civ 409 上诉庭先例。而执行外国裁决书的权力来源是《Arbitration Act 1996》之 Section 103(3)。这些已经在本章之 5.1 段有介绍,英国法院除仲裁程序本身有问题外可考虑不予协助或执行的唯一理由是无法通过英国公共政策的"安全阀"。

这特别是在 1958 年《纽约公约》下,外国仲裁的公约裁决书都应该被公约国的法院尊重与得到承认与执行,这是公约国的国际承诺与责任。只有极少数理由才能拒绝承认与执行公约裁决书,而与本段内容关系比较大的是《纽约公约》之 Article V(2)(b)的执行地的公共政策。在本章之 5.5.1 段介绍的 Missouri Steamship Co, Re(1889)42 Ch. D. 321 上诉庭先例已经提到在普通法下是局限在"刑事犯罪、邪恶与不道德"(criminal、wicked or immoral nature)的情况才会令英国法院不予协助执行涉外合约或外国法院判决。这样,虽然对公约裁决书的执行多了一个理由或借口去严格协助执行,但涉及国际上的道德与共同秩序,也不应该因此对国际仲裁在涉及国际的刑事犯罪、邪恶与不道德行为有不同与更宽容的对待。

在国际商业的范畴,笔者马上想到这种情况会是为欺诈/欺骗而伪造文件,或向政府官员或公职人士行贿疏通关系。这种事在外国发生是英国法院管辖不了的,但相信在绝大部分的外国法律下也不可能去对这种行为宽容并合法化。所以涉外合约的形成、履行或合约目的在该合约的管辖法下应是非法在绝大部分情况下毫无疑问。

这样剩下要考虑的只是不一定与违反法律等同(特别违反外国的法律更不一定是英国的非法)的公共政策。首先要指出的是在执行仲裁裁决的课题下,非法与公共政策问题实际上是一回事,所有非法的背后都是公共政策问题。在 Omnium de Traitement et de Valorisation SA v. Hilmarton Ltd(1999)2 Lloyd's Rep 222 先例,Timothy Walker 大法官就说:"In his reply however Mr. Dunning(原告代表大律师)said that … there is a distinction to be made between performance being illegal and performance being contrary to public policy. I entirely disagree. They are but two strands of the same principle."

这将带来几方面的问题,首先是涉及如非一般程度的"非法/违规"的贪污腐败,也明显违反英国根本性公共政策,有关争议是否可通过双方约定的解决争议办法,以仲裁"私了"? 这涉及非法是否可仲裁(arbitrable)的问题。接下来会讨论的问题是:(1)如果可以,这种涉嫌贪污腐败的争议,对发展中国家而言,去外国国家法院(如英国或新加坡商业法庭)解决或通过国际仲裁解决孰优孰劣?(2)如果在仲裁中败诉(事实是在国际仲裁中发展中国家当事人败诉的几率很高),败诉方在裁决书执行时,能否在执行法院重复提出贪污腐败违反公共政策作为抗拒并要求重审?(3)英国法院与其他支持仲裁的法院,仍然有一些理论协助执行涉及贪污腐败的公约裁决书,如当事人双方同意将所有争议通过仲裁解决,而仲裁庭已经审理了有关的争议/争端;如果对仲裁庭的裁决不服,为何不去监督法院寻求救济? 监督法院已经审理过并已经拒绝对裁决书作出救济,执行法院不应再质疑。

6.1 严重非法/违反公共政策的争议可否仲裁

可仲裁性(arbitrable)的课题在笔者的《仲裁法:从 1996 年英国仲裁法到国际商务仲裁》一书第六章有详及,不去重复。在此只针对欺诈/欺骗与同样或更严重的欺骗国家民众的贪污腐败[54]的非法与违反公共政策的可仲裁性去进一步探讨。看来,这种涉及严重非法与影响公共利益的争议能否以仲裁"私了",在英国的近代史是有很不同的看法与改变。这可先节录《Kerr on Fraud and Mistake》(1920 年,第 5 版)一书之 382 页所说:"In cases where fraud is charged, the Court will in general refuse to send the dispute to arbitration, if the party charged in fraud desires a public inquiry. But where the objection to arbitration is by the party charging the fraud, the Court will not necessarily accede to it, and will never do so, unless a prima facie case of fraud is proved … So disputes between partners where a prima facie case of fraud is set up should not as a rule be referred to arbitration."

另外还可以仲裁立法的改变显示出来,首先是在 1996 年立法前的《Arbitration Act 1950》之 Section 24(2)中说:"Where an agreement between any parties provides that disputes which may arise in the future between them shall be referred to arbitration, and **a dispute which so arises involves the question whether any such party has been guilty of fraud**, the High Court shall, so far as may be necessary to enable that question to be determined by the High Court, have power to order that the agreement shall cease to have effect and power to give leave to revoke the authority of any arbitrator or umpire appointed by or by virtue of the agreement."(加黑部分是笔者的强调)

早在 Permavox Ltd v. Royal Exchange Assurance(1939)64 Lloyd's Rep 145 先例中,Greaves-Lord 大法官说:"(fraud) should be tried in open court and in the light of day."这表示在很长一段时间,涉外合约(早年主要是集中在国际航运与国际商品买卖)约定在伦敦仲裁,只要争议涉及欺诈,当事人就可去向英国法院申请令仲裁协议/条文失效与否定仲裁员的权力,让法院审理有关争议。

这也可体现在 Heyman v. Darwins Ltd(1942)AC 356 贵族院先例中,Macmillan 勋爵说:"If there has never been a contract at all, there has never been as part of it an agreement to arbitrate. The greater includes the less. Further, a claim to set aside a contract on such grounds as fraud, duress or essential error cannot be the subject-matter of a reference under an arbitration clause in the contract sought to set aside."

但到了《Arbitration Act 1996》的立法,再没有类似的条文去剥夺欺诈/欺骗的可

---

[54] 例如,美国的司法部(Department of Justice)对付欺诈的部门(Fraud Section),主要的两个小组一个是针对国际贪污腐败的"FCPA(Foreign Corrupt Practices Act) Unit",另一个是针对所有其他商业、公司与市场的各种不同手法的欺诈/欺骗的"MIMF(Market Integrity and Major Frauds) Unit"。

仲裁性,而 Section 7 更是以立法明确说明仲裁协议/条文在“独立原则”(separability)下,不受主合约/基础合约(这可以是英国本地或者是涉外合约)的无效、不存在或失效的影响,说:“**Separability of arbitration agreement.** Unless otherwise agreed by the parties, an arbitration agreement which forms or was intended to form part of another agreement (whether or not in writing) shall not be regarded as invalid, non-existent or ineffective because that other agreement is invalid, or did not come into existence or has become ineffective, and it shall for that purpose be treated as a distinct agreement.”

这样一来,欺诈/欺骗与欺诈性误述可使合约无效在 1996 年的立法下看来是可仲裁去“私了”。但本来英国法律(或任何其他国家的法律)在不允许剥夺法院的管辖权的大前提下,或多或少对以仲裁解决双方当事人的涉及非法的争议有所局限。在 Soleimany v. Soleimany (1999) QB 785 上诉庭先例中,Waller 大法官给出了另一个例子,说:“The English Court would not recognise an agreement between highwaymen (拦路抢劫的强盗) to arbitrate their differences any more than it would recognise the original agreement to split the proceeds.”

另在 Westacre Investments Inc v. Jugoimport SPDR Holding Co Ltd (1999) QB 740 一审判决中,Colman 大法官举的例子是非法买卖毒品可卡因,说:“The conceptual foundation of this submissions leads to the result that ... say an international contract for the sale and illegal importation of cocaine, which contains and ICC arbitration clause, an ICC award in favour of the seller in respect of the unpaid purchase price of the drugs must be treated as insulated from the substantive agreement for the purposes of the public policy exception to the enforcement of Convention awards and indeed at common law.”

在一个没有被报道的 O'Callaghan v. Coral Racing Ltd (unreported, 19 November 1998) 上诉庭先例中,案情涉及一位职业赌徒 O' Callaghan 先生与一家球赛博彩庄家 Coral Racing Ltd 之间在 4 场球赛的投注所产生的争议。双方同意去仲裁,而之后败诉的 O' Calleghan 却向法院质疑裁决书。上诉庭判该球赛的博彩协议是非法(违反《Gaming Act 1845》之 section 18)与无效的,而仲裁协议作为非法无效的博彩协议的部分,也无法独立生存。Hirst 大法官说:“(仲裁协议) must be treated as part and parcel of the void agreement, and so cannot survive independently.”

在上述举的三个先例可察觉到公共政策的不肯定与不稳定。在涉及国际贪污腐败的 Westacre Investments Inc v. Jugoimport SPDR Holding Co Ltd 先例与涉及走私的 Soleimany v. Soleimany 上诉庭先例的仲裁条文与可仲裁性被法院接受。但涉及在道德上远比贪污腐败更可能被大众或国际社会接受的“赌球”的 O'Callaghan v. Coral Racing Ltd 上诉庭先例,仲裁协议就与博彩协议一并被判决无效。

这个矛盾的结果产生的原因可能是赌球涉及的是英国本地的法律与非法行为,但前两个先例是外国发展中国家(科威特与伊朗)法律的非法履行,所以内外有别。

其他产生的疑问是在千变万化类别的“非法”争议中,可仲裁与不可仲裁“私了”

的分水岭是什么？怎样判断？笔者认为，对政府官员或公职人员的贪污腐败/以不正当手段疏通关系，相比抢劫或贩毒对整体国际社会与民众道德的败坏与伤害，在程度上有过之而无不及。

新加坡仲裁法针对可仲裁性的局限是在《International Arbitration Act》(Cap. 143A)第11条第1款规定："Any dispute which the parties have agreed to submit to arbitration under an arbitration agreement may be determined by arbitration unless it is contrary to public policy to do so."

6.2　法院或仲裁审理欺诈/欺骗与贪污腐败争议孰优孰劣

笔者认为处理商业欺诈/欺骗与贪污腐败/以不正当手段疏通关系的案件，更适合由法院审理，而不是以仲裁"私了"。

6.2.1　公开与公众监督[55]

欺诈或贪污腐败案件中的受害人会希望案件在法院审理。所以《Arbitration Act 1950》之 Section 24(2)才会规定，如果作为欺诈受害人的原告希望法院公开审理解决争议，但受仲裁条文约束，可以向法院申请命令仲裁协议无效与撤回仲裁员。

公开与公众监督的威慑力只会更大，因为接下来要面对的可能就不只是民事诉讼而是政府机构跟进的刑事调查(如根据《Bribery Act 2010》)或规管。但仲裁这种私人与机密的程序，显然没有这种威慑力，公司或个人在行事时也会更加没有忌惮。

这一点投资仲裁也有了警觉，虽然投资仲裁一直相比商业仲裁透明度更高，近年也不断推进进一步的透明化。2017年联合国《基于条约的投资者与国家间仲裁透明度公约》(以下简称《毛里求斯公约》)生效，2014年《联合国贸易法委员会关于以条约为基础的投资者与国家间仲裁透明度的规则》将适用在所有被告是签约国的新投资仲裁中。2016年10月，国际投资争端解决中心(以下简称ICSID)正式启动了新一轮规则修订工作。2022年1月20日，ICSID向其行政理事会提交了修订后的一系列规则供表决并在之后获得批准。这些规则于2022年7月1日生效。根据此次修订的《ICSID Convention Arbitration Rule》之 Rule 62、Rule 63 与《ICSID Additional Facility Arbitration Rules》之 Rule 73 的规定，如果当事人没有在60天内明确反对，将被视为同意公布仲裁庭的决定、命令与裁决。

但即便如此，公众对于投资仲裁的关注度也远远比不上对法院判决的关注度，因此监督程度依然有限。更不用说以上公约只适用于投资仲裁，对于大量的国际商业仲裁来说仍没有帮助。

6.2.2　法院判决成为普通法的一部分与永久纪录

英国法院在一审审理证据(主要是文件证据与口头证据)并认定事实，然后把有关的法律套用在事实上去作出决定。在欺诈/欺骗与贪污腐败的案件中，有关法律地位是已经明了，所以真正重要的是通过证据去找出事实真相。如果认定有外国政府

[55]　见笔者《证据法：国际规管与诉讼中的证据攻防》一书第四章之1.1段。

官员或国企高管贪污腐败的行为，其法律地位在本章讲得很清楚了，如 Lemenda Trading Co Ltd v. African Middle East Petroleum Co Ltd(1988) QB 448 上诉庭先例与《Bribery Act 2010》。

虽然在法院诉讼，败诉方或不满意一审结果的当事人是可以自由去上诉的，但上诉庭不能去取证重审。由于法律问题在这种案件一般不是问题，上诉庭能起的作用不大。但在笔者的《证据法：基础理论、口头证据与专家证据》一书第三章之 3.1.2 段与第六章之 4.1 段有详及，上诉庭对一审的事实认定与双方证据（特别是双方的专家意见证据）取舍的理由会严格监督。一旦理由不充分或说不通，就会下令重审或去推翻一审判决：见 Ellison v. Glencore Services(UK) Ltd(2016) EWCA Civ 407 上诉庭先例。

这相比在伦敦仲裁（与其他绝大部分仲裁地点）的法律，确定仲裁庭认定的最终事实与约束性相差太远了：见 Lesotho Highlands Development Authority v. Impregilo SpA(2005) UKHL 43 贵族院先例。由于认定是否违反外国法律、是非法或合法等的争议是事实方面的问题，所以一般是要通过外国法专家在开庭审理时作为专家证人协助仲裁庭。而仲裁庭如果"错判"，也不像法院的判决会上诉与受到严格监督。这就无可避免地使仲裁庭成员在认定贪污腐败案件的事实时没有什么压力，错判也经常发生。这种心态或心理上的压力与法院的一审法官是有极大的差别的。此外，仲裁的机密性也让仲裁员可以放心。

一旦涉及英国法院，由于任何判决都会永久进入普通法的系统，英国法院有责任对英国政府进行监督与纠正，所以对本地政府官员的贪污腐败与以不正当手段疏通关系或为私利不合法游说丝毫不能宽待。但显然英国法院在监督与纠正外国的同类案件会无能为力，正如在 Westacre Investments Inc v. Jugoimport SPDR Holding Co Ltd (2000) QB 288 上诉庭先例中，Waller 大法官说："...so far as public policy is concerned ... the English court is concerned with the integrity of its own system, and concerned that its executive power is not abused. ...If the court were concerned with a domestic arbitration and citizens of this country, I would have thought that if a party were to come before the English court and seek to prove that an agreement was unenforceable because it was in fact an agreement to pay a bribe, in addition to the contract not being enforced by the English court, the papers would be sent to the Director of Public Prosecutions. There is no such sanction available in relation to an agreement between foreign citizens."

虽然对外国贪污腐败的案件法院无法进行监督与纠正，但从维持国际道德最起码标准的角度来看，英国法院不应该名正言顺地在普通法系统下为发生在英国本地与国际（特别是发展中国家）的贪污腐败案件订下两套完全不同（一紧一松）的准则。但这种顾虑在机密的国际仲裁中是无须关心与担忧的。通过国际仲裁，英国法院在协助执行裁决书时有了另一个借口，就是《纽约公约》下承认与协助执行外国公约裁决书是更重要与压倒性（overriding importance）的公共政策。

6.2.3 欺诈/欺骗与贪污腐败/以不正当手段疏通关系需要更完整与可信度高的证据

在国际仲裁,即使是涉及欺诈/欺骗与贪污腐败/以不正当手段疏通关系的案件,举证责任仍是只需要满足民事诉讼的标准。但由于这些是严重指控,相比一般侵权(negligence/wrong-doings)会带来的违反小心谨慎责任(duty of care)的指控发生的内在可能性较低(至少对英国本地而言),所以即使只要满足平衡可能性的举证责任,也需要更完整与可信度高的证据才会成功。

这些说法可见 Three Rivers District Council v. Bank of England(No. 3)(2001) UKHL 16 贵族院先例,Hope 勋爵说:"the facts referred to might have inferred dishonesty but were consistent with innocence, it was not to be presumed that the defendant had been dishonest."

另可见 B(Children)(Sexual Abuse: Standard of Proof), Re(2008) UKHL 35 与 Bank St Petersburg PJSC v. Arkhangelsky(2020) EWCA Civ 408 等先例。在后者上诉庭先例中,Males 大法官说:"fraud and dishonesty are inherently improbable ...cogent evidence is required for their proof, since it was predicated on the notion that people do not usually act dishonestly..."

所以,被英国法院假设"内在不可能"(inherently improbable)发生贪污腐败/以不正当手段疏通关系,作为受害方的发展中国家的公司/企业举证就会有困难。但在国际仲裁中,虽然走的对抗制诉讼程序与英国法院是大同小异,但在强制披露文件与提供证人让对方律师严苛交叉盘问的能力方面,如果不配合的阻吓力比起英国法院是差远了。有经验的国际仲裁员知道,如果当事人不想披露可能对他们严重不利的文件,他们会有各种理由(如常见是声称没有这些文件)去抗拒披露。仲裁庭往往就不像法院能够有更多的办法去严格强制他们。这会是各种原因造成的,如仲裁整体的商业化令仲裁庭一般不愿意得罪双方当事人;当事人代表律师即使是英国律师也不像法院的"法院官员"(officer of the court)般有责任去坦率披露;仲裁庭不像法院般有太大的权力与勇气,如在不披露文件下去撤销索赔或抗辩/反索赔;仲裁庭的成员会来自不同法系或没有这些做法(披露不利自己一方的文件或交叉盘问)的国家或地区。

在举证标准(standard of proof)方面,可节录在 Jus Mundi 的 2022 年 2 月 17 日由 Dr Ana Gerdau de Borja Mercereau、Shirin Gurdova 与 Dr Affef Ben Mansour 合著的《Corruption》一文,其中有提到国际仲裁的仲裁员各有不同对待贪污腐败案件的举证责任标准,说:"Several tribunals have applied a balance of probabilities(or preponderance of evidence) standard of proof with caution, often requiring robust evidence of corruption. Some tribunals applied a 'heightened' standard of proof for allegations of corruption or required 'clear and convincing' evidence of corruption. Fewer tribunals have applied a criminal law standard of proof 'beyond reasonable doubt.' Finally, others have adopted a less-formalistic approach and chose to refrain from applying a specific standard of proof. Generally, tribunals have considered that the party alleging corruption must prove a causal link between the corruption and the investment."国际仲裁对国际贪污腐败案件的举证责任/标准是不肯定与不稳定的。国际仲裁的仲裁员不太可能愿意接受在本章之5.3段提到的根据间接证据/环境证据,也就是通过所谓的"红旗测试"(Red Flags test)去认定贪污腐败的行为。

6.2.4　英国法院的民事拘押程序(committal proceedings)

英国法院的民事诉讼法下CPR 81规定:"(1) If the court finds the defendant in contempt of court, the court may impose a period of imprisonment (an order of committal), a fine, confiscation of assets or other punishment permitted under the law."

立法针对的藐视法院的行为主要是不服从(disobedience)与干扰(interference),这包括了各种妨碍司法公正行为,不严格遵守法院的禁令与命令,提交法院并签署了"真实声明"(statement of truth)的证人证言、宣誓书或全面搜查与披露文件的声明等被发觉有虚假内容等行为。此立法中藐视法院不是一个刑事犯罪,但法院可以对被告做出监禁、罚款或没收财产等惩罚。

这可介绍Super-Max Offshore Holdings, Actis Consumer Groming Products Limited v. Ramesh Malhotra (2020) EWHC 1130 (Comm)先例,案情涉及印度生产的Super-Max刀片,该生产公司(第一原告SMOH)由被告的父亲建立,被告本人曾经是该公司的首席执行官。而第二原告ACGPL是一个基金,在SMOH投资了高达2.25亿美元,但投资的条件是有可退出并让SMOH回购的选择权。本来大家的希望业务良好并可以让包括ACGPL在内的投资方的投资有一个很好的回报,但结果事与愿违。这导致产生争议与一连串的诉讼,包括在印度法院的诉讼与LCIA的仲裁等。在ACGPL与SMOH的申请下,英国法院向被告作出各种禁令/命令。在接下来提起的拘押程序中,英国法院判被告存在共达30次之多的藐视法院行为,判被告监禁15个月。这些藐视法院的行为包括了违反法院禁令、提交的证人证言有虚假内容、干扰证人等。

相比在国际仲裁中,熟悉程序与做法的人士可以马上看到仲裁庭对这种藐视行为能够做出的阻吓与法院是有天壤之别的。

6.2.5　协助执行《纽约公约》下公约裁决书成为支持仲裁国家的压倒性公共政策

笔者已经在本章多次提到,英国在1975年通过立法承认1958年《纽约公约》后,逐渐发展到已经把执行外国公约裁决书(convention award)视为超越一切的公共政策,认为必须协助执行公约裁决书。这样,在决定是否协助执行一个国际裁决书时,即使涉及国际贪污腐败与以不正当手段疏通关系(只要这发生在外国而不是本地)是违反另一个至关重要的公共政策,法院在权衡下仍是优先协助执行国际公约裁决书。

在带出这压倒性重要说法的Westacre Investments Inc v. Jugoimport SPDR Holding Co Ltd(2000)QB 288 上诉庭先例的一审中，Colman 大法官明确说："On balance, I have come to the conclusion that the public policy of sustaining international arbitration awards on the facts of this case outweighs the public policy in discouraging international commercial corruption."

在 R v. V(2008)EWHC 1531(Comm)先例，Steel 大法官也重复说："... the public policy of sustaining international arbitration awards on the facts of this case outweighs the public policy in discouraging international commercial corruption."

另也可见新加坡 AJU v. AJT(2011)SGCA 41 上诉庭先例，法院把适用法是泰国法且履行所发生的非法行为发生在泰国的合约，与适用法是新加坡法的合约区别对待。后者才算是新加坡的公共政策，也是新加坡法院可以理会的法律问题。

这表示涉及贪污腐败或以不正当手段疏通关系的商业案件只要避开国际仲裁，如争议解决是在外国的国际商业法庭进行，就可以避开英国对 1958 年《纽约公约》的公共政策，有机会在申请英国法院协助执行时，采用 Soleimany v. Soleimany(1999)QB 785 上诉庭先例中 Waller 大法官在附带意见中提出，但之后在 Westacre Investments Inc v. Jugoimport SPDR Holding Co Ltd 先例中没有被多数意见接受的"两步测试"(two stage test)，带来对外国贪污腐败重审的机会。

总而言之，笔者认为针对欺诈/欺骗与贪污腐败/以不正当手段疏通关系的案件，看来在英国(新加坡或美国等)法院审理应比在国际仲裁优越得多(这是针对受害方而言)。这样即使涉及这种非法与违反公共政策的案件，相信其中一个最大的困难是很多国家无法接受去其他国家法院作为当事人接受审理。相对来说，接受"私了"与机密的国际仲裁面子上就好得多。但认为去国际仲裁就可以保住面子往往只是掩耳盗铃。

6.3　仲裁员是否有管辖权去审理欺诈/欺骗或贪污腐败的争议

换一个角度，撇开在本章之 6.1 段探讨的可仲裁性的公共政策，而另从管辖权(jurisdiction)的角度去探讨这个问题。在普通法下，针对无效合约，曾被视为合约条文之一的仲裁条文也一并无效，也就是再也不会有仲裁或仲裁员可以有管辖权去审理该无效合约的争议。在 Overseas Union Insurance Ltd v. AA Mutual International Insurance Co Ltd(1998)2 Lloyd's Rep 63 先例中，Evans 大法官说这是权威说法并符合逻辑："owes as much to logic as it does to authority."

但在 Harbour Assurance Co(UK)Ltd v. Kansa General International Insurance Co Ltd(1993)QB 701 上诉庭先例[56]中，在国际环境越来越支持仲裁的情况下，有了重大的改变。该先例的非法涉及违反英国的《Insurance Companies Acts 1974 & 1981》，被告在没有注册与获批准下在英国进行再保险(reinsurance)业务。上诉庭在该先例中再次确定当时仍是不肯定与有不同说法的仲裁协议独立原则。反正这些支持仲裁

---

〔56〕 案情介绍可见笔者的《仲裁法：从 1996 年英国仲裁法到国际商务仲裁》一书第五章之 5 段。

独立原则的先例(另包括如 Heyman v. Darwins Ltd[1942]AC 356;Bremer Vulcan v. South India Shipping Corporation Ltd[1981]2 WLR 141 等贵族院先例),也都已经被收纳在立法的《Arbitration Act 1996》之 Section 7 了。

但 Harbour Assurance Co(UK)Ltd v. Kansa General International Insurance Co Ltd 上诉庭先例的非法在严重程度上与贪污腐败的非法不可用日而语。在著名的 Fiona Trust & Holding Corp v. Privalov(2007)UKHL 40 贵族院先例中,在《Arbitration Act 1996》生效后,首次有机会去考虑这个特定的疑问,即在一份说得通是贪污腐败的合约下,有关争议是否由仲裁去解决。虽然在这著名的仲裁方面的权威先例中,被大家熟悉与强调的主要是对传统解释仲裁协议/条文的考虑有了根本性改变。以前的法律默示不允许剥夺法院的管辖权,如果想改为由仲裁去解决,就要写清楚,这包括仲裁的方方面面,特别是可以管辖的争议类别与范围。但在开始大力支持仲裁后,Fiona Trust & Holding Corp v. Privalov 贵族院先例确定了在是否清楚明示仲裁员有权管辖的争议类别与范围方面,一个有效的仲裁协议或条文的文字/措辞再也不像以前这么重要,如索赔的诉因是侵权或是复原/不当得利,是否被包括在仲裁协议的范围内。只要是双方约定去仲裁,解释仲裁协议或条文的起点就是"假设双方意图把所有会出现的争议去一站式解决"(a presumption of 'one stop' dispute resolution is to be applied)。

在 Fiona Trust & Holding Corp v. Privalov 的一系列先例中,英国法院要宣示(declaration)的是,在面对表面合理或说得通被指称是通过行贿诱导产生的合约,并在发觉后被撤销合约,在一般通用的仲裁条文下有关争议可否或应否以仲裁解决?下文分析这个疑问。

6.3.1　仲裁的独立原则

独立原则(separability)的课题在笔者的《仲裁法:从 1996 年英国仲裁法到国际商务仲裁》一书第五章有详尽介绍,不重复。只再次节录英国《Arbitration Act 1996》立法之 Section 7 说:"**Separability of arbitration agreement.** Unless otherwise agreed by the parties, an arbitration agreement which forms or was intended to form part of another agreement(whether or not in writing) shall not be regarded as invalid, non-existent or ineffective because that other agreement is invalid, or did not come into existence or has become ineffective, and it shall for that purpose be treated as a distinct agreement."

立法条文明示了主合约即使是失效(invalid)、不存在[57](non-existent)或失去功能(ineffective),也不影响仲裁协议的有效性。这表示绝大部分本书所针对的有关合约无效或可使无效的课题如可诉误述/虚假陈述、可诉错误、不当影响、胁迫等,都不影响以仲裁解决争议。在独立原则下,仲裁协议变为一个独立的合约,不受主合约有效性的影响。

---

〔57〕如双方是否有一致想法(consensus ad idem 或 meeting of minds),或是否存在真正有效对价(considerations)或满足构成合约的其他要件等的争议。

但即使仲裁协议/条文已由立法确认是独立的，仍需要确认在发生争议时从客观与表面看有主合约存在（即使有效性或是否真正存在是有争议），否则会面对从哪个主合约“独立”，仲裁要解决的是什么争议等的疑问。

6.3.2　Fiona Trust & Holding Corp v. Privalov（2007）UKHL 40 贵族院先例

Fiona Trust & Holding Corp v. Privalov 贵族院先例针对的是被告 Privalov 向英国法院申请中止 Fiona Trust 在法院试图阻止 Privalov 启动伦敦仲裁的行动，让仲裁可以推进。但这被一审法院拒绝，所以 Privalov 上诉到上诉庭并且成功改变了一审结果。其中 Longmore 大法官认为即使争议涉及贪污腐败的非法，在独立原则下与在本章之6.3段介绍的 Harbour Assurance Co（UK）Ltd v. Kansa General International Insurance Co Ltd（1993）QB 701 上诉庭先例所针对的非法令再保险合约无效，虽然非法的严重性有天渊之别但没有本质不同，说：“no argument for saying that a separable arbitration clause cannot be invoked for the purpose of resolving the issue whether bribery occurred. In this connection an allegation of bribery is（and should be）no different from the allegation of initial illegality in Harbour v Kansa.”

接下来上诉去了贵族院，上诉庭的判决被支持。其中 Hoffmann 勋爵说：

“The … question is whether，in view of the allegation of bribery，the clause is binding upon the owners. … if they（指 Fiona Trust）are right about the bribery，they were entitled to rescind the whole contract，including the arbitration clause. The arbitrator therefore has no jurisdiction and the dispute should be decided by the court.

The principle of separability enacted insection 7 means that the invalidity or rescission of the main contract does not necessarily entail the invalidity or rescission of the arbitration agreement. **The arbitration agreement must be treated as a ‘distinct agreement’ and can be void or voidable only on grounds which relate directly to the arbitration agreement**. …

…In the present case，it is alleged that the main agreement was in uncommercial terms which，together with other surrounding circumstances，give rise to the inference that an agent acting for the owners was bribed to consent to it. But that does not show that he was bribed to enter into the arbitration agreement…. Mr Butcher QC（Fiona Trust 代表大律师）said that but for the bribery，the owners would not have entered into any charter with the charterers and therefore would not have entered into an arbitration agreement. But that is in my opinion exactly the kind of argument which section 7 was intended to prevent. … **the arbitration agreement can be invalidated only on a ground which relates to the arbitration agreement and is not merely a consequence of the invalidity of the main agreement**.”（加黑部分是笔者的强调）

另 Hope 勋爵也说：“The appellants’（指 Fiona Trust）argument was not that there was no contract at all，but that they were entitled to rescind the contract including the arbitration agreement because the contract was induced by bribery. Allegations of that kind, if sound, may affect the validity of the main agreement. But they do not undermine the validity of the arbitration agreement as a distinct agreement. **The doctrine of separability requires direct impeachment of the arbitration agreement before it can be set aside.**"(加黑部分是笔者的强调)

这表示质疑主合约或基础合约的有效性不影响在独立原则下的仲裁协议/条文的有效性。但如果连仲裁协议/条文的有效性或是否存在也受质疑,独立原则就不再适用了,所有争议都只能是由适格法院(competent court)去审理了。

6.3.3　质疑独立原则下的仲裁协议/条文的有效性

上小段提到独立原则从客观与表面看是有主合约或基础合约的存在(即使有效性或是否真正存在是有争议),才会带来仲裁协议或条文需要"独立"去解决有关主合约的争议。所以在独立原则下,仅是质疑主合约的有效性,但不质疑仲裁协议,无法避免仲裁而成功把有关争议(主要是涉及贪污腐败)交出给法院审理。

但什么情况才算是同时质疑仲裁协议或条文的有效性?这种极端的例子可先举一个"临时仲裁协议"(ab hoc arbitration agreement),例如在出了争议后(如船舶碰撞)双方达成协议去伦敦仲裁"私了",并同意委任一位有丰富海事经验的人士作为独任仲裁员。在法律上,这仲裁协议与其他的合约是完全一样的,必须满足产生一个有效合约的要件,也可以受到各种影响合约效力的因素(vitiating factors)如误述、错误、胁迫等影响。该仲裁协议也可以因违约/毁约、受阻等原因而被终止。这样,一旦此临时仲裁协议的有效性受到质疑,这些争议就只能由法院审理了。这带来一个与有关主合约有效性的微妙区别。已经说到过,在仲裁中经常会争议有关主合约是否有效的是涉及合约可使无效或合约被终止的情况。这表示主合约虽然在启动仲裁时已经无效,但主合约(与仲裁协议/条文)曾一度存在与有效过。所以在独立原则下,主合约即使无效,也不影响仲裁协议独立于主合约有效。但在较罕有的主合约从来没有存在过的情况下,说仲裁协议独立说不通。从何而来与怎样来?恐怕无法回答。这样,质疑主合约从来未存在过也会同时去质疑仲裁协议的有效性。

这也是类同在近年来热门的仲裁协议的"管辖权"(jurisdiction)与"可采纳性"(admissibility)的区分:见 Emirates Trading Agency LLC v. Prime Mineral Exports Private Limited(2014)EWHC 2104(Comm);BBA v. BAZ(2020)SGCA 53;BTN v. BTP(2020)SGCA 105;The "Leonidas"(2021)2 Lloyd's Rep 165;Republic of Sierra Leone v. SL Mining Ltd(2021)EWHC 286(Comm);NWA & Ors v. NVF & Ors(2021)EWHC 2666(Comm);T v. B(2021)HKCFI 3645;DHL Project & Chartering Ltd v. Gemini Ocean Shipping Co Ltd(2022)EWCA Civ 1555 等先例。

在 DHL Project & Chartering Ltd v. Gemini Ocean Shipping Co Ltd 上诉庭先例中,Males 大法官区分为"仲裁协议的形成"(contract formation)与"仲裁协议的有效性"(contract validity)。前者才真正涉及管辖权的问题,而如果认定的事实确是合约从

来没有产生过,合约内的仲裁条文也是同样命运,独立原则也就无从说起了。

在 Albon v. Naza Motor Trading Sdn Bhd(2007)EWCA Civ 1124 上诉庭先例中,案情涉及 Albon 先生的公司在 1997 年 3 月开始向 Naza Motor 提供有关英国与马来西亚之间汽车进出口业务的代理服务。双方的代理合约是一份在英国订立与适用英国法的合约。在 2005 年 8 月 10 日,Albon 在英国法院向 Naza Motor 提起诉讼,但在 2006 年 2 月,Naza Motor 在马来西亚的吉隆坡国际仲裁中心(KLRCA)启动了仲裁。Naza Motor 的依据是双方在 2003 年 7 月 29 日在吉隆坡签了一个合资协议(以下简称 JVA),内有马来西亚仲裁条文。Naza Motor 也向英国法院申请中止法院程序,让双方的争议可以通过马来西亚仲裁解决。但 Albon 指称该 JVA 是伪造文件。

在一审法院,Lightman 大法官考虑了双方的证据,包括双方的证人证言,认定 Albon 对该 JVA 是伪造的,且并不是他的签字。部分理由包括 Naza Motor 提供的有关文件中没有任何地方提到过 JVA,并且有其他蛛丝马迹。伪造一份合约确实是容易,但伪造完整的相关文件如合约的谈判就难于登天。Lightman 大法官说以《Arbitration Act 1996》之 Section 9 之"Stay of legal proceedings"下申请中止法院程序让给仲裁解决双方争议,Naza Motor 必须证明双方有表面看来是同意了的仲裁协议,法院也满意该仲裁协议不是"空与无效、无法操作或不能履行"(null and void, inoperative, or incapable of being performed),才会中止法院程序。Lightman 大法官最后决定先要由英国法院审理该 JVA 的真实性时说:"I do not think that it would be just in all the circumstances of this case to require Mr Albon to submit himself to the Arbitration Proceedings in Malaysia unless and until the validity of the JVA has been decided against him here."

在接下来另一个申请,Lightman 大法官也向 Naza Motor 发出一个禁止推进 KLRCA 仲裁命令(anti-arbitration injunction)。这些决定在 Naza Motor 上诉后被上诉庭支持。

简单总结来说,上述先例就显示了在伪造合约的质疑,只要表面站得住脚,仲裁协议/条文也同时受到牵连,无法"独立"于主合约了。同样,独立原则也不适用将仲裁协议/条文与主合约一起考虑,而双方对有否跨越谈判与达成合约的分水岭有争议[58]的情况。此外,也不适用在"这并非是我的协议"[59](*non est factum*)或"对对方订约方的身份有错误理解"[60](mistaken identity)的争议,这可再多举一些权威说法与其他的案例。

在 Harbour Assurance Co(UK)Ltd v. Kansa General International Insurance Co Ltd

---

〔58〕 见本书第七章之 6 段。这是说客观看是否已经跨过了谈判的阶段,这与本章之 6.3.1 段提到的是否没有达成一致意见,或是是否存在有效对价或满足其他构成合约的要件有微妙不同。

〔59〕 见本书第七章之 16 段。

〔60〕 见本书第七章之 12 段。

(1993)QB 701 上诉庭先例的一审中,Steyn 大法官说:"Once it be became accepted that the arbitration clause is a separate agreement, ancillary to the contract, the logical impediment to referring an issue of the invalidity of the contract to arbitration disappears. Provided that **the arbitration clause itself is not directly impeached(e. g. by a non est factum plea), the arbitration agreement is as a matter of principled legal theory capable of surviving the invalidity of the contract**."(加黑部分是笔者的强调)

而在上诉庭中,Hoffmann 大法官说:"There will obviously be cases in which a claim that no contract came into existence necessarily entails a denial that there was any agreement to arbitrate. **Cases of non est factum or denial that there was a concluded agreement, or mistake as to the identity of the other contracting party suggest themselves as examples**. But there is no reason why every case of initial invalidity should have this consequence ..."(加黑部分是笔者的强调)

在《Arbitration Act 1996》生效后的 Fiona Trust & Holding Corp v. Privalov(2007) UKHL 40 贵族院先例中,Hope 勋爵说:"... as Longmore LJ said in ... the Court of Appeal's judgment, this case is different from **a dispute as to whether there was ever a contract at all**. As everyone knows, an arbitral award posses no binding force except that which is derived from the joint mandate of the contracting parties. Everything depends on their contract, and if there was no contract to go to arbitration at all an arbitrator's award can have no validity. So, where the arbitration agreement is set out in the same document as the main contract, the issue whether there was an agreement at all may indeed affect all parts of it. Issues as to whether the **entire agreement was procured by impersonation or by forgery, for example, are unlikely to be severable from the arbitration clause**."(加黑部分是笔者的强调)

再接下来介绍的是 The "Pacific Champ"(2013) EWHC 470(Comm)先例,案情涉及常见的争议类别,[61]就是船东与承租人以电邮往来谈判,有否达成有效与有约束性的租约。在此先例,船东说没有达成租约,但承租人不同意并指控船东违约/毁约。在伦敦仲裁中,仲裁庭判船东败诉,双方已达成租约。船东以《Arbitration Act 1996》之 Section 67 上诉,要求法院重审管辖权,指称双方如果没有达成租约,也就不会有仲裁协议。Eder 大法官在重审后,认定双方并没有达成租约,所以没有仲裁协议/条文,仲裁庭也就没有管辖权去作出该裁决书,所以要被撤销。Eder 大法官说:"it is my conclusion that there was no consensus and therefore no binding contract ... that there was no arbitration agreement. It follows therefore that HMM's(船东) challenge concerning the tribunal's jurisdiction under s. 67 of the 1996 Act succeeds, and the Award must be set aside or varied ..."

---

[61] 见本书第七章之 6 段。

再接下来是近期的 DHL Project & Chartering Ltd v. Gemini Ocean Shipping Co Ltd(2022)EWHC 181(Comm)先例,案情与 The “Pacific Champ”先例大同小异,也是在租约的谈判中,双方有否达成一致想法。争议的重点是“subject shippers/receiver's approval”是否是有效合约成立的先决条件(condition precedent)〔62〕。Jacobs 大法官在重审管辖权争议后也是得出与 Eder 大法官同样判法。此先例再上诉到上诉庭[(2022)EWCA Civ 1555],也是支持一审。

这又回到本段关注的贪污腐败与以不正当手段疏通关系带来的合约能否摆脱独立原则去英国法院公开审理而不是以仲裁“私了”的问题。已经提到过,如果以欺诈/欺骗与欺诈性误述令合约可使无效是不能回避“独立”的仲裁协议/条文。很多争议都需要通过仲裁去认定/裁定,如是否有一个可诉欺诈性误述或只是严重疏忽?如果有,是否仍能够撤销合约或是因各种障碍如无法回复到原状(restitutio in integrum)〔63〕导致受害方只能有损失赔偿的救济等。看来,只有能够成功证明有关的仲裁协议/条文根本没有产生过、存在过,才能够摆脱要通过机密的仲裁来处理贪污受贿的问题,笔者看到一种可能并将在接下来介绍。

6.3.4 质疑贪污腐败人士的授权

在上段的介绍下,是否从另一个不同诉因会有更好机会去回避仲裁协议而让法院审理?这就是授权(warrant of authority)的争议,也就是通过这种行贿带来的合约,行贿的外国公司应该知道受贿的政府官员或企业领导是不会有宪法或一般法律或企业的授权[无论是真正授权(actual authority)或表见授权(ostensible authority)]去订立这种合约。这样,合约就从来未存在过,自然也不存在仲裁协议,从而也就不需要争议仲裁协议独立与否了。

在 Fiona Trust & Holding Corp v. Privalov(2007)UKHL 40 贵族院先例中,没有太多去针对授权问题。在上诉庭中,虽然 Fiona Trust 代表大律师有提出并依赖《Bowstead & Reynolds on Agency》一书说:“Unless otherwise agreed, authority to act as agent includes only authority to act for the benefit of the principal.”

Longmore 大法官只简短地说:“… Professor Reynolds is correct to observe there that a transaction such as a contract procured by bribery is, as regards the principal, void as being unauthorised. But that is no argument for saying that a separable arbitration clause cannot be invoked for the purpose of resolving the issue whether bribery occurred.”

在贵族院,Hoffmann 勋爵针对独立原则不再适用的情况以是否有授权的争议作为例子,并与伪造合约相提并论说:

“Of course there may be cases in which the ground upon which the main agreement

〔62〕 见笔者《合约的解释:规则与应用》一书第二章之 2 段。

〔63〕 见本书第三章之 5 段。

is invalid is identical with the ground upon which the arbitration agreement is invalid. For example, if the main agreement and the arbitration agreement are contained in the same document and one of the parties claims that he never agreed to anything in the document and that his signature was forged, that will be an attack on the validity of the arbitration agreement. But the ground of attack is not that the main agreement was invalid. It is that the signature to the arbitration agreement, as a ' distinct agreement' , was forged. **Similarly, if a party alleges that someone who purported to sign as agent on his behalf had no authority whatever to conclude any agreement on his behalf, that is an attack on both the main agreement and the arbitration agreement.**

On the other hand, **if** (as in this case) the allegation is that **the agent exceeded his authority** by entering into a main agreement in terms which were not authorized or for improper reasons, that is not necessarily an attack on the arbitration agreement. It would have to be shown that **whatever the terms of the main agreement or the reasons for which the agent concluded it, he would have had no authority to enter into an arbitration agreement**. Even if the allegation is that there was no concluded agreement (for example, that terms of the main agreement remained to be agreed) that is not necessarily an attack on the arbitration agreement.[64] If the arbitration clause has been agreed, the parties will be presumed to have intended the question of whether there was a concluded main agreement to be decided by arbitration. "(加黑部分是笔者的强调)

Hoffmann 勋爵的例子是如果有骗子假冒是某公司的代理人,他根本没有任何授权去订立合约,公司是不受约束的,也不存在独立或不独立的仲裁协议可去约束公司。这是 Hope 勋爵在同一先例有说:"Issues as to whether the **entire agreement was procured by impersonation** or by forgery ... are unlikely to be severance from the arbitration clause. "(加黑部分是笔者的强调)

Hoffmann 勋爵接下来举例说如果争议只是在代理人超越了公司的授权去订立合约,如在著名的 The "Ocean Frost" (1986) AC 717 贵族院先例中,只是质疑主合约,不是质疑独立的仲裁协议/条文。超越授权充其量是令已经存在的合约无效,因为公司可以去追认(ratify)[65]代理人的授权。

---

〔64〕 这似乎与上一段介绍的 The "Pacific Champ" (2013) EWHC 470 (Comm) 与 DHL Project & Chartering Ltd v. Gemini Ocean Shipping Co Ltd (2022) EWHC 181 (Comm) 先例有矛盾。根据这两个先例,如果 A 与 B 订立合约,客观看主合约还在谈判阶段,同样没有仲裁协议。笔者认为这两个先例针对的是中间没有代理人/经纪人或代理人没有越权的情况,而这一段 Hoffmann 勋爵针对的是代理越权的情况。也就是虽然 A 告诉代理人仍在考虑某些条文,但代理人越权向 B 说"没问题"或"确认",在这种情况下 A 与 B 争议是否存在有效合约或代理人是否有表见授权,仲裁协议仍然在独立原则下有效。

〔65〕 见笔者《提单及其他付运单证》(2016 年)一书第三章之 2.6 段。

公司的领导或高管只是该法人的代理人,他们贪污腐败的行为显然不会有真正授权。行贿的外国公司也肯定知道受贿的领导或高管没有合法授权,所以谈不上有表见授权,也不受《Companies Act 1985》之 Section 35A 的保护,该立法条文这样规定:"In favour of a person dealing with a company **in good faith**, the power of the board of directors to bind the company ... shall be deemed to be free of any limitation under the company's constitution."(加黑部分是笔者的强调)

这样,这种情况与伪造合约没有区别,仲裁协议或条文是否存在或有效性受质疑,独立原则不适用。这可举较近期的 Criterion Properties Plc v. Stratford UK Properties LLC(2004)UKHL 28 贵族院先例为例,案中原告 Criterion 是一家英国上市公司,它在 1998 年与被告美国公司 Oaktree 成立的项目公司 Stratford(以下简称 Oaktree)订立投资与股东合约(investment and shareholders agreement,以下简称 ISA)成立合伙企业投资房地产项目。在 ISA 下 Oaktree 占股 85%,主要负责为购买地产项目出资,而 Criterion 公司占股 15%,除了提供少部分出资外,主要负责地产项目的管理工作。在双方的合作下,也成功于 1998 年完成了几次地产项目的投资。到了 2000 年 3 月,双方另签了一份 ISA 的附加协议(second supplemental agreement,以下简称 SSA),而该 SSA 则是争议的合约。据 Criterion 公司的董事总经理 Aubrey Glaser 先生所称,该 SSA 签订的背景是 Criterion 公司面临敌意收购,为了阻止该敌意收购,Criterion 公司在 SSA 中设计了一个毒丸计划(poison pill)或"埋地雷",也即如果 Criterion 公司的管理权易主或者 Glaser 先生不再担任董事或者受雇于 Criterion 公司,Oaktree 有权要求 Criterion 公司购买其在合伙企业中的全部股份,而购买价格是一个对 Criterion 公司非常不利的价格。在 SSA 签订的前一日,敌意收购的买家放弃了对 Criterion 公司的收购。2001 年 4 月 Glaser 先生被 Criterion 公司辞退,Oaktree 行使 SSA 下的权利,要求 Criterion 公司买下它在合伙企业中的全部股份,售价为 400 万英镑。Criterion 公司主张 Glaser 先生是在公司不知情与没有公司授权下签订的该 SSA,所以公司不受约束,从而向法院申请判 SSA 无效。与此同时,Oaktree 则向法院申请要求 Criterion 公司实际履行 SSA。Scott 勋爵说:"This case turns, in my opinion, on the 'authority' issue. If Mr Glaser(Criterion 前董事总经理)and Mr Palmer(Criterion 前公司秘书与董事)either had actual authority to conclude the SSA, given by a person or body with power to confer that authority ... or, if they did not have actual authority, had apparent authority to do so, then I can see no reason why the SSA should not be held enforceable against Criterion. If, on the other hand, Mr Glaser and Mr Palmer had neither actual nor apparent authority to conclude the SSA, then the SSA could not be held enforceable against Criterion. Mr Glaser and Mr Palmer might be liable to Oaktree for breach of warranty of authority, but the SSA would not be Criterion's contract.... Both Hart J(一审法官)and the Court of Appeal thought that the SSA was clearly contrary to the commercial interests of Criterion. Hart J thought that Oaktree must have known, or be taken to have known, that

that was so. I do not wish to be taken to be saying that knowledge of this sort on the part of Oaktree, or knowledge by Oaktree that Mr Glaser and Mr Palmer were, in signing the SSA, in breach of the duty they owed to Criterion, would be irrelevant to the authority issue. **If a person dealing with an agent knows that the agent does not have actual authority to conclude the contract or transaction in question, the person cannot rely on apparent authority**. Apparent authority can only be relied on by someone who does not know that the agent has no actual authority. And **if a person dealing with an agent knows or has reason to believe that the contract or transaction is contrary to the commercial interests of the agent's principal, it is likely to be very difficult for the person to assert with any credibility that he believed the agent did have actual authority. Lack of such a belief would be fatal to a claim that the agent had apparent authority**."(加黑部分是笔者的强调)

并不是所有涉及贪污腐败的案件,都可以用合约是没有真正与表见授权订立的抗辩。只有没有该行贿与受贿的行为本来是不会产生合约的情况,才能使用没有授权来质疑仲裁协议/条文独立性与有效性。如 Hoffmann 勋爵所讲,仅是越权(如 Fiona Trust & Holding Corp v. Privalov 先例)的争议并不足以否定仲裁协议/条文的独立性原则。但根据 Scott 勋爵以上所讲,如果对委托人(国家或企业)没有商业利益或有害(甚至是灾难),就很难以代理人(代表国家的官员或企业领导)有表见授权推搪。特别是在对方合约方知情时更是如此,而贪污腐败正是这样的情况。这样看来在 Fiona Trust & Holding Corp v. Privalov 先例无论是上诉庭还是贵族院越权的判法可能有问题。

6.4　英国本地仲裁裁决书涉及欺诈/欺骗与贪污腐败合约的质疑

在伦敦仲裁中,案情涉及外国(主要是发展中国家)的欺诈/欺骗与贪污腐败/以不正当手段疏通关系的案件,作为英国本地的裁决书也有法院对外国公约裁决书一样的制衡或安全阀。这就是裁决书本身或附属的主合约涉及非法与违反英国公共政策,而在外国的合约履行地发生欺诈/欺骗与贪污腐败行为显然就是典型例子。贪污腐败行为如果直接与裁决本身有关,如曾向仲裁员行贿而取得胜诉,这个裁决书在有证据支持指控仲裁程序不公正的情况下,就根本无法被判定有效或获得协助执行。贪污腐败/以不正当手段疏通关系如果只是涉及主合约,也是实体法下的非法。如果伦敦仲裁的主合约适用英国法,是一份"英国法合约",那么就是英国法下的非法。如果伦敦仲裁的主合约适用外国法,就要看外国法下是否非法。

欺诈/欺骗与贪污腐败案件在巴黎、日内瓦、瑞典、新加坡、中国香港特区等国家和地区或仲裁机构如 ICC、SIAC、HKIAC、ICSID 仲裁,并在取得胜诉裁决书之后向英国法院申请承认与协助执行,发展中国家抗拒执行的主要依据就是违反了英国公共政策,这在公约裁决书方面已在本章多处如 5.4 段有详及。

而在英国本地伦敦的仲裁中,也同样要面对英国公共政策的制衡。这在《Arbitration Act 1996》之 Section 68(2)(g),是说:"Serious irregularity means an irregularity of one or more of the following kinds which the court considers has caused or will cause substantial injustice to the applicant —... the award being obtained by fraud or the award or the way in which it was procured being contrary to public policy."

在笔者的《仲裁法:从开庭审理到裁决书的作出与执行》一书第八章之2.10段有说到这立法条文所针对的三个方面是:(1)欺诈取得裁决书;(2)裁决书是违反公共政策;(3)在取得裁决书的仲裁过程中有违反公共政策的行为。(1)与(3)的违反英国公共政策只涉及仲裁的程序,如(1)的以伪证取得胜诉的裁决书,而(3)可以中国香港的 JJ Agro Industries(P)Ltd v. Texuna International Ltd(1992)2 HKLR 391 先例涉及绑架证人改变他的证言等为例。这两方面都已在该书第八章之2.10.1与2.10.2段详及,不在此重谈。这里关心的只是(2)的裁决书违反英国公共政策,也就是裁决书针对的主合约涉及贪污腐败/以不正当手段疏通关系了。

毕竟,在绝大部分的情况下仲裁条文只是主合约的其中一条条文,硬把该条文视为独立于主合约的一个仲裁协议是法律假想出来让仲裁庭对主合约的有效性争议有管辖权去审理与裁定的说法。可以说"独立原则"只是在 Harbour Assurance Co(UK) Ltd v. Kansa General International Insurance Co Ltd(1993)QB 701 上诉庭先例后才开始发展与建立起来。

6.4.1 非法的公共政策在协助执行英国本地与国际公约裁决书中的异同

在现实中,无论是在《Arbitration Act 1996》之 Section 68(2)(g)下撤销一份伦敦裁决书,或是 Section 103(3)下拒绝承认与协助执行一份外国公约裁决书,英国法院在面对以外国贪污腐败抗拒执行时是同样对待。所以本章接下来的6.5、6.6等段的内容将对之一并介绍。

已经在本书第八章之7.5段介绍过,Patel v. Mirza(2016)UKSC 42 最高院先例针对的是英国法下合约非法的问题,涉外合约的非法虽然不被 Patel v. Mirza 先例特别针对,也同样会适用基于多因素判断的方法(factors-based approach)的精神,考虑多方面因素后作判断,而不是死板地看是否违反法律等。但可以肯定的是,Patel v. Mirza 先例没有考虑在《Arbitration Act 1996》之 Section 103 执行仲裁裁决书时涉及的公共政策/非法问题,而且更是存在支持国际公约裁决书的重要公共政策考虑,因此看来并不会直接受 Patel v. Mirza 先例的影响。在笔者看来,只有是根据仲裁庭在裁决书中认定的事实,英国法院需要初步质询/判断〔66〕(preliminary inquiry)该公约裁决书是否违背英国本地公共政策时,才会涉及 Patel v. Mirza 先例中的基于多因素判断有关的非法。

〔66〕 这是指 Waller 大法官在 Soleimany v. Soleimany(1999)QB 785 上诉庭先例作为附带意见中提出,但之后在 Westacre Investments Inc v. Jugoimport SPDR Holding Co Ltd(2000)QB 288 先例中没有被多数意见接受的"两步测试"(two stage test)之一的"初步质询",之后觉得有必要才去第二步的"全面质询"。这也表示对仲裁庭对贪污受贿的事实认定有一定的监督的说法也已经被否定。

这也是涉及贸仲裁决书向英国法院申请协助执行的 RBRG v. Sinocore International(2018)EWCA Civ 838 上诉庭先例的说法,可以节录 Hamblen 大法官所说如下:

"In my judgment Patel v Mirza does not affect the principles to be applied when considering recognition and enforcement under section 103,... Patel v Mirza will be relevant to whether, on the facts found, there is any illegality as a matter of English law. The policy considerations taken into account for the purpose of that determination may overlap with those to be considered under section 103, but Patel v Mirza neither purports to nor does it consider or decide the proper approach to be taken in section 103(3) cases. In particular:

(1) Prior to Patel v Mirza it is clear that a distinct approach applied in the context of a challenge to enforcement of arbitration award under s. 103(3), compared to the enforcement of a substantive claim.

(2) In Patel v Mirza the Supreme Court did not consider any of the authorities on illegality and public policy in the context of section 103(3). These authorities were not cited in argument, nor were they referred to in the judgment. There is nothing in the judgment to suggest that the Supreme Court contemplated that the approach it set out might also be applicable in the context of section 103(3).

(3) There are sound justifications for taking a different approach to substantive claims and enforcement claims, reflecting the different role performed by the court in each circumstance...

(4) It may be that Patel v Mirza has moved the jurisprudence on illegality as a defence to a substantive claim rather closer to the multifactorial approach that has always applied in the context of illegality as a public policy defence to enforcement, but the context and the relevant factors remain different. In particular, as the authorities make clear, there is always a strong public policy in support of enforcement."

6.4.2　伦敦仲裁裁决书在《Arbitration Act 1996》下的三种救济

英国法院作为伦敦仲裁的监督法院(supervisory court)在《Arbitration Act 1996》下是在三方面作出监督与协助去给予本地裁决书各种救济,这包括:(1) Section 67,管辖权(jurisdiction)方面法院才有最后的决定权;(2) Section 68,仲裁程序有"严重不正常"(serious irregularity)并造成"严重不公平"(serious injustice),这在 Section 68(2)(g)包括了违反英国公共政策,法院有权去撤销裁决书;(3) Section 69,裁决书如果错判英国法律,会有机会在批准下向法院上诉(leave to appeal on points of law)。

这些救济会与欺诈/欺骗与贪污腐败/以不正当手段疏通关系的案件有一点关系。例如 Section 67 的管辖权质疑(可见本章之 6.3 段)与 Section 68(2)(g)有关的违反英国公共政策。另外在一个英国法合约中,即使是在外国的贪污腐败/以不正当手段疏通关系的案件事实上被认定时,也会在英国适用法如《Bribery Act 2010》下非法。如果伦敦仲裁庭裁定没有非法,败诉的发展中国家的企业或有机会成功以 Section 69 申请上诉法院试图改变仲裁庭对法律错判(error of law)的裁决。此外,在证据的处理方面,如果在没有证据下去认定没有非法的事实或指鹿为马,[67]将会成为法律的问题。这里只节录 Stephenson 大法官在 GKN v. Matbro(1976)2 Lloyd's Rep 555 先例中所说:"Bearing in mind,... that the Court is bound by the arbitrator's finding of fact and cannot review them unless they are unsupported by any evidence ..."另在 Gillespie Bros & Co v. Thompson Bros & Co(1922)13 Lloyd's Rep 519 先例中,Atkin 大法官说:"... there is no evidence on which the facts could be found, because that would be a mere error in law."

Section 69 的救济是英国仲裁法的例外,与《联合国示范法》(UNCITRAL Model Law)要求国家法院不要去插手仲裁案件的实质争议(substantive issues),主要是事实或法律的争议/争端,是十分不一致的。这也是英国不被视为"示范法国家"的一个重要原因。在面对贪污腐败/以不正当手段疏通关系的案件时,英国《Arbitration Act 1996》之 Section 69 的救济或协助对受害的发展中国家的保护作用恐怕微乎其微。即使是英国法合约与去伦敦仲裁,仲裁庭如果不认定存在这种行为或证明不了,英国法院作为监督法院对受害方的救济的门槛仍低不了。

6.4.3 英国本地裁决书的执行:R v. V(2008)EWHC 1531(Comm)先例

接下来介绍的 R v. V 先例是适用英国法以伦敦作为仲裁地的 ICC 仲裁。该先例的案情是 R 与由 F 先生控制的 BVI 公司 V 订立合约,该合约表面看来是一份咨询协议(consultancy agreement)。在该协议下 F 先生为 R 的分公司在与利比亚国有石油公司谈判中提供建议与帮助,合约中泛泛地说:"Whereas R desires to use the Consultant to advise and assist(R 附属公司)in its negotiations with NOC(National Oil Company of Libya)with the purpose of obtaining for(R 附属公司)the approval of the development plans and production quotas submitted for the discoveries in Blocks NC 186, NC 187 and M4 ... in terms and conditions acceptable for(R 附属公司)."

之后开发计划获得批准,但 R 在支付了 V 首期的顾问费后,就过河拆桥拒绝再支付,这引发了这个伦敦 ICC 仲裁。R 提出的一个抗辩理由就是该合约涉及贿赂,在利比亚法律下非法与违反英国公共政策。

但仲裁庭最后裁定该合约在利比亚法律下合法与不违反英国的公共政策。R 为此根据《Arbitration Act 1996》之 Section 68(2)(g)的仲裁程序有了"严重不正常"向英国法院申请撤销裁决书。

虽然此先例涉及的是英国本地裁决书而不是公约裁决书,但法院仍然遵从了 Westacre Investments Inc v. Jugoimport SPDR Holding Co Ltd(2000)QB 288 上诉庭先例的多数意见判决。毕竟在考虑撤销英国裁决书或协助执行外国裁决书带来的疑惑

[67] 见本书第一章之 2.6.4.2.2 段。

是一样的，就是在仲裁庭已经认定与裁定有关合约并不是非法与符合英国公共政策的情况下，法院能否或应否进一步看仲裁庭判对或判错，这需要深入重审，如同法院在 Section 67 下针对管辖权争议的上诉一样需要去重审。[68] 这样，特别是没有仲裁庭在审理时看不到的迟来新证据，会否是让仲裁败诉方有了“第二次机会推倒重来”(second bite of the cherry)的不公平现象与仲裁不再是终局。另外，重审也不科学，会劳民伤财并带来严重的司法延误。审理 R v. V 先例的 Steel 大法官决定跟从 Westacre Investments Inc 先例多数意见(Waller 大法官有不同看法)的判决，在针对是否违反英国公共政策而撤销英国本地裁决书时与针对 Section 68(2)(g)同样考虑。换言之，针对这方面的争议(也就是在外国发生的贪污腐败与/以不正当手段疏通关系是否违反英国公共政策)，监督法院与执行法院是同样做法与考虑。这些做法与考虑(包括法院是否去重审仲裁庭已经是认定与裁定的结果、有否新证据的出现等)稍后在 6.5 段会详论。在此，只先节录 Steel 大法官所说：

“The difficulty with the concept of some form of preliminary inquiry[Waller 大法官在 Soleimany v. Soleimany(1999) QB 785 先例建议的“两步测试”之一“初步质询”，之后觉得有必要才去第二步的“全面质询”]is of course assessing how far that inquiry has to go. This must be all the more so where R does not seek to deploy any new evidence(let alone evidence not available at the time of the original reference). ...

In short, **it is correct in my judgment to accord the award full faith and credit**, even if it were appropriate to embark on any form of preliminary inquiry. In doing so I recognise that the questions posed in Soleimany are unlikely to be exhaustive. But is it legitimate to put into the balancing exercise as between finality and illegality any general examination of the merits of the illegality allegation? ...

Even if such an inquiry was to take place, it is to be noted that the majority in Westacre accepted that Colman J had accorded ‘an appropriate level of opprobrium’ at which to place commercial corruption if such it was. ...

As regards the strength of the case, it would on ordinary principles(**accepting the quality of the tribunal** and the extensive reasons furnished as part of the award) be illegitimate to treat the potential issue estoppel as undermined because of the fact that the tribunal was arguably wrong and thus allowing the point to be re-argued. ...

In the result, **by reason of the decision in Westacre which is binding on me and in respect of which there is no material factual distinction from the present case, I conclude that R has failed to establish that the award or its enforcement can be challenged on public policy grounds**.”(加黑部分是笔者的强调)

---

[68] 见笔者《仲裁法：从 1996 年英国仲裁法到国际商务仲裁》一书第五章之 8.7.5 段。

6.5　仲裁败诉方于裁决书执行时在执行法院重复提出贪污腐败作为抗辩

这种已经是仲裁庭全面审理后，也可能被监督法院考虑过决定不撤销裁决书，如果在执行法院再去重提贪污腐败的争辩，就肯定会被视为有第二次机会甚至第三次机会推倒重来，被不少国家的执行法院视为无理取闹或是没有遵守国际商务游戏的精神。

但这种想法是有问题的，因为这是1958年《纽约公约》的规定，执行法院如果不考虑本国的公共政策才会是"失职"。虽然《纽约公约》只说是"可以"(may)而不是"必须"(must)考虑，全球所有的国家或地区因为不同的国情，如历史、宗教、种族、政治、文化背景、经济条件、社会发展等因素而有不同的公共政策，《纽约公约》保留这一点就是为了保护各个国家不同的公共政策。这样，仲裁庭或外国法院（无论是监督法院或其他执行法院）决定了有关合约或交易是否非法与违反公共政策，而另一个执行法院在不再考虑有关的裁决是否违反本国公共政策下就去承认与执行该公约裁决书，这等于是把决定本国公共政策权力交给(delegate)国际仲裁庭或外国法院，显然不符合《纽约公约》的精神，也是执行国家法院失职的表现。

针对英国法院在作为对本地仲裁裁决书的监督法院或对外国的公约裁决书的执行法院，在《Arbitration Act 1996》之Section 68(2)(g)或Section 103赋予的权力下，面对仲裁庭已经审理与决定了的贪污腐败/以不正当手段疏通关系的争议，应如何处理的课题，笔者可以从三个不同方面进一步分析。

6.5.1　英国作为监督或执行法院不愿意重审仲裁庭审理过的贪污腐败案件

在大力支持仲裁下，法院很抗拒这种找第二次机会将仲裁推倒重来并劳民伤财的行为。

其他也会包括英国法院的审理法官很多打算将来退休后做仲裁员，所以在他们的小圈子中，彼此都相互认同与尊重，很不愿意去重审。例如在R v. V(2008)EWHC 1531(Comm)先例中，Steel大法官（他已经是转行为全职仲裁员多年）说："it is correct in my judgment to accord the award full faith and credit"。

6.5.2　贪污腐败有重大新证据的重要性

英国法院不愿意拒绝执行裁决书（特别是国际的）的一个可以理解的原因是如果在仲裁审理过贪污腐败的案件，再容许败诉方以大同小异的陈述/争辩与证据在执行法院重审一次，是毫无意义与劳民伤财的做法。而这种被视为毫无意义的尝试推翻重来的第二次机会，就凸显了新证据(new evidence)的重要。这新证据显然是指在裁决书作出后才被发觉或可以被发觉的重大证据，因为在这之前已经被发觉或可以被发觉，就应该提交给仲裁庭考虑，监督或执行法院也就不必重审。这方面的权威先例是Ladd v. Marshall(1954)1 WLR 1489上诉庭先例，Denning大法官说："To justify the reception of fresh evidence or a new trial, there conditions must be fulfilled: first, it must be shown that the evidence could not have been obtained with reasonable diligence for use at the trial; secondly, the evidence must be such that, if given, it would probably have an important influence on the result of the case, though it need not be decisive; thirdly, the evidence must be such as is presumably to be believed, or in other words, it must be apparently credible, though it need not be incontrovertible."

这法院对新证据的地位如果适用在英国本地仲裁,更是在《Arbitration Act 1996》之 Section 73(1)规定不准去后来引入新证据,说:

"(1) If a party to arbitral proceedings takes part, or continues to take part, in the proceedings without making, either forthwith or within such time as is allowed by the arbitration agreement or the tribunal or by any provision of this Part, any objection—(a) that the tribunal lacks substantive jurisdiction, (b) that the proceedings have been improperly conducted, (c) that there has been a failure to comply with the arbitration agreement or with any provision of this Part, or (d) that there has been any other **irregularity affecting the tribunal** or the proceedings, **he may not raise that objection later, before** the tribunal or **the court, unless he shows that, at the time he took part or continued to take part in the proceedings, he did not know and could not with reasonable diligence have discovered the grounds for the objection.**"(加黑部分是笔者的强调)

新证据的重要在很多先例有提到,在此只挑几个介绍。在 R v. V(2008) EWHC 1531(Comm)先例,Steel 大法官说:"The difficulty with the concept of some form of preliminary inquiry is of course assessing how far that inquiry has to go. This must be all the more so where R does not seek to deploy any new evidence (let alone evidence not available at the time of the original reference). ..."

另在 Honeywell International Middle East Ltd v. Meydan Group LLC(2014) EWHC 1344(TCC)先例中,案情涉及原告 Honeywell 在一个迪拜仲裁中胜诉后在英国寻求协助执行裁决书。败诉的 Meydan 以合约是涉及在履行地阿联酋贪污腐败与秘密佣金等非法行为违反英国公共政策为由,在《Arbitration Act 1996》之 Section 103(3)下抗拒执行。但该争议/争端与相关的证据在仲裁时已经存在,只是因为缺席没有提出。这样,虽然这不严格是对贪污腐败的争议,有推翻重来的第二次机会,但仍不算有了新证据让执行法院去审查。Ramsey 大法官说:"Even if I had not come to that conclusion or if I had found that the allegation of bribery was one which should be dealt with by hearing oral evidence, it is clear that the relevant evidence of bribery was available to Meydan at the time of the arbitration. However at that stage Meydan decided not to participate in the Arbitration or raise the allegations in that Arbitration. As stated in Westacre ... the condition to be fulfilled before a party can rely on evidence of fraud in an application to set aside leave to enforce an award will be 'that the evidence to establish the fraud was not available to the party alleging the fraud at the time of the hearing before the arbitrators'. In this case I consider that that this condition was not fulfilled because the evidence to establish the alleged bribery was available to and could have been deployed by Meydan before the arbitrators made their award and the fact that Meydan did not participate in the arbitration does not, in my judgment, affect that position."

再在 National Iranian Oil Co v. Crescent Petroleum Co International Ltd (2016) EWHC 510 (Comm) 先例,Burton 大法官说:"To my mind what is particularly important is ... the absence of any fresh evidence which might have been some justification for refusing to enforce the award."

但在 Nigeria v. Process & Industrial Developments Limited (2020) EWHC 2379 (Comm) 先例中由于有新证据,法院同意去考虑对裁决书的救济并重审仲裁庭已经裁决的在尼日利亚向政府官员行贿的指控与违反英国公共政策的争议。在该先例尼日利亚在伦敦仲裁败诉,裁决书命令赔偿本金加上利息高达 100 亿美元。案情涉及尼日利亚与被告(以下简称 P&ID)之间签订的一份天然气处理合约(gas processing agreement,以下简称 GSPA)。P&ID 是一家 BVI 公司,公司本身没有资产,它背后是两个爱尔兰人。伦敦仲裁庭针对管辖权争议、责任与赔偿金额共作出 3 个裁决书,而最后的赔偿金额裁决书在 2017 年 1 月 31 日作出。在拖了 3 年半后,尼日利亚向英国法院申请延长时间让它以《Arbitration Act 1996》之 Section 67 与 68(2)(g) 寻求救济,撤销裁决书。

在伦敦仲裁在 2015 年 7 月 17 日作出针对责任并判尼日利亚败诉的部分裁决书后,尼日利亚的司法部部长在 2016 年 2 月开始向 P&ID 进行调查,发现很多涉及贪污腐败的问题,如 P&ID 在尼日利亚银行提取大量现款(77 万美元加上其他本地货币)看来是为了行贿,涉及受贿的前政府官员的口供书(包括一位 Tijani 先生承认收取贿赂与 P& ID 代支付儿子婚礼费用)等。在尼日利亚拖延了实在太久后才申请法院根据《Arbitration Act 1996》之 Section 80(5) 延期允许向法院申请救济的案件中,尼日利亚必须出示很有可能存在贪污腐败案件,能够在全面审理时证明。所以即使延期申请,也有 34 位证人。另尼日利亚也要证明无法在仲裁中有证据提出与支持有关 P& ID 贪污腐败的指控,所以出了裁决书之后才能首次提出质疑仲裁庭的管辖权与贪污腐败,尼日利亚是没有过错或故意拖延。这样,才满足《Arbitration Act 1996》之 Section 73(1) 的要求,不会被认为失去了质疑裁决书的权利。

反正最后 Cranston 大法官对两点都满意,判尼日利亚可以获得延期去申请救济,说:"The delay in this case is extraordinary and weighs heavily on the side of the balance against an extension. In my view, however, other factors bring it down in favour of an extension. As I have explained, the delay is not in my view the result of a deliberate decision made because of some perceived advantage, and in all the circumstances Nigeria has acted reasonably. Given the strong prima facie case of fraud which I have concluded Nigeria has established, the position is along the lines ... where ... identified the substantial injustice an applicant would suffer in respect of the underlying dispute if deprived of the opportunity of making a challenge should an extension of time be refused ..."

6.5.3　执行法院质询/审查仲裁庭对贪污腐败争议决定的程度

最后要谈的方面是英国法院作为监督或执行裁决书的法院，如果要对争议重审，什么是恰当的做法？

当然，执行法院再质询（inquire）或审查（review）有关贪污腐败的争议，就带来了质询/审查程度的问题。这可以只停留在查阅该裁决书的分析与仲裁庭决定的理由，或是好像《Arbitration Act 1996》之 Section 67 所针对的管辖权争议，英国监督法院必须重新审理有关争辩与证据（包括以前没有提交的证据），不理会也不受仲裁庭对自己管辖权在一个"管辖权裁决书"（jurisdictional award）的初步决定的约束。

这看来有三种不同程度的质询/审查：

1. 在几乎所有这种类别案件的监督或执行法院已经是在做的事情，就是通过查阅仲裁庭的裁决书中对贪污腐败争议的决定给出的理由。今天英国本地或国际仲裁的裁决书，都要求仲裁庭为他们的决定给理由。固然，经常会有裁决书给的理由不足。对待英国本地裁决书，在《Arbitration Act 1996》之 Section 70（4）下，作为监督法院有权下令仲裁庭多给充分的理由。[69] 但对待外国的公约裁决书要求英国法院协助执行，就没有这个权力对外国仲裁庭指指点点了。法院就只能决定协助或不协助执行，毕竟判决必须有充分理由支持也是司法公正与透明的公共政策。

但也不要求仲裁庭把每一个双方的争辩与/或证据都在裁决书写出来，否则很多裁决书都会很厚。正如在 PT Transportasi Gas Indonesia v. ConocoPhillips（Grissik）Ltd（2016）EWHC 2834（Comm）先例，Cooke 大法官说："It is clear that a Tribunal does not have to set out each step by which it reaches its conclusions or deal with every point made by a party in an arbitration. Nor does a Tribunal fail to deal with an issue that it decides without giving reasons. … the approach of the court is to read the award in a 'reasonable and commercial way expecting, as is usually the case, that there will be no substantial fault that can be found with it'."

但这样一来，如果英国执行法院在面对被告败诉方的抗拒，指称仲裁庭错判与遗漏了很多重要关于贪污腐败的事实与证据时，如果只看裁决书的表面内容，往往看不出裁决书是否如败诉方所言的般仲裁庭错判甚至是严重错判，贸然协助执行不符合英国的公共政策。正如在 Westacre Investments Inc v. Jugoimport SPDR Holding Co Ltd（2000）QB 288 上诉庭先例中，Waller 大法官说："… if the defendants（仲裁败诉的被告）were not to be allowed to go behind the award and were not to be allowed to establish facts inconsistent with the findings of the … arbitrators."

2. 在 Soleimany v. Soleimany（1999）QB 785 上诉庭先例中，Waller 大法官在附带意见中曾提出对协助执行外国裁决书的"两步测试"，也就是先"初步质询"与如果发现有必要再进行后续的"全面质询"，说："In our view, an enforcement judge, if there is

---

〔69〕　在笔者《仲裁法：从开庭审理到裁决书的作出与执行》一书第七章之 2.5 段有详细介绍。

prima facie evidence from one side that the award is based on an illegal contract, **should inquire further to some extent.** Is there evidence on the other side to the contrary? Has the arbitrator expressly found that the underlying contract was not illegal? Or is it a fair inference that he did reach that conclusion? Is there anything to suggest that the arbitrator was incompetent to conduct such an inquiry? May there have been collusion or bad faith, so as to procure an award despite illegality? Arbitrations are, after all, conducted in a wide variety of situations; not just before high-powered tribunals in international trade but in many other circumstances. We do not for one moment suggest that the judge should conduct a full-scale trial of those matters in the first instance. That would create the mischief which the arbitration was designed to avoid. **The judge has to decide whether it is proper to give full faith and credit to the arbitrator's award. Only if he decides at the preliminary stage that he should not take that course does he need to embark on a more elaborate inquiry into the issue of illegality.**"（加黑部分是笔者的强调）

在以上节录内容中提到了初步质询仍会涉及很多事实，如根据实际案情可能包括：(1)另一方是否提出了相反的证据反驳？(2)仲裁庭是否在仲裁程序中经过深思熟虑后，已经给出事实认定合约非法或合法？(3)仲裁庭得出结论是否属于合理推断？(4)仲裁庭是否有权或适格进行这样的认定？(5)是否存在合谋恶意用仲裁方式掩盖非法交易？等等。

Waller 大法官看来是希望区分法院考虑实质争议与法院考虑执行仲裁裁决书的不同程度的审理，而在执行过程中只需要"初步质询"。但在笔者看来，初步质询不免仍然是需要当事人提供大量证据，令执行法院仍然要重新在一定程度上开启对事实的审理。这样，到什么程度是恰当的"初步"不容易决定与掌控。正如 Steel 大法官在 R v. V (2008) EWHC 1531 (Comm) 先例说："The difficulty with the concept of some form of preliminary inquiry is of course assessing how far that inquiry has to go."

另在英国的对抗制诉讼制度下，双方代表律师会尽他们的努力把所有对己方有利的事实证据都展示出来支持自己的案件，不会理会只是"初步"审理就收敛。所以即使是"初步质询"也不会与"全面质询"有区别，反正就是重审一次。

所以之后在 Westacre Investments Inc v. Jugoimport SPDR Holding Co Ltd 先例中"两步测试"没有被多数意见接受也不奇怪，Mantell 大法官这样说："... in the obiter passage cited by Waller L. J. from the judgment in Soleimany v. Soleimany ... it seems to have been suggested that **some kind of preliminary inquiry short of a full scale trial** should be embarked upon whenever 'there is prima facie evidence from one side that the award is based on an illegal contract ...' For my part **I have some difficulty with the concept and even greater concerns about its application in practice**, ... it seems to me that any such preliminary inquiry in the circumstances of the present case must inevitably lead to the same conclusion, namely, that the attempt to reopen the facts should be rebuffed.... **The seriousness of the alleged illegality** to which Waller LJ gives weight **is not, in my judgment, a factor to be considered at the stage of deciding whether or not to mount a full-scale inquiry.** ”(加黑部分是笔者的强调)

3. 不去“两步测试”,也没有“初步质询”,如果英国法院作为执行法院真是在1958年《纽约公约》下去认真把关与“不失职”,去质询/审查外国公约裁决书对政府官员或企业领导是否有行贿与是否违反英国公共政策,就只剩下是全面审理了。

这种审理是把所有在仲裁已经有提供与审理过的证据重新审理,并且审理的往往更多,如“新证据”。如果仲裁的败诉方视为重要的事实与证据不被仲裁庭关注,在裁决书也不去提及,也就有了另一个机会向审理法官展示,会得出另一个结果/结论也是有可能的。反正在全面审理、披露与交叉盘问的法院对抗制诉讼下,即使是比较隐蔽的行贿行为,也会能把背后涉及的严重贪污腐败暴露出来。

但问题是这样做会带来昂贵的费用与严重的延误,如在 National Iranian Oil Co v. Crescent Petroleum Co International Ltd(2016)EWHC 510(Comm)先例中有提到针对贪污腐败争议在仲裁庭的开庭就长达30天,如果法院去重审就另会要更长的6~8周的时间,这就需要考虑与权衡是否值得与成比例(proportionality)。笔者看来,对严重败坏国际道德的行贿行为,应去大力打击而不是协助执行。

6.6　英国法院支持涉及贪污腐败的裁决书的若干理论

6.6.1　仲裁是双方同意将所有的争议通过仲裁“私了”,后果自负

仲裁是双方通过合约去同意以此作为替代法院强制管辖的解决双方争议的办法。只以 Bremer Vulcan v. South India Shipping Corporation Ltd(1981)2 WLR 141 贵族院先例去区分法院与仲裁在双方发生争议时以对抗性诉讼去解决争议的不同权力来源与做法,其中 Scarman 勋爵说:“... arbitration is consensual and litigation compulsory in so far as the respondent(or defendant)is concerned, both are judicial processes of an adversarial character. ”

Diplock 勋爵说了不少有关仲裁是双方为了避开法院诉讼而同意通过以仲裁“私了”的做法,如:“The consensual aspect of arbitration is that the parties have agreed that instead of the court resolving a dispute an arbitration will ...”;“The conduct of an arbitration is almost entirely consensual. ”;“The consensual basis of an arbitration is radically different from that of plaintiff and defendant in litigation in the courts. ”

所以经常见到与听到对仲裁不满意的当事人向法院寻求协助或救济,支持国际仲裁的法院会说这是你们的选择,后果要自负。败诉方在面对本地或国际裁决书被强制执行时作出抗拒,提出仲裁庭对严重的欺诈/欺骗与贪污腐败错判,英国执行法院也难逃有这种想法,甚至在判决中显示出来。在 Omnium de Traitement et de Valorisation SA v. Hilmarton Ltd(1999)2 Lloyd's Rep 222 先例,Walker 大法官说:“... the fact that English law would or might have arrived at a different result is nothing to the point. Indeed, the reason for the different result is that ... the parties chose ... Swiss arbitration. If anything, this consideration dictates (as a matter of policy of the upholding of international arbitral awards) that the award should be enforced. ”

另可以 BBA v. BAZ(2020) SGCA 53 新加坡上诉庭先例为例，Quentin Loh 大法官说：“We repeat the views of this court in AKN and another v ALC and others and other appeals [2015] 3 SLR 488… see to similar effect Soh Beng Tee & Co Pte Ltd v Fairmount Development Pte Ltd [2007] 3 SLR(R) 86 … that: A critical foundational principle in arbitration is that the parties choose their adjudicators. **Central to this is the notion of party autonomy**. Just as the parties enjoy many of the benefits of party autonomy, so too **must they accept the consequences of the choices they have made**. **The courts do not and must not interfere in the merits of an arbitral award and, in the process, bail out parties who have made choices that they might come to regret**, or offer them a second chance to canvass the merits of their respective cases. This important proscription is reflected in the policy of minimal curial intervention in arbitral proceedings, a mainstay of the Model Law and the IAA … ”（加黑部分是笔者的强调）

6.6.2 仲裁庭成员可信可靠

英国法院在 1958 年《纽约公约》下或《Arbitration Act 1996》之 Section 103 下考虑对涉及欺诈/欺骗与贪污腐败的外国公约裁决书是否以违反英国公共政策为由拒绝执行，其中一个重要考虑因素是仲裁庭是否可信可靠。正如 Waller 大法官在 Soleimany v. Soleimany(1999) QB 785 上诉庭先例中提出“两步测试”的初步质询，其中就包括对仲裁员是否可信可靠去处理这种严重的指控或争议作出审查，毕竟国际仲裁员的素质是良莠不齐的，说：“In our view, an enforcement judge, if there is prima facie evidence from one side that the award is based on an illegal contract, should inquire further to some extent. … **Is there anything to suggest that the arbitrator was incompetent to conduct such an inquiry**? May there have been collusion or bad faith, so as to procure an award despite illegality? Arbitrations are, after all, conducted in a wide variety of situations; not just before **high-powered tribunals** in international trade but in many other circumstances… ”（加黑部分是笔者的强调）

如果在初步质询下发觉该外国裁决书没有理由或充分理由，又或是说理不通等，均可以判断出外国的裁决书在质量上会有问题。英国法院作为执行的法院无法监督这些外国裁决书，但至少可以做的是行使权力去进一步全面审理这个涉及欺诈/欺骗与贪污腐败的争议，才决定是否违反英国公共政策而可去拒绝协助执行。

国际知名仲裁员针对不是在英国本地发生的欺诈/欺骗与贪污腐败的争议作出的国际裁决书，英国执行法院就难免会先入为主对裁决书决定有信心与感觉可靠。在 R v. V(2008) EWHC 1531 (Comm) 先例，Steel 大法官说：“The arbitrators have expressly found that the contract was not illegal. The tribunal is made up of arbitrators who are well known, experienced and highly competent and who are fully familiar with the international commercial law scene. ... it is correct in my judgment to accord the award full faith and credit ..."

6.6.3 监督法院才是当事人选择去监督仲裁庭有否错判的法院

英国作为执行法院在面对抗拒执行裁决书的败诉方,首先会想到的问题是如果败诉方对仲裁庭的裁决不满意,为何不去监督法院寻求救济？而如果监督法院已经审理并拒绝作出救济,执行法院是否应该再去质疑？在 Minmetals Germany GmbH v. Ferco Steel Ltd(1999)CLC 647 先例中,案情涉及 CIETAC 裁决书在英国法院申请协助执行。该裁决书也曾被仲裁败诉的 Ferco Steel 向北京的监督法院申请撤销,但不成功。Colman 大法官解释国际仲裁的机制,即 1958 年《纽约公约》的设计,是当事人对他们选择的仲裁庭作出的裁决书如果不满意与觉得有缺陷,就必须去他们选择的仲裁地法院,也就是监督法院寻求救济。而后来在全球不同地点的执行法院就在此主政策(cardinal policy)下认为对监督法院已经审理并拒绝作出救济的,就更不应再去质疑。Colman 大法官说:

"In international commerce a party who contracts into an agreement to arbitrate in a foreign jurisdiction is bound not only by the local arbitration procedure but also by the supervisory jurisdiction of the courts of the seat of the arbitration. **If the award is defective or the arbitration is defectively conducted** the party who complains of the defect **must in the first instance pursue such remedies as exist under that supervisory jurisdiction**. That is because by his agreement to the place in question as the seat of the arbitration he has agreed not only to refer to all disputes to arbitration but that the conduct of the arbitration should be subject to that particular supervisory jurisdiction. Adherence to that part of the agreement must, in my judgment, be **a cardinal policy consideration by an English court considering enforcement of a foreign award.**

In a case where a remedy for an alleged defect**is applied for from the supervisory court, but is refused, leaving a final award undisturbed, it will therefore normally be a very strong policy consideration before the English courts** that it has been conclusively determined by the courts of the agreed supervisory jurisdiction that the award should stand. Just as great weight must be attached to the policy of sustaining the finality of international awards so also must great weight be attached to the policy of sustaining the finality of the determination of properly referred procedural issues by the courts of the supervisory jurisdiction. ... any suggestion that under the guise of allegations of substantial injustice procedural defects in the conduct of an arbitration which have already been considered by the supervisory court should be re-investigated by the English courts on an enforcement application is to be most strongly deprecated."(加黑部分是笔者的强调)

最后可介绍中国香港特区的 Gao Haiyan v. Keeneye Holdings Ltd(2011)HKCA 459 上诉庭先例,案情涉及一个西安仲裁委的裁决书在香港特区法院申请协助执行。

此先例并不涉及本章主要针对的贪污腐败/以不正当手段疏通关系，而涉及仲裁败诉的被告抗拒执行，指称西安仲裁违反了程序公正，这违反了香港特区的公共政策。一审的 Reyes 大法官同意这是违反公共政策并拒绝协助执行。但这判决被上诉庭推翻，主要的理由就是该裁决书已经被败诉方尝试在西安的监督法院申请撤销但不成功。上诉庭的邓国桢大法官认为 Reyes 大法官没有给西安监督法院拒绝去撤销该裁决书的事实足够分量的考虑，说："It is also relevant to note that, where, as here, the court with the supervisory jurisdiction has refused to set aside the Award and has upheld its validity, the result of a refusal to enforce the Award, can be extremely unjust.... I have referred to the Respondents' unsuccessful attempt to set aside the Award before the supervisory court.... The fact that the Xian Court has refused to set aside the Award for bias is relevant to the enforcement court's decision on enforcement of the Award. ...I believe Reyes J should have given more weight to the decision of the Xian Court."

以上所讲可以看出虽然有《纽约公约》设计出来的主政策，但 R v. V(2008) EWHC 1531(Comm)先例显示了在今天主要仲裁中心所在地的监督法院支持仲裁终局性的大政策下，显然对仲裁庭错判不会起到监督的作用。

6.7　执行国际公约裁决书时考虑的英国公共政策小结

6.7.1　权威书籍的小结

节录《Dicey, Morris & Collins, The Conflict of Laws》(2018 年，第 15 版)一书之 16-160 段，针对英国法院的态度小结如下：

"English law recognises an important public policy in the enforcement of arbitral awards, and the courts will only refuse to do so ... in a clear case. **A controversial question**, which has been the subject of several recent decisions, **is the extent to which it may be contrary to English public policy to enforce a foreign arbitral award** rendered on the basis of an underlying contract the enforcement of which (as distinct from enforcement of the arbitral award) might be contrary to English public policy. The following principles can be derived from the authorities.

First, it is legitimate for the court, in considering whether a foreign arbitral award should not be enforced on the ground of public policy, to take account of the underlying contract on which the award is based. (英国法院完全有权在审视有关主合约的基础上，考虑在英国公共政策下是否协助执行外国仲裁裁决书。)

Second, if that contract is in itself contrary to public policy (e. g. the classic case of a contract to share the proceeds of crime) the award may be refused enforcement on the ground of public policy. (如果主合约本身就违反公共政策，法院当然就可以基于公共政策的理由拒绝协助执行裁决书：见 Soleimany v. Soleimany[1999]QB 785 上诉庭先例。)

Third, it is important to distinguish between domestic public policy in English law;

and considerations of international public policy applied by the English courts so as to disapply foreign law or refuse to enforce an arbitral award, as the case may be. Thus the mere fact that English law would have arrived at a different result does not of itself justify the application of English public policy.（如果在英国本地法律或公共政策下认为应该有不同判法，并不是用来拒绝执行仲裁裁决书的理由。只有在国际共识的公共政策下，英国法院才会拒绝协助执行外国裁决书。）

Fourth, the mere fact that the performance of the contract may be illegal in the place of performance, without more, will not render an award on the basis of such a contract unenforceable in England, where the contract is legal by its applicable law and by the lex arbitri.［仲裁庭会根据合约的准据法以及仲裁地法判断与认定合约是否属于非法。而英国法院不能仅仅因为合约在履行地可能非法而拒绝执行合约：见 Westacre Investments Inc v. Jugoimport SPDR Holding Co Ltd（2000）QB 288 先例。］

Fifth, if it is apparent on the face of the award that the contract was made with the intention of violating the law of a foreign friendly State, then the enforcement of an award rendered on the basis of such a contract may be contrary to English public policy.［如果裁决书表面显示了主合约的目的是在友好国家采取非法行为，该裁决书的执行会是违反英国公共政策：见 Foster v. Driscoll（1929）1 KB 470 先例。］

Sixth, the court has to perform a balancing exercise between the finality that should prima facie exist particularly for those that agree to have their disputes arbitrated, against the policy of ensuring that the enforcement power of the English court is not abused: the nature of, and strength of the case for, the illegality, and the extent to which it can be seen that the asserted illegality was addressed by the arbitral tribunal are factors in the balancing exercise between the competing public policies of finality and illegality.（法院是在每一个不同案件去权衡裁决书的终局性与案件所涉非法的性质与严重性，以及仲裁庭在裁决书中如何针对该非法的指控，以此去决定这两个起冲突的公共政策哪个优先。）”（加黑部分是笔者的强调）

6.7.2 《纽约公约》Article V（2）（b）的公共政策应包括国际贪污腐败与欺诈/欺骗

需要指出是 1958 年《纽约公约》之 Article V（2）（b）提到的公共政策，明确针对的是法院地的公共政策，让执行法院在履行国际公约责任时有一个“安全阀”。执行法院可考虑的不是申请协助执行的公约裁决书中被仲裁庭认定与裁定主合约适用法或履行地的公共政策，或是另一个执行国法院考虑过的公共政策，因为大家的公共政策会不完全一样。这可以节录 Westacre Investments Inc v. Jugoimport SPDR Holding Co Ltd（2000）QB 288 上诉庭先例，Waller 大法官所说如下：“... it is relevant that the English court is considering the enforcement of an award, and not the underlying contract. **The English court takes cognisance of the fact that the underlying contract, on the**

facts as they appear from the award and its reasons, does not infringe one of those rules of public policy where the English court would not enforce it whatever its proper law or place of performance. It is entitled to take the view that such domestic public policy considerations as there may be, have been considered by the arbitral tribunal. It is legitimate to conclude that **there is nothing which offends English public policy if an arbitral tribunal enforces a contract which does not offend the domestic public policy under either the proper law of the contract or its curial law**, even if English domestic public policy might have taken a different view. "(加黑部分是笔者的强调)

《纽约公约》之 Article V(2)(b)的"执行地公共政策"应包括公约裁决书所针对的实体争议是涉及贪污腐败,正如在 PT Asuransi Jasa Indonesia (Persero) v. Dexia Bank SA(2006) SGCA 41 新加坡先例中,Chan Sek Keong 大法官小结了过往先例中哪些是《纽约公约》所指的公共政策,可以节录如下:"Although the concept of public policy of the State is not defined in the Act or the Model Law, the general consensus of judicial and expert opinion is that public policy under the Act encompasses **a narrow scope**. In our view, **it should only operate** in instances where the upholding of an arbitral award would "**shock the conscience**" (see Downer Connect Ltd v Pot Hole People Ltd (CIV 2003 - 409 - 002878, 19 May 2004, unreported)), or is "**clearly injurious to the public good or ... wholly offensive to the ordinary reasonable and fully informed member of the public**" (see Deutsche Schachbau v Shell International Petroleum Co Ltd [1987] 2 Lloyd's Rep 246 ...), or where it **violates the forum's most basic notion of morality and justice**: see Parsons & Whittemore Overseas Co Inc v Societe Generale de L'Industrie du Papier (RAKTA) 508 F 2d, 969 (2nd Cir, 1974).... This would be consistent with the concept of public policy that can be ascertained from the preparatory materials to the Model Law. As was highlighted in the Commission Report (A/40/17), at para 297 (referred to in A Guide to the UNCITRAL Model Law on International Commercial Arbitration: Legislative History and Commentary by Howard M Holtzmann and Joseph E Neuhaus [Kluwer, 1989] at 914): In discussing the term 'public policy', it was understood that it was not equivalent to the political stance or international policies of a State but comprised the fundamental notions and principles of justice... **It was understood that the term 'public policy', which was used in the 1958 New York Convention** and many other treaties, **covered fundamental principles of law and justice in substantive** as well as procedural **respects. Thus, instances such as corruption, bribery or fraud and similar serious cases would constitute a ground for setting aside**.... "(加黑部分是笔者的强调)

在上述介绍下,《纽约公约》之 Article V(2)(b)的公共政策,可以肯定公约的意图是作为执行地的英国法院应该拒绝承认与不去协助执行一个涉及贪污腐败/以不正当手段疏通关系的公约裁决书。这意图也可在本章之6.4段提到的《联合国示范法》的工作会议(travaux preparatoires)报告中所说的包括贪污腐败与欺诈/欺骗的行为应可去撤销裁决书。

6.7.3 对英国法院协助执行涉及欺诈/欺骗与贪污腐败的公约裁决书的批评

英美国家这几十年的法律演变为现在可令部分贪婪的公司更隐蔽、快捷、直接与有效地掠夺发展中国家的财富的手段。这演变包括以下几点:

1. 仲裁协议的"独立原则"把所有的争议(包括贪污腐败与欺诈/欺骗)让仲裁庭"一站式"与"终局性"去解决。

2. 仲裁的机密性与"小圈子"隐秘操作。

3. 英美等国主宰了国际仲裁,包括代表律师、仲裁员、专家证人、国际上受欢迎的仲裁机构的负责人、监督法院与受欢迎的执行地法院的法官等。

4. 如果仲裁庭有管辖权认定特定事实,该认定就应该得到尊重。即使监督或执行法院根据仲裁败诉方提供的证据有不同意见,也不能篡夺仲裁庭的地位与权力。对于事实问题仲裁庭的裁决就是决定性的,无论仲裁庭对事实的认定是对或错,都不应该重审,为了省钱与快捷必须"一裁终局"。

5. 在《纽约公约》下支持执行裁决书是压倒性的公共政策(overriding policy)更为重要。笔者感受到从 Lemenda Trading Co Ltd v. African Middle East Petroleum Co Ltd(1988)QB 448 与 Soleimany v. Soleimany(1999)QB 785 等先例,过渡到 Westacre Investments Inc v. Jugoimport SPDR Holding Co Ltd(2000)QB 288 先例的一审 Colman 大法官与上诉庭的多数意见,英国法院在取态与政策上开始有了重要的改变。其中 Colman 大法官明确说:"... the importance of sustaining the finality of international arbitration awards in a jurisdiction which is the venue of more international arbitrations than anywhere else in the world ... On balance, I have come to the conclusion that the public policy of sustaining international arbitration awards on the facts of this case outweighs the public policy in discouraging international commercial corruption."

另在 R v. V(2008)EWHC 1531(Comm)先例,Steel 大法官也说得直白:"the public policy of sustaining international arbitration awards on the facts of this case outweighs the public policy in discouraging international commercial corruption."

6. 在 Soleimany v. Soleimany 上诉庭先例中,三位大法官考虑了 Westacre Investments Inc v. Jugoimport SPDR Holding Co Ltd 先例的 Colman 大法官一审判决后,得出的决定在笔者看来与 Lemenda Trading Co Ltd v. African Middle East Petroleum Co Ltd 上诉庭先例一致,其认为如果案件表面显示了主合约的目的涉及在外国友好国家的非法(Lemenda Trading Co Ltd v. African Middle East Petroleum Co Ltd 先例涉及在卡塔尔以不正当手段疏通关系,Soleimany v. Soleimany 先例中的合约涉及伊朗的走私漏税),英国法院就应该以对待外国法院判决的同样大原则与做法去对待仲裁裁决书,不认为因为有仲裁协议的独立性就可去分隔,说:"it is in our view inconceiv-

able that an English court would enforce an award made on a joint venture agreement between bank robbers, any more than it would enforce an agreement between highwaymen,.... Where public policy is involved, the interposition of an arbitration award does not isolate the successful party's claim from the illegality which gave rise to it."

Waller 大法官在 Soleimany v. Soleimany 上诉庭先例中的看法与他在 Westacre Investments Inc v. Jugoimport SPDR Holding Co Ltd 上诉庭先例中的少数意见一致,但不再代表英国法律的地位,说:"**I have reached a different conclusion** to that of the judge(一审的 Colman 大法官). **I disagree** with him as to the appropriate level of opprobrium at which to place commercial corruption. **It seems to me that the principle against enforcing a corrupt bargain of the nature of this agreement**,... as being based on public policy of **the greatest importance** and almost certainly recognised in most jurisdictions throughout the world. I believe it **important that the English court is not seen to be turning a blind eye to corruption on this scale**.... I also believe that the judge did not sufficiently consider the extent to which the case now presented on bribery was examined by the arbitration tribunal. When one examines **the circumstances of this case one can see that in truth the bribery issue has not been ventilated properly before the Swiss arbitral tribunal**."(加黑部分是笔者的强调)

7. 但在 Westacre Investments Inc v. Jugoimport SPDR Holding Co Ltd 上诉庭先例后,[70] 只要通过国际仲裁,英国法院就可以通过将案件下放给仲裁员,实际上不再理会主合约涉及外国非法与贪污腐败/以不正当手段疏通关系争议的案件了。这样,也就不会对英国法律制度下对非法(illegality)、违背道德的对价不生诉权(ex turpi causa non orbiter action)、欺诈超越一切(fraud unravels all)等标准与定位造成任何影响。

8. 英国法院严重夸大了英国坚决反对欺诈/欺骗与贪污腐败/以不正当手段疏通关系公共政策与另一个在《纽约公约》下协助执行可能涉及这种严重非法但被仲裁庭错判了的公约裁决书的公共政策之间的潜在矛盾。把后者的公共政策视为压倒性

---

〔70〕 此重要上诉庭先例的多数意见已是目前英国在协助执行外国公约裁决书的《Arbitration Act 1996》之 Section 103(3)下的法律地位,有不少之后的先例受约束与跟从:可见 Omnium de Traitement et de Valorisation SA v. Hilmarton Ltd(1999)2 Lloyd's Rep 222;DDT Trucks of North America Ltd v. DDT Holdings Ltd(2007)EWHC 219(Comm);HJ Heinz Co Ltd v. EFL Inc(2010)EWHC 1203(Comm);Pencil Hill Ltd v. US Citta Di Palermo SpA(2016)1 WLUK 262;National Iranian Oil Co v. Crescent Petroleum Co International Ltd(2016)EWHC 510(Comm);PT Transportasi Gas Indonesia v. ConocoPhillips(Grissik)Ltd(2016)EWHC 2834(Comm);RBRG v. Sinocore International(2018)EWCA Civ 838;Carpatsky Petroleum Corp v. PJSC Ukrnafta(2018)EWHC 2516(Comm);Eastern European Engineering Ltd v. Vijay Construction(Pty)Ltd(2018)EWHC 2713(Comm);Nigeria v. Process & Industrial Developments Limited(2020)EWHC 2379(Comm);Sterling v. Rand(2020)EWHC 2899(Ch);Lenkor Energy Trading DMCC v. Puri(2021)EWCA Civ 770 等先例。

去超越前者更是在《纽约公约》之 Article V(2)(b)下的失职。至于怎样能知道错判而不是简单说一句对仲裁庭成员有信心就了事,也不应是种困难。Waller 大法官在 Soleimany v. Soleimany 上诉庭先例与在 Westacre Investments Inc v. Jugoimport SPDR Holding Co Ltd 上诉庭先例中的少数意见中提出的"两步测试",也就是先"初步质询"与如果发现有必要再进行后续的"全面质询",就会是可行的做法。英国也不会对这种做法陌生,上诉庭对一审法院的事实认定进行监督已是历史悠久,如果发觉很可能是错判,就会插手一审对事实的认定,撤销判决或下令重审。这在笔者的《证据法:基础理论、口头证据与专家证据》一书第三章之 3 段有详论,不重复。

9. 笔者也认为英国法律导致很多说法或原则说不通或分水岭模糊。例如,本章之 6.1 段的"可仲裁性"。1958 年《纽约公约》只是无数的国际公约之一,也只在 1975 年才被英国立法。为何将协助执行视为压倒性政策独大,而针对国际贪污腐败的国际公约如《OECD Anti-Bribery Convention》《United Nations Convention against Corruption》等要靠边站?更不如说是,《纽约公约》之 Article V(2)(b)本来就没有要去靠边站,可以同时兼顾两方面的公共政策。

10. 其他。近年来法国法院在《纽约公约》下协助执行涉及在发展中国家贪污腐败/以不正当手段疏通关系的外国公约裁决书,看来有完全相反的想法与做法。这在下一小段会进一步介绍。

6.8　国际执行非常依赖具体法院的态度

胜诉方取得一个在仲裁地点是《纽约公约》签约国的裁决书后,就可以在全球共 170 个国家申请承认与协助执行这个公约裁决书。但往往实际需要去的是英美等国,因为这些地方最可能找到败诉方的资产,或在这些普通法管辖地能申请到全球冻结令等有效手段迫使敌对方投降或仲裁败诉方支付裁决债务。

显然,不同的执行法院在本国公共政策的不同考虑下去提供或拒绝协助执行外国公约裁决书,也是《纽约公约》所允许的。但近年来法国法院看来有了不同的想法、看法,接下来将进一步介绍。

6.8.1　巴黎上诉庭在 Sorelec v. Libya 与其他同类案件的判决

接下来在 Sorelec v. Libya(Paris Court of Appeal, 17 November 2020 No. 18/02568)案件中,法国法院在三个主要方面确立了与英国法律不同之处。这包括:(1)依据 2003 年联合国公约《United Nations Convention against Corruption》与 1997 年《OECD Convention against corruption》,确立禁止对政府官员行贿是国际上的共识,说:"the prohibition of bribery of public officials is one of the principles which violation cannot be disregarded by the French legal system, even in an international context. It is therefore a matter of international public policy."(2)巴黎上诉庭确认可以根据环境证据或"红旗测试"(Red Flags test)去裁定/认定有关的主合约是否涉嫌贪污腐败。(3)即使有关贪污腐败/以不正当手段疏通关系的争议没有在仲裁程序与审理中提起,也不影响巴黎上诉庭去重审,说:"compliance with the French conception of international public policy implies that domestic courts have jurisdiction over any alleged infringement of international public policy even if such infringement was not raised during the arbitration proceedings and the arbitrators did not discuss this issue with the parties."

该案的案情是1979年法国公司Sorelec与利比亚教育部订立了一份建造教育设施的建筑合约。履行合约过程中发生争议，双方于2003年签订了一份和解协议。利比亚政府没有履行该份和解协议，Sorelec根据法国与利比亚两国签订的双边投资协定（bilateral investment treaty或简称BIT）中的仲裁条文于2013年对利比亚政府提起了ICC仲裁，索赔1.09亿欧元加利息。在仲裁期间，利比亚司法部与后来的临时政府与Sorelec又进一步签订了另外一份最终和解协议。2017年12月20日，仲裁庭将双方签订的最终和解协议加入部分裁决书中，裁定利比亚在裁决书做出后的45日内支付2.3亿欧元，如果逾期未予支付，仲裁庭将会发出一份最终裁决书，判利比亚赔偿4.52亿欧元。根据上述的介绍，可以看到Sorelec最终能获得自己最初索赔金额4倍还多的赔偿。

利比亚于2018年1月26日向巴黎上诉庭申请要求废除该ICC的仲裁裁决书，其中一个理由是"红旗测试"下有力、精准与一致的因素显示出最终和解协议是Sorelec通过贿赂利比亚政府官员而获取的，根据法国《民事诉讼法典》的规定，这是违反国际公共政策的行为。这些"红旗测试"所包括的间接证据/环境证据有：（1）根据监察贪污腐败的国际非政府组织透明国际（Transparency International）与利比亚审计署（利比亚的金融管理部门）发布的报告，当时利比亚政府官员贪污腐败成风。（2）利比亚司法部在签署最终和解协议前根本没有遵守利比亚法律所要求的审批程序。（3）尽管该最终和解协议的后果对整个利比亚的财政都会有重要的影响，但没有任何书面证据（包括书信往来、开会的会议记录等）显示双方在签订最终和解协议前有进行过谈判与磋商。（4）尽管当时利比亚的财政状况已经千疮百孔，但最终和解协议的条文满足了所有Sorelec的索赔请求，极端一面倒得对Sorelec有利。（5）最终和解协议在仲裁的最后阶段才签订，这对利比亚一方去保护法律费用与降低诉讼风险没有任何的好处，而且仲裁庭的裁决结果不会比最终和解协议更差。

Sorelec反对这些"红旗测试"的证据被法院采纳，理由是：在程序上，这些证据与主张没有在仲裁程序中提出；在实体上，这些证据不足以证明存在贪污腐败。

针对证据的可采纳性问题，巴黎上诉庭认为根据2003年《联合国反腐败公约》与1997年OECD公约中所反映出的对于贪污腐败问题所达至的国际共识来看，无论是从本国还是国际的角度，打击政府官员的贪污腐败是无法被忽视。所以，打击贪污腐败应该作为一个国际公共政策来支持与保护。根据之前的一些案件的判决，Sorelec针对证据可采纳的抗辩被驳回。

在实体上，巴黎上诉庭遵循了SA Ancienne Maison Marcel Bauche v. Indagro（Paris Court of Appeal, 27 September 2016, No. 15/12614）案件的判法，认为法院可以收集所有法律上与事实上认定非法所需要的信息，来综合判断承认与执行仲裁裁决书是否会有效与实质上地破坏国际公共政策。上诉庭认为这与执行地法院要克制与避免去审查裁决书的实体判决并不矛盾,并且又一次确认“红旗测试”的方法来以环境证据证明政府官员贪污腐败。

该案的判决与巴黎上诉庭之前在 Alexander Brothers Ltd(HK SAR)v. Alston Transport SA 决定仲裁裁决书的执行时的案件判决结果一致,即如果存在有力、精准与一致性的证据证明裁决书令一份被贪污腐败所污染的合约被执行,法院有理由去撤销该裁决。

最后,在 2022 年 3 月 23 日,法国最高院在 Belokon v. Kyrgyzstan(Cass. Civ. 1ère, 23 March 2022,No. 17 – 17.981)中确认了巴黎上诉庭在上述介绍的一系列判决中的测试标准与态度。此案件有关在 2010 年后,吉尔吉斯斯坦政府以本地 Manas 银行涉嫌参与前总理库尔曼别克·巴基耶夫的洗钱活动为由对银行采取监管,5 年后银行破产。银行背后的老板是拉脱维亚商人 Valeri Belokon。Belokon 先生在 2011 年开始了投资仲裁(仲裁地是巴黎),指称所谓的参与洗钱活动是子虚乌有,吉尔吉斯斯坦政府的行为属于间接征收。仲裁庭在 2014 年作出裁决,判 Belokon 先生胜诉并驳回了吉尔吉斯斯坦关于 Belokon 先生参与洗钱与存在贪污腐败行为的抗辩。仲裁庭说尽管能感觉到银行的一些现金交易非常可疑,但没有实质证据证明银行参与了洗钱。特别是吉尔吉斯斯坦曾经两次起诉 Belokon 先生,但都没有判 Belokon 先生有罪。

吉尔吉斯斯坦随即向巴黎上诉庭申请撤销裁决书,上诉庭判即使在有限的证据也能有力、精准与一致地显示了 Belokon 先生有从银行的行贿行为与参与洗钱活动中获利。上诉庭认为承认裁决书违反了反洗钱的国际公共政策,因此撤销了裁决书。

Belokon 先生上诉,法国最高院确认了上诉庭的判决。在 2003 年《联合国反腐败公约》等国际公约下,反洗钱是广泛的国际共识,因此属于法国的核心国际公共政策之一。法国最高院也确认了上诉庭的角色并非重审 Belokon 先生的索赔,而只是决定承认裁决书是否违反法国的公共政策,而上诉庭在考虑时也不局限于双方递交给仲裁庭的证据。法国最高院也提到,在撤销裁决书时无需证明刑事犯罪确实存在,而只需要显示有违反国际公共政策的特征。所以在笔者看来这不仅是在审查裁决书的程度上拓宽了,举证标准也降低了。

而在此最高院先例后不久,巴黎上诉庭在 2022 年 4 月 5 日在 Le Groupement Santullo Sericom Gabon v. Gabon(Paris Court of Appeal,4 April 2022,No. 20/03242)先例中,再次以贪污腐败为由撤销了一个 1.8 亿美元的 ICC 投资仲裁裁决书。针对贪污腐败,仲裁庭在裁决时适用的是“红旗测试”,但认为加蓬共和国并没有指出足够数量的“红旗”支持其主张。而上诉庭在考虑了一连串的可疑交易(如合约对加蓬一面倒的不利),仲裁原告与加蓬政府高官的资金往来,在裁决书作出后瑞士的调查证实仲裁原告存在对加蓬政府高官的行贿行为等后,认定有足够的证据证明合约被贪污腐败污染,并以违反国际公共政策撤销了裁决书。

在笔者看来，巴黎法院通过一系列符合逻辑并且有说服力的判决持续向全世界的仲裁圈释放出要从是否符合打击国际贪污腐败的公共政策方面对裁决书进行监管的强烈信号。

6.8.2 国际执行涉及贪污腐败裁决书的小结

作为小结，只节录在 2021 年 6 月 8 日于 Global Arbitration Review 刊登的有关国际贪污腐败的仲裁裁决书在国际执行的"Substantive Grounds for Challenge"一文的内容：

"A significant development affecting the enforcement of arbitral awards is **the emergence of fraud and corruption as substantive grounds for challenge**. In **some jurisdictions, courts seem willing to relax the traditionally stringent standard for reviewing awards to revisit allegations of fraud or corruption or to consider them for the first time.**

To remain within the legal framework established by the UNCITRAL Model Law and the New York Convention, **courts have relied on public policy to reject awards** that are **tainted by fraud or corruption, not only in the arbitral process itself but also in the underlying transaction**. Again, courts are free to disregard an award if they believe it violates their own state's public policy. As a general matter, an award is contrary to public policy if it is repugnant to fundamental notions of justice or morality, or if it contravenes important national interests. Because of its inherent vagueness, the public policy defence seems to provide the greatest latitude for courts to overturn infirm awards.

For now, **French courts seem to be leading the charge against fraud or corruption in international arbitration**. ...

In 2020, the Paris Court of Appeal set aside two ICC awards[71] rendered in favour of a French construction company against Libya, finding fraudulent collusion between the French company and a public official in the procurement of the underlying contract. It bears noting that corruption had not been alleged during the arbitration even though the facts relied on before the Court were available at the time. Still, the Court found that enforcing an award infected with corruption would be contrary to international public policy. Because of the difficulty of proving actual corruption through direct evidence, **French courts have developed a circumstantial evidence standard based on 'serious, precise and consistent indicia'.**

The Hague Court of Appeal adopted a similar approach in a 2019 case[72] (in which

---

〔71〕 见 Sorelec v. Libya (Paris Court of Appeal, 17 November 2020 No. 18/02568) 判决。

〔72〕 见 Bariven SA v. Wells Ultimate Service LLC, The Hague Court of Appeal, 22 October 2019, ECLI: NL: GHDHA: 2019: 2677 判决。

it **refused to enforce an award because of ' strong indications' of corruption during the procurement of the underlying contract**. The Court ruled that it had the power to assess independently whether the contract had been procured through corruption based on evidence that had been dismissed by the tribunal on procedural grounds, as well as facts that occurred after the award was rendered. It held that the general premise that an enforcement proceeding is not to be treated as a disguised appeal should not prevent compliance with a fundamental rule of law, such as the prohibition against corruption.

This **' red flags' methodology seems to have originated with the concept of ' warning signs' under the US Foreign Corrupt Practices Act. It also mirrors the ' badges of fraud' analysis developed in the common law tradition**, an approach that US courts continue to use in various contexts. Despite these links to US law, it remains to be seen whether US courts will follow a similar approach. ..."(加黑部分是笔者的强调)

法国法院看来是希望建立一个更平等与更美好、和平的国际环境，所以在执行涉及贪污腐败的国际公约裁决书的态度上发生了重大改变，这应该大力欢迎。但只是停留在法国法院的改变是远远不够的。毕竟伦敦与纽约是更重要的裁决书执行地。而法国法院态度的改变，反而增加了英国法院执行裁决书的业务量，因为更多仲裁胜诉方会去英国而不是去法国要求协助执行了。

6.9　英国协助执行涉及贪污腐败与其他非法的裁决书的先例介绍

6.9.1　Soleimany v. Soleimany(1999)QB 785 先例

在较早前多次提到的 Soleimany v. Soleimany 上诉庭先例中，有关交易涉及当事人一起从伊朗出口/走私波斯地毯到英国等地销售，在合约中约定了由贝丝丁/犹太教宗教法庭(Beth Din)根据犹太教法律仲裁。当事人事后对于销售所得如何分成产生争议，因此开始仲裁。并无争议的是此出口生意因违反伊朗出口与关税法律而非法。仲裁庭也认定有关交易违反伊朗法律，但是在犹太教法律下仍然愿意执行原告诉求，并给出原告胜诉的裁决书。原告之后在英国执行仲裁裁决时，就遇上被告主张有关交易非法、违反英国公共政策，因此根据当时的《Arbitration Act 1950》之 Section 26，英国法院不应该执行。这说法得到上诉庭支持，而上诉庭这样判的关键是作为执行地法院，就必须考虑英国的公共政策。而既然仲裁庭已经认定交易非法，而执行原告诉求就变成执行这个非法交易，英国法院是不会予以执行的。虽然此案件已经通过仲裁获得裁决书，但这并没有将原告诉求/索赔与其非法行为分割开来，通过仲裁并不会使得执行原告诉求变得有什么不同。可以节录 Waller 大法官所说如下："Even if we were wrong in the view already expressed that an arbitration agreement between robbers(for example) to arbitrate their disputes would itself be void, it is in our view inconceivable that an English court would enforce an award made on a joint venture agreement between bank robbers, any more than it would enforce an agreement between highwaymen...**Where public policy is involved, the interposition of an arbitration award does not isolate the successful party's claim from the illegality which gave rise to it.**"(加黑部分是笔者的强调)

也因此可以说,此先例这样的判法,关键就是仲裁庭认定交易非法,而既然诉求/索赔无法与非法行为分割,即使是通过仲裁程序给出裁决,披上这一层合法的面纱,也不应该影响英国法院不会执行。

但这也带出了进一步的问题,如果仲裁庭对事实的认定是主合约不涉及非法,英国法院作为执行法院应该如何考虑?毕竟作出该裁决书的仲裁庭会错判,作为执行地的英国法院要为本土的公共政策把关,是不会也不应该只简单看裁决书的认定与简单裁定有关交易是非法或不非法。即使法院可以看裁决书表面的原因或解释,但在败诉方抗拒执行的争辩下,往往是发觉裁决书原因并不充分与不令人满意,只让执行法院的疑团加大。对此问题 Waller 大法官也提出了自己的附带意见(obiter),即本章之 6.5.3 段介绍的初步质询与全面质询的两步测试。

但 Waller 大法官的附带意见(没有作为先例的约束力)中的"两步测试"指引,已在 Westacre Investments Inc v. Jugoimport SPDR Holding Co Ltd(2000) QB 288 上诉庭先例中被否定。在后来的案例中,包括近期的 RBRG v. Sinocore International(2018) EWCA Civ 838 先例与 Betamax Ltd v. State Trading Corporation(Mauritius)(2021) UKPC 14 先例等,都遵从 Westacre Investments Inc v. Jugoimport SPDR Holding Co Ltd 上诉庭先例的判法,确立公约裁决书的终局性。

6.9.2 Westacre Investments Inc v. Jugoimport SPDR Holding Co Ltd(2000) QB 288 先例

Westacre Investments Inc v. Jugoimport SPDR Holding Co Ltd 上诉庭先例在笔者《仲裁法:从开庭审理到裁决书的作出与执行》一书第十二章之 6.8.5.1 段有过简单介绍。此先例的背景是 1989 年南斯拉夫公司 Jugoimport 与其他被告,包括政府部门(故接下来统称被告为南斯拉夫)向科威特销售军事设备,在合约中还包括了一间巴拿马公司 Westacre 作为南斯拉夫的顾问(就是代理人/中间人),会根据签订的合约金额收取佣金。有关合约约定适用瑞士法律,约定争议在日内瓦通过 ICC 仲裁解决。事后南斯拉夫违约/毁约,因此当事人之间开始仲裁。南斯拉夫在仲裁中主张 Westacre 贿赂了科威特政府官员,让政府官员利用影响力促成南斯拉夫的交易,交易也因此非法而无效/不可执行。但仲裁庭在考虑了双方提供的证据后,对事实的认定是:尽管该政府官员可能确实利用了自己的影响力促成交易,但提供的证据未能证明所指称的贿赂,故南斯拉夫败诉,需要支付 Westacre 佣金。

在上诉到瑞士法院后,南斯拉夫进一步提出新的论点与证据,主张 Westacre 根本是该科威特政府官员的公司,专门用来收取名为佣金实为贿赂的金钱,一旦执行合约就变成帮助实现贪污受贿。法院考虑了双方的陈词与证据,也听取了仲裁庭成员给出的陈述,认为在仲裁程序中这一点看来完全没有被提到,[73]在仲裁程序中针对的是贿赂是否存在的问题。尽管法院认可,如果南斯拉夫提出的主张得到证明,确实会导致合约在瑞士法下无效,但是这新主张实际上与仲裁中认定的事实并不配合。而仲裁程序本身并无不妥(如当事人也有足够的机会陈述案件、提供证据等),只要仲裁庭在事实认定的过程中并无违反自然公正的公共政策,法院也愿意尊重仲裁庭的认定,因此最后支持了仲裁庭的判法。

后来 Westacre 在英国申请协助执行裁决书,作为执行法院的英国法院再次遇到了南斯拉夫以违反公共政策作出的抗辩,这一次南斯拉夫提供了一份涉案人员的誓章(affidavit),以证明当事人根本从头到尾都知道顾问合约的核心内容就是让该科威特政府官员利用不正当的影响促成交易。这样就是合约目的是采用不正当影响促成交易(而不仅仅是仲裁中主张的贿赂)而违反科威特法律与公共政策,因此要求法院不予协助执行。此主张是否可以对抗裁决书的执行被法院作为初步争议(preliminary issue)进行审理。[74]

案情从表面看来与本章之 5.5.6 段介绍的 Lemenda Trading Co Ltd v. African Middle East Petroleum Co Ltd(1988)QB 448 先例有类似之处。该先例涉及的是在卡塔尔通过支付佣金让中间人游说政府官员拿到石油供应合约,英国法院认定此行为的性质既违反了执行地(英国)的公共政策,同时也违反了履行地(卡塔尔)的公共政策,因此在国际睦仪/礼让的公共政策下拒绝执行。但一个重要的不同是 Lemenda 先例的争议是在英国法院审理,而 Westacre Investments Inc v. Jugoimport SPDR Holding Co Ltd 先例是英国法院协助执行公约裁决书时要考虑的公共政策(并接下来发展成为压倒性)。

该先例的一审[(1999)QB 740],尚未有 Soleimany v. Soleimany(1999)QB 785 上诉庭先例中 Waller 大法官的不同看法与判法,包括建议的“两步测试”。Colman 大法官在一审为今后英国法院协助执行外国公约裁决书演变为压倒性公共政策所给出的小结如下:

“The effect of the authorities is in my judgment as follows.

---

〔73〕 这一点的判法与在本章之 6.8.2 段介绍的 Sorelec v. Libya(Paris Court of Appeal,17 November 2020 No. 18/02568)法国巴黎上诉庭案件的判法完全不同。打击贪污腐败与其他一般的争辩并不一样,是属于有国际共识的公共政策,道德上是不应该以技术性的“一事不再审”(issue estoppel)问题去绕过。

〔74〕 在审理过程中,南斯拉夫还进一步要求修改文书请求与提交证人证言,主张在仲裁过程中多位证人提供伪证。但针对这问题,在纽约公约下执行裁决书时,一般不允许提供新证据进行重新审理,除非有关证据可信而且分量很重、在仲裁中提出会实质影响仲裁庭的裁决。但这有重要前提条件,有关证据必须是“新”证据,如果该证据在仲裁程序或者是仲裁地监督法院审理过程中有机会提出但没有提出的,事后是不应该在执行法院再被考虑的,这也是禁反言规则(estoppel)。而此先例中南斯拉夫就未能成功显示在仲裁程序或监督法院的上诉程序中这些证据(证人证言)无法被获得,也因此在英国法院的执行程序中不允许再提交此类证据。

(i) Where it is alleged that an underlying contract is illegal and void and that an arbitration award in respect of it is thereby unenforceable**the primary question is whether the determination of the particular illegality alleged fell within the jurisdiction of the arbitrators.**

(ii) There is no general rule that, where an underlying contract is illegal at common law or by reason of an English statute, an arbitration agreement, which is ancillary to that contract is incapable of conferring jurisdiction on arbitrators to determine disputes arising within the scope of the agreement including disputes as to whether illegality renders the contract unenforceable.

(iii) Whether such an agreement to arbitrate is capable of conferring such jurisdiction depends upon whether the nature of the illegality is such that, in the case of statutory illegality the statute has the effect of impeaching that agreement as well as the underlying contract and, in the case of illegality at common law, public policy requires that disputes about the underlying contract should not be referred to arbitration.

(iv) When, at the stage of enforcement of an award, it is necessary for the court to determine whether the arbitrators had jurisdiction in respect of disputes relating to the underlying contract, the court must consider the nature of the disputes in question. If the issue before the arbitrators was whether money was due under a contract which was indisputably illegal at common law, an award in favour of the claimant would not be enforced for it would be contrary to public policy that the arbitrator should be entitled to ignore palpable and indisputable illegality. If, however, there was an issue before the arbitrator whether the underlying contract was illegal and void, the court would first have to consider whether, having regard to the natureof the illegality alleged, it was consistent with the public policy which would, if illegality were established, impeach the validity of the underlying contract, that the determination of the issue of illegality should be left to arbitration. If it was not consistent, the arbitrators would be held to have no jurisdiction to determine that issue.

(v) **If the court concluded that the arbitration agreement conferred jurisdiction to determine whether the underlying contract was illegal and by the award the arbitrators determined that it was not illegal, prima facie the court would enforce the resulting award.**

(vi) If the party against whom the award was made then sought to challenge enforcement of the award on the grounds that, on the basis of facts not placed before the arbitrators, the contract was indeed illegal, **the enforcement court would have to consider whether the public policy against the enforcement of illegal contracts outweighed the countervailing public policy in support of the finality of awards in general and of**

awards in respect of the same issue in particular."(加黑部分是笔者的强调)

Colman 大法官的判法看来非常强调协助执行有效国际仲裁裁决书的公共政策,相比较之下不鼓励国际商业贪污腐败行为的公共政策被认为较为次要。这宽松的态度也被质疑,如在 National Iranian Oil Co v. Crescent Petroleum Co International Ltd (2016) EWHC 510(Comm)先例中,代表伊朗国有石油公司的大律师向英国法院申请在《Arbitration Act 1996》之 Section 68(2)(g)下撤销裁决书,试图说服法院 Colman 大法官的判决已是不合时宜,说:"... public policy is not a closed category, and that public opinion and legislative approach has hardened in recent years against conduct which constitutes corruption or bribery such that, for example, a court would no longer form the same view as Colman J in Westacre Investments Inc v. Jugoimport-SPDR Ltd, whereby he concluded that the public policy of sustaining international arbitration awards ... outweighed the public policy in discouraging international commercial corruption."

这表示在 Colman 大法官的判法下,只要确定审理的仲裁庭是对有关贪污腐败的争议有管辖权,既然在仲裁中已经认定不存在贪污腐败,执行法院就根本无需再继续考虑是否事实上有这种行为(即使有新证据)。一审的结果是南斯拉夫以违反科威特公共政策试图对抗裁决书执行的主张就被驳回了。

案件上诉到上诉庭,多数意见(Mantell 大法官与 Hirst 大法官,Waller 大法官持不同意见)支持了一审 Colman 大法官与对公共政策的权衡的判法,尤其是反对在此阶段引入与考虑新证据,持多数意见的大法官们表示不认同应该采取 Soleimany v. Soleimany 上诉庭先例中"两步测试"的做法。Mantell 大法官还明确拒绝了将非法程度的严重性纳入初步质询的考虑因素中,此时应该只考虑仲裁裁决的作出是否应该被完全支持,至于非法程度严不严重只有在认为有理由不能完全支持仲裁裁决书的情况下,才需要考虑在英国公共政策下是否因为严重非法导致不可执行。Mantell 大法官说:It is of crucial importance to evaluate both the majority decision in the arbitration and the ruling of the Swiss Federal Tribunal, Swiss Law being both the proper law of the contract and the curial law of the arbitration and Switzerland, like the United Kingdom, being a party to the New York Convention. From the award itself it is clear that bribery was a central issue. The allegation was made, entertained and rejected. Had it not been rejected the claim would have failed, Swiss and English public policy being indistinguishable in this respect. Authority apart, in those circumstances and without fresh evidence I would have thought that there could be no justification for refusing to enforce the award. ... in the obiter passage cited by Waller LJ from the judgment in Soleimany v. Soleimany ... seems to have been suggested that some kind of preliminary inquiry short of a full scale trial should be embarked upon whenever 'there is prima facie evidence from one side that the award is based on an illegal contract ...' For my part I have some difficulty with the concept and even greater concerns about its application in practice, ... I so conclude by reference to the criteria given by way of example in Soleimany v. Soleimany itself. **First**, there was evidence before the tribunal that this was a straightforward, commercial contract. **Secondly, the arbitrators specifically found that the underlying contract was not illegal. Thirdly, there is nothing to suggest incompetence on the part of the arbitrators**. Finally, there is no reason to suspect collusion or bad faith in the obtaining of the award. **The seriousness of the alleged illegality** to which Waller LJ gives weight **is not**, … **a factor to be considered at the stage of deciding whether or not to mount a full-scale inquiry.** It is something to be taken into account as part of the balancing exercise between the competing public policy considerations of finality and illegality which can only be performed in response to the second question, if it arises, namely, should the award be enforced?"（加黑部分是笔者的强调）

6.9.3 Omnium de Traitement et de Valorisation SA v. Hilmarton Ltd (1999) 2 Lloyd's Rep 222 先例

稍后的 Omnium de Traitement et de Valorisation SA v. Hilmarton Ltd 先例也已经在笔者的《仲裁法：从开庭审理到裁决书的作出与执行》一书第十二章之 6.8.5.2 段有介绍，不打算在此详细介绍。简单地说，Omnium de Traitement et de Valorisation（以下简称 OTV）委任 Hilmarton 帮助从阿尔及利亚政府处获取合约。委任合约适用瑞士法，并约定在瑞士仲裁。仲裁庭认定此先例中这种代理人/中间人疏通政府官员促成交易违反阿尔及利亚立法，但并不涉及贿赂行为。而瑞士法下纯粹是利用个人影响疏通关系与促成合约并不属于会导致无效/不可执行的非法。在仲裁中 Hilmarton 胜诉。

而与 Westacre Investments Inc v. Jugoimport SPDR Holding Co Ltd (2000) QB 288 先例中败诉方先在瑞士监督法院寻求救济不同的是，此先例中裁决书并没有在瑞士监督法院寻求救济，Hilmarton 直接在英国法院申请执行，但这区别看来并没有什么影响，英国高院执行了仲裁裁决。Walker 大法官说："It may well be that an English arbitral tribunal, chosen by the parties, and applying English law as chosen by the parties, would have reached a different result. It may well be that such a tribunal would have dismissed [Hilmarton]'s claim, applying the full rigour of the principle stated by Viscount Simonds in Regazzoni v. K. C. Sethia (1944) Ltd … But I am not adjudicating upon the underlying contract. **I am deciding whether or not an arbitration award should be enforced in England.** In this context it seems to me that (absent a finding of fact of corrupt practices which would give rise to obvious public policy considerations) the fact that English law would or might have arrived at a different result is nothing to the point. Indeed, the reason for the different result is that Swiss law is different from English law, and **the parties chose Swiss law and Swiss arbitration. If anything, this consideration dictates (as a matter of policy of the upholding of international arbitral awards) that the award should be enforced. … reliance on Soleimany … was in my view misplaced**. In that case, it was apparent from the face of the award that the arbitrator was dealing with **an illicit enterprise** for smuggling carpets out of Iran. It was quite simply a smuggling contract. The case thus clearly fell into the category of cases where as a matter of public policy no award would be enforced by an English Court, and the whole of the judgment … has to be read in that context. **The element of corruption or illicit practice** was present [in Soleimany] which, on the **arbitrator's unchallengeable finding of fact** in this case, **was not present here.**"(加黑部分是笔者的强调)

上述节录部分也提到了与 Soleimany v. Soleimany(1999)QB 785 上诉庭先例的区别。在 Soleimany v. Soleimany 先例中,仲裁庭认定了有关交易/主合约违反伊朗法律,但仍然作出原告胜诉的裁决书。而在此先例中,仲裁庭认定并不存在贿赂的行为,在瑞士法下没有非法。但笔者觉得这些区分都只是借口,如果仲裁庭认定贿赂的行为,也通常代表 Hilmarton 应该败诉,不存在需要英国法院协助执行的情况了。

6.9.4 National Iranian Oil Co v. Crescent Petroleum Co International Ltd(2016) EWHC 510(Comm)先例

在 National Iranian Oil Co v. Crescent Petroleum Co International Ltd 先例中,原告是伊朗国有石油公司(National Iranian Oil Co,以下简称 NIOC),而被告则是阿联酋的新月石油公司(Crescent Petroleum)的两家子公司(以下简称 Crescent)。双方签订了一份长达 25 年的天然气供应合约(gas supply and purchase contract,以下简称 GSPC),约定适用伊朗法与伦敦仲裁。事后 NIOC 没有按照合约供应任何天然气,导致 Crescent 开始仲裁索赔巨额损失。

NIOC 的主要抗辩是此合约是 Crescent 通过贿赂的手段获取,并以此质疑合约的效力与仲裁庭的管辖权。但在仲裁中仲裁庭认定的事实是 Crescent 尽管讨论过采取贿赂等手段,但最后 NIOC 并没有足够证据证明 Crescent 有去实施。所以,裁决书裁定 NIOC 的非法抗辩不成功,GSPC 有效与有约束力。

这样 NIOC 就在英国监督法院申请撤销该伦敦仲裁裁决书,重要主张就是在《Arbitration Act 1996》之 Section 68(2)(g)中,英国法院可以根据违反英国公共政策去撤销裁决书。但英国法院驳回了 NIOC 的申请,支持了裁决书。

可以节录 Burton 大法官的小结与判决如下:

"I reach the following conclusions:—

(1) English public policy applies so as to lead a court to refuse to enforce an illegal contract, even if not illegal at relevant foreign law, such as a contract to pay a bribe. The contract cannot be enforced because ex turpi causa haud oritur actio: out of a disgraceful cause an action cannot arise. The supply contract enforced by the Arbitrators was not and is not suggested to be an illegal contract, and the action to enforce it does not arise out of a disgraceful cause. [重申英国公共政策是在不能从非法行为获利、违背道德的对价不生诉权的大原则下,一份在本土或外国非法的合约如去行贿(如支付给政府官员

或国企领导控制的公司秘密佣金）是不会被执行的。但此先例要执行的天然气供应合约并不是这类非法的合约，该合约产生的诉权谈不上有任何不道德。]

（2）There is no English public policy requiring a court to refuse to enforce a contract procured by bribery. A court might decide to enforce the contract at the instance of one of the parties. It is not that the contract is unenforceable by reason of public policy, but that the public policy impact would not relate to the contract but to the conduct of one party or the other. [英国公共政策并不要求法院拒绝执行一份涉及贿赂的合约。因为合约本身可能并不非法，只是通过非法手段获得的。公共政策针对的是一方或其他人士的非法行为，让做出非法行为的一方不能因此获利，而不是令合约本身不可执行。在一些情况（如在无辜方/受害方的申请）下，法院会执行一份涉及贿赂的合约。例如，天然气市场大跌，NIOC 可能要求被告履行 GSPC，此时法院就会协助执行。[75]]

（3）There is certainly no English public policy to refuse to enforce a contract which has been preceded, and is unaffected, by a failed attempt to bribe, on the basis that such contract, or one or more of the parties to it, have allegedly been tainted by the precedent conduct.... There may be many contracts which have been preceded by undesirable conduct on one side or other or both-lies, fraud, threats and worse-but the Court would not interfere with a contract entered into by such parties, even if one or more of those parties had committed criminal acts for which they could be prosecuted, unless the contract itself was illegal and unenforceable, or one or more of the acts of such parties induced the contract, in which case it might be voidable at the instance of an innocent party so induced. [英国的公共政策不会拒绝执行一份一方或其他当事人曾经试图去行贿但不果的合约。现实中会有很多合约在订立前的谈判阶段，曾经有过一方或双方当事人做过一些不如意与不道德的行为，如说谎、欺诈/欺骗、威胁或更坏的行为（如行贿），但英国法院不会干预这种合约。如果合约的形成、履行或目的非法，法院可以主动拒绝执行。[76] 或者谈判中的不道德的行为导致了合约形成，救济是受害方/无辜方有权去令合约无效，如果受害方/无辜方确实撤销了合约，法院就不会执行合约。]

（4）In any event, in this case, the conclusion to which the Arbitrators came was that the GSPC was not procured by bribery, after full consideration and evidence. The English Court should not interfere with the Arbitrators' decision under s. 68, or s. 103, without fresh evidence of which there is none, or save in very exceptional circumstances, of which there are none...[仲裁庭的认定与裁定是 GSPC 并非通过贿赂获取，英国监督（或作为执行）

---

[75] 这方面的课题可见 Honeywell International Middle East Ltd v. Meydan Group LLC（2014）EWHC 1344（TCC）与 Wilson v. Hurstanger（2007）1 WLR 2351 等先例。

[76] 在本书第八章之 1.2 段提到即使是当事人都没有用“非法理论”去提出抗辩，只要根据当事人披露的事实被法院发现合约非法，就不应该执行合约。

法院是不应该去干预这个裁决书终局的裁定,另 NIOC 也没有提供新证据。]”

6.9.5 RBRG v. Sinocore International(2018)EWCA Civ 838 先例

此先例已在本书第三章之 8.2.2 段有介绍过,但仍在此进一步详尽介绍。在 RBRG v. Sinocore International 先例中,英国公司(RBRG)向中国公司(Sinocore)购买冷轧钢卷(steel coils)。该 CIF 买卖合约中约定以不可撤销信用证方式付款,以及货物付运日期即提单日期为 2010 年 7 月底前。同时合约约定适用中国法,争议交由北京 CIETAC 仲裁。

RBRG 依照合约约定在一家荷兰银行开出信用证,信用证的内容也与买卖合约一致,即提单装船日期为 7 月 31 日前。随后 Sinocore 于 7 月 5 日与 7 月 6 日安排货物付运,并将载有真实货物装船日期的装船通知告知了 RBRG。这时 RBRG 在未获得 Sinocore 同意的情况下单方面指示荷兰银行更改信用证的内容,将货物装船日期变为 2010 年 7 月 20 日至 30 日。这是开玩笑的,RBRG 明知货物已经装船,这时把信用证单方面改为提单不可能符合的付运日期,等于是说“我不给钱”。信用证也是一份荷兰银行与 Sinocore 之间承诺支付的合约,如果单方面可改变付运或货物装船日期,那荷兰银行可否改变信用证从“不可撤销”为“可撤销”?或结汇要求的单证增加 5 项其他类别单证,都是 Sinocore 无法获得的?

RBRG 这样做看起来是由于钢材的市场价格大跌,在履行中给 Sinocore 找麻烦,看 Sinocore 是否懂行并有水平化解,如果不懂就有可能做出一些不恰当的行为,从而给 RBRG 机会合法从合约中脱身。而后来发生的事情也确实让 RBRG 打响如意算盘。

Sinocore 收到荷兰银行发出的修改版信用证后并没有提出异议,如回应一句简单的内行话:“你作为开证人不能单方面改变信用证,我作为受益人从来没有答应过。”相反,在稍后交单给荷兰银行进行结汇时,交出的提单上的付运日期为 7 月 20 日与 21 日。提单上的装船日期显然与真实装船的 7 月 5 日与 6 日的事实不相符,是伪造的。RBRG 知道真实的装船日期,早已备妥并马上在荷兰法院成功以虚假单证为由申请“止付禁令”阻止荷兰银行付款。

Sinocore 在收不到货款、RBRG 不理睬、货物已经付运、租用的船舶需要尽快还船与 RBRG 对货物在市场转卖设置障碍等多重压力下,最终血本无归。

在之后的 CIETAC 仲裁中,RBRG 指称 Sinocore 在 7 月 5 日、7 月 6 日已真正付运货物,但伪造日期更晚的提单令买卖合约无法履行,于是向 Sinocore 索赔因此带来的损失。

最后仲裁庭认定 RBRG 单方面修改信用证属于在先的违约/毁约行为,也是令合约无法履行的直接原因。至于 Sinocore 伪造提单日期的行为,只可以说是为了欺诈荷兰银行。但在买卖合约下 Sinocore 对 RBRG 并不存在任何欺诈,RBRG 对于真实的装船日期一直很清楚。而单方面修改信用证才是与 Sinocore 后来收不到货款、

的主张要成立,需要与 Sinocore 提交伪造提单的行为有因果关系,这就必须改变仲裁中仲裁庭对因果关系的认定。但既然没有证据与理由认为仲裁庭作出裁定的程序有问题(如违反自然公正),就不应该重新考虑仲裁庭根据中国法作出的裁决结果。(2)RBRG 在履行合约以及仲裁程序中的主张都是 Sinocore 同意修改信用证,因此 Sinocore 未能提供符合修改后的信用证的提单。但仲裁庭在没有证据证明下,认定的是 RBRG 单方面修改。现在 RBRG 实际上是要法院通过不同理由来改判仲裁庭对事实的认定,这是说不通的。(3)根据仲裁庭认定的事实,买卖合约本身不涉及任何违反中国法或英国法的因素。(4)此先例中顶多存在一个试图欺诈但未成功的情节,并未真正有人受骗,也并没有人根据伪造的提单付款。有关提单也从未进入流通而影响商业社会对提单、信用证的信心。因此看来并不能说 Sinocore 有从自己的非法行为中获利。(5)这样失败的欺诈行为最多只是一个附带(collateral)情节或因素,与双方的争议关系/联系不大。或者是根本不涉及有关公共政策,或者即使涉及某些公共政策,在权衡之下也不足以让法院拒绝执行。

Sinocore 虽然最后"惨胜",但据悉 RBRG 后来破产了,这也意味着 Sinocore 即使拿到胜诉裁决书也会是一场空。如果 Sinocore 对英美合约法与信用证业务熟悉(UCP600 下开证人与开证行不能在没有受益人同意下单方面修改信用证,这也是基础的合约法理念),从而告知荷兰银行不能修改,仍然根据真实的提单在信用证下结汇,笔者不认为荷兰银行会拒绝。这样,Sinocore 完全可以拿到合约中以高昂价格出售的钢材的货款了。

6.9.6 Betamax Ltd v. State Trading Corporation(Mauritius)(2021) UKPC 14 先例

在 Betamax Ltd v. State Trading Corporation(Mauritius)英国枢密院先例中,State Trading Corporation(STC)是毛里求斯国企,需要通过油轮进口石油产品。2009 年毛里求斯当地家族与新加坡的船舶管理公司合作,共同设立了毛里求斯公司 Betamax。有关的交易是 Betamax 订购了油轮,并同时与 STC 签订 15 年期的包运合约(Contract of Affreightment ,以下简称 COA),从印度运输石油产品前往毛里求斯。COA 约定新加坡国际仲裁中心仲裁,但仲裁地在毛里求斯。

船舶在 2011 年开始履行 COA,但到了 2015 年毛里求斯政府新内阁上台,提出当年的 COA 签订不符合毛里求斯法律,STC 也随后终止了合约。Betamax 因此开始仲裁,主张 STC 违约/毁约,索赔 COA 下的损失。STC 提出了多方面的抗辩,重要的一点是 2006 年毛里求斯就针对国家采购行为有了针对性的立法《Public Procurement Act 2006》,后来还有规章《Public Procurement Regulations 2008》。而 COA 应适用这些法律,并需要获得毛里求斯中央采购局(Central Procurement Board)的批准,但此先例中的 COA 从未获得过批准,因此非法。

仲裁庭通过对毛里求斯法以及对 COA 性质与内容的解释,认定此先例中的 COA 属于立法下的豁免类别,不需要中央采购局的批准。这样,也就根本不存在

STC 所指的非法。因此裁定 STC 败诉,应支付 Betamax 超过 1.15 亿美元的预期损失赔偿。

面对如此巨大的仲裁裁决金额,STC 就在仲裁地(毛里求斯)的监督法院申请撤销裁决书。根据毛里求斯法律,此先例中这类仲裁会适用《International Arbitration Act 2008》(以下简称 IAA),该立法主要基于《联合国示范法》(UNCITRAL Model Law)。IAA 之 Section 39(2)(b)(ii)跟从了示范法之 Article 34,可以节录如下:"(2)An arbitral award may be set aside by the Supreme Court only where —(b)the Court finds that —(i)the subject matter of the dispute is not capable of settlement by arbitration under Mauritius Law;(ii)**the award is in conflict with the public policy of Mauritius**;(iii)the making of the award was induced or affected by fraud or corruption;or(iv)a breach of the rules of natural justice occurred during the arbitral proceedings or in connection with the making of the award by which the rights of any party have been or will be substantially prejudiced."(加黑部分是笔者强调)

经过审理后,毛里求斯最高院撤销了裁决书,最高院根据对毛里求斯法律以及对 COA 的解释,认为 COA 并不属于毛里求斯法律下的豁免类别,必须先获得中央采购局批准。这类没有获得批准就进行的交易,是明目张胆的违法行为,属于违反了毛里求斯的公共政策可不予执行。[78]

案件被进一步上诉到英国枢密院,当事人之间对于毛里求斯最高院可以解释毛里求斯立法、明确毛里求斯的公共政策没有什么疑问。但此案件中的问题是裁决书能否被执行,这涉及了几个步骤:(1)毛里求斯最高院是否有权重新审理与改变仲裁庭对事实与/或法律的认定/裁定。(2)如果有权重新审理与改变,就还要再进一步考虑是否实质上在毛里求斯法下非法。

针对问题(1),就需要看仲裁地的监督法院根据有关立法到底有怎样的权力。此先例中适用的毛里求斯 IAA,基本上基于《联合国示范法》制定的,并且规定对于立法的解释也要参考示范法的解释,也就是仲裁庭对事实与法律的认定/裁定有终局效力。

枢密院再次强调了国际仲裁的终局性的大原则,Thomas 勋爵说:"The issue in this appeal is the scope of section 39(2)(b)(ii)of the International Arbitration Act in relation to a decision of an arbitral tribunal which decided that a contract was not illegal on the basis of its interpretation of legislative provisions and regulations that were applica-

---

〔78〕 毛里求斯最高院给出的测试标准是:"The breach of the legal provisions must be flagrant, actual and concrete. But it is not any legal breach which would suffice to set aside the enforcement of an award. The threshold is quite high; it should be the breach of a fundamental legal principle, a breach which disregards the essential and broadly recognised values which form part of the basis of the national legal order, and a departure from which will be incompatible with the State's legal and economic system."而此先例中涉及的公共政策被最高院认为足以满足前述测试。

ble to a contract. … More likely, as appears from the decided cases and observations made in them, are cases where the **arbitral tribunal has expressly considered issues** which have required the arbitral tribunal to inquire **into circumstances suggesting illegality** and set out their reasons for holding as a matter of fact and of law that there was no illegality. In cases of that kind, **the arbitral tribunal's decision on fact and on law is a decision for the arbitral tribunal, if within its jurisdiction; if it holds that the contract is not illegal, then that decision will be final, in the absence of fraud, a breach of natural justice or any other vitiating factor.** There may be some exceptional cases, where the court under the Model Law provision may be entitled to review the decision on legality, but it is not easy to think of such a case arising in practice…. "(加黑部分是笔者的强调)

Thomas 勋爵接下来也提到毛里求斯的采购法与采购规章要求的中央采购局的批准显然主要是为了公开透明与防止贪污腐败(看来这也暗示了 Betamax 与 STC 的 15 年 COA 背后会有猫腻),但仲裁庭已经认定的事实或裁定的法律(包括解释毛里求斯的立法条文)是终局性的,监督法院也不能去改变。毕竟,毛里求斯的 IAA 也就是《联合国示范法》,不像英国的《Arbitration Act 1996》之 Section 69 可去重审与改变仲裁庭对法律问题的裁定。而作为监督法院的毛里求斯最高院,根据 IAA 只是有权力以违反公共政策为由撤销该裁决书。但即使仲裁庭错误解释有关采购法的立法条文,也不是违反公共政策方面的问题。

由于判词太长在此不节录,只说英国枢密院也对问题(2)给了说法,也就是完全同意仲裁庭对毛里求斯采购法的立法条文的解释是可以豁免该 15 年的 COA。

7. 反贪污腐败条文

发展中国家与企业(部分会是上市公司)有责任去保护自己的国民、纳税人、股东、雇员等有关人士的利益,提升自己的良好管治水平、国际商业道德与诚实正直等。另外,要在一定程度上保证订立合约的外国公司是正规、善意与可信赖的商业对手。这样,应可考虑在订立合约(特别是长期合约)时,像加入不可抗力条文(force majeure clause)、完整合约条文/不依赖条文(entire agreement clause/Non-reliance clause)、免责条文(exemption clause)等惯用条文(boiler-plate clauses)一样,强制要求必须加入这种"反贪污腐败条文"(anti-corruption clause)。其中明确约定,一旦在订立合约前与履行合约期间对存在贪污腐败行为有任何合理怀疑,发展中国家或企业(或是任何一方合约方)可以选择终止合约。

这种条文甚至可以延伸去使用在所有有关的合约,如雇佣员工合约、自己或对方雇用的分包商、分买方或分卖方、顾问、律师、[79]代理人、经纪人或中间人(subcontractor, reseller/sub-buyer, consultants, representatives, agents, lawyers, advisers)等第三人的合约等。

这里最著名的是国际商会(International Chambers of Commerce, 以下简称ICC) 2012年的"ICC Anti-corruption Clause"。[80] 该反贪污腐败条文的详尽介绍,可见ICC发表的[81](ICC Publication No. 740E, ISBN:978-92-842-0175-4)。条文可节录如下:

"Each Party hereby undertakes that, at the date of the entering into force of the Contract, itself, its directors, officers or employees have not offered, promised, given, authorized, solicited or accepted any undue pecuniary or other advantage of any kind (or implied that they will or might do any such thing at any time in the future) in any way connected with the Contract and that it has taken reasonable measures to prevent subcontractors, agents or any other third parties, subject to its control or determining influence, from doing so. [合约各方保证在合约生效之日,合约方本身、合约方的董事、管理人员或雇员没有以与合约有关联的任何方式提供、保证、给出、授权、索求或接受任何不当的金钱或任何其他好处(或默示他们将来会或可能会做这样的事情),并且已经采取合理方式[82]阻止其能控制或有决定性影响力的分合约方、代理人或其他第三人这样做。]

The Parties agree that, at all times in connection with and throughout the course of the Contract and thereafter, they will comply with and that they will take reasonable measures to ensure that their subcontractors, agents or other third parties, subject to their control or determining influence, will comply with Part I of the ICC Rules on Combating Corruption 2011, which is hereby incorporated by reference into the Contract, as if written out in the Contract in full. [合约方同意在与合约相关时间(包括订立合约前)、整个合约履行过程和之后的任何时间,都会遵守并采取合理措施确保受他们控制或有绝对性影响力的分合约方、代理人或其他第三人遵守合并进合约的《ICC Rules on Comba-

[79] 见Nayyar v. Denton Wilde Sapte (2009) EWHC 3218 (QB)先例。

[80] ICC早在1977年已经有了《ICC Rules on Combating Corruption》,这是世界上最早发表的防范贪污腐败的规则与指引。在《OECD Convention on Combating Bribery of Foreign Public Officials in International Business Transactions 1997》与《United Nations Convention against Corruption 2003》等国际公约生效后,加上其他实务上的经验与发展,ICC在2011年重写了1977年的反贪污腐败规则,并之后在2012年拟定了此模板条文以供国际商业企业、公司或相关组织使用或参考。

[81] 见< https://iccwbo.org/content/uploads/sites/3/2012/10/ICC-Anti-corruption-Clause.pdf >。

[82] 相比只是宽松的合理方式的说法,这里可以更明确地要求合约方要采取的方式,如要求雇用前要尽职调查、明示要求作出保证不雇用前政府官员等。或是在与第三人订立的合约中要求第三人(包括其董事、管理人员、雇员)陈述与保证没有在过去、现在与将来进行任何贪污腐败行为或雇佣任何人士进行贪污腐败行为,并且同意如果将来公司有合理怀疑可以雇佣外部机构审核其账户(包括私人账户)。

ting Corruption 2011》。]

If a Party, as a result of the exercise of a contractually-provided audit right, if any, of the other Party's accounting books and financial records, or otherwise, brings evidence that the latter Party has been engaging in material or several repeated breaches of the provisions of Part I of the ICC Rules on Combating Corruption 2011, it will notify the latter Party accordingly and require such Party to take the necessary remedial action in a reasonable time and to inform it about such action. If the latter Party fails to take the necessary remedial action, or if such remedial action is not possible, it may invoke a defence by proving that by the time the evidence of breach(es) had arisen, it had put into place adequate anti-corruption preventive measures, as described in Article 10 of the ICC Rules on Combating Corruption 2011, adapted to its particular circumstances and capable of detecting corruption and of promoting a culture of integrity in its organization. If no remedial action is taken or, as the case may be, the defence is not effectively invoked, the first Party may, at its discretion, either suspend the Contract or terminate it, it being understood that all amounts contractually due at the time of suspension or termination of the Contract will remain payable, as far as permitted by applicable law. [如果一方合约方 A 在行使合约权利审计对方 B 的账簿与财务记录时，发现 B 重度参与或多次重复违反了《ICC Rules on Combating Corruption 2011》的规定，应通知 B 有关事宜并要求其在合理时间内采取补救措施并通知 A。如果 B 采取补救措施不成功，或不可能采取补救措施[83]，B 在面对违约的证据时，可以自己已经采取了《ICC Rules on Combating Corruption 2011》之 Article 10 中描述的足够的（根据有关的情况、自己监测贪污腐败行为与推动公司正直风气的能力）反贪污腐败措施作为抗辩。如果 B 没有采取补救措施，或前述的抗辩不成功，A 可以行使裁量权中止或取消合约。只要法律允许，此时双方在合约项下应支付的款项仍要支付。

---

[83] "可补救"与"不可能补救"的违约可去令合约被终止在 Telchadder v. Auckland Holding Limited (2014) UKSC 57 最高院先例中有详及。一般而言，违反承诺都会可以补救。例如，没有按时支付一笔钱就可去加上延误的利息去事后支付作出补救。但涉及合约的"禁止性承诺"（negative covenant），也就是一方合约方承诺不会做某些事情，曾有看法是违约后是不可能补救。但在 Rugby School (Governors) v. Tannahill (1935) 1 QB 87 上诉庭先例中，涉及租客把租用房屋组织他人卖淫，被发觉后就停业，但这是不是补救？上诉庭 O'Connor 大法官说："To stop doing what is forbidden by a negative covenant may or may not remedy the breach even if accompanied by compensation in money. Thus to remove the window boxes and pay for the repair of any damage done will remedy the breach, but to stop using the house as a brothel will not, because the taint lingers on and will not dissipate within a reasonable time."也就是说，组织他人卖淫的违约不可能补救，这也难以金钱赔偿补救去回复到违约前的地位，例如该房屋是无法在合理时间内恢复声誉可去转租别人、跌价或甚是无人问津等。违约（或在此针对的贪污受贿行为）是否可以补救是要现实去看每次不同的事实，这包括事件的严重性、或补救加上金钱赔偿是否足够真正恢复到原状等。

如果是履行过程中出现一些低层次与不严重的贪污腐败行为，可能没有必要令合约终止/无效，可以只去要求采取补救措施。另外，如果是通过贪污腐败行为获取合约很难说有什么补救措施，可以在合约中明确写明如果发现有关行为，受害方可撤销合约，令它们无效。]

Any entity, whether an arbitral tribunal or other dispute resolution body, rendering a decision in accordance with the dispute resolution provisions of the Contract, shall have the authority to determine the contractual consequences of any alleged non-compliance with this ICC Anti-corruption Clause. [仲裁庭（如 ICC 仲裁）或其他合约约定的争议解决机构有权决定没有遵守此 ICC 反贪污腐败条文而产生的合约后果。但是笔者已经在上文讲过，这样的约定对发展中国家是不利的。所以在订约自由下可以反其道而行之，在合约或 BIT 中约定如果有表面证据显示涉及贪污腐败，争议应交由或任何一方当事人可以选择交由法院（可以是英国商事法院或其他国家的商事法院）审理，甚至规定举证只需要满足本章之 5.3 段介绍的"红旗测试"标准。]"

上面提到的《ICC Rules on Combating Corruption 2011》之 Article 10 中涉及公司防止员工贪污腐败行为的合规（Corporate Compliance Programme）包括以下措施：

"a) expressing a strong, explicit and visible support and commitment to the Corporate Compliance Programme by the Board of Directors or other body with ultimate responsibility for the Enterprise and by the Enterprise's senior management ("tone at the top");

b) establishing a clearly articulated and visible policy reflecting these Rules and binding for all directors, officers, employees and Third Parties and applying to all controlled subsidiaries, foreign and domestic;

c) mandating the Board of Directors or other body with ultimate responsibility for the Enterprise, or the relevant committee thereof, to conduct periodical risk assessments and independent reviews of compliance with these Rules and recommending corrective measures or policies, as necessary. This can be done as part of a broader system of corporate compliance reviews and/or risk assessments;

d) making it the responsibility of individuals at all levels of the Enterprise to comply with the Enterprise's policy and to participate in the Corporate Compliance Programme;

e) appointing one or more senior officers (full or part time) to oversee and coordinate the Corporate Compliance Programme with an adequate level of resources, authority and independence, reporting periodically to the Board of Directors or other body with ultimate responsibility for the Enterprise, or to the relevant committee thereof;

f) issuing guidelines, as appropriate, to further elicit the behavior required and to deter the behavior prohibited by the Enterprise's policies and programme;

g) exercising appropriate due diligence, based on a structured risk management approach, in the selection of its directors, officers and employees, as well as of its Business Partners who present a risk of corruption or of circumvention of these Rules;

h) designing financial and accounting procedures for the maintenance of fair and accurate books and accounting records, to ensure that they cannot be used for the purpose of engaging in or hiding of corrupt practices;

i) establishing and maintaining proper systems of control and reporting procedures, including independent auditing;

j) ensuring periodic internal and external communication regarding the Enterprise' santi-corruption policy;

k) providing to their directors, officers, employees and Business Partners, as appropriate, guidance and documented training in identifying corruption risks in the daily business dealings of the Enterprise as well as leadership training;

l) including the review of business ethics competencies in the appraisal and promotion of management and measuring the achievement of targets not only against financial indicators but also against the way the targets have been met and specifically against the compliance with the Enterprise's anti-corruption policy;

m) offering channels to raise, in full confidentiality, concerns, seek advice or report in good faith established or soundly suspected violations without fear of retaliation or of discriminatory or disciplinary action. Reporting may either be compulsory or voluntary; it can be done on an anonymous or on a disclosed basis. All bona fide reports should be investigated;

n) acting on reported or detected violations by taking appropriate corrective action and disciplinary measures and considering making appropriate public disclosure of the enforcement of the Enterprise's policy;

o) considering the improvement of its Corporate Compliance Programme by seeking external certification, verification or assurance; and

p) supporting collective action, such as proposing or supporting anti-corruption pacts regarding specific projects or anti-corruption long term initiatives with the public sector and/or peers in the respective business segments."

8. 国际基金/第三方资助基金的国际监管

在本章之6.2.2段提到了第三方资助(Third-Party Funding，以下简称TPF)对今天针对发展中国家的投资仲裁会产生的影响。这也在近期受到国际上部分国家的关注，可简单介绍以便于大家明白问题所在。

TPF 在澳大利亚出现后非常迅速地成为国际上另一个高利润、高回报、涉及亿万美元的新兴行业，TPF 公司目前主要在英国、美国与加拿大。对 TPF 的批评显而易见是促进了大量本来不会推进的投资仲裁，特别是针对发展中国家的投资仲裁。

目前，政府几乎没有对 TPF 的监管，位于英国伦敦的诉讼第三方资助联会（Association of Litigation Funders）仅有 12 家成员，也更不用说代表 TPF 自己与其背后的英美资本的自律协会在这种自我监管下制定的行为守则能有多大作用。2022 年，欧洲议会首先提出了对 TPF 的监管，监管建议包括：将 TPF 从资助的案件胜诉金额中抽取的回报比例限制在 40%，必须承担败诉要赔偿对方胜诉方的诉讼/仲裁费用，对资助的当事人有诚信责任（fiduciary duty）等。

联合国国际贸易法委员会（以下简称 UNCITRAL）也有工作小组研究如何改革投资仲裁，并将在 2026 年的大会上对改革建议进行表决，改革建议其中包括成立投资争议法庭（multilateral investment court）并设上诉机制去替代投资仲裁。这被批评是建立了另一个小型的国际法院（mini-international court of justice），在没有类似 1958 年《纽约公约》的情况下在全球执行判决也成问题。

对发展中国家而言，笔者相信这方向是好事且具有启发性。发展中国家也无须太害怕会影响外来投资，一般在深思熟虑后希望去长期投资的外国公司，都不会轻易向主权国家启动投资仲裁，也不会希望通过贪污受贿等不法手段去获取合约等。

第十章　胁　　迫

1. 胁迫、不当影响与不合情理/显失公平交易概述

本章与下一章主要讨论的三种不同理论(doctrine)都针对谈判地位不对等而令合约可使无效(voidable)的情况。这三种理论是:胁迫(duress)、不当影响(undue influence)与不合情理/显失公平交易(unconscionable transaction)。

1.1　合约双方谈判地位不对等的三种不同理论

胁迫是普通法理论,针对的情况是在订约过程中一方向另一方施加了不被法律所允许或接受为恰当的压力,基于此压力导致合约产生,因此普通法会给予合约可使无效的救济。很显然的问题就是,什么压力才不会被法律所接受?这个问题并不容易,什么是可被接受也随着社会发展、道德观念与公共政策的变化而有所变化。例如最早期只认可对人的人身胁迫(duress of the persons),后来对货物、财产的胁迫(duress of goods)也能构成胁迫。

近年来,胁迫的范围一直在扩张,连纯粹经济上的压力也会不被接受为合法压力(lawful pressure)而构成经济胁迫(economic duress),如一方威胁(threaten)说除非对方加价否则会违约不交货等。甚至近期是已经开始有一些案件在合法行为所造成的压力下提出一些错误要求,也被认为是不法或不恰当(illegitimate)并足以构成经济胁迫。

不当影响是衡平法救济(equitable remedy),针对的情况是一方当事人滥用自己对另一方的影响力,如向对方弱势方实际施加影响,或由于当事人之间关系应当履行某些坦诚的义务(如披露)但未能履行,因此产生了实际的不当影响(actual undue influence);或者是根据双方的关系与最后不公平的合约条文内容推定不当影响(presumed undue influence),导致合约产生。

不当影响发展起来的一个重要原因是早期普通法胁迫理论过于狭窄,而在一些案件中如果不给类似救济会产生不公平合理的结果,也因此有说法将不当影响称为衡平法胁迫[1](equitable duress)。例如,在 Morris v. Burroughs(1737)1 Atk 399 先

---

〔1〕 这叫法有点不伦不类,毕竟胁迫是普通法理论,这可见 PIAC v. Times Travel(2021)UKSC 40 最高院先例中 Burrows 勋爵的评论。

例中考虑到父母对子女(尤其是未成年子女)的特殊影响,父母与子女订立的明显不利于子女的协议就被撤销。这种情况父母并没什么对人或财物施加压力的行为,但是不给救济显然不是个公平合理的结果。而今天胁迫范围逐渐扩张之后,就逐渐开始与不当影响有大量重叠之处,尤其是实际上不当影响需要证明是什么不当影响的行为,这与胁迫可以说是非常类似的。但不当影响仍然有自己的不同之处,尤其是在推定不当影响中,并不会要求证明有什么特定的施加压力/不当影响行为,根据双方关系与合约内容就已经足够导致合约可使无效。所以,不当影响仍然是除了胁迫外有可能成功的武器。另外,除了商业合约,不当影响理论在遗产继承等领域还有广泛应用,但与本书关系不大,不会在本书中进行讨论。

不合情理/显失公平的交易,则是另一种衡平法救济,目的与不当影响一样是去保护弱势方不在经济上被剥削(to protect the vulnerable from economic harm)。针对的情况是一方当事人处于特殊不利地位(special disadvantage),如文盲或者精神有问题,另一方当事人利用对方弱势方的这个不利地位订立了非常不利于对方的合约。这对弱势方不利的合约在实质内容远不止是不合理(unreasonable),而是十分苛刻的(oppressive),令衡平法法院的审理法官感觉到震惊良心。如在 Alec Lobb v. Total Oil GB(1985)1 WLR 173 上诉庭先例中,一审的 Peter Millett 大法官说:"the resulting transaction was not merely hard or improvident but overreaching and oppressive."

不合情理交易与不当影响的异同可节录《Duress, Undue Influence and Unconscionable Dealing》(2019 年,第 3 版)一书之 15 – 002 段说:"... The doctrine of **unconscionable dealing** has some similarities with other doctrines such as **duress**, **undue influence** and abuse of confidence. However, unconscionable dealing is distinct and separate from the other doctrines. For example, undue influence has been distinguished from unconscionability ... on the ground that **undue influence is concerned with the quality of the consent of the weaker party** ... whereas **unconscionable dealing is concerned** to provide relief '**against an unfair advantage gained** by an unconscientious use of power by a stronger party against a weaker'. ... Unconscionable dealing allows the courts to 'interfere with agreements the parties have freely concluded'. ..."

按以上英文,也可以这样区分这三种理论:胁迫与不当影响是针对订立合约时的"程序不公平"(procedural unfairness),因为在谈判过程中原告弱势方受到不法/不恰当压力(illegitimate pressure)或不当影响(undue influence)。但"不合情理交易"是"实质不公平"(substantive unfairness),是订立的合约内容对弱势方严重不公平。

总的看来,很多案件的事实都会与这三种不同的理论沾得上边,所以也经常会在同一诉讼同时作为诉因之一。但是在商业合约(特别是国际商业)领域,往往除了胁迫理论外,衡平法的不当影响与不合情理交易理论是没有太大关系的,因为法律上双方当事人都被假设为在知识水平方面平起平坐、各自能够保护自己的利益,不存在某一方处于特殊不利地位。而在普通法中,没有针对"谈判地位不对等"(unequal bargaining power)的说法或理论,正如 Templeman 勋爵在 Biustany v. Pigott(1995)69 P& CR 298 枢密院先例中说:"Unequal bargaining power or objectively unreasonable terms provide no basis for equitable interference in the absence of unconscientious or extortionate abuse of power where exceptionally, and as a matter of common fairness, 'it was not right that the strong should be allowed to push the weak to the wall'."

从以上的简短介绍可以看到,这三类导致合约可使无效的理论尽管是区别来自普通法理论与衡平法理论,但实际适用在不同案件事实时存在很多重叠与类似的情况,大量案件中的当事人也确实往往选择同时提出这几种诉因支持自己的案件。在 Lloyds Bank Ltd v. Bundy(1975)QB 326 先例中,Denning 勋爵一度提过针对不对等谈判地位,法院应当专门统一为一个理论给予救济,但最后被 National Westminster Bank Plc v. Morgan(1985)AC 686 贵族院先例否定,认为法院不好处理这种有千奇百怪的不对等谈判地位的案件,这社会问题应由政府通过立法去解决。

对此问题可节录《Duress, Undue Influence and Unconscionable Dealing》(2019 年,第 3 版)一书之 1-001 段所说如下:"Although each doctrine is a distinct ground of relief with its own requirements, limitations and remedies, there is considerable overlap between them. It is therefore possible that all three may be applicable on the facts of a particular case and it is not uncommon for all three doctrines to be pleaded in the alternative in the same case. The overlap between the doctrines led Lord Denning MR, in Lloyds Bank Ltd v. Bundy, to suggest that the doctrines should all be unified into one general doctrine under the name of 'inequality of bargaining power'. But that suggestion was firmly rejected by Lord Scarman in National Westminster Bank Plc v. Morgan. Rejection of a wider umbrella doctrine means that the various grounds for relief remain separate and distinct."

至于在现实情况,这三类理论的不同适用在《Civil Fraud》(2018 年,第 1 版)一书之 15-005 段也有介绍:"Duress is a creature of the common law and undue influence is a creature of equity. Nevertheless, many of the factual circumstances which in practice arise allow for both types of claim, and also for a third type of claim called 'unconscionable dealing'. Because, however, of the practical way in which the claim for undue influence can be applied, in particular where the burden can in certain circumstances be placed on the defendant to prove that the influence exercised was not undue, undue influence has become a much more prevalent claim deployed in fraud cases, and tends to be at the forefront of many claimants' arguments, particularly where there is a more 'human' element to the alleged misconduct."

以上是说由于不当影响会被法院"推定"[2](presumption)而将举证责任转移给

---

〔2〕 见本书第十一章之 1.4.2 段。

被告。特别在有欺诈味道的案件中，因为受害方原告有更困难的法定举证责任加上这种案件的隐蔽性，特别是在社会上一般的没有“斗争经验”的人士，更是难以胜任。所以，能够转移举证责任给被告，让他去说服审理法官不存在不当影响，相比胁迫更有优越性。另重申胁迫是普通法救济，而不当影响与不合情理/显失公平交易是衡平法救济。对“走出去”参与国际商业活动的中国公司的区别是，由于合约双方被假设是都有同等水平，这三种由于谈判不对等造成交易与合约可使无效的救济会有很不同的后果。

不当影响与不合情理/显失公平交易是衡平法，法院会行使裁量权去决定是否给予衡平救济，所以中国公司在上述假设下，不会被视为不当影响的弱势方，更不会被视为有特殊不利地位的一方当事人。Hoffmann 勋爵在 Union Eagle Ltd v. Golden Achievement Ltd（1997）AC 514 枢密院先例中给出了权威说法。法院在商业合约（特别是国际商业合约）中不应该考虑衡平救济以避免出现不肯定与搞乱商业关系和安排。所以笔者只会在第十一章简短介绍这方面课题。

1.2　不合情理/显失公平与合约的肯定性大原则之间的矛盾

作为衡平法救济的“不当影响”与“不合情理交易”显然重点是针对有关合约的订立是否是不合情理/显失公平（unconscionable）。毕竟，人与人之间的影响是无处不在的，双方在地位、财力、供求、议价能力、知识水平等方面经常并不对等。与胁迫的不法/不恰当压力一样道理，在任何交易与订立合约的每一步，各种压力都是无处不在的，有必要局限在“不法/不恰当”的压力才构成可诉胁迫。所以，衡平法会做出救济的不当影响必须是不合情理/显失公平。

《Duress，Undue Influence and Unconscionable Dealing》（2019 年，第 3 版）一书之 7－005 段表明：“It is not every kind of influence that will be enough to give ground for relief in equity. As Lord Nichols has said，in everyday life people constantly seek to influence the decisions of others. In many cases there is nothing wrong with such exercise of influence. … it now seems settled that to establish undue influence，it must be shown that there was an unconscionable exercise of influence …”

即使是普通法救济的胁迫，也与不合情理/显失公平的衡平法理论有关系。例如胁迫的要求是施压方向受压方作出威胁（threat）与/或提出错误要求（wrongful demand），而这些综合看来是应该受到谴责的言行与衡平法的不合情理/显失公平的不同表述在实质上没有太大的区别。再说，不少主张胁迫的案件也会同时主张不当影响作为替代诉因。毕竟，衡平法救济比普通法会更有弹性与宽松得多。例如，普通法下的“不合法”行为类别会比衡平法窄得多，很多在社会上或道德上不能被接受的行为，在普通法下并非非法或不法，但在衡平法下就不可以被接受。又如，胁迫只针对施压方直接向受压方施加不当压力，但不当影响理论包括了不当影响来自第三人的情况。所以经常会有可能原告主张的胁迫不成立，但不当影响却成立了。

所以，如果更宽松解释何谓“不合情理/显失公平”的理论，会与胁迫或不当影响重叠太多,也难怪上段提到有主张是把针对谈判不对等的三种理论合并为一个理论。

接下来本段想探讨的主要问题是不合情理/显失公平的理论与普通法下的合约法有正面与严重的相互矛盾与冲突。英国合约法(特别是商业合约的法律)追求订约自由(freedom of contract)、合约的肯定性(certainty)、明确性(clarity)、可预测性(predictability)、神圣性(sanctity)与合约承诺必须绝对/严格履行等至高无上的大原则是众所周知的。

早在 Vallejo v. Wheeler(1774)1 Cowp 143 先例中,Mansfield 勋爵就已经说商法的肯定性至关重要,否则商人将无所适从:"speculators in trade then know what ground to go upon"。

同样说法在后来无数先例中被重述,在针对"合法行为胁迫"(lawful act duress)的 PIAC v. Times Travel(2021)UKSC 40 最高院权威先例中,商业合约的肯定性、明确性与神圣性的重要性被多次提到。Burrows 勋爵说:"Within the realm of commercial contracts, with which we are here concerned, English law has a long-standing reputation for certainty and clarity..."

针对"不合情理/显失公平"给予救济(无论是以胁迫、不当影响或不合情理交易)使合约无效,在道德与社会层面看来完全公平合理(just and fair)但如果通过艰辛、耗时与花费高昂的谈判订立的商业合约可以轻易被对方合约方事后以"不合情理/显失公平"使其无效,并不是好事。正如在《Duress, Undue Influence and Unconscionable Dealing》(2019 年,第 3 版)一书之名 3-029 段中所说:"**The danger of uncertainty**... the courts apply unconscionable conduct ... with caution, since it is a vague and imprecise concept with a potential to lead to confusion with the doctrine of unconscionable dealing as an independent ground for setting aside a transaction. ..."

因此,审理法院在考虑不合情理/显失公平行为或交易的案件时,需要采取非常严格的态度,看法律是否能够划分清楚明确,尽量局限在越过了分水岭/红线非要给予救济的过分/异于寻常的案件(egregious fact cases),以避免与合约法的肯定性起冲突。

涉及"不合情理/显失公平"理论去给予衡平法救济,在 Earl of Chesterfield v. Jansen(1750)2 Ves Sen 125;Fry v. Lane(1888)40 Ch. D. 312;Cresswell v. Potter(1978)1 WLR 255 等早期先例中,只局限在保护"贫穷与无知"(poor and ignorant)的弱势方被对方占便宜。但在 Cresswell v. Potter 先例中,Megarry 大法官从英国社会的改变(例如文盲基本上消失)出发,也认同说可以放宽让其他弱势方寻求救济,说:"What has to be considered is, first, whether the plaintiff is poor and ignorant; second, whether the sale was at a considerable undervalue; and third, whether the vendor had independent advice. I am not, of course, suggesting that these are the only circumstances which will suffice; thus **there may be circumstances of oppression or abuse of confidence which will invoke the aid of equity**."(加黑部分是笔者的强调)

"不合情理/显失公平"理论在 Multiservice Bookbinding Ltd v. Marden(1979)Ch 84 先例中被进一步放宽,Browne-Wilkinson 大法官说:

"In my judgment a bargain cannot be unfair and unconscionable unless one of the parties to it has imposed the objectionable terms in a **morally reprehensible manner**, that is to say, in a way which affects his conscience.

The classicexample of an unconscionable bargain is where advantage has been taken of a young, inexperienced or ignorant person to introduce a term which no sensible well-advised person or party would have accepted. But **I do not think the categories of unconscionable bargains are limited: the court can and should intervene where a bargain has been procured by unfair means**."(加黑部分是笔者的强调)

看来,只要是社会道德上应该受到谴责的交易或行为就属予不合情理/显失公平。这也被后来的先例所认同,如在 Alec Lobb v. Total Oil GB(1985)1 WLR 173 上诉庭先例中,Millett 大法官说:"... not only that the terms of the transaction were harsh or oppressive, but that 'one of the parties to it has imposed the objectional terms in **a morally reprehensive manner, that is to say, in a way which affects his conscience**' ... where I pointed out that there must be some impropriety, both **in the conduct** of the stronger party **and in the terms of the transaction** itself ..."(加黑部分是笔者的强调)

但只要是"社会道德上应该受到谴责的行为或交易"就给救济会带来问题,并最终与保护合约的肯定性与可预测性大原则起矛盾。这包括:(1)从"贫穷与无知"放宽到针对"社会道德上受谴责"会否步子迈得太快、太大?(2)这也难逃会受个别审理法官的主观看法影响。(3)"不合情理/显失公平"理论本质上是空泛的大道理,感觉是为"要做好人"建立一套理论,并细化成为制度与成千上万条规则让公众清楚明了怎么样做是合法的"好人"与怎样做就会是犯法的"坏人",但这实际上是做不到的。正如在新加坡的 BOM v. BOK(2018)SGCA 83 上诉庭先例中,Andrew Phang 大法官说:"... the chief weakness of the doctrine of unconscionability is that it is a rather general and vague doctrine that does not furnish sufficient legal criteria in order to enable the court to apply it so as to arrive at a just and fair result in the case at hand."

看来对衡平救济的"不当影响"与"不合情理交易"的理论更有关系,特别是后者。本质上,施压方施加不法/不恰当压力与误述方(misrepresentor)作出事实的误述去导致合约产生的道理是一致的,都涉及施压方/误述方主动的错误行为并偏离或扭曲了受害方原告的订约自由与意愿。但近年来有了"合法行为胁迫"(lawful act duress)的延伸,就带来了如何考虑"不合情理/显失公平"理论的问题,毕竟欺诈性误述、非法行为胁迫等本就会是不合情理/显失公平行为,不被法律接受。

合法行为胁迫是否可以被接受为英国法律与怎样去划出合理、清楚无误与现实可行的分水岭/红线是近年来颇有争议的话题。反对的有不少,毕竟压力无处不在。既然压力"合法",法律仍应考虑救济显然对刚提到的合约大原则冲击太大,从而带来英国商法的不肯定与不可预测的问题。反对引入合法行为胁迫的其他普通法国家有新加坡、澳大利亚与新西兰。而更多反对的是法律学者，在此可节录《The Principles of the Law of Restitution》（2015 年，第 3 版）一书之 218 段如下："... despite the recent explicit recognition that a lawful threat can still be an illegitimate threat for economic duress, the better view is that only unlawful threats should suffice. **A lawful threat may still result in restitution, but only ... if the more stringent test of unconscionability is satisfied. This ensures that the law does not intervene unacceptably in commercial markets.** Where a defendant has obtained a benefit as a result of an unlawful threat which caused the benefit to be transferred, it is appropriate for restitution to be awarded. Where **the benefit was obtained as the result of a lawful threat, it is only appropriate to award restitution where the defendant's conduct is characterised as unconscionable** ..."（加黑部分是笔者的强调）

也就是普通法没有必要引入合法行为胁迫，如果在罕有发生的过分/异于寻常的案件是施压方通过合法手段去向对方获得完全不合理与不合情理/显失公平的好处，也可以通过衡平法的"不合情理交易"［或推定不当影响的 II（B）类别〔3〕］，对何谓"公平合理"有更高门槛去解决。

但认同引入合法行为胁迫的说法也不少，毕竟已经有这方面先例的存在，是普通法的一部分。另外，刑法（《Theft Act 1968》之 Section 21）也承认合法行为胁迫（只要是敲诈，不管施加的压力是合法或非法），民商法也得跟上。

反正，在近期的 PIAC v. Times Travel 最高院先例中已经肯定了英国法律有合法行为胁迫。接下来的工作就是去摸索建立一套明确与实际可行的制度与规则划下对合法行为胁迫的红线与确立构成要件了，并尽量多加关卡以减少对商业合约肯定性与可预测性的大原则的影响。

1.3 需要保护弱势方的无知是指法律知识

最后是多处讲到的"水平"或"知识水平"，例如英国法律推定的发展中国家有同样的水平，指的是法律水平，与高科技（rocket science）毫无关系。英国是法治社会，各种活动都发展出了或正在发展出一套客观看合乎情理与现实可行的法律去规管。所以在这三种不同的谈判不对等情况，受压方或弱势方有否、能否与被通知否［例如主要在妻子为丈夫提供担保〔4〕（surety wives）的案件］寻找称职与独立的律师寻求法律意见是决定的主要因素之一。一旦有了律师从旁建议与协助，就很难成功主张自己是受压方或弱势方了。

这在几乎每个涉及不当影响与不合情理/显失公平的交易的案例中都有提到这一点。信手拈来，在 JP Morgan Chase Bank v. Springwell Navigation Corporation

---

〔3〕 见本书第十一章之 1.4.2.2.2 段。

〔4〕 可见在本书第五章之 6.3.3.2 段与第十一章之 1.4 段的详细介绍。

(2008)EWHC 1186(Comm)先例中,Gloster 大法官说:"… his(主张受不当影响的 Springwell)second signature acknowledging that Chase had **advised him to take independent legal advice** regarding the contents and effect of the Memorandum of Deposit. … they were highly experienced and astute businessmen who were well versed in concluding commercial contracts and who were fully capable(if they bothered to read the relevant terms)of understanding both the significance of agreeing contractual terms and the meaning and effect of the terms which they agreed. **If they required legal advice,they were fully capable of taking it**."(加黑部分是笔者的强调)

另在 National Westminster Bank Plc v. Morgan(1985)AC 686 贵族院先例中,Scarman 勋爵说:"The bank suggested,very wisely and fairly,that Mrs. Morgan should take legal advice …"

最后在 Chagos Islanders v. Attorney General(2003)EWHC 2222(QB)先例中,Ouseley 大法官说:"The Claimants were unable to discover with reasonable diligence that the Defendants had behaved fraudulently and unconscionably at an earlier stage because they were **uneducated**,trusting,**without access to pre-legal advice** and effectively under the control of the Defendants who had misled … at all stages as to their rights and status."(加黑部分是笔者的强调)

2. 胁　迫

不妨先节录在《Chitty on Contract》(2021 年,第 34 版)一书之 10 – 003 段对胁迫的简单概述:"A contract which has been entered as the result of duress may be avoided by the party who was threatened. It has long been recognised that a threat to the victim's person may amount to duress;it is now established that the same is true of wrongful threats to his property,including threats to seize his goods,and of wrongful or illegitimate threats to his economic interests,at least where the victim has no practical alternative but to submit. In each case the wrongful or illegitimate threat must have had some causal effect on his decision to enter the contract,but the causal requirements may differ between the various kinds of duress. In cases of economic duress,it is submitted that the victim must also show that they had no practical(or unreasonable)alternative to submission to the challenged contract."

简单而言,胁迫是一种可使合约无效的救济。胁迫的诉因类别不是合约(contractual)或侵权(tortious),而可以归类为不当得利(unjust enrichment)。涉及的情况是一方(可称为施压方)施加不法/不恰当压力(illegitimate/improper pressure),导致对方(可称为受压方)缺乏其他合理选择(absence of reasonable alternative choice),被迫订立他本来不愿意订立的合约与/或作出支付/转让金钱或财产等,法律就允许受压方事后撤回给出的允诺或同意,让订立的合约可使无效与复原(restitution),把支付的金钱或转让的财产取回。这节录在《Civil Fraud》(2018 年,第 1 版)一书之 15.034 段,针对什么是胁迫,说:"The legal concept of duress embraces the situation where a person takes a step — for instance the payment of money, or the entry into a contract — which is procured by the exercise of pressure or threats, such that the will of the complainant(受压方), although not destroyed, is illegitimately coerced, so that it cannot be said that he took the relevant step voluntarily."

接下来在 15 - 037 段针对胁迫的救济,说:"... Duress is a basis for avoiding the relevant transaction(and hence avoiding any executory obligations) and, so far as necessary, obtaining restitution of any monies paid or property transferred as a result of the duress. In this sense, duress is a part of the wider law of unjust enrichment. Hence duress may be pleaded as a defence to a claim on a contract or as a form of cause of action seeking recovery of property and/or declaratory relief; the complainant may be either defendant or claimant. But a contract induced by duress ... is not void ab initio; it is voidable and so the usual bars to rescission are potentially applicable."

法律承认多种形式的胁迫,包括对人身的胁迫、对财产的胁迫以及经济胁迫。

本书主要探讨的只是民事/商事合约关系中的胁迫。在英国法下刑事案件中受胁迫是抗辩一些犯罪指控的抗辩理由,背后的原理与民事合约的胁迫是类似的,但是判断标准等方面有一些区别。

3. 胁迫是对订约自由意志的偏离

传统对胁迫(以及不当影响[5])的理解,是认为胁迫的存在导致受胁迫一方的自由意志(will)被"超越/压倒"(overbear)或完全消灭/摧毁(destroy),或者给出的允诺或同意并非该人士自愿(voluntary)。这说法可见 Barton v. Armstrong(1976) AC 104 贵族院先例,Wilberforce 勋爵与 Simon 勋爵说:"The action is one to set aside an apparently complete and valid agreement on the ground of duress. The basis...is, thus, that though there was apparent consent there was no true consent to the agreement: that the a-

[5] 不当影响有一大类情况是一方通过根据自己与对方的关系,滥用自己能造成的影响,逼迫(coercion)对方,诱导合约的产生。这与胁迫在案情上是类似的,今天也会主要适用普通法胁迫的原则处理。但不当影响的范围要比胁迫大,这会在本书第十一章之 1.1 段介绍。不当影响在今天更关注施加影响一方是否有衡平过错(equity wrong)、显失公平(unconscionable)行为,这与胁迫关注的是受胁迫一方的订约意图是否受限有所不同。另外胁迫是普通法理论,而不当影响是衡平法理论;这也导致在被告可以采用的抗辩与救济手段等会有一些区别。

greement was not voluntary."

这样的要求往往是较为严格的,必须是压倒与达到并非受压方自愿的程度。但这说法的问题是,胁迫的后果应当如何?毕竟一个有效的合约,必须是双方在自由意志下订立的。如果胁迫的后果是完全消灭了自由意志,合约自始就没有达成,对抗合约成立的抗辩应该是"这并非我的协议"[6](*non est factum*),合约自始无效(*void ab initio*)。这与一贯认为胁迫带来的只是可使无效合约的后果是不一致的。[7]

而且在这样的说法下,只要根据事实认定受压方确实因为胁迫而没有任何选择(如被施压方用枪指着要求签字),合约就因为有这严重缺陷而没有成立,这变成事实问题(issue of fact)。但根据过往判例可以看到,对于胁迫还要考虑胁迫本身是否有非法性、因果关系等法律问题(issue of law)或事实与法律混合问题(mixed issue of fact and law)。

因此,近年来更偏向另一种解读,即认为胁迫本质上并非要求完全消灭自由意志,只是偏离(deflection):见 Huyton SA v. Peter Cremer GmbH & Co(1999)1 Lloyd's Rep 620 先例等。胁迫导致选择受限,受压方仍然是自主作出的选择,只不过必须"两害相权取其轻"("choice between evils")。

在这样的解读下,合约可以视为有效成立(不会因为完全缺乏自由意志或意愿而自始无效),但法律给予受压方合法撤销合约的救济,允许撤销不受法律保护的允诺与同意。这有点类似于欺诈获取允诺或同意的后果,而与"这并非我的协议"的自始无效后果是不同的。在 Lynch v. DPP of Northern Ireland(1975)AC 653 贵族院先例中,Simon 勋爵说:"Similarly with duress in the English law of contract. Duress again deflects, without destroying, the will of one of the contracting parties. There is still an intention on his part to contract in the apparently consensual terms; but there is coactus volui[8] on his side. The contrast is with non est factum. The contract procured by duress is therefore not void: it is voidable-at the discretion of the party subject to duress."

The "Universe Sentinel"(1983)1 AC 366 贵族院先例[9]中,Diplock 勋爵也给出了类似的解读,指出胁迫是指受压方的允诺或同意是在施压方的压力下做出的,受压方可以撤回自己的允诺或同意。Diplock 勋爵说:"It is, however, in my view crucial to the decision of the instant appeal to identify the rationale of this development of the com-

---

[6] 见本书第七章之 16 段。

[7] 当然如果可以根据事实认定一方当事人根本没有真正意愿作出允诺或同意,就会属于"这并非我的协议"的抗辩,合约自始无效,而不需要根据胁迫抗辩合约可使无效了。有关无效与可使无效的区别,可见本书第三章之 6.3.1 段。

[8] 拉丁文"*coactus volui*"的简单英语解释是:"I consented under compulsion",即被强制而同意。

[9] 与此先例的案情类似的 The "Evia Luck"(1992)2 AC 152 贵族院先例可见本章之 7.1 段的介绍。

mon law.〔10〕It is not that the party seeking to avoid the contract which he has entered into with another party,or to recover money that he has paid to another party in response to a demand,did not know the nature or the precise terms of the contract at the time when he entered into it or did not understand the purpose for which the payment was demanded. The rationale is that **his apparent consent was induced by pressure exercised upon him by that other party which the law does not regard as legitimate,with the consequence that the consent is treated in law as revocable unless approbated either expressly or by implication after the illegitimate pressure has ceased to operate on his mind.** It is a rationale similar to that which underlies the avoidability of contracts entered into and the recovery of money exacted under colour of office,〔11〕or under undue influence or in consequence of threats of physical duress.〔12〕”(加黑部分是笔者的强调)

简单再举一个例子,就是在 The “Siboen” and The “Sibotre”(1976)1 Lloyd’s Rep 293 先例中,承租人向船东期租了 2 艘船舶。承租人知道船东需要依赖租金偿还船舶的贷款,而由于市场价格下跌,一旦失去承租人,船东就可能面临船舶贷款断供的风险。承租人借此机会与船东谈判,欺诈/虚假陈述自己没有实质资产,如果船东不降租金自己就唯有破产与违约,船东最后可能什么也拿不到,以此逼迫并成功使船东同意降低租金。此先例以欺诈为由撤销合约(见本书第三章的介绍)。但 Kerr 大法官也提到了经济胁迫(economic duress)也能有合约可使无效的后果,但此先例中压力并没有完全“压倒”或摧毁自由意志,因此拒绝给予胁迫的救济。在当时虽然已经有了经济胁迫的说法与讨论,但还没有权威确认。尤其是在可以欺诈给予救济的情况下,Kerr 大法官也不需要再以经济胁迫给予救济。但到了经济胁迫已经得到大量发展的今天来看,承租人给予船东的压力是欺诈方式的不法压力,再加上能够显示是由于此压力导致船东被迫接受降低租金,或者说是因为压力导致自由意志“偏离”、缺乏合理选择,就也足以构成经济胁迫了。在《Chitty on Contract》(2021 年,第 34 版)一书之 10 – 020 段这样评论该先例说:“In the event,however,he(The “Siboen” and The “Sibotre”先例中审理案件的 Kerr 大法官)denied relief on this ground because the owner’s consent or will was not vitiated by the pressures,which were only normal commercial pressures. In light of the discussion of Lynch’s case(刚刚节录的 Lynch v. DPP of Northern Ireland 贵族院先例中 Simon 勋爵的说法)… this ground of decision seems dubious;the question which the learned judge ought to have asked himself

〔10〕 此先例中涉及的是现代发展起来的经济胁迫(economic duress),而不仅仅是传统的对人生的胁迫。见本章之 5.4 段的介绍。

〔11〕 这是指本章之 11 段介绍的情况。

〔12〕 在这方面的原理上,无论是属于普通法救济(legal remedy)的人身或经济胁迫,还是属于衡平法救济(equity remedy)的不当影响(undue influence)都是一样的。

was not whether the owners' consent was negatived by the pressure, but whether the pressure was permissible pressure to exert. Given his finding that the pressure was based on fraud, it would seem that duress should have been a further ground for relief, although in the circumstances it would have been immaterial, given that relief was available for fraud."

4. 胁迫:不法压力与压力导致没有合理选择

胁迫是帮助受到不被法律接受的压力的受压方可以摆脱合约。针对什么时候压力不被法律所接受,必须划出一条分水岭/红线来。

毕竟在竞争激烈的商业活动中,实际上常常有各种不同类型的压力,这些压力本身甚至很多时候都是被法律所接受甚至是支持的。典型的例子就是在合约要约中,实际上都会暗含着压力,例如A允诺以较高的价格销售一批紧俏的货物给B,并要求B必须在24小时内回复,这显然是合法合理的。这样的例子还有很多,例如租船中船舶过了合约所订的销约期(cancelling date)[13]仍未能抵达装港或交船港,承租人以此威胁除非船东同意减低运费否则解约。又例如买卖合约约定货物最迟装船日期,超过此日期未装船买方可解约,但货物未能在该日期前装船,买方借机威胁要求减低货价否则解约。这些情况中,承租人或买方行使合约赋予自己的权利,完全正当与合法。毕竟,作为受压方的船东或卖方可以不就范,接受租约或买卖合约被解约。但如果受压方觉得让步在经济上更划算,与施压方订立新合约去减低运费或货价肯定有效,而且不能也不应该事后允许以胁迫为由撤销。

所以在普通法权威先例的说法是胁迫必须同时满足两个要件(pre-conditions):(1)受压方的订约自由意志由于压力而受限;(2)施加的压力有非法性(illegitimacy)。如果涉及经济胁迫,还强调必须多一个要件,即(3)受压方没有其他合理选择。

这可节录 The "Universe Sentinel"(1983)1 AC 366 先例中,Scarman 勋爵说:"The authorities...reveal two elements in the wrong of duress:(1)**pressure amounting to compulsion of the will** of the victim;and(2)the **illegitimacy of the pressure exerted**. There must be pressure, the practical effect of which is **compulsion or the absence of choice**. Compulsion is variously described in the authorities as coercion or the vitiation of consent. The class case of duress is, however, not the lack of will to submit but the victim's intentional submission arising from the realisation that there is no other practical choice open to him...The absence of choice can be proved in various ways, e. g. by pro-

---

〔13〕 关于销约期问题,可见杨大明律师的《期租合同》一书第三十四篇之34.1段的介绍。

test, by the absence of independent advice,〔14〕or by a declaration of intention to go to law to recover the money paid or the property transferred...〔15〕But none of these evidential matters goes to the essence of duress. The victim's silence will not assist the bully, if the lack of any practical choice but to submit is proved."(加黑部分是笔者的强调)

类似说法可见 R v. Attorney General for England and Wales(2003) UKPC 22 枢密院先例, PIAC v. Times Travel(2021) UKSC 40 最高院先例等。在此仅节录 PIAC v. Times Travel 先例, Burrows 勋爵说:"Where it is alleged that one contracting party(the defendant) has induced the other contracting party(the claimant) to enter into the contract between them by duress, the case law has laid down that there are **two essential elements** that a claimant needs to establish in order to succeed in a claim for rescission of the contract. The **first is a threat(or pressure exerted) by the defendant that is illegitimate**. The **second is that that illegitimate threat(or pressure) caused the claimant to enter into the contract**. As Lord Goff said, **in the context of economic duress** ... there is a **third element. This is that the claimant must have had no reasonable alternative** to giving in to the threat(or pressure)."(加黑部分是笔者的强调)

5. 胁迫的不同类型

5.1 三大胁迫类型的发展

传统普通法对于胁迫的定义是非常狭窄的,仅包括一些极端的针对人身的逼迫(coercion)。在19世纪时强调必须对受压方有实际或威胁将施行暴力(violence)或监禁(imprisonment),才被认定为胁迫。这在后来稍有扩大,出现了对财物的胁迫(duress to goods),例如船东非法留置货物,此时法律允许取回额外被迫支付金钱的救济。

相比之下,衡平法法院在处理背后道理近似的不当影响〔16〕案件时,会根据个别案件公平合理进行判断,在标准上比较宽松,救济不限于对人身或对财物的胁迫。1976年以来,法院在不少完全不涉及对人身的胁迫的案件中,也开始给予了普通法

〔14〕是否获取了独立(法律)意见,这看来类比衡平法下的显失公平交易(unconscionable bargains)。显失公平针对的不是不法压力,而纯粹是强势方利用了弱势方的特殊不利地位(如精神疾病或药物作用等失去判断能力)而在弱势方没有独立法律意见的情况下,签订了对弱势方过分、压迫/苛刻的合约。今天经济胁迫虽然被作为胁迫看待,但有衡平法的来源与背景,在涉及的案件事实情况上也会与衡平法的显失公平或不当影响有很多重叠之处。

〔15〕这是受压方在证据上应当进行的准备,如要当下提出抗议说明虽然这么做但是"under protest",或说明虽然现在同意付钱但保留权力将来索赔。

〔16〕见本书第十一章之1段的介绍。

胁迫的救济，逐步建立起来了经济胁迫的说法。近年来，更是出现了“合法行为胁迫”的说法。

先说英国法下的普通法与衡平法。早期英国有两类法院，即普通法法院与衡平法法院，衡平法法院主要处理适用各类严格普通法原则会带来不公平的案件，并建立自己的一套理论与救济。当事人可以根据自己的需求选择在哪一个法院进行诉讼。例如合约的当事人违约，无辜方可以在普通法法院索赔损害赔偿（damages），而如果损害赔偿不够则可以在衡平法法院申请履约指令（specific performance）。而一旦出现衡平法与普通法的冲突，便有著名的衡平法优先[17]（equity prevails）的法律格言（legal maxim），毕竟每一个案件的公平正义的结果是法律所追求的终极目标。而如果普通法法院的权限不足，衡平法法院会填补。当然在英国《Judicature Act 1873》后，早已不再区分普通法法院和衡平法法院，无论是衡平法问题还是普通法问题，都由同一个法院系统一并处理。也因此，今天英国法院在案件中可以同时根据衡平法与普通法进行判案，如给予各类损害赔偿同时也给出各种禁令。但是普通法与衡平法仍然有不少区别，例如相比普通法，衡平法主要是基于各类法律格言，更关注公平正义的大原则而不拘泥于具体的规则，很多概念都较为模糊（有时候法院甚至不愿意进行太具体的定义以免限制了自己的权限），甚至被普通法认为过于不肯定与不被普通法原则接纳。这并非本书重点，也不在此详细展开。

也能想到在胁迫的发展过程中，尤其是经济胁迫的原则、要件与测试，非常受到衡平法的影响。在开始发展经济胁迫的 Barton v. Armstrong（1976）AC 104 贵族院先例中，Wilberforce 与 Simon 勋爵这样说：“... out of the various means by which consent may be obtained-advice, persuasion, influence, inducement, representation, commercial pressure-the law has come to select some which it will not accept as a reason for voluntary action: fraud, abuse of relation of confidence, undue influence, **duress or coercion**. In this **the law, under the influence of equity**, has developed from the old common law conception of duress-threat to life and limb-and it has arrived at the modern generalisation ... ‘subjected to an improper motive for action’”[18]（加黑部分是笔者的强调）

这些影响主要来自不当影响，特别是 Rookes v. Barnard（1964）AC 1129 贵族院先例带来了现在对不当影响的理论，以及不合情理/显失公平（unconscionable）理论，这两者会在本书第十一章介绍。这在不少先例的判词中也都有提到，例如在 The “Universe Sentinel”（1983）1 AC 366 贵族院先例中，Diplock 勋爵在讨论经济胁迫背后的

---

〔17〕 这在《Judicature Act 1873》中有立法规定。今天则可见《Senior Court Act 1981》之 Section 49：“Subject to the provisions of this or any other Act, every court exercising jurisdiction in England or Wales in any civil cause or matter shall continue to administer law and equity on the basis that, wherever there is any conflict or variance between the rules of equity and the rules of the common law with reference to the same matter, the rules of equity shall prevail.”

〔18〕 有关施压方的主观动机对于是否构成不法压力的影响，可见本章之 7.2.2 段的介绍。

原理时说："It is a rationale similar to that which underlies the avoidability of contracts entered into and the recovery of money … or under undue influence or in consequence of threats of physical duress."

The"Evia Luck"(1992)2 AC 152 先例与 Huyton SA v. Peter Cremer GmbH & Co (1999)1 Lloyd's Rep 620 先例提到压力如果涉及不法威胁或构成不合情理行为就会是不当压力。类似地，较近期的 Borrelli v. Ting(2010) UKPC 21 枢密院先例与 The "Cenk Kaptanoglu"(2012) EWHC 273(Comm) 先例在给予受压方救济时都考虑了施压方的行为是否不合情理。

在笔者看来，普通法救济与衡平法救济仍然有不少区别，如普通法救济不会适用衡平法抗辩的理由，如怠慢[19](laches)不会给予救济、净手规则(clean hands)等。而且普通法救济倾向于根据满足法律规定的要件(例如好像疏忽侵权的要件[20])就给予救济，而不是在每个案件都根据具体案情的不同判断是否公平正义，也因此更强调需要划出红线(red lines)的要件才能让法律有肯定与可预测的测试标准。也只有这样才能满足在社会交往，尤其是商业往来中对于明确与肯定这大原则的要求。因此虽然普通法胁迫引入了这些衡平法的概念与说法，以适应今天社会尤其是商业社会的要求，但未必可以完全采用衡平法理论中的测试标准。

本章接下来会分别详细讨论这几种类型的不法压力。

5.2 针对人身的胁迫(duress of the persons)

《Chitty on Contract》(2021 年，第 34 版)一书之 10－017 段介绍了针对人身的胁迫，说："Duress of the person may consist in violence to the person, or threats of violence, or in imprisonment whether actual or threatened. The threat of violence need not be directed at the claimant(受压方): a threat of violence against the claimant's spouse or near relation suffices and a threat against the claimant's employees has been held to constitute duress. It is suggested that a threat against even a stranger should be enough if the claimant genuinely believed that submission was the only way to prevent the stranger from being injured or worse."

简单而言，针对人身的胁迫是指实际进行或威胁进行的暴力或监禁行为，而目标对象则可以是当事人，或当事人的配偶、近亲属，或可能是雇员或甚至是其他受压方关心的第三人等。

在国际商业社会中，针对人身的胁迫逼迫签合约的相对少一些，但也不是没有。例如在 Barton v. Armstrong(1976) AC 104 先例中，就涉及原告主张被告雇佣了一个臭名昭著的罪犯，威胁说如果不满足被告要求签订合约就杀了原告。又如在 Antonio v. Antonio(2010) EWHC 1199(QB) 先例中，原告与被告原本是夫妻，妻子经营一家成

---

〔19〕 但普通法救济有索赔时效的问题。

〔20〕 疏忽侵权救济的要件见本书第一章之 2.1.1 段的介绍。

功的设计公司。但丈夫发现妻子有外遇,就雇佣了一个长期被希腊通缉与希望被引渡的杀手,该杀手长期出入住宅与设计公司。当妻子外遇对象在回到希腊寻求庇护时,庇护外遇对象的人士都将被谋杀。丈夫以此要挟,并且后来成功让妻子转让了设计公司50%股份给自己。法院认定存在针对人身的胁迫,转股的合约可撤销。还如近期的 Al Nehayan v. Kent(2018)EWHC 333(Comm)先例,〔21〕其涉及双方合资在希腊开办酒店业务,但后来双方关系破裂,一方要买断另一方在业务中的所有利益,逼迫对方签订协议时就威胁说"blood would be shed if necessary"以及威胁说"这样下去的结果是你我都不希望看到的"等。或者是 Singh v. Redford(2018)EWHC 2390(Ch)先例,其涉及较小规模的商业合作,双方关系破裂后,一方威胁另一方及其家人。

当然即使是针对人身的胁迫,也需要有非法性质。一般的暴力或监禁也都是不法压力,但仍然要根据事实进行判断。例如在 R v. Attorney General for England and Wales(2003)UKPC 22 先例中,原告曾经是英国陆军特种空勤团 SAS(Special Air Service,英国精英特种作战队)成员,在海湾战争期间还作为 B20 小队的一员被空投敌后执行特种作战任务。〔22〕此先例中,原告想要撤销自己在 1996 年签署的保密协议,理由就是自己受国防部的"威胁",如果不签署就会被强制离开精英团 SAS,回到以前的部队编制(这类做法通常是用来惩罚违反 SAS 纪律或者不再适合担任 SAS 队员的军人)。枢密院判这并非非法威胁,毕竟国防部有权调动军人的编制与部署,也因此不会由于胁迫导致合约可使无效。

5.3 针对财物的胁迫(duress of goods)

5.3.1 威胁扣押或扣留财物

早在 18 世纪,就有案件判如果施压方错误地扣押(seizure)或扣留(detention)财物,逼迫受压方支付金钱,受压方即使为了拿回财物而付钱,事后只要证明自己才是真正拥有或对财物有占有权的人士,就可以在普通法下追回这笔支付的金钱。例如,在 Astley v. Reynolds(1731)2 Str 915 先例中,原告把财物出质给当铺,但在赎回时当铺要求额外利息,否则不会交还财物,原告思考再三还是先支付了额外利息赎回财物,之后再起诉当铺要求归还金钱,这就得到了法院的支持。

另在 Maskell v. Horner(1915)3 KB 106 上诉庭先例中,Reading 勋爵说:"If a person pays money, which he is not bound to pay, under the compulsion of urgent and press-

---

〔21〕 案情在本书第一章之 2.7.4.3 段有介绍。

〔22〕 1991 年海湾战争期间,英国 B20 小队被空投敌后执行特种作战任务,但行动失败,被伊拉克武装部队发现与追捕。一共 8 名成员中只有 1 名成功逃离,3 名在逃亡过程中死亡,4 名被抓捕(包括此先例中原告)并受到严刑拷打,直到战后才被释放回英国。之后有成员与队伍指挥官以此事件出版书籍,包括著名的《Bravo Two Zero》等,还被改编为电视、电影播放。但其他成员(包括此先例中原告)以及军队都广泛对此不满,认为其中有诋毁其他幸存成员与死亡成员的部分。但由于缺乏保密协议,国防部对此无能为力。因此之后军人大规模请愿,导致国防部在 1996 年要求所有作战队成员签署保密协议,以防再次出现此类事件。

ing necessity or of seizure, actual or threatened, of his goods he can recover it as money had and received. The money is paid not under duress in the strict sense of the term, as that implies duress of person, but under the pressure of seizure or detention of goods which is analogous to that of duress."

在早期的案件中，曾经一度区分此时由于只是对财物的胁迫而非对人身的胁迫，因此没有合约可使无效的救济，而只是可以取回额外支付的金钱：见古老的 Skeate v. Beale (1841) 113 ER 688 先例。[23] 但今天看来已经不再有这样的区分。一方面的原因是在现代趋向宽松的法律下不太说得通为什么要有这样的区分，在 The "Evia Luck" (1992) 2 AC 152 先例中，Goff 勋爵在附带意见中也认为此先例在今天不再是正确的法律了。另一方面的原因则是今天类似的事实除了可以依赖对财物的胁迫，都可以依赖经济胁迫的说法，而经济胁迫的测试中不存在这样的区分。

不妨介绍 The "Alev" (1989) 1 Lloyd's Rep 138 先例。此先例中原告是"Alev"轮的船东，将船舶期租给了承租人二船东。二船东装船了一批货物，签发了运费预付提单，该提单也已经背书转让给了被告（目的港的货方/提单持有人）。问题是二船东经济困难，没有继续支付期租租金，但是由于预付租金的提单约束船东与货方/提单持有人，船东仍然有义务将货物运送到目的地港。船东因此与二船东以及货方展开谈判，在船东表示除非同意否则拿不到货物的威胁下，货方同意支付港口费用、卸货费用，以及放弃一切针对船东的索赔权利，也放弃扣船的权利等。但是在船舶到达卸港卸货后，货方扣船并主张因胁迫而要求撤销自己与船东之间的约定。高院判这既是经济胁迫也是针对财物的胁迫，因此合约无效。毕竟船东有义务将货物送达目的地与交货，明知如此仍然提出额外要求，并且威胁要扣押货方的货物，是不法压力。Hobhouse 大法官说："... it is clear that the agreement falls within the principles of economic duress and for that matter duress of goods. The plaintiffs did make a threat which was illegitimate, and if it be relevant, they know it be illegitimate. They were under an obligation to carry the cargo to ... and deliver it there to the defendants. They had no right to refuse to do so or to assert any inconsistent right over the goods. They did refuse to

---

[23] 此先例中，被告拖欠了应支付给原告的租金，因此原告扣押了被告的财物并打算出售以抵扣租金，而被告则同意如果原告不再扣押财物，自己会支付欠下的租金，但在原告将财物归还后，被告没有按约定支付，并主张原告扣押财物行为的威胁导致不得已同意支付。法院判对财物的扣押不会使得合约无效，也因此被判应当支付全部租金。判词中还区分了对人身的威胁与对财物的威胁的不同后果，认为对人身威胁的程度严重，但对财物胁迫的程度较低以及对自由意志的影响没有这么大，因此在对财物威胁的情况中仍然要视乎情况，如果有其他合理选择（如向法院申请命令）就不会让合约无效："the distinction pointed out between duress of, or menace to, the person, and duress of goods. The former is a constraining force, which not only takes away the free agency, but may leave no room for appeal to the law for a remedy; a man, therefore, is not bound by the agreement which he enters into under such circumstances; but the fear that goods may be taken or injured does not deprive any one of his free agency who possesses that ordinary degree of firmness which the law requires all to exert..."

carry the goods to...and delivery them to the defendants unless the defendants met their demands. They did assert a dominion over the defendant's goods; they refused to recognize the defendants' right to have the goods. The consent of the defendants was overborne..."

对中国货方而言,The "Alev"先例就是很好的应对例子,只要货物安全抵达卸港,在卸港法院(中国法院)有类似法律与做法,就可以采取同样行动,强制卸货、要求退还已经支付的金钱与宣告撤销"新合约"。

除此之外,还有常常发生的情形,例如承租人未支付运费、租金或装港滞期费等,(在提单合约没有条文许可留置的情况下)船东非法在卸港或港外留置无辜货方的货物。即使卸港没有健全的法院系统可以很快申请到命令强制船东卸货,而只能先支付船东索要的金钱换来卸货,事后也一样可以起诉撤销该"和解"协议并取回金钱。有关这种船东行使留置权留置货物是否合法的问题可见《程租合约》一书第十二章之3段,杨大明律师《期租合同》一书第四十篇之40.3.6段以及《提单与其他付运单证》一书之3.4.10段。

在本章之12.2.1.2段介绍的Gulf Azov Shipping Co Ltd v. Idisi(2001)EWCA Civ 505先例中,也涉及非法扣押船舶的对财物的胁迫。

5.3.2 威胁损毁财物

除了扣押和扣留货物以外,如果是威胁要损毁财物,今天一般也被认为可以构成非法压力。在本章之3段已经介绍过的The "Siboen" and The "Sibotre"(1976)1 Lloyd's Rep 293先例中,Kerr大法官在附带意见中就提到说以损毁房屋或名画为要挟逼迫签订租约,是可以基于胁迫提出索赔请求的:"he(被告代表大律师)submitted that although money paid under duress to goods is recoverable, a contract can only be set aside for duress to the person but not in any other case of duress ... I do not think that English law is as limited as submitted... For instance, if I should be compelled to sign a lease or some other contract for a nominal but legal sufficient consideration under an imminent threat of having my house burnt down or a valuable picture slashed, though without any threat of physical violence to anyone, I do not think that the law would uphold the agreement. I think that a plea of coercion or compulsion would be available in such cases..."

5.4 经济胁迫(economic duress)

这种类型的可诉胁迫(actionable duress),可以说在20世纪70年代才正式被接受。在Pao On v. Lau Yiu Long(1980)AC 614枢密院先例中,Scarman勋爵说:"There is nothing contrary to principle in recognising economic duress as a factor which may render a contract voidable."

在之后的几十年间,国际商业活动中频繁发生以威胁违约(threatening breach of contract)逼迫对方达成新合约或支付金钱,对方事后想要撤销或拿回金钱的争议,这些大量案例就发展了经济胁迫的理论。

顾名思义,经济胁迫是通过针对弱势方(无论是在经济上、商业上其他方面)施加不法/不恰当压力(illegitimate pressure)而获取利益。在今天国际商事活动中,以暴力针对人身的胁迫订约的极端例子毕竟很少,出现胁迫的争议绝大多数都是经济胁迫。但法律并不阻止自我谋利(self-interest),这是普遍的人性,在商业社会更是如此。构成违法的经济胁迫,必须涉及施压方向受压方以"不法/不恰当"(包括应该受到谴责与不合情理/显失公平)的言行施加压力,并提出"错误"的要求谋取利益。经济胁迫的权威定义不少,都是大同小异,先挑一个最近的 Instagroup Limited v. David Carroll & Others(2022)EWHC 464(QB)先例中的例子,Nigel Cooper QC 大法官说:

"In order to establish economic duress, it is necessary to establish the following elements: i) The making of an **illegitimate … threat** by one party; ii) Sufficient **causation between the threat and the threatened party entering into the contract** or making the non-contractual threat; and iii) The **lack of any reasonable alternative** to the threatened party giving into the threat.

The illegitimacy of a threat is to be determined by focusing on the nature and justification of the demand made by the threatening party having regard to, among other things, the behaviour of the threatening party (including the pressure it applied) and the circumstances of the threatened party. **The law generally accepts that the pursuit of commercial self-interest is justified in commercial bargaining and a demand which is motivated by commercial self-interest will in general be justified**. A threat will be illegitimate if it amounts to reprehensible or unconscionable conduct, …"(加黑部分是笔者的强调)

与相对简单的对人身的胁迫或对财物的胁迫不同,经济或商业上的压力在表现形式上是相当多样的。例如,支付方利用收款方在财政上的困境逼迫收款方接受相比原合约约定更低的价格才不去拖延;一方以违反原合约、不再履行义务作为威胁,逼迫对方接受新要求;工会罢工或威胁罢工,逼迫雇主重新与雇员订立新合约;船东在装港装运易腐货时临时要求增加运费,否则拒装或拒签提单,逼迫承租人提前支付依约本应在卸货 30 天后才结算的装港滞期费;以及在"无效果无报酬"(no cure no pay)救助中,救助方逼迫被救船舶签订报酬额过高的救助协议;[24] 甚至在一些特别的案情中,采取完全合法行为导致受压方处于不利地位然后敲竹杠等。

经济胁迫在国际商业活动最常出现的情况是涉及威胁违约的不法/不恰当威吓,可以在每天都在发生的大同小异的案件中随便挑一个介绍。在 Kolmar Group AG v. Traxpo Enterprises Pvt Ltd(2010)EWHC 113(Comm)先例中,原告为了转售给一个急需甲醇的重要客户,作为买方向作为卖方的被告购买一批甲醇,已经约定了数量、货价、以及交货期,也已经定下了运货的船舶。然而签订合约后市场上甲醇供不应求价格飙升,导致被告事后提出无法按照合约约定提供货物。被告给出了"爱要不要"

〔24〕 见 The "Port Caledonia" and The "Anna"(1903)P 184 先例。

(take it or leave it)的两个选择:一个是按照合约价格交易,但只能提供数量少得多的货物,并且逼迫原告支付因此产生的超过 100 万美元的船舶空仓费(dead freight);另一个则是可以提供较多数量的货物,但销售价格要比合约约定高得多。

对于原告而言,在当时的情况下即使被涨价也不得不选择拿到更多货物,无法提供货物给自己的重要客户既导致原告商誉受损,也会影响原告与重要客户的后续生意。而且仅仅在这一单与重要客户的协议下,如果未能按约提供货物将要面临的索赔就可能超过 200 万美元。如果接受被告的违约/毁约,要从市场上购买其他甲醇来满足货物供应,不要说交货期的问题,能不能买到都有疑问,而且价格肯定会高得离谱。除此以外,在与被告商谈期间,运输的船舶早已到港靠泊,每天都会产生 2 万美元的滞期费,还要再加上换泊位的费用等额外港口费用,因此必须马上做决定。相比之下,虽然看起来原告可以选择的法律行动有不少,但都谈不上"足够"补救,也因此原告在按被告要求加价拿到货物后,以经济胁迫寻求救济。

被告既施加了威胁违约的不法压力,而且还因此导致原告在没有其他"合理"选择下只能接受被告的无理要求,就能构成经济胁迫。

以经济胁迫为理由给予救济最早出现在一些美国的案例中。但近几十年来英国法很快通过一系列先例确立了足以构成胁迫的地位:见 Barton v. Armstrong(1976) AC 104;The "Siboen" and The "Sibotre"(1976)1 Lloyd's Rep 293;The "Atlantic Baron"(1979)1 Lloyd's Rep 89;Pao On v. Lau Yiu Long;Burmah Oil Co v. Bank of England(1980) AC 1090;The "Universe Sentinel"(1983)1 AC 366;B&S Contracts and Design Ltd v. Victor Green Publications Ltd(1984) ICR 419;The "Alev"(1989)1 Lloyd's Rep 138;The "Evia Luck"(1992)2 AC 152;CTN Cash and Carry Ltd v. Gallagher Ltd (1994)4 All ER 714;Huyton SA v. Peter Cremer GmbH & Co(1999)1 Lloyd's Rep 620;DSND Subsea Ltd v. Petroleum Geo-Services ASA(2000) BLR 530;Carillion Construction Ltd v. Felix(UK) Ltd(2001) BLR 1;Adam Opel GmbH v. Mitras Automotive UK Ltd(2007) EWHC 3205(QB);Kolmar Group AG v. Traxpo Enterprises Pvt Ltd;Borrelli v. Ting(2010) UKPC 21;The "Cenk Kaptanoglu"(2012) EWHC 273(Comm);Burger King Corp v. King Franchises Ltd(2013) EWHC 1761(Comm);Ryan v. Tiuta International Ltd(2014)11 WLUK 703;Bonhams 1793 Ltd v. Cavazzoni(2014) EWHC 682 (QB);Salekipour v. Parmar(2017) EWCA Civ 2141;Al Nehayan v. Kent(2018) EWHC 333(Comm);Chaggar v. Chaggar(2018) EWHC 1203(QB);Barclays Bank Plc v. Borkhatria(2018) EWHC 1326(Comm);Rock Advertising Ltd v. MWB Business Exchange Centres Ltd(2018) UKSC 24;McDonagh v. Bank of Scotland Plc(2019)4 WLR 12;Breakshore v. Forbes(2020)12 WLUK 170;Rotamead Ltd v. Durston Scaffolding Ltd (2020) EWHC 2738(TCC);Adare Finance DAC v. Yellowstone Capital Management SA (2020) EWHC 2760(Comm);Morely v. Royal Bank of Scotland Plc(2021) EWCA Civ 338;Rhino Enterprises Properties Ltd, Re(2021) EWHC 2533(Ch);Safe-T-Systems

Holdings Ltd v. ILR Safety CC(2021)EWHC 2992(Ch);Kings Solutions Group Ltd,Re (2021)EWCA Civ 1943;Instagroup Limited v. David Carroll & Others 先例等。

在 The “Evia Luck”贵族院先例中 Goff 勋爵就已经说英国法下经济胁迫的存在已经被广泛接受:“... it is now accepted that economic pressure may be sufficient to amount to duress for this purpose, provided at least that the economic pressure may be characterised as illegitimate and has constituted a significant cause inducing the plaintiff to enter into the relevant contract...”

5.4.1 合约双方重新谈判更改合约的原因与英国法律的地位

5.4.1.1 国际商业社会经常发生经济胁迫案件的原因

商业合约的履行,尤其是中、长期合约,往往是在订约时觉得是对自己有利或双赢的交易。但履行到中途,这一美好愿望就因为各种突发事件或情况变化而出现履行困难已是屡见不鲜。例如在船舶建造合约中,原材料价格或工资上涨、法律或规定的改变,或合约约定的付款货币汇率下跌等,导致船厂从预期的获得微薄利润变了亏本或严重亏损。又如房地产开发项目中途地产市场崩溃,开发商的现金流有了困难无法支付承建商,与/或触发了融资银行与接受抵押担保的借贷合约下的违约条款等。在这种情况下,受影响的合约方 X(船厂或开发商)是可以困难履行下去的(如自己想办法去注资改善公司现金流),但现实中更会发生的是向对方合约方 Y(如订购船舶的船东、融资银行或承建商)主张将无力继续履行有关合约,并企图哀求或迫使对方更改合约(variation)如提高造船价格、承建商与/或银行接受分期支付或还债等。

X 的行为属于违约/毁约,Y 可以接受后终止有关合约并索赔损失。但也会有不少案件中的 Y 不想这样做。这样 Y 就需要回应 X 的更改合约的诉求了,但 Y 会要求 X 满足一些条件作为交换,也好让 Y 有交代(即使是想帮助 X)。这都需要双方通过重新谈判来解决困难,并希望最后能够成功订立一个更改的(或新的)合约去替代原来的旧合约。谈判的过程中难免有漫天要价、吹嘘、施加压力、不抖出自己底牌等惯常手法。期间,X 的吹嘘或施加压力的言行都会有危险犯错,如欺诈性误述或不法/不恰当压力的胁迫等。毕竟,X 讨价还价的唯一底牌就是履行合约困难,也就是威胁违约/毁约。

5.4.1.2 更改合约的障碍:法律对交换有实质价值对价的坚持

除了谈判中施加压力,有效更改合约的要件之一是对价(consideration)。[25] 这样,X 与 Y 达成的新合约就需要看双方是否有交换对价。会是明确有对价的情况如 X 为了顺利获得 Y 同意提高造船价格或可以分期支付/还债等,承诺为合约的继续

〔25〕 合约更改必须有对价支持有悠久的普通法历史:见 Stilk v. Myrick(1809)2 Camp 317 等先例。有关此课题,与这方面法律的一些不明确之处,在《合约的履行、弃权与禁反言》一书第三章之 2.4.3 段与第四章之 12.1.2 段有详论。

履行提供个人担保(personal guarantee)。又如X承诺为Y加建一艘船舶并定价优惠等。但也有很大可能X的承诺只是向Y保证(或再度保证)去尽力履行原合约的责任,不会再回来向Y提额外要求,这是否是对价,就有很大的争议:见Foakes v. Beer(1884)9 App Cas 605;Williams v. Roffey Bros & Nicholls(Contractors)Ltd(1991)1 QB 1;In re Selectmove Ltd(1995)1 WLR 474等先例。

这些千变万化的情况,只能说如果Y提出的条件也在谈判后被X接受是有真正价值,这更改合约会实质上是你情我愿所达成的。例如,X承诺为Y以优惠价格稍后加建一艘船舶。相反,X最终没有接受任何Y的条件或只是做出一些微小承诺,就有更强的味道是Y在压力下屈服或更改合约没有真正的对价。而X与Y相互交换了有实质价值的对价(特别是看来足够的对价)达成更改合约,后来Y因其他原因想以不法/不恰当压力反悔试图使更改合约无效,也困难得多。因为Y在X承诺了有实质价值的对价下接受更改,清楚显示了你情我愿,更难满足经济胁迫的三个要件中的受压与签约之间的因果关系,更像是Y完全自愿签订合约。但在有实质价值的对价交换的更改合约的情况,出现这种争议是比较少见。针对是否有实质价值对价与胁迫的关系,还可见《Chitty on Contract》(2021年,第34版)一书之10-025段:"... the fact that there was some consideration does not rule out the question of duress. Where the consideration is only trifling, it is suggested that its inadequacy may be relevant in establishing that the variation of the contract has been secured by improper pressure."

更常见的情况是没有对价交换的更改合约,当有关合约顺利履行完毕,Y就会回想到多给X敲了一笔钱或损失(因为被迫同意延迟支付/还债)。Y对更改合约的反悔也会在没有顺利履行完毕,如更改后的合约在履行中发生其他重大事件而受阻。反正只要X的履行告一段落,Y就会反悔了。这样,Y想复原到原合约,就必须令更改合约无效,这就至少会带来"对价"与"胁迫"的争议。

5.4.1.3 发生突发事件/情况变化令合约履行困难而更改合约在英国法律的总结

在英国法律下,针对这种经常在合约履行困难时双方试图去找出变通做法与达成合约更改的情况,法律地位可以简单描述如下:

1. 法律地位是合约必须严格或绝对履行。只有发生订约时无法预见的外来突发事件导致合约无法履行,或合约方的共同合约目的发生根本性改变,此时构成受阻[26](frustration)令合约自动终止。因事件受影响的X(船厂或地产开发商)也没有义务继续履行了,这与违约/毁约或损失赔偿无关,有了损失也只是各自自己承担。但只在非常有限与极端情况下,才会涉及受阻理论。而且发生的突发事件是否足够令合约真正受阻会存在模糊与富有争议,需要由法院或仲裁庭审理进行事实认定后才能确定下来。这样,X与Y仍是有很大可能走同样的路,谈判找出变通做法(例如,船厂在发生突发

---

〔26〕 有关受阻理论,见《合约的履行、弃权与禁反言》一书第二章。

事件如船舶主体部分被有关当局禁止出口令船舶建造不下去,看是否可改建为海上平台或其他类型船舶等)与更改合约。

2. 当事人可以用明示条文约定改变不令人满意的法律默示地位,以明示条文去针对合约履行期间可以合理预见但说不准会否发生、不愿意接受某种情况变化时的风险。这对合约主要负责履行的一方(如工程合约的承建商、或运输合约的承运人)特别重要,订约时必须谨慎。

至于明示条文写明如何应对,如何调整与分摊风险,〔27〕典型的就例如不可抗力条文(force majeure clause),类似的条文还包括是针对延误的时间延长条文(extension of time clause),或者是针对市场价格波动的价格调整条文(price escalation clause)等。根据这些条文的约定,发生特定事件(如地震、洪水、罢工等)可以中止履行某些义务,而不构成违约/毁约。又例如市场有巨大波动时,如市场价格超出一定比例就按照市场某日价格重新定价。这样会相对明确与肯定,也可以比默示地位包括更多种类的情况。

但如果履行真出了突发事件或情况变化,X 与 Y 又是走同样的谈判道路去寻找变通办法与更改合约。多了对有关条文如何解释的争议,好处是双方同意更改后的合约更像是和解合约,面对诉讼或潜在的诉讼各让一步,在存在有效的对价方面是更明确。

3. 更改合约的对价问题直到近期的 Rock Advertising Ltd v. MWB Business Exchange Centres Ltd(2018)UKSC 24 最高院先例仍未解决。此先例中 MWB 在伦敦运营办公室,将其中一间办公室有偿许可给 Rock 使用。在合约中约定了一条不允许口头更改签字合约的"书面更改条文"(No Oral Modification Clause)。Rock 经营困难,到了 2012 年已经欠下多期许可费未支付。在 2012 年 2 月,Rock 的董事与 MWB 的高管/信贷控制员(credit controller)达成口头约定,允许 Rock 在 2 月到 10 月间先以低于合约约定的金额支付许可费,而与原合约约定之间差额以及已经欠下的许可费,则分摊到之后的许可期间按月额外支付。换言之,对 MWB 而言,口头协议下支付的总金额与原合约下的总金额差别不大,只有一些因为推迟支付导致的利息差别。Rock 也实际按新口头协议支付了 2 月的许可费,但之后 MWB 高层有不同想法,仍然根据原合约终止合约与驱逐了 Rock,因此双方对于口头协议是否有效产生争议。

双方争议焦点问题在于:(1)书面更改条文是否可以被口头协议改变;(2)如果可以,此先例中的口头协议更改是否有对价支持。最高院支持了书面更改条文的效力,也就是口头协议无效,因此不需要继续考虑对价问题。但对于对价问题上不清楚的法律地位,最高院的 Sumption 勋爵说:"That makes it unnecessary to deal with consideration. It is also, I think, undesirable to do so. The issue is a difficult one. The only consideration which MWB can be said to have been given for accepting a less advanta-

〔27〕 这方面在笔者《合约的解释:规则与应用》一书第十三章之 1 段有详细介绍。

geous schedule of payments was(i)the prospect that the payments were more likely to be made if they were loaded onto the back end of the contract term, and(ii)the fact that MWB would be less likely to have the premises left vacant on its hands while it sought a new licensee. These were both expectations of practical value, but neither was a contractual entitlement. In Williams v Roffey Bros & Nicholls(Contractors)Ltd[1991]1 QB 1, the Court of Appeal held that an expectation of commercial advantage was good consideration. The problem about this was that practical expectation of benefit was the very thing which the House of Lords held not to be adequate consideration in Foakes v Beer(1884) 9 App Cas 605 ... There are arguable points of distinction, although the arguments are somewhat forced. A differently constituted Court of Appeal made these points in In re Selectmove Ltd[1995]1 WLR 474, and declined to follow Williams v Roffey. The reality is that any decision on this point is likely to involve a re-examination of the decision in Foakes v Beer. It is probably ripe for re-examination. But if it is to be overruled or its effect substantially modified, it should be before an enlarged panel of the court and in a case where the decision would be more than obiter dictum."

因此,在这种困难情况下双方无论是以口头或书面更改合约,即使继续履行下去对 X 与 Y 均有好处,但缺乏 X 给 Y 什么有实质价值的对价时,是否属于有效的更改仍然存在疑问。

4. 英国法也在试图解决这个问题,双方更改后的新合约如果因为对价出问题,可以由禁反言理论来补救,尤其是承诺性禁反言[28](promissory estoppel)。在更改合约后,即使因为缺乏对价而无效,但依赖更改合约而受损害的当事人仍可以要求救济。在 Rock Advertising Ltd v. MWB Business Exchange Centres Ltd 最高院先例中,Sumption 勋爵说:"(不执行更改合约的一方当事人)carries with it the risk that a party may act on the contract as varied, for example by performing it, and then find itself unable to enforce it. It will be recalled that both the Vienna Convention and the UNIDROIT model code qualify the principle that effect is given to(原合约条文), by stating that a party may be precluded by his conduct from relying on such a provision to the extent that the other party has relied(or reasonably relied)on that conduct. In some legal systems this result would follow from the concepts of contractual good faith or abuse of rights. In England, the safeguard against injustice lies in the various doctrines of estoppel. This is not the place to explore the circumstances in which a person can be estopped from relying on a contractual provision laying down conditions for the formal validity of a variation. ..."

5. 另有权威说法是建议在过往先例中严格要求更改合约的对价,一个重要的公共政策考虑是用来保护在更改合约时受到了施压方不恰当的压力,从而在没有什么

---

〔28〕 有关禁反言的课题见《合约的履行、弃权与禁反言》一书第四章之 12.1 段。

有实质意义的对价交换下就同意更改合约的合约方。然而,因为早年在商业上的不恰当压力只被局限在对人身(或对财物)的胁迫,所以如果没有对价要求的保护,受压方就求助无门。但今天胁迫理论既然已经扩展到了经济胁迫,可以足够给予救济。因此,更好的做法是让胁迫理论解决更改合约是否有效的问题。同时,对更改合约是否有对价的问题上可以宽松对待,只要受压方 Y 在同意更改合约时有一些利益(如希望继续履行原合约)就已经足够。对此可节录《Chitty on Contract》(2021 年,第 34 版)一书之 6－072 段,说:"The insistence in the earlier cases on the stricter requirement of legal benefit or detriment no longer seems justified(if it ever was)by the need to protect B from the undue pressure that A might exert by refusing to perform their original contract;for this need can now be met by the expanding concept of duress. This provides a more satisfactory solution of the present problem since it invalidates promises only where actual duress is established. Where this is not the case,and the promise has in fact conferred a benefit on the promisor by performing the original contract,there seems to be no good reason for refusing to enforce the new promise and it can be argued that the requirement of consideration should be treated as satisfied."

5.4.2　构成经济胁迫的三个要件

相比之下,针对人身与财物的胁迫都较为明显是不合法行为(稍后会介绍),而经济胁迫纯粹是经济上的压力。

至于构成经济胁迫的要件(pre-conditions),在本章之 5.4 段已经有提到。在另一个 DSND Subsea Ltd v. Petroleum Geo-Services ASA(2000)BLR 530 先例也有同样的说法,三个要件是:(1)压力的不法性,(2)经济压力与受压方签订合约或付款之间的因果关系,(3)压力造成受压方没有其他合理选择的后果。Kerr 大法官说:"The ingredients of actionable duress are that there must be pressure,(a)whose practical effect is that there is compulsion on,or a lack of practical choice for,the victim,(b)which is illegitimate,and(c)which is a significant cause inducing the claimant to enter into the contract…"

在 PIAC v. Times Travel(2019)EWCA Civ 828 上诉庭先例[29]中,Davids Richard 大法官说:"… three necessary ingredients for a successful claim. **First**,there must be illegitimate pressure applied to the claimant. **Second**,the pressure must be a significant cause inducing the claimant to enter into the contract. **Third**,the practical effect of the pressure is that there is compulsion on,or a lack of practical choice for,the claimant."(加黑部分是笔者的强调)

而在 Kolmar Group AG v. Traxpo Enterprises Pvt Ltd(2010)EWHC 113(Comm)

---

〔29〕　此先例已经有 PIAC v. Times Travel(2021)UKSC 40 贵族院先例的判法,给出的是类似说法也已经在本章之 4 段节录,不在此重复。

先例中,高院的 Christopher Clarke 还针对经济胁迫总结了如下四点:

1. 在今天英国法下通过过往先例已经明确了经济上的压力,如果是被认定有不法性,以及能够满足与签订合约有因果关系,即"要不是"测试,就足以认定胁迫:"Economic pressure can amount to duress, provided it may be characterised as illegitimate and has constituted a 'but for' cause inducing the claimant to enter into the relevant contract or to make a payment..."

2. 如果施压方的威胁是违约行为(尤其是该方知道自己的威胁是违约行为时),多半会被认定为属于不法:"a threat to break a contract will generally be regarded as illegitimate, particularly where the defendant must know that it would be in breach of contract if the threat were implemented..."

当然,这还会需要考虑是否真实相信自己地位,如较早提到的双方对一条"不可抗力条文"有争议,各持己见(即使之后在这点败诉);是否情况发生了严重变化,见极罕见的违约不被法院认为是不法压力的胁迫的 DSND Subsea Ltd v. Petroleum Geo-Services ASA 先例;是否仅仅陈述自己的困难等因素,会令威胁被法院视为可以接受或并非恶意(bad faith)。

3. 还需要考虑受压方是否有"合理选择",如是否可以抵抗压力,实际可以选择事后通过法律行动索赔已经足够补救,如果没有合理选择,就是很强的证据证明受压方的签约或付款行为是威胁所导致:"it is relevant to consider whether the claimant had a 'real choice' or 'realistic alternative' and could, if it had wished, equally well have resisted the pressure and, for example, pursued practical and effective legal redress. If there was no reasonable alternative, that may be very strong evidence in support of a conclusion that the victim of the duress was in fact influenced by the threat."

在经济胁迫中尤其需要用必须没有其他合理选择限制构成胁迫的情况,如明明应该有其他办法(如申请法院命令或在市场上买到替代的货物等)而不用屈服,但受压方由于各种原因轻易就放弃,事后再想以胁迫寻求救济是不会得到支持的。

4. 受压方是否有提出抗议,是有关威胁是否导致签约或付款的考虑因素之一。当然即使没有抗议,也可能存在胁迫:"the presence, or absence, of protest, may be of some relevance when considering whether the threat had coercive effect. But, even the total absence of protest does not mean that the payment was voluntary."

这些标签化的看法就像《证据法:国际规管与诉讼中的证据攻防》一书第十三章之 3.3 段介绍的无损害规则下滥用"无损害"(without prejudice)的措辞/文字一样,太多商人滥用。"抗议"被滥用虽然较少见,但即使是加上,如果案情显示受压方实在有太多其他合理的选择,不必马上向施压方无条件投降,就算有抗议也没有用。相反,受压方没有提出"抗议"但案情明显是胁迫下被迫答应城下之盟,也是无妨。更不用说受压方会有合乎情理的原因不抗议,如受压方不敢当时就抗议,担心抗议后反而更加得罪施压方:见 The "Atlantic Baron" (1979) 1 Lloyd's Rep 89 先例。

因此一般是否有“抗议”的标签并非决定性的，而只是证据之一，需要结合案情整体看待。

6.“可诉胁迫”要件之一：压力的非法性、作出威胁与错误要求

英国法下的一般说法是能够构成“可诉胁迫”（actionable duress）的压力需要是非法、不法与/或不恰当。Wilberforce 勋爵与 Simon 勋爵在 Barton v. Armstrong（1976）AC 104 贵族院先例中说：“…in life…many acts are done under pressure, sometimes overwhelming pressure, so that one can say that the actor had no choice but to act. Absence of choice in this sense does not negate consent in law: for this **the pressure must be one of a kind which the law does not regard as legitimate.**”（加黑部分是笔者的强调）

6.1　非法（illegal）、不法（unlawful）与不恰当的区别

在开始讨论前可先简单介绍两个一般都被称为“非法”的英文“illegal”与“unlawful”，其实两者有本质上的不同。“illegal”严格是指做出了已经是在形式、技术与程序上法律禁止实施的行为。而“unlawful”则是做出了法律没有授权允许或许可（permitted）进行的行为。换言之，“illegal”针对的仅仅是法律禁止采取的行为，而有一些行为虽然没有被法律禁止，但在社会与道德层面与/或在民事范畴的公平合理下不能被接受，这些并非“illegal”行为，但可以是“unlawful”行为。所以“unlawful”也经常会适用在正统、嫡系血缘、正当等，如“已满 18 岁的合法年龄”（lawful age）、“遗产的合法继承人”（lawful heir）等。显然，“unlawful”在范围上更广泛，可以肯定的是一个“illegal”的威胁肯定是“unlawful”的威胁。

在本书，“illegal”被称为“非法”，“unlawful”被称为“不法”，但是他们的反义词“legal”与“lawful”都统称为“合法”而无法在中文上详细区分。在本书第八章有关“非法”在英文可见是针对“illegality”，这包括触犯或违反立法、普通法与/或公共政策的行为。

本章胁迫主要针对的是不被法律接受为是恰当的压力，统称为“不法/不恰当压力”（illegitimate pressure），这包括社会上、道德上或国际上视为不容或不恰当的压力（improper pressure），所以使用“unlawful”或用另一个意思更广泛的近义词“illegitimate”来形容。

简单举一个例子就是违约行为一般不会是非法行为，因为合约条文是当事人之间的约定，法律并不禁止违约。甚至有“有效益违约”[30]（effective breach）的说法；

---

〔30〕 见笔者《损失赔偿与救济》一书第十二章之 4.1 段。

以及合约义务可分为两种的说法:(1)履行作为首要义务,(2)用金钱作为替代赔偿的次要义务。[31]

但以违约行为施加压力是被英国法律普遍认为是不法行为,[32]因为施压方往往是估计到对方作为受压方会让步才去施压,也就是乘人之危,不会出现向受压方好好说"我必须违约,但愿意赔偿你所有损失,并为此提供担保"的情况。这样,这种违约的压力显然是应该受到谴责与不合情理/显失公平,去施加的压力也难逃是"不法/不恰当"。

但仍会有例子是违约行为仍被认定是合法压力,例如较早介绍的 DSND Subsea Ltd v. Petroleum Geo-Services ASA(2000)BLR 530 先例。所以有说法是施压方以违约行为相逼,仍不能说死是不法/不恰当压力,虽然这种情况的案件会是很少。

6.2 针对"不法/不恰当压力"的权威说法

但困难的问题在于哪些压力会被认为属于胁迫理论下的不法/不恰当的压力?在英国法下要关注两方面因素:(1)施压方的威胁;与(2)是否提出错误要求。

首先是在 The "Universe Sentinel"(1983)1 AC 366 贵族院先例中,Scarman 勋爵说:"In determining what is legitimate two matters may have to be considered. The first is as to the **nature of the pressure**. In many cases this will be decisive, though not in every case. and so the second question may have to be considered, namely, **the nature of the demand** which the pressure is applied to support."(加黑部分是笔者的强调)

1. 压力/威胁的性质,例如看威胁是否本就是刑事犯罪行为,[33]带来的压力也难逃是不法/不恰当压力。

2. 即使是以合法行为进行威胁,也可能构成不法压力,典型的情况就是以做出合法行为(例如做好公民检举揭发犯罪)进行敲诈勒索(blackmail)。毕竟这样的行为甚至可以构成刑事犯罪,没理由不会属于民事错误。

在民事诉讼中,根据 Scarman 勋爵的说法,也就是一方面会看威胁本身的性质是

---

〔31〕 见笔者《损失赔偿与救济》一书第十一章之 1.1 段。

〔32〕 在《Duress, Undue Influence and Unconscionable Dealing》(2019 年,第 3 版)一书之 3-003 段,提到了有意见认为违约并非不法:见 Greater Fredericton Airport Authority Inc v. NAV Canada(2008)290 DLR(4th)405 加拿大先例。

〔33〕 刑事犯罪中的敲诈勒索本就是非常严重的罪行,英国法下敲诈勒索可见《Theft Act 1968》之 Section 21:"**Blackmail.** (1) A person is guilty of blackmail if, with a view to gain for himself or another or with intent to cause loss to another, he **makes any unwarranted demand with menaces**; and for this purpose a demand with menaces is unwarranted unless the person making it does so in the belief—(a) that he has reasonable grounds for making the demand; and (b) that the use of the menaces is a proper means of reinforcing the demand. (2) **The nature of the act or omission demanded is immaterial**, and it is also **immaterial whether the menaces relate to action to be taken by the person making the demand**. (3) A person guilty of blackmail shall on conviction on indictment be liable to imprisonment for a term not exceeding fourteen years."(加黑部分是笔者的强调)

什么。例如说:“除非你同意打折扣把货物卖给我,否则我打断你的腿。”威胁打断对方的腿本身就非法(甚至是触犯刑法),这带来的压力在民事案件中来看也一般就都是不法/不恰当的。至于提出的要求是否合理(也就是要求打折扣),作为第二步去看是否不法/不恰当。

而即使不是不法/不恰当的威胁,另接下来要看的方面就是施压方要求的是什么?如果是错误要求,也可能令整件事看来是不合情理/显失公平(unconscionable)而被认定属于不法压力。例如,合法行为的敲诈勒索,如施压方向对方受压方说:“除非你同意转 20 万元给我,否则我就向你家人举报那天看到你出轨的事情。”通风报信行为并非非法或不法,但是以此要挟支付金钱,仍然是不法/不恰当压力,属于可诉胁迫。Atkin 勋爵在 Thorne v. Motor Trade Association(1937)AC 797 最高院先例有如下经典说法:“The ordinary blackmailer normally threatens to do what he has a perfect right to do — namely, communicate some compromising conduct to a person whose knowledge is likely to affect the person threatened … **What he has to justify is not the threat, but the demand of money**.”(加黑部分是笔者的强调)

Scarman 勋爵的说法也获得了较为近期的 R v. Attorney General for England and Wales(2003)UKPC 22 枢密院先例的肯定,Hoffmann 勋爵还总结了过往先例中的两个因素:(1)一般而言任何形式的不法(unlawful)行为的威胁都会被认为属于不法压力;(2)合法(lawful)行为的威胁,但向受压方提出错误要求,从而变成不法/不恰当的压力。有关判决可节录如下:“The legitimacy of the pressure must be examined from two aspects: **first, the nature of the pressure** and **secondly, the nature of the demand which the pressure is applied to support**…Generally speaking, the threat of any form of unlawful action will be regarded as illegitimate. On the other hand, that fact that the threat is lawful does not necessarily make the pressure legitimate.”(加黑部分是笔者的强调)

在本书第八章介绍了民事案件中什么时候适用非法理论(doctrine of illegality)。在 Patel v. Mirza(2016)UKSC 42 最高院先例后,普通法非法案件是要基于多因素判断(factors-based approach)。但针对胁迫理论而言,Patel v. Mirza 先例中的这些因素与判断方法是否同样可以借鉴,在 PIAC v. Times Travel(2021)UKSC 40 最高院先例中已经明确拒绝了将多因素判断引入胁迫理论。

6.3 因素之一:不法/不恰当的威胁(unlawful threat)

只简单节录《Duress, Undue Influence and Unconscionable Dealing》(2019 年,第 3 版)一书之 3-009 段所说如下:

“**Threat of unlawful action is illegitimate** The general rule is that ‘the threat of any form of unlawful action will be regarded as illegitimate’. An action is unlawful, and so can constitute duress, if it is a criminal offence, a tort or a breach of contract. In some cases, the threat itself may constitute the tort of intimation. [34] In D & C Builders v. Rees (1966) 1 WLR 288, a builder in financial difficulties accepted a cheque for a sum smaller than the amount owed to him in full satisfaction of the debt. The creditor accepted the settlement after the wife of the debtor had told him that: 'We will pay you nothing, unless you accept £ 300 in settlement'. The Court of Appeal held that the agreement was unenforceable for want of consideration. [35] ... Lord Denning MR went further, to hold that there was no accord on the ground that the creditor's assent had been procured by duress. The pressure was brought about by the threats made by the debtor's wife, and the threat amounted to the tort of intimidation. ... held that 'no person can insist on a settlement procured by intimidation'.

The question whether the defendant's conduct was unlawful, and therefore illegitimate, is not confined to threats that are unlawful under domestic law. It extends to acts or threats of actions by a sovereign state that is unlawful under international law. Thus in a contract that is governed by English law, the English courts can entertain a defence of duress by a sovereign state based on allegations that it entered into the impugned contract as a result of acts or threats of violence by another sovereign state that are unlawful under international law.

There is no difficult where the act or the threat of action amounts to a criminal offence or a tort. However, there has been some controversy as to whether a threat to breach a contract will always be illegitimate."

6.4 因素之二:错误/不合理[36]的要求(**wrongful/unreasonable demand**)

对此可先简单节录《Duress, Undue Influence and Unconscionable Dealing》(2019年,第3版)一书之3-009段所说如下:

"**Unreasonable demands** Even where there are unanticipated supervening events for which the defendant is not responsible, for a threat to breach a contract to be legitimate the demand must be reasonable. It is not legitimate for a party to exploit the change of circumstances to make an unreasonable demand. In B&S Contracts and Design Ltd v. Victor

---

[34] 有关恐吓侵权(tort of intimation),可见本章之12.2段。

[35] 在商业社会,经常发生的不法/不恰当压力是威胁受压方在原合约作出对施压方有利的更改(如提高或减少约定价格),更改后合约的有效性在事后常受到是否有对价以及是否存在胁迫的影响,见本章之5.4.1段。

[36] 本段标题虽然仍是以"不合理"要求,以配合紧接下来的《Duress, Undue Influence and Unconscionable Dealing》一书的节录内容。但合法行为威胁时根据要求是否合理作为能否构成不法/不恰当压力的标准已在PIAC v. Times Travel (2021) UKSC 40最高院先例被否定,这在本章之8.4.1段有介绍。但笔者也无意在此(与本章其他段节)删除"不合理要求",只在此加上对这一点上普通法的最近发展的解释。

Green Publications Ltd …, a threatened breach of contract was illegitimate because there was no justification for the demand. The parties were faced with strike action by the contractor's workforce, which was refusing to work unless it was paid a certain sum. The contractor(施压方) was prepared to pay the men what they were demanding, but said they did not have the money available to do so. The complainant(受压方) offered to help to make the money available by paying the contractor an advance on the contract price, but the contractor refused to accept the payment as an advance and insisted on the complainant paying the money as an extra payment instead. The Court of Appeal held that the threat of breach of contract unless the complainant paid the extra sum was 'thoroughly unreasonable behaviour' and therefore illegitimate.

It is a different matter where the demand is reasonable in the circumstances. In DSNDSubsea Ltd v. Petroleum Geo-Services ASA, faced with unforeseen circumstances, for which the contract had not made provision, one party DSND(施压方) demanded a variation of the contract and suspended work in order to support its demand. It was held that in the circumstances of the case, even if that suspension of work was a breach of contract, it 'did not amount to illegitimate pressure. It was reasonable behaviour by a contractor(施压方) acting bona fide in a very difficult situation'. The breach of contract(suspension of work) was not illegitimate because it was used to support a reasonable demand (resolution of the insurance/indemnity question). However, the court made it clear that the breach of contract would have been illegitimate if it had been used to support a demand which in the circumstances was unreasonable. Thus, Dyson J said that if DSND had said that they would not resume work 'until the compensation issue was resolved' that would have been illegitimate pressure. In the circumstances of the case, suspension of work(breach of contract) was reasonable if done for the purpose of achieving resolution of the insurance/indemnity problem. It was not reasonable if the reason for it 'was the desire to put pressure on PGS(受压方) to meet DSND's demands for compensation."

在 B& S Contracts and Design Ltd v. Victor Green Publications Ltd(1984) ICR 419 上诉庭先例中,B&S 与 Victor Green 签订合约,为 Victor Green 建造某展会中的展台。问题出在原告聘用自己已经破产的子公司的前雇员来建造,前雇员狮子大开口要求原告支付一笔额外的遣散费,否则就要罢工。而一旦罢工,工程会被拖延可能赶不上展会,这会让 Victor Green 面对严重的商誉损失与巨额索赔。于是 Victor Green 知道工人要求额外的遣散费与威胁罢工而 B&S 现金流有问题后,向 B&S 提出提前支付 4500 英镑的工程费。但 B&S 起初听错了,以为 Victor Green 在合约的工程费上去多支付 4500 英镑,表示自己愿意另掏出 4500 英镑,凑够 9000 英镑满足工人的要求。但在进一步澄清下,B&S 才知道 Victor Green 只是"预付"不是"多付"后,就表示不接受预付的提议。最终 Victor Green 屈服,支付了 4500 英镑,但在工程完毕后,Victor

Green 在工程费尾款中扣下 4500 英镑。于是 B& S 开始诉讼追讨欠款，而 Victor Green 主张是这 4500 英镑是在经济胁迫下支付的。一审与上诉庭均判是胁迫，虽然 B& S 没有直说，但是默示或是隐蔽地威胁了如果 Victor Green 不拿出这笔钱，就不会继续履行合约，这提出的是错误与不合理（当时还是这个标准）要求。从该先例的案情也可以看出法律水平高与保留对自己有利的证据的重要性。法院判存在非法压力时，非常依赖 Victor Green 说的“你让我别无选择”。此外，合约中有一条不可抗力条文，其中包括罢工。因此如果 B&S 在之前谈判时以此作为停工的依据，而不是在诉讼时才提出，即使最终不被法院支持，认为不能依赖该不可抗力条文，也很有可能被法院认定谈判时 B& S 并非恶意要求，而是想与 Victor Green 共同解决目前的困难。[37]

另外在本章之 7.2.1.2 段介绍的 DSND Subsea Ltd v. Petroleum Geo-Services ASA（2000）BLR 530 先例中，涉及的压力是中止工作的违约行为，[38]但考虑到提出的要求（及时解决一个重大事故）被认为是完全公平合理而非错误，最后综合认定不是不法/不恰当压力，不构成经济胁迫。

7. 不法行为的威胁

近期的 PIAC v. Times Travel（2021）UKSC 40 最高院先例将不法/不恰当压力（illegitimate pressure）分成两大类型来讨论：一类是不法行为（unlawful act）造成的不法压力（unlawful pressure），另一类则是本身威胁合法（lawful threat）但由于以此施加压力要求是错误的（wrongful demand）因此综合来看属于不法/不恰当压力的情况。在下文中也将按这两部分，并结合刚刚谈到的这些需要考虑的因素分别进行讨论。

7.1 犯罪或侵权的威胁属于不法压力

一般而言如果威胁涉及的是犯罪（crime）或侵权（tort），基本上都会属于不法压力。犯罪行为与侵权行为的定义也非常广泛，在现实社会一些过火的威胁也经常会发生。

威胁犯罪包括各种类型的犯罪，可以是十分严重的如 Barton v. Armstrong（1976）AC 104 先例中以杀人为威胁。有说法是如果施压方的威胁是构成刑事犯罪，而并非仅为民事错误（civil wrong）时，就严重得多，不再需要考虑受压方是否有其他合理选择。

民事范畴的侵权行为包括各种类型的侵权（如对人身的侵权或很多不同种类的经济侵权、欺诈、误述、恶意诉讼、串谋侵权等）。本章之 3 段提到的 The “Siboen” and The “Sibotre”（1976）1 Lloyd’s Rep 293 先例以欺诈性误述进行威胁就足以构成

---

〔37〕 见本章之 7.2.2 段。

〔38〕 见笔者《合约的履行、弃权与禁反言》一书第一章之 3.10 段。

非法的压力。

本章之3段提到的 The "Universe Sentinel"(1983)1 AC 366先例涉及的是被立法免责的侵权行为,类似案情即方便旗船舶在西方国家被国际运输工人公会(International Transport Workers Federation,以下简称ITF)抵制装卸,要求船东额外付钱的先例还有不少。例如,The "Evia Luck"(1992)2 AC 152贵族院先例中,船舶在瑞典港口因为遇上抵制装卸,导致船东与ITF签订协议(包括定期向ITF支付会费等)。这些抵制装卸行为在瑞典法下其实是受到当地法律保护的合法行为。但由于协议约定适用英国法,因此英国法院就以英国法来判断ITF的抵制行为是否属于不法压力(而不是根据行为所在地法律判断是否"合法"),而在协议适用法/准据法即英国法下抵制(boycott)船舶行为无论是在英国还是其他地方,都可以被认为是不法压力与构成胁迫,因此最终给出肯定答案,协议被撤销以及要求ITF归还船东之前支付的金钱。Goff勋爵说:"Accordingly in the present case we look to English law,as the proper law,to discover whether the contract may,as a matter of principle,be affected by duress and,if so,what constitutes duress for this purpose;what impact such duress must have exercised upon the formation of the contract;and what remedial action is available to the innocent party. We know,of course,that by English law a contract induced by duress is voidable by the innocent party;and that one form of duress is illegitimate economic pressure,including the blacking or the threat of blacking of a ship. I can see **no reason in principle why,prima facie at least,blacking or the threat of blacking a ship should not constitute duress** for this purpose,wherever it is committed-whether within the English jurisdiction or overseas;for in point of fact its impact upon the contract does not depend upon the place where the relevant conduct occurs."(加黑部分是笔者的强调)

7.2 威胁违约是否为不法/不恰当压力

以犯罪或侵权行为进行威胁时,构成不法压力一般没什么问题。但已经在本章之6.1段提到,普通法下威胁违约(threaten breach of contract)也通常是不法/不恰当行为:见 Kolmar Group AG v. Traxpo Enterprises Pvt Ltd(2010)EWHC 113(Comm);The "Cenk Kaptanoglu"(2012)EWHC 273(Comm)等先例。

但也要看看施加压力是否应受谴责与不合情理,显然不能每一次威胁说我不干了,就变成不法压力。毕竟违约方难逃赔偿损失的"次要义务",在"有效益违约"的说法下,违约方说明将把无辜方恢复到合约被履行的经济地位,并马上作出部分支付以表诚意,就不像有不法或不恰当压力的味道。

另在某些存在法律争议,如合约受阻或不可抗力条文等争议,双方各持己见,不去或无法履行下去。最后败诉方X的坚持己见即使错误,也难说死是不法/不恰当压力。毕竟,不同案件都会有自己的特殊情况与事实。例如,X曾经坚持说不干了,而同时建议Y去合作马上取得法院或仲裁庭命令或宣示,但被Y拒绝;或是,X在一审胜诉,只是在后来的上诉被技术上推翻;等。反正在这种各自有不同事实的案情下,是难说 X 的坚持,虽然最后被认定违约,是不法/不恰当压力。

问题是每一个不同案件的案情,何时构成不法/不恰当压力,何时是合法压力的分水岭或红线如何划分?例如:(1)卖方 X,在如市场价格飙升时,提出说除非买方 Y 的对价(买卖合约规定的货物价格)加倍,否则不会供货。(2)另一个极端会是,X 坦率向 Y 说明因为某些内部原因而无法再履行合约,合约有针对性的"议定赔偿条文"(liquidated damage clause)并建议支付该笔款项,以取得 Y 同意提前终止合约。(3)更常见的是 X 与 Y 对事实或法律地位有争议,可以是 X 坚持说我认为合约应该如何解释(但其实是错误理解),所以无须履行某些燃眉之急的事情,但 Y 有不同理解。这导致 X 与 Y 的争议要按约定的仲裁条文解决。但这需要时间,所以 X 与 Y 更现实的是通过谈判并最后达成如何过渡或甚是终局的解决办法。客观看 X 的坚持有理有据,公平合理,因为争议涉及一个完全可争议的案件(arguable case)。(4)在(3)的情况下,在谈判过程中,X 觉察 Y 很需要 X 的让步去马上履行,所以乘机提出苛刻的条件,甚至是与双方争议无关的好处。

反正最后 Y 在抗议下(或没有异议下)接受 X 的要求并达成新的更改合约(还会涉及法律鼓励与支持双方尽量对争议和解的公共政策)去替代原合约。但后来事过境迁,觉得吃了亏的 Y 反悔,就带来该新合约可否以 X 的胁迫而可使无效?但显然在上述举的少数例子,已明显看到 X 在与 Y 谈判中的做法(即提出要求所作出的威胁与施加的压力),可以是合情合理,也有完全不当与不可接受的情况。

在过往先例中出现了针对"合法"或"不法/不恰当"的判断标准与考虑因素非常多不同的说法,有说法认为英国法院在判断威胁违约是否属于施加不法/不恰当压力时,会综合考虑这些所有有关因素进行判断。对此可节录《Duress, Undue Influence and Unconscionable Dealing》(2019 年,第 3 版)一书之 3-004 段所说如下:"A number of tests have been suggested as the key to determining whether a threatened breach of contract is illegitimate. **One** is whether the defendant is threatening to breach the contract because he is unable to perform it due to circumstances of his own making, as opposed to a warning that because of a change in circumstances not due to his fault, he is unable to perform as agreed. A **second** test is whether the threat was made in bad faith. A **third** is whether the agreement resulting from the threat is substantively unfair. **However**, it has been argued that **no single test can reconcile all the English cases on the point**. It is submitted that this is because the cases are not based on a single test, but rather on a wider approach which involves a number of factors. Each test seeks to capture an important aspect of the features the court should be concerned with. So, each has its proper place, but none is comprehensive. **The approach adopted by the English courts is a wider one** that takes each test into account as one of a number of factors, rather than as a single touchstone that is alone decisive. According to this wider approach, **the factors that the courts take into account when deciding whether a particular threat to break a con-**

tract is illegitimate includes: whether **the demand is made because of a significant change in circumstances** affecting performance of the contract; whether the threat is made to support **a demand that is reasonable** in the circumstances and whether the **demand is made in good faith**."(加黑部分是笔者的强调)

以上提到了三个不同的主要因素的测试标准与考虑:(1)是否确实发生了并非由于施压方导致与合约没有明确针对的严重突发事件/情况变化,让施压方无路可走履行不下去?(2)施压方的威胁是否存在"恶意"?例如,是否是乘人之危,明知对方非接受不可。(3)最后达成的更改合约是否公平合理?

法院并不是死板地根据任何一个主要因素得出结论,而会根据具体案情考虑大量的所有其他因素后进行分析与平衡,才决定施压方的压力是否"不法/不恰当"。

接下来区别进一步探讨这三个主要因素。

7.2.1　考虑因素之一:是否发生严重突发事件/情况变化让施压方履行不下去或十分困难

尤其是在中、长期合约履约中途可能发生严重突发事件/情况变化(serious change of circumstances)导致合约履行不下去,合约没有明确把风险分摊给合约的履约方(承建商、承运人等),也不涉及履约方的过错。即使勉强履行下去,也将带来各种其他严重的问题,例如原本预计的工期会有延误,这对双方而言都不是好事。所以履约方干脆停工并试图找对方寻找变通办法与合约更改,期间履约方(或施压方)并没有向对方做出过火的言行,仅仅是多次提醒对方不解决问题对双方都没有好处。

7.2.1.1　在合约中已经预见与分摊风险或风险是履约方自己的过错导致

外部营商环境往往风平浪静,但仍会出现这种施压方以违约或威胁违约向受压方要求更改合约与让步的情况。原因通常是施压方在订约时算错账、合约条件对其不利、施压方对整个交易安排不妥善等。如本章之7.2段提到的卖方X在市场价格飙升时(如因为货物短缺上涨了20%)提出除非买方Y对价(买卖合约规定的货物价格)加倍,否则不会供货,这就是典型的例子。

这背后导致的原因不外是如下几点:(1)有关市场飙升的风险已经在买卖合约分摊给了卖方;(2)施压方可以试图把这完全可预期的市场风险在合约以明示条文转嫁给对方;(3)市场变化让施压方多花钱,赚钱变亏本不是可以令合约受阻,[39]更不可以在订约后才试图把亏的钱转嫁给对方,甚至借机敲一笔;(4)市场飙升的是生产货物的原材料,如建造的船舶所需要的钢材市场飙升而令成本大涨。这里会涉及卖方(船厂)的过错与整个安排有疏漏,例如没有及时以对冲或预先订下供应合约把主要的原材料价格稳定下来;等等。

可以说上述原因都不是真正意义上的"严重突发事件/情况变化"。在《Duress, Undue Influence and Unconscionable Dealing》(2019年,第3版)一书之3-005段说到

---

〔39〕 见《合约的履行、弃权与禁反言》一书第二章之7.4段。

在三种情况下不是“严重突发事件/情况变化”,说:“Changed circumstances that could justify a threat to breach a contract will occur only in rare cases. It will not be enough where the circumstances:(a) were foreseen and the risk allocated in the contract;or(b) although unanticipated at the time of the contract, are self-induced;or(c) do not affect the defendant's performance in a sufficiently serious manner.”

以上节录内容中所说这些“严重突发事件/情况变化”很少见、不会轻易让威胁违约合法化的三点因素也很容易理解:(1)风险是否已经被预见,在合约中是否已经分摊了风险,这就不是“突发情况”。双方在你情我愿下分摊了风险,施压方就不应在发生了风险后再找理由或借口不履行合约向对方施压,重新分摊风险。施压方如果仍刻意(或无知)向受压方威胁违约,就难以说是合情合理与合法。(2)确实没有预料到,但是情况变化本就是因为施压方自己行为所导致,此时施压方再威胁违约就会被认为属于不法压力。这也是配合法律的大原则,订约方不能从自己的错误行为中获利。[40] (3)情况变化必须非常严重到实际影响施压方履行合约的能力,在受阻理论[41]与可诉错误理论[42]中也有同样与一致的要件。这也很好理解,如果任何一点轻微的情况变化都允许施压方可以随便威胁违约、拿到更多利益是说不通的。

这样,如果履约方/施压方以违约或威胁违约(如停止继续履行)逼迫对方就难逃是不法/不恰当压力了。

有大量威胁违约被判属于不法/不恰当压力的先例,在本章中也介绍了多个此类先例中,例如本章之5.3.1段介绍的The “Alev”(1989)1 Lloyd's Rep 138先例中运费预付提单下船东威胁不将货物运送到卸港;本章之10.4段介绍的Adam Opel GmbH v. Mitras Automotive UK Ltd(2007) EWHC 3205(QB)先例中汽车零件供应商断供;本章之12.2.1.1段介绍的Kolmar Group AG v. Traxpo Enterprises Pvt Ltd(2010) EWHC 113(Comm)先例中买卖合约下的卖方在市场价格飙升时威胁拒绝供货等。在此只多提以下先例:

1. 在TA Sundell & Sons Pty Ltd v. Emm Yannoulatos(Overseas) Pty Ltd(1956)56 SR(NSW)323澳大利亚先例中,被告是矿产供应链中的一个商人,根据合约按双方约定的价格向后续的买方销售矿产。但之后矿产市场价格飙升,被告就表示希望加价,否则自己无法供应矿产。甚至为了表示诚意可以让买方来查看自己的账目,显示自己的加价完全合理。这仍然被法院判决属于不法压力,构成经济胁迫。

2. 在The “Atlantic Baron”(1979)1 Lloyd's Rep 89先例中,涉及的是作为原告的船东与作为被告的韩国现代船厂签订了一个油轮造船合约,合约价格以美元计价

---

〔40〕 解释合约时,假设订约方不能从自己的错误行为中获利,见《合约的解释:规则与应用》一书第四章之10段。

〔41〕 见《合约的履行、弃权与禁反言》一书第二章之7.3段。

〔42〕 见本书第七章之8段。

与分期付款。在建造过程中,美元出现了10%的大幅贬值,船厂提出除非船东同意提高10%的造价,否则就要终止合约。当时船东正与壳牌石油公司协商一个非常赚钱的油轮租船合约,很希望船舶尽快建造完成,因此在电文中同意了船厂的要求。但电文加上了"无损害我们的权利"(without prejudice to our rights)的条件,这也被仲裁庭认定是船厂未警惕这个保留条款。船东为了不得罪船厂,不敢说得更明白用"抗议下(同意支付)"(under protest)的措辞/文字,因为害怕船厂不会接受有条件的同意。

在后来支付的分期付款中,船东也确实提高了10%。而在接收船舶后,船东不再有压力,马上就开始诉讼要求拿回自己额外支付的10%。

在造船合约中,最后造价的美元汇率下跌,而船舶造价如船厂的成本(包括工资、原材料等)都是韩元或其他货币,这样船厂能赚取的利润从微利要变成亏本了。这固然是不幸的情况,但合约中双方同意与选择采用美元计价已经把汇率的风险默示分摊给了船厂。从另一角度看,就是如果美元汇率大涨,相信船厂也不会自觉把这笔意外之财与船东分享。再说,现在也有很多衍生品工具可减免这种风险,或在一些成本建造中主要的合约(如钢材的供应合约)中针对性做出保障(如也以美元计价)等。

3. 在 Atlas Express Ltd v. Kafco (Importers and Distributors) Ltd (1989) QB 833 先例中,原告是一家运输公司,被告是一家提供篮子的小供应商。被告与当时英国零售巨头(Woolworths)签订供应合约,并与原告签订协议由原告提供运输服务。但是原告拖车到了被告门口时,告诉被告除非加价否则就要拒绝履行。法院认定当时原告知道被告必须得及时送货才能保障自己的业务能做下去,而且被告在当时的情况很难及时找到替代的运输商。因此虽然当时被告答应会支付额外金钱,但这构成不法压力,被法院判定为经济胁迫,合约无效。

4. 在 Carillion Construction Ltd v. Felix (UK) Ltd (2001) BLR 1 先例中,原告承建一项工程,部分工程项目被分包给被告。被告有分包工期延误的违约行为,导致整个项目的完工时间已经非常接近原告向业主承诺的工期。被告在知道这情况后,就威胁说自己工期可能进一步延误要求拿到更多好处,这威胁违约就被认为属于不法压力。

7.2.1.2 发生合约无法预见的严重突发事件/情况变化

威胁违约一般都是不法/不恰当压力,但遇上订约时"无法预见"(unforeseeable)也不是任何一方过错的突发事件/情况变化就是例外。这道理也容易理解。遇上这种情况,履行受影响一方也不是想要违约/毁约、拒绝履行,只是按照原来的预期履行非常困难,需要重启谈判,以解决此问题。而对方合约方也想要合约继续履行,此时双方经过谈判与协商达成新合约合情合理、情有可原。例如建造工程中,合约约定分包商需要使用的特定标准的材料因为突发事件缺货,分包商与总承建商就需要谈判解决问题,要么延长完工时间、等待市场上货物恢复供应后继续保证质量,要么就接受采用市场上有现货的另一套较低标准的材料但可以保证工期。分包商无法按合约约定标准继续建造,本身也可争辩并非违约/毁约行为(如可能属于不可抗力条文)。这样,分包商作为施压方向总承建商谈判与协商。而看是什么工程(如建造足球世界杯的足球场或是重要与长期使用的基础设施),对于总承建商(与背后的雇主)而言,可能是保障工期顺利完工比质量更重要,或是反过来,工程质量是重要得多。反正在最后达成的更改合约,施压方也获得了满意的解决方案,如约定等待市场供应恢复或以合约规定的另一个进口与昂贵的材料替代,另多支付施压方工程费用与放弃工程延误的损失赔偿等。这样的新合约就是情有可原的了,总承建商也不能成功事后反悔。

但难免在谈判的过程中,各自用上惯常的谈判技巧,履约方可能采取了过火、激烈的威胁,但也可能没有过火的言行,只是说合约难以履行下去,或即使勉强履行下去,也带来各种其他问题,对双方而言都不是好事,所以必须寻找变通办法或更改合约。如果履约方言行不过火,会被审理法官(或仲裁庭)客观上认为是"善意"与"完全合理与情有可原"的威胁与施压。毕竟在威胁时,施压方或受压方都是心里没底,毕竟不可控的严重突发事件/情况变化在合约条文中没有明确针对,到底会是什么法律地位也是未知数。所以受影响的施压方威胁说无法履行下去会是善意或至少不是恶意,也难以质疑,毕竟在谈判时拒绝履行合约的做法可能最后在法律上是站得住脚的。

这类"无法预见"的情况在现实看来也应该是不多,接近合约受阻的突发事件本就不多。众所周知在普通法重点支持合约有效性与肯定性态度下,受阻令合约自动终止很难成立。由于不少中、长期合约都会加进一条不可抗力条文(force majeure clause)或履行困难条文(hardship clause),内容中列出一长串双方控制不了与无法精准预测的将来可能发生的突发事件/情况变化,如战争、政府/法律干预、地震、火山爆发、不可预见的坏天气等。可以说,这种是可以预见的,但合约不明确、完整、清楚与足以分摊风险,仍不阻止受阻理论的适用。[43] 正如《Chitty on Contracts》(2021 年,第 34 版)一书之 26 - 090 段的脚注中说:"Many events are foreseeable but neither party assumes the risk of their occurrence. Death is the classic example. The death of an employee during the currency of his employment contract is a foreseeable event but it operates to discharge the contract of employment because neither party assumes the risk of its occurrence."

履行时发生了严重的情况改变是无法预见或是双方在订约时根本没有想到与合约没有针对的,本质上更会是接近"共同错误"[44](只是本章针对的事件发生在履约期间而不是订约前)下双方不知道或错误理解了订约时的严重影响合约的事实与/

---

〔43〕 见《合约的履行、弃权与禁反言》一书第二章之 7.2.2 段。

〔44〕 见本书第七章之 13 段。

或法律地位。只是相比共同错误下想让合约自始无效(void ab initio),此时双方都希望继续履行合约,也已经在履行的半途了,所以进行谈判与协商以达成更改的新合约。这种做法合情合理、情有可原,但难免在谈判的过程中,各自用上惯常的谈判技巧,主要履约方会违约或威胁违约也是难免。

在少有的违约与威胁违约但不被认定为不法/不恰当压力的 DSND Subsea Ltd v. Petroleum Geo-Services ASA(2000)BLR 530 先例中,案情涉及 DSND 为 PGS 建设某海底工程项目,由 PGS 提供特定部件,再由 DSND 负责安装。履行中途发现该部件在还从来没有进行过本应进行的海底测试时就需要马上安装,但这样的做法带来了额外的安装花费,也有更高的安装风险与可能带来严重后果。这是双方在订立合约时都没有预见到的,合约也没有明示或默示分摊了这个风险或情况。例如,PGS 没有在合约中保证(或误述)有关海底有否进行过测试,当然 DSND 也没有问,因为预见不到在稍后的履行中会有此技术上的问题。

面对此严重问题,DSND 暂缓安装,要求 PGS 重新讨论保险与补偿,双方也签订了更改与补充原合约的一份谅解备忘录(MOU),重新约定有关事宜。但 DSND 暂缓或停止履行合约在英国法律下是违约行为,正如 Dyson 大法官说:"The Contract did not contain a provision which entitled DSND to suspend work. The Contract simply did not make provision for a situation such as occurred. ... I would say that the suspension of work on the RTIAs(特定部件)pending resolution of the insurance/indemnity question,... it was a breach of contract..."

事件过后,PGS 就提出根据原合约条文 DSND 无权暂缓安装,自己签订 MOU 是因为受到 DSND 暂缓安装的不法压力,应该给予胁迫的救济。但 Dyson 大法官从案件的所有因素综合来看,不认同 DSND 的违约行为构成不法/不恰当压力。原因包括了在本章之 7.2 段提到的三个主要因素,即本段介绍的合约履行面对了在合约订立时无法预见也没有针对的严重突发事件/情况变化,在后两段还会区别介绍施压方 DSND 的压力被认定是善意,和 DSND 提出的要求与订立的 MOU 是公平合理的。

另一个例子是在 McIntyre v. Nemesis DBK Ltd(2009)NZCA 329 新西兰先例中,双方约定共同开发一片土地,并委任被告作为经理人负责申请批文、管理与开发等工作,但是在开发过程中遇上了当地政府处理有关工作的人士的消极对待与不配合。这样就导致开发工作远远超出了双方订约时的预期,而给被告的报酬相比于工作远远不够。此时被告反复要求加薪并且威胁说撂挑子不干了,但这威胁违约的行为就没有被视为不法压力。

这道理在 R v. Attorney General for England and Wales(2003)UKPC 22 枢密院先例的新西兰一审(HC AK CP 641/98 6 December 2000)中也有体现,Salmon 大法官提到说:"There are **no definitive criteria for determining whether pressure is legitimate or illegitimate**. The criterion most commonly resorted to is that of 'awfulness'. Thus, where the pressure consists of an unlawful act or a threat to commit an unlawful act, then prima facie the pressure is illegitimate. Although the criterion of lawfulness is useful, it cannot be definitive. If it were, the inquiry would be directed to the lawfulness of the pressure rather than to its legitimacy. It follows that **some instances of unlawful pressure may be legitimate and that some instances of lawful pressure may be illegitimate**. An example of the former might be **a party's threat to break a contract when a change in circumstances beyond their control has meant that they are genuinely unable to perform**…."(加黑部分是笔者的强调)

7.2.2 考虑因素之二:施压方的威胁是否存在恶意

过往有先例将施压方是善意还是恶意纳入考虑范畴。例如在施压方威胁违约后,受压方妥协与让步达成原合约的更改,但事后反悔以自己是由于施压方的违约或威胁违约行为而受到不法/不恰当压力所导致,要求撤销更改合约。但也有较罕见的案件,在认定所有有关事实后判违约或威胁违约不构成不法/不恰当压力,所以并不是经济胁迫。以下可以介绍两个这方面的先例:

1. 在 Huyton SA v. Peter Cremer GmbH & Co(1999)1 Lloyd's Rep 620 先例中,案情涉及一票 FOB 货物买卖,卖方(Peter Cremer)销售一批小麦给买方(Huyton),双方同意以托收(Cash Against Documents)方式付款,买方应当在卖方交齐一系列文件后支付货款。而买方(实是分买方)实际上也已经在苏丹港以"无单放货"收到与接收了货物(小麦),但在支付方面买方认为卖方提供的文件有多处不符而拒付。卖方主张买方的收货行为默示放弃了拒绝文件的权利,而买方则主张未能提供符合买卖合约约定要求的文件无须支付货款,卖方坚持不提交或无法提交文件是违约/毁约行为。后来双方都主张对方行为属于违约/毁约,也根据合约约定的争议解决方式开始了伦敦仲裁。在仲裁中途双方达成协议,买方会根据卖方提供的文件付款,但卖方需要放弃一切针对买方的船舶装港滞期费等费用索赔。在买方支付货款后,卖方马上主张买方拒绝支付的行为是实际或威胁违约/毁约的不法行为,自己签订和解协议是受到经济胁迫。

在此先例中,Mance 大法官指出法律大原则确实是要保护双方当事人善意达成的和解协议。但如果一方(如买方)根本不认为自己有可争辩案件,就是恶意拒绝支付,这就根本不能算作真正的达成和解。另一方面即使是买方善意真实相信自己地位,也仍然有可能属于不法压力。Mance 大法官说:"**The law** will of course **be cautious about re-opening an apparent compromise made in good faith on both sides**. But it seems, on the one hand, questionable whether a 'compromise' achieved by one party who does not believe that he had at least an arguable case is a compromise at all — though it may be upheld if there is other consideration…; and, on the other hand, **difficult to accept that illegitimate pressure applied by a party who believes bona fide in his case could never give grounds for relief against an apparent compromise.**"(加黑部分是笔者的强调)

最后针对此先例中的情况，Mance 大法官认为买卖合约下是在卖方提交恰当的文件后买方才有付款义务，即使买方已经取货也不改变此合约的约定。固然如果卖方确实无法提交恰当文件导致没有获得支付，卖方可以要求买方归还产权仍属于自己的货物，而此先例没有证据显示买方（或分买方）无法归还货物，这仍然是做得到的。因此在客观看买方有站得住脚的拒付理由，双方在仲裁中途达成的和解协议有对价，也看不出买方有恶意（并不真实相信自己有可争辩的案件），法律应当保护和解协议。再说，卖方签订和解协议时也不是没有其他合理选择，例如把伦敦仲裁推进下去并取得最后裁决。

2. 另在本章之上一段介绍的 DSND Subsea Ltd v. Petroleum Geo-Services ASA（2000）BLR 530 先例中，Dyson 大法官就指出即使原合约下 DSND 暂缓安装的行为属于违约/威胁违约，但 DSND 的行为完全是情有可原的善意行为，并不属于不法压力。Dyson 大法官说："The Contract did not contain a provision which entitled DSND to suspend work. The Contract simply did not make provision for a situation such as occurred. If it were necessary so to hold, I would say that the suspension of work … pending resolution of the insurance/indemnity question, **even if it was a breach of contract, and even if it amounted to pressure, did not amount to illegitimate pressure. It was reasonable behaviour by a contractor acting bona fide in a very difficult situation.**"（加黑部分是笔者的强调）

所以《Duress, Undue Influence and Unconscionable Dealing》（2019 年，第 3 版）一书之 3-010 到 3-011 段就提到施压方威胁违约，这威胁是善意或恶意是考虑有否成立的经济胁迫的因素之一，说："There is now a line of cases holding that **good or bad faith is relevant factor in determining whether a threat to breach a contract is illegitimate**… Good or bad faith is not the single test which alone determines whether or not a threat is illegitimate. It is only one of a number of factors to be considered by the court in assessing the illegitimacy of a threat to breach a contract. Thus a threatened breach of contract **may constitute duress even though it was made in good faith**…"

众所周知在英国合约法中没有"善意"的说法，但这也不代表英国法在个别类别的合约或行为没有善意的要求，如关系合约（relational contract）、行使合约的裁量权（exercise of discretion）与投标（tenders）等。[45] 所以法律对善意并不是一片空白。

是否构成胁迫不是以施压方意图或动机为标准的主观测试（subjective test）。毕竟无论施压方背后的意图或动机如何，受压方感受到的压力是一样的，就是施压方不履行合约的承诺。现实也常会是施压方主观认为自己的做法（施加压力与提出的要求）合情合理与善意，但实是对法律的无知（如不知道对有关风险分摊的默示地位、合约承诺与履行是严格责任等）。施压方自以为有可争辩的理由，也不向称职律师

---

[45] 见本书第一章之 2.6 段与笔者《合约的解释：规则与应用》一书第九章的详细介绍。

咨询,就向受压方以威胁违约施加压力,即使是自己真实相信的善意,也无济于事。对法律无知并不是理由,特别在法律已假设了国际商业人士有同等水平与知识的情况下。在判断是否构成违约/毁约行为时采用客观测试(objective test):见 The "Nanfri "(1978)2 Lloyd's Rep 132 贵族院先例中,不法/不恰当压力更是如此。

根据本章之 5.4.1.3 与 7.2 与本段的介绍,从客观判断以违约或威胁违约施加压力会出现"善意"或至少不是"恶意"的情况会是有一些重要的指引,如:(1)本章之 7.2.1 段的介绍,是否真正发生严重突发事件/情况变化,而令双方需要寻找变通办法与更改合约。(2)谈判期间,履约方并没有过火的言行,或主要只是陈述自己的困难情况,或在充分考虑双方的共同利益下提出建议、解决办法。另外,施压方在谈判时不要误述,这会是欺诈性误述,会有可令更改合约无效的后患。(3)提出的要求与达成的更改合约(或和解协议)看来公平合理,如主要针对当前困难的解决,不涉及让施压方乘人之危在其他方面获利。另外,撇开足够或是否属于真正的对价问题,但从结果来看对受压方肯定有或多或少的实际好处。

但"善意"本质上是一个泛泛的理念,仍然存在不肯定之处,包括善意与恶意明确的界限,如何衡量善意/恶意与其他因素之间的权重也非常模糊。而且于违约或威胁违约(本身就是表面证据显示是不法/不恰当压力),施压方就需要有很有说服力的证据去显示不是恶意而是善意了。有关这善意或恶意的考虑因素与不肯定,最后可节录《Chitty on Contract》(2021 年,第 34 版)一书之 10 - 054 段作为小结:"It is thus difficult to state with confidence whether a threat of a breach of contract will ever be regarded as legitimate and,if so,in what circumstances. It is submitted that deliberate exploitation of the victim's position with a view to gaining some advantage,particularly one unrelated to the contract and to which the threatening party knows he is not entitled is clearly illegitimate. At the other end of the scale,an apparent threat should not be treated as illegitimate if it was really no more than a true statement that,unless the demand is met,the party making it will be unable to perform. The difficult case is that of the party who has a genuine belief that he is entitled to the amount demanded. It is submitted that by analogy to the cases in which it has been held that there is consideration for a compromise of a claim which is in fact bound to fail if the party making the claim honestly and reasonably believed in its validity,a party who honestly and not unreasonably believes that he has a legal claim is not acting in bad faith by demanding what he thinks is due. A court should hesitate to find that the demand was illegitimate. It is also suggested that a demand made in good faith in the sense that the party demanding has a genuine belief in the moral strength of his claim-for example,because he has encountered serious and unexpected difficulties in performing and will suffer considerable hardship if his demand is not met;or to correct an acknowledged imbalance in the existing contract-may in some circumstances also be treated as legitimate."

7.2.3 考虑因素之三:达成的更改合约是否公平合理

已经在本章之6.4段提到了压力的不法性不仅仅看威胁本身的性质,也要结合要求是否错误/公平合理来看待。因此不难想到在威胁违约的情况中,施压方要求的到底是什么也是考虑因素之一。例如在DSND Subsea Ltd v. Petroleum Geo-Services ASA(2000)BLR 530先例中,在出现当事人没有预料到的突发事件后,DSND提出的重新协调合约没有针对的费用与保险的要求被认为是完全合理,不属于不法压力。

作为对比则可见B&S Contracts and Design Ltd v. Victor Green Publications Ltd (1984)ICR 419先例。该先例的案情已经在本章之6.4段介绍,只说法院判B& S要求多支付4,500英镑的行为远远偏离公平合理,此先例中的威胁违约也被认定属于不法压力。

对于"走出去"的中国公司而言,也要能够判断什么是合理要求。因为是否合理的判断标准,是国际商业规则中客观看待的合理。这套规则与中国法的做法在大方向上类似,但具体细节上存在不少差异。例如,国际上更强调意思自治与合约的肯定性,但中国法会强调当事人道德上的善意与允许事后由法院更改当事人的合约等。又例如在民事案件中,针对误述、假文件等问题,如何设定系统性、明确与稳定的标准还在发展之中。

7.2.4 陈述自己的困难情况和威胁违约

在合约履行过程中,由于客观情况的变化(如市场价格或需求的变动)导致一方履行困难的情况屡见不鲜。很常见的是,履行困难的一方寻求对方的谅解,对如何继续履行合约进行谈判,而如果能够达成和解协议或更改原合约,并且双方继续按新的做法履行显然是理想的。如果对方不同意和解或更改,或者同意了和解或更改,但事后提出存在不法行为(威胁违约)胁迫想要撤销,就会带来麻烦了。

综合来看,施压方此时在语境下表达的是什么意思就显得非常重要。在本章之7.2段中已经多次提到言行不应该"过火"与需要有水平掌握轻重。如果谈判过程中的意思客观来看是以违约作为威胁,就很可能是不法行为。但如果纯粹是陈述履行合约的困难事实,请求对方的宽限进行谈判,客观来看并不是在"威胁"对方,就可能不属于胁迫。这不仅仅是用了什么措辞/文字,而要看整体的事实背景与语境。

在Williams v. Roffey Bros & Nicholls(Contractors)Ltd(1991)1 QB 1先例[46]中,建造合约的分包商低估了一些工作的价格,因此很可能无法根据合约约定的时间完成工作。而总承建商为了确保总的建造不发生延误,主动允诺与同意支付更多金钱,以避免自己因延误而要向业主支付高昂的议定赔偿或者是为了保证自己在业界的名声。此时如果分包商说除非加钱,否则就会继续拖延工期或干脆不干了,这就会被认为是威胁而导致属于胁迫。但此先例中加钱的要求实际上是总承建商在了解情况后,为了保证工期自己提出的,最后也没有被认定是不法压力的威胁违约。

---

〔46〕 此先例可见《合约的履行、弃权与禁反言》一书第三章之2.4.3.3段有介绍。

在 DSND Subsea Ltd v. Petroleum Geo-Services ASA(2000) BLR 530 先例中,根据原合约条文,DSND 无权暂缓安装有关设备,因此如果 DSND 在谈判时坚持除非有保险或补偿,否则自己不会开工,这就会属于施加不法压力。但是法院根据谈判前后的书面记录,以及双方会面交谈时的证人证言,综合事实后认定 DSND 并没有给出任何这样压迫性的措辞文字,双方纯粹是为了共同的利益考虑如何解决问题,协商的气氛也非常融洽。DSND 只不过是出于对于额外的花费与风险的合理担心而暂缓安装。实际上合约当事人也是自愿重新约定了新合约。Dyson 大法官说:"The question of compensation had been the subject of negotiations since late July. Work on the riser installation was about to begin. It was clearly in the interests of both parties that this matter be resolved as soon as possible. I do not accept that DSND told PGS at the meeting of 24th or 25th that they would not resume work on the RTIAs until the compensation issue was resolved. That would clearly have been a flagrant breach of contract, and, if pressure, it would in my view have been illegitimate pressure. Mr Hirsti(DSND 的证人,当时代表 DSND 进行协商)said that he knew that DSND had no right to suspend work for such a reason. It is significant that the suspension of work was limited to the RTIA assembly. That is explicable if the reason for it was the concern about going offshore without a resolution of the insurance/indemnity problem. It is not reasonably explicable if the reason for suspension of work was the desire to put pressure on PGS to meet DSND's demands for compensation."

这里能看到证据的重要性。一些精明狡猾的商人会在文件中仅仅陈述自己的困难,措辞上从不过火,但通过电话或见面以口头沟通进行威胁,并事后在诉讼(或仲裁)中否认给出过任何威胁。受压方如果没有及时对通话录音,就会没有足够证据证明胁迫。所以受压方要保存证据,最好是事后马上通过当场文件对通话内容进行重述,自己是抗议之下接受对方要求等。这样有白纸黑字的文件证明,就有更大机会向法院/仲裁庭说明当时发生的情况与对方采取的威胁行为,而不至于最后输掉官司。

8. 合法行为的威胁

8.1 合法行为构成不法/不恰当压力

合法行为(lawful act)一般而言是不会构成不法压力(illegitimate pressure),任何人士坚持维护自己的法律权利与地位没有什么不妥。例如买卖双方价格谈不拢,就不能强买强卖。或是在合约的履行中有了争议,一方向另一方提起仲裁。

另一种情况的例子,就是合法扣船[47]后,船东提供担保或其他方式解除扣船,事后显然不能说合法扣船属于胁迫,而要求撤回担保等。早在 Liverpool Marine Credit Co v. Hunter(1868)LR 3 Ch. App. 479 先例中,Chelmsford 大法官说:"… if a man pays money or gives securities(which is the same thing in effect)to redeem his goods from the custody of the law, that is not a case of duress, nor can he recover back his money or defend himself from proceedings taken to enforce the securities which he has paid or given under legal compulsion."

在传统上不法压力才能构成胁迫,虽然这些年来胁迫理论一直在不断扩张,但如果扩张到合法行为都能构成不法压力,会带来不稳定并不可预测,毕竟这会否认双方达成的表面看来你情我愿的合约。合法行为的压力实际上无处不在,如果任意扩张就难以划出清楚、合情合理的分水岭。也因此一些其他普通法国家或地区的判决拒绝将经济胁迫延伸到合法行为:见澳大利亚的 Australia and New Zealand Banking Group Ltd v. Karam(2005)NSWCA 344 先例。

为了给商业社会带来普通法的稳定与可预测,更好的办法看来是将胁迫限制在相对肯定的不法行为胁迫。至于合法行为的威胁造成的不公平,毕竟是少数情况,则留给衡平法对个别案件有否不合情理/显失公平去处理,而在商业社会中要满足不合情理/显失公平理论的救济标准是非常严格的:见本章之 1 段与本书第十一章之 1.7 段的介绍。对此可节录《The Principles of the Law of Restitution》(2015 年,第 3 版)一书之 218 段如下:"… despite the recent explicit recognition that a lawful threat can still be an illegitimate threat for economic duress, the better view is that only unlawful threats should suffice. A lawful threat may still result in restitution, but only … if the more stringent test of unconscionability is satisfied. This ensures that the law does not intervene unacceptably in commercial markets. Where a defendant has obtained a benefit as a result of an unlawful threat which caused the benefit to be transferred, it is appropriate for restitution to be awarded. Where the benefit was obtained as the result of a lawful threat, it is only appropriate to award restitution where the defendant's conduct is characterised as unconscionable …"

8.1.1 确定英国法有合法行为胁迫的 PIAC v. Times Travel(2021)UKSC 40 最高院先例

在 PIAC v. Times Travel 最高院先例中,最高院的大法官一致认可了英国法下,合法行为构成不法压力尽管非常有争议,但答案应是肯定的,而且已经获得英国法上的地位。多数意见认可 Burrows 勋爵给出的以下四个原因:[48]

1. 合法行为能够构成不法压力与过往先例中的判法并不存在冲突,尤其是过去

---

[47] 有关扣船的问题,可见杨良宜的《海事法》(1999 年)一书第一章。

[48] Burrows 勋爵给出的是少数意见,但多数意见中认可与同意该几点原因。

先例中针对胁迫的威胁或压力提到的都是更广泛的“不恰当”(illegitimate)一词而不是“不法”[49](unlawful)。

英国法会允许一些虽然合法,但是整体来看因为各种社会、道德上的原因被认为不恰当与构成胁迫的行为,这也带来了如何判断不恰当的困难问题。例如本章之8.4.4段提到的购买救命药物时,卖方明知买方非买不可时恶意提高100倍价格出售,这就会是不会被社会道德所接受,但 PIAC v. Times Travel 先例否定了单纯以社会道德是否可接受作为判断标准,纯粹提价行为并不构成合法行为胁迫。稍后在本章之8.3与8.4段会详细解释这方面问题。

2. 根据案例与立法都明确刑事的敲诈勒索会包括合法威胁,如威胁会将对方想要极力隐瞒但是真实的消息告诉媒体报刊,或者是向警方报告对方的犯罪行为等,以此获得自己想要的利益。而类似原理的民事胁迫却不会包括合法威胁造成的不法压力是说不通的。《Theft Act 1968》之 Section 21(1)中针对敲诈勒索罪的重点是以恫吓(menaces)或威胁方式提不当要求[50](unwarranted demand),即无论威胁行为是否合法。

在 PIAC v. Times Travel 先例 Burrows 勋爵说:“... it would be very odd for the civil law of duress not to include threats of lawful acts when the criminal law of blackmail does so.”

3. 在一些早期先例中,就有判决认定合法行为的威胁、施加压力也会使得受压方有权撤销合约、取回支付的金钱:见本章之8.2.1.1段会介绍的 Williams v. Bayley (1866) LR 1 HL 200 与 Mutual Finance Co Ltd v. John Wetton & Sons Ltd (1937) 2 KB 389 等先例。这些早期先例在当时被作为不当影响[51]案件,是因为当时普通法胁迫只包括对人身的胁迫,或者是针对财物的胁迫而想要取回支付的额外金钱的情况。这些先例中的威胁,如威胁要将犯罪信息透露给警方,既没有对人身的胁迫也没有对财物的胁迫,因此只能采用衡平法的不当影响理论对普通法胁迫理论的不足进行弥补。但在今天来看,虽然威胁与不当影响在很多案件中十分接近甚至被混为一谈,但前者是普通法,后者是衡平法。在不当影响中往往涉及当事人之间有影响力关系,但胁迫会适用于任何合约关系。有说法就是在有经济胁迫后,应该被认为包括在合法行为中。这也是为什么今天有不少人士认为不当影响应该只是针对有影响力关系的情况。Burrows 勋爵说:“Although these cases may have used the language of undue influence, it is clear that they were not concerned with the standard case of undue influence... Rather one was looking at actual undue influence where the influence was being exerted by a lawful threat. ... there is no reason to hive off those earlier cases from duress by

[49] 这两者之间的区分见本章之6.1段。

[50] 有关立法条文见本章之6.2段的脚注。

[51] 不当影响见本书第十一章之1段介绍,与胁迫的区别也可见本书第十一章之1.1段的介绍。

labelling them as cases on undue influence. On the contrary, the underlying element is identical-it is an illegitimate, albeit lawful, threat-and it is therefore rational today to treat them as examples of duress(albeit not economic duress)."

4. 在今天的普通法胁迫发展起来以后,在较近期先例中也有一些先例指出即使是合法行为也可以给予撤销合约、复原等救济:见 CTN Cash and Carry Ltd v. Gallaher Ltd(1994)4 All ER 714;Alf Vaughan & Co Ltd v. Royscot Trust Plc(1999)1 All ER (Comm)856;Borrelli v. Ting(2010)UKPC 21;The "Cenk Kaptanoglu"(2012)EWHC 273(Comm);Marsden v. Barclays Bank Plc(2016)EWHC 1601(QB);The Flying Music Co Ltd v. Theater Entertainment SA(2017)EWHC 3192(QB);Al Nehayan v. Kent (2018)EWHC 333(Comm)等先例。

在 PIAC v. Times Travel 最高院先例中,Burrows 勋爵还给出了如下针对合法行为构成胁迫的总结:"One can summarise the analysis of the law set out in this judgment as follows:(i)Lawful act duress, including lawful act economic duress, exists in English law. (ii)Three elements need to be established for lawful act economic duress: an illegitimate threat; sufficient causation; and that the threatened party had no reasonable alternative to giving in to the threat. [合法行为经济胁迫需要证明以下三点:采用的是不法/不恰当威胁(逼迫受压方满足自己提出的要求),足够的因果关系,以及受压方没有其他合理选择只能被迫答应。](iii)As the threat is lawful, the illegitimacy of the threat is determined by focusing on the justification of the demand. (以要做出合法行为相威胁,因此此时是否有不法压力主要关注的是提出的是什么要求。Burrows 勋爵还给出少数意见说,分水岭就在于要求是否是"恶意";如果是,就能构成合法行为胁迫。[52])(iv)A demand motivated by commercial self-interest is, in general, justified. Lawful act economic duress is essentially concerned with identifying rare exceptional cases where a demand, motivated by commercial self-interest, is nevertheless unjustified. (在商业合约谈判中,提出要求的动机是为了自己的商业利益一般不会被认为不正当。正常商业谈判中,为了自己的商业利益而想尽一切合法手段逼迫对方也是现实

[52] 这就是 Burrows 勋爵的总结中提到的第五点:"In relation to a demand for a waiver by the threatened party of a claim against the threatening party, a demand is unjustified, so that the lawful act economic threat is illegitimate, where, first, the threatening party has deliberately created, or increased, the threatened party's vulnerability to the demand and, secondly, the 'bad faith demand' requirement is satisfied. The demand is made in bad faith where the threatening party does not genuinely believe that it has any defence (and there is no defence) to the claim being waived."但贵族院的其他大法官的多数意见在这一点上与 Burrows 勋爵有分歧,因为 Burrows 勋爵引入了"恶意要求"作为判断标准,如果不是真实相信自己有合理抗辩理由的情况下逼迫对方弃权就属于不法压力。但多数意见否定此标准,认为并不因为恶意要求就一定属于不法压力。而在多数意见给出的案件类型中,"用应受谴责的手段操纵对方处于弱势地位并逼迫对方不得不放弃索赔",实际上也不考虑施压方的主观想法是"善意"还是"恶意"。这可见本章之 8.4.3 段的介绍。

的实际做法,轻易出现这样的行为都会构成不法压力导致胁迫、达成的合约无效,与商业现实是不配合的。合法行为经济胁迫针对的只是少数例外案件中,施压方为了自己的商业利益提出的要求被法律认为是不正当的情况。)"

8.1.2 重点看是否属于错误要求

这些合法行为能够构成不法压力,也可以解释得通。尤其是今天的说法是压力的不法性要关注威胁的性质与要求是否合理,因此一种情况就是合法行为但伴随错误要求(wrongful demand)而变成不法压力,即敲诈勒索。而敲诈勒索的性质,实际上是原本合法行为整体看来变成了敲诈勒索的不法行为。

另一种情况则是本章开头已经提到的在今天快速发展的经济胁迫案件中,实际上大量受到衡平法的影响,法院会看有关施压方的行为与提出的要求是否应受谴责(reprehensive),是否不合情理/显失公平(unconscionable)。在个别案件的案情下,法官认为行为加上要求虽然合法但应受谴责、不合情理,整体来看虽然仍然是合法行为,但压力变成了不法/不恰当压力。在 PIAC v. Times Travel(2021)UKSC 40 最高院先例中,Hodge 勋爵说:"… the courts have developed the common law doctrine of duress to include lawful act economic duress by drawing on the rules of equity in relation to undue influence and treating as 'illegitimate' conduct which, when the law of duress was less developed, had been identified by equity as giving rise to an agreement which it was unconscionable for the party who had conducted himself or herself in that way to seek to enforce. In other words, morally reprehensible behaviour which in equity was judged to render the enforcement of a contract unconscionable in the context of undue influence has been treated by English common law as illegitimate pressure in the context of duress."

但这显然存在的问题是在商业社会的合约关系中引入考虑公平合理与是否不合情理/显失公平,会带来极大不肯定、不稳定、不可预测,分水岭应该如何划分?而这分水岭必须要作出划分。这方面问题在英国普通法下目前还没有肯定说法,没有给出明确的标准,并留待将来先例的完善。但在大原则上是十分明确的,并不愿意太扩张合法行为经济胁迫的说法,只会是一些非常例外的情况才会给予胁迫的救济。

PIAC v. Times Travel 最高院先例多数意见除了认定过去先例中建立起来与在下段会介绍的两种类型合法行为胁迫外,并没有继续拓展出判断标准。看来是希望具体的判断标准通过后续一个又一个先例逐步根据具体(以及考虑什么才是法律框架下能够做到的"公平正义")情况作判断,在后期有了大量先例后再进行总结与归纳,没必要在早期阶段就给出判断标准。而在目前阶段为了尽量保持商业合约的肯定性与可预测性,对待合法行为胁迫的态度会非常局限与严格,要求尽量不会超出过去的两种类型。Hodge 勋爵说:"The boundaries of the doctrine of lawful act duress are not fixed and the courts should approach any extension with caution, particularly in the context of contractual negotiations between commercial entities. In any development of the doctrine of lawful act duress it will also be important to bear in mind not only that analogous remedies already exist in equity, such as the doctrines of undue influence and unconscionable bargains, but also the absence in English law of any overriding doctrine of good faith in contracting or any doctrine of imbalance of bargaining power."

8.2 目前合法行为胁迫的两种类型

PIAC v. Times Travel (2021) UKSC 40 最高院先例提到,在过去先例中建立起来以下两类合法行为胁迫:(1)类似敲诈勒索的情况。这类案件中的法律相对稳定与清楚,毕竟因为本就有敲诈勒索等刑事或侵权法律针对这种行为。(2)采用应受谴责的手段(这可以是违约、欺诈性误述等)操纵对方处于弱势地位并逼迫对方不得不同意施压方的错误要求,如放弃索赔("using illegitimate means to manoeuvre the claimant into a position of weakness to force him to waive his claim")。

Hodge 勋爵说:"... it was the combination of (i) the existence of legal claims by B against A and (ii) the manoeuvring by A of B by reprehensible means into a vulnerable position where it had no alternative but to waive its pre-existing rights that amounted to illegitimate pressure."

这第二种类型具体针对的就是 Borrelli v. Ting (2010) UKPC 21 枢密院先例与 The "Cenk Kaptanoglu" (2012) EWHC 273 (Comm) 先例中的情况,见稍后介绍。

8.2.1 敲诈勒索

以做出合法行为相威胁,但实际上构成敲诈勒索(blackmail),这就会属于不法压力与可以构成胁迫。敲诈勒索的情况也千变万化,但较为常见的是威胁将对方或对方家人的非法犯罪行为报告给警方,或者是将真实信息告诉媒体报刊等。这些情况也可以发生在商业活动中。

还如在 The "Italia Express" (1992) 2 Lloyd's Rep 216 先例中,"Italian Express"轮在希腊港口爆炸沉没,船东向保险人劳合社的索赔被拒绝,双方就船东是否故意把船弄沉产生争议。船东的表弟曾经对一次谈话进行了录音,记录了与潜水员等人士讨论如何在船底安装炸药弄沉船舶的计划,事后表弟就用以将录音带交出作为威胁向船东敲诈勒索金钱,但未能成功。[53] 可以想到如果船东受压之下真的交钱平息事件,在拿到保险赔偿后或各种原因拿不到赔偿(如保险公司倒闭),也会以胁迫为由向表弟要求拿回金钱。

虽然威胁采取的行为本身是合法行为甚至是一个良好市民应该采取的行为,但整体看敲诈勒索行为是非法的。例如,本章之 8.1.1 段已经节录的《Theft Act 1968》之 Section 21(1)中,规定得非常广泛,任何以恫吓、威胁行为提不当的要求都可以构成敲诈勒索。

---

〔53〕 此先例最后录音是被交给了保险人劳合社,但由于表弟无法出庭作证,导致在当时的证据规则下属于传闻证据最后也未能被法院采纳:见《证据法:基础理论、口头证据与专家证据》一书第八章之 3 段。

8.2.1.1 早期的敲诈勒索案件

一些英国早期判例就涉及过此类问题。这类案件中往往涉及很多导致合约效力出问题的理由。例如威胁要举报对方犯罪行为和证据,这可能暗示了会有监禁的惩罚,被认定为属于针对人身的胁迫。如果以不举报非法犯罪行为作为"对价"达成合约,还可能由于非法理论(illegality doctrine)导致合约不可执行。[54] 在一些早期先例中,由于不属于针对人身或财物的威胁,因此只给予不当影响的衡平法救济。

例如在 Williams v. Bayley(1866) LR 1 HL 200 先例中,银行持有原告儿子伪造的文书,逼迫原告将财产抵押给银行才归还伪造的文书,法院判抵押协议可使无效。类似的还可见 Mutual Finance Co Ltd v. John Wetton & Sons Ltd(1937)2 KB 389 等先例。

当然如果敲诈勒索的威胁涉及针对了人身,如可能有监禁后果等情况,仍然会适用针对人身的胁迫。在 Kaufman v. Gerson(1904)1 KB 591 先例中,丈夫挪用了原告的金钱,此挪用行为在法国会构成刑事犯罪。原告可以起诉丈夫要求赔偿,但知悉妻子有资产,就威逼利诱妻子,在法国与妻子达成协议,由妻子归还这笔金钱,原告则不提起诉讼,也不会向有关机构举报。[55] 事后作为施压方的原告在英国法院执行协议,但被上诉庭拒绝。上诉庭认为协议是被逼迫产生的,虽然协议本身适用法国法,而在法国法下此行为并不非法,但在英国一样认为此协议是由于胁迫所导致,因此在公共政策下也不会予以执行。

8.2.1.2 恶意诉讼的侵权

敲诈勒索中,一种在商业社会很常见的情况是施压方威胁对方要开始诉讼或索赔,并敲诈对方。这里可以先区分一下涉及恶意诉讼(malicious prosecution)的侵权行为,如明知没有合理的理据而恶意提起的诉讼。传统英国法下恶意诉讼主要针对刑事诉讼,但今天看来,民事诉讼也可能属于恶意诉讼:见 Willers v. Joyce(2016) UKSC 43 最高院先例。一旦涉及恶意诉讼就是侵权行为,是不法行为构成的不法压力与胁迫,也不需要依赖本小段针对的合法行为胁迫了。

8.2.1.3 有合理理据开始民事诉讼是合法行为

提出民事诉讼,显然如果威胁或实际已经提起诉讼一方是由于各种各样的原因(如对方侵权或违反合约自己要索赔损失等)有合理的理据提起诉讼,也证明不了原告没有合理理据去这样做,没有理由认为这样的行为是错误的或构成不法压力。寻求救济本就是法律赋予的权利。

也因此后来如果达成和解,只要双方都是善意的,和解协议会得到法律的支持与

---

[54] 一般公共政策不会允许当事人(这与公诉人代表政府与嫌疑人/被告达成辩诉交易不同)自己达成协议解决刑事诉讼,尤其是涉及严重的刑事犯罪时。最多也只允许当事人自己和解有关民事部分的责任。

[55] 此先例还可见本书第九章之 5.5.2 段的介绍。

保护，不会轻易就认定不法压力：见本章之7.2.2段已经介绍过的 Huyton SA v. Peter Cremer GmbH & Co(1999)1 Lloyd's Rep 620先例。例如，双方都善意和解谈判时，一方即使"威胁"说达不成我方的和解要求就要继续推进诉讼，也不属于不法压力。

但这种情况下如果提出错误要求，或者根据具体的案件事实施压方的行为应受谴责，是否可以在这些特别情况中认定存在不法压力而给予经济胁迫的救济？

目前这方面的先例看来非常少见，但是从原理上来说是有可能存在的。《Chitty on Contract》(2021年，第34版)一书之10-065段说："It is likely that a threat to institute civil proceedings which is not unlawful in itself can also constitute duress for present purposes, if it is coupled (for instance) with a wholly unjustified demand, or if it is made in special circumstances (for instance) in which the defendant has a particular fear of the publicity which may follow from a claim."

例如在 Drew v. Daniel(2005)EWCA Civ 507上诉庭先例中，家族生意产生纠纷，被告逼原告退出家族生意，在原告年事已高、非常恐惧任何形式的对抗、很害怕上法庭这类事宜的情况下，被告通过威胁起诉要挟原告达到目的。法院根据此先例的特殊案情认为在公平的原则下给予了救济。虽然最后采用的是衡平法的不当影响理论，但看来如果具体案情采用胁迫理论争辩，也同样有可能成功。

8.2.2 用应受谴责的手段操纵对方处于弱势地位并逼迫对方不得不放弃索赔

在过往的合法行为胁迫的案例中，这种情况有两个著名的先例，可以分别进行介绍。它们都涉及施压方的威胁与要求，独立来看是合法行为。例如威胁拒绝签一些文件、拒绝同意做某件事、拒绝作出协助等，而提出的要求是受压方必须同意放弃向施压方索赔欠下债务或损失的权利。这本来是国际商业社会经常发生的事情，法律不应该也不会插手。但在受压方需要施压方签文件、同意做某事或给予协助时，受压方其实已经是无路可走，所以只能答应施压方的要求。重要的是，受压方的无路可走正是施压方在同一个事件中通过一连串的不法手段(如伪造文件、违约、欺诈性误述等)造成的。

8.2.2.1 先例之一：Borrelli v. Ting(2010)UKPC 21枢密院先例

Borrelli v. Ting枢密院先例中，涉及的事实背景是在1999年底雅佳控股(Akai)被发现经营有严重问题资不抵债，被香港特区法院命令破产。此先例中的原告主要是代表雅佳的清算人(liquidator)。被告是时任雅佳董事长和CEO的丁谓[56](James Henry Ting)。清算人在清算过程中困难重重，一方面是缺乏足够资金继续清算，另

[56] 丁谓创立了善美(Semi-tech)公司，并曾经因收购美国超过150年历史的胜家(Singer)缝纫机生产商并成功将公司扭亏为盈，被称为"公司医生"。但后来迅速扩张收购大量公司，其中就包括日本雅佳，善美之后也更名为雅佳控股。但后来被曝光，从1999年到2000年，雅佳控股一年亏损135亿港元，之后丁谓也因此被称为"亏损之王"。

一方面是公司缺乏账簿与记录，而丁谓极度不合作。

为了筹集清算资金，清算人计划将雅佳控股在港交所上市的股票转售给第三人，并已经与第三人拟定了相关协议。根据有关公司法与公司章程规定，此转售需要在有至少 3/4 股权股东参与的股东会议上获得多数票。丁谓通过自己控制的两家公司持有的股权，已经足够使得天平偏向反对出售。而一旦无法出售，清算人很快就没有资金推进清算了。

有关会议在 2002 年 11 月 25 日于香港特区召开，丁谓控制的公司由律师代理出席，但是因为委托手续不足，律师不能作为代理人投票。当时丁谓人在上海，马上让其控制的公司在香港特区伪造、倒签了委托文件（如伪造了丁谓在文件上的签字），以满足投票手续。针对这重要投票是否有效的问题就开始了在法院的诉讼。法院在审理过程中遇到了很多问题，包括有两任审理法官因为丁谓与其控制公司的反对而主动回避，有一任审理法官在审理中途手骨折而退出审理等，导致诉讼程序一路延长迟迟得不到结果。

这带来的问题就是，根据转售的相关协议，在 2002 年 12 月 31 日之前雅佳如果还没有通过决议，第三人公司有选择权不再购买股票。而当时雅佳曝光的困境与信息越来越多，港交所已经明确不会允许股票再被转售给其他人士。而且随着进一步的曝光，股权显然越来越没有价值。如果继续拖下去，转售计划多半要泡汤，也就没有资金推进清算了。在这样的情况下，涉及清算程序的多方人士在 2002 年 12 月 30 日签订了一份和解协议，根据和解协议，清算人必须放弃所有针对丁谓与其控制的两间公司的索赔。在和解协议后，丁谓就放弃了对转售投票的反对。也能想到，事后清算人就主张经济胁迫导致和解协议可使无效，以向丁谓与其控制的公司索赔。

案件上诉到枢密院，枢密院认定存在经济胁迫。在枢密院看来影响判决的一个重要因素就是丁谓（及其控制的控股公司）被认定是恶意采取行动阻止转售计划。Saville 勋爵说：

"… finding of particular importance is that James Henry Ting procured the opposition to the scheme（转售计划）by …（两间丁谓控制的控股公司）'solely so as to defeat …（转售计划）with the desire and intention of thereby depriving the liquidators of funds with a view to preventing any further investigation of his conduct of the affairs of the company' … In other words, James Henry Ting's opposition was not made in good faith, but for an improper motive.

… In the view of the Board（指枢密院，Judicial Committee of the Privy Council）James Henry Ting's failure to provide any assistance to the liquidators; his opposition to the scheme; and his resort to forgery and false evidence in order to further that opposition amount to unconscionable conduct on his part … by agreeing to withdraw the opposition to the scheme James Henry Ting did no more than he should have done from the outset, had he acted in good faith rather than in an attempt to avoid responsibility for his conduct of the affairs of Akai Holdings Ltd.

The Board is of the view that in the present case the liquidators**entered into the settlement agreement as the result of the illegitimate means** employed by James Henry Ting,namely by opposing the scheme for no good reason and in using forgery and false evidence in support of that opposition,all in order to prevent the liquidators from investigating his conduct of the affairs of Akai Holdings Ltd or making claims against him arising out of that conduct. As the Board has already observed,by adopting these means James Henry Ting **left the liquidators with no reasonable or practical alternative but to enter into the settlement agreement.** "(加黑部分是笔者的强调)

在 PIAC v. Times Travel(2021)UKSC 40 最高院先例中,多数意见对此先例的解读是:(1)丁谓采取了应受谴责、不合情理/显失公平的非法行为(包括违反作为破产公司的董事、高管配合清算人的职责,以及伪造文书、恶意投反对票等行为),通过这些行为"操纵"导致清算人处在了非常弱势的地位;(2)最后逼得清算人缺乏其他合理选择而只能签署和解协议放弃追究丁谓与其控制公司的责任。在这种情况下诱导合约产生的行为(两间公司放弃反对转售计划)虽然是合法行为,但综合来看仍然属于不法压力,会给予胁迫的救济。

8.2.2.2 先例之二:The "Cenk Kaptanoglu"(2012)EWHC 273(Comm)先例

The "Cenk Kaptanoglu"先例的案情是船东同意将"Cenk Kaptanoglu"轮程租给承租人,在合约中没有约定可以替代船舶履行。但在承租人不知情的情况下,船东将"Cenk Kaptanoglu"轮租赁给了第三人导致无法履行与承租人租约下约定的航次。这是违约/毁约行为,承租人如果选择此时接受违约/毁约,合约即告终止,承租人也可以去市场寻找替代船舶并向船东索赔损失,特别是租用更昂贵的替代船舶带来的损失。

船东也承认是自己搞错,一船两租,但提出自己可以提供替代船舶,并赔偿由于未能提供租约约定的履约船舶带来的对承租人的损失,如替代船舶会迟于原定船舶抵达装港等带来的延误损失。承租人因此没有马上接受违约/毁约与自己寻找其他替代船舶履行,而是等待船东提供替代船舶继续履行原租约。

之后船东提名了一艘替代履行的船舶,并且表示愿意在运费上打折。承租人同意替代的船舶与打折运费,但是保留向船东索赔违约导致的所有损失的权利,并之后与卸货港的实际收货人修改了关联的货物买卖的条文(如由于延迟付运要修改交货时间与降低货物价格等)。

但问题是签订使用替代船舶履行的和解协议时,船东抛出了一个"爱要不要"的要约,要求承租人必须放弃所有对原租约的索赔,才可以接受折扣运费的替代船舶履行。承租人此时就面临进一步困境,如果不接受这个要约,变成之前的工夫全部白费,而且关联的货物买卖合约下自己将无法履行(买方是否愿意进一步修改是另一回事了,完全可以认为是承租人的违约/毁约并开始索赔)。面临这样的困境,承租人在提出抗议的前提下接受要约。事后则开始仲裁,主张船东的行为构成不法压力与经济胁迫,并得到仲裁庭支持。但船东行为是否构成不法压力这个法律问题被上诉到英国高院。

高院 Cooke 大法官的判法是,根源问题是船东在原租约下的违约/毁约,这不法或受谴责的行为导致承租人处在一个没有其他合理选择的地位(否则就要面临买卖合约下的巨大损失),此时船东虽然以不派替代船舶的合法行为(因为原租约是没有这个合约责任,而一船两租只是过去的违约行为)相威胁,但提出的让承租人放弃索赔的要求脱离了公平合理,这样综合来看应该属于不法压力。Cooke 大法官说:

"… it would be very odd if pressure could be brought about by a threatened breach of contract, which did amount to an unlawful act but not by a past breach, coupled with conduct since that breach, which drove the victim of the breach into a position where it had no realistic alternative but to waive its rights in respect of that breach, in order to avoid further catastrophic loss…

it is clear that the arbitrators took the view that the **owners had manoeuvred the charterers into the position they were in, following the breach, in order to drive a hard bargain**. The charterers had no realistic practical alternative but to submit to the pressure …

… As I have already said, the pressure created by the owners in their demand for a waiver of rights by the charterers has to be seen both in the light of their repudiatory breach and in the light of their subsequent conduct, including their deliberate refusal to comply with the assurances they had previously given about providing a substitute vessel and paying full compensation in respect of that breach. **Their refusal to supply the substitute vessel to meet the charterers' needs, in circumstances which they had created by their breach and their subsequent misleading activity**, unless the charterers waived their rights, could readily be found by the arbitrators to amount to 'illegitimate pressure'. In my judgment, not only was that a finding which the arbitrators could properly reach when applying the correct test in law, … it was the right decision on the facts of this case."(加黑部分是笔者的强调)

类似的情况还会发生在其他的行业中,如在一个工程合约中,一个日进斗金的商场因为风暴损坏了顶棚而需要紧急维修。也正由于急切需要尽快修缮完成继续正常营业,在商场与总承建商的合约中对工程延误约定了很高的每天议定赔偿。总承建商将脚手架的工程交给了一个分包商完成,分包商也知道此工程的紧急性。但由于分包商成功拿到了另一个更赚钱的脚手架工程,人手被派遣优先完成另一份工作。这样就导致商场顶棚的维修工期延误了。在这个阶段,总承建商尚有机会另寻其他公司完成脚手架工程,但是分包商告诉总承建商自己愿意另安排人手(第三人)完成工程,同时也愿意对导致的延误作出赔偿。因此,总承建商与分包商同意延长原完工日期。但之后分包商改变主意,要求总承建商放弃所有对自己延误的索赔与赔偿要求，否则不会安排第三人开工。这样，面对与商场合约下严格的工期要求与高昂的议定赔偿，总承建商感觉无路可走，只能答应了分包商的要求。这就与 The “Cenk Kaptanoglu” 的情况非常类似了，也是分包商的违约在先，并操纵总承建商处于进退两难的困局，看来总承建商在稍后工程完毕后，可以依赖合法行为胁迫推翻对分包商的承诺。

8.2.3　PIAC v. Times Travel（2021）UKSC 40 最高院先例

最后可以介绍 PIAC v. Times Travel 最高院先例。此先例中是占有市场优势地位甚至垄断地位的一方，施加压力给对方并诱导产生合约，是否构成不法压力的问题。在此先例中最高院同时也面对了要不要继续扩张已经建立的两种类型合法行为胁迫，以及要扩张的话怎样划出分水岭/红线的问题。

此先例中的被告航空公司（Pakistan International Airlines Corp，以下简称 PIAC）独家经营英国到巴基斯坦之间的直航航线。PIAC 在英国委任了很多票务代理，原告（Times Travel）也是其中一家家庭经营的小型票务代理。很容易想到，占据谈判优势地位的 PIAC 与所有代理签订的代理合约都是全面有利于 PIAC 的。

根据代理合约，代理按销售的机票数量获取佣金（与/或奖金），因此代理能够获取的利润非常依赖自己能够销售的机票数量。合约下双方有权提前一个月通知后终止合约。2012 年，PIAC 与大量票务代理之间都发生了佣金争议，这令 PIAC 全面更新与改变了自己的代理制度。

PIAC 原本每两周提供 300 张票给 Times Travel，但在佣金争议出现后，PIAC 就大幅度削减机票数量至 60 张，并且说考虑要终止代理合约。后来 PIAC 就提供了新的代理合约，新合约一方面降低了佣金，另一方面要求 Times Travel 必须放弃在原代理合约下对 PIAC 就佣金的诉权。只要 Times Travel 接受新合约，PIAC 就恢复机票供应。Times Travel 只是家庭经营的小型公司，如果只能卖这么一点票，只能关门大吉，无奈之下只能同意新合约。新合约签订后，PIAC 也把机票数量恢复到正常水平。

事后 Times Travel 开始诉讼想要索赔原合约下的佣金，这就必须先推翻新合约中的弃权条文，Times Travel 主张经济胁迫而可使该条文无效。这带来的问题就是 PIAC 的行为是否能够构成不法压力。双方对于 PIAC 缩减机票数量与根据原合约的终止条文通知结束合作等行为都是并非违约的合法行为没有争议。

上诉庭［（2019）EWCA Civ 828］判这并不是不法压力，重要的判断理由是采取合法行为的 Times Travel 没有任何恶意。而在上诉到最高院后，最高院一样是判不构成经济胁迫，但理由有所不同。

最高院的多数意见认可根据过往先例已经建立的两类合法行为胁迫。多数意见并没有说不存在其他情况的合法行为胁迫，需要留待后续先例发展出判断的具体标准，但是明确指出商业环境中要达到不法压力的情况会非常少（“extremely limited”）的。

这样，此先例中的情况既不是敲诈勒索，也没有显示出 PIAC 有任何应受谴责的行为。不像是 Borrelli v. Ting(2010)UKPC 21 枢密院先例与 The “Cenk Kaptanoglu”(2012)EWHC 273(Comm)先例中施压方都是有错在先,包括伪造文件与违约等来令受压方陷入困境。因此 PIAC 根据自己独家经营航线的市场优势地位逼迫 Times Travel 签订协议放弃索赔,并不属于被认可的两种合法行为胁迫的类型。从案情来看 PIAC 的所作所为纯粹是依赖它的市场优势地位为了自己的利益来向票务代理施加压力,没理由扩张出新的合法行为胁迫类型,也因此 Times Travel 败诉。Hodge 勋爵说:“... it would **be rare that in a commercial context the use by A of lawful pressure to induce B to concede to a demand would amount to economic duress**. Significantly, there are **no findings** that PIAC(被告)**had used any reprehensible means** such as were evident in Borrelli and The Cenk K, to manoeuvre Times Travel into a position of increased vulnerability in order to exploit that vulnerability. PIAC gave notice on 14 September 2012 that Times Travel's contract would be terminated at the end of October 2012. On 17 September PIAC cut Times Travel's(原告)fortnightly allocation of tickets from 300 to 60, as under its existing contract it was entitled to do. At the meeting on 24 September 2012 PIAC gave Times Travel a 'take it or leave it' option: to sign the new agreement with the waiver and thus regain its prior allocation of tickets, or its agency would come to an end on the expiry of the existing contract. While this entailed hard-nosed commercial negotiation that exploited PIAC's position as a monopoly supplier, **it did not involve the reprehensible means of applying pressure which gave rise to the findings of lawful act economic duress** in Borrelli and The Cenk K. There are also **no findings that PIAC acted in bad faith** in making the demands which it did...”(加黑部分是笔者的强调)

8.3 谈判中利用优势地位获取商业利益不是不法压力

在商业社会中,显然占据优势地位的一方会尽可能获取更多商业利益,这做法也无可厚非,尤其是施加压力是采用了合法行为时,没有理由影响合约的有效性。目前英国法下较为明确的是,一方利用自己的市场优势甚至是垄断地位,逼迫对方在商业上让步,即使这看来在道德上有问题或做法在社会大众看来不被接受,也不会属于不法压力。可以节录 PIAC v. Times Travel(2021)UKSC 40 最高院先例,Hodge 勋爵说:“... there is **no doctrine of inequality of bargaining power and no general principle of good faith in contracting in English law**. A commercial party in negotiation with another commercial party is entitled to use its bargaining power to obtain by negotiation contractual rights which it does not have until the contract is agreed. A powerful commercial party, such as a monopoly supplier or monopoly purchaser, can impose onerous terms, for example demanding a premium, as a condition for entering into a transaction with another party.”(加黑部分是笔者的强调)

现实商业社会中当事人在合约谈判时,谈判力量往往都不对等,甚至力量强弱还会随时发生变化。例如,买卖市场上,由于市场的波动,有时会是买方优势,有时变成卖方优势。即使在一些通常一方占优的情况,如雇佣合约中雇主往往有压倒性的谈判力量,但如果是市场上人手短缺,或者是有经验的高管、技术人才等,在面对雇主时也会有很强的谈判力量。而如果是一些做法不被社会大众接受,因此特别需要对特定类型的弱势方予以结构性保护,则通过立法中少数的强制性条文,或者是雇佣法、反不正当竞争法等立法针对。通过普通法在个别案件调整与"拉平"一般商业合约中双方不对等的谈判力量,并没有实际意义,也很难做到。

PIAC v. Times Travel 先例的判法也是过往英国法院的一致判法,这会在接下来的段节介绍。

8.3.1 CTN Cash and Carry Ltd v. Gallaher Ltd(1994)4 All ER 714 上诉庭先例

在 CTN Cash and Carry Ltd v. Gallaher Ltd 上诉庭先例中,被告 Gallaher 是某品牌香烟的独家代理,定期向原告 CTN 供应香烟,也向 CTN 提供信贷融通(credit facility)。每一次香烟供应都是单独的合约,Gallaher 没有持续性的合约义务提供额外的供应或信贷融通。在一次香烟供应中,Gallaher 搞错交货地点,将货物送到了 CTN 的另一个仓库而不是约定的仓库。Gallaher 同意重新送货,但在没来得及有任何进一步行动前,这批香烟被小偷从 CTN 仓库中偷走。Gallaher 主张此时货物遗失的风险是由 CTN 承担,要求 CTN 依照合约支付货价,而如果 CTN 拒绝据付款,就不会再继续提供信贷融通。需要信贷融通的 CTN 在压力之下答应付款,但事后以经济胁迫为由要求取回这笔金钱。

审理案件的 Steyn 大法官指出此案件的三方面特质:(1)此案件不涉及受保护的关系,双方都是商人,并不涉及对消费者的特别保护。Gallaher 拒绝将来提供货物,或拒绝提供信贷融通,不是违约/毁约,都是合法的商业行为。(2)Gallaher 是香烟的独家代理,实质是有市场垄断地位。但不会仅仅因为个别合约谈判时谈判力量的不对等,就导致原本不是胁迫的行为变成胁迫。Steyn 大法官说:"The fact that the defendants were in a monopoly position cannot therefore by itself convert what is not otherwise duress into duress."(3)特别重要的一点是根据事实来看,Gallaher 在此先例中虽然有错误的想法,但确实善意地有真实信念(genuine belief)即香烟被偷走的风险由 CTN 承担,因此自己有权要求 CTN 支付被偷走的香烟的货价,施加压力的动机纯粹是为了自己的商业利益。可以节录 Steyn 大法官所说如下:"A third, and critically important, characteristic of the case is the fact that the defendants **bona fide thought** that the goods were at the risk of the plaintiffs and that the plaintiffs owed the defendants the sum in question. The defendants exerted commercial pressure on the plaintiffs in order to obtain payment of a sum which they bona fide considered due to them. The defendants' **motive in threatening withdrawal of credit facilities was commercial self-interest** in obtaining a sum that they considered due to them."(加黑部分是笔者的强调)

综合这三点后,Steyn 大法官判在这样的商业领域,虽然本身合法行为也可能导致胁迫后果或不法压力,但会是极为少见的例外情况,尤其是当显示施压方提出要求是善意与有真实信念时。显示善意通常是证人的口头证据说明自己当时相信自己有权这样做(即使有问过律师,也可以主张法律业务特免权拒绝披露律师意见的内容),如 Gallaher 以为即使把香烟送错了交货地点,但仍是给了 CTN,CTN 作为买方或受托人(bailee)应小心谨慎照顾,Gallaher 并不知道送错的仓库是欠缺保安等。最后谁对谁错虽然可以通过诉讼决定,但为了肯定性与避免诉讼的麻烦与费用,如果可以用合法压力逼迫对方达成和解协议就最好不过了。一旦法院接受施压方是善意地提出自己的要求,多半不属于不法压力、不构成胁迫。

在此先例中 Gallaher 是香烟的独家代理,每一次供货都是与 CTN 的单独合约交易,因此作出的威胁即取消以后的信贷融通,或者以后不再供货,完全都是合法行为。而 Gallaher 提出的要求,即要求 CTN 根据合约支付货款,这是 Gallaher 真实地相信自己根据合约有权获取的(而且很重要的是没有相反证据证明 Gallaher 的其他思想状态如恶意想要敲一笔),这并无不当之处。也因此综合来看,并不应该属于不法压力。在此上诉庭先例中的大法官们也是这样判法。最后节录 Steyn 大法官的判词如下:

"We are being asked to extend the categories of duress of which the law will take cognisance. That is not necessarily objectionable, but it seems to me that **an extension capable of covering the present case, involving 'lawful act duress' in a commercial context in pursuit of a bona fide claim, would be a radical one with far-reaching implications**. It would introduce a substantial and undesirable element of uncertainty in the commercial bargaining process. Moreover, it will often enable bona fide settled accounts to be reopened when parties to commercial dealings fall out. The aim of our commercial law ought to be to encourage fair dealing between parties. But it is a mistake for the law to set its sights too highly when the critical inquiry is not whether the conduct is lawful but whether it is morally or socially unacceptable.[57] That is the inquiry in which we are engaged. In my view there are policy considerations which militate against ruling that the defendants obtained payment of the disputed invoice by duress.

Outside the field of protected relationships, and **in a purely commercial context, it might be a relatively rare case in which 'lawful act duress' can be established**. And it might be **particularly difficult to establish duress if the defendant bona fide consid-**

---

〔57〕 也一度有先例对 Steyn 大法官说法的解读,是其实仍然要考虑道德与社会是否接受的问题,如 The "Cenk Kaptanoglu" (2012) EWHC 273 (Comm) 先例等。但这说法在 PIAC v. Times Travel (2019) EWCA Civ 828 上诉庭先例中已经被明确拒绝:"I have already made clear my disagreement with an analysis of Steyn LJ's judgment that sees his reference to whether conduct is morally or socially acceptable as extending the concept of lawful act duress beyond the case of the demand made in bad faith."

ered that his demand was valid. In this complex and changing branch of the law I deliberately refrain from saying 'never'. But as the law stands, I am satisfied that the defendants' conduct in this case did not amount to duress."(加黑部分是笔者的强调)

即使如此,CTN Cash and Carry Ltd v. Gallaher Ltd 先例可以说仍然是给合法行为经济胁迫打开一个发展的窗口。什么样的合法行为能够构成不法压力?尤其是还提到了是否对自己的要求有真实信念(或善意)的说法,这是否意味着真实信念变成需要考虑的因素或测试标准?

8.3.2 Holyoake v. Candy(2017)EWHC 3397(Ch)先例

类似的争议还可以再介绍 Holyoake v. Candy 先例,此先例中原告是一名地产开发商,想要在伦敦重新开发一幢 1868 年的古建筑(Grosvenor Gardens House)用作豪华住宅公寓。为了购买产权与开发,原告 H 先生获取多笔贷款。其中有一笔1200 万英镑的贷款是通过自己在大学时就结识的著名豪华地产开发商 Candy 兄弟获得,具体的贷款合约是与 Candy 兄弟控制的公司(CPC Group Limited,以下简称 CPC)签订。

虽然 H 先生与 Candy 兄弟私交甚笃,在急需资金的情况下 CPC 甚至提供的是无担保贷款,但仍然要求 H 先生必须保持超过 1.2 亿英镑的净资产并提供相应证明,并加上消极担保(negative security)条文不允许 H 先生在订约后未经许可的情况下以资产向其他人提供任何形式的担保。

在合约签订后,从 H 先生提供的文件中 CPC 主张 H 先生的净资产并没有达到贷款合约的要求,而且还发现其实事后 H 先生抵押了一些资产,因此 CPC 提出违约条文(default clause)已经被触发,自己有权要求 H 先生马上还款付息。在 CPC 威胁要开始诉讼、已经发出了索赔函的情况下,双方进行会议商谈,并重新约定了一系列协议。例如在补充协议下,H 先生承认自己确实对贷款合约违约与付款期限已至,并且还需要用一些其他资产作为债务担保,作为回报 CPC 则会给予一些额外还款时间宽限。

然而事后 H 先生仍然未能在补充协议下按期还款。H 先生最后与 CPC 签订和解协议,H 先生会出售尚未开发的古建筑,并从售价中向 CPC 支付包括贷款本金与利息、贷款协议与补充协议下允诺的最低利润分成、因为贷款合约的违约而延期付款的费用以及为了追讨金钱 CPC 支付的律师费等,共计 3700 万英镑。

之后 H 先生在法院提起诉讼,一项主张就是补充协议、和解协议都是受胁迫下订立的,因此要求归还支付的金钱,以及还要求损失的利润等赔偿,总索赔金额达到 1.32亿英镑。在这个争议下,显然核心问题就是 CPC(或 Candy 兄弟)是否施加了不法压力?

针对此问题,双方提供了大量的证据,包括当时的书信往来,也对一些关键会议上到底说了什么提供了口头证据。经过开庭审理后,法官认定了 CPC 确实进行了大量的威胁的说法。例如在会面中威胁说要"take a wrecking ball to your assets and leave you with nothing...",或者是说要尽一切可能达到自己的目的,以及还有要通知

H 先生的其他债权人等。而这些说法主要造成的实质影响就是会开始诉讼（如一旦开始公开诉讼，消息灵通的业界也肯定都会知道 H 先生的经济情况不乐观），而这也确实会给 H 先生带来重大的麻烦甚至是灾难性后果。

而 Nugee 大法官的判法是，这些实际上都是 CPC 作为债权人的合法行为，而利用自己的优势地位尽可能获取利益并不被认为是不法压力，即使是确实会给 H 先生带来严重后果也不改变这个地位。Nugee 大法官这样说：

"I find that the critical factor in his decision to sign the Supplemental Loan Agreement was the threat of litigation and the consequences which he saw that as entailing. That means the substantive question is whether CPC were justified in threatening to bring proceedings against him. The essence of economic duress is the use of illegitimate pressure: **I do not see that it can amount to economic duress for a creditor who believes that he has an accrued cause of action against a debtor to threaten to bring proceedings, even if the result is likely to be disastrous for the debtor, and even if the creditor spells out in strong language why it will be disastrous.** In fact in the present case I have already concluded that Mr Holyoake was in default under the Loan Agreement, and it must follow that **CPC were entitled to bring proceedings. If they were entitled to bring them, they were entitled to threaten to bring them**.

Since I have found that it was the threat of litigation that was the critical factor in Mr Holyoake's decision, I do not think the other matters raised at the meeting, or any intemperate language used, change the analysis. ...

... In these circumstances I find that none of the agreements entered into by Mr Holyoake are voidable for economic duress. The reality is that once he had signed the Loan Agreement, with its requirement for minimum net assets of £ 120m, he was always at risk of CPC taking a tough line and calling an event of default and hence he was always vulnerable to being sued, and very much more so after granting the Aeriance charges（违反贷款合约中消极担保条文，将一些资产抵押给第三人 Aeriance）. It was that threat of litigation which I have found was the effective cause of his agreeing to the terms of the Supplemental Loan Agreement, and it remained that threat which at every stage persuaded him to agree to the terms required by CPC for the successive extensions of time and other agreements that he wanted."（加黑部分是笔者的强调）

当然在笔者看来，Candy 兄弟实际上是非常精明与狡猾的合法高利贷商人。H 先生借了 1200 万英镑，但在相当短的时间内还了超过 3700 万英镑，连待开发的地产都丧失了。但 Candy 兄弟是在有水平的基础上，在规则范畴内占尽便宜。例如，在会议中的谈话内容，Candy 兄弟也只是说要针对 H 先生的财产采取严厉手段，在审理法官看来这也能解释得通主要会采取一些商业上的合法手段（主要就是开始诉讼），也并不针对 H 先生的人身。这种情况下，尽管涉及一些有严重后果的威胁，并不改变并非不法压力的结果。Candy 兄弟的要求是签订新的补充协议(以及之后的和解协议),实际上是重组债务,从中获取更多利益,以及要求提供资产担保等方式降低 H 先生无法还债的风险,这个安排也合情合理,在商业社会中也是常见的做法。

从另一个方面也显示出这类案件中证据的重要性。例如,此先例中的书信往来中没有什么过火的说法,又如通过证人证言解释了会面时口头说法到底意味着什么(如"wrecking ball"到底是指的什么?是否仅仅是合法的诉讼行为等)。而相比之下,H 先生作为证人被认为可信度存疑,就难以证明 CPC 与 Candy 兄弟在仅仅采取合法行为施加商业压力外还存在不法压力。

8.3.3 Instagroup Limited v. David Carroll & Others(2022)EWHC 464(QB)先例

此先例的案情涉及原告 Instagroup 向被告 Carroll 先生(与另一位 Barclay 先生)的 Warmspace 公司(主要业务是为房屋安装保温层)供应保温材料。由于 Warmspace 的财政问题与 Carroll 希望退休正在与第三人谈判收购公司,所以希望 Instagroup 不要停止供货,并接受让 Warmspace 对欠下的债务分期付款。Instagroup 在 2015 年 5 月 7 日的会议中要 Carroll 与 Barclay 签下个人担保才肯分期付款供货。

但之后 Warmspace 没有准时分期付款,到了 2016 年年底,已经累积了 1.3 万英镑的欠款。而到了 2017 年 2 月,Warmspace 已经进入破产管理(administration)。这也导致在 2 月底,Instagroup 的代表律师发函向两位担保人要求支付 Warmspace 欠下的 1.526 万英镑的债务。

之后,Instagroup 与 Barclay 达成和解并以汤姆林命令[58]在法院记录在案,但向 Carroll 的诉讼仍持续。Carroll 的抗辩有以下方面:(1)担保合约是在经济胁迫下签订的;(2)Instagroup 曾作出欺诈性误述诱导合约的产生(主要是指称在 5 月 7 日,Instagroup 代表曾说"将来是不会执行这一份担保合约的,签了也不用怕");(3)其他如对价、禁反言等,是与本章没有关系的抗辩。

针对经济胁迫,从案情看来是在商业上完全正常做法与合理的要求,Instagroup 谈不上有任何"不法/不恰当"的言行与"错误"的要求,除非 Instagroup 真有作出过欺诈性误述。但由于没有当场文件证据,仅是凭双方的口头证据是各说各的,双方的多年前(会议是 2015 年)的回忆也不再可靠,所以判经济胁迫不成立。Nigel Cooper QC 大法官说:

"The pleaded threat alleged by Mr. Carroll is that at the meeting on 07 May 2015 Mr. Robson and Mr. Milne(Instagroup 的代表)told him and Mr. Barclay that unless they signed the credit account application forms, Instagroup would stop supplying insulation materials to Warmspace and take immediate steps to enforce Warmspace's obligations. This threat, it is said, was made in circumstances where Instagroup knew that the supply of insulation materials was critical to the survival of Warmspace's business. ...

---

[58] 有关汤姆林命令,可见《证据法:国际规管与诉讼中的证据攻防》一书第四章之 1.7.6 段。

Against the background described…, it is unsurprising that Mr. Robson and Mr. Milne explained to Mr. Carroll and Mr. Barclay that they would require them to give personal guarantees by signing the credit account application forms. …

It is no doubt true that Mr. Carroll and Mr. Barclay did feel by August 2015 that they had no choice but to sign the credit account application forms but this was because they wanted to go ahead with the management buyout. They knew that to do this they required the support of Instagroup and that Instagroup required them to sign the credit account application forms. **The evidence before me reveals a process of commercial negotiation between Instagroup and Warmspace from May 2015 until the guarantees were signed in August 2015 that is not unusual and does not show Mr. Robson or Mr. Milne making demands which could be described as reprehensible or unconscionable. The request for the personal guarantees was one, which would be justified by the commercial self-interest of Instagroup**."(加黑部分是笔者的强调)

8.3.4 衡平法法院不"拉平"商业合约不对等的谈判地位

衡平法的不当影响理论确实会考虑不对等的谈判地位:见 National Westminster Bank Plc v. Morgan(1985)AC 686 先例。但这类不对等地位有比较多的限制,主要适用在社会上的不平等问题,而不太出现在商业社会中。正如本章之1段已经提到,在国际商业社会中,法院往往假设这些参加国际业务的商业主体在地位与能力上都是对等的:见 The Libyan Investment Authority v. Goldman Sachs International(2016) EWHC 2530(Ch)先例。这样实际上以地位不对等导致不当影响、不合情理/显失公平理论的衡平法救济并不多见。英国法院总体的态度也很明显是抗拒通过法院判例"拉平"与处理商业社会中不对等的谈判地位,即使是不利于市场竞争的垄断性行为、消费者的弱势等问题,也最好是留待立法解决。在 National Westminster Bank Plc v. Morgan 先例中,Scarman 勋爵说:"The doctrine of undue influence has been sufficiently developed not to need the support of a principle which by its formulation in the language of the law of contract is not appropriate to cover transactions of gift where there is no bargain. The fact of an unequal bargain will, of course, be a relevant feature in some cases of undue influence. But it can never become an appropriate basis of principle of an equitable doctrine which is concerned with transactions 'not to be reasonably accounted for on the ground of friendship, relationship, charity, or other ordinary motives on which ordinary men act'. And even in the field of contract I question whether there is any need in the modern law to erect a general principle of relief against inequality of bargaining power. Parliament has undertaken the task-and it is essentially a legislative task-of enacting such restrictions upon freedom of contract as are in its judgment necessary to relieve against the mischief: for example, the hire-purchase and consumer protection legislation, of which the Supply of Goods (Implied Terms) Act 1973, Consumer Credit Act 1974,

Consumer Safety Act 1978, Supply of Goods and Services Act 1982 and Insurance Companies Act 1982 are examples. I doubt whether the courts should assume the burden of formulating further restrictions."

8.3.5 胁迫理论不考虑谈判地位不对等的权威说法

在近期的 PIAC v. Times Travel(2021)UKSC 40 最高院先例中,多数意见指出普通法下针对商业合约就没有不对等谈判地位或善意的理论。法院的态度向来是即使有必要对不对等谈判地位给予救济也应该以立法解决。因此在商业合约谈判中施加压力,在绝大部分情况下也不会被认为达到不法压力的标准。虽然确实存在合法行为构成胁迫,但在商业社会中这种情况是非常少的。Hodge 勋爵说:

"In negotiating a commercial contract each party to the negotiations seeks to obtain contractual entitlements which he or she does not possess unless and until the parties agree the terms of the contract. Inequality of bargaining power means that one party in the negotiation of a commercial contract may be able to impose terms on a weaker party which a party of equal bargaining power would refuse to countenance. Equally, a party in a strong bargaining position, such as a monopoly supplier, may refuse outright to enter into a contract which the weaker party desires or may impose terms which the weaker party considers to be harsh. **The courts have taken the position that it is for Parliament and not the judiciary to regulate inequality of bargaining power where a person is trading in a manner which is not otherwise contrary to law**.(在商业合约谈判中,双方都是需要先答应对方提出的条件,才能获得合约权利。而不对等的谈判地位,意味着商业合约谈判中的强势方可以向弱势方任意提出条件,而如果双方谈判地位对等同样的条件是不可能被答应的。或者换个角度说,强势方可以任意拒绝弱势方的要求。英国法院的态度是,对于商业合约谈判中的谈判地位不对等,除非是采取了其他非法行为,否则应该由立法机关立法规管,而不是由司法系统来纠正。)

The English law of contract seeks to protect the reasonable expectations of honest people when they enter into contracts. It is an important principle which is applied to the interpretation of contracts... But, in contrast to many civil law jurisdictions and some common law jurisdictions, **English law has never recognised a general principle of good faith in contracting**. Instead, English law has relied on piecemeal solutions in response to demonstrated problems of unfairness...[英国合约法会保护诚实的当事人在签订合约时的合理预期,在解释合约时这也是重要的考虑因素与原则。但是与一些其他国家/地区的做法不同,英国合约法不认可存在一般适用的善意原则。而对于可能导致的实际不对等与不合理,英国法则是通过对特定类型的案件与不同的理论(如弃权、禁反言、解释合约的规则等)予以单独保护。]

The absence of**these doctrines restricts the scope for lawful act economic duress in commercial life**. In chapter 5 of his book, 'The Use and Abuse of Unjust Enrichment'

(Oxford 1991) Professor Jack Beatson … discussed the development of the modern doctrine of economic duress and the severe limitations on its application in commercial negotiation. At pp 129 – 130 he explained the basic approach of the common law in these terms: 'All that is not prohibited is permitted and there is no general doctrine of abuse of rights. If therefore a person is permitted to do something, he will generally be allowed to do it for any reason or for none. In the context of contractual negotiations this position enables people to know where they stand and provides certainty as to what is acceptable conduct in the bargaining process but it does leave many forms of socially objectionable conduct unchecked. Again, this is soundly based for judges should not, as a general rule, be the arbiters of what is socially unacceptable and attach legal consequences to such conduct.' He suggested … that **the scope for lawful act duress in contractual negotiations was 'extremely limited'. I agree.** (也是由于缺乏这些理论,限制了商业社会中合法行为经济胁迫能适用的范畴。Beatson 大法官在其书籍中指出在普通法下法无禁止皆自由,而且也不存在'滥用权利'的说法,因此当事人如果合法行为,无论是出于什么原因、什么目的行使该权利都是当事人的自由。在商事合约谈判中,这样的地位能使得当事人明确知道自己地位如何,给谈判中什么能做、什么不能做带来肯定性与稳定性。不可否认这确实会导致一些社会、道德上无法接受的行为失去监督与管制。但是也很明确的是,一般情况下的确不应该由法官来判断什么是社会、道德上无法接受,并根据判断赋予相应法律后果。这样,也能理解为什么'合法行为胁迫'必须只能限制在特别有限的情况中。)

'Anson's Law of Contract', 31st ed (2020) … similarly recognises this restrictive approach to the law of duress in contractual negotiations …: 'It is not ordinarily duress to threaten to do that which one has a right to do, for instance to refuse to enter into a contract or to terminate a contract lawfully. In the cut-and-thrust of business relationships various types of pressure may be brought to bear in differing situations. … [A] contracting party will not be permitted to escape from its contractual obligations merely because it was coerced into making a contract by fear of the financial consequences of refusing to do so. Although **this approach leaves many forms of socially objectionable conduct unchecked, as a general rule the determination of when socially objectionable conduct which is not in itself unlawful should be penalized is for the legislature rather than the judiciary.**' (《Anson's Law of Contract》一书中也提到类似说法,在合约谈判过程中胁迫理论的适用是非常有限的。一般情况下威胁采取自己有权采取的行为并不是胁迫,如完全可以拒绝达成合约,或者是合法终止合约。但另一方面,则是不允许合约方仅仅因为害怕不达成合约会有金钱上的损失等后果时,就主张属于被逼迫签约从而逃脱应尽的合约义务。这也确实放任了一些不被社会接受的行为,但这些行为应该由立法机关通过立法解决。)

Against this**commercial background** the pressure applied by a negotiating party will **very rarely come up to the standard of illegitimate pressure or unconscionable conduct**. It will therefore be **a rare circumstance** that a court will find lawful act duress in the context of commercial negotiation.(也因此在商业谈判中施加的压力,几乎不太能满足不法压力或不合情理行为的标准,这也是为什么商业谈判中合法行为胁迫几乎不太出现的原因。)”(加黑部分是笔者的强调)

8.4 过往有关合法行为胁迫的若干考虑因素

已经介绍过,针对商业合约中的合法压力胁迫,法院会尽量做出限制,但仍然存在什么是所说的“少数例外”的问题。经济胁迫目前如何划出分水岭,什么时候是法院可接受的压力,什么时候又变成不法压力仍然处在较为不稳定的发展阶段。但在PIAC v. Times Travel(2021)UKSC 40 最高院先例前的有关先例中,对此有一些关于判断标准的建议与说法。例如在《Duress, Undue Influence and Unconscionable Dealing》[2019 年,第3 版(2021 年第1 次增补)]一书之3-021 段提到了多种(相比其他类别的胁迫如对人身、对财物或经济胁迫,以便把门开得更窄)的考虑因素或要件:“In earlier cases, the courts considered a range of factors to determine whether the exercise of lawful pressure was illegitimate. These include:(1) whether the claimant had a reasonable alternative;[59](2) whether a threat of criminal proceedings was used to apply moral pressure;[60](3) whether the threat was made in bad faith;[61](4) whether the pressure was applied to support an unjustified or unreasonable demand;[62] and(5) whether the defendant's conduct is unconscionable.[63]”

但在PIAC v. Times Travel 最高院先例后,多数意见确认已经介绍过的两种情况属于合法行为胁迫:(1)敲诈勒索;(2)以应受谴责手段操纵对方处于弱势地位后,以合法行为逼迫对方放弃索赔与/或答应其他错误要求。但多数意见并没有否定将来会发展出更多类型的合法行为胁迫,只是没有明确合法行为胁迫的判断标准如何,特别是何时属于错误要求导致变成非法压力。也因此对此问题可再多进行一些介绍。

需要特别指出的是,这不是针对本章之8.2.2 段介绍的第(2)类情况,即Borrelli v. Ting(2010)UKPC 21 与The “Cenk Kaptanoglu”(2012)EWHC 273(Comm)先例中的情况,而是针对合法行为何时构成非法压力的一般测试标准应该如何设立的问题,即完全合法行为的威胁下提出要求何时属于“错误”? 例如,施压方采取的合法行为可以是在本章之8.3 段的施压方利用市场优势地位,又或者由于原合约的条文如施

[59] 见本章之10 段的可诉胁迫要件三。

[60] 见本章之8.2.1 段的类似情况。

[61] 见本章之8.4.3 段。

[62] 见本章之8.1.2 与8.4.1 段。

[63] 胁迫理论的发展过程中受到不当影响理论等衡平法理论的影响,有不少案件中都提到了将是否不合情理/显失公平等问题作为考虑因素。这见本章之5.1 段以及8.1.2 段等的介绍。

压方有权行使一个十分有利的权利/选择权而带来优势,对受压方而言这些压力简直是要了他的命等千变万化的情况。此时如果施压方提出的要求十分过分,而受压方无路可走只能答应,受压方是否可以事后反悔?如果可以,“十分过分”要求的分水岭/红线应如何划分?

已经在本章之8.1.2段提到,法院判断是否构成合法行为胁迫时,重点看是否属于错误要求。以下可以简单介绍一些过往先例中提到过的是否属于错误要求的考虑因素。

8.4.1 施压方超出商业的正常要求

过去有说法是,一个标准可以看是否显著超出合法商业交易的正常要求(beyond normal commercial demand)。例如在《Chitty on Contract》(2015年,第32版)一书之8-046段曾经说:“Threatening to carry out something perfectly within one's right will not normally amount to duress; for instance, a party who relies on his existing contractual rights to drive a hard bargain is not, on that ground alone, guilty of economic duress. But there can be no doubt that even a threat to commit what would otherwise be a perfectly lawful act may be improper if the threat is **coupled with a demand which goes substantially beyond what is normal or legitimate in commercial arrangements.**”(加黑部分是笔者的强调)

在较近期的Al Nehayan v. Kent(2018)EWHC 333(Comm)先例[64]中,除了人身胁迫之外,被迫出售自己在合资企业中的利益的原告主张自己签订退出经营的框架协议,以及签署本票(promissory note)也是由于经济胁迫,因此可使无效。针对本段要讨论的课题,Leggatt大法官提出了一个“特定最低标准”(“certain minimum standard”)的说法。但Leggatt大法官没有进一步解释这里提到的施压方提出要求的特定最低标准如何衡量,只是在后续段落中提到了考虑是否是错误要求时,要看是否有客观合理的基础支持(通常就是指法律基础,也会涉及商业上是否有合理基础),合理人士是否会认为不应该采用这样的威胁来满足自己的要求。Leggatt大法官说:“In civil as well as in criminal law, the state of mind of the defendant is naturally a relevant consideration where the question is whether the defendant has acted wrongfully. But the factors which render a contract defective and make it just to require contractual benefits to be restored are not limited to cases where the defendant has acted wrongfully. They include, for example, cases where a party lacks capacity or where one party is under the undue influence of the other, even though such influence may not involve any wrongdoing. They may also, in principle, include cases where the defendant has exploited a position of extreme vulnerability on the part of the claimant to induce the claimant to agree to a wholly unreasonable demand. There **is no reason why**, in this context, **the availability of**

[64] 案情在本书第一章之2.7.4.3段有介绍。

relief should depend on the defendant's own perception of whether his conduct was justified. On the contrary, as in other cases where **the law sets limits to freedom of contract by requiring the parties to observe certain minimum standards of behaviour**, the appropriate arbiter of those standards is the independent judgment of the court. ...On this basis a demand coupled with a threat to commit a lawful act will be regarded as illegitimate if (a) **the defendant has no reasonable grounds for making the demand** and (b) **the threat would not be considered by reasonable and honest people to be a proper means of reinforcing the demand.**"（加黑部分是笔者的强调）

但是在 PIAC v. Times Travel（2019）EWCA Civ 828 上诉庭先例中，上诉庭拒绝了 Leggatt 大法官提出的考虑客观是否“合理”（合理基础支持与合理人士认同）的说法。理由主要是出于政策上的考虑。客观上的合理性对于英国法而言并不是一个陌生的概念，很多情况中都会考虑客观合理性，在平衡之下也接受这样做法所必然带来的一定程度的不肯定，如涉及的是根据法律标准来判断一个索赔是否有合理理据等。但是上诉庭认为，在复杂多变的商业交往中，合法行为施压提要求被事后客观认定“不合理”就变成不法压力，并导致合约可使无效的胁迫救济，会带来难以清楚划分合理与否的分水岭的困难，以及导致商业合约效力存疑与不肯定的严重后果。而且最后判断商业交往中涉及私权利行使是否客观合理，要让不熟悉商业也没有渠道获取公众意见的法官来判断，也并不理想。上诉庭的 David Richards 大法官说：

"My conclusion on the central legal issue is that **the doctrine of lawful act duress does not extend to the use of lawful pressure to achieve a result to which the person exercising pressure believes in good faith it is entitled, and that is so whether or not, objectively speaking, it has reasonable grounds for that belief.** The common law and equity set tight limits to setting aside otherwise valid contracts. In this way undesirable uncertainty in a commercial context is reduced.... But that will not be the case in the much more common situation of a party using lawful commercial pressure in support of a purely commercial demand. There is no yardstick by which to judge such demands, save those that can be set out in legislation such as that applying to consumer contracts. Such demands are a matter of negotiation against the background of the pressures operating on both parties.

The relevant considerations go beyond uncertainty. **In judging the use of lawful acts or threats of lawful acts as commercial pressure, there is a sharp distinction between such use to pursue demands made in good faith and those made in bad faith.** As I earlier mentioned, a lack of good faith on the part of a contracting party is a feature in a number of the grounds on which contracts may be avoided. Rescission on grounds of fraudulent misrepresentation or unconscionable transaction are examples. It is a clear criterion involving conduct which all can agree is unacceptable and which is a fact capable of proof, often as it happens by reference to the lack of any reasonable grounds for the belief. By contrast, **not only is reasonableness in this context a standard of very uncertain content but it is also very unclear why or on what basis the common law should hold that a party with a private law right**, whose exercise is not subject to any overriding duty, **cannot use it to achieve a purpose which is both lawful and advanced in good faith**."(加黑部分是笔者的强调)

在 PIAC v. Times Travel(2021) UKSC 40 最高院先例中,Burrows 勋爵也同样对引入客观合理去看待施压方提的要求是否合法持反对意见,主张这样说法不肯定:"It is my view, with respect, that those tests risk rendering the law on lawful act duress too uncertain and would potentially jeopardise the stability of the English law of contract. ... alive to those risks and trusts the courts can draw a stable line as to what, for example, constitutes a demand that goes substantially beyond what is normal."

在最新版的《Chitty on Contract》(2021 年,第 34 版)一书之 10 - 056 段看来也是删除了本段开头节录的提议。笔者也觉得这样的分析是正确的,不应该以客观来看商业上是否合理作为判断标准,毕竟所有案件都多少可以争辩是否合理,这会带来不肯定与不稳定。

8.4.2 合法行为的威胁与所提出的要求之间是否成比例

这说法看来主要针对的情况是施压方利用自己占有的市场优势地位(如垄断地位),逼迫受压方签订合约,而合法行为的威胁与所要求的"合法"利益之间不成比例的情况。

在 CPR 改革中能看到法院在近年来开始逐渐更多考虑成比例(disproportionate demand)问题。在 CPR 之前的做法,往往是为了保证与维护司法系统的纯洁性,口号是"以任何代价追求正义"(Justice at all costs)。但在 CPR 改革时,Woolf 勋爵就提出这样的做法固然提升了司法系统的正义与纯洁,但代价太高让一般平民根本无力承担,也就失去意义了。因此在 CPR 就特别引入与强调了成比例的概念。当然相比这里所说的商业合约中成比例,在 CPR 下要相对简单得多,考虑的只是诉讼费用(与延误)相比于案件争议的金额、复杂程度等是否成比例。例如金额很小的争议就尽量简化诉讼程序。

但"成比例"也不是传统英国合约法中的概念。在近年来虽然开始引入成比例的说法,如在有关惩罚性条款(penalty clause)的 Cavendish Square Holdings BV v. Makdessi(2015) UKSC 67 最高院先例中,或者是在有关非法理论的 Patel v. Mirza (2016) UKSC 42 最高院先例等。在显然不成比例的极端案件中也是容易区分的,但是具体分水岭如何划分、模棱两可的案件中如何处理,这方面尚没有肯定与清楚的原则与测试标准。在 PIAC v. Times Travel(2021) UKSC 40 最高院先例中,少数意见的 Burrows 勋爵也指出这会带来不肯定与不稳定的问题:"it is far from clear how disproportionality would work in the context of a case like the present; and, more generally, one can anticipate that there would be great uncertainty in the working out of a disproportionality idea in the general context of lawful act economic duress."

成比例也就是能够在这两者之间"掌握轻重"。比如同样是 Holyoake v. Candy (2017) EWHC 3397(Ch) 先例的案情，在 H 先生触发违约条文后，Candy 兄弟以要求全额还款付息、将 H 先生欠下巨额债务的情况告知其他债权人与开始诉讼作为威胁，假设几种不同的例子：(1) 极端的例子就是要求 H 先生将其名下所有地产都低价出售给自己，后半辈子还债，这就是一个不成比例的要求，会被认为属于错误要求与能够构成胁迫。(2) 在该先例中实际发生的是重组债务等要求，这些看来是正常的商业行为（尽管结果对 H 先生不利）很难说是不成比例。(3) 模棱两可的例子，就比如假设要求的是额外增加 1 厘的利息，这可能是成比例，如果继续增加下去，变成额外的 2 厘、3 厘，加到什么程度会变成不成比例？

这问题就是在没有先例的经验确认规则（如哪些是需要考虑的因素，每个因素的重量如何等）的情况下，对轻重如何掌握是尺度也相差很大。这也是为什么在这个阶段引入成比例问题会导致不肯定与不稳定，尤其是在复杂、千变万化的商业社会中，倾向于不采用这样的做法。

而且胁迫的后果是非常严重的合约可使无效、决定"生死"，与 CPR 下成比例只是针对程序问题、费用多少的问题有所不同。这看来也是 Burrows 勋爵认为这给商业社会带来不肯定与大力反对该案上诉庭判法中引入成比例作为考虑因素的原因之一。

8.4.3　施压方的恶意要求

在本章之 5.4.2 段与 7.2.2 段介绍了在不法行为威胁中，违约/威胁违约的不法行为是否属于不法/不恰当压力的问题时，需要考虑施压方违约/威胁违约是善意还是恶意，如果是恶意就多半属于不法压力了。而本段考虑的善意/恶意稍有不同，针对的是合法行为威胁，没有违约/威胁违约的不法行为。在这种情况下，重点就变成要看提出的要求是否恶意（bad faith demand）。

在本章之 6 段有提到，由于合法行为威胁是否会变为不法压力，重点看施压方提出的要求是否错误，而在本章之 8.3.1 段也介绍了提出的要求以客观看商业上是否合理的测试标准并不被 PIAC v. Times Travel (2021) UKSC 40 最高院先例接受，这就带来施压方提出的要求是否恶意的更高标准测试的疑问。在该先例中，少数意见的 Burrows 勋爵就提出了一种恶意要求测试作为判断标准，但这测试没有被该先例中多数意见接受。

尽管如此，由于在过往先例中常常都提到会考虑"善意"/"恶意"，在将来根据先例发展，合法行为胁迫的测试标准也仍然存在重新细化与设定这方面的标准的可能性，因此为了完整，会简单介绍 Burrows 勋爵提出的标准，与在此先例中不接受的原因。

8.4.3.1　Burrows 勋爵的恶意要求测试

在本章之 8.3.1 段介绍的 CTN Cash and Carry Ltd v. Gallaher Ltd (1994) 4 All ER 714 先例将是否善意提出要求作为重要的考虑因素。Steyn 大法官还解释说这里的善意,针对的是施压方是否有真实信念(genuine belief)受压方欠下了债务(在该先例中还包括认为货物被偷走的风险由受压方承担),这样用合法商业行为威胁以要求获取这些应得的利益不会被认为属于不法压力。可以重复节录 Steyn 大法官所说如下:"A third, and **critically important**, characteristic of the case is the fact that the **defendants bona fide thought** that the goods were at the risk of the plaintiffs and that the plaintiffs owed the defendants the sum in question. The defendants **exerted commercial pressure on the plaintiffs in order to obtain payment of a sum which they bona fide considered due to them.**"(加黑部分是笔者的强调)

到了 PIAC v. Times Travel(2021) UKSC 40 最高院先例中,持少数意见的 Burrows 勋爵正是依赖 CTN Cash and Carry Ltd v. Gallaher Ltd 先例的说法,提出了在判断合法行为是否可以构成不法/不恰当压力时,采用是否有真实信念为标准的恶意要求测试,合法行为要构成不法/不恰当压力必须涉及施压方的恶意。而在 PIAC v. Times Travel 先例中,按照 Burrows 勋爵的说法就是因为没能证明施压方(航空公司)的恶意,导致不会属于不法压力,说:"Given that 'good faith' can be used in different senses, it is important to clarify that what was here meant was that, albeit mistakenly, the defendants genuinely believed that they were contractually owed the payment demanded. The case may therefore be said to establish what I shall refer to hereinafter as the 'bad faith demand' requirement. This requirement can be expressed as follows. In the context we are focusing on-of **a demand for what is claimed to be owing**, or analogously, as on the facts of this case, **a demand for the waiver of a claim**-it is a **necessary requirement** for establishing lawful act economic duress that the demand is made in bad faith in the particular sense that the **threatening party does not genuinely believe that it is owed what it is claiming to be owed or does not genuinely believe that it has a defence to the claim being waived by the threatened party.**"(加黑部分是笔者的强调)

在具体的测试标准上,Burrows 勋爵看来还提出了两种不同情况:

1. 第一种针对的是 Borrelli v. Ting(2010) UKPC 21 枢密院先例与 The "Cenk Kaptanoglu"(2012) EWHC 273(Comm)先例这类被多数意见认可属于合法行为胁迫的案件。这类案件中要求施压方首先故意造成或增加了受压方的不利处境,其次要求施压方还提出恶意要求,这就会构成不法压力。Burrows 勋爵说:"... Taken together, what Borrelli v Ting and Progress Bulk Carriers (The "Cenk Kaptanoglu") can be taken to have established is that, in relation to a demand for a waiver by the threatened party of a claim against the threatening party, the demand is unjustified, so that the lawful act economic threat is illegitimate where: **first, the threatening party has deliberately created, or increased, the threatened party's vulnerability to the demand**; and, **secondly, the 'bad faith demand' requirement is satisfied (ie the threatening party does not genuinely believe that it has a defence, and there is no defence, to the claim being**

waived)."(加黑部分是笔者的强调)

Burrows 勋爵这样的测试标准,可以解释 Borrelli v. Ting 枢密院先例与 The "Cenk Kaptanoglu"的判法。这两个先例都多少有故意行为造成了原告脆弱(vulnerable)的困境。[65] 其次就是在这两个先例中施压方都不会有真实信念自己有对抗受压方索赔的抗辩。例如,Borrelli v. Ting 先例中的丁谓没有什么理由抵抗清盘人继续调查与向丁谓及其控制的公司追偿,The "Cenk Kaptanoglu"先例中的船东面对承租人对明确不过的船东原先一船两租的违约索赔也不存在什么抗辩的理由。

2. Burrows 勋爵还提出了第二种更进一步的测试标准,就是即使施压方并没有故意造成受压方的脆弱困境,但只要明知受压方处于脆弱困境时,还提出了恶意要求,也能构成不法压力。

但是大量商业交往,尤其是在合约尚未达成的谈判过程中,有水平的商人都是在摸底/试探与经过专业人士尽职调查的情况下,施加合法商业压力。这样,为了避免此类一般都视为正当的情况也被包括在内,Burrows 勋爵提出这测试必须加多一道门槛,也就是双方已经有一定的关系如合约关系,有已经存在的法律权利或义务(existing legal rights or duty)。此时施压方提出对这些法律义务或权利的要求,如将合约同意的价格提高一倍,或者是要求放弃对过去合约下索赔的权利,就可以判断是否"恶意"了。也就是可以客观看待,由施压方提供证据显示提出的要求背后的法律基础,并根据证据判断这理由是否可以接受为有真实信念。

相比之下,如果双方原本没有合约关系,如双方首次接触谈判交易并试图达成合约,只要你情我愿就没有不妥。即使是一方占有优势地位(如垄断某高科技产品),明知开出的价格远远超出正常市场价格或卖给其他人士的价格,但弱势的买方没有其他选择,只能仍然硬着头皮愿意达成买卖合约。这种情况不涉及"恶意要求",事后买方无法主张卖方的合法行为胁迫导致合约无效。

Burrows 勋爵说:

"... it is possible to go one step further in one's interpretation of the reasoning in CTN Cash and Carry... **Although one cannot say that the defendants had deliberately created, or increased, the claimants' vulnerability** (as one could in Borrelli v Ting and Progress Bulk Carriers and on the facts of this case), the defendants must have known that the claimants were in an exceptionally vulnerable position because of the defendants' monopoly position. If one then adds to that the postulated satisfaction of the 'bad faith demand'

---

〔65〕 有关案情已经在本章之 8.2.2 段介绍,不在此详细介绍。就如在 Borrelli v. Ting 先例中破产清算公司的股东通过伪造文件、恶意投票等不法手段反对公司股权转售,造成无法通过转售筹措清算资金的清算人无法继续清算程序,此时股东用不继续投反对票的合法行为诱导清算人放弃索赔。又如在 The "Cenk Kaptanoglu"先例中,船东将约定出租给承租人的船舶租给了第三人是不法的违约/毁约行为,造成临近交货时间承租人找不到运输船舶就可能失去重要客户与面对巨额索赔,此时船东再提出可以提供替代船舶(这本身是合法行为)诱导承租人放弃针对船东索赔。

requirement-so that, on the facts, the defendants would have been dishonestly claiming that the money was owing under the contract when they knew it was not-there is a compelling analogy to the facts of Borrelli v Ting and Progress Bulk Carriers. Although it is not necessary to decide this point in this case, I am of the view that, had the facts otherwise been the same but the 'bad faith demand' requirement had been satisfied in CTN Cash and Carry, the demand would have been unjustified thereby rendering the threat illegitimate.

...**The law on lawful act economic duress would be far too wide if, generally, the illegitimacy of the threat turned on whether the threatening party did, or did not, bona fide believe that it was entitled to what was demanded**. For example, a party (A) negotiating a contract with another party (B) may threaten (lawfully) not to supply goods unless B pays A money. Plainly economic duress could not be made out (there would otherwise be a risk of undermining ordinary contractual negotiations) even if it could be shown that A did not genuinely believe itself entitled to the money demanded from B. Indeed, it is obvious that, until the contract has been concluded, A has no contractual entitlement to what is demanded. Put another way, **the 'bad faith demand' requirement is dependent on there being an existing legal right and duty between the parties (whether contractual or otherwise) which provides a clear and certain standard against which alleged bad faith of the threatening party can be assessed**. Without that tie to an existing legal right and duty, the 'bad faith demand' requirement loses its force as being underpinned by a workable standard of dishonesty: the bad faith demand is concerned with either a dishonest assertion of an existing right or the dishonest removal (by waiver) of an existing right. It also loses its force as providing a clear and certain means of controlling the scope of lawful act economic duress and of distinguishing a demand that is unjustified from one that is made in ordinary commercial bargaining."(加黑部分是笔者的强调)

Burrows 勋爵还引用了《Goff & Jones: The Law of Unjust Enrichment》(2016 年，第9版)一书之 10－70 段针对 CTN Cash and Carry Ltd v. Gallaher Ltd 先例的评论[66]:"If the claimants could have shown that when the defendants made their threat they knew that the goods were at the defendants' risk, then the claimants would surely have succeeded, for the money would then have been extorted from them, and commercial self-interest is not unbridled."

在这样的测试标准下，如 CTN Cash and Carry Ltd v. Gallaher Ltd 上诉庭先例中的案情，施压方并非故意造成受压方的困境(并非故意送错仓库、导致货物被偷走)，事后合法行为提出要求时也有真实信念，因此并非不法压力。而如果情况有所变化，

---

〔66〕 在该权威书籍的最新版(2022 年，第 10 版)中，因为 PIAC v. Times Travel(2021) UKSC 40 最高院先例的判决，这段内容被删除。

施压方在提出要求时明知货物被偷走的风险并非由受压方承担,按照 Burrows 勋爵的标准这就应该属于不法压力了。

8.4.3.2 多数意见否定了 Burrows 勋爵的测试

已经提到 Burrows 勋爵提出的恶意测试的标准被最高院多数意见的大法官拒绝。多数意见认为 CTN Cash and Carry Ltd v. Gallaher Ltd(1994)4 All ER 714 上诉庭先例并不是对什么时候有不法压力给了一个判断标准,只是否定性的判法,也就是占有垄断地位的公司在商业谈判中利用自己地位要求更多商业利益不是不法压力,这种情况在现实社会也会频繁发生。Steyn 大法官的说法,充其量也只能理解为如果处于市场垄断地位的被告不诚实地宣称自己有权获得原告支付,再加上后续合法行为有可能构成不法压力,但仍然并非一定,既非充分也非必要条件。不能说只要是没有真实信念,就会导致不法压力。Hodge 勋爵说:"The implication of his judgment (Steyn 大法官的判法) may be that the dishonest assertion of a pre-existing entitlement to payment accompanied by a threat to carry out a lawful act, such as to withdraw credit arrangements on future contracts or to refuse to enter into further contracts, could amount to lawful act duress as a form of an abuse of right."

以是否恶意作为判断标准是给合法行为胁迫引入了思想状态[67](state of mind)作为考虑因素。但在 PIAC v. Times Travel(2021)UKSC 40 最高院先例中,多数意见只认可目前存在两类合法行为胁迫。除了第一类敲诈勒索外,第二类"用应受谴责的手段操纵对方处于弱势地位并逼迫对方不得不放弃索赔",实际上是不用考虑施压方提出要求的主观想法是"善意"还是"恶意",没有主观想法的因素。

在多数意见说法下,分析在 CTN Cash and Carry Ltd v. Gallaher Ltd 上诉庭先例中,是因为占有垄断地位的被告并没有采取应受谴责的手段如欺诈性误述等操纵原告处于弱势地位,被告利用自己的优势地位占尽商业利益就不是不法压力,也无须考虑此时被告是善意还是恶意。即使被告明知香烟的遗失风险应由自己承担,仍然执意或恶意要求原告对这批香烟付钱,这也不是不法压力。

这样的解读下,可以在需要肯定性与可预测性的合约法下,避开了涉及善意/恶意、主观/客观的问题。Hodge 勋爵指出,在商业环境中,追求最大化利益的精明商人常常都多少有"恶意",也很少没有任何说得出的真实信念,无论是对是错。Hodge 勋爵说:"A 'bad faith demand' based on an asserted pre-existing entitlement may not be a rare occurrence in commercial life. Discreditable behaviour can be a feature of commercial activity."

Hodge 勋爵在判词中还继续给出了为什么不同意 Burrows 勋爵引入"恶意要求"的三点重要理由,可以节录如下:

"First, it would be difficult to anchor the extension in any recognised legal principle.

〔67〕 有关思想状态可见《证据法:基础理论、口头证据与专家证据》一书第十章。

Where B(受压方)is induced by A(施压方)'s fraudulent representation to meet its demand,B may have a claim against A under the tort of deceit. But that is not the circumstance envisaged in CTN(CTN Cash and Carry Ltd v. Gallaher Ltd 先例)or by the Court of Appeal in this case. Where B is induced to meet A's demand because of the stark inequality of bargaining power which gives B no effective choice but to meet the demand which B knows is not justified,it is not obvious to me that,without more,B could have a claim for economic duress in the absence of a general principle of good faith in contracting or a doctrine of imbalance of bargaining power,neither of which currently exists. It is difficult in principle to distinguish such a circumstance from a circumstance in which A makes an exorbitant demand in the course of negotiations as a condition for entering into contractual relations with B.(合法行为威胁与采用欺诈性误述等行为诱导合约是两码事。反而是与在谈判中利用自己优势地位获取更多利益并无不同,在英国普通法下没有善意或拉平谈判地位不对等的说法与救济,这种纯粹以自己优势地位获取更大利益、没有什么错误行为,不应该构成经济胁迫。)

Secondly,in the absence of an underlying principle,the extension of lawful act duress in this way would create unwanted uncertainty. There is,in my view,force in the concern that the extension of the concept of lawful act duress would risk creating unacceptable uncertainty in the sphere of commercial transactions... Lord Burrows seeks to avoid such uncertainty through the construct of the bad faith demand,but I do not accept that,without more,lawful act economic duress would exist even if there were such a bad faith demand. In my view the doctrine is more limited in the context of commercial relations.(由于对商业交易的合约关系带来的巨大不肯定与不稳定,多数意见非常抗拒扩大合法行为威胁能构成胁迫的案件类型。目前涉及合法行为胁迫只限于本章前文中已经介绍的两大类情况。)

Thirdly,the extension of lawful act duress in this way might be of limited utility. This isbecause,first,commercial organisations may enter into a dispute or commence litigation without an informed idea of their legal rights or any intention of seeking judicial resolution but with the aim of reaching a settlement of the dispute on better terms than are currently on offer. The vast majority of commercial disputes do not go to trial and are not expected to do so. Each organisation may have to reach its own view as to its entitlements and resolve the dispute accordingly. Secondly,it would be very difficult for B to establish its case because B would have to demonstrate A's subjective bad faith. The application of legal rules to a particular factual circumstance,such as when risk passes on a contract of sale,commonly involves questions of legal judgment on which legal advisers may reasonably differ. A party may be advised that it has an arguable case but that the application of the law to the facts of that case is uncertain. A party may proceed to make a claim on the basis of legal advice of a percentage chance of success. What is envisaged in the 'bad faith demand' requirement in this context is that there is little, if any, uncertainty as to A's lack of entitlement, and that A makes its demand in the knowledge that it does not have the legal entitlement which it claims. B would succeed in its claim for lawful act duress only if it established that A did not genuinely believe that it had that entitlement. [这样扩大合法行为胁迫的范围，对于商业实践的帮助与指导意义也不大。首先是出现商业争议时当事人未必理解自己的法律权利或地位，而只是想要达成一个更有利于自己的解决方案。有时候即使开始诉讼也只是为了与对方达成更有利于自己的和解协议，大部分的诉讼都走不到庭审阶段。其次，要证明施压方的真实信念（恶意或善意要求），不是一件容易的事情。更不用说更常见的情况是一出现争议，当事人往往咨询律师之后根据律师的意见行事，哪怕是再差的案件，有经验和有水平的律师多少能找出一线生机或至少是说得过去的理由，差别只是胜诉几率高低而已。因此按照律师意见行事的商人很难说是没有真实信念自己有所主张的权利。]

I therefore do not accept that the lawful act doctrine could be extended to a circumstance in which, without more, a commercial organisation exploits its strong bargaining power or monopoly position to extract a payment from another commercial organisation by an assertion in bad faith of a pre-existing legal entitlement which the other organisation believes or knows to be incorrect."

以上节录内容最后一段就提到，综合以上三点来看，判决不接受将合法行为胁迫扩张到以必须存在恶意要求作为判断标准，商业机构利用自己优势或垄断地位，即使恶意主张自己存在已有的某些法律权利，以此向其他商业机构提出各种要求，包括要求支付金钱或好处，也不是胁迫。

除此以外，哪怕是将是否恶意作为考虑因素，多数意见也不认可将恶意仅仅限于是否有真实信念。Hodge 勋爵说也要综合看施压方的行为，包括提的是什么要求，提要求的事实背景等，说："In both cases it was the combination of the probable or at least possible validity of B（受压方）'s claim against A（施压方）combined with A's behaviour of that nature which gave rise to the court's conclusion that the waiver had been obtained through the application of illegitimate pressure. In other words, bad faith is potentially relevant both to the content of the demand and to the context in which A makes its demand."

8.4.4 施压方的要求是不合情理/显失公平

例如，卖方 A 手中有市场十分短缺的货物（如救命的药品），明知道奇货可居，而买方 B 特别紧急需要，加上 A 一贯与 B 关系一般，所以想趁机敲竹杠。最后 B 无奈以 10 倍价格买下，但事后也知道 A 在同一时间只以一半价格把同样的货物卖给 C、D 与 E。这样，B 能否以 A 恶意要求 10 倍价格，主张合法行为胁迫？如果可以，会否法律过分干预正常商业活动？而且分水岭在哪里？10 倍不成，5 倍或 3 倍可以吗？

A 与 B 关系一般,但与 C、D 与 E 关系好要不要考虑? 如果要考虑,如何设定标准与量化?

施压方提出的错误要求的程度是否严重到不合情理/显失公平(unconscionable demand)占受压方的便宜在 PIAC v. Times Travel(2021)UKSC 40 最高院先例前的少数合法行为胁迫案件中,也常被提到与在一些案件中被作为考虑因素之一,可节录《Duress,Undue Influence and Unconscionable Dealing》(2019 年,第 3 版)一书之 3-030 段所说:"In Alf Vaughan & Co v. Royscot Trust(1999)1 All ER(Comm)856,it was held that it was not unconscionable for a party **to threaten lawful action in order to support a demand for a higher price** than that offered by the victim of the threat. ... In other words,the mere fact of using the threat of lawful action in order to support a demand for a better price in a commercial transaction did not make the conduct unconscionable and the threat illegitimate. In that case ... **there was no finding that the owner had grossly overpriced the goods**. By contract,in Harrison v. Halliwell Landau,His Honour Judge Eccles QC ... said that a threat of lawful action could be regarded as illegitimate ..."(加黑部分是笔者的强调)

只针对 Harrison v. Halliwell Landau(2004)EWHC 1316(QB)先例多讲几句。此先例的案情简单而言是在一个诉讼案件中 Halliwell Landau 律师所曾代表 Harrison 夫妇,但中途双方关系破裂,Harrison 夫妇也终止了 Halliwell Landau 的服务。之后 Halliwell Landau 向 Harrison 夫妇提起诉讼追讨欠下的律师费用,Harrison 夫妇则以律师的疏忽作为抗辩与反索赔。但在开庭审理前,双方达成和解并以汤姆林命令[68](Tomlin Order)在法院记录在案,条件是 Harrison 夫妇支付共 60,000 英镑,首期10,000英镑在 3 个月内支付,余款按每月 2000 英镑分期支付。但 Harrison 夫妇没有支付首期,并试图以合法行为胁迫推翻和解协议与撤销汤姆林命令。作为施压方的 Halliwell Landau 推进诉讼的行为显然是合法行为,不是不法/不恰当压力的经济胁迫。而且还有几方面问题导致 Harrison 夫妇的主张显然无法成功,例如没有尽快主张救济,可被视为确认(affirmation)了由于胁迫而可使无效的和解协议;又如 Harrison 夫妇作为受压方并不缺乏其他合理选择,也就是可以不和解与让诉讼推进下去。而在此先例中,还有一个重要的问题是在分析了有关的诉讼与和解金额后,法院不认为 Halliwell Landau 占了 Harrison 夫妇的大便宜,远没有严重到"不合情理/显失公平"的地步。Eccles 大法官说:"In my view the only other consideration that might persuade the court that this case should fall into **the relatively rare category of 'lawful act' duress** justifying an order setting aside the agreement of 25 July 2001(和解协议) would be if it could be established that **the terms were so manifestly disadvantageous as to make it unconscionable for Halliwell Landau to retain the benefit of them**.... In my

[68] 有关汤姆林命令,可见《证据法:国际规管与诉讼中的证据攻防》一书第四章之 1.7.6 段。

judgment, without expressing any view about the likely outcome had the case been fought to the end, the settlement was far from being manifestly and unconscionably disadvantageous."(加黑部分是笔者的强调)

"不合情理/显失公平"本是十分含糊与不精确的衡平法说法,与支持商业合约的肯定、稳定与可预测性的法律大原则有直接冲突,也会带来与本书第十一章介绍的不合情理/显失公平交易的混乱。正如在《Duress, Undue Influence and Unconscionable Dealing》(2019 年,第 3 版)一书之 3-029 段说:"**The danger of uncertainty** A threat of lawful action may be illegitimate if the threatener's conduct is unconscionable. However, the courts apply unconscionable conduct in this context with caution, since it is a vague and imprecise concept with a potential to lead to confusion with the doctrine of unconscionable dealing as an independent ground for settling aside a transaction. ..."

但在 PIAC v. Times Travel 最高院先例后,已经是把在本章之 8.2.2 段介绍的 Borrelli v. Ting (2010) UKPC 21 与 The "Cenk Kaptanoglu" (2012) EWHC 273 (Comm) 先例中的情况整体来看视为属于"不合情理/显失公平",接受属于合法行为胁迫。这类案件中其实是施压方在同一个事件中通过一连串的应受谴责的手段(多数是不法甚至非法手段,如伪造文件、违约、欺诈性误述等)造成受压方无路可走,最后逼迫受压方不得不答应自己的要求。而且,最高院多次强调了商业合约肯定性的重要大原则。这样看来,在不涉及过往应受到谴责手段时,即使采取合法行为胁迫的方式"敲竹杠"、漫天开价与完全不理会还价,恶意要求买药救命的买方支付 10 倍、20 倍或更高 100 倍的价格,即使单看要求是不合情理/显失公平,也不会构成合法行为胁迫,要想改变这种不乐见的社会现象,就只能靠立法、行政命令与手段了。

8.4.5 小结

虽然 PIAC v. Times Travel (2021) UKSC 40 最高院先例没有否定在本章之 8.2 段的两种类型的合法行为胁迫以外,会在将来的案例中发展出其他新冒出来的类型,但也没有划出"错误要求"是要错到什么程度才令"合法行为"威胁蜕变为"不法/不恰当压力"与构成"合法行为胁迫"。如果连极端到"恶意要求"也不被最高院多数大法官接受,可能会给商业合约的肯定性与稳定性带来负面影响,合法行为胁迫的案件将来也很难再会有新的类别出现。

或者说,只剩下在施压方提出的错误要求属于违反刑法(可能也包括侵权)时,才有可能被接受为合法行为胁迫,毕竟民商法需要与刑法同步。[69]

8.5 其他国家与地区的判法

在 PIAC v. Times Travel (2021) UKSC 40 最高院先例中还总结了目前普通法国家与地区有关合法行为胁迫的不同判法:

1. 澳大利亚对于是否存在合法行为胁迫,看来没有明确的一致判法。Crescendo

[69] 非法理论中也是同样道理,民商法需要与刑法同步,也可见本书第八章之 1.1 段。

Management Pty Ltd v. Westpac Banking Corp(1988)19 NSWLR 40;Mitchell v. Pacific Dawn Pty Ltd(2011) QCA 98;Electricity Generation Corp v. Woodside Energy Ltd (2013) WASCA 36;Morgan Stanley Wealth Management Australia Pty Ltd v. Detata (No. 3)(2018) WASC 32;Doggett v. Commonwealth Bank of Australia(2015) VSCA 351;Braam v. BBC Hardware(2020)VSCA 164 等先例中认可合法行为胁迫。但 Australia and New Zealand Banking Group Ltd v. Karam(2005)NSWCA 344;May v. Brahmbhatt(2013)NSWCA 309 先例拒绝了存在合法行为胁迫的说法,将胁迫限于不法行为,而如果在个别案件可以符合不当影响或不合情理/显失公平理论则可以寻求衡平法救济,这是另一回事了。

对于利用自己市场优势地位通过谈判获取更多商业利益,这与 CTN Cash and Carry Ltd v. Gallaher Ltd(1994)4 All ER 714 先例中的情况类似,一般不认为属于不法压力。例如在 Smith v. William Charlick Ltd(1924)34 CLR 38 先例中,当时的澳大利亚小麦局(Australian Wheat Board,但后来已经私有化)销售小麦给被告,后来威胁说除非被告对过往已经支付的几批小麦额外多支付一些金钱(当然也找出了一些理由支持,如小麦价格上涨,是为了给种植小麦的农民合理补偿等,因此可争辩说不是恶意的),否则以后不会再与被告签订新的供应合约。这被法院判不是胁迫。

2. 新西兰跟从英国 The "Universe Sentinel"(1983)1 AC 366 贵族院先例的说法,认可合法行为胁迫:见 Magsons Hardware Ltd v. Concept 124 Ltd(2011)NZCA 559 先例中,并且将合法行为胁迫的判断标准等同于不合情理/显失公平理论。

同样利用市场优势地位获取商业利益也不被认为有什么不恰当之处:见 McIntyre v. Nemesis DBK Ltd(2009)NZCA 329 先例。在较近期的 Dold v. Murphy(2020) NZCA 313 上诉庭先例中,一家旅游公司收到了以 1.1 亿多澳元的总价收购其全部股份的要约,对方的出价非常好,同时要求在 5 天内签订合约。持有旅游公司 93.8% 股权的两位大股东欣然接受,但持有 6.2% 股权的小股东要求大股东答应从最后收到的金钱额外分 400 万澳元给自己,否则不会同意对方收购。面对小股东的最后通牒,以及不及时接受要约就可能再也没有这么好的机会,大股东只能答应小股东的要求。事后大股东以经济胁迫为由要求小股东退回 400 万澳元。法院的判法是,首先小股东行使自己股东权利的行为没有违反该公司的股东协议,因此这是股东的合法行为,而仅仅是商业投机,并不是不法压力,不构成胁迫。

在笔者看来这样的判法也很符合现实,这类小股东"行使权利"要求更多利益的行为在公司收购中屡见不鲜,商业活动中这样的行为也通常都被接受,如果这都能构成合法行为胁迫看来是会范围过于广泛了。

3. 加拿大是认可经济胁迫的:见 Martel Building Ltd v. Canada(2000)2 SCR 860 先例等。但与英国法不同的是,对于经济胁迫中是否以不法/不恰当压力为判断,有不同说法。支持必须有不法/不恰当压力的见 Stott v. Merit Investment Corpn(1988) 63 OR(2d)545;Techform Products Ltd v. Wolda(2001)206 DLR(4th)171 等先例。也

有先例认为英国法下什么时候会变成不法/不恰当压力不够清楚,因此对此有所抗拒:见 Greater Fredericton Airport Authority Inc v. NAV Canada(2008)290 DLR(4th)405;Burin Peninsula Community Business Development Corpn v. Grandy(2010)327 DLR(4th)752 等先例。

加拿大法律与英国的不同是在合约履行有“善意”(bona fide / good-faith)的要求:见在加拿大最高院的 Bhasin v. Hrynew(2014)3 SCR 494 先例。这样对于合法行为胁迫看来会更类似接下来介绍的美国法的地位。Hodge 勋爵对此的介绍说:“… the decision of the Canadian Supreme Court in Bhasin v Hrynew… to recognise a general organising **principle of good faith in contractual performance** may have a significant influence on the direction of Canadian jurisprudence on the doctrine of economic duress. … the **courts can give relief from provisions in agreements which are ‘highly unreasonable or very unfair’ and that the test for duress is one of unfairness or unconscionability**…”(加黑部分是笔者的强调)

4. 美国法下,《Restatement(Second)of Contracts》(1981 年,2020 年 6 月更新)之 Section 176 中,针对美国法下的所谓不恰当威胁(improper threat)给出如下几种情况:

“(1)A threat is improper if(a)what is threatened is a crime or a tort,or the threat itself would be a crime or a tort if it resulted in obtaining property,(用犯罪或侵权行为威胁,或威胁获取财产本身已经构成犯罪或侵权)(b)what is threatened is a criminal prosecution,(见本章之 8.2.1 段介绍的敲诈勒索案件)(c)what is threatened is the use of civil process and the threat is made in bad faith,or(d)the threat is a breach of the duty of good faith and fair dealing under a contract with the recipient.

(2)A threat is improper if the resulting exchange is not on fair terms,and(此时针对的并非威胁本身,而针对的是最后达成的合约/交易结果是否公平,而且还至少要满足以下三点要求其中任意一个,才会属于不恰当威胁)(a)the threatened act would harm the recipient and would not significantly benefit the party making the threat,(b)the effectiveness of the threat in inducing the manifestation of assent is significantly increased by prior unfair dealing by the party making the threat,or(c)what is threatened is otherwise a use of power for illegitimate ends.”

Hodge 勋爵对以上内容评论说:“The first heading addresses unlawful act duress. The second heading is the equivalent of the … lawful act duress cases… The fourth heading is influenced by the general duty of good faith and fair dealing in contract …,which does not have its counterpart in English law. Little guidance can therefore be gained from the fourth heading in the Restatement on the question of lawful act duress in English law.”

简单而言,在一些大原则上美国法与英国法有类似之处,如非法犯罪行为、侵权行为、威胁刑事诉讼、恶意威胁民事诉讼(敲诈勒索)都被认为是不恰当威胁。但由于美国(上一段介绍的加拿大法律也是一样)有关商业的法律中存在善意概念,例如《Uniform Commercial Code》之 Section 1 – 304 说:"Every contract or duty within the Uniform Commercial Code imposes an obligation of good faith in its performance and enforcement."又如《Restatement (Second) of Contracts》之 Section 205 也有类似说法:"Every contract imposes upon each party a duty of good faith and fair dealing in its performance and its enforcement."也因此对于是否属于不恰当威胁,尤其是一般违约/毁约的威胁时,是否善意与公平交易变成关键问题,会由于善意而可以偏离原合约约定的条文。但在严格要求执行合约与没有一般性的善意责任的英国法下不会有这样的弹性,也因此就带来很多方面的不同,但这里不再进一步分析。

5. 大陆法国家也有胁迫理论,但是否包括合法行为胁迫并不明确。《UNIDROIT Principles of International Commercial Contracts》(2016 年)采用的措辞/文字是不正当的威胁(unjustified threat),针对了两种情况。第一种是威胁行为本身不正当即非法行为胁迫。第二种是采用有关行为逼迫受压方订立合约整体来看不正当,这看来可以将敲诈勒索类型的胁迫也包括在内,但是这是否可以广泛地包括更多其他类型的合法行为胁迫是不清楚的。可以节录 Article 3.2.6,说:"ARTICLE 3.2.6 (Threat) A party may avoid the contract when it has been led to conclude the contract by the other party's **unjustified threat** which, having regard to the circumstances, is so imminent and serious as to leave the first party no reasonable alternative. In particular, **a threat is unjustified** if the act or omission with which a party has been threatened is wrongful in itself, **or it is wrongful to use it as a means** to **obtain the conclusion of the contract**."(加黑部分是笔者的强调)

9."可诉胁迫"要件之二:因果关系

一旦确定有不法压力的存在,接下来就要看该胁迫有否产生实际作用。这也很好理解,即使有不法压力的存在,如果受压方原本就要签订合约,也没理由给予这会带来严重后果的胁迫的救济。

现实中也有多种原因导致原本就愿意订立合约的情况。例如,施压方给出的要约,或者提供交换的对价足够,并非只是象征式(purely technical)。又如受压方不想破坏长期的业务关系。再如原合约中已经获利颇丰,受压方注意到情况(如市场价格、对方的经济状况等)的变化,愿意做出一些让步。这些事实情况会是千变万化的。

9.1 因果关系的不同程度

这里所说不法压力与合约的订立之间必须有"一定"的因果关系,是因为在今天的判法下，不同类型的胁迫对因果关系的要求也有不同。例如对人身的胁迫因果关系的要求会非常低，而且转移举证责任。而对财物的胁迫或是经济胁迫往往就需要胁迫足以构成重要因素（significant cause）或满足要不是测试，这些将在本段稍后详细介绍。在此只节录《Goff & Jones：The Law of Unjust Enrichment》（2022 年，第 10 版）一书之 10 – 37 段，说："… it is generally accepted that the principle governing causation in duress to the person are exceptional，and that the default position is that it is for the claimant to show that the duress amounted to **a 'significant cause'** of the conferral of the benefit."（加黑部分是笔者的强调）

因果关系是一个复杂的课题，在各种不同法律关系之中，针对责任问题与针对损失问题的因果关系也不尽相同。有关损失的因果关系可见《损失的赔偿与救济》一书第四章。本段主要针对的是有关是否要给予不法压力以胁迫救济的因果关系，即责任上的因果关系问题。

为了帮助理解，不妨在开头先根据事实的不同，按因果关系的远近、紧密程度简单区分以下几种不同情况。

9.1.1　程度之一：没有关系且没有受到影响

举一个日常生活中买水果的例子。某人路过一个水果摊买水果，该水果摊名为优质水果摊，但他买水果时从来没有注意到水果摊叫什么名字，或者即使确实留意到是名为优质水果摊但不认为这个名字就代表水果的真正品质。水果摊的名称与买水果的行为并没有因果关系。

在本段针对的不法/不恰当经济压力，也就是施压方所施加的压力对名义上的"受压方"一点影响都没有，受压方本来就已经决定要与施压方签订有关合约。

9.1.2　程度之二："确实有考虑到"或原因之一

同样是买水果的例子，在水果摊买水果确实是有考虑到这个水果摊距离家很近，但是又并没有达到"要不是距离这么近，就不会在这个水果摊买"的程度。例如其实距离差不多的还有好几家水果摊，又如其实去这家水果摊买纯粹是因为与老板熟悉，甚至因此即使这家水果摊搬迁到了远处仍然会驱车前往。这种情况下，距离近这个因素其实是无法满足"要不是"（but for）测试的，而只能说在过往买水果时确实是考虑了这个因素，这说法可以称之为"确实有考虑到"（actively in mind）。

而在较近期的一些有关误述的先例中，如 Raiffeisen Zentralbank Osterreich AG v. Royal Bank of Scotland Plc（2010）EWHC 1392（Comm）先例等在此基础上还提到了要不是欺诈性误述，被误述方"有可能采取不同行为"（"might have acted differently"）的说法。在 BV Nederlandse Industrie Van Eiprodukten v. Rembrandt Enterprises Inc（2019）EWCA Civ 596 上诉庭先例中，Longmore 大法官就说这两者没什么不同，并且针对"确实有考虑到"解释说："If it means no more than being actively present in the mind of the representee…it is perhaps a convenient shorthand. But if it means that the court cannot make up its mind on inducement and therefore decides as a matter of law to give the representee the benefit of the doubt, it is not a helpful concept because that would be contrary to the law as I conceive it to be…"

在笔者看来无论是以上哪一种说法,实质上都是在欺诈性误述[70](或在本章之5.2段介绍的针对人身的胁迫)的因果关系中对"要不是"测试的放松,也就是并不需要能够证明说"要不是"欺诈性误述存在,就不会签订合约的程度。只要陈述方未能证明被陈述方完全不知道误述的存在、根本没有受影响或没有考虑过误述,就应当认为满足这方面的因果关系要求了。

测试的放松是法律在政策上的考虑,相比违约或侵权行为只是疏忽等原因所导致,更要打击欺诈或涉及暴力等故意/恶意的不法行为。这可节录在 Al Nehayan v. Kent(2018)EWHC 333(Comm)先例中,Leggatt 大法官说:"Dealing with the question(涉及的问题是不当得利的经济胁迫去撤销合约的因果关系在程度上是否与恐吓侵权的索赔损失一样)as one of principle, however, it seems to me that the same test must apply. I reach that conclusion because the **justification for applying a weaker test of causation than the ordinary 'but for' test in cases of physical duress is one of policy**. It is the policy of English law to **impose more extensive liability on intentional wrongdoers than on careless or other less culpable defendants**: see e. g. Smith New Court Securities Ltd v Scrimgeour Vickers(Asset Management)Ltd[1997]AC 254,…(Lord Steyn). By the same standard, where physical threats are made, the interest of the law in deterring violence and the grave nature of such wrongdoing justifies setting a low threshold for inferring that a threat of violence has adversely affected the claimant. This policy is equally applicable where the issue is whether the defendant's conduct has caused damage to the claimant as where the issue is whether the conduct has caused the claimant to enter into a contract which has conferred a benefit on the defendant. Thus, considerations both of policy and consistency require that the test should be the same in each case."(加黑部分是笔者的强调)

除此以外更困难的问题还出现在并非明确的"陈述",而是通过言行举止表现出来的默示陈述,此时是否"确实有考虑到"更加有争议。毕竟在简单的情况下,例如拍卖会上竞拍者举牌,通过行为表达自己有意愿与有能力出价购买,就显然没理由质疑拍卖行确实考虑到了这些默示的陈述。但在 Leeds City Council and Ors v. Barclays Bank plc and Anor(2021)EWHC 363(Comm)先例[71]中,关于银行是否对于 LIBOR 有误述的问题,并没有明确的陈述,而需要通过双方交流的复杂背景与通讯("a web of dealings … against the background of a web of prior communications written and oral…")推断是否有默示陈述,此时是否"确实考虑到"就很有争议,而原告/被陈述

---

〔70〕 有关欺诈所需要的因果关系,在本书第一章之1.3.6段有介绍。

〔71〕 此先例可见本书第三章之9.4.2段。

方没能显示自己意识到(consciously aware)这些默示陈述更不用说考虑到,就无法满足误述的因果关系。

9.1.3 程度之三:满足"要不是"测试

例如买方对价格敏感,而水果摊的水果是市场最低价,可以说"要不是价格这么优惠,不会在这个水果摊买"。又如某附近的水果摊是唯一销售一种进口水果的店铺,"要不是只有你这里有这种水果,不会在这个水果摊买"。

事件与结果之间事实上的因果关系,采用经典的"要不是"(but for)测试,在英国法下,尤其是侵权法中不是一个陌生的概念。绝大部分的因果关系要求,例如疏忽侵权中的因果关系,都采用要不是测试。一般来说,要不是发生了原因就不会发生结果,原因是结果产生的必要条件,原因与结果之间的因果关系就足以满足"要不是"测试。这也可见"要不是"测试的拉丁文的说法"*causa sine qua non*",英文简单翻译是"cause without which"。

9.1.4 程度之四:多重原因/同步原因

现实与复杂的国际商业活动中会发生的事情也不会太简单,一个重大交易的签约或支付决定的背后往往会有多重原因(multiple causes)/同步原因(concurrent cause),对方的不法/不恰当压力只是原因之一。这与本章之9.1.2段的"原因之一"的区别是这多重或同步原因任何一个单独存在,都足够满足这"要不是"测试,毕竟要不是测试并不是一个太难满足的测试,而这些原因的同时存在共同影响了签订合约或支付一笔金钱的决定。

例如再以买水果的例子,家里一定要买水果,马上要封城,加上附近没有其他水果摊或其他水果摊已经被抢购一空,只剩下次货。此时如果水果摊施加不法/不恰当压力临时抬价,将本来电话询价中说好的价格抬高一倍,买方最后决定接受。这接受非要买水果不可的结果,就可以从中挑出多个多重或同步原因,个别都能满足事实上的"要不是"测试。

如果这些多重或同步原因中有一些相对而言是特别重要或占主导地位,此时会被称为主导或决定性原因(predominant/decisive reason)。

在以上这些关系的基础上,可以接下来讨论胁迫行为与想撤销的合约之间的因果关系需要紧密到什么程度,才可以构成胁迫并造成可撤销合约的后果。

9.2 对人身的胁迫:原因之一就已经足够

针对人身的胁迫,有说法是因果关系可以类比欺诈来考虑。这背后的原因涉及政策上的考虑,在本章之9.1.2段已介绍。简单来说,只要发现签约过程涉及欺诈,就会导致合约失去根基。早在Reynell v. Sprye(1852)1 De GM & G 660先例中,Cranworth勋爵说:"Once make out that there has been anything like deception, and no contract resting in any degree on that foundation can stand."这也是在对这类恶行零容忍的公共政策下,普通法给出了在因果关系上异常宽松的标准。

对人身的胁迫看来是一样的,只需要不法压力与合约的签订沾上边,就已经足够。只需要是原因之一,甚至有多重原因的情况下都不需要是重要的原因,更不需要是主导/决定性原因。这说法与类比可见 Barton v. Armstrong(1976)AC 104 枢密院先例中,Cross 勋爵说:"...If on the other hand Barton relied on the misrepresentation Armstrong(施压方)could not have defeated his claim to relief by showing that there were other more weighty causes which contributed to his decision to execute the deed,for in this field the court does not allow an examination into the relative importance of contributory causes. ... the same rule should apply in cases of duress and that if Armstrong's threats were 'a' reason for Barton(受压方)'s executing the deed he is entitled to relief even though he might well have entered into the contract if Armstrong had uttered no threats to induce him to do so..."

另可节录 Wilberforce 勋爵与 Simon 勋爵更详细与清楚的说法如下:"...the next necessary step would be to **establish the relationship between the illegitimate means used and the action taken**... we are prepared to accept the test proposed by the majority... that **the illegitimate means used was a reason(not the reason,nor the predominant reason nor the clinching reason)why the complainant acted as he did.** We are also prepared to accept that a decisive answer is not obtainable by asking the question whether the contract would have been made even if there had been no threats because,even if the answer to this question is affirmative,that does not prove that the contract was not made because of the threats."(加黑部分是笔者的强调)

换言之,此时不需要满足"要不是"测试,即并不能说"要不是威胁就不会签约"。所以,如果以合法手段业已足够说服对方签约,但仍掌握不好轻重、过火地作出人身威胁,这是很愚蠢的事情,只会让对方在事后改变主意、依赖胁迫撤销合约。

针对人身的胁迫不需要属于主导原因的说法还可见较近期的 Singh v. Redford(2018)EWHC 2390(Ch)先例中,Martin Roger 大法官说:"It is enough that duress be a contributory cause of the transfer of a benefit by a claimant to a defendant,without it being the sole or operative cause."

另外在举证责任方面也一样类比欺诈,由施压方证明不法压力根本对受压方没有造成任何影响,根本不是签订合约或支付金钱的任何原因。可以节录 Barton v. Armstrong 枢密院先例中,Cross 勋爵所说如下:"If Barton(受压方)had to establish that he would not have made the agreement but for Armstrong's(施压方)threats,then their Lordships would not dissent from the view that he had not made out his case. But no such onus lay on him. On the contrary it was for Armstrong to establish,if he could,that the threats which he was making and the unlawful pressure which he was exerting for the purpose of inducing Barton to sign the agreement and which Barton knew were being made and exerted for this purpose in fact contributed nothing to Barton's decision to sign."

举证责任也在此先例中起到了决定性作用。毕竟要证明受压方完全没有受到任何胁迫因素的影响,在签约时根本没考虑过胁迫的问题,是非常困难的。

较近期的 Antonio v. Antonio(2010)EWHC 1199(QB)先例也跟从与确认了此说法:"It follows that,at least in the case of duress of the person,a contracting party who proves that such threats were made for the purpose of inducing the contract(and that they were taken seriously)need prove no more. The burden then falls on the counterparty who made the threats to prove that the threats were not even 'a' reason why the victim entered the contract. It also follows from the above analysis that,in contrast with the position which probably applies in cases of economic duress,it is not necessary for the victim of threats to the person to demonstrate that they had no practical alternative but to enter the contract in question."

9.3 针对财物的胁迫:类比经济胁迫与采用重要原因/"要不是"测试

有关针对财物的胁迫因果关系的权威先例不多,有说法是类比经济胁迫的因果关系,需要满足威胁是最后交易/合约的重要原因(significant cause)或满足"要不是"测试(but for test)。有关经济胁迫的因果关系会在下一段详细介绍,在此仅节录《Chitty on Contract》(2021 年,第 34 版)一书之 10-032 段如下:"In cases of duress to goods,it seems that the threatened seizure must have been a significant cause of the victim's agreeing to the contract or payment. Thus,the victim will not be entitled to avoid the contract if he had an effective alternative remedy,for example to be obtain an injunction to prevent the seizure,though it is recognised that a legal remedy may be of no avail if the victim has a urgent need for the goods. **The victim** will also be **unable to avoid the contract if it was a 'voluntary settlement'** of the other party's claim. The meaning of this is not wholly clear but it appears that relief will be denied if the threat was not the reason for the victim agreeing to the other party's demand. Nor is it clear exactly what is meant by 'significant cause'. **Relief will be denied if** the threat did not influence the victim at all,so that **it was not even 'one of the reasons' for the victim agreeing to the other party's demand**. On the other hand,it seems **unlikely** that the courts **will apply the analogy of fraud as they do in cases of duress to the persons**. Thus the victim will not have the benefit of the reversed burden of proof in the same way as the victim of duress to the person nor that it will suffice that the threat was merely 'one reason' for his actions or 'present to his mind'. **It seems likely that the victim must show that,'but for' the threat,he would not have entered the contract**. We will see that it has been said that this is the appropriate test of causation in economic duress and,given **the similarity of duress of goods and economic duress,the same test of causation seems appropriate**."(加黑部分是笔者的强调)

9.4 经济胁迫中的因果关系:必须是重要原因、满足“要不是”测试

针对经济胁迫(不论是不法行为或合法行为导致的胁迫)就比较复杂,因为在商业社会经常发生。所以在因果关系上必须比针对人身的胁迫收紧,否则会导致影响商业合约的肯定性。否则只因为其中一方在谈判时说过一句涉及经济压力过火与不必要,就可以否定合约的有效性。这带来了经济胁迫中威胁必须是达成交易/合约的“重要原因”(significant cause)的说法,这可见 The “Evia Luck”(1992)2 AC 152 先例中,Goff 勋爵说:“… it is now accepted that economic pressure may be sufficient to amount to duress for this purpose, provided at least that the **economic pressure may be characterised as illegitimate** and **has constituted a significant cause** inducing the plaintiff to enter into the relevant contract…”(加黑部分是笔者的强调)

但什么时候算是“重要原因”并没有明确说法。如果不法/不恰当压力与最后订立的合约之间没有任何关系,这显然不够。但是再往上需要达到什么程度就不明确了。毕竟经济胁迫的说法也是相对近期才发展起来:见 Barton v. Armstrong(1976)AC 104 枢密院先例。

到了 Huyton SA v. Peter Cremer GmbH & Co(1999)1 Lloyd's Rep 620 先例(此先例的事实已在本章之 7.2.2 段有介绍),Mance 大法官就提出 Goff 勋爵所说的“重要原因”实际上是“要不是”测试。也提到在不同案情下会有的变化,如存在多重或同步原因(multiple/concurrent causes)时,虽然除了不法/不恰当经济压力属于重要或决定性原因,还另有其他一个或多个重要原因(如必须在某期限前完成交易,否则会受到惩罚或蒙受重大损失),而这些原因各自独立存在都可满足与订立合约之间的“要不是”测试,这足够满足因果关系。

但毕竟“要不是”测试并不是一个困难的测试标准,例如复杂商事交易中会有大量因素都可以满足要不是测试。也因此在不少案件中,虽然因果关系上较为宽松地以“要不是”测试为标准,但并不能因为满足“要不是”测试就认为构成经济胁迫,例如尽管可以证明要不是因为不法压力不会订立合约,但其实是受压方太容易屈服,这就把经济胁迫的门槛设得太低了。因此,在经济胁迫中还强调要进一步看在当时受压方是否存在接受订立合约外的其他真正可行的选择(如可以申请法院命令与获得足够的法律救济),这会在本章之 10 段介绍。Mance 大法官说:“The use of the phrase ‘a significant cause’ by Lord Goff in The Evia Luck … suggests that this relaxed view of causation〔72〕 in the special context of duress to the person cannot prevail in the less serious context of economic duress. **The minimum basic test of subjective causation in economic duress ought, it appears to me, to be a ‘but for’ test.** The illegitimate pressure must have been such as **actually caused the making of the agreement**, in the sense that it would not otherwise have been made either at all or, at least, in the terms in which it

〔72〕 对人身的胁迫在因果关系上只要求是“原因之一”就已经足够:见本章之 9.2 段的介绍。

was made. In that sense, **the pressure must have been decisive or clinching**. There may of course be cases where a common-sense relaxation, even of a but for requirement is necessary, for example in the event of an agreement induced by **two concurrent causes, each otherwise sufficient to ground a claim of relief**, in circumstances where each alone would have induced the agreement, so that it could not be said that, but for either, the agreement would not have been made. On the other hand, it also seems clear that the application of a simple 'but for' test of subjective causation in conjunction with a requirement of actual or threatened breach of duty could lead too readily to relief being granted. It would not, for example, cater for the obvious possibility that, although the innocent party would never have acted as he did, **but for the illegitimate pressure, he nevertheless had a real choice and could, if he had wished, equally well have resisted the pressure** and, for example, pursued alternative legal redress."(加黑部分是笔者的强调)

这说法在今天英国法的后续先例中得到了跟从,在本章之5.4.2段提到的Kolmar Group AG v. Traxpo Enterprises Pvt Ltd(2010) EWHC 113(Comm)先例中,Christopher Clarke大法官的小结中也显然明确了会采用"要不是"测试的地位。在更近期的先例中如Al Nehayan v. Kent(2018) EWHC 333(Comm)等都是类似判法,Leggatt大法官说:"The test of causation differs according to the nature of the duress. Where the illegitimate pressure involves a threat of violence, it is sufficient that the threat was 'a' reason for entering into the contract, even if the person threatened might well have entered into the contract without the threat... On the other hand, in cases of economic duress the ordinary test of causation applies which generally requires the claimant to show that he or she would not have entered into the contract 'but for' the defendant's act."

另外在经济胁迫(对财物的胁迫也是类似)的举证责任方面,由于还没有更高级法院的先例,并不明确到底举证责任是否会如同对人身的胁迫一样,在受压方证明不法压力的存在、属于考虑的原因之一后,施压方承担举证责任证明对方在签约时完全没有考虑过此因素。

英国法下,至少在Huyton SA v. Peter Cremer GmbH & Co先例中,Mance大法官看来是不同意经济胁迫中举证责任由被告承担,也就是作为原告的受压方要证明不法压力、因果关系、没有其他合理选择。Mance大法官说:"The **onus of proof in respect of economic duress is another relatively unexplored area**... The Privy Council's recognition of, not merely the prima facie factual inference, but of an apparent **shifting of the legal onus, cannot, I think, be transposed automatically to the context of the more recently developed tort of economic duress**. Threats to the person are, by definition, mala fide acts. Economic duress, as this case shows, embraces situations where the party applying what can, at least with hindsight, be shown to have economic pressure held the view quite reasonably at the time that he was entitled to do so. There is, also, as indicated above, **a major difference between the substantive test of causation in cases of threats to the person and in cases of economic duress**. Leaving aside cases of fraud and fraudulent misrepresentation, mentioned in Barton v. Armstrong, the law normally treats the party seeking relief in respect of a breach of contract or seeking to set aside a bargain on grounds, such as innocent misrepresentation, as under a legal onus to prove his case on causation. **The particular facts may give rise to an inference of loss or inducement, which may shift a factual onus to the other party, but the underlying legal onus remains at the end of the day on the party seeking relief**... It would seem to me, as presently advised, that **this could represent the appropriate general approach in cases of economic duress**.... "(加黑部分是笔者的强调)

但针对经济胁迫的因果关系与举证责任,其他普通法国家与地区看来也有不一样的做法,如澳大利亚与新西兰就都有先例判采用更宽松的只要属于原因之一。澳大利亚可见 Crescendo Management Pty Ltd v. Westpac Banking Corp (1988) 19 NSWLR 40; Electricity Generation Corp v. Woodside Energy Ltd (2013) WASCA 36; Morgan Stanley Wealth Management Australia Pty Ltd v. Detata (No. 3) (2018) WASC 32 等先例。新西兰先例可见 Pharmacy Care Systems Ltd v. Attorney General (2004) NZCA 187 等先例。另是举证责任方面,在澳大利亚 Crescendo Management Pty Ltd v. Westpac Banking Corp 先例中就对所有胁迫一致对待,由施压方承担举证责任证明受压方没有受到影响。在此不再展开。

9.5 对因果关系的证明与会打断关系的因素

不妨用 Pao On v. Lau Yiu Long (1980) AC 614 枢密院先例来显示今天英国法下对胁迫证明会考虑到的一些因素。该先例涉及针对一家香港私人公司的股权转让交易,该公司的重要资产是某个在建的地产项目。原告是该私人公司的股东,被告是一家香港上市公司的大股东,想要通过上市公司收购该地产项目。因此在 1973 年,原告与被告控制的上市公司达成合约出售私人公司股权。根据合约约定,上市公司不支付金钱对价,而是向原告增发上市公司的股票。为了防止上市公司股票价格的急剧波动与下跌,双方在合约约定了禁售期,在 1974 年 4 月底之前原告必须至少持有一定比例的增发股票不得出售。

双方还签订"补充协议",约定在禁售期满后,被禁售的股票定价 2.5 美元出售给被告。但签订协议后原告醒悟过来,这补充协议虽然保护自己免于任何股价下跌的风险,但同时如果股价上涨,自己也拿不到任何好处。因此原告表示除非撤销补充协议,另重新订立一份"担保协议"来补偿股价下跌损失,否则自己不会继续按主合约转让股权给上市公司。

面对原告威胁,被告在此时显然是有选择的,例如可以将其言行认为是违约/毁约并开始诉讼与获得法律救济等。但是被告担心此时提起诉讼其实无法在短期内解决问题。而且如果被告与上市公司关于地产项目的主合约交易不按计划或尽快完成,市场、投资人、融资银行等可能对上市公司的信心大减等,因此决定答应原告的要求。被告与原告撤销了原本的补充协议,然后签订了新的担保协议,约定的内容仍然是在禁售期满后被告会购买原告的股票,但内容变成如果届时股价低于2.5美元则会补偿差价,即底价是2.5美元但上不封顶。

之后主合约的交易正常进行,原告也获取了上市公司的股票。但是禁售期满前股票价格下跌,因此原告想要依赖担保协议寻求被告的补偿,被告则提出了经济胁迫作为抗辩。

在此先例中,原告威胁不履行主合约,已经在本章之7.2段介绍过这是不法行为,会构成不法/不恰当压力(illegitimate pressure)。被告在答应与原告签订担保协议时,也显然是考虑了原告的威胁违约、不出售该私人公司股权给上市公司的行为。但涉及经济胁迫时,会是更不容易去认定到底在受压方心里是什么原因最后驱动了他去签订协议。所以,还会需要考虑一系列的其他事实证据,如重要的会看受压方是否有其他合理选择等。Scarman勋爵说:"Duress, whatever form it takes, is a coercion of the will so as to vitiate consent. Their Lordships agree … that in a contractual situation commercial pressure is not enough. There must be present some factor 'which could in law be regarded as a coercion of his will so as to vitiate his consent.' … In determining whether there was a coercion of will such that there was no true consent, it is material to inquire whether the person alleged to have been coerced **did or did not protest**; whether, at the time he was allegedly coerced into making the contract, he **did or did not have an alternative course open to him such as an adequate legal remedy**; whether he **was independently advised**; and whether **after entering the contract he took steps to avoid it**."(加黑部分是笔者的强调)

以上节录内容中提到的因素可以简单分段介绍如下。

9.5.1 是否作出过抗议

可先节录《Chitty on Contract》(2021年,第34版)一书之10-054段:"Here the behaviour of the victim, for example whether he protests, will be relevant. First… it will go to causation: if the victim pays without protest, that may be evidence that he was not influenced by the threat. But secondly, payment without protest may leave the demanding party believing that the justice of his demand is admitted, whereas it will be harder for him to prove that he was acting in good faith if he ignores the victim's protests."

在签订合约过程中存在抗议(protest)是受到了逼迫的很好的证据。例如在签约前就用一份电邮写明自己签约,关键原因是因为对方给予的压力,自己是迫不得已才愿意签订合约,这就是很好的当场证据,也显然有助于证明"要不是"施压方的压力,是不会达成合约的。抗议也不需要有特定的形式或措辞/文字,无论是书面或其他言行,或者通过代理人表达的言行等都可以,关键要是结合语境看待表达出了"抗议"的意思。例如,The "Atlantic Baron"(1979) 1 Lloyd's Rep 89先例中,受压方船东向船厂的电文中写的是“无损害我们的权利”(without prejudice to our rights)。

在 XS Racing & Event Marketing Ltd v. Sunseeker Europe AG & Co KG(2005) EWHC 3023(Comm)先例中,David Steel 大法官认定不存在经济胁迫时,就特别指出受压方在当时没有提出任何抗议:“In considering whether this is made out on the facts, there will be various material considerations, including the nature of the illegitimacy and the degree of the commercial pressure exerted by the threat; the good or bad faith of the party making the threat; the availability of an alternative course of action; **presence or absence of protest**, and the acceptance or otherwise of the consequences of the agreement. ... **It is very striking that no contemporary complaint was made**...”(加黑部分是笔者的强调)

要注意抗议只不过是证据之一,在其他证据不够明确时可以依赖是否有抗议作为关键证据。但抗议并非必要条件,不是说必须有抗议才属于逼迫导致订约意图受限。没有抗议的原因也会有很多,如会觉得不值得与毫无意义,或如过去有一些先例中涉及沟通不顺畅联络不上,〔73〕又如根本是一方刻意避开通讯,〔74〕还如施压方威胁违约,受压方非常希望继续履行、真正把事情“搞定”,如 Pao On v. Lau Yiu Long (1980) AC 614 枢密院先例中的情形,此时还要提出抗议,可能会是反而“刺激”施压方不合作,或拖延要求更多,对自己也是不利的。因此早在 Maskell v. Horner(1915)3 KB 106 上诉庭先例中,Reading 勋爵就说:“I do not think that the mere fact of a payment under protest would be sufficient to entitle the plaintiff to succeed; but I think that **it affords some evidence**, when accompanied by other circumstances, that the payment was not voluntarily made to end the matter.”(加黑部分是笔者的强调)

9.5.2 是否本就愿意甚至打算签订合约

在 Pao On v. Lau Yiu Long(1980) AC 614 枢密院先例中,在施压方威胁违约时,受压的被告其实可以将之视为违约/毁约并开始法律诉讼寻求救济,而被告没有选择这样做,是进行了全盘商业考虑之后,自己决定重新与原告签订新合约。看来可能的考虑是,只要上市公司能够成功拿到地产项目,无论是原补充协议还是新担保协议实际上对被告而言差别不大甚至并不重要。在此先例中香港上诉庭就是认定被告是在完整考虑过了有关事实后,自己选择不进行诉讼,而且是评估了给担保的风险后自己愿意作出的商业决定。枢密院最后也认可并没有给予经济胁迫的救济。

这就涉及了是否有其他合理选择(reasonable alternative/choice)的问题,有说法这是经济胁迫的要件之一,将在本章之 10 段进一步介绍。在这里仅针对所有类别的胁迫都需要满足的“因果关系”要件,但有否其他合理选择与此要件是息息相关。如果是有的情况下,很可能就影响到无法满足“要不是”测试了。此时即使不存在不法

〔73〕 见 TD Keegan Ltd v. Palmer(1961)2 Lloyd's Rep 449 先例。

〔74〕 见 Atlas Express Ltd v. Kafco(Importers and Distributors) Ltd(1989) QB 833 先例。

压力,受压方仍然会出于其他原因(如商业考虑)签订合约。

在更近期的 Morley(t/a Morley Estates)v. Royal Bank of Scotland Plc(2021)EWCA Civ 338 上诉庭先例中,原告 Morley(Morley 先生及其控制的公司)是地产开发商,经营方式主要是从银行贷款开发商业地产项目后出租给商业客户,然后用租金偿还贷款与获取利润。2006 年 Morley 先生用自己的一批商业地产开发项目作为抵押,向被告银行(RBS)获得 7500 万英镑的贷款,还款期为 2009 年 12 月。在此贷款合约下,RBS 只有有限追索权(recourse),如果 Morley 未能按期还款,只能通过变卖抵押的地产项目、收取的租金、利率对冲协议(interest hedging agreement)等追索,而不能直接向 Morley 先生个人追索。贷款合约下,RBS 也加上了针对多种事项的违约条文(default clause),一旦发生条文中所陈述的情况,RBS 有权要求全额偿还贷款。此先例中比较重要是有一条"loan to value"条文(以下简称 ITV 条文),要求未清偿贷款余额不低于被抵押的地产项目总价值的一定百分比。

2007 年开始地产项目价值下跌,触发了 ITV 条文。RBS 先是允许 Morley 以支付金钱换取 RBS 不行使要求全额还款的权利。双方关于重组贷款(restructure loan)的谈判一直在进行但未达成协议。双方就此僵持不下,而到了 2009 年对地产项目估值只有 5940 万英镑(远低于借出的 7500 万英镑),违反 ITV 条文。这种情况下对于 RBS 而言,确实可以行权,但是从商业上考虑,在此市场下跌时,RBS 看来是更倾向于与 Morley 重新达成一份让 RBS 满意的重组贷款协议。这背后原因很多,例如 RBS 要行使抵押权利,就需要委任接管人(receiver)区别在市场上公开出售地产项目,这耗费不菲,会导致本就不多的资产价值雪上加霜。另一方面则是 Morley 预测由其继续开发,之后市场回暖后资产价值会重新升值,作为回报 Morley 还可以再分多一部分将来资产收益给 RBS 来换取宽限,希望 RBS 给自己更多信心与时间。对于 RBS 而言,如果在之后再行使抵押权利,经过开发后的资产也能更有价值,尤其是自己对将来地产市场的上涨也有信心。

双方在各自都有律师与各类专业人士的帮助下,就此进行了长时间的谈判。包括在超过了 2009 年 12 月的还款期、Morley 未能还款后还在继续谈判。双方也各自都向对方施加压力。例如 RBS 内部的会议记录显示明明是想要跟 Morley 达成重组贷款协议,但谈判过程中会坚持如果达不成协议就要行使贷款合约下的抵押权利、拿走全部资产。在面对 RBS 提出要求,想要多收取将来资产项目收益,Morley 拒不同意,并"威胁"自己会"撂挑子"不干,干脆让 RBS 收走所有资产,反正在没有个人担保的情况下,RBS 也没法向 Morley 先生个人追索。最后到了 2010 年,Morley 对于重组贷款提出了多个方案,其中一个方案就是 Morley 赎回部分资产,而剩余部分资产则转予 RBS 子公司。经过多次交锋,双方也是根据此方案最后达成重组贷款协议,Morley 会支付 2050 万英镑并保留部分地产项目,剩余地产项目则会被打包转让给 RBS 子公司。在继续开发多年后,Morley 主张涉及经济胁迫要求撤销。

法院对谈判时的事实证据审核后认定,在 Morley 未能按时偿债时双方已经开始沟通，双方都是商业主体也各自有能力照顾自己利益。双方也一直有律师代表，谈判内容也是经过深思熟虑的结果。在谈判过程中，双方也是各显神通，如 Morley 自己也打算给予 RBS 社会舆论的压力。而对于此先例中主张的 RBS 施加的压力而言，主要是 RBS 坚持万一谈判不成功，就要行权、以 Morley 无力偿债为由委任接管人等手段，但这都谈不上属于不法/不恰当压力，仅仅是坚持了自己的合约与法律地位：见本章之 8.3 段的介绍。

更重要的是，最后解决方案的实际内容根本是 Morley 自己预先提出来的，是艰苦谈判的结果。从双方各自提出的要求对比最后合约条文来看，双方都有不小的让步与妥协。在这过程中双方也都有律师等专业人士的代表与建议，也都有充分时间考虑。从事后 Morley 向其他银行寻求融资过程中 Morley 自己的陈述来看，对于这份重组贷款协议的描述也是认为根本来自 Morley 自己的想法，而且认为是达成合意甚至是对 Morley 有利的解决方案。综合来看，一审与上诉庭均认定 Morley 并不是被逼迫签订合约。这样无论压力本身是否不法/不恰当，经济胁迫主张都不会成立。

9.5.3　是否获取了独立意见

涉及经济胁迫时，受压方如果无知、无能，也不清楚情况与自己的地位与有什么其他合法选择，被施压方稍加不法/不恰当压力后就很快订约或支付金钱。从满足经济胁迫的三个要件之一的因果关系与"要不是测试"看来，就会是明显不过不法压力与受压方的屈服有因果关系，正如在《Duress, Undue Influence and Unconscionable Dealing》(2019 年，第 3 版）一书之 4 - 028 段所说："... Where the complainant(受压方)did not receive legal advice and did not understand the circumstances before entering into the transaction the court may infer that the threat had a causative effect on the decision to do as the threatener(施压方)demanded."

相反，如果受压方在面对不法压力向律师咨询后变成充分了解自己的地位与有什么其他选择，再回来向施压方屈服与接受错误要求，反而会带来因果关系有了中断的可能，因为看起来像是受压方在充分了解后选择"缴械投降"，特别是在可以说当时有其他的选择时。在该书之 4 - 028 段接下来说："Conversely, where the complainant received legal advice before deciding to enter into the transaction, the court may infer that his decision to go ahead with the transaction was not induced by the threat. ... where a person who has received legal advice, and is thus aware of an easy legal remedy, decides to agree to the defendant's demand, instead of pursuing the easy legal remedy, the court is less likely to accept that his assent was caused by the defendant's threat."

在 Hennessy v. Craigmyle & Co Ltd(1986) ICR 461 上诉庭先例中，一审的工业裁判庭(industrial tribunal)判胁迫的指控不成立，因为自称的受压方在咨询了律师后完全明白屈服的后果，说："was well aware of the consequences of his action, he had taken legal advice and in the circumstances he had decided to accept ..."

上诉庭的 Donaldson 大法官说："… all the tribunal was doing was to point out that the duress was not of such an order as to deprive the applicant（受压方）of his understanding of the situation. It did not say that his understanding the situation was, of itself, fatal to his claim to be entitled to avoid the settlement. It was merely one of many factors to be taken into account."

但不要因此就认为不委任懂行与称职的律师总算有了好处，即更容易去满足因果关系与"要不是测试"，而咨询了律师后变得更困难建立因果关系。这是断章取义，这可从以下几方面来讨论：

1. 满足因果关系与"要不是"测试只是证明经济胁迫的三个要件之二，不懂的受压方如果自己乱来，就会在要件之三的缺乏其他合理选择过不了关。例如"走出去"的商业人士如果不懂法律，怎么会知道施压方的拒绝履行合约在涉及明确的"明示承诺不会做的事情"（negative covenant）时，其实很容易与很快就可以向法院取得禁令也就可以强制履行。受压方甚至不会知道经济胁迫是需要满足这个要件之三。

2. 即使满足因果关系的要件，无知的受压方是否咨询过律师、清楚自己法律地位也只是证据之一，还有很多其他重要的事实需要证明。例如，是否提出过抗议？显然，无知的受压方是不会警觉去这样做。他们也更可能在表面看来很爽快地向施压方无条件屈服时，使用的措辞/文字不当，更能显示是自愿接受错误要求。他们也更有可能被精明的施压方套出一些不该说的话等。

3. 即使咨询了律师，也要看不同案件千变万化的事实才能真正判断因果关系。例如咨询了律师并在大家深思熟虑后，清楚了受压方的法律地位是没有其他合理或甚至是可行的选择，只有先向施压方屈服是在经济上与现实可行的最佳选择。现实中有律师在背后，受压方也不太可能很爽快、看起来"自愿"接受施压方的要求，通常都是经过争辩之后显示没有办法之下才接受要求。有了这些事实与证据，岂非更明确不法/不恰当压力与受压方决定接受要求之间的因果关系。

简单举个例子，在本章之 5.3.1 段介绍过的 The "Alev"（1989）1 Lloyd's Rep 138 先例中，受压方在获取了律师意见后，认为可以有其他途径解决问题（如申请禁令，或事后索赔），但是这些办法都有困难而且无法解决货物被扣押的燃眉之急，可以认为是并不实际有其他合理选择（至少在法律方面）。此时受压方签订城下之盟，显然不因为已有第三人独立意见而得不到胁迫的救济。

9.5.4 签约后是否试图推翻合约或是确认

如果合约是被迫签订，在紧急的情况过后，常识看来就会开始寻求办法纠正原本的错误了。而如果没有任何表示，而是正常履行合约，甚至是持续长时间地履行合约，客观看来就会是即使有这些不法/不恰当压力，受压方其实也没有把这当一回事，即因果关系不成立。

例如，在刚刚提到的 Morley（t/a Morley Estates）v. Royal Bank of Scotland Plc（2021）EWCA Civ 338 上诉庭先例中，在开发商 Morley 与银行 RBS 签订借贷的解决

方案之后,Morley 长期都没有提出任何问题,甚至在后续向其他银行(HSBC)融资借贷的过程中,在文件中还解释说:"These were properties which were previously secured under an RBS facility. This was a consensual deal and one which was driven by us rather than RBS..."这类行为就很可能被用来显示合约并非被逼迫产生了。

胁迫的救济是可使无效,因此受压方可以选择让合约无效,或者是继续履行,对合约的确认(affirmation)。[75] 因此合约如果被长期正常履行也没有反对与抗议,就会是确认。在本章之 7.2.1.1 段已经介绍过案情的 The "Atlantic Baron"(1979)1 Lloyd's Rep 89 先例中,就涉及受压的船东持续履行与支付金钱、没有继续抗议的行为被认为对涨价了 10% 的新合约的确认,不能事后再以胁迫撤销合约,在此仅节录 Mocatta 大法官所说:"I have come to the conclusion that the important points here are that **since there was no danger at this time in registering a protest, the final payments were made without any qualification and were followed by a delay until July 31, 1975**, before the owners put forward their claim, the correct inference to draw, taking an objective view of the facts, is that the action and **inaction of the owners can only be regarded as an affirmation** of the variation in June 1973 of the terms of the original contract by the agreement to pay the additional 10 per cent."(加黑部分是笔者的强调)

这种情况,在部分"走出去"的中国公司身上经常发生。由于不懂而不警觉自己有这方面的权利。也有时候虽然会知道自己可以有胁迫的救济,但抓不住出击的时机,因为对国际商业游戏规则不熟悉犹豫不决。

9.6 胁迫"诱导"合约产生/支付采用客观还是主观标准

针对在某案件的受压方是自愿行为,即其他原因驱动了向施压力屈服,不主要是施压方的不法/不恰当压力,在考虑是否胁迫"诱导"合约产生/支付金钱时早年曾有先例判是客观测试。客观看合理人士会选择其他方式而不是签订合约或支付金钱,这是有争议的。这就会带来在个别案件受压方当时是感觉"无路可走"下接受向施压方投降,但在诉讼被施压方争辩说受压方应可走其他法律或现实可行的路,无须去投降,选择投降肯定有其他背后原因。而审理法官或仲裁员也"客观"接受了施压方的说法。但看来,这客观测试不被接受,在《Goff & Jones: The Law of Unjust Enrichment》(2022 年,第 10 版)一书之 10-72 段说:"... Significantly, there is no case in the books where a party has failed because a reasonable person in his position would have sought some other remedy. On the contrary, the case law demonstrates, more often than not, that no other remedy would have been adequate."

换言之,现在是对受压方的主观测试,因为只是他在不法压力下感觉到无路可走。而每一个自然人在受压下都有不同反应,有些更怕事、但也有些更能抗压。这可

---

[75] 关于合约确认,可见笔者《合约的履行、弃权与禁反言》一书第一章之 7 段的介绍。这也可能构成禁反言(estoppel)/弃权(waiver)而不能再依赖胁迫而要求撤销合约。

节录《Duress, Undue Influence and Unconscionable Dealing》(2019 年,第 3 版)一书之 4 – 014 段说:"Under the modern approach, the question is whether the illegitimate pressure induced the complainant to enter into the agreement, not whether it would have induced a reasonable person to enter into the agreement. … As Sir Richard Henn Collins MR said in Kaufman v. Gerson (1904) 1 KB 591, it does not matter what particular form of illegitimate pressure is used, 'so long as the will is coerced … Some persons would be more easily coerced by moral pressure, such as was exercised here, than by the threat of physical violence'."

使用主观测试显然是更不容易判断,因为受压方在当时脑子里的想法是只有他才知道。但不是没有办法,笔者的《证据法:基础理论、口头证据与专家证据》一书第十章之 1 段有提到。

这样,就可以看到在本章之 9.5 段节录了 Scarman 勋爵在 Pao On v. Lau Yiu Long (1980) AC 614 枢密院先例所说的认定受压方是否在经济胁迫下无路可走,并非自愿下去签订协议或支付一笔钱,最后的标准是看不法/不恰当压力是否是受压方签订合约的重要原因,但在认定是否属于被诱导、是否成立经济胁迫的因果关系时一样要结合一系列的客观的其他事实证据以作印证,[76] 包括是否作出过抗议、是否获取了独立意见/法律意见等。而其中受压方是否有其他合理的法律或现实可行的选择,更是十分重要的事实去证明是"无路可走"或"有路可走"。

10. "经济胁迫"要件之三:受压方缺乏其他合理选择

这个要件容易理解,如果受压方完全有其他合理选择 (reasonable alternative/choice),而不需要"屈服"于施压方的不法/不恰当压力接受错误要求,就难以说服客观第三人(审理法官或仲裁员)"受压方"是受到胁迫而订立合约或支付一笔金钱。毕竟,即使施压方施加的压力完全合法合理,如是因为成本增加而需要在新合约每吨提价 10 元,受压的买方如果有其他合理选择,相信买方也不会接受提价。例如货物不着急或无关紧要,就会选择暂时先不买;又例如有多个其他卖方排着队希望以原合约价格出售同样的货物。

更不用说法律如果接受构成胁迫,接下来的救济就是合约可使无效 (voidable)。这是普通法很不希望的结果,因为大原则是尽力支持商业合约的肯定性与可预测性,而不是轻易使合约无效,让自称是"受压方"的人士从中获利(否则也不会主张胁

---

[76] 关于这主观与客观混合的测试,可参考笔者《证据法:基础理论、口头证据与专家证据》一书第十章之 5 段。

迫)。虽然对人身的胁迫的构成中没有这个要件,但在考虑个别案件的不同情况时,也会考虑到这个因素。换言之,受压方完全可以选择说“不”。这样,即使是受压方主张存在对人身的胁迫也不一定被接受,没有偏离受压方订约的自由意志。

但人身的胁迫是类同欺诈性误述/欺骗侵权的公共政策不容的行为。所以后者可通过事实的推定放宽受害方(受压方或被误述方)对成立要件的举证责任,如在本书第一章之1.3.6段讲到对诱导与依赖要件的推定,转移了举证责任。

而经济胁迫在现实的商业社会频频发生,通常不涉及“非法”或“不法”,而是不法/不恰当的违约或威胁违约,不涉及公共政策。所以为了防止不断扩张的危险并影响商业合约/和解协议的肯定性,有必要加以额外的限制或要件。所以才有了在本章之4段与5.4段提到的受压方需要举证证明已满足这第三个要件的说法。

10.1　有否其他合理选择在经济胁迫中的重要性

照说受压方完全有其他合理与足够的选择,即使在要件二的因果关系下的“要不是”测试,相信也过不了关。这与损失赔偿计算的原则之一的因果关系是一样道理,如果最后造成的损失是新介入事件即原告受害方自己的行为所导致,就会中断因果关系。这在《损失赔偿与救济》一书第四章之9.2.1至9.2.4段也区别给了一些例子如:受害方自由选择投机不及时在市场卖出或买入替代货物;受害方穷困而做出不正常的选择;受害方选择不及时接受治疗等。而因果关系中断了,也就无需再去追究最后的损失受害方到底有否/能否合理减损了。[77]

在笔者看来,经济胁迫下的“受压方缺乏其他合理选择”与损失计算的“受害方有否合理减损”是类似。因为首先要满足因果关系的要件,也就是在本章之6段已经介绍构成胁迫需要一方施加不法/不恰当压力(通常是不法行为威胁造成的压力),受压方在无路可走下签订合约或支付一笔钱的情况下才会给予救济。而受压方有其他合理选择就会中断因果关系了。

例如买卖合约的卖方威胁说不加价我就不发货,此时买方完全有其他合理选择(如足够的时间诉讼索赔取回损失,或者将这视为违约/毁约而在市场上马上可以找到合理价格的替代货物,甚至当时就有其他卖方在向该买方兜售),但买方是考虑后更愿意让步达成新合约。这样,能在“要不是”测试去特定考虑买方是否有其他合理的法律或现实可行的选择,会更能判断买方接受加价的新合约更倾向是订约自由意志没有偏离,或是真正受压导致。

但“要不是”测试是一个要求不高的测试,很多不同的案情都足以满足。例如虽然客观来看当时对有经验与法律水平的人士而言其实有其他合理选择,但受压方因为相对无知、怕麻烦等原因而没有这样做,施压方一施加压力就轻易缴械投降,在要不是测试上也足以满足。但对于经济胁迫而言,这样将大量增加这类案件,给商业社会带来太多不确定。所以增加这第三点,让受压方解释为什么没有其他合理选择或

---

〔77〕　见笔者《损失赔偿与救济》一书第五章的介绍。

其他选择为什么不是合理选择,就可以将大量这类案件拦在门外。

在 Huyton SA v. Peter Cremer GmbH & Co(1999)1 Lloyd's Rep 620 先例中,Mance 大法官说:"… it also seems clear that the application of a simple 'but for' test of subjective causation in conjunction with a requirement of actual or threatened breach of duty could lead too readily to relief being granted. It would not, for example, cater for the obvious possibility that, although the innocent party would never have acted as he did, but for the illegitimate pressure, he nevertheless had a real choice and could, if he had wished, equally well have resisted the pressure and for example, pursued alternative legal redress."

除了因果关系以外,如果受压方有其他合理选择不去理会,也是很能帮助去推断这不是不法/不恰当的压力。毕竟胁迫给予救济的原理,就是因为压力导致签订合约一方缺乏合理选择,压迫、限制了自由意志。例如 Tucker 大法官在 Atlas Express Ltd v. Kafco(Importers and Distributors)Ltd(1989)QB 833 先例中说:"… economic duress was present which 'vitiates(受压方)apparent consent to the agreement."

或 Kerr 大法官在 The "Siboen" and The "Sibotre"(1976)1 Lloyd's Rep 293 先例中说:"The consent of(受压方)was overborne by compulsion so as to deprive him of any animus contrahendi."

又或是 Scarman 勋爵在 Pao On v. Lau Yiu Long(1980)AC 614 枢密院先例中说:"… the basis of such recognition is that it must amount to coercion of the will, which vitiates consent. It must be shown that the payment made or the contract entered into was not a voluntary act."

10.2 存在其他合理选择是否为要件或只是考虑因素之一

对其他合理选择是要件三或只是作为整体考虑经济胁迫的要件一/二的因素在过往先例中存在分歧。有说法是经济胁迫缺乏其他合理选择只不过是与很多其他因素(如有没有独立意见、抗议等)一并是证明胁迫的证据性事实,直到最近有了权威定论。

这里的区别是:如果是要件,受压方就必须满足,否则经济胁迫的主张无法成立。而且,受压方作为原告也必须在一开始的文书请求/索赔请求中就加入有关的重要事实,否则会有危险被作为施压方的被告申请提前撤销索赔请求。[78] 但如果只是作为可诉胁迫能否成立的考虑因素之一,正如其他的考虑因素一样,证明不了或满足不了平衡的可能性也不是一定成立不了经济胁迫,因为还会有其他证明(如向施压方作出过抗议)可满足胁迫与因果关系。

可先节录《Duress, Undue Influence and Unconscionable Dealing》(2019 年,第 3 版)一书之 4-022 段说:"**A third requirement for economic duress**? Judicial opinion

---

〔78〕 见笔者《证据法:国际规管与诉讼中的证据攻防》一书第六章之 4 段。

is divided on this issue. Some English cases hold that the absence of a practical alternative goes to the essence of duress and that it is a requirement for a claim based on duress or economic duress. But there is another line of cases deciding that the absence of a practical alternative is one of the factors which the court takes into account as a matter of evidence alongside other factors, such as protest and independent advice. It is submitted that the evidential approach is to be preferred. ..."

认为是否有其他合理选择只是考虑因素之一,作为证据性事实看待的,可见 Huyton SA v. Peter Cremer GmbH & Co(1999)1 Lloyd's Rep 620 先例中,Mance 大法官说:"It is **not necessary to go as far as to say that it is an inflexible third essential ingredient of economic duress that there should be no or no practical alternative course open to the innocent party**. But it seems, as I have already indicated, self-evident that relief may not be appropriate, if an innocent party decides, as a matter of choice, not to pursue an alternative remedy which any and possibly some other reasonable persons in his circumstances would have pursued. **Relief may perhaps also be refused, if** he has made no protest and conducted himself in a way which showed that, for better or for worse, **he was prepared to accept and live with the consequences, however unwelcome**..."(加黑部分是笔者的强调)

Mance 大法官提到是否存在其他合理选择只是考虑因素之一,如果确实没有其他合理选择,只是有很强的证据显示受压方是受到了压力逼迫或偏离自由意志,在"无路可走"下接受施压方的错误要求,而不是经济胁迫的"要件",变为经济胁迫必须跨越的分水岭/红线之一。

在较近期的 Kolmar Group AG v. Traxpo Enterprises Pvt Ltd(2010)EWHC 113(Comm)先例中,Christopher Clarke 大法官也同意说:"... it is relevant to consider whether the claimant had a 'real choice' or 'realistic alternative' and could, if it had wished, equally well have resisted the pressure and, for example, pursued practical and effective legal redress. **If there was no reasonable alternative, that may be very strong evidence in support of a conclusion that the victim of the duress was in fact influenced by the threat**."(加黑部分是笔者的强调)

在更近期的 Al Nehayan v. Kent(2018)EWHC 333(Comm)先例中,也说没有其他合理选择只不过是可以考虑的因素之一,用来加强证明:(1)压力属于不法/不恰当的有力证据;(2)因果关系,而不是说经济胁迫比对人身胁迫要多一个必须满足的要件。Leggatt 大法官说:"It is sometimes said to be a further requirement of economic duress that the claimant had no reasonable alternative to giving in to the illegitimate pressure. The alternative view, which ... was accepted by Christopher Clarke J in Kolmar Group AG v Traxpo Enterprises Pvt Ltd ... is that **the absence of any reasonable alternative is not an absolute requirement but rather is very strong evidence of whether**

the claimant was induced by the threat or other illegitimate pressure to enter into the contract. It is also, as it seems to me, **a relevant factor in determining whether use of pressure was illegitimate** in cases where the defendant has not acted or threatened to act unlawfully and the allegation of duress is based on exploitation of the claimant's situation to make an unjustified demand."(加黑部分是笔者的强调)

但在近期权威的 PIAC v. Times Travel(2021)UKSC 40 最高院先例中,说法仍是没有其他合理选择是构成经济胁迫必须满足的第三个要件。Burrows 勋爵说:"It is also important that, **in the context of economic duress**(but the position appears to be different in respect of other forms of duress...), there **is a third element**. This is that the claimant **must have had no reasonable alternative** to giving in to the threat(or pressure)..."(加黑部分是笔者的强调)

针对这方面的分歧,可以节录《Chitty on Contract》(2021 年,第 34 版)一书之 10-044 段作为总结,说:"Nevertheless, it is submitted that the existence of no reasonable alternative for the victim but to submit to the threat and demand should be regarded as an independent and additional requirement of duress since it goes to the very essence of the jurisdiction."

以及在 10-046 段所说:"On the one hand, it is argued that while the victim will seldom obtain relief if they had a reasonable alternative, this is because they will fail to convince the court that they would not have entered the contract but for the threat. On the other hand, the House of Lords and lower courts, and some writers, have argued that **it is a necessary ingredients of economic duress. It is submitted that the latter are correct**."(加黑部分是笔者的强调)

这样看来,针对经济胁迫,受压方缺乏其他合理选择仍是三个要件之一。在较早提到的《Duress, Undue Influence and Unconscionable Dealing》一书有不同说法是因为其出版在 PIAC v. Times Travel 最高院先例前。所以,中国公司面对这种对方以违约/威胁违约并提出错误要求的情况,要注意这方面,包括收集证据证明自己有去寻找与考虑了其他合理选择。因为在主张经济胁迫的索赔请求中就需要加入这些重要事实。

10.3 其他合理的现实与法律救济的选择

受压方有没有其他合理与足够的选择针对两个方面:

1. 现实可行的选择:如 Mocatta 大法官在 The "Atlantic Baron"(1979)1 Lloyd's Rep 89 先例说:"There was no practical possibility of placing a substitute order for a ship to be delivered to meet the cancelling date of the Shell charterparty."又如货物买卖中卖方作为施压方拒绝按时交货,在市场上涨时强迫买方接受自己的要求,在知道买方急于要这票货物的情况下漫天抬价,但作为受压方的买方很容易在市场买到更便宜价格的同样货物,根本无须向卖方屈服接受多支付一笔完全不成比例的抬价。

2. 法律救济的选择：如 Kerr 大法官在 B&S Contracts and Design Ltd v. Victor Green Publications Ltd（1984）ICR 419 上诉庭先例中说：“the consequences of a refusal would be serious and immediate so that there is no reasonable alternative open such as legal redress.”或 Scarman 勋爵在 Pao On v. Lau Yiu Long（1980）AC 614 枢密院先例中说：“whether at the time（受压方）was alleged coerced into making the contract, he did or did not have an alternative course open to him such as an adequate legal remedy.”

在法治社会或法治的环境下，面对问题显然就应该寻求法律救济。虽然，法律行动通常昂贵、耗时与有不确定性，在受压方面对不法/不恰当压力时往往是“远水救不了近火”。例如在 The “Atlantic Baron”先例中，Mocatta 大法官说：“（受压方船东）might have claimed damages against（施压方船厂）with all the inherent unavoidable uncertainties of litigation, but in view of the position of the owners vis-à-vis their relationships with Shell（承租人）it would be unreasonable to hold that this is the course they should have taken.”

在《Goff & Jones：The Law of Unjust Enrichment》（2022 年，第 10 版）一书之 10－32 段提到在大部分情况下法律救济都不太“足够”：“… the delay, expense and uncertainty of legal process would prevent most legal remedies from being called ‘adequate’…”

但会有情况是受压方是可以有简易的法律救济（easy remedy）如申请履约指令或禁令，但完全没有去尝试或考虑，而只是希望息事宁人、省律师费用与麻烦，对施压方不成比例的要求屈服。这就会有问题了。

10.4 涉及其他合理选择的先例

正由于是否有其他合理选择是经济胁迫要满足的要件，因此在涉及胁迫的案件中，都不可避免地需要满足这一点。本书介绍的多个先例都已经提到过这方面问题，如 The “Atlantic Baron”（1979）1 Lloyd’s Rep 89；The “Universe Sentinel”（1983）1 AC 366；B&S Contracts and Design Ltd v. Victor Green Publications Ltd（1984）ICR 419；The “Alev”（1989）1 Lloyd’s Rep 138；XS Racing & Event Marketing Ltd v. Sunseeker Europe AG & Co KG（2005）EWHC 3023（Comm）；Kolmar Group AG v. Traxpo Enterprises Pvt Ltd（2010）EWHC 113（Comm）；Borrelli v. Ting（2010）UKPC 21；The “Cenk Kaptanoglu”（2012）EWHC 273（Comm）先例等。

以下只介绍 Adam Opel GmbH v. Mitras Automotive UK Ltd（2007）EWHC 3205（QB）先例，以便更好地理解这方面课题。原告 Adam Opel 是通用汽车（General Motor）的子公司，从供应商处购买零件制造汽车。而作为某零件（保险杠支架）的独家供应商的被告 Mitras 与 Adam Opel 签订合约提供该种保险杠支架。但在 2001 年开始制造后，Adam Opel 到了 2005 年打算更换汽车设计并换另一种保险杠支架，因此告知 Mitras 将在 2006 年 8 月终止合约。Mitras 就主张自己提供零件原本是以 12 年为基础的，这从合约中提供的优惠价格也能看出明显是基于长期与大量供应的前提，因此要求 Adam Opel 支付 56 万英镑加上提高 2006 年开始已经提供（以及到 8 月为止尚待提供)的产品的价格。Adam Opel 则主张根据自己计算,平摊下来只愿意额外支付不到 2 万英镑给 Mitras。Mitras 威胁如果不答应这个要求,就会马上停止供货,例如 Mitras 威胁 Adam Opel 说:"You have a choice of either accepting the price or procuring the goods elsewhere..."

Adam Opel 马上就向法院单方面(ex parte/without notice)申请禁令,但法院拒绝给出单方面禁令而要求给予 Mitras 通知后,双方有机会在法院争辩后再作决定。这样 Adam Opel 也没有再继续推进法律行动,但 Mitras 消息很灵通,很快知道了 Adam Opel 曾经向法院申请禁令,就立刻断供。为了保障汽车生产不停滞,Adam Opel 不情愿地支付了金钱与答应了 Mitras 要求,Mitras 才恢复供应。而后来在不再需要 Mitras 的供应之后,在 2006 年 10 月 Adam Opel 索赔已经支付的金钱,并以经济胁迫作为理由。Mitras 的重要抗辩,就是 Adam Opel 在后来完全可以继续申请禁令,这是合理的其他选择,因此不能获得经济胁迫的救济。

但 Mitras 的抗辩被驳回,David Donaldson 大法官判 Adam Opel 如果继续在法院申请,即使要送达给 Mitras 让双方都参与,仍然有可能获得成功。但是这救济途径并不"足够"。毕竟即使继续法院申请,能否成功申请到仍存在风险。也完全能想到可能会面临很多问题,如如果合约中约定的供应数量,使用的是"合理"、或者是 Adam Opel "所需"这类供应合约中常见的措辞时,由于合约条文的不确定性法院未必愿意在此中间阶段就给出禁令,而且禁令的措辞如何写会是恰当?这风险相比于 Adam Opel 由于马上就缺少零件而停产所带来的危害,可能是完全不成比例。也因此判继续法院申请,虽然确实是其他选择,但并不"足够",因此不能作为 Mitras 威胁停供所带来的不法/不恰当压力的抗辩,也就可以得到经济胁迫的救济了。

11. 权限假托/政府胁迫(duress colore officii)

本小段将简单讨论政府或公共机构滥用职权或越权向民众/公司收取不该收取的费用的问题。此课题涉及与本书关系不大的公法(public law)与复杂的税务法律,所以不会详细介绍。在此简单介绍的原因是英美政府机构的收费/罚款(如规管机构的天文数字罚款等)与税务(如货物进口税等或其他名目繁多的税收)等问题也会影响中国公司。如果有关收费或征税的立法与规定因违反公约等在后来被推翻,或公共机构是在错误理解立法与规定下征收,中国公司多缴纳或错误支付了有关的费用或税务,事后发现时,可否要求政府机构退还、复原?如果能,是以什么理由或诉因?这类案件会涉及庞大的金额,例如在 Woolwich Equitable Building Society v. Inland Revenue Commissioners(1993)AC 70 贵族院先例中的涉案金额是 7600 万英镑;Test Claimants in the FII Group Litigation v. Revenue and Customs Commissioners(2020)UKSC 47[以下简称 FII(SC)(2020)]最高院先例涉及的集体诉讼案件,潜在多缴纳的税款更是多达50亿英镑。这也不奇怪,因为英国的公司税最高可达45%,还要加上复息与预缴等。

在过往先例中民众/公司提出退还的重要理由就是公司(或自然人)并非自愿支付或自愿达成协议(如与规管机构在讨价还价下达成的和解协议)。如果公司是自愿支付(特别是在知道无须支付或十分怀疑的情况下仍想要息事宁人而支付),即使后来知道是错误支付而想反悔,也会被视为"赠与"[79](gift),也难去主张支付是本章的可诉胁迫(actionable duress)。这样,退还错误支付或撤销协议的要求就是难上加难了。正如在 Maskell v. Horner(1915)3 KB 106 上诉庭先例中,Reading 勋爵说:"If a person with knowledge of the facts pays money, which he is not in law bound to pay, and in circumstances implying that he is paying it voluntarily to close the transaction, he cannot recover it. Such a payment is in law like a gift, and the transaction cannot be reopened. If a person pays money, which he is not bound to pay, under the compulsion of urgent and pressing necessity or of seizure, actual or threatened, of his goods he can recover it as money had and received. The money is paid not under duress in the strict sense of the term, as that implies duress of person, but under the pressure of seizure or detention of goods which is analogous to that of duress. Payment under such pressure establishes that the payment is not made voluntarily to close the transaction."

11.1 政府或公共机构多/错误征收费用或税款的救济

在早年先例中,英国法将多缴纳或错误支付给政府或公共机构的费用或税收视为在胁迫下支付(或达成协议),因此给予救济。这胁迫不要求政府或公共机构真正通过威胁将罚款或收取高息等行为去施加压力,而是存在"推定胁迫"(presumption of duress),正如在 Steele v. Williams(1853)8 Ex 625 先例中的判决提要说:"when money is paid under an illegal demand, colore officii, the payment can never be voluntary."

法律有这个推定是因为政府与民众的关系不平等。正如 Abbott 大法官在 Morgan v. Palmer(1824)2 B & C 729 上诉庭先例中说:"One party has the power of saying to the other, 'that which you require shall not be done except upon the conditions which I choose to impose', no person can contend that they stand upon anything like an equal footing."

换言之,根据胁迫理论要求政府或公共机构退还多缴纳或错误支付的金钱不是问题。但只有是针对税款,英国法律是没有这个法律的推定,而是要根据事实证明缴纳不是自愿而是在胁迫(早年只承认对人身与财物的胁迫)下进行。例如 Maskell v. Horner(1915)3 KB 106 上诉庭先例涉及是否多缴纳税务的问题,就是通过证据显示存在将货物充公的威胁,也就是证明了对财物的胁迫,而不是在权限假托理论下推定

---

〔79〕 见本书第七章之7.1.1段与11.3段。

胁迫。因为税务局针对一般税务(除了有些特殊的税务如货物进口税),能够强制执行的唯一手段就是提起或威胁提起诉讼。提起诉讼完全是合法手段,加上受压的纳税人大可以选择诉讼作为合理选择而无需投降,谈不上是受税务局的胁迫。而如果纳税人因为怕打官司或各种其他原因而提前投降作出支付,看来更像是自愿支付。

这可节录《Duress, Undue Influence and Unconscionable Dealing》(2019 年,第 3 版)一书之 5 - 017 段说:"In the case of payments made by way of **tax or similar levies**, recovery on the ground of duress was **only available where the payment was made in response to a threat made by public authority(other than a threat to institute legal proceedings)**. … The idea was that since the public authority could only enforce payment by legal proceedings, the payer could take the opportunity of challenging the legality of the demand by legal process. In other words, the complainant(声称自己是受压方的纳税人)had a reasonable alternative other than to pay. If they decided instead to give in to the unlawful demand, **the payment was regarded as voluntary so that recovery on the ground of duress was not available.** In William Whiteley Ltd v. The King(1909)101 L. T. 741, the restitution claim failed on this ground. … Walton J dismissed the claim on the ground that the moneys were paid voluntarily and therefore could not be recovered back on the ground of duress. He concluded that ' there was nothing in this case which amounted to compulsion'. "(加黑部分是笔者的强调)

英国普通法在错误征税这方面给予狭窄救济的法律地位不被其他普通法国家认同,如美国的 Atchison, Topeka & Santa Fe Railway Co v. O' Connor 223 US 289 (1911); Gaar, Scott & Co v. Shannon 223 US 468(1911)等先例;澳大利亚的 Sargood Bros v. The Commonwealth(1910)11 CLR 258 先例;加拿大的 Kingstreet Investments Ltd v. New Brunswick(Finance)(2007)1 SCR 3 最高院先例等。

11.2　Woolwich Equitable Building Society v. Inland Revenue Commissioners (1993) AC 70 贵族院先例:政府越权下必须退还多缴纳或错误支付的税款

不当得利[80](unjust enrichment)理论中的重要先例之一的 Woolwich Equitable Building Society v. Inland Revenue Commissioners(以下简称 Woolwich)贵族院先例为错误征税另打开了一条十分宽松的救济的渠道。该先例简单的案情是原告(房屋互助协会)对被告(税务局)根据《Income Tax(Building Societies) Regulations 1986》税务规则征收的税款作出了支付。但原告其实不认为需要支付,只是觉得拒付会带来对名誉或将来累积额外利息的不良影响。为了避免被当作是"自愿"支付,原告马上向

[80]　这是 Goff 勋爵在 Lipkin Gorman v. Karpnale Ltd(1991)2 AC 548 贵族院先例后发展起来的理论,并把以前 150 年以来各种不同名称或理由的复原(restitution)案例归纳在此理论。这课题在本书第三章之 5.4.3 段、第七章之 7.1 段与笔者的《合约的履行、弃权与禁反言》一书第五章之 4 段也有介绍。

法院申请司法复核,并在支付时说明是"无损害":"you should be aware that we are presently seeking leave to commence proceedings in connection with the regulations and accordingly this payment is made without prejudice to any right to recover any payments made pursuant to the regulations which may arise as a result of legal proceedings ..."此先例一审判是该税务规则是越权与无效。这就带来被告税务局是否要退还这笔错误支付的税款与利息的争议。该争议一直上诉到贵族院。

首先可诉胁迫被认定不适用,因为即使已经有了经济胁迫的说法,税务局也没有任何言行可被解释为是明示或默示施加了不法/不恰当压力。其次是针对可诉错误,由于这是法律错误(mistake of law),在本书第二章之6.4段介绍直到Kleinwort Benson Ltd v. Lincoln City Council(1999)2 AC 349(以下简称"Kleinwort Benson")贵族院先例后才明确对法律错误有救济。

这样在当时的普通法下,原告即使是在抗议下支付了不应该缴纳的税款,仍无法要求税务局退还。唯一可行的办法是在支付前与税务局达成合约,约定如果法院稍后认定是多付或错付,税务局就要退还。

税务局不是商人可以去讨价还价的地方,多付或错付的税款(加上利息)的退还也一直是立法针对的事宜,毕竟税务问题关乎国家政策与公共财政。在Woolwich贵族院先例中,Keith勋爵就介绍了一些针对税务的立法:"... the considerable number of instances which exist of Parliament having legislated in various fields to define the circumstances under which payments of tax not lawfully due may be recovered, and also in what situations and upon what terms interest on overpayments of tax may be paid. Particular instances are section 33 of Taxes Management Act 1970 as regards overpaid income tax, corporation tax, capital gains tax and petroleum revenue tax; section 24 of the Finance Act 1989 as regards value added tax; section 29 of the Finance Act 1989 as regards excise duty and car tax; section 241 of the Capital Transfer Tax Act 1984 as regards inheritance tax; and section 13(4) of the Stamp Act 1891(54 &55 Vict. c. 39) as regards stamp duty. Mention may also be made of section 9 of the General Rate Act 1967 which, as described above was, considered by this House in Reg. v. Tower Hamlets London Borough Council, Ex parte Chetnik Developments Ltd. [1988] AC 858."

但在立法没有规定的情况下,税务局行使裁量权来决定退税问题,就会发生困难了。毕竟,多年后退还一大笔税款与利息会严重影响政府的财政。更不用说税务局作为政府机构也不会在没有法律依据的情况下批准退钱。

在Woolwich贵族院先例中,Goff勋爵代表多数意见指出不退还税款对原告十分不公道,在法治社会中原告处于困难情况下采取的都是恰当的行为(如在税务局要求下就支付,但明示保留了权利,并马上申请司法复核等)。如果原告确实是错误支付,没理由不退还。因为等待立法改变将会遥遥无期,所以多数意见决定由法院通过普通法先例来改变这个不公平的法律地位。但在错误理论与胁迫理论不适用的情况下,另开了一个渠道,以税务局错误征收税款是欠缺国家议会授权的越权行为(ultra vires)为由,给予普通法下复原、归还不当得利的救济。Goff 勋爵说:"... it is one of the most fundamental principles of our law-enshrined in a famous constitutional document, the Bill of Rights 1688 — that taxes should not be levied without the authority of Parliament; and full effect can only be given to that principle if the return of taxes exacted under an unlawful demand can be enforced as a matter of right."

这也是所谓的"Woolwich 原则",Goff 勋爵接下来说:"I would therefore hold that **money paid by a citizen to a public authority in the form of taxes or other levies paid pursuant to an ultra vires demand by the authority is prima facie recoverable by the citizen as of right**. As at present advised, I incline to the opinion that this principle should extend to embrace cases in which the tax or other levy has been wrongly exacted by the public authority not because the demand was ultra vires but for other reasons, for example because the authority has misconstrued a relevant statute or regulation."(加黑部分是笔者的强调)

可说"Woolwich 原则"是 Goff 勋爵建立的不当得利理论中的另一个重要部分。此理论希望把过往很多不同案情下判"复原"的先例统一起来,建立一个独立的理论与设定一致的要件,成为民事领域合约法与侵权法外的第三类别权利与义务。正如 Steyn 勋爵在 Banquet Financiere de la Cite v. Parc (Battersea) Ltd & Ors (1999) 1 AC 221 贵族院先例中所说:"unjust enrichment ranks next to contract and tort as part of the law of obligations. It is an independent source of rights and obligations."

另可节录《Goff & Jones: The Law of Unjust Enrichment》(2022 年,第 10 版)一书之 1-08 至 1-09 段说:

"Whatever the underlying justifications for the award of restitution in these cases, the **'unjust' element in 'unjust enrichment' is simply a 'generalisation of all the factors which the law recognises as calling for restitution'**. In other words, unjust enrichment is not an abstract moral principle to which the courts refer when deciding cases; it is **an organising concept that groups decided cases on the basis that they share a set of common features**, namely that in all of them [被告] has been enriched by the receipt of a benefit gained at [原告]'s expense in circumstances that the law deems to be unjust.

The reasons why the courts have held [被告]'s enrichment to be unjust vary from one set of cases to another and this diversity seems to have been what Lord Sumption had in mind when he said in Patel v Mirza that 'English law **does not have a unified theory of restitution**'."(加黑部分是笔者的强调)

根据以上所说,简单而言不当得利理论的四个要件是:(1)被告(在此先例是英国税务局)有否得利(Has the defendant been enriched)?(2)该得利是否是基于原告付出的代价(Was the enrichment at the claimant's expense)?(3)该得利是否不当(Was the enrichment unjust)? (4)被告有否抗辩的原因(Are there are any defences available to the defendant)? 例如在"Woolwich 原则"下,时效已过(time barred)就是一个重要的抗辩。

这四个要件在 Investment Trust Companies v. Revenue and Customs Commissions (2018) AC 275 先例中,被 Reed 勋爵形容为:"[the] four questions are ... for ease of exposition. They are intended to ensure a structured approach to the analysis of unjust enrichment, by identifying the essential elements in broad terms. If they are not separately considered and answered, there is a risk that courts will resort to an unstructured approach driven by perceptions of fairness, with consequent uncertainty and unpredictability."

但持少数意见的 Keith 勋爵大力反对,他认为法院"以判例立法"(judicial legislation)对待税务问题是过分侵犯了国家议会的工作范畴。[81] 不少后来的先例也依从或参照了 Woolwich 原则,如:Norwich City Council v. Stringer (2001) 33 HLR 15; FJB Chalke Ltd v. Revenue and Customs Commissioners (2010) EWCA Civ 313; Test Claimants in the FII Group Litigation v. Revenue and Customs Commissioners (2012) UKSC 19; Littlewoods Retail Ltd v. Revenue and Customs Commissioners (2015) EWCA Civ 515; Ipswich Town Football Club Co Ltd v. Chief Constable of Suffolk (2017) EWHC 375 (QB); Lone v. Hounslow LBC (2019) EWCA Civ 2206; Vodafone Ltd v. Office of Communication (2020) EWCA Civ 183; Surrey CC v. Lincolnshire Clinical Commissioning Group (2020) EWHC 3550 (QB); Test Claimants in the FII Group Litigation v. Revenue and Customs Commissioners (2020) UKSC 47 等先例。

11.3 Deutsche Morgan Grenfell Group plc v. Inland Revenue Commissioners (2006) UKHL 49 贵族院先例:法律错误下必须退还多缴纳或错误支付的税款

在本书第二章之 6.4 段介绍的 Kleinwort Benson 贵族院先例判决法律错误(mistake of law)也等同于普通法下的事实错误后,向税务局要求退还多缴纳或错误支付的税款又多了一种途径,即以可诉错误作为诉因,在普通法下要求归还不当得利,无论错误是事实错误(如计算错了)或法律错误:见本书第七章之 7.1.3 段介绍的 Deutsche Morgan Grenfell Group plc v. Inland Revenue Commissioners(以下简称"DMG")贵族院先例。

简单重复此先例,案情关于英国税法《Income and Corporation Taxes Act 1988》(后来绝大部分条文都已经被《Income Tax Act 2007》与《Corporation Tax Act 2010》替代)。该立法规定如果母公司和子公司都在英国,在集团公司合并报税下,子公司向母公司支付股息时是豁免缴纳预缴公司税(advanced corporation tax),但对母公司在英国以外的其他欧盟成员国的公司则没有这种豁免。欧洲法院认为该区别对待的法律规定是违反欧盟法律,并要求英国政府对此做出纠正。这样,大量纳税人要求税务局退还过往多年(英国是在 1973 年已经加入欧盟)来多缴纳或错误支付的公

---

[81] Keith 勋爵(与 Jauncey 勋爵)反对多数意见判决的原因,可见本书第二章之 6.4.2 段。

司税。

税务局的主要抗辩就是对于错误缴纳税款而需要退税的问题,在 Woolwich Equitable Building Society v. Inland Revenue Commissioners(1993) AC 70 贵族院先例以后,权威法律地位就是 Woolwich 原则,而在 Kleinwort Benson 贵族院先例中,Goff 勋爵在附带意见中提到 Woolwich 原则与法律错误是两套完全不同的理论,都可但归类为不当得利(unjust enrichment)。所以在适用 Woolwich 原则的情况下,法律错误就不适用。而 Woolwich 原则适用的话,原告索赔在 1993 年至 1996 年期间多缴纳的税款就受 6 年立法时效的约束,并因该时效已过而要被法院驳回。这样,原告为了解决时效问题,就提出了法律错误(mistake of law)的诉因,因为"错误"在立法时效的计算是从发现错误或者合理勤勉可以发现错误开始起算,可以保护此先例索赔的时效。因此原告主张法律错误与 Woolwich 原则中的政府越权(ultra vires)可以同时作为不当得利诉因中"不当因素"(unjust factors)来适用。根据双方的争辩,法院主要解决了以下三个问题:(1)Kleinwort Benson 贵族院先例确立的法律错误可以复原是否适用于税务?贵族院的答案是肯定的。(2)贵族院在考虑税务问题是否要被排除在 Kleinwort Benson 贵族院先例中确立的法律错误的适用范围以外这个问题时,也分析如果将税务问题作为适用的例外(exceptions),这带来对税务局与其他政府/公共机构的不同对待。做出这种区分的标准或理由何在?贵族院显然并不支持这种例外,因为正在建立的不当得利理论很难对这种例外划出分水岭/红线。(3)针对退税问题,Woolwich 原则的越权是否是唯一的诉因与不当得利的救济?上诉庭接受税务局的立场,认为 Woolwich 原则唯一适用。贵族院推翻了上诉庭的判决,支持原告的主张。贵族院认为 Woolwich 原则与法律错误是两个证明得利是不当的"不当因素",而这些不当因素在同一个案件完全可以同时提出。因法律错误带来的不公平,不会因为存在其他的不当得利的因素而受限制或被排除。

此先例贵族院以 4 比 1 的多数意见,推翻了上诉庭判决,判 DMG 胜诉,可以法律错误要求税务局退还多缴纳与错误支付的公司税。

11.4 纳税人的选择或替代诉因:"Woolwich 原则"和"DMG 原则"

这样在普通法下(撇开立法允许退还的情况),对于多缴纳或错误支付了税款的纳税人而言,就存在两个可行的诉因,各有千秋,也有不同的适用,纳税人可以选择对自己有利的诉因或同时提出作为替代诉因(alternate cause of action),也对政府有不同程度的弊端(两个原则的诉因都难会对政府有利)。

11.4.1 "Woolwich 原则"的利弊

"Woolwich 原则"适用广泛,不需要任何不法/不恰当压力,甚至不需要税务局提出过支付的要求,更不需要有对事实或法律的错误(虽然多数重大的退税案件都会涉及法律错误)。

但由于这原则(虽然 DMG 原则也应该是一样)是根据"不当得利"得出的,所以会有“改变地位”[82](change of position)作为抗辩理由的可能,目前没有见到政府有以此作为抗辩。

技术上来看证明越权相比于证明错误(包括是否存在与在什么时间发现)更加容易。但 Woolwich 原则有一个最大的弊端就是受立法时效 6 年的约束。而在税务问题中,原告往往是在缴税的多年后才发现多缴或错缴。这样,Woolwich 原则的适用就有局限性。

11.4.1.1 是否只适用在多缴纳或错误支付税款

Woolwich 原则是否适用在税款以外政府/公共机构错误征其他收的费用或罚款看来并不明确。照理说,政府越权应该适用在所有政府的收费。看来这也是法律委员会(Law Commission)的看法,在 1994 年《Restitution:Mistakes Of Law And Ultra Vires Public Authority Receipts And Payments》(Law Com No. 227)报告之 6.42 段中表明:“We believe that the crucial element is that the payment is collected by any person or body which is operating outside its statutory authority, that is, it is acting ultra vires.”

但在 Woolwich 贵族院先例中,多数意见的判决并没有说清楚,只说针对“in the form of taxes or other levies”。

在后来的 DMG 贵族院先例与 Test Claimants in the FII Group Litigation v. Revenue and Customs Commissioners(2012)UKSC 19 最高院先例中,Walker 勋爵也提出过这方面的问题,但没有答案,只在后一个先例重申针对税款时说:“We should restate the Woolwich principle so as to cover all sums paid to a public authority in response to (and sufficiently casually connected with) an apparent statutory requirement to pay tax which (in fact and in law) is not lawfully due.”

Norwich City Council v. Stringer(2001)33 HLR 15 上诉庭先例涉及房屋津贴(housing benefit),判是适用“胁迫”,不适用“Woolwich 原则”。这在《Duress, Undue Influence and Unconscionable Dealing》(2019 年,第 3 版)一书之 5 - 030 段有简要提及原因,说:“One reason for the decision(上诉庭决定)that the claim fell outside the Woolwich principle was that the local authority's demand for a refund was not a demand in the nature of a demand for tax which was backed by the coercive power of the state and which put the citizen at a disadvantage with the state. It was explained that the demand for payment in that case was different from a tax demand which a citizen is bound to pay on pain of penalty. However, although the payment fell outside the scope of the Woolwich principle, it was within the scope of duress. If the payment had been made because the local authority had made threats of unlawful action to back its unlawful demand for payment, then it may have been possible to establish duress.”

另在 Waikato Regional Airport v. Attorney General(2003)UKPC 50 枢密院先例

---

[82] 这方面在笔者的《合约的履行、弃权与禁反言》一书第五章之 4 段有介绍。

中，新西兰一审的 Wild 大法官判政府向原告机场收取的“边防费”(border control costs)不合法，在考虑适用“Woolwich 原则”与政府胁迫(duress colore officii)后判是后者适用，这一审判决被枢密院支持。

《Duress, Undue Influence and Unconscionable Dealing》(2019 年，第 3 版)一书之 5－030 段的最后部分对这两个不同原则或说法会带来的不同结果说：“The distinction between a claim based on duress and one based on the Woolwich principle may also be significant in terms of defences. This may be the case, for example, if the law were to recognise special defences to the Woolwich principle as a response to concerns about serious disruption to public finances resulting from Woolwich claims, since such defences are likely to be confined to the recovery of tax or similar charges within the Woolwich principle, they may not apply to claims based on duress to recover money paid otherwise than by way of tax or similar charges.”

11.4.1.2　适用 6 年的立法时效

立法《Limitation Act 1980》针对索赔时效，例如 Section 5 针对合约说：“An action founded on simple contract shall not be brought after the expiration of six years from the date on which the cause of action accrued.”但该立法中并没有针对不当得利。

事实上在《Limitation Act 1980》之 Section 2(7)规定立法时效一般并不适用在衡平法救济(equitable remedy)，只有衡平法与普通法的救济类似时，才会类比适用立法索赔时效：“This section shall not apply to any claim for specific performance of a contract or for an injunction or for other equitable relief, except in so far as any provision thereof may be applied by the court by analogy in like manner …”

因此衡平法救济一般仍然只受限于衡平法的怠慢(laches)理论等，要求原告尽快提出申请，否则法院会行使裁量权拒绝给予衡平法救济。而针对不当得利的问题就是，不当得利的复原有的是普通法救济，有的是衡平法救济。

而《Goff & Jones: The Law of Unjust Enrichment》(2022 年，第 10 版)一书提出，普通法不当得利一般应该适用 Section 5 的 6 年立法时效，只有纯粹衡平法的不当得利复原(如不当影响[83]的复原)仍然由怠慢理论处理，可以节录该书之 33－07 段与 33－12 段如下：“It followed that unless a different period is laid down by the 1980 Act or some other statute, **the limitation period affecting common law claims in unjust enrichment is six years… Where no limitation statute applies to an equitable claim**, and no analogy with a statutory rule can be drawn, **an equitable claim will not be time-barred at all unless the doctrine of laches applies**. … It does not operate as a technical rule, but as a discretionary bar to a claim for equitable relief where the claimant has delayed in prosecuting his claim to the disadvantage of the defendant (or a third party) such

〔83〕 见本书第十一章。

that the balance of justice favours withholding relief to the claimant. ... the court considers all the circumstances and then exercises its discretion whether or not to allow the claim to proceed."(加黑部分是笔者的强调)

在近期的先例中也有类似说法,尤其是涉及一般合约撤销后的复原与归还不当得利(例如本书针对的非欺诈性误述),应该适用 Section 5 条文。在 Sixteenth Ocean Gmbh & Co KG v. Société Générale(2018)EWHC 1731(Comm)先例中,Peter MacDonald Eggers QC 大法官说:"The 1980 Act does not refer to claims in restitution or for unjust enrichment. Nevertheless, the application of this provision to claims in restitution, at least where the claim in restitution is related to an express or implied contract, has been acknowledged by the Supreme Court. Certainly, it has been held that claims for money had and received are subject to section 5 of the 1980 Act(Westdeutsche Landesbank Girozentrale v Islington London Borough Council[1994]4 All ER 890)..."

回到本段针对的 Woolwich 原则不当得利复原,由于是普通法不当得利,因此看来会明确适用此条文,FII(SC)(2020)最高院先例也予以确认。Reed 与 Hodge 勋爵说:"Restitutionary claims for the recovery of money are normally subject under English law to a limitation period of six years from the date when the cause of action accrued, on the basis that they are founded on simple contract within the meaning of section 5 of the Limitation Act 1980..."

11.4.2 DMG 原则的利弊

DMG 原则对希望向税务局要求退还多缴纳或错误支付税款的纳税人是好事,也与 Woolwich 原则一样可广泛适用,除了要求案情必须涉及法律错误。但这在大部分重大的退税案件都不是问题,往往涉及关税法、税务规则或税务局做法违反宪法、人权法、国际公约,或税务局错误理解有关立法多征收或错误征收了税款时,都构成法律错误。

现实中退还税款的案件涉及事实错误(mistake of fact)的不多,如果有,涉及的金钱也不会多,在时间上也会很快被发现并解决。但一旦有了 DMG 原则的法律错误,对政府的影响就大了。因为政府向民众征收的税项,都涉及庞大的金额。如果多年后某项税收被法院判是违法征收,需要退还给社会上众多的纳税人(公司法人与自然人),涉及的金钱就会是天文数字。这会给政府财政带来极大的压力,怎么样去寻找这笔钱退还也会是大问题。

而更令政府头痛的是相比 Woolwich 原则的 6 年时效,DMG 原则的时效就有危险大幅度被延长,这是因为在《Limitation Act 1980》之 Section 32(1)(c)是说可诉错误的时效是从错误被发现后才起算,这可节录《Limitation Act 1980》之 Section 32(1)(c):"... where in the case of any action for which a period of limitation is prescribed by this Act, either—(c) the action is **for relief from the consequences of a mistake**; the period of limitation shall not begin to run until the plaintiff has discovered the fraud, concealment or mistake (as the case may be) or could **with reasonable diligence have discovered it**."(加黑部分是笔者的强调)

可以想到是英国政府十分抗拒,各种方法无所不用,这主要包括改变立法与在法院争取对《Limitation Act 1980》立法之 Section 32(1)(c)条文做出更有利政府的解释。这也体现在近年来对这个立法解释最重要的几个最高院先例中,将在接下来介绍。

11.5 《Limitation Act 1980》之 Section 32(1)(c)下可延长 6 年时效的争议

DMG 原则或可诉错误比 Woolwich 原则在时效计算上要更优越。因为在 DMG 先例中,贵族院判法律错误与事实错误的时效一样,可以根据《Limitation Act 1980》之 Section 32(1)(c),在有关的法律错误被发现后才起算 6 年时效。

在本书第七章之 17.1 段与 17.2 段已经介绍了该 1980 年立法之 Section 32(1)(c)。简单而言 Woolwich 原则根据不当得利成立时起算时效(通常也就是受害方支付以及获利方收到金钱之时),而如果涉及的是可诉错误,根据立法可以延后到发现或合理勤勉可以发现有值得起诉的索赔(worthwhile claim)时起算:见 FII(SC)(2020)最高院先例。

在 Test Claimants in the FII Group Litigation v. Revenue and Customs Commissioners 集体诉讼案件(以下简称 FII 案件)中,这个区别就特别重要。因为英国 1973 年税务改革规定公司税收制度中对公司的股息/分红预缴公司税(advanced corporation tax),直到 1999 年才废除此税务规则。而这一规则下有多种规则由于给予英国设立的公司优待,涉及违反欧盟法律中的资本流动自由(free movement of capital)与设立自由(freedom of establishment)。这包括已经提到的《Income and Corporation Taxes Act 1988》中如果母公司和子公司都在英国合并报税豁免预缴公司税的条文等。从 2001 年就开始就有欧洲法院(Court of Justice of the European Union)判决认定这税务规则下有条文违反欧盟法律:见 Hoechst case(Metallgesellschaft Ltd v. Inland Revenue Commissioners, Hoechst AG v. Inland Revenue Commissioners)(Joined Cases C-397/98 and C-410/98)(2001) ECR I-1727 先例。在 2006 年,FII 案件的集体诉讼更是针对更多与更广泛的税务规则条文,经欧洲法院认定违反欧盟法律:见 Test Claimants in the FII Group Litigation v. Inland Revenue Commissioners (Case C-446/04) (2006) ECR I-11753 欧洲法院先例。这样一来,出现了大量要求英国政府退还早至 1973 年以来(英国也是在 1973 年加入欧盟/欧共体)多缴纳税款的诉讼,在 FII 案件中涉及的总金额可能就超过 50 亿英镑。

如果根据 Woolwich 原则要求归还,显然绝大部分税务付款由于早在 1999 年以前支付,到了此先例中案件开始(于 2003 年作出集体诉讼命令)时,早已经超过了一般的 6 年索赔时效,因此根据 Woolwich 原则起诉是无法成功的。但是按照 DMG 原则起诉,就可以根据 1980 年立法之 Section 32(1)(c)延长索赔时效,起算点无论是 2001 年欧洲法院作出 Hoechst case 判决时,还是 2006 年最高院先例确认 DMG 原则时,或是2006年欧洲法院针对FII案件作出判决时,6年时效均没有届满。

英国税务局自然是抗拒的,因为这么庞大的退税,另加上复息,会带来政府财政上的困境。这样,就只剩时效可作为税务局减少退还税款抗辩的唯一出路。在DMG先例一审([2003]EWHC 1779[Ch])判决允许退还法律错误导致多缴纳的税款后,英国就马上于2003年9月宣布会专门立法排除这类可诉法律错误案件中延长索赔时效的Section 32(1)(c)适用,并马上有了《Finance Act 2004》之Section 320(1)。到了2006年DMG贵族院先例确认了DMG原则后,英国更是进一步订立有追溯力的《Finance Act 2007》之Section 107明确了排除的意图,换言之就是不想退税。但是在Test Claimants in the FII Group Litigation v. Revenue and Customs Commissioners (2012)UKSC 19最高院先例中,多数意见认为这两个立法条文均违反了欧盟法律。在2013年12月12日,这两次立法也分别被欧洲法院判违反欧盟法律。

这样,英国政府唯一的出路只剩下质疑DMG先例实属错判,尤其是针对《Limitation Act 1980》之Section 32(1)(c)应该如何解释,提出了一系列争议,与本段内容有关的几个重要争议就是:(1)该立法条文是否可以适用在DMG原则的法律错误的案件中?是否Kleinwort Benson先例与DMG先例都错判了,因为立法的本意只是针对事实错误,根本没有想去针对法律错误?(2)如果可以适用,应该如何认定何时"发现"(discover)法律错误并开始起算6年?(3)什么时候才算是立法中所说的"合理勤勉"(reasonable diligence)可以发现法律错误?

11.5.1 1980年立法是否可以解释为包括法律错误

Section 32(1)(c)条文显然是针对事实错误的案件。但问题是《Limitation Act 1980》是合并了《Limitation Act 1939》、针对人命伤亡(personal injury)的《Limitation Act 1963》与针对潜在损失(latent damages)的《Limitation Act 1986》。在1939年的早期立法中就已经加入与Section 32(1)(c)立法条文一样内容的条文(Section 26[c]),而当时普通法下错误理论并不包括法律错误,在Kleinwort Benson贵族院先例后才明确扩张到包括法律错误。所以在1980年的立法(与更早在1939年的立法)中所针对的"错误"并不包括法律错误。但这就带来另一个问题,就是按立法目的、本质与采用的措辞/文字应该如何解释,是狭窄还是宽松解释。毕竟不少立法不会只想停留在当时的时空,而是希望持续适用以及与时俱进,所谓的"always speaking"。这方面权威的说法体现在Royal College of Nursing of the UK v. Department of Health and Social Security(1981)AC 800贵族院先例中,Wilberforce勋爵说:"In interpreting an Act of Parliament it is proper, and indeed necessary, to have regard to the state of affairs existing, and known by Parliament to be existing, at the time. It is a fair presumption that Parliament's policy or intention is directed to that state of affairs. ... when a new state of affairs, or a fresh set of facts bearing on policy, comes into existence, the courts have to consider whether they fall within the Parliamentary intention. They may be held to do so, if they fall within the same genus of facts as those to which the expressed policy has been formulated. They may also be held to do so if there can be detected a clear purpose in the legislation which can only be fulfilled if the extension is made. How liberally these principles may be applied must depend upon the nature of the enactment, and the strictness or otherwise of the words in which it has been expressed. The courts should be less willing to extend expressed meanings if it is clear that the Act in question was designed to be restrictive or circumscribed in its operation rather than liberal or permissive. They will be much less willing to do so where the subject matter is different in kind or dimension from that for which the legislation was passed. In any event there is one course which the courts cannot take, under the law of this country; they cannot fill gaps; they cannot by asking the question 'What would Parliament have done in this current case-not being one in contemplation-if the facts had been before it?' attempt themselves to supply the answer, if the answer is not to be found in the terms of the Act itself."

Section 32(1)(c)的立法目的就是保护错误理论中的受害方,不至于因为错误稍后才被发现而错过时效无法索赔导致不公平,这样看来法律错误似乎应该一样适用。DMG 贵族院先例就是这样的判法,针对 1980 年立法之 Section 32(1)(c),Hope 勋爵解释说这事实错误与法律错误背后原理与性质是一样的,没理由在时效问题上要区分对待:"… the right way forward is not to distort the common law of restitution by artificially limiting the scope of Kleinwort Benson but for the legislature to stop time running indefinitely in mistake cases…There seems to be no good reason why cases of mistake of fact, the nature of which and the occasion for the discovery of which can vary greatly, should not be treated in the same way for limitation purposes as mistakes of law. Relief from the general six year time limit could be given in either case where the mistake was induced by the payee's words or conduct."

FII(SC)(2020)先例也对这说法予以支持,原因很多,包括:(1)从立法的措辞/文字来看,在立法时虽然没有针对法律错误,但采用的措辞/文字是广泛的,可以解释为包括法律错误。(2)从立法的目的来看,该立法条文是为了帮助错误理论适用时难以及时开始诉讼的原告。而无论是法律错误还是事实错误,原告遇到的是完全相同的困境。(3)如果解释为包括法律错误,在后果上对一般商业合约的影响也是有限的,英国法本来就以肯定性而闻名,法院一贯以来都倾向于不更改一般法律地位,因此这类法律错误的案件相对有限,再加上稍后还会介绍此先例还将在发现或合理勤勉可以发现法律错误的时间点提前到值得起诉的索赔(worthwhile claim)之时,更是会大大减少这类案件,不太会有大量退税的陈年旧案被翻出来。

Hodge 勋爵与 Reed 勋爵说:"… The rationale of section 32(1)- to postpone the commencement of the limitation period in respect of a claim for relief from the consequences of a mistake where, as a result of the mistake, the claimant could not reasonably have known of the circumstances giving rise to his cause of action at the time when it accrued-applies with equal force to a mistake of law as to a mistake of fact. To construe the provision in a sense which excluded such claims would not be consistent with Parliament's intention to relieve claimants from the necessity of complying with the time bar which would apply in the absence of section 32(1), at a time when they could not reasonably be expected to do so. Nor would such a construction reflect the ordinary meaning of the language which Parliament used: a mistake of law is, and always was, a 'mistake' in the ordinary sense of the word. … For these reasons, although there is undeniable force in the argument that section 32(1)(c) should be construed as being confined to mistakes of fact, the balance of the arguments in our view favours giving the language of section 32(1)(c) its ordinary meaning, so that it is applicable also to actions for relief from the consequences of a mistake of law. That approach to the construction of the provision best gives effect to Parliament's intention to relieve claimants from the necessity of complying with a time limit at a time when they cannot reasonably be expected to do so, and does not have unacceptable consequences for the legal certainty which the 1980 Act is primarily designed to protect. …"

大力反对的少数意见(Briggs、Sales、Carnwath 勋爵)认为 1939 年立法本意是为了索赔时效的肯定性,只针对当年的事实错误,在立法文字上也是刻意与其他两种推迟起算的情况(欺诈与隐瞒)不同,也被 Phillips-Higgins v. Harper(1954)1 QB 411 先例判定为狭窄的解释。[84] 但 Kleinwort Benson 贵族院先例承认法律错误后,如果包括在 Section 32(1)(c)适用范围,就与立法本意是为了排除拖延太久的索赔案件与该条文应该狭窄解释等起直接冲突。因为这与事实错误很不一样,普通法一有改变就有追溯力,就令过去几十年甚至上百年已经是了结的交易、合约或支付都可以大量的"复活",也不受 6 年时效影响,因为是从法律错误被发现的那一天才起算时效。这里只说这个少数意见也获得了很多法律学者的支持。

11.5.2 "发现错误"的时间点

这样也就要具体考虑如何适用 Section 32(1)(c)条文,而关键问题就是,什么时候才是发现或合理勤勉可以发现错误(has discovered the mistake)?

在事实错误的案件中,这看来是清楚与明确的,问题只在不同案件中如何通过原告提供的证据去证明他最早能在何时发现或可以发现他拥有有关的诉因(accrued cause of action),并起算 6 年时效。但在法律错误的案件中,这就存在困难了,尤其是法律错误是法院判决对长期与稳定的法律地位有了改变,或者是法院判某些法律规则违反宪法、公约等,可以说直到法院判决之前,原本大家认为的法律地位并没有错误。

---

〔84〕 见本书第七章之 17.1 段。

11.5.2.1 “发现理论”(discoverable doctrine)适用在欺诈、刻意隐瞒、事实错误、人身伤亡与潜在损失

在《Limitation Act 1980》之 Sections 11、14 与 32 下，已经有大量先例明确了如何认定在哪一天开始起算 6 年时效(无论是合约或侵权)，也就是受害方可以提起诉讼并作出索赔请求的一天。这可称为是“索赔请求测试”(Statement of Claim test)：见 Johnson v. Chief Constable of Surrey (1992) 10 WLUK 225；C v. Mirror Group Newspapers (1997) 1 WLR 131；Paragon Finance Plc v. DB Thackeray & Co (1999) 1 All ER 400；The “Kriti Palm” (2006) EWCA Civ 1601；Arcadia Group Brands Ltd v. Visa Inc (2015) EWCA Civ 883 等先例。

这里只节录部分权威判词，首先是在有关欺诈的 Law Society v. Sephton & Co (2004) EWCA Civ 1627 上诉庭先例中，Neuberger 大法官说：“As the judge(一审法官) said, a claimant does not ‘**discover**’ **a fraud until he has** ‘**material sufficient to enable him properly to plead it**’. Authoritative guidance on that topic was given by Millett LJ in Paragon Finance plc v DB Thakerar & Co…: ‘The question is not whether the plaintiffs should have discovered the fraud sooner; but whether they could with reasonable diligence have done so. The burden of proof is on them. They must establish that they could not have discovered the fraud without exceptional measures which they could not reasonably have been expected to take. In this context the length of the applicable period of limitation is irrelevant.…”(加黑部分是笔者的强调)

另在针对隐瞒的 Arcadia Group Brands Ltd v. Visa Inc 上诉庭先例中，Etherton 大法官说：“… one looks at the words in section 32(1)(b), ‘any fact relevant to the plaintiff’s right of action’. It seems to me that those words must mean any fact which **the plaintiff has to prove to establish a prime facie case**.’ …Johnson’s case, the Mirror Group Newspaper case and The Kriti Palm are clear authority, binding on this court, for the following principles applicable to section 32(1)(b) of the 1980 Act: (1) a ‘fact relevant to the plaintiff’s right of action’ within section 32(1)(b) is a fact without which the cause of action is incomplete; (2) facts which merely improve prospects of success are not facts relevant to the claimant’s right of action; (3) facts bearing on a matter which is not a necessary ingredient of the cause of action but which may provide a defence are not facts relevant to the claimant’s right of action.”(加黑部分是笔者的强调)

也是在针对隐瞒的 The “Kriti Palm”上诉庭先例中，Rix 大法官说：“… it is clear from authority that the statutory words ‘any fact relevant to a plaintiff’s right of action’ are to be given a narrow rather than a wide interpretation. Thus in Johnson v Chief Constable of Surrey …, where the claim was in false imprisonment and the police had deliberately concealed facts relevant to the absence of reasonable cause, this court accepted the defendant’s submission that ‘**the relevant fact must be a fact without which the cause**

of action is incomplete', contrasting a fact relevant to an action and to a right of action … Thus Rose LJ said '**Facts which improve prospects of success are not … facts relevant to his right of action'** … He accepted that the interpretation was a narrow one…Russell LJ agreed, saying …: 'Accordingly, whilst I acknowledge that **the new facts might make the plaintiff's case stronger or his right to damages more readily capable of proof they do not in my view bite upon the 'right of action' itself**. And Neill LJ emphasised that although absence of reasonable cause was an element in the tort of false imprisonment, the 'gist of the action' is in the imprisonment itself, which establishes a prima facie case and puts the burden of proving justification on the defendant. **Therefore the statutory words 'must mean any fact which the plaintiff has to prove to establish a prima facie case'**."(加黑部分是笔者的强调)

另 Buxton 大法官也说:"as Rix LJ emphasises, Johnson stands as authority for the proposition that what **must be concealed is something essential to complete the cause of action**. It is not enough that evidence that might enhance the claim is concealed, provided that the claim can be properly pleaded without it. **The court** therefore **has to look for the gist of the cause of action that is asserted, to see if that was available to the claimant without knowledge of the concealed material**. In Johnson the plaintiff sought to bring a claim of false imprisonment against the police, and discovered more than six years after his arrest that the police had, allegedly, concealed from him material that demonstrated that they had had no genuine belief in his guilt. Neill LJ said …'the gist of the action of false imprisonment is the mere imprisonment. The plaintiff need not prove that the imprisonment was unlawful or malicious; he establishes a prima facie case if he proves that he was imprisoned by the defendant. The onus is then shifted to the defendant to prove some justification for it.'"(加黑部分是笔者的强调)

在涉及隐瞒与人身伤亡的 Kimathi v. Foreign and Commonwealth Office (2018) EWHC 1169 (QB) 先例中, Stewart 大法官说:"It seems to me that the present authorities on the definition of 'any fact relevant to the [Claimant's] right of action' must be followed. This is not only because they are binding upon this court and cannot be properly distinguished, or explained away so as to give a broader construction, but also for the following reasons: (a) The Limitation Act 1980 provides a bar whereby stale claims should not be litigated after a fixed period of time. The consequences of harsh results arising from the application for such fixed periods are alleviated by 'knowledge' provisions in sections 11 – 14 for personal injury Claimants and section 14A for Claimants with other rights of action. (b) Section 32 deals with a specific situation, namely postponing the limitation period in cases of fraud, deliberate concealment or an action for relief from the consequences of mistakes. (c) Personal injury Claimants also have the (albeit discretionary)provision in section 33. (d) For the purposes of section 32(1)(b), if **a Claimant has the knowledge to plead his or her cause of action**, then that is sufficient to obviate any adverse consequences of deliberate concealment by the Defendant. (e) **To suggest that there has to be 'some consideration of the prospect of success' is not only contrary to authority, it is also something which wholly lacks clarity and would lead to a substantial increase in litigation**. Any attempted widening of the appropriate test was expressly outlawed by the Court of Appeal in the Arcadia case…"(加黑部分是笔者的强调)

在近期涉及欺诈性诱导投资的 European Real Estate Debt Fund(Cayman)Ltd(In Liquidation)v. Treon(2021)EWHC 2866(Ch)先例中,Miles 大法官针对 Section 32(1)的"发现"一词总结说:

"This section has been considered in a number of cases which were reviewed in OT Computers Limited v Infineon Technologies AF[2021]EWCA Civ 501. The following points … are relevant for the present dispute:

i) **The state of knowledge which a claimant must have in order for it to have discovered the concealment has for the most part been regarded as the knowledge sufficient to enable it to plead a claim**. More recent authority such as Test Claimants in the FII Group Litigation v Revenue and Customs Commissioners[2020]UKSC 47 … **suggests that time should begin to run from the(possibly earlier)point when the claimant knows, or could with reasonable diligence know, about the mistake with sufficient confidence to justify embarking on the preliminaries to the issue of proceedings**, such as submitting a claim to the proposed defendant, taking advice and collecting evidence. (**I shall apply the statement of claim test**, as it is not clearly established on the authorities whether the potentially more liberal test applies to fraud claims. In any event the parties did not suggest that the slight differences in the test would materially affect the outcome.)

ii) Whichever of these tests is applied, 'there will be cases where discovery of the relevant facts**involves a process over a period of time as pieces of information become available**. In such cases it may be **difficult to identify the precise point of time at which a claimant exercising reasonable diligence could have discovered enough, either to plead a claim or … to begin embarking on the preliminaries to the issue of proceedings**'…

iii) The following passage from Paragon Finance Plc v DB Thakerar[1999]1 ALL ER 400 has been treated as authoritative: 'The question is not whether the plaintiffs should have discovered the fraud sooner; but**whether they could with reasonable diligence have done so. The burden of proof is on them**. They must establish that they could not have discovered the fraud without exceptional measures which they could not reasonably have been expected to take.... '

iv) In OT Computers Males LJ said..., ... although **the question what reasonable diligence** requires ...(接下来的内容与本章之11.5.3.2段有关,将在该段节录)"(加黑部分是笔者的强调)

11.5.2.2 "发现"在"索赔请求测试"的重点

从上述少量节录的权威说法,可以得出以下几个重点:

1.《Limitation Act 1980》立法的本意与政策上是去排除拖延太久的民事诉讼(stale claims),虽然部分案件(特别是涉及被告恶意欺诈或隐瞒的案件)因为受害方往往不能及时发现他们拥有的诉因或谁是被告,所以需要网开一面。但立法本意仍不是让这些受害方"拥抱他们的权利去睡觉"(to sleep on their rights),所以对什么时间算是"发现"应是去狭窄解释。

2.将受害方的原告作出索赔请求的时间作为"发现"的恰当时间点,是因为如果索赔请求显示不了一个有重要事实支持的表面站得住脚的诉因(prima facie cause of action),就会被被告申请法院提前撤销索赔(strike out claim)。[85] 在Arcadia Group Brands Ltd v. Visa Inc(2015)EWCA Civ 883上诉庭先例中,Etherton大法官说:"what is sufficient knowledge to constitute discovery within section 32(1) depends on the particular facts. More importantly, for the purposes of this appeal, the point has no relevance to proceedings such as the present ones where **a complete cause of action has been pleaded, the particulars of claim are endorsed with a statement of truth, and it is accepted that no new facts necessary to complete the cause of action have been discovered during the previous six years**. I agree with the defendants' submission that it is logically inconsistent for the claimants both to assert that the particulars of claim plead a complete cause of action and cannot be **struck out for failing to disclose reasonable grounds for bringing the claim or for otherwise being an abuse of the court's process** and yet also to contend that, for the purposes of the 'statement of claim' test ..."

另在Nomura International Plc v. Granada Group Ltd(2007)EWHC 642(Comm);先例中,Cooke大法官说:"If a claimant cannot do that which is necessary to prosecute the claim by setting out the basis of it, even in a rudimentary way, a claimant has no business to issue a Claim Form at all 'in the hope that something may turn up'."

3.加上原告需要为请求的事实(pleaded facts)向法院作出保证,也就是要签署"真实声明"(statement of truth)。[86] 以及像在欺诈等诉讼中,英国律师都受到专业

---

〔85〕 见笔者《证据法:国际规管与诉讼中的证据攻防》一书第六章之4段。

〔86〕 见笔者《证据法:基础理论、口头证据与专家证据》一书第二章之1.3段。

守则的约束在没有满足客户已掌握足够证据前不肯提起指控被告欺诈的诉讼。[87]这一切都清楚显示原告是“发现”了他拥有的诉因。

4. 举证责任在原告,他需要证明在平衡的可能性下,无法更早发现需要提起索赔诉讼的重要事实并拿到证据。这涉及 Section 32(1)(c)下原告有“合理勤勉”义务去调查取证尽早发现有关事实的立法要求,这将稍后分段探讨。

5. 不是关键性支持诉因的重要事实,可称为是“次要事实”(secondary matters)与“发现”无关。在绝大部分诉讼中,是持续不断(甚至直到开庭审理时)进行调查取证、文件披露等。这可以在提起诉讼前(毕竟“发现”起算时效仍有 6 年时间)或甚是在诉讼程序中进行。确实,已经掌握了重要事实的表面证据不代表原告不需要去进一步加强证据与/或调整主张(会是要去更改索赔请求)以更好说服审理法官与提升胜诉机会,特别是被告出来抗辩并提供反驳的证据,但原告“发现”他的诉因的时间点早已过去。

6. 原告对有关事实带来的法律权利与后果(legal implication)的了解与“发现”无关,也就是如果原告可以掌握可去提起诉讼的重要事实,就算不知道自己有诉因,不影响已经可以“发现”并起算 6 年时效。例如,原告几年前就已经在医院检查时发现因为接触有毒石棉患上间皮瘤(mesothelioma),[88]但是不知道可以索赔。直到几年后与工友聚会才知道可以索赔,于是向律师咨询并知悉根据《The Compensation Act 2006》之 Section 3 是可以向任何一个令他接触石棉的雇主索赔。这时效应该从发现患上间皮瘤起算,而不是从咨询律师意见知道他的权利时才起算。这可节录在 HF Pension Trustees(1999)PNLR 894 先例中,Jonathan Parker 大法官所说:“In my judgment, however, in cases under section 14A as in personal injury cases, mere ignorance that the known facts may give rise to a claim in law cannot postpone the running of time under the 1980 Act. As I read the sections and the authorities, both section 14 and section 14A are concerned exclusively with matters of fact provable by evidence, as opposed to matters of(English)law, in respect of which evidence is not admissible.”

另在 Booker v. RR Financial Services UK Ltd(2016)EWHC 3186(Ch)先例中,Master Matthews 法官也说:“… it is wrong to look at when the claimant first becomes aware that he has a legal claim; that is to say, when he has first drawn the correct legal inference, or a possibly correct legal inference, from the primary facts. That is the wrong focus. The correct focus is on the primary facts.”

7. 其他诉讼(或仲裁)案件认定的相关事实也显然与“发现”本案要提起诉讼所需要掌握的重要事实的时间点无关。其他案件被认定的事实充其量会是加强自己主张的事实,变得更可信与有说服力。例如在同一宗庞氏骗局中,原告不应该等待其他

---

〔87〕 见本书第三章之 8.2.4 段。

〔88〕 关于石棉造成的大量人身伤亡案件,可见笔者《损失赔偿与救济》一书第四章之 4.3.3 段与第八章。

受害方胜诉后才(更有信心)提起诉讼,但届时掌握重要事实的时间与6年时效也早已过去。这方面可见 Johnson v. Chief Constable of Surrey(1992)10 WLUK 225;HF Pension Trustees;Sandhu v. Revenue and Customs Commissioners(2017)EWHC 60(QB)等先例。

8. 而其他相关诉讼的法律问题,更是和本案的“发现”与起算6年时效的议题无关。索赔请求只需要说明与主张诉因有关的重要事实,无需请求或争辩法律。[89] 其他相关诉讼裁定的法律,只是对原告有帮助与让原告有信心推进诉讼。

11.5.2.3 DMG 贵族院先例针对“发现理论”在法律错误的不同测试

Kleinwort Benson 贵族院先例改变了长期以来的法律定论,也就是法律错误是不会有救济的,并进一步判《Limitation Act 1980》之 Section 32(1)(c)也适用于法律错误。这就带来了确立什么是“发现”错误的时间点的困难,因为上小段介绍了时间点是原告可发现或掌握提起诉讼/作出索赔请求所需要的重要事实(material facts)时。但法律错误不存在重要事实,这样“索赔请求测试”看来并不适用。

而且,法律错误的案件往往会在后来有更高层次的法院去推翻现在的法律地位或说法,尤其是历史悠久的一般法律地位更是去贵族院(今天的最高院)才会推翻改判,如 Kleinwort Benson 贵族院先例。而在这之前的法律地位(只有事实错误),即使是有了法律学者或一审法院的批评或求变,如果原告敢去提起诉讼并主张法律错误的诉因要求救济,被告也会申请撤销索赔并可能被法院支持,因为这被视为滥用程序(abuse of process),索赔请求没有显示有一个站得住脚/表面可争辩的诉因。

因为会有以上所讲的困难,所以在 DMG 贵族院先例中,才会将6年时效起算的时间点放在发现或合理勤勉可以发现法律的真正地位时。而真正地位也就是判决已经是司法系统终局地位(如未能拿到上诉批文或者已经是最高院判决)。在 FII(SC)(2020)最高院先例中,Reed 与 Hodge 勋爵这样总结 DMG 先例的判法:

“In considering the application of section 32(1)(c), Lord Hoffmann stated ... that the ‘reasonable diligence’ proviso depended upon **the true state of affairs being there to be discovered**: ‘In this case, however, **the true state of affairs was not discoverable until the Court of Justice**(欧洲法院)**pronounced its judgment**. One might make guesses or predictions, especially after the opinion of the Advocate General. This gave DMG sufficient confidence to issue proceedings. But they could not have discovered the truth because the truth did not yet exist. **In my opinion, therefore, the mistake was not reasonably discoverable until after the judgment had been delivered**.’

This statement is based on a number of premises. One is that a mistake of law is a ‘mistake’ within the meaning of section 32(1)(c), as had been held in Kleinwort Benson, and therefore falls within the ambit of the discoverability test. ... Lord Hoffmann’s

[89] 见笔者《证据法:国际规管与诉讼中的证据攻防》一书第七章之6段。

statement also assumes that ‘discovery’, within the meaning of section 32(1), means the ascertainment of the truth, and that, ... **judicial decisions which establish a point of law thereby bring the truth into existence for the first time**..."(加黑部分是笔者的强调)

在本章之11.5段已经提到,根据FII(SC)(2020)最高院先例的事实,起算点无论是2006年DMG先例的贵族院判决,还是2001年或2006年欧洲法院的判决,在2003年集体诉讼命令时都没有超出6年索赔时效。

11.5.2.4 FII(SC)(2020)最高院先例:"值得起诉的索赔测试"

DMG贵族院先例的测试带来的问题在上诉到FII(SC)(2020)最高院先例后重新得到考虑。最高院的多数意见否定了DMG先例的判法,接受了DMG先例中唯一持不同意见的Brown勋爵的观点,认为"发现"法律错误的测试是:"as soon as a paying party recognises that a worthwhile claim arises that he should not after all have made the payment and accordingly is entitled to recover it ... he has ‘discovered’ the mistake within the meaning of section 32."

最高院考虑的原因很多,仅挑几点简单介绍如下:

1. 立法时效一般规定是从诉因产生之时起算,无论当时是否存在争议,或该诉因是否已经有足够的证据支持等,如不能说等到原告咨询了律师、调查取证完成、十拿九稳之后才起算时效。Section 32(1)(c)的推迟起算只是为了保护欺诈、刻意隐瞒与错误案件中无法及时知道诉因存在与起诉的受害方原告。如果法律错误是按照知道真实地位作为标准来看,这相当于是让原告明确会胜诉后才开始计算,这与立法本意是相悖的。

2. 以真实地位作为起算时间,在逻辑上也有问题。司法系统中必须先有当事人提起诉讼,才会涉及法院审理与判决决定法律地位到底如何。因此可以说是否真正有法律错误是无法提前发现,只有等到第一个原告起诉获得最后判决结果后才能有"真正地位"。但第一个原告又会因为没有确定的司法系统判决,主张法律错误可能属于滥用程序而被撤销,永远不会有法律的"真正地位",这也会发展成一个"鸡生蛋,蛋生鸡"的问题。

3. 逻辑上还有其他混乱与不一致的问题,如在考虑是否法律错误时,理论说法就是事后法院判决后,可以将缴纳税款时的法律地位"视为"(deemed)与事后的法律地位一致,因此缴纳税款属于错误与应该复原。但是在考虑时效时,又变成只有在事后法院判决结果后才是真正法律地位。

在综合考虑后,最高院多数意见认为从更符合立法目的与公平的角度来看,起算时间应该是解释为原告合理勤勉可以发现诉因的时间点,或者说就是原告应该发现自己有一个值得起诉的索赔的时间点。Reed与Hodge勋爵说:"The purpose of the postponement effected by section 32(1) is to ensure that a claimant is not disadvantaged, so far as limitation is concerned, by reason of being unaware of the circumstances giving rise to his cause of action as a result of fraud, concealment or mistake. That purpose is achieved, where the ingredients of the cause of action include his having made a mistake of law, if time runs from the point in time when he knows, or could with reasonable diligence know, that he made such a mistake '**with sufficient confidence to justify embarking on the preliminaries to the issue of a writ, such as submitting a claim to the proposed defendant, taking advice and collecting evidence**'; or, as Lord Brown put it in Deutsche Morgan Grenfell... **he discovers or could with reasonable diligence discover his mistake in the sense of recognising that a worthwhile claim arises**. We do not believe that there is any difference of substance between these formulations, each of which is helpful and casts light on the other."(加黑部分是笔者的强调)

毕竟只要找到在某一个时间点上,原告发现或可以发现自己是拥有诉因(或潜在诉因),原告就应该自己考虑是否要起诉的问题,已经足够满足1980年立法条文中推迟起算索赔时效的目的,那么就应该从这个时间点就开始起算。

例如在此先例中的情况,英国有关税务法律规则与欧盟法律相悖的问题的讨论已经有一段时间,真正确认这一系列法律规则错误的案件也经过了一系列的欧洲法院的判决。例如在Hoechst case(Metallgesellschaft Ltd v. Inland Revenue Commissioners, Hoechst AG v. Inland Revenue Commissioners)(Joined Cases C-397/98 and C-410/98)(2001)ECR I-1727欧洲法院先例中,早在1995年就已经起诉,而且这是被媒体广泛报道的公开信息。这就要根据证据来看原告到底在什么时候知道这方面的情况,甚至也不仅仅是1995年知道已经有他人起诉时,还有可能是在更早时原告自己就已经先发现这方面的法律问题,只不过是打算等别人先测试了"水温"之后谋定而后动。这种情况下没有理由不从根据证据可以显示原告发现了真正存在可争辩的法律错误、属于值得起诉的索赔(即使当时并不能确定结果)与可以说服法院有一个可争辩的诉因(不会被提前撤销)时起算。但在此先例中,由于在前几审中并没有针对这方面的事实问题,最高院没有凭空揣测,而是判发回一审重审。

这样的判法纠正了DMG先例认定的法律错误的"发现"时间点,因为"值得起诉的索赔测试"(worthwhile claimtest)在本质上与"索赔请求测试"接近,可以说是在一定程度上把6年时效的起算提前了。毕竟1980年立法是排除拖延太久的索赔,延后时效所针对的是诉因,不是有关法律的"真正地位"。如延迟到有法院终局判决才算是"发现",原告才提起诉讼也就不是正常的诉讼与审理,而会是简易判决(summary judgment),这从逻辑与道理上都说不过去。

11.5.2.5 "发现值得起诉的索赔"的时间点

有不少批评说在千变万化的案件中确立什么算是"值得起诉"的时间点,是一个模糊、不可捉摸、不肯定、富争议、不实际与/或难以操作的判断标准。在FII(SC)(2020)最高院先例中,多数判决也没有给出太多的指引,只是将该先例的"发现"应是在哪一天,即值得起诉的一天,发还给一审法院去认定。

会有案件是很快就能判断会存在法律错误,值得提起诉讼,根本不需要去涉及

1980 年立法之 Section 32(1)(c),从诉因产生起算的 6 年时效已绰绰有余。例如 Woolwich 贵族院先例与 Ipswich Town Football Club Co Ltd v. Chief Constable of Suffolk(2017)EWHC 375(QB)先例中,都是原告在作出支付时就已经认为错误。

又或是,一位纳税人在无知的情况下支付了税款,但多年后咨询了律师知道法律错误,这不影响他在支付时已应能判断存在法律错误,Section 32(1)(c)不考虑无知或疏懒,也不会因此可以延长时效

但在其他情况下的法律错误,所谓的"错误"是后来普通法的发展,有追溯力的案例所导致,实是会在方方面面都带来问题。例如在本书第七章之 7.2.3 段有"将来法律地位改变对诉讼/仲裁签订妥协/和解协议的影响",就涉及和解协议由于将来法律地位的改变而令双方原先订立的大量和解协议都以共同错误(common mistake)理解订约时的法律而自动无效的问题。Jeremy Philip Elston v. Lawrence King, Sue Roscoe(trustees in bankruptcy of Jeremy Philip Elston)(2020)EWHC 55(Ch)先例区分了两种不同的改变法律地位的情况与不同的对待,区别视为双方的"自愿承担法律变化风险"与不会导致和解协议无效,或是"真正错误理解法律"令和解协议无效。在此针对的确立什么时间点"发现"法律错误并值得去提起诉讼,也可类似地区分为两种情况在接下来介绍:

1. 一种情况是谈不上有一个悠久、权威性与稳定的法律地位,如在不同的一审法院有不同判法。或甚是一个新颖的税法或税例尚没有在法院考验过,只有专业内(如会计师、税务律师等)有一些看法。纳税人如果作出支付就应该知道法律仍在初步发展阶段,支付时对该法律的认知会在之后有所改变的几率相对高。这样,会否 Section 32(1)(c)的"发现"一天也就是支付的一天? 向法院提起诉讼也可以显示出有一个合理基础的诉因(reasonable grounds for bringing the claim)而不会被撤销?

2. 困难会是在法律地位已经是悠久、权威性与稳定的另一种情况,即所谓的"settled state of law"。这样,纳税人在支付时根本想也没想过会是法律错误下的支付,说是"法律错误"纯粹是普通法的判例是有追溯力。例如在 Kleinwort Benson 贵族院先例中,一般法律人士都不会想到贵族院的轻微多数意见作出改变历史悠久与稳定的"对法律理解错误规则"(mistake of law rule)。所以这"错误"是被"视为"(deemed)与"人为拟定"(artificial)的,完全谈不上是纳税人在支付时真正的错误。这样,正常情况下纳税人与他的专业团队都不会质疑法律的地位,直到 DMG 先例或 FII 案件在有了欧洲法院判违反欧盟法律的公开报道后才警觉法律的"真正地位"(true state)有了改变。这样,如果要把"发现"去找出纳税人有了一个更早的"值得起诉的索赔"的时间点,也只能是通过"视为"与"人为拟定"找出这一天了。这里"视为发现"的一天是:"The claimant knows, or could with reasonable diligence know, that he made such a mistake with sufficient confidence to justifying embarking on the preliminaries to the issue of a writ…"

这是纳税人作为原告的举证责任,他要提供证据。在 FII(SC)(2020)最高院先

例中，Reed 与 Hodge 勋爵说这些证据是：

"... In practice ... in cases where the claimant has made a payment on the basis of **a mistaken understanding of the law which has resulted from ignorance, the mistake will normally have been discoverable immediately, by seeking legal advice**. Section 32(1) only has effect where a mistake could not have been discovered at the time of the payment with the exercise of reasonable diligence. On the other hand, where **the payment was made in reliance on a precedent that was subsequently overruled, or an understanding of the law that was later altered by a judicial decision**, the question will be whether the claim was brought within the prescribed **period beginning on the date when it was discoverable** by the exercise of reasonable diligence that **the basis of the payment was legally questionable**, so as to give rise to a worthwhile claim to restitution. Depending on the circumstances, **it may be difficult to identify a specific date**, but doubtful cases can be resolved by bearing in mind that the burden of proof lies on the claimant to prove that his claim was brought within the prescribed limitation period.

...**The focus of that evidence is likely to be upon developments in legal understanding within the relevant category of claimants and their advisers**... Thus, in the circumstances of the present case, ... there being a reasonable prospect that the limitation period could be deferred until the time when 'a well advised multi-national group based in the UK would have had good grounds for supposing that it had a valid claim to recover ACT levied contrary to EU law' .... **Evidence in relation to matters of this kind may well include expert evidence concerning the state of understanding of the law within the relevant categories of professional advisers during the relevant period**.

It is true that this approach involves a more nuanced inquiry than a mechanical test based on the date on which an authoritative appellate judgment determined the point in issue. But it would be**unduly pessimistic to conclude at this stage that it will prove to be unworkable in practice, or too uncertain in its operation** to be acceptable."（加黑部分是笔者的强调）

但针对第二点这是十分笼统的指引，Reed 与 Hodge 勋爵自己也知道会是实际没法操作，只是不想太早下定论。这表示只针对法律错误，Section 32(1)(c)的"发现"将来需要有更明确的指导才可行。但法律错误在本质上与事实错误、欺诈与隐瞒等有很大的不同，不会有一些事实可去证明"发现"的门槛（threshold）或路标（signpost）。法律本来也只有法律专业人士才会掌握，不是一般商人可"发现"有错误的。而且，法律本质上是意见，即使是有了明确的法律地位，也难逃不断在法律圈子里有异议。如 FII(SC)(2020)最高院先例判决公开后，笔者就见到不少法律学者对之进行批评。该先例本身就是 4:3 的多数意见，而且少数意见被笔者视为强而有力。这样，是否代表已经到了 Section 32(1)(c)的"发现"时间点？或是，目前是过不了提起诉讼与索赔请求测试的关卡,相信一定会被法院视为滥用法律程序而被撤销。但批评与异议要到什么程度才会满足这关卡?会否是要有案例的审理法官提出一些没有约束力的批评,或是权威书籍如《Chitty on Contracts》呼吁对该法律作出变化,法院才不视为要求改变是滥用法律程序。

难怪少数意见的 Briggs 勋爵大力反对,认为 Section 32(1)(c)根本不应适用在法律错误的立法时效,说:"Plainly, there may be a very long period when a rule of law is taken to be established by professional practice or judicial decisions before the threshold of discoverability proposed by Lord Brown to suggest it might be wrong is crossed. ...The test of discoverability proposed by Lord Brown is itself very uncertain, in a way that the test for discoverability of whether there has been a mistake as a matter of fact is not. The identification of a point in time, earlier than when the relevant claim was actually launched, when such **a claim became worth pursuing requires a deeply speculative process of hypothetical fact-finding**. ... The application of his test will often require a wide-ranging investigation at trial of something as **inherently vague and intangible as the state of professional opinion as it changes year by year over what may be a very long period. It is unclear whether expert evidence would be of much assistance for such a speculative investigation into legal history**. Moreover, the more one focuses on what was reasonable to expect of one claimant or particular type of claimant, as distinct from the general understanding of the legal profession, the greater the range of cases in which the court will have to produce speculative and uncertain judgments as to whether the relevant threshold of discoverability has been passed. Again, therefore, this tends to undermine the principle of certainty which Parliament and the LR Committee intended should be upheld."(加黑部分是笔者的强调)

看来针对法律错误的"发现"理论应会有后续案例去进一步澄清这方面的法律地位。

11.5.2.6 Jazztel Plc v. Revenue and Customs Commissioners(2022)EWCA Civ 232 上诉庭先例

很快就有了此上诉庭先例去适用确立的针对法律错误的"发现"理论。案情是有关一种名为"stamp duty reserve tax"(SDRT)的税项,原告 Jazztel Plc 在 2000 年至 2008 年都支付了这笔税款。在第一次支付(金额是 1,819,060 英镑)前,已有委任的律师(年利达律师事务所)在 1999 年 12 月 22 日以电文警告原告说此税项有问题,会违反欧盟法律,大致上是因为其他国家没有征收或少征收,也影响货物在欧盟的自由流转,但也提到涉及的金额去与税务局争议要花费的律师费用会是得不偿失。

原告最后仍是在 2000 年 1 月 7 日的最后限期支付了这笔税款,但通过年利达去保留权利。年利达也在当天发信函给税务局说:"(原告的支付是)merely to avoid any interest or penalties if, notwithstanding our view on the European law issues, these

SDRT charges were ultimately found to be applicable."

年利达更在 2000 年 1 月 11 日向税务局的一位主管跟进了投诉。而欧洲法院是在 2009 年的 HSBC Holdings Plc v. Revenue and Customs Commissioners(Case C-569/07)(2009)ECR I-9047 先例中判英国的 SDRT 违反了欧盟法律。

到了 2013 年 12 月 19 日,原告向税务局提起诉讼,要求退还多年支付的 SDRT。显然 1980 年立法之 Section 32(1)(c)不是从 2009 年起算 6 年时效,而是从更早的合理勤勉可以发现的时间点起算。双方争议的时间点是:原告主张是 2009 年欧洲法院的判决,因为虽然早在 1999 年 12 月已经有年利达的警告,但一审法院已经认定原告对法律(有关税法)可能错误的怀疑只是"轻微"(marginal),也就是低于 50%,谈不上是"发现"了一个可去提起诉讼的诉因。但被告税务局认为早在 2000 年 1 月年利达就已经是"发现"了法律的错误。双方大律师部分争辩可节录如下:

"Mr Baldry(被告税务局代表大律师)submitted that the correspondence between Linklaters(年利达),Jazztel and HMRC(被告税务局)in December 1999 and January 2000 establishes that Jazztel 'discovered' its mistake within the meaning of section 32(1)of the 1980 Act or, failing that, that it could have done so with reasonable diligence.... True it may be that Linklaters said that any attack on the charge 'would be very strongly resisted by the UK Inland Revenue' and that 'There must be doubts about whether this is worth pursuing' ..., but such matters do not bear on whether Jazztel was in a position to 'embark on the preliminaries' or even whether a 'worthwhile claim' had arisen. Time begins to run under section 32...While mere suspicion that SDRT might not be payable would not of itself suffice to start time running, if you have been advised of a potential argument and made a claim on that basis, you have inevitably reached the relatively low threshold for 'discovery'.

In contrast, Mr Grodzinski(原告代表大律师)argued that time does not begin to run under section 32 of the 1980 Act until a claimant recognises, or could with reasonable diligence have recognised, that he has a 'worthwhile' claim.... For a mistake of law to have been 'discovered', Mr Grodzinski said, the claimant must believe in the truth of an assertion that a mistake has been made. In the present case, far from Jazztel so believing, the Judge has made unchallenged findings to the effect that ... in HSBC Holdings ... in 2009, Jazztel had no more than a 'marginal' doubt as to whether SDRT was due, not 'serious' doubts, and, that being so, Linklaters' letter to Mr Halsey(税务局主管)of 11 January 2000 cannot matter. Further, it is impossible for this court to arrive at a conclusion as to whether Jazztel could with reasonable diligence have discovered its mistake."

上诉庭判定由于年利达在 2000 年 1 月 11 日给税务局的信函是根据有关的税务规则去正式作出投诉,这虽然比不上法院正式启动诉讼,但如果在这时间点原告仍说是没有"发现"自己有一个诉因太牵强。所以,本来上诉庭必须依从一审对事实的认定，也就是原告对法律可能错误的怀疑只是“轻微”，但从年利达信函投诉的事实与证据看来，“发现”的时间点是在2000年1月11日，这也代表原告在2000年至2008年前期大部分的支付都已经过了时效。Newey 大法官说：

“But for Linklaters' letter to Mr Halsey(税务局主管) of 11 January 2000, however, we would have accepted that Jazztel had not discovered its mistake at that stage. Although Linklaters had alerted Jazztel on 22 December 1999 to the fact that there might be grounds for questioning the SDRT charges on the basis of EU law, the Judge found that Jazztel's state of mind remained predominantly that the tax was due and that such doubt as it had was 'marginal'. Moreover, as Mr Grodzinski stressed, there is no challenge to that finding. In the circumstances, we do not think the advice which Linklaters gave on 22 December can of itself be said to have led Jazztel to know of its mistake 'with sufficient confidence to justify embarking on the preliminaries to the issue of a writ' or to 'recognis[e] that a worthwhile claim arises'.

On 11 January 2000, however, Linklaters sent HMRC on Jazztel's behalf a letter formally requesting the return of the £ 1,819,060 which it had paid. That letter constituted a 'claim' for the purposes of the SDRT Regulations and so affected Jazztel's legal position. ... Further, the 11 January letter correctly identified the basis on which the SDRT regime could be impugned, as was later held in HSBC Holdings...

...Even so, it seems to us that Jazztel must be taken to have 'discovered' its mistake for the purposes of section 32(1) of the 1980 Act by the time Linklaters sent the 11 January 2000 letter on its behalf. The letter shows that, by then, Jazztel was alive to the grounds on which SDRT would prove not to have been payable and was in a position to claim repayment. While the company did not follow up the letter with any legal proceedings, it did not have to: the SDRT Regulations allowed it to make a legally effective 'claim' by letter. It appears to us that, **just as a person who has issued a claim form cannot be heard to suggest that he lacked the requisite knowledge for the purposes of the 1980 Act, Jazztel cannot be heard to suggest that it had not discovered its mistake when it had already succeeded in making a 'claim' for repayment under regulation 14 of the SDRT Regulations**. ... it is not open to someone who has made a claim under the SDRT Regulations to recover an overpayment to say that he has not yet discovered that he could make one.

In the circumstances, it is in our view possible to determine from the existing materials, without the need for any further hearing, that the present proceedings are statute-barred...**Jazztel must be considered to have sufficiently 'discovered' by 11 January 2000 that it had a claim to recover its SDRT payments**.”(加黑部分是笔者的强调)

在此先例中，也没有发生在上一小段提到的双方通过法律专家证人去证明在整个时间段(2000年至2009年)会不会出现更恰当“发现”的时间点的昂贵、不可捉摸与不肯定的做法,这是因为此先例在1999年12月与2000年1月发生的年利达律师事务所、原告 Jazztel Plc 与被告税务局通讯往来的事实可去重点针对,无需大海捞针在之后的八九年去挑一个“视为发现”的时间点。所以还要等待更多先例去考验 FII (SC)(2020)最高院先例对法律错误的“发现理论”作出的多数判决是否实际可行。

但此先例仍受到了一贯反对 Kleinwort Benson 先例、DMG 先例与 FII(SC)(2020)先例的判法的法律学者的批评,也就是《Limitation Act 1980》之 Section 32(1)(c)的立法本意与现实做法都不应该被解释为是包括法律错误,并无可避免地带来了一连串很牵强才能去解释的问题。在《Law Quarterly Review》2022年版第535页,牛津大学的两位老师发表的《Between rocks and hard places:limitation, privilege, and mistake of law》一文就指出在此上诉庭先例中,原告与年利达之间的通迅往来涉及“法律业务特免权”[90](legal professional privilege),因此没有披露,如果披露,在“挑选樱桃规则”[91](cherry picking rule)下就要全部披露。此时原告就会陷入两难:一方面,原告有举证责任,而对法律的错误理解往往涉及律师,也就是享有特免权。另一方面,原告又不会想要全面披露特免权文件。在此先例中,刚巧年利达给税务局的信函不存在特免权的问题比较容易解决。但有了三个贵族院/最高院的判决,普通法去改正是不可能的,所以该文希望早日以立法作出改变去排除 Section 32(1)(c)适用在法律错误中。

11.5.3 纳税人合理勤勉可以发现

无论是欺诈还是错误等立法推迟起算时效的情况,显然不是无限优待原告,设定的时间点都根据原告的情况,代入合理的客观标准,原告可以发现诉因(或潜在诉因)存在的时间点。

11.5.3.1 合理勤勉(reasonable diligence)的标准

在《Limitation Act 1980》中多处体现了这样的立法目的与精神。例如在针对人身伤害案件的 Section 11(4):“the period applicable is three years from... the date of knowledge(if later) of the person injured.”

在 Section 14(3)解释 Section 11 中的知情(knowledge)说:“For the purposes of this section a person's knowledge includes knowledge which he might reasonably have been expected to acquire—(a) from facts observable or ascertainable by him; or (b) from facts ascertainable by him with the help of medical or other appropriate expert advice which it is reasonable for him to seek; but a person shall not be fixed under this subsection with knowledge of a fact ascertainable only with the help of expert advice so long as he has taken all reasonable steps to obtain (and, where appropriate, to act on) that

---

〔90〕 见笔者《证据法:国际规管与诉讼中的证据攻防》一书第九章。

〔91〕 见笔者《证据法:国际规管与诉讼中的证据攻防》一书第十二章之4段。

advice."

在本段针对的 Section 32(1)中的措辞/文字是："… the period of limitation shall not begin to run until the plaintiff has discovered the fraud, concealment or mistake (as the case may be) or could with reasonable diligence have discovered it."虽然用的文字是发现(discover)，但与知情的意思是类似的，在判断标准上也是相近的。

这类案件需要合理勤勉作为客观的标准，在过往一些欺诈案件中早已经有过指引。[92] 作为依赖立法延迟起算时效条文的原告，需要承担举证责任，证明自己已经采取了合理勤勉的行为了解真相与调查情况等，但直到某一个时间点才发现欺诈。客观的标准在于，需要假设一位人士拥有与原告类似的人力与资源，合理地想要调查欺诈，何时能够发现。这就可以排除受害方无知、疏懒与鲁莽等立法无意保护的情况。可重复节录 Millett 大法官在 Paragon Finance plc v. DB Thakerar & Co(1999)1 All ER 400 上诉庭先例对这方面的权威说法，如下："The question is not whether the plaintiffs should have discovered the fraud sooner; but whether they could with reasonable diligence have done so. The burden of proof is on them. They must establish that they could not have discovered the fraud without exceptional measures which they could not reasonably have been expected to take. In this context the length of the applicable period of limitation is irrelevant. … the six-year limitation period did not provide the relevant standard. … **the test was how a person carrying on a business of the relevant kind would act if he had adequate but not unlimited staff and resources and were motivated by a reasonable but not excessive sense of urgency.** I respectfully agree."(加黑部分是笔者的强调)

在 Law Society v. Sephton & Co(2004)EWCA Civ 1627 上诉庭先例中，Neuberger 大法官还提出原告要满足合理勤勉的标准，需要自己有动力找出真相并采取行动主动调查，说："… it is inherent in s32(1) of the 1980 Act… that there must be an assumption that the claimant desires to discover whether or not there has been a fraud. Not making any such assumption would rob the effect of the word 'could', as emphasised by Millett LJ(上一段节录的 Millett 大法官的说法), of much of its significance. Further, the concept of 'reasonable diligence' carries with it the notion of a desire to know, and, indeed, to investigate."

在 FII(SC)(2020)最高院先例中，Reed 与 Hodge 勋爵说："…The **standard of reasonable diligence** is how **a person carrying on a business of the relevant kind would act**, on the assumption that **he desired to know** whether or not he had made a mistake, if he had adequate but not unlimited staff and resources and was motivated by a reasonable **but not excessive sense of urgency**. The question is not whether the claimant

---

[92] 见笔者《证据法：基础理论、口头证据与专家证据》一书第十章之5段。

should have discovered the mistake sooner, but whether he could with reasonable diligence have done so. **The burden of proof is on the claimant.** He must establish **on the balance of probabilities that he could not have discovered the mistake without exceptional measures which he could not reasonably have been expected to take.**"(加黑部分是笔者的强调)

11.5.3.2 以原告的具体情况客观测试"合理勤勉可以发现"

在 Section 32(1)(c)中采用的措辞/文字是"合理勤勉可以"("… could with reasonable diligence have… ")。近期就有一些先例针对这应该是主观测试(subjective test)还是客观测试(objective test)进行讨论。

主观测试就会是针对真正原告(actual claimant),看原告的水平、能力,甚至其他人不知道的一些个人问题,如懒散、贫穷、不肯或不能花钱调查等,看原告可以发现法律错误的时间。显然,与客观合理人士都会发现的时间相比,真正原告发现的时间点要更迟了。

而纯粹客观的测试,就是要假设一位合理与称职的原告(hypothetical claimant),不理会有关先例中的真正原告到底情况如何。例如在已经介绍过的 Hoechst case (Metallgesellschaft Ltd v. Inland Revenue Commissioners, Hoechst AG v. Inland Revenue Commissioners)(Joined Cases C-397/98 and C-410/98)(2001) ECR I-1727 欧洲法院先例中,早在 1995 年就已经起诉,而且这是被媒体广泛报道的公开信息。此时假设的合理称职原告就应该已经可以发现了。

看来,近期先例明确了 Section 32(1)(c)下,由于加上了"合理勤勉"的措辞/文字,是需要客观来看真正原告的实际与具体情况如何。例如先要看原告是一家小公司还是身经百战的大型跨国公司,再根据合理的小公司/跨国公司的标准,在假设有动力了解与发现的情况下,比照原告的行为是否已经达到了客观合理勤勉的标准,或者如果能够达到标准,应该在什么时候可以发现法律错误。配合上一段欧洲法院判决的例子,一般纳税的大公司/跨国公司有自己的法律部门/公司法务,可以在当时就发现支付给税务局的金钱可能存在法律错误。而小型公司没有公司法务,一旦有任何法律问题都是委任外部律师,也不会跟进税务问题,更不会知道重要的法律案件的发展,实际上能够发现交付的公司税是法律错误的时间就要迟一些。当然也不会迟太多,法院是不会容忍小公司不找律师无限拖延下去。

接下来可介绍两个这方面的先例,可先节录 Adams v. Bracknell Forest(2005)1 AC 76 贵族院先例中,Scott 勋爵说:"In my opinion, be taken to be a reference to knowledge which **a person in the situation of the claimant**, ie an adult who knows he is illiterate(该先例涉及原告因为有读写障碍是一个文盲), **could reasonably be expected to acquire**. Personal characteristics such as shyness and embarrassment, which may have inhibited the claimant from seeking advice about his illiteracy problems but which would not be expected to have inhibited others with a like disability, should be left out of the equation. **It is the norms of behaviour of persons in the situation of the claimant that should be the test.** "(加黑部分是笔者的强调)

第二个是在 OT Computers Ltd(in liquidation) v. Infineon Technologies AG(2021) EWCA Civ 501 上诉庭先例中，Males 大法官说："Commenting on this decision in Hussain v Mukhtar[2016] EWHC 424 (QB), Martin Chamberlain QC (sitting as a deputy High Court judge) suggested that this did not mean that **personal characteristics such as naïveté and inexperience** in financial matters **should be taken into account as to do so would involve a departure from the objective standard which the cases require**. I would agree that personal traits or characteristics bearing on the likelihood of the particular claimant discovering facts which a person in his position could reasonably be expected to discover, such as **whether the claimant is slothful, naive, shy, nervous, uncurious or ill-informed, are not relevant**. But **it does not necessarily follow … that the claimant must be assumed to be someone or something which he is not**.… "(加黑部分是笔者的强调)

接下来 Males 大法官指出"合理勤勉"的考虑要查问两个方面：(1)原告如果是一个合理细心的人士，应该已经能够了解与知悉哪些信息，是否会导致应去作进一步的调查以找出真相；(2)在一个合理勤勉的调查能发现什么问题。这些都是事实问题，需要证据来支持。Males 大法官说："… although the question **what reasonable diligence requires may have to be asked at two distinct stages**, (1) whether there is anything to put the claimant on notice of a need to investigate **and**(2) what a reasonably diligent investigation would then reveal, … Although some of the cases have spoken in terms of reasonable diligence only being required once the claimant is on notice that there is something to investigate(the 'trigger'), it is more accurate to say that the requirement of reasonable diligence applies throughout. At the **first stage** the claimant must be reasonably attentive so that he becomes aware(or is treated as becoming aware) of the things **which a reasonably attentive person in his position would learn**. At the **second stage**, he is taken to know those things **which a reasonably diligent investigation would then reveal**. Both questions are questions of fact and will depend on the evidence. To that extent, an element of uncertainty is inherent in the section. … while the use of **the words 'could with reasonable diligence' make clear that the question is objective**, in the sense that the section is concerned with **what the claimant could have learned and not merely with what he did in fact learn**, the question remains what the claimant … could have learned if he had exercised such reasonable diligence. **That must refer to the actual claimant … and not to some hypothetical claimant.** "(加黑部分是笔者的强调)

而回到本段讨论的纳税人因为法律错误而多缴纳税款的问题，在 FII(SC)(2020)最高院先例中，Reed 与 Hodge 勋爵在判词中指出，英国法下一般法律地位的改变通常不会是完全出乎意料的突然改变,而通常是已经在法律界或甚是社会面经过了一段时间甚至是长时间的讨论与辩论。在讨论中通常不少人士都会参与,对这方面有关注的律师甚至是原告自己都能在这个过程中了解到消息。因此原告用证据显示自己是在什么时候最早可以发现了可能有值得起诉的法律错误时,被告就可以根据原告的具体情况(如公司的规模),加上事实证据(如原告的法务就是积极参与有关法律变更讨论的人士,已经与其他开始准备诉讼的人士展开这方面合作等)来从客观的角度看是否可以在"合理勤勉"下更早"发现"该法律错误。Reed 与 Hodge 勋爵这样说:"If the limitation period can begin to run at a time when a claim is uncertain of success, then, in addition to the logical problem discussed earlier, there is also a lack of realism in treating the date of a judicial decision authoritatively establishing the true state of the law as the earliest date when the claimant discovers, or **could with reasonable diligence discover, the mistake in question**. In the first place, the courts do not act on their own initiative, but only when their jurisdiction is invoked: normally, by the issuing of a claim. A point of law could often have been decided earlier, if a claim had been brought at an earlier time. Secondly, thinking about **the law evolves over time. Developments in judicial thinking, in particular, do not take place in a vacuum**. Judgments are the culmination of an evolution of opinion within a wider legal community, to which practitioners, universities, legal journals and the judiciary all contribute. And it is **not only judges who are influenced by that evolving body of opinion**. Claimants and their advisers respond to the same developments in their understanding of the state of the law, and their decisions **as to whether or not worthwhile claims may exist**. It is therefore **possible to investigate how legal thinking on a particular question** (for example, in the present case, whether the UK tax treatment of dividends received by UK-resident companies from non-resident subsidiaries was compatible with EU law) **developed over time, and to ascertain, by means of evidence, the time by which a reasonably diligent person in the position of the claimant** (such as, in the present case, a UK-based multi-national company) **could have known of a previous mistake of law, to the extent of knowing that there was a real possibility that such a mistake had been made, and that a worthwhile claim could therefore be made on that basis.** This line of thought suggests that **the focus of attention under section 32(1)** of the 1980 Act should not be on judicial decisions, but **on the claimant's ability to discover that he had a worthwhile claim**."(加黑部分是笔者的强调)

在后来涉及刻意隐瞒与欺诈的 ECU Group plc v. HSBC Bank plc (2021) EWHC 2875 (Ch) 先例中,Moulder 大法官就确认了对事实错误与法律错误的两种不同测试,说:"The approach adopted in these cases of fraud, like that proposed by Lord Brown **for cases of mistake, treats the relevant date, for the purposes of the commencement of**

the limitation period,not as the date when the Claimant knows or can establish the truth, but **as the date when he can recognise that a worthwhile claim arises**,in Lord Brown's formulation,**or can plead a statement of claim**,in the formulation preferred in the fraud cases."(加黑部分是笔者的强调)

12. 胁迫的救济

有说法是"可诉胁迫"(actionable duress)的救济只是去撤销合约(因为偏离了受压方的订约自由意志)与复原/不当得利(无论是否涉及合约)。在 Investec Bank (Channel Islands)Ltd v. Retail Group Plc(2009)EWHC 476(Ch)先例中,Sales 大法官说:"... it remains the case that the primary object of a plea of economic duress in relation to a contract is to avoid the contract,which is a legal consequence significantly different from establishing a cause of action in damages. ..."

另在 Al Nehayan v. Kent(2018)EWHC 333(Comm)先例中,Leggatt 大法官说:"The doctrine of duress has developed as a ground for rescinding a contract and for claiming restitution based on unjust enrichment. In principle ... the circumstances in which a contract may be rescinded and the defendant required to restore a benefit received from the claimant may not coincide with those in which the claimant is entitled to recover damages for loss caused by a wrongful act of the defendant. It therefore seems to me with respect that the view ... must be correct that conduct amounting to duress will not necessarily give rise to liability in tort."

涉及因为胁迫撤销合约,把双方复原到合约没有出现过的地位是有必要的。虽然胁迫的救济主要是撤销合约,但也不一定涉及合约,有时受压方会在不法威胁下交出财物或支付金钱。这样,在不当得利的大原则下,施压方也必须退还财物或金钱。这可节录《Duress,Undue Influence and Unconscionable Dealing》(2019 年,第 3 版)一书之 28 -082 段所说:"Where the claimant(受压方)paid money or transferred property to the defendant(施压方)in circumstances where there was no contract so that the remedy of rescission is not available,the traditional remedy for the claimant is an action for restitution of the money or property. ... This remedy allows the claimant simply to recover money paid to the defendant under duress and is not dependant on rescission of a contract. Recovery is simply based on unjust enrichment. The defendant has been enriched by the money received from the complainant(受压方). The enrichment is at the expense of the complainant who paid it,and the enrichment is unjust because it was gained by means of the wrong of duress."

至于撤销合约的救济,今天比较明确的是,一旦认定存在胁迫,合约是可使无效

(voidable)而并非自始无效(void ab initio)。受压方有选择权,可以言行或时隔太久确认合约的有效性并必须继续履行,或可以选择撤销合约。但如果在合约涉及会伤害无辜第三人等无法回复到原状(restitutio in integrum)的情况,法院就可能不会允许撤销合约。这些方面都在本书第三章之5至8段有详论,不重复。只节录《Chitty on Contract》(2021年,第34版)一书之10-068段:"... it now seems clearly established that a contract entered into under duress is voidable and not void, consequently a person who has entered into a contact under duress may either affirm or avoid such contract after the duress has ceased, and if he has voluntarily acted under it with a full knowledge of all the circumstances he may be held bound on the ground of ratification, or if after escaping from duress he takes no steps to set aside the transaction he may be found to have affirmed it.〔93〕The agreement must be avoided as a whole: the claimant cannot rescind a just promissory note that was an inseparable part of a large agreement that he has not sought to rescind.〔94〕"

胁迫是普通法课题,像欺诈性误述一样,受害方撤销合约是普通法救济(common law rescission)。这与适用在衡平救济的撤销合约(equitable rescission)有一定的区别。但在现实中看来影响不大,在此简单说是因为英国普通法与衡平法法院在《Judicature Acts 1873》合并后,已经有足够的弹性去处理,这将在本章之12.1.2段详细介绍。

衡平救济适用于曾经与胁迫有十分密切关系的不当影响,〔95〕以及其他很多类别的衡平过错(equitable wrong)中,如违反诚信/信义义务、违反信托、滥用信任等。

由于普通法与衡平法下对胁迫的撤销合约救济不一定可行,也不一定可去充分补偿受害方,所以就要涉及以金钱向受压方/受害方赔偿的问题了。在普通法下(主要是合约或侵权关系)是有金钱损失赔偿(pecuniary damages),〔96〕但合约下的损失赔偿针对的是合约履行的违约,作为替代首要合约义务的次要合约义务。而胁迫是合约产生本身有缺陷,导致合约无效,这就与合约的损失赔偿无关了。这样,不存在继续履行合约,也不涉及违约与损失赔偿了。而即使是在受压方在选择行使权利去使合约无效,并向施压方作出通知〔97〕之前已经发生了的违约行为与造成的损失,也不再是损失赔偿。因为一旦选择撤销合约,就等于合约从未产生过,只是在复原下以金钱作出调整以回复到原本没有合约的地位。

---

〔93〕 见本章之7.2.1.1段已经介绍过的The "Atlantic Baron" (1979) 1 Lloyd's Rep 89先例。

〔94〕 见Al Nehayan v. Kent (2018) EWHC 333 (Comm)先例,有关案情见本书第一章之2.7.4.3段。关于不能只撤销整套交易中的个别合约,可见本书第三章之4段。

〔95〕 在本章之1.1段已经讲过,在早年胁迫只局限在人身与财物胁迫时,不当影响与胁迫十分接近,有说法将不当影响称为衡平法胁迫(equitable duress)。

〔96〕 有关损失赔偿的课题,可见笔者《损失赔偿与救济》一书。

〔97〕 见Car and Universal Finance Ltd v. Caldwell (1965) 1 QB 525等先例与本书第三章之6.3.1.1段。

另外,胁迫本身不被视为侵权行为而归类在不当得利,所以胁迫除了撤销合约与复原外,也不涉及侵权的损失赔偿。这方面可节录《Duress, Undue Influence and Unconscionable Dealing》(2019 年,第 3 版)一书之 28 - 089 段:

"**Is duress a tort**? There is a divergence of judicial opinion on the question of whether duress is a tort for which damages may be recovered. In Dimskal Shipping Co SA v. International Transport Workers Federation (The "Evia Luck") (1992) 2 AC 152, ... Lord Goff stated that under English law **conduct which may amount to duress may not necessary constitute a tort**. Conduct does not have to be tortious to constitute duress. Similarly, in the earlier case of Universe Tankships of Monrovia v. ITWF (The "Universe Sentinel") (1983) 1 AC 366, Lord Diplock said that duress 'is not a tort per se; the form that that duress takes may or may not, be tortious. **The remedy to which economic duress** gives rise **is not an action for damages but an action for restitution of property or money exacted under such duress and the avoidance of any contract that had been induced by it**; but where the particular form taken by the economic duress used is itself a tort, the restitutional remedy ... is one which the plaintiff is entitled to pursue as an alternative remedy to an action for damages in tort.'

According to this view, **damages for duress are available only where the particular form of duress amounts to a tort, such as intimidation**.

However, in the same case, Lord Scarman took the view that any form of duress is actionable as a tort provided that it causes damage or loss. He said that it was established that 'Duress, if proved, not only renders voidable a transaction into which a person has entered under compulsion but is actionable as a tort, if it causes damage or loss.'

What is clear is that a claimant who is induced to enter into a contract by the exercise of duress can recover damage in tort where the conduct which constitutes duress also amounts to an independent cause of action in tort such as wrongful detention, interference with contractual rights or intimidation. ... However, the position is less clear where the conduct which constitutesduress does not amount to an independent tort."(加黑部分是笔者的强调)

以上看来,受压方如果想在胁迫下主张金钱的损失赔偿,就需要寻找另一个侵权的同步诉因,并以该诉因支持损失赔偿。这在现实中也不困难,因为施压方作出的造成不法/不恰当压力的威胁,也经常是涉及经济侵权的行为,特别是与胁迫的要件是十分相似的恐吓侵权(tort of intimidation)。

可以说,胁迫如果得不到撤销合约的救济就让受压方/受害方两手空空,没有任何其他救济也说不通。以上对胁迫救济的介绍,可节录《Chitty on Contract》(2021 年,第 34 版)一书之 10 - 071 段作为小结:"Since it now appears clear that a threat to break a contract may, in appropriate circumstances, constitute unlawful duress in the law of contract, so that a variation of the contract thereby obtained may be voidable as a matter of contract law, it would seem that **the doctrines of duress and intimidation are based on similar principles**. (It is, of course, also clear that a threat to commit a crime or a tort may equally constitute both duress in contract law, and intimidation in tort law.), If this is correct, it may be that, even **where a person has affirmed a contract which is voidable for duress, damage could still be recovered in tort**... It is arguable that this conclusion makes it all the more necessary to recognise that damages may be recovered for duress; for otherwise ... the plaintiff who has lost his right to avoid will be left without any remedy for a wrongful act; but two decisions at first instance have held that economic duress does not itself give rise to liability in damages, if it does not amount to intimidation or some other wrong.[98]"(加黑部分是笔者的强调)

接下来,笔者在本段将分别介绍以下几点:(1)作为胁迫主要或是唯一救济的撤销合约权利,在普通法与衡平法下救济的差异与近期的趋向。(2)与胁迫经常同步作为损失赔偿诉因的恐吓侵权。(3)与胁迫曾经是有十分密切关系的不当影响,由于是衡平法的救济,虽然也同样会面临与胁迫一样的问题,也就是撤销合约不可行或不足以补偿受害方的损失,但可以作出类似普通法损失赔偿的"衡平赔偿"[99](equitable compensation)和交出利润[100](account for profit)等金钱救济。

12.1 撤销胁迫产生的合约

撤销(rescission)合约在本书第三章已经有十分详尽的介绍,不在此重复。只准备在此简单介绍在本书第三章之1段与第四章之5.1段都有提到的撤销合约的权利到底是不是"自助救济"(self-help),或是必须先由法院批准或行使裁量权?这看来在近期先例仍有混乱,如在本书第四章之5.3.2段介绍的SK Shipping Plc v. Capital VLCC 3 Corp(2020)EWHC 3448(Comm)先例与上诉庭([2022]EWCA Civ 231)的不同意见。

此先例与本书第四章之5.3.1段介绍的The"Lucy"(1983)1 Lloyd's Rep 188先例的混乱是由于《Misrepresentation Act 1967》立法针对撤销合约没有清楚说明理念是根据普通法撤销或衡平法撤销。笔者在此会稍为详尽介绍这两种不同撤销在历史上因不同的普通法法院与衡平法法院执行而带来的一定区别,并展望两个不同法院在《Judicature Act 1873》[101]合并后英国法院会怎么样处理。

---

[98] 这两个案件即本段前文中提到的Investec Bank(Channel Islands)Ltd v. Retail Group Plc(2009)EWHC 476(Ch)先例与Al Nehayan v. Kent(2018)EWHC 333(Comm)先例。

[99] 本书第六章之11段有简单的介绍。

[100] 本书四章之4.2.2.3.6段有简单的介绍。

[101] 这在本书多处提到,如本书第三章之1段。

12.1.1 普通法与衡平法撤销合约的不同做法

由于普通法的欺诈、胁迫,衡平法的不当影响、不合情理交易等都有非常悠久的历史,而各自都会可以撤销合约与需要复原,因此目的与理念都不一样的普通法法院和衡平法法院[102]各自发展出了一套撤销合约与复原的做法。它们的做法也在多处都存在不同。笔者在此只针对以下主要的两点。

12.1.1.1 自助救济与法院的裁量权

普通法撤销合约是自助救济(self-help remedy),只要受害方向对方给出通知[103]就可以撤销合约:见 Reese River Silver Mining Co Ltd v. Smith(1869)LR 4 HL 64;Abram Steamship Co Ltd v. Westville Shipping Co Ltd(1923)AC 773 等先例。

如果合约相对方对此有质疑当然可以在法院开始诉讼,但诉讼是确认受害方撤销合约的权利与做法,而并非由法院决定撤销合约,在其中法院并没有裁量权决定是否应该撤销,而实际上只是宣示与确认受害方是否真正有权(如可诉误述或胁迫是否成立)。合约实际上在受害方作出通知时已经撤销,覆水难收。在 TSB Bank Plc v. Camfield(1995)1 WLR 430 先例中,Roch 大法官说:"The right to set aside or rescind the transaction is that of the representee(受害方),not that of the court. The court's role in a disputed case will be to decide whether the representee has lawfully rescinded the transaction or is entitled to rescind it. Normally,if the representee is entitled to rescind the legal charge,that will have been effected by the representee's pleading(没有提前通知,在诉讼中通过文书请求告知对方也是通知)that the transaction has been or should be set aside;that is to say,the transaction would have been set aside before the matter reaches the court. The court is not being asked to grant equitable relief;nor is it,in my view,granting equitable relief to which terms may be attached."

但如果一项权利并非法律权利(普通法),需要依赖衡平法法院法官的裁量权(discretion),因此衡平法撤销合约并非"自助权利",受害方必须先向法院申请,由法官考虑是否给予救济。这可见 Erlanger v. New Sombrero Phosphate Co(1878)3 App Cas 1218 先例中,Blackburn 勋爵说:"a Court of Equity requires that those who come to it to ask its active interposition to give them relief..."

也只有在法院行使裁量权,给出判决给予撤销合约的救济后,合约才真正被撤销。在较近期的 Johnson v. EBS Pensioner Trustees Ltd(2002)EWCA Civ 164 上诉庭先例中,依赖的是滥用信任[104]的衡平法理论,Dyson 大法官就提到依赖这些衡平法理论时,取决于法院的裁量权:"... In relation to rescission... whatever the position in

[102] 例如在 Cheese v. Thomas(1994)1 WLR 129 先例中,Donald Nicholls 大法官说:"equity as a court of conscience will look at all the circumstances and do what fairness requires"

[103] 见本书第三章之 6.1.1 段。

[104] 见本书第十一章之 1.5 段的简单介绍。

relation to a claim to rescind based on misrepresentation, **the right to rescission on grounds of undue influence**, abuse of confidence or breach of fiduciary duty **depends on the exercise of the discretion by the court to intervene in the enforcement of legal rights**."(加黑部分是笔者的强调)

衡平法下法官的裁量权,包括决定是否撤销合约。甚至是为了在无法完全复原的情况下达到实际公平[105](practical justice),还可以决定是否对撤销合约加以条件(如交出利润、保护无辜第三人利益等):见 O'Sullivan v. Management Agency and Music Ltd(1985)QB 428;Cheese v. Thomas;Smith v. Cooper(2010)EWCA Civ 722 等先例。

12.1.1.2 对复原的要求严格与宽松

除此以外,还有一个重要区别在于对于复原的要求。传统普通法合约的复原要求较为严格。衡平法撤销合约与复原(如根据不当影响或不合情理要求撤销合约与复原),一贯是较为宽松的。虽然衡平法法院不允许对损失作出金钱赔偿(这是普通法法院的权力范围),但有广泛的裁量权允许采取各种各样的方式以达到在个别案件的实际公平,如交出利润,允许已经贬值的部分减免(allowance),或者允许以金钱对无法反复原的标的进行补偿(equitable compensation):见 Dunbar Bank Plc v. Nadeem(1998)3 All ER 876 先例。这方面的权威说法可节录 Blackburn 勋爵在早期的 Erlanger v. New Sombrero Phosphate Co 先例中所说:"… **a Court of Equity could not give damages**, and, unless it can rescind the contract, can give no relief. And, on the other hand, it can take accounts of profits, and make allowance for deterioration. And I think the practice has always been for a Court of Equity to give this relief whenever, by the exercise of its powers, **it can do what is practically just**, though it cannot restore the parties precisely to the state they were in before the contract."(加黑部分是笔者的强调)

普通法下的复原(如针对欺诈、胁迫的复原)就较为严格,要求实物归还(restitution in specie),即必须退回实际的资产而不能用其他方式(如交易不是金钱,就不能用金钱替代),如果做不到就有可能不允许撤销合约,只能根据普通法下可能存在的其他诉因索赔损失:见 Clarke v. Dickson(1858)120 ER 463 先例。即使资产有贬值,也不妨碍撤销与复原:见 Newbigging v. Adam(1888)13 App Cas 308;Armstrong v. Jackson(1917)2 KB 822 等先例。只有一些特别情况,如被告有欺诈等行为时才会稍有放松:见 Hulton v. Hulton(1917)1 KB 813 等先例。

发展到今天,由于必须实物归还可能导致各种各样的不公平与不实际的问题,普通法对待撤销合约与复原也开始有宽松的倾向,但到什么程度还不明朗。例如,原告获得的交易标的是被告提供的服务,交易完成、服务已经(或部分)提供后显然这不

---

[105] 见本书第三章之 5.2 段。

可能实物归还,但因此就不给予救济说不过去。例如一方向另一方提供装饰,撤销合约后也不必将已经完成的装饰部分拆除,但允许对冲需要归还的费用:见 Do Ferguson & Associates v. Sohl(1992)62 BLR 95 先例。

又如在 Smith New Court Securities Ltd v. Scrimgeour Vickers(Asset Management) Ltd(1994)1 WLR 1271 先例中,案情在本书第三章之 5.3.1 段有详细介绍,只说原告买方主张被告有误述想要撤销股票买卖合约,但是因为已经转卖了自己手中的股票,所以反复原只能去市场以低价另买入同样的股票。但上诉庭说不行,这不是以原来的一批股票去复原。而案件上诉到贵族院时因为原告放弃撤销合约的请求也就不再有这方面的争议,但 Brown-Wilkinson 勋爵看来是在类似的情况下,完全可以从市场上购买股票作为反复原:"As to the first rule referred to by the Court of Appeal, the reasons why … abandoned their claim to rescind were not explored before your Lordships. I will therefore say nothing about the point save that if the current law in fact provides(as the Court of Appeal thought) that there is no right to rescind the contract for the sale of quoted shares once the specific shares purchased have been sold, the law will need to be closely looked at hereafter. Since in such a case other, **identical, shares can be purchased on the market, the defrauded purchaser can offer substantial restitutio in integrum which is normally sufficient.** "(加黑部分是笔者的强调)

回到胁迫,相对而言胁迫案件中看来较少遇到反复原是否需要回复到原状(restitutio in integrum)的问题,因为大部分案情是原告受到不法压力签订新合约或更改合约,向对方施压方支付额外金钱。事后主张胁迫的原告也只需要干脆撤销合约,要求对方退回金钱即可。加上法律要求不法压力一过,受压方立即行动,否则会被视为确认新合约:见 The "Atlantic Baron"(1979)1 Lloyd's Rep 89 先例。所以,时间不会相隔太久,回复到原状比较容易,特别是相比其他影响合约效力的因素,如欺诈性误述会是合约履行很久后才被受害方/被误述方发现。

12.1.2 现在弹性的做法

撤销合约与复原/反复原是个复杂与仍然在不断发展的课题。[106] 只节录《Duress, Undue Influence and Unconscionable Dealing》(2019 年,第 3 版)一书之 28-004 段说到《Judicature Act 1873》将英国普通法法院与衡平法法院合并,导致今天的法院同时行使两种不同的救济,包括本小段针对的胁迫可撤销合约。有部分法官认为两种救济不必再去区分,可合并使用。但多数法官还是不同处理,看涉及的是普通法过错(legal wrong)还是衡平过错(equitable wrong):"Historically, the law of rescission on

[106] 有关反复原的课题可见近期的 School Facility Management Ltd v. Governing Body of Christ the King College(2021)EWCA Civ 1053 先例中,不在此展开。

the ground of vitiating factors[107] developed along the jurisdictional divide of common law and equity. The question whether the fusion of the administration of law by the Judicature Act of 1873 and 1875 resulted in a fusion of the separate rules of rescission at common law and in equity is controversial. Some judges have expressed the view that the pre-Judicature Acts distinction between common law and equitable rules of rescission no longer apply. However **the majority of the authorities indicate that the two regimes continue to exist, each with its separate rules**. … the common law rules on rescission apply where the ground for rescission is a common law vitiating factor (such as fraud or duress) and the rules of equity apply where the ground for rescission is a vitiating factor in equity (such as undue influence and unconscionable dealing). **However by virtue of equity's concurrent jurisdiction, all the vitiating factors that are recognised as grounds for rescission at common law are also grounds for rescission in equity**."(加黑部分是笔者的强调)

上述节录是说欺诈与胁迫是适用普通法撤销合约,但不当影响适用更有弹性与灵活性的衡平法撤销。另在最后加黑一句提到了法院的"equity's concurrent jurisdiction"把这两种不同的撤销视为同一码事。这也可以节录该书之28-018段来解释,并带出今天对可诉胁迫救济的做法:

"**The modern position: flexible approach.** Section 9 of the Senior Court Act 1981, which reproduces the effect of s. 25(11) of the Judicature Act 1873, provides that 'Wherever there is any conflict or variance between the rules of equity and the common law with reference to the same subject matter, **the rules of equity shall prevail'.**

In Halpern v. Halpern, in relation to the requirement of restitutio in integrum, Carnwath LJ argued that**since duress and undue influence deal with very much the same subject matter**, the **rules of equity should prevail** in relation to any difference between common law rescission for duress and rescission for undue influence in equity. He suggested that there should be **no difference in principle between rescission for duress and rescission for other vitiating factors such as undue influence**. If this approach is adopted it would mean not only that the requirement of restitutio in integrum applies to rescission for duress but also that in the case of **rescission for duress the requirement of restitutio in integrum is to be applied following the flexible approach of equity**."(加黑部分是笔者的强调)

以上是说,根据《Senior Court Act 1981》之Section 9,在普通法法院与衡平法法院合并后,对于同一事项如果有了冲突就应以衡平法优先。这样由于构成胁迫与不

---

[107] 英国法下影响合约效力的因素(vitiating factors)就是本书介绍的误述、胁迫、不当影响、非法、错误等。

当影响的要件几乎一样，而不当影响是衡平法，所以胁迫在撤销时可以采用灵活与有弹性的做法。

这说法根据 Halpern v. Halpern(2007) EWCA Civ 291 上诉庭先例，有关案情在本书第三章之 5.3.3 段已经有介绍，不重复，只节录 Carnwath 大法官所说如下："Returning to the question posed by the preliminary issue in this case, a definitive response is not possible or appropriate, until the facts have been found. **I would be inclined to agree** with the deputy judge **that rescission for duress should be no different in principle from rescission for other 'vitiating factors'**. However, the **practical effect of counter-restitution… will depend on the circumstances of the particular case**. In the present case, if … the defendants are able to establish that their consent to **the compromise agreement was procured by improper pressure** (**whether that is characterised as duress or undue influence**), **it would be surprising if the law could not provide a suitable remedy**. The form of the remedy, **whether equitable or tortious**, is a matter which cannot sensibly be decided until the facts are known, not only as to the nature and effect of the improper pressure, but also as to the identity and significance of the documents destroyed."(加黑部分是笔者的强调)

只是关于这一点，在 Halpern v. Halpern 先例后不再有先例针对与跟从，更不用说给出更权威的说法。毕竟，衡平法与普通法之间的谁更优先，仍是在很多地方不明确。但它是上诉庭先例中，可以肯定说是英国法律在针对可诉胁迫的救济，可适用衡平救济，特别是当撤销合约是明确的。

英国法下这些烦琐的区分是来自于本身的历史发展与长期判法的制约，而对于中国法来说，完全可以根据中国特色发展出一套一致性地针对所有情况的法律。而且在中国法下也有公平合理的大原则，只要在熟悉后认为衡平法中有值得借鉴的理论内容，就可以吸收，提炼其中最配合实际、全面可解答任何问题、不存在相互矛盾、说理性强、逻辑性强与客观是公平合理的部分进行立法，就可以发展出更先进的国际法律制度了。

12.1.3　不允许用合约条文排除胁迫的救济

法律不允许在因胁迫达成的合约条文中加入措辞/文字排除事后主张胁迫。例如，在 Borrelli v. Ting(2010) UKPC 21 枢密院先例中原告受压之下达成和解协议放弃对被告的诉权，即使有关的措辞/文字写得非常宽松甚至可以解释为放弃了对以不法手段(例如不法压力)诱导和解协议的诉权，但这不影响事后原告以胁迫起诉要求撤销合约。这与明示条文超越默示地位不同，不允许以胁迫手段诱导合约产生背后存在公共政策的支持，这与本书第三章之 8.3 段介绍的不能用合约来排除欺诈性误述救济的道理是一样的。Saville 勋爵说："It was also submitted that the Settlement Agreement(此先例中涉及经济胁迫达成的合约，有关案情见本章之 8.2.2.1 段的介绍) was so widely drafted that it excluded the right of the Liquidators to withdraw their agreement, even on the basis that it had been procured by illegitimate means. The Board (枢密院) reject this submission, which necessarily involves a further unacceptable proposition, namely that it is possible, by the use of illegitimate means, to obtain a binding agreement from which the party subject to the duress cannot withdraw."

12.2 恐吓侵权:辅助胁迫索赔金钱损失

首先介绍是胁迫与恐吓侵权(tort of intimidation)的不同诉因之间的关系,这可节录《Civil Fraud》(2018 年,第 1 版)一书之 5 - 006 段:

"Intimidation is also a wrong which is allied to the doctrine of duress ... **Duress is not a tort...**, **but is** instead part of **the law of unjust enrichment and also provides a basis for avoidance of a contract** or other transaction. It will often be the case that the doctrine of duress, which appears to be based on wider foundations than the tort of intimidation ..., provides a sufficient basis for the claimant to obtain adequate redress. Indeed in some cases **a claim in intimidation will be capable of being asserted as an alternative to a claim in duress and the two claims will succeed or fail together**. Nonetheless the two concepts are separate: 'The use of economic duress is not a tort in itself, though the particular form that some economic duress takes may amount to a tort. The **remedy to which economic duress gives rise is not an action for damages but an action for restitution of property or money extracted under such duress and the avoidance of any contract that is induced by it**. In some cases the economic duress may amount to a tort, in which case the restitutionary remedy for money had and received is merely an alternative remedy to an action for damages in tort. The two are however distinct.'[108]

Hence, where the claimant has suffered loss which is wider than the transmission of benefits to the defendant pursuant to a contract said to be procured by duress, then **the claimant will have to resort to the tort of intimidation**."(加黑部分是笔者的强调)

至于一些权威先例的说法,首先可节录在 Investec Bank (Channel Islands) Ltd v. Retail Group Plc (2009) EWHC 476 (Ch) 先例中 Sales 大法官所说:"The primary object of a plea of economic duress in relation to a contract is to avoid the contract, which is a legal consequence significantly different from establishing a cause of action in damages. So far as a cause of action in damages is to be made out, I can see no proper basis in principle why it should be on any basis other than a pleading of facts and matters sufficient to establish a cause of action for the tort of intimidation."

另在 Berezovsky v. Abramovich (2011) EWCA Civ 153 上诉庭先例的一审([2010] EWHC 647 [Comm])中, Colman 大法官说:

---

[108] 这节录的是 Cooke 大法官在 Progress Bulk Carriers Ltd v. Tube City IMS LLC (2012) EWHC 273 (Comm) 先例中的说法。

"Lord Diplock observed(在 The "Universe Sentinel" [1983] 1 AC 366 贵族院先例)：— The use of economic duress to induce another person to part with property or money is not a tort per se; **the form that the duress takes may, or may not, be tortious**. The remedy to which economic duress gives rise is not an action for damages but an action for restitution of property or money exacted under such duress and the avoidance of any contract that had been induced by it; but where the particular form taken by the economic duress used is itself a tort, the restitutional remedy for money had and received by the defendant to the plaintiff's use is one which the plaintiff is entitled to pursue as an alternative remedy to an action for damages in tort.

It is argued that these statements of the law point to the view that, **if the duress in question causes loss and damage not compensatable by restitution, it gives rise to a claim for damages in tort. That tort would be intimidation**....

That the precise limits of duress as a tort are ill-defined, particularly **where there is lawful act duress**, is recognised by the judgment of Steyn LJ in CTN Cash and Carry Ltd v Gallaher Ltd...**It merely establishes that if the threats are made in good faith, there can be no tort**."(加黑部分是笔者的强调)

最后在 Al Nehayan v. Kent(2018) EWHC 333(Comm)先例，[109] Leggatt 大法官说："I agree with Sales J when he said in Investec Bank(Channel Islands) Ltd v The Retail Group plc ...I would simply add that there may, depending on the facts, be other bases for claiming damages than the tort of intimidation...In the present case I am nonetheless satisfied that each of the three bases on which I have found that Mr Kent(受压方) would have been entitled to rescind the Framework Agreement and the promissory note does also give rise to claim for damages."

12.2.1 受压方需要辅助的情况

看来，这两种不同诉因在不少案件中是可以同时出现的，不同诉因只是因为本质上不同。已经在本章之 2 段与 12 段介绍过，经济胁迫本质是"不当得利"，救济只是回复到合约没有产生过的地位。不当得利的诉因不一定是被告有法律过错(legal wrong)，所以不涉及索赔损失的救济。而"恐吓"的侵权是法律过错，救济是索赔恐吓造成或带来的损失，与撤销合约的选择权扯不上关系。这样，受压方的原告就可以同时提出这两种诉因或作为替代，就可以撤销合约、复原与索赔损失均不落空了：见 Kolmar Group AG v. Traxpo Enterprises Pvt Ltd(2010) EWHC 113(Comm)；Al Nehayan v. Kent(2018) EWHC 333(Comm)等先例。

会有撤销合约可能有困难或受压方蒙受的损失是复原也不足以补偿的情况，因此会需要根据其他案情可以套用的侵权诉因才能去索赔损失，特别与胁迫关系密切

[109] 案情在本书第一章之 2.7.4.3 段有介绍。

与通常可行的就是恐吓侵权。可以主张胁迫与撤销合约并同时索赔损失,或在《Chitty on Contract》(2021 年,第 34 版)一书之 10 – 071 段还提出即使没有或因为各种原因(如受压方已经确认合约)而无法撤销合约,可以单纯起诉索赔损失,有关段落已经在本章之 12 段节录,不在此重复。

以下会介绍两个先例中,以帮助理解。

12.2.1.1 Kolmar Group AG v. Traxpo Enterprises Pvt Ltd(2010)EWHC 113 (Comm)先例

在本章之 5.4 段已经介绍了的 Kolmar Group AG v. Traxpo Enterprises Pvt Ltd 先例中的案件是经常在国际商品买卖合约发生的案件。市场经常有严重波动急剧上升或下跌,此时已经订立了合约的卖方或买方会作出违约/毁约的威胁要求抬价或减价。在此只简单重复此先例的案情,原告为了转售给一个急需甲醇的重要客户,作为买方向作为卖方的被告购买一批甲醇。而签订合约后市场上甲醇供不应求价格飙升,导致被告无法按照合约约定提供货物。被告给出了"爱要不要"的两个选择:一个是按照合约价格交易,但只能提供数量少得多的货物,并且逼迫原告支付因此产生的超过 100 万美元的船舶空仓费;另一个则是可以提供较多数量的货物,但销售价格要比合约约定高得多。

法院认定存在经济胁迫,作为受压方的 FOB 买方可去撤销抬价的更改合约与以复原取回支付了的额外(相比原合约)金钱(约 150 万美元)。另买方也蒙受其他相关损失,如作为施压方的卖方在买方同意抬价前拒绝装船带来的移船费用与滞期费等,也同时以恐吓威胁成功索赔。

12.2.1.2 Gulf Azov Shipping Co Ltd v. Idisi(2001)EWCA Civ 505 先例

另在 Gulf Azov Shipping Co Ltd v. Idisi 先例中,也是同样撤销合约之外还以侵权[虽然不是以恐吓威胁,而是非法扣押(unlawful detention)]成功索赔损失。案情涉及原告船东的船舶从印度付运两台钻机(drilling rigs)到尼日利亚,提单约定伦敦仲裁。但是到达卸港时发现货物装载在甲板上的部分丢失。船东抗辩是在航程中遇上的风暴中丢失了,所以可对此货损免责。[110] 被告收货人不接受这个说法,并在尼日利亚开始诉讼索赔,金额高达 1700 万美元,并同时扣押船舶与船员。对于在尼日利亚的诉讼,被告在英国法下违反了提单中约定的伦敦仲裁,原告应很容易向英国法院申请到止诉禁令[111](anti-suit injunction),但能否向在尼日利亚的被告执行是另一码事。而扣押船舶是面对货损货差的收货人都会尽快采取的对物诉讼[112](in rem action)以取得诉前担保[113](pre-action security)。在此先例的问题是被告同时扣押

〔110〕 见笔者《提单与其他付运单证》(2016 年)一书第五章之 12.3 段。

〔111〕 见笔者《提单与其他付运单证》(2016 年)一书第四章之 2.4.8.1 段。

〔112〕 见笔者《仲裁法:从 1996 年英国仲裁法到国际商务仲裁》一书第十二章之 7.12.4 段。

〔113〕 见笔者《仲裁法:从 1996 年英国仲裁法到国际商务仲裁》一书第十二章之 7.12 段。

了大部分船员，不准离开尼日利亚，这明显是非法。事实上，船东曾以人权法向尼日利亚联邦法院起诉，并成功获得宣示判决扣押船员是违反他们的自由（personal liberty/freedom of movement），但看来也没有完全得到执行。

船东互保协会（船舶的责任保险人）在事故开始就有参与并与被告谈判，愿意提供100万～150万美元的担保以交换放船与放人，但不会对这个视为漫天要价的1700万美元索赔金额提供全部担保。在双方的僵持之下，船舶与部分船员被扣押了超过21个月，直到双方最后达成300万美元的和解协议并提供了银行担保后才被放行。

船东/互保协会在收到船舶离开的信息后，再也无所畏惧，立即向英国法院申请冻结令[114]（freezing injunction）禁止银行支付这300万美元，接着以胁迫要求法院撤销和解协议。一审与上诉庭都支持了船东，以简易判决判船东是在扣押船舶特别是扣押船员的胁迫（这会是对人身与财物的胁迫）之下才与被告达成和解协议，因此撤销和解协议。此外法院还以非法扣押的侵权判被告要赔偿损失（主要是船期损失）约420万美元再加上约77万美元的利息。

12.2.2 经济胁迫与恐吓侵权：善意及不恰当等方面的异同

当然，会有少数经济胁迫的案件是不涉及另一个侵权的诉因。正如上述节录的Berezovsky v. Abramovich（2011）EWCA Civ 153上诉庭先例的一审（[2010] EWHC 647 [Comm]），Colman大法官说“威胁”（threat）如果是善意，就不会是侵权。经济胁迫的善意或不存在恶意的情况在本章之7.2.2段有介绍，如DSND Subsea Ltd v. Petroleum Geo-Services ASA（2000）BLR 530先例。

在本章之6.1段谈到社会上、道德上与国际上视为不容也属于不恰当的压力（improper pressure），可以构成胁迫，另也在本章之8段谈到合法行为胁迫（lawful act duress）。在本章之8.3.1段介绍的CTN Cash and Carry Ltd v. Gallaher Ltd（1994）4 All ER 714上诉庭先例中，Steyn大法官针对英国法律下合法行为威胁可以构成胁迫时说：

“I also readily accept that the fact that the defendants have used lawful means does not by itself remove the case from the scope of the doctrine of economic duress. Professor Birks, in his ‘Introduction to the Law of Restitution’ … lucidly explains: ‘**Can lawful pressures also count**? This is a difficult question, because, **if the answer is that they can, the only viable basis for discriminating between acceptable and unacceptable pressures is not positive law but social morality**. In other words, the judges must say what pressures (though lawful outside the restitutionary context) are improper as contrary to prevailing standards. That makes the judges, not the law or the legislature, the arbiters of social evaluation. On the other hand, **if the answer is that lawful pressures are al-**

[114] 见笔者《证据法：国际规管与诉讼中的证据攻防》一书第三章。

ways exempt, those who devise outrageous but technically lawful means of compulsion must always escape restitution until the legislature declares the abuse unlawful. It is tolerably clear that, at least where they can be confident of a general consensus in favour of their evaluation, **the courts are willing to apply a standard of impropriety rather than technical unlawfulness**.'

And there are a number of cases where English courts have accepted that a threat may be illegitimate when coupled with a demand for payment even if the threat is one of lawful action. See Thorne v. Motor Trade Association [1937] AC 797 …; Mutual Finance, Limited v. John Wetton & Sons, Limited [1937] 2 KB 389; Universe Tankships Inc. of Monrovia v. International Transport Workers Federation, 'The Universe Sentinel' [1983] 1 AC 366 … On the other hand, Goff and Jones, 'The Law of Restitution', third edition, at p. 240, observed that English courts have wisely not accepted any general principle that a threat not to contract with another, except on certain terms, may amount to duress."(加黑部分是笔者的强调)

在本章之 8.2.3 段介绍的 PIAC v. Times Travel(2021) UKSC 40 最高院先例中,进一步明确了可以有合法行为胁迫,只是收紧了这一类胁迫的范围,除了敲诈勒索外,也只有"用应受谴责的手段操纵对方处于弱势地位并逼迫对方不得不放弃索赔"这类案件。

但在恐吓侵权看来威胁必须"不法",正如《Civil Fraud》(2018 年,第 1 版)一书之 5-023 段所说:"… to threaten to do that which you have a right to do cannot constitute the tort of intimidation. As Lord Reid said in Rookes v. Barnard: 'there is a chasm between what you have a legal right to do and doing what you have no legal right to do, and there seems to me to be the same chasm threatening to do what you have a legal right to do and threatening to do what you have no legal right to do'."

而除了犯罪、侵权、违约/毁约或违反信义义务等的不法行为外,其他在法律上仅仅被视为"不恰当",如因为社会、道德因素等而不恰当,此时以这些行为威胁看来是不足以构成恐吓侵权。这可节录在 Berezovsky v. Abramovich 先例的一审中,Colman 大法官所说:"**Whether a threat of conduct towards a claimant which is neither a crime, nor a tort, nor a breach of contract or of fiduciary duty is capable of founding a claim in tort**, even if made for the purpose of damaging the claimant, with the effect that he is induced to act in such a way that he suffers loss, is, **in my view, extremely doubtful**. No decision of the English courts has gone that far and **it is, in my view, very improbable** that the law will develop in that way. For that would render substantial areas of trade competition vulnerable to potential tortious liability. However, if outside the field of legitimate competition, such threats were made exclusively in order to inflict loss on the claimant, it may be that the courts will provide a remedy going beyond restitution and going as far as damages. That said, this must be regarded as a difficult but developing area of law. Since the development and application of legal principle in this field depends heavily on the findings of fact."(加黑部分是笔者的强调)

从上述节录可以看到 Colman 大法官关心引入不涉及非法、侵权、违约或违反信义义务外的恐吓,会与鼓励合法的商业竞争有矛盾。毕竟,商业竞争经常会涉及同行竞争的一方刻意去伤害另一方的利益,岂非全都会带来侵权的责任。

再说,这方面的不同也说得过去:经济胁迫主要针对受压方的订约自由意志的偏离,所以要给予可以撤销合约与复原的救济。经济胁迫主要不是追究施压方的过错,虽然经常会是这种情况。但恐吓侵权是恐吓方犯了法律过错,受恐吓方可向其提起诉讼索赔损失。

12.2.3 恐吓侵权

12.2.3.1 "经济恐吓侵权"

恐吓侵权好像早期的人身胁迫一样,主要是针对暴力(physical violence)与真正威胁。直到 1964 年,恐吓这种侵权很少适用,也不受关注。《Clerk & Lindsell on Torts》(2020 年,第 23 版)一书之 23 - 70 段说:"Intimidation as a tort has its origin in threats of violence and was, until relative recently, regarded as 'a rare and peculiar cause of action'. Thus, in a case which for over a century excited little interest. ..."

但之后 Rookes v. Barnard(1964) AC 1129 贵族院先例认定以违约胁迫对方也可以构成恐吓。这样,也就带来了现在不少的"经济恐吓侵权"(tort of economic intimidation)案件,毕竟,威胁违约/毁约在商业社会是司空见惯的情况。在该贵族院先例中,Reid 勋爵说:"threatening a breach of contract may be a much more coercive weapon than threatening a tort ... and if there is no technical reason requiring a distinction between different kinds of threats, I can see no other ground for making any such distinction. ... no difference in principle between a threat to break a contract and a threat to commit a tort."

另 Devlin 勋爵也说:"(Could find) nothing differentiate a threat of a breach of contract from a threat of physical violence or any other illegal threat."

Rookes v. Barnard 贵族院先例确立的"经济恐吓侵权"也带来在 Barton v. Armstrong(1976) AC 104 贵族院先例后发展起来的"经济胁迫",成为 20 世纪 90 年代建立起来的"经济侵权"[115](economic tort)理论的重要说法之一。

12.2.3.2 恐吓侵权的两种类型:两方或三方的要件

恐吓侵权的情况可先简单节录《Clerk & Lindsell on Torts》(2020 年,第 23 版)一书之 23 - 62 段:"In Rookes v Barnard, Lord Devlin accepted that there are two forms of the tort of intimidation. The first form, often called 'two-party intimidation' will be com-

---

[115] 见本书第八章之 2.1 段的介绍。

mitted by a defendant **who intentionally causes loss to a claimant by making a threat** that could be phrased 'unless you act in this way(that will cause you loss),I will carry out this threat',with the **result that the claimant acts in the required way and suffers loss**. ... Rookes v Barnard itself involved the second form,often called 'three-party intimidation'. A defendant will commit this form of the tort if,**with the intention of causing loss to the claimant**,he delivers a threat to B that he will commit an act,or use means,**unlawful** as against B,as a result of which B does or refrains from doing some act which he is entitled to do,thereby causing loss to the claimant."(加黑部分是笔者的强调)

以上显示了恐吓侵权可分两种:第一种是恐吓方A是意图去伤害受恐吓方B,这可称为是"两方恐吓",利益受损的B可以作为原告索赔;第二种是A意图去伤害第三人C,而不是受恐吓方B,这可称为"三方恐吓",利益受损的C可以作为原告索赔。

至于恐吓侵权的构成要件,在涉及工会与属于"三方恐吓"的Morgan v. Fry(1968)2 QB 710上诉庭先例中,Denning勋爵说:"... there must be a threat by one person to use unlawful means(such as violence or a tort or a breach of contract)so as to compel another to obey his wishes;and the person so threatened must comply with the demand rather than risk the threat being carried into execution. In such circumstances the person damnified by the compliance can sue for intimidation."

而在属于"两方恐吓"的Berezovsky v. Abramovich(2011)EWCA Civ 153上诉庭先例中,Longmore大法官提到了"两方恐吓"侵权的要件:"For the purposes of this case therefore the essential ingredients of the tort of intimidation are:— 1)a threat by the defendant(D)to do something unlawful or 'illegitimate';2)the threat must be intended to coerce the claimant(C)to take or refrain from taking some course of action;3)the threat must in fact coerce C to take such action;4)loss or damage must be incurred by C as a result."

可见无论是"三方恐吓",还是"两方恐吓",前三个要件是完全相同的,唯一的区别在于第四个要件中"三方恐吓"蒙受损失的不是受恐吓方而是第三人。

从以上说法可以看到,恐吓侵权(特别是"两方恐吓")与本章之6段至10段介绍的构成胁迫(尤其是不法行为胁迫)的要件是很类似的,而英国20世纪70年代发展与确认了经济胁迫后更是有大量经济胁迫案件同时看来也能构成恐吓侵权。因为两者的核心都是以可诉的非法/不法威胁(actionable threat),逼迫受害方做一些他不愿意做的事,所以以胁迫要求撤销合约之余,往往也可以同时起诉恐吓侵权索赔损失。

有关恐吓侵权的权威先例Rookes v. Barnard(1964)AC 1129贵族院先例是属于"三方恐吓"的案件。在此先例中,一家公司B与工会A的集体劳资协议(collective agreement)中,约定不发动员工罢工。同时A还与B有不成文约定,只能聘用工会成员。而一名公司雇员C看来是与A有矛盾,退出了工会。A就逼迫B解雇该雇员

C,威胁说如果不解雇,就会发动罢工,最后导致 B 不得不解雇 C。C 随后就以恐吓侵权作为诉因起诉了 A 索赔损失,并获得了贵族院的支持。

有关“三方恐吓”的商业案件,可介绍 Global Asset Capital Inc & Ors v. Aabar Block SARL & Ors(2016) EWHC 298(Comm)先例。该先例是本书第三章之 4.3.2 段介绍的 Marme Inversiones 2007 SL v. NatWest Markets Plc (2019) EWHC 366 (Comm)先例涉及的交易的一些后续发展。在 2008 年金融海啸后,Marme 公司与其实际控制人 Glenn Maud 先生(本案的两位原告之一,以下简称 Maud)在和西班牙最大的国际银行桑坦德银行合作投资位于西班牙马德里的金融城地产项目后深陷债务危机。苏格兰皇家银行(以下简称 RBS)是给 Marme 公司和 Maud 提供融资的主要银行。2010 年,RBS 将其对 Marme 公司与 Maud 个人提供的两项贷款的债权(包括 Maud 为贷款提供的个人担保)转让给 Aabar 公司与 Robert Tchenguiz 先生(以下简称 Tchenguiz)所控制的 Edgeworth 公司。随后在 Marme 公司和 Maud 无法清偿贷款与利息的债务后,Aabar 与 Edgeworth 在英国法院开始了一系列诉讼,其中包括 2014 年向法院申请 Maud 个人破产。Maud 不想破产,因为一旦进入破产程序,他就会对名下所有的资产(最主要的就是金融城项目,也包括他个人提供担保的资产)失控。为了解决与 Aabar 和 Edgeworth 的债务,Maud 希望在两家对冲基金的支持下达成本案所涉的债务重整,即由原告 Global Asset Capital(以下简称 GAC)从 Aabar 手中买回针对 Marme 公司和 Maud 的两项贷款的部分债权。

Maud 主张 GAC 和 Aabar 于 2015 年 5 月 6 日达成了购买债权的协议,但 Aabar 不同意双方有达成过任何协议。而本案的第三被告 Tchenguiz,Maud 主张 Tchenguiz 想要迫使 Marme 和 Maud 将对金融城的控制权交出给他,所以他不仅不同意相关的安排,并且以威胁 Aabar 将对其提起诉讼的方式去阻挠 Aabar 与 Marme 公司和 Maud 进行债务重整,这构成恐吓侵权。看来,这是一个涉及三方的恐吓侵权,恐吓方是 Tchenguiz,被恐吓方是 Aabar,利益受损方则是 GAC 与 Maud。

本案高院的 Walker 大法官面对的申请之一是 Tchenguiz 要求以简易判决提前撤销 GAC 与 Maud 提出的恐吓侵权的索赔。Tchenguiz 主张 Maud 无法证明恐吓侵权的要件,包括以不法手段进行威胁以及 Tchenguiz 是否为了损害 GAC 与 Maud 的利益而对 Aabar 进行威胁。

已经在本章之 12.2.2 段提到,恐吓侵权必须是非法/不法威胁。在没有任何站得住脚的诉因下提起诉讼是滥用诉讼程序,滥用诉讼程序的确能构成“不法”威胁,如果 Maud 可以证明 Tchenguiz 是滥用诉讼程序,目的是让 Aabar 在威胁下因惧怕打官司而放弃债务重整,那看来并不是完全没有理据。Walker 大法官认为原告在修改诉讼请求的基础上仍然有一个可以审理的诉因。而关于是否是为了损害 Maud 利益的问题,Walker 大法官也认为在 Maud 可以满足其他恐吓侵权的要件下,证明该目的也是完全有可能。所以 Walker 大法官驳回了 Tchenguiz 提前撤销索赔请求的简易判决申请。

"两方恐吓"的案件在过去不多,但近期也开始多了,如 Elite Property Holdings Ltd v. Barclays Bank Plc(2017)EWHC 2030(QB);Morley(t/a Morley Estates)v. Royal Bank of Scotland Plc(2021)EWCA Civ 338 等先例。后一个先例的案情在本章之 9.5.2 段有详尽介绍,针对的是经济胁迫。但已经提到,经济胁迫与恐吓两个不同诉因的核心是一样的。所以在该先例中,也有同样篇幅针对恐吓侵权。

在此先例中,原告 Morley 先生主张该偿债协议是在 RBS 的恐吓下订立的,因为在 2010 年 7 月的一次会议上 RBS 威胁要将 Morley 先生的资产在委任破产接管人之前就按照预包装(pre-pack)破产程序出售,这会令这些地产的价值大打折扣。而这会构成非法,因为抵押债权人有责任善意以一个最合理价格出售或处置抵押品,[116] 这可见:Cuckmere Brick Co Ltd v. Mutual Finance Ltd(1971)Ch 949;Tse Kwong Lam v. Wong Chit Sen(1983)1 WLR 1349 等先例。这可节录一审的 Kerr 大法官判词的有关部分,如下:"The claimant relies heavily on alleged threats by the bank to breach its duties as mortgagee of the properties in the portfolio, to which I have just referred. His submissions start with the uncontroversial proposition that a mortgagee must, in selling the security, obtain the best price reasonably obtainable ...I turn to consider what threat or threats, if any, were or were not made at the meeting ... Would it be lawful for the bank to carry out the threat? Before addressing that important question, for completeness I must mention the suggested threat ... that unless the claimant signed up to a consensual deal, the bank would appoint receivers on the Monday to sell the portfolio on a pre-pack basis to West Register at an undervalue and/or without proper market testing and/or for an improper purpose. ... I agree with Mr Sinclair(被告 RBS 银行的代表大律师)that there is no evidence that threat ... was made, ...It is, indeed, inherently unlikely that a bank employee would say he intended to sell a mortgaged asset at an undervalue or without proper market testing. If he did, a finding of bad faith would be likely to follow."

换言之,Kerr 大法官的认定是 RBS 没有做出过这样的不法威胁,而有关的预包装出售只是为了减少出售费用,在商业上完全说得通:"The pre-pack nature of the sale, said Mr Sinclair, was rational and envisaged for the proper commercial purpose of minimising transaction costs."所以,恐吓侵权也是与经济胁迫一样,原告都败诉。

笔者只多提一句,在今天经济下行时经常发生的债权人(如银行)与债务人之间的重整债务谈判,如果银行讲话过了火,就有构成恐吓的危险。

12.2.3.3 恐吓侵权的"威胁"(threat)

先节录《Clerk & Lindsell on Torts》(2020 年,第 23 版)一书之 23 – 64 段:"The word 'threat', together with other words such as 'coercion' or even 'intimidation', has

---

[116] 关于抵押权人/债权人/银行在出售被抵押的财产时的责任,可见笔者《船舶融资与抵押》一书第五章之 4.3.1 段与 4.3.2 段的详细介绍。

often been applied to **utterances** which are quite **lawful and give rise to no liability**. A threat, for our purposes, is something which puts pressure on the person to whom it is addressed to take a particular course of action, something by means of which that person is 'improperly coerced'. A threat is an intimidation by one to another that unless the latter does or does not do something the former will do something which the latter will not like. The **threat must be coercive, it must be of the 'or else' kind**. It must be capable of being effective, to produce the desired result, and be more than 'idle abuse', something to be taken seriously. ..."（加黑部分是笔者的强调）

在 JT Stratford & Sons v. Lindley (No. 1) (1965) AC 269 贵族院先例中，Denning 勋爵指出一个威胁的同时要提出要求，受恐吓方也必须被逼迫（coerces）接受与屈服，这相当于侵权的要件之一是造成有关联性的损失，[117] 说："... capable of being expressed in the form, 'I will hit you unless you do what I ask,' or 'if you do what I forbid you to do.' A bare threat without a demand does not to my mind amount to the tort of intimidation. If a man says to another, 'I am going to hit you when I get you alone,' it is undoubtedly a threat; and an injunction can be obtained to restrain him from carrying out his threat. But the threat itself does not give rise to a claim for damages. It is only when he delivers the blow that it is actionable; and then as an assault, not as intimidation."

这种威胁也必须涉及不法的行为（unlawful act），如违反刑法、侵权、违约或违反信义义务。Colman 勋爵在 Berezovsky v. Abramovich (2010) EWHC 647 (Comm) 先例的说法已经在本章之 12.2.2 段节录，不再重复。

12.2.3.4　威胁与警告（warning）的区别

可诉威胁（actionable threat）不只是一个警告：见 Gaskell v. Lancashire and Cheshire Miners' Federation (1912) 28 TLR 518; Santen v. Busnach (1913) 29 TLR 214; Rookes v. Barnard (1964) AC 1129 等先例。

但这两者不容易区分，主要是看恐吓方讲话的艺术、当时的环境/语境与不同审理法官的印象。"威胁"会是恐吓方话讲得坦率与直白，如"你不这样做，我就要你的命"。"警告"会是如"你不这样做，对你的健康不是太好"。当然这"警告"如果来自一位医生，就完全没有问题；如果来自一位黑社会组织人员，就应是威胁了。但如果不是在这两个极端，就会是不好区分了。这难度类似在本书第六章 6.5 段去区分什么是专业人士提供的是"意见"（advice）或是"信息"（information）一样。[118] 只节录

---

[117] 见本书第六章之 1.3.1 段。

[118] 在本书第六章之 9.1.3 段也提到在 Manchester Building Society v. Grant Thornton UK LLP (2021) UKSC 20 最高院先例否定了"信息"与"意见"之分，转而要在不同的案件中分析责任的目的以及违反责任带来的后果与损失。

《Clerk & Lindsell on Torts》(2020 年,第 23 版)一书之 23 - 65 段:"The need for **some coercive element is the basis for the distinction between a ' threat ' and a ' warning '**, a distinction which is difficult to apply but which is well founded on authority. Thus, in Rookes v. Barnard, it was noted that what had been said was a threat and not ' merely informing BOAC(受恐吓方) that the men would strike if their terms were not accepted '. If all that a union official(恐吓方) does is to inform an employer that men will or may strike, that is not intimidation ..."(加黑部分是笔者的强调)

12.2.3.5 必须是恐吓方意图伤害受恐吓方

在《Civil Fraud》(2018 年,第 1 版)一书之 5 - 032 段也有提到恐吓侵权是恐吓方必须有意图(intentional)去逼迫受恐吓方,说:"**Intention to coerce**: Intimidation is a tort of intentionality. Hence it must be proved that the defendant intended by his words that the claimant be coerced into taking a step or desisting from taking a step which he would otherwise not have taken (or would have taken, as the case may be). This aspect of intention is inherent within the notion of coercion. As Lord Denning MR put it in JT Stratford & Son v. Lindley, the threat ' must be intended to coerce a person into doing something that he is unwilling to do or not doing something that he wishes to do '. More recently, the need for an intention to coerce was recognised by the Court of Appeal in Berezovsky v. Abramovich. ..."

该书接下来也指出恐吓方的逼迫也必须是意图要伤害主张恐吓侵权的原告(这可以是两方恐吓的受恐吓方或三方恐吓的第三人),说:"**Intention to cause loss**: It also seems that an intention to injure (in the sense of causing loss to) the claimant is necessary. ..."

12.3 衡平法的金钱救济

在本书第三章之 5.2 段与 5.4.2 段已经介绍过衡平法复原中,并不像普通法复原一样严格要求实物归还、严格回复到原状,而只需要做到实际公平。而做到实际公平的办法,就包括"以金钱反复原"(pecuniary counter-restitution)。在 BV Nederlandse Industrie Van Eiprodukten v. Rembrandt Enterprises Inc (2018) EWHC 1857 (Comm) 先例中就提到的"以钱代货"或以金钱反复原的说法。例如可以是要求交出利润或者是以金钱做替代,以帮助撤销合约与达到复原的目的。

但除了撤销与复原的救济外,衡平法下还可以有不需要撤销合约、独立的救济手段,无须撤销合约,而只是用金钱赔偿。尤其是在撤销与复原确实有困难(例如涉及无辜第三人的合约),相比之下其他救济手段更合适时。例如交出利润就可以作为独立的救济,类似的还有衡平赔偿(equitable compensation)。这类救济手段通常适用在违反信托义务(breach of trust)、信义义务/诚信责任(breach of fiduciary duty)或滥用信任(abuse of confidence)等案件中。

针对本书要针对的胁迫、不当影响与不合情理/显失公平交易救济,在《Duress,

Undue Influence and Unconscionable Dealing》(2019 年,第 3 版)一书之 28 - 001 段提到说:"**The principal remedy for duress, undue influence** or unconscionable dealing **is rescission**. ... In certain cases **where rescission is not the appropriate remedy** the court may order **an account for profits as an alternative**. ... In cases where neither rescission nor account of profits would be appropriate, **equitable compensation may be awarded** as an alternative form of relief, depending on the particular ground for relief."(加黑部分是笔者的强调)

在不当影响与不合情理交易这两种衡平救济中,在严格回复到原状有困难时可以用交出利润、金钱替代辅助复原没有疑问,但是否可以单独适用交出利润与衡平赔偿、不撤销合约是有疑问的,会在本章稍后介绍。

而在胁迫案件中,虽然有先例提出不应该再区分衡平法复原与普通法复原,因此胁迫的复原可以无须严格恢复原状,像衡平法复原一样用各种方式如用金钱辅助复原:见本章之 12.1.2 段已经介绍的 Halpern v. Halpern(2007)EWCA Civ 291 上诉庭先例。但这判法的法律地位与带来的影响尚不明确,如是否意味着绝大部分情况下因为都可以宽松地用金钱救济辅助达到实际公平,因此都可以撤销合约与复原?更麻烦的问题是,如果最后复原仍然难以做到,是否可以进一步扩张,将衡平法的这些独立救济也一样适用到胁迫理论中?而目前的看法仍是胁迫的救济只是撤销与复原,而要单独索赔损失只能倚靠例如恐吓侵权等其他诉因。

12.3.1　交出利润(account for profit)

首先针对交出利润的金钱救济,在独立作为救济手段时,不需要撤销合约与复原,只是要求被告将在衡平过错行为中的获利交出给原告受害方。作为"良心"的衡平法法院,在针对不同案件时是会有很大的裁量权在不同的救济中寻找最适合的一种。

普通法(特别是侵权)下也有以被告的获利来计算的损失赔偿方式,即"返还性损失"(restitutionary damages),这在《损失赔偿与救济》一书第一章之 7 段有介绍,同时也介绍了只适用在需要去阻止对方"不当得利"的案件,并介绍了一些著名案例如违反机密的 Attorney General v. Blake(2001)1 AC 268 贵族院先例,不在此重复。另在本书第四章之 4.2.2.3.6 段也针对欺诈性误述是否可以要求交出利润有简单介绍。毕竟这与普通法下损失赔偿的复原大原则(compensatory principle)有直接冲突,所以只有比较极端的案件才会适用这种交出利润的损失赔偿方式。

交出利润的救济适用类别的案件主要是一些侵权如违反诚信/信义义务、侵入土地(trespass to land)、知识产权侵权(infringement of intellectual property rights)、侵占或非法干预货物(conversion, wrongful interference of goods)等。显然,这些类别的案件都不涉及或适合撤销合约与复原的救济。

其中交出利润多在违反信义义务或滥用信任案件中被用作救济手段。这也可以理解,在本书第一章之 2.7 段与第十一章之 1.5 段也已经介绍过这是特别特殊的关系。例如上市公司与委任的董事,后者作为受信人(fiduciary)时,违反了信义义务如挪用(不管是否善意)公款或借用公司关系牟利。毕竟,在这种违反或过错,撤销合约与复原的救济往往是不适用。要求董事交出所得利润给公司的救济在 Regal(Hastings)v. Gulliver(1967)2 AC 134 贵族院先例中,Russell 勋爵说:"The rule of equity which insists on those, **who by use of a fiduciary position make a profit, being liable to account for that profit, in no way depends on fraud, or absence of bona fides**; or upon such questions or considerations as whether the profit would or should otherwise have gone to the plaintiff, or whether the profiteer was under a duty to obtain the source of the profit for the plaintiff, or whether he took a risk or acted as he did for the benefit of the plaintiff, or whether the plaintiff has in fact been damaged or benefited by his action. The liability arises from the mere fact of a profit having, in the stated circumstances, been made. **The profiteer, however honest and well-intentioned, cannot escape the risk of being called upon to account.**"(加黑部分是笔者的强调)

另 Sankey 勋爵也说:"The general rule of equity is that no one who has duties of a fiduciary nature to perform is allowed to enter into engagements in which he has or can have a personal interest conflicting with the interests of those whom he is bound to protect. If he holds any property so acquired as trustee, he is bound to account for it to his cestui que trust."

而交出利润是否可以拓展到所有其他类型的衡平法救济存在疑问,特别是已经有确立了的适合救济时。例如在本书第三章之 5.2.2 段介绍的 O'Sullivan v. Management Agency and Music Ltd(1985)QB 428 上诉庭先例中,当事人之间涉及不当影响,而法院最后给出救济是既可撤销合约,被告也要交出利润。这就带来了是否意味着不当影响案件除了撤销合约与复原外,可加上或单独以交出利润作为救济手段的疑问。[119] 但该先例即使是不当影响案件,也涉及信义关系以加强法院作出交出利润的救济的理据。这方面仍然存在争议,目前看来更倾向于肯定的说法。对此不展开,仅仅节录《Duress, Undue Influence and Unconscionable Dealing》(2019 年,第 3 版)一书之 28-060 到 28-061 段所说如下:

"The remedy of account of profits enables the claimant to recover from the defendant any profits which the defendant has gained as a result of their wrongdoing. In some cases the remedy is available as a supplement to the remedy of rescission to allow the court to achieve restitutio in integrum, ... In such a case the account is simply an ancillary measure to facilities the main relief of rescission. However, in other cases an account of profits is ordered because rescission is not the appropriate remedy in the circumstances of the case. In such a case, the order for account of profits is itself the main remedy... **It is**

---

[119] 同样的疑问也体现在衡平赔偿(equitable compensation)的救济,这在接下来之 12.3.2.2 段有详及。

settled proposition that the remedy of account of profits is available for breach of fiduciary duty or abuse of confidence. It is less settled whether it is available for undue influence...It was held that **in O' Sullivan itself the parties were in a fiduciary relationship**. The question may therefore arise whether the power to order accounts to be taken is limited to cases of undue influence or unconscionability where there is a fiduciary relationship between the parties. Dunn LJ(该先例中的大法官)seemed to be of the clear view that the power exercised in that case was one available in cases where the parties were in a fiduciary relationship.

However, since the other members of the court concluded more generally that the principle is applicable to a case of undue influence, **it is arguable that the principle applies to all cases of undue influence, including cases where the parties are not in a fiduciary relationship.** "(加黑部分是笔者的强调)

上述节录的最后一句说是"可争辩"(arguable)不当影响的救济是不必涉及信义关系也可以作出交出利润的救济,但要等待更权威的案例来明确这一点。至于接下来介绍的衡平赔偿,则倾向于对不当影响与不合情理交易不可给予这种衡平救济。

这方面的混乱在笔者看来主要是需要做出各种衡平救济的侵权类别太多,而过往先例针对不同类别各有视为最合适的衡平救济。而不当影响(与不合情理交易)一贯只是撤销合约与复原(宽松与弹性处理),不延伸去交出利润(与衡平赔偿)。这样,衡平法法院虽然希望对审理的个别案件去达至公平合理,也不希望偏离以往先例太远,丧失肯定性。在这方面谨慎是因为会与合约和侵权的损失赔偿大原则起冲突,即只是让受害方回复到合约被履行或侵权没有发生的地位,而不是惩罚对方或让受害方赚一笔。

12.3.2 衡平赔偿(equitable compensation)

但会有情况是被告没有利润可以交出,例如被告公司董事挪用公款投资,结果血本无归。在这种情况下,上小段介绍的"交出利润"的衡平救济就行不通,而需要判被告作出衡平赔偿以让原告受害方获得救济。

衡平赔偿主要适用在信托关系(trust relationship),或者是关系有类似之处的信义关系,以及滥用信任等案件:见 Nocton v. Lord Ashburton(1914)AC 932;Longstaff v. Birtles(2002)1 WLR 470[120]等先例。在 Nocton v. Lord Ashburton 贵族院先例中,Haldane 勋爵说:"Courts of Equity had jurisdiction to direct accounts to be taken, and in proper cases to order the solicitor(违反信义义务的律师)to replace property improperly acquired from the client(客户), or to make compensation if he had lost it by acting in breach of a duty which arose out of his confidential relationship to the man(客户)who had trusted him."

---

[120] 有关案情可见本书第五章之7.1段。

衡平赔偿的发展主要是在信托关系，资产是由受托人(trustee)持有，但实际的衡平权益(equity interest)是属于受益人(beneficiary)。而一般信托中往往受益人众多，权利归属也很复杂。因此在受托人违背了信托义务(如没有严格按照信托文件的规定处置资产，或者是干脆挪用了资产)，[121]最合适的做法是让信托资产回复到原本地位，这样也不至于因此产生与各个不同受益人之间的复杂问题。但拥有资产法律产权的受托人处置资产后，很可能不能用撤销合约等方式来复原，这会影响无辜第三人利益(如有关资产以市价卖给了第三人)。因此衡平法发展出的做法就是无须考虑撤销与复原，而是让受益人以金钱对信托资产作出赔偿，这就被称为衡平赔偿。

在 Target Holdings Ltd v. Redferns(a firm)(1996) AC 421 贵族院先例中，Browne-Wilkinson 勋爵说："The equitable rules of compensation for breach of trust have been largely developed in relation to such traditional trusts, where **the only way in which all the beneficiaries' rights can be protected is to restore to the trust fund what ought to be there**. In such a case the basic rule is that a trustee in breach of trust must restore or pay to the trust estate either the assets which have been lost to the estate by reason of the breach or compensation for such loss. **Courts of Equity did not award damages but, acting in personam, ordered the defaulting trustee to restore the trust estate**: see Nocton v. Lord Ashburton ... If specific restitution of the trust property is not possible, then the liability of the trustee is to pay sufficient compensation to the trust estate to put it back to what it would have been had the breach not been committed... Equitable compensation for breach of trust is designed to achieve exactly what the word compensation suggests: **to make good a loss in fact suffered by the beneficiaries and which, using hindsight and common sense, can be seen to have been caused by the breach.**"(加黑部分是笔者的强调)

也可节录《Chitty on Contract》(2021 年，第 34 版)一书之 21 - 143 段的介绍，特别强调了衡平赔偿是针对违反信义义务的救济，这与衡平损失[122](equitable damages)是两码事："The acceptance of a general notion of equitable compensation is a fairly recent development, at any rate in England and Wales. **The phrase refers to a monetary award for loss caused by breach of fiduciary duty**, and is to be distinguished from 'equitable damages', a phrase that can be used of an award of damages in lieu of specific

---

[121] 会有情况是双方之间存在信托关系/信义关系，但同时有合约关系，如律师与客户之间。通常律师违反的并非信义义务而是专业疏忽的合约关系：见 Bristol and West Building Society v. Mothew(1998) Ch 1 先例。这样，赔偿金额的计算、遥远性等，包括本书第六章介绍的 SAMMCO 原则都适用。但如果律师违反的是信义义务(这种情况对律师应是不多，他们有严格的专业操守)，如在本书第六章之 11.1 段介绍的 Main v. Giambrone & Law(2017) EWCA Civ 1193 上诉庭先例中，就适用衡平救济，包括是衡平赔偿在计算上的优待。

[122] 见《损失赔偿与救济》一书第十二章之 1.3 至 1.5 段与本书第四章之 5.4 段。

performance under Lord Cairns' Act,[123] which used to be regarded by some as the only clear occasion in which a court of Equity could give monetary judgment. **Equitable compensation is plainly an appropriate remedy for loss caused where an agent acts disloyally or a fiduciary in breach of fiduciary duty.** "(加黑部分是笔者的强调)

12.3.2.1 衡平赔偿的内容与普通法损失的异同

衡平赔偿的目的是实施了衡平过错行为的被告(如未能履行义务的受托人)必须将无辜方回复到没有过错的地位,这实际上与普通法中对待欺诈在损失方面的救济手段是类似的:见 Nocton v. Lord Ashburton(1914) AC 932 先例。[124]

衡平赔偿看来是为了阻吓受托人违反义务,在计算方面没有严格的因果关系与可预见性的要求。例如在很早期就已经有先例判信托受托人违反信托义务后,产生的损失无论是否可以预见都需要承担:见 Caffrey v. Darby(1801)6 Ves Jun 488 先例。

Target Holdings Ltd v. Redferns(a firm)(1996) AC 421 先例也提到只需要满足因果关系上的"要不是"测试,[125]而无需考虑遥远性等问题。例如信托资产是公司股票,但在作为被告的受托人懈怠、基本不参与董事会会议的情况下,董事会决议公司将参与某些风险极高的商业行为最后导致严重亏损,此时真正近因其实是董事会(其他董事)的共同行为,但由于被告自己违反了信托义务,因此一样要用金钱赔偿全数损失、将信托资产(公司股票)回复到原本地位。Browne-Wilkinson 勋爵这样说:"Even if the immediate cause of the loss is the dishonesty or failure of a third party, the trustee is liable to make good that loss to the trust estate if, but for the breach, such loss would not have occurred... Thus the common law rules of remoteness of damage and causation do not apply. However there does have to be some causal connection between the breach of trust and the loss to the trust estate for which compensation is recoverable, viz. the fact that the loss would not have occurred but for the breach..."

对于衡平赔偿与普通法赔偿的异同,只多节录 Swindle v. Harrison(1997)4 All ER 705 先例中 Evans 大法官所说:"At common law, damages on what may be called the restitutionary basis are awarded when the plaintiff was induced to enter into a transaction by the defendant's fraud... Similar principles have been developed by the courts of equity, and the authorities show that similar results have been achieved. When the breach of duty falls within the rather wider category of inequitable conduct which equity regards as fraud,[126] then the defendant's liability in damages is measured in the same way as if

---

〔123〕 见本书第四章之5.4.2段。

〔124〕 此先例可见本书第五章之7.1段的介绍。

〔125〕 甚至"要不是"测试也有说法可以放松:见富有争议的 Canson Enterprise Ltd v. Boughton & Co(1991) 85 DLR(4th)129 先例。

〔126〕 见本书第十一章之1段的脚注1对衡平法欺诈比普通法欺诈更广泛的解释。

fraud was proved at common law."

以及在该先例中,Hobhouse 勋爵也说:

"Equitable compensation may be awarded for breach of fiduciary duty. As observed in a number of the cases cited, the restitutionary obligation imposed on those who owe trustee or fiduciary duties is more strict than the common law obligation to pay damages for contractual or tortious negligence.

In considering the extent of liability for breach of fiduciary duty, it is not always necessary to consider all the matters which may be relevant in determining the extent of liability to pay damages for negligence. Foreseeability and remoteness of damage are, in general, irrelevant to restitutionary remedies for breach of trust or breach of fiduciary duty. The liability is to make good the loss suffered by the beneficiary of the duty. It is, however, necessary to address the issue of causation. Although equitable compensation, whether awarded in lieu of rescission or specific restitution or whether simply awarded as monetary compensation, is not damages, it is still necessary... to show that the loss suffered has been caused by the relevant breach of fiduciary duty. Liability is not unlimited."

《Duress, Undue Influence and Unconscionable Dealing》(2019 年,第 3 版)一书之 28－071 段综合以上的说法小结说衡平赔偿由于不考虑遥远性与可预见性,加上衡平救济的本质,因此会比普通法的违约或疏忽侵权的赔偿更广泛:"There has been some controversy as to the extent to which equitable compensation resembles or differs from common law damages. However, it is now clear that equitable compensation for breach of fiduciary duty is different from common law damages for breach of contract or for negligence. **The main difference is that equitable compensation is restitutionary in character**, in that it seeks to restore the complainant to the position in which they would have been if the breach had not been committed. Moreover, some of the common law rules of **limitation like foreseeability and causation do not apply**. This means that **the liability of a defendant in breach of fiduciary duty is more extensive than that of a defendant liable for negligence or breach of contract.**"(加黑部分是笔者的强调)

12.3.2.2 衡平赔偿的扩张与适用

而衡平赔偿在近年来看来还有扩张的趋势,例如在较近期的 Li Sau Ying v. Bank of China(Hong Kong)Ltd(2004)7 HKCFAR 579 香港终审法院先例中,Scott 勋爵说今天衡平赔偿广泛适用在涉及衡平过错(equitable wrong)的案件:"It is certainly correct that as a general proposition, equitable compensation can be ordered to be paid by a wrongdoer against whom some equitable wrong has been established."

但这样就带来了相当多类型案件中是否可以采用独立的衡平赔偿作为救济的争议。毕竟衡平过错的类型很多且缺乏清晰明确的说法,甚至法院在过往案例中刻意没有给出明确定义与范围，例如在 Tate v. Williamson(1866) LR 2 Ch. App. 55 先例中，Chelmsford 勋爵说："... the courts have always been careful not to fetter this useful jurisdiction by defining the exact limits of its exercise."

而针对本书要针对的两类衡平法诉因，即第十一章介绍的不当影响与不合情理交易，是否可以采用衡平赔偿作为救济的问题，与本章之 12.3.1 段提到的 O'Sullivan v. Management Agency and Music Ltd(1985) QB 428 上诉庭先例后，是否可以采用交出利润作为救济的问题类似，可以简单介绍如下。

12.3.2.2.1　不当影响

今天针对不当影响(undue influence)理论的原理尽管存在争议，但主要说法就是必须涉及衡平过错行为，滥用了影响力：见 Royal Bank of Scotland Plc v. Etridge(No. 2)(2001) UKHL 44 贵族院先例。

这样不当影响理论的救济，除了传统的复原(包括以金钱辅助复原)外，是否可以不撤销合约而索赔金钱损失就带来疑问。这方面常被用来支持可以采用衡平赔偿的案件是本书第三章之 5.2.3 段介绍的 Mahoney v. Purnell(1996) 3 All ER 61 先例。该先例中有信义/诚信关系的岳父与女婿合伙开公司经营酒店生意，事后女婿打算把岳父挤出生意，在 1988 年达成协议以 20 万英镑买断岳父的股份，但一转头在 1989 年就用 327.5 万多英镑售出了酒店。这样岳父主张不当影响要求撤销合约，但公司已经破产复原有困难。法院最后根据 Nocton v. Lord Ashburton(1914) AC 932 先例判应该同样给予衡平赔偿的救济并撤销了合约。

但是该先例的判法仍然被主流意见认为并不是将衡平赔偿扩张到在不当影响案件中适用，而只是用金钱赔偿辅助复原。《Chitty on Contracts》(2021 年，第 34 版)一书之 10 – 136 段说："In Mahoney v. Purnell, May J held that equitable compensation ... is also available in such circumstances and the plaintiff could recover the value of what he had transferred, giving credit for what he had received. .... **Doubt has been expressed whether equitable compensation is available in every case of undue influence, or only those in which there is a fiduciary relationship of a narrower sort**, such as between solicitor and client or beneficiary and trustee...It has been argued persuasively that 'equitable compensation' in this context should be understood as referring to pecuniary restitution of any unjust enrichment, which is appropriate in cases of undue influence. **The case shows not that equitable compensation may be given when restitution is impossible, so much as that rescission need not be prevented by the fact that property cannot be returned in specie; as between the parties it may be effected in money**."(加黑部分是笔者的强调)

在近期的 De Sena v. Notaro(2020) EWHC 1031(Ch) 先例中，涉及无法复原的问题时，Paul Matthews 大法官也是将这两种不同救济分开对待："I have no hesitation in saying that it would not be an appropriate case, even if a case of undue influence approved, for undoing the demerger transaction, because the parties cannot be restored now to the position that they would have been in. Whether in such a case some other remedy could be awarded, such as equitable compensation, is another matter."

12.3.2.2.2 不合情理/显失公平交易

要构成不合情理交易(unconscionable bargain),强势方必须采取了应受谴责的手段(reprehensible means)利用弱势方的特殊不利地位,并达成对弱势方过分、苛刻、震惊法院良心的交易。[127] 既然涉及应受谴责的手段,或许也可以说这属于衡平过错。

但是英国法下给予不合情理交易的救济是撤销与复原,过往先例中没有给予过衡平赔偿。《Duress, Undue Influence and Unconscionable Dealing》(2019 年,第 3 版)一书之 28-070 段这样说:"It would appear that in English law equitable compensation is not normally available for unconscionable conduct. Even where the transaction is rescinded as an unconscionable bargain, damages may not be awarded to compensate for loss suffered as a result of entering into the transaction, as opposed to adjustments needed to achieve restitutio in integrum...."

在 Norwich Union Life Insurance Society v. Qureshi (1998) CLC 1605 先例中,Rix 大法官也说单纯是不合情理的行为,并不带来金钱赔偿的救济。如果是该行为加上交易结果构成不合情理交易,法院会给予的也只是撤销与复原的救济。Rix 大法官说:"... it in essence amounts to an assertion that ... unconscionable conduct constituted in itself an independent cause of action which would found relief in respect of the losses caused thereby. I do not think that such an independent cause of action has been pleaded, and I doubt that it could be made good if pleaded, or that the doctrine whereby equity will set aside unconscionable bargains can be stretched that far."

因此可以总结以上所说,看来今天的主要说法仍然是在不当影响、不合情理交易中,并不能适用衡平赔偿。法院的救济仍然是撤销合约与复原,当然对于复原可以用金钱替代与辅助复原。

对于胁迫而言,尽管今天在 Halpern v. Halpern (2007) EWCA Civ 291 上诉庭先例提出在复原方面可以采取衡平法做法宽松对待,即以金钱辅助复原等,但这地位可以说尚有待后续先例的发展与确认。至于衡平赔偿,如果可以认定属于胁迫行为,看来也可以归类为衡平过错,但与不当影响、不合情理一样目前还没有说法可以进一步扩张胁迫的救济手段,胁迫仍然仅仅只限于撤销与复原,要索赔损失只能依赖恐吓侵权等其他诉因了。

---

[127] 显失公平交易的要件,可见本书第十一章之 2.2 段。

第十一章　不当影响与不合情理/显失公平交易

1. 不 当 影 响

简单而言,不当影响(undue influence)理论是为了防止强势方滥用(abuse)自己对弱势方的影响,衡平法会给予弱势方救济,通过不当影响达成的合约可使无效(voidable)。这被当作是欺诈[1]的一种:见 Dunbar Bank Plc v. Nadeem(1998)3 All ER 876;CIBC Mortgages plc v. Pitt(1994)1 AC 200 等先例。

涉及不当影响(以及本章后文中会介绍的不合情理/显失公平理论)的案件有很多。个人、家庭之间施加的不当影响较为常见,如不当影响方面权威的 Royal Bank of Scotland Plc v. Etridge(No.2)(2001)UKHL 44 先例就涉及妻子为了丈夫的债务抵押自己在夫妻家庭住房中的权利,事后主张受到不当影响要求撤销。[2]

还如各类赠与案件,或者遗产继承[3]案件中遗嘱人(特别是神志也已经不甚清醒的老年人)订立遗嘱将遗产大部分都分给护工或在遗嘱人临终前对其会有影响的人士而非自己配偶、子女。即使当时有律师在场,但他不是遗嘱人的律师而是遗嘱受益人的律师。

在商业活动中,除非能证明像胁迫一样实际施加了什么不当的影响,否则虽然理论上不当影响理论确实可以适用,但由于假设双方实际地位对等,就导致一般无法依赖不当影响理论:见本章之 1.7 段的介绍。而今天以不当影响作为诉因(之一)的案件,有很大一部分是因为在 2008 年金融海啸过后,很多投资者损失惨重,就根据与银行之间签订的投资协议起诉银行。由于这些案件往往涉案金额比较大,损失惨重的

---

〔1〕 普通法的欺诈侵权(tort of deceit)在本书第三章有涉及,定义是在著名的 Derry v. Peek(1889)14 App Cas 337 贵族院先例。显然 A 要证明 B 是有不诚实的思想状态并不容易,而衡平法欺诈(equitable fraud)就只需要法院以证明了的事实推定 B 会是不诚实,范围也广泛得多。这可节录在 Hart v. O'Connor(1985)AC 1000 枢密院先例中,Brightman 勋爵说:"'Fraud' in its equitable context does not mean, or is not confined to, deceit; 'it means an unconscientious use of the power arising out of these circumstances and conditions' of the contracting parties"

〔2〕 也可见本书第五章之 6.3.3.2 段的介绍。

〔3〕 遗产继承案件中的不当影响案例很多,与一般案件中的不当影响在有些地方并不一致。但这与本书关系不大,后文中也不专门针对此类案件进行介绍。

投资人要想尽一切可能的办法弥补损失，才将包括不当影响理论在内的各种不同的诉因都扯在一起作为替代的理由，如合约下是否有信义义务/诚信责任（fiduciary obligations），银行是否滥用了投资者的信任与信心（trust and confidence），是否违背公平交易的原则，或者是否存在利用了投资者的弱点等。但这类案件都难以成功，如在本章之1.7段介绍的JP Morgan Chase Bank v. Springwell Navigation Corporation（2008）EWHC 1186（Comm）先例与更近期的The Libyan Investment Authority v. Goldman Sachs International（2016）EWHC 2530（Ch）先例等。

1.1 不当影响、不合情理/显失公平交易与胁迫

在本段提及的不当影响与稍后涉及的不合情理/显失公平交易，都是重要的导致合约可使无效的衡平法理论。而不当影响与本书第十章涉及的胁迫的目的有类似之处，都涉及不允许采取非法压力/不当影响（如威胁）导致受压方/弱势方的订约自由意志（contractual free will）有了偏离（deflection），所以要允许从被胁迫或不当影响下订立的合约中脱身。

特别在早年，胁迫理论的适用仍然很狭窄，只包括非法造成对人身或财物上的逼迫（physical coercion）等。所以会有情况是在普通法下可以接受或合法的行为，但在特定的案情下，作为"良心法律"的衡平法认为不道德与不合情理，就可以支援普通法，更广泛与全面地以不当影响作出救济以弥补胁迫理论的不足：见Williams v. Bayley（1866）LR 1 HL 200先例中，Mutual Finance Co Ltd v. John Wetton & Sons Ltd（1937）2 KB 389先例等。正如在Dunbar Bank Plc v. Nadeem（1998）3 All ER 876上诉庭先例中，Millett大法官说："The court of equity is a court of conscience. It sets aside transactions obtained by the exercise of undue influence because such conduct is unconscionable."

但随着对胁迫理论的放宽，主要是20世纪70年代后认可经济胁迫[4]（economic duress）以及合法行为也可以构成非法压力，作为衡平救济的不当影响从在胁迫不可行时支援胁迫理论变为同时是替代诉因。虽然如果胁迫不成立，往往是实际不当影响也不会成立：见Holyoake v. Candy（2017）EWHC 3397（Ch）先例与KHS Farm Ltd v. KSH Plant Ltd（2021）EWHC 1986（Ch）先例等。在KHS Farm Ltd v. KSH Plant Ltd先例中，Mark West大法官说："If the plea of duress fails on the pleaded grounds, as I have held that it does, by the same token the plea of undue influence, which relies on exactly the same factual averments, must also fall.... **An unsuccessful case in duress cannot be rebadged and relaunched as a good case in undue influence if it relies on exactly the same factual allegations**. To paraphrase Nugee J in Holyoake v. Candy, **the plea of actual undue influence does not add anything to the plea of duress** and it cannot succeed if the plea of duress fails on the facts."（加黑部分是笔者的强调）

---

〔4〕 见本书第十章之5.4段。

但他们之间也有明显的不同。例如与胁迫相比,由于不当影响还可以是推定不当影响(presumed undue influence),此时不需要实际证明存在施加影响或压力,甚至可以确实没有采取什么威胁或行为,仅仅由于当事人之间存在特殊关系,就足以构成影响。

其他重要的不同也显而易见,如胁迫理论不追究施压方与受压方之间的权力或地位的比较。毕竟可能会有一位穷光蛋在无路可走时暴力胁迫一位富豪订立一份捐赠合约。但不当影响或不合情理/显失公平交易是关心双方之间的权力与地位,尽量为可被推断受到不当影响或是订立的合约对其十分不利的一方(这也通常是处于弱势的一方)在面对强势方时,作出衡平救济。又如雇主与低级别雇员之间,如果是雇员提起的诉讼多半是主张受到不当影响,但如果是雇主提起诉讼一般就是主张受到胁迫了。

相比胁迫理论,不当影响与不合情理/显失公平交易的两个理论,可以说是更为接近了。正如在 Lawrence v. Poorah(2008)UKPC 21 枢密院先例中,Walker 勋爵说:"they share a common root-equity's concern to protect to the vulnerable from economic harm."

所以相比普通法的胁迫理论,这两个衡平法的理论更常见在同一案件的案情,去作为同一码事处理。正如在 Louth v. Diprose(1992)175 CLR 621 先例中,Brennan 大法官说:"the similarity between the two jurisdictions gives to cases arising in the exercise of one jurisdiction an analogous character in cases involving the same points in the other jurisdiction."

而如果不当影响与不合情理/显失公平交易之间,一个成立不了,另一个也帮不上忙。例如在 R v. Attorney General for England and Wales(2003)UKPC 22 枢密院先例中,Hoffmann 勋爵说:"if the transaction was not such as to give rise to an inference that it had not been unfairly obtained by a party in a position to influence the other, it must follow that the transaction cannot be independently attacked as unconscionable."

而如果不合情理交易可以成立,替代的不当影响也能成立。这可节录《Duress, Undue Influence and Unconscionable Dealing》(2019 年,第 3 版)一书之 20-011 段提及 Credit Lyonnais Bank Nederland NV v. Burch(1997)1 All ER 144 上诉庭先例时,说:"In many cases, the facts giving rise to unconscionable dealing may also be sufficient to constitute undue influence."

这两个理论的要件基本上一样或接近,只是重心与形式不一样。例如不合情理/显失公平交易,不仅是合约一面倒对弱势方不利,也涉及强势方的不合情理行为如明知道弱势方有"特殊不利"(special disadvantage)去取巧。正如在 Alec Lobb v. Total Oil GB(1983)1 WLR 87 先例中所说的"in some morally culpable manner",或在加拿大的 Cain v. Clarica Life Insurance Co(2005)ABCA 437 先例中的"knowingly taking advantage of(弱势方)vulnerability."

1.2 不当影响的定义

定义不当影响不容易。本来人与人之间的交往,无论是大小事情,都会希望去影响并说服其他人士,又或是被其他人士说服。在这个过程中,双方都要施加一些压力或影响力来帮助说服对方。这压力是否管用也往往因人而异,会有人很有主见与抗压能力强,故此很难被说服。但也会有人因为没有主见、不谨慎或是愚昧,稍加压力或影响力就轻易被说服。所以法律(即使是衡平法理论)为这种社会上千变万化情况划一条"红线"明确什么是恰当的影响与什么是法律不允许的不当影响是不容易的。正如 Clyde 勋爵在 Royal Bank of Scotland Plc v. Etridge(No. 2)(2001)UKHL 44 贵族院先例中说不当影响是"not easy to define"。但在该针对不当影响的重要先例中,Nicholls 勋爵给了一个简短的定义,说:"One of the grounds of relief developed by the courts of equity as a court of conscience. The objective is to ensure that the influence of one person over another is not abused."

另在 National Westminster Bank Plc v. Morgan(1985)AC 686 贵族院先例中,Scarman 勋爵说一方加害他能影响的另一方:"It is not a vague 'public policy' but specifically the victimisation of one party by the other."

在更早期的 Allcard v. Skinner(1887)36 Ch. D. 145 上诉庭先例中,案情涉及原告在加入一个宗教组织后把自己所有的财产(约 8000 英镑)全数贡献给了组织。在几年后退出,希望以她受了不当影响去把这笔财产取回。Lindley 大法官就有了一个著名的解释,说:"The principle must be examined. What then is the principle? Is it that it is right and expedient to save persons from the consequences of their own folly? or is it that it is right and expedient to save them from being victimised by other people? In my opinion the doctrine of undue influence is founded upon the second of these two principles. **Courts of equity have never set aside gifts on the ground of the folly, imprudence, or want of foresight** on the part of donors. The courts have always repudiated any such jurisdiction…It would obviously be to encourage folly, recklessness, extravagance and vice if persons could get back property which they foolishly made away with…On the other hand, **to protect people from being forced, tricked or misled in any way by others** into parting with their property is one of the most legitimate objects of all laws; and the equitable doctrine of undue influence has grown out of and been developed by the necessity of grappling with insidious forms of spiritual tyranny and with the infinite varieties of fraud."(加黑部分是笔者的强调)

在此著名先例中可见不同案件的困难,假设原告只是捐了 5 英镑或 10 英镑给宗教组织,显然仍是受了影响。但如果捐款金额是合理的,虽然原告仍是受了影响才会去捐款,但也不会是"不当"影响。更可能是原告出于自己的自由意志,而衡平法是不会想对此作出救济。这在 Tufton v. Sperni(1952)2 TLR 516 上诉庭先例中,Evershed 大法官说:"Extravagant liberality and immoderate folly do not of themselves provide a passport to equitable relief."

但在 Allcard v. Skinner 先例中,在各种因素权衡下,主要是贡献了原告几乎所有的财产,显然受宗教的不当影响,因为这么极端的行为是自身愚昧解释不通的,法院就给予了衡平救济。此时由于这样的行为超出了合理与正常的人一般动机之下会采取的行为,因此"需要解释"(call for explanation),法院就推定受到的影响"不当",接受捐赠的宗教组织需要反证有关行为背后有恰当理由,并非"不当"。Lindley 大法官说:"But if the gift is so large as not to be reasonably accounted for on the ground of friendship, relationship, charity, or other **ordinary motives on which ordinary men act**, the burden is upon the donee to support the gift."(加黑部分是笔者的强调)

最后可节录《Chitty on Contracts》(2021 年,第 34 版)一书之 10-072 段对不当影响的概述如下:"The equitable doctrine of undue influence is a comprehensive phrase covering cases in which a transaction between two parties who are in a particular type of relationship may be set aside if the transaction is the result of an abuse of the relationship. Normally, the relevant relationship is one of trust and confidence, but it may also include relationships of emotional or physical dependency. If the claimant shows that the other party obtained it by abusing the relationship, this, as we shall see, is often termed 'actual undue influence', but it is better to refer to such cases as one in which undue influence is actually (or directly) proved. A transaction may also be set aside in the absence of direct proof if claimant shows the existence of a relationship of trust and confidence with the other party, and that the transaction is one that 'calls for explanation'. Then there will be an evidential presumption that the transaction was the result of undue influence and unless the presumption is rebutted, the transaction may be set aside."

1.3 不当影响是衡平救济

1.3.1 支援普通法的衡平救济

早期的衡平法法院[也称"良心法院"(court of conscience)]发展起来是为了针对个别案件的不公平(injustice/unfairness)或不合情理(unconscionable),赋予当事人新的权利或给予衡平救济,这是追求大局肯定性的普通法解决不了的。例如,创立了信托(trust),并在财产的普通法产权(legal title)外赋予财产的受益人一个衡平法产权(equitable title)。又如在违约/毁约中,受害方在普通法下的救济只是金钱的损失赔偿。但这在个别案件不解决受害方的问题或将会面对的并非金钱赔偿可以弥补的损失,更需要的是违约方继续履行有关的合约。这样,衡平法就发展出"履约指令"[5](specific performance)的救济:如 Walsh v. Lonsdale (1882) 21 Ch. D. 9 上诉庭先例。又如在诽谤或侵犯专利等案件中,受害方蒙受的伤害可以通过普通法获得赔偿。但为了避免将来再次侵犯,就需要衡平法以"禁令"(injunction)作出救济了。禁

[5] 见笔者《损失赔偿与救济》一书第十二章的详细介绍。

令的衡平救济今天也已是发展到方方面面，如被视为法院核武器的“财产冻结令”[6]（Mareva injunction 或 Freezing Order）、搜查令[7]（Anton Pillar 或 Search Order）等。

但衡平法也追求普通法的肯定性与可预测性，所以也从针对个别案件的不同案情去主持公平合理，变为像普通法一样遵从先例与受约束，并发展出不少衡平法理论（equitable doctrines），虽然核心思想仍是针对不公平与/或不合情理的案件。所以在 National Funds Assurance Company，Re（1878）10 Ch. D. 118 上诉庭先例中，Jessel 大法官说：“（equity is not）a court of conscience but rather a court of law.”

不当影响是衡平法理论，用作防止一方滥用自己对另一方的影响。在 Holyoake v. Candy（2017）EWHC 3397（Ch）先例中，Nugee 大法官说：“The doctrine of undue influence is one of the doctrines developed by equity to protect the vulnerable and weak, and as the word ‘influence’ suggests, the paradigm cases are cases where one party to a transaction has acquired a position of influence or ascendancy over another. Many of the cases are therefore concerned with a relationship where A reposes trust or confidence in B, and B abuses that relationship.”

作为衡平法理论，就需要在不同案件的案情事实上去看这影响是否“不当”/“不合情理”。

1.3.2　何为“不当”

首先是“不当”（undue）或“衡平法过错”（equitable wrong），又是在千变万化与每一个案件的事实都有微妙的差异，定义（或去划一条红线）是不容易。在 National Bank of Montreal v. Stuart（1911）AC 120 先例中，Macnagthen 勋爵说：“It is difficult to determine in any case the point at which the influence of one mind upon another amounts to undue influence.”

另在 Royal Bank of Scotland Plc v. Etridge（No. 2）（2001）UKHL 44 贵族院先例中，Nicholls 勋爵说：“It is impossible to be more precise or definitive. The circumstances in which one person acquires influence over another, and the manner in which influence may be exercised, vary too widely to permit of any more specific criterion.”

看来，影响是否是“不当”是要从强势方 A 与弱势方 B 的角度同时考虑。从 B 的角度是去看订约自由意志是否受到不当影响；从 A 的角度是去看施加的影响是否不恰当、不合情理，包括是否有过错如误述或胁迫等。要成立不当影响，这两个要件

---

[6] 见笔者《证据法：国际规管与诉讼中的证据攻防》一书第三章的详细介绍。

[7] 见笔者《证据法：国际规管与诉讼中的证据攻防》一书第二章之 3 段的详细介绍。

缺一不可。[8] 例如,说是 B 的订约自由意志受到影响,但 A 的言行没有任何可以挑得出毛病,就不会有“无辜不当影响”(innocent undue influence)的说法。订立有关的合约更有可能是 B 自己的问题,如愚昧,而其他合理人士是不会受到影响的。

这可先节录一些先例的说法,首先是 Hobhouse 勋爵在 Royal Bank of Scotland Plc v. Etridge(No. 2)贵族院先例中所说:“It is **an equitable wrong committed by the dominant party** against the other which makes it unconscionable for the dominant party to enforce his legal rights against the other. It is typically **some express conduct overbearing the other party's will**. It is capable of including conduct which might give a defence at law, for example, duress and misrepresentation.”(加黑部分是笔者的强调)

另在 Drew v. Daniel(2005) EWCA Civ 507 上诉庭先例中,Ward 大法官说:“... her will(受到影响方的订约自由意愿)was overborne ... It remains for me to consider whether ... there was evidence of(施加影响方)overt acts of improper pressure or coercion or persuasive conduct. ...”

最后可节录在《Duress, Undue Influence and Unconscionable Dealing》(2019 年,第 3 版)一书之 7 - 006 段:“... It is submitted that the doctrine of undue influence ... is both complainant-sided(弱势方)and defendant-sided(强势方). It is complainant-sided because it is concerned with the impairment of the complainant's free will. However, it is also defendant-sided because it judges the nature of the defendant's conduct to determine whether it is improper or unconscientious. The question whether the exercise of influence is 'undue' turns on both the effect of the influence on the complainant's free will and the manner in which it was exercised(whether unconscionable). To put it differently, as the law now stands, there is no such thing as 'innocent undue influence', where the complainant's free will is impaired in circumstances where the defendant's conduct cannot be castigated as unconscionable...”

另该书之 8 - 024 段也说:“The basis of the court's intervention in cases of undue influence is ... **to protect against victimisation**. Since victimisation is the 'unconscientious use of ... power', it is clear that the use of the word 'victimisation' in connection with relief for undue influence is intended to make it plain that, in addition to the first requirement(impaired autonomy of the complainant), there **must also be unconscionable use of influence** by the defendant. This is the approach that English law has adopted ....

---

[8] 过去对于不当影响的性质一直存在不同说法,是关键在于 B 的自由意志被影响(无论 A 是否有衡平法过错),还是在于 A 采取了衡平法过错/不合情理的行为(而 B 自由意志被影响仅仅有证据价值,并非必要要件)。而在《Duress, Undue Influence and Unconscionable Dealing》(2018 年,第 3 版)一书提出的看法是构成不当影响这两者必须同时存在,见稍后节录的该书之 7 - 006 段,本书也以该书的说法为准。仅仅从效果上来看,A 以不合情理的行为影响了 B,实际上也会影响 B 的自由意志。

For there to be undue influence, there must be, ... improper or unconscionable conduct on the part of the defendant. This means that there will be no undue influence if the court finds that the defendant's conduct is not unconscionable. In determining **whether in the particular case the defendant's conduct is unconscionable the court will consider a wide range of issues**, including whether the defendant took an unfair advantage of the position of weakness of the complainant or opportunistically exploited his own position of advantage. **In many cases where the complainant's free will is impaired the defendant's conduct will also be unconscionable**. ..."(加黑部分是笔者的强调)

1.4 区分两种不当影响

《Duress, Undue Influence and Unconscionable Dealing》(2019年,第3版)一书之7-007-7-008段这样说:

"**Two forms of unacceptable conduct** It is generally accepted that there are two forms of unacceptable conduct for which relief may be available on the ground of undue influence. One 'comprises overt acts of improper pressure or coercion such as unlawful threats'. This area is also occupied by common law duress as developed in modern times. The other form of undue influence 'arises out of a relationship between two persons where one has acquired over another a measure of influence, or ascendancy, of which the ascendant person then takes unfair advantage'

This second form concerns insidious forms of unacceptable conduct. Equity long recognized the need to protect parties from abuse of influence acquired in a relationship in the absence of overt acts of persuasion. However, without overt acts, proof of such abuse of influence would be difficult, if not impossible. Conscious of this difficulty, equity afforded the complainant(受到影响方/原告) in these 'relationship' cases some help in the form of presumptions.... "

以上是说不当影响根据证明方式的不同可分为实际不当影响(actual undue influence)与推定不当影响(presumed undue influence)两类。过去不当影响案件中会区分这两类案件甚至作为不同诉因看待,因此同样是不当影响但背后的性质与原理有不少不同说法。但经过 Royal Bank of Scotland Plc v. Etridge(No. 2)(2001)UKHL 44 贵族院先例后已经统一为目前的说法,这两者仅仅是证明的方式不同而已,Clyde 勋爵说:"I question the wisdom of the practice which has grown up... of attempting to make classifications of cases of undue influence. That concept is in any event not easy to define. ... It is something which can be more easily recognised when found than exhaustively analysed in the abstract. Correspondingly the attempt to build up classes or categories may lead to confusion. The confusion is aggravated if the names used to identify the classes do not bear their actual meaning. Thus on the face of it a division into cases of 'actual' and 'presumed' undue influence appears illogical. It appears to confuse definition and proof. There is also room for uncertainty whether the presumption is of the existence of an influence or of its quality as being undue. I would also dispute the utility of the further sophistication of subdividing 'presumed undue influence' into further categories. All these classifications to my mind add mystery rather than illumination."

这两类在法定举证责任(burden of proof)上是一样的,也就是都是由弱势方在平衡的可能性(balance of probabilities)下证明不当影响必须满足的两个要件(弱势方自由意志受影响以及强势方有衡平法过错行为滥用了影响力)。[9] 但第二类推定不当影响[10]中,会涉及由于双方的关系可以推定影响,以及由于最后达成的协议"需要解释"而推定不当,这样便产生了举证责任转移,由强势方反证不存在不当影响,而不是由主张不当影响的弱势方来举证。可节录 Royal Bank of Scotland Plc v. Etridge(No.2)先例中,Nicholls 勋爵说:"Whether a transaction was brought about by the exercise of undue influence is a question of fact. Here, as elsewhere, the general principle is that he who asserts a wrong has been committed must prove it. The burden of proving an allegation of undue influence rests upon the person who claims to have been wronged. This is the general rule. The evidence required to discharge the burden of proof depends on the nature of the alleged undue influence, the personality of the parties, their relationship, the extent to which the transaction cannot readily be accounted for by the ordinary motives of ordinary persons in that relationship, and all the circumstances of the case. ...This use of the term 'presumption' is descriptive of a shift in the evidential onus on a question of fact. When a plaintiff succeeds by this route he does so because he has succeeded in establishing a case of undue influence. The court has drawn appropriate inferences of fact upon a balanced consideration of the whole of the evidence at the end of a trial in which the burden of proof rested upon the plaintiff. The use, in the course of the trial, of the forensic tool of a shift in the evidential burden of proof should not be permitted to obscure the overall position."

具体而言,这两类不当影响区别是:

1. 实际不当影响,需要证明强势方的不合情理/衡平法过错行为。这主要就是弱势方能够证明强势方公然以不当或非法威胁施加影响力。随着本书第十章介绍的胁

---

〔9〕 有关举证责任的问题,可见《证据法:基础理论、口头证据与专家证据》一书第七章之1至4段。

〔10〕 有关推定(presumption),以及本章后文会提到的是否可反驳(rebuttable),法律推定与证据推定等课题,见《证据法:基础理论、口头证据与专家证据》一书第七章之6.1段的介绍。简单而言,法律推定是根据法律的规定(force of law),一旦发生某类一致的事实或情况时,就可以对事实进行推定,不会再有进一步裁量的问题。而事实推定是在特定案件中,根据已经认定的事实(包括承认的事实或双方没有异议的事实等),凭常识与逻辑(common sense and logic)推理出的结果,这会是根据具体的案件事实而千变万化,也是审理法官的裁量问题。推定可反驳,针对的则是即使已经作出推定,当事人如果有证据能够反驳、证明相反的事实,可以推翻原本推定的事实。

迫的扩大与延伸，施加压力与影响力之间已经区别不大，不当影响的强势方也是违法胁迫下的施压方。

这类实际不当影响也包括根据双方之间的关系，导致强势方需要承担一些特定义务，如必须坦诚地披露，而未能履行这些义务就变成实际的不当影响。或者是该关系中强势方完全处在支配地位，对弱势方予取予求，如强势方有长期暴力欺凌弱势方的历史，此时从这些环境证据也可以证明不合情理/衡平法过错行为。

在 The Libyan Investment Authority v. Goldman Sachs International(2016) EWHC 2530(Ch)先例中，Rose 大法官说："The claimant can prove actual undue influence if he can point to specific instances of unconscionable conduct or he can rely on a presumption that undue influence has occurred because certain circumstances have arisen. Within actual undue influence there are also two strands. The first is where there has been an improper threat of some kind. …For this kind of actual undue influence there is no need to establish any particular relationship between the parties. … The second kind of actual undue influence is where the nature of the relationship between the parties to the disputed transactions is such as to place on the stronger party a duty to behave to the vulnerable party with candour and fairness. If the stronger party then acts in breach of that duty, the transaction can be set aside for undue influence. I shall refer to the relationship that can form the basis of a claim of actual undue influence as a 'protected relationship'…"

2. 推定不当影响是针对双方有特殊关系(special relationship)或影响力关系，如信心与信任(trust and confidence)的关系就推定存在"影响"，以及在此基础上最后达成的交易并非合理与正常的人一般动机之下会达成的交易/"需要解释"就推定"不当"。

例如夫妻之间，这影响力无处不在，妻子对赚钱养家的丈夫言听计从。丈夫影响妻子订立合约如把她名下的居住房屋抵押给银行作为丈夫贷款融资的担保，就往往不涉及特别的言行去影响妻子。这样，就需要推定存在潜在的不当影响以保护这些社会上弱势群体。也就是需要执行有关合约并主张没有受到不当影响的银行去推翻这个推定。[11] 这可节录在 Smith v. Cooper(2010) EWCA Civ 722 上诉庭先例中，Lloyd 大法官所说："If … the presumption of undue influence applies, that is to say, the court will presume that the transaction was procured by undue influence exercised by one party over the other, in other words by the abuse by the one of the position of influence that he has over the other. In such a case it is then up to the one party to prove that the transaction was not procured by an abuse of his position of influence but was rather the free exercise of the will of the other party as a result of full, free and informed thought….

---

〔11〕 可见在本书第五章之6.3.3.2段介绍的作为普通家庭主妇的妻子为丈夫贷款提供担保(surety wives)的案件。

Full understanding of the transaction is of course necessary but by no means sufficient, because the problem is lack of independence, not lack of understanding."

银行推翻这个不当影响的推定，惯常做法是在妻子签订抵押协议前建议她先去找一位律师取得独立意见。这除了可以让妻子知道签下去后果严重外，也可以在一定程度上摆脱丈夫的影响力，如丈夫通常会安慰说"你放心、没事、相信我"等。《Duress, Undue Influence and Unconscionable Dealing》(2019年，第3版)一书之12-008段说："It has long been accepted that the presumption of undue influence may be rebutted by proof that the transaction was entered into after its nature and effect had been fully explained to the complainant(受推定不当影响的妻子)by independent qualified person(独立的律师)... So proof that the complainant received independent advice before entering into the impugned transaction(抵押协议)is one of the matters that a court takes into account in weighing all the evidence to determine whether the presumption of undue influence has been rebutted. However, although independent legal advice is an important factor, it is not necessarily a decisive factor in every case. ...

1.4.1 实际不当影响的要件

Hobhouse勋爵在Royal Bank of Scotland Plc v. Etridge(No. 2)(2001)UKHL 44贵族院先例中针对实际不当影响(actual undue influence)时说："Actual undue influence ... is an equitable wrong committed by the dominant party against the other which makes it unconscionable for the dominant party to enforce his legal rights against the other. It is typically some express conduct overbearing the other party's will. It is capable of including conduct which might give a defence at law, for example, duress and misrepresentation. Actual undue influence does not depend upon some preexisting relationship between the two parties though it is most commonly associated with and derives from such a relationship. He who alleges actual undue influence must prove it."

在BCCI v. Aboody(1990)1 QB 923先例中，Slade大法官提到了需要证明实际不当影响要证明四方面内容：(1)强势方有能力影响弱势方；(2)确实施加了影响；(3)该影响属于"不当"影响；(4)该影响导致交易达成。可以节录相关内容如下："... we think that a person relying on a plea of actual undue influence must show that(a) the other party to the transaction(or someone who induced the transaction for his own benefit)had the capacity to influence the complainant; (b) the influence was exercised; (c) its exercise was undue; (d) its exercise brought about the transaction."

《Duress, Undue Influence and Unconscionable Dealing》(2019年，第3版)一书之8-001段说："For a claim to succeed on the ground of actual undue influence it must be shown that the intention of the complainant(弱势方)to enter into the transaction was secured by some unacceptable form of persuasion, especially overt acts of improper pressure such as unlawful threats. Thus, for a claim to succeed on the ground of actual undue influence, it must be established that (a) the complainant's free will was impaired, (b) there was impropriety in the defendant's conduct and, in terms of causation, (c) the improper conduct constituted by (a) and (b) were part of the process by which the complainant's consent to the transaction was obtained."

以上所讲的实际不当影响理论的要件有以下三个(与 Slade 大法官的四个要件没有本质区别):(1)弱势方达成交易的意图或订约自由意志被强势方影响;(2)强势方有衡平法过错、不合情理行为,滥用了地位、影响力;(3)不当影响与最后达成交易(合约)之间存在因果关系。

1.4.1.1 要件之一:订约自由意志受影响

《Duress, Undue Influence and Unconscionable Dealing》(2019 年,第 3 版)一书之 8-004 段说:"In considering whether the complainant's free will was impaired by overt acts of pressure or persuasion the court must consider a wide range of facts. In any given case there will be 'a vast penumbra of facts which bear upon the question whether actual undue influence was exerted'. This includes the personalities of the parties. It is important for the court to know whether the complainant was particularly vulnerable, for example, because of age, mental or physical illness. The impact of a given act of pressure may be different depending on the personality of the complainant to whom it is directed. A threat of court action, for example, will not have the same effect on an experienced businessman ... as it would on an old lady anxious to avoid confrontation. Therefore, it is difficult to divide acts of pressure into those that will impair the free will of the complainant, and so could constitute undue influence, and those that would not. All that can be said is that for an overt act of pressure to impair the free will of the complainant it must overcome his will ...."

以上段落中提到自由意志是否被影响,很依赖具体的案件事实。例如,当事人双方的个人特质如何。毕竟同样是面对诉讼的威胁,对一个惯于诉讼、身经百战的商人和一个害怕卷入任何纠纷、缺乏知识与胆小的市民或老人来说,效果是完全不同的。也因此这会需要考虑案件中的具体人士是否被影响(而不是看一般合理人士处于弱势方地位是否会受到影响):见 Brocklehurst Estate, Re (1978) Ch 14 先例。又例如弱势方看起来是在受压之下仓促地签订合约,是没机会也不像是经过深思熟虑的,但其实弱势方已经向称职律师紧急获取了独立法律意见,一样可以推断自由意志没有被影响。

还可以节录该书之 8-019 段对一些过往先例中判自由意志没有被影响的概述如下:"In most cases where there is no overt act of pressure but it is not regarded as sufficient to overcome the complainant's will, the reason will be because either the pressure is ordinary family or commercial pressure or because the complainant was convinced by the acts of persuasion... However it must be borne in mind that some cases may involve a mixture of both, as where ordinary family pressure contributes to persuade the complainant that to enter into the impugned transaction was the right thing to do."

以上提到的通常认为自由意志没有被影响的两种情况:(1)有关影响只不过是正常、合法的商业压力;(2)弱势方实际上是被强势方用道理说服,自己做的决定。例如丈夫对妻子坦诚说没有这笔贷款家里经济困难,连孩子下一笔学费都交不起,妻子就会是深思熟虑之下做出的决定:见 Barclays Bank Plc v. O'Brien(1994)1 AC 180 先例。

另外如果是根据双方关系认为强势方没有履行自己坦诚的义务等情况,或者是在完全支配的关系中,此时显然弱势方也就不是在自己独立与知情的判断下达成交易:见 Lloyds Bank Ltd v. Bundy(1975)QB 326 先例与 BCCI v. Aboody(1990)1 QB 923 先例等。

1.4.1.2　要件之二:不恰当与不合情理的影响

不同案件中合约是否是通过不当影响而产生是要客观去看有关案情的很多不同因素。主要是以下几个方面:

1. 强势方是否知道弱势方的弱点,并通过影响施压或诱导订立合约取巧?这可节录《Duress, Undue Influence and Unconscionable Dealing》(2019 年,第 3 版)一书之 8 – 25 段:"… A defendant can hardly be said to have exploited the complainant's weakness or to have taken unfair advantage of the complainant's weakness if he was not aware of what he was exploiting or taking unfair advantage of. … Such knowledge is assumed in most cases where the complainant's consent is impaired by illegitimate threats, bullying, deliberate concealment or domination."

2. 弱势方的订约自由意志被影响,也是显示存在不合情理的证据。

3. 强势方无意伤害弱势方利益不是对不当影响的抗辩。《Duress, Undue Influence and Unconscionable Dealing》(2019 年,第 3 版)一书之 8 – 030 段说:"Where the complainant's consent is procured by the defendant's conduct which is otherwise improper or unconscionable, the conduct does not cease to be unconscionable merely because the defendant had no intention to injure the complainant. …"

该段也举了 Banks v. The Cheltenham Co-operative Dairy Co Ltd(1911)29 NZLR 979 新西兰先例与 BCCI v. Aboody(1990)1 QB 923 先例作为依据。

4. 不当影响不像不合情理/显失公平交易(unconscionable transaction/dealing),不要求订立的合约是不平衡(imbalance)或一面倒倾向强势方的利益。虽然受不当影响订立合约的弱势方通常订立"不平等条约"时才会向法院申请衡平救济,但这只是作为显示弱势方自由意志受到影响以及强势方施加的影响"不当"的证据,而不是成立不当影响的要件之一。也因此虽然过去一度有争议,但 CIBC Mortgages plc v. Pitt(1994)1 AC 200 贵族院先例已经明确实际不当影响并不需要证明最后达成的交易是否对弱势方不利。这只是理论,毕竟基本不可能是合约对受到不当影响的弱势方有利。这可节录《Duress, Undue Influence and Unconscionable Dealing》(2019年,第3版)一书之8-039段:"... it is now accepted that it is **not a requirement for relief on the ground of actual undue influence that the transaction must be disadvantageous to the party influenced**. If the basis of the court's intervention in cases of undue influence was to allow the plaintiff to throw off a disadvantage which they have assumed because their freedom was impaired by the defendant's influence, then it would have made sense for there to be a disadvantage. But since ... the court intervenes simply because the defendant's unconscionable conduct prevented the claimant from bringing a free and independent mind to the transaction, there is no need to show disadvantage. **The object of the doctrine is to protect the complainant's freedom of choice from the defendant's misuse of his influence over the complainant. ...**"

不当影响作为衡平法或良心法院的考虑,显然对不合情理还要看很多其他因素,这是在每一个案件都会有差异。例如,A向B威胁将提起诉讼(或仲裁)解决双方的争议,这在法治社会完全是合法的言行,不涉及不当影响理论。虽然这种威胁即使在国际商业环境下也在很多情况下行得通或造成影响,令B让步,如订立和解协议。但这不会是不当影响,因为是保护弱势群体的理论,而B作为商业主体,无论是大公司还是小公司,都无论如何不会被视为弱势群体,衡平法是不会给予救济。

但换为A是侄子,B是年迈的姑母,A知道B在这个年龄会怕事与怕打官司,就以启动诉讼威胁B作出让步,订立合约,这就会是不当影响了[也会同时是经济胁迫(economic duress)]:见Daniel v. Drew(2005)EWCA Civ 507先例。

1.4.1.3 要件之三:因果关系

《Duress, Undue Influence and Unconscionable Dealing》(2019年,第3版)一书之8-033段说:"Where is has been established that the influence exercised by the defendant is undue, relief may nevertheless be refused if the undue influence did not cause the complainant to enter into the impugned transaction. It is generally accepted that for a transaction to be set aside on the ground of undue influence, it must be shown that it was brought about by the alleged undue influence. Since undue influence is a species of fraud, the analogy with fraud and duress suggests that for causation to be established, the undue influence need not be the principal reason for the complainant entering into the transaction; it need only be 'a reason'. ...."

曾经一度有BCCI v. Aboody(1990)1 QB 923先例认为应当采用"要不是"测试(but for test),即要不是存在不当影响,不会达成交易。换言之,如果可以证明无论是否有不当影响的存在,受影响一方都会出于其他原因达成交易,事后就不可以依赖不当影响的救济。Slade大法官说:"... it would not be appropriate for the court to exercise this jurisdiction in a case where the evidence establishes that on balance of probabilities the complainant would have entered into the transaction in any event."

但在更近期的先例中，将实际不当影响[12]类比为欺诈，可称为衡平欺诈（equitable fraud），不会轻易让实施了错误行为的骗子逃脱自己的责任。因此这类案件中的因果关系会非常宽松地有利于弱势方，只要在交易达成过程中涉及了不当影响，就会给予救济，不用额外考虑其他因素了。类似的做法已经在本书第十章之9.2段有介绍，即对人身胁迫只需要是原因之一就已经足够。这在本书第一章之1.3.6段介绍欺诈性误述时也说对于欺诈性误述存在受害方/被误述方有被诱导与依赖的事实推定（presumption），在此不再重复。在CIBC Mortgages plc v. Pitt（1994）1 AC 200先例中，Browne-Wilkinson勋爵说："Actual undue influence is a species of fraud. Like any other victim of fraud, a person who has been induced by undue influence to carry out a transaction which he did not freely and knowingly enter into is entitled to have that transaction set aside as of right."

跟从这样判法的可见UCB Corporate Services Ltd v. Williams（2002）EWCA Civ 555与Hewitt v. First Plus Financial Group Plc（2021）EWCA Civ 312等先例。在Hewitt v. First Plus Financial Group Plc先例中，Briggs大法官这样说："It has never been part of the proof of undue influence that, but for the relevant abuse of trust, the impugned transaction would not have been entered into. The right to set aside the transaction arises not because, on a but for causation analysis, it would otherwise have been avoided, but because of the equitable wrong constituted by the abuse of confidence was part of the process by which the victim's consent to it was obtained."

因此目前英国法的地位是，只要存在实际不当影响并且该影响确实与最后达成交易有关，就足以构成不当影响令交易可使无效。这样，对强势方而言要对此进行抗辩，就需要证明不当影响与弱势方达成交易是完全无关。而BCCI v. Aboody先例中针对因果关系采用"要不是"测试对实际不当影响太严格，不再适用。最后节录《Chitty on Contracts》（2021年，第34版）一书之10－099段说："In case of fraud, the fraud must have induced the contract; by analogy it would seem that actual undue influence must have contributed to the claimant's decision to enter the contract. ... Presumably it would follow also that the same presumption applies as in fraud, so that it will be for the stronger party to show that the undue influence had no impact at all on the complainant's decision."

1.4.2 推定不当影响的要件

1.4.2.1 以推定克服证明上的困难

已经在本章之1.4段介绍过在不少案件中当事人之间存在关系（如夫妻与子女、

---

[12] 这里只针对了实际不当影响，但在Royal Bank of Scotland Plc v. Etridge（No. 2）（2001）UKHL 44贵族院先例后应该说这两类不当影响只是证明方式有区别，因此可以说推定不当影响案件中，也应是类似地位。而且本段开头也已经提到推定不当影响案件中有推定不需要太关注因果关系问题。

律师与客户等），导致强势方可以通过不当影响而达成交易，但弱势方难以实际证明强势方采取了什么公然的影响。而大量的这类案件都因此不给予救济是说不通的，所以为了克服这些证据上的空缺，衡平法理论允许采用推定的方式对“影响”与“不当”区别予以证明。

可先节录《Duress, Undue Influence and Unconscionable Dealing》（2019 年，第 3 版）一书之 10 – 001 段如下：“**A pre-existing relationship** Unlike actual undue influence, presumed undue influence requires proof of pre-existing relationship between the parties. … the party who seeks to rely on the presumption of undue influence must prove not only that there was a pre-existing relationship between the parties, but also that the relationship was one where the alleged wrongdoer acquired influence over the complainant.”

还可节录 Royal Bank of Scotland Plc v. Etridge（No. 2）（2001）UKHL 44 贵族院先例中，Nicholls 勋爵说：“Proof that the complainant placed **trust and confidence** in the other party in relation to the management of the complainant's financial affairs, **coupled with a transaction which calls for explanation**, will normally be sufficient, failing satisfactory evidence to the contrary, to discharge the burden of proof. On proof of these two matters the stage is set for the court to infer that, **in the absence of a satisfactory explanation, the transaction can only have been procured by undue influence**. In other words, proof of **these two facts is prima facie evidence that the defendant abused the influence he acquired in the parties' relationship**. He preferred his own interests. He did not behave fairly to the other. So the evidential burden then shifts to him. It is for him to produce evidence to counter the inference which otherwise should be drawn.”（加黑部分是笔者的强调）

也就是双方之间有特殊关系，再结合交易“需要解释”才能说得通，就可以推定不当影响（presumed undue influence）。而实际上这里是两方面推定：

1. 首先是原告先提供证据证明一部分事实，根据这些事实可以推定存在特殊关系（special relationship）或称影响力关系（relationship of influence），如信任与信心关系（trust and confidence）等。在这关系下，会认为另一方必然对原告施加了影响（注意这里仅仅是影响，而非不当影响）。

当然需要额外指出的是，虽然常见说的是信任与信心关系，但不当影响原则会根据案件千变万化，也有先例中涉及占有优势谈判地位的一方滥用另一方的弱势地位等情况。因此《Chitty on Contracts》一书中也单独以“影响力关系”称呼。然而这些千变万化的案件的核心内容是一致的，即通过事实可以推定存在不当影响导致交易。可以节录 Royal Bank of Scotland Plc v. Etridge（No. 2）先例中，Nicholls 勋爵所说：

“The law has long recognised **the need to prevent abuse of influence in these 'relationship' cases despite the absence of evidence of overt acts of persuasive con-**

duct. The types of relationship, such as parent and child, in which this principle falls to be applied cannot be listed exhaustively. Relationships are infinitely various. Sir Guenter Treitel QC has rightly noted that **the question is whether one party has reposed sufficient trust and confidence in the other**, rather than whether the relationship between the parties belongs to a particular type: see Treitel, The Law of Contract, 10th ed(1999), pp 380 – 381. For example, the relation of banker and customer will not normally meet this criterion, but exceptionally it may: see National Westminster Bank Plc v Morgan[1985] AC 686, 707 – 709.

Even this test is not comprehensive. The principle is not confined to cases of abuse of trust and confidence. It also includes, for instance, cases where a vulnerable person has been exploited. Indeed, there is no single touchstone for determining whether the principle is applicable. Several expressions have been used in an endeavour to encapsulate the essence: trust and confidence, reliance, dependence or vulnerability on the one hand and ascendancy, domination or control on the other. None of these descriptions is perfect. None is all embracing. Each has its proper place. "(加黑部分是笔者的强调)

2. 但有影响也未必就有可使无效的后果,必须是"不当"。此时如果交易是合理与正常的人在一般动机之下(ordinary motives of ordinary persons)不会达成的,或者说是"需要解释"的,就可以推定影响"不当"。在此推定下,举证责任转移,应由交易对方(或施加影响的第三人)提供证据反证交易并没有受到不当影响,解释交易完全说得通。反证的证据就如原告曾经获取过第三人(如律师)的独立意见后才订立合约等。

1.4.2.2 两种推定不当影响

在什么情况下才能推定有影响力关系的存在,过去先例的判法中进一步区分了两类不同的情况。在 Barclays Bank Plc v. O' Brien(1994)1 AC 180 贵族院先例中, Browne-Wilkinson 勋爵说:

"… Presumed undue influence

In these cases the complainant only has to show, in the first instance, that there was a relationship of trust and confidence between the complainant and the wrongdoer of such a nature that it is fair to presume that the wrongdoer abused that relationship in procuring the complainant to enter into the impugned transaction. … therefore there is no need to produce evidence that actual undue influence was exerted in relation to the particular transaction impugned: once a confidential relationship has been proved, the burden then shifts to the wrongdoer to prove that the complainant entered into the impugned transaction freely, for example by showing that the complainant had independent advice. Such a confidential relationship can be established in two ways, viz.,

… (**A**) **Certain relationships**(for example solicitor and client, medical advisor and patient) **as a matter of law** raise the presumption that undue influence has been exercised.

...(**B**) Even if there is no relationship falling within ...(A), if the complainant **proves the de facto existence of a relationship** under which the complainant generally reposed trust and confidence in the wrongdoer, the existence of such relationship raises the presumption of undue influence. In ...(B) case therefore, in the absence of evidence disproving undue influence, the complainant-succeed in setting aside the impugned transaction merely by proof that the complainant reposed trust and confidence in the wrongdoer without having to prove that the wrongdoer exerted actual undue influence or otherwise abused such trust and confidence in relation to the particular transaction impugned."(加黑部分是笔者的强调)

另在《Duress, Undue Influence and Unconscionable Dealing》(2019年,第3版)一书之10-001段,说:"In the proof of a relationship of influence, the law draws a distinction between **two classes** of case. **The first comprises relationships where the existence of influence is presumed**. The claimant only needs to prove that a particular type of relationship existed between the parties (such as the relationship of parent and child) and the law presumes, irrebuttably,[13] that the relationship is one in which one party acquired influence over another. This class of relationship is commonly **referred to as class 2A relationships**. The **second class, class 2B relationships**, covers all relationships where no presumption of influence arises, so that **the existence of influence has to be proved**. ..."

简单而言,上述内容中提到的A类别,是只要属于法律承认(通常是有先例确立)的特定类别,如原本有诚信/信义关系[14]的情况或父母与未成年子女关系,就属于有推定影响力的关系。也就是弱势方需要证明的只是双方之间属于此类关系,如父女之间的关系。而B类别则是要根据具体的案件事实推定存在影响力关系,也就是弱势方需要通过个别不同案情的证据证明自己对强势方有信任与信心或被强势方支配等,例如老人与私人护工之间的关系。

但进行这样详细区分的做法在Royal Bank of Scotland Plc v. Etridge (No. 2) (2001) UKHL 44先例中也有批评,认为这反而带来不肯定、不稳定。例如Clyde勋爵说:"There is also room for uncertainty whether the presumption is of the existence of an influence or of its quality as being undue. I would also dispute the utility of the further sophistication of subdividing 'presumed undue influence' into further categories. All these classifications to my mind add mystery rather than illumination."

在中国香港特区的Lo Sau Ying v. Bank of China (HK) Ltd (2005) 1 HKLRD 106

[13] 但今天不认为这是不可反驳的推定,这方面可见本章之1.4.2.2.1段的介绍。

[14] 见本书第一章之2.7段的详细介绍。

先例中,Scott 勋爵也说:"I do not wish to leave this issue without expressing the hope that in future cases, where undue influence has to be proved but where the relationship between the parties is not a relationship that falls within … Class 2A category, the parties will concentrate on whether the evidence justifies the inference that, on a balance of probabilities, the impugned transaction was procured by undue influence, that is to say, by an abuse by the allegedly dominant party of the trust and confidence reposed in him by the allegedly subservient party. References in such cases to, and attempts to invoke the assistance of, an alleged evidential presumption of undue influence are, in my opinion, likely to be, as they have been in this case, a source of confusion and an impediment to the evaluation of the available evidence."

可以想得到在今天人与人之间的复杂关系,已经不像早年一样可以"一刀切"。具体的情况千变万化,如同样是父母与子女,子女未成年属于 A 类别可以推定有影响。但其实父母与子女根本从来不住在一起,或是继子女关系非常冷淡。或者是子女已经成年,此时按理会属于 B 类别,但如果子女刚成年、经济与父母无法脱离,也仍然可能属于 A 类别。再例如如果事实上该成年子女痴呆,要求子女进行举证是多少有点强求了。另一方面则是没有什么明确区分 A 类别与 B 类别的理由,如未婚妻与未婚夫之间可以法律推定,但是在夫妻之间又明确不能法律推定;又如父母与未成年子女之间可以法律推定,但是与祖父母之间看来又没有明确的案件支持可以法律推定。这看来也是今天有不少对这种区分的批评的重要原因。

而且无论是 A 类别还是 B 类别,都要先证明双方关系,只不过是 B 类别需要额外证明一些其他事实显示弱势方对强势方的信任与信心。但在实际案件中,双方显然针对的问题在于是否存在影响力关系,也无论是 A 类别还是 B 类别,强势方都会举证显示双方之间关系不够紧密甚至是并没有什么关系用以反驳推定,而弱势方会举证显示自己在关系中的弱势与被支配状况。这导致在最后开庭审理时,双方提供的证据是不会由于属于不同类别而有太大差异。也就是按现在的说法,在举证责任上 A 类别与 B 类别确实存在区别,但实际上由于双方都会举证,最后实际提供的证据未必有什么不同。[15]

另一个问题则是由于 A 类别中的特定类别通常需要信任与信心,导致与需要信任与信心的诚信/信义关系混淆在一起,也确实在大量这类别案件中都可以构成诚信关系。但是 A 类别的设立是为了证据上的目的,是用来克服弱势方证明不当影响的困难,相比之下诚信关系针对的是实体法,在意义与范畴也要广泛得多,违反诚信关系、滥用信任(abuse of confidence)的做法上也与不当影响不尽相同。[16]

这可节录《Duress, Undue Influence and Unconscionable Dealing》(2019 年,第 3

〔15〕 这方面可见在《证据法:基础理论、口头证据与专家证据》一书第七章之 3.4 段也有介绍。

〔16〕 滥用信任可见本章稍后之 1.5 段的介绍。

版)一书之 10-001 段:"Some commentators place the doctrine of presumed undue influence within a wider framework of fiduciary obligations. According to this view, where a relationship of trust and confidence exists between the parties it gives rise to fiduciary duties on the part of the party in whom trust and confidence is reposed to prefer the other party's interest over his own. This conflates presumed undue confidence with the doctrine of abuse of confidence … It is different from the jurisprudential basis of presumed undue influence in English law. Its conceptual basis is evidential, as the presumption is raised to bridge an evidential gap. The objective is to assist the complainant in the process of proving undue influence, by shifting the burden of proof; it is not to establish a breach of fiduciary duty. Therefore, to raise the presumption, what must be proved is that there was a relationship of influence, not merely a relationship of trust and confidence. …"

从以上所讲,笔者相信将来无须再去斟酌到底是 A 或 B 类别的关系。只需要在每一个案件的不同案情考虑是否显示了弱势方确实对强势方(无论是什么关系类别)有信心与信任或受到支配等,并会受到不当影响订立合约,就可作出推断了。因此在《Chitty on Contracts》(2021 年,第 34 版)一书之 10-106 段就提出按照这样的趋势(主要是最高院的大法官如 Clyde 勋爵与 Scott 勋爵的评论),将来可能也不再详细区分如继续扩张 A 类别,总之就是看案件中双方当事人之间是否有信任与信心,或一方支配另一方等。A 类别顶多是可以跟从过往先例中,认为原告与被告存在这样的关系的可反驳推定。可以节录该书之 8-082 段所说如下:"These statements might be taken as hints that in future the courts will abandon altogether the separate category of 'presumed influence' and simply ask in each case whether the relationship was one of trust and confidence or of domination, or at least treat the fact that a case falls within … A as raising no more than a rebuttable presumption that there was a relationship of trust and confidence between the parties."

1.4.2.2.1 A 类别的法律推定

已经在上一段提到现在的趋势是无须再区分到底是 A 类别还是 B 类别的案件,但为了完整仍在本段介绍什么特殊关系属于 A 类别。A 类别主要是当事人之间有一些特定类别关系时。这些关系例如父母与未成年子女[17]、监护人与被监护人[18]、信

---

〔17〕 见 Wright v. Vanderplank(1855)2 K&J 1 先例。而且在子女与父母的交易中,如果是子女刚刚成年,看来也有一样的推定:见 Pauling's Settlement Trusts, Re(1964)Ch 303 等先例。

〔18〕 见 Hylton v. Hylton(1754)2 Ves Sen 547;Taylor v. Johnston(1882)19 Ch. D. 603 等先例。关键在于监护人是否仍然控制被监护人的财产或行为:见 Hatch v. Hatch(1804)9 Ves 292 先例。《Chitty on Contracts》(2021 年,第 34 版)一书之 10-110 段还介绍了多种此类关系的情况,如代行父母义务者(in loco parentis)与子女之间:见 Archer v. Hudson(1844)7 Beav 551 先例;继母与继女:见 Powell v. Powell(1900)1 Ch 243 先例;甚至是遗嘱执行人与受益人之间:见 Grosvenor v. Sherratt(1860)28 Beav 659 先例等。

托受托人与受益人[19]、律师与客户[20]、医生与病人[21]等,还如较近期的Hackett v. Crown Prosecution Service(2011)EWHC 1170(Admin)先例提到一方签署了给另一方的授权委托书。在这些有信义/诚信关系的人士之间,就推定未成年子女、被监护人、受益人、客户、病人,在达成交易时,受到了父母、监护人、信托受托人、律师、医生的影响。这类情况被认为是法律推定(legal presumption),或者也有说法叫作"不可反驳的推定不当影响"(irrebuttable presumed undue influence)。

在Royal Bank of Scotland Plc v. Etridge(No.2)(2001)UKHL 44贵族院先例中,Nicholls勋爵说:"The law has adopted a sternly protective attitude towards certain types of relationship in which one party acquires influence over another who is vulnerable and dependent and where, moreover, substantial gifts by the influenced or vulnerable person are not normally to be expected. Examples of relationships within this special class are parent and child, guardian and ward, trustee and beneficiary, solicitor and client, and medical adviser and patient. In these cases **the law presumes, irrebuttably, that one party had influence over the other.** The complainant need not prove he actually reposed trust and confidence in the other party. It is sufficient for him to prove the existence of the type of relationship."(加黑部分是笔者的强调)

针对Nicholls勋爵以上的说法,值得一提以下两点:

1. 这类案件中,是法律推定影响力关系,在此关系下认为一方会对另一方有影响。但有影响未必属于不当影响,仍然需要证明存在"不当",但弱势方没有再额外证明影响力关系的举证责任。

2. 虽然Nicholls勋爵提到这里的推定是不可反驳(irrebuttable)的,在《Goff & Jones:The Law of Unjust Enrichment》(2022年,第10版)一书之11-48段不同意这样的说法:"Although Lord Nicholls said that an 'irrebuttable' presumption is raised in respect of the special categories of relationship, we share Sir Kim Lewison's extra-judicial view[22] that this is unnecessary and unprincipled, and that a rebuttable presumption would be preferable."

这也能够理解,毕竟不可反驳的法律推定在法律中只是极少数的情况,往往发生在即使有证据也只会与推定的结果一致,或者是有很强的公共政策不允许推翻推定的事实的情况,但这里推定影响力关系的情况显然不符合。例如,律师与客户之间进行交易,固然可以推定律师对客户有影响,但如果可以提供证据显示客户本就是该类

---

[19] 见Elis v. Barker(1871)LR 7 Ch. App. 104;Benningfield v. Baxter(1866)12 App Cas 167等先例。

[20] 律师与客户之间有信义/诚信关系。有说法是律师与客户之间的交易需要善意:见Moody v. Cox and Hatt(1917)2 Ch 71等先例。

[21] 见Mitchell v. Homfray(1881)8 QBD 587;Radcliffe v. Price(1902)18 TLR 466等先例。

[22] 这是指Lewison大法官的"Under the Influence"(2011)RLR 1一文。

交易中身经百战的商人,也受过法律训练,显然在这段关系中谁影响谁还不好说,没理由就不允许认定事实真相。也因此笔者也同意《Goff & Jones: The Law of Unjust Enrichment》一书与 Lewison 大法官的观点,即使涉及这些特定类别,也只是可反驳的法律推定存在影响力关系。毕竟任何看起来是"真理"的事情事后都可能会推翻,而且也往往存在例外。

有一些关系,则在过往先例中明确判不属于可以法律推定的特定类别,这些关系包括:(1)夫妻之间:见 Bank of Montreal v. Stuart(1911)AC 120;Barclays Bank Plc v. O'Brien(1994)1 AC 180;Royal Bank of Scotland Plc v. Etridge(No. 2)等先例。但有说法是未婚妻依赖未婚夫的关系可以属于特定类别。[23] (2)兄弟姐妹之间:见 Pesticcio v. Huet(2004)EWCA Civ 372 先例。(3)父母与已经脱离父母的成年子女之间:见 Leeder v. Stevens(2005)EWCA Civ 50 等先例。

1.4.2.2.2　B 类别的事实推定

在可以推定影响力的关系中,从 A 类别逐渐扩展到根据事实而千变万化的 B 类别。例如在 Tufton v. Sperni(1952)2 TLR 516 先例中,Raymond Evershed 大法官就指出推定影响力关系不会限于特定类别说:"... refute the suggestion that, to create the relationship of confidence, the person owing the duty must be found clothed in the recognisable garb of a guardian, trustee, solicitor, priest, doctor, manager, or the like."

正因为需要根据具体的案件事实做判断,所以会导致千变万化的情况。在过往先例中,也有不少法官纷纷表示过不愿意将这类衡平救济适用的案情定义得太受限制。例如 Lloyds Bank Ltd v. Bundy(1975)QB 326 上诉庭先例中,Eric Sachs 大法官说:"Everything depends on the particular facts, and such a relationship has been held to exist in unusual circumstances as between purchaser and vendor, as between great uncle and adult nephew, and in other widely differing sets of circumstances. Moreover, it is neither feasible nor desirable to attempt closely to define the relationship, or its characteristics, or the demarcation line showing the exact transition point where a relationship that does not entail that duty passes into one that does."

这也显示出 B 类别应用的情况是非常多的。例如,叔侄之间的关系不属于 A 类别,但是叔叔年老后常年由侄子照顾,最后将大量财产赠与或遗赠给侄子,一毛钱都不留给亲生子女,也因此子女要依赖不当影响申请撤销赠与、遗赠。即使是在商业关系中理论上也可以适用,如即使是买卖合约中一般要求买方自己小心(caveat emp-

---

[23] 见 Lloyd Bank Ltd, Re(1931)1 Ch 289 先例。Maugham 大法官说:"(未婚妻)A young woman engaged to be married is in a very different position. In most cases she does not interest herself in her future pecuniary position as between herself and her husband. In general, she reposes the greatest confidence in her future husband; otherwise she would not marry him. In many, if not most, cases she would sign almost anything he put before her."

tor,"let the buyer beware"),但是如果是长期有合作关系,且实际上是买方处在弱势就可能适用。例如,买方知识水平低下,双方也都知道实际上不懂的买方长期以来依赖卖方(如依赖卖方的稳定供货、对货物进行挑选),买方也由于信任与依赖卖方而一贯接受卖方的所有货物并作出支付,而且此争议交易中买方也是根本没有考虑就接受了卖方出售的远远偏离正常市场价格的货物。此时理论上是有可能成功显示双方之间有影响力关系、能推定卖方施加了影响的。

尽管如此,可以看到在过往先例中,往往涉及用以下两大类事实证明双方之间的影响力关系:

1. 双方之间有一定的关系,根据证据显示在关系下弱势方对强势方有信任与信心,或在关系中强势方占支配地位。这说法可见 Tate v. Williamson(1866)LR 2 Ch. App. 55 先例中,Chelmsford 勋爵所说:"Wherever two persons stand in such a relation that, while it continues, confidence is necessarily reposed by one, and the influence which naturally grows out of that confidence is possessed by the other, and this confidence is abused, or the influence is exerted to obtain an advantage at the expense of the confiding party, the person so availing himself of his position will not be permitted to retain the advantage, although the transaction could not have been impeached if no such confidential relation had existed."

例如,在 Turkey v. Awadh(2005)EWCA Civ 382 先例中,当事人分别是住在英国的父亲,以及住在沙特、几乎不会英文的女儿与女婿,所有事情都依赖父亲。再加上过去当事人之间有一系列交易的历史,法院就认定存在影响力关系。但此先例最终判最后交易完全说得通,因此虽然有影响,但并非不当,不当影响并未真正成立。

但在社会与商业关系中大家都只各自考虑自己的利益,所以一般也不会推断影响力关系。银行与客户的关系就是特别明显的,银行与公司之间往往双方对等、在商场上各自盘算,不会存在什么信任与信心、被支配的情况。但银行与自然人之间,就会有时因自然人是弱势方、对银行有信任与信心的情况,需要保护自然人了。因此在 Lloyds Bank Ltd v. Bundy 上诉庭先例中就通过证据显示,是种地的农民长期为开公司的儿子提供担保,与银行经理有了长期关系,依赖熟悉的银行经理的建议,此时银行经理也应该向父亲解释主债务人(儿子公司)的情况,或者是让父亲寻求独立意见,这样导致产生推定属于有影响力的关系,有关交易被撤销。

但在 National Westminster Bank Plc v. Morgan(1985)AC 686 贵族院先例中,夫妻按揭购房后无力还贷,丈夫找到一家愿意提供融资的银行,银行经理与妻子讨论后由妻子在借贷合约上签字,事后妻子主张不当影响,法院认定未能提供证据证明妻子与银行的关系有什么超出一般正常商业往来中的银行与客户关系,仅仅有关系并不导致出现能推定不当影响的影响力关系。

2. 根据特定交易的内容进行推定。有时候虽然双方原本之间没有历史上交易推断出有影响力关系,但在一个看起来是临时、一次性的交易中,交易本身非常离奇与不寻常,也因此可以推定有影响力关系。对此可以介绍一个表面上是商业交易的 Macklin v. Dowsett(2004)EWCA Civ 904 上诉庭先例。

此先例中 D 先生穷困潦倒,住在大篷车中,也没什么经济来源,[24]但拥有一块土地。这块土地上特别有价值的是政府批准允许建造房屋,但必须在特定期限前开工。D 先生显然无力开工,因此将土地产权出售给 M 先生,只保留 0 租金的终身租赁权/保有权[25](life tenancy)。有了这笔资金,D 先生偿还了自己以前的大量债务,并且初步打下地基保护了建造许可。但问题是在 M 先生与 D 先生之间还有期权协议,约定如果 D 先生无法在 3 年内完成建造,M 先生就可以行权以 5000 英镑买断终身租赁权。这协议的意义就显然是 M 先生在剥削 D 先生了,毕竟 D 先生根本无力继续建造房屋,而这终身租赁权的价值远远不止 5000 英镑。

一审法官认定双方之间不存在影响力关系,理由很多,包括 D 先生也不是傻瓜,看清了合约条文仍然愿意签订协议。还包括一个重要理由是在土地转让协议后 D 先生与 M 先生之间实际上是土地产权人与承租人的关系,在他们之间的利益根本是冲突的,谈不上影响力关系:"... be extremely difficult to imagine any case in which the necessary relationship of trust and confidence, or of ascendancy and dependency, could arise against that background."

但是这说法在上诉庭被改判,认为从交易内容上来看,D 先生当时迫切需要 M 先生的经济支持至少先打下地基。而打下地基也不仅仅是 D 先生获益,打定主意侵吞土地的 M 先生才是真正最后获益的人。而期权协议下处于弱势地位的 D 先生显然不可能建造房屋,实际上是同意以仅仅 5000 英镑就转让终身保有权。综合考虑事实之下认为可以至少表面推定有影响力关系的存在。

而这看来也意味着,关注交易内容有两方面用途:(1)显示交易中弱势方处在被支配地位;(2)接下来会介绍的最后达成的交易"需要解释"。

从此先例也能看得出,由于根据事实推定,因此特别依赖个别案件的案情,也依赖具体审理法官的裁量与想法。

也因此不在这里过多介绍,只简单列举部分近期先例中判出现过影响力关系的情况:(1)流行歌手与经纪人:见 O' Sullivan v. Management Agency and Music Ltd (1985)QB 428 先例;[26](2)农场经理人与农场主:见 Credit Lyonnais Bank Nederland NV v. Burch(1997)1 All ER 144 先例;(3)成年母子:见 Abbey National Plc v. Stringer (2006)EWCA Civ 338 先例;(4)侄孙与叔祖:见 Goodchild v. Bradbury(2006)EWCA

---

〔24〕 因此也有说法是,这种情况更适合采用本章之 2 段的不合情理/显失公平原则。

〔25〕 简单而言,是一方在有生之年仍然像承租人一样拥有土地的使用权(但会根据合约而有限制,例如可以限制原告不得转让给他人等),该权利期限就是直到该方去世。一旦去世,使用权会转回给土地所有权人。

〔26〕 在本书第三章之 5.2.2 段有详细介绍。

Civ 1868 先例;(5)护工与被照顾的雇主:见 Murphy v. Rayner(2011)EWHC 1(Ch)先例等。

1.4.2.3 合理与正常人的一般动机和需要解释

已经介绍过,能够证明有影响力关系并不够,还需要进一步显示影响的“不当”。毕竟就算是有影响力的关系,也不能简单“一刀切”将所有交易都认为受不当影响,否则父母与子女、律师与客户之间的任何交易与合约全都留下“后患”,都被推定为“不当”影响可使无效,这也是难以接受的。所以,在 A 类别或被弱势方证明是 B 类别的有影响力关系,仍需要多走一步,也就是弱势方要证明其他合理与正常人一般动机(ordinary motives of ordinary persons)下不会订立这种合约,或者说是“需要解释”。在 Royal Bank of Scotland Plc v. Etridge(No. 2)(2001)UKHL 44 贵族院先例中,Nicholls 勋爵说:“... It would be absurd for the law to presume that every gift by a child to a parent, or every transaction between a client and his solicitor or between a patient and his doctor, was brought about by undue influence unless the contrary is affirmatively proved. Such a presumption would be too far-reaching.”

接下来就是第二步推定,即推定存在“不当”,这就转移了举证责任,由强势方证明不存在什么“不当”。在 Royal Bank of Scotland Plc v. Etridge(No. 2)贵族院先例中,Nicholls 勋爵说:“The evidence required to discharge the burden of proof depends on the nature of the alleged undue influence, the personality of the parties, their relationship, the extent to which the transaction **cannot readily be accounted for by the ordinary motives of ordinary persons in that relationship**, and all the circumstances of the case.”(加黑部分是笔者的强调)

曾经一度有一些先例提到“不当”需要达到交易明显不利(manifest disadvantage)的程度:见 National Westminster Bank Plc v. Morgan(1985)AC 686 贵族院先例。在该先例中,法院认定有关借贷交易本身看来公平合理,不存在明显不利,就拒绝了推定不当影响。

法院认定明显不利时会考虑的因素就包括价值不菲的赠与,或者是明显偏离市场价格的销售等。但仅是这样的标准也会有问题,如赠与可能发生在关系紧密的人士之间,如夫妻结婚纪念日,一方赠与另一方一颗昂贵的宝石,表面看来也是明显不利的,但是否可以推定不当影响呢?

因此在 CIBC Mortgages plc v. Pitt(1994)1 AC 200 贵族院先例中,就判交易对原告不利并非不当影响的必须要素。在 Royal Bank of Scotland Plc v. Etridge(No. 2)贵族院先例中也明确指出 CIBC Mortgages plc v. Pitt 判法背后的大原则是正确的,但更倾向于 Lindsay 大法官在 Allcard v. Skinner(1887)36 Ch. D. 145 先例中的说法:“But if the gift is so large as not to be reasonably accounted for on the ground of friendship, relationship, charity, or other ordinary motives on which ordinary men act, the burden is upon the donee to support the gift.”

法院有必要配合现实,也就是应当根据具体的事实来判断是否是根据双方关系一般会达成的交易。这是要根据不同的案情,例如双方本来就是非常亲密的朋友关系,在朋友婚礼上送一大笔"份子钱"很正常。或者是本就是虔诚的教徒,许愿事后用一大笔钱"还愿",也是正常情理之中的情况。但如果是如同 Allcard v. Skinner 先例中一样将自己身家性命全部都交给教会,就不是合理与正常的人会有的一般行动了。

以上所讲可以节录 Royal Bank of Scotland Plc v. Etridge(No. 2)贵族院先例,Nicholls 勋爵解释这背后的原理时说:"The law would out of touch with everyday life if the presumption were to apply to every Christmas or birthday gift by a child to a parent, or to an agreement whereby a client or patient agrees to be responsible for the reasonable fees of his legal or medical adviser. The law would be rightly open to ridicule, for transactions such as these are unexceptionable. They do not suggest that something may be amiss. **So something more is needed before the law reverses the burden of proof, something which calls for an explanation.** When that something more is present, the greater the disadvantage to the vulnerable person, the more cogent must be the explanation before the presumption will be regarded as rebutted."(加黑部分是笔者的强调)

因此如果根据双方关系,至少表面看来是正常交易,就不太容易推断"不当":见涉及家族争产的 Turkey v. Awadh(2005)EWCA Civ 382 先例。女儿女婿常住迪拜,在伦敦通过按揭购置一处房产后,出租给父亲居住。后来父亲与女儿女婿签订契约,约定由父亲帮助女儿女婿偿还包括房屋按揭在内的债务,而女儿女婿则转让该房产的长期使用权给父亲。在父亲还债后,女儿女婿拒绝履行契约转让使用权。法院通过事实推定存在信任与信心关系,但是有关交易的内容根据双方的关系表面来看完全解释得通,正常的父亲与女儿女婿之间(其他合理与正常人的一般动机)也会有同样的交易,也就拒绝推定存在不当影响,无须父亲反驳自己没有不当、交易没有受影响。

至于根据关系来判断要考虑的因素,需要综合考虑多方面事实,会包括双方之间关系的性质、关系的历史、具体交易的金额、交易对当事人的影响等。BCCI v. Aboody(1990)1 QB 923 先例针对的是担保,上诉庭关注了担保人/保证人实际面临的风险,与保证人提供担保所能获得的利益:"... must depend on two factors, namely (a) the seriousness of the risk of enforcement to the giver, in practical terms, and (b) the benefits gained by the giver in accepting the risk."

还可节录较近期的 Pesticcio v. Huet(2004)EWCA Civ 372 先例,Mummery 大法官说:"The court scrutinises the circumstances in which the transaction, under which benefits were conferred on the recipient, took place and the nature of the continuing relationship between the parties, rather than any specific act or conduct on the part of the recipient."

回到本章之1.4段提到的英国作为普通家庭主妇的妻子为丈夫贷款提供担保(surety wives)的例子,今天看来 Royal Bank of Scotland Plc v. Etridge(No. 2)贵族院先例中 Nicholls 勋爵的看法是如果是正常夫妻关系,双方经济利益绑定密切,或者一方是家里主要收入来源,如果丈夫融不到资妻子也活不下去,看来即使妻子同意交易将房产或其他利益抵押贷款,并不太会推定不当影响。

1.4.2.4 反驳推定的证据

对不当影响的推定,都只是可反驳的推定,因此对方可以提出证据反驳。在 Royal Bank of Scotland Plc v. Etridge(No. 2)(2001)UKHL 44 贵族院先例中,Nicholls 勋爵说:"The onus shifts to the defendant. Unless the defendant introduces evidence to counteract the inference of undue influence that the complainant's evidence justifies, the complainant will succeed."

至于用证据反驳推定的目标,就是弱势方其实没有受到不当影响。例如既然已经建议第三方律师向弱势方解释交易的性质与内容,弱势方根本是在完整、自由与知情的考虑后做出的独立自主的决定,可以说未必存在什么真正影响,也谈不上有什么不当之处了。在 Inche Noriah v. Shaik Allie Bin Omar(1929)AC 127 枢密院先例中,Hailsham 勋爵说:"It is necessary for the donee to prove that the gift was the result of the free exercise of independent will. The most obvious way to prove this is by establishing that the gift was made **after the nature and effect of the transaction had been fully explained** to the donor by some independent and qualified person so completely as to **satisfy the Court that the donor was acting independently of any influence from the donee and with the full appreciation of what he was doing**; and in cases where there are no other circumstances this may be **the only means by which the donee can rebut the presumption.**"(加黑部分是笔者的强调)

在 Zamet v. Hyman(1961)1 WLR 1442 先例中,Evershed 勋爵说:"... the onus is cast upon those who support the document of establishing affirmatively that the woman (作为弱势方的妻子为丈夫的贷款提供担保)executed this document not merely understanding its effect but as a result of **full, free and informed thought** about it."(加黑部分是笔者的强调)

在 Smith v. Cooper(2010)EWCA Civ 722 先例中,Lloyd 大法官说:"If that is shown ..., the presumption of undue influence applies, that is to say, the court will presume that the transaction was procured by undue influence exercised by one party over the other, in other words by the abuse by the one of the position of influence that he has over the other. In such a case it is then up to the one party to prove that the transaction was not procured by an abuse of his position of influence but was rather the free exercise of the will of the other party as a result of full, free and informed thought. Lord Nicholls' phrase 'in the absence of satisfactory explanation' ... refers to the dominant party satisfying this burden of showing that the transaction was not procured by undue influence."

而具体到需要哪些证据，就要依赖案件事实而定与会有不同的证明方式，重点是显示弱势方对事情进行了深思熟虑，或"完整、自由与知情的考虑"。不当影响案件会是与本书第十章之3段介绍的胁迫情况一样，弱势方会是知道自己签的是什么只不过两害相权取其轻，也会是并不知道自己签字意味着什么，特别当涉及一大笔资产的处理时。也因此如果通过证据显示弱势方实际上根本是在知情的情况下，进行过自由的深思熟虑仍是决定"明知山有虎，偏向虎山行"，可以用来反驳不当影响的推定。

而其中最常见的证明方式就是弱势方在交易前从第三人处获取了称职(competent)与独立(independent)意见。这第三人通常就是律师，但也可以是其他适当的专业人士，如会计师、测量师等。这特别是在妻子(弱势方)为丈夫提供担保的情况下，银行往往有更多的责任采取行动，以防止丈夫误述或对妻子有不当影响，一个惯常做法就是建议担保人妻子在签署担保合约前，先自己委任律师取得独立法律意见与解释担保合约的本质与后果。[27] 在 Royal Bank of Scotland Plc v. Etridge(No. 2)贵族院先例中，Nicholls 勋爵说："Proof that the complainant received advice from a third party before entering into the impugned transaction is one of the matters a court takes into account when weighing all the evidence. The weight, or importance, to be attached to such advice depends on all the circumstances. In the normal course, advice from a solicitor or other outside adviser can be expected to bring home to a complainant a proper understanding of what he or she is about to do. But a person may understand fully the implications of a proposed transaction, for instance, a substantial gift, and yet still be acting under the undue influence of another. Proof of outside advice does not, of itself, necessarily show that the subsequent completion of the transaction was free from the exercise of undue influence. Whether it will be proper to infer that outside advice had an emancipating effect, so that the transaction was not brought about by the exercise of undue influence, is a question of fact to be decided having regard to all the evidence in the case."

该意见首先应是独立意见，律师如果提供意见给双方(通常就是银行委任的律师)，反驳推定的证据重量就会很低。因为一位律师如果同时为双方服务，即使不考虑利益冲突，也很可能被认为不独立：见 Smith v. Cooper 上诉庭先例。在 Royal Bank of Scotland Plc v. Etridge(No. 2)贵族院先例中，Hobhouse 勋爵甚至提到说，如果律师是在妻子与要求签字的银行经理会面时在场，而不是与妻子单独会面，都会导致对反驳推定的证据重量不够。

其次也很容易理解的是，意见必须是衡量了综合的情况后，称职与诚实地给出的深思熟虑的意见(considered opinion)。例如，为了什么债务给担保，担保是否有上

---

〔27〕 这在本书第五章之6.3.3.2段也有介绍。

限，担保的风险与后果如何，是否可能导致什么严重情况如无家可归等。因此如果律师给出的意见并未考虑完整的事实，或者是该意见本身有疏漏，反驳的重量也很低。可以节录在 Inche Noriah v. Shaik Allie Bin Omar 枢密院先例中，Hailsham 勋爵说：“... it must be given with a knowledge of all relevant circumstances and must be such as a competent and honest adviser would give if acting solely in the interests of the donor.”

对于强势方而言，也不需要证明弱势方确实考虑了独立与称职的意见。毕竟，是否完成交易是弱势方自己的决定，律师只不过是提供建议。在 Royal Bank of Scotland Plc v. Etridge (No. 2) 先例中，Nicholls 勋爵说：“Thus, in the present type of case it is not for the solicitor to veto the transaction by declining to confirm to the bank that he has explained the documents to the wife and the risks she is taking upon herself. If the solicitor considers the transaction is not in the wife's best interests, he will give reasoned advice to the wife to that effect. But **at the end of the day the decision on whether to proceed is the decision of the client, not the solicitor**. A wife is not to be precluded from entering into a financially unwise transaction if, for her own reasons, she wishes to do so. That is the general rule. There may, of course, be exceptional circumstances where it is glaringly obvious that the wife is being grievously wronged. In such a case the solicitor should decline to act further.”（加黑部分是笔者的强调）

一般情况下一方即使没有获取独立法律意见，也并不代表什么，不强制要求一方建议另一方寻求独立意见：见 R v. Attorney General for England and Wales (2003) UKPC 22 先例与 Wollenberg v. Casinos Austria International Holding GmbH (2011) EWHC 103 (Ch) 先例等。在 R v. Attorney General for England and Wales 先例中，Hoffmann 勋爵说：“The absence of independent legal advice may or may not be a relevant matter according to the circumstances. It is not necessarily an unfair exploitation of a relationship for one party to enter into a transaction with the other without ensuring that he has obtained independent legal advice. On the other hand, the transaction may be such as to give rise to an inference of undue influence even if the induced party was advised by an independent lawyer and understood the legal implications of what he was doing.”

这也很容易理解，即使是妻子为丈夫提供担保，也会根据事实如当事人的具体情况而千变万化。例如，妻子自己就是退休法官，为丈夫提供担保看来没什么理由需要获取独立法律意见。又如，妻子的精神状况根本不理解律师在说什么，哪怕寻求了独立意见也不会有什么用。当然最后到了案件开庭审理时，是可以根据当事人的出庭作证表现澄清到底是否会需要律师意见以及律师意见是否真的有用等问题。毕竟在高水平的交叉盘问下弱势方的水平高低、是否真正是“弱势”，很容易被察觉。

1.5　诚信/信义关系以及滥用信任理论

与不当影响常常被认为是很近似的，还有另一个理论：滥用信任。这涉及的是在诚信/信义关系（fiduciary relationship）时，就会认为委托人 A 给予受信人（fiduciary）

B 以“信任与信心”(trust and confidence)。诚信/信义关系已经在本书第一章之 2.7 段有介绍,简单而言主要有两类:

1. 一类是已经通过过往先例的判法明确属于诚信关系的情况,如:律师与客户之间:见 Hilton v. Booth & Eastwood(2005) UKHL 8 先例等;信托关系的受托人与受益人之间:见 Dougan v. Macpherson(1902) AC 197 先例等;在委托人与代理人之间:见 Kelly v. Cooper(1993) AC 205 先例等。

2. 另一类则是根据具体的案件事实可以认定确实存在诚信关系:见 Kyrris v. Oldham(2003) EWCA Civ 1506 先例等。

诚信关系实际上是不平等的关系,在此关系中 A 由于托付了自己的信任与信心,因此在面对 B 时非常弱势与易受伤害(vulnerable)。例如,B 会知道很多 A 的机密信息,A 对 B 会是没有防备心理,凡事都交给 B 处理。在他们之间进行交易时,A 对 B 会没有对陌生第三人一样的戒心。甚至也不仅仅是善意这么简单,在诚信关系中 A 会完全相信 B 在行事时以 A 的利益为先。这导致 B 很容易可以占 A 的便宜。

因此衡平法为了保护诚信关系中弱势与易受伤害的 A,发展出滥用信任理论(abuse of confidence),给 B 以更沉重的义务。B 必须对 A 的利益“无保留、全心全意与专一的效忠”(undivided, exclusive and single-minded loyalty),必须优先考虑 A 而不是自己的利益。例如与 A 签订合约,就要采取合理措施降低由于诚信关系带来的 A 的弱势,让 A 好像是与陌生第三人交易一样看待此次交易。而且事后如果 A 主张自己与 B 之间的交易不妥,必须由 B 给出足够证据证明自己已经履行了恰当的义务,其实已经考虑了 A 的利益、以 A 的利益为先。

这些义务会根据具体事实千变万化,本章也不主要针对这些内容。[28] 可以只简单节录《Duress, Undue Influence and Unconscionable Dealing》(2019 年,第 3 版)一书之 14-019 段介绍的一些义务/责任,例如,B 必须显示已经终止了诚信关系或告知了 A 自己在交易中会获利并获得 A 的真正同意;向 A 全面披露关于交易的所有重要事实;虽然交易相对方是 B 自己,但 B 没有优先考虑自己的利益,尽职勤勉地为 A 拿到了最优的待遇;最终交易内容公平等。可以节录该段内容如下:“This requires the fiduciary to show that: (i) they terminated the fiduciary relationship or informed their principal of their interest in the transaction and obtained the principal's consent; (ii) they made a full disclosure of all other material facts; (iii) they exercised all due diligence to get the best deal for the principal against themselves; and (iv) the transaction itself was a fair one.”

如果 B 能够证明自己确实履行了应尽义务,采取了恰当措施,最后达成的交易法院会予以执行:见 Wollenberg v. Casinos Austria International Holding GmbH(2011) EWHC 103(Ch)先例。但是如果 B 未能有足够证据证明已经履行了义务,就会认定

---

[28] 有部分内容,如需要披露重要事实等问题,也在本书第五章之 7 段提到。

交易涉及衡平过错,这样合约效力就有问题了。早在古老的 Gibson v. Jeyes(1801)6 Ves Jr 266 先例中,Eldon 勋爵说:"I answer, in that great rule of the Court, that he, who bargains in matter of advantage with a person placing confidence in him is bound to shew, that a reasonable use has been made of that confidence; a rule applying to trustees, attorneys, or any one else."

在 CIBC Mortgages Plc v. Pitt(1994)1 AC 200 先例中,Browne-Wilkinson 勋爵说:"... long standing principle laid down in the abuse of confidence cases viz. the law requires those in a fiduciary position who enter into transactions with those to whom they owe fiduciary duties to establish affirmatively that the transaction was a fair one ... The abuse of confidence principle is founded on considerations of general public policy, viz. that in order to protect those to whom fiduciaries owe duties as a class from exploitation by fiduciaries as a class, the law imposes a heavy duty on fiduciaries to show the righteousness of the transactions they enter into with those to whom they owe such duties."

滥用信任是要防止诚信关系中受信人滥用信任,而不当影响则防止不当利用影响力。不当影响中的弱势方无论是通过实际证明强势方施加了不当影响,还是根据事实、证据或双方之间的关系推定存在不当影响,都要证明"不当"影响的存在。但滥用信任案件中,A 不需要证明受信人 B 采取了什么行为,而是由 B 证明自己履行了诚信关系下的应尽义务。

但在他们之间,尤其是在推定不当影响时确实有非常明显的类似之处。推定不当影响时,也是根据当事人之间的影响力关系以及最后达成交易需要解释推定不当影响的存在,并由强势方提出证据证明自己交易完全没有不当影响。而信任与信心关系或诚信关系一般也都属于影响力关系。因此,一旦涉及诚信关系,A 既可以依赖滥用信任理论要求 B 证明履行了义务、不存在滥用信任,也可以类似地依赖推定不当影响要求 B 证明最后交易并没有受到不当影响。如果 B 无法证明,最后的结果一样都导致合约可使无效。

也因此过往不少先例也并不对这两者进行严格区分,两种理论之间的做法被互相套用。例如在针对不当影响的权威案件 Royal Bank of Scotland Plc v. Etridge(No. 2)(2001)UKHL 44 贵族院先例中,Hobhouse 勋爵就将滥用信任的说法套用在推定不当影响中:"Presumed undue influence is different in that it necessarily involves some legally recognised relationship between the two parties. As a result of that relationship one party is treated as owing a special duty to deal fairly with the other. It is not necessary for present purposes to define the limits of the relationships which give rise to this duty... Such legal relationships can be described as relationships where one party is legally presumed to repose trust and confidence in the other—the other side of the coin to the duty not to abuse that confidence."

但也有不少先例并没有混淆这两者。对此《Duress, Undue Influence and Unconscionable Dealing》(2019 年,第 3 版)一书之 14 - 054 段说:"Not all judges treat the two doctrines as the same. Thus, even though in Etridge Lord Hobhouse conflated the two doctrines, Lord Scott... treated them as separate. In an earlier case, Lord Wilberforce and Lord Simon... assumed that they were separate. In any event, authority apart, there are important differences between the two."

无论在原理上防止诚信关系中的滥用信任与推定不当影响中的滥用影响力到底有多大区别,实际上确实会存在不同:(1)在举证问题上,滥用信任中的原告只需要证明存在诚信关系,而推定不当影响中除了要证明关系的存在外,还需要证明"交易需要解释"才能推定不当影响的存在。(2)推定不当影响也不仅仅局限在存在诚信关系的情况:见本章之 1.4.2.2 段的介绍。(3)具体的救济方面,出现滥用信任时就可以索赔衡平赔偿(equitable compensation),无论是否撤销与复原。但不当影响的救济是撤销合约,[29] 只有在难以复原时用金钱来辅助复原。但今天也有说法是在不当影响案件中也可以用衡平赔偿。[30]

1.6 衡平救济:合约可使无效

不当影响的衡平救济是合约可使无效(voidable),这可简单节录《Chitty on Contracts》(2021 年,第 34 版)一书之 10 - 132 段所说:"A transaction entered into as a result of undue influence is voidable and not void. The right to rescind on the ground of undue influence may be lost either by express affirmation of the transaction by the victim, by estoppel or by delay amounting to proof of acquiescence."

至于撤销合约(rescission of contract)与复原(restitution),或确认合约(affirmation of contract)等课题,已经在本书第三章针对误述/虚假陈述的救济时有详及,同样适用在不当影响的救济,所以不重复。

不当影响(与不合情理交易)的内容很多与十分复杂,但这些衡平法律与商业(特别是国际商业)活动关系不大,所以此处不再赘述。

1.7 不当影响不适用在对等的国际商业关系

这些衡平法律与商业(特别是国际商业)活动关系不大的原因在本书第十章之 1 段已经介绍,这里只简单重复。不当影响与商业活动看似应该有密切关系,特别是交易一边是英国本国的弱势方(自然人或中小公司法人),另一边是强势方(财雄势大或垄断性的大公司/跨国公司)。确实针对本国,英国已经是通过各种立法(与普通法)保护本土的弱势人士,特别是自然人,包括消费者、劳工、残疾人士等。但即使是针对本国的商业活动,中小公司也不受保护。原因是对抗制诉讼与普通法(如"买方自己小心"、没有自动披露责任等)的法治理念也是同样的精神,包括商业合约的肯

---

〔29〕 不当影响与经济胁迫(economic duress)本质上非常类似,而后者的主要救济就是撤销合约,这在本书第十章之 12 段有详细介绍。

〔30〕 见本书第十章之 12.3 段。

定性、可预测性、订约自由与当事人意思自治。所以即使商业人士实力不对等，如本国的大公司与中小公司订立合约，也不会以不当影响判合约可使无效。

至于国际商业活动，更是早在这方面“内外有别”。

衡平法院的理论与做法是主持公平、保护弱势方，认为涉及不当影响与/或不合情理交易的合约可使无效。不当影响的理论涉及当事人之间有特别关系/影响力关系（influential relationship）、弱势方依赖与信任强势方，不合情理交易理论更是当事人之间必须有一方处在特殊不利地位（special disadvantage），这些关系基本上针对的主要是并非同等知识与能力的“关系”。不当影响与不合情理交易都很重视当事人之间的知识水平与经验是否存在差异、弱势方是否有特别的欠缺。

所以英国法律虽然只有一套，理论上也可以主张不当影响或不合情理交易。在 Strydom v. Vendside Ltd（2009）EWHC 2130（QB）先例中，Blair 大法官说：“Equity will intervene in any case where there has been unconscionable behaviour.”但因为有了这假设，在极少数敢去套用不当影响或不合情理/显失公平的国际商业案件的弱小当事人，都会“头破血流”，如较近期的 The Libyan Investment Authority v. Goldman Sachs International（2016）EWHC 2530（Ch）先例等。

在 Union Eagle Ltd v. Golden Achievement Ltd（1997）AC 514 枢密院先例中也提到说尽管衡平救济理论上是在什么案件中都可以适用的，表面看来也有显然好处可以根据每一个具体案件的案情考虑公平合理、不合情理/显失公平的问题，但是在商业活动中，这样要考虑个别案件中不合情理/显失公平的做法必然带来无法被接受的不稳定、不肯定。甚至有说法是在商业案件中应该排除衡平救济，这样才能解决因为理论上存在这些救济而导致的诉讼风险，与因此给商业社会带来的不肯定。Hoffmann 勋爵说：

“The boundaries of the equitable jurisdiction to relieve against contractual penalties and forfeitures are in some places imprecise.... The notion that the court's jurisdiction to grant relief is ‘unlimited and unfettered’（per Lord Simon of Glaisdale in Shiloh Spinners Ltd v Harding [1973] AC 691）was rejected as a ‘beguiling heresy’（简单翻译是表面看来很有欺骗性的歪理邪说）by the House of Lords in The Scaptrade ... [1983] 2 AC 694[31] ...It is worth pausing to notice why it continues to beguile and why it is a heresy. It has the obvious merit of allowing the court to impose what it considers to be a fair solution in the individual case. **The principle that equity will restrain the enforcement of legal rights when it would be unconscionable** to insist upon them has an attractive breadth. But the reasons why **the courts have rejected such generalisations** are founded

〔31〕 The “Scaptrade”（1983）2 Lloyd's Rep 253 贵族院先例中，此先例中判在期租合约中，法院没有给予衡平法“Relief Against Forfeiture”救济的权利，有关判法可见杨大明律师的《期租合约》一书第十八篇之 18.7 段的介绍。

not merely upon authority … but also **upon practical considerations of business**. These are, in summary, that in many forms of transaction it is of great importance that if something happens for which the contract has made express provision, the parties should know with certainty that the terms of the contract will be enforced. **The existence of an undefined discretion to refuse to enforce the contract on the ground that this would be 'unconscionable' is sufficient to create uncertainty**. Even if it is most unlikely that a discretion to grant relief will be exercised, its mere existence enables litigation to be employed as a negotiating tactic. The realities of commercial life are that this may cause injustice which cannot be fully compensated by the ultimate decision in the case.

The considerations of this nature, which led the House of Lords in The Scaptrade to reject the existence of an equitable jurisdiction to relieve against the withdrawal of a ship for late payment of hire under a charterparty, … was cited with approval by the House…Of course **the same need for certainty** is not present in all transactions and the difficult cases have involved attempts to define the jurisdiction in a way which will enable justice to be done in appropriate cases without **destabilising normal commercial relationships.** …"(加黑部分是笔者的强调)

还可以节录《Goff & Jones: The Law of Unjust Enrichment》(2022年,第10版)一书之11-66段,评论与建议说今天应该避免用衡平法的不合情理/显失公平理论影响商业合约肯定性:"We think it undesirable that the courts should enjoy an unfettered power to rewrite contracts simply because the substantive terms appear to be unfair. Unconscionability and inequality of bargaining power are elusive and mercurial concepts which mean different things to different people…It is 'seldom in any negotiation that the bargaining powers of the parties are absolutely equal' and this fact alone should not suffice to show that a contractual provision 'is objectively unreasonable'. To bring the rules affecting unconscionable bargains into play, the claimant must additionally demonstrate that he suffered from a special disadvantage that compromised his judgmental capacity, which entailed some inherent deficiency or inadequacy and was not sourced in his relationship with the defendant (in which case mere in equality of bargaining power would suffice)."

最后节录在《Civil Fraud》(2018年,第1版)一书之15-004段,说到商业社会,除了经济胁迫这唯一可去针对极端案件的安全阀外,很少会是适用不当影响的诉因,说:"In what might be called purely commercial situations, claims for undue influence or duress are less common than in personal or family situations, for the simple reason that it is expected that commercial parties of full capacity are able to stand up for themselves. Commercial life would soon falter if claims based on actionable pressure were too readily allowed. Nonetheless 'economic duress' is now a recognized form of claim, providing an important legal safety valve where conduct falls outside what is considered to be legally acceptable, albeit that the incidents of its successful deployment are relatively rare."

以上看来也只有在社会上一些非常特别类型、英国本土需要保护有特殊不利的弱势人士,特别是自然人如老人、贫穷与无知、文盲、精神存在问题、残疾人士等,或者是一些特别的社会问题如夫妻购买共有住房等,可以允许一定程度的不稳定、不肯定,才能允许这些个别案件中根据公平合理给衡平救济。今天虽然不当影响与不合情理/显失公平交易的理论并没有在商业合约中被排除,但适用会非常受限并被法院抗拒,在国际商业更是如此。

以下会介绍几个在商业关系下主张不当影响、滥用信任与不合情理交易的先例,但在这些先例中有关的主张都没有成功。

1.7.1 JP Morgan Chase Bank v. Springwell Navigation Corporation (2008) EWHC 1186 (Comm) 先例

JP Morgan Chase Bank v. Springwell Navigation Corporation 先例的案情涉及原告投资人(是一家投资公司,但背后的资金来源是希腊船东)在新兴市场投资了7亿美元债券,但因为亚洲金融危机而蒙受严重损失,试图向提供投资意见的摩根大通银行提起诉讼并索赔损失。有关的案情背景在笔者《证据法:基础理论、口头证据与专家证据》一书第九章之2.5.2.4段有详细介绍。该先例的关键争议之一是摩根大通银行能否依赖协议中十分详尽的"完整合约条文"(Entire Agreement Clause)与"没有依赖条文"[32](Non-reliance Clause),这在笔者《合约的解释:规则与应用》一书第十三章之2.4.9段有详细介绍,这里不再重复。

因为涉案金额很大,所以损失惨重的原告为了弥补损失将各种不同的诉因都扯在一起作为替代的理由,如合约下是否有信义义务/诚信责任,银行是否公平交易,是否滥用了投资者的信任与信心,利用了投资者的弱点等。

原告主张虽然投资顾问与客户之间没有法律推定的诚信关系,但根据此先例的事实,原告与被告之间应存在诚信关系。第一,被告有诚信责任披露所有合约文件中的重要事实并向原告解释。第二,被告有责任披露其以牺牲原告的利益为代价赚取不正常的巨额收益。第三,被告有责任避免利益冲突与披露其在多个交易中的利益。

但法院并没有支持原告的主张,虽然被告作为原告账户持有的证券的保管人可能对原告有某些特定的诚信责任,但是没有原告主张的全面的诚信责任。原告知道被告(包括被告集团的其他银行/公司)是部分交易的相对方有自己的经济利益,甚至很多合约文件中特别强调了被告可能在相关交易中获利。原告虽然确实依赖或"信任"被告雇员(Justin Atkinson先生,不仅与原告家族建立了友谊还被介绍给了其他希腊航运家族)的观点、推荐与建议,但在商业关系下,仅仅是一方"信任"另一方

[32] 关于完整合约条文与没有依赖条文,在本书第一章之1.3.8段与本书第四章之6.6段也有详细介绍。

是不会导致产生诚信关系。"信任"一词与"建议"一样可以代表很多意思。原告毫无疑问确实"信任"被告会以在商业上恰当的方式行事,但这不代表原告有任何合理预期是被告在与原告的商业交往中会将自己的利益置于原告之下。所以被告对原告没有广泛的诚信责任。

至于公平交易、滥用了投资者的信任与信心与利用了投资者的弱点、不当影响的替代争议,法院只是简单说从有关的事实背景看不适用。

1.7.2　Holyoake v. Candy(2017)EWHC 3397(Ch)先例

Holyoake v. Candy 先例已经在本书第十章之 8.3.2 段介绍胁迫理论时有详细介绍,原告(H 先生)为自己开发的地产项目融资,从熟人 Candy 兄弟控制的被告公司 CPC 处获得无担保贷款 1200 万英镑。但 H 先生行为触发贷款协议中的违约条文。因此 CPC 以此为由要求更多利益,包括先签订补充协议明确 H 先生承认违约,以及 H 先生会为此贷款提供资产担保,换取 CPC 的宽限。之后 H 先生仍然未能按期还款的情况下,更是逼 H 先生达成和解协议,出售地产项目,并从售价中支付3700 多万英镑给 CPC 作为和解金额。

H 先生起诉要求撤销补充协议与和解协议,原因就是 CPC 在这两个协议谈判时,都威胁说过谈不拢就会采取一切手段(主要是开始诉讼、将 H 先生的欠债的情况告知原告其他债权人等)。已经介绍过 H 先生依赖胁迫理论的主张被法院拒绝,因为通过证据认定 CPC 所威胁的"一切手段"是有权采取的合法行为,虽然确实会给 H 先生带来严重后果,利用优势地位尽可能获取利益并不被认为是不法压力(illegitimate pressure)。而 H 先生同时依赖不当影响理论中的实际不当影响,也一样被法院拒绝。

法院指出此案件中的情况,可以说基本不太会适用推定不当影响,双方之间有根本利益冲突,也是平等主体的商业交易,不存在影响力关系。但确实仍然有可能存在实际不当影响,这与胁迫的情况是非常类似的,也就是施加了威胁、不恰当压力从而可能是不当影响。但既然已经认定不存在法律会给予救济的非法压力、驳回了胁迫的主张,实际不当影响的主张也完全可以以类似理由驳回。Nugee 大法官说:

"The next pleaded claim is that the same threats, intimidation and coercion as are relied on as constituting duress also constituted actual undue influence in equity. At first sight this is slightly surprising. ...In the present case it is not suggested that the relationship between CPC and Mr Holyoake was either such as to give rise to a presumption of undue influence or was a protected relationship...The case is solely put as one of actual threats, menaces and coercion. ... there is in such a case a considerable overlap with the common law doctrine of duress, and indeed Chitty ... suggests these cases are now probably better viewed as cases of illegitimate pressure(covered by the doctrine of duress).

In these circumstances it is not clear to me what, if anything, the plea of actual undue influence adds to the plea of duress, or how it could succeed if, as I have held, the plea of duress fails on the facts... I have found that the substantive threat that caused Mr Holyoake to enter into the Supplemental Loan Agreement and the series of subsequent agreements was the threat by CPC to litigate. If, as I have held, that was not illegitimate pressure for the purposes of the law of duress, it was in my judgment equally not undue influence for the purposes of the equitable doctrine. I hold that none of the agreements were voidable for actual undue influence. ”

1.7.3 The Libyan Investment Authority v. Goldman Sachs International (2016) EWHC 2530 (Ch) 先例

在 The Libyan Investment Authority v. Goldman Sachs International 先例中，原告（以下简称 LIA）是利比亚的主权基金（sovereign wealth fund）。利比亚长期被制裁，直到 2003 年联合国解除制裁，以及 2004 年美国解除制裁后，利比亚通过出售石油等产品获得不少资产并交由 LIA 投资管理。这样大批银行盯上了 LIA 手中的资金，纷纷想要提供金融服务。最后 LIA 选择了与被告（以下称高盛）合作，投资一批复杂的合成衍生品交易（synthetic derivative trades），所有交易也都加了金融杠杆（leveraged）。

在这些交易中，在交易日 LIA 向高盛支付一笔金钱，获得特定公司股票价格的敞口（exposure），如果相比交易日股票价格，在到期日（maturity dates）股票价格上涨，则高盛需要向 LIA 支付此价格差，如果更低则高盛不需要支付。换言之，实际上 LIA 并不是购买股票本身，而只是购买了“看多”股票价格的机会，只有在股票价格高涨到差值会超过自己支付的金钱时才有利润。但凡股票价格不够高涨，都不会获得真正利润。甚至一旦股票价格持平甚至下跌，LIA 就会亏损甚至血本无归了。

此先例涉及多笔交易，这些交易中大部分的交易日是在 2008 年 1 月到 4 月之间，此时由于经济危机发生的可能性，股票价格已经在短期有了大幅下跌，LIA 看来是想要赌一手这只是市场价格的短期波动很快会反弹（这也是当时不少人士的想法），因此进行了这些交易看多，将到期日设定在 2011 年。在这些交易中，LIA 在交易日总计向高盛支付了 12 亿美元，涉及的股票价值约 52 亿美元。但后来金融海啸爆发，显然 LIA 在这些交易中血本无归。因此 LIA 向法院提起诉讼，申请撤销这些交易，并要求高盛退还交易日支付的金钱（12 亿美元）。LIA 的主要诉因是不当影响，其次则是不合情理交易。

LIA 主张在交易期间有以下几方面的事实：（1）LIA 对这类交易的了解不多，处在无知、水平低的状态。LIA 根本不了解有关交易的性质，一直都以为自己是在购买股票，并不清楚一旦股票价格下跌将会血本无归的风险。（2）高盛与 LIA 之间逐渐建立了超出一般投行与投资人的关系。高盛经过一系列行为，如长期派遣雇员常驻 LIA，结交 LIA 的雇员并提供培训、建议与帮助等，与 LIA 建立了信任与信心的关系。实际上高盛一直像是 LIA 的内部公司银行一样，因此 LIA 完全依赖高盛的意见与建议，信任高盛以 LIA 的利益行事，才达成涉案交易。（3）有关交易的定价不公平，高盛从中获取了巨额利润。交易根本是豪赌式的，性质上来说完全不适合作为主权基金的 LIA 的需求。(4)针对其中一次特定交易,LIA 还主张高盛为了达成协议,用允许 LIA 副主席的家人在高盛进行实习诱导,不当影响副主席"就范"。

法院同意如果可以用证据证明以上事实,是有可诉的不当影响与/或不合情理交易的。但是根据双方提供的证据来看,首先是针对实际不当影响方面,认定了高盛用各类好处拉拢 LIA、提供实习工作给副主席家人的诱导合约行为不属于不当影响。其次针对推定不当影响,则是认定 LIA 并非完全无知与水平低的主体;为了拉生意高盛作为投行提供一些额外的好处(如培训、意见与建议等)并没有超出一般投行与客户的关系,因此不存在信任与信心关系。

而且针对最后的交易内容,法官审核了高盛针对这些交易的投资利润、定价策略等后,认定交易本身也并不需要解释。因此不当影响方面是为败诉。

针对不合情理/显失公平,则主要需要显示合约一方有严重劣势(贫穷、无知、缺乏独立意见等),而且另一方利用此劣势采用道德上应受谴责(reprehensible / morally culpable)、震惊法院良心(shocks the conscience of the court)的手段,导致最后签订的合约明显对劣势方而言过分(overreaching)与/或过于压迫/苛刻(oppressive),此时法院会考虑撤销合约,这方面可见本章之 2 段。由于已经提到普通法对双方知识水平、谈判力量的假设,而此先例中法院对事实的认定也符合此假设,不合情理/显失公平的诉因也同样被驳回。

除此以外,笔者还想要再次强调的是,除非是如针对消费者等已经有立法保护的情形,现在英国法对商业合约的态度较为明确,即以最大可能支持当事人的订约自由。除非有非常明确的良好理由偏离,如可以明确证明 LIA 在决策时高盛有不恰当的行为(贪污受贿、欺诈性误述等),否则是不会给予撤销合约的严重后果的。而这也凸显了采用误述原则撤销合约的好处,如需要证明的事实相对明确与可以证明,也未必一定需要欺诈性误述、不一定需要证明被告有衡平过错行为等,也因此不奇怪的是今天不少案件中如果可以选择误述作为诉因,都会将其作为主要的诉因。

1.7.4 Nature Resort Ltd v. First Citizens Bank Ltd(2022) UKPC 10 先例

在 Nature Resort Ltd v. First Citizens Bank Ltd 先例中,公司 Nature Resort Ltd(以下简称 NRL)是被专门设立用来持有与开发一个特立尼达和多巴哥共和国[33](Republic of Trinidad and Tobago)的不动产(The Culloden Estate)项目。卖方 Patrick Dankou 先生(也是 NRL 的唯一股东)向买方 Simon Paler 先生与 Christopher James 先生出售 75% 的 NRL 股权。买方为了融资需要向银行借贷,而银行要求用项目作为抵押担保,这得到了持有项目的 NRL(以及卖方)的同意。[34]

在此多方交易中,律师 Richard Wheeler 先生有多个委托工作:(1)担保合约下,

[33] 此先例中各方均认可该国家关于不当影响的法律与英国法是一致的。

[34] 因此这还涉及被收购方对收购方提供经济援助非法的问题。类似问题见本书第八章之 11.5.4.2 段的介绍。但此问题并非此上诉争议焦点,不在这里详细介绍。

受银行委托准备合约文件。(2)股权买卖合约下,同时受买卖双方委托准备合约,以及协助买方准备向卖方付款的本票。而且律师过去就与 NRL/卖方有紧密的关系,即律师曾是 NRL 的董事,曾经受卖方委托准备遗嘱等。

后来买方未能按约偿还贷款,银行就行使自己在抵押合约下的权利,公开出售项目。NRL 就提出反对,要求撤销抵押担保合约。一个主要理由就是抵押合约的签订,NRL/卖方受到了律师的不当影响。

在抵押担保合约下,显然律师只不过是第三人,并非合约当事人。但是此先例中在抵押担保合约下律师可以被认为是银行的代理人,或者可以认为银行对律师行为有推定知情,因此如果确实是律师施加了不当影响,撤销合约不存在障碍。在此仅节录此先例中 Briggs 与 Burrows 勋爵针对第三人不当影响的总结如下:"In a three-party situation, where there is undue influence by B over A such that A enters into a transaction with C, the transaction will be voidable by A provided that C had notice of the undue influence or that B was acting as C's agent in procuring the transaction. The concept of notice, and how it applies in this context, was explained in detail in Etridge. That the law of agency has a role to play in the context of undue influence was accepted in cases..."

而从 NRL 提供的证据上来看,并没有实际证明律师有什么公然的不合情理/衡平法过错行为,因此并非实际不当影响。焦点集中在是否属于推定不当影响的问题上。

针对推定不当影响必须满足的两点要求(双方之间存在影响力关系,最后达成交易并非合理与正常的人士在一般动机下的行为/需要解释),高院、上诉庭、枢密院均认为并不能同时满足这两点,因此不当影响并不成立。但它们各自意见稍有不同,可以简单节录各个法院的判决思路如下:

1. 特立尼达和多巴哥高院(Pemberton 大法官)判既没有影响力关系、交易也解释得通。认定并不存在影响力关系:(1)首先是在律师与 NRL(或卖方)之间曾经是律师与客户的关系,这本应属于根据特定关系就可以推定的 A 类别。但是在争议的抵押担保协议下,律师并未受 NRL 委托,因此并非特定类别。(2)其次是这次具体的交易中,也并没有证据显示 NRL 对律师有什么特别的依赖,NRL(与卖方)对律师有信任与信心。Pemberton 大法官认定:"It is clear that [Mr Wheeler] had no significant part to play in discussing, negotiating or dispensing advice for the important transactions which are the bases for the case at bar."因此也无法从事实上推断存在影响力关系。

最后达成的抵押担保协议也被认为可以解释得通:(1)对于担保协议而言,律师只不过是第三方,并没有从中获利;(2)通过达成担保协议,卖方实际上是获得了自己想要的商业利益的,尤其是得以从买方支付的金钱中支付收益给背后隐名投资人与清偿了 NRL 的公司债务。

2. 特立尼达和多巴哥上诉庭(Mendonça, Mohammed 与 des Vignes 大法官)判定

存在推定不当影响但被银行以证据成功反驳。针对影响力关系，上诉庭判定 NRL（与卖方）向来是律师（与其律所）的客户，这足够建立影响力关系。针对达成的交易则强调相比于 NRL 的唯一资产（不动产项目）面临在买方不按时还款可能被银行出售的巨大风险下，NRL 并没有什么真正的利益，因此属于需要解释的情况。

但是卖方是精明的商人，也充分了解签订抵押担保协议所带来的巨大风险，尤其是在知道通过达成抵押担保协议与促成股权交易后，卖方仍然持有的 25% 股权的价值还会有巨大提升，因此在平衡的可能性下认定卖方其实是在充分、知情的考虑过后，纯粹是自己的自由意愿签订合约，成功反驳不当影响的推定。Mendonça 大法官说："Mr Dankou entered into the mortgage transaction on his own free will knowing what he was doing and fully appreciating the risks involved."

3. 英国枢密院认为不应该推定不当影响。枢密院认为类似此先例中的情况，商业行为中律师同时接受或曾经接受过双方当事人委托的情况相当常见，如土地交易或融资借贷中都经常出现，在类似情况下当事人事后发现交易对自己不利，是否都可以主张推定不当影响？英国枢密院就担心特立尼达和多巴哥上诉庭的判法会造成商业社会中此类合约的不肯定、不稳定，因此特意针对性地说这种情况下订立的合约，绝少能够构成推定不当影响。枢密院尤其指出这种交易中常常发生的情况是：（1）律师除了正常收费外没有其他利益；（2）这类交易中尽管会出现一方获取了更多利益，或者事后发现其实交易对一方有利的情况，但往往根据交易当时的情况都能解释得通。例如，此先例中的情况在枢密院看来就其实更倾向于高院对事实的解读，认为上诉庭看法过于片面，只强调了 NRL 没拿到什么实际利益，而忽视了抵押担保合约会给卖方带来的巨大好处，而实际控制 NRL 的卖方在这样的利益面前愿意达成抵押担保协议完全是说得通的。

可以节录枢密院所说如下：

"The Board has concerns that the reasoning of the Court of Appeal may lead to the view that, in many situations where a solicitor (or attorney) is providing professional advice to a client, and the client then enters into a disadvantageous commercial transaction with a third party, the client would be able to invoke the law on undue influence (including the law of agency) to set aside the transaction. **There are many instances where, for example, the solicitor is acting for both a purchaser of land and a lender of the money for the purchase where that relationship should not operate to give rise to a presumption of undue influence for either client to be used against the other**. This is so where the solicitor does not obtain any personal benefit (beyond his normal fees) from the transaction.

In the Board's view, **where the other party to the transaction is not the solicitor obtaining some benefit from the client but is rather a third party, an ordinary commercial transaction such as a mortgage, entered into by a person engaged in busi-**

ness, should rarely be regarded as one that is not readily explicable on ordinary motives, merely because it is, or turns out to be, disadvantageous. It is readily explicable that the client will enter into such a transaction without being under the undue influence of the solicitor.

...In the Board's view the Court of Appeal was wrong to ignore this bigger picture and therefore wrong to take the view that the deed of mortgage was not readily explicable. Although unnecessary for our decision, it follows that, in the Board's view, **there was no presumption of undue influence that needed to be rebutted in this case**. In this respect(ie that the transaction was readily explicable), the Court of Appeal was incorrect and the first instance judge was correct."（加黑部分是笔者的强调）

2. 不合情理/显失公平交易

2.1　简介

如果一个交易或合约中，双方当事人中有一方是处于明显的特殊不利地位（special disadvantage）的弱势方，最后交易内容对弱势方过分（overreaching）或苛刻（oppressive），而且强势方采取了道德上应受谴责的方式（reprehensible means/morally culpable manner）利用弱势方的不利地位，强行将这些不合情理/显失公平的内容加入合约，衡平法就会考虑给予弱势方以不合情理/显失公平交易的衡平救济（equitable remedy）。

背后的公共政策与原理，在一些古老的衡平法先例中就有提到，双方之间必须有合理程度的对等地位，才能达成真正你情我愿的有效合约：见 Longmate v. Ledger (1860) 2 Giff 157 等先例。也因此如果弱势方存在特殊不利地位，导致强势方可以获取不公平优势，衡平法法院就会考虑给予救济，合约可使无效。

另可节录早期的 James v. Kerr (1889) 40 Ch. D. 449 先例，说是达到弱势方任凭强势方摆布的程度就会给予救济："the ground for relief in equity arising from the position of **mercy of the lenders**（强势方的贷款人）poverty and necessity in which the Plaintiff was, which put him practically at the, whatever terms they chose to exact."（加黑部分是笔者的强调）

近期说法可见 Lloyds Bank Ltd v. Bundy (1975) QB 326 先例，Denning 勋爵说："as a matter of common fairness, it is not right that the strong should be allowed to push the weak to the wall..."

在其他普通法国家如澳大利亚先例中，看来关注的是不利地位是否严重到令弱势方不能考虑什么才是符合自己最佳利益，Commercial Bank of Australia v. Amadio (1983) 151 CLR 447 先例说："... the disabling condition or circumstance is one which seriously affects the ability of the innocent party to make a judgment as to his own best interests."

在接下来的段节将简单讨论今天英国法院会给出不合情理/显失公平救济的原理与测试标准或要件。在此先节录十分近期的 PIAC v. Times Travel(2021)UKSC 40 最高院先例,Hodge 勋爵对不合情理/显失公平原则的简单总结:"... the equitable doctrine of unconscionable bargains has been applied where B is at a serious disadvantage relative to A through 'poverty, or ignorance, or lack of advice or otherwise' so that circumstances existed of which unfair advantage could be taken; A exploited B's weakness in a morally culpable manner; and the resulting transaction was not merely hard or improvident but overreaching and oppressive... Examples of unconscionable transactions include circumstances in which A knowingly negotiates an agreement with B while B is elderly, unwell and intoxicated ... and where a poor, illiterate and unwell person is induced to enter into a disadvantageous transaction without advice and in great haste ... In Fry v Lane (1888) 40 Ch D 312, Kay J summarised the then existing case law in these terms ...: 'where a purchase is made from a poor and ignorant man at a considerable undervalue, the vendor having no independent advice, a Court of Equity will set aside the transaction.' He held that the circumstances of poverty, ignorance and lack of independent advice impose on the purchaser the burden of showing that the purchase was fair, just and reasonable. Unequal bargaining power does not suffice; it is necessary for the claimant to show that unconscientious advantage has been taken of his or her disabling condition or circumstances: Boustany v Pigott (1993) 69 P & CR 298 (JCPC)... Extortionate bargains can be struck down or varied in other circumstances; see, for example, The Port Caledonia and the Anna [1903] P 184 in which the court drastically reduced a claim for salvage where a ship's captain in an emergency had been forced to accept an extortionate offer from a tug captain for the provision of salvage services. But the rules relating to salvage may depend on specialties of maritime law ..."

2.2 成立标准或要件

今天被接受的所谓"Alec Lobb criteria"是根据 Alec Lobb v. Total Oil GB(1985)1 WLR 173 上诉庭先例,[35]一审([1983]1 WLR 87)的 Peter Millett 大法官总结了不合情理/显失公平原则下法院会插手合约内容的三个要件,这三个要件必须同时满足,法院才会考虑插手,这说法被上诉庭支持。这三个要件是:(1)一方当事人有特殊不利地位;(2)交易内容对一方过分、苛刻、震惊法院良心;(3)强势方采用道德上应受谴责方式利用对方不利地位。

可节录 Peter Millett 大法官所说如下:"**First, one party has been at a serious disadvantage to the other, whether through poverty, or ignorance, or lack of advice, or**

[35] 有关案情已经在本书第八章之 11.5.3.2 段有介绍,不重复。

otherwise, so that circumstances existed of which unfair advantage could be taken: see, for example, Blomley v. Ryan ..., where, to the knowledge of one party, the other was by reason of his intoxication in no condition to negotiate intelligently; **secondly, this weakness of the one party has been exploited by the other in some morally culpable manner**: see, for example, Clark v. Malpas (1862) 4 De G. F. & J. 401, where a poor and illiterate man was induced to enter into a transaction of an unusual nature, without proper independent advice, and in great haste; and **thirdly, the resulting transaction has been, not merely hard or improvident, but overreaching and oppressive.** Where there has been a sale at an undervalue, the under-value has almost always been substantial, so that it calls for an explanation, and is in itself indicative of the presence of some fraud, undue influence, or other such feature. In short, there must, in my judgment, **be some impropriety, both in the conduct of the stronger party and in the terms of the transaction itself** (though the former may often be inferred from the latter in the absence of an innocent explanation) which in the traditional phrase 'shocks the conscience of the court,' and makes it against equity and good conscience of the stronger party to retain the benefit of a transaction he has unfairly obtained."(加黑部分是笔者的强调)

该先例是一个国际商业案件,显然原告 Alec Lobb 要证明是一个不合情理/显失公平交易并获得衡平救济是绝不容易的。所以 Alec Lobb 虽然提出了这个主张,但被一审与上诉庭否定,这里背后的原因会稍后讨论。

另也可节录在 Boustany v. Pigott (1995) 69 P & CR 298 枢密院先例中,Templeman 勋爵基本上一致的说法:"(1) It is not sufficient to attract the jurisdiction of equity to prove that a bargain is hard, unreasonable or foolish; it must be proved to be unconscionable, in the sense that 'one of the parties to it has imposed the objectionable terms in a morally reprehensible manner, that is to say, in a way which affects his conscience' ... (2) 'Unconscionable' related not merely to the terms of the bargain but to the behaviour of the stronger party, which must be characterised by some moral culpability or impropriety ... (3) Unequal bargaining power or objectively unreasonable terms provide no basis for equitable interference in the absence of unconscientious or extortionate abuse of power where exceptionally, and as a matter of common fairness, 'it was not right that the strong should be allowed to push the weak to the wall' ... (4) A contract cannot be set aside in equity as 'an unconscionable bargain' against a party innocent of actual or constructive fraud. Even if the terms of the contract are 'unfair' in the sense that they are more favourable to one party than the other ('contractual imbalance'), equity will not provide relief unless the beneficiary is guilty of unconscionable conduct ... (5) In situations of this kind it is necessary for the plaintiff who seeks relief to establish unconscionable conduct, namely that unconscientious advantage has been taken of this disabling condition or circumstances …"

最后可节录一些权威书籍对构成不合情理交易要件的说法，先是在《Duress, Undue Influence and Unconscionable Dealing》(2019 年，第 3 版)一书之 15－004 段说："**The Alec Lobb criteria** … the court identified three criteria for relief on the ground of unconscionable dealing. These are that:(a)'one party has been at a serious disadvantage to the other, whether through poverty, or ignorance, or lack of advice, or otherwise, so that the circumstances existed of which unfair advantage could be taken';(b) This weakness of the complainant(弱势方)was 'exploited by the other(party)in some morally culpable manner';and(c)'the resulting transaction must have been, not merely hard or improvident, but overreaching and oppressive.' After a period of some uncertainty and confusion as to the unconscionability criteria in English law … the Alec Lobb criteria now commands the support of the overwhelming majority of modern English authorities. …"

最后节录《Chitty on Contracts》(2021 年，第 34 版)一书之 10－164 段所说如下："The doctrine of unconscionable bargains seems to be limited in three ways. The first is that the bargain must be oppressive to the complainant in overall terms;the second that it may only apply when the complaint was suffering from certain types of bargaining weakness;and the third that the other party must have acted unconscionably in the sense of having knowingly taken advantage of the complainant."

2.3 不当影响与不合情理交易的区分

区分这两种衡平救济有点不容易，因为表面看来十分相似，甚至包括普通法救济的胁迫，都有说法是对不合情理交易给予救济的"一揽子"/"雨伞"理论(umbrella doctrine)：可见 BOM v. BOK(2018)SGCA 83 新加坡上诉庭先例。

这稍有不同说法的诉因或主张会是不当影响，主要针对订立合约的过程或程序方面是否有"不当"，其中最重要的是利用特殊关系(special relationship)/影响力关系(relationship of influence)，导致弱势方因为这种关系订约自由意志(contractual free will)被影响。至于合约内容是否是正常交易，只不过是证明或推定程序存在"不当"的证据。

但如果主张是不合情理交易，主要针对或针对之一是交易与合约内容对一方过分、苛刻、震惊法院良心。在《Duress, Undue Influence and Unconscionable Dealing》(2019 年，第 3 版)一书说要件之一是："the resulting transaction must have been, not merely hard or improvident, but overreaching and oppressive." 另在《Chitty on Contracts》(2021 年，第 34 版)一书的说法是"the bargain must be oppressive to the complainant in overall terms"。

这可节录在 Irvani v. Irvani(2000)1 Lloyd's Rep 412 先例中，Buxton 大法官所说："Undue influence is concerned with the prior relationship between the contracting parties, and with whether that was the motivation or reason for which the bargain was entered into. Unconscionable bargain is, as its title suggests, concerned with the nature and circumstances of the bargain itself, and can arise without there being any relationship, outside that of the immediate contract, between the parties, significantly different from the circumstances of a case of undue influence..."

所以在 Hart v. O'Connor(1985)AC 1000 枢密院先例中，提出不当影响针对的是程序不公平(procedural unfairness)，而不合情理交易可以称之为合约实质内容上的不公平/不平衡(contractual unfairness/imbalance)。因此与不当影响理论不同，无须理会双方之间是什么关系。Brightman 勋爵说："If a contract is stigmatised as 'unfair', it may be unfair in one of two ways. It may be unfair by reason of the unfair manner in which it was brought into existence; a contract induced by undue influence is unfair in this sense. It will be convenient to call this '**procedural unfairness.**' It may also, in some contexts, be described (accurately or inaccurately) as 'unfair' by reason of the fact that the terms of the contract are more favourable to one party than to the other. In order to distinguish this 'unfairness' from procedural unfairness, it will be convenient to call it '**contractual imbalance.**' The **two concepts may overlap. Contractual imbalance may be so extreme as to raise a presumption of procedural unfairness**, such as undue influence or some other form of victimisation. Equity will relieve a party from a contract which he has been induced to make as a result of victimisation. **Equity will not relieve a party from a contract on the ground only that there is contractual imbalance not amounting to unconscionable dealing.** Of the three indicia of unfairness... the first was contractual imbalance and the second and third were procedural unfairness."(加黑部分是笔者的强调)

2.4 交易过分/苛刻与采用了道德上应受谴责方式

在 Alec Lobb v. Total Oil GB(1985)1 WLR 173 上诉庭先例中，由于这是一个国际商业案件，Alec Lobb 也确实委任了自己的律师与会计师全程协助交易的谈判。这样，Alec Lobb 主张受到不当影响就很难说得通了，只能以合约内容对他过分、苛刻与一面倒，是一个不合情理的交易为由寻求救济。但一审的 Peter Millett 大法官不同意只看这一点，说："The plaintiffs ... submitted that the transaction of lease and lease-back was a harsh and unconscionable bargain of a kind which a court of equity will not allow to stand. In such a case the court is concerned, not with the reality of the weaker party's consent, but with the conduct of the stronger; for the word 'unconscionable' seems to relate both to the terms of the bargain and to the behaviour of the stronger party. It is not enough to show that the bargain was a hard or unreasonable one ...I can find **nothing whatever for criticism in the defendants' conduct**. The plaintiff company was **advised throughout by its own solicitors and accountants**, who were completely independent of the defendants. The defendants were not to know that Mr. Lobb had not taken his advisers into his confidence, and had neither asked for not received comprehensive legal and financial advice.... They **did not press Mr. Lobb for a quick decision**; there was **no undue haste**. On the contrary, it was Mr. Lobb and his solicitors who urged speed; the defendants were somewhat dilatory, though the delay was due in part to their own internal administrative procedures. They were unenthusiastic; they did not regard the deal as particularly favourable to them. They recognised the advantage of securing the outlet; but they had had the site professionally valued, and were advised that they were paying a realistic price.... "(加黑部分是笔者的强调)

上诉庭的 Dunn 大法官同意说:

"(Alec Lobb 的代表大律师) conceded that he could not bring himself within any of the established categories of equitable relief, but ... submitted that the circumstances of this case disclosed **a classic case of inequality of bargaining power of which the defendants had taken advantage by entering into the transaction, although he did not suggest any pressure or other misconduct on their part**. He submitted that if it was necessary to categorise the grant of relief sought, it was **an unconscionable bargain**. He ... sought to distinguish the instant case ... that here the plaintiffs were under a compelling necessity to accept the loan, so that **misconduct by the defendants was unnecessary**. The fact of their impecuniosity, that they were already tied to the defendants by mortgages, that there was no other source of finance, and that they could not sell the equities of redemption under the mortgages without giving up trading, coupled with the knowledge of the defendants of those facts rendered the transaction unconscionable, and placed the onus upon the defendants to show that its terms were fair and reasonable.

I find myself**unable to accept** those arguments. Mere impecuniosity has never been held a ground for equitable relief. In this case **no pressure was placed upon the plaintiffs**. On the contrary the defendants were reluctant to enter into the transaction. The plaintiffs **took independent advice from their solicitors and accountants**. They went into the transaction **with their eyes open**, and it was of benefit to them because they were enabled to continue trade from the site for a number of years. In my view **the judge was right to refuse equitable relief.** "(加黑部分是笔者的强调)

这"Alec Lobb criteria"也在后来的先例中被普遍跟从,如在 Chagos Islanders v. Attorney General (2003) EWHC 2222 (QB) 先例中,Ouseley 大法官总结说:"...(原告大律师) submitted that what was necessary for a party to make unconscientious use of its superior position or superior bargaining power to the detriment of someone suffering from special disability or disadvantage. **This weakness had to be exploited in some morally culpable manner, leading to an oppressive transaction**. These propositions are drawn from the judgement of Mr Peter Millett QC in Alec Lobb Ltd v. Total Oil Ltd ... This decision was affirmed in the Court of Appeal ...;the principles were not in dispute but the Court emphasized the need for unconscientious behaviour rather than a mere disparity of bargaining power. That point was not at issue."(加黑部分是笔者的强调)

换言之,即使是合约内容或条件过分、苛刻与一面倒,也不满足不合情理交易的要件,而必须在谈判的过程中涉及道德上应受谴责的行为或衡平法过错。

举例更容易说清楚,如A将自己随意在路边古董摊买的小物件便宜卖给B,而双方实际上都对古董是外行或一知半解,即使A事后发现该古董是价值连城的真品,但该交易中双方相比之下不存在不利地位,也就不能依赖不合情理/显失公平理论。换一换案情,A是外行,但B是专家,B心知肚明捡了一个大便宜,知道A做了冤大头。但这买卖交易仍不是不合情理,A不能在发现该古董是真品价值连城后试图否定该合约。在本书的第五章之1段也介绍了英国普通法下B没有自动披露或提醒A的责任。再换一下案情仍是A是外行,处理祖先遗留下来的一件不起眼的小物件,于是慕名向专家B查问。B虽然在心里偷笑,但对A说这应是赝品,有买家肯出100元就已经是运气。这样,A最终干脆以50元卖了给B,省得白跑一趟。但后来发现该小物件是真品古董、价值连城,这样既有非常不公平的合约,又涉及了B的衡平过错行为,就可以成功否定该买卖合约了,依赖的诉因可以包括不合情理交易、不当影响、推定欺诈(constructive fraud)/衡平法欺诈(equitable fraud)等。

2.5 谈判地位不对等与有特殊不利地位

最后介绍满足不合情理交易的衡平救济的三个要件中,没有谈到的"一方当事人有特殊不利地位(special disadvantage)"。首先说明是谈判地位不对等并导致交易与合约内容有相应的倾斜,是无可避免的现实,在国际商业活动中尤其如此。这不是衡平法要去救济的情况,毕竟作出救济就要否定有关的合约或重写合约了。但这是对订约自由与合约的肯定性、稳定性与可预测性的致命打击。

所以有说法是仅是谈判地位不对等是远不够的,只是在极端情况下,也就是弱势方是有"特殊不利地位"时才会有衡平救济。早期说法是贫穷与无知,后续也有不少先例解释得很广泛,无论是贫穷、知识水平、年龄、精神状态、订约时是否处在正常人警觉的状态等因素都可能被认为有关系。如贫穷[36]与无知:[37]见Proof v. Hines (1735) Cas T Talb 111;Evans v. Llewellin(1787)1 Cox 333;Fry v. Lane(1888)40 Ch. D. 312等先例。年老、生病而且文盲:见Clark v. Malpas(1862)4 De GF & J 401先例。年幼而且毫无经验:见Earl of Aylesford v. Morris(1873)LR 8 Ch. App. 484等先例。

---

〔36〕 在Cresswell v. Potter(1978)1 WLR 255先例中,现代对贫穷(poor)的定义应该是"低收入人群"(lower income group)而不需要是赤贫(destitute)。但什么是低收入人群仍有一定的客观标准,不是当事人自己说自己收入低,或者相比对方当事人贫穷就可以。

〔37〕 在Cresswell v. Potter先例说无知(ignorant)的定义应该是"没有受过高等教育"(less highly educated)。

早期这种案件与商业活动有关系的只是各类海事救助(salvage)案件,遇难船舶处在危险状态签订救助合约,即使施救人士(salvor)不是胁迫或不当影响,遇难船舶也会去签下对自己十分不利与一面倒的救助合约,遇难船舶就可以事后主张不合情理撤销合约:见 The "Port Caledonia" and The "Anna"(1903)P 184 先例。当然在引入劳氏救助合约(Lloyd's Open Form)[38]的做法后这问题也不再存在。

2.5.1　结构性的谈判地位不对等应由政府通过立法解决

谈判地位不对等很多时候主要由于弱势方对法律的无知。所以,弱势方有否被提醒或实际有否机会咨询独立与称职律师被视为弱势方有否受到不当影响或是否有特殊不利的一个重要因素。

谈判地位不取决于公司大小或市场的变化。从整个社会的进步来看,也不应该压制水平高的商业人士以帮助水平低的商业人士。但无可避免地会出现严重不对等谈判地位是结构性的,弱势方无法依赖自己提高水平去改变现状,典型的就是消费者与垄断公司之间的谈判地位,这就只能以立法伸出援手了。

虽然在 Lloyds Bank Ltd v. Bundy(1975)QB 326 先例中,Denning 勋爵一度提过针对不公平谈判地位(inequality of bargaining power)法院应当专门建立理论给予救济,但他也说:"Now let me say at once that in the vast majority of cases a customer who signs a bank guarantee or a charge cannot get out of it. **No bargain will be upset which is the result of the ordinary interplay of forces**. There are many hard cases which are caught by this rule. Take the case of a poor man who is homeless. He agrees to pay a high rent to a landlord just to get a roof over his head. The common law will not interfere. It is left to Parliament. Next take the case of a borrower in urgent need of money. He borrows it from the bank at high interest and it is guaranteed by a friend. The guarantor gives his bond and gets nothing in return. The common law will not interfere. Parliament has intervened to prevent moneylenders charging excessive interest. But it has never interfered with banks."(加黑部分是笔者的强调)

接下来在本书第十章之 8.3.4 段介绍过 National Westminster Bank Plc v. Morgan(1985)AC 686 贵族院先例,其中更是明确说明对于谈判地位问题,英国法院倾向于不插手,这应当是由政府考虑的政策性问题,即使要解决也是通过立法解决。Scarman 勋爵说:"... in the field of contract I question whether there is any need in the modern law to erect a general principle of relief against inequality of bargaining power. Parliament has undertaken the task — and it is essentially a legislative task — of enacting such restrictions upon freedom of contract as are in its judgment necessary to relieve against the mischief: for example, the hire-purchase and consumer protection legislation, of which the Supply of Goods (Implied Terms) Act 1963, Consumer Credit Act 1974, Consumer Safety

[38]　关于劳氏救助合约,可见本书第七章之 13.4 段的详细介绍。

Act 1978, Supply of Goods and Services Act 1982 and Insurance Companies Act 1982 are examples. I doubt whether the courts should assume the burden of formulating further restrictions."

但是今天的大量的在方方面面的立法以保护订约方不会因为结构性的弱势而被迫签订不合情理的合约,仍是无法解决所有的问题。所以在立法没有规定或无法涵盖的情况下,不合情理/显失公平理论仍然可以被依赖去解决一部分问题。以下简单介绍涉及不合情理交易争议的例子。

2.5.2 Strydom v. Vendside Ltd(2009)EWHC 2130(QB)先例

一般情况下,工人与工会之间不会有特殊不利地位的问题。但是在较为近期的 Strydom v. Vendside Ltd 先例中,事实背景是当时英国因为出现大量矿工因工罹患震动白指症,作为个体非常弱势的矿工非常依赖工会帮助找索赔顾问为自己的伤病索赔。英国政府为了解决大量劳工问题实际上与索赔顾问签订了协议,索赔顾问代理索赔案件会得到政府支付费用,但并不禁止索赔顾问额外收费。此先例中原告就是一名矿工,刚刚从工会退出,但没有其他门路而只能依赖工会推荐、出资与控制的索赔顾问,并与索赔顾问签订风险代理合约,胜诉后需要向索赔顾问支付一笔金钱。最后原告也的确胜诉并支付了费用,但事后发现索赔顾问实际上可以从政府收到费用,因此起诉想要拿回金钱。法院根据这特殊事实背景认为原告与工会/索赔顾问相比确实处在不利地位,但是合约本身虽然对索赔顾问非常有利、多赚很多钱,但对原告矿工而言这合约顶多是不合理的,并没有过分、苛刻,只是正常的风险代理的合约条件。而且工会/索赔顾问虽然没有自动披露自己其实会从政府收钱的事实,但这并没有构成道德上应受谴责的行为。因此依赖不合情理交易要求撤销合约的申请被拒绝。

可节录 Blair 大法官所说:

"In summary, therefore, before the court will consider setting a contract aside as an unconscionable bargain, **one party has to have been disadvantaged** in some relevant way as regards the other party, that **other party must have exploited that disadvantage in some morally culpable manner**, and the **resulting transaction must be overreaching and oppressive**. No single one of these factors is sufficient-**all three elements must be proved**, otherwise the enforceability of contracts is undermined... Where all these requirements are met, the burden then passes to the other party to satisfy the court that the transaction was fair, just and reasonable ...

As to the first requirement, the Judge accepted that there was inequality of bargaining power between a former miner looking for advice and trusting the union to look out for his interests, and the union offering to pursue the miner's claim on its own terms and for its own benefit. ... But, he held, it was essential that the outcome was oppressive to the Claimant, and that in addition the Defendant must have acted unconscionably. As to unconscionable behavior, he said: 'Neither the consequences of the contract nor the conduct of the Defendant's, even if regarded as reprehensible, qualifies for that sort of relief. To turn failure to disclose(索赔顾问的被告没有披露会向政府收钱) into conduct which will allow the Court to intervene in equity in my judgment is to take the powers of the Court too far ...'.

...Furthermore, I think that ... the third element identified in Lobb, namely that the transaction was oppressive, was not shown on the facts of this case. ... before it will be treated as an unconscionable bargain, a contract must be oppressive to the complainant in its overall terms. The question is whether the contract was oppressive, not whether it was unreasonable...The question must, I think, be determined on the facts as they are at the time the contract is entered into, and from the perspective of the disadvantaged contracting party. Whilst I have considerable sympathy with the Claimant's submissions, ... the fact is that he had to pay a fee because he was seeking union representation and was no longer paying his union dues, the fee was payable only in the event of a successful settlement, and it was capped at £ 300. It is correct that the union was also to receive a fee from the DTI, and that this activity turned out to be very profitable given the number of claims that were handled. But legitimate public concern on this ground does not render the contract 'oppressive' in the legal sense as regards the Claimant. ..."(加黑部分是笔者的强调)

2.5.3 China Finance & Assets Management Ltd v. Lafe Properties (Hong Kong) Ltd (2015) HKEC 300 中国香港特区先例

在中国香港特区的 China Finance & Assets Management Ltd v. Lafe Properties (Hong Kong) Ltd 先例中,案情涉及被告(背后是广州的 Guangzhou Lafe Electronic Components Co Ltd)为了发展位于广东番禺的地产项目需要融资,原告作为中间人向被告介绍愿意向其贷款的公司,并从中抽取25%的服务费。在双方的委托贷款咨询合约(Commissioned Financing Consultation Agreement)中,约定在双方订立合约后被告就要先给原告一张2500万港元的支票作为首期服务费。之后原告兑现支票时,发现支票已经被被告取消了,于是开始向被告提起诉讼。

被告提出几个抗辩理由,其中包括这个交易是过分、苛刻与一面倒的。被告争辩说如果按照原告对合约的解释,即使被告没有获得任何贷款,原告仍可以保留这2500万港币,这显然是不合情理的交易。

看来被告的主张难以站得住脚,因为合约条件对被告十分不利与不合理并不是不合情理交易,毕竟是在双方你情我愿的情况下订立的。能够获得衡平救济,需要是极端的情况。更不用说审理案件的大法官对该合约的解释有不同看法,认为连不利与不合理也谈不上。大法官指出原告证人在开庭时也同意如果在被告没有任何过错的情况下,原告无法帮被告找到贷款,这笔2500万港元要退回给被告。另外,即使原告不同意退回,大法官也认为合约中有这样的默示,并且被告无论如何都可以"完全得不到对价的好处"[39]（a total failure of consideration）为由去取回这笔金钱。所以这样看来，整个合约的商业安排无论如何都不能说是"过分、苛刻与震惊法院良心"。

此外，衡平救济的三个要件的另两个，即被告作为弱势方有特殊不利地位与原告采用道德上应受谴责方式，也是远无法满足的。大法官说被告是一家新加坡上市公司的联营公司，有关的委托贷款咨询合约由被告的管理层与公司法务（被假设是有对等水平）审核过，很难证明这合约是不合情理交易与合约可使无效的："Lafe HK was a subsidiary of a listed company managed by experienced businessmen. The relevant agreements had been examined by Lafe's management and in-house legal counsel. On this basis there can be little scope for contending that a transaction it freely entered into ought to be set aside as an unconscionable bargain...In any event, on my findings, Lafe HK has failed to prove any relevant assurance which was reneged upon or other culpable conduct on the part of China Finance."

3. 谈判与订约地位不对等在国际商业案件中没有救济

英国法院根据不合情理/显失公平理论干预、重写商业合约，显然会冲击订约自由大原则与牺牲合约的肯定性/可预测性，所以除非是特别例外的情况，英国法院绝不会轻易用这方面的衡平救济（这包括本章针对的不当影响与不合情理交易）来干预合约，尤其是国际商业合约。本章之1.7.1段介绍的JP Morgan Chase Bank and Others v. Springwell Navigation Corporation（2008）EWHC 1186（Comm）先例、1.7.2段介绍的The Libyan Investment Authority v. Goldman Sachs International（2016）EWHC 2530（Ch）先例与在2.4段介绍的Alec Lobb v. Total Oil GB（1985）1 WLR 173上诉庭先例等都显示出这个取态。

按理说不少最不发达国家的公司或自然人在事实上不难去证明与认定是处在弱势或特殊不利地位，完全可以符合这方面衡平救济的要件。例如在本章之2.2段介绍的构成不合情理交易的三个要件中，（1）与（2）都完全可以套用。即使直接证据不能满足法定举证责任，但在"红旗测试"（Red Flags test）下就能够认定根据平衡的可能性有这种行为。从英国社会的道德标准与角度看，这种行为是道德上应受谴责，应是不难在这些交易或合约给予衡平救济。这样看来，外国（发展中国家）就要明白英国法律（可延伸至普通法体系）在这方面的衡平救济是内外有别的。

这方面认知有偏差的危险在中国很显著，因为中国法律有诚实信用原则。而诚实信用原则又被称为是民商事法律中的"帝王条款"或"帝王规则"，一切民商事活动

---

〔39〕 见本书第七章之13.5段。

都受到该帝王条款的约束。如《民法典》第 7 条规定:“民事主体从事民事活动,应当遵循诚信原则,秉持诚实,恪守承诺。”《民法典》第 151 条规定:“一方利用对方处于危困状态、缺乏判断能力等情形,致使民事法律行为成立时显失公平的,受损害方有权请求人民法院或者仲裁机构予以撤销。”而原《合同法》第 54 条第 1 款更是规定可以变更合约:“下列合同,当事人一方有权请求人民法院或者仲裁机构变更或者撤销:……(二)在订立合同时显失公平的。一方以欺诈、胁迫的手段或者乘人之危,使对方在违背真实意思的情况下订立的合同,受损害方有权请求人民法院或者仲裁机构变更或者撤销。”

笔者确实也知悉有不少商业/国际商业案件(无论是法院诉讼或仲裁),在涉及不当影响或不合情理/显失公平交易时,都会获得救济(撤销或变更/重写有关合约)。所以在习惯这种做法下,“走出去”的中国公司涉及涉外贸易时,一旦选择适用法是普通法,就必须了解在本书第十章之 1 段已经介绍过的会假设双方知识水平、谈判地位对等,谈不上是弱势方或是有特殊不利地位的一方去订立不合情理的商业合约。通过普通法/国际商法的学习,带着两套思维“走出去”,才可以真正(不是在英国法下推定或假设)与西方国家的公司或自然人在合约谈判地位中实现对等。

案 例 目 录